MW01204719

Hoover's Handbook of

Private Companies

2009

HOOVERS™

A D&B COMPANY

Austin, Texas

Hoover's Handbook of Private Companies 2009 is intended to provide readers with accurate and authoritative information about the enterprises covered in it. Hoover's researched all companies and organizations profiled, and in many cases contacted them directly so that companies represented could provide information. The information contained herein is as accurate as we could reasonably make it. In many cases we have relied on third-party material that we believe to be trustworthy, but were unable to independently verify. We do not warrant that the book is absolutely accurate or without error. Readers should not rely on any information contained herein in instances where such reliance might cause financial loss. The publisher, the editors, and their data suppliers specifically disclaim all warranties, including the implied warranties of merchantability and fitness for a specific purpose. This book is sold with the understanding that neither the publisher, the editors, nor any content contributors are engaged in providing investment, financial, accounting, legal, or other professional advice.

The financial data (Historical Financials sections) in this book are from the companies profiled or from trade sources deemed to be reliable. Hoover's, Inc., is solely responsible for the presentation of all data.

Many of the names of products and services mentioned in this book are the trademarks or service marks of the companies manufacturing or selling them and are subject to protection under US law. Space has not permitted us to indicate which names are subject to such protection, and readers are advised to consult with the owners of such marks regarding their use. Hoover's is a trademark of Hoover's, Inc.

10 9 8 7 6 5 4 3 2 1

Publishers Cataloging-in-Publication Data

Hoover's Handbook of Private Companies 2009

    Includes indexes.

    ISBN 978-1-57311-128-7

    ISSN 1073-6433

    1. Business enterprises — Directories. 2. Corporations — Directories.

HF3010 338.7

Hoover's Company Information is also available on the Internet at Hoover's Online (www.hoovers.com). A catalog of Hoover's products is available on the Internet at www.hooversbooks.com.

The Hoover's Handbook series is produced for Hoover's Business Press by:

Sycamore Productions, Inc.
5808 Balcones Drive, Suite 205
Austin, Texas 78731
info@sycamoreproductions.com

Cover design is by John Baker. Electronic prepress and printing are by Jostens, Inc., Clarksville, Tennessee.

U.S. AND WORLD BOOK SALES

Hoover's, Inc.
5800 Airport Blvd.
Austin, TX 78752
Phone: 512-374-4500
Fax: 512-374-4538
e-mail: orders@hoovers.com
Web: www.hooversbooks.com

EUROPEAN BOOK SALES

William Snyder Publishing Associates
5 Five Mile Drive
Oxford OX2 8HT
England
Phone & fax: +44-186-551-3186
e-mail: snyderpub@aol.com

Hoover's, Inc.

ABOUT HOOVER'S, INC. – THE BUSINESS INFORMATION AUTHORITY™

Hoover's, a D&B company, provides its customers the fastest path to business with insight and actionable information about companies, industries, and key decision makers, along with the powerful tools to find and connect to the right people to get business done. Hoover's provides this information for sales, marketing, business development, and other professionals who need intelligence on U.S. and global companies, industries, and the people who lead them. Hoover's unique combination of editorial expertise and one-of-a-kind data collection with user-generated and company-supplied content gives customers a 360-degree view and competitive edge. This information, along with powerful tools to search, sort, download, and integrate the content, is available through Hoover's (http://www.hoovers.com), the company's premier online service. Hoover's is headquartered in Austin, Texas.

Abbreviations

AFL-CIO – American Federation of Labor and Congress of Industrial Organizations

AMA – American Medical Association

AMEX – American Stock Exchange

ARM – adjustable-rate mortgage

ASP – application services provider

ATM – asynchronous transfer mode

ATM – automated teller machine

CAD/CAM – computer-aided design/ computer-aided manufacturing

CD-ROM – compact disc – read-only memory

CD-R – CD-recordable

CEO – chief executive officer

CFO – chief financial officer

CMOS – complimentary metal oxide silicon

COO – chief operating officer

DAT – digital audiotape

DOD – Department of Defense

DOE – Department of Energy

DOS – disk operating system

DOT – Department of Transportation

DRAM – dynamic random-access memory

DSL – digital subscriber line

DVD – digital versatile disc/digital video disc

DVD-R – DVD-recordable

EPA – Environmental Protection Agency

EPROM – erasable programmable read-only memory

EPS – earnings per share

ESOP – employee stock ownership plan

EU – European Union

EVP – executive vice president

FCC – Federal Communications Commission

FDA – Food and Drug Administration

FDIC – Federal Deposit Insurance Corporation

FTC – Federal Trade Commission

FTP – file transfer protocol

GATT – General Agreement on Tariffs and Trade

GDP – gross domestic product

HMO – health maintenance organization

HR – human resources

HTML – hypertext markup language

ICC – Interstate Commerce Commission

IPO – initial public offering

IRS – Internal Revenue Service

ISP – Internet service provider

kWh – kilowatt-hour

LAN – local-area network

LBO – leveraged buyout

LCD – liquid crystal display

LNG – liquefied natural gas

LP – limited partnership

Ltd. – limited

mips – millions of instructions per second

MW – megawatt

NAFTA – North American Free Trade Agreement

NASA – National Aeronautics and Space Administration

Nasdaq – National Association of Securities Dealers Automated Quotations

NATO – North Atlantic Treaty Organization

NYSE – New York Stock Exchange

OCR – optical character recognition

OECD – Organization for Economic Cooperation and Development

OEM – original equipment manufacturer

OPEC – Organization of Petroleum Exporting Countries

OS – operating system

OSHA – Occupational Safety and Health Administration

OTC – over-the-counter

PBX – private branch exchange

PCMCIA – Personal Computer Memory Card International Association

P/E – price to earnings ratio

RAID – redundant array of independent disks

RAM – random-access memory

R&D – research and development

RBOC – regional Bell operating company

RISC – reduced instruction set computer

REIT – real estate investment trust

ROA – return on assets

ROE – return on equity

ROI – return on investment

ROM – read-only memory

S&L – savings and loan

SCSI – Small Computer System Interface

SEC – Securities and Exchange Commission

SEVP – senior executive vice president

SIC – Standard Industrial Classification

SOC – system on a chip

SVP – senior vice president

USB – universal serial bus

VAR – value-added reseller

VAT – value-added tax

VC – venture capitalist

VoIP – Voice over Internet Protocol

VP – vice president

WAN – wide-area network

WWW – World Wide Web

Contents

Companies Profiled

Companies Profiled (continued)

Companies Profiled (continued)

Companies Profiled (continued)

Companies Profiled (continued)

About Hoover's Handbook of Private Companies 2009

Privately held enterprises are major players in the US economy (giant food processor Cargill or insurer State Farm, for example), and our mission with this volume is to fill the information gap that exists around some private enterprises. Finding current, relevant information can be a challenge, as many of these organizations see secrecy as a competitive strategy. In this 14th edition of *Hoover's Handbook of Private Companies*, we have done for you the tough work of compiling these hard-to-find facts.

We consider this volume to be one of the premier sources of business information on privately held enterprises in the US. It features the facts on 900 of the largest and most influential of those enterprises. Entries feature overviews of company operations, up to five years of financial information, product information, and lists of company executives as found in Hoover's huge database of company information. Some larger and more visible companies will feature an additional History section.

HOOVER'S ONLINE FOR BUSINESS NEEDS

In addition to Hoover's widely used MasterList and Handbooks series, comprehensive coverage of more than 40,000 business enterprises is available in electronic format on our Web site at www.hoovers.com. Our goal is to provide our customers the fastest path to business with insight and actionable information about companies, industries, and key decision makers, along with the powerful tools to find and connect to the right people to get business done. Hoover's has partnered with other prestigious business information and service providers to bring you all the right business information, services, and links in one place.

We welcome the recognition we have received as the premier provider of high-quality company information — online, electronically, and in print — and continue to look for ways to make our products more available and more useful to you.

Hoover's Handbook of Private Companies is one of our four-title series of handbooks that covers, literally, the world of business. The series is available as an indexed set, and also includes *Hoover's Handbook of American Business*, *Hoover's Handbook of World Business*, and *Hoover's Handbook of Emerging Companies*. This series brings you information on the biggest, fastest-growing, and most influential enterprises in the world.

We believe that anyone who buys from, sells to, invests in, lends to, competes with, interviews with, or works for a company should know all there is to know about that enterprise. Taken together, this book and the other Hoover's products and resources represent the most complete source of basic corporate information readily available to the general public.

HOW TO USE THIS BOOK

This book has four sections:

1. "Using Hoover's Handbooks" describes the contents of our profiles and explains the ways in which we gather and compile our data.

2. "A List-Lover's Compendium" contains lists of the largest and fastest-growing private companies. The lists are based on the information in our profiles, or compiled from well-known sources.

3. The company profiles section makes up the largest and most important part of the book — 900 profiles of major private enterprises, arranged alphabetically.

4. Three indexes complete the book. The first sorts companies by industry groups, the second by headquarters location. The third index is a list of all the executives found in the Executives section of each company profile.

As always, we hope you find our books useful. We invite your comments via phone (512-374-4500), fax (512-374-4538), mail (5800 Airport Boulevard, Austin, Texas 78752), or e-mail (custsupport@hoovers.com).

The Editors,
Austin, Texas,
November 2008

Using Hoover's Handbooks

SELECTION OF THE COMPANIES PROFILED

The 900 enterprises profiled in this book include the largest and most influential private enterprises in America. Among them are:

- private companies, from the giants (Cargill and Koch) to the colorful and prominent (Helmsley Enterprises and L.L. Bean)
- mutuals and cooperative organizations owned by their customers (State Farm Insurance, Ace Hardware, Ocean Spray Cranberries)
- not-for-profits (Red Cross, Kaiser Foundation Health Plan, Smithsonian Institution)
- joint ventures (Motiva Enterprises, Dow Corning)
- partnerships (PricewaterhouseCoopers, Baker & McKenzie)
- universities (Columbia, Harvard, University of California)
- government-owned corporations (US Postal Service and New York City's Metropolitan Transportation Authority)
- and a selection of other enterprises (National Basketball Association, AFL-CIO, Texas Lottery Commission).

ORGANIZATION

The profiles are presented in alphabetical order. You will find the commonly used name of the enterprise at the beginning of the profile; the full, legal name is found in the Locations section. If a company name is also a person's name, such as Henry Ford Health System or Mary Kay, it will be alphabetized under the first name; if the company name starts with initials, for example, L.L. Bean or S.C. Johnson, look for it under the combined initials (in the above examples, LL and SC, respectively).

Basic financial data are listed under the heading Historical Financials. The annual financial information contained in the profiles is current through fiscal year-ends occurring as late as August 2008. We have included certain nonfinancial developments, such as officer changes, through October 2008.

OVERVIEW

In the first section of the profile, we have tried to give a thumbnail description of the company and what it does. The description will usually include information on the company's strategy, reputation, and ownership. We recommend that you read this section first.

HISTORY

This extended section, which is available for some of the larger and more well-known companies, reflects our belief that every enterprise is the sum of its history and that you have to know where you came from in order to know where you are going. While some companies have limited historical awareness, we think the vast majority of the enterprises in this book have colorful backgrounds. We have tried to focus on the people who made the enterprises what they are today. We have found these histories to be full of twists and ironies; they make fascinating reading.

EXECUTIVES

Here we list the names of the people who run the company, insofar as space allows. In the few cases where available, we have shown the ages and pay of key officers. In some instances the published data is for the previous year although the company has announced promotions or retirements since year-end. The pay represents cash compensation, including bonuses, but excludes stock option programs.

Although companies are free to structure their management titles any way they please, most modern corporations follow standard practices. The ultimate power in any corporation lies with the shareholders, who elect a board of directors, usually including officers or "insiders," as well as individuals from outside the company. The chief officer, the person on whose desk the buck stops, is usually called the chief executive officer (CEO). Often, he or she is also the chairman of the board.

As corporate management has become more complex, it is common for the CEO to have a "right-hand person" who oversees the day-to-day operations of the company, allowing the CEO plenty of time to focus on strategy and long-term issues. This right-hand person is usually designated the chief operating officer (COO) and is often the president of the company. In other cases one person is both chairman and president.

A multitude of other titles exists, including chief financial officer (CFO), chief administrative officer, and vice chairman. We have always tried to include the CFO, the chief legal officer, and the chief human resources or personnel officer.

The people named in the Executives section are indexed at the back of the book.

The Executives section also includes the name of the company's auditing (accounting) firm, where available.

LOCATIONS

Here we include the company's full legal name and its headquarters, street address, telephone and fax numbers, and Web site, as available. The back of the book includes an index of companies by headquarters locations.

In some cases we have also included information on the geographic distribution of the company's business, including sales and profit data. Note that these profit numbers, like those in the Products/Operations section below, are usually operating or pretax profits rather than net profits. Operating profits are generally those before financing costs (interest income and payments) and before taxes, which are considered costs attributable to the whole company rather than to one division or part of the world. For this reason the net income figures (in the Historical Financials section) are usually much lower, since they are after interest and taxes. Pretax profits are after interest but before taxes.

Headquarters for companies that are incorporated in Bermuda, but whose operational headquarters are in the US, are listed under their US address.

PRODUCTS/OPERATIONS

This section contains selected lists of products, services, brand names, divisions, subsidiaries, and joint ventures. We have tried to include all of a company's major lines and all familiar brand names.

The nature of this section varies by company and the amount of information contained in Hoover's storehouse of business information. If the company publishes sales and profit information by type of business, we have included it.

COMPETITORS

In this section we have listed companies that compete with the profiled company. This feature is included as a quick way to locate similar companies and compare them. The universe of competitors includes all public companies and all private companies with sales in excess of $500 million. In a few instances we have identified smaller private companies as key competitors.

HISTORICAL FINANCIALS

Here we have tried to present as much data about each enterprise's financial performance as we could compile in the allocated space. The information varies somewhat from industry to industry and is less complete in the case of private companies that do not release data. (We have always tried to provide annual sales and employment, although in some instances those numbers are simply not available.) There are a few industries, venture capital and investment banking, for example, for which revenue numbers are not reported as a rule. In the case of private companies that do not publicly disclose financial information, we have sometimes used estimates of sales and other statistics when reliable sources are available.

The following information is generally present.

A five-year table, with relevant annualized compound growth rates, covers:
- Sales — fiscal year sales (year-end assets for most financial companies)
- Net income — fiscal year net income (before accounting changes)
- Net profit margin — fiscal year net income as a percent of sales (as a percent of assets for most financial firms)
- Employees — fiscal year-end or average number of employees

The information on the number of employees is intended to aid the reader interested in knowing whether a company has a long-term trend of increasing or decreasing employment. As far as we know, we are the only company that publishes this information in print format.

The numbers on the left in each row of the Historical Financials section give the month and the year in which the company's fiscal year actually ends. Thus, a company with a March 31, 2008, year-end is shown as 3/08. The last item in the Financials section is a graph, which for private companies shows net income, or, if that is unavailable, sales.

Key year-end statistics are included in this section for insurance companies and companies required to file reports with the SEC. They generally show the financial strength of the enterprise, including:
- Debt ratio (long-term debt as a percent of shareholders' equity)
- Return on equity (net income divided by the average of beginning and ending common shareholders' equity)
- Cash and cash equivalents
- Current ratio (ratio of current assets to current liabilities)
- Total long-term debt (including capital lease obligations)
- Fiscal year sales for financial institutions.

Hoover's Handbook of

Private Companies

A List-Lover's Compendium

The 300 Largest Companies by Sales in
Hoover's Handbook of Private Companies 2009

Rank	Company	Sales ($ mil.)	Rank	Company	Sales ($ mil.)	Rank	Company	Sales ($ mil.)
1	Cargill, Incorporated	120,439	51	Dairy Farmers of America	11,100	101	University of Texas System	6,468
2	Koch Industries	98,000	52	Harrah's Entertainment	10,825	102	Providence Health & Services	6,348
3	US Postal Service	74,973	53	The Trump Organization	10,700	103	Performance Food	6,305
4	State Farm	61,600	54	CCA Global Partners	10,200	104	Trinity Health	6,300
5	Chrysler LLC	59,700	55	Reyes Holdings	10,100	105	New York City Health and Hospitals	6,213
6	Cellco Partnership	43,900	56	Capital Group Companies	9,900	106	Peter Kiewit Sons'	6,200
7	Carlson Companies	39,800	57	Wakefern Food	9,900	107	Colonial Group	6,200
8	Kaiser Foundation Health Plan	37,800	58	Blue Cross (MI)	9,849	108	Major League Baseball	6,100
9	Kaiser Permanente	37,800	59	Enterprise Rent-A-Car	9,500	109	Thrivent Financial	6,081
10	Bechtel Group	27,000	60	Dollar General	9,495	110	Aleris International	5,990
11	HCA Inc.	26,858	61	Liberty Media	9,423	111	Ryerson Inc.	5,909
12	Liberty Mutual	25,961	62	TVA	9,244	112	University of Michigan	5,821
13	PricewaterhouseCoopers	25,150	63	Land O'Lakes	8,925	113	Hexion Specialty Chemicals	5,810
14	Mars, Incorporated	25,000	64	Topco Associates	8,800	114	Freescale Semiconductor	5,722
15	Motiva Enterprises	24,400	65	S.C. Johnson	8,750	115	Associated Wholesale Grocers	5,700
16	Federal Reserve System	23,540	66	Army and Air Force Exchange	8,705	116	MacAndrews & Forbes	5,700
17	Publix Super Markets	23,194	67	Catholic Health Initiatives	8,603	117	Gulf States Toyota	5,700
18	Deloitte Touche Tohmatsu	23,100	68	Federal Home Loan Bank of Atlanta	8,429	118	Metropolitan Transportation Authority	5,666
19	Nationwide Mutual Insurance	22,797	69	Catholic Healthcare West	8,402	119	Hy-Vee, Inc.	5,600
20	Northwestern Mutual Life Insurance	21,355	70	The Regence Group	8,372	120	Keystone Foods	5,580
21	Ernst & Young Global	21,160	71	Blue Shield Of California	8,364	121	Allegis Group	5,570
22	New York Life Insurance	21,123	72	QuikTrip Corporation	8,300	122	Racetrac Petroleum	5,520
23	IGA, Inc.	21,000	73	Transammonia, Inc.	8,300	123	Meadowbrook Meat Company	5,500
24	U.S. Foodservice	20,200	74	Southern Wine & Spirits	8,300	124	Guardian Industries	5,470
25	KPMG International	19,810	75	State University of New York	8,151	125	Boise Cascade	5,414
26	C&S Wholesale Grocers	19,500	76	Cumberland Farms	8,100	126	Bloomberg L.P.	5,400
27	Massachusetts Mutual Life Insurance	18,744	77	CDW Corporation	8,100	127	McKinsey & Company	5,330
28	Teacher Retirement System of Texas	18,002	78	Hilton Hotels	8,090	128	Pension Benefit Guaranty Corporation	5,325
29	Flying J Inc.	16,200	79	Bill & Melinda Gates Foundation	8,082	129	Unisource Worldwide	5,300
30	University of California	15,465	80	First Data Corporation	8,051	130	Graybar Electric	5,258
31	NBC Universal	15,416	81	Giant Eagle	8,020	131	Kohler Co.	5,230
32	Cox Enterprises	15,033	82	Energy Future Holdings	7,992	132	Apex Oil	5,200
33	FMR LLC	14,900	83	Advance Publications	7,970	133	Save Mart Supermarkets	5,100
34	USAA	14,418	84	Menard, Inc.	7,800	134	Avaya Inc.	5,100
35	Health Care Service Corporation	14,348	85	Sutter Health	7,651	135	Tribune Company	5,063
36	SemGroup, L.P.	14,200	86	Guardian Life Insurance	7,648	136	Wawa, Inc.	5,050
37	Penske Corporation	14,000	87	Horizon Healthcare	7,527	137	Pacific Mutual	5,049
38	Meijer, Inc.	13,900	88	New York State Lottery	7,175	138	Pro-Build Holdings	5,000
39	Toys "R" Us	13,794	89	Alticor Inc.	7,100	139	Gulf Oil	5,000
40	H-E-B	13,500	90	NewYork-Presbyterian Healthcare	7,060	140	Southwire Company	4,980
41	Platinum Equity	13,500	91	Love's Travel Stops	7,000	141	Dow Corning	4,940
42	Ascension Health	13,489	92	Sinclair Oil	7,000	142	Stanford University	4,905
43	TIAA-CREF	13,187	93	Marmon Group	6,990	143	SunGard Data Systems	4,901
44	Chevron Phillips Chemical	12,986	94	Dole Food	6,931	144	Center Oil	4,900
45	ARAMARK	12,384	95	National Football League	6,900	145	Blue Cross (NC)	4,900
46	MidAmerican Energy	12,376	96	Mayo Foundation	6,898	146	Adventist Health System	4,835
47	JM Family Enterprises	12,200	97	American Family Insurance	6,868	147	Auto-Owners Insurance Group	4,802
48	BCD Travel	12,000	98	Gordon Food Service	6,700	148	Kinray Inc.	4,800
49	Tenaska, Inc.	11,600	99	Yale University	6,651	149	AllianceBernstein L.P.	4,720
50	Knight inc	11,500	100	Realogy Corporation	6,492	150	NUMMI	4,699

SOURCE: HOOVER'S, INC., DATABASE, NOVEMBER 2008

Rank	Company	Sales ($ mil.)	Rank	Company	Sales ($ mil.)	Rank	Company	Sales ($ mil.)
151	OSI Group	4,620	201	Parsons Corporation	3,600	251	California State University System	2,900
152	Neiman Marcus	4,601	202	Tishman Realty & Construction	3,560	252	General Parts	2,870
153	Charmer Sunbelt	4,600	203	H.T. Hackney	3,550	253	University of Washington	2,853
154	University of Pennsylvania	4,569	204	Georgia Lottery	3,519	254	Securian Financial	2,852
155	Wegmans Food Markets	4,500	205	CalPERS	3,514	255	DeBruce Grain	2,830
156	Kingston Technology	4,500	206	Harvard University	3,482	256	Medline Industries	2,830
157	Ergon, Inc.	4,490	207	Henry Ford Health System	3,470	257	Cornell University	2,826
158	Massachusetts State Lottery	4,480	208	Grant Thornton International	3,461	258	Columbia University	2,820
159	Sheetz, Inc.	4,410	209	Advocate Health Care	3,457	259	Dot Foods	2,810
160	Brightstar Corp.	4,400	210	Raley's	3,450	260	BJC HealthCare	2,800
161	National Basketball Association	4,400	211	Ashley Furniture	3,430	261	Amsted Industries	2,800
162	Hallmark Cards	4,400	212	Burlington Coat Factory Warehouse	3,424	262	Lefrak Organization	2,800
163	Hearst Corporation	4,380	213	Schneider National	3,400	263	Vanguard Health Systems	2,791
164	CH2M HILL Companies	4,376	214	Oxbow Corporation	3,400	264	Reader's Digest	2,786
165	Catholic Health East	4,365	215	Sammons Enterprises	3,375	265	Western & Southern Financial	2,779
166	RNDC Texas	4,320	216	ServiceMaster	3,357	266	National Hockey League	2,747
167	Washington Companies	4,300	217	Factory Mutual Insurance	3,356	267	CUNA Mutual	2,741
168	Perdue Incorporated	4,300	218	Structure Tone	3,330	268	Salt River Project	2,739
169	The Scoular Company	4,300	219	Schwan Food	3,300	269	Vanderbilt University	2,733
170	Levi Strauss	4,266	220	Swift Transportation	3,270	270	Grocers Supply	2,720
171	Mutual of Omaha	4,242	221	Bonneville Power Administration	3,269	271	LPL Financial	2,718
172	Clark Enterprises	4,220	222	Black & Veatch	3,200	272	Services Group of America	2,700
173	Battelle Memorial Institute	4,181	223	Port Authority of NY & NJ	3,192	273	Quintiles Transnational	2,700
174	Salvation Army	4,157	224	Red Cross	3,175	274	Ag Processing	2,685
175	OSI Restaurant Partners	4,150	225	Goodwill Industries	3,164	275	Bass Pro Shops	2,650
176	Jones Financial Companies	4,147	226	JELD-WEN, inc.	3,160	276	Rich Products	2,650
177	Eby-Brown Company	4,100	227	E. & J. Gallo Winery	3,150	277	Chick-fil-A	2,641
178	Booz Allen Hamilton	4,100	228	Glazer's Wholesale Drug	3,150	278	JE Dunn Construction	2,634
179	Ohio State University	4,090	229	Golub Corporation	3,140	279	ABC Supply	2,630
180	ESPN, Inc.	4,031	230	Unified Grocers	3,133	280	University of Chicago	2,624
181	Roundy's Supermarkets	4,000	231	JohnsonDiversey, Inc.	3,130	281	BI-LO, LLC	2,620
182	The Renco Group	4,000	232	84 Lumber	3,100	282	Leprino Foods	2,620
183	Global Hyatt	4,000	233	Pennsylvania Lottery	3,089	283	The Vanguard Group	2,600
184	Ace Hardware	3,971	234	Berry Plastics	3,055	284	U.S. Central Federal Credit Union	2,599
185	Whiting-Turner Contracting	3,970	235	International Data Group	3,020	285	Sentry Insurance	2,588
186	SIRVA, Inc.	3,970	236	US Oncology	3,001	286	George E. Warren Corporation	2,586
187	Red Apple Group	3,950	237	NASCAR	3,000	287	University of California, Davis	2,571
188	University of Illinois	3,900	238	Sabre Holdings	3,000	288	Momentive Performance Materials	2,538
189	Consolidated Electrical Distributors	3,900	239	WinCo Foods	3,000	289	University of Southern California	2,524
190	Carpet One	3,900	240	Golden State Foods	3,000	290	Follett Corporation	2,520
191	Manor Care	3,890	241	J.R. Simplot	3,000	291	Hensel Phelps Construction	2,520
192	Michaels Stores	3,862	242	Andersen Corporation	3,000	292	Cooper-Standard Automotive	2,511
193	Delta Dental Plan	3,830	243	Central National-Gottesman	3,000	293	World Wide Technology	2,500
194	Belk, Inc.	3,825	244	Sports Authority	2,980	294	Quality King Distributors	2,500
195	Texas Lottery	3,775	245	Gilbane, Inc.	2,970	295	Schnuck Markets	2,500
196	Catholic Healthcare Partners	3,715	246	Alex Lee	2,920	296	DeMoulas Super Markets	2,500
197	Stater Bros.	3,674	247	New York Power Authority	2,906	297	Truman Arnold	2,500
198	Sisters of Mercy Health System	3,654	248	University of Alabama System	2,900	298	Bausch & Lomb	2,500
199	University of Wisconsin	3,628	249	Schreiber Foods	2,900	299	TA Delaware	2,500
200	Walsh Group	3,600	250	McCarthy Building Companies	2,900	300	Harvard Pilgrim Health Care	2,498

The 300 Largest Employers in
Hoover's Handbook of Private Companies 2009

Rank	Company	Employees	Rank	Company	Employees	Rank	Company	Employees
1	US Postal Service	684,762	51	Army and Air Force Exchange	43,658	101	University of Pennsylvania	23,704
2	Express Employment	375,000	52	Adventist Health System	43,000	102	Freescale Semiconductor	23,200
3	ARAMARK	250,000	53	Bechtel Group	42,500	103	Federal Prison Industries	23,152
4	Carlson Companies	160,000	54	West Corporation	42,000	104	Wheaton Franciscan Services	23,000
5	Cargill, Incorporated	160,000	55	Michaels Stores	42,000	105	University of Nebraska	23,000
6	Kaiser Permanente	159,766	56	Knowledge Learning	42,000	106	Save Mart Supermarkets	23,000
7	PricewaterhouseCoopers	146,767	57	Liberty Mutual	41,000	107	The Trump Organization	22,450
8	Deloitte Touche Tohmatsu	146,600	58	Golden Horizons	41,000	108	Schneider National	22,216
9	Publix Super Markets	144,000	59	Delaware North Companies	40,000	109	OSI Group	22,000
10	Hilton Hotels	135,000	60	Menard, Inc.	40,000	110	Schwan Food	22,000
11	University of California	127,368	61	Ohio State University	39,120	111	SavaSeniorCare	22,000
12	KPMG International	123,322	62	Jones Financial Companies	38,100	112	Saint Barnabas Health Care System	22,000
13	Ernst & Young Global	121,000	63	University of Michigan	37,925	113	USAA	22,000
14	Ascension Health	107,000	64	Genesis HealthCare	37,700	114	CH2M HILL Companies	22,000
15	IGA, Inc.	92,000	65	Wegmans Food Markets	37,602	115	Swift Transportation	21,900
16	Global Hyatt	90,000	66	Giant Eagle	37,000	116	Vanderbilt University	21,502
17	Goodwill Industries	87,444	67	Catholic Healthcare Partners	36,925	117	Marmon Group	21,500
18	Harrah's Entertainment	87,000	68	Penske Corporation	36,000	118	24 Hour Fitness	21,410
19	State University of New York	83,547	69	Nationwide Mutual Insurance	36,000	119	Cooper-Standard Automotive	21,123
20	Cox Enterprises	81,693	70	Red Cross	35,000	120	Perdue Incorporated	21,000
21	Koch Industries	80,000	71	City University of New York	33,460	121	Roundy's Supermarkets	21,000
22	University of Texas System	73,329	72	Freeman Decorating Services	32,200	122	Quintiles Transnational	21,000
23	Toys "R" Us	72,000	73	Kohler Co.	32,000	123	University of New Mexico	20,210
24	Dollar General	71,500	74	Life Care Centers	31,153	124	Battelle Memorial Institute	20,000
25	Cellco Partnership	69,000	75	University of California, Davis	30,086	125	Lifetouch Inc.	20,000
26	Metropolitan Transportation Authority	68,628	76	Kellwood Company	30,000	126	MacAndrews & Forbes	19,800
27	State Farm Mutual	68,000	77	Waffle House	30,000	127	Lone Star Steakhouse	19,750
28	Meijer, Inc.	67,000	78	Advocate Health Care	30,000	128	Tribune Company	19,600
29	Enterprise Rent-A-Car	66,700	79	Duke University Health System	29,826	129	University of Minnesota	19,274
30	Chrysler LLC	66,409	80	Advance Publications	29,100	130	Bally Total Fitness	19,200
31	Sitel Corporation	66,000	81	ServiceMaster	29,000	131	Federal Reserve System	19,159
32	Catholic Health Initiatives	65,296	82	Asplundh Tree Expert	28,606	132	Amtrak	19,000
33	H-E-B	63,000	83	Laureate Education	28,500	133	Liberty Media	19,000
34	Manor Care	61,700	84	University of Wisconsin	28,345	134	Booz Allen Hamilton	19,000
35	Salvation Army	59,651	85	University of Washington	28,198	135	Guardian Industries	19,000
36	Mayo Foundation	54,914	86	Sisters of Mercy Health System	28,000	136	Adventist Health	18,823
37	Catholic Health East	54,000	87	Grant Thornton International	27,861	137	University of Alabama System	18,785
38	Hy-Vee, Inc.	54,000	88	U.S. Foodservice	27,160	138	Claire's Stores	18,700
39	NewYork-Presbyterian Healthcare	53,562	89	First Data Corporation	27,000	139	National Institutes of Health	18,627
40	Chick-fil-A	50,000	90	Texas A&M University System	26,876	140	HCA Inc.	18,600
41	Wakefern Food	50,000	91	BJC HealthCare	26,622	141	University of Rochester	18,531
42	Catholic Healthcare West	50,000	92	Burlington Coat Factory Warehouse	26,580	142	Guardsmark, LLC	18,500
43	Platinum Equity	50,000	93	Belk, Inc.	26,375	143	Vanguard Health Systems	18,500
44	Mars, Incorporated	48,000	94	Metromedia Company	25,500	144	Indiana University	18,427
45	FMR LLC	46,400	95	University of Illinois	24,513	145	University of Wisconsin-Madison	18,374
46	Dole Food	45,000	96	University of California, San Diego	24,187	146	Stater Bros.	18,000
47	Providence Health & Services	45,000	97	University of Missouri	24,013	147	Hobby Lobby	18,000
48	Sutter Health	44,828	98	Day & Zimmermann	24,000	148	Nypro Inc.	18,000
49	Trinity Health	44,500	99	Golub Corporation	23,892	149	Central Parking	18,000
50	California State University System	44,000	100	JELD-WEN, inc.	23,750	150	University of Southern California	18,000

SOURCE: HOOVER'S, INC., DATABASE, NOVEMBER 2008

Rank	Company	Employees	Rank	Company	Employees	Rank	Company	Employees
151	Neiman Marcus	18,000	201	Alticor Inc.	13,000	251	Foster Poultry Farms	10,000
152	General Parts	18,000	202	Andersen Corporation	13,000	252	Sequa Corporation	10,000
153	Avaya Inc.	18,000	203	Keystone Foods	13,000	253	WinCo Foods	10,000
154	SunGard Data Systems	17,900	204	Bausch & Lomb	13,000	254	Milliken & Company	10,000
155	Henry Ford Health System	17,489	205	Friendly Ice Cream	12,800	255	J.R. Simplot	10,000
156	MidAmerican Energy	17,200	206	Acapulco/El Torito Restaurants	12,701	256	Dow Corning	10,000
157	Hearst Corporation	17,070	207	MediaNews Group	12,700	257	Allegis Group	10,000
158	Pro-Build Holdings	17,000	208	Berry Plastics	12,700	258	REI	10,000
159	Ashley Furniture	17,000	209	Brookshire Grocery	12,700	259	Stanford University	9,821
160	Ilitch Holdings	17,000	210	Amscan Holdings	12,569	260	Pella Corporation	9,800
161	C&S Wholesale Grocers	17,000	211	Taylor Corporation	12,500	261	NTK Holdings	9,800
162	BI-LO, LLC	17,000	212	Estes Express Lines	12,374	262	Catalent Pharma Solutions	9,800
163	Health Care Service Corporation	16,500	213	TVA	12,013	263	Anderson News	9,800
164	Wawa, Inc.	16,426	214	Gordon Food Service	12,000	264	Cengage Learning	9,800
165	Vanderbilt University Medical Center	16,230	215	K-VA-T Food Stores	12,000	265	Black & Veatch	9,600
166	Lefrak Organization	16,200	216	Quad/Graphics, Inc.	12,000	266	Guitar Center	9,540
167	Flying J Inc.	16,000	217	BCD Travel	12,000	267	Affinia Group	9,507
168	ShopKo Stores	16,000	218	Alsco, Inc.	12,000	268	Kaleida Health	9,500
169	ClubCorp USA	16,000	219	Massachusetts Mutual Life Insurance	12,000	269	Big Y Foods	9,500
170	New York University	16,000	220	Houchens Industries	12,000	270	Boston University	9,225
171	Hallmark Cards	15,900	221	S.C. Johnson	12,000	271	Amsted Industries	9,200
172	Sports Authority	15,825	222	Yale University	11,750	272	Ceridian Corporation	9,177
173	McKinsey & Company	15,600	223	Discount Tire	11,630	273	APi Group	9,000
174	Cornell University	15,558	224	Levi Strauss	11,550	274	Sabre Holdings	9,000
175	Raley's	15,500	225	Parsons Brinckerhoff	11,500	275	Capital Group Companies	9,000
176	Schnuck Markets	15,500	226	Zachry Group	11,500	276	Infor Global Solutions	9,000
177	Harvard University	15,302	227	Sheetz, Inc.	11,500	277	US Oncology	9,000
178	Volunteers of America	15,000	228	The Vanguard Group	11,500	278	Crown Equipment	9,000
179	Peter Kiewit Sons'	15,000	229	JohnsonDiversey, Inc.	11,500	279	TIC Holdings	9,000
180	Whataburger	15,000	230	Mashantucket Pequot Tribal Nation	11,500	280	US Investigations Services	9,000
181	Turner Industries	15,000	231	Parsons Corporation	11,500	281	Blue Cross (MI)	8,945
182	Sentara Healthcare	15,000	232	White Castle	11,451	282	Grocers Supply	8,900
183	New York Life Insurance	14,847	233	The Renco Group	11,400	283	Aleris International	8,800
184	University of Chicago	14,772	234	Yucaipa Companies	11,000	284	Solo Cup	8,700
185	Station Casinos	14,500	235	ADESA, Inc.	11,000	285	Land O'Lakes	8,700
186	Spectrum Health System	14,400	236	TA Delaware	11,000	286	Reyes Holdings	8,700
187	Barnes & Noble College Bookstores	14,400	237	TPG Capital	11,000	287	Graybar Electric	8,600
188	Bashas' Inc.	14,300	238	Alex Lee	10,900	288	W. L. Gore & Associates	8,500
189	Sensata Technologies	14,246	239	OSI Restaurant Partners	10,900	289	Ardent Health	8,500
190	Columbia University	14,113	240	Michigan State University	10,900	290	Realogy Corporation	8,500
191	Bass Pro Shops	14,000	241	U.S. Xpress	10,885	291	Key Safety Systems	8,500
192	Koch Foods	14,000	242	Iasis Healthcare	10,826	292	American Family Insurance	8,482
193	Fry's Electronics	14,000	243	Bloomberg L.P.	10,800	293	Dartmouth-Hitchcock Alliance	8,392
194	International Data Group	13,640	244	SAS Institute	10,737	294	Sandia National Laboratories	8,300
195	ContiGroup Companies	13,500	245	QuikTrip Corporation	10,500	295	Haworth, Inc.	8,000
196	University of Kentucky	13,500	246	Walsh Group	10,500	296	Heico Companies	8,000
197	GNC Corporation	13,239	247	Mohegan Tribal Gaming Authority	10,400	297	Yates Companies	8,000
198	Panda Restaurant Group	13,000	248	Southern Wine & Spirits	10,300	298	Pratt Industries	8,000
199	DeMoulas Super Markets	13,000	249	Ritz Camera Centers	10,150	299	Follett Corporation	8,000
200	Academy Sports & Outdoors	13,000	250	Boise Cascade	10,042	300	Bose Corporation	8,000

The *Inc.* 500 Fastest-Growing Private Companies in America

Rank	Company	Headquarters	Sales Growth Increase (%)*	Rank	Company	Headquarters	Sales Growth Increase (%)
1	Senior Whole Health	Cambridge, MA	31,525.4	51	LEVEL5	Atlanta, GA	2,998.9
2	Eliason Inc.	St. Germain, WI	24,391.8	52	Solvern Innovations	Glen Burnie, MD	2,900.5
3	The Snack Factory	Skillman, NJ	18,371.3	53	Trace Communications	Indianapolis, IN	2,896.2
4	Torres Advanced Enterprise Solutions	Arlington, VA	16,455.8	54	Nantero	Woburn, MA	2,833.0
5	GroupGemstone	Las Vegas, NV	15,465.1	55	Signature Foods	Pendergrass, GA	2,814.2
6	Just Like Sugar	Las Vegas, NV	13,212.7	56	Industriaplex	Alpharetta, GA	2,750.7
7	Greenline Industries	Larkspur, CA	10,941.8	57	LeGacy Resource Corporation	Brentwood, TN	2,750.2
8	Zorch	Chicago, IL	10,822.2	58	Stallion Oilfield Services	Houston, TX	2,660.1
9	Harley Stanfield	Washington, DC	9,744.7	59	ProfitPoint	Franklin, TN	2,642.0
10	Amir Amirfar and Associates	Irvine, CA	8,353.1	60	Salt Lake Mailing & Printing	Salt Lake City, UT	2,639.2
11	Glispa Media	New York, NY	8,140.2	61	iTrendz	Edison, NJ	2,637.6
12	Hollingsworth Capital Partners	Clinton, TN	7,256.4	62	SaltWorks	Woodinville, WA	2,629.7
13	BlueStar Energy Services	Chicago, IL	6,988.3	63	Innovative Foods	Wilmington, MA	2,626.8
14	Bridgepoint Education	San Diego, CA	6,794.1	64	Bill Me Later	Timonium, MD	2,573.5
15	beBetter Networks	Charleston, WV	6,674.7	65	Ahura Scientific	Wilmington, MA	2,525.8
16	Carahsoft Technology	Reston, VA	6,551.3	66	NeatReceipts	Philadelphia, PA	2,519.0
17	Red Ventures	Charlotte, NC	5,863.8	67	Enrich IT	Alpharetta, GA	2,515.9
18	Cameron Hughes Wine	San Francisco, CA	5,754.1	68	SellingSource	Las Vegas, NV	2,494.0
19	Succeed Corp.	Mesa, AZ	5,598.5	69	OnDemand Resources	Great Falls, VA	2,460.1
20	WebHouse	Rockville Centre, NY	5,452.5	70	Pepperjam	Wilkes-Barre, PA	2,447.5
21	HostGator	Houston, TX	5,297.7	71	CPX Interactive	Westbury, NY	2,402.8
22	Agistix	Redwood City, CA	5,214.7	72	Temporary Housing Directory	Plano, TX	2,393.8
23	SolutionSet	Palo Alto, CA	5,168.8	73	FireFold	Concord, NC	2,379.1
24	StrataLight Communications	Los Gatos, CA	5,125.7	74	JBCStyle	New York, NY	2,348.3
25	Woot	Carrollton, TX	4,988.5	75	Craig Technologies	Cape Canaveral, FL	2,338.7
26	Premier Payment Systems	Lombard, IL	4,790.5	76	1 Source Consulting	Germantown, MD	2,337.5
27	Ticket Software	Vernon, CT	4,737.3	77	Incisent Technologies	Chicago, IL	2,320.3
28	ESC Select	Amherst, NY	4,646.8	78	Smart Destinations	Boston, MA	2,290.8
29	Merchant Processing Services	New York, NY	4,481.5	79	DesignerPlumbingOutlet.com	Palm Beach Gardens, FL	2,227.8
30	Hardwire	Pocomoke City, MD	4,405.6	80	PN Hoffman	Washington, DC	2,212.6
31	Skullcandy	Park City, UT	4,077.4	81	Electronic Payments	Calverton, NY	2,208.2
32	Vizio	Irvine, CA	4,056.9	82	RealNet Investments	Portland, OR	2,185.5
33	Financial Intelligence	Mountain View, CA	3,913.4	83	Flu Busters	Roswell, GA	2,156.5
34	AdBrite	San Francisco, CA	3,856.1	84	High Street Partners	Annapolis, MD	2,128.3
35	ForeclosuresDaily.com	Largo, FL	3,838.5	85	iContact	Durham, NC	2,114.3
36	LHR Technologies	Pasadena, TX	3,822.1	86	Shoe Metro	San Diego, CA	2,099.6
37	Groupware Technology	Campbell, CA	3,777.6	87	Rockett Interactive	Cary, NC	2,093.5
38	Milestone Metals	Fairfax, VA	3,579.6	88	The Analysis Group	Falls Church, VA	2,078.6
39	FURminator	Fenton, MO	3,505.8	89	Search Wizards	Atlanta, GA	2,066.2
40	WineCommune	Oakland, CA	3,460.2	90	Logical Innovations	Richmond, VA	2,053.8
41	CPO Commerce	Pasadena, CA	3,396.0	91	Latshaw Drilling & Exploration	Tulsa, OK	2,045.5
42	Capital City Technologies	Suwanee, GA	3,330.6	92	Solar Liberty	Buffalo, NY	2,022.7
43	Santur	Fremont, CA	3,311.6	93	Triplefin	Cincinnati, OH	2,021.6
44	Service Financial	Milwaukee, WI	3,239.4	94	Simplicity Group	Springville, UT	1,982.7
45	Walz Certified Mail Solutions	Temecula, CA	3,231.3	95	Solid Source Realty	Roswell, GA	1,972.3
46	Interbank FX	Salt Lake City, UT	3,224.6	96	The Coding Source	Los Angeles, CA	1,965.1
47	Integrity Asset Management	Louisville, KY	3,217.9	97	National Retirement Partners	San Juan Capistrano, CA	1,907.5
48	Revel Consulting	Bellevue, WA	3,063.6	98	Credant Technologies	Addison, TX	1,907.3
49	Delivery Agent	San Francisco, CA	3,059.1	99	American Bancard	Boca Raton, FL	1,903.8
50	Pandigital	Dublin, CA	3,048.4	100	2Pi Solutions	Washington, DC	1,902.7

*Average annual sales growth measured over a three-year period.

SOURCE: *INC.*, SEPTEMBER 2008

The *Inc.* 500 Fastest-Growing Private Companies in America (continued)

Rank	Company	Headquarters	Sales Growth Increase (%)	Rank	Company	Headquarters	Sales Growth Increase (%)
101	Dogswell	Los Angeles, CA	1,896.9	151	Morgan Borszcz Consulting	Ashburn, VA	1,498.2
102	Royal Buying Group	Lisle, IL	1,896.2	152	MindFire	Irvine, CA	1,492.3
103	Volusion	Simi Valley, CA	1,893.4	153	Laurand Associates	Great Neck, NY	1,483.8
104	DVS Group	Poughkeepsie, NY	1,886.3	154	Optimal Solutions Group	Hyattsville, MD	1,458.7
105	LaborLawCenter	Garden Grove, CA	1,885.8	155	Thrustmaster of Texas	Houston, TX	1,456.7
106	Modern Concrete	Elko, NV	1,868.0	156	Integrity Capital Partners	Bethesda, MD	1,454.6
107	Sales Partnerships	Westminster, CO	1,864.9	157	Reliant Technologies	Mountain View, CA	1,449.3
108	Tango Office Environments	Bellevue, WA	1,850.7	158	Mark/Ryan Associates	Schaumburg, IL	1,447.9
109	Genband	Plano, TX	1,829.4	159	Skywire Software	Frisco, TX	1,425.6
110	Genesis Today	Austin, TX	1,828.1	160	AgileThought	Tampa, FL	1,421.4
111	MasterPlans	Portland, OR	1,797.0	161	SANBlaze Technology	Maynard, MA	1,417.5
112	Fusion Solutions	Addison, TX	1,785.4	162	Pentadyne	Chatsworth, CA	1,415.0
113	Global Business Consulting Services	Edison, NJ	1,768.0	163	CouponCabin	Hoffman Estates, IL	1,414.7
114	Signature Genomic Laboratories	Spokane, WA	1,766.4	164	Ideal Innovations	Arlington, VA	1,413.7
115	Advanced Interactive Sciences	Oldsmar, FL	1,766.4	165	Secure-24	Southfield, MI	1,412.7
116	Sting Surveillance	Henderson, NV	1,754.3	166	Infoscitex	Waltham, MA	1,411.3
117	Embassy International	Dallas, TX	1,725.1	167	Ranon Construction	Deerfield Beach, FL	1,406.4
118	Virpie	Southbury, CT	1,724.0	168	Cymphonix	Sandy, UT	1,398.7
119	Nfinity	Atlanta, GA	1,706.8	169	Infra-Strategy	Chicago, IL	1,398.1
120	TORC Financial	New York, NY	1,705.6	170	Suntiva Executive Consulting	Falls Church, VA	1,391.8
121	Salient Mobility	Atlanta, GA	1,675.9	171	Pariveda Solutions	Dallas, TX	1,391.5
122	Strategic Resources International	Parlin, NJ	1,671.7	172	Survey Analytics	Seattle, WA	1,389.7
123	Epic MedStaff Services	Dallas, TX	1,665.6	173	TGaS Advisors	East Norriton, PA	1,380.3
124	Hillery Holding	Boston, MA	1,662.4	174	CCI	Milwaukee, WI	1,377.3
125	iCrossing	Scottsdale, AZ	1,661.5	175	Acclaim Technical Services	Huntington Beach, CA	1,367.1
126	Ward Media	New York, NY	1,660.6	176	Concerro	San Diego, CA	1,365.5
127	Earth Resources Technology	Annapolis Junction, MD	1,656.8	177	Libsys	Naperville, IL	1,356.0
128	Credit Solutions	Richardson, TX	1,656.1	178	Source Abroad	Inglewood, CA	1,355.3
129	Meridian Partners	Miami Beach, FL	1,653.2	179	elQnetworks	Acton, MA	1,354.7
130	VST Consulting	Iselin, NL	1,634.5	180	Seastone	Provo, UT	1,343.3
131	Synoptek	Santa Ana, CA	1,633.2	181	Mercom	Pawleys Island, SC	1,332.5
132	Bamko	Los Angeles, CA	1,630.8	182	Bridgevine	Vero Beach, FL	1,325.6
133	Electronic Cash Systems	Rancho Santa Margarita, CA	1,621.1	183	BabyEarth	Round Rock, TX	1,319.3
134	BIAS Corp.	Atlanta, GA	1,619.2	184	Smarsh	Portland, OR	1,318.1
135	Intensus Engineering	Cold Spring, NY	1,607.7	185	Business Financial Publishing	Washington, DC	1,303.7
136	Solusia	Atlanta, GA	1,607.6	186	Texas Energy Holdings	Dallas, TX	1,301.8
137	RideSafely.com	Bensalem, PA	1,593.8	187	Energy Services Providers	Pittsfield, MA	1,299.3
138	Implantable Provider Group	Alpharetta, GA	1,583.6	188	Eved Services	Skokie, IL	1,286.4
139	On Time Electric & Air	Austin, TX	1,582.2	189	Catapult Consultants	McLean, VA	1,286.3
140	Synacor	Buffalo, NY	1,572.8	190	Bomgar	Ridgeland, MS	1,282.0
141	OraMetrix	Richardson, TX	1,565.5	191	Centuria	Dulles, VA	1,277.9
142	Oil Chem Technologies	Sugar Land, TX	1,564.5	192	Brian Taylor International	Griffin, GA	1,273.7
143	Bridge Business & Property Brokers	Bohemia, NY	1,562.5	193	eZanga.com	Middletown, DE	1,273.6
144	Calnet	Reston, VA	1,553.2	194	The Centurion Group	Colorado Springs, CO	1,266.7
145	Sensor Technologies	Red Bank, NJ	1,526.2	195	EA Hunter Transportation	Cincinnati, OH	1,244.9
146	NorthStar Systems International	San Francisco, CA	1,519.2	196	Wexley School for Girls	Seattle, WA	1,244.8
147	Splice Communications	San Mateo, CA	1,509.7	197	BSN	Boca Raton, FL	1,244.7
148	MobileDemand	Hiawatha, IA	1,507.2	198	Rigdon Marine	Houston, TX	1,243.3
149	DestinationWeddings.com	Framingham, MA	1,504.8	199	Kirtas Technologies	Victor, NY	1,242.2
150	GWL Construction	Atlanta, GA	1,498.3	200	Integrated Wave Technologies	Fremont, CA	1,241.7

Rank	Company	Headquarters	Sales Growth Increase (%)	Rank	Company	Headquarters	Sales Growth Increase (%)
201	MotionPoint	Coconut Creek, FL	1,231.6	251	Globoforce	Southborough, MA	1,041.0
202	WilDon Solutions	Washington, DC	1,229.4	252	BuilderFusion	Orem, UT	1,036.8
203	Computer System Designers	Oklahoma City, OK	1,223.7	253	Xymogen	Orlando, FL	1,032.1
204	Big Fish Games	Seattle, WA	1,222.6	254	Adayana	Minneapolis, MN	1,030.1
205	VisionIT	Detroit, MI	1,221.7	255	SalesQuest	Lawrence, MA	1,026.9
206	Aviation Network Services	Atlanta, GA	1,211.8	256	MediaWhiz	New York, NY	1,026.5
207	Midwest Recreational Clearinghouse	Cannon Falls, MN	1,209.0	257	Bills.com	San Mateo, CA	1,021.8
208	Reliable Review Services	Boca Raton, FL	1,202.6	258	brass|MEDIA	Corvallis, OR	1,020.1
209	The Siegel Group	Las Vegas, NV	1,202.6	259	Atlanta Pediatric Therapy	Atlanta, GA	1,015.7
210	One Technologies	Dallas, TX	1,189.6	260	MDI Access	Alsip, IL	1,014.2
211	Hydra	Beverly Hills, CA	1,189.1	261	Borrego Solar Systems	Berkeley, CA	1,008.9
212	TEAM Technologies	Cedar Falls, IA	1,188.3	262	Viva Vision	San Diego, CA	1,008.1
213	Zebra Imaging	Austin, TX	1,188.2	263	OneCommand	Cincinnati, OH	1,006.7
214	Gantech	Columbia, MD	1,184.1	264	Fire & Flavor	Bogart, GA	1,005.2
215	Single Digits	Manchester, NH	1,176.4	265	ReStockIt.com	Hollywood, FL	1,002.1
216	The Saxon Group	Sugar Hill, GA	1,174.3	266	Customer Effective	Greenville, SC	1,000.7
217	Summit Tech Consulting	Atlanta, GA	1,150.5	267	Planet Shoes	Waltham, MA	999.0
218	Speridian Technologies	Albuquerque, NM	1,150.3	268	Colarelli Construction	Colorado Springs, CO	996.3
219	Ovation Health & Life Services	Dallas, TX	1,147.0	269	Health Diagnostics	Melville, NY	995.6
220	DSP Clinical Research	Parsippany, NJ	1,143.7	270	Mainline Contracting	Durham, NC	993.8
221	Workforce Solutions Group	Foothill Ranch, CA	1,139.1	271	Intellego	Davie, FL	993.5
222	Outsource Manufacturing	Carlsbad, CA	1,138.3	272	Net Matrix Solutions	Houston, TX	992.8
223	Strada Capital	Irvine, CA	1,131.0	273	CFO Selections	Bellevue, WA	988.2
224	Miles Consulting	Folsom, CA	1,130.8	274	Multivision	Fairfax, VA	988.0
225	Keystone Property Group	Bala Cynwyd, PA	1,128.4	275	Gotham Dream Cars	New York, NY	986.2
226	Infusionsoft	Gilbert, AZ	1,128.1	276	Options University	Boca Raton, FL	985.7
227	Insight Sourcing Group	Norcross, GA	1,125.9	277	CMR Construction & Roofing	Indianapolis, IN	985.5
228	Sahni Enterprises	Norcross, GA	1,125.3	278	R&B Films	New Hyde Park, NY	984.4
229	Advanced Systems Resources	Miami Beach, FL	1,125.0	279	Projectline Services	Seattle, WA	980.4
230	Venture Technologies Group	Philadelphia, PA	1,123.9	280	DMS International	Silver Spring, MD	977.5
231	Bad Boy Enterprises	Natchez, MS	1,123.3	281	Roys & Associates	Los Angeles, CA	976.8
232	RAC Enterprise	Hazleton, PA	1,117.7	282	Market Tech	Scotts Valley, CA	972.7
233	Complete Office	Seattle, WA	1,111.2	283	Canvas On Demand	Raleigh, NC	972.2
234	ERP Analysts	Dublin, OH	1,109.4	284	Millennium Pharmacy Systems	Wexford, PA	967.6
235	Affordable Health Insurance	Arlington Heights, IL	1,100.0	285	MicroTech	Vienna, VA	965.6
236	Insitu	Bingen, WA	1,097.9	286	One Call Now	Troy, OH	962.7
237	String Real Estate Information Services	Washington, DC	1,096.6	287	Sittercity	Chicago, IL	961.9
238	Alphaport	Cleveland, OH	1,094.8	288	Oak Grove Technologies	Raleigh, NC	959.7
239	Achieve Internet	San Diego, CA	1,088.8	289	InTouch Health	Santa Barbara, CA	958.0
240	Buycastings.com	Dayton, OH	1,088.8	290	Troon Construction	Mesa, AZ	955.5
241	Rosenberg Communications	Rockville, MD	1,082.7	291	MindLeaf Technologies	Bedford, MA	954.9
242	Blue Sun Biodiesel	Golden, CO	1,077.7	292	Alpha Card Services	Huntingdon Valley, PA	948.2
243	Wpromote	El Segundo, CA	1,076.4	293	Sunray Enterprise	Atlanta, GA	947.4
244	American Unit	Frisco, TX	1,073.2	294	TalentBurst	Natick, MA	947.0
245	Prime Technology Group	King of Prussia, PA	1,072.7	295	Acronis	Burlington, MA	946.6
246	nGroup	Fort Mill, SC	1,072.5	296	AtLast Fulfillment	Denver, CO	943.9
247	Corporate Call Center	Blue Bell, PA	1,070.6	297	BleekerVigesaa General Contractors	Brighton, CO	943.1
248	K4 Solutions	Falls Church, VA	1,067.3	298	Logistic Dynamics	Amherst, NY	938.6
249	Controlled Air	Kingsport, TN	1,063.2	299	Idleaire Technologies	Knoxville, TN	937.5
250	SRS	Gallatin, TN	1,051.6	300	BlackLine Systems	Calabasas, CA	932.7

The *Inc.* 500 Fastest-Growing Private Companies in America (continued)

Rank	Company	Headquarters	Sales Growth Increase (%)
301	TopCoder	Glastonbury, CT	927.6
302	Pets United	Hazleton, PA	926.0
303	Nxtbook Media	Lancaster, PA	922.4
304	National Trade Supply	Indianapolis, IN	916.4
305	Edible Arrangements International	Wallingford, CT	915.8
306	ESET	San Diego, CA	915.6
307	Adams, Evens & Ross	Kennesaw, GA	914.6
308	SPADAC	McLean, VA	914.5
309	Online Commerce Group	Montgomery, AL	912.9
310	Triton Products	Solon, OH	909.4
311	LinguaLinx	Schenectady, NY	904.1
312	Emma	Nashville, TN	902.2
313	Turning Technologies	Youngstown, OH	900.3
314	PowerPay	Portland, ME	899.0
315	Rimm-Kaufman Group	Charlottesville, VA	897.2
316	Wholesale Interiors	Bensenville, IL	893.0
317	RigNet	Houston, TX	892.4
318	Rapid Product Development Group	San Diego, CA	892.2
319	MacUpdate	Traverse City, MI	891.9
320	Vaco	Brentwood, TN	890.8
321	iFAX Solutions	Philadelphia, PA	890.7
322	Media Two Interactive	Clayton, NC	890.0
323	Innovative Management & Technology Services	Fairmont, WV	888.9
324	Doba	Orem, UT	884.9
325	M. K. Smith Builders	Charleston, SC	884.7
326	GlobalTranz	Phoenix, AZ	884.4
327	Zipcar	Cambridge, MA	883.3
328	Schoolwires	State College, PA	882.8
329	Sensis	Los Angeles, CA	879.8
330	Bandwidth Consulting	Costa Mesa, CA	877.5
331	Eight Crossings	Sacramento, CA	875.2
332	REC Solar	San Luis Obispo, CA	869.1
333	TDC Systems Integration	Smyrna, GA	867.4
334	C&Z Enterprises	Pflugerville, TX	866.6
335	Fusion Holdings	Bountiful, UT	860.9
336	Adlucent	Austin, TX	857.0
337	Norvax	Chicago, IL	856.9
338	C.L. Carson	Austin, TX	856.2
339	eClinicalWorks	Westborough, MA	855.2
340	Luxspan	Campbell, CA	854.7
341	LandAirSea Systems	Cary, IL	854.5
342	ServerPlex Networks	San Mateo, CA	854.4
343	Universal Mind	Westfield, MA	853.9
344	ACI Estate	Doylestown, PA	851.9
345	Sajan	River Falls, WI	848.5
346	Leading Edge Recovery Solutions	Chicago, IL	845.8
347	ClickSpeed	Overland Park, KS	843.0
348	Brian Cork Human Capital	Roswell, GA	842.6
349	Austin GeoModeling	Austin, TX	840.3
350	ScienceLogic	Reston, VA	840.2
351	Platinum Builders	New Carlisle, IN	839.6
352	Cactus Custom Analog Design	Chandler, AZ	838.9
353	Winshuttle	Bothell, WA	838.5
354	Allied PhotoChemical	Kimball, MI	834.3
355	MaxisIT	Edison, NJ	832.8
356	Fishbowl Inventory	Orem, UT	831.6
357	Monoprice	Rancho Cucamonga, CA	829.4
358	ISTS Worldwide	Fremont, CA	825.0
359	Customized Energy Solutions	Philadelphia, PA	824.2
360	Virtue Group	Alpharetta, GA	822.2
361	Cantaloupe Systems	Berkeley, CA	822.0
362	We Buy Houses	South Holland, IL	818.6
363	The Select Group	Raleigh, NC	816.2
364	AspireHR	Plano, TX	815.4
365	Integrated Environmental Restoration Services	Tahoe City, CA	812.9
366	Street Legal Industries	Oak Ridge, TN	810.9
367	H2O Audio	San Diego, CA	810.3
368	Apogee Search	Austin, TX	809.5
369	BlueRadios	Englewood, CO	809.3
370	Steadfast Networks	Chicago, IL	806.9
371	Enjoy Life Foods	Schiller Park, IL	805.4
372	Perazzi Apparel	Tucker, GA	805.2
373	LogiXML	McLean, VA	804.3
374	ACFN Franchised	San Jose, CA	801.3
375	USfalcon	Morrisville, NC	800.5
376	Environmental Services of North America	Dearborn, MI	799.8
377	Hunt Consulting	Laurel, MD	799.7
378	Logisolve Consulting	Minneapolis, MN	799.2
379	ProConcepts International	Colorado Springs, CO	795.6
380	Antennas Direct	Eureka, MO	795.4
381	Crown Asset Management	Duluth, GA	791.4
382	First Western Financial	Denver, CO	791.2
383	Extreme Molding	Watervliet, NY	789.5
384	Guidant Financial Group	Bellevue, WA	788.6
385	Skip Hop	New York, NY	786.2
386	GetMyHomesValue.com	Lancaster, PA	785.7
387	Defender Direct	Indianapolis, IN	785.0
388	HealthDataInsights	Las Vegas, NV	782.9
389	Ethertronics	San Diego, CA	780.9
390	The Great Gourmet	Federalsburg, MD	780.5
391	MicroAgility	Plainsboro, NJ	779.4
392	Heritage Web Solutions	Provo, UT	778.2
393	Neudesic	Irvine, CA	778.2
394	Krozak Information Technologies	Silver Spring, MD	777.9
395	Accelera Solutions	Falls Church, VA	777.7
396	Energy Recovery	San Leandro, CA	775.1
397	The Research Associates	New York, NY	771.9
398	JH Global Services	Greenville, SC	771.6
399	Hire Methods	Jacksonville, FL	771.4
400	Slone Partners	Miami Beach, FL	770.5

Rank	Company	Headquarters	Sales Growth Increase (%)	Rank	Company	Headquarters	Sales Growth Increase (%)
401	Application Development Resources	Alpharetta, GA	768.7	451	BEC Electric	Huntington Beach, CA	700.3
402	Verisae	Minneapolis, MN	768.5	452	Bluefish Wireless Management	Indianapolis, IN	698.2
403	Global Analytics Corporation	Waterbury, CT	768.3	453	Passageways	West Lafayette, IN	697.1
404	SyApps	Herndon, VA	766.4	454	Talyst	Bellevue, WA	696.6
405	Allcare Dental Management	Buffalo, NY	764.2	455	Select Engineering	Tulsa, OK	696.5
406	AuctionDrop	Menlo Park, CA	763.7	456	America's Incredible Pizza Company	Springfield, MO	693.1
407	Ponds & Sons Construction	Lodge, SC	760.0	457	MIG & Co.	New York, NY	691.5
408	RMCN Credit Services	McKinney, TX	759.6	458	TaxBreak	Gadsden, AL	689.0
409	Surf Cowboy	Vancouver, WA	758.6	459	HemCon Medical Technologies	Portland, OR	688.4
410	PCN Strategies	Washington, DC	757.5	460	3K Technologies	Santa Clara, CA	686.6
411	GDI	Oakbrook Terrace, IL	757.1	461	ProfitFuel	Austin, TX	683.0
412	Chesapeake Solar	Jessup, MD	754.1	462	Liberty Power	Fort Lauderdale, FL	682.6
413	PriceSpective	Blue Bell, PA	753.6	463	Texzon Utilities	Waxahachie, TX	682.6
414	Spinnaker	Denver, CO	752.5	464	Artemis Woman	Wilton, CT	679.7
415	Kaleidescape	Sunnyvale, CA	747.6	465	Adaequare	Centerville, OH	679.5
416	T Coombs and Associates	Springfield, VA	746.2	466	Elontec	Phoenix, AZ	676.4
417	APG	Reston, VA	743.9	467	Synechron	Piscataway, NJ	675.2
418	Abbott's Custom Printing	Las Vegas, NV	743.4	468	Packet Digital	Fargo, ND	673.9
419	XCEL Solutions	Matawan, NJ	743.1	469	Ascendant Technology	Austin, TX	669.5
420	AtTask	Orem, UT	740.4	470	Metrofuser	Roselle, NJ	669.4
421	iGoDigital	Indianapolis, IN	738.5	471	BackOffice Associates	South Harwich, MA	669.0
422	Social Smoke	Arlington, TX	737.6	472	Medical Solutions	Omaha, NE	667.8
423	Trancos	Redwood City, CA	737.4	473	Bradley Excavating	Colorado Springs, CO	666.1
424	Bay Microsystems	San Jose, CA	737.1	474	Stokes Dock	Osage Beach, MO	664.3
425	Clearlink	Salt Lake City, UT	737.0	475	American Solar Electric	Scottsdale, AZ	662.0
426	Ultimo Software Solutions	San Jose, CA	737.0	476	Red F	Charlotte, NC	660.2
427	Contract Office Installations	Posen, IL	735.2	477	Presidium Learning	Reston, VA	658.9
428	Xenosoft Technologies	Dallas, TX	734.8	478	Chicagoland Transportation Solutions	Hoffman Estates, IL	654.4
429	Mindshare Technologies	Salt Lake City, UT	733.7	479	Custom HBC Corporation	Waconia, MN	653.9
430	Malcap Mortgage	Brentwood, TN	733.4	480	CorePartners	Frederick, MD	650.0
431	MedValue	Oak Brook, IL	732.9	481	Engenuity Financial	Sandy, UT	649.5
432	Prime Property Investors	Northbrook, IL	732.3	482	Strike Construction	Spring, TX	649.5
433	Southern Light	Mobile, AL	732.0	483	LightWedge	Nantucket, MA	649.4
434	Intelligent Logistics	Round Rock, TX	730.9	484	Green Beans Coffee	Larkspur, CA	644.4
435	Ogando Associates	Fort Lauderdale, FL	730.7	485	Quintech Security Consultants	Summerville, SC	644.0
436	Piston Automotive	Redford, MI	730.4	486	Assured Information Security	Rome, NY	643.5
437	DOMA Technologies	Virginia Beach, VA	727.6	487	Single Path	Lombard, IL	642.5
438	A-T Solutions	Fredericksburg, VA	725.9	488	NextAce	Anaheim, CA	642.4
439	5Linx Enterprises	Rochester, NY	724.7	489	Drain Doctors	Tampa, FL	641.7
440	Pop Labs	Houston, TX	724.4	490	ICSN	Riverside, CA	641.3
441	S4	Burlington, MA	723.3	491	NETE Solutions	McLean, VA	639.1
442	Queen Anne Window & Door	Seattle, WA	722.8	492	CSN Stores	Boston, MA	639.1
443	Netlink	Madison Heights, MI	720.5	493	Clovis	Bethesda, MD	637.4
444	Working Person's Store	Lakeville, IN	717.3	494	iSeatz.com	New Orleans, LA	636.3
445	Urbancode	Cleveland, OH	715.6	495	Talent Connections	Roswell, GA	634.9
446	Ceteris	Chicago, IL	705.0	496	JSMN International	Jersey City, NJ	633.4
447	Vinculums	Costa Mesa, CA	704.7	497	MurTech Consulting	Independence, OH	632.0
448	Bandwidth.com	Cary, NC	703.4	498	MIR3	San Diego, CA	625.8
449	Decypher Technologies	San Antonio, TX	700.6	499	Absorbent, Ink.	Lawrence, KS	625.8
450	Specialty Fertilizer Products	Belton, MO	700.5	500	Samuel Engineering	Greenwood Village, CO	625.0

The *Forbes* Largest Private Companies in the US

Rank	Company	Sales ($ mil.)	Rank	Company	Sales ($ mil.)	Rank	Company	Sales ($ mil.)
1	Cargill	110,630	51	Hexion Specialty Chemicals	5,810	101	Consolidated Electrical Distributors	3,900
2	Koch Industries	98,000	52	Freescale Semiconductor	5,720	102	Manor Care	3,890
3	Chrysler	59,700	53	Gulf States Toyota	5,700	103	Michaels Stores	3,860
4	GMAC Financial Services	31,490	54	Allegis Group	5,600	104	Belk	3,830
5	PricewaterhouseCoopers	28,190	55	Keystone Foods	5,580	105	Roundy's Supermarkets	3,800
6	Mars	27,400	56	RaceTrac Petroleum	5,520	106	Stater Bros.	3,740
7	Bechtel	27,000	57	MBM	5,500	107	Booz Allen Hamilton	3,700
8	HCA	26,860	58	Guardian Industries	5,470	108	Brightstar	3,660
9	Ernst & Young	24,520	59	Bloomberg	5,400	109	Walsh Group	3,600
10	Publix Super Markets	23,190	60	McKinsey & Co.	5,330	110	Tishman Construction	3,560
11	US Foodservice	20,160	61	International Automotive Components	5,310	111	HT Hackney	3,550
12	C&S Wholesale Grocers	19,450	62	Unisource Worldwide	5,300	112	VWR Funding	3,540
13	H.E. Butt Grocery	15,500	63	Graybar Electric	5,260	113	Berry Plastics	3,540
14	Fidelity Investments	14,900	64	Kohler	5,230	114	WinCo Foods	3,520
15	Cox Enterprises	14,590	65	Avaya	5,100	115	Eby-Brown	3,460
16	Flying J	14,320	66	Mansfield Oil	5,100	116	Raley's	3,450
17	Toys "R" Us	13,790	67	Save Mart Supermarkets	5,100	117	InterTech Group	3,450
18	Meijer	13,650	68	Tribune Company	5,060	118	Ashley Furniture Industries	3,430
19	Platinum Equity	13,500	69	Wawa	5,050	119	Burlington Coat Factory	3,420
20	Aramark	13,200	70	Pro-Build Holdings	5,000	120	Schneider National	3,400
21	Enterprise Rent-A-Car	13,100	71	SunGard Data Systems	4,980	121	ServiceMaster	3,360
22	TransMontaigne	12,250	72	Southwire	4,980	122	Structure Tone	3,330
23	JM Family Enterprises	12,200	73	Kinray	4,800	123	Golden State Foods	3,300
24	Tenaska Energy	11,600	74	NewPage	4,660	124	Schwan Food	3,300
25	Love's Travel Stops	11,460	75	OSI Group	4,620	125	Swift Transportation	3,270
26	Reyes Holdings	11,200	76	DeBruce Grain	4,620	126	Black & Veatch	3,200
27	Harrah's Entertainment	10,830	77	Neiman Marcus Group	4,600	127	International Data Group	3,200
28	Capital Group Cos.	9,900	78	Charmer Sunbelt Group	4,600	128	Jeld-Wen	3,160
29	Dollar General	9,500	79	Kingston Technology Company	4,500	129	Glazer's Wholesale Drug	3,150
30	Performance Food Group	9,480	80	Wegmans Food Markets	4,500	130	E&J Gallo Winery	3,150
31	S.C. Johnson & Son	8,750	81	Ergon	4,490	131	Golub	3,140
32	Transammonia	8,340	82	Sheetz	4,410	132	84 Lumber	3,100
33	Southern Wine & Spirits	8,300	83	J.R. Simplot	4,400	133	LPL Investment Holdings	3,100
34	CDW	8,150	84	Hearst	4,380	134	Boise Cascade	3,080
35	Cumberland Farms	8,100	85	CH2M Hill Cos.	4,380	135	JohnsonDiversey	3,040
36	Hilton Hotels	8,090	86	Levi Strauss & Co.	4,360	136	Andersen	3,000
37	QuikTrip	8,090	87	Carlson Cos.	4,360	137	Central National-Gottesman	3,000
38	First Data	8,050	88	Republic National Distributing	4,320	138	Sabre Holdings	3,000
39	Giant Eagle	8,020	89	Perdue	4,300	139	US Oncology	3,000
40	Energy Future Holdings	7,990	90	Scoular	4,300	140	Sports Authority	2,980
41	Advance Publications	7,970	91	Washington Cos.	4,300	141	Gilbane	2,970
42	Murdock Holding Company	7,900	92	Clark Enterprises	4,220	142	Alex Lee	2,920
43	Menard	7,800	93	Hallmark Cards	4,170	143	McCarthy Building Cos.	2,900
44	Alticor	7,100	94	Edward Jones	4,150	144	Sammons Enterprises	2,900
45	Sinclair Oil	7,000	95	OSI Restaurant Partners	4,150	145	Schreiber Foods	2,900
46	Gordon Food Service	6,700	96	Global Hyatt	4,000	146	Parsons	2,900
47	Aleris International	6,600	97	Renco Group	4,000	147	General Parts	2,870
48	Hy-Vee	6,270	98	Whiting-Turner Contracting	3,970	148	Medline Industries	2,830
49	Peter Kiewit Sons'	6,240	99	McJunkin Red Man	3,950	149	Cooper-Standard Automotive	2,810
50	Colonial Group	6,200	100	Red Apple Group	3,950	150	Dot Foods	2,810

SOURCE: *FORBES*, NOVEMBER 26, 2008

Rank	Company	Sales ($ mil.)	Rank	Company	Sales ($ mil.)	Rank	Company	Sales ($ mil.)
151	Amsted Industries	2,800	201	Houchens Industries	2,290	251	Warren Equities	1,940
152	Vanguard Health Systems	2,790	202	Milliken & Co.	2,270	252	Goodman Manufacturing	1,930
153	Reader's Digest Association	2,790	203	J.F. Shea	2,260	253	Frank Consolidated Enterprises	1,930
154	Grocers Supply	2,720	204	Baker & Taylor	2,260	254	Barnes & Noble College Booksellers	1,930
155	Flex-N-Gate	2,720	205	ShopKo Stores	2,250	255	J. D. Heiskell & Co.	1,920
156	Quintiles Transnational	2,700	206	J M Smith	2,220	256	Apex Oil	1,910
157	Services Group of America	2,700	207	Anderson Cos.	2,210	257	D&H Distributing	1,900
158	Bass Pro Shops	2,650	208	Brookshire Grocery	2,200	258	Newegg Inc.	1,900
159	J.E. Dunn Construction Group	2,630	209	UniGroup	2,200	259	Parsons Brinckerhoff	1,900
160	ABC Supply	2,630	210	Young's Market	2,200	260	Conair	1,900
161	Bi-Lo Holdings	2,620	211	U.S. Oil	2,190	261	Drummond	1,890
162	Leprino Foods	2,620	212	Bose	2,180	262	American Tire Distributors Holdings	1,880
163	Rich Products	2,600	213	Skadden, Arps	2,170	263	Shamrock Foods	1,860
164	Hensel Phelps Construction	2,520	214	Heico Cos.	2,170	264	Metals USA	1,860
165	Follett	2,520	215	Bashas'	2,160	265	Rexnord	1,850
166	AMC Entertainment	2,500	216	SAS Institute	2,150	266	Electro-Motive Diesel	1,830
167	Bausch & Lomb	2,500	217	Affinia Group	2,140	267	Merit Energy	1,830
168	Demoulas Super Markets	2,500	218	M. A. Mortenson	2,140	268	Catalent Pharma Solutions	1,830
169	Quality King Distributors	2,500	219	Life Care Centers of America	2,120	269	Crown Equipment	1,830
170	Schnuck Markets	2,500	220	Hunt Consolidated/Hunt Oil	2,120	270	Guthy-Renker	1,800
171	Tower Automotive	2,500	221	Solo Cup	2,110	271	ICC Industries	1,800
172	Truman Arnold Cos.	2,500	222	CompuCom Systems	2,100	272	Koch Foods	1,800
173	World Wide Technology	2,500	223	J.M. Huber	2,100	273	Rooney Holdings	1,800
174	Graham Packaging Holdings	2,490	224	TIC Holdings	2,100	274	Arctic Slope Regional	1,780
175	Golden Living	2,490	225	Zachry Construction	2,100	275	Great Lakes Cheese	1,780
176	Travelport	2,490	226	Ingram Industries	2,100	276	Hobby Lobby Stores	1,770
177	Ben E. Keith	2,460	227	Fagen	2,080	277	Soave Enterprises	1,770
178	O'Neal Steel	2,440	228	Univision Communications	2,070	278	Red Chamber Group	1,760
179	WinWholesale	2,430	229	Genesis HealthCare	2,070	279	Rooms To Go	1,750
180	W.L. Gore & Associates	2,400	230	Iasis Healthcare	2,070	280	Austin Industries	1,750
181	Maines Paper & Food Service	2,400	231	Academy Sports & Outdoors	2,060	281	Columbia Sussex	1,730
182	Mary Kay	2,400	232	Quad/Graphics	2,050	282	Reynolds and Reynolds	1,730
183	Petco Animal Supplies	2,400	233	Wilbur-Ellis	2,010	283	Kum & Go	1,720
184	Rosen's Diversified	2,400	234	Dresser	2,010	284	Bradco Supply	1,700
185	G-I Holdings	2,380	235	Brasfield & Gorrie	2,010	285	McWane	1,700
186	Biomet	2,380	236	Latham & Watkins	2,010	286	Taylor	1,700
187	NTK Holdings	2,370	237	Foster Farms	2,000	287	Vertis	1,700
188	Asplundh Tree Expert	2,370	238	Holiday Cos.	2,000	288	Duane Reade	1,690
189	Fry's Electronics	2,350	239	Hunt Construction Group	2,000	289	Education Management	1,680
190	West Corp.	2,350	240	Ma Labs	2,000	290	Continental Grain	1,680
191	Software House Intl.	2,330	241	Plastipak Holdings	2,000	291	K-VA-T Food Stores	1,660
192	Delaware North Cos.	2,310	242	Sun Products	2,000	292	Ardent Health Services	1,650
193	Discount Tire	2,310	243	Select Medical	1,990	293	Tang Industries	1,650
194	Boston Consulting Group	2,300	244	Yates Cos.	1,980	294	Carpenter	1,650
195	Ebsco Industries	2,300	245	Day & Zimmermann	1,980	295	Ceridian	1,650
196	Guitar Center	2,300	246	Roll International	1,980	296	Bain & Co.	1,640
197	HP Hood	2,300	247	Vizio	1,970	297	Vought Aircraft Industries	1,630
198	Infor	2,300	248	Sequa	1,960	298	Crowley Maritime	1,620
199	Oxbow	2,300	249	Swinerton	1,960	299	L.L. Bean	1,620
200	Smart & Final	2,300	250	Thorntons	1,940	300	Knowledge Learning	1,620

The *Forbes* Largest Private Companies in the US (continued)

Rank	Company	Sales ($ mil.)
301	The Brock Group	1,620
302	Weitz	1,610
303	SSA Marine	1,610
304	Camac International	1,600
305	Haworth	1,600
306	International Specialty Products	1,600
307	ViewSonic	1,600
308	HealthMarkets	1,600
309	KAR Holdings	1,590
310	CC Industries	1,590
311	Sigma Plastics Group	1,580
312	Towers Perrin	1,570
313	Suffolk Construction	1,570
314	Maritz	1,560
315	GNC	1,550
316	Dart Container	1,540
317	Ilitch Holdings	1,520
318	Turner Industries Group	1,520
319	Pinnacle Foods	1,510
320	Claire's Stores	1,510
321	Bartlett & Co.	1,510
322	U.S. Xpress Enterprises	1,510
323	Marsh Supermarkets	1,500
324	Cook Group	1,500
325	Interstate Battery System	1,500
326	The Kraft Group	1,500
327	Pella	1,500
328	Les Schwab Tire Centers	1,480
329	Dunavant Enterprises	1,480
330	Brand Energy	1,480
331	DPR Construction	1,470
332	Michael Foods	1,470
333	Berwind	1,470
334	Buffets	1,460
335	Personal Communications Devices	1,450
336	Station Casinos	1,450
337	Jones Day	1,440
338	Gate Petroleum	1,440
339	Laureate Education	1,420
340	Barton Malow	1,400
341	Micro Electronics	1,400
342	Landmark Media Group	1,400
343	Estes Express Lines	1,400
344	Sidley Austin	1,390
345	Freeman	1,380
346	White & Case	1,370
347	Dawn Food Products	1,370
348	Wirtz	1,370
349	MediaNews Group	1,360
350	Printpack	1,360

Rank	Company	Sales ($ mil.)
351	API Group	1,350
352	New Balance Athletic Shoe	1,350
353	David Weekley Homes	1,340
354	Honickman Affiliates	1,330
355	Big Y Foods	1,330
356	Affinion Group	1,320
357	GSC Enterprises	1,320
358	Kirkland & Ellis	1,310
359	Foodarama Supermarkets	1,310
360	Bozzuto's	1,300
361	Brookshire Brothers	1,300
362	Dean Health System	1,300
363	FHC Health Systems	1,300
364	MWH	1,300
365	Schottenstein Stores	1,300
366	Swagelok	1,300
367	Euramax International	1,300
368	The Flintco Companies	1,290
369	P.C. Richard & Son	1,290
370	NCO Group	1,290
371	24 Hour Fitness Worldwide	1,280
372	Ash Grove Cement	1,270
373	SavaSeniorCare	1,270
374	Visant	1,270
375	Beall's	1,270
376	Forever 21	1,260
377	Goya Foods	1,260
378	Amscan Holdings	1,250
379	Pepper Construction Group	1,240
380	TeamHealth	1,230
381	Holder Construction	1,230
382	Associated Materials	1,200
383	Advanced Drainage Systems	1,200
384	ASI	1,200
385	Barry-Wehmiller Companies	1,200
386	Deseret Management	1,200
387	Henkels & McCoy	1,200
388	Keane	1,200
389	Topa Equities	1,200
390	Warren Equipment	1,200
391	Weil, Gotshal & Manges	1,200
392	Nypro	1,190
393	MTD Products	1,190
394	Hoffman	1,190
395	Mayer Brown	1,180
396	Ritz Camera Centers	1,180
397	Sherwood Food Distributors	1,180
398	Alsco	1,160
399	Gould Paper	1,160
400	Alberici	1,150

Rank	Company	Sales ($ mil.)
401	Mountaire Farms	1,150
402	Williamson-Dickie Manufacturing	1,150
403	A. G. Spanos Cos.	1,130
404	Remy International	1,130
405	Marc Glassman	1,130
406	Simmons Bedding	1,130
407	Central Parking	1,120
408	Goss International	1,110
409	Indalex	1,110
410	William Lyon Homes	1,110
411	Blue Tee	1,100
412	Beaulieu of America Group	1,100
413	Booz & Company	1,100
414	Hilmar Cheese	1,100
415	National Gypsum	1,100
416	Pliant	1,100
417	Extended Stay Hotels	1,090
418	McKee Foods	1,090
419	Crete Carrier	1,080
420	Safety-Kleen Systems	1,070
421	Sutherland Lumber	1,070
422	Orgill	1,070
423	Inserra Supermarkets	1,060
424	Lifetouch	1,050
425	North Pacific Group	1,040
426	Stewart's Shops	1,040
427	Ryan Companies	1,040
428	Morgan Lewis & Bockius	1,030
429	Newark Group	1,030
430	BrandsMart USA	1,030
431	Coastal Pacific Food Distributors	1,020
432	Pittsburgh Glass Works	1,010
433	Sierra Pacific Industries	1,010
434	ValleyCrest Landscape Cos.	1,010
435	Crescent Electric Supply	1,000
436	Davisco Foods International	1,000
437	Kellwood	1,000
438	Key Safety Systems	1,000
439	MGA Entertainment	1,000
440	Walbridge Aldinger	1,000
441	Wells' Dairy	1,000

Top 20 Universities

Ranked by composite score, including such factors as graduation and retention rates, faculty resources, and student-to-faculty ratio.

SOURCE: *U.S. NEWS AND WORLD REPORT*, AUGUST 21, 2008

Top 20 US Foundations

Rank	Name	State	Assets ($ mil.)
1	Bill & Melinda Gates Foundation	WA	38,921.0
2	The Ford Foundation	NY	13,798.8
3	J. Paul Getty Trust	CA	10,133.4
4	The Robert Wood Johnson Foundation	NJ	10,102.9
5	The William and Flora Hewlett Foundation	CA	9,284.9
6	W. K. Kellogg Foundation	MI	8,403.0
7	Lilly Endowment Inc.	IN	7,734.9
8	The David and Lucile Packard Foundation	CA	6,594.5
9	The Andrew W. Mellon Foundation	NY	6,539.9
10	Gordon and Betty Moore Foundation	CA	6,409.3
11	John D. and Catherine T. MacArthur Foundation	IL	6,178.2
12	The California Endowment	CA	4,773.8
13	The Rockefeller Foundation	NY	3,810.3
14	The Kresge Foundation	MI	3,329.9
15	The Annie E. Casey Foundation	MD	3,326.1
16	The Starr Foundation	NY	3,300.6
17	Tulsa Community Foundation	OK	3,136.7
18	Carnegie Corporation of New York	NY	3,073.8
19	The Duke Endowment	NC	2,981.7
20	Robert W. Woodruff Foundation, Inc.	GA	2,716.0

SOURCE: THE FOUNDATION CENTER (WWW.FOUNDATIONCENTER.ORG), SEPTEMBER 11, 2008

Top 20 US Law Firms

Rank	Law Firm	2007 Gross Revenue ($ mil.)
1	Skadden, Arps, Slate, Meagher & Flom	2,170.0
2	Latham & Watkins	2,005.5
3	Baker & McKenzie	2,188.0
4	Jones Day	1,441.0
5	Sidley Austin	1,386.0
6	White & Case	1,373.0
7	Kirkland & Ellis	1,310.0
8	Greenberg Traurig	1,200.0
9	Mayer Brown	1,183.0
10	Weil, Gotshal & Manges	1,175.0
11	DLA Piper	1,134.5
12	Morgan, Lewis & Bockius	1,033.0
13	Sullivan & Cromwell	985.0
14	McDermott Will & Emery	978.0
15	Paul, Hastings, Janofsky & Walker	975.0
16	Simpson Thacher & Bartlett	966.0
17	Wilmer Cutler Pickering Hale and Dorr	944.0
18	O'Melveny & Myers	934.0
19	Shearman & Sterling	921.0
20	Gibson, Dunn & Crutcher	907.5

SOURCE: *AMERICAN LAWYER*, MAY 1, 2008

Top 20 Tax & Accounting Firms by US Revenue

Rank	Firm	Headquarters	2007 US Revenue ($ mil.)
1	Deloitte & Touche	New York	9,850.0
2	Ernst & Young	New York	7,561.0
3	PricewaterhouseCoopers	New York	7,463.8
4	KPMG	New York	5,357.0
5	RSM/McGladrey & Pullen	Bloomington, MN	1,389.3
6	Grant Thornton	Chicago	1,074.6
7	BDO Seidman	Chicago	589.0
8	CBiz/Mayer Hoffman McCann	Cleveland	500.7
9	Crowe Group	Oak Brook Terrace, IL	457.4
10	BKD	Springfield, MO	322.0
11	Moss Adams	Seattle	317.0
12	UHY Advisors	Chicago	277.3
13	Plante & Moran	Southfield, MI	271.2
14	Clifton Gunderson	Peoria, IL	228.0
15	J.H. Cohn	Roseland, NJ	215.0
16	Virchow Krause & Co.	Madison, WI	202.1
17	Reznick Group	Bethesda, MD	197.4
18	Dixon Hughes	High Point, NC	178.0
19	LarsonAllen	Minneapolis	173.0
20	Rothstein, Kass & Co.	Roseland, NJ	131.5

SOURCE: *ACCOUNTING TODAY*, APRIL 11, 2008

Hoover's Handbook of

Private Companies

The Companies

24 Hour Fitness

If you're holding too much weight, 24 Hour Fitness Worldwide has the solution. It owns and operates more than 400 fitness centers that offer aerobic, cardiovascular, and weight lifting activities to the company's more than 3 million members. Some facilities also feature squash, racquetball, and basketball courts; swimming pools; steam and sauna rooms; tanning rooms; and whirlpools. It is one of the only fitness chains open 24 hours a day. The centers are located in more than 15 states in the US, as well as throughout Asia. Forstmann Little & Co owns 24 Hour Fitness.

The chain has a history of linking with sports stars to open co-branded clubs such as 24 Hour Fitness — Lance Armstrong and 24 Hour Fitness — Derek Jeter. In addition, the company is a partner of the NBC reality TV show *The Biggest Loser*.

The firm was founded in 1983 by chairman Mark Mastrov. Financier Theodore J. Forstmann acquired the company for $1.6 billion in 2005.

EXECUTIVES

CEO: Carl C. Liebert III
President, Asia: Colin Heggie
EVP and CFO: Jeffrey N. (Jeff) Boyer, age 50
Chief Marketing Officer: Tony Wells
Divisional VP Operations: Chris Smith
VP Fitness Operations: Derek Gallup
Auditors: Deloitte & Touche

LOCATIONS

HQ: 24 Hour Fitness Worldwide, Inc.
12647 Alcosta Blvd., 5th Fl., San Ramon, CA 94583
Phone: 925-543-3100   **Fax:** 925-543-3200
Web: www.24hourfitness.com

Selected Club Locations
Asia
  Hong Kong
  Malaysia
  Singapore
  Taiwan
US
  Arizona
  California
  Colorado
  Florida
  Hawaii
  Kansas
  Missouri
  Nebraska
  New Jersey
  Nevada
  New York
  Oregon
  Tennessee
  Texas
  Utah
  Washington

PRODUCTS/OPERATIONS

Selected Amenities
Baby sitting
Basketball courts
Cardio equipment
Group exercise classes
Personal trainers
Swimming pools
Weight training equipment

Selected Co-branded Clubs
Andre Agassi Signature Clubs
Lance Armstrong Signature clubs
Magic Johnson Signature Clubs
Shaquille O'Neal Signature Clubs

COMPETITORS

Bally Total Fitness	Lady of America
Crunch Fitness	Physical Property Holdings
Curves International	The Sports Club
Equinox Holdings	World Gym
Gold's Gym	YMCA
Jazzercise	YWCA

HISTORICAL FINANCIALS
Company Type: Private

Income Statement   FYE: December 31

	REVENUE ($ mil.)	NET INCOME ($ mil.)	NET PROFIT MARGIN	EMPLOYEES
12/07	1,280	—	—	21,410
12/06	1,840	—	—	11,000
12/05	1,077	—	—	19,660
12/04	1,004	—	—	—
12/03	1,000	—	—	16,000
Annual Growth	**6.4%**	**—**	**—**	**7.6%**

Revenue History

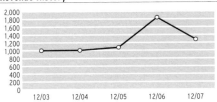

84 Lumber

With its utilitarian stores (most don't have heat or air conditioning), 84 Lumber has built itself up to be a leading low-cost provider of lumber and building materials and services. Through some 380 stores in more than 35 states the company, which is the nation's largest privately held building-materials supplier, sells lumber, siding, drywall, windows, and other supplies, as well as kits to make barns, play sets, decks, and even homes. Its 84 Components subsidiary operates about a dozen manufacturing plants that make floor and roof trusses and wall panels. Its stores are mainly in the East, Southeast, and Midwest; the firm also sells products internationally. CEO Joseph Hardy Sr. founded 84 Lumber in 1956.

The slump in the new home construction market has hit 84 Lumber like a two-by-four to the head. To date in 2008 the building supplies retailer has closed and consolidated more than 50 stores across the US, including some in core markets. It has also mothballed several of its component plants until market conditions improve. The downturn has preempted plans to open 125 new stores by the end of 2009, thereby extending its reach to more than 40 states.

Although 84 Lumber was founded to serve professionals, the retailer had attempted to attract more do-it-yourself (DIY) consumers before refocusing its efforts on professional builders and

remodelers (about 95% of sales). As a result, it is particularly vulnerable to the downturn in housing starts. To carry it through the housing slump, the company has negotiated two five-year financing packages totaling $590 million.

While the professional market is less profitable and more cyclic than the DIY segment, it has the advantage of being less crowded with big-box competitors, such as The Home Depot and Lowe's.

The company has also expanded to provide professional services, including financing, risk insurance, and travel through 84 Travel. Its 84 Lumber Installed Sales Services business provides installation services for windows, doors, and framing and roofing jobs.

To foster growth and better manage the company, the building materials retailer has split into two divisions (northeastern and southeastern) and added a Midwest region.

HISTORY

In 1956 Joseph Hardy Sr. opened the first 84 Lumber store in Eighty Four, Pennsylvania, a town near Pittsburgh. Hardy epitomized the bare-bones approach, keeping a tight rein on his company and paying cash for new building sites.

The strategy was successful, and for the next two decades 84 Lumber prospered, growing steadily to more than 350 stores in the early 1980s. But the 1980s brought trouble, not only for 84 Lumber but also within the Hardy family. Paul Hardy, the second-eldest son, left the company after continued sparring with Hardy Sr. Another son, Joe Hardy Jr., seemed to be his father's handpicked successor: He had worked for 84 Lumber since 1967, rising to the level of COO. However, Joe Jr. and Joe Sr. clashed and under pressure from his father, Joe Jr. resigned in 1988.

Joe Sr. also underwent a transformation during this time, opening his once-tight purse strings to buy himself an honorary English title — lord of the manor of Henley-in-Arden — for about $170,000. In 1987 he paid $3.1 million to purchase a retreat in southwestern Pennsylvania, the Nemacolin Woodlands. He placed the renovation of the resort (at the cost of some $100 million) in the hands of his daughter Maggie, who was in her early twenties at the time.

While Hardy was transforming, so was 84 Lumber. The company started moving away from its traditional approach in an attempt to gain a piece of the budding yuppie market. This approach, along with an ill-timed expansion, led to a loss of customers and falling profits. Earnings fell from $52 million in 1987 to $22 million in 1989.

84 Lumber started to right itself in 1991. Hardy transferred stock to Maggie, his heir apparent. While running luxury resort Nemacolin Woodlands, Maggie strove to emulate her father's business style, including obscenity-laced staff meetings. 84 Lumber shut stores and returned to its basic operating scheme as a low-cost provider of lumber in small towns. The company also added do-it-yourself (DIY) building kits for kitchens and baths that year, and it expanded that DIY concept a year later in 1992, with home building kits.

Under new president Maggie, 84 Lumber's sales topped the $1 billion mark in 1993 and the company refocused on its professional contractor customers. The company first shipped its building materials internationally in 1996 (to New Zealand) and added customers in China, South Korea, Switzerland, and Australia in the late 1990s.

In 1997 84 Lumber opened Maggie's Building Solutions Showroom, a 7,500-sq.-ft. remodeling center featuring upscale home products. By that year 84 Lumber was the US's largest dealer of building supplies to professional contractors.

In a further effort to attract contractors' business, 84 Lumber introduced a builder financing program in 1999 and began converting some of its stores to an 84-Plus store format, in which its traditional lumberyard setup is matched with a 10,000-sq.-ft. hardware store.

In an effort to reach more professionals, the firm increased outside sales staff by 25% in 2000.

The next year the company bought 15 stores from Payless Cashways, which went out of business, a move that extended 84 Lumber's operations to Oklahoma, Nevada, and Nebraska.

The company added two red-letter dates to its company history in 2002. On April 3 of that year, 84 Lumber opened 20 new stores throughout the US, increasing its store count by 5%. Thanks in part to added revenue from those stores, on December 7, 2002, company cash registers went past the $2 billion mark in sales for the year.

In June 2004 84 Lumber opened a distribution center in Auburn, New York. The facility supplies vinyl siding and roofing materials to stores in Rochester and Syracuse.

To help fund its future growth, in May 2007 the company completed a $200 million sale/lease-back deal with Spirit Finance Corporation covering 53 stores and a manufacturing facility. Also in May 84 Lumber acquired two Denver-area companies (JAC & Co. and Front Range Panel).

Between January and April 2008, the building supplies retailer closed or consolidated more than 50 stores across the US.

EXECUTIVES

CEO: Joseph A. Hardy Sr.
President: Maggie Hardy Magerko
CFO: Dan Wallach
EVP, Store Operations: Frank Cicero
EVP: Mark Garboski
SVP, National Sales: Brian Sento
VP, Marketing and Corporate Communications:
 Jeff Nobers
VP, Human Resources: Jim Guest
VP, Installed Sales: Mike McCrobie
VP, Store Operations, Northeast Division: Ed McKenzie
Director Purchasing: Mitch Wagner
Director Diversity and Inclusion: Angeles Valenciano
Designer: Allen Robinson
Manager, Public Relations: Robyn Hall
Manager, Operations: Kristen Jansanti

LOCATIONS

HQ: 84 Lumber Company
 1019 Rte. 519, Eighty Four, PA 15330
Phone: 724-228-8820   **Fax:** 724-228-8058
Web: www.84lumber.com

PRODUCTS/OPERATIONS

Selected Products

Doors	Roofing
Drywall	Room additions
Flooring	Siding
Insulation	Skylights
Lumber	Trim
Plywood	Trusses
Project kits	Ventilation
Barns	Windows
Decks and play sets	
Garages	
Houses	
Kitchens	
Play sets	

COMPETITORS

Ace Hardware
Builders FirstSource
Building Materials Holding
Carter Lumber
Do it Best
Foxworth-Galbraith Lumber
Futter Lumber
Grossman's
HD Supply
Lowe's
McCoy Corp.
Menard
Stock Building Supply
Sutherland Lumber
True Value

HISTORICAL FINANCIALS
Company Type: Private

Income Statement   FYE: First Sunday following December 31

	REVENUE ($ mil.)	NET INCOME ($ mil.)	NET PROFIT MARGIN	EMPLOYEES
12/07	3,100	—	—	7,000
12/06	3,920	—	—	9,500
12/05	4,000	—	—	10,500
12/04	3,460	—	—	8,000
12/03	2,538	—	—	6,500
Annual Growth	5.1%	—	—	1.9%

Revenue History

A&E Networks

You might say this company is trying to give TV viewers a new perspective on things. A&E Television Networks owns and operates a leading portfolio of cable television channels, including its flagship A&E and History networks. Reaching more than 95 million US homes, A&E offers a mix of reality-based programming, investigative shows, and documentaries. The History channel offers non-fiction programming focused on culture, military history, and science. Other niche interest channels include Bio and History International. A&E's networks reach more than 235 million subscribers in 125 countries. The company is a joint venture between Hearst (37.5%), Disney ABC Cable (37.5%), and NBC Universal Cable (25%).

A&E Television has been focused on expanding its audience and attracting younger viewers by shifting the type and mix of programming on its flagship channels. A&E, which built its reputation mostly on the strength of syndicated *Law & Order* reruns (a franchise it lost in 2003), has

been leaning heavily on syndicated crime series such as *The Sopranos* and *CSI: Miami*. It began a transformation in 2008 under the marketing tag line "Real life. Drama." to feature more reality-based programming such as *Gene Simmons Family Jewels* and *Intervention*, as well as original series *The Cleaner*.

Reality television has also taken root at the History channel, once popularly known as "The Hitler Channel" for its frequent airings of WWII documentaries. The network is hoping to broaden its appeal with shows such as *Ax Men* and *Ice Road Truckers*, as well as science show *The Universe*.

The transformation of A&E Television's channels has come under the watch of Abbe Raven, who was promoted to CEO in 2005.

EXECUTIVES

President and CEO: Abbe Raven
SEVP: Whitney Goit II
EVP and CFO: Gerard Gruosso
EVP Enterprises: Steve Ronson
EVP National Ad Sales: Melvin (Mel) Berning
SVP and Controller: Andy Lemaire
SVP and General Counsel: Anne Atkinson
SVP Ad Sales Operations and Administration:
 Mona Tropeano
SVP Affiliate Sales: David Zagin
SVP Corporate Outreach and Chief Historian:
 Libby Haight O'Connell
SVP Human Resources: Rosalind Clay Carter
SVP Production and Broadcast Operations: Bill Harris
SVP Revenue Management: Michael Peretz
VP Public Affairs and Communication: Michael Feeney
President, The History Channel: Daniel E. (Dan) Davids
**President and General Manager, A&E Network and
 Biography Channel:** Robert (Bob) DiBitetto

LOCATIONS

HQ: A&E Television Networks
 235 E. 45th St., New York, NY 10017
Phone: 212-210-1400   **Fax:** 212-210-1308
Web: www.aetn.com

PRODUCTS/OPERATIONS

Operating Units

A&E Network
AETN Consumer Products (home videos, magazines,
 CDs, and e-commerce)
AETN International
The Biography Channel
Crime & Investigation Network
Crime & Investigation Network (Australia)
The History Channel
The History Channel en Español
The Military History Channel
History Channel International

COMPETITORS

Discovery Communications
E! Entertainment Television
Fox Entertainment
MTV Networks
National Geographic
NBC Universal Cable
Rainbow Media
Scripps Networks
Showtime Networks
Starz Entertainment
Turner Broadcasting

AARP

Turn 50 and the doors of the AARP will open for you, as they have for more than 35 million current members. On behalf of its members, the not-for-profit AARP acts as an advocate on public policy issues, publishes information (including the monthly *AARP Bulletin* and the bimonthly *AARP The Magazine*), promotes community service, and works with business partners to offer products and services (including discounts on insurance and travel). The group is organized into some 3,500 local chapters throughout the US. Royalties from businesses eager to reach AARP members account for about 40% of the group's revenue; membership dues ($12.50 per year) account for about 25%.

AARP may not be the most exclusive club around, but it is one of the most powerful. As the largest advocacy group in the US, the organization has a loud (and sometimes feared) voice on Capitol Hill, in part because older people tend to vote in greater relative numbers than many other segments of the population. AARP policy recommendations address such issues as the national budget, Medicare, elder abuse, and Social Security.

The group has worked to attract baby boomers with its 50+ campaign, a five-year plan begun in 2000. In 2003 AARP developed a 10-year agenda designed to address the effects of the first wave of boomers reaching age 65 in 2011. Concerns for the 50+ set include Medicare reforms, improved consumer protections and financial security, and employment opportunities for older workers. As concerns about funding for Social Security become more urgent, AARP intends to continue to make its voice heard.

In 2007 AARP announced plans to expand its insurance offerings, through partnerships with Aetna and UnitedHealth Group. The AARP-branded products includes policies designed to supplement Medicare coverage and policies intended to cover people ages 50 to 64.

HISTORY

Ethel Andrus, a retired Los Angeles high school principal who founded the National Retired Teachers Association (NRTA) in 1947, founded the American Association of Retired Persons (AARP) in 1958 with the assistance of Leonard Davis, a New York insurance salesman who had helped her find an underwriter for the NRTA. The new organization's goal: to "enhance the quality of life" for older Americans and "improve the image of aging."

Andrus offered members the same low rates for health and accident insurance provided to NRTA members. She also started publishing AARP's bimonthly magazine, *Modern Maturity*, in 1958. The organization's first local chapter opened in Youngstown, Arizona, in 1960. Still an insurance man, Davis formed Colonial Penn Insurance in 1963 to take over the AARP account. Andrus led the AARP and its increasingly powerful lobby for the elderly until her death in 1967.

With criticism of Colonial Penn mounting in the 1970s (critics charged the organization was little more than a front for the insurance company), Prudential won AARP's insurance business in 1979. The NRTA merged with AARP in 1982, and the following year it lowered the membership eligibility age from 55 to 50. The organization continued to expand its offerings, adding an auto club and financial products such as mutual funds and expanded insurance policies. The organization also started a federal credit union for members in 1988, but despite rosy projections, it ceased operations two years later.

AARP forked over $135 million to the IRS in 1993 as part of a settlement regarding the tax status of profits from some of its activities, but the dispute remained unresolved. AARP switched insurance providers again in 1996 (New York Life) and started offering discounted legal services. Also that year, AARP said it would let HMOs offer managed-care services to members. The plan drew objections over its potential violation of Medicare anti-kickback laws and AARP developed a revised payment plan in 1997.

AARP's image was bruised in 1998 when Dale Van Atta wrote a scathing account of the organization, *Trust Betrayed: Inside the AARP.* The book accused the organization of operating out of lavish accommodations, acting as a shill for businesses to hawk their wares, and concealing a drop in membership. The next year, recognizing that nearly a third of its members were working, the organization dropped the American Association of Retired Persons moniker and began to refer to itself by the AARP abbreviation.

To end the long-running dispute with the IRS, AARP reached a settlement over its alleged profit-making enterprises by creating a new taxable subsidiary called AARP Services in 1999. The following year AARP initiated a five-year plan to attract aging baby boomers. AARP launched its new *My Generation* magazine in 2001; two years later the organization combined *My Generation* with its *Modern Maturity* magazine to form a single publication: *AARP The Magazine*.

In 2005 the group's lobbying efforts focused on Social Security reform proposals and a new prescription drug benefit for Medicare recipients.

EXECUTIVES

Chairman: Bonnie M. Cramer
CEO: William D. (Bill) Novelli
COO: Thomas C. Nelson
CFO: Robert R. Hagans Jr., age 49
President and Director: Jennie Chin Hansen
President-Elect and Director: W. Lee Hammond
EVP Policy and Strategy: John Rother
EVP Social Impact: Nancy LeaMond
EVP Member Value: Shereen Remez
Group Executive Officer for State and National Initiatives: Christopher W. (Chris) Hansen
Chief People Officer: Ellie Hollander
General Counsel: Joan S. Wise
Chief Brand Officer: Emilio Pardo
Chief Communications Officer: Kevin Donnellan
Publications Director: Cathy Ventura-Merkel
Senior Manager, Media Relations: Michelle Alvarez
Co-Lead and EVP, AARP Services: Jean Alexander
Co-Lead and EVP, AARP Services: John Wider
President, AARP Foundation: Robin Talbert
President, AARP Financial (AFI): Richard (Mac) Hisey
Auditors: KPMG LLP

LOCATIONS

HQ: AARP
    601 E St. NW, Washington, DC 20049
Phone: 202-434-7700   **Fax:** 202-434-7710
Web: www.aarp.org

PRODUCTS/OPERATIONS

2007 Sales

	$ mil.	% of total
Royalties	497.6	43
Membership dues	249.4	21
Advertising	121.5	10
Investment income	80.0	7
Federal & other grants	82.4	7
Contributions	49.2	4
Program income	90.9	8
Other	2.9	—
Total	**1,173.9**	**100**

Selected Operations and Programs

AARP Andrus Foundation (gerontology research)
AARP Bulletin (monthly news update)
AARP Driver Safety (classroom refresher)
AARP Legal Services Network
AARP Services (taxable product management, marketing and e-commerce subsidiary)
AARP The Magazine (bimonthly magazine)
Financial Planning
Public Policy Institute
Research Information Center
Senior Community Service Employment Program
Tax-Aide

HISTORICAL FINANCIALS

Company Type: Not-for-profit

Income Statement

FYE: December 31

	REVENUE ($ mil.)	NET INCOME ($ mil.)	NET PROFIT MARGIN	EMPLOYEES
12/07	1,174	10	0.8%	—
12/06	1,010	(31)	—	—
12/05	936	—	—	—
12/04	878	—	—	—
12/03	770	—	—	—
Annual Growth	**11.1%**	—	—	—

2007 Year-End Financials

Debt ratio: —   Current ratio: —
Return on equity: 3.1%   Long-term debt ($ mil.): —
Cash ($ mil.): —

Net Income History

Aavid

Aavid Thermalloy is avid about keeping cool. The company makes heat sinks, fans, heat spreaders, liquid cooling products, cooling assemblies, and other devices used in computer, networking, and industrial electronic systems. Aavid Thermalloy's Applied Thermal Technologies subsidiary provides thermal management systems consulting and design services. Customers include 3M, Agilent, Dow Chemical, General Motors, IBM, andLockheed Martin. The company has manufacturing facilities in China, Italy, Mexico, and the US. Heat Holdings, which is controlled by private investment firm Willis Stein & Partners, owns Aavid Thermalloy.

In 2006 ANSYS acquired Aavid for about $565 million in cash and stock. ANSYS bought the company to obtain Aavid's Fluent subsidiary, which makes computational fluid dynamics (CFD) software for analyzing heat transfer. The Aavid thermal management product line, Aavid Thermalloy, was spun off to the company's existing shareholders, including Willis Stein, and operates as a standalone business.

The Applied Thermal Technologies unit was spun off in 2001 to establish a separate corporate brand for its services. The subsidiary works with Fluent and ANSYS to provide design tools for its consulting clients.

EXECUTIVES

Chairman, President, and CEO:
 Bharatan R. (Bart) Patel, $645,501 pay
COO: Michael Flander
CFO: Brian A. Byrne, age 60, $332,824 pay
VP General Counsel: John W. Mitchell, age 59
Managing Director, Europe: Luca Rossi
Auditors: Ernst & Young LLP

LOCATIONS

HQ: Aavid Thermalloy, LLC
 70 Commercial St., Ste. 200, Concord, NH 03301
Phone: 603-224-9988   **Fax:** 603-223-1790
Web: www.aavid.com

Aavid Thermalloy has operations in China, Germany, India, Italy, Mexico, Singapore, Taiwan, the UK, and the US.

PRODUCTS/OPERATIONS

Selected Products and Services

Thermal Products
 Services
  Consulting
  Thermal management systems design
 Thermal management products
  Fans
  Heat sinks, fan heat sinks, and heat spreaders
  Interface materials and attachment accessories
  Liquid cooling and phase change devices

COMPETITORS

Hon Hai
MAYA Heat Transfer Technologies
Molex
NMB Technologies
SEMX
TAT Technologies
Wakefield Thermal Solutions

ABC Supply

American Builders & Contractors Supply Co. (better known as ABC Supply) has put roofs over millions of heads. A leading supplier of roofing, siding, windows, gutters, doors, and other exterior building products, ABC Supply operates about 380 outlets in 46 states and the District of Columbia. It carries its own brand of products under the Amcraft name, and also offers products from outside vendors. The privately held company, which markets its products mostly to small and medium-sized professional contractors, was founded in 1982 by its former chairman and CEO the late Ken Hendricks, the son of a roofer.

Hendricks died in late 2007 and was succeeded as chief executive by David Luck, who joined the firm as president and COO in 1998.

ABC Supply's goal is to grow to 500 branches and $5 billion in sales (up from about $3 billion in 2006) by 2012.

In 2004 the company acquired Paco Building Supply (distributor of exterior siding and windows in Missouri) and Mansion Supply (a New Jersey window company).

ABC Supply is one of about 20 diverse companies owned by Hendricks Holding Company.

EXECUTIVES

President, CEO, and Director: David A. Luck
CFO, Treasurer, and Director: Kendra A. Story
EVP, Secretary, and Director: Diane M. Hendricks, age 61
SVP Strategic Marketing and Planning: Keith Rozolis, age 45
VP Branch Operations: Kevin Hendricks
VP and CIO: Kathy Murray
VP Merchandising and Purchasing: Brent Fox
VP; President Mule-Hide Products: Kim Hendricks
Regional VP, Midwest: Jim Welch
Regional VP, Northeast: Tom Kuchan
Regional VP, Southeast: Phil Gentry
Regional VP, West: John Simonelli
Regional VP, Southwest: John Yonkin
Managing Partner: Darin Richardson
Auditors: Ernst & Young LLP

LOCATIONS

HQ: American Builders & Contractors Supply Co., Inc.
 1 ABC Pkwy., Beloit, WI 53511
Phone: 608-362-7777   **Fax:** 608-362-2717
Web: www.abc-supply.com

PRODUCTS/OPERATIONS

Selected Products

Roofing materials
Siding materials
Tools and equipment
Windows and doors

COMPETITORS

Beacon Roofing
Bradco Supply
Building Materials Holding
Emco Corporation
Guardian Building Products Distribution
HD Supply
Huttig Building Products
Lowe's
North Pacific Group
Pacific Coast Building Products
PrimeSource Building

HISTORICAL FINANCIALS
Company Type: Private

Income Statement

	REVENUE ($ mil.)	NET INCOME ($ mil.)	NET PROFIT MARGIN	EMPLOYEES
12/07	2,630	53	2.0%	5,243
12/06	2,990	—	—	5,431
12/05	2,597	—	—	5,144
12/04	2,042	—	—	4,128
12/03	1,793	—	—	4,128
Annual Growth	10.1%	—	—	6.2%

Revenue History

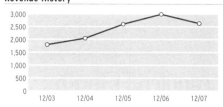

Academy Sports & Outdoors

Academy Sports & Outdoors is near the head of the class among sporting goods retailers. The company is one of the top full-line sporting goods chains in the US with more than 100 stores in about a dozen states throughout the South and Southwest. Academy's low-frills stores carry clothing, shoes, and equipment for almost any sport and outdoor activity, including camping, golf, hunting, fishing, and boating. The company, which also operates a catalog operation, dates back to a San Antonio tire shop opened by Max Gochman in 1938. The business moved into military surplus items and during the 1980s began focusing on sports and outdoor merchandise. The Gochman family still owns Academy.

The regional sporting goods chain is expanding by building larger stores (up to 82,000 sq. ft.) and opening outlets in new markets, such as Georgia and Missouri. To support its expansion, in late 2007 the retailer began building a second distribution center in Georgia. Currently, all of its stores are supplied from the company's facility in Katy, Texas.

Academy's merchandising strategy focuses on multiple price points to compete with discounters, including Wal-Mart, on the low end as well as pricier specialty stores like Foot Locker.

The chain has also begun selling higher-end products, including the Callaway, TaylorMade, and NIKE brands of golf equipment.

EXECUTIVES

Chairman and CEO: David Gochman
President: Rodney (Rod) Faldyn
EVP Corporate Development: Michelle McKinney
EVP General Merchandise Manager: Robert Frennea
EVP General Merchandise Manager: Beth Menuet
EVP and General Counsel: Elise Neal
VP Marketing and Advertising: Carl Main
VP Store Operations: Kevin Chapman
VP Loss Prevention: Joe Matthews
VP Store Merchandising: Bruce Meunier

LOCATIONS

HQ: Academy Sports & Outdoors, Ltd.
1800 N. Mason Rd., Katy, TX 77449
Phone: 281-646-5200 **Fax:** 281-646-5000
Web: www.academy.com

COMPETITORS

Bass Pro Shops
Cabela's
Dick's Sporting Goods
Finish Line
Foot Locker
Golf Galaxy
Golfsmith
Hibbett Sports

Kmart
REI
Sears
Sports Authority
Sportsman's Warehouse
Target
Wal-Mart

Acapulco/El Torito Restaurants

This company is a real combinación grande. Real Mex Restaurants operates and franchises more than 220 Mexican restaurants in California and more than a dozen other states. Its flagship El Torito chain has about 80 locations offering full-service Mexican dining, while its chain of about 100 Chevys Fresh Mex (operated through Chevys Restaurants) provides a more laid-back, cantina atmosphere. Real Mex also operates more than 30 full-service Acapulco restaurants featuring California-Mexican cuisine. Smaller concepts include Casa Gallardo, GuadalaHarrys, and Las Brisas. About 190 of the restaurants are company-owned. Real Mex is owned by private equity firm Sun Capital Partners.

The company has been focused mostly on improving results at its existing restaurants while driving additional traffic through renewed marketing efforts. It also has added a handful of new eateries to its estate but plans for more vigorous expansion of its flagship Chevys and El Torito chains.

The El Torito banner had originally been operated by doomed restaurateur Prandium, which sold the Mexican concept to private equity firm Bruckmann, Rosser, Sherrill & Co. (BRS) in 2000. Real Mex was formed to build a portfolio of dining concepts, and it acquired Chevys in 2005 along with the Fuzio Universal Pasta chain (sold in 2007). Sun Capital, which also owns bagel outlet Bruegger's Enterprises, Italian chain Fazoli's, Garden Fresh, and Souper Salad, acquired the company in 2006.

EXECUTIVES

President and CEO: Frederick (Fred) Wolfe
EVP and CFO: Steven (Steve) Tanner
SVP Human Resources: Steve Wallace
SVP Research and Development and Executive Chef: Roberto (Pepe) Lopez
SVP Information Technology: John Koontz
VP Facilities and Construction: Mark Turpin
VP Marketing: Julie Koenig-Browne
VP and Controller: Kathleen Burkett
President, Real Mex Foods: Carlos Angulo
SVP Operations, El Torito and Acapulco: Ray Garcia
SVP Operations, Chevys: Nick Mayer
Auditors: Grant Thornton LLP

LOCATIONS

HQ: Real Mex Restaurants, Inc.
5660 Katella Ave., Ste. 100, Cypress, CA 90630
Phone: 562-346-1200 **Fax:** 562-346-1469
Web: www.realmexrestaurants.com

2007 Locations

	No.
US	
California	157
Missouri	13
Illinois	6
Arizona	5
New Jersey	5
Oregon	5
Maryland	4
New York	4
Virginia	4
Washington	4
Florida	3
Louisiana	2
Nevada	2
Indiana	1
Minnesota	1
South Dakota	1
International	
Japan	8
Turkey	3
United Arab Emirates	1
Total	**229**

PRODUCTS/OPERATIONS

2007 Sales

	$ mil.	% of total
Restaurants	523.3	92
Franchising	3.7	1
Other	38.2	7
Total	**565.2**	**100**

2007 Locations

	No.
Company-owned	188
Franchised & licensed	41
Total	**229**

Selected Restaurants

Acapulco
Casa Gallardo Mexican Restaurant
Chevys Fresh Mex
El Paso Cantina
El Torito
El Torito Grill
GuadalaHarry's
Las Brisas
WhoSong & Larry's

COMPETITORS

Applebee's
Brinker
Carlson Restaurants
Cheesecake Factory
Chipotle
Darden

Hooters
Houlihan's
OSI Restaurant Partners
Romacorp
Ruby Tuesday

HISTORICAL FINANCIALS

Company Type: Private

Income Statement

FYE: Last Sunday in December

	REVENUE ($ mil.)	NET INCOME ($ mil.)	NET PROFIT MARGIN	EMPLOYEES
12/07	565	(24)	—	12,701
12/06	565	(14)	—	12,769
12/05	534	13	2.5%	—
12/04	327	14	4.2%	—
Annual Growth	20.0%	—	—	(0.5%)

2007 Year-End Financials

Debt ratio: 106.2%
Return on equity: —
Cash ($ mil.): —

Current ratio: —
Long-term debt ($ mil.): 173

Net Income History

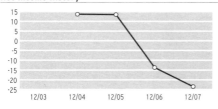

Accredited Home Lenders

Accredited Home Lenders is willing to give credit where it's due . . . or not. The mortgage banker originates, acquires, services, and sells mostly subprime single-family mortgages for homebuyers throughout the US who may not otherwise qualify. It operates through a network of independent mortgage brokers. Private equity firm Lone Star Funds bought Accredited Home Lenders for some $400 million in 2007. The fund invested an additional $100 million of working capital in the company shortly after the deal was finalized.

Like most of its peers, Accredited Home Lenders took a serious hit amidst the credit market turmoil of 2007 and 2008. The company laid off more than half its staff, closed all but one of its US operations centers, and exited the Canadian market outright (which it had entered just four years before that). Lone Star Funds acquired the assets of Bear Stearns Residential Mortgage (BSRM), which also originates conforming in addition to noncomforming loans, and merged it into Accredited Home Lenders' operations. BSRM CEO Jeff Walton took the helm of the combined company.

Before the meltdown in the subprime mortgage industry, which has seen several of Accredited Home Lenders' peers file for bankruptcy protection, retrench, or have their funding pulled out from under them, the company had been on the grow. It boosted its wholesale and retail operations with the purchase of Aames Investment and its approximately 75 retail branches, as well as three regional wholesale offices. The company also created Accredited Mortgage Loan REIT to invest in and manage mortgage assets.

EXECUTIVES

CEO: Jeff Walton
President, COO, and Director: Joseph J. Lydon, age 47, $925,673 pay
EVP and Secretary: Stuart D. (Stu) Marvin, age 46, $1,082,168 pay (partial-year salary)
CIO: Larry Murphy, age 64
General Counsel: David E. Hertzel, age 51
Director, Human Resources and Administration: Joseph F. (Joe) Weinbrecht, age 60
Director, Corporate Communications: Richard W. (Rick) Howe

Director, Internal Audit and Quality Control:
Richard D. Romero
Director, Marketing: Roxane W. Helstrom, age 49
Director, Operations: Jeffrey W. (Jeff) Crawford, age 51,
$588,341 pay
Auditors: Squar, Milner, Peterson, Miranda &
Williamson, LLP

LOCATIONS

HQ: Accredited Home Lenders Holding Co.
15090 Ave. of Science, Ste. 200,
San Diego, CA 92128
Phone: 212-355-4449   **Fax:** 866-558-4920
Web: www.accredhome.com

COMPETITORS

Citigroup
Countrywide Financial
First Republic Preferred Capital
Lendmark Financial Services
Long Beach Mortgage

HISTORICAL FINANCIALS

Company Type: Private

Income Statement

FYE: December 31

	ASSETS ($ mil.)	NET INCOME ($ mil.)	INCOME AS % OF ASSETS	EMPLOYEES
12/06	11,349	(206)	—	4,200
12/05	9,853	155	1.6%	2,762
12/04	6,688	131	2.0%	2,694
12/03	3,501	100	2.9%	2,056
12/02	1,807	29	1.6%	1,294
Annual Growth	58.3%	—	—	34.2%

2006 Year-End Financials

Equity as % of assets: 4.9%   Long-term debt ($ mil.): 10,429
Return on assets: —   Sales ($ mil.): 1,072
Return on equity: —

Net Income History

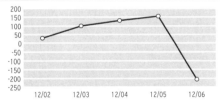

Ace Hardware

Luckily, Ace has John Madden up its sleeve.
Despite the growth of warehouse-style competitors, Ace Hardware has remained a household
name, thanks to ads featuring Madden, a former
Oakland Raiders football coach and TV commentator. By sales the company is the #1 hardware co-operative in the US, ahead of Do It Best. Ace
dealer-owners operate more than 4,600 Ace Hardware stores, home centers, and lumber and building materials locations in all 50 US states and
about 60 other countries. From about 15 warehouses Ace distributes such products as electrical and plumbing supplies, garden equipment,
hand tools, housewares, and power tools. Ace's
paint division is a major paint manufacturer in
the US.

It also makes its own brand of paint and offers
thousands of other Ace-brand products. In addition to its own-brand paints, Ace began offering
Benjamin Moore products in its stores in 2006.
Ace additionally provides training programs
and advertising campaigns for its dealers. Ace
dealers own the company and receive dividends
from Ace's profits.

Challenged by big-box chains such as The
Home Depot and Lowe's, Ace unveiled its Next
Generation store concept, which involves signage with detailed product descriptions and different flooring to set off departments, among
other features. The company is also focusing on
opening smaller neighborhood stores to entice
customers who would rather not drive to edge-of-town big-box chains. In its most ambitious
expansion plan to date, Ace Hardware will add
150 to 200 stores.

The company is also increasing the size of its
stores. The average store is 10,000 sq. ft., but
newer stores are about 14,000 sq. ft. To support
store growth in the West, Ace is expanding its
distribution center in Prescott Valley, Arizona.

In mid-2007 CEO Ray Griffith sent a letter to
its retailers, saying the company was considering changing from a cooperative to a traditional
corporation to become more competitive and to
better fuel growth.

Shortly after, the company announced a
$154 million accounting shortfall uncovered
while Ace prepared to convert formats. It then
called off the conversion as it researched the error.

Following a review, the company determined
that a mid-level employee made the accounting
error accidentally. Ace plans to restore equity
within two years.

HISTORY

A group of Chicago-area hardware dealers —
William Stauber, Richard Hesse, Gern Lindquist,
and Oscar Fisher — decided in 1924 to pool their
hardware buying and promotional costs. In 1928
the group incorporated as Ace Stores, named in
honor of the superior WWI fliers dubbed aces.
Hesse became president the following year, retaining that position for the next 44 years. The
company also opened its first warehouse in 1929,
and by 1933 it had 38 dealers.

The organization had 133 dealers in seven
states by 1949. In 1953 Ace began to allow dealers to buy stock in the company through the Ace
Perpetuation Plan. During the 1960s Ace expanded into the South and West, and by 1969 it
had opened distribution centers in Georgia and
California — its first such facilities outside
Chicago. In 1968 it opened its first international
store in Guam.

By the early 1970s the do-it-yourself market
began to surge as inflation pushed up plumber
and electrician fees. As the market grew, large
home center chains gobbled up market share
from independent dealers such as those franchised through Ace. In response, Ace and its
dealers became a part of a growing trend in the
hardware industry — cooperatives.

Hesse sold the company to its dealers in 1973
for $6 million (less than half its book value), and
the following year Ace began operating as a co-operative. Hesse stepped down in 1973. In 1976
the dealers took full control when the company's
first Board of Dealer-Directors was elected.

After signing up a number of dealers in the
eastern US, Ace had dealers in all 50 states by

1979. The co-op opened a plant to make paint in
Matteson, Illinois, in 1984. By 1985 Ace had
reached $1 billion in sales and had initiated its
Store of the Future Program, allowing dealers to
borrow up to $200,000 to upgrade their stores
and conduct market analyses. Former head
coach John Madden of the National Football
League's Oakland Raiders signed on as Ace's
mouthpiece in 1988.

A year later the co-op began to test ACENET,
a computer network that allowed Ace dealers to
check inventory, send and receive e-mail, make
special purchase requests, and keep up with
prices on commodity items such as lumber. In
1990 Ace established an International Division to
handle its overseas stores. (It had been exporting products since 1975.) EVP and COO David
Hodnik became president in 1995. That year the
co-op added a net of 67 stores, including a three-store chain in Russia. Expanding further internationally, Ace signed a five-year joint-supply
agreement in 1996 with Canadian lumber and
hardware retailer Beaver Lumber. Hodnik added
CEO to his title in 1996.

Ace fell further behind its old rival, True
Value, in 1997 when ServiStar Coast to Coast
and True Value merged to form TruServ (renamed True Value in 2005), a hardware giant
that operated more than 10,000 outlets at the
completion of the merger.

Late in 1997 Ace launched an expansion program in Canada. (The co-op already operated distribution centers in Ontario and Calgary.) In
1999 Ace merged its lumber and building materials division with Builder Marts of America to
form a dealer-owned buying group to supply
about 2,700 retailers. In 2000 Ace gained 208
member outlet stores, but saw 279 member outlets terminated. The next year it gained 220, but
lost 255.

Sodisco-Howden bought all the shares of Ace
Hardware Canada in February 2003. To better
serve international members, Ace opened its first
international buying office, in Hong Kong, in
April 2004.

In all, the company added 131 new stores in
2005. That year, after 33 years with the company, David F. Hodnik retired as president and
CEO of Ace Hardware. He was succeeded by COO
Ray A. Griffith.

EXECUTIVES

Chairman: J. Thomas (Tom) Glenn
President and CEO: Ray A. Griffith, age 53
CFO: Dorvin D. Lively, age 48
EVP: Rita D. Kahle
SVP, General Counsel, and Secretary:
Arthur J. (Art) McGivern
SVP, International and Paint: David F. (Dave) Myer
VP, Business Development: John Venhuizen, age 36
VP, Information Technology: Michael G. (Mike) Elmore
VP, Retail Operations: Kenneth L. (Ken) Nichols
VP, Merchandising, Marketing, and Advertising:
Lori L. Bossmann
**VP, Retail Development, New Business, and Company
Stores:** Michael A. (Mike) Zipser
VP, Human Resources: Jimmy Alexander
VP, Retail Support: William J. (Bill) Bauman
VP, Supply Chain: Daniel C. (Dan) Prochaska
Director, Advertising and Brand Development:
Paula K. Erickson
Director, Global Retail Operations: Angel L. Garcia
Manager, New Business: Bill Jablonowski
Manager, Advertising: Frank Rothing
Specialty Business Manager: Russ Goerlitz
Auditors: KPMG LLP

LOCATIONS

HQ: Ace Hardware Corporation
2200 Kensington Ct., Oak Brook, IL 60523
Phone: 630-990-6600   **Fax:** 630-990-6838
Web: www.acehardware.com

COMPETITORS

84 Lumber	Menard
Akzo Nobel	Northern Tool
Benjamin Moore	Orgill
Building Materials Holding	Reno-Depot
Costco Wholesale	Sears
Do it Best	Sherwin-Williams
Fastenal	Stock Building Supply
Grossman's	Sutherland Lumber
Handy Hardware Wholesale	True Value
Home Depot	United Hardware
Kmart	Distributing
Lowe's	Wal-Mart
McCoy Corp.	

HISTORICAL FINANCIALS

Company Type: Cooperative

Income Statement			FYE: Saturday nearest December 31	
	REVENUE ($ mil.)	NET INCOME ($ mil.)	NET PROFIT MARGIN	EMPLOYEES
12/07	3,971	87	2.2%	4,800
12/06	3,770	107	2.8%	5,000
12/05	3,466	100	2.9%	4,976
12/04	3,289	102	3.1%	5,000
12/03	3,159	101	3.2%	5,100
Annual Growth	5.9%	(3.6%)	—	(1.5%)

2007 Year-End Financials

Debt ratio: 76.3%   Current ratio: —
Return on equity: 43.5%   Long-term debt ($ mil.): 172
Cash ($ mil.): —

Net Income History

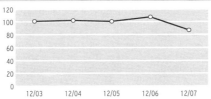

Activant Solutions

Activant Solutions wants all parts of a business holding hands, singing in perfect harmony. The company provides enterprise resource planning (ERP) software for more than 30,000 small and medium-sized businesses in the automotive parts aftermarket, hardware and home center, wholesale trade, and lumber and building materials industries.

Activant's software automates functions such as inventory management, parts selection, general accounting, and point-of-sale analysis. Customers have included members of the Ace Hardware, True Value, and Do it Best cooperatives.

Activant has grown through its acquisitions of enterprise resource planning software maker Speedware (March 2005) and the assets of The Systems House (May 2005), a developer of soft-

ware for distributors in the automotive aftermarket and office products industries.

Later in 2005, Activant bought distribution software maker Prophet 21, which became its wholesale distribution unit, in a deal worth $215 million.

In 2007 the company purchased Eclipse, the distribution management software unit of Intuit, for $100 million. The move expanded Activant's product offerings for electrical and plumbing wholesale distributors.

The company has operations throughout the US as well as in Canada, Ireland, and the UK.

EXECUTIVES

Chairman: Robert B. Henske, age 46
President, CEO, and Director: Pervez A. Qureshi, age 51
EVP Wholesale Distribution: Kevin V. Roach
EVP Hardlines and Lumber: Paul H. Salsgiver
SVP and CFO: Kathleen M. (Kathy) Crusco, age 42
SVP Sales Hardlines and Lumber: Scott B. Hanson, age 53
SVP Business Development: Mary Beth Loesch, age 45, $326,323 pay
SVP Finance and Treasurer: Christopher J. Speltz, age 45
SVP Human Resources: Beth A. Taylor
SVP Corporate Strategic Accounts:
  Stephen A. (Steve) McLaughlin, age 50
SVP Product Development: William (Bill) Wilson, age 49, $364,998 pay
SVP Marketing Hardlines and Lumber:
  Stephen L. (Steve) Bieszczat, age 52
SVP Corporate Development: David F. Petroni, age 40
VP, General Counsel, and Secretary: Timothy F. Taich
Auditors: Ernst & Young LLP

LOCATIONS

HQ: Activant Solutions Inc.
7683 Southfront Rd., Livermore, CA 94551
Phone: 925-449-0606
Web: www.activant.com

Activant Solutions Holdings has offices in Canada, France, Ireland, the UK, and the US.

PRODUCTS/OPERATIONS

Selected Products

Automotive
  Activant A-DIS (warehouse management)
  Activant J-CON (inventory management and electronic purchasing)
  Activant The Paperless Warehouse (warehouse operations management system)
  Activant PRISM (distribution management system)
  Activant Ultimate (centralized business solution)
Industry Solutions
  Activant CSD (building materials management system)
  Activant Eagle (comprehensive set of Windows applications business management software)
  Activant Falcon (management system for large multi-location lumber and building material dealers)
  Activant Gemini (ERP system for multi-store hardware and lumber retail stores)

COMPETITORS

AutoZone
CAM Commerce Solutions
Catalyst International
Genuine Parts
i2 Technologies
Intuit
JDA Software
Reynolds and Reynolds
Wrenchead, Inc.

ADESA, Inc.

ADESA (Auto Dealers Exchange Services of America) doesn't sell cars, it sells fleets of cars to dealers. The company offers used- and salvage-vehicle redistribution services to automakers, lessors, and dealers in the US, Canada, and Mexico. ADESA operates about 60 used-vehicle auctions and more than 40 salvage auctions; it also offers such ancillary services as logistics, inspections, evaluation, titling, and settlement administration. The company collects fees from buyers and sellers on each auction and from its extra services. Its AFC (Automotive Finance Corporation) unit offers dealer floorplan financing services. In mid-2007 ADESA was acquired by an investment group for $3.7 billion.

The $3.7 billion bid — from Kelso & Company, GS Capital Partners, ValueAct Capital, and Parthenon Capital — included about $700 million in debt. The group plans on integrating ADESA's operations with Insurance Auto Auctions, a fellow automotive salvage auction provider (and rival of ADESA) owned by members of the investment group. KAR Holdings is the newly created parent that holds both ADESA and Insurance Auto Auctions.

In January 2008 ADESA acquired Dent Demon, a paintless dent repair service in Indiana. Other reconditioning services provided by ADESA include body work, detailing, glass repair, light mechanical work, tire and key replacement, and upholstery repair. In June 2008 it acquired Live Global Bid (LGB), a provider of Internet-based auction software and services. (ADESA, which uses LGB's technology, previously owned about 18% of the firm.)

The company agreed in September 2008 to sell its real estate portfolio to First Industrial Realty Trust for $82 million. ADESA will lease back the land at eight of the sites, as ADESA wanted more financial flexibility to reinvest funds back into its core business.

Founded in 1989, ADESA was acquired by electric power distributor ALLETE in 1996 and spun off in 2004.

EXECUTIVES

President and CEO: James P. (Jim) Hallett, age 51
COO: Tom Caruso
EVP Operations and Finance: Paul Lips
EVP Customer Strategies and Analytics: Tom Kontos
EVP Sales and Marketing: Robert (Bob) Rauschenberg
EVP International Markets and Managing Director ADESA Canada: Benjamin Skuy
EVP Corporate Development: Warren Byrd
EVP Western Region: Kenny Osborn
SVP Operations and Strategic Improvement:
  David Vignes
VP; President, ADESA Canada: Brian J. Warner, age 39
VP Commercial Sales and Operations: Jeff Bescher
VP e-Business Sales and Operations: Jason Ferreri
VP Legal: Michelle Mallon
VP Marketing: Carol Sewell
Auditors: KPMG LLP

LOCATIONS

HQ: ADESA, Inc.
13085 Hamilton Crossing Blvd., Carmel, IN 46032
Phone: 317-815-1100   **Fax:** 317-249-4651
Web: www.adesa.com

Autobytel
Columbus Fair Auto Auction
Copart
Cox Enterprises
D-A Auto Auction
eBay
Pennsylvania Auto Dealers' Exchange
Ritchie Bros. Auctioneers

HISTORICAL FINANCIALS

Company Type: Subsidiary

Income Statement				FYE: December 31
	REVENUE ($ mil.)	NET INCOME ($ mil.)	NET PROFIT MARGIN	EMPLOYEES
12/07	1,103	44	4.0%	11,000
12/06	1,104	126	11.4%	11,915
12/05	969	126	13.0%	10,740
12/04	932	105	11.3%	10,418
12/03	912	115	12.6%	—
Annual Growth	4.9%	(21.3%)	—	1.8%

Net Income History

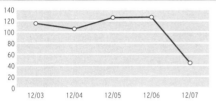

Advance Publications

Advance Publications gets its marching orders from the printed page. A leading US newspaper publisher, Advance owns daily newspapers in some 20 cities around the country, including *The Star-Ledger* (New Jersey), *The Cleveland Plain Dealer*, and its namesake *Staten Island Advance*. It also owns American City Business Journals (more than 40 weekly papers) and Parade Publications (*Parade Magazine* Sunday insert). The company is a top magazine publisher through its Condé Nast unit. Aside from print publishing, Advance is a major online publisher through its Advance Internet network of local news sites; Advance additionally owns television assets. Samuel "Si" Newhouse Jr. and his brother, Donald, own the company.

The company's Condé Nast unit publishes such popular titles as *Allure, Gourmet, Golf Digest*, and *Vanity Fair*. Internet properties such as Epicurious (food and dining) and Concierge (travel) are run through its CondéNet unit. Trade journal publisher Fairchild Publications (*Women's Wear Daily*) is also a division of Condé Nast.

The company has interests in cable television through affiliate Advance/Newhouse Communications, which owns cable systems operator Bright House Networks through a partnership with Time Warner Cable. Advance/Newhouse also controls 33% of Discovery Communications (DCI) after joining with partner Discovery Holding to spin off the cable broadcasting venture to the public.

Things at the *Star-Ledger* are not rosy. It suffers from declining advertising sales and about 200 of the paper's roughly 750 staffers have been offered buyouts. A possible closure or sale of the paper is on the horizon.

HISTORY

Solomon Neuhaus (later Samuel I. Newhouse) got started in the newspaper business after dropping out of school at age 13. He went to work at the *Bayonne Times* in New Jersey and was put in charge of the failing newspaper in 1911; he managed to turn the paper around within a year. In 1922 he bought the *Staten Island Advance* (founded in 1886) and formed the Staten Island Advance Company in 1924. After buying up more papers, he changed the name of the company to Advance Publications in 1949. By the 1950s the company had local papers in New York, New Jersey, and Alabama.

In 1959 Newhouse bought magazine publisher Condé Nast as an anniversary gift for his wife. (He joked that she had asked for a fashion magazine, so he bought her *Vogue*.) His publishing empire continued to grow with the addition of the *Times-Picayune* (New Orleans) in 1962 and *The Cleveland Plain Dealer* in 1967. In 1976 the company paid more than $300 million for Booth Newspapers, publisher of eight Michigan papers and *Parade Magazine*.

Newhouse died in 1979, leaving his sons Si and Donald to run the company, which encompassed more than 30 newspapers, a half-dozen magazines, and 15 cable systems. The next year Advance bought book publishing giant Random House from RCA. Si resurrected the Roaring Twenties standard *Vanity Fair* in 1983 and added *The New Yorker* under the Condé Nast banner in 1985. The Newhouses scored a victory over the IRS in 1990 after a long-running court battle involving inheritance taxes. Condé Nast bought Knapp Publications (*Architectural Digest*) in 1993 and Advance later acquired American City Business Journals in 1995.

In 1998 the company sold the increasingly unprofitable Random House to Bertelsmann for about $1.2 billion. It later bought hallmark Internet magazine *Wired* (though it passed on Wired Ventures' Internet operations). That year revered *New Yorker* editor Tina Brown, credited with jazzing up the publication's content and increasing its circulation, left the magazine; staff writer and Pulitzer Prize winner David Remnick was named as Brown's replacement.

In 1999 Advance joined Donrey Media Group (now called Stephens Media Group), E.W. Scripps, Hearst Corporation, and MediaNews Group to purchase the online classified advertising network AdOne (later named PowerOne Media). It also bought Walt Disney's trade publishing unit, Fairchild Publications, for $650 million. In 2000 the company shifted *Details* from Condé Nast to Fairchild and relaunched the magazine as a fashion publication. Later that year the company announced it would begin creating Web versions of its popular magazine titles.

In 2001 Condé Nast bought a majority stake in Miami-based Ideas Publishing Group (Spanish language versions of US magazines; its name was later changed to Condé Nast Americas). Also

that year Advance bought four golf magazines, including *Golf Digest*, from the New York Times Company for $430 million. Condé Nast picked up *Modern Bride* magazine from PRIMEDIA in 2002 for $52 million.

Richard Diamond, a Newhouse relative who'd been publisher of the *Staten Island Advance* since 1979, died in 2004.

EXECUTIVES

Chairman and CEO; Chairman, Condé Nast Publications: Samuel I. (Si) Newhouse Jr., age 80
Chairman and CEO: Donald E. Newhouse, age 79
CFO; President Advance Finance Group LLC: Thomas S. (Tom) Summer, age 54
CEO Conde Nast: Charles H. (Chuck) Townsend
Chairman and CEO, American City Business Journals: Ray Shaw, age 74
Chairman, CEO, and Publisher, Parade Publications: Walter Anderson
Chairman, Advance.net: Steven Newhouse, age 50
President Advance Internet: Peter Weinberger
President CondéNet: Sarah Chubb
SVP Consumer Marketing; SVP Circulation, Condé Nast Publications: Peter A. Armour
Publisher, Staten Island Advance: Caroline Harrison

LOCATIONS

HQ: Advance Publications, Inc.
950 Fingerboard Rd., Staten Island, NY 10305
Phone: 212-286-2860   **Fax:** 718-981-1456
Web: www.advance.net

PRODUCTS/OPERATIONS

Broadcasting and Communications
Bright House Networks
Discovery Communications (33%, cable TV channel)

Magazine Publishing
Conde Nast Publications
    Fairchild Publications

Selected Newspaper Publishing
American City Business Journals (about 40 weekly titles in some 20 states)
    Sporting News
    Street & Smith's Sports Business Group
Newhouse Newspapers (more than 30 papers across the US)
    The Birmingham News (Alabama)
    The Oregonian (Portland)
    The Plain Dealer (Cleveland)
    The Star-Ledger (Newark, NJ)
    Staten Island Advance (New York)
    The Times-Picayune (New Orleans)
Parade Publications

Selected Online Publishing
Advance Internet
    al.com (Alabama)
    cleveland.com
    MassLive.com (Massachusetts)
    MLive (Michigan)
    NJ.com (New Jersey)
    NOLA.com (New Orleans)
    OregonLive.com
    PennLive.com (Pennsylvania)
    SILive (New York)
    syracuse.com (New York)
CondéNet
    Concierge (travel information)
    Epicurious (recipes and fine dining)
    STYLE.com (fashion and beauty)

COMPETITORS

American Express	McClatchy Company
American Media	Meredith Corporation
Crain Communications	New York Times
E. W. Scripps	News Corp.
Essence Communications	Newsweek
F+W Publications	North Jersey Media
Forbes	Reader's Digest
Freedom Communications	Reed Elsevier Group
Gannett	Rodale
Gruner + Jahr	Time Inc.
Hearst Corporation	Tribune Company
Johnson Publishing	Washington Post
Lagardère Active	Wenner Media
Martha Stewart Living	

HISTORICAL FINANCIALS
Company Type: Private

Income Statement — FYE: December 31

	ESTIMATED REVENUE ($ mil.)	NET INCOME ($ mil.)	NET PROFIT MARGIN	EMPLOYEES
12/07	7,970	—	—	29,100
12/06	7,700	—	—	28,000
12/05	7,315	—	—	30,000
Annual Growth	4.4%	—	—	(1.5%)

Revenue History

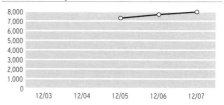

Advanced Drainage Systems

Advanced Drainage Systems' work isn't down the drain, it *is* the drain. The company manufactures high density polyethylene (HDPE) pipes for use in drainage systems for residential and commercial construction projects. Advanced Drainage Systems' plastic products include culverts, drains, fittings, gaskets, grates, screens, leaching chambers, and storm sewers. Customers include mining and timber operations and companies specializing in construction of highways and waste management systems. Advanced Drainage Systems products are also found under some of the more fabled athletic fields and complexes in the US, such as Augusta National, Dodger Stadium, and Lambeau Field.

In 2005 Advanced Drainage Systems acquired regional rival Hancor, creating the world's largest HDPE corrugated plastic pipe company.

The company, which was founded in 1966, operates 40 domestic and international manufacturing facilities. It also has 30 distribution centers in the US.

EXECUTIVES

Chairman, President, and CEO:
 Joseph A. (Joe) Chlapaty, age 62
CFO: Mark B. Sturgeon
EVP; VP Marketing Hancor Inc.: Bob Klein
EVP; VP Manufacturing Hancor Inc.: Jim Baich
EVP Engineering; VP Engineering Hancor Inc.:
 Tom Fussner
Director Marketing: Tori Durliat
Director International Operations: Ewout Leeuwenburg

LOCATIONS

HQ: Advanced Drainage Systems, Inc.
 4640 Trueman Blvd., Hilliard, OH 43026
Phone: 614-658-0050   **Fax:** 614-658-0204
Web: www.ads-pipe.com

COMPETITORS

Charlotte Pipe & Foundry
CONTECH
Diamond Plastics
Enerfab
J-M Manufacturing
NACO Industries
NIBCO
PW Eagle

HISTORICAL FINANCIALS
Company Type: Private

Income Statement — FYE: December 31

	REVENUE ($ mil.)	NET INCOME ($ mil.)	NET PROFIT MARGIN	EMPLOYEES
12/07	1,200	—	—	4,000
12/06	1,200	—	—	3,900
12/05	1,200	—	—	3,800
Annual Growth	0.0%	—	—	2.6%

Revenue History

Advanced Lighting Technologies

And then there was metal halide light. Advanced Lighting Technologies' (ADLT) metal halide simulates sunlight more closely than other lighting technologies. Through subsidiary Venture Lighting, ADLT makes metal halide lamps ranging from 50 to 2,000 watts. Other lighting products include lamp components, power supplies, and lamp-making equipment. A vertically integrated company, ADLT makes the metal halide salts used in its own products; metal halide salts are also sold to other manufacturers. ADLT's Deposition Sciences subsidiary makes passive optical telecommunications devices and deposition coating equipment. The company is 99%-owned by Saratoga Partners.

In 2007 ADLT bought Auer Lighting GmbH of Germany. A maker of components for digital projection, stage, medical, and automotive lighting, Auer Lighting had sales of about $74 million in 2006.

ADLT emerged from Chapter 11 in late 2003 and was taken private after an investment from Saratoga Lighting Holdings, an affiliate of the New York-based private equity investment firm Saratoga Partners.

EXECUTIVES

Chairman: Robert Cizik
CEO and Director: Wayne R. Hellman, $2,210,478 pay
COO and Director: Sabu Krishnan, $477,789 pay
EVP, CFO, and Treasurer: Wayne J. Vespoli, $319,039 pay
VP: Lee A. Bartolomei, $300,000 pay
VP: James L. Schoolenberg, $302,769 pay
Corporate Communications: Lisa Barry
Auditors: Grant Thornton LLP

LOCATIONS

HQ: Advanced Lighting Technologies, Inc.
 32000 Aurora Rd., Solon, OH 44139
Phone: 440-519-0500   **Fax:** 440-519-0501
Web: www.adlt.com

2006 Sales

	$ mil.	% of total
US	98.3	60
UK	30.2	18
Australia	14.3	9
Canada	14.0	9
Other countries	7.0	4
Total	**163.8**	**100**

COMPETITORS

Corning	Magnetek
El Products	Nortel Networks
GE	OSRAM
JDS Uniphase	Philips Electronics
LSI Industries	SLI Holdings International

Advanstar Communications

Advanstar Communications offers a constellation of business-to-business publishing and marketing services related to fashion, life sciences, and powersports. The company has a portfolio of nearly 70 print publications and directories and some 150 electronic publications and Web sites. It stages more than 90 expositions and conferences annually. Titles include *Motor Age*, *Medical Economics*, and *Dermatology Times*; trade shows include apparel show MAGIC Marketplace; and marketing offerings include direct mail services and custom publishing. A consortium of investors led by private-equity firm Veronis Suhler Stevenson owns Advanstar.

The company was previously owned by DLJ Merchant Banking Partners III, the merchant banking affiliate of Donaldson, Lufkin & Jenrette (now part of Credit Suisse Group). In 2007 Veronis Suhler Stevenson acquired the firm for more than $1 billion; Citigroup Private Equity and New York Life Capital Partners were co-sponsors in the deal.

EXECUTIVES

Chairman: James M. (Jim) Alic
CEO and Board Member: Joseph (Joe) Loggia,
$935,273 pay
EVP Corporate Development: Eric I. Lisman, age 50,
$362,000 pay
EVP Healthcare, Pharmaceutical, and Science:
R. Steven (Steve) Morris
EVP Powersports and Automotive:
Daniel M (Danny) Phillips, $325,000 pay
EVP Finance and CFO: Theodore S. (Ted) Alpert,
$71,154 pay (partial-year salary)
EVP Licensing, Market Development, and Europe:
Georgiann DeCenzo
EVP Fashion; President, Magic International:
Chris DeMoulin
EVP Exhibitions: Anthony (Tony) Calanca
VP and General Counsel: Ward D. Hewins
VP Human Resources: Nancy Nugent
VP, Treasurer, and Controller: Shelbie O'Brien
Director Corporate Marketing: Lorelyn Eaves
Manager Corporate Marketing and Communications:
Susannah George
Auditors: PricewaterhouseCoopers LLP

LOCATIONS

HQ: Advanstar Communications Inc.
6200 Canoga Ave., 2nd Fl.,
Woodland Hills, CA 91367
Phone: 818-593-5000   **Fax:** 818-593-5020
Web: www.advanstar.com

PRODUCTS/OPERATIONS

Selected Products and Services

Marketing services
  Classified advertising
  Database marketing
  Direct mail services
  Directories
  Guides and reference books
  Reprints
Trade, business, and professional publications
Trade shows and conferences

Selected Trade Shows and Conferences

International Powersports Dealer Expo (powersports
  accessories trade show)
MAGIC Marketplace (men's apparel trade show)

Selected Publications

Auto Body Repair News
Dental Product Reports
Dermatology Times
DIRTsports
Medical Economics
Motor Age
Pharmaceutical Technology

COMPETITORS

Access Intelligence
BravoSolution US
Crain Communications
Fairchild Publications
Freeman Decorating Services
George P. Johnson
Hanley Wood
Harte-Hanks
IHS
Informa
International Data Group
Lebhar-Friedman
McGraw-Hill
The Nielsen Company
Penton Media
Reed Elsevier Group
Thomas Publishing
United Business Media
Wolters Kluwer

HISTORICAL FINANCIALS

Company Type: Private

Income Statement

FYE: December 31

	REVENUE ($ mil.)	NET INCOME ($ mil.)	NET PROFIT MARGIN	EMPLOYEES
12/06	324	(42)	—	1,000
12/05	289	9	3.0%	1,000
12/04	381	(67)	—	1,400
12/03	326	(70)	—	1,400
12/02	307	(124)	—	1,200
Annual Growth	1.3%	—	—	(4.5%)

Net Income History

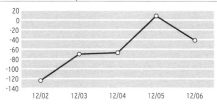

Adventist Health

Not simply waiting around for the advent of good health, Adventist Health operates 18 hospital systems (with about 2,800 beds) in the western portion of the US. Its health care systems — sprinkled throughout California, Hawaii, Oregon, and Washington — also include physicians' clinics and outpatient centers. Additionally, the organization runs more than a dozen home health care agencies and has established a handful of joint-venture nursing homes in California, Oregon, and Washington. Adventist Health maintains strong ties to the Seventh-day Adventist Church but is independently owned. A sister organization, Adventist Health System, operates in the central and southern parts of the country.

The organization works with its own churches and those of other denominations to offer such preventive health services as medical screenings, immunizations, and health education. It also operates a network of more than 20 rural health clinics in California, offering primary and specialty medical care, dental services, and other types of care to underserved regions.

In 2007 Adventist Health sold its Paradise Valley Hospital in National City, California, to Prime Healthcare Services. It is maintaining a presence in the community, however, by building a nursing home there.

EXECUTIVES

Chairman: Jere D. Patzer
Vice Chairman: Ricardo Graham
President, CEO, and Director: Robert G. Carmen
SVP and CFO: Douglas E. Rebok
EVP, COO, and Director: Larry D. Dodds
VP and Treasurer: Rodney Wehtje
SVP: Scott Reiner
VP and Chief Nursing Officer: Gloria Bancarz
VP Clinical Effectiveness and Chief Medical Officer:
Keith R. Doram
VP and CIO: Alan Soderblom
Auditors: Ernst & Young LLP

LOCATIONS

HQ: Adventist Health
2100 Douglas Blvd., Roseville, CA 95661
Phone: 916-781-2000   **Fax:** 916-783-9909
Web: www.adventisthealth.org

Selected Facilities

California
  Central Valley General Hospital (Hanford)
  Feather River Hospital (Paradise)
  Frank R. Howard Memorial Hospital (Willits)
  Glendale Adventist Medical Center (Glendale)
  Hanford Community Medical Center (Hanford)
  Redbud Community Hospital (Clearlake)
  San Joaquin Community Hospital (Bakersfield)
  Selma Community Hospital (Selma)
  Simi Valley Hospital (Simi Valley)
  Sonora Regional Medical Center (Sonora)
  South Coast Medical Center (Laguna Beach)
  St. Helena Hospital (Deer Park)
  Ukiah Valley Medical Center (Ukiah)
  White Memorial Medical Center (Los Angeles)
Hawaii
  Castle Medical Center (Kailua)
Oregon
  Adventist Medical Center (Portland)
  Tillamook County General Hospital (Tillamook)
Washington
  Walla Walla General Hospital (Walla Walla)

COMPETITORS

Catholic Healthcare West
HCA
Kaiser Permanente
Legacy Health System
LifePoint Hospitals
Los Angeles County Health Department
Memorial Health Services
Providence Health & Services
Sisters of Charity of Leavenworth
Sutter Health
Tenet Healthcare

Adventist Health System

One of the country's largest faith-based hospital systems, not-for-profit Adventist Health System runs about 40 hospitals and 15 nursing homes, as well as more than 20 home health care agencies. Its acute care hospitals have more than 6,300 beds combined, and its long-term care facilities offer more than 2,000 beds. While it operates in 10 states (mostly in the South and Midwest), Florida is a key market: The organization's Florida division includes 17 hospitals located throughout the state, with the seven-campus Florida Hospital serving Central Florida via more than 1,400 beds. The health system is sponsored by the Seventh-Day Adventist Church as part of that denomination's legacy of providing health care.

EXECUTIVES

Chairman: Walter L. Wright
President, CEO, and Director: Donald L. Jernigan,
age 61
**President and CEO, Florida Hospital and Florida
Division:** Lars D. Houmann, age 48
President and CEO, Multi-State Division:
Richard K. (Rich) Reiner

CFO: Terry D. Shaw
CIO and Director: Brent G. Snyder
SVP Administration: Robert R. Henderschedt
SVP and Treasurer: Gary C. Skilton
SVP Clinical Effectiveness and Chief Medical Officer:
  Loran D. Hauck
SVP Finance and Senior Financial Officer:
  Paul C. Rathbun
SVP Managed Care: John R. Brownlow
SVP Finance: Lewis A. Seifert
**VP Business Development and Risk Management and
  Chief Compliance Officer; Director:** Sandra K. Johnson
VP Human Resources: Donald G. (Don) Jones
VP Legal Services: T. L. Trimble

LOCATIONS

HQ: Adventist Health System
  111 N. Orlando Ave., Winter Park, FL 32789
Phone: 407-647-4400   **Fax:** 407-975-1469
Web: www.ahss.org

Selected Facilities

Colorado
  Avista Adventist Hospital (Louisville)
  Littleton Adventist Hospital (Littleton)
  Parker Adventist Hospital (Parker)
  Porter Adventist Hospital (Denver)

Florida
  Florida Hospital
    Florida Hospital Altamonte (Altamonte Springs)
    Florida Hospital Apopka
    Florida Hospital Celebration Health (Celebration)
    Florida Hospital Kissimmee
    Florida Hospital East Orlando
    Florida Hospital Orlando
    Florida Hospital Winter Park
  Florida Hospital DeLand
  Florida Hospital Fish Memorial (Orange City)
  Florida Hospital Flagler (Palm Coast)
  Florida Hospital Heartland Medical Center (Sebring)
    Florida Hospital Lake Placid
    Florida Hospital Wauchula
  Florida Hospital Oceanside (Ormond Beach)
  Florida Hospital Ormond Memorial (Ormond Beach)
  Florida Hospital Waterman (Tavares)
  Florida Hospital Zephyrhills

Georgia
  Gordon Hospital (Calhoun)
  Emory-Adventist Hospital (Smyrna)

Illinois
  Adventist Bolingbrook Medical Center (Bolingbrook)
  Adventist GlenOaks Hospital (Glendale Heights)
  Adventist Hinsdale Hospital (Hinsdale)
  Adventist La Grange Memorial Hospital (La Grange)

Kansas
  Shawnee Mission Medical Center (Shawnee Mission)

Kentucky
  Manchester Memorial Hospital (Manchester)

North Carolina
  Park Ridge Hospital (Fletcher)

Tennessee
  Jellico Community Hospital (Jellico)
  Takoma Regional Hospital (Greeneville)

Texas
  Central Texas Medical Center (San Marcos)
  Huguley Memorial Medical Center (Fort Worth)
  Metroplex Hospital (Killeen)
  Rollins-Brook Community Hospital (Lampasas)

Wisconsin
  Chippewa Valley Hospital (Durand)

COMPETITORS

Ascension Health
Catholic Health Initiatives
Catholic Healthcare Partners
Community Health Systems
HCA
Mount Sinai Medical Center of Florida
Orlando Health
Tenet Healthcare

HISTORICAL FINANCIALS

Company Type: Not-for-profit

Income Statement

FYE: December 31

	REVENUE ($ mil.)	NET INCOME ($ mil.)	NET PROFIT MARGIN	EMPLOYEES
12/07	4,835	360	7.5%	43,000
12/06	4,969	325	6.5%	43,000
12/05	4,637	251	5.4%	43,000
12/04	4,379	236	5.4%	—
12/03	4,086	203	5.0%	44,000
Annual Growth	4.3%	15.4%	—	(0.6%)

2007 Year-End Financials

Debt ratio: —   Current ratio: —
Return on equity: 11.9%   Long-term debt ($ mil.): —
Cash ($ mil.): —

Net Income History

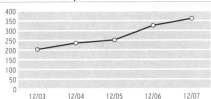

Advocate Health Care

Advocating wellness in Chicagoland from Palos Heights to Palatine, Advocate Health Care is an integrated health care network with more than 200 sites serving the Chicago area. Advocate's operations include ten acute and specialty care hospitals (including Christ Medical Center, Hope Children's Hospital, and Lutheran General Hospital) with 3,500 beds, as well as community health clinics and home health care and hospice services. The health system includes physician medical groups with nearly 500 members, as well as thousands of affiliated doctors.

Advocate also has teaching affiliations with area medical schools, such as the University of Illinois at Chicago, and is part of a clinical laboratory joint venture, ACL Laboratories, with Aurora Health Care. ACL provides analytical and diagnostic testing services for the two companies' facilities.

In 2008 Advocate Health Care agreed to acquire the 200-bed Condell Medical Center for $180 million. Condell Medical had been seeking a buyer due to financial difficulties. Advocate Health Care plans to expand Condell's emergency services and patient capacity.

Advocate Health Care has ties to both the United Church of Christ and the Evangelical Lutheran Church in America. The organization was formed in 1995.

EXECUTIVES

President and CEO: James H. (Jim) Skogsbergh
EVP and COO: William P. (Bill) Santulli
EVP and Chief Medical Officer: Lee B. Sacks
SVP and CIO: Bruce Smith
SVP Strategic Planning and Growth: Scott Powder
SVP Human Resources: Ben Grigaliunas
SVP Communications: Anthony (Tony) Mitchell
SVP and CFO: Dominic J. Nakis

SVP Mission and Spiritual Care:
  Rev Jerry A. Wagenknecht
Chief Legal Officer and General Counsel:
  Gail D. Hasbrouck
Director Public Relations: Mike Maggio
**Director Operations and Support, Advocate Health
  Centers:** Linda Escobar
Director Communications and Government Relations:
  Virgil Giles
Chairperson, Advocate Charitable Foundation:
  Tom Shirey
CEO, Advocate Health Partners: Marty Manning, age 53
Auditors: Ernst & Young

LOCATIONS

HQ: Advocate Health Care
  2025 Windsor Dr., Oak Brook, IL 60523
Phone: 630-572-9393   **Fax:** 630-990-4752
Web: www.advocatehealth.com

PRODUCTS/OPERATIONS

Selected Operations

Advocate Bethany Hospital
Advocate Christ Medical Center
Advocate Good Samaritan Hospital
Advocate Good Shepherd Hospital
Advocate Health Centers
Advocate Home Health Services
Advocate Hope Children's Hospital
Advocate Illinois Masonic Medical Center
Advocate Illinois Masonic Physician Group
Advocate Lutheran General Hospital
Advocate Lutheran General Children's Hospital
Advocate Medical Group
Advocate Physician Partners
Advocate South Suburban Hospital
Advocate Trinity Hospital

COMPETITORS

Alexian Brothers Health System
Children's Memorial Hospital
Covenant Ministries
Evanston Northwestern Healthcare
HCA
Hospital Sisters Health System
Lake Forest Hospital Foundation
Loyola University Health System
Mercy Hospital and Medical Center
Northwest Community Healthcare
Northwestern Memorial HealthCare
Pronger Smith
Provena Health
Rush System for Health
SSM Health Care
University of Chicago Medical Center

HISTORICAL FINANCIALS

Company Type: Not-for-profit

Income Statement

FYE: December 31

	REVENUE ($ mil.)	NET INCOME ($ mil.)	NET PROFIT MARGIN	EMPLOYEES
12/07	3,457	—	—	30,000
12/06	3,268	—	—	29,100
12/05	2,974	—	—	29,600
12/04	2,780	—	—	24,500
12/03	2,716	—	—	25,000
Annual Growth	6.2%	—	—	4.7%

Revenue History

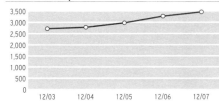

Aerospace Corporation

A not-for-profit company, The Aerospace Corporation provides space-related research, development, and advisory services, primarily for US government programs. Its chief sponsor is the US Air Force, and its main customers have included the Space and Missile Systems Center of Air Force Space Command and the National Reconnaissance Office. Other clients have included NASA and the National Oceanic and Atmospheric Administration, as well as commercial enterprises, universities, and international organizations. Areas of expertise include launch certification, process implementation, systems engineering, and technology application. The Aerospace Corporation was established in 1960.

Officially, the company operates a federally funded research and development center, or FFRDC, for the Air Force. The Aerospace FFRDC is one of more than 40 established to help government agencies with tasks related to aviation, defense, energy, health and human services, space, and tax administration.

EXECUTIVES

Chair: Donald L. Cromer, age 72
President, CEO, and Director: Wanda M. Austin
EVP: Joe M. Straus
SVP Operations and Support Group:
 Jerry M. (Mike) Drennan
SVP, General Counsel, and Secretary: Gordon J. Louttit
SVP Engineering and Technology Group:
 Rami R. Razouk
SVP Systems Planning and Engineering:
 Rand H. Fisher
SVP National Systems Group: Manuel De Ponte
VP, CFO, and Treasurer: Dale E. Wallis
VP Civil and Commercial Operations: Gary P. Pulliam
VP Program Assessment: John R. Wormington
VP Space Launch Operations: Ray F. Johnson
VP Space Program Operations: David J. Gorney
VP and CIO: William C. (Willie) Krenz
VP National Systems Group: Bernard W. Chau
VP Space Operations, Requirements and Technology:
 Catherine J. Steele
Auditors: Deloitte & Touche LLP

LOCATIONS

HQ: The Aerospace Corporation
 2350 E. El Segundo Blvd., El Segundo, CA 90245
Phone: 310-336-5000   **Fax:** 310-336-7055
Web: www.aero.org

HISTORICAL FINANCIALS

Company Type: Not-for-profit

Income Statement

	REVENUE ($ mil.)	NET INCOME ($ mil.)	NET PROFIT MARGIN	EMPLOYEES
				FYE: September 30
9/07	790	—	—	3,942
9/06	720	—	—	3,800
9/05	664	—	—	3,000
Annual Growth	9.1%	—	—	14.6%

Revenue History

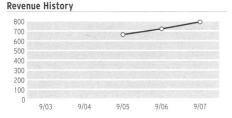

Affinia Group

Affinia Group caters to those with an affinity for car parts. The company is a leading designer, manufacturer, and distributor of aftermarket vehicular components. "Aftermarket" refers to the network of vendors existing to sell vehicle components intended to replace the stock manufacturer's parts. Affinia's products, which are sold in 19 countries worldwide, consist of brake, filtration, and chassis parts and are made for passenger cars; sport utility vehicles (SUVs); light, medium, and heavy trucks; and off-highway vehicles. Its brand names are well-known in the industry and include AIMCO, McQuay-Norris, Nakata, Quinton Hazell, Raybestos, and WIX.

Its brake (cylinders, hardware and hydraulics, drums, shoes, pads, and more) and filtration (oil, fuel, air, and other filters) products account for more than 80% of sales.

Affinia's customers, who are primarily large aftermarket distributors and retailers (who then sell to professional technicians and installers), include CARQUEST, NAPA, and Federated Auto Parts. In addition, the company provides private-label and co-branded components for Federated and Automotive Distribution Network (ADN).

EXECUTIVES

Chairman: Larry W. McCurdy, age 72
President, CEO, and Director: Terry R. McCormack, age 56, $600,000 pay
SVP, General Counsel, and Secretary: Steven E. Keller, age 48, $275,000 pay
SVP and CFO: Thomas H. Madden, age 57, $275,000 pay
VP Business Architecture: Jerry A. McCabe, age 59
VP Human Resources: Timothy J. Zorn, age 54
VP and CIO: James E. Burdiss, age 56
VP Commercial Distribution, Europe:
 Rod Ashby-Johnson, age 63
VP Commercial Distribution, South America:
 Jorge C. Schertel, age 56
President, Global Brake and Chassis Group:
 H. David Overbeeke
President, Global Filtration: Keith A. Wilson, age 45, $310,625 pay
Auditors: Deloitte & Touche LLP

LOCATIONS

HQ: Affinia Group Intermediate Holdings Inc.
 1101 Technology Dr., Ann Arbor, MI 48108
Phone: 734-827-5400   **Fax:** 734-827-5402
Web: www.affiniagroup.com

COMPETITORS

Cardone Industries	Federal-Mogul
CLARCOR	Genuine Parts
Cummins	Honeywell International
Donaldson Company	United Components

HISTORICAL FINANCIALS

Company Type: Private

Income Statement

	REVENUE ($ mil.)	NET INCOME ($ mil.)	NET PROFIT MARGIN	EMPLOYEES
				FYE: December 31
12/07	2,138	6	0.3%	9,507
12/06	2,160	(5)	—	10,497
12/05	2,132	(30)	—	11,678
12/04	2,089	24	1.1%	12,400
Annual Growth	0.8%	(37.0%)	—	(8.5%)

2007 Year-End Financials

Debt ratio: 138.2%	Current ratio: —
Return on equity: 1.5%	Long-term debt ($ mil.): 597
Cash ($ mil.): —	

Net Income History

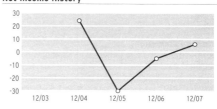

Affinity Group

Recreation is serious business for Affinity Group (AGI). The direct marketing firm sells goods and services through its clubs, such as Good Sam, Coast to Coast, President's Club (which provides discounts for the RV crowd), and Golf Card (discounts for green fees). In 28 states, it runs about 75 Camping World retail stores, which sell RV products (air conditioners, sanitation systems, repair items, and furnishings) not usually found in general merchandise stores. AGI also organizes related trade shows and publishes magazines and travel guides, from which it derives subscription fees and ad sales revenue. Chairman Steve Adams is the majority owner of both AGI and, through another entity, RV retailer FreedomRoads.

Its clubs boast some 1.9 million members. AGI also has 5.3 million in aggregate circulation, as well as 1 million in paid circulation, for its 38 publications.

EXECUTIVES

Chairman: Stephen Adams, age 70
President, CEO, and Director: Michael A. Schneider, age 53, $100,000 pay
EVP Powersports Media: Dick Hendricks
SVP and CFO: Thomas F. Wolfe, age 46, $185,000 pay
SVP Human Resources: Laura A. James, age 51
SVP Business Development and General Counsel, Camping World: Brent Moody, age 46, $320,404 pay
SVP Media: Joe Daquino
SVP Products and Services: Prabhuling Patel, age 61
CEO and President, Camping World:
 Marcus A. Lemonis, age 34
COO Camping World: Mark J. Boggess, age 52, $101,923 pay (prior to title change)
President, E-Commerce, Camping World:
 Kenneth Marshall, age 48, $314,346 pay
President, Affinity Clubs: Grant Miller
Director Internet Marketing: Leslie Pfingston
Auditors: Ernst & Young LLP

LOCATIONS

HQ: Affinity Group, Inc.
 2575 Vista Del Mar, Ventura, CA 93001
Phone: 805-667-4100   **Fax:** 805-667-4419
Web: www.affinitygroup.com

PRODUCTS/OPERATIONS

2007 Sales

	% of total
Retail	57
Membership services	27
Publications	16
Total	**100**

Selected Publications

American Rider
ATV Sport
Bass & Walleye Boats
Boating Industry
Camping Life
Cruising Rider
MotorHome
Powerboat
PowerSports Business
Rider
RV Business
RV View
SnowGoer
Snowmobile
Snow Week
Thunder Press-North
TrailerBoats
Trailer Life
Ultimate Snowmobile Buyers Guide
Watercraft World
Woodall's Tenting Directory
Woodall's Specials

COMPETITORS

International Leisure
Kampgrounds of America
Outdoor Resorts
REI
Thousand Trails

HISTORICAL FINANCIALS

Company Type: Private

Income Statement

	REVENUE ($ mil.)	NET INCOME ($ mil.)	NET PROFIT MARGIN	EMPLOYEES	FYE: December 31
12/07	562	19	3.4%	2,003	
12/06	515	(5,731)	—	2,006	
12/05	486	11	2.2%	1,842	
12/04	465	10	2.2%	1,800	
12/03	425	24	5.7%	1,701	
Annual Growth	7.2%	(6.2%)	—	4.2%	

2007 Year-End Financials

Debt ratio: —
Return on equity: —
Cash ($ mil.): —
Current ratio: —
Long-term debt ($ mil.): 283

Net Income History

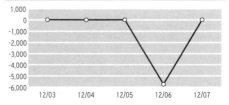

AFL-CIO

Talk about spending a long time in labor: The AFL-CIO (American Federation of Labor and Congress of Industrial Organizations) has been at it for more than a century. The AFL-CIO is an umbrella organization for more than 50 autonomous national and international unions representing more than 10 million workers — ranging from actors and airline pilots to marine engineers and machinists — and fights to improve wages and working conditions. The organization charters 51 state federations and nearly 580 central labor councils. Union members generally receive about 30% higher pay and more benefits than nonmembers.

The organization's membership has been decreasing because of the decline in manufacturing jobs and the increased use of temporary workers and automation. Despite president John Sweeney's aggressive plans to increase recruiting, the Teamsters and the Service Employees International Union (SEIU) left the AFL-CIO in 2005 over the issues of plummeting membership and the future course of the labor movement. They took 3.3 million members with them.

HISTORY

The American Federation of Labor (AFL) was formed in 1886 in Columbus, Ohio, by the merger of six craft unions and a renegade craft section of the Marxist-oriented Knights of Labor. Samuel Gompers, a New York cigar factory worker who headed the AFL until his death in 1924, initiated the AFL's pragmatic focus: to work within the economic system to increase wages, improve working conditions, and abolish child labor.

Gompers' successes incensed employers, whose arsenal, supported by the US courts and public opinion, included injunctions, government-backed police forces to crush strikes, and the Sherman Anti-Trust Act (used to assail union monopoly powers).

WWI's production needs boosted AFL membership to 4 million by 1919. Labor clashes with management were widespread in the 1920s amid the fear of Bolsheviks. As part of open-shop drives, employers replaced strikers with southern African-Americans and Mexican workers.

The Great Depression brought more supportive public and pro-labor laws, including the National Industrial Recovery Act (NIRA, 1933), which allowed union organizing and collective bargaining. After NIRA was declared unconstitutional, the Wagner Act (1936) restated many of NIRA's provisions and established the legal basis for unions.

Union power split in 1935 when AFL coal miner John L. Lewis began organizing unskilled workers. Lewis and his allies, expelled from the AFL, formed the Congress of Industrial Organizations (CIO, 1938) and enjoyed success in unionizing the auto, steel, textile, and other industries. By 1946 the AFL and CIO had 9 million and 5 million members, respectively.

Amid postwar concern over rising prices, communist infiltration, and union corruption, Congress passed the Taft-Hartley Act in 1947 (which outlawed closed shops). The new climate of hostility led the AFL (headed by plumber George Meany) and the CIO (headed by autoworker Walter Reuther) to merge in 1955. The AFL-CIO soon expelled the Teamsters and other unions on

charges of corruption. (The Teamsters reaffiliated in 1987.)

AFL-CIO membership jumped after President Kennedy gave federal employees the right to unionize (1962); state, county, and municipal workers soon followed.

Union membership, which peaked in the mid-1940s with more than a third of the US labor force, was particularly hurt by a jump in imported goods in the 1970s and automation's triumph over manual labor in the 1980s. Legislation supported by the AFL-CIO included a law requiring 60 days' notice for plant closings (1988) and the Family Medical Leave Act (1993). But labor lost its battle against NAFTA (North American Free Trade Agreement), which it feared would export jobs to Mexico.

In 1995 John Sweeney, former head of the Service Employees International Union (SEIU), became president of the AFL-CIO in its first contested election. Under Sweeney the union spent $35 million in advertising in 1996 to draw attention to issues. After years with little focus on organizing, in 1997 the AFL-CIO launched a massive campaign to organize construction, hospital, and hotel workers in Las Vegas, and committed a third of its budget to recruiting and reorganizing. It supported the Teamsters' successful strike against UPS in 1997 and in 1998 threw its weight behind the Air Line Pilots Association's walkout on Northwest Airlines. It approved a restructuring plan in 1999 and the next year spent significant time and money rallying members all across the US in support of losing presidential candidate Al Gore. In 2002 AFL-CIO announced its pledge of $750 million to create affordable housing in New York City.

At the group's 2005 convention, the Teamsters and the SEIU broke ranks over Sweeney's inability to stem the tide of falling membership. They joined a rival group, Change to Win Coalition, led by SEIU's Andrew Stern.

EXECUTIVES

President: John J. Sweeney, age 74
EVP: Arlene Holt Baker
Secretary and Treasurer: Richard L. Trumka, age 59
General Counsel: Jonathan Hiatt

LOCATIONS

HQ: AFL-CIO
815 16th St. NW, Washington, DC 20006
Phone: 202-637-5000 **Fax:** 202-637-5323
Web: www.aflcio.org

PRODUCTS/OPERATIONS

Selected Trades and Workers Represented

Acting	Industrial trades
Airline pilots	Maritime trades
Broadcasting	Metal trades
Building trades	Mining
Education	Music
Electrical trades	Office employees
Engineering	Police
Farmworkers	Postal employees
Firefighters	Restaurant employees
Flight attendants	Teachers
Food trades	Transportation trades
Government workers	Utility workers
Hotel employees	Writers

Ag Processing

Soy far, soy good for Ag Processing (AGP), one of the largest soybean processors in the US. AGP's chief soybean products include vegetable oil and commercial animal feeds. The agricultural cooperative provides grain marketing and transportation services for its members. The cooperative also offers corn-based ethanol and soybean oil-based bio-fuels, fuel additives, and solvents. AGP processes some 15,000 acres of soybeans a day from its members' farms. The co-op's owners include approximately 250,000 member-farmers in the US and Canada. Mostly Midwestern farmers, AGP's members are represented through about 200 local and regional co-ops.

AGP also turns its products into food ingredients, such as lecithin and meat extenders for ground beef. To capitalize on new EPA emission limits and mandates, the co-op lobbies to increase retail demand for ethanol. Additionally, AGP is promoting methyl ester, a by-product of soy oil refining, for use as a clean fuel and fuel additive, agricultural spray, and non-toxic solvent to replace petroleum-based products.

In 2007 the co-op's board rejected a hostile take-over bid made by Ag Processors Alliance (APA). (APA was formed exclusively to take over AGP and consisted of the leadership of Ag and Food Associates of Omaha, an investment banking firm that manages the project on behalf of an investment group that has a specific interest and expertise in agricultural operations.)

HISTORY

Seeking strength in numbers, Ag Processing (AGP) was formed in 1983 when agricultural cooperatives Land O' Lakes and Farmland Industries merged their money-losing soybean operations into similarly struggling Boone Valley Cooperative.

Separately, AGP's six soybean mills had been unable to compete successfully against each other and larger corporations. The entire industry had been hampered by the Soviet grain embargoes imposed by the US in 1973 and 1979, and US government policies had contributed to increased competition from heavily subsidized soy producers in Argentina and Brazil. Soy exports from the US had fallen dramatically, leading to a production capacity surplus.

Collectively, AGP was able to attract a stronger management staff than its predecessors had; it hired 21-year Archer Daniels Midland (ADM) veteran James Lindsay as CEO and general manager. With operations scattered over four states, AGP placed its headquarters in Omaha, Nebraska — chosen for its central location and close proximity to the co-op's main bank.

In its first two years, AGP cut employee rolls by 20% and scaled back production, thus trimming costs and squeezing higher prices for finished products. A turnaround came quickly, and in 1985 members received a dividend from the co-op's $8 million pretax profit. That year AGP purchased two Iowa plants from AGRI Industries.

AGP dismantled two plants in 1987. By the next year the co-op witnessed an increase in domestic demand and had resumed selling to the Soviet Union. It generated additional sales by further processing soybean oil into food-grade products like hydrogenated oil and lecithin.

With an eye on diversification and value-added products, by 1991 AGP had expanded to eight soybean plants and two vegetable oil refineries; it also acquired the feed and grain business of International Multifoods that year through an 80%-owned joint venture with ADM. The acquisition included 29 feed plants in the US and Canada, 26 retail centers, 18 grain elevators, and the brands Supersweet and Masterfeeds. In 1994 AGP formed feed manufacturer Consolidated Nutrition, a 50-50 joint-venture with ADM.

Consolidated Nutrition introduced a Swine Operations program in 1996. The program quickly grew through the development of PORK PACT, a partnership to serve pork producers. (The co-op has since exited the swine business.) The next year AGP's grain division sold nine grain elevators in Ohio and Indiana to Cargill. That year the co-op gained control of Venezuelan feed manufacturer Proagro.

By 1998 passage of the Freedom to Farm Act and growing demand had spurred soybean planting. The co-op in 1998 opened an additional processing plant in Emmetsburg, Iowa, followed by another in Eagle Grove, Iowa. AGP sold off its pet food operations in 1998 to Windy Hill, which was later acquired by Doane Pet Care Enterprises. Also that year Consolidated Nutrition combined its Master Mix and Supersweet feed brands into the Consolidated Nutrition label.

In 1999 the company added the Garner-Klemme-Meservey cooperative to its grain operations. It opened a new plant late that year in St. Joseph, Missouri, to make value-added products such as hardfat (used in emulsifiers).

In 2001 AGP sold its 50% share of Consolidated Nutrition to ADM. In 2002 the co-op's Masterfeeds business acquired four feed mills and a merchandising operation from Saskatchewan Wheat Pool (now Viterra). In 2003 AGP opened the Port of Grays Harbor vessel-loading terminal in Aberdeen, Washington.

The company formed a subsidiary, AgGrowth Products, to market crop nutrients manufactured by Bio Tech Nutrients in 2005. Also that year, the company announced facility expansions for its ethanol, biodiesel, and soybean processing operations.

EXECUTIVES

Chairman: Bradley T. (Brad) Davis
Vice Chairman: Lowell D. Wilson
CEO and General Manager: Martin P. (Marty) Reagan
SVP and Corporate Controller: Tim E. Witty
SVP Corporate and Member Relations:
  Michael L. Maranell
SVP Engineering and Environment:
  Charles A. Janiszewski
SVP Human Resources: Judith V. Ford
SVP Transportation: Terry J. Voss
SVP Marketing and Soybean and Corn Processing:
  Gregory (Greg) Twist
SVP Industrial Products and Government Relations:
  John B. Campbell
SVP Refined Vegetable Oils: David E. Tegeder
SVP Operations and Research: Richard P. Copeland
VP, Corporate General Counsel, and Assistant Secretary: Larry J. Steier
Treasurer, Secretary, and Director: Dean B. Isaacson
Director International Trade and Business Development: Pete Mishek
Auditors: Deloitte & Touche LLP

LOCATIONS

HQ: Ag Processing Inc
  12700 W. Dodge Rd., Omaha, NE 68154
Phone: 402-496-7809   **Fax:** 402-498-2215
Web: www.agp.com

PRODUCTS/OPERATIONS

Selected Brands

AMINOPLUS (dairy feed additive)
BYN (crop nutrient)
Masterfeeds (feeds, Canada)
Progtinal/Proagro (poultry and feed, Venezuela)
SOYGOLD (bio-diesel, solvents, fuel additives)

Selected Exported Products

Barley
Corn
Distillers dried grains (DDGS)
Feeding Peas
High-protein soybean meal
Lecithin
Low-protein soybean meal
Oats
Soybean hulls
Soybean oil
Soybeans
Sunflowers
Wheat

Selected Operations

Commercial feeds
Food (lecithin, soybean oil, vegetable oil)
Grain
Industrial products (ethanol, methyl ester)
Soybean processing

COMPETITORS

Abengoa Bioenergy
ADM
ADM Alliance Nutrition
AGRI Industries
Agrium
Andersons
Badger State Ethanol
Bunge Limited
Bunge Milling
Cargill
CHS
Corn Products
  International
Crop Production Services
DeBruce Grain
Griffin Industries
GROWMARK
J. D. Heiskell & Company
Lake Area Corn Processors
Land O'Lakes Purina Feed
Liberty Vegetable Oil
Little Sioux Corn
  Processors
MFA
Omega Protein
Owensboro Grain
Riceland Foods
Scoular
Southern States
SunOpta

HISTORICAL FINANCIALS

Company Type: Cooperative

Income Statement

FYE: August 31

	REVENUE ($ mil.)	NET INCOME ($ mil.)	NET PROFIT MARGIN	EMPLOYEES
8/07	2,685	76	2.8%	950
8/06	2,361	63	2.7%	1,000
8/05	2,350	42	1.8%	1,000
8/04	2,664	26	1.0%	—
8/03	2,127	11	0.5%	1,500
Annual Growth	6.0%	61.9%	—	(10.8%)

2007 Year-End Financials

Debt ratio: 27.8%   Current ratio: —
Return on equity: 15.9%   Long-term debt ($ mil.): 134
Cash ($ mil.): —

Net Income History

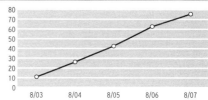

A.G. Spanos

Spanning the land from California to Florida, A.G. Spanos Companies bridges many operations: from building, managing, and selling multi-family housing units to constructing master-planned communities, to developing land, to building commercial space. The firm currently has around 20 multifamily properties in seven states. Operations include luxury apartments in the Sunbelt, some 2 million square feet of office and retail space, master-planned and mixed-use development, and property management. Alex Spanos, owner of the NFL's San Diego Chargers, operates the company with his sons Dean (president and CEO) and Michael Spanos (EVP).

In 1951 Alex Spanos quit his job as a baker at his father's bakery to found his first business, A.G. Spanos Agricultural Catering Service. He moved into real estate in 1956 and built his first apartment building in 1960. The firm has built more than 100,000 apartments in 18 states since its founding.

EXECUTIVES

Chairman and Founder: Alexander Gus (Alex) Spanos, age 85
President and CEO: Dean A. Spanos, age 58
CFO: Jeremiah T. Murphy, age 64
EVP: Michael A. Spanos, age 46
EVP: Charlie Raffo
VP Marketing and Sales: Nick Faklis
Director, Public Relations and Communications: Natalia Orfanos

LOCATIONS

HQ: A. G. Spanos Companies
10100 Trinity Pkwy., 5th Fl., Stockton, CA 95219
Phone: 209-478-7954   **Fax:** 209-473-3703
Web: www.agspanos.com

Apartment Complexes

	No.
California	7
Texas	5
Florida	2
Georgia	2
Kansas	2
Nevada	2
Arizona	1
Total	**21**

PRODUCTS/OPERATIONS

Other Ownership Interests

Bell Wine Cellars
San Diego Chargers National Football League Team
Spanos Berberian Wine Company

COMPETITORS

Avatar Holdings
Castle & Cooke
Engle Homes
Irvine Company
SunCor Development
Trammell Crow Residential

Alabama Farmers Cooperative

Alabama Farmers Cooperative (AFC) provides farmers in the Yellowhammer State a full range of agricultural supplies and services, including feed, fertilizer, seed, grain storage, and marketing, along with home-gardening items such as seeds and hardware. The co-op, which boasts 46 member associations, also serves members in parts of Florida, Georgia, and Mississippi. AFC owns Bonnie Plant Farms, one of the largest suppliers of vegetable plants and annual flowers in the US. Its Anderson's Peanuts division was sold to Birdsong in 2007. Originally called the Tennessee Valley Fertilizer Cooperative, it was established in 1936.

EXECUTIVES

Chairman: Larry Bennich
Vice Chairman: Lawrence Smith
President and CEO: Tommy Paulk
Secretary, Treasurer, and CFO: Dan Groscost
EVP and COO: Roger Pangle
EVP and COO, BioLogic: Bobby Cole
VP and Manager, Cooperative Financial Services: Bill Eubanks
VP and General Manager, Anderson's Peanut: Dennis Finch
VP Management Services: James Fudge
VP Grain: John Gamble
VP Feed, Farm, and Home: Steve Moore
VP and General Manager, Bonnie Plant Division: Dennis Thomas
VP Human Resources: Tina Johnson
Director Public Relations and Advertising: Jim Allen
Corporate Controller and President, BioLogic: Albert (Al) Cheatham Jr.
CIO: Wayne Holt

LOCATIONS

HQ: Alabama Farmers Cooperative, Inc.
121 Somerville Rd. SE, Decatur, AL 35601
Phone: 256-353-6843   **Fax:** 256-350-1770
Web: www.alafarm.com

PRODUCTS/OPERATIONS

Sales Segments

Grain
Feed, Farm, and Home
    Feed
    Animal Health
    Lawn and Garden
    Hardware and TBA
Peanut
Gin
Plant

COMPETITORS

Ag Processing
Andersons
CHS
Jimmy Sanders
Scoular
Southern States
Tennessee Farmers Co-op

HISTORICAL FINANCIALS

Company Type: Cooperative

Income Statement

FYE: May 31

	REVENUE ($ mil.)	NET INCOME ($ mil.)	NET PROFIT MARGIN	EMPLOYEES
5/07	260	—	—	2,300
5/06	255	—	—	2,300
5/05	267	—	—	—
5/04	286	—	—	—
5/03	324	—	—	—
Annual Growth	**(5.4%)**	**—**	**—**	**0.0%**

Revenue History

Alberici Corporation

Alberici helped shape the St. Louis skyline; it now sets its sights — or its construction sites — across North America. Alberici Corporation, parent of Alberici Constructors (formerly J.S. Alberici Construction Co.), encompasses a group of enterprises with a presence in North America, South America, and Europe. Operations include construction services, building materials, and steel fabrication and erection units. Alberici offers general contracting, design/build, construction management, demolition, and specialty contracting services. It also offers facilities management. The Alberici family still holds the largest share of the employee-owned firm, founded in 1918 by John S. Alberici.

The company has a joint venture with the Washington Division of URS Corporation to build a cement plant in Missouri for Holcim (US). The plant will be one of the largest in the world.

EXECUTIVES

Chairman: John S. Alberici
President; President, Alberici Constructors, Inc.: Gregory J. (Greg) Kozicz
CFO, Alberici Group: Gregory T. (Greg) Hesser
SVP, Administration and Contract Review, Alberici Group: James E. (Jim) Frey
SVP, Business Acquisition: Steven E. (Steve) Olson
CIO and VP, Support Services, Alberici Group: Frank C. Kropiunik
COO, Alberici Constructors, Inc.: Leroy J. Stromberg
General Manager, Hillsdale Structures, Alberici Constructors, Ltd. (Canada): Jeff Tyers
VP and General Manager, Hillsdale Fabricators: Michael W. (Mike) Burke
VP, Employee Services, Alberici Group: Denay Davis
VP and General Counsel: Trevor Ladner
Diversity Manager, St. Louis: Chris Enriquez

LOCATIONS

HQ: Alberici Corporation
8800 Page Ave., St. Louis, MO 63114
Phone: 314-733-2000   **Fax:** 314-733-2001
Web: www.alberici.com

PRODUCTS/OPERATIONS

Selected Markets

Automotive
Building
Health care
Industrial
Manufacturing/Food and Beverage
Water and Wastewater Treatment

COMPETITORS

Aker Construction
Barton Malow
Bechtel
Black & Veatch
DPR Construction
Fluor
Fred Weber
Hensel Phelps
 Construction
Hoffman Corporation
Hunt Construction

Jacobs Engineering
McCarthy Building
Parsons Corporation
Perini
Peter Kiewit Sons'
TIC Holdings
Turner Corporation
Walbridge Aldinger
Walsh Group
Washington Division
Zachry Group

Albertsons LLC

Call it the incredible shrinking grocery chain. Albertsons LLC (formerly Albertson's) is all that's left of what was once the nation's #2 supermarket operator. Stung by competition, the 2,500-store chain sold itself in mid-2006 to a consortium that included rival grocer SUPERVALU, drugstore chain CVS, investment firm Cerberus Capital Management, and Kimco Realty for about $9.7 billion. SUPERVALU and CVS cherry picked the company's best supermarket and drugstore assets. Subsequent divestments (most notably 132 stores in Northern California and another 50 stores in Florida) have left the company with 250-plus Albertsons supermarkets and about 115 Express fuel centers in about half a dozen states.

Albertsons' remaining stores are located in the Southwest (Arizona, New Mexico, and El Paso, Texas), Florida, Louisiana, and Texas. However, Albertsons has sold about half of its supermarkets in Florida to Publix Super Markets, leaving the grocer with just about 45 stores in the Sunshine State. The grocery chain exited the Oklahoma market in mid-2007.

Albertsons, in May 2008, agreed to sell 72 of its Express fuel centers in Arizona, Colorado, Louisiana, and Texas to Valero Energy Corp. The company wants to focus its energies on its core grocery and pharmacy business.

Incursions into the grocery market from nontraditional players, including Wal-Mart Supercenters and Costco Wholesale, hurt the grocery chain's performance and led to the decision to sell the company. (Both Wal-Mart and Costco had overtaken Albertson's 4.9% share of the grocery market.) The recruitment in 2001 of General Electric veteran Lawrence R. Johnston as chairman and CEO of the company failed to save the grocery chain.

Other investors in Albertsons LLC include Schottenstein Stores, Lubert-Adler Partners, and Klaff Realty LP.

HISTORY

J. A. "Joe" Albertson, Leonard Skaggs (whose family ran Safeway), and Tom Cuthbert founded Albertson's Food Center in Boise, Idaho, in 1939. Albertson, who left his position as district manager for Safeway to run the store, thought big from the start. The 10,000-sq.-ft. store was not only eight times the size of the average competitor, it also offered an in-store butcher shop and bakery, one of the country's first magazine racks, and homemade "Big Joe" ice-cream cones. The men ended their partnership in 1945, the year Albertson's was incorporated, and by 1947 it operated six stores in Idaho.

The company opened its first combination food store and drugstore, a 60,000-sq.-ft. superstore, in 1951 and began locating stores in growing suburban areas. Albertson's went public to raise expansion capital in 1959 and by 1960 had 62 stores in Idaho, Oregon, Utah, and Washington. The food retailer acquired Greater All American Markets (1964), a grocery chain based in Downey, California, and Semrau & Sons (1965) of Oakland, which aided the company's thrust into the California market.

Albertson's and the Skaggs chain (by this time run by L. S. Skaggs Jr.) reunited temporarily in 1969, financing six Skaggs-Albertson's food-and-drug-combination stores. (The partnership dissolved in 1977, with each side taking half of the units.) By 1986 the company had reached $5 billion in sales, a fivefold increase over 1975.

The company purchased 74 Jewel Osco combination food stores and drugstores (mostly in Arkansas, Florida, Oklahoma, and Texas) from American Stores in 1992. Co-founder Albertson died in 1993 at age 86.

In 1997 the United Food and Commercial Workers union, which represents supermarket employees, sued Albertson's, alleging the company forced employees to work overtime without pay. (It was settled in 1999, resulting in a $22 million charge.)

In 1999 the grocer revisited its roots when it acquired American Stores (Skaggs' successor), which operated more than 1,550 stores in 26 states. To obtain regulatory approval for the $12 billion deal, Albertson's sold 145 stores in overlapping markets in three states (most were in California).

In 2001 Larry Johnston, former CEO of GE Appliances, took over as chairman and CEO of Albertson's. Facing increasing competition (especially from Wal-Mart), Johnston announced in March 2002 aggressive restructuring plans that included job cuts and closing 95 stores in underperforming markets, specifically Memphis and Nashville, Tennessee, and Houston and San Antonio, Texas. Albertson's exited the New England drugstore market in 2002 when it sold 80 New England Osco stores to Brooks Pharmacy.

A four-and-a-half month strike by grocery workers in Southern California ended in March 2004. The dispute pitted workers' demands for continued generous health care coverage vs. management's call for cost cuts to remain profitable in the face of Wal-Mart's entry into the Southern California grocery market. In April Albertson's completed the acquisition of JS USA Holdings, which runs Shaw's and Star Markets stores in New England, from UK grocer J Sainsbury. The deal to buy Shaw's was worth about

$2.4 billion (cash and leases). In September Albertson's gained a toehold in the gourmet-food market with the purchase of Bristol Farms, the operator of about a dozen upscale food markets in Southern California.

In June 2006 Albertson's was sold to a consortium that included SUPERVALU, CVS, Cerberus Capital Management, and Kimco for about $9.7 billion. Following the acquisition and the divvying up of Albertson's assets, the surviving company went private and changed its name to Albertsons LLC. Concurrently, Johnston left Albertsons and was succeeded by Robert Miller, chairman of drugstore chain Rite Aid and the former head of Fred Meyer for eight years in the 1990s. Of the company's 27 price-impact Super Saver stores, 25 closed their doors in mid-2006. Also, in June, the company put about 45 stores on the auction block. (It was announced in late 2006 that discount apparel retailer Ross Stores would acquire these stores.)

In February 2007 Albertsons sold 132 grocery stores and two distribution centers in Northern California and Nevada to Save Mart Supermarkets for an undisclosed amount. Other recent closings include stores in Texas, in the Dallas-Fort Worth, Austin, and Longview markets; Colorado; and Oklahoma.

Albertsons also sold eight of its stores in Wyoming to SUPERVALU in January 2008. The divestments continued in September with the sale of 49 supermarkets in Florida to Publix Super Markets for about $500 million.

EXECUTIVES

Chairman: Howard S. Cohen, age 61
CEO: Robert (Bob) Miller
CFO: Richard J. (Rick) Navarro, age 56
SVP Distribution Operations: Michael (Mike) McCarthy
SVP Human Resources and Labor Relations:
 Andrew Scoggin
SVP Marketing and Merchandising: Mark Butler
SVP and General Counsel: Paul Rowan
CIO: Mark Bates
Chief Strategic Officer: Justin Dye
President, Dallas/Ft. Worth Division: William Emmons
President, Florida: Wayne A. Denningham
President, Southwest: Robert (Bob) Colgrove

LOCATIONS

HQ: Albertsons LLC
 250 Parkcenter Blvd., Boise, ID 83706
Phone: 208-395-6200   **Fax:** 208-395-6349
Web: albertsonsmarket.com

COMPETITORS

Costco Wholesale
H-E-B
IGA
King Soopers
Kmart
Kroger
Publix
Rite Aid
Safeway
SAM'S CLUB
Walgreen
Wal-Mart
Whole Foods
Winn-Dixie

Aleris International

Aleris International was formed in 2004 when aluminum recycler IMCO Recycling bought Commonwealth Industries. It got a lot bigger with the 2006 acquisition of Corus Group's downstream aluminum operations and has continued to grow through acquisitions. Its rolled and extruded products unit makes alloy aluminum sheet from recycled metal as well as extruded profiles for the construction and engineering markets. Aleris' recycling unit processes recycled aluminum (beverage cans and scrap) and metal alloys (aluminum scrap and other metals). It operates in China, the Americas, and throughout Europe. In 2006 Texas Pacific Group acquired Aleris for about $3.5 billion in cash and assumed debt.

Aleris International paid $150 million for ALSCO Metals, a supplier of aluminum building products that had annual sales of somewhere near $300 million. Also in 2005 Aleris bought aluminum rolled products and recycling assets from Ormet for $133 million. The next year the company acquired the extruded product operations of Corus for nearly a billion dollars. It kept on aquiring in 2007, too, when Aleris bought Wabash Alloys from Connell LP.

Aleris also used to recycle zinc to make galvanized steel, paint, and chemicals. Following the Wabash Alloys deal it sold that business to Votorantim Metais for about $300 million. The move allowed Aleris to concentrate on its aluminum operations as well as to pay down some of the debt accumulated from all the acquisitions.

The name Aleris is meant to combine *alliance*, *aluminum*, and *era*.

EXECUTIVES

Chairman, President, and CEO:
Steven J. (Steve) Demetriou, age 49, $2,457,000 pay
EVP and CFO: Kevin L. Brown, age 48
EVP; President, Aleris Europe: Roeland Baan, age 50
EVP Corporate Development and Strategy:
Sean M. Stack, age 41
EVP, General Counsel, and Secretary:
Christopher R. Clegg, age 50
SVP and Controller: Scott A. McKinley, age 46
SVP; President, Aleris Rolled and Extruded Products, Europe: Alfred Haszler, age 62
SVP and Chief Accounting Officer: Joseph M. Mallak, age 42
SVP and General Manager, Rolled Products North America: K. Alan Dick
Auditors: Ernst & Young LLP

LOCATIONS

HQ: Aleris International, Inc.
25825 Science Park Dr., Ste. 400,
Beachwood, OH 44122
Phone: 216-910-3400   **Fax:** 216-910-3650
Web: www.aleris.com

Aleris International operates from facilities in Asia, Europe, and North and South America.

2007 Sales

	$ mil.	% of total
North America		
US	2,978.4	50
Other countries	237.8	4
Europe	2,345.7	39
Asia	211.1	4
South America	194.9	3
Other regions	13.0	—
Total	**5,989.9**	**100**

PRODUCTS/OPERATIONS

2007 Sales

	$ mil.	% of total
Global rolled & extruded products	4,305.0	70
Global recycling	1,808.5	30
Adjustments	(123.6)	—
Total	**5,989.9**	**100**

COMPETITORS

Alcoa
David J. Joseph
Kaiser Aluminum
Norsk Hydro ASA
Novelis
Quanex Building Products
Rio Tinto Alcan

HISTORICAL FINANCIALS

Company Type: Private

Income Statement				FYE: December 31
	REVENUE ($ mil.)	NET INCOME ($ mil.)	NET PROFIT MARGIN	EMPLOYEES
12/07	5,990	(126)	—	8,800
12/06	4,749	70	1.5%	8,500
12/05	2,429	74	3.1%	4,200
12/04	1,227	(24)	—	3,200
12/03	892	(1)	—	1,788
Annual Growth	61.0%	—	—	48.9%

2007 Year-End Financials

Debt ratio: 322.5%
Return on equity: —
Cash ($ mil.): —
Current ratio: —
Long-term debt ($ mil.): 2,744

Net Income History

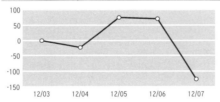

Alex Lee

Wholesale groceries is only part of the story for this company. Alex Lee is a leading wholesale distributor of food and other products to retailers and food service operators. Through Merchants Distributors, Inc. (MDI), it supplies food and related merchandise to more than 600 retailers in about 10 states, mostly in the Southeast. Its Institutional Food House (IFH) unit is a foodservice supplier serving customers in the hospitality industry. Alex Lee also operates a chain of more than 100 grocery stores through Lowe's Food Stores, and it provides warehousing services through Consolidation Services. Alex and Lee George started the company in 1931; the George family continues to control Alex Lee.

The company joined with Canadian meat processor Vantage Foods to open a $21 million meat packaging plant in 2007. The facility serves Alex Lee's grocery stores, as well as its MDI wholesale distribution operation.

Alex Lee began diversifying its operations in the 1960s when it acquired IFH. It bought the Lowe's Food chain in 1984 and formed its Consolidation Services warehousing and logistics outsourcing subsidiary in 1998.

EXECUTIVES

Chairman and CEO: Boyd L. George, age 66
President: Dennis G. Hatchell
EVP and CFO: Ronald W. Knedlik
VP, Human Resources: Glenn DeBiasi
VP, Information Systems: Jay Schwarz
President, Institution Food House:
David A. (Dave) Stansfield
President, Lowes Foods: Curtis L. Oldenkamp

LOCATIONS

HQ: Alex Lee, Inc.
120 4th St. SW, Hickory, NC 28602
Phone: 828-725-4424   **Fax:** 828-725-4435
Web: www.alexlee.com

COMPETITORS

Ahold USA
Associated Wholesale Grocers
Ben E. Keith
C&S Wholesale
H.T. Hackney
Ingles Markets
Kroger
K-VA-T Food Stores

MAINES
McLane
Nash-Finch
Performance Food
Ruddick
SUPERVALU
SYSCO
U.S. Foodservice
Winn-Dixie

Alfa Mutual

Alfa Corporation wants to be the top dog in the Alabama insurance pack. As a subsidiary of the Alfa Mutual group of companies (Alfa Mutual Insurance, Alfa Mutual Fire Insurance, and Alfa Mutual General Insurance), Alfa Corporation provides personal property/casualty insurance in a dozen central and southeastern states. It also offers life insurance policies in Alabama, Georgia, and Mississippi. The company enjoys a pooling arrangement between all of the Alfa companies. President and chairman Jerry Newby is also president of the Alabama Farmers Federation, which founded the company in 1946.

Alfa makes the majority of its money on personal auto and homeowners insurance, and it holds a healthy market share of the property/casualty market in Alabama. However, the company does engage in non-insurance activities, including consumer lending, real estate investment and sales, and other financial services.

Acquisitions have helped to expand Alfa's territory. In 2005 the company acquired The Vision Insurance Group (Tennessee) to expand its personal lines business. The new subsidiary is named Alfa Vision Insurance Corporation. In early 2007 the company acquired what had been Virginia Mutual (Virginia) and folded it into Alfa Alliance Insurance Corporation.

The Alfa Mutual group of companies owned 54% of Alfa Corporation until 2008 when it acquired the rest of the company and took it private.

EXECUTIVES

Chairman, President, and CEO: Jerry A. Newby, age 60, $330,167 pay
EVP Marketing: Herman T. Watts, age 60, $182,909 pay
EVP Operations and Assistant Treasurer: C. Lee Ellis, age 56, $225,164 pay
SVP and CIO: John T. Jung, age 61, $228,535 pay
SVP, CFO, and Chief Investment Officer:
  Stephen G. Rutledge, age 49, $153,960 pay
SVP, General Counsel, and Secretary: H. Al Scott, age 52
SVP Corporate Development: Al Schellhorn, age 43
SVP Claims: W. Jerry Johnson, age 52
SVP Human Resources: Thomas E. Bryant, age 61
SVP Underwriting: Wyman Cabaniss, age 56
SVP Life and Loan Operations: Robert Robison, age 49
Auditors: PricewaterhouseCoopers LLP

LOCATIONS

HQ: Alfa Corporation
  2108 E. South Blvd., Montgomery, AL 36116
Phone: 334-288-3900   **Fax:** 334-613-4709
Web: www.alfains.com

PRODUCTS/OPERATIONS

2007 Revenues

	$ mil.	% of total
Property/casualty insurance	625.9	75
Life insurance	88.9	11
Net investment income	94.8	11
Net realized investment losses	(1.1)	—
Other income	27.7	3
Total	**836.2**	**100**

COMPETITORS

ACE Limited
AIG
Allstate
Atlantic American
Chubb Corp
Cotton States Insurance
GEICO
National Security Group
Progressive Corporation
Prudential
Safeco
State Farm

HISTORICAL FINANCIALS

Company Type: Private

Income Statement

	ASSETS ($ mil.)	NET INCOME ($ mil.)	INCOME AS % OF ASSETS	EMPLOYEES
12/07	2,642	94	3.5%	4,923
12/06	2,534	106	4.2%	4,161
12/05	2,382	99	4.2%	0
12/04	2,223	89	4.0%	—
12/03	2,045	79	3.8%	—
Annual Growth	**6.6%**	**4.5%**	**—**	**—**

FYE: December 31

2007 Year-End Financials

Equity as % of assets: 33.2%   Long-term debt ($ mil.): 101
Return on assets: 3.6%   Sales ($ mil.): 836
Return on equity: 11.0%

Net Income History

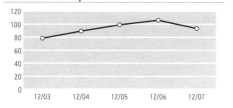

Alion Science and Technology

Ah, Alion! Alion Science and Technology creates an alliance between science, technology, and big government. Alion is a development and research company that provides consulting and technology services primarily to federal agencies. The majority of its revenues come from contracts with the US Department of Defense (DoD), especially the Navy. Its areas of specialty include marine and naval architecture and engineering, wargaming, lab support and chemical decontamination, wireless operations, military transformation, wireless communications engineering, and more. Employee-owned Alion operates from offices and facilities throughout the US, generally near government military bases and other installations.

Alion counts on the US government for nearly all of its business, but the company has said that it plans on expanding its client base to include more civilian agencies and to build its organization through acquisitions.

To this end, the company in 2006 made a series of acquisitions including the purchase of program management and engineering services firm Anteon from General Dynamics. Other purchases that year included software and systems engineering firm BMH Associates, enterprise IT and management consultancy Washington Consulting, and the high-speed vessel design technology assets of Australia-based International Catamaran Designs (INCAT).

The company acquired the assets of logistics and inventory tracking firm LogConGroup in 2007. The deal expands the company's high-value asset and identification and tracking operations. LogConGroup's technology incorporates RFID and other high-tech tracking systems.

EXECUTIVES

Chairman and CEO: Bahman Atefi, age 54
EVP and COO: Stacy Mendler, age 44
Group SVP: Richard Meidenbauer
Group SVP: Roger Bagbey
SVP, Acting CFO, Assistant Treasurer, and Executive Director Financial Operations: Michael J. Alber, age 50
SVP Engineering and Integration Solutions: Scott Fry, age 58
SVP Administration: Gary N. Armstutz
SVP Defense Operations Integration: Rob Goff, age 61
SVP Corporate Development: Sidney I. (Sid) Firstman
SVP Engineering and Information Technology:
  Walter (Buck) Buchanan, age 57
SVP, General Counsel, and Secretary:
  James C. (Jim) Fontana, age 49
Manager Corporate Development: Steve Kimmel
Chief Administrative Officer: Patricia A. Weaver
Director Marketing and Communications:
  Peter J. Jacobs
Auditors: KPMG LLP

LOCATIONS

HQ: Alion Science and Technology Corporation
  1750 Tysons Blvd., Ste. 1300, McLean, VA 22102
Phone: 703-918-4480   **Fax:** 703-714-6508
Web: www.alionscience.com

PRODUCTS/OPERATIONS

2007 Sales

	$ mil.	% of total
Naval architecture & marine engineering	296.7	40
Defense operations	151.3	21
Systems engineering	77.9	11
Chemical, biological, nuclear & environmental sciences	70.3	10
Modeling & simulation	52.4	7
Information technology	39	5
Industrial technology solutions	31.6	4
Wireless communications	18.4	2
Total	**737.6**	**100**

COMPETITORS

Accenture
Battelle Memorial
BearingPoint
Booz Allen
CACI International
CAE Inc.
Capgemini
Computer Sciences Corp.
EDS
Evans & Sutherland
GE
General Dynamics
IBM
Lockheed Martin
ManTech
MTC Technologies
Northrop Grumman
Perot Systems
SAIC
SI International
SRA International
Unisys

HISTORICAL FINANCIALS

Company Type: Private

Income Statement

	REVENUE ($ mil.)	NET INCOME ($ mil.)	NET PROFIT MARGIN	EMPLOYEES
9/07	738	(43)	—	3,400
9/06	509	(31)	—	3,575
9/05	369	(40)	—	2,508
9/04	270	(15)	—	1,880
9/03	166	(13)	—	1,604
Annual Growth	**45.2%**	**—**	**—**	**20.7%**

FYE: September 30

2007 Year-End Financials

Debt ratio: —   Current ratio: —
Return on equity: —   Long-term debt ($ mil.): 549
Cash ($ mil.): —

Net Income History

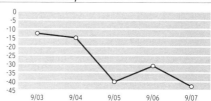

Allbritton Communications

This company has a real affinity for the Alphabet Network. Allbritton Communications is a leading television broadcaster with about 10 TV stations all affiliated with Walt Disney's ABC network. The stations serve markets in Alabama, Arkansas, Oklahoma, Pennsylvania, South Carolina, and Virginia, as well as Washington, DC. The company also owns and operates a 24-hour cable news channel (NewsChannel 8) that serves the nation's capitol, and it publishes *The Politico*, a newspaper that targets members of Congress, congressional staffers, and others interested in politics. Joe Allbritton started the family-owned business in 1975.

The company launched *The Politico* in 2007 as part of an effort to expand its media profile in Washington, DC. Originally announced as *The Capitol Leader*, the paper and companion Web site hired *Washington Post* reporter Jim VandeHei to serve as executive editor and later added such talent as *Time* magazine White House correspondent Mike Allen.

EXECUTIVES

Chairman and CEO: Robert L. Allbritton, age 38, $550,000 pay
Vice Chairman, President, and COO: Frederick J. (Fred) Ryan Jr., age 52, $475,000 pay
EVP and Director: Barbara B. Allbritton, age 70
SVP and CFO: Stephen P. Gibson, age 42, $350,000 pay
SVP Legal and Strategic Affairs and General Counsel: Jerald N. Fritz, age 56, $340,000 pay
VP and Controller: Elizabeth A. Haley
VP Sales: James C. Killen Jr., age 45, $368,750 pay
Auditors: PricewaterhouseCoopers LLP

LOCATIONS

HQ: Allbritton Communications Company
1000 Wilson Blvd., Ste. 2700, Arlington, VA 22209
Phone: 703-647-8700   **Fax:** 703-236-9268

PRODUCTS/OPERATIONS

2007 Sales

	% of total
Local & national advertising	84
Subscriber fees	4
Political ads	4
Trade & barter	3
Network compensation	2
Other	3
Total	**100**

Selected Operations

Television stations
KATV (Little Rock, AR)
KTUL (Tulsa, OK)
WBMA (Birmingham, AL)
WCFT (Tuscaloosa, AL)
WCIV (Charleston, SC)
WHTM (Harrisburg, PA)
WJLA (Washington, DC)
WJSU (Anniston, AL)
WSET (Roanoke-Lynchburg, VA)
Other
NewsChannel 8 (cable news channel; Washington, DC)
The Politico (newspaper)

COMPETITORS

E. W. Scripps
Equity Media
Fox Entertainment
Gannett
Hearst-Argyle Television
Media General
National Journal
National Review
NBC
News World Communications
Nexstar Broadcasting
Schurz Communications
Sinclair Broadcast Group
Tribune Company
Washington Post

HISTORICAL FINANCIALS

Company Type: Private

Income Statement

FYE: September 30

	REVENUE ($ mil.)	NET INCOME ($ mil.)	NET PROFIT MARGIN	EMPLOYEES
9/07	226	23	10.0%	1,046
9/06	223	(17)	—	972
9/05	200	14	6.8%	960
9/04	203	14	6.7%	936
9/03	203	—	—	936
Annual Growth	**2.8%**	**18.4%**	**—**	**2.8%**

2007 Year-End Financials

Debt ratio: —
Return on equity: —
Cash ($ mil.): —
Current ratio: —
Long-term debt ($ mil.): 484

Net Income History

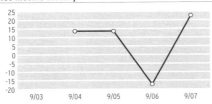

Allegis Group

Clients in need of highly skilled technical and other personnel might want to take the pledge of Allegis. One of the world's largest staffing and recruitment firms, Allegis Group operates from more than 300 offices in North America and Europe. Among its operating companies are Aerotek (engineering, automotive, and scientific professionals for short- and long-term assignments), Stephen James Associates (recruitment for accounting, financial, and cash management positions), and TEKsystems (information technology staffing and consulting). Chairman Jim Davis helped found the company (originally known as Aerotek) in 1983 in order to provide contract engineering personnel to two clients in the aerospace industry.

Allegis consolidated its Mentor 4 subsidiary (human resources and accounting recruitment) into Aerotek in 2006 in an effort to strengthen its operating structure for providing professional and financial staffing services. Mentor 4 changed its name to Aerotek Professional Services.

In 2008 Allegis expanded its geographical footprint when it acquired legal search firm Major, Lindsey & Africa and India-based IT recruitment firm TVA Infotech Pvt., Ltd.

Other Allegis units include sales support outsourcer MarketSource.

EXECUTIVES

Chairman: James C. (Jim) Davis
CFO: Paul Bowie
EVP Human Resources: Neil Mann
CIO: Kevin Apperson
General Counsel: Randy Sones
President, Aerotek: Tom Thornton

LOCATIONS

HQ: Allegis Group, Inc.
7301 Parkway Dr., Hanover, MD 21076
Phone: 410-579-4800   **Fax:** 410-540-7556
Web: www.allegisgroup.com

PRODUCTS/OPERATIONS

Selected Subsidiaries

Aerotek
Aerotek Automotive
Aerotek Aviation, LLC
Aerotek CE
Aerotek Commercial Staffing
Aerotek E&E
Aerotek Energy Services
Aerotek Professional Services
Aerotek Scientific, LLC
Allegis Group Canada
Allegis Group Europe
Allegis Group Services
Major, Lindsey & Africa
MarketSource, Inc
Stephen James Associates
TEKsystems

COMPETITORS

Adecco
ASG Renaissance
CDI
Innovative Management Solutions Group
Kelly Services
Manpower
MPS
Randstad Holding
RDL Corporation
Robert Half
Snelling Staffing
Spherion
Volt Information

HISTORICAL FINANCIALS

Company Type: Private

Income Statement

FYE: December 31

	REVENUE ($ mil.)	NET INCOME ($ mil.)	NET PROFIT MARGIN	EMPLOYEES
12/07	5,570	—	—	10,000
12/06	5,000	—	—	8,000
12/05	4,400	—	—	7,000
12/04	3,600	—	—	6,000
12/03	2,750	—	—	4,600
Annual Growth	**19.3%**	**—**	**—**	**21.4%**

Revenue History

Alliance Laundry

Laundry day can't come often enough for Alliance Laundry Holdings (ALH). Through its wholly owned subsidiary, Alliance Laundry Systems, the company makes commercial laundry equipment used in laundromats, multi-housing laundry facilities (apartments, dormitories, military bases), and on-premise laundries (hotels, hospitals, prisons). Its washers and dryers are made under the brands Speed Queen, UniMac, Huebsch, IPSO, and Cissell. They're sold in North America and in 90 countries. Investment firm Teachers' Private Capital (private equity arm of Ontario Teachers' Pension Plan) acquired more than 91% of ALH for about $450 million in 2005. The company was founded in 1908.

To expand its laundry business overseas, ALS in mid-2006 bought Laundry System Group NV's Commercial Laundry Division headquartered in Belgium. The division, which has operations in the US and Belgium, makes and markets commercial washer/extractors, ironers, and tumble dryers under the Ipso and Cissell names. During 2008 ALS is considering strategic acquisitions — domestically and internationally.

EXECUTIVES

Chairman: Lee L. Sienna, age 55
President, CEO, and Director:
  Thomas F. (Tom) L'Esperance, age 59, $753,472 pay
SVP Sales and Marketing: Jeffrey J. (Jeff) Brothers, age 61, $253,424 pay
VP and CFO: Bruce P. Rounds, age 51, $278,620 pay
VP and Corporate Controller: Robert T. Wallace, age 51
VP Strategic Projects: William J. Przybysz, age 62, $259,574 pay
VP and General Manager, Ripon Operations:
  R. Scott Gaster, age 55, $253,396 pay
VP, Chief Legal Officer, and Secretary: Scott L. Spiller, age 57, $240,356 pay
VP Engineering: Robert J. Baudhuin, age 46
VP European Operations: Jean-Marc Vandoorne, age 38
Treasurer and Assistant Secretary: Jeffrey Thoms
Auditors: PricewaterhouseCoopers LLP

LOCATIONS

HQ: Alliance Laundry Holdings LLC
119 Shepard St., Ripon, WI 54971
Phone: 920-748-3121   **Fax:** 920-748-4334
Web: www.comlaundry.com

2007 Sales

	$ mil.	% of total
Commercial laundry	317.4	72
European operations	85.4	19
Service parts	51.8	12
Consumer laundry	19.4	4
Worldwide eliminations	(30.7)	(7)
Total	**443.3**	**100**

PRODUCTS/OPERATIONS

2007 Sales

	$ mil.	% of total
Equipment & service parts	435.2	98
Equipment financing	8.1	2
Total	**443.3**	**100**

COMPETITORS

American Dryer
Electrolux
GE Consumer & Industrial
Miele
Whirlpool

HISTORICAL FINANCIALS

Company Type: Private

Income Statement

FYE: December 31

	REVENUE ($ mil.)	NET INCOME ($ mil.)	NET PROFIT MARGIN	EMPLOYEES
12/07	443	10	2.2%	1,653
12/06	366	(3)	—	1,517
12/05	297	(1)	—	1,312
12/04	281	12	4.2%	1,312
12/03	268	16	5.9%	1,309
Annual Growth	**13.4%**	**(11.2%)**	**—**	**6.0%**

2007 Year-End Financials

Debt ratio: 241.6%   Current ratio: —
Return on equity: 7.7%   Long-term debt ($ mil.): 341
Cash ($ mil.): —

Net Income History

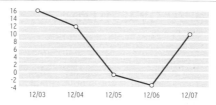

AllianceBernstein L.P.

AllianceBernstein has tons of funds. As one of the world's largest investment managers, the company (formerly Alliance Capital Management) administers about 80 domestic and international mutual funds. It serves such institutional investors as pension funds, foundations, endowments, government entities, and insurance firms. For retail investors, the company provides private client services, managed accounts, annuities, retirement plans, and college savings plans. AllianceBernstein also owns money manager and research firm Sanford C. Bernstein. French insurer AXA holds nearly 60% of AllianceBernstein; publicly traded AllianceBernstein Holding owns more than 30%.

Active in North America, Europe, Australia, and the Far East, AllianceBernstein has offices in nearly 50 cities in 25 countries. A majority of the company's new accounts come from overseas.

Long known as a growth investor, AllianceBernstein is trying to cast itself in a more conservative light. Institutional customers — which include public retirement funds in approximately 40 states and employee benefit plans — account for almost half of the firm's approximately $600 billion in assets under management, most of which are invested in fixed income and value equity products.

The company changed its name to AllianceBernstein in 2006 to highlight its relationship with the respected research house Sanford C. Bernstein.

HISTORY

Alliance Capital Management began in 1962 as the management department of Donaldson, Lufkin & Jenrette (now part of Credit Suisse (USA)). The company opened its first international office in the UK in 1978. Also that year the company introduced its first money market fund. In 1983 the company debuted its first mutual fund. The Equitable acquired Alliance as part of its DLJ acquisition in 1985.

In an attempt to raise money, cash-strapped Equitable sold 40% of the company in a 1988 public offering of Alliance stock. The company acquired Shields Asset Management in 1994 and bought Cursitor-Eaton two years later. Poor performance of the Cursitor unit forced the company to take a $121 million charge in 1997.

In 1998 the Taxpayer Relief Act of 1997 removed Alliance's Master Limited Partnership tax status and increased the company's tax rate to that of a regular partnership, a 3.5% increase. The next year the company organized a holding company and transferred its operations and old name to a new limited partnership, Alliance Capital Management Holding, to help provide tax relief for parent company The Equitable (renamed AXA Financial in 1999).

The firm continued to bolster its reputation as a global investor, expanding its operations in Asia, Europe, the UK, and South America, where it targeted privatized pension funds. As deregulation opened the Japanese mutual fund market in 1998, the company worked to rapidly establish a major presence there. Alliance's global vision played into the strategy of its ultimate parent, AXA. As one of the world's largest insurers, AXA began building its brand, using Alliance to help establish itself in global financial services.

In 2000 the company bought money manager Sanford C. Bernstein, a firm noted for its research.

In 2003 Alliance came under investigation as instances of improper market-timing trades came to light. The firm's president, the head of its mutual fund distribution unit, and some additional employees were ousted amidst the scandal. In late 2003, the company reached a $600 million settlement with regulators, also agreeing to cut its fund fees and freeze the rates at that level for a five-year period.

AllianceBernstein sold its cash management business to Federated Investors in 2005; the sale included the assets under management of 22 third-party-distributed money-market funds.

EXECUTIVES

Chairman and CEO: Lewis A. (Lew) Sanders, age 61, $275,002 pay
President, COO, and Director:
  Gerald M. (Jerry) Lieberman, age 61, $4,250,000 pay
EVP and Chief Investment Officer: Sharon E. Fay, age 47, $4,050,000 pay
EVP, Head of AllianceBernstein Blend Strategies, and Chief Investment Officer — Style Blend:
  Seth J. Masters, age 48
EVP and CTO: Lawrence H. (Larry) Cohen, age 46
EVP, Director of Global Fixed Income, and Co-Chief Investment Officer — Fixed Income:
  Douglas J. (Doug) Peebles, age 42
EVP, Director Global Quantitative Research, Co-Head of Alternative Investments, and Chief Investment Officer — Global Diversified Funds: Mark R. Gordon, age 54
EVP and Chief Investment Officer, Fixed Income:
  Jeffrey S. (Jeff) Phlegar, age 41
EVP and General Counsel: Laurence E. Cranch, age 61
EVP and Head of Client Services and Marketing:
  David A. Steyn, age 48
EVP; Head of Bernstein Global Wealth Management:
  Thomas S. Hexner, age 51
EVP, Head of Global Value Equities, and Chairperson, US Large Cap Value Equity Investment Policy Group:
  Marilyn G. Fedak, age 61, $4,140,769 pay
EVP and CEO, AllianceBernstein Limited; Head, Global/International Growth Equities:
  Christopher M. Toub, age 48

EVP and Head of US Large-Cap Growth:
James G. Reilly, age 46
EVP and Global Head of Growth Equities:
Lisa A. Shalett, age 44
EVP; Executive Managing Director, AllianceBernstein Investments: Marc O. Mayer, age 50
EVP; Chairman and CEO, SCB LLC: James A. Gingrich, age 49
EVP and Head of Institutional Investments:
Gregory J. Teneza, age 41
SVP and CFO: Robert H. Joseph Jr., age 60, $1,225,000 pay
Chairman, Private Client Investment Policy Group:
Dianne F. Lob
Auditors: PricewaterhouseCoopers LLP

LOCATIONS

HQ: AllianceBernstein L.P.
1345 Avenue of the Americas, New York, NY 10105
Phone: 212-969-1000   **Fax:** 212-969-2229
Web: www.alliancebernstein.com

PRODUCTS/OPERATIONS

2007 Sales

	$ mil.	% of total
Investment advisory & services fees	3,386.2	72
Distribution revenues	473.4	10
Institutional research services	423.5	9
Dividend & interest income	284.0	6
Other	152.6	3
Total	**4,719.7**	**100**

2007 Sales by Segment

	$ mil.	% of total
Retail services	1,521.2	32
Institutional investment services	1,481.9	31
Private client services	960.7	21
Institutional research services	423.5	9
Other	332.4	7
Total	**4,719.7**	**100**

2007 Assets Under Management

	% of total
Institutional investment services	63
Retail services	23
Private client services	14
Total	**100**

COMPETITORS

Affiliated Managers Group	Janus Capital
AIG	Legg Mason
AIG Retirement Services	MFS
American Century	Neuberger Berman
BlackRock	Nuveen
Eaton Vance	Principal Financial
Federated Investors	Raymond James Financial
FMR	T. Rowe Price
Franklin Resources	UBS Financial Services
GAMCO Investors	The Vanguard Group
ING	Waddell & Reed
Invesco	

HISTORICAL FINANCIALS

Company Type: Private

Income Statement				FYE: December 31
	ASSETS ($ mil.)	NET INCOME ($ mil.)	INCOME AS % OF ASSETS	EMPLOYEES
12/07	9,369	1,260	13.5%	5,580
12/06	10,601	1,109	10.5%	4,914
12/05	9,491	868	9.1%	4,312
12/04	8,779	705	8.0%	4,100
12/03	8,172	330	4.0%	4,096
Annual Growth	3.5%	39.8%	—	8.0%

2007 Year-End Financials

Equity as % of assets: 48.5%	Long-term debt ($ mil.): 534
Return on assets: 12.6%	Sales ($ mil.): 4,720
Return on equity: 27.7%	

Net Income History

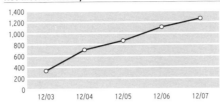

Allied Systems

Carrying more than 9 million cars, trucks, and SUVs every year, Allied Systems Holdings leads the North American automobile-hauling market. Subsidiary Allied Automotive Group moves vehicles with a fleet of about 4,000 tractor-trailer rigs, which it operates from about 90 terminals in the US and Canada. Vehicles are transported from manufacturing plants, railway distribution points, ports, and auctions to auto dealers and car rental companies. Automakers, including industry leaders such as Chrysler, Ford, General Motors, Honda, and Toyota, are the company's main customers. Investment firm Yucaipa Companies owns a controlling stake in Allied Systems Holdings.

Yucaipa participated in a financial restructuring of Allied Systems Holdings and wound up with a controlling interest when the holding company emerged from Chapter 11 bankruptcy protection in May 2007.

Success in the car-hauling business is tied directly to new vehicle production and sales, and slumping sales for the top US-based automakers have put the brakes on Allied's earnings. The company cited a drop in new vehicle production, an increase in fuel costs, and wage and benefit obligations to unionized employees as reasons for its bankruptcy filing, which came in July 2005.

A new labor agreement with the Teamsters accompanied Allied Systems Holdings' exit from Chapter 11. With its debt restructured and its financial picture improved, the company will aim to maintain its market share by holding onto its longstanding customers.

Through its Axis Group unit, Allied Systems Holdings provides vehicle-related logistics services, but the actual hauling of cars, trucks, and SUVs accounts for the vast majority of the company's overall sales.

Allied Systems Holdings has worked over the years to incorporate Christian values into its business. Toward that end, the company has assigned a chaplain to each of its terminals to counsel employees as requested.

EXECUTIVES

Chairman: Robert J. Rutland, age 66, $432,586 pay
President, CEO, and Director: Mark Gendregske, age 47
EVP and CFO: Thomas H. (Tom) King, age 52, $321,080 pay
EVP, General Counsel, and Secretary: Thomas M. Duffy, age 46, $434,699 pay
SVP and Director: Guy W. Rutland IV, age 43

SVP Field Operations: Joseph V. (Joe) Marinelli, age 46, $236,043 pay
SVP Human Resources: Brenda Ragsdale
SVP Information Systems: Larry G. Parks
SVP Maintenance and Procurement: Robert Ferrell
SVP Service Operations: Keith M. Rentzel
VP and Treasurer: Scott D. Macaulay
VP Business Development: John W. Kreisler
President, Axis Group: John Harrington
Auditors: KPMG LLP

LOCATIONS

HQ: Allied Systems Holdings, Inc.
2302 Parklake Dr., Bldg. 15, Ste. 600, Atlanta, GA 30345
Phone: 404-373-4285   **Fax:** 404-370-4206
Web: www.alliedholdings.com

COMPETITORS

Burlington Northern Santa Fe	Norfolk Southern
Cassens	United Road Services
CSX	UPS Supply Chain Solutions
Jack Cooper Transport	Waggoners Trucking
JHT Holdings	

HISTORICAL FINANCIALS

Company Type: Private

Income Statement				FYE: December 31
	REVENUE ($ mil.)	NET INCOME ($ mil.)	NET PROFIT MARGIN	EMPLOYEES
12/06	894	—	—	5,600
12/05	893	—	—	—
12/04	895	—	—	6,400
12/03	866	—	—	6,200
12/02	898	—	—	6,600
Annual Growth	(0.1%)	—	—	(4.0%)

Revenue History

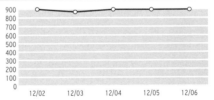

Allstates WorldCargo

No relation to insurance giant Allstate, Allstates WorldCargo uses its "good hands" to provide freight forwarding and logistics services. The company arranges the transportation of its customers' cargo by plane, ship, and truck. Rather than maintaining its own transportation assets, Allstates WorldCargo uses a network of air, ocean, and over-the-road carriers. The company operates from a network of about 20 offices in the US, and it maintains agents and relationships with freight forwarders in Europe, South America, and the Asia/Pacific region. Freight forwarding within the US accounts for most of the company's sales. Company founder Joseph Guido owns 58% of Allstates WorldCargo.

To grow, Allstates World Cargo intends to continue to invest in information technology. The company has implemented systems that improve its ability to track freight and manage inventory.

Besides its freight forwarding business, Allstates WorldCargo generates revenue from a subsidiary, Audiogenesis Systems, that distributes protective clothing and other safety equipment to employees of a pharmaceutical company.

Audiogenesis Systems bought Allstates Air Cargo in a reverse acquisition in 1999, and the combined company took the name Allstates WorldCargo. Guido, a former freight supervisor for AMR's American Airlines, founded Allstates Air Cargo in 1961.

CEO Sam DiGiralomo, a veteran employee of Audiogenesis and its predecessor, Genesis Safety Systems, owns 12% of Allstates WorldCargo.

EXECUTIVES

President and CEO: Sam DiGiralomo, age 64, $294,153 pay
EVP, COO, and Director: Barton C. Theile, age 61, $294,153 pay
CFO, Secretary, Treasurer, and Director: Craig D. Stratton, age 56, $185,000 pay
Auditors: Cowan, Gunteski & Co., P.A.

LOCATIONS

HQ: Allstates WorldCargo, Inc.
 4 Lakeside Dr. South, Forked River, NJ 08731
Phone: 609-693-5950 **Fax:** 609-693-5550
Web: allstates-worldcargo.com

2007 Sales

	$ mil.	% of total
Domestic	57.4	77
International	17.5	23
Total	**74.9**	**100**

COMPETITORS

BAX Global	Lakeland Industries
CEVA Logistics	Menlo Worldwide
C.H. Robinson Worldwide	Mine Safety Appliances
DHL	UPS Supply Chain
Expeditors	Solutions
FedEx Trade Networks	UTi Worldwide
GeoLogistics	

HISTORICAL FINANCIALS

Company Type: Private

Income Statement

FYE: September 30

	REVENUE ($ mil.)	NET INCOME ($ mil.)	NET PROFIT MARGIN	EMPLOYEES
9/07	75	0	0.4%	93
9/06	71	0	0.1%	85
9/05	69	1	0.9%	97
9/04	55	0	0.4%	93
9/03	46	(1)	—	98
Annual Growth	**12.8%**	—	—	**(1.3%)**

2007 Year-End Financials

Debt ratio: 295.1%   Current ratio: —
Return on equity: 48.8%   Long-term debt ($ mil.): 2
Cash ($ mil.): —

Net Income History

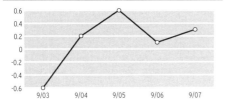

Alsco, Inc.

Alsco tells its clients, "It pays to keep clean," and then provides uniforms, linens, and related products and services in 10 countries to achieve that goal. The company (whose name stands for American linen supply company) supplies towels, linens, and uniforms to the medical and hospitality industries, among others. It also manufactures, rents, and sells uniforms, provides workplace restroom services, launders specialized garments, and manages gown rooms at high-tech sites.

The company expanded in 2006 by buying the assets of National Linen and Uniform Service. Founded in 1889 by George Steiner, Alsco is owned and operated by the Steiner family.

EXECUTIVES

Co-President: Kevin Steiner
Co-President: Robert Steiner
CFO: Jim Kearns
VP Operations, Alsco North America: Steve Larson
Director Human Resources: Tim Weiler
Director Information Systems: Larry Tomsic
Director Sales and Marketing: Jim Divers
Manager National Sales: Russ Meredith

LOCATIONS

HQ: Alsco, Inc.
 505 E. South Temple, Salt Lake City, UT 84102
Phone: 801-328-8831 **Fax:** 801-363-5680
Web: www.alsco.com

PRODUCTS/OPERATIONS

Selected Products and Services

Cold weather gear
Drum covers
Dust bags
Filter belts
Garments
Gown room management
Gowns
Hospitality/restaurant apparel
Kitchen matting
Laundry
Medical apparel
Restroom service
Restroom supplies
Towel service
Towels
Uniform rental
Uniform sales
Vacuum filters

COMPETITORS

Angelica Corporation
ARAMARK
Cintas
Crothall Services
Davis Service
Ecolab
G&K Services
Healthcare Services
ISS A/S
JohnsonDiversey
Rentokil Initial
ServiceMaster
Sodexo USA
Superior Uniform Group
Swisher Hygiene
Tranzonic
UniFirst

Alticor Inc.

At the core of Alticor, there is Amway. Alticor was formed in 2000 as a holding company and operates five businesses: direct-selling giant Amway, Web-based sales firm Quixtar, Amway Hotel Corp. (corporate development for Alticor and affiliates), upscale cosmetics company Gurwitch Products, and Access Business Group (manufacturing, logistics services). Access Business' biggest customers are Amway and Quixtar, but Access also serves outsiders. Amway, which accounts for most of Alticor's revenues, sells more than 450 different products through 3 million independent distributors. Quixtar sells Amway and other products online. Alticor is owned by Amway founders, the DeVos and Van Andel families.

Alticor expanded its cosmetics portfolio by inking a deal in July 2006 to acquire Gurwitch Products from The Neiman Marcus Group. Gurwitch, the licensee of Laura Mercier cosmetics, makes and markets luxury cosmetics and skin care items. As part of the deal, Gurwitch Products became a wholly owned subsidiary of Alticor. The acquisition gives Alticor a foothold in upscale cosmetics and offers its hefty direct sales ranks growth opportunities. For Gurwitch the deal breathes new life into its Laura Mercier business.

The company also owns the Amway Grand Plaza Hotel, located in Grand Rapids, Michigan. The hotel houses the state's first AAA Five-Diamond-designated restaurant, the 1913 Room.

EXECUTIVES

Chairman: Steve Van Andel
President: Doug DeVos
EVP and CFO: Russell A. (Russ) Evans
EVP; EVP, Quixtar and EVP, Amway Corporation: Jim Payne
VP, Public Policy: Richard Holwill
VP Human Resources: Kelly Savage
Chief Marketing Officer: Candace Matthews
Corporate General Counsel: Michael Mohr
Corporate Communications: Mike Smith
CEO, Gurwitch Products: Janet Gurwitch
EVP, Greater China and Southeast Asia, Amway: Eva Cheng
President and Representative Director, Japan and Korea, Amway: David D. Ussery

LOCATIONS

HQ: Alticor Inc.
 7575 Fulton St. East, Ada, MI 49355
Phone: 616-787-1000 **Fax:** 616-682-4000
Web: www.alticor.com

PRODUCTS/OPERATIONS

Selected Amway Products

Catalog Products
 Appliances
 Electronics
 Fashions
 Home furnishings
 Office supplies
 Toys
Home Care Products
 Dishwashing liquid
 Laundry detergent
 Multi-purpose cleaner
Home Living/Home Tech Products
 Cookware
 Water-treatment systems

Nutrition and Wellness Products
    Beverages
    Dietary supplements
    Meals
    Snacks
    Weight-control products
Personal Care Products
    Body washes
    Deodorants
    Hair care products
    Lotions
    Toothpaste
Skin Care and Cosmetics Products
    Cleansers
    Color cosmetics
    Moisturizers
    Toners

COMPETITORS

Avon	Kao
Bath & Body Works	L'Oréal
Brown-Forman	MacAndrews & Forbes
CCL Industries	Mary Kay
Clorox	Newell Rubbermaid
Colgate-Palmolive	Nikken
Daiei	Nu Skin
Estée Lauder	PFSweb
Fingerhut	Procter & Gamble
Forever Living	S.C. Johnson
GNC	Shaklee
Henkel	Tupperware
Johnson & Johnson	Unilever

American Bar Association

The American Bar Association (ABA) doesn't have anything to do with alcohol, except maybe defending drunk drivers. The ABA seeks to promote improvements in the American justice system and develop guidelines for the advancement of the legal profession and legal education. It provides law school accreditation, continuing legal education, legal information, and other services to assist legal professionals.

Its roster of more than 400,000 members includes judges, court administrators, law professors, and nonpracticing lawyers. All lawyers in good standing with any US state or territory bar are eligible for membership. The ABA cannot discipline lawyers, nor can it enforce its rules; it can only develop guidelines.

The ABA releases about 100 books and 60 magazines, journals, and newsletters through its ABA Publishing division. Popular materials run the gamut of topics, from administrative practices for lobbyists to immigration law guides for criminal lawyers to leadership and empowerment for women lawyers. Publications are for sale on the ABA's Web site.

HISTORY

One hundred lawyers from 21 states met in Saratoga, New York, in 1878 and drafted the constitution for the American Bar Association. As the ABA grew over the next hundred years, it came to influence the direction of legal education and the nomination and confirmation of judicial candidates. This brought the ABA into the political arena where its stance on controversial issues politicized the group and opened it to charges of partisan bias.

Its activities also have led to lawsuits (imagine that), including a 1993 suit by the Massachusetts School of Law claiming that the ABA's law school accreditation practices impinged on the university's right to set school policy. The Justice Department agreed, saying the ABA's requirements raised costs without improving educational quality, so in 1995 the association changed its accreditation process.

Its influence over judicial nominations took a beating in 1997 when the Senate Judiciary Committee announced that it would no longer await ABA pronouncements before acting on a nomination. The ABA's accreditation process came under fire again in 1998 when the government agency that oversees educational accreditation agencies threatened to penalize or terminate the ABA unless its accreditation policies complied with federal law. Supreme Court Justice Clarence Thomas levied his own attack in 1999 by charging that the ABA's political platforms compromised its objectivity in reviewing judicial nominations.

The ABA joined with the Federal Bar Association in 2001 to support a pay increase for federal judges. In 2002 the ABA voted to recommend that alleged terrorists tried before military tribunals should be guaranteed the same legal protections as criminal defendants in US courts.

EXECUTIVES

President: William H. Neukom, age 66
Executive Director and COO: Henry F. White Jr.
CFO: Kenneth J. Widelka
Secretary: Armando Lasa-Ferrer
Chair, House of Delegates: William (Bill) Hubbard
Auditors: Ernst & Young LLP

LOCATIONS

HQ: American Bar Association
    321 N. Clark St., Chicago, IL 60610
Phone: 312-988-5000   **Fax:** 312-988-5177
Web: www.abanet.org

PRODUCTS/OPERATIONS

Selected Commissions, Forums, and Other Groups

Board of Elections
Business Law
Central European and Eurasian Law Initiative
Coalition for Justice
Commission on Domestic Violence
Commission on Mental and Physical Disability Law
Commission on Racial and Ethnic Diversity in the Profession
Commission on Women in the Profession
Coordinating Committee on Gun Violence
Council on Racial and Ethnic Justice
Death Penalty Moratorium Implementation Project
Forum on Affordable Housing and Community Development Law
Forum on Entertainment and Sports Industries
Judicial Division
Law Student Division
Office of the President
Section of Administrative Law and Regulatory Practice
Section of Antitrust Law
Section of Labor and Employment Law
Senior Lawyers Division
Standing Committee on Judicial Independence
Standing Committee on Lawyers' Professional Liability
Standing Committee on Legal Assistants
Standing Committee on Pro Bono and Public Service
Young Lawyers Division

HISTORICAL FINANCIALS
Company Type: Association

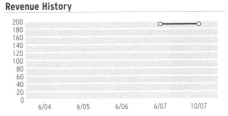

Income Statement				FYE: August 31
	REVENUE ($ mil.)	NET INCOME ($ mil.)	NET PROFIT MARGIN	EMPLOYEES
10/07*	191	—	—	900
6/07	191	—	—	900
Annual Growth	0.0%	—	—	0.0%

*Fiscal year change

Revenue History

200	
180	
160	
140	
120	
100	
80	
60	
40	
20	
0	6/04 6/05 6/06 6/07 10/07

American Cancer Society

The American Cancer Society (ACS) works as a firefighter for your lungs. Dedicated to the elimination of cancer, the not-for-profit organization is staffed by professionals and more than 2 million volunteers at some 3,400 local units across the country. ACS is the largest source of private cancer research funds in the US. Recipients of the society's funding include more than 40 Nobel Prize laureates. In addition to research, the ACS supports detection, treatment, and education programs. The organization encourages prevention efforts with programs such as the Great American Smokeout. Patient services include moral support, transportation to and from treatment, and camps for children who have cancer.

The ACS has generated considerable income by marketing its name for antismoking nicotine patches and orange juice, and is contemplating even more lucrative deals. Programs account for about 70% of expenses; the rest goes to administration and fund raising.

The organization has seen double-digit growth in online monetary gifts, although online giving still is a small percentage of overall giving.

HISTORY

Concerned over the lack of progress in detecting and treating cancer, a group of 10 physicians and five laymen met in New York City in 1913 to form the American Society for the Control of Cancer (ASCC). Because public discussion of cancer was taboo, the group struggled with how to educate people without raising unnecessary fears. Some physicians even preferred keeping knowledge of the disease from the public. In the 1920s the ASCC began sponsoring cancer clinics and collecting statistics on the disease. By 1923 some states reported improvements in early diagnosis and treatment. In 1937 the ASCC started its first nationwide public education program, with the help of volunteers known as the Women's Field

Army. President Franklin Roosevelt named April National Cancer Control Month, a practice since followed by every president.

By 1944 some cancer rates were rising but the word "cancer" still couldn't be mentioned on radio. Mary Lasker, wife of prominent ad executive Albert Lasker, was instrumental in getting information about cancer broadcast. At her insistence, in 1945 the newly renamed American Cancer Society began donating at least 25% of its budget to research. The society raised $4 million in its first major national fund-raising campaign.

The link between smoking and lung cancer became known after a study in the early 1950s by ACS medical director Charles Cameron. That information became part of the Surgeon General's Report of 1964. In 1973 an ACS branch in Minnesota held the first Great American Smokeout to encourage people to quit smoking.

The ACS backed the 1971 congressional bill that inaugurated the War on Cancer. The society was attacked in the 1970s for emphasizing cures rather than prevention because, critics claimed, research would reveal environmental causes from industrial products made by companies with connections to ACS directors. In the 1970s and 1980s, the ACS backed tougher restrictions on tobacco and, in response to earlier criticism, directed research toward prevention as well as treatment. The society played a major role in the 1989 airline smoking ban.

John Seffrin, a former Indiana University professor, was named CEO of ACS in 1992. The first of several genetic breakthroughs came in the 1990s when ACS grantees isolated genes believed to be responsible for triggering various types of cancer. In 1995 the ACS accused the tobacco industry of infiltrating its offices in the 1970s and using its papers to aid in the early marketing of low-tar cigarettes.

In 1996 the ACS announced that new data showed a drop in the US cancer death rate for the first time ever. The ACS entered agreements with SmithKline Beecham (NicoDerm antismoking patches) and the Florida Department of Citrus in 1996 to allow the use of the American Cancer Society name in marketing.

The proposed $369 billion settlement between the attorneys general of 40 states and the tobacco industry was big news in 1997. The ACS had wanted more concessions, such as a $2-per-pack tax increase, more power for industry regulation by the FDA, and underage use rate-reduction targets for smokeless tobacco products as stringent as those for cigarettes.

In 1998 the ACS launched a $5 million national advertising campaign to combat what it saw as "misleading" information spread by the tobacco industry. It argued before the Supreme Court in 1999 to help the FDA gain control over cigarette production and distribution. In 2000 ACS restructured its $50-million-a-year research program to increase the size of individual grants; it also awarded its largest-ever award, $1.7 million, to study the side effects of cancer treatment. ACS filed petitions to the FDA the next year urging it to regulate new tobacco products marketed as being safer than traditional cigarettes. In 2002 ACS and The Robert Wood Johnson Foundation launched the Center for Tobacco Cessation to help people quit smoking. ACS published strategic guides the following year to help countries in the early stages of tobacco control.

EXECUTIVES

Chair: Marion E. Morra
Vice Chair: George W. P. Atkins
CEO: John R. Seffrin
President and Director: Elmer E. Huerta
Chair-Elect and Director: G. Van Velsor Wolf Jr.
President-Elect and Director:
  Elizabeth T. H. (Terry) Fontham
Immediate Past President: Richard C. Wender
Senior Director Communications and Media Advocacy:
  Steven C. Weiss
Treasurer and Director: Nancy Brakensiek
Chief Medical Officer: Otis W. Brawley, age 47
First VP: Alan G. Thorson
Second VP: Edward E. Partridge
Auditors: Ernst & Young LLP

LOCATIONS

HQ: American Cancer Society, Inc.
  1599 Clifton Rd. NE, Atlanta, GA 30329
Phone: 404-320-3333   **Fax:** 404-982-3677
Web: www.cancer.org

PRODUCTS/OPERATIONS

Selected Programs and Grants

Patient Services Programs
  Children's Camps (for children and teens with cancer; some for siblings)
  Hope Lodge (housing assistance)
  I Can Cope (education and support classes on living with cancer)
  Look Good . . . Feel Better (cosmetics and beauty techniques for women experiencing side effects of cancer treatment)
  Man To Man Prostate Cancer Support
  Pamphlets and brochures for cancer patients and their families
  Reach to Recovery (support for women with breast cancer and their families)
  Road to Recovery (transportation services)
Public Education Programs
  Great American Smokeout (national stop-smoking-for-a-day event)
  Making Strides Against Breast Cancer (fund-raiser)
  Relay for Life (fund-raiser)
Research Grants and Awards
  Clinical research professorships
  Clinical research training grants
  Institutional research grants
  Postdoctoral fellowships
  Research opportunity grants
  Research professorships

HISTORICAL FINANCIALS

Company Type: Not-for-profit

Income Statement
FYE: August 31

	REVENUE ($ mil.)	NET INCOME ($ mil.)	NET PROFIT MARGIN	EMPLOYEES
8/07	1,172	114	9.7%	7,000
8/06	1,038	169	16.2%	—
8/05	978	—	—	—
Annual Growth	9.5%	(32.5%)	—	—

2007 Year-End Financials

Debt ratio: 4.8%   Current ratio: —
Return on equity: 7.4%   Long-term debt ($ mil.): 76
Cash ($ mil.): —

Net Income History

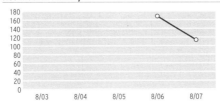

180				
160				
140				
120				
100				
80				
60				
40				
20				
0				
	8/03	8/04	8/05	8/06	8/07

American Crystal Sugar

Call it saccharine, but for American Crystal Sugar, business is all about sharing. This sugar-beet cooperative is owned by some 2,900 growers in the Red River Valley of North Dakota and Minnesota. Farming more than one-half million owned and contracted acres of cropland. American Crystal, formed in 1899 and converted into a co-op in 1973, divides the 35-mile-wide valley into five districts, each served by a processing plant. The plants produce sugar, molasses, and beet pulp. American Crystal's products are sold internationally to industrial users and to retail and wholesale customers under the Crystal name, as well as under private labels through marketing co-ops United Sugars and Midwest Agri-Commodities.

Company subsidiary, Sidney Sugars, operates a processing facility in Montana. Sidney owns a plant in Wyoming that is leased to another sugar cooperative. American Crystal holds the controlling interest in the corn-sweetener joint venture, ProGold, which leases its facility to Cargill, for the production of high-fructose corn syrup.

The company also sells agri-products and sugar-beet seeds.

EXECUTIVES

Chairman: David J. Kragnes, age 55
President and CEO: David A. Berg, age 53, $364,818 pay
COO: Joseph J. (Joe) Talley, age 47, $359,219 pay
VP Finance and CFO: Thomas S. Astrup, age 39, $306,091 pay
VP Administration: Brian F. Ingulsrud, age 44, $267,515 pay
Director Factory Operations, Crookston:
  David A. Walden, $275,628 pay
Director Business Development: David L. Malmskog, age 50
Director Government Affairs: Kevin Price
Secretary and General Counsel: Daniel C. Mott, age 48
Treasurer and Assistant Secretary: Samuel S. M. Wai, age 53
Public Relations Manager: Jeff Schweitzer
Manager Human Resources: Sharon Connell
Controller, Chief Accounting Officer, Assistant Treasurer, and Assistant Secretary: Teresa Warne
Auditors: Eide Bailly LLP

LOCATIONS

HQ: American Crystal Sugar Company
  101 N. Third St., Moorhead, MN 56560
Phone: 218-236-4400   **Fax:** 218-236-4422
Web: www.crystalsugar.com

PRODUCTS/OPERATIONS

2007 Sales

	$ mil.	% of total
Sugar	1,197.2	98
Leasing	24.9	2
Total	**1,222.1**	**100**

Selected Joint Ventures and Subsidiaries

Joint Venture
  Midwest Agri-Commodities
  Progold L.L.C.
  United Sugars Corporation
Subsidiary
  Crab Creek Sugar Company
  Sidney Sugars Incorporated

COMPETITORS

ADM	Nippon Beet Sugar
Alberto-Culver	NutraSweet
Alexander & Baldwin	Südzucker
Amalgamated Sugar	SMBSC
C&H Sugar	Sterling Sugars
Cargill	Sugar Cane Growers
Cumberland Packing	Cooperative of Florida
Florida Crystals	Sugar Foods
Imperial Sugar	Tate & Lyle
M A Patout	U.S. Sugar
Merisant Worldwide	Western Sugar Cooperative
Michigan Sugar Company	

HISTORICAL FINANCIALS

Company Type: Cooperative

Income Statement

FYE: August 31

	REVENUE ($ mil.)	NET INCOME ($ mil.)	NET PROFIT MARGIN	EMPLOYEES
8/07	1,222	601	49.2%	1,380
8/06	1,006	445	44.3%	1,306
8/05	966	373	38.7%	1,337
8/04	1,033	473	45.8%	1,359
8/03	829	362	43.6%	1,231
Annual Growth	10.2%	13.5%	—	2.9%

2007 Year-End Financials

Debt ratio: 44.2%
Return on equity: 172.2%
Cash ($ mil.): —
Current ratio: —
Long-term debt ($ mil.): 158

Net Income History

700		
600		
500		
400		
300		
200		
100		
0		
8/03	8/04	8/05	8/06	8/07

American Family Insurance

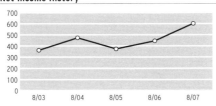

Even confirmed bachelors can get insured through American Family Insurance. The company specializes in property/casualty insurance, but also offers life, health, and homeowners coverage, as well as investment and retirement-planning products. The company operates in nearly 20 states, primarily in the Midwest and Western US. It is among the largest US mutual companies that concentrates on auto insurance (State Farm is the biggest). American Family Insurance also provides coverage for apartment owners, restaurants, contractors, and other businesses. Through the company's consumer finance division, agents can also offer their customers home equity and personal lines of credit.

American Family Insurance sells its products through a network of nearly 4,000 independent agents. Unlike many of its competitors, the company has said it has no plans to demutualize and has steadily grown its equity and assets.

Where property/casualty insurers along US coastlines were hard hit during the 2005 hurricane season, American Family rode that year out comfortably. However the company paid out $1.1 billion in storm losses in the wake of hail and windstorms that hit the midwestern US during 2006.

HISTORY

In 1927 Herman Wittwer founded Farmers Mutual Automobile Insurance to sell coverage to Wisconsin farmers. As farms became mechanized in the 1920s, the insurance market grew. Low-density rural traffic reduced the potential for accidents, a fact that attracted Wittwer and others, such as State Farm (founded in 1922) to serve the similar markets. Wittwer also noted that rural Wisconsin's severe winters made cars unusable for a good part of the year, further reducing risk.

Farmers Mutual grew despite the Depression and WWII, spreading to Minnesota (1933); Missouri (1939); Nebraska and the Dakotas (1940); and Indiana, Iowa, and Kansas (1943). The war years were generous to insurers: Rising incomes allowed people to insure their cars, but rationing programs limited use of the cars. The postwar suburban boom — when cars became a necessity rather than a luxury — also helped auto insurers.

Growing prosperity for single-earner households in the 1950s helped boost the demand for life insurance. In 1958 Farmers Mutual formed American Family Life Insurance. The company wrote $1.6 million in insurance on its first day in the life insurance business. During that decade, Farmers Mutual moved into Illinois.

The 1960s brought growth and change. To capture more auto business, it founded American Standard Insurance to write nonstandard auto insurance. The firm also launched consumer finance operations for insurance customers and noncustomers alike, departing from standard industry practice by selling through agents rather than offices. In 1963, in recognition of its growing diversification, Farmers Mutual changed its name to American Family Mutual Insurance.

During the 1970s and 1980s, the firm strengthened its infrastructure and added regional offices. It moved into Arizona and later formed American Family Brokerage to fill in gaps in its own coverage by obtaining insurance for clients through other insurers.

During this period American Family suffered cultural pains. It moved beyond its traditional rural clientele and into the urban unknown as it sought to increase its market share. In 1981 community groups questioned whether the company was adequately serving racially mixed neighborhoods. In 1988 the US Justice Department began investigating allegations that the firm engaged in redlining (offering inferior or no service for minority neighborhoods); a class-action suit based on similar claims was filed in 1990. The suit went all the way to the Supreme Court, which ruled that insurance sales must comply with the Fair Housing Act.

The company had begun rectifying its practices before the case was decided. Nevertheless, when American Family settled the case in 1995, it agreed to pay a $14.5 million settlement plus

about $2 million in court costs. Part of the settlement was to compensate people who had suffered from the company's discrimination. But most of the money went to fund community programs begun in 1996 to promote home ownership among minorities. In 1997 trouble came from within and without: One lawsuit claimed the company falsely promised to shrink premiums as policies earned dividends, and two dissident agents filed a civil complaint for wrongful termination (the latter case was settled the next year).

The company's profits tumbled in 1998 due to severe storms in Minnesota and Wisconsin. The next year American Family expanded its operations in Colorado and moved into Cleveland.

In 2000 Wisconsin was again pounded by hail, high winds, and floods. American Family Insurance announced $100 million in expected losses from the event. Streamlining claims processing, the company closed nine of its offices in 2001.

American Family Insurance grew its policy count by almost 10% in 2002 but the volatile stock market hurt the company's net result. By 2004 the company had regained financial strength to the tune of $4.2 billion in policyholder equity, primarily due to record gains in operations.

EXECUTIVES

Chairman and CEO: David R. Anderson
President, COO, and Director: Jack C. Salzwedel
CFO and Treasurer: Daniel R. Schultz
EVP: Alan E. Meyer
EVP: Bradley J. Gleason
EVP: Mary L. Schmoeger
Chief Legal Officer and Secretary: James F. Eldridge
VP Broker/Dealer: Paulette L. Siebers
VP Claims: Mark V. Afable
VP Life, Variable Products, and Health: M. Jeffrey Bosco
VP Legal: Christopher S. Spencer
VP Office Administration: Annette S. Knapstein
VP Personal Lines: Joseph J. Zwettler
VP Public Relations: Richard A. Fetherston
VP Commercial-Farm/Ranch: Gerry W. Benusa
VP and Controller: Kari E. Grasee
VP Government Affairs and Compliance:
  Scott J. Seymour
VP Human Resources: Daniel J. Kelly
VP Education: Betty A. Bergquist
Auditors: PricewaterhouseCoopers LLP

LOCATIONS

HQ: American Family Insurance Group
  6000 American Pkwy., Madison, WI 53783
Phone: 608-249-2111   **Fax:** 608-243-4921
Web: www.amfam.com

PRODUCTS/OPERATIONS

2007 Revenues

	$ mil.	% of total
Property & casualty premiums	5,925.8	86
Investment income	569.4	8
Life premiums	317.3	5
Finance charges	10.0	—
Other	45.4	1
Total	**6,867.9**	**100**

Selected Subsidiaries

American Family Financial Services, Inc. (AFFS)
American Family Insurance Company
American Family Life Insurance Company (AFLIC)
American Family Mutual Insurance Company
American Family Securities, LLC.
American Standard Insurance Company of Wisconsin

COMPETITORS

AIG	Nationwide
Allstate	Ohio Casualty
American Financial	Old Republic
Cincinnati Financial	Progressive Corporation
General Casualty	Prudential
The Hartford	Safeco
Liberty Mutual	State Farm
Lincoln Financial Group	Travelers Companies
Mutual of Omaha	USAA

HISTORICAL FINANCIALS
Company Type: Mutual company

Income Statement

FYE: December 31

	ASSETS ($ mil.)	NET INCOME ($ mil.)	INCOME AS % OF ASSETS	EMPLOYEES
12/07	16,004	82	0.5%	8,482
12/06	15,477	24	0.2%	8,237
12/05	14,637	672	4.6%	8,135
12/04	13,641	564	4.1%	8,238
12/03	12,239	155	1.3%	8,100
Annual Growth	6.9%	(14.7%)	—	1.2%

2007 Year-End Financials

Equity as % of assets: 31.5%   Long-term debt ($ mil.): —
Return on assets: 0.5%   Sales ($ mil.): 6,868
Return on equity: 1.7%

Net Income History

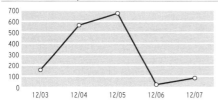

American Library Association

Shhhh! The American Library Association (ALA) is a not-for-profit that works to develop, promote, and improve library and information services. Governed by an elected council, the ALA works with libraries of all types, from public to academic to prison. The more than 66,000-member organization consists of 11 divisions, as well as affiliated organizations and chapters in all 50 states, all working to advance ALA causes, such as Banned Books Week, an annual event promoting awareness about efforts to ban certain books from libraries. The ALA's Washington, DC, branch office tries to influence federal legislative policy to ensure the public's right to free access to information. The group was founded in 1876.

EXECUTIVES

President: Loriene Roy
President-Elect: Jim Rettig
Executive Director: Keith Michael Fiels
Associate Executive Director for Finance:
 Gregory (Greg) Calloway
Director Human Resources: Dorothy Ragsdale
Treasurer: Rodney M. Hersberger

LOCATIONS

HQ: American Library Association
 50 E. Huron St., Chicago, IL 60611
Phone: 312-944-6780   **Fax:** 312-440-9374
Web: www.ala.org

HISTORICAL FINANCIALS
Company Type: Association

Income Statement

FYE: August 31

	REVENUE ($ mil.)	NET INCOME ($ mil.)	NET PROFIT MARGIN	EMPLOYEES
8/07	44	—	—	260

American Media

If you've sighted Elvis or Bigfoot recently, or better yet Paris Hilton, you might want to contact one of these papers. American Media is the nation's top publisher of tabloid newspapers and magazines, including *National Enquirer* and *Star*. It also publishes women's health magazine *Shape*, as well as a number of other magazines such as *Flex, Men's Fitness*, and *Natural Health*. In addition to publishing, American Media offers distribution services to other publishers to get their periodicals in the racks at supermarkets throughout the US and Canada. American Media is owned by EMP Group LLC, a holding company controlled by private equity firms Evercore Partners and Thomas H. Lee.

American Media has struggled for the past several years with declining readership and advertising, despite attempts to revamp its core publications, *Star* and *National Enquirer*, into celebrity gossip papers. It announced in 2007 plans to halt print publication of *Weekly World News*, though the tabloid will continue to cover Bigfoot, UFOs, and other "news" online. The company also labors under mounting debt as a result of its $350 million acquisition of several fitness magazines from Weider Publications (formerly part of Weider Health & Fitness) in 2003.

Looking to recover, American Media has put several of its titles on the auction block, including *Country Weekly, Muscle & Fitness, Flex, Muscle & Fitness Hers*, and Spanish language paper *Mira!* The company hopes the sale will help it focus on its core publications and it plans to use the funds to pay down debt. American Media also moved the editorial headquarters of the *Enquirer* from New York City back to Florida as part of a cost-cutting move.

EXECUTIVES

Chairman and CEO: David J. Pecker, age 56,
 $1,500,000 pay
President and COO: John J. Miller, age 54
EVP and CFO: Dean D. Durbin, age 55
EVP and Chief Marketing Officer: Kevin Hyson, age 58
EVP Consumer Marketing: David W. (Dave) Leckey,
 age 55
EVP: John Swider, age 48

SVP Special Projects and Business Affairs:
 John M. Hughes
SVP and Chief Accounting Officer: Saul M. Kredi,
 age 39
SVP and Group Publisher, Fit Pregnancy, Natural Health, Shape, and Country Weekly: Diane Newman
VP Corporate Sales: Gary Berger
VP and Publisher, Star Magazine: David Jackson
Human Resources: Ken Slivken
Editor-at-Large: Bonnie Fuller, age 51
Editor-in-Chief, The National Enquirer: David Perel
President and CEO, DSI: Michael J. (Mike) Porche,
 age 51, $500,000 pay
Auditors: Deloitte & Touche LLP

LOCATIONS

HQ: American Media, Inc.
 1000 American Media Way, Boca Raton, FL 33464
Phone: 561-997-7733
Web: www.americanmediainc.com

PRODUCTS/OPERATIONS

2007 Sales

	% of total
Circulation	57
Advertising	35
Other	8
Total	**100**

2007 Sales

	% of total
Newspapers	29
Celebrity publications	26
Women's health & fitness	16
Distribution services	6
Other	23
Total	**100**

Selected Publications

Newspapers
 Globe
 National Enquirer
 National Examiner
Celebrity publications
 Country Weekly
 Star
Women's health and fitness
 Fit Pregnancy
 Shape
Other
 Flex
 Men's Fitness
 Mira!
 Muscle & Fitness
 Muscle & Fitness Hers
 Natural Health
 Sun

COMPETITORS

Bauer Publishing USA
Condé Nast
Goodman Media Group
Lagardère Active
Meredith Corporation
Northern and Shell
Radar Media
Rodale
Time Inc.
Wenner Media

American Medical Association

The AMA knows whether there's a doctor in the house. The American Medical Association (AMA) prescribes the standards for the medical profession. The membership organization's activities include advocacy for physicians, promoting ethics standards in the medical community, and improving health care education. Policies are set by the AMA's House of Delegates, which is made up mainly of elected representatives. The AMA also publishes books and products for physicians, is a partner in the Medem online physician network, sells medical malpractice insurance, and helps doctors fight legal claims. The organization was founded in 1847 to establish a code of medical ethics. The AMA has about 240,000 members.

EXECUTIVES

CEO and EVP: Michael D. Maves
COO: Bernard L. Hengesbaugh
President: Nancy H. Nielsen
President-Elect: J. James Rohack
SVP Finance and CFO: Denise Hagerty
SVP Human Resources and Corporate Services:
  Robert W. (Bob) Davis
**SVP Scientific Publications and Multimedia
  Applications, and Chief Editor, JAMA:**
  Catherine D. De Angelis
SVP Publishing and Business: Robert A. Musacchio
SVP Professional Standards: Modena H. Wilson
SVP and Chief Marketing Officer: Marietta Parenti
SVP Advocacy Group: Richard A. Deem
General Counsel: Jon Ekdahl
CTO: Michael J. Berkery
Auditors: Deloitte & Touche LLP

LOCATIONS

HQ: American Medical Association
  515 N. State St., Chicago, IL 60610
Phone: 312-464-5000   **Fax:** 312-464-4184
Web: www.ama-assn.org

PRODUCTS/OPERATIONS

2007 Revenues

	$ mil.	% of total
Royalties & credentialing products	63.3	22
Book & product sales	47.9	17
Membership dues	45.3	16
Advertising	34.5	12
Insurance commissions	32.7	11
Subscriptions	17.1	6
Investments	14.8	5
Other publishing revenue	20.1	7
Grants & other	11.7	4
Sponsored revenue	1.4	—
Equity in profit of unconsolidated subsidiary	0.7	—
Total	**289.5**	**100**

HISTORICAL FINANCIALS
Company Type: Association

Income Statement				FYE: December 31
	REVENUE ($ mil.)	NET INCOME ($ mil.)	NET PROFIT MARGIN	EMPLOYEES
12/07	290	50	17.4%	1,121
12/06	286	25	8.8%	1,114
12/05	280	—	—	—
12/04	270	—	—	—
12/03	256	—	—	—
Annual Growth	**3.1%**	**99.6%**	**—**	**0.6%**

2007 Year-End Financials
Debt ratio: —   Current ratio: —
Return on equity: 14.8%   Long-term debt ($ mil.): —
Cash ($ mil.): —

Net Income History

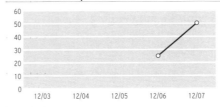

American Seafoods

With operations in the northern Pacific and Atlantic oceans as well as catfish farming and processing sites in the southern US, American Seafoods Group has cast a wide net. The company offers frozen and processed fish such as Alaska pollock, Pacific whiting, Pacific cod, sea scallops, and farm-raised catfish. It operates its own fleet of ships that processes and freezes the catch while at sea, as well as a fleet of transport trucks. American Seafoods' land-based operations take place in Alabama and Massachusetts, as well as in Japan. It sells its fish under the American Pride, Frionor, and Southern Pride brand names. Its value-added products include surimi, breaded and battered filets, and nuggets.

American Seafoods' customers include foodservice and food retailing companies worldwide. Much of the company's fish is sold to restaurants and other foodservice outlets for use in breaded or battered-fish entrees. It also harvests fish eggs (roe) for sale to markets in Japan.

EXECUTIVES

Chairman and CEO: Bernt O. Bodal, age 54,
  $854,766 pay
CFO and Treasurer: Brad D. Bodenman, age 44,
  $508,790 pay
Chief Legal Officer and General Counsel:
  Matthew D. Latimer, age 39, $404,665 pay
VP Sales: Robert Hatcher
VP Sales: Thomas Wilson
VP Treasury and Compliance: Glenn Sumida
VP Human Resources: Tammy French
VP IT: Dar Khalighi
**President, American Pride Seafoods, American
  Seafoods International, and Southern Pride Catfish:**
  John Cummings, age 52
President, American Seafoods Company:
  Inge Andreassen, age 44, $782,500 pay
Auditors: KPMG LLP

LOCATIONS

HQ: American Seafoods Group LLC
  Marketplace Tower, 2025 1st Ave., Ste. 900,
  Seattle, WA 98121
Phone: 206-374-1515   **Fax:** 206-374-1516
Web: www.americanseafoods.com

PRODUCTS/OPERATIONS

Selected Operations
American Seafoods Company
American Seafoods Company Dutch Harbor
American Seafoods Company Seattle Warehouse
American Seafoods Europe ApS
American Seafoods International
American Seafoods Japan
Pacific Longline Company
Southern Pride Catfish

Selected Products and Species Used
Fishmeal
  Alaska pollock
  Pacific Whiting
  Yellowfin sole
Fillet block
  Alaska pollock
  Pacific cod
  Pacific whiting
Headed + Gutted (H+G)
  Flathead sole
  Rock sole
  Yellowfin sole
Roe
  Alaska pollock
  Pacific cod
Shatterpack fillets
  Alaska pollock
  Pacific cod
Surimi
  Alaska pollock
  Pacific whiting

COMPETITORS

Alyeska Seafoods	Pacific Seafood
Arrowac Fisheries	Pescanova
Icelandic Group	Red Chamber Co.
Icicle Seafoods	Seafreeze
Maruha Nichiro	Thai Union
Nippon Suisan Kaisha	Trident Seafoods
Ocean Beauty Seafoods	

American Tire

American Tire Distributors Holdings' business starts where the rubber meets the road. The company, through its American Tire Distributors unit, is one of the largest tire wholesalers in the US. Offerings include the flagship brands of industry leaders Bridgestone, Continental, Goodyear, and Michelin, as well as budget brands and private-label tires. Tires account for about 90% of the company's sales.

American Tire Distributors also distributes custom wheels and tire service equipment. It maintains about 85 distribution centers that serve independent tire dealers, retail chains, and auto service facilities in more than 35 states. Investment firm Investcorp owns the company.

Investcorp bought American Tire Distributors in 2005 and, in conjunction with the acquisition, formed American Tire Distributors Holdings.

American Tire Distributors has grown steadily over the years by acquiring smaller, regional players, and that pattern has continued under the company's new ownership. In 2005 American Tire Distributors gained operations in seven western states when it bought Wholesale Tire. In 2006, American Tire Distributors bought Golden State Tire and Silver State Tire (California and Nevada), as well as Samaritan Wholesale Tire (Minnesota and Wisconsin). The company continued its buying habits in 2007, with purchases of tire distributors in Texas, Florida, and Colorado.

Besides growing through acquisitions, American Tire Distributors hopes to gain revenue by selling more of its brands to dealers in its network.

EXECUTIVES

Chairman and CEO: Richard P. (Dick) Johnson, age 60, $1,625,000 pay
President and COO: William E. (Bill) Berry, age 53, $985,000 pay
EVP and CFO: David L. Dyckman, age 43
EVP, General Counsel, and Secretary:
  J. Michael (Mike) Gaither, age 55, $582,500 pay
EVP Sales: Daniel K. (Dan) Brown, age 54, $552,500 pay
EVP Procurement: Phillip E. (Phil) Marrett, age 57, $537,500 pay
SVP Marketing: Ron Sinclair
SVP Sales: Roland Boyette
SVP Operations: John Flowers
SVP Procurement: Dan Seitler
SVP Administration and Pricing: Jason Shannon
Auditors: PricewaterhouseCoopers LLP

LOCATIONS

HQ: American Tire Distributors Holdings, Inc.
  12200 Herbert Wayne Ct., Ste. 150,
  Huntersville, NC 28078
Phone: 704-992-2000   **Fax:** 704-992-1384
Web: www.americantiredistributors.com

PRODUCTS/OPERATIONS

2007 Sales

	% of total
Tires	89
Custom wheels	6
Related automotive service equipment	3
Tools and supplies	2
Total	**100**

Selected Products

Equipment and supplies (including valve stems, auto lifts)
Tires
Wheel covers
Wheel Wizard (computer program allowing customers to virtually see wheel types on their vehicle)

COMPETITORS

Dealer Tire
TBC
TCI Tire Centers
Treadways
Wal-Mart

HISTORICAL FINANCIALS

Company Type: Private

Income Statement			FYE: Saturday closest to Dec. 31	
	REVENUE ($ mil.)	NET INCOME ($ mil.)	NET PROFIT MARGIN	EMPLOYEES
12/07	1,878	1	0.1%	2,400
12/06	1,578	(5)	—	2,100
12/05	1,151	(2)	—	2,127
12/04	1,282	25	1.9%	2,071
12/03	1,113	16	1.4%	1,894
Annual Growth	14.0%	(45.6%)	—	6.1%

2007 Year-End Financials

Debt ratio: —   Current ratio: —
Return on equity: 0.6%   Long-term debt ($ mil.): —
Cash ($ mil.): —

Net Income History

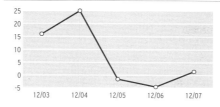

American United Mutual Insurance

There are 50 states, but only OneAmerica. American United Mutual Insurance Holding Company is primarily a life insurer whose operating units do business under the OneAmerica Financial Partners banner. The company offers individual life insurance, disability and long-term-care coverage, and annuities. For businesses the company offers employee benefits, medical stop loss coverage, retirement plans, and group life insurance. Its subsidiaries include American United Life Insurance, The State Life Insurance Company, OneAmerica Securities, Pioneer Mutual Life Insurance, and R.E. Moulton. The company operates in 49 states and Washington, DC.

The insurer restructured into mutual holding company ownership in 2000, a move that has not only given it a more favorable tax status, but has allowed it to form and acquire stock subsidiaries.

Flagship insurer American United Life was formed in the 1936 merger of United Mutual Life Insurance and American Central Life Insurance.

As OneAmerica, the company has an appetite for acquisitions. Purchases include the life, long-term-care, and annuity business of Golden Rule Insurance (2005); medical stop-loss insurer R.E. Moulton and the group life and disability insurance business of The Union Central Life Insurance Company (2003); and Pioneer Mutual Life Insurance (2002).

American United Mutual Insurance Company exited the reinsurance business in 2002.

EXECUTIVES

Chairman, President, and CEO: Dayton H. Molendorp, age 61
SVP and Chief Actuary: David A. Brentlinger
SVP Individual Operations: Mark A. Wilkerson
VP, Employee Benefits Division: Leonard A. Cavallaro
President, State Life and Director: Richard L. Merrill
CFO, OneAmerica Financial: J. Scott Davison
SVP Corporate Finance, OneAmerica Financial:
  Constance E. Lund
SVP Human Resources, OneAmerica Financial:
  Mark C. Roller
SVP Investments, OneAmerica Financial: G. David Sapp
SVP Retirement Services, OneAmerica Financial:
  William F. Yoerger
General Counsel and Corporate Secretary, OneAmerica Financial: Thomas M. Zurek
Auditors: PricewaterhouseCoopers LLP

LOCATIONS

HQ: American United Mutual Insurance Holding Company
  1 American Sq., Indianapolis, IN 46206
Phone: 317-285-1111   **Fax:** 317-285-1728
Web: www.aul.com

PRODUCTS/OPERATIONS

2007 Revenues

	$ mil.	% of total
Net investment income	534.3	48
Premiums & other considerations	344.4	31
Policy & contract charges	190.4	17
Realized investment gains (losses)	(2.7)	—
Other income	37.4	4
Total	**1,103.8**	**100**

Selected Subsidiaries and Affiliates

American United Life Insurance Company (life insurance and annuities)
OneAmerica Securities, Inc. (broker and investment advisor)
Pioneer Mutual Life Insurance Company (individual life insurance and annuities)
R.E. Moulton, Inc. (stop-loss insurance; group life, health and disability insurance)
The State Life Insurance Company (individual long-term care insurance)

COMPETITORS

Aetna	Northwestern Mutual
CNA Financial	Ohio National
John Hancock Financial	Principal Financial
Lincoln Financial Group	Prudential
MassMutual	Reliance Standard
MetLife	Securian Financial
Mutual of America	Security Benefit Group
Nationwide Financial	Unity Mutual Life
New York Life	

HISTORICAL FINANCIALS

Company Type: Mutual company

Income Statement				FYE: December 31
	ASSETS ($ mil.)	NET INCOME ($ mil.)	INCOME AS % OF ASSETS	EMPLOYEES
12/07	19,921	88	0.4%	—
12/06	18,491	68	0.4%	—
12/05	17,607	62	0.4%	—
12/04	15,028	56	0.4%	1,800
12/03	14,041	62	0.4%	1,730
Annual Growth	9.1%	9.4%	—	4.0%

2007 Year-End Financials

Equity as % of assets: 6.6%   Long-term debt ($ mil.): —
Return on assets: 0.5%   Sales ($ mil.): 1,104
Return on equity: 6.9%

Net Income History

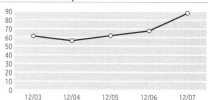

Ampacet Corporation

Ampacet helps manufacturers of plastic products show their true hues with its custom color and additive concentrates. Using polyethylene, polypropylene, polyamide, and polyester resins, Ampacet makes compounds, concentrates, and masterbatches that enable those manufacturers to produce consistent colors and chemical characteristics for their extruded and molded products. Globally, the company is #2 behind Ciba Specialty Chemicals in the market for color concentrates. Its additives are used in food and industrial packaging, pipe and conduit, wire and cable, and other plastic products. Ampacet was founded in 1937, and the family of the late Norman Alexander, one-time chairman of Sequa Corporation, owns the firm.

Alexander bought Ampacet, then known as American Molding Powder Co., in 1954. (Ampacet is actually short for American Molding Powder acetate.) Ampacet operates from facilities in the Americas, Europe, and Asia.

EXECUTIVES

President and CEO: Robert A. DeFalco
SVP Finance: Joel Slutsky
SVP and General Manager, North America:
  Robert J. Fielding
VP Engineering: Sam Bhoumik
VP Sales North America and Export: Robert J. Lammie
General Manager, Ampacet South America: Yves Carette
VP Technical: Christian Carnevali
Executive Director Assets and Process: Daniel Peruzzo
Senior Director Procurement: Jack Chaszar
Senior Director Manufacturing: John Waters
**Senior Director Strategy and Development and
  Strategic Accounts:** Michael M. Gaudio
Senior Director Human Resources:
  Robert K. (Bob) Oakes
Senior Director Business Development: Frank Iannotti

LOCATIONS

HQ: Ampacet Corporation
  660 White Plains Rd., Tarrytown, NY 10591
Phone: 914-631-6600   **Fax:** 914-631-7197
Web: www.ampacet.com

Ampacet has manufacturing plants in Asia, Europe, and North and South America.

COMPETITORS

A. Schulman
Americhem
Ciba Specialty Chemicals
Clariant
DuPont
Ferro
PolyOne
Spartech

Amscan Holdings

Amscan Holdings caters to the party animal in all of us. The company designs, makes, and distributes party goods, including balloons, invitations, piñatas, stationery, and tableware to party superstores and other retailers worldwide. On the retail side of the business, Amscan owns or franchises about 955 party supply stores in the US, Puerto Rico, and Dubai under the Party City, Party America, and Factory Card & Party Outlet banners, among others. Amscan makes party items and buys the rest from other manufacturers, primarily in Asia. It has production and distribution facilities in Asia, Australia, Europe, and North America. Berkshire Partners and Weston Presidio acquired Amscan in 2004.

Amscan has grown its retail business through three major acquisitions in 2005 (Party City), 2006 (Party America), and 2007 (Factory Card & Party). Other company-owned chains include Halloween USA and The Paper Factory.

Amscan's purchase in November 2007 of Factory Card & Party Outlet was valued at $72 million. Amscan plans to continue to operate the chain as a separate entity, with its own brand, mix of merchandise, and growth strategy.

In mid-2008 the company sold four retail stores in the Salt Lake City market to Zurcher's Merchandise Company, a regional operator of party stores. In return, Zurcher's and Amscan entered into a seven-year supply agreement under which Zurcher's agreed to purchase more merchandise from Amscan.

While generating some 5% of its revenue from international operations, Amscan is banking on opportunities in Europe, Mexico, Canada, Asia, and the UK to push that percentage upward. Its plans include broadening its distribution network, expanding its retail reach, and creating custom accessories to localize its offerings.

Berkshire and Weston Presidio sold a 38% stake in the company to global buyout fund Advent International in August 2008.

EXECUTIVES

Chairman: Robert J. (Rob) Small, age 41
CEO and Director: Gerald C. (Jerry) Rittenberg, age 56, $1,500,000 pay
President, COO, and Director: James M. Harrison, age 56, $1,350,000 pay
CFO: Michael A. Correale, age 50, $357,700 pay
VP Marketing: Craig Leaf
VP Marketing, Amscan Inc.: Mark Sifferlin
CIO: Michael Mostrom
Controller: John Conlon
Human Resources Manager: Laura Bucci
Credit Manager: Vita Spano
Customer Service: Rose Giagrande
Purchasing: Jim Dotti
Auditors: Ernst & Young LLP

LOCATIONS

HQ: Amscan Holdings, Inc.
  80 Grasslands Rd., Elmsford, NY 10523
Phone: 914-345-2020   **Fax:** 914-345-3884
Web: www.amscan.com

2007 Sales

	$ mil.	% of total
Domestic	1,191.3	94
Foreign	80.0	6
Adjustments	(23.9)	—
Total	**1,247.4**	**100**

PRODUCTS/OPERATIONS

2007 Stores

	No.
Company-owned	673
Franchised	283
Total	**956**

2007 Sales

	$ mil.	% of total
Retail	794.1	56
Wholesale	626.5	44
Adjustments	(173.1)	—
Total	**1,247.4**	**100**

Selected Products

Party goods
  Candles
  Cascades and centerpieces
  Crepe
  Cutouts
  Decorative and solid color tableware
  Flags and banners
  Guest towels
  Latex balloons
  Party favors
  Party hats
  Piñatas
Metallic balloons
  Sing-A-Tune
  SuperShapes
  Bouquets
  18-inch standard
Stationery
  Baby and wedding memory books
  Decorative tissues
  Gift wrap, bows, and bags
  Invitations, notes, and stationery
  Photograph albums
  Ribbons
  Stickers and confetti
Gifts
  Ceramic giftware
  Decorative candles
  Decorative frames
  Mugs
  Plush toys
  Wedding accessories and cake tops

COMPETITORS

American Greetings
Celebrate Express
CSS Industries
CTI Industries
Garden Ridge
Hallmark
iParty
Kmart
Michaels Stores
Solo Cup
Target
Walgreen
Wal-Mart

HISTORICAL FINANCIALS

Company Type: Private

Income Statement			FYE: December 31	
	REVENUE ($ mil.)	NET INCOME ($ mil.)	NET PROFIT MARGIN	EMPLOYEES
12/07	1,247	19	1.5%	12,569
12/06	1,015	6	0.6%	8,138
12/05	418	12	2.9%	6,720
12/04	399	8	1.9%	1,750
12/03	403	17	4.3%	1,900
Annual Growth	32.7%	2.9%	—	60.4%

Debt ratio: 155.6%   Current ratio: —
Return on equity: 5.2%   Long-term debt ($ mil.): 584
Cash ($ mil.): —

Net Income History

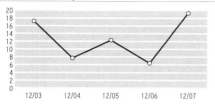

LOCATIONS

HQ: Amsted Industries Incorporated
  2 Prudential Plaza, 180 N. Stetson St., Ste. 1800,
  Chicago, IL 60601
Phone: 312-645-1700   **Fax:** 312-819-8494
Web: www.amsted.com

Amsted Industries has 47 manufacturing facilities in 11 countries.

PRODUCTS/OPERATIONS

Selected Products

Construction and industrial products
  Closed circuit cooling towers
  Cooling towers
  Ductile iron pressure pipe and fittings
  Evaporative condensers
  Ice thermal storage units
  Roller chains
Railroad products
  Center plates
  Constant contact side bearings
  Couplers and connectors
  Draft gears and cushion units
  Draft sills
  Locomotive draft gears
  Rail anchors
  Springs
  Tapered roller bearings
  Truck systems
  Wheels
Vehicular products
  Aluminum and iron wheel hubs
  Aluminum castings
  Automatic transmission reaction plates
  Brake drums
  Fifth wheels
  Molded plastic components
  One-way clutches
  Piston pins
  Powder metal parts
  Steering column components

Selected Divisions

ASF-Keystone (cast steel freight car components, hot coiled steel springs and buffers, discharge gates, draft and draw gears, dynamic brake components, valves)
Baltimore Aircoil Company (cooling towers, evaporative condensers, heat exchangers, ice thermal storage systems, industrial fluid coolers)
Brenco, Incorporated (railroad track anchoring systems, tapered roller bearings)
Burgess-Norton Mfg. Co. (gray and ductile iron castings, piston pins, powder metal parts, rocker arms and assemblies)
Consolidated Metco, Inc. (aluminum permanent mold and die castings, axle hubs, door sill assemblies, fifth wheels and assemblies, instrument panels, sleeper cab accessories, spring brake flanges and pistons, structural molded plastic products, suspension components, transmission housings)
Diamond Chain Company (roller chain)
Griffin Pipe Products Co.(ductile iron pressure pipe and fittings, ductile iron sewer pipe)
Griffin Wheel Co. (cast steel railroad wheels)
Means Industries, Inc. (automatic transmission reaction plates, one-way clutches, stamped metal components, steering column components, transmission components)

COMPETITORS

ALSTOM	Japan Steel Works
BorgWarner	L. B. Foster
CAF	Lamson & Sessions
Columbus Stainless	McWane
Evapco	Portec
Faiveley	Timken
Graham Corporation	Tower Tech
Greenbrier Rail Services	U.S. Pipe
Gunite	U.S. Tsubaki

Amsted Industries

Wilbur and Orville Wright's first flight might never have succeeded without an assist from Amsted Industries' Diamond Chain subsidiary. A maker of roller chains for a variety of equipment and machinery, Diamond Chain also produced the propeller chain for the Wright brothers' aircraft. The company has three main segments, selling its products to industrial distributors, locomotive and railcar manufacturers, and automotive OEMs. Employee-owned Amsted Industries has nearly 50 plants worldwide. North American customers account for 85% of the company's sales.

Amsted's other subsidiaries include ASF-Keystone (side frames, bolsters, and cast steel freight car components), Griffin Pipe Products (ductile iron pressure and sewer pipe), and Means Industries (automotive steering and transmission components).

In 2007 the US Department of Justice reached an agreement with Amsted Industries requiring the company to divest certain assets from its 2005 acquisition of FM Industries. The acquisition removed Amsted's only competitor in new end-of-car cushioning units used in the railroad industry, according to Justice. Customers complained to the government that prices had increased following Amsted's purchase of FM, which had been a subsidiary of Progress Rail Services.

Since Amsted has only one facility producing the units, the Justice Department is requiring the company to grant a perpetual license for the relevant intellectual property to any company that wants to compete with Amsted in making the railroad equipment.

EXECUTIVES

Chairman, President, and CEO: W. Robert Reum, age 65
VP Finance and CFO: Stephen Gregory
VP People: Shirley J. Whitesell
VP and Treasurer: Matthew J. Hower
VP, General Counsel, and Secretary: Stephen R. Smith
President, Amsted Rail: John Wories Jr.
President, Baltimore Aircoil: Steven S. Duerwachter
President Business Systems, Amsted Rail: Dave Liming
President, Consolidated Metco: Ed Oeltjen
President, Burgess-Norton: Brett Vasseur
President, Griffin Pipe Products: Paul T. Ciolino
President, Means Industries, Inc.: D. W. (Bill) Shaw
Controller: Steven E. Obendorf
Auditors: PricewaterhouseCoopers

Amtrak

America's ambivalence toward intercity rail travel is reflected in Amtrak. The National Railroad Passenger Corporation, better known as Amtrak, carries more than 25 million passengers a year throughout the US. Along with its intercity offerings, Amtrak provides or supports commuter rail services in several major markets. Overall, the company's system includes about 21,000 route miles of track, most of which is owned by freight railroads. Ridership has been rising, but Amtrak, a for-profit company, has never been profitable. The rail carrier, which is controlled by the US Department of Transportation, depends on subsidies from the federal government to maintain its operations.

Some government officials have called for Amtrak to be self-sufficient, and the railroad's annual requests for federal money tend to be the subject of considerable debate in Congress. After a Bush administration proposal to end subsidies, break up Amtrak, and turn over passenger rail operations to local authorities failed to gain traction, rising gasoline prices led some lawmakers to push for an increase in Amtrak appropriations. The same price increases that cause more travelers to consider the train as an alternative to the car, however, affect Amtrak in the form of higher diesel fuel costs.

To boost revenue, Amtrak has been investing in its infrastructure, particularly in the northeastern US, where the company owns most of the track that it uses in the Boston-to-Washington, DC corridor. Another focus has been a route between Philadelphia and Harrisburg, Pennsylvania, where Amtrak has worked with state authorities to make improvements needed to enable the railroad to offer higher-speed service. High-demand routes in California, the Chicago area, and the Pacific Northwest also have been targeted for upgrades.

Amtrak's system spans 46 states (Alaska, Hawaii, South Dakota, and Wyoming are excluded), as well as the District of Columbia and three Canadian provinces. The company's trains serve more than 500 destinations altogether.

HISTORY

US passenger train travel peaked in 1929, with 20,000 trains in operation. But the spread of automobiles, bus service, and air travel cut into business, and by the late 1960s only about 500 passenger trains remained running in the country. In 1970 the combined losses of all private train operations exceeded $1.8 billion in today's dollars. That year Congress passed the Rail Passenger Service Act, which created Amtrak to preserve America's passenger rail system. Although railroads were offered stock in the corporation for their passenger equipment, most just wrote off the loss.

Amtrak began operating in 1971 with 1,200 cars, most built in the 1950s. Although the company lost money from the outset ($153 million in 1972), it continued to be bankrolled by Uncle Sam, despite much criticism. Amtrak ordered its first new equipment in 1973, the year it also began taking over stations, yards, and service staff. The company didn't own any track until 1976, when it purchased hundreds of miles of right-of-way track from Boston to Washington, DC.

After a 1979 study showed Amtrak passengers to be by far the most heavily subsidized travelers in the US, Congress ordered the company to better utilize its resources. The 1980s saw Amtrak leasing its rights-of-way along its tracks in the Northeast corridor to telecommunications companies, which installed fiber-optic cables, and beginning mail and freight services for extra revenue.

In the early 1990s Amtrak faced a number of challenges: Midwest flooding, falling airfares, and safety concerns over a number of rail accidents, particularly the 1993 wreck of the Sunset Limited near Mobile, Alabama, in which 47 people were killed (the worst accident in Amtrak's history). In 1994 Amtrak's board of directors (at Congress' behest) adopted a plan to be free of federal support by 2002. In 1995 the company began planning high-speed trains for its heavily traveled East Coast routes.

In 1997 Amtrak finalized agreements to buy the high-speed cars and locomotives central to its self-sufficiency plan. It initiated an effort to haul more freight, and it had its first profitable offering: the Metroliner route between New York and Washington, DC.

Amtrak's board of directors was replaced by Congress in 1997 with a seven-member Reform Board appointed by President Clinton. Chairman and president Thomas Downs resigned that year, and Tommy Thompson, then governor of Wisconsin, took over as chairman. Former Massachusetts governor Michael Dukakis was named vice chairman, and George Warrington stepped in as Amtrak's president and CEO.

Technical problems in 1999 delayed Amtrak's introduction of the Acela high-speed train in the Northeast until late 2000, when service began in the Boston-Washington corridor. In 2001 Amtrak pitched a 20-year plan, involving an annual outlay of $1.5 billion in federal funds, for expanding and modernizing its passenger service to help alleviate highway and airport congestion nationwide.

Thompson left the Amtrak board in 2001 after he was named US secretary of health and human services.

Realizing Amtrak would not meet its end-of-the-year deadline to be self-sufficient, in 2002 the Amtrak Reform Council sent a proposal to Congress that Amtrak be divided into three groups: one to oversee operations and funding, a second to maintain certain Amtrak-owned tracks and properties, and a third to operate trains. It also called for competition to be allowed on some passenger routes within two to three years.

Also in 2002 Warrington resigned and was replaced by David Gunn, who formerly headed the metropolitan transit systems in New York and Toronto. Gunn began moving to cut costs, and he worked to secure new federal money to avert a threatened shutdown of rail service in July 2002. In 2004 the company exited the mail-carrying business, which had not been profitable.

Gunn was fired in November 2005, however, and chief engineer David Hughes was named interim president and CEO. He left the company after Alexander Kummant was made president and CEO in September 2006.

EXECUTIVES

President, CEO, and Director: Alexander K. Kummant, age 46
COO: William L. (Bill) Crosbie
CFO: William H. Campbell
VP, General Counsel, and Corporate Secretary: Eleanor D. Acheson
VP Strategic Partnerships and Business Development: Anne Witt
VP Security Strategy and Special Operations: William Rooney
VP Government Affairs and Corporate Communications: Joseph H. (Joe) McHugh
VP Human Resources and Diversity Initiatives: Lorraine A. Green
VP Labor Relations: Joseph M. Bress
VP Procurement and Materials Management: Michael J. Rienzi
VP Marketing and Product Management: Emmett H. Fremaux
VP Planning and Analysis: Roy Johanson
CIO: Ed Trainor
Inspector General: Fred E. Weiderhold
Auditors: KPMG LLP

LOCATIONS

HQ: National Railroad Passenger Corporation
60 Massachusetts Ave. NE, Washington, DC 20002
Phone: 202-906-3000   **Fax:** 202-906-3306
Web: www.amtrak.com

PRODUCTS/OPERATIONS

2007 Sales

	$ mil.	% of total
Passenger-related	1,730.9	80
Commuter	117.4	6
State capital payments	2.0	—
Other	302.3	14
Total	**2,152.6**	**100**

COMPETITORS

AirTran Holdings	JetBlue
AMR Corp.	Northwest Airlines
Continental Airlines	Southwest Airlines
Delta Air Lines	UAL
Frontier Airlines	US Airways
Greyhound	

HISTORICAL FINANCIALS

Company Type: Government-owned

Income Statement

FYE: September 30

	REVENUE ($ mil.)	NET INCOME ($ mil.)	NET PROFIT MARGIN	EMPLOYEES
9/07	2,153	(1,121)	—	19,000
9/06	2,043	(1,068)	—	19,000
9/05	1,886	(1,192)	—	19,000
9/04	1,865	(1,309)	—	19,700
9/03	2,077	(1,274)	—	22,000
Annual Growth	**0.9%**	**—**	**—**	**(3.6%)**

Net Income History

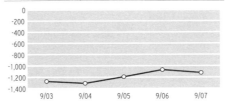

AmWINS Group

AmWINS is rarely at a loss when it comes to insurance. The company is among the largest wholesale insurance brokers in the US (along with Swett & Crawford and Crump). The group sells insurance products — including property/casualty, group benefits, and specialty coverage — to retail brokers across the country. It also provides underwriting of specialty insurance products for niches including armored cars, broadcasters, and Domino's franchise owners. The company also offers additional services such as administration and actuarial services for some products. Private equity firm Parthenon Capital acquired a majority stake in AmWINS in 2005.

The company's property/casualty brokerage division accounts for nearly three-quarters of sales; however, its fastest-growing unit is its group benefits business, which provides group health and life insurance products to businesses through retail brokerages. The division also administers retiree health plans, provides claims administration, and offers pharmacy benefit management services.

AmWINS in 2005 acquired Stewart Smith Group, the US wholesale insurance unit of Willis Group Holdings; the transaction was part of an industry-wide trend in which retail insurance brokers (such as Willis) divested wholesale holdings to remove any appearance of a conflict of interest. Other recent acquisitions, including the 2006 purchases of Texas-based WEB-TPA and the policy administration operations of CBCA, have strengthened the company's growing group benefits division.

The company's holdings of niche underwriters was bolstered with its 2007 purchase of London American General Agency, which provides commercial transportation underwriting for limousines and truckers.

Former chairman Ernie Telford and CEO Steve DeCarlo founded American Wholesale Insurance Group in 2002 by combining several specialty wholesale insurance firms. AmWINS proposed an initial public offering in 2006, but withdrew its registration in 2007.

EXECUTIVES

CEO: M. Steven (Steve) DeCarlo, $785,000 pay
President: W.H. (Skip) Cooper
President, Group Benefits Division: Samuel H. (Sam) Fleet, $1,695,583 pay
President, Specialty Underwriting Division: J. Scott Reynolds
VP, CFO, and Secretary: Scott M. Purviance, $340,000 pay
General Counsel: Donna L. Hargrove
Director of Human Resources: Kristin L. Downey
Director Program Development: Ben Francavilla
Auditors: PricewaterhouseCoopers LLP

LOCATIONS

HQ: AmWINS Group, Inc.
4725 Piedmont Row Dr., Ste. 600,
Charlotte, NC 28210
Phone: 704-749-2700   **Fax:** 704-943-9000
Web: www.amwins.com

AmWINS has offices throughout the US.

PRODUCTS/OPERATIONS

Selected Subsidiaries and Affiliates

Americana Program Underwriters, Inc.
BrokerNetUSA
National Employee Benefit Companies
Specialty Programs & Facility Managers, Inc. (SPFM)
The American Equity Underwriters, Inc
WEB-TPA
Woodus K. Humphrey & Co., Inc.

COMPETITORS

CRC Insurance
Crump Group
Swett & Crawford

HISTORICAL FINANCIALS

Company Type: Private

Income Statement

FYE: December 31

	REVENUE ($ mil.)	NET INCOME ($ mil.)	NET PROFIT MARGIN	EMPLOYEES
12/06	185	—	—	976
12/05	142	—	—	976
12/04	85	—	—	695
12/03	58	—	—	—
Annual Growth	47.1%	—	—	18.5%

Revenue History

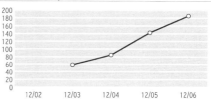

Anaheim Ducks

Officially these Ducks are no longer Mighty, but they are still pretty good. Formerly known as The Mighty Ducks of Anaheim, the Anaheim Ducks Hockey Club joined the National Hockey League as an expansion team in 1993. Anaheim made its first playoff appearance in 1997 and reached the Stanley Cup finals in 2003 (losing to the Dallas Stars); the team captured its first NHL championship in 2007. The Ducks franchise was originally granted to entertainment goliath Walt Disney, which named the team after its 1992 hockey film, *The Mighty Ducks*. Billionaire Henry Samueli, who co-founded computer chip maker Broadcom, and his wife Susan purchased the franchise from Disney in 2005.

Samueli changed the name of the team for the start of the 2006-07 season to help market the hockey franchise to new fans. Also getting a name change, the team's home ice became the Honda Center in 2006 when American Honda Motor Co. signed a 15-year, $60 million naming rights deal. The arena was formerly known as the Arrowhead Pond of Anaheim.

Steadily improving on the ice, and at the box office, since the labor dispute that scotched the 2004-05 NHL season, the Ducks finally made a successful Stanley Cup run during the 2006-07 season with the help of newly acquired players

Scott Niedermayer, Chris Pronger, and Teemu Selanne. The previous season the team reached the Western Conference finals but eventually lost that series to the Edmonton Oilers.

Samueli, meanwhile, has been suspended by the NHL pending the outcome of a criminal case involving stock options backdating at Broadcom. The former chairman of the company has been charged with lying to investigators looking into the $2.2 billion financial scandal.

Disney's short-lived flirtation with professional sports, which also included the Anaheim Angels baseball team (now carrying the labor-intensive moniker Los Angeles Angels of Anaheim), was a strategy designed to create new revenue streams while providing programming for its television stations. ABC and ESPN, both Disney-owned networks, paid $600 million for the television rights to NHL games, but ratings were so poor that they dropped out of the broadcast scheme following the 2004 season. The media company sold the Angels in 2003.

EXECUTIVES

CEO; Chairman, Anaheim Arena Management:
Michael Schulman
EVP and COO; President and CEO, Anaheim Arena Management: Tim Ryan
EVP and General Manager: Brian P. Burke, age 53
SVP and Chief Marketing Officer: Bob Wagner
VP Sales and Marketing: Steve Obert
VP Finance: Doug Heller
VP Human Resources: Kim Kutcher
Head Coach: Randy Carlyle
Director Broadcasting: Aaron Teats
Director Media and Communications: Alex Gilchrist
Director Fan Development: Matt Savant
Director Finance: Mike McGee
Director Human Resources: Jenny Price
Director Marketing: Tracie Jones
Director Sales and Marketing: Michael Williams

LOCATIONS

HQ: Anaheim Ducks Hockey Club, LLC
2695 E. Katella Ave., Anaheim, CA 92806
Phone: 714-704-2700   **Fax:** 714-704-2754
Web: www.anaheimducks.com

The Anaheim Ducks play at the 17,250-seat capacity Honda Center in Anaheim, California.

PRODUCTS/OPERATIONS

Championship Trophies
Stanley Cup (2007)
Clarence S. Campbell Bowl (2003, 2007)

COMPETITORS

Dallas Stars
Los Angeles Kings
Phoenix Coyotes
San Jose Sharks

HISTORICAL FINANCIALS

Company Type: Private

Income Statement

FYE: June 30

	REVENUE ($ mil.)	NET INCOME ($ mil.)	NET PROFIT MARGIN	EMPLOYEES
9/07	89	—	—	—
9/06	75	—	—	—
9/05	0	—	—	—
9/04	54	—	—	—
9/03	59	—	—	—
Annual Growth	10.8%	—	—	—

Revenue History

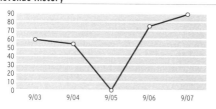

Andersen Corporation

Windows of opportunity open daily for Andersen, a leading and well-known maker of wood-clad windows and patio doors in the US. Andersen offers window designs from hinged, bay, and double-hung to skylight, gliding, and picture windows. It operates more than 100 Renewal by Andersen window replacement stores in around 35 states. Andersen's EMCO Doors subsidiary makes storm and screen doors. Through independent and company-owned distributorships (including its Andersen Logistics division), Andersen sells to homeowners, architects, builders, designers, and remodelers. The company is owned by the Andersen family, the Andersen Foundation, and company employees.

Andersen competes in the marketplace by building strong brand recognition for its products. The company offers products that are available in more than 600,000 unique shapes and styles; it builds some 12 million doors and windows annually from more than 15 factories.

Acquisitions, too, play an important role in the company's growth strategy. In 2006 it bought rival Silver Line Building Products, a maker of vinyl window products. The move is a departure for Andersen, which had hitherto concentrated on its wooden windows. Vinyl is the fastest-growing segment of the window industry. The previous year, the company bought Eagle Window & Door, a maker of aluminum clad windows and patio doors.

Other units include Canada-based roof window and skylight maker and distributor Dashwood Industries, and specialty window manufacturer KML Windows. Through its Aspen Research subsidiary, Andersen analyzes composite materials development, product life-cycle management, and waste elimination and reclamation.

Andersen's annual profit-sharing program has been in operation since it was established in 1914, with the exception of the Depression-era years from 1929 to 1936.

HISTORY

Danish immigrant Hans Andersen and his two sons, Fred and Herbert, founded Andersen in 1903. Andersen's first words in English, "All together, boys," became the company motto. Andersen arrived in Portland, Maine, in 1870 and worked as a lumber dealer and manufacturer. In the 1880s he bought a sawmill in St. Cloud, Minnesota, and later managed one in Hudson, Wisconsin. When the Hudson mill owners asked him to let workers go during the off season, Andersen refused and then resigned. He subsequently launched his own lumber business — Andersen Lumber Company — in 1903 and hired some of the men who had been laid off. He opened a second lumberyard, in Afton, Minnesota, in 1904.

Andersen and his sons revolutionized the window industry in the early 1900s by introducing a standardized window frame with interchangeable parts. Buoyed by success, the Andersens sold their lumberyards in 1908 to focus on the window-frame business. (Andersen purchased lumberyards again in 1916 before exiting the lumberyard business for good in the 1930s.) Around 1913 the company moved from Hudson to South Stillwater (now Bayport), Minnesota.

Thrifty Hans launched the company's first (and the US's third) profit-sharing plan shortly before his death in 1914. Herbert became VP, secretary, treasurer, and factory manager, and Fred became president. Herbert died in 1921 (at age 36), but Fred proved to be a versatile and capable successor. Among his accomplishments, Fred came up with the tag line "Only the rich can afford poor windows."

In 1929 the company changed its name to Andersen Frame Corporation. In the following decade Andersen introduced a number of innovations, including Master Frame (a frame with a locked sill joint, 1930); a casement window, the industry's first complete factory-made window unit (1932); and a basement window (1934). The company adopted its current name in 1937.

Andersen introduced the gliding window concept in the early 1940s. It also launched the Home Planners Scrap Book consumer ad campaign in 1943. During the 1950s Andersen's new products included the Flexivent awning window, which featured welded insulating glass that served as an alternative to traditional storm windows. In the 1960s the company produced a gliding door and introduced the Perma-Shield system. The system featured easy-to-maintain vinyl cladding to protect wood frames from weathering. By 1978 Perma-Shield products accounted for three-quarters of sales. Fred, who had run the company as president until 1960 and had subsequently held the positions of chairman and chairman emeritus, died in 1979 at age 92.

Between 1984 and 1994 the company increased its sales threefold by introducing additional customized and state-of-the-art products, including patio doors. In 1995 it launched Renewal by Andersen, a retail window-replacement business.

Andersen acquired former long-term strategic partner Aspen Research (materials testing, research, and product development) in 1997. In 1998 company veteran Donald Garofalo succeeded Andersen's president and CEO Jerold Wulf, who retired after 39 years with the company. Andersen reinforced its company-owned distributorships in 1999 when it bought millwork distributors Morgan Products (now Andersen Logistics) and Independent Millwork.

Expanding its product offerings, Andersen purchased privately held EMCO Enterprises (storm doors and accessories, Iowa) in 2001. Other acquisitions from about 1993 to 2003 have included Dashwood Industries (windows, skylights, roof windows, doors; Canada) and KML Windows (architectural windows and doors, Canada). The company also opened a new production facility in Menomonie, Wisconsin.

At the close of 2002, Andersen's COO James Humphrey was promoted to president, becoming the company's ninth president; he gained the added role of chief executive the next year. Garofalo retained the position of vice chair of the board; he later became chair of the board. Andersen celebrated its 100th year in 2003, publishing a book on its history, and the company kicked off a community project to build 100 Habitat for Humanity homes throughout North America over the next five years.

Andersen completed construction of a 150,000-sq.-ft. facility for wood composite profile extrusion in North Branch, Minnesota in 2004. The company shut down its plant in White Bear Lake and relocated approximately 40 employees to North Branch. Andersen also reorganized its distribution centers.

EXECUTIVES

Chairman: Donald L. Garofalo
President and CEO: James E. (Jim) Humphrey, age 57
EVP and COO: Jay Lund
SVP and CFO: Philip (Phil) Donaldson
SVP Human Resources and Corporate Administration: Mary D. Carter
SVP Research, Technology, and Engineering: Mary J. Schumacher
SVP and General Counsel: Alan Bernick
VP Marketing: J. Glasnapp
Director, Corporate Communications: Maureen McDonough
Director, Marketing Communications and Services: Frank Quadflieg
President and CEO, Silver Line: T. Randall (Randy) Iles
President, Renewal by Andersen: Craig Evanich
VP Sales: Vic Springer

LOCATIONS

HQ: Andersen Corporation
   100 4th Ave. North, Bayport, MN 55003
Phone: 651-264-5150   **Fax:** 651-264-5107
Web: www.andersenwindows.com

PRODUCTS/OPERATIONS

Selected Products and Brands

Doors
   Patio doors
      Art glass
      Frenchwood Collection (gliding, hinged, and outswing)
      Narroline gliding patio doors
      Perma-Shield gliding patio doors
   Screen doors
   Storm doors
Windows
   Aluminum-clad
   Art glass
   Awning
   Basement
   Bay and bow
   Casement
   Double-hung
   Fixed
   Gliding
   Horizontal sliding
   Picture
   Skylights and roof windows
   Transom
   Utility
   Wood
   Wood-clad

Selected Companies

Andersen Logistics
Aspen Research Corporation (R&D of composite materials, adhesives, and coatings)
Dashwood Industries Ltd. (roof windows and skylights, distribution, Canada)
Eagle Window & Door (aluminum clad wood windows and patio doors)
EMCO Doors (all-season/storm doors and accessories)
KML Windows Inc. (architecturally designed windows and entranceways, Canada)
Silver Line Building Products (vinyl windows and patio doors)

COMPETITORS

GBO
JELD-WEN
Marshfield DoorSystems
MI Windows and Doors
Owens Corning Sales
Pella
Ply Gem
Royal Group
Sierra Pacific Industries
Simonton Windows, Inc.
Thermal Industries

HISTORICAL FINANCIALS

Company Type: Private

Income Statement				FYE: December 31
	ESTIMATED REVENUE ($ mil.)	NET INCOME ($ mil.)	NET PROFIT MARGIN	EMPLOYEES
12/07	3,000	—	—	13,000
12/06	3,000	—	—	14,000
12/05	3,000	—	—	16,000
12/04	2,500	—	—	8,500
12/03	2,000	—	—	8,000
Annual Growth	10.7%	—	—	12.9%

Revenue History

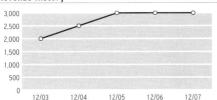

Anderson News

Anderson News is the cover girl of the magazine wholesale industry. The company is one of the top US magazine distributors. It distributes thousands of magazine titles to about 40,000 outlets in 45 states, including bookstores, mass merchants, grocery stores, discount retailers, and just about any place that sells books and magazines. The company distributes best-selling books and comics as well. Anderson News also owns Liquid Digital Music, an online music download service used by retailers like Wal-Mart and Amazon.com. Anderson News was founded in 1917 by CEO Charles Anderson's grandfather; it is still family owned. The founding Anderson family also runs the #3 US bookstore chain, Books-A-Million.

Changes in the magazine industry have forced Anderson News, along with other magazine wholesalers, to modify some practices. Some magazine publishers have made their newsstand copy prices so low that it is difficult for the wholesalers to make a profit. As a result, Anderson News has cut the number of low cover price titles it carries, especially those priced under $2.50.

EXECUTIVES

Chairman: Joel R. Anderson
President and CEO: Charles (Charlie) Anderson, age 69
SVP, Finance: John Campbell
VP, Information Systems: Sadie Kelley
Human Resources Administrator: Carl Boley

LOCATIONS

HQ: Anderson News, LLC
     6016 Brookvale Ln., Ste. 151, Knoxville, TN 37919
Phone: 865-584-9765   **Fax:** 865-584-7769
Web: www.andersonnews.com

COMPETITORS

American Media	Jim Pattison Group
AMREP	Levy Home Entertainment
Hudson News	Source Interlink
Ingram Industries	

HISTORICAL FINANCIALS

Company Type: Private

Income Statement

	ESTIMATED REVENUE ($ mil.)	NET INCOME ($ mil.)	NET PROFIT MARGIN	EMPLOYEES
12/07	2,210	—	—	9,800
12/06	2,350	—	—	10,000
12/05	2,696	—	—	12,100
12/04	1,300	—	—	8,400
12/03	1,100	—	—	7,000
Annual Growth	19.1%	—	—	8.8%

FYE: December 31

Revenue History

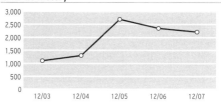

Anthony & Sylvan Pools

Pooling resources is second nature to Anthony & Sylvan Pools Corporation. The company, created through the 1996 union of industry leaders Anthony Pools and Sylvan Pools, installs custom in-ground concrete swimming pools for private residences. The company has roots dating back to 1946 and has installed more than 360,000 pools during its history. It operates a network of more than 35 company-owned locations, consisting of sales and design centers, pool and spa renovation centers, and retail service centers that sell pool accessories such as chemicals, heaters, filters, pumps, and pool toys. The company is active in Texas, Nevada, and 10 East Coast states.

Anthony & Sylvan Pools became a division of pool equipment manufacturer Essef Corporation in 1997. It was then spun off to shareholders of Essef as part of that company's acquisition by Pentair two years later. A buyout by management took Anthony & Sylvan Pools private in 2004.

EXECUTIVES

Chairman and CEO: Stuart D. Neidus, age 57
COO: Richard E. Mills
President: Howard P. Wertman, age 63
EVP and CFO: Martin Iles
VP Human Resources: Ken F. Sloan
VP Sales: Thomas J. Casey
VP Management Information Systems: Bill Meyerowitz
VP, Secretary, and General Counsel: Michael Sprenger
Auditors: KPMG LLP

LOCATIONS

HQ: Anthony & Sylvan Pools Corporation
     Mt. Vernon Sq., 6690 Beta Dr., Ste. 300,
     Mayfield Village, OH 44143
Phone: 440-720-3301   **Fax:** 440-720-3303
Web: www.anthonysylvan.com

COMPETITORS

Centex	Paddock Pool
Hayward Industries	Pentair Water
Leslie's Poolmart	Pool Corp.

Anvil Holdings

Despite its name, it likely won't require metal shaping to get this imprinting job done. Anvil Holdings, which operates primarily through its subsidiary Anvil Knitwear, makes and markets activewear for men, women, and children that it sells to screen printers, private label brand owners, and distributors in the US. In addition to its apparel offerings (primarily short- and long-sleeve T-shirts), Anvil also makes bags, caps, robes, and towels. Before they're purchased, Anvil's products are typically embellished with characters, designs, or logos. The company's brands include Anvil Logo, Anvil, Cotton Deluxe, chromaZONE, and Towels Plus by Anvil, as well as private labels manufactured for other companies.

Anvil relies on distributors such as Alpha, Broder Bros., and Gauss Sales. The apparel maker has operations worldwide, including facilities in North Carolina and South Carolina as well as Nicaragua and Honduras.

The company completed a financial restructuring in early 2007 that involves the elimination of some $200 million in debt. The restructuring allows Anvil to make plans to add new facilities, brands, and styles. Soon thereafter, Anvil debuted a 100% organic T-shirt line as its foray into the lucrative organic-apparel market alongside the likes of American Apparel.

EXECUTIVES

Chairman and CEO: Anthony Corsano, age 46, $632,154 pay
EVP Finance and CFO: Frank Ferramosca, age 51, $344,231 pay
EVP Sales: Frank D. Keeney, age 55
EVP, Chief Administrative Officer, and General Counsel: Caterina Conti
EVP Marketing: Ellen Singer
EVP Manufacturing: Chris Binnicker
Auditors: Deloitte & Touche LLP

LOCATIONS

HQ: Anvil Holdings, Inc.
     228 E. 45th St., 4th Fl., New York, NY 10017
Phone: 212-476-0300   **Fax:** 212-476-0323
Web: www.anvilknitwear.com

PRODUCTS/OPERATIONS

Selected Products

Basic T-shirts
Organic T-shirts
Caps
Towels
Robes
Dri-release performance shirts

COMPETITORS

adidas	Gildan Activewear
Fila USA	Hanesbrands
Fruit of the Loom	SanMar
The Gap	Under Armour

Apex Oil

Always at the top of its game, Apex Oil sells, stores, and distributes petroleum products. Its range of refined products includes asphalt, kerosene, fuel oil, diesel fuel, heavy oil, gasoline, and bunker fuels. The company's terminals are located on the East Coast and Gulf Coast, in California, and in the Midwest. Internationally, Apex Oil has a terminal in Caracas, Venezuela, and has additional activities in Bermuda, Monaco, and the Netherlands. The company's subsidiaries include Apex Towing, a tug boat and barge business, and Petroleum Fuel and Terminal, a storage and truck rack operation. Apex Oil is controlled by CEO Tony Novelly.

Apex Oil was founded in 1932 by Samuel Goldstein. Apex Oil paid $550 million for Clark Oil and Refining in 1981. Financially strapped, it sold that company in 1994.

EXECUTIVES

CEO: P. Anthony (Tony) Novelly, age 64
President and Bulk Activity, Heavy Oil: Edwin L. (Ed) Wahl
EVP and General Counsel: Douglas D. Hommert
VP and Treasurer: John L. Hank Jr.
Controller: Jeffrey D. Baltz
Terminal Manager: Ken Fenton
Credit: Laura Seymour
Director IT: Dave Paul
Human Resources and Benefits: Julie Cook

LOCATIONS

HQ: Apex Oil Company, Inc.
     8235 Forsyth Blvd., Ste. 400, Clayton, MO 63105
Phone: 314-889-9600   **Fax:** 314-854-8539
Web: www.apexoil.com

PRODUCTS/OPERATIONS

Major Products

Asphalt
Bunker fuels
Diesel fuel
Fuel oil
Gasoline
Heavy oil
Kerosene

Selected Subsidiaries and Affiliates

Apex Towing Company (tugs & barges)
Clark Oil Trading Company
Petroleum Fuel and Terminal Co. (storage and truck racks)

APi Group

Holding company APi Group has a piece of the action in five business sectors: construction services, fire protection, special systems, manufacturing, and materials distribution. APi has more than 25 subsidiaries, which operate as independent companies. Services provided by the company's construction subsidiaries include energy conservation; electrical, industrial, and mechanical contracting; industrial insulation; and overhead door installation. Other units install fire protection systems, fabricate structural steel, and distribute building materials. The family-owned company was founded by Reuben Anderson, father of chairman Lee Anderson.

EXECUTIVES

Chairman: Lee R. Anderson Sr., age 64
President and CEO: Russell (Russ) Becker
VP Construction: Jerry Pederson
President and CEO, ANCO Products: Ray Plagens
President, Communication Systems: Ted Barker
President, Doody Mechanical:
 Michael J. (Mike) Stillman
President, Jamar: Mike McParlan
President, APi Distribution: Jack Schwartz
President, Northern Fire & Communication:
 Chuck Thompson
President and CEO, Grunau: Paul Grunau

LOCATIONS

HQ: APi Group, Inc.
 2366 Rose Place, St. Paul, MN 55113
Phone: 651-636-4320 **Fax:** 651-636-0312
Web: www.apigroupinc.com

APi Group has more than 100 offices, plants, and warehouses in the US, Canada, and the UK.

PRODUCTS/OPERATIONS

Selected Subsidiaries

Fabrication and Manufacturing
 Anco Products, Inc. (flexible air ducts)
 Industrial Fabricators, Inc. (industrial silencers)
 LeJeune Steel Company (structural steel fabrication)
 Wisconsin Structural Steel Company

Fire Protection Systems
 Alliance Fire Protection, Inc.
 Davis-Ulmer Sprinkler Company
 Security Fire Protection Company
 United States Fire Protection Company
 VFP Fire Systems, Inc.
 Viking Automatic Sprinkler Company
 Vipond Fire Protection, Inc. (Canada)
 Vipond Fire Protection, Ltd. (UK)
 Western States Fire Protection, Inc.

Materials Distribution
 APi Distribution (insulation and construction materials)
 ASDCO (construction materials)
Specialty Construction Services
 APi Construction Company (industrial insulation)
 APi Electric (electrical contracting)
 APi Supply, Inc. (rental, sales, service of aerial work platforms)
 Classic Industrial Services, Inc. (full-service merit shop specialty contractor)
 Doody Mechanical, Inc. (mechanical contracting, including heating, ventilation, and air-conditioning)
 Garage Door Store (residential and commercial garage and specialty doors)
 Grunau Company, Inc. (mechanical and fire protection systems)
 Industrial Contractors, Inc. (energy industry contracting)
 The Jamar Company (mechanical and specialty contracting)
 Larson Electric Systems, Inc. (electrical contracting)
 Twin City Garage Door Company (installation and servicing of overhead doors)
Systems
 APi Systems Group (fire and gas detection and security systems provider)
 Communications Systems, Inc. (security systems integration)
 Halon Banking Systems
 Northern Fire & Communication (fire alarm and communications equipment)
 Vipond Systems Group, Inc. (fire alarm and communications equipment)

COMPETITORS

ADT Worldwide
Comfort Systems USA
EMCOR
Integrated Electrical Services
Irex
John E. Green
TDIndustries
Team
Turner Industries

HISTORICAL FINANCIALS

Company Type: Private

Income Statement

FYE: December 31

	ESTIMATED REVENUE ($ mil.)	NET INCOME ($ mil.)	NET PROFIT MARGIN	EMPLOYEES
12/07	1,000	—	—	9,000
12/06	900	—	—	5,000
Annual Growth	11.1%	—	—	80.0%

Revenue History

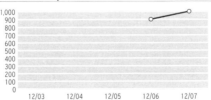

	12/03	12/04	12/05	12/06	12/07
1,000					

Appleton Papers

Appleton Papers hasn't fallen far from the tree. The company manufactures and distributes a variety of specialty paper products. Its top product is carbonless paper (sold under the NCR Paper brand), which is used for business forms. Appleton also makes thermal paper and related products that are used in point-of-sale receipts and coupons, tickets (including event, lottery, and transportation tickets), and labels. Other units make security products (checks, security-printed vouchers, and counterfeit-resistant documents) and plastic packaging films for use in the food processing, household goods, and industrial products industries. Appleton is owned by its employees.

The company restructured its operations in 2005 to streamline costs and position the company for growth. It also acquired packaging company New England Extrusion that year. Other subsidiaries include American Plastics and C&H Packaging. In 2008 Appleton sold BemroseBooth to American Industrial Acquisition Corporation, a private equity firm.

In 2007 the company sought, and received, help from the federal government regarding dumping of paper products by foreign companies. Appleton has contended that companies in China, Germany, and South Korea are selling thermal paper products in the US at prices below what it costs them to make. The company also decided it would focus its operational efforts on its core North American products. Part of that plan includes the sale of its Bemrose subsidiary, which it had acquired with the hopes of expanding into the UK market.

Employees own Appleton through a holding company, Paperweight Development. Money from employee retirement savings plans was used to fund Paperweight Development's purchase of Appleton from ArjoWiggins (then known as Arjo Wiggins Appleton) in 2001.

EXECUTIVES

Chairman, President, and CEO: Mark R. Richards, $714,234 pay
President, Technical Papers Division: Walter Schonfeld
VP Finance and CFO: Thomas J. Ferree
VP and General Manager, International Division:
 Sarah T. Macdonald
VP and General Manager, Performance Packaging:
 M. Kathleen (Kathy) Bolhous
VP Business Development: Ted E. Goodwin
VP Marketing and Strategy: Kent E. Willetts
VP Operations, Technical Papers Division:
 David B. Williams
Auditors: PricewaterhouseCoopers LLP

LOCATIONS

HQ: Appleton Papers Inc.
 825 E. Wisconsin Ave., Appleton, WI 54912
Phone: 920-734-9841 **Fax:** 920-991-7365
Web: www.appletonideas.com

PRODUCTS/OPERATIONS

2007 Sales

	$ mil.	% of total
Technical papers		
Coated solutions	572.0	59
Thermal papers	257.1	27
Security papers	32.3	3
Performance packaging	101.8	11
Total	**963.2**	**100**

Selected Products

Coated solutions
  Carbonless paper
    Credit card receipts
    Invoices
    NCR Paper
  Coated products
    Design and print applications
    Point-of-sale displays
Thermal and advanced technical products
  Non-thermal products
  Thermal business products
    Point-of-sale receipts and coupons
    Label products
    Lotteries and gaming tickets
    Tags for airline baggage
    Tickets
Security products
  Business documents
  Checks
  Government documents
Secure and specialized print services
  High-integrity mailing and niche publishing
  Mass transit and car parking tickets
  Security printed vouchers and payment cards
Performance packaging
  Flexible packaging materials
  Multilayered films

COMPETITORS

ArjoWiggins
Asia Pulp & Paper
Bemis
Boise Cascade
Cascades Inc.
Communisis
Curwood
De La Rue
Glatfelter
Kanzaki Specialty Papers
MeadWestvaco
Mitsubishi Paper Mills
Nippon Paper
Oji Paper
Pliant
Printpack
Ricoh
Rio Tinto Alcan
R.R. Donnelley
Winpak

HISTORICAL FINANCIALS

Company Type: Private

Income Statement

FYE: Saturday nearest December 31

	REVENUE ($ mil.)	NET INCOME ($ mil.)	NET PROFIT MARGIN	EMPLOYEES
12/07	963	(6)	—	3,001
12/06	1,087	11	1.0%	3,144
12/05	1,047	(3)	—	3,238
12/04	990	(25)	—	3,406
12/03	862	11	1.3%	3,348
Annual Growth	2.8%	—	—	(2.7%)

2007 Year-End Financials

Debt ratio: 227.5%
Return on equity: —
Cash ($ mil.): —
Current ratio: —
Long-term debt ($ mil.): 240

Net Income History

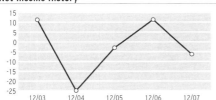

ARAMARK

Keeping employees fed and clothed is one mark of this company. ARAMARK is the world's #3 foodservice provider (behind Compass Group and Sodexo) and the #2 uniform supplier (behind Cintas) in the US. It offers corporate dining services and operates concessions at many sports arenas and other entertainment venues, while its ARAMARK Refreshment Services unit is a leading provider of vending and beverage services. The company also provides facilities management services. Through ARAMARK Uniform and Career Apparel, the company supplies uniforms for health care, public safety, and technology workers. Founded in 1959, ARAMARK is owned by an investment group led by chairman and CEO Joseph Neubauer.

A leader in its industry, the company continues to look for opportunities to expand not only its client base, but also to expand the number of services it supplies for its existing customers. For new business, ARAMARK is targeting such industry segments as correctional facilities and health care operators.

It is also keen on international expansion with a focus on Europe and Japan, as well as the burgeoning market in China. Already operating in the country through subsidiary Bright China Service, ARAMARK in 2006 acquired Beijing-based food services outfit Golden Collar. The following year, the company was selected to provide foodservices for the 2008 Olympics in Beijing.

With backing from such investment firms as CCMP Capital, Thomas H. Lee Partners, and Warburg Pincus, Neubauer took the company private in 2007 for $8.3 billion, including the assumption of $2 billion in debt. (The executive already owned 40% of ARAMARK.) The deal marked the second such transaction for the company, having been taken private by Neubauer and a management group in the 1980s.

EXECUTIVES

Chairman and CEO: Joseph (Joe) Neubauer, age 66, $2,750,000 pay
EVP, General Counsel, and Secretary: Bart J. Colli, age 59, $942,800 pay
EVP Human Resources: Lynn B. McKee, age 52, $917,800 pay
EVP and CFO: L. Frederick Sutherland, age 55, $1,042,800 pay
EVP, ARAMARK Business and Industry Facility Services: Joseph J. Tinney Jr.
EVP; President Domestic Food, Hospitality, and Facilities: Andrew C. Kerin, age 44, $975,850 pay
EVP; President ARAMARK International: Ravi K. Saligram, age 51, $917,800 pay
EVP; President ARAMARK Uniform and Career Apparel: Thomas J. (Tom) Vozzo, age 45, $893,750 pay
SVP; President, ARAMARK Business, Sports, and Entertainment: John R. (Jack) Donovan Jr.
SVP, Controller, and Chief Accounting Officer: John M. Lafferty, age 63
SVP Corporate Communications and Public Affairs: Ronald (Ron) Iori
SVP and CIO: David S. Kaufman
SVP and Treasurer: Christopher S. (Chris) Holland, age 41
Associate VP Investor Relations: Bobbi Chaville
Auditors: KPMG LLP

LOCATIONS

HQ: ARAMARK Corporation
ARAMARK Tower, 1101 Market St.,
Philadelphia, PA 19107
Phone: 215-238-3000   **Fax:** 215-238-3333
Web: www.aramark.com

PRODUCTS/OPERATIONS

2007 Sales

	$ mil.	% of total
Food & support services		
Domestic	8,433.4	68
International	2,276.1	18
Uniform & career apparel	1,674.8	14
Total	**12,384.3**	**100**

Selected Operations

Food and support services
  ARAMARK College and University Services
  ARAMARK Convention Centers
  ARAMARK Correctional Institution Services
  ARAMARK Facilities Management
  ARAMARK Food Services
  ARAMARK Harrison Lodging (conference centers)
  ARAMARK Healthcare
  ARAMARK Higher Education
  ARAMARK Innovative Dining Solutions
  ARAMARK National Events
  ARAMARK Parks and Resorts
  ARAMARK Refreshment Services (vending services)
  ARAMARK School Support Services
  ARAMARK Sports and Entertainment Services
Uniform and career apparel
  ARAMARK Cleanroom Services
  ARAMARK Uniform & Career Apparel
  Galls (tactical equipment and apparel)

COMPETITORS

ABM Industries	Elior
Alsco	G&K Services
Autogrill	Healthcare Services
Centerplate	ISS A/S
Cintas	ServiceMaster
Compass Group	Sodexo
Delaware North	UniFirst

HISTORICAL FINANCIALS

Company Type: Private

Income Statement

FYE: Friday nearest September 30

	REVENUE ($ mil.)	NET INCOME ($ mil.)	NET PROFIT MARGIN	EMPLOYEES
9/07	12,384	31	0.2%	250,000
9/06	11,621	261	2.2%	240,000
9/05	10,963	289	2.6%	240,000
9/04	10,192	263	2.6%	242,500
9/03	9,448	301	3.2%	200,000
Annual Growth	7.0%	(43.4%)	—	5.7%

2007 Year-End Financials

Debt ratio: 415.2%
Return on equity: 2.1%
Cash ($ mil.): —
Current ratio: —
Long-term debt ($ mil.): 5,891

Net Income History

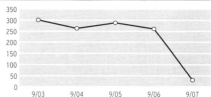

Archstone

Archstone (formerly Archstone-Smith) is the cornerstone of Tishman Speyer and Lehman Brothers' real estate partnership. Acquired by Tishman and Lehman for $22 billion in 2007, the firm is one of the largest apartment investment companies in the US, behind Equity Residential and AIMCO. It owns about 70,000 apartment units in areas such as Washington, DC (about 40% of its portfolio); Southern California; New York City; and Boston. Archstone operates under the Archstone brand name (garden-style units) and the Charles E. Smith name (high-rises). The company also offers extended-stay properties through Oakwood Worldwide. Lehman's filed for bankruptcy in 2008 and could sell some $32 billion in real estate assets.

Before the Chapter 11 bankruptcy, which was brought on by the subprime mortgage crisis, Lehman and Archstone already had begun selling off assets in the San Francisco area to raise cash.

In 2005 Archstone acquired a portfolio of 36 apartment communities from affiliates of furnished and corporate housing provider Oakwood for some $1.5 billion. It also bought three high-rise apartment buildings in Manhattan and began construction on a fourth. The company dipped its toe in European real estate, buying an 11-building portfolio in Germany in anticipation of the nation's economic recovery and privatization of multifamily housing.

Archstone continued its expansion in Manhattan in 2006 with the purchase of a 13-story apartment building for $110 million.

That year the REIT expanded its holdings in Germany with the acquisition of Deutsche WohnAnlage GmbH (deWAG) for $649 million.

Then-named Archstone Communities, the company acquired DC-based apartment property owner Charles E. Smith Residential in 2001.

EXECUTIVES

Chairman and CEO: R. Scot Sellers, age 51, $2,500,000 pay
COO: Charles E. (Chaz) Mueller Jr., age 44, $380,000 pay
President, U.S. Operations: Jack R. Callison, age 37
CFO: Gerald R. (Gerry) Morgan, age 44
General Counsel and Secretary: Caroline Brower, age 58, $335,000 pay
Chief Development Officer; President, Charles E. Smith Residential Division: Alfred G. (Al) Neely, age 60, $787,500 pay
SVP, East Region: Matthew T. Smith
Associate General Counsel: Thomas S. Reif
Auditors: KPMG LLP

LOCATIONS

HQ: Archstone
9200 E. Panorama Cir., Ste. 400,
Englewood, CO 80112
Phone: 303-708-5959   **Fax:** 303-708-5999
Web: www.archstoneapartments.com

2007 Markets

	% of total
Washington, DC	41
Southern California	22
San Francisco area	14
New York City area	9
Boston	7
Seattle	5
Other (Chicago, Southeast Florida, Houston, Denver)	2
Total	**100**

COMPETITORS

AIMCO
AMLI Residential
Associated Estates Realty
AvalonBay
BRE Properties
Colonial Properties
Equity Residential
Essex Property Trust
Gables Residential Trust
Intergroup
Lincoln Property
Post Properties
UDR

HISTORICAL FINANCIALS

Company Type: Private

Income Statement
FYE: December 31

	REVENUE ($ mil.)	NET INCOME ($ mil.)	NET PROFIT MARGIN	EMPLOYEES
12/06	1,134	727	64.2%	2,666
12/05	947	616	65.1%	2,703
12/04	873	542	62.1%	2,640
12/03	900	434	48.2%	2,730
12/02	1,082	315	29.1%	3,450
Annual Growth	1.2%	23.3%	—	(6.2%)

2006 Year-End Financials

Debt ratio: 117.0%
Return on equity: 13.9%
Cash ($ mil.): 368
Current ratio: —
Long-term debt ($ mil.): 6,452

Net Income History

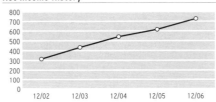

Arctic Slope Regional Corporation

The Inupiat people have survived the Arctic for centuries, and now they're surviving in the business world. The Inupiat-owned Arctic Slope Regional Corporation (ASRC) was set up to manage 5 million acres on Alaska's North Slope after the Alaska Native Claims Settlement Act in 1971 cleared the way for oil development in the area. ASRC gets more than two-thirds of sales from its energy services subsidiary (ASRC Energy Services) and its petroleum refining and marketing unit (Petro Star). Other operations include construction, engineering, and governmental services.

ASRC represents eight villages on the north slope of Alaska: Anaktuvuk Pass, Atqasuk, Barrow, Kaktovik, Nuiqsut, Point Hope, Point Lay, and Wainwright.

EXECUTIVES

Chairman: Rex A. Rock Sr.
Vice Chairman: Molly Pederson
President, CEO, and Director:
Roberta (Bobbi) Quintavell
SEVP and COO: Mark Kroloff
EVP and CFO: Kristin Mellinger
First VP and Director: George Sielak
Second VP and Director: George T. Kaleak
Third VP and Director: Raymond Paneak
VP and General Counsel: Alma McClellan Upicksoun
VP Administration and Shareholder Relations:
Flossie Chrestman
VP Government Affairs: Oliver Leavitt
VP Shareholder Development and Treasury Operations and Director: Crawford Patkotak
VP Human Resources: David White
VP Corporate Development: Craig Floerchinger
VP Communications and Public Relations:
Carol Richards
Secretary and Director: Patsy Aamodt
Auditors: KPMG LLP

LOCATIONS

HQ: Arctic Slope Regional Corporation
3900 C St., Ste. 801, Anchorage, AK 99503
Phone: 907-339-6000   **Fax:** 907-339-6028
Web: www.asrc.com

Arctic Slope Regional Corporation has US offices in Alaska, Arizona, California, Maryland, New Mexico, and Oregon. It also has operations in Mexico and Venezuela.

PRODUCTS/OPERATIONS

2007 Sales

	$ mil.	% of total
Petroleum refining & marketing	655.2	37
Energy & construction services	620.1	35
Technical contract services	462.7	26
Other	39.5	2
Total	**1,777.5**	**100**

Selected Subsidiaries

Energy services
Alaska Petroleum Contractors
ASRC Energy Services
ASRC Parsons Engineering, LLC.
Global Power and Communications
Houston Contracting Company-Alaska, Ltd.
Natchiq Sakhalin Ltd.
Omega Service Industries, Inc.
Tri Ocean Engineering, Ltd.

Engineering and construction
Arctic Slope Construction, Inc.
ASCG, Inc.
ASCG Inspection, Inc.
ASCG of New Mexico
McLaughlin Water Engineers, Ltd.
SKW/Eskimos, Inc.

Manufacturing
Puget Plastics Corporation
Puget Plastics S.A. de C.V. (Mexico)
Triquest Puget Plastics, LLC

Petroleum refining and marketing
Kodiak Oil Sales Inc. (North Pacific Fuel)
Petro Star, Inc.
Petro Star Valdez, Inc. (Valdez refinery)
Sourdough Fuel, Inc.
Valdez Petroleum Terminal (North Pacific Fuel)

Technical Services
Arctic Slope World Services, Incorporated
ASRC Aerospace Corp.
ASRC Communications, Ltd.

Other operations
Alaska Growth Capital Bidco Inc.
Barrow Cable Television
Eskimos, Inc.
Tundra Tours, Inc.

COMPETITORS

ACS Group	Schlumberger
Baker Hughes	Smith International
Halliburton	Tesoro
Nabors Industries	Tesoro Alaska
Noble	T-Mobile USA

HISTORICAL FINANCIALS

Company Type: Private

Income Statement   FYE: December 31

	REVENUE ($ mil.)	NET INCOME ($ mil.)	NET PROFIT MARGIN	EMPLOYEES
12/07	1,778	208	11.7%	6,000
12/06	1,701	206	12.1%	6,000
12/05	1,567	128	8.1%	6,000
12/04	1,201	(17)	—	6,500
12/03	1,029	5	0.5%	6,458
Annual Growth	14.6%	155.2%	—	(1.8%)

2007 Year-End Financials

Debt ratio: 7.6%
Return on equity: 36.3%
Cash ($ mil.): —

Current ratio: —
Long-term debt ($ mil.): 51

Net Income History

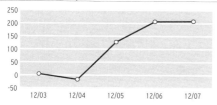

Ardent Health

Ardent Health Services is passionate about healing the body. The company operates ten acute care hospitals in the southern US, primarily located in New Mexico, where the company operates as the Lovelace Health System, and in Oklahoma, where Ardent Health Services does business as Hillcrest Healthcare System. The company's facilities also include physician group practices and medical laboratories. Lovelace Health also operates a health plan that serves some 190,000 members in New Mexico. Welsh, Carson, Anderson & Stowe owns a controlling stake in Ardent Health Services.

The company sold off its 20 behavioral health care facilities to Psychiatric Solutions in 2005 in order to focus on the dozen or so acute care hospitals it owned. The company had announced plans to grow by acquiring additional acute care hospitals, but it has since instead sold off several facility interests. Ardent sold its interest in Lexington, Kentucky's Samaritan Hospital to partner Associated Healthcare Systems later that same year.

Ardent sold its stake in Summit Hospital in Baton Rouge, Louisiana, to the Ochsner Clinic Foundation in 2007. Ardent has also consolidated inpatient care at its downtown Albuquerque location, leaving only outpatient services at its Gibson, New Mexico, hospital.

A deal with Oklahoma State University will transfer ownership of the Oklahoma State University Medical Center from Ardent to a public trust in 2009.

Ardent was founded in 1993 as Behavioral Healthcare Corporation (BHC), which had six behavioral treatment centers at the outset. Investment firm Welsh, Carson, Anderson & Stowe acquired majority ownership of BHC in 2001 and renamed the company.

EXECUTIVES

President and CEO: David T. Vandewater, age 54
CFO: Kerry Gillespie
SVP Financial Operations: Jim Schnuck
SVP, General Counsel, and Secretary:
 Steven C. Petrovich
SVP Human Resources and Administration:
 Neil Hemphill
VP and CIO: Mark Gillum
VP Communications: Kevin Gwin
Chief Accounting Officer: Clint B. Adams
President, Albuquerque Division: Ron Stern
President, Oklahoma Division: Earl Denning
Auditors: KPMG LLP

LOCATIONS

HQ: Ardent Health Services LLC
 1 Burton Hills Blvd., Ste. 250, Nashville, TN 37215
Phone: 615-296-3000   **Fax:** 615-296-6351
Web: www.ardenthealth.com

PRODUCTS/OPERATIONS

Selected Operations

Hillcrest HealthCare System (Oklahoma)
 Bailey Medical Center
 Cushing Regional Hospital
 Henryetta Medical Center
 Hillcrest Medical Center
 OSU Medical Center
Lovelace Sandia Health System (New Mexico)
 Lovelace Health Plan
 Lovelace Healthcare Center — Gibson
 Lovelace Medical Center
 Lovelace Rehabilitation Hospital
 Lovelace Westside Hospital
 Lovelace Women's Hospital

COMPETITORS

Catholic Health Initiatives
CIGNA
Community Health Systems
MedCath
Presbyterian Healthcare Services
Saint Francis Health System
St. John Health System

HISTORICAL FINANCIALS

Company Type: Private

Income Statement   FYE: December 31

	REVENUE ($ mil.)	NET INCOME ($ mil.)	NET PROFIT MARGIN	EMPLOYEES
12/07	1,650	—	—	8,500
12/06	1,670	—	—	9,942
12/05	1,731	—	—	8,800
12/04	1,607	—	—	15,900
12/03	1,320	—	—	10,100
Annual Growth	5.7%	—	—	(4.2%)

Revenue History

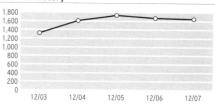

Arizona Chemical

Arizona Chemical is always pining for more business. The company is among the world's largest fractionators (separators) of crude tall oil (from the Swedish word *talloja*, or pine oil). Tall oil is a by-product of paper making. The company manufactures such pine tree-based chemicals as fatty acids, rosin esters, and terpenes. These chemicals are used to manufacture a wide variety of products, including adhesives, household cleaners, hydraulic fluids, inks, paints, personal care products, and plastics.

Arizona Chemical was formed in 1930 by paper products maker International Paper (IP) and American Cyanamid and now is owned by private equity group Rhone Capital after being sold in early 2007 by IP.

The company operates a number of manufacturing plants in the US and Europe; it also maintains R&D facilities in the US as well as in the Netherlands. Its sales offices and distribution centers are in Asia, Europe, Latin America, and the US.

In mid-2005 International Paper announced a corporate reorganization, which included putting Arizona Chemical on the block. That sale, to Rhone Capital for $485 million, was completed in late 2006.

EXECUTIVES

President and CEO: Gerald C. Marterer
VP and CFO: David Broadbent
VP Human Resources and Communications:
 David (Dave) Cowfer
VP and Managing Director Europe: Juhani Tuovinen
VP and General Counsel: Bo Segers
VP; General Manager, North America: Gary Reed
VP Tax and Treasury: Glenda Haynes
Auditors: Deloitte & Touche LLP

LOCATIONS

HQ: Arizona Chemical Company
 4600 Touchton Rd. East, Ste. 500,
 Jacksonville, FL 32246
Phone: 904-928-8700   **Fax:** 904-928-8779
Web: www.arizonachemical.com

Arizona Chemical's US plants are in Florida, Georgia, and Ohio. The company also has plants in Finland, France, Sweden, and the UK.

PRODUCTS/OPERATIONS

Selected Products and Brands

Adhesives
 Dispersions
 Hot melt polyamides
 Hydrocarbon-based adhesive resins
 Rosin tackifiers
 Terpene resin tackifiers

Inks and Coatings
 Additives
 Hydrocarbon-based ink resins
 Polyamides
 Resinates
 Rosin resins
Oleochemicals
 Dimer acids
 Ester products
 Hydrogenated castor oil derivatives (CENWAX)
 Oleo fatty acids
 Tall oil products
 Terpenes
Special Products
 Arizona polymer additives
 Digital ink resins (Unirez)
 Specialty gellants (Uniclear)

COMPETITORS

Akzo Nobel
Eastman Chemical
Georgia-Pacific Chemicals
Hercules
MeadWestvaco

HISTORICAL FINANCIALS

Company Type: Private

Income Statement				FYE: December 31
	REVENUE ($ mil.)	NET INCOME ($ mil.)	NET PROFIT MARGIN	EMPLOYEES
12/07	1,000	—	—	1,400
12/06	769	—	—	1,400
12/05	692	—	—	1,600
12/04	672	—	—	1,600
12/03	625	—	—	1,600
Annual Growth	12.5%	—	—	(3.3%)

Revenue History

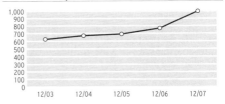

Army and Air Force Exchange

Be all that you can be and buy all that you can buy at the PX (Post Exchange). The Army and Air Force Exchange Service (AAFES) runs more than 3,000 facilities — including PXs and BXs (Base Exchanges) — at US Army and Air Force bases in more than 30 countries (including Iraq), 49 US states, and five US territories. Its outlets range from tents to shopping centers that have retail stores, fast-food outlets (brand names like Burger King and Taco Bell), movie theaters, beauty shops, and gas stations. AAFES serves active-duty military personnel, reservists, retirees, and their family members. Although it is a government agency under the DOD, it receives less than 5% of its funding from the department.

While the AAFES receives very little federal money, it pays neither taxes nor rent to occupy US government property. Its retail prices average about 20% less than the competition, and about two-thirds of AAFES's profits go into Morale, Welfare, and Recreation (MWR) programs for amenities such as libraries and youth centers. Other profits are used to renovate or build new stores. Active military personnel head AAFES, but its staff consists mostly of military family members and other civilians.

AAFES shops are facing increased competition from Wal-Mart Stores, which is luring soldiers off base with its low prices. To better compete with discounters, AAFES has begun adding dollar sections to about 150 of its stores worldwide.

AAFES is a multi-channel retailer offering catalog and online shopping as well as retail stores. The online store offers more than 30,000 items.

HISTORY

During the American Revolution, peddlers known as sutlers followed the Army, selling items such as soap, razors, and tobacco. The practice lasted until after the Civil War, when post traders replaced sutlers. This system was replaced in 1889 when the War Department authorized canteens at military bases.

The first US military exchanges were established in 1895, creating a system to supply military personnel with personal items on US Army bases around the world. The exchanges were run independently, with each division creating a Post Exchange (PX) to serve its unit. The post commander would assign an officer to run the PX (usually along with other duties) and would decide how profits were spent.

In 1941 the Army Exchange Service was created, and the system was reorganized. A five-member advisory committee made up of civilian merchandisers was created to provide recommendations for the reorganization. The restructuring made the system more like a chain store business. The independent PXs were bought by the War Department from the individual military organizations that ran them. Civilian personnel were brought in to staff the PXs, and a brigadier general was named to head an executive staff made up of Army officers and civilians that provided centralized control of the system. The Army also created a special school to train officers to run the PXs.

Sales at the PXs skyrocketed during WWII; a catalog business was added so soldiers could order gifts to send home to their families. The Department of the Air Force was established in 1947, and the exchange system organization was renamed the Army and Air Force Exchange Service (AAFES) the next year.

In 1960 the government allowed the overseas exchanges to provide more luxury items in an effort to keep soldiers from buying foreign-made goods. By the time the military had been cranked up again for the Vietnam War, big-ticket items such as TVs, cameras, and tape recorders were among the exchanges' best-sellers. In 1967 AAFES moved its headquarters from New York City to Dallas.

By 1991 the exchanges were open to the National Guard and the Reserve; AAFES's customer base had grown to 14 million. When the military began downsizing during the 1990s following the end of the Cold War, AAFES's customer base shrank by 35%.

AAFES stores sold more than $12 million in pornographic materials in 1995. The House of Representatives passed the Military Honor and Decency Act the next year prohibiting the sale of pornography on US military property, including AAFES stores; this ban was struck down as unconstitutional in 1997. That year AAFES was approved as a provider of medical equipment covered by federal CHAMPUS/TRICARE insurance. It also created a Web site to offer online shopping in 1997.

The Supreme Court upheld the 1996 porn ban in 1998; the Pentagon banned the sale of more than 150 sexually explicit magazines (such as Penthouse), while a military board permitted the continued sale of certain publications (including Playboy). Maj. Gen. Barry Bates took over as AAFES's Commander and CEO in 1998. To better battle other retailers, that year AAFES announced its stores would offer best-price guarantees, matching prices of local stores and refunding price differences if customers found lower prices within 30 days of buying products.

In 1999 AAFES expanded to Macedonia and Kosovo, providing its services to military personnel in Operation Joint Guardian. In 2000 Bates was replaced as AAFES commander and CEO by Maj. Gen. Charles J. Wax.

Maj. Gen. Kathryn Frost became commander and CEO when Wax stepped down in August 2005.

Brigadier General Keith L. Thurgood assumed duties as AAFES Commander on August 2007.

EXECUTIVES

Chairman: Richard Y. Newton III
Commander: Keith L. Thurgood
Deputy Commander and Director, Equal Opportunity: Francis L. (Fran) Hendricks
Chief Staff: Thomas M. Baker
COO: Michael P. (Mike) Howard
CFO: Harold Lavender
CTO: Dale Linebarger
General Counsel: Eric Weiss
SVP Human Resources: James Moore
SVP Sales: Maggie Burgess
SVP Marketing: Mat Dromey
SVP Real Estate: Dan Metsala
VP Business Transformation: Robin Price
VP Corporate Compliance: Shelton Irick
VP Main Stores and Softlines Division: Alicia Scott
VP Main Stores and Hardlines Division: Ana Middleton
VP Real Estate: Mike Gividen
VP Sales: Ed Bouley
Corporate Communications Chief: William D. Thurmond
Executive Secretary: Gregg Cox
Commander's Assistant and Senior Enlisted Advisor: Bryan Eaton
Auditors: Ernst & Young LLP

LOCATIONS

HQ: Army and Air Force Exchange Service
 3911 S. Walton Walker Blvd., Dallas, TX 75236
Phone: 214-312-2011   **Fax:** 214-312-3000
Web: www.aafes.com

PRODUCTS/OPERATIONS

Selected Merchandise and Services

Barber and beauty shops
Books, newspapers, and magazines
Catalog services
Class Six stores
Concessions
Food facilities (mobile units, snack bars, name-brand fast-food franchises, and concession operations)
Gas stations and auto repair
Military clothing stores
Movie theaters
Retail stores
Vending centers

COMPETITORS

7-Eleven	Kroger
Amazon.com	METRO AG
Best Buy	Sears
Costco Wholesale	Supercuts
J. C. Penney	Target
Kmart	Wal-Mart

HISTORICAL FINANCIALS

Company Type: Government agency

Income Statement			FYE: Saturday nearest January 31	
	REVENUE ($ mil.)	NET INCOME ($ mil.)	NET PROFIT MARGIN	EMPLOYEES
1/08	8,705	442	5.1%	43,658
1/07	8,921	428	4.8%	45,000
1/06	8,667	378	4.4%	45,000
1/05	8,352	474	5.7%	48,000
1/04	7,905	485	6.1%	47,323
Annual Growth	2.4%	(2.3%)	—	(2.0%)

2008 Year-End Financials

Debt ratio: —
Return on equity: —
Cash ($ mil.): —
Current ratio: —
Long-term debt ($ mil.): 0

Net Income History

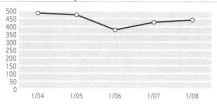

Ascension Health

Ascension Health has ascended to the pinnacle of not-for-profit health care. As the largest Catholic hospital system in the US, and thus one of the top providers of charity care in the nation, the organization's health care network consists of more than 60 general hospitals along with a dozen long-term care acute care, rehabilitation, and psychiatric hospitals. Ascension Health also operates nursing homes, community clinics, and other health care providers. Its network of medical facilities spans 19 states and the District of Columbia. The organization's facilities have more than 16,700 licensed beds.

Consistent with its not-for-profit status, Ascension Health provides millions of dollars in "community benefit," a vaguely defined term that includes charity care to the indigent and uninsured, costs not covered by Medicaid, and other community health programs. Ascension Health recorded more than $800 million in community benefit costs in 2007.

Ascension Health is engaged in system-wide efforts to improve patient safety at its facilities, vowing to reduce preventable deaths from hospital-acquired infections, surgical and drug complications, birth trauma injuries, and other avoidable circumstances. The organization also advocates for expanded access to health care and has set a goal of guaranteed access to care in all its markets by the year 2020. It is working in partnership with local governments and private

groups (persuading doctors to add some uninsured patients to their rolls, for instance) to achieve that goal.

But alongside its role as a mission-driven organization, Ascension Health is also a large business, and it has used its business savvy to make it one of the nation's largest and most successful health care organizations.

It has consistently pruned money-losing operations, including the divestiture in 2006 of St. Joseph Hospital of Augusta, Georgia, to Triad (now part of Community Health Systems).

And it has been snapping up hospitals and health systems to expand its geographic footprint and market share. It bought Eastern Health System, a three-hospital group in Birmingham, in 2007 and merged it with its existing St. Vincent's Health System. The same year it became co-owner of Via Christi Health System in Wichita, Kansas, and it has also agreed to an affiliation of its Columbia St. Mary's system in Milwaukee with Froedtert & Community Health. A plan to enter the Boston market by acquiring Caritas Christi fell through in 2007.

Additionally, Ascension Health in 2007 joined with two other Catholic hospital companies, Catholic Health Initiatives and Catholic Health East, to form a venture capital fund that invests in health care start-ups. It was the second such venture for Ascension Health, which set up a wholly owned fund in 2001. The funds invest in emerging technologies that have the potential to improve health care delivery, but that will also reap financial rewards for Ascension Health and its partners.

HISTORY

The Daughters of Charity order was formed in France in 1633 when St. Vincent de Paul recruited a rich widow (St. Louise de Marillac) to care for the sick on battlefields and in their homes.

Elizabeth Ann Seton, America's first saint (canonized 1974), brought the order to the US. In 1809 Seton earned the title of Mother and started the Sisters of Charity. The Sisters adopted the vows of the Daughters of Charity, adding "service" to them in 1812.

The Sisters officially became part of the Daughters of Charity in 1850. The Daughters cared for soldiers during the Civil War and were responsible for training Florence Nightingale. In the late 1800s the Daughters pioneered exclusive provider arrangements (similar to today's managed care contracts) with railroads, lumber camps, and the like. During the next 100 years, the order furthered its mission of caring for the sick and the poor. To support their efforts, the nuns founded hospitals (44 by 1911), schools, and other charity centers.

In 1969 the charity association formed a health care services cooperative, which became the Daughters of Charity National Health System (DCNHS).

DCNHS operated as two regional institutions (one based in Maryland, the other in Missouri) until 1986, when the systems merged. The first task was to balance their holy mission with the need to make money. With competition from managed care companies increasing, DCNHS responded by cutting staff and diversifying into nursing homes and retirement centers.

The Daughters of Charity's western unit combined its six hospitals in California with Mullikin Centers (a physician-owned medical group) in 1993 to form one of the largest health care associations in the state.

DCNHS expanded its network in 1995 by merging its hospitals with and becoming a co-sponsor of San Francisco-based Catholic Healthcare West. That year it joined with Catholic Relief Services to operate a hospital in war-torn Angola.

In 1996 DCNHS dropped a proposed merger of its struggling 221-bed Carney Hospital in Boston with Quincy Hospital because the municipally owned Quincy facility was required by law to provide abortions. Instead, DCNHS sold Carney Hospital to Caritas Christi Health Care System (owned by the Boston Roman Catholic archdiocese), one of about a dozen hospital sales by DCNHS in the mid-1990s.

DCNHS reorganized its leadership in 1997, creating SVP positions for system direction and policy and for program development to strengthen and update its programs. In 1998 Sister Irene Kraus, who had founded DCNHS and led it through its expansion, died.

In 1999 DCNHS merged with fellow Catholic caregiver Sisters of St. Joseph Health System, then Michigan's largest health care system, to form Ascension Health.

In 2000 Ascension saw the collapse of a five-hospital merger in Florida between subsidiary St. Vincent's Health System and Baptist Health System. The organization also launched the Voice for the Voiceless initiative, which combines private monies and federal grants to fund programs for the uninsured in Detroit, New Orleans, and Austin, Texas.

In response to rising health care costs, Ascension merged with national Catholic health care provider Carondelet Health System in 2003.

EXECUTIVES

Chairman: John O. (Jack) Mudd
President and CEO: Anthony R. (Tony) Tersigni, age 57
President, Non-Acute Care Operations: Laura S. Kaiser
COO: Robert J. (Bob) Henkel, age 54
SVP and CFO: Anthony J. (Tony) Speranzo
SVP and CIO: Sherry L. Browne
SVP and Chief Risk Officer: James K. Beckmann Jr.
SVP Legal Services and General Counsel: Joseph R. Impicciche
SVP and Chief Supply Chain Officer: Michael T. (Mike) Langlois
SVP Mission Integration: Sister Maureen McGuire
SVP, Governance and Sponsor Relations: Rex P. Killian
SVP Leadership Development & Succession Planning: Andrew W. Allen
SVP, Corporate Responsibility: John Nusbaum
VP Communications: Steve LeResche
VP Research and Development: Hyung Tai Kim
Chief Medical Officer: David B. Pryor
Chief Strategy Officer: John D. Doyle
Auditors: Ernst & Young LLP

LOCATIONS

HQ: Ascension Health
4600 Edmundson Rd., St. Louis, MO 63134
Phone: 314-733-8000 **Fax:** 314-733-8013
Web: www.ascensionhealth.org

Selected Hospitals

Alabama
Providence Hospital (Mobile)
St. Vincent's Hospital (Birmingham)
Arizona
Carondelet Holy Cross Hospital
Carondelet St. Joseph's Hospital (Tucson)
Carondelet St. Mary's Hospital (Tucson)
Arkansas
DePaul Health Center (Dumas)
St. Elizabeth Health Center (Gould)
Connecticut
Hall-Brooke Behavioral Health Services (Westport)
St. Vincent's Medical Center (Bridgeport)

District of Columbia
    Providence Hospital
Florida
    Sacred Heart Children's Hospital (Pensacola)
    Sacred Heart Hospital of the Emerald Coast (West
        Destin)
    Sacred Heart Hospital of Pensacola (Pensacola)
    Sacred Heart Women's Hospital (Pensacola)
    St. Vincent's Medical Center (Jacksonville)
Georgia
    Walton Rehabilitation Hospital (Augusta)
Idaho
    St. Joseph Regional Medical Center (Lewiston)
Illinois
    Saint Anthony Hospital (Chicago)
Indiana
    Saint John's Health System (Anderson)
    St. Elizabeth Ann Seton Hospital (Boonville)
    St. Joseph Hospital (Kokomo)
    St. Mary's Warrick Hospital (Boonville)
    St. Vincent Carmel Hospital
    St. Vincent Clay Hospital (Brazil)
    St. Vincent Frankfort Hospital
    St. Vincent Jennings Hospital (North Vernon)
    St. Vincent Indianapolis Hospital
    St. Vincent Mercy Hospital (Elwood)
    St. Vincent Randolph Hospital (Winchester)
    St. Vincent Williamsport Hospital
Louisiana
    The Daughters of Charity Health Center (New Orleans)
Maryland
    Sacred Heart Hospital (Cumberland)
    St. Agnes HealthCare (Baltimore)
Michigan
    Borgess-Lee Memorial Hospital (Dowagiac)
    Borgess Medical Center (Kalamazoo)
    Borgess-Pipp Health Center (Plainwell)
    Brighton Hospital
    CareLink of Jackson
    Genesys Regional Medical Center (Grand Blanc)
    Providence Hospital (Southfield)
    St. John Hospital and Medical Center (Detroit)
    St. John Macomb Hospital (Warren)
    St. John North Shores Hospital (Harrison Township)
    St. John Oakland Hospital (Madison Heights)
    St. Mary's of Michigan Medical Center (Saginaw)
    St. Mary's of Michigan — Standish Hospital
    St. Joseph Health System (Augres)
Missouri
    St. Joseph Medical Center (Kansas City)
    St. Mary's Medical Center (Blue Springs)
New York
    Mount St. Mary's Hospital and Health Center
        (Lewiston)
    Our Lady of Lourdes Memorial Hospital (Binghamton)
    St. Mary's Hospital (Amsterdam)
    St. Mary's Hospital (Troy)
Pennsylvania
    Good Samaritan Regional Medical Center (Pottsville)
Tennessee
    Baptist Hickman Community Hospital (Centerville)
    Baptist Hospital (Nashville)
    Middle Tennessee Medical Center (Murfreesboro)
    Saint Thomas Health Services System (Nashville)
Texas
    Brackenridge Hospital (Austin)
    Dell Children's Medical Center of Central Texas
        (Austin)
    Providence Health Center (Waco)
    Seton Edgar B. Davis (Luling)
    Seton Highland Lakes (Burnet)
    Seton Medical Center (Austin)
    Seton Northwest Hospital (Austin)
    Seton Southwest Hospital (Austin)
Washington
    Lourdes Medical Center (Pasco)
Wisconsin
    Columbia St. Mary's (Milwaukee)
    Columbia St. Mary's Ozaukee Campus (Mequon)
    Orthopaedic Hospital of Wisconsin (Glendale)
    Sacred Heart Rehabilitation Institute (Milwaukee)

COMPETITORS

Catholic Health East
Catholic Health Initiatives
Catholic Healthcare Partners
Catholic Healthcare West
Community Health Systems
Detroit Medical Center
Golden Horizons
HCA
Health Management Associates
HealthSouth
Henry Ford Health System
Kindred Healthcare
Life Care Centers
MedStar Health
Tenet Healthcare
Trinity Health (Novi)
Universal Health Services
University of Maryland Medical System

HISTORICAL FINANCIALS
Company Type: Not-for-profit

Income Statement				FYE: June 30
	REVENUE ($ mil.)	NET INCOME ($ mil.)	NET PROFIT MARGIN	EMPLOYEES
6/08	13,489	—	—	107,000
6/07	12,322	—	—	106,000
6/06	11,263	—	—	106,000
6/05	10,861	—	—	107,000
6/04	10,046	—	—	106,000
Annual Growth	7.6%	—	—	0.2%

Revenue History

14,000
12,000
10,000
8,000
6,000
4,000
2,000
0
        6/04   6/05   6/06   6/07   6/08

Ashley Furniture

Not to be confused with Laura Ashley, this Ashley is more interested in peddling leather, hardwood, and bedding than toile and chenille. Ashley Furniture Industries, one of the nation's largest furniture manufacturers, makes and imports upholstered furniture, as well as leather and hardwood pieces. It has manufacturing plants and distribution centers throughout the country and overseas. Ashley licenses its name to more than 300 Ashley Furniture HomeStores located in the US, as well as Canada, Mexico, Central America, and Japan. These stores are independently owned and sell only Ashley Furniture-branded products. Founded by Carlyle Weinberger in 1945, Ashley Furniture is owned by father-and-son duos Ron and Todd Wanek and Chuck and Ben Vogel.

The company has three operating divisions: Ashley Casegoods, Ashley Upholstery, and Millennium. About 45% of the company's furniture is manufactured in Asia. Overall, Ashley maintains 3 million sq. ft. of manufacturing facilities spanning six locations.

Under a trademark usage agreement with sofabed retailer Jennifer Convertibles, three Ashley Furniture HomeStores are scheduled to open in New York. The first store opened in 2007, with a second in 2008.

The company cut about 200 jobs from its Mississippi production plants in 2008, saying it made the reduction to stay competitive. The housing slowdown coupled with reduced consumer spending have created less demand for furniture.

In 2005 the owners — Vogels and Waneks — settled a long-running lawsuit out of court. In November 2002 the Vogels (who own 25% of Ashley Furniture) filed a lawsuit against the Waneks (who own 75%), alleging that the Waneks were trying to squeeze the Vogel father and son out of the business by offering to buy out their share of the business at a "grossly depressed and unfair price." (Based on 2001 sales of $1.09 billion, the Vogels said their share in Ashley was worth more than $200 million. Ashley later logged sales of $2.04 billion in 2004.)

EXECUTIVES

Chairman: Ronald G. (Ron) Wanek
President and CEO: Todd Wanek
President, Casegoods Division: Rob Hoffman
CFO: Dale Barneson
CIO: Dwain Jansson
Director of Corporate Marketing: Stacy Roshto
Credit Manager: Jim Evanson
Human Resources Manager: Jim Dotta

LOCATIONS

HQ: Ashley Furniture Industries, Inc.
    1 Ashley Way, Arcadia, WI 54612
Phone: 608-323-3377   **Fax:** 608-323-6008
Web: www.ashleyfurniture.com

COMPETITORS

Bassett Furniture
Berkline/BenchCraft
Bombay Brands
Brown Jordan
    International
Ethan Allen
Euromarket Designs
Furniture Brands
    International
Havertys

Home Meridian
Hooker Furniture
IKEA
Kimball International
Klaussner Furniture
La-Z-Boy
Natuzzi
Rowe Fine Furniture
Williams-Sonoma

HISTORICAL FINANCIALS
Company Type: Private

Income Statement				FYE: December 31
	ESTIMATED REVENUE ($ mil.)	NET INCOME ($ mil.)	NET PROFIT MARGIN	EMPLOYEES
12/07	3,430	—	—	17,000
12/06	3,120	—	—	14,600
12/05	2,550	—	—	13,400
12/04	2,000	—	—	11,000
12/03	1,700	—	—	9,300
Annual Growth	19.2%	—	—	16.3%

Revenue History

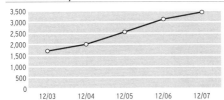

3,500
3,000
2,500
2,000
1,500
1,000
500
0
        12/03   12/04   12/05   12/06   12/07

ASI Computer Technologies

ASI Computer Technologies is a wholesale distributor of computer software, hardware, and accessories. It offers more than 8,000 products, including PCs, modems, monitors, networking equipment, and storage devices. ASI sells to more than 20,000 resellers throughout North America. The company's vendor partners include such companies as AMD, Intel, Microsoft, Samsung, and Western Digital. Its services include custom systems integration and contract assembly. The company also markets a line of computer devices and configures custom computer systems under its own Nspire brand.

ASI Computer Technologies' customers include resellers, retailers, systems integrators, and OEMs. It has operations in the Americas and Asia.

EXECUTIVES

Chairman and CEO: Marcel Liang
President: Christine Liang
VP Marketing: Kent Tibbils
VP Business Development: Henry Chen
VP Storage Development: Bill Orlowski
VP NA Sales: Rhea Moore
Director Product Management: Cathy Wang
Director Operations: Mike Jackson
Director Technical Services: Vince Tartalia

LOCATIONS

HQ: ASI Computer Technologies, Inc.
48289 Fremont Blvd., Fremont, CA 94538
Phone: 510-226-8000   **Fax:** 510-226-8858
Web: www.asipartner.com

PRODUCTS/OPERATIONS

Selected Products

Accessories
Cables
Cameras
Cases
CD-ROM drives
Central processing units
Controller cards
DVD drives
Fans
Floppy drives
Hard drives
Keyboards
Memory
Mice
Modems
Monitors
Motherboards
MP3 players
Multimedia products
Network connectivity products
Notebooks
Optical drives
PCs
Power supplies
Printers
Projectors
Removable drives and media
Scanners
Software
Sound cards
Speakers
Storage devices
Tape back-up products
Video cards
Zip drives

COMPETITORS

Agilysys
Arrow Electronics
Avnet
Bell Microproducts
CompuCom
D&H Distributing
Dell
En Pointe
Flextronics
Hewlett-Packard
IBM
Ingram Micro
Merisel
MicroAge
MTM Technologies
New Age Electronics
SED International
Softmart
Software House
Supercom
SYNNEX
Tech Data

HISTORICAL FINANCIALS

Company Type: Private

Income Statement				FYE: December 31
	REVENUE ($ mil.)	NET INCOME ($ mil.)	NET PROFIT MARGIN	EMPLOYEES
12/07	1,300	—	—	800
12/06	1,110	—	—	850
12/05	1,110	—	—	600
12/04	1,060	—	—	500
12/03	1,200	—	—	550
Annual Growth	2.0%	—	—	9.8%

Revenue History

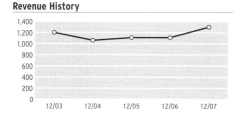

Asplundh Tree Expert

How much wood would a woodchuck chuck, if a woodchuck could chuck wood? A lot, if the woodchuck were named Asplundh. Asplundh is one of the world's leading tree-trimming businesses, clearing tree limbs from power lines for utilities and municipalities throughout the US and in Canada, Australia, and New Zealand.

Asplundh also offers utility-related services such as line construction, meter reading, and pole maintenance; in addition, the company has branched out into fields such as billboard maintenance, traffic signal and highway lighting construction, and vegetation control for railroads and pipelines. The Asplundh family owns and manages the company, which was founded in 1928.

In 2008 Asplundh sold its Central Locating Service unit, which finds and marks underground utility lines, to a group led by investment firm Kohlberg & Company. Kohlberg at the same time acquired a Central Locating Service rival, SM&P Utility Resources, and the utility locating companies have been combined as components of a new company, United States Infrastructure, in which Asplundh holds a minority stake.

EXECUTIVES

Chairman and CEO: Christopher B. Asplundh
President: Scott M. Asplundh
Treasurer and Secretary: Joseph P. Dwyer
Manager Field Personnel: Ryan Swier
Manager Corporate Communications: Patti Chipman

LOCATIONS

HQ: Asplundh Tree Expert Co.
708 Blair Mill Rd., Willow Grove, PA 19090
Phone: 215-784-4200   **Fax:** 215-784-4493
Web: www.asplundh.com

COMPETITORS

Arbor Tree Surgery
Davey Tree
Quanta Services

HISTORICAL FINANCIALS

Company Type: Private

Income Statement				FYE: December 31
	REVENUE ($ mil.)	NET INCOME ($ mil.)	NET PROFIT MARGIN	EMPLOYEES
12/07	2,370	—	—	28,606
12/06	2,400	—	—	28,831
12/05	2,366	—	—	24,000
12/04	2,080	—	—	28,638
12/03	1,800	—	—	28,948
Annual Growth	7.1%	—	—	(0.3%)

Revenue History

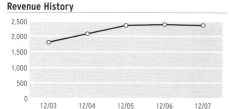

Associated Electric Cooperative

Associated Electric Cooperative makes the connection between power and cooperatives. The utility provides transmission and generation services to its six member/owner companies, which in turn provide power supply services to 51 distribution cooperatives in three Midwest states. (The distribution cooperatives have a combined customer count of more than 850,000.) Associated Electric operates 9,217 miles of power transmission lines and has more than 5,500 MW of generating capacity from interests in primarily coal- and gas-fired power plants and from wholesale energy transactions with other regional utilities.

Founded in 1961, Associated Electric supplies wholesale power to 39 distribution cooperatives in Missouri, three in southeast Iowa, and nine in northeast Oklahoma.

EXECUTIVES

President, Board of Directors: O. B. Clark
VP, Board of Directors: Emery O. Geisendorfer Jr.
CEO and General Manager: James J. Jura
CFO: David W. McNabb
Special Assistant to the CEO and General Manager: Michael M. (Mike) Miller
Special Assistant to the CEO and General Manager: Keith E. Hartner
General Counsel: Patrick A. Baumhoer
Secretary: R. Layne Morrill
Treasurer: Charles C. Baile
CIO: Ronald H. Murphy
Director Human Resources: David P. Stump
Director Power Production: Duane D. Highley
Director Engineering and Operations: Roger S. Clark
Director Member Services and Corporate Communications: Joseph E. Wilkinson
Auditors: KPMG LLP

LOCATIONS

HQ: Associated Electric Cooperative Inc.
2814 S. Golden, Springfield, MO 65801
Phone: 417-881-1204   **Fax:** 417-885-9252
Web: www.aeci.org

PRODUCTS/OPERATIONS

Member Transmission and Distribution Cooperatives

Central Electric Power Cooperative
KAMO Power
M&A Electric Power Cooperative
Northeast Missouri Electric Power Cooperative
NW Electric Power Cooperative Inc.
Sho-Me Power Electric Cooperative

COMPETITORS

Ameren
Empire District Electric
Great Plains Energy
Westar Energy

HISTORICAL FINANCIALS

Company Type: Cooperative

Income Statement				FYE: December 31
	REVENUE ($ mil.)	NET INCOME ($ mil.)	NET PROFIT MARGIN	EMPLOYEES
12/07	909	21	2.3%	645
12/06	865	16	1.8%	640
12/05	873	11	1.2%	640
12/04	798	18	2.2%	620
12/03	756	11	1.4%	591
Annual Growth	4.7%	17.9%	—	2.2%

2007 Year-End Financials

Debt ratio: 385.6%   Current ratio: —
Return on equity: 6.8%   Long-term debt ($ mil.): 1,170
Cash ($ mil.): —

Net Income History

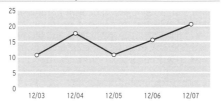

Associated Materials

Vinyl has never gone out of style at Associated Materials Incorporated (AMI). AMI makes and distributes vinyl siding and windows, as well as aluminum and steel siding, aluminum trim coil, and accessories. Products are sold primarily in the US and Canada, and bear such brand names as Alside, Gentek, and Revere. The home repair and remodeling markets make up about 65% of sales; the rest is new construction sales. AMI's approximately 125 supply centers generate 70% of sales, primarily to contractors. AMI also distributes building products made by other OEMs, and makes UltraGuard-branded vinyl fencing and railing. AMI is indirectly owned by AMH Holdings, which is controlled by Investcorp and Harvest Partners.

The company increased its market presence and its product line with the 2003 purchase of Gentek Holdings and its Gentek Building Products subsidiaries for about $118 million. AMI took over the vinyl, aluminum, and steel siding and vinyl windows business that Gentek ran through distribution centers in the Mid-Atlantic region of the US and in Canada.

Raw materials that are used in AMI's products — vinyl resin, aluminum, steel, glass, window hardware, and packaging materials — are purchased through contracts with resin suppliers.

Vinyl siding makers such as AMI compete for exterior wall cladding business with fiber cement, stone veneer, stucco, brick, and other masonry manufacturers. Particularly in the Southwest US, the economic climate of the vinyl siding industry has declined, causing companies such as AMI and rivals Ply Gem Industries and CertainTeed to close manufacturing plants. AMI plans to relocate some of its extrusion lines to facilities in the Northeast and Midwest, where demand for vinyl siding is greater.

EXECUTIVES

Chairman: Ira D. Kleinman, age 51
President and CEO: Thomas N. (Tom) Chieffe, age 50
SVP Operations: Warren J. Arthur, age 40
VP Sales: David L. King
VP Human Resources: John F. Haumesser, age 43, $216,252 pay
VP, CFO, Treasurer, and Secretary: Cynthia L. (Cyndi) Sobe, age 40
President, Alside Supply Centers: Robert M. Franco, age 54, $292,500 pay
Auditors: Ernst & Young LLP

LOCATIONS

HQ: Associated Materials Incorporated
3773 State Rd., Cuyahoga Falls, OH 44223
Phone: 330-929-1811   **Fax:** 330-922-2354
Web: www.associatedmaterials.com

Associated Materials has plants in Arizona, Iowa, New Jersey, North Carolina, Ohio, Texas, and Washington in the US, as well as in Ontario and Quebec, Canada.

PRODUCTS/OPERATIONS

2007 Sales

	$ mil.	% of total
Vinyl windows	418.1	35
Vinyl siding	285.8	24
Metal products	220.2	18
Third-party manufactured products	203.7	17
Other	76.3	6
Total	**1,204.1**	**100**

COMPETITORS

Alcoa Home Exteriors
Andersen Corporation
CertainTeed
James Hardie Industries
JELD-WEN
Louisiana-Pacific
Owens Corning Sales
Ply Gem
Royal Group
Silver Line Building Products
Timber Truss Housing Systems

HISTORICAL FINANCIALS

Company Type: Private

Income Statement				FYE: Saturday nearest December 31
	REVENUE ($ mil.)	NET INCOME ($ mil.)	NET PROFIT MARGIN	EMPLOYEES
12/07	1,204	40	3.3%	3,625
12/06	1,250	33	2.7%	5,009
12/05	1,174	22	1.9%	3,872
12/04	1,094	(11)	—	3,137
12/03	780	25	3.1%	3,173
Annual Growth	11.5%	12.8%	—	3.4%

2007 Year-End Financials

Debt ratio: 73.4%   Current ratio: —
Return on equity: 13.8%   Long-term debt ($ mil.): 226
Cash ($ mil.): —

Net Income History

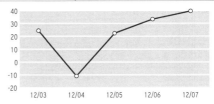

Associated Milk Producers

Associated Milk Producers Inc. (AMPI) might wear a cheesy grin, but it churns up solid sales. The dairy cooperative transforms more than 5 billion pounds of milk into butter, cheese, and fluid milk and other dairy products each and every year. A regional co-op with some 4,000 member/farmers from Iowa, Minnesota, Missouri, Nebraska, North and South Dakota, and Wisconsin, AMPI operates 12 manufacturing plants. Aside from its own AMPI and State brands, Associated Milk Producers makes private-label products for food retailers and foodservice companies. It also makes dairy ingredients for food manufacturers.

AMPI has upgraded its upper-Midwestern processing plants to produce additional value-added dairy products such as shredded cheese, aseptic-packaged cheese sauces (in coated cardboard containers for stable shelf life), and individually wrapped butter pats.

AMPI's 93,000-sq.-ft. plant in New Ulm, Minnesota, is the biggest butter barn in the US and was originally able to whip up nearly 20,000 pounds of butter per hour. However, a fire at the plant in 2004 melted nearly 3 million pounds of butter and left the facility badly damaged. AMPI has since rebuilt the plant. It reopened in 2005.

In 2007 AMPI acquired cheese and milk producing co-op, Cass-Clay Creamery, located in North Dakota. Consisting of farmers in Wisconsin, Minnesota, Iowa, Nebraska, Missouri, South Dakota, North Dakota and Montana, the acquisition added some 200 members to AMPI.

EXECUTIVES

Chairman: Paul Toft
Vice Chairman: Roger Lyon
President and CEO: Mark Furth
Director Human Resources: Jeff Davies
Director Communications and Government Relations:
 Sheryl Doering Meshke
Director Fluid Marketing: Neil Gulden
Director Marketing: Jim Walsh
Director Quality Assurance: Tom Honce
Treasurer and Director: Dale Hoffman
Secretary and Director: Phil Johnson
Assistant General Manager: Donn DeVelder

LOCATIONS

HQ: Associated Milk Producers Inc.
 315 N. Broadway, New Ulm, MN 56073
Phone: 507-354-8295   **Fax:** 507-359-8651
Web: www.ampi.com

PRODUCTS/OPERATIONS

Selected Products

Butter
Cheese
Cheese sauce
Dry milk
Fluid milk
Instant milk
Pudding

COMPETITORS

Bel Brands USA
BelGioioso Cheese
California Dairies Inc.
Dairy Farmers of America
Dairylea
Dean Foods
Foremost Farms
Great Lakes Cheese
Kraft Foods
Land O'Lakes
Leprino Foods
Marathon Cheese
MMPA
Prairie Farms Dairy
Saputo
Saputo Cheese USA Inc.
Sargento
Schreiber Foods

Associated Press

This just in: The Associated Press (AP) is reporting tonight and every night wherever news is breaking. AP is one of the world's largest newsgathering organizations, with about 240 news bureaus in nearly 100 countries. It provides news, photos, graphics, and audiovisual services that reach people daily through print, radio, television, and the Web. In addition to traditional news services, it operates international television news service APTN (AP Television News), photo archives, and an interactive news service (AP Digital). It also offers advertising management and distribution services. The not-for-profit cooperative is owned by 1,500 US daily newspaper members.

The company serves 1,700 newspapers and 5,000 radio and television outlets in the US, as well as newspaper, radio, and television subscribers internationally. In recent years AP has shifted its focus from providing content to newspapers; some of the company's biggest customers now include new media outlets, including cable broadcasters and Web portals such as Yahoo! and Google. AP's Online Video Network (OVN) service provides news video to AP member and customer Web sites.

With print publishing struggling against declining readership and the rise in popularity of digital media, AP consolidated its print, broadcast, and digital sales and marketing units in 2008. The restructuring was part of an effort to streamline the distribution of news that it hopes will lead to greater efficiencies. Also in response to new media formats, AP joined with Nintendo in 2007 to launch a news channel for the game maker's Wii console.

A group of New York newspapers founded the AP in 1846 in order to chronicle the US-Mexican War more efficiently.

HISTORY

The Associated Press traces its roots to 1846, when *New York Sun* publisher Moses Yale Beach agreed to share news arriving by telegraph about the Mexican-American War with four other New York newspapers. The cooperative news gathering effort was later established as the AP, which began selling wire reports to other papers and started creating regional associations. Adapting to changing technologies and public interests, AP began covering sports, financial, and public interest stories in the 1920s and was selling news reports to radio stations in the 1940s. Advancements during WWII included using transatlantic cable and radio-teletype circuits to deliver news and photos.

In the late 1960s AP and Dow Jones introduced services to improve business and financial reporting. AP improved photo delivery, reception, and storage in the 1970s with the advent of Laserphoto and the Electronic Darkroom. It began transmitting news by satellite and offering color photographs to newspapers in the 1980s. In 1985 Louis Boccardi took over the job as president and CEO of AP.

AP adjusted to the media-heavy culture of the 1990s by launching the APTV international news video service and the All News Radio network in 1994. It then moved onto the Internet with The WIRE in 1996 and began offering online access to its Photo Archive in 1997. It bought Worldwide Television News in 1998, combining it with APTV to form AP Television News Limited (APTN). The following year it purchased the radio news contracts of UPI after the rival organization announced it was getting out of broadcast news.

In 2000 AP created an Internet division, AP Digital, to focus on marketing news to online providers. The cooperative continued its Internet focus the following year, launching AP Online en Español (news for Spanish-language Web sites) and AP Entertainment Online (multimedia entertainment news for Web sites). Also that year AP bought the Newspaper Industry Communication Center from the Newspaper Association of America.

In 2002 the company launched an expanded editorial partnership with Dow Jones Newswires, increasing the amount of financial news distributed on AP wires. Later that year it acquired Capitolwire, a provider of state government news. Boccardi stepped down as CEO in 2003,
handing the reigns to former *USA TODAY* publisher Tom Curley.

In 2004 AP relocated from Rockefeller Plaza (its home for the last 65 years) to a new headquarters on the west side of Manhattan that features a 105,000-sq.-ft. newsroom and serves as a central hub of digital news streams.

The company moved to strengthen its sports information coverage in 2005, merging its AP MegaSports operation with News Corporation's STATS, Inc., to form STATS, LLC, a 50-50 joint venture that provides sports-related information, content, and statistical analysis.

EXECUTIVES

Chairman: William D. (Dean) Singleton, age 57
President and CEO: Thomas (Tom) Curley, age 59
SVP and CFO: Kenneth J. (Ken) Dale, age 51
SVP and Director Newspapers and New Media Markets:
 Thomas R. (Tom) Brettingen
SVP and Executive Editor: Kathleen Carroll
SVP Global Technology and VP Product Development:
 Lorraine Cichowski
SVP Global Product Development: Jane Seagrave
SVP International Business: James M. (Jim) Donna,
 age 61
SVP Americas Media Markets and Global New Media:
 Sue Cross
VP; Managing Director, International Television:
 J. Eric Braun, age 58
VP and Director Corporate Communications: Ellen Hale
VP and Director Broadcast Division:
 James R. Williams III
VP and Director Strategic Planning: James M. Kennedy
VP and General Counsel: Srinandan (Sri) Kasi, age 42
VP Business Operations, US Newspaper Markets:
 John O. Lumpkin
VP Human Resources: Jessica Bruce, age 42
VP Images: Ian Cameron
VP Newspaper Markets: Thomas E. Slaughter
VP Marketing Operations: Joy Jones
Senior Managing Editor: Mike Silverman, age 63
Director Media Relations: Jack Stokes
Auditors: Ernst & Young LLP

LOCATIONS

HQ: The Associated Press
 450 W. 33rd St., New York, NY 10001
Phone: 212-621-1500   **Fax:** 212-621-5447
Web: www.ap.org

PRODUCTS/OPERATIONS

Selected Products and Services

AP Digital News (Internet and wireless news delivery)
AP Images (photo services)
APTN (AP Television News, international television news service)
ENPS (electronic news production system)
Online Video Network (video content distribution)
STATS (sports-related content)

COMPETITORS

Agence France-Presse
Bloomberg L.P.
Business Wire
Comtex News
Corbis
Dow Jones
E. W. Scripps
Gannett
Getty Images
New York Times
PR Newswire
Reuters
Tribune Company
UPI

Associated Wholesale Grocers

Associated Wholesale Grocers (AWG) knows its customers can't live by bread and milk alone. One of the largest US retailer-owned cooperatives, AWG supplies more than 2,300 member-stores in more than 20 states from eight distribution centers with a wide array of grocery items, produce, and fresh meats, along with other retail merchandise and specialty services for in-store delis and bakeries. AWG has also developed its own grocery store concepts, including Country Mart and Homeland. In addition, the co-op offers a variety of business services to its members, including advertising and marketing programs, insurance, retail systems support, and store design. AWG was founded by a group of independent grocers in 1924.

In a bid to expand its territory and operations, the cooperative acquired a distribution center in Ft. Worth from Albertsons in 2007, along with more than 20 Albertsons retail locations in Oklahoma. As part of the deal, AWG took over supplying Albertsons locations in Arkansas, Louisiana, and Texas; it also rebranded some of the stores under its Homeland banner.

AWG is also continuing to build sales for its private-label products such as Best Choice and Always Save. In addition to marketing the products as lower cost alternatives to brand-name products, the co-op has been investing in efforts to make sure the quality of its private-label items matches competing national brands.

HISTORY

About 20 Kansas City, Kansas-area grocers met in a local grocery in 1924 and organized the Associated Grocers Company to get better deals on purchases and advertising. They elected J. C. Harline president, and each chipped in a few hundred dollars to make their first purchases. It took a while to find a manufacturer who would sell directly to them; a local soap maker was finally convinced, and others gradually followed.

In 1926 the group was incorporated as Associated Wholesale Grocers (AWG). It outgrew two warehouses in four years, finally moving to a 16,000-sq.-ft. facility big enough to add new lines and more products. Membership doubled between 1930 and 1932 as grocers moved from ordering products a year ahead to the new wholesale concept, and members took seriously the slogan: "Buy, Sell, Buy Some More." They met every week to plan how to sell their products, and buyer and advertising manager Harry Small gave sales presentations and advertising ideas (his trade-in plan for old brooms sold more than two train-carloads of brooms in two weeks). Heavy newspaper advertising also paid off; AWG topped $1 million in sales in 1933.

The cooperative made its first acquisition in 1936, buying Progressive Grocers, a warehouse in Joplin, Missouri; a second warehouse named Associated Grocers was acquired the next year in Springfield, Missouri. AWG continued building and expanding warehouses, and annual sales were at $11 million by 1951.

Louis Fox became CEO in 1956. Fox maximized year-end rebates for members, led several acquisitions, and formed a new subsidiary for financing stores and small shopping centers where AWG members had a presence (Supermarket Developers). Sales increased nearly fifteen fold to over $200 million in his first 15 years.

James Basha, who succeeded Fox when he retired in 1984, saw sales reach $2.4 billion by his own retirement in 1992.

Basha was followed by former COO Mike DeFabis, once a deputy mayor of Indianapolis, who orchestrated several acquisitions. The purchases included 41 Kansas City-area stores — most of which were quickly bought by members — from bankrupt Food Barn Stores in 1994 and 29 Oklahoma stores and a warehouse from Safeway spinoff Homeland Stores in 1995 (members bought all the stores).

AWG's nonfood subsidiary, Valu Merchandisers Co., was established in 1995; its new Kansas warehouse began shipping health and beauty aids and housewares the following year to help members battle big discounters. Members narrowly defeated a proposal in late 1996 to convert the cooperative into a public company. Proponents promptly petitioned for a second vote, which was defeated early the next year.

AWG veteran Doug Carolan succeeded DeFabis in 1998, becoming only the fifth CEO in the cooperative's history. The company bought five Falley's and 33 Food 4 Less stores in Kansas and Missouri from Fred Meyer in 1998 for $300 million. In a break with tradition, AWG began operating the stores rather than selling them to members.

In 2000, after a months-long labor dispute with the Teamsters was resolved, Carolan left AWG. The company's CFO, Gary Phillips, was named president and CEO later that year. In 2001 the company debuted a new format, ALPS (Always Low Price Stores) — small stores that carry a limited selection of grocery top-sellers. Also that year AWG's Kansas City division began distributing to more than 10 new stores that had formerly been served by Fleming, the #1 US wholesale food distributor.

In 2002 supermarket operator Homeland Stores, which operates stores in Oklahoma, emerged from bankruptcy as a fully owned subsidiary of AWG. AWG formed a new subsidiary, Associated Retail Grocers, to oversee Homeland and its Falley's chain.

As a result of the 2003 sale of Fleming Companies' wholesale distribution business, AWG picked up food distribution centers in Nebraska (two), Oklahoma (one), and Tennessee (two) and general-merchandise distribution centers in Tennessee and Kansas.

Introducing a "dollar" section in its stores in 2004 proved successful, leading AWG to expand the category to more than 1,000 food and non-food items. The following year it merged the corporate offices of its Homeland and Food 4 Less chains.

AMG took steps to expand its capacity and its territory in 2007 when it acquired a distribution center in Ft. Worth from Albertsons. The cooperative also took on supply operations for Albertsons locations in Arkansas, Louisiana, and Texas.

EXECUTIVES

Chairman: Bob Hufford
President and CEO: Gary A. Phillips, age 61
EVP and CFO: Robert C. (Bob) Walker
EVP Marketing: Jerry Garland, age 57
EVP, Operations Wholesale: Michael (Mike) Rand
SVP, Grocery Products: Dennis Kinser, age 63
SVP, General Counsel, and Corporate Secretary: Frances Pellegrino Puhl, age 58
SVP, Perishables: Lucky Hicks
SVP Real Estate and Store Engineering: Scott Wilmoski, age 55
SVP and Division Manager, Nashville: Milton Milam
SVP and Division Manager, Kansas City: William A. (Bill) Quade
SVP and Division Manager, Oklahoma: Steve Arnold
SVP and Division Manager, Kansas City: Gary Jennings
VP, Corporate Human Resources: Frank Tricamo
VP, Corporate Sales: Bill Lancaster, age 68
VP Corporate Sales Development: Stephen G. (Steve) Dillard
VP, Corporate Controller: Gary Koch
President and CEO, Benchmark Insurance Company: Bill Morrison
CIO: Keith Martin
Auditors: KPMG LLP

LOCATIONS

HQ: Associated Wholesale Grocers, Inc.
   5000 Kansas Ave., Kansas City, KS 66106
Phone: 913-288-1000   **Fax:** 913-288-1587
Web: www.awginc.com

COMPETITORS

Affiliated Foods
Affiliated Foods Midwest
Alex Lee
Associated Grocers, Inc.
C&S Wholesale
Grocers Supply
GSC Enterprises
H.T. Hackney
IGA
Kroger
McLane
Nash-Finch
SUPERVALU
Wal-Mart

HISTORICAL FINANCIALS

Company Type: Cooperative

Income Statement

FYE: Last Saturday in December

	REVENUE ($ mil.)	NET INCOME ($ mil.)	NET PROFIT MARGIN	EMPLOYEES
12/07	5,700	—	—	—
12/06	5,000	—	—	—
12/05	5,000	—	—	—
12/04	4,570	—	—	—
12/03	3,721	—	—	6,171
Annual Growth	**11.3%**	—	—	—

Revenue History

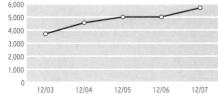

A.T. Kearney

With roots going back to the founding of McKinsey & Company in 1926, A.T. Kearney has established a place for itself in the management consulting pantheon. Today's A.T. Kearney operates from offices in more than 30 countries around the world. It offers consulting in a variety of areas, including growth strategies, IT strategies, and supply chain management. Clients have come from a wide range of industries, including automotive, financial services, health care, and utilities. A.T. Kearney is owned by its management team. The consulting firm took its current name in 1946 from that of Andrew T. Kearney, one of McKinsey's first partners.

A.T. Kearney hopes to grow by using its geographic reach to gain more business from clients with operations in multiple countries. As part of an environmental sustainability initiative, the firm aims to expand its use of collaborative technology to reach across geographic regions, in order to reduce consultants' travel and thus minimize the firm's overall carbon footprint. Lessons from the internal sustainability efforts are being applied to the firm's work for its customers, particularly on issues related to supply chains.

At the same time, A.T. Kearney is once again flexing its muscles as an independent consultancy after having operated under the wing of systems integrator and data management company Electronic Data Systems (EDS), from 1995 until it was acquired by managers in 2006.

EDS and A.T. Kearney did not enjoy a particularly smooth road together. Although the pairing enabled A.T. Kearney to grow, a cultural divide became apparent. The consulting firm began losing autonomy, and partners found their compensation reduced to levels more in line with those of executives at a public company.

The acquisition by the management team in January 2006 did not include the firm's executive search unit, which EDS sold to an investment group, or A.T. Kearney's former maintenance, repair, and operations management group, which EDS retained.

EXECUTIVES

Chairman and Managing Officer: Paul A. Laudicina, age 56
COO; Managing Director, Asia Pacific: John Yoshimura
CFO: Dan A. DeCanniere
Managing Director, North America:
  Michael J. (Mike) Tower, age 44
Chief Human Resources Officer: Peter (Pete) Pesce, age 57
General Counsel: Mark Berlind
Partner, London: Phil Dunne
Partner, Madrid: Dirck Forquignon
Partner, Automotive Practice, Detroit: Bill Windle
Partner, Singapore: Mui Fong Goh
Principal, Brussels: Mario Goethals
Principal, Madrid: Javier Navarro
Manager, São Paulo: João Pedro Castelo Branco
Auditors: KPMG LLP

LOCATIONS

HQ: A.T. Kearney, Inc.
  222 W. Adams St., Chicago, IL 60606
Phone: 312-648-0111   **Fax:** 312-223-6200
Web: www.atkearney.com

PRODUCTS/OPERATIONS

Selected Practice Areas

Enterprise services transformation
Growth strategies
Innovation and complexity management
IT strategies
Merger strategies
Strategic supply management
Supply chain management
Supply management services

COMPETITORS

Accenture
Bain & Company
BearingPoint
Booz Allen
Boston Consulting
Capgemini
Celerant Consulting
Computer Sciences Corp.
Deloitte Consulting
IBM Global Services
McKinsey & Company
PA Consulting
Roland Berger

HISTORICAL FINANCIALS

Company Type: Private

Income Statement

FYE: December 31

	REVENUE ($ mil.)	NET INCOME ($ mil.)	NET PROFIT MARGIN	EMPLOYEES
12/07	785	—	—	2,500
12/06	798	—	—	2,500
12/05	700	—	—	2,500
12/04	806	—	—	—
12/03	846	—	—	4,000
Annual Growth	(1.9%)	—	—	(11.1%)

Revenue History

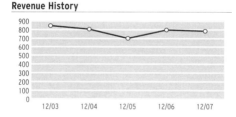

Atlanta Spirit

This company serves spirited Atlanta sports fans. Atlanta Spirit owns and operates two of the city's professional sports franchises, the Atlanta Hawks basketball team and the Atlanta Thrashers hockey team. The Hawks were founded in 1946, joined the National Basketball Association in 1949, and moved to Atlanta from St. Louis in 1968. The Thrashers joined the National Hockey League as an expansion franchise in 1999. Atlanta Spirit also operates Philips Arena, the home of both its teams. The sports investment partnership includes entrepreneurs Steve Belkin, Bruce Levenson, and Michael Gearon, Jr.

Belkin and his partners have been embroiled in a public feud over the ownership of Atlanta Spirit since late in 2005. After a lawsuit, an injunction, and power plays of all sorts over the signing of guard Joe Johnson, Belkin originally agreed to sell his 30% stake in Atlanta Spirit to the other owners but he has been battling in the courts over how to effect the sale.

Amid the turmoil, CEO Bernie Mullen left Atlanta Spirit in early 2008, followed by CFO Bill Duffy as well as several other top executives. A committee handles day-to-day operations at the company, reporting to the estranged ownership group.

Atlanta Spirit acquired the sports franchises in 2004 for $250 million from Turner Sports, a unit of Time Warner's Turner Broadcasting.

EXECUTIVES

Owner: Michael Gearon Jr.
SVP Broadcast and Corporate Partnerships:
  Tracy White
VP and Chief Legal Officer: T. Scott Wilkinson
VP Basketball: Dominique Wilkins
VP Public Relations: Arthur Triche
VP Operations: Patrick Lane
VP Marketing, Advertising, and Branding: Jim Pfeifer
VP Strategic Planning: Ailey Penningroth
VP Community Development: LaVerne Henderson
Counsel: Melissa Linsky
Director Basketball Operations: Mike McNeive
Director Media Relations: Jon Steinberg
President, Philips Arena: Bob Williams
SVP Booking and Events, Philips Arena: Trey Feazell

LOCATIONS

HQ: Atlanta Spirit, LLC
  101 Marietta St. NW, Ste. 1900, Atlanta, GA 30303
Phone: 404-878-3800
Web: www.atlantaspirit.com

COMPETITORS

Atlanta Braves
Atlanta Falcons
Atlanta Motor Speedway
Six Flags Over Georgia

HISTORICAL FINANCIALS

Company Type: Private

Income Statement

FYE: December 31

	REVENUE ($ mil.)	NET INCOME ($ mil.)	NET PROFIT MARGIN	EMPLOYEES
12/07	139	—	—	—
12/06	134	—	—	—
12/05	87	—	—	—
12/04	83	—	—	—
12/03	78	—	—	—
Annual Growth	15.5%	—	—	—

Revenue History

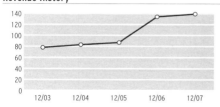

Atlantic Express Transportation

Driving with thousands of schoolchildren in the back seat, or rows of seats, doesn't bother Atlantic Express Transportation. The company serves about 105 school districts throughout the US with a fleet of some 5,100 vehicles. School bus services account for about 90% of the company's sales. In addition, Atlantic Express provides paratransit services (transportation of people with disabilities) in New York City and offers charter, express, and fixed-route bus services, mainly as a contractor for New York's Metropolitan Transportation Authority. Investment firm Greenwich Street Capital owns a controlling stake in Atlantic Express, which was founded in 1968.

Contracts with the New York City Department of Education, which represent a little more than half of the company's overall revenue, have been extended through 2010. Typically Atlantic Express has been able to renew contracts in order to ensure a steady revenue stream — more than 95% of its contracted revenue comes from customers who have worked with the company for five years or longer.

EXECUTIVES

Chairman: Peter Frank, age 60, $300,000 pay
President, CEO, and Director: Domenic Gatto, age 59, $1,173,694 pay
COO, Secretary, and Treasurer: Jerome (Jerry) Dente, age 62, $202,166 pay
CFO: Nathan Schlenker, age 69, $421,325 pay
EVP: Noel Cabrera, age 48
Auditors: BDO Seidman, LLP

LOCATIONS

HQ: Atlantic Express Transportation Corp.
7 North St., Staten Island, NY 10302
Phone: 718-442-7000   **Fax:** 718-442-7672
Web: www.atlanticexpress.com

Selected Operating Locations
California
Illinois
Massachusetts
Missouri
New Jersey
New York
Pennsylvania

PRODUCTS/OPERATIONS

2008 Sales

	$ mil.	% of total
School bus	386.3	89
Paratransit & transit	47.2	11
Total	**433.5**	**100**

COMPETITORS

FirstGroup America
MV Transportation
National Express Group
STA
Veolia Transportation

HISTORICAL FINANCIALS
Company Type: Private

Income Statement
FYE: June 30

	REVENUE ($ mil.)	NET INCOME ($ mil.)	NET PROFIT MARGIN	EMPLOYEES
6/08	434	(34)	—	7,600
6/07	429	(17)	—	7,600
6/06	414	(30)	—	8,100
6/05	364	(42)	—	—
6/04	364	57	15.6%	—
Annual Growth	**4.5%**	**—**	**—**	**(3.1%)**

2008 Year-End Financials

Debt ratio: —   Current ratio: —
Return on equity: —   Long-term debt ($ mil.): 191
Cash ($ mil.): —

Net Income History

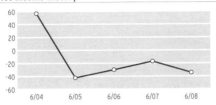

Atrium Companies

Atrium Companies produces aluminum and vinyl windows and patio doors, and "woodn't" have it any other way — not after selling its wood window and door business. Customers include retail centers, lumberyards, builders, and wholesalers for both new construction and remodeling markets. Atrium also offers installation and repair services. Since its founding in 1948, Atrium has grown to include window- and door-making facilities, vinyl and aluminum extrusion operations, and other operations throughout the US and Canada. The company's acquisition of Canada-based North Star Vinyl Windows and Doors in 2007 deepened its product line.

Atrium has spent much of the past decade reconfiguring its holdings by buying and selling operations. In 2007 it sold its Miniature Die Casting (MDC) subsidiary, which makes window hardware, to Advanced Global Technologies. The move was a reversal of sorts — it had acquired MDC in 2003 as part of a vertical integration initiative.

Also in 2007 Atrium closed a plant in Connecticut, as well as several offices in Florida as part of its shift from a direct-to-dealer sales model to independent distributors. The latter move was prompted by a drop in housing starts in Florida, traditionally one of the strongest real estate markets. In 2008 it said it would consolidate factories in California and Arizona, closing the Arizona plant and laying off workers.

EXECUTIVES

Chairman: Larry T. Solari, age 65
President and CEO: Gregory T. (Greg) Faherty
EVP and CFO: Madhusudan A. (Sudan) Dewan
EVP and COO: Robert E. Burns
SVP, Human Resources: D. D. (Gus) Agostinelli
SVP, General Counsel, and Secretary:
Philip J. (Phil) Ragona
VP, Information Technology: Roger Santone
VP, Logistics: Harold Krane
VP, Marketing: Mark Gallant
President, R. G. Darby and Total Trim: Cliff Darby, age 38
President, Superior Engineered Products:
Bob Rodriguez
Auditors: Deloitte & Touche LLP

LOCATIONS

HQ: Atrium Companies, Inc.
3890 W. Northwest Hwy., Ste. 500, Dallas, TX 75220
Phone: 214-630-5757   **Fax:** 214-630-5001
Web: home.atrium.com

PRODUCTS/OPERATIONS

Selected Subsidiaries
Danvid Window Company
Dow-Tech Plastics
HR Windows
North Star Windows & Doors
R.G.Darby Co., Inc.
Superior Engineered Products Corporation
Thermal Industries Inc.

COMPETITORS

Andersen Corporation	MW Manufacturers
Drew Industries	Pella
GBO	Ply Gem
Installux	Sierra Pacific Industries
International Aluminum	Silver Line
JELD-WEN	Building Products
Masonite Canada	Simonton Windows, Inc.
MI Windows and Doors	Therma-Tru
Milgard Manufacturing	

HISTORICAL FINANCIALS
Company Type: Private

Income Statement
FYE: December 31

	REVENUE ($ mil.)	NET INCOME ($ mil.)	NET PROFIT MARGIN	EMPLOYEES
12/07	700	—	—	5,100
12/06	840	—	—	6,000
12/05	800	—	—	7,000
12/04	800	—	—	6,300
12/03	598	—	—	6,100
Annual Growth	**4.0%**	**—**	**—**	**(4.4%)**

Revenue History

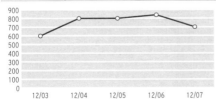

Attorneys' Title Insurance Fund

Sunshine State attorneys know where to go for title insurance services. Attorneys' Title Insurance Fund (The Fund) provides property title insurance products to its 6,000 member attorneys throughout Florida. (Title insurance protects real estate buyers and sellers against loss resulting from defective titles.) The Fund is owned by a business trust created in 1947. Membership in the trust is limited to Florida attorneys, although The Fund serves non-member customers as well. Products include title insurance underwriting, property information, property ownership verification, real estate closing software, and a variety of industry-related marketing tools.

The company is experiencing some financial difficulties due to a downturn in the Florida (and nationwide) real estate market in 2007, and it has responded by making efforts to cut costs.

The Fund is the controlling shareholder of National Attorneys' Title Assurance Fund, which provides title insurance in Indiana.

EXECUTIVES

Chairman: Charles S. Isler III
President: Charles J. Kovaleski
SVP Financial Services and Treasurer: Jimmy R. Jones
SVP Legal Services, General Counsel, and Corporate Secretary: R. Norwood Gay III
SVP Branch Operations: Sharon K. Priest
SVP Employee and Member Services: B. Gwen Geier
SVP Information Services: Jeannie L. Calabrese
SVP Marketing Services: Michael R. Hammond
VP Legal Services and Associate General Counsel: W. Theodore (Ted) Conner
VP Special Legal Services: G. Robert Arnold
VP Underwriting: Patricia P. Jones
VP and Special Projects Manager: Sue Ellen Woodward
Auditors: PricewaterhouseCoopers LLP

LOCATIONS

HQ: Attorneys' Title Insurance Fund, Inc.
6545 Corporate Centre Blvd., Orlando, FL 32822
Phone: 407-240-3863 **Fax:** 407-240-0750
Web: www.thefund.com

PRODUCTS/OPERATIONS

2007 Sales

	$ mil.	% of total
Insurance premiums	86.9	61
Title information revenue	27.3	19
Realized investment gains	15.4	11
Investment income	6.0	4
Real estate sales	3.7	2
Secondary mortgage sales	0.8	1
Other	3.5	2
Total	**143.6**	**100**

COMPETITORS

Fidelity National Financial
First American
Investors Title
LandAmerica Financial Group
North American Title
Old Republic
Stewart Information Services
Ticor Title Co.
Title Resource Group
United General Title Insurance

HISTORICAL FINANCIALS
Company Type: Private

Income Statement
FYE: December 31

	ASSETS ($ mil.)	NET INCOME ($ mil.)	INCOME AS % OF ASSETS	EMPLOYEES
12/07	381	(8)	—	819
12/06	366	26	7.1%	850
12/05	333	31	9.3%	821
12/04	282	33	11.7%	844
12/03	243	26	10.8%	875
Annual Growth	11.9%	—	—	(1.6%)

2007 Year-End Financials

Equity as % of assets: 47.6%   Long-term debt ($ mil.): 0
Return on assets: —   Sales ($ mil.): 144
Return on equity: —

Net Income History

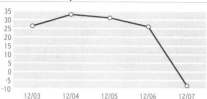

Austin Industries

Belying its name, Austin Industries is actually based in Dallas. The company provides civil, commercial, and industrial construction services in the South and Southwest. Its oldest subsidiary, Austin Bridge & Road, provides road, bridge, and parking lot construction across Texas. (It built the longest bridge in Texas, the Queen Isabella Causeway.) Subsidiary Austin Commercial builds office buildings, technology sites, hospitals, and other commercial projects. The group's Austin Industrial provides construction, maintenance, and electrical services for the chemical, refining, power, and manufacturing industries. The employee-owned company, which prides itself on its employee relations, was founded in 1918.

In fact, countering the traditional view of the construction industry, Austin Industries is committed to diversity. The company has been named Construction Corporation of the Year by the Dallas-Fort Worth Minority Business Council seven times; other awards include General Contractor of the Year (Black Contractors Association) and Corporate Advocate of the Year (Hispanic Contractors Association). It has a unit devoted to diversity affairs, which seeks women-owned, minority-owned, and disadvantaged companies to do business with or provide mentorship for.

Austin Bridge & Road's largest project is a four-level interchange in Texarkana, Texas. The $180 million project also calls for work on 10 miles of frontage roads and reconstruction of several area bridges.

EXECUTIVES

President and CEO: Ronald J. (Ron) Gafford, age 57
President, Austin Bridge & Road: James R. (Jim) Andoga
President, Austin Commercial: David B. Walls
President, Austin Industrial: Barry Babyak
VP Finance and CFO: Paul W. Hill
VP Human Resources and Treasurer: James (Jim) Schranz
Co-General Counsel: Charles Hardy
Co-General Counsel: Elaine E. Nelson
CIO: Stan Smith
Corporate Controller: Dana Bartholomew
Director Corporate Communications: Lori Elise Brakhage
Manager Communications: Kay Bishop

LOCATIONS

HQ: Austin Industries, Inc.
3535 Travis, Ste. 300, Dallas, TX 75204
Phone: 214-443-5500
Web: www.austin-ind.com

Austin Industries and its operating companies have about 20 offices in Alabama, Arizona, California, Florida, Georgia, New Mexico, and Texas.

PRODUCTS/OPERATIONS

Selected Projects and Customers

Bridge & Road
  Elm Fork (railroad bridge, Dallas)
  Port Isabella Causeway (Cameron County, TX)
  Texarkana, IH-30 (bridges, turnarounds, flyover ramps; Texarkana, TX)
  Westpark Tollway (flyover ramps, Houston)
Austin Commercial
  ACME Brick Headquarters (Ft. Worth, TX)
  AMD Fab 25 (Austin, TX)
  AMD Lone Star Campus (Austin)
  American Airlines Terminal, Miami International Airport
  Burlington Northern Santa Fe Command Station and Headquarters (Ft. Worth)
  Dallas Convention Center (2002 expansion)
  Federal Reserve Automation System Consolidation (data center, Dallas)
  Marriott Hotel & Golf Club (Ft. Worth)
  Museum of Living Art at the Forth Worth Zoo
  Presbyterian Hospital of Plano Tower III (Plano, TX)
  Taylor Place (ASU dormitories, Phoenix)
  TCU Recreation Center (Ft. Worth)
  UNT Chemistry Building (Denton, TX)
  UNT School of Public Health (Ft. Worth)
  UT Applied Computational Engineering & Sciences Building (Austin)
  UT Executive Education and Conference Center (Austin)
  UT Southwestern Medical Center T. Boone Pickens Biomedical Building and Conference Center (Dallas)
  W Austin
Austin Industrial
  Augusta Service Company (contract services)
    DSM Chemicals
    DSM Resins
    Nylon Polymer
    W.R. Grace
  BP Exploration, Gas-to-Liquids Test Facility (Nikiski, AK)
  Nordic Biofuels Ethanol Plant (Ravenna, NE)

COMPETITORS

Balfour Beatty	J.F. Shea
Bechtel	JGC
Beck Group	MYR Group
Brasfield & Gorrie	Peter Kiewit Sons'
Choate Construction	Rooney Holdings
Flint Industries	Shaw Group
Fluor	Skanska
Granite Construction	Sundt
Halliburton	Swinerton
Hardin Construction	Turner Corporation
Hensel Phelps	Turner Industries
Construction	Vecellio & Grogan
Hunt Construction	Zachry Group
JC General Contractors	

HISTORICAL FINANCIALS

Company Type: Private

Income Statement

FYE: December 31

	REVENUE ($ mil.)	NET INCOME ($ mil.)	NET PROFIT MARGIN	EMPLOYEES
12/07	1,700	—	—	5,600
12/06	1,310	—	—	6,000
12/05	1,359	—	—	6,000
12/04	1,230	—	—	5,300
12/03	1,200	—	—	6,000
Annual Growth	9.1%	—	—	(1.7%)

Revenue History

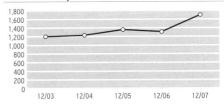

Autocam Corporation

Members of both the UAW and the AMA use Autocam's products. The company makes precision components for the automotive and medical device industries. Autocam makes parts used in automotive air bags, brake systems, electric motors, fuel systems, and power steering systems. The company's medical components are used in the manufacture of stents, joint implants, DNA testing equipment, and ophthalmic and surgical devices. Autocam also offers machined components for power tools. Investment firm Aurora Capital Group sold Autocam in 2004 to investors including GS Capital, Roger Penske, and Autocam CEO John Kennedy.

Aurora Capital Group's investment in Autocam paid off handsomely. The investment firm paid $20 million for the company in 2000 and sold it for about $390 million.

Penske, a former race car driver and the CEO of Penske Corporation, is investing in Autocam through private equity fund Transportation Resource Partners, which focuses on companies engaged in transportation and related services.

Major Autocam customers have included Tier 1 auto industry suppliers ZF Friedrichshafen, Delphi, TRW Automotive, and Robert Bosch.

EXECUTIVES

President and CEO: John C. Kennedy, $500,600 pay
COO, North American Operations: John R. Buchan, $286,985 pay
COO, International Operations: Jonathan B. DeGaynor
COO, South American Operations: Eduardo Renner de Castilho, $275,000 pay
CFO, Secretary, and Treasurer: Warren A. Veltman, $273,446 pay
VP Sales and Marketing: Thomas K. O'Mara, $239,446 pay
Director Human Resources: Jim Wojczynski
Quality Assurance: Greg Coberly
Purchasing Manager: June Doyle
Auditors: Deloitte & Touche LLP

LOCATIONS

HQ: Autocam Corporation
4436 Broadmoor SE, Kentwood, MI 49512
Phone: 616-698-0707 **Fax:** 616-698-6876
Web: www.autocam.com

PRODUCTS/OPERATIONS

Selected Automotive Products

Steering system components
Input shafts
Pinions
Pump shafts
Sleeves
Torsion bars
Fuel system components
Armatures
Cores
Guides
Housings
Needles
Plungers
Pole pieces
Pump shafts
Seats
Spacers
Tubes
Valves
Braking system components
Armatures
Inlet tubes
Support tubes
Valve inserts
Valve seats
Electric motors
Armature shafts
Gear boxes
Worm gears
Air bag systems
Adapters
Collars
Diffusers
Pistons
Projectiles

COMPETITORS

Autoliv
Boston Scientific
Dana Corporation
DENSO
Hilite International
Key Safety Systems
Mark IV
Medtronic
Remy
Smiths Group
Visteon

Auto-Owners Insurance Group

There's more to Auto-Owners Insurance Group than the name implies. In addition to auto coverage, the company provides a range of personal property/casualty and life insurance products including disability and annuities. The company operates through its aptly named subsidiaries (including Auto-Owners Life Insurance, Home-Owners Insurance, and Property-Owners Insurance). Its Southern-Owners Insurance subsidiary offers property/casualty insurance in Florida. Auto-Owners Insurance Group also sells commercial auto, liability, and workers' compensation policies.

Established in 1916, the company operates in 25 states nationwide and is represented by some 6,000 independent agents.

Most of the company's revenues come from Florida and Michigan. Auto-Owners is focused on growing its business by establishing strong relationships with independent agents and by diversifying its product offerings.

EXECUTIVES

CEO and Chairman: Roger L. Looyenga
President: Ron Simon
EVP: Jeffrey F. Harrold

LOCATIONS

HQ: Auto-Owners Insurance Group
6101 Anacapri Blvd., Lansing, MI 48917
Phone: 517-323-1200 **Fax:** 517-323-8796
Web: www.auto-owners.com

PRODUCTS/OPERATIONS

Selected Subsidiaries

Auto-Owners Insurance Company
Auto-Owners Life Insurance Company
Home-Owners Insurance Company
Owners Insurance Company
Property-Owners Insurance Company
Southern-Owners Insurance Company

COMPETITORS

ACE Limited
AIG
Allstate
ANPAC
Century-National Insurance
Farmers Group
GEICO
Hanover Insurance
Mercury General
MetLife
Progressive Corporation
Prudential
Safeco
State Farm
Travelers Companies

HISTORICAL FINANCIALS
Company Type: Private

Income Statement
FYE: December 31

	ASSETS ($ mil.)	NET INCOME ($ mil.)	INCOME AS % OF ASSETS	EMPLOYEES
12/07	13,903	467	3.4%	3,400
12/06	13,005	634	4.9%	3,400
12/05	11,912	623	5.2%	3,300
12/04	10,835	191	1.8%	3,270
Annual Growth	8.7%	34.8%	—	1.5%

2007 Year-End Financials
Equity as % of assets: 40.0%
Return on assets: 3.5%
Return on equity: 8.8%
Long-term debt ($ mil.): —
Sales ($ mil.): 4,802

Net Income History

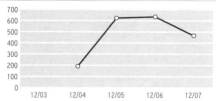

Avaya Inc.

Avaya helps to tie the corporate world together. The company's communication equipment and software integrates voice and data services for customers including large corporations, government agencies, and small businesses. Avaya's office phone systems incorporate IP telephony, messaging, Web access, and interactive voice response. The company offers a wide array of consulting, integration, and managed services through its Avaya Global Services unit. It sells directly and through distributors, resellers, systems integrators, and telecom service providers. Avaya was acquired by Silver Lake Partners and TPG Capital for $8.2 billion in 2007.

Consolidation in the telecommunications equipment sector had fueled speculation that Avaya was a takeover target, either for private equity investors or competitors such as Cisco Systems and Nortel Networks. Silver Lake and TPG paid $17.50 a share to purchase Avaya.

Avaya, which has increased its multinational enterprise accounts in recent years, has grown its direct sales force to better serve larger customers. Second tier enterprise accounts are handled by a combination of direct and channel partners, and small and medium businesses are served primarily through channel partners.

The company has supplemented its internal product development with a string of acquisitions. It bought audio conferencing systems maker Spectel in late 2004, and Nimcat Networks, a developer of peer-to-peer communications software, in 2005. Avaya acquired mobile device communications software developer Traverse Networks in 2006.

Avaya continues to sell traditional communications equipment with an eye toward helping customers with legacy voice products migrate to converged, IP-based systems.

EXECUTIVES

Interim President and Interim CEO: Charles H. (Charlie) Giancarlo, age 50
COO and Director: Michael C. Thurk, age 55, $1,073,076 pay
CFO: Thomas M. (Tom) Manley, age 47
Chief Administrative Officer: Pamela F. Craven, age 53, $844,278 pay
Chief Marketing Officer: Jocelyne J. Attal
SVP and CIO: Lorie Buckingham, age 48
SVP Manufacturing, Logistics, and Procurement: Francis M. Scricco, age 58, $810,113 pay
SVP, Human Resources: Roger C. Gaston, age 49
SVP, Strategy and Technology: Karyn Mashima, age 54
SVP and President, Global Communications Solutions: Stuart Wells
SVP Global Sales; President Field Operations: Todd A. Abbott, age 48
SVP, Global Sales: Charles (Charlie) Ill, age 50
SVP, Global Business Operations: Micky S. Tsui
VP, Treasurer and Investor Relations: Matthew W. Booher
Auditors: PricewaterhouseCoopers LLP

LOCATIONS

HQ: Avaya Inc.
211 Mount Airy Rd., Basking Ridge, NJ 07920
Phone: 908-953-6000 **Fax:** 908-953-7609
Web: www.avaya.com

PRODUCTS/OPERATIONS

Selected Products
Global Communications Solutions
Communications systems
Appliances, Mobile, and Small Systems Division (traditional and IP phones, wireless devices, phone accessories)
Customer Service Applications Division (contact center hardware and software)
Unified Communications Division (Avaya Communications Portal, modular messaging, multimedia conferencing, video, IP soft phones)
Converged voice applications
Media gateways
Media servers
Session Initiation Protocol (SIP) enablement services
Voice and data infrastructure management tools
Voice application software
Avaya Global Services
Applications design and integration
Business communications strategy development and planning
Communications support and network monitoring
Globalization planning
IP migration
Managed business communications services
Security consulting and integration

COMPETITORS

3Com
Aastra Technologies
Accenture
Active Voice
Alcatel-Lucent
Aspect Software
Cisco Systems
Computer Sciences Corp.
Comverse Technology
Ericsson
IBM Global Services
Microsoft
Mitel Networks
NEC
Nokia Siemens Networks
Nortel Networks
Panasonic Corporation of North America
Siemens AG
Unisys

Bad Boy Worldwide Entertainment Group

From music to fashion to food, Bad Boy Worldwide Entertainment Group sells attitude and image. The company oversees the business interests of its founder, owner, and CEO Sean "Diddy" Combs, a music impresario, fashion designer, and business mogul. Combs' core business is Bad Boy Records, founded in 1994 with Craig Mack and the late Notorious B.I.G., which produces such artists as Yung Joc, Danity Kane, and Cassie, as well as the music of Diddy himself. The label is 50% owned by Warner Music Group (WMG). Combs also markets branded clothing through Sean John Clothing and operates two upscale restaurants called Justin's (named after Combs' oldest son) in New York City and Atlanta.

Bad Boy Records was originally a joint venture between Combs and Arista Records, an imprint of Sony Music Entertainment (formerly Sony BMG). Arista, however, eventually dropped the label due to lagging sales. Bad Boy Records formed a partnership with WMG in 2005 to distribute albums through its Atlantic Records unit. The $30 million distribution deal gave WMG a 50% stake in the record company.

Diddy, who has also gone by the monikers Puffy, Puff Daddy, and most recently P. Diddy, is active in film and TV projects. His company has teamed with MTV Networks to produce TV shows such as the reality series *Making the Band*, *Taquita & Kaui*, and *Run's House*. In addition Diddy partnered with HBO for *P. Diddy Presents: The Bad Boys of Comedy*.

In late 2007 Diddy signed a multiyear deal to develop Diageo's Ciroc vodka brand for a 50-50 share in the profits.

EXECUTIVES

Chairman and CEO, Bad Boy Worldwide Entertainment Group and Sean John Clothing; CEO, Blue Flame Marketing and Advertising: Sean (Diddy) Combs, age 38
CFO: Derek Ferguson
Chief Marketing Officer: Jon Cropper
President, Bad Boy Records: Harve Pierre
SVP Radio Promotion, Bad Boy Records: Mel Smith
Senior Director A and R, Bad Boy Records: Conrad Dimanche
National Director Mix Show and Club Promotion, Bad Boy Records: Henry Polanco
Director A and R, Bad Boy Records: Shannon Lawrence

LOCATIONS

HQ: Bad Boy Worldwide Entertainment Group
1710 Broadway, New York, NY 10019
Phone: 212-381-1540 **Fax:** 212-381-1599
Web: www.badboyonline.com

PRODUCTS/OPERATIONS

Selected Operations
Blue Flame Marketing + Advertising
Justin's (restaurant)
Music
Bad Boy Records
Daddy's House Studios
Janice Combs Management
Janice Combs Music Publishing
Sean John Clothing

COMPETITORS

Armani
Capitol Records
Columbia Records
Epic Records
FUBU
Hugo Boss
Interscope Geffen A&M
Island Def Jam
Motown Records
Roc Apparel
Rush Communications
Tommy Boy
Zomba

Badger State Ethanol

Badger State Ethanol hopes to badger gasoline consumers into using its ethanol. The company manufactures fuel-grade ethanol (a performance-enhancing gasoline additive derived from processing corn into ethyl alcohol) at the rate of 40 million gallons per year at its plant in Monroe, Wisconsin. Its ethanol is marketed through distributor Murex; the firm has also opened a retail fuel station. Badger State Ethanol also sells 128,000 tons a year of distiller's grains (an animal feed supplement) and carbon dioxide, two by-products of ethanol production. The company was formed in 2000 and opened its ethanol plant in 2002.

EXECUTIVES

Chairman, President, and General Manager:
Gary L. Kramer, age 59, $125,000 pay
CFO: James (Jim) Leitzinger, age 52, $78,355 pay
VP and Director: David Kolsrud, age 59
Commodity Manager: Erik Huschitt
Director, Distiller's Sales and Marketing:
George Drewry
Secretary and Director: Nathan (Nate) Klassy
Office Manager: Cindy Sigafus
Plant Manager: Kurt Koller
Manager Maintenance: Bill Jacobson
Administrative Assistant and Safety Director:
Laurie Cannova
Auditors: Grant Thornton LLP

LOCATIONS

HQ: Badger State Ethanol, LLC
820 W. 17th St., Monroe, WI 53566
Phone: 608-329-3900   **Fax:** 608-329-3866
Web: www.badgerstateethanol.com

COMPETITORS

Abengoa Bioenergy
ADM
Ag Processing
Cargill
Iogen Corporation
Iroquois Bio-Energy
Lake Area Corn Processors
Little Sioux Corn Processors
Methanex
Northern Growers
Pacific Ethanol
Texas Petrochemicals
United Wisconsin

Bain & Company

Bain aims to be ready when corporate titans need a little direction. One of the world's leading management consulting firms, Bain & Company offers a wide array of services aimed at increasing efficiency and streamlining business processes. The firm also consults on strategic business issues, such as potential mergers and acquisitions and private equity investments; services include due-diligence preparation. In addition, Bain consultants address topics such as information technology, marketing, and performance improvement. The firm operates from more than 35 offices in about two dozen countries. It was founded in 1973 by Boston Consulting Group alumnus Bill Bain.

As companies have become more savvy about what consulting firms can and cannot do, as well as more sensitive to costs, they have started to demand smaller engagements that will provide specific business improvements and less "big picture" consulting. For its part, Bain measures success by its ability to improve clients' financial results.

Although founded by the same individuals, Bain & Company and investment firm Bain Capital are separate entities.

EXECUTIVES

Chairman: Orit Gadiesh, age 57
Worldwide Managing Director: Steve Ellis
VP and CFO: Leonard C. Banos
VP, France: Bertrand Pointeau
Treasurer: Andrew J. Frommer
Senior Director: Catherine Lemire
Director of Human Capital: Elizabeth Corcoran
Director Public Relations: Cheryl Krauss
Head, Asia-Pacific Private Equity Practice:
Chul-Joon Park
Chief Investment Officer and Partner, Boston:
Steve Schaubert

LOCATIONS

HQ: Bain & Company, Inc.
131 Dartmouth St., Boston, MA 02116
Phone: 617-572-2000   **Fax:** 617-572-2427
Web: www.bain.com

PRODUCTS/OPERATIONS

Selected Practice Areas

Change management
Corporate renewal
Corporate strategy
Cost and supply chain management
Customer strategy and marketing
Growth strategy
IT
Mergers and acquisitions
Organization
Performance improvement
Private equity

COMPETITORS

Accenture	IBM
A.T. Kearney	Keane
BearingPoint	McKinsey & Company
Booz Allen	Oliver Wyman
Boston Consulting	PA Consulting
Capgemini	Perot Systems
Computer Sciences Corp.	Roland Berger
Deloitte Consulting	Towers Perrin

HISTORICAL FINANCIALS

Company Type: Private

Income Statement

FYE: December 31

	ESTIMATED REVENUE ($ mil.)	NET INCOME ($ mil.)	NET PROFIT MARGIN	EMPLOYEES
12/07	1,640	—	—	4,083
12/06	1,310	—	—	3,550
12/05	1,130	—	—	3,200
Annual Growth	20.5%	—	—	13.0%

Revenue History

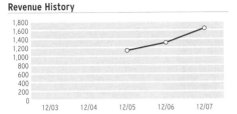

Baker & McKenzie

Baker & McKenzie believes big is good and bigger is better. One of the world's largest law firms, it has about 3,600 attorneys practicing from some 70 offices — from Bangkok to Berlin to Buenos Aires — in almost 40 countries. It offers expertise in a wide range of practice areas, including antitrust, intellectual property, international trade, mergers and acquisitions, project finance, and tax law. Baker & McKenzie's client list includes big companies from numerous industries, including banking and finance, construction, and technology, as well as smaller enterprises. The firm was founded in 1949.

Baker & McKenzie is known for the geographic scope of its practice — some 80% of the firm's attorneys work outside the US. The firm touts its widespread network of offices as an advantage for clients with multinational interests.

The vast scale of Baker & McKenzie's operations increases the firm's exposure to liability, however, and that concern led Baker & McKenzie to reorganize itself as a Swiss Verein in 2004. Under the new structure, which is used by accounting firms such as Deloitte Touche Tohmatsu, Baker & McKenzie's member firms operate as separate entities, insulating the parent firm from liability. Baker & McKenzie was the first international law firm to organize itself under a Verein structure.

HISTORY

Russell Baker traveled from his native New Mexico to Chicago on a railroad freight car to attend law school. Upon graduation in 1925 he started practicing law with his classmate Dana Simpson under the name Simpson & Baker. Inspired by Chicago's role as a manufacturing and agricultural center for the world and influenced by the international focus of his alma mater, the University of Chicago, Baker dreamed of creating an international law practice. He began developing an expertise in international law, and in 1934 Abbott Laboratories retained him to handle its worldwide legal affairs. Baker was on his way to fulfilling his dream.

Baker joined forces with Chicago litigator John McKenzie in 1949, forming Baker & McKenzie. In 1955 the firm opened its first foreign office in Caracas, Venezuela, to meet the needs of its expanding US client base. Over the next 10 years it branched out into Asia, Australia, and Europe, with offices in London, Manila, Paris, and Tokyo. Baker's death in 1979 neither slowed the firm's growth nor changed its international character. The next year it expanded into the Middle East and opened its 30th office in 1982 (Melbourne). To manage the sprawling law firm, Baker & McKenzie created the position of chairman of the executive committee in 1984.

In late 1991 the firm dropped the Church of Scientology as a client, losing an estimated $2 million in business. It was speculated that pressure from client Eli Lilly (maker of the drug Prozac, which Scientologists actively oppose) influenced the decision. In 1992 Baker & McKenzie was ordered to pay $1 million for wrongfully firing an employee who later died of AIDS. (The case became the basis for the 1993 film *Philadelphia*.) The firm fought the verdict but eventually settled for an undisclosed amount in 1995.

In 1994 Baker & McKenzie closed its Los Angeles office (the former MacDonald, Halsted & Laybourne; acquired 1988) amid considerable rancor. Also that year a former secretary at the firm received a $7.1 million judgment for sexual harassment by a partner. (A San Francisco Superior Court judge later reduced the award to $3.5 million.)

John Klotsche, a senior partner from the firm's Palo Alto, California, office, was appointed chairman in 1995. The following year the firm began a major expansion into California's Silicon Valley as part of an initiative to serve technology companies around the world. It also expanded its Warsaw, Poland, office through a merger with the Warsaw office of Dickinson, Wright, Moon, Van Dusen & Freman.

In 1998 Baker & McKenzie formed a special unit in Singapore to deal with business generated by the financial troubles in Asia. The opening of offices in Taiwan and Azerbaijan in 1998 brought the firm's total number of offices to 59. Klotsche stepped down in 1999 as the firm celebrated its 50th anniversary; Christine Lagarde replaced him. In early 2001 Baker & McKenzie created a joint venture practice with Singapore-based associate firm Wong & Leow. Also that year it merged with Madrid-based Briones Alonso y Martin to create the largest independent law firm in Spain.

Lagarde stepped down as executive chairman in 2004, and John Conroy was chosen to lead the firm.

EXECUTIVES

Chairman: John J. Conroy Jr.
COO: Greg Walters
CFO: Robert S. Spencer
Chief Global Press Officer: Judith Green
General Counsel: Edward J. Zulkey
Regional Operating Officer, Asia Pacific: Paul Malliate
Regional Operating Officer, Europe, Middle East, and Central Asia: Kate Stonestreet
Regional Operating Officer, Latin America: Leon J. Sacks
Regional Operating Officer, North America: Joseph Plack

Managing Partner, North American Region and Executive Committee Member: David P. Hackett
Chairman, Australian Offices and Executive Committee Member: David Jacobs
Global Director Marketing: David Tabolt
Global Director Global Information Systems: Martin Telfer
Manager Marketing, North America: Heidi Bouldin
Senior Public Relations Coordinator: Jessica Benzon

LOCATIONS

HQ: Baker & McKenzie
1 Prudential Plaza, 130 E. Randolph Dr., Ste. 2500, Chicago, IL 60601
Phone: 312-861-8800   **Fax:** 312-861-2899
Web: www.bakernet.com

PRODUCTS/OPERATIONS

Selected Practice Areas

Antitrust and trade
Banking and finance
Corporate
Dispute resolution
Employment
Insurance
Intellectual property
International/commercial
IT/communications
Major projects and project finance
Pharmaceuticals and health care
Real estate, construction, environment, and tourism
Tax

COMPETITORS

Clifford Chance
DLA Piper
Jones Day
Kirkland & Ellis
Latham & Watkins
Mayer Brown
McDermott Will & Emery
Shearman & Sterling
Sidley Austin
Skadden, Arps
Sullivan & Cromwell
Weil, Gotshal
White & Case

HISTORICAL FINANCIALS

Company Type: Private

Income Statement

FYE: June 30

	REVENUE ($ mil.)	NET INCOME ($ mil.)	NET PROFIT MARGIN	EMPLOYEES
6/07	1,829	—	—	—
6/06	1,522	—	—	9,503
6/05	1,352	—	—	8,500
6/04	1,228	—	—	8,400
6/03	1,134	—	—	8,401
Annual Growth	12.7%	—	—	4.2%

Revenue History

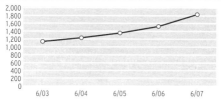

Baker & Taylor

If you've strolled through a library recently, you likely saw a lot of Baker & Taylor (B&T) without knowing it. The #1 book supplier to libraries, B&T primarily serves two types of markets. Its core business distributes books, calendars, music, and DVDs to thousands of school, public, and specialty libraries worldwide. The firm's retail unit supplies storefront and Internet retailers, as well as independent booksellers, with a million book titles and about 311,000 DVD, and CD titles. On the Internet (which formerly operated as Informata.com), B&T offers B2B e-commerce fulfillment services. Investment firm Willis Stein & Partners sold the company to Castle Harlan.

Castle Harlan bought B&T in 2006 for about $455 million for its direct-to-home distribution for Internet retailers and its library-based business model. Castle Harlan believes B&T's library business and its Internet retailing wholesale segment will continue to grow, spurring the deal to buy the company.

B&T's YBP Library Services unit offers acquisition and collection management support services to libraries. B&T's fulfillment customers include companies such as Amazon.com and barnesandnoble.com. The retail unit also handles the company's international operations.

B&T offers automatic shipping of books by popular authors (mailed as soon as they are published), and its J.A. Majors Company subsidiary is a major supplier of medical books to the educational and professional health markets.

The company acquired most of Advanced Marketing Services' assets in 2007, boosting its customer service offerings.

EXECUTIVES

Chairman and CEO: Thomas I. (Tom) Morgan, age 54
President: Marshall A. (Arnie) Wight
EVP and CFO: Jeff Leonard
EVP Strategic Business Development: Robert C. Nelson, age 46
SVP Operations: Gary Dayton
SVP Information Systems Development: Dan Johnson
SVP Information Technology: Matt Carroll
SVP Entertainment Group: Frank Wolbert
SVP Merchandising: Jean Srnecz
SVP Retail and International Sales: William (Bill) Preston
SVP; COO, YBP Library Services: Gary M. Shirk
President, Baker & Taylor Institutional: George Coe
President, Baker & Taylor Retail: David K. Cully, age 48

LOCATIONS

HQ: Baker & Taylor, Inc.
2550 W. Tyvola Rd., Ste. 300, Charlotte, NC 28217
Phone: 704-998-3100   **Fax:** 704-998-3316
Web: www.btol.com

PRODUCTS/OPERATIONS

Selected Products and Services

Calendars and accessories
Cataloging database (B&T MARC)
CD-ROM and Internet database and ordering software (Title Source II)
CDs, DVDs, and videos
Hardcover and paperback books
Library acquisition and collection management services (YBP Library Services)
Medical books (J.A. Majors Company)
Spoken-word media
Standing-order service (Compass)

COMPETITORS

Alliance Entertainment
Dawson Holdings
East Texas Distributing
Educational Development
Follett
Handleman
Ingram Industries
Levy Home Entertainment
Media Source
Navarre
Rentrak
Source Interlink

Baker Botts

Baker Botts is a Lone Star legal legend. The law firm's history stretches back to 1840, when founding partner Peter Gray was admitted to the bar of the Republic of Texas. The firm became Baker & Botts after Walter Browne Botts and James Addison Baker, great-grandfather of former US secretary of state and current partner James A. Baker III, joined the partnership. Today, the firm has some 750 lawyers in about 10 offices. Over the years Baker Botts has represented numerous clients from the energy industry, including Exxon Mobil and Halliburton. The firm practices in such areas as corporate, intellectual property, and tax law.

EXECUTIVES

Managing Partner: Walter J. (Walt) Smith
CFO: Lydia Companion
Chief Administrative Officer: Mark White
Director Client Relations: Catherine Austin
Director Information Technology: Mark Hendrick
Director Knowledge Services: Tracy Hallenberger
Director Human Resources: Roger Walter
Director Attorney Recruiting and Development:
 Rachel Koenig
Manager Public Relations: Michael A. (Mike) Cinelli

LOCATIONS

HQ: Baker Botts L.L.P.
 1 Shell Plaza, 910 Louisiana St., Houston, TX 77002
Phone: 713-229-1234   **Fax:** 713-229-1522
Web: www.bakerbotts.com

Selected Office Locations

Austin, Texas
Beijing
Dallas
Dubai, United Arab Emirates
Hong Kong
Houston
London
Moscow
New York
Riyadh, Saudi Arabia
Washington, DC

PRODUCTS/OPERATIONS

Major Practice Areas

Corporate
Environmental
Global Projects
Intellectual Property
Litigation
Tax

COMPETITORS

Akin Gump
Andrews Kurth
Bracewell & Patterson
Fulbright & Jaworski
Thompson and Knight
Vinson & Elkins

HISTORICAL FINANCIALS
Company Type: Partnership

Income Statement

	REVENUE ($ mil.)	NET INCOME ($ mil.)	NET PROFIT MARGIN	EMPLOYEES
12/07	578	—	—	—
12/06	503	—	—	—
12/05	365	—	—	—
12/04	420	—	—	1,601
12/03	394	—	—	1,582
Annual Growth	10.0%	—	—	1.2%

FYE: December 31

Revenue History

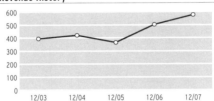

Baker, Donelson

Law firm Baker, Donelson, Bearman, Caldwell & Berkowitz has grown beyond its Southern roots to represent clients with stakes in national and international issues as well as local and regional matters. The firm boasts more than 500 attorneys and public policy advisers in almost 20 offices, which are concentrated in the southeastern US; it also operates out of Washington, DC, and Beijing. Baker, Donelson's practice areas include public policy, health care, securities, and intellectual property. The firm was founded in 1888.

EXECUTIVES

Chairman and CEO: Ben C. Adams
President, COO, and CFO; Shareholder, Memphis:
 Jerry Stauffer
Executive Director: James M. (Jim) Hughes
CIO: John D. Green
Controller: Ronnie Drumwright
**Co-Leader, Securities and Corporate Governance
 Practice Group:** Tonya Grindon
**Co-Leader, Securities and Corporate Governance
 Practice Group:** Mark Carlson
Chief Business Development Officer: Telisha Hoffman
General Counsel; Shareholder, Memphis: Sam Blair
**Director Professional Development; Shareholder,
 Birmingham:** Susan S. Wagner
Director Human Resources and Operations:
 Caroline W. Boswell
Media Contact: Johanna Burkett

LOCATIONS

HQ: Baker, Donelson, Bearman, Caldwell
 & Berkowitz, PC
 165 Madison Ave., First Tennessee Bldg.,
 Memphis, TN 38103
Phone: 901-526-2000   **Fax:** 901-577-2303
Web: www.bakerdonelson.com

PRODUCTS/OPERATIONS

Selected Practice Areas

Antitrust
Bankruptcy and creditors' rights
Business and technology
Business and transactions
Construction
Eminent domain
Employee benefits and executive compensation
Environmental, health and safety
Equipment leasing
Estate planning
Health law
Immigration
Intellectual property
Labor and employment
Litigation
Public policy
Transportation

COMPETITORS

Alston & Bird
Carlton Fields
Nelson Mullins Riley & Scarborough
Powell Goldstein
Troutman Sanders
Womble Carlyle

Bally Total Fitness

Business is working out for Bally Total Fitness Holding. The company is one of the largest fitness center operators in the US, with about 400 facilities located in the US, Mexico, South Korea, China, and the Caribbean. The clubs operate under the Bally Total Fitness and Bally Sports Clubs brands. Bally's members have access to pools, aerobic programs, running tracks, and racquet courts, as well as personal trainers and sports medicine services. Bally also markets private-label nutritional products and sells health-related products in most of its clubs, as well as in retail outlets. The company is controlled by hedge-fund operator Harbinger Capital.

The troubled gym operator is looking to start anew after emerging from Chapter 11 bankruptcy in 2007. Bally was forced to reorganize with the help of an influx of capital from Harbinger Capital due to mounting debts and losses. Its bankruptcy was also spurred by an internal investigation that uncovered problems with accounting practices, forcing the company to restate its earnings from 2000 to 2004.

To start getting back into financial shape, the company sold its Toronto, Ontario, facilities to Extreme Fitness and GoodLife Fitness Centres for some $18 million. The disposal came a year after Bally sold Crunch Fitness and Garilla Sports chain, among other clubs, to fitness club veteran Marc Tascher and a private equity group for $45 million in cash.

Former 24 Hour Fitness chief Mike Sheehan was named CEO in 2008.

EXECUTIVES

Interim Chairman: Don R. Kornstein, age 56
CEO and Director: Michael (Mike) Sheehan, age 46
COO: Michael A. Feder, age 61
SVP Sales and Interim Chief Marketing Officer:
 John H. Wildman
SVP, Secretary, and General Counsel:
 Marc D. Bassewitz, age 50, $575,000 pay
SVP Membership Services: Julie Adams, age 61
SVP Operations: Thomas S. Massimino, age 47
SVP Finance and Corporate Development and CFO:
 William G. (Bill) Fanelli, age 45, $440,000 pay
SVP and CIO: Gail J. Holmberg, age 51
SVP Customer Care and Member Services:
 Teresa R. Willows, age 48
VP and Treasurer: Katherine L. (Kathy) Abbott
Auditors: KPMG LLP

LOCATIONS

HQ: Bally Total Fitness Holding Corporation
 8700 W. Bryn Mawr Ave., Chicago, IL 60631
Phone: 773-380-3000   **Fax:** 773-693-2982
Web: www.ballyfitness.com

PRODUCTS/OPERATIONS

Selected Amenities

Aerobic exercise rooms
Courts (basketball, racquetball, and squash)
Free-weight areas
In-club retail stores (BFIT Essentials)
Indoor jogging tracks
Lap pools
Nutritional products
Personal training services
Physical therapy centers
Sauna and steam facilities

COMPETITORS

24 Hour Fitness	Lady of America
Crunch Fitness	Life Time Fitness
Curves International	Physical Property Holdings
Equinox Holdings	The Sports Club
Gold's Gym	Town Sports International
Health Fitness	World Gym
Jazzercise	YMCA
Jenny Craig	YWCA

HISTORICAL FINANCIALS

Company Type: Private

Income Statement

FYE: December 31

	REVENUE ($ mil.)	NET INCOME ($ mil.)	NET PROFIT MARGIN	EMPLOYEES
12/06	1,059	43	4.1%	19,200
12/05	1,071	(10)	—	21,600
12/04	1,048	(30)	—	23,200
12/03	954	(646)	—	—
12/02	968	4	0.4%	23,000
Annual Growth	2.3%	87.3%	—	(4.4%)

2006 Year-End Financials

Debt ratio: —   Current ratio: 0.08
Return on equity: —   Long-term debt ($ mil.): 247
Cash ($ mil.): 35

Net Income History

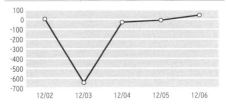

BancTec, Inc.

BancTec keeps tabs on all sorts of financial transactions. The company offers electronic processing systems, software, and services for government agencies, banks, utility and telecommunications companies, and other organizations that do high-volume financial transactions. BancTec's systems and software capture and process checks, bills, and other documents; products include digital archiving systems, workflow software, and scanners. BancTec's services include cost estimates and contingency planning, resource use, systems integration, and maintenance. Founded in 1972, BancTec is owned by investment firm Welsh, Carson, Anderson & Stowe, which took BancTec private in 1999.

Banctec's installed systems process more than 10 billion checks annually, serving 10 of the largest banks in the US. The company's 2,000 customers span more than 50 countries and process more than 50 million documents daily using BancTec's products and services.

EXECUTIVES

Chairman and CEO: J. Coley Clark, age 63, $558,156 pay
SVP and CFO: Jeffrey D. (Jeff) Cushman, age 46,
 $429,551 pay
SVP and Chief Administrative Officer: Lin M. Held
SVP; President, Europe, Middle East, and Africa:
 Michael D. (Mike) Peplow
SVP and CTO: Mark D. Fairchild
**SVP Strategy and Business Development; President,
 Information Technology Service Management:**
 Brendan P. Keegan
SVP Corporate Marketing; President, Americas:
 Michael D. Fallin
VP Worldwide Marketing: Chuck Corbin
VP Sales, Americas: Richard Mason
VP Technology and Portfolio Management:
 Neil Snowdon
VP Investor Relations: Kathy M. Costner
President, DocuData Solutions: Brian Rathe
Auditors: Deloitte & Touche LLP

LOCATIONS

HQ: BancTec, Inc.
 2701 E. Grauwyler Rd., Irving, TX 75061
Phone: 972-821-4000   **Fax:** 972-821-4823
Web: www.banctec.com

PRODUCTS/OPERATIONS

Selected Products

Check processing
 Check repair and preprocessing system (CheckMender)
 High-speed archiving system (OpenARCHIVE)
 Item processing transport (X-Series Transport,
  E-Series Transport)
Document management
 Document organization system (ImageFIRST Office)
 Electronic data management applications (eFIRST)
 Image processing and workflow tools (Plexus)
 Image quality assurance application (Image Sentry)
 Scanning (DocuScan and S-Series Scanner)
 Workflow automation (FloWare)
Payment processing
 Remittance processing suite (PayCourier)

COMPETITORS

EDS	Jack Henry
Equifax	NCR
First Data	Top Image Systems
Fiserv	Total System Services
IBM	Unisys

HISTORICAL FINANCIALS

Company Type: Private

Income Statement

FYE: December 31

	REVENUE ($ mil.)	NET INCOME ($ mil.)	NET PROFIT MARGIN	EMPLOYEES
12/07	390	(6)	—	2,526
12/06	380	(1)	—	2,670
12/05	345	(7)	—	2,750
12/04	361	(17)	—	3,000
12/03	379	18	4.7%	3,100
Annual Growth	0.7%	—	—	(5.0%)

2007 Year-End Financials

Debt ratio: 1.1%   Current ratio: —
Return on equity: —   Long-term debt ($ mil.): 1
Cash ($ mil.): —

Net Income History

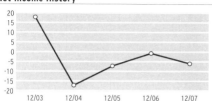

Barnes & Noble College Bookstores

Barnes & Noble College Bookstores is the scholastic sister company of Barnes & Noble (B&N), the US's largest bookseller. Started in 1873, the company operates more than 600 campus bookstores nationwide, selling textbooks, trade books, school supplies, collegiate clothing, and emblematic merchandise. Universities, medical and law schools, and community colleges hire Barnes & Noble College Bookstores to replace traditional campus cooperatives. (The schools get a cut of the sales.) Its College Marketing Network division offers on-campus marketing opportunities to businesses. B&N's chairman, Leonard Riggio, owns a controlling interest in the company.

Barnes & Noble College Bookstores often goes above and beyond when it takes over an old co-op location, adding Starbucks cafes, media centers where students can try out high-tech gadgets like laptops and handheld devices from Dell and Apple, and school-related decor like the eight-person rowing scull suspended from the ceiling at Georgia Tech's bookstore.

EXECUTIVES

Chairman: Leonard S. Riggio, age 67
President: Max J. Roberts
EVP: Bill Maloney
VP Book Merchandising: Jade Roth
VP Finance: Barry Brover
VP General Merchandise: Joel Friedman
VP Marketing: Janine von Juergensonn
Auditors: BDO Seidman, LLP

LOCATIONS

HQ: Barnes & Noble College Bookstores, Inc.
120 Mountain View Blvd., Basking Ridge, NJ 07920
Phone: 908-991-2665 **Fax:** 908-991-2846
Web: www.bkstore.com

COMPETITORS

Amazon.com
Borders
Ecampus.com
Follett
Nebraska Book
Wal-Mart

Bartlett and Company

When the cows come home, Bartlett and Company will be ready. The company's primary business is grain merchandising, but it also runs cattle feedlots, mills flour, and sells feed and fertilizer. Bartlett operates grain storage facilities, terminal elevators, and country elevators in the midwestern US, including locations in Kansas, Iowa, Missouri, and Nebraska. Bartlett also operates flour mills and feed stores in the Midwest and along the East Coast; its cattle operations are based in Texas. The Bartlett and Company Grain Charitable Foundation makes financial gifts to local causes. Founded in 1907 as Bartlett Agri Enterprises, the company is still owned by the founding Bartlett family.

EXECUTIVES

Chairman: Paul D. Bartlett Jr.
President and CEO: James B. (Jim) Hebenstreit, age 61
VP, Secretary, and Treasurer: Arnold F. (Arnie) Wheeler
VP Human Resources: Bill Webster
CIO: Jack Moran
President, Bartlett Milling and Bartlett Cattle:
John Gillcrist
President, Bartlett Grain: William J. Fellows

LOCATIONS

HQ: Bartlett and Company
4800 Main St., Ste. 1200, Kansas City, MO 64112
Phone: 816-753-6300 **Fax:** 816-753-0062
Web: www.bartlettandco.com

PRODUCTS/OPERATIONS

Selected Subsidiaries
Bartlett Cattle Company, L.P.
Bartlett Grain Co Southwest, L.P.
Bartlett Grain Company, L.P.
Bartlett Milling Company, L.P.
Bartlett Specialty Grains

COMPETITORS

ADM
Ag Processing
AzTx Cattle
Cactus Feeders
Cargill
CHS
ContiGroup
DeBruce Grain
Friona Industries
GROWMARK
King Ranch
Scoular

HISTORICAL FINANCIALS

Company Type: Private

Income Statement

FYE: December 31

	REVENUE ($ mil.)	NET INCOME ($ mil.)	NET PROFIT MARGIN	EMPLOYEES
12/07	1,510	—	—	700
12/06	1,100	—	—	750
Annual Growth	37.3%	—	—	(6.7%)

Revenue History

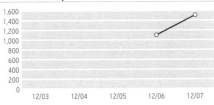

1,600				
1,400				
1,200				
1,000				
800				
600				
400				
200				
0				
12/03	12/04	12/05	12/06	12/07

Barton Malow

Barton Malow scores by building end zones and home plates. The construction management and general contracting firm with 13 offices around the US and in Mexico also makes points for its schools, hospitals, offices, and plants. Services range from planning to completion on projects in 37 states and Washington, DC. These include Atlanta's Phillips Arena, Boston's Shriners Hospital, and General Motors' Truck Product Center.

The company provides architecture and engineering services, and the Barton Malow Rigging unit installs process equipment and machinery. President Ben Maibach III and his family own a majority stake in the company, which Carl Osborn Barton began as C.O. Barton Company in Detroit in 1924.

In 2008 Barton Malow bought L.C. Gaskins Construction Company, which is based in Jacksonville, Florida. The new company will operate as Gaskins, a Barton Malow Company and specialize in the federal market sector. Barton Malow has focused on growing its operations in northern Florida with projects including public schools, and health care facilities. It also built the Baseball Grounds at Jacksonville for the city of Jacksonville.

EXECUTIVES

Chairman, President, and CEO: Ben C. Maibach III
EVP and COO: Lester (Les) Snyder III
EVP, Chief Legal Officer, and Secretary:
Thomas (Tom) Porter
SVP and CFO: Lori R. Howlett
SVP Southern and Western Regions:
Aleksei (Alex) Ivanikiw
SVP Eastern Region: Phil Kirby
SVP Sports Facilities: Harvey Oliva
VP Higher Education: Todd Ketola
VP Health Facilities: Donald (Don) Davis
Chief Marketing Officer: Sheryl B. Maibach
CIO: Phil Go
Public Relations Manager: Anne-Marie Poltorak
Auditors: Grant Thornton LLP

LOCATIONS

HQ: Barton Malow Company
26500 American Dr., Southfield, MI 48034
Phone: 248-436-5000 **Fax:** 248-436-5001
Web: www.bmco.com

PRODUCTS/OPERATIONS

Primary Services
Architecture/Planning
Building Information Management (BIM)
Concrete Trades
Construction Management
Design/Build
Facility Audits
Facility Services
General Contracting
Interior Design
Interiors Trades
Preconstruction
Program Management
Rigging/Millwright
Technology Consulting

COMPETITORS

Alberici
BE&K
Clark Enterprises
Fluor
Gilbane
Hensel Phelps Construction
H.J. Russell
Hunt Construction
M. A. Mortenson
McCarthy Building
Skanska USA Building
Turner Corporation
Walbridge Aldinger
Walsh Group
Whiting-Turner
Zachry Group

Bashas' Inc.

Bashas' has blossomed in the Arizona desert. The food retailer has grown to about 165 stores located primarily in Arizona, as well as a few stores in California and New Mexico. Its holdings include Bashas' traditional supermarkets, AJ's Fine Foods (gourmet-style supermarkets), and about a dozen Food City supermarkets (which cater to Hispanics in southern Arizona). It also operates a handful of Dine Markets in the Navajo Nation ("dine" means "the people" in Navajo) and offers natural and organic items through 50 Natural Choice in-store departments. The company was founded in 1932 and is still owned by the Basha family.

Citing economic pressures, including rising gas prices and penny-pinching customers, Bashas' shut down its online grocery shopping and delivery service — called Groceries On The Go — in May 2008. The service was used by less than 1% of the grocery chain's customers.

The third-largest grocery retailer in Arizona, Bashas' trails rivals Fry's Food Stores (owned by The Kroger Co.) and Wal-Mart. Bashas' outspoken CEO Eddie Basha has likened the Wal-Mart juggernaut to an economic blitzkrieg. Wal-Mart has more than 50 locations in Arizona.

Bashas' opened its first free-standing natural foods store in Tucson in May 2007. The new format — called Ike's Farmers' Market — specializes in organic and natural foods.

In early 2007, the supermarket operator acquired Phoenix wine retailer Sportsman's Fine Wine and Spirits, the operator of three retail stores and a wine storage facility.

EXECUTIVES

Chairman and CEO: Edward N. (Eddie) Basha Jr., age 70
Vice Chairman and SVP Real Estate: Johnny Basha
President and COO: Mike Proulx
SVP Finance and CFO: James (Jim) Buhr
SVP Human Resources: Michael Gantt
SVP Legal and Financial Affairs: Edward N. Basha III
SVP Logistics: Mike Basha
SVP Marketing, Sales, and Merchandising:
 Christie Frazier-Coleman
SVP Retail Operations: Ralph Woodward
SVP Support Services: Ike Basha
SVP Warehouse and Distribution: Sonny Felix
Public Relations: Alison Bendler

LOCATIONS

HQ: Bashas' Inc.
 22402 S. Basha Rd., Chandler, AZ 85248
Phone: 480-895-9350   **Fax:** 480-895-5371
Web: www.bashas.com

PRODUCTS/OPERATIONS

2007 Stores

	No.
Bashas'	83
Food City	63
AJ's Fine Foods	11
Sportman's Wine & Spirits	3
Ike's Farmers' Market	1
Total	**161**

COMPETITORS

Fry's Food
Safeway
SUPERVALU
Trader Joe's
Wal-Mart
Whole Foods

HISTORICAL FINANCIALS
Company Type: Private

Income Statement				FYE: December 31
	REVENUE ($ mil.)	NET INCOME ($ mil.)	NET PROFIT MARGIN	EMPLOYEES
12/07	2,160	—	—	14,300
12/06	2,080	—	—	14,299
12/05	2,500	—	—	14,300
12/04	2,000	—	—	14,100
12/03	1,800	—	—	13,200
Annual Growth	4.7%	—	—	2.0%

Revenue History

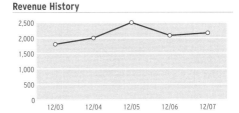

Bass Pro Shops

Bass Pro Shops (BPS) knows how to reel in shoppers. Each of more than 50 Outdoor World stores in the US and Canada covers about 280,000 sq. ft. The cavernous outlets sell boats, campers, equipment, and apparel for most outdoor activities and offer features such as archery ranges, fish tanks, snack bars, and video arcades. The first Outdoor World store (in Missouri) has been one of the state's biggest tourist attractions since it opened in 1981. It owns Tracker Marine (boat manufacturing) and American Rod & Gun (sporting goods wholesale) and runs an 850-acre resort in the Ozark Mountains. Founder John Morris owns BPS.

The company introduced its private-label credit card in partnership with GE Consumer Finance in three markets in 2005.

BPS catches shoppers at home with its seasonal and specialty catalogs, online operations, and through its TV and radio programs.

The outdoor products retailer opened about 10 new stores in 2006. The company has taken steps to appeal to more female consumers and launched its first catalog targeting women in 2007.

EXECUTIVES

Founder: John L. (Johnny) Morris
President and COO: James (Jim) Hagale
VP and CFO: Toni Miller
VP, Construction: Sean Easter
VP, Human Resources: Mike Roland
VP, Marketing: Stan Lippleman
Director Corporate Public Relations and Conservation: Martin MacDonald
Manager Corporate Public Relations and Outdoor Education: Larry Whitely
Corporate Maintenance Manager: Mark Kueck
CIO: Shawn Morin

LOCATIONS

HQ: Bass Pro Shops, Inc.
 2500 E. Kearney, Springfield, MO 65898
Phone: 417-873-5000   **Fax:** 417-873-4672
Web: www.basspro.com

PRODUCTS/OPERATIONS

Other Operations

American Rod & Gun (sporting goods wholesale)
Bass Pro Shops (sporting goods catalog)
Bass Pro Shops Collections (catalog aimed at women)
Bass Pro Shops Outdoor World (magazine and radio and TV programs)
Big Cedar Lodge (resort)
Outdoor World (retail stores)
Tracker Marine (sport boat manufacturing)

COMPETITORS

Academy Sports & Outdoors	Orvis Company
Cabela's	REI
Cruise America	Sears
Dick's Sporting Goods	Sports Authority
Gander Mountain	Sportsman's Guide
Hibbett Sports	Sportsman's Warehouse
Kmart	Wal-Mart
L.L. Bean	West Marine
MarineMax	Winmark

HISTORICAL FINANCIALS
Company Type: Private

Income Statement				FYE: December 31
	ESTIMATED REVENUE ($ mil.)	NET INCOME ($ mil.)	NET PROFIT MARGIN	EMPLOYEES
12/07	2,650	—	—	14,000
12/06	2,660	—	—	13,000
12/05	1,915	—	—	12,500
12/04	2,050	—	—	11,300
12/03	1,600	—	—	10,700
Annual Growth	13.4%	—	—	7.0%

Revenue History

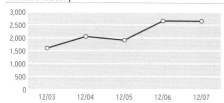

Battelle Memorial Institute

When you use a copier, hit a golf ball, or listen to a CD, you're using technologies developed by Battelle Memorial Institute. The not-for-profit trust operates one of the world's largest research enterprises, with more than 20,000 scientists, engineers, and staff serving some 1,100 corporate and government customers each year. Owning its own research facilities in the US and Switzerland, Battelle also manages or co-manages several Department of Energy-sponsored labs, including Brookhaven National Laboratory, Oak Ridge National Laboratory, Idaho National Laboratory, and Pacific Northwest National Laboratory. The family of Gordon Battelle, an early leader in the steel industry, established the institute in 1929.

While contract research and development remains the core activity of the company, Battelle is becoming more and more involved in managing laboratory operations for the government. Battelle operates Idaho National Laboratory through Battelle Energy Alliance, a partnership formed with BWX Technologies, Washington Group International, Electric Power Research Institute, and a consortium of universities including MIT, Ohio State, and the University of Idaho.

Through its Battelle Ventures subsidiary, the company also serves as a nesting ground for new businesses formed to commercialize discoveries and technologies Battelle owns or has rights to.

Originally formed to promote metallurgy and related industries, the institute — which conducts nearly $4 billion in research and development each year — has diversified into researching other areas such as agriculture, energy, software, and medicine. Among other notable milestones, Battelle's research was instrumental in developing the photocopy machine, optical digital recording (used with compact discs), and bar codes.

HISTORY

Battelle Memorial Institute was founded with a $1.5 million trust willed by Gordon Battelle, who died in 1923. Battelle was a champion of research for the advancement of humankind, and before taking his father's place as president of several Ohio steel mills, he had funded a former university professor's successful work to extract useful chemicals from mine waste. Battelle's mother, upon her death in 1925, left the institute an additional $2.1 million. The institute opened in 1929.

The institute took on perhaps the most important project in its history in 1944 when it helped an electronics company's patent lawyer, Chester Carlson, find practical uses for his invention, called xerography. Eventually Battelle developed the first photocopy machine, and in 1955 it sold the patent rights for the machine to Haloid (now Xerox) in exchange for royalties.

During WWII Battelle worked on uranium refining for the Manhattan Project, and in the early 1950s it established the world's first private nuclear research facility. The company also set up operations in Germany and Switzerland.

The tax man came knocking in 1961, questioning the tax-free status of some of Battelle's activities. The organization eventually had to pay $47 million. In 1965 Battelle developed a coin with a copper core and a copper-and-nickel-alloy cladding for the US Treasury.

As the result of a ruling that reinterpreted a clause in Gordon Battelle's will, in 1975 the institute gave $80 million to philanthropic enterprises. This ruling, coupled with the taxes that the organization was still unaccustomed to paying, forced Battelle to reexamine its strategy.

Battelle co-developed the Universal Product Code (the bar code symbol found today on nearly all consumer goods packaging) in the 1970s. The institute also landed a lucrative contract from the US Department of Energy (DOE) to manage its commercial nuclear waste isolation program.

In 1987 Battelle chose Douglas Olesen — a 20-year veteran of the institute — to replace retiring CEO Ronald Paul. The company signed an extension with the DOE in 1992 to run its Pacific Northwest Laboratory (which it has operated since 1965).

An Ohio court in 1997 approved a seven-page agreement with the institute outlining the key principles that must be followed according to Gordon Battelle's will. This agreement replaced the 1975 decree and ended more than 20 years of scrutiny by the state attorney general's office.

In 1998 the DOE contracted Brookhaven Science Associates — a partnership between the State University of New York and Battelle — to operate Brookhaven National Laboratory. That year a Battelle contract to dispose of Vietnam War-era napalm drew national attention when subcontractor Pollution Control Industries backed out of the project, citing safety concerns. Under Battelle's direction, Houston-based GNI Group took the 3.4 million gallons of napalm off the US Navy's hands.

Battelle and the University of Tennessee in 1999 won a five-year contract to operate the US government's Oak Ridge National Laboratory. That year the institute made several breakthroughs in cancer research, including FDA approval to test an inhalation delivery system for treating lung cancer.

In 2000 the company spun off OmniViz (data mining software) and Battelle Pulmonary Therapeutics (pulmonary and drug delivery technology) as wholly owned subsidiaries. In 2001

Battelle chose former Kodak EVP and chief technology officer Carl Kohrt to replace Olesen.

Battelle and several partners, including BWX Technologies, Washington Group International, and Electric Power Research Institute, won a 10-year contract in 2004 to operate Idaho National Laboratory, a facility established to focus on nuclear energy research and related technologies.

EXECUTIVES

Chairman: John B. McCoy Jr.
President and CEO: Carl F. Kohrt, age 64
EVP and CFO: I. Martin Inglis
SVP and Director, Idaho National Laboratory, Global Laboratory Operations: John J. Grossenbacher
SVP Corporate Relations: Anthony T. Hebron
SVP, General Counsel, and Secretary: Russell P. (Russ) Austin
SVP, International Partnerships: Richard C. Adams
SVP; President, Energy Technology Global Business: Donald P. McConnell
SVP; President, National Security Global Business: Stephen E. Kelly
SVP, Organizational Development: Robert W. Smith Jr.
Director Congressional Affairs for Science and Technology Programs: Paul Doucette, age 33
SVP; President, Health and Life Sciences Global: Barbara L. Kunz
SVP; Director, Oak Ridge National Laboratory, Global Laboratory Operations: Thomas E. Mason
Manager National Media Relations: Katy Delaney, age 42
Treasurer: Gwendolyn C. Von Holten
President and CEO, Bluefin Robotics: David Kelly

LOCATIONS

HQ: Battelle Memorial Institute
505 King Ave., Columbus, OH 43201
Phone: 614-424-6424   **Fax:** 614-424-5263
Web: www.battelle.org

PRODUCTS/OPERATIONS

Selected Laboratories and Research Facilities
Battelle Eastern Science and Technology Center (Aberdeen, MD)
Brookhaven National Laboratory (Upton, NY)
Human Factors Transportation Center (Seattle)
Idaho National Laboratory (Idaho Falls, ID)
Marine Science Laboratory (Sequim, WA)
Oak Ridge National Laboratory (Oak Ridge, TN)
Battelle Duxbury Operations (Duxbury, MA)
Pacific Northwest National Laboratory (Richland, WA)

Selected Inventions
Exploded-tip paintbrush (nylon brush for Wooster Brush Co., 1950)
Golf ball coatings (1965)
Heat Seat (microwaveable stadium cushion, 1990s)
Holograms (work began in the 1970s)
Insulin injection pen (for Eli Lilly, 1990s)
Oil spill outline monitor (1992)
PCB-cleaning chemical process (1992)
Photocopy machine (with Haloid, 1940s)
Plastic breakdown process (1990s)
"Sandwich" coins (copper/copper and nickel alloy cladding design for US Treasury, 1965)
SenSonic toothbrush (with Teledyne/WaterPik, 1990s)
Smart cards (cards embedded with tiny computer chips that store information, 1980s)
Universal Product Code (co-creator; bar code, 1970s)

HISTORICAL FINANCIALS

Company Type: Not-for-profit

Income Statement

FYE: September 30

	REVENUE ($ mil.)	NET INCOME ($ mil.)	NET PROFIT MARGIN	EMPLOYEES
9/07	4,181	8	0.2%	20,000
9/06	3,815	42	1.1%	20,000
9/05	3,445	30	0.9%	20,000
9/04	2,864	21	0.7%	9,034
9/03	1,317	10	0.7%	8,900
Annual Growth	33.5%	(3.0%)	—	22.4%

2007 Year-End Financials

Debt ratio: —
Return on equity: 0.9%
Cash ($ mil.): —

Current ratio: —
Long-term debt ($ mil.): —

Net Income History

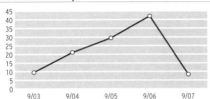

Bausch & Lomb

Eyes are the windows to profit for Bausch & Lomb. The eye care company is best known as a leading maker of contact lenses and lens care solutions (including the PureVision and ReNu brands). In addition to its lens products, Bausch & Lomb makes prescription and over-the-counter ophthalmic drugs through its pharmaceuticals division, while its surgical unit makes equipment for cataract, refractive, and other ophthalmic surgeries. Bausch & Lomb markets its products in more than 100 countries worldwide. The company was acquired by private equity firm Warburg Pincus in 2007, in a deal worth about $4.5 billion plus assumption of debt.

For a time after agreeing to the acquisition, Bausch & Lomb kept its options open, saying it planned to consider better offers if they came along. One rival offer, valued at more than $4 billion, came from competing eye care company Advanced Medical Optics, but the company later withdrew the bid.

Warburg Pincus is hoping to get a good deal with Bausch & Lomb, whose stock plummeted following a worldwide recall of a popular lens care solution, but which also has perhaps the best-known brand name in the eye care business. Not long after the takeover, former Johnson & Johnson executive Gerald Ostrov was brought in to lead the company, replacing outgoing CEO Ronald Zarrella.

Bausch & Lomb had halted sales of its ReNu with MoistureLoc lens care solution in 2006, following an outbreak of serious fungal eye infections. Expenses associated with the recall hurt the company's bottom line, as well as its stock price; Bausch & Lomb is also facing consumer lawsuits over the incident.

The company has boosted its surgery business in order to cash in on the boom in cataract and corrective eye surgeries. It acquired intraocular lens maker eyeonics, which makes products used to surgically replace cataract-affected lenses, in 2008. The year before it introduced a new cataract surgery system, called Stellaris, that requires a smaller incision (1.8 mm) than incisions used in earlier cataract surgeries.

Bausch & Lomb also continues to develop new contact lens products, including its Nike MAXSIGHT tinted lens, which is designed to improve vision during athletic activities.

Bausch & Lomb's pharmaceuticals division makes prescription and over-the-counter ophthalmic drugs, as well as vitamins for ocular health. Its vitamin product line includes products for age-related macular degeneration and dry eye; the company expanded its portfolio in 2007 with a vitamin for diabetics. The division also sells prescription anti-inflammatory/anti-infective Zylet and plans to develop more proprietary prescription drugs over the long term.

HISTORY

In 1853 German immigrant Jacob Bausch opened a small store in Rochester, New York, to sell European optical imports. Henry Lomb soon became a partner by lending Bausch $60.

Bausch & Lomb's first major breakthrough came with Bausch's invention of Vulcanite (a hard rubber) eyeglass frames. The company fitted the frames with European lenses and by 1880 had a New York City sales office. Bausch & Lomb later began making microscopes, binoculars, and telescopes.

The company incorporated in 1908 as Bausch & Lomb Optical Co. In 1912 Jacob's son, William Bausch, became one of the few to make optical-quality glass in the US. During WWI, Bausch & Lomb supplied the military with lenses for binoculars, searchlights, rifle scopes, and telescopes.

The Army Air Corps commissioned the company in 1929 to create lenses to reduce sun glare for pilots. Bausch & Lomb responded with Ray-Ban sunglasses; they were made available to the public in 1936 and went on to become a company mainstay. Bausch & Lomb went public in 1938.

The company won an Oscar in the 1950s for its Cinemascope lens; it won government contracts for lenses used in satellite and missile systems in the 1960s. Bausch & Lomb also bought such firms as Ferson Optics (1968) and Reese Optical (1969). It began concentrating on contact lenses after the FDA approved its soft lenses in 1971.

In 1981 Daniel Gill, who had helped build the soft contact lens business, became CEO. He sold the company's prescription eyeglass services and industrial instruments units and diversified into medical products and research.

Earnings soared in the 1990s with foreign expansion and acquisitions, including Steri-Oss (dental implants); the Curel and Soft Sense skin care lines from S.C. Johnson & Son; Award, a Scottish manufacturer of disposable contacts (1996); and Arnette Optic Illusions sport sunglasses (1996).

However, Gill's insistence on double-digit growth contributed to a dubious ethical climate in which some executives used questionable tactics to put more sales on the books. This led to an SEC probe (closed in 1997 with no fines or penalties assessed) and a shareholder lawsuit (settled in 1997 for $42 million). That year, the company also paid $1.7 million to settle a class action lawsuit alleging Bausch & Lomb was marketing one type of contact lens under several different product names with varying prices. Gill resigned under fire in 1995 and was replaced by outside director William Waltrip; he turned the reins over to William Carpenter in 1997.

Noncore divisions were sold (oral care and dental implant businesses in 1996; skin care line to Kao subsidiary Andrew Jergens in 1998) in a $100 million restructuring program, and 1,900 jobs were cut. The company entered the cataract and refractive surgery market, buying Chiron's vision unit in 1998 and ophthalmic diagnostic technology company Orbtek in 1999.

To focus on eye care, in 1999 the company sold its sunglasses unit to Luxottica, Amplifon S.p.A., and Charles River Laboratories to an affiliate of Donaldson, Lufkin & Jenrette, now Credit Suisse First Boston (USA). Bausch & Lomb then consolidated its manufacturing operations and cut its workforce.

Facing off with rivals Johnson & Johnson and Novartis' CIBA Vision unit over its new PureVision extended-wear lenses, the company withdrew disputed product ads after an FDA warning in 1999. Ronald Zarrella became chairman and CEO of Bausch & Lomb in 2001, after seven years with General Motors.

Bausch & Lomb was taken private by private equity firm Warburg Pincus in 2007, in a deal worth about $4 billion. A few months later, in early 2008, Zarrella retired as CEO and chairman and was replaced by former Johnson & Johnson executive Gerald Ostrov.

EXECUTIVES

Chairman Emeritus: Ronald L. Zarrella, age 58
Chairman and CEO: Gerald M. Ostrov, age 58
SVP and CFO: Efrain Rivera, age 52
SVP Customer Service and Information Technology and CIO: Alan H. Farnsworth, age 56
SVP and President, Asia Region: Dwain L. Hahs, age 56
SVP Global Operations and Engineering: Gerhard Bauer, age 52
SVP Research and Development and Chief Scientific Officer: Praveen Tyle, age 48
Corporate VP, Communications and Investor Relations: Barbara M. Kelley, age 62
Corporate VP and Chief Medical Officer: Brian Levy, age 55
Corporate VP, Global Vision Care and Commercial Operations in Canada and Latin America: Angela J. Panzarella, age 50
Corporate VP, U.S. Pharmaceutical and Surgical Businesses: Gary M. Phillips, age 42
Corporate VP, Global Surgical: Henry C. Tung, age 49
Corporate VP and Chief Technology Officer: John W. Sheets Jr.
Corporate VP; Global President, Pharmaceuticals: Fleming Ornskov, age 50
Corporate VP; President, Europe, Middle East, and Africa: John H. Brown
Corporate VP; President, Asia Pacific: David N. Edwards
Corporate VP and Chief Human Resources Officer: Paul H. Sartori
VP, Human Resources, Global Research and Development: Michelle Graham
VP; President, U.S. Vision Care Businesses: Robert J. Moore, age 51
VP and General Counsel: A. Robert D. Bailey, age 45
Corporate Secretary: Jean F. Geisel
Director Investor Relations: Daniel L. Ritz
Auditors: PricewaterhouseCoopers LLP

LOCATIONS

HQ: Bausch & Lomb Incorporated
1 Bausch & Lomb Place, Rochester, NY 14604
Phone: 585-338-6000   **Fax:** 585-338-6007
Web: www.bausch.com

PRODUCTS/OPERATIONS

Selected Products and Brands
Contact lens
  Boston GP (hard contact lenses)
  Medalist II (two-week disposable lenses)
  Nike MAXSIGHT (tinted sports lenses)
  PureVision
  SofLens59 (two-week replacement soft contact lenses)
  SofLens Multi-Focal (bifocal soft contact lenses)
  SofLens One Day (disposable soft contact lenses)
  SofLens Toric (soft contact lenses for astigmatism)
Lens care
  ReNu
Pharmaceuticals
  Alrex (anti-inflammatory)
  Liposic (dry eye)
  Lotemax (anti-inflammatory)
  Ocuvite (ocular vitamins)
  Zylet (anti-inflammatory and anti-infective)
Cataract and vitreoretinal
  Akreos (foldable intraocular lens)
  Crystalens (intraocular lens for cataract surgery)
  SofPort (foldable intraocular lens)
  Stellaris (cataract surgery system)
Refractive surgery
  Zyoptix (LASIK system)

COMPETITORS

Advanced Medical Optics
Advanced Vision Research
Akorn
Alcon
Allergan
CIBA Vision
CooperVision
Escalon Medical
Essilor International
LaserSight
Merck
Paradigm Medical
Pfizer
STAAR Surgical
Vistakon

HISTORICAL FINANCIALS
Company Type: Private

Income Statement				FYE: Last Saturday in December
	REVENUE ($ mil.)	NET INCOME ($ mil.)	NET PROFIT MARGIN	EMPLOYEES
12/07	2,500	—	—	13,000
12/06	2,292	—	—	13,000
12/05	2,354	—	—	—
12/04	2,232	—	—	—
12/03	2,020	—	—	—
Annual Growth	5.5%	—	—	0.0%

Revenue History

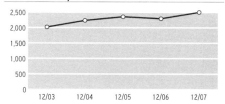

BCD Travel

When E.T. phoned home, BCD Travel would have been there to provide flight and booking information. Operating in more than 1,300 locations in 90-plus countries, BCD Travel is a leading provider of corporate travel services. Its Travel-Net Portal offers personalized travel information and services, including real-time flight status, hotel rates, weather, and maps. The company also offers travel consulting services through its Advito unit. Chairman John Fentener van Vlissingen's BCD Holdings owns BCD Travel, which was formed when WorldTravel BTI and The Travel Company were integrated in 2006.

BCD Holdings also owns Park 'N Fly (specializes in off-airport parking), TRX (transaction processing and data integration), and Airtrade (leisure travel). In 2007 BCD Travel moved its headquarters from Atlanta to the Netherlands.

After trying to come up with a way to travel together, WorldTravel BTI's co-owners, UK travel management giant Hogg Robinson and BCD Holdings, decided to go their own ways in January 2006. BCD Holdings wound up in control, and it subsequently acquired British corporate travel agency The Travel Company and integrated it with WorldTravel BTI.

EXECUTIVES

Chairman: John A. Fentener van Vlissingen, age 69
President and COO: John Snyder
CFO: Stephan Baars
EVP Products, Technology, and Supplier Relations: Dee Runyon
EVP Global Business Solutions, Sales and Marketing: Louise Miller
SVP Marketing: Melanie Garrett
VP Online Technology Solutions: Ross Atkinson
VP Human Resources, Americas: Nancy Pavey
Managing Director and SVP Growth and Emerging Markets: Greg O'Neil
Senior Director Marketing, Americas: Thad Slaton
CEO, BCD Travel and BCD N.V.: Johan G. (Joop) Drechsel, age 52
President, Asia Pacific: Michael A. (Mike) Buckman, age 55
President, Americas: Danny Hood
President, EMEA Region: Ilona de March
President, UK and Ireland: Mike Walley
President, Affiliates Program: Ted Cromwell
President, BCD Meeting and Incentives: Scott Graf

LOCATIONS

HQ: BCD Travel
Europalaan 400, 3526 KS Utrecht, The Netherlands
Phone: +31-20-562-1800   **Fax:** +31-20-548-1101
US HQ: 1055 Lenox Park Blvd., Ste. 400,
Atlanta, GA 30319
US Phone: 404-841-6600   **US Fax:** 404-814-2983
Web: www.bcdtravel.com

COMPETITORS

Ambassadors International
American Express
Carlson Wagonlit
JTB
Kuoni Travel
Ovation Travel Group
Thomas Cook
Travel Franchise Group
TUI
Tzell Travel Group

Beaulieu Group

Doing business as Beaulieu of America, Beaulieu Group is rolling into a room near you with products that primarily include berber, commercial, and indoor/outdoor (non-woven, turf) carpet. Chances are you may have had Beaulieu underfoot at some point; the company is the third-largest carpet manufacturer in the world. Major customers for its carpets include home improvement chains The Home Depot and Lowe's Companies. Consumer brands include Beaulieu, Coronet, and Hollytex; the company markets commercial products under the Bolyu (high-end), Cambridge (value), and Aqua (hospitality) brands.

Beaulieu of America operates facilities in Canada, Mexico, and the US.

Chairman and CEO Carl Bouckaert and his wife, Mieke, whose family made carpets in Europe, founded Beaulieu in 1978. The Bouckaerts diversified into tufting carpet in 1984. The company is still controlled by the Bouckaert family.

EXECUTIVES

Chairman and CEO: Carl M. Bouckaert
President and COO: Ralph Boe
CFO: Tom Weisser
EVP Sales and Marketing: Pete Ciganovich
VP Marketing: Mike McAllister
Director Human Resources: Bernadette Martin

LOCATIONS

HQ: Beaulieu Group, L.L.C.
1502 Coronet Dr., Dalton, GA 30720
Phone: 706-695-4624   **Fax:** 706-695-6237
Web: www.beaulieugroup.com

COMPETITORS

Armstrong World Industries
Dixie Group
Interface, Inc.
Milliken
Mohawk Industries
Shaw Industries

HISTORICAL FINANCIALS

Company Type: Private

Income Statement				FYE: December 31
	ESTIMATED REVENUE ($ mil.)	NET INCOME ($ mil.)	NET PROFIT MARGIN	EMPLOYEES
12/07	1,100	—	—	5,850
12/06	1,200	—	—	6,500
12/05	1,100	—	—	8,300
Annual Growth	0.0%	—	—	(16.0%)

Revenue History

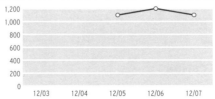

Bechtel Group

Whether the job is raising an entire city or razing a nuclear power plant, you can bet the Bechtel Group will be there to bid on the business. The engineering, construction, and project management firm is the US's #1 contractor (ahead of Fluor) per *Engineering News-Record*. It operates worldwide and has participated in such historic projects as the construction of Hoover Dam and the cleanup of the Chernobyl nuclear plant. Bechtel's Oil, Gas & Chemical business unit and Bechtel National, its government contracts group, are its leading revenue producers. The group is in its fourth generation of leadership by the Bechtel family, with chairman and CEO Riley Bechtel at the helm.

Bechtel has made a name for itself by participating in mega-projects. In addition to providing its core project management and design services, it offers such services as environmental restoration and remediation, telecommunications infrastructure (installing cable-optic networks and constructing data centers), and project financing through Bechtel Enterprises.

Bechtel National is the prime contractor for design and construction of the Hanford Vitrification Plant in Washington State, one of the DOE's most complex cleanup projects. The project's aim is to treat 53 million gallons of high-level radioactive waste stored at the Hanford site.

Among Bechtel's more traditional (perhaps notorious) infrastructure projects is its involvement in the "Big Dig," Boston's Central Artery/Tunnel project. Bechtel, in a joint venture with Parsons Brinckerhoff, has served as lead contractor on the $14.6 billion project, which has been the subject of much dispute over cost overruns and safety issues. After a death occurred in which the ceiling collapsed on a motorist, the National Transportation Safety Board said that Bechtel was partially at fault. Bechtel/Parsons Brinckerhoff paid a $450 million settlement which included a provision removing any criminal liability.

In Europe, the group has expanded its rail business by working on High Speed One, the high-speed rail line connecting London with the Channel Tunnel and the UK's first major new railroad project in a century. It is also managing the upgrade of the UK's West Coast main line and has joined a consortium to renovate part of London's 140-year-old subway. The group provides telecommunications services to US government entities through its Bechtel Federal Telecoms unit.

Bechtel has completed projects in some 50 countries on all seven continents. It was one of the companies that received contracts to help rebuild Iraq's infrastructure beginning in 2003, but it exited that country in 2006 as its contracts expired.

HISTORY

In 1898 25-year-old Warren Bechtel left his Kansas farm to grade railroads in the Oklahoma Indian territories, then followed the rails west. Settling in Oakland, California, he founded his own contracting firm. Foreseeing the importance of roads, oil, and power, he won big projects such as the Northern California Highway and the Bowman Dam. By 1925, when he incorporated his company as W.A. Bechtel & Co., it ranked as the West's largest construction company. In 1931 Bechtel helped found the consortium that built Hoover Dam.

Under the leadership of Steve Bechtel (president after his father's death in 1933), the company obtained contracts for large infrastructure projects such as the San Francisco-Oakland Bay Bridge. Noted for his friendships with influential people, including Dwight Eisenhower, Adlai Stevenson, and Saudi Arabia's King Faisal, Steve developed projects that spanned nations and industries, such as pipelines in Saudi Arabia and numerous power projects. By 1960, when Steve Bechtel Jr. took over, the company was operating on six continents.

In the next two decades, Bechtel worked on transportation projects — such as San Francisco's Bay Area Rapid Transit (BART) system and the Washington, DC, subway system — and power projects, including nuclear plants. After the 1979 Three Mile Island accident, Bechtel tried its hand at nuclear cleanup. With nuclear power no longer in vogue, it focused on other markets, such as mining in New Guinea (gold and copper, 1981-84) and China (coal, 1984). Bechtel's Jubail project in Saudi Arabia, begun in 1976, raised an entire industrial port city on the Persian Gulf.

The US recession and rising developing-world debt of the early 1980s sent Bechtel reeling. It cut its workforce by 22,000 and stemmed losses by piling up small projects.

Riley Bechtel, great-grandson of Warren, became CEO in 1990. After the 1991 Gulf War, Bechtel extinguished Kuwait's flaming oil wells and worked on the oil-spill cleanup. That decade it also worked on such projects as the Channel tunnel (Chunnel) between England and France, a new airport in Hong Kong, and pipelines in the former Soviet Union.

Bechtel was part of the consortium contracted in 1996 to build a high-speed passenger rail line between London and the Chunnel. International Generating (InterGen), Bechtel's joint venture with Pacific Gas and Electric (PG&E), was chosen to help build Mexico's first private power plant. In 1996 Bechtel bought PG&E's share of InterGen, then sold a 50% stake in InterGen to a unit of Royal Dutch Shell in early 1997.

In 1998 Bechtel joined Battelle and Electricité de France in project management of a long-term plan to stabilize the damaged reactor of the Chernobyl nuclear plant in Ukraine.

The next year Bechtel was hired to decommission the Connecticut Yankee nuclear plant. It also won contracts with Internet companies, including failed online grocer Webvan, to build a series of 26 automated grocery warehouses in the US in a deal worth nearly $1 billion. However, only four were completed before Webvan fizzled in mid-2001.

Bechtel expanded its telecommunications operations in 2001 to provide turnkey network implementation services in Europe, the Middle East, and Asia. In 2002 Bechtel was once again called on to work on the UK's rail system, taking over management of the upgrade of the West Coast main line from financially troubled Railtrack. As part of a consortium with UK facilities management giants Jarvis and Amey, Bechtel began work that year on a 30-year project to modernize part of London's aging subway system.

In 2005 Bechtel and joint venture partner Shell Oil sold InterGen, its power production joint venture, to AIG Highstar Capital for about $1.75 billion.

EXECUTIVES

Chairman Emeritus: Stephen D. (Steve) Bechtel Jr., age 83
Chairman and CEO: Riley P. Bechtel, age 54
Vice Chairman, President, and COO: Adrian Zaccaria
CFO and Director: Peter Dawson
EVP and Director: Bill Dudley
SVP and Manager, Human Resources: Mary Moreton
VP, Engineering, Procurement & Construction Functions and Manager, Sigma 6: Carl Rau
General Counsel, Secretary and Director: Judith Miller
CIO and Manager Information Systems and Technology: Geir Ramleth
President, Power Global Business Unit and Director: Tim Statton
President, Oil, Gas, and Chemicals: Jim Jackson
President, Bechtel Systems & Infrastructure, Inc.: Scott Ogilvie
EVP Strategy, Marketing, and Business Development, Bechtel Systems and Infrastructure: Craig Weaver
SVP and Principal Deputy Lab Director, Los Alamos National Laboratory: John T. Mitchell
Manager, Oil, Gas, and Chemicals: Jim Illich
Manager, Corporate Media Relations: Jonathan Marshall
Auditors: PricewaterhouseCoopers LLP

LOCATIONS

HQ: Bechtel Group, Inc.
  50 Beale St., San Francisco, CA 94105
Phone: 415-768-1234   **Fax:** 415-768-9038
Web: www.bechtel.com

Bechtel Group operates worldwide from offices in a dozen states in the US, along with international offices in Australia, Brazil, Canada, Chile, China, Egypt, France, India, Indonesia, Japan, Korea, Malaysia, Mexico, Peru, the Philippines, Qatar, Russia, Saudi Arabia, Singapore, Thailand, Turkey, the United Arab Emirates, and the UK.

PRODUCTS/OPERATIONS

Selected Services

Construction
Engineering
Financing and development
Procurement
Project management
Safety
Technology

Selected Markets

Civil infrastructure (airports, rail, highways, heavy civil)
Communications (wireless and other telecommunications)
Mining and metals
Oil, gas, and chemicals (Design and construction for chemical, petrochemical, LNG and natural gas plants, and pipelines)
Power electrical (gas, oil, coal, and nuclear power plants)
U.S. Government Services (defense, space, demilitarization, security, nuclear, and environmental restoration and remediation services)

COMPETITORS

Aker Solutions	Marelich Mechanical
AMEC	Parsons Corporation
Balfour Construction	Perini
Black & Veatch	Peter Kiewit Sons'
Bouygues	RWE
CH2M HILL	Schneider Electric
Chiyoda Corp.	Shaw Group
EIFFAGE	Siemens AG
Fluor	Skanska
Foster Wheeler	SNEF
Halliburton	Technip
HOCHTIEF	Uhde
Hyundai Engineering	URS
ITOCHU	VINCI
Jacobs Engineering	Washington Division
Kajima	Weston
Lummus Technology	

HISTORICAL FINANCIALS

Company Type: Private

Income Statement

FYE: December 31

	REVENUE ($ mil.)	NET INCOME ($ mil.)	NET PROFIT MARGIN	EMPLOYEES
12/07	27,000	—	—	42,500
12/06	20,500	—	—	40,000
12/05	18,100	—	—	40,000
12/04	17,378	—	—	40,000
12/03	16,337	—	—	44,000
Annual Growth	**13.4%**	**—**	**—**	**(0.9%)**

Revenue History

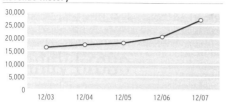

Belden & Blake

It may sound like a law firm, but Belden & Blake is in fact an energy company that obeys the laws of supply and demand in the oil and gas market. It acquires properties, explores for and develops oil and gas reserves, and gathers and markets natural gas in the Appalachian and Michigan basins. In 2007 Belden & Blake reported interests in 4,470 wells, leases on 571,141 net acres, and it owned and operated 1,620 miles of gas gathering lines. The company had estimated proved reserves of 258.1 billion cu. ft. of gas equivalent. Belden & Blake is controlled by Capital C Energy Operations, itself controlled by EnerVest Ltd.

EXECUTIVES

Chairman and CEO: Mark A. Houser, age 46
President, CFO, and Director: James M. Vanderhider, age 49
SVP, COO, and Director: Kenneth (Ken) Mariani, age 46
VP Accounting: Frederick J. Stair, age 48, $145,948 pay
VP Land and Secretary: Barry Lay, age 48
Auditors: Deloitte & Touche LLP

LOCATIONS

HQ: Belden & Blake Corporation
  1001 Fannin St., Ste. 800, Houston, TX 77002
Phone: 713-659-3500

Belden & Blake has operations in Kentucky, Michigan, New York, Ohio, Pennsylvania, and West Virginia.

PRODUCTS/OPERATIONS

2007 Sales

	$ mil.	% of total
Oil & gas	114.4	91
Gas gathering & marketing	10.3	8
Other	1.0	1
Total	**125.7**	**100**

COMPETITORS

Cabot Oil & Gas
Equitable Resources
Petroleum Development
Quicksilver Resources
Range Resources
Sharpe Resources

HISTORICAL FINANCIALS

Company Type: Private

Income Statement				FYE: December 31
	REVENUE ($ mil.)	NET INCOME ($ mil.)	NET PROFIT MARGIN	EMPLOYEES
12/07	126	(35)	—	0
12/06	159	52	32.8%	0
12/05	155	17	11.1%	134
12/04	102	13	12.5%	180
12/03	109	(2)	—	305
Annual Growth	3.6%	—	—	—

2007 Year-End Financials

Debt ratio: 284.8%
Return on equity: —
Cash ($ mil.): —

Current ratio: —
Long-term debt ($ mil.): 291

Net Income History

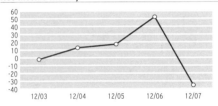

Belk, Inc.

Belk is busy bulking up. Already the nation's largest privately owned department store chain, Belk now operates about 300 stores in some 15 states, following its 2006 purchase of the Parisian chain from Saks. Previously, Belk acquired Saks' McRae's and Proffitt's divisions. Belk stores are located primarily in the Southeast and Mid-Atlantic (the Carolinas and Georgia) states and offer mid-priced brand-name and private-label apparel, shoes, jewelry, cosmetics, gifts, and home furnishings. Its stores usually anchor malls or shopping centers in small to medium-sized markets and target 35-to-54-year-old middle- and upper-income women. The Belk family runs the show and owns most of the company.

Belk has completed the re-branding of 25 of the Parisian stores acquired from Saks in October 2006 to the Belk banner. (Previously, it sold four of the acquired stores to The Bon-Ton Stores and disposed of about a dozen others.) In 2008 the company plans to open about a dozen new stores and complete expansions at another dozen locations. Belk is focusing its expansion efforts in medium-sized markets and suburbs surrounding large cities.

The retailer also launched its own fine jewelry business in 2007 under the "Belk and Co. Fine Jewelers" name and operates jewelry departments under that brand in about half of its stores.

HISTORY

William Henry Belk didn't mind being known as a cheapskate. At 26 he opened his first store, New York Racket, in 1888 in Monroe, North Carolina. He nicknamed the tiny shop "The Cheapest Store on Earth" and created the slogan "Cheap Goods Sell Themselves." In 1891 Belk convinced his brother John to give up a career as a doctor and join him in the retail business.

The new company, Belk Brothers, opened stores in North and South Carolina, often with partners who were family members or former employees, resulting in many two-family store names such as Belk-Harry and Hudson-Belk.

The Belks formed a partnership with the Leggett family (John's in-laws) in 1920. But feuding between the two families led to a split in 1927. The Leggetts agreed that the Belk family could keep a 20% share of the Leggett stores. John died the next year.

A strict no-credit policy worked in William's favor during the Depression, when he was able to buy out his more lenient competitors for rock-bottom prices. The shrewd businessman grew the chain from 29 stores in 1929 to about 220 stores by 1945, employing concepts such as a no-haggling policy and easy returns. William died in 1952.

That year one of his six children, William Henry Jr., opened a Belk-Lindsey store in Florida using a new format that featured, among other things, an Oriental design. Most of his siblings balked at the store's new look, but William Jr. opened another store in 1953 following the same format.

Two years later four of William Jr.'s siblings — John, Irwin, Tom, and Sarah — cut ties with the Florida stores and formed Belk Stores Services to organize their other stores. Angry at the rebuke, William Jr. and another brother, Henderson, sued the rest of the family, but they later dropped the lawsuit. In 1956 Belk Stores, with John at the helm, bought out 50-store rival chain Effird.

John had political ambitions and was elected mayor of Charlotte, North Carolina, in 1969, despite attempts by his brother William Jr. to foil the campaign. He remained mayor until 1977. Tom became the company's president in 1980.

Belk Stores continued to hold its own in the 1980s against larger department store chains on the prowl for acquisitions, but the company was stung by family discord and a loose ownership structure. Some relatives sold Belk stores to competitors such as Proffitt's (now Saks Inc.) and Dillard's. Irwin and his family, discouraged about the company's direction, sold their stock to John. In 1996 the Leggetts came back into the fold when Belk Stores bought out their 30-store chain.

Tom died in 1997 after complications from gall bladder surgery. His three sons, Tim, Johnny, and McKay, stepped up as co-presidents but continued to answer to their uncle John, the CEO. Also in 1997 Belk Stores closed its struggling 13 Tags off-price outlets.

A year later the firm reorganized and brought all 112 separate corporations under one company, streamlining the company's accounting (previously it had to fill out tax forms for all 112 businesses) and other operations. Soon after, Belk consolidated its 13 divisional offices into four regional units. Also in 1998 it traded several store locations with Dillard's.

In 1999 Belk formed Belk National Bank in Georgia to manage its credit card operations. The company closed four of its distribution centers in 2001, consolidating their operations into its new Blythewood, South Carolina, center.

The company opened nine new department stores in 2002 and shut down two others. In 2003 it opened eight stores and completed major renovation on four existing stores.

After serving over 50 years as the company's CEO and close to 25 years as chairman, John Belk retired in May 2004. Nephew Tim Belk was named the new chairman and CEO, and his brothers McKay and Johnny were promoted to co-presidents of the company.

In July 2005 Belk acquired the Proffitt's and McRae's department store business from Saks Inc. for about $622 million. At the time, Proffitt's/McRae's operated 47 stores in 11 southeastern states.

In January 2006, Belk sold its private-label credit card business, with about $300 million in receivables, to an affiliate of GE Consumer Finance, for about $321 million. (Concurrently, GE Consumer Finance purchased the Proffitt's and McRae's proprietary credit card account from HSBC.) In October Belk paid $285 million for Saks Inc.'s. 38-store Parisian department store chain, which has a presence in nine states in the Midwest and Southeast.

The company's acquisition of Migerobe, Inc. in June 2006 for about $19 million brought another niche for the retailer. Migerobe had leased and operated fine jewelry departments in 35 of Belk's stores. In early 2007 Belk began expanding its fine jewelry operations when its contract with Finlay Fine Jewelry Corp. expired. Belk hired a couple of Migerobe executives to lead its jewelry team.

In 2007 the company trimmed its store count by about a dozen stores and exited the Indiana and Ohio markets.

EXECUTIVES

Chairman and CEO: Thomas M. (Tim) Belk Jr., age 53, $816,784 pay
Co-President, COO, and Director: John R. (Johnny) Belk, age 49, $716,944 pay
Co-President, Chief Merchandising Officer, and Director: H. W. McKay Belk, age 51, $716,944 pay
President, Merchandising and Marketing: Mary R. Delk, age 56, $738,313 pay
President Merchandising and Marketing: Kathryn (Kathy) Bufano, age 55
EVP and CFO: Brian T. Marley, age 51, $527,692 pay
EVP, General Counsel, and Secretary: Ralph A. Pitts, age 54, $625,203 pay
EVP and General Merchandise Manager, Shoes: David Neri
EVP Human Resources: Stephen J. (Steve) Pernotto
EVP, Private Brands: Paul Thum Suden
EVP, Real Estate and Store Planning: William L. (Bill) Wilson, age 54
EVP Systems: Robert K. (Roddy) Kerr Jr.
EVP and General Merchandising Manager, Men's and Home: David B. Zant, age 51
SVP Finance and Controller: Adam M. Orvos, age 43
SVP, Sales Promotion and Marketing: Paul Michelle
Chairman, Belk, Inc. Northern Division: Bob Greiner
Chairman, Belk's Central Division: David Stovall
Auditors: KPMG LLP

LOCATIONS

HQ: Belk, Inc.
2801 W. Tyvola Rd., Charlotte, NC 28217
Phone: 704-357-1000   **Fax:** 704-357-1876
Web: www.belk.com

	No.
North Carolina	72
Georgia	46
South Carolina	37
Florida	30
Alabama	23
Tennessee	23
Virginia	20
Mississippi	16
Texas	11
Other states	25
Total	**303**

PRODUCTS/OPERATIONS

2008 Sales

	% of total
Women's apparel	37
Cosmetics, shoes & accessories	30
Men's apparel	17
Home	10
Children's apparel	6
Total	**100**

Selected Private Labels

Biltmore Estate for Your Home
Cook's Tools
Home Accents
J.Khaki
Kim Rogers
Madison Studio
Mary Jane's Farm
Meeting Street
ND (New Directions)
Pro Tour
Red Camel
Saddlebred
W.H. Belk

COMPETITORS

Dillard's	Stein Mart
J. C. Penney	Target
Kohl's	TJX Companies
Macy's	Wal-Mart
Sears	

HISTORICAL FINANCIALS

Company Type: Private

Income Statement			FYE: Saturday nearest January 31	
	REVENUE ($ mil.)	NET INCOME ($ mil.)	NET PROFIT MARGIN	EMPLOYEES
1/08	3,825	96	2.5%	26,375
1/07	3,685	182	4.9%	28,900
1/06	2,969	137	4.6%	23,200
1/05	2,447	124	5.1%	17,900
1/04	2,265	112	4.9%	17,200
Annual Growth	14.0%	(3.7%)	—	11.3%

2008 Year-End Financials

Debt ratio: 52.3%
Return on equity: 7.1%
Cash ($ mil.): 187

Current ratio: 2.59
Long-term debt ($ mil.): 726

Net Income History

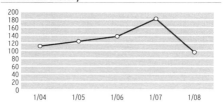

Ben E. Keith

Ben E. Keith is your bud if you like eating out and drinking brew. A leading food and beverage distributor, the company supplies restaurants, hotels, schools, and other institutional foodservice operators in six Southern states with more than 20,000 food and non-food products from its six distribution centers. Ben E. Keith is also one of the largest Anheuser-Busch distributors, delivering beer to customers in some 60 Texas counties. Founded in 1906 as Harkrider-Morrison, the company assumed its current name in 1931 in honor of Benjamin Ellington Keith, who served as the firm's president until 1959. It is controlled by Robert and Howard Hallam.

The company has been expanding its foodservice operation, opening a new distribution facility in Amarillo in 2007. The company also plans to build another facility in Houston.

EXECUTIVES

Chairman and CEO: Robert Hallam
President and COO: Howard Hallam
CFO and Treasurer: Mel Cockrell
VP and Controller: Jerry Hall
Corporate Secretary and General Counsel:
 Stewart D. (David) Greenlee
Director Human Resources: Sam Reeves
President, Ben E. Keith Beers: Kevin Bartholomew
President, Ben E. Keith Foods: Michael (Mike) Roach
EVP Marketing, Purchasing, and National Accounts, Ben E. Keith Foods: Jim Lavender
SVP Sales, Ben E. Keith Foods: Ron Boyd
Director Produce and Dairy and Sales Training, Ben E. Keith Foods: David Werner

LOCATIONS

HQ: Ben E. Keith Company
 601 E. 7th St., Fort Worth, TX 76102
Phone: 817-877-5700   **Fax:** 817-338-1701
Web: www.benekeith.com

Selected Distribution Locations

Beverage division
 Abilene, TX
 Commerce, TX
 Dallas
 Denton, TX
 Llano, TX
 Palestine, TX
 Waco, TX
Food division
 Albuquerque, NM
 Amarillo, TX
 Dallas
 Little Rock, AR
 Oklahoma City
 San Antonio

COMPETITORS

Brown Distributing
Clark National
Glazer's Wholesale Drug
Glazier Foods
MAINES
McLane Foodservice
Meadowbrook Meat Company
MillerCoors
Molson Coors
Performance Food
RNDC Texas
Silver Eagle
Southern Wine & Spirits
SYSCO
UniPro Foodservice
U.S. Foodservice

Berry Plastics

Berry Plastics Group makes bunches and bunches of plastic products. Its operating subsidiary, Berry Plastics Corporation, is a leading maker of injection-molded plastic products. The company makes containers, closures, and consumer products such as plastic drink cups and housewares. Its containers are made to hold items ranging from dairy products and chemicals to prescriptions and personal care products. Apollo Management and Graham Partners acquired Berry Plastics from Goldman Sachs and J.P. Morgan for $2.25 billion in September 2006. The company then moved into the flexible packaging industry by merging with another Apollo-controlled company, Covalence Specialty Materials.

Covalence is the former plastics and adhesives business of Tyco that was also acquired by Apollo in 2006. The two Apollo-controlled companies combined in a stock-for-stock merger transaction in April 2007, with the surviving entity retaining the Berry Plastics name. The Covalence business includes trash bags, stretch films, liners, film products, and specialty adhesives and added approximately 30 manufacturing facilities in the US, as well as over half a dozen plants in Belgium, Canada, India, and Mexico.

Shortly after the Covalence transaction was completed, Berry Plastics acquired another flexible packaging firm, Rollpak Corporation, and it sold its UK business, Berry Plastics UK Ltd., to Plasticum Group for $10 million.

Products of Berry Plastics' closures unit include overcaps for aerosol cans, as well as caps for mouthwash and detergent containers. Fast-food restaurants, convenience stores, and stadiums use the company's plastic drink cups.

Early in 2008, the company acquired Captive Holdings; Captive Plastics, the primary subsidiary, makes bottles and closures for the food and beverage industries. The acquisition expands Berry Plastics' product mix, in line with its strategy of growing through acquisitions in recent years.

The company expanded its closure operations through the 2005 acquisitions of Kerr Group and Mexican injection molding firm Euromex Plastics. A new group subsidiary, technical services provider Berry Global Services, was formed in 2007. Also in 2007 the company picked up Rollpak Corporation, which makes flexible films. Berry Plastics anticipates the acquisition will bolster its institutional can liner operations.

Apollo Management owns approximately 72% of the company; minority stakeholder Graham Partners (10%) is a middle-market private equity firm, sponsored by Graham Group, that specializes in acquiring industrial manufacturers. Prior to its Apollo-led acquisition, the holding entity for Berry Plastics Corporation was named BPC Holding Corporation.

EXECUTIVES

Chairman and CEO: Ira G. Boots, age 53, $755,072 pay
President and COO: Ralph Brent Beeler, age 54, $619,153 pay
EVP, CFO, Secretary, and Treasurer:
 James M. Kratochvil, age 51, $485,795 pay
EVP and Controller: Mark Miles
President, Rigid Open Top Division:
 Glenn Adam Unfried, $273,867 pay
President, Rigid Closed Top Division:
 Randall J. Hobson, $273,705 pay
Media Relations: Diane Tungate
Auditors: Ernst & Young LLP

LOCATIONS

HQ: Berry Plastics Corporation
101 Oakley St., Evansville, IN 47710
Phone: 812-424-2904   **Fax:** 812-424-0128
Web: www.berryplastics.com

Berry Plastics has production facilities in Belgium, Canada, India, Italy, Mexico, and the US.

PRODUCTS/OPERATIONS

Selected Products

Open top containers
  Drink cups
  Housewares
    Bowls
    Outdoor flowerpots
    Pitchers
    Plates
    Tumblers
  Containers
    Building products
    Chemicals
    Dairy
    Food products
Closed top containers
  Closures and overcaps
    Aerosol overcaps
    Child resistant
    Continuous thread
    Cups and spouts (for liquid laundry detergent)
    Dispensing
    Dropper bulb assemblies
    Fitments and plugs (for medical applications)
    Tamper evident
  Prescription vials and bottles
    Personal care
    Pharmaceuticals
    Spice containers
    Vitamins & nutritionals
  Tubes
    Plastic squeeze (for personal care products)
Flexible packaging
  Can liners
  Cloth tapes
  Custom and plastic film products
  Foil tapes
  Pipeline corrosion protection tapes
  Plastic sheeting
  Private-label trash bags
  Stretch films

COMPETITORS

AEP Industries
Alcoa
AptarGroup
Berlin Packaging
Dart Container
Dopaco
Graham Packaging
Huhtamäki
Inteplast
International Paper
Intertape Polymer
Letica
Omni Industries Holdings
Owens-Illinois
Polytainers
Portola Packaging
Rexam
Sigma Plastics
Silgan White Cap
Solo Cup
WinCup

HISTORICAL FINANCIALS

Company Type: Private

Income Statement

	REVENUE ($ mil.)	NET INCOME ($ mil.)	NET PROFIT MARGIN	EMPLOYEES
9/07*	3,055	(116)	—	12,700
12/06	1,432	(75)	—	6,600
12/05	1,170	20	1.7%	6,800
12/04	814	23	2.8%	4,550
12/03	552	13	2.4%	4,700
Annual Growth	53.4%	—	—	28.2%

FYE: September 30

*Fiscal year change

Net Income History

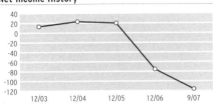

Bertucci's Corporation

New Englanders in need of a taste of Italy can turn to Bertucci's. The company owns and operates more than 90 Italian casual-dining establishments operating under the Bertucci's Brick Oven Ristorante banner. The restaurants, located in about a dozen states primarily in the Northeast, feature a wide array of Tuscan-style dishes, including pasta, chicken, and seafood dishes, as well as appetizers and desserts. It also offers premium, brick oven pizza. In addition to its flagship chain, Bertucci's operates about a half dozen Vinny T's of Boston casual dining spots in Massachusetts. Chairman Benjamin Jacobson controls the company through his Jacobson Partners holding company.

While Bertucci's is slowly expanding its chain through a modest building campaign, it is mostly focused on upgrading its existing locations with a new look designed to evoke the feel of a Tuscan trattoria. The new look has been accompanied with new menu items and marketing campaign.

The company became a multi-concept operator in 2006 when it acquired the Vinny T's of Boston chain from Buca di Beppo operator BUCA for about $6 million.

EXECUTIVES

Chairman and Treasurer: Benjamin R. (Ben) Jacobson, age 63
Vice Chairman and CEO: Stephen V. Clark, age 54, $548,077 pay
COO: Francis Christman
President, CFO, and Director: David G. Lloyd, age 44, $451,615 pay
SVP Marketing: Maria Feicht
VP and Controller: Dan E. Shea
VP Construction: Lewis P. Holt, age 54
VP and Executive Chef: Stefano Cordova
VP Information Technology: James D. (Jim) Lux, age 42
VP Purchasing and Distribution: Kevin Connelly
Director Culinary Operations: Martha Leahy
Director Employee Benefits, Relations, and Licensing: Bryan Schwanke
Auditors: Deloitte & Touche LLP

LOCATIONS

HQ: Bertucci's Corporation
155 Otis St., Northborough, MA 01532
Phone: 508-351-2500   **Fax:** 508-393-8046
Web: www.bertuccis.com

COMPETITORS

Applebee's
Back Bay Restaurant
BRAVO! Development
Brinker
BUCA
California Pizza Kitchen
Carino's Italian Grill
Carlson Restaurants

Cheesecake Factory
Darden
O'Charley's
OSI Restaurant Partners
P.F. Chang's
Ruby Tuesday
Uno Restaurants

HISTORICAL FINANCIALS

Company Type: Private

Income Statement

	REVENUE ($ mil.)	NET INCOME ($ mil.)	NET PROFIT MARGIN	EMPLOYEES
12/06	226	—	—	7,645
12/05	205	—	—	6,546
12/04	200	—	—	6,307
12/03	186	—	—	6,275
12/02	162	—	—	6,060
Annual Growth	8.7%	—	—	6.0%

FYE: Wednesday nearest December 31

Revenue History

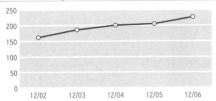

Berwind Corporation

It's an ill wind indeed that blows Berwind no good. Founded in 1886 to mine Appalachian coal, Berwind began leasing its mining operations in 1962 to fund investments in new ventures. Berwind Corporation gives autonomy to the management teams of its portfolio companies while adding investment fuel to their financial fires. The company's portfolio includes Elmer's Products, maker of Elmer's Glue, Krazy Glue, and other products; specialty chemicals companies CRC and Colorcon; and promotional products firm National Pen. The Berwind family owns Berwind Corporation.

Berwind Property Group (or BPG Properties) owns more than 30 million sq. ft. of residential, multi-family, student, retail, hotel, and industrial properties. In 2008 BPG bought Boston Capital Real Estate Investment Trust, which owns around a dozen apartment buildings totalling 2.7 million sq. ft.

Berwind's venture capital arm, Inflection Point Ventures (IPV), funds early-stage telecommunications and information technology concerns. Another unit, Berwind Natural Resources, still holds coal, natural gas, and timber rights in Kentucky, Pennsylvania, Virginia, and West Virginia.

The company takes full ownership of its investment companies. It looks for target companies that show steady growth, international operations, and companies with high growth margins.

EXECUTIVES

President and CEO: Michael McClelland
CFO: Van Billet, age 53
CEO, Consumer Group; CEO, Elmer's Products:
Timothy M. (Tim) Callahan

LOCATIONS

HQ: Berwind Corporation
   3000 Centre Sq. West, 1500 Market St.,
   Philadelphia, PA 19102
Phone: 215-563-2800   **Fax:** 215-575-2314
Web: www.berwind.com

PRODUCTS/OPERATIONS

Selected Operations

Berwind Natural Resources (land and resource
   management)
Colorcon (specialty chemical products)
CRC Industries (specialty chemical products)
Elmer's Products (consumer adhesives)
Inflection Point Ventures (venture capital)
National Pen Co. (promotional products)

COMPETITORS

Apollo Advisors
Berkshire Income Realty
Bruckmann, Rosser, Sherrill & Co.
Jordan Company
Vulcan

HISTORICAL FINANCIALS

Company Type: Holding company

Income Statement

	ESTIMATED REVENUE ($ mil.)	NET INCOME ($ mil.)	NET PROFIT MARGIN	EMPLOYEES
12/07	1,470	—	—	3,565
12/06	1,710	—	—	3,500
12/05	1,629	—	—	3,500
Annual Growth	(5.0%)	—	—	0.9%

FYE: December 31

Revenue History

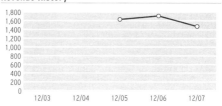

Best Western

Western hospitality has really spread. Begun in 1946 by hotelier M. K. Guertin and named for its California origins, Best Western has more than 4,000 independently owned and operated hotels (including 2,200-plus in the US, Canada, and the Caribbean), making it the world's largest hotel brand (by number of rooms). Hotels sport its flag in about 80 countries; Australia and the UK have the most outside the US. Best Western is organized as a not-for-profit membership association, with most of its sales coming from monthly fees and annual dues.

The company is expanding its global presence, especially in Asia, where the chain plans to have more than 200 hotels by 2010. In addition, through a licensing agreement in India, Best Western also expects to add 100 new hotels per year there through the next decade.

EXECUTIVES

Chairman: Charles (Charlie) Helm
Vice Chairman: Roman J. Jaworowicz
President and CEO: David T. Kong
CFO: Mark Straszynski
SVP Distribution and CIO: Scott Gibson
SVP Brand Quality and Member Services: Ric Leutwyler
SVP Marketing and Sales: Dorothy Dowling
VP and General Counsel: Kris Schloemer
VP International Operations: Suzi Yoder MacDonald
VP Human Resources: Barbara Bras
VP Worldwide Sales: Kevin Kluts
VP Marketing: Renee Ryan
Director External Communications: David Trumble
Secretary and Treasurer: Dave Francis
Auditors: Mukai, Greenlee & Company, P.C.

LOCATIONS

HQ: Best Western International, Inc.
   6201 N. 24th Pkwy., Phoenix, AZ 85016
Phone: 602-957-4200   **Fax:** 602-957-5641
Web: www.bestwestern.com

COMPETITORS

Accor
Choice Hotels
HVM
InterContinental Hotels
La Quinta
Marriott
Scandic Hotels
ShoLodge
Sunburst Hospitality
Wyndham Worldwide

HISTORICAL FINANCIALS

Company Type: Association

Income Statement

	REVENUE ($ mil.)	NET INCOME ($ mil.)	NET PROFIT MARGIN	EMPLOYEES
11/07	221	(3)	—	1,134
11/06	206	4	2.0%	1,076
11/05	199	(2)	—	1,066
11/04	190	(4)	—	1,200
11/03	179	4	2.2%	1,200
Annual Growth	5.5%	—	—	(1.4%)

FYE: November 30

Net Income History

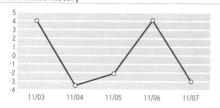

Big Y Foods

Why call it Big Y? Big Y Foods began as a 900-sq.-ft. grocery at a Y intersection in Chicopee, Massachusetts. It now operates about 55 supermarkets throughout Massachusetts and Connecticut. Most of its stores are Big Y World Class Markets, offering specialty areas such as bakeries and floral shops, as well as banking. The rest consist of Big Y Supermarkets and a single gourmet food and liquor store called Table & Vine in Springfield, Massachusetts. Some Big Y stores provide child care, dry cleaning, photo processing, and even propane sales, and their delis and Food Courts offer to-go foods. Big Y is owned and run by the D'Amour family and is one of New England's largest independent supermarket chains.

Jumping on the organic and natural foods bandwagon, in 2006 Big Y created a new store format called Fresh Acres. About half the size of a typical Big Y World Class Market, the 30,000-sq.-ft. store offers fresh, natural, and easy-to-prepare foods.

EXECUTIVES

Chairman and CEO: Donald H. D'Amour
President and COO: Charles L. D'Amour
CFO: William (Bill) White
SVP Merchandising: Daniel (Dan) Lescoe
VP Sales: Phillip J. (Phill) Schneider
VP Corporate Communications:
   Claire H. D'Amour-Daley
VP Employee Services: Jack Henry
VP Information Systems: John N. Sarno
VP Marketing and Corporate Strategies:
   Antonio F. Gomes
VP Fresh Foods: Michael P. D'Amour
Michael S. Gold
VP Store Operations: William P. Hogan
Auditors: Deloitte & Touche LLP

LOCATIONS

HQ: Big Y Foods, Inc.
   2145 Roosevelt Ave., Springfield, MA 01102
Phone: 413-784-0600
Web: www.bigy.com

2008 Stores

	No.
Massachusetts	30
Connecticut	27
Total	**57**

Selected Products and Services

Babysitting
Bakery
Banking
Bottle redemption
Coin sorting and counting
Deli
Dry cleaning
Florist
General merchandise
Gourmet food
Knife sharpening
Liquor
Lottery tickets
Meat
Money orders
Phone cards
Photo processing
Postage stamps
Poultry
Produce
Propane
Seafood
Sushi
Western Union
Wine

COMPETITORS

Costco Wholesale
Cumberland Farms
DeMoulas Super Markets
Golub
Hannaford Bros.

Shaw's
Stop & Shop
SUPERVALU
Target
Wal-Mart

Bill & Melinda Gates Foundation

You don't have to be one of the world's richest men to make a difference with your charitable gifts — but it helps. Established by the chairman of Microsoft and his wife, the Bill & Melinda Gates Foundation works in developing countries to improve health and reduce poverty and in the US to support education and libraries nationwide and children and families in the Pacific Northwest. With an endowment of about $38 billion, the foundation is the largest in the US, and it's getting bigger. Investor Warren Buffett has announced plans to give the Bill & Melinda Gates Foundation about $30 billion worth of Berkshire Hathaway stock.

The Buffett gift will be spread over a number of years. The $30 billion figure represents the value of the stock when the gift was announced in June 2006, so the actual amount may be different — especially if the value of Berkshire Hathaway stock continues to increase as it has under Buffett's stewardship. Buffett's 2006 and 2007 gifts to the Bill & Melinda Gates Foundation were worth about $1.6 billion and $1.7 billion, respectively.

With the Buffett giving program comes a challenge, however: Starting in 2009, the foundation will have to annually give away 100% of Buffett's contribution from the previous year. Not a bad problem to have, but the foundation is working to expand its staff and revamp its processes in order to take advantage of the new

opportunity. Global economic development efforts are expected to gain additional support.

As part of its response to the Buffett gift, the foundation restructured itself in November 2006. Its assets were transferred to the Bill & Melinda Gates Foundation Trust, which will receive future contributions of Berkshire Hathaway stock and will be overseen by the Gateses as trustees. Money will pass from the trust to the Bill & Melinda Gates Foundation, which will make grants. Buffett joined the Gateses as a trustee of the Bill & Melinda Gates Foundation — but not of the asset trust, thus separating him from decisions about the disposition of the trust's Berkshire Hathaway shares.

At the same time, the foundation announced that it would give away all of its assets within 50 years of the deaths of Buffett, then 76, Bill Gates, then 51, and Melinda Gates, then 42. Gates previously had said he would like to give away most of his fortune while he is still living, and he is scaling back his duties at Microsoft in order to spend more time at the foundation.

The Gates Foundation is co-funding a study called *The Joys and Dilemmas of Wealth,* scheduled for release in the fall of 2008. The study will survey American households worth $25 million or more with the goal of encouraging charitable giving by the rich.

Jeff Raikes, a 27-year Microsoft veteran, succeeded Patty Stonesifer as CEO of the Bill & Melinda Gates Foundation in September 2008. Raikes will oversee rapid expansion of the foundation, which is expected to double in size to about 1,000 employees.

HISTORY

Bill Gates created the William H. Gates Foundation in 1994 with $106 million. During the next four years, he added about $2 billion to the charity. He appointed his father the head of the foundation, which at first was housed in Bill Gates Sr.'s basement. In 1997 Gates established the Gates Learning Foundation (originally called the Gates Library Foundation), a philanthropic effort to improve library systems. It was Gates' goal to improve technology and Internet access at libraries, which some critics saw as a way for him to plant Microsoft software at libraries nationwide. Patty Stonesifer, a former executive at Microsoft, ran the organization from an office above a pizza parlor.

Bill and his wife, Melinda French Gates, contributed some $16 billion to the foundation in 1999. In 2000 Gates decided to merge his two charity programs into one entity, the Bill & Melinda Gates Foundation, to be run by the elder Gates and Stonesifer.

In early 2000 Gates made another $5 billion gift of stock to the foundation. Also that year the foundation pledged $10 million toward construction of an underground visitors center at Capitol Hill in Washington, DC. The Bill & Melinda Gates Foundation donated another $10 million in 2001 to be awarded over three years to the Hope for African Children Initiative, to help African children affected by AIDS. In 2002 the Bill & Melinda Gates Foundation pledged more than $100 million over 10 years to reduce the spread of AIDS in India. The foundation awarded a $70 million grant to the departments of genome sciences and bioengineering at the University of Washington in 2003.

The Bill & Melinda Gates Foundation donated $750 million to be given over 10 years to the Global Alliance for Vaccines & Immunization in

2005. This follows a $750 million gift to the organization when it was established in 2000.

In 2006 investor Warren Buffett announced plans to give the Bill & Melinda Gates Foundation about $30 billion over a number of years.

In September 2008 Patty Stonesifer, who had served as CEO of the foundation since its inception, was succeeded by Jeff Raikes, a 27-year Microsoft veteran.

EXECUTIVES

Co-Chair: William H. (Bill) Gates III, age 52
Co-Chair: Melinda F. Gates, age 43
Co-Chair: William H. (Bill Sr.) Gates Sr., age 82
CEO: Jeffrey S. (Jeff) Raikes, age 50
COO: Cheryl M. Scott, age 56
CFO: Alexander S. Friedman
President, Global Development Program:
Sylvia Matthews Burwell, age 42
President, Global Health Program:
Tadataka (Tachi) Yamada, age 62
President, U.S. Program: Allan C. Golston
Chief Administrative Officer: Martha Choe
CIO: David Fennell
General Counsel and Secretary: Connie Collingsworth
Managing Director Public Policy: Geoffrey Lamb
Director Global Health Policy and Advocacy, Global Health Program: Joe Cerrell
Director Advocacy and Policy, U.S. Program:
Greg Shaw
Director Research and Evaluation: David J. Ferrero
Director Avahan India AIDS Initiative, Global Health Program: Ashok Alexander
Director Education, U.S. Program: Jim Shelton
Director Financial Services for the Poor, Global Development Program: Bob Christen
Director Operations, U.S. Program: Diane de Ryss
Chief Communications Officer: Heidi Sinclair
Auditors: KPMG LLP

LOCATIONS

HQ: Bill & Melinda Gates Foundation
1551 Eastlake Ave. East, Seattle, WA 98102
Phone: 206-709-3100 **Fax:** 206-709-3180
Web: www.gatesfoundation.org

PRODUCTS/OPERATIONS

2007 Revenue

	$ mil.	% of total
Net investment income	4,953.0	61
Contributions	3,129.3	39
Total	**8,082.3**	**100**

Selected Beneficiaries

Alliance for Cervical Cancer Prevention ($3.9 million over two years)
Gay City Health Project ($30,000 over three years)
Global Alliance for Vaccines & Immunization ($1.5 billion over 15 years)
Global Health Council ($4.8 million over three years)
Helen Keller International ($5 million over five years)
International Planned Parenthood Federation ($8.8 million over five years)
International Tuberculosis Foundation ($1.9 million over five years)
International Vaccine Institute ($40 million over five years)
Library and Information Commission ($4.2 million over one year)
National Institute of Child Health and Human Development ($15 million over five years)
Oxfam ($2.9 million over four years)
Pacific Institute for Women's Health ($1 million over three years)
Population Council ($4 million over two years)
Portland Children's Museum ($600,000 over three years)
United Negro College Fund ($1 billion over 20 years)
US Fund for UNICEF ($15 million over five years)

HISTORICAL FINANCIALS
Company Type: Foundation

Income Statement

	REVENUE ($ mil.)	NET INCOME ($ mil.)	NET PROFIT MARGIN	EMPLOYEES
12/07	8,082	—	—	626
12/06	5,704	—	—	457
12/05	1,864	—	—	270
12/04	3,344	—	—	234
12/03	4,010	—	—	184
Annual Growth	19.2%	—	—	35.8%

Revenue History

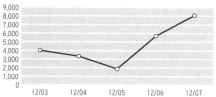

BI-LO, LLC

To buy low, try BI-LO. BI-LO operates about 225 supermarkets in North and South Carolina, Georgia, and Tennessee. Many of BI-LO's stores house pharmacies and some boast Starbucks Café kiosks. Brands include national names, the BI-LO private-label banner, Finast health and beauty products, Southern Hearth Bakery items, and Vince's deli meats and meals-to-go. The firm was founded in 1961 by Frank Outlaw. Dutch grocery giant Royal Ahold, which entered the US market with its 1977 buy of BI-LO, sold the regional grocery chain and its smaller sister supermarket chain Bruno's Supermarkets to Dallas-based investment firm Lone Star Funds in 2005.

That year BI-LO Holdings (the parent company of BI-LO, LLC and Bruno's Supermarkets) signed a third-party distribution agreement with grocery distributor C&S Wholesale Grocers. Under the agreement, BI-LO and Bruno's sold their warehouses located in Alabama, South Carolina, and Tennessee to New Hampshire-based C&S, which became the grocery distributor to both chains.

Also in 2005 BI-LO Holding sold or closed about 115 BI-LO and Bruno's stores in the southeastern US to focus on its strongest markets.

Lone Star, after separating the two business so each chain could better focus on itself, announced in 2007 that both chains were for sale. However, turmoil in the credit markets caused Lone Star to take BI-LO off the market later in the year.

The regional grocery chain opened its first Super BI-LO store in North Carolina in March 2008. The "super" stores boast expanded products selections, including plenty of organic and natural foods, and measure about 58,000 square feet. The grocer has opened about 15 Super BI-LO stores since launching the format in South Carolina in 2005. Several traditional BI-LO stores

are slated to be converted to the Super BI-LO format in 2008.

Brian Hotarek, a former CFO at Ahold USA and Stop & Shop, was named president and CEO of the company in January 2007. He succeeded Dean Cohagan, who retired. Cohagan had served as BI-LO CEO since 2001.

EXECUTIVES

President and CEO: Brian W. Hotarek, age 62
EVP and CFO: Brian P. Carney, age 47
EVP Marketing and Merchandising: Tye Anthony
EVP Store Operations: John Symons
SVP Finance and Treasurer: Ken Jones
VP Brand Marketing and Sales Planning: John Gianakas
VP Information Management: Carol deWitt
VP Operations Support: Dwayne Goodwin
VP Sales Development: Mark Jerosko
VP Strategic Planning and Analysis: John Croft
VP Legal and General Counsel: Dwane Bryant
VP Human Resources and Diversity: Ken Peterson
Executive Director Charities: Carol Browning
Director Corporate Communications: Joyce Smart
Director Sales Planning and Corporate Brands: Mike Mannion
Auditors: Deloitte Accountants

LOCATIONS

HQ: BI-LO, LLC
   208 BI-LO Blvd., Greenville, SC 29607
Phone: 864-213-2500   **Fax:** 864-234-6999
Web: www.bi-lo.com

PRODUCTS/OPERATIONS

Selected Brand Names
BI-LO
Finast Gold Star Meats
Southern Home
Top Care health and beauty products
Walter's Produce

COMPETITORS

BJ's Wholesale Club	Piggly Wiggly Carolina
Costco Wholesale	Publix
CVS Caremark	Rite Aid
Food Lion	Ruddick
Harris Teeter	Walgreen
Ingles Markets	Wal-Mart
Kroger	Winn-Dixie
K-VA-T Food Stores	

HISTORICAL FINANCIALS
Company Type: Private

Income Statement

	REVENUE ($ mil.)	NET INCOME ($ mil.)	NET PROFIT MARGIN	EMPLOYEES
12/07	2,620	—	—	17,000
12/06	4,750	—	—	23,000
12/05	4,264	—	—	23,500
Annual Growth	(21.6%)	—	—	(14.9%)

Revenue History

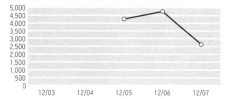

Biomet, Inc.

When the leg bone and the knee bone don't connect so well anymore, Biomet may have a solution. Orthopedic specialists use the medical devices made by Biomet, whose wares include reconstructive products (hips, knees, and shoulders), fixation devices (bone screws and pins), orthopedic support devices, dental implants, and operating-room supplies. Through its EBI subsidiary, the firm also sells electrical bone-growth stimulators and external devices, which are attached to bone and protrude from the skin. Subsidiary Biomet Microfixation markets implants and bone substitute material for craniomaxillofacial surgery. In 2007 Biomet was acquired by a group of private equity firms for more than $11 billion.

The private equity consortium includes Blackstone Group, Goldman Sachs Capital Partners, Kohlberg Kravis Roberts, Texas Pacific Group, and former CEO Dane Miller. UK medical device company Smith & Nephew had also made a bid but was rejected in favor of the slightly lower private equity offer.

Biomet had been on the auction block for more than a year. It had hired Morgan Stanley in 2006 to help it consider its options, shortly after long-time CEO Miller abruptly resigned amid disappointing earnings results.

In the year that followed, Biomet also revealed that it had backdated some stock options given to executives, a scandal that predictably resulted in some top-level resignations, shareholder lawsuits, and a restatement of earnings. Department of Justice officials also were investigating Biomet (along with several rivals) over payments to orthopedic surgeons who use the company's hip and knee replacements; the company settled with the DOJ in 2007, agreeing to pay about $27 million in fines.

Reconstructive devices account for some 70% of Biomet's sales, and the US is its biggest market (about 60% of sales); Europe accounts for more than 25%. The company distributes its products in some 70 countries worldwide, but it is looking to expand its geographical presence, particularly in Asia and Latin America.

The acquisition of Interpore, a maker of orthopedic biomaterials and specialty fixation devices, expanded the company's product offering within the reconstructive surgery market. But Biomet had difficulty integrating the acquisition, which became part of EBI, and its poor performance hurt the company's earnings overall. Strong sales of its core reconstructive implants (such as knee replacements) have buoyed the company, however.

HISTORY

In 1977 Niles Noblitt, Dane Miller, and two others established Biomet to design orthopedic products, a field then dominated by divisions of large pharmaceutical companies; the founders hoped that Biomet (the name links "biological" and "metal") could — because of its focus and small size — grow unhindered by bureaucratic red tape. The company's discovery that contractors making Biomet-designed products were selling them to competitors inspired the move into manufacturing.

Biomet went public in 1982. The company acquired Orthopedic Equipment in 1985, gaining access to the UK market. In 1988 it engineered the hostile takeover of Electro-Biology. Biomet acquired Effner GmbH (orthopedic devices, Germany) in 1991 and Walter Lorenz Surgical Instruments in 1992. Two years later the company acquired Kirschner Medical, a producer of joint-replacement products for hips, knees, and shoulders. Biomet founded Biomet Europe in 1995 to strengthen and centralize its international marketing effort. In 1996 the company was hit with a $36 million judgment in a patent dispute. The award was vacated three years later.

In 1998 the company formed a 50/50 joint venture with Merck KGaA to distribute orthopedic products in Europe. The deal gave Biomet its first crack at licensing both Merck's existing biomaterial orthopedic products (outside Europe) and future products developed by the joint venture.

The company continued moving into genetically engineered products with a 1999 agreement to distribute tissue-repair and -regeneration products developed by Selective Genetics. It also bought Implant Innovatives (later renamed 3i), which sells dental reconstructive implants. Also that year Biomet lost a breach of contract suit (relating to a distribution agreement) brought by Orthofix, which won a $49 million judgment.

In 2000 Biomet introduced a host of new products, including the SpineLink Cervical System, the Opti-rom Elbow Fixator, and the RC Needle Kit. The company continued to push out new products the following year.

After nearly 30 years at Biomet, Dane Miller retired as president and CEO in March 2006. Daniel P. Hann served in the top spot on an interim basis until Jeffrey Binder was appointed president and CEO of Biomet early the following year.

EXECUTIVES

Chairman: Niles L. Noblitt, age 55, $614,100 pay
President, CEO, and Director: Jeffrey R. Binder, age 45
SVP and CFO: Daniel P. (Dan) Florin, age 44
SVP; President of Biomet 3i, Inc. (formerly Implant Innovations, Inc.): Steven F. Schiess, age 48
SVP; President Biomet SBU Operations: Gregory W. Sasso, age 46
SVP Biomet Orthopedics Commercial Operations: William C. Kolter, age 49
SVP; President, Biomet Trauma and Biomet Spine: Glen A. Kashuba, age 44
SVP, General Counsel, and Secretary: Bradley J. Tandy, age 49
SVP Operations: Richard J. Borror Jr., age 49
SVP Human Resources: Darlene K. Whaley, age 50
President, International Operations: Roger P. van Broeck, age 58
President, Biomet Sports Medicine: David A. Nolan Jr.
President, Biomet Biologics: Stuart G. Kleopfer
President, Walter Lorenz Surgical: David Josza
President International: Wilber C. Boren
President Orthopedics: Jon Serbousek, age 47
Director, Corporate Communications: Barbara Goslee
Auditors: Ernst & Young LLP

LOCATIONS

HQ: Biomet, Inc.
56 E. Bell Dr., Warsaw, IN 46582
Phone: 574-267-6639   **Fax:** 574-267-8137
Web: www.biomet.com

PRODUCTS/OPERATIONS

Selected Product Lines

Reconstructive products
  Bone cement
  Dental reconstructive implants
  Joint replacement systems
Fixation products
  Craniomaxillofacial fixation systems
  Electrical stimulation devices (non-spinal)

External fixation devices
Internal fixation devices (nails, plates, screw, and pins)
Spinal products
  Orthobiologics (allograft)
  Spinal fusion stimulation systems
  Spinal fixation products
Other
  Arthroscopy products
  Operating room supplies
  Orthopedic soft goods and braces

Selected Subsidiaries

Biomet 3i, Inc. (dental reconstructive implants)
Biomet Biologics, Inc. (orthobiologics)
Biomet Europe B.V. (Netherlands, European headquarters)
Biomet Microfixation, Inc. (craniomaxillofacial fixation systems)
Biomet Orthopedics, Inc. (joint replacements)
Biomet Sports Medicine, Inc. (arthroscopy products)
EBI, L.P. (dba Biomet Trauma and Biomet Spine, external fixation and electrical stimulation devices)

COMPETITORS

Aesculap, Inc. USA
Arthrex
ArthroCare
Astra Tech (Sweden)
Codman & Shurtleff
CONMED Corporation
DePuy
DJO
Ethicon
Exactech
Medtronic Sofamor Danek
Nobel Biocare
Orthofix
OrthoLogic
Smith & Nephew
Straumann
Stryker
Synthes
Wright Medical Group
Zimmer Holdings

HISTORICAL FINANCIALS

Company Type: Private

Income Statement

FYE: May 31

	REVENUE ($ mil.)	NET INCOME ($ mil.)	NET PROFIT MARGIN	EMPLOYEES
5/08	2,135	(964)	—	7,220
5/07	2,107	336	15.9%	6,506
5/06	2,026	406	20.0%	4,075
5/05	1,880	352	18.7%	6,100
5/04	1,615	326	20.2%	—
Annual Growth	7.2%	—	—	5.8%

2008 Year-End Financials

Debt ratio: 128.7%
Return on equity: —
Cash ($ mil.): —
Current ratio: —
Long-term debt ($ mil.): 6,225

Net Income History

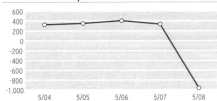

Birds Eye Foods

Whether from a bird's eye or with eyes on the bottom line, the view is excellent at Birds Eye Foods. As one of the top US makers of frozen vegetables, the company's namesake brand is the market leader, offering some 500 different products. The company also makes pie fillings (Comstock, Wilderness), chili and chili ingredients (Brooks, Nalley), salad dressings (Bernstein's, Nalley), and salty snacks (Husman's, Snyder of Berlin, Tim's). In addition to the retail food sector, the company also supplies foodservice and industrial-market customers. Birds Eye is owned by investment firm Vestar Capital Partners.

Increasing the number of offerings in its value-added line of products, the company introduced Steamfresh, complete microwaveable meals, with single-serve portions introduced in 2006 and Meals for Two in 2007.

Headquartered in Rochester, New York, Birds Eye has operations in Minnesota, Michigan, Pennsylvania, Washington, and Wisconsin. The company's products are available in all 50 US states.

EXECUTIVES

Chairman, President, and CEO: Neil Harrison, age 55
EVP Business Optimization, CFO, and Secretary: Earl L. Powers, age 62, $505,444 pay
EVP Specialty Food Group: Carl W. Caughran, $436,579 pay
SVP Frozen Sales: Robert G. Montgomery, $393,880 pay
SVP Administration: Lois Warlick-Jarvie
SVP Frozen Supply Chain: Ron Trine
VP and Controller: Linda Nelson
VP Quality Systems Management: Kurt Buckman
General Counsel and Assistant Secretary: Elizabeth J. Robinson
Auditors: Deloitte & Touche LLP

LOCATIONS

HQ: Birds Eye Foods, Inc.
90 Linden Oaks, Rochester, NY 14625
Phone: 585-383-1850   **Fax:** 585-385-2857
Web: www.birdseyefoods.com

PRODUCTS/OPERATIONS

Selected Brands

Bernstein's Salad Dressings
Birds Eye
Birds Eye Fresh
Birds Eye Steamfresh
Birds Eye Voila!
Brooks
Comstock
C&W
Freshlike
Greenwood Beets
Husman's
McKenzie's
Nalley
Riviera
Snyder of Berlin
Tim's Cascade Snacks
Wilderness

Allens
Bush Brothers
Campbell Soup
ConAgra
Del Monte Foods
Dole Food
Eden Foods
Frito-Lay
General Mills
Gorton's
Graceland Fruit
Hain Celestial
Hanover Foods
Heinz
J & J Snack Foods
Kellogg U.S. Snacks
Kettle Foods
Kraft Foods
Lakeside Foods
Lance Snacks
National Frozen Foods
Nestlé USA
NORPAC
Old Dutch Foods
Pacific Coast Producers
Pictsweet
Pinnacle Foods
San Antonio Frozen Vegetables
Seabrook Brothers
Seneca Foods
Small Planet Foods
Smith Frozen Foods
Symons Frozen Foods
Twin City Foods
Unilever
United Natural
Victoria Packing
Willow Wind Organic Farms

BJC HealthCare

BJC HealthCare operates about a dozen hospitals — including Barnes-Jewish Hospital, Boone Hospital Center, and Christian Hospital — and some 100 primary care and specialty health facilities in and around St. Louis. BJC HealthCare's facilities all together have more than 3,500 beds. Specialized services include hospice and home health care, behavioral health, and outpatient services, along with long-term care at a handful of nursing facilities. The company's BarnesCare and OccuMed subsidiaries offer occupational health care and workers' compensation services. BJC HealthCare has several hospitals affiliated with Washington University School of Medicine.

In addition to its general acute care hospitals, BJC HealthCare operates St. Louis Children's Hospital, a leader in pediatric care, and the Rehabilitation Institute of St. Louis, which provides inpatient and outpatient rehab services in partnership with HealthSouth. BJC also manages Clay County Hospital, a 22-bed Critical Access facility in rural southern Illinois.

After a long, contentious battle with rival SSM Health Care System, the hospital operator won approval in 2004 to build a new hospital in O'Fallon, one of Missouri's fastest-growing cities. Called Progress West HealthCare Center, the new hospital opened early in 2007.

The company has also expanded several of its hospital facilities in recent years, including St. Louis Children's Hospital, Alton Memorial Hospital, and Missouri Baptist Medical Center. BJC

HealthCare is also investing in medical research facilities.

BJC HealthCare is the product of the June 1993 merger of Barnes-Jewish and Christian Health Services.

EXECUTIVES

Chairman: Paul McKee Jr.
President and CEO: Steven H. Lipstein
SVP and Interim President Jefferson Memorial Hospital: Ronald G. Evens
SVP and CFO: Kevin V. Roberts
SVP and General Counsel: Michael A. (Mike) DeHaven
Senior Executive Officer; President, St. Louis Children's Hospital: Lee F. Fetter
VP and CIO: David A. Weiss
VP Chief Learning Officer: JoAnn Shaw
VP Capital Asset Management: Robert W. Cannon
VP Corporate and Public Communications: June McAllister Fowler
VP Center for Health Care Quality and Effectiveness: W. Claiborne Dunagan
VP and Chief Human Resources Officer: Carlos Perea
Group President: Sandra A. Van Trease, age 47
President Christian Hospital: Ronald B. (Ron) McMullen
President Barnes-Jewish Hospital: Andrew Ziskind
President Barnes-Jewish St. Peters Hospital: C. David Ross
President Barnes-Jewish West County Hospital: Pat Mohrman
President Missouri Baptist Hospital-Sullivan: Tony L. Schwarm
President Missouri Baptist Medical Center: Joan R. Magruder
President Boone Hospital Center: Daniel J. Rothery
President Progress West HealthCare Center: John D. Antes
President Parkland Health Center: Richard L. Conklin
President Alton Memorial Hospital: Dave Braasch
President BJC Medical Group: Jack Davidson

LOCATIONS

HQ: BJC HealthCare
  4444 Forest Park Ave., St. Louis, MO 63108
Phone: 314-286-2000   **Fax:** 314-286-2060
Web: www.bjc.org

Selected Facilities
Illinois
  Alton Memorial Hospital (Alton)
  Eunice C. Smith Home (Alton)
  Clay County Hospital (Flora)
Missouri
  Barnes-Jewish Extended Care (St. Louis)
  Barnes-Jewish Hospital (St. Louis)
  Barnes-Jewish St. Peters Hospital (St. Peters)
  Barnes-Jewish West County Hospital (St. Louis)
  Boone Hospital Center (Columbia)
  Christian Hospital (St. Louis)
  Missouri Baptist Hospital-Sullivan
  Missouri Baptist Medical Center (St. Louis)
  Parkland Health Center (Farmington)
  Progress West HealthCare Center (O'Fallon)
  Rehabilitation Institute of St. Louis
  St. Louis Children's Hospital
  Village North Retirement Community (Florissant)

COMPETITORS

Alexian Brothers Health System
Ascension Health
Carle Clinic
Catholic Health Initiatives
CHRISTUS Health
HCA
Saint Luke's Health System
Sisters of Mercy Health System
SSM Health Care
St. Anthony's Medical Center
Tenet Healthcare

Black & Veatch

Black & Veatch provides the ABCs of construction, engineering, and consulting. The international group is one of the largest private companies in the US. Targeting infrastructure development for the energy, water, services, and telecommunications markets, the group engages in all phases of building projects, including design and engineering, financing and procurement, and construction. Among its services are environmental consulting, operations and maintenance, security design and consulting, management consulting, and IT services. Projects include coal, nuclear, and combustion turbine plants; drinking water and coastal water operations; and wireless and broadband installation.

The company acquired MJ Gleeson's engineering division for £36 million in 2006. The move boosted Black & Veatch's water industry business.

Black & Veatch has moved into ethanol fuel production with plans to build a renewable fuels plant. The plant will convert switch grass, wood waste, corn stubble, and other plant waste into fuel, which is cheaper than using corn. Other alternative fuels operations include solar, ocean, and wind energy.

The group's operations in the global water markets affect water quality and quantity throughout the water cycle: from source to treatment, to delivery, to wastewater collection and treatment. A key player in water treatment and wastewater treatment design, Black & Veatch's water sector division works with utilities, governments, and industries worldwide.

Founded in 1915 in Kansas City, Missouri, by engineers E. B. Black and Tom Veatch, the firm is now employee-owned and has more than 100 offices worldwide.

EXECUTIVES

Chairman, President, and CEO: Leonard C. (Len) Rodman
EVP, CFO, and Director: Karen L. Daniel, age 50
Chief Administrative Officer: Howard G. Withey
Chief Human Resources Officer: Shirley Gaufin
SVP, CTO, and Chief Knowledge Officer: John G. Voeller
SVP and Director, Black & Veatch Nuclear Group: Steve Rus
SVP, Enterprise Management Solutions (EMS): Michael A. (Mike) Elzey
President and CEO, B&V Energy; Director: O. H. (Dean) Oskvig
President, BV Solutions Group, Information Sector: Gerald J. White
President, Enterprise Management Solutions: Rodger E. Smith
President, Federal Services Division, Information Sector: David F. (Dave) Guyot
President, Telecommunications Division, Information Sector: Martin G. Travers
President and CEO, Black & Veatch Water; Director: Daniel W. (Dan) McCarthy
President, Strategic Sales & Marketing: Kim I. Mastalio
President, Construction & Procurement: Hal E. Smith
VP, Corporate Marketing, Branding, and Communications: Corrine Smith
Auditors: KPMG LLP

LOCATIONS

HQ: Black & Veatch Holding Company
  8400 Ward Pkwy., Kansas City, MO 64114
Phone: 913-458-2000   **Fax:** 913-458-2934
Web: www.bv.com

PRODUCTS/OPERATIONS

Market Sectors

Energy
  Air Quality Control
  Coal
  Combustion Turbine
  Gas, Oil & Chemicals
  Hydropower
  IGCC
  Nuclear
  Power Delivery
  Renewables
Water
  Conveyance Systems and Tunneling Services
  Drinking Water
  Hydropower
  River & Coastal Management
  Wastewater
  Water Resources
Telecommunications
  Broadband Wireline
  Enterprise Networks
  Utility Automation
  Wireless
Management Consulting
  Integrated Strategy Development
  Process Improvement
  Technology Application Services
Federal
  Civil Works
  Disaster Support
  Facilities
  Federal Design Build
  Management Programs
  Security
Environmental
  Air Quality
  Compliance Management
  Due Diligence
  Field Studies/Investigations
  Permitting
  Prevention Plans
  Remediation
  Siting
  Water/Wastewater
  Watershed Analysis & Restoration

COMPETITORS

AECOM
AMEC
Bechtel
Burns and Roe
CH2M HILL
EA Engineering
Fluor
Foster Wheeler
HNTB Companies
Louis Berger
Malcolm Pirnie
McDermott
Michael Baker
MWH Global
Parsons Brinckerhoff
Parsons Corporation
Shaw Group
SNC-Lavalin
Tetra Tech
TIC Holdings
Washington Division
Zachry Group

HISTORICAL FINANCIALS

Company Type: Private

Income Statement

FYE: December 31

	REVENUE ($ mil.)	NET INCOME ($ mil.)	NET PROFIT MARGIN	EMPLOYEES
12/07	3,200	—	—	9,600
12/06	2,200	—	—	8,600
12/05	1,573	—	—	7,500
12/04	1,400	—	—	6,800
12/03	1,400	—	—	6,200
Annual Growth	23.0%	—	—	11.6%

Revenue History

Bloomberg L.P.

What do you do when you've conquered Wall Street? You become mayor of the city the famous financial district calls home. After leading his financial news and information company to success, Michael Bloomberg left to lead the Big Apple in 2002. The company's core product is the Bloomberg Professional, a service terminal that provides real-time, around-the-clock financial news, market data, and analysis. Bloomberg is among the world's largest providers of such devices. The company also has a syndicated news service, publishes books and magazines, and disseminates business information via TV (Bloomberg Television), radio, and the Web. Michael Bloomberg founded the company in 1981; he owns about 70% of the firm.

Bloomberg Professional serves some 250,000 customers in more than 150 countries. Terminals account for some 85% of the company's business. The company charges a monthly fee per terminal for multiple system clients; its data can also be found on PCs and BlackBerrys. Bloomberg also distributes financial news and information through other media channels in an effort to build its brand and keep up with fierce competition.

Such competition only intensified when Thomson bought Reuters for $17 billion in 2008 to form the world's largest financial data company. The acquisition created Thomson Reuters, which commands 34% of the financial data market; Bloomberg trails at a close second, with 33%.

Months after the Thomson Reuters deal closed, Bloomberg hired Norman Pearlstine, the former top editor of Time and The Wall Street Journal, to the newly created position of chief content officer of Bloomberg. The move emphasizes the company's focus on its editorial staff, which has nearly doubled from 1,200 employees in 2001 to 2,300 in 2008.

Other recent management shifts include the 2008 hiring of Daniel Doctoroff (a former deputy mayor under Bloomberg) as president of the company, and the departure of former CEO Lex

Fenwick, who stepped down to oversee Bloomberg Ventures, an offshoot of the company that pursues new business opportunities. Later that year the company hired former Sony BMG Chairman and NBC News President Andrew Lack to run its multimedia operations, overseeing Bloomberg News' radio, television, and interactive divisions. Lack's hiring is another move in Bloomberg's corporate strategy of boosting business areas other than its terminals.

In 2005 the company left Park Avenue and moved into the new Bloomberg Tower on Lexington Avenue. The 53-story building is also home to retail and residential space. There is speculation that Mayor Bloomberg, who was re-elected in 2005, will sell the business when he leaves the mayor's office in 2009 to pursue more philanthropic endeavors.

Merrill Lynch is a major shareholder, with a 20% stake in the company. The investment firm has plans to sell its interest back to Bloomberg for an estimated $4.5 billion.

HISTORY

By the mid-1970s ambitious Michael Bloomberg had worked his way up to head of equity trading and sales at New York investment powerhouse Salomon Brothers. He left Salomon in 1981, just after the firm went private, cashing out with $10 million for his partnership interest.

Bloomberg founded Innovative Marketing Systems and spent the next year developing the Bloomberg terminal, which allowed users to manipulate bond data. In 1982 he pitched it to Merrill Lynch, which bought 20 machines. Regular production of the terminals began in 1984, and in 1985 Merrill Lynch invested $39 million in the company to gain a 30% stake. The company prospered during the 1980s boom, and over time the data, not the machines, became the heart of the business, which was renamed Bloomberg L.P. in 1986.

The company weathered the stock market crash of 1987, opening offices in London and Tokyo. Bloomberg made its entry into news-gathering and delivery in 1990 when Bloomberg News began broadcasting on its terminals. The company built its news organization from scratch, hiring away reporters from such publications as *The Wall Street Journal* and *Forbes*. Bloomberg bought a New York radio station in 1992 and converted it to an all-news format. The next year it built an in-house TV studio and created a business news show for PBS. A satellite TV station followed in 1994, along with the *Bloomberg Personal Finance* magazine.

In 1995 Bloomberg began offering business information via its Web site. The company also introduced the Bloomberg Tradebook, an electronic securities-trading venue designed to compete with Instinet. (In 1997 Tradebook was approved by the SEC for use in connection with some Nasdaq-listed stocks.) Bloomberg also started offering its services to subscribers in a PC-compatible format and selling its data to other news purveyors, such as LexisNexis (an online information service).

In 1996 the company went further into financial publishing, issuing *Swap Literacy: A Comprehensive Guide* and *A Common Sense Guide to Mutual Funds*. That year Michael Bloomberg bought back 10% of the company from Merrill Lynch for $200 million, giving Bloomberg L.P. an estimated market value of $2 billion. The company agreed in 1997 to supply the daytime programming for New York TV station WPXN.

When Bridge Information Systems bought Dow Jones Markets from Dow Jones in 1998, Bridge surpassed Bloomberg in number of financial information terminals installed, bumping Bloomberg from the #2 spot into third place. But Bloomberg continued expanding its offerings through strategic agreements with Internet companies such as America Online and CNET Networks, and through the introduction of new magazines such as *Bloomberg Money* in 1998, as well as *On Investing* and *Bloomberg Wealth Manager* in 1999.

Also in 1999 Bloomberg secured a deal with the Australian stock exchange that would allow its terminals to facilitate international order routing into the Australian market. The company also expanded its presence in the Spanish-language market through its agreement with CBS Telenoticias to produce a TV news program (*Noticiero Financiero*). In 2000 Bloomberg joined with Merrill Lynch to make Merrill Lynch's institutional e-commerce portal available to Bloomberg customers. The company shuttered its *Bloomberg Personal Finance* magazine in early 2003. The next year Bloomberg announced that it would provide financial programming to E! Entertainment Television during the early morning on weekdays in a three-year deal.

EXECUTIVES

Founder: Michael R. (Mike) Bloomberg, age 66
Chairman: Peter T. Grauer, age 62
President and Director: Daniel L. (Dan) Doctoroff
Director Worldwide Sales: Thomas (Tom) Secunda
Editor-in-Chief and Head News:
  Matthew (Matt) Winkler, age 52
Head Sales, Americas: Max Linnington
Chief Content Officer: Norman Pearlstine
CEO, Multimedia Group: Andrew R. (Andy) Lack, age 61
Head Global Corporate Communications:
  Judith A. Czelusniak
Head Sales, Europe, Africa, Middle East:
  Jean-Paul (J.P.) Zammitt
Head Sales, Asia and Pacific: Gerard Francis

LOCATIONS

HQ: Bloomberg L.P.
  731 Lexington Ave., New York, NY 10022
Phone: 212-318-2000   **Fax:** 917-369-5000
Web: www.bloomberg.com

PRODUCTS/OPERATIONS

Selected Products and Services
Bloomberg Hardware (terminal includes keyboard, flat-panel monitors, and audio/video conferencing tools)
Bloomberg Markets Magazine (content for and about professional investors)
Bloomberg News (syndicated news service)
Bloomberg Press (book publishing)
Bloomberg Professional (24-hour, real-time financial information system)
  Bloomberg Data License (financial database service)
  Bloomberg Roadshows (presentation service)
  Bloomberg Tradebook (equities trading technology)
  Bloomberg Trading Systems (Bloomberg information combined with trading technology)
Bloomberg Radio (syndicated radio news service)
Bloomberg Television (24-hour news channel and syndicated reports)
Bloomberg.com (Web site)

COMPETITORS

Agence France-Presse	Intuit
Associated Press	MarketWatch
Dow Jones	Morningstar
FactSet	Pearson
Financial Times	TheStreet.com
Forbes	Thomson Reuters
Interactive Data	

HISTORICAL FINANCIALS
Company Type: Private

Income Statement
FYE: December 31

	REVENUE ($ mil.)	NET INCOME ($ mil.)	NET PROFIT MARGIN	EMPLOYEES
12/07	5,400	—	—	10,800
12/06	4,700	—	—	9,500
12/05	4,100	—	—	8,200
12/04	3,500	—	—	8,000
12/03	3,250	—	—	8,200
Annual Growth	13.5%	—	—	7.1%

Revenue History

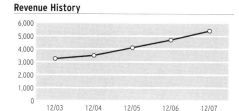

Blue Cross and Blue Shield Association

The rise of managed health care has had some of its members singing the blues, but the Blues, with nearly 100 million members nationwide, aren't complaining. The Blue Cross and Blue Shield Association is a federation of independent health insurance companies who license the Blue Cross and Blue Shield brand names. Member companies — of which there are about 40 — own the rights to sell Blue-branded health plans within defined regions. The Association coordinates some national programs such as BlueCard, which allows members of one franchisee to have coverage in other service areas, and the Federal Employee Program, which covers more than half of federal government employees, retirees, and their families.

These days, most of the Blues companies are healthy and profitable, after a tough decade in the 1990s that led to a continuing series of rate hikes, as well as consolidation, conversions to for-profit status, and product innovations, among other strategies.

WellPoint, the largest Blues company and the largest for-profit health insurer in the nation, has grown by buying up for-profit Blues plans (or converting them to for-profit status). It has also acquired a number of non-Blue subsidiaries, such as Lumenos, though it is required to get two-thirds of its insurance revenue from Blue products to keep its Blue Cross Blue Shield license.

The pace of for-profit conversions has slowed, as state regulators have become increasingly wary of signing off on the procedure. The rosy financial situation of most of the not-for-profit Blues has also taken away a key incentive for for-profit conversion — access to capital markets.

Consolidation among Blues plans continues, however. Health Care Service Corporation added its fourth not-for-profit Blues plan (Blue Cross and Blue Shield of Oklahoma) in 2005. And Highmark and Independence Blue Cross have agreed to merge, in a deal that would give the resulting company dominant market share in Pennsylvania.

As profits at the Blues companies have grown, the Association and its franchisees have come in for criticism over high executive pay and other perceived excesses.

HISTORY

Blue Cross was born in 1929, when Baylor University official Justin Kimball offered schoolteachers 21 days of hospital care for $6 a year. A major plan feature was a community rating system that based premiums on the community claims experience rather than members' conditions.

The Blue Cross symbol was devised in 1933 by Minnesota plan executive E. A. van Steenwyck. By 1935 many of the 15 plans in 11 states used the symbol. Many states gave the plans nonprofit status, and in 1936 the American Hospital Association formed the Committee on Hospital Service (renamed the Blue Cross Association in 1948) to coordinate them.

As Blue Cross grew, state medical societies sponsored prepaid plans to cover doctors' fees. In 1946 they united under the aegis of the American Medical Association (AMA) as the Associated Medical Care Plans (later the Association of Blue Shield Plans).

In 1948 the AMA thwarted a Blue Cross attempt to merge with Blue Shield. But the Blues increasingly cooperated on public policy matters while competing for members, and each Blue formed a not-for-profit corporation to coordinate its plan's activities.

By 1960 Blue Cross insured about a third of the US. Over the next decade the Blues started administering Medicare and other government health plans, and by 1970 half of Blue Cross' premiums came from government entities.

In the 1970s the Blues adopted such cost-control measures as review of hospital admissions; many plans even abandoned the community rating system. Most began emphasizing preventive care in HMOs or PPOs. The two Blues finally merged in 1982, but this had little effect on the associations' bottom lines as losses grew.

By the 1990s the Blues were big business. Some of the state associations offered officers high salaries and perks but still insisted on special regulatory treatment.

But as lower-cost plans attracted the hale and hearty, the Blues' customers became older, sicker, and more expensive. With their quasi-charitable status and outdated rate structures, many Blues lost market share.

The Blues fought back by updating their technology and rate structures, merging among themselves, creating for-profit subsidiaries, forming alliances with for-profit enterprises, or (in some cases) dropping their not-for-profit status and going public — while still using the Blue Cross Blue Shield name.

Blue Cross of California became the first chapter to give up its tax-free status when it was bought by WellPoint Health Networks, a managed care subsidiary it had founded in 1992. In a 1996 deal, WellPoint became the chapter's parent and converted it to for-profit status, assigning all of the stock to a public charitable foundation which received the proceeds of its subsequent IPO. WellPoint also bought the group life and health division of Massachusetts Mutual Life Insurance.

The for-profit switches picked up in 1997. Blue Cross of Connecticut merged with insurance provider Anthem (now WellPoint), and other mergers followed. Half the nation's Blues formed an alliance called BluesCONNECT, competing with national health plans by offering employers one nationwide benefits organization. The association also pursued overseas licensing agreements in Europe, South America, and Asia, assembling a network of Blue Cross-friendly caregivers aiming for worldwide coverage.

In 1998 Blues in more than 35 states sued the nation's big cigarette companies to recoup costs of treating smoking-related illnesses. In a separate lawsuit, Blue Cross and Blue Shield of Minnesota received nearly $300 million from the tobacco industry. In 1999 Anthem moved to acquire or affiliate with Blues in Colorado, Maine, and New Hampshire.

In 2000, after years of discussions, the New York attorney general permitted Empire Blue Cross and Blue Shield to convert to for-profit status.

In 2004 Anthem (now called WellPoint) and WellPoint Health Networks announced plans to merge, becoming the largest for-profit health insurer in the nation. WellPoint acquired Empire Blue Cross and its parent WellChoice in 2005.

EXECUTIVES

President and CEO: Scott P. Serota
SVP and Chief Medical Officer: Allan M. Korn
SVP and Chief Information Officer: Doug Porter
SVP, Corporate Secretary, and General Counsel: Roger G. Wilson
SVP Human Resources and Administrative Services: William (Bill) Colbourne
SVP National Programs: Steve W. Gammarino
SVP Policy and Representation: Mary Nell Lehnhard
SVP Strategic Services: Maureen Sullivan
VP Federal Relations: Jack Ericksen
VP, Deputy General Counsel, and Assistant Corporate Secretary; Managing Director, BlueShield Ventures, Inc: Paul F. Brown
VP Legislative and Regulatory Policy: Alissa Fox
VP Inter-Plan Programs: Frank Coyne
VP and Chief Technology Officer: William B. O'Loughlin
VP Business Informatics and Blue Health Intelligence: Shirley S. Lady
VP China Development: Ted Li
VP Business Development: Jody Voss
VP Federal Employee Program: Jena L. Estes
VP Brand Strategy and Marketing Services: Jennifer Vachon
Executive Director External Affairs: Jeff Smokler
Director External Affairs: Kelly Miller
Director External Affairs: Paul Cholette
Auditors: PricewaterhouseCoopers LLP

LOCATIONS

HQ: Blue Cross and Blue Shield Association
225 N. Michigan Ave., Chicago, IL 60601
Phone: 312-297-6000   **Fax:** 312-297-6609
Web: www.bcbs.com

PRODUCTS/OPERATIONS

2007 Health Care Members

	Members (mil.)	% of total
PPO	65.8	62
HMO	15.8	18
Traditional indemnity	12.9	14
POS (point-of-service)	4.8	6
Total	**99.3**	**100**

Selected Blue Cross and Blue Shield Licensees

Arkansas Blue Cross and Blue Shield
Blue Cross and Blue Shield of Alabama
Blue Cross and Blue Shield of Arizona
Blue Cross and Blue Shield of Delaware
Blue Cross and Blue Shield of Florida
Blue Cross and Blue Shield of Kansas
Blue Cross and Blue Shield of Louisiana
Blue Cross and Blue Shield of Massachusetts
Blue Cross and Blue Shield of Michigan
Blue Cross and Blue Shield of Minnesota
Blue Cross and Blue Shield of Mississippi
Blue Cross and Blue Shield of Kansas City
Blue Cross and Blue Shield of Montana
Blue Cross and Blue Shield of Nebraska
Blue Cross and Blue Shield of North Carolina
Blue Cross and Blue Shield of North Dakota
Blue Cross of Northeastern Pennsylvania
Blue Cross and Blue Shield of Rhode Island
Blue Cross and Blue Shield of South Carolina
Blue Cross and Blue Shield of Tennessee
Blue Cross and Blue Shield of Wyoming
Blue Cross and Blue Shield of Vermont
Blue Shield of California
Capital BlueCross (Pennsylvania)
CareFirst
   CareFirst Blue Cross and Blue Shield (District of Columbia)
   CareFirst Blue Cross and Blue Shield of Maryland
Excellus BlueCross BlueShield of New York
Hawaii Medical Service Association
Health Care Service Corporation
   Blue Cross and Blue Shield of Illinois
   Blue Cross and Blue Shield of New Mexico
   Blue Cross and Blue Shield of Oklahoma
   Blue Cross and Blue Shield of Texas
HealthNow New York
   BlueCross and BlueShield of Western New York
   BlueShield of Northeastern New York
Highmark Blue Cross Blue Shield (Pennsylvania)
   Mountain State Blue Cross and Blue Shield (West Virginia)
Horizon Blue Cross and Blue Shield of New Jersey
Idaho Blue Cross
Independence Blue Cross (Pennsylvania)
   La Cruz Azul de Puerto Rico
Premera Blue Cross (Alaska and Washington)
The Regence Group
   Regence BlueCross and BlueShield of Oregon
   Regence BlueCross BlueShield of Utah
   Regence BlueShield of Idaho
   Regence BlueShield (Washington)
Triple-S (Puerto Rico)
Wellmark
   Wellmark Blue Cross and Blue Shield of South Dakota
   Wellmark Blue Cross and Blue Shield of Iowa
WellPoint
   Anthem Blue Cross and Blue Shield of Colorado
   Anthem Blue Cross and Blue Shield of Connecticut
   Anthem Blue Cross and Blue Shield of Indiana
   Anthem Blue Cross and Blue Shield of Kentucky
   Anthem Blue Cross and Blue Shield of Maine
   Anthem Blue Cross and Blue Shield of Nevada
   Anthem Blue Cross and Blue Shield of New Hampshire
   Anthem Blue Cross and Blue Shield of Ohio
   Anthem Blue Cross and Blue Shield of Virginia
   Blue Cross and Blue Shield of Georgia
   Blue Cross and Blue Shield of Missouri
   BlueCross BlueShield of Wisconsin
   California Blue Cross
   Empire Blue Cross and Blue Shield of New York

COMPETITORS

Aetna
AMERIGROUP
Centene
CIGNA
Coventry Health Care
Health Net
Humana
Kaiser Foundation Health Plan
Molina Healthcare
UnitedHealth Group
WellCare

Blue Cross (LA)

The Bayou State's largest health insurer, Blue Cross and Blue Shield of Louisiana provides health insurance products and related services to more than 1 million members across Louisiana. Established in 1934, the company is an independent licensee of the Blue Cross and Blue Shield Association and has offices throughout the state. Blue Cross and Blue Shield of Louisiana offers point-of-service, PPO, supplemental Medicare, and traditional health care plans, as well as the Blue*Saver* high-deductible plan with a health savings account. Its HMO Louisiana subsidiary offers an HMO plan that provides some out-of-network benefits. Customers include both individuals and employer groups.

In addition to medical coverage, Blue Cross and Blue Shield of Louisiana sells group life and disability insurance through its Southern National Life Insurance Company subsidiary.

Despite disruptions caused by Hurricane Katrina in 2005, the company has managed to continue growing its medical membership. As a result of the storm, however, it has had to reconstitute its provider network, which was decimated when Katrina shut down hospitals and forced doctors and other health care providers to relocate outside the state.

EXECUTIVES

Chairman: Virgil Robinson Jr.
Vice Chair: Kathy Sellers Johnson
EVP and CFO: Peggy B. Scott
SVP and CIO: Worachote (Ob) Soonthornsima
SVP and Chief Marketing Officer: Mike Reitz
SVP and General Counsel: Michele Calandro
SVP, Benefits Administration: Mike Hayes
SVP, Human Resources: Todd G. Schexnayder
SVP, Medical Economics: Sabrina Heltz
SVP, Provider and Community Relations: Richard Williams
VP, Administrative Services: Charles Gilbert
VP, Application Development: Parnell Bourgeois
VP, Benefits Administration: Thomas Cross
VP, Benefits Administration, HMO Louisiana and Blue Cross and Blue Shield of Louisiana: Allison Young
VP, Corporate Communications: John Maginnis
VP, eROC Project: Sam Griffin
VP, Network Administration: Dawn Cantrell
VP and Chief Actuary: Brian Small
VP, Provider Reimbursement: Steve Cunningham
Secretary: Ann H. Knapp
Statewide Director, Individual Sales: Brian Keller
Director, Customer Engagement and IT Strategic Planning: Laura Landry
Director, Facility Reimbursement: Sandra Jones

LOCATIONS

HQ: Blue Cross and Blue Shield of Louisiana
5525 Reitz Ave., Baton Rouge, LA 70809
Phone: 225-295-3307   **Fax:** 225-295-2054
Web: www.bcbsla.com

COMPETITORS

Aetna
CIGNA
Coventry Health Care
Health Net
Humana
UnitedHealth Group

HISTORICAL FINANCIALS

Company Type: Not-for-profit

Income Statement

	REVENUE ($ mil.)	NET INCOME ($ mil.)	NET PROFIT MARGIN	EMPLOYEES
12/07	1,946	66	3.4%	1,600
12/06	1,764	78	4.4%	1,555
12/05	1,626	111	6.8%	—
12/04	1,497	81	5.4%	—
12/03	1,351	58	4.3%	—
Annual Growth	9.6%	3.3%	—	2.9%

FYE: December 31

2007 Year-End Financials

Debt ratio: —   Current ratio: —
Return on equity: 11.3%   Long-term debt ($ mil.): —
Cash ($ mil.): —

Net Income History

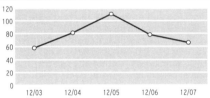

Blue Cross (MA)

The dominant health insurer in the Bay State, Blue Cross and Blue Shield of Massachusetts covers nearly 3 million members. The company, an independent licensee of the Blue Cross and Blue Shield Association, offers a variety of individual and employer-sponsored health care plans, including HMO (HMO Blue), PPO (Blue Care Elect), and point-of-service (Blue Choice) plans, as well as various hybrid options and personal spending accounts to cover out-of-pocket costs. Blue Cross and Blue Shield of Massachusetts also provides dental, vision, and prescription drug coverage. It was founded in 1937.

In response to sweeping health care reforms passed in Massachusetts in 2006, Blue Cross and Blue Shield of Massachusetts introduced several new products (called Commonwealth Choice plans) intended for individuals required to purchased insurance coverage under the new law.

The company has also been pushing information technology as a means to keep medical costs

lower and improve care. In 2008, for example, it partnered with Google Health, the online medical records initiative of Google, to allow its members to import their insurance claims into their Google Health profiles.

EXECUTIVES

Chairman, President, and CEO:
Cleve L. Killingsworth Jr., age 55
EVP and CFO: Allen P. Maltz
EVP and Chief Legal Officer: Sandra L. (Sandy) Jesse
EVP Sales, Marketing, and Information Technology:
Stephen R. Booma
EVP Health Care Services: Andrew Dreyfus
SVP and CIO: Carl J. Ascenzo
SVP Corporate Relations: Fredi Shonkoff
SVP and Chief Physician Executive: John A. Fallon
SVP and Chief Strategy Officer: Vinod K. (Vin) Sahney
SVP and Chief Human Resources Officer:
Ann S. Anderson
VP Public, Government, and Regulatory Affairs:
Jay Curley
Chief of Staff, Executive Office Senior Vice President:
John Schoenbaum
Auditors: Ernst & Young LLP

LOCATIONS

HQ: Blue Cross and Blue Shield of Massachusetts, Inc.
LandMark Center, 401 Park Dr., Boston, MA 02215
Phone: 617-246-5000   **Fax:** 617-246-4832
Web: www.bcbsma.com

PRODUCTS/OPERATIONS

Selected Health Plans

Access Blue (open access HMO plan)
Blue Care Elect (PPO plan)
Blue Choice (point-of-service plan)
Blue Medicare PFFS PlusRx (private-fee-for-service Medicare Advantage plan)
Consumer Choice Blue (high-deductible plan with personal spending account)
Essential Blue YA (low-cost, young adult plan)
HMO Blue (statewide managed care)
Medex (Medicare supplemental plan)
Medicare HMO Blue (Medicare Advantage plan)
Medicare PPO Blue (Medicare Advantage plan)

COMPETITORS

Aetna
CIGNA
ConnectiCare
Dental Service of Massachusetts
Fallon Community Health Plan
Harvard Pilgrim
Health New England
MVP Health Plan
Neighborhood Health Plan
Tufts Health Plan

HISTORICAL FINANCIALS

Company Type: Not-for-profit

Income Statement

	REVENUE ($ mil.)	NET INCOME ($ mil.)	NET PROFIT MARGIN	EMPLOYEES
12/07	227	146	64.3%	3,878
12/06	2,098	157	7.5%	3,983
12/05	1,977	128	6.5%	4,038
12/04	4,928	243	4.9%	—
12/03	4,497	265	5.9%	3,545
Annual Growth	(52.6%)	(13.9%)	—	2.3%

FYE: December 31

2007 Year-End Financials

Debt ratio: 0.0%   Current ratio: —
Return on equity: 21.8%   Long-term debt ($ mil.): 0
Cash ($ mil.): —

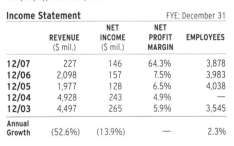

Net Income History

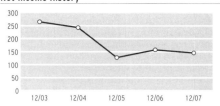

Blue Cross (MI)

Blue Cross Blue Shield of Michigan is Michigan's leading health benefits organization, serving more than 4.6 million members residing in the state or employed by companies headquartered there. The company's insurance offerings include traditional indemnity, PPO, and POS plans, in addition to its Blue Care Network HMO plans. It also offers consumer-directed Flexible Blue plans paired with health savings accounts, as well as options for individual buyers and Medicare beneficiaries. The not-for-profit organization is an independent licensee of the Blue Cross and Blue Shield Association.

Like most health plans, Blue Cross Blue Shield of Michigan has combated the rise of health care costs with a combination of rate hikes, new product offerings that shift the burden of cost to members, and programs that encourage healthy lifestyles and the use of lower-cost alternatives such as generic drugs.

It entered the Medicare Part D market in 2006, offering prescription drug plans to seniors. It also revamped its product lineup for individual buyers that year and acquired the M-CARE health plan from the University of Michigan Health System.

The organization has also launched a long-term care insurance subsidiary, called Life-Secure, which is licensed throughout most of the country.

HISTORY

The history of prepaid medical care began in 1929, when Baylor University Hospital administrator Justin Kimball developed a plan to offer schoolteachers 21 days of hospital care for $6 a year. Fundamental to the plan was a community rating system, which based premiums on the community's claims experience rather than subscribers' conditions.

A similar program was started in Michigan in 1938 when a group of hospitals formed the Michigan Society for Group Hospitalization, which became the Michigan Hospital Service and later became a chapter of the national Blue Cross association. The health care plan was funded by local hospitals and private grants. (A group of private donors, including Oldsmobile automotive founder Ransom Olds, loaned the group $5,000.)

The state insurance commission approved tax-exempt status for the Michigan Blue Cross in 1939. Nine days after opening a three-person office in Detroit, Blue Cross landed its first customer, insurance company John Hancock Mutual Life. John Hancock's Detroit branch manager became the first subscriber, paying

$1.90 per month for 21 days of hospitalization coverage for his family of eight.

Due in part to the addition of Chrysler, Ford, and General Motors to its health plans, Blue Cross grew from less than 1 million members in the 1940s to more than 3 million in the 1950s. In 1945 it began to offer coverage for individuals; 14 years later the association started to offer policies to seniors who were ineligible for group coverage. Blue Cross took over operation of Michigan's Medicare program in 1966.

Michigan's Blue Cross merged with longtime partner Blue Shield in 1975 to create Blue Cross Blue Shield of Michigan, with a total of 5 million subscribers. Blue Shield, a prepayment plan that covered doctors' services, had been started in 1939 by the Michigan State Medical Society (a group of Michigan physicians).

As overseas competition forced automakers to cut their employment rolls, Blue Cross Blue Shield of Michigan's membership contracted. BCBSM chairman John McCabe, realizing the need to generate additional revenue, pushed for an end to the company's not-for-profit status in the 1980s but was rejected by the Michigan legislature. This failure was at least partially behind McCabe's resignation in 1987.

The struggling Michigan Blues moved toward profitability in 1994 when the state legislature specially authorized its $291 million purchase of the for-profit State Accident Fund, the state's workers' compensation program. It also lost its large but hard-to-manage state Medicare contract to Blue Cross Blue Shield of Illinois (now Health Care Service Corporation). In 1996 the company reorganized, with a division for Michigan residents and one for nationwide accounts. In 1997 BCBSM continued its efforts to increase revenue by acquiring private health management company Preferred Provider Organization of Michigan, which operates in Michigan and nearby states. BCBSM president and CEO Richard Whitmer announced that he was willing to compete with other Blues in bordering states.

In 1998 Blue Cross Blue Shield of Michigan consolidated four regional HMOs into a single statewide HMO, the Blue Care Network. Costs of the merger and growing losses in drug coverage constrained earnings, but were counterweighted by returns on assets invested in the stock market. In 1999 and 2000 the company rankled Detroit's small business owners with double-digit premium hikes.

Blue Cross Blue Shield of Michigan sold its for-profit subsidiary Preferred Provider Organization of Michigan to regional health plan provider HMS Healthcare in 2004.

EXECUTIVES

Chairman: Gregory A. (Greg) Sudderth
Vice Chairman: Spencer C. Johnson
President and CEO: Daniel J. Loepp
EVP and CFO; President, Emerging Markets:
  Mark R. Bartlett
EVP, Health Care Value Enhancements: Kevin L. Seitz
SVP, Health Care Value and Provider Affiliation and Chief Medical Officer: Thomas L. Simmer
SVP and General Counsel: Lisa S. DeMoss
SVP, Group Sales and Corporate Marketing:
  Kenneth R. (Ken) Dallafior
SVP and Chief Actuarial Officer: J. Paul Austin
SVP, Subsidiary Operations; President and CEO, Blue Care Network of Michigan: Jeanne H. Carlson
SVP Human Resources: Darrell E. Middleton
SVP, Hospital and Contracting Relations:
  Robert Milewski
SVP, Network Relations, Contracting, and Pharmacy Services: Michael R. Schwartz

SVP, Subsidiary Operations; President and CEO, Accident Fund Insurance Company of America:
  Elizabeth R. Haar, age 39
SVP and CIO: Joseph H. Hohner
VP and Deputy General Counsel, Corporate Practice Group: Jeffrey P. Rumley
VP, Corporate and Financial Investigations:
  Gregory W. Anderson
VP, Corporate Communications: R. Andrew Hetzel
VP, Federal Programs: Catherine Schmitt
VP, Medical Care Management Operations:
  Karen A. Maher
VP, Subsidiary Operations; President and CEO, DenteMax: Rick V. Morrone
VP, Employee Services: Kathryn Elston
VP, Corporate Services: Audrey Harvey
VP, Claims and BlueCard Operations: Chris Maier
VP, Chief of Staff and Corporate Strategy and Performance: Amy Tattrie
VP and Treasurer: Carolynn Walton
VP, Corporate Secretary and Services: Tricia Keith
President and CEO, LifeSecure Holdings: E. Lisa Wendt
Auditors: Deloitte & Touche LLP

LOCATIONS

HQ: Blue Cross Blue Shield of Michigan
  600 E. Lafayette Blvd., Detroit, MI 48226
Phone: 313-225-9000   **Fax:** 313-225-5629
Web: www.bcbsm.com

PRODUCTS/OPERATIONS

Selected Products

BCN Advantage (Medicare Advantage HMO)
Blue Care Network (HMO)
Blue Choice (point-of-service plan)
Blue Preferred PPO
Blue Preferred Plus PPO
First Dollar (traditional indemnity plan)
Flexible Blue (consumer-directed plan)
Individual Care Blue (individual health plan)
LifeSecure (long-term care insurance)
Medicare Plus Blue (Medicare Advantage plan with prescription drug coverage)
Value Blue (basic health coverage for individuals)

COMPETITORS

Aetna
CIGNA
Health Alliance Plan of Michigan
HealthPlus of Michigan
Humana
OmniCare Health Plan
Total Health Care
UnitedHealth Group

HISTORICAL FINANCIALS

Company Type: Not-for-profit

Income Statement

	REVENUE ($ mil.)	NET INCOME ($ mil.)	NET PROFIT MARGIN	EMPLOYEES
12/07	9,849	177	1.8%	8,945
12/06	8,687	243	2.8%	7,047
12/05	8,151	295	3.6%	—
12/04	8,044	411	5.1%	—
12/03	13,716	368	2.7%	8,500
Annual Growth	(7.9%)	(16.7%)	—	1.3%

FYE: December 31

2007 Year-End Financials

Debt ratio: —   Current ratio: —
Return on equity: 6.1%   Long-term debt ($ mil.): —
Cash ($ mil.): —

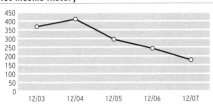

Net Income History

Blue Cross (NC)

Blue Cross and Blue Shield of North Carolina (BCBSNC) provides health care insurance products and related services to about 3.5 million members in North Carolina. The company's health plans include Blue Care (HMO) and Blue Options (PPO), as well as consumer-directed plans that couple a high-deductible policy with a health savings account. BCBSNC also provides dental, life, disability, long-term care, and Medicare supplemental insurance, as well as prescription drug coverage. The company's Partners National Health Plans subsidiary offers Medicare Advantage health plans. BCBSNC is a licensee of the Blue Cross and Blue Shield Association.

North Carolina's largest health insurer, the company maintains a provider network that includes nearly 5,000 primary care doctors, 15,000 specialists, and more than 100 hospitals.

Like many health insurers, BCBSNC is focused on enlisting its members in health improvement programs — including fitness programs and health screenings — that it hopes will lower medical costs over the long run.

EXECUTIVES

Chairman: Jeffrey L. Houpt
President, CEO, and Trustee:
  Robert J. (Bob) Greczyn Jr.
COO: J. Bradley (Brad) Wilson
CFO: Daniel E. (Dan) Glaser
SVP and CIO: John Sternbergh
SVP Human Resources: Fara Palumbo
SVP Commercial and Governmental Operations:
  Ian Gordon
Chief Administrative Officer, General Counsel, and Corporate Secretary: Maureen K. O'Connor
Chief Sales and Marketing Officer: John T. Roos
VP Community Relations; President, BCBSNC Foundation: Kathy Higgins
VP Corporate Communications: Lynne Garrison
VP Document Operations and Electronic Solutions:
  Josh Duffy
VP Operations and Director Communications, BCBSNC Foundation: Danielle Breslin
Auditors: PricewaterhouseCoopers LLP

LOCATIONS

HQ: Blue Cross and Blue Shield of North Carolina
  5901 Chapel Hill Rd., Durham, NC 27707
Phone: 919-489-7431   **Fax:** 919-765-7818
Web: www.bcbsnc.com

PRODUCTS/OPERATIONS

Selected Products
Dental Blue (dental insurance)
Blue Advantage (PPO)
Blue Care (HMO)
Blue Medicare Supplement (Medicare supplemental coverage)
Blue Medicare Rx (Medicare prescription drug coverage)
Blue Medicare HMO (Medicare Advantage plan)
Blue Medicare PPO (Medicare Advantage plan)
Blue Options (high-deductible plan with health savings account)

COMPETITORS
Aetna
Celtic Insurance
CIGNA HealthCare of North Carolina
Coventry Health Care
North Carolina Mutual
UnitedHealth Group

HISTORICAL FINANCIALS
Company Type: Not-for-profit

Income Statement				FYE: December 31
	REVENUE ($ mil.)	NET INCOME ($ mil.)	NET PROFIT MARGIN	EMPLOYEES
12/07	4,900	—	—	4,700
12/06	4,407	—	—	4,000
Annual Growth	11.2%	—	—	17.5%

Revenue History

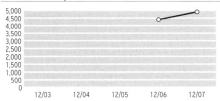

Blue Diamond Growers

Blue Diamond Growers is one nutty business. Some 3,000 California almond growers belong to the cooperative, which is a top global player in the tree nut market. The company sells almonds and almond products, hazelnuts, macadamia, pistachio, and other nuts to food and candy makers, the foodservice industry, and food retailers. Blue Diamond Growers has developed products such as Almond Breeze, an almond-based, lactose-free milk substitute; Nut Thins crackers; and special cuts and flavored varieties of the nuts. The co-op, formed in 1910, sells its products throughout the US and in more than 90 other countries. It operates processing plants, receiving stations, and retail nut stores in California and Oregon.

In response to consumer demand for healthier products, the company has introduced 100-calorie portion packs and a line of oven-roasted nuts. In 2000 Blue Diamond Growers purchased the world's largest macadamia nut producer, MacFarms of Hawaii; it later sold it to Sparks Corp. and Greater Pacific Food Holdings in 2003.

EXECUTIVES
Chairman: Clinton Shick
Vice Chairman: Dale Van Groningen
President and CEO: Douglas D. Youngdahl
CFO: Robert S. Donovan
General Manager Industrial Sales and Operations: Kim Kennedy
Manager Credit and Accounts Receivable: Elaine Dykhouse
Manager Marketing: Jennifer Pfanner
Manager Materials: David Hills
Director Member Relations: Dave Baker
Director Industrial Sales: Rex Lake
Director Marketing: Al Greenlee
Director Public Affairs: Susan Brauner
Human Resources, Salida Office: Sheryl Guzman
Auditors: KPMG LLP

LOCATIONS
HQ: Blue Diamond Growers
1802 C St., Sacramento, CA 95814
Phone: 916-442-0771   **Fax:** 916-446-8461
Web: bluediamond.com

COMPETITORS
Calcot
Diamond Foods
Dole Food
Golden West Nuts
Mauna Loa Macadamia Nut Corp.
Meridian Nut Growers
ML Macadamia Orchards
Paramount Farms
Primex International
Stewart & Jasper Orchards
Tejon Ranch

Blue Shield Of California

Blue Shield of California (a.k.a. California Physicians' Service) provides health insurance products and related services to some 3.2 million members in the state of California. The not-for-profit organization's health insurance products include HMO, preferred provider organization (PPO), dental, and a Medicare supplemental plan. Accidental death and dismemberment, executive medical reimbursement, life insurance, vision, and short-term health plans are provided by the company's Blue Shield of California Life & Health Insurance subsidiary. Blue Shield of California has more than 20 locations across California.

Blue Shield of California is a Blue Cross and Blue Shield Association member. The company was established in 1939 by the California Medical Association House of Delegates. The company's provider network has grown to include some 60,000 primary and specialty physicians and 350 hospitals.

The company has come under fire from California agencies and lawmakers, including the Los Angeles city attorney, for the alleged improper rescinding of customer policies after they become ill.

EXECUTIVES
President and CEO and Chairman: Bruce G. Bodaken
EVP and CFO: Heidi Kunz, age 52
EVP Customer Services and Corporate Marketing: Bob Novelli
SVP and Chief Medical Officer: Alan Sokolow
SVP Vice President & Chief Executive, Individual, Small Group and Government Business Unit: Karen Vigil
SVP and Chief Actuary: Edward C. (Ed) Cymerys
SVP and CIO: Elinor C. MacKinnon
SVP General Counsel and Corporate Secretary: Seth A. Jacobs
SVP and CEO, Large Group Business Unit: Paul Markovich
SVP Human Resources: Marianne Jackson
SVP Network Services: David S. Joyner
VP Deputy General Counsel and Chief Compliance Officer: Charles Sweeris
VP Customer Service Appeals and Grievances: Rob Geyer
VP Finance and Consumer Operations: Kathi Lucke
VP Human Resources, Customer Services, and Corporate Marketing: Cindy Bottenhagen
VP Medical Operations and Health Care Services: Debby Naegle
VP Pharmacy Services: Nancy Stalker
VP and Corporate Controller: Christopher Gorecki
VP eBusiness Strategy and Execution: Jan Vorfeld
VP Producer Sales, Individual, Small Groups and Government Business Unit: Brent Hitchings
VP Talent Acquisition and Human Resources Support: Priscilla Muniz
VP Corporate Marketing: Doug Biehn
VP Mid to Large Sector Sales, Southern California, Large Group Business Unit: Jim Elliott
VP CalPERS Business Unit: Tom McCaffery
VP Mid to Large Sector Sales, Northern California, Large Group Business Unit: Thad Roake
VP Government Affairs: Mark Weideman
President and CEO Blue Shield of California Foundation: Crystal Hayling

LOCATIONS
HQ: Blue Shield Of California
50 Beale St., San Francisco, CA 94105
Phone: 415-229-5000   **Fax:** 415-229-5070
Web: www.blueshieldca.com

COMPETITORS
Aetna	Kaiser Foundation Health
CIGNA	Molina Healthcare
Delta Dental Plan	UnitedHealth Group
Health Net of California	WellPoint

HISTORICAL FINANCIALS
Company Type: Not-for-profit

Income Statement				FYE: December 31
	REVENUE ($ mil.)	NET INCOME ($ mil.)	NET PROFIT MARGIN	EMPLOYEES
12/07	8,364	318	3.8%	4,500
12/06	8,150	382	4.7%	4,500
12/05	7,519	330	4.4%	4,300
12/04	6,846	334	4.9%	—
12/03	6,203	314	5.1%	4,200
Annual Growth	7.8%	0.3%	—	1.7%

Net Income History

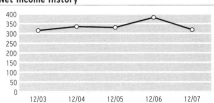

Blue Tee

Blue Tee has stayed out of the rough through diversification. Oooperating through its subsidiaries, the company distributes steel and scrap metal and manufactures a variety of industrial equipment. Blue Tee's Brown-Strauss Steel subsidiary is a leading distributor of steel products (beams, pipe, tubing) in the western US.

Other operations include AZCON (scrap metal sales and rail cars and parts), GEFCO (portable drilling rigs), Standard Alloys (pump parts), and Steco (dump-truck trailers). Union Tractor provides replacement parts for construction and transportation equipment in western Canada.

Blue Tee is owned by its employees.

EXECUTIVES

Chairman and CEO: Richard A. Secrist
President and COO: William M. Kelly, age 57
SVP Finance and Secretary: David P. Alldian
Group VP, Metals Operations: Richard A. Secrist Jr.
Controller: Thomas Caruso
Treasurer and Assistant Secretary: Jerry D'Auria
Assistant Controller: Annette Marino D'Arienzo

LOCATIONS

HQ: Blue Tee Corp.
250 Park Ave. South, New York, NY 10003
Phone: 212-598-0880   **Fax:** 212-598-0896
Web: www.bluetee.com

Blue Tee has operations in the US and Canada.

PRODUCTS/OPERATIONS

Selected Subsidiaries

AZCON Corporation (ferrous and nonferrous scrap; rail cars, locomotives, and parts; relay and reroll rail)
Brown-Strauss Steel (steel distribution, including angles, beams, channels, pipe, and tubing)
GEFCO (The George E. Failing Company, portable drilling rigs)
PUMPSTAR (truck-mounted concrete boom pumps)
Southco, Inc. (distribution of pipe and reinforcing bar)
Standard Alloys (pump parts and repairs)
Steco (dump trailers, transfer trailers, and trailer parts)
Union Tractor Ltd. (Canada)
    Delta Warehouses (replacement parts for construction and transportation equipment)
    United Diesel Injection (parts and service for fuel-injection systems and turbochargers)

COMPETITORS

A. M. Castle
APi Group
Dover Corporation
Furukawa
Kreher Steel
OmniSource
Philip Services
Reliance Steel
RTI International Metals
Russel Metals
Supreme Industries
Trinity Industries
TTX
Utility Trailer
Wescast Industries

HISTORICAL FINANCIALS
Company Type: Private

Income Statement
FYE: December 31

	REVENUE ($ mil.)	NET INCOME ($ mil.)	NET PROFIT MARGIN	EMPLOYEES
12/07	1,103	33	2.9%	1,050
12/06	852	36	4.2%	—
12/05	699	23	3.3%	—
12/04	741	36	4.9%	—
12/03	379	5	1.2%	—
Annual Growth	30.6%	62.2%	—	—

Net Income History

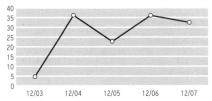

	12/03	12/04	12/05	12/06	12/07

Boise Cascade

Boise Cascade Holdings manufactures and distributes lumber, plywood, particleboard, and engineered products such as wood I-joists and laminated lumber. It also operates about 30 wholesale building material distribution centers throughout the US that sell a broad line of building materials, including those made by the company. To better focus on its core wood products and building materials distribution businesses, the firm has sold its paper and packaging and newsprint businesses, as well as its timberland assets. Formerly part of Boise Cascade Corporation (now OfficeMax), Boise Cascade Holdings is controlled by the private investment firm Madison Dearborn Partners through Forest Products Holdings, L.L.C.

In February 2008 Boise Cascade Holdings (BCH) sold its paper, packaging and newsprint, and transportation businesses, which now operate as publicly traded Boise Inc., to Aldabra. (BCH owns about 49% of Boise Inc's. shares following the sale.) The slowdown in the US housing market led to lower sales in 2007 vs. 2006 for the remaining wood products and building materials distribution business segments.

To reduce outstanding debt, the company sold its US timberland assets (2.2 million acres in Alabama, Idaho, Louisiana, Minnesota, Oregon, and Washington) to investment company Forest Capital Partners for $1.65 billion in 2005. The transaction included an agreement in which Forest Capital will supply fiber and wood products to Boise Cascade's mills and manufacturing plants.

Boise Cascade had a long history as Boise Cascade Corporation; however, the corporation's paper, forest products, and timber assets were purchased by Madison Dearborn Partners in late 2004, forming BCH. During this transaction, the old Boise Cascade Corporation's office products distribution business changed its name to OfficeMax Incorporated.

OfficeMax owns 20% of BCH; management and Madison Dearborn Partners own the rest.

HISTORY

Boise Cascade got its start as the old Boise Cascade Corporation in 1957 with the merger of two small lumber companies — Boise Payette Lumber Company (based in Boise, Idaho) and Cascade Lumber Company (Yakima, Washington). The business diversified in the 1960s under the leadership of Robert Hansberger, moving into office-products distribution in 1964. A number of acquisitions followed, including Ebasco Industries (1969), a consulting, engineering, and construction firm. By 1970 Boise Cascade had made more than 30 buys to diversify into building materials, paper products, real estate, recreational vehicles (RVs), and publishing.

In the early 1970s the company suffered a timber shortage as its access to public timberlands dwindled. Its plans to develop recreational communities in California, Hawaii, and Washington met opposition from residents, causing Boise Cascade to scrap all but six of the 29 projects.

In 1972 high costs related to the remaining projects left the company in debt. John Fery replaced Hansberger as president that year and sold companies not directly related to the company's core forest-product operations.

In the late 1980s and early 1990s, Boise sold more nonstrategic operations, including its Specialty Paperboard Division in 1989. It sold more than half of its corrugated-container plants in 1992 to focus on manufacturing forest products and distributing building materials and office supplies.

Boise Cascade also sold its wholesale office-product business in 1992 to focus on direct sales to big buyers such as IBM and Boeing. The company sold off its Canadian subsidiary, Rainy River Forest Products, during 1994 and 1995. Resurgent paper prices resulted in a profit in 1995, Boise Cascade's first since 1990.

Also in 1995, in a move into the international paper market, Boise Cascade signed a joint venture agreement with Shenzhen Leasing to form Zhuhai Hiwin Boise Cascade, a Chinese manufacturer of carbonless paper. That year it sold a minority stake in Boise Cascade Office Products (BCOP) to the public.

The company sold its coated-papers business to paper and packaging heavyweight Mead in 1996 for $639 million. The following year Boise began harvesting its first quick-growth cotton-wood trees (specially grown to cut the cost of harvesting from traditional slow-growth hardwood plantations). Also in 1997 BCOP bought Jean-Paul Guisset, an office-products direct marketer in France. Although this acquisition boosted sales and increased the company's European presence, company profits suffered that year because of weak paper prices.

The low price of paper in 1998 prompted the company to close four sawmills and a research and development center. Restructuring costs associated with the closures and a fire at the company's Medford, Oregon, plywood plant led to a net income loss for the year.

In 1999 Boise bought Wallace Computer Services, a contract stationer business, and broadened its building-supply distribution network nationwide by acquiring Furman Lumber, a building-supplies distributor. In 2000 Boise Cascade completed the purchase of the 19% of Boise Office Solutions that it didn't already own. The company also sold its European office products operations for $335 million and then turned around and purchased the Blue Star Business Supplies Group of US Office Products in Australia and New Zealand for about $115 million.

Because of the decline in federal timber sales, in 2001 the company closed its plywood mill and lumber operations in Emmett, Idaho, and a sawmill in Cascade, Idaho. In 2002 lagging profits prompted Boise to implement cost-cutting procedures. In 2003 the company pinned its hopes for growth on the office product segment with the acquisition of OfficeMax for nearly $1.2 billion in cash and stock. The deal put Boise Cascade's office products business on par with industry leaders Staples and Office Depot. The deal would also seriously alter the way the company began to run its business (office products versus timber and wood products) in the future.

Investment firm Madison Dearborn Partners purchased Boise Cascade's paper, forest products, and timberland assets for $3.7 billion in October 2004 and changed the name of the company to Boise Cascade Holdings, L.L.C. Thomas Stephens became the new CEO. The firm filed an IPO registration statement and converted from a Delaware limited liability company to a Delaware corporation named Boise Cascade Company, but canceled the IPO in May 2005. It converted back to a limited liability company status and reinstated its Boise Cascade Holdings, L.L.C. name in December 2005.

In February 2008 the firm sold its paper, packaging and newsprint, and transportation businesses, which now operate as publicly traded Boise Inc., to Aldabra for about $1.6 billion.

EXECUTIVES

Chairman and CEO: W. Thomas (Tom) Stephens, age 65, $1,000,000 pay
EVP, Paper and Packaging and Newsprint: Alexander Toeldte, age 48, $500,000 pay
SVP and CFO: Thomas E. Carlile, age 56, $425,000 pay
SVP, Paper: Miles A. Hewitt, age 49
SVP, Building Materials Distribution: Stanley R. (Stan) Bell, age 61, $370,000 pay
SVP, Wood Products: Thomas A. (Tom) Lovlien, age 52, $341,667 pay
VP, Boise Engineered Wood Products: Tom Corrick
VP, Office Papers, Boise Paper: Robert (Rob) Sommer
VP, Boise Paper, Uncoated Freesheet Papers: George Jendrzejewski
VP and Controller: Samuel K. Cotterell, age 56
VP, General Counsel, and Secretary: Karen E. Gowland, age 46
VP and CIO, Information Services: Robert Egan, age 43
VP and General Manager, Boise Packaging: Judith M. (Judy) Lassa
VP, Boise Newsprint: Robert E. (Bob) Strenge
VP, Corporate Planning: Robert Tracy
VP and Treasurer: Wayne M. Rancourt, age 42
VP, Communications, Performance Management, and Organizational Development: Virginia Aulin
VP, Investor Relations and Public Policy: Robert McNutt
VP and Operations Manager, Boise Building Materials Distribution: Nick A. Stokes
VP and Region Manager, Minnesota Operations: Terry W. Ward
Manager, Market Pulp, Boise Paper: Ric Sandstrom
Auditors: KPMG LLP

LOCATIONS

HQ: Boise Cascade Holdings, L.L.C.
1111 W. Jefferson St., Ste. 900, Boise, ID 83702
Phone: 208-384-6161
Web: www.bc.com

PRODUCTS/OPERATIONS

2007 Sales

	$ mil.	% of total
Building materials distribution	2,564.0	47
Paper	1,596.2	29
Wood products	1,010.2	19
Packaging & newsprint	783.1	14
Adjustments	(540.0)	(9)
Total	**5,413.5**	**100**

Selected Products and Operations

Building material distribution
  Composite decking
  Engineered wood products (EWP)
  Framing accessories
  Insulation
  Lumber
  Oriented strand board (OSB)
  Plywood
  Roofing
  Siding
Wood
  Dimension lumber
  Engineered wood products (EWP)
  Laminated veneer lumber
  Plywood
  Ponderosa pine lumber

COMPETITORS

84 Lumber
BlueLinx
Builders FirstSource
Georgia-Pacific
Guardian Building Products Distribution
HD Supply
Lowe's
Pacific Coast Building Products
Potlatch
PrimeSource Building
Stock Building Supply
Temple-Inland
Weyerhaeuser

HISTORICAL FINANCIALS

Company Type: Private

Income Statement

	REVENUE ($ mil.)	NET INCOME ($ mil.)	NET PROFIT MARGIN	EMPLOYEES
12/07	5,414	128	2.4%	10,042
12/06	5,780	72	1.2%	10,191
12/05	5,907	121	2.0%	10,155
12/04	5,735	94	1.6%	10,494
12/03	4,654	(47)	—	—
Annual Growth	**3.9%**	**—**	**—**	**(1.5%)**

FYE: December 31

2007 Year-End Financials

Debt ratio: 115.3%   Current ratio: —
Return on equity: 14.3%   Long-term debt ($ mil.): 1,113
Cash ($ mil.): —

Net Income History

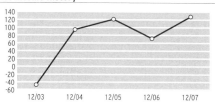

Boler Company

This Boler wants trucks to ride smoothly in their lanes. The holding company's main subsidiary, Hendrickson, makes truck and trailer suspension systems and auxiliary axle systems for the commercial heavy-duty vehicle market. Hendrickson's stamping division makes truck bumpers and stamped components, and its spring division manufactures steel flat-leaf and parabolic taper-leaf springs. Hendrickson primarily sells to OEMs in North America, but it also distributes products to Australia, Mexico, Europe, and Asia. Boler, which acquired Hendrickson in 1978, has been attempting to grow its international presence.

During 2007, the company made two acquisitions that have expanded its manufacturing capacity. It bought the trailer axle business of bankrupt Dana Corporation, which gave Hendrickson additional operations in the US, Canada, and China. Near the end of that year it also bought Watson and Chain Manufacturing, which makes truck drive-axle suspensions and related products. Watson and Chain Manufacturing will operate as an independent subsidiary.

EXECUTIVES

Chairman: John M. Boler
President and CEO: Matthew J. Boler
President and CEO, Hendrickson: Gary Gerstenslager
VP North American Sales and Marketing, Hendrickson: Baine Adams
VP and General Manager, Hendrickson Trailer Suspension Systems: Perry Bahr
VP International Operations, Hendrickson: Mike Keeler
VP and General Manager, Hendrickson Truck Systems Group: Doug Sanford
VP Human Resources, Hendrickson: Dave Templeton
VP International Business Development, Hendrickson: John Parr
Director, Marketing and Communications: Mark Slingluff

LOCATIONS

HQ: The Boler Company
500 Park Blvd., Ste. 1010, Itasca, IL 60143
Phone: 630-773-9111   **Fax:** 630-773-9121
Web: www.hendrickson-intl.com

COMPETITORS

American Axle & Manufacturing
ArvinMeritor
Dana Corporation
Magna International
TA Delaware
Tenneco
Wozniak Industries

Bonneville Power Administration

Bonneville Power Administration (BPA) keeps the lights on in the Pacific Northwest. The US Department of Energy power marketing agency operates a 15,440-mile high-voltage transmission grid that delivers about 35% of the electrical power consumed in the region. The electricity that BPA wholesales is generated primarily by 31 federal hydroelectric plants and one private nuclear facility. BPA also purchases power from other hydroelectric, gas-fired, and wind and solar generation facilities in North America. Founded in 1937, the utility sells power primarily to public and investor-owned utilities, as well as some industrial customers.

EXECUTIVES

Administrator and CEO: Stephen J. (Steve) Wright, age 44
Deputy Administrator: Steven G. (Steve) Hickok, age 59
COO: Anita Decker
EVP, Internal Business Systems: Kimberly (Kim) Leathley
EVP, Finance and CFO: David J. Armstrong
EVP, Planning and Governance: Charles E. (Chuck) Meyer
EVP and General Counsel: Randy A. Roach
SVP, Transmission Business Line: Mark W. Maher
SVP, Employee and Business Resources: Terence G. (Terry) Esvelt
SVP, Power Services: Paul E. Norman
SVP, Transmission Services: Vickie A. VanZandt
VP, Information Technology and CIO: Larry D. Buttress
VP, Environment, Fish and Wildlife: Gregory K. Delwiche
VP, Field Services, Transmission Business Line: Frederick M. (Fred) Johnson
VP, National Relations: Jeffrey K. (Jeff) Stier
VP, Strategic Planning: Pamela J. (Pam) Marshall
Chief Public Affairs Officer: Christy Brannon
Political Strategy and Public Affairs Manager: Carolyn Whitney
Chief Technical Officer: Scott Ducar
Manager Construction and Maintenance Services: John McGhee
Communication and Liaison: Sonya Tetnowski
Chief Compliance Officer: Keshmira McVey
Human Resources Diversity and EEO: Godfrey Beckett
Tribal Relations: John Smith
Chief Risk Officer: Eric Larson
Chief Press Officer: Ed Mosey
CIO: Brian Furumasu
Auditors: PricewaterhouseCoopers LLP

LOCATIONS

HQ: Bonneville Power Administration
905 NE 11th Ave., Portland, OR 97208
Phone: 503-230-3000   **Fax:** 503-230-5884
Web: www.bpa.gov

Bonneville Power Administration carries electricity to California, Idaho, Montana, Nevada, Oregon, Utah, Washington, and Wyoming.

COMPETITORS

AEP	IDACORP
AES	NW Natural
Avista	PacifiCorp
Black Hills	PG&E
CenterPoint Energy	Portland General Electric
Duke Energy	Puget Energy
Dynegy	Sempra Energy

HISTORICAL FINANCIALS
Company Type: Government-owned

Income Statement
FYE: September 30

	REVENUE ($ mil.)	NET INCOME ($ mil.)	NET PROFIT MARGIN	EMPLOYEES
9/07	3,269	457	14.0%	2,896
9/06	3,419	611	17.9%	2,923
9/05	3,268	487	14.9%	3,028
9/04	3,198	504	15.8%	3,153
9/03	3,612	555	15.4%	3,121
Annual Growth	(2.5%)	(4.7%)	—	(1.9%)

2007 Year-End Financials

Debt ratio: 93.1%
Return on equity: 7.1%
Cash ($ mil.): —
Current ratio: —
Long-term debt ($ mil.): 6,262

Net Income History

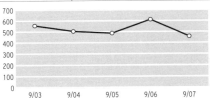

9/03	9/04	9/05	9/06	9/07

Booz Allen Hamilton

Consultants at Booz Allen Hamilton aim to help US government agencies operate more efficiently at home and abroad. The firm provides a wide range of management consulting and technology integration services; its specialties include information technology, operations, organization and change, program management, strategy, and systems engineering. Booz Allen has worked for such agencies as the Department of Defense, the Federal Aviation Administration, and the Internal Revenue Service. Investment firm The Carlyle Group owns a majority interest in the consulting firm, which traces its roots to 1914.

Though focused on US government clients, Booz Allen nevertheless undertakes a variety of engagements. Key markets include civil government agencies responsible for energy, finance, health, and transportation, as well as defense and national security agencies. Clients also include international development entities, such as the World Bank, and nongovernmental organizations, such as foundations and universities.

Booz Allen formerly worked for commercial as well as government clients. But the firm separated its commercial- and government-related businesses in July 2008 as part of a deal in which The Carlyle Group paid about $2.5 billion for control of the government arm, which retained the Booz Allen name. The firm's commercial arm was spun off as a separate entity, Booz & Company, which is owned by its officers.

The goal of the separation was to enable each operating business to better focus on its core market. Just as the commercial and government units did when they operated under common ownership, however, Booz Allen and Booz & Company will work together on engagements when it makes sense to do so.

HISTORY

Edwin Booz graduated from Northwestern University in 1914 with degrees in economics and psychology and started a statistical analysis firm in Chicago. After serving in the army during WWI, he returned to his firm, renamed Edwin Booz Surveys. In 1925 Booz hired his first full-time assistant, George Fry, and in 1929 he hired a second, James Allen. By then the company had a long list of clients, including U.S. Gypsum, the *Chicago Tribune*, and Montgomery Ward, which was losing a retail battle with Sears, Roebuck and Co.

In 1935 Carl Hamilton joined the partnership, and a year later it was renamed Booz, Fry, Allen & Hamilton. The firm prospered well into the next decade by providing advice based on "independence that enables us to say plainly from the outside what cannot always be said safely from within," according to a company brochure.

During WWII the firm worked increasingly on government and military contracts. Fry opposed the pursuit of such work for consultants and left in 1942. The firm was renamed Booz, Allen & Hamilton. Hamilton died in 1946, and the following year Booz retired (he died in 1951), leaving Allen as chairman. He successfully steered the firm into lucrative postwar work for clients such as Johnson Wax, RCA, and the US Air Force.

A separate company, Booz, Allen Applied Research, Inc. (BAARINC), was formed in 1955 for technical and government consulting, including missile and weaponry work, as well as consulting with NASA. By the end of the decade, *Time* had dubbed Booz Allen "the world's largest, most prestigious management consultant firm." The partnership was incorporated as a private company in 1962, and in 1967 commissioner Pete Rozelle requested its services for the merger of the National Football League and American Football League.

When Allen retired in 1970, Charlie Bowen became the new chairman, and the company went public. However, as the economy stalled during the energy crisis, spending for consultants plunged. Jim Farley replaced Bowen in 1975, and the company was taken private again in 1976. A turnaround was engineered, and the firm was soon helping Chrysler through its historic bailout and developing strategies for the breakup of AT&T.

Booz Allen again experienced trouble in the 1980s after Farley instituted a competition to select his successor. Michael McCullough was eventually chosen in 1984, but the 10-month election process turned into a dogfight that pitted partner against partner, taking an enormous toll on morale. McCullough began restructuring the firm along industry lines, creating a department store of services in an industry characterized by boutique houses. The turmoil was too much, and by 1988 nearly a third of the partners had quit.

William Stasior became chairman in 1991 and reorganized Booz Allen yet again, splitting it down public and private sector lines. Allen died in 1992, the same year the firm moved to McLean, Virginia. The company began privatization work in the former Soviet Union and in Eastern Europe in 1992 and continued to emphasize government business, including contracts with the IRS (1995) for technology modernization and with the General Services Administration (1996) to provide technical and management support for all federal telecommunications users.

In 1998 the company won a 10-year, $200 million contract with the US Defense Department to establish a scientific and technical data warehouse. Ralph Shrader was appointed CEO in early 1999; Stasior retired as chairman later that year. Booz Allen acquired Scandinavian consulting firm Carta in 1999 and formed a venture capital firm for startups with Lehman Brothers in 2000. The company announced in late 2000 that it would spin off Aestix, its e-commerce business, but reconsidered amid a general economic slowdown and hostile IPO market. (The unit was integrated back into Booz Allen in 2002.)

Booz Allen saw an increase in work related to defense and national security after the terrorist attacks of September 11, 2001. Engagements included work related to the reconstruction of Iraq (as a subcontractor on telecommunications projects managed by Lucent), and in 2003 Booz Allen was awarded a contract from the Health Resources and Services Administration to help establish and operate a bioterrorism technical support center.

In 2008 Booz Allen spun off its commercial consulting business as an independent firm, Booz & Company. The spinoff was part of a transaction in which investment firm The Carlyle Group acquired a controlling interest in the Booz Allen's government-related consulting business, which retained the Booz Allen name.

EXECUTIVES

Chairman and CEO: Ralph W. Shrader, age 63
President, US Government Business:
 Dennis O. Doughty
SVP and Chief Administrative Officer:
 Samuel R. (Sam) Strickland
SVP, Chief Legal Officer, Secretary, and Director:
 C. G. Appleby
Lead VP, Information Technology, Security Market:
 James (Jim) Manchisi
VP and CIO: Frank S. Smith III
VP and Chief Personnel Officer: Horacio Rozanski
VP, Intellectual Capital Officer, and Client Service Officer, Civil Market Entitlement Agencies:
 Nancy Hardwick
VP and Director: Francis J. (Jimmy) Henry
VP and Director: Lloyd W. Howell Jr.
VP and Director: Christopher M. (Chris) Kelly
VP and Director: John D. Mayer
VP and Principal Manager, Diplomacy and International Development Business: Donald L. (Don) Pressley
VP and Head, Information Analysis Center:
 Robert J. (Bob) Lamb
VP and Head, Economic and Business Analysis:
 Robert Makar
VP, Advanced Enterprise Integration:
 Gregory G. (Greg) Wenzel
Auditors: Deloitte & Touche LLP

LOCATIONS

HQ: Booz Allen Hamilton Inc.
 8283 Greensboro Dr., McLean, VA 22102
Phone: 703-902-5000   **Fax:** 703-902-3333
Web: www.boozallen.com

PRODUCTS/OPERATIONS

Selected Markets

Civil government
 Benefits and entitlements
 Federal finance
 International development and diplomacy
Defense
 Air Force
 Army
 Joint staff and combatant commands
 Navy and Marine Corps
 Office of the Secretary of Defense and defense agencies
 Space

Energy
Environment
Health
 Health informatics
 Health not-for-profit/nongovernmental organizations
 International public health
 US public health
Homeland security
Intelligence
Law enforcement
Not-for-profit/nongovernmental organizations
Transportation
 Aviation infrastructure
 Highways and automotive technology
 Passenger rail and mass transit

Selected Practice Areas

Assurance and resilience
Economic and business analysis
Information technology
Modeling and simulation
Organization and strategy
Supply chain and logistics
Systems engineering and integration

COMPETITORS

Accenture
A.T. Kearney
BAE SYSTEMS
Bain & Company
BearingPoint
Boston Consulting
CACI International
Capgemini
Computer Sciences Corp.
Deloitte Consulting
EDS
General Dynamics
IBM
Lockheed Martin
MAXIMUS
McKinsey & Company
Northrop Grumman
PA Consulting
PRTM Management
Raytheon
Towers Perrin
Unisys

HISTORICAL FINANCIALS

Company Type: Private

Income Statement

FYE: March 31

	REVENUE ($ mil.)	NET INCOME ($ mil.)	NET PROFIT MARGIN	EMPLOYEES
3/07	4,100	—	—	19,000
3/06	3,700	—	—	17,300
3/05	3,300	—	—	16,000
3/04	2,700	—	—	14,000
3/03	2,300	—	—	11,300
Annual Growth	15.5%	—	—	13.9%

Revenue History

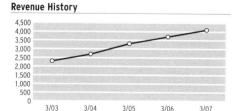

Bose Corporation

Bose has been making noise in the audio products business for some time. The firm is one of the world's leading manufacturers of speakers for the home entertainment, automotive, and pro audio markets. It makes a variety of consumer models for stereo systems and home theaters, including its compact Wave radio system. For sound professionals, Bose offers loudspeakers and amplifiers, as well as products designed for musicians. Bose sells its products at 100-plus factory and showcase stores and through affiliated retailers. The company is using its expertise to branch out into other markets. Founder Amar Bose, a former professor of electrical engineering at Massachusetts Institute of Technology, owns the company.

The company has eight manufacturing plants and 16 international subsidiaries. One new subsidiary, ElectroForce Systems Group, offers advanced test instruments for materials research and product development.

Bose has built a reputation for making high-quality products through its commitment to research in electronics and acoustical engineering. The expertise of its engineers proved invaluable to the Boston Convention & Exhibition Center, which brought in Bose to revamp its public address system.

Its research focus has taken the company into new fields in recent years: Bose has been developing an electromagnetic suspension system for automobiles since the 1980s and in 2004 it acquired testing equipment maker EnduraTEC. Taking advantage of the popularity of Apple's iPod, Bose introduced the SoundDock digital music system in 2004.

EXECUTIVES

Chairman and CEO: Amar G. Bose, age 76
President: Bob Maresca
VP Finance and CFO: Daniel A. Grady, age 67
VP Engineering: Joseph (Joe) Veranth
VP Finance and Assistant Treasurer:
 Herbert W. Batchelder
VP Human Resources: John C. Ferrie
VP Manufacturing: Bryan Fontaine
VP Research and Director: Thomas A. Froeschle
VP; President, Bose Japan: Sumiyoshi Sakura
VP Bose Europe: Nic A. Merks
General Manager, Bose Corporation India:
 Ratish Pandey
General Manager, EnduraTEC Systems Group:
 Ed Moriarty
Chief Engineer and Director, Bose Live Music Technology Group: Ken Jacob
General Counsel and Secretary: Mark E. Sullivan
Director of Americas Professional Systems Division:
 Mitch Nollman
Director Information Security: Terri Curran
Director of Public Relations: Carolyn Cinotti
Media Relations: Joanne Berthiaume
CIO: Rob Ramrath
Auditors: PricewaterhouseCoopers LLP

LOCATIONS

HQ: Bose Corporation
 The Mountain, Framingham, MA 01701
Phone: 508-879-7330   **Fax:** 508-766-7543
Web: www.bose.com

PRODUCTS/OPERATIONS

Selected Products

Automotive sound systems
Aviation and military headsets
Home entertainment
  Headphones and headsets
  Home stereo speakers
  Home theater speakers
  Multimedia speakers
  Outdoor and marine speakers
  Wave systems
Professional audio
  Amplifiers
  Loudspeakers

COMPETITORS

Boston Acoustics
Cambridge SoundWorks
Eminence Speaker
Harman International
JVC KENWOOD
Klipsch
Koss
Mitek Corporation
Phoenix Gold
Pioneer Corporation
Polk Audio
QSC Audio
Rockford
Sony USA
SpeakerCraft
Stanton Group
Telex Communications

Boston Consulting Group

Global corporations are willing to give much more than a penny for the thoughts of Boston Consulting Group (BCG). One of the world's top-ranked consulting practices, BCG operates from about 65 offices in more than 35 countries in the Americas, Europe, and the Asia/Pacific region. The firm's 3,900 consultants offer a wide array of services, mainly to large corporate clients. BCG's practice areas include branding and marketing, corporate finance, globalization, and information technology. Founded in 1963 by industry pioneer Bruce Henderson, the firm is owned by its employees.

BCG is noted for developing consulting concepts such as "time-based competition" (rapid response to change) and "deconstruction" (an end to vertical integration).

Over the years, CEO Hans-Paul Bürkner has worked to distinguish the firm from competitors such as McKinsey & Company and Bain & Company in an effort to win consulting engagements in a tight economy. One area of focus is China, where BCG intends to expand its staff.

EXECUTIVES

Chairman Emeritus: John S. Clarkeson, age 65
Chairman: Carl W. Stern, age 62
President and CEO: Hans-Paul Bürkner
CFO: Debbie Simpson
Senior Partner and Managing Director: Dieter Heuskel
Senior Partner and Managing Director:
  Michael Silverstein
Senior Partner and Managing Director: Rich Lesser
Senior Partner and Managing Director:
  Antonella Mei-Pochtler
Senior Partner and Managing Director: Takashi Mitachi
Senior Partner and Managing Director: Michel Fredeau
Chairman, North and South America:
  Steven H. (Steve) Gunby
Chairman, Asia Pacific: John Wong

Chairman, Europe and Middle East: Bjørn Matre
Global Leader, Practice Areas: Ron Nicol
Media Contact US: Eric Gregoire

LOCATIONS

HQ: The Boston Consulting Group Inc.
  1 Exchange Place, 6th Fl., Boston, MA 02109
Phone: 617-973-1200   **Fax:** 617-973-1399
Web: www.bcg.com

Selected Office Locations

Americas
Atlanta
Boston
Buenos Aires
Chicago
Dallas
Detroit
Houston
Los Angeles
Mexico City
Miami
Monterrey
New York
San Francisco
Santiago
São Paulo
Toronto
Washington, DC

Europe and Middle East
Abu Dhabi
Amsterdam
Athens
Barcelona
Berlin
Brussels
Budapest
Cologne
Copenhagen
Dubai
Düsseldorf
Frankfurt
Hamburg
Helsinki
Kiev

Asia/Pacific region
Auckland
Bangkok
Beijing
Hong Kong
Jakarta
Kuala Lumpur
Melbourne
Mumbai
Nagoya
New Delhi
Seoul
Shanghai
Singapore
Sydney
Taipei
Tokyo

Lisbon
London
Madrid
Milan
Moscow
Munich
Oslo
Paris
Prague
Rome
Stockholm
Stuttgart
Vienna
Warsaw
Zürich

PRODUCTS/OPERATIONS

Selected Practice Areas

Branding
Corporate finance
E-commerce
Globalization
Information technology
Innovation
Intellectual property
Marketing and sales
Operations
Organization
Post-merger integration
Strategy

COMPETITORS

Accenture
Arthur D Little
A.T. Kearney
Bain & Company
BearingPoint
Booz Allen
Computer Sciences Corp.
Deloitte Consulting
EDS
IBM
McKinsey & Company
Monitor Group
PA Consulting
Perot Systems
PRTM Management
Roland Berger
Towers Perrin

HISTORICAL FINANCIALS

Company Type: Private

Income Statement

FYE: December 31

	ESTIMATED REVENUE ($ mil.)	NET INCOME ($ mil.)	NET PROFIT MARGIN	EMPLOYEES
12/07	2,332	—	—	6,000
12/06	1,800	—	—	6,270
12/05	1,500	—	—	5,500
Annual Growth	24.7%	—	—	4.4%

Revenue History

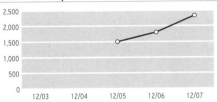

Boston Red Sox

You might say this team is now a curse on the other teams in Major League Baseball. Boston Red Sox Baseball Club operates one of the oldest and most storied franchises in the major leagues, notable for its 86-year championship drought popularly attributed to "The Curse of the Bambino." The team broke The Curse in 2004 when it won the World Series, then won its seventh championship three years later. Throughout its struggles, though, the Sox have continued to enjoy strong support from hometown fans at venerable Fenway Park, the oldest pro baseball stadium in the country. The franchise was founded as a charter member of the American League in 1901; it has been owned by John Henry since 2002.

Boston's rise to the top of baseball has come mostly thanks to the deep pockets of its owner, who has spent lavishly to stock the BoSox roster with talent. Before making its run for the 2007 World Series, the team signed Japanese pitcher Daisuke Matsuzaka to a six-year, $52 million contract (plus a $51 million "negotiating fee" paid to Matsuzaka's former team, the Sebu Lions) and later inked former Los Angeles Dodger J. D. Drew to a five-year, $70 million deal. The Red Sox have the second highest payroll in the majors, behind their hated rivals the New York Yankees.

Henry, who previously controlled the Florida Marlins, and his partners (which include The New York Times) paid about $660 million for the storied franchise, a record sum for a baseball team. The new ownership group upgraded the team's 90-year-old stadium with new concessions areas and seats atop the Green Monster — the left field wall which measures 37 feet high. Additional upgrades came in 2008 with additional seating. Plans have also been announced to replace the wooden seats in the stadium's grandstand section.

The partnership, known as New England Sports Ventures, also owns an 80% stake in New England Sports Network along with Boston Bruins owner Jeremy Jacobs.

EXECUTIVES

Principal Owner: John W. Henry
Chairman: Thomas C. (Tom) Werner
Vice Chairman: David I. Ginsberg
Vice Chairman: Phillip H. Morse
President and CEO: Larry Lucchino, age 63
COO: Mike Dee
EVP and General Manager: Theo Epstein
SVP Corporate Relations and Executive Director, Red Sox Foundation: Meg Vaillancourt
SVP Fenway Affairs: Lawrence C. (Larry) Cancro
SVP Sales and Marketing: Samuel (Sam) Kennedy
SVP Planning and Development: Janet Marie Smith
VP and CFO: Robert C. (Bob) Furbush
VP and Club Counsel: Elaine Weddington Steward
VP Player Personnel: Benjamin P. (Ben) Cherington, age 31
VP Human Resources and Administration: Mary Sprong
VP Public Affairs: Susan Goodenow
VP Media Relations: John C. Blake
VP Business Operations: Jonathan Gilula
VP and Club Counsel: Jennifer Flynn
VP Ticketing: Ron Bumgarner
Director Event Operations: Jeffrey E. (Jeff) Goldenberg
Director Facilities Management:
  Thomas L. (Tom) Queenan
Director Minor League Operations: Raquel S. Ferreira
Director Security and Emergency Services:
  Charles Cellucci
Medical Director: Thomas J. Gill
Manager: Terry John Francona

LOCATIONS

HQ: Boston Red Sox Baseball Club Limited Partnership
  4 Yawkey Way, Boston, MA 02215
Phone: 617-267-9440   **Fax:** 617-375-0944
Web: boston.redsox.mlb.com

The Boston Red Sox play at 39,928-seat capacity Fenway Park in Boston.

PRODUCTS/OPERATIONS

Championship Titles
World Series (1903, 1912, 1915-16, 1918, 2004, 2007)
American League Pennant (1903-04, 1912, 1915-16, 1918, 1946, 1967, 1975, 1986, 2004, 2007)

COMPETITORS

Baltimore Orioles
New York Yankees
Tampa Bay Rays
Toronto Blue Jays

HISTORICAL FINANCIALS

Company Type: Private

Income Statement

	REVENUE ($ mil.)	NET INCOME ($ mil.)	NET PROFIT MARGIN	EMPLOYEES
12/07	263	—	—	—
12/06	234	—	—	—
12/05	206	—	—	—
12/04	220	—	—	—
12/03	190	—	—	—
Annual Growth	8.5%	—	—	—

FYE: December 31

Revenue History

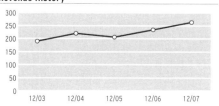

Boston University

With colleges and universities thick on the ground in Boston, Boston University accounts for more than a hill of beans. Founded as a Methodist seminary in 1839, Boston University (BU) has about 32,000 students and 3,800 faculty at its campus on the banks of the Charles River. The private university has some 20 graduate and undergraduate schools and colleges, including schools of education, law, management, medicine, social work, and theology. BU also supports a number of research programs, such as the Center for Space Physics and the Center for Human Genetics. Nobel laureates Elie Wiesel, Derek Walcott, and Sheldon Glashow are among BU's more than 3,500 faculty members.

EXECUTIVES

Chairman: Robert A. Knox, age 56
President and Trustee: Robert A. Brown, age 56
Provost: David K. Campbell
Provost, Medical Campus: Karen H. Antman
EVP and Chief Administrative Officer:
  Joseph P. Mercurio
VP Financial Affairs and Treasurer:
  Kenneth G. Condon, age 60
VP and General Counsel: Todd L. C. Klipp
VP Government and Community Affairs:
  Edward M. King
VP Marketing and Communications: Stephen P. Burgay
VP Planning, Budgeting, and Information:
  Marvin F. Cook
VP Operations: Gary W. Nicksa
VP Enrollment and Student Affairs: Anne W. Shea
VP Administrative Services: Peter Fiedler
VP Financial Affairs and Treasurer: Martin J. Howard
VP Development and Alumni Relations:
  Scott G. Nichols
VP Interim Information Systems and Technology:
  Michael Krugman
Chief Investment Officer: Pamela L. Peedin
Dean of Students: Kenneth Elmore
Auditors: PricewaterhouseCoopers LLP

LOCATIONS

HQ: Boston University
  1 Sherborn St., Boston, MA 02215
Phone: 617-353-2000   **Fax:** 617-353-4048
Web: www.bu.edu

PRODUCTS/OPERATIONS

Selected Schools and Colleges
College of Arts and Sciences
College of Communication
College of Engineering
College of General Studies
Goldman School of Dental Medicine
Graduate School of Arts and Sciences
Metropolitan College (continuing education)
Sargent College of Health & Rehabilitation Sciences
School of Education
School of Hospitality Administration
School of Law
School of Management
School of Medicine
School of Public Health
School of Social Work
School of Theology
The University Professors Program

Boy Scouts of America

Scouts enter dens as Tigers and eventually take flight as Eagles. Boy Scouts of America (BSA), one of the nation's largest youth organizations, has some 3 million youth members and more than 1 million adult leaders in its ranks. BSA offers educational and character-building programs emphasizing leadership, citizenship, personal development, and physical fitness. In addition to traditional scouting programs (Tiger, Cub, Webelos, and Boy Scouts, ranging up to Eagle rank), it offers the Venturing program for boys and girls ages 14-20. BSA generates revenue through membership and council fees, supply and magazine sales, and contributions. The organization was founded by Chicago publisher William Boyce in 1910.

BSA programs remain popular, but membership growth in the organization's units has stalled. The organization has a strategic plan that involves reaching out to new groups of parents and students. For example, it has studied African-American, Asian, and Hispanic families in order to best determine how to attract more youth and volunteers from those groups. It has also analyzed Generation X and Millennial parents, in order to determine how to best bring scouting to their families.

In 2000 the US Supreme Court ruled that the organization could legally bar homosexuals from becoming troop leaders, and since then BSA has been involved in legal battles over access to charitable funds and public meeting locations.

EXECUTIVES

President: John Gottschalk, age 64
National Commissioner: Tico A. Perez
International Commissioner: Wayne Perry
Chief Scout Executive: Robert J. (Bob) Mazzuca
COO and Assistant Chief Scout Executive:
  Wayne Brock
CFO and Assistant Chief Scout Executive: Jim Terry
EVP: Rex W. Tillerson, age 56
VP: Richard L. (Rick) Burdick
VP Human Resources: James S. Turley
VP Development: Drayton McLane Jr., age 72
VP Council Solutions: Terrence P. (Terry) Dunn
VP Marketing: Nathan Rosenberg
VP: Earl G. Graves Sr., age 73
VP Outdoor Adventures: Jack Furst
VP Supply: O. Temple Sloan Jr., age 69
VP Administration: Randall Stephenson
Treasurer: Aubrey B. Harwell Jr., age 65
Auditors: PricewaterhouseCoopers LLP

LOCATIONS

HQ: Boy Scouts of America
  1325 W. Walnut Hill Ln., Irving, TX 75015
Phone: 972-580-2000   **Fax:** 972-580-7870
Web: www.scouting.org

PRODUCTS/OPERATIONS

2007 Youth Membership

	No.
Cub scout age	1,687,986
Boy scout age	913,588
High school age	254,259
Total	**2,855,833**

HISTORICAL FINANCIALS

Company Type: Not-for-profit

Income Statement

FYE: December 31

	REVENUE ($ mil.)	NET INCOME ($ mil.)	NET PROFIT MARGIN	EMPLOYEES
12/07	175	32	18.4%	500
12/06	195	65	33.2%	500
12/05	181	26	14.3%	500
12/04	270	—	—	500
12/03	298	—	—	500
Annual Growth	(12.5%)	11.7%	—	0.0%

2007 Year-End Financials

Debt ratio: —
Return on equity: 4.6%
Cash ($ mil.): —
Current ratio: —
Long-term debt ($ mil.): —

Net Income History

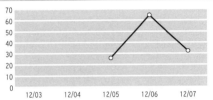

Bozzuto's Inc.

Bozzuto's is a leading wholesale grocery distribution company that supplies food and non-food products to independent supermarkets belonging to the IGA network in Maryland, New Jersey, New York, Pennsylvania, and in New England. The company distributes a full line of grocery items, including meat products, produce, and frozen food, as well as household goods and other general merchandise. It carries goods sold under both the IGA and Hy-Top labels, in addition to national brands. Bozzuto's also owns about 10 supermarkets in Connecticut and Massachusetts operating under the Adams Super Food Stores banner. The company, founded in 1945, is owned and operated by the Bozzuto family.

EXECUTIVES

Chairman, President, and CEO: Michael A. Bozzuto
EVP Retail Development: George Motel
SVP Merchandising, Advertising, and Procurement: Steve Heggelke
VP Finance: Robert H. (Bob) Wood
VP Deli, Bakery, and Dairy: Robert Cohen
VP Information Technology: John Keeley
VP Sales: Dan Brock
Corporate Secretary and Assistant Treasurer: Patricia S. (Pat) Houle
Director Human Resources: Lilly Branco
Director Advertising and Communication: Amy Yeager

LOCATIONS

HQ: Bozzuto's Inc.
275 School House Rd., Cheshire, CT 06410
Phone: 203-272-3511   **Fax:** 203-250-2954
Web: www.bozzutos.com

COMPETITORS

Associated Grocers of New England
Associated Wholesalers
C&S Wholesale
Krasdale Foods
McLane
Nash-Finch
Pine State Trading
Shaw's
Stop & Shop
SUPERVALU
Wakefern Food

Bradco Supply

Bradco Supply offers construction contractors everything they need to put a roof over their clients' heads. The company distributes roofing, siding, windows, and other building materials through about 145 locations in 30 states under several names, including Admiral Building Products, Bak-A-Lum, and FlexMaster. It is one of the nation's largest distributors of roofing materials for commercial use. Bradco also exports its construction materials to the Caribbean, Europe, Latin America, and the Middle East. The company has grown by acquiring smaller roofing material businesses. In 2008 private equity firm Advent International acquired a majority interest in Bradco Supply from its founder Barry Segal and family.

Segal, who founded Bradco Supply in 1966 and had served as its CEO, retired following completion of the Advent deal in August 2008. Segal's sons Brad and Martin will remain with the company as president and vice president, respectively. The Segal family retained a minority stake in the business.

In late 2007 Bradco Supply acquired Admiral Building Products, a major Firestone roofing materials distributor with five locations in New England. Admiral Building Products founder Ted Boylan joined Bradco Supply as its CEO, succeeding Barry Segal.

EXECUTIVES

CEO: Ted Boylan
President: Bradley (Brad) Segal
CFO: Joe Stacy
VP: Martin Segal
Accounting Manager: Susan Biunno
Accounts Payable Manager: Bob Ripp
Facilities Manager: Skip Roberts
Fleet Manager: Kevin Tremmel
Information Systems Manager: Joe Hradil
Operations Manager: Joe Revello
Marketing Manager: Paul Barsa
Vendor Relations Manager: Steve Kubicka
Real Estate Manager: Mark Singer
General Counsel: Michael L. Weinberger
Credit Manager: George Waeckel
Audit Manager: Joe Iannini
Procurement Manager: Jon Hauge
Human Resources Manager: Andrew Fullerton

LOCATIONS

HQ: Bradco Supply Corp.
34 Englehard Ave., Avenel, NJ 07001
Phone: 732-382-3400   **Fax:** 732-382-6577
Web: www.bradcosupply.com

PRODUCTS/OPERATIONS

Selected Subsidiaries

Admiral Building Products (roofing materials)
Bak-A-Lum (building materials, cabinets, countertops)
Bradco Metals (metal roofing systems)
Bradco Tapered Express (tapered roof design)
East Coast (commercial and residential roofing)
FlexMaster (building products)
Posey Steel & Supply (metals and building materials)

COMPETITORS

ABC Supply
Beacon Roofing
CRH
Guardian Building Products
Huttig Building Products
North Pacific Group
PrimeSource Building

HISTORICAL FINANCIALS

Company Type: Private

Income Statement

FYE: December 31

	REVENUE ($ mil.)	NET INCOME ($ mil.)	NET PROFIT MARGIN	EMPLOYEES
12/07	1,700	—	—	2,600
12/06	1,920	—	—	3,100
12/05	1,760	—	—	3,200
12/04	1,340	—	—	3,250
12/03	995	—	—	2,000
Annual Growth	14.3%	—	—	6.8%

Revenue History

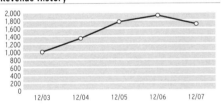

Brasfield & Gorrie

If the South will rise again, Brasfield & Gorrie should have something to do with it. One of the leading construction companies in the Southeast, Brasfield & Gorrie builds high rises and hotels, bridges and churches, hospitals and malls. Other projects include industrial plants, water and wastewater treatment facilities and schools. Commercial and industrial construction together account for most of its revenues; the company is a leading health care facilities contractor. Brasfield & Gorrie provides general contracting, design/build, and construction management services. Founded in 1922 by Thomas C. Brasfield, the company was sold to owner Miller Gorrie (chairman and CEO) in 1964.

Projects include the I-59/I-20 replacement bridge in Alabama that was destroyed in 2004 when a tanker truck carrying diesel fuel crashed and burned. Brasfield & Gorrie and the other contractors replaced the bridge almost a month ahead of schedule.

Brasfield & Gorrie has offices in Atlanta; Birmingham, Alabama; Nashville, Tennessee; Jacksonville and Orlando, Florida; and Raleigh, North Carolina.

EXECUTIVES

Chairman and CEO: M. Miller Gorrie, age 72
President: M. James (Jim) Gorrie
VP and COO: Jeffrey I. (Jeff) Stone
CFO: Randall J. Freeman
CIO: Tom Garrett
VP and General Counsel: Charles (Chip) Grizzle
President, East Region: Rob Taylor
President, Corporate Planning and Administration:
 Stan Starnes
Director Operations: Marty Hardin
Auditors: PricewaterhouseCoopers

LOCATIONS

HQ: Brasfield & Gorrie, LLC
 3021 7th Ave. South, Birmingham, AL 35233
Phone: 205-328-4000   **Fax:** 205-251-1304
Web: www.brasfieldgorrie.com

PRODUCTS/OPERATIONS

Portfolio

Clubhouses
Education
Healthcare
Industrial
Mixed-Use
Multi-Family
Office
Parking
Religious
Retail
Sports & Leisure
Treatment

COMPETITORS

Alberici
B. L. Harbert
Barton Malow
BE&K
Beck Group
Bovis Lend Lease
Brice Building
Choate Construction
Doster Construction
Hardin Construction
H.J. Russell
Hoar Construction
McCarthy Building
Skanska USA Building
Turner Corporation
Whiting-Turner

HISTORICAL FINANCIALS

Company Type: Private

Income Statement   FYE: December 31

	REVENUE ($ mil.)	NET INCOME ($ mil.)	NET PROFIT MARGIN	EMPLOYEES
12/07	2,006	—	—	3,000
12/06	1,980	—	—	2,939
12/05	1,645	—	—	2,743
12/04	1,260	—	—	2,267
12/03	1,040	—	—	2,301
Annual Growth	17.9%	—	—	6.9%

Revenue History

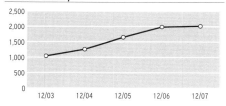

Brightstar Corp.

Brightstar shines in the constellation of telecommunications distributors. The company distributes wireless communications products, including cell phones and accessories, wireless data equipment, and prepaid wireless products. It also offers inventory management, logistics, fulfillment, customized packaging, and assembly services. Brightstar distributes cell phones made by the likes of Motorola, Kyocera, Samsung, LG, and Sony Ericsson. Brightstar operates facilities in more than 40 countries. It sells to network operators, retailers, and resellers.

EXECUTIVES

Chairman, President, and CEO: R. Marcelo Claure
COO; President, Global Solutions: George Appling
CFO: Dennis Strand
SVP and Corporate Controller: Arlene Vargas, age 39
CTO: David A, (Dave) Stritzinger
VP, Fixed Wireless Solutions: Jaime Narea, age 49
VP, Global Marketing and Press Relations: Sally Lange
CEO, Brightstar US: Denise Gibson
President, Middle East, Africa, and India:
 Javier Villamizar, age 34
Senior Director, Product Management: Elias J. Kabeche, age 40
Director, Business Development and Venture Solutions: Andres Chisco
President and COO, Brightstar US: Michael (Mike) Cost
President, Brightstar Europe: Rod Millar
President, Brightstar Latin America:
 Juan Carlos Archila
President, Integrated Supply Chain Solutions:
 Harry Lagad
Corporate Treasurer and Cash Conversion Cycle Officer: Oscar J. Fumagali
Auditors: Deloitte & Touche LLP

LOCATIONS

HQ: Brightstar Corp.
 9725 NW 117th Ave., Ste. 300, Miami, FL 33178
Phone: 305-421-6000
Web: www.brightstarcorp.com

COMPETITORS

Axesstel
Brightpoint Inc.
CLST
Hello Direct
InfoSonics
Ingram Micro
Phones International
SED International
Tech Data
Telular
TESSCO
Tricell

HISTORICAL FINANCIALS

Company Type: Private

Income Statement   FYE: December 31

	REVENUE ($ mil.)	NET INCOME ($ mil.)	NET PROFIT MARGIN	EMPLOYEES
12/07	4,400	—	—	3,500
12/06	3,590	—	—	1,684
12/05	2,252	—	—	1,441
Annual Growth	39.8%	—	—	55.8%

Revenue History

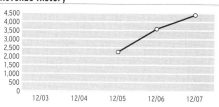

Bristol West Holdings

Looking for auto coverage? Go west, young man — or east, north, or south. Bristol West Holdings sells non-standard private passenger insurance; that is, insurance for those who have trouble getting standard coverage because of bad driving records, age, limited financial resources, and the like. The company operates in some 37 states through about 10,000 agents.

Though the majority of Bristol West's customers buy minimum liability policies, the company also offers collision and comprehensive coverage, as well as medical payments coverage that pays for health care costs related to automobile accidents.

Farmers Group, a unit of Zurich Financial Services, acquired Bristol West in 2007. Affiliates of Kohlberg Kravis Roberts had taken the company public in 2004 and owned about 40% of Bristol West until the Farmers Group takeover.

EXECUTIVES

President and CEO: Simon J. Noonan, age 43
SVP and CFO: Robert D. Sadler, age 44
SVP and CIO: John L. Ondeck, age 47
SVP Chief Legal Officer, and Corporate Secretary:
 George G. O'Brien, age 51
SVP Business Integration: George N. Christensen, age 61
SVP Claims: James J. Sclafani Jr., age 48, $340,656 pay
SVP Human Resources: Nila J. Harrison, age 43
SVP Operations: Anne M. Bandi, age 50
SVP Product Research and Development:
 Brian J. Dwyer, age 50
SVP Product Management: Ronald E. Latva, age 42
SVP Product Management: Audrey E. Sylvan, age 43
SVP Marketing: Douglas R. Burtch
Auditors: Deloitte & Touche LLP

LOCATIONS

HQ: Bristol West Holdings, Inc.
 5701 Stirling Rd., Davie, FL 33314
Phone: 954-316-5200   **Fax:** 954-316-5275
Web: www.bristolwest.com

COMPETITORS

Affirmative Insurance
AIG
Allstate
Direct General
GEICO
Infinity Property & Casualty
Mercury General
Nationwide
Progressive Corporation
Safeco
State Farm

HISTORICAL FINANCIALS

Company Type: Private

Income Statement

FYE: December 31

	ASSETS ($ mil.)	NET INCOME ($ mil.)	INCOME AS % OF ASSETS	EMPLOYEES
12/06	945	42	4.5%	1,154
12/05	893	55	6.1%	1,205
12/04	1,041	61	5.9%	1,288
12/03	778	34	4.3%	1,285
12/02	633	12	1.8%	—
Annual Growth	10.5%	38.3%	—	(3.5%)

2006 Year-End Financials

Equity as % of assets: 37.8%
Return on assets: 4.6%
Return on equity: 12.1%
Long-term debt ($ mil.): 100
Sales ($ mil.): 661

Net Income History

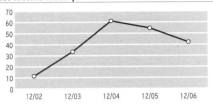

70				
60				
50				
40				
30				
20				
10				
0				
12/02	12/03	12/04	12/05	12/06

Broadcast Music, Inc.

If you are a composer or musician, Broadcast Music, Inc. (BMI) is here to see that your royalties are paid. The not-for-profit organization collects licensing fees from a host of outlets and venues (such as radio stations, TV programs, Web sites, restaurants, and nightclubs) and distributes them to the more than 350,000 songwriters, composers, and music publishers it represents. Its catalog of compositions includes more than 6.5 million works by a diverse range of artists including the Dixie Chicks, Marilyn Manson, Willie Nelson, Sting, and Shania Twain.

BMI is working to eliminate online piracy and ensure that its clients get a cut of the proceeds when their music is downloaded on the Internet. The organization monitors music played over the Web and has created a digital licensing center to license music played online. BMI's New Media unit also makes deals related to the use of music in podcasts and mobile phone ringtones.

EXECUTIVES

Chairman: Cecil L. Walker
President, CEO, and Director: Del R. Bryant
EVP and COO: John Cody
SVP and CFO: Bruce Esworthy
SVP and General Counsel: Marvin Berenson
SVP International: Ron Solleveld
SVP Licensing: Michael O'Neill
SVP Operations and Information Technology: Bob Barone
SVP Performing Rights: Alison Smith
SVP Writer/Publisher Relations: Phillip R. Graham

VP Corporate Relations: Robbin Ahrold
VP Film and TV Relations, Los Angeles: Doreen Ringer Ross
VP New Media and Strategic Development: Richard Conlon
VP, Treasurer, and Financial Planning: Angelo Bruno
VP and Controller: Gary Cannizzo
VP Operations and Information Technology: Milt Laughlin
VP Corporate Planning: Jodi H. Saal
Senior Director Media Relations and Business Communications: Jerry Bailey
Promotions Director: Claudette (Candi) Shand

LOCATIONS

HQ: Broadcast Music, Inc.
320 W. 57th St., New York, NY 10019
Phone: 212-586-2000   **Fax:** 212-245-8986
Web: www.bmi.com

Broadcast Music has offices in Atlanta; Los Angeles; Miami; Nashville, Tennessee; and New York, as well as in London and San Juan, Puerto Rico.

PRODUCTS/OPERATIONS

Selected Artists Represented

The Beach Boys
The Beatles
Chuck Berry
David Bowie
Brooks & Dunn
James Brown
Dave Brubeck
Mariah Carey
Eric Clapton
Sheryl Crow
Dixie Chicks
Eagles
Eminem
Elton John
Kid Rock
Little Richard
Jennifer Lopez
Marilyn Manson
matchbox twenty
Tim McGraw
Sarah McLachlan
Moby
Willie Nelson
Santana
Smash Mouth
Sting
Shania Twain

HISTORICAL FINANCIALS

Company Type: Not-for-profit

Income Statement

FYE: June 30

	REVENUE ($ mil.)	NET INCOME ($ mil.)	NET PROFIT MARGIN	EMPLOYEES
6/08	901	—	—	—
6/07	839	—	—	—
6/06	779	—	—	—
6/05	728	—	—	—
6/04	673	—	—	700
Annual Growth	7.6%	—	—	—

Revenue History

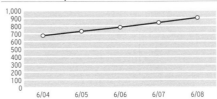

1,000				
900				
800				
700				
600				
500				
400				
300				
200				
100				
0				
6/04	6/05	6/06	6/07	6/08

Broder Bros.

Selling clothes had been in the genes of sportswear distributor Broder Bros. for years. Begun as a haberdashery in 1919, it evolved from making hats and gloves to distributing imprintable sportswear, such as golf shirts, T-shirts, sweatshirts, and jerseys. The firm sells trade brands (Hanes), exclusive brands (adidas Golf), and private labels and operates under the Broder, Alpha, and NES units. Its private labels include Devon & Jones, Desert Wash, Harvard Square, and others. Customers, mostly small US retailers, order merchandise through seasonal catalogs or online. Private investment firm Bain Capital has held a majority interest of the company since May 2000, when the Broder family sold the firm.

Since being acquired by Bain Capital, Broder Bros. has been busy adding to its portfolio. The company acquired the assets of Amtex Imports, a competitor based in Northlake, Illinois, for $6.8 million in September 2006.

The company caters to some 80,000 customers. These include advertising specialty companies, screen printers, embroiderers, and specialty retailers who purchase Broder Bros. products to embellish for its clients.

EXECUTIVES

President, CEO, and Director: Thomas Myers, age 59, $176,038 pay (prior to promotion)
SVP Operations: Norman Hullinger, age 48, $294,231 pay
CFO: Martin J. Matthews, age 36
VP, Human Resources: Richard Emrich
PR Contact: Anne Rivers
VP Pricing Administration: Jon Hays, $175,385 pay
VP Marketing: Girisha Chandraraj, age 33
VP Purchasing: Robert Lackman, age 52
Auditors: PricewaterhouseCoopers LLP

LOCATIONS

HQ: Broder Bros., Co.
6 Neshaminy Interplex, 6th Fl., Trevose, PA 19053
Phone: 215-291-6140   **Fax:** 800-521-1251
Web: www.broderbros.com

PRODUCTS/OPERATIONS

2007 Sales

	$ mil.	% of total
Alpha	442.6	48
Broder	370.8	40
NES	115.7	12
Total	**929.1**	**100**

2007 Sales

	% of total
Trade brands	75
Private label brands	16
Exclusive or near-exclusive brands	9
Total	**100**

COMPETITORS

Anvil Holdings
Delta Apparel
Drew Pearson Marketing
Fruit of the Loom
Gildan Activewear
Hanesbrands
PremiumWear
Russell Corporation
VF

HISTORICAL FINANCIALS

Company Type: Private

Income Statement

FYE: December 31

	REVENUE ($ mil.)	NET INCOME ($ mil.)	NET PROFIT MARGIN	EMPLOYEES
12/07	929	(124)	—	1,743
12/06	959	(8)	—	1,799
12/05	978	—	—	1,571
12/04	877	—	—	1,498
12/03	488	—	—	—
Annual Growth	17.5%	—	—	5.2%

2007 Year-End Financials

Debt ratio: —
Return on equity: —
Cash ($ mil.): —
Current ratio: —
Long-term debt ($ mil.): 338

Net Income History

Brookshire Grocery

By selling staples, specialties, and Southern hospitality, Brookshire Grocery Co. has grown into a chain of about 155 Brookshire's, Super 1 Food, and Olé Foods supermarkets in Texas, Arkansas, Louisiana, and Mississippi. The company also owns three distribution centers, a dairy, and SouthWest Foods, its private label manufacturing unit. Brookshire's stores average about 40,000 sq. ft., while its warehouse-style Super 1 Foods stores average 80,000 sq. ft. More than 110 of Brookshire Grocery's stores have pharmacy departments. Originally part of the Brookshire Brothers grocery chain (dating back to 1921), the company split from it in 1939. The Brookshire family is still among the company's owners.

To better compete with Wal-Mart Supercenters, among other rivals, the Texas grocer has added its own Health & Harmony line of organic and natural foods and other specialty food items, and is touting low prices. To that end, its newest store format is named ALPS (for Always Low Price Store), a discount-store prototype. The regional grocer also seeks to please the state's sizable Hispanic population with a pair of Olé Foods stores, which cater to Hispanic shoppers.

CEO Marvin Massey retired in 2007. He was succeeded by Rick Rayford, a 35-year veteran and former EVP of Brookshire Grocery.

EXECUTIVES

CEO: Rick Rayford
EVP and Chief Retail Operations Officer: Johnny Skelton
EVP, CFO, and Controller: Tim King
SVP and CIO: Gary Butler
SVP and Category Management Officer: Randy Duke
SVP Super 1 Foods Division: Pete Leung
SVP and Chief Marketing Officer: Rick Ellis
SVP Corporate Development: Greg Nordyke

VP Category Management Grocery: Ron Oran
VP Category Management, Merchandising: Roger Story
VP Corporate Asset Protection: Ed Van Fleet
VP Distribution: Hugh Kirksey
VP Manufacturing: James (Jim) Pitner
VP Materials Management: Jerry Nick
VP Category Management, Fresh Foods: Chris Mooney
VP Category Management, General Merchandise and Nonfoods: Kevin Santone

LOCATIONS

HQ: Brookshire Grocery Company
1600 W. South West Loop 323, Tyler, TX 75701
Phone: 903-534-3000   **Fax:** 903-534-2206
Web: www.brookshires.com

PRODUCTS/OPERATIONS

2008 Stores

	No.
Brookshire's Food Stores	124
Super 1 Foods	30
Olé Foods Stores	2
ALPS (Always Low Price)	1
Total	**157**

Selected Private-Label Brands

Brookshire's Meats (deli and other meats)
Dairy Pride (dairy products)
Economize (milk)
Flavor Pride (beverages)
Goldenbrook Farms (premium dairy and frozen foods)
Premier Mountain (water)
Tasty Bakery (baked goods)
Sunnybrook Farms (fresh produce)

COMPETITORS

E-Z Mart Stores
Fiesta Mart
H-E-B
Kmart
Kroger
Minyard Group
Randall's
SUPERVALU
Target
Wal-Mart
Whole Foods

Brookstone, Inc.

Need an office putting green? How about an alarm clock that projects the outside temperature on the ceiling? Then Brookstone is the place for you. It sells gifts, gadgets, and other doodads targeted primarily toward men through more than 300 stores in more than 40 states, the District of Columbia, and Puerto Rico. The company's functional yet unique product categories include health and fitness, home and office, outdoor living, and travel and auto. Brookstone also sells online and through catalogs Brookstone and Hard-To-Find Tools. Because most of Brookstone's sales are gifts, it operates temporary kiosks during the busy Father's Day and December holiday seasons. The company is owned by Osim International.

Quirky, high-quality items range from a $30 meat thermometer to a $3,000 Ms. Pac-Man arcade game, with most of its products bearing the Brookstone name.

With the demise of competitor Sharper Image, Brookstone in 2008 capitalized on the situation, with a limited-time offer giving holders of Sharper Image gift cards a 25% discount on items. (Sharper Image, now called TSIC, has since closed its retail stores, but continues to sell its products in other stores.)

A consortium led by fellow lifestyle products company Osim International acquired the company for $417.2 million and took it private in 2005. Osim is based in Singapore; its US subsidiary is Osim Health Focus. Other consortium members include Singapore-based investment firm Temasek Holdings and US private equity firm JW Childs Associates. The new owners did away with the Gardeners Eden chain.

EXECUTIVES

Chairman: Ron Sim Chye Hock, age 48
President and CEO: Louis (Lou) Mancini, $487,500 pay (partial-year salary)
EVP Finance and Administration, CFO, Treasurer, and Secretary: Philip W. Roizin, age 48, $400,000 pay
EVP Store Operations: George H. Sutherland, age 46
SVP Business Development: Jim Rabbitt
VP and General Manager, Direct Marketing: Gregory B. (Greg) Sweeney, age 52, $350,000 pay
VP Distribution and Logistics and CIO: Steven P. Brigham, $300,000 pay
VP Human Resources: Carol A. Lambert, age 53
VP Marketing: Steven C. Strickland, age 44
VP and General Merchandising Manager: M. Rufus (Rudy) Woodard Jr., age 50, $350,000 pay
National Corporate Sales Manager: Amy Sheehy
Auditors: Ernst & Young LLP

LOCATIONS

HQ: Brookstone, Inc.
1 Innovation Way, Merrimack, NH 03054
Phone: 603-880-9500   **Fax:** 603-577-8005
Web: www.brookstone.com

PRODUCTS/OPERATIONS

Selected Categories and Products

Health and fitness
  Bath
  Climate Control
  Fitness
  Massage
  Personal Care
  Sleep Comfort
  Tempur-Pedic
Home and office
  Bedroom
  Desk & Office
  Electronics
  Games
  Kitchen
  Lighting
  Telescopes & Optical
  Wine & Bar
Outdoor living
  Barbecue
  Hammocks & Furniture
  Lawn & Garden
  Outdoor Decor
  Pool & Beach
  Sports & Games
Travel and auto
  Auto Accessories
  Auto Care
  Clocks & Appliances
  Garage
  Luggage
  Travel Accessories

COMPETITORS

Bed Bath & Beyond	RadioShack
Best Buy	RedEnvelope
Eddie Bauer Holdings	Relax the Back
Hammacher Schlemmer	Restoration Hardware
Levenger	SkyMall
Linens 'n Things	Smith & Hawken
L.L. Bean	TSIC
Neiman Marcus	Williams-Sonoma

HISTORICAL FINANCIALS
Company Type: Private

Income Statement
FYE: Saturday nearest December 31

	REVENUE ($ mil.)	NET INCOME ($ mil.)	NET PROFIT MARGIN	EMPLOYEES
12/07	563	6	1.1%	3,504
12/06	512	2	0.3%	3,278
12/05*	441	(4)	—	—
1/05	499	21	4.3%	3,016
1/04	434	18	4.1%	2,905
Annual Growth	6.7%	(22.3%)	—	4.8%

*Fiscal year change

2007 Year-End Financials
Debt ratio: 65.7%   Current ratio: —
Return on equity: 2.4%   Long-term debt ($ mil.): 175
Cash ($ mil.): —

Net Income History

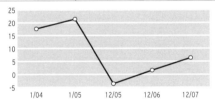

Bureau of National Affairs

The Bureau of National Affairs (BNA) is a leading provider of legal and regulatory information. The company publishes advisory and research reports, books, newsletters, and other publications covering economic, health care, labor, public policy, and tax issues for professionals in business and government. It has a staff of 600 reporters, editors, and legal experts who gather information from around the country. BNA delivers its information online and through print and electronic products, some available through subscription services such as LexisNexis and Thomson Reuter's Westlaw. It also produces financial planning and tax software (BNA Software) and provides commercial printing services (McArdle Printing).

Other subsidiary companies include Tax Management Inc. (information for tax planning and compliance needs), Institute of Management and Administration (practical information for

lawyers, accountants, and human resources professionals), and Kennedy Information (information for professionals in management consulting, executive recruiting, and investor relations).

Founded in 1929, BNA was incorporated in its present form as an employee-owned company in 1946. It is the country's oldest fully employee-owned company.

EXECUTIVES

Chairman: Sandra C. Degler, age 68
Chairman and CEO: Paul N. Wojcik, age 59, $571,789 pay
President, COO, and Director; President, Tax Management: Gregory C. McCaffery, age 47, $385,598 pay
VP, Corporate Secretary, and Director: Cynthia J. Bolbach, age 60
VP, General Counsel, and Director: Eunice L. Bumgardner, age 47, $212,126 pay
VP Resource Management: Carol A. Clark, age 51, $257,402 pay
VP and CFO: Robert P. Ambrosini, age 51
President, BNA Washington: Elizabeth (Betti) Brown
President, BNA International: Alan Edmunds
President, STF Services: Michael Smith
President, Kennedy Information and Institute of Management Administration (IOMA): Joseph Bremner
President, McArdle Printing: Lisa Arsenault
Treasurer: Gilbert S. Lavine, age 56
Controller: James R. Schneble, age 53
Manager Financial Planning and Analysis, Assistant Treasurer, and Director: Paul A. Blakely, age 50
Group Publisher, Tax Management and Director: Darren P. McKewen, age 46
Auditors: BDO Seidman, LLP

LOCATIONS

HQ: The Bureau of National Affairs, Inc.
1801 S. Bell St., Arlington, VA 22202
Phone: 703-341-3000   **Fax:** 800-253-0332
Web: www.bna.com

PRODUCTS/OPERATIONS

2007 Sales

	$ mil.	% of total
Publishing	289.5	82
Printing	35.7	10
Software	27.0	8
Total	**352.2**	**100**

Selected Subsidiary Companies
BNA Washington Inc.
BNA International Inc.
Institute of Management and Administration, Inc.
Kennedy Information, Inc.
The McArdle Printing Co., Inc.
STF Services Corp.
Tax Management Inc.

COMPETITORS
BLS
CCH Incorporated
EB
H&R Block
Informa
Inside Washington Publishers
National Journal
Reed Elsevier Group
Thomson Reuters
US Census Bureau
Wolters Kluwer

HISTORICAL FINANCIALS
Company Type: Private

Income Statement
FYE: December 31

	REVENUE ($ mil.)	NET INCOME ($ mil.)	NET PROFIT MARGIN	EMPLOYEES
12/07	352	88	25.0%	1,719
12/06	345	20	5.7%	1,728
12/05	329	24	7.3%	1,729
12/04	321	23	7.0%	1,802
12/03	312	16	5.2%	1,878
Annual Growth	3.1%	52.9%	—	(2.2%)

2007 Year-End Financials
Debt ratio: 101.9%   Current ratio: —
Return on equity: 499.6%   Long-term debt ($ mil.): 34
Cash ($ mil.): —

Net Income History

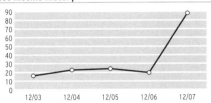

Burlington Coat Factory Warehouse

Burlington Coat Factory Warehouse has two *de facto* mottos: "not affiliated with Burlington Industries" (thanks to a 1981 trademark-infringement lawsuit settlement) and "We sell more than coats." The company operates about 400 no-frills retail stores offering current, brand-name clothing at less than standard retail price. Although it is one of the nation's largest coat sellers, it also sells children's apparel, bath items, furniture, gifts, jewelry, linens, and shoes. The business operates under the names Burlington Coat Factory (98% of sales), Cohoes Fashions, MJM Designer Shoes, and Super Baby Depot in some 45 states.

Founded in 1972, Burlington was acquired by affiliates of buyout firm Bain Capital in 2006. Under the terms of the buyout, Bain Capital acquired all of Burlington Coat Factory's outstanding shares for about $2.1 billion. (The family of founder Monroe Milstein owned 62% of Burlington Coat Factory prior to the acquisition.)

The retailer is best known for its year-round selection of about 10,000 to 20,000 discounted coats (compared to about 1,500 to 2,000 coats at the typical department store). Burlington Coat Factory takes less of a markup than its department store competition and has lower profit margins than other clothing retailers. It buys the coats early in the season (up to five months before department store rivals) to lock in lower prices. Burlington Coat Factory prefers to lease existing buildings and refurbish rather than build new stores, keeping overhead low. Unlike other off-price retailers, it buys directly from manufacturers and does not rely on leftovers or closeouts. The company also sells merchandise on the Internet at burlingtoncoatfactory.com and babydepot.com.

As part of its growth plan, the off-price retailer has acquired the rights for up to 24 leases from Value City Department Stores owner Retail Ventures. The stores, located in Ohio, Pennsylvania, New Jersey, and Maryland, are slated to open under the Burlington Coat Factory banner in the fall of 2008 through spring 2009.

In fiscal year 2006 the company opened three MJM Designer Shoes stores. The company's two stand-alone Luxury Linens stores were shut down and instead operate as departments within Burlington Coat Factory stores.

HISTORY

Russian-Jewish immigrant Abe Milstein and a partner started coat wholesaler and manufacturer Milstein and Feigelson in 1924. Abe's son, Monroe, was a quick study. He graduated from New York University with a business degree in 1946 at age 19 and started his own coat and suit wholesaling business called Monroe G. Milstein, Inc. His mother provided free labor at her son's company six days a week to keep the business alive. Abe ended his partnership in 1953 and joined his son's business.

Family relations were strained temporarily in 1972, when Monroe disregarded his father's advice not to buy a faltering coat factory outlet store in Burlington, New Jersey. (Abe believed that his son did not have enough retailing experience.) Monroe, however, thought owning a retail store would provide a guaranteed sales outlet for their merchandise, and he bought Burlington Coat Factory for $675,000 (using $60,000 of his wife Henrietta's savings). His company also adopted the Burlington Coat Factory Warehouse moniker as its own.

To become less dependent on the season-specific coat business, the company soon expanded its merchandise mix by adding a children's division (started by Henrietta, deceased in 2001) and subleased departments. It opened a second store in Long Island, New York, in 1975.

Settling a trademark dispute with fabric maker Burlington Industries in 1981, Burlington Coat Factory agreed to say in advertising — as it does to this day — that the two companies are not affiliated. The 31-store company went public two years later, using the money it raised to open almost 30 stores that year. As part of its expansion in the 1980s, Burlington Coat Factory opened stores in warmer climates such as Texas and Florida.

The firm tried to grow through acquisitions that decade but failed in its attempts to buy a number of department store retailers. It made a successful bid in 1989 for New York discount retailer Cohoes.

Burlington Coat Factory's sales topped the $1 billion mark for the first time in fiscal 1993. Also that year the company bought Boston-based off-price family apparel chain Decelle. It then opened its first store outside the US (in Mexico) and tried new stand-alone store concepts based on successful in-store departments such as Luxury Linens and Baby Depot. A warm winter in 1994 hurt the company: Profits fell by two-thirds, and it sold off inventory for two years afterward.

The company pulled a line of men's parkas in late 1998 after a Humane Society investigation revealed that the coats were trimmed with hair from dogs killed inhumanely in China. Burlington Coat Factory launched a baby gift registry in 2000, and later that year opened a silk floral division in selected stores. In 2001 the company acquired 16 stores formerly occupied by bankrupt Montgomery Ward. Burlington Coat Factory began operating MJM Designer Shoes in fiscal 2002, opening nine of the stand-alone specialty shoe stores. The company closed its Decelle stores in 2003 but converted most of them to the Burlington Coat Factory and Cohoes names while launching 25 new stores in 2004 (most under the Burlington Coat Factory moniker).

In 2005 the company opened two Super Baby Depot stores. Burlington Coat Factory was acquired by the Boston-based private equity firm Bain Capital Partners in April 2006 for about $2.1 billion.

EXECUTIVES

President, CEO and Director: Mark A. Nesci, age 52
EVP, General Counsel, and Secretary: Paul C. Tang, age 55, $277,115 pay
SVP Information Systems: Brad H. Friedman
SVP Supply Chain: Charles (Charlie) Guardiola
CFO and Chief Accounting Officer: Todd Weyhrich, age 45
Chief Marketing Officer: Garry Graham
CTO: Michael (Mike) Prince
President Merchandising, Planning, Allocation and Marketing: Jack E. Moore Jr., age 53
VP, Chief Accounting Officer and Treasuree: Robert L. (Bob) LaPenta Jr., age 54
VP and Senior Divisional Merchandise Manager: Steven (Steve) Koster, age 59
VP Fashion and Branding: Jason Somerfield
VP Advertising: H. Robert Greenbaum
VP Baby Depot: David Cestaro
VP Facilities Management: Jerry Lupia
VP Logistics: Lorenzo Figueroa
VP Operations and Administration: Albert (Al) Cuccorelli
VP Real Estate: Robert Grapski, age 57, $279,807 pay
VP Recruiting: Sarah Orleck
VP e-Learning and Task Management: Gloria Johnson
VP Store Planning: Gerry Incollingo
VP Warehousing and Distribution: David Sanford
Director Human Resources: Judy Mascio
Auditors: Deloitte & Touche LLP

LOCATIONS

HQ: Burlington Coat Factory Warehouse Corporation
1830 Rte. 130, Burlington, NJ 08016
Phone: 609-387-7800   **Fax:** 609-387-7071
Web: www.burlingtoncoatfactory.com

PRODUCTS/OPERATIONS

2008 Stores

	No.
Burlington Coat Factory	379
MJM Designer Shoes	15
Cohoes Fashions	2
Super Baby Depot	1
Total	**397**

Selected Store Banners

Burlington Coat Factory (off-price clothing, accessories, linens, bath items, gifts)
Cohoes Fashions (upscale apparel and accessories)
MJM Designer Shoes (designer and fashion shoes)
Super Baby Depot (accessories, clothes, furniture for babies and toddlers)

COMPETITORS

Babies "R" Us	Macy's
Bed Bath & Beyond	Nordstrom
Belk	Payless ShoeSource
Bon-Ton Stores	Retail Ventures
Dillard's	Ross Stores
Dress Barn	Saks Inc.
DSW	Sears
Filene's Basement	Stein Mart
Gottschalks	Syms
J. C. Penney	Target
Kohl's	TJX Companies
Linens 'n Things	Wal-Mart

HISTORICAL FINANCIALS

Company Type: Private

Income Statement   FYE: Saturday nearest May 31

	REVENUE ($ mil.)	NET INCOME ($ mil.)	NET PROFIT MARGIN	EMPLOYEES
5/08	3,424	(49)	—	26,580
5/07	3,442	(47)	—	28,005
5/06	3,439	67	1.9%	26,500
5/05	3,200	106	3.3%	25,000
5/04	2,878	68	2.3%	24,000
Annual Growth	**4.4%**	**—**	**—**	**2.6%**

2008 Year-End Financials

Debt ratio: 457.5%   Current ratio: —
Return on equity: —   Long-term debt ($ mil.): 1,480
Cash ($ mil.): —

Net Income History

Burns & McDonnell

It may sound like a law firm, but Burns & McDonnell provides construction services, not legal advice. One of the leading design firms in the US, the company provides engineering, architectural, and design/build services for the aviation, defense, environmental, utilities, and other markets. The group has about 20 offices throughout the US, as well as locations in several other countries. It ranks among the top 10 designers for the power industry; more than one-third of its revenues are earned from projects for that market. In 2006 the company created its tenth business unit to offer architectural, engineering, and related services to the health care industry.

Burns & McDonnell's other divisions include aviation, energy, environmental, and infrastructure units.

The company was founded in Kansas City in 1898 by Clinton Burns and Robert McDonnell. The employee-owned firm's first major project (secured in 1900) was a combined water and light plant for Iola, Kansas.

EXECUTIVES

Chairman: Joel A. Cerwick
President and CEO: Greg M. Graves, age 50
SVP and General Manager, Infrastructure Group:
James (Jim) Foil
VP, Treasurer, and CFO: Mark Taylor
VP and General Counsel: Gerard T. (Gerry) Bukowski
VP and Chief Administrative Officer: Denny Scott
VP and Chief Technical Officer: Greg Gould
VP, Business and Technology Services Group: Jeff Greig
VP, Healthcare and Research Facilities Group:
Rick Keeler
VP, Environmental Group: Stephen (Steve) Linneman
VP, Environmental Studies and Permitting Group:
Dale Trott
President, Aviation and Facilities Group:
David Yeamans
President, Construction Group: Don Greenwood
President, Energy Group: Ray Kowalik
President, Process and Industrial Group:
John E. Nobles
**President, Electrical Transmission and Distribution
Group:** Walt Womack
President, Regional Office Group: Paul Fischer
Manager, Marketing Communications: Roger Dick

LOCATIONS

HQ: Burns & McDonnell, Inc.
9400 Ward Pkwy., Kansas City, MO 64114
Phone: 816-333-9400   **Fax:** 816-822-3412
Web: www.burnsmcd.com

COMPETITORS

Bechtel
Black & Veatch
Burns and Roe
Fluor
Foster Wheeler
HNTB Companies
Michael Baker
Parsons Corporation
Sargent & Lundy
Shaw Group
Terracon
URS
Washington Division

HISTORICAL FINANCIALS

Company Type: Private

Income Statement

FYE: September 30

	REVENUE ($ mil.)	NET INCOME ($ mil.)	NET PROFIT MARGIN	EMPLOYEES
9/07	1,000	850	85.0%	2,800
9/06	905	760	84.0%	—
9/05	638	—	—	—
Annual Growth	25.2%	11.8%	—	—

Net Income History

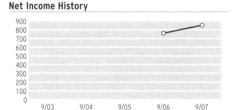

California Dairies Inc.

Herding dairies to give them greater "ag"-gregate strength has made California Dairies one of the largest dairy cooperatives in the US. California Dairies' 626 members provide the co-op with 16 billion pounds of milk a year. Its plants process milk, cheese, butter, and powdered milk. California Dairies' subsidiaries include Challenge Dairy Products (retail and foodservice butter products) and Los Banos Foods (cheddar cheese ingredients for food manufacturing). California Dairies is also a majority owner of DairyAmerica, Inc., which markets dairy products, including some 60% of all the milk powder produced in the US. The company exports its products to some 40 countries worldwide.

California Dairies was formed as the result of the 1999 merger of three California dairy cooperatives — California Milk Producers, the Danish Creamery Association, and San Joaquin Valley Dairymen.

EXECUTIVES

Chairman: George Borba
First Vice Chairman: Tony Mendes
Second Vice Chairman: Gerben Leyendekker
President and CEO: Richard Cotta
SVP and COO: Keith Gomes
SVP and CFO: Joe Heffington
VP Human Resources: Holly Misenhimer
VP Operations, Turlock and Los Banos Plants:
Eric Snoke
Secretary and Director: Steve Maddox
Director Information Technology: Scott McDonald
Treasurer and Director: Duane Matheron

LOCATIONS

HQ: California Dairies Inc.
2000 N. Plaza Dr., Visalia, CA 93291
Phone: 559-625-2200   **Fax:** 559-625-5433
Web: www.californiadairies.com

PRODUCTS/OPERATIONS

Selected Milk Powder Products
Dry buttermilk
Extra grade sweet cream
Grade A sweet cream
Dry whole milk
Extra grade 26%
Extra grade 28.5%
Non-fat dry milk
Extra grade low heat
Extra grade medium heat
Extra grade high heat
Grade A low heat
Grade A medium heat
Grade A high heat

COMPETITORS

Agri-Mark	Foremost Farms
Agropur Cooperative	Foster Dairy Farms
AMPI	Humboldt Creamery
Berkeley Farms	J.M. Swank
Dairy Farmers of America	Kraft Food Ingredients
Dairy Manufacturers	Land O'Lakes
Danisco A/S	Main Street Ingredients
Darifair Foods	Nestlé
Darigold, Inc.	Northwest Dairy
Dean Foods	Schreiber Foods
Denali Flavors	Sodiaal
Emmi	

California State University System

California State University (CSU) turns students into teachers. The university traces its roots to the state's teaching colleges and trains about 85% of California's teachers and staff. CSU is neck-and-neck with the State University of New York (SUNY) as the nation's largest university system. With some baby boomers' children reaching college age and college participation increasing among adults, CSU's student body has grown to about 415,000. The system has campuses in about 20 cities, including Bakersfield, Los Angeles, San Francisco, and San Jose. CSU primarily awards bachelor's and master's degrees in nearly 250 subject areas, leaving higher levels of study to the University of California (UC) system.

CSU is developing strategies to cope with an expected enrollment increase of about 40% through 2010 — what it calls Tidal Wave II. The first wave started with more than 20,000 additional students flooding the system in the fall of 2001. To battle the crippling influx of new students, CSU has begun offering distance education programs in which students are taught via teleconferencing and the Internet. Other strategies involve adding a summer semester to create year-long schooling, and expanding the use of off-campus centers.

HISTORY

In 1862 San Francisco's Normal School, a training center for elementary teachers, became California's first state-founded school for higher education. Six students attended its first classes, but there were 384 by 1866. It later moved to San Jose to escape the bustle of San Francisco.

In the late 1880s State Normal Schools opened in Chico, San Diego, and San Francisco, followed in 1901 by California State Polytechnic Institute, which offered studies in agriculture, business, and engineering. Other new colleges included Fresno State (1911) and Humboldt State (1913). Most of the schools offered four-year programs and admitted any student with eight years of grammar school education.

The Normal Schools were renamed Teachers Colleges in 1921 to reflect their role in teacher education. Two years later the colleges began awarding bachelor of arts degrees in education. In 1935 the schools were renamed State Colleges and expanded into liberal arts. In 1947 they were authorized to confer master's degrees in education.

After WWII, students on the GI Bill helped increase enrollment, and campuses opened in Los Angeles, Sacramento, and Long Beach. The prospect of the first baby boomers reaching college age prompted the founding of more campuses in the late 1950s. Russia's 1957 launch of Sputnik spurred additional focus on science and math at all education levels. The next year the colleges began awarding master's degrees in subjects unrelated to teacher education.

During the Red Scare, the system's first chancellor, Buell Gallagher, was accused by the press of being soft on communism. Other faculty were subpoenaed to appear before the House Committee on Un-American Activities.

In 1961 the system became the California State Colleges (CSC) and the board of trustees was created, giving the schools more independence from state government. In 1969 student and faculty groups seeking ethnic studies departments went on strike in San Francisco; the unrest closed the campus.

In 1972 CSC became known as the California State University and Colleges. Ten years later it adopted California State University as its name.

Barry Munitz became chancellor in 1991, taking over a system that had become oppressive due to a heavy-handed administration. Munitz, who came from corporate America, brought his business sense to the university and increased private fund raising, among other activities. He used words like "consumer" and "product" to describe his job. Munitz also increased tuition, which caused enrollments to drop from 1991-1995.

CSU added two new campuses in 1995, including CSU Monterey Bay, the first military base to be converted into a university since the end of the Cold War.

In 1997 Charles Reed was named to replace Munitz as chancellor, effective the following year. That year CSU proposed the California Educational Technology Initiative (CETI), a plan to build high-speed computer and telephone networks linking its campuses. CETI failed in 1998 after Microsoft and other investors pulled out. In 1999, after lengthy contract negotiations between Reed and faculty members failed to produce accord over teacher salaries and employment conditions, Reed imposed his own merit-based plan. The faculty responded with official rebukes and a vote of no confidence in Reed. The two sides eventually settled on a new three-year contract with provisions that salary and benefits may be negotiated annually.

The rancor over pay continued in 2000 when the California Faculty Association issued a report claiming women were discriminated against and the merit system was inherently unfair. CSU issued its own report denying the charges. In 2001 Reed, stirring up more controversy, began a new quest that would allow CSU to offer doctorate degrees. The move was bitterly opposed by the competing University of California system. In 2002 CSU started a program funded by a federal grant to reduce the harmful effects of alcohol on its students.

EXECUTIVES

Chair: Roberta Achtenberg
Vice Chair: Jeffrey L. Bleich
Chancellor and Ex-Officio Board Member:
  Charles B. Reed, age 67, $362,500 pay
Executive Vice Chancellor and Chief Academic Officer:
  Gary W. Reichard, $262,008 pay
Executive Vice Chancellor and CFO: Richard P. West,
  $280,056 pay
Interim Vice Chancellor, Human Resources:
  Gail E. Brooks
Special Assistant to the Chancellor: Jackie McClain,
  $246,186 pay
Chief of Staff: William Dermody
Associate Chief of Staff: Sandra B. George
Associate Vice Chancellor, Academic Affairs:
  Keith O. Boyum
Assistant Vice Chancellor, Advocacy and Institutional
  Relations: Karen Yelverton-Zamarripa
Assistant Vice Chancellor, Federal Relations: Jim Gelb
Assistant Vice Chancellor, Public Affairs: Claudia Keith
General Counsel: Christine Helwick, age 61,
  $230,002 pay
Director, Media Relations: Clara Potes-Fellow
Auditors: KPMG LLP

LOCATIONS

HQ: California State University System
  401 Golden Shore St., Long Beach, CA 90802
Phone: 562-951-4000   **Fax:** 562-951-4956
Web: www.calstate.edu

California State University has campuses in 23 cities.

California State University Campuses

California Maritime Academy
California Polytechnic State University, San Luis Obispo
California State Polytechnic University, Pomona
California State University
  Bakersfield
  Channel Islands
  Chico
  Dominguez Hills
  East Bay
  Fresno
  Fullerton
  Long Beach
  Los Angeles
  Monterey Bay
  Northridge
  Sacramento
  San Bernardino
  San Marcos
  Stanislaus
Humboldt State University
San Diego State University
San Francisco State University
San Jose State University
Sonoma State University

PRODUCTS/OPERATIONS

Selected Majors

Agriculture	History
Anthropology	Latin American studies
Asian studies	Mathematics
Business administration	Nursing
Chemistry	Philosophy
Communications	Physics
Computer science	Psychology
Economics	Public administration
Education	Theater arts

California Steel Industries

California Steel Industries (CSI) doesn't use forensic evidence, but its work does involve a steel slab. The company uses steel slab produced by third parties to manufacture steel products such as hot-rolled and cold-rolled steel, galvanized coils and sheets, and electric resistance weld (ERW) pipe. Its customers include aftermarket automotive manufacturers, oil and gas producers, roofing makers, tubing manufacturers, and building suppliers. CSI serves the western region of the US. The company operates slitting, shearing, coating, and single-billing services for third parties. Japan's JFE Holdings and Brazilian iron ore miner Companhia Vale do Rio Doce (Vale) each own 50% of CSI.

It buys more than two-thirds of its steel slab from ArcelorMittal subsidiary Lazaro Cardenas, in Mexico; ArcelorMittal Tubarão, in Brazil; and Australia's Bluescope Steel. The purchased slab is transported to the Port of Los Angeles and then sent by train to CSI's facilities. Effectively all of its products are sold within the US.

EXECUTIVES

Chairman: Masakazu Kurushima, age 59, $454,932 pay
President and CEO: Vicente Wright, age 55
EVP and CFO: Ricardo Bernandes, age 44, $347,538 pay
EVP Operations: Tashiyuki (Ted) Tamai, age 56,
  $342,031 pay
VP Administration and Corporate Secretary:
  Brett Guge, age 53, $315,256 pay
VP Commercial: James (Jim) Wilson, age 58,
  $320,323 pay
Manager Communications: Kyle Schulty
Manager Customer Service, Tubular Products
  Commercial: Martha Martinez
Manager Tubular Products Commercial: Ray Dubreuil
Manager Original Equipment Mfg.: Bob Swist
Auditors: Ernst & Young LLP

LOCATIONS

HQ: California Steel Industries, Inc.
  14000 San Bernardino Ave., Fontana, CA 92335
Phone: 909-350-6200   **Fax:** 909-350-6398
Web: www.californiasteel.com

California Steel Industries sells steel products in 11 states in the western US.

PRODUCTS/OPERATIONS

2007 Production

	% of total
Hot Rolled	38
Galvanized	38
Electric Resistance Welded (ERW) pipe	14
Cold Rolled	10
Total	**100**

COMPETITORS

AK Steel Holding Corporation
Evraz Steel Mills, Inc.
Nucor
O'Neal Steel
Steel Dynamics
Steelscape
Ternium Mexico
USS-POSCO Industries

HISTORICAL FINANCIALS

Company Type: Joint venture

Income Statement				FYE: December 31
	REVENUE ($ mil.)	NET INCOME ($ mil.)	NET PROFIT MARGIN	EMPLOYEES
12/07	1,283	(1)	—	933
12/06	1,359	109	8.0%	931
12/05	1,234	43	3.5%	938
12/04	1,257	109	8.7%	944
12/03	764	5	0.6%	921
Annual Growth	13.9%	—	—	0.3%

2007 Year-End Financials

Debt ratio: 53.9%   Current ratio: —
Return on equity: —   Long-term debt ($ mil.): 177
Cash ($ mil.): —

Net Income History

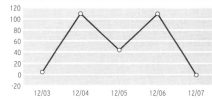

Callison Architecture

Callison Architecture provides services such as architectural design, consulting, graphic and interior design, and master planning for retail, mixed-use, multifamily residential, hospitality, health care, and corporate projects all over the world. The company, founded in 1975, also has a division dedicated to consulting and technical audit services for data centers and mission-critical facilities. A new real estate analysis and planning service was added in 2007. Callison's US clients have included Boeing, The Gap, Hewlett-Packard, Microsoft, NIKE, Nordstrom, Starwood Hotels and Resorts, and Washington Mutual.

International clients include the Bank of China, Harrods (UK), Mass Transit Railway Corporation (Hong Kong), IKEA (Sweden), Falabella Department Store (Chile), The Seibu Department Stores (Japan), LG Department Stores (Korea), and Central Pattana (Thailand).

Callison has offices around the world including Seattle, New York, Los Angeles, Dallas, Shanghai, and London. The company opened an office in Mexico City in 2007 after acquiring AGI Mexico — a small, full-service design firm.

World Architecture magazine ranked Callison as the top retail design firm in the US in 2008, a position which the company has held since 2003.

EXECUTIVES

CEO and Board Member: William B. (Bill) Karst
President and Board Member: Robert J. (Bob) Tindall
COO and Board Member: Steve Epple
EVP/Principal and Board Member: John Bierly
EVP/Principal and Board Member: Paula Stafford

LOCATIONS

HQ: Callison Architecture, Inc.
   1420 5th Ave., Ste. 2400, Seattle, WA 98101
Phone: 206-623-4646   **Fax:** 206-623-4625
Web: www.callison.com

Callison Architecture has principal US offices in Seattle, New York, and Santa Monica, California. It has international offices in London and Shanghai.

PRODUCTS/OPERATIONS

Selected Services

Architecture
Feasibility and development analysis
Fixture design
Graphic design
Interior design
Landlord services
Master planning
Medical planning
Operational analysis
Program management
Programming
Purchasing
Real estate consulting
Sustainable design
Tenant strategy and planning
Visual merchandising
Workplace consulting

Selected Projects

Campus planning
Corporate offices
Health care facilities and research laboratories
Hotels, resorts, and golf communities
Multi-family residential projects
Stores, shopping centers, theaters, and entertainment
   facilities
Urban mixed-use developments

COMPETITORS

A. Epstein and Sons	Kohn Pedersen Fox
Anshen+Allen	NBBJ
Cannon Design	RMJM Hillier
Gensler	Skidmore Owings
HOK	Zimmer Gunsul Frasca

HISTORICAL FINANCIALS

Company Type: Private

Income Statement

FYE: September 30

	REVENUE ($ mil.)	NET INCOME ($ mil.)	NET PROFIT MARGIN	EMPLOYEES
9/07	185	—	—	800
9/06	130	—	—	750
9/05	103	—	—	550
9/04	77	—	—	450
9/03	68	—	—	—
Annual Growth	28.3%	—	—	21.1%

Revenue History

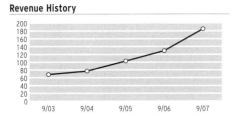

CalPERS

California's public-sector retirees already have a place in the sun; CalPERS gives them the money to enjoy it. CalPERS is the California Public Employees' Retirement System, the largest public pension system in the US. It manages retirement and health plans for more than 1.5 million beneficiaries (employees, retirees, and their dependents) from more than 2,600 government agencies and school districts. Even though the system's beneficiaries are current or former employees of the Golden State, CalPERS brings its influence to bear in all 50 states and beyond.

With more than $240 billion in assets in its investment funds, CalPERS uses its clout to sway such corporate governance issues as company performance, executive compensation, and even social policy. In the absence of a strong federal effort to purge corporations of corruption, CalPERS has often acted as a force for reform, urging companies to remove conflicts of interest and make themselves more accountable to shareholders, employees, and the public. CalPERS is also a powerful negotiator for such services as insurance; rates established by the system serve as benchmarks for employers throughout the nation.

Most of CalPERS' revenue comes from its enormous investment program: It has interests in US and foreign securities, oil and energy, real estate, and even hedge funds and venture capital activities. CalPERS has steadily increased its investments in private equity, looking to take ownership stakes in more firms. It owns stake in such prestigious entities as the Carlyle Group, Apollo Management, and Blackstone.

During the coming years CalPERS may be forced to sell assets, as it is expected to be hit with a wave of early retirements by middle-aged workers. The fund plans to sell some of its US stocks in exchange for emerging markets such as India and China. CalPERS is also eyeing new sectors such as infrastructure.

CalPERS' board consists of six elected, three appointed, and four designated members (the director of the state's Department of Personnel Administration, the state controller, the state treasurer, and a member of the State Personnel Board). The board has seen its share of disputes, on issues ranging from staff salaries to how to invest assets. The public and sometimes nasty donnybrooks have led to the exodus of several key personnel.

HISTORY

The state of California founded CalPERS in 1931 to administer a pension fund for state employees. By the 1940s the system was serving other public agencies and educational institutions on a contract basis.

When the Public Employees' Medical and Hospital Care Act was passed in 1962, CalPERS added health coverage. The fund was conservatively managed in-house, with little exposure to stocks. Despite slow growth, the state used the system's funds to meet its own cash shortfalls.

CalPERS became involved in corporate governance issues in the mid-1980s, when California treasurer Jesse Unruh became outraged by corporate greenmail schemes. In 1987 he hired as CEO Wisconsin pension board veteran Dale Hanson, who led the movement for corporate accountability to institutional investors.

In the late 1980s CalPERS moved into real estate and Japanese stocks. When both crashed around 1990, Hanson came under pressure. CalPERS was twice forced to take major writedowns for its real estate holdings and turned to expensive outside fund managers, but its investment performance deteriorated and member services suffered.

Legislation in 1990 enabled CalPERS to offer long-term health insurance. Governor Pete Wilson's 1991 attempt to use $1.6 billion from CalPERS to help meet a state budget shortfall resulted in legislation banning future raids. CalPERS made its first direct investment in 1993, an energy-related infrastructure partnership with Enron.

CalPERS suffered in the 1994 bond crash. That year Hanson resigned amid criticism that his focus on corporate governance had depressed fund performance. The system moved to an indexing strategy.

CalPERS eased its corporate relations stance, creating a separate office to handle investor issues and launching an International Corporate Governance Program. However, the next year CalPERS was uninvited from a KKR investment pool because of criticism of its fund management and fee structure.

In 1996 the system teamed with the Asian Development Bank to invest in the Asia/Pacific region; it took a major hit in the Asian financial crisis the next year, but used the downturn as an opportunity to expand its position there in undervalued stocks. In 1998 CalPERS pressured foreign firms to adopt more transparent financial reporting methods.

In 2000 the system raised health care premiums almost 10% to keep up with rising care costs. It widened the scope of its direct investments with stakes in investment bank Thomas Weisel Partners (10%) and asset manager Arrowstreet Capital (15%); it also moved into real estate development, buying Genstar Land Co. with Newland Communities, and announcing plans to invest in high-tech firms focused on B2B online real estate services. CalPERS said that year it would sell off more than $500 million in tobacco holdings; it then invested the same amount in five biotech funds, its first foray into the sector.

In 2001 California state controller and CalPERS board member Kathleen Connell successfully sued the system for not following state-sanctioned rules regarding pay increases. CalPERS was forced to cut salaries for investment managers, a move that prompted chief investment officer Daniel Szente to resign.

In 2003 CalPERS agreed to a record $250 million settlement relating to an age-discrimination suit brought by the Equal Employment Opportunity Commission. Also that year CalPERS clamored for (and got) the resignation of New York Stock Exchange (NYSE) chairman Richard Grasso. CalPERS and others claimed Grasso's pay of $140 million a year made it impossible for him to effectively monitor the exchange's member companies for corruption.

In another row, CalPERS in 2003 sued the NYSE and several specialist firms, including Bear Wagner Specialists, Fleet Specialist, LaBranche & Co, and Van der Moolen Holding's Van Der Moolen Specialists USA. The suit accused the exchange and the specialists of using the trading system for their own gain at the expense of investors. CalPERS found itself on the receiving end of a corporate governance issue in 2004 when a media group sued, demanding CalPERS make public the fees it pays to venture capital firms and hedge funds. CalPERS settled the suit by disclosing the fees.

Also in 2004 the president of CalPERS' board, Sean Harrigan, was ousted when the State Personnel Board voted to remove him as its representative. Harrigan had drawn the ire of the business community because of his labor ties and because, under his leadership, the board had withheld votes for directors of most of the companies in which CalPERS invests.

EXECUTIVES

President, Board: Rob Feckner
VP, Board: Robert F. Carlson
CEO: Fred R. Buenrostro Jr., age 56
Deputy Executive Officer, Operations:
 Gloria Moore Andrews
Deputy Executive Officer, Benefits Administration:
 Jarvio A. Grevious
Chief Operating Investment Officer: Anne Stausboll
Assistant Executive Officer, Public Affairs:
 Patricia K. Macht
Assistant Executive Officer, Administrative Services:
 John Hiber
Assistant Executive Officer, Information Technology Services: Ronald E. (Gene) Reich
Assistant Executive Officer, Actuarial and Employer Services Branch: Kenneth W. Marzion
Assistant Executive Officer, Member and Benefit Services Branch: Kathie Vaughn
Brad W. Pacheco
Chief Actuary: Ronald L. (Ron) Seeling
Chief Compliance Officer: Sherry Johnstone
Chief Investment Officer: Russell Read
Chief, Benefit Services Division: Donna Lum
Chief, Customer Service and Education Division:
 Ron Kraft
Chief, Member Services: Darryl Watson
Chief, Policy & Program Development: Ken Nitschke
General Counsel: Peter H. Mixon
Auditors: Macias, Gini & Company LLP

LOCATIONS

HQ: California Public Employees' Retirement System
 Lincoln Plaza, 400 Q St., Sacramento, CA 95811
Phone: 916-795-3829   **Fax:** 916-795-4001
Web: www.calpers.ca.gov

COMPETITORS

AIG Retirement	Morgan Stanley
AllianceBernstein	Nationwide Financial
AXA Financial	Principal Financial
Charles Schwab	Putnam
Citigroup Global Markets	Raymond James Financial
FMR	State Street
Franklin Resources	T. Rowe Price
Janus Capital	TIAA-CREF
Legg Mason	UBS Financial Services
Merrill Lynch	USAA
MFS	The Vanguard Group

C&S Wholesale Grocers

C&S Wholesale Grocers is at the bottom of the food chain — and likes it that way. The company is New England's largest food wholesaler and second in the US (behind SUPERVALU), delivering groceries to some 5,000 independent supermarkets, major supermarket chains (including Safeway), mass marketers, and wholesale clubs. The company distributes more than 53,000 items, including groceries, produce, and non-food items from its more than 70 distribution centers in a dozen states. Israel Cohen founded C&S Wholesale with Abraham Siegel in 1918. The company is still owned by Cohen's family, led by chairman and CEO Richard Cohen.

C&S Wholesale has become a giant in the wholesale distribution business through its focus on serving retail chains with a variety of services allied to distribution. The company's affiliated ES3 logistics business provides warehousing and supply-chain management services for such retailers as Pathmark and Safeway, and also for food manufacturers such as Unilever. Its diversified portfolio of services not only offers a lucrative stream of revenue, but it has also helped protect the company from bankruptcies in the retail grocery industry.

In C&S 2008 partnered with The Great Atlantic & Pacific Tea Co. (A&P) in a 10-year deal to combine their supply agreements into one. The deal, which includes Pathmark's supply agreement, represents an effort for both companies to streamline their distribution operations.

The company has been creative in the mergers and acquisitions arena as well. The company in 2005 acquired about 100 retail stores from BI-LO and Bruno's and is operating the stores under the Southern Family Markets banner. It plans to use the stores as a foothold into the southeastern market, as well as a platform for developing new supply-chain processes.

HISTORY

Israel Cohen and Abraham Siegel began C&S Wholesale Grocers in 1918 in Worcester, Massachusetts. Cohen ran the company for more than 50 years after buying out Siegel in 1921. It became a family concern in 1972 when Cohen turned the company over to his son Lester, who soon brought in his sons, Jim and Rick.

C&S Wholesale expanded over the years, growing along with its customers. It had $98 million in sales in 1981, the year its skyrocketing growth began. Also in 1981 Rick, now the company's chairman, president, and CEO, engineered a move to Brattleboro, in southern Vermont, where it had better access to interstate highways and a larger workforce.

After attending a seminar hosted by management whiz Tom Peters, in 1987 Cohen set up self-managed teams of three to eight employees who would act as small business units responsible for a customer's order from the time it was received to when it was delivered. Team members were paid for the amount of time they worked and were given bonuses for error-free operations and penalties for errors or damaged goods. His plan saw an immediate response in terms of increased sales, and by 1992 C&S Wholesale had more than $1 billion in sales. Rick bought out his father in 1989 and the next year became the company's single shareholder when he bought out his brother.

C&S Wholesale started its produce business in 1990 (by 1994 it was the major purchaser of locally grown fruits and vegetables) and began making plans to build an 800,000-sq.-ft. refrigerated warehouse near a scenic highway in Brattleboro. It ran up against environmentalists and Vermont's Act 250 environmental impact law, and eventually dropped its original plan, opting instead to expand at its headquarters.

In 1992 the wholesaler offered plans for a smaller, revised warehouse, but again met opposition. After a two-year battle, C&S Wholesale gave up and said it would build elsewhere. (Most of its employees and warehouses are now in Massachusetts and New Jersey.)

The following year C&S Wholesale welcomed 127 Grand Union stores and several East Coast Wal-Mart stores as customers. The next year the company picked up another 103 Grand Union stores; Grand Union said it was closing two distribution centers and shifting distribution to C&S Wholesale in a deal worth $500 million a year. A $650 million-per-year contract with Edwards stores was inked in 1996, the year C&S Wholesale's sales topped $3 billion.

The company acquired ice-cream distributor New England Frozen Foods in 1997. Continuing its move toward the mid-Atlantic, C&S Wholesale took over the distribution and supply operations of New Jersey-based grocery chain Pathmark Stores in 1998 for $60 million. In 1999 C&S Wholesale purchased Shaw's Supermarkets' Star Markets' wholesale division and moved into Pennsylvania with a facility in York.

In 2001 the company, through affiliate GU Markets, bought most of the assets of one of its biggest customers, bankrupt The Grand Union Company. C&S acquired about 170 of Grand Union's 197 stores in the purchase. It transferred most of the stores to third-party purchasers.

In 2002 C&S Wholesale formed a new holding company, called C&S Holdings, and reorganized its management to better oversee its various businesses. That summer the company acquired the grocery distribution operations of TOPS Markets, which until 2007 was a division of Dutch supermarket giant Royal Ahold.

C&S acquired the New England operations of SUPERVALU in 2003. President and COO Edward Albertian resigned in 2004 after just three years with the company. He was replaced by Ron Wright, a 20-year veteran with the company. In 2005 C&S acquired the warehouse facilities and distribution functions of supermarket chains BI-LO and Bruno's. Later that year C&S subsidiary Southern Family Markets bought more than 100 BI-LO and Bruno's stores.

EXECUTIVES

Chairman and CEO: Richard B. (Rick) Cohen
EVP Distribution and Supply Chain Management: Nat Silverman
EVP, General Counsel, and Secretary: Michael (Mike) Newbold
EVP Process Engineering and CIO: Joe Caracappa
EVP Operations: Scott Charlton
EVP Human Resources: Bruce Johnson
EVP and CFO: Chris Kreidler
EVP Procurement and Merchandising: Robert (Bob) Palmer
SVP Merchandising, Supply Chain, and Trade Relations: Tracy Moore
SVP Corporate Construction and Engineering: Dennis Mead
SVP Chain Sales and Customer Service: Marilyn Tillinghast
SVP Finance and Accounting: Jim Weidenheimer
SVP Perishables: Michael Papaleo
SVP Strategic Planning: William Hamlin
SVP Transportation: Michelle Livingstone
SVP Warehouse Operations: Peter Fiore
SVP and General Manager, Southern Family Markets: Jeffrey Burkhead
SVP Warehousing: Jeff Hoban
SVP Facilities, Maintenance, Construction, and Engineering: Richard Tannenbaum
VP Merchandising: Zena Tessier
VP Produce: Albert Grimaldi
CTO: Mike Schmitt

LOCATIONS

HQ: C&S Wholesale Grocers, Inc.
7 Corporate Dr., Keene, NH 03431
Phone: 603-354-7000   **Fax:** 603-354-4690
Web: www.cswg.com

PRODUCTS/OPERATIONS

Selected Customers
A&P Food Mart
Big Y Foods
BJ's Warehouse
Demoulas
Giant Food Stores
Great American
Pathmark
Safeway
SavMart/Foodmax
Shaw's
Stop and Shop

COMPETITORS

Alex Lee	H.T. Hackney
Associated Wholesale	Kroger
Grocers	McLane
Associated Wholesalers	Nash-Finch
Bozzuto's	SUPERVALU
GSC Enterprises	Wakefern Food

HISTORICAL FINANCIALS

Company Type: Private

Income Statement
FYE: September 30

	REVENUE ($ mil.)	NET INCOME ($ mil.)	NET PROFIT MARGIN	EMPLOYEES
9/07	19,500	—	—	17,000
9/06	18,000	—	—	20,000
9/05	15,200	—	—	18,000
9/04	13,600	—	—	12,000
9/03	13,500	—	—	9,000
Annual Growth	9.6%	—	—	17.2%

Revenue History

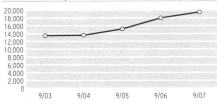

Capital Group Companies

If asset management companies were described like potential romantic partners in lonely hearts ads, The Capital Group Companies would definitely be marriage material. The mutual fund firm, founded in 1929, is quiet (they don't advertise or grant many interviews), conservative (known for consistent performance), and faithful (most of its investments and its executives are long-term). Among its dislikes are hierarchy, star traders, and fads. Subsidiary Capital Research and Management manages The American Funds, a family of about 30 mutual funds that ranks among the largest groups of mutual funds by assets in the US.

The American Funds benefited from investors shuffling their investments to more reliable firms amid recent mutual fund scandals. However, in 2005 the company came under scrutiny from the SEC and National Association of Securities Dealers (NASD) regarding allegations that it engaged in a practice known as directed brokerage (or "pay to play") — rewarding commissions on trades to high-performing brokerage firms instead of keeping those commissions in shareholder accounts. The Capital Group was slapped with a $5 million fine the following year.

Other Capital Group units offer funds in Canada and Europe, manage assets for institutional clients, and perform recordkeeping for small-company retirement plans.

EXECUTIVES

President: Philip de Toledo
SVP and Treasurer; SVP, Capital International: Jim Brown
SVP, Capital International; Research Director, Capital Global Private Equity: Lam Nguyen-Phuong
SVP, Capital International: Koenraad C. Foulon
VP, Capital International Research: Ashley Dunster
VP, Capital International Research: Stewart Gibson

Chairman and Portfolio Manager, Capital Guardian: Shelby Notkin
Chairman, Capital Group International and Capital Guardian Trust Company: David I. Fisher
Chairman, Capital International: Shaw B. Wagener
President, Personal Investment Management, Capital Guardian: John B. Emerson
Chief Administrative Officer, Personal Investment, Capital Guardian: Karen Skinner-Twomey
Director of Media Relations: Chuck Freadhoff

LOCATIONS

HQ: The Capital Group Companies, Inc.
333 S. Hope St., 53rd Fl., Los Angeles, CA 90071
Phone: 213-486-9200   **Fax:** 213-486-9217
Web: www.capgroup.com

COMPETITORS

AIG	Invesco
AllianceBernstein	MFS
American Century	Principal Financial
AXA Financial	Prudential
Charles Schwab	Putnam
FMR	T. Rowe Price
Franklin Resources	The Vanguard Group

CapRock Communications

CapRock Communications provides satellite communications services where others fear to tread. The company's network enables the secure transmission of voice-over-IP, data, and video primarily for customers operating in remote locations and/or harsh environments such as offshore drilling platforms or mining sites. Clients come from such industries as construction, maritime, military, mining, and oil and gas exploration. The company's SeaAccess Communications service provides broadband networking to ships at sea. CapRock maintains and operates a global communications network in cooperation with other satellite fleet operators. The company was founded in 1981 as IWL Communications.

CapRock operates international teleports in Brazil, Indonesia, the UK, and the US, and has operations centers in Angola, Brazil, Mexico, Norway, and the US.

The company in 2007 acquired Arrowhead Global Solutions, a supplier of communications systems and services to the federal government and military agencies, in a move to boost the company's expertise in systems integration, engineering, and construction.

Also that year, CapRock expanded into Australia with the opening of a sales and support office in Perth. The new location is intended to increase access to and improve service for the energy, maritime, and mining industries in the region.

EXECUTIVES

Chairman and CEO: Peter Shaper
President and COO: Bryan L. Olivier, age 35
SVP Global Customer Support: Keith Johnson
CFO: Hank M. Winfield
VP Global Energy Services Sales: Aldo Rodriguez
VP and General Counsel: Alan B. Aronowitz
VP Global Engineering: Ron Long
VP Corporate Development: Bill Weakley

VP and General Manager, North America: Ron Wagnon
COO and President, Global Energy Services:
Douglas A. Tutt
President, Arrowhead Global Solutions:
Thomas E. (Tom) Eaton Jr.
President, Maritime: Tore Hilde
VP SATCOM Division, Arrowhead Global Solutions:
David A. Cavossa
**Managing Director, European, Middle Eastern, and
African Operations:** Eduardo Correa
General Manager, SE Asia Region: Ian Ford

LOCATIONS

HQ: CapRock Communications, Inc.
4400 S. Sam Houston Pkwy. East,
Houston, TX 77048
Phone: 832-668-2300   **Fax:** 832-668-2388
Web: www.caprock.com

COMPETITORS

AT&T	QUALCOMM
Globalstar	RigNet
Iridium Satellite	Stratos
ORBCOMM	Telenor

HISTORICAL FINANCIALS

Company Type: Private

Income Statement

	REVENUE ($ mil.)	NET INCOME ($ mil.)	NET PROFIT MARGIN	EMPLOYEES
12/07	235	—	—	650
12/06	119	—	—	450
12/05	104	—	—	392
12/04	91	—	—	388
12/03	51	—	—	210
Annual Growth	46.8%	—	—	32.6%

FYE: December 31

Revenue History

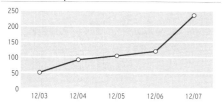

CareerBuilder LLC

CareerBuilder constructs new careers by bringing employers and potential employees together through the Web. The firm's CareerBuilder Network consists of flagship site careerbuilder.com, as well as dozens of affiliated career sites, including iVillage.com, CollegeClub.com, and Experience.com. CareerBuilder.com allows job seekers access to the Mega Job Search to peruse more than 1.6 million job openings, and more than 300,000 employers tap into its database consisting of over 26 million resumes. The company also conducts surveys and polls through the Web paneling of its vast database. Newpaper publisher Gannett owns a controlling stake in CareerBuilder, which was founded in 1995.

In early 2008, CareerBuilder expanded its product offerings when it launched Personified, an independent consulting firm focusing on the relationship between a company's hiring practices and its work performance. Personified provides employee acquisition and retention, recruitment outsourcing, corporate culture development, and employment branding services.

Besides Gannett, which owns a 51% stake in CareerBuilder, the job site's shareholders include newspaper companies Tribune (31%) and McClatchy (14%), plus Microsoft (4%).

The Microsoft investment, made in 2007, enabled CareerBuilder to extend its partnership with MSN Careers through 2013. Under the agreement, CareerBuilder will pay MSN more than $440 million over seven years in order to be featured as the Web site's primary job search engine.

EXECUTIVES

President, CEO, and Director:
Matthew W. (Matt) Ferguson
COO: Brent Rasmussen
CFO: Kevin Knapp
CTO: Eric Presley
VP Business Development: Hope Gurion
VP Consumer Marketing: Richard Castellini
VP Corporate Marketing: Jason Lovelace
VP Human Resources and Senior Career Advisor:
Rosemary Haefner
VP International Finance: Mark S. Hoyt
President International Group: Farhan Yasin
President Personified: Mary Delaney
Director Consumer Products: Liz Harvey
Director Strategic Services: Jennifer Seith
Head of Lesjeudis.com: Cedric Barbier
General Counsel: Alex Green
Media Contact: Jennifer Sullivan

LOCATIONS

HQ: CareerBuilder LLC
200 N. LaSalle St., Ste. 1100, Chicago, IL 60631
Phone: 773-527-3600   **Fax:** 773-399-6313
Web: www.careerbuilder.com

COMPETITORS

craigslist
Dice
HotJobs
Kelly Services
Monster.com

HISTORICAL FINANCIALS

Company Type: Joint venture

Income Statement

	REVENUE ($ mil.)	NET INCOME ($ mil.)	NET PROFIT MARGIN	EMPLOYEES
12/07	768	—	—	2,000
12/06	672	—	—	1,800
12/05	495	—	—	1,500
12/04	280	—	—	900
12/03	160	—	—	550
Annual Growth	48.0%	—	—	38.1%

FYE: December 31

Revenue History

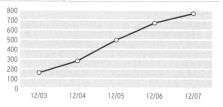

Cargill, Incorporated

Cargill may be private, but it's highly visible. The US's second largest private corporation (after Koch Industries), Cargill's diversified operations include grain, cotton, sugar, petroleum and financial trading; food processing; futures brokering; health and pharmaceutical products; agricultural services such as animal feed and crop protection; and industrial products, including biofuels, oils and lubricants, starches, and salt. The company is one of the leading grain producers in the US, and its Excel unit is one of the top US meatpackers. Cargill's brands include Diamond Crystal (salt), Gerkens (cocoa), Honeysuckle White (poultry), Sterling Silver (fresh meats), and Nutrena (dog and cat food).

Being private doesn't mean Cargill is cut off from the world. The agribusiness giant has operations in 65 countries throughout the world. Along with its grain and meatpacking businesses, Cargill is a commodity trader. It is also a global supplier of oils, syrups, flour, and other products used in food processing.

Long the largest private company in the US, it lost the #1 title in 2005 when conglomerate Koch Industries acquired forest products maker Georgia-Pacific Corp. But Cargill is still a powerhouse. It is involved in petroleum trading, financial trading, futures brokering, and shipping. It formed a joint venture with Hormel Foods to market fresh beef, along with pork, under the Always Tender brand. Cargill is also a major US supplier for McDonald's, providing the burger behemoth with eggs, oils, sauces, and beef products.

Diving into the US's health care morass, in 2006 Cargill announced the formation of Harvest Health, a Cargill-funded health care plan for grain farmers. The company contributes up to $5,450 per family or $2,700 per individual per year in exchange for which the farmer contributes up to 25% of his or her annual corn or soybean crop. Cargill said it set up the program because it kept hearing from farmers that health care costs were squeezing their profits and because it guarantees a more predictable grain supply for the company.

Looking to growing markets, the company acquired a 100% ownership of Chinese xanthan gum operation Zibo Cargill Huanghelong Bioengineering (ZCHB) in 2006 by buying out its joint venture partner in ZCHB, Shandong Huanghelong Group.

Long-time CEO Warren Staley retired in 2007. Cargill's board chose 33-year company veteran, president and COO, Gregory Page, to replace Staley. Page stated that he hopes to make Cargill, an historically tight-lipped company, more visible. (Later that year, Page was appointed chairman of the company.)

Twice during the month of October 2007, the company was forced to recall meat products because of *E. coli* contamination. The first involved more than 800,000 pounds of frozen beef patties. More than 1 million pounds of fresh ground beef was involved in the second recall.

Late in 2007 Cargill introduced Meadowlands Farms ground beef at food retailers throughout the US, marking the company's first foray into the nationally branded hamburger market. Further adding to its retail and foodservice meat products, in 2008 Cargill acquired turkey processor, Willow Brook Foods.

HISTORY

William W. Cargill founded Cargill in 1865 when he bought his first grain elevator in Conover, Iowa. He and his brother Sam bought grain elevators all along the Southern Minnesota Railroad in 1870, just as Minnesota was becoming an important shipping route. Sam and a third brother, James, expanded the elevator operations while William worked with the railroads to monopolize transport of grain to markets and coal to farmers.

Around the turn of the century, William's son William S. invested in a number of ill-fated projects. William W. found that his name had been used to finance the projects; shortly afterward, he died of pneumonia. Cargill's creditors pressed for repayment, which threatened to bankrupt the company. John MacMillan, William W.'s son-in-law, took control and rebuilt Cargill. It had recovered by 1916 but lost its holdings in Mexico and Canada. MacMillan opened offices in New York (1922) and Argentina (1929), expanding grain trading and transport operations.

In 1945 Cargill bought Nutrena Mills (animal feed) and entered soybean processing; corn processing began soon after and grew with the demand for corn sweeteners. In 1954 Cargill benefited when the US began making loans to help developing countries buy American grain. Subsidiary Tradax, established in 1955, became one of the largest grain traders in Europe. A decade later, Cargill began trading sugar by purchasing sugar and molasses in the Philippines and selling them abroad.

Cargill made its finances public in 1973 (as a requirement for its unsuccessful takeover bid of Missouri Portland Cement), revealing it to be one of the US's largest companies, with $5.2 billion in sales. In the 1970s it expanded into coal, steel, and waste disposal and became a major force in metals processing, beef, and salt production.

To placate family heirs who wanted to take Cargill public, CEO Whitney MacMillan, grandson of John, created an employee stock plan in 1991 that allowed shareholders to cash in their shares. He also boosted dividends and reorganized the board, reducing the family's control. MacMillan retired in 1995 and non-family member Ernest Micek became CEO and chairman.

The firm bought Akzo Nobel's North American salt operations in 1997, becoming the #2 US salt company. Cargill bulked up its grain trading business by acquiring the grain export operations of Continental Grain in 1999. Micek resigned as CEO that year and was replaced by Warren Staley. Also in 1999 Cargill fessed up to misappropriating some genetic seed material from rival Pioneer Hi-Bred, killing the $650 million sale of its North American seed assets to Germany's AgrEvo.

In a move to focus on its core agribusinesses, Cargill sold four steel mills (including North Star Steel) to Canadian company Gerdau Ameristeel in 2004. Also in 2004, in conjunction with Monsanto, Cargill announced the introduction of a low-linolenic soybean, which can be used to produce soybean oil that helps reduce trans-fats in food products. Also that year Cargill combined its crop-nutrition segment with phosphate fertilizer maker IMC Global to form a new, publicly traded company called Mosaic. Cargill owns about 66% of the company. This is the first time privately held Cargill has ventured into the public sector.

In 2005 Cargill acquired The Dow Chemical Company's interest in the two companies' 50-50 plastics business joint venture, Cargill Dow LLC,

and renamed it NatureWorks. That year it also broke ground for its first oil refinery in Russia.

In 2008 Cargill added to its sugar business, announcing the construction of its first sugar refinery. Located in Louisiana and with a 1 million ton-per-year capacity, the refinery is part of the company's strategy to expand its sweetener offerings. Although it already trades raw sugar in China, Switzerland, Holland, and the US and operates sugar export terminals in Brazil, the refinery is Cargill's first foray into directly producing the commodity. The operation is a 50-50 joint venture between Cargill and the Louisiana agricultural cooperative, Sugar Growers and Refiners (SUGAR).

EXECUTIVES

Chairman and CEO: Gregory R. (Greg) Page, age 56
Vice Chairman: F. Guillaume (Bassy) Bastiaens, age 65
Vice Chairman: David W. Raisbeck, age 58
EVP: David M. Larson
EVP Cargill Europe: Henricus M. (Henk) Mathot
SVP and CFO: David W. MacLennan, age 49
SVP: Richard D. Frasch, age 53
SVP: David W. Rogers
SVP: Paul D. Conway
SVP: William A. (Bill) Buckner
Corporate VP and Treasurer: Jayme D. Olson
Corporate VP, Information Technology: Rita J. Heise
Corporate VP, Corporate Affairs: Bonnie E. Raquet
Corporate VP, Transportation and Product Assurance: Frank L. Sims, age 57
Corporate VP, Research and Development: Christopher P. (Chris) Mallett
Corporate VP, General Counsel, and Corporate Secretary: Steven C. Euller
Corporate VP and CTO: Ronald L. Christenson
Corporate VP and Controller: Galen G. Johnson, age 61
Corporate VP, Human Resources: Peter Vrijsen, age 54
VP, Environment, Health, and Safety: LaRaye Osborne
VP, Plant Operations for Global Food and Engineering: Tom Hayes
President, Cargill Ag Horizons U.S.: Dan Dye
President, Cargill Meat Solutions and President, Cargill Beef: Bill Rupp, age 47
President, Cargill Energy, Transportation, and Industrial Group: Tom Intrator
President, Value Added Meat: John O'Carroll
President, Ocean Transportation: Gert Jan Vandenakker
President, Cargill Beef: John Keating
President, Cargill Meat Solutions and President, Cargill Case Ready Beef: Jody Horner
Auditors: KPMG LLP

LOCATIONS

HQ: Cargill, Incorporated
15407 McGinty Rd. West, Wayzata, MN 55391
Phone: 952-742-7575   **Fax:** 952-742-7393
Web: www.cargill.com

PRODUCTS/OPERATIONS

Selected Products and Services

Agriculture and Animal Nutrition
  Agricultural commodity trading
  Animal nutrition
  Crop production
  Sugar refining
Financial and Risk Management
  Investment
  Risk Management
Food
  Baking and cereals
  Beverages
  Chocolates and confections
  Dairy products
  Health, nutrition, and organic
  Meat and poultry
  Prepared foods
  Salt
  Snacks

Health and Pharmaceutical
  Health, nutrition, and organic
  Pharmaceuticals
Industrial
  Biobased polyols
  Biofuels
  Deicing products and surface overlays
  Fermentation solutions
  Oils and lubricants
  Power and gas
  Salt
  Soy-based candle waxes
  Starches and derivatives
  Steel and ferrous raw materials

Selected Joint Ventures and Operations

Freeman's of Newent Ltd (chicken processing, UK)
Frontier Agriculture (UK)
Horizon Milling
NatureWorks LLC
Progressive Baker
Renessen Feed & Processing
Seara (pork and poultry processing, Brazil)
Sun Valley (chicken processing, UK)

COMPETITORS

Abengoa Bioenergy	King Arthur Flour
ADM	Koch Industries, Inc.
Ag Processing	Kraft Foods
Amalgamated Sugar	Lake Area Corn Processors
American Animal Health	Land O'Lakes
American Crystal Sugar	Land O'Lakes Purina Feed
American Steel	Mars, Incorporated
Asia Food & Properties	Merisant Worldwide
Aventine	Michigan Sugar Company
Badger State Ethanol	Monsanto Company
BASF SE	Morton Salt
Bayer Animal Health	Nestlé Purina PetCare
Beef Products	Nippon Steel
BioFuel	Northern Growers
Blyth	Nucor
Bunge Limited	NutraSweet
C&H Sugar	Omega Protein
Casco	Pacific Ethanol
Chaparral Energy	Palm Restaurants
CHS	Perdue Incorporated
COFCO	Pfizer
Coleman Natural Foods	Phibro Animal Health
ConAgra	Raeford Farms
ContiGroup	Rohm and Haas
Corn Products	Royal Canin
International	RSG
Cumberland Packing	Südzucker
Dean Foods	Sara Lee Food & Beverage
Del Monte Foods	Schering-Plough
Doane Pet Care	Sime Darby
Dow Chemical	SMBSC
DuPont	Smithfield Foods
DuPont Agriculture &	Sterling Sugars
Nutrition	Sugar Cane Growers
Eight in One Pet Products	Cooperative of Florida
Ellison Meat Company	Sugar Foods
Evialis	Tate & Lyle
Faultless Starch	Tate & Lyle Ingredients
Florida Crystals	Teva Pharmaceuticals
General Mills	United Salt
Hershey	United States Steel
Hill's Pet Nutrition	U.S. Microbics
Holly Sugar	U.S. Sugar
Iams	Viterra Inc.
Imperial Sugar	Western Beef
IOI	Western Sugar Cooperative
JBS	Yankee Candle

HISTORICAL FINANCIALS

Company Type: Private

Income Statement

	REVENUE ($ mil.)	NET INCOME ($ mil.)	NET PROFIT MARGIN	EMPLOYEES
5/08	120,439	3,951	3.3%	160,000
5/07	88,266	2,343	2.7%	158,000
5/06	75,208	1,537	2.0%	149,000
5/05	71,066	2,103	3.0%	124,000
5/04	62,907	1,331	2.1%	101,000
Annual Growth	17.6%	31.3%	—	12.2%

FYE: May 31

2008 Year-End Financials

Debt ratio: —
Return on equity: 22.1%
Cash ($ mil.): —

Current ratio: —
Long-term debt ($ mil.): —

Net Income History

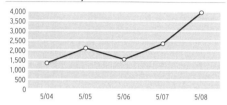

4,000				
3,500				
3,000				
2,500				
2,000				
1,500				
1,000				
500				
0	5/04	5/05	5/06	5/07	5/08

Carlson Companies

Carlson Companies began in 1938 as the Gold Bond Stamp Company, but has evolved into a leisure services juggernaut. The company owns 55% of travel giant Carlson Wagonlit. Its Carlson Hotels Worldwide owns and operates more than 950 hotels in some 70 countries under brands such as Radisson, Country Inns & Suites By Carlson, and Park Plaza; its Carlson Restaurants Worldwide includes the T.G.I. Friday's chain. A specialist in relationship marketing, Carlson Marketing offers services such as sales promotion and customer loyalty programs. Chairman Marilyn Carlson Nelson and director Barbara Carlson Gage, daughters of founder Curtis Carlson, each own half of the company.

The company formerly owned a variety of leisure and franchise travel holdings, including cruise-specialty operations Cruise Holidays, Sea-Master Cruises, and Cruise Specialists, as well as online operations such as CruiseDeals.com and SinglesCruise.com, through its Carlson Leisure Group. However, in 2008 those assets were sold to Carlson Leisure Group's management team. Also in 2008 Carlson Wagonlit president and CEO Hubert Joly replaced Marilyn Carlson Nelson as CEO of Carlson Companies. Nelson remains chairman.

The Carlsons are one of the first families of business in Minnesota, and Nelson regularly makes the list of the most powerful women in corporate America. She and her son Curtis Nelson are engaged in a legal battle. The younger heir was fired from his position as COO of the company and is suing his mother, asking for a larger share of the company and claiming he deserves the CEO position. Carlson Nelson claims that her son is not suited for the position, citing his past problems with alcohol and substance abuse in a countersuit.

HISTORY

Curtis Carlson, the son of Swedish immigrants, graduated from the University of Minnesota in 1937 and went to work selling soap for Procter & Gamble in the Minneapolis area. In 1938 he borrowed $55 and formed Gold Bond Stamp Company to sell trading stamps. His wife, Arleen, dressed as a drum majorette and twirled a baton to promote the concept. By 1941 the company had 200 accounts. Business was slowed by WWII but took off in the 1950s. During the 1960s the company began diversifying into other enterprises such as travel, marketing, hotels, and real estate.

Gold Bond Stamp bought the Radisson Hotel in Minneapolis in 1962 and began expanding the chain. The company adopted the Carlson Companies name in 1973. Carlson Companies continued expanding its holdings during the 1970s, buying the 11-unit T.G.I. Friday's chain, as well as a chain of Country Kitchen family restaurants (sold in 1997).

In 1979 Carlson bought First Travel Corp., which owned travel agency Ask Mr. Foster and Colony Hotels. Carlson Companies slowed the pace of its acquisitions in the 1980s. Hired in 1984, Juergen Bartels changed the hospitality division's strategy from building and owning hotels to franchising and managing them. This enabled Carlson to weather the crash that followed the 1980s hotel building boom.

The company took T.G.I. Friday's public to fund expansion in 1983, but it reacquired all outstanding shares in 1989. It launched its cruise ship business in 1992, when the luxury liner SSC *Radisson Diamond* set sail.

Carlson made a major international advance in 1994 when it formed joint venture Carlson Wagonlit Travel, with France's Accor. In 1997 it expanded into the luxury hotel business when it bought Regent International from Four Seasons. In a nod to its roots, the company also unveiled the Gold Points Reward guest loyalty system to reward customers who frequent its hotels and restaurants.

In 1998 Curtis Carlson appointed his daughter, Marilyn Carlson Nelson, as the company's chief executive (he remained chairman). The following year Carlson Companies merged its UK leisure travel business with UK-based travel and financial services firm Thomas Cook. Founder Curtis Carlson died that year and Nelson added chairman to her title. The company later filed to spin off its T.G.I. Friday's unit as Carlson Restaurants Worldwide.

Carlson Companies sold its 22% stake in Thomas Cook Holdings in 2001 to German tour company C&N (which then changed its name to Thomas Cook AG). In mid-2001 the company bought 52-unit Asian restaurant chain Pick Up Stix. The following year Carlson Companies announced a major expansion initiative into the Asia/Pacific region. The company bought customer-based business strategy firm Peppers & Rogers in 2003, and the next year completed the purchase of the business travel subsidiary of Maritz Travel.

In early 2008 the company sold several leisure and franchise travel holdings that operated under the Carlson Leisure Group banner. Later that year Hubert Joly replaced Marilyn Carlson Nelson as CEO. Nelson remains chairman.

EXECUTIVES

Chairman: Marilyn Carlson Nelson, age 68
President and CEO: Hubert Joly, age 49
EVP and CFO: Trudy Rautio, age 55
EVP Business Unit Liaison; President and CEO, Carlson Marketing: Jeffrey A. (Jeff) Balagna, age 47
EVP Human Resources: Jim T. Porter
EVP: William A. (Bill) Van Brunt
SVP Enterprise Sales: Fay Beauchine
VP and Chief Communications Officer: Kim Olson
VP and Treasurer: John M. Diracles Jr.
VP Business Process Improvement: Joseph Dehler
VP Corporate Audit: Suzanne H. Riesterer
VP Corporate Human Resources: Charles Montreuil
VP Responsible Business, Carlson Hotels Worldwide: Carmen Baker
VP Enterprise Transformation and Integration: Steve Geiger
VP Executive Communications: Douglas R. Cody
VP External Affairs: Deborah Cundy
VP Finance and Chief Accounting Officer: Robert Kleinschmidt
VP Financial Shared Services, Carlson Shared Services: Jim Hotze
VP Human Resources Shared Services, Carlson Shared Services: Greg Peters
VP Leadership and Organizational Development: Rick Clevette
VP Legal and Corporate Secretary: Ralph Beha
VP Relationship Management and Development: Kathy Hollenhorst
VP Tax: Linda Lewison
VP Technology, Carlson Shared Services: Paula Winkler
President and CEO, Carlson Hotels Worldwide and CEO, Regent: Jay S. Witzel, age 60
President and CEO, Carlson Restaurants Worldwide: Richard T. Snead, age 57
President, Carlson Hotels Worldwide, The Americas: Paul S. Kirwin
President, Carlson Cruises Worldwide; President and CEO, Regent Seven Seas Cruises: Mark S. Conroy
President, Carlson Family Foundation: Barbara Carlson Gage
President, Carlson Real Estate Company: Matt Van Slooten
President and CEO, Carlson Wagonlit Travel: Douglas (Doug) Anderson, age 53

LOCATIONS

HQ: Carlson Companies, Inc.
701 Carlson Pkwy., Minnetonka, MN 55305
Phone: 763-212-4000   **Fax:** 763-212-2219
Web: www.carlson.com

PRODUCTS/OPERATIONS

Selected Operations

Hotel brands
   Country Inns & Suites By Carlson
   Park Inn Hotels
   Park Plaza Hotels & Resorts
   Radisson Hotels & Resorts
   Regent International Hotels
Marketing
   Carlson Marketing Group
Restaurants
   Pick Up Stix
   T.G.I. Friday's
Travel
   Carlson Wagonlit Travel (55%)

HISTORICAL FINANCIALS

Company Type: Private

Income Statement				FYE: December 31
	REVENUE ($ mil.)	NET INCOME ($ mil.)	NET PROFIT MARGIN	EMPLOYEES
12/07	39,800	—	—	160,000
12/06	37,100	—	—	176,000
12/05	34,400	—	—	—
12/04	30,700	—	—	190,000
12/03	20,900	—	—	—
Annual Growth	17.5%	—	—	(5.6%)

Revenue History

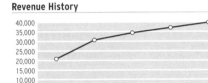

The Carlyle Group

The Carlyle Group, with more than $80 billion under management, is one of the world's largest private investment firms. Undertakings include management-led buyouts, minority equity investments, real estate, venture capital, and leveraged finance opportunities in the aerospace and defense, automotive and transportation, consumer and retail, and energy and power industries. Other sectors it focuses on include financial services, health care, industrial, infrastructure, real estate, technology, and telecommunications and media. Since its founding in 1987, the firm has made more than 775 investments; it maintains offices in about 20 countries and oversees some 60 private equity funds.

Affiliate Carlyle Capital went under in 2008 when creditors, including some of the world's biggest investment banks, began liquidating their assets. The company had invested in triple-A rated mortgages but did not have enough collateral to cover its debt. Carlyle Group extended a $150 million line of credit to the company, but ultimately, the lifeline wasn't enough.

Later that year it closed yet another hedge fund, Blue Wave, when its assets fell by one-third.

However, in the spirit of making lemonade from lemons, that year the company formed a new fund to invest in troubled securities, companies, and other distressed investments.

Formerly a list of who's-who in aerospace and defense, Carlyle has unloaded many of its assets in the sector, retooled its management board, and made its undertakings more transparent, in part due to suspicions regarding its dealings with Saudi investors (including the bin Laden family) in a post-9/11 world.

Out are the likes of former US President George H.W. Bush, former British Prime Minister John Major, former Secretary of State James Baker, and former US Secretary of Defense Frank Carlucci. They have been replaced by business leaders such as Lou Gerstner, the former IBM chairman and CEO, former SEC chairman Arthur Levitt, and David Calhoun, a former vice chairman of GE.

Carlyle is not completely severing its political ties, however. In 2008 the company announced plans to pay some $2.5 billion for a majority stake in the government operations of Booz Allen Hamilton, which provides consulting services to the US Department of Defense and other government agencies at home and abroad.

Although the majority of its money is in North America, Carlyle also has investments in Asia and Europe, and has been making inroads in Australia, Latin America, North Africa, and Russia. The company traditionally has been known for turning small acquisitions into big companies, but the recent boom in private equity investing has seen Carlyle make bigger and bigger deals. It has stakes in some 200 firms, including Dunkin' Brands, Hawaiian Telcom, Hertz, and SS&C Technologies.

California Public Employees' Retirement System (CalPERS) owns more than 5% of Carlyle; the Abu Dhabi government owns another 7.5%. The rest is owned by a group of individuals, most of whom are managing directors at Carlyle.

HISTORY

In 1987 T. Rowe Price director Edward Mathias brought together David Rubenstein, a former aide to President Carter; Stephen Norris and Daniel D'Aniello, both executives with Marriott; William Conway Jr., the CFO of MCI; and Greg Rosenbaum, a VP with a New York investment firm. They pooled their experience along with a load of money from T. Rowe Price Associates, Alex. Brown & Sons (now Deutsche Banc Alex. Brown), First Interstate (acquired by Wells Fargo), and Pittsburgh's Mellon family to form a buyout firm.

Named after the Carlyle Hotel in New York, the firm opted to make Washington, DC, its headquarters so it wouldn't get lost in the crowd of New York investment firms. The company spent its first years investing in a mish-mash of companies, using Norris' and D'Aniello's Marriott experience to focus primarily on restaurant and food service companies (including Mexican restaurant chain Chi-Chi's).

In 1989 it wooed the well-connected Frank Carlucci, who had served as President Reagan's secretary of defense, to join the group. Soon thereafter, Carlyle began making more high-profile deals. That year it acquired Coldwell Banker's commercial real estate operations (sold 1996) and Caterair International, Marriott's airline food services (sold 1995).

Carlucci helped redirect the firm's focus to the downsizing defense industry. Among its targets were Harsco (1990), BDM International (1991), and LTV's missile and aircraft units (1992). Carlyle helped overhaul their operations and make them attractive (for the right price) to the industry's elite, including Boeing and Lockheed Martin.

As the company's reputation grew, so did its cast of players. Among its new backers were James Baker and Richard Darman (both Reagan and Bush administration alums) and investor George Soros, who chipped some $100 million into the Carlyle Partners L.P. buyout fund. With the help of its "access capitalists" such as Baker and Saudi Prince al-Waleed bin Talal (the firm helped add to his fortune in a 1991 Citicorp stock transaction), Carlyle made deals in the Middle East and Western Europe (including a bailout of Euro Disney) in the mid-1990s.

While the firm continued to be a side in the iron triangle, acquiring such defense companies as aircraft castings maker Howmet in 1995, it picked up a grab bag of holdings, such as natural food grocer Fresh Fields Markets (1994; sold 1996); the quick turnaround helped build Carlyle's war chest. The firm also began investing in industrial-cleanup companies, seeing increased government spending as a major opportunity for profit. In 1999 the firm acquired automobile engine parts manufacturer Honsel International Technologies in Germany's first public-to-private transaction. (It later sold this investment to Ripplewood Holdings in 2004.)

The company added more than 50 businesses to its portfolio in 2007. Just more than half of these investments are in US-based companies, but Carlyle also put its money in foreign ventures, ranging from a sporting goods manufacturer in China to real estate portfolios in Italy to an after-school tutoring institute in Korea. Carlyle also joined with Bain Capital and Clayton, Dubilier & Rice to buy HD Supply, the wholesale construction supply business of The Home Depot, for around $8.5 billion.

In 2008 Carlyle arranged to sell steelmaker John Maneely Company to Russian firm Novolipetsk Steel for some $3.5 billion. It also announced plans to buy De La Rue's cash systems division for some £360 million in 2008. The operations include branch teller automation, desktop coin and banknote counters, and cash and other dispenser mechanisms.

EXECUTIVES

Founding Partner and Managing Director; Chairman, Carlyle Investment Committees:
William E. Conway Jr., age 56
Founding Partner and Managing Director:
Daniel A. D'Aniello
Founding Partner and Managing Director:
David M. Rubenstein
Managing Director and CFO: Peter H. Nachtwey
Managing Director and General Counsel:
Jeffrey W. Ferguson
Managing Director and Chief Accounting Officer:
Curt Buser
Managing Director, Investor Relations: Roman Pelka
Senior Advisor Asia, Europe, Japan and U.S. Buyout Funds: Louis V. (Lou) Gerstner Jr., age 66
Senior Advisor, Europe Buyout, Aerospace & Defense:
Julian Browne
Senior Advisor, U.S. Buyout, Aerospace & Defense:
Thomas A. (Tom) Corcoran, age 63
Senior Advisor: Arthur Levitt Jr., age 77
Senior Advisor: Thomas F. (Mack) McLarty III, age 62
Senior Advisor, U.S. Buyout and U.S. Venture and Growth Capital, Technology & Business Services:
Charles O. Rossotti, age 67
Senior Advisor, U.S. Buyout, Aerospace & Defense, Automotive & Transportation, and Industrial:
David L. Squier, age 62
Senior Advisor, U.S. Buyout, Aerospace & Defense:
William W. (Bill) Boisture Jr.
Senior Advisor, Financial Services:
James H. (Jim) Hance Jr., age 63

President and CEO, LifeCare Holdings:
G. Wayne McAlister, age 61
Co-Head, Financial Services Investments:
Oliver Sarkozy, age 38
Principal and COO, Carlyle Capital Corporation:
Claudia K. Fox
Principal; Director and Corporate Spokesman:
Christopher W. Ullman
Principal and Chief Compliance Officer: Ralph F. Mittl

LOCATIONS

HQ: The Carlyle Group
1001 Pennsylvania Ave. NW, Washington, DC 20004
Phone: 202-729-5626   **Fax:** 202-347-1818
Web: www.carlyle.com

US Offices

Charlotte, NC
Denver
Los Angeles
New York
Newport Beach, CA
San Francisco
Washington, DC

International Offices

Barcelona
Beijing
Beirut
Cairo
Dubai
Frankfurt
Hong Kong
Istanbul
London
Luxembourg
Mexico City
Milan
Munich
Mumbai
Paris
São Paulo
Seoul
Shanghai
Singapore
Stockholm
Sydney
Tokyo
Warsaw

PRODUCTS/OPERATIONS

Selected Portfolio Companies

Aerospace and Defense
  ARINC
  Aerostructures Corporation
  Combined Systems, Inc.
  NP Aerospace Limited
  Standard Aero Holdings, Inc.
  Vought Aircraft Industries, Inc.
  Wesco Aircraft Hardware Corp.
Automotive
  AxleTech International Holdings, Inc.
  Edscha AG (Germany)
  Rhythm Corporation (Japan)
  United Components, Inc.
  United Road Towing, Inc.
Consumer and Retail
  Britax Childcare Holdings Limited (child car safety
    seats, UK)
  China Pacific Insurance (Group) Co. Ltd.
  Dunkin' Brands
  IMO Car Wash Group
  Mattress Giant Corporation
  Oriental Trading Company
Energy and Power
  CDM Resource Management Ltd.
  Frontier Drilling ASA (Norway)
  Legend Natural Gas (natural gas and crude oil
    exploration)
  Magellan Midstream Partners, L.P.
  Phoenix Exploration Company LP
  Stallion Oilfield Services

Health Care
  Acufocus, Inc.
  Cellutions, Inc.
  Claris Lifesciences Limited (India)
  Endius, Inc.
  The Innovation Factory
  InteliStaf Group, Inc.
  MultiPlan, Inc.
  NeoVista, Inc.
  Primary Health, Inc.
  Transport Pharmaceuticals, Inc.
Industrial
  Comark Building Systems, Inc.
  Custom Alloy (France)
  Goodyear Engineered Products
  John Maneely Company
  Sanitors, Inc.
  Specialty Manufacturing Company
  StrionAir, Inc.
Technology and Business Services
  Adesso Systems, Inc.
  Archetype Solutions, Inc.
  AuthenTec, Inc.
  Command Information, Inc.
  Compusearch Software Systems
  Cube Optics AG (Germany)
  Flexcom Company Limited (South Korea)
  Freescale Semiconductor, Inc.
  Grant Street Group
  Ingenio
  Jazz Semiconductor, Inc.
  Liquid Engines, Inc.
  Panasas, Inc.
  Solsoft, Inc.
  SS&C Technologies, Inc.
  TradeBeam Holdings, Inc.
  USBX, Inc.
  ZCom Company Limited (China)
Telecom and Media
  Actelis Networks, Inc.
  AMC Entertainment, Inc.
  Aprovia (business publishing, France)
  Hawaiian Telecom
  Hispanic Teleservices Corporation
  Insight Communications, Inc.
  The Nielsen Company
Other
  TVK Gemi Yapim (50%, shipbuilding, Turkey)

COMPETITORS

Blackstone Group	Investcorp
CD&R	KKR
Forstmann Little	Thomas H. Lee Partners
Goldman Sachs	TPG
HM Capital Partners	

Carolina Hurricanes

Carolina Hurricanes Hockey Club is a professional hockey franchise that represents North Carolina in the National Hockey League. The team earned its first and only Stanley Cup championship in 2006. Originally founded in 1971 as the New England Whalers of the World Hockey Association (WHA), the team joined the NHL as the Hartford Whalers in 1979. Peter Karmanos, founder and chairman of Compuware, led a group that acquired the team in 1994, relocating it first to Greensboro, North Carolina, before settling in Raleigh in 1999.

Returning to the ice after the 2004-05 season was scuttled by the NHL player lockout, the Canes blew into the playoffs and secured its second Eastern Conference title in 2006, beating the Buffalo Sabres in seven games. Carolina then overcame the Edmonton Oilers to win the National Hockey League title after another seven-game series. The franchise made its first Stanley Cup finals appearance in 2002, losing to the Detroit Red Wings.

The Whalers originally represented Boston before moving to Hartford, Connecticut, in 1975. The Hartford Whalers later joined the NHL in 1979 after the WHA folded.

EXECUTIVES

CEO and Governor: Peter (Pete) Karmanos Jr., age 65
President and General Manager: Jim Rutherford
CFO: Michael (Mike) Amendola
Director Information Technology: Glenn Johnson
Director Food and Beverage: Chris Diamond
Director Ticket Sales: Kyle Prairie
Marketing Coordinator: Laura Caso

LOCATIONS

HQ: Carolina Hurricanes Hockey Club
1400 Edwards Mill Rd., Raleigh, NC 27607
Phone: 919-467-7825   **Fax:** 919-462-7030
Web: www.caneshockey.com

The Carolina Hurricanes play at 18,680-seat capacity RBC Center in Raleigh, North Carolina.

PRODUCTS/OPERATIONS

Championship Trophies

Stanley Cup (2006)
Prince of Wales Trophy (2002, 2006)

COMPETITORS

Atlanta Thrashers
Florida Panthers
Tampa Bay Lightning
Washington Capitals

HISTORICAL FINANCIALS

Company Type: Private

Income Statement

FYE: June 30

	REVENUE ($ mil.)	NET INCOME ($ mil.)	NET PROFIT MARGIN	EMPLOYEES
6/07	68	—	—	—
6/06	72	—	—	—
6/05	0	—	—	—
6/04	52	—	—	—
6/03	57	—	—	—
Annual Growth	4.5%	—	—	—

Revenue History

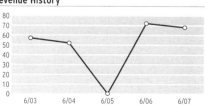

Carpenter Co.

It's a cushy job for Carpenter Co., making polyurethane foam and chemicals and polyester fiber used as cushioning by the automotive, bedding, floor covering, packaging, and furniture industries. The company started out making foam rubber; it now also manufactures air filters, expanded polystyrene building materials, and a tire fill product used as a replacement for air in off-road construction vehicles. Carpenter also sells consumer products — which include craft fiber products, mattress pads, and pillows — through retailers. The company has facilities throughout North America and Europe. Carpenter, which was founded in 1948 by E. Rhodes Carpenter, is owned by chairman and CEO Stanley Pauley.

EXECUTIVES

CEO: Stanley F. Pauley
COO: Stanley Yukevich
CFO: Michael (Mike) Lowery
Human Resources: Rich Trownsell
Managing Director, Dumo: Hendrick Kesteloot

LOCATIONS

HQ: Carpenter Co.
   5016 Monument Ave., Richmond, VA 23230
Phone: 804-359-0800   **Fax:** 804-353-0694
Web: www.carpenter.com

Carpenter has manufacturing facilities throughout Europe and North America.

PRODUCTS/OPERATIONS

Selected Products

Air filter media
Bedding
Carpet cushion
Chemicals
Chemical systems
Consumer products
Expanded polystyrene systems
Flexible foam packaging
Furniture
Polyester fiber
Tire products

COMPETITORS

British Vita
Dash Multi-Corp
Foamex International
Henry Company
MTI Global
Owens Corning Sales
PMC Global
The Woodbridge Group

HISTORICAL FINANCIALS

Company Type: Private

Income Statement

FYE: December 31

	REVENUE ($ mil.)	NET INCOME ($ mil.)	NET PROFIT MARGIN	EMPLOYEES
12/07	1,650	—	—	5,900
12/06	1,710	—	—	5,675
12/05	1,456	—	—	5,900
12/04	1,300	—	—	6,000
12/03	1,200	—	—	6,000
Annual Growth	**8.3%**	—	—	**(0.4%)**

Revenue History

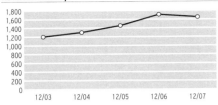

	12/03	12/04	12/05	12/06	12/07

Carpet One

When one needs carpet, one can shop at Carpet One, the #1 seller of floor covering (ahead of big-box retailers Home Depot and Lowe's) with more than 1,000 independently owned and operated locations that reach across Canada, New Zealand, and throughout the US. Besides carpet and area rugs, Carpet One peddles bamboo, ceramic, cork, exotic wood, hardwood, laminate, and vinyl floor coverings. The company's exclusive brands include Good Housekeeping, relax it's LEES, Mirror Lake Laminate, and Hanover Hills Hardwood, as well as Liz Claiborne. Founded in 1985 with some 13 member stores, today the co-operative is the largest division of CCA Global Partners.

EXECUTIVES

President: Evan Hackel
VP Marketing and Advertising: Stan Langer
VP Member Relations: Sally Kelly
VP Merchandising: Sands Woody
VP Operations: Eileen Shapiro
VP Public Relations and Licensing: Terri Daniels
VP Retail: David Hendler
VP Store Design: Theresa Fisher
VP Carpet One Canada: Baxter Freake
General Manager Australia and New Zealand:
   Scott Wegener

LOCATIONS

HQ: Carpet One
   670 N. Commercial St., Manchester, NH 03101
Phone: 800-450-7595   **Fax:** 603-626-3444
Web: carpetone.com

COMPETITORS

Abbey Carpet
Costco Wholesale
Home Depot
IKEA
J. C. Penney
Kohl's
Lowe's
Macy's
Menard
SAM'S CLUB
Sears
Target
Wal-Mart

Catalent Pharma Solutions

Catalyst + talent = Catalent. At least, that's the brand Catalent Pharma Solutions is trying to convey. The company develops, manufactures, and sells oral (soft and hardshell capsules), topical (ointment applicators), sterile (syringes), and inhaled (nasal sprays) forms of drug delivery products to pharmaceutical companies in nearly 100 countries. Catalent also manufactures different types of packaging: bottles, pouches, and strips used to hold tablet, powder, and liquid medicines. The company was formed in 2007 when The Blackstone Group acquired Cardinal Health's pharmaceutical technologies segment for $3.3 billion. Catalent now operates 30 facilities worldwide and generates $1.7 billion in annual revenue.

As an independent company, Catalent recently established a strategic direction by reorganizing its business into three main segments: oral technologies, sterile technologies, and packaging technologies. The company announced that it would close a facility in New Mexico and another in France (which manufactured hormone products) because neither were core to its future growth. In its place, Catalent opened a facility near Belgium specifically designed to double the production of prefilled flu vaccine syringes, thereby enhancing its sterile technologies business. Already it operates prefilled syringe plants in North Carolina and France, which are helping the company keep pace with customer demand in Europe, Japan, and the US.

Catalent also expects to benefit from collaborative agreements with such pharmaceutical companies as ALK-Abello, which is funding a new line of tablet-based allergy products. Using Catalent's Zydis oral dissolving tablet technology, ALK-Abello clinically demonstrated that its allergy vaccine, GRAZAX, can be consumed orally by patients rather than injected. Commercial production of the new line is scheduled to start at Catalent's Swindon, UK, facility in 2010.

EXECUTIVES

Chairman and Interim CEO: George L. Fotiades, age 54
SVP and CFO: Matthew M. (Matt) Walsh, age 41
SVP, Global Sales: David Heyens
SVP and General Counsel: Samrat (Sam) Khichi
VP and General Manager, Global Clinical Supplies:
   Frank Lis
Group President, Packaging Services:
   Tracy Ken Tsuetaki
Group President, Sterile Technologies:
   Richard Yarwood
Group President, Oral Technologies: Thomas Stuart
Media Relations: Cornell Stamoran
Auditors: Ernst & Young LLP

LOCATIONS

HQ: Catalent Pharma Solutions, Inc.
   14 Schoolhouse Rd., Somerset, NJ 08873
Phone: 732-537-6200   **Fax:** 732-537-6480
Web: www.catalent.com

HISTORICAL FINANCIALS

Company Type: Private

Income Statement				FYE: June 30
	REVENUE ($ mil.)	NET INCOME ($ mil.)	NET PROFIT MARGIN	EMPLOYEES
6/08	1,828	(540)	—	9,800
6/07	1,704	(125)	—	10,000
6/06	1,612	51	3.2%	—
6/05	1,517	14	0.9%	—
Annual Growth	6.4%	—	—	(2.0%)

Net Income History

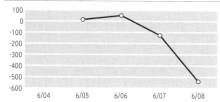

Catholic Health East

Catholic Health East marries the physical and the spiritual in its vast network of not-for-profit health care facilities. As one of the top religious health systems in the country, Catholic Health East carries out its mission of healing the sick through more than 30 hospitals, about 40 nursing homes and long-term acute care facilities, and about 20 senior living facilities. Operating health systems all along the East Coast from Maine to Florida, Catholic Health East also runs behavioral health facilities and is one of the country's largest providers of home health care services. The health care organization is sponsored by 10 congregations of nuns.

Catholic Health East was founded in 1998 when three regional Catholic health systems joined forces. It has since grown its network by adding affiliated hospitals to its network, including the 2008 addition of Saint Michael's Medical Center in Newark, New Jersey.

In 2006 the organization sold its Mercy Hospital of Pittsburgh (now UPMC Mercy) to UPMC.

HISTORY

It was three easy pieces that made up Catholic Health East in 1997. Allegany Health System, Eastern Mercy Health System, and Sisters of Providence Health System operated almost entirely in separate, but adjacent, geographic areas on the East Coast, overlapping only in Florida.

Catholic Health East's history goes as far back as 1831, when the Sisters of Mercy was founded in Dublin, Ireland, by Catherine McAuley, who established a poorhouse using her inheritance.

Some of the sisters hopped the Pond in 1843, establishing the first Catholic hospital in the US, the Mercy Hospital of Pittsburgh, four years later. Over the years the Sisters of Mercy expanded throughout the US. By 1991 there were 25 Sisters of Mercy congregations; they united that year under the newly formed Institute of the Sisters of Mercy of the Americas.

The Sisters of Providence came from Kingston, Ontario, to found the first hospital in Holyoke, Massachusetts. Having established their own ministry, the sisters in Holyoke became a separate congregation in 1892. The congregation expanded slowly, moving into North Carolina in 1956, eventually forming the Sisters of Providence Health System.

A Polish nun, Mother Colette Hilbert, formed a new congregation in Pittsburgh in 1897 after the other members of her former parish were recalled to Poland. The new congregation entered health care in 1926, establishing a home for the elderly in New York. In honor of Hilbert's favorite saint, the order became the Franciscan Sisters of St. Joseph in 1934.

The Franciscan Sisters of St. Joseph and the Sisters of Mercy united to form the ministry that became Pittsburgh Mercy Health System in 1983. In 1986 the congregations formed Eastern Mercy Health System as a holding company for the health concern. The consolidation served to cut costs, as well as to preserve the organization's religious mission.

The Franciscan Sisters of Allegany congregation got its start in 1859 teaching children in Buffalo, New York. In 1883 the order took over St. Elizabeth Hospital in Boston, expanding its health care services ministry throughout New York, New Jersey, and Florida by the 1930s. In 1986 the sisters organized the operations as Allegany Health System.

In the early 1990s Catholic health care systems underwent a round of consolidation. Allegany Health Systems and Eastern Mercy Health Systems combined services, aiming to lower costs through economies of scale.

The mid-1990s also brought consolidation, but this time operational costs weren't the major problem; Catholic health systems across the nation were facing a shortage of sisters. To have a sufficient number of sisters to keep the "Catholic" in Catholic health care, the three health systems merged in 1997, becoming Catholic Health East.

After the merger, the company continued to build its network through acquisitions, including Mercy Health in Miami (1998) and a suffering, secular Cooper Health System in Camden, New Jersey (1999). In 2000 it gained control of two troubled hospitals in Palm Beach, Florida, only to sell them the following year. Catholic Health East remains focused on reducing costs as it expands.

EXECUTIVES

Chairperson: Jacquelyn Kinder
President and CEO: Robert V. Stanek
EVP and COO: Mark O'Neil
EVP and CFO: Peter L. (Pete) DeAngelis Jr.
EVP and Chief Medical Officer: Thomas L. Garthwaite, age 58
EVP, Mission Integration: Sister Juliana M. Casey
EVP, Northeast: Judith M. (Judy) Persichilli
EVP, Strategic Ministry Development: Sister Kathleen Popko
EVP, Southeast: Howard Watts
VP, Legal Services and General Counsel: Michael C. Hemsley

VP, Risk Management Services and Chief Risk Officer: Theodore Schlert
President and CEO, Mercy Hospital Miami: John C. Johnson
President and CEO, St. Mary Medical Center: Greg Wozniak
President and CEO, St. Joseph of the Pines, Southern Pines, North Carolina: Ken Cormier
President and CEO, Continuing Care Management Services Network: John Capasso
Executive Director, Global Health Ministry: Sister Mary Jo McGinley
Director Human Resources and Administration: Susan Tillman-Taylor
CIO: Donette Herring
Auditors: PricewaterhouseCoopers LLP

LOCATIONS

HQ: Catholic Health East
3805 W. Chester Pike, Ste. 100,
Newtown Square, PA 19073
Phone: 610-355-2000   **Fax:** 610-271-9600
Web: www.che.org

Selected Facilities

Alabama
   Mercy Medical (rehabilitation and nursing care, Daphne)
Connecticut
   Mercy Community Health (nursing care and senior living facilities, West Hartford)
Delaware
   St. Francis Healthcare Services (Wilmington)
Florida
   BayCare Health Systems (Clearwater)
   Holy Cross Hospital (Fort Lauderdale)
   Mercy Hospital (Miami)
Georgia
   Saint Joseph's Health System (Atlanta)
   St. Mary's Health Care System, Inc. (Athens, GA)
Massachusetts
   Sisters of Providence Health System (Springfield)
Maine
   Mercy Health System of Maine (Portland)
New Jersey
   Lourdes Health System (Camden)
   Saint Michael's Medical Center (Newark)
   St. Francis Medical Center (Trenton)
New York
   Catholic Health System (Buffalo)
   St. James Mercy Health System (Hornell)
   St. Peter's Health Care Services (Albany)
North Carolina
   St. Joseph of the Pines (senior living facility, Southern Pines)
Pennsylvania
   Maxis Health System (Carbondale)
   Mercy Health System of Southeastern Pennsylvania (Conshohocken)
   St. Mary Medical Center (Langhorne)

COMPETITORS

HISTORICAL FINANCIALS
Company Type: Not-for-profit

Income Statement
FYE: December 31

	REVENUE ($ mil.)	NET INCOME ($ mil.)	NET PROFIT MARGIN	EMPLOYEES
12/07	4,365	255	5.8%	54,000
12/06	4,183	199	4.8%	50,000
12/05	4,246	219	5.2%	43,000
12/04	4,035	205	5.1%	43,000
12/03	5,700	—	—	43,000
Annual Growth	(6.5%)	7.5%	—	5.9%

2007 Year-End Financials
Debt ratio: 45.7%   Current ratio: —
Return on equity: 8.9%   Long-term debt ($ mil.): 1,357
Cash ($ mil.): —

Net Income History

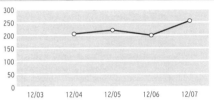

	12/03	12/04	12/05	12/06	12/07

Catholic Health Initiatives

For Catholic Health Initiatives (CHI), returning sick people to good health is more than a business: It's a mission. Formed in 1996 through the merger of three Catholic hospital systems, the giant not-for-profit organization is the second largest Catholic hospital operator in the US, just behind Ascension Health. It operates some 70 hospitals and more than 40 long-term care, assisted-living, and senior residential facilities in about 20 states from Washington to Maryland. Its hospitals range from large urban medical centers to small critical access hospitals in rural areas. All told, the health system has more than 14,000 acute care beds. It is sponsored by a dozen different congregations of nuns.

The organization grew in 2007 through several new affiliations. It bought 38-bed Enumclaw Regional Hospital, which became part of Washington State's Franciscan Health System; and its Kentucky-based Saint Joseph HealthCare system gained Mary Chiles Hospital, later renamed Saint Joseph Mount Sterling. CHI's largest addition, however, came with the proposed affiliation of Saint Clare's Health System, a four-hospital system operating in northwest New Jersey.

Catholic Health Initiatives, along with other not-for-profit hospitals, came under some pressure from Congress in 2006, as federal officials tried to determine whether such hospitals provided enough benefit to their communities (by treating the poor and uninsured, among other things) to earn their tax-exempt status. In anticipation of increased congressional scrutiny, CHI adopted an updated system for reporting their contributions to their communities; the system was developed by the Catholic Health Association, an organization of not-for-profit health systems to which CHI belongs.

HISTORY

In 1860 the Sisters of St. Francis established a hospital in Philadelphia, laying the foundation for a larger health care organization. In 1981 Franciscan Health System was formally established to be a national holding company for Catholic hospitals and related organizations. By the mid-1990s the system consisted of 12 member and two affiliate hospitals and 11 long-term-care facilities located in the mid-Atlantic states and the Pacific Northwest.

Sisters of Charity of Cincinnati and the Sisters of St. Francis Perpetual Adoration of Colorado Springs co-sponsored The Sisters of Charity Health Care Systems, incorporated in 1979 as a multi-institutional health care network. By the mid-1990s the system included 20 hospitals in Colorado, Kentucky, Nebraska, New Mexico, and Ohio.

Three congregations collaborated to form Catholic Health Corporation in 1980, one of the first such health care partnerships between religious communities within the Roman Catholic Church in the US. By 1996 this coalition operated 100 health care facilities in 12 states.

The development of modern managed care health care systems put pressure on the smaller Catholic hospital operations, so the three systems established Catholic Health Initiatives (CHI) in 1996 as a national entity serving five geographic regions. Patricia Cahill, a lay health care veteran who previously served the Archdiocese of New York, was appointed president and CEO of CHI. The following year CHI absorbed the 10-hospital Sisters of Charity of Nazareth Health Care System, based in Bardstown, Kentucky (founded in a log cabin in 1812).

That year CHI continued to seek new partnerships to improve efficiency. With Alegent Health it formed provider network Midwest Select with nearly 200 hospitals, marketing discounted rates to businesses. CHI allied with the Daughters of Charity to form for-profit joint venture Catholic Healthcare Audit Network to provide operational, financial, compliance, and information systems audits, as well as due diligence reviews. CHI also joined insurance joint venture NewCap Insurance with the Daughters of Charity and Catholic Health East; the firm allowed CHI to operate independently of commercial insurers.

CHI made a secular tie-in with the University of Pennsylvania Health System in 1998, whereby the university's system would offer care through five Catholic hospitals (CHI made plans to transfer these hospitals to Catholic Health East in 2001). The next year CHI announced its first loss, due to lackluster performance in the Midwest. During 2000 the company responded by streamlining operations and changing management, resulting in a positive bottom line. In 2001 it sold three hospitals in Pennsylvania, one in Delaware, and one in New Jersey to Catholic Health East.

EXECUTIVES

President and CEO: Kevin E. Lofton
EVP and COO: Michael T. Rowan
Chief Administrative Officer: Michael L. Fordyce
SVP and Chief Medical Officer: John F. Anderson
SVP and Chief Human Resource Officer, Kentucky: Herbert J. Vallier
SVP Advocacy: M. Colleen Scanlon
SVP Communications: Joyce M. Ross
SVP Finance and Treasury and CFO: Colleen M. Blye
SVP and General Counsel: Paul G. Neumann
SVP Mission: Rev Thomas R. Kopfensteiner
SVP Performance Management: Susan E. Peach
SVP Sponsorship and Governance: Sister Peggy Ann Martin
SVP Supply Chain: Phillip W. Mears
SVP Strategy and Business Development: John F. DiCola
SVP and Group Executive Officer: Deborah M. Lee-Eddie
SVP Operations, Minnesota: Larry A. Schulz
SVP Information Technology and Chief Information Officer: Christopher J. Macmanus
SVP and Group Executive Officer: David J. Goode
SVP and Chief Risk Officer, Kentucky: Mitch H. Melfi
SVP Operations: Gary S. Campbell
SVP and Division Executive Officer: Jeffrey S. Drop
SVP and Chief Nursing Officer: Kathleen D. Sanford
Director, Public Policy: Marcia Desmond
Director, Communication Services: Peg O'Keefe
Auditors: Ernst & Young LLP

LOCATIONS

HQ: Catholic Health Initiatives
1999 Broadway, Ste. 2600, Denver, CO 80202
Phone: 303-298-9100   **Fax:** 303-298-9690
Web: www.catholichealthinit.org

Selected Facilities and Operations
Arkansas
  St. Vincent Health System
    St. Anthony's Medical Center (Morrilton)
    St. Vincent Doctors Hospital (Little Rock)
    St. Vincent Infirmary Medical Center (Little Rock)
    St. Vincent Medical Center North (Sherwood)
    St. Vincent Rehabilitation Hospital (Sherwood)
Colorado
  Centura Health
    Centura Senior Services
      Centura Senior Life Center (Denver)
      The Gardens at St. Elizabeth (Denver)
      Medalion Retirement Center (Colorado Springs)
      Namaste Alzheimer Center (Colorado Springs)
      Progressive Care Center (Canon City)
      Villa Pueblo (Pueblo)
      The Villas at Sunny Acres (Denver)
    Penrose-St. Francis Health Services
      Penrose Community Hospital (Colorado Springs)
      Penrose Hospital (Colorado Springs)
      St. Francis Health Center (Colorado Springs)
    St. Anthony Hospitals
      St. Anthony Central Hospital (Denver)
      St. Anthony Granby Medical Center
      St. Anthony North Hospital (Westminster)
      St. Anthony Summit Medical Center (Frisco)
    St. Mary-Corwin Medical Center (Pueblo)
    St. Thomas More Hospital (Canon City)
  Mercy Regional Medical Center (Durango)
Idaho
  Mercy Medical Center (Nampa)
Iowa
  Alegent Health
    Alegent Health-Mercy Hospital (Corning)
    Alegent Health-Mercy Hospital (Council Bluffs)
  Mercy Health Network
    Bishop Drumm Retirement Center (Johnston)
    Mercy Clinics (Des Moines)
    Mercy College of Health Sciences (Des Moines)
    Mercy Court (Des Moines)
    Mercy Medical Center — Centerville
    Mercy Medical Center — Des Moines
    Mercy Park Apartments (Des Moines)

Kansas
  Central Kansas Medical Center (Great Bend)
    St. Joseph Memorial Hospital (Larned)
  St. John's Maude Norton Memorial Hospital
    (Columbus)
  St. Catherine Hospital (Garden City)
Kentucky
  Continuing Care Hospital, Inc. (Lexington)
  Flaget Memorial Hospital (Bardstown)
  Jewish Hospital and St. Mary's HealthCare (with
    Jewish Hospital HealthCare Services)
    Our Lady of Peace (Louisville)
    Sts. Mary & Elizabeth Hospital (Louisville)
  Marymount Medical Center (London)
  Our Lady of the Way Hospital (Martin)
  Saint Joseph HealthCare
    Saint Joseph Berea Hospital
    Saint Joseph Hospital (Lexington)
    Saint Joseph Hospital East (Lexington)
    Saint Joseph Hospital Mount Sterling (Mt. Sterling)
Maryland
  St. Joseph Medical Center (Towson)
Minnesota
  LakeWood Health Center (Baudette)
  St. Francis Medical Center (Breckenridge)
  St. Francis Home (Breckenridge)
  St. Joseph's Area Health Services (Park Rapids)
  Unity Family Healthcare (dba St. Gabriel's Healthcare)
    Albany Area Hospital and Medical Center
    Alverna Apartments (Little Falls)
    St. Camillus Place (Little Falls)
    St. Otto's Care Center (Little Falls)
Missouri
  St. John's Regional Medical Center (Joplin)
  St. John's Rehabilitation Center (Joplin)
Nebraska
  Alegent Health (joint venture with Immanuel
    Healthcare System)
    Alegent Health-Bergan Mercy Medical Center
      (Omaha)
  Good Samaritan Health Systems
    Richard H. Young Hospital (Kearney)
  Saint Elizabeth Health Systems
    Saint Elizabeth Regional Medical Center (Lincoln)
  Saint Francis Medical Center (Grand Island)
  St. Mary's Community Hospital (Nebraska City)
New Mexico
  St. Joseph Community Health (Albuquerque)
North Dakota
  CHI North Dakota
    Carrington Health Center (Carrington)
    Lisbon Area Health Services
    Mercy Hospital (Valley City)
    Oakes Community Hospital
  Mercy Hospital (Devils Lake)
  Mercy Medical Center (Williston)
  St. Joseph's Hospital and Health Center (Dickinson)
  Villa Nazareth Corporation
    Friendship (Fargo)
    Riverview Place (Fargo)
Ohio
  Premier Health Partners
    Good Samaritan Hospital (Dayton)
    The Maria-Joseph Center (Dayton)
  TriHealth
    Good Samaritan Hospital (Cincinnati)
Oregon
  Holy Rosary Medical Center (Ontario)
  Mercy Medical Center
    Linus Oakes, Inc. (Roseburg)
  St. Anthony Hospital (Pendleton)
  St. Elizabeth Health Services (Baker City)
Pennsylvania
  St. Joseph Health Ministries (Lancaster)
  St. Joseph Regional Health Network
    St. Joseph Living Care Center (Reading)
    St. Joseph Medical Center (Reading)

South Dakota
  St. Mary's Healthcare Center
    Gettysburg Medical Center
    Maryhouse Long-term Care Facility (Pierre)
    ParkWood Retirement Apartments (Pierre)
    Oahe Manor (Gettysburg)
    Oahe Villa (Gettysburg)
    St. Mary's Hospital (Pierre)
Tennessee
  Memorial Health Care System
    Memorial Hospital (Chattanooga)
    Memorial North Park Hospital (Hixson)
Washington
  Franciscan Health System
    Enumclaw Regional Hospital (Enumclaw)
    St. Clare Hospital (Lakewood)
    St. Francis Hospital (Federal Way)
    St. Joseph Medical Center (Tacoma)
Wisconsin
  Franciscan Villa (South Milwaukee)

COMPETITORS

Adventist Health System
Allina Hospitals
Ascension Health
Baptist Health (Arkansas)
Baptist Healthcare System
BryanLGH Medical Center
Catholic Healthcare Partners
Denver Health and Hospital Authority
Exempla Healthcare
Golden Horizons
HCA
Health Alliance
Kettering Medical Center Network
Life Care Centers
MedCath
Memorial Hospital of Colorado Springs
Methodist Health System
MultiCare Health System
OhioHealth
Tenet Healthcare
Universal Health Services
University of Colorado Hospital

HISTORICAL FINANCIALS

Company Type: Not-for-profit

Income Statement

FYE: June 30

	REVENUE ($ mil.)	NET INCOME ($ mil.)	NET PROFIT MARGIN	EMPLOYEES
6/07	8,603	1,020	11.9%	65,296
6/06	8,077	687	8.5%	65,070
6/05	7,091	461	6.5%	54,044
6/04	6,121	770	12.6%	53,459
6/03	6,072	203	3.3%	54,975
Annual Growth	9.1%	49.7%	—	4.4%

2007 Year-End Financials

Debt ratio: 37.1%
Return on equity: 14.7%
Cash ($ mil.): —
Current ratio: —
Long-term debt ($ mil.): 2,725

Net Income History

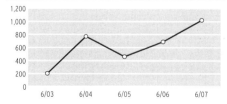

Catholic Healthcare Partners

Say "Amen" to the healing powers of Catholic Healthcare Partners (CHP). One of the nation's largest not-for-profit health systems, CHP offers health care services, primarily in Ohio but also in Indiana, Kentucky, Pennsylvania, and Tennessee through some 100 organizations. Facilities include about 30 hospitals, more than a dozen long-term care facilities, housing for the elderly, and wellness centers. CHP also offers physician practices and hospice and home health care. The system is co-sponsored by the Sisters of Mercy communities of Cincinnati and Dallas, Pennsylvania; the Sisters of the Humility of Mary of Villa Maria, Pennsylvania; the Franciscan Sisters of the Poor; and Covenant Health Systems.

Catholic Healthcare Partners organizes its operations into nine regions to better serve the communities where its facilities are located.

EXECUTIVES

Chairman: Anthony L. Barbato
Vice Chairman: James C. (Jim) Patton
President and CEO: Michael D. Connelly
EVP, Chief Administrative Officer: Jane Durney Crowley
COO: A. David Jimenez
SVP and CFO: William Shuttleworth
SVP and CIO: Rebecca (Becky) Sykes
SVP and General Counsel: Michael A. Bezney
SVP, Talent Management and Diversity: Jon C. Abeles
SVP, Insurance and Physician Services:
  R. Jeffrey Copeland
SVP, Mission and Values Integration:
  Sister Doris Gottemoeller
SVP; President and CEO, Humility of Mary Health Partners: Robert W. (Bob) Shroder
SVP; President and CEO, Mercy Health Partners — Northeast Region: James E. (Jim) May
SVP; President and CEO, Mercy Health Partners — Northern Region: Steven L. (Steve) Mickus
SVP; President and CEO, Mercy Health Partners — Southwest Ohio Region: Thomas S. Urban
SVP; President and CEO, St. Mary's Health Partners and Mercy Health Partners — Kentucky Region: Debra K. London
SVP; President and CEO, West Central Ohio Health Partners and St. Rita's Medical Center: James P. Reber
SVP, Human Resources: John Starcher
Auditors: Ernst & Young LLP

LOCATIONS

HQ: Catholic Healthcare Partners
  615 Elsinore Place, Cincinnati, OH 45202
Phone: 513-639-2800 **Fax:** 513-639-2700
Web: www.health-partners.org

PRODUCTS/OPERATIONS

Regions

Community Health Partners (North Central Ohio)
Community Mercy Health Partners
Humility of Mary Health Partners (Northeast Ohio)
Mercy Health Partners Kentucky/Indiana Region
Mercy Health Partners Northeast Region (Northeast Pennsylvania)
Mercy Health Partners Northern Region (Northwest Ohio and Southern Michigan)
Mercy Health Partners Southwest Ohio Region
St. Mary's Health Partners (Eastern Tennessee)
West Central Ohio Health Partners

COMPETITORS

Ascension Health
Catholic Health Initiatives
HCA
Kindred Healthcare
OhioHealth
Tenet Healthcare
Universal Health Services

HISTORICAL FINANCIALS

Company Type: Not-for-profit

Income Statement

FYE: December 31

	REVENUE ($ mil.)	NET INCOME ($ mil.)	NET PROFIT MARGIN	EMPLOYEES
12/07	3,715	97	2.6%	36,925
12/06	3,511	136	3.9%	34,280
12/05	3,361	154	4.6%	35,000
12/04	3,158	171	5.4%	—
12/03	2,874	—	—	30,524
Annual Growth	6.6%	(17.3%)	—	4.9%

2007 Year-End Financials

Debt ratio: 73.7%
Return on equity: 4.4%
Cash ($ mil.): —

Current ratio: —
Long-term debt ($ mil.): 1,624

Net Income History

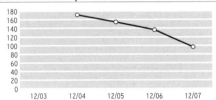

Catholic Healthcare West

Catholic Healthcare West (CHW) has steadily grown to become the largest private, not-for-profit health care provider in the state of California. Sponsored by eight congregations of nuns, CHW operates a network of more than 40 acute care facilities located in the Golden State and, to a lesser extent, in Arizona and Nevada. Those facilities house more than 8,000 acute care beds, as well as nearly 1,000 skilled nursing beds. CHW also provides home health care and hospice services through agencies in California and Nevada. Founded in 1986, CHW is the official health care provider of the San Francisco Giants.

CHW is expanding some facilities and adding new ones in high-growth areas. In 2006 it opened Mercy Gilbert Medical Center in Gilbert, Arizona, as well as a third campus for its Las Vegas-area St. Rose Dominican Hospitals. The following year, the organization added Saint Mary's Regional Medical Center in Reno, Nevada, to its stable of hospitals.

In 2004 CHW joined other Catholic hospitals in announcing plans to charge uninsured patients the same rates charged to patients on Medicare, Medicaid, and other government-funded health care programs. The announcement came, in part, as a response to criticism that hospitals across the country charge uninsured patients much higher rates for services and aggressively seek payment.

In 2006 CHW settled a class action lawsuit alleging that the company overcharged uninsured patients for the services they received. As part of the settlement, CHW agreed to give hundreds of millions of dollars in refunds and bill adjustments to more than 750,000 patients.

With both clergy and laity on its board, CHW has grown by consolidating both religious-group affiliated and community hospitals.

HISTORY

Catholic Healthcare West traces its roots to 1857, when the Sisters of Mercy founded St. Mary's Hospital in San Francisco. The order expanded in that area, and in 1986 two different communities of the Sisters of Mercy merged their hospitals into an organization with one retirement home and 10 hospitals from the Bay Area to San Diego. Declining membership in Roman Catholic religious orders, combined with consolidation in the field, led the orders to see merger as their only route to survival.

Rising medical costs, slow payers, and merger expenses dropped the organization's combined net income to $20 million in 1988 (from nearly $58 million in 1986). One of the hardest-hit CHW affiliates was Mercy Healthcare Sacramento, which lost $4.2 million between 1986 and 1987. In 1988 Mercy Healthcare restructured along regional lines.

The next year the Sisters of St. Dominic brought two hospitals into the alliance. CHW launched the Community Economic Assistance program, which provided $220,000 in grants to 16 human service and health care agencies in its first year.

CHW continued to add facilities, including AMI Community Hospital in Santa Cruz, California, in 1990. Since CHW already owned the area's only other acute care hospital, Dominican Santa Cruz Hospital, CHW in 1993 was ordered not to acquire any more acute care hospitals in Santa Cruz County without FTC approval.

As the trend toward managed care became a stampede in the 1990s, CHW moved more into preventive care and began reining in costs through productivity improvement plans. It continued to add hospitals, including tax-supported institutions trying to compete with national for-profit systems.

The network increased its medical clout in 1994 by allying with San Diego-based Scripps, one of the state's largest HMO systems. In 1995 the Daughters of Charity Province of the West realigned its six-hospital operation with CHW. The next year the Dominican Sisters (California), Dominican Sisters of St. Catherine of Siena (Wisconsin), and Sisters of Charity of the Incarnate Word allied their California hospitals with CHW. New community hospitals included Bakersfield Memorial, Sierra Nevada Memorial (Grass Valley), and Sequoia Hospital (Redwood City).

Charity and cost-consciousness clashed in 1996 when union members staged a walkout to protest nonunion outsourcing of vocational nursing, housekeeping, and kitchen jobs. This dispute was settled, but CHW continued to be a target for union organizers, with a bitter battle against the Service Employees International Union (SEIU) starting in 1998.

CHW agreed in 1996 to merge with Samaritan Health Systems (now Banner Health System) in a move that would have made CHW one of the US's top five providers, but the deal fell apart in 1997. In 1998 CHW merged with UniHealth, a group with eight facilities in Los Angeles and Orange counties. Mounting costs forced CHW to post a loss, and in 1999 it cut some managerial positions and reorganized to recover.

The year 2000 brought CHW more problems with labor relations: SEIU argued that the organization was resistant to unionization. Continued losses led the organization to implement major restructuring the following year, as its 10 regional divisions were consolidated into four.

In 2001 CHW stepped up donations, grants, and other sponsorship efforts designed to benefit areas served by its hospitals and clinics. However, the rapid expansion that made the system a name in the California health care industry also left it bloated. Rising health care costs and trouble with its physician management groups cut deeply into earnings. Management casualties occurred as CHW reorganized that year.

Two years later the company parted ways with one of its sponsoring organizations, the Franciscan Sisters of the Sacred Heart of Frankfort, Illinois. The sponsorship ended when CHW closed St. Francis Medical Center of Santa Barbara. However, the hospital operator that fiscal year posted its first operating profit since 1996.

The hospital operator continued to expand its California presence in 2004, acquiring two hospitals from Universal Health Services: French Medical Center in San Luis Obispo and Arroyo Grande Community Hospital in Arroyo Grande. The two facilities combined added almost 180 beds.

EXECUTIVES

Chair: Jarrett Anderson
Vice Chair: Tessie Guillermo
President, CEO, and Director: Lloyd H. Dean, age 57
EVP and Co-COO: Marvin O'Quinn
EVP and Co-COO: William J. (Bill) Hunt
EVP and CFO: Michael D. Blaszyk
SVP and Chief Administrative Officer: Elizabeth Shih
SVP and Chief Medical Officer: Robert Wiebe
SVP Human Resources: Ernest Urquhart
SVP and Chief Strategy Officer: Charles P. Francis
SVP and General Counsel: Derek F. Covert
SVP Managed Care: John Wray
SVP Sponsorship and Mission Integration:
Bernita McTernan
SVP and CIO: Benjamin R. (Ben) Williams
CEO, St. Mary's Medical Center: Ken Steele
President, Marian Medical Center:
Charles (Chuck) Cova, age 52
President, Mercy San Juan Medical Center:
Michael (Mike) Uboldi
Media Relations: Tricia Griffin
Auditors: Deloitte & Touche LLP

LOCATIONS

HQ: Catholic Healthcare West
185 Berry St., Ste. 300, San Francisco, CA 94107
Phone: 415-438-5500   **Fax:** 415-438-5724
Web: www.chwhealth.org

Selected Facilities

Arizona
Barrow Neurological Institute (Phoenix)
Chandler Regional Hospital
Mercy Gilbert Medical Center
St. Joseph's Hospital and Medical Center (Phoenix)

California
  Arroyo Grande Community Hospital
  Bakersfield Memorial Hospital
  California Hospital Medical Center (Los Angeles)
  Community Hospital of San Bernardino
  Dominican Hospital (Santa Cruz)
  French Hospital Medical Center (San Luis Obispo)
  Glendale Memorial Hospital and Health Center
  Marian Medical Center (Santa Maria)
  Mark Twain St. Joseph's Hospital (San Andreas)
  Mercy General Hospital (Sacramento)
  Mercy Hospital of Bakersfield
  Mercy Hospital of Folsom
  Mercy Medical Center Merced
  Mercy Medical Center Mt. Shasta
  Mercy Medical Center Redding
  Mercy San Juan Medical Center (Carmichael)
  Mercy Southwest Hospital (Bakersfield)
  Methodist Hospital of Sacramento
  Northridge Hospital Medical Center
  Oak Valley Hospital (Oakdale)
  San Gabriel Valley Medical Center
  Sequoia Hospital (Redwood City)
  Sierra Nevada Memorial Hospital (Grass Valley)
  St. Bernardine Medical Center (San Bernardino)
  St. Dominic's Hospital (Manteca)
  St. Elizabeth Community Hospital (Red Bluff)
  Saint Francis Memorial Hospital (San Francisco)
  St. John's Pleasant Valley Hospital (Camarillo)
  St. John's Regional Medical Center (Oxnard)
  St. Joseph's Behavioral Health Center (Stockton)
  St. Joseph's Medical Center (Stockton)
  St. Mary Medical Center (Long Beach)
  St. Mary's Medical Center (San Francisco)
  Woodland Healthcare
Nevada
  Saint Mary's Regional Medical Center (Reno)
  St. Rose Dominican Hospital Rose de Lima Campus
    (Henderson)
  St. Rose Dominican Hospital San Martín Campus (Las
    Vegas)
  St. Rose Dominican Hospital Siena Campus
    (Henderson)

PRODUCTS/OPERATIONS

Sponsoring Organizations

Auburn Regional Community of the Sisters of Mercy
  (California)
Burlingame Regional Community of the Sisters of Mercy
  (California)
Congregation of the Dominican Sisters of St. Catherine
  of Siena of Kenosha (Wisconsin)
Congregation of the Sisters of Charity of the Incarnate
  Word (Houston, TX)
Sisters of Mercy of the Americas
Sisters of St. Dominic, Congregation of the Most Holy
  Rosary (Adrian, MI)
Sisters of St. Francis of Penance and Christian Charity,
  St. Francis Province (Redwood City, CA)
Sisters of the Third Order of St. Dominic, Congregation
  of the Most Holy Name (San Rafael, CA)

COMPETITORS

Adventist Health
Banner Health
HCA
Kaiser Permanente
Los Angeles County Health Department
Memorial Health Services
Shasta Regional Medical Center
St. Joseph Health System
Stanford University Medical
Sutter Health
Tenet Healthcare
Universal Health Services

HISTORICAL FINANCIALS
Company Type: Not-for-profit

Income Statement
FYE: June 30

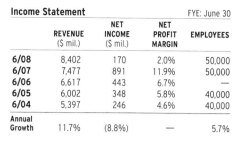

	REVENUE ($ mil.)	NET INCOME ($ mil.)	NET PROFIT MARGIN	EMPLOYEES
6/08	8,402	170	2.0%	50,000
6/07	7,477	891	11.9%	50,000
6/06	6,617	443	6.7%	—
6/05	6,002	348	5.8%	40,000
6/04	5,397	246	4.6%	40,000
Annual Growth	11.7%	(8.8%)	—	5.7%

2008 Year-End Financials
Debt ratio: 92.4%   Current ratio: —
Return on equity: 4.1%   Long-term debt ($ mil.): 4,003
Cash ($ mil.): —

Net Income History

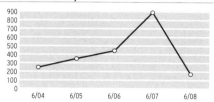

Cavaliers Operating Company

This business hardly has a carefree attitude towards roundball. The Cavaliers Operating Company owns and operates the Cleveland Cavaliers professional basketball team and its home court, Quicken Loans Arena. The Cavs joined the National Basketball Association in 1970 as part of an expansion that included the Portland Trail Blazers and Buffalo Braves (now the Los Angeles Clippers). Though losing records have been more the norm for the team in the past, things have been looking up for Cleveland since drafting high school sensation LeBron James in 2003. The family of original owner Gordon Gund owns part of the team but Quicken Loans founder Dan Gilbert holds the majority.

In addition to providing a much needed spark on the court, the arrival of James in Cleveland also helped spur increased ticket sales. The team clinched its first ever conference title in 2007, though the Cavs fell to the San Antonio Spurs in the NBA Finals.

With the Cavs fortunes on the rise, the Gund family sold a majority stake in the team to Gilbert for about $365 million in 2005. He changed the name of the operating company from Cavaliers/Gund Arena Company later that year. In addition to the Gunds, hip hop star Usher owns a minority stake in the team.

EXECUTIVES

Chairman: Daniel B. (Dan) Gilbert
Vice Chairman: David B. Katzman, age 43
CEO: Mark Stornes
President: Len Komoroski
General Manager: Danny Ferry
EVP Corporate Sales and Broadcasting: Kerry Bubolz
EVP: Roy Jones
SVP Communications: Tad Carper
SVP Marketing: Tracy Marek
Head Coach: Mike Brown
Assistant Coach: Hank Egan
Assistant General Manager: Chris Grant, age 36
Assistant General Manager: Lance Blanks
Senior Director Broadcasting Services:
  Dave Dombrowski
Director Human Resources: Farrell Finnin
Director Team Security: Marvin Cross
Director Player Development and Assistant Coach:
  Chris Jent

LOCATIONS

HQ: Cavaliers Operating Company, LLC
  1 Center Ct., Cleveland, OH 44115
Phone: 216-420-2000   **Fax:** 216-420-2101
Web: www.nba.com/cavaliers

The Cleveland Cavaliers play at 20,562-seat capacity Quicken Loans Arena in Cleveland.

PRODUCTS/OPERATIONS

Championship Titles
Eastern Conference Champions (2007)

COMPETITORS

Chicago Bulls
Detroit Pistons
Indiana Pacers
Milwaukee Bucks

HISTORICAL FINANCIALS
Company Type: Private

Income Statement
FYE: October 31

	REVENUE ($ mil.)	NET INCOME ($ mil.)	NET PROFIT MARGIN	EMPLOYEES
10/07	152	—	—	—
10/06	115	—	—	—
10/05	102	—	—	—
10/04	93	—	—	—
10/03	72	—	—	—
Annual Growth	20.5%	—	—	—

Revenue History

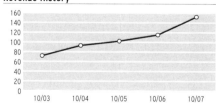

CCA Global Partners

Business is "floor"ishing at CCA Global Partners. Formerly Carpet Co-op, the firm operates more than 3,600 retail stores in the US and abroad in the floor covering and various other specialties. Many stores operate under the Carpet One name; other names include Flooring America, Flooring One, ProSource, and International Design Guild (high-end showrooms). The world's largest floor covering retailer (with stores in the US, Canada, Australia, and New Zealand), Carpet One is the exclusive US marketer of Bigelow and the LEES For Living carpet brands. CCA Global has also made forays into bicycle retailing, mortgage banking, and men's formalwear. Executives Howard Brodsky and Alan Greenberg founded the co-op in 1984.

CCA Global's Lenders One division operates as an aggregator of mortgage money. Its Lighting One division (bought by CCA in 2001) has about 100 locations selling lamps, ceiling fans, and accessories. The Biking Solution — a network of more than 225 bicycle stores in 42 states — sells Giant brand bicycles, as well as other bicycle brands, parts, and accessories.

In 2006 the company added South Africa to its list of global sites when Durban-based Top Carpet & Tile, with 90 stores, joined the group.

In 2003 CCA Global expanded into formalwear with its acquisition of Tuxedo America Group, a cooperative of more than 300 independently owned retailers of men's formalwear. Today the independent retailers are known collectively as Savvi Formalwear and operate more than 400 stores.

EXECUTIVES

Chairman and Co-CEO: Howard Brodsky
Co-CEO: Richard W. (Rick) Bennet III, age 55
President: Sandy Mishkin
COO: Bob Wilson
CFO: Ed Muchnick
SVP Training: Brian Metcalf
VP Information Technology: John Lauderbach
Chief Product Officer: Charlie Dilks
Chief Marketing Officer: Dean Marcarelli
CEO, FloorExpo: David Gheesling
CEO, Lender's One: Scott Stern
President, Carpet One Floor & Home: Evan Hackel
President, Flooring Services: George Holder
President, Flooring America: Vinnie Virga
President, Flooring Canada: Jim Duff
President and COO, FloorExpo: Jay Smith
President, International Design Guild; President, Savvi Formalwear: Christopher P. (Chris) Ramey
President, Lender's One: Tim Stern
President, Lighting One: Michael (Mike) Cherico, age 41
President, ProSource: David Kraeling
President, Rug Décor: Scott Hayim
President, Carpet One Floor & Home: Eric Demaree
COO, Lender's One: Barry Sandweiss
SVP, Stone Mountain's Flooring Outlet, GCO Flooring Outlet and Floor Trader: Tony Greco
Director Human Resources: Lisa Miles

LOCATIONS

HQ: CCA Global Partners
4301 Earth City Expwy., St. Louis, MO 63045
Phone: 314-506-0000   **Fax:** 314-291-6674
Web: www.ccaglobal.com

PRODUCTS/OPERATIONS

Selected Companies
US Flooring
  Carpet One
  FloorExpo
  Flooring America
  International Design Guild
  ProSource Wholesale Floorcoverings
  Rug Décor
  Stone Mountain's Carpet Mill Outlet/GCO Carpet Outlet
International Flooring
  Carpet One (Canada, Australia, New Zealand)
  Flooring One (UK)
  Flooring Canada (Canada)
Bicycle Retail
  The Biking Solution
Mortgage Banking
  Lenders One
Specialty Lighting
  Lighting One
Men's Formalwear
  Savvi Formalwear

COMPETITORS

Abbey Carpet
After Hours Formalwear
Formal Specialist
Home Depot
Lowe's
Macy's
Menard

CDW Corporation

CDW Corporation takes more orders than Beetle Bailey. The firm offers some 100,000 computer products, mostly through catalogs, telesales, and the company's Internet and extranet Web sites. Brands include Adobe, Apple, Cisco, Lenovo, Samsung, ViewSonic, and others. In addition to computers, CDW also sells items such as printers, software, accessories, and networking products from companies including Hewlett-Packard, IBM, Microsoft, Sony, and Xerox. Almost all of CDW's sales come from private business and public sector customers. Founded in 1984, CDW was acquired in 2007 by private equity firm Madison Dearborn Partners for about $7.3 billion.

CDW shareholders, including company founder and chairman emeritus Michael Krasny who owned nearly 22% of CDW, received $87.75 per share in cash from Madison Dearborn for their shares.

The firm acquired IT solution provider Berbee Information Networks in late 2006 in a bid to enhance its advanced technology products and services offerings. The purchase brought with it several large enterprise customers within the corporate, health care, education, and state and local government sectors.

CDW continues to expand its public sector business, which accounts for about a third of sales, through its CDW Government subsidiary. The division sells exclusively to government (federal, state, and local) and education customers.

HISTORY

Michael Krasny started Computer Discount Warehouse at his kitchen table in 1984. Weary of selling used cars at his father's Chicago lot (though he did like using his programming skills to computerize the dealership), Krasny quit and had to sell his own computer to raise cash. A classified ad in the *Chicago Tribune* generated phenomenal response, and Krasny sold his computer almost immediately.

When the calls kept coming in, he bought more computers and sold them to people responding to the original ad, and his mail-order business was under way. Krasny chose new, stripped-down IBM clones, packaged them with monitors and printers, and advertised them as used computer systems. Because PCs were still in their infancy and because customers were lost in the technology, computer setup and repair became a large part of the early business.

CDW launched its first catalog in 1987. Figuring that some buyers would shy away from purchasing costly PC systems by mail, Krasny in 1990 opened his first retail showroom (one of two) in Chicago.

The company went public in 1993 after changing the name to CDW Computer Centers. By then it had intensified its push into the corporate market, which featured bulk purchases and solid repeat business. Sales that year nearly doubled from 1992. CDW launched an Internet site in 1995. The next year it expanded its telemarketing-based sales strategy and began taking online orders. Also in 1996 the company enlarged its Chicago showrooms.

Intense marketing and low prices boosted sales in 1997 with multimedia products, data storage devices, PCs, software, and video products as the fastest sellers. That year the company relocated its offices (and one of its showrooms) to a larger facility in Vernon Hills, Illinois. CDW pushed past the $1 billion mark for the first time in 1997, logging sales of nearly $1.3 billion. The following year the company formed CDW Government, a subsidiary set up to focus on sales to government and education institutions.

In May 2001 Krasny assumed the role of chairman emeritus; CEO John Edwardson added chairman to his duties. In May 2003 shareholders approved a decision to change the company name to CDW Corporation.

In October 2006 CDW completed the acquisition of privately held Berbee Information Networks for $184 million. A year later CDW was itself acquired by private equity firm Madison Dearborn Partners for about $7.3 billion. The firm's shares were delisted on October 12, 2007.

EXECUTIVES

Chairman and CEO: John A. Edwardson, age 59, $760,629 pay
EVP Sales; President CDW Government: James R. (Jim) Shanks, age 43, $320,639 pay
EVP: Paul S. Shain, age 45
SVP and CFO: Ann E. Ziegler, age 50
SVP Operations, Logistics, and Customer Services: Douglas E. (Doug) Eckrote, age 43, $260,639 pay
SVP, General Counsel, and Corporate Secretary; Secretary, CDW Government: Christine A. (Chris) Leahy, age 43
SVP and Chief Coworker Services Officer: Dennis G. Berger, age 43
SVP and CIO: Jonathan J. (Jon) Stevens, age 38

Group VP Public Sector, CDW Government:
  Christina V. (Chris) Rother
Group VP: Gregory L. (Greg) Sliwicki
VP and Controller: Sandra M. (Sandy) Rouhselang
VP Investor Relations: Cindy T. Klimstra
VP and Chief Marketing Officer: Mark J. Gambill, age 48
Director Information Technology: K. C. Tomsheck
Media Relations Manager: Gary Ross
Auditors: PricewaterhouseCoopers LLP

LOCATIONS

HQ: CDW Corporation
  200 N. Milwaukee Ave., Vernon Hills, IL 60061
Phone: 847-465-6000
Web: www.cdw.com

PRODUCTS/OPERATIONS

COMPETITORS

Amazon.com
Apple
ASAP Software
AT&T
Austin Ribbon & Computer
Best Buy
Buy.com
Circuit City
CompuCom
Costco Wholesale
Dell
EDS
Fry's Electronics
Gateway, Inc.
GTSI
Hewlett-Packard
IBM
Insight Enterprises
Micro Electronics
Newegg
Office Depot
OfficeMax
PC Connection
PC Mall
PC Warehouse
Pomeroy IT
Softchoice
Software House
Staples
SunGard Availability Services
SunGard Higher Education
Systemax
Verizon
Wal-Mart
Zones

HISTORICAL FINANCIALS

Company Type: Private

Income Statement

FYE: December 31

	REVENUE ($ mil.)	NET INCOME ($ mil.)	NET PROFIT MARGIN	EMPLOYEES
12/07	8,100	—	—	6,900
12/06	6,786	—	—	5,500
12/05	6,292	—	—	4,300
12/04	5,738	—	—	—
12/03	4,665	—	—	—
Annual Growth	14.8%	—	—	26.7%

Revenue History

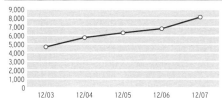

Cellco Partnership

Cellco Partnership, which does business as Verizon Wireless, is the #2 US wireless phone operator (after rival AT&T Mobility), serving nearly 66 million customers nationwide. The company also offers mobile voice services, including text messaging, multimedia content, and mobile Web services. Verizon Wireless began operations in 2000 when Bell Atlantic and Vodafone combined their US wireless assets. It gained GTE's US wireless operations when Bell Atlantic bought GTE to form Verizon Communications, which owns 55% of the company; Vodafone owns 45%. In June 2008 the company announced plans to purchase ALLTEL in a $28.1 billion deal that would make Verizon Wireless the top wireless provider in the US.

In order to gain approval from the US Department of Justice for the acquisition, Verizon will exit about 100 US markets through the divestiture of assets in areas where Alltel also has operations.

The company's network uses CDMA (code division multiple access) digital technology enabling next-generation wireless data and interactive services. It was one of the first US wireless carriers to provide a nationwide broadband data service, which it calls EV-DO technology.

Verizon Wireless has teamed up with Qualcomm subsidiary MediaFLO for the development of real-time mobile TV broadcast services. In 2007 it unveiled a mobile TV service featuring eight 24-hour subscription-based broadcasts. It also is working with Microsoft to further develop and market wireless data services. Verizon Wireless announced plans in 2007 that would see V Cast Music become the the mobile platform for a music service joint venture between MTV Networks and RealNetworks called Rhapsody America. The next year it acquired Rural Cellular — a provider of cellular service in smaller markets — for about $2.6 billion.

Bowing to market pressures in 2007, Verizon Wireless announced that it would allow subscribers to use phones purchased somewhere other than Verizon Wireless retail stores to make calls on its network.

EXECUTIVES

President, CEO, and Director: Lowell C. McAdam
EVP and COO; President, CEO, and Director, Rural Cellular: Jack D. Plating, age 55
VP and CFO; VP, CFO, and Director, Rural Cellular: John Townsend, age 45, $499,138 pay
VP and Chief Marketing Officer:
  Michael P. (Mike) Lanman
VP Business Development, Cellco Partnership and Rural Cellular: Margaret P. (Molly) Feldman, age 50
VP Legal and External Affairs, General Counsel, and Secretary: Steven E. Zipperstein, age 48, $799,375 pay
VP Human Resources: Martha Delehanty, age 41
VP Corporate Communications: James J. (Jim) Gerace, age 43
CIO: Ajay Waghray
Region President, Upstate New York: Marquett Smith
President, Washington-Baltimore-Virginia Region:
  Michael (Mike) Maiorana
President, Midwest Area: Marni Walden
President, South Area: Jim McGean
President, West Area: Roger Gurnani
President, Northeast Area: David J. Small
SVP and CTO, Cellco Partnership and Rural Cellular: Anthony J. (Tony) Melone Sr., age 48
Auditors: Deloitte & Touche LLP

LOCATIONS

HQ: Cellco Partnership
  1 Verizon Way, Basking Ridge, NJ 07920
Phone: 908-559-2000
Web: www.verizonwireless.com

PRODUCTS/OPERATIONS

Selected Services

Equipment sales
Location-based services
Mobile voice
Mobile Web
Paging
PCS (personal communications services)
Push-to-talk voice service
Ringback tones
Text and picture messaging
Wireless broadband
Wireless business services

COMPETITORS

ALLTEL	T-Mobile USA
AT&T Mobility	U.S. Cellular
Sprint Nextel	

HISTORICAL FINANCIALS

Company Type: Joint venture

Income Statement

FYE: December 31

	REVENUE ($ mil.)	NET INCOME ($ mil.)	NET PROFIT MARGIN	EMPLOYEES
12/07	43,900	—	—	69,000
12/06	38,000	—	—	67,000
12/05	32,301	—	—	55,700
12/04	27,662	—	—	49,800
12/03	22,489	—	—	43,900
Annual Growth	18.2%	—	—	12.0%

Revenue History

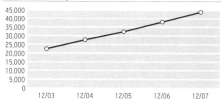

Cengage Learning

Cengage Learning provides courseware, specialized content, and learning services for businesses, educational institutions, government agencies, and individuals. Its offerings include online reference databases, distance learning and test preparation courses, corporate training courses, and materials for specific academic disciplines. Cengage Learning offers educational products under the Wadsworth, South-Western, Course Technology, Delmar, Gale, Prometric, and NETg names. In June 2008 the company puchased the Houghton Mifflin College Division (HM College) for about $750 million.

The company was acquired by Apax Partners and Omers Capital Partners in July 2007.

Through its Delmar brand, the company also purchased PAL Publications in 2008; Delmar is a provider of education and training for the electrical and technical trades.

EXECUTIVES

Chairman: David H. (Dave) Shaffer, age 65
President and CEO: Ronald G. (Ron) Dunn, age 61
COO and CFO: Jerry V. Elliott, age 47
EVP: William D. Rieders
SVP and CTO: Ray F. Lowrey
SVP Human Resources: Adrian Butler
President, Academic and Professional Group:
 Charles Siegel
President and CEO, EMEA: Jill Jones
President, Gale: Patrick C. Sommers, age 50
President, Nelson Education: Greg Pilon
General Counsel: Ken Carson
Director Corporate Communications: Lindsay Brown
Auditors: PricewaterhouseCoopers LLP

LOCATIONS

HQ: Cengage Learning
 200 First Stamford Place, Ste. 400,
 Stamford, CT 06902
Phone: 203-965-8600 **Fax:** 800-487-8488
Web: www.cengage.com

Cengage Learning has offices in Australia, Brazil, Canada, Mexico, Puerto Rico, Singapore, Spain, the UK, and the US.

PRODUCTS/OPERATIONS

Selected Businesses

Course Technology (line of print and technology-based
 courses for business and technology)
Delmar Learning (tailored learning materials for health
 care, technology, trade, and career education)
Gale (content databases for libraries, schools, and
 Internet users)
Heinle (language learning materials)
Nelson (Canada-based online educational resource
 publisher for education, business, and government))

COMPETITORS

Global Knowledge
Pearson Education
PLATO Learning
Reed Elsevier Group
Renaissance Learning

Saba Software
Scholastic
SkillSoft
SumTotal

Center Oil

Center Oil's core business is peddling petroleum. The company is one of the largest private wholesale distributors of gasoline and other petroleum products to customers primarily in the eastern region of the US. Center Oil owns eight storage terminals capable of storing more than 2 million barrels of petroleum products. It also has access to 36 terminals in 10 states, as well as access to the Magellan, Texas Eastern, Kinder Morgan Chicago, and Kaneb pipeline systems. Its products are also distributed through a fleet of ships, barges, and trucks.

Center Oil was established in 1986 by president and CEO Gary Parker. The company is one of the largest privately held companies in the St. Louis metropolitan area.

EXECUTIVES

President and CEO: Gary R. Parker, age 58
Secretary and General Counsel:
 Michael C. Aufdenspring
Treasurer and Head Human Resources:
 Richard I. (Rick) Powers

Controller: Joseph (Joe) Beck
Finance Manager: Brian Skoff
Sales Manager, Truck Sales: Rob Kraeger
**Manager Operations and Scheduling — Supply and
 Distribution:** Jerry Jost
Manager Business Development: Richard Hollocher
Manager IT: Eric Pitts
Cash Management, Truck Sales: Lisa Wolff
Assistant Finance Manager: Todd Garland
Assistant Manager IT: Kostadin Todorov

LOCATIONS

HQ: Center Oil Company
 600 Mason Ridge Center Dr., St. Louis, MO 63141
Phone: 314-682-3500 **Fax:** 314-682-3599
Web: www.centeroil.com

COMPETITORS

Apex Oil
Colonial Group
George Warren
Gulf Oil
U.S. Oil

HISTORICAL FINANCIALS

Company Type: Private

Income Statement

FYE: December 31

	REVENUE ($ mil.)	NET INCOME ($ mil.)	NET PROFIT MARGIN	EMPLOYEES
12/07	4,900	—	—	46
12/06	5,400	—	—	45
12/05	4,800	—	—	46
Annual Growth	1.0%	—	—	0.0%

Revenue History

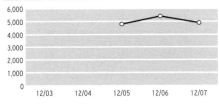

Central National-Gottesman

All the news that's fit to print (or at least some of it) shows up on a good portion of Central National-Gottesman's products. The family-owned papermaker distributes pulp, paper, paperboard, and newsprint in more than 75 countries worldwide. In addition to its North American operations, the company operates about 20 international offices in countries located in Asia, Europe, and Latin America. The Central National-Gottesman network includes the Lindenmeyr family of companies, which specialize in the distribution of fine paper, as well as papers for books and magazines.

The company's extensive list of suppliers includes paper industry leaders International Paper (#1) and Weyerhaeuser.

Central National-Gottesman was founded in New York in 1886 to provide raw materials for papermaking. By the 1950s it had begun operating internationally with established offices in Europe and South America.

EXECUTIVES

President and CEO: Kenneth L. Wallach
VP, Human Resources: Louise Caputo
Treasurer: Steven Eigen

LOCATIONS

HQ: Central National-Gottesman Inc.
 3 Manhattanville Rd., Purchase, NY 10577
Phone: 914-696-9000 **Fax:** 914-696-1066
Web: www.cng-inc.com

COMPETITORS

Clifford Paper
International Paper
Midland Paper
Pope & Talbot

RIS the paper house
Smurfit-Stone Container
Unisource

HISTORICAL FINANCIALS

Company Type: Private

Income Statement

FYE: December 31

	REVENUE ($ mil.)	NET INCOME ($ mil.)	NET PROFIT MARGIN	EMPLOYEES
12/07	3,000	—	—	1,000
12/06	2,700	—	—	850
12/05	2,300	—	—	850
12/04	2,000	—	—	775
12/03	1,900	—	—	850
Annual Growth	12.1%	—	—	4.1%

Revenue History

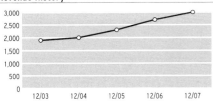

Central Parking

If you park your car in a central location, you might very well be doing business with Central Parking. A leading parking provider, the company oversees more than 2,800 facilities with about 1.3 million spaces, primarily in the US and Canada. Its facilities serve high-traffic locations such as airports, office buildings, and stadiums. Along with operating parking lots and garages, the company provides shuttle transportation and valet parking, plus parking meter enforcement and collection under contracts with cities. It also serves as a consultant for parking facility operators. A group of private equity firms bought Central Parking in May 2007.

The $726 million buyout — led by affiliates of Kohlberg & Co. LLC, Lubert-Adler LP, and Chrysalis Capital Partners LP — came amid an effort by Central Parking to enhance profitability by exiting smaller US markets and less-promising international locations. In August 2007 the company sold its operations in Europe, which had accounted for less than 5% of overall sales. It has retained its operations in several Latin American countries.

To grow, Central Parking has been working to win contracts in major US metropolitan areas, particularly at airports, and on gaining national accounts from big customers such as hotels and property management companies.

EXECUTIVES

President and CEO: Emanuel J. Eads, $617,153 pay
EVP: James H. Bond, $489,775 pay
EVP: Gregory J. (Greg) Stormberg, $600,329 pay
SVP: Alan J. Kahn, $621,370 pay
SVP and CFO: John I. Hill
SVP: Hector Chevalier
SVP: Robert L. Cizek
SVP Human Resources: Donald N. Holmes
SVP: Gregory D. (Greg) Maxey
SVP and General Counsel: Benjamin F. Parrish Jr.
President, USA Parking: William H. Bodenhamer Jr., $454,720 pay
Secretary: Henry J. Abbott
Auditors: KPMG LLP

LOCATIONS

HQ: Central Parking Corporation
2401 21st Ave. South, Ste. 200, Nashville, TN 37212
Phone: 615-297-4255   **Fax:** 615-297-6240
Web: www.parking.com

COMPETITORS

ABM Industries
Ace Parking
Diamond Parking
Impark
Macquarie Infrastructure Company
Parking Company of America
Standard Parking

Centric Group

This company makes sure the world has enough balloons, baggage, and beverages. Centric Group is a holding company for several manufacturing and distribution businesses. Its Betallic unit manufactures latex and Mylar balloons sold through florist shops and other gift retailers. The company's TGR Group, meanwhile, manufactures luggage and other travel bags under such brands as Callaway Golf and Victorinox. In addition, Centric serves commissaries at correctional facilities with snacks, beverages, and other food and non-food items through its Keefe Group. The company was formed in 1974 as part of Enterprise Rent-A-Car and spun off in 1999. It is still controlled by the Taylor family.

Longtime CEO Doug Albrecht retired early in 2008 and was replaced by a triumvirate, including CFO John O'Connell, COO Jim Theiss, and chairman Andy Taylor (who also serves as CEO of Enterprise).

EXECUTIVES

Chairman: Andrew C. (Andy) Taylor, age 60
Vice Chairman and CFO: John T. O'Connell, age 51
President and COO: Jim Theiss, age 49
VP and Corporate Controller: Vicki S. Altman
VP and General Manager, TRG Group: Nathan Schulte
VP Human Resources: Cynthia M. (Cindy) Murdoch
President, Betallic: Bob Boedeker
President and COO, Keefe Group: Jeff Donnelly
EVP and General Manager, Keefe Commissary Network: John Puricelli
VP and General Manager, Courtesy Products: Mark Schwarz
VP Corporate Market, TRG Group: Andrew Spellman

LOCATIONS

HQ: Centric Group, L.L.C.
1260 Andes Blvd., St. Louis, MO 63132
Phone: 314-214-2700   **Fax:** 314-214-2766
Web: www.centricgp.com

PRODUCTS/OPERATIONS

Selected Operations

Betallic (latex and Mylar balloon manufacturing)
Courtesy Products (hospitality beverage services and supplies)
Keefe Group
    Access Catalog Company
    Keefe Commissary Network (corrections facility commissary supplier)
    Keefe Supply Company (wholesale foodservice distribution)
TRG Group (travel baggage and athletic footwear manufacturing)

COMPETITORS

ABL Management
Amscan
ARAMARK
CTI Industries
Good Source
Guest Supply
Rawlings
Samsonite
Tumi
US Balloon Manufacturing

HISTORICAL FINANCIALS

Company Type: Private

Income Statement

	ESTIMATED REVENUE ($ mil.)	NET INCOME ($ mil.)	NET PROFIT MARGIN	EMPLOYEES
12/07	750	—	—	2,300
12/06	700	—	—	2,000
12/05	600	—	—	1,600
Annual Growth	**11.8%**	**—**	**—**	**19.9%**

Revenue History

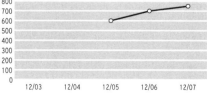

Ceridian Corporation

Problems with payroll? Trouble with taxes? Ceridian wants to help. The company's Human Resource Solutions segment provides payroll processing, tax filing, benefits administration, and other human resources services to more than 110,000 employers (and their 25 million employees), mainly in the US but also in Canada and the UK. Ceridian's other business unit, Comdata, issues and processes payments for credit, debit, and stored value cards (gift cards and employee expense cards), primarily for companies in the trucking and retail industries. Investment firm Thomas H. Lee Partners and insurer Fidelity National Financial own Ceridian, which they acquired in November 2007 for $5.3 billion.

Ceridian generates human resources business through its sales force and via marketing alliances with consulting firms and other providers of outsourced business services. Before it went private, the company hoped to grow by acquiring complementary businesses. It expanded its work-life offerings in 2006 by buying Leade Health, a weight- and stress-management coaching company. The next year, Ceridian bought Inter-Tax, a provider of fuel tax compliance services, to augment Comdata's transportation-related business.

Ceridian operates out of seven offices across Canada, the UK, and the US.

EXECUTIVES

Chairman, President, and CEO: Kathryn V. (Kathy) Marinello, age 52
EVP and CFO: Gregory J. (Greg) Macfarlane
EVP and CTO: Perry H. Cliburn, age 49
EVP Human Resources: Kairus K. Tarapore, age 46
EVP Quality and Service Operations: Michael F. Shea, age 42
EVP, General Counsel, and Secretary: Michael W. Sheridan
SVP and Associate General Counsel: Albert J. Bart
SVP Ceridian Small Business: Vincent (Vinny) Mottola
SVP Implementation: Liza Sayre
SVP Human Resources and Payroll Account Management: Greg Hawes
SVP Ceridian Benefit Services: John Shade
SVP Human Resources and Payroll Services: Steven Rodriguez
SVP Human Resource Outsourcing: Keith Strodtman
SVP LifeWorks Commercial: Zachary Meyer
SVP U.S. Human Resource Solutions: Nancy L. Hanna
VP and General Manager, Ceridian Recruiting Solutions: Craig Julien
VP and General Manager, Comdata's Fuel Management Services: Randy Morgan
VP Ceridian Retirement Plan Services: Glenn Dial
VP Investor Relations: Craig Manson
VP Marketing Communications: Keith Peterson
President, Comdata: Brett Rodewald
President, Ceridian Canada: David (Dave) MacKay
EVP and President, Ceridian International: Jim Burns
EVP and General Manager, Stored Value Systems: Thomas L. (Tom) Recktenwald
Director, Public Relations, Ceridian U.S.: Peter (Pete) Stoddart

LOCATIONS

HQ: Ceridian Corporation
3311 E. Old Shakopee Rd., Minneapolis, MN 55425
Phone: 952-853-8100   **Fax:** 952-853-4430
Web: www.ceridian.com

PRODUCTS/OPERATIONS

Selected Products and Services
Compliance resources and services
Corporate health and wellness programs
Employee assistance programs
Employee benefits administration
Employee productivity management
Employee retention and rewards
Government solutions
Human resources management and HRO
Payroll processing and tax filing
Recruiting and screening services
Time and labor management

COMPETITORS

Administaff	Hewitt Associates
ADP	Northgate Information
Barrett Business Services	Solutions
CBIZ	Paychex
C.H. Robinson Worldwide	Sage Software
CompuPay.	Spherion
EDS	TeamStaff
First Data	Ultimate Software
Fleetcor	Wright Express
Gevity HR	

HISTORICAL FINANCIALS
Company Type: Private

Income Statement
FYE: December 31

	REVENUE ($ mil.)	NET INCOME ($ mil.)	NET PROFIT MARGIN	EMPLOYEES
12/07	1,700	—	—	9,177
12/06	1,565	—	—	9,579
12/05	1,459	—	—	9,433
12/04	1,320	—	—	—
12/03	1,214	—	—	—
Annual Growth	8.8%	—	—	(1.4%)

Revenue History

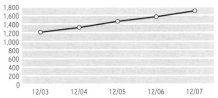

1,800				
1,600				
1,400				
1,200				
1,000				
800				
600				
400				
200				
0				
12/03	12/04	12/05	12/06	12/07

CH2M HILL Companies

Catchy, no. Descriptive, yes. CH2M HILL's name is culled from its founders — Cornell, Howland, Hayes, and Merryfield — plus HILL, from its first merger. The group is organized into three divisions: civil infrastructure, industrial, and federal. Its civil infrastructure group designs and builds water and wastewater systems, airports, highways, and other transportation infrastructures. Federal services include nuclear and environmental cleanup projects and US government facility operations. Industrial operations include engineering, procurement, and construction for private-sector companies in the chemical, energy, and life sciences industries. Clients include the US Department of Defense and the US Navy.

CH2M HILL provides its services to both domestic and international clients, although the US accounts for the vast majority of its revenues. The company's revenues are also fairly evenly distributed amongst its three divisions, with the industrial segment accounting for about 40%.

The company expects to see continued growth in this particular segment partially due to key acquisitions in 2007 of two energy services companies, troubled Alaskan oil and gas services firm VECO and Colorado pipeline contractor Trigon EPC. The industrial segment is also being driven by several engineering, procurement, and construction contracts with major US utility companies to build power generation facilities.

CH2M HILL, along with partners Laing O'Rourke and Mace Ltd., won a $190 million contract to oversee construction on sports venues and infrastructures for the 2012 Olympic Games in London. CH2M HILL's team beat out three other major rivals for the job: AMEC plc, Balfour Beatty plc, and Jacobs Engineering Group; Bechtel Group; and Bovis Lend Lease, Kellogg, Brown & Root, Capita Symonds, and Franklin & Andrews. Among CH2M HILL's responsibilities will be to make the 2012 Games the most environmentally-friendly in history by using recycled construction materials, incorporating wind energy, and reducing carbon dioxide emissions.

Founded in 1946, CH2M HILL has operations in more than 30 countries. The company is owned by its employees.

EXECUTIVES

Chairman and CEO: Ralph R. Peterson, age 63, $1,650,000 pay
Vice Chairman and Chief Marketing Officer: Donald S. (Don) Evans, age 57
President and COO; Acting President and Group CEO, Industrial Group: Lee A. McIntire, age 58
President and Group Chief Executive, Federal: Nancy R. Tuor, age 59
President, North America Operations: William T. Dehn, age 61
President, Energy and Chemicals: Garry M. Higdem, age 54, $812,900 pay
President and Group Chief Executive, International: Thomas G. (Tom) Searle, age 51
President, Transportation: Michael D. (Mike) Kennedy, age 55
President, Water: Robert W. (Bob) Bailey, age 52
President, Enterprise Management Solutions: Jeff Akers
President and Group Chief Executive, Civil Infrastructure: Mark A. Lasswell, age 53
President, Power: Don Zabilansky
President, Electronics and Advanced Technology: Randall I. (Randy) Smith
President, Environmental: Gene Lupia
President, Manufacturing: Michael Gearhart
President, Nuclear Business Services: Mark Spears
President and Group Chief Executive, Industrial: Michael (Mike) McKelvy
President, Operations and Maintenance: Elisa Speranza
President, Government Facilities and Infrastructure: Fred Brune
President, Industrial Systems: Steve Gelman
President, Idaho Cleanup Project: Robert Iotti
SVP, CFO, and Director: M. Catherine Santee, age 46, $2,006 pay
SVP, Enterprise Management Solutions: Mike Underwood
SVP and Chief Human Resource Officer: Robert C. (Bob) Allen
SVP, Director of Operations, Environmental Services, and Director: Michael A. Szomjassy, age 57

Chairman, CH2M HILL International: Robert G. (Bob) Card, age 55
President and CEO, CH2M HILL Hanford Group: John Fulton
Director, Health, Safety, Security and Environment: Keith Christopher
CIO: Robert (Bob) Bullock
Chief Legal Officer: Margaret B. McLean
Director, External Communications: John Corsi
Auditors: KPMG LLP

LOCATIONS

HQ: CH2M HILL Companies, Ltd.
9191 S. Jamaica St., Englewood, CO 80112
Phone: 303-771-0900   **Fax:** 720-286-9250
Web: www.ch2m.com

2007 Sales

	% of total
US	85
International	15
Total	**100**

PRODUCTS/OPERATIONS

2007 Sales

	$ mil.	% of total
Federal	1,246.2	28
Civil infrastructure	1,445.3	33
Industrial	1,684.7	39
Total	**4,376.2**	**100**

Selected Subsidiaries
CH2M HILL Alaska, Inc.
CH2M HILL Canada, Inc.
CH2M HILL Constructors, Inc.
CH2M HILL Engineers, Inc.
CH2M HILL Hanford, Inc.
CH2M HILL, Inc.
CH2M HILL International, Ltd.
Operations Management International
VECO Corporation

COMPETITORS

AECOM
Bechtel
Black & Veatch
Earth Tech
Environmental Resources Management Ltd
Fluor
Foster Wheeler
Jacobs Engineering
MWH Global
Parsons Brinckerhoff
Parsons Corporation
Perini
Shaw Group
Tetra Tech
URS

HISTORICAL FINANCIALS
Company Type: Private

Income Statement
FYE: December 31

	REVENUE ($ mil.)	NET INCOME ($ mil.)	NET PROFIT MARGIN	EMPLOYEES
12/07	4,376	66	1.5%	22,000
12/06	4,007	39	1.0%	17,000
12/05	3,152	82	2.6%	18,363
12/04	2,715	32	1.2%	14,000
12/03	2,154	24	1.1%	14,000
Annual Growth	19.4%	29.0%	—	12.0%

Debt ratio: 40.0%   Current ratio: —
Return on equity: 15.9%   Long-term debt ($ mil.): 185
Cash ($ mil.): —

Net Income History

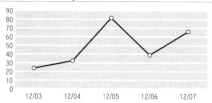

Charmer Sunbelt

The Charmer Sunbelt Group is one of the biggest swigs in its business sector. A leading wine and spirits wholesaler, the company operates through a number of joint ventures and subsidiaries, including Charmer Industries (New York), Premier Beverage (Florida), Reliable Churchill (Maryland), and Ben Arnold-Sunbelt Beverage (South Carolina). Charmer Sunbelt also distributes non-alcoholic products such as bottled water.

Division management bought the group from McKesson (drugs and sundries wholesaler) and took it private in 1988. Descendants of founder Herman Merinoff own and operate the company.

In 2007 the company combined Charmer Industries' metro New York operations with those of Peerless Importers to form a new entity, Empire Merchants.

EXECUTIVES

Vice Chairman and CEO: Charles (Charlie) Merinoff, age 51
EVP, COO, and CFO: Gene Luciano
EVP Sales and Marketing: Joe Davolio
Corporate VP and CIO: Bill Healey
Corporate VP Marketing: Katherine Nicholls, age 41
Corporate VP Sales: Greg Baird
VP Human Resources: Ann Giambusso
Chairman, Capital Wine and Spirits Company: Robert Storey
Chairman, R and R Marketing: Howard Jacobs
Chairman and CEO, Reliable Churchill: James (Jim) Smith
Vice Chairman, Charmer Industries, Connecticut Distributors, and Service-Universal Distributors: Steven M. Drucker, age 54
CEO, Empire Merchants: E. Lloyd Sobel, age 51
CEO, Empire Merchants North: Jay Andretta
President and CEO, R and R Marketing: Jon Maslin
President and CEO, United Distributors of Delaware: J. Paul Tigani
President, Alabama Sales and Mississippi Sales: Steve Young
President, Alliance Beverage Distributing Company: Robert Smith
President, Associated Distributors: D.J. (Jimmy) Rogers
President, Augustan Wine Imports: Proal Perry
President, Bacchus Importers: Bruce Gearhart
President, Ben Arnold Beverage Company: William Tovell

President, Beverage Distributors Company: Robert Catalani
President, Capital Wine and Spirits: Kevin Karcher
President, Connecticut Distributors: Andrew Hillman
President, Distinctive Wines and Spirits: Bill Cosmos
President, Premier Beverage Company: Bob Drinon
President, Prestige Wines Distributors: Bill McConnell
President, Commonwealth Wines and Spirits: Tom Coleman
President and COO, Reliable Churchill; President, Washington Wholesale Liquor: Kevin Dunn
Corporate Marketing and Communications Assistant Manager: Ashley Wilkinson

LOCATIONS

HQ: The Charmer Sunbelt Group
60 E. 42nd St., New York, NY 10165
Phone: 212-699-7000   **Fax:** 212-699-7099
Web: www.charmer-sunbelt.com

Selected States of Operation
Alabama
Arizona
Colorado
Connecticut
Delaware
The District of Columbia
Florida
Illinois
Maryland
Mississippi
New Jersey
New York
North Carolina
Pennsylvania
South Carolina
Virginia

PRODUCTS/OPERATIONS

Selected Joint Ventures and Partnership Companies
Alabama Sales Company, LLC
Alliance Beverage Distributing Co. (Arizona)
Associated Distributors, LLC (Virginia)
Ben Arnold Beverage Co. (South Carolina)
Beverage Distributors Corp. (Colorado)
Commonwealth Wine & Spirits (Massachusetts)
Empire Merchants (New York)
Mississippi Sales Co., LLC
R&R Marketing, LLC (New Jersey)
United Distributors of Delaware

COMPETITORS

Allied Beverage Group
Bacardi USA
Constellation Brands
Georgia Crown
Glazer's Wholesale Drug
Johnson Brothers
National Distributing
National Wine & Spirits
Southern Wine & Spirits
Tarrant Distributors
United States Beverage
W. J. Deutsch
Young's Market

Chevron Phillips Chemical

A coin toss determined which company's name would go first when Chevron and Phillips Petroleum (now ConocoPhillips) formed 50-50 joint venture Chevron Phillips Chemical Company in 2000. Among the largest US petrochemical firms, the company produces ethylene, propylene, polyethylene, and polypropylene — sometimes used as building blocks for the company's other products such as pipe. Chevron Phillips Chemical also produces aromatics such as benzene and styrene, specialty chemicals such as acetylene black (a form of carbon black), and mining chemicals. The company has several petrochemicals joint ventures in the Middle East (including Saudi Chevron Phillips Company, 50%, and Qatar Chemical Company, roughly 50%).

Chevron Phillips Chemical is North America's largest producer of high-density polyethylene (HDPE) — used in blow/injection molding, plastic bags and pipes, and films. Chevron Phillips Chemical also is near the top in styrene, ethylene, and aromatics production.

Chevron Phillips Chemical Company LP is the US operating subsidiary of CPChem, which also includes foreign ventures, mainly those in Asia and the Middle East. Chevron Phillips Chemical Company LP accounts for most of its parent's revenues.

In 2008 Chevron Phillips Chemical combined its styrene and polystyrene business in the Americas with that of Dow Chemical to form a 50-50 joint venture. The JV, called Americas Styrenics, will combine Dow's much larger business with Chevron Phillips Chemical's ability to provide feedstocks for the production of styrene monomer and polystyrene.

EXECUTIVES

President and CEO: Greg C. Garland, age 50, $542,158 pay
SVP Olefins and Polyolefins: Timothy G. (Tim) Taylor, $612,133 pay
SVP, General Counsel, and Secretary: Craig B. Glidden, $556,654 pay
SVP, CFO, and Controller: Greg G. Maxwell, $497,901 pay
SVP Manufacturing: Rick L. Roberts
SVP Specialties, Aromatics, and Styrenics: Mark Haney
VP Human Resources: Don F. Kremer
VP and Treasurer: Joseph M. (Joe) McKee
VP Technology: Mary Jane Hagenson
VP Environment, Health, and Safety: Greg Hanggi
CIO: Larry R. Frazier
General Manager Corporate Communications: Stan Sehested
Media and Management Communications: Brian Cain
Styrenics General Manager; President and CEO, Americas Styrenics: Tim Roberts
Human Resources; VP Human Resources and Public Affairs, Americas Styrenics: Doug Chauveaux
Auditors: Ernst & Young LLP

LOCATIONS

HQ: Chevron Phillips Chemical Company LLC
10001 6 Pines Dr., The Woodlands, TX 77380
Phone: 832-813-4100   **Fax:** 800-231-3890
Web: www.cpchem.com

Chevron Phillips Chemical Company operates more than 30 manufacturing facilities and about a half dozen research and technical centers, including facilities in Belgium, Brazil, Colombia, China, Qatar, Puerto Rico, Saudi Arabia, Singapore, South Korea, and the US.

PRODUCTS/OPERATIONS

2007 Sales

	% of total
Olefins & polyolefins	67
Aromatics & styrenics	28
Specialty products	5
Total	**100**

Selected Products

Olefins and polyolefins
  Ethylene
  Polyethylene
  Polyethylene pipe
  Polypropylene
  Propylene
Aromatics and styrenics
  Benzene
  Cumene
  Cyclohexane
  Paraxylene
  Styrene
Specialty products
  Acetylene black
  Alpha olefins
  Dimethyl sulfide
  Drilling specialty chemicals
  High-purity hydrocarbons and solvents
  Mining chemicals
  Neohexene
  Performance and reference fuels
  Polyalpha olefins
  Polystyrene

Selected Joint Ventures

Chevron Phillips Singapore Chemicals (Private) Limited
  (50%)
CPChem/BP Solvay Polyethylene (50%)
K.R. Copolymer, Co., Ltd. (60%)
Phillips Sumika Polypropylene Company (60%)
Qatar Chemical Company Ltd. (Q-Chem)
Saudi Chevron Phillips Company (50%)
Shanghai Golden Phillips Petrochemical Co. Ltd. (40%)

COMPETITORS

Dow Chemical
DuPont
Equistar Chemicals
ExxonMobil Chemical
KRATON
LyondellBasell
NOVA Chemicals
SABIC
Sasol
Sterling Chemicals
Sunoco Chemicals
Westlake Chemical

HISTORICAL FINANCIALS

Company Type: Joint venture

Income Statement

	REVENUE ($ mil.)	NET INCOME ($ mil.)	NET PROFIT MARGIN	EMPLOYEES
12/07	12,986	719	5.5%	5,500
12/06	12,330	1,349	10.9%	5,150
12/05	11,038	853	7.7%	5,150
12/04	9,558	605	6.3%	5,300
12/03	7,018	7	0.1%	5,451
Annual Growth	**16.6%**	**218.4%**	**—**	**0.2%**

FYE: December 31

2007 Year-End Financials

Debt ratio: 28.8%   Current ratio: —
Return on equity: 17.1%   Long-term debt ($ mil.): 1,199
Cash ($ mil.): —

Net Income History

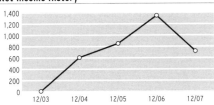

Chevy Chase Bank

Chevy Chase Bank is ready for prime time. It is one of the largest financial institutions in the greater Washington, DC area with a network of more than 200 branches and 1,000 ATMs. The savings bank offers traditional deposit products such as checking and savings accounts, CDs, and IRAs, in addition to investment management services, insurance, and credit cards. Its loan portfolio is dominated by residential mortgages (around 80% of all loans) and also includes consumer, commercial, and construction loans. The bank also runs a car rental business.

In 2008 Chevy Chase Bank shuttered some 50 branches inside Giant Food stores. It also announced plans to close some of its traditional branches as well.

Chairman and CEO B. Francis Saul II, who founded the bank in 1969 and also heads retail real estate firm Saul Centers, controls Chevy Chase Bank through various entities.

EXECUTIVES

Chairman and CEO: B. Francis Saul II, age 75
Vice Chairman: Alexander R.M. Boyle
Vice Chairman: B. Francis Saul III, age 46
EVP and General Counsel: Thomas H. McCormick, age 57
EVP and CFO: Stephen R. Halpin
EVP and CIO: Robert H. Spicer II
EVP and Chief Lending Officer: George P. Clancy Jr.
EVP, Retail Banking: W. Scott McSween
President, Chevy Chase Trust: Peter M. Welber
President, ASB Capital Management: Daniel B. Mulvey
President, B.F. Saul Mortgage Company:
  Robert D. Broeksmit
Director, Human Resources: Russ McNish

LOCATIONS

HQ: Chevy Chase Bank, F.S.B.
  7501 Wisconsin Ave., Bethesda, MD 20814
Phone: 240-497-4600   **Fax:** 240-497-4110
Web: www.chevychasebank.com

PRODUCTS/OPERATIONS

2007 Sales

	% of total
Interest	
Loans	62
Mortgage-backed securities	5
Other	2
Noninterest	
Deposit servicing fees	13
Servicing, securitization, & mortgage banking income	12
Asset management fees	3
Other	3
Total	**100**

COMPETITORS

Bank of America
BB&T
Citibank
M&T Bank
PNC Financial
Provident Bankshares
Sandy Spring Bancorp
SunTrust
TD Bank USA
Wachovia Corp

HISTORICAL FINANCIALS

Company Type: Private

Income Statement

FYE: September 30

	ASSETS ($ mil.)	NET INCOME ($ mil.)	INCOME AS % OF ASSETS	EMPLOYEES
9/07	15,107	55	0.4%	4,817
9/06	14,158	78	0.6%	4,506
9/05	14,262	108	0.8%	4,101
9/04	13,287	134	1.0%	3,714
9/03	11,796	80	0.7%	4,000
Annual Growth	**6.4%**	**(8.7%)**	**—**	**4.8%**

2007 Year-End Financials

Equity as % of assets: 5.5%   Long-term debt ($ mil.): —
Return on assets: 0.4%   Sales ($ mil.): 898
Return on equity: 6.8%

Net Income History

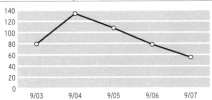

CHG Healthcare

Medical practices without a doctor in the house look to CHG Healthcare Services to find them one. The company, formerly CompHealth Group, provides locum tenens (physician staffing) services, recruiting physicians in 35 specialties for temporary and permanent assignments at hospitals and medical practices throughout the US. It offers temporary placement of nurses and allied health professionals, including physician assistants, pharmacists, and radiology technicians. CHG Healthcare operates under the names CompHealth, Weatherby Locums, Destination Healthcare Staffing, Foundation Medical Staffing, and RN Network. In December 2006 investment firm J.W. Childs acquired the company for more than $300 million.

EXECUTIVES

President and CEO: Michael R. Weinholtz, $389,583 pay
COO: Donald D. (Don) DeCamp
CFO: Sean Dailey, $273,833 pay
VP Business Development: Brian Dunn
VP Marketing: John Genna
Director Internet Services: Glen Thomson
Corporate Communications and Public Relations:
  Mary Biljanic
Auditors: KPMG LLP

LOCATIONS

HQ: CHG Healthcare Services, Inc.
6440 South Millrock Dr., Ste. 175,
Salt Lake City, UT 84171
Phone: 801-930-3000 **Fax:** 801-930-4517
Web: www.chghealthcare.com

COMPETITORS

AMN Healthcare
Cejka Search
Cross Country Healthcare
InteliStaf Healthcare
Medical Staffing Network
On Assignment
TeamStaff

Chicago Bulls

If you mess with these Bulls on the court, you might get the horns. Chicago Professional Sports owns and operates the Chicago Bulls professional basketball team, which boasts six NBA championships thanks to five-time MVP Michael Jordan. His charismatic presence not only set a high-water mark for Chicago between 1991 and 1998, but also helped increase the popularity of the league. The team was started by Dick Klein and joined the National Basketball Association in 1966. Real estate developer Jerry Reinsdorf has owned the Bulls since 1985. He also owns Chicago's United Center (along with Chicago Blackhawks owner the Wirtz Corporation) and the Chicago White Sox baseball team.

While the Bulls maintain a loyal following in the Windy City, Reinsdorf has shouldered much of the blame for the lack of championship performances since His Airness left the team in 1998. (Some still blame the owner and then general manager Jerry Krause for driving away Jordan and head coach Phil Jackson.)

Head coach Scott Skiles was replaced by Jim Boylan after a disappointing start to the 2007-08 season; Boylan was let go at the end of the campaign. Skiles had led the Chicago bench for four seasons.

Reinsdorf earned his seventh championship title as a team owner when his White Sox won the World Series in 2005.

EXECUTIVES

Chairman: Jerry Reinsdorf, age 72
EVP Basketball Operations: John Paxson
EVP Business Operations: Steve Schanwald
SVP Financial and Legal: Irwin Mandel
VP Ticket Sales: Keith Brown
Controller: Stu Bookman
Senior Director Public and Media Relations:
Tim Hallam
Senior Director of Ticket Operations: Joe O'Neil
Director of Community Affairs: Bob (Butterbean) Love
Director of Community Relations: David Kurland
Director of Ticket Sales: David Dowd
Equipment Manager: John Ligmanowski
Manager Purchasing: Ben Adair
Assistant Coach and Advance Scout: Mike Wilhelm
Director Player Personnel: Gar Forman

LOCATIONS

HQ: Chicago Professional Sports Corporation
United Center, 1901 W. Madison St.,
Chicago, IL 60612
Phone: 312-455-4000 **Fax:** 312-455-4189
Web: www.nba.com/bulls

The Chicago Bulls play at the 21,711-seat capacity United Center in Chicago.

PRODUCTS/OPERATIONS

Championship Titles

NBA Championship (1991-93, 1996-98)
NBA Eastern Conference Champions (1991-93, 1996-98)

COMPETITORS

Cavaliers
Detroit Pistons
Indiana Pacers
Milwaukee Bucks

HISTORICAL FINANCIALS

Company Type: Private

Income Statement
FYE: July 31

	REVENUE ($ mil.)	NET INCOME ($ mil.)	NET PROFIT MARGIN	EMPLOYEES
7/07	161	—	—	—
7/06	149	—	—	—
7/05	136	—	—	—
7/04	123	—	—	—
7/03	119	—	—	—
Annual Growth	7.8%	—	—	—

Revenue History

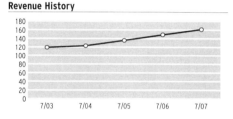

Chick-fil-A

Beloved by bovines, Chick-fil-A operates one of the nation's largest fast-food chains that specializes in chicken dishes. Boasting about 1,400 restaurants in almost 40 states, the chain offers chicken entrees, sandwiches, and salads, along with its popular waffle fries and fresh-squeezed lemonade. It is made up primarily of free-standing units that offer drive-through service, as well as dine-in seating, but it also has a significant number of mall-based stores. Chick-fil-A also licenses its concept to foodservice and concessions operators. The chain was started in 1946 by chairman S. Truett Cathy; a devout Baptist, he insists on a policy that all Chick-fil-A restaurants be closed on Sundays.

Chick-fil-A has been ramping up its expansion efforts the past few years, focusing especially on new free-standing units; it added about

---

80 locations during 2007. Looking to drive additional traffic to its eateries, the company has also been investing significantly in product development efforts to expand and refresh the chain's menu. New items rolled out in 2008 have included an expanded line of salads and new wrap-style sandwiches.

The company has been a big sponsor of athletic events, including the annual Chick-fil-A Bowl (formerly the Chick-fil-A Peach Bowl), one of the top post-season college football games. It also supports leadership training and scholarship programs through the WinShape Foundation.

Unlike most fast-food franchises, Chick-fil-A owns most of its restaurants and licenses franchisees to run the units for a fixed annual income plus a share in the profits. This unique arrangement lowers the initial cost to its franchisees and has resulted in less operator turnover than in other chains.

The company also operates two full-service restaurant concepts, Chick-fil-A Dwarf Houses and Truett's Grill.

HISTORY

S. Truett Cathy began his restaurant career in 1946 by opening a 24-hour diner called the Dwarf Grill (it only had 10 stools and four tables) in a suburb of Atlanta. It was there that he perfected a quick-cooked chicken sandwich. He ventured into the rapidly growing fast-food industry more than 20 years later, when in 1967 he convinced a local shopping mall to make room for the first Chick-fil-A unit. There he found a successful niche, and for nearly 20 years the company placed its units exclusively inside malls, especially in the South.

Chick-fil-A moved slowly at first, opening just six stores from 1968 to 1970. In 1974 it opened 14 new restaurants. It really hit its stride in the early 1980s, opening 101 units during the first two years of the decade (a store every eight days). Chick-fil-A Dwarf House, the chain's first full-service restaurant, opened in 1985.

As mall construction slowed and competition increased, the company began looking at alternatives. It began licensing in 1992, entering into agreements with Georgia Tech and Clemson University. The following year Chick-fil-A established its first drive-through-only outlet.

In an effort to extend its brand name, Chick-fil-A signed on as a sponsor for the Ladies Professional Golf Association in 1995 and college football's Peach Bowl in 1996. Also that year it opened its first airport store (at Atlanta's Hartsfield International) and expanded internationally with a unit in Durban, South Africa. In 1999 the company continued aggressive expansion, opening 88 new restaurants (56 of them standalone units).

Dan Cathy, son of the founder, was named president and COO of Chick-fil-A in 2001. In 2002 the company's number of free-standing units surpassed the number of its mall locations.

In early 2004 Chick-fil-A opened its first free-standing restaurant in Southern California. It also expanded its breakfast menu that year. In 2006 the company's sponsorship and marketing efforts got a boost when the Chick-fil-A Peach Bowl was renamed the Chick-fil-A Bowl.

EXECUTIVES

Chairman: S. Truett Cathy, age 87
President and COO: Dan T. Cathy, age 55
SVP Design and Construction: Perry A. Ragsdale
SVP Finance, and CFO: James B. (Buck) McCabe
SVP Marketing and Chief Marketing Officer:
 Steve A. Robinson
SVP Operations: Timothy P. (Tim) Tassopoulos
SVP Real Estate and General Counsel:
 Bureon E. Ledbetter Jr.
SVP; President, Dwarf House: Donald M. (Bubba) Cathy
VP and Assistant General Counsel: B. Lynn Chastain
VP and CIO: Jonathan B. (Jon) Bridges
VP and Controller: Philip A. Barrett
VP Brand Development: William F. (Woody) Faulk
VP Business Analysis: Roger E. Blythe Jr.
VP Human Resources: Dee Ann Turner
VP Operations Services: Stephen G. Mason
VP Public Relations: Donald A. (Don) Perry
VP Purchasing and Distribution: Younger D. Newton II
VP Real Estate: Erwin C. Reid
VP Sales Development: Barry V. White
VP Field Operations, Northern Region: David G. Salyers
VP Training and Development: T. Mark Miller

LOCATIONS

HQ: Chick-fil-A, Inc.
 5200 Buffington Rd., Atlanta, GA 30349
Phone: 404-765-8038
Web: www.chick-fil-a.com

COMPETITORS

AFC Enterprises
American Dairy Queen
Arby's
Burger King
Cajun Operating Company
CKE Restaurants
Jack in the Box
Kahala
KFC
McDonald's
Quiznos
Sonic Corp.
Subway
Wendy's
Whataburger
YUM!

HISTORICAL FINANCIALS
Company Type: Private

Income Statement

	REVENUE ($ mil.)	NET INCOME ($ mil.)	NET PROFIT MARGIN	EMPLOYEES
12/07	2,641	—	—	50,000
12/06	2,275	—	—	45,000
12/05	1,975	—	—	40,924
Annual Growth	15.6%	—	—	10.5%

FYE: December 31

Revenue History

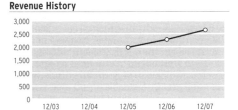

Children's Medical Center of Dallas

Sick kiddos in northern Texas who need specialized care don't have to travel far to find it. Children's Medical Center of Dallas treats children from birth to age 18 with various medical needs. Specialties include craniofacial deformities, cystic fibrosis, gastroenterology, and heart disease. Children's Medical Center is also a major pediatric transplant center for bone marrow, heart, kidney, and liver. The hospital has some 410 beds and is the pediatric teaching facility for the University of Texas Southwest medical program. Children's Medical Center also operates a network of some 50 outpatient clinics in and around Dallas.

The hospital operates Dallas County's only pediatric emergency room. Its Physicians for Children affiliate provides primary health care services to children living in the county's underserved areas.

In 2007 Children's opened an expansive outpatient center; future plans include the addition of an inpatient facility in Plano, Texas.

EXECUTIVES

President and CEO: Christopher J. Durovich
EVP Development: T.W. Hudson Akin
SVP Operations: Doug Hock
SVP Business Development and Ambulatory Services:
 Patricia U. (Pat) Winning
SVP: James W. Herring
SVP: Julio Perez Fontan
CFO: Ray Dziesinski
Chief Medical Officer: Tom Zellers
CIO: Pamela Arora
VP Ambulatory Services: Christopher Dougherty
VP Ancillary Services: Brett Daniel Lee
VP Facilities Management: Louis Saksen
VP Legal Affairs: Anne E. Long
VP Quality: Fiona Howard Levy
VP Public Affairs: Betsy Field MacKay
Manager Media Relations: Rachel Blacketer
Auditors: Ernst & Young LLP

LOCATIONS

HQ: Children's Medical Center of Dallas
 1935 Motor St., Dallas, TX 75235
Phone: 214-456-7000   **Fax:** 214-456-2197
Web: www.childrens.com

COMPETITORS

Baylor University Medical Center
Dallas County Hospital District
Dell Children's Medical Center
HCA
Shriners Hospitals For Children
St. Jude Children's Research Hospital
Tenet Healthcare
Texas Children's Hospital

HISTORICAL FINANCIALS
Company Type: Not-for-profit

Income Statement

	REVENUE ($ mil.)	NET INCOME ($ mil.)	NET PROFIT MARGIN	EMPLOYEES
12/07	640	92	14.3%	4,800
12/06	580	88	15.2%	4,500
12/05	514	51	10.0%	—
12/04	448	44	9.9%	—
12/03	418	—	—	—
Annual Growth	11.2%	27.4%	—	6.7%

FYE: December 31

2007 Year-End Financials

Debt ratio: 24.6%   Current ratio: —
Return on equity: 10.5%   Long-term debt ($ mil.): 227
Cash ($ mil.): —

Net Income History

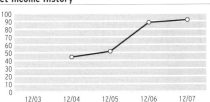

Chrysler LLC

The divorce is final: Daimler got the Mercedes and Chrysler got the minivan. After almost a decade of trying to make the most audacious merger in automotive history work, Daimler-Chrysler is now Daimler and Chrysler. In 2007 private equity concern Cerberus Capital Management bought Chrysler for about $7.4 billion — or about one-fifth of the $37 billion Daimler paid in 1998.

In addition to its eponymous Chrysler brand, the company also controls the Dodge and Jeep marques. Specific models include Chrysler 300, Dodge Ram pickups, and Jeep Grand Cherokee. The company offers financing to both consumers and dealers through Chrysler Financial Services LLC.

The DaimlerChrysler experiment looked good on paper, but the "merger of equals" never lived up to its promise. The plan had been to leverage Chrysler's mass market expertise with Daimler's engineering prowess and quality. But none of that ever came to fruition. Throughout their tumultuous relationship, Daimler and Chrysler were never simultaneously healthy, and in 2007 the cries of angry DaimlerChrysler investors became impossible to ignore any longer.

So what's next? Cerberus says it is in the car business for the long haul, although the automotive world's hot topic du jour is a possible GM-Chrysler merger. GM would like to get its hands on Chrysler's money (a reported $11.7 billion), customer base, and financing arm. The potential problems, however, are immense. The proposed merger would create an almost unmanageable stable of car brands (something GM is already fighting) and an enormous network of dealers.

More potential synergies include automotive financial services. Cerberus led a group of investors in 2006 that bought a 51% stake in GMAC,

GM's financing arm. GMAC, combined with Chrysler Financial Services, could create competitive advantages for both carmakers and both lenders.

Another scenario being bandied about is a stronger alliance with Nissan. The Japanese carmaker is said to be interested in acquiring a 20% stake in Chrysler. The two car companies have already agreed to build vehicles for one another. Nissan will manufacture a small, fuel efficient car that will bear the Chrysler name, while the replacement for the Nissan Titan pickup will be made by Chrysler. The new car is scheduled to hit the road in 2010, with the truck expected the following year.

Whatever Cerberus plans to do with it, Chrysler has a long way to go. The company lost $1.5 billion and $1.6 billion in 2006 and 2007, respectively, and Cerberus has to find a way to stop the bleeding. This will be hard, as much of the carnage is being caused by something that can't be fixed quickly — a lack of small cars. The Caliber is the smallest car Chrysler makes, and it's not very small.

To make its strategy work Cerberus has tapped Robert Nardelli as the new CEO. The former GE executive, who left The Home Depot under a cloud in early 2007, succeeded Thomas LaSorda as CEO of Chrysler; LaSorda was named vice chairman and president. While Nardelli doubled Home Depot's sales during his six years as chairman and CEO, his imperious ways with shareholders, his alienation of customers and employees, a steadily declining stock price, and the size of his hefty compensation package (which he was unwilling to reduce when requested to do so by the board) led to his ouster at Home Depot.

In a move aimed at bumping up its retail business, Chrysler announced in mid-2008 that it would no longer lease automobiles in the US. It also said it will discontinue four less-gas-friendly models in 2009: Chrysler branded Crossfire, PT Cruiser, and Pacifica, and the Dodge Magnum. Chrysler is not ready to give up on large SUVs, however. In 2009 the company will introduce hybrid versions of its Dodge Durango and Chrysler Aspen. The carmaker has also announced that 2010 will bring an all-electric vehicle to the Chrysler stable of vehicles.

The company announced in late 2008 that it would reduce its salaried workforce by 25%. Chrysler hopes to achieve the reduction through buyouts, layoffs, and early retirement offers. Earlier, in a cost-cutting move, Chrysler asked for a 5% cost reduction from all of its non-production suppliers. The measure, which went into effect June 1, 2008, will last for one year. Additionally, the company has reduced its capacity by more than a third. While not yet back in the black, the company's finances appear to be taking a positive turn.

Currently Cerberus currently owns about 80% of Chrysler, and Daimler retains the rest; however, Daimler is in talks to sell its remaining stake to Cerberus.

HISTORY

When the Maxwell Motor Car Company went into receivership in 1920, a bankers' syndicate hired Walter Chrysler, former Buick president and General Motors (GM) VP, to reorganize it.

Chrysler became president in 1923 and in 1924 introduced his own car, the Chrysler, which borrowed from WWI aircraft in the design of its six-cylinder engine. The next year Chrysler took over Maxwell and renamed it after himself.

In 1928 the company acquired Dodge and introduced the low-priced Plymouth and the more luxurious DeSoto. Its research and development budget never decreased during the Depression, and innovations included overdrive and a three-point engine suspension on rubber mountings. In 1933 Chrysler's sales surpassed Ford's, and two years later Walter retired.

To minimize costs, Chrysler kept the same car models from 1942 until 1953, while other makers were adding yearly style modifications. The company lost market share and slipped to third place by 1950.

Chrysler misjudged customer demands in the 1960s, when it introduced small cars, and again in the 1970s, when it maintained production of large cars, resulting in massive losses. Facing the prospect of bankruptcy, Chrysler negotiated $1.5 billion in loan guarantees from the federal government and brought in Lee Iacocca, former Ford president (and the man behind the Ford Mustang), as CEO in 1978.

Iacocca became one of the most visible CEOs ever, appearing in TV commercials, publishing his autobiography, and making an issue of Japanese trading practices. Chrysler reorganized, closed several plants, and cut its workforce; by 1983 it had repaid all guaranteed loans, seven years ahead of schedule. The next year it introduced the first minivan.

The company diversified, buying Gulfstream Aerospace (corporate jets, sold 1990), E.F. Hutton Credit, and Finance America for a total of $1.2 billion. In 1986 Chrysler created a joint venture with Mitsubishi (Diamond-Star, sold 1993) to sell Mitsubishi cars in the US, and the following year it purchased American Motors. Between 1989 and 1991 Chrysler bought Thrifty, Snappy, Dollar, and General car rental agencies.

Corporate raider Kirk Kerkorian bought about 10% of Chrysler in 1990. An economic downturn in 1992 forced the carmaker to sell nonautomotive assets. Iacocca stepped down as chairman late that year and was replaced by GM's head of European operations, Robert Eaton.

Making progress on its pledge to shed some noncore businesses, Chrysler in 1996 sold most of its aerospace and defense holdings to Raytheon for $475 million. In 1997 the automaker sold its electronics unit, Pentastar Electronics, to investment group PEI Acquisition and spun off the Dollar Thrifty Group, which operates Dollar Rent A Car and Thrifty Rent-A-Car.

The next year Daimler-Benz agreed to acquire Chrysler in a deal worth an estimated $37 billion. The purchase marked the largest takeover of a US firm by a foreign buyer to that time. The deal brought a windfall for Chrysler execs; for instance, chairman Robert Eaton got an estimated $70 million in stock and cash.

In 2006 Chrysler announced a deal with Chery Automobile of China for a small car based on modifications to one of Chery's domestic models. It will be branded as a Dodge, Chrysler, or Jeep. The cars will be sold in Europe, India, and China, and will become the first Chinese car imported into the US.

EXECUTIVES

Chairman and CEO: Robert L. (Bob) Nardelli
Vice Chairman and CEO, Chrysler Financial: Thomas F. Gilman
Vice Chairman and Co-President: Thomas W. (Tom) LaSorda, age 54
Vice Chairman and Co-President: James E. (Jim) Press, age 61
EVP Manufacturing: Frank J. Ewasyshyn, age 56
EVP Human Resources and Communications: Nancy A. Rae, age 50
EVP Procurement: John P. Campi
EVP Product Development: Frank O. Klegon, age 56
EVP North America, Sales and Marketing, Service and Parts: Steven J. (Steve) Landry, age 49
EVP International Sales, Marketing, and Business Development: Michael Manley, age 44
SVP and CFO: Ronald E. Kolka, age 48
SVP External Affairs and Public Policy: W. Frank Fountain Jr., age 63
SVP, CIO, and Treasurer: Jan A. Bertsch, age 50
SVP Global External Affairs and Public Policy: Robert G. Liberatore
VP, General Counsel, and Secretary: Holly Leese
VP and Chief Marketing Officer: Deborah Wahl Meyer, age 45
VP Employee Relations: Al Iacobelli
VP Union Relations: Kenneth J. McCarter, age 60
VP External Affairs and Public Policy: John Bozzella
VP Design: Ralph Gilles
CEO, Global Electric Motor Cars and Chairman, Global Engine Manufacturing Alliance: Bruce D. Coventry
President, Mopar, Global Service and Parts: Simon Boag, age 43
CEO, Asia Operations: Philip F. (Phil) Murtaugh
COO, Chrysler Financial: Darryl R. Jackson, age 47
Executive Director, Corporate Diversity Office: Monica E. Emerson
President, Global Engine Manufacturing Alliance: Bruce Baumbach
Executive Director Multi Brand Marketing and Agency Relations: Christine MacKenzie, age 51
Executive Director Communications: Lori McTavish
Director Dodge Brand and SRT Global Marketing: Michael J. Accaviti, age 49
Director International Marketing and Communications: Judith K. Wheeler
Director Jeep Brand Marketing and Global Communications: John D. Plecha
Chief Customer Officer: Douglas G. Betts
Interior and Exterior Designer: Akino Tsuchiya, age 37
Lead Economist: Paul Traub

LOCATIONS

HQ: Chrysler LLC
1000 Chrysler Dr., Auburn Hills, MI 48326
Phone: 248-576-5741
Web: www.chryslerllc.com

PRODUCTS/OPERATIONS

Selected Products

Chrysler
  Cirrus
  Concorde
  Sebring
  Town & Country
Dodge
  Caravan
  Neon
  Ram
  Stratus
  Viper
Eagle
  Talon
Jeep
  Grand Cherokee
  Jamboree
Plymouth
  Breeze
  Grand Voyager
  Neon
  Voyager

Selected Subsidiaries and Affiliates
Chrysler do Brasil Ltda.
Chrysler Financial Corp. (loans and leasing plans)
Chrysler Japan Sales Limited
Chrysler Motors de Venezuela, SA
Chrysler Realty Corp.
Chrysler Sales & Services (Thailand) Ltd.
New Venture Gear Inc. (64%, auto parts)

COMPETITORS

BMW	Mazda
Daimler	Nissan
Fiat	Peugeot
Ford Motor	Renault
Fuji Heavy Industries	Saab Automobile
General Motors	Saab Automobile USA
Honda	Suzuki Motor
Isuzu	Toyota
Kia Motors	Volkswagen

HISTORICAL FINANCIALS
Company Type: Private

Income Statement
FYE: December 31

	REVENUE ($ mil.)	NET INCOME ($ mil.)	NET PROFIT MARGIN	EMPLOYEES
12/07	59,700	—	—	66,409
12/06	62,160	—	—	77,778
12/05	59,355	—	—	—
12/04	67,515	—	—	—
Annual Growth	(4.0%)	—	—	(14.6%)

Revenue History

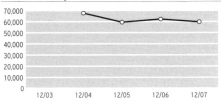

Chugach Electric Association

Deriving its name from an old Eskimo tribal word, Chugach Electric Association generates, transmits, distributes, and sells electricity in Alaska's railbelt region. This area extends from the coastal Chugach Mountains into central Alaska and includes the state's two largest cities (Anchorage and Fairbanks). The member-owned cooperative utility has 530 MW of generating capacity from its natural gas-fired and hydro-electric power plants. Serving 80,300 metered retail locations, Chugach Electric, the largest electric utility in Alaska, also sells wholesale power to other municipal and cooperative utilities in the region.

Chugach Electric was formed in 1948 as a Rural Electrification Administration cooperative to create an electrical distribution system to meet the growing power needs of the Greater Anchorage region.

EXECUTIVES
Chairman: Liz Vazquez
CEO: Bradley W. Evans, age 53
CFO: Michael R. Cunningham, age 58
Acting SVP Power Delivery: Edward Jenkin, age 47
Acting SVP Strategic Planning and Corporate Affairs: Ron Vecera, age 50
Acting SVP Power Supply: Paul Risse, age 53
VP Human Resources: Mary Tesch
Director Informational Services: David Smith
Public Relations Contact: Patti Bogan
General Counsel: Carol Johnson
Auditors: KPMG LLP

LOCATIONS
HQ: Chugach Electric Association, Inc.
5601 Electron Dr., Anchorage, AK 99518
Phone: 907-563-7494   **Fax:** 907-762-4678
Web: www.chugachelectric.com

PRODUCTS/OPERATIONS

2007 Sales

	$ mil.	% of total
Retail		
Residential	76.9	30
Commercial	72.6	28
Wholesale	97.8	38
Other	10.1	4
Total	**257.4**	**100**

COMPETITORS
SEMCO Energy

HISTORICAL FINANCIALS
Company Type: Cooperative

Income Statement
FYE: December 31

	REVENUE ($ mil.)	NET INCOME ($ mil.)	NET PROFIT MARGIN	EMPLOYEES
12/07	257	3	1.1%	348
12/06	268	10	3.7%	348
12/05	226	10	4.2%	356
12/04	201	8	3.8%	355
12/03	184	6	3.4%	353
Annual Growth	8.8%	(17.6%)	—	(0.4%)

2007 Year-End Financials
Debt ratio: 231.3%
Return on equity: 1.9%
Cash ($ mil.): —
Current ratio: —
Long-term debt ($ mil.): 345

Net Income History

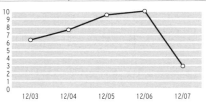

Circus and Eldorado Joint Venture

Circus and Eldorado Joint Venture owns and operates the Silver Legacy Resort Casino in Reno, Nevada. The Silver Legacy, which features a 19th-century silver-mining theme, offers a more than 85,000-sq.-ft. casino with about 1,600 slot machines and nearly 70 table games. The casino's hotel boasts some 1,700 guest rooms and 140 penthouse and hospitality suites. Silver Legacy also houses six restaurants. Circus Circus Hotel and Casino owner MGM MIRAGE and Eldorado Resorts each own 50% of the company. (MGM MIRAGE's stake was owned by Mandalay Resort Group until MGM bought Mandalay in 2005. Its share is held through Galleon, Inc.)

The company markets the Silver Legacy to a select group of patrons, including preferred casino customers, convention groups, and specialty Internet travel groups.

EXECUTIVES
CEO; General Manager, Silver Legacy: Gary L. Carano, age 55, $400,000 pay
Secretary; Executive Director Marketing, Silver Legacy: Glenn T. Carano, age 52, $400,000 pay
Assistant General Manager, Silver Legacy: Bruce C. Sexton, age 54, $217,553 pay
Controller and Chief Accounting and Financial Officer; CFO Silver Legacy: Stephanie D. Lepori, age 37, $130,053 pay
Auditors: Deloitte & Touche LLP

LOCATIONS
HQ: Circus and Eldorado Joint Venture
407 N. Virginia St., Reno, NV 89501
Phone: 775-325-7401   **Fax:** 775-325-7330
Web: www.silverlegacyreno.com

PRODUCTS/OPERATIONS

2007 Sales

	% of total
Casino	48
Hotel	25
Food & beverage	22
Other	5
Total	**100**

COMPETITORS

Boomtown	MGM Grand Hotel
Boyd Gaming	Monarch Casino
Coast Casinos	Monte Carlo Resort
Hard Rock Hotel	& Casino
Harrah's Entertainment	Sands Regent

HISTORICAL FINANCIALS
Company Type: Joint venture

Income Statement
FYE: December 31

	REVENUE ($ mil.)	NET INCOME ($ mil.)	NET PROFIT MARGIN	EMPLOYEES
12/07	178	9	4.8%	2,110
12/06	159	9	5.8%	2,175
12/05	149	—	—	2,160
12/04	154	—	—	2,105
12/03	152	—	—	2,061
Annual Growth	4.0%	(8.6%)	—	0.6%

2007 Year-End Financials
Debt ratio: 115.1%
Return on equity: 6.2%
Cash ($ mil.): —

Current ratio: —
Long-term debt ($ mil.): 160

Net Income History

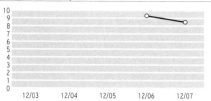

| | 12/03 | 12/04 | 12/05 | 12/06 | 12/07 |

Citizens Bancorp

Citizens Bancorp is the holding company for Citizens Bank, which offers traditional banking services through about a dozen branches in western Oregon. Its retail offerings include regular savings and checking accounts, money market and NOW accounts, CDs, IRAs, and home mortgages. The bank also offers safe-deposit boxes and online banking and bill payment. It is mainly a business lender, with commercial mortgages making up the largest portion of its loan portfolio. Loans to farmers for land, operations, and equipment are a growing part of Citizens Bank's business.

EXECUTIVES

Chairman: Jock Gibson, age 66
President, CEO, and Director, Citizens Bancorp and Citizens Bank: William V. (Bill) Humphreys Sr., age 60, $252,240 pay
EVP and CFO, Citizens Bank: Lark E. Wysham, age 58, $131,836 pay
EVP and COO, Citizens Bank:
William F. (Bill) Hubel Jr., age 52, $129,826 pay
EVP and Chief Lending Officer, Citizens Bank:
Steven R. (Steve) Terjeson, age 51, $125,394 pay
VP and Human Resources Manager, Citizens Bank:
Bobbie Carter
Assistant VP and Manager, Merchant Services, Citizens Bank: Ranee McDougal
Auditors: Symonds, Evans & Company, P.C.

LOCATIONS

HQ: Citizens Bancorp
275 SW 3rd St., Corvallis, OR 97339
Phone: 541-752-5161   **Fax:** 541-757-3546
Web: www.citizensebank.com

PRODUCTS/OPERATIONS

2007 Sales

	$ mil.	% of total
Interest		
Loans	21.3	80
Securities	2.3	9
Other	0.4	1
Noninterest		
Service charges on deposit accounts	1.1	4
BankCard income	0.5	2
Other	1.1	4
Total	**26.7**	**100**

COMPETITORS

Bank of America
Cascade Bancorp
KeyCorp
Pacific Continental
Sterling Financial (WA)

Umpqua Holdings
U.S. Bancorp
Washington Federal
Washington Mutual
Wells Fargo

HISTORICAL FINANCIALS
Company Type: Private

Income Statement

	ASSETS ($ mil.)	NET INCOME ($ mil.)	INCOME AS % OF ASSETS	EMPLOYEES
12/07	361	6	1.7%	132
12/06	359	6	1.5%	127
12/05	339	5	1.6%	131
12/04	335	4	1.3%	137
12/03	326	5	1.5%	136
Annual Growth	**2.5%**	**5.1%**	**—**	**(0.7%)**

FYE: December 31

2007 Year-End Financials
Equity as % of assets: —
Return on assets: 1.7%
Return on equity: —

Long-term debt ($ mil.): —
Sales ($ mil.): 27

Net Income History

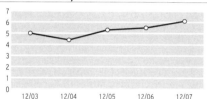

| | 12/03 | 12/04 | 12/05 | 12/06 | 12/07 |

City University of New York

The City University of New York (CUNY) is the big "U" in the Big Apple. The college has 20 campuses in the five boroughs of New York City and is the US's largest urban university system. About 460,000 undergraduate, graduate, and continuing education students (from 164 countries) are enrolled at CUNY, which has 11 senior colleges, six community colleges, a doctoral-granting graduate school, a law school, the School of Professional Studies, and The Sophie Davis School of Biomedical Education. Its 1,400 academic programs range from specialized, career-oriented courses to traditional liberal arts curricula. CUNY employs some 6,100 full-time teaching faculty members.

CUNY has made some big changes, including tougher admission standards that critics feared would hurt the university's ethnic diversity, a hallmark of the school (enrollment numbers have proven otherwise). Notable CUNY alumni include novelist Oscar Hijuelos, General Colin Powell, comedian Jerry Seinfeld, and 11 Nobel laureates.

As with many public universities throughout the US, CUNY is enduring tough times econom-ically. In order to free up the money to hire more full-time professors, the university has had to end a 10-year tradition of not charging four-year students for the last semester of their senior year.

CUNY opened its Graduate School of Journalism in September 2006.

HISTORY

The New York State Legislature first created a municipal college system in New York City in 1926, when it formed the New York City Board of Higher Education to manage the operations of the City College of New York and Hunter College. City College's roots were established in 1847 when New York passed a referendum creating the Free Academy, a tuition-free school. Hunter College was founded in 1870 as a women's college, and it was the first free teachers college in the US.

The Board of Higher Education authorized City College to create the Brooklyn Collegiate Center (a two-year men's college) in 1926; Hunter established a similar two-year women's branch in Brooklyn. Four years later the schools merged to create the Brooklyn College of the City of New York, the city's first public, co-ed liberal arts college. Other schools added to the municipal system included Queens College (1937), New York City Community College (1947), Staten Island Community College (1955), Bronx Community College (1957), and Queensborough Community College (1958).

The state legislature renamed New York City's municipal college system The City University of New York (CUNY) in 1961 and ordered its board of trustees to expand the system's facilities and scope. One of the first actions was to create a graduate school. CUNY chartered a number of new schools during the 1960s, including Richmond College (1965), York College (1966), Medgar Evers College (1968), and several community colleges. CUNY took over management of the New York State Institute of Applied Arts and Sciences (renamed New York City Technical College) in 1964 and established the John Jay College of Criminal Justice. CUNY became affiliated with Mount Sinai School of Medicine in 1967.

Despite its expansion, the university system had difficulty keeping up with demand, particularly after 1970, when it established an open admissions policy for all New York City high school graduates. Richmond College and Staten Island Community College became the College of Staten Island in 1976. Both CUNY and the City of New York ran into serious financial problems in the mid-1970s, spelling the end of CUNY's tradition of free undergrad tuition for New York City residents. To increase state financial support for CUNY, the legislature signed the City University Governance and Financing Act in 1979.

The City University School of Law held its first classes in 1983. The following year the state board of regents authorized CUNY to offer a doctor of medicine degree. CUNY's law school received accreditation from the American Bar Association in 1992. Since abandoning the free enrollment policy in the 1970s, the university's tuition continued to increase. In 1992, after presenting a nearly $600 increase in tuition, CUNY initiated its "last semester free" program, whereby four-year students did not have to pay tuition for the last semester of their senior year.

After several years of budget cuts and steadily increasing enrollment, CUNY declared a state of financial emergency in 1995. The following year

New York's Governor George Pataki proposed new budget cuts, and in 1997 he called for tuition hikes. CUNY's board of trustees introduced a resolution calling for the elimination of remedial education programs at the senior college level in 1998. The state Board of Regents approved the plan in 1999 (most remedial classes were phased out by 2001). Matthew Goldstein was appointed chancellor in 1999 and has worked to increase CUNY's budget to hire more full-time faculty.

EXECUTIVES

Chairperson: Benno C. Schmidt Jr.
Vice Chairperson: Philip A. Berry, age 58
Chancellor: Matthew Goldstein
Executive Vice Chancellor, Academic Affairs and Provost: Selma Botman
Executive Vice Chancellor and Chief Operating Officer: Allan H. Dobrin
Senior Vice Chancellor, Legal Affairs and General Counsel: Frederick P. Schaffer
Senior Vice Chancellor, University Relations and Secretary: Jay Hershenson
Vice Chancellor, Facilities Planning, Construction, and Management: Iris Weinshall
Vice Chancellor, Academic Administration and Planning: Michael J. Zavelle
Vice Chancellor, Budget and Finance: Ernesto Malave
Vice Chancellor, Faculty and Staff Relations: Brenda Richardson Malone
Vice Chancellor, Faculty and Staff Relations: Gloriana Waters
CIO: Brian Cohen
Dean, Academic Affairs: Ann Cohen
Dean, Institutional Research and Assessment: David Crook
Dean, The Executive Office: Robert Ptachik
Dean, Undergraduate Education: Judith Summerfield
Director, Media Relations: Michael Arena
VP, Student Affairs and Enrollment: Marcela Katz Armoza, age 54
Director, Human Resources, Central Office: Sonia Pearson
Auditors: KPMG LLP

LOCATIONS

HQ: The City University of New York
535 E. 80th St., New York, NY 10075
Phone: 212-794-5555   **Fax:** 212-209-5600
Web: www.cuny.edu

The City University of New York has schools serving the Bronx, Brooklyn, Manhattan, Queens, and Staten Island boroughs of New York City.

PRODUCTS/OPERATIONS

Selected Senior Colleges

Bernard M. Baruch College
Brooklyn College
City College
City University School of Law at Queens College
The College of Staten Island
The Graduate School and University Center
Herbert H. Lehman College
Hunter College
John Jay College of Criminal Justice
Medgar Evers College
New York City College of Technology
Queens College
York College

Selected Community Colleges

Borough of Manhattan Community College
Bronx Community College
Hostos Community College
Kingsborough Community College
LaGuardia Community College
Queensborough Community College

Claire's Stores

If the difference between men and boys is the price of their toys, for young women and girls, it may be the price of their accessories. For thrifty, fashion-conscious females ages 7 to 27, Claire's Stores is the queen of costume jewelry, handbags, and hair bows. Claire's operates more than 3,000 boutiques, primarily in malls, that include Claire's and Icing by Claire's. The chain is present in all 50 US states, Puerto Rico, the US Virgin Islands, and Canada, and about 10 European countries. Founded by Rowland Schaefer and later run by his daughters, Bonnie and Marla Schaefer, Claire's Stores was sold to an affiliate of the New York-based private equity firm Apollo Management for $3.1 billion in 2007.

Prior to the sale, the Schaefer family was the company's majority shareholder and controlled about a third of Claire's voting power. Apollo Advisors appointed Eugene Kahn, formerly the CEO of The May Department Stores, as the chain's new chief executive replacing co-CEOs Bonnie and Marla.

Claire's operates about 900 stores in the UK, Ireland, France, Spain, Portugal, Belgium, Switzerland, Austria, the Netherlands, and Germany. In Japan, Claire's Nippon runs about 200 stores through a 50-50 joint venture with AEON CO. Expanding its global footprint, Claire's franchises about 165 stores in the Middle East, Russia, Turkey, Poland, South Africa, and Guatemala. Some two-thirds of Claire's products are imported from China.

Despite declining sales, Claire's continues to add stores at home and overseas. Between 70 and 80 company-owned stores, primarily in Europe, are planned in fiscal 2009, as well as about 15 stores in Japan and another 20 new shops operated by franchisees.

Claire's has sought to extend its retail reach beyond the tween (ages 7 to 11) and teen markets by appealing to young girls (ages 3 to 5) through its Claire's Club brand and its Icing format targeted at the college set and young women (ages 18 to 27) entering the workforce. The retailer's jewelry and accessories (hair goods, handbags, small leather goods, and cosmetics) are typically priced between $2 and $24.

EXECUTIVES

Chairman: Peter P. Copses, age 50
CEO and Director: Eugene S. (Gene) Kahn, age 57
EVP: James (Jim) Conroy, age 37
SVP and CFO: J. Per Brodin, age 46
SVP and Corporate General Counsel: Rebecca Orand
SVP and CIO: E. Keith Pickens
SVP Franchise Operations: Bruce Marshall
VP Corporate Communications and Investor Relations: Marisa F. Jacobs
President, Claire's North America: John A. Zimmerman, age 49
President and Managing Director, Claire's Europe: Mark G. Smith, age 49
COO, Claire's Europe: Ingrid Osmundsen
Chief Administrative Officer, Claire's North America: Joseph A. DeFalco
SVP Store Operations, Claire's North America: Colleen Collins
SVP and General Merchandise Manager, Claire's North America: Michael Rosa
Chief Merchandise Officer: Joan E. Munnelly
Auditors: KPMG LLP

LOCATIONS

HQ: Claire's Stores, Inc.
3 SW 129th Ave., Pembroke Pines, FL 33027
Phone: 954-433-3900   **Fax:** 954-433-3999
Web: www.clairestores.com

2008 Sales

	% of total
North America	65
International	35
Total	**100**

2008 Stores

	No.
North America	2,135
Europe	905
Total	**3,040**

PRODUCTS/OPERATIONS

2008 Sales

	% of total
Jewelry	54
Accessories	46
Total	**100**

Selected Stores

Afterthoughts
Claire's
Claire's Accessories
Claire's Boutiques
Claire' Club
Icing

COMPETITORS

Alloy, Inc.	Monsoon
The Buckle	Pacific Sunwear
Charlotte Russe Holding	Target
Charming Shoppes	TJX Companies
Deb Shops	Tween Brands
dELiA*s	Urban Outfitters
Fingerhut	Wal-Mart
Forever 21	Wet Seal
Hot Topic	

HISTORICAL FINANCIALS

Company Type: Private

Income Statement

FYE: Saturday nearest January 31

	REVENUE ($ mil.)	NET INCOME ($ mil.)	NET PROFIT MARGIN	EMPLOYEES
1/08	1,511	(43)	—	18,700
1/07	1,481	189	12.7%	18,500
1/06	1,370	172	12.6%	18,000
1/05	1,279	143	11.2%	17,500
1/04	1,133	115	10.2%	16,000
Annual Growth	7.5%	—	—	4.0%

2008 Year-End Financials

Debt ratio: 390.5%
Return on equity: —
Cash ($ mil.): —
Current ratio: —
Long-term debt ($ mil.): 2,363

Net Income History

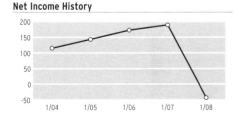

Clark Enterprises

Like Clark Kent, this firm holds some super powers. Clark Enterprises, one of the largest privately held companies in the Washington, DC area, holds interests in real estate, private equity, venture capital, and construction companies. Its real estate holdings include some 5 million sq. ft. of office space, 15,000 residential units, and 300,000 sq. ft. of warehouse space. The Clark Construction Group, its flagship subsidiary with more than $2 billion in annual revenue, is a top US contractor that performs construction management, general contracting, design, and consulting services. Other units include residential builder Seawright Homes and highway construction company Shirley Contracting.

Chairman and CEO James Clark owns the company, which was founded in 1972.

In 2007 Clark Construction and construction giant Balfour Beatty won a federal contract to build a spy complex for the CIA.

Clark Realty Capital also is working to develop a $2.5 billion, 40-acre mixed use project with parkland, offices, and housing in Washington, DC, called Poplar Point.

EXECUTIVES

Chairman and CEO: A. James Clark
President and COO: Lawrence C. Nussdorf, age 45
EVP; Managing Director, CNF Investments LLC: Robert J. (Bob) Flanagan, age 51
SVP and General Counsel: Rebecca L. Owen
VP and General Counsel: Michael J. Mintz
Chairman, Clark Construction Group: Peter C. Forster
President, Clark Construction Group: Dan T. Montgomery
President, Clark Realty Builders: Glenn Ferguson
President, Clark Realty Capital: Douglas (Doug) Sandor
President and CEO, Atkinson Construction: Scott Lynn
President, Seawright Corp.: D. Stephen Seawright
President and CEO, Shirley Contracting: Michael Post
Principal, CNF Investments LLC: Joe Del Guercio
Head of Asset Management Group: Alexandra Lee
Deputy General Counsel: David H. Brody
Executive Assistant to President and Office Manager: Connie Pumphrey

LOCATIONS

HQ: Clark Enterprises, Inc.
7500 Old Georgetown Rd., 15th Fl.,
Bethesda, MD 20814
Phone: 301-657-7100   **Fax:** 301-657-7263
Web: www.clarkenterprisesinc.com

PRODUCTS/OPERATIONS

Selected Subsidiaries

The Clark Construction Group, LLC. (commercial, institutional, and heavy construction)
Clark Realty Builders, LLC (residential building)
Clark Realty Capital, LLC (residential development)
Clark Realty Management, LLC (property management)
CNF Investments LLC (private equity investment)
Seawright Homes, LLC (single-family homes, high rise condos, rental apartments)
Shirley Contracting (highway and heavy construction)

COMPETITORS

Barton Malow
Bovis Lend Lease
Donohoe Companies
Fluor
Forest City Enterprises
Gilbane
Hensel Phelps
Hunt Construction
Palomar Ventures
Peter Kiewit Sons'
RFE Investment Partners
Skanska
Turner Corporation
Whiting-Turner

HISTORICAL FINANCIALS

Company Type: Private

Income Statement				FYE: December 31
	REVENUE ($ mil.)	NET INCOME ($ mil.)	NET PROFIT MARGIN	EMPLOYEES
12/07	4,220	—	—	4,200
12/06	3,220	—	—	4,200
12/05	2,844	—	—	4,200
12/04	2,800	—	—	3,200
12/03	2,750	—	—	4,200
Annual Growth	11.3%	—	—	0.0%

Revenue History

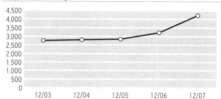

ClubCorp USA

This company makes its green from the green — the golf green, that is. ClubCorp is the world's largest operator of golf courses and private clubs with more than 150 facilities throughout the US and four international locations. Its resorts and golf courses include such well known venues as Firestone Country Club (Akron, Ohio), The Homestead (Hot Springs, Virginia), and Mission Hills Country Club (Rancho Mirage, California). ClubCorp also operates private business and sports clubs. Robert Dedman started the company in 1957. It is owned by private equity firm KSL Capital Partners.

ClubCorp has been investing in improvements for its current properties while keeping an eye out for new facilities to acquire. In 2008 it acquired Seville Golf & Country Club in Gilbert, Arizona, and it opened a new water park at its Clubs of Kingwood in Texas.

KSL Capital acquired ClubCorp for about $1.8 billion in 2006. The investment firm already had investments in several resort properties, including the Doral Golf Resort in Florida and La Costa Resort and Spa in California. Eric Affeldt, a founding member of KSL Capital, took over as president and CEO of ClubCorp following the acquisition. As part of the deal, the Dedman family, which previously controlled 70% of the company, retained ownership of the historic Pinehurst Resort & Country Club in North Carolina.

EXECUTIVES

President and CEO: Eric L. Affeldt, age 50
EVP New Business Development: Douglas T. Howe, age 50
EVP Sales: Frank C. Gore, age 56
EVP Finance: Angela A. Stephens
EVP Business Development: David B. Woodyard
EVP Operations: John H. Longstreet
EVP Sales and Marketing: Jamie Walters
EVP Golf and Country Club Division: Mark Burnett
EVP and CIO: Daniel T. (Dan) Tilley
EVP People Strategy, General Counsel, and Secretary: Ingrid Keiser
SVP Purchasing: William T. (Bill) Walden
SVP Strategic Growth: Paul A. Golden
SVP Integrated Revenue: Mark Murphy
VP Golf Course Management: Douglas Miller
VP Corporate Communications: Rich Lakers
Auditors: Deloitte & Touche LLP

LOCATIONS

HQ: ClubCorp USA, Inc.
3030 LBJ Fwy., Ste. 600, Dallas, TX 75234
Phone: 972-243-6191   **Fax:** 972-888-7558
Web: www.clubcorp.com

PRODUCTS/OPERATIONS

Selected Clubs and Resorts

Country clubs and golf courses
  Brookhaven Country Club (Dallas)
  Country Club of Hilton Head (South Carolina)
  Cozumel Country Club (Mexico)
  Firestone Country Club (Akron, OH)
  Golden Bear Golf Club at Indigo Run (Hilton Head, SC)
  Greenbrier Country Club (Chesapeake, VA)
  The Hills Country Club at Lakeway (Austin, TX)
  Hunter's Green Country Club (Tampa)
  Indian Wells Country Club (California)
  Nags Head Golf Links (North Carolina)
  Nicklaus Golf Club at LionsGate (Overland Park, KS)
  Piedmont Golf Club (Haymarket, VA)
Resorts
  Barton Creek Resort (Austin, TX)
  The Homestead (Hot Springs, VA)
Business and sports clubs
  Boston College Club
  Buckhead Club (Atlanta)
  Capital Club (Beijing)
  Citrus Club (Orlando, FL)
  City Club of Washington (Washington, DC)
  City Club on Bunker Hill (Los Angeles)
  Crescent Club (Memphis)
  Nashville City Club (Tennessee)
  One Ninety One Club (Atlanta)
  Plaza Club (Houston)
  Pyramid Club (Philadelphia)
  Renaissance Club (Detroit)
  Tower Club (Dallas)
  University of Texas Club (Austin)

COMPETITORS

American Golf
Arnold Palmer Golf Management, LLC
Club Med
Four Seasons Hotels
Hilton Hotels
Hyatt
KemperSports
Marriott
Starwood Hotels & Resorts
Troon Golf

HISTORICAL FINANCIALS
Company Type: Private

Income Statement
FYE: December 31

	REVENUE ($ mil.)	NET INCOME ($ mil.)	NET PROFIT MARGIN	EMPLOYEES
12/07	898	—	—	16,000
12/06	1,020	—	—	18,000
12/05	1,028	—	—	18,300
12/04	944	—	—	18,500
12/03	912	—	—	19,000
Annual Growth	(0.4%)	—	—	(4.2%)

Revenue History

1,200				
1,000				
800				
600				
400				
200				
0	12/03	12/04	12/05	12/06	12/07

Colonial Group

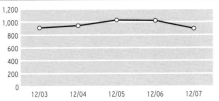

Colonial Group presides over an empire of oil and gas and shipping-related companies in the Southeastern US. The group provides storage and distribution services for liquid and dry bulk products, including bulk chemicals, motor fuels, industrial fuel oil, and retail gas. It also provides ship bunkering, commercial shipping, and tug and barge services. Colonial Group also operates more than 70 gas stations and convenience stores in Georgia, North Carolina, and South Carolina through its Enmark Stations unit. In addition, subsidiary Georgia Kaolin Terminals provides storage facilities for customers in the US kaolin industry.

The company was founded in 1921 as American Oil Company by Raymond Demére, grandfather of president Robert Demére, Jr. The enterprise was renamed Colonial Oil Industries in 1933.

EXECUTIVES
President: Robert H. Deméré Jr., age 59
CFO: Francis A. (Frank) Brown, age 56
CTO: Jeff Mathews
VP Operations: William Baker
Director Human Resources: David (Dave) Deason
Employment Manager: Butch Almeida

LOCATIONS
HQ: Colonial Group Inc.
101 N. Lathrop Ave., Savannah, GA 31415
Phone: 912-236-1331   **Fax:** 912-235-3881
Web: www.colonialgroupinc.com

Colonial Group operates throughout the Southeastern US.

PRODUCTS/OPERATIONS

Selected Subsidiaries
Chatham Towing Company, Inc. (tugboat and barge services)
Colonial Chemical Solutions, Inc. (products and services for food, chemical process, and basic chemical industries)
Colonial Energy, Inc. (natural gas supplies)
Colonial Marine Industries, Inc. (ship brokerage, chartering, and management)
Colonial Oil Industries, Inc. (oil pipelines and terminals)
Colonial Towing, Inc. (d/b/a Sun State Towing, tugboat and barge services)
Colonial Terminals, Inc. (liquid and dry bulk storage facilities)
Compliance Systems, Inc. (safety and compliance services)
Enmark Stations, Inc. (gas stations and convenience stores)
Georgia Kaolin Terminals, Inc. (marine terminal management)

COMPETITORS
Apex Oil
A.T. Williams
Center Oil
Jordan Oil Company
Mountain Empire Oil

Colorado Avalanche

This Avalanche is breaking loose on ice sheets across the National Hockey League. The Colorado Avalanche represents the Denver area in the NHL and boasts two Stanley Cup championships, its last in 2001. A perennial contender for the playoffs, the team draws regular sellout crowds at its Pepsi Center home arena. The franchise was founded in 1972 as the Quebec Nordiques of the World Hockey League and joined the NHL in 1979. It relocated to the Rocky Mountain state in 1995. Wal-Mart heir Stan Kroenke bought the team and the Pepsi Center in 2000 through Kroenke Sports Enterprises. He also owns the Denver Nuggets basketball team and has a stake in the St. Louis Rams football team.

EXECUTIVES
Owner: E. Stanley (Stan) Kroenke
President: Pierre Lacroix, age 49
General Manager: Francois Giguere, age 42
Head Coach: Tony Granato, age 44
Assistant Coach: Jacques Cloutier, age 44
SVP Communications and Team Services: Jean Martineau
SVP Sports Finance: Mark Waggoner
VP Community Relations: Deb Dowling-Canino
VP Player Personnel: Michel Goulet
Chief Scout: Jim Hammett
Senior Director of Human Resources: Cheryl Miller
Director of Hockey Operations: Eric Lacroix
Director of Player Development: Craig Billington
Director of Player Personnel: Brad Smith

LOCATIONS
HQ: Colorado Avalanche, LLC
Pepsi Center, 1000 Chopper Circle,
Denver, CO 80204
Phone: 303-405-1100   **Fax:** 303-575-1920
Web: www.coloradoavalanche.com

The Colorado Avalanche play at the 18,000-seat capacity Pepsi Center in Denver.

PRODUCTS/OPERATIONS

Championship Trophies
Stanley Cup (1996, 2001)
Clarence S. Campbell Bowl (1996, 2001)
Presidents' Trophy (1997, 2001)

COMPETITORS
Calgary Flames
Edmonton Oilers
Minnesota Wild
Vancouver Canucks

HISTORICAL FINANCIALS
Company Type: Private

Income Statement
FYE: June 30

	REVENUE ($ mil.)	NET INCOME ($ mil.)	NET PROFIT MARGIN	EMPLOYEES
6/07	79	—	—	—
6/06	81	—	—	—
6/05	0	—	—	—
6/04	99	—	—	—
6/03	88	—	—	—
Annual Growth	(2.7%)	—	—	—

Revenue History

100				
90				
80				
70				
60				
50				
40				
30				
20				
10				
0	6/03	6/04	6/05	6/06	6/07

Colt's Manufacturing

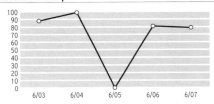

The Colt .45 may have won the West, but it took a New York investment firm to save Colt's Manufacturing from a post-Cold War decline in weapons sales and tough foreign competition. Through its subsidiaries, Colt's Manufacturing makes handguns (Cowboy, Defender) and semi-automatic rifles (M-4). The company has distributors throughout Europe, Asia, and Australia. Founded in 1836 by Samuel Colt, the company is about 85%-owned by investment firm Zilkha & Co., which has been reviving the company since 1994 when it bought the firm out of bankruptcy.

With the firearms industry taking cover from safety and health care expense-related lawsuits filed by cities and counties across the US, Colt's is discontinuing a number of handguns it makes for the consumer market.

The company spun off its "smart gun" division as iColt, but the division closed soon after. Another spinoff, small arms manufacturer Colt Defense, filed papers to go public in 2005 but the IPO did not go forward as planned.

HISTORY

After waiting four years for a patent, Samuel Colt started the Patent Arms Manufacturing Company in 1836 to make his revolutionary handgun, a revolver. The newfangled gun was slow to catch on (the company went bankrupt in 1842), but it gained fame after being adopted by the Texas Rangers. The US Army delegated Capt. Samuel Walker to work with Colt to improve the design, and sales of the resulting "Walker Colt" enabled Colt to set up a factory in Hartford, Connecticut.

In 1851 the company was the first American manufacturer to open a plant in England. Four years later Patent Arms Manufacturing was renamed Colt's Patent Fire Arms Manufacturing Co. Colt was a millionaire when he died in 1862 at age 47.

Colt's introduced the six-shot Colt .45 Army Model, "the gun that won the West," in 1873. More products followed, including machine guns and automatic pistols designed by inventor John Browning. Colt's widow sold the firm to an investor group in 1901.

Business boomed during both world wars, but by the 1940s labor strife and outmoded equipment began to take a toll, and Colt's lost money during the last years of WWII. In 1955 the struggling firm was acquired by conglomerate Penn-Texas. In 1959 Colt's patented the M-16 rifle; in 10 years it sold a million units to the US military.

During the Vietnam War the company flourished, but the 1980s brought low-end competition and shrinking defense orders. Colt's sales were hurt when the US government replaced the Colt .45 as the standard-issue sidearm for the armed forces. A three-year strike prompted the Army to shift manufacturing of its M-16 to Belgium's FN Herstal in 1988.

Two years later Colt's was acquired by private investors and a Connecticut state pension fund and was renamed Colt's Manufacturing. Sales remained flat, however, forcing the company to seek bankruptcy protection in 1992. There Colt's remained until New York investment firm Zilkha & Co. bailed it out in 1994, reorganizing the company. The new management made an offer for rival FN Herstal in 1997, but the deal was blocked by the Belgian government and fell through. Late that year the company won a contract to supply M-4 rifles to the Army.

Colt's bought military weapons specialist Saco Defense, maker of MK 19 and Striker grenade launchers, in 1998. Also that year Steven Sliwa succeeded retiring CEO Ronald Stewart.

As US cities began suing Colt's and other makers of firearms in attempts to recover safety and health expenses attributed to gun violence, the company stepped up lobbying in 1999 and said it would increase gun safety efforts, including development of its "smart gun" technology.

A restructuring in 1999 ended most of Colt's consumer handgun business. It also spun off its smart gun technology as a separate company, iColt. Sliwa left to head iColt, and retired US Marine Lieutenant General William Keys was named president and CEO of Colt's. Also in 1999 Colt's bought Ultra-Light Arms, a maker of upscale hunting rifles, and said it would buy Heckler & Koch, a small arms manufacturer based in Germany. By 2000 the company had withdrawn iColt (investors didn't seem interested in a lawsuit laden industry) and stepped away from the Heckler & Koch deal. The company continues to focus on weapons for the military and police, but in 2001 it lost out to CAPCO Inc. in a bid for a contract to upgrade M-16 rifles used by the Air Force.

EXECUTIVES

Chairman: Donald Zilkha
President and CEO: William M. (Bill) Keys
Director Human Resources: Mike Magouirk
Director Marketing: Mike Reissig
Director Materials: John Ibbotson

LOCATIONS

HQ: Colt's Manufacturing Company, LLC
545 New Park Ave., West Hartford, CT 06110
Phone: 860-236-6311   **Fax:** 860-244-1442
Web: www.coltsmfg.com

COMPETITORS

Browning Arms
Fabbrica D'Armi Pietro Beretta
Glock
Marlin Firearms
Mauser-Werke
Remington Arms
Ruger
SIG
Smith & Wesson Holding

HISTORICAL FINANCIALS

Company Type: Private

Income Statement

FYE: December 31

	REVENUE ($ mil.)	NET INCOME ($ mil.)	NET PROFIT MARGIN	EMPLOYEES
10/07*	12	—	—	86
6/07	12	—	—	86
Annual Growth	0.0%	—	—	0.0%

*Fiscal year change

Revenue History

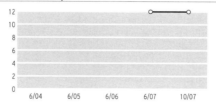

| | 6/04 | 6/05 | 6/06 | 6/07 | 10/07 |

Columbia Forest Products

Columbia Forest Products is one of North America's largest manufacturers of hardwood plywood, veneer, and laminated products as well as hardwood logs. The employee-owned company makes products used in cabinets, architectural millwork, commercial fixtures, and more. Columbia Forest Products specializes in Northern Appalachian hardwoods. Its rotary veneer is used by the cabinetry, door, furniture, and decorative plywood industries. The company sells its products to original equiment manufacturers, wholesale distributors, and mass merchandisers. Columbia Forest Products began in 1957 with a plywood plant in Oregon and has grown to operate around a dozen plants in the US and Canada.

The company sold its wood flooring plants to Mohawk Industries, one of its flooring distributors. The four plants — three in the US and one in Malaysia — had been operating at a loss. Later in 2007 it also closed its Canadian particleboard plant, citing low prices, high energy costs, and reduced demand. However, it said it would spend $3 million on improvements to a hardwood mill that would allow it to increase production.

The company converted all of its veneer-core hardwood plywood plants to formaldehyde-free manufacturing processes in 2005. Its new glues are based on a nontoxic soy-based adhesive. In 2007 Columbia Forest Products became the exclusive distributor of adhesive producer Hercules Inc.'s formaldehyde-free glues to the composite wood industry.

EXECUTIVES

Chairman: Arnold Curtis
President and CEO: Harry L. Demorest
EVP and CFO: Clifford (Cliff) Barry
EVP Special Projects: Ed Woods
EVP Columbia Flooring: Greg Pray
VP Strategic Planning: Phill Guay
VP MIS: Frank Leipzig
President, Plywood and Veneer: Brad Thompson

LOCATIONS

HQ: Columbia Forest Products Inc.
7820 Thorndike Rd., Greensboro, NC 27409
Phone: 336-605-0429
Web: www.columbiaforestproducts.com

PRODUCTS/OPERATIONS

Selected Products

Hardwood logs (cherry, maple, poplar, red oak, walnut, white oak)
Hardwood plywood (aromatic cedar, decorative interior veneers and panels)
Hardwood veneers

COMPETITORS

Georgia-Pacific
Louisiana-Pacific
Norbord
Plum Creek Timber
Potlatch
Roseburg Forest Products
Sierra Pacific Industries
Temple-Inland
West Fraser Timber
Weyerhaeuser

HISTORICAL FINANCIALS
Company Type: Private

Income Statement
FYE: December 31

	REVENUE ($ mil.)	NET INCOME ($ mil.)	NET PROFIT MARGIN	EMPLOYEES
12/07	1,000	—	—	4,500
12/06	1,000	—	—	4,000
12/05	1,050	—	—	4,000
Annual Growth	(2.4%)	—	—	6.1%

Revenue History

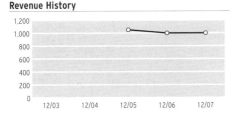

| | 12/03 | 12/04 | 12/05 | 12/06 | 12/07 |

Columbia University

Predating the American Revolution, Columbia University (founded as King's College in 1754) is the fifth-oldest institution of higher learning in the US. With a student population of more than 24,600 and a main campus spread across 36 acres in Manhattan, Columbia's 15 schools and colleges grant undergraduate and graduate degrees in about 100 disciplines, including its well-known programs in journalism, law, and medicine. The Ivy League university's more than 3,500-member faculty has included nearly 70 Nobel laureates, as well as former Vice President Al Gore. Columbia, which operates four sites in New York City and one in Paris, also has a strong reputation for research.

Columbia has forged affiliations with nearby institutions such as Barnard College, Teachers College, and Union Theological and The Jewish Theological seminaries. Columbia-Presbyterian Medical Center, the result of more than 75 years of partnership between Columbia and New York Presbyterian Hospital, helped pioneer the concept of academic medical centers.

Columbia's list of alumni includes such luminaries as Yankee great Lou Gehrig, Supreme Court Justice Ruth Bader Ginsberg, and President Franklin Roosevelt. The university has gone to the alumni well (and others sources) often over the past 10 years, resulting in an endowment valued at about $5 billion.

HISTORY

Created by royal charter of King George II of England, the university was founded in 1754 as King's College. Its first class of eight students met in a schoolhouse adjacent to Trinity Church (in what is now Manhattan). Some of the university's earliest students included Alexander Hamilton and John Jay. King's College was renamed Columbia College in 1784, a name that symbolized the patriotic mind-set of the age.

The college moved to 49th Street and Madison Avenue in 1849. The School of Law was founded in 1858, followed by the predecessor to the School of Engineering and Applied Science in 1864. The Graduate School of Arts and Sciences was established in 1880, and Columbia became affiliated with Barnard College in 1889.

Columbia College became Columbia University in 1896, and the following year it moved to its present location, the former site of the Bloomingdale Insane Asylum. Columbia continued to expand during the early 20th century. It added the School of Journalism in 1912 with funding from publishing magnate Joseph Pulitzer. Other additions included the School of Business (1916), the School of Public Health (1921), and the School of International and Public Affairs (1946).

Dwight Eisenhower became president of Columbia in 1948, retaining the position until becoming President of the United States in 1953. During the late 1960s Columbia gained a reputation for student political action, and in 1968 students closed down the university for several days in protest of the Vietnam War.

Facing financial woes, an escalating New York City crime rate, and contention among its faculty, Columbia struggled to maintain its reputation during the 1970s and 1980s. With this challenge as a backdrop, the university continued to evolve, welcoming its first co-ed freshman class in 1983.

Still facing economic pressures and reductions in government research spending, Columbia was forced to cut costs, eliminating its linguistics and geography departments in 1991. George Rupp became Columbia's president in 1993. Columbia took over operation of the controversial Biosphere 2 laboratory in Arizona in 1996 (the university had been associated with the lab since 1994, when it formed a consortium with other universities to overhaul the ailing science experiment).

By the late 1990s Columbia had begun to recover from its financial and academic decline. Under the leadership of president Rupp, the university improved its fund-raising efforts and became more selective in student admissions. Microsoft founder Bill Gates donated $50 million to Columbia's School of Public Health in 1999 for research into the prevention of death and disability from childbirth in developing countries. That year Columbia created Morningside Ventures, a for-profit company focused on producing educational materials.

The university partnered in 2000 with the British Library, Cambridge University Press, the London School of Economics, the New York Public Library, and the Smithsonian to form another for-profit venture, Fathom.com, a site offering online access to various scholarly resources from each institution. Although the Web site served more than 65,000 people, Fathom.com shut down in 2003. Columbia refocused its online efforts through its Columbia Digital Knowledge Ventures (DKV), a Web site created in 2000, but updated to include e-learning tools in 2003.

In 2001, the National Science Foundation awarded Columbia a $90,000 grant to gather personal accounts and create an oral history piece on the World Trade Center attacks of September 11. In 2002 Columbia University received a pledge of $8 million from Bernard Spitzer for stem cell research to develop new treatments for Parkinson's disease and other neurological disorders. Also that year Lee Bollinger replaced Rupp as president.

EXECUTIVES

Chair Emeritus: David J. Stern, age 66
Chair: William V. (Bill) Campbell, age 68
Vice Chair: Michael E. Patterson, age 57
President and Trustee: Lee C. Bollinger, age 61
Provost: Alan Brinkley
SEVP: Robert A. Kasdin, age 49
EVP Health and Biomedical Sciences:
  Gerald D. Fischbach
EVP Research: David I. Hirsh
EVP Government and Community Affairs:
  Maxine F. Griffith
EVP University Development and Alumni Relations:
  Susan K. Feagin
EVP Finance: Anne R. Sullivan
EVP and Secretary: Jerome Davis
EVP Communications: David M. Stone
EVP Facilities: Joseph A. Ienuso
EVP Student and Administrative Services:
  Jeffrey F. Scott
VP Human Resources: Lucinda (Cindy) Durning
President, New Teachers College: Susan H. Fuhrman, age 64
Dean, Columbia Law School: David M. Schizer, age 36
Dean, Columbia Business School: R. Glenn Hubbard, age 50
Dean, Career Development: Kavita Sharma
General Counsel: Elizabeth J. Keefer
Treasurer: Gail Hoffman
Controller: Cheryl Ross
Auditors: PricewaterhouseCoopers LLP

LOCATIONS

HQ: Columbia University
  2960 Broadway, New York, NY 10027
Phone: 212-854-1754   **Fax:** 212-749-0397
Web: www.columbia.edu

PRODUCTS/OPERATIONS

Schools, Colleges, and Affiliated Institutions

Undergraduate Schools
  Columbia College
  Engineering and Applied Science
  General Studies
    Postbaccalaureate Premedical Program
Graduate and Professional Schools
  Architecture, Planning and Preservation
  Arts
  Arts and Sciences
  Business
  Continuing Education
  Dental and Oral Surgery
  Engineering and Applied Science
  International and Public Affairs
  Journalism
  Law
  Medicine
  Nursing
  Public Health
  Social Work
Affiliated Institutions
  Barnard College
  Jewish Theological Seminary
  Teachers College
  Union Theological Seminary

CompuCom Systems

CompuCom Systems urges clients to leave the IT management to them. The company provides infrastructure management services encompassing desktops, servers, networks, data centers, and security. Its application services include consulting, implementation, and custom development. CompuCom also offers third-party hardware and software management services, handling the procurement, configuration, deployment, and support of products from such providers as Apple, Microsoft, IBM, Hewlett-Packard, and Sun Microsystems. The company markets primarily to medium and large enterprises in North America. Court Square Capital Partners acquired CompuCom for $628 million in 2007.

Court Square purchased CompuCom, along with the managed services business of Vanguard Managed Solutions, from Platinum Equity. It merged Vanguard and CompuCom after the acquisition.

In 2008 CompuCom purchased the North American operations of Netherlands-based IT services provider Getronics. The deal served to significantly increase CompuCom's presence in the US and Canada, as well as in Mexico.

EXECUTIVES

President and CEO: James W. Dixon
COO: Jeffrey E. Frick
CFO: Michael Simpson
SVP, Enterprise Sales: William D. (Bill) Barry
SVP, Human Resources: Joe Valdes
SVP, Transition and Integration: Timothy Shea
SVP, Sales and Service Delivery: Kevin Shank
SVP ITO Business Development: Rocco Musumeche
VP, Marketing: Jim Arnold
Chief Strategy Officer: John F. McKenna
CTO: David W. Hall
Corporate Communications Director:
Stephanie Leonard
President, Application Services Division:
Richard T. (Rick) Jorgenson

LOCATIONS

HQ: CompuCom Systems, Inc.
7171 Forest Ln., Dallas, TX 75230
Phone: 972-856-3600   **Fax:** 972-856-5395
Web: www.compucom.com

COMPETITORS

Accenture	Hewlett-Packard
Agilysys	High Point Solutions
ASI Computer	IBM
Technologies	Ingram Micro
Avnet	Merisel
Bell Industries	MicroAge
Bell Microproducts	MoreDirect
Black Box	New Age Electronics
CDW	Pomeroy IT
CompUSA	SARCOM, Inc.
Computech Systems	Siemens AG
Computer Sciences Corp.	Softmart
CSI Computer Specialists	Software House
Dimension Data	Tech Data
EDS	Unisys
En Pointe	Westcon
GTSI	ZT Group

HISTORICAL FINANCIALS

Company Type: Private

Income Statement

	REVENUE ($ mil.)	NET INCOME ($ mil.)	NET PROFIT MARGIN	EMPLOYEES
12/07	1,500	—	—	7,700

FYE: December 31

Conair Corporation

Counterintelligence has shown that Conair has a place in many bathrooms and kitchens. Personal products by Conair, Rusk, and Jheri Redding include curling irons, hair dryers, mirrors, shavers, and salon products designed for both home and professional salon use. Its garment care products include fabric steamers, irons, and presses. Conair also sells Interplak electric toothbrushes and Scünci hair accessories. Products are sold at discount chains, department stores, and mass merchants (Bed Bath & Beyond, Target, Wal-Mart) throughout the US. Lee Rizzuto, who founded Conair in 1959 with his parents, pleaded guilty to tax evasion in 2002.

The company is a top-selling brand of hair accessories at food, drug, and discount retailers. To secure its spot at the top, Conair has been adding brand names, through acquisitions, to its portfolio. Having bought the Scünci hair accessories business, Conair has been expanding the Scünci brand into hair appliances and taking it to overseas markets. In early 2007 Conair acquired Connecticut's Franzus Company LLC to extend its reach into travel appliances and other items, as well as expand its market into Europe where Conair sells BaByliss haircare appliances.

To increase its domestic and international reach, Conair in September 2007 bought Allegro Manufacturing, based in California. The manufacturer of cosmetic and travel organizer bags had expanded into making diaper bags, bath items, small luggage, and pet accessories in recent years. The deal gave Conair a foothold in more than 20 countries where Allegro trades — such as the UK, France, Mexico, Canada, and Australia — and ownership of Allegro's manufacturing plants in China and the Philippines.

Conair also manufactures and distributes hairstyling appliances (hair dryers, curling irons, and straightening irons) for teen girls marketed under teenage superstars Mary-Kate and Ashley Olsen's eponymous brand. Conair launched its Infiniti line of haircare tools in 2006.

EXECUTIVES

Co-President: Ronald T. Diamond
Co-President: Barry Haber
CFO: Dennis Ling
SVP Finance: Pat Yannotta
SVP Administration: John Mayorek
VP Chemical Product Development: Lou Salce
VP Research and Development: Jules Nachtigal
VP Marketing, New Product Development:
Martin A. Cohen
VP Advertising and Communications: Robert Dixon
VP, Treasurer and Assistant Secretary: John Vele
VP, General Counsel and Secretary: Ricard Margulies

LOCATIONS

HQ: Conair Corporation
1 Cummings Point Rd., Stamford, CT 06902
Phone: 203-351-9000
Web: www.conair.com

PRODUCTS/OPERATIONS

Selected Brands

BaByliss
Conair
ConairPro
Cuisinart
Grand Finale
Interplak
Jheri Redding
Pollenex
Rusk
Scünci
Waring

Selected Divisions and Products

Conair Appliance Manufacturing (worldwide production)
Conair Packaging (health and beauty aid products)
Consumer Toiletries (hair care products)
Cuisinart (kitchen appliances)
Interplak (electric toothbrushes)
Personal Care (hair dryers, curling irons, health and
wellness appliances)
Professional Products (toiletries and appliances for salon
use)
Rusk (hair care products)
Scünci International (hair accessories)
Waring (kitchen appliances)

Selected Subsidiaries

Conair Consumer Products (Canada)
Continental Conair (Hong Kong)

COMPETITORS

Alberto-Culver	Newell Rubbermaid
Applica	Philips Electronics
Claire's Stores	Philips Oral
Global-Tech Appliances	Procter & Gamble
Goody	Revlon
Helen of Troy	Salton
John Paul Mitchell	Spectrum Brands
L'Oréal	The Stephan Co.
National Presto Industries	

HISTORICAL FINANCIALS

Company Type: Private

Income Statement

	REVENUE ($ mil.)	NET INCOME ($ mil.)	NET PROFIT MARGIN	EMPLOYEES
12/07	1,900	—	—	4,060
12/06	1,700	—	—	3,367
12/05	1,488	—	—	3,459
12/04	1,340	—	—	3,331
12/03	1,277	—	—	4,000
Annual Growth	10.4%	—	—	0.4%

FYE: December 31

Revenue History

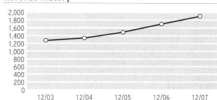

Concentra Inc.

Concentra concentrates on keeping employees healthy. The company's main business is providing occupational health care services through its network of more than 300 medical centers in 40 states, as well as at numerous workplace clinics across the country. Services provided at the centers include pre-employment screening, injury care, vaccinations, and physical therapy. The company also provides a suite of services (which it calls Auto Injury Solutions) to property/casualty insurers, offering bill review, claims processing, and other services related to auto injury cases. Concentra is owned by private equity firm Welsh, Carson, Anderson & Stowe.

Concentra has been paring down its operations geared toward insurers in order to focus on the provision of health care services. In 2007 it sold its workers' compensation services businesses to Coventry Health Care. The divested operations provided medical bill review, repricing, and pharmacy benefit management services to insurers. The same year it spun off its Concentra Network Services division, which provided cost containment services to health insurers, into a newly formed company called Viant. And the previous year it sold First Notice Systems, at the time part of the Network Services unit, to The Innovation Group.

With those divestitures complete, Concentra is focusing its energies on managing and growing its health services business, providing occupational health services through its nationwide group of worksite clinics and standalone medical centers. It is expanding into the realm of urgent care as well, offering walk-in care to the general public at an increasing number of its medical centers.

The company has grown its portfolio of clinics by acquiring occupational health clinics and opening up centers of its own. It bought two clinics in Birmingham in 2007, for instance. It had previously acquired Occupational Health + Rehabilitation, expanding its network by 27 locations into new markets in six states.

EXECUTIVES

Chairman: Daniel J. (Dan) Thomas, age 49, $607,896 pay
CEO: James M. (Jim) Greenwood, age 47, $339,204 pay
President and COO: W. Keith Newton
EVP, CFO, and Treasurer: Thomas E. (Tom) Kiraly, age 48, $359,591 pay
EVP and Chief Medical Officer: W. Tom Fogarty
EVP and General Counsel: Mark A. Solls
SVP Human Resources and Compliance Officer: Tammy S. Steele
SVP Sales and Account Management: Jay B. Blakey
SVP Medical Operations: William R. Lewis
SVP and CIO: Suzanne C. Kosub
SVP Accounting and Finance: Su Zan Nelson
SVP Marketing and Communications: John A. deLorimier
SVP Medical Operations: John R. Anderson
President, Diversified Services Operations: A. Michael McCollum
President, Auto Injury Services: Matthew K. Elges
Auditors: PricewaterhouseCoopers LLP

LOCATIONS

HQ: Concentra Inc.
 5080 Spectrum Dr., Ste. 1200 West, Addison, TX 75001
Phone: 972-364-8000 **Fax:** 972-387-0019
Web: www.concentra.com

PRODUCTS/OPERATIONS

Selected Services

Auto Injury Solutions
On-site medical clinics
Physical exams
Physical therapy
Urgent care
Workers' compensation injury care
Worksite vaccinations and other preventive services

COMPETITORS

Carle Clinic	Hooper Holmes
CorVel	Physiotherapy Associates
Crawford & Company	RTW
eScreen	U.S. Physical Therapy
First Advantage	Walgreen
First Health Group	

HISTORICAL FINANCIALS

Company Type: Private

Income Statement

FYE: December 31

	REVENUE ($ mil.)	NET INCOME ($ mil.)	NET PROFIT MARGIN	EMPLOYEES
12/07	832	—	—	—
12/06	1,299	—	—	11,585
12/05	1,155	—	—	11,285
12/04	1,102	—	—	10,370
12/03	1,051	—	—	10,000
Annual Growth	(5.7%)	—	—	5.0%

Revenue History

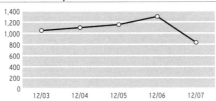

The Conference Board

The Conference Board is as serious as it sounds. The not-for-profit membership organization focuses on increasing the effectiveness of businesses through its nearly 110 member councils. It does research on corporate citizenship and governance, HR issues, and strategic planning and sponsors conferences, makes forecasts, and publishes economic reports and other products. In addition to research and executive action reports, it publishes *The Conference Board Review*, a magazine for senior executives, and newsletters for US, European, and Asian members. The organization traces its roots to 1916 when a group of business leaders banded together to bolster public confidence in business and quiet growing labor unrest.

EXECUTIVES

Chairman: Douglas R. Conant, age 57
Vice Chairman: Josef Ackermann, age 60
Vice Chairman: Harry M. J. Kraemer Jr., age 53
Vice Chairman: Nandan M. Nilekani, age 53
Vice Chairman: Anne M. Tatlock, age 68
CEO: Jonathan Spector

President: Gail D. Fosler, age 60
EVP and COO: Joan S. Dargery
SVP Human Resources and Chief Diversity Officer: Toni L. Riccardi
VP and Chief Economist: Bart Van Ark
General Counsel and Corporate Secretary: Sophia A. Muirhead
Director Communications: Frank Tortorici
Trustee; President and CEO, The Conference Board of Canada: Anne Golden
Auditors: Ernst & Young LLP

LOCATIONS

HQ: The Conference Board, Inc.
 845 3rd Ave., New York, NY 10022
Phone: 212-759-0900 **Fax:** 212-980-7014
Web: www.conference-board.org

HISTORICAL FINANCIALS

Company Type: Not-for-profit

Income Statement

FYE: June 30

	REVENUE ($ mil.)	NET INCOME ($ mil.)	NET PROFIT MARGIN	EMPLOYEES
6/07	61	—	—	300
6/06	56	—	—	200
6/05	51	—	—	—
6/04	46	—	—	210
6/03	44	—	—	—
Annual Growth	8.3%	—	—	12.6%

Revenue History

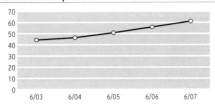

Connecticut Lottery

The Connecticut Lottery gives residents of the Constitution State a chance to amend their incomes. The organization operates a variety of scratch-off instant games and daily numbers games (Cash 5, Nightly Numbers, Play 4). It also offers Classic Lotto twice-a-week jackpot games and the multistate Powerball Lottery. Players who buy Instant Powerball TV Game scratch-off tickets also are eligible to win a chance to get their 15 minutes of fame by competing on *Powerball Instant Millionaire*, a weekly lottery game show operated by the Multi-State Lottery Association. The Connecticut Lottery pays out about 60% of lottery revenue in prizes and about 30% to Connecticut's general fund.

The company has given back more than $5.5 billion to the state's general fund. The Connecticut Lottery employs Cashman + Katz of Glastonbury, Connecticut to manage its $5 million advertising and public relations budget.

EXECUTIVES

Interim CEO and CFO: John A. Ramadei
EVP: Marvin Steinberg
VP Sales and Marketing: Dennis D. Chapman
VP Operations and Administration: Barbara A. Porto
Director Sales: Gloria G. Donnelly
Director Security: Alfred W. Dupuis
Director Information Systems: Michael J. Hunter
Director Communications and Public Relations: Diane Patterson
Director Human Resources: Karen M. Mehigen
Corporate Counsel and Director Government Affairs: James F. McCormack
Drawing Coordinator: Richard Wiszniak
Lottery Ambassador: Bill Hennessey
Auditors: UHY LLP

LOCATIONS

HQ: Connecticut Lottery Corporation
777 Brook St., Rocky Hill, CT 06067
Phone: 860-713-2000   **Fax:** 860-713-2805
Web: www.ctlottery.org

PRODUCTS/OPERATIONS

Selected Games

Cash 5
Classic Lotto
Mid-day 3
Mid-day 4
Play 4
Powerball
Powerball Instant Millionaire
Scratch-off games

COMPETITORS

Loto-Québec
Mashantucket Pequot
Massachusetts State Lottery
New Hampshire Lottery
New Jersey Lottery
New York State Lottery
Pennsylvania Lottery

HISTORICAL FINANCIALS

Company Type: Government-owned

Income Statement

FYE: June 30

	REVENUE ($ mil.)	NET INCOME ($ mil.)	NET PROFIT MARGIN	EMPLOYEES
6/07	979	—	—	130
6/06	994	—	—	130
6/05	960	—	—	130
6/04	912	—	—	120
6/03	858	—	—	120
Annual Growth	3.3%	—	—	2.0%

Revenue History

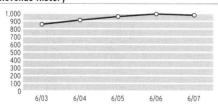

Connell Limited Partnership

Limited partnership, unlimited appetite for growth. Connell Limited Partnership acquires and operates manufacturing companies with growth opportunities in the aluminum alloy and industrial equipment sectors. Connell's primary businesses, Anchor Danly (die sets and die makers' supplies) and Yuba Heat Transfer (heat transfer equipment), serve customers in the aerospace, appliance, automotive, electronics, and power and process industries. Connell started operating in 1987. The company has sold its Wabash Alloys subsidiary (aluminum recycling) to Aleris International.

EXECUTIVES

Chairman: Margot Connell
President and CEO: Francis A. (Frank) Doyle III, age 59
VP and CFO: Kurt J. Keady
VP, Legal and Environmental: John Curtin
VP, Human Resources: Catherine R. Gallagher
VP, Operations: John Andy

LOCATIONS

HQ: Connell Limited Partnership
1 International Place, Boston, MA 02110
Phone: 617-737-2700   **Fax:** 617-737-1617
Web: www.connell-lp.com

Connell Limited Partnership has manufacturing plants in Canada, Mexico, and the US.

COMPETITORS

Aleris International
Anchor Lamina
Commercial Metals

Consolidated Container

Being flexible allowed Consolidated Container to can its former name (Continental Can). Consolidated Container is one of the largest manufacturers of rigid plastic containers in the US. The company markets its products to the dairy, water, agricultural, food, and industrial chemical industries and manufactures containers for a variety of products, including water, milk, ketchup, salsa, soap, motor oil, antifreeze, insect repellent, fertilizers, and medical supplies. Dean Foods and Procter & Gamble are major customers. Consolidated Container was formed when Suiza Foods merged its plastics business with Reid Plastics.

All told, the company operates more than 70 manufacturing plants and produces about 7 billion packages annually.

Other major customers of Consolidated Container include Coca-Cola North America, Colgate-Palmolive, Kroger, Nestlé Waters North America, National Dairy Holdings, PepsiCo, and Scotts.

Consolidated Container expanded its West Coast operations in 2005 by acquiring two California-based companies, Mayfair Plastics and STC Plastics. The next year it acquired two factories from Quintex, a manufacturer of injection-molded and blow-molded plastics. Later in 2006, Consolidated Container bought the assets of Kentucky-based MAB Group, which makes blow-molded plastic beverage bottles.

The company continued its buying streak the following year with agreements to purchase Whitmire Container (two blow-molded plastics plants in the South) and Mesa Industries (nine plants in the Southeast). The Mesa Industries deal was completed in July 2007.

EXECUTIVES

Chairman: James P. (Jim) Kelley
Vice Chairman: B. Joseph Rokus
President, CEO, and Director: Jeffrey M. Greene, $423,077 pay
CFO: Richard P. Sehring, $335,231 pay
SVP General Counsel and Secretary: Louis Lettes, $242,692 pay
SVP Operations Services and Procurement: Robert Keith Brower, $335,692 pay
SVP Beverage and Industrial Container Group: Robert Walton, $295,692 pay
SVP Consumer Packaging Group: Eustace M. Horton
VP Information Services: Beth Duncan
Auditors: Deloitte & Touche LLP

LOCATIONS

HQ: Consolidated Container Company LLC
3101 Towercreek Pkwy., Ste. 300, Atlanta, GA 30339
Phone: 678-742-4600   **Fax:** 678-742-4750
Web: www.ccclc.com

Consolidated Container has 57 manufacturing plants in North America.

PRODUCTS/OPERATIONS

Selected Products

Antifreeze containers
Bleach bottles
Dishwashing liquid bottles
Edible oil containers
Fertilizer containers
Fruit juice bottles
Insect repellent containers
Ketchup bottles
Laundry detergent bottles
Maple syrup containers
Milk bottles
Motor oil containers
Salsa bottles
Water bottles
Windshield wash solvent bottles

COMPETITORS

Ball Corporation
Crown Holdings
Graham Packaging
KRONES
Owens-Illinois
Plastipak Holdings, Inc.
RPC Group
Silgan
Silgan Plastics Corporation

HISTORICAL FINANCIALS

Company Type: Private

Income Statement

FYE: December 31

	REVENUE ($ mil.)	NET INCOME ($ mil.)	NET PROFIT MARGIN	EMPLOYEES
12/07	858	—	—	3,400
12/06	858	—	—	4,000
12/05	846	—	—	3,300
12/04	761	—	—	3,500
12/03	740	—	—	4,000
Annual Growth	3.8%	—	—	(4.0%)

Revenue History

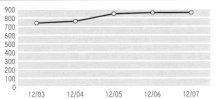

Consolidated Electrical Distributors

Electrical equipment wholesaler Consolidated Electrical Distributors (CED) has US distribution wired. With more than 500 locations nationwide, the family-owned business is one of the largest distributors of electrical products in the country. CED supplies load centers, panelboards, transformers, switches, motor controls, drives, and similar products to residential and commercial contractors and industrial customers. Founded in 1957 as The Electric Corporation of San Francisco, the company has grown by acquiring electrical distributors; since it usually keeps the acquired firm's name and management team, CED now does business under about 80 names. The Colburn family owns CED.

While CED continues to pursue acquisitions, the company's ranking among the leading US electrical distributors has fallen in recent years, as its peers have bulked up bigger with aggressive acquisition strategies. The company now ranks fourth among the biggest distributors, behind Rexel, Inc.; WESCO International, and Graybar Electric. Sonepar USA ranks fifth and is pressuring CED.

In late 2007 CED acquired US Electrical Services and its Electrical Wholesalers subsidiary.

EXECUTIVES

President: H. Dean Bursch
CFO: Jeff Wofford
Secretary: David C. Verbeck
Treasurer: John D. Parish
PC Manager: Mike Uggla

LOCATIONS

HQ: Consolidated Electrical Distributors, Inc.
31356 Via Colinas, Ste. 107,
Westlake Village, CA 91362
Phone: 818-991-9000   **Fax:** 818-991-6842
Web: www.cedcareers.com

Consolidated Electrical Distributors has more than 500 US locations in 45 states.

PRODUCTS/OPERATIONS

Selected Products

Adjustable-frequency drives
Circuit breakers
Control transformers
Load centers
Metering equipment
Motor control centers
Open starters/contractors
Panelboards
Power outlet panels
Pushbuttons
Relays
Safety switches
Starters
Switchboards
Switchgear
Timers
Transformers

COMPETITORS

Anixter International	One Source Distributors
Border States Electric	Premier Farnell
Electrocomponents	Rexel Canada
Fastenal	Rexel CLS
General Cable	Rexel, Inc.
Gexpro	Sonepar USA
Graybar Electric	Stuart C. Irby
HD Supply	SUMMIT Electric Supply
Hubbell	Turtle & Hughes
Kirby Risk	United Electric Supply
McJunkin Red Man	Walters Wholesale Electric
McNaughton-McKay	WESCO International
North Coast Electric	W.W. Grainger

HISTORICAL FINANCIALS

Company Type: Private

Income Statement

FYE: December 31

	ESTIMATED REVENUE ($ mil.)	NET INCOME ($ mil.)	NET PROFIT MARGIN	EMPLOYEES
12/07	3,900	—	—	6,160
12/06	3,280	—	—	5,200
12/05	2,800	—	—	5,200
12/04	2,600	—	—	5,200
12/03	2,300	—	—	5,000
Annual Growth	14.1%	—	—	5.4%

Revenue History

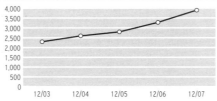

Consumers Union

Consumers Union of United States (CU) inspires both trust and fear. Best known for publishing *Consumer Reports* magazine, the independent not-for-profit organization also serves as a consumer watchdog through other print publications (newsletters and guides), radio and TV reports, and on the Web (ConsumerReports.org). Its subscriber site rates products ranging from candy bars to cars. CU tests and rates thousands of products annually through its National Testing and Research Center, which conducts laboratory testing and survey research. CU accepts no advertising and derives income from the sale of *Consumer Reports* and other services, and from noncommercial contributions, grants, and fees.

CU has revamped its *Consumer Reports* publication with additional content and a new look aimed at improving the magazine's layout and organization. It has also launched a new magazine, *ShopSmart*, aimed at women who want a quick read on consumer items such as food, beauty products, and home and yard products.

The organization testifies before legislative and regulatory entities and files lawsuits on behalf of consumers. CU is governed by an 18-member board. Board members are elected by CU members and meet three times a year. To preserve its independence, CU does not permit its ratings or comments to be used commercially.

EXECUTIVES

President and CEO: James A. (Jim) Guest
EVP: Joel Gurin
SVP Information Products: John J. Sateja
VP and CFO: Richard B. (Rich) Gannon
VP and Technical Director: Jeffrey A. (Jeff) Asher
VP Administration and Human Resources: Richard (Rick) Lustig
VP Publishing: Jerry Steinbrink
VP and Editorial Director: Kevin McKean
VP and CTO: Rahul Belani
VP and General Counsel: Eileen B. Hershenov
Senior Scientist: Edward (Ned) Groth
Senior Director and Controller: Connie Tucker
Senior Director, Treasury and Chief Investment Officer: Eric Wayne
Director, Human Resources: Milca Esdaille
Auditors: KPMG LLP

LOCATIONS

HQ: Consumers Union of United States, Inc.
101 Truman Ave., Yonkers, NY 10703
Phone: 914-378-2000   **Fax:** 914-378-2900
Web: www.consumersunion.org

Consumers Union of United States performs most product tests at its National Testing and Research Center, a renovated warehouse in Yonkers, New York. It has public policy and advocacy offices in Austin, Texas; San Francisco; and Washington, DC, and an Auto Test Division in East Haddam, Connecticut.

PRODUCTS/OPERATIONS

2007 Sales

	$ mil.	% of total
Subscriptions	208.0	81
Investment income	26.3	10
Contributions	18.2	7
Other	2.7	2
Total	**255.2**	**100**

Content Areas
Autos
Electronics
Finance
Health and family
Home

Selected Offerings
Magazines and newsletters
  Consumer Reports Magazine
  Consumer Reports Money Advisor (newsletter)
  Consumer Reports on Health (newsletter)
  ShopSmart
TV and radio
  Consumer Reports on TV (video segments)
  CR Radio (daily radio feature)
Web sites
  ConsumerReports.org

COMPETITORS

Consumers' Research	National Technical Systems
Hearst Corporation	Reader's Digest
International Data Group	Reed Elsevier Group
J.D. Power	Shopping.com
Kelley Blue Book	Underwriters Labs

HISTORICAL FINANCIALS
Company Type: Not-for-profit

Income Statement
FYE: May 31

	REVENUE ($ mil.)	NET INCOME ($ mil.)	NET PROFIT MARGIN	EMPLOYEES
5/07	255	11	4.2%	560
5/06	216	12	5.7%	519
5/05	197	—	—	450
Annual Growth	13.9%	(12.9%)	—	11.6%

2007 Year-End Financials
Debt ratio: 48.3%
Return on equity: 11.6%
Cash ($ mil.): —
Current ratio: —
Long-term debt ($ mil.): 47

Net Income History

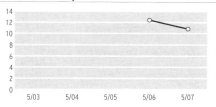

	5/03	5/04	5/05	5/06	5/07

The Container Store

With its packets, pockets, and boxes, The Container Store has the storage products niche well-contained. Its merchandise ranges from backpacks to recipe holders. The home organization pioneer operates about 45 stores in more than 15 states, mostly in major cities in California, Colorado, Georgia, Illinois, Maryland, New York, and Texas. The stores carry more than 9,000 items; the firm's Elfa brand wire shelving (manufactured in Sweden) accounts for about one-fifth of sales. The company touts a low employee-turnover rate, thanks in part to high wages. Founded in 1978, Leonard Green & Partners acquired a majority stake in The Container Store in mid-2007.

Leonard Green & Partners acquired the stake from Garrett Boone, the company's chairman and co-founder, and his family. The deal places The Container Store in the investment firm's portfolio alongside the likes of Rite Aid and Neiman Marcus Group. Leonard Green & Partners, as part of the deal, retained the retailer's top management and will run the company within arm's reach. Employees also have an ownership stake in the company. Boone took on the title of chairman emeritus with the deal.

Boone and CEO Kip Tindell met in 1969 working in a Montgomery Ward paint department and opened their first store in Dallas in 1978.

The Container Store is expanding in new and existing markets, including Little Rock, Arkansas, and in Plano, Texas, the company's home state. New stores are slated to open in Arizona, Minnesota, and Ohio in the fall of 2008.

EXECUTIVES

Chairman Emeritus: Garrett Boone
Chairman and CEO: Kip Tindell
President: Melissa Reiff
CFO: Jodi L. Taylor, age 45
Chief Merchandising Officer and Director: Sharon Tindell
VP and Chief Technology Officer: Thomas (Tom) Birmingham
VP Buying: Mona Williams
VP Marketing: Casey Priest
VP Marketing: Lucy Witte
VP Stores: John Thrailkill
VP Visual Merchandising: Peggy Doughty
VP Stores: Eva Gordon

LOCATIONS

HQ: The Container Store Inc.
  500 Freeport Pkwy., Coppell, TX 75019
Phone: 972-538-6000   **Fax:** 972-538-7623
Web: www.containerstore.com

COMPETITORS

Bed Bath & Beyond	Pier 1 Imports
ClosetMaid	Restoration Hardware
Euromarket Designs	Sterilite
Garden Ridge	Target
Home Depot	Tupperware
IKEA	Wal-Mart
Linens 'n Things	Williams-Sonoma
Newell Rubbermaid	ZAG Industries

CONTECH

CONTECH Construction Products keeps the gutters going. The company makes, distributes, and installs civil engineering products related to environmental storm water, drainage, bridges, and earth stabilization, serving clients working on commercial, industrial, public, and large-scale residential projects. Products range from retaining walls and water-detention vaults to storm water pipes and bridges in a variety of types for vehicular or pedestrian use. CONTECH Construction Products has a national sales organization of more than 350 people, as well. Apax Partners acquired the company in 2006.

CONTECH Construction Products has grown through acquisition, buying about 20 companies since 1999.

The acquisition deal by Apax Partners included roughly $330 million and the assumption of $670 million in debt for a net cost of more than $1 billion. Its acquisition by Apax Partners poises CONTECH Construction Products for further growth, both organically and through acquisitions. The company in 2007 announced plans to make its first overseas acquisition.

Members of the management hold minority ownership interests in the recapitalized firm.

EXECUTIVES

Chairman: Patrick M. Harlow
President and CEO: Ronald C. (Ron) Keating
SVP and CFO: Jeffrey S. (Jeff) Lee
SVP Marketing and Development; President, Stormwater Solutions: Richard G. (Rick) Stepien
SVP and Chief Administrative and Development Officer: Michael M. Rafi
VP Operations: Micheal (Mike) Mihelck
VP and General Counsel: Thomas Singer
Director Human Resources: Karen Luther
Chief Engineer: Darrell Sanders
Media Contact: Jessica Noll
President, CONTECH Sales and Marketing: Steve R. Spanagel
President, CONTECH Bridges and Walls: Thomas P. Slabe

LOCATIONS

HQ: CONTECH Construction Products Inc.
  9025 Centre Pointe Dr., Ste. 400,
  West Chester, OH 45069
Phone: 513-645-7000   **Fax:** 513-645-7993
Web: www.contech-cpi.com

CONTECH Construction Products has regional offices in California, Florida, Georgia, Indiana, Kansas, Maryland, Ohio, Oregon, and Texas; it has operations in all 50 states.

PRODUCTS/OPERATIONS

Selected Products and Brands
Bridges
  BEBO
  CON/SPAN
  Continental
  Steadfast
Hard armor
  A-Jacks
  Armorflex
Retaining walls
  Keystone
Storm water management
  Enviropod
  Optimizer
  StormFilter
  Vortechs

COMPETITORS

Advanced Drainage Systems
Charlotte Pipe & Foundry
Cretex
Hanson Pipe
Lafarge North America
Lehigh Cement
MANCO
Rinker Materials

HISTORICAL FINANCIALS

Company Type: Private

Income Statement

FYE: June 30

	REVENUE ($ mil.)	NET INCOME ($ mil.)	NET PROFIT MARGIN	EMPLOYEES
6/07	950	—	—	2,000
6/06	942	—	—	2,150
6/05	750	—	—	1,819
Annual Growth	12.5%	—	—	4.9%

Revenue History

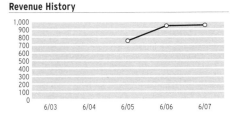

1,000				
900				
800				
700				
600				
500				
400				
300				
200				
100				
0				
	6/03	6/04	6/05	6/06	6/07

ContiGroup Companies

Knowing its place on the food chain, ContiGroup Companies (CGC) focuses on meat production. CGC operates through subsidiary Wayne Farms, a major poultry processor, and Five Rivers Ranch Cattle Feeding, a 50-50 joint venture with Smithfield Foods that is one of the world's largest feedlot enterprises. Overseas, it has interests in flour milling, animal feed production, and pork and poultry processing. CGC's investment arm, ContiInvestments, manages diverse holdings. Chairman and CEO Paul Fribourg (a descendant of founder Simon Fribourg) and his family own CGC.

CGC entered the Five Rivers joint venture with Smithfield Foods in 2005. The two companies combined their respective feedlot operations to form the new entity, which operates 10 cattle feedlots with a capacity of more than 1 million head of beef cattle in Colorado, Idaho, Kansas, Oklahoma, and Texas. CGC contributed six of the 10 feedlots, which were previously operated by its former ContiBeef subsidiary.

Smithfield Foods agreed to sell the Five Rivers feedlot operation to JBS in 2008. In order to make the sale, Smithfield offered to buy CGC's 50% interest in the Five Rivers feed lot operation for some 2 million shares of Smithfield stock.

Overseas, the company has extensive operations including ContiLatin in the Caribbean and Latin America. It owns feed and flour mills in the French West Indies; a flour mill in Haiti (as a joint venture with the Haitian government); a shrimp farm and hatchery in Ecuador; and poultry operations in Peru and Venezuela.

Through its ContiAsia operations, it has businesses in feed milling, animal husbandry, and poultry production and processing in China. Its Asian joint ventures include Conti Chia Tai International, a 50-50 joint venture with Charoen Pokphand, Thailand's largest agricultural company. It operates feed mills and premix plants.

The company's other Asian joint ventures include The Conti Feed (China) Group, which is majority owned by ContiGroup and includes five premix and feed production sites, as well as warehouse and distribution sites; the Great Wall

Northeast Asia Corporation (in which CGC owns a minority interest), consisting of poultry processing plants, feed mills, broiler-breeder farms and hatcheries, and food manufacturing facilities; and ContiAsia Meat Merchandising, headquartered in Hong Kong, which sells frozen poultry, pork and other meat products from the US and other countries. It is the marketing operation for Sanderson Farms and Wayne Farms' poultry products in Hong Kong and China.

ContiInvestments has holdings in food and agribusiness companies, as well as in insurance, health care, financial services, transportation, and computer systems and software.

HISTORY

Simon Fribourg founded a commodity trading business in Belgium in 1813. It operated domestically until 1848, when a drought in Belgium forced it to buy large stocks in Russian wheat.

As the Industrial Revolution swept across Europe and populations shifted to cities, people consumed more traded grain. In the midst of such rapid changes, the company prospered. After WWI, Russia, which had been Europe's primary grain supplier, ceased to be a major player in the trading game, and Western countries picked up the slack. Sensing the shift, Jules and Rene Fribourg reorganized the business as Continental Grain and opened its first US office in Chicago in 1921.

Throughout the Depression the company bought US grain elevators, often at low prices. Through its purchases, Continental Grain built a North American grain network that included major locations like Kansas City, Missouri; Nashville, Tennessee; and Toledo, Ohio.

In Europe, meanwhile, the Fribourgs were forced to endure constant political and economic upheaval, often profiting from it (they supplied food to Republican forces during the Spanish Civil War). When Nazis invaded Belgium in 1940, the Fribourgs were forced to flee, but they reorganized the business in New York City after the war.

Following the war, Continental Grain pioneered US grain trade with the Soviets. The company went on a buying spree in the 1960s and 1970s, acquiring Allied Mills (feed milling, 1965) and absorbing many agricultural and transport businesses, including Texas feedlots, a bakery, and the Quaker Oats agricultural products unit.

During the 1980s Continental Grain sold its baking units (Oroweat and Arnold) and its commodities brokerage house. Amid an agricultural bust, it formed ContiFinancial and other financial units.

Michel Fribourg stepped down as CEO in 1988 and was succeeded by Donald Staheli, the first outside CEO. The company entered a grain-handling and selling joint venture with Scoular in 1991. Three years later Staheli added the title of chairman, and Michel's son Paul became president. Continental Grain sold a stake in ContiFinancial (home equity loans and investment banking) to the public in 1996. Also in 1996 the firm formed ContiInvestments, an investment arm geared toward the parent company's areas of expertise.

That year Continental Grain and an overseas affiliate (Arab Finagrain) agreed to pay the US government $35 million, which included a $10 million fine against Arab Finagrain, to settle a fraud case involving commodity sales to Iraq.

Paul succeeded Staheli as CEO in 1997. The company bought Campbell Soup's poultry processing units that year, and in 1998 it bought a 51% stake in pork producer/processor Premium Standard Farms. Meanwhile, ContiFinancial diversified into retail home mortgage and home equity lending.

Continental Grain sold its commodities marketing business in 1999 to #1 grain exporter Cargill. With its grain operations gone, the company renamed itself ContiGroup Companies.

During 2000 ContiFinancial declared bankruptcy, and ContiGroup sold its Animal Nutrition Division (Wayne Foods) to feed manufacturer Ridley Inc. for $37 million. Later that year Premium Standard Farms doubled its processing capacity with the purchase of Lundy Packing Company. Chairman emeritus Michel Fribourg, the founder's great-great-grandson, died in 2001. That year ContiSea, the salmon and seafood processing joint venture between ContiGroup and Seaboard, was sold to Norway's Fjord Seafood, giving ContiGroup a significant share of Fjord.

To better focus on its food and agribusiness holdings, in 2003 ContiGroup sold off its ContiChem LPG business.

EXECUTIVES

Chairman, President, and CEO: Paul J. Fribourg, age 54
EVP Human Resources and Information Systems: Teresa E. McCaslin
EVP Investments and Strategy and CFO; President, ContiInvestments: Michael J. Zimmerman, age 57
EVP: David A. Tanner
CEO, Wayne Farms: Elton Maddox
SVP and Managing Director, ContiAsia: Nicholas W. Rosa
VP and General Manager, ContiLatin: Brian Anderson

LOCATIONS

HQ: ContiGroup Companies, Inc.
277 Park Ave., New York, NY 10172
Phone: 212-207-5930   **Fax:** 212-207-5499
Web: www.contigroup.com

PRODUCTS/OPERATIONS

Selected Business Units and Operations

ContiAsia (feed milling, pork production, and poultry production; China)
ContiInvestments, LLC (investment management)
ContiLatin (feed and flour milling, poultry operations, and shrimp farming; Caribbean and Latin America)
Five Rivers Ranch Cattle Feeding LLC (joint venture with Smithfield Foods, cattle feedlot operations)
Wayne Farms, LLC (poultry production)

COMPETITORS

ADM	JR Simplot
Agri Beef	Kent Feeds
Alico	King Ranch
AzTx Cattle	Land O'Lakes Purina Feed
Bachoco	National Beef
Butterball	New Market Poultry
Cactus Feeders	Northern Pride
Cagle's	Perdue Incorporated
Cargill	Petaluma Poultry
Cargill Meat Solutions	Pilgrim's Pride
CHS	Ridley Inc.
ConAgra	Rose Acre Farms
Cooper Farms	Sam Kane Beef Processors
Fremont Beef	Sanderson Farms
Golden Belt Feeders	Seaboard
Hormel	Smithfield Beef Group
Iowa Turkey Growers	Smithfield Foods
JBS Swift	Tyson Foods
Jennie-O	U.S. Premium Beef

Continuous Computing

Continuous Computing just wants to ensure steady, continuous communications throughout your entire network. The company provides a variety of software, hardware, and services that telecommunications equipment manufacturers use to deploy communications networks and services. Continuous Computing's products include protocol software, rackmount hardware systems, and platform management software. The company also provides professional services such as consulting, custom development, program management, and training. Continuous Computing was founded in 1998.

EXECUTIVES

Chairman: Randall R. (Randy) Lunn, age 57
President, CEO, and Director: Mike Dagenais
SVP Sales and Field Operations: Brian Brown
VP Corporate Strategy: Garrett Choi
VP, Marketing and Business Development: Brian Wood
VP and Managing Director, Continuous Computing India: Pradeep Malhotra
VP, Engineering: Amit Agarwal
VP, Finance: Bill Dow
VP, General Counsel, and Secretary: Larry Nishnick
VP Manufacturing Operations: Robert Telles
CTO: Michael (Mike) Coward
Chief Engineer and Acting Manager, Embedded Software: Wurzel Parsons-Keir
Principal Architect: Chuck Hill
Principal Architect: James Radley

LOCATIONS

HQ: Continuous Computing Corporation
9380 Carroll Park Dr., San Diego, CA 92121
Phone: 858-882-8800   **Fax:** 858-777-3388
Web: www.ccpu.com

COMPETITORS

Kontron
Mercury Computer
Motorola, Inc.
Performance Technologies
RadiSys

Cooper-Standard Automotive

When it comes to cars, Cooper-Standard Automotive upholds its standards. The company was created when Cooper Tire & Rubber acquired The Standard Products Company (1999) and Siebe Automotive (2000). The company's body and chassis division makes noise, vibration, and heat control systems, as well as interior sealing systems. Cooper-Standard's fluid systems division manufactures various tubes and hoses used in braking, fuel, and emissions systems. Its customers have included automakers Chrysler, Ford Motor, and General Motors. Cooper-Standard Automotive operates about 75 manufacturing facilities worldwide.

An entity formed by private equity firm Cypress Group and Goldman Sachs Capital Part-

ners bought the company from Cooper Tire for $1.17 billion late in 2004.

In 2005 Cooper-Standard agreed to buy the automotive brake and fuel tubing business of ITT Industries for $205 million. The deal was completed early in 2006.

The following year the company agreed to buy a factory in Mexico owned by Ford. Later in 2007 Cooper-Standard bought Metzeler Automotive Profile Systems (MAPS), a maker of automotive sealing systems. MAPS has factories in Belgium, Germany, Italy, and Poland, as well as joint venture operations in China and India.

Early in 2008 Cooper-Standard put the finishing touches on an Indian portion of the (MAPS) deal when it secured a majority interest in Metzeler Automotive Profiles India Pte. Ltd. (MAP India), a maker of automotive sealing systems (Toyoda Gosei is Cooper-Standard's partner in the venture). With the deal Cooper-Standard becomes India's largest maker of automotive sealing systems; it already sits on that throne in North America and China.

As part of the milestone Asian expansion, Cooper-Standard plans to shift away from its two division structure — body and chassis systems and fluid systems — and split its Asian operations off as a separate segment.

EXECUTIVES

Chairman: James S. (Jim) McElya
President and CEO: Edward A. (Ed) Hasler
VP and CFO: Allen J. Campbell
VP Information Technology: Brian J. O'Loughlin
VP, General Counsel, and Secretary: Timothy W. Hefferon
VP Corporate Controller: Helen T. Yantz
VP Investor Relations and Corporate Communications: Scott Finch
VP and Treasurer: Timothy Griffith
President, Global Fluid Systems: Larry J. Beard, age 58
Auditors: Ernst & Young

LOCATIONS

HQ: Cooper-Standard Automotive Inc.
39550 Orchard Hill Place, Novi, MI 48375
Phone: 248-596-5900   **Fax:** 248-596-6535
Web: www.cooperstandard.com

PRODUCTS/OPERATIONS

Selected Products

Fluid Systems
ABS block lines
Chassis brake lines
Engine oil-cooling subsystems
Flexible brake lines
Fuel, brake, and vapor subsystems
Fuel fill/vent hose
Fuel quick connects
Fuel supply and return lines
High-pressure and suspension lines
Hydraulic clutch lines
Noise-reduction technology
Pedal assemblies
Power steering cooler
Power steering quick connects
Power steering reservoir hoses
Pressure and return lines
Rack cylinder tubes
Remote reservoirs
Throttle position sensors
Torque position sensors
Transmission oil-cooling subsystems
Vacuum brake hoses
Vapor control lines

NVH (Noise, Vibration, Heat) Control Systems
Body cushions
Engine mounts
Hydromounts
Powertrain isolators
Torque struts
Transmission mounts
Sealing Systems
Convertible roof sealing
Door seals
Glass run channel assemblies
Hood seals
Inner and outer belt weatherstrip assemblies
Lower door seals
Mirror corner seals
Quarter window trim molding
Sealing systems
Sunroof sealing and trim
Trunk lid seals

COMPETITORS

Aisin Seiki	Robert Bosch
ArvinMeritor	Tenneco
Delphi Corp.	Valeo
Federal-Mogul	Visteon

HISTORICAL FINANCIALS

Company Type: Private

Income Statement				FYE: December 31
	REVENUE ($ mil.)	NET INCOME ($ mil.)	NET PROFIT MARGIN	EMPLOYEES
12/07	2,511	(151)	—	21,123
12/06	2,164	(8)	—	16,266
12/05	1,827	9	0.5%	13,429
12/04	1,859	83	4.5%	13,605
12/03	1,662	—	—	—
Annual Growth	10.9%	—	—	15.8%

2007 Year-End Financials

Debt ratio: 405.2%   Current ratio: —
Return on equity: —   Long-term debt ($ mil.): 1,088
Cash ($ mil.): —

Net Income History

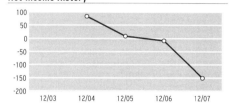

Corbis Corporation

If a picture is worth a thousand words, then Corbis has lots to say. The company's archive of more than 100 million images is one of the largest in the world, along with that of rival Getty Images. Corbis licenses its images — contemporary and archival photography, art, illustrations, and footage — for commercial and editorial use in print and electronic media. Customers can find and license images via the company's Web site. Corbis also offers artist representation (matching photographers with assignments), rights services (securing rights to images controlled by third parties), and media management (hosting of others' digital content). Microsoft cofounder Bill Gates owns Corbis, which he founded in 1989.

Highlights of the Corbis archive include images from Ansel Adams, the Bettmann Collection, the Smithsonian Institution, and the Andy Warhol Foundation.

However, big-name collections like those of Corbis and Getty face a growing competitive threat from so-called microstock agencies, which receive images from amateur photographers and license them for as little as $1 apiece. (By contrast, the average cost of an image from the Corbis collection is about $250.) To keep up, Corbis in 2007 launched the SnapVillage online marketplace, where images cost between $1 and $50. In addition, Corbis is offering licensing options tailored for Internet and mobile phone applications, and in 2007 it expanded its image licensing business by buying Canada-based Veer.

To help generate new sales, Corbis is deploying business development teams in major media markets worldwide. At the same time, it is consolidating many of its customer service functions at centers in Europe and North America and closing some facilities in smaller markets. The changes were part of an effort, announced in 2007, to streamline the company's global sales organization. More than 280 jobs were eliminated, which reduced the company's workforce to about 1,075; in September 2008, Corbis said it would eliminate another 175 jobs over 12 months.

Overall, Corbis has about 20 offices in about a dozen countries in the Asia/Pacific region, Europe, and North America. It does business in more than 50 countries altogether.

The company's growth initiatives are being overseen by a new CEO. Steve Davis stepped down in 2007 after 10 years at the helm and president Gary Shenk succeeded him.

HISTORY

Bill Gates founded Interactive Home Systems (later Continuum Productions) in 1989 and began buying rights to digitize images from museums, archival collections, private collectors, and publications. The company changed its name to Corbis Corporation in 1995 and bought one of the world's largest collections of photos, the Bettmann Collection, which ranges from images of prehistoric cave drawings to the pre-1991 photo library of United Press International. That year it also bought the rights to Russia's Hermitage Museum collection (3 million works). Such moves prompted concern about the extent of Gates' control over world art treasures.

Corbis acquired exclusive rights to works from wilderness photographer Ansel Adams in 1996 (about 40,000 images). Also that year it reached a licensing agreement with the Mariners' Museum in Newport News, Virginia (with 650,000 photographic images). The company lost several key employees in 1997, including CEO Doug Rowan, during its struggle to pin down a strategic direction. Co-presidents Anthony Rojas and Steve Davis replaced Rowan.

Corbis agreed to license the photographs of Jack Moebes in 1998, who captured the southern Civil Rights Movement of the 1960s. The company bought royalty-free digital image provider Digital Stock that year. The next year it more than doubled its collection when it acquired Sygma.

Corbis purchased TempSports (1.8 million images covering worldwide sports events) in 2000. It also launched a documentary film division. It continued to diversify its offerings the next year when it acquired moving image company Sekani.

Corbis opened Corbis Japan as a joint venture with Japanese image provider amana in 2002 to focus exclusively on the Japanese market, leveraging Corbis' own collection of international images with amana's Japanese image collection. That year the company also opened Corbis Germany. Late in 2002 Corbis moved its headquarters from Bellevue, Washington, to Seattle. Rojas stepped down as co-president that year, leaving Davis in charge.

In 2005 Corbis purchased the Roger Richman Agency, a licensing agency representing deceased figures such as Albert Einstein, Sigmund Freud, the Marx Brothers, Steve McQueen, and Vivien Leigh. The acquisition of Roger Richman combined Corbis' existing historical archive images with the ability to secure the rights to license the persona of a dead celebrity; it also was a move toward expansion into the agency business.

After 14 years with Corbis, Davis left the company in 2007 to pursue other interests, and president Gary Shenk was promoted to CEO.

EXECUTIVES

Chairman: William H. (Bill) Gates III, age 52
CEO: Gary Shenk
CFO: Barry Allen
SVP Corporate Development and General Counsel: Jim Mitchell
SVP Rights Services: Mark Sherman
SVP Networks: Nairn Nerland
SVP Sales: Ivan Purdie, age 35
SVP Products: Don Wieshlow
SVP Human Resources: Vivian Farris
VP Branded Content Licensing: David Reeder
VP Sales, Europe: Philippe Bagot
Director Communications: Dan Perlet
Director Marketing, Corbis London: Matt Burgess
Program Manager Marketing: Anne-Sophie Duchamp
Senior Manager Creative Intelligence: Amber Calo
President, Veer: Brad Zumwalt
Auditors: Deloitte & Touche

LOCATIONS

HQ: Corbis Corporation
    710 2nd Ave., Ste. 200, Seattle, WA 98104
Phone: 206-373-6000   **Fax:** 206-373-6100
Web: www.corbis.com

COMPETITORS

AG Interactive
Agence France-Presse
Associated Press
Broadcaster
Getty Images
Jupitermedia
MediaVast
National Geographic
New York Times
PR Newswire
Reuters
Rex Features
Sipa Press
Zuma Press

HISTORICAL FINANCIALS

Company Type: Private

Income Statement				FYE: December 31
	REVENUE ($ mil.)	NET INCOME ($ mil.)	NET PROFIT MARGIN	EMPLOYEES
12/07	76	—	—	1,050
12/06	251	—	—	1,100
12/05	228	—	—	—
Annual Growth	(42.3%)	—	—	(4.5%)

Revenue History

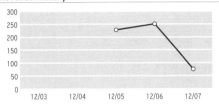

Cornell University

To excel at Cornell, you'll need every one of your brain cells. The Ivy League university has been educating young minds since its founding in 1865. Its more than 20,000 students can select undergraduate, graduate, and professional courses from 14 colleges and schools. In addition to its Ithaca, New York, campus the university has medical programs in New York City and Doha, Qatar. Cornell's faculty includes a handful of Nobel laureates, and the university has a robust research component studying everything from animal health to space to waste management; the university's 20 libraries hold more than 7 million volumes. Notable alumni include author E. B. White and US Supreme Court Justice Ruth Bader Ginsburg.

Cornell awarded the nation's first university degree in veterinary medicine and first doctorates in electrical engineering and industrial engineering. It awarded the world's first degree in journalism (and taught the first university course in that subject), and established the first four-year schools of hotel administration and industrial and labor relations.

EXECUTIVES

Chairman Emeritus: Austin H. Kiplinger
Chairman Emeritus: Harold Tanner
Chairman: Peter C. Meinig
President: David J. Skorton
EVP Finance and Administration: Stephen T. (Steve) Golding
VP Financial Affairs and CFO: Joanne M. DeStefano
VP Human Resources: Mary G. Opperman
VP Information Technologies: Polley Ann McClure
VP Student and Academic Services: Susan H. Murphy, age 56
VP University Communications: Thomas W. Bruce
VP Government and Community Relations: Stephen P. Johnson
Interim Provost: David R. Harris
Dean, Students: Kent L. Hubbell
Dean, Graduate School: Alison G (Sunny) Power
University Counsel and Secretary: James J. Mingle
University Librarian: Anne R. Kenney
University Controller: Anne Shapiro
Chief Investment Officer: James Walsh
Auditors: KPMG LLP

PRODUCTS/OPERATIONS

Selected Colleges and Schools

Undergraduate
College of Agriculture and Life Sciences
College of Architecture, Art, and Planning
College of Arts and Sciences
College of Engineering
School of Hotel Administration
College of Human Ecology
School of Industrial and Labor Relations
Graduate and Professional
College of Veterinary Medicine
Graduate School
Johnson Graduate School of Management
Law School
Weill Graduate School of Medical Sciences (New York City)
Weill Medical College (New York City and Doha, Qatar)

Corporation for Public Broadcasting

This organization is made possible by a grant from the federal government and by support from viewers like you. The Corporation for Public Broadcasting (CPB) is a private, not-for-profit corporation (not a government agency) created by the federal government that receives appropriations from Congress to help fund programming for more than 1,000 member-owned stations of the Public Broadcasting Service, National Public Radio, Public Radio International, and other organizations. The organization's funding is often a political hot potato and frequently a target of officials and critics opposed to government funding of educational, informational, and cultural programming. CPB was created by Congress in 1967.

CPB has struggled in recent years to answer critics' demands that it take a fair and objective stance when funding programming for PBS and other public broadcasting operations. A 2005 report by the CPB inspector general recommended the organization conduct regular reviews of the programs it funds for objectivity and balance, but the "fairness doctrine" has yet to be implemented while the CPB continues to study how such a policy should be created.

The IG report was issued in the wake of allegations that then-chairman Kenneth Tomlinson was improperly using his position to promote certain types of programming. Tomlinson, a Republican, had tried to correct what he considered a liberal bias in public broadcasting by focusing on shows with a conservative slant, including a news program featuring *The Wall Street Journal*'s conservative editorial board. The show aired for about 15 months before PBS pulled the plug; Tomlinson resigned in 2005.

A controversial documentary funded by the CBP called *Islam vs. Islamists* was rejected by PBS in 2007 on the grounds that it fell short of its editorial standards, prompting inquiries from Congress about the use of taxpayer money for projects that never make it to the airwaves. Part of the film, re-titled *Muslims Against Jihad*, was later aired by FOX News.

Taking on much of the heat at CPB is Patricia Harrison, a former co-chairwoman of the Republican National Committee who was named CEO in 2005. Her appointment was criticized on the grounds that she will inject partisanship into the CPB.

Some on Congress have proposed abolishing appropriations for the CBP altogether. However, an effort in 2005 to reduce funding met with such public outcry that the House ultimately restored about $100 million in funds that were originally cut. Contributions from CPB represent about 15% of public broadcasting's revenue.

HISTORY

As commercial radio began to fill the radio dial, the FCC in 1945 reserved 20 channels from 88 FM to 92 FM for noncommercial, educational broadcasts. The first public television station started broadcasting in 1953, and by 1965 there were 124 public TV stations across the country. To help allocate government funds to these public TV and radio stations, Congress created the Corporation for Public Broadcasting (CPB) in 1967. CPB created the Public Broadcasting Service (PBS) in 1969 and National Public Radio (NPR) in 1970.

CPB has always been politically controversial; critics have often charged it with elitism, cultural bias, and liberalism. When Republicans gained control of Congress in 1994, their laundry list of grievances included government cultural spending. They were foiled in their effort to eliminate funding for CPB, however, in part because of public support for public television. Congress still cut funding by $100 million, forcing CPB to reduce its staff by almost 25% and introduce performance criteria for stations seeking grant money, including listenership and community financial support minimums.

Robert Coonrod was promoted to CEO in 1997. The following year Congress approved additional funding to help public television's transition from analog to digital broadcasting. Frank Cruz was appointed chairman of CPB in 1999. At about the same time, increased funding for 2003 (funding is approved two years in advance) was threatened when it was discovered that some PBS stations were giving their mailing lists to the Democratic party for fundraising purposes. Nevertheless, funding for CPB was increased in the 2001 budget.

In late 2001 businesswoman Katherine Milner Anderson was voted in as chairman, taking over for Cruz (who remained on the board). After serving two consecutive terms as chairman, Anderson was replaced by veteran journalist Kenneth Tomlinson in 2003.

CPB's funding was approved at $350 million for 2002 and $365 million for 2003. Coonrod left the company the following year. Former COO Kathleen Cox and CPB agreed to a one-year contract for her to serve as president and CEO. However, she left the post after nine months.

Chairman Tomlinson resigned in 2005 amid allegations that he violated CPB policies by using his position to get funding for programs with a conservative political view. That same year, former Republican National Committee co-chairwoman Patricia Harrison was named the new CEO of the CPB.

EXECUTIVES

Chair: Cheryl F. Halpern
Vice Chair: Gay Hart Gaines
President and CEO: Patricia de Stacy (Pat) Harrison
EVP and COO: Vincent Curren
EVP and Senior Adviser to the President:
Frederick L. DeMarco
Treasurer and CFO: William P. Tayman Jr.
SVP and General Counsel:
H. Westwood (West) Smithers Jr.
SVP Business Affairs: Steven J. Altman
SVP Educational Programming and Services:
Peggy O'Brien
SVP Media: Andrew L. Russell
SVP Television Programming: Greg Diefenbach
SVP Corporate and Public Affairs: Michael Levy
SVP System Development and Media Strategy:
David B. Liroff
SVP Radio: Bruce Theriault
SVP System Development and Media Strategy:
Mark Erstling
VP Public Media Engagement: Cheryl Head
VP Government Affairs: Tim Isgitt
Corporate Secretary: Teresa Safon
Ombudsman: Ken A. Bode
Auditors: PricewaterhouseCoopers LLP

LOCATIONS

HQ: Corporation for Public Broadcasting
401 9th St. NW, Washington, DC 20004
Phone: 202-879-9600 **Fax:** 202-879-9700
Web: www.cpb.org

PRODUCTS/OPERATIONS

Selected Affiliations

American Public Television (programs for public television)
Independent Television Service (independent creative programming for public TV)
National Public Radio (radio programming distribution)
Public Broadcasting Service (TV distribution)
Public Radio International (international radio distribution)

HISTORICAL FINANCIALS

Company Type: Not-for-profit

Income Statement

FYE: September 30

	REVENUE ($ mil.)	NET INCOME ($ mil.)	NET PROFIT MARGIN	EMPLOYEES
9/07	511	(31)	—	100
9/06	510	(6)	—	97
9/05	480	(2)	—	100
9/04	445	11	2.5%	—
9/03	426	30	7.1%	100
Annual Growth	4.7%	—	—	0.0%

2007 Year-End Financials

Debt ratio: 0.0% Current ratio: —
Return on equity: — Long-term debt ($ mil.): 0
Cash ($ mil.): —

Net Income History

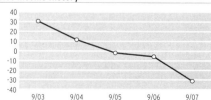

Cox Enterprises

The Cox family has been working at this enterprise for more than 100 years. One of the largest media conglomerates in the US, family-owned Cox Enterprises publishes more than 30 daily and non-daly newspapers through Cox Newspapers, and owns 15 TV stations through Cox Television. It also owns Cox Communications (which was a public company until a Cox Enterprises buyout in late 2004), one of the US's largest cable systems with more than 6 million subscribers. Other operations include 95% of Cox Radio, owner of about 80 radio stations in nearly 20 markets; Manheim, which sells 10 million vehicles through auctions worldwide; marketing subsidiary Cox Target Media; and a majority stake in AutoTrader.com.

Cox Communications is the company's biggest revenue generator (more than half of sales). The company's focus in this arena includes offering more and more broadband Internet services, VoIP (Voice over Internet Protocol) digital telephone services, and digital video recorders and related entertainment-on-demand services.

In addition to its cable system, Cox Enterprises has been spending a lot of money and time driving on the information superhighway. The firm operates AutoTrader.com in conjunction with Manheim, a profitable Internet operation and one of the world's largest used-car auctioneers.

In 2008 the company purchased online advertising firm Adify Corporation for about $300 million. Adify provides technology and services that help clients build and operate targeted ad networks. Later that year Cox announced plans to sell its newspapers in North Carolina, Colorado, and Texas, as well as Valpak, a direct-mail advertising operation that is part of Cox Target Media. The divestiture is part of the company's plan to focus on the Internet and other new technologies.

Ranked on *Forbes'* list of the richest Americans, Anne Cox Chambers, daughter of founder James Cox, controls the company. Her late sister Barbara Cox Anthony (mother of chairman and CEO James Kennedy) died in 2007.

HISTORY

James Middleton Cox, who dropped out of school in 1886 at 16, worked as a teacher, reporter, and congressional secretary before buying the *Dayton Daily News* in 1898. In 1905 he acquired the nearby *Springfield Press-Republican* and then took up politics, serving two terms in the US Congress (1909-1913) and three terms as Ohio governor (1913-1915; 1917-1921). He even ran for president in 1920 (his running mate was future President Franklin Roosevelt) but lost to rival Ohio publisher Warren G. Harding.

Once out of politics, Cox began building his media empire. He bought the *Miami Daily News* in 1923 and founded WHIO (Dayton, Ohio's first radio station). He bought Atlanta's WSB ("Welcome South, Brother"), the South's first radio station, in 1939 and added WSB-FM and WSB-TV, the South's first FM and TV stations, in 1948. Cox founded Dayton's first FM and TV stations

(WHIO-FM and WHIO-TV) the next year, and *The Atlanta Constitution* joined his collection in 1950. Cox died in 1957.

The company continued to expand its broadcasting interests in the late 1950s and early 1960s. It was one of the first major broadcasting companies to expand into cable TV when it purchased a system in Lewistown, Pennsylvania, in 1962. The Cox family's broadcast properties were placed into publicly held Cox Broadcasting in 1964. Two years later its newspapers were placed into privately held Cox Enterprises, and the cable holdings became publicly held Cox Cable Communications. The broadcasting arm diversified, buying Manheim Services (auto auctions, 1968), Kansas City Automobile Auction (1969), and TeleRep (TV ad sales, 1972).

Cox Cable had 500,000 subscribers in nine states when it rejoined Cox Broadcasting in 1977. Cox Broadcasting was renamed Cox Communications in 1982, and the Cox family took the company private again in 1985, combining it with Cox Enterprises. James Kennedy, grandson of founder James Cox, became chairman and CEO in 1987.

Expansion became the keyword for Cox in the 1990s. The company merged its Manheim unit with the auto auction business of Ford Motor Credit and GE Capital in 1991. It also formed Sprint Spectrum in 1994, a partnership with Sprint, TCI (now part of AT&T), and Comcast to bundle telephone, cable TV, and other communications services (Sprint bought out Cox in 1999). Then, in one of its biggest transactions, Cox bought Times Mirror's cable TV operations for $2.3 billion in 1995 and combined them with its own cable system into a new, publicly traded company called Cox Communications. The following year it spun off its radio holdings into a public company called Cox Radio.

To expand its online presence, the company formed Cox Interactive Media in 1996, establishing a series of city Web sites and making a host of investments in various Internet companies, including Career Path, ExciteHome, iVillage, MP3.com, and Tickets.com. Cox also applied the online strategy to its automobile auction businesses, establishing AutoTrader.com in 1998 and placing the Internet operations of Manheim Auctions (now just Manheim) into a new company, Manheim Interactive, in 2000.

In 2002 Cox dropped plans to expand its local Internet city guide business nationwide and moved its Interactive Media operations to other parts of the company. Two years later, fed up with the demands of running a publicly traded cable company, Cox bought the 38% of Cox Communications that it didn't already own for $8.5 billion.

EXECUTIVES

Chairman and CEO; Chairman, Cox Communications and Cox Radio: James C. Kennedy, age 60
Vice Chairman: G. Dennis Berry, age 63
President and COO: Jimmy W. Hayes, age 55
EVP and CFO: John M. Dyer, age 53
EVP Administration: Timothy W. (Tim) Hughes
SVP Finance: Richard J. Jacobson
SVP Investments and Administration: John G. Boyette
SVP Strategic Investments and Real Estate Planning: Dale Hughes
SVP Human Resources: Marybeth H. Leamer

VP and Controller: David J. Head
VP Government Affairs: Joab M. (Joey) Lesesne III
VP and CIO: Gregory B. (Greg) Morrison
VP and Treasurer: Susan W. Coker
VP and General Tax Counsel: Preston B. Barnett
VP Corporate Communications and Public Affairs: Roberto I. Jimenez
VP Business Development: J. Lacey Lewis
VP Legal Affairs, General Counsel, and Corporate Secretary: Andrew A. (Andy) Merdek
VP Marketing: Deborah E. (Debby) Ruth
Senior Director, Marketing and Creative Services: Winston Warrior
President, Cox Newspaper and Cox Auto Trader: Sanford H. (Sandy) Schwartz, age 55
President and CEO, Cox Radio: Robert F. (Bob) Neil, age 49
President and CEO, Manheim Auctions: Dean H. Eisner
President, Cox Communications: Patrick J. (Pat) Esser
President, Cox Television: Andrew S. Fisher

LOCATIONS

HQ: Cox Enterprises, Inc.
6205 Peachtree Dunwoody Rd., Atlanta, GA 30328
Phone: 678-645-0000   **Fax:** 678-645-1079
Web: www.coxenterprises.com

PRODUCTS/OPERATIONS

2007 Sales

	$ mil.	% of total
Cox Communications	8,300	55
Manheim	3,300	22
Cox Newspapers	1,400	9
Cox Television	670	5
AutoTrader.com	918	6
Cox Radio	445	3
Total	**15,033**	**100**

Selected Operations

Cox Communications (cable television systems)
Manheim (online auto auctions)
Cox Newspapers
  Daily Newspapers
    The Atlanta Journal-Constitution
    Austin American-Statesman (Texas)
    Dayton Daily News (Ohio)
    The Daily Advance (Elizabeth City, NC)
    The Daily Reflector (Greenville, NC)
    The Daily Sentinel (Grand Junction, CO)
    The Daily Sentinel (Nacogdoches, TX)
    Longview News-Journal (Texas)
    The Lufkin Daily News (Texas)
    The Middleton Journal (Ohio)
    News Messenger (Marshall, TX)
    Palm Beach Daily News (Florida)
    The Palm Beach Post (Florida)
    Rocky Mount Telegram (North Carolina)
    Springfield News Sun (Ohio)
    Waco Tribune-Herald (Texas)
  Cox Custom Media (commercial newsletters)
  PAGAS Mailing Services
  Valpak (direct mail advertisements)
Cox Television
  Television Stations
    KFOX (El Paso, TX; FOX)
    KICU (San Francisco/San Jose, CA; independent)
    KIRO (Seattle, CBS)
    KRXI (Reno, NV; FOX)
    KTVU (Oakland/San Francisco, CA; FOX)
    PCNC (cable channel, Pittsburgh, independent)
    WAXN (Charlotte, NC; independent)
    WFTV (Orlando, FL; ABC)
    WHIO (Dayton, OH; CBS)
    WJAC (Johnstown, PA; NBC)
    WPXI (Pittsburgh, NBC)
    WRDQ (Orlando, FL; independent)
    WSB-TV (Atlanta, ABC)
    WSOC (Charlotte, NC; ABC)
    WTOV (Steubenville, OH; NBC)
Cox AutoTrader (automobile classified publications and sites)

Cox Radio
 Atlanta (WBTS-FM, WSB-AM, WSB-FM)
 Birmingham, AL (WBHJ-FM, WBHK-FM, WZZK-FM)
 Bridgeport/New Haven, CT (WEZN-FM)
 Dayton, OH (WHIO-AM, WHKO-FM)
 Greenville/Spartanburg, SC (WJMZ-FM)
 Honolulu (KRTR-FM, KXME-FM)
 Houston (KLDE-FM)
 Jacksonville (WAPE-FM, WFYV-FM, WKQL-FM)
 Long Island, NY (WBAB-FM, WBLI-FM)
 Louisville, KY (WRKA-FM, WVEZ-FM)
 Miami (WEDR-FM, WHQT-FM)
 New Haven, CT (WPLR-FM)
 Orlando, FL (WHTQ-FM, WWKA-FM)
 Richmond, VA (WKLR-FM)
 San Antonio (KCYY-FM, KISS-FM, KONO-FM)
 Stamford/Norwalk, CT (WEFX-FM, WNLK-AM)
 Tampa (WDUV-FM, WWRM-FM)
 Tulsa, OK (KRAV-FM, KRMG-AM, KRTQ-FM, KWEN-FM)

COMPETITORS

Advance Publications
Belo Corp.
CBS Corp
Clear Channel
Columbus Fair Auto Auction
Comcast
D-A Auto Auction
Disney
E. W. Scripps
Gannett
Hearst Corporation
McClatchy Company
Media General
Morris Communications
New York Times
News Corp.
Ticketmaster
Time Warner Cable
Tribune Company
Washington Post

HISTORICAL FINANCIALS

Company Type: Private

Income Statement

FYE: December 31

	REVENUE ($ mil.)	NET INCOME ($ mil.)	NET PROFIT MARGIN	EMPLOYEES
12/07	15,033	—	—	81,693
12/06	13,200	—	—	80,000
12/05	12,000	—	—	77,000
12/04	11,552	—	—	77,000
12/03	10,700	—	—	77,000
Annual Growth	8.9%	—	—	1.5%

Revenue History

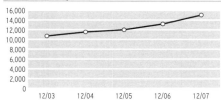

Crain Communications

These Crains have been whooping it up in the publishing business for almost 100 years. Crain Communications publishes some 30 business, consumer, and trade journals worldwide, mostly in North America and Europe. Its portfolio includes *AutoWeek, TelevisionWeek,* and *RCR Wireless News,* as well as its flagship publication *Advertising Age.* Crain also publishes business journals in four major US cities (Chicago, Cleveland, Detroit, and New York City), operates trade shows, and publishes trade content online. Its Crain News Service provides business news and information to other media outlets. The founding Crain family continues to own and operate the company.

Crain Communications has built up its stable of trade journals over time, focusing on, and in most cases ultimately dominating, particular niche markets. Its *AutoWeek* and *Automotive News* are must-reads for anyone following the auto manufacturing industry, *Pensions & Investments* is the go-to source for financial services professionals, and *Advertising Age* (also known by the shortened moniker *AdAge*) is the bible for creatives and marketers.

The company has continued to expand its portfolio of titles, launching *Business Insurance Europe* in 2006. The following year, Crain acquired *Plastics & Rubber Weekly* along with several industry conferences from UK-based trade publisher Emap. Also in 2007, the company shuttered two underperforming international publications, *Crain's Mexico* and *Crain's Monterrey.*

EXECUTIVES

Chairman; Publisher and Editor-in-Chief, Automotive News, Automotive News Europe, and Crain's Detroit Business; Editor-in-Chief, AutoWeek, Plastics News, Rubber & Plastics News, Tire Business, and Waste News: Keith E. Crain
President; Editor-in-Chief, Advertising Age, Crain's Chicago Business, Crain's New York Business, and TelevisionWeek: Rance E. Crain
EVP Operations: William A. (Bill) Morrow
SVP and Group Publisher: Gloria Scoby
Group VP Technology, Manufacturing, and Circulation: Robert C. (Bob) Adams
VP Distribution: Joyce McGarvy
VP Finance: Thomas M. (Tom) Marantette Jr.
VP Human Resources: Laura Anger
VP Manufacturing and Production: Dave Kamis
CIO: Paul Dalpiaz
Director Corporate Circulation: Patrick Sheposh
Secretary and Assistant Treasurer: Merrilee P. Crain
Treasurer and Assistant Secretary: Mary Kay Crain

LOCATIONS

HQ: Crain Communications Inc
 1155 Gratiot Ave., Detroit, MI 48207
Phone: 313-446-6000 **Fax:** 313-446-1616
Web: www.crain.com

Crain Communications has more than a dozen offices in Akron and Cleveland, Ohio; Boston; Chicago; Denver; Detroit; Irvine, Los Angeles, and San Francisco, California; Nashville, Tennessee; New York City; and Washington, DC; and in London, Munich, and Tokyo.

PRODUCTS/OPERATIONS

Selected Publications

Advertising Age
American Coin-Op
American Drycleaner
American Laundry News
Automobilwoche (Germany)
Automotive News
AutoWeek
BtoB
Business Insurance
Crain's Chicago Business
Crain's Cleveland Business
Crain's Detroit Business
Crain's New York Business
Creativity
European Rubber Journal
FinancialWeek
InvestmentNews
Modern Healthcare
Pensions & Investments
Plastics News
RCR Wireless News
Rubber & Plastics News
TelevisionWeek
Tire Business
Urethanes Technology International
Waste News
Workforce Management

COMPETITORS

Advanstar	Lebhar-Friedman
American City Business Journals	McGraw-Hill
	Nielsen Business Media
Dow Jones	Penton Media
Forbes	Reed Business
Informa	

Crown Equipment

The jewels in the crown of Crown Equipment Corporation are electric heavy-duty lift trucks used for maneuvering goods in warehouses and distribution centers. A market leader, the company's products include narrow-aisle stacking equipment, powered pallet trucks, and forklift trucks. Its equipment can move 4-ton loads and stack pallets nearly 45 feet high. Crown Equipment sells its products globally through retailers. The company, founded in 1945 by brothers Carl and Allen Dicke, originally made temperature controls for coal furnaces. It began making material-handling equipment in the 1950s. The Dicke family still controls Crown Equipment.

Crown offers customers a wide range of electric fork lift trucks (from hand pallet trucks to very narrow-aisle (VNA) turret trucks) and extensive maintenance and repair services through its global dealer network.

EXECUTIVES

Chairman Emeritus: James F. Dicke
Chairman and CEO: James F. Dicke II, age 60
President: James F. Dicke III, age 35
SVP, Manufacturing: David J. Besser
SVP: Donald E. Luebrecht
SVP: James D. Moran

VP and CFO: Kent W. Spille
VP and General Counsel: John G. Maxa
VP, Human Resources: Randall W. (Randy) Niekamp
VP, Development and Information Services:
 Mark A. Manuel
VP International Accounts: David J. Kerr
VP, Manufacturing Operations: David L. Beddow
Auditors: Deloitte & Touche

LOCATIONS

HQ: Crown Equipment Corporation
 44 S. Washington St., New Bremen, OH 45869
Phone: 419-629-2311   **Fax:** 419-629-2900
Web: www.crown.com

PRODUCTS/OPERATIONS

Selected Products

Hand pallet trucks
Narrow-aisle reach trucks
Rider pallet trucks
Sit-down counterbalanced trucks
Stand-up counterbalanced trucks
Stockpickers
Tow tractors
Walkie pallet trucks
Walkie stackers

COMPETITORS

Briggs Equipment
Cascade Corporation
Caterpillar
CLARK Material
Hyundai Heavy Industries
Jungheinrich
Komatsu
Linde Material Handling
NACCO Industries
NACCO Materials Handling
Nissan Forklift
Toyota Material Handling

Cumberland Farms

Once a one-cow dairy, Cumberland Farms now operates a network of about 1,000 convenience stores and gas stations in about a dozen eastern seaboard states from Maine to Florida. The company operates its own grocery distribution and bakery operations to supply its stores, as well. Cumberland owns a two-thirds limited partnership in petroleum wholesaler Gulf Oil, giving it the right to use and license Gulf trademarks in Delaware, New Jersey, New York, most of Ohio, Pennsylvania, and the New England states. The first convenience-store operator in New England, Cumberland was founded in 1939 by Vasilios and Aphrodite Haseotes. The Haseotes' children, including chairman Lily Haseotes Bentas, own the company.

In August 2008 Joseph Petrowski was appointed CEO of the company and Bentas assumed the position of chairman.

The company's Wholesale Petroleum Division, its partnership with Gulf Oil, has given it a more than 300-strong network of franchised Gulf and Exxon gasoline stations.

EXECUTIVES

Chairman: Lily Haseotes Bentas
CEO: Joseph H. (Joe) Petrowski
President and COO: Harry J. Brenner
SVP, Retail Operations: Daniel D. Phaneuf
VP and Corporate Controller: William Barnes
VP, Information Technology: John Carroll
VP Human Resources: Patricia Firing
**Chief Legal and Administrative Officer, General
 Counsel, and Corporate Secretary:** Mark G. Howard
Corporate Marketing Manager: Mike Esposito
Manager, Fleet Administration Department:
 Edward Potkay
Manager Training Systems and Development:
 Sheree Beissner
Administrative Secretary: Debra Sprout
Senior Corporate Recruiting and Staffing Supervisor:
 Stephen Dolinich
President, Cumberland Farms Retail: Ari Haseotes
President and CEO, Gulf Oil: Ronald R. (Ron) Sabia

LOCATIONS

HQ: Cumberland Farms, Inc.
 777 Dedham St., Canton, MA 02021
Phone: 781-828-4900   **Fax:** 781-828-9624
Web: www.cumberlandfarms.com

PRODUCTS/OPERATIONS

Selected Operations

Convenience stores
Gas stations
Grocery distribution
Bakery operations
Gas wholesaler

COMPETITORS

7-Eleven	Golub
BP	Motiva Enterprises
Chevron	Racetrac Petroleum
DeMoulas Super Markets	Sheetz
Exxon	Stewart's Shops
Gate Petroleum	Stop & Shop
Getty Realty	Wawa, Inc.

CUNA Mutual

CUNA Mutual knows a thing or two about credit unions, having served them and their members since 1935. The company provides insurance (such as credit insurance and health benefit packages) for the credit unions themselves, as well as consumer products like homeowners and crop insurance that the institutions can offer to members. Participants in CUNA Mutual's MemberCONNECT program, for instance, can offer auto and homeowners insurance provided jointly by CUNA and its partner Liberty Mutual. CUNA also provides credit unions with software and marketing support for bringing in new members and advisory services for growing their investments. It operates throughout the US and in some foreign markets.

Under CEO Jeff Post (appointed in 2005), CUNA Mutual has streamlined its business in response to a consolidating marketplace and revamped its sales and customer service operations. In addition to reducing its workforce and outsourcing some jobs, it opened a new customer operations center in Fort Worth and reorganized its sales team so that each of its credit union customer accounts

has a single sales contact. It also merged two of its insurance subsidiaries, CUNA Mutual Insurance Society and CUNA Mutual Life Insurance, in 2007 to realize tax savings.

Additionally, the company has been expanding its products and services offered to credit unions and their members. It introduced specialized crop insurance in 2006, partnering with Texas-based crop insurer Producers Ag Insurance Group (Pro Ag); CUNA Mutual acquired a minority stake in Pro Ag in 2007. It also expanded its partnership with Liberty Mutual in 2007 to offer workers' compensation insurance to its credit union customers, and it has plans to expand its product offering in the areas of retirement plans, student loans, auto loans, and agricultural insurance.

CUNA Mutual established a new European headquarters in Dublin in 2008 and announced expansion plans in Europe. It has other international operations in Australia, Canada, Latin America, and South Korea.

The company has had contentious relations with its Wisconsin-based union employees, who have balked at repeated workforce reductions and movement of union jobs out of Wisconsin. The union (the Office and Professional Employees Union) and CUNA Mutual signed a four-year contract in 2008 designed to patch up some of their differences.

EXECUTIVES

Chairman: Loretta M. Burd
Vice Chairman: C. Alan Peppers
President, CEO, and Director: Jeff Post
EVP and CFO: Jeffrey D. (Jeff) Holley
EVP and Chief Products Officer: David Lundgren
EVP and Chief Sales Officer: Robert (Bob) Trunzo
EVP and Chief Investment Officer: David Marks
SVP Customer Operations: Rick R. Roy
**SVP Consumer Products and Head, Consumer
 Insurance:** Andy Napoli
SVP and Chief Ethics and Compliance Officer:
 Steve Koslow
VP Human Resources and Talent Acquisition:
 Ryan Dull
VP Communications: Jim Buchheim
CIO: Tom Gosnell
Auditors: Deloitte & Touche LLP

LOCATIONS

HQ: CUNA Mutual Group
 5910 Mineral Point Rd., Madison, WI 53705
Phone: 608-238-5851
Web: www.cunamutual.com

PRODUCTS/OPERATIONS

2007 Sales

	$ mil.	% of total
Life & health premiums	1,262	45
Property/casualty premiums	712	25
Net investment income	452	16
Net realized investment losses	(70)	—
Contract charges	82	3
Other	303	11
Total	**2,741**	**100**

Selected Products and Services

Products and services for credit union members
 CU Choice Lending Protection
 CUNA Brokerage Services
 IRA services
 Loanliner.com (Internet lending)
 MemberCONNECT auto and homeowners insurance
 Member's Choice credit life and disability insurance
 Mortgage insurance
 Trust services

Products and services for credit unions
  Business auto insurance
  Credit union bonds
  Executive benefit packages
  Group health and life insurance
  Investment advisory services
  Loan marketing programs
  Retirement plans
  Risk management services
  Workers' compensation insurance

COMPETITORS

Bankers Bank
Nexity
Online Resources
PrimeVest
SEI Investments
U.S. Central

HISTORICAL FINANCIALS
Company Type: Mutual company

Income Statement   FYE: December 31

	ASSETS ($ mil.)	NET INCOME ($ mil.)	INCOME AS % OF ASSETS	EMPLOYEES
12/07	15,202	184	1.2%	4,500
12/06	15,046	187	1.2%	5,500
12/05	14,574	124	0.9%	5,500
12/04	14,004	136	1.0%	6,000
12/03	12,885	134	1.0%	6,000
Annual Growth	4.2%	8.2%	—	(6.9%)

2007 Year-End Financials

Equity as % of assets: 11.8%   Long-term debt ($ mil.): 0
Return on assets: 1.2%   Sales ($ mil.): 2,741
Return on equity: 10.0%

Net Income History

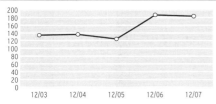

Cutter & Buck

Relatively unknown less than a decade ago, Cutter & Buck has climbed onto the leader board of the nation's top makers of golf apparel. Cutter & Buck sells men's and women's golf apparel and other sportswear through golf pro shops, resorts, and specialty stores throughout North America, as well as to corporate accounts. It sells its products in other countries through distributors. Most of its sales come from men's apparel. Cutter & Buck divides its apparel into two lines: the ephemeral fashion line, with brighter colors, and the seasonless and less-expensive classics line. Its corporate marketing division puts company logos on products for corporate golf events and recognition programs. New Wave Group AB owns the company.

Cutter & Buck aims to please both experienced golfers and those who don't know the difference between a birdie and a bogey. The company has stared down the rival lines of Greg Norman (by Reebok) and Jack Nicklaus by making attire featuring natural fabrics, detailed embroidery, and a casual look that can be worn on the golf course as well as at the office or for casual occasions unrelated to the sport. Its Annika Collection is named after famed golfer Annika Sorenstam and features colorful women's golf attire.

The company's executive ranks were reshuffled in early 2006, when CEO Tom Wyatt resigned. Ernie Johnson, then SVP and CFO with 30 years in finance and operations, was appointed to replace him.

Sweden-based New Wave Group AB acquired the company in 2007 for $156 million, in order to boost its upscale golf offerings. New Wave Group plans to give Cutter & Buck a stronger presence in Europe.

Taking advantage of greater customer awareness of environmental issues, the company began selling organic cotton shirts in 2008 for a price slightly higher than non-organic cotton shirts.

EXECUTIVES

Chairman: Douglas G. (Doug) Southern, age 63
CEO and Director: Ernest R. (Ernie) Johnson, age 55, $242,426 pay (prior to promotion)
President: Tim Cronin
VP, CFO, and Secretary: Michael Gats, age 49, $169,339 pay
VP, Design and Merchandising: Julie Snow, age 37, $209,242 pay
VP and General Manager, Golf, Corporate, International/Domestic Licensing: Brian C. Thompson, age 38, $211,099 pay
VP, Global Sourcing and Distribution: Jon P. Runkel, age 49, $164,509 pay (prior to promotion)
Auditors: Ernst & Young LLP

LOCATIONS

HQ: Cutter & Buck Inc.
  701 N. 34th St., Ste. 400, Seattle, WA 98103
Phone: 206-830-6812   **Fax:** 206-448-0589
Web: www.cutterbuck.com

COMPETITORS

Ashworth
Hartmarx
J. Crew
Lands' End
Nautica Enterprises
NIKE
Perry Ellis International
Phillips-Van Heusen
Polo Ralph Lauren
PremiumWear
Reebok
Sport-Haley
Tommy Hilfiger

Dairy Farmers of America

The members of the Dairy Farmers of America (DFA) are partners in cream. DFA is one of the world's largest dairy cooperatives, with more than 18,000 members in 48 US states. The co-op produces some 34% of the US milk supply with an annual pool of more than 61 billion pounds of milk. Along with fresh and shelf-stable fluid milk, the co-op also produces cheese, butter, whey, dried milk powder, and other dairy products for industrial, wholesale, and retail customers worldwide. DFA seeks strength by adding value-added products and looks for joint ventures to distribute its milk and milk-based food ingredients to wider regions.

DFA is a major supplier to the #1 US milk processor, Dean Foods. It also owns 50% of another US milk powerhouse, National Dairy Holdings. DFA's American Dairy Brands group makes and markets Borden cheeses, and its Formulated Dairy Food Products group bottles up Starbucks' Frappuccino coffee drink. In addition, the co-op provides marketing, research and development, and legislative lobbying on behalf of its members.

American dairy farmers have had to come to terms with consolidation in the retail industry, dissolving government milk price supports, and increased foreign competition. To better compete with other dairy processors and soften the swings of the commodity markets, DFA has invested heavily in facilities and joint ventures to process its fluid milk into value-added products and high-end dairy-based ingredients.

DFA's sheer size makes it a frequent target of antitrust investigations. Investigations have sought, for example, to determine if the cooperative bullied farmers and smaller cooperatives to join it, and paid out below-market prices to its members.

HISTORY

Mid-America Dairymen (Mid-Am), the largest of the cooperatives that merged to form Dairy Farmers of America (DFA), was born in 1968. At that time, several Midwestern dairy co-ops banded together to attack common economic problems, such as reduced government subsidies, price drops resulting from a rising milk surplus, dealer consolidation, and improvements in production, processing, and packaging. The merging organizations — representing 15,000 dairy farmers — were Producers Creamery Company (Springfield, Missouri), Sanitary Milk Producers (St. Louis), Square Deal Milk Producers (Highland, Illinois), Mid-Am (Kansas City, Missouri), and Producers Creamery Company of Chillicothe (north central Missouri).

During the early 1970s Mid-Am struggled with internal restructuring. Most dairy farmers and co-ops were hit hard by the energy crisis and the government's decision to allow increased dairy imports in 1973, the same year the US Justice Department filed an antitrust suit against Mid-Am. (A judge cleared the co-op 12 years later.)

In 1974 Mid-Am lost almost $8 million on revenues of $625 million, chalked up to record-high feed prices, a weakened economy, a milk surplus, and a massive inventory loss. Co-op veteran Gary Hanman was named CEO that year. Over the next two years, Mid-Am cut costs, sold corporate frills, downsized management, and began marketing more of its own products under the Mid-America Farms label, thus reducing dependency on commodity sales.

Mid-Am expanded its research and development efforts throughout the 1980s. The co-op opened its services to farmers in California and New Mexico in 1993, and a series of mergers in 1994 and 1995 nearly doubled its size. In 1997 it purchased some of Borden's dairy operations, including rights to the valuable Elsie the Cow and Borden's trademarks.

Wary of falling milk prices, Mid-Am merged with Western Dairymen Cooperative, Milk Marketing, and the Southern Region of Associated Milk Producers at the end of 1997 to form DFA. Hanman moved into the seat of CEO at the new co-op. DFA began a series of joint ventures with the #1 US dairy processor, Suiza Foods.

DFA added California Gold (more than 330 farmers, 1998) and Independent Cooperative Milk Producers Association (730 dairy farmer members in Michigan and parts of Ohio and Indiana, 1999). In another joint venture with Suiza, in early 2000 DFA sold its 50% stake in the US's #3 fluid milk processor, Southern Foods, in exchange for 34% of a new company named Suiza Dairy Group.

After mollifying the government's antitrust fears, DFA acquired the butter operations of Sodiaal North America in 2000. It then molded all its butter businesses into a new entity, Keller's Creamery. However, another acquisition did not fare as well. The same year, DFA acquired controlling interest in Southern Belle Dairy only to have the merger challenged three years later by the Department of Justice. Arguing that the merger formed a monopoly in school milk sales in several states, the Department of Justice filed suit, which a federal judge later dismissed.

During 2001 the cooperative went in with Land O'Lakes 50-50 to purchase a cheese plant from Kraft. Later in the year as Suiza Foods acquired Dean Foods (and took on its name), DFA sold back its stake in Suiza Dairy Group to the new Dean Foods. DFA then teamed up with a group of dairy investors to form a new 50/50 joint venture, National Dairy Holdings, which received 11 processing plants from Dean Foods as part of the exchange for Suiza Dairy.

Weak milk prices and a drop in demand during 2002 caused DFA's revenues to slide. DFA has typically grown by inviting smaller dairy co-ops to merge with it, including the Black Hills Milk Producers Cooperative in 2002. However, to better secure milk sources for its customers in the northeastern US, that same year DFA welcomed two regional co-ops, Dairylea and St. Albans, to join as members. The two co-ops remain as separate but affiliated organizations.

At the beginning of 2005 DFA acquired full ownership of what had been a joint venture in Keller's Creamery. Longtime president and CEO Hanman retired at the end of 2005; he was replaced by company veteran Rick Smith.

EXECUTIVES

Chairman: James P. (Tom) Camerlo
President and CEO: Richard P. (Rick) Smith
SVP Accounting: Joel Clark
SVP and Legal Counsel: David A. Geisler
SVP Finance: David Meyer
SVP Marketing and Industry Affairs: John J. Wilson
SVP and COO, Southwest Area: David C. Jones
SVP Strategy and Internal Development: Jay Waldvogel
VP Quality Assurance and Regulatory Affairs: James F. (Jim) Carroll
VP and COO, Central Area: Randall S. (Randy) McGinnis
VP and COO, Western Area: David L. Parrish
VP and COO, Mountain Area: Greg Yando
VP Human Resources: Annette Regan
VP Corporate Communications and Member Relations: Monica Coleman
VP Regulatory and Dairy Policy: Jim Hahn
President, Dairy Food Products: Mark Korsmeyer
COO, Mideast Area: Glenn Wallace
COO, Northeast Area: Gregory I. (Greg) Wickham
COO, Southeast Area: Sonia Fabian
Government Relations: Sam Stone
Member Relations: Melissa Lascon
Auditors: Deloitte & Touche LLP

LOCATIONS

HQ: Dairy Farmers of America, Inc.
10220 N. Ambassador Dr., Kansas City, MO 64153
Phone: 816-801-6455   **Fax:** 816-801-6456
Web: www.dfamilk.com

PRODUCTS/OPERATIONS

Selected Brands

Borden
Breakstone's
CalPro
Enricco
Falfurrias
Golden
Hotel BarJacobo
Keller's
Mid-America Farms
Plugra
Apoer AhKW

Selected Products

Butter
Cheese dips
Cheeses
Coffee creamer
Condensed milk
Cream
Dehydrated dairy products
Infant formula
Nonfat dry milk powder
Shelf-stable nutritional beverages
Whey products

COMPETITORS

AMPI	Kraft Foods
Arla Foods	Kraft North America
Berkeley Farms	Lactalis
California Dairies Inc.	Land O'Lakes
ConAgra	Leprino Foods
Darigold, Inc.	Marathon Cheese
Dean Foods	Mayfield Dairy Farms
Farmland Dairies	Northwest Dairy
Fonterra	Prairie Farms Dairy
Foremost Farms	Quality Chekd
Friendship Dairies	Saputo
Garelick Farms	Sargento
Glanbia plc	Schreiber Foods
Great Lakes Cheese	Unilever
Humboldt Creamery	

HISTORICAL FINANCIALS

Company Type: Cooperative

Income Statement

FYE: December 31

	REVENUE ($ mil.)	NET INCOME ($ mil.)	NET PROFIT MARGIN	EMPLOYEES
12/07	11,100	—	—	4,000
12/06	7,899	—	—	4,000
12/05	8,909	—	—	—
12/04	8,954	—	—	—
12/03	6,933	—	—	4,000
Annual Growth	12.5%	—	—	0.0%

Revenue History

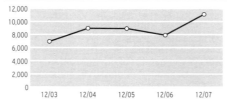

Dakota Growers Pasta

Dakota Growers Pasta Company is trying to put an *al dente* in the noodle market. The company is a supplier of branded and private-label pasta products and flours to retail, foodservice, and ingredient companies in North America. Its brand names include Dreamfields, Pasta Growers, Pasta Sanita, Primo Piatto, and Zia Briosa. It also sells organic pasta under the Dakota Growers Pasta label and provides customers with private-label services. The company started out in 1991 as a wheat-growers cooperative; it became a private corporation in 2002. In 2004 the company took over New World Pasta's foodservice unit and now distributes the Ronzoni, Prince, San Giorgio, and Mrs. Weiss pasta brands to the foodservice sector.

The company's products are distributed throughout the US. Customer U.S. Foodservice accounts for approximately 12% of sales. Dakota Growers operates production plants in Minnesota and North Dakota.

EXECUTIVES

Chairman: John S. (Jack) Dalrymple III, age 59
Vice Chairman: John D. Rice Jr., age 53
President and CEO: Timothy J. Dodd, age 52, $272,229 pay
CFO: Edward O. Irion, age 36, $176,628 pay
Auditors: Eide Bailly LLP

LOCATIONS

HQ: Dakota Growers Pasta Company, Inc.
1 Pasta Ave., Carrington, ND 58421
Phone: 701-652-2855   **Fax:** 701-652-3552
Web: www.dakotagrowers.com

PRODUCTS/OPERATIONS

2007 Sales

	% of total
Retail	49
Foodservice	31
Ingredients	20
Total	**100**

COMPETITORS

ADM	Horizon Milling
American Italian Pasta	Italgrani
Barilla	Kraft Foods
Bay State Milling	Nestlé
Campbell Soup	New World Pasta
ConAgra	Rossi Pasta
Hodgson Mill	

HISTORICAL FINANCIALS

Company Type: Private

Income Statement

FYE: July 31

	REVENUE ($ mil.)	NET INCOME ($ mil.)	NET PROFIT MARGIN	EMPLOYEES
7/07	191	7	3.5%	435
7/06	172	4	2.6%	416
7/05	156	3	1.6%	409
7/04	145	0	0.2%	367
7/03	137	(0)	—	388
Annual Growth	8.7%	—	—	2.9%

Debt ratio: 82.8%   Current ratio: —
Return on equity: 11.6%   Long-term debt ($ mil.): 41
Cash ($ mil.): —

Net Income History

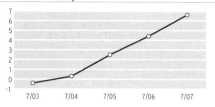

Dallas Cowboys

Legend has it that there's a hole in the roof of Texas Stadium so God can watch his favorite team. Dallas Cowboys Football Club operates the famed Dallas Cowboys professional football franchise, one of the most popular teams in the National Football League and the winner of a record five Super Bowl titles (a mark it shares with the San Francisco 49ers and Pittsburgh Steelers). The franchise, often called "America's Team," was founded in 1960 by Clint Murchison Jr. and Bedford Wynne and competed for the NFL championship twice in that decade (losing both times to the Green Bay Packers). Oilman Jerry Jones has owned the team since 1989.

The Cowboys franchise has become one of the more financially successful teams in the NFL with the help of its legions of fans buying tickets and merchandise. To keep those fans coming through the turnstiles, Jones has spared little expense acquiring talent for the Cowboys roster.

During 2007 the franchise was stunned when head coach Bill Parcells announced his retirement after four seasons in Dallas, but his replacement, former San Diego Chargers defensive coordinator Wade Phillips, coached the Cowboys to the best record in the NFC that season. (The team lost to the New York Giants in the divisional round of the playoffs, however.) Parcells, the famed coach who led the Giants to Super Bowl titles in 1986 and 1990, had presided over two playoff seasons in Big D.

To expand the team's revenue-generating potential, the Cowboys are building a new $1 billion retractable-roof stadium in nearby Arlington (home of the Texas Rangers' ballpark) that will seat 80,000 fans (expandable to 100,000 people for other events). The city of Arlington agreed to put up about $325 million of the cost. The new facility will replace the team's aging Texas Stadium home in nearby Irving, one of the smaller venues in the league.

EXECUTIVES

Owner, President, and General Manager:
Jerral W. (Jerry) Jones, age 65
EVP, COO, and Director Player Personnel:
Stephen Jones, age 44
EVP and Chief Sales and Marketing Officer:
Jerry Jones Jr., age 39
EVP Brand Management; President, Charities:
Charlotte Jones Anderson, age 42
Head Coach: Wade Phillips, age 61
SVP Sales and Marketing: Greg McElroy
CFO: George Mitchell
Director Football Operations: Bruce Mays
Director Public Relations: Rich Dalrymple
General Counsel: Alec Scheiner
Chief Diversity Officer: Vincent Thomson
Director College and Pro Scouting: Tom Ciskowski
Controller: David Frey

LOCATIONS

HQ: Dallas Cowboys Football Club, Ltd.
1 Cowboys Pkwy., Irving, TX 75063
Phone: 972-556-9900   **Fax:** 972-556-9304
Web: www.dallascowboys.com

The Dallas Cowboys play at 65,675-seat capacity Texas Stadium in Irving, Texas.

PRODUCTS/OPERATIONS

Championship Titles
Super Bowl Championships
  Super Bowl XXX (1996)
  Super Bowl XXVIII (1994)
  Super Bowl XXVII (1993)
  Super Bowl XII (1978)
  Super Bowl VI (1972)
NFC Championship (1970-71, 1975, 1977-78, 1992-93, 1995)
NFC East Champions (1970-71, 1973, 1976-79, 1981, 1985, 1992-96, 1998, 2007)
NFL Eastern Conference Champions (1966-67)
NFL Capitol Division Champions (1967-69)

COMPETITORS

New York Giants
Philadelphia Eagles
Washington Redskins

HISTORICAL FINANCIALS

Company Type: Private

Income Statement   FYE: February 28

	REVENUE ($ mil.)	NET INCOME ($ mil.)	NET PROFIT MARGIN	EMPLOYEES
2/08	269	—	—	—
2/07	242	—	—	—
2/06	235	—	—	—
2/05	231	—	—	—
2/04	205	—	—	—
Annual Growth	7.0%	—	—	—

Revenue History

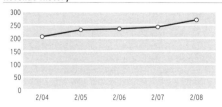

Dallas Mavericks

This basketball franchise has bucked its image as a losing team. The Dallas Mavericks joined the National Basketball Association in 1980 but struggled to find success for much of its history. Under current owner Mark Cuban, though, the team has become a regular contender for the playoffs. A talented roster that included such players as Dirk Nowitzki and Josh Howard earned the franchise's first trip to the NBA finals in 2006 (a loss to the Miami Heat). The Dallas basketball team was formed by millionaire Donald Carter; Cuban, an Internet billionaire, has owned the Mavs since 2000.

Since becoming a franchise owner, Cuban has developed a reputation as an outspoken critic of game officiating and commissioner David Stern, and has been regularly fined by the league for his comments and courtside antics. His sometimes outrageous behavior has made him a popular figure among fans, however, and has helped raise the profile of the Mavericks.

Head coach Avery Johnson was let go after the 2007-08 season. He had led the team to four consecutive playoff appearances, however the Mavs advanced to the NBA Finals only once during that span.

Cuban paid about $280 million to buy the team; he also shares ownership of Center Operating Company, which owns and operates the American Airlines Center, with Dallas Stars owner Tom Hicks. The forthright billionaire co-founded online broadcasting pioneer broadcast.com and sold it to Yahoo! for about $5 billion in 1999.

EXECUTIVES

Owner: Mark Cuban
President and CEO: Terdema L. Ussery II, age 49
President Basketball Operations: Donnie Nelson
Head Coach: Rick Carlisle, age 49
SVP Human Resources: Buddy Pittman
SVP Corporate Sponsorships: George Killebrew
VP and CFO: Floyd Jahner
VP Merchandising: Steve Shilts
VP Operations and Arena Development: Steve Letson
VP Ticket Sales and Services: George Prokos
Controller: Ronnie Fauss
Director of Marketing: Paul Monroe
Director Basketball Development: Rolando Blackman
Director of Scouting: Amadou Gallo Fall
Director of Technology and Information Systems:
Ken Bonzon
Corporate Promotions and Events Manager:
Geoffrey Pence
Player Relations Manager: Tiffany Farha

LOCATIONS

HQ: Dallas Mavericks
The Pavilion, 2909 Taylor St., Dallas, TX 75226
Phone: 214-747-6287   **Fax:** 214-752-3860
Web: www.dallasmavericks.com

The Dallas Mavericks play in the 21,041-seat capacity American Airlines Center in Dallas.

PRODUCTS/OPERATIONS

Championship Titles
Western Conference Champions (2006)

COMPETITORS

Houston Rockets
Memphis Grizzlies
New Orleans Hornets
San Antonio Spurs

HISTORICAL FINANCIALS
Company Type: Private

Income Statement
FYE: June 30

	REVENUE ($ mil.)	NET INCOME ($ mil.)	NET PROFIT MARGIN	EMPLOYEES
6/07	140	—	—	—
6/06	140	—	—	—
6/05	124	—	—	—
6/04	117	—	—	—
6/03	117	—	—	—
Annual Growth	4.6%	—	—	—

Revenue History

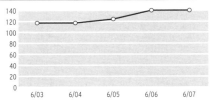

D&H Distributing

D&H Distributing sells computer and electronics products in the US and Canada. Its product portfolio includes computers and peripherals, electronic components, data storage devices, printing and imaging equipment, software, mobile devices, gaming systems, home appliances, surveillance systems, and digital music players. Clients include small and large resellers and retailers, system builders, and college bookstores. D&H also targets schools and government agencies. Suppliers include Hewlett-Packard, Intel, and Microsoft. D&H has been employee-owned since 1999.

In 2008 the company reported significant growth in its gaming and home entertainment divisions, which distribute such products as digital music players, home theater systems, and high-definition gaming consoles.

D&H was founded in 1918 as a tire retreader; the company entered the electronics business in 1926. Dave Schwab and Harry Spector were the original D&H.

The company opened its first international subsidiary in Canada in 2007.

EXECUTIVES

Chairman and CEO: Israel (Izzy) Schwab
President Emeritus: Gary Brothers
Co-President: Daniel (Dan) Schwab
Co-President: Michael (Mike) Schwab
EVP and Treasurer: James F. (Jimmy) Schwab
VP Sales: Jeff Davis
VP and Controller: Robert J. Miller Jr.
VP Purchasing: Rob Eby
VP Marketing: Mary Campbell
Senior Director Purchasing: Tina Fisher

LOCATIONS

HQ: D&H Distributing Co.
2525 N. 7th St., Harrisburg, PA 17110
Phone: 717-236-8001   **Fax:** 717-255-7838
Web: www.dandh.com

COMPETITORS

Agilysys
Arrow Electronics
ASI Computer Technologies
Avnet
Elcom International
Electrograph Systems
Ingram Micro
Merisel
New Age Electronics
Sayers
SED International
Sirius Computer Solutions
Solarcom Capital
Supercom
SYNNEX
Tech Data
ZT Group

Dart Container

Dart Container is a world cup winner — not in soccer, but in foam cups and containers. (It commands about half of the global market in foam cups.) The company uses a secret method of molding expandable polystyrene to make its products, which include cups, lids, dinnerware, and cutlery for customers such as hospitals, schools, and restaurants. To cut costs, Dart Container builds its own molding machinery and operates its own distribution trucks. The firm sells its recycled polystyrene to companies that make such items as insulation material and egg cartons. The Dart family controls the company.

The company runs four polystyrene-recycling plants and operates in the US and through subsidiaries in Argentina, Australia, Canada, Mexico, and the UK.

The king of cups has a simple strategy — secrecy. The Darts never patented the cup-making machine they developed; this allowed them to avoid revealing how it works. Most of the company's factory workers have never seen the machines, and the firm's salespeople are not allowed inside the plants. After years of legal battles in the 1990s and early 2000s, the Darts have reached an agreement regarding alleged discrepancies in the family inheritance. The terms of the settlement are, naturally, secret.

HISTORY

William F. Dart founded a Michigan firm to make steel tape measures in 1937. Dart's son William A. started experimenting with plastics in 1953, and in the late 1950s the two devised a cheap way to mold expandable polystyrene and built a cup-making machine. Dart Container was incorporated in Mason, Michigan, in 1960 and shipped its first cups that year. By the late 1960s the rising demand for plastic-foam products sparked an increase in R&D. In 1970 the company built a plant in Corona, California.

It was a family feud in the making in 1974, as William F. divided the business among his grandsons — Tom, Ken, and Robert — in separate trusts that named William A. trustee for all. Tom branched out in 1975 and founded oil and gas company Dart Energy, which was later absorbed into Dart Container. William F. died the next year. Following the oil market crash of the early 1980s, Tom went through a sticky divorce and

admitted to cocaine abuse. His father temporarily removed him as head of Dart Energy in 1982, and the next year the entire family underwent group psychiatric counseling.

The family reorganized its assets in 1986, giving Ken and Robert the cup business and Tom the energy business plus $58 million in cash. In 1987 Ken began to swell the family fortune with a series of successful investments. Better tax rates motivated Dart family members to move to Sarasota, Florida, in 1989. They set up shop in an unmarked building behind a sporting-goods store. By the late 1980s Dart Container commanded more than 50% of the worldwide market for foam cups.

In 1990 the company paid $250,000 to settle a factory worker's minority discrimination lawsuit. The next year Ken bought 11% of the Federal Home Loan Mortgage Corp. (Freddie Mac), as well as portions of Salomon and Brazil's foreign debt. According to Tom, that year Ken also financed brain research in hopes of finding a way to keep his brain alive after the death of his body in an attempt to avoid future estate taxes.

Tom sued his brothers and father in 1992 for allegedly cheating him out of millions in trust money in the 1986 reorganization. Ken turned a $300 million investment into $1 billion by selling the Freddie Mac shares. The next year he and Robert renounced their US citizenship to avoid paying taxes. Ken also made a failed attempt to block the restructuring of Brazil's debt (of which Dart owned 4%). That year Ken's new $1 million Sarasota home was firebombed (the case remains unsolved), and Robert moved to Britain, where he soon filed for divorce.

Ken began hiring bodyguards, and he moved his family to the Cayman Islands in 1994. Dart then shelled out $230,000 to settle yet another discrimination case. In 1995 Tom was fired from Dart Energy, and Ken tried — and failed — to return to the US as a diplomat of Belize. In 1996 Tom accused Judge Donald Owens of being biased in favor of William A. The judge succumbed to the pressure in 1997 and removed himself from the proceedings, only to be ordered back on the case by Michigan's Court of Appeals. The lawsuit was settled in 1998 before going to trial, but the terms were kept secret. The following year saw yet another series of lawsuits for the container company. In 1999 Dart Container filed an appeal to an IRS demand to pay $31 million in back taxes from 1994 and late penalties. The legal wrangling continued through 2001, but in 2002 the company agreed to pay $26 million to settle the issue.

A slight shift in its operational practices occurred in 2005 when employees at the company's unionized Corona, California, plant voted to end its union contract. The move came as a result of management-style changes that valued worker input more than in the past. Also, in an effort to support operations at the Corona facility, Dart opened a new facility in Tijuana, Mexico, in 2007.

EXECUTIVES

Chairman: William Dart
President: Kenneth B. Dart
CEO: Robert C. Dart
VP Administration and General Counsel: Jim Lammers
VP Manufacturing: Dan Calkins
VP Manufacturing: John M. Murray
VP Technology: Ralph MacKenzie
Director Human Resources: Mark Franks
Director Sales: Robert Williams
Treasurer: Kevin Fox

LOCATIONS

HQ: Dart Container Corporation
500 Hogsback Rd., Mason, MI 48854
Phone: 517-676-3800   **Fax:** 517-676-3883
Web: www.dartcontainer.com

Dart Container has manufacturing operations in Argentina, Australia, Canada, Mexico, the UK, and the US.

PRODUCTS/OPERATIONS

Selected Products

Clear containers
Container lids
Deli containers and lids
Dinnerware
Foam cups
Hinged containers
Paper cups and lids
Plastic cups and lids
Plastic cutlery

Selected Services

CARE (Cups Are REcyclable) Program (provides densifier to larger customers to compact their polystyrene, which Dart then picks up)
Foam-Recycling (four plants in Canada, Florida, Michigan, and Pennsylvania and a drop-off site in Georgia)
Recycla-Pak (provides small-volume businesses with cup-shipping containers that double as recycling bins)

COMPETITORS

Berry Plastics Corporation
Huhtamäki
NOVA Chemicals
Smurfit-Stone Container
Solo Cup
Sonoco Products
Temple-Inland
WinCup

HISTORICAL FINANCIALS

Company Type: Private

Income Statement				FYE: December 31
	ESTIMATED REVENUE ($ mil.)	NET INCOME ($ mil.)	NET PROFIT MARGIN	EMPLOYEES
12/07	1,540	—	—	5,840
12/06	1,510	—	—	5,640
12/05	1,388	—	—	5,200
12/04	1,250	—	—	5,000
12/03	1,200	—	—	5,000
Annual Growth	6.4%	—	—	4.0%

Revenue History

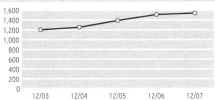

Dartmouth-Hitchcock Alliance

It's not a scholastic organization, nor is it a private investigation agency — it's simply a group of medical providers. The Dartmouth-Hitchcock Alliance provides a wide range of health care services to residents of Massachusetts, New Hampshire, and Vermont through a network of about a dozen community hospitals, home health care agencies, and mental health centers. Each member of the Alliance is an independently owned and operated not-for-profit organization with its own board of directors. Collaborative services provided by Dartmouth-Hitchcock include procurement, human resources, information technology, and finance, as well as the coordination of facility policies and planning.

EXECUTIVES

President: Nancy Formella
COO: Stephen LeBlanc
CFO: Richard Showalter

LOCATIONS

HQ: Dartmouth-Hitchcock Alliance
1 Medical Center Dr., Lebanon, NH 03756
Phone: 603-650-5000   **Fax:** 603-650-8765
Web: www.dhalliance.org

COMPETITORS

Beth Israel Deaconess Medical Center
Boston Medical Center
Brigham and Women's Hospital
Cambridge Health Alliance
CareGroup
Caritas Christi
Children's Hospital Boston
Massachusetts General Hospital

Datatel, Inc.

Datatel doesn't care if you're a Bruin, a Hurricane, or a Longhorn as long as you've got data that needs managing. The company, which serves higher education institutions across the country, makes software that manages information about students, finances, financial aid, human resources, and advancement. The company's software products streamline such processes as enterprise resource planning, e-recruitment, and alumni communications, serving more than 700 institutions throughout North America. Datatel was founded in 1968 by Ken Kendrick and Tom Davidson: they sold the company in 2005 to members of their exective team (backed by Thoma Cressey Equity Partners and Trident Capital).

EXECUTIVES

President and CEO: John F. Speer III
CFO: Kevin M. Boyce, age 33
VP, Finance: Virginia L. (Ginger) Piercy
VP, Professional Services: Elizabeth A. Murphy
VP, Software Development: Thomas A. (Tom) Reynolds
VP, Strategic Planning and Marketing: Jayne W. Edge
VP, Sales: David J. Gutch
Sales Director: Steve Boller
Director, Product Management: Sue Kumpf
Director, Business Development: Jose Cabrera
Director, Marketing Executive and Consultant Programs: Ana Borray
Senior Product Manager, Financial Solutions: Moira Kirkland
Public Affairs: Carly Isaac

LOCATIONS

HQ: Datatel, Inc.
4375 Fair Lakes Ct., Fairfax, VA 22033
Phone: 703-968-9000   **Fax:** 703-968-4573
Web: www.datatel.com

COMPETITORS

Blackbaud
Blackboard
Jenzabar
SunGard Higher Education

HISTORICAL FINANCIALS

Company Type: Private

Income Statement				FYE: December 31
	REVENUE ($ mil.)	NET INCOME ($ mil.)	NET PROFIT MARGIN	EMPLOYEES
12/07	123	—	—	550
12/06	108	—	—	547
Annual Growth	13.6%	—	—	0.5%

Revenue History

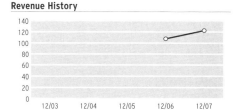

Daubert Industries

For Daubert Industries, metal health is the top concern. Its three subsidiaries protect metals by different methods. Daubert Cromwell makes VCI (volatile corrosion inhibitors) protective coatings for almost every metal — ferrous, nonferrous, and multi-metal. Its transparent coatings protect metal that is stored or shipped until it is unwrapped and the coatings break down. ECP (Entire Car Protection) offers paints, carpet dyes, detailing products, and under-the-hood cleaners for automobiles. Daubert Chemical focuses on developing corrosion prevention, industrial anti-skid, and sound-deadening coatings. Daubert Industries was formed in 1935 by George Daubert, whose decendants still control the company.

EXECUTIVES

Chairman: Peter D. Fischer
Vice Chairman: Andrew M. Fischer
Vice Chairman: Harry A. (Fritz) Fischer III
President and CEO: M. Lawrence Garman
SVP Finance and Administration and CFO: Peter Miehl
VP, Treasurer, and Secretary: John R. Cosbey
President and CEO, Daubert Cromwell:
Martin J. Simpson, age 43
President and CEO, Daubert Chemical: Michael Dwyer
EVP Operations, Daubert Chemical: Mark Pawelski
VP Business Development, Daubert Chemical:
Glenn Bilek
VP Sales, Daubert Chemical: Richard Bramwell
VP Technology, Daubert Chemical: Richard Lauterbach
Director, Human Resources, Daubert Chemical:
Ginny Winkelmann
Auditors: McGladrey & Pullen, LLP

LOCATIONS

HQ: Daubert Industries, Inc.
1333 Burr Ridge Pkwy., Ste. 200,
Burr Ridge, IL 60521
Phone: 630-203-6800   **Fax:** 630-203-6907
Web: www.daubert.com

Daubert has manufacturing operations in Illinois. It has distributors throughout Canada and the US.

PRODUCTS/OPERATIONS

Selected Operations and Products

Corrosion prevention coatings
    Industrial anti-skid coatings
    Penetrating oil
    Sound deadening coatings
        Coating papers — ferrous metals
        Coating papers — nonferrous and multi-metals
Liquid coating — ferrous and nonferrous metals
    Buffers
    Car soaps, shampoos, detergents
    Chamois and wash mits
    Cleaners, solvents, degreasers
    Lubricants and protectants
    Paint
    Paint correction compounds
    Underhood cleaners
    Vinyl, plastic, carpet dyes
    Wax specialty applicators

COMPETITORS

Atlantis Plastics   General Magnaplate
Bodycote   Quaker Chemical
Enerchem International

Davey Tree

Business at The Davey Tree Expert Company is as green as grass. The company's roots extend back to 1880 when John Davey founded the horticultural services company, which branched into residential, commercial, utility, and other natural resource management services. Among the services Davey offers are the treatment, planting, and removal of trees, shrubs, and other plant life; landscaping; tree surgery; and the application of fertilizers, herbicides, and insecticides. Other services include line clearing for public utilities, urban and utility forestry research and development, and environmental planning. Pacific Gas and Electric accounts for almost 10% of sales. Davey has been employee-owned since 1979.

EXECUTIVES

Chairman: R. Douglas Cowan, age 67, $446,539 pay
(prior to title change)
President, CEO, and Director: Karl J. Warnke, age 56,
$361,539 pay (prior to promotion)
EVP, CFO, and Secretary: David E. Adante, age 56,
$246,500 pay
EVP Operations: Patrick M. (Pat) Covey, age 44
EVP Operations: Steven A. Marshall, age 56
SVP; General Manager, Davey Tree Surgery Company:
Howard D. Bowles, age 64, $200,851 pay
**SVP and General Manager, Residential and Commercial
Services:** C. Kenneth Celmer, age 61, $207,846 pay
VP and CTO: Roger C. Funk, age 63
**VP and General Manager, Commercial Landscape
Services:** George M. Gaumer, age 55
VP and Controller: Nicholas R. Sucic, age 61
Treasurer: Joseph R. Paul, age 46
CIO: Tom Countryman
Manager Corporate Communications: Sandra Reid
Auditors: Ernst & Young LLP

LOCATIONS

HQ: The Davey Tree Expert Company
1500 N. Mantua St., Kent, OH 44240
Phone: 330-673-9511   **Fax:** 330-673-9843
Web: www.davey.com

2007 Sales

	$ mil.	% of total
US	451.1	89
Canada	55.0	11
Total	**506.1**	**100**

PRODUCTS/OPERATIONS

2007 Sales

	$ mil.	% of total
Utility services	247.7	49
Residential & commercial services	222.8	44
Other	35.6	7
Total	**506.1**	**100**

COMPETITORS

Arbor Tree Surgery   UGL Unicco
Asplundh   ValleyCrest Companies
TruGreen Landcare

HISTORICAL FINANCIALS

Company Type: Private

Income Statement

FYE: December 31

	REVENUE ($ mil.)	NET INCOME ($ mil.)	NET PROFIT MARGIN	EMPLOYEES
12/07	506	18	3.6%	5,600
12/06	468	14	3.0%	5,500
12/05	432	13	3.1%	5,200
12/04	399	12	3.1%	5,000
12/03	346	9	2.5%	5,100
Annual Growth	**10.0%**	**20.1%**	**—**	**2.4%**

2007 Year-End Financials

Debt ratio: —   Current ratio: —
Return on equity: 20.5%   Long-term debt ($ mil.): —
Cash ($ mil.): —

Net Income History

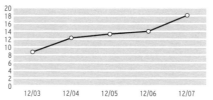

David and Lucile Packard Foundation

One of the wealthiest philanthropic organizations in the US, The David and Lucile Packard Foundation primarily provides grants to not-for-profit entities operating in three areas: conservation and science; children, families, and communities; and population. The foundation has approximately $6.2 billion in assets and in 2006 awarded nearly $225 million in national and international grants, with an extra focus on Northern California's Monterey, San Mateo, Santa Clara, and Santa Cruz counties. The late David Packard (co-founder of Hewlett-Packard) and his wife, the late Lucile Salter Packard, created the foundation in 1964. Their children now run the organization.

EXECUTIVES

Chairman: Susan Packard Orr
Vice Chairman: Nancy Packard Burnett
Vice Chairman: Julie E. Packard
President and CEO: Carol S. Larson, age 51
VP and CFO: George A. Vera, age 64
VP and Director Communications: Chris DeCardy
Secretary and General Counsel: Barbara P. Wright,
age 56
Director, Children, Families, and Communities:
Lois Salisbury
Acting Director, Population: Sono Aibe
Director, Conservation and Science: Walter Reid
Auditors: Deloitte & Touche LLP

LOCATIONS

HQ: The David and Lucile Packard Foundation
300 2nd St., Los Altos, CA 94022
Phone: 650-948-7658   **Fax:** 650-948-5793
Web: www.packard.org

HISTORICAL FINANCIALS

Company Type: Foundation

Income Statement

FYE: December 31

	REVENUE ($ mil.)	NET INCOME ($ mil.)	NET PROFIT MARGIN	EMPLOYEES
12/07	591	252	42.6%	—
12/06	829	588	70.9%	—
12/05	646	462	71.4%	—
12/04	74	—	—	—
12/03	1,501	—	—	83
Annual Growth	**(20.8%)**	**(26.2%)**	**—**	**—**

2007 Year-End Financials

Debt ratio: —   Current ratio: —
Return on equity: 3.9%   Long-term debt ($ mil.): —
Cash ($ mil.): —

Net Income History

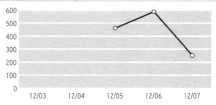

David Weekley Homes

A development home developed to *your* taste? David Weekley Homes can do it. Founded in 1976, it is one of the largest privately owned homebuilders in the US, annually building around 4,600 single-family detached homes that range from about 1,500 sq. ft. to 5,000 sq. ft. Weekley builds homes from hundreds of floor plans and offers custom upgrades. Prices range from the $100,000s to more than $800,000s. The firm's average home price is $275,000.

The company builds in its own planned communities in Texas, Colorado, and the Southeast and Mid-Atlantic. Founder and chairman David Weekley owns the firm.

As with most builders in the nation, David Weekley Homes has been affected by the subprime mortgage collapse as well as the general oversupply of new housing. The company has been hit with high foreclosure rates in its Florida, Denver, and Dallas markets, although other regions have not been as badly affected.

To combat the decline in sales, the company has cut prices (its average home price has dropped) and added incentives.

EXECUTIVES

Chairman: David M. Weekley
CEO: John Johnson
CFO: Stuart Bitting
CIO: Heather Humphrey
VP Design: Bob Rhode
VP Human Resources: Michael (Mike) Brezina
VP Marketing: Natalie Harris
VP Operations: Mike Humphrey
VP Supply Chain Services: Bill Justus
Director Finance: John Bena
Communications Coordinator: Cindy Haynes
Auditors: Ernst & Young LLP

LOCATIONS

HQ: David Weekley Homes
1111 N. Post Oak Rd., Houston, TX 77055
Phone: 713-963-0500   **Fax:** 713-963-0322
Web: www.davidweekleyhomes.com

Markets

Atlanta	Jacksonville
Austin, TX	Orlando, FL
Bluffton/Hilton Head, SC	Palm Coast, FL
Charleston, SC	Panama City, FL
Charlotte, NC	Phoenix
Dallas/Fort Worth	Port Charlotte, FL
Denver	Raleigh, NC
Fort Myers, FL	San Antonio
Greenville, NC	Tallahassee, FL
Houston	Tampa

COMPETITORS

Beazer Homes	Mercedes Homes
Centex	M/I Homes
Choice Homes	NVR
D.R. Horton	Pulte Homes
Engle Homes	Rottlund
Highland Homes	The Ryland Group
Hovnanian Enterprises	Standard Pacific
KB Home	Toll Brothers
Kimball Hill inc	TOUSA
Lennar	WL Homes
M.D.C.	

HISTORICAL FINANCIALS

Company Type: Private

Income Statement

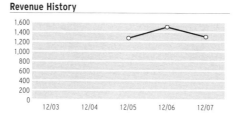

	REVENUE ($ mil.)	NET INCOME ($ mil.)	NET PROFIT MARGIN	EMPLOYEES
12/07	1,300	—	—	1,221
12/06	1,500	—	—	1,446
12/05	1,272	—	—	1,466
Annual Growth	1.1%	—	—	(8.7%)

FYE: December 31

Revenue History

Davidson Companies

Employee-owned Davidson Companies offers investment banking, asset management, and travel services in more than a dozen (mostly northwestern) states through its five subsidiaries. The company's flagship firm, D.A. Davidson & Co., was founded in 1935 and offers financial advice and a range of investment products. Davidson Trust Co. was acquired by the Davidson companies in 1986 and provides estate planning and wealth management to individuals and organizations. Davidson Investment Advisors offers portfolio management, while Davidson Travel is a full-service travel agency.

In 2005 D.A. Davidson expanded its bond trading business by acquiring the Kirkpatrick Pettis family of companies from Mutual of Omaha. The various Kirkpatrick Pettis units operate as divisions or subsidiaries of various Davidson companies, but retain the Kirkpatrick Pettis name.

EXECUTIVES

Chairman: Ian B. Davidson, age 76
Vice Chairman: Vincent M. (Vinney) Purpura
President and CEO: William A. (Bill) Johnstone
SVP and CFO: Tom Nelson
SVP, Chief Market Strategist, and Director, Private Client Research: Fred Dickson
SVP and Regional Director, Western Region Branches: Jim Kerr
SVP and Regional Director, Eastern Region Branches: Gerry Meyer
SVP and Director, Institutional Research: John Rogers
SVP and Director, Private Client Services: Jordan Werner
SVP and Managing Director Equity Capital Markets: Doug Woodcock
VP and Director, Human Resources: Dan McLaughlin
Associate VP, Public Relations: Jacquie Burchard
Vice Chairman, D.A. Davidson & Co.: L. C. (Jack) Petersen
President, Davidson Trust: Arthur P. Sims
Auditors: KPMG LLP

LOCATIONS

HQ: Davidson Companies
8 3rd St. North, Great Falls, MT 59401
Phone: 406-727-4200   **Fax:** 406-791-7238
Web: www.dadco.com

Davidson Companies has operations in Arizona, California, Colorado, Florida, Idaho, Illinois, Kansas, Minnesota, Missouri, Nebraska, Oklahoma, Oregon, Utah, Washington, and Wyoming.

COMPETITORS

Charles Schwab	Green Manning & Bunch
Commonwealth Financial Network	McAdams Wright
	Merrill Lynch
Edward Jones	Piper Jaffray

HISTORICAL FINANCIALS

Company Type: Private

Income Statement

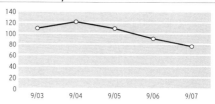

	REVENUE ($ mil.)	NET INCOME ($ mil.)	NET PROFIT MARGIN	EMPLOYEES
9/07	76	—	—	—
9/06	90	—	—	—
9/05	109	—	—	866
9/04	121	—	—	800
9/03	109	—	—	700
Annual Growth	(8.8%)	—	—	11.2%

FYE: September 30

Revenue History

Dawn Food Products

A muffin at Starbucks, a cookie from Mrs. Fields, a Weight Watchers low-cal blueberry muffin, or a warm donut from Krispy Kreme — it's all just another day in the kitchens at Dawn Food Products. The company provides more than 4,000 pre-baked and fully baked grain products, such as cakes, muffins, cookies, donuts, and artisan breads, as well as all the fixings for bakery products, including bases, fillings, frozen dough, icings, ingredients, and mixes for the food industry. Its customers include food manufacturers, foodservice companies, institutional bakeries, restaurants, retail outlets, and supermarkets.

In 2004 the company acquired the bakery business of Bunge North America. It added California cookie-maker, Countryside Baking, to its list of holdings in 2006.

Dawn has manufacturing and distribution sites worldwide, including 31 US locations, six Canadian locations, and four Mexican locations, as well as operations in Africa, Asia, Europe, Oceania, and South America. It has more than 40,000 customers located worldwide, including in North and Central America and Europe.

Dawn Food is owned and operated by the founding Jones family.

EXECUTIVES

Chairman: Ronald L. (Ron) Jones
Co-Chairman: Miles E. (Mike) Jones
CEO: Carrie L. Jones-Barber
VP, Distribution Services and Sales: Erik Riswick
VP Principal Accounts: Richard L. (Rick) Dahlin
National Replenisher Manager: Aaron Jones
Manager, National Accounts: Sam Barber
Product Manager: Sarah Jones
Project Manager: Dave Barry
President, U.S. Bakery Products: David (Dave) Kowal
President, Global Business Processes: Jerry Baglien
President, Global Resources: Tom Harmon
President, Dawn International: Ken Hall

LOCATIONS

HQ: Dawn Food Products, Inc.
   3333 Sargent Rd., Jackson, MI 49201
Phone: 517-789-4400   **Fax:** 517-789-4465
Web: www.dawnfoods.com

PRODUCTS/OPERATIONS

Selected Products

Batters
Breadings
Brownies
Cakes
   Crème
   Pound
Cinnamon rolls
Coatings
Cookies
Croissants
Danish
Donuts
Extracts, emulsions, and colors
Fillings
Frozen dough
Glazes
Ice cream bases
Ice cream toppings
Icings
   Butter cream
   Donut and pastry
   Specialty
Mixes
   Biscuit
   Pancake
   Scone
   Waffle
Mexican products
Muffins
Non-dairy icings, fillings, and toppings
Puff dough
Ready-to-finish donuts and cakes
Ready-to-sell cakes, donuts and muffins
Spreads and smears
Sweet dough
Toppings
   Dessert
   Ice cream

COMPETITORS

BakeMark	King Arthur Flour
Bell Flavors & Fragrances	King's Hawaiian
Best Brands	Maple Leaf Foods
Blendex	McCormick & Company
Bridgford Foods	Ottens Flavors
Chef Solutions	Pepperidge Farm
Chelsea Milling	Ralcorp Frozen Bakery
Columbia Bakeries	Products
ConAgra Foods Ingredients	Rich Products
Denali Flavors	Sara Lee
Flowers Foods	Sara Lee Food & Beverage
General Mills	Sara Lee Foodservice
George Weston	Sensient Dehydrated
Gonnella Baking	Flavors
Hayward Enterprises, Inc.	Smucker
Interstate Bakeries	Tropical Nut & Fruit

HISTORICAL FINANCIALS

Company Type: Private

Income Statement   FYE: December 31

	REVENUE ($ mil.)	NET INCOME ($ mil.)	NET PROFIT MARGIN	EMPLOYEES
12/07	1,370	—	—	3,950
12/06	1,250	—	—	4,000
12/05	1,110	—	—	3,850
Annual Growth	11.1%	—	—	1.3%

Revenue History

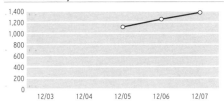

Day & Zimmermann

Day & Zimmermann offers services as distinct as day and night. The company provides engineering and construction, design, plant maintenance, security, staffing, munitions decommissioning, validation, and asset management services worldwide. A top global contractor, Day & Zimmermann provides operations, contract support, and maintenance services to US and foreign governments, as well as commercial customers. Its Day & Zimmerman NPS unit maintains half of the US's nuclear plants. Technical staffing subsidiary Yoh Services specializes in filling IT, engineering, and health care positions. Founded in 1901, Day & Zimmermann is owned and managed by the Yoh family, which has headed the firm for three generations.

Day & Zimmerman was busy in 2007. Its acquisition of Atlantic Services, Inc., expanded its presence in the power services sector and makes it the primary services provider for nearly half of all US nuclear power plants.

It also acquired Reliable Security Guard Agency Inc., which it folded into its Day & Zimmermann Security Services division. The company formed a joint venture with SAP services provider Dassian, Day & Zimmermann Dassian LLC, that will market project and contract management solutions.

It also acquired the rest of American Ordnance, a munitions manufacturer and cleanup firm, that it didn't already own from General Dynamics.

Not to be left out, Yoh acquired rival Sci-Tek Professionals, which places scientists in clinical and research positions.

In 2008 Day & Zimmerman merged its Hawthorne Army Depot with Special Operations Consulting, a private security training firm, to train soldiers for deployment.

EXECUTIVES

Chairman and CEO: Harold L. (Hal) Yoh III, age 48
President, Munitions: Michael H. Yoh
SVP, General Counsel, and Secretary:
   William R. (Bill) Hamm
VP Finance and CFO: Joseph W. (Joe) Ritzel

VP and CIO: Anthony J. Bosco Jr.
VP Human Resources: Diana M. Newmier
VP Government Affairs: James (Jim) Hickey
VP Planning and Strategy: Lisa Carr
Director Branding, Marketing, PR Strategy, and Programs: Maureen Omrod
President and CEO, Commercial and Public: Joseph J. Ucciferro
President, Engineering and Field Services: Michael J. (Mick) McAreavy
President, Government Services: Larry Ames
President, Power Services: Michael P. McMahon
President, Security Services and Validation Services: John J. Sacht
President and CEO, Yoh: William C. (Bill) Yoh
President, Mason & Hanger: Ted Daniels
President, DZNPS: Gary McKinney
Auditors: Deloitte & Touche

LOCATIONS

HQ: The Day & Zimmermann Group
   1500 Spring Garden St., Philadelphia, PA 19130
Phone: 215-299-8000   **Fax:** 215-299-8030
Web: www.dayzim.com

PRODUCTS/OPERATIONS

Selected Subsidiaries

Hawthorne Corporation (government services)
Mason & Hanger (architecture, engineering, and construction)
Yoh Services (temporary and long-term job placement in IT, medical, scientific, and other industries)

Selected Services

Commercial services
   Architecture, engineering and plant services
   Maintenance and modification services
   Security services
   Talent and outsourcing services
Government services
   Architecture, engineering, and construction services
   DOD equipment maintenance and facilities services
   Facilities management and operations
   Munitions products
   Munitions logistics and demilitarization
   Security services
   Talent and outsourcing services
   Validation services

COMPETITORS

Adecco	Manpower
Babcock & Wilcox Nuclear	McCarthy Building
Power	Parsons Corporation
Bechtel	Peter Kiewit Sons'
CDI	URS
Fluor	Washington Division
Jacobs Engineering	WS Atkins

HISTORICAL FINANCIALS

Company Type: Private

Income Statement   FYE: December 31

	REVENUE ($ mil.)	NET INCOME ($ mil.)	NET PROFIT MARGIN	EMPLOYEES
12/07	2,200	—	—	24,000
12/06	1,900	—	—	23,000
12/05	1,600	—	—	20,000
Annual Growth	17.3%	—	—	9.5%

Revenue History

DeBruce Grain

Got a few bushels of wheat and no place to keep it? DeBruce Grain stores, handles, and sells grain and fertilizer for the agribusiness industry. The company owns and operates 26 grain elevators in six US states, boasting a total storage capacity of 101 million bushels, four fertilizer-distribution terminals, and seven retail fertilizer operations in Iowa and Texas. DeBruce also markets wholesale fertilizer. The company also has a facility in Guadalajara, Mexico, which serves DeBruce's international customers. Owner and CEO Paul DeBruce founded the company in 1978.

DeBruce paid a $685,000 fine over a 1998 explosion of its Haysville, Kansas, facility — at the time the largest grain elevator in the world. The explosion killed seven workers. The site never reopened.

EXECUTIVES

CEO: Paul DeBruce
President: Larry Kittoe
CFO: Curt Heinz
General Director, DeBruce Grain De México:
 Cristopher Brown

LOCATIONS

HQ: DeBruce Grain, Inc.
 4100 N. Mulberry Dr., Kansas City, MO 64116
Phone: 816-421-8182   **Fax:** 816-584-2350
Web: www.debruce.com

DeBruce has grain elevators located in Iowa, Kansas, Kentucky, Texas, and Mexico.

PRODUCTS/OPERATIONS

Selected Business Units

Creston Bean Processing LLC
DeBruce Feed Ingredients Inc.
DeBruce Fertilizer Inc.
DeBruce Grain Inc.
DeBruce Risk Services
DeBruce Transportation Inc.

COMPETITORS

ADM
Ag Processing
Bartlett and Company
Bunge Limited
Cargill
CHS
Grain Processing Corporation
Owensboro Grain
Scoular
Stewart Grain
Wheeler Brothers

Delaware North Companies

This company makes few concessions when it comes to selling hot dogs and sodas at the ball game. Delaware North is a leading provider of foodservices and hospitality at airports, sports stadiums, and tourist destinations throughout the US and in a handful of other countries. Its Sportservice division operates concessions at more than 50 major and minor league sporting arenas, while its Travel Hospitality Services division runs concessions and retail operations at more than 25 airports. In addition, Delaware North provides hospitality services at several tourist destinations, and it operates Boston's TD Banknorth Garden. The family-owned company was founded in 1915 by brothers Charles, Louis, and Marvin Jacobs.

Delaware North's sports concessions unit boasts an impressive list of clients, including Busch Stadium in St. Louis, Soldier Field in Chicago, and famed Wembley National Stadium in the UK. Its parks and resorts division serves tourists at such destinations as the Grand Canyon, Kennedy Space Center Visitor Complex, and Yellowstone. In 2008 Sportservice inked a 10-year deal to provide concessions at the new stadium in the Meadowlands that will host the New York Giants and the New York Jets football teams. The 82,000-seat facility is slated to open in 2010.

The company has been eyeing expansion of its gaming operations, which include a handful of pari-mutuel racetracks with casinos. In 2008 its Gaming & Entertainment unit opened a greyhound racing track in Daytona Beach, Florida. It is also in the running to acquire a license to operate a casino at New York's Aqueduct Racetrack.

In addition to running his family's concession and entertainment empire, CEO Jeremy Jacobs controls the Boston Bruins professional hockey team.

EXECUTIVES

Chairman and CEO: Jeremy M. Jacobs Sr.
President and COO: Charles E. (Chuck) Moran Jr., age 57
CFO: Karen L. Kemp
EVP: Louis M. (Lou) Jacobs
EVP; Chairman, Delaware North Companies Sportservice Corporation: Jeremy M. Jacobs Jr.
EVP Delaware North and Boston Bruins:
 Charles M. (Charlie) Jacobs
VP, General Counsel, and Secretary: Bryan J. Keller
VP Human Resources: Eileen Morgan
VP and Controller: Bruce W. Carlson
VP Corporate Communications and Public Relations: Wendy A. Watkins
President, Delaware North Companies Gaming and Entertainment: William J. Bissett, age 59
President, Delaware North Companies Hospitality Group: Dennis J. Szefel, age 57
President, Delaware North Companies Boston and TD Banknorth Garden: John A. Wentzell
President and General Manager, Wheeling Island Gaming: Robert D. (Bob) Marshall Jr., age 43
President, Delaware North Companies Parks and Resorts: Kevin T. Kelly
President, Delaware North Companies Sportservice: Rick Abramson

LOCATIONS

HQ: Delaware North Companies, Inc.
 40 Fountain Plaza, Buffalo, NY 14202
Phone: 716-858-5000   **Fax:** 716-858-5479
Web: www.delawarenorth.com

PRODUCTS/OPERATIONS

Selected Operations

Hospitality services
 Delaware North Companies Parks & Resorts
  (foodservices and lodging)
 Delaware North Companies Sportservice (stadium foodservices and concessions)
 Delaware North Companies Travel Hospitality Services (airport foodservices and concessions)
Other
 Delaware North Companies Gaming & Entertainment (pari-mutuel racing and casino facilities)
 TD Banknorth Garden (sports and entertainment venue, Boston)

Selected Sports and Entertainment Arenas Served

Busch Stadium (St. Louis)
Cleveland Browns Stadium
Comerica Park (Detroit)
Edward Jones Dome (St. Louis)
Great American Ball Park (Cincinnati)
HSBC Arena (Buffalo, New York)
Jacobs Field (Cleveland)
Miller Park (Milwaukee)
Nationwide Arena (Columbus, Ohio)
PETCO Park (San Diego)
Ralph Wilson Stadium (Buffalo, New York)
Rangers Ballpark in Arlington (Texas)
Rogers Centre (Toronto)
Soldier Field (Chicago)
St. Pete Times Forum (Tampa)
TD Banknorth Garden (Boston)
US Cellular Field (Chicago)
Wembley National Stadium (London)

COMPETITORS

ARAMARK
Centerplate
Culinaire International
Global Spectrum
Guest Services
HMSHost
Levy Restaurants
SMG Management
Sodexo

HISTORICAL FINANCIALS

Company Type: Private

Income Statement				FYE: December 31
	REVENUE ($ mil.)	NET INCOME ($ mil.)	NET PROFIT MARGIN	EMPLOYEES
12/07	2,000	—	—	40,000
12/06	2,040	—	—	50,000
12/05	2,000	—	—	40,000
12/04	1,700	—	—	30,000
12/03	1,700	—	—	30,000
Annual Growth	4.1%	—	—	7.5%

Revenue History

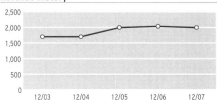

Deloitte Touche Tohmatsu

This company is "deloitted" to make your acquaintance, particularly if you're a big business in need of accounting services. Deloitte Touche Tohmatsu (doing business as Deloitte) is one of accounting's Big Four, along with Ernst & Young, KPMG, and PricewaterhouseCoopers. Deloitte offers traditional audit and fiscal-oversight services from some 70 member firms in more than 140 countries. It also provides human resources, tax, and technology services, as well as services to governments and lending agencies working in emerging markets, including China and India. Units include Deloitte & Touche (the US accounting arm) and Deloitte Consulting. Consulting accounts for more than 20% of Deloitte's revenues.

Deloitte is an umbrella organization over partnerships that have historically operated on a country-by-country basis. Deloitte in 2006 embarked on a "clustering" program, uniting member firms in such emerging growth areas as the former Soviet republics, Latin America, Southeast Asia, and the Caribbean, as well as in more traditional Deloitte markets (such as Switzerland and the UK, which are combining their practices). The program is designed to leverage the strengths of the member firms and broaden their capabilities.

In 2003 Italian dairy foods manufacturer Parmalat filed for bankruptcy in the midst of a $12 billion financial scandal, then dropped Deloitte as its auditor. Parmalat sued Deloitte in 2004, claiming its auditing procedures were inadequate and should have uncovered the fraud at Parmalat earlier. Deloitte settled the case for $149 million in 2007.

In 2008 the company's life sciences consulting unit acquired Recombinant Capital, now operating as Deloitte Recap. The business operates a life sciences subscription database and advisory service with 20 years of industry data.

HISTORY

In 1845 William Deloitte opened an accounting office in London, at first soliciting business from bankrupts. The growth of joint stock companies and the development of stock markets in the mid-19th century created a need for standardized financial reporting and fueled the rise of auditing, and Deloitte moved into the new field. The Great Western Railway appointed him as its independent auditor (the first anywhere) in 1849.

In 1890 John Griffiths, who had become a partner in 1869, opened the company's first US office in New York City. Four decades later branches had opened throughout the US. In 1952 the firm partnered with Haskins & Sells, which operated 34 US offices.

Deloitte aimed to be "the Cadillac, not the Ford" of accounting. The firm, which became Deloitte Haskins & Sells in 1978, began shedding its conservatism as competition heated up; it was the first of the major accountancy firms to use aggressive ads.

The firm spent the 1980s and 1990s pursuing a strategy of using accountants and consultants in concert to provide seamless service in auditing, accounting, strategic planning, information technology, financial management, and productivity.

In 1989 Deloitte Haskins & Sells joined the flamboyant Touche Ross (founded 1899) to become Deloitte & Touche. Touche Ross's Japanese affiliate, Ross Tohmatsu (founded 1968) rounded out the current name. The merger was engineered by Deloitte's Michael Cook and Touche's Edward Kangas, in part to unite the former firm's US and European strengths with the latter's Asian presence. Cook continued to oversee US operations, with Kangas presiding over international operations. Many affiliates, particularly in the UK, rejected the merger and defected to competing firms.

As auditors were increasingly held accountable for the financial results of their clients, legal action soared. In the 1990s Deloitte was sued because of its actions relating to Drexel Burnham Lambert junk bond king Michael Milken, the failure of several savings and loans, and clients' bankruptcies.

Nevertheless, in 1995 the SEC chose Michael Sutton, the firm's national director of auditing and accounting practice, as its chief accountant. That year Deloitte formed Deloitte & Touche Consulting to consolidate its US and UK consulting operations; its Asian consulting operations were later added to facilitate regional expansion. Deloitte Consulting became Deloitte's fastest-growing line, offering strategic and management consulting in addition to information technology and human resources consulting services.

Increasingly, though, Deloitte and its peers came under fire for their combined accounting/consulting operations; regulators and observers wondered whether accountants could maintain objectivity when they were auditing clients for whom they also provided consulting.

In 1996 the firm formed a corporate fraud unit (with special emphasis on the Internet) and bought PHH Fantus, the leading corporate relocation consulting company. The next year Deloitte and Thurston Group (a Chicago-based merchant bank) teamed up to form NetDox, a system for delivering legal, financial, and insurance documents via the Internet.

The Asian economic crisis hurt overseas expansion in 1998, but provided a boost in restructuring consulting. In 1999 the firm sold its accounting staffing service unit (Resources Connection) to its managers and Evercore Partners, citing possible conflicts of interest with its core audit business. Also Kangas stepped down as CEO to be succeeded by James Copeland.

In 2001 the SEC forced Deloitte & Touche to restate the financial results of Pre-Paid Legal Services. In an unusual move, Deloitte & Touche publicly disagreed with the SEC's findings.

The accountancy put some old trouble to bed in 2003 when it agreed to pay $23 million to settle claims it had been negligent in its auditing of failed Kentucky Life Insurance, a client in the 1980s. Later that year the UK's High Court found Deloitte negligent in audits related to the failed Barings Bank; however, the ruling was considered something of a victory for the accountancy because it essentially cleared Deloitte of the majority of charges against it and effectively limited its financial liability in the matter.

Copeland retired from the global CEO's office that year and handed the reins over to Bill Parrett, who had formerly served as managing director for the US and the Americas. Parrett was succeeded in 2007 by Jim Quigley.

EXECUTIVES

Chairman: John P. Connolly
CEO: James H. (Jim) Quigley, age 56
Deputy CEO, Clients; Executive Member, United Kingdom: Stephen (Steve) Almond
CFO: Jeffrey P. (Jeff) Rohr
Global Managing Partner Tax, EMEA Managing Partner and Executive Member: Alberto E. Terol
Global Managing Partner, Regulatory and Risk and Executive Member, US: Jeffrey K. (Jeff) Willemain
Global Managing Partner Services and M&A and Executive Member, US: Jerry P. Leamon
Global Managing Partner Talent and Executive Member, United Kingdom: Vassi Naidoo
Global Managing Partner Consulting and Executive Member, US: Ainar D. Aijala Jr.
Executive Member and Country Leader, United States: Barry Salzberg, age 54
Executive Member and Global Managing Partner, DTT Operations: Manoj P. Singh
Chief Human Resources Officer: James H. (Jim) Wall
General Counsel: Philip Rotner
Director Global PR and CEO Communications: Madonna Jarrett
Global Brand and Marketing Director: Luis Gallardo
Chief Diversity Officer: Jane Allen
Chief Strategy Officer: Mumtaz Ahmed

LOCATIONS

HQ: Deloitte Touche Tohmatsu
1633 Broadway, New York, NY 10019
Phone: 212-489-1600   **Fax:** 212-489-1687
Web: www.deloitte.com/dtt

2007 Sales

	% of total
Americas	50
Europe/Middle East/Africa	40
Asia/Pacific/Japan	10
Total	**100**

PRODUCTS/OPERATIONS

2007 Sales

	% of total
Audit	48
Consulting	22
Tax	22
Financial advisory services	8
Total	**100**

2007 Sales by Industry

	% of total
Financial services	23
Consumer business	19
Manufacturing	15
Telecom, media & technology	14
Energy & resources	8
Life sciences	7
Public sector	7
Aviation & transport	2
Other	5
Total	**100**

Selected Products and Services
Audit
  Auditing services
  Global offerings services
  International financial reporting conversion services
Consulting
  Enterprise applications
  Human capital
  Outsourcing
  Strategy and operations
  Technology integration
Enterprise Risk Services
  Capital markets
  Control assurance
  Corporate responsibility and sustainability
  Internal audit
  Regulatory consulting
  Security and privacy services

Financial Advisory
    Corporate finance
    Forensic services
    Reorganization services
    Transaction services
    Valuation services
Merger and Acquisition Services
Tax
    Corporate tax
    Global tax compliance
    Indirect tax
    International assignment services
    International tax
    M&A transaction services
    Research and development credits
    Tax publications
    Tax technologies
    Transfer pricing

COMPETITORS

Accenture	H&R Block
BDO International	KPMG
Booz Allen	Marsh & McLennan
Boston Consulting	McKinsey & Company
Capgemini	PricewaterhouseCoopers
EDS	Towers Perrin
Ernst & Young Global	Watson Wyatt
Grant Thornton	

HISTORICAL FINANCIALS
Company Type: Partnership

Income Statement
FYE: May 31

	REVENUE ($ mil.)	NET INCOME ($ mil.)	NET PROFIT MARGIN	EMPLOYEES
5/07	23,100	—	—	146,600
5/06	20,000	—	—	135,000
5/05	18,200	—	—	121,283
5/04	16,400	—	—	115,000
5/03	15,100	—	—	119,237
Annual Growth	11.2%	—	—	5.3%

Revenue History

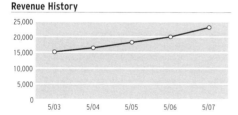

Delta Dental Plan

Delta Dental of California doesn't just help keep the mouths of movie stars clean. A not-for-profit organization, the company is a member of the Delta Dental Plans Association and has affiliates nationwide. Delta Dental of California provides dental coverage through HMOs, preferred provider plans (PPOs), and such government programs as the TRICARE Retiree Dental Program and California's Healthy Families Program. It also offers vision coverage through its DeltaVision program. The company serves about 16 million enrollees in California; its programs cover more than one-third of California residents.

Delta Dental of California has formed a holding company organization with other Delta Dental members, including Delta Dental of Pennsylvania and Delta Dental Insurance Company; together the affiliated companies serve about 23 million members in some 15 states across the US.

Delta Dental of California also provides information technology services to other Delta Plan affiliates across the nation through its for-profit subsidiary, DeltaNet.

EXECUTIVES

President and CEO: Gary D. Radine
EVP and COO; President, Delta Dental Insurance Company: Anthony S. (Tony) Barth, age 44
EVP and CFO: Michael J. Castro
EVP and CIO: Patrick S. Steele, age 54
EVP and Chief Dental Officer: Marilynn Belek
EVP and Chief Legal Officer: Robert G. Becker
SVP and Associate General Counsel: Charles Lamont
SVP Sales and Marketing: Belinda Martinez
SVP State Government Programs: Michael Kaufmann
SVP Federal Services: Lowell Daun
Group VP, Dental Affairs: Cathye Smithwick
VP Sales: MohammadReza Navid, age 36
VP and Enterprise Controller: Alicia Weber
Director Public Affairs: Jeff Album
Coordinator Employee/Spanish Communications: Michelle Wagner

LOCATIONS

HQ: Delta Dental of California
    100 1st St., San Francisco, CA 94105
Phone: 415-972-8300   **Fax:** 415-972-8466
Web: www.deltadentalca.org

PRODUCTS/OPERATIONS

Selected Products
DeltaCare USA (group and individual dental HMOs)
Delta Dental PPO
Delta Dental Premier (fee-for-service plan)
DeltaVision (group vision HMO)

COMPETITORS

Aetna	MetLife
CIGNA	SafeGuard Health
First Dental Health	WellPoint
Health Net	Western Dental Services

DeMoulas Super Markets

The Demoulas supermarket chain is ripe with family history all rolled up into numerous Market Baskets. Demoulas Super Markets runs some 60 grocery stores under the Market Basket banner in Massachusetts and New Hampshire. One store still operates under the "DeMoulas" banner. The grocery retailer also manages real estate interests. Market Basket supermarkets are typically located in shopping centers with other retail outlets, including properties owned by the company through its real estate arm, Retail Management and Development (RMD), Inc. Begun as a mom-and-pop grocery store, the Demoulas

sons transformed the chain into a traditional, yet modern, concept.

The company was founded in 1954 when brothers George and Telemachus "Mike" Demoulas bought their parents' mom-and-pop grocery. The men agreed that, upon one brother's death, the other would care for the deceased's family and maintain the firm's 50-50 ownership. In 1990 George's family alleged that Mike had defrauded them of all but 8% of the company's stock. The 10-year court battle was decided in favor of George's family, giving it 51% of the company. By then Mike had resigned as CEO and he died in 2003 at age 82.

EXECUTIVES

President: Arthur Demoulas
EVP: James Miamis
VP, Finance and Treasurer: Donald Mulligan
VP, Grocery Sales and Merchandising: Joseph Rockwell
VP and Treasurer, Retail Management and Development Inc.: Michael Kettenbach
Corporate Counsel: Sumner Darman
Director, Operations: Bill Marsden
Payroll Administrator: Lucille Lopez
Coffee and Beverage Buyer: Jim Lacourse

LOCATIONS

HQ: Demoulas Super Markets Inc.
    875 East St., Tewksbury, MA 01876
Phone: 978-851-8000   **Fax:** 978-640-8390

2007 Stores

	No.
Massachusetts	34
New Hampshire	24
Total	**58**

PRODUCTS/OPERATIONS

Selected Banners
Market Basket
DeMoulas

COMPETITORS

Big Y Foods	IGA
BJ's Wholesale Club	Shaw's
Costco Wholesale	Stop & Shop
Cumberland Farms	SUPERVALU
Golub	Trader Joe's
Hannaford Bros.	Wal-Mart

HISTORICAL FINANCIALS
Company Type: Private

Income Statement
FYE: December 31

	ESTIMATED REVENUE ($ mil.)	NET INCOME ($ mil.)	NET PROFIT MARGIN	EMPLOYEES
12/07	2,500	—	—	13,000
12/06	2,200	—	—	13,000
12/05	2,000	—	—	12,000
12/04	1,950	—	—	—
12/03	1,950	—	—	12,900
Annual Growth	6.4%	—	—	0.2%

Revenue History

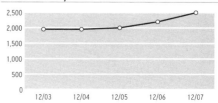

Denver Nuggets

You might say this team has the perfect moniker when the name of the game is taking the rock to the hole. The Denver Nuggets professional basketball franchise was formed by trucking magnate J. W. "Bill" Ringsby in 1967 as the Denver Rockets (renamed in 1974), a charter member of the American Basketball Association. Since joining the National Basketball Association in 1976, the team has had little postseason success, although the signing of star forward Carmelo Anthony in 2004 has helped put Denver back in playoff contention, boosting attendance at the team's Pepsi Center arena the past few seasons. Wal-Mart heir Stan Kroenke has owned the team since 2000.

Under new head coach George Karl (formerly with the Milwaukee Bucks), the team drove to its first division title in 18 years during the 2005-06 season. Hopes that the Nuggets might strike the mother lode were cut short, however, when the team lost its first round series to the Los Angeles Clippers in five games.

Through his Kroenke Sports Enterprises, Kroenke also owns the Colorado Avalanche professional hockey team and Denver's Pepsi Center. In addition, he has a substantial stake in the St. Louis Rams football team.

EXECUTIVES

Owner: E. Stanley (Stan) Kroenke
Head Coach: George Karl, age 57
Assistant Coach/Player Development: John Welch, age 45
Director Basketball Administration: Lisa Johnson
Director Media Relations: Eric Sebastian
Director Player Services: Tim Dixon
Director Basketball Operations: Greg Knight, age 29
VP Basketball Operations: Mark Warkentien, age 53
VP Player Personnel: Rex Chapman
Advanced Scout: Chad Iske, age 30

LOCATIONS

HQ: Denver Nuggets
1000 Chopper Circle, Denver, CO 80204
Phone: 303-405-1100   **Fax:** 303-575-1920
Web: www.nba.com/nuggets

The Denver Nuggets play at the 19,099-seat capacity Pepsi Center in Denver.

COMPETITORS

Minnesota Timberwolves
Oklahoma City Thunder
Portland Trail Blazers
Utah Jazz

HISTORICAL FINANCIALS
Company Type: Private

Income Statement

	REVENUE ($ mil.)	NET INCOME ($ mil.)	NET PROFIT MARGIN	EMPLOYEES
6/07	104	—	—	—
6/06	100	—	—	—
6/05	94	—	—	—
6/04	89	—	—	—
6/03	75	—	—	—
Annual Growth	8.5%	—	—	—

FYE: June 30

Revenue History

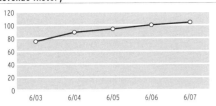

Derive Technologies

Derive Technologies provides infrastructure development, maintenance, security implementation, and other network integration services. The company also provides consulting services, with expertise in such areas as information storage and wireless technologies. It serves the advertising, education, financial services, government, health care, legal, retail, and transportation sectors. The company installs and maintains IT products from a variety of vendors, including CA, Cisco Systems, Citrix Systems, Hewlett-Packard, IBM, Microsoft, and VERITAS Software. Derive Technologies was founded in 1987.

EXECUTIVES

CEO: Kirit Desai
COO: Lawrence Marcus
EVP Sales: Mitchell Martinez
VP Business Development and Marketing: John Wood
VP Sales: Madhu Royal
VP Solutions: William (Bill) Eggers
VP: Howard Bergman
CTO: Darius Stafford
Director Services: Steve Weissman

LOCATIONS

HQ: Derive Technologies LLC
116 John St., New York, NY 10038
Phone: 212-363-1111   **Fax:** 212-363-3107
Web: www.derivetech.com

COMPETITORS

ePlus
Software House
Westcon

Desert Schools FCU

One of the largest credit unions in Arizona, Desert Schools Federal Credit Union operates about 60 branch locations in the Phoenix area, serving more than 325,000 members. Established in 1939 by a group of 15 teachers, the credit union offers banking products and services, including checking and savings accounts, IRAs, and CDs; it also provides online banking services. Subsidiary Desert Schools Financial Services sells insurance products and investment services. Membership is available to any individual living, working, or attending church or school in Gila, Maricopa, or Pinal counties.

EXECUTIVES

Chairman: Claudette M. Gronksi
Vice Chairman: Mary Pat Garry
President and CEO: Susan C. Frank
EVP: Jeffrey D. Meshey
Assistant VP Marketing: Cathy Graham
Treasurer: Robert R. Little
Auditors: McGladrey & Pullen, LLP

LOCATIONS

HQ: Desert Schools Federal Credit Union
148 N. 48th St., Phoenix, AZ 85034
Phone: 602-433-7000
Web: www.desertschools.org

PRODUCTS/OPERATIONS

2007 Sales

	$ mil.	% of total
Interest		
Loans to members	147.5	62
Investments & cash equivalents	29.2	12
Noninterest		
Service charges & other fees	52.4	22
Net gains on sales of loans	5.2	2
Other	4.2	2
Total	**238.5**	**100**

COMPETITORS

AmTrust Bank
Bank of America
Compass Bancshares
JPMorgan Chase
Marshall & Ilsley
Washington Mutual
Western Alliance
Zions Bancorporation

HISTORICAL FINANCIALS
Company Type: Not-for-profit

Income Statement

FYE: December 31

	ASSETS ($ mil.)	NET INCOME ($ mil.)	INCOME AS % OF ASSETS	EMPLOYEES
12/07	3,020	30	1.0%	1,300
12/06	2,885	40	1.4%	1,300
12/05	2,570	36	1.4%	1,134
12/04	2,212	28	1.3%	1,000
12/03	1,979	27	1.4%	700
Annual Growth	11.2%	1.9%	—	16.7%

2007 Year-End Financials

Equity as % of assets: 11.5%   Long-term debt ($ mil.): 210
Return on assets: 1.0%   Sales ($ mil.): 239
Return on equity: 8.9%

Net Income History

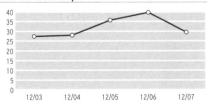

Dewey & LeBoeuf

International law firm Dewey & LeBoeuf has 1,400 lawyers in about 25 offices worldwide. One of the leading law firms headquartered in New York, Dewey & LeBoeuf's areas of expertise include antitrust, bankruptcy, government investigations, real estate, tax, and trade law, as well as mergers and acquisitions. The firm is the result of the October 2007 merger between law firms Dewey Ballantine and LeBoeuf, Lamb, Greene & MacRae. Dewey Ballantine was initially founded in 1909; the Dewey in the name refers to former partner Thomas Dewey, a three-term New York governor and two-time Republican presidential nominee in the 1940s. LeBoeuf Lamb was established in 1929.

The LeBoeuf Lamb transaction comes on the heels of a proposed merger that couldn't be completed. In late 2006, Dewey Ballantine was set to combine with San Francisco-based Orrick, Herrington & Sutcliffe; however, the deal fell through after key partners at Dewey left. The deal would have created Dewey Orrick, a firm with 1,500 lawyers and some $1 billion in annual revenue.

Still, the firm is satisfied with the results of the merger with LeBoeuf Lamb, and by late 2008, it managed to fully integrate the two firms' managerial and technical infrastructure.

EXECUTIVES

Chairman: Steve H. Davis
Executive Director: Stephen DiCarmine
COO: Dennis D'Alessandro
CFO: Joel I. Sanders
Chief Administrative Officer: Thomas F. Van Buskirk
Chief Human Resources Officer:
 Jason S. (Jay) Dinwoodie
Chief Practice Services Officer: Herb Thomas
Chief Administrative Officer: Julia Sherlock
Chief Marketing Officer: Sophie Aldred
Secretary: Carol A. McCrystal
Director Pro Bono: Scot H. Fishman
CIO: Peter Owings

LOCATIONS

HQ: Dewey & LeBoeuf LLP
 1301 Avenue of the Americas, New York, NY 10019
Phone: 212-259-8000   **Fax:** 212-259-6333
Web: www.deweyleboeuf.com

PRODUCTS/OPERATIONS

Selected Practice Areas

Antitrust
Bank and Institutional Finance
Bankruptcy Litigation
Business Solutions and Governance
Compensation, Benefits and Employment
Competition/EU
Corporate Finance
Employment Litigation
Energy Litigation
Energy Regulatory
Environmental, Health and Safety
Environmental Litigation
Insurance Regulatory
Insurance/Reinsurance
Intellectual Property Litigation
International Arbitration
International Litigation
International Trade
IT and IP Transactions
Legislative and Public Policy
Mergers and Acquisitions

Private Equity
Project Finance
Real Estate
Securities, Mergers and Acquisitions, and Corporate
 Governance Litigation
Sports Litigation
Structured Finance
Tax
Tax Controversy and Litigation
White Collar Criminal Defense and Investigations
Wealth Management

COMPETITORS

Baker & McKenzie
Cleary Gottlieb
Cravath, Swaine
Davis Polk
Fried, Frank, Harris
Jones Day
Kirkland & Ellis
Shearman & Sterling
Skadden, Arps
White & Case
Willkie Farr

HISTORICAL FINANCIALS

Company Type: Partnership

Income Statement

FYE: September 30

	REVENUE ($ mil.)	NET INCOME ($ mil.)	NET PROFIT MARGIN	EMPLOYEES
9/07	1,009	—	—	—
9/06	409	—	—	—
9/05	350	—	—	—
9/04	381	—	—	—
9/03	374	—	—	—
Annual Growth	28.1%	—	—	—

Revenue History

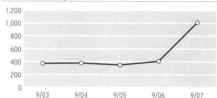

Dickinson Financial

Drop and give me a twenty. Dickinson Financial is the holding company for Bank Midwest, as well as a group of military banks: Armed Forces Bank, Armed Forces Bank of California, SunBank, Southern Commerce Bank, and Academy Bank. Bank Midwest operates about 70 branches in Kansas and Missouri. The military banking group operates from some 120 locations on or around military bases in about 20 states. The banks offer traditional deposit and lending products: savings, checking, money market, and retirement accounts; lines of credit; and CDs. The Dickinson family owns Dickinson Financial.

Commercial real estate loans (including agricultural, construction, development, and multi-family residential loans) account for about two-thirds of Dickinson Financial's loan portfolio. Commercial, residential mortgage, and consumer loans make up the remainder.

EXECUTIVES

Chairman: Ann K. Dickinson
CEO; President and CEO, Bank Midwest; Chairman, Armed Forces Bank, Armed Forces Bank of California, and Southern Commerce Bank: Rick L. Smalley
President; SVP Bank Midwest; Director, Armed Forces Bank: Amy Dickinson Holewinski
SEVP; EVP Commercial Real Estate Lending, Bank Midwest; Director, Academy Bank and Armed Forces Bank: Dan L. Dickinson
SEVP; SEVP, Southern Commerce Bank; EVP, Commercial Business Lending, Bank Midwest; Director, Academy Bank and Armed Forces Bank: Paul P. Holewinski
SEVP and Chief Lending Officer, Bank Midwest: Randall M. Nay
SVP and Senior Counsel; VP Bank Midwest: Jane A. Dickinson
Chairman, President, and CEO, Academy Bank; President and CEO, Armed Forces Bank; President, CEO, and Secretary, Armed Forces Bank of California: Donald C. Giles

LOCATIONS

HQ: Dickinson Financial Corporation
 1100 Main St., Ste. 350, Kansas City, MO 64105
Phone: 816-471-9800   **Fax:** 816-412-0022
Web: www.bankmw.com

PRODUCTS/OPERATIONS

2007 Sales

	$ mil.	% of total
Interest		
Loans	321.1	60
Securities	30.5	6
Other	9.8	3
Noninterest		
Service charges on deposit accounts	116.5	22
Other	43.4	9
Total	**521.3**	**100**

COMPETITORS

Commerce Bancshares
UMB Financial
U.S. Bancorp
USAA

HISTORICAL FINANCIALS

Company Type: Private

Income Statement

FYE: December 31

	ASSETS ($ mil.)	NET INCOME ($ mil.)	INCOME AS % OF ASSETS	EMPLOYEES
12/07	5,579	105	1.9%	2,179
12/06	4,705	107	2.3%	2,002
12/05	4,022	76	1.9%	1,901
12/04	3,509	62	1.8%	1,726
12/03	3,509	49	1.4%	1,723
Annual Growth	12.3%	21.0%	—	6.0%

2007 Year-End Financials

Equity as % of assets: 10.8%   Long-term debt ($ mil.): 362
Return on assets: 2.0%   Sales ($ mil.): 521
Return on equity: 19.0%

Net Income History

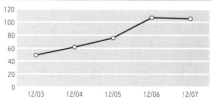

Discount Tire

Concerned about that upcoming "re-tire-ment"? Discount Tire Co., one of the largest independent tire dealers in the US, can provide several options. With about 680 stores in nearly 20 states, the company sells such leading brands as Michelin, Goodyear, and Uniroyal, as well as wheels (Enkei, Konig, Weld Racing). Discount Tire operates mostly in the West, Midwest, and Southwest. Some of the company's West Coast stores operate as America's Tire Co. because of a name conflict. Customers can search for tires by make and model on the company's Web site. Chairman and owner Bruce Halle founded the company in 1960 with six tires — four of them recaps.

The company is one of the country's fastest-growing tire dealers. Discount Tire opened more than 30 stores from August 2006 to August 2007. One of its top rivals, Tire Kingdom, is also adding stores at a similar pace.

Discount Tire has a mail-order division for customers who do not live near a retail store.

EXECUTIVES

Chairman: Bruce T. Halle
Vice Chairman: Gary T. Van Brunt
CEO: Tom Englert
COO: Steve Fournier
CFO: Christian Roe
EVP and Chief Administrative Officer: Bob Holman

LOCATIONS

HQ: Discount Tire Co. Inc.
20225 N. Scottsdale Rd., Scottsdale, AZ 85255
Phone: 480-606-6000   **Fax:** 480-951-8619
Web: www.discounttire.com

COMPETITORS

BFS Retail & Commercial	Sears
Commercial Tire	TBC
Les Schwab Tire Centers	TCI Tire Centers
Monro Muffler Brake	Tire Distribution Systems
Penske	VIP
Pep Boys	Wal-Mart

HISTORICAL FINANCIALS

Company Type: Private

Income Statement				FYE: December 31
	REVENUE ($ mil.)	NET INCOME ($ mil.)	NET PROFIT MARGIN	EMPLOYEES
12/07	2,310	—	—	11,630
12/06	2,060	—	—	10,980
12/05	1,856	—	—	10,100
12/04	1,670	—	—	9,500
12/03	1,541	—	—	9,500
Annual Growth	10.7%	—	—	5.2%

Revenue History

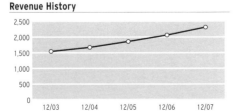

Dole Food

Bananas might be Dole Food's favorite fruit because they have "a-peel," but as the world's largest producer of fresh fruits and vegetables, it grows and markets much more than the slipper-peeled fruit. The company is the world's top producer of bananas (158 million boxes a year) and the #2 producer of pineapples (behind Fresh Del Monte Produce). It also markets citrus, table grapes, dried fruits, nuts, and freshly cut flowers. Dole offers value-added products (packaged salads, novelty canned pineapple shapes) to insulate itself from fluctuating commodity markets. Sourcing from some 75 countries, Dole sells more than 200 products in more than 90 countries worldwide.

Along with being the world's largest producer of fresh fruits and vegetables, The company holds the #1 spot in North American market share for bananas, iceberg lettuce, celery, cauliflower, and packaged fruit products. Dole is also a world-leading producer of freshly cut flowers, offering some 500 different floral varieties.

Dole has been introducing convenience-oriented products such as bagged vegetables, ready-to-eat salads, and individual fruit serving packaged in plastic cups and bowls, as well as niche products such as organic bananas. It has had good luck with its Wildly Nutritious brand of frozen fruit blends. It continues to add to its distribution channels, with a significant share of its products now available in drug and convenience stores, club stores, and mass merchandisers.

The company began test marketing the placement of vending machines in schools in 2007, offering students healthier eating options such as fresh fruit and fruit bowls.

Dole director David DeLorenzo took the helm as president and CEO in 2007. Chairman David Murdock took the company private in 2003 and is its sole owner.

HISTORY

James Dole embarked on an unlikely career in a faraway land when he graduated from Harvard College in 1899 and sailed to Hawaii. He bought 61 acres of farmland for $4,000 in 1900 and the next year organized the Hawaiian Pineapple Company, announcing that the island's pineapples would eventually be in every US grocery store.

Others had tried and failed to sell fresh fruit to the mainland. Dole decided he would succeed by canning pineapples. He built his first cannery in 1903 and introduced a national magazine advertising campaign in 1908 designed to make consumers associate Hawaii with pineapples (then considered exotic fruits).

In 1922 Dole expanded his production by buying the island of Lanai, where he set up a pineapple plantation. He financed the purchase by selling a third interest in Hawaiian Pineapple to Waialua Agricultural Company, which was part of Castle & Cooke (C&C). Samuel Castle and Amos Cooke, missionaries to Hawaii, formed C&C in 1851 to manage their church's failing depository, which supplied outlying mission posts with staple goods. In 1858 they entered the sugar business and within 10 years served as agents for several Hawaiian sugar plantations and the ships that carried their cargoes.

C&C gained control of Hawaiian Pineapple in 1932 when it acquired an additional 21% interest in the business. The company began using

the Dole name on packaging the next year. Dole became chairman of the board of the reorganized company in 1935 but pursued other business interests until he retired in 1948.

Hawaiian Pineapple was run separately until C&C bought the remainder in 1961. The company started pineapple and banana farms in the Philippines in 1963 to supply markets in East Asia. C&C began importing bananas when it purchased 55% of Standard Fruit of New Orleans in 1964. (It purchased the remainder four years later.)

Heavily in debt and limping from two hostile takeover attempts, C&C agreed in 1985 to merge with Flexi-Van, a container leasing company. The merger brought with it needed capital, Flexi-Van owner David Murdock (who became C&C's CEO), and a fleet of ships to transport produce. Murdock began trimming back, leaving C&C with its fruit and real estate operations. He then decided to end all pineapple operations on Lanai to concentrate on tourist properties. (The company took a $168 million write-off on them in 1995, when it spun off its real estate and resort operations as Castle & Cooke.)

C&C became Dole Food in 1991. The company expanded at home and internationally, adding SAMICA (dried fruits and nuts, Europe, 1992), Dromedary (dates, US, 1994), Chiquita's New Zealand produce operations (1995), and SABA Trading (60%, produce importing and distribution, Sweden, 1998; Dole acquired 100% of SABA in 2005).

In 1995 Dole sold its juice business to Seagram's Tropicana Products division, keeping its pineapple juices and licensing the Dole name to Seagram. (PepsiCo bought Tropicana in 1998.) Dole entered the fresh-flower trade in 1998 by acquiring four major growers and marketers. It is now the world's largest producer of freshly cut flowers.

A worldwide banana glut, Hurricane Mitch, and severe freezes in California hit the company hard in late 1998. The next year Dole launched cost-cutting measures, which by early 2000 had ripened into better earnings. Nonetheless, cutbacks and disposals continued throughout 2001.

In 2002 Murdock made a cash and debt takeover bid for the company worth about $2.5 billion. However, at least one minority shareholder was dissatisfied with the offer and filed a proposal calling for Murdock's resignation. The company rejected Murdock's $29.50 per share offer and negotiated with him regarding a larger price-per-share offer. In December Dole and Murdock finally signed a merger agreement. The deal, which gave stockholders $33.50 per share in cash, was approved by company stockholders in March 2003 and left Murdock in sole control of the company.

In 2004 Lawrence Kern, Dole's president and COO, left the company; chairman, CEO, and sole owner Murdock took over as president. In 2004 CFO Richard Dahl became president. Also in 2004 the company acquired frozen fruit manufacturer J.R. Wood, Inc., which it renamed Dole Packaged Frozen Foods, Inc. It also acquired fresh berry producer Coastal Berry Company (now Dole Berry Company) in 2004, making Dole a top North American strawberry producer.

In 2006 Dole paid almost $42 million in cash to Jamaica Producers Group for the remaining 65% that it did not already own of Jamaica Producers' subsidiary JP Fruit Distributors.

EXECUTIVES

Chairman: David H. Murdock, age 85
President, CEO, and Director: David A. DeLorenzo, age 61
EVP, Chief of Staff, and Director: Roberta Wieman, age 62
EVP Corporate Development, and Director: Scott A. Griswold, age 54
EVP, General Counsel, Corporate Secretary, and Director: C. Michael Carter, age 64, $1,012,500 pay
SVP Manufacturing: Danko Stambuk
SVP Marketing and Sales: Brad C. Bartlett
SVP Worldwide Human Resources and Industrial Relations: Sue Hagen
VP and CFO: Joseph S. Tesoriero, age 54, $525,000 pay
VP, Corporate Controller, and Chief Accounting Officer: Yoon J. Hugh
VP Eastern Seaboard Sourcing: Peter Gilmore
VP, Marketing, Dole Packaged Foods: Dave Spare
VP, Sales and Marketing, Foodservice: Chris Lock
VP, Worldwide Applied Research: Thomas Farewell
VP, Marketing and Communications: Marty Ordman
President, Dole Fresh Fruit: Michael J. Cavallero
Auditors: Deloitte & Touche LLP

LOCATIONS

HQ: Dole Food Company, Inc.
1 Dole Dr., Westlake Village, CA 91362
Phone: 818-879-6600   **Fax:** 818-879-6615
Web: www.dole.com

2007 Sales

	$ mil.	% of total
US	2,773.4	40
Japan	590.8	8
Euro zone countries		
Sweden	474.2	7
Germany	470.7	7
UK	331.9	5
Other	808.2	12
Canada	263.1	4
Other countries	1,218.7	17
Total	**6,931.0**	**100**

PRODUCTS/OPERATIONS

2007 Sales

	$ mil.	% of total
Fresh fruit	4,737.0	68
Fresh vegetables	1,059.4	15
Packaged foods	1,023.2	15
Fresh-cut flowers	110.2	2
Other	1.2	—
Total	**6,931.0**	**100**

Divisions and Selected Products

Fresh fruit

Apples	Kiwi	Papayas
Bananas	Lemons	Pears
Cherries	Mangoes	Pineapples
Cranberries	Melons	Raspberries
Grapefruit	Nectarines	Strawberries
Grapes	Oranges	Tangelos

Fresh vegetables

Artichokes	Green cabbage	Romaine
Asparagus	Iceberg lettuce	lettuce
Broccoli	Mushrooms	Snow peas
Carrots	Onions	Spinach
Celery	Plantains	Yucca root
Field greens		

Packaged foods
Canned mandarin-orange segments
Canned mixed fruits
Canned pineapple
Pineapple juice
Pineapple orange banana juice
Pineapple orange juice

Fresh-cut flowers
Alstroemeria
Aster, Butterfly
Aster, Matsumoto
Campanula
Carnations
Chrysanthemums
Delphiniums
Freesia
Gerber daisies
Gypsophilia
Kangaroo Paws
Monks Hood
Roses
Snapdragon
Stock
Statice
Sunflowers
Tulips

COMPETITORS

A. Duda & Sons	National Grape Cooperative
Bakkavor	Naturipe Farms
BBI Produce	The Nunes Company
Blue Diamond Growers	Ocean Mist Farms
C&D Fruit and Vegetable	Ocean Spray
Calavo Growers	O'Leary Potato
Cargill Kitchen Solutions	Orchard House Foods
Chiquita Brands	Peace River Citrus
Cranberries Limited	Products
Del Monte Foods	Performance Food
Dixie Growers	Pictsweet
Four Seasons Produce	Pro-Fac
Frank Capurro & Son	Ready Pac
Fresh Del Monte Produce	River Ranch Fresh Foods
Fresh Kist Produce	Salyer American
Frontera Produce	Seneca Foods
Fyffes	Snokist Growers
Golden West Nuts	Stewart & Jasper Orchards
Harry's Fresh Foods	Sun Growers
John Sanfilippo & Son	Sun World International
Lake Placid Groves	Sunkist
Mann Packing Company	Sunsweet Growers
Maui Land & Pineapple	Tanimura & Antle
Mauna Loa Macadamia Nut	Taylor Fresh Foods
Meridian Nut Growers	Tejon Ranch
ML Macadamia Orchards	Tropicana
Moonlight Packing	UniMark Group
Nash Produce	Worldwide Fruit

HISTORICAL FINANCIALS

Company Type: Private

Income Statement

FYE: Saturday nearest December 31

	REVENUE ($ mil.)	NET INCOME ($ mil.)	NET PROFIT MARGIN	EMPLOYEES
12/07	6,931	(58)	—	45,000
12/06	6,172	(89)	—	47,000
12/05	5,871	—	—	72,000
12/04	5,316	—	—	64,000
12/03	4,773	—	—	59,000
Annual Growth	**9.8%**	**—**	**—**	**(6.5%)**

2007 Year-End Financials

Debt ratio: 712.7%   Current ratio: —
Return on equity: —   Long-term debt ($ mil.): 2,316
Cash ($ mil.): —

Net Income History

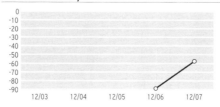

Dollar General

Dollar General's at ease with living off the crumbs of Wal-Mart. The retailer commands a chain of more than 8,200 discount stores in about 35 states, primarily in the southern and eastern US, the Midwest, and the Southwest. Offering basic household items such as cleaning supplies and health and beauty aids, as well as some apparel and food, the firm targets low-, middle-, and fixed-income customers. Its stores are generally located in small towns off the radar of giant discounters. Its big-city stores (about 30% of its total) are situated in lower-income neighborhoods. About a third of its stores' goods are priced at $1 or less. Dollar General was taken private by affiliates of KKR and Goldman Sachs in 2007.

Other investors included Citi Private Equity, an investment arm of Citigroup Inc.

Historically one of the country's fastest-growing retailers, Dollar General's pace of new store openings has slowed. (After adding more than 500 stores in 2006, the company plans to add only about 200 new stores in 2008.) CEO Rick Dreiling, who joined the firm following its acquisition by KKR, plans to focus on developing the chain's private-label business and its pricing and merchandising strategies.

Because Dollar General's customers typically live in small towns (fewer than 20,000 people), the company doesn't advertise. It only sends out direct mailings to announce new stores. Dollar General caters to customers who find shopping at its small, bare-bones stores (about 6,900 sq. ft.) easier and quicker than at super-sized competitors such as Wal-Mart (which are often much farther away). However, as Wal-Mart grows, its retail presence is being felt in more and more of Dollar General's markets.

In 2003 the company launched a new retail concept called Dollar General Market: larger stores (averaging 17,250 sq. ft.) that sell fresh produce and a range of refrigerated, frozen, and nonperishable foods in addition to its core merchandise. It currently operates about 55 Dollar General Market stores.

EXECUTIVES

Chairman: Michael M. Calbert, age 45
CEO and Director: Richard W. (Rick) Dreiling, age 54
President and Chief Strategy Officer: David L. (Dave) Beré, age 54
Division President Store Operations and Store Development: Kathleen R. Guion, age 56, $426,683 pay (prior to promotion)
EVP and CFO: David M. Tehle, age 51, $480,019 pay
EVP and General Counsel: Susan S. Lanigan, age 45, $473,525 pay (prior to promotion)
SVP General Merchandise Manager: James W. (Jim) Thorpe
SVP and Controller: Anita C. Elliott, age 43
SVP Store Operations: Thomas H. (Tom) Mitchell
SVP Real Estate and Store Development: Gayle Aertker
SVP and Chief People Officer: Bob Ravener
SVP and CIO: Ryan Boone
SVP Supply Chain: John Flanigan
SVP Global Strategic Sourcing: Rod Birkins
VP Human Resources: Jeffrey R. (Jeff) Rice, age 41
Director Investor Relations: Emma Jo Kauffman
Corporate Secretary and Chief Compliance Officer: Christine Connolly
Spokeswoman: Tawn Earnest
Auditors: Ernst & Young LLP

LOCATIONS

HQ: Dollar General Corporation
  100 Mission Ridge, Goodlettsville, TN 37072
Phone: 615-855-4000   **Fax:** 615-855-5252
Web: www.dollargeneral.com

2008 Stores

	No.
Texas	969
Georgia	464
North Carolina	467
Ohio	465
Alabama	446
Florida	415
Pennsylvania	393
Tennessee	403
Louisiana	326
Illinois	306
Missouri	309
South Carolina	316
Indiana	302
Kentucky	300
Oklahoma	271
Mississippi	256
Virginia	243
Michigan	238
New York	223
Arkansas	224
Iowa	170
West Virginia	149
Kansas	144
Wisconsin	88
Nebraska	80
Maryland	57
Arizona	51
New Mexico	42
Other states	105
Total	**8,222**

PRODUCTS/OPERATIONS

2008 Sales

	% of total
Highly consumable	67
Seasonal	16
Home products	9
Basic clothing	8
Total	**100**

Selected Merchandise

Basic apparel
Cleaning supplies
Dairy products
Frozen foods
Health and beauty aids
Housewares
Packaged foods
Seasonal goods
Stationery

COMPETITORS

99 Cents Only
Big Lots
Costco Wholesale
CVS Caremark
Dollar Tree
Family Dollar Stores
Fred's
Kmart
Retail Ventures
Rite Aid
Target
TJX Companies
Variety Wholesalers
Walgreen
Wal-Mart

HISTORICAL FINANCIALS

Company Type: Private

Income Statement

FYE: Friday nearest January 31

	REVENUE ($ mil.)	NET INCOME ($ mil.)	NET PROFIT MARGIN	EMPLOYEES
1/08	9,495	(13)	—	71,500
1/07	9,170	138	1.5%	71,500
1/06	8,582	350	4.1%	64,500
1/05	7,661	344	4.5%	63,200
1/04	6,872	301	4.4%	57,800
Annual Growth	**8.4%**	—	—	**5.5%**

2008 Year-End Financials

Debt ratio: 158.2%
Return on equity: —
Cash ($ mil.): —

Current ratio: —
Long-term debt ($ mil.): 4,279

Net Income History

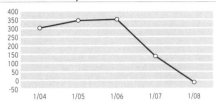

Dot Foods

Dot Foods, the largest foodservice redistributor in the US, started out in business as one station wagon that hauled dairy goods around and went by the name of Associated Dairy Products. The company now owns more than 700 trucks (under the name Dot Transportation) that distribute some 70,000 products including food, flatware, serve ware, and janitorial supplies from some 700 manufacturers to its customers — more than 3,300 foodservice distributors. Dot has about 10 distribution facilities located across the country. Its edotfoods unit offers ordering and fulfillment services online. The company also sells food ingredients to dairies, bakeries, confectioners, meat processors, and other food manufacturers.

EXECUTIVES

Chairman: Patrick F. (Pat) Tracy
CEO and Director: John M. Tracy
President, COO, and Director: Joe Tracy
CFO: William H. (Bill) Metzinger
SVP, General Counsel, Secretary, and Director:
  James W. (Jim) Tracy, age 53
VP Business Development: Michael A. (Mike) Buckley
VP Distribution Centers: John Long
VP Human Resources: Mike Hulsen
VP Information Technology: Mark Read
VP Marketing: Scott C. Stamerjohn
VP, Quality: Dan Koch
VP Sales: Michael J. (Mike) Duggan, age 57
VP Customer Development: Dick Tracy
Controller: Thomas L. (Tom) Tracy
Corporate Communications Manager: Suzanne Kassing
President, Tracy Family Foundation: Jean Buckley

LOCATIONS

HQ: Dot Foods, Inc.
  1 Dot Way, Mount Sterling, IL 62353
Phone: 217-773-4411   **Fax:** 217-773-3321
Web: www.dotfoods.com

COMPETITORS

Associated Wholesalers
Bi-Rite Restaurant Supply
C.D. Hartnett
Federated Group
McLane Foodservice
Purity Wholesale Grocers

HISTORICAL FINANCIALS

Company Type: Private

Income Statement

FYE: December 31

	REVENUE ($ mil.)	NET INCOME ($ mil.)	NET PROFIT MARGIN	EMPLOYEES
12/07	2,810	—	—	3,168
12/06	2,490	—	—	2,916
12/05	2,164	—	—	2,746
12/04	1,930	—	—	2,500
12/03	1,573	—	—	2,200
Annual Growth	**15.6%**	—	—	**9.5%**

Revenue History

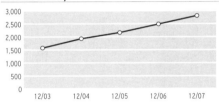

Dow Corning

Dow Corning knows about cooperation. The company began as a joint venture of chemical titan Dow and glass giant Corning in 1943 and ranks among the longest lasting partnerships of its kind in the US. Dow Corning produces more than 7,000 silicone-based products such as adhesives, insulating materials, and lubricants for aerospace, automotive, and electrical uses. Because silicone does not conduct electricity, it is also used in its hard polycrystalline form (silicon) as the material on which semiconductors are built. Its products are also used in the production of photovoltaic cells used to produce solar energy. With plants worldwide, the company sells more than half of its products outside the US.

Moving outside its traditional position in polymeric silicones, the company acquired the holographic data storage business of Aprilis in 2006. The acquired division, now called DCE Aprilis, operates as a separate Dow Corning subsidiary.

Through its Xiameter brand and Web site, Dow Corning sells products online to more than 80 countries. Launched in 2000, Xiameter serves customers that order in large volumes and require less customer service attention. Now Dow Corning (through both its eponymous brand and the Xiameter brand) achieves 30% of its sales online, more than twice the industry average.

HISTORY

Dow Corning was founded in 1943 as a joint venture between Dow Chemical and Corning Glass Works. Corning, founded by Amory Houghton in 1875, provided Thomas Edison with glass for the first light bulbs. It developed Pyrex heat-resistant glass in 1915.

Corning made its first silicone resin samples in 1938. It teamed with a group of Dow Chemical scientists who were also working on silicone products in 1940. Dow Chemical president Willard Dow and Corning Glass Works president Glen Cole shook hands on the idea of a joint venture in 1942, and 10 months later Dow Corning was formed. Its first product, the engine grease DOW CORNING 4, enabled B-17s to fly at 35,000 feet (a major contribution to the Allied war effort). In 1945 DOW CORNING 35 (an emulsifier used in tire molds) and Pan Glaze (which made baking pans stick-proof and easier to clean) were instant successes on the home front.

Dow Corning expanded rapidly in international markets and in 1960 set up Dow Corning International to handle sales and technical service in markets outside North America. By 1969 the company had operations worldwide.

Dow Corning's first breast implants went on the market in 1964. Over the next three decades, Dow Corning and other silicone makers sold silicone breast implants to more than a million women in the US. In the early 1980s breast-implant recipients began suing Dow Corning and other implant makers, claiming that the silicone gel in the implants leaked and caused health problems. Dow Corning, the leading implant maker, defended the devices as safe. The company stopped making implants in 1992, after the Food and Drug Administration called for a moratorium on silicone-gel implants.

In 1993 Baxter International, Bristol-Myers Squibb, and Dow Corning offered $4.2 billion to settle thousands of claims. The corporation declared bankruptcy in 1995 to buy time for financial reorganization. A federal judge stripped Dow Chemical of its protection from direct liability, and the company was later ordered to pay a Nevada couple $4.1 million in damages (other jurisdictions did not follow suit). Dow Corning sold its Polytrap polymer technology to Advanced Polymer, maker of polymer-based pharmaceutical delivery systems, in 1996. The following year the company sold Bisco Products, its silicone-foam business, to Rogers Corporation for $12 million.

Dow Corning's $3.7 billion bankruptcy reorganization plan, offered in 1997, allowed for $2.4 billion to be set aside to settle most implant lawsuits against the corporation. However, a federal bankruptcy judge found legal flaws in the proposal and refused to allow claimants to vote on it. In 1998 Dow Corning upped the ante to $4.4 billion — $3 billion to the silicone claimants and the rest to creditors.

Both sides later agreed to a $3.2 billion compensation package, and in 1999 the plan received approval from a bankruptcy judge and creditors. However, the settlement stalled when the judge ruled that women who disagreed with the settlement could sue Dow Chemical and Corning (Dow Corning appealed). Despite its court battles, in 2000 the company acquired the 51% of Universal Silicones & Lubricants (high-tech lubricants and silicone sealants) it did not own and renamed the company Dow Corning India.

In early 2004, a bankruptcy court judge ruled that the re-approved settlement would go through. The move allowed the money Dow Corning set aside for the settlement to be dispersed to claimants and for the company to exit Chapter 11, which finally occurred in the middle of that year.

EXECUTIVES

Chairman, President, and CEO: Stephanie A. Burns, age 54
EVP, Office of the CEO: Christopher J. (Chris) Bowyer
VP and CFO; President, Americas Area: Joseph D. (Don) Sheets
VP and Chief Human Resources Officer: Derek A. O'Malley-Keyes
VP, General Counsel, and Secretary: Sue K. McDonnell
VP Chief Engineer: Brett W. Able
VP Specialty Chemicals; President, Asia Area: Jean-Marc Gilson
VP Strategic Programs: Allan C. (Harry) Ludgate
VP and European Area President: Bruno J. Sulmon
VP, CTO, and Executive Director Science and Technology: Gregg A. Zank
VP and General Manager, Core Products: Robert D. (Bob) Hansen
VP and General Manager, Advanced Technologies and Ventures: Marie N. Eckstein
VP Asia; General Manager, Service Enterprise Unit: Thomas H. (Tom) Cook
Chief Marketing Officer and Executive Director Marketing and Sales: Brian Chermside
Executive Director and CIO: Abbe M. Mulders
Executive Director and Chief Communications Officer: Janet M. Botz
Auditors: PricewaterhouseCoopers LLP

LOCATIONS

HQ: Dow Corning Corporation
2200 W. Salzburg Rd., Midland, MI 48640
Phone: 989-496-4000   **Fax:** 989-496-4393
Web: www.dowcorning.com

Dow Corning operates about 30 manufacturing sites and about 15 R&D centers worldwide.

PRODUCTS/OPERATIONS

Selected Products and Applications

Aerospace
  Adhesives
  Encapsulants
  Exotic composite materials
  Greases
  High-purity fluids
  Primers
  Protective coatings
  Sealants
Automotive
  Body components
  Brake systems
  Chassis
  Electrical components
  Electronic components
  Engine/drivetrain
  Exterior lighting
  Fuel systems
Chemical and Material Manufacturing
  Auto appearance chemicals
  Industrial release agents
  Materials treatment
  Process aid antifoams
  Pulp manufacturing
Cleaning Products
  Dry cleaning
  Laundry detergents
  Polishes and hard surface cleaners
Coatings and Plastics
  Caulks
  Coatings
  Sealants

Electrical/Electronics
  Adhesives and sealants
  Conformal coatings
  Dielectric gels
  High-voltage insulators
  Hyperpure polycrystalline silicon
  Interlayer dielectric and passivation materials
  Liquid transformer fluid
  Silicone encapsulants
  Silicone grease for insulators
  Silicone RTV coating for insulators
  Silicone rubber insulators
  Thermally conductive adhesives
Food and Beverage
  Defoamers
  Packaging
Health Care
  Hydrocephalus shunts
  Pacemaker leads
  Tubing for dialysis
Paper Manufacturing and Finishing
  Release coatings for label-backing paper, pressure-sensitive adhesives, and paper coatings
Personal Care
  Materials for deodorants, cosmetics, and lotions
Plastics
Textiles
  Waterproofing agents

COMPETITORS

3M
Asahi Glass
Bayer MaterialScience
Bostik
Cytec Engineered Materials
Evonik Degussa
Formosa Plastics
H.B. Fuller
Hexcel
Honeywell Specialty Materials
Shin-Etsu Chemical
Wacker Chemie

HISTORICAL FINANCIALS

Company Type: Joint venture

Income Statement

FYE: December 31

	REVENUE ($ mil.)	NET INCOME ($ mil.)	NET PROFIT MARGIN	EMPLOYEES
12/07	4,940	—	—	10,000
12/06	4,392	—	—	9,000
12/05	3,879	—	—	—
12/04	3,373	—	—	—
12/03	2,873	—	—	8,200
Annual Growth	14.5%	—	—	5.1%

Revenue History

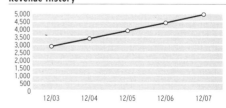

DreamWorks SKG

DreamWorks woke up to media consolidation. Created in 1994 by filmmaker Steven Spielberg, animation guru Jeffrey Katzenberg, and recording industry maven David Geffen, DreamWorks produces movies and TV shows (*Tropic Thunder*, *Las Vegas*). Initially an experiment in creating a diversified media company, DreamWorks struggled with any business beyond filmed entertainment and shed its other operations, including arcade business GameWorks (a venture with SEGA and Universal Pictures) and a music label (sold to Universal Music). Money maker DreamWorks Animation was spun off to shareholders. DreamWorks was sold to Paramount in 2006, but two years later separated from Paramount through backing from Reliance Entertainment.

Katzenberg left the company to head DreamWorks Animation when that company was spun off in 2004. Two years later Paramount lured former Universal Pictures chairman Stacey Snider into the fold as co-chairman and CEO of DreamWorks. (She shared the chairman title with Geffen.) The move further cemented the turnaround of Paramount's executive suite, as Snider had a proven box office track record at Universal with such hits as *Meet the Fockers* and *The Bourne Supremacy*. Under Snider's lead DreamWorks churned out commercial successes in 2007, including *Transformers*, *Norbit*, *Blades of Glory*, and *Disturbia*. Its summer 2008 release, *Tropic Thunder*, also did well at the box office.

However, perhaps feeling that they hadn't been appreciated by their Viacom (Paramount's parent company) owners, despite the fact that DreamWorks played a large role in catapulting Paramount from fifth place in 2006 to first in market share in 2007, DreamWorks principals left Paramount in 2008. In order to finance their departure, Spielberg raised about $1.2 billion through the formation of a partnership with India's Reliance Entertainment. (Reliance is investing some $500 million in equity, with another $700 million in debt coming from JPMorgan Chase. Geffen is not joining the venture.)

The deal follows more than two years of DreamWorks operating as part of Paramount. Viacom bought DreamWorks for $1.6 billion and placed it under Paramount's purview. As part of that deal, Paramount took over distribution rights to all DreamWorks Animation films for seven years starting in 2006. In addition, to minimize the financial risk, Paramount sold the DreamWorks' library of about 60 films for $900 million to a private investment fund led by billionaire George Soros. Paramount gets to keep a small stake in the library, retains the rights to distribute the titles for five years, and also has an option to buy the films back.

Before the Paramount acquisition, the DreamWorks live-action movie unit had generated successes such as *Dreamgirls* and *Munich*; however, DreamWorks Animation turned out to be the firm's most successful business. Its series of *Shrek* films surpassed previous records as one of the most successful animated franchises of all time. The company spun off DreamWorks Animation in an effort to better compete with rival Pixar. DreamWorks no longer holds any ownership interest in the animation company.

EXECUTIVES

Chairman: Roger A. Enrico, age 63
Co-Chairman and CEO: Stacey Snider
Co-Chairman: David Geffen, age 65
COO: Ann Daly, age 51
President, Production: Adam Goodman
Co-Head DreamWorks Television: Justin Falvey
Co-Head DreamWorks Television: Darryl Frank
Co-Head Motion Picture Division: Laurie MacDonald
Co-Head Motion Picture Division: Walter Parkes, age 52
Head Distribution Operations: Mark Christiansen
Head Distribution Sales: Donald Harris
Head Non-Theatrical Distribution: Joan Filippini
Head Theatrical Marketing Services: Patricia Gonzalez
Head Sales, Canada: Don Popow
Head Sales, Central Division: Kyle Davies
Head Sales, Eastern Division: Joe Sabatino
Legal: Andrew Chang
General Counsel and Secretary: Katherine Kendrick, age 47

LOCATIONS

HQ: DreamWorks SKG
　　1000 Flower St., Glendale, CA 91201
Phone: 818-733-7000　　**Fax:** 818-695-7574
Web: www.dreamworks.com

PRODUCTS/OPERATIONS

Selected Films and Television Shows

DreamWorks Pictures
　Almost Famous (2000)
　American Beauty (1999)
　Amistad (1997)
　Antz (1998)
　A Beautiful Mind (2001, co-produced with Universal Studios)
　Catch Me if You Can (2002)
　Chicken Run (2000, co-produced with Aardman Animation)
　Deep Impact (1998, co-produced with Paramount Pictures)
　Disturbia (2007)
　Dreamgirls (2006)
　Galaxy Quest (1999)
　Gladiator (2000, co-produced with Universal Studios)
　House of Sand and Fog (2003)
　Match Point (2005)
　Memoirs of a Geisha (2005)
　Minority Report (2002)
　Mouse Hunt (1997)
　Munich (2005)
　Norbit (2007)
　Old School (2003)
　The Prince of Egypt (1998)
　The Ring (2002)
　The Ring Two (2005)
　Road to Perdition (2002)
　Road Trip (2000)
　Saving Private Ryan (1998, co-produced with Paramount Pictures)
　Seabiscuit (2003, co-produced with Paramount Pictures)
　Shark Tale (2004)
　Shrek (2001)
　Shrek 2 (2004)
　The Terminal (2004)
　Transformers (2007)
　Tropic Thunder (2008)
　War of the Worlds (2005, co-produced with Paramount Pictures)
DreamWorks Television
　Boomtown (2002-2003)
　The Contender (2005)
　Father of the Pride (2004)
　Freaks and Geeks (1999-2000)
　The Job (2001)
　Las Vegas (2003-present)
　Oliver Beene (2003)
　Spin City (1996-2002)
　Undeclared (2001)

COMPETITORS

Fox Filmed Entertainment
Lionsgate
Lucasfilm
MGM
Miramax
Sony Pictures Entertainment
Universal Pictures
Warner Bros.

The Drees Company

Drees Co. is a leading homebuilder in Cincinnati and one of the top private builders in the US. Customers may choose from homes that range from about $100,000 to more than $900,000. It also builds condominiums, apartments, and commercial buildings through its nine divisions. The company is expanding through acquisitions such as the addition of the homebuilding assets of Zaring National in Cincinnati (Zaring Premier Homes), Indianapolis, and Nashville, Tennessee, and Ausherman Homes (renamed Drees) in Frederick, Maryland (near Washington, DC). The Drees Co. offers financing through its First Equity Mortgage subsidiary.

The Drees Co. also purchases land to develop as homesites in southeastern Indiana, northern Kentucky, Maryland, North Carolina, Ohio, Tennessee, Texas, eastern West Virginia, and Washington, DC.

A family-operated enterprise since its founding by Theodore Drees in 1928, the Drees Co. is run by the third generation of the Drees family.

EXECUTIVES

Chairman: Ralph Drees
President and CEO: David Drees
EVP and CFO: Mark Williams
VP Human Resources: Effie McKeehan
VP Marketing: Barbara Drees Jones
Secretary and Treasurer: Lawrence G. Herbst
President, Dallas West Division: Greg Dawson
President, Southern Region: Mike Rubery
President, Midwest Region: Terry Sievers
President, Dallas East Division: David Harbin
President, Indianapolis Division: Steve Masuccio
President, Premier Region: Dan Jones
President, Nashville Division: Ron Schroeder

LOCATIONS

HQ: The Drees Company
　　211 Grandview Dr., Ste. 300,
　　Fort Mitchell, KY 41017
Phone: 859-578-4200　　**Fax:** 859-341-5854
Web: www.dreeshomes.com

Division Office Locations

Austin (Texas)
Cincinnati (Fort Mitchell, KY)
Cleveland (North Canton, OH)
Dallas (Irving, TX)
Dayton (Centerville, OH)
Indianapolis (Indiana)
Jacksonville (Florida)
Nashville (Brentwood, TN)
Raleigh (North Carolina)
Washington, DC (Alexandria, VA)

COMPETITORS

Centex
D.R. Horton
Engle Homes
Fischer Homes
KB Home

Lennar
M/I Homes
Pulte Homes
The Ryland Group

Dresser, Inc.

Is your energy business all dressed up with no place to flow? Not if Dresser can help it. The company, formerly Dresser Industries (and once a part of Halliburton), makes flow control products (valves, actuators, meters, fittings, and the like for oil and gas exploration), measurement systems (gas pumps and point of sale terminals made by business unit Dresser Wayne for gas stations and convenience stores), and power systems (Waukesha engines and Roots blowers and compressors). Dresser serves companies in the oil and gas, power generation, transportation, chemical, and process industries. The company maintains a presence in more than 100 countries, with manufacturing or support facilities in more than 20.

Dresser was acquired by an investment consortium led by Riverstone Holdings in mid-2007. Other members of the consortium include First Reserve Corporation, Lehman Brothers, and The Carlyle Group. First Reserve was already an investor, owning more than 90% of Dresser as of 2005 when Dresser announced plans for an IPO. After delays related to accounting problems, Dresser called off the IPO in 2006. Shortly after, the company said it would explore strategic options, including a possible sale of the company.

In late 2005 the company sold its On/Off valve business, which primarily served the oil and gas exploration industry, to Cooper Cameron (now Cameron International) for more than $220 million. While the On/Off business had accounted for about a fifth of Dresser's total sales, its margins were low. Also in 2005 the company sold Dresser Instruments, which makes pressure gauges, transmitters, and temperature switches, to KPS Special Situations Funds. Dresser sold the businesses to concentrate on its more profitable operations.

The company then expanded through several small acquisitions in 2006 and 2007, including Dresser Wayne's purchase of software provider Performance Retail; Dresser Piping Specialties' acquisition of Blackhawk Industries, a maker of fluid fittings; and Dresser Root's purchase of engineering and design firm ESCOR, which focuses on control systems for wastewater treatment systems, a core focus of Dresser Root.

EXECUTIVES

President, CEO, and Board Member: John P. Ryan
SVP and CFO: Robert D. (Bob) Woltil
SVP Corporate Development: J. Scott Matthews
SVP and General Counsel: Linda Rutherford
SVP Human Resources: Mark J. Scott
VP Corporate Development: Scott Coleman
VP Investor Relations and Corporate Communications: Jenny Haynes
VP and CIO: Darren F. Whitney
President, Waukesha Engine: Thomas J. Laird
President, Dresser Wayne, Fuel Dispenser Business Unit: Neil H. Thomas

President, Dresser Roots, Blower Business Unit: John S. Parrish
President, Dresser Natural Gas Solutions, Engine Business Unit: Daniel E. Jezerinac
President, Dresser Masonellan, Control Valve Business Unit: Andrew Norman
President, Dresser Consolidated, Pressure Relief Valve Business Unit: J. Richard Fentem
Corporate Secretary and Associate General Counsel: David M. Dolan
Corporate Controller and Chief Accounting Officer: Jennifer L. Botter, age 42
Treasurer: Richard T. Kernan
Auditors: PricewaterhouseCoopers LLP

LOCATIONS

HQ: Dresser, Inc.
  15455 Dallas Pkwy., Ste. 1100, Addison, TX 75001
Phone: 972-361-9800   **Fax:** 972-361-9903
Web: www.dresser.com

PRODUCTS/OPERATIONS

Selected Brands and Products

Andco
Becker
Blackhawk
Consolidated
Masoneilan
Mooney
Piping Specialties
RCS Actuators
REDQ Regulators
Roots Blowers
Roots Meters
Roots Provers
Texstream Pumps
Waukesha Engine
Wayne

COMPETITORS

Cameron International
Caterpillar
CIRCOR International
Curtiss-Wright Flow
  Control
Danaher
Datamarine
Elster American Meter
Emerson Electric
Flowserve
Gilbarco

IDEX
Ingersoll-Rand
ITT Corp.
Kerr Machine Company
Pentair
Radiant Systems
Rotork
SPX
Tokheim
Tyco
Velan

HISTORICAL FINANCIALS

Company Type: Private

Income Statement				FYE: December 31
	REVENUE ($ mil.)	NET INCOME ($ mil.)	NET PROFIT MARGIN	EMPLOYEES
12/07	2,000	—	—	6,400
12/06	1,830	—	—	6,100
12/05	1,700	—	—	6,500
12/04	1,992	—	—	8,800
12/03	1,657	—	—	8,300
Annual Growth	4.8%	—	—	(6.3%)

Revenue History

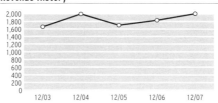

Drummond Company

Drummond does business from the ground down. The company operates the Shoal Creek underground coal mine in Alabama and the Pribbenow surface coal mine in Colombia. Drummond's ABC Coke unit produces foundry coke, which is used mainly in the automotive, construction, and sugar industries, at a plant in Alabama. In addition, Drummond develops housing communities and office parks in Alabama, California, and Florida. H. E. Drummond began his company in 1935 on land homesteaded by his mother; eventually his five sons entered the business. The Drummond family still owns and manages the company.

EXECUTIVES

Chairman and CEO: Garry N. Drummond Sr., age 66
Vice Chairman: E. A. (Larry) Drummond
SVP and CFO: Jack Stilwell
SVP Mining: Richard Mullen
VP Facilities Engineering: Gene Honeycutt
VP Mine Engineering and Underground Operations: Mike Butts
President, ABC Coke Division: John M. Pearson
President, Drummond Coal Sales: George E. Wilbanks
President, Drummond, Ltd.: Augusto Jimenez
General Counsel: Bruce C. Webster
Human Resources: B. Blackburn
Treasurer and Executive Assistant to the CEO: Matt Brown

LOCATIONS

HQ: Drummond Company, Inc.
  1000 Urban Center Dr., Ste. 300,
  Birmingham, AL 35242
Phone: 205-945-6300   **Fax:** 205-945-6440
Web: www.drummondco.com

PRODUCTS/OPERATIONS

Selected Operations

ABC Coke (coke plant; Jefferson County, Alabama)
Liberty Park (real estate development; Birmingham, Alabama)
Mina Pribbenow (coal, Colombia)
Oakbridge (real estate development; Lakeland, Florida)
Puerto Drummond (port facilities, Colombia)
Rancho La Quinta (real estate development; La Quinta, California)
Shoal Creek Mine (coal; Jefferson County, Alabama)

COMPETITORS

Alliance Resource
Arch Coal
CONSOL Energy
Massey Energy
Oxbow
Peabody Energy
Penn Virginia
Sherritt International
Walter Industries
Westmoreland Coal

HISTORICAL FINANCIALS
Company Type: Private

Income Statement

FYE: December 31

	REVENUE ($ mil.)	NET INCOME ($ mil.)	NET PROFIT MARGIN	EMPLOYEES
12/07	1,890	—	—	5,600
12/06	1,770	—	—	5,100
12/05	1,798	—	—	5,100
Annual Growth	2.5%	—	—	4.8%

Revenue History

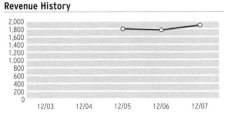

Duane Reade

Duane Reade is the Big Apple of drugstores. Named after the two streets where its first store was located, the company is the market leader in densely populated Manhattan. In all, the company operates about 230 stores in New York and about a dozen in New Jersey. Many of the company's stores are in high-traffic Manhattan (giving the firm more sales per square foot than any other US drugstore chain). Duane Reade's stores vary greatly in size (1,600-14,700 sq. ft.). The company sells prescription drugs, but about half of sales come from items such as over-the-counter medications, food and beverages, and health and beauty aids. Duane Reade was taken private in mid-2004 by equity group Oak Hill Capital Partners.

Oak Hill Capital is led by Texas investor Robert Bass. In return for each share, stockholders received $16.50 in cash for a transaction valued at about $700 million — including debt — for the company.

The drugstore chain has new leadership with John Lederer joining the firm as chairman and CEO in April 2008. Lederer is a former president of the Canadian supermarket chain Loblaw.

Much of Duane Reade's growth has been through new store openings, including what it terms "planned cannibalization," where new stores are opened near crowded older stores to relieve traffic. In 2007 the drugstore chain acquired eight Gristedes supermarkets in Manhattan, which were converted to Duane Reade stores.

While the company has slowed the pace of its store openings in recent years, it has introduced new in-store services, including professional tooth whitening and diet planning. Duane Reade is also experimenting with ATM-like movie vending machines, coffee kiosks, and "Skin Fitness Centers" to boost sales.

The firm buys most of its non-pharmacy products directly from manufacturers and distributes those items through its warehouses in New Jersey and Queens. Duane Reade fills about 1,700 called-in prescriptions a day from its midtown central fill station. The company also offers more than 800 private-label products (including its "apt.5" line of cosmetics).

New York's ban on smoking in some public places has cut into the chain's front-end sales.

A ruling by the National Labor Relations Board could force the regional drugstore chain to pay out more than $25 million in unpaid benefit contributions to its unionized employees. The ruling is part of an ongoing labor dispute between Duane Reade and 2,600 members of Local 338, which the company no longer recognizes.

EXECUTIVES
Chairman and CEO: John A. Lederer, age 52
SVP and CFO: John K. Henry, age 58
SVP and Chief Merchandising Officer:
 Joseph C. Magnacca
SVP Human Resources and Administration:
 Vincent A. Scarfone, age 50
SVP Store Operations: Charles R. (Chuck) Newsom, age 57
SVP Supply Chain: Mark W. Scharbo
SVP and General Counsel: Michelle D. Bergman, age 41
VP and Controller: Chris A. Darrow
VP Finance: Anthony M. Goldrick
VP Distribution: Don Yuhasz
VP Marketing: Jeffrey Thompson
VP Real Estate: Mark Bander
VP and CIO: Marc Saffer
Auditors: PricewaterhouseCoopers LLP

LOCATIONS
HQ: Duane Reade Inc.
 440 9th Ave., New York, NY 10001
Phone: 212-273-5700   **Fax:** 212-244-6527
Web: www.duanereade.com

2007 Stores

	No.
New York	231
New Jersey	11
Total	**242**

PRODUCTS/OPERATIONS

Selected Merchandise and Services
Automated teller machines
Cosmetics
Food and beverage items
Greeting cards
Health and beauty aids
Hosiery
Housewares
Lottery ticket sales
Nutritional products
Over-the-counter medications
Photo supplies
Photofinishing
Prescription drugs
Seasonal merchandise
Tobacco products
Vitamins

COMPETITORS

A&P
CVS Caremark
drugstore.com
Rite Aid
Walgreen

HISTORICAL FINANCIALS
Company Type: Private

Income Statement

FYE: Saturday nearest December 31

	REVENUE ($ mil.)	NET INCOME ($ mil.)	NET PROFIT MARGIN	EMPLOYEES
12/07	1,687	(88)	—	6,700
12/06	1,585	(79)	—	6,100
12/05	1,590	(100)	—	6,100
12/04	1,598	(52)	—	6,300
Annual Growth	1.8%	—	—	2.1%

Net Income History

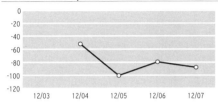

Duchossois Industries

The only thing this family of companies has in common is the Duchossois family, the owners of Duchossois Industries, Inc (DII). The holding company, pronounced Deshy-swa, focuses its interests in the industrial, consumer products, and technology sectors. Subsidiary The Chamberlain Group is the world's top maker of residential and commercial door openers, and it is a leading maker of access control products. AMX Corporation performs systems integration while other companies offer awnings, AV equipment, Internet-based access control, and lighting products. DII also owns an early stage IT venture capital fund and holds a minority stake in horse racetrack Churchill Downs.

It should come as no surprise that the company has bought and sold large portions of its portfolio over the years. DII's current strategy is "lifestyle improvements for the home and office." To that end, it's looking to expand its existing portfolio of consumer goods, access control, and systems integration companies. The company also hopes to diversify by adding firms that have a niche product, strong management team, and intellectual property.

In 2007-2008 DII picked up seven additions, including a UK-based AV control manufacturer. It also moved AMX into Asia, opening a sales and distribution office in Singapore.

EXECUTIVES
Chairman: Richard L. Duchossois, age 86
CEO: Craig J. Duchossois, age 63
President and COO: Robert L. (Bob) Fealy, age 56
EVP and CFO: Michael E. Flannery
CEO, The Chamberlain Group: J. David Rolls
EVP, Administration, The Chamberlain Group:
 Mark Tone
Hiring Manager, The Chamberlain Group:
 Melanie Ditore
VP, Information and Technology, The Chamberlain Group: David Banaszak

LOCATIONS

HQ: Duchossois Industries, Inc.
 845 N. Larch Ave., Elmhurst, IL 60126
Phone: 630-279-3600   **Fax:** 630-530-6091
Web: www.duch.com

PRODUCTS/OPERATIONS

Selected Subsidiaries and Affiliates

AMX Corporation (systems integration)
Brivo Systems (access control)
Churchill Downs, Inc. (25%, horse racing and
   entertainment)
Duchossois Technology Partners (venture capital)
Durasol Systems (retractable awnings)
The Chamberlain Group, Inc. (access control)

COMPETITORS

Gadco
GE
Griffon
Microchip Technology
NTK Holdings
Overhead Door
Sanwa Shutter
Somfy
Stanley Works
Wayne-Dalton

Duke University Health System

Antibodies inside ya dukin' it out? Better get to the Duke University Health Center — no, no, not the campus infirmary, the Medical Center. At the core of the Duke University Health System is the Duke University Hospital. The system also includes two community hospitals in Durham (Durham Regional Hospital) and Raleigh (Duke Raleigh Hospital), North Carolina. Its network of medical facilities provides such services as primary and specialty care, home and hospice care, clinical research, and public education programs. The total bed capacity of all three hospitals combined is 1,544. Duke University Health Center is part of Duke University Medical School.

EXECUTIVES

President and CEO: Victor J. Dzau, age 62
SVP, CFO, and Treasurer: Kenneth C. Morris
SVP Clinical Affairs; CEO, Duke University Hospital:
 William J. Fulkerson Jr.
**VP, Ambulatory Care; Executive Director, Duke Private
 Diagnostic Clinic and Duke Patient Revenue
 Management Organization:** Paul R. Newman
**VP, Business Development and Chief Strategic
 Planning Officer; Vice Chancellor, Medical Center
 Integrated Planning:** Molly K. O'Neill
**VP, Diagnostic Services and CIO; VP, Diagnostic
 Services and CIO, Duke University Medical Center:**
 Asif Ahmad
VP, Medical Affairs: Michael Cuffe
Chief Patient-Safety Officer: Karen Frush
**Vice Chancellor, Academic Affairs, Duke University
 Medical Center and Dean, Duke University School of
 Medicine:** Robert Sanders (Sandy) Williams, age 59
**Vice Chancellor, Science and Technology, Duke
 University Medical Center:** Peter C. Agre

**Vice Chancellor, Nursing Affairs; Dean, Duke
 University School of Nursing:** Catherine Lynch Gilliss
Vice Chancellor, Clinical Research: Robert Califf
CEO, Duke Health Raleigh Hospital:
 Douglas B. (Doug) Vinsel, age 55

LOCATIONS

HQ: Duke University Health System
 3701 Duke Medical Center, Durham, NC 27706
Phone: 919-684-8111
Web: dukehealth.org

COMPETITORS

Cumberland County Hospital System
Danville Regional Medical Center
FirstHealth of the Carolinas
Morehead Memorial Hospital
Moses Cone Health
Novant Health
Rex Healthcare
Rowan Regional Medical Center
UNC Hospitals
University Health Systems of Eastern Carolina
Wake Forest University Baptist Medical Center
WakeMed
Wesley Long Community Hospital

Dunavant Enterprises

King Cotton is alive and well in Memphis. Homegrown Dunavant Enterprises is one of the largest cotton traders in the world. Dunavant was founded in 1960 by William Dunavant, his son Billy (who is allergic to cotton), and Samuel T. Reeves. (The elder Dunavant died shortly after the founding, and Reeves left in 1995 to form Pinnacle Trading.) The company, which grew by selling aggressively to China and the Soviet Union, maintains offices in Africa, Asia, Australia, Europe, Latin America, and the southern US. Other operations include cotton ginning, trucking, warehousing, real estate development, and commodities trading. Dunavant Enterprises is owned by the Dunavant family and company employees.

Dunavant handles some 6 million bales of cotton per year. It has cotton warehouses in the US and Australia, and ginning operations in Zambia, Uganda, Mozambique, and Australia.

EXECUTIVES

Chairman: William B. (Billy) Dunavant Jr.
President and CEO: William B. Dunavant III
Manager, Human Resources: Mike Andereck
Secretary and General Counsel:
 William (Bill) Stubblefield
President, Dunavant of California: Roger Glaspey

LOCATIONS

HQ: Dunavant Enterprises, Inc.
 3797 New Getwell Rd., Memphis, TN 38118
Phone: 901-369-1500   **Fax:** 901-369-1608
Web: www.dunavant.com

COMPETITORS

Calcot	Southwestern Irrigated
Cargill	Cotton
J.G. Boswell Co.	Staplcotn
King Ranch	Weil Brothers Cotton
Plains Cotton	

Dunkin' Brands

Doughnuts and ice cream make sweet bedfellows at Dunkin' Brands. The company is a multi-concept foodservice franchisor, with more than 13,000 locations in 50 countries, including its popular Dunkin' Donuts and Baskin-Robbins chains. With more than 7,000 shops in 30 countries (4,400 of which are in North America), Dunkin' Donuts is the world's leading chain of donut shops. Baskin-Robbins is a leading seller of ice cream and frozen snacks with its nearly 6,000 outlets (about half are located in the US). About 1,100 locations offer a combination of the company's brands. Dunkin' Brands is owned by a group of private investment firms.

Formerly part of UK-based beverage maker Allied Domecq, Dunkin' Brands was acquired for $2.4 billion in 2006 by investment firms Bain Capital, The Carlyle Group, and Thomas H. Lee Partners. The UK-distiller had been acquired the previous year by French beverage maker Pernod Ricard, which sold the restaurant business to focus on its core drinks operations.

The now private company has major expansion plans for its popular donut chain. Dunkin' Brands has unveiled a small-format Dunkin' Donuts store that should lower the cost of construction for franchisees, and it hopes to use other formats including kiosks and carts located inside supermarkets and other retail stores. Internationally, the company plans to open about 100 Dunkin' Donuts outposts in Taiwan by 2017.

Another way Dunkin' Brands is reaching consumers in the grocery store aisles is through a licensing deal with Procter & Gamble, under which the food manufacturing giant is distributing Dunkin' Donuts-branded coffee to retailers. Late in 2007 Dunkin' Brands sold its Togo's sandwich chain, with more than 250 units, to private equity firm Mainsail Partners. Founded in 1971, Togo's had been acquired by Allied Domecq in 1997.

CEO Jon Luther, who formerly ran AFC Enterprises' Popeyes Chicken & Biscuits chain, has been leading the quick-service franchising operation since 2003. He was originally brought in by Allied Domecq to re-energize the restaurant chains.

EXECUTIVES

Chairman and CEO: Jon L. Luther, age 64
Chief Administrative Officer: Paul Leech
**President and Chief Brand Officer, Dunkin' Donuts
 Worldwide:** Will A. Kussell, age 50
CFO: Kate S. Lavelle
SVP Communications: Margery B. Myers
VP and Treasurer: Bonnie M. Monahan, age 45
VP Global Research and Development:
 Michael O'Donovan
Chief Legal Officer and General Counsel:
 Stephen (Steve) Horn, age 61
Chief Multibrand and New Market Entry Officer:
 Tom Wyczawski
Chief Creative and Innovation Officer:
 Joseph (Joe) Scafido
Executive Chef and Director Culinary Development:
 Stan Frankenthaler
Chief Communications and Public Affairs Officer:
 Stephen J. Caldeira, age 50
CIO: Daniel J. (Dan) Sheehan, age 42
Auditors: KPMG Audit Plc

LOCATIONS

HQ: Dunkin' Brands, Inc.
   130 Royall St., Canton, MA 02021
Phone: 781-737-3000   **Fax:** 781-737-4000
Web: www.dunkinbrands.com

COMPETITORS

Ben & Jerry's
Bruegger's
Burger King
Dairy Queen
Dippin Dots
Einstein Noah Restaurant Group
FOCUS Brands
Freshëns
Friendly Ice Cream
Jamba
Kahala
Krispy Kreme
Marble Slab
McDonald's
Mrs. Fields Famous Brands
Starbucks
Tim Hortons
Wendy's

Duquesne Light Holdings

As energy markets deregulate, Duquesne Light Holdings (formerly DQE) is restructuring PDQ. Its principal subsidiary, regulated utility Duquesne Light, distributes electricity to 580,000 customers in southwestern Pennsylvania. The company has been divesting noncore assets to concentrate on its power utility and energy services businesses; it changed its name in 2003 to mark the shift. In 2006 Duquesne Light Holdings acquired Atlantic City Electric's 108 MW ownership interests in the Keystone and Conemaugh coal-fired power plants. The next year a consortium led by Macquarie Infrastructure Partners and Diversified Utilities and Energy Trust acquired Duquesne Light for about $3 billion in cash and debt.

As part of the divestment of noncore operations, Duquesne Light Holdings has sold its propane distribution and e-commerce assets, as well as its AquaSource water and wastewater subsidiary. Most of the AquaSource assets were sold to Philadelphia Suburban (now Aqua America).

EXECUTIVES

Chair: Robert P. Bozzone, age 74
Vice Chair: Doreen E. Boyce
President, CEO and Director: Morgan K. O'Brien, age 48, $911,690 pay
SVP and COO: Joseph G. (Joe) Belechak
SVP and CFO: Stevan R. Schott, age 45, $387,616 pay
SVP and Chief Legal and Administrative Officer: Maureen L. Hogel, age 48, $449,480 pay
SVP and Chief Strategic Officer: James E. Wilson, age 43, $288,320 pay
VP and Treasurer; President, DQE Financial: William F. Fields, age 58
Media Relations: Joseph Vallarian
Auditors: Deloitte & Touche LLP

LOCATIONS

HQ: Duquesne Light Holdings, Inc.
   411 7th Ave., Pittsburgh, PA 15219
Phone: 412-393-6000   **Fax:** 412-393-5517
Web: www.duquesnelight.com

COMPETITORS

Allegheny Energy
Dominion Resources
Equitable Resources
Exelon
FirstEnergy
PPL
UGI

E. & J. Gallo Winery

E. & J. Gallo Winery brings merlot to the masses. The company is one of the world's largest wine makers thanks in part to its inexpensive jug and box brands, including Carlo Rossi, Peter Vella, and Boone's Farm brands. The vintner owns seven wineries and about 20,000 acres of California vineyards. It is the leading US exporter of California wine, selling its some 60 brands in more than 90 countries across the globe. Among its premium wines and imports are those of Gallo Family Vineyards Sonoma Reserve and the Italian wine, Ecco Domani. For those who prefer a little more kick to their imbibing, Gallo distills several lines of brandy and one gin label.

Gallo once only sold wine in the low-to-moderate price range, but now sells across a wide price range, from alcohol-added wines and wine coolers to upscale varietals that fetch more than $50 a bottle. It has successfully expanded premium wines such as Turning Leaf and Frei Brothers, which don't have the Gallo name on the label. It also imports wines from Argentina, Australia, France, Germany, Italy, New Zealand, Spain, and South Africa.

The company has tried new approaches to marketing its products, such as sponsoring pro volleyball tournaments. It also rebranded its California wines as the "Gallo Family Vineyards" and removed the Ernest & Julio tag from its packaging. In 2008 it began producing wines under the MARTHA STEWART VINTAGE label. Offering three varieties — chardonnay, cabernet sauvignon, and merlot — the label is a limited-release product consisting of 15,000 cases.

In addition to using its own grapes, Gallo buys the fruit from other Sonoma County growers. Its 2002 purchase of fellow Sonoma County vintner Louis M. Martini Winery marked the first time Gallo bought another winery rather than land or wine labels. Gallo invested about $1 million in capital improvements at the winery and ramped up production of cabernet under the Martini label. Along with brewing wine and spirits, the company makes its own labels and bottles at its subsidiary, Gallo Glass.

Founded in 1933, the company is still owned and operated by the Gallo family.

HISTORY

Giuseppe Gallo, the father of Ernest and Julio Gallo, was born in 1882 in the wine country of northwest Italy. Around 1900 he and his brother, Michelo (they called themselves Joe and Mike), traveled to America seeking fame and fortune in San Francisco. Both brothers became wealthy growing grapes and anticipating the growth of the market during Prohibition (homemade wine was legal and popular).

Giuseppe's eldest sons, Ernest and Julio, worked with their father from the beginning, but their relationship was strained. The father was reluctant to help his sons, particularly Ernest, in business. However, the mysterious murder-suicide that ended the lives of Giuseppe and his wife in 1933 eliminated that problem; the sons inherited the business their father had been unwilling to share.

From then on Ernest ran the business end, assembling a large distribution network and building a national brand, while Julio made the wine and Joe Jr., the third, much younger, brother, worked for them. In the early 1940s Gallo opened bottling plants in Los Angeles and New Orleans, using screw-cap bottles, which then seemed more hygienic and modern than corks. Gallo lagged during WWII, when alcohol was diverted for the military. Under Julio's supervision, it upgraded its planting stock and refined its technology.

In an attempt to capitalize on the sweet wines popular in the 1950s, Gallo introduced Thunderbird, a fortified wine (its alcohol content boosted to 20%), in 1957. In the 1960s Gallo spurred its growth by heavily advertising and keeping prices low. It introduced Hearty Burgundy, a jug wine, in 1964, along with Ripple. Gallo introduced the carbonated, fruit-flavored Boone's Farm Apple Wine in 1969, creating short-term interest in "pop" wines.

The company introduced its first varietal wines in 1974. In the 1970s Gallo field workers switched unions, from the United Farm Workers to the Teamsters. Repercussions included protests and boycotts, but sales were largely unaffected. From 1976 to 1982 Gallo operated under an FTC order limiting its control over wholesalers. The order was lifted after the industry's competitive balance changed.

Through the 1970s and 1980s, Gallo expanded its production of varietals; in 1988 it began adding vintage dates to labels. But it also kept a hand in the lower levels of the market, introducing Bartles & Jaymes wine coolers.

Gallo began a legal battle in 1986 with Joe, who had been eased out of the business, over the use of the Gallo name. In 1992 Joe lost the use of his name for commercial purposes. Julio died the next year when his Jeep overturned on a family ranch.

In 1996 rival Kendall-Jackson sued Gallo for trademark infringement over Gallo's new wine brand, Turning Leaf, claiming Gallo copied its Vintner's Reserve bottle and label. A jury ruled in Gallo's favor in 1997; a federal appeals court supported that decision in 1998.

In 2000 Gallo announced plans to promote wine-cooler market leader Bartles & Jaymes with a new advertising campaign, although the category continued to wane. The next year Gallo expanded the technological end of the wine business. Gallo's research team patented a number of tools licensed to winemakers around the world; one tool, for example, can diagnose a sick vine in a matter of hours, rather than years.

The purchase of Louis M. Martini Winery in Napa Valley in 2002 furthered Gallo's expansion into premium wines. In 2004 it bought the brand name and stocks of San Jose-based wine producer Mirassou Vineyards, one of the oldest wineries in California, and Santa Barbara company Bindlewood Weste Winery. In 2005 Gallo added Grape Links, Inc., maker of Barefoot Cellars, to its stable of holdings.

Ernest Gallo died in 2007 at the age of 97.

EXECUTIVES

Co-President and CEO: Joseph E. (Joe) Gallo, age 66
Co-President: James E. (Jim) Coleman, age 73
Co-President: Robert J. (Bob) Gallo, age 73
EVP and General Counsel: Jack B. Owens
VP Marketing and Chief Marketing Strategist: Gerald (Gerry) Glasgow
VP Viticulture: Nick Dokoozlian
VP and CIO: Kent Kushar
VP Communications: George Marsden
VP and General Manager, Europe: Devinder Singh
VP Public Relations: Susan Hensley
VP Grower Relations: Greg Coleman
VP Sales and Administration: Peter Abate
Director Environmental Affairs: Chris Savage
Senior Marketing Director: Stephanie Gallo, age 36
Director, National Trade Development: Joseph (Joe) Farnan
Director, Wine Education and Hospitality: Patrick Dodd
Senior Manager Public Relations: Michael J. Heintz

LOCATIONS

HQ: E. & J. Gallo Winery
600 Yosemite Blvd., Modesto, CA 95354
Phone: 209-341-3111
Web: www.gallo.com

PRODUCTS/OPERATIONS

Selected Brands

Spirits
E. & J. VS Brandy
E. & J. VSOP Brandy
E. & J. XO Brandy
New Amsterdam Gin

Wine

Anapamu	Ghost Pines
André	Hornsby's
Ballatore	Indigo Hills
Barefoot Bubbly	Liberty Creek
Barefoot Cellars	Livingston Cellars
Bartles & Jaymes	Louis M. Martini
Bella Sera	MacMurray Ranch
Black Swan	Marcelina
Boone's Farm	Martn Côdax
Bridlewood Estate	Maso Canali
Winery	Mattie's Perch
Carlo Rossi	McWilliam's
Cask & Cream	Mirassou
Clarendon Hills	Peter Vella
Dancing Bull	Pölka Dot
DaVinci	Rancho Zabaco
Don Miguel Gascon	Red Bicyclette
Ecco Domani	Red Rock Winery
Frei Brothers	Redwood Creek
Frutézia	Sebeka
Gallo Family	Tisdale Vineyards
Vineyard Estate	Turning Leaf
Gallo Family Vineyard	Turning Leaf
Single Vineyard	Sonoma Reserve
Gallo Family Vineyard	Whitehaven
Sonoma Reserve	Wild Vines
Gallo Family Vineyard	William Hill Estate
Twin Valley	Wycliff Sparkling

COMPETITORS

Asahi Breweries	LVMH
Bacardi	Newton Vineyard
Bacardi USA	Pernod Ricard
Bronco Wine Co.	Premier Pacific
Brown-Forman	Ravenswood Winery
Concha y Toro	R.H. Phillips
Constellation Wines	Scheid Vineyards
Diageo	Sebastiani Vineyards
Diageo Chateau & Estate	Sunview Vineyards
Wines	Taittinger
Foster's Americas	Terlato Wine
Foster's Group	Trinchero Family Estates
GIV	UST Inc.
Heaven Hill Distilleries	Vincor
Kendall-Jackson	Wine Group
Kirin Holdings Company	

HISTORICAL FINANCIALS

Company Type: Private

Income Statement

	ESTIMATED REVENUE ($ mil.)	NET INCOME ($ mil.)	NET PROFIT MARGIN	EMPLOYEES
12/07	3,150	—	—	5,000
12/06	2,700	—	—	4,600
12/05	2,700	—	—	4,400
12/04	3,000	—	—	—
12/03	2,000	—	—	4,600
Annual Growth	12.0%	—	—	2.1%

FYE: December 31

Revenue History

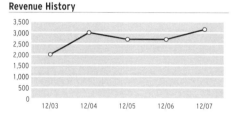

EBSCO Industries

Few portfolios are more diverse than that of EBSCO Industries (short for Elton B. Stephens Company). Among the conglomerate's more than 40 information services, manufacturing, and sales subsidiaries are magazine subscription and fulfillment firms, a fishing lure manufacturer, a rifle manufacturer, a specialty office and computer furniture retailer, and a real estate company. Its main businesses revolve around the publishing industry: EBSCO operates a subscription management agency and is one of the largest publishers of digital information. It has a database of more than 300,000 title listings from more than 78,000 publishers worldwide. The family of founder Elton B. Stephens Sr. owns the company.

EBSCO provides bulk subscription services for print and electronic journals, technical reports, books, and other publications to schools, libraries, and professional offices. It offers sales, promotion, telemarketing, and fulfillment services to publishers, and it owns commercial printers and supplies bindery and packaging products.

Among EBSCO's eclectic subsidiaries are PRADCO Fishing, which makes fishing lures; Valley Joist, which produces steel construction

materials; Vulcan Industries, which makes point-of-purchase displays; Knight & Hale, which makes hunting accessories; specialty furniture makers H. Wilson and Luxor; and real estate unit EBSCO Development.

The aquisitive company's recent purchases include Hallmark Data Systems, a provider of subscription fulfillment services to business-to-business magazines; Lindy Little Joe, a sportfishing products company; and independent insurance agency ANB Insurance Services.

HISTORY

During the 1930s Elton B. Stephens Sr. put himself through college selling magazine subscriptions. Although he later earned a law degree, Stephens thought he could make more money selling magazines. Stephens and his wife, Alys, formed Military Service Co. in 1944 to sell magazines, binders, and display racks to the US military.

Early in his career Stephens suggested that he'd like to own five companies so that he'd have a fallback if one failed. He set about fulfilling his wish, forming Metal Fabricators and Finishers (now Vulcan Industries) in 1946, Vulcan Binder & Cover (now Vulcan Information Packaging) in 1947, and Vulcan Enterprises (now Directional Advertising Services) in 1954.

In 1958 the businesses were combined under the name EBSCO Industries, Inc. (the name is an acronym for Elton B. Stephens Company). In 1960 EBSCO acquired Chicago's Hanson-Bennett Magazine Agency, and in 1967 it bought Los Angeles' National Publications and binder manufacturer The Burkhardt Co. of Detroit.

Stephens retired as president of the company in 1971, and his son James took over. The following year EBSCO bought the Franklin Square Agency and Ziff-Davis' subscription service, doubling the volume of EBSCO Subscription Services. EBSCO started its Publisher Promotion and Fulfillment service and added operations in Europe in 1975.

EBSCO acquired Valley Joist (metal construction products) in 1976 and H. Wilson Co. (audiovisual and computer furniture) in 1977. EBSCO Curriculum Materials and EBSCO Reception Room Subscription Services were formed in 1979 and 1980, respectively. Purchases in 1980 included Metro Press (now EBSCO Graphics), National Billiard, and PRADCO (fishing lures).

In 1981 Elton began a second career at age 70 when he founded Alabama Bancorp.

Under James's direction, EBSCO continued to grow through acquisitions and startups. It bought Four Seasons (promotional clothing and other items, 1983) and NSC International (binding and laminating products, 1984). The company formed electronic database publisher EBSCO Electronic Information (now EBSCO Publishing, 1986) and bought Bomber Bait (1988).

After a short breather, the company acquired Luxor (school and library furniture) in 1992. That year the various Vulcan operations were combined in a new facility in Moody, Alabama. The company acquired Dynamic Information (later EBSCO Document Services) in 1994. The following year it bought Northeast Looseleaf (now part of Vulcan Information Packaging), and in 1996 it formed EBSCO Magazine Express.

The next year EBSCO bought Fred Arbogast, maker of the Jitterbug and Hula Popper fishing lures, and hunting game-call maker Knight & Hale. In 1998 the company bought Network Support, a Canadian maker of document imaging and management software, and closed down its document delivery unit. That year EBSCO Development Company was formed, beginning plans for Mount Laurel — a traditional neighborhood development. In 1999 EBSCO Publishing revealed Searchasaurus, an online search engine for children. The following year EBSCO formed EBSCOPrint.com to sell promotional products via the Internet.

In order to handle its insurance needs in-house, in 2001 EBSCO acquired insurance firm S.S. Nesbitt & Co. In 2003 EBSCO acquired the European operations of RoweCom, a company that provided libraries with an online service giving subscribers access to more than 240,000 periodicals.

James Stephens announced in 2004 that he would step down as CEO in 2005 and appointed company executive Dixon Brooke Jr. (James's brother-in-law) as his replacement.

In 2005 EBSCO expanded its medicine and consumer health data with the acquisition of the assets of HealthGate Data's patient content repository business for $8.1 million in cash.

EXECUTIVES

Chairman: James T. (J.T.) Stephens
President and CEO: F. Dixon Brooke Jr.
VP and CFO: Richard L. (Rick) Bozzelli
VP and Chief Accounting Officer: Carol M. Johnson
VP and Manager Acquisitions: David Walker
VP and General Manager, Administrative Services: Becky Caldarello
VP and General Manager, Corporate Communications: Joe K. Weed
VP and General Manager, Human Resources and Training: John Thompson
VP and General Manager, Information Systems and Services: John R. Fitts
President, EBSCO Information Services: Allen Powell
President, EBSCO Publishing: Timothy R. (Tim) Collins

LOCATIONS

HQ: EBSCO Industries Inc.
 5724 Hwy. 280 East, Birmingham, AL 35242
Phone: 205-991-6600   **Fax:** 205-995-1636
Web: www.ebscoind.com

PRODUCTS/OPERATIONS

Selected Operations

Information Services
 EBSCO Information Services (reference databases, online journals, and subscription services)
 EBSCO Publishing (database publishing and information retrieval services)
 EBSCO Subscription Services (subscription services for libraries and institutions)

Manufacturing
 EBSCO Media (commercial printer)
 Knight & Hale Game Calls
 Knight Rifles
 Luxor (specialty furniture for offices, schools, libraries, and health care facilities)
 PRADCO Outdoor Brands (fishing lures, fishing line, and related products)
 Valley Joist (steel joists, girders, and metal decks for the construction industry)
 Vitronic (promotional products)
 Vulcan Industries (point-of-purchase displays)
 Vulcan Information Packaging (binders, tabs, and packaging for albums, software, and videotapes)
 Wayne Industries (point-of-purchase advertising and signs)

Sales
 EBSCO Development Co. (real estate development)
 EBSCO Magazine Express (direct-marketing subscription agency)
 EBSCO Realty (real estate broker)
 EBSCO Reception Room Subscription Services (subscription services for professional offices)
 EBSCO TeleServices (telemarketing services)
 Military Service Company (producer and manufacturers' representative serving military base exchanges)
 NSC International (distribution of binding and laminating systems)
 Publisher Promotion and Fulfillment (promotion and fulfillment services)
 Publishers' Warehouse (publishers' warehousing and shipping service)
 S.S. Nesbitt & Co. (insurance)
 Vulcan Service (magazine subscription sales)

COMPETITORS

AMREP
APAC Customer Services
Bowne
Brunswick Corp.
Dai Nippon Printing
HALO Holding
Johnson Outdoors
McGraw-Hill
Quebecor
Reed Elsevier Group
Roanoke Bar Division
R.R. Donnelley
Scholastic
Simon Worldwide
Thomson Reuters
TRG Customer Solutions

Eby-Brown Company

Eby-Brown makes its money on such vices as munchies and nicotine. The company is a leading convenience-store supplier that distributes more than 16,000 products to about 12,000 customers in 28 states mostly east of the Mississippi. It operates eight distribution centers that supply such items as beverages, candy and snack foods, frozen and refrigerated foods, tobacco products, and general merchandise. In addition, the company offers advertising and promotion services for its customers. Eby-Brown was founded in 1887 by the Wake family, which continues to own the company.

Looking to expand into the prepared foods segment, Eby-Brown in 2007 launched a new division called Wakefield Sandwich Company. The new unit supplies fresh, prepared sandwiches and breakfast sandwiches, along with related warmers and other display equipment.

EXECUTIVES

Co-President: Richard W. (Dick) Wake, age 54
Co-President: Thomas G. (Tom) Wake, age 48
CFO: Mark Smetana
EVP Cigarette Purchasing: Jode Bunce
VP Business Development: Ron Coppel
VP Merchandising, Groceries, School Supplies, Automotive Oils and Accessories, Kraft, Non-edible, and Miscellaneous: Tom Cinnamon
VP Merchandising, Foodservice (Fresh foods, Condiments, Fresh and Frozen Sandwiches, Roller Grill, Beverages, Fountain, Frozen Beverage, Dispensed Beverage, Water, Isotonic, Juice, Tea, Coffee, and Cappuccino): Sharon Kuncl

VP Merchandising, Candy, Cookies, Crackers, Snacks, Nuts, and Meat Snacks: John Scardina
VP Merchandising, Health and Beauty Care, Tobacco (non-cigarettes), Tobacco Papers, Proprietary Paper and Store Supplies, Food Service Supplies, Institutional Paper and Cups, Institutional Fountain and Supplies, Blades, Razors, and Shavers: Mike Wierzbicki
Manager Human Resources: Steve Bundy
CIO: Kevin Reilly
Auditors: Deloitte & Touche

LOCATIONS

HQ: Eby-Brown Company, LLC
 280 W. Shuman Blvd., Ste. 280,
 Naperville, IL 60566
Phone: 630-778-2800   **Fax:** 630-778-2830
Web: www.eby-brown.com

COMPETITORS

AMCON Distributing
C&S Wholesale
Core-Mark
GSC Enterprises
H.T. Hackney
McLane
Nash-Finch
S. Abraham & Sons
Spartan Stores
SUPERVALU
Wal-Mart

Edelman

If image truly is everything, then Edelman may be one of the most indispensable companies around. The PR firm is the largest independent agency in the industry, conducting work for heavy hitters such as General Motors and Microsoft. With more than 45 offices worldwide, the company provides its services through 15 practices (including financial communications and investor relations, corporate affairs, diversity marketing, litigation, and public affairs) covering five industries. Edelman has fiercely guarded its independent status despite the still-growing trend toward consolidation. Chairman Daniel Edelman owns the company. It bought Silicon Valley PR firm A&R Partners (now called A&R Edelman) in 2006.

The acquisition of A&R Edelman, Silicon Valley's leading technology PR firm, significantly augmented Edelman's global technology practice. As a result, Edelman believes its technology practice will become its third largest, after consumer and health care.

Although Edelman has been primarily a PR firm (through PR21 and the Edelman agency) the company also dabbles in advertising through its Blue Worldwide unit. In addition, Edelman owns three other specialty agencies: First&42nd (management consulting), Bioscience Communications (medical education and publishing), and StrategyOne (research).

Edelman's independence is not without a price; the company competes with the PR segments of the large advertising and marketing conglomerates and must do so without the opportunities to raise capital that publicly held companies enjoy.

EXECUTIVES

Chairman: Daniel J. Edelman
President and CEO: Richard W. Edelman
CFO, US: Michael Sloan
EVP and Creative Director: Camille DeSantis
EVP and Director, Financial Communications: Jeff Zilka
EVP and General Manager, San Francisco:
 Catherine Ogilvie
EVP and Regional General Manager, Southwest:
 Teresa Henderson
**EVP and Global Leader, Corporate Social Responsibility
 and Sustainability:** Christopher (Chris) Deri
EVP Customer Publishing: Howard Lalli
EVP and General Manager, Sacramento:
 Steven (Steve) Telliano
EVP and Director Editorial Services: Dan Santow
EVP, Edelman Change and Employee Engagement:
 Jerilan Greene
EVP Global Public Affairs: Anthony Blankley
EVP Media Relations: Cheryl Cook
**EVP, Head, Crisis and Risk Communications and
 Public Affairs:** Nick Archer
Managing Director, U.S. Human Resources:
 Laura Smith

LOCATIONS

HQ: Edelman
 200 E. Randolph Dr., 63rd Fl., Chicago, IL 60601
Phone: 312-240-3000   **Fax:** 312-240-2900
Web: www.edelman.com

PRODUCTS/OPERATIONS

Practice Areas

Corporate
Design
Governance Advisors
Diversified Services
Crisis and Issues
Diversity Solutions
Editorial Services
Employee Management
Interactive Solutions
Financial and Investor Relations
Food
Litigation
Marketing
Public Affairs
Sports and Entertainment

Industries Served

Consumer Brands
Financial Services
Health
Industrial
Technology

COMPETITORS

Burson-Marsteller	Ketchum
Cohn & Wolfe	Manning Selvage
Euro RSCG	Ogilvy Public Relations
Fleishman-Hillard	Porter Novelli
Harrison, Elliott & Brown	Ruder Finn
Hill & Knowlton	Waggener Edstrom
Hoffman Agency	Weber Shandwick
KCSA	

HISTORICAL FINANCIALS

Company Type: Private

Income Statement

FYE: June 30

	REVENUE ($ mil.)	NET INCOME ($ mil.)	NET PROFIT MARGIN	EMPLOYEES
6/07	403	—	—	3,100
6/06	355	—	—	2,599
6/05	291	—	—	2,069
6/04	255	—	—	—
Annual Growth	16.4%	—	—	22.4%

Revenue History

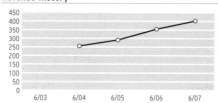

Electro-Motive Diesel

What do manufacturer Electro-Motive Diesel (EMD) and 1970s band Grand Funk Railroad have in common? They both want you to do the locomotion! EMD designs, builds, sells, and services diesel-electric locomotives for commercial railroad use, including commuter, freight, industrial, intercity passenger, and mining. The company has the largest installed base of diesel-electric locomotives in the world; its products are sold in more than 70 countries. EMD also provides diesel engines to the marine, oil drilling, and power generation markets. The company was founded in 1922 as Electro-Motive Engineering. Greenbriar Equity and Berkshire Partners bought EMD from General Motors in 2005.

EMD acquired ITS Rail Services in 2007 in an attempt to expand its aftermarket services both in the US and abroad. The company is currently struggling to take back market share from its biggest competitor, General Electric, which now has more than 60% of the North American locomotive market.

GE has spent many years and many more dollars investing in its locomotive business, while GM neglected EMD.

EXECUTIVES

Chairman: Jerry Greenwald
President and CEO: John Hamilton
VP and General Manager International Business:
 Albert Enste
VP and Chief Mechanical Officer: Gary Griffiths
Regional Sales VP: Frank Ward
**Director Area Sales, Australia, New Zealand, and SE
 Asia:** Matthew Dunwoodie
**Senior Manager, International Aftermarket Sales and
 Administration:** Salvador E. Rangel
Manager Country, China: Maxine Chen
Country Manager, China: William Yu
Interim Locomotive Sales Manager: Scott Garman
Managing Director, EMD Locomotive Technologies P.:
 Ajay Sinha
Product Manager: Kevin Bahnline
Manager Locomotive Sales and Marketing:
 John Cavanaugh

LOCATIONS

HQ: Electro-Motive Diesel, Inc.
 9301 West 55th St., La Grange, IL 60525
Phone: 800-255-5355   **Fax:** 708-387-6626
Web: www.emdiesels.com

Electro-Motive Diesel operates sales offices in China, Germany, India, and the US.

PRODUCTS/OPERATIONS

Selected Products

Locomotives
 Freight (JT42CWRM, SD70ACe, SD70M-2)
 Passenger (Euro 4000)
OEM Parts
 Diesel engines
 Digital video recorders
 Lash adjusters
 Valve bridges

COMPETITORS

Cummins Power Generation
GE
MISCOR Group
Sulzer

HISTORICAL FINANCIALS

Company Type: Private

Income Statement

FYE: December 31

	REVENUE ($ mil.)	NET INCOME ($ mil.)	NET PROFIT MARGIN	EMPLOYEES
12/07	1,830	—	—	2,740
12/06	1,710	—	—	2,640
12/05	1,030	—	—	2,640
Annual Growth	33.3%	—	—	1.9%

Revenue History

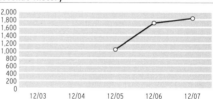

Elgin National Industries

Managing more than 15 businesses is all in a day's work for Elgin National Industries (ENI), which operates a diverse group of manufacturing and engineering services companies. The company makes highly engineered products such as centrifuges, fasteners, and electrical switch gear equipment and it provides bulk materials handling systems, as well as design, engineering, procurement, and construction management services for mineral processors.

The electric utility, industrial equipment, mining, and mineral processing industries use ENI's products and services. It has operations across the US and in Australia, Indonesia, India, and Poland.

In 2007 a majority stake in ENI was purchased by private equity fund GFI Energy Ventures.

EXECUTIVES

Chairman and CEO: Fred C. Schulte, age 59,
$595,229 pay
President, COO, and Director: Charles D. Hall, age 67,
$550,332 pay
VP, CFO, Treasurer, and Director: Wayne J. Conner,
age 53, $379,727 pay
VP, Controller, and Secretary: Lynn C. Batory, age 47,
$247,729 pay
VP, Manufacturing: David Hall, $247,729 pay
Auditors: McGladrey & Pullen, LLP

LOCATIONS

HQ: Elgin National Industries, Inc.
2001 Butterfield Rd., Ste. 1020,
Downers Grove, IL 60515
Phone: 630-434-7200   **Fax:** 630-434-7272
Web: www.eni.com

PRODUCTS/OPERATIONS

Selected Subsidiaries

Elgin Engineering and Construction
Roberts & Schaefer — USA
Roberts & Schaefer — Australia
Roberts & Schaefer — Poland
Soros Associates
TransService, Inc.

Elgin Equipment Group
Centrifugal & Mechanical Industries
Centrifugal Services, Inc.
Clinch River Corporation
Mining Controls, Inc.
Norris Screen and Manufacturing Inc.
Tabor Machine Company

Elgin Fastener Group
Best Metal Finishing, Inc.
Chandler Products
Elgin Fasteners International
Leland Powell Fasteners, Inc.
Ohio Rod Products
Precision Screw & Bolt

COMPETITORS

Illinois Tool Works
Indel
Morton Industrial Group
NACCO Industries
Sumitomo Heavy Industries
Synalloy
Toyota Material Handling

Elkay Manufacturing

Someone's in the kitchen with Dinah, and it's Elkay Manufacturing. Elkay makes sinks, cabinets, drinking fountains, faucets, water coolers, and water filtration products. The family-owned company sells residential and commercial stainless steel sinks under such names as Harmony, The Mystic, and Elite Gourmet. It also offers kitchen accessories (colanders, cutting boards, soap dispensers). Elkay began making cabinets in 1993. Brands include Yorktowne, Medallion, and MasterCraft. Elkay is the parent of a dozen privately held companies and one joint venture, Elkay Pacific Rim (water dispensing). Elkay Manufacturing was founded in 1920 by the Katz family to make sinks for butlers' pantries and sculleries.

EXECUTIVES

Chairman and CEO: Ronald C. (Ron) Katz
President and COO: John P. (Jack) Edl
VP and CFO: Timothy J. (Tim) Bondy
VP, Human Resources: Walter E. Reilly
**VP Trade Sales and Market Development Plumbing
Products, West Region:** Mark Whittington
**VP Engineering and Sink and Faucet Product
Development:** Stephen C. (Steve) Rogers
Managing Director Global Business Development:
Richard H. Dickson
Manager, Research and Development: Wally Moran
President Cabinetry: Tom Cook
President Plumbing Products: R. James (Jim) Scott
**President North American Operations, Plumbing
Products:** Stanley Bandur
Auditors: Ernst & Young

LOCATIONS

HQ: Elkay Manufacturing Company
2222 Camden Ct., Oak Brook, IL 60523
Phone: 630-574-8484   **Fax:** 630-574-5012
Web: www.elkay.com

PRODUCTS/OPERATIONS

Selected Products

Drinking fountains
Faucets
Kitchen cabinets
Residential and commercial sinks
Sink accessories (including colanders, cutting boards,
drain trays, soap dispensers)
Sink tops, countertops, and drainboards
Water coolers
Water filters

Selected Subsidiaries and Affiliates

Elkay Pacific Rim Sdn. Bhd. (50%; water coolers and
dispensers; joint venture with Formosa Prosonic
Equipment)
Halsey Taylor (water coolers and drinking fountains)
MasterCraft Cabinets, Inc.
Medallion Cabinetry, Inc.
Phylrich International (decorative plumbing products)
Revere (stainless steel kitchen sinks)
Yorktowne, Inc.

COMPETITORS

American Woodmark	Kohler
AquaCell	MAAX
Armstrong World	Masco
Industries	MasterBrand Cabinets
Black & Decker	Moen
Jacuzzi Brands	RSI Holding Corporation

Emigrant Bank

Emigrant Bank has built its business around the huddled masses longing to save. The bank, which also has four regional Emigrant Savings Bank affiliates in the Bronx, Brooklyn, Queens, and Long Island, serves retail and commercial customers in the New York metropolitan area from some 35 branches. It offers online banking nationwide through its Emigrant*Online* service. The bank provides standard products such as checking and savings accounts, CDs, IRAs, and credit and debit cards. New York Private Bank & Trust is Emigrant Bank's wealth management

division; Emigrant Financial Services offers mutual funds and life insurance. Emigrant Mortgage originates home loans in about a dozen Eastern states.

One- to four-family residential mortgages account for the largest portion of Emigrant Bank's loan portfolio, followed by commercial and industrial loans and multifamily residential mortgages.

The bank offers commercial real estate lending services through its Emigrant Funding unit. Emigrant Business Credit provides equipment financing. Emigrant Bank also has a Fine Art Financing division that lends money to clients using art or antiques as collateral. The bank's Emigrant Capital unit makes direct investments in private companies with annual sales between $20 million and $100 million.

One of the largest privately owned banks in the US, Emigrant Bank is controlled by the family of chairman and CEO Howard Milstein. It was founded by Irish emigrants in 1850.

EXECUTIVES

Chairman and CEO: Howard P. Milstein
SVP and Chief Marketing Officer: Ted Morehouse
SVP and Chief Credit Officer: Patricia Goldstein
Managing Director, Emigrant Realty Finance:
Chris Grey
Managing Director, Emigrant Realty Finance:
David Feingold

LOCATIONS

HQ: Emigrant Bank
5 E. 42nd St., New York, NY 10017
Phone: 212-850-4521   **Fax:** 212-850-4372
Web: www.emigrant.com

COMPETITORS

Astoria Financial
Bank of America
Capital One
Citigroup
Dime Community Bancshares
JPMorgan Chase
New York Community Bancorp
Signature Bank
TD Bank USA
Washington Mutual

HISTORICAL FINANCIALS

Company Type: Private

Income Statement

	REVENUE ($ mil.)	NET INCOME ($ mil.)	NET PROFIT MARGIN	EMPLOYEES
12/07	771	112	14.5%	809
12/06	640	162	25.3%	773
12/05	534	—	—	848
Annual Growth	20.2%	(30.6%)	—	(2.3%)

2007 Year-End Financials

Debt ratio: —   Current ratio: —
Return on equity: 13.2%   Long-term debt ($ mil.): 590
Cash ($ mil.): —

Net Income History

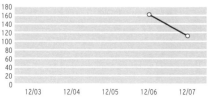

Encyclopædia Britannica

Encyclopædia Britannica thinks it knows everything, and it probably does. The company publishes reference works including its flagship 32-volume *Encyclopædia Britannica* (first published in 1768) and *Great Books of the Western World*. It also publishes a variety of dictionaries (*Merriam Webster's Collegiate Dictionary*, *Merriam Webster's Biographical Dictionary*) through its Merriam-Webster subsidiary. Most of the company's products are available online (Britannica.com), as well as on CD-ROM and DVD. The company also publishes Britannica Online School Edition, a reference site for students and teachers. Swiss financier Jacob Safra (a nephew of the late banking king Edmond Safra) owns the company.

Its Britannica.com Web site offers access for a fee to its entire collection of encyclopedia articles, an editorially reviewed Web site directory, and third-party content from *The New York Times* and other providers. Britannica's site also features an online store where users can buy its print and interactive products.

Trying a new approach to reach consumers, the company began selling its products on TV home shopping network QVC.

EXECUTIVES

Chairman: Jacob E. (Jacqui) Safra
President: Jorge Cauz, age 45
EVP, Secretary, and General Counsel: William J. Bowe
SVP and Editor: Dale Hoiberg
SVP Consumer Sales: Daniel W. (Dan) Smith, age 36
SVP Corporate Development: Michael Ross
SVP International: Leah Mansoor
VP Operations and Finance: Richard Anderson
Corporate Communications Director: Tom Panelas
Executive Technology Director: Tom Lang
Direct Marketing Manager: Christine Hodgson
President and Publisher, Merriam-Webster: John Morse
Auditors: PricewaterhouseCoopers

LOCATIONS

HQ: Encyclopædia Britannica, Inc.
  331 N. La Salle St., Chicago, IL 60610
Phone: 312-347-7159 **Fax:** 312-294-2104
Web: corporate.britannica.com

Encyclopædia Britannica makes its headquarters in Chicago and maintains offices in London; New Delhi; Paris; Seoul; Sydney; Taipei, Taiwan; Tel Aviv; and Tokyo.

PRODUCTS/OPERATIONS

Selected Products
Digital
  Britannica.com
  Britannica Online School Edition
Print
  Britannica Student Encyclopedia
  Encyclopædia Britannica
  Great Books of the Western World
  Merriam Webster's Collegiate Dictionary
  My First Britannica

COMPETITORS

Cengage Learning
Dow Jones
Editis
Franklin Electronic Publishers
Houghton Mifflin Harcourt
LexisNexis
McGraw-Hill
Microsoft
National Geographic
Pearson
Random House
Scholastic Library Publishing
Time Inc.
Wikimedia Foundation
World Book

Energy Future Holdings

Energy Future Holdings' (formerly TXU) has seen the future and it works —powered by electricity. The company is the largest nonregulated retail electric provider in Texas (TXU Energy), with more than 2 million customers, and through its Luminant unit it has a generating capacity of more than 18,300 MW from its interests in nuclear and fossil-fueled power plants in the state. Energy Future Holdings has regulated power transmission and distribution operations through Oncor Electric Delivery. In 2007 the company was acquired in a $45 billion leveraged buyout by an investor group led by Goldman Sachs, Kohlberg Kravis Roberts, and Texas Pacific Group.

Oncor Electric Delivery operates the largest distribution and transmission system in Texas, providing power to more than 3 million electric delivery points over more than 115,000 miles of transmission and distribution lines. Luminant's power operations include 2,300 MW of nuclear and 5,800 MW of coal-fueled generation capacity. It is also the largest purchaser of wind-generated electricity in Texas.

In 2006 the company teamed up with InfrastruX Group to form the InfrastruX Energy Services joint venture in a 10-year, $8.7 billion agreement to provide for utility infrastructure and management services.

In 2007 Luminant joined The FutureGen Alliance, non-profit consortium of global electric utilities and coal companies working with the US Department of Energy to site and develop FutureGen, a first-of-a-kind coal-fueled power plant with near-zero emissions.

HISTORY

The first North Texas electric power company was founded in Dallas in 1883. Another was built in 1885 in Fort Worth. From these and other small power plants, three companies grew to serve most of the state: Texas Power & Light (TP&L, incorporated in 1912), Dallas Power & Light (DP&L, 1917), and Texas Electric Service (TES, 1929). Texas Utilities Company, called TU, was formed in 1945 as a holding company for the three utilities.

In the 1940s, TU began leasing large lignite coal reserves, and in 1952 formed Industrial

Generating to mine lignite and operate a coal-fired power plant. TU, after pioneering lignite-burning technology in the 1960s, opened the first of nine large lignite units in 1971. In 1974 it began building the Comanche Peak nuclear plant near Fort Worth.

DP&L, TES, TP&L, and Industrial Generating joined in 1984 as Texas Utilities Electric (TU Electric). The mining company was renamed Texas Utilities Mining.

The Nuclear Regulatory Commission wouldn't license Comanche Peak in 1985, citing design and construction faults, but finally granted the license in 1990. TU bought out its construction partners after much wrangling over multibillion-dollar cost overruns.

In 1993 TU bought Southwestern Electric Service (now TXU SESCO), another Texas electric utility. Accounting changes resulted in a loss for TU in 1995. However, it did gain entry to the telecom arena, buying a 20% stake in the Texas operations of wireless PCS provider PrimeCo. (The company sold the PrimeCo stake in 1999.) TU expanded its telecom holdings in 1997 when it acquired phone company Lufkin-Conroe (now part of TXU Communications).

TU headed down under in 1996, buying Australian electric company Eastern Energy (now part of TXU Electricity). It purchased gas dealer ENSERCH (now TXU Gas), which brought substantial energy services and trading assets on board, including Texas' largest gas utility, Lone Star Gas.

Despite a windfall tax levied by the UK's Labor Party, TU bought British utility The Energy Group (now TXU Europe) for about $10 billion in 1998. Back in Texas the 1999 Legislature approved retail competition for the electric industry, beginning in 2002. Also in 1999 Texas Utilities restructured its operations and began using the name TXU Corp. It officially changed its name the next year.

In 2000 TXU acquired Norweb Energi, United Utilities' electricity and gas supply business, which added some 1.8 million electricity customers and 400,000 gas customers in the UK. TXU also contributed the stock of its telecommunications companies to Pinnacle One Partners in exchange for a 50% stake and about $960 million. Other efforts to reduce debt and streamline operations include TXU's sale of its natural gas processing operations, UK gas metering business, and interests in a Czech utility and North Sea gas fields.

In 2001 TXU acquired a 50% stake in Stadtwerke Kiel, its first utility in Germany (where TXU Europe was already trading energy), and it agreed to sell two gas-fired power plants (2,300 MW) in Texas to Exelon for $443 million (completed in 2002). TXU Europe sold two UK power stations (3,000 MW) in 2001 and sold its Eastern Electricity distribution unit and its interest in joint venture 24seven in 2002.

In 2002 retail electric competition began in Texas, and TXU responded by separating TXU Electric's regulated and nonregulated operations. TXU Electric's name was changed to TXU US Holdings, which also took over TXU SESCO's electric operations.

TXU sold TXU Europe's retail supply and generation operations to UK utility Powergen in late 2002 due to poor market conditions. Shortly after, TXU Europe filed for bankruptcy protection, and TXU wrote off its investment in the unit. The following year, TXU sold the northeastern US gas marketing operations of TXU Energy to UGI.

Continuing with its effort to reduce debt and focus on core utility businesses, TXU sold subsidiary TXU Communications to private telecom firm Consolidated Communications and its TXU Fuel (gas transportation) unit to Energy Transfer Partners. The company sold TXU Gas to Atmos Energy for $1.9 billion in 2004; the transaction included the company's gas transportation and storage assets.

The company announced plans to form a wholesale energy marketing joint venture with Credit Suisse First Boston in 2004; however, the two firms later decided not to pursue the venture. Energy Future Holdings has also outsourced its information technology functions to Capgemini Energy LP, a unit of Capgemini.

EXECUTIVES

Non-Executive Chairman: Donald L. (Don) Evans, age 61
Advisory Chairman: James A. (Jim) Baker III, age 77
President, CEO, and Director: John F. Young, age 51
EVP and General Counsel: Robert C. (Rob) Walters, age 50
EVP and CFO: Paul M. Keglevic, age 54
EVP Energy Future Holdings: M. Rizwan (Riz) Chand, age 44
EVP; COO Luminant: Michael T. (Mike) McCall, age 50
EVP; Chief Executive, Luminant Construction: Charles R. (Chuck) Enze, age 54
Director Investor Relations: Tim Hogan
Chairman and CEO, Oncor: Robert S. (Bob) Shapard, age 52
President and CEO, Luminant: David A. Campbell, age 39
President and COO, Oncor: Rob D. Trimble
CEO TXU Energy: James A. (Jim) Burke, age 39
Chief Marketing Officer, TXU Energy: Dan Valentine
General Counsel, TXU Energy: Cecily S. Gooch
Auditors: Deloitte & Touche LLP

LOCATIONS

HQ: Energy Future Holdings Corp.
1601 Bryan St., Dallas, TX 75201
Phone: 214-812-4600
Web: www.energyfutureholdings.com

Energy Future Holdings has energy operations in North America, primarily in Texas.

PRODUCTS/OPERATIONS

2007 Sales

	$ mil.	% of total
Retail electric	6,156	55
Wholesale electric	2,142	19
Other	330	3
Regulated delivery	2,519	23
Adjustments	(3,155)	—
Total	**7,992**	**100**

COMPETITORS

AEP	First Choice Power
AEP Texas Central	FPL Group
AEP Texas North	Gexa Energy
AES	Green Mountain Energy
Atmos Energy	Mirant
Brazos Electric	NRG Energy
Calpine	ONEOK
CenterPoint Energy	Reliant Energy
Direct Energy	Southwestern Electric
Duke Energy	Power
El Paso Electric	Strategic Energy
Entergy	Texas Gas Transmission

HISTORICAL FINANCIALS

Company Type: Private

Income Statement

FYE: December 31

	REVENUE ($ mil.)	NET INCOME ($ mil.)	NET PROFIT MARGIN	EMPLOYEES
12/07	7,992	(637)	—	7,600
12/06	10,856	2,552	23.5%	7,262
12/05	10,437	1,722	16.5%	7,615
12/04	9,308	485	5.2%	—
12/03	11,008	582	5.3%	—
Annual Growth	**(7.7%)**	**—**	**—**	**(0.1%)**

2007 Year-End Financials

Debt ratio: 577.5%
Return on equity: —
Cash ($ mil.): —
Current ratio: —
Long-term debt ($ mil.): 38,603

Net Income History

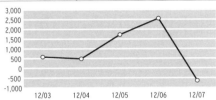

	12/03	12/04	12/05	12/06	12/07

(chart values: 3,000 to -1,000 scale)

Enterprise Rent-A-Car

This Enterprise helps customers to boldly go where they might not have gone before they rented a fresh set of wheels. A leading US car rental company, Enterprise Rent-A-Car maintains a fleet of some 711,000 vehicles from nearly 7,000 locations — more than 6,000 in the US and another 900 in Canada, Germany, Ireland, and the UK. Unlike rivals such as Hertz and Avis, which operate primarily from airports, Enterprise focuses on customers whose own cars are in the shop or who need a rental for vacations or other special occasions. Enterprise, which acquired rival Vanguard Car Rental, is controlled by chairman and CEO Andrew Taylor, whose father, Jack Taylor, founded the company in 1957.

The mid-2007 purchase of Vanguard Car Rental created an on-and-off-airport car rental powerhouse with nearly 10,700 locations and 1.1 million vehicles, further separating Enterprise from the rest of its rivals. Vanguard manages the successful Alamo Rent A Car and National Car Rental brands, operating from more than 3,800 locations, mostly at airports. The newly acquired business will be operated as a separate subsidiary for now.

More than 90% of Enterprise's car rental business comes from customers in their home cities, as opposed to travelers.

In addition to its primary car rental operations, Enterprise leases vehicles and manages fleets for other companies (Enterprise Fleet Services), rents trucks (from more than 90 locations), and sells used cars.

HISTORY

In 1957 Jack Taylor, the sales manager for a Cadillac dealership in St. Louis, hit on the idea that leasing cars might be an easier way to make money than selling them. Taylor's idea sounded good to his boss, Arthur Lindburg, who agreed to set Taylor up in the leasing business. In return for a 50% pay cut, Taylor received 25% of the new enterprise, called Executive Leasing, which began in the walled-off body shop of a car dealership.

In the early 1960s Taylor started renting cars for short periods as well as leasing them. When his leasing agents expressed annoyance with the rental operation, Taylor turned that business over to Don Holtzman. Holtzman realized that his 17-car rental operation was too little to take on industry giants like Hertz and Avis; instead, he concentrated on the "home city" or replacement market. He offered competitive rates to insurance adjusters who needed to find cars for policyholders whose vehicles were damaged or stolen.

Propelled by court decisions that required casualty companies to pay for loss of transportation, Taylor expanded from his St. Louis base in 1969 with a branch office in Atlanta. Since another car leasing outfit in Georgia was already named Executive, Taylor changed the name of his company to Enterprise Rent-A-Car.

The company expanded into Florida and Texas in the early 1970s, targeting garages and body shops that performed repairs for insured drivers. Oil price shocks of that period compelled Taylor to diversify his operations. In 1974 Enterprise acquired Keefe Coffee and Supply, a supplier of coffee, packaged foods, and beverages to prison commissaries. To service *FORTUNE* 1000 companies wanting to lease or buy more than 50 vehicles, the company started Enterprise Fleet Services in 1976.

Enterprise acquired Courtesy Products (coffee and tea for hotel guests) in 1980, and the following year sales reached the $100 million mark. It acquired ELCO Chevrolet in 1986, the same year it formed Crawford Supply (hygiene products for prisons). Taylor bought out the Lindburg family's interest in Enterprise the next year. In 1989 Enterprise raised its brand recognition with a national TV campaign that focused on an older and higher-income audience by showing its commercials exclusively on CBS. Also in the late 1980s, the company began targeting "discretionary rentals" to families with visiting relatives or with children home for the holidays.

Taylor's son, Andrew, became CEO of Enterprise in 1991, and sales topped $1 billion for the first time. By 1994 sales had passed $2 billion, and the company had expanded into Canada and the UK. By 1996 Enterprise had a fleet of more than 300,000 vehicles. That year it opened several locations in the UK. In 1997 the company opened locations in Ireland, Germany, Scotland, and Wales.

In 1998 Enterprise battled other rental firms over use of the advertising tagline, "We'll pick you up," which it had trademarked. Rent-A-Wreck lost a court case over the matter; Hertz settled with Enterprise over use of the phrase.

The company more than doubled the number of its airport locations in 1999 in an attempt to woo occasional travelers (rather than hard-core corporate fliers). Also that year the Taylor family split off their non-automotive operations (including companies involved in prison supplies, hotel amenities, a golf course, mylar balloons, and athletic shoes) as Centric Group.

In 2001 the company's COO, Donald Ross, became the first non-Taylor to be promoted to president after Jack Taylor was named chairman emeritus and Andrew gave up the president title to assume the company's chairmanship while remaining CEO.

In August 2007 Enterprise bought rival Vanguard Car Rental Group from Cerberus Capital Management. Vanguard manages the Alamo Rent A Car and National Car Rental brands.

EXECUTIVES

Chairman and CEO: Andrew C. (Andy) Taylor, age 60
Vice Chairman: Donald L. (Don) Ross, age 64
President and COO: Pamela M. (Pam) Nicholson, age 48
EVP and CFO: William W. (Bill) Snyder
SVP and CIO: Craig Kennedy
SVP and Chief Administrative Officer: Lee R. Kaplan
SVP Car Sales: Tim Walsh
SVP European Operations: James (Jim) Burrell
SVP Fleet Management: Steven E. (Steve) Bloom
SVP Human Resources: Edward (Ed) Adams
SVP Rental: Jim Runnels
VP Corporate Communications: Christy Conrad
VP Corporate Responsibility and Communications: Pat Farrell
VP Marketing Communications: Brian Curtin
VP and Treasurer: Rose Langhorst
President, National Car Rental and Alamo Rent A Car: Greg R. Stubblefield
President, Enterprise Rent-A-Car Foundation: Jo Ann Taylor Kindle
Auditors: Ernst & Young LLP

LOCATIONS

HQ: Enterprise Rent-A-Car Company
600 Corporate Park Dr., St. Louis, MO 63105
Phone: 314-512-5000   **Fax:** 314-512-4706
Web: www.enterprise.com

PRODUCTS/OPERATIONS

Selected Operations
Alamo Rent A Car
Enterprise Car Sales (used car sales)
Enterprise Fleet Services (vehicle leasing and fleet management services)
Enterprise Rent-A-Car
Enterprise Rent-A-Truck
National Car Rental

COMPETITORS

Avis Budget
Avis Europe
Dollar Thrifty Automotive
Hertz
PHH Arval
Rent-A-Wreck
Sixt

HISTORICAL FINANCIALS
Company Type: Private

Income Statement

	REVENUE ($ mil.)	NET INCOME ($ mil.)	NET PROFIT MARGIN	EMPLOYEES
7/07	9,500	—	—	66,700
7/06	9,000	—	—	75,700
7/05	8,230	—	—	61,000
7/04	7,400	—	—	57,300
7/03	6,900	—	—	53,500
Annual Growth	8.3%	—	—	5.7%

FYE: July 31

Revenue History

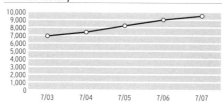

Ergon, Inc.

When it comes to work, Ergon (named after the Greek word for work) has it covered. Ergo, Ergon operates in six major business segments: asphalt and emulsions; information technology (embedded computing); oil and gas; real estate; refining and marketing; and transportation and terminaling. In addition to providing a range of petroleum products and services, the company manufactures and markets computer technology services and sells road maintenance systems, including emulsions and special coatings. Ergon also provides truck, rail, and marine transport services and sells residential and commercial real estate properties.

Ergon's Asphalt and Emulsions business is a leading innovator in the asphalt industry. It delivers high-performance, polymer-modified binders to asphalt suppliers throughout the inland waterways system via Ergon unit Magnolia Marine Transport. In 2007 the unit acquired Innovative Adhesives Company, a leading maker of specialty asphalt coatings and adhesives, located in Kansas City, Kansas.

EXECUTIVES

CEO: Leslie B. Lampton Sr.
CFO: A. Patrick (Pat) Busby
President, Asphalt Division: Bill Lampton
VP Environment, Health, and Safety, Ergon Refining: Paul Young
VP Marine Operations, Magnolia Marine Transport: Roger Harris
VP: Baxter Burns
Director Communications: Jim Temple
Human Resources Manager: Daphne Williams

LOCATIONS

HQ: Ergon, Inc.
2829 Lakeland Dr., Ste. 2000, Jackson, MS 39232
Phone: 601-933-3000   **Fax:** 601-933-3350
Web: www.ergon.com

PRODUCTS/OPERATIONS

Major Operations
Asphalt and Emulsions
Crafco, Inc.
Ertech, Inc.
Information Technology (Embedded Computing)
Diversified Technology, Inc.
Oil and Gas
Lampton-Love, Inc.
Real Estate
Ergon Properties, Inc.

Refining and Marketing
Ergon Refining, Inc.
Lion Oil Company
Transportation and Terminaling
Ergon Terminaling, Inc.
Ergon Trucking, Inc.
Magnolia Marine Transport Company

COMPETITORS

AmeriGas Partners
Ferrellgas Partners
Kirby Corporation
Koch Industries, Inc.
Marathon Oil

HISTORICAL FINANCIALS
Company Type: Private

Income Statement

	ESTIMATED REVENUE ($ mil.)	NET INCOME ($ mil.)	NET PROFIT MARGIN	EMPLOYEES
12/07	4,490	—	—	2,500
12/06	4,110	—	—	2,500
12/05	3,000	—	—	2,500
12/04	2,680	—	—	2,300
12/03	2,000	—	—	2,300
Annual Growth	22.4%	—	—	2.1%

FYE: December 31

Revenue History

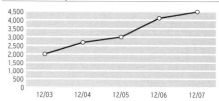

Ernst & Young Global

Accounting may actually be the *second*-oldest profession, and Ernst & Young is one of the oldest practitioners. Ernst & Young is also one of the world's Big Four accounting firms (third in revenue behind PricewaterhouseCoopers and Deloitte Touche Tohmatsu, ahead of KPMG). It has some 700 offices providing auditing and accounting services in 140 countries. The firm also provides legal services and services relating to emerging growth companies, human resources issues, and corporate transactions (mergers and acquisitions, IPOs, and the like). Ernst & Young has one of the world's largest tax practices, serving multinational clients that have to comply with multiple local tax laws.

Ernst & Young offers its services to a vast range of industries, including asset management, biotech, mining, and hotel and leisure. The company's financial reporting segment offers an IFRS/GAAP comparison so companies can compare and contrast the international and US accounting standards.

It's not all so stodgy, however. The company hands out an Entrepreneur of the Year award annually; in 2007 it went to Cirque du Soleil founder Guy Laliberté.

HISTORY

In 1494 Luca Pacioli's *Summa di Arithmetica* became the first published text on double-entry bookkeeping, but it was almost 400 years before accounting became a profession.

In 1849 Frederick Whinney joined the UK firm of Harding & Pullein. His ledgers were so clear that he was advised to take up accounting, which was a growth field as stock companies proliferated. Whinney became a name partner in 1859 and his sons followed him into the business. The firm became Whinney, Smith & Whinney (WS&W) in 1894.

After WWII, WS&W formed an alliance with Ernst & Ernst (founded in Cleveland in 1903 by brothers Alwin and Theodore Ernst), with each firm operating on the other's behalf across the Atlantic. Whinney merged with Brown, Fleming & Murray in 1965 to become Whinney Murray. In 1979 Whinney Murray, Turquands Barton Mayhew (also a UK firm), and Ernst & Ernst merged to form Ernst & Whinney.

But Ernst & Whinney wasn't done merging. Ten years later, when it was the fourth-largest accounting firm, it merged with #5 Arthur Young, which had been founded by Scotsman Arthur Young in 1895 in Kansas City. Long known as "old reliable," Arthur Young fell on hard times in the 1980s because its audit relationships with failed S&Ls led to expensive litigation (settled in 1992 for $400 million).

Thus the new firm of Ernst & Young faced a rocky start. In 1990 it fended off rumors of collapse. The next year it slashed payroll, even thinning its partner roster. Exhausted by the S&L wars, in 1994 the firm replaced its pugnacious general counsel, Carl Riggio, with the more cost-conscious Kathryn Oberly.

In the mid-1990s Ernst & Young concentrated on consulting, particularly in software applications, and grew through acquisitions. In 1996 the firm bought Houston-based Wright Killen & Co., a petroleum and petrochemicals consulting firm, to form Ernst & Young Wright Killen. It also entered new alliances that year, including ones with Washington-based ISD/Shaw, which provided banking industry consulting, and India's Tata Consulting.

In 1997 Ernst & Young was sued for a record $4 billion for its alleged failure to effectively handle the 1993 restructuring of the defunct Merry-Go-Round Enterprises retail chain (it settled for $185 million in 1999). On the heels of a merger deal between Coopers & Lybrand and Price Waterhouse, Ernst & Young agreed in 1997 to merge with KPMG International. But Ernst & Young called off the negotiations in 1998, citing the uncertain regulatory process they faced.

The firm reached a settlement in 1999 in lawsuits regarding accounting errors at Informix and Avis Budget Group and sold its UK and southern African trust and fiduciary businesses to Royal Bank of Canada (now RBC Financial Group).

In 2000 Ernst & Young became the first of the (then) Big Five firms to sell its consultancy, dealing it to France's Cap Gemini Group for about $11 billion. The following year the UK accountancy watchdog group announced it would investigate Ernst & Young for its handling of the accounts of UK-based The Equitable Life Assurance Society. The insurer was forced to close to new business in 2000 because of massive financial difficulties.

Ernst & Young made headlines and gave competitors plenty to talk about in 2002 when closely held financial records were made public during a divorce case involving executive Rick Bobrow (who in 2003 abruptly retired as global CEO after just a year on the job).

Also in 2002 the firm allied with former New York City mayor Rudy Giuliani to launch a business consultancy bearing the Giuliani name. Ernst & Young later helped the venture to build its investment banking capabilities by selling its corporate finance unit (as well as its stake in Giuliani Partners) to that firm in 2004.

With the collapse of rival Andersen in 2002, Ernst & Young boosted its legal services, assembling some 2,000 lawyers in dozens of countries.

But the firm faced Andersen-style trouble of its own as client suits against auditors became more common in the wake of corporate scandals at Enron and other troubled companies. Both Avis Budget Group, Inc. (formerly Cendant) and HealthSouth sued Ernst & Young in connection with alleged accounting missteps in 2004.

In 2005 Ernst & Young's UK arm emerged victorious from a torrid legal battle with insurer Equitable Life, which in 2003 had sued the accountancy for professional negligence related to work performed when Ernst & Young was its auditor. Another highlight for that year was the fee bonanza fueled by changes in international accounting standards required by the Sarbanes-Oxley Act in the US.

EXECUTIVES

Chairman and CEO, Ernst & Young International and Ernst & Young L.L.P.: James S. (Jim) Turley, age 53
Vice Chair, Tax: Sam Fouad
Vice Chair, Transaction Advisory Services: Dave Read
Vice Chair, Assurance and Advisory Business Services: John Murphy
Global Vice Chair, Strategy and Regulatory Affairs: Beth A. Brooke
COO: John Ferraro
Global Managing Partner, Client Service and Accounts: Herman Hulst
Global Managing Partner, Quality and Risk Management: Sue Frieden
Global Managing Partner, Operations and Finance: Jeffrey H. (Jeff) Dworken
Global Managing Partner, People: Pierre Hurstel
Managing Partner, Client Service and Accounts, UK and NEMIA: Thomas P. (Tom) McGrath
Global Director, Automotive: Michael S. (Mike) Hanley
Insurance Practice Leader: Peter R. (Pete) Porrino
European Pharmaceuticals Leader: Patrick J.P. Flochel

LOCATIONS

HQ: Ernst & Young Global Limited
Becket House, 1 Lambeth Palace Rd.,
London SE1 7EU, United Kingdom
Phone: +44-20-7951-2000   **Fax:** +44-20-7951-1345
US HQ: 5 Times Sq., New York, NY 10036
US Phone: 212-773-3000   **US Fax:** 212-773-6350
Web: www.ey.com

Ernst & Young International has approximately 700 offices in 140 countries.

PRODUCTS/OPERATIONS

Selected Services

Assurance and Advisory
  Actuarial services
  Audits
  Accounting advisory
  Business risk services
  Internal audit
  Real estate advisory services
  Technology and security risk services

Emerging Growth Companies
  Corporate finance services
  Mergers and acquisitions advisory
  Operational consulting
  Strategic advisory
  Transactions advisory
Human Capital
  Compensation and benefits consulting
  Cost optimization and risk management
  Transaction support services
Law
  Corporate and M&A
  Employment
  Finance
  Information technology services
  Intellectual property
  International trade and anti-trust
  Litigation and arbitration
  Real estate
Tax
  Global tax operations
  Indirect tax
  International tax
Transactions
  Capital management
  Corporate development advisory
  Financial and business modeling
  M&A advisory
  Post-deal advisory
  Strategic finance
  Transaction management
  Valuation

COMPETITORS

Baker Tilly International
BDO International
Deloitte
Grant Thornton International
Horwath International
KPMG
Moore Stephens International
PKF International
PricewaterhouseCoopers

HISTORICAL FINANCIALS

Company Type: Partnership

Income Statement				FYE: June 30
	REVENUE ($ mil.)	NET INCOME ($ mil.)	NET PROFIT MARGIN	EMPLOYEES
6/07	21,160	—	—	121,000
6/06	18,400	—	—	114,000
6/05	16,902	—	—	106,650
6/04	14,547	—	—	100,601
6/03	13,136	—	—	103,000
Annual Growth	12.7%	—	—	4.1%

Revenue History

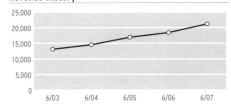

ESPN, Inc.

ESPN is a superstar of the sports broadcasting world. The company is the leading cable sports broadcaster, reaching more than 97 million US homes with its stable of channels, including ESPN, ESPN2 (sporting events, news, and original programming), and ESPN Classic (historical sports footage). It also creates original programming for TV and radio and lends content for ESPN.com (operated by Disney Online), one of the most popular sports sites on the Internet. Its international operations extend the ESPN brand to another 190 countries. ESPN is 80% owned by Walt Disney (through ABC); Hearst has a 20% stake.

The network has become more than just a leading sports outlet on TV: ESPN's popularity is so vast it is a force to be reckoned with in popular culture, spurring catch phrases ("Boo-yah!") and launching athletes into celebrity status. Through ESPN Original Entertainment, the broadcaster has pushed into original programming with talk shows (*Pardon the Interruption*), series television, and specials.

To reach that stage, ESPN has worked tirelessly to extend its power and influence throughout sports and entertainment. It holds broadcasting contracts with Major League Baseball, the National Basketball Association, and the National Football League, as well as NASCAR and college sports conferences. In 2008 the cable sports channel inked a 15-year deal with the Southeastern Conference (SEC) worth more than $2 billion to air football and basketball games.

ESPN took over *Monday Night Football* from sister company ABC in 2006. ABC lost about $150 million a year on the venerable program, and the network decided it would fare better on cable. ESPN agreed to pay the NFL $1.1 billion a year (for eight years) for the broadcasting rights. ABC also turned over its sports programming arm (ABC Sports) to ESPN, which now airs games on ABC under the ESPN banner.

In addition to the big ticket sports, ESPN has been increasing its coverage of minor sports leagues, including Major League Lacrosse and Major League Soccer. It also has an equity stake in the Arena Football League (acquired in 2006) and extended its AFL broadcasting contract for five more years. Outside the US, ESPN owns and operates the North American Sports Network, which it plans to re-brand as ESPN America in 2009.

The network was launched in 1979 under the name Entertainment and Sports Programming Network; it adopted the new name — ESPN — in 1985.

EXECUTIVES

President, ESPN, Inc and ABC Sports; Co-Chairman, Disney Media Networks; Chairman, ESPN, Inc:
George W. Bodenheimer, age 49
EVP and CFO: Christine Driessen
EVP Administration: Ed Durso
EVP Content: John Skipper
EVP News, Talent, and Content Operations:
Steve Anderson
EVP Multimedia Sales: David Rotem
EVP Sales and Marketing: Sean H. R. Bratches
EVP Production: Norby Williamson
EVP Program Planning and Development: David Berson
EVP Programming and Acquisitions: John Wildhack
EVP and CTO: Chuck Pagano

SVP and General Counsel: David Pahl
SVP Communications: Chris LaPlaca
SVP Human Resources: Daryl Smith
President, Disney and ESPN Networks Affiliate Sales and Marketing: Ben Pyne
President, ESPN/ABC Sports Customer Marketing and Sales: Ed Erhardt

LOCATIONS

HQ: ESPN, Inc.
ESPN Plaza, 935 Middle St., Bristol, CT 06010
Phone: 860-766-2000   **Fax:** 860-766-2213
Web: espn.go.com

PRODUCTS/OPERATIONS

Selected Operations

ESPN (sporting events and news channel)
ESPN Classic (archival sports footage channel)
ESPN Deportes (Spanish-language sports network)
ESPN Enterprises (new business venture development)
ESPN HD (high-definition channel)
ESPN International
ESPN On Demand (video on demand programming)
ESPN Original Programming (original content for cable channels)
ESPN Radio
ESPN *The Magazine* (print magazine)
ESPN2 (sporting events and news channel)
ESPN2HD (high-definition channel)
ESPNEWS (24-hour sports news channel)
ESPNU (college sports)

COMPETITORS

Big Ten Network
CBS
Comcast SportsNet
Fox Entertainment
Madison Square Garden
NBC
NESN
Turner Broadcasting
VERSUS
YES Network

Esselte Corporation

Write it, print it, staple it, drop it in a folder, and store it in a filing cabinet — Esselte is there for each step. Manufacturer of more than 30,000 products, the company is a leading manufacturer of office supplies worldwide. Esselte makes paper-based filing and document management items (files, binders, folders, covers), workspace products (staplers, letter trays), and computer accessories under the Esselte, Leitz, Oxford, Pendaflex, and Xyron brands. Customers range from wholesalers and direct marketers to office superstores and mass retailers. J. W. Childs Associates bought Esselte in 2002.

The company has five main divisions — Esselte Americas, Esselte Europe, Creative, Asia Pacific, and X Product Development — that serve consumers in more than 120 countries.

Esselte brought on new president and CEO Gary Brooks in 2006. Brooks had been head of the firm's US filing division. Former Esselte CEO and president Magnus Nicolin, who'd been chief since the J. W. Childs acquisition, resigned to explore other ventures.

Esselte has grown worldwide through its strategic purchases. Its acquisition activity began with the 2003 purchase of Scottsdale, Arizona-based Xyron, a binding and laminating company. Esselte has been repositioning Xyron's products from the office to the creative marketplace, which is growing with the popularity of scrapbooking. A year later Esselte acquired EJA CZ in the Czech Republic and Universal Trade Stationers in Ireland.

In 2007 Xyron cut some 25 jobs from its Scottsdale, Arizona facility, as part of a restructuring.

Esselte sold its DYMO labeling systems unit, which didn't fit into its overall strategy, to Newell Rubbermaid in 2005. Newell Rubbermaid paid $730 million in cash for the unit.

EXECUTIVES

President and CEO: Gary J. Brooks
SVP and CFO: Richard A. (Rich) Douville
SVP, Human Resources: James (Jim) O'Leary
SVP Sales; Europe: Nigel Gunn
SVP, Business Development, Chief Innovation Officer; President Asia/Pacific; President Creative Division:
Sean Fernandez
SVP and President, China Operations: Kelvin Yao
VP and Corporate Controller: Joseph Keyes
VP Far East Sourcing: Dennis Tow
VP Global IT: Mark Katz
President, Creative Division: Chuck Ensign
Director Public Relations: Chris Curran
Media Relations Contact: Sharon Mann

LOCATIONS

HQ: Esselte Corporation
5 High Ridge Park, Ste. 205, Stamford, CT 06905
Phone: 203-658-1730   **Fax:** 203-658-1731
Web: www.esselte.com

2007 Sales

	% of total
Europe	55
North America	40
Asia/Pacific/Latin America	5
Total	**100**

PRODUCTS/OPERATIONS

Selected Products

Creative
  Adhesive application
  Image transfer products
  Laminate application
Filing
  Arch files
  Concertina files
  File folders
  Indices
  Plastic pockets
  Presentation folders
  Ring binders
  Suspension files
Workspace
  Binding and lamination equipment
  Desk accessories
  Letter trays
  Magazine files
  Perforators
  Staplers
Other Products
  Computer accessories
  Printer supplies

COMPETITORS

ACCO Brands   Fiskars
Acme United   MeadWestvaco
Avery Dennison   Smead
Cardinal Brands   TAB Products

Estes Express Lines

Estes Express Lines is a multiregional less-than-truckload (LTL) freight hauler. (LTL carriers consolidate freight from multiple shippers into a single trailer.) The company operates a fleet of about 6,600 tractors and 22,800 trailers from a network of about 200 terminals throughout the US. Estes Express offers service in Canada through ExpressLINK alliance partner TST Overland Express; it works with other companies to offer service in the Caribbean and in Mexico. Founded by W. W. Estes in 1931, the company is owned and operated by the Estes family.

To supplement its LTL business, Estes Express offers airfreight forwarding, equipment leasing, expedited delivery, supply chain management, truckload transportation, and warehousing services.

Estes Express has gradually expanded its service territory over the years, and in March 2008 the company opened terminals in the remaining states where it did not already have them: Iowa, Minnesota, Nebraska, North Dakota, South Dakota, and Wisconsin. Previously, Estes Express had served the upper Midwest through an alliance with Lakeville Motor Express.

To expand the territory it directly served to include the western US, Estes Express took full ownership of G.I. Trucking in July 2005. Estes Express had been a major shareholder of the California-based carrier since 2001, when Estes Express combined with G.I. Trucking executives to buy G.I. Trucking from Arkansas Best.

EXECUTIVES

President and CEO: Robey W. (Rob) Estes Jr., age 56
EVP and COO: William T. (Billy) Hupp
EVP and COO, Estes Air Forwarding: Scott Fisher
Treasurer and CFO: Gary D. Okes
VP Corporate Operations: John T. (Junior) Johnson
VP Corporate Communications: Trish Garland
VP Human Resources: Thomas Donahue
VP Fleet Services: Ray G. Williams
VP Safety: Paul J. Dugent
VP Corporate Sales: Chuck Parker
VP Information Services: Hugh Camden
VP Safety: Curtis Carr
VP National Accounts: Lewis Mustian
Corporate Secretary: Stephen E. Hupp
Manager Strategic Communications: Paula Evans
Auditors: Joyner, Kirkham, Keel & Robertson, P. C.

LOCATIONS

HQ: Estes Express Lines, Inc.
3901 W. Broad St., Richmond, VA 23230
Phone: 804-353-1900   **Fax:** 804-353-8001
Web: www.estes-express.com

COMPETITORS

AAA Cooper Transportation
Arkansas Best
Averitt Express
Con-way Freight
FedEx Freight
Old Dominion Freight
Penske Truck Leasing
R+L Carriers
Ryder System
Saia, Inc.
UPS Freight
Vitran
YRC Worldwide

HISTORICAL FINANCIALS

Company Type: Private

Income Statement

	REVENUE ($ mil.)	NET INCOME ($ mil.)	NET PROFIT MARGIN	EMPLOYEES
12/07	1,395	—	—	12,374
12/06	1,447	—	—	13,824
12/05	1,149	—	—	13,051
12/04	1,000	—	—	—
12/03	865	—	—	10,027
Annual Growth	**12.7%**	—	—	**5.4%**

FYE: December 31

Revenue History

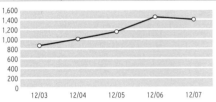

Euramax International

When it comes to RV components and parts, Euramax International takes it to the max, both in Europe and the US. Through subsidiary holdings, the company produces aluminum, steel, vinyl, and fiberglass products for OEMs (commercial panel makers and RV and other transportation industry manufacturers), distributors, contractors, and home centers. The company has in-house coil-coating capabilities for supplying aluminum sidewalls to RV makers and steel siding to manufactured housing customers. Euramax makes a majority of the aluminum sidewalls used annually by RV makers in the US. Euramax International is controlled by Goldman Sachs & Co.

Euramax International was established in 1996 when Alumax Inc., in order to fund acquisitions in its core aluminum businesses, sold Alumax Fabricated Products, Inc. to Citicorp Venture Capital Ltd. (U.S.) and CVC European Capital Partners.

Euramax acquired Berger Holdings (now Berger Building Products) in 2003.

Citigroup Venture Capital sold Euramax to Goldman Sachs & Co. and members of Euramax's management in 2005.

EXECUTIVES

President, CEO, and Director: Mitchell B. Lewis, age 45
VP, CFO, and Secretary: R. Scott Vansant, age 45
President, Gutter Suppliers and ADP:
Scott R. Anderson, age 45
President, Amerimax Home Products: P. Dudley Rowe, age 49
President, Amerimax Building Products: Nick E. Dowd, age 50
President, Berger Building Products: David Stewart
President, Ellbee: Nigel Smailes
President, Fabral: Paul K. Emert Jr.
Managing Director, Coated Products: Rob Dresen, age 53
Managing Director, Euramax Industries:
Aloyse R. Wagener, age 60
Auditors: Ernst & Young LLP

LOCATIONS

HQ: Euramax International, Inc.
5445 Triangle Pkwy., Ste. 350, Norcross, GA 30092
Phone: 770-449-7066   **Fax:** 770-449-7354
Web: www.euramax.com

Euramax International operates facilities in France, the Netherlands, the UK, and the US.

PRODUCTS/OPERATIONS

Selected Products

Aluminum shower and bath enclosures
Aluminum or vinyl windows and doors
Aluminum RV/caravan doors, windows, and sidewalls
Metal and vinyl raincarrying systems
Metal wall and roof systems
Patio products
Roofing accessories
Soffit and facia systems
Specialty coated coil

COMPETITORS

Atwood Mobile
Bodycote
Butler Manufacturing
NCI Building Systems
Worthington Industries

HISTORICAL FINANCIALS

Company Type: Holding company

Income Statement

	REVENUE ($ mil.)	NET INCOME ($ mil.)	NET PROFIT MARGIN	EMPLOYEES
12/07	1,300	—	—	3,471
12/06	1,210	—	—	3,300
12/05	1,068	—	—	3,200
12/04	965	—	—	2,700
12/03	744	—	—	2,600
Annual Growth	**15.0%**	—	—	**7.5%**

FYE: Last Friday of December

Revenue History

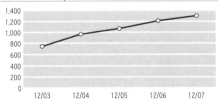

Evergreen Holdings

Through subsidiary Evergreen International Aviation, Evergreen Holdings soars over green lands. Evergreen International Aviation itself operates through several units, including Evergreen International Airlines, which transports cargo for government and commercial customers with a fleet of Boeing 747 freighters. Evergreen Aviation Ground Logistics Enterprise provides ground handling services at US airports. Other Evergreen units offer helicopter transportation services; maintain, repair, and overhaul aircraft; sell and lease aircraft; and engage in farming. Del Smith, a former Air Force pilot and crop duster, owns a controlling stake in the company, which he founded in 1960.

Over the years the Air Force's Air Mobility Command has been a major customer of Evergreen International Airlines. The carrier hauls hazardous materials and other sensitive cargo for the Air Force; in addition, it transports general cargo for customers such as airlines and freight forwarders, often under ACMI (aircraft, crew, maintenance, and insurance) contracts.

Evergreen Holdings has stakes not only in the present and the future of aviation, but also in its past. A museum outside the company's headquarters houses Howard Hughes' Spruce Goose and other vintage aircraft.

EXECUTIVES

Chairman and CEO: Delford M. (Del) Smith, age 76, $5,801,045 pay
President and Director; President and Director, Evergreen International Aviation: Timothy G. Wahlberg, age 60, $152,917 pay
President, Evergreen Helicopters International: James A. Porter, age 59
President, Evergreen Helicopters: David Rath
President, Evergreen International Airlines and Systems LogistiX and Director, Evergreen International Aviation: Brian T. Bauer, age 38, $143,109 pay
President, Fixed Wing: Michael A. Hines
President, Evergreen Helicopters of Alaska: Sabrina Ford
President, Evergreen Helicopters International: Dan Blanchard
SVP Sales and Marketing, Evergreen International Airlines and Director, Evergreen International Aviation: Ranjit Seth, age 41, $133,000 pay
Auditors: GHP Horwath, PC

LOCATIONS

HQ: Evergreen Holdings, Inc.
3850 Three Mile Ln., McMinnville, OR 97128
Phone: 503-472-9361   **Fax:** 503-472-1048
Web: www.evergreenaviation.com

COMPETITORS

AAR Corp.
Air Methods
Air T
Air Transport Services Group
Aircraft Service International
Arrow Air
ASTAR Air Cargo
Atlas Air Worldwide
Bristow Group Inc
CHC Helicopter
GATX
GE Commercial Aviation Services
Goodrich Corporation
Grand Aire
Kalitta Air
Keystone Helicopter
Menzies Aviation
Mercury Air Group
PHI, Inc.
Servisair
Swissport USA, Inc.
WFS

Express Employment

When you need a worker fast, Express Employment Professionals delivers. Formerly known as Express Personnel Services, the professional staffing company provides work for some 350,000 employees from about 600 offices across Australia, Canada, South Africa, and the US. In addition to temporary staffing, it provides professional placement and contract staffing through Express Professional Staffing and offers workplace services (consulting, training, development) through Express Business Solutions. Founded in 1983, the company is owned by founders William Stoller (vice chairman) and Robert Funk (CEO).

EXECUTIVES

Chairman and CEO: Robert A. Funk
Vice Chairman: William H. (Bill) Stoller, age 32
EVP Operations, CFO and Director: Thomas N. Richards
EVP Sales and Director: Bob Fellinger
SVP Administration and Human Resources: Carol Lane
SVP Public Relations: Linda C. Haneborg
SVP Franchise Support and Information Services: Terri Weldon
VP and Controller: Sharon Patric
VP Federal Accounts: Marshall Lee
VP Financial Analysis: L. Edward Taylor
VP Franchising: Nikki Sells
VP Sales and Marketing: Linda Sasser

LOCATIONS

HQ: Express Employment Professionals
8516 Northwest Expwy., Oklahoma City, OK 73162
Phone: 405-840-5000   **Fax:** 405-717-5669
Web: www.expresspros.com

PRODUCTS/OPERATIONS

Selected Staffing Fields
Express Personnel
  General labor
  Government
  Health care
  Industrial
  Office and clerical
  Scientific
  Technical
Express Professional
  Accounting and financial
  Engineering and manufacturing
  Health care
  Human resources
  Information technology
  Sales and marketing
  Technical

COMPETITORS

Adecco
Administaff
ADP TotalSource
Barrett Business Services
Butler International
Gevity HR
Kelly Services
Manpower
MPS
Randstad Holding
Robert Half
Spherion
Volt Information

HISTORICAL FINANCIALS
Company Type: Private

Income Statement

	REVENUE ($ mil.)	NET INCOME ($ mil.)	NET PROFIT MARGIN	EMPLOYEES
12/07	2,000	—	—	375,000
12/06	1,800	—	—	350,000
12/05	1,550	—	—	300,000
Annual Growth	**13.6%**	**—**	**—**	**11.8%**

FYE: December 31

Revenue History

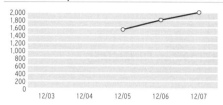

Express, LLC

Right from the runway is the Express way. Express operates more than 620 men's, women's, and dual-gender stores in the US that sell trendy private-label apparel and accessories. (Its fashions are styled to have an international influence and modern appeal.) Express also sells denim and lingerie. Its brand was extended to menswear, again, when former parent company Limited Brands converted its Structure stores and reunited both labels to re-create Express Men's in 2002. More recently, amid declining sales, Express has been closing stores and converting its men's and women's stores to dual-gender outlets. Limited Brands, which launched Express in 1980, sold the chain to Golden Gate Capital in mid-2007.

Golden Gate Capital (GGC) acquired a 75% interest in the chain in July 2007 for about $425 million. (Limited Brands retained a 25% stake in Express.) GGC kept the Express name and the company remained based in Columbus, Ohio. However, GGC replaced Jay Margolis — who headed Express as president of Limited Brands' apparel group — with the appointment of Michael Weiss as CEO. Weiss, who led Express for most of his 23 years with the company, retired in 2004.

Sales at Express stores have declined in recent years, as have those of its former sister company Limited Stores, which has also been sold to another private equity firm. Limited Brands said it sold both chains in order to focus on its better performing intimate apparel and personal care businesses (Victoria's Secret and Bath & Body Works). Express accounted for about 15% of Limited Brands' sales.

Over the past two years more than 200 Express shops have been closed.

EXECUTIVES

President and CEO: Michael A. Weiss, age 67
CFO: Matt Mollering
EVP Marketing: Lisa A. Gavales

LOCATIONS

HQ: Express, LLC
   1 Limited Pkwy., Columbus, OH 43230
Phone: 614-415-4000   **Fax:** 614-415-7440
Web: www.expressfashion.com

COMPETITORS

Abercrombie & Fitch	Guess?
American Eagle Outfitters	J. C. Penney
AnnTaylor	Kenneth Cole
bebe stores	Kohl's
Charlotte Russe Holding	Macy's
Charming Shoppes	Target
Dillard's	TJX Companies
Donna Karan	Wet Seal
The Gap	

HISTORICAL FINANCIALS
Company Type: Private

Income Statement				FYE: Saturday nearest January 31
	REVENUE ($ mil.)	NET INCOME ($ mil.)	NET PROFIT MARGIN	EMPLOYEES
1/08	1,800	—	—	—
1/07	1,749	—	—	—
1/06	1,794	—	—	—
1/05	1,913	—	—	—
1/04	2,071	—	—	—
Annual Growth	(3.4%)	—	—	—

Revenue History

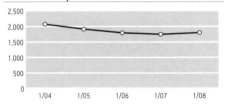

Factory Mutual Insurance

If you're looking to protect your corporation, turn your insurance dial to FM Global. Factory Mutual Insurance (operating as FM Global) provides commercial and industrial property insurance and a variety of risk management services, ranging from all-risk programs to specialized products for ocean cargo and machinery equipment, as well as property loss prevention engineering and research. FM Global operates through such subsidiaries as Affiliated FM Insurance, FM Global Cargo, and Mutual Boiler Re. In addition to the US, the company has offices in Asia, Australia, Canada, Europe, and South America.

FM Global operates a business model that promotes proactive loss prevention rather than actuarial loss predictions. The company helps its clients improve and strengthen facilities, minimizing the damage that can result from such events as fires, explosions, and hurricanes. Its engineering expertise is provided by FM Global Research Campus, a research and testing complex. The company's TSB Loss Control Consultants provides emergency response training for its customers.

EXECUTIVES

Chairman and CEO: Shivan S. Subramaniam
EVP: Ruud H. Bosman
EVP: Brian J. Hurley
SVP Commercial Lines: Carol G. Barton
SVP Underwriting and Reinsurance: Jonathan W. Hall
SVP Engineering and Research: Thomas A. Lawson
SVP Finance: Jeffrey A. Burchill
SVP Human Resources: Enzo Rebula
SVP Information Services: Jeanne R. Lieb
SVP International Division: Kenneth W. Davey
SVP Investments: Paul E. LaFleche
SVP Law and Governmental Affairs: John J. Pomeroy
SVP Marketing and Training:
   Christopher (Chris) Johnson
SVP Claims: Gerardo L. Alonso
Auditors: Ernst & Young LLP

LOCATIONS

HQ: Factory Mutual Insurance Company
   1301 Atwood Ave., Johnston, RI 02919
Phone: 401-275-3000   **Fax:** 401-275-3029
Web: www.fmglobal.com

PRODUCTS/OPERATIONS

2007 Sales

	$ mil.	% of total
Net premiums	2,949.6	88
Investment income	368.4	11
Fees	37.8	1
Total	**3,355.8**	**100**

Selected Subsidiaries

Affiliated FM Insurance Company
Corporate Insurance Services
FM Approvals
FM Global Cargo
FM Global Research
Mutual Boiler Re
TSB Loss Control Consultants, Inc.

COMPETITORS

ACE Limited
AIG
Allianz
CNA Financial
Endurance Specialty
The Hartford
HSB Group
Nationwide
Specialty Underwriters' Alliance
Travelers Companies
Western World Insurance
Zurich Financial Services

HISTORICAL FINANCIALS
Company Type: Mutual company

Income Statement				FYE: December 31
	ASSETS ($ mil.)	NET INCOME ($ mil.)	INCOME AS % OF ASSETS	EMPLOYEES
12/07	13,030	928	7.1%	4,500
12/06	12,268	737	6.0%	4,900
12/05	11,090	635	5.7%	4,700
12/04	9,484	558	5.9%	4,700
12/03	8,250	666	8.1%	4,400
Annual Growth	12.1%	8.6%	—	0.6%

Equity as % of assets: 48.1%   Long-term debt ($ mil.): 0
Return on assets: 7.3%   Sales ($ mil.): 3,356
Return on equity: 16.3%

Net Income History

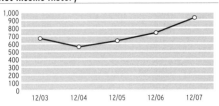

Federal Home Loan Bank of Atlanta

Where do banks in the southeastern US bank? Federal Home Loan Bank of Atlanta. More than 1,200 commercial banks, credit unions, insurance companies, and thrifts in the southeast bank at the institution, which calls itself FHLBank Atlanta. It's one of 12 Federal Home Loan Banks in the Federal Home Loan Bank System and is cooperatively owned by its member institutions, ranging in size from organizations with less than $5 million in assets to "super-regionals" with more than $125 billion. Institutions are required to purchase capital stock in the bank to be members. A government-sponsored enterprise, it funds residential mortgages and community development loans.

The bank's territory includes Alabama, Florida, Georgia, Maryland, North Carolina, South Carolina, Virginia, and Washington, DC.

The Federal Housing Finance Board, an independent federal government agency, supervises and regulates the bank.

EXECUTIVES

Chairman: Scott C. Harvard, age 53
Vice Chairman: James Thomas Johnson, age 61
President and CEO: Richard A. Dorfman, age 62
EVP and CFO: Steven J. Goldstein, age 56
EVP, General Counsel, Chief Strategy Officer, and Corporate Secretary: Jill Spencer, age 56
EVP and Director Financial Management:
   W. Wesley (Wes) McMullan, age 44
EVP and Chief Credit Officer: Kirk R. Malmberg, age 47
EVP and CIO: Marian M. Lucia
SVP and Director Internal Audit: Richard A. Patrick
SVP and Director of Member Sales and Trading:
   Praveen Jha
SVP Staff Services: Cathy C. Adams, age 48
SVP and Treasurer: Andrew B. Mills
First VP, Accounting and Controller:
   J. Daniel (Dan) Counce
First VP, Human Resources: M. Bryan DeLong
Auditors: PricewaterhouseCoopers LLP

LOCATIONS

HQ: Federal Home Loan Bank of Atlanta
   1475 Peachtree St., NE, Atlanta, GA 30309
Phone: 404-888-8000   **Fax:** 404-888-5648
Web: www.fhlbatl.com

PRODUCTS/OPERATIONS

2007 Sales

	$ mil.	% of total
Interest		
Advances	6,270.3	74
Other	2,145.5	26
Noninterest	13.5	—
Total	**8,429.3**	**100**

COMPETITORS

Fannie Mae
FHLB Chicago
Freddie Mac
Ginnie Mae
MoneyGram International

HISTORICAL FINANCIALS

Company Type: Member-owned banking authority

Income Statement				FYE: December 31
	ASSETS ($ mil.)	NET INCOME ($ mil.)	INCOME AS % OF ASSETS	EMPLOYEES
12/07	189,746	445	0.2%	362
12/06	140,758	414	0.3%	349
12/05	143,239	344	0.2%	339
12/04	134,013	294	0.2%	—
Annual Growth	12.3%	21.1%	—	3.3%

2007 Year-End Financials

Equity as % of assets: 4.2%
Return on assets: 0.3%
Return on equity: 6.3%
Long-term debt ($ mil.): —
Sales ($ mil.): 8,429

Net Income History

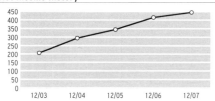

Federal Prison Industries

Some businesses benefit from captive audiences; this company benefits from captive employees. Federal Prison Industries (FPI), known by its trade name UNICOR, uses prisoners to make products and provide services, mainly for the US government. More than 21,000 inmates (about 18% of the total eligible inmate population) are employed in nearly 110 FPI factories in prisons across the US. UNICOR, which is part of the Justice Department's Bureau of Prisons, manufactures products such as office furniture, clothing, beds and linens, electronics equipment, and eyewear. It also offers services including data entry, bulk mailing, laundry services, recycling, and refurbishing of vehicle components.

Federal law mandates that government buyers consider UNICOR products before they consider competing products from the private sector. In 2006 the US House of Representatives over-

whelmingly approved a bill to remove this mandate; the bill has yet to be considered by the US Senate. If it passes, it would introduce a new dimension of competition for UNICOR.

UNICOR is also allowed to sell services (but not products) to the private sector. FPI is benefiting from a growing prison population and the cheap cost of its labor (pay ranges from 23 cents to $1.15 per hour). The company is also tapping into the commercial market by offering services. Self-supporting, UNICOR is overseen by a governing board that is appointed by the US president.

Its largest customers include the US Departments of Defense (which buys nearly all of its furniture from UNICOR), Homeland Security, and Justice, and the Social Security Administration.

Unlike most manufacturers these days that look to establish facilities in developing countries, UNICOR tries to leverage its low labor costs and actually looks for labor-intensive products to make.

HISTORY

FPI was established by President Franklin Roosevelt in 1934 to teach job skills at men's and women's federal prisons. During WWII, 95% of FPI's output was dedicated to the war effort — the company's products included parachutes and munitions. In the late 1950s and early 1960s, FPI built or renovated structures at 18 of the 31 federal prisons. In 1974 it established regional sales offices, and in 1977 it took the name UNICOR.

Although self-supporting, UNICOR remained necessarily inefficient because of its goal to put as many inmates as possible to work. However, as the prison population increased, the company underwent rapid expansion and added skilled services in the 1980s.

UNICOR put its product catalog online in 1996. The next year the Senate authorized a study of ways to make UNICOR more competitive, after private businesses had complained that the booming prison population, low wages (23 cents to $1.15 per hour), and government preferential treatment gave UNICOR an unfair advantage. Legislation to force FPI to bid against the private sector for government contracts was brought before Congress in 1999; at the same time, a bill was introduced to allow the company to offer its products to the private sector. Meanwhile, FPI began selling services such as data entry to private-sector customers.

In 2003 Dell Computer dropped UNICOR as the vendor for its computer recycling program.

EXECUTIVES

Chairman: David D. Spears
Vice Chairman: Donald R. Elliott
CEO: Harley G. Lappin
COO: Steve Schwalb
Sales Manager, Office Furniture, South and Southwest: Katherine Allen
Sales Manager, Office Furniture, Southeast: Diane Stabinski
Design Manager, Office Furniture Sales Offices, Alabama: Amy McGowan
Product Manager, Clothing and Textiles: Bill Young
Program Manager Business Development: Lark Conatser
Administrator, Customer Service Center: Randy Toy
Assistant Director, Human Resources: Keith Hall
Controller: Bruce Long
Auditors: KPMG LLP

LOCATIONS

HQ: Federal Prison Industries, Inc.
320 1st St. NW, Bldg. 400, Washington, DC 20534
Phone: 202-305-3500   **Fax:** 202-305-7340
Web: www.unicor.gov

Federal Prison Industries operates 106 factories at more than 70 prisons in the US.

PRODUCTS/OPERATIONS

2007 Sales

	$ mil.	% of total
Electronics	326.3	34
Clothing & textiles	175.3	19
Fleet management	156.4	16
Office furniture	116.0	12
Services	34.8	4
Industrial products	32.8	3
Recycling	11.2	1
Other	105.1	11
Total	**957.8**	**100**

Selected Products

Electronics
  Electrical cables (both braided and cord assemblies)
  Electrical components and connectors
  Lighting systems
  Wire harness assemblies and circuit boards
Clothing and textiles
  Apparel
  Draperies and curtains
  Embroidery and screen printing on textiles
  Mattresses, bedding, linens, and towels
Office furniture
  Casegoods and training table products
  Filing and storage products
  Office furniture and accessories
  Office system products
  Packaged office solutions
  Seating products
Fleet management
  Fleet management customized services
  New-vehicle retrofit services
  Rebuilt and refurbished vehicle components
Industrial products
  Custom fabricated industrial products, lockers, and
    storage cabinets
  Dorm and quarters furnishings and packaged room
    solutions
  Industrial racking catwalks, mezzanines, and shelving
  Optical eyewear (safety and prescription)
  Replacement filters
  Security fencing
Services
  Assembly and packing services
  Call center and order fulfillment services
  Distribution and mailing services
  Document conversion
  Laundry services
Recycling
  Recycling of electronic components
  Reuse and recovery of usable components for resale

COMPETITORS

Avnet
CPAC
Deere
Federal Signal
Haworth, Inc.
Herman Miller
HNI
Kimball International
Matthews International
Mine Safety Appliances
Molex
Steelcase
Tyco
WestPoint Home Inc

HISTORICAL FINANCIALS

Company Type: Government agency

Income Statement

FYE: September 30

	REVENUE ($ mil.)	NET INCOME ($ mil.)	NET PROFIT MARGIN	EMPLOYEES
9/07	958	46	4.8%	23,152
9/06	774	17	2.2%	21,205
9/05	834	65	7.7%	19,720
9/04	879	64	7.2%	19,337
9/03	722	2	0.3%	20,274
Annual Growth	7.3%	118.8%	—	3.4%

2007 Year-End Financials

Debt ratio: 0.0%
Return on equity: 10.0%
Cash ($ mil.): —

Current ratio: —
Long-term debt ($ mil.): 0

Net Income History

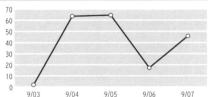

Federal Reserve System

Where do banks go when they need a loan? To the Federal Reserve System, which sets the discount interest rate, the base rate at which its member banks may borrow. Known as the Fed, the system oversees a network of 12 Federal Reserve Banks located in major US cities; these in turn regulate banks in their districts and ensure they maintain adequate reserves. The Fed also clears money transfers, issues currency, and buys or sells government securities to regulate the money supply. Through its powerful New York bank, the Fed conducts foreign currency transactions, trades on the world market to support the US dollar's value, and stores gold for foreign governments and international agencies.

By setting the discount rate and the federal funds rate (the rate at which banks borrow from each other), the Fed influences the pace of lending and, many believe, the pace of the nation's economy itself.

A seven-member Board of Governors oversees the Fed's activities. The board was chaired by former Ayn Rand compadre Alan Greenspan from the Reagan administration until 2006. As chairman under four different presidents, Greenspan wielded more power than perhaps any Fed chief in history, and securities markets rose and fell on his every word. Greenspan was replaced by former chairman of President Bush's Council of Economic Advisers and Fed board member, Ben Bernacke. As his predecessor did during the economic downturn earlier, Bernacke agressively cut the discount interest rate in an effort to jumpstart the economy.

However, in 2008 the US faced an economic crisis as severe as any seen since the Great De-

pression that claimed numerous victims including Bear Stearns (the Fed brokered and assisted its purchase by JPMorgan Chase) and Lehman Brothers. Together with Secretary of the Treasury Henry Paulson, Bernanke pushed for the passage of a $700 billion rescue plan, the largest in history.

The Fed also eased up its dollar swap facilities with top European central banks in an effort to provide liquidity and meet demand for the dollar overseas.

Fed board members are appointed by the US president and confirmed by the Senate for one-time 14-year terms, staggered at two-year intervals to prevent political stacking. The seven governors comprise the majority of the 12-person Federal Open Market Committee, which determines monetary policy. The five remaining members are reserve bank presidents who rotate in one-year terms, with New York always holding a place. Although the Fed enjoys significant political and financial freedom, the chairman is required to testify before Congress twice a year. National member banks must own stock in their Federal Reserve Bank, though it is optional for state-chartered banks.

HISTORY

When New York's Knickerbocker Trust Company failed in 1907, it brought on a panic that was stemmed by J. P. Morgan, who strong-armed his fellow bankers into supporting shaky New York banks. The incident showed the need for a central bank.

Morgan's actions sparked fears of his economic power and spurred congressional efforts to establish a central bank. After a six-year struggle between eastern money interests and populist monetary reformers, the 1913 Federal Reserve Act was passed. Twelve Federal Reserve districts were created, but New York's economic might ensured it would be the most powerful.

New York bank head Benjamin Strong dominated the Fed in the 1920s, countering the glut of European gold flooding the US in 1923 by selling securities from the Fed's portfolio. After he died in 1928, the Fed couldn't stabilize prices. Such difficulty, along with low rates encouraging members to use Fed loans for stock speculation, helped set the stage for 1929's crash.

During the Depression and WWII, the Fed yielded to the demands of the Treasury to buy bonds. But after WWII it sought independence, using Congress to help free it from Treasury demands. This effort was led by chairman William McChesney Martin, with the assistance of New York bank president Alan Sproul (also a rival for the chairmanship). Martin diluted Sproul's influence by governing by consensus with the other bank leaders.

The Fed managed the economy successfully in the postwar boom, but it was stymied by inflation in the late 1960s. In the early 1970s the New York bank also faced the collapse of the fixed currency exchange-rate system and the growth of currency trading. Its role as foreign currency trader became even more crucial as the dollar's value eroded amid rising oil prices and a slowing economy.

The US suffered from double-digit inflation in 1979 as President Jimmy Carter appointed New York Fed president Paul Volcker as chairman. Volcker, believing that raising interest rates a few points would not suffice, allowed the banks to raise their discount rates and increased bank reserve requirements to reduce the money sup-

ply. By the time inflation eased, Ronald Reagan was president.

During the 1980s and 1990s, US budget fights limited options for controlling the economy through spending decision, so the Fed's actions became more important. Its higher profile brought calls for more access to its decision-making processes. Alan Greenspan took over as chairman in 1987 after being designated by Reagan (and reappointed by presidents George H. W. Bush, Bill Clinton, and George W. Bush). He stepped down during the second Bush administration, and was replaced by Ben Bernanke.

While the US economy seemed immune to the Asian currency crisis of 1997 and 1998, the Federal Reserve remained relatively quiescent. But when Russia defaulted on some of its bonds in 1998, leading to the near-collapse of hedge fund Long-Term Capital Management, the New York Federal Reserve Bank brokered a bailout by the fund's lenders and investors.

This led in 1999 to new guidelines for banks' risk management. The next year the Fed faced up to the Internet age, taking a look at e-banking supervision. After raising interest rates to stave off inflation during the go-go late 1990s, the Fed cut rates an unprecedented 11 times in 2001 (to a 40-year low of 1.75%) to help spur the flagging post-boom economy.

Rate changes, and following economic changes, continued with a low of 1% in 2003. In all, rates were adjusted a total of 18 times between 2002 and 2006.

EXECUTIVES

Chairman: Ben S. Bernanke, age 54
Vice Chairman: Donald L. Kohn, age 65
Assistant to the Board and Chief Spokesperson: David W. Skidmore
Assistant to the Board for Public Information: Rosanna (Rose) Pianalto-Cameron
Assistant to the Board: Winthrop P. Hambley
General Counsel, Legal Division: Scott G. Alvarez
President, Federal Reserve Bank of Dallas: Richard W. Fisher
President, Federal Reserve Bank of New York: Timothy F. Geithner
President, Federal Reserve Bank of Kansas City: Thomas M. (Tom) Hoenig, age 62
President, Federal Reserve Bank of Richmond: Jeffrey M. (Jeff) Lacker, age 53
President, Federal Reserve Bank of Cleveland: Sandra Pianalto, age 54
President, Federal Reserve Bank of Minneapolis: Gary H. Stern
President, Federal Reserve Bank of Philadelphia: Charles I. Plosser, age 57
President, Federal Reserve Bank of San Francisco: Janet L. Yellen, age 62
President and CEO, Federal Reserve Bank of Atlanta: Dennis P. Lockhart, age 59
President, Federal Reserve Bank of Chicago: Charles L. (Charlie) Evans, age 50
President and CEO, Federal Reserve Bank of Boston: Eric S. Rosengren, age 50
President and CEO, Federal Reserve Bank of St. Louis: James B. Bullard, age 47
Comptroller of the Currency: John C. Dugan
Secretary: Jennifer J. Johnson
Director, Division of Banking Supervision and Regulation: Roger T. Cole
Director, Division of Consumer and Community Affairs: Sandra F. Braunstein
Director, Office of Board Members, and Assistant to the Board: Michelle A. Smith
Director, Division of Monetary Affairs: Brian F. Madigan
Inspector General: Elizabeth A. Coleman
Auditors: PricewaterhouseCoopers LLP

LOCATIONS

HQ: Federal Reserve System
20th Street and Constitution Avenue NW,
Washington, DC 20551
Phone: 202-452-3000
Web: www.federalreserve.gov

Federal Reserve Banks

Atlanta
Boston
Chicago
Cleveland
Dallas
Kansas City, Missouri
Minneapolis
New York
Philadelphia
Richmond, Virginia
St. Louis
San Francisco

Feed The Children

Tuppence a bag might feed some birds, but it takes more to feed growing children. Feed The Children (FTC) is a not-for-profit Christian charity that distributes food, medicine, and other items. In the US, FTC accepts bulk contributions of surplus food from businesses, packages it in various ways at six main facilities nationwide, and distributes it to food banks, homeless shelters, churches, and other organizations that help feed the hungry. Overseas, FTC works with organizations, such as schools, orphanages, and churches to provide food, medical supplies, clothing, and educational support to the needy. Larry and Frances Jones founded FTC in 1979.

While FTC has focused its efforts on feeding children, the organization also concentrates on supplying them with support through outreach programs. FTC launched an educational initiative named H.E.L.P. (or Homeless Education and Literacy Program), which works with homeless outreach coordinators in elementary and middle schools to provide students with school supplies, books, and personal-care items, in addition to food.

EXECUTIVES

Chairman: Dwight Powers
Founder, President, and CEO: Larry Jones
CFO: Christy Tharp
EVP: Frances Jones
VP and General Counsel: Larri Sue Jones
VP International Public Relations: Steven Whetstone
VP Management Information Systems: Larry Correa
VP Human Relations: Richard Gray
VP Operations: Travis Arnold
Auditors: McGladrey & Pullen, LLP

LOCATIONS

HQ: Feed The Children, Inc.
333 N. Meridian Ave., Oklahoma City, OK 73107
Phone: 405-942-0228   **Fax:** 405-945-4177
Web: www.feedthechildren.org

PRODUCTS/OPERATIONS

2007 Support and Revenue

	$ mil.	% of total
Gifts-in-kind	823.2	86
Contributions	113.4	12
Other	18.5	2
Total	**955.1**	**100**

2007 Distribution Expenditures

	% of total
Program services	83
Fundraising	13
Management & support services	4
Total	**100**

HISTORICAL FINANCIALS
Company Type: Not-for-profit

Income Statement

FYE: June 30

	REVENUE ($ mil.)	NET INCOME ($ mil.)	NET PROFIT MARGIN	EMPLOYEES
6/07	955	402	42.0%	—
6/06	664	(11)	—	—
6/05	861	—	—	—
6/04	967	—	—	160
6/03	576	—	—	160
Annual Growth	**13.5%**	**—**	**—**	**0.0%**

2007 Year-End Financials

Debt ratio: 0.0%
Return on equity: —
Cash ($ mil.): —
Current ratio: —
Long-term debt ($ mil.): 0

Net Income History

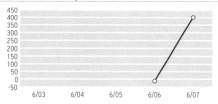

Feld Entertainment

A lot of clowning around has helped Feld Entertainment become one of the largest live entertainment producers in the world. The company entertains people through its centerpiece, Ringling Bros. and Barnum & Bailey Circus, which visits about 90 locations. Feld also produces several touring ice shows, including Disney On Ice shows such as *Finding Nemo* and *High School Musical: The Ice Tour*. Chairman and CEO Kenneth Feld, whose father, Irvin, began managing the circus in 1956, owns the company and personally oversees most of its productions. Ringling Bros. and Barnum & Bailey Circus made its first performance in 1871.

Feld Entertainment's circus, ice, and stage shows have played in 50 countries, and approximately 25 million people see the company's productions each year.

Throught its history, the company has engaged in some high-profile battles with animal rights activists who claim that the Ringling Bros. and Barnum & Bailey Circus' use of an elephant-herding tool known as a bullhook injures elephants. The company opened the Ringling Bros.

---

and Barnum & Bailey Center for Elephant Conservation in 1995.

In 2008 Feld expanded with the purchase of Live Nation Motor Sports from concert producer Live Nation for some $175 million. The deal adds car races and monster-truck events such as Monster Jam to Feld's operations.

HISTORY

When 5-year-old Irvin Feld found a $1 bill in 1923, he told his mother, "I'm going to buy a circus." He started by working the sideshows of traveling circuses before settling in Washington, DC, in 1940. Feld, who was white, opened the Super Cut-Rate Drugstore in a black section of the segregated city with the backing of the NAACP. In 1944 he opened the Super Music City record store and started his own record company, Super Disc. Feld and his brother Israel also began promoting outdoor concerts. When rock and roll became popular in the 1950s, Feld promoted Chubby Checker and Fats Domino, among others.

Feld came a step closer to his dream in 1956 when he began managing the Ringling Bros. and Barnum & Bailey Circus for majority owner John Ringling North. North's circus traced its roots back to 1871 and P. T. Barnum's Grand Traveling Museum, Menagerie, Caravan, and Circus. Barnum's circus merged with James Bailey's circus in 1881, creating Barnum & Bailey. In 1907 Bailey's widow sold Barnum & Bailey to North's uncles, the Ringling brothers, who had started their circus in 1884.

Among Feld's suggestions to North was moving the circus into air-conditioned arenas, saving $50,000 a week because 1,800 roustabouts were no longer needed to set up tents. Feld continued to promote music acts, but he suffered a serious blow in 1959 when three of his stars — Buddy Holly, Ritchie Valens, and J. P. Richardson (the Big Bopper) — died in a plane crash.

Feld's dream of owning a circus finally was realized in 1967 when he and investors paid $8 million for Ringling Brothers. He fired most of the circus' performers and opened a Clown College to train new ones. Feld bought a German circus the following year to obtain animal trainer Gunther Gebel-Williams (who then spent the next 30 years with Ringling Brothers). Feld split Ringling into two units in 1969, so he could book it in two parts of the country at the same time and double his profits. Feld took the company public that year.

Feld and the other stockholders sold the circus to Mattel in 1971 for $47 million in stock; Feld stayed on as manager and held on to the lucrative concession business, Sells-Floto. He persuaded Mattel to buy the Ice Follies, Holiday on Ice, and the Siegfried & Roy magic show in 1979. Mattel sold the circus back to Feld in 1982 for $22.5 million, along with the ice shows and the magic show. Feld died two years later, and his son Kenneth became head of the company. A chip off the old block, Kenneth fired almost all the circus performers when he took over.

In an attempt to leverage the Barnum & Bailey brand, the company opened four retail store locations in 1990, but the venture failed and the stores were closed two years later. A constant target of animal rights activists, Feld began backing conservation efforts on behalf of the endangered Asian elephant and established the Center for Elephant Conservation in Florida in 1995. The next year the company changed its name to Feld Entertainment.

Under increasing pressure as the company's creative guru and managerial boss, Feld hired Turner Home Entertainment executive Stuart Snyder as president and COO in 1997 so he could focus on the creative side of the business. That focus produced Barnum's Kaleidoscape in 1999, an upscale version of the original circus, featuring specialty acts, gourmet food, plush seats, and audience interaction. Plus, for the first time since 1956, a Feld circus was performed under a tent. (The company later shut down the tour of the Kaleidoscape.) Snyder resigned later in 1999.

In an effort to inject new life into the 130-year-old Ringling Bros. and Barnum & Bailey Circus, Feld Entertainment launched two new marketing campaigns (one aimed at adults, the other aimed at children) in 2001.

In 2001 a district court judge dismissed a complaint filed against the company by several animal activist groups that claimed that Feld Entertainment didn't comply with federal regulations regarding the care of Asian elephants. The lawsuit was reinstated in early 2003 due to a procedural technicality. A former Ringling Bros. employee is a co-plaintiff in the lawsuit.

Feld Entertainment's popular Siegfried & Roy show suffered a tragedy in 2003 when Roy Horn was mauled by a white tiger during a performance. He later suffered a stroke that left him partially paralyzed, and the Siegfried & Roy show is closed indefinitely.

In 2004 the company battled a potential ban on exotic animal acts in Denver. A 15-year-old student led the charge, getting the initiative on the ballot. Feld hired political consultants and handily defeated the measure by a 72% vote.

In 2008 the company acquired Live Nation Motor Sports.

EXECUTIVES

Chairman and CEO: Kenneth J. (Ken) Feld, age 59
President, COO, and Director: Michael Shannon
CFO and Director: Michael (Mike) Little
EVP: Alana Feld
EVP: Nicole Feld
SVP Chief Marketing Officer: Rob Desatnick
SVP North America Event Marketing and Sales: Jeff Meyer
SVP International Sales and Business Development: Robert McHugh
VP and Deputy General Counsel: Julie Alexa Strauss
VP Creative Development: Jerry Bilik
VP Animal Stewardship: Bruce Read
VP Human Resources: Kirk McCoy
VP Government Relations: Tom Albert
VP Sponsorship: Jason Bitsoff
VP Corporate Communications: Stephen (Steve) Payne
CTO: Neal Grunsey
National Director Public Relations, Ringling Bros.: Enrico Dinges

LOCATIONS

HQ: Feld Entertainment, Inc.
8607 Westwood Center Dr., Vienna, VA 22182
Phone: 703-448-4000   **Fax:** 703-448-4100
Web: www.feldentertainment.com

PRODUCTS/OPERATIONS

Selected Attractions

Disney On Ice
Finding Nemo
High School Musical: The Ice Tour
Monsters, Inc.
Princess Classics
The Incredibles
Three Jungle Adventures
Walt Disney's 100 Years of Magic

Feld Entertainment Motor Sports
Monster Jam
Ringling Bros. and Barnum & Bailey Circus

COMPETITORS

CIE
Cirque du Soleil
Harlem Globetrotters
HIT Entertainment
Indy Racing League
Live Nation
NASCAR
On Stage Entertainment
Renaissance Entertainment
Six Flags
TBA Global

Fellowes, Inc.

Fellowes (formerly Fellowes Manufacturing Company) produces office products that can organize or obliterate. The leading maker of paper shredders (Powershred, Micro-shred), it also makes computer and office accessories, such as ergonomic wrist rests, multimedia storage, and other accessories. As a licensee of Body Glove International (maker of high-tech surf and scuba gear), Fellowes offers fashionable Body Glove cases for mobile phones and iPods. Fellowes' products are sold through office retailers and mass merchants, as well as online. Still owned and run by the Fellowes family, the company was started in 1917 when Harry Fellowes paid $50 for Bankers Box, a maker of storage boxes for bank records.

Fellowes in mid-2006 agreed to acquire the Perma corrugated storage box business from ACCO Brands.

The company continued to expand in core markets in 2007, opening joint ventures in China and Russia to increase global distribution of products. Its Chinese operation has one of the largest shredder manufacturing facilities in the world.

EXECUTIVES

Chairman and CEO: James (Jamie) Fellowes
EVP and COO: Joseph T. (Joe) Koch
EVP and Chief Supply Chain Officer: James (Jim) Lewis
EVP Global Human Resources: Lyn Bulman
VP and General Manager, Mobile Technology Accessories: Mark Martin
VP Sales and Planning: Jeff Nielson, age 41
CIO: Jeff Tietz
Director, Corporate Marketing Communications: Maureen Moore
Marketing Manager: John Fellowes
President, Global Sales: Robert (Bob) Compagno
President, Fellowes Europe: Andrea Davis

LOCATIONS

HQ: Fellowes, Inc.
1789 Norwood Ave., Itasca, IL 60143
Phone: 630-893-1600   **Fax:** 630-893-1683
Web: www.fellowes.com

PRODUCTS/OPERATIONS

Selected Products

Business machines
Binding machines and supplies
Laminating machines and supplies
Paper shredders and supplies
Desktop and office essentials
Cleaning supplies
Copy holders
Dust covers
Headsets
Keyboard managers
Mice, keyboards, and trackballs
Monitor and CPU accessories
Monitor/LCD enhancers
Printer stands
Surge protection
Tool kits
Wrist rests
Media labeling and storage
CD storage
CD wallets
CD/DVD labeling
DVD storage
Multimedia storage
Video storage
Mobile accessories
Camera cases
Cellular accessories
Laptop accessories
PDA accessories
Tablet PC accessories

COMPETITORS

ACCO Brands
Cummins-American
Escalade
Esselte
Lane Industries
Newell Rubbermaid
Smead

FHC Health Systems

FHC Health Systems makes life just a little bit easier, providing behavioral health care services to millions of people through its subsidiary companies. Its ValueOptions subsidiary offers managed behavioral care for companies, health plans, and state agencies, including employee assistance plans and mental health and substance abuse services. Rx Innovations provides institutional pharmacy services for long-term care facilities and other treatment centers. Its FirstLab subsidiary offers drug testing and employment screening. FHC sold its Alternative Behavioral Services subsidiary, which offered residential psychiatric care and case management services, to Psychiatric Solutions for about $200 million.

Other businesses include the Corporation for Standards and Outcomes, which focuses on performance management for public agency programs, and StayStat, which offers Web-based practice management tools.

The company was founded by chairman and CEO Ronald I. Dozoretz.

EXECUTIVES

Chairman and CEO; Chairman and CEO, FirstLab: Ronald I. Dozoretz
EVP Administration and Operations; CEO, Alternative Behavioral Services: Edward C. Irby Jr.
SVP and Chief Legal Officer: Adam Easterday
SVP Human Resources: Carol Dalton Cash
President and CEO, StayStat: Michael A. Taylor
President, FirstLab: Dennis J. Bennett
CEO, ValueOptions: Barbara B. Hill, age 55
COO, ValueOptions: Michele D. Alfano
EVP and CTO; CIO, ValueOptions: Bob Esposito
VP, Marketing and Communications, ValueOptions: Thomas (Tom) Warburton
Chief Administrative Officer, ValueOptions: Tom Brown

LOCATIONS

HQ: FHC Health Systems, Inc.
240 Corporate Blvd., Norfolk, VA 23502
Phone: 757-459-5100   **Fax:** 757-459-5219
Web: www.fhchealthsystems.com

PRODUCTS/OPERATIONS

Selected Subsidiaries

Corporation for Standards and Outcomes (CS&O, outcome and accountability software)
FirstLab (drug testing and employment screening services)
Rx Innovations (institutional pharmacy services)
StayStat (physician practice software and services)
ValueOptions (managed behavioral care)

COMPETITORS

Comprehensive Care
Horizon Health
Magellan Health
Mental Health Network
Premier Behavioral Solutions

HISTORICAL FINANCIALS

Company Type: Private

Income Statement   FYE: December 31

	REVENUE ($ mil.)	NET INCOME ($ mil.)	NET PROFIT MARGIN	EMPLOYEES
12/07	1,300	—	—	4,500
12/06	1,400	—	—	4,549
12/05	1,600	—	—	8,100
12/04	1,500	—	—	8,500
12/03	1,300	—	—	8,198
Annual Growth	0.0%	—	—	(13.9%)

Revenue History

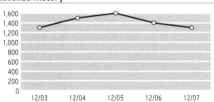

1,600				
1,400				
1,200				
1,000				
800				
600				
400				
200				
0	12/03	12/04	12/05	12/06	12/07

First Data Corporation

Paper, plastic, or Internet — First Data moves the money. The company covers virtually all the bases when it comes to transaction processing and funds transfer. Primary segments include commercial services and financial services, (merchant and debit network processing, check verification, prepaid cards, statement and card processing), and First Data International. Through its integrated payment segment, the company also provides official checks and money orders, remote clearing, and similar services. Subsidiary TeleCheck provides paper check processing services, although the use of paper checks has been dropping steadily.

Investment firm KKR bought First Data in 2007. The deal valued the company at some $29 billion. As part of the acquisition, First Data announced plans to consolidate operations and close about a dozen offices. Following the acquisition by KKR, First Data merged its Commercial Services and Financial Institutions segments.

The company continued its acquisitive ways that year, with deals including Brazilian payment processor Check Forte and Wells Fargo's Instant Cash business, which provides debit card and ATM processing services to community financial institutions in some 20 states.

First Data is also party to several joint ventures and link-ups. In 2008 it formed an alliance with Allied Irish Bank for AIB Merchant Services, expanding its card processing operations in Ireland. First Data also owns 49% of payments processor Chase Paymentech Solutions (JPMorgan Chase owns the rest). The two firms, however, have agreed to end the joint venture by the end of the 2008 and will operate separate transaction processing businesses.

That year the company announced plans to buy prepaid gift card provider Interactive Communications in a deal that could total some $1 billion. The move will put First Data ahead in the lucrative prepaid market. InComm has deals with retailers including Starbucks and Blockbuster, among others.

Also in 2008, First Data strengthened its European business with the acquisition of a 50% stake in the inter-bank processing business of multi-bank entity Trionis (formerly European Savings Banks Financial Services, or EUFISERV). The Belgium-based operation's products are marketed through First Data's European division and through Trionis as a whole.

EXECUTIVES

Chairman and CEO: Michael D. Capellas, age 54
SEVP; President, First Data USA: Edward A. (Ed) Labry III, age 44, $750,000 pay (prior to title change)
EVP and CFO: Philip M. Wall, age 50
EVP Marketing and Communications: Grace Chen Trent, age 38
EVP and Chief Strategy Officer: Thomas R. Bell Jr., age 47
EVP; President, International Operations: David Yates, age 45
EVP, General Counsel, and Secretary: David R. (Dave) Money, age 52
EVP Human Resources: Peter W. Boucher, age 53
SVP Investor Relations: Silvio Tavares
SVP Processing and Product Sales, First Data Resources: Kyle Thomas
SVP Sales: O. B. Rawls IV
SVP and Chief Accounting Officer: Gregg Sonnen, age 49

Director, Corporate Communications: Nancy Etheredge
CTO: Robert P. (Bob) DeRodes, age 58
President, First Data Debit Services: Todd B. Strubbe, age 42
President, Asia Pacific: Nigel Lee
President, First Data International, Latin America and Canada: Peter Harrington
President, Merchant Services: Brian Mooney
Auditors: Ernst & Young LLP

LOCATIONS

HQ: First Data Corporation
6200 S. Quebec St., Greenwood Village, CO 80111
Phone: 303-488-8000   **Fax:** 303-967-7000
Web: www.firstdatacorp.com

2007 Sales

	% of total
US	80
Other countries	20
Total	**100**

PRODUCTS/OPERATIONS

2007 Sales

	$ mil.	% of total
Transaction & processing fees		
Merchant services	2,871.9	35
Check services	403.7	5
Card services	1,874.1	23
Other	369.5	5
Investment income, net	(75.1)	—
Product sales & other	839.4	10
Reimbursable debit network fees & other	1,767.9	22
Total	**8,051.4**	**100**

2007 Sales By Segment

	% of total
First Data Commercial Services	51
First Data Financial Institution Services	23
First Data International	19
Integrated Payment Systems	2
Corporate & Other	5
Total	**100**

COMPETITORS

Atos Origin
Cardtronics
Deluxe Corporation
Discover
ECHO, Inc.
Elavon
Fidelity National Information Services
Fiserv
Global Payments
Litle & Co.
MasterCard
Total System Services
US Postal Service
Visa Inc

HISTORICAL FINANCIALS

Company Type: Private

Income Statement   FYE: December 31

	REVENUE ($ mil.)	NET INCOME ($ mil.)	NET PROFIT MARGIN	EMPLOYEES
12/07	8,051	159	2.0%	27,000
12/06	7,076	1,513	21.4%	29,000
12/05	10,568	1,717	16.3%	33,000
12/04	10,013	1,875	18.7%	32,000
12/03	8,400	1,409	16.8%	29,000
Annual Growth	(1.1%)	(42.0%)	—	(1.8%)

2007 Year-End Financials

Debt ratio: 330.6%
Return on equity: 1.9%
Cash ($ mil.): —

Current ratio: —
Long-term debt ($ mil.): 22,574

Net Income History

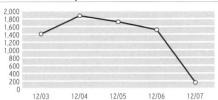

First Interstate BancSystem

This Treasure State bank wants to be your treasury. First Interstate BancSystem is the holding company for First Interstate Bank, First Western Bank and The First Western Bank Sturgis, which have around 70 branches in Montana, South Dakota, and Wyoming.

First Interstate offers individuals and businesses traditional banking services, including deposit accounts, insurance, and agricultural, consumer, commercial, and mortgage loan products. It also offers trust and wealth management services. Commercial real estate loans make up more than 25% of the bank's loan portfolio; other loans include farm and home loans.

The company also owns i_Tech, a provider of information processing services for financial institutions and ATMs. It acquired First Western Bank Sturgis and First Western Data in 2008, gaining nearly 20 branches and a presence in South Dakota.

The Scott family, which includes brothers Thomas (chairman), James (vice chairman), and Homer (board member), controls First Interstate BancSystem.

EXECUTIVES

Chairman: Thomas W. Scott, age 64
Vice Chairman: James R. Scott, age 58
President, CEO, and Director: Lyle R. Knight, age 62, $826,922 pay
EVP and CFO: Terrill R. Moore, age 55, $311,231 pay
EVP and Chief Credit Officer: Edward Garding, age 58, $212,231 pay
EVP and Chief Administrative Officer: Robert A. Jones, age 57, $196,311 pay
EVP and Chief Banking Officer: Gregory A. Duncan, age 52
SVP and Branch Administration Officer: Ralph K. Cook, age 62, $162,153 pay
SVP and Chief Marketing Officer: Neil W. Klusmann
SVP and CIO: Kevin Guenthner
Auditors: McGladrey & Pullen, LLP

LOCATIONS

HQ: First Interstate BancSystem, Inc.
401 N. 31st St., Billings, MT 59116
Phone: 406-255-5390   **Fax:** 406-255-5160
Web: www.firstinterstatebank.com

PRODUCTS/OPERATIONS

2007 Sales

	$ mil.	% of total
Interest		
Loans, including fees	272.5	65
Securities	47.4	11
Other	5.7	1
Noninterest		
Service charges, commissions & fees	24.2	6
Technology services	19.1	5
Service charges on deposit accounts	17.8	4
Wealth management	11.7	3
Loan origination & sales	11.2	3
Other	8.4	2
Total	**418.0**	**100**

COMPETITORS

Glacier Bancorp
U.S. Bancorp

HISTORICAL FINANCIALS

Company Type: Private

Income Statement				FYE: December 31
	ASSETS ($ mil.)	NET INCOME ($ mil.)	INCOME AS % OF ASSETS	EMPLOYEES
12/07	5,217	69	1.3%	1,858
12/06	4,974	76	1.5%	1,608
12/05	4,562	55	1.2%	1,576
12/04	4,217	45	1.1%	1,574
12/03	3,880	41	1.1%	1,617
Annual Growth	7.7%	13.9%	—	3.5%

2007 Year-End Financials

Equity as % of assets: 8.5%
Return on assets: 1.3%
Return on equity: 16.1%

Long-term debt ($ mil.): 5
Sales ($ mil.): 418

Net Income History

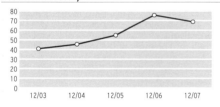

Flying J Inc.

Flying J puts out a welcome mat for truckers in North America. From its beginnings in 1968 with four locations, the company has become a leading distributor of diesel fuel and truck-stop operator in the US — with 220-plus amenity-loaded Flying J Travel Plazas and fuel stops in some 40 US states and Canada. Flying J goes beyond the usual truck-stop fare (food, fuel, showers) by offering extra services, including banking, bulk-fuel programs, communications (wireless Internet connections), fuel cost analysis, insurance, and truck fleet sales. The company also owns Longhorn Pipeline Holdings, the operator of a 700-mile-long pipeline across Texas. Founder and chairman Jay Call died in a plane crash in 2003.

Flying J plans to add another 30 truck stops to its North American network in the coming years.

Longhorn Pipeline Holdings (LPH), which Flying J acquired in August 2006, is undergoing an expansion of its pumping capacity from 72,000 barrels per day to about 125,000 barrels per day. The upgrade is expected to be completed by early 2009. (The capacity increase is the next increment to reach the ultimate capacity of 225,000 bpd.) LPH also owns a terminal that has more than 1 million barrels of storage.

Flying J, together with oil-and-gas company Shell Canada, opened its first co-branded travel plaza in Edmonton in June 2005. Currently the company operates about a half a dozen co-branded travel plazas in five Canadian provinces and plans to continue to grow in Canada. Shell Canada has been the official fuel supplier to Flying J in Canada since 1998.

The company's Big West Oil subsidiary operates a refinery in Bakersfield, California, which it purchased from Shell Oil in 2005. Flying J plans to double the plant's gasoline output by late 2008 from its current production capacity of 68,000 barrels per day. Big West also operates a smaller refinery in Utah.

EXECUTIVES

President and CEO: J. Phillip (Phil) Adams
EVP, Big West Oil (Refining): Fred L. Greener, age 52
SVP, Supply and Distribution and Petroleum Marketing: Richard D. Peterson
SVP Highway Hospitality: Jim Baker
CFO and Treasurer: Robert L. Inkley, age 44
VP, General Counsel and Secretary: James Dester
VP Transportation and Communication Services; President, Longhorn Pipeline Operations: Jeff Foote
VP, Real Estate: Ronald R. (Ron) Parker
VP, Supply/Refining: Daniel Bohman
CIO: Bron McCall
Director, Human Resources: Jerry Beckman
Director Marketing: Virginia Parker
Director Supply and Distribution: John Hillam
Director Wholesale Petroleum Marketing: Rocky Edelman
President and COO, Flying J Oil & Gas Inc.: John R. Scales
President and CEO, Transportation Alliance Bank: JJ Singh
President, Flying J Enterprise Solutions: Michael Wadsworth

LOCATIONS

HQ: Flying J Inc.
1104 Country Hills Dr., Ogden, UT 84403
Phone: 801-624-1000   **Fax:** 801-624-1587
Web: www.flyingj.com

2008 Locations

	No.
US	167
Canada	53
Total	**220**

PRODUCTS/OPERATIONS

Selected Products and Services

Advertising services
Banking and ATMs
Bulk-fuel programs
Calling cards
Credit cards
Fleet financing
Food
Freight matching
Fuel
Insurance
Load and equipment postings
Lube centers
Motels
Restaurants
Showers and laundry facilities
Truck washes

HISTORICAL FINANCIALS

Company Type: Private

Income Statement

FYE: January 31

	REVENUE ($ mil.)	NET INCOME ($ mil.)	NET PROFIT MARGIN	EMPLOYEES
1/08	16,200	—	—	16,000
1/07	11,350	—	—	16,300
1/06	9,450	—	—	14,600
1/05	5,910	—	—	13,000
1/04	5,586	—	—	12,000
Annual Growth	30.5%	—	—	7.5%

Revenue History

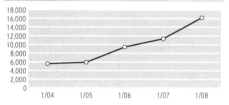

FMR LLC

FMR is *semper fidelis* (ever faithful) to its core business. The financial services conglomerate, better known as Fidelity Investments, is one of the world's largest mutual fund firms. Serving more than 23 million individual and institutional clients, Fidelity manages more than 300 funds and has more than $1.5 trillion of assets under management. It also operates a leading online discount brokerage and has more than 100 investor centers in the US and Canada, as well as locations in Europe and Asia. The founding Johnson family controls FMR; Abigail Johnson, CEO Ned Johnson's daughter and perhaps his successor (not to mention one of the richest women in America), is the company's largest single shareholder.

Fidelity's nonfund offerings include life insurance, trust services, securities clearing, and retirement services. It is one of the largest administrators of 401(k) plans, and the firm continues to grow this segment, which includes other services related to benefits outsourcing. The company had been reluctant to give direct investment advice to 401(k) plan participants, but under pressure from customers struck an agreement with Financial Engines Inc., which now provides those services to Fidelity's clients.

FMR has private equity investments in telecommunications firm COLT Telecom Group and transportation company BostonCoach, among others. Like many institutional investors, Fidelity uses its clout to sway the boards of com-

panies in which it has significant holdings. In 2007 the company's Fidelity Equity Partners arm launched a $500 million buyout fund that targets middle-market firms involved in media, software, health care, and service industries in North America and Europe.

FMR also holds about a 15% stake in venerable British investment bank Lazard, which it acquired in 2005.

HISTORY

Boston money management firm Anderson & Cromwell formed Fidelity Fund in 1930. Edward Johnson became president of the fund in 1943, when it had $3 million invested in Treasury bills. Johnson diversified into stocks, and by 1945 the fund had grown to $10 million. In 1946 he established Fidelity Management and Research to act as its investment adviser.

In the early 1950s Johnson hired Gerry Tsai, a young immigrant from Shanghai, to analyze stocks. Placed in charge of Fidelity Capital Fund in 1957, Tsai's brash, go-go investment strategy in such speculative stocks as Xerox and Polaroid paid off; by the time he left to form his own fund in 1965, he was managing more than $1 billion.

The Magellan Fund started in 1962. The company entered the corporate pension plans market (FMR Investment Management) in 1964, and retirement plans for self-employed individuals (Fidelity Keogh Plan) in 1967. It began serving investors outside the US (Fidelity International) in 1968.

Holding company FMR was formed in 1972, the same year Johnson gave control of Fidelity to his son Ned, who vertically integrated FMR by selling directly to customers rather than through brokers. In 1973 he formed Fidelity Daily Income Trust, the first money market fund to offer check writing.

Peter Lynch was hired as manager of the Magellan Fund in 1977. During his 13-year tenure, Magellan grew from $20 million to $12 billion in assets and outperformed all other mutual funds. Fidelity started Fidelity Brokerage Services in 1978, becoming the first mutual fund company to offer discount brokerage.

In 1980 the company launched a nationwide branch network and in 1986 entered the credit card business. The Wall Street crash of 1987 forced its Magellan Fund to liquidate almost $1 billion in stock in a single day. That year FMR moved into insurance by offering variable life, single premium, and deferred annuity policies. In 1989 the company introduced the low-expense Spartan Fund, targeted toward large, less-active investors.

Magellan's performance faded in the early 1990s, dropping from #1 performer to #3. Most of Fidelity's best performers were from its 36 select funds, which focus on narrow industry segments. FMR founded London-based COLT Telecom in 1993. In 1994 Johnson gave his daughter and heir apparent, Abigail, a 25% stake in FMR.

Jeffrey Vinik resigned as manager of Magellan in 1996, one of more than a dozen fund managers to leave the firm that year and the next. Robert Stansky took the helm of the $56 billion fund, which FMR decided to close to new investors in 1997. Fidelity had a first that year when it went with an outside fund manager, hiring Bankers Trust (now part of Deutsche Bank) to manage its index funds.

FMR did some housecleaning in the late 1990s. It sold its Wentworth art galleries (1997)

and *Worth* magazine (1998). Despite continued management turnover, it entered Japan and expanded its presence in Canada.

In 1999 the firm teamed with Internet portal Lycos (now part of Terra Networks) to develop its online brokerage. FMR opened savings and loan Fidelity Personal Trust Co. in 2000.

In 2006 the company announced that it would pay $42 million into its mutual funds after an internal investigation showed that some of its traders had allegedly guided business to brokers who had given the traders gifts. The SEC later slapped FMR with an $8 million fine.

EXECUTIVES

Chairman and CEO: Edward C. (Ned) Johnson III
President: Rodger A. Lawson, age 61
EVP and CFO: Clare S. Richer
EVP and Director, Corporate Affairs: Thomas E. Eidson
EVP, Fidelity Human Resources: D. Ellen Wilson
President, Fidelity Employer Services Company: Abigail P. (Abby) Johnson, age 46
President, Fidelity Registered Investment Advisor Group: John W. Callahan
President, Fidelity Human Resources Services Company: Jim MacDonald
President, Fidelity Real Estate: Sarah K. Abrams
President, Pembroke Real Estate: Stephen M. Bell
President, Registered Investment Advisor Group: William C. (Bill) Carey
President, Investment Services, Fidelity Management & Research: Dwight D. Churchill
President, Devonshire Investors: Timothy T. Hilton, age 54
President, Fidelity Strategic Initiatives: Robert A. Lawrence
President, National Financial: Norman R. Malo
President, Fidelity Personal Investments: Steven P. (Steve) Akin
General Counsel: Marc Gary
Interim Chief Administrative Officer: John Remondi
Auditors: PricewaterhouseCoopers LLP

LOCATIONS

HQ: FMR LLC
82 Devonshire St., Boston, MA 02109
Phone: 617-563-7000   **Fax:** 617-476-6150
Web: www.fidelity.com

HISTORICAL FINANCIALS

Company Type: Private

Income Statement
FYE: December 31

	REVENUE ($ mil.)	NET INCOME ($ mil.)	NET PROFIT MARGIN	EMPLOYEES
12/07	14,900	—	—	46,400
12/06	12,870	—	—	41,900
Annual Growth	15.8%	—	—	10.7%

Revenue History

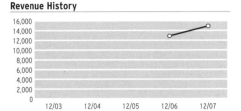

Foley & Lardner

Though most famous for its cheese, Wisconsin has another thing going for it: lawyers. Foley & Lardner, the largest and oldest law firm in Wisconsin, has nearly 1,000 lawyers and has expanded far beyond its Milwaukee base with offices in more than 15 other US cities (including four in Florida and six in California). In addition, Foley & Lardner has international offices in Brussels, Shanghai, and Tokyo. The firm, founded in 1842, has one of the nation's leading health law practices and an increased focus on its intellectual property practice; other areas of expertise include business law, litigation, regulatory issues, and tax planning.

In mid-2008, Foley & Lardner opened an office in Shanghai. (It had already established a presence in China in the past, having conducted legal work for the Chinese government.) The firm hopes its specialized intellectual property practice will help separate itself from other law firms with an international presence.

EXECUTIVES

Chairman and CEO: Ralf-Reinhard (Ralf) Böer
Managing Partner: Stanley S. (Stan) Jaspan
Executive Director and COO: Darrell R. Ohlhauser
CFO: Tom L. Budde
CIO: Douglas D. (Doug) Caddell
Chief Marketing Officer: Kyle J. Heath
Chief Human Resources Officer: Marilyn L. Lagerman
Operating Officer, Business Law Department:
 Gregory P. (Greg) Marren
Operating Officer, Health Law Department and Business Development Manager: James E. Greeley
Operating Officer, Intellectual Property Department:
 Marion E. Baker
Operating Officer, Litigation Department:
 Armand C. Go
COO, Regulatory Department: Robert J. (Bob) Parker
Senior Public Relations Manager: Jocelyn Brumbaugh
Director Administration and Operations:
 Joseph A. Shapiro

LOCATIONS

HQ: Foley & Lardner LLP
 777 E. Wisconsin Ave., Milwaukee, WI 53202
Phone: 414-271-2400   **Fax:** 414-297-4900
Web: www.foley.com

Office Locations

Boston
Brussels
Chicago
Detroit
Jacksonville, FL
Los Angeles
Madison, WI
Milwaukee
New York
Orlando, FL
Palo Alto, CA
Sacramento, CA
San Diego
San Francisco
Shanghai
Silicon Valley, CA
Tallahassee, FL
Tampa
Tokyo
Washington, DC

PRODUCTS/OPERATIONS

Selected Practice Areas

Antitrust
Appellate
Bankruptcy and Business Reorganizations
Construction
Consumer Financial Services Litigation
Corporate Compliance and Enforcement
Distribution and Franchise
Energy Regulation
Family Law
General Commercial Litigation
Immigration, Nationality, and Consular Law Services
Insurance and Reinsurance Litigation
Labor and Employment
Media Law
Securities Enforcement and Litigation
White Collar Defense

COMPETITORS

Baker & McKenzie	Quarles & Brady
Holland & Knight	Shearman & Sterling
Jones Day	Skadden, Arps
McDermott Will & Emery	

HISTORICAL FINANCIALS

Company Type: Partnership

Income Statement
FYE: January 31

	REVENUE ($ mil.)	NET INCOME ($ mil.)	NET PROFIT MARGIN	EMPLOYEES
1/08	720	—	—	2,621
1/07	668	—	—	2,527
1/06	611	—	—	2,405
1/05	543	—	—	2,305
1/04	523	—	—	—
Annual Growth	8.3%	—	—	4.4%

Revenue History

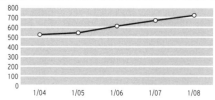

Follett Corporation

Not all kids like to read, but (fortunately for Follett) by the time they reach college, they don't have a choice. Follett is the #1 operator of US college bookstores with more than 750 campus bookshops across the nation, as well as Canada. The company's business groups, which reach about 60 countries, also provide books and audiovisual materials to grade school and public libraries, library automation and management software, textbook reconditioning, and other services. Follett acquired its smaller online rival Varsity Group in 2008, complementing its own efollett.com Web site that sells new and used college textbooks. The Follett family has owned and managed the company for four generations.

Follett paid about $3.8 million to acquire publicly held Varsity Group in a deal that closed in April 2008. Varsity Group, based in Washington, DC, is an online college retailer and provider of marketing services to colleges. Follett is counting on the virtual bookstore's e-commerce expertise to help it grow its online business.

In addition to books, Follett's campus stores sell items such as clothing, school supplies, and software. The company has capitalized on the growing trend of universities farming out operations to independent operators.

HISTORY

Follett began in 1873 as a small bookstore opened by the Rev. Charles Barnes in his Wheaton, Illinois, home. By 1893 a recession had rocked the business, and Barnes sought investment from his wife's family, for which he gave up controlling interest. Sales topped $237,000 in 1899.

Initially hired by Barnes in 1901 to help move the store to a new location in Chicago, 18-year-old C. W. Follett stayed on as both salesman and stock clerk. Barnes retired the following year and left the business to his son William and his father-in-law, John Wilcox, who was a major shareholder. In 1917 C. W. bought into the company when William moved to New York (he started what became one of Follett's biggest competitors, Barnes & Noble), and he renamed it J. W. Wilcox & Follett Company. Wilcox died in 1923, and C. W. bought the Wilcox family shares and shortened the name to Wilcox & Follett.

C. W.'s sons were brought into the business, and each was instrumental in shaping the company's future. Garth created Follett Library Resources, a wholesale service for libraries. Dwight started the elementary textbook publishing division. But Robert would have the most influence: He began wholesaling college textbooks, which led to the establishment of Follett College Stores and Follett Campus Resources.

Wilcox & Follett expanded throughout the Depression. During WWII it began publishing kids' books, which were in demand because of a metal toy shortage. C. W. died in 1952 and Dwight took over. Five years later the firm organized into divisions; Follett was created as the parent company. During the 1960s Follett developed the first multi-racial textbook series. Dwight built the company to $50 million in annual sales by 1977, when he retired. His son Robert succeeded him and led Follett through tremendous growth in the 1980s.

In 1983 the company sold its publishing division to Esquire Education Group; using funds from this sale, it began acquiring college book-store chains such as Campus Services. In 1989 Follett developed Tom-Tracks, a computerized textbook system for college bookstores. A year later the company acquired Brennan College Service, adding 57 stores to its chain. Robert's son-in-law Richard Traut, named chairman in 1994, was the first person without the Follett name to hold that position. By 1994 Tom-Tracks had been installed in over 500 bookstores across the country. That year Follett introduced Sneak Preview Plus, a CD-ROM product designed to enhance the acquisition process in libraries.

The company acquired used-textbook reseller Western Textbook Exchange (1996), juvenile-book distributor Book Wholesalers (1997), and coursepack printer CAPCO (1998). In early 1998 Follett reorganized its corporate struc-ture by market segments, establishing three di-visions: the Elementary/High School Group, the Higher Education Group, and the Library Group. Later that year the Follett Campus Re-sources unit agreed to pay the University of Tennessee $380,000 after the school discovered that the firm had been underpaying students in a book-buyback program for several years. Adding to its bevy of campus bookstores, it signed a contract the same year to build a $5 million bookstore at the University of Texas at Arlington.

Also in 1998 CFO Kenneth Hull replaced Richard Litzsinger as CEO. Follett launched efollett.com in early 1999 to sell college text-books online. That year Hull became chairman upon Richard Traut's departure. In November 2000 Christopher Traut became CEO; Hull re-mained chairman.

In April 2001 Hull retired, and Mark Litzsinger succeeded him as chairman.

In April 2008, Follett acquired the online col-lege textbook seller Varsity Group for about $3.8 million.

EXECUTIVES

Chairman: R. Mark Litzsinger
President and CEO: Christopher D. (Chris) Traut, age 44
EVP Finance and CFO: Kathryn A. Stanton
EVP Human Resources: Richard Ellspermann
VP and Chief Information Security Officer: Joe Agnew
President, BWI: John Nelson
President, Follett Educational Distribution Group: Robert Mallo, age 48
President, Follett Educational Services: Todd Litzsinger
Prersident, Follett Technology Solutions and International Group: Chuck Follett, age 52
President, Follett Software Company: Tom Schenck
President, Higher Education Group: Thomas A. (Tom) Christopher
COO, TetraData: Martin Brutosky

LOCATIONS

HQ: Follett Corporation
2233 West St., River Grove, IL 60171
Phone: 708-583-2000   **Fax:** 708-452-9347
Web: www.follett.com

PRODUCTS/OPERATIONS

Selected Company Divisions

Elementary/High School Group
  Follett Educational Services (K-12 textbooks and workbooks)
  Follett Software Company (library automation)
Higher Education Group
Library Group
  Book Wholesalers, Inc. (BWI, public libraries)
  Follett Library Resources (school libraries)
  VarsityBooks.com (online textbooks)

COMPETITORS

Amazon.com	Educational Development
Baker & Taylor	Ingram Industries
Barnes & Noble	MBS Textbook Exchange
College Bookstores	Nebraska Book
barnesandnoble.com	Time Warner
Brodart	Wal-Mart
Ecampus.com	

Foodarama Supermarkets

Foodarama Supermarkets thinks its cus-tomers deserve world-class grocery stores. A member of the Wakefern Food purchasing and distribution cooperative, the company operates about 25 ShopRite supermarkets in central New Jersey. The majority of Foodarama's stores are classified by the company as World Class, mean-ing they are larger than 50,000 sq. ft. and offer amenities such as international foods, in-store bakeries, kosher sections, snack bars, and phar-macies. Foodarama also operates two liquor stores, a garden center, a food processing facil-ity (which supplies its stores with meat and pre-pared foods), and a bakery. The founding Saker family took the company private in 2006.

Foodarama owns nearly 16% of Wakefern Food, the New Jersey-based co-op that owns the ShopRite name and provides advertising, pur-chasing, warehousing, and distribution services to more than 200 member stores.

The company continues to upgrade older stores and plans to open new ones under its larger World Class store format.

The Sakers include Foodarama chairman Joseph Saker and his son Richard, who has suc-ceeded his father as president and CEO of the company. In mid-2006 a group led by Richard Saker launched a $25 million tender offer for the shares of the company it did not already own. In July of that year Foodarama shareholders gave the Saker bid a green light, tendering 91% of the outstanding shares of the company. (In May 2006 Foodarama rejected a buyout offer from supermarket magnate Ron Burkle's Yucaipa Companies, which controls Foodarama rival Pathmark Stores.)

EXECUTIVES

President and Director: Richard J. Saker, $577,548 pay
SVP, Financial Administration, Assistant Secretary and Assistant Treasurer: Joseph C. (Joe) Troilo
SVP Real Estate and Store Development: Edward Turkot
SVP, Sales and Merchandising: Carl L. Montanaro, $192,751 pay
SVP Operations and Director: Thomas A. Saker
VP, CFO, Treasurer and Assistant Secretary: Thomas H. Flynn
Secretary: Joseph J. Saker Jr., $170,939 pay
Auditors: Amper, Politziner & Mattia, P.C.

LOCATIONS

HQ: Foodarama Supermarkets, Inc.
922 Hwy. 33, Bldg. 6, Ste. 1, Freehold, NJ 07728
Phone: 732-462-4700   **Fax:** 732-294-2322

COMPETITORS

A&P	Kings Super Markets
Acme Markets	Pathmark Stores
BJ's Wholesale Club	Stop & Shop
Costco Wholesale	Walgreen
Cumberland Farms	Wal-Mart
CVS Caremark	Wawa, Inc.
Food Circus Super Markets	Wegmans
Inserra Supermarkets	

Ford Foundation

As one of the US's largest philanthropic organ-izations, The Ford Foundation can afford to be generous. The foundation offers grants to indi-viduals and institutions around the world that work to meet its goals of strengthening demo-cratic values, reducing poverty and injustice, promoting international cooperation, and ad-vancing human achievement. The Ford Founda-tion's charitable giving has run the gamut from A (Association for Asian Studies) to Z (Zanzibar International Film Festival). The foundation has an endowment of about $12 billion. It no longer has stock in Ford Motor Company or ties to the founding Ford family.

The Ford Foundation gives to a variety of causes in one of three areas: Asset Building and Community Development (designed to help ex-pand opportunities for the poor and reduce hardship); Peace and Social Justice (to promote peace and the rule of law, human rights, and freedom); and Knowledge, Creativity, and Free-dom (aimed at strengthening education and the arts and at building identity and community).

The foundation has offices worldwide and is governed by an international board of trustees.

The Ford Foundation has offices in New York City, as well as Beijing; Cairo; Hanoi, Vietnam; Jakarta, Indonesia; Johannesburg; Lagos, Nige-ria; Mexico City; Moscow; Nairobi, Kenya; New Delhi; Rio de Janeiro; and Santiago, Chile.

HISTORY

Henry Ford and his son Edsel gave $25,000 to establish The Ford Foundation in Michigan in 1936, followed the next year by 250,000 shares of nonvoting stock in the Ford Motor Company. The foundation's activities were limited mainly to Michigan until the deaths of Edsel (1943) and Henry (1947) made the foundation the owner of 90% of the automaker's nonvoting stock (cata-pulting the endowment to $474 million, the US's largest).

In 1951, under a new mandate and president (Paul Hoffman, former head of the Marshall Plan), Ford made broad commitments to the promotion of world peace, the strengthening of democracy, and the improvement of education. Early education program grants overseen by Uni-versity of Chicago chancellor Robert Maynard Hutchins ($100 million between 1951 and 1953) helped establish major international programs (e.g., Harvard's Center for International Legal Studies) and the National Merit Scholarships.

Under McCarthyite criticism for its experi-mental education grants, the foundation in 1956 granted $550 million (after selling 22% of its Ford shares) to noncontroversial recipients such as liberal arts colleges and not-for-profit hospitals. The organization's money set up the Radio and Television Workshop (1951); public TV support became a foundation trademark.

International work, begun in Asia and the Middle East (1950) and extended to Africa (1958) and Latin America (1959), focused on education and rural development. The foundation also supported the Population Council and research in high-yield agriculture with The Rockefeller Foundation.

In the early 1960s Ford targeted innovative approaches to employment and race relations. McGeorge Bundy (former national security adviser to President John Kennedy), named president of the foundation in 1966, increased the activist trend with grants for direct voter registration; the NAACP; public-interest law centers serving consumer, environmental, and minority causes; and housing for the poor.

The early 1970s saw support for black colleges and scholarships, child care, and job training for women, but by 1974 inflation, weak stock prices, and overspending had eroded assets. Programs were cut, but continued support for social justice issues led Henry Ford II to quit the board in 1976.

Under lawyer Franklin Thomas (named president in 1979), Ford established the nation's largest community development support organization, Local Initiatives Support. Thomas, the first African-American to lead the foundation, was a catalyst in a series of meetings between white and black South Africans in the mid-1980s.

Thomas stepped down in 1996, and new president Susan Berresford, formerly EVP, consolidated the foundation's grant programs into three areas: Asset Building and Community Development; Peace and Social Justice; and Education, Media, Arts, and Culture. In the late 1990s Ford was surpassed by various other foundations and had to relinquish its 30-year title as the biggest charitable organization in the US.

In 2000 the foundation announced its largest grant ever, the 10-year, $330 million International Fellowship Program to support graduate students studying in 20 countries.

After the September 11, 2001, terrorist attacks, the foundation joined other philanthropic organizations in providing disaster relief. It made grants of $10 million in New York and more than $1 million in Washington, DC.

Berresford retired in early 2008.

EXECUTIVES

Chair: Kathryn S. Fuller, age 61
President and Trustee: Luis A. Ubiñas
EVP, Secretary, and General Counsel: Barron M. Tenny
VP and Chief Investment Officer: Linda B. Strumpf
VP, Asset Building and Community Development:
 Pablo J. Farías
VP, Communications: Marta L. Tellado
VP, Knowledge, Creativity, and Freedom:
 Alison R. Bernstein
VP Peace and Social Justice Program: Maya Harris
Deputy VP, Special Initiative on HIV/AIDS:
 Jacob A. Gayle
Deputy VP, Program Management: David B. Chiel
Treasurer, Comptroller, and Director, Financial Services: Nicholas M. Gabriel
Director, Human Resources: Bruce D. Stuckey
Assistant Secretary and Associate General Counsel:
 Nancy P. Feller
Program Officer Media and Cultural Policy:
 Jenny Toomey
Auditors: PricewaterhouseCoopers LLP

LOCATIONS

HQ: The Ford Foundation
 320 E. 43rd St., New York, NY 10017
Phone: 212-573-5000 **Fax:** 212-351-3677
Web: www.fordfound.org

PRODUCTS/OPERATIONS

Program Area Grants

Asset Building and Community Development
 Community and Resource Development
 Economic Development

Knowledge, Creativity, and Freedom
 Education, Sexuality, Religion
 Media, Arts, and Culture

Peace and Social Justice
 Governance and Civil Society
 Human Rights

HISTORICAL FINANCIALS

Company Type: Foundation

Income Statement

FYE: September 30

	REVENUE ($ mil.)	NET INCOME ($ mil.)	NET PROFIT MARGIN	EMPLOYEES
9/07	2,198	1,393	63.4%	600
9/06	1,312	623	47.5%	600
9/05	1,588	908	57.2%	550
9/04	1,319	729	55.3%	500
9/03	261	609	233.5%	450
Annual Growth	70.4%	23.0%	—	7.5%

2007 Year-End Financials

Debt ratio: — Current ratio: —
Return on equity: 11.1% Long-term debt ($ mil.): —
Cash ($ mil.): —

Net Income History

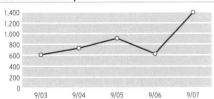

EXECUTIVES

President: David E. (Dave) Fuhrmann
VP Business Development and Industry Relations:
 Joseph Weis
VP Manufactured Products: Douglas (Doug) Wilke
VP Member Services and Milk Marketing:
 Mike Pronschinske
Director Communications and Employee Development:
 Joan Behr
Director Human Resources Corporate: Joe Chenoweth
Director Sales and Marketing, Ingredient:
 Keith Gretenhart
Director Sales and Marketing, Cheese:
 Patrick Mathiowetz
Director Planning and Business Services:
 Tim Greenway
Director Corporate Production Planning: Al Larson
Director Operations: Mark Peterson
Director Technology: Brian Cords
Auditors: PricewaterhouseCoopers LLP

LOCATIONS

HQ: Foremost Farms USA, Cooperative
 E10889A Penny Ln., Baraboo, WI 53913
Phone: 608-355-8700 **Fax:** 608-355-8699
Web: www.foremostfarms.com

Foremost Farms serves farmers in Illinois, Indiana, Iowa, Michigan, Minnesota, Ohio, and Wisconsin.

PRODUCTS/OPERATIONS

Selected Products

Butter
Buttermilk
Cheese
Cream
Eggnog
Fluid milk
Ingredients
 Feed
 Food
 Nutritional
 Pharmaceutical
 Specialty
Juice and drinks
Sour cream

COMPETITORS

AMPI	MMPA
California Dairies Inc.	National Dairy Holdings
Century Foods	Prairie Farms Dairy
Dairy Farmers of America	Quality Chekd
Dairylea	Saputo
Dean Foods	Sargento
Land O'Lakes	Schreiber Foods
Leprino Foods	

HISTORICAL FINANCIALS

Company Type: Cooperative

Income Statement

FYE: December 31

	REVENUE ($ mil.)	NET INCOME ($ mil.)	NET PROFIT MARGIN	EMPLOYEES
12/07	1,600	—	—	1,400
12/06	1,246	—	—	1,523
12/05	1,419	—	—	1,540
Annual Growth	6.2%	—	—	(4.7%)

Revenue History

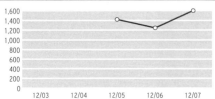

Foremost Farms

No jokes about "herd mentality," please. Foremost Farms USA (owned by some 3,000 dairy farmers in Wisconsin and six other Midwestern states) is a major dairy cooperative. From 20 plants, the co-op churns some 5 billion pounds of milk per year into solid and fluid dairy products for industrial, retail, and foodservice customers. Its biggest sector is cheese, with a 2006 production of almost 500 million pounds. Foremost's retail brands include Golden Guernsey Dairy and Morning Glory. The co-op also produces private-label products for retailers.

To reduce dependence on commodity products, Foremost also manufactures value-added items, such as flavored milk drinks, and pharmaceutical-grade lactose and whey-based ingredients.

Forever 21

You don't have to be 21 or older to shop at Forever 21's stores — you just need your wallet. The retailer operates 400-plus mainly mall-based stores in the US and Canada under the Forever 21, Forever XXI, and For Love 21 banners. The retailer, which helped pioneer fast fashion, offers cheap and chic apparel and accessories for women and junior girls. Most of its trendy apparel is private label and made in Southern California. Forever XXI stores are larger than classic Forever 21 shops and offer men's and women's fashions, as well as lingerie, footwear, cosmetic items, and other accessories. CEO Don Chang and his wife founded the company as Fashion 21 in 1984.

The fast-growing fast-fashion chain plans to open more than 70 stores and expand about 20 others over the next few years. Also the company has made a bid to acquire the remaining 150 or so stores of bankrupt retailer Mervyn's. Forever 21 is attracted to Mervyn's prime real estate. (Indeed, the company bid for the same sites back in 2004 when Mervyn's former parent Target Corp. was selling them, but lost at auction.)

Internationally, Forever 21 also has two stores in the United Arab Emirates and one in Singapore. The firm is exploring expansion opportunities in South Korea, Russia, and the UK.

The size of the retailer's stores has increased from about 15,000 sq. ft. (on average) to include many 40,000-sq.-ft. boutiques. Going forward the company plans to construct even larger stores, eventually spanning 90,000 sq. ft. and anchoring malls in select locations. The increase in scale matches Forever 21's aspiration to evolve from a purveyor of teen fashion to a youth-lifestyle retail concept.

Forever 21 has also grown by launching new concepts and acquiring other chains. The company bought 44 Rampage stores, valued at $14 million, from Charlotte Russe in late 2006. Also in 2006 Forever 21 launched Twenty One, a line of denim-based men's wear. Previously, in March 2005 the chain acquired the assets of bankrupt teen retailer Gadzooks for about $33 million. The purchase of 150 Gadzooks stores in 36 states greatly expanded Forever 21's retail presence. Also in 2005 it launched an accessories-only format, called For Love 21, which has since grown to about a dozen locations.

In mid-2003 the company extended its reach in the junior market by acquiring Reference Clothing Co. Reference had a similar product offering of inexpensive trendy clothes; all of its stores were converted into Forever 21 stores.

The speed at which Forever 21 goes to market with new merchandise has led to potential copyright trouble for the company. Designers, manufacturers, and competitors, including Diane von Furstenberg and rival chain bebe stores, have filed a slew of lawsuits that allege the fast-fashion chain has copied prints, logos and specific designs that belong to them.

Under fire from the animal rights activist group People for the Ethical Treatment of Animals (PETA), Forever 21 has banned clothing with fur from its shelves.

EXECUTIVES

CEO: Do Won (Don) Chang, age 48
SVP and CFO: Lawrence (Larry) Meyer
Head Buyer: Jin Sook Chang
Human Resources Manager: Kate Chun

LOCATIONS

HQ: Forever 21, Inc.
2001 S. Alameda St., Los Angeles, CA 90058
Phone: 213-741-5100   **Fax:** 213-741-5161
Web: www.forever21.com

COMPETITORS

Abercrombie & Fitch	H&M
American Eagle Outfitters	Old Navy
bebe stores	Target
Charlotte Russe Holding	Urban Outfitters
Charming Shoppes	Wal-Mart
Claire's Stores	Wet Seal
dELiA*s	Zara
The Gap	

HISTORICAL FINANCIALS

Company Type: Private

Income Statement

FYE: December 31

	REVENUE ($ mil.)	NET INCOME ($ mil.)	NET PROFIT MARGIN	EMPLOYEES
12/07	1,300	—	—	—
12/06	1,050	—	—	—
Annual Growth	23.8%	—	—	—

Revenue History

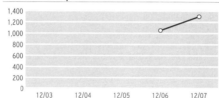

Forever Living Products

Forever Living Products International might not lead you to immortality, but its aloe-vera-based health care products are intended to improve your well-being. The firm sells aloe vera drinks, as well as aloe-vera-based aromatherapy products, cosmetics, dietary and nutritional supplements, lotion, soap, and tooth gel products. Owner Rex Maughan also owns aloe vera plantations in the Dominican Republic, Mexico, and Texas; Aloe Vera of America, a processing plant; and Forever Resorts' US resorts and marinas, including Dallas-area Southfork Ranch (of *Dallas* TV show fame). Forever Living Products, founded in 1978, sells its goods through a global network of some 8.8 million independent distributors.

Subsidiary Forever Resorts has about 50 locations (lodges and marinas) in the US, Europe, and Africa. It also offers luxury houseboat rentals at about a dozen marinas in the southwestern US.

EXECUTIVES

Chairman and CEO: Rex Gene Maughan
Vice Chairman and CFO: Rjay Lloyd
EVP: Navaz Ghaswala
President: Gregg Maughan
SVP Sales, North America: Harold Greene
SVP Human Resources and Risk Management:
Glen B. Banks

VP Finance: Dave Hall
VP Information Technology: Steve Itami
VP European Operations: Aidan O'Hare
VP Latin America: Garin Breinholt

LOCATIONS

HQ: Forever Living Products International, Inc.
7501 E. McCormick Pkwy., Scottsdale, AZ 85258
Phone: 480-998-8888   **Fax:** 800-455-3503
Web: www.foreverliving.com

PRODUCTS/OPERATIONS

Selected Products

Aloe drinks
Bee products
Nutrition
Personal care
Skin care
Sonya Colour collection
Weight loss

COMPETITORS

Alticor
Amway
Avon
Body Shop
Burt's Bees
GNC
Jafra
Mannatech
Nature's Sunshine
NBTY
Neways
Shaklee
Sunrider
Whole Foods

Forsythe Technology

Forsythe Technology believes it has the foresight to provide valuable business and information technology consulting services. The company helps businesses and government agencies manage their IT infrastructure, providing services ranging from strategy to implementation and support. It also provides leasing and other financial services. Serving clients from offices throughout the US and western Canada, the company works with vendors such as Cisco Systems, Hewlett-Packard, and Sun Microsystems. Forsythe Technology customers have included Aflac, Outback Steakhouse, and TriZetto.

Richard Forsythe founded the employee-owned company in 1971 as Forsythe McArthur Associates, starting off with $200 and a telephone on a dining room table. Today it is one of the largest employee-owned companies in the US.

In 2004 the company acquired security services firm National Business Group, which expanded Forsythe's offerings in the area of IT risk management. The company expanded into the Canadian market with its purchase of Information Security Technology in 2007. Forsythe acquired storage systems integrator More Group in 2008.

EXECUTIVES

Chairman: Richard A. (Rick) Forsythe
President, CEO and Director; President and Director, Forsythe Solutions: William P. (Bill) Brennan, age 52
EVP, CFO, and Director; President, Forsythe McArthur: Albert L. (Al) Weiss
SVP, General Counsel, Secretary, and Director: R. Thomas (Tom) Hoffman
SVP and Sales Manager, Financial Services: John D. Carcone
SVP, Systems Solutions and Technology Products: Michael J. (Mike) Qualley
SVP and Chief Accounting Officer: Thomas R. (Tom) Ehmann, age 55
SVP Marketing and Sales Operations: James G. (Jim) Bindon
SVP Human Resources: Julie A. Fusco Nagle
SVP Emerging Technologies and Director: Michael P. Conley, age 39
SVP Sales Administration: Michelle M. Coffield, age 41
Corporate Communications Manager: Kyra Auslander

LOCATIONS

HQ: Forsythe Technology, Inc.
 7770 Frontage Rd., Skokie, IL 60077
Phone: 847-213-7000   **Fax:** 847-213-7922
Web: www.forsythe.com

COMPETITORS

Affiliated Computer Services
ATEL Capital
Black Box
Blackwell Consulting
CDW
Computer Sciences Corp.
Dell
EDS
Electro Rent
ePlus
FAEF
GATX
GCI Systems
HP Technology Solutions Group
IBM Global Services
ICON Capital
Keane
Meridian Group
ORIX
Perot Systems
Sayers
Unisys

HISTORICAL FINANCIALS

Company Type: Private

Income Statement
FYE: December 31

	REVENUE ($ mil.)	NET INCOME ($ mil.)	NET PROFIT MARGIN	EMPLOYEES
12/07	629	—	—	808
12/06	604	—	—	718
12/05	518	—	—	619
12/04	449	—	—	639
12/03	444	—	—	549
Annual Growth	9.1%	—	—	10.1%

Revenue History

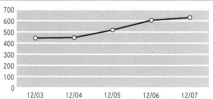

Foster Poultry Farms

It doesn't matter if Henny Penny is having hot flashes, Foster Poultry Farms never uses hormones. The company's vertically integrated operations see chickens and turkeys from the incubator to grocers' meat cases, delis, and freezers (under the Foster Farms brand). In addition to hatching, raising, slaughtering, and processing chickens and turkeys for the retail grocery and foodservice industries, the company grinds its own feeds. Already #1 in its home state, Foster Poultry Farms grew larger with the 2001 purchase of the chicken operations of a local rival, Zacky Farms.

Max and Verda Foster founded the company in 1939; it is still owned and operated by the Foster family, which also owns and operates sister company Foster Dairy Farms.

EXECUTIVES

CEO: Ron Foster
President, Poultry: Don Jackson
SVP and CFO: John Landis
SVP and General Counsel: Randy Boyce
SVP and CIO: Dave Weinmeister
SVP Human Resources: Tim Walsh
SVP Retail Sales: Bob Kellert
SVP Marketing: Bob Wangerien
VP Marketing: Greta Janz
VP Supply Chain: Dan Huber
VP Processing, Fresh Poultry: Richie King
VP Sales and Marketing, Foodservice: Brad Moore
Treasurer: Regina King

LOCATIONS

HQ: Foster Poultry Farms
 1000 Davis St., Livingston, CA 95334
Phone: 209-357-1121   **Fax:** 209-394-6342
Web: www.fosterfarms.com

PRODUCTS/OPERATIONS

Selected Products

Cooked frozen chicken
Cooked frozen turkey
Corn dogs
Fresh chicken
Fresh turkey
Hot dogs
Individually frozen chicken
Lunchmeats
Savory servings

COMPETITORS

Bell & Evans
Butterball
Cagle's
Cooper Farms
Eberly Poultry
Fair Oaks Farms
Hormel
Jennie-O
Murphy-Brown
New Market Poultry
Northern Pride
Perdue Incorporated
Pilgrim's Pride
Plainville Farms
Raeford Farms
Randall Foods
Sanderson Farms
Shelton's
Tyson Foods
Wayne Farms LLC
West Liberty Foods

HISTORICAL FINANCIALS

Company Type: Private

Income Statement
FYE: December 31

	ESTIMATED REVENUE ($ mil.)	NET INCOME ($ mil.)	NET PROFIT MARGIN	EMPLOYEES
12/07	1,890	—	—	10,000
12/06	1,800	—	—	10,500
12/05	1,730	—	—	10,000
12/04	1,660	—	—	10,000
12/03	1,520	—	—	11,000
Annual Growth	5.6%	—	—	(2.4%)

Revenue History

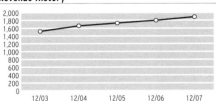

Frank Consolidated Enterprises

Frank Consolidated Enterprises has an old lease on life. A holding company for its Wheels subsidiary, the firm is a pioneer of the auto leasing concept, and provides fleet management services — administrative, management, and financing services to help clients maintain vehicle fleets. Overall, the company manages more than 250,000 vehicles. It operates in the US as Wheels and in other countries through Fleet Synergy International, an alliance of international fleet management and leasing companies.

Wheels was founded in 1939 by a Chicago auto dealer named Zollie Frank. The Frank family owns and runs the company.

EXECUTIVES

Chairman: Elaine S. Frank
President and CEO: James S. (Jim) Frank
SVP Finance and Operations, CFO, and Director, Wheels: Mary Ann O'Dwyer, age 52
SVP Sales, Marketing, and Account Management, Wheels: Scott Pattullo
VP Client Relations, Wheels: Norman Din
VP Customer Service Operations, Wheels: Christine Steinberg
VP Finance, Wheels: Shlomo Y. Crandus
VP Human Resources, Wheels: Joan Richards
VP International Sales, Wheels: Peter Egan
VP IT and CIO: Steve Loos
VP Sales, Wheels: Prentiss Harvey
CEO, Fleet Logistics International: Peter Soliman

LOCATIONS

HQ: Frank Consolidated Enterprises, Inc.
 666 Garland Place, Des Plaines, IL 60016
Phone: 847-699-7000   **Fax:** 847-699-6494
Web: www.wheels.com

Automotive Rentals
Donlen
Emkay
Enterprise Rent-A-Car
GE Fleet Services
Holman Enterprises
PHH Arval
Sixt

FreedomRoads, L.L.C.

Home, home on the road, where the semis and the SUVs play . . . that's how this company would sing it. The company sells about 20 brands of new and used RVs at some 60 FreedomRoads dealerships in nearly 30 states and online at RVs.com. Its Camping World unit runs 70-plus accessory stores for RV owners and camping buffs. FreedomRoads also provides financing and service for RVs. The firm grows by buying existing dealerships. To that end, the company acquired Sonny's Camp-N-Travel and in 2007 rebranded it as Camping World RV Sales. Chairman and CEO Marcus Lemonis founded FreedomRoads in 2003. It is owned, indirectly, by Steve Adams, chairman of RV products company Affinity Group.

EXECUTIVES

President and CEO: Marcus A. Lemonis, age 34
COO: Mark J. Boggess, age 52, $101,923 pay
CFO: Roger Nuttall
EVP and CIO: Matthew Baden
EVP Business Development and General Counsel: Brent Moody, age 46
SVP Human Resources: Gene Schrecengost
SVP Communication and Marketing: Diana Ardelean
Chief Marketing Officer: Tamara Ward
President, E-Commerce: Kenneth Marshall, age 48, $314,346 pay
President, Retail Operations: John A. Sirpilla
President, RV Dealer Group: Craig Jensen
Director, Motor Sports, RV Dealer Group: Kurt Hunt

LOCATIONS

HQ: FreedomRoads, L.L.C.
250 Parkway Dr., Ste. 320, Lincolnshire, IL 60069
Phone: 847-808-3000   **Fax:** 847-808-7015
Web: www.freedomroads.com

FreedomRoads operates about 60 RV dealerships and 70 Camping World stores in Alabama, Arizona, California, Colorado, Florida, Georgia, Illinois, Indiana, Kentucky, Louisiana, Michigan, Minnesota, New Hampshire, New Jersey, New Mexico, New York, Nevada, North Carolina, Ohio, Oklahoma, Oregon, Pennsylvania, South Carolina, Tennessee, Texas, Utah, Virginia, and Washington State.

COMPETITORS

Cruise America
General RV
Giant Inland Empire RV
La Mesa RV
Lazy Days RV Center

HISTORICAL FINANCIALS
Company Type: Private

Income Statement
FYE: December 31

	REVENUE ($ mil.)	NET INCOME ($ mil.)	NET PROFIT MARGIN	EMPLOYEES
12/07	1,650	—	—	4,000
12/06	1,600	—	—	3,500
12/05	1,500	—	—	3,200
12/04	1,200	—	—	—
Annual Growth	11.2%	—	—	11.8%

Revenue History

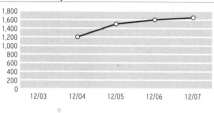

Freeman Decorating Services

Freeman Decorating Services knows there's no business like the trade show business. Doing business simply as "Freeman," the firm stages thousands of conventions, corporate meetings, expositions, and trade shows every year and prepares exhibits for its clients. Its operations include event design and production, Party Time Rentals (equipment rental for events in Canada), and Stage Rigging (theatrical rigging). The company's AVW/TELAV unit specializes in providing audio and visual technology and equipment used for meetings and events. Freeman was founded by D.S. "Buck" Freeman in 1927; the company is owned by the Freeman family (including chairman Donald Freeman) and company employees.

In 2007 Freeman acquired Chicago-based ProActive, Inc., an event marketing and communications firm.

Freeman has about 70 offices in 41 cities in the US and Canada.

EXECUTIVES

Chairman: Donald S. Freeman Jr.
President and CEO: Joseph V. (Joe) Popolo Jr.
EVP and COO: John F. O'Connell
EVP and CFO: Ellis Moseley
EVP Sales, Corporate Accounts: Bob Moore
EVP, Executive Sales Group: Bob Lozier
EVP, Human Resources: Albert Chew
EVP, Operations: Jay Atherton
EVP Sales, Exposition Services: Barry Rappaport
SVP, Nevada Region: Steve Hagstette
VP and Treasurer: William H. Baxley
VP and Controller: Bob Liles
VP Marketing: Carrie Freeman Parsons
President and COO, AVW-TELAV Audio Visual USA: Craig Smith
Corporate Director of Marketing and Communications: Ellen Beckert

LOCATIONS

HQ: Freeman Decorating Services, Inc.
1600 Viceroy, Ste. 100, Dallas, TX 75235
Phone: 214-445-1000   **Fax:** 214-445-0200
Web: www.freemanco.com

PRODUCTS/OPERATIONS

Selected Operations

Freeman Decorating
Budgeting
Event design
Rental furnishings and carpeting
Sign and graphics production
Theme decor
Freeman Exhibit
Exhibit production and design
Modular exhibit rental programs
Stage Rigging
Theatrical rigging

Selected Clients

American Heart Association
Anheuser-Busch, Inc.
Mary Kay Cosmetics
Microsoft Corp.
National Association of Home Builders
National Automobile Dealers Association
National Cable TV Association
Republican National Convention
Starbucks Corp.
Texas Association of School Boards
Texas Instruments

COMPETITORS

Audio Visual Services
Czarnowski
Dynasty Gaming
Exhibit Enterprises
Exhibitgroup/Giltspur
George P. Johnson
GES
GL events
Innovative Display & Design
Sparks Marketing Group
Viad
Virtual Meeting

Freescale Semiconductor

Freescale Semiconductor just wants to be free. Freescale, formerly Motorola's Semiconductor Products Sector, is one of the oldest and most diverse makers of microchips in the world. It produces many different kinds of chips for use in automobiles, computers, industrial equipment, wireless communications and networking equipment, and other applications. The company's global client roster includes such blue-chip companies as Alcatel-Lucent, Bosch, Cisco Systems, Fujitsu, Hewlett-Packard, QUALCOMM, and Siemens; former parent Motorola remains a substantial customer, representing around 24% of sales.

Following a strategic review in 2008 by CEO Rich Beyer and senior executives, Freescale made plans to sell or spin off its cellular handset chipset products business. The product line, which includes audio chips, baseband processors, power management devices, and radio-frequency (RF) transceivers, accounts for about 20% of the company's sales. Freescale and Motorola amended their contractual obligations as a result, with Motorola no longer required to meet minimum purchase commitments.

Motorola's woes in the cellular handset market, where it has dropped to #3 in the world (behind Nokia and Samsung Electronics) and it is being challenged for the third spot by Sony Ericsson and LG Electronics, weighed heavily on Freescale. The former parent accounted for about 94% of sales in Freescale's Cellular segment.

Two years after going public, Freescale went private in a 2006 buyout valued at $17.6 billion. Perhaps looking to be freed from the headaches of being a publicly held company, Freescale was acquired by an investment group consisting of The Blackstone Group, The Carlyle Group, Permira Advisers, and Texas Pacific Group, in the largest private-equity transaction in the technology sector since the $11.3 billion acquisition of SunGard Data Systems in 2005. A consortium of Apax Partners, Bain Capital, KKR, and Silver Lake Partners were said to have submitted a competing bid.

Freescale is focusing on the automotive, multimedia, and networking markets for growth. To revamp operations for more efficiency as a freestanding company, Freescale reduced its headcount significantly, discontinued product lines, and consolidated manufacturing operations.

In 2008 the company acquired another Austin-based chip maker, SigmaTel, for around $110 million in cash in the first significant strategic move by Freescale since the big buyout.

Later that year the Motorola spinoff spun off its magnetoresistive random-access memory (MRAM) business as a new company, EverSpin Technologies. Freescale retained an equity stake in EverSpin and will continue to develop embedded products based on the MRAM technology.

HISTORY

Freescale is the successor to the Semiconductor Products Sector (SPS) of electronics giant Motorola, which began as a supplier of radio products in 1928. Motorola began offering semiconductors in 1953, just six years after the invention of the transistor. As of the late 1950s, Motorola used nine-tenths of the semiconductors it produced in its own wide variety of electronic gear. Already a leader in automotive radios, during the 1950s and 1960s Motorola introduced many designs for semiconductor-based automotive electronics, a market in which it is still one of the foremost players.

Early in the 1960s, Motorola pioneered the epitaxial method of semiconductor wafer production, in which silicon crystals are grown layer by layer onto wafers; epitaxy became an industry-standard process that still endures. By the late 1960s, Motorola sold $200 million per year of its chips, and vied with fellow industry titan Texas Instruments as the top chip maker in the world.

Motorola entered the microprocessor (MPU) market in 1974 with its 8-bit 6800 model, which was used in computers, video games, and automotive systems. (Intel had introduced the first MPU in 1971.) While Intel and Advanced Micro Devices ultimately captured most of the market for computer processors, Motorola went on to become a top maker of embedded processors for many kinds of electronic equipment, especially portable devices such as wireless phones (in which Motorola has always been a world leader) and PDAs.

In 1979 the company introduced a 16-bit MPU, successors of which were used in the 1980s in early models of Apple's Macintosh computer. Motorola introduced its first 32-bit MPU in 1984. In 1991 Motorola began collaborating with IBM on the PowerPC family of processors, which powered Macintoshes for the next 15 years. (Apple then switched to Intel processors for Macs.) In 1995 Motorola debuted its DragonBall line of processors designed for portable consumer electronics applications.

SPS lost nearly $4 billion in 2001 and 2002 amid the worst downturn in semiconductor industry history. Late in 2003 Motorola announced plans to spin off SPS as a separate company; it subsequently dubbed the unit Freescale Semiconductor. Initially Motorola named veteran SPS executive Scott Anderson to lead Freescale, but several months later it appointed long-time IBM veteran Michel Mayer as CEO. (Anderson remained president and COO until 2005.)

Freescale debuted on the New York Stock Exchange in mid-2004. Motorola owned most of it until late in 2004, when it distributed its stake to Motorola shareholders.

The company sold a wafer fabrication plant (fab) in China to Shanghai-based SMIC in 2004. It sold its timing products group to Integrated Device Technology the following year.

Freescale's wireless operations got a boost early in 2005 when the company acquired the assets of PrairieComm, a developer of software and chipsets for cellular phones. That same year it also acquired the assets of content processing semiconductor developer Seaway Networks.

Freescale agreed to a $17.6 billion buyout by a consortium of private equity firms in September 2006, which was approved by shareholders two months later, and the transaction was completed in late 2006.

After leading the company through its IPO and the buyout, CEO Michel Mayer stepped down in early 2008. Freescale named Rich Beyer, the CEO of Intersil, to succeed Mayer as chairman and CEO.

EXECUTIVES

Chairman and CEO: Richard M. (Rich) Beyer, age 59
SVP and CFO: Alan Campbell, age 49
SVP, General Counsel, and Secretary: John D. Torres, age 49
SVP and Chairman, Asia-Pacific: Joe Yiu
SVP and Chairman Europe, Middle East & Africa (EMEA) Region: Denis Griot
SVP and General Manager, Japan: Tsuneo Takahashi
SVP Business Operations, Corporate Communications and Marketing Services: Janelle S. (Jan) Monney, age 51
SVP Human Resources and Security: Kurt Twining, age 52
SVP and Chief Sales and Marketing Officer: Henri Richard, age 49
SVP and Chief Development Officer: Sandeep Chennakeshu, age 49
VP and Chief Accounting Officer: Daryl E. Raiford, age 45
VP and CIO: Sam Coursen
VP and Treasurer: Greogory J. Heinlein, age 44
Investor Relations: Mitch Haws
Auditors: KPMG LLP

LOCATIONS

HQ: Freescale Semiconductor, Inc.
 6501 William Cannon Dr. West, Austin, TX 78735
Phone: 512-895-2000
Web: www.freescale.com

Freescale Semiconductor has facilities in Denmark, France, Germany, Hong Kong, India, Ireland, Israel, Japan, Malaysia, Romania, Russia, the UK, and the US.

2007 Sales

	$ mil.	% of total
Asia/Pacific		
Singapore	1,800	32
Hong Kong	745	13
Japan	282	5
Taiwan	66	1
US	1,493	26
Europe		
Germany	639	11
France	197	3
UK	158	3
Sweden	61	1
Other regions	281	5
Total	**5,722**	**100**

PRODUCTS/OPERATIONS

2007 Sales

	$ mil.	% of total
Microcontroller Solutions	1,878	33
Cellular Products	1,217	21
Networking & Multimedia	1,121	20
RF, Analog & Sensors	1,048	18
Other	458	8
Total	**5,722**	**100**

Selected Semiconductor Products

8-, 16-, and 32-bit microcontrollers (MCUs)
Analog
 Power management integrated circuits (ICs)
 Power switching ICs
 Network transceivers
Application-specific Standard Products (ASSPs)
 Digital video encoders
 Display drivers
Clock drivers
Digital signal processors
Embedded processors
Memory
 Content-addressable memory
 Magnetoresistive random-access memory (MRAM)
Networking processors
Radio-frequency
 Amplifier ICs and modules
 Transistors
Sensors
Wireless receivers and transmitters

COMPETITORS

AMD	Microchip Technology
Analog Devices	National Semiconductor
Atmel	NVIDIA
Avago Technologies	NXP
Broadcom	ON Semiconductor
Cavium Networks	QUALCOMM CDMA
Conexant Systems	Renesas
Cypress Semiconductor	RF Micro Devices
IBM Microelectronics	Sensata
Infineon Technologies	STMicroelectronics
Intel Corp.	Texas Instruments
Linear Technology	VIA Technologies
LSI Corp.	Vishay Intertechnology
Marvell Technology	ZiLOG
Maxim Integrated Products	

HISTORICAL FINANCIALS

Company Type: Private

Income Statement				FYE: December 31
	REVENUE ($ mil.)	NET INCOME ($ mil.)	NET PROFIT MARGIN	EMPLOYEES
12/07	5,722	(1,607)	—	23,200
12/06	6,363	—	—	24,000
12/05	5,843	—	—	22,700
12/04	5,715	—	—	22,200
12/03	4,864	—	—	22,300
Annual Growth	4.1%	—	—	1.0%

Revenue History

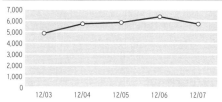

Friendly Ice Cream

Screaming ice cream lovers can soothe their pipes at Friendly Ice Cream. The company operates a chain of more than 500 family-style restaurants in more than 15 states that specialize in frozen dairy dessert treats. Among fan favorites are Friendly's Fribble shakes, the Royal Banana Split Sundae, and Chocolate Covered Berry Patch desserts. In addition to ice cream, the restaurants serve breakfast, lunch, and dinner — mostly traditional American fare such as sandwiches and burgers. Most of the chain's locations are company-operated. Friendly's also distributes ice cream and other frozen desserts through some 4,000 supermarkets and other retail sites. The company was acquired by Sun Capital Partners in 2007.

The investment firm took Friendly's private for almost $340 million and plans to invest in efforts to expand the chain, which has been struggling of late due mostly to budget-conscious families curtailing their restaurant dining. As part of its reorganization strategy, the company sold more than 160 properties in a sale-leaseback deal that netted about $40 million.

In addition to Friendly's, Sun Capital owns such dining businesses as Bruegger's Enterprises and Garden Fresh, and it purchased the Smokey Bones Barbeque chain from Darden Restaurants in 2007.

George Condos, formerly the marketing chief at Dunkin' Donuts (one of the chains under the Dunkin' Brands umbrella), was appointed CEO in 2007 prior to the company going private. He replaced John Cutter, who had unexpectedly resigned the previous year.

EXECUTIVES

President and CEO: George M. Condos, age 52
EVP Administration, CFO, Treasurer, and Assistant Clerk: Paul V. Hoagland, age 55, $359,430 pay
SVP Company Operations: John Bowie
VP, General Counsel, and Clerk: Gregory A. Pastore, age 43, $215,200 pay
VP Human Resources: Garrett J. Ulrich, age 57, $247,600 pay
VP Marketing: George (Skip) Weldon
Senior Director Investor Relations:
Deborah (Debbie) Burns
Director Corporate Communications: Maura C. Tobias
Controller: Florence Tassinari, age 44
Auditors: Ernst & Young LLP

LOCATIONS

HQ: Friendly Ice Cream Corporation
1855 Boston Rd., Wilbraham, MA 01095
Phone: 413-731-4000   **Fax:** 413-731-4471
Web: www.friendlys.com

COMPETITORS

American Dairy Queen
Ben & Jerry's
Bob Evans
Brinker
Bruster's
Buffets Holdings
Carlson Restaurants
Carvel
CBRL Group
Cold Stone Creamery
Darden
Denny's
DineEquity
Dreyer's
Dunkin
Eat'n Park
McDonald's
Nestlé
Perkins & Marie Callender's
Ruby Tuesday

HISTORICAL FINANCIALS

Company Type: Private

Income Statement				FYE: Last Sunday in December
	REVENUE ($ mil.)	NET INCOME ($ mil.)	NET PROFIT MARGIN	EMPLOYEES
12/06	532	5	0.9%	12,800
12/05	531	(27)	—	12,700
12/04	575	(3)	—	14,500
12/03	580	10	1.8%	16,000
12/02	570	6	1.1%	15,000
Annual Growth	(1.8%)	(5.7%)	—	(3.9%)

2006 Year-End Financials

Debt ratio: —
Return on equity: —
Cash ($ mil.): 26
Current ratio: 0.85
Long-term debt ($ mil.): 227

Net Income History

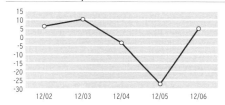

Fry's Electronics

Trying to catalog all the things this superstore carries could fry your brain. Fry's Electronics is a leading big-box retailer of computers, consumer electronics, and appliances with 30-plus stores in about 10 states. The chain's extensive inventory includes computer software and components, magazines, movies and music, refrigerators, small appliances, stereo equipment, and televisions. In addition, each store typically stocks a variety of snacks and other impulse items. The technogeek's dream store began in 1985 as the brainchild of CEO John Fry (with brothers Randy and Dave) and EVP Kathryn Kolder. The Fry brothers, who got their start at Fry's Food Stores, still own the company.

Its mammoth stores, some swallowing almost 200,000 sq. ft., cater to the intensely technical shopper. Fry's stores stock more than 50,000 low-priced electronic items and are known for their decor and displays. Each follows a theme, from *Alice in Wonderland* to a UFO crash site. The selection ranges from silicon chips to potato chips, from *Byte* to *Playboy,* and high-speed PCs (plus software and peripherals) to hair dryers (and other health and beauty items).

In addition to its retail outlets, Fry's sells electronics at Frys.com, replacing Outpost.com (its online subsidiary acquired in 2001). The company also offers dial-up and high-speed Internet access services in more than 40 states.

Fry's stores' extensive inventories are said to be the company's strongest draw, unlike its reputation for poor customer service. This reputation, combined with Fry's bemoaned system for returning items, has left the company a target of many gripe-filled Web sites.

HISTORY

The Fry brothers — David, John, and Randy — wear genes stitched of retailing. Their father, Charles, started Fry's Food Stores supermarket chain in the 1950s in South Bay, California. The 40-store chain was sold for $14 million in 1972 to Dillion (now part of grocery store giant The Kroger Co.) before Charles' progeny heard the retail calling.

Charles gave each of his sons $1 million from the sale of the supermarkets. His oldest, John, who had gained technical expertise while running the supermarket's computer system, convinced his siblings of the viability of a hard-core computer retail store. The brothers pooled their funds and in 1985 started the first in Sunnyvale, California, along with Kathryn Kolder (now EVP). They added a store in Fremont in 1988; the Palo Alto store was completed two years later.

John mixed his supermarket sales experience with a sharp marketing acumen, selling prime shelf space at smart prices to suppliers. He stocked the stores with everything for a computer user's survival and slashed prices. The first Los Angeles-area store opened in 1992; a second one opened the following year. Hiring an ex-Lucasfilm designer, John spent $1 million on each location, decorating stores like medieval castles, Mayan temples, Wild West saloons, and other individual fantasy themes.

In 1994 the Los Angeles computer retail market began to see increased competition from nationwide discount computer superstores. The next year Fry's responded by opening a new store in Woodland Hills with an *Alice in Wonderland* motif. It was the first Southern California Fry's Electronics store to offer appliances and an expanded music department.

The chain continued to gain notoriety for the contempt it seemed to show its customers. Local Better Business Bureaus started ranking Fry's "unsatisfactory" because the stores would not respond to complaints. Patrons with a beef were usually met by security guards; there were scores of hidden surveillance cameras, and employees were promised bonuses for talking customers out of cash returns.

Still the company thrived, turning over its inventories twice as fast as competitors. One customer who sued Fry's for injuries allegedly received at the hands of store security guards went back for deals soon thereafter. Fry's went on an expansion frenzy in 1996, opening new California stores in Burbank, San Jose, and Anaheim. Moving beyond its Pacific roots, the company in 1997 spent $118 million to buy six of Tandy's failed Incredible Universe retail mega-outlets in Arizona, Oregon, and Texas. The company also won a legal battle with Frenchy Frys, a Seattle vending machine maker, for the right to own and use the frys.com URL. The company in 1998 continued to restructure its new stores into Fry's outlets.

Fry's opened a new store (complete with gushing oil derricks) in Houston in 2001. That year it pulled out of a deal to acquire all of the assets of technology products marketer Egghead.com and bought competitor Cyberian Outpost instead. In 2003 Fry's set up shop in Las Vegas; the entrance features a two-story neon slot machine.

In October 2006 the company (finally) launched Frys.com, although it has owned the domain name since 1997.

EXECUTIVES

CEO: John Fry
President: William R. (Randy) Fry
CFO and CIO: David (Dave) Fry
EVP Business Development: Kathryn (Kathy) Kolder
VP Merchandising and Advertising: Ohmar Siddiqui
Controller: Chris Scheiber
Director of Human Resources: Karen Schultz
Community Relations Manager: Manuel Valerio
Legal Department Manager: Lisa McIntire

LOCATIONS

HQ: Fry's Electronics, Inc.
600 E. Brokaw Rd., San Jose, CA 95112
Phone: 408-487-4500   **Fax:** 408-487-4741
Web: www.frys.com

PRODUCTS/OPERATIONS

Selected Products

Appliances (coffeemakers, blenders, vacuums)
Cameras
CD players
Computer components (hard drives, routers)
Computers (PCs, notebooks)
DVD players
DVDs
MP3 players
Office products (printers, copiers, fax machines)
PDAs
Software
Toys
Video games

COMPETITORS

Amazon.com	Newegg
Apple	Office Depot
Best Buy	PC Mall
Buy.com	PC Warehouse
CDW	RadioShack
Circuit City	Staples
CompUSA	Trans World Entertainment
Dell	Tweeter Newco
GameStop	Wal-Mart
Gateway, Inc.	Zones
Hastings Entertainment	

HISTORICAL FINANCIALS

Company Type: Private

Income Statement				FYE: December 31
	ESTIMATED REVENUE ($ mil.)	NET INCOME ($ mil.)	NET PROFIT MARGIN	EMPLOYEES
12/07	2,350	—	—	14,000
12/06	2,610	—	—	12,000
12/05	2,340	—	—	12,000
12/04	2,250	—	—	6,500
12/03	2,100	—	—	6,000
Annual Growth	2.9%	—	—	23.6%

Revenue History

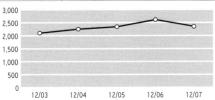

Gate Petroleum

Gate Petroleum swings many ways. The company runs a chain of about 225 Gate Food Post stores in Florida, Georgia, Kentucky, Louisiana, North Carolina, South Carolina, and Virginia that sell gas and groceries and offer fleet management services. The firm is also a wholesale fuel distributor to customers throughout the Southeast. The company is also active in the real estate and construction materials businesses. In Florida Gate owns several private clubs, office buildings, and business parks. Subsidiary Gate Concrete has plants in six states that make and sell concrete and building materials. CEO Herbert Peyton, who founded the company in 1960, owns the majority of Gate Petroleum Company.

Gate Petroleum's private clubs include the Epping Forest Yacht Club, the Ponte Vedra Inn & Club, and the Ponte Vedra Lodge & Club. It is also developing a huge residential and commercial complex in Jacksonville, Florida.

EXECUTIVES

Chairman and CEO; President, Gate Marketing Co.:
Herbert H. (Herb) Peyton
VP Finance: P. Jeremy Smith
VP, Payroll: Mary Ann Bright
VP, Real Estate; President GL National: Ken Wilson
Director, Human Resources: Denise Gaitanzis

Chairman, Gate Marketing Co.: Wayne Levitt
President, Gate Marketing Co.: Mitchell Rhodes
VP, Development, Gate Marketing Co.: George Nail
Director, Fleet Services, Gate Marketing Co.: Jim Beck

LOCATIONS

HQ: Gate Petroleum Company
9540 San Jose Blvd., Jacksonville, FL 32257
Phone: 904-737-7220   **Fax:** 904-732-7660
Web: www.gatepetro.com

PRODUCTS/OPERATIONS

Selected Operations

Gate Construction Materials (architectural and structural precast/prestressed concrete)
Gate Fuel Service (petroleum distribution)
Gate Petroleum Marketing (gas station/convenience stores)
Real Estate (investment)
Resorts (Florida, resorts & clubs)

COMPETITORS

7-Eleven
Chevron
Cumberland Farms
Exxon
The Pantry
Publix
Racetrac Petroleum
Royal Dutch Shell

General Parts

Feel free to salute General Parts, distributor of replacement automotive parts, supplies, and tools for every make and model of foreign and domestic car, truck, bus, and farm or industrial vehicle. The firm operates the CARQUEST auto parts distribution network of some 40 distribution centers, and owns about 1,400 of CARQUEST's 3,400 auto parts stores across the US, Canada, and Mexico. The company sells its parts to DIY mechanics, professional installers, body shops, farmers, and fleet owners (commercial customers account for most sales). General Parts has been growing through acquisitions. The company, founded in 1961 by college student Temple Sloan, owns CARQUEST Canada.

EXECUTIVES

Chairman and CEO: O. Temple Sloan Jr., age 69
President and COO: O. Temple Sloan III
CFO: John Gardner
EVP Marketing and Merchandising: Dale Ward, age 58
EVP Store Group: Jerry Colley, age 51
EVP Product Management: Robert Blair
SVP Product Management; President, CARQUEST:
Todd Hack
SVP Marketing: Ray Birden
VP Product Management: Randall Long
Chief People Officer: John Dibenedetto
Logistics: Michael Pughes
Operations Manager: Danny Wusterbath

LOCATIONS

HQ: General Parts, Inc.
2635 Millbrook Rd., Raleigh, NC 27604
Phone: 919-573-3000   **Fax:** 919-573-3553

COMPETITORS

Advance Auto Parts
Applied Industrial Technologies
AutoZone
CSK Auto
Dorman Products
Hahn Automotive
Keystone Automotive
Pep Boys
Sears

HISTORICAL FINANCIALS

Company Type: Private

Income Statement

FYE: December 31

	ESTIMATED REVENUE ($ mil.)	NET INCOME ($ mil.)	NET PROFIT MARGIN	EMPLOYEES
12/07	2,870	—	—	18,000
12/06	2,400	—	—	24,500
12/05	2,250	—	—	23,000
12/04	2,000	—	—	20,000
12/03	1,800	—	—	13,500
Annual Growth	12.4%	—	—	7.5%

Revenue History

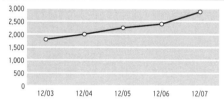

Genesis HealthCare

Genesis HealthCare Corporation cares for people when care is what counts. Genesis HealthCare operates about 200 assisted living and skilled nursing facilities in 13 states in the eastern US. Its facilities have about 26,000 beds total. Genesis HealthCare's rehabilitation division provides speech, physical, and occupational therapy services through contracts with health care providers in nearly 20 states. The company also offers respiratory therapy, adult day care, Alzheimer's care, dialysis, and home and hospice care. Genesis HealthCare was taken private in 2007 by a group of private equity investors from Formation Capital and the private equity arm of real estate investment firm J. E. Roberts.

Genesis HealthCare has grown by developing its specialty services, including its transitional care facilities and rehabilitation contract services. Medicaid and Medicare payments account for more than 75% of the company's revenues.

The company is continuing to grow through regional acquisitions. Genesis HealthCare has announced that it intends to acquire Haven Healthcare, with 27 facilities in the northeastern US.

Genesis HealthCare was formed as a spinoff of NeighborCare in 2003. In early 2007 investment firms Formation Capital and JER Partners announced a plan to purchase Genesis HealthCare. Fillmore Capital Partners countered with a higher offer, prompting Formation and JER to increase their offer, which was accepted in mid-2007.

EXECUTIVES

CEO: George V. Hager Jr., age 52, $895,700 pay
EVP and COO: Robert A. (Mike) Reitz, age 57, $432,000 pay
EVP and CFO: James V. (Jim) McKeon III, age 43, $437,500 pay
EVP and President, Southern Area: David C. (Dave) Almquist, age 53, $365,500 pay
EVP and President, Northeast Area: Richard P. (Dick) Blinn, age 53, $354,500 pay
EVP and President, Central Area: Paul D. Bach
SVP and CIO: Richard L. (Rich) Castor
SVP Administration: Richard (Rich) Pell Jr., age 59
SVP, Clinical Practice and Outcomes Management Group: Irene Fleshner
SVP, General Counsel, and Corporate Secretary: Eileen M. Coggins, age 43
SVP Planning and Development: Barbara J. Hauswald, age 48
SVP Human Development: Arthur T. (Bud) Locilento Jr., age 64
President, Genesis Rehab Services: Dan Hirschfeld
Director Investor Relations: Lori Mayer
Auditors: KPMG LLP

LOCATIONS

HQ: Genesis HealthCare Corporation
101 E. State St., Kennett Square, PA 19348
Phone: 610-444-6350   **Fax:** 610-925-4000
Web: www.genesishcc.com

Genesis HealthCare Corporation has skilled nursing and assisted living facilities in Connecticut, Delaware, Maine, Maryland, Massachusetts, New Hampshire, New Jersey, North Carolina, Pennsylvania, Rhode Island, Vermont, Virginia, and West Virginia.

PRODUCTS/OPERATIONS

2007 Revenues

	% of total
Medicaid	50
Medicare	28
Private pay & insurance	22
Total	**100**

COMPETITORS

Golden Horizons
HealthSouth
Kindred Healthcare
Manor Care
Sunrise Senior Living

Genmar Holdings

Genmar Holdings trolls for sales by cruising the pleasure boat market with a line of luxury yachts, recreational powerboats, and fishing boats. The company builds more than 250 different boat models, ranging in size from 60-foot yachts (servants not included) to fishing skiffs. Its brands include Glastron, Ranger, and Wellcraft. Genmar markets its boats through more than 1,000 independent dealers in the US and 30 other countries. The company, which is a combination of 13 different boat manufacturing brands acquired over 25 years, is controlled by chairman Irwin Jacobs, an investor and former corporate raider.

With economic woes putting the squeeze on US markets for things like fishing boats and yachts, the company is relying heavily on its international sales, especially at the upper end of the spectrum. Yacht brands Marquis and Carver get about 40% of their sales from overseas. Buoyed by those sales, the company in early 2008 announced a $27 million expansion in its yacht operations, including a new plant in Green Bay, Wisconsin.

For those who can't afford multi-million dollar yachts, Genmar also said in late 2008 that it would launch a line of less expensive aluminum boats as part of a new unnamed company from a factory set to open in early 2010.

After laying off about 60 workers in Florida and then moving production out of Florida (citing high taxes and workers compensation costs) to its Tennessee and Minnesota plants early in 2008, the company laid off an undisclosed number of people at its plants in Minnesota and elsewhere later in the year.

Genmar sold its Aluminum Boat Companies unit (Crestliner, Lowe, and Lund brands) to fellow boat maker Brunswick in 2004.

Genmar was founded in 1978.

EXECUTIVES

Chairman: Irwin L. Jacobs
President and COO: Roger R. Cloutier II
SVP, Purchasing: Ronald V. Purgiel
Corporate Communications: Mark Helgren

LOCATIONS

HQ: Genmar Holdings, Inc.
80 S. 8th St., Minneapolis, MN 55402
Phone: 612-337-1965   **Fax:** 612-337-1994
Web: www.genmar.com

PRODUCTS/OPERATIONS

Selected Brands

Carver Yachts
Champion
Four Winns
Glastron
Hydra Sports
Larson
Marquis
Ranger
Seaswirl
Stratos
Triumph
Wellcraft
Windsor Craft

COMPETITORS

Bénéteau
Brunswick Boat
Duckworth Boat Works
Fountain Powerboat
Marine Products
Sea Fox Boats
Yamaha Motor

George E. Warren Corporation

By barge, by pipeline, by tank truck, by George; George E. Warren is a major private wholesale distributor of petroleum in the eastern US. Founded in Boston by George E. Warren in 1907 as a coal and oil distributor, it moved to Florida in 1989. The company distributes product mostly by barge and pipeline, though it uses some tank trucks as well. Warren has distribution facilities in the southeastern and southwestern US. It distributes products including ethylene and heating oil to various industries. President and CEO Thomas Corr owns the company.

George E. Warren is one of the largest private companies in Florida. In addition to its Vero Beach office, the wholesale fuel distributor also has an office in the UK.

EXECUTIVES

President and CEO: Thomas L. Corr
CFO and Controller: Michael E. George
Director Human Resources: Cheryl Ernst

LOCATIONS

HQ: George E. Warren Corporation
   3001 Ocean Dr., Vero Beach, FL 32963
Phone: 772-778-7100   **Fax:** 772-778-7171
Web: www.gewarren.com

COMPETITORS

Center Oil
ConocoPhillips
Crown Central
Exxon
Martin Resource Management
Penn Octane
Sun Coast Resources
Williams Companies

Georgia Lottery

Lottery fans with an eye toward education may have Georgia on their minds. Established in 1993, the Georgia Lottery has contributed more than $9 billion to the state's education coffers. In addition to the HOPE program, which has helped some 1 million students attend college with lottery-funded scholarships, the lottery helps finance a pre-kindergarten program and public school capital improvements. More than 7,500 retailers throughout Georgia sell tickets for lottery games, including instant-ticket, on-line, and keno-style games, and a powerball-like game aptly named Mega Millions. In its first year the Georgia Lottery reached $1.1 billion in sales and has been growing ever since.

EXECUTIVES

Chairman: George Anthony (Tony) Campbell, age 56
President and CEO: Margaret R. DeFrancisco, age 58
SVP Finance, Planning, and Development:
   Joan Schoubert

SVP and General Counsel: Kurt Freedlund
SVP Administration: Gerald Mecca
CTO: Daniel Johnson
VP Applied Technology: Larry Sipes
VP Corporate Affairs: J.B. Landroche
VP Financial Management: Sharman Lawrence
VP Legal Affairs: Rosemarie Morse
VP Security: Mar-D Greer
VP Marketing: James Hutchinson
VP Human Resources: Doug Parker
VP Sales: Jack Dimling
VP Customer Operations: Teri Rosa
Auditors: Deloitte & Touche LLC

LOCATIONS

HQ: Georgia Lottery Corporation
   250 Williams St., Ste. 3000, Atlanta, GA 30303
Phone: 404-215-5000   **Fax:** 404-215-8983
Web: www.galottery.com

COMPETITORS

Florida Lottery
Multi-State Lottery
Virginia Lottery

HISTORICAL FINANCIALS

Company Type: Government-owned

Income Statement				FYE: June 30
	REVENUE ($ mil.)	NET INCOME ($ mil.)	NET PROFIT MARGIN	EMPLOYEES
6/08	3,519	—	—	279
6/07	3,422	—	—	266
6/06	2,960	—	—	260
6/05	2,922	—	—	—
6/04	2,710	—	—	—
Annual Growth	6.8%	—	—	3.6%

Revenue History

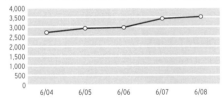

Georgia Tech

The Georgia Institute of Technology, commonly known as Georgia Tech, is one of the country's top engineering schools for both graduate and undergraduate students. The university also offers degrees in the Colleges of Architecture, Sciences, Computing, and Management, and the Ivan Allen College of Liberal Arts. It has an enrollment of more than 16,000 students. The school is also renowned for its scientific and technological research, receiving more than $355 million in research awards annually. Georgia Tech was founded in 1885 as the Georgia School of Technology.

EXECUTIVES

President: G. Wayne Clough, age 66
SVP Administration and Finance: Robert K. Thompson
VP Academic Affairs and Provost: Jean-Lou Chameau, age 54
Vice Provost Distance Learning and Professional Education: William J. Wepfer
Vice Provost Research and Dean of Graduate Studies: Charles Liotta
Vice Provost Institutional Development: Jack R. Lohmann
Vice Provost Undergraduate Studies and Academic Affairs: Anderson Smith
Associate Vice Provost, Associate VP, and CIO: John Mullin
Associate VP Facilities: Chuck Rhode
Associate VP Financial Services: Joel E. Hercik
Associate VP Human Resources: Chuck Donbaugh

LOCATIONS

HQ: Georgia Institute of Technology
   225 North Ave. NW, Atlanta, GA 30332
Phone: 404-894-5051   **Fax:** 404-894-1277
Web: www.gatech.edu

HISTORICAL FINANCIALS

Company Type: School

Income Statement				FYE: June 30
	REVENUE ($ mil.)	NET INCOME ($ mil.)	NET PROFIT MARGIN	EMPLOYEES
6/07	997	60	6.1%	5,370
6/06	879	18	2.0%	—
6/05	826	—	—	—
6/04	896	—	—	—
6/03	500	—	—	—
Annual Growth	18.8%	245.1%	—	—

2007 Year-End Financials

Debt ratio: 40.4%   Current ratio: —
Return on equity: 6.3%   Long-term debt ($ mil.): 398
Cash ($ mil.): —

Net Income History

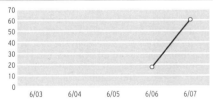

Getty Images

With an eye out for the big picture, visual content provider Getty Images is a major supplier of creative (stock) and editorial still and moving images and illustrations, as well as music. It also offers photo services for corporate clients. The company targets four main markets: advertising and graphic design firms; editorial organizations, such as newspapers, magazines, and online publishers; corporate communications departments; and film and broadcast producers. Getty Images, which distributes its products online, has customers in more than 100 countries around the world; most of its sales come from outside the US. In mid-2008, Getty Images was acquired by private equity firm Hellman & Friedman.

Hellman & Friedman paid about $2.4 billion, including assumed debt, for the company. The deal was struck a few months after Getty Images had announced that it had hired advisers to help the company evaluate ways to increase shareholder value. Its profits and its share price had been slumping, in part because of increased competition from low-cost image providers.

Before it was taken private, Getty Images was expanding its image library quickly through acquisitions. In April 2007 the company completed its purchase of WireImage, a leading provider of celebrity- and entertainment-related images for editorial use, for about $200 million. Included in the deal were WireImage affiliates FilmMagic and ContourPhotos, along with the companies' parent, MediaVast. Also in 2007, Getty Images entered the music licensing business by acquiring Pump Audio, a provider of independent music used in advertising, broadcast, film, and other applications.

The transaction came on the heels of two 2006 acquisitions by Getty Images: Ireland-based Pixel Images, the parent company of visual content providers Stockbyte and Stockdisc, for $135 million; and iStockphoto, a company that deals mainly in micropayment transactions and makes images available for use for as little as $1, for $50 million. Getty Images is maintaining the Web sites for iStockphoto, Pump Audio, and WireImage as part of an effort to broaden its Web presence.

Besides acquisitions, the company's growth strategies have included boosting its presence in non-English speaking markets and strengthening its offerings in the micropayment market. With backing from Hellman & Friedman, Getty Images hopes to continue its expansion push.

EXECUTIVES

Chairman: Mark H. Getty, age 47
CEO and Director: Jonathan D. Klein, age 47
EVP and COO: Nicholas E. (Nick) Evans-Lombe, age 41
SVP and CFO: Thomas (Tom) Oberdorf, age 50
SVP Business Development, Emerging Markets Sales, and Asia/Pacific Sales: Jeffrey L. (Jeff) Beyle, age 46
SVP Sales, North America: Michael D. Teaster, age 41
SVP Sales, Europe: Lee Martin
SVP Human Resources and Facilities and Interim SVP Marketing: James C. (Jim) Gurke, age 52
SVP and General Counsel: John J. Lapham, age 40
SVP Technology; CEO, iStockphoto: Bruce T. Livingstone, age 36
VP Communications: Caroline Andoscia
Director Investor Relations: Alan Pickerill
Auditors: PricewaterhouseCoopers LLP

LOCATIONS

HQ: Getty Images, Inc.
601 N. 34th St., Seattle, WA 98103
Phone: 206-925-5000   **Fax:** 206-925-5001
Web: www.gettyimages.com

2007 Sales

	$ mil.	% of total
US	342.6	40
UK	120.6	14
Germany	73.1	8
France	48.6	6
Other countries	272.7	32
Total	**857.6**	**100**

COMPETITORS

AG Interactive	New York Times
Agence France-Presse	PR Newswire
Associated Press	Reuters
Corbis	Rex Features
Jupitermedia	Sipa Press
National Geographic	Zuma Press

HISTORICAL FINANCIALS

Company Type: Private

Income Statement
FYE: December 31

	REVENUE ($ mil.)	NET INCOME ($ mil.)	NET PROFIT MARGIN	EMPLOYEES
12/07	858	126	14.7%	1,935
12/06	807	130	16.2%	1,750
12/05	734	150	20.4%	1,823
12/04	622	107	17.1%	—
12/03	523	64	12.2%	—
Annual Growth	**13.1%**	**18.4%**	**—**	**3.0%**

2007 Year-End Financials

Debt ratio: —
Return on equity: 9.4%
Cash ($ mil.): 364
Current ratio: 1.05
Long-term debt ($ mil.): —

Net Income History

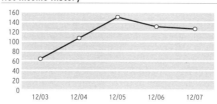

G-I Holdings

G-I Holdings has a kung-fu grip on the roofing materials business. Also known under its former name GAF Corporation, G-I and its subsidiary Building Materials Corporation of America make flashing, vents, and complete roofing systems. It makes residential shingles and commercial asphalt roofing under the Timberline, Everguard, and Ruberoid brands. Other products include natural stone, ornamental ironwork, and ducting. G-I Holdings is in bankruptcy protection due to asbestos liability claims. Chairman Samuel Heyman owns the company and affiliate specialty chemicals manufacturer International Specialty Products Inc.

Perhaps reflecting the moxie of its chairman, G-I Holdings turned around and countersued the law firms that represented asbestos victims, saying their tactics violated the company's right to political speech.

In 2007 G-I Holdings also accused now-defunct consulting firm L. Tersigni Consulting of overbilling it for work done in relation to its asbestos bankruptcy case. The Department of Justice is investigating.

Subsidiary Building Materials Corporation acquired rival ElkCorp in 2007, beating out Carlyle Group. Elk was merged into the company's GAF Materials business.

EXECUTIVES

Chairman, G-I Holdings and Building Materials Corporation of America: Samuel J. (Sam) Heyman, age 66
CFO: John F. Rebele, age 53
VP Human Resources: Gary Schneid

LOCATIONS

HQ: G-I Holdings Inc.
1361 Alps Rd., Wayne, NJ 07470
Phone: 973-628-3000

PRODUCTS/OPERATIONS

Selected Brands

Camelot
Country Mansion
Drill-Tec
EnergyCote
EnergyGuard
EverGuard
FireOut
GAFGLAS
Grand Canyon
Grand Sequoia
Grand Timberline
GrandSlate
LeakBuster
Lexsuco
Marquis WeatherMax
Matrix
Mineral Shield
ROOFMatch
Royal Sovereign
Ruberoid
Sentinel
Slateline
Timberline 30
TOPCOAT

COMPETITORS

CertainTeed
Johns Manville
JPS Industries
NCI Building Systems
Owens Corning Sales
Saint-Gobain

HISTORICAL FINANCIALS

Company Type: Private

Income Statement
FYE: December 31

	REVENUE ($ mil.)	NET INCOME ($ mil.)	NET PROFIT MARGIN	EMPLOYEES
12/07	2,380	—	—	4,200
12/06	1,970	—	—	3,600
12/05	1,956	—	—	3,700
12/04	1,770	—	—	3,700
12/03	1,608	—	—	3,500
Annual Growth	**10.3%**	**—**	**—**	**4.7%**

Revenue History

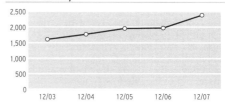

Giant Eagle

Giant Eagle has its talons firmly wrapped around parts of Pennsylvania and Ohio. The grocery chain, a market leader in Pittsburgh and eastern Ohio, operates about 160 company-owned stores and some 65 franchised supermarkets, as well as about 145 GetGo convenience stores (which feature fresh foods and sell gas at discounted prices through the fuelperks! program). Many Giant Eagle stores feature video rental, banking, photo processing, dry cleaning services, and ready-to-eat meals. Giant Eagle is also a wholesaler to licensed stores and sells groceries to other retail chains. CEO David Shapira is the grandson of one of the men who founded the company in 1931. The founders' families own Giant Eagle.

As with other birds of the retailing feather, Giant Eagle's supermarkets carry private-label merchandise (Market District, Giant Eagle, and Nature's Basket brands) and nonfood items; many have pharmacies. To promote its private-label goods, which return higher profits to the retailer, Giant Eagle in 2008 launched an in-store/online publication called "G." G will be published four to six times a year, with each issue featuring eight to 12 pages detailing how the store's private-label brands can simplify and enrich shoppers' lives.

The supermarket chain, which also has limited operations in Maryland and West Virginia, has shifted the start of its weekly sales specials from Sunday to Thursday to match its customers' changing shopping patterns and better compete with nontraditional grocery chains, such as Costco Wholesale and Wal-Mart. Giant Eagle has also cut prices on 750 national-brand and private-label items in its Pittsburgh-area stores. Previously, the grocery chain reduced the cost an average of 7% on some 3,000 items to better compete with discount grocery chains.

The company's goal is to grow Giant Eagle food and drug sales through a combination of acquisitions and organic growth. To that end, in late 2006 Giant Eagle acquired nearly 20 stores in northeastern Ohio from rival TOPS Markets. Previous purchases include Giant Eagle's successful bid for the remaining assets of bankrupt discount drugstore chain Phar-Mor. It also acquired and converted eight Big Bear grocery stores in the Columbus area from bankrupt supermarket operator Penn Traffic.

HISTORY

When Joe Porter, Ben Chait, and Joe Goldstein sold their chain of 125 Eagle grocery stores in Pittsburgh to Kroger in 1928, the agreement stated that the men would have to leave the grocery business for three years. In retrospect, Kroger should have made the term last for the length of their lives, because in 1931 the three men joined the owners of OK Grocery — Hyman Moravitz and Morris Weizenbaum — and launched a new chain of grocery stores called Giant Eagle. Eventually, the chain would knock Kroger out of the Pittsburgh market.

Although slowed by the Great Depression, the chain expanded, fighting such large rivals as Acme, A&P, and Kroger for Pittsburgh's food shoppers. The stores were mom-and-pop operations with over-the-counter service until they

began converting to self-service during the 1940s. Store sizes expanded to nearly 15,000 sq. ft. in the 1950s. During that time Giant Eagle, with about 30 stores, launched Blue Stamps in answer to Green Stamps and other loyalty programs.

It phased out trading stamps in the 1960s in lieu of everyday low prices. To accommodate its growth, in 1968 Giant Eagle acquired a warehouse in Lawrenceville, Pennsylvania, that more than doubled its storage area. Also that year the firm opened its first 20,000-sq.-ft. Giant Eagle store.

During the inflationary 1970s Giant Eagle introduced generic items and began offering the Food Club line, a private-label brand, in conjunction with wholesaler Topco. It continued its expansion, and by 1979 it had become Pittsburgh's #1 supermarket chain, as chains such as Kroger, Acme, and A&P were leaving the city. In 1981 Giant Eagle, with 52 stores, acquired Tamarkin, a wholesale and retail chain in Youngstown, Ohio, part-owned by the Monus family. The purchase moved it into the franchise business, and later that year the first independent Giant Eagle store opened in Monaca (outside Pittsburgh).

The Tamarkin purchase brought together Mickey Monus and Giant Eagle CEO David Shapira, grandson of founder Goldstein. In 1982 they created Phar-Mor, a deep-discount drugstore chain (Wal-Mart's Sam Walton once said it was the only competitor he truly feared). From a single store in Niles, Ohio, Phar-Mor grew rapidly to 310 outlets in 32 states in the early 1990s.

Phar-Mor president Monus helped found the World Basketball League (WBL) in 1987 and became the owner of three teams. In 1992 an auditor discovered two unexplainable Phar-Mor checks to the WBL totaling about $100,000. Investigators soon uncovered three years of overstated inventories and a false set of books; Shapira (who was also CEO of Phar-Mor), Giant Eagle owners (which held a 50% stake in Phar-Mor until 1992), and other investors had been duped of more than $1 billion. Shapira fired Monus and other executives on July 31, 1992. The next day the WBL folded; about two weeks after that Phar-Mor filed for Chapter 11 bankruptcy. A mistrial in 1994 couldn't save Monus from prison; he was reindicted in 1995 and sentenced to 20 years (later reduced to 12).

Giant Eagle made its largest acquisition in 1997, paying $403 million for Riser Foods, a wholesaler (American Seaway Foods) with 35 company-owned stores under the Rini-Rego Stop-n-Shop banner. The stores were converted to the Giant Eagle banner in 1998 (another 18 independent Stop-n-Shop stores were also converted).

In 2000 Giant Eagle opened several stores in Columbus, Ohio. The grocer moved into Maryland in 2001 when it acquired six Country Market stores in Maryland and Pennsylvania. Also in 2001, the grocer founded ECHO Real Estate Services Co. to develop retail, housing, and golf course projects.

In 2002 Giant Eagle was among the winning bidders for the remaining assets of bankrupt Phar-Mor, acquiring leases to 10 Phar-Mor stores and the inventory and prescription lists for 27 stores.

In mid-2005 the grocery chain acquired four CoGo convenience stores, which it converted to its fast-growing GetGo banner. In late 2006 Giant Eagle acquired nearly 20 stores in northeastern Ohio from rival TOPS Markets.

EXECUTIVES

Chairman, President, and CEO:
David S. (Dave) Shapira, age 66
Vice-Chairman: Raymond (Ray) Burgo
EVP, Sales: Laura Karet
SVP and CFO: Mark Minnaugh
SVP and CIO: Russell (Russ) Ross
SVP, Distribution and Logistics: Larry Baldauf
SVP, Marketing: Kevin Srigley
SVP, Real Estate: Shelly Sponholz
SVP, Marketing: Brett L. Merrell
VP, Application Engineering: Mike Krugle
VP, Meat, Seafood, and Prepared Foods: Ed Steinmetz
VP, Columbus Operations: David (Dave) Daniel
VP, Fuels and Convenience: Daniel (Dan) Pastor
VP, Logistics: Bill Parry
VP, Pharmacy: Randy Heiser
VP, Retail Operations: Bill Artman
Director, Marketing: Rob Borella
Director, Human Resources Services: Vicki Clites

LOCATIONS

HQ: Giant Eagle, Inc.
101 Kappa Dr., Pittsburgh, PA 15238
Phone: 412-963-6200   Fax: 412-968-1617
Web: www.gianteagle.com

2008 Stores

	No.
Ohio	121
Pennsylvania	98
West Virginia	2
Maryland	2
Total	**223**

PRODUCTS/OPERATIONS

2008 Stores

	No.
Company-owned	158
Franchised	65
Total	**223**

Selected Private-Label Brands

Giant Eagle
Market District
Nature's Basket

Selected Services

Bakery
Banking services
Childcare
Deli department
Dry cleaning
Fresh seafood
Greeting cards
Pharmacy
Photo developing
Ready-to-eat meals
Ticketmaster outlet
Video rental

COMPETITORS

7-Eleven
Costco Wholesale
CVS Caremark
Giant Food
Heinen's
IGA
Kroger
Shop 'n Save
SUPERVALU
Target
Uni-Marts
Walgreen
Wal-Mart
Wegmans
Weis Markets
Whole Foods

Gibson Guitar

Real pickers put Gibson Guitar on a pedestal. Though it trails top guitar maker Fender, Gibson builds instruments that are held in unparalleled esteem by many guitarists, including top professional musicians. The company's most popular guitar is the legendary Les Paul. Gibson also makes guitars under such brands as Epiphone, Kramer, and Steinberger. In addition to guitars, the company makes pianos through its Baldwin unit, Slingerland drums, Tobias bass, Wurlitzer vending machines and jukeboxes, and Echoplex amplifiers, as well as many accessory items. Company namesake Orville Gibson began making mandolins in the late 1890s. Gibson Guitar is owned by executives Henry Juszkiewicz and David Berryman.

Gibson's core business continues to focus on challenging such rivals as Fender, Martin, and Taylor for a greater share of the guitar market. To get the word out about its products and attract customers, the company has traditionally relied on word-of-mouth between players and endorsement deals with top-selling musicians. However, Gibson struck a lucrative marketing deal with Universal Studios in 2005, acquiring the naming rights to the 33-year-old Universal Amphitheatre at the company's Southern California theme park. The 10-year deal, worth about $14 million, not only gives the instrument maker brand visibility in an important market but also opens the door to product placement in TV and film projects.

The company's long-range sights, though, are set on top musical instrument maker Yamaha. Through its acquisition of famous brand names, from Baldwin to Wurlitzer, and its reintroduction of others, such as Epiphone, Gibson has expanded its product lines beyond the core guitar market and continues to develop new product lines. Juszkiewicz sees a lot of potential in using technology to update designs that have not significantly changed since the 1950s. The firm introduced a digital guitar in 2004 that looks and feels like a conventional electric guitar but converts string vibrations into a data stream using Gibson's proprietary MaGIC (media-accelerated global information carrier) technology. The company also hopes to license MaGIC to manufacturers for use in consumer electronics.

Gibson's growth also has expanded the business from its Nashville roots and it now boasts a global presence. The company has a manufacturing plant in China to make Epiphone guitars and it has a majority stake in Baldwin Zhongshan China, a joint venture formed in 2004 with Zhongshan Yue Hua Piano and Musical Instruments. To strengthen its foothold in China and significantly expand its manufacturing capacity there, Gibson in late 2006 acquired a major player in China's piano market — Dongbei Piano Co., Ltd. Gibson renamed the firm Baldwin-Dongbei Piano & Musical Instruments Co., Ltd. In 2005 the company acquired full ownership of Gibson Med, a key European distributor based in Milan, Italy. In July 2006 Gibson acquired Deutsche Wurlitzer from Nelson Group Overseas after years of litigation between the two regarding use of the Wurlitzer name. The deal brings Wurlitzer Jukebox and Vending Electronics into Gibson's fold.

In North America, Gibson is expanding its manufacturing capacity in Canada, as well as its Gibson Acoustic division. In mid-2007 the instrument manufacturer acquired Canada's Garrison Guitars, which is best known for the Griffiths Active Bracing System and its innovative guitar construction. Gibson plans to use the purchase to boost its median-priced guitar portfolio and grab a larger share of the acoustic guitar market. As part of the agreement, Gibson will expand Garrison's factory in Newfoundland.

Juszkiewicz and Berryman bought Gibson for $5 million in 1986.

EXECUTIVES

Chairman and CEO, Gibson Guitar and Baldwin Piano:
Henry E. Juszkiewicz, age 54
President: David H. (Dave) Berryman
EVP Outreach Marketing: Caroline Galloway
SVP Sales and Marketing Administration:
Roger Mitchell
VP Chief Global Sales: Dana Barrette
CFO: Tom Beyer
CTO: Michael Johnson
General Counsel: Barbara O'Connell
General Manager, Custom Division:
Richard (Rick) Gembar
General Manager, Gibson USA: Jim Bitterle
General Manager, Gibson Acoustic: Doug Koffinke
General Manager, Epiphone: Jim Rosenberg
Auditors: Grant Thornton

LOCATIONS

HQ: Gibson Guitar Corp.
309 Plus Park Blvd., Nashville, TN 37217
Phone: 615-871-4500   **Fax:** 615-889-5509
Web: www.gibson.com

PRODUCTS/OPERATIONS

Selected Products
Amplifiers
Guitars
Pianos and consumer products
Other products
  Accessories
  Equipment
    Echoplex (sound processing equipment)
    Maestro (guitar effects pedals)
    Oberheim (sound processing equipment)

COMPETITORS

All A Cart Manufacturing	Korg
Allen Organ Company	LaSiDo
C. F. Martin & Co.	Line 6
Carvin	LOUD Technologies
CASIO COMPUTER	The Music Link
Crane Co.	Musicorp
D'Addario	Peavey Electronics
Ernie Ball	PRS
Fender Musical	QSC Audio
Instruments	Rickenbacker
Ford Gum & Machine	Roland Corporation
Company	Samick
GHS	St. Louis Music
Harman International	Steinway
Hoshino (U.S.A.)	Taylor Guitars
Kaman Music	US Music
Kawai	Whirlpool
K.H.S. Musical Instrument	Yamaha

Gilbane, Inc.

Family-owned Gilbane has been the bane of its rivals for four generations. Subsidiary Gilbane Building provides construction management, contracting, and design and build services to construct office buildings, manufacturing plants, schools, prisons, and more for the firm's governmental, commercial, and industrial clients. Landmark projects include work on the National Air and Space Museum, Lake Placid's 1980 Winter Olympics facilities, and the World War II memorial and Capitol Visitors Center in Washington, DC. Another subsidiary, Gilbane Development Company, develops and finances public and private projects and acts as a property manager. William Gilbane founded the firm in 1873.

The company also includes Gilbane University, an in-house training program that offers more than 500 courses to assist new employees with construction and technical skills development. In 2007 Gilbane spent nearly $8 million to train its employees and views the investment as a way to attract and retain its workforce.

EXECUTIVES

Chairman: Paul J. Choquette Jr., age 69
President and CEO; Chairman and CEO, Gilbane Building Company: Thomas F. (Tom) Gilbane Jr., age 60
VP; President and CEO, Gilbane Development: Robert V. Gilbane
VP; President and COO, Gilbane Building Company: William J. Gilbane Jr., age 61
VP: Robert C. Zerbe
VP and Regional Operations Manager, Delaware: Stephen J. O'Connor

LOCATIONS

HQ: Gilbane, Inc.
7 Jackson Walkway, Providence, RI 02903
Phone: 401-456-5800   **Fax:** 401-456-5936
Web: www.gilbaneinc.com

PRODUCTS/OPERATIONS

Selected Markets
Aviation
Corporate
Criminal justice
Cultural
Education
Government
Health care
Life sciences
Pharmaceutical
Public assembly
Recreation
Sports
Technology
Transportation

COMPETITORS

Barton Malow	KBR
BE&K	M. A. Mortenson
Bechtel	McCarthy Building
Bernards Brothers	Parsons Corporation
Bovis Lend Lease	Perini
Centex	Skanska USA Building
Clark Enterprises	Structure Tone
Fluor	Swinerton
Hunt Construction	Turner Corporation
Jacobs Engineering	Whiting-Turner

Company Type: Private

Income Statement
FYE: December 31

	REVENUE ($ mil.)	NET INCOME ($ mil.)	NET PROFIT MARGIN	EMPLOYEES
12/07	2,970	—	—	2,180
12/06	2,790	—	—	2,024
12/05	2,832	—	—	1,800
12/04	2,580	—	—	1,757
12/03	2,100	—	—	1,700
Annual Growth	9.1%	—	—	6.4%

Revenue History

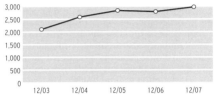

Glazer's Wholesale Drug

Glazer's Wholesale Drug, named during Prohibition when only drugstores and drug wholesalers could deal in liquor, is a wholesale distributor of alcoholic beverages. In Texas it is the largest company of its kind and one of the largest wine and spirits distributors in the US. The company distributes Robert Mondavi wines, Brown-Forman and Bacardi spirits, and Diageo products. CEO Bennett Glazer and his family own Glazer's. The company's origins date back to the early 1900s when the Glazer family sold flavored soda water, which it distributed using horse-drawn wagons.

Growth is Glazer's game. In 2003 Glazer's bought a 50% stake in Union Beverage Co. (a subsidiary of National Wine & Spirits, Inc.) to move distribution into Illinois. Later that year the company became the sole provider of Diageo brands in Dallas and Houston as part of Diageo's consolidation of its Texas distributors. Glazer's has been acquiring wholesalers and distributors in the Midwest, including Mid-Continent Distributor (Missouri). Glazer's is expanding in Oklahoma, having bought Reliance Wine & Spirits Co. It also has purchased Hirst Imports Co. In Arkansas, Glazer's is consolidating three distributors: Little Rock-Silbernagel, Barrett Hamilton, and Strauss Distributors. In the Midwest it bought up Olinger Distributors.

Founded in Dallas in 1933, the third generation of Glazers run this family-owned business.

EXECUTIVES

Chairman and Treasurer: R.L. Glazer
Chairman and CEO: Bennett J. Glazer
President: Jerry Cargill
EVP and COO: Mike Maxwell
EVP and Director: Barkley J. Stuart
EVP and Director: Mike Glazer
EVP and CFO: Cary Rossel

SVP Corporate Strategy and Business Intelligence: Louis Zweig
SVP Off-Premise National Accounts; President, Southwest Region: Don Pratt
SVP Growth and Business Development: Mike Lakusta
SVP Operations, Finance, and Administration: Phil Meacham
SVP Marketing: Jim Reichardt
SVP Human Resources and Development: Kristin Snyder
Director Human Resources: Rusty Harmount

LOCATIONS

HQ: Glazer's Wholesale Drug Company, Inc.
14911 Quorum Dr., Ste. 400, Dallas, TX 75254
Phone: 972-392-8200   **Fax:** 972-702-8508
Web: www.glazers.com

PRODUCTS/OPERATIONS

Selected Operations
Advantage Wine Sales & Marketing
Alliance Beverage Distributing Company (50-50 joint venture with Charmer Sunbelt Arizona)
Glazer's Domains & Estates
In Vie

COMPETITORS

Allied Beverage Group
Ben E. Keith
E. & J. Gallo
Gambrinus
Georgia Crown
Hensley & Company
Johnson Brothers
National Distributing
National Wine & Spirits
Premier Beverage Company
Republic National Distributing Company
Southern Wine & Spirits
Sunbelt Beverage
Tarrant Distributors
Wirtz Corporation
Young's Market

HISTORICAL FINANCIALS
Company Type: Private

Income Statement
FYE: December 31

	REVENUE ($ mil.)	NET INCOME ($ mil.)	NET PROFIT MARGIN	EMPLOYEES
12/07	3,150	—	—	5,900
12/06	3,000	—	—	5,800
12/05	2,900	—	—	5,800
12/04	2,800	—	—	5,800
12/03	2,200	—	—	5,500
Annual Growth	9.4%	—	—	1.8%

Revenue History

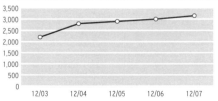

Global Hyatt

Travelers interested in luxury lodgings can check in for the Hyatt touch. Global Hyatt is one of the world's top operators of full-service luxury hotels and resorts with more than 700 locations in some 40 countries. Its core Hyatt Regency brand offers hospitality services targeted primarily to business travelers and upscale vacationers. The firm also operates properties under the names Grand Hyatt, Park Hyatt, Hyatt Place, Hyatt Summerfield Suites, Hyatt Resorts, and Andaz. Its resort destinations offer golf, spas, and other upmarket rest and relaxation activities. Although Global Hyatt was formed in 2004, the Hyatt chain traces its roots back to 1957. It is owned by the wealthy Pritzker family of Chicago.

As part of an ongoing effort to restructure H Group Holding, the holding company that oversees the family's various business enterprises, Global Hyatt was formed to consolidate the Pritzker's hospitality interests. The reorganization brought together the operations of Hyatt Hotels Corporation (domestic hotels), Hyatt International (international hotels), Hyatt Equities (hotel ownership), and Hyatt Vacation Ownership (timeshares) under one umbrella. In 2007, Hyatt launched Andaz, a new luxury hotel brand.

Global Hyatt has been busy expanding beyond the luxury segment, investing in the growth of its Hyatt Place banner, a new brand designed to attract younger travelers with wireless Internet access, flat screen televisions, and contemporary interiors. The limited-service chain was rebranded from AmeriSuites, a banner Hyatt acquired in 2005 from Prime Hospitality. The company is also growing its Hyatt Summerfield Suites chain, an upscale all-suite/extended-stay brand previously known as Summerfield Suites (acquired from The Blackstone Group in 2006).

As part of an effort to focus on its growth businesses, the company sold its U.S. Franchise Systems subsidiary in 2008 to Wyndham Worldwide for about $150 million. The unit, acquired in 2000, operated the smaller Hawthorn Suites and Microtel Inns & Suites chains.

HISTORY

Nicholas Pritzker left Kiev for Chicago in 1881, where his family's ascent to the ranks of America's wealthiest families began. His son A. N. left the family law practice in the 1930s and began investing in a variety of businesses. He turned a 1942 investment (Cory Corporation) worth $25,000 into $23 million by 1967. A. N.'s son Jay followed in his father's wheeling-and-dealing footsteps. In 1953, with the help of his father's banking connections, Jay purchased Colson Company and recruited his brother Bob, an industrial engineer, to restructure a company that made tricycles and US Navy rockets. By 1990 Jay and Bob had added 60 industrial companies, with annual sales exceeding $3 billion, to the entity they called The Marmon Group.

The family's connection to Hyatt hotels was established in 1957 when Jay Pritzker bought a hotel called Hyatt House, located near the Los Angeles airport, from Hyatt von Dehn. Jay added five locations by 1961 and hired his gregarious youngest brother, Donald, to manage the hotel company. Hyatt went public in 1967, but the move that opened new vistas for the hotel chain was the purchase that year of an 800-room hotel in Atlanta that both Hilton and Marriott had turned down.

John Portman's design, incorporating a 21-story atrium, a large fountain, and a revolving rooftop restaurant, became a Hyatt trademark.

The Pritzkers formed Hyatt International in 1969 to operate hotels overseas, and the company grew rapidly in the US and abroad during the 1970s. Donald Pritzker died in 1972, and Jay assumed control of Hyatt. The family decided to take the company private in 1979. Much of Hyatt's growth in the 1970s came from contracts to manage Hyatt hotels built by other investors. When Hyatt's earnings on those contracts shrank in the 1980s, the company launched its own hotel and resort developments under Nick Pritzker, a cousin to Jay and Bob. In 1988, with US and Japanese partners, it built the Hyatt Regency Waikoloa on Hawaii's Big Island for $360 million — a record at the time for a hotel.

The Pritzkers took a side-venture into air travel in 1983 when they bought bedraggled Braniff Airlines through Hyatt subsidiaries as it emerged from bankruptcy. After a failed 1987 attempt to merge the airline with Pan Am, the Pritzkers sold Braniff in 1988.

Hyatt opened Classic Residence by Hyatt, a group of upscale retirement communities, in 1989. The company joined Circus Circus (now part of MGM MIRAGE) in 1994 to launch the Grand Victoria, the nation's largest cruising gaming vessel. The next year, as part of a new strategy to manage both freestanding golf courses and those near Hyatt hotels, the company opened its first freestanding course: an 18-hole, par 71 championship course in Aruba.

President Thomas Pritzker, Jay's son, took over as Hyatt chairman and CEO following his father's death in early 1999. In 2000 Hyatt announced plans to join rival Marriott International in launching an independent company to provide an online procurement network serving the hospitality industry. The Pritzker family that year led a buyout of U.S. Franchise Systems (sold to Wyndham Worldwide in 2008). The following year the company announced plans to build a 47-story skyscraper in downtown Chicago. Construction for the new building, named the Hyatt Center, began at the end of 2002.

In 2004 the Pritzker family consolidated its hospitality holdings to form Global Hyatt Corporation. The following year the company bought the AmeriSuites limited-service hotel chain from Prime Hospitality.

Mark Hoplamazian, president of The Pritzker Organization, a merchant-banking firm serving the family's business activities, took over as president and CEO in 2006; Thomas Prtizker remained chairman.

EXECUTIVES

Chairman, Global Hyatt and Hyatt International: Thomas J. (Tom) Pritzker, age 58
Vice Chairman; Chairman and CEO, Hyatt Development and Hyatt Equities: Nicholas J. (Nick) Pritzker
President and CEO: Mark S. Hoplamazian, age 44
CFO: Harmit Singh
EVP Global Real Estate and Development: Stephen G. (Steve) Haggerty
SVP and General Counsel: Susan T. Smith, age 53
SVP Real Estate and Development, The Americas: James R. (Jim) Abrahamson, age 49
SVP Real Estate and Development, North America Division, Western Region: Christopher (Chris) Ivy
SVP Real Estate and Development, North America Division, Eastern Region: David Tarr
Chief Marketing Officer: Thomas F. (Tom) O'Toole, age 50
VP Corporate Communications: Katie Meyer
VP Finance: Kirk A. Rose, age 48
Director Corporate Public Relations: Lori Alexander

President, Hyatt Hotels: Edward W. Rabin Jr., age 61
President, Hyatt International: Bernd O. Chorengel
EVP and COO, Hyatt Hotels: Chuck Floyd, age 47
SVP Field Operations, Hyatt Hotels: Pete Sears
VP Human Resources, Hyatt Hotels: Doug Patrick
VP Marketing, Hyatt Hotels: Amy Weyman
SVP Operations, North America, Hyatt Hotels and Resorts: David R. Phillips
SVP Brand Communication, Hyatt Hotels and Resorts: Amy Curtis-McIntyre

LOCATIONS

HQ: Global Hyatt Corporation
71 S. Wacker Dr., Chicago, IL 60606
Phone: 312-750-1234   **Fax:** 312-750-8550
Web: www.hyatt.com

PRODUCTS/OPERATIONS

Selected Brands
Andaz (luxury hotels)
Hyatt Regency (core hotel format)
Hyatt Summerfield Suites (extended stay)
Hyatt Vacation Ownership (timeshares)

COMPETITORS

Accor
Carlson Hotels
Club Med
Four Seasons Hotels
Hilton Hotels
InterContinental Hotels
LXR Luxury Resorts
Marriott
Millennium & Copthorne Hotels
Sonesta International Hotels
Starwood Hotels & Resorts
Wyndham Worldwide

GNC Corporation

What's good for the customer is good for GNC Corporation (formerly General Nutrition Centers). With more than 6,150 company-owned and franchised outlets in all 50 US states and Canada and franchised stores in some 50 foreign markets, GNC is the leading nutritional-supplements retail chain devoted solely to items such as vitamins and dietary products. The company also has about 1,350 stores within Rite Aid drugstores and makes Rite Aid private-label products. GNC has been closing underperforming stores located in the US. GNC's online partner is drugstore.com. In 2007 Apollo Advisors sold the firm to Ontario Teachers' Pension Plan and Ares Management, a US private equity firm, for about $1.6 billion.

Previously, GNC had filed to go public in June 2006, but withdrew the offering two months later citing market conditions. (GNC had planned to offer 23.5 million shares at $16-$18 a share.)

Facing increased competition from mass merchants like Wal-Mart, which advertise low prices, GNC has worked to shed its "muscle head" image by redesigning all of its US stores, which measure between 1,000 and 2,000 sq. ft. By attracting more women and seniors into its shops, the company hopes to increase its share of the nutritional supplement market. The company has also pumped up its Web site, gnc.com, with

e-commerce capabilities; the site is operated by GSI Commerce.

A deal inked in August 2007 with Rite Aid extends its previous 1998 agreement to build GNC LiveWell stores-within-a-store. As part of the partnership extension, GNC will create 1,125 more stores within Rite Aid locations nationwide by the end of 2014.

GNC's private-label brands (about 48% of sales) include Mega Men and Pro Performance targeted at 18-to-49-year-old males and Body Answers, a diet product marketed to women. In addition to providing Rite Aid with private-label vitamins and nutritional supplements, GNC produces a line of co-branded vitamins and supplements for Rite Aid called PharmAssure.

EXECUTIVES

Chairman: Norman Axelrod, age 55
CEO and Director: Joseph (Joe) Fortunato, age 54, $399,519 pay
President, Chief Merchandising and Marketing Officer, and Director: Beth J. Kaplan, age 49
EVP and CFO: Michael Nuzzo
EVP Store Operations and Development: Tom Dowd, age 44
SVP, Human Resources and Customer Service: Eileen D. Scott, age 51
SVP Manufacturing: Michael Locke, age 62, $235,355 pay
SVP, Product Development and National Sales Director: Margaret A. Peet
SVP, Chief Legal Officer, and Secretary: Gerald J. Stubenhofer Jr., age 38
SVP Scientific Affairs: Guru Ramanathan, age 44
Senior Director, Corporate Communications: Benjamin Pratt
Auditors: PricewaterhouseCoopers LLP

LOCATIONS

HQ: GNC Corporation
300 6th Ave., Pittsburgh, PA 15222
Phone: 412-288-4600   **Fax:** 412-288-4764
Web: www.gnc.com

2007 Stores

	No.
US	
Company-owned	2,598
Within Rite Aid	1,358
Franchised	978
Canada	147
International	1,078
Total	**6,159**

PRODUCTS/OPERATIONS

2007 Sales

	No.
Retail	75
Franchise	16
Manufacturing & wholesale	9
Total	**100**

2007 US Retail Sales

	$ mil.	% of total
Vitamins, minerals & herbal supplements	431.7	41
Sports nutrition products	376.6	36
Diet products	152.4	14
Other	94.0	9
Total	**1,054.7**	**100**

Selected Proprietary Brand Names
Body Answers
Mega Men
Preventive Nutrition
Pro Performance
Ultra Mega

COMPETITORS

Alticor	Planet Organic Health
Bactolac Pharmaceutical	Safeway
Bayer AG	Shaklee
CVS Caremark	Slim-Fast
Duane Reade	Sunrider
Forever Living	Trader Joe's
Jenny Craig	Tree of Life
Kroger	United Natural
Mannatech	VS Holdings
NAI	Walgreen
Nature's Sunshine	Wal-Mart
NBTY	Whole Foods
Nu Skin	Wyeth
Pfizer	

HISTORICAL FINANCIALS

Company Type: Private

Income Statement

FYE: December 31

	REVENUE ($ mil.)	NET INCOME ($ mil.)	NET PROFIT MARGIN	EMPLOYEES
12/07	1,553	(32)	—	13,239
12/06	1,487	37	2.5%	12,707
12/05	1,318	18	1.4%	12,415
12/04	1,345	42	3.1%	13,618
12/03	1,430	(585)	—	14,251
Annual Growth	2.1%	—	—	(1.8%)

Net Income History

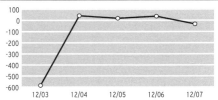

Go Daddy

Go Daddy, go! Go Daddy provides individuals and businesses with domain name registration, Web site hosting, and related services and software such as spam-protected e-mail, secure socket layer (SSL) certificates, and Web-site creation tools. With its discounted pricing on domain names and hosting services, Go Daddy has become the largest domain registrar in the world, with more than 29 million domain names. The company has affiliates that address market niches in site registration and hosting, including Domains By Proxy and Wild West Domains, all of which are accredited by ICANN, the international regulatory body for the public Internet. CEO Bob Parsons owns the company, which he founded in 1997.

The company has experienced rapid growth in its short history, and has raised its public profile in recent years with an advertising campaign that has included controversial Super Bowl commercials.

Go Daddy filed to go public in 2006, but later withdrew, citing unfavorable market conditions.

EXECUTIVES

Chairman and CEO: Robert R. (Bob) Parsons
President and COO: Warren J. Adelman, age 42
EVP: Barbara J. (Barb) Rechterman
CFO: Michael J. Zimmerman
General Counsel: Christine N. Jones
VP Marketing: Theresa J. (Teri) D'Hooge
VP Corporate Development and Policy:
Timothy J. (Tim) Ruiz
VP Technical Operations and Chief Information Security Officer: Neil G. Warner
Communications Manager: Nick Fuller
Auditors: Ernst & Young LLP

LOCATIONS

HQ: The Go Daddy Group, Inc.
14455 N. Hayden Rd., Ste. 219,
Scottsdale, AZ 85260
Phone: 480-505-8800   **Fax:** 480-505-8844
Web: www.godaddy.com

PRODUCTS/OPERATIONS

Selected Services

Domain name registration, auctions, tranfers
E-commerce tools
E-mail management
Security management
Web site development tools and hosting

COMPETITORS

Google	United Internet
Microsoft	Verio
Network Solutions	VeriSign
Register.com	Web.com Inc
Tucows	Yahoo!

Golden Horizons

GGNSC Holdings is a holding company doing business as Golden Horizons. The firm operates hundreds of nursing homes and assisted living facilities across the US, most of them company-owned and others leased. Its company-owned facilities go by the name Golden Living, while its leased ones operate under the Beverly brand, a nod to the company's former existence as Beverly Enterprises. All told, Golden Horizons runs about 350 nursing homes and 20 assisted living centers. It was taken private in 2006, when private investor Fillmore Capital Partners bought it for more than $2 billion. It subsequently changed its name to Golden Horizons and re-branded all its company-owned operations under the "Golden" moniker.

In addition to its senior living facilities, Golden Horizons has several other subsidiaries that provide auxiliary health services and administrative services to its own and third-party nursing facilities. Its auxiliary services unit, called Golden Innovations, offers rehabilitation, hospice, staffing, and other services under a number of names, including Aegis, Asera, Aedon, and Vizia Design. Golden Ventures is the name of the company's administrative services division.

Beginning in early 2005 investor group Formation Capital, which owned 8% of Beverly, proposed a $1.5 billion takeover, but the unsolicited bid was rejected. Beverly then put itself on the auction block and a bidding war ensued between North American Senior Care and Formation Capital. However, it was Fillmore Capital that eventually won out.

In 2006 the company settled an investigation by the Justice Department, which had alleged that its erstwhile medical equipment subsidiary MK Medical had fraudulently billed Medicare and Medi-Cal (a California social service program) without doing the proper paperwork. The company agreed to pay $20 million to federal and state authorities to keep the issue from going to court.

HISTORY

In 1963 Utah accountant Roy Christensen founded Beverly as three convalescent hospitals near Beverly Hills, California. The emergence of Medicare and Medicaid in the 1960s fueled the firm's growth. Beverly also dabbled in mirrors, plastics, real estate, and printing before going public in 1966.

Beverly sobered up to losses and industrywide overexpansion by the early 1970s. The company turned to investment firm Stephens to ward off a takeover. Beverly doubled in size in 1977, buying Leisure Lodges nursing homes from Stephens in exchange for 23% of Beverly. Acquisitions pushed Beverly into the #1 nursing home spot by 1983 (by then, Stephens had sold out for a tidy profit). Beverly also diversified, starting its Pharmacy Corporation of America (PCA) institutional pharmacy unit.

Management later wrestled with labor unrest, allegations of patient neglect (including the company's implication in patients' deaths in California and Minnesota), and systemic problems with Medicaid. Beverly again turned to Stephens in the late 1980s to ward off another takeover and to shake up management.

An inventive late 1980s plan to restructure debt by selling nursing homes cast a cloud over some of those involved in it, including lawyers from Little Rock's Rose Law Firm (William Kennedy and Vince Foster, who would later become White House counsels, and Webster Hubbell, who would become an assistant attorney general before being convicted of financial irregularities at Rose). A loophole let Beverly sell unprofitable Arkansas and Iowa nursing homes to not-for-profit shell organizations, which bought them with funds raised through tax-free bonds. An $86 million sale was completed in Iowa. After public outcry, the Arkansas deal was killed by then-Governor Bill Clinton.

In 1990 Beverly's headquarters moved to Arkansas, near Stephens' Little Rock home. Beverly decentralized management of its 883 nursing homes (a move it would later try to use to shield it from liability in labor violations) and began selling some assets. In the mid-1990s Beverly sought relief in higher-margin businesses (post-acute care hospitals, pharmacy services, rehab and respiratory therapy). In 1996 Beverly backed out of managed care; divestitures included PCA. Beverly also exited Texas' punitive regulatory environment, selling 49 nursing homes in the state.

In 1993 the National Labor Relations Board (NLRB) concluded the company had illegally stifled workers' attempts to organize; a similar complaint was filed in 1996. (The company dismissed the NLRB's decisions as "fundamentally flawed.") In 1998 the company filed, then withdrew, a slander suit against a Cornell professor who characterized Beverly as "one of the nation's most notorious labor-law violators."

Beverly set records for punitive damages in 1997 and 1998, suffering $70 million and $95 million judgments (later reduced to $54 million and $3 million, respectively) relating to patient neglect.

Having whittled its nursing homes down to about 560 in 1999 and losing the top spot to Sun Healthcare, Beverly braced itself for a period of austerity as Medicare inaugurated its per-procedure billing method in 1999, the same year the federal government announced it was investigating Beverly's Medicare billings back to 1990. The government charged that Beverly was systematically falsifying records to defraud Medicare. As a result, in 2000 the firm agreed to pay $175 million in restitution (paid over eight years through Medicare reimbursement garnishments) and sell 10 facilities belonging to a California-based subsidiary that were disqualified from federal health insurance programs as part of their punishment for falsifying reimbursement claims.

In 2002 Beverly shed its Florida operations due to high insurance-liability costs in the state. Beverly divested its Washington and Arizona operations, and reduced its California operations by 50% due to patient liability costs.

In 2004 Beverly sold more than 80 nursing homes and its MATRIX Rehabilitation subsidiary, which operated outpatient therapy clinics specializing in occupational health and sports medicine. The nursing home divestitures were part of Beverly's strategy to offset the decline in Medicare payments caused by the government's decision, implemented in 1999, to reimburse operators per procedure, not actual costs.

More sales were completed that year as the company pursued more profitable eldercare service businesses such as hospices. In August 2004 Beverly completed the purchase of Hospice USA, which offers hospice services in 18 locations in Alabama, Mississippi, and Tennessee.

EXECUTIVES

President and CEO: Neil Kurtz
EVP and CFO: Richard D. Skelly Jr.
EVP and Chief Administrative Officer:
Lawrence (Larry) Deans, age 53
SVP and Treasurer: Michael Morton
SVP, Controller, and Chief Accounting Officer:
Belinda Marcotte
SVP and Chief Legal Officer: David Beck, age 53
**SVP Government Relations & International
Development:** Jack MacDonald
SVP Sales and Marketing: Harold A. (Hal) Price
SVP Procurement; President, Ceres Purchasing:
Ramon Rodriguez, age 47
SVP Clinical Services and Quality of Life Programs:
Andrea J. Ludington, age 62
SVP Compliance, Golden Ventures: Becky Bodie
SVP Human Resources & Administration:
Michael Karicher, age 39
SVP Skilled Nursing Facility: Kevin Roberts, age 55
SVP and CIO: John Derr
SVP Litigation: Paul Killeen
SVP State Government Relations: Paul Goss
President and CEO, Golden Innovations:
Cindy H. Susienka
President, Aegis Acute Rehab and Aegis Therapies:
Martha J. Schram
President, AseraCare Hospice: Robert Donovan

LOCATIONS

HQ: GGNSC Holdings LLC
1000 Fianna Way, Fort Smith, AR 72919
Phone: 479-201-2000   **Fax:** 479-201-1101
Web: www.goldenliving.com/Golden+Ventures

COMPETITORS

Assisted Living Concepts	Mariner Health Care
Emeritus Corporation	National HealthCare
Extendicare	Odyssey HealthCare
Five Star Quality Care	Skilled Healthcare Group
Genesis HealthCare	Sun Healthcare
Kindred Healthcare	Sunrise Senior Living
Life Care Centers	VITAS Healthcare
Manor Care	

HISTORICAL FINANCIALS

Company Type: Private

Income Statement

FYE: December 31

	ESTIMATED REVENUE ($ mil.)	NET INCOME ($ mil.)	NET PROFIT MARGIN	EMPLOYEES
12/07	2,490	—	—	41,000
12/06	2,500	—	—	40,000
Annual Growth	(0.4%)	—	—	2.5%

Revenue History

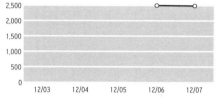

2,500				
2,000				
1,500				
1,000				
500				
0				
	12/03	12/04	12/05	12/06	12/07

Golden State Foods

You might say this company helps make the Golden Arches shine. Golden State Foods is a leading food service supplier that primarily supplies McDonald's restaurants with more than 130 products, including beef patties, Big Mac sauce (which it helped formulate), buns, ketchup, and mayonnaise. It distributes goods to more than 20,000 quick-service eateries from about 15 distribution centers, including one in Egypt. In addition, the company runs a non-profit organization, the GSF Foundation, that supports local charities focused on helping children and families. Founded in 1947 by the late William Moore, Golden State Foods is controlled by Wetterau Associates, an investment group led by CEO Mark Wetterau.

The company is a leading supplier to about 9,300 McDonald's locations throughout the US and works closely with the fast-food giant to maintain standards. The two companies have enjoyed a long relationship that began in the 1950s and was later sealed with a handshake between Moore and fast-food pioneer Ray Kroc in the 1960s. As an indication of McDonald's loyalty to its suppliers, they continue to do business without the benefit of a long-term contract.

Golden State has a joint venture with Salinas, California-based grower Taylor Fresh Foods, through which it supplies McDonald's with fresh produce.

While the Golden Arches is still the company's main customer, Golden State Foods has diversified its customer base in the past several years and now supplies outposts of other fast food chains, including Arby's, KFC, and Popeyes. It

also provides paper products and baked goods to some Starbucks locations.

During 2006 the company opened a new distribution center in City of Industry, California; the 270,000-sq.-ft. facility is the largest in the McDonald's supply chain. Golden State Foods also acquired two additional facilities from HAVI Group in Illinois and Wisconsin that year.

Wetterau led a management buyout of the company in 2004, acquiring the 50% stake formerly owned by investment firm Yucaipa Companies.

HISTORY

In 1947 William Moore founded Golden State Meat, a small meat-supply business that served restaurants and hotels in the Los Angeles area. In 1954 he added several new clients to his business — franchisees of a new chain of hamburger stands called McDonald's that was founded in San Bernardino, California in 1948. In 1961 Ray Kroc, a franchisee from Illinois, bought out the founding McDonald brothers, and the next year he moved to California to oversee a massive expansion in that state.

Moore and Kroc met, were mutually impressed, and became friends. Moore, at first, tried to get Kroc to buy him out, but Kroc's view of McDonald's did not include micromanaging its supply operations. He wanted to find suppliers the company could trust, and preferred smaller ones that weren't intent on breaking into the retail market. Golden State's relationship with McDonald's was sealed by a handshake between Kroc and Moore.

Moore and a partner bought a McDonald's franchise in 1965; two years later they had five. When Moore's partner died, McDonald's bought the units back for stock, which Moore later sold, using the proceeds to finance a new meat processing plant and warehouse. In 1969 Golden State Meat incorporated as Golden State Foods.

In 1972, after the new facilities were completed, Moore introduced the idea of total distribution. In addition to processing and distributing meat (by now delivered as frozen patties rather than fresh meat, which had limited delivery ranges in the 1950s and 1960s), Moore began supplying most of the needs of the McDonald's stores, making and delivering ketchup, mayonnaise, packaging, and syrup base for soft drinks. This allowed clients to reduce the number of weekly deliveries they received from as many as 30 to about three. The company went public in 1972, and two years later it dropped all of its other clients to cater exclusively to McDonald's.

Golden State grew in the 1970s, supplying a large share of the millions of McDonald's hamburgers sold every day. Moore died in 1978. Soon thereafter, a group of executives led by newly appointed CEO James Williams began exploring the possibility of taking the company private. In 1980, with backing from Butler Capital, they paid $29 million for the company, which then had sales of $330 million.

During the next decade Golden State expanded its relationship with McDonald's (and with the buying co-ops that supply stores operated by franchisees), opening facilities in other parts of the country. In 1990 the owners of Golden State tried to cash out by putting the company up for sale, but they withdrew it from the market within two years.

Golden State moved its headquarters from Pasadena to Irvine in 1992. In 1996 the company opened a distribution center in Portland, Oregon, and international expansion followed.

Yucaipa and Wetterau Associates, whose management hailed from a major Midwestern food wholesaler sold to SUPERVALU in 1992, bought Golden State in 1998 for about $400 million. The purchase represented Yucaipa's first significant acquisition outside the supermarket arena. James Williams, who had been with Golden State Foods for 38 years and served as its CEO for more than two decades, resigned in 1999. He was replaced by Mark Wetterau, a partner in Wetterau Associates along with his brother Conrad Wetterau.

In early 2004 Wetterau bought the 50% stake in Golden State Foods held by investor Ron Burkle and his Yucaipa investment firm for $110 million.

EXECUTIVES

Chairman, President, and CEO: Mark S. Wetterau, age 49
Vice Chairman: Michael L. (Mike) Waitukaitis
Corporate SEVP Operations: Frank Listi
CFO: Richard D. (Rich) Moretti
Corporate VP Human Resources: Steve Becker
Corporate VP International: Phillip Crane
Corporate VP Worldwide Sales and Marketing: Larry McGill
Corporate SVP; President, Distribution Group: Robert (Bob) Jorge
Corporate VP; President, Liquid Products Group: John Pooley
Corporate VP and General Counsel: John Page
Corporate VP Finance: Bill Sanderson
CIO: Pandora Ovanessian
Group VP Meat Products Group: Wayne Morgan
Group VP National Accounts: Brian Dick
Group VP McDonald's Business: Paul Sestak
VP Global Quality and Food Safety: Marty Hudak-Roos
Senior Corporate Communications Director: Shellie Frey

LOCATIONS

HQ: Golden State Foods Corp.
18301 Von Karman Ave., Ste. 1100, Irvine, CA 92612
Phone: 949-252-2000   **Fax:** 949-252-2080
Web: www.goldenstatefoods.com

Selected Distribution Locations

Cairo, Egypt
City of Industry, CA
Greensboro, NC
Henderson, NV
Lemont, IL
Lexington, SC
Phoenix
Portland, OR
Rochester, NY
San Antonio
Suffolk, VA
Sumner, WA
Waipahu, HI
Whitewater, WI

COMPETITORS

JR Simplot
Keystone Foods
MAINES
Martin-Brower
McLane Foodservice
Meadowbrook Meat Company
OSI Group LLC
Performance Food
Reyes Holdings
Services Group of America
Shamrock Foods
SYSCO
UniPro Foodservice
U.S. Foodservice

HISTORICAL FINANCIALS

Company Type: Private

Income Statement

FYE: December 31

	REVENUE ($ mil.)	NET INCOME ($ mil.)	NET PROFIT MARGIN	EMPLOYEES
12/07	3,000	—	—	3,000
12/06	2,600	—	—	2,800
12/05	2,375	—	—	2,500
12/04	2,200	—	—	2,500
12/03	2,100	—	—	2,500
Annual Growth	9.3%	—	—	4.7%

Revenue History

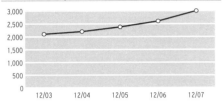

Golden State Warriors

These Warriors call the hardwood floor their battlefield. The Golden State Warriors professional basketball team has had a long and storied history since joining the Basketball Association of America (now the National Basketball Association) as a charter member in 1946. Originally formed as the Philadelphia Warriors by Eddie Gottlieb, the team moved to San Francisco in 1962 before relocating across the bay in 1971. The Warriors franchise boasts three league championships, its last in 1975. A 12-year streak of losing seasons has made it a challenge for the team to attract crowds at Oakland Arena (known as The Arena in Oakland). Former cable mogul Chris Cohan has controlled the franchise since 1995.

Cohan has drawn heavy criticism during his tenure as Warriors owner for the team's lack of success. Following yet another dismal outing during the 2005-06 season, the team brought in former Dallas Mavericks coach Don Nelson as head coach to replace Mike Montgomery, who was hired in 2004. Nelson previously coached the Warriors from 1988 to 1995, leading the team to its last playoff appearance in 1994.

In addition to Cohan, the team's ownership includes four Silicon Valley investors — Michael Marks (CEO of Flextronics), John Thompson (Symantec Corporation CEO), and venture capital investors Jim Davidson and Fred Harman — who acquired a 20% stake in the Warriors in 2004.

EXECUTIVES

Owner and Managing Member: Christopher Cohan
President: Robert Rowell
EVP Business Development: Neda Barrie
EVP Basketball Operations: Chris Mullin
EVP Team Marketing: Travis Stanley
Head Coach: Don Nelson, age 68
VP Finance: Dwayne Redmon
VP Ticket and Premium Sales: Ben Shapiro
Senior Executive Director Marketing and Game Presentation: Joe Azzolina
Executive Director Arena Operations: Terry Robinson
Executive Director Broadcasting: Dan Becker

Executive Director Public Relations: Raymond Ridder
Executive Director Human Resources: Erika Brown
Pro Scout: Mike Riley

LOCATIONS

HQ: Golden State Warriors
1011 Broadway, Oakland, CA 94607
Phone: 510-986-2200   **Fax:** 510-452-0132
Web: www.nba.com/warriors

The Golden State Warriors play at the 19,596-seat capacity Oakland Arena.

PRODUCTS/OPERATIONS

Championship Titles

NBA Champions (1947, 1956, 1975)
Western Conference Champions (1975)
Western Division Champions (1964, 1967)
Eastern Division Champions (1947-48, 1956)

COMPETITORS

Los Angeles Clippers
Los Angeles Lakers
Phoenix Suns
Sacramento Kings

HISTORICAL FINANCIALS

Company Type: Private

Income Statement

FYE: June 30

	REVENUE ($ mil.)	NET INCOME ($ mil.)	NET PROFIT MARGIN	EMPLOYEES
6/07	103	—	—	—
6/06	89	—	—	—
6/05	81	—	—	—
6/04	76	—	—	—
6/03	70	—	—	—
Annual Growth	10.1%	—	—	—

Revenue History

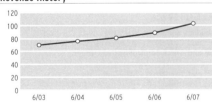

Golub Corporation

Supermarket operator The Golub Corporation offers tasty come-ons such as table-ready meals, gift certificates, automatic discount cards, and a hotline where cooks answer food-related queries. Golub operates about 115 Price Chopper supermarkets in Connecticut, Massachusetts, New Hampshire, upstate New York, northeastern Pennsylvania, and Vermont. It also runs Mini Chopper service stations and convenience stores. Golub discontinued its HouseCalls home delivery service in 2001 but is giving home delivery another try. Brothers Bill and Ben Golub founded the company in 1932. Today the Golub family runs the company and owns 45% of the grocery chain; employees own slightly more than 50%.

In a major expansion for the regional grocery chain, in late 2007 Golub announced that it planned to build as many as 30 new Price Chopper stores in the Northeast over the next three to four years.

In a bid to recapture business lost to takeout restaurants, Price Chopper began testing the home delivery of pizza, chicken wings, fried chicken, submarine sandwiches and other prepared foods at its store in Troy in the fall of 2007. Price Chopper, rival Hannaford, and other regional supermarket chains have been increasing their in-store offerings of prepared meals for busy shoppers. Home delivery is a logical extension.

In 2006 Price Chopper partnered with ProHealth Physicians to open a health clinic in its new store in Putnam, Connecticut.

EXECUTIVES

Chairman: Lewis Golub
President and CEO: Neil M. Golub, age 70
EVP and COO: Jerel T. (Jerry) Golub, age 49
EVP, Secretary and General Counsel:
  William J. Kenneally
SVP, Finance, Treasurer, and CFO: John Endres
SVP, Distribution and Transportation:
  Renato (Ron) Cellupica
VP and Corporate Controller: Carol L. Cillis
VP, Human Resources: Margaret Davenport
VP, Merchandising: Joe Kelley
VP, Operations: Mark E. Boucher
VP, Public Relations and Consumer Services:
  Mona J. Golub, age 43
VP, Real Estate: Donald (Don) Orlando
VP, Strategic Initatives: Jim Mizeur
CIO: Richard Bauer
Auditors: PricewaterhouseCoopers LLP

LOCATIONS

HQ: The Golub Corporation
  501 Duanesburg Rd., Schenectady, NY 12306
Phone: 518-355-5000   **Fax:** 518-379-3536
Web: www.pricechopper.com

2007 Stores

	No.
New York	71
Massachusetts	14
Vermont	13
Connecticut	8
Pennsylvania	8
New Hampshire	2
Total	**116**

COMPETITORS

7-Eleven
A&P
ALDI
Big Y Foods
BJ's Wholesale Club
Costco Wholesale
Cumberland Farms
DeMoulas Super Markets
Hannaford Bros.
Penn Traffic
Shaw's
Stop & Shop
Target
TOPS Markets
Wal-Mart
Wegmans

Goodman Global

While a good man may be hard to find, *this* Goodman makes it easy to find comfort with its residential and light commercial HVAC products. The company manufactures heating, ventilation, and air conditioning (HVAC) products, including split-system air conditioners and heat pumps, gas furnaces, packaged units, air handlers, and evaporator coils. It sells products under the Goodman, Amana, and Quietflex brands through some 150 company-operated distribution centers and about 700 independent distributor locations throughout North America. Investment firm Hellman & Friedman bought the company in 2008.

Goodman Global had gone public in 2006, but another private equity firm, Apollo Advisors, held 40% of the company before it was sold to Hellman & Friedman.

The company operates distribution centers in such key growth states as Arizona, California, Florida, Nevada, and Texas. Company centers and direct sales generate about 60% of revenues; its top 10 independent distributors account for a little more than 20% of its total sales.

In addition to independent distributors, Goodman Global's customers include contractors who install residential and light commercial HVAC products, national homebuilders, and other national accounts. The company sells to contractors mainly through its distribution network.

Goodman Global was founded in 1975 by Harold Goodman to manufacture flexible duct for simplifying the installation of central air conditioning systems. The company entered the air conditioning equipment distribution business in 1980; two years later, it entered the air conditioning equipment manufacturing business.

EXECUTIVES

Chairman: Charles A. Carroll, age 57, $1,004,166 pay
President, CEO, and Director: David L. (Dave) Swift
EVP and CFO: Lawrence M. Blackburn, age 52,
  $426,900 pay
EVP, Human Resources: Donald R. King, age 50,
  $311,927 pay
EVP, Secretary, and General Counsel: Ben D. Campbell,
  age 49, $346,152 pay
SVP and CIO: Terrance M. Smith, age 57
SVP, Independent Distribution: Peter H. Alexander,
  age 68
SVP, Logistics and Business Development:
  Samuel G. Bikman, age 38
SVP, Marketing: Gary L. Clark, age 44
SVP, Operations: William L. Topper, age 50
SVP and President, Company Owned Distribution:
  James L. Mishler, age 52
VP, Corporate Controller, and Treasurer: Mark M. Dolan,
  age 47
VP, Investor Relations: Richard J. Bajenski, age 53
Auditors: Ernst & Young LLP

LOCATIONS

HQ: Goodman Global, Inc.
  5151 San Felipe, Ste. 500, Houston, TX 77056
Phone: 713-861-2500   **Fax:** 713-861-3207
Web: www.goodmanmfg.com

COMPETITORS

Carrier
Lennox
Paloma
Trane Inc.

HISTORICAL FINANCIALS

Company Type: Private

Income Statement

	REVENUE ($ mil.)	NET INCOME ($ mil.)	NET PROFIT MARGIN	EMPLOYEES
12/07	1,936	—	—	
12/06	1,795	—	—	4,878
12/05	1,565	—	—	4,997
12/04	1,318	—	—	4,816
12/03	1,193	—	—	
Annual Growth	12.9%	—	—	0.6%

FYE: December 31

Revenue History

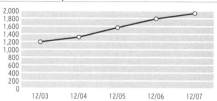

Goodwill Industries

Goodwill Industries International supports the operations of more than 185 independent Goodwill chapters worldwide. Though known mainly for its 2,100-plus thrift stores, the organization focuses on providing rehabilitation, job training, placement, and employment services for people with disabilities and others. Goodwill is one of the world's largest providers of such services, as well as one of the world's largest employers of the physically, mentally, and emotionally disabled. Support for the organization's programs comes mainly from sales of donated goods, both at the retail stores and through an online auction site, as well as from contract work and from government grants. Goodwill was founded in 1902.

The organization's online shopping and auction site, shopgoodwill.com (launched in 1999), sold more than 2.6 million items and rang up nearly $12 million in sales in 2007.

EXECUTIVES

Chairman: David Hadani
President and CEO: Jim Gibbons
COO: Steve Krotonsky
VP Employee Related Services: Miriam Johnson
VP, Member Relations: Dave Barringer
VP Planning: Linda Chandler
Treasurer: Michael B. Sullivan
Director Media Relations: Christine Nyirjesy-Bragale
Manager Media Relations: Lauren Lawson
Auditors: Deloitte & Touche

LOCATIONS

HQ: Goodwill Industries International, Inc.
  15810 Indianola Dr., Rockville, MD 20855
Phone: 301-530-6500   **Fax:** 301-530-1516
Web: www.goodwill.org

PRODUCTS/OPERATIONS

2007 Revenue

	$ mil.	% of total
Retail	1,900.	60
Industrial & service contract work	624.5	20
Mission services	474	15
Public & private support	65	2
Other	100	3
Total	**3,163.5**	**100**

HISTORICAL FINANCIALS
Company Type: Not-for-profit

Income Statement				FYE: December 31
	REVENUE ($ mil.)	NET INCOME ($ mil.)	NET PROFIT MARGIN	EMPLOYEES
12/07	3,164	—	—	87,444
12/06	2,903	—	—	86,375
12/05	2,650	—	—	82,185
12/04	2,390	—	—	80,142
12/03	2,210	—	—	82,370
Annual Growth	**9.4%**	**—**	**—**	**1.5%**

Revenue History

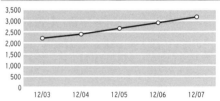

Gordon Food Service

This company caters to the tastes of American and Canadian food service operators alike. Gordon Food Service (GFS) is a leading food service supplier in North America with more than a dozen distribution centers in the US and Canada. It offers more than 15,000 food and non-food products (both nationally branded and private-label items) to some 45,000 customers in 15 US states and throughout Canada. It serves schools, restaurants, and other institutions. The company also sells food and supplies through more than 100 GFS Marketplace stores, which are open to the public, in five Midwestern states and Florida. Tracing its roots back to 1897, GFS is owned by the Gordon family.

EXECUTIVES

Chairman: Paul Gordon
CEO: Dan Gordon
CFO: Jeff Maddox
President: Jim Gordon
EVP, US: Tony Groll
Secretary and Treasurer: John Gordon Jr.
Director Marketing and Procurement, US: Rob VanRenterghem
Director Marketing and Procurement, Canada: Todd Baker
Director Sales, US: Paul LaLonde
Customer Marketing Specialist: Ken Wasco
President, GFS Canada: Frank Geier

LOCATIONS

HQ: Gordon Food Service
333 50th St. SW, Grand Rapids, MI 49501
Phone: 616-530-7000   **Fax:** 616-717-7600
Web: www.gfs.com

COMPETITORS

Ben E. Keith
Clark National
Costco Wholesale
I Supply
MAINES
McLane Foodservice
Meadowbrook Meat Company
Performance Food
Services Group of America
Sherwood Food
SYSCO
UniPro Foodservice
Unisource
U.S. Foodservice

Goss International

Goss International always has some pressing news. The company operates through its Goss Graphic Systems subsidiary, making web-offset printing presses for newspapers and commercial printers, as well as advertising insert presses. Goss offers its presses, related parts, and services (sensitive to publishing schedules) through sales offices and plants in North America, Europe, and Asia. The company serves newspaper publishers in more than 120 countries. Customers include *The Asahi Shimbun* (Japan), *The People's Daily* (China), and *The Financial Times* (UK). Investment firm Stonington Partners controls the company.

The company is one of three companies still manufacturing web presses in the US, the others being Didde Press Systems (part of Stolle Machinery) and Web Press Corp.

In 2004 Goss acquired Heidelberg Web Systems from Heidelberger Druckmaschinen, doubling its annual sales in the process.

The company dates back to 1885, when it was founded in Chicago as Goss Printing Press Company by brothers Fred and Sam Goss. Rockwell International Corp. bought Goss in 1969 and sold it in 1996 to Stonington Partners for about $600 million.

EXECUTIVES

CEO: Bob Brown
COO: Jochen Meissner
EVP and CFO: Joseph P. Gaynor III
SVP, Global Sales: Dick Schultz
SVP: Greg Blue
Director, Training and Technical Publications: Peter Farmer
General Sales Manager, UK and Eire: Ian McLeod
Regional Sales Manager, Northeast Region, The Americas: Bruce Barna
Manager, Commercial Press Audits: Geoff Adamson
Recruiting, Human Resources: Angela Lewis

LOCATIONS

HQ: Goss International Corporation
3 Territorial Ct., Bolingbrook, IL 60440
Phone: 630-755-9300   **Fax:** 630-755-9301
Web: www.gossinternational.com

Goss International has US manufacturing operations in Cedar Rapids, Iowa, and international operations in China, France, Germany, Japan, and the UK.

PRODUCTS/OPERATIONS

Selected Products

Advertising-insert presses (C700, Magnum)
Aftermarket parts
Commercial presses (G18, G25, M16)
Large newspaper presses (Colorliner, Newsliner)
Small newspaper presses (Community, Universal)

COMPETITORS

Baldwin Technology	Mitsubishi Heavy
Dainippon Screen	Industries
FUJIFILM Graphic Systems	Pamarco Technologies
Koenig & Bauer	QuadTech
MAN AG	Quipp
Manugraph DGM	Ryobi Ltd.
MEGTEC Systems	

HISTORICAL FINANCIALS
Company Type: Private

Income Statement				FYE: December 31
	ESTIMATED REVENUE ($ mil.)	NET INCOME ($ mil.)	NET PROFIT MARGIN	EMPLOYEES
12/07	1,110	—	—	4,000
12/06	1,140	—	—	4,100
12/05	1,100	—	—	4,100
Annual Growth	**0.5%**	**—**	**—**	**(1.2%)**

Revenue History

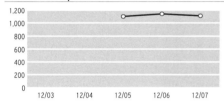

Gould Paper

Paper is as good as gold for Gould Paper, one of the largest privately owned distributors of printing and fine papers in the US. The company, owned by the Gould family, distributes and sells paper for multiple markets including fine papers, commercial printing, lithography, newsprint, direct mail, catalogs, envelopes, and specialty papers. Gould also supplies paperboard and packaging grades, and it has paper converting operations. The company sells 2 million tons of paper products annually. It operates from about 20 locations in Canada and the US; subsidiaries P3/Saleshurst, WWF, and Price & Pierce focus on sales in Europe and the Asia/Pacific.

The company has overseas locations in France, Finland, the UK, New Zealand, Singapore, Hong Kong, China, the Philippines, and the United Arab Emirates.

Harry Gould Sr. (father of chairman, president, CEO, and owner Harry Gould Jr.) formed the company in 1924. Gould Paper has expanded over the years by acquiring other paper companies. In 2006 it bought Missouri-based Boone Paper Company to enhance its position in the Midwest market; it also acquired Florida-based Southern Paper, Inc. to expand its presence in that region. Boone Paper was merged into the BRW Paper subsidiary.

Later in 2006 Gould Paper acquired the western Canadian merchant operations of Cascades Resources from PaperlinX. The Cascades Resources operations were renamed Gould Paper (Canada) in 2007.

EXECUTIVES

Chairman, President, and CEO: Harry E. Gould Jr.
EVP and CFO: Carl Matthews
SVP, Price & Pierce: Rick E. Moore
VP and CIO: Robert (Bob) Bunsick
VP, Secretary, and Treasurer: Patrick Mullen
VP, Integrated Supply Chain: Paul Collins
VP and President, Metro: Dean Marabeti
VP, Sales: Joseph DeSopo
Director, Human Resources: Barbara O'Grady
President, BRW Paper, Dallas: Gale Woellfer
President, Gould Business Products Division: Michael Negri
President, Distribution: Robert (Bob) Weil
President, National: Mike Duncan
President, Metro Division: Mike Trachtenberg
President, Canada: Jim Dunn
President, BRW Paper, Kansas: Jim Rehor
President, Gould Office Papers: Peter Tilearcio

LOCATIONS

HQ: Gould Paper Corporation
11 Madison Ave., New York, NY 10010
Phone: 212-301-0000   **Fax:** 212-481-0067
Web: www.gouldpaper.com

COMPETITORS

Bradner Central	RIS the paper house
Cascades Inc.	Sappi Fine Paper
Clifford Paper	Unisource
Horizon Paper	United Stationers
Midland Paper	West Coast Paper
National Envelope	xpedx

HISTORICAL FINANCIALS

Company Type: Private

Income Statement

FYE: December 31

	REVENUE ($ mil.)	NET INCOME ($ mil.)	NET PROFIT MARGIN	EMPLOYEES
12/07	1,160	—	—	431
12/06	1,150	—	—	464
12/05	1,240	—	—	374
12/04	1,210	—	—	410
12/03	1,100	—	—	400
Annual Growth	1.3%	—	—	1.9%

Revenue History

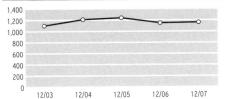

Goya Foods

Whether you call 'em *frijoles* or *habichuelas*, beans are beans, and Goya's got 'em. Goya Foods produces some 1,500 Hispanic and Caribbean grocery items, including canned meats, canned and dried beans, fruit nectars, oils, olives, rice, seasonings and sauces, plantain and yucca chips, and frozen entrees. It sells many different types of rice and some 30 types of beans and peas. The company's brands include Goya and Canilla. It also sells beverages such as tropical fruit nectars and juices, tropical sodas, and coffee. Goya is owned by one of the richest Hispanic *familias* in the US, the Unanues, who founded the company in 1936.

Goya has historically served the Hispanic communities in the northeastern US and Florida, having mostly Cuban, Dominican, and Puerto Rican customers. The company now has products geared toward the tastes of Hispanics in California and the Southwest who have roots in Mexico, the Caribbean, and Central and South America. An added plus is that the growing taste for ethnic foods across the US has fueled Goya's growth beyond its Hispanic roots. In addition, its "all-in-one-aisle" product placement in food stores has proven very successful.

Continued growth at Goya is a way of life for the company. However, it still faces competition from food giants such as Kraft Foods, which have lines of Hispanic specialty products. It's also challenged by food manufacturers located in Mexico, who are turning north to tap the pocketbooks of US consumers. Goya is one of the largest Hispanic-owned companies in the US.

Food retailers carrying Goya products in the US include Wal-Mart, H-E-B, Soriana, Chedraui, and Casa Ley.

In 2007 Goya began distributing about 40 of its products in major Mexican cities, including Guadalajara, Monterrey, and Mexico City. The move marked the first time the company entered the Mexican food market. That year it also began marketing a line of organically grown beans; varieties include kidney, black, pinto, and navy beans, along with chick peas.

Turning to markets farther afield, in 2008 the company entered into an agreement with Golden Dragon to market and distribute Goya products in China.

HISTORY

Immigrants from Spain by way of Puerto Rico, husband and wife Prudencio Unanue and Carolina Casal founded Unanue & Sons in New York City in 1936. The couple imported sardines, olives, and olive oil from Spain, but when the Spanish Civil War (1936-1939) interrupted supply lines, they began importing from Morocco.

In 1949 the company established a cannery in Puerto Rico; the Puerto Rican imports were distributed to local immigrants from the West Indies. Each of the couple's four sons eventually joined the family business, and in 1958 the firm relocated to Brooklyn. The company took its current name, Goya Foods, in 1962 when the family bought the Goya name — originally a brand of sardines — for $1.

The oldest Unanue son, CEO Charles, was fired from Goya in 1969 — and subsequently cut out of Prudencio's will — when he spoke out about an alleged tax evasion scheme. (Legal wrangling between Charles and the rest of the family continued into the late 1990s.) Goya moved to its present New Jersey headquarters in 1974.

Another son, Anthony, died in 1976, as did Prudencio. That year Joseph, another sibling, was named president and CEO. Along with his brother Francisco (Frank), president of Goya Foods de Puerto Rico, he began a cautious expansion campaign by adding traditional products to the company's existing line of Latin, Caribbean, and Spanish favorites.

Buoyed by the growing popularity of Mexican food, in 1982 Goya began distributing its products in Texas, targeting the region's sizable Mexican and Central American population. At first, the move proved a disaster. Goya's products were not suited to the Mexican palate, which generally preferred spicier food. Likewise, a similar strategy to capture a portion of Florida's huge Cuban market share initially met with only moderate success, but Goya persevered, eventually turning the tables in its favor.

During the 1980s the company also attempted to woo the non-Hispanic market. While Goya's cream of coconut — a key ingredient in piña coladas — found a broader market, its ad campaign featuring obscure actress Zohra Lampert did little to attract a large following of non-Hispanic customers.

Success in that market came in the 1990s. America's interest in the reportedly healthier "Mediterranean diet" boosted sales of Goya's extra-virgin olive oil. Recommendations for low-fat, high-fiber diets prompted the company's launch of the "For Better Meals, Turn to Goya" advertising campaign — its first in English — in 1992.

Three years later the company released a line of juice-based beverages. In 1996 Goya sponsored an exhibition of the works of the Spanish master Goya at the New York Metropolitan Museum of Art. Continuing its efforts to reach out to non-Hispanics and English-dominant Hispanics, in 1997 the company began including both English and Spanish on the front of its packaging.

To lure more snackers, the next year Goya added yucca (a.k.a. cassava) chips to its line. In 1999 Goya began packaging its frozen entrees in microwaveable trays. In 2001 it bought a new factory in Spain.

In 2002 Goya added 12 flavors (including guava, mandarin orange, and tamarind) to its line of Refresco Goya Fruit Sodas, thus joining the beverage industry trend toward offering more diverse flavors. In 2002 the president of the company's Puerto Rican division, Francisco J. Unanue, died.

In 2004 long-time chairman, CEO, and president Joseph Unanue and his son, COO Andy Unanue, were forced out of family-owned Goya by Joseph's two nephews, Robert I. and Francisco R. Unanue. Robert is now president and Francisco took over the Florida division of the company. Lawsuits to regain control of the company filed by Joseph followed but were eventually dropped.

In 2005 the company celebrated its 70th year in business and opened an online e-store.

EXECUTIVES

President: Robert I. (Bob) Unanue, age 54
SVP Purchasing, European Operations, and Marketing, Sales, and Advertising: Joseph F. Perez
VP Logistics and Operations: Peter J. Unanue
VP MIS: David Kinkela
VP Sales & Marketing: Conrad O. Colon
VP and General Manager, Goya Foods Puerto Rico: Carlos Unanue
VP Operations, Goya Foods Puerto Rico: Jorge Unanue
VP Finance: Miguel Lugo
VP Goya Foods Texas and General Manager Goya Foods of California: Evelio Fernandez
VP and General Counsel: Carlos Ortiz
VP Traffic: Rebecca Rodriguez
Director, Human Resources: Tony Rico
Director, Public Relations: Rafael Toro
Director, Purchasing Goya Foods Florida: Tom Unanue
Director, DSD Sales: John Hernandez
National Sales Manager: Eric Bray
President, Florida Division: Francisco R. (Frank) Unanue

LOCATIONS

HQ: Goya Foods, Inc.
100 Seaview Dr., Secaucus, NJ 07096
Phone: 201-348-4900   **Fax:** 201-348-6609
Web: www.goya.com

Goya has some 15 plants located in the Dominican Republic, Puerto Rico, Spain, and the US.

PRODUCTS/OPERATIONS

Selected Products

Beverages
  Café Goya
  Coconut water
  Refresco (fruit-flavored sparkling water)
  Malta (malt beverage)
  Nectars and juices (apple, apricot, banana, guanabana, guava, mango, passion fruit, papaya, peach, pear, pear/passion, pineapple, pineapple/guava, pineapple/passion, strawberry, strawberry/banana, tamarind, tropical fruit punch)
  Tropical sodas (apple, coconut, cola champagne, fruit punch, ginger beer, grape, guaraná, guava, lemon lime, mandarin orange, pineapple, strawberry, tamarind)

Foods and Other Products
  Beans (black-eyed peas, chick peas, lentils, refried)
  Bouillon
  Cookies
  Cooking sauces
  Cooking wine
  Cornmeal
  Devotional candles
  Flour
  Frozen foods
  Marinades
  Meat (chorizo, corned beef, potted, Vienna sausage)
  Olive oil
  Olives
  Pasta
  Plantain chips
  Rice
  Salsa
  Seafood (canned bonito, mackerel, pulpo, sardines, tuna)
  Seasonings
  Spices
  Tomato sauce
  Yucca chips

COMPETITORS

American Rice
Authentic Specialty Foods
Azteca Corn Products
B&G Foods
Bolner's Fiesta Products
Bush Brothers
Campbell Soup
Casa de Oro Foods
Chiquita Brands
ConAgra
Del Monte Foods
Dole Food
Don Miguel Mexican Foods
Don Pancho Authentic Mexican Foods
El Dorado Mexican Food Products
Frito-Lay
General Mills
Grupo Bimbo
Heinz
Herdez
Hormel
Kellogg
Kraft Foods
La Flor
La Reina
La Tortilla Factory
McCormick & Company
Nestlé
Ole' Mexican Foods
Pro-Fac
Ralcorp
Reser's
Riceland Foods
Riviana Foods
Ruiz Foods Inc.
Ruiz Mexican Foods
Seneca Foods
Taco Bell
Unilever
World Finer Foods

HISTORICAL FINANCIALS

Company Type: Private

Income Statement

FYE: December 31

	ESTIMATED REVENUE ($ mil.)	NET INCOME ($ mil.)	NET PROFIT MARGIN	EMPLOYEES
12/07	1,260	—	—	3,000
12/06*	1,190	—	—	3,000
5/05	750	—	—	2,500
5/04	850	—	—	2,500
5/03	750	—	—	2,500
Annual Growth	13.8%	—	—	4.7%

*Fiscal year change

Revenue History

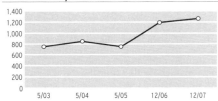

Grande Communications

Grande Communications' grand vision is to become a big player in Texas telecommunications. The company provides bundled telephone services, Internet access, and cable television to more than 140,000 residential and business customers over its own fiber-optic network. Grande Communications also provides wholesale communications services to other telecoms and ISPs. The company has operations in Austin-San Marcos, Corpus Christi, Dallas, Houston, Midland-Odessa, San Antonio, and Waco. Grande's investors include Whitney & Co. (22% of voting power), The Centennial Funds (17%), and Austin Ventures (7%).

Grande Communications expanded with the acquisition of broadband services provider ClearSource in 2002 and it expanded its fiber-optic network by purchasing assets from utility firms that are exiting the telecommunications market. These acquisitions include 3,000 fiber-miles of network from C3 Communications, a unit of American Electric Power (AEP). This purchase expanded the company's network from the Rio Grande Valley of South Texas to parts of Oklahoma, Arkansas, and Louisiana, and connects Texas' major markets, including Houston, Dallas, Austin, San Antonio, and Corpus Christi.

Grande Communications got a jump start on its operations in 2000 with the purchase of San Marcos, Texas-based integrated network services provider Thrifty Call.

EXECUTIVES

Chairman, President, and CEO: Roy H. Chestnutt, age 48, $486,779 pay (partial-year salary)
COO: W.K.L. (Scott) Ferguson Jr., age 49, $210,140 pay
CFO: Michael L. (Mike) Wilfley, age 52, $236,999 pay
SVP Marketing: Miguel Lecuona
VP and General Manager, Austin: Harris Bass
VP and General Manager, San Antonio: Carlos del Castillo
VP Network Services: Jared P. Benson
VP Corporate Finance: Richard Robuck
VP Network Operations and Engineering: Brady Adams
VP People and Culture: Kay Stroman
VP Retail Operations: Mark Machen
VP Retail Operations: J. Lyn Findley
Treasurer: Douglas T. (Doug) Brannagan
Auditors: Ernst & Young LLP

LOCATIONS

HQ: Grande Communications Holdings, Inc.
401 Carlson Cir., San Marcos, TX 78666
Phone: 512-878-4000   **Fax:** 512-878-4010
Web: www.grandecom.com

PRODUCTS/OPERATIONS

Selected Services

Broadband Internet access
Cable TV
Local telephone access
Long-distance
Network services
  Data services
  Managed services
  Switched carrier services
Wholesale services

COMPETITORS

AT&T
Cable One
CenturyTel
Charter Communications
Comcast Cable
Cox Communications
DIRECTV
DISH Network Corporation
Suddenlink Communications
Time Warner Cable
Verizon
Vonage

HISTORICAL FINANCIALS
Company Type: Private

Income Statement

	REVENUE ($ mil.)	NET INCOME ($ mil.)	NET PROFIT MARGIN	EMPLOYEES
12/07	197	(51)	—	831
12/06	190	(142)	—	810
12/05	195	(90)	—	835
12/04	179	(55)	—	873
12/03	182	(38)	—	811
Annual Growth	2.1%	—	—	0.6%

FYE: December 31

2007 Year-End Financials

Debt ratio: 296.9%
Return on equity: —
Cash ($ mil.): —
Current ratio: —
Long-term debt ($ mil.): 204

Net Income History

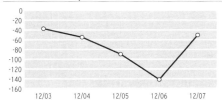

Grant Thornton International

Grant Thornton International is a kid brother to the Big Four. The umbrella organization of accounting and management consulting firms operates from more than 520 offices in more than 110 countries, making it one of the top second-tier companies that trail behind the biggest of the big guys (Deloitte Touche Tohmatsu, Ernst & Young Global, KPMG International, and PricewaterhouseCoopers). More than 60% of its member firms' clients are private companies. The company offers assurance, tax, business risk, corporate advisory, and other services to public and private companies. By virtue of the consolidation in the industry, Grant Thornton is the longest-lived, same-name organization in the world.

Like other second-tier firms, the company concentrates its auditing efforts on mid-cap public, large private, and entrepreneurial companies, leaving the big boys to the Big Four. However, Grant Thornton has seen some doors opened by rules sparked by Enron and other scandals of the early 2000s: Mandates that companies use separate providers for auditing and some types of consulting and advisory have helped Grant Thornton step in with specialist services for clients who continued to use Big Four firms as their auditors.

Grant Thornton has been focusing on developing business in emerging markets, particularly in Asia, Europe, and Latin America. (The accountancy is particularly keen to boost its presence in China.) Member firms have been working to increase cross-border cooperation by pooling resources and cutting costs.

HISTORY

Cameron, Missouri accountant Alexander Grant founded Alexander Grant & Co. in 1924 with William O'Brien. They built their firm in Chicago and concentrated on providing services to midwestern clients.

In the 1950s and 1960s, the firm began expanding both domestically and internationally. Alexander Grant & Co. continued to focus on manufacturing and distribution companies.

In 1973 O'Brien died. In 1979 the company began publishing its well-known (and sometimes controversial) index of state business climates. An attempt to merge with fellow second-tier accounting firm Laventhol & Horwath failed that year. The next year Grant Thornton International was formed when Alexander Grant & Co. and its British affiliate, Thornton Baker, combined their offices around the world to form a network. The UK and US branches, however, kept their respective names.

The 1980s brought turmoil and change for the firm. Financial scandals led investors and the government to hold accounting firms liable for their audits. Along with the (then) Big Six, Alexander Grant & Co. was hit with several lawsuits alleging fraud and cover-ups. One case marred the firm's squeaky-clean image and caused dozens of clients to jump ship: Just days after Alexander Grant issued it a clean audit, a Florida trading firm was shut down by the SEC. Jilted investors sued to reclaim lost money; Alexander Grant settled for $160 million. Chairman Herbert Dooskin and other leaders also left the company; although they denied it was because of the scandal, their departures left Alexander Grant rudderless during a critical time.

Meanwhile, the company merged with Fox & Co. to create the US's #9 accounting firm. With scandal-scared partners leaving (and taking clients), Fox looked to the merger to shore up its reputation. But Alexander Grant's auditing troubles led some Fox partners and clients to flee from the merged company.

After the fallout from the lawsuits and the merger, the company began rebuilding, taking on new clients, reclaiming lost ones, and refocusing on midsized companies. In 1986 both Alexander Grant & Co. and Thornton Baker took the Grant Thornton name.

The early 1990s recession reduced accounting revenues but increased demand for management consulting. As political and economic barriers fell during the decade, Grant Thornton International grew. The firm entered emerging markets in Africa, Asia, Europe, and Latin America. In 1998 the Big Six became the Big Five; Grant Thornton added refugee firms and partners to its global network. In 1999 the firm's US branch entertained merger offers from H&R Block and PricewaterhouseCoopers, but instead announced plans to reposition itself as a corporate services firm to better compete.

In 2000 the company pulled out of its advisory position to companies involved in controversial diamond mining in war-torn portions of Africa. It also agreed to merge its UK operations with those of HLB Kidsons; the merged firm retained the Grant Thornton name.

The following year, after disagreements about strategy, US CEO Dom Esposito resigned. UK partner David McDonnell was named the global CEO. In 2002, Grant Thornton grew by picking up pieces of Andersen that fell away as a result of the Enron scandal. Andersen's fall also winnowed out Grant Thornton's competitors (at

least in the numeric sense), as the Big Five became the Big Four.

Like Andersen before it, Grant Thornton felt the red-hot glare of unwanted media attention as Italian food giant Parmalat (a former auditing client) fell into bankruptcy amidst an Enron-style scandal in late 2003. Grant Thornton's Italian unit had remained the auditor for Parmalat subsidiary Bonlat, which played a central role in the unfolding scandal. The Italian affiliate, which has been expelled from Grant Thornton's global network, maintains it was a victim of fraud in the case. Parmalat in 2004 filed suit against the Italian accountancy, claiming two of its partners were involved in the fraud; the two also face criminal charges.

EXECUTIVES

Global CEO: David C. McDonnell
COO: Mike Starr
Global Leader Member Firm Network: Gabriel Azedo
Global Leader Assurance Services: Ken Sharp
Global Leader Tax Services: Ian Evans
Global Leader Specialist Advisory Services: Scott Barnes
Global Leader Privately Held Business Services: Alex MacBeath
Global Director Marketing Communications: Jon Geldart
National Managing Partner Industry Practices: Robert (Bob) Leavy
Executive Director Member Firm Relations: Sören Carlsson
Executive Director Public Policy: April Mackenzie
Director Worldwide Quality Control and CFO: Barry Barber
Director, Client Service, Grant Thornton Corporate Finance: Tim Blois
Director, Human Resources: Annemarie Wade
International Director of Development: Paul Andrews
Head of International and European Services: Andrew Godfrey
Head, Professional Practices Group, London: Peter Gamson
Head Communications: Kate Speirs

LOCATIONS

HQ: Grant Thornton International
175 W. Jackson Blvd., 20th Fl., Chicago, IL 60604
Phone: 312-856-0200   **Fax:** 312-602-8099
Web: www.gti.org

PRODUCTS/OPERATIONS

Selected Services

Assurance
Corporate finance
Corporate recovery and business reorganization
International tax
PRIMA (people and relationship issues in management)

COMPETITORS

Baker Tilly International
BDO International
Deloitte
Ernst & Young Global
KPMG
McGladrey & Pullen
McKinsey & Company
Moore Stephens International
PricewaterhouseCoopers
RSM McGladrey

Graybar Electric

There's no gray area when it comes to describing Graybar Electric's main business: it's one of the largest distributors of electrical products in the US. Purchasing from thousands of manufacturers, the employee-owned company distributes more than 1 million types of electrical and communications components, including wire, cable, and lighting products. Its customers include electrical contractors, industrial plants, power utilities, and telecommunications providers. Subsidiary Graybar Financial Services offers equipment leasing and financing, as well as complete project funding. Graybar Electric gets most of its sales in the US, with a small portion derived from Canada, Mexico, and Puerto Rico.

Graybar maintains distribution networks — each comprising a main facility and supporting branch locations — in 13 regional districts throughout the US. Its distribution facilities are supported by 10 warehouses. Graybar's largest group of customers, electrical contractors, account for about half of the company's sales. It has more than 160,000 customers.

To help bring supply, distribution, and inventory costs down, the company uses electronic data interchange and supplier-assisted inventory management. Graybar has looked to new technologies to streamline its supply chain. In 2004 the company completed a multi-year project to implement an enterprise resource planning (ERP) system that links its entire network of warehouses and distribution facilities.

The company stocks products made by more than 4,000 manufacturers.

HISTORY

After serving as a telegrapher during the Civil War, Enos Barton borrowed $400 from his widowed mother in 1869 and started an electrical equipment shop in Cleveland with George Shawk. Later that year Elisha Gray, a professor of physics at Oberlin College who had several inventions (including a printing telegraph) to his credit, bought Shawk's interest in the shop, and the firm moved to Chicago, where a third partner joined.

The company incorporated as the Western Electric Manufacturing Co. in 1872, with two-thirds of the company's stock held by two Western Union executives. As the telegraph industry took off, the enterprise grew rapidly, providing equipment to towns and railroads in the western US.

Gray and his company missed receiving credit for inventing the telephone in 1875 when Gray's patent application for a "harmonic telegraph" reached the US Patent Office a few hours after Bell's application for his telephone. However, the telephone and the invention of the light bulb in 1879 opened new doors for Western Electric. The company began to grow into a major corporation, selling and distributing a variety of electrical equipment, including batteries, telegraph keys, and fire-alarm boxes. By 1900 the firm was the world's #1 maker of telephone equipment.

Western Electric formed a new distribution business in 1926, Graybar Electric Co. (from "Gray" and "Barton"), the world's largest electrical supply merchandiser. In 1929 employees bought the company from Western Electric for $3 million in cash and $6 million in preferred stock. During the 1930s it marketed a line of appliances and sewing machines under the Graybar name.

In 1941 the company bought the outstanding shares of stock from Western Electric for $1 million. Graybar Electric was a vital link between manufacturers and US defense needs during WWII. Its men and equipment wired the Panama Canal with telephone cable; it also helped the US military during the Korean conflict and the Vietnam War.

By 1980 Graybar Electric had reached nearly $1.5 billion in sales. Business was hurt when construction slowed in the late 1980s and the early 1990s, and the company reorganized in 1991, closing regional offices and cutting jobs. Rebounding in 1992 as the US economy improved, Graybar acquired New Jersey-based Square Electric Co.

In 1994 the company acquired a minority interest in R.E.D. Electronics, a Canadian data communications and computer networking company, and realigned its operations into two business segments: electrical products and communications and data products.

In 1995 Graybar Electric formed the Solutions Providers Alliance with wholesale distributors Kaman Industrial Technologies, VWR Scientific Products, and Vallen Corporation. In 1996 AT&T's Global Procurement Group named the company as one of only three suppliers for its electrical products. The next year Graybar Electric upped its stake in one of its Canadian operations, Harris & Roome Supply Limited.

Graybar Electric in 1998 opened a subsidiary in Chile and formed a joint venture, Graybar Financial Services, with Newcourt Financial (formerly AT&T Capital). The next year Graybar Electric bought the Connecticut-based electrical wholesaler Frank A. Blesso, Inc., and it expanded its distribution partnership with wire and cable manufacturer Belden Electronics in 2000.

In 2001 Graybar opened a new distribution location in northeastern Pennsylvania. The following year Graybar increased its presence in the telecommunications industry when it inked a deal to distribute products made by Copper Mountain Networks, a US-based broadband equipment manufacturer.

The company received a five-year contract in 2003 from Los Angeles County to provide electrical supplies to local and state governments, school districts, and other tax-funded agencies participating in the US Communities program. US Communities is a government buying cooperative established in 1999.

During 2004 Graybar won several contracts from the Defense Logistics Agency, worth a total of $195 million over two years.

Graybar signed a three-year supply contract in 2005 with Premier Purchasing Partners, a group purchasing organization for the health care industry.

In 2006 Graybar opened new locations in Kent, Washington, and Wallingford, Connecticut.

EXECUTIVES

Chairman, President, and CEO: Robert A. Reynolds Jr., age 59, $535,608 pay
SVP, CFO, and Director: D. Beatty D'Alessandro, age 47, $200,193 pay
SVP US Business: Dennis E. DeSousa, age 49, $248,904 pay
SVP Operations and Director:
  Lawrence R. (Larry) Giglio, age 53, $341,250 pay
SVP Sales and Marketing, Electrical and Director:
  Richard D. Offenbacher, age 57, $225,391 pay
SVP, Secretary, General Counsel, and Director:
  Matthew W. Geekie
SVP Sales and Marketing, Communication and Data:
  Kathleen M. Mazzarella, age 48
VP and Treasurer: Jon N. Reed, age 51
VP and Controller: Martin J. Beagen, age 51
VP, Human Resources: Jack F. Van Pelt, age 69
President and CEO, Graybar Electric Canada and Director: F. H. Hughes, age 61
Auditors: Ernst & Young LLP

LOCATIONS

HQ: Graybar Electric Company, Inc.
  34 N. Meramec Ave., St. Louis, MO 63105
Phone: 314-573-9200   **Fax:** 314-573-9455
Web: www.graybar.com

Graybar Electric operates primarily in North America, with warehouses in California, Florida, Georgia, Illinois, Massachusetts, Missouri, North Carolina, Ohio, Texas, and Virginia.

2007 Sales

	% of total
US	95
Other countries	5
Total	**100**

PRODUCTS/OPERATIONS

2007 Sales

	% of total
Electrical contractors	48
Voice & data communications	20
Commercial & industrial	19
Other	13
Total	**100**

Selected Products

Ballasts
Batteries
Cable
Conduit
Connectors
Emergency lighting
Enclosures
Fiber optic cable
Fittings
Fluorescent lighting
Fuses
Hand tools
Hangers/fasteners
Heating and ventilating equipment
Industrial fans
Lighting
Lubricants
Paints
Patch cords
Smoke detectors
Testing and measuring instruments
Timers
Transfer switches
Transformers
Utility products
Wire

COMPETITORS

Anixter International	Premier Farnell
Asia Pacific Wire & Cable	Rexel, Inc.
Communications Supply	Richardson Electronics
Communications Systems	Sonepar USA
Consolidated Electrical	SUMMIT Electric Supply
Gexpro	Tech Data
Hagemeyer	United Electric Supply
HD Supply	WESCO International
HWC	W.W. Grainger

HISTORICAL FINANCIALS
Company Type: Private

Income Statement				FYE: December 31
	REVENUE ($ mil.)	NET INCOME ($ mil.)	NET PROFIT MARGIN	EMPLOYEES
12/07	5,258	83	1.6%	8,600
12/06	5,009	57	1.1%	8,400
12/05	4,288	17	0.4%	7,800
12/04	4,080	14	0.3%	7,700
12/03	3,803	9	0.2%	7,900
Annual Growth	8.4%	77.0%	—	2.1%

2007 Year-End Financials
Debt ratio: 24.1%   Current ratio: —
Return on equity: 18.1%   Long-term debt ($ mil.): 115
Cash ($ mil.): —

Net Income History

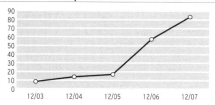

Great Lakes Cheese

Great Lakes Cheese understands the power of provolone, the charm of cheddar, and the goodness of gruyere. The firm manufactures and distributes natural and processed cheeses and cheese spreads, including varieties such as cheddar, colby, Swiss, mozzarella, and provolone. It also makes premium cheese Adams Reserve New York Cheddar. Great Lakes packages shredded, chunked, and sliced cheese for deli, bulk, and food service sale under the Great Lakes, Adams Reserve, and private-label and store brands. With seven manufacturing plants, the Great Lakes Cheese distributes its products, which are sold in deli and dairy cases, throughout the US.

In addition to its domestic production, Great Lakes imports cheese including havarti, blue, fontina from Denmark, gouda from Holland, emmentaler and gruyere from Switzerland, and jarlsberg from Norway. Its bulk products include blue, boursin, feta, goat, gorgonzola, grated Italian, and smoked cheeses.

Chairman Hans Epprecht, a Swiss immigrant, founded the firm in 1958 as a Cleveland bulk-cheese distributor. Epprecht and Great Lakes employees own the company.

EXECUTIVES
Chairman: Hans Epprecht, age 78
President and CEO: Gary Vanic
CFO: Russell (Russ) Mullins
VP, Sales: Bill Andrews
VP and General Manager, Co-Packing Operations: John W. Epprecht
VP, Supply Chain and Manufacturing: Craig Filkouski
VP, Packaging: Richard (Dick) Metzler
VP Human Resources: Beth Wendell
VP Procurement: Kurt L. Epprecht
Director, Information Services: Ron Barlow

LOCATIONS
HQ: Great Lakes Cheese Company, Inc.
17825 Great Lakes Pkwy., Hiram, OH 44234
Phone: 440-834-2500   **Fax:** 440-834-1002
Web: www.greatlakescheese.com

PRODUCTS/OPERATIONS

Selected Products
Domestic cheese	Imported cheese
American	Blue
Cheddar	Boursin
Colby	Brie
Cream	Emmenthaler
Hot pepper	Feta
Jack	Fontina
Mozzarella	Goat
Provolone	Gorgonzola
Swiss	Gouda
	Gruyere
	Havarti
	Jarlsberg

COMPETITORS
American Milk Products
AMPI
Bel Brands USA
BelGioioso Cheese
Cheesemakers, Inc.
Dairy Farmers of America
Ellsworth Cooperative
Hickory Farms
Kraft Foods
Land O'Lakes
Leprino Foods
Marathon Cheese
Masters Gallery
Original Herkimer County Cheese Company
Saputo
Sargento
Schreiber Foods
Specialty Cheese Company
Swiss-American
Tillamook County Creamery Association
Tropical Cheese Industries
Uplands Cheese Company, Inc.

HISTORICAL FINANCIALS
Company Type: Private

Income Statement				FYE: December 31
	REVENUE ($ mil.)	NET INCOME ($ mil.)	NET PROFIT MARGIN	EMPLOYEES
12/07	1,700	—	—	1,700
12/06	1,700	—	—	1,700
12/05	1,375	—	—	1,700
12/04	1,375	—	—	1,700
12/03	965	—	—	1,700
Annual Growth	15.2%	—	—	0.0%

Revenue History

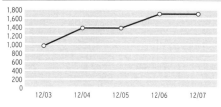

Greatwide Logistics

Greatwide Logistics Services has brought together a world of freight transportation and logistics companies. Greatwide's operating units, assembled through a series of acquisitions, provide dedicated transportation, in which drivers and equipment are assigned to a customer long-term; distribution logistics; truckload freight brokerage; and truckload freight transportation, largely via independent owner-operators. Overall, Greatwide can call upon a fleet of some 5,500 tractors and 1,700 trailers, and the company maintains about 3.6 million sq. ft. of warehouse space at facilities throughout the US. Investcorp owns a majority interest in Greatwide.

Two other investment firms, Fenway Partners and Dallas-based Hicks Holdings, own minority stakes in the logistics company. Fenway, which first invested in what is now Greatwide in 2000, sold most of its interest in the company to Investcorp and Hicks Holdings for $730 million in December 2006.

To maintain its growth, Greatwide intends to continue to cultivate relationships with agents that help market its services and truck owner-operators that help provide them. The company believes it can generate better investment returns by maintaining its "asset-light" business model than it could by investing extensively in transportation equipment and infrastructure.

EXECUTIVES
Chairman: Thomas O. (Tom) Hicks, age 62
President, CEO, and Director: Raymond B. (Ray) Greer
CFO: Stephen P. (Steve) Bishop
EVP Corporate Development: Jim Hartman
SVP, General Counsel, and Secretary: John N. Hove
Chief Commercial Officer: Richard M. (Dick) Metzler
Chief Risk Officer: Jeffery H. (Jeff) Lester
VP Business Development: Jim Kitz
VP Human Resources, Dedicated Transport: Kyle Killingsworth
VP Corporate Development and Integration: Jamie Pierson
President, Distribution Logistics: Vincent F. (Vin) Gulisano
President and CEO, Freight Brokerage: Douglas G. (Doug) Clark
President and COO, Dedicated Transport: John Simone
President, Truckload Management: Joe Chandler

LOCATIONS
HQ: Greatwide Logistics Services, Inc.
12404 Park Central Dr., Ste. 300S, Dallas, TX 75251
Phone: 972-228-7300   **Fax:** 972-228-7328
Web: www.greatwide.com

COMPETITORS
Arrow Trucking
Boyd Bros. Transportation
C.H. Robinson Worldwide
Crete Carrier
CRST Malone
J.B. Hunt
Landstar System
Ryder System
Schneider National
Swift Transportation
Transplace
UPS Supply Chain Solutions
U.S. Xpress
UTi Worldwide

HISTORICAL FINANCIALS

Company Type: Private

Income Statement

	REVENUE ($ mil.)	NET INCOME ($ mil.)	NET PROFIT MARGIN	EMPLOYEES
12/07	1,140	—	—	3,000
12/06	1,200	—	—	3,000
12/05	1,087	—	—	2,800
Annual Growth	2.4%	—	—	3.5%

FYE: December 31

Revenue History

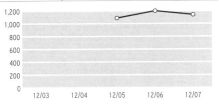

Green Bay Packers

On the frozen tundra of Lambeau Field, the Green Bay Packers battle for pride in the National Football League. The team, founded in 1919 by Earl "Curly" Lambeau, has been home to such football icons as Bart Starr, Ray Nitschke, and legendary coach Vince Lombardi. The Packers boast a record 12 championship titles, including three Super Bowl victories (its last in Super Bowl XXXI after the 1996 season). The team is also the only community-owned franchise in American professional sports, being a not-for-profit corporation with about 112,000 shareholders. The shares do not increase in value nor pay dividends, and can only be sold back to the team. No individual is allowed to own more than 200,000 shares.

Win or lose, Green Bay remains a very popular team: Regular season games have been sold out since 1960 and the waiting list for season tickets boasts about 78,000 names. Nationally, the team regularly places near the top of popularity polls, and it is one of the top NFL teams in terms of merchandise sales.

The Packers lost one of its biggest stars of recent history in 2008 when three-time MVP quarterback Brett Favre was traded to the New York Jets after retiring early that year and then attempting a comeback. He had led the team to a 13-3 regular season record the previous year, though a bid for the Super Bowl ended with a loss to the New York Giants in the NFC Championship game. Favre had played for Green Bay since 1992, winning one championship title and earning nearly every meaningful NFL passing record.

The Packers selected Mark Murphy to replace retiring CEO Bob Harlan at the beginning of 2008. The hiring came after a previous succession plan involving former president and COO John Jones was scuttled. (Concerns about Jones' management abilities were initially reported as the reason for the sea change, though an official statement later cited health concerns arising from Jones' 2006 emergency open heart surgery.) A former NFL player and NFL Players Association executive, Murphy previously served as athletic director at Northwestern University.

HISTORY

In 1919 Earl "Curly" Lambeau helped organize a professional football team in Green Bay, Wisconsin, with the help of George Calhoun, the sports editor of the *Green Bay Press-Gazette*. At 20 years old, Lambeau was elected team captain and convinced the Indian Packing Company to back the team, giving the squad its original name, the Indians. The local paper, however, nicknamed the team the Packers and the name stuck. Playing on an open field at Hagemeister Park, the team collected fees by passing the hat among the fans. In 1921 the franchise was admitted into the American Professional Football Association (later called the National Football League), which had been organized the year before.

The Packers went bankrupt after a poor showing its first season in the league and Lambeau and Calhoun bought the team for $250. With debts continuing to mount, *Press-Gazette* general manager Andrew Turnbull helped reorganize the team as the not-for-profit Green Bay Football Corporation and sold stock at $5 a share. Despite winning three straight championships from 1929-31, the team again teetered on the brink of bankruptcy, forcing another stock sale in 1935. With fortunes on and off the field dwindling, Lambeau retired in 1950 after leading the team to six NFL championships (prior to the creation of the Super Bowl which pitted the NFL against rival American Football League). A third stock sale was called for that year, raising $118,000. City Stadium (renamed Lambeau Field in 1965) was opened in 1957. In 1959 the team hired New York Giants assistant Vince Lombardi as head coach.

Under Lombardi, the Packers dominated football in the 1960s, winning five NFL titles with such players as Bart Starr and Ray Nitschke. The team defeated the Kansas City Chiefs in the first Super Bowl after the 1966 season. Lombardi resigned after leading Green Bay to victory over the Oakland Raiders in Super Bowl II. (Following his death in 1970, NFL commissioner Pete Rozelle named the league's championship trophy the Vince Lombardi trophy.)

The team again fell into mediocrity following the departure of Lombardi. Former MVP Starr was called upon to coach in 1974 but couldn't turn the tide before he was released in 1983. Forrest Gregg, another former Packer great, took over but was also unsuccessful in four seasons at the helm.

Bob Harlan, who had joined the Packers as assistant general manager in 1971, became president and CEO in 1989. He hired Ron Wolf as general manager in 1991, who in turn hired Mike Holmgren as head coach early the next year. With a roster including Brett Favre, Reggie White, and Robert Brooks, the Packers posted six straight playoff appearances and won its third Super Bowl (and 12th NFL title) in 1997. A fourth stock sale (preceded by a 1,000:1 stock split) netted the team more than $24 million.

After Holmgren resigned in 1999 (he left to coach the Seattle Seahawks), former Philadelphia Eagles coach Ray Rhodes tried to lead the team but lasted only one dismal season. In 2000 Mike Sherman, a former Holmgren assistant, was named the team's 13th head coach. Prompted by falling revenue, the team announced plans to renovate Lambeau Field, and voters in Brown County later approved a sales tax

increase to help finance the $295 million project. (The work was completed in 2003.) The next year Wolf retired and coach Sherman added general manager to his title. The team also signed quarterback Favre to a 10-year, $100 million contract extension.

While Sherman managed to lead the team to the playoffs in four of his first five seasons, the Packers were a disappointing 2-4 in postseason play. The team hired Ted Thompson from Seattle in 2005 to take over the general manager duties. That season turned out to be one of the worst in recent team history, however, and Sherman was replaced as head coach by San Francisco 49ers assistant coach Mike McCarthy in 2006.

The Packers rebounded during the 2007 season, reaching the NFC Championship game. (Green Bay lost to the New York Giants.) That off-season in 2008, the Packers underwent a change in the front office as Harlan retired as CEO and was replaced by Mark Murphy, a former NFL player and athletic director at Northwestern University. Favre announced his retirement that same year but attempted a comeback during the summer; he was later traded to the New York Jets.

EXECUTIVES

Chairman Emeritus: Robert E. (Bob) Harlan, age 72
President, CEO, and Director: Mark H. Murphy, age 53
EVP, General Manager, and Director of Football Operations: Ted Thompson, age 55
SVP Marketing and Sales: Laura Sankey, age 43
VP and Director: John J. Fabry
VP Administration and General Counsel: Jason Wied, age 36
VP Administration and Player Finance: Russ Ball, age 49
VP Finance: Vicki Vannieuwenhoven, age 42
VP Organizational and Staff Development: Betsy Mitchell
Head Coach: Michael (Mike) McCarthy
Secretary and Director: Peter M. Platten III, age 68
Treasurer and Director: Larry L. Weyers, age 63
Controller: Duke Copp
Director of Administrative Affairs: Mark Schiefelbein
Director of College Scouting: John Dorsey, age 48
Director of Marketing and Corporate Sales: Craig Benzel
Director of Pro Personnel: Reggie McKenzie, age 45
Director of Public Relations: Jeff Blumb
Team Historian: Lee Remmel, age 84
Manager Human Resources: Nicole Ledvina
Auditors: Wipfli Ullrich Bertelson LLP

LOCATIONS

HQ: The Green Bay Packers, Inc.
Lambeau Field Atrium, 1265 Lombardi Ave.,
Green Bay, WI 54304
Phone: 920-569-7500   **Fax:** 920-569-7301
Web: www.packers.com

The Green Bay Packers play at 72,928-seat capacity Lambeau Field in Green Bay, Wisconsin.

PRODUCTS/OPERATIONS

Championship Titles
Super Bowl Championships
  Super Bowl XXXI (1997)
  Super Bowl II (1968)
  Super Bowl I (1967)
NFL Championships (1929-31, 1936, 1939, 1944, 1961-62, 1965-67)
NFC Championships (1996-97)
NFC North Division (2002-04, 2007)
NFC Central Division (1972, 1995-97)
NFL Western Conference (1936, 1938-39, 1944, 1960-62, 1965-67)

HISTORICAL FINANCIALS
Company Type: Not-for-profit

Revenue History

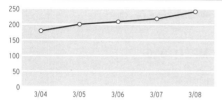

Grocers Supply

Need crackers in Caracas or vanilla in Manila? Grocers Supply Co. distributes groceries near and far. The company (not to be confused with fellow Texas distributor GSC Enterprises) supplies food, health and beauty items, household products, and school and office supplies to nearly 2,000 convenience stores and grocery retailers, as well as some 200 schools, within a 350-mile radius of Houston. The company's international division, meanwhile, ships supplies to oil company operations, US embassies, and other customers around the world. It also owns Fiesta Mart, a chain of ethnic food stores. Grocers Supply was founded by Joe Levit in 1923; his family, led by president Max Levit, continues to own the company.

Looking to expand its retail base, Grocers Supply in 2008 agreed to acquire nearly 40 grocery stores from Minyard Food Stores. The deal includes the 23-unit Carnival Food Stores chain, most of which will be converted to Fiesta Mart locations.

EXECUTIVES
President: Max S. Levit
SVP and CFO: Michael (Mike) Castleberry
SVP Buying: Tom Becker
SVP Sales: David R. (Dave) Hoffman
SVP Operations: Robert Hunt
SVP Financial Services: Jim Nelson
VP Real Estate: James Arnold
VP Human Resources: Deborah Howard
VP Sales: Jim Davenport
Controller: Bill Stewart
Auditors: PricewaterhouseCoopers

LOCATIONS
HQ: The Grocers Supply Co., Inc.
3131 E. Holcombe Blvd., Houston, TX 77221
Phone: 713-747-5000   **Fax:** 713-746-5611
Web: www.grocerssupply.com

COMPETITORS
Affiliated Foods
Associated Grocers, Inc.
Associated Wholesale Grocers
C&S Wholesale
GSC Enterprises
H-E-B
Kroger
McLane
Nash-Finch
Randall's
SUPERVALU
Wal-Mart

HISTORICAL FINANCIALS
Company Type: Private

Income Statement				FYE: December 31
	ESTIMATED REVENUE ($ mil.)	NET INCOME ($ mil.)	NET PROFIT MARGIN	EMPLOYEES
12/07	2,720	—	—	8,900
12/06	2,510	—	—	8,800
12/05	1,900	—	—	2,000
Annual Growth	19.6%	—	—	111.0%

Revenue History

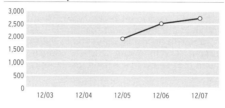

GSC Enterprises

GSC Enterprises brings the groceries to the grocery store. Doing business as Grocery Supply Company (not to be confused with Grocers Supply Co.), the wholesale distributor supplies more than 4,500 independently owned convenience stores, grocers, discounters, and other retailers and wholesalers in about 15 states, mostly in the Southwest, Southeast, and Midwest. GSC stocks and distributes tobacco, grocery items, prepared foods (Chicago Style Pizza, Chester Fried Chicken, Deli-Fast Foods), and other items. In addition, its Fidelity Express subsidiary sells money orders in retail stores. Ken McKenzie, Curtis McKenzie, and Woodrow Brittain started GSC in 1947; the McKenzie family continues to own the company.

The company's Fidelity Express division primarily serves the small, often rural, independent merchants and small grocery chains that also make use of its distribution services. The company has also expanded its financial services offerings: in addition to processing more than $2.5 billion in money orders annually, Fidelity Express now provides walk-in bill payment services and processing for more than 50 companies consisting primarily of utilities and electric cooperatives.

EXECUTIVES
Chairman: Michael K. (Mickey) McKenzie
President and CEO: Michael J. Bain
VP, Finance and CFO: Kerry Law
VP, Information Technology: Jerry Donaho
VP, Marketing and Trade Relations: Steve Shing
VP, Risk Management and Employee Services: Janet Price
VP, Sales: Monty Covington
VP, Distribution: Billy Key
VP, Systems and Planning: Ryan McKenzie
Corporate Counsel: Steve Rutherford
Secretary: Melissa Bernard
Director, Human Resources: Theresa Patterson

LOCATIONS
HQ: GSC Enterprises, Inc.
130 Hillcrest Dr., Sulphur Springs, TX 75482
Phone: 903-885-0829   **Fax:** 903-885-6928
Web: www.grocerysupply.com

COMPETITORS
Affiliated Foods
Alex Lee
Associated Wholesale Grocers
Brenham Wholesale
C&S Wholesale
C.D. Hartnett
Eby-Brown
First Data
Grocers Supply
H.T. Hackney
McLane
MoneyGram
Nash-Finch
Spartan Stores
SUPERVALU

HISTORICAL FINANCIALS
Company Type: Private

Income Statement				FYE: Saturday nearest December 31
	REVENUE ($ mil.)	NET INCOME ($ mil.)	NET PROFIT MARGIN	EMPLOYEES
12/07	1,320	—	—	1,200
12/06	1,230	—	—	1,200
12/05	1,174	—	—	1,150
Annual Growth	6.0%	—	—	2.2%

Revenue History

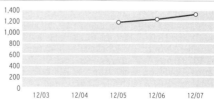

Guardian Industries

Giving its customers a break would never occur to Guardian Industries, one of the world's largest glassmakers. With more than 60 facilities on five continents, Guardian primarily produces float glass and fabricated glass products for the automobile and construction markets. It also makes architectural glass, fiberglass, and automotive trim parts. Through its Guardian Building Products Distribution division, the company operates building supply distribution centers throughout North America. President and CEO William Davidson took Guardian Industries public in 1968 and bought it back for himself in 1985. Davidson is also the managing partner of the Detroit Pistons NBA team.

Guardian has been expanding primarily through international acquisitions and by increasing its already significant position in the building materials business. The company added business in Egypt (a stake in Egyptian Glass Company) and has been opening float glass plants and treatment facilities on a regular basis. It added float plants in Poland (2002), the UK (2003), and Mexico (2004), as well as other international and domestic locations, and it announced new developments in Russia and the United Arab Emirates in 2006.

In 2008 the company bought auto parts manufacturer Siegel-Robert Automotive through its Guardian Automotive subsidiary.

HISTORY

Guardian Glass Company began as a small maker of car windshields in Detroit in 1932 during the Great Depression. The company spent the 1930s and 1940s building its business to gain a foothold in glassmaking, historically one of the world's most monopolized industries. In 1949 PPG Industries and Libbey-Owens-Ford (now owned by the UK's Pilkington) agreed to stop their alleged monopolistic activity. William Davidson took over Guardian Glass from his uncle in 1957. As president, he tried to boost the enterprise's standing in the windshield niche, but PPG and Libbey-Owens-Ford refused to sell him raw glass. That year Guardian Glass filed for bankruptcy to reorganize.

The company emerged from bankruptcy in 1960 (the same year Pilkington developed the float process for glassmaking), and in 1965 it was hit with its first patent-infringement lawsuit. Three years later the company went public, changed its name to Guardian Industries, and was refused a license to use Pilkington's float technology. Guardian began an aggressive acquisition strategy in 1969, and in 1970 it hired Ford's top glass man (who knew the float process) and proceeded to build its first float-glass plant in Michigan. PPG sued Guardian in 1972. Davidson bought the Detroit Pistons in 1974. He applied a do-or-die style that might best be illustrated by the 1979 firing of Piston's coach Dick Vitale, who claims Davidson axed him on his own front doorstep while a curbside limo waited with the motor running.

In 1980 Guardian started making fiberglass and began hiring former workers from insulation maker Manville to duplicate that company's patented technology for fiberglass insulation. Manville successfully sued Guardian in 1981.

Guardian opened a Luxembourg plant that year. Pilkington sued Guardian in 1983, but the case was settled out of court three years later. Davidson took Guardian private in 1985, and in 1988 he bought an Indiana auto trim plant. He also built The Palace of Auburn Hills sports arena in 1988.

The 1990s brought more international expansion for Guardian, with plants added in India, Spain, and Venezuela. It also set up a distribution center in Japan, a country known for its tight control of the glass industry. In 1992 Guardian bought OIS Optical Imaging Systems, a maker of computer display screens. Guardian moved its headquarters to Auburn Hills, Michigan, in 1995. Its 1996 purchase of Automotive Moulding boosted its position in the auto plastics and trim market.

Guardian booted its OIS Optical Imaging Systems unit in 1998, citing ongoing losses. That year the company's fiberglass subsidiary bought 50% of building materials buying group Builder Marts of America, giving Guardian a foothold in the markets for lumber and roofing products. Also in 1998 Davidson made a failed attempt to buy the Tampa Bay Lightning hockey team.

In 1999 Guardian bought Siam Guardian Glass Ltd. from Siam Cement Plc, the company's partner in Thailand. The next year Guardian acquired Cameron Ashley Building Products (renamed Ashley Aluminum), a distributor with more than 160 branches in the US and Canada. In 2002 the company expanded to Poland where it built a float glass plant; Guardian also opened float glass plants in the UK in 2003 and in Mexico in 2004.

In 2005 Guardian introduced ClimaGuard SPF, a residential glass product that blocks 99.9% of UV rays with no visible reduction in light transmission. The following year the company acquired the assets of Heartland Insulation.

EXECUTIVES

President and CEO: William M. (Bill) Davidson, age 84
EVP: Ralph J. Gerson
VP Human Resources: Bruce Cummings
Group VP Finance and CFO: Jeffrey A. Knight
President and CEO, Automotive Products Group: D. James Davis
President, Building Products Group: Duane H. Faulkner
President, Glass Group: Russell J. Ebeid
Managing Director, Latin America: Mark LaCasse
Managing Director, Asian Operations: Chuck Croskey
Managing Director, European Operations: Jim Moore

LOCATIONS

HQ: Guardian Industries Corp.
    2300 Harmon Rd., Auburn Hills, MI 48326
Phone: 248-340-1800   **Fax:** 248-340-9988
Web: www.guardian.com

PRODUCTS/OPERATIONS

Selected Products and Services

Architectural Glass
    Custom fabrication
    Float glass
    Insulating glass
    Laminated glass
    Mirrors
    Patterned glass
    Reflective coated glass
    Tempered glass

Automotive Systems
    Bodyside (mud flaps, wheel covers)
    Front and rear end (grilles, rub strips)
    Side window (door-frame moldings)
    Windshield (window-surround moldings)
Guardian Building Products
    Aluminum screen doors
    Carports
    Ceiling tile
    Door frames
    Doors
    Fiberglass insulation
    Formica
    Metal roofing
    Patio covers
    Plywood
    Rebar
    Sheetrock
    Storm doors
    Windows
Guardian Fiberglass
    Fiberglass insulation
Retail Auto Glass
    Auto glass
    Auto glass repair and replacement
    Insurance claim processing

COMPETITORS

Apogee Enterprises
Asahi Glass
AUTOGLASS
Belron US
Corning
CRH
Dura Automotive
Johns Manville
Magna Donnelly
Nippon Sheet Glass
Owens Corning Sales
Pilkington
PPG
Saint-Gobain
SCHOTT
United Glass
Vitro

HISTORICAL FINANCIALS

Company Type: Private

Income Statement

	ESTIMATED REVENUE ($ mil.)	NET INCOME ($ mil.)	NET PROFIT MARGIN	EMPLOYEES
12/07	5,470	—	—	19,000
12/06	5,330	—	—	19,000
12/05	5,000	—	—	19,000
Annual Growth	4.6%	—	—	0.0%

FYE: December 31

Revenue History

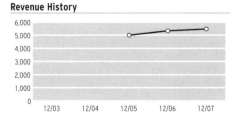

Guardian Life Insurance

When your guardian angel fails you, there's Guardian Life Insurance Company of America. The mutual company, owned by its policy holders, offers life insurance, disability income insurance, and — more recently — retirement programs to individuals and businesses. Guardian's employee health indemnity plans provide HMO, PPO, and dental and vision plans, as well as disability plans. In the retirement area, the company offers the Park Avenue group of mutual funds and annuity products, managed by its Guardian Investor Services. Guardian also offers estate planning and education savings programs.

To meet competition in the quickly deregulating financial services area, the company is building its wealth management capabilities to target baby boomers getting ready for retirement. It created broker-dealer Park Avenue Securities and launched Guardian Trust Company to offer trust and investment management services. The company has also added long-term care insurance to its product line.

Guardian has also grown through acquisition, buying complementary firms, such as disability insurance specialist Berkshire Life Insurance and RS Investments (investment management).

HISTORY

Hugo Wesendonck came to the US from Germany in 1850 to escape a death sentence for his part in an abortive 1848 revolution. After working in the silk business in Philadelphia, he moved to New York, which was home to more ethnic Germans than any city save Berlin and Vienna.

In 1860 Wesendonck and other expatriates formed an insurance company to serve the German-American community. Germania Life Insurance was chartered as a stock mutual, which paid dividends to shareholders and policy owners. Wesendonck was its first president.

The Civil War blocked the company's growth in the South, but it expanded in the rest of the US and by 1867 even operated in South America.

After the Civil War, many insurers foundered from high costs. Wesendonck battled this by implementing strict cost controls and limiting commissions, allowing the company to continue issuing dividends and rebates on its policyholders' premiums.

In the 1870s Germania opened offices in Europe, and for the next few decades much of the company's growth was there. By 1910, 46% of sales originated in Europe. The company's target clientele in the US decreased between the 1890s and WWI as German immigration slowed, and its market share dropped from ninth in 1880 to 21st in 1910.

During WWI the company lost contact with its German business. Prodded by anti-German sentiment in the US, the company changed its name to The Guardian Life Insurance Company of America in 1917. After WWI the company began winding down its German business (a process that lasted until 1952).

In 1924 Guardian began mutualizing but could not complete the process until 1944 because of probate problems with a shareholder's estate.

After WWII, Guardian offered noncancelable medical insurance (1955) and group insurance (1957). The company formed Guardian Investor Services in 1969 to offer mutual funds; two years later it established Guardian Insurance & Annuity to sell variable contracts. In 1989 it organized Guardian Asset Management to handle pension funds.

In 1993, as indemnity health costs rose, the company moved into managed care via its membership in Private Healthcare Systems, a consortium of commercial insurance carriers offering managed health care products and services. This allowed Guardian to offer HMO and PPO products. It later sold its interest in Private Healthcare Systems to Multiplan in 2006.

Guardian entered a joint marketing agreement in 1995 with HMO Physicians Health Services, which contracts with physicians and hospitals in the New York tri-state area. In 1996 the company acquired Managed Dental Care of California and an interest in Physicians Health Services.

Facing deregulation and consolidation in the financial services area, as well as the demutualization of some of its largest competitors, Guardian in the late 1990s decided to add depth to its employee benefits lines and breadth to its wealth management lines.

In 1999 Guardian formed its broker-dealer subsidiary and received a thrift license to facilitate creation of a trust business. Acquisitions included Innovative Underwriters Services, Fiduciary Insurance Co. of America, and managed dental care companies First Commonwealth and First Choice Dental Network. In 2001 the company moved to boost its disability business with the purchase of Berkshire Life Insurance.

EXECUTIVES

President, CEO, and Director: Dennis J. Manning
EVP and COO: K. Rone Baldwin
EVP Finance, Risk and Operational Excellence, CFO, and Director: Robert E. Broatch
EVP and Corporate Actuary: Armand M. de Palo
EVP and Chief Transformation Officer: Gary B. Lenderink
EVP Equity Products: Bruce C. Long
EVP, Corporate Secretary, and Director: Joseph A. Caruso
EVP and Chief Investment Officer; President, The Park Avenue Portfolio: Thomas G. Sorell
EVP Individual Products Distribution: Margaret W. (Meg) Skinner
EVP Retirement Products and Services: Scott Dolfi
EVP Individual Life and Disability: Deanna M. Mulligan, age 43
SVP Individual Markets: David W. Allen
SVP Group Pensions: Dennis P. Mosticchio
SVP Human Resources: James D. (Jim) Ranton
SVP Corporate Marketing: Nancy F. Rogers
SVP and CIO: Frank Wander
SVP and Chief Actuary: Barbara L. Snyder
SVP Corporate Finance and Treasurer: Barry Belfer
SVP and Corporate Controller: John Flannigan
SVP and Chief Communications Officer: Richard Jones
VP and General Counsel: John Peluso
Auditors: PricewaterhouseCoopers LLP

LOCATIONS

HQ: The Guardian Life Insurance Company of America
7 Hanover Sq., New York, NY 10004
Phone: 212-598-8000   **Fax:** 212-919-2170
Web: www.guardianlife.com

Guardian Life Insurance Company of America has operations throughout the US.

PRODUCTS/OPERATIONS

Selected Subsidiaries and Affiliates
Berkshire Life Insurance Company of America
First Commonwealth, Inc.
Guardian Baillie Gifford Limited
The Guardian Insurance & Annuity Company, Inc.
Guardian Investor Services LLC
Guardian Trust Company, FSB
Innovative Underwriters, Inc.
Managed Dental Care (California)
Managed DentalGuard, Inc. (New Jersey)
Managed DentalGuard, Inc. (Texas)
Park Avenue Life Insurance Company
Park Avenue Securities LLC

COMPETITORS

Aetna
AIG American General
Allstate
AXA Financial
Charles Schwab
CIGNA
Citigroup
CNA Financial
FMR
The Hartford
John Hancock Financial Services
Liberty Mutual
Lincoln Financial Group
MassMutual
MetLife
Mutual of Omaha
Nationwide
New York Life
Northwestern Mutual
Pacific Mutual
Principal Financial
Prudential
UBS Financial Services
UnitedHealth Group
Unum Group
USAA

HISTORICAL FINANCIALS

Company Type: Mutual company

Income Statement
FYE: December 31

	ASSETS ($ mil.)	NET INCOME ($ mil.)	INCOME AS % OF ASSETS	EMPLOYEES
12/07	28,328	292	1.0%	5,000
12/06	26,719	376	1.4%	5,000
12/05	24,807	375	1.5%	5,000
12/04	23,336	286	1.2%	5,000
12/03	21,671	218	1.0%	5,500
Annual Growth	6.9%	7.6%	—	(2.4%)

2007 Year-End Financials

Equity as % of assets: 13.2%   Long-term debt ($ mil.): —
Return on assets: 1.1%   Sales ($ mil.): 7,648
Return on equity: 8.1%

Net Income History

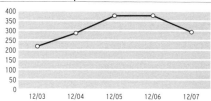

Guardsmark, LLC

When FBI agents leave Quantico, they go to Guardsmark. The company, a leading employer of former FBI agents, provides security services to companies in the financial, health care, transportation, and utility industries. Guardsmark offers security guards, private investigation, and drug testing services. The company also conducts background checks (employment, education, and criminal history) and consults with architects and builders to design security programs. Guardsmark operates in some 400 cities. Chairman and president Ira Lipman owns the company, which he founded in 1963.

Lipman also publishes *The Limpan Report*, a monthly newsletter targeting security management that provides up-to-date analysis of security issues such as terrorism, workplace violence, and computer security.

Guardsmark has more than 150 offices throughout the US, Canada, Puerto Rico, the UK, France, and Singapore.

EXECUTIVES

Chairman and President: Ira A. Lipman, age 67
Vice Chairman, CFO, and Treasurer: Jeffrey B. Westcott
EVP and Group Executive: Gustave K. Lipman
SVP and Group Executive: Don K. Pettus
SVP and Secretary: Joshua S. (Josh) Lipman
SVP Sales, Security Division: John F. Clark
VP: M. Benjamin Lipman, age 31
VP and General Counsel: Gareth C. (Gary) Leviton
Auditors: PricewaterhouseCoopers LLP

LOCATIONS

HQ: Guardsmark, LLC
10 Rockefeller Plaza, New York, NY 10020
Phone: 212-765-8226   **Fax:** 212-603-3854
Web: www.guardsmark.com

PRODUCTS/OPERATIONS

Selected Services
Background screening
Consulting
  Security program surveys
Facility design
  Technical and physical security infrastructure
Investigations
  Undercover agents
Security services
  Individualized protection of client assets
  Uniformed officers
Specialized services
  Computer crime programs
  Executive protection
  Emergency operations
  White-collar crime programs

COMPETITORS

ADP Screening and Selection
AlliedBarton Security
ChoicePoint
Command Security
Kroll
Kroll Background Screening
Quest Diagnostics
TransNational Security
Wackenhut
Whelan Security

Guitar Center

What AutoZone is to the garage, Guitar Center is to the garage band. The nation's #1 retailer of guitars, amplifiers, drums, keyboards, and pro-audio equipment operates more than 210 stores in 40-plus US states. Brands include Fender, Roland, Yamaha, and Sony. Guitar Center stores also sell music-related computer hardware and software, and used instruments. Its American Music Group division operates about 95 Music & Arts Center stores that specialize in the sale and rental of band and orchestral instruments. The music retailer acquired ailing Dennis Bamber in early 2007. Later that same year Guitar Center was taken private by the investment firm Bain Capital Partners (BCP) for about $2.1 billion.

No stranger to retailing, BCP has investments in companies including Toys "R" Us, Michaels, Stores, and Burlington Coat Factory.

After a decade of rapid growth as a public company, privately-owned Guitar Center plans to slow down the pace of new store openings and to focus instead on improving operations and internal efficiencies.

Operating in a highly fragmented industry (where the top five retailers account for only about 25% of total sales) the company leverages its size to undersell — and sometimes flush out — its mostly mom-and-pop competitors. It also buys up ailing music retailers. To that end, Guitar Center's Musician's Friend subsidiary purchased all of the assets of bankrupt Dennis Bamber (dba The Woodwind & The Brasswind), including its inventory of band and orchestra instruments and music123.com and related Web sites for about $27 million in February 2007. Musician's Friend is the largest direct response retailer of musical instruments in the US. Previous acquisitions include four Hermes Music stores in Texas in 2006. The stores were converted to the Guitar Center banner and strengthened the retailer's business with the Hispanic community.

Guitar Center stores range in size from 12,000 to 30,000 sq. ft., and the majority of the company's retail store customers are professional/aspiring musicians in large metropolitan areas. The company started opening smaller stores (8,000 to 10,000 sq. ft.) to cater to its secondary markets and operates about 35 stores under this format.

The company's original Hollywood store, founded in 1964, features the Rock Walk, a sidewalk tribute to 200 musicians and music pioneers.

HISTORY

"Ladies and gentlemen . . . the Beatles!" Ed Sullivan's introduction, barely audible over the hysterical screams of the audience, and the subsequent performance by the Fab Four sent American youths scurrying for electric guitars. Former car salesman Wayne Mitchell, who was running a chain of music stores at the time, was actually pushed into the fray. A supplier told him if he wanted to keep selling organs, he would have to stock the Beatles' signature Vox amplifiers as well. Mitchell converted an old movie theater next door to his Hollywood shop, stocked it with Vox amps, and opened the first Guitar Center in 1964 on Sunset Boulevard.

Guitar Center opened its second store, in San Francisco, in 1972. Mitchell died in 1983, and former music products wholesaler Raymond Scherr acquired a majority interest in Guitar Center (reduced to about 8% after the company

went public). Two years later the Hollywood Rock Walk was established in front of the original Guitar Center; it features cemented handprints and plaques honoring rock's most influential musicians and instrument makers and has become a tourist destination.

The company went public in 1997 (recapitalization the previous year created a $72 million loss). Guitar Center tripled in size between 1995 and 1998. It opened stores in highly populated areas buzzing with band activity, including Los Angeles, San Francisco, Boston, and Chicago.

In 1999 longtime employees Larry Thomas and Marty Albertson were named co-CEOs of the company. In addition to these titles, Thomas became chairman and Albertson was named president. In June Guitar Center bought Musician's Friend, a leading catalog and Internet retailer of musical instruments, for $48.3 million (including over $18 million in debt assumption). The company has converted seven of Musician's Friend's nine stores to Guitar Centers and is keeping the mail order and e-commerce business under the Musician's Friend moniker, which it operates as a separate business.

Guitar Center acquired New York-based American Music Group (12 band instrument retail stores, two mail-order catalogs, and a music accessory distributor) in April 2001 for almost $17 million. In 2002 American Music acquired M&M MUSIC, which operates five band instrument stores and serves more than 200 schools in the Southeast.

In January 2004, the company's direct response division, Musician's Friend, was named to Internet Retailer's Best of the Web 2004, as one of the country's top 50 retailing Web sites. In late 2004 chairman and co-CEO Larry Thomas stepped down in order to spend more time promoting music education. He remains on the board as chairman emeritus. Co-CEO and president Marty Albertson was named chairman and CEO.

In mid-2005, Guitar Center bought Maryland-based Music & Arts Center, a musical instrument chain that caters to beginners, and added it to its American Music Group division. The chain added 80-plus locations flying the Music & Arts Center banner. The following year Guitar Center bought four Hermes Music stores in Brownsville, Laredo, McAllen, and San Antonio, Texas for about $11 million.

In February 2007 Guitar Center acquired all of the assets of Dennis Bamber (dba The Woodwind & The Brasswind) out of bankruptcy for about $30 million. Guitar Center itself was acquired by the private equity firm Bain Capital Partners in October 2007 and its shares delisted from the NASDAQ stock exchange.

EXECUTIVES

Chairman and CEO: Marty P. Albertson, $954,042 pay
President and COO: Gregory A. (Greg) Trojan, age 48
EVP and Chief Marketing Officer: Norman Hajjar
EVP and CFO: Erick Mason, $399,250 pay
  (prior to title change)
EVP and Chief Logistics Officer: William (Bill) Deeney
EVP and CIO: John Zavada
EVP and General Merchandise Manager: Jay Wanamaker
EVP International Development and Proprietary Brands: David Angress
EVP, Chief Administrative Officer, General Counsel, and Secretary: Leland (Lee) Smith, $338,625 pay
EVP Sales and Stores: Mark Galster
SVP Human Resources: Dennis Haffeman
SVP Information Systems: Edward Chan
SVP Strategic Development: Andrew (Andy) Heyneman

VP, Marketing Communications: Jack Sonni
VP Merchandising, Guitar and Amp Division: Keith Brawley
VP, Purchasing, Musical Instruments Division: Eric Spitzer
CEO, Music & Arts Center: Kenneth (Kenny) O'Brien, age 51, $360,500 pay
CEO, Musician's Friend: Robert Eastman, age 48, $543,018 pay
President and COO, Musician's Friend: Craig Johnson
EVP Merchandising, Musician's Friend: Gene Joly
EVP Marketing, Musician's Friend: Stephen Zapf
Auditors: KPMG LLP

LOCATIONS

HQ: Guitar Center, Inc.
5795 Lindero Canyon Rd.,
Westlake Village, CA 91362
Phone: 818-735-8800 **Fax:** 818-735-8822
Web: www.guitarcenter.com

PRODUCTS/OPERATIONS

Selected Products and Brands

Accessories (cables, strings, microphones, picks, stands, straps)
Amplifiers (Ampeg, Crate, Fender, Marshall, Mesa Boogie, S.W.R., Vox)
Band and orchestral instruments and accessories (Blessing, Buffet, DEG, Gemeinhardt, Jupiter, Leblanc, Rico, Selmer, Schiller, Yamaha)
Computer-related recording products (sound cards, sound libraries, recording software)
Guitars (Fender, Gibson, Ibanez, Martin, Ovation, PRS, Taylor, Yamaha)
Keyboards (Alesis, Emu, Ensoniq, Korg, Kurzweil, Roland, Yamaha)
Percussion instruments (Drum Workshop, Pearl, Premier, Remo, Sabian, Tama, Yamaha, Zildjian)
Pro audio/DJ and recording equipment (Alesis, Digidesign, JBL, Mackie, Panasonic, Roland, Sony, Tascam, Yamaha)
Used and vintage products (instruments, technology products)

COMPETITORS

Best Buy	Schmitt Music
Costco Wholesale	Sweetwater
Fletcher Music Centers	Target
Full Compass Systems	Wal-Mart
Sam Ash Music	

HISTORICAL FINANCIALS

Company Type: Private

Income Statement				FYE: December 31
	REVENUE ($ mil.)	NET INCOME ($ mil.)	NET PROFIT MARGIN	EMPLOYEES
12/07	2,300	—	—	9,540
12/06	2,030	—	—	9,540
12/05	1,783	—	—	8,154
12/04	1,513	—	—	—
12/03	1,275	—	—	—
Annual Growth	**15.9%**	**—**	**—**	**8.2%**

Revenue History

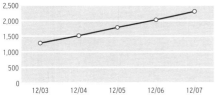

Gulf Oil

Gulf Oil bridges the gap between petroleum producers and retail sales outlets. The petroleum wholesaler distributes gasoline and diesel fuel to about 2,400 Gulf-brand stations in 11 northeastern states. Gulf Oil, which owns and operates 12 storage terminals, also distributes motor oils, lubricants, and heating oil to commercial, industrial, and utility customers. The company has alliances with terminal operators in areas in the Northeast where it does not have a proprietary terminal. Gulf Oil boasts one of the oldest and most recognizable brands in the oil business.

Gulf Oil traces its roots to the famous 1901 oil strike in Spindletop, Texas. At one time one of the largest integrated oil concerns in the world, Gulf Oil Corporation restructured into seven operating companies in the 1970s, the bulk of which were acquired by Chevron in 1984.

EXECUTIVES

President and CEO: Ronald R. (Ron) Sabia
SVP and CFO: Jayne Fitzpatrick
VP and CIO: Sorin Hilgen
Chief Administrative Officer: Robert (Bob) Far
Director Credit Card Services: Marge McDonnell
Director Human Resources: Karen Channel

LOCATIONS

HQ: Gulf Oil Limited Partnership
275 Washington St., Ste. 300, Newton, MA 02458
Phone: 617-454-9300 **Fax:** 617-884-0637
Web: www.gulfoil.com

Gulf Oil operates in 11 northeastern US states.

PRODUCTS/OPERATIONS

Selected Products

Antifreeze
Gasoline
Grease
Heating oil
Kerosene
Synthetic lubricants
Transmission fluid
Zinc-free oils

COMPETITORS

BP
CITGO
Consolidated Beacon
Exxon
Getty Petroleum Marketing
Global Partners
Hess Corporation
Motiva Enterprises
Sunoco

Gulf States Toyota

Even good ol' boys buy foreign cars from Gulf States Toyota (GST). One of only two US Toyota distributors not owned by Toyota Motor Sales (the other is JM Family Enterprises' Southeast Toyota Distributors), the company distributes cars, trucks, and sport utility vehicles in Arkansas, Louisiana, Mississippi, Oklahoma, and Texas. GST has expanded its vehicle processing center in Houston to handle Toyota Tundra pickup trucks built in nearby San Antonio.

Founded in 1969 by Thomas Friedkin and still owned by The Friedkin Companies, GST distributes new Toyotas, parts, and accessories to around 145 dealers in Texas and other states in the region. GST plans to move to a new headquarters in west Houston.

The Toyota distributor plans to open a second vehicle processing center in Temple, Texas in 2011. The new facility will be built in Temple's Rail Park at Central Pointe, offering access to the Burlington Northern Santa Fe railroad yard. It's expected to employ more than 500 people and process and ship about 100,000 Toyota and Scion vehicles annually via rail.

EXECUTIVES

President and General Manager: Toby Hynes
CFO: Frank Gruen
SVP Marketing: J.C. Fassino
VP Human Resources: Dominic Gallo
VP Sales Operations: Tom Bittenbender
Director Administration: David Copeland
Marketing Support Senior Manager: Eric Williamson

LOCATIONS

HQ: Gulf States Toyota, Inc.
7701 Wilshire Place Dr., Houston, TX 77040
Phone: 713-580-3300 **Fax:** 713-580-3332

COMPETITORS

BMW	Kia Motors
Daimler	Mazda
David McDavid Auto Group	Nissan North America
Ford Motor	Volkswagen
General Motors	Volvo
Honda	

HISTORICAL FINANCIALS

Company Type: Private

Income Statement				FYE: December 31
	ESTIMATED REVENUE ($ mil.)	NET INCOME ($ mil.)	NET PROFIT MARGIN	EMPLOYEES
12/07	5,700	—	—	1,275
12/06	4,600	—	—	1,200
12/05	4,600	—	—	1,200
12/04	4,000	—	—	3,500
12/03	3,800	—	—	3,100
Annual Growth	**10.7%**	**—**	**—**	**(19.9%)**

Revenue History

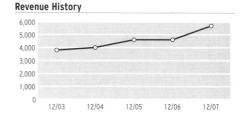

Gundle/SLT Environmental

Oil and water don't mix, and Gundle/SLT Environmental (GSE) plans to keep it that way. The company makes and installs synthetic liners used to prevent groundwater contamination. Waste-management firms, mining companies, and industrial businesses, among others, use these liners at garbage dumps and water-containment facilities. Its solid waste containment services generated more than half of its revenue. The company makes high-density polyethylene smooth-sheet liners, as well as textured sheets and geosynthetic clay liners. The US accounts for about half of sales. Private equity firm Code Hennessy & Simmons bought GSE and took it private in 2004.

At the beginning of 2006 Gundle/SLT acquired the operating assets of the Chilean company SL Limitada, which will open the South American market even further. Its primary products are geomembranes marketed to the mining, solid waste, and water management industries.

That same year, the company expanded its product line with the purchase of the assets of ProGreen Sport Surfaces, which provides synthetic turf for athletic fields for educational institutions and governmental organizations.

EXECUTIVES

Chairman: Daniel J. (Dan) Hennessy, age 50
President, CEO, and Director: Samir T. Badawi, age 68, $465,000 pay
Managing Director, Asia/Pacific: James T. (Jim) Steinke, age 61, $210,000 pay
VP, Corporate Counsel, and Secretary: C. Wayne Case
VP and General Manager, Europe/Middle East/Africa Operations: Paul A. Firrell, age 41, $283,910 pay
VP, CFO, and Assistant Secretary: Ernest C. (Ernie) English Jr., age 55, $209,000 pay (prior to promotion)
VP and General Manager, North American Operations: Gerald E. (Gerry) Hersh, age 64, $204,000 pay
VP Engineering and Quality Control: Ed Zimmel
VP Technical Sales: Boyd J. Ramsey
VP Sales and Marketing: Stephen T. (Steve) Eckhart
VP and CIO: Daniel E. (Dan) Mastin
VP and Corporate Controller: Richard H. Watts
VP Manufacturing: Don E. Bohac
Auditors: Ernst & Young LLP

LOCATIONS

HQ: Gundle/SLT Environmental, Inc.
19103 Gundle Rd., Houston, TX 77073
Phone: 281-443-8564   **Fax:** 281-230-2504
Web: www.gseworld.com

Gundle/SLT Environmental has manufacturing operations in Australia, Canada, Chile, Egypt, Germany, Thailand, the UK, and the US.

2006 Sales

	$ mil.	% of total
US	184.4	49
Europe	77.1	21
Latin & South America	42.1	11
Far East/Pacific Rim	37.9	10
Africa & Middle East	25.7	7
Other	6.1	2
Total	**373.3**	**100**

PRODUCTS/OPERATIONS

2006 Sales

	$ mil.	% of total
Solid Waste Containment	196.2	53
Liquid Containment	71.9	19
Mining	64.4	17
Other applications	40.8	11
Total	**373.3**	**100**

Selected Products

Concrete protection liners
Drainage nets
Geocomposites
Geosynthetic clay liners
Vertical barrier walls

Selected Subsidiaries

Bentofix Technologies (USA) Inc.
Bentofix Technologies, Inc. (Canada)
GSE Australia Pty Ltd
GSE Clay Lining Technology Co.
GSE Lining Technology (Canada) LTD
GSE Lining Technology Company Ltd.
Hyma/GSE Lining Technology Co. (Egypt)
Hyma/GSE Manufacturing Co. (Egypt)

COMPETITORS

Baker Hughes
Bechtel
BJ Services
Black & Veatch
Butyl Products
Fluor
Halliburton
McDermott
Nabors Industries
Peter Kiewit Sons'
Raytheon
Schlumberger
Smith International
Weatherford International

HISTORICAL FINANCIALS

Company Type: Private

Income Statement

FYE: December 31

	REVENUE ($ mil.)	NET INCOME ($ mil.)	NET PROFIT MARGIN	EMPLOYEES
12/06	373	3	0.7%	928
12/05	318	1	0.2%	1,033
12/04	288	2	0.7%	1,045
Annual Growth	**13.9%**	**11.8%**	**—**	**(5.8%)**

2006 Year-End Financials

Debt ratio: 227.8%
Return on equity: 3.5%
Cash ($ mil.): —
Current ratio: —
Long-term debt ($ mil.): 163

Net Income History

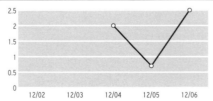

Guthy-Renker

What do Kathie Lee Gifford, Cindy Crawford, Victoria Principal, and Tony Robbins have in common? Each has starred in a program produced by Guthy-Renker, one of the largest infomercial producers in the US. The electronic retailing company pursues marketing opportunities through direct TV, cable and satellite, mail, and telemarketing. Its pitch people hawk a variety of goods and services, including skin care products and cosmetics such as Proactive Solution (the company's primary category), fitness equipment, and motivational tapes. Guthy-Renker was founded in 1988 by co-CEOs Bill Guthy and Greg Renker, after being spun off from Guthy's Cassette Productions Unlimited (CPU).

EXECUTIVES

Founding Principal: William (Bill) Guthy
Founding Principal: Greg Renker
EVP and COO: Kevin Knee
EVP: Ben Van De Bunt

LOCATIONS

HQ: Guthy-Renker Corporation
41-550 Eclectic St., Ste. 200,
Palm Desert, CA 92260
Phone: 760-773-9022   **Fax:** 760-733-9016
Web: www.guthy-renker.com

PRODUCTS/OPERATIONS

Selected Infomercials

The Dean Martin Celebrity Roasts
Get The Edge motivational (hosted by Tony Robbins)
Meaningful Beauty skin care (hosted by Cindy Crawford)
Natural Advantage skin care (hosted by Kathie Lee Gifford)
Principal Secret skin care (hosted by Victoria Principal)
Pro-Activ Solutions skin care (hosted by Elle Macpherson, Jessica Simpson, and Vanessa Williams)
Sheer Cover make-up (hosted by Leeza Gibbons)
Winsor Pilates weight loss (hosted by Daisy Fuentes and Mary Winsor)
Youthful Essence skin care (hosted by Susan Lucci)

COMPETITORS

Aloette	QVC
Avon	Ronco
Gaiam	Thane International
HSN	ValueVision Media

HISTORICAL FINANCIALS

Company Type: Private

Income Statement

FYE: December 31

	REVENUE ($ mil.)	NET INCOME ($ mil.)	NET PROFIT MARGIN	EMPLOYEES
12/07	1,800	—	—	—
12/06	1,500	—	—	825
12/05	1,500	—	—	825
Annual Growth	**9.5%**	**—**	**—**	**0.0%**

Revenue History

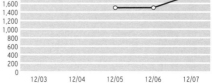

Haights Cross Communications

Haights Cross Communications helped students buckle down on their studies. The company, which has put all of its business assets up for sale, was once a leading publisher of test preparation and supplemental education materials. Its imprints included Buckle Down, Sundance Publishing, and Triumph Learning. Aimed mostly at the K-12 market, its materials included competency tests, supplemental reading instruction, and skills assessments. Haights Cross also published audio books for libraries through its Recorded Books business, as well as continuing medical education (CME) products through its Oakstone imprint.

The decision to put the company up for sale came after a lengthy corporate review initiated as part of a recapitalization effort in 2007. Later that year Paul Crecca replaced founder and CEO Peter Quandt, who resigned.

Rowman & Littlefield Publishing, a Maryland-based academic publisher, acquired the company's Sundance/Newbridge unit in 2008. That same year private equity firm Boston Ventures Management purchased its Oakstone Publishing business.

Haights Cross Communications sold its products to approximately 150,000 customers, including educators and school systems, public and school libraries, and medical professionals.

EXECUTIVES

Chairman: Eugene I. (Gene) Davis, age 53
President, CEO, CFO, and Director; President, Haights Cross Operating: Paul J. Crecca, age 50, $476,110 pay
EVP; President, Triumph Learning: Kevin M. McAliley, age 48, $493,804 pay
SVP and CFO: Mark Kurtz, age 43
SVP Finance and Planning: Melissa L. Linsky, age 49
VP Market Research: Julie Latzer
President and General Manager, Buckle Down Publishing: Thomas (Tom) Emrick
President, Oakstone Publishing: Nancy McMeekin, age 53
President, Options Publishing: Barbara Russell, age 60
President, Sundance/Newbridge Educational Publishing: Paul A. Konowitch, age 53, $328,079 pay (prior to title change)
Publisher and Executive Editor, Oakstone: Dean Celia
President, Recorded Books: Scott Williams, age 47
Auditors: Ernst & Young LLP

LOCATIONS

HQ: Haights Cross Communications, Inc.
10 New King St., Ste. 102, White Plains, NY 10604
Phone: 914-289-9400   **Fax:** 914-289-9401
Web: www.haightscross.com

PRODUCTS/OPERATIONS

2007 Sales

	$ mil.	% of total
Test-prep & intervention	86	37
Library	85	36
Medical education	34	15
K-12 supplemental education	27	12
Total	**232.0**	**100**

COMPETITORS

HarperCollins
Houghton Mifflin Harcourt
McGraw-Hill
National Geographic
Pearson Education
Random House
Scholastic
Simon & Schuster
Time Life

HISTORICAL FINANCIALS

Company Type: Private

Income Statement

FYE: December 31

	REVENUE ($ mil.)	NET INCOME ($ mil.)	NET PROFIT MARGIN	EMPLOYEES
12/07	232	64	27.4%	855
12/06	222	(73)	—	821
12/05	211	(44)	—	822
12/04	171	(26)	—	700
12/03	162	(2)	—	645
Annual Growth	**9.4%**	**—**	**—**	**7.3%**

2007 Year-End Financials

Debt ratio: —   Current ratio: —
Return on equity: —   Long-term debt ($ mil.): 290
Cash ($ mil.): —

Net Income History

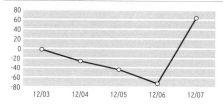

Hallmark Cards

As the #1 producer of warm fuzzies, Hallmark Cards is the Goliath of greeting cards. The company's cards are sold under brand names such as Hallmark, Shoebox, and Ambassador and can be found in more than 43,000 US retail stores. (About 3,700 stores bear the Hallmark Gold Crown name; the majority of these stores are independently owned). Hallmark also offers electronic greeting cards, gifts, and flowers through its Web site. In addition to greeting cards, the company owns crayon manufacturer Crayola (formerly Binney & Smith), a controlling stake in cable broadcaster Crown Media, and Kansas City's Crown Center real estate development. Members of the founding Hall family own two-thirds of Hallmark.

While Hallmark has risen to the top tier in the industry, changes in the ways that people interact and communicate have created new challenges for the company. Sales have been fairly stagnant the past few years, leading Hallmark to continue to downsize its workforce as part of a cost saving effort; in 2008 it consolidated production at two printing plants in Kansas, eliminating several jobs at plants in Toronto, Arkansas, and at its Sunrise Publications subsidiary in Indiana.

Product development has been key for its traditional card business. Hallmark has had success with a line of musical cards (Cards With Sound) and now sells cards featuring short animated videos. The high-tech products, along with a new line of humorous cards, have helped boost the traditional card business. Hallmark's Crayloa business, meanwhile, continues to enjoy success and rising sales thanks to strong back-to-school sales and such new products Color Wonder Sprayer and Color Explosion Spinner. The subsidiary was recast under its famous brand name in 2007.

Another of its makeover effort has been an initiative to update its Gold Crown stores. The company hopes a new design and layout will reflect a homier image and differentiate the outlets from other retail shops. Hallmark also launched a women's lifestyle periodical called *Hallmark Magazine* and acquired the assets of Paramount Cards, a Rhode Island-based card manufacturer.

HISTORY

Eighteen-year-old Joyce Hall started selling picture postcards from two shoe boxes in his room at the Kansas City, Missouri, YMCA in 1910. His brother Rollie joined him the next year, and the two added greeting cards to their line in 1912. The brothers opened Hall Brothers, a store that sold postcards, gifts, books, and stationery, but it was destroyed in a 1915 fire. The Halls got a loan, bought an engraving company, and produced their first original cards in time for Christmas.

In 1921 a third brother, William, joined the firm, which started stamping the backs of its cards with the phrase "A Hallmark Card." By 1922 Hall Brothers had salespeople in all 48 states. The firm began selling internationally in 1931.

Hall Brothers patented the "Eye-Vision" display case for greeting cards in 1936 and sold it to retailers across the country. The company aired its first radio ad in 1938. The next year it introduced a friendship card, displaying a cart filled with purple pansies. The card became the company's best-seller. During WWII Joyce Hall persuaded the government not to curtail paper supplies, arguing that his greeting cards were essential to the nation's morale.

The company opened its first retail store in 1950. The following year marked the first production of *Hallmark Hall of Fame,* TV's longest-running dramatic series and winner of more Emmy awards than any other program. Hall Brothers changed its name to Hallmark Cards in 1954 and introduced its Ambassador line of cards five years later.

Hallmark introduced paper party products and started putting *Peanuts* characters on cards in 1960. Donald Hall, Joyce Hall's son, was appointed CEO in 1966. Two years later Hallmark opened Crown Center, which surrounded company headquarters in Kansas City. Disaster struck in 1981 when two walkways collapsed at Crown Center's Hyatt Regency hotel, killing 114 and injuring 225.

Joyce Hall died in 1982, and Donald Hall became both chairman and CEO. Hallmark acquired Crayola Crayon maker Binney & Smith in 1984. It introduced Shoebox Greetings, a line of nontraditional cards, in 1986. Irvine Hockaday replaced Donald Hall as CEO the same year (Hall continued as chairman).

The company joined with Information Storage Devices in 1993 to market recordable greeting cards. The following year it acquired film production company RHI Entertainment, renaming the unit Hallmark Entertainment. Hallmark unveiled its Web site, Hallmark.com, in 1996 and began offering electronic greeting cards.

Hallmark's 1998 acquisition of UK-based Creative Publications boosted the company into the top spot in the British greeting card market. That same year it purchased Sunrise Publications. The following year the company acquired portrait studio chain The Picture People (sold in 2005) and Christian greeting card maker DaySpring Cards. It also acquired a stake in cable channel Odyssey, which was later renamed the Hallmark Channel (now operated by Crown Media).

The company began testing overnight flower delivery in the US just in time for Valentine's Day 2000. Hockaday retired as president and CEO at the end of 2001; vice chairman Donald Hall Jr. took the additional title of CEO in early 2002.

Hallmark decided to move some of its IT operations in 2004 to Affiliated Computer Services in a seven-year deal worth $230 million; the Dallas-based company opened a center near the Hallmark headquarters to handle the work. Binney & Smith changed its name to Crayola in 2007.

EXECUTIVES

Chairman: Donald J. Hall
Vice Chairman, President, and CEO:
 Donald J. (Don) Hall Jr., age 52
EVP and General Counsel: Brian E. Gardner, age 55
SVP Human Resources: Tom Wright
SVP Greetings: Steve Hawn
SVP Public Affairs and Communication: Steve Doyal, age 59
SVP Customer Development: Steve Paoletti
SVP Creative: Teri Ann Drake
VP Marketing Strategy: Jay Dittmann
VP Trade Development: Vince G. Burke
President and CEO, Crayola: Mark J. Schwab
President, Personal Expression Group: David E. Hall, age 45
President, Retail: James E. (Jim) Boike
VP Sales, Hallmark Insights: Kimberly Hanson
Public Relations Director, Public Affairs and Communications: Julie O'Dell

LOCATIONS

HQ: Hallmark Cards, Inc.
 2501 McGee St., Kansas City, MO 64108
Phone: 816-274-5111   **Fax:** 816-274-5061
Web: www.hallmark.com

PRODUCTS/OPERATIONS

Selected Brands

Keepsake (holiday ornaments and other collectibles)
Mahogany (products celebrating African-American heritage)
Nature's Sketchbook (cards and gifts)
Shoebox (greeting cards)
Sinceramente (Spanish-language greeting cards)
Tree of Life (products celebrating Jewish heritage)

Selected Subsidiaries

Crayola (crayons and markers)
Crown Center Redevelopment (retail complex)
Crown Media Holdings (pay television channels, 95%)
DaySpring Cards (Christian greeting cards)
Hallmark Insights (business and consumer gift certificates)
Halls Merchandising (department store)
Image Arts (discount greeting card distribution)
Irresistible Ink (handwriting and marketing service)
Litho-Krome (lithography)
William Arthur (invitations, stationery)

COMPETITORS

1-800-FLOWERS.COM	Enesco
American Greetings	Faber-Castell
Amscan	International Greetings
Andrews McMeel Universal	iParty
BIC	MEGA Brands
Blyth	NobleWorks
Build-A-Bear	Party City
Clinton Cards	SPS Studios
CSS Industries	Syratech
Dixon Ticonderoga	Taylor Corporation

HISTORICAL FINANCIALS

Company Type: Private

Income Statement

FYE: December 31

	REVENUE ($ mil.)	NET INCOME ($ mil.)	NET PROFIT MARGIN	EMPLOYEES
12/07	4,400	—	—	15,900
12/06	4,100	—	—	16,000
12/05	4,200	—	—	18,000
12/04	4,400	—	—	18,000
12/03	4,300	—	—	18,000
Annual Growth	**0.6%**	**—**	**—**	**(3.1%)**

Revenue History

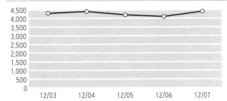

Hampton Affiliates

As a vertically integrated lumber company, Hampton Affiliates knows trees from the seedling to the stud. One of Oregon's top timber firms, Hampton produces about 1.9 billion board feet of softwood lumber yearly through seven sawmills. The company has nearly 170,000 acres of timberland and owns tree farms and mills in Oregon, Washington, and British Columbia. It also manages nearly 300,000 acres of publicly owned forest land in British Columbia. Through its Hampton Distribution Companies division, it distributes doors, windows, and other building materials. Hampton supplies homebuilding centers through its stud lumber and distribution operations. The company has its own railcar fleet to transport its products.

L. M. "Bud" Hampton founded the company in 1942, and the Hampton family continues to own the enterprise.

During 2002 the company acquired Darrington Lumber Mills and completed a timberland exchange of 92,000 acres. In 2004 the company added 12,000 acres in Northwest Oregon through its purchase of Wilson River Tree Farm. It also closed its Fort Hill sawmill that year due to uncertain supply and market conditions. Hampton Affiliates sold its Lane Stanton Vance hardwoods distribution business to BlueLinx in 2005.

Hampton Affiliates expanded its production capabilities in 2006 when it acquired a majority interest in Babine Forest Products and Decker

Lake Forest Products' sawmills in British Columbia. A year after their acquisition, the plants slashed production by about 40% in response to a slowdown in the lumber market.

EXECUTIVES

Chairman: Michael P. Hollern, age 63
CEO: Steven J. (Steve) Zika
CTO: Andy McNiece
VP Finance and CFO: Robert Bluhm
VP Manufacturing: Bruce Mallory
Controller: Arvid Lacy
Director Human Resources: Dave Salmon
Director of Distribution and Financial Analysis, HDC Sacramento: Chris Walton

LOCATIONS

HQ: Hampton Affiliates
 9600 SW Barnes Rd., Ste. 200, Portland, OR 97225
Phone: 503-297-7691   **Fax:** 503-203-6607
Web: www.hamptonaffiliates.com

Hampton Affiliates owns sawmills in Oregon and Washington and distribution facilities in California.

PRODUCTS/OPERATIONS

Selected Products

Clear and industrial lumber
Dimensional lumber
Engineered wood
Panel products
Residential doors
Siding and trim
Stud lumber
Timbers
Wood windows

COMPETITORS

Canfor	Potlatch
Cascades Inc.	Roseburg Forest Products
Deltic Timber	Sierra Pacific Industries
Georgia-Pacific	Simpson Investment
International Paper	West Fraser Timber
Louisiana-Pacific	Western Forest Products
Plum Creek Timber	Weyerhaeuser

Harman Management

This company helped a colonel get started in the chicken business. Harman Management, one of the largest franchisees of KFC (a division of YUM! Brands), was founded by Leon Harman — the first person to buy a franchise from the chain's founder, Colonel Sanders. The company now has more than 340 fried chicken units in California, Colorado, Utah, and Washington, along with several locations co-branded with Taco Bell, Pizza Hut, and A&W units. Harman, who ran a cafe in Salt Lake City, was awarded his franchise in 1952. He coined the name Kentucky Fried Chicken and popularized the concept of selling the chicken in a bucket.

EXECUTIVES

Chairman Emeritus: Jackie Trujillo, age 72
Chairman and CEO: James D. (Jim) Olson
COO: Vern Wardle
VP Finance: James S. Jackson
VP Operations: James (Jim) Beglin
Director Human Resources: Shawn Brady
Director Real Estate: Karen Bellini
Director Information Systems: Jonathan Packer

LOCATIONS

HQ: Harman Management Corporation
199 1st St., Ste. 212, Los Altos, CA 94022
Phone: 650-941-5681   **Fax:** 650-948-7532

COMPETITORS

American Dairy Queen	Fresh Enterprises
Arby's	In-N-Out Burgers
Burger King	Jack in the Box
Cajun Operating Company	McDonald's
Chick-fil-A	Popeyes
Chipotle	Quiznos
CKE Restaurants	Subway
Del Taco	Wendy's
El Pollo Loco	

HISTORICAL FINANCIALS

Company Type: Private

Income Statement

FYE: June 30

	REVENUE ($ mil.)	NET INCOME ($ mil.)	NET PROFIT MARGIN	EMPLOYEES
6/07	450	—	—	—
6/06	437	—	—	—
6/05	411	—	—	—
6/04	391	—	—	13,500
6/03	377	—	—	13,000
Annual Growth	4.5%	—	—	3.8%

Revenue History

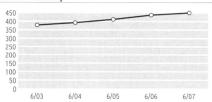

	6/03	6/04	6/05	6/06	6/07
450					
400					
350					
300					
250					
200					
150					
100					
50					
0					

Harpo, Inc.

Everyone knows Oprah Winfrey is an exceptional businesswoman; there's no need to Harpo on it. Unrelated to the silent Marx brother, Harpo controls the entertainment interests of talk show host/actress/producer Oprah Winfrey. *The Oprah Winfrey Show* is the highest-rated TV talk show in history, seen in almost every US market and in 120 countries. Harpo also produces feature films (*Beloved*, which also starred Winfrey) and made-for-TV movies (*Their Eyes Were Watching God*), as well as radio content distributed by SIRIUS XM Radio. In print, the company publishes *O, The Oprah Magazine* with Hearst Magazines, which boasts a circulation of about 2.4 million. Winfrey founded Harpo in 1986.

With her entertainment empire showing no signs of losing strength, Winfrey ranks among one of the top paid and most powerful celebrities in entertainment. She was also the first black woman to join the ranks of *Forbes* magazine's list of billionaires.

The crown jewel in Oprah's holdings is by far her talk show, which reaches about 8 million viewers per day in the US, about three-fourths of whom are women. The celebrity media mogul

had announced she would end *The Oprah Winfrey Show* in 2006, the 20th anniversary of the program; however, she has since signed a new contract to keep it on the air into 2011. (Winfrey claims she will retire that year as well.)

Continuing to build its portfolio of media holdings, Harpo launched *The Rachael Ray Show* starring Food Network star Rachael Ray in 2006. Pairing celebrity interviews and Ray's culinary talents, the show has quickly gained a loyal following. Harpo also produces the popular *Dr. Phil* show (starring celebrity therapist Dr. Phil McGraw), which is distributed by King World along with *Oprah* and *Rachael Ray*.

The company has also partnered with Discovery Communications to launch a new cable channel called OWN: The Oprah Winfrey Network. Slated to launch in 2009, the network will replace Discovery's existing Discovery Health Channel.

Winfrey previously owned a significant stake in women's cable channel operator Oxygen Media, which was acquired in 2007 by NBC Universal. The Oxygen network airs her *Oprah After the Show* program, where viewers can see the candid conversations Oprah has with her studio audience. Fans of Oprah can also keep up with the show via the oprah.com Web site.

HISTORY

Oprah Winfrey began her broadcasting career in 1973 at age 19 as a news anchor at Nashville's WTVF-TV. She became an evening news co-anchor in Baltimore in 1976, where she was recruited to co-host WJZ-TV's local talk show *People Are Talking*. She moved to Chicago in the early 1980s to host ABC affiliate WLS-TV's *AM Chicago*, which quickly became the city's top morning talk show. It was renamed *The Oprah Winfrey Show* in 1985.

Winfrey's performance in Steven Spielberg's *The Color Purple* in 1985 (her first ever acting role) won her an Oscar nomination and boosted her ratings when *The Oprah Winfrey Show* debuted nationally in 138 cities the following year, thanks to a syndication deal with King World Productions secured by her agent (later Harpo's president and COO) Jeffrey Jacobs. Harpo was founded that year.

Winfrey obtained full ownership of her program in 1988. Two years later Harpo Films was created, and Winfrey bought a Chicago studio to produce *Oprah*, becoming only the third woman to own her own production studio (Mary Pickford and Lucille Ball were the others). She introduced the popular Oprah's Book Club in 1996. Also that year Texas cattlemen filed a lawsuit claiming she had caused a drop in beef futures prices after a show on the UK outbreak of mad cow disease (Winfrey didn't emphasize that the disease had not appeared in the US). But jurors ruled in her favor in early 1998. Winfrey also renewed her contract that year until the 2001-2002 TV season.

In 1998 Winfrey agreed to produce original programming for Oxygen, a new cable network for women launched by Oxygen Media, in exchange for an equity stake. (The network was acquired by NBC Universal in 2007.) CBS bought King World in 1999, and the deal gave King World stockholder Winfrey a $100 million stake in CBS (later bought by Viacom and now part of CBS Corporation). The following year Winfrey launched with Hearst Magazines her own magazine (*O, The Oprah Magazine*) that focuses on relationships, health, and fashion.

In 2002 the talk show diva decided that Oprah's Book Club would be an occasional, instead of a regular, segment on her TV program (much to the dismay of many book publishers). In addition, a spin-off talk show hosted by Dr. Phil McGraw (a regular on the Oprah show) premiered that year. In 2003 Winfrey announced that she was reviving her book club (with an emphasis on classic literature rather than books authored by contemporary writers). She also signed a contract to keep her TV program on the air into 2008. The next year Winfrey extended the contract even further, striking a deal to keep gabbing until 2011.

In 2006 Harpo launched another celebrity-hosted talk show, *The Rachael Ray Show* starring Food Network star Rachael Ray.

EXECUTIVES

Chairman: Oprah G. Winfrey, age 54
CFO: Douglas J. (Doug) Pattison
President, Harpo Productions: Tim Bennett
President, Harpo Films: Kate Forte
President, The Oprah Winfrey Network (OWN):
Robin Schwartz
EVP Creative Services, Development Group:
Ellen Rekieten
EVP Marketing and Development, Development Group:
Harriet Seitler
EVP: Eric Logan
VP Communications: Lisa Halliday
General Counsel: William L. (Bill) Becker
General Manager, Harpo Radio: John R. Gehron, age 62
Executive Producer, The Oprah Winfrey Show:
Sheri Salata
Co-Executive Producer, The Oprah Winfrey Show:
Lisa Erspamer

LOCATIONS

HQ: Harpo, Inc.
110 N. Carpenter St., Chicago, IL 60607
Phone: 312-633-1000   **Fax:** 312-633-1976
Web: www.oprah.com

PRODUCTS/OPERATIONS

Selected Operations

Harpo Entertainment Group
Harpo Films
    Amy & Isabelle (2001)
    Beloved (1998)
    Oprah Winfrey Presents: Before Women Had Wings (1997)
    Oprah Winfrey Presents: The Wedding (1998)
    Overexposed (1992)
    Their Eyes Were Watching God (2005)
    There Are No Children Here (1993)
Harpo Productions
    Dr. Phil
    Oprah After the Show
    Oprah Winfrey Presents: David and Lisa (1998)
    Oprah Winfrey Presents: Tuesdays with Morrie (1999)
    The Oprah Winfrey Show
    The Rachael Ray Show
    The Women of Brewster Place (1989)
Harpo Print
    O, The Oprah Magazine (joint venture with Hearst Corporation)
    O, At Home (periodic issues)
Harpo Radio (satellite radio content)
Harpo Video
Oprah's Angel Network (charitable organization)
Oprah's Book Club (reading club featured on *The Oprah Winfrey Show*)
Oprah Boutique (consumer products)
Oprah.com

HISTORICAL FINANCIALS

Company Type: Private

Income Statement				FYE: December 31
	REVENUE ($ mil.)	NET INCOME ($ mil.)	NET PROFIT MARGIN	EMPLOYEES
12/07	345	—	—	410
12/06	325	—	—	370
12/05	290	—	—	341
12/04	275	—	—	—
12/03	275	—	—	250
Annual Growth	5.8%	—	—	13.2%

Revenue History

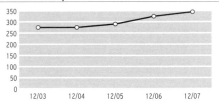

Harrah's Entertainment

Harrah's Entertainment likes to spread its bets. The world's largest gaming company, Harrah's owns, operates, and/or manages about 50 casinos (under such names as Bally's, Caesars, Harrah's, Horseshoe, and Rio), primarily in the US and the UK. Operations include casino hotels, dockside and riverboat casinos, and Native American gaming establishments. Harrah's acquired rival Caesars Entertainment for $9.4 billion in cash, stock, and debt. The deal cemented Harrah's as the world's #1 gaming company, jumping over the merged MGM MIRAGE/Mandalay combination. To appease regulators, Harrah's sold its Harrah's Tunica and East Chicago casinos to Colony Capital. The firm is owned by Apollo Advisors and TPG Capital.

Harrah's facilities boast more than 3 million sq. ft. of casino space and some 38,000 hotel rooms and suites. The company derives 70% of its revenues from gambling at its casinos; its locations are in Illinois, Indiana, Iowa, Louisiana, Mississippi, Missouri, Nevada, New Jersey, and Pennsylvania. Las Vegas properties include Harrah's Las Vegas, Rio All-Suite Hotel & Casino, Caesars Palace, Bally's Las Vegas, Flamingo Las Vegas, Paris Las Vegas, Imperial Palace Hotel & Casino, and Bill's Gamblin' Hall & Saloon.

Harrah's also owns and operates the World Series of Poker tournament and brand, and manages three casinos on Indian reservations (in Arizona, California, and North Carolina).

Internationally, the company has a presence in Canada, Egypt, South Africa, and the UK. In addition, Harrah's has teamed with joint venture partners to develop and open casinos in the Bahamas and Spain.

In 2008 the company was acquired by private-equity firms Apollo and TPG for about $17 billion plus the assumption of about $11 billion in debt. As a result of the deal, Harrah's stock ceased trading on the New York Stock Exchange, the Chicago Stock Exchange, and the Philadelphia Stock Exchange.

HISTORY

William Harrah and his father founded their first bingo parlor in Reno, Nevada, in 1937. Using the income from that business, Harrah opened his first casino, Harrah's Club, in downtown Reno in 1946. In 1955 and 1956 he bought several clubs in Stateline, Nevada (near Lake Tahoe). Harrah built the company by using promotions to draw middle-class Californians to his clubs.

During the 1960s the entrepreneur expanded his operations in Lake Tahoe, and in 1968 he built a 400-room hotel tower in Reno. Harrah's went public in 1971. After Harrah's death in 1978, the company expanded outside Nevada by building a hotel and casino in Atlantic City, New Jersey.

Holiday Inns bought Harrah's in 1980 for about $300 million. The hotelier already owned a 40% interest in River Boat Casino, which operated a casino next to a Holiday Inn in Las Vegas. When Holiday Inns acquired the other 60% of the casino/hotel in 1983, Harrah's took over its management. Holiday Inns became Holiday Corporation in 1985. The following year UK brewer Bass PLC put up $100 million for 10% of Holiday Corporation.

In 1990 Bass acquired the Holiday Inn hotel chain for $2.2 billion. The rest of Holiday Corporation, including Harrah's, was renamed Promus under chairman Michael Rose.

In the early 1990s Harrah's built a casino on Ak-Chin Indian land near Phoenix and opened riverboat casinos in Joliet, Illinois; Shreveport, Louisiana; and North Kansas City, Missouri. In 1995 Promus spun off its hotel operations as Promus Hotel Corporation and changed the name of its casino business to Harrah's Entertainment.

Also in 1995 Harrah's gambled and lost. Big. Its New Orleans casino was shelved even before it was finished — a victim of Louisiana's Byzantine politics. Eager for the right to build what would be a $395 million, 200,000-sq.-ft. casino in the heart of the city, Harrah's had made a number of ill-advised concessions to state and municipal officials. It agreed not to offer hotel rooms or food at the casino (foregoing about 20% of anticipated revenues) and promised to make an annual $100 million minimum payment to the state, in addition to 19% of the casino's revenues. In the end the fiasco's price tag reached $900 million (only half of which went to casino construction costs), and Harrah's put the project into bankruptcy to stop the bleeding. (It resumed construction in 1999 and finally opened the casino at the end of the year.)

In 1997 Rose retired as chairman and was replaced by CEO Philip Satre. In 1998 Harrah's bought competitor Showboat, with properties in Las Vegas and Atlantic City, and management of a New South Wales, Australia, casino.

In early 1999 Harrah's bought Rio Hotel & Casino, which operates one upscale casino on the Las Vegas Strip, for about $525 million. In 2000 the company bought riverboat casino operator Players International for $425 million.

Harrah's purchasd Harveys Casino Resorts, with four locations in Colorado, Iowa, and Nevada, for $675 million in 2001. (It sold the Colorado location in 2002.) The 452-room Harrah's Atlantic City hotel tower was opened in 2002. Also that year it began construction of a second, 800-room tower at its Atlantic City Showboat casino. Later in 2002 Harrah's acquired Louisiana Downs, a Thoroughbred racetrack in Bossier City, for $157 million. Harrah's subsequently turned Louisiana Downs into a full-blown casino.

In 2004 Harrah's acquired casino operator Horseshoe Gaming for $1.45 billion. The purchase added the properties to Harrah's portfolio (Hammond, Indiana; Bossier City, Louisiana; and Tunica, Mississippi). In order to gain regulatory approval for the purchase, Harrah's later sold its Harrah's Shreveport casino to Boyd Gaming for $190 million.

The following year Harrah's completed a monster-sized deal, the $9.4 billion acquisition of rival Caesars Entertainment, which rocketed the company to the top of the gaming world.

In 2005 Harrah's bought the Imperial Palace, one of the last few independent casinos on the Las Vegas Strip, for $370 million.

The effects of Hurricane Katrina were felt at the company's Biloxi and Gulfport, Mississippi locations, which suffered extensive damage. Harrah's sold the Gulfport location, such as it was, and rebuilt the Biloxi site, which re-opened in 2006. That year Harrah's sold its Flamingo Laughlin hotel-casino and an undeveloped land parcel in Atlantic City to American Real Estate Partners. It also purchased casino operator London Clubs International for $586 million. London Clubs operates seven UK casinos, as well as two in Egypt and one in South Africa.

EXECUTIVES

Chairman, President, and CEO: Gary W. Loveman, age 47
CFO: Jonathan S. Halkyard, age 43, $420,740 pay
SVP and General Counsel:
Stephen H. (Steve) Brammell, age 50, $486,923 pay (prior to title change)
SVP Business Development: Richard E. (Rich) Mirman, age 41
SVP Communications and Government Relations:
Janis L. (Jan) Jones, age 58
SVP and Chief Marketing Officer: David W. Norton, age 39
SVP Operations, Products, and Services:
Anthony F. (Tony) Santo
SVP Human Resources: Mary H. Thomas, age 41
CIO and SVP Innovation, Gaming, and Technology:
Timothy S. (Tim) Stanley, age 42
SVP Slots: Kenneth M. Weil
SVP, Controller, and Chief Accounting Officer:
Anthony D. (Tony) McDuffie
SVP, Las Vegas Operations; SVP and General Manager, Rio All-Suite Hotel & Casino: Marilyn G. Winn
SVP and General Manager, Harrah's Laughlin:
Wade Faul
SVP and General Manager, Harrah's New Orleans Casino: Jim Hoskins
VP Public Policy and Communications: Marybel Batjer, age 52
VP, Secretary, and Associate General Counsel:
Michael D. Cohen
VP Harrah's Operating Company:
Michael (Mike) O'Hagan
Chief Litigation Officer: Michael Kostrinsky
Auditors: Deloitte & Touche LLP

LOCATIONS

HQ: Harrah's Entertainment, Inc.
1 Caesars Palace Dr., Las Vegas, NV 89109
Phone: 702-407-6000 **Fax:** 702-407-6037
Web: www.harrahs.com

PRODUCTS/OPERATIONS

2007 Sales

	$ mil.	% of total
Casino	8,831	70
Food & beverage	1,699	13
Rooms	1,354	11
Management fees	81	1
Other	696	5
Promotional allowances	(1,836)	—
Total	**10,825**	**100**

US Properties

Atlantic City, New Jersey
    Harrah's Atlantic City
    Showboat Atlantic City
    Bally's Atlantic City
    Caesars Atlantic City
Bossier City, Louisiana
    Louisiana Downs
    Horseshoe Bossier City
Chester, Pennsylvania
    Harrah's Chester
Chicago, Illinois area
    Harrah's Joliet (Illinois)
    Horseshoe Hammond (Indiana)
Council Bluffs, Iowa
    Harrah's Council Bluffs
    Horseshoe Council Bluffs
Indiana
    Caesars Indiana
Kansas City, Missouri
    Harrah's North Kansas City
Lake Tahoe, Nevada
    Harrah's Lake Tahoe
    Harveys Lake Tahoe
    Bill's Lake Tahoe
Las Vegas, Nevada
    Harrah's Las Vegas
    Rio
    Caesars Palace
    Paris Las Vegas
    Bally's Las Vegas
    Flamingo Las Vegas
    Imperial Palace
    Bill's Gamblin' Hall & Saloon
Laughlin, Nevada
    Harrah's Laughlin
Reno, Nevada
    Harrah's Reno
Metropolis, Illinois
    Harrah's Metropolis
Mississippi Gulf Coast
    Grand Casino Biloxi
New Orleans, Louisiana
    Harrah's New Orleans
St. Louis, Missouri
    Harrah's St. Louis
Tunica, Mississippi
    Horseshoe Tunica
    Grand Casino Tunica
    Sheraton Casino & Hotel

International Properties

Egypt
    London Club Cairo-Nile
    Rendezvous Cairo-Ramses
Ontario, Canada
    Casino Windsor
Punta del Este, Uruguay
    Conrad Punta del Este Resort and Casino
South Africa
    Emerald Safari
United Kingdom
    Golden Nugget
    Rendezvous Casino
    The Sportsman
    Fifty
    Rendezvous Brighton
    Rendezvous Southend-on-Sea
    Manchester235
    The Casino at the Empire
    Alea Nottingham
    Alea Glasgow

Other Operations

Casinos managed for Indian tribes
    Harrah's Ak-Chin (Phoenix, Arizona)
    Harrah's Cherokee (Cherokee, North Carolina)
    Harrah's Rincon (San Diego, California)
Racetracks
    Bluegrass Down (Paducah, KY)
    Louisiana Downs (Bossier City)
    Turfway Park (50%; Simpson County, KY)
World Series of Poker

COMPETITORS

Ameristar Casinos
Boyd Gaming
Isle of Capri Casinos
Kerzner International
Mashantucket Pequot
MGM MIRAGE
Pinnacle Entertainment
President Casinos
Station Casinos
Trump Resorts

HISTORICAL FINANCIALS

Company Type: Private

Income Statement

FYE: December 31

	REVENUE ($ mil.)	NET INCOME ($ mil.)	NET PROFIT MARGIN	EMPLOYEES
12/07	10,825	619	5.7%	87,000
12/06	9,674	536	5.5%	85,000
12/05	7,111	236	3.3%	85,000
12/04	4,548	368	8.1%	46,600
12/03	4,323	293	6.8%	41,000
Annual Growth	**25.8%**	**20.6%**	**—**	**20.7%**

2007 Year-End Financials

Debt ratio: 187.6%
Return on equity: 9.8%
Cash ($ mil.): —
Current ratio: —
Long-term debt ($ mil.): 12,430

Net Income History

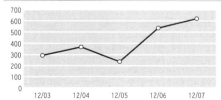

Harvard Pilgrim Health Care

If Harvard Pilgrim Health Care were any more New England-centric, it would have to be located on Plymouth Rock. A leading provider of health benefits in Massachusetts, the not-for-profit organization also offers plans to residents of New Hampshire and Maine. It has more than 1 million members enrolled in its HMO, PPO, point-of-service, and Medicare Advantage plans. Those members have access to a regional network of about 135 hospitals and 28,000 doctors and other providers. Harvard Pilgrim Health Care also targets multi-state employers with its Choice Plus and Options PPO plans, offered through a partnership with UnitedHealth.

In addition to its direct insurance offerings, the company provides third-party administrative services for self-insured plans. It has been growing this part of its business through acquisitions, including the purchases of regional third-party administrators Health Plans (in 2005) and Benefit Plan Management (2006).

Harvard Pilgrim Health Care upgraded its Medicare-related offerings in 2007, replacing its HMO plan with a Medicare Advantage private-fee-for-service plan (branded First Seniority Freedom), which it makes available in several Massachusetts and New Hampshire counties.

It has also begun enrolling Massachusetts residents in low-cost coverage plans as part of the state's mandate, passed in 2006, that requires every resident to have health insurance.

EXECUTIVES

President, CEO, and Director:
Charles D. (Charlie) Baker Jr.
COO: Bruce M. Bullen
CFO: James M. DuCharme
SVP Health Services and Chief Medical Officer:
Roberta Herman
SVP Information Technology and Operations and CIO:
Deborah A. Norton
SVP and General Counsel: Laura S. Peabody
SVP Actuarial Services and Chief Actuary: Gary H. Lin
SVP Sales and Customer Service: Vincent (Vin) Capozzi
SVP, Controller, Corporate Accounting, and Treasury:
Marie Montgomery
VP Medical Management: Judith H. Frampton
VP Customer and Member Service: Lynn A. Bowman
VP Human Resources: Deborah Hicks
VP Marketing: Dana Rashti
President, Health Plans: William R. (Bill) Breidenbach
Auditors: PricewaterhouseCoopers LLP

LOCATIONS

HQ: Harvard Pilgrim Health Care, Inc.
93 Worcester St., Wellesley, MA 02481
Phone: 617-509-1000 **Fax:** 617-509-7590
Web: www.harvardpilgrim.org

Harvard Pilgrim Health Care operates in Maine, Massachusetts, and New Hampshire.

PRODUCTS/OPERATIONS

2007 Revenues

	% of total
Net investment income	66
Net underwriting gains	34
Total	**100**

Selected Products

Best Buy HSA PPO (high-deductible plan)
Choice Plus PPO (with UnitedHealth)
First Seniority Freedom (Medicare Advantage private-
  fee-for-service plan)
Harvard Pilgrim Core Coverage (HMO)
Harvard Pilgrim POS (point-of-service plan)
Harvard Pilgrim PPO (preferred provider organization)
Options PPO (with UnitedHealth)

COMPETITORS

Aetna	Health New England
Blue Cross (MA)	MVP Health Plan
CIGNA	Neighborhood Health
ConnectiCare	Tufts Health Plan
Fallon Community Health	

HISTORICAL FINANCIALS

Company Type: Not-for-profit

Income Statement   FYE: December 31

	REVENUE ($ mil.)	NET INCOME ($ mil.)	NET PROFIT MARGIN	EMPLOYEES
12/07	2,498	46	1.8%	—
12/06	2,488	71	2.8%	—
12/05	2,200	74	3.4%	—
12/04	2,300	39	1.7%	—
12/03	2,100	44	2.1%	1,400
Annual Growth	4.4%	0.8%	—	—

2007 Year-End Financials

Debt ratio: 0.0%   Current ratio: —
Return on equity: 12.2%   Long-term debt ($ mil.): 0
Cash ($ mil.): —

Net Income History

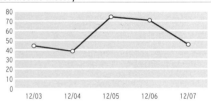

Harvard University

Many parents dream of sending their children to Harvard; and at more than $30,000 a year (undergraduate), some even dream of being able to afford it. Harvard, the oldest institution of higher learning in the US, is home to Harvard College (undergraduate studies) and 10 graduate schools, including the Harvard Business, Law, and Medical Schools. The Radcliffe Institute for Advanced Study at Harvard was created when Radcliffe College and Harvard University merged in 1999. Harvard has about 20,000 students, about half of whom are enrolled in graduate programs. Harvard's endowment of more than $29 billion is the largest of any university in the world. (Yale ranks #2.)

It's usually a toss-up whether Harvard or one of its Ivy League rivals Princeton or Yale will rank at the top of the list of America's premiere schools or programs, but the university's reputation for academic excellence is well-founded. More than 40 Harvard faculty members have won Nobel Prizes over the years. Additionally, among Har-

vard's alumni are more than a half dozen US presidents — John Adams, John Quincy Adams, Rutherford B. Hayes, John F. Kennedy, Franklin Delano Roosevelt, Theodore Roosevelt, and George W. Bush.

Harvard's controversial 27th president Lawrence H. Summers resigned at the end of the 2005-06 academic year. Derek Bok, who served as president of the university from 1971 to 1991, succeeded Summers on an interim basis. Drew G. Faust was named as the school's 28th president (and first woman to hold the job) effective July 1, 2007.

HISTORY

In 1636 the General Court of Massachusetts appropriated 400 pounds sterling for the establishment of a college. The first building was completed at Cambridge in 1639 and was named for John Harvard, who had willed his collection of about 400 books and half of his land to the school. The first freshman class had four students.

During its first 150 years, Harvard adhered to the education standards of European schools, with emphasis on classical literature and languages, philosophy, and mathematics. It established its first professorship in 1721 (the Hollis Divinity Professorship) and soon after added professorships in mathematics and natural philosophy. In 1783 the school appointed its first professor of medicine.

Harvard updated its curriculum in the early 1800s, after professor Edward Everett returned from studying abroad with reports of the modern teaching methods in Germany. The university established the Divinity School in 1816, the Law School in 1817, and two schools of science in the 1840s.

In 1869 president Charles Eliot began engineering the development of graduate programs in arts and sciences, engineering, and architecture. He raised standards at the medical and law schools and laid the groundwork for the Graduate School of Business Administration and the School of Public Health. Radcliffe College was founded as "Harvard Annex" in 1879, 15 years after a group of women had begun studying privately with Harvard professors in rented rooms.

Harvard's enrollment, faculty, and endowment grew tremendously throughout the 20th century. The Graduate School of Education opened in 1920, and the first undergraduate residential house opened in 1930. In the 1930s and 1940s, the school established a scholarship program and a general education curriculum for undergraduates. During WWII Harvard and Radcliffe undergraduates began attending the same classes.

A quota limiting the number of female students was abolished in 1975, and in 1979 Harvard introduced a new core curriculum. Princeton-educated Neil Rudenstine became president in 1991 and vowed to cut costs and to seek additional funding so that no one should be denied a Harvard education for financial reasons.

Harvard made dubious headlines during its 1994-95 academic year, enduring a bank robbery in Harvard Square, three student suicides, and one murder-suicide. The following year Harvard paid a fine of $775,000 after the US Attorney's Office claimed the school's pharmacy had not properly controlled drugs, including antidepressants and codeine cough syrup. The fine was the largest ever paid in the US under the Controlled Substance Act.

In 1998 Harvard's endowment fund acquired insurance services firm White River in one of

the largest direct investments ever made by a not-for-profit institution. Also that year the school altered some of its graduation processes and introduced stress-reducing programs in the wake of another student suicide.

In 1999 Radcliffe College merged with Harvard and the Radcliffe Institute for Advanced Study at Harvard was established. In 2000 president Neil Rudenstine announced he would step down in 2001. Former US Treasury Secretary Lawrence Summers replaced him.

EXECUTIVES

President: Drew Gilpin Faust
Provost: Steven E. (Steve) Hyman
EVP: Edward C. Forst, age 47
VP Finance and CFO: Elizabeth Mora
VP Administration: Sally H. Zeckhauser
VP Government, Community, and Public Affairs:
  Alan J. Stone
VP Human Resources: Marilyn M. Hausammann
VP and General Counsel: Robert I. Iuliano
Acting VP Alumni Affairs and Development:
  Robert Cashion
VP Policy: A. Clayton Spencer
President and CEO, Harvard Management Company:
  Jane Mendillo
Auditors: PricewaterhouseCoopers LLP

LOCATIONS

HQ: Harvard University
  University Hall, Cambridge, MA 02138
Phone: 617-495-1000   **Fax:** 617-495-0754
Web: www.harvard.edu

PRODUCTS/OPERATIONS

Selected Programs & Schools

Undergraduate
  Harvard College
Graduate
  Graduate School of Arts and Sciences
  Graduate School of Design
  Graduate School of Education
  Harvard Business School
  Harvard Divinity School
  Harvard Law School
  Harvard Medical School
  Harvard School of Public Health
  John F. Kennedy School of Government
  School of Dental Medicine

Haworth, Inc.

Designers at Haworth sit at their cubicles and think about . . . more cubicles. The company is one of the top office furniture manufacturers in the US, competing with top rivals Steelcase and HNI Corporation. Haworth offers a full range of furniture known for its innovative design, including partitions, desks, chairs, tables, and storage products. Brands include Monaco, Patterns, PLACES, and X99.

Dilbert and other long-suffering office drones have Haworth to thank for inventing the pre-wired partitions that make today's cubicled workplace possible. Haworth is owned by the family of Gerrard Haworth, who founded the company in 1948.

The company sells its products worldwide through more than 600 dealers. It has about 30 manufacturing locations and 60 showrooms around the world.

Haworth, known as an aggressive competitor, has been expanding its presence in Europe and Asia, mostly through acquisitions and new manufacturing plants. Operations include Germany's Roeder, Spain's Kemen, and Canada's SMED and Groupe Lacasse. It opened plants in China and India in recent years.

An extended decline in the office furniture industry forced the company to consolidate operations, including relocating its US manufacturing from four states (Arkansas, North Carolina, Pennsylvania, and Texas) to three plants in Michigan.

EXECUTIVES

Chairman: Richard G. (Dick) Haworth
President and CEO: Franco Bianchi
VP Business Groups, Global Architectural Interiors and Wood Solutions: Paul K. Smith
VP Global Interior Architecture and Wood Products Business Groups; President, Haworth Ltd.: Gary Scitthelm
VP Global Finance: John Mooney
VP Global Customer Service and Customer Processes: Al Lanning
VP Global Information Services: Ann M. Harten
VP Global Marketing and Sales Support: Mabel Casey
VP Global Manufacturing: Robert J. (Bob) Stander
VP Global Human Resources: Pamela Wright Armstrong
VP Global Sales: Bob Kimball
President, Groupe Lacasse: François Giroux
Senior Corporate Communications Administrator: Dave Adamski

LOCATIONS

HQ: Haworth, Inc.
 1 Haworth Center, Holland, MI 49423
Phone: 616-393-3000   **Fax:** 616-393-1570
Web: www.haworth.com

Haworth operates in more than 120 countries throughout the Americas, Asia, the Caribbean, Europe, and the Middle East.

PRODUCTS/OPERATIONS

Products
Desks and casegoods
Files and storage
Seating
Systems
Tables
Work tools

Selected Brands
Accolade
Compose
Dashboards
Galerie
Hello
if
Improv
Jump Stuff
LOOK
Monaco
Orlando
PLACES
PREMISE
Prescott
RACE
Tally
Tas
Tempo
Tripoli
UniGroup
Varia
X99

COMPETITORS
CFGroup
Global Group
Herman Miller
HNI
Inscape corp
KI
Kimball International
Knoll, Inc.
Neutral Posture
Norstar Office Products
Steelcase
Teknion
Trendway
Virco Mfg.

HISTORICAL FINANCIALS
Company Type: Private

Income Statement

	REVENUE ($ mil.)	NET INCOME ($ mil.)	NET PROFIT MARGIN	EMPLOYEES
12/07	1,660	—	—	8,000
12/06	1,480	—	—	8,000
12/05	1,400	—	—	7,500
12/04	1,260	—	—	7,500
12/03	1,230	—	—	9,000
Annual Growth	7.8%	—	—	(2.9%)

FYE: December 31

Revenue History

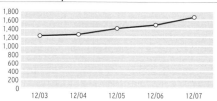

HCA Inc.

The largest for-profit hospital operator in the US, HCA (also known as Hospital Corporation of America) operates about 170 acute care, psychiatric, and rehabilitation hospitals in the US and abroad. It also runs about 100 ambulatory surgery centers, as well as diagnostic imaging, cancer treatment, and outpatient rehab centers that form health care networks in many of the communities it serves. The company has facilities in about 20 states, with about three-quarters of its hospitals located in the southern US. (About 70 are in Florida and Texas.) The hospital giant's HCA International operates six hospitals in the UK. In 2006 a group of investors took the company private in a $30 billion leveraged buyout.

The private investor group included HCA co-founder Thomas Frist Jr., as well as Bain Capital, Kohlberg Kravis Roberts, the private equity arm of Merrill Lynch, and other members of HCA management.

Most of HCA's hospitals are in high-growth urban and suburban markets, and the vast majority are medical-surgical hospitals. (It has five psychiatric facilities and one rehabilitation hospital.) The company divested 10 rural hospitals over the course of 2005 and 2006 in order to focus on its key markets. Four Virginia and West Virginia facilities went to LifePoint Hospitals in 2006; it had sold five non-urban hospitals in Louisiana, Oklahoma, Tennessee, and Washington to Capella Healthcare the previous year.

Divestitures have taken place overseas as well. In 2007 the company sold off its two Swiss hospitals to a division of private equity firm Colony Capital.

The company plans to grow in its selected markets by acquiring hospitals and by luring patients to its existing facilities with high-quality care and a broad range of services. It is particularly interested in expanding its outpatient offerings, as well as specialty services in high-margin fields such as orthopedics and cardiology.

HCA also tries to take advantage of its national scale (and its position as the leading health care provider in many communities) to negotiate advantageous purchasing contracts, as well as favorable deals with managed care companies. Its attempts to demand rate increases in some renegotiated contracts with UnitedHealth in 2006, however, led to a bitter dispute that was finally resolved late that year, but not before UnitedHealth filed suit against HCA for alleged anti-competitive practices.

Like most hospital operators, HCA has had to deal with the rising rate of uninsured patients it treats, a phenomenon that leads to increasing amounts of bad debt when patients can't pay their bills. To combat the problem (and in response to criticism over how the hospital industry bills the uninsured), HCA instituted a discount plan for such patients in 2005.

EXECUTIVES

Chairman and CEO: Jack O. Bovender Jr., age 63, $1,404,959 pay
President, COO, and Director: Richard M. Bracken, age 55, $817,667 pay
EVP and CFO: R. Milton Johnson, age 51, $578,373 pay
SVP: Victor L. Campbell, age 61
SVP and CIO; President, HCA Information Technology & Services: Noel Brown Williams, age 53
SVP and General Counsel: Robert A. (Bob) Waterman, age 54, $569,988 pay
SVP Human Resources: John M. Steele, age 53
SVP Quality and Chief Medical Officer: Jonathan B. (Jon) Perlin, age 47
VP and Corporate Secretary: John M. Franck II
VP Investor Relations: Mark Kimbrough
President, Financial Services Group: Beverly B. Wallace, age 57
President, Central Group: William P. (Paul) Rutledge
President, Eastern Group: Charles J. (Chuck) Hall, age 55
President, Western Group: Samuel N. (Sam) Hazen, age 48, $569,981 pay
Auditors: Ernst & Young LLP

LOCATIONS

HQ: HCA Inc.
 1 Park Plaza, Nashville, TN 37203
Phone: 615-344-9551   **Fax:** 615-344-2266
Web: www.hcahealthcare.com

2007 Locations

	No.
US	
Florida	37
Texas	35
Georgia	13
Tennessee	13
Louisiana	10
Virginia	10
Colorado	7
Missouri	6
Utah	6
California	5
Kansas	4
Nevada	3
South Carolina	3
Idaho	2
Kentucky	2
New Hampshire	2
Oklahoma	2
Alaska	1
Indiana	1
Mississippi	1
Other countries	
England	6
Total	**169**

PRODUCTS/OPERATIONS

2007 Sales

	% of total
Managed care & other insurers	53
Medicare	24
Uninsured	10
Medicaid	5
Managed Medicare	5
Managed Medicaid	3
Total	**100**

2007 Sales

	% of total
Western group	42
Eastern group	31
Central group	23
Corporate & other	4
Total	**100**

COMPETITORS

Adventist Health
Adventist Health System
Ascension Health
Banner Health
Baylor Health
Catholic Health Initiatives
Catholic Healthcare West
CHRISTUS Health
Community Health Systems
Health Management Associates
HealthSouth
Kaiser Permanente
Psychiatric Solutions
SSM Health Care
Tenet Healthcare
Trinity Health (Novi)
Universal Health Services

HISTORICAL FINANCIALS

Company Type: Private

Income Statement

FYE: December 31

	REVENUE ($ mil.)	NET INCOME ($ mil.)	NET PROFIT MARGIN	EMPLOYEES
12/07	26,858	874	3.3%	18,600
12/06	25,477	1,036	4.1%	186,000
12/05	24,455	1,424	5.8%	191,100
12/04	23,502	1,246	5.3%	191,400
12/03	21,808	1,332	6.1%	188,000
Annual Growth	5.3%	(10.0%)	—	(43.9%)

2007 Year-End Financials

Debt ratio: —
Return on equity: —
Cash ($ mil.): —
Current ratio: —
Long-term debt ($ mil.): 27,000

Net Income History

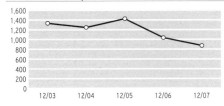

Health Care Service Corporation

Health Care Service Corporation (HCSC) has the Blues in Chicago and the Southwest. A licensee of the Blue Cross and Blue Shield Association, HCSC consists of four regional Blue health plans: Blue Cross Blue Shield of Illinois, Blue Cross and Blue Shield of Texas, Blue Cross and Blue Shield of New Mexico, and Blue Cross Blue Shield of Oklahoma. The mutually owned company provides group and individual health plans —including traditional indemnity plans, managed care programs, and Medicare supplemental coverage — to more than 11 million members, a majority of them in Illinois. Through some non-blue subsidiaries, HCSC sells life and disability insurance, as well as annuities.

Its life insurance companies include Fort Dearborn Life Insurance and Colorado Bankers Life Insurance. Together, the companies operate as the Preferred Financial Group.

The not-for-profit company has grown through strategic acquisitions of independent Blue Cross companies, as well as other health and insurance firms that complement the company's core product offerings. It began in the 1930s with its Blue Cross operations in Illinois, but since 1998 has added Blue plans in Texas (1998), New Mexico (2001), and Oklahoma (2005). Its acquisition strategy has allowed HCSC to benefit from economies of scale.

HCSC has also been focused on better information technology as a means to improve health care costs. It has introduced online enrollment and health care management tools, as well as a comprehensive care management system (called Blue Care Connection) which integrates and analyzes data from claims forms, health care providers, and patients themselves, in order to reduce costs and inefficiencies. Additionally, in 2008 it acquired health care IT firm MEDecision, which provides health care management software and data analytics services to doctors and managed care companies.

Though the company has about half a million Medicare beneficiaries enrolled in supplemental health care plans, the company has been cautious about expanding into full-fledged Medicare Advantage plans. Its New Mexico, Oklahoma, and Texas operations do offer Medicare Advantage products in some markets, however.

HISTORY

The seeds of the Blue Cross organization were sown in 1929 when an official at Baylor University Hospital in Dallas began offering school-teachers 21 days of hospital care for $6 a year. Fundamental to its coverage was a community rating system, which based premiums on the community's claims experience rather than subscribers' conditions.

In 1935 Elgin Watch Co. owner Taylor Strawn, Charles Schweppe, and other Chicago civic leaders pooled resources to form Hospital Services Corporation to provide the same type of coverage. (The firm adopted the Blue Cross symbol in 1939.) Employees of the Rand McNally cartography company were the first to be covered by the plan.

Soon, four similar plans were launched in other Illinois towns. Between 1947 and 1952, Hospital Services Corp. and these other four joined forces, offering coverage nearly statewide.

Meanwhile, Blue Shield physician's fee plans in several cities were incorporated as Illinois Medical Service. Hospital Services Corp. and Illinois Medical Service operated independently but shared office space and personnel.

A 1975 change in state legislation let the entities merge to become Health Care Service Corp. (HCSC), which offered both Blue Cross and Blue Shield coverage. Following the merger, the company's board of directors (which had been primarily composed of care providers) became dominated by consumers, which helped HCSC become more responsive to its members.

For the next six years, the state denied HCSC any rate increases, leaving it with a frighteningly low $12 million in reserves in 1982.

HCSC achieved statewide market presence in 1982 when it merged with Illinois' last independent Blue Cross plan, Rockford Blue Cross. In 1986, as managed care swept through the health care industry, only 14% of HCSC's members were enrolled in managed care plans. HCSC created its Managed Care Network Preferred point-of-service plan in 1991; the idea caught on with both employers and individuals and enrollment skyrocketed. By 1994 more than two-thirds of the firm's subscribers participated in some sort of managed care plan. That year it picked up Medicare payment processing for the state of Michigan.

In 1995 HCSC and Blue Cross and Blue Shield of Texas (BCBST) formed an affiliation they hoped would culminate in a merger, giving the combined company $6 billion in sales and reserves of more than $1 billion. Texas consumer groups objected to the merger, claiming that Texas residents own BCBST and that Texans should be compensated for the transfer of ownership — especially since BCBST had received state tax breaks for decades in exchange for accepting all applicants. (A Texas judge ruled in favor of the merger in 1998.)

Citing high risks and low margins, HCSC in 1997 dropped its Medicare payment processing contract, which it had held for some 30 years. The next year HCSC agreed to pay $144 million after it pleaded guilty to covering up its poor performance in processing Medicare claims.

In 1998 HCSC acquired Blue Cross and Blue Shield of Texas.

In 2000 HCSC bought Aetna's NylCare of Texas, giving it large, profitable HMOs in Houston and Dallas. The next year it bested Anthem (now WellPoint) and Wellmark in wooing the troubled Blue Cross Blue Shield of New Mexico. And in 2005 it acquired Blue Cross and Blue Shield of New Mexico.

228

EXECUTIVES

Chairman: Milton Carroll, age 57
CEO: Raymond F. McCaskey, age 64
President and COO: Patricia A. (Pat) Hemingway Hall, age 54
EVP Plan Operations: Martin G. Foster
EVP Internal Operations: Colleen F. Reitan, age 49
SVP and CFO: Denise A. Bujack
SVP and CIO: Brian Hedberg
SVP and Chief Legal Officer:
Deborah Dorman-Rodriguez
SVP and Chief Medical Officer: Paul B. Handel
SVP and Chief Human Resources Officer:
Patrick F. O'Conner
SVP, Audit, Compliance, Security, Corporate Compliance Officer, and Corporate Privacy Officer:
Tara Dowd Gurber
SVP, Strategy, Planning, and Enterprise Process Management: Karen Chesrown
VP and Treasurer: Brian A. Kennedy
VP Public Affairs: Robert Kieckhefer
President, Blue Cross and Blue Shield of Illinois:
Paul S. Boulis
President, Blue Cross and Blue Shield of New Mexico:
Elizabeth A. Watrin
President, Blue Cross and Blue Shield of Oklahoma:
Wyndham Kidd Jr.
President, Blue Cross and Blue Shield of Texas:
Darren Rodgers
President and CEO, Life and Subsidiary Operations:
Anthony F. (Tony) Trani
Auditors: Ernst & Young LLP

LOCATIONS

HQ: Health Care Service Corporation
300 E. Randolph St., Chicago, IL 60601
Phone: 312-653-6000 **Fax:** 312-819-1220
Web: www.hcsc.com

PRODUCTS/OPERATIONS

Selected Products and Services

Annuities
Dental insurance
Disability insurance
Indemnity insurance
Life insurance
Managed health care plans
Supplemental Medicare coverage
Prescription drug coverage

Selected Subsidiaries

Blue Cross and Blue Shield of Illinois
Blue Cross and Blue Shield of New Mexico
Blue Cross and Blue Shield of Oklahoma
Blue Cross and Blue Shield of Texas
Dental Network of America
Hallmark Services Corporation
Preferred Financial Group
Colorado Bankers Life Insurance Company
Fort Dearborn Life Insurance Co.

COMPETITORS

Aetna
Aflac
AMERIGROUP
CIGNA
Guardian Life
Health Alliance Medical Plans
Health Net
HealthSpring
Humana
Kaiser Foundation Health Plan
MetLife
Molina Healthcare
Mutual of Omaha
New York Life
Prudential
UnitedHealth Group
ValueOptions
WellPoint

HISTORICAL FINANCIALS

Company Type: Mutual company

Income Statement

FYE: December 31

	REVENUE ($ mil.)	NET INCOME ($ mil.)	NET PROFIT MARGIN	EMPLOYEES
12/07	14,348	—	—	16,500
12/06	12,972	—	—	16,500
12/05	11,714	—	—	14,000
12/04	10,629	—	—	—
12/03	8,190	—	—	13,000
Annual Growth	15.0%	—	—	6.1%

Revenue History

HealthMarkets, Inc.

HealthMarkets lets the self-employed shop for better insurance. The company offers health and life insurance through its MEGA Life and Health Insurance, Chesapeake Life Insurance Company, and other subsidiaries. Its targeted customers are the self-employed, association groups, and small businesses. Other services include third-party administrative and distribution services for health care providers and other insurers. HealthMarkets is expanding its product line to include health spending accounts (HSAs), high deductible health plans (HDHPs), and Medicare supplemental insurance. The company changed its name from UICI to Health Markets in 2006 after being acquired by a consortium led by the Blackstone Group.

Blackstone Group holds 52% of the company. Other investors include Goldman Sachs Capital Partners (22%) and DLJ Merchant Banking Partners (11%). The acquisition deal paid out $1.6 billion to former shareholders and the investors put up approximately $985 million in equity.

The company markets policies through a sales force consisting of some 1,900 independent contractors in 44 states. Health insurance policies account for more than 85% of the company's revenue.

HealthMarkets is focusing on its businesses geared to serve the self-employed and has exited its less profitable financial services businesses. It also sold off its Star HRG division (health insurance for hard-to-insure employees) and its Student Insurance division in 2006. In 2008 the company announced that it would sell off substantially all of its life insurance businesses to Wilton Reassurance Company. The sale will include The Chesapeake Life Insurance Company, Mid-West National Life Insurance Company of Tennessee, and The MEGA Life and Health Insurance Company.

EXECUTIVES

Chairman: Allen F. Wise, age 65
Vice Chairman: William J. (Bill) Gedwed, age 52
President and CEO: Phillip J. (Phil) Hildebrand, age 55
EVP and CFO: Steven P. (Steve) Erwin, age 65
EVP and General Counsel, HealthMarkets, The MEGA Life and Health Insurance Company, Mid-West National Life Insurance Company of Tennessee:
Michael A. (Mike) Colliflower, age 53
EVP and Chief Administrative Officer: Anurag Chandra, age 31
Treasurer and Controller:
Maria Consuelo (Connie) Palacios
SVP Human Resources: Vicki Cansler
SVP and CIO; EVP, Mid-West National Life Insurance Company of Tennessee: Marc F. (Frank) Jackson
SVP Budget, Planning, and Analysis: K. Alec Mahmood
SVP Operations; SVP, Mid-West National Life Insurance Company of Tennessee: John E. Hunter
Auditors: KPMG LLP

LOCATIONS

HQ: HealthMarkets, Inc.
9151 Boulevard 26, North Richland Hills, TX 76180
Phone: 817-255-5200 **Fax:** 817-255-5390
Web: www.healthmarkets.com

PRODUCTS/OPERATIONS

2007 Sales

	$ mil.	% of total
Premiums		
Health	1,311.7	82
Life	70.5	5
Investment income	103.0	6
Other income	106.6	7
Gains on sale of investments	3.5	—
Total	1,595.3	100

Selected Subsidiaries

Mid-West National Life Insurance Company of Tennessee
The Chesapeake Life Insurance Company
The MEGA Life and Health Insurance Company
ZON Re USA LLC (82.5%)

COMPETITORS

Aflac
Atlantic American
Guarantee Trust

HCSC
Torchmark
USHEALTH Group

HISTORICAL FINANCIALS

Company Type: Private

Income Statement

FYE: December 31

	REVENUE ($ mil.)	NET INCOME ($ mil.)	NET PROFIT MARGIN	EMPLOYEES
12/07	1,595	70	4.4%	2,000
12/06	2,147	238	11.1%	1,800
12/05	2,121	—	—	2,700
Annual Growth	(13.3%)	(70.5%)	—	(13.9%)

2007 Year-End Financials

Debt ratio: 157.1%
Return on equity: 16.9%
Cash ($ mil.): —

Current ratio: —
Long-term debt ($ mil.): 481

Net Income History

Hearst Corporation

Like founder William Randolph Hearst's castle, The Hearst Corporation is sprawling. Through Hearst Newspapers, the company owns some 15 daily newspapers (such as the *San Francisco Chronicle* and the *Houston Chronicle*) and 50 weekly newspapers. Its Hearst Magazines publishes some 20 US consumer magazines (*Cosmopolitan, Esquire*) with nearly 200 international editions. Hearst has broadcasting operations through majority-owned Hearst Argyle Television. Its Hearst Entertainment & Syndication unit includes a syndication service (King Features), a newspaper production service (Reed Brennan), and stakes in cable networks (A&E, ESPN). The Hearst Corporation is owned by the Hearst family, but managed by a board of trustees.

Hearst publishes information for automotive, electronic, pharmaceutical, and finance industries through its Hearst Business Media segment.

Through its Hearst Interactive Media unit, the company makes strategic investments in online properties such as drugstore.com, and Gather. In 2007 Hearst ponied up about $100 million to acquire UGO Entertainment, which operates a Web site targeting young men.

Hearst's top magazine title, *Cosmopolitan*, is published in about 35 languages and sold in more than 100 countries, making it the largest magazine franchise in the world. The company publishes magazines in the UK through subsidiary The National Magazine Company. Hearst also has interests in over 60 daily and 100 non-daily newspapers owned by MediaNews Group, which include the *Denver Post* and *Salt Lake Tribune*.

Although the company no longer owns Hearst Castle (deeded to the State of California in 1951), it has extensive real estate holdings. Projects include the Hearst Ranch in San Simeon, California, and the Hearst Tower in New York.

Former president and CEO Victor F. Ganzi resigned his position in 2008. The company cited "irreconcilable policy differences" with the Board of Trustees over the company's future direction as the reason for his leaving. Vice chairman (and previous company head) Frank A. Bennack, Jr., reassumed the role of CEO as the company looks for a permanent replacement.

Upon his death, William Randolph Hearst left 99% of the company's common stock to two charitable trusts controlled by a 13-member board that includes five family and eight non-family members. The will includes a clause that allows the trustees to disinherit any heir who contests the will.

HISTORY

William Randolph Hearst, son of a California mining magnate, started as a reporter — having been expelled from Harvard in 1884 for playing jokes on professors. In 1887 he became editor of the *San Francisco Examiner,* which his father had obtained as payment for a gambling debt. In 1895 he bought the *New York Morning Journal* and competed against Joseph Pulitzer's *New York World*. The "yellow journalism" resulting from that rivalry characterized American-style reporting at the turn of the century.

Hearst branched into magazines (1903), film (1913), and radio (1928). Also during this time it created the Hearst International News Service (it was sold to E.W. Scripps' United Press in 1958 to form United Press International). By 1935 Hearst was at its peak, with newspapers in 19 cities, the largest syndicate (King Features), international news and photo services, 13 magazines, eight radio stations, and two motion picture companies. Two years later Hearst relinquished control of the company to avoid bankruptcy, selling movie companies, radio stations, magazines, and later, most of his San Simeon estate. (Hearst's rise and fall inspired the 1941 film *Citizen Kane.*)

In 1948 Hearst became the owner of one of the US's first TV stations, WBAL-TV in Baltimore. When Hearst died in 1951, company veteran Richard Berlin became CEO. Berlin sold off failing newspapers, moved into television, and acquired more magazines.

Frank Bennack, CEO since 1979, expanded the company, acquiring newspapers, publishing firms (notably William Morrow, 1981), TV stations, magazines (*Redbook,* 1982; *Esquire,* 1986), and 20% of cable sports network ESPN (1991). Hearst branched into video via a joint venture with Capital Cities/ABC (1981) and helped launch the Lifetime and Arts & Entertainment cable channels (1984).

In 1992 Hearst brought on board former Federal Communications Commission chairman Alfred Sikes, who quickly moved the company onto the Internet. In 1996 Randolph A. Hearst passed the title of chairman to nephew George Hearst (the last surviving son of the founder, Randolph died in 2000). Broadcaster Argyle Television merged with Hearst's TV holdings in 1997 to form publicly traded Hearst-Argyle Television.

In 1999 Hearst combined its HomeArts Web site with Women.com to create one of the largest online networks for women. In addition, it joined with Oprah Winfrey's Harpo Entertainment to publish *O, The Oprah Magazine* (launched in 2000).

The company sold its book publishing operations to News Corp.'s HarperCollins unit in 1999. It also agreed to buy the *San Francisco Chronicle* from rival Chronicle Publishing. That deal was called into question over concerns that the *San Francisco Examiner* would not survive and the city would be left with one major paper. To resolve the issue, the next year Hearst sold the *Examiner* to ExIn (a group of investors affiliated with the Ted Fang family and other owners of the *San Francisco Independent*). Also in 2000 Hearst bought the UK magazines of Gruner + Jahr, the newspaper and magazine unit of German media juggernaut Bertelsmann.

In mid-2002 Victor Ganzi took over as CEO and president following Bennack's retirement from these positions. Hearst further expanded its potent stable of magazines in 2003 by purchasing *Seventeen* magazine from PRIMEDIA. Hearst also became a major player in yellow page publishing with its 2004 purchase of White Directory Publishers, one of the largest telephone directory companies in the US.

In 2006 Hearst backed MediaNews when that company paid $1 billion to acquire four newspapers (including the *San Jose Mercury News*, the *Contra Costa Times*, and the *St. Paul Pioneer Press)* from McClatchy. Hearst purchased a 30% interest in MediaNews Group the next year — an investment that did not include any of MediaNews' San Francisco holdings.

CEO Victor Ganzi left the company in 2008.

EXECUTIVES

Chairman: George R. Hearst Jr., age 80
Vice Chairman and Interim CEO: Frank A. Bennack Jr., age 75
SVP and CFO: Ronald J. Doerfler, age 66
SVP and Chief Legal and Development Officer: James M. Asher
SVP; President, Hearst Newspapers: George B. Irish
VP; President and CEO, Hearst Magazines International; EVP, Hearst Magazines: George J. Green
VP; EVP, Hearst Entertainment and Syndication: Bruce L. Paisner
Chairman and Editorial Director, SmartMoney: Edwin A. Finn Jr.
President and CEO, Hearst-Argyle Television: David J. Barrett, age 60
President, Hearst Business Media: Richard P. Malloch
President, Hearst Interactive Media: Kenneth A. Bronfin, age 48
President, Hearst Magazines: Cathleen P. (Cathie) Black, age 63
VP, Hearst Interactive Media: Michael Dunn
Executive Director Corporate Communications; VP Communications, Hearst Magazines: Paul Luthringer
VP; EVP and Deputy Group Head, Hearst Business Media: Steven A. Hobbs, age 48

LOCATIONS

HQ: The Hearst Corporation
300 W. 57th St., New York, NY 10019
Phone: 212-649-2000 **Fax:** 212-649-2108
Web: www.hearstcorp.com

PRODUCTS/OPERATIONS

Selected Operations

Hearst Broadcasting
  Hearst-Argyle Television (majority owned)
Hearst Business Media
  Black Book
  Diversion
  Electronic Products
  First DataBank
  MOTOR Magazine
Hearst Entertainment & Syndication
  A&E Television Networks (joint venture with ABC & NBC)
    A&E
    The Biography Channel
    The History Channel
    History Channel International
  ESPN (20%)
  King Features Syndicate
  Hearst Entertainment (content library and production operations)
  Lifetime Entertainment Services (with Walt Disney Company)
    Lifetime Movie Network
    Lifetime Online
    Lifetime Television
  New England Cable News (with Comcast)
  Reed Brennan Media Associates (production services for newspapers)
Hearst Interactive Media
  Circles (online loyalty marketing programs)
  drugstore.com (online pharmacy site)
  Gather (social networking)
  Hire.com (job site)

Hearst Magazines
  CosmoGIRL!
  Cosmopolitan
  Country Living
  Esquire
  Good Housekeeping
  Harper's BAZAAR
  House Beautiful
  Marie Claire
  O, The Oprah Magazine (with Harpo)
  Popular Mechanics
  Quick & Simple
  Redbook
  Seventeen
  SmartMoney (with Dow Jones)
  Teen
  Weekend
Hearst Newspapers
  Albany Times Union (New York)
  Houston Chronicle
  Huron Daily Tribune (Michigan)
  Laredo Morning Times (Texas)
  Midland Daily News (Michigan)
  San Antonio Express-News
  San Francisco Chronicle
  Seattle Post-Intelligencer
Other Operations
  Real estate

COMPETITORS

Advance Publications	McClatchy Company
Andrews McMeel Universal	McGraw-Hill
Bauer Publishing (UK)	Meredith Corporation
Belo Corp.	New York Times
Bertelsmann	News Corp.
Bloomberg L.P.	Reader's Digest
Cox Enterprises	Reed Elsevier Group
Dennis Publishing	Rodale
Disney	Seattle Times
E. W. Scripps	Time Warner
Freedom Communications	Tribune Company
Gannett	Viacom
IPC Group	Washington Post
Lagardère	Yellow Book USA
Liberty Media	

HISTORICAL FINANCIALS

Company Type: Private

Income Statement				FYE: December 31
	ESTIMATED REVENUE ($ mil.)	NET INCOME ($ mil.)	NET PROFIT MARGIN	EMPLOYEES
12/07	4,380	—	—	17,070
12/06	4,520	—	—	17,062
12/05	4,550	—	—	17,016
12/04	4,000	—	—	16,667
12/03	4,100	—	—	20,000
Annual Growth	1.7%	—	—	(3.9%)

Revenue History

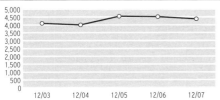

H-E-B

The Muzak bounces between Tejano and country, and the warm tortillas and marinated fajita meat are big sellers at H. E. Butt Grocery (H-E-B). Texas' largest private company and the #1 food retailer in South and Central Texas, H-E-B owns more than 300 supermarkets, including a growing number of large (70,000 sq. ft.) gourmet Central Market stores in major metropolitan areas and more than 80 smaller (24,000-30,000 sq. ft.) Pantry Foods stores, often in more rural areas. H-E-B also has about 30 upscale and discount stores in Mexico. H-E-B processes some of its own bread, dairy products, meat, and tortillas. The 100-year-old company is owned by the Butt family, which founded H-E-B in Kerrville, Texas, in 1905.

To cement its #1 spot in Central Texas and fend off Wal-Mart, which is expanding its supercenter presence in the region, H-E-B has begun opening huge H-E-B Plus stores, which range in size from 109,000 to nearly 200,000 sq. ft. and devote about 40% of their space to nonfood items, including casual furniture, cooking equipment, and electronics. The Wal-Mart-sized stores have opened in the San Antonio and Austin markets, where H-E-B has acquired stores from ailing rival Albertsons to bolster its position. By purchasing Albertsons stores and expanding its own, H-E-B now operates some 45 stores in fast-growing Central Texas.

Since entering the Houston market in 2001, the Texas grocery chain has invested heavily to open about a dozen large combination food and drug stores, while closing some of its smaller Pantry supermarkets in the area. To gain an edge on its competition, H-E-B plans to incorporate aspects of its upscale Central Market format, including cafes, into the new Houston stores. To that end, in mid-July 2006 H-E-B opened its largest store in the Houston area: a 125,000-sq.-ft. combination H-E-B food and drug store and Central Market hybrid.

H-E-B currently operates eight Central Market stores in five Texas markets. The Texas grocery chain's newest format, Mi Tienda, debuted in Pasadena, Texas, in October 2006. The Hispanic-themed store features a Mexican-style bakery and other amenities designed to appeal to Latino shoppers.

H-E-B is familiar with the tastes of Latinos as about half of its market is Hispanic. South of the border, the grocery company's Mexican subsidiary Supermercados Internacionales HEB has moved into Monterrey's more affluent neighborhoods, with stores operating under the H-E-B banner and the Economax name (a discount supermarket format).

More than 40% of the H-E-B stores have gasoline outlets, and about 190 have pharmacies. The retailer recently opened its first Payless Express shoe department in a Laredo store and has plans to open more.

In the fall of 2006 H-E-B launched a program to fill prescriptions for 500 generic drugs for $5 each. The move is an attempt to match rival Wal-Mart's $4 generic drug program. The company moved further into the medical arena with the introduction of in-store medical clinics run by RediClinic in select H-E-B locations.

H-E-B has introduced a new line of baby products and extended its line of Central Market Organics and All Natural products to about 150 H-E-B stores.

HISTORY

Charles C. Butt and his wife, Florence, moved to Kerrville, in the Texas Hill Country, in 1905, hoping the climate would help Charles' tuberculosis. Since Charles was unable to work, Florence began peddling groceries door-to-door for A&P. Later that year she opened a grocery store, C. C. Butt Grocery. However, Florence, a dyed-in-the-wool Baptist, refused to carry such articles of vice as tobacco. The family lived over the store, and all three of the Butt children worked there. The youngest son, Howard, began working in the business full-time in his teens and took over the business after WWI.

By adopting modern marketing methods such as price tagging (and deciding to sell tobacco), the Butts earned enough to begin expanding. In 1927 Howard opened a second store in Del Rio in West Texas, and over the next few years he opened other stores in the Rio Grande Valley. The company gained patron loyalty by making minimal markups on staples. It moved from Kerrville to Harlingen, Texas, in 1928 (it moved to Corpus Christi, Texas, in 1940 and to San Antonio in 1985).

The company began manufacturing foods in the 1930s and invested in farms and orchards. In 1935 Howard (who had adopted the middle name Edward) rechristened the chain the H. E. Butt Grocery Company (H-E-B). He put his three children to work for the company, grooming son Charles for the top spot after Howard Jr. took over the H. E. Butt Foundation from his mother.

While other chains updated their stores during the 1960s, H-E-B plodded. Howard Sr. resigned in 1971 and Charles took over, bringing in fresh management. But this was not enough. Studies showed that the reasons for its lagging market share were its refusal to stock alcohol and its policy of Sunday closing; it abandoned these policies in 1976. It also drastically undercut competitors, driving many independents out of business. H-E-B emerged the dominant player in its major markets.

H-E-B's first superstore, a 56,000-sq.-ft. facility offering general merchandise, photofinishing, and a pharmacy, opened in Austin, Texas, in 1979, and the company concentrated on building more superstores over the next decade.

In 1988 H-E-B launched its H-E-B Pantry division, which remodeled and built smaller supermarkets, mostly in rural Texas towns. Three years later it launched another format, the 93,000-sq.-ft. H-E-B Marketplace in San Antonio, which included restaurants. It also opened the upscale Central Market in Austin with extensive cheese, produce, and wine departments in 1994 (it later opened similar stores in San Antonio, Houston, and Dallas).

Chairman and CEO Charles retired as president in 1996, and James Clingman became the first non-family member to assume the office. That year H-E-B opened its first non-Texas store in Lake Charles, Louisiana. In 1997 it opened its first Mexican store in an affluent area of Monterrey, followed the next year by a discount supermarket there under the Economax banner. In 2001 H-E-B opened its first store — a Central Market — in the Dallas/Fort Worth area.

In 2002 the company also acquired five San Antonio stores from Albertsons and reopened them as H-E-B stores in August and September. Clingman retired in 2003.

In early 2004 H-E-B opened its first H-E-B Plus store in San Juan, Texas. In 2005 the Texas grocer celebrated its centennial.

EXECUTIVES

Chairman and CEO: Charles C. Butt, age 68
COO: Robert D. (Bob) Loeffler, age 53
EVP, Food Manufacturing, Procurement, and Merchandising: Steve Harper
SVP, General Manager, Central Texas: Jeff Thomas
SVP and General Merchandise, Manager, San Antonio Region: Greg Souquette
SVP, Real Estate Facilities Alliance and Services: Todd Piland
SVP, Operations, Central Market, and Dallas-Fort Worth Region: Stephen Butt
SVP, Procurement and Merchandising Strategy: Harvey McCoy
SVP, Supply Chain and Logistics: Kenneth (Ken) Allen
Group VP, Manufacturing: Bob McCullough
Group VP, Marketing, Advertising, and Branding: Cory J. Basso
Group VP, Public Affairs and Diversity: Winell Herron
VP, Information Solutions: Shawn Sedate
VP, Petroleum Marketing: James Aulds
VP, Quality Assurance and Environmental Affairs: William (Bill) Fry, age 63
Chief Strategic Officer: Craig Boyan, age 42
Director, Public Affairs: Shelley Parks
Treasurer: Megan Rooney
CIO: Gavin L. Gallagher
President, H-E-B Houston and Central Market Stores: Scott McClelland, age 51

LOCATIONS

HQ: H. E. Butt Grocery Company
646 S. Main Ave., San Antonio, TX 78204
Phone: 210-938-8000 **Fax:** 210-938-8169
Web: www.heb.com

H. E. Butt Grocery Company operates 300-plus grocery stores and gas stations throughout Texas and in Mexico. The company also operates bakeries; a photo processing lab; and meat, milk, and ice cream plants.

PRODUCTS/OPERATIONS

Selected Private Label Brands

Central Market All Natural
Central Market Organics
H-E-B Brand
Hill Country Fare

Selected Store Formats

Central Market (about 70,000 sq. ft., upscale supermarkets with expanded organic and gourmet foods; located in major metropolitan markets)
Economax (discount supermarkets, Mexico)
Gas 'N Go (gas stations)
H-E-B (large supermarkets)
H-E-B Marketplace (large supermarkets with specialty departments)
H-E-B Pantry (24,000-30,000 sq. ft., no-frills supermarkets with basic groceries; often located in rural or suburban areas)
H-E-B Plus (109,000-200,000 sq. ft., extensive nonfood sections)

COMPETITORS

7-Eleven	Kmart
Brookshire Brothers	Kroger
Chedraui	Minyard Group
Comerci	Randall's
Costco Wholesale	Rice Food Markets
CVS Caremark	Soriana
Fiesta Mart	Target
Foodarama Supermarkets	Walgreen
Gerland's Food Fair	Wal-Mart
Grupo Corvi	Wal-Mart de México
IGA	Whole Foods

HISTORICAL FINANCIALS

Company Type: Private

Income Statement

FYE: October 31

	REVENUE ($ mil.)	NET INCOME ($ mil.)	NET PROFIT MARGIN	EMPLOYEES
10/07	13,500	—	—	63,000
10/06	12,400	—	—	60,000
10/05	11,500	—	—	60,000
10/04	10,500	—	—	60,000
10/03	10,700	—	—	56,000
Annual Growth	6.0%	—	—	3.0%

Revenue History

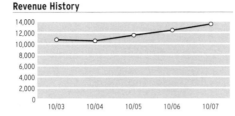

HISTORICAL FINANCIALS

Company Type: Private

Income Statement

FYE: December 31

	ESTIMATED REVENUE ($ mil.)	NET INCOME ($ mil.)	NET PROFIT MARGIN	EMPLOYEES
12/07	2,170	—	—	8,000
12/06	2,100	—	—	8,000
12/05	2,500	—	—	11,000
12/04	1,750	—	—	9,500
12/03	1,470	—	—	8,000
Annual Growth	10.2%	—	—	0.0%

Revenue History

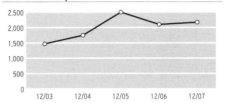

Heico Companies

Heico Companies specializes in buying distressed companies and turning them around. The firm, which typically invests for the long haul, owns interests in about 40 companies, several of them Rust Belt-based manufacturing concerns that founder Michael Heisley acquired during the 1980s. Heico's holdings include CopperCom, Davis Wire, Canadian steelmaker Ivaco, and heavy industrial equipment maker Pettibone. Heico also has interests in companies in the plastics, food, and telecommunications industries. Heisley, who launched Heico in 1979, also controls the NBA's Memphis Grizzlies but is looking to sell his stake.

EXECUTIVES

Chairman Emeritus: Michael E. Heisley, age 67
Chairman: Emily Heisley Stoeckel
President and CEO: E. A. (El) Roskovensky
EVP and CFO: Lawrence G. Wolski

LOCATIONS

HQ: Heico Companies LLC
70 W. Madison St., Ste. 5600, Chicago, IL 60602
Phone: 312-419-8220 **Fax:** 312-419-9417

COMPETITORS

Blackstone Group
CD&R
HM Capital Partners
KKR
KPS Capital Partners
Leonard Green
Thomas H. Lee Partners
TPG
Wingate Partners

Heifer Project

It's not just a handout; it's a new way of life. Heifer Project International (known as Heifer International) runs more than 860 projects that help millions of impoverished families become self-sufficient. Recipients are located in 125 countries around the world, including 28 US states. The non-profit organization provides more than 25 different kinds of breeding livestock and other animals (bees, rabbits, ducks) that can be used for food, income, or plowing power, in addition to training in sustainable agriculture techniques. In exchange, the family agrees to pass on not only the animals' first female offspring to another needy family, but their knowledge, too.

In early 2008 Heifer International received a four-year, more-than-$42-million grant from the Bill & Melinda Gates Foundation. The grant, which is the largest single grant to the foundation in its history, was dog-eared to fund a project to help poor rural East African farmers double their incomes by increasing the production of high-quality raw milk they can sell to dairies.

Heifer International was established in 1944 by Dan West, who had worked helping feed the hungry during the Spanish Civil War.

EXECUTIVES

President and CEO: Jo Luck, age 67
SVP Institution Building: Tanya Wright
SVP Programs: James (Jim) De Vries
SVP Finance and Administration: James Neal
SVP Development: Donna Jared
VP Communications and Marketing: Tom Peterson
Senior Director Marketing: Mike Matchett
Director Finance: Kit Smith
Auditors: BKD, LLP

LOCATIONS

HQ: Heifer Project International
1 World Ave., Little Rock, AR 72202
Phone: 800-422-0474 **Fax:** 501-907-2902
Web: www.heifer.org

HISTORICAL FINANCIALS

Company Type: Not-for-profit

Income Statement

FYE: June 30

	REVENUE ($ mil.)	NET INCOME ($ mil.)	NET PROFIT MARGIN	EMPLOYEES
6/07	118	—	—	345
6/06	99	—	—	307
6/05	83	—	—	—
6/04	69	—	—	304
6/03	58	—	—	—
Annual Growth	19.5%	—	—	4.3%

Revenue History

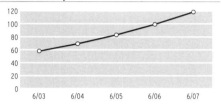

Helmsley Enterprises

"Infamous" doesn't begin to cover Helmsley Enterprises and its former chairman, the late Leona Helmsley. The company holds the real estate empire amassed by the late Harry Helmsley over a period of 50 years. Leona, who was dubbed the "Queen of Mean" in her heyday, served time for tax evasion and had interests in such high-profile properties as the Helmsley Park Lane and the Helmsley Windsor. Other holdings include apartment buildings and millions of square feet of New York real estate, as well as a lease on the Empire State Building. The portfolio was valued at $5 billion before Harry Helmsley's death in 1997. Leona Helmsley sold more than $2 billion worth of property between 1997 and her death in 2007.

At its apex, Helmsley's real estate empire included interests in more than 25 million sq. ft. of office space, more than 20,000 apartments, some 7,500 hotel rooms, 50 retail projects, warehouse space, land, garages, restaurants, and real estate companies. To keep the money in the family, the properties were managed by Helmsley-Spear (then 99%-owned by Helmsley, sold in 1997) and Helmsley-Noyes.

Helmsley has quietly sold a number of properties over the years, many at a premium in New York's stratospheric real estate market. The hotels may have lost some of their cachet; Helmsley hotels no longer hold coveted slots on the *Zagat Survey of Top U.S. Hotels*, and occupancy levels are below those of Manhattan's new trendy boutique hotels.

In the complex world of high-end New York real estate, in 2006 Helmsley signed deals with business partners/business rivals/family feud members Irving Schneider and the Malkin family, in which she bought out Schneider's share in the Empire State Building and other towers for $100 million.

HISTORY

In 1925 Harry Helmsley began his career as a Manhattan rent collector; the work, then done in person, taught him to evaluate buildings and acquainted him with their owners. During the Depression, Helmsley obtained property at bargain prices. He paid $1,000 down for a building with a $100,000 mortgage and later quipped that he did so to provide a job for his father, whom he hired as superintendent. In 1946 he sold the building for $165,000.

In the late 1940s Helmsley teamed up with lawyer Lawrence Wien. Helmsley located properties; Wien financed them through a device of his own invention, the loan syndicate. Prominent properties Helmsley bought into in the 1950s included the Flatiron (1951), Berkeley (1953), and Equitable (1957) buildings. He moved into management in 1955 with the purchase of Leon Spear's property management firm. In 1961 Helmsley bought the Empire State Building for $65 million and sold it to Prudential for $29 million with a 114-year leaseback (which expires in 2075); a public offering for the newly created Empire State Building Co. made up the balance.

In the mid-1960s Helmsley moved into property development, erecting office buildings and shopping centers. He bought the 30-building Furman and Wolfson trust, borrowing $78 million of the $165 million price on the strength of his reputation — the largest signature loan ever.

In 1969 Spear introduced Helmsley to Leona Roberts, a real estate broker who had sold Spear an apartment. Helmsley hired Leona and promoted her to SVP at his Brown, Harris, Stevens real estate brokerage. He divorced his wife and married Leona in 1971. In 1974 he leased an historic building and delegated the renovation to Leona (who built the company's hotel business). The Helmsley Palace opened in 1980 (now the New York Palace, sold 1993).

As Harry's health began to fail in the 1980s, Leona gained control of the empire. Maintenance deteriorated, bookkeeping went lax, and the couple's lavish spending became notorious. In 1988 they were charged with tax evasion. Harry was ruled incompetent to stand trial, but in 1989 Leona was convicted, fined $7.1 million, and sentenced to jail. She spent 21 months incarcerated, the last part of it in a halfway house.

After her 1994 release, Leona was banned from management of the hotels by laws forbidding felon involvement in businesses that serve liquor. She became more involved in the management of Harry's interests and began reshuffling assets, moving management contracts from Helmsley-Spear to Helmsley-Noyes, and selling buildings.

A 1995 suit brought by Harry's partners in Helmsley-Spear accused Leona of looting the company by depriving it of management contracts and loading it with debt to render worthless their right to buy the company under a 1970 option agreement.

In 1997 Harry died, and Leona announced she would sell the 125-property Helmsley portfolio. Wien's son-in-law Peter Malkin, partner in 13 top-notch Manhattan buildings, contested the control granted to her by Harry's will. They resolved their differences late that year. Leona also settled her differences with the Helmsley-Spear partners in 1997, agreeing to sell them the firm for less than $1 million.

Leona sold her favorite, the Helmsley Building on 230 Park Place, in 1998 to the Bass family on condition the building retain the name. That year, partly to avoid estate taxes, she formed the

Harry and Leona Helmsley Foundation, a charity to which she contributed more than $30 million in 1999.

Leona moved closer to a deal in 2000 to buy back the Empire State Building from then-owner Donald Trump and partners. The following year Malkin moved to challenge her, forming a plan to buy the skyscraper himself; Leona vowed to block his proposal. In 2002 Trump agreed to sell the building to Malkin for $57.5 million.

Leona died at her home in Greenwich, Connecticut, in 2007 at the age of 87.

EXECUTIVES

SVP and General Counsel: Harold A. Meriam
VP and CFO: Abe Wolf
Human Resources Director: Yogesh Mathur
Auditors: Eisner & Lubin LLP

LOCATIONS

HQ: Helmsley Enterprises, Inc.
230 Park Ave., New York, NY 10169
Phone: 212-679-3600   **Fax:** 212-953-2810

COMPETITORS

Accor	Ritz-Carlton
Four Seasons Hotels	Shorenstein
Hyatt	SL Green Realty
JMB Realty	Tishman
Lefrak Organization	Trammell Crow Company
Lincoln Property	The Trump Organization
Macklowe Properties	Vornado Realty
Marriott	

Henry Ford Health System

In 1915 automaker Henry Ford founded the hospital that forms the cornerstone of southeastern Michigan's not-for-profit Henry Ford Health System (HFHS), a hospital network that is also involved in medical research and education. The system's half-dozen hospitals — including the flagship Henry Ford Hospital, as well as Henry Ford Wyandotte Hospital and mental health facility Kingswood Hospital — hold more than 2,000 beds. HFHS also operates a 1,000 doctor-strong medical group, as well as nursing homes, hospice and home health care providers, and a medical supply retailer. The system's Health Alliance Plan of Michigan provides managed care and health insurance to about 550,000 members.

HFHS previously had a joint venture with Bon Secours Health System, called Bon Secours Cottage Health Services, which operated Cottage Hospital and Bon Secours Hospital, both located northeast of Detroit. However, in 2007 HFHS became the sole owner of Cottage Hospital, while Detroit's Beaumont Hospitals acquired Bon Secours Hospital.

That same year, HFHS acquired full ownership of St. Joseph's Healthcare, a 435-bed hospital system headquartered in Clinton Township that it had previously operated through a joint venture with Trinity Health. HFHS subsequently changed the acquired system's name to Henry Ford Macomb Hospitals.

HFHS is also building a new 300-bed acute care facility in West Bloomfield.

Affiliated with Wayne State University's School of Medicine, the health system is a leading education and research center, with ongoing research in areas such as stroke, heart disease, cancer, and diabetes.

EXECUTIVES

President Emeritus: Gail L. Warden, age 69
President and CEO: Nancy M. Schlichting, age 54
EVP and COO: Robert G. (Bob) Riney
EVP; CEO, Henry Ford Medical Group: Mark A. Kelley
SVP and CFO: James M. Connelly
SVP and CIO: Arthur Gross
SVP Clinical Affairs; Chairman, Department of Internal Medicine, Henry Ford Medical Group: John Popovich
SVP Philanthropy: Gary E. Rounding
SVP and Chief Quality Officer; Chief Medical Officer, Henry Ford Hospital: William A. Conway
SVP Marketing and Public Relations: Rose Glenn
Chief Nursing Officer: Constance J. Cronin
Director Recruitment and Human Resources Services: Jocelyn Giangrande
President and CEO, Henry Ford Hospital and Health Network: Anthony (Tony) Armada

LOCATIONS

HQ: Henry Ford Health System
1 Ford Place, Detroit, MI 48202
Phone: 313-876-8700   **Fax:** 313-876-9243
Web: www.henryfordhealth.org

PRODUCTS/OPERATIONS

Selected Operations

Hospitals
Henry Ford Hospital
Henry Ford Macomb Hospitals
Henry Ford Cottage Hospital
Henry Ford Wyandotte Hospital
Kingswood Hospital (mental health care)
Other
Health Alliance Plan of Michigan (health plan)
Henry Ford Continuing Care (nursing homes)
Henry Ford Health Products (medical supply retailer)
Henry Ford Home Health Care
Henry Ford Medical Group

COMPETITORS

Blue Cross (MI)
Crittenton Hospital
Detroit Medical Center
HealthPlus of Michigan
McLaren Heath Care
OmniCare Health Plan
St. John Health
Total Health Care
Trinity Health (Novi)
William Beaumont Hospital

HISTORICAL FINANCIALS

Company Type: Not-for-profit

Income Statement				FYE: December 31
	REVENUE ($ mil.)	NET INCOME ($ mil.)	NET PROFIT MARGIN	EMPLOYEES
12/07	3,470	106	3.0%	17,489
12/06	3,250	135	4.2%	16,000
12/05	3,049	112	3.7%	14,900
12/04	2,846	16	0.6%	13,000
12/03	2,600	—	—	12,700
Annual Growth	7.5%	87.7%	—	8.3%

2007 Year-End Financials

Debt ratio: —   Current ratio: —
Return on equity: 8.8%   Long-term debt ($ mil.): —
Cash ($ mil.): —

Net Income History

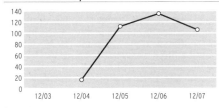

Hensel Phelps Construction

Hensel Phelps Construction builds it all, from the courthouse to the big house. Launched as a homebuilder by founder Hensel Phelps in 1937, the employee-owned general contractor focuses on design/build and construction management services for institutional and commercial projects, including prisons, airports, hotels, government and corporate complexes, convention centers, sport arenas, laboratories, and more. It also works on transportation, educational, residential, and health care projects. Major clients have included the US Army Corps of Engineers, IBM, Computer Sciences Corporation, United Airlines, The University of Texas, NASA, and Whole Foods. Hansel Phelps has eight regional offices throughout the US.

EXECUTIVES

Chairman and CEO: Jerry L. Morgensen
President and COO: Jeffrey (Jeff) Wenaas
EVP Eastern Division: Mark T. Baugh
VP Finance and CFO: Stephen J. (Steve) Carrico
VP and General Counsel: Eric L. Wilson
Auditors: KPMG LLP

LOCATIONS

HQ: Hensel Phelps Construction Co.
420 6th Ave., Greeley, CO 80632
Phone: 970-352-6565   **Fax:** 970-352-9311
Web: www.henselphelps.com

COMPETITORS

Balfour Construction
C.F. Jordan
CH2M HILL
Clark Construction Group
Dick Corporation
Fluor
Gilbane
Hunt Construction
Jacobs Engineering
KBR

M. A. Mortenson
McCarthy Building
PCL
Perini
Rooney Holdings
Skanska USA Building
Turner Corporation
Walbridge Aldinger
Walsh Group
Whiting-Turner

HISTORICAL FINANCIALS

Company Type: Private

Income Statement				FYE: December 31
	REVENUE ($ mil.)	NET INCOME ($ mil.)	NET PROFIT MARGIN	EMPLOYEES
12/07	2,520	—	—	2,727
12/06*	2,130	—	—	2,534
5/05	1,728	—	—	2,324
5/04	1,800	—	—	2,500
5/03	1,872	—	—	2,500
Annual Growth	7.7%	—	—	2.2%

*Fiscal year change

Revenue History

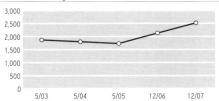

Hexion Specialty Chemicals

Hexion Specialty Chemicals is the world's largest thermosetting resins (or thermosets) maker, ahead of Georgia-Pacific. Thermosets add a desired quality (heat resistance, gloss, adhesion, etc.) to a number of different paints and adhesives. Hexion also is among the largest makers of formaldehyde and other forest product resins, epoxy resins, and raw materials for coatings and inks. In 2007 the company agreed to buy Huntsman for $10.5 billion. However, with the deal yet to be closed a year later, Hexion has attempted to pull out of the transaction. Apollo Management controls more than 90% of Hexion.

The company's business is divided into four segments. The Epoxy and Phenolic Resins unit is by far the largest, accounting for nearly half of sales. It sells its products to the auto, aerospace, electronics, and oil and gas industries. The next largest is the Formaldehyde and Forest Products Resins segment, whose products go into lumber, plywood, particle board, herbicides, and catalysts. The Coatings and Inks segment includes acrylic and polyester resins, versatic acids, and resins and additives for inks. These products are used in paints and coatings for the automotive, marine, construction, and maintenance industries, as well as in printing inks.

The final unit is the company's smallest. The Performance Products segment makes encapsulated substrates used for oil field services, as well as in foundries.

Hexion made the Coatings and Inks unit somewhat larger in 2006 with the acquisition of the decorative coatings and adhesives business of Rhodia. It then further strengthened the segment with the purchase of the inks and adhesive resins business of Akzo Nobel for just over $100 million. In 2007 the company continued to add to its European business with the acquisition of Arkema's urea formaldehyde resins operations.

The offer for Huntsman came soon after LyondellBasell had bid $9.5 billion for Huntsman. That company eventually backed down, and Huntsman and Hexion agreed to the deal. In the months after the agreement, though, Huntsman's earnings continued to dip, and the credit market continued to tank. Those factors led Hexion and Apollo to conclude that the combination of the two companies was no longer viable. They filed suit to break the agreement in mid-2008; Huntsman didn't agree with Hexion and Apollo's conclusion and filed a suit of its own, naming Apollo, rather than Hexion, as its target. The judgement, when it came, favored Huntsman, citing language in the original agreement that tilted the balance in Huntsman's favor, largely because Huntsman had backed out of the LyondellBasell deal to go with Apollo and Hexion. Eventually, Apollo contributed $540 million to Hexion to help it finance the closing of the deal, which should happen shortly.

Private investment goliath Apollo formed Hexion in 2005 when it combined the former Borden Chemical, Resolution Performance Products, Resolution Specialty Materials, and Bakelite. All these companies had been owned by Apollo prior to Hexion's founding.

EXECUTIVES

Chairman: Peter R. Huntsman
Vice Chairman: Marvin O. Schlanger, age 59
President and CEO: Craig O. Morrison, age 52, $1,598,033 pay
COO: Donald J. Stanutz
EVP, CFO, and Director: William H. (Bill) Carter, age 54, $1,049,214 pay
EVP; President, Epoxy and Phenolic Resins: Joseph P. (Jody) Bevilaqua, age 52, $550,452 pay
EVP; President, Coatings and Inks: Sarah R. Coffin, age 55, $463,104 pay
EVP; President, Forest Products Division: Dale N. Plante
EVP Environmental Health and Safety: Richard L. Monty, age 60
EVP Procurement: Nathan E. Fisher, age 42
EVP Human Resources: Judith A. (Judy) Sonnett, age 49
EVP and General Counsel: Mary Ann Jorgenson, age 67
VP Manufacturing: C. Hugh Morton, age 54, $430,080 pay (prior to title change)
VP Public Affairs: Peter F. (Pete) Loscocco
Director Investor Relations: John Kompa
Auditors: PricewaterhouseCoopers LLP

LOCATIONS

HQ: Hexion Specialty Chemicals, Inc.
180 E. Broad St., Columbus, OH 43215
Phone: 614-225-4000
Web: www.hexionchem.com

Hexion Specialty Chemicals operates 100 manufacturing facilities worldwide and sells to more than 100 countries.

2007 Sales

	$ mil.	% of total
US	2,466	42
The Netherlands	1,194	21
Germany	399	7
Canada	330	6
Other countries	1,421	24
Total	**5,810**	**100**

PRODUCTS/OPERATIONS

2007 Sales

	$ mil.	% of total
Epoxy & Phenolic Resins	2,424	42
Formaldehyde & Forest Products Resins	1,663	28
Coatings & Inks	1,330	23
Performance Products	393	7
Total	**5,810**	**100**

COMPETITORS

Akzo Nobel	Dynea
Arizona Chemical	ExxonMobil Chemical
Arkema US	Georgia-Pacific
Ashland	MeadWestvaco
BASF SE	Mitsui Chemicals
Celanese	Nan Ya Plastics
Dainippon Ink	Reichhold
Dow Chemical	

HISTORICAL FINANCIALS

Company Type: Private

Income Statement

FYE: December 31

	REVENUE ($ mil.)	NET INCOME ($ mil.)	NET PROFIT MARGIN	EMPLOYEES
12/07	5,810	(65)	—	6,400
12/06	5,205	(109)	—	6,900
12/05	4,470	(87)	—	7,000
12/04	2,019	(114)	—	6,900
12/03	782	(83)	—	—
Annual Growth	**65.1%**	—	—	**(2.5%)**

2007 Year-End Financials

Debt ratio: —
Return on equity: —
Cash ($ mil.): —
Current ratio: —
Long-term debt ($ mil.): 3,635

Net Income History

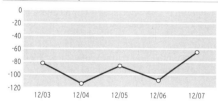

Hillman Companies

If you were to *label* it, the *key* to success — according to distributor The Hillman Companies — is doing things by the *numbers*. Operating through subsidiary The Hillman Group, it distributes small hardware such as fasteners, keys, signs, letters, numbers, and identification tags to home centers, hardware stores, pet stores, and grocery stores. Hillman distributes items from about 600 suppliers through nearly a dozen distribution centers in the US and Canada. It also makes and distributes its own key duplication and engraving systems. Customers include Wal-Mart, Home Depot, Lowe's, Sears, and PetSmart.

In 2007 Hillman Companies expanded its presence in Florida by purchasing All Points Industries, which specializes in distributing fasteners for hurricane protection. In early 2006 the company acquired SteelWorks, a manufacturer of

metal sheets, rods, and shapes, for $34 million. It plans to continue future growth through strategic acquisitions in existing or new markets.

Investment firm Allied Capital acquired The Hillman Companies in 2001; private equity company Code Hennessy & Simmons (CHS) bought Hillman in 2004 for about $510 million.

Code Hennessy & Simmons owns 55% of the company's voting stock; the Ontario Teachers' Pension Plan controls 31%.

EXECUTIVES

Chairman: Peter M. Gotsch, age 43
President, CEO, and Director: Max W. Hillman Jr., age 62, $436,126 pay
CFO and Secretary: James P. Waters, age 47, $212,831 pay
President, The Hillman Group: Richard P. Hillman, age 60, $330,417 pay
SVP Engraving, The Hillman Group: George L. Heredia, age 50, $286,644 pay
SVP National Account Sales, The Hillman Group: Terry R. Rowe, age 54, $248,601 pay
Auditors: Grant Thornton LLP

LOCATIONS

HQ: The Hillman Companies, Inc.
10590 Hamilton Ave., Cincinnati, OH 45231
Phone: 513-851-4900   **Fax:** 513-851-4997
Web: www.hillmangroup.com

The Hillman Companies operates facilities in Canada and the US.

2007 Sales

	$ mil.	% of total
US	429.6	96
Canada	7.3	2
Mexico	2.5	1
Other countries	6.2	1
Total	**445.6**	**100**

PRODUCTS/OPERATIONS

2007 Sales

	$ mil.	% of total
Fasteners	230.9	52
Keys	79.4	18
Engraving	39.1	9
Letters, numbers & signs	37.7	8
Threaded rod	30.7	7
Code cutter	5.1	1
Builders hardware	2.6	1
Other	20.1	4
Total	**445.6**	**100**

Selected Products and Services

Anchors
Bolts
Brads
Fasteners
In-store service
Keys
Key duplication systems
Letters
Merchandising systems
Metal shapes
Numbers
Nuts
Picture hanging wire
Screws
Signs
Tacks
Tags
Threaded rods
Washers

HISTORICAL FINANCIALS

Company Type: Private

Income Statement				FYE: December 31
	REVENUE ($ mil.)	NET INCOME ($ mil.)	NET PROFIT MARGIN	EMPLOYEES
12/07	446	(10)	—	2,055
12/06	424	(8)	—	1,897
12/05	383	(4)	—	1,853
12/04	352	(19)	—	1,794
12/03	318	(5)	—	1,760
Annual Growth	8.8%	—	—	4.0%

2007 Year-End Financials

Debt ratio: 1,020.9%   Current ratio: —
Return on equity: —   Long-term debt ($ mil.): 229
Cash ($ mil.): —

Net Income History

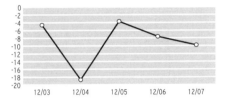

Hilton Hotels

If you need a bed for the night, Hilton Hotels has a few hundred thousand of them. One of the largest hoteliers in the world, the company's lodging empire includes about 2,800 hotels and resorts in more than 80 countries operating under such names as Doubletree, Embassy Suites, and Hampton, as well as its flagship Hilton brand. Many of its hotels serve the mid-market segment, though its Hilton and Conrad hotels offer full-service, upscale lodging. In addition, its Homewood Suites chain offers extended-stay services. The company franchises many of its hotels; it owns the Waldorf-Astoria and the New York Hilton. Private equity firm The Blackstone Group bought Hilton in 2007 for about $20 billion plus debt.

The Blackstone deal represents the biggest private equity buyout in the hotel industry. As a result of the acquisition, the equity firm will assume about $6 billion in debt, bringing the total purchase price to some $26 billion. Blackstone already owns hotel assets such as LaQuinta Inns and Suites and LXR Luxury Resorts & Hotels (operated by WHM). The new parent will transition some of its own luxury brands to the Hilton name. Blackstone also plans significant

growth for Hilton in the US, as well as an international expansion through partnerships, rather than direct investment.

Hilton's largest chain is its Hampton Inn and Hampton Inn & Suites, with about 1,400 locations offering moderately priced rooms with limited amenities. Nearly all its Hampton hotels are operated by franchisees or by the company under management contracts with third-party owners. At the other end of the scale, its Hilton and Conrad chains offer luxury services and distinctive locations. Its Hilton Grand Vacations subsidiary operates more than 30 time-share vacation resorts located mostly in Florida.

In 2006 the company acquired Hilton International, the lodging operations of UK-based Hilton Group (now Ladbrokes). The $5.7 billion deal re-unified the Hilton Hotel brand throughout the world and added about 400 new locations to Hilton's portfolio. The purchase solidified the company's plans for significant international expansion. The company additionally brought into the Hilton fold about 80 LivingWell Health Clubs and more than 140 hotels operating under the Scandic brand. Following the acquisition, Hilton in 2007 sold its Scandic Hotels business to private equity firm EQT for $1.1 billion.

The company has introduced a new brand of luxury hotels, the Waldorf-Astoria Collection. The elite brand debuted with New York's Waldorf-Astoria, along with three luxury resorts newly managed by Hilton: the Grand Wailea Resort Hotel & Spa in Hawaii; the Arizona Biltmore Resort & Spa in Phoenix, and La Quinta Resort & Club in La Quinta, California.

After leading the company for more than a decade, CEO Stephen Bollenbach stepped down at the end of 2007 to become CEO at troubled home builder KB Home, though he'll remain co-chairman of the hotel business through 2010. Christopher J. Nassetta was appointed as Bollenbach's replacement.

The family of co-chairman William Barron Hilton, son of founder Conrad Hilton, owned about 5% of the company before it was acquired by Blackstone in 2007.

HISTORY

Conrad Hilton got his start in hotel management by renting out rooms in his family's New Mexico home. He served as a state legislator and started a bank before leaving for Texas in 1919, hoping to make his fortune in banking. Hilton was unable to shoulder the cost of purchasing a bank, however, but recognized a high demand for hotel rooms and made a quick change in strategy, buying his first hotel in Cisco, Texas. Over the next decade he bought seven more Texas hotels.

Hilton lost several properties during the Depression, but began rebuilding his empire soon thereafter through the purchase of hotels in California (1938), New Mexico (1939), and Mexico (1942). He even married starlet Zsa Zsa Gabor in 1942 (they later divorced, of course). Hilton Hotels Corporation was formed in 1946 and went public. The company bought New York's Waldorf-Astoria in 1949 (a hotel Hilton called "the greatest of them all") and opened its first European hotel in Madrid in 1953. Hilton paid $111 million for the 10-hotel Statler chain the following year.

Hilton took his company out of the overseas hotel business in 1964 by spinning off Hilton International and began franchising the following year to capitalize on the well-known Hilton name. Barron Hilton, Conrad's son, was appointed president in 1966 (he became chairman upon Conrad Hilton's death in 1979). Hilton bought two Las Vegas hotels (the Las Vegas Hilton and the Flamingo Hilton) in 1970 and launched its gaming division. The company returned to the international hotel business with Conrad International Hotels in 1982 and opened its first suite-only Hilton Suites hotel in 1989.

Hilton expanded its gaming operations in the 1990s, buying Bally's Casino Resort in Reno in 1992 and launching its first riverboat casino, the Hilton Queen of New Orleans, in 1994. Two years later it acquired all of Bally Entertainment, making it the largest gaming company in the world. Also that year, Stephen Bollenbach, the former Walt Disney CFO who negotiated the $19 billion acquisition of Capital Cities/ABC, was named CEO — becoming the first non-family member to run the company.

Hilton formed an alliance with Ladbroke Group in 1997 (later Hilton Group, owner of Hilton International and the rights to the Hilton name outside the US) to promote the Hilton brand worldwide. With a downturn in the gambling industry translating into sluggish results in Hilton's gaming segment, the company spun off its gaming interests as Park Place Entertainment (later Caesars Entertainment, now owned by Harrah's) in 1998.

In 1999 Hilton made a massive acquisition with the $3.7 billion purchase of Promus Hotel Corp. At the end of 2002 the company formed a $400 million venture with CNL Hospitality (now CNL Hotels & Resorts) to buy and refurbish hotel properties.

Following an extended downturn in the hospitality business brought on by recession and post-9/11 fears about terrorism, Hilton began to invest in refurbishments for many of its properties and added about 150 locations in 2004.

Two years later the company re-unified the Hilton Hotels brand internationally by acquiring Hilton International from Hilton Group (now Ladbrokes) for about $5.7 billion.

In 2007 the company was acquired by The Blackstone Group, and Christopher J. Nassetta replaced Bollenbach as CEO.

EXECUTIVES

Chairman: William Barron Hilton, age 81
President, Global Operations; CEO, Hilton International: Ian R. Carter, age 46, $2,906,543 pay
CFO: Thomas C. Kennedy, age 42
EVP; CEO, Americas and Global Brands: Thomas L. (Tom) Keltner, age 61
EVP Global Distribution Services and Shared Brand Services, and CIO: James T. (Tim) Harvey, age 48
EVP, General Counsel, and Corporate Secretary: Madeleine A. Kleiner, age 55, $1,025,000 pay
EVP; CEO, Hilton Grand Vacations: Antoine Dagot
EVP Americas Operations, Sales, and Revenue Management: Kenneth M. (Ken) Smith
EVP and General Counsel: Richard M. Lucas
EVP Human Resources, Diversity, and Administration: Molly McKenzie-Swarts
SVP and Treasurer: Mariel A. Joliet
SVP Development and Finance: Ted Middleton
SVP Sales and Development: Bob Dirks
SVP Global Communications and Public Relations: Ellen D. Gonda
SVP Customer Loyalty: Adam Burke
VP Corporate Communications: Kathy Shepard
VP Investor Relations: Atish Shah

President, Conrad Hotels: Clem Barter
President and CEO: Christopher J. (Chris) Nassetta, age 45
President Global Development and Real Estate: Steven R. (Steve) Goldman, age 46
President, Middle East and Asia Pacific: Koos Klein
President, Hilton Grand Vacations: Mark Wang
Auditors: Ernst & Young LLP

LOCATIONS

HQ: Hilton Hotels Corporation
9336 Civic Center Dr., Beverly Hills, CA 90210
Phone: 310-278-4321 **Fax:** 310-205-7678
Web: www.hiltonworldwide.com

PRODUCTS/OPERATIONS

Selected Brands

Conrad Hotels & Resorts
Doubletree
Embassy Suites Hotels
Hampton Inn
Hampton Inn & Suites
Hilton
Hilton Garden Inn
Hilton Grand Vacations Club
Homewood Suites by Hilton

Selected Owned Hotels

Chicago's Palmer House Hilton
The Hilton Hawaiian Village on Waikiki Beach
Hilton San Francisco on Union Square
The New York Hilton
The Waldorf Astoria

COMPETITORS

Accor North America
Best Western
Carlson Hotels
Choice Hotels
Fairmont Raffles
Four Seasons Hotels
Hyatt
InterContinental Hotels
Marriott
Starwood Hotels & Resorts
Wyndham Worldwide

HISTORICAL FINANCIALS

Company Type: Private

Income Statement

	REVENUE ($ mil.)	NET INCOME ($ mil.)	NET PROFIT MARGIN	EMPLOYEES
12/07	8,090	121	1.5%	135,000
12/06	8,162	572	7.0%	105,000
12/05	4,437	460	10.4%	61,000
12/04	4,146	238	5.7%	—
12/03	3,819	164	4.3%	—
Annual Growth	20.6%	(7.3%)	—	48.8%

2007 Year-End Financials

Debt ratio: 407.4%
Return on equity: 2.7%
Cash ($ mil.): —
Current ratio: —
Long-term debt ($ mil.): 21,177

Net Income History

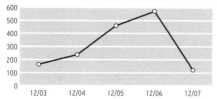

Hobby Lobby

If something wicker this way comes, Hobby Lobby Stores may be the source. The firm operates about 400 stores in more than 30 states and sells arts and crafts supplies, baskets, beads, candles, frames, home-decorating accessories, and silk flowers. The #3 craft and fabric retailer (behind Michaels Stores and Jo-Ann Stores), it prefers to set up shop in second-generation retail sites (such as vacated supermarkets and superstores). Sister companies supply Hobby Lobby stores with merchandise, received from its Oklahoma distribution facility. CEO David Green, who owns the company with his wife Barbara, founded Hobby Lobby in 1972 and operates it according to biblical principles, including closing stores on Sunday.

About a dozen new Hobby Lobby stores, also known as Hobby Lobby Creative Centers, were planned for 2008.

The company also has operations in China, Hong Kong, and the Philippines. It recently expanded its 3.4 million sq. ft. of manufacturing, corporate office, and distribution space in Oklahoma City. Hobby Lobby makes its own candle and scented products, craft supplies, home furnishings, and other products, which are supplied by affiliated companies, including Crafts, Etc!, and Hemispheres. Crafts, Etc!, Hemispheres, and Christian products maker Mardel are all housed at the expanded Oklahoma facility.

Hobby Lobby began as a picture frame manufacturing company.

EXECUTIVES

CEO: David Green
President and Director of Real Estate: Steven Green, age 41
SVP and CFO: John Cargill
SVP Operations: Ken Haywood
VP Advertising: John Schumacher
VP Construction: Steve Seay
VP Legal: Peter Dobelbower
Director of Recruiting: Bill Owens

LOCATIONS

HQ: Hobby Lobby Stores, Inc.
7707 SW 44th St., Oklahoma City, OK 73179
Phone: 405-745-1100 **Fax:** 405-745-1547
Web: www.hobbylobby.com

PRODUCTS/OPERATIONS

Selected Products

Arts and crafts supplies
Baskets
Candles
Cards
Furniture
Home accent pieces
Jewelry-making supplies
Model kits
Needlework
Party supplies
Picture frames and framing
Rubber stamping supplies
Scrapbooking supplies
Seasonal items
Sewing materials (fabric, patterns, notions)
Silk flowers
Wearable art

Selected Affiliates

Bearing Fruit Communications (Christian advertising agency)
Crafts, Etc! (online sales and wholesale distribution of domestic and imported arts, crafts, and jewelry-making and hobby materials to Hobby Lobby and other retailers)
Hemispheres (home furnishings and accessories stores)
HL Construction (remodels and redesigns sites to become Hobby Lobby stores)
Hong Kong Connection (China sourcing and buying office)
Mardel Christian Office & Educational Supply (Christian materials, office supplies, and educational products)

COMPETITORS

A.C. Moore	Jo-Ann Stores
Burnes Home Accents	Kirkland's
Family Christian Stores	Longaberger
Garden Ridge	Michaels Stores
Hancock Fabrics	Old Time Pottery
HobbyTown USA	Target
Home Interiors & Gifts	Wal-Mart

HISTORICAL FINANCIALS

Company Type: Private

Income Statement

FYE: December 31

	REVENUE ($ mil.)	NET INCOME ($ mil.)	NET PROFIT MARGIN	EMPLOYEES
12/07	1,800	—	—	18,000
12/06	1,620	—	—	17,500
12/05	1,500	—	—	17,000
12/04	1,400	—	—	16,000
12/03	1,300	—	—	15,000
Annual Growth	8.5%	—	—	4.7%

Revenue History

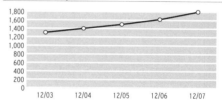

Holiday Companies

Wholesaling and sporting goods retailing have both taken a vacation at Holiday Companies. The firm sold its Fairway Foods distribution business in 2000; its Gander Mountain sporting goods chain went public in 2004. Today, Holiday Companies operates about 400 Holiday Stationstores (about 100 of which are franchised) in a dozen states, from Michigan to Washington and Alaska. These stores sell gas supplied by the company's Erickson Petroleum subsidiary, as well as Blue Planet gasoline (low-sulfur fuel available in Minnesota). The company was founded in 1928 as a general store in a small Wisconsin town by two Erickson brothers, whose descendants still own and run the company.

EXECUTIVES

Chairman and CEO: Ronald A. (Ron) Erickson, age 71
Vice Chairman and VP: Gerald Erickson
President and COO: Brent G. Blackey, age 49
VP and CIO: Randy Skare
VP Merchandising: Dave Yamaguchi
VP Human Resources: Robert S. (Bob) Nye
VP Petroleum Supply and Distribution, Holiday Stationstores: Richard (Dick) Mills
VP Operations: Rick Johnson
VP Sales and Marketing: Brian Hooks
Auditors: Ernst & Young LLP

LOCATIONS

HQ: Holiday Companies
4567 American Blvd. West, Bloomington, MN 55437
Phone: 952-830-8700   **Fax:** 952-830-8864
Web: holidaystationstores.com

COMPETITORS

7-Eleven   Kroger
Casey's General Stores   Marathon Petroleum
Couche-Tard   QuikTrip
Exxon   TravelCenters of America

HISTORICAL FINANCIALS

Company Type: Private

Income Statement			FYE: December 31
	ESTIMATED REVENUE ($ mil.)	NET INCOME ($ mil.)	NET PROFIT MARGIN	EMPLOYEES
12/07	2,000	—	—	4,600
12/06	1,820	—	—	4,410
12/05	1,742	—	—	4,200
12/04	1,310	—	—	4,000
12/03	1,200	—	—	4,000
Annual Growth	13.6%	—	—	3.6%

Revenue History

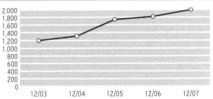

Honickman Affiliates

Honickman Affiliates doesn't mind bottling its creative juices. The firm is one of the nation's largest privately owned bottlers — bottling and distributing soft drinks primarily in Maryland, New Jersey, New York, Ohio, and Virginia. A major bottler of Pepsi-Cola and Dr Pepper Snapple Group brands including 7 UP, it also sells Canada Dry, Mott's, Snapple, and South Beach Beverage Company's SoBe beverages. It distributes Coors beers in New York and brews up private-label soft drinks. Chairman and owner Harold Honickman started the company in 1957, with his father-in-law building a bottling plant for him.

EXECUTIVES

Chairman: Harold A. Honickman
CEO: Jeffrey A. (Jeff) Honickman, age 51
CFO: Walt Wilkinson
President, Pepsi-Cola and Canada Dry: Robert Brockway
Director Human Resources: June Raufer
Data Processing: Gwen Dolceamore
Corporate Safety Director: Jeffrey Brody

LOCATIONS

HQ: Honickman Affiliates
8275 Rte. 130, Pennsauken, NJ 08110
Phone: 856-665-6200   **Fax:** 856-661-4684

COMPETITORS

Cott   Pepsi Bottling Ventures
G & J Pepsi-Cola Bottlers   Philadelphia Coca-Cola
National Beverage   Polar Beverages
Pepsi Bottling

HISTORICAL FINANCIALS

Company Type: Private

Income Statement				FYE: December 31
	ESTIMATED REVENUE ($ mil.)	NET INCOME ($ mil.)	NET PROFIT MARGIN	EMPLOYEES
12/07	1,330	—	—	5,000
12/06	1,280	—	—	5,000
12/05	1,215	—	—	5,000
12/04	1,130	—	—	5,000
12/03	1,100	—	—	5,000
Annual Growth	4.9%	—	—	0.0%

Revenue History

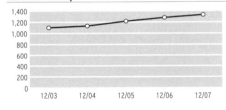

Horizon Healthcare

Horizon Healthcare Services (dba Horizon Blue Cross Blue Shield of New Jersey) is New Jersey's top health insurance provider, serving about 3.5 million members. The not-for-profit company, a licensee of the Blue Cross and Blue Shield Association, offers traditional indemnity and managed care plans, including HMO, PPO, POS, and Medicare Advantage plans. It also provides dental and behavioral health coverage and, through subsidiary Horizon Casualty Services, manages workers' compensation claims. The company's Horizon NJ Health subsidiary participates in the state of New Jersey's Medicaid program. And its Rayant Insurance Agency sells life and disability insurance coverage.

Horizon Healthcare's largest single account is New Jersey's State Health Benefits Program, which covers state government workers. The company also covers federal employees through the Blue Cross and Blue Shield Association's Federal Employee Program.

Like all US health insurers, Horizon Healthcare continually grapples with the problem of rising health care costs. It is trying to keep costs under control in a number of ways, including via lower-cost, consumer-directed products (branded Horizon MyWay) that place more financial and decision-making responsibility on the policyholder. The company is also trying to keep its members healthy with programs that promote fitness, provide reminders for health screenings, and help members manage chronic diseases.

Horizon Healthcare jumped on the Medicare prescription drug bandwagon in 2006, introducing a Medicare Part D program at the beginning of the year. Other growing businesses within the company include its dental plan (which boasts more than a million members) and its workers' compensation managed care programs offered through Horizon Casualty Services.

The company provides dental coverage in New York and Pennsylvania, in addition to its dental offerings in New Jersey. In 2007 the company changed the name of its dental business in New York and Pennsylvania to Rayant. (At the same time its Horizon Healthcare Insurance Agency, which provides life and disability insurance, became Rayant Insurance Agency.) Horizon had previously offered health insurance in New York as well, but it decided to exit that market in 2006.

Horizon Healthcare Services has occasionally flirted with the idea of converting from a not-for-profit entity to a for-profit corporation. It decided in 2005 to retain its not-for-profit status for the time being, but in 2008 announced it was taking steps towards conversion.

EXECUTIVES

Chairman: Vincent J. Giblin
President, CEO, and Director: William J. Marino, age 64
EVP and COO: Robert A. Marino
SVP, Administration, CFO, and Treasurer: Robert J. Pures
SVP, General Counsel, and Secretary: John W. Campbell
SVP Service: Jackie R. Jennifer
SVP Market Business Units: Christopher M. Lepre
SVP, Information Technology and CIO: Mark Barnard
VP, Corporate Marketing and Communications: Lawrence B. Altman
VP, Strategy and Development: Donna M. Celestini
VP, Health Affairs and Chief Medical Officer: Richard G. Popiel
VP, Human Resources: Margaret Coons
President and COO, Horizon NJ Health: Karen L. Clark
CEO, Horizon Healthcare of NJ: Christy W. Bell
Director, Public Affairs, Corpoarte Marketing and Communications: Thomas W. Rubino
Auditors: PricewaterhouseCoopers LLP

LOCATIONS

HQ: Horizon Healthcare Services, Inc.
3 Penn Plaza East, Newark, NJ 07101
Phone: 973-466-4000   **Fax:** 973-466-4317
Web: www.horizon-bcbsnj.com

PRODUCTS/OPERATIONS

2007 Revenue

	$ mil.	% of total
Operating revenue		
Insured premiums	7,009.9	93
Administrative service fee income	345.7	5
Other operating revenue	28.1	—
Investment income	140.3	2
Net realized gains on investments	2.5	—
Total	**7,526.5**	**100**

2007 Membership

	No. of members (thousands)
Large group customers	1,795
State Health Benefits Program	594
Small group customers	407
Medicaid members	332
Individuals	151
Federal Employees Program	125
Medicare Advantage members	55
Total	**3,459**

COMPETITORS

Aetna
AmeriHealth
CIGNA
Health Net
Healthfirst
Healthplex
MetLife
Oxford Health

HISTORICAL FINANCIALS

Company Type: Not-for-profit

Income Statement

FYE: December 31

	REVENUE ($ mil.)	NET INCOME ($ mil.)	NET PROFIT MARGIN	EMPLOYEES
12/07	7,527	161	2.1%	5,200
12/06	6,730	180	2.7%	4,700
12/05	6,025	214	3.5%	4,400
12/04	5,504	173	3.1%	4,400
12/03	5,082	171	3.4%	4,600
Annual Growth	10.3%	(1.5%)	—	3.1%

2007 Year-End Financials

Debt ratio: —
Return on equity: 10.3%
Cash ($ mil.): —

Current ratio: —
Long-term debt ($ mil.): —

Net Income History

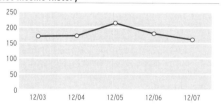

Houchens Industries

Houchens Industries is a supermarket of businesses as well as an operator of supermarkets. The diversified company runs about 175 grocery stores under the Houchens, Food Giant, IGA, Piggly Wiggly, and Buy Low banners. Its 220 Save-A-Lot discount grocery stores in a dozen states offer limited selections and cover 15,000 sq. ft. or less. Houchens also owns about 40 Jr. Foods convenience stores and two dozen Tobacco Shoppe discount cigarette outlets, mostly in Kentucky and Tennessee. It sold cigarette maker Commonwealth Brands in 2007. Other businesses include construction, financial services, real estate, and recycling. Founded as BG Wholesale in 1918 by Ervin Houchens, the firm is 100% owned by its employees.

Employee-owned since 1988, Houchens has amassed a diverse portfolio of companies over the years through acquisitions. The company looks to buy assets that have sound management and history of providing good cash flow that can be bought at a reasonable price.

Its most recent acquisition was Chicago-based Tampico Beverages, a maker of refrigerated juice drinks and punches sold in more than 36 countries, for an undisclosed amount in July 2008. Tampico supplies beverages to grocery and convenience stores, as well as quick-serve restaurants. In March 2008 Houchens purchased the Kentucky-based brokerage and financial services firm J.J.B. Hilliard, W.L. Lyons (Hilliard Lyons for short), Inc. from The PNC Financial Services Group to form a new company called HL Financial Services. In 2007 the company sold its Commonwealth Brands cigarette division to Britain's Imperial Tobacco for $1.9 billion. Houchens owned the business for about six years. In the grocery arena, Houchens acquired Food Giant Supermarkets, the operator of 90 Food Giant and Piggly Wiggly supermarkets in eight states, in mid-2004. In late 2004 the company also acquired Scotty's Contracting & Stone — a Central Kentucky highway-construction company — in a stock swap between the two employee-owned companies. Connected with the Scotty's transaction, Houchens also bought TS Trucking.

Other acquisitions made by the Houchens Insurance Group include the purchase of the assets of rival Synaxis Van Meter Insurance Agency Inc. and Employers Risk Services Inc., both in 2006.

The regional grocery chain is undertaking a number of banner conversions, including the renaming of about five of its IGA stores to the newer Crossroads IGA format; Houchens-banner stores to Hometown IGA; and Jr. Foods convenience stores to IGA Express. It's also increasing the number of IGA Super Savers it operates. It is also looking to grow its retail grocery business through continued acquisitions. To that end, in June 2008 the firm acquired Buehler Foods, the operator of 22 BUY LOW grocery stores in Illinois, Indiana, and Kentucky.

Houchens is the nation's largest Save-A-Lot licensee. True to its name, the chain focuses on lower-income shoppers and competes with other discount grocers such as fast-growing ALDI. (Grocery retailer and wholesaler SUPERVALU is the parent company of Save-A-Lot.)

EXECUTIVES

Chairman and CEO: James (Jimmie) Gipson
President: Spencer Coates
CFO: Gordon Minter
Director of Benefits: Sharon Grooms
Director of Marketing and Merchandising: Alan Larsen
Information Systems Manager: Terry Cornell

LOCATIONS

HQ: Houchens Industries Inc.
700 Church St., Bowling Green, KY 42102
Phone: 270-843-3252   **Fax:** 270-780-2877

COMPETITORS

7-Eleven
ALDI
Ameriprise
Charles Schwab
Citigroup
Cumberland Farms
Delhaize America
Dole Food
Dr Pepper Snapple Group
E*TRADE Financial
Edward D. Jones
Faygo
Florida's Natural
FMR
Goya
John Hancock Financial Services
Jugos del Valle
Kroger
K-VA-T Food Stores

Meijer
Mott's
Nestlé
Ocean Spray
Odwalla
Old Orchard
Raymond James Financial
Sheetz
Smokin Joes
Sunkist
Sunny Delight
TD Ameritrade
Tree Top
Tropicana
Vector Group
Veryfine
Wal-Mart
Weis Markets
Welch's
Winn-Dixie

Houghton Mifflin

Alice Cooper's 1972 album *School's Out* probably doesn't get much play around the offices of Houghton Mifflin. A top publisher of textbooks for the K-12 markets, the company also offers trade and reference books for adults and children, such as the *American Heritage Dictionary*. Divisions include McDougal Littell (textbooks), Riverside Publishing (educational testing), and Great Source (supplemental school materials). In 2007 it acquired several businesses from Harcourt, another K-12 publisher, creating subsidiary Houghton Mifflin Harcourt Publishing Company. Houghton Mifflin sold its College Division in 2008. Houghton Mifflin is owned by Irish holding company Houghton Mifflin Riverdeep Group PLC.

The publisher currently relies heavily on its K-12 publishing business. However, its trade fiction and nonfiction lines, although small, still produce the occasional best seller. Hits have included *The Gourmet Cookbook,* Philip Roth's *The Plot Against America,* and children's book *The Polar Express.*

In 2007 the company purchased several Harcourt businesses from Reed Elsevier. The deal included the acquisition of Harcourt Education, Harcourt Trade, and Greenwood-Heinemann for about $4 billion, strengthening Houghton Mifflin's position in the US educational publishing market. (Reed Elsevier sold other Harcourt brands, including international publishing business Harcourt Education Ltd., to education firm Pearson.) Houghton Mifflin sold its College Division to Cengage Learning (formerly Thomson Learning) for $750 million in cash in order to become exclusively a publisher of K-12, trade, and reference titles.

Throughout its long history, the company has had several changes of ownership. The most recent occurred with the formation of Houghton Mifflin Riverdeep Group PLC, a holding company created in 2006 to purchase Houghton Mifflin from affiliates of private investment firms Thomas H. Lee Partners, Bain Capital, and The Blackstone

Group, and members of Houghton Mifflin's management. The deal, worth some $5 billion total, was the result of a reverse takeover by Dublin-based courseware publisher HM Rivergroup. The entity renamed itself Houghton Mifflin Riverdeep Group after it combined Houghton Mifflin with its Riverdeep holdings.

EXECUTIVES

CEO: Anthony (Tony) Lucki, age 60
President and COO: Gerald T. Hughes
EVP; President, Assessment Group: Sylvia Metayer
EVP and Chief Publishing Officer: Donna Lucki
EVP and Chief Human Resources Officer: Ciara Smyth
EVP and General Counsel: Bill Bayers
SVP and CFO: Michael Muldowney
SVP Operations: Greg DuMont
SVP, Clerk, Secretary, and General Counsel:
  Paul D. Weaver, age 58
SVP Educational and Governmental Affairs:
  Maureen DiMarco
SVP Finance: Stephen Tapp
President, Great Source Education Group:
  Steven Zukowski
**President, Houghton Mifflin Harcourt Trade and
  Reference Publishers:** Gary Gentel
President, Houghton Mifflin Harcourt College Division:
  Kristine Clerkin
**President, Houghton Mifflin Harcourt International
  Publishers:** Patricia Tutunjian
**President, Houghton Mifflin Harcourt Learning
  Technology:** Scott Kirkpatrick
**President, Houghton Mifflin Harcourt School
  Publishers:** Michael Lavelle
President, McDougal Littell: Rita H. Schaefer, age 47
President, The Riverside Publishing Company:
  Richard Swartz
Auditors: PricewaterhouseCoopers LLP

LOCATIONS

HQ: Houghton Mifflin Company
  222 Berkeley St., Boston, MA 02116
Phone: 617-351-5000   **Fax:** 617-351-1105
Web: www.hmco.com

PRODUCTS/OPERATIONS

Selected Operations
Pre-K-12 Publishing
  Houghton Mifflin Harcourt
  Great Source (supplemental education materials)
  McDougal Littell (secondary textbooks)
  The Riverside Publishing Company (testing materials)
Trade and Reference Publishing

COMPETITORS

Educational Testing Service
Everyday Learning
Goodheart-Willcox
Hachette Book Group
HarperCollins
John Wiley
McGraw-Hill
Merriam-Webster
Pearson
Questar Assessment
Random House
Scholastic
Verlagsgruppe Georg von Holtzbrinck
W.W. Norton

Houston Rockets

Houston basketball fans really blast off for this team. The Houston Rockets joined the National Basketball Association in 1967 as the San Diego Rockets, a franchise first awarded to Bob Breitbard. After moving to Houston in 1971, the team reached the NBA Finals twice before finally winning back-to-back championship titles in 1994 and 1995. The Rockets roster has been graced with such Hall of Fame players as Clyde Drexler, Moses Malone, and Hakeem Olajuwon. In 2003 the franchise took up residence at Houston's Toyota Center. Former Wall Street securities trader Leslie Alexander has owned the team since 1993.

While the Rockets have been perennial playoff contenders the past several years, the team has mostly failed to advance past the first or second round. At the end of the 2006-07 season, head coach Jeff Van Gundy was fired and replaced by former Sacramento Kings coach Rick Adelman. A former NBA player, Adelman had originally been drafted by the San Diego Rockets.

EXECUTIVES

Owner: Leslie L. Alexander, age 66
CEO: Thaddeus B. (Tad) Brown
CFO: Marcus Jolibois
General Manager: Daryl Morey
Head Coach: Rick Adelman, age 62
SVP Basketball Operations and Athletic Trainer:
  Keith Jones
VP Human Resources: Vivian L. Mora
VP and General Manager, Toyota Center:
  R. Douglas (Doug) Hall, age 42
VP Player Personnel: Dean Cooper
General Counsel: Rafael Stone
Director Broadcasting: Joel Blank
Director Marketing Operations: Ken Sheirr
Director Community Relations: Sarah Joseph
Director Corporate Services: Frances Castaneda
Director Media Relations: Nelson Luis

LOCATIONS

HQ: Houston Rockets
  1510 Polk St., Houston, TX 77002
Phone: 713-758-7200   **Fax:** 713-758-7315
Web: www.nba.com/rockets

The Houston Rockets play in the 18,300-seat capacity Toyota Center in Houston.

PRODUCTS/OPERATIONS

Titles
NBA Champions (1994-95)
Western Conference Champions (1981, 1986, 1994-95)

COMPETITORS

Dallas Mavericks
Memphis Grizzlies
New Orleans Hornets
San Antonio Spurs

HISTORICAL FINANCIALS
Company Type: Private

Income Statement
FYE: June 30

	REVENUE ($ mil.)	NET INCOME ($ mil.)	NET PROFIT MARGIN	EMPLOYEES
6/07	149	—	—	—
6/06	142	—	—	—
6/05	141	—	—	—
6/04	125	—	—	—
6/03	82	—	—	—
Annual Growth	16.1%			

Revenue History

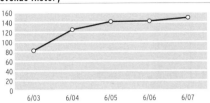

Howard University

Howard University is a predominantly African-American university that enrolls some 10,800 students. The school offers nearly 80 undergraduate majors and about 100 graduate degrees in areas such as engineering, education, dentistry, law, medicine, history, political science, music, and social work. Notable alumni include choreographer Debbie Allen, former US Supreme Court Justice Thurgood Marshall, former New York City mayor David Dinkins, Nobel Laureate Toni Morrison, and singer Roberta Flack. Established in 1867, the school was named after one of its founders, General Oliver O. Howard, a Civil War hero who was Commissioner of the Freedman's Bureau.

EXECUTIVES

Chairman: Addison B. Rand, age 63
Vice Chairwoman: Renee Higginbotham-Brooks
President: Sidney A. Ribeau, age 60
General Counsel: Norma Leftwich
SVP, CFO, and Treasurer: Sidney H. Evans Jr.
SVP and Secretary: Artis G. Hampshire-Cowan
**SVP Strategic Planning, Operations and External
  Affairs and CTO:** Hassan Minor
SVP Health and Sciences: Donald E. Wilson
**Acting SVP Academic Matters and Dean, School of Law
  and:** Kurt L. Schmoke, age 58
VP University Advancement: Virgil E. Ecton
Dean, Graduate School: Orlando L. Taylor
Dean, Student Life and Activities: Tonya L. Guillory
Director Admissions: Linda Sanders-Hawkins
Executive Communications Manager: Grace Virtue

LOCATIONS

HQ: Howard University
  2400 6th St. NW, Washington, DC 20059
Phone: 202-806-6100
Web: www.howard.edu

HP Hood

HP Hood is busily trying to cream its competition — with coffee cream, ice cream, sour cream, and whipping cream. The company, a leading US dairy producer, also makes fluid milk, cottage cheese, and juices. Its home turf is New England, where it is one of the few remaining dairies to offer home milk delivery. Hood's products are available at chain and independent food retailers, convenience stores, and to food service purveyors. In addition to its own brands, the company makes private-label, licensed, and franchise dairy products; Hood also owns regional dairy producers Kemps and Crowley Foods. The company operates more than 20 manufacturing plants throughout the US.

Hood has licensing agreements for branded products such as LACTAID, Nesquik, Coffee-mate, Stonyfield Farm, Arizona FRESH Iced Tea, and Southern Comfort Eggnog. It also makes Wal-Mart's private brand of coffee creamer and the official ice cream and frozen novelties of the Boston Red Sox, with flavors like Fenway Fudge and Green Monster Mint.

One of the company's most successful offerings is the Simply Smart line of fat-free and low-fat milks; another is the dairy beverage, Calorie Countdown. Although introduced back in the low-carb diet craze, Calorie Countdown products continue to be popular.

Hood has been expanding its portfolio of brands and regional operations through a series of strategic acquisitions. It purchased California's Crystal Cream & Butter Co. in 2007, cementing its West Coast operations. The following year the company acquired the Brigham's ice cream brand and product lines. (An outside investment group acquired Brigham's chain of ice cream shops, striking a licensing deal with Hood to continue using the popular name.)

Harvey P. Hood founded the company in 1846 as a one-man milk-delivery service. The family of CEO John Kaneb controls the company.

EXECUTIVES

Chairman, President, and CEO: John A. Kaneb, age 73
CFO: Gary R. Kaneb
EVP Sales: James F. (Jim) Walsh
SVP Research and Development, Engineering, and Procurement: Mike J. Suever
SVP Operations: H. Scott Blake
SVP and General Counsel: Paul C. Nightingale
VP Human Resources: Bruce W. Bacon
VP and Treasurer: Theresa M. Bresten
VP and Controller: James A. Marcinelli
VP Public Relations and Government Affairs: Lynne M. Bohan
Director Information Systems: Jack Billiel
Director Marketing: Chris Ross
President and CEO, Kemps: James B. (Jim) Green

LOCATIONS

HQ: HP Hood LLC
6 Kimball Ln., Lynnfield, MA 01940
Phone: 617-887-3000   **Fax:** 617-887-8484
Web: www.hphood.com

PRODUCTS/OPERATIONS

Selected Brands
Crowley Foods
  Axelrod
  Crowley
  Heluva Good
  Maggio
  Penn Maid
  Rosenberger's
HP Hood
  Calorie Countdown
  HP Hood
  Lactaid (licensed)
  New England Creamery
  Simply Smart
  Stonyfield Farm (licensed)
Kemps
  Brown Velvet
  Cascadian Farm
  IttiBitz
  Kemps
  Mid-America Farms
  Yo-J

Selected products
Buttermilk
Coffee cream
Cottage cheese
Cream
Eggnog
Frozen novelties
Ice cream
Iced tea
Juices
Lactose-free milk
Lemonade
Milk
Non-dairy creamer
Sour cream

COMPETITORS

Agri-Mark	National Dairy Holdings
AMPI	Odwalla
Coca-Cola North America	Old Orchard
Dairy Farmers of America	Organic Valley
Dean Foods	Stew Leonard's
Dole Food	Sunny Delight
Dreyer's	Tree Top
Florida's Natural	Tropicana
Friendship Dairies	Unilever
Garelick Farms	Veryfine
Guida's	Welch's
Land O'Lakes	
Maryland & Virginia Milk Producers	

HISTORICAL FINANCIALS
Company Type: Private

Income Statement
FYE: December 31

	REVENUE ($ mil.)	NET INCOME ($ mil.)	NET PROFIT MARGIN	EMPLOYEES
12/07	2,300	—	—	4,500
12/06	2,500	—	—	5,400
12/05	2,300	—	—	5,000
12/04	2,300	—	—	4,850
12/03	2,200	—	—	5,000
Annual Growth	1.1%	—	—	(2.6%)

Revenue History

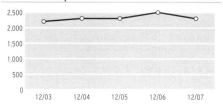

H.T. Hackney

The H.T. Hackney Company began delivering goods to small grocers by horse and buggy in 1891; it now supplies more than 20,000 independent grocers and convenience stores in about 20 states east of the Mississippi. H.T. Hackney distributes more than 25,000 items, including frozen food, tobacco products, health and beauty items, and deli products. In addition, it owns bottled water producer Natural Springs Water Group, and the company is involved in furniture manufacturing through subsidiaries Holland House and Volunteer Fabricators. H.T. Hackney is owned by chairman and CEO Bill Sansom.

EXECUTIVES

Chairman and CEO: William B. (Bill) Sansom, age 66
VP and COO: Dean Ballinger
VP and CFO: Mike Morton
VP Administration: Leonard Robinette
VP Sales: Tommy Thomas

LOCATIONS

HQ: H.T. Hackney Company
502 S. Gay St., Knoxville, TN 37902
Phone: 865-546-1291   **Fax:** 865-546-1501
Web: www.hthackney.com

COMPETITORS

Alex Lee	GSC Enterprises
AMCON Distributing	McLane
Associated Wholesale Grocers	Nash-Finch
C&S Wholesale	S. Abraham & Sons
Core-Mark	Spartan Stores
Eby-Brown	SUPERVALU

Hunt Consolidated

Hunt Consolidated is a holding company for the oil and real estate businesses of Ray Hunt, son of legendary Texas wildcatter and company founder H.L. Hunt. Founded in 1934 (reportedly with H.L.'s poker winnings), Hunt Oil is an oil and gas production and exploration company with primary interests in North and South America. Hoping to repeat huge discoveries in Yemen, Hunt is exploring in Canada, Ghana, Madagascar, and Oman. Signaling a new strategic direction, in 2007 Hunt Oil struck a deal with Iraqi officials to explore for oil in Iraq's semi-autonomous Kurdish region. Hunt Realty handles commercial and residential real estate investment management activities.

Hunt Oil and its affiliates restructured in 1986 and formed Hunt Consolidated as a holding company, in order to better manage the Hunt family's diverse interests.

It has teamed up with Repsol YPF and SK Corporation on an exploration project in Peru, and has expanded its Canadian operations.

EXECUTIVES

Chairman, President, and CEO: Ray L. Hunt, age 64
SVP and CFO: Donald (Don) Robillard
SVP and General Counsel: Richard A. Massman
SVP and Assistant General Counsel: W. Kirk Baker
SVP Financial Administration: Harry Dombroski
SVP Corporate Development: Thomas A. (Tom) Meurer
SVP; President, Hunt Investment Corporation:
Chris Kleinert
SVP Corporate Affairs and International Relations:
Rt. Hon. Jeanne L. Phillips
VP and CIO: Kevin P. Campbell
VP Human Resources: Paul Hoffman
VP and Treasurer: Donna German
VP Environment, Health, and Safety: Scott Rolseth
President, Hunt Power; SVP, Hunt Oil Company:
Hunter Hunt, age 40

LOCATIONS

HQ: Hunt Consolidated Inc.
Fountain Place, 1445 Ross at Field, Ste. 1400,
Dallas, TX 75202
Phone: 214-978-8000   **Fax:** 214-978-8888
Web: www.huntoil.com

PRODUCTS/OPERATIONS

Selected Subsidiaries and Affiliates

Hunt Oil Company (integrated oil company)
Hunt Oil Company of Canada
Hunt Power L.P. (utility projects and services)
Hunt Private Equity Group
Hunt Realty Corporation (acquires real estate and
manages investments)
Hunt Refining Co. Inc.
Hunt Ventures, L.P. (diversified investments)
Yemen Hunt Oil Co.

COMPETITORS

Anadarko Petroleum
BP
Exxon
Lincoln Property
Murphy Oil
Nexen
Royal Dutch Shell
TOTAL

HISTORICAL FINANCIALS

Company Type: Private

Income Statement

	ESTIMATED REVENUE ($ mil.)	NET INCOME ($ mil.)	NET PROFIT MARGIN	FYE: December 31 EMPLOYEES
12/07	2,120	—	—	3,000
12/06	2,130	—	—	3,000
12/05	2,300	—	—	3,000
Annual Growth	(4.0%)	—	—	0.0%

Revenue History

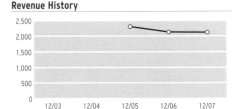

Hy-Vee, Inc.

Give Hy-Vee a high five for being one of the largest privately owned US supermarket chains, despite serving some modestly sized towns in the Midwest. The company runs about 225 Hy-Vee supermarkets in states including Illinois, Iowa, Kansas, Minnesota, Missouri, Nebraska, and South Dakota. About half of its supermarkets are in Iowa, as are most of its 25-plus Hy-Vee (formerly Drug Town) drugstores. It distributes products to its stores through several subsidiaries, including Lomar Distributing (specialty foods), Perishable Distributors of Iowa (fresh foods), and Florist Distributing (flowers). Charles Hyde and David Vredenburg founded the employee-owned firm in 1930. The company name is a combination of the founders' names.

Hy-Vee spent more than $200 million in 2006 to open new supermarkets and to relocate or expand existing stores. Although Hy-Vee is in no hurry to grow, the chain is seeking to expand gradually in several markets in the Midwest, including Chicago, Minneapolis, and Madison, Wisconsin. To that end, the regional grocery chain is building a 90,000-square-foot store on the site of an old Kmart in Madison. The opening of the Madison store (expected in 2009) will mark Hy-Vee's entry into a new state for the first time in nearly 20 years.

The company has also announced that it will try a smaller format store (about 20,000-25,000 sq. ft., with no pharmacies) in selected locations.

Going beyond traditional grocery fare, the company has been focusing on adding Hy-Vee Gas convenience units (some 80 locations include these), wine and spirits stores, pharmacies, and Hy-Vee HealthMarket departments. The grocery retailer began selling prepaid mobile phones in late 2007. Many Hy-Vee stores also have seasonal garden centers. Store brands include Hy-Vee, Grand Selections, Health Market, and Midwest County Fare.

In a bid to get its customers to eat well, Hy-Vee employs more than 120 dietitians in its stores.

The company renamed its Drug Town stores Hy-Vee Drugstores to capitalize on Hy-Vee's strong brand recognition in the region. The company has begun opening walk-in medical clinics in its supermarkets through a partnership with Sioux City, Iowa-based Curaquick Clinics. The partnership dissolved in 2007 and Hy-Vee may find a replacement clinic company to continue to offer the service.

EXECUTIVES

Chairman Emeritus: Ronald D. (Ron) Pearson, age 67
Chairman, President, CEO, and COO:
Richard N. (Ric) Jurgens
EVP: Raymond (Ray) Stewart
EVP: Ken Waller
SVP, CFO, and Treasurer: John Briggs
SVP, Corporate Procurement and Logistics: Ron Taylor
SVP, Human Resources: Jane Knaack-Esbeck
SVP, Retail Operations: Randy Edeker, age 43
VP, Management Information Systems: Eric Smith
VP, Marketing: Paula Correy, age 42
VP, Perishables: Jon Wendel, age 45
**VP, Petroleum Marketing, General Merchandise, and
Pharmacy:** Tom Watson
Assistant VP, Communications: Ruth Comer
President, Perishable Distributors of Iowa:
Andy McCann
Auditors: McGladrey & Pullen, LLP

LOCATIONS

HQ: Hy-Vee, Inc.
5820 Westown Pkwy., West Des Moines, IA 50266
Phone: 515-267-2800   **Fax:** 515-267-2817
Web: www.hy-vee.com

PRODUCTS/OPERATIONS

Selected Subsidiaries

D & D Foods, Inc. (salads, dips, and meats)
Florist Distributing, Inc. (flowers, plants, and florist
supplies)
Hy-Vee Weitz Construction, L.C. (construction)
Lomar Distributing, Inc. (specialty foods)
Midwest Heritage Bank, FSB (banking)
Perishable Distributors of Iowa, Ltd. (meat, fish, seafood,
and ice cream)
The Meyocks Group, Inc. (branding and marketing
communications)

COMPETITORS

ALDI	Nash-Finch
Associated Wholesale Grocers	Niemann Foods
	Rite Aid
Ball's Food	Roundy's Supermarkets
Casey's General Stores	Save-A-Lot Food Stores
CVS Caremark	SUPERVALU
Dahl's Foods	Target
Fareway Stores	Walgreen
Kmart	Wal-Mart
Kroger	

Iasis Healthcare

If you're sick in the suburbs, IASIS Healthcare provides a medical oasis. The company owns and operates about 15 acute care hospitals and one behavioral health facility (more than 2,600 beds total) in Arizona, Florida, Louisiana, Nevada, Texas, and Utah. IASIS also operates several outpatient facilities and other centers providing ancillary services, such as radiation therapy, diagnostic imaging, and ambulatory surgery. Its Health Choice Arizona subsidiary is a Medicaid managed health plan that serves about 125,000 individuals in Arizona. An investor group led by Texas Pacific Group owns the company.

IASIS is growing both by acquiring and building new facilities. It generally looks for hospitals that have between 100 and 400 beds and that are located in fast-growing urban and suburban areas.

The company purchased Glenwood Regional Medical Center in West Monroe, Louisiana, in 2007 and estimates it will spend $30 million on renovations at the facility in the first four years of owning it. It also built a new hospital in the Phoenix area (Mountain Vista Medical Center) that opened its doors in 2007.

In addition to expanding its portfolio of facilities, the company is adding services and upgrading equipment and facilities at its existing hospitals. Among other things, it looks to expand its higher-margin specialty medical and surgical offerings, add capacity to its emergency rooms, and upgrade diagnostic imaging and robotic surgical equipment.

IASIS Healthcare consolidated its two Port Arthur hospitals into the new Medical Center of Southeast Texas, which opened in 2005.

EXECUTIVES

Chairman and CEO: David R. White, age 60
President and COO: Sandra K. McRee, age 51
CFO and Principal Financial Officer: W. Carl Whitmer, age 43
VP, Treasurer, and Chief Accounting Officer: John M. Doyle, age 47
VP Corporate Communications and Marketing: Tomi Galin
VP Ethics and Business Practices: Peter Stanos, age 44
VP Clinical Operations: Tedd Adair
VP Human Resources: Russ Follis
CIO: Brian Loflin
Corporate Controller: Sean Tussey
Secretary and General Counsel: Frank A. Coyle, age 43
President, Texas and Louisiana Markets: Jim McKinney, age 54
President, Utah Market: Kirk Olsen, age 58
President, Florida Market: James Purcell, age 57
Auditors: Ernst & Young LLP

LOCATIONS

HQ: IASIS Healthcare LLC
117 Seaboard Ln., Bldg. E, Franklin, TN 37067
Phone: 615-844-2747   **Fax:** 615-846-3006
Web: www.iasishealthcare.com

Selected Facilities

Davis Hospital and Medical Center (Layton, UT)
Glenwood Regional Medical Center (West Monroe, LA)
Jordan Valley Hospital (West Jordan, UT)
Memorial Hospital of Tampa (Tampa, FL)
Mesa General Hospital (Mesa, AZ)
North Vista Hospital (Las Vegas, NV)
Odessa Regional Medical Center (Odessa, TX)
Palms of Pasadena Hospital (St. Petersburg, FL)
Pioneer Valley Hospital (West Valley City, UT)
St. Luke's Medical Center (Phoenix, AZ)
St. Luke's Behavioral Hospital (Phoenix, AZ)
Salt Lake Regional Medical Center (Salt Lake City, UT)
Southwest General Hospital (San Antonio, TX)
Tempe St. Luke's Hospital (Tempe, AZ)
The Medical Center of Southeast Texas (Port Arthur, TX)
Town & Country Hospital (Tampa, FL)

PRODUCTS/OPERATIONS

2007 Sales

	$ mil.	% of total
Acute care operations	1,399	76
Premiums (Health Choice)	451	24
Total	**1,850**	**100**

COMPETITORS

Banner Health
BayCare Health System
Bayfront Health
Bon Secours Health
Catholic Healthcare West
CHRISTUS Health
Desert Springs Hospital
HCA
Intermountain Health Care
John C. Lincoln Health Network
MedCath
Tampa General Hospital
University Community Health
University Health System
Valley Hospital
Vanguard Health Systems

HISTORICAL FINANCIALS

Company Type: Private

Income Statement

FYE: September 30

	REVENUE ($ mil.)	NET INCOME ($ mil.)	NET PROFIT MARGIN	EMPLOYEES
9/07	1,850	42	2.2%	10,826
9/06	1,626	40	2.4%	8,877
9/05	1,524	41	2.7%	8,800
9/04	1,387	(32)	—	9,000
9/03	1,088	21	1.9%	8,200
Annual Growth	**14.2%**	**19.2%**	**—**	**7.2%**

2007 Year-End Financials

Debt ratio: —
Return on equity: 6.2%
Cash ($ mil.): —
Current ratio: —
Long-term debt ($ mil.): —

Net Income History

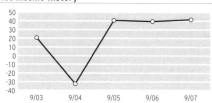

ICC Industries

ICC Industries is helping the world look brighter, smell better, and live healthier. The company trades basic and specialty chemicals globally. Operating through a number of subsidiaries, ICC Industries is an international maker of chemicals (Dover Chemical), plastics (Primex), and pharmaceutical products; it also trades and distributes nutritional supplements and food ingredients. Its main subsidiary, ICC Chemical, maintains trading and marketing offices throughout the world. The Farber family, including chairman John Farber, owns ICC.

EXECUTIVES

Chairman: John J. Farber, age 82
Vice Chairman: Sandra Farber
President: John Oram
VP and CFO: Blaise Sarcone
VP and Treasurer: Susan Abinder
VP and General Counsel: Paul Falick
President and CEO, ICC Chemical and Fallek Chemical: William Brunger
President, Primex Plastics Corporation: Mike Cramer
President, Dover Chemical Corporation: Dwain S. Colvin
President and CEO, Frutarom: Ori Yehudai, age 53

LOCATIONS

HQ: ICC Industries Inc.
460 Park Ave., New York, NY 10022
Phone: 212-521-1700   **Fax:** 212-521-1970
Web: www.iccindustries.com

ICC Industries has offices in Asia, Europe, Latin America, the Middle East, and North America.

PRODUCTS/OPERATIONS

Selected Operations and Products

Azur S.A.
  Coatings
  Lacquers
  Paints
  Putties
  Synthetic resins
  Thinners
Dover Chemical Corporation
  Brominated and bromochlorinated flame retardants
  Chlorinated paraffins
  Lubricant additives
  Metallic stearates
  Organo-phosphites
  Specialty alkyl phenols
  Surfactants
Frutarom Industries Ltd. (37%)
  Botanicals
  Citrus derivatives
  Flavors for foods and beverages
  Natural flavor ingredients
  Protected amino acids
  Seasonings
  Spice oleoresins
Primex Plastics Corporation
  Plastic Sheets
    Antistatic, weatherable, conductive, and UV inhibited sheet
    Mono- and multilayer extruded and coextruded sheet (made from polystyrene, polyester, polyethylene, polypropylene, and acrylonitrile butadiene styrene)
    Print-grade sheet
    Polypropylene and polyethylene twin wall sheet
    Sheets produced under white room conditions
Coral Plastics Enterprises Inc.
  Polystyrene and polystyrene light lens material
O'Neil Color and Compounding Corp.
  Custom-color compounded resins
  Custom-color matched and standard color concentrates
  Custom compounding
  Mineral fillers
  Plastic additives (antiblocks, antistatic, ultraviolet inhibitors, and processing aids and flame retardants)
Pace Industries, Inc.
  Polystyrene and polyolefin sheet for specialty industries
  Print-grade sheet
Woodruff Corporation
  Custom packaging
  Reusable returnable containers
  Silk-screened indoor and outdoor signs

COMPETITORS

Ashland Distribution
Atlantis Plastics
Formosa Plastics
HELM U.S.
International Flavors
Lipo Chemicals
LyondellBasell
Nagase
R.T. Vanderbilt
Synthetech
Teva Pharmaceuticals
Univar USA

Company Type: Private

Income Statement

	REVENUE ($ mil.)	NET INCOME ($ mil.)	NET PROFIT MARGIN	EMPLOYEES
12/07	1,800	—	—	1,700
12/06	1,370	—	—	1,525
12/05	1,342	—	—	1,700
Annual Growth	15.8%	—	—	0.0%

FYE: December 31

Revenue History

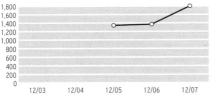

ICON Health & Fitness

ICON Health & Fitness has brawn as one of the leading US makers of home fitness equipment. Its products primarily include treadmills, elliptical trainers, and weight benches. Brands include HealthRider, NordicTrack, and ProForm. ICON also offers fitness accessories and commercial fitness gear. It makes most of its products in Utah and sells them through retailers, infomercials, the Web, and its catalog Workout Warehouse. Sears has an exclusive license to sell NordicTrack brand products and apparel. The company was founded as a housewares importer in 1977.

Sears has been ICON's largest customer since 1985; it accounted for about 40% of net sales in 2006. The company sells its products internationally and has facilities in Canada, China, and Europe, in addition to the US.

The company has changed its products to keep up with the entertainment needs of its customers. For example, an entertainment version of its NordicTrack treadmill comes with a built-in TV, an MP3 port, stereo speakers, and a digital personal trainer.

ICON shut its Clearfield, Utah, manufacturing facility in early 2007, laying off about 250 workers. The company moved most Utah manufacturing to its main plant in Logan, in order to achieve greater efficiency.

Bain Capital, Credit Suisse, and founders Scott Watterson and Gary Stevenson collectively own over 90% of ICON.

EXECUTIVES

Chairman and CEO: David J. Watterson, age 47, $726,000 pay
President and Chief Merchandising Officer:
Matthew N. Allen, age 42, $480,000 pay
COO: M. Joseph Brough, age 42, $413,850 pay
CFO: S. Fred Beck, age 48, $545,667 pay
SVP, Research and Development: Jace Jergensen, age 43
SVP, Manufacturing: Jon M. White, age 58

VP, Business Development: Lynn C. Brenchley
VP, Imports, Transportation, and New Business Development: Jeff Carmignani
VP, Purchasing: Douglas L. Clausen
VP, Design: William T. Dalebout, age 58
Secretary and General Counsel: Brad H. Bearnson, age 52
President, ICON Canada: Richard Hebert, age 61, $578,950 pay
President, ICON Europe: Giovanni Lato, $303,540 pay
Operations Manager, ICON Europe:
Daniele Di Carmine, age 49, $248,255 pay
Director, NordicTrack Retail Stores: David Packham
Auditors: PricewaterhouseCoopers LLP

LOCATIONS

HQ: ICON Health & Fitness, Inc.
1500 S. 1000 West, Logan, UT 84321
Phone: 435-750-5000 **Fax:** 435-750-3917
Web: www.iconfitness.com

PRODUCTS/OPERATIONS

Selected Products

Ellipticals
Exercise bikes
Free weights
Home gyms
Treadmills
Weight benches

Selected Brands

Epic
Free Motion Fitness
Gold's Gym (licensed)
HealthRider
Image
JumpKing
NordicTrack
ProForm
Reebok (licensed)
Weider

COMPETITORS

Cybex International	Life Fitness
Easton-Bell Sports	Nautilus
Escalade	Orthometrix
Fitness Quest	Precor
Keys Fitness	

IGA, Inc.

IGA grocers are independent, but not alone. The world's largest voluntary supermarket network, IGA has about 4,000 stores, including members in some 45 US states and more than 40 other countries on six continents. Collectively, its members are among North America's leaders in terms of supermarket sales. IGA (for either International or Independent Grocers Alliance, the company says) is owned by about 35 worldwide distribution companies, including SUPERVALU. Members can sell IGA Brand private-label products (over 2,300 items) and take advantage of joint operations and services, such as advertising and volume buying. Some stores in the IGA alliance, which primarily cater to smaller towns, also sell gas.

About two-thirds of IGA's total stores are located outside the US. As the first US grocer in China and Singapore, the company has plans for some 1,000 IGA-affiliated stores in China. IGA is also present in Europe with operations in Poland and Spain.

In 2006 the company reorganized by splitting itself into three companies: IGA USA, IGA Global, and the IGA Coca-Cola Institute. All three operate under IGA, Inc. As a result of the reorganization, Thomas Haggai became chairman and CEO of IGA International, and Mark Batenic — formerly of Clemens Markets — joined the company as chairman, president, and CEO of IGA USA. (Previously, IGA realigned its corporate structure in 2001.)

By separating IGA's domestic stores from its stores overseas, the company hopes to improve communications among IGA's US retailers.

One of Batenic's first moves was to establish a presence for IGA in San Francisco with the acquisition of eight supermarkets there from Ralphs Grocery.

IGA claims that it doesn't try to fight large chains such as Wal-Mart and Publix, instead preferring to keep the focus on its own niche of hometown and family-owned grocery stores.

EXECUTIVES

Chairman and CEO: Thomas S. Haggai
SVP Procurement and Private Brands: David S. Bennett
SVP Retail and Business Development: Doug Fritsch
VP Finance and CFO: John Collins
VP Marketing, Branding and Business Development:
James J. (Jim) Walz
VP Administration, Events, and Communication:
Barbara G. Wiest
VP, Information Technology: Nick Liakopulos
Chairman, President, and CEO IGA USA:
Mark K. Batenic
EVP, IGA International, and President, IGA Institute:
Paulo Goelzer
Senior Director Marketing, Branding, and Business Development, IGA USA: Jim Walz
Public Relations Contact: Ashley M. Page

LOCATIONS

HQ: IGA, Inc.
8725 W. Higgins Rd., Chicago, IL 60631
Phone: 773-693-4520 **Fax:** 773-693-4532
Web: www.igainc.com

PRODUCTS/OPERATIONS

Selected Joint Operations and Services

Advertising
Community service programs
Equipment purchase
IGA Brand (private-label products)
IGA Grocergram (in-house magazine)
Internet services
Marketing
Merchandising
Red Oval Family (manufacturer/IGA collaboration on sales, marketing, and other activities)
Volume buying

COMPETITORS

A&P	H-E-B
Albertsons	Ito-Yokado
Associated Wholesale Grocers	Kroger
	Meijer
BJ's Wholesale Club	Penn Traffic
C&S Wholesale	Publix
Carrefour	Roundy's Supermarkets
Casino Guichard	Royal Ahold
Coles Group	Safeway
Daiei	Spartan Stores
Dairy Farm International	Wakefern Food
Delhaize	Wal-Mart
George Weston	Winn-Dixie
Hannaford Bros.	

HISTORICAL FINANCIALS

Company Type: Holding company

Income Statement				FYE: December 31
	ESTIMATED REVENUE ($ mil.)	NET INCOME ($ mil.)	NET PROFIT MARGIN	EMPLOYEES
12/07	21,000	—	—	92,000
12/06	21,000	—	—	92,000
Annual Growth	0.0%	—	—	0.0%

Revenue History

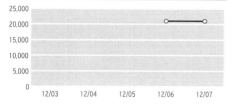

Ilitch Holdings

This holding company rules over a Caesar, tames Tigers, and takes flight on the ice. Ilitch Holdings controls the business interests of Mike and Marian Ilitch and their family, which includes the Little Caesars pizza chain, the Detroit Tigers baseball team, and the Detroit Red Wings hockey team. The holding company also oversees Olympia Entertainment, an entertainment company that owns Detroit's Fox Theatre and operates Comerica Park, Joe Louis Arena, and Cobo Arena. Its Blue Line Foodservice Distribution unit is a leading supplier of food and equipment to restaurant operators (including Little Caesars operators). The Ilitches started Little Caesars in 1959 and formed Ilitch Holdings in 1999.

With a growing pizza chain and two successful sports franchises, the Ilitch family has been riding high the past few years and made it onto the *Forbes* richest people list for the first time in 2007. Little Caesars has been expanding rapidly, posting sales gains the past several years, while the Red Wings franchise (acquired in 1982) won its 11th Stanley Cup championship in 2008. The Tigers baseball team (1992) managed to win the American League pennant in 2006, the franchise's first since 1984.

The family has continued to invest in real estate in downtown Detroit, reportedly as part of an effort to construct a new arena for its hockey team. Bolstering those rumors, the Ilitches hired Dana Warg from Anschutz Entertainment Group (AEG, part of The Anschutz Company) as CEO of Olympia Entertainment. Warg had overseen facilities operations for AEG, including the Staples Center in Los Angeles.

EXECUTIVES

Chairman: Michael (Mike) Ilitch, age 78
Vice Chairwoman: Marian Ilitch
President and CEO: Christopher (Chris) Ilitch
CFO: Scott Fisher
VP Corporate Communications: Karen Cullen
VP Human Resources: Joni C. Nelson
VP Tax Affairs: John M. Kotlar
CIO: Todd Seroka
President and CEO, Detroit Tigers: Dave Dombrowski
President, Champion Foods: John Schaible
President, Little Caesars Enterprises:
 David (Dave) Scrivano, age 41
President, Little Caesars Pizza Kit Fundraising Program: Joan Rivard
President, Olympia Development: Atanis Ilitch
President, Olympia Entertainment: Dana Warg, age 60
President, Blue Line Foodservice Distribution:
 Matthew Ilitch
General Manager, Detroit Red Wings: Ken Holland,
 age 52

LOCATIONS

HQ: Ilitch Holdings, Inc.
 2211 Woodward Ave., Detroit, MI 48201
Phone: 313-983-6600   **Fax:** 313-983-6094
Web: www.ilitchholdings.com

PRODUCTS/OPERATIONS

Selected Operations

Entertainment venues
 Olympia Entertainment
  Fox Theatre (Detroit)
 Uptown Entertainment (film theaters; Birmingham,
  Michigan)
Food services
 Blue Line Foodservice Distribution
 Champion Foods
 Hockeytown Cafe
 Little Caesars Pizza
Sports teams
 Detroit Red Wings (hockey)
 Detroit Tigers (baseball)

COMPETITORS

Detroit Lions
Live Nation
Palace Sports & Entertainment

HISTORICAL FINANCIALS

Company Type: Holding company

Income Statement				FYE: December 31
	ESTIMATED REVENUE ($ mil.)	NET INCOME ($ mil.)	NET PROFIT MARGIN	EMPLOYEES
12/07	1,520	—	—	17,000
12/06	1,480	—	—	17,000
12/05	1,500	—	—	12,000
Annual Growth	0.7%	—	—	19.0%

Revenue History

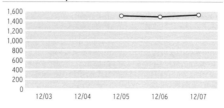

Indalex Holdings

Its alloys may be soft, but don't try to muscle in on Indalex's business. Operating as Indalex Aluminum Solutions, the company manufactures soft alloy aluminum products such as fabricated aluminum conduit, aluminum profiles, and secondary aluminum billets, which in turn are sold to the automotive, construction, consumer durables, and electrical industries. (Some 95% of the products made by Indalex are custom orders.) Indalex operates extrusion facilities and cast houses across Canada and the US. Formerly a subsidiary of Honeywell, Indalex was acquired by Sun Capital Partners in 2006.

Honeywell acquired Indalex's former parent company, Novar, in early 2005, but never intended to keep Indalex, which didn't fit well within its core businesses. The automation and materials giant agreed to sell Indalex to private investment group Sun Capital Partners later in the year, and the deal was concluded early in 2006. Honeywell got $425 million in the transaction.

The company sold its 25% stake in Asia Aluminum Group in 2007 to OK Spring Roll Limited Partnership; the deal was reported to be worth more than $150 million. Indalex used about $70 million to pay down debt.

EXECUTIVES

President, CEO, and Director:
 Timothy R.J. (Tim) Stubbs, age 41
COO: John R. Bagnuolo, age 47
CFO and Director: Patrick Lawlor, age 44
SVP Human Resources: Dale Tabinowski, age 60
SVP Sales, National Accounts: Joseph Valvo, age 54
SVP Sales and Marketing: Keith Burlingame, age 51
VP and General Manager, West Operations:
 Ronald L. Kline, age 45
VP Planning and Supply Chain: James Piperato, age 49
VP Operations Effectiveness: Sat Adusumilli

LOCATIONS

HQ: Indalex Holdings Finance, Inc.
 75 Tristate International Ste. 450,
 Lincolnshire, IL 60069
Phone: 847-810-3000   **Fax:** 847-295-3851
Web: www.indalex.com

2007 Sales

	$ mil.	% of total
US	903.4	82
Canada	199.3	18
Other countries	2.7	—
Total	**1,105.3**	**100**

COMPETITORS

Acme Alliance
Alcoa
Anchor Harvey
General Extrusions
Ohio Valley Aluminum Company
Ross Aluminum
Tower Extrusions
West Irving Die

HISTORICAL FINANCIALS
Company Type: Private

Income Statement
FYE: December 31

	REVENUE ($ mil.)	NET INCOME ($ mil.)	NET PROFIT MARGIN	EMPLOYEES
12/07	1,105	(7)	—	2,700
12/06	1,243	(22)	—	3,000
Annual Growth	(11.1%)	—	—	(10.0%)

Net Income History

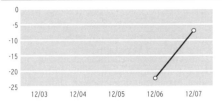

Indiana Pacers

This team sets the tempo on the basketball court. Pacers Basketball, which does business as Pacers Sports & Entertainment, owns and operates the Indiana Pacers professional basketball franchise of the National Basketball Association, along with Indianapolis' Conseco Fieldhouse, the team's home arena. The franchise was formed in 1967 as a charter member of the American Basketball Association by a group of investors that included Richard Tinkman (who also helped found the ABA) and joined the NBA in 1976. A perennial playoff contender, the team claims just one appearance in the NBA Finals. The sports franchise is owned by shopping-center magnates Melvin and Herbert Simon; they purchased the Pacers in 1983.

After failing to make the playoffs for the first time in a decade, the team fired head coach Rick Carlisle following the 2006-07 season. Jim O'Brien, formerly coach of the Philadelphia 76ers, was hired as his replacement. Carlisle had coached the Pacers for four years, reaching the Eastern Conference finals in 2004.

Longtime team president Donnie Walsh resigned from the Pacers in 2008, taking the top front office job with the troubled New York Knicks. Herb Simon was named the new CEO of Pacers Sports with famed Hoosier State native and former Celtics star Larry Bird remaining as head of basketball operations. Front office veteran David Morway was later promoted to general manager.

In addition to the NBA team, Pacers Basketball controls the Indiana Fever of the WNBA. The Simon family founded Simon Property Group, the top mall operator in the US.

EXECUTIVES
Co-Owner, Chairman, and CEO: Herbert (Herb) Simon, age 73
Co-Owner: Melvin Simon, age 81
President: Jim Morris
President, Basketball Operations: Larry Bird, age 51
COO: Rick Fuson
Head Coach: Jim O'Brien

SVP Finance and CFO: Kevin Bower
SVP and General Manager: David Morway
SVP Marketing: Larry Mago
VP Player Relations: Sam Perkins
VP Human Resources: Donna Wilkinson
VP Corporate and Public Relations: Greg Schenkel
Director Player Personnel: Mel Daniels
Director Scouting: Joe Ash
Director Community Relations: Kelli Towles

LOCATIONS
HQ: Pacers Basketball Corporation
125 S. Pennsylvania St., Indianapolis, IN 46204
Phone: 317-917-2500 **Fax:** 317-917-2599
Web: www.nba.com/pacers

The Indiana Pacers play at the 18,345-seat capacity Conseco Fieldhouse in Indianapolis.

PRODUCTS/OPERATIONS

Titles
Eastern Conference Champions (2000)

COMPETITORS
Cavaliers
Chicago Bulls
Detroit Pistons
Milwaukee Bucks

HISTORICAL FINANCIALS
Company Type: Private

Income Statement
FYE: June 30

	REVENUE ($ mil.)	NET INCOME ($ mil.)	NET PROFIT MARGIN	EMPLOYEES
6/07	107	—	—	—
6/06	110	—	—	—
6/05	108	—	—	—
6/04	104	—	—	—
6/03	94	—	—	—
Annual Growth	3.3%	—	—	—

Revenue History

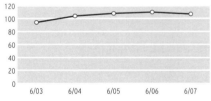

Indiana University

Indiana University has been schooling Hoosiers since 1820. With a total student population of some 100,000, the university offers more than 1,000 associate, baccalaureate, master's, professional, and doctoral degree programs at eight campuses: flagship institution IU-Bloomington; regional campuses in Fort Wayne, Gary, Kokomo, New Albany, Richmond, and South Bend; and an urban campus in Indianapolis that is operated jointly with Purdue University.

An 1820 statute created the Indiana Seminary, the predecessor to Indiana University. In 1828 the legislature changed the name of the institution to Indiana College, and in 1838 it established Indiana University.

EXECUTIVES
President, Board of Trustees: Stephen L. Ferguson
President: Michael A. McRobbie
EVP and Provost Indiana University Bloomington: Karen Hanson
EVP and Chancellor, IU-Purdue University Indianapolis: Charles R. Bantz
VP and CFO: Neil D. Theobald
VP and Chief Administrative Officer: J. Terry Clapacs
VP and General Counsel: Dorothy J. Frapwell
VP Institutional Development and Student Affairs: Charlie Nelms
VP University Relations: Michael M. Sample
Chancellor, IU-Purdue University Fort Wayne: Michael A. Wartell
Chancellor, IU Northwest: Bruce W. Bergland
Chancellor, IU South Bend: Una Mae Reck
Chancellor, IU Southeast: Sandra R. Patterson-Randles
Executive Director Marketing: Lisa Townsend
Treasurer: MaryFrances McCourt
Auditors: Indiana State Board of Accounts

LOCATIONS
HQ: Indiana University
107 S. Indiana Ave., Bloomington, IN 47405
Phone: 812-855-4848 **Fax:** 812-855-9972
Web: www.indiana.edu

Indiana University has campuses in Bloomington, Fort Wayne, Gary, Indianapolis, Kokomo, New Albany, Richmond, and South Bend, Indiana.

HISTORICAL FINANCIALS
Company Type: School

Income Statement
FYE: June 30

	REVENUE ($ mil.)	NET INCOME ($ mil.)	NET PROFIT MARGIN	EMPLOYEES
6/07	1,754	175	10.0%	18,427
6/06	1,625	123	7.6%	18,373
6/05	1,546	119	7.7%	21,664
6/04	1,494	115	7.7%	15,000
6/03	1,374	—	—	15,000
Annual Growth	6.3%	15.2%	—	5.3%

2007 Year-End Financials
Debt ratio: —
Return on equity: 8.3%
Cash ($ mil.): —
Current ratio: —
Long-term debt ($ mil.): —

Net Income History

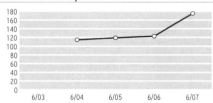

Infor Global Solutions

Before manufacturers and distributors get products to the shelf, Infor gets software to their computers. Infor Global Solutions supplies customers with enterprise resource planning, business intelligence, relationship management, demand management, supply chain planning, and warehouse management software.

Infor targets customers in such industries as automotive, chemicals, consumer packaged goods, food and beverage processing, metal fabrication, and pharmaceuticals. Its client list includes Bristol-Myers Squibb, Cargill, Coca-Cola Enterprises, GlaxoSmithKline, Grohe, Heinz, and TRW. Infor is backed by Golden Gate Capital and Summit Partners.

Infor has used a string of acquisitions to quietly become one of the leading vendors of business software. In 2005 Infor purchased two providers of software for the manufacturing industry, MAPICS ($347 million) and Formation Systems. Its buying spree continued in 2006, when it snatched up asset management software supplier Datastream Systems ($216 million), enterprise software provider SSA Global Technologies ($1.36 billion), and financial and performance management software developers Systems Union Group and Extensity. The company expanded its offerings with the acquisitions of Workbrain (workforce management) and Hansen Information Technologies (enterprise applications for local government agencies) in 2007.

Infor has a history of growing and changing its business with acquisitions. It was formed in 2002 when Golden Gate Capital and Parallax Capital Partners bought the process manufacturing software business of Systems & Computer Technology. Formerly called Agilisys, the company changed its name to Infor after acquiring German enterprise resource planning software provider infor business solutions AG in 2004.

EXECUTIVES

Chairman and CEO: C. James (Jim) Schaper
EVP and COO: Robin Pederson
EVP and CFO: Raghavan (Raj) Rajaji
SVP, General Counsel, and Secretary:
Gregory M. Giangiordano
SVP, Human Resources: Glenn Goldberg
SVP, Mergers, Acquisition, and Integration:
Kevin Samuelson
SVP, Global Marketing: Rick Parker
SVP, Product Development, Support, and Maintenance:
Ken Walters
Chief Technology Officer: Bruce Gordon
President, Americas Region: Jerry Rulli
President, EMEA: Keith Deane
President, Asia/Pacific: Lawrence Y. H. Chan

LOCATIONS

HQ: Infor Global Solutions, Inc.
13560 Morris Rd., Ste. 4100, Alpharetta, GA 30004
Phone: 678-319-8000   **Fax:** 678-319-8682
Web: www.infor.com

COMPETITORS

American Software	Lawson Software
AspenTech	Manhattan Associates
CDC Corp.	Microsoft
CDC Software	Oracle
EDS	QAD
Epicor Software	RedPrairie
i2 Technologies	SAP
JDA Software	

Ingram Entertainment

Companies selling books and CDs might get the star treatment, but Ingram Entertainment doesn't mind a supporting role. The company is one of the largest independent video, DVD, and computer game distributors in the US. In addition, Ingram distributes software, audio books, electronics, and used videos and games. From some 15 sales and distribution centers, Ingram serves more than 10,000 video stores, mass retailers, drugstores, and supermarkets. The company also operates AccessIngram.com, a business-to-business e-commerce site,. and creates and maintains personalized Web sites for its customers through its MyVideoStore.com offering. Ingram Entertainment was spun off from family-owned Ingram Industries in 1997.

Ingram customers include leading retailers such as 7-Eleven, Amazon.com, Barnes & Noble, and Best Buy.

DVDs account for 75% of the company's sales.

EXECUTIVES

Chairman and President: David B. Ingram, age 45
EVP and CFO: William D. (Donnie) Daniel
EVP Purchasing and Operations: Robert W. (Bob) Webb
SVP Finance and Treasurer: Jeffrey D. (Jeff) Skinner
SVP Sales and Marketing: Bob Geistman
SVP and CIO: Mark D. Ramer
VP Human Resources: Susan Gritton
VP Sales: Bill Bryant
Auditors: PricewaterhouseCoopers

LOCATIONS

HQ: Ingram Entertainment Holdings Inc.
2 Ingram Blvd., La Vergne, TN 37089
Phone: 615-287-4000   **Fax:** 615-287-4982
Web: www.ingramentertainment.com

PRODUCTS/OPERATIONS

2007 Sales

	% of total
DVDs	75
Video games, electronics & accessories	24
Audio books	1
Total	**100**

Products

Accessories
  Adapters
  Blank tapes
  Cleaning products
  Controllers
  Head cleaners
  Memory cards
  Repair kits
  Rewinders
  Security tags
  Storage cases
Audio books
DVDs
Electronics
Previously viewed videos
Video games
Videos

COMPETITORS

Alliance Entertainment	KOCH Entertainment
Baker & Taylor	MTI Home Video
East Texas Distributing	Navarre
FLHE	Rentrak
Handleman	Source Interlink
Image Entertainment	

HISTORICAL FINANCIALS
Company Type: Private

Income Statement
FYE: December 31

	REVENUE ($ mil.)	NET INCOME ($ mil.)	NET PROFIT MARGIN	EMPLOYEES
12/07	813	—	—	670
12/06	764	—	—	685
12/05	839	—	—	747
Annual Growth	(1.6%)	—	—	(5.3%)

Revenue History

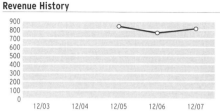

Ingram Industries

Ingram Industries is heavy into books and boats. Ingram Book Group is one of the largest wholesale book distributors in the US; it ships books, as well as music, DVDs, and videos to retail outlets. It also ships internationally through its Ingram International arm. Ingram Marine Group operates Ingram Barge and ships grain, ore, and other products through about 4,000 barges and 100 boats. The Ingram family, led by chairman Martha (Rivers) Ingram (one of America's wealthiest active businesswomen), owns and runs Ingram Industries and controls about 20% of the shares of Ingram Micro (a top computer products wholesaler).

Martha Ingram succeeded her husband Bronson Ingram as chairman and CEO in 1995.

Ingram Book Group (operating out of four fulfillment centers) is also a leading distributor to libraries, and the entire book division accounts for over half of Ingram Industries' total sales. Its Lightning Source subsidiary is a leader in print-on-demand services with over 400,000 titles (including e-books) from more than 4,300 publishing partners.

The company acquired Coutts Information Services in late 2006, in order to boost its academic library supply business.

HISTORY

Orrin Ingram and two partners founded the Dole, Ingram & Kennedy sawmill in 1857 in Eau Claire, Wisconsin, on the Chippewa River, about 50 miles upstream from the Mississippi River. By the 1870s the company, renamed Ingram & Kennedy, was selling lumber as far downstream as Hannibal, Missouri.

Ingram's success was noticed by Frederick Weyerhaeuser, a German immigrant in Rock Island, Illinois, who, like Ingram, had worked in a sawmill before buying one of his own. In 1881 Ingram and Weyerhaeuser negotiated the formation of Chippewa Logging (35% owned by up-river partners, 65% by down-river interests), which controlled the white pine harvest of the Chippewa Valley. In 1900 Ingram paid $216,000 for 2,160 shares in the newly formed Weyer-haeuser Timber Company. Ingram let his sons and grandsons handle the investment and formed O.H. Ingram Co. to manage the family's interests. He died in 1918.

In 1946 Ingram's descendants founded Ingram Barge, which hauled crude oil to the company's refinery near St. Louis. After buying and then selling other holdings, in 1962 the family formed Ingram Corp., consisting solely of Ingram Barge. Brothers Bronson and Fritz Ingram (the great-grandsons of Orrin) bought the company from their father, Hank, before he died in 1963, and in 1964 they bought half of Tennessee Book, a textbook distributing company founded in 1935. In 1970 they formed Ingram Book Group to sell trade books to bookstores and libraries.

Ingram Barge won a $48 million Chicago sludge-hauling contract in 1971, but later the company was accused of bribing city politicians with $1.2 million in order to land the contract. The brothers stood trial in 1977 for authoriz-ing the bribes; Bronson was acquitted, but the court convicted Fritz on 29 counts. Before Fritz entered prison (he served 16 months of a four-year sentence), he and his brother split their company. Fritz took the energy operations and went bust in the 1980s. Bronson took the barge and book busi-nesses and formed Ingram Industries.

The new company formed computer products distributor Ingram Computer in 1982 and be-tween 1985 and 1989 bought all the stock of Micro D, a computer wholesaler. Ingram Com-puter and Micro D merged to form Ingram Micro. In 1992 it acquired Commtron, the world's #1 wholesaler of prerecorded videocassettes, and merged it into Ingram Entertainment.

When Bronson died in mid-1995, his wife Martha (the PR director) became chairman and began a restructuring. Ingram Industries closed its non-bookstore rack distributor (Ingram Mer-chandising) in 1995 and sold its oil-and-gas ma-chinery subsidiary (Cactus Co.) in 1996. It spun off Ingram Micro in 1996, followed in 1997 by In-gram Entertainment. Ingram Industries pur-chased Christian books distributor Spring Arbor that year and also introduced an on-demand book publishing service (Lightning Print).

The company in late 1998 agreed to sell its book group to Barnes & Noble for $600 million, but FTC pressure killed the deal in mid-1999. With customers and competitors increasing distribu-tion capacity in the western US, a resulting drop in business led Ingram Industries to cut more than 100 jobs at an Oregon warehouse in 1999.

In early 2000 Ingram renamed Lightning Print as Lightning Source. Also that year Ingram announced plans to distribute products other than books for e-tailers (starting with gifts). In March 2001 Ingram took over the specialty-book distribution for Borders.

In July 2002 Ingram completed its acquisi-tion of Midland Enterprises LLC, a leading US inland marine transportation company that in-cludes The Ohio River Company LLC and Orgulf Transport LLC. In an effort to streamline its distribution network, in mid-2002 Ingram Book Group consolidated its eight distribution centers into four super centers, including a new facility in Pennsylvania.

In late 2003 the company's Lightning Source subsidiary celebrated the printing of its 10 mil-lionth book.

The company sold its Permanent General In-surance business (which covers high-risk drivers in about seven states) to Capital Z Financial Ser-vices Partners and PGC Holdings in late 2004.

EXECUTIVES

Chairman: Martha R. Ingram, age 72
Vice Chairman; Chairman, Ingram Book Group:
  John R. Ingram, age 47
President and CEO; Chairman, Ingram Barge
  Company: Orrin H. Ingram II, age 47
EVP and CFO: Mary K. Cavarra
VP Human Resources: Dennis Delaney
President and CEO, Ingram Barge: Craig E. Philip
President and CEO, Lightning Source: J. Kirby Best
President and CEO, Ingram Digital Group:
  James R. Gray
President and CEO, Ingram Book Group:
  David (Skip) Prichard
President, Ingram Library Services and Managing
  Director, Coutts Information Services:
  Joseph P. (Joe) Reynolds
CEO, VitalSource: Frank A. Daniels III
COO, Ingram Digital Ventures: Michael F. Lovett
SVP Global Sales, Lightning Source: David Taylor
VP and General Manager, Tennessee Book Company:
  Randy S. Collignon
VP Client Acquisitions, Ingram Publisher Services:
  Janet McDonald
VP National Accounts, Ingram Book Group: Jeff McCall
VP Business Development, Far East Region, Ingram
  Digital Group: Richard L. (Rich) Rosy
VP Sales and Client Services, Lightning Source:
  Ron Powers
VP Sales, Ingram Book: Daniel T. (Dan) Sheehan

LOCATIONS

HQ: Ingram Industries Inc.
  1 Belle Meade Place, 4400 Harding Rd.,
  Nashville, TN 37205
Phone: 615-298-8200   **Fax:** 615-298-8242
Web: www.ingrambook.com

PRODUCTS/OPERATIONS

Selected Operations

Ingram Book Group
  Ingram Book Company (wholesaler of trade books and
    audiobooks)
  Ingram Customer Systems (computerized systems and
    services)
  Ingram Fulfillment Services (book shipping)
  Ingram International (international distribution of
    books and audiobooks)
  Ingram Library Services (distributes books,
    audiobooks, and videos to libraries)
  Ingram Periodicals (direct distributor of specialty
    magazines)
  Lightning Source (on-demand printing and electronic
    publishing)
  Spring Arbor Distributors (products and services for
    Christian retailers)
  Tennessee Book Company (Tennessee school system
    textbook depository)
Ingram Marine Group
  Custom Fuel Services (provides midstream fueling
    services to inland marine operations)
  Ingram Barge (ships grain, ore, and other products)
  Ingram Materials (produces construction materials
    such as sand and gravel)

COMPETITORS

American Commercial Lines
Anderson News
Baker & Taylor
Follett
Hudson News
Jim Pattison Group
Kirby Corporation
Levy Home Entertainment
Media Source
Safeco
Thomas Nelson
Times Publishing Limited

HISTORICAL FINANCIALS

Company Type: Private

Income Statement				FYE: December 31
	ESTIMATED REVENUE ($ mil.)	NET INCOME ($ mil.)	NET PROFIT MARGIN	EMPLOYEES
12/07	2,100	—	—	5,700
12/06	1,810	—	—	5,200
12/05	2,539	—	—	5,200
12/04	2,310	—	—	5,767
12/03	2,200	—	—	6,730
Annual Growth	(1.2%)	—	—	(4.1%)

Revenue History

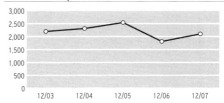

Inland Real Estate Group

Feeling at sea in the real estate business? Go Inland. The Inland Real Estate Group invests in neighborhood, community, power, lifestyle, and single-tenant retail centers as well as office and in-dustrial properties. The group includes public and private real estate investment trusts Inland Real Estate Corporation (focusing on properties in Chicago and Minneapolis), Inland Western Re-tail Real Estate Trust (US and Canada), and Inland American Real Estate Trust (also US and Canada). Its Inland Real Estate Exchange Corporation lets investors exchange properties for capital gains benefits. Inland Real Estate Group owns and manages some 500 properties comprising more than 100 million sq. ft. of commercial space.

The group buys, sells, and develops properties in metropolitan areas throughout the US. It has a joint venture with Juliet Companies to develop retail shopping centers in the western US, par-ticularly the Las Vegas area.

It sold Inland Retail Real Estate Trust to De-velopers Diversified Realty for $6.2 billion in 2007. That year affiliated REIT Inland American Real Estate Trust acquired Winston Hotels, Inc.

In 1967 teacher Daniel Goodwin (CEO) teamed up with three friends (also teachers) and pooled $1,000 to start the group.

EXECUTIVES

Chairman and CEO: Daniel L. (Dan) Goodwin, age 64
Vice Chairman: G. Joseph (Joe) Cosenza
CFO: Alan Kremin
EVP, General Counsel, and Vice Chairman:
  Robert H. Baum
Director, Human Resources: Nora O'Conner
President and CEO, Inland Western Retail Real Estate
  Trust: Michael O'Hanlon
President, Inland Commercial Mortgage Corporation:
  Michael S. Poe, age 36
President, Inland Mortgage Corporation:
  Raymond E. Peterson

**President, Inland Real Estate Development
Corporation:** Anthony A. Casaccio
President, Inland Real Estate Sales: Jonathan J. Stein
SVP, Inland Mortgage Capital Corporation:
Leslie Lundin
SVP, Inland Real Estate Acquisitions: Karen Kautz
SVP, Inland Real Estate Development Corporation:
Matthew G. Fiascone
SVP, Inland Real Estate Acquisitions: Lou Quilici

LOCATIONS

HQ: The Inland Real Estate Group of Companies, Inc.
2901 Butterfield Rd., Oak Brook, IL 60523
Phone: 630-218-8000   **Fax:** 630-218-4957
Web: www.inlandgroup.com

The Inland Group operates primarily in the Chicago
area, but also has offices in Arizona, California, Florida,
Georgia, Indiana, Maryland, Michigan, Minnesota, New
Hampshire, New Jersey, New York, North Carolina,
Pennsylvania, Tennessee, Texas, Utah, and Wisconsin.

COMPETITORS

CNL Financial
Forest City Enterprises
JMB Realty
Jones Lang LaSalle
Lincoln Property
Prime Group Realty
W. P. Carey

Inserra Supermarkets

The Big Apple need never be short of apples (or
oranges, for that matter), thanks to Inserra Supermarkets. Inserra owns and operates 20-plus
ShopRite supermarkets and superstores in
northern New Jersey and southeastern New York
State (most are in Westchester and Rockland
counties). Inserra's superstores feature bagel
bakeries, cafes, and pharmacies. The regional
grocery chain also offers banking services in selected stores through agreements with Pough-
keepsie Savings Bank, Statewide Savings Bank,
and others. Owned by the Inserra family, the retailer is one of more than 40 members that make
up cooperative Wakefern Food, the owner of the
ShopRite name.

The regional supermarket operator opened a
new 70,000-sq.-ft. store in Lodi, New Jersey, in
early 2008. The upscale store is one of Inserra's
largest supermarkets and includes an upscale
bakery department, floral section, fresh sushi, international gourmet cheeses, and full-service
meat, seafood, and pharmacy departments.

Previously, it had closed a ShopRite supermarket in West Haverstraw, New York, in May 2007.

EXECUTIVES

Chairman, President, and CEO: Lawrence R. Inserra Jr.
CFO: Theresa Inserra
VP and Operations Director: Steve Chalas
Human Resources Director: Marie Larson

LOCATIONS

HQ: Inserra Supermarkets, Inc.
20 Ridge Rd., Mahwah, NJ 07430
Phone: 201-529-5900   **Fax:** 201-529-1189

COMPETITORS

A&P
D'Agostino Supermarkets
Food Circus Super Markets
Gristede's Foods
Hannaford Bros.
Key Food
King Kullen Grocery
Kings Super Markets
Man-dell
Stop & Shop
Trader Joe's
Western Beef

HISTORICAL FINANCIALS

Company Type: Private

Income Statement

	REVENUE ($ mil.)	NET INCOME ($ mil.)	NET PROFIT MARGIN	EMPLOYEES
12/07	1,050	—	—	3,500
12/06	1,030	—	—	4,000
12/05	1,030	—	—	4,000
Annual Growth	1.0%	—	—	(6.5%)

FYE: December 31

Revenue History

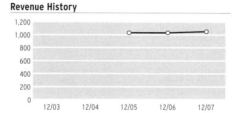

Insight Communications

Insight Communications had the foresight to
jump on an industry trend and turn its cable TV
systems into broadband networks. The firm's
cable system (formerly a joint venture with Comcast known as Insight Midwest) serves about
650,000 subscribers in the Midwest, with the
majority of customers in Kentucky. Insight upgraded its networks for two-way communications so it can offer interactive digital video and
high-speed data services, including cable modem
Internet access. Adding telephony to its list of
services, the company has a deal with AT&T that
provides co-branded broadband phone service.

Both Insight and Comcast had the right to
dissolve the Insight Midwest partnership after
2005. Comcast's indication that it would do so
was one factor that contributed to management's
decision to take Insight Communications private in 2005.

Comcast acted on its impulse in 2007, splitting
the joint venture and taking more than 680,000
basic-cable subscribers with it.

EXECUTIVES

Chairman: Sidney R. Knafel, age 77, $250,000 pay
Vice Chairman and CEO: Michael S. Willner, age 54
President, COO, and Director: Dinesh C. (Dinni) Jain,
age 43
EVP and CFO: John Abbot, age 44
EVP Central Operations and CTO: Hamid R. Heidary,
age 50
EVP Field Operations: Christopher (Chris) Slattery,
age 39
SVP and Chief Accounting Officer: Daniel Mannino
SVP, General Counsel, and Secretary: Elliot Brecher,
age 41
SVP Communications: Sandra D. (Sandy) Colony
SVP Human Resources: Jim Morgan
SVP Brand Strategy and Programming:
Pamela Euler Halling
SVP Operations: John W. (Woody) Hutton
SVP Product Management: Paul Meltzer
VP Marketing: Steven Eliasof
Auditors: Ernst & Young LLP

LOCATIONS

HQ: Insight Communications Company, Inc.
810 7th Ave., New York, NY 10019
Phone: 917-286-2300   **Fax:** 917-286-2301
Web: www.insight-com.com

PRODUCTS/OPERATIONS

Selected Services

Basic, premium, and pay-per-view cable TV
programming
Cable modem-based Internet access
Interactive digital video
Telephone services

COMPETITORS

AT&T
Cable One
Charter Communications
Comcast
Cox Communications
DIRECTV
DISH Network Corporation
Mediacom Communications
Rainbow Media
Time Warner Cable

HISTORICAL FINANCIALS

Company Type: Private

Income Statement

	REVENUE ($ mil.)	NET INCOME ($ mil.)	NET PROFIT MARGIN	EMPLOYEES
12/07	1,400	—	—	2,569
12/06	1,263	—	—	4,035
12/05	1,118	—	—	3,829
Annual Growth	11.9%	—	—	(18.1%)

FYE: December 31

Revenue History

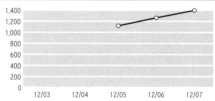

International Data Group

International Data Group (IDG) is a publishing giant with digital appeal. The world's top technology publisher, IDG produces more than 300 magazines and newspapers (including *PC World* and *CIO*) in 85 countries and in dozens of languages. In addition to publishing, IDG provides technology market research through its IDC unit, and the company also produces technology-focused industry events. The company offers career services through sites such as ITcareers.com, and operates 450 Web sites featuring technology content. Chairman Patrick McGovern founded IDG in 1964.

IDG produces more than 750 industry events, including Macworld Conference & Expo and LinuxWorld Conference & Expo. The company's IDC research unit has more than 900 analysts in more than 60 countries. Its IDG News Service is a 24-hour news organization that reports on IT news to the company's online network from bureaus around the world. In addition, IDG provides international brand marketing services for IT companies and media agencies through its IDG Global Services unit.

HISTORY

Patrick McGovern began his career in publishing as a paperboy for the *Philadelphia Bulletin.* As a teenager in the 1950s, McGovern was inspired by Edmund Berkeley's book *Giant Brains; or Machines That Think.* He later built a computer and won a scholarship to MIT. There he edited the first computer magazine, *Computers and Automation.* McGovern started market research firm International Data Corporation in 1964 after interviewing the president of computer pioneer UNIVAC. Three years later he launched *Computerworld,* and within a few weeks the eight-page tabloid had 20,000 subscribers. Combined under the name International Data Group, McGovern's company reached $1 million in sales by 1968.

Taking the "International" in its name to heart, IDG began publishing in Japan in 1971 and expanded to Germany in 1975. Following the collapse of communism, the company had 10 publications in Russia and Eastern Europe by 1990. That year two teenage hackers broke into the company's voice mail system and erased orders from customers and messages from writers. The prank cost IDG about $2.4 million. Also in 1990, IDG launched IDG Books Worldwide (renamed Hungry Minds in 2000), which hit it big the next year with *DOS for Dummies.*

With the technology boom of the 1990s, competition in tech publishing heated up. By 1993 several of IDG's magazines, including *InfoWorld, Macworld,* and *PC World,* began losing ad pages to rivals Ziff-Davis and CMP Media. To help stem advertiser attrition, IDG started an incentive program tied to its new online service. In 1995 IDG bought a stake in software companies Architect Software (now ExciteHome) and Netscape (now owned by America Online) as part of its move toward Internet-based services.

In 1996 IDG launched *Netscape World: The Web,* a magazine covering the Internet, and introduced more than 30 industry newsletters delivered by e-mail. The company also bought *PC Advisor,* the UK's fastest-growing computer magazine. IDG kicked off its online ad placement service, Global Web Ad Network, in 1997. That year IDG merged *Macworld* with rival Ziff-Davis' *MacUser* in a joint venture called Mac Publishing.

In 1998 IDG pledged $1 billion in venture capital for high-tech startups in China. It also introduced new publications in China, including a Chinese edition of *Cosmopolitan* (with Hearst Magazines) and *China Computer Reseller World.* Later that year the company launched *The Industry Standard* and spun off 25% of IDG Books to the public.

In 1999 it sold a 20% stake in Industry Standard Communications (renamed Standard Media International) to private investors and began laying plans for a possible spinoff in 2000. However, a weakening economy and slowing ad sales in 2000 quieted those plans.

The next year both Standard Media and Hungry Minds announced staff cuts and restructuring. IDG eventually sold its majority interest in Hungry Minds to John Wiley & Sons for about $90 million. Standard Media filed for bankruptcy and liquidated its assets, some of which were bought by IDG. The company also purchased Ziff Davis' 50% stake in their joint venture Mac Publishing. In 2002 IDG CEO Kelly Conlin left the business and was replaced by company executive Pat Kenealy, who had previously founded the now-defunct *Digital News* magazine.

EXECUTIVES

Chairman and CEO: Patrick J. (Pat) McGovern
CFO: Ted Bloom
EVP Online: Colin Crawford
VP Human Resources: Piper Sheer
Director Communications and Marketing Programs: Howard Sholkin
Director Corporate Communications: Susanna Hinds
President and CEO, CXO Media: Michael (Mike) Friedenberg
President and CEO, IDC: Kirk Campbell
President, CEO, and Publisher, Computerworld: Matthew Sweeney
President and CEO, IDG International Publishing Services: David F. Hill
CEO IDG Communications: Bob Carrigan
President, IDG Entertainment: Daniel (Dan) Orum
President, IDG Global Solutions: John P. O'Malley
Auditors: Deloitte & Touche LLP

LOCATIONS

HQ: International Data Group, Inc.
1 Exeter Plaza, 15th Fl., Boston, MA 02116
Phone: 617-534-1200   **Fax:** 617-423-0240
Web: www.idg.com

PRODUCTS/OPERATIONS

Selected Operations

IDC (market research)
IDG Communications List Services
IDG Events & Conferences
IDG Global Solutions
IDG News Service
IDG Publications (periodical publishing)
IDG Recruitment Solutions (employment services)
IDG Research Services Group
IDG.net (online publications hub)

Selected Events

Bio-IT World Conference & Expo
CIO 100
ComNet Conference & Expo
DEMO
IDC Directions
LinuxWorld Conference & Expo
Macworld Conference & Expo

Selected Periodicals

Bio-IT World
Channel World
CIO
CSO
Computerworld
DigitalWorld
GamePro
InfoWorld
Macworld
Network World
PC World

COMPETITORS

1105 Media	Jupitermedia
Advanstar	The Nielsen Company
CBS Interactive	Penton Media
CMP Media	Reed Elsevier Group
Editis	SourceForge
Forrester Research	SYS-CON Media
Future plc	TechTarget
Gartner	United Business Media
IHS	Ziff Davis Media

International Specialty Products

If you've washed, shaved, and groomed, then you've probably shared a chemical experience with the folks at International Specialty Products (ISP). The company, also called ISP Chemco, makes about 300 types of specialty chemicals, including food and pharmaceutical ingredients, personal care, and fine chemicals, industrial chemicals (like butanediol for fibers and plastics), and minerals products. ISP also makes waterproofing agents, moisturizers, and preservatives for personal care products such as sunscreen and hair care products. Chairman Samuel Heyman owns ISP; after watching the company's stock dive in 2002, Heyman took ISP private.

After the going-private transaction was complete, ISP went shopping. The company bought Germinal S.A., a South American food ingredients company, and Ameripol Synpol's elastomers plant in Texas. The company operates throughout North and South America, Europe, and Asia.

Heyman and ISP waged and lost, in 2003, a proxy fight for control of Hercules, of which ISP owned 10%. ISP sold most of its shares in Hercules later that year.

EXECUTIVES

Chairman: Samuel J. (Sam) Heyman, age 66
President and CEO: Sunil Kumar, $1,374,725 pay
EVP, General Counsel, and Secretary: Richard A. Weinberg, age 45
EVP Finance and Treasurer: Susan B. Yoss
SVP Sales and General Manager, Asia: Warren Bishop
SVP and Commercial Director, Americas: Ron Brandt
SVP Sales and Commercial Director, Europe: Roger J. Cope
SVP Research and Development and Latin America: Lawrence Grenner
SVP Global Marketing and Sales: Stephen R. Olsen
SVP Operations, Specialty Chemicals Division: Steven E. Post
SVP EMEA: Philip Strenger
VP and CIO: Ken Morris
VP Human Resources: Marianne Spencer
Manager Communications: Michelle Evans
Auditors: KPMG LLP

LOCATIONS

HQ: International Specialty Products, Inc.
 1361 Alps Rd., Wayne, NJ 07470
Phone: 973-628-4000   **Fax:** 973-628-4423
Web: www.ispcorp.com

International Specialty Products has operations in Asia,
Europe, North America, and South America.

PRODUCTS/OPERATIONS

Selected Products and Applications

Specialty chemicals
 Fine chemicals
  Specialized products (agricultural, biotechnology,
   imaging, and pharmaceutical markets)
  Flunixin Meglumine (animal analgesic)
  Milotane (cancer treatment)
  Pharmaceutical intermediates (cholesterol control,
   heart and kidney disease, and viral infections)
  Pheromones (used for insect control)
 Food and beverage
  Beer
  Cheese sauces
  Fruit fillings
  Health drinks
  Salad dressings
 Performance chemicals
  Acetylene-based polymers (Agriculture, coatings,
   detergents, electronics, imaging, metalworking)
  Advanced materials (aerospace, defense, electronics,
   and powder metallurgy industries)
  Vinyl ether monomers
 Personal care
  Hair care
   Conditioning agent (hair conditioning rinses)
   Fixative resins (holding power for gels, hairsprays,
    and mousses)
   Stabilizers (shampoo)
   Thickeners (shampoo)
  Skin care
   Adhesive (facial cleansing strips)
   Emollients (body and facial moisturizers)
   Moisturizers
   Preservatives
   Ultraviolet light-absorbing chemicals
   Waterproofing agents (eyeliners and sun screen)
 Pharmaceutical
  Antiseptics
  Cough syrups
  Denture adhesives
  Injectionable prescription drugs and serums
  Prescription and over-the-counter tablets
  Toothpastes
Industrial chemicals
 Coatings
 Electronics cleaning
 High-performance plastics
 Lubricating oil and chemical processing
Minerals
 Colored roofing granules (asphalt roofing shingles)

COMPETITORS

3M
Albemarle
BASF SE
Cognis
CP Kelco
CPAC
DuPont Canada
Evonik Degussa
Hercules
Penford
Stepan
Yule Catto

HISTORICAL FINANCIALS
Company Type: Private

Income Statement

	REVENUE ($ mil.)	NET INCOME ($ mil.)	NET PROFIT MARGIN	EMPLOYEES
12/07	1,600	—	—	3,300
12/06	1,500	—	—	3,100
12/05	1,360	—	—	3,100
12/04	1,023	—	—	2,600
12/03	893	—	—	2,800
Annual Growth	15.7%	—	—	4.2%

FYE: December 31

Revenue History

Interstate Batteries

Interstate Battery System of America offers a
battery of batteries. The company can provide
the electrical juice for everything from cellular
phones and laptops to automobiles, boats, and
lawn equipment. Interstate Battery has 300-plus
distributors throughout North America; consumers can purchase Interstate Battery's products at more than 200,000 retail locations,
including a growing number of Interstate All
Battery Centers. The company makes the official
replacement battery for the vehicles of companies such as Land Rover, Subaru, and Toyota. Interstate Battery sponsors the Joe Gibbs Racing
team on the NASCAR circuit. Chairman Norm
Miller owns the company.

Interstate sells batteries that carry its own
brand as well as products with manufacturers' labels. Johnson Controls supplies Interstate's automotive line.

The company was founded in Dallas in 1952
by John Searcys. He started the company by
selling replacement batteries in service stations
on consignment.

EXECUTIVES

Chairman: Norm Miller
President and CEO: Carlos Sepulveda, age 50
VP, Corporate Accounting and Services:
 Lisa Huntsberry
VP, Advertising and Public Relations: Charles Suscavage
VP, All Battery and E-Commerce: Mickey Elam
VP, Independent Distributor Development: Jeff Haddock
VP, Information Technology and CIO: Merv Tarde
VP, Interstate Owned Territories: Alex Louis
**VP, Human Resources and PowerCare, and General
 Counsel:** Walter (Walt) Holmes
VP, Marketing: Dennis Brown
VP, National Accounts: William (Billy) Norris
VP, Supply Chain Management: Chris Antoniou
Director, Public Relations: Jane Koenecke

LOCATIONS

HQ: Interstate Battery System of America, Inc.
 12770 Merit Dr., Ste. 400, Dallas, TX 75251
Phone: 972-991-1444   **Fax:** 972-458-8288
Web: www.ibsa.com

Interstate Battery System of America has distributors in
Canada, the Dominican Republic, Guam, Jamaica,
Puerto Rico, and the US.

PRODUCTS/OPERATIONS

Selected Applications

Automotive/truck
Calculators
Camcorders
Cellular phones
Chargers
Commercial equipment
Computers/laptops
Cordless phones
Cordless tools
Flashlights
Household batteries
Lawn and garden
Marine/RV
Medical equipment
Motorcycles
Pagers
Photo batteries
Radio batteries
Sealed lead/SLA
Watches

COMPETITORS

Advance Auto Parts
AutoZone
Costco Wholesale
Genuine Parts
Kmart
O'Reilly Automotive
Pep Boys
Sears
Target
Wal-Mart

HISTORICAL FINANCIALS
Company Type: Private

Income Statement

	REVENUE ($ mil.)	NET INCOME ($ mil.)	NET PROFIT MARGIN	EMPLOYEES
4/08	1,500	—	—	1,415
4/07	1,000	—	—	1,275
4/06	1,000	—	—	1,400
4/05	755	—	—	1,251
4/04	700	—	—	900
Annual Growth	21.0%	—	—	12.0%

FYE: April 30

Revenue History

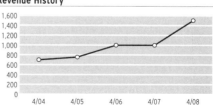

Irvine Company

At The Irvine Company, everything goes according to plan — the *master* plan! The real estate investment company plans and designs office, retail, and residential villages in San Diego, Los Angeles, Silicon Valley, and Orange County. Its portfolio includes 400 office buildings, 40 retail centers, and 90 apartment communities, as well as several hotels, marinas, and golf clubs, not to mention The Irvine Ranch, one of the largest planned communities in the US. The ranch has some 260,000 residents and covers 93,000 acres, a drop from its original 120,000 acres back in the mid-1800s, when James Irvine bought out the debts of Mexican land-grant holders. Chairman Donald Bren, an American billionaire, owns the company.

The Irvine Company's portfolio includes Irvine Spectrum, one of the nation's largest high-tech research and business centers, encompassing some 40 million sq. ft. It also owns Irvine Apartment Communities, a residential management firm that owns and operates about 90 apartment complexes. The University of California, Irvine is built on company-donated land.

Bren has continued the 40-year-old master plan created by the Irvine Foundation (the former parent of The Irvine Company), which calls for gradual development of its rigorously planned communities. The plan — which has so far helped form the communities of Laguna Beach, Newport Beach, Orange, and Tustin, as well as centerpiece Irvine — has entered its final phase (set for completion around 2040), but the company faces increasing political opposition to its plans from area residents, who tend to become development-weary after they get their piece of The Irvine Ranch. In a move to prevent unchecked growth, the company has stopped selling desirable Irvine Spectrum land to small commercial building developers.

With most of its developments complete, The Irvine Company has increasingly focused on property investment and management. In addition to Irvine Spectrum, the company has been overseeing the development, marketing, leasing, and management of Fashion Island in Newport Beach, McCarthy Center in Silicon Valley, Symphony Towers in San Diego, and Fox Plaza in West Los Angeles.

HISTORY

A wholesale merchant in San Francisco during the gold rush, James Irvine and two others assembled vast holdings in Southern California in the mid-1800s by buying out the debts of Mexican and Spanish land-grant holders. Irvine bought his partners' shares in 1876 and passed the ranch of 120,000 acres to his son, James II, upon his death in 1886. Eight years later James II incorporated the ranch as The Irvine Company and began turning it into an agribusiness empire, shifting from sheep ranching to cash crop farming.

James II owned the ranch and company until the 1930s, when the death of his son, James III, prompted him to transfer a controlling interest in the company to the not-for-profit Irvine Foundation. James III's wife Athalie, and daughter Joan, inherited 22% of Irvine.

In 1959 company president Myford Irvine, a grandson of James I and uncle to Joan, was found dead from two shotgun wounds. Officials ruled it a suicide, but others weren't so sure.

With Athalie and Joan's encouragement, the company donated land in the early 1960s for construction of the University of California, Irvine. The company would continue contributing to educational and philanthropic causes as well as donating property for green space to improve Orange County's suburban areas.

The 1960s also saw the Irvine Foundation forming its definitive master plan for prearranged communities and marked the company's entry into the real estate development sector. The plan was designed to anticipate and control growth, with provisions for green space and a mix of pricing levels.

Superrich firebrand Joan, who had long accused Irvine Foundation officers of serving their own interests at the expense of other stockholders, lobbied Congress in the late 1960s to change tax laws pertaining to the foundation. Along with a group of investors led by Donald Bren, Alfred Taubman, and Herbert Allen, Joan trumped a bid by Mobil Oil and in 1977 wrested control of the company from the foundation.

When California's real estate market went sour in 1983, Bren bought out his fellow shareholders, and increased his ownership stake from 34% to 95%. Joan returned to court to protest the price, gaining extra money when the court valued the land at $1.4 billion.

In 1993 Bren sought cash from his holdings by offering apartment developments as a real estate investment trust (REIT), Irvine Apartment Communities.

Orange County's record-setting bankruptcy in 1994 (the county lost $1.7 billion in risky investments) threatened the value of The Irvine Company's property portfolio, most of which is located in Orange County. Thanks in part to a frothy economy and settlements from brokerage firms, Orange County and The Irvine Company were spared another 1983-esque bust.

In 1996 Bren bought the company's remaining stock. As part of its expansion into R&D, retail, and office properties in the Silicon Valley area, The Irvine Company opened an office in San Jose the next year, followed by its Eastgate Technology Park in San Diego in 1998. An industrywide slide in REIT stock prices prompted Bren to take Irvine Apartment Communities private in 1999.

The company continued to expand its retail and office holdings into the aughts — including the purchase of Century City's Fox Plaza. In 2002 the Irvine City Council approved The Irvine Company's plans to develop the last phase of the company's master plan (to be completed in 2040) — bringing over 12,000 homes, 730,000 sq. ft. of retail space, and 6.57 million sq. ft. of industrial space to the city's Northern Sphere area.

EXECUTIVES

Chairman: Donald L. Bren, age 76
Vice Chairman and CEO: Michael D. McKee, age 62
EVP: Clarence W. Barker
SVP and CFO: Marc Ley, age 40
SVP Urban Planning and Design: Robert N. Elliott
SVP Corporate Affairs: Tony Russo
SVP Legal Affairs and Risk Management; Secretary:
  Patricia Frobes, age 61
VP Commercial Land Sales: Larry Williams
VP Community Affairs: Robin Leftwich
VP Capital Markets: Robert (Rob) Lang
VP Development, San Diego: Thomas Sullivan, age 55
VP Finance, Resort Properties: Thomas Keeney
VP Leasing, San Diego: Steve Center
VP Marketing, Resort Properties: Michael Donahue,
  age 54
President, Community Development:
  Daniel (Dan) Young
President, Apartment Communities: Max L. Gardner,
  age 51
President, Office Properties: Richard I. (Rick) Gilchrist,
  age 63
President, Retail Properties: Keith Eyrich
President, Resort Properties: Ralph Grippo
President, Office Properties: E. Valjean Wheeler

LOCATIONS

HQ: The Irvine Company
  550 Newport Center Dr., Newport Beach, CA 92660
Phone: 949-720-2000   **Fax:** 949-720-2218
Web: www.irvinecompany.com

The Irvine Company owns about 44,000 acres of land in Orange County, California, including the City of Irvine and parts of Anaheim, Laguna Beach, Newport Beach, Orange, and Tustin. It also owns properties in Los Angeles, San Diego, and San Jose.

PRODUCTS/OPERATIONS

Selected Divisions

Investment Properties Group
  Apartment communities
  Commercial land sales
  Resort properties (hotels, marinas, and golf courses)
  Office properties
  Retail properties
Irvine Community Development
  Agricultural operations
  Land sales and management
  Residential development sales

COMPETITORS

California Coastal Communities
C.J. Segerstrom & Sons
Corky McMillin
D.R. Horton
Intergroup
KB Home
Kilroy Realty
The Koll Company
Majestic Realty
MBK Real Estate
Mission West Properties
Newhall Land
Rancho Mission Viejo
Tejon Ranch
Western National Group

HISTORICAL FINANCIALS

Company Type: Private

Income Statement   FYE: June 30

	ESTIMATED REVENUE ($ mil.)	NET INCOME ($ mil.)	NET PROFIT MARGIN	EMPLOYEES
6/07	150	—	—	2,000

It's Just Lunch

It's Just Lunch (IJL) doesn't offer high-tech hook-ups. The matchmaking service sets up busy, professional singles for lunch dates based on personal interviews instead of the much maligned introduction videos or online dating pools. The company, which franchises nearly 100 offices in the US, Singapore, Canada, Australia, Europe, and the Caribbean, charges singles around $1,000 for a series of dates (prices vary by location). It boasts having arranged more than 2 million dates since its inception. Founder Andrea McGinty established the company in 1992 after her fiancé jilted her weeks before their wedding. She sold IJL to The Riverside Company in 2006.

Catering to young professional women, the men who use the services often feel that they get the shaft in terms of personalized service (and not in the good way).

EXECUTIVES

Chairman: Matt Schaffer
CEO: Kevin Bazner
President and Chief Marketing Officer: Irene LaCota
SVP: Nancy Kirsch
VP: Alana Beyer
VP: Melissa Brown
VP: Jennifer Pannucci

LOCATIONS

HQ: It's Just Lunch International LLC
75430 Gerald Ford Dr., Ste. 207,
Palm Desert, CA 92211
Phone: 760-779-0101   **Fax:** 760-779-9191
Web: www.itsjustlunch.com

Selected Franchise Locations

Albuquerque	Minneapolis
Austin	New York City
Charlotte	San Antonio
Chicago	St. Louis
Madison	St. Paul

COMPETITORS

eHarmony.com	Spark Networks
FastCupid	Together Management
Lavalife	Various, Inc.
Match.com	Yahoo!

Jacobs Entertainment

Jacobs Entertainment wants you to come out and play. The company operates The Lodge Casino and Gilpin Casino in Black Hawk, Colorado; and the Gold Dust West Casinos in Reno, Carson City, and Elko, Nevada. The company also has about 20 truck stop video gaming facilities throughout Louisiana, and the Colonial Downs horseracing track in New Kent, Virginia; and eight satellite pari-mutuel wagering locations throughout Virginia. Chairman and CEO Jeffrey Jacobs owns 50% of the company. His father, Richard Jacobs, who co-founded Jacobs Entertainment, owns the other half.

The company offers hotel rooms at its casino locations in Black Hawk, Reno, and Carson City.

In 2006 Jacobs Entertainment expanded with the purchase of Piñon Plaza in Carson City. The property was subsequently re-branded as Gold Dust West-Carson City. Also that year the company remodeled and improved the entrance and access to The Lodge Casino. Its Elko, Nevada casino opened in 2007.

EXECUTIVES

Chairman, CEO, Secretary, and Treasurer:
Jeffrey P. Jacobs, age 54, $750,000 pay
President: Stephen R. Roark, age 60, $457,000 pay
COO: Michael T. Shubic, age 54, $315,000 pay
CFO: Brett A. Kramer, age 39
EVP: Stanley Politano
President, Pari-Mutuel Wagering Operations:
Ian M. Stewart, age 53, $325,000 pay
Auditors: Deloitte & Touche LLP

LOCATIONS

HQ: Jacobs Entertainment, Inc.
17301 W. Colfax Ave., Ste. 250, Golden, CO 80401
Phone: 303-215-5200   **Fax:** 303-215-5219
Web: www.bhwk-hr.com

2007 Sales

	% of total
Louisiana	46
Colorado	28
Virginia	13
Nevada	12
Total	**100**

PRODUCTS/OPERATIONS

2007 Sales

	$ mil.	% of total
Gaming		
Casino	144.7	38
Truck stops	64.3	17
Pari-mutuel	41.3	11
Convenience store - fuel	81.3	21
Convenience store - other	11.1	3
Food & beverage	29.3	8
Hotel	4.4	1
Other	5.4	1
Total	**381.8**	**100**

Selected Operations

Colonial Downs Racetrack
Gilpin Casino
Gold Dust West-Carson City
Gold Dust West-Elko
Gold Dust West-Reno
The Lodge Casino
Louisiana Truck Plazas

COMPETITORS

Ameristar Casinos
Boyd Gaming
Harrah's Entertainment
Isle of Capri Casinos
MGM MIRAGE
Penn National Gaming
Pinnacle Entertainment
Station Casinos

HISTORICAL FINANCIALS

Company Type: Private

Income Statement

FYE: December 31

	REVENUE ($ mil.)	NET INCOME ($ mil.)	NET PROFIT MARGIN	EMPLOYEES
12/07	382	5	1.3%	2,200
12/06	339	(11)	—	1,100
12/05	234	(5)	—	1,585
12/04	190	5	2.6%	1,365
12/03	172	3	1.6%	1,365
Annual Growth	22.1%	16.7%	—	12.7%

2007 Year-End Financials

Debt ratio: 1,052.9%
Return on equity: 16.8%
Cash ($ mil.): —
Current ratio: —
Long-term debt ($ mil.): 298

Net Income History

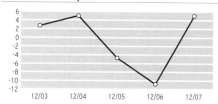

Jacuzzi Brands

Aaah, that feels good. Jacuzzi Brands makes the eponymous whirlpool baths, spas, and showers (it also sells bath products under the Sundance and Astracast brands) that soothe the aches and pains of customers in the US, Europe, Middle East, and South America. Besides spas, products include toilets and sinks, accessories such as bath pillows and heating kits, steam showers, and other Romanesque bathroom necessities. Investment firm Apollo Management acquired Jacuzzi Brands for about $1.25 billion in early 2007. Apollo then transferred Jacuzzi's institutional plumbing business, Zurn Industries, to its RBS Global division.

The purchase price of the transaction included $990 million for Jacuzzi's shareholders and the assumption of $260 million in debt. Immediately after the deal closed, Apollo Management sold the Zurn plumbing business to RBS Global, an Apollo portfolio company that does business as Rexnord, for about $942 million in cash. The company now operates through its Jacuzzi Bath, Jacuzzi Spa, and Sundance Spa units.

Later in 2007 Jacuzzi Brands entered the specialty mattress arena by forming a partnership with Thurmo-Pudic USA, which subsequently changed its name to Jacuzzi Sleep Systems.

EXECUTIVES

President and CEO: Thomas D. Koos
CFO: Glen Ferguson
VP Human Resources: Kevin Clegg
VP and Global Controller: David Hellman
VP Industrial Design and New Product Engineering: Erica Moir
President and CEO, Spa Division: Jonathan Clark
President, Jacuzzi Whirlpool Bath: Robert I. Rowan, age 48

Chief Marketing Officer: Michelle Cervantez
CIO: Sharon Solomon
Senior Director e-Marketing: William (Bill) Smelley
Director Marketing Communications and Strategy:
 Dawn Wells
Communications Manager: Anthony Pasquarelli
Auditors: Ernst & Young LLP

LOCATIONS

HQ: Jacuzzi Brands Corporation
 13925 City Center Dr., Ste. 200,
 Chino Hills, CA 91709
Phone: 909-606-1416
Web: www.jacuzzibrands.com

COMPETITORS

Clarion Bathware   Ridgewood
Geberit   Sanitec
Kohler   TOTO
Mansfield Plumbing   Villeroy & Boch
Moen

Jazzercise, Inc.

Jazzercise has shown people how to shake their booties toward fitness for more than 30 years. The company's franchised fitness classes, taught by more than 6,000 instructors, blend jazz dancing with an aerobic workout for nearly a half million students worldwide. Jazzercise makes money through franchise fees as well as the sale of clothing, books, and other merchandise online and through catalogs.

The company's JM DigitalWorks unit produces Jazzercise workout tapes and provides video production services to other clients. Its Jazzertogs division offers fitness apparel and accessories. CEO Judi Sheppard Missett, a professional dancer, founded Jazzercise in 1969 and began franchising in 1980.

EXECUTIVES

CEO: Judi Sheppard Missett, age 64
COO and CFO: Sally Baldridge
EVP: Shanna Missett Nelson, age 39
VP International Operations and Corporate Events:
 Kenny Harvey
VP Marketing: Kathy Missett
VP Sales: Kelly Sweeney
VP Technology: Brad Jones
Director Management Information Systems: David West
Director Human Resources: Rick Colson
Director Public Relations: Denice Menard
Marketing Coordinator: Amanda Carson

LOCATIONS

HQ: Jazzercise, Inc.
 2460 Impala Dr., Carlsbad, CA 92010
Phone: 760-476-1750   Fax: 760-602-7180
Web: www.jazzercise.com

PRODUCTS/OPERATIONS

Selected Operations

Jazzertogs, A Division of Jazzercise (catalog clothing and
 book sales)
JM DigitalWorks, A Division of Jazzercise (exercise tapes
 and video production for clients)

Class Formats

Body Sculpting by Jazzercise (abdominal, arm, and leg
 muscle toning)
Cardio Quick by Jazzercise (short class)
Circuit Training by Jazzercise (weights)
Jazzercise (dance exercise)
Jazzercise Plus (longer workouts)
Jr. Jazzercise! (ages 6-11)
Personal Touch Jazzercise (one-on-one training)
Simply-Lite (physically restricted)
Step by Jazzercise (step aerobics)
Team Dance (preteens and teens)

COMPETITORS

24 Hour Fitness
Bally Total Fitness
Curves International
Gold's Gym
The Sports Club
Town Sports International Holdings
YMCA
YWCA

HISTORICAL FINANCIALS

Company Type: Private

Income Statement

FYE: June 30

	REVENUE ($ mil.)	NET INCOME ($ mil.)	NET PROFIT MARGIN	EMPLOYEES
6/08	93	—	—	161

J.B. Poindexter & Co.

No matter what you're hauling, J.B. Poindexter & Co. has got you covered. Through its Morgan Corporation subsidiary, the company makes medium-duty commercial van bodies that are mounted on truck chassis made by other manufacturers. A separate unit, Morgan Olson, makes bodies for step vans. J.B. Poindexter's truck accessories unit makes pickup bed enclosures such as tonneaus and campers under brands including Leer and LoRider. The company's specialty manufacturing group includes subsidiaries EFP (expandable foam plastics), Specialty Vehicle Group (funeral coaches and other funeral vehicles) and MIC Group (precision metal parts, casting, and machining). Chairman and CEO John B. Poindexter owns the company.

Morgan Corp.'s customers include rental companies, such as AMERCO's U-Haul International; leasing companies, such as Penske Truck Leasing; and operators of fleets of delivery vehicles, such as FedEx and UPS. Morgan Corp. sells its products through a network of more than 180 distributors and dealers.

J.B. Poindexter expanded its MIC Group in 2007 with the acquisition of three precision machining operations: Richard's Manufacturing, Tarlton Supply Company, and Machine & Manufacturing I.

Early in 2006 J.B. Poindexter acquired Eagle Coach; that business combined with the operations of Federal Coach (acquired in 2005), make up the company's Specialty Vehicle Group.

EXECUTIVES

Chairman, President, and CEO: John B. Poindexter,
 age 63
SVP, Operations: Joseph M. Fiamingo, age 57
VP, Administration and Assistant Secretary:
 Larry T. Wolfe, age 59, $382,383 pay
VP, Business Development: Andrew Foskey, age 39,
 $350,000 pay
VP, Finance, Secretary, and Treasurer:
 Robert S. Whatley, age 56
VP, Quality and Process: Frank Meterko
VP, Information Technology: Rick Maus
President, EFP Corporation: William (Bill) Flint Jr.,
 age 56
President, Morgan Corporation: Norbert Markert
President, Specialty Manufacturing Group:
 Nelson Byman, $424,901 pay
President, Truck Accessories: Bruce Freeman, age 53,
 $384,964 pay
President, Morgan Olson: Patrick (Pat) Warmington,
 age 53
President, Specialty Vehicle Group: Robert Whitehouse,
 age 52

LOCATIONS

HQ: J.B. Poindexter & Co., Inc.
 1100 Louisiana, Ste. 5400, Houston, TX 77002
Phone: 713-655-9800   Fax: 713-951-9038
Web: www.jbpoindexter.com

PRODUCTS/OPERATIONS

2007 Sales

	$ mil.	% of total
Morgan	332.9	42
Specialty Manufacturing	195.2	25
Truck Accessories	155.6	20
Morgan Olson	110.3	14
Adjustments	(1.8)	—
Total	792.2	100

COMPETITORS

Fleetwood Enterprises
Foamex International
Kidron
Lund International
Master Precision Machining
RKI
Royal Truck Body
Supreme Industries
Utilimaster
Utility Trailer

HISTORICAL FINANCIALS

Company Type: Private

Income Statement

FYE: December 31

	REVENUE ($ mil.)	NET INCOME ($ mil.)	NET PROFIT MARGIN	EMPLOYEES
12/07	792	(1)	—	4,227
12/06	795	9	1.1%	4,500
12/05	668	5	0.8%	4,000
12/04	585	10	1.7%	—
12/03	411	9	2.2%	3,000
Annual Growth	17.8%	—	—	9.0%

Net Income History

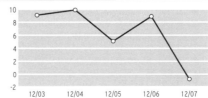

JCM Partners

At the upper end of the Golden State is where you'll find JCM Partners, which invests in, renovates, manages, markets, and sells multifamily residential and commercial real estate in Northern California. It owns about 45 properties, including nearly 40 apartment communities (containing a total of about 5,000 units), one multi-tenant office/retail property, two office properties, and four industrial properties. Nearly half of JCM Partners' residential properties are located in Sacramento County; the remainder are in San Joaquin, Solano, Stanislaus, and Contra Costa counties (the Central Valley and the San Francisco metro area).

JCM Partners plans to continue to focus its portfolio on apartments, punctuated with commercial properties within the same geographical markets. The firm is the result of a reorganization of IRM Corporation, which emerged from bankruptcy in 2000.

Executives and management collectively own 12% of the company.

EXECUTIVES

Chairman: Michael W. Vanni, age 68
Vice Chairman: Marvin J. Helder, age 58
President, CEO, Secretary, and Manager: Gayle M. Ing, age 57
COO: Brian S. Rein, age 50, $325,000 pay
CFO: Douglas W. Toovey, age 51
Auditors: Moss Adams, LLP

LOCATIONS

HQ: JCM Partners, LLC
    2151 Salvio St., Ste. 325, Concord, CA 94520
Phone: 925-676-1966   **Fax:** 925-676-1744

2006 Properties

	No.
Apartment	
Sacramento	18
Fairfield/Vacaville	5
Modesto/Turlock	5
Tracy/Manteca	4
Concord/Antioch	3
Stockton	3
Commercial	
Bay Area	7
Total	**45**

PRODUCTS/OPERATIONS

2006 Sales

	$ mil.	% of total
Rental	50.9	93
Rental settlement	2.2	4
Interest	1.9	3
Total	**55.0**	**100**

COMPETITORS

A.G. Spanos
Archstone
AvalonBay
BRE Properties
Equity Residential
Intergroup
Pacific Property Company
UDR

HISTORICAL FINANCIALS
Company Type: Private

Income Statement
FYE: December 31

	REVENUE ($ mil.)	NET INCOME ($ mil.)	NET PROFIT MARGIN	EMPLOYEES
12/06	55	8	14.7%	191
12/05	47	16	33.7%	191
12/04	50	6	11.7%	205
12/03	52	2	3.1%	222
12/02	51	1	1.2%	—
Annual Growth	1.8%	91.7%	—	(4.9%)

Net Income History

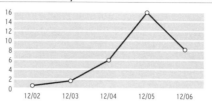

JE Dunn Construction

JE Dunn Construction Group prides itself on getting the job done. Owned by descendants of founder John E. Dunn, the firm holds a group of construction companies, including flagship J. E. Dunn Construction and Atlanta-based R.J. Griffin & Company. The group builds institutional, commercial, and industrial structures. It also provides construction and program management and design/build services. J. E. Dunn Construction, which ranks among the top 10 US general builders, was one of the first contractors to offer the construction management delivery method. Major projects it has completed include the IRS complex and world headquarters for H&R Block in Kansas City.

A bigwig particularly in the Midwest, JE Dunn won a major contract from the US Army Corps of Engineers to build a regional correction facility at Fort Leavenworth, Kansas, that will replace smaller prisons in Texas, Kentucky, and Oklahoma. The facility is expected to open in 2010. The firm regularly bids on federal government projects.

EXECUTIVES

Chairman Emeritus: William H. Dunn Sr.
Chairman: Robert A. (Bob) Long
Vice Chairman and Treasurer: Stephen D. (Steve) Dunn
President and CEO: Terrence P. (Terry) Dunn
CFO and EVP Finance: Gordon E. Lansford III
EVP General Counsel, and Secretary: Casey S. Halsey
EVP Marketing: Gregory E. Nook
EVP Purchasing and Warehouse Operations:
 William H. (Bill) Dunn Jr.
SVP, Human Resources: Richard E. (Rick) Beyer

President and CEO, J.E. Dunn Construction Company:
 Jack P. Nix Jr.
President and CEO, J.E. Dunn Rocky Mountain:
 Steve Hamline
President, CEO, and Treasurer of J.E. Dunn South Central: Gregg A. Lynch
President, CEO, Treasurer, and Secretary of J.E. Dunn Northcentral: Kenneth A. Styrlund
President and CEO, J.E. Dunn Northwest:
 Frederick S. Shipman III
President and CEO, RJ Griffin & Company:
 Steven A. (Steve) Touchton

LOCATIONS

HQ: JE Dunn Construction Group, Inc.
    929 Holmes, Kansas City, MO 64106
Phone: 816-474-8600   **Fax:** 816-391-2510
Web: www.jedunn.com

JE Dunn Construction has 16 offices throughout the US: Atlanta; Austin, Dallas, and Houston, Texas; Charlotte, North Carolina; Colorado Springs and Denver, Colorado; Des Moines, Iowa; Kansas City, Missouri; Minneapolis; Nashville, Tennessee; Orlando, Florida; Phoenix; Portland, Oregon; Seattle; and Topeka, Kansas.

COMPETITORS

Alberici
Bovis Lend Lease
Clark Enterprises
Hensel Phelps Construction
Hunt Construction
McCarthy Building
Perini
Rudolph & Sletten
Skanska USA Building
Sundt
Turner Corporation
Washington Division
The Weitz Company, LLC
Whiting-Turner

HISTORICAL FINANCIALS
Company Type: Private

Income Statement
FYE: December 31

	REVENUE ($ mil.)	NET INCOME ($ mil.)	NET PROFIT MARGIN	EMPLOYEES
12/07	2,634	—	—	4,100
12/06	2,563	—	—	3,000
12/05	2,305	—	—	3,000
12/04	1,633	—	—	3,000
12/03	1,497	—	—	3,000
Annual Growth	15.2%	—	—	8.1%

Revenue History

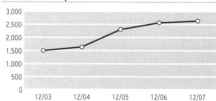

JELD-WEN, inc.

JELD-WEN can improve your outlook by providing new windows and doors for your home or by offering accommodations at a scenic resort. A leading manufacturer of windows and doors (some designed to withstand hurricane winds), JELD-WEN offers aluminum, vinyl, and wood windows; interior and exterior doors; garage doors; swinging and sliding patio doors; and door frames and moldings. It sells its products mainly in North America, Europe, and Australia. If you get tired of looking out your own doors and windows, JELD-WEN owns several resorts and communities in Oregon and Idaho, including Oregon's Eagle Crest Resort and Idaho's Silver Mountain Resort.

The company sold its 56-store home improvement outlet chain Grossman's (now Grossman's Bargain Outlet) to E.C. Barton in 2006.

Chairman Richard Wendt and his siblings founded JELD-WEN in 1960.

EXECUTIVES

Chairman: Richard L. Wendt, age 77
President and CEO: Roderick C. (Rod) Wendt
EVP and CFO: Douglas P. (Doug) Kintzinger
EVP and COO: Robert Turner
SVP External Affairs: Ron Saxton
VP and Treasurer: Karen Hoggarth
Marketing Director, Europe: Joanne Mitchell
General Manager, Retail Distribution, Denver: Glen Macy
General Manager, Window Division: Tom Takach
Corporate Communications Manager: Teri Cline
Office Services Manager, Marketing Department: Cindy Rowe
Sports Marketing Manager: Gina Monterossi

LOCATIONS

HQ: JELD-WEN, inc.
401 Harbor Isles Blvd., Klamath Falls, OR 97601
Phone: 541-882-3451   **Fax:** 541-885-7454
Web: www.jeld-wen.com

PRODUCTS/OPERATIONS

Selected Products
Doors
  Exterior (wood, custom fiberglass, fiberglass, and steel)
  Garage (wood composite)
  Interior (wood, custom-carved, molded, and flush)
  Patio (wood, vinyl, aluminum, and steel)
Millwork
  Columns
  Posts
  Spindles
  Stair parts
Windows
  Aluminum clad wood
  Energy-efficient
  Replacement
  Wood

Resorts and Communities
Brasada Ranch (Oregon)
Eagle Crest Resort (Oregon)
Harbor Isles (Oregon)
Ridgewater (Oregon)
The Running Y Ranch Resort (Oregon)
Silver Mountain Resort (Idaho)
Yarrow Living (Oregon)

COMPETITORS

Andersen Corporation
Designer Doors
Installux
Marshfield DoorSystems
NTK Holdings
Pella
Sierra Pacific Industries
Simonton Windows, Inc.
Wyndham Vacation

HISTORICAL FINANCIALS

Company Type: Private

Income Statement

FYE: December 31

	ESTIMATED REVENUE ($ mil.)	NET INCOME ($ mil.)	NET PROFIT MARGIN	EMPLOYEES
12/07	3,160	—	—	23,750
12/06	3,160	—	—	23,750
12/05	2,600	—	—	25,000
12/04	2,300	—	—	21,000
12/03	2,200	—	—	21,000
Annual Growth	9.5%	—	—	3.1%

Revenue History

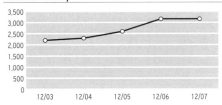

J.F. Shea Co.

J.F. Shea didn't build Shea Stadium but it could have. The family-owned construction and real estate company takes on commercial and civil engineering projects and offers design/build services through its flagship group, J.F. Shea Construction. The group's heavy civil engineering division builds tunnels and water treatment and water storage facilities. J.F. Shea's seven other companies offer residential construction and mortgage services, aggregate supply, concrete foundation construction and machinery, venture capital, and golf courses. The company's prominent Shea Homes builds a variety of planned communities and other residences in seven states.

The Shea family owns J.F. Shea, which was founded as a plumbing company in 1881. Over the course of its history, the company has worked on engineering icons like the Hoover Dam and the Golden Gate Bridge in addition to San Francisco's urban transit system, the Bay Area Rapid Transit (BART).

Current projects include a water purification and desalination project in Southern California (with Tetra Tech) and a tunnel and expansion project for the New York City subway system with a consortium that includes Skanska and Schiavone Construction.

EXECUTIVES

Chairman: John F. Shea
President and CEO: Peter O. Shea Jr., age 41
CFO and Secretary: James G. (Jim) Shontere
EVP; President, J.F. Shea Construction: Peter O. Shea
EVP: Edmund H. Shea Jr.
VP Taxes: Ron Lakey
Treasurer: Robert R. O'Dell
Senior Technical Manager: Mike Little
Director, Finance: Andy Roundtree
President and CEO, Shea Homes: Bert Selva

LOCATIONS

HQ: J.F. Shea Co., Inc.
655 Brea Canyon Rd., Walnut, CA 91789
Phone: 909-594-9500   **Fax:** 909-594-0917
Web: www.jfshea.com

PRODUCTS/OPERATIONS

Major Units
BlueStar Resort & Golf (golf course in Scottsdale, Arizona)
J.F. Shea Construction, Inc. (commercial buildings, subways, and civil engineering projects)
  J.F. Shea Heavy Civil Engineering (bridges, tunnels, and transit systems)
Reddin3g Construction (sand, gravel, asphalt, and concrete products; highway construction)
Reed Manufacturing (concrete guns and pumps and concrete-placing equipment)
Shea Homes LP (residential units, developed and master-planned communities)
Shea Mortgage (mortgage lender)
Shea Properties LLC (apartment, industrial, and commercial building management)
Venture Capital (investment firm)

COMPETITORS

Austin Industries	Michael Baker
Bechtel	Parsons Corporation
Black & Veatch	Perini
Centex	Peter Kiewit Sons'
Dick Corporation	Pulte Homes
D.R. Horton	The Ryland Group
Fluor	Shapell Industries
Granite Construction	Shaw Group
Halliburton	Standard Pacific
Hyundai Engineering	Technip
Jacobs Engineering	Tutor-Saliba
KB Home	URS
Lennar	Washington Division
M.D.C.	Zachry Group

HISTORICAL FINANCIALS

Company Type: Private

Income Statement

FYE: December 31

	REVENUE ($ mil.)	NET INCOME ($ mil.)	NET PROFIT MARGIN	EMPLOYEES
12/07	2,260	—	—	2,200
12/06	3,180	—	—	2,700
12/05	3,429	—	—	3,299
12/04	3,080	—	—	2,668
12/03	2,597	—	—	2,685
Annual Growth	(3.4%)	—	—	(4.9%)

Revenue History

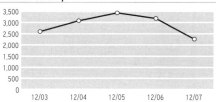

JM Family Enterprises

JM Family Enterprises is a family affair. JM, owned by the family of founder James Moran, is a holding company (Florida's second-largest private company, in fact, after Publix Super Markets) with about a dozen automotive-related businesses, including the world's largest-volume Lexus retailer, JM Lexus, in Margate, Florida. JM's major subsidiary, Southeast Toyota Distributors, is the nation's largest independent Toyota and Scion distribution franchise, delivering Toyota cars, trucks, and SUVs to more than 165 dealers in Alabama, Florida, Georgia, Texas, and Ohio. Following the recent retirement of chairwoman Pat Moran, daughter of the firm's founder, the company is run by CEO Colin Brown.

Among JM Family's other subsidiaries, software marketer JM Solutions acquired Orlando-based DealerUps, a software firm specializing in customer-relations management, in January 2007 for an undisclosed sum.

JM&A Group provides insurance and warranty services to retailers nationwide. World Omni Financial handles leasing, dealer financing, and other financial services for US auto dealers and is one of the largest auto finance firms in the US.

JM Family Enterprises is one of the largest woman-owned companies in the US and consistently ranks in the top half on *FORTUNE* magazine's 100 Best Companies to Work For list on the strength of on-site medical, fitness, and day-care centers.

Pat Moran, who succeeded her father as chairman of the company, retired in early 2007. She remains a director of the diversified family-owned automotive firm. The chairman's post was eliminated upon her retirement.

HISTORY

Jim Moran first became visible as "Jim Moran, the Courtesy Man" in Chicago TV advertisements in the 1950s. At that time he ran Courtesy Motors, where he was so successful as the world's #1 Ford dealer that *Time* magazine put his picture on its cover in 1961.

Moran had entered the auto sales business after fixing up and selling a car for more than three times the price he had paid for it. That profit was much better than what he made at the Sinclair gas station he had bought, so he opened a used-car lot. Later, he moved to new-car sales when he bought a Hudson franchise (Ford had rejected him).

Seeing the promise of TV advertising, in 1948 Moran pioneered the forum for Chicago car dealers, not only as an advertiser and program sponsor but also as host of a variety show and a country/western music barn dance. The increased visibility positioned Moran as Hudson's #1 dealer, but the sales tactics at Courtesy Motors earned an antitrust suit that was settled out of court.

In 1955 Moran started with Ford and, with his TV influence as host of *The Jim Moran Courtesy Hour,* he became the world's #1 Ford dealer in his first month.

He moved to Florida in 1966 after being diagnosed with cancer and given one year to live. Successfully fighting the disease, he bought a Pontiac franchise and later started Southeast Toyota Distributors. In 1969 he formed JM Family Enterprises.

Legal problems cropped up in 1973 when the IRS investigated a Nassau bank serving as a tax haven for wealthy Americans. Moran and three Toyota executives were linked to the bank, and in 1978 Moran was indicted for tax fraud. When an immunity deal fell through, Moran pleaded guilty to seven tax fraud charges in 1984 and was sentenced to two years (suspended), fined more than $12 million, and ordered to perform community service. Moran's legal problems threatened his association with Toyota and were blamed for causing his stroke in 1983.

JM's legal problems continued in the 1980s, partly because of the imposition of auto import restrictions. To get more cars to sell, some Southeast Toyota managers encouraged auto dealers to file false sales reports. Some North Carolina dealers resisted and one sued, settling out of court for $22 million. Other dealers alleged racketeering and fraud on the part of Southeast Toyota, and by the beginning of 1994, JM had paid more than $100 million in fines and settlements for cases stretching back to 1988. In spite of that, Toyota renewed its contract with the company in 1993, a year ahead of schedule.

Pat Moran succeeded her father as JM president in 1992. Between 1991 and 1994 three suits were filed against Jim and Southeast Toyota alleging racism against blacks in establishing Toyota dealerships. All three suits were settled.

Jim teamed with Wayne Huizenga in 1996 to launch a national chain of used-car megastores under the name AutoNation USA, which Jim expected would draw buyers to his own auto dealerships. (AutoNation USA's first store was built just two blocks from JM's Coconut Creek Lexus Dealership.) Jim's interest in AutoNation USA was converted into a small percentage (less than 5%) of Republic Industries stock after Huizenga merged AutoNation into waste hauler Republic Industries (now called AutoNation) in 1997.

In late 1998 JM embarked on a national strategy to expand its presence outside the Southeast, establishing an office in St. Louis that handles indirect consumer leasing.

In 2000 Jim became honorary chairman while Pat was given the chairman position and continued as CEO; COO Colin Brown was named president. Also that year the company was named the 51st Best Company to Work For in the United States by *FORTUNE* magazine. The company's rank in the Best Company to Work For list rose to 20th place in 2001.

In March 2003 Brown assumed the CEO title, with Pat Moran continuing in the chairman position. In 2004 the company ranked first in the nation in dealer service contract satisfaction according to J.D. Power and Associates and sat at 25 on *FORTUNE*'s Best Company to Work For list.

In early 2007 Pat Moran retired. In April of that year, founder and honorary chairman James Moran died at the age of 88.

EXECUTIVES

President and CEO: Colin Brown
EVP and CFO: Mark S. Walter
EVP; President, JM&A Group: Louis Feagles
EVP; President, JMsolutions: Scott Barrett
EVP; President, JM & A Group: Forrest Heathcott
EVP; President, World Omni Financial Corporation: Brent Burns
EVP, CIO, Chief Administrative Officer; President, JM Service Center: Ken Yerves
EVP; President, Southeast Toyota Distributors LLC; President, JM Lexus: Ed Sheehy, age 47
SVP World Omni Financial Corp.: Frank Armstrong
SVP: Jan Moran

VP and Treasurer: Cheryl Scully
VP Aviation and Marine: George Kokinakis
VP Learning and Organizational Development: Lisa Wheeler
VP Technology Delivery and Architecture: Rajeev Ravindran
VP and General Manager, JM Lexus: Jim Dunn
VP Sales and Strategic Alliances, JM&A Group: T. Michael (Mike) Casey
VP and Chief Division Counsel, JM Service Center: Caren Snead Williams
VP JM Service Center: Eduardo Rivera
VP Government Relations: Sonya R. Deen
VP Medical Services: Richard Luceri

LOCATIONS

HQ: JM Family Enterprises, Inc.
100 Jim Moran Blvd., Deerfield Beach, FL 33442
Phone: 954-429-2000   **Fax:** 954-429-2300
Web: www.jmfamily.com

JM Family Enterprises operates auto retail, distribution, leasing, and financing businesses across the US, mainly in Alabama, Florida, Georgia, and North and South Carolina.

PRODUCTS/OPERATIONS

Selected Subsidiaries

Finance and Leasing
  Centerone Financial Services
  World Omni Financial Corp.

Insurance, Marketing, Consulting, and Related Companies
  Courtesy Insurance Company
  Fidelity Insurance Agency, Inc.
  Fidelity Warranty Services, Inc.
  Jim Moran & Associates, Inc.
  JM&A Group (auto service contracts, insurance)
  J.M.I.C. Life Insurance Co.

Retail Car Sales
  JM Lexus

Software
  JMsolutions (customer relationship management software)

Vehicle Processing and Distribution
  SET Inland Processing
  SET Parts Supply and Distribution
  SET Port Processing
  SET Westlake Processing
  Southeast Toyota Distributors, LLC

COMPETITORS

AutoNation	Hendrick Automotive
CarMax	Holman Enterprises
Ed Morse Auto	Island Lincoln-Mercury
Gulf States Toyota	Penske Automotive Group

HISTORICAL FINANCIALS

Company Type: Private

Income Statement

FYE: December 31

	REVENUE ($ mil.)	NET INCOME ($ mil.)	NET PROFIT MARGIN	EMPLOYEES
12/07	12,200	—	—	4,700
12/06	11,100	—	—	4,600
12/05	9,400	—	—	4,300
Annual Growth	13.9%	—	—	4.5%

Revenue History

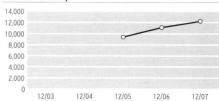

J.M. Huber

As great as toothpaste, paint, and tires may be, J.M. Huber claims to make them even better. Hard to believe, we know. Founded in 1890 by Joseph M. Huber and still owned by his heirs, the company makes specialty additives and minerals used to thicken and improve the cleaning properties of toothpaste, the brightness and gloss of paper, the strength and durability of rubber, and the flame retardant properties of wire and cable. The diverse company also makes oriented strand board (a plywood substitute), explores for and produces oil and gas, and provides technical and financial services. Huber also makes hydrocolloids (thickeners for gums) through subsidiary CP Kelco.

Huber also manages approximately 500,000 acres of timberland in Maine and the southeastern US, and has oil and gas operations in Texas, Colorado, Kansas, Utah, and Wyoming.

Huber acquired a minority stake in CP Kelco from Hercules in 2004, and then turned around and bought the rest of the company from Lehman Brothers later that same year. The company has since combined its Noviant (hydrocolloids) business with CP Kelco; the two subsidiaries operate under the CP Kelco brand.

EXECUTIVES

Chairman, President, and CEO: Peter T. Francis
CFO: Jeffrey (Jeff) Prosinski
CIO: Vincent Solano
VP and General Counsel: Ed Castorina
VP Human Resources: Niall Mulkeen
VP Chief Communications and Public Affairs Officer: Robert (Bob) Currie
CEO, Demica: Phillip Kerle
President, CP Kelco: Donald (Don) Rubright
President, Huber Engineered Materials: Michael (Mike) Marberry
President, Huber Engineered Woods LLC: Brian Carlson
President and CEO, Shelterwood Financial Services LLC: William Rankin
President, Huber Energy: Ralph Schofield

LOCATIONS

HQ: J.M. Huber Corporation
333 Thornall St., Edison, NJ 08837
Phone: 732-549-8600   **Fax:** 732-549-7256
Web: www.huber.com

J. M. Huber Corporation has operations in Asia, Europe, Latin America, and North America.

PRODUCTS/OPERATIONS

Selected Operations

Engineered Materials
  CP Kelco (food, pharmaceutical, household, and industrial gums)
    Noviant (carboxymethyl cellulose, hydrocolloids for paper, food, hygiene, and industrial uses)
  Huber Engineered Materials (engineered minerals and specialty chemicals)
  Huber Engineered Woods (high-performance specialty woods, including oriented strand board)
Natural Resources
  Huber Energy (oil and gas acquisition, exploration, and production)
  Huber Timber (timberland management)
Technology-based Services
  Demica (trade receivables securitization)
  Huber Resources Corporation (yield maximization from timberland)
  Shelterwood Financial Services LLC (investment management and business consulting)

COMPETITORS

ADM
Baker Hughes
Danisco A/S
Evonik Degussa
Georgia-Pacific
Imerys
Kerry Group
Minerals Technologies
Occidental Petroleum

HISTORICAL FINANCIALS

Company Type: Private

Income Statement

FYE: December 31

	REVENUE ($ mil.)	NET INCOME ($ mil.)	NET PROFIT MARGIN	EMPLOYEES
12/07	2,100	—	—	4,500
12/06	2,220	—	—	5,000
12/05	2,300	—	—	5,000
12/04	2,400	—	—	5,000
12/03	1,805	—	—	4,850
Annual Growth	3.9%	—	—	(1.9%)

Revenue History

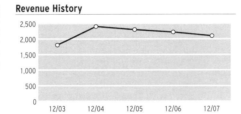

Johnny Rockets

Hep cats still hang out at Johnny Rockets restaurants, where U-shaped counters, padded booths, table-top jukeboxes, and white uniforms salute the classic American diner. The Johnny Rockets Group operates and franchises more than 200 restaurants in 30 states and a dozen other countries that specialize in such classic diner fare as hamburgers, malts, fries, and apple pie. About two-thirds of the locations are operated by franchisees. The chain was founded by Ronn Teitelbaum, who opened the first Johnny Rockets on Los Angeles' fashionable Melrose Avenue in 1986. The company was acquired by RedZone Capital, an investment fund led by Washington Redskins owner Dan Snyder, in 2007.

Snyder purchased Johnny Rockets from Apax Partners with plans to fund an aggressive expansion campaign. With the deep pockets of its new owner, the chain hopes to add 1,000 new locations by 2012. It also launched a new concept called Johnny Rockets Express, a smaller-format eatery designed for airports, malls, and other high-traffic locations. In addition, Johnny Rockets inked a deal with Six Flags (another business controlled by Snyder) to open more than 25 restaurants at its amusement parks.

Longtime CEO Michael Shumsky resigned in 2007 and was replaced by former Buffalo Wild Wings executive Lee Sanders.

Teitelbaum, who died of brain cancer in 2000, was an award-winning men's fashion retailer for nearly 20 years before he tried his hand at the restaurant business. He first sold Johnny Rockets in 1995 to an investor group led by Patricof & Co. (later Apax Partners).

EXECUTIVES

Chairman: Christopher J. (Chris) Ainley
President and CEO: Lee Sanders, age 54
CFO: John Fuller
SVP Franchise Sales and Development: Dave Eberle
VP Operations: Brett Babick
VP Development: Shelley Donovan
Director Design and Construction: Mike Shotzbarger
Director Human Resources: Terri Pattello
Marketing Manager: Chad Bailey
Controller: Denise Campos
Franchise Development: Christopher Sheets
Auditors: Ernst & Young LLP

LOCATIONS

HQ: The Johnny Rockets Group, Inc.
25550 Commercentre Dr., Ste. 200,
Lake Forest, CA 92630
Phone: 949-643-6100   **Fax:** 949-643-6200
Web: www.johnnyrockets.com

COMPETITORS

Applebee's
Brinker
Bubba Gump Shrimp
California Pizza Kitchen
Carlson Restaurants
Cheesecake Factory
Darden
Denny's
Fuddruckers
OSI Restaurant Partners
Red Robin
Ruby Tuesday
Steak n Shake

HISTORICAL FINANCIALS

Company Type: Private

Income Statement

FYE: April 30

	REVENUE ($ mil.)	NET INCOME ($ mil.)	NET PROFIT MARGIN	EMPLOYEES
4/08	231	—	—	—
4/07	209	—	—	—
4/06	199	—	—	—
4/05	177	—	—	—
4/04	147	—	—	—
Annual Growth	12.0%	—	—	—

Revenue History

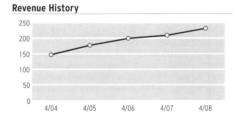

Johnson Publishing

Snubbed by advertisers when he founded his company 60 years ago, the late John Johnson pushed his magazine company to the front of the pack. Led by its flagship publication, *Ebony*, family-owned Johnson Publishing Company is a black-owned global publishing firm. The company also publishes *Jet* and operates the JPC Book Division. In addition, Johnson Publishing produces a line of cosmetics (Fashion Fair Cosmetics) marketed for African-American women, and each year it hosts the Ebony Fashion Fair, a traveling fashion show that raises money for scholarships and charities in cities across the US and Canada.

The company's book division features titles such as *The New Ebony Cookbook* and the more controversial *Forced Into Glory: Abraham Lincoln's White Dream.*

In 2007 the company formed the EBONY/JET Entertainment Group to oversee the creation and distribution of branded entertainment content through theatrical, broadcast, cable, and digital (video on demand and mobile) platforms.

Johnson Publishing is owned and controlled by family members of founder Johnson, who died in 2005. His daughter, Linda Johnson Rice, handles the day-to-day operations as president and CEO. His wife Eunice produces the Ebony Fashion Fair.

HISTORY

John H. Johnson launched his publishing business in 1942 while he was still in college in Chicago. The idea for a black-oriented magazine came to him while he was working part-time for Supreme Life Insurance Co. of America, where one of his jobs was to clip magazine and newspaper articles about the black community. Johnson used his mother's furniture as collateral to secure a $500 loan and then mailed $2 charter subscription offers to potential subscribers. He received 3,000 replies and used the $6,000 to print the first issue of *Negro Digest,* patterned after *Reader's Digest.* Circulation was 50,000 within a year.

Johnson started *Ebony* magazine in 1945 (which gained immediate popularity and is still the company's premier publication) and launched *Jet* in 1951, a pocket-sized publication containing news items and features. In the early days Johnson was unable to obtain advertising, so he formed his own Beauty Star mail-order business and advertised its products (dresses, wigs, hair care products, and vitamins) in his magazines. He won his first major account, Zenith Radio, in 1947; Johnson landed Chrysler in 1954, only after sending a salesman to Detroit every week for 10 years. For 20 years, *Ebony* and *Jet* were the only national publications targeting blacks in the US.

By the 1960s Johnson had become one of the most prominent black men in the US. He posed with John F. Kennedy in 1963 to publicize a special issue of *Ebony* celebrating the Emancipation Proclamation. US magazine publishers named him Publisher of the Year in 1972. Johnson launched *Ebony Jr!* (since discontinued) in 1973, a magazine designed to provide "positive black images" for black preteens. His first magazine, *Negro Digest* (renamed *Black World*), became known for its provocative articles, but its circulation dwindled from 100,000 to 15,000. Johnson retired the magazine in 1975.

Unable to find the proper makeup for his *Ebony* models, Johnson founded his own cosmetics business, Fashion Fair Cosmetics, that year, which carved out a niche beside Revlon (which introduced cosmetic lines for blacks) and another black cosmetics company, Johnson Products (unrelated) of Chicago. By 1982 Fashion Fair sales were more than $30 million.

The company got into broadcasting in 1972 when it bought Chicago radio station WGRT (renamed WJPC; that city's first black-owned station). It added WLOU (Louisville, Kentucky) in 1982 and WLNR (Lansing, Illinois; re-launched in 1991 as WJPC-FM) in 1985. By 1995, however, it had sold all of its stations.

Johnson and the company sold their controlling interest in the last minority-owned insurance company in Illinois (and Johnson's first employer), Supreme Life Insurance, to Unitrin (a Chicago-based life, health, and property insurer) in 1991. That year the company and catalog retailer Spiegel announced a joint venture to develop fashions for black women. The two companies launched a mail-order catalog called *E Style* in 1993 and an accompanying credit card the next year.

Johnson Publishing launched its South African edition of *Ebony* in 1995. Johnson was awarded the Presidential Medal of Freedom in 1996. The next year, however, circulation of *Ebony* fell 7% as mainstream magazines began covering black issues more thoroughly and a host of new titles appeared. In response, the company restructured its ventures and closed its *E Style* catalog. Johnson Publishing retired *Ebony Man* (launched in 1985) in 1998 and *Ebony South Africa* in 2000.

In 2002 John Johnson named his daughter Linda Johnson Rice as CEO of the company; Johnson kept the title of chairman and publisher. John Johnson died at the age of 87 in 2005.

EXECUTIVES

Chairman and CEO: Linda Johnson Rice, age 50
Vice Chairman and General Counsel:
  June Acie Rhinehart
SVP and Associate Publisher, Advertising: Jeff Burns Jr.
SVP and Midwest Advertising Director:
  Dennis H. Boston
SVP Fashion Fair Cosmetics: J. Lance Clark
VP and CFO: Treka Owens
VP and Director Manufacturing and Sales:
  Tammy E. Rollé
VP and Director Western Advertising: Barbara E. Rudd
VP and Editorial Director, EBONY and JET Magazines:
  Bryan Monroe
VP Multimedia Resources: Pamela Cash Menzies
Assistant VP Licensing: Lisa M. Butler
Assistant VP and Director Human Resources:
  Sheila Jenkins
Secretary and Treasurer; Producer and Director,
  EBONY Fashion Fair: Eunice W. Johnson
Director Corporate Communications: Wendy E. Parks
Director Information Technology: Eric Haynes
Director National Marketing: Raquel Graham Crayton
Director Research: Aeisha Powell
Director Circulation: Robert S. Acquaye
Group Publisher: Kenard E. Gibbs
Senior Corporate Counsel: Renée Cogdell Lewis
Chief of Digital Strategy: Eric Easter
Executive Editor Emeritus, EBONY: Lerone Bennett Jr.
President and COO; President and COO Fashion Fair
  Cosmetics: Anne S. Ward, age 36

LOCATIONS

HQ: Johnson Publishing Company, Inc.
  820 S. Michigan Ave., Chicago, IL 60605
Phone: 312-322-9200   **Fax:** 312-322-0918
Web: www.johnsonpublishing.com

PRODUCTS/OPERATIONS

Selected Operations

Book publishing
Fashion and beauty products
  Ebony Fashion Fair (traveling fashion show)
  Fashion Fair Cosmetics (color cosmetics, fragrances, skincare)
Magazines
  Ebony
  Jet

COMPETITORS

Advance Publications
Alberto-Culver
Avon
BET
Earl G. Graves
Essence Communications
Estée Lauder
Forbes
Hearst Magazines
LFP
L'Oréal
Mary Kay
Meredith Corporation
Revlon
Time Inc.

HISTORICAL FINANCIALS

Company Type: Private

Income Statement

FYE: December 31

	REVENUE ($ mil.)	NET INCOME ($ mil.)	NET PROFIT MARGIN	EMPLOYEES
12/07	453	—	—	503
12/06	458	—	—	1,100
12/05	496	—	—	1,707
12/04	498	—	—	—
12/03	489	—	—	2,000
Annual Growth	(1.9%)	—	—	(29.2%)

Revenue History

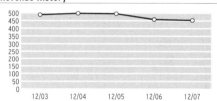

JohnsonDiversey, Inc.

JohnsonDiversey is the industrial-strength version of S.C. Johnson & Son. Split off from the well-known private company in 1999, JohnsonDiversey provides professional commercial cleaning, hygiene, pest control, and food sanitation products to retailers, building service contractors, hospitality firms, and foodservice operators. It is the #2 global industrial and institutional cleaning products firm (behind Ecolab), selling its products in more than 170 countries, with Europe representing more than half of its sales. It operates across 33 manufacturing facilities located in almost 25 countries. The Johnson family controls two-thirds of the company; Unilever controls the rest.

The firm changed its name from S.C. Johnson Commercial Markets to JohnsonDiversey in 2002 after acquiring DiverseyLever, Unilever's industrial cleaning business. The acquisition of DiverseyLever more than doubled the company's sales.

In November 2005 JohnsonDiversey announced a corporate restructuring, cutting its worldwide work force by 10% over the next two to three years. As a result, the company began exiting its services to health and hospitality customers, though it will continue to sell products to them. JohnsonDiversey will also be closing a number of factories. Plants in Cambridge, Maryland and East Stroudsburg, Pennsylvania closed in 2006, eliminating 500 workers.

In association with the 2005 restructuring plan, JohnsonDiversey sold its Auto-Chlor branch operations, a unit that sold dishwashing systems and laundry and kitchen chemicals, for about $70 million in late 2007. Its Polymer unit, which made acrylic resins used in printing, packaging, and adhesives, was sold to BASF in mid-2006.

EXECUTIVES

Chairman: Samuel Curtis (Curt) Johnson III, age 52, $693,750 pay
President, CEO, and Director: Edward F. (Ed) Lonergan, age 48, $941,667 pay
EVP and CFO: Joseph F. (Joe) Smorada, age 61, $460,000 pay
SVP and Chief Scientific Officer, Research Development and Engineering:
Stephen A. (Steve) Di Biase, age 55
SVP Global Value Chain: Gregory F. Clark, age 54
SVP and Chief Marketing Officer: Nabil Shabshab, age 42
SVP Corporate Affairs and Director, Office of the President: John W. Matthews, age 48
SVP Global Human Resources: James W. (Jim) Larson, age 55
SVP, General Counsel, and Secretary: Scott D. Russell, age 45
VP and Corporate Treasurer: Lori P. Marin, age 46
VP and CIO: Matt Peterson, age 43
VP and Corporate Controller: P. Todd Herndon, age 42
Auditors: Ernst & Young LLP

LOCATIONS

HQ: JohnsonDiversey, Inc.
8310 16th St., Sturtevant, WI 53177
Phone: 262-631-4001   **Fax:** 262-631-4282
Web: www.johnsondiversey.com

2007 Sales

	$ mil.	% of total
Europe	1,617.0	52
Americas		
North America	798.6	25
Latin America	226.9	7
Asia		
Japan	281.7	9
Asia/Pacific	224.5	7
Adjustments	(18.6)	—
Total	**3,130.1**	**100**

COMPETITORS

Arrow-Magnolia
Clorox
Colgate-Palmolive
Dow Chemical
Ecolab
Kimberly-Clark
NCH
Procter & Gamble
Zep Inc.

HISTORICAL FINANCIALS
Company Type: Private

Income Statement   FYE: December 31

	REVENUE ($ mil.)	NET INCOME ($ mil.)	NET PROFIT MARGIN	EMPLOYEES
12/07	3,130	(87)	—	11,500
12/06	2,928	118	4.0%	11,000
12/05	3,310	(167)	—	12,000
12/04	3,169	14	0.4%	12,000
12/03	2,948	24	0.8%	13,000
Annual Growth	**1.5%**	**—**	**—**	**(3.0%)**

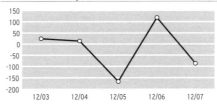

Net Income History

Jones Day

Legal leviathan Jones Day ranks as one of the world's largest law firms, providing counsel to about half of the *FORTUNE* 500 companies. It has some 2,300 attorneys in about 30 offices worldwide. Outside the US, Jones Day has offices in the Asia/Pacific region and in Europe. The firm's practice areas include capital markets, government regulation, intellectual property, real estate, and tax. Jones Day has counted Bridgestone/Firestone, General Motors, IBM, RJR Nabisco, and Texas Instruments among its clients. The firm traces its roots to the Cleveland law partnership founded by Edwin Blandin and William Rice in 1893.

EXECUTIVES

Managing Partner: Stephen J. Brogan
Partner, Government Regulation, Washington:
Andrew B. (Andy) Steinberg
Global Public Communications Manager:
David R. Petrou
Asia Business Development Manager: Lance Godard
Europe Business Development Manager: Sylvie Marchal
Firm Lateral Recruiting Manager: Kristin G. Edwards

LOCATIONS

HQ: Jones Day
North Point, 901 Lakeside Ave.,
Cleveland, OH 44114
Phone: 216-586-3939   **Fax:** 216-579-0212
Web: www.jonesday.com

PRODUCTS/OPERATIONS

Selected Practice Areas

Antitrust and competition law
Banking and finance
Business restructuring and reorganization
Capital markets
Employee benefits and executive compensation
Energy delivery and power
Environmental, health, and safety
Government regulation
Health care
Intellectual property
International litigation and arbitration
Issues and appeals
Labor and employment
Mergers and acquisitions
Oil and gas
Private equity
Product liability and tort litigation
Real estate
Securities and shareholder litigation and SEC enforcement
Tax
Trial practice

COMPETITORS

Akin Gump
Baker & McKenzie
Cleary Gottlieb
Clifford Chance
Davis Polk
Kirkland & Ellis
Latham & Watkins
Mayer Brown
McDermott Will & Emery
Shearman & Sterling
Sidley Austin
Skadden, Arps
White & Case

HISTORICAL FINANCIALS
Company Type: Partnership

Income Statement   FYE: December 31

	REVENUE ($ mil.)	NET INCOME ($ mil.)	NET PROFIT MARGIN	EMPLOYEES
12/07	1,441	—	—	—
12/06	1,310	—	—	4,977
12/05	1,285	—	—	4,850
Annual Growth	**5.9%**	**—**	**—**	**2.6%**

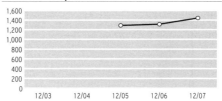

Revenue History

Jones Financial Companies

This isn't your father's broker. Well, maybe it is. The Jones Financial Companies is the parent of Edward Jones, an investment brokerage network catering to individual investors. Most of its clients are retirees and small-business owners in rural communities and suburbs. The "Wal-Mart of Wall Street" has thousands of satellite-linked offices in all 50 states plus Canada and the UK. Brokers preach a conservative buy-and-hold approach, offering relatively low-risk investment vehicles such as government bonds, blue-chip stocks, and high-quality mutual funds. The company also sells insurance and engages in investment banking, underwriting and distributing securities for corporate and municipal clients.

Edward Jones' network of more than 10,000 offices — many of them with a single broker — makes it one of the largest brokerage networks in the world. The firm embraces technology, maintaining one of the industry's largest satellite networks (including a dish for each office).

Preferring to groom brokers internally, the firm accepts applicants with no previous experience, trains them extensively, and monitors investment patterns to prevent account churning and trading in risky low-cap stocks. Before they are given such luxuries as office space or assistants, new brokers must make 1,000 cold calls in their chosen community. Edward Jones' investment in training, backed by what's perceived to be old-school values and strong ethics, seems to be paying off: The firm is consistently ranked among *FORTUNE* magazine's "100 Best Companies to Work For."

The Jones Companies is the only major financial services firm still organized as a partnership, and it has said it has no plans to go public.

HISTORY

Jones Financial got its start in 1871 as bond house Whitaker & Co. In 1922 Edward D. Jones (no relation to the Edward D. Jones of Dow Jones fame) opened a brokerage in St. Louis. In 1943 the two firms merged.

Jones' son Edward "Ted" Jones Jr. joined the firm in 1948. Under Ted's leadership (and against his father's wishes), the company focused on rural customers, opening its first branch in the Missouri town of Mexico in 1955 and beginning its march across small-town America. Ted took over as managing partner in 1968, masterminding the company's small-town expansion. (The Wal-Mart comparison is apt; Ted Jones and Sam Walton were good friends.)

Almost from the start, the firm hammered home a conservative investment message focusing on blue-chip stocks and bonds. It expanded steadily throughout the years, adding offices with such addresses as Cedarburg, Wisconsin, and Paris, Illinois.

In the 1970s Edward D. Jones moved into underwriting, with clients including Southern Co., Citicorp, and Humana. (It got burned in the mid-1980s on one such deal, when the SEC accused the company of fraud in a bond offering for life insurer D.H. Baldwin Co., which later filed for bankruptcy.)

The company's technological bent was spurred in 1978 after its Teletype network couldn't handle the demand generated by the firm's 220 offices. As a stopgap, the company nixed use of the Teletype for stock quotes, telling its brokers to call Merrill Lynch's toll-free number instead.

Managing partner John Bachmann took over from Ted Jones in 1980. (Bachmann started at the company as a janitor.) A follower of management guru Peter Drucker, Bachmann inculcated the company's brokers with Drucker's customer- and value-oriented principles.

Edward D. Jones began moving into the suburbs and into less-than-posh sections of big cities in the mid-1980s. In 1986 the company started a mortgage program, but the plan was never successful and was ended in 1988. The company weathered the 1987 stock market crash (many brokerages did not), albeit with thinner profit margins.

In 1990 Ted Jones died. The first half of the decade was a time of great expansion for the company as it doubled its number of offices. In 1993 the company opened an office in Canada.

In 1994 Jones Financial's acquisition of Columbia, Missouri-based thrift Boone National gave it the ability to offer trust and mortgage services to its clients, which helped sales as Jones started facing competition from Merrill Lynch in its small-town niche. The company's rapid expansion and relatively expensive infrastructure (all those one-person offices add up) began to eat at the bottom line, and in 1995 Bachmann stopped expansion so the firm could catch its breath.

In 1997 Edward Jones (which had unofficially dropped its middle "D" to boost name recognition) moved overseas, opening its first offices in the UK, a prime expansion target for the company. The next year the firm teamed up with Mercantile Bank to offer small-business loans. Jones resumed its expansionist push in 1999 and 2000, adding offices in all its markets.

In 2004 Edward Jones was one of several brokerage firms investigated for allegedly failing to disclose the incentives its brokers received for certain mutual fund sales. To settle the matter, the firm paid a $75 million penalty distributed to Edward Jones customers; also, managing partner Douglas Hill was required to step down in 2005 as part of an agreement with a US District Attorney investigating the matter.

The company sold its lone banking subsidiary, Boone National Savings and Loan, which had four branches in Columbia, Missouri, to Commerce Bancshares in 2006.

EXECUTIVES

CEO and Managing Partner: James D. (Jim) Weddle, age 54, $184,954 pay
General Partner, Canadian Operations: Gary D. Reamey, age 52, $159,954 pay
General Partner, Operations, Service, Information Systems, and Human Resources: Norman L. Eaker, age 52, $184,954 pay
General Partner, Products, Services, and Marketing: Brett Campbell, age 48
General Partner, United Kingdom Operations: Tim Kirley, age 53
General Partner, Legal and Compliance: James Tricarico Jr., age 55
Chief Market Strategist: Alan F. Skrainka
CIO: Vinny Ferrari
Principal, Financial Advisor Training and Development: Dann Timm
Principal, Service: Randy Haynes
Principal, Compliance: Pamela (Pam) Cavness
Principal, Internal Audit: Tony Damico
Principal, Human Resources: Ken Dude
Management Development: Robert (Bob) Virgil Jr.
Auditors: PricewaterhouseCoopers LLP

LOCATIONS

HQ: The Jones Financial Companies, L.L.L.P.
   12555 Manchester Rd., Des Peres, MO 63131
Phone: 314-515-2000   **Fax:** 314-515-2622
Web: www.edwardjones.com

PRODUCTS/OPERATIONS

2007 Sales

	$ mil.	% of total
Commissions	1,858.2	45
Asset fees	1,098.6	27
Account & activity fees	441.0	11
Principal transactions	384.6	9
Interest & dividends	309.4	7
Investment banking	34.7	1
Other	20.3	—
Total	**4,146.8**	**100**

COMPETITORS

Charles Schwab
Citigroup
E*TRADE Financial
FMR
Legg Mason
Morgan Stanley
National Financial Partners
Oppenheimer Holdings
Piper Jaffray
Raymond James Financial
T. Rowe Price
TD Ameritrade
UBS Financial Services
Wachovia Securities

HISTORICAL FINANCIALS

Company Type: Partnership

Income Statement

FYE: December 31

	REVENUE ($ mil.)	NET INCOME ($ mil.)	NET PROFIT MARGIN	EMPLOYEES
12/07	4,147	—	—	38,100
12/06	3,518	—	—	34,300
12/05	3,190	—	—	32,400
12/04	2,891	—	—	31,400
12/03	2,539	—	—	29,200
Annual Growth	13.0%	—	—	6.9%

Revenue History

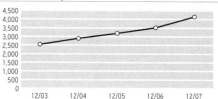

J.R. Simplot

J.R. Simplot hopes you'll have fries with that. Potato potentate J. R. "Jack" Simplot simply shook hands with McDonald's pioneer Ray Kroc in the mid-1960s, and his company's french fry sales have sizzled ever since. The company still remains the major french fry supplier for McDonald's and supplies Burger King, KFC, and Wendy's, as well. It produces more than 3 billion pounds of french fries and hash browns annually, making it one of the world's largest processors of frozen potatoes. The company sells its potato products mainly to food service customers under Simplot and private-label brands.

Along with potatoes, J.R. Simplot also produces fruits and vegetables under the RoastWorks and Simplot Classic labels. The company's spuds sprouted other businesses as well, including cattle ranches and feedlots (which use feed made from potato peels). Its AgriBusiness Group mines phosphates (for fertilizer and feed) and silica. The company's Turf and Horticulture Group produces grass and turf seed and fertilizer.

In 2008 the company acquired Washington State-based H&R Ag, an agricultural retailer that supplies crop nutrition and protection products to farmers. With operations in Washington and Oregon, H&R fits into the Simplot intended strategy to expand into new key products, services, and areas in the Northwest US.

In addition to the US, Simplot has foreign operations in Australia, Canada, China, Europe, Korea, Mexico, and Guatemala.

Founder Jack Simplot died in 2008. Officially retired from the company in 1994, he was one of the wealthiest people in America.

Since 1979 the company has been sponsoring the Simplot Games, an athletic competition held each February at Idaho State University. The games feature track-and-field events, in an indoor venue, for high school athletes from Canada and the US. Several participants have gone on to international competition as Olympians.

HISTORY

J.R. Simplot was born in Dubuque, Iowa, in 1909. His family moved to the frontier town of Declo, Idaho, about a year later. Frustrated with school and an overbearing father, Simplot dropped out at age 14 and moved to a local hotel, where he made money by paying cash for teachers' wage scrip, at 50 cents on the dollar. Simplot then got a bank loan using the scrip as collateral and moved into farming, first by raising hogs and then by growing potatoes. He met Lindsay Maggart, a leading farmer in the area, who taught him the value of planting certified potato seed, rather than potatoes.

Simplot purchased an electric potato sorter in 1928 and eventually dominated the local market by sorting for neighboring farms. By 1940 his company, J.R. Simplot, operated 33 potato warehouses in Oregon and Idaho. The company moved into food processing in the 1940s, first by producing dried onions and other vegetables for Chicago-based Sokol & Co. and later by producing dehydrated potatoes. Between 1942 and 1945 J.R. Simplot produced more than 50 million pounds of dehydrated potatoes for the US military. During the war the company also expanded into fertilizer production, cattle feeding, and lumber. It moved to Boise, Idaho, in 1947.

In the 1950s J.R. Simplot researchers developed a method for freezing french fries. In the mid-1960s Simplot persuaded McDonald's founder, Ray Kroc, to go with his frozen fries, a handshake deal that practically guaranteed Simplot's success in the potato processing industry. By the end of the 1960s Simplot was the largest landowner, cattleman, potato grower, and employer in the state of Idaho. He also had established fertilizer plants, mining operations, and other businesses in 36 states, as well as in Canada and a handful of other countries.

During the oil crisis of the 1970s, J.R. Simplot began producing ethanol from potatoes. However, Simplot's empire-building was not without its rough edges. In 1977 he pleaded no contest to federal charges that he failed to report his income, and the next year he was forced to settle charges that he manipulated Maine potato futures.

The company entered the frozen fruit and vegetable business in 1983. Other ventures included using wastewater from potato processing for irrigation and using cattle manure to fuel methane gas plants. Simplot set up a Chinese joint venture in the 1990s to provide processed potatoes to McDonald's and other customers in East Asia.

The company bought the giant ZX cattle ranch near Paisley, Oregon, in 1994. Simplot retired from the board of directors that year to become chairman emeritus; Stephen Beebe was named president and CEO. The 1995 acquisition of the food operations of Pacific Dunlop (now Ansell) led to the creation of Simplot Australia, one of the largest food processors in Australia. Its 1997 stock swap with I. & J. Foods Australia enlarged the subsidiary's frozen food menu.

In 1999 the company sold its Simplot Dairy Products cheese business to France's Besnier Group, and it teamed with Dutch potato processor Farm Frites to enter new markets. In 2000 it launched agricultural Web site planetAg, bought the turf grass seed assets of AgriBioTech, and added the US potato operations of Nestlé to its pantry.

In 2002 Simplot sold its Australian pudding maker Big Sister to the Fowlers Vacola Group and its Agrisource grain company to a private buyer. That same year Beebe retired and Lawrence Hlobik, president of the company's agribusiness unit, was named CEO. The company closed its only meat-processing plant in 2003.

After being out of the dehydrated potato business for more than 30 years, Simplot acquired the dehydrated potato granule business of Nestlé USA in 2004; in addition, it reached an agreement with Idaho Fresh-Pak to distribute that company's dehydrated potatoes.

In 2004 the company began offering zero-gram trans-fat french fries, called Infinity Fries, for the foodservice market.

In 2005 J. R. Simplot and his wife, Esther, donated their former hilltop home in Boise to the State of Idaho; the structure became the governor's mansion for the state, which previously didn't have an official residence for the governor's family.

Also that year, Simplot stopped producing fertilizer-grade ammonium nitrate; the material can be used to produce devastating explosions, as in the 1995 terrorist attack on the federal building in Oklahoma City.

J. R. Simplot died in 2008.

EXECUTIVES

Chairman: Scott R. Simplot
President, CEO, and Director:
  Lawrence S. (Larry) Hlobik
SVP Finance and CFO: Annette Elg
SVP, Corporate Secretary, and General Counsel:
  Terry Uhling
SVP Retail Operations, AgriBusiness Group:
  Dave DuFault
VP Mining and Manufacturing: Martin Hunt
VP Human Resources: Erin Nuxoll
VP Marketing, Food Group: Alan Kahn
VP Sales, Food Group: Steve Patterson
VP and CIO: Roger Parks
VP Public Relations: Fred Zerza
Director Corporate Communications and Public Relations: Rick Phillips
Director National YUM Brands Accounts: Tim Long
Director Energy and Natural Resources:
  Don Sturdevandt
Manager Marketing Solutions, AgriBusiness:
  Kristi Smith
Manager Consumer Focus Marketing, Food Products:
  Anne Newton
President, Food Group: Kevin Storms
President, AgriBusiness Group: Bill Whitacre

LOCATIONS

HQ: J.R. Simplot Company
  999 Main St., Ste. 1300, Boise, ID 83702
Phone: 208-336-2110   **Fax:** 208-389-7515
Web: www.simplot.com

PRODUCTS/OPERATIONS

Selected Operating Groups

Agriculture Group
  Simplot Feed Ingredients
  Simplot Grower Solutions
  Simplot Plant Nutrients
Food Group
  Avocados
  Other fruits
  Potatoes
  Roastworks
  Vegetables
Industrial Group
  Simplot Industrial Products
  Simplot Silica Sand
Land & Livestock Group
  Simplot Cattle Feeding
  Simplot Farming Operations
  Simplot Ranching Operations
  Simplot Grain Facilities
  Western Stockmen's

Turf & Horticulture Group
  APEX
  BEST
  Jacklin
  Simplot Partners

COMPETITORS

ADM	Golden State Foods
Agri Beef	Heinz
Bayer CropScience	Idaho Supreme Potatoes
Birds Eye	King Ranch
Cactus Feeders	Martin-Brower
Calavo Growers	McCain Foods
Cargill	Michael Foods, Inc.
ConAgra	PotashCorp
ContiGroup	Pro-Fac
Del Monte Foods	Scotts Miracle-Gro
Dow AgroSciences	Scoular
Fairmount Minerals	Seneca Foods
Friona Industries	Tejon Ranch
General Mills	U. S. Silica
Golden Belt Feeders	West Central Co-op

Kaiser Foundation Health Plan

Kaiser Foundation Health Plan aims to be the emperor of the HMO universe. With more than 8.5 million members in nine states and the District of Columbia, it is one of the largest not-for-profit managed health care companies in the US. Kaiser has an integrated care model, offering both hospital and physician care through a network of hospitals and physician practices operating under the Kaiser Permanente name. Members of Kaiser health plans have access to hospitals and some 400 other health care facilities operated by Kaiser Foundation Hospitals and Permanente Medical Groups, associations consisting of about 13,000 doctors.

California is the company's largest market, accounting for some 75% of its members. It also operates in Colorado, Georgia, Hawaii, Maryland, Ohio, Oregon, Virginia, Washington, and the District of Columbia.

Kaiser's strategy for growth and profitability consists of strengthening its integrated care model via increased use of technology and construction of new health care facilities.

HISTORY

Henry Kaiser — shipbuilder, war profiteer, builder of the Hoover and Grand Coulee dams, and founder of Kaiser Aluminum — was a bootstrap capitalist who did well by doing good. A high school dropout from upstate New York, Kaiser moved to Spokane, Washington, in 1906 and went into road construction. During the Depression, he headed the consortium that built the great WPA dams.

It was in building the Grand Coulee Dam that, in 1938, Kaiser teamed with Dr. Sidney Garfield, who earlier had devised a prepayment health plan for workers on California public works projects. As Kaiser moved into steelmaking and shipbuilding during WWII (turning out some 1,400 bare-bones Liberty ships — one per day at peak production), Kaiser decided healthy workers produce more than sick ones, and he called on

Garfield to set up on-site clinics funded by the US government as part of operating expenses. Garfield was released from military service by President Roosevelt for the purpose.

After the war, the clinics became war surplus. Kaiser and his wife bought them — at a 99% discount — through the new Kaiser Hospital Foundation. His vision was to provide the public with low-cost, prepaid medical care. He created the health plan — the self-supporting entity that would administer the system — and the group medical organization, Permanente (named after Kaiser's first cement plant site). He then endowed the health plan with $200,000. This health plan, the classic HMO model, was criticized by the medical establishment as socialized medicine performed by "employee" doctors.

But the plan flourished, becoming California's #1 medical system. In 1958 Kaiser retired to Hawaii and started his health plan there. But physician resistance limited national growth; HMOs were illegal in some states into the 1970s.

As health care costs rose, Congress legalized HMOs in all states. Kaiser expanded in the 1980s; as it moved outside its traditional geographic areas, the company contracted for space in hospitals rather than build them. Growth slowed as competition increased.

Some health care costs in California fell in the early 1990s as more medical procedures were performed on an outpatient basis. Specialists flooded the state, and as price competition among doctors and hospitals heated up, many HMOs landed advantageous contracts. Kaiser, with its own highly paid doctors, was unable to realize the same savings and was no longer the best deal in town. Its membership stalled.

To boost membership and control expenses, Kaiser instituted a controversial program in 1996 in which nurses earned bonuses for cost-cutting. Critics said the program could lead to a decrease in care quality; Kaiser later became the focus of investigations into wrongful death suits linked to cost-cutting in California (where it has since beefed up staffing and programs) and Texas (where it has agreed to pay $1 million in fines).

In 1997 Kaiser and Washington-based Group Health Cooperative of Puget Sound formed Kaiser/Group Health to handle administrative services in the Northwest. Kaiser also tried to boost membership by lowering premiums, but the strategy proved *too* effective: Costs linked to an unwieldy 20% enrollment surge brought a loss in 1997 — Kaiser's first annual loss ever.

A second year in the red in 1998 prompted Kaiser to sell its Texas operations to Sierra Health Services. It also entered the Florida market via an alliance with Miami-based AvMed Health Plan. In 1999 Kaiser announced plans to sell its unprofitable North Carolina operations (it closed the deal the following year).

In 2000 Kaiser announced plans to charge premiums for its Medicare HMO, Medicare Advantage, to offset the shortfall in federal reimbursements. Kaiser also responded to rising costs by selling its unprofitable operations in North Carolina (2000) and Kansas (2001). In 2001 the company's hospital division bought the technology and assets of defunct Internet grocer Webvan in an effort to increase its distribution activity. Also that year the son of a deceased anthrax victim sued a Kaiser facility for failing to recognize and treat his father's symptoms.

Kaiser Permanente hopes to be a permanent leader in US health care. The not-for-profit entity is among the largest integrated health care systems in the US. The company offers health care services through a network of nearly 14,000 physicians belonging to Permanente Medical Groups; 32 medical centers and more than 415 medical offices that form the Kaiser Foundation Hospitals; and the Kaiser Foundation Health Plan, which covers some 8.7 million lives (most of which are in California). Kaiser Permanente is primarily bi-coastal, active in California, Colorado, Georgia, Hawaii, Maryland, Ohio, Oregon, Virginia, Washington, and Washington, DC.

The company's empire is divided into geographic regions: Northern California, Southern California, Colorado, Georgia, Hawaii, Mid-Atlantic States (Maryland, Virginia, and Washington, DC), Ohio, and Oregon/Washington. Although Kaiser Permanente owns hospitals only in California, Hawaii, and Oregon, it operates clinics in several states and provides services to its members in the other areas it operates through contracts with health care facilities. The company has an alliance with Group Health Cooperative that extends its network in the Pacific Northwest.

To better serve its roughly 3.3 million participants in Northern California (nearly 40% of its total enrollment), Kaiser Permanente reorganized its operations in the region, forming eight service areas, each with a major Kaiser-affiliated medical center at its core. The company is doling out a fair amount of money in the state, spending more than $1.2 billion to build four new hospitals and bring its facilities up to earthquake safety codes. Two new medical centers opened in the region (near San Francisco) in 2007. Kaiser is also expanding its operations by building new facilities in Southern California, Oregon, and Georgia.

In addition to providing health care plans and services, Kaiser Permanente conducts medical research and offers health education to the communities it serves. The organization is also something of a pioneer in health care administration: Its automated electronic medical records system is accessible to members and physicians and should help the company reap significant cost savings. Kaiser is spending some $3 billion over 10 years (from 2003 through 2013) on administrative technology. All of the company's facilities use the HealthConnect system for administration and business functions. In addition, all of Kaiser's outpatient clinics use electronic medical records; its hospitals are gradually implementing the system.

EXECUTIVES

Chairman and CEO: George C. Halvorson
Senior Medical Director, Permanente Federation: Francis J. Crosson
EVP and CFO: Kathy Lancaster
EVP Health Plan Operations: Arthur M. Southam
EVP Health Plan and Hospital Operations Kaiser Foundation Health Plan, Inc. and Kaiser Foundation Hospitals: Bernard J. Tyson

EXECUTIVES

Chairman and CEO: George C. Halvorson
EVP Strategic Planning and CFO: Kathy Lancaster
EVP Health Plan Operations: Arthur M. Southam
EVP Health Plan and Hospital Operations: Bernard J. Tyson, age 47
Chief Compliance Officer; Director: Daniel P. (Dan) Garcia
SVP, Quality and Clinical Systems Support: Louise L. Liang
SVP, Community Benefit; CEO, KP Cal: Raymond J. (Ray) Baxter
SVP Research and Policy Development: Robert M. Crane
SVP Human Resources: Laurence G. O'Neil
SVP Brand Strategy, Communications, and Public Relations: Diane Gage Lofgren
SVP and General Counsel: Steven (Steve) Zatkin
SVP and CIO: Philip (Phil) Fasano
VP and Treasurer: Tom Meier
VP, Clinical Information System (CIS) Project: Bruce Turkstra
Executive Director, The Permanente Federation; Board Member: John H. Cochran Jr.
Auditors: KPMG LLP

LOCATIONS

HQ: Kaiser Foundation Health Plan, Inc.
1 Kaiser Plaza, Oakland, CA 94612
Phone: 510-271-5800   **Fax:** 510-271-6493
Web: www.kaiserpermanente.org

COMPETITORS

Aetna
AMERIGROUP
Blue Cross of California
Blue Shield Of California
CareFirst
CIGNA
Community Health Plan of Washington
Coventry Health Care
First Choice Health
Group Health Cooperative (Puget Sound)
Hawaii Medical Service Association
Health Net
Humana
Molina Healthcare
Oregon Dental
Premera Blue Cross
Regence
Regence BlueShield
Sharp Health Plan
UnitedHealth Group
WellCare
WellPoint

HISTORICAL FINANCIALS

Company Type: Subsidiary

Income Statement

FYE: December 31

	REVENUE ($ mil.)	NET INCOME ($ mil.)	NET PROFIT MARGIN	EMPLOYEES
12/07	37,800	—	—	159,766
12/06	34,400	—	—	156,000
12/05	31,100	—	—	—
12/04	28,000	—	—	—
12/03	25,300	—	—	54,300
Annual Growth	10.6%	—	—	31.0%

Revenue History

SVP Research and Policy Development:
Robert M. Crane
SVP Quality and Clinical Systems Support, Kaiser Foundation Health Plan and Hospitals: Louise L. Liang
SVP and General Counsel: Steven (Steve) Zatkin
SVP and CIO: Philip (Phil) Fasano
SVP National Sales and Account Management:
Thomas A. Curtin Jr.
SVP Customer Service and Program Management:
Jerry Coy
Auditors: KPMG LLP

LOCATIONS

HQ: Kaiser Permanente
1 Kaiser Plaza, Oakland, CA 94612
Phone: 510-271-5800   **Fax:** 510-267-7524
Web: www.kaiserpermanente.org

Local Operating Markets

Colorado Region
 Boulder
 Colorado Springs
 Denver
Georgia Region
 Atlanta
Hawaii Region
 Hawaii
 Kauai
 Maui
 Oahu
Mid-Atlantic States Region
 Baltimore
 Northern Virginia
 Suburban Maryland
 Washington, DC
Northern California Region
 East Bay
 Fresno
 Golden Gate
 North East Bay
 South Bay
 Stanislaus County
 Valley
Ohio Region
 Akron
 Cleveland
Oregon/Washington
 Portland (includes Salem/Longview)
Southern California Region
 Coachella Valley
 Inland Empire
 Kern County
 Metropolitan Los Angeles/West Los Angeles
 Orange County
 San Diego County
 The Valleys
 Tri-Central
 Western Ventura County

COMPETITORS

Adventist Health
Aetna
Blue Cross
Catholic Health Initiatives
Catholic Healthcare Partners
Catholic Healthcare West
CIGNA
The Cleveland Clinic
HCA
Humana
Prince William Health System
Scripps
St. Joseph Health System
Sutter Health
Swedish Health Services
Tenet Healthcare
UnitedHealth Group
ValleyCare Health System

HISTORICAL FINANCIALS
Company Type: Not-for-profit

Income Statement

	REVENUE ($ mil.)	NET INCOME ($ mil.)	NET PROFIT MARGIN	EMPLOYEES
12/07	37,800	2,200	5.8%	159,766
12/06	34,400	1,400	4.1%	156,853
12/05	31,100	—	—	148,884
12/04	28,000	—	—	140,356
12/03	25,300	—	—	147,000
Annual Growth	10.6%	57.1%	—	2.1%

Net Income History

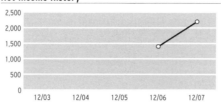

Kaleida Health

Kaleida Health tries to catch you if you fall somewhere in the Snow Belt. Operating five acute-care facilities with some 1,200 beds total, Kaleida Health serves the residents of western New York. The health system's hospitals are Buffalo General Hospital, The Women & Children's Hospital of Buffalo, DeGraff Memorial Hospital, Millard Fillmore Gates Circle Hospital, and Millard Fillmore Suburban Hospital. Primary care needs are met through a network of community and school-based clinics. Kaleida Health also operates four skilled nursing care facilities and provides home health care. To help train future medical professionals, Buffalo General Hospital is a teaching affiliate of the State University of New York.

In 2007 Kaleida Health was ordered by the State of New York to consolidate with fellow Buffalo-based hospital Erie County Medical Center, but both facilities have resisted merging due to a slew of legal, financial, and employment issues.

The following year the two health care organizations reached an agreement to unite under a governing board (the Western New York Healthcare System board) made up of representatives from both companies and the community while continuing to operate their hospitals separately.

EXECUTIVES

Chair: Edward F. Walsh Jr.
President, CEO, and Director: James R. (Jim) Kaskie, age 55
EVP and COO: Connie Vari
EVP and Chief Medical Officer: Margaret Paroski
EVP Human Resources: Eric (Rick) Pogue
CFO: Joseph (Joe) Kessler
SVP Human Resources: David R. Whipple, age 51
SVP Legal Services and General Counsel: Robert Nolan
VP Ambulatory Services and Business Development; Interim President, Millard Fillmore Gates Circle Hospital: Donald (Don) Boyd

VP Public Relations and Government Affairs:
Michael P. (Mike) Hughes
VP Long Term Care: Maureen Caruana
Auditors: KPMG LLP

LOCATIONS

HQ: Kaleida Health
100 High St., Buffalo, NY 14203
Phone: 716-859-5600   **Fax:** 716-859-3323
Web: www.kaleidahealth.org

PRODUCTS/OPERATIONS

Selected Facilities

Buffalo General Hospital
DeGraff Memorial Hospital
Millard Fillmore Gates Circle Hospital
Millard Fillmore Suburban Hospital
Women and Children's Hospital of Buffalo

COMPETITORS

Catholic Health East
Community General
Lifetime Health
Oneida Healthcare Center
St. Joseph's Hospital Health Center
SUNY Upstate Medical University
United Health Services Hospitals
Unity Health System

HISTORICAL FINANCIALS
Company Type: Not-for-profit

Income Statement

	REVENUE ($ mil.)	NET INCOME ($ mil.)	NET PROFIT MARGIN	EMPLOYEES
12/06	1,000	50	5.0%	9,500
12/05	935	26	2.8%	9,500
12/04	872	8	0.9%	10,000
12/03	824	2	0.2%	9,724
Annual Growth	6.7%	192.0%	—	(0.8%)

Net Income History

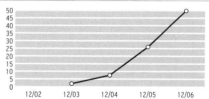

Kellogg Foundation

Charitable grants from W.K. Kellogg Foundation are grrrrrrrrreat! Founded in 1930 by cereal industry pioneer Will Keith Kellogg, the foundation provides more than $280 million in grants annually to a variety of programs focused on youth and education, health, food systems and rural development, and philanthropy and volunteerism. Most of its grants go to initiatives in the US, though it also makes grants throughout Latin America and Africa as well. The work of the W.K. Kellogg Foundation is supported by a related trust; together, the foundation and the trust have assets of about $7 billion — mainly in Kellogg Company stock.

Charity really does begin at home for the W.K. Kellogg Foundation, which allocated nearly a quarter of its US grant money (more than $56 million) to activities in Michigan in 2006.

W.K. Kellogg Foundation is guided by its founder's desire "to help people help themselves" and prefers to support programs that offer long-term solutions rather than quick handouts.

Though they share a founder and a home city, the Kellogg Foundation and the Kellogg Company are governed independently.

HISTORY

Born in 1860, Will Keith Kellogg began his career with jobs as a stock boy and traveling broom salesman. He also worked as a clerk (and, later, bookkeeper and manager) at the Battle Creek Sanitarium, a renowned homeopathic hospital where his older brother, John Harvey Kellogg, was physician-in-chief. The brothers' experiments to improve vegetarian diets led to a happy accident in 1894 that resulted in the first wheat flakes. In 1906 W.K. Kellogg started the Battle Creek Toasted Corn Flake Company. Through marketing genius and innovative products, Kellogg's company became a leader in the industry.

A philanthropist by inclination, Kellogg established the Fellowship Corporation in 1925 to build an agricultural school and a bird sanctuary, as well as to set up an experimental farm and a reforestation project. He also gave $3 million to hometown causes, such as the Ann J. Kellogg School for disabled children, and for the construction of an auditorium, a junior high school, and a youth recreation center.

After attending a White House Conference on Child Health and Protection, Kellogg established the W.K. Kellogg Child Welfare Foundation in 1930. A few months later he broadened the focus of the charter and renamed the institution the W.K. Kellogg Foundation. That year the foundation began its landmark Michigan Community Health Project (MCHP), which opened public health departments in counties once thought too small and poor to sustain them. In 1934 Kellogg placed more than $66 million in Kellogg Company stock and other investments in a trust to fund his foundation.

During WWII the foundation expanded its programming to Latin America, funding advanced schooling for dentists, physicians, and other health professionals. After the war, it broadened its programming to include agriculture to help war-torn Europe. It funded projects in Germany, Iceland, Ireland, Norway, and the UK. Following Kellogg's death in 1951, the organization began providing support for graduate programs in health and hospital administration, as well as for rural leadership and community colleges.

During the 1970s the foundation lent its support to the growing volunteerism movement and to aiding the disadvantaged, with a special emphasis on programs for minorities. A review of operations in the late 1970s led the Kellogg Foundation to reassert its emphasis on health, education, agriculture, and leadership. The foundation also expanded its programs to southern Africa.

In 1986 the Kellogg Foundation began funding the Rural America Initiative — a series of 28 projects meant to develop leadership, train local government officials, and revitalize rural areas. William Richardson became president and CEO of the foundation in 1995, leaving his post as president of The Johns Hopkins University. Also during the 1990s the foundation supported the

Community-Based Public Health Initiative, which assisted universities in educating public health professionals by presenting community-based approaches to students and faculty.

In 1998 the organization announced a five-year, $55 million plan to bring health care to the nation's poor and homeless. Also that year it gave Portland State University a $600,000 grant to develop its Institute for Nonprofit Management. In 1999 the Kellogg Foundation started its first geographically based program, pledging $15 million in grants for development of Mississippi River Delta communities in Arkansas, Louisiana, and Mississippi. In 2001 the foundation pledged an additional $20 million to support economic growth in the region through the Emerging Markets Partnership. In 2002 the Kellogg Foundation awarded about $2 million in grants to SPARK (Supporting Partnerships to Assure Ready Kids) to help prepare low-income children for starting school. The organization funded a national campaign to improve men's health in 2003.

After a decade as president and CEO, Richardson stepped down in 2005. Sterling Speirn, who had led the San Mateo, California-based Peninsula Community Foundation since 1990, took over as president and CEO of the Kellogg Foundation in January 2006.

EXECUTIVES

Chair: Cynthia H. Milligan, age 61
President and CEO: Sterling Speirn, age 60
SVP and Corporate Secretary: Gregory A. Lyman
SVP Programs: James E. McHale
VP Finance and Treasurer: La June Montgomery-Talley
VP and Chief Investment Officer: Paul J. Lawler
VP Programs: Richard M. Foster
VP Programs: Gail D. McClure
VP Programs: Gail C. Christopher
VP Programs: Anne B. Mosle
VP Programs: Gregory B. Taylor
General Counsel and Assistant Corporate Secretary: Mary Carole Cotter
Director Human Resources: Norman (Norm) Howard
Director Policy: Sheri A. Brady
Director Program Learning: Kathleen A. Zurcher
Director Technology: Timothy L. Dechant
Director Public Affairs: Diane E. Price
Auditors: Deloitte & Touche LLP

LOCATIONS

HQ: W.K. Kellogg Foundation
1 Michigan Ave. East, Battle Creek, MI 49017
Phone: 269-968-1611 **Fax:** 269-968-0413
Web: www.wkkf.org

2006 Grants

	$ mil.	% of total
US	235.3	82
Southern Africa	28.2	10
Latin America & the Caribbean	23.3	8
Total	**286.8**	**100**

HISTORICAL FINANCIALS

Company Type: Foundation

Income Statement

FYE: August 31

	REVENUE ($ mil.)	NET INCOME ($ mil.)	NET PROFIT MARGIN	EMPLOYEES
8/07	424	—	—	192
8/06	364	—	—	193
8/05	250	—	—	—
8/04	328	—	—	—
8/03	277	—	—	203
Annual Growth	**11.2%**	**—**	**—**	**(1.4%)**

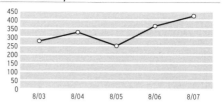

Revenue History

Kellwood Company

Who would be one of the most dominant apparel makers in the US? Kellwood would. It generates the highest percentage of its sales from women's wear, including its Koret and Sag Harbor lines. It also produces men's and children's clothes and hats. Other Kellwood brands include Kelty, Baby Phat, Phat Farm, and Sierra Designs. The company sells its products through department stores, mass retailers, specialty boutiques, and catalogs. Kellwood has gained a foothold in new niches and grown through acquisitions, including Vince, Briggs New York, Group B Clothing, Romance du Jour, Phat Fashions, Gerber Childrenswear, Royal Robbins, and Hanna Andersson. The company was taken private by Sun Capital Partners in 2008.

Kellwood became a portfolio of the private equity firm in February 2008 following Sun Capital's second run at the apparel maker. (Kellwood had rejected a previous offer proffered in September 2007.) The purchase price was $544 million, about the same amount as the first offer. In July 2008 Robert Skinner, Jr., chairman, president, and CEO, was replaced by Michael Kramer as president and CEO. Kramer hails from Abercrombie & Fitch, Apple Retail, and The Limited, among other firms.

As part of its business strategy, Kellwood has been restructuring and cutting its less profitable private-label and small-volume business while expanding its presence through high-margin acquisitions and licensing agreements.

To focus on its more promising consumer lifestyle brands, Kellwood exited or sold a few operating divisions. The reorganization included a jettison of its private label menswear, Intimate Apparel Group (Biflex, LA Intimates, and Dotti divisions), and Kellwood New England (David Brooks and Pink Poodle brands). The company finalized its restructuring efforts by selling its Biflex Intimates Group to Industrial Renaissance.

Kellwood has continued to focus on its licensing revenue — consisting of deals with Accessory Network Group, Calvin Klein, Claiborne, and Phillips-Van Heusen — by partnering with Henry Jacobson LLC in 2007 to make a line of Henry Jacobson shirts, which sell at better specialty and department stores. Kellwood inked a deal in November 2007 to make and distribute Perry Ellis and Perry Ellis Portfolio dress shirts through its distribution division, as well as its Hong Kong-based Smart Shirts Ltd. manufacturing subsidiary. The same month Kellwood announced an agreement it inked to sell its Smart Shirts manufacturing operation to Youngor Group Co., Ltd., for $120 million in cash.

To expand its men's sportswear segment, Kellwood bought the upscale contemporary brand

Hollywould, a maker of footwear, apparel, and accessories, in late 2006.

Looking to extend its reach in the recreation and leisure products area, the company bought rugged outdoors wear unit Royal Robbins from Phoenix Footwear Group in July 2007 for about $40 million. As part of the agreement, Royal Robbins was folded into Kellwood's American Recreation Products division. Kellwood also expanded its upscale offerings with the acquisition of children's apparel maker and retailer Hanna Andersson in mid-2007 for about $175 million. The company planned to open 60 Hanna Andersson stores in the next five years.

EXECUTIVES

President and CEO: Michael W. Kramer, age 43
COO: W. Lee Capps III
CFO: Gregory W. (Greg) Kleffner
EVP, Secretary, and General Counsel: Keith Gyrpp
SVP Retail Outlet: Paul Thomasset
VP Human Resources: J. David (Dave) LaRocca
VP and CIO: Michael M. Saunders
VP Strategy and Chief Marketing Officer:
  George Sokolowski
VP Treasurer and Investor Relations:
  Samuel W. Duggan II
VP Business Development and Special Projects:
  Stephen Walmsley
VP Retail: Bob Ross
Senior Manager Corporate Communications:
  Erin Haggerty

LOCATIONS

HQ: Kellwood Company
  600 Kellwood Pkwy., Chesterfield, MO 63017
Phone: 314-576-3100   **Fax:** 314-576-3460
Web: www.kellwood.com

PRODUCTS/OPERATIONS

Selected Brands and Licenses
Baby Phat
Briggs New York
David Meister (licensed)
Gerber (licensed)
Phat Farm
XOXO (licensed)
Koret
Sag Harbor
Dorby
My Michelle
Vince
Calvin Klein (licensed)
Liz Claiborne dresses & suits (licensed)
O Oscar
Kelty
Sierra Designs
Nautica (licensed)
Claiborne
Northern Isles
Royal Robbins
Hanna Andersson
Hollywould

COMPETITORS

Bernard Chaus	Liz Claiborne
Capital Mercury Apparel	Oxford Industries
Coleman	Perry Ellis International
Columbia Sportswear	Phillips-Van Heusen
Donna Karan	Polo Ralph Lauren
Fruit of the Loom	St. John Knits
Hartmarx	Tommy Hilfiger
Johnson Outdoors	VF
Jones Apparel	Warnaco Group
Levi Strauss	W.L. Gore

HISTORICAL FINANCIALS
Company Type: Private

Income Statement
FYE: January 31

	REVENUE ($ mil.)	NET INCOME ($ mil.)	NET PROFIT MARGIN	EMPLOYEES
1/07	1,962	31	1.6%	30,000
1/06	2,062	(38)	—	30,000
1/05	2,556	66	2.6%	—
1/04	2,347	71	3.0%	—
1/03	2,205	42	1.9%	28,000
Annual Growth	(2.9%)	(7.0%)	—	1.7%

2007 Year-End Financials
Debt ratio: 76.6%   Current ratio: 2.95
Return on equity: 5.0%   Long-term debt ($ mil.): 487
Cash ($ mil.): 341

Net Income History

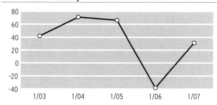

Kentucky Lottery

Kentucky's grass may be blue, but many Kentuckians prefer green — the kind they can stuff into their wallets. For optimists looking to bag some bucks, the Kentucky Lottery offers numbers games (Pick 3, Pick 4, Lotto South) and an array of scratch-off and pull-tab games (Hot Cherries, NutQuacker, Bluegrass Highway). Kentucky also offers the multistate Powerball game. About a quarter of the lottery's proceeds go to education grants and scholarships, literacy programs for adults and children, and Kentucky's General Fund. Launched in 1989, the lottery has introduced new games as it deals with competition from nearby casinos and Tennessee's new lottery. The lottery has raised some $2 billion for the state coffers.

EXECUTIVES

Chairman: Keith Griffee
Vice Chairman: Ray DeSloover
President and CEO: Arthur L. (Arch) Gleason Jr.
Kentucky State Treasurer: Jonathan Miller
EVP and COO: Margaret (Marty) Gibbs
SVP Finance and Administration: Howard Kline
SVP Marketing and Sales: Steve Casebeer
SVP Security: Bill Hickerson
SVP Information Technology: Gary Ruskowski
SVP Internal Audit and Information Security:
  Gale Vessels
SVP, General Counsel, and Corporate Secretary:
  Mary Harville
**VP Communications, Government, and Public
  Relations:** Chip Polston
VP Human Resources: Church Saufley

LOCATIONS

HQ: Kentucky Lottery Corporation
  1011 W. Main St., Louisville, KY 40202
Phone: 502-560-1500   **Fax:** 502-560-1670
Web: www.kylottery.com

The Kentucky Lottery Corporation has regional offices in Bowling Green, Jefferson, Lexington, Louisville, Madisonville, and Prestonsburg, Kentucky.

PRODUCTS/OPERATIONS

Selected Games
Numbers Games
  Kentucky Cash Ball
  Kentucky Powerball
  Lotto South
  Pick 3
  Pick 4
Pull-Tabs
  Aces High
  Cherry Fever
  Paper or Plastic
  Winners Club
Scratch-offs
  Bluegrass Stash
  Instant Cash
  Livin' Lucky
  Roulette Riches
  Snow Dough
  What's Your Number?
  Winning 7's

COMPETITORS

Churchill Downs
Hoosier Lottery
Illinois Lottery
The Trump Organization
Virginia Lottery

HISTORICAL FINANCIALS
Company Type: Government-owned

Income Statement
FYE: June 30

	REVENUE ($ mil.)	NET INCOME ($ mil.)	NET PROFIT MARGIN	EMPLOYEES
6/07	757	(1)	—	—
6/06	743	(13)	—	—
6/05	707	—	—	—
6/04	725	—	—	204
6/03	674	—	—	204
Annual Growth	3.0%	—	—	0.0%

Net Income History

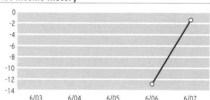

Key Safety Systems

This Key won't start your car, but it will protect the occupants. Key Safety Systems is a leading maker of air bags and air bag components. The company also makes steering wheels and seat belts. Key Safety Systems' line of air bag products includes sensors, inflators, driver-side and steering-wheel air bag combinations, and side-impact air bag systems. The company supplies air bag systems to most of the world's carmakers. Key Safety Systems also makes a line of interior trim products, including automatic and manual shift knobs, parking brake handles, shift and brake boots, armrest covers, and pull handles. The company is controlled by investment firm Crestview Partners.

Carlyle Management Group, the turnaround arm of investment firm The Carlyle Group, bought Key Safety Systems (then known as BREED Technologies) in April 2003. Carlyle Management principal Edward Ewing became CEO and soon announced sweeping cost-cutting plans. The company cut 3,500 jobs across its global operations (27% of the workforce) and negotiated for price breaks from its suppliers.

The company changed its name to Key Safety Systems in 2003 and was folded into Key Automotive Group, which also includes Key Plastics.

In 2004 Carlyle Management, led by Ewing, split off from Carlyle Group to form a new company, Ewing Management. In 2007 private equity group Crestview Partners, in cooperation with Key Safety Systems' management, bought the company from Ewing Management. Terms of the deal were not disclosed, but in 2006 Key Safety Systems had sales of more than $1 billion. The deal did not include Key Plastics.

Later in 2007 Key Safety Systems moved to expand its global footprint when it formed joint venture KSS-ABHISHEK Safety Systems Pvt., Ltd. with Indian partner Abhishek Auto Industries. Based just outside Delhi, India, KSS-ABHISHEK Safety Systems will provide safety systems to the rapidly growing Indian automotive market, as well as for global export.

EXECUTIVES

Chairman: Sir Nicholas V. (Nick) Scheele, age 63
CEO: Jason Luo
SVP and CFO: Dave Smith
SVP Legal: Stuart D. Boyd
SVP Global Sales and Marketing:
 Ronald (Ron) Feldeisen Jr.
SVP Global Human Resources: Larry Casey
SVP Global Purchasing: Steve Dubuc
SVP Global Technology: Wendell C. Lane Jr.
CTO: Mark Wehner
President and COO, Global Airbags: Greg Heald
President and COO, Global Steering Wheels &
 Seatbelts: Jim Scarpa

LOCATIONS

HQ: Key Safety Systems, Inc.
 7000 Nineteen Mile Rd., Sterling Heights, MI 48314
Phone: 586-726-3800   **Fax:** 586-726-4150
Web: www.keysafetyinc.com

PRODUCTS/OPERATIONS

Selected Products
Airbag systems, inflators, and modules
Armrest covers
Electronics (crash sensors)
Parking brake handles
Seat-belt systems
Shift and brake boots
Shift knobs
Steering wheels

COMPETITORS

Analog Devices	OZ Italy Wheel
Autocam	PerkinElmer
Autoliv	Robert Bosch
DENSO	SensoNor
Fondmetal	Siemens AG
Honeywell International	Temic
Motorola, Inc.	Texas Instruments
Oki Electric	Tokai Rika

HISTORICAL FINANCIALS
Company Type: Private

Income Statement
FYE: December 31

	REVENUE ($ mil.)	NET INCOME ($ mil.)	NET PROFIT MARGIN	EMPLOYEES
12/07	1,000	—	—	8,500
12/06	1,030	—	—	8,700
12/05	1,100	—	—	9,000
12/04	1,100	—	—	8,000
12/03	1,100	—	—	10,000
Annual Growth	(2.4%)	—	—	(4.0%)

Revenue History
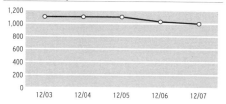

Keystone Foods

Beef is just one of the cornerstones of this food company. Keystone Foods is one of the largest makers of hamburger patties and processed poultry, with more that 28 distribution and processing centers located throughout the world. A major supplier to McDonald's restaurants, Keystone serves nearly 30,000 restaurants worldwide with hamburgers, chicken wings, breast fillets, and chicken patties, as well as fish and pork products. Keystone also provides custom distribution and logistics services to thousands of customers throughout the world. Chairman Herb Lotman owns the company, which began as a beef-boning business in the 1960s.

Keystone has distribution centers in the US, Europe, Asia/Pacific, the Middle East, Australia, and New Zealand. A supplier to McDonald's since 1969, Keystone developed McDonald's chicken nugget in the late 1970s.

EXECUTIVES

Chairman: Herbert (Herb) Lotman, age 74
President and CEO: Jerry Dean
EVP and CFO: John Coggins
SVP USA Poultry: Keith Lewis
SVP Business Development: Ken Brown
SVP and Controller: Paul McGarvie
VP Human Resources and Communications:
 Jerry Gotro
VP USA Distribution: Ken Wierman
VP Quality Assurance and Food Safety: Dane Bernard
VP Research and Development: Chandler Horton
VP USA Beef: Gregg Berens
VP Operations, USA Poultry: Tim Lawson
VP Sales and Marketing, USA Poultry: Jerry Wilson
Auditors: Ernst & Young LLP

LOCATIONS

HQ: Keystone Foods LLC
 300 Barr Harbor Dr., Ste. 600,
 West Conshohocken, PA 19428
Phone: 610-667-6700   **Fax:** 610-667-1460
Web: www.keystonefoods.com

COMPETITORS

ConAgra
Golden State Foods
Lopez Foods
MAINES
Martin-Brower
McLane Foodservice
OSI Group LLC
Perdue Incorporated
Pilgrim's Pride
Reyes Holdings
Royal Ahold
Services Group of America
SYSCO
Tyson Foods
UniPro Foodservice

HISTORICAL FINANCIALS
Company Type: Private

Income Statement
FYE: December 31

	ESTIMATED REVENUE ($ mil.)	NET INCOME ($ mil.)	NET PROFIT MARGIN	EMPLOYEES
12/07	5,580	—	—	13,000
12/06	3,310	—	—	8,000
12/05	3,119	—	—	7,800
12/04	3,000	—	—	7,800
12/03	2,800	—	—	6,500
Annual Growth	18.8%	—	—	18.9%

Revenue History
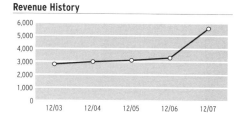

Kings Super Markets

Kings Super Markets has severed all ties to the British monarchy. The regional supermarket chain operates about 25 upscale grocery stores in northern New Jersey and a single store in Garden City, New York. Formerly owned by UK clothing retailer Marks and Spencer, which first put Kings up for sale in 1999, the chain was finally sold — after several unsuccessful attempts — in 2006 to a pair of New York-based private equity firms (Angelo, Gordon & Co. and MTN Capital Partners) and Bruce Weitz, a former CEO of Duane Reade, for about $61 million. Kings Super Markets was founded in 1936.

After the ebb and flow of negotiations had settled, Weitz — who succeeded Dan Portnoy as CEO of the company in August 2006 — announced that Kings had big expansion plans slated for the next five years. The firm's plan includes remodeling existing stores and opening new ones, as well as shopping for single stores or groups of two or three or more. The regional grocery chain also wants to launch an online shopping site.

After putting Kings on the block in 1999, in 2000 M&S opted to keep Kings. An agreement was reached in mid-2002 to sell the company to D'Agostino Supermarkets for $160 million. However, the deal fell through when D'Agostino failed to obtain financing. Talks were then opened with New York-based grocer Gristede's Foods, which offered $120 million for Kings, but that deal also failed to materialize.

EXECUTIVES

Chairman: James A. (Jim) Demme
President and CEO: Bruce Weitz
CFO: Patrick Dentato
EVP Merchandising and Marketing: Fred Brohm
VP Produce and Floral: Paul Kneeland
VP Human Resources: Cherie Bliwise
Senior Director, Marketing and Sales Promotion: Patricia Mikell
Senior Director, Store Operations: Rich Durante
Senior Director, Grocery, Dairy, and Frozen Foods Merchandising: Vince Colatriano
Manager, Community Relations and Consumer Affairs: Cheryl Good
Manager, Loss Prevention, Safety, and Risk: Craig T. Frank
Auditors: PricewaterhouseCoopers LLP

LOCATIONS

HQ: Kings Super Markets, Inc.
700 Lanidex Plaza, Parsippany, NJ 07054
Phone: 973-463-6300   **Fax:** 973-463-6512
Web: www.kingswebsite.com

2007 Stores

	No.
New Jersey	25
New York	1
Total	**26**

COMPETITORS

A&P
Costco Wholesale
Inserra Supermarkets
Stop & Shop
Target
Village Super Market
Wal-Mart
Whole Foods

Kingston Technology

Kingston Technology cuts a regal figure in the realm of memory. The company is a top maker of memory modules — circuit boards loaded with DRAM or other memory chips that increase the capacity and speed of printers and computers. Kingston also makes flash memory cards used in portable electronic devices, such as digital still cameras, MP3 players, and wireless phones. Kingston has taken on some manufacturing chores for customers through its sister company Payton Technology, which runs a specialized factory that tests and packages memory chips before assembling them into customized memory modules. Founders John Tu (president and CEO) and David Sun (COO) own the company.

Tu and Sun promote a casual atmosphere and treat employees as members of an extended family. (Their work cubicles are identical to their employees'.) Since 1996 they have given more than $100 million in bonuses to workers; in some cases the bonuses have amounted to three times the employees' annual salaries.

Kingston is known for its friendliness to business partners. It is sometimes the first to receive scarce components during shortages, thanks to the relations it enjoys with its suppliers.

In late 2002 the company inked a long-term deal with German chip heavyweight Infineon, under which Infineon is to supply much of Kingston's DRAM needs and Kingston is to provide Infineon with contract manufacturing and engineering services. (In 2006 Infineon spun off its memory chip business as Qimonda, retaining majority ownership of the new venture.)

In 2003 Kingston made a $50 million investment in DRAM maker Elpida Memory.

In 2005 Kingston formed a Japanese joint venture, Tera Probe, with Elpida, Advantest, and Powertech Technology, to provide wafer testing services. Kingston's Japanese subsidiary invested ¥3 billion (about $27 million) in Tera Probe, taking an equity stake of around 27%. Tera Probe will serve Elpida and other Japanese semiconductor manufacturers.

HISTORY

Kingston Technology was founded in 1987 by Shanghai-born John Tu and Taiwan-born David Sun, both of whom had moved to California in the 1970s. The pair met in 1982 and started a memory upgrade company called Camminton Technology in Tu's garage. Sales had reached $9 million by 1986, when they sold the business to high-tech firm AST Research for $6 million. The two invested their money in stock market futures but suffered heavy losses when the market crashed in 1987.

That year PC makers were producing computers that lacked the memory needed to run the latest, hottest software, so Tu and Sun sprang into action. With just $4,000 in cash, they started another company that converted inexpensive, outdated chips into memory upgrades. Tu, who was educated in Europe, wanted to call the company Kensington after the gardens in London. A mouse pad company had that name, so Kingston was chosen.

Tu had doubts about the new company and bet Sun a Jaguar that it wouldn't survive the first year of operations. Sun won the car (which he later gave to a veteran employee who dreamed of owning one) and within two years the company

had sold nearly $40 million worth of products. In 1989 Kingston began making memory system upgrades; a year later it started producing processor upgrades.

The company was #1 on *Inc.* magazine's list of fastest-growing private US companies in 1992. The next year Kingston began marketing networking and storage products. Its vendor-friendly policy paid off that year, when demand for semiconductors far outstripped supply. Suppliers kept shipping to the company even when orders for other buyers were delayed.

In 1996 SOFTBANK paid $1.5 billion for 80% of the company but promised to preserve its culture and retain all management — including Tu and Sun — and employees. Sun and Tu set aside $100 million for employee bonuses.

In 1998 Kingston opened its first foreign manufacturing facilities, in Ireland and Taiwan. Also in 1998, in a unique arrangement suggesting that SOFTBANK overpaid when it bought Kingston, Tu and Sun agreed to forgo SOFTBANK's final $333 million payment. The following year Tu and Sun bought back SOFTBANK's stake for about $450 million. Also in 1999 the company opened a manufacturing plant in Malaysia.

After years of making computer storage devices, Kingston in 2000 formed a separate company, StorCase Technology, which specializes in storage equipment. The following year Kingston discontinued its Peripheral Products Division's offerings.

Also in 2001 Kingston launched a joint venture (and opened a new plant) in China with computer maker China GreatWall Computer Shenzhen Company.

Annual revenues topped $2 billion for the first time in 2004.

In 2005 Kingston completed an expansion of its plant in Shanghai, increasing its production capacity from 1.5 million modules per month to 5 million modules per month. The company went over the $3 billion mark in sales for the year.

Kingston topped $4 billion in sales for 2007.

EXECUTIVES

President and CEO: John Tu, age 66
COO: David Sun
CFO: Koichi Hosokawa
SVP Sales and Marketing: Mike Sager
VP Sales: John Holland
VP Administration (HR): Daniel Hsu
Digital Storage Product Manager: Mike Kuppinger
Senior Technology Manager: Mark Tekunoff

LOCATIONS

HQ: Kingston Technology Company, Inc.
17600 Newhope St., Fountain Valley, CA 92708
Phone: 714-435-2600   **Fax:** 714-435-2699
Web: www.kingston.com

Kingston Technology has operations in Australia, China, France, Germany, India, New Zealand, Taiwan, the UK, and the US.

PRODUCTS/OPERATIONS

Selected Products

Flash memory cards (CompactFlash, DataFlash, MultiMediaCard)
Memory modules and add-on boards
Standard memory modules (ValueRAM)

COMPETITORS

Acer	Micron Technology
Amkor	Mosel Vitelic
ASE Test	Netlist
Buffalo Technology	Numonyx
Centon Electronics	PNY Technologies
Dataram	Samsung Electronics
Elpida Memory	SanDisk
Entorian	Silicon Storage
Hynix	SMART Modular
IM Flash Technologies	STEC
Intel Corp.	Unigen
Lexar	Viking InterWorks
MA Laboratories	Wintec

HISTORICAL FINANCIALS

Company Type: Private

Income Statement

FYE: December 31

	REVENUE ($ mil.)	NET INCOME ($ mil.)	NET PROFIT MARGIN	EMPLOYEES
12/07	4,500	—	—	4,500
12/06	3,700	—	—	4,000
12/05	3,000	—	—	2,900
12/04	2,400	—	—	2,000
12/03	1,800	—	—	2,200
Annual Growth	25.7%	—	—	19.6%

Revenue History

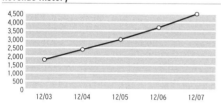

Kinray Inc.

Kinray, the US's top private wholesale drug distributor, is nothing if not independent. It provides generic, branded, and repackaged drugs, health and beauty products, medical equipment, vitamins and herbals, and diabetes-care products. The distributor also offers some 800 private label products under the Preferred Plus Pharmacy brand. It serves more than 3,000 independent pharmacies in eight northeastern US states; its customers also include long-term care facilities and specialty pharmacies. The firm was founded in 1944 by Joseph Rahr. His son, CEO and president Stewart Rahr, has owned Kinray since 1975.

Like its bigger rivals McKesson, Cardinal Health, and AmerisourceBergen, Kinray had depended on speculative buying (the practice of stocking up on drugs it anticipated were about to go up in price) for much of its rapid growth. That mode of operation took a hit since Bristol-Myers Squibb was sued by the SEC over the practice in 2005. It is also facing stiff competition from mail-order pharmacies.

In response, Kinray is focusing more on selling higher-margin generic drugs, a big part of its business, and private-label home health care products. It also offers merchandising and marketing programs, including retail pricing consultation, shelf-labeling and promotional materials, and more, and offers online ordering and inventory management through its Weblink system.

Kinray and other small distributors face a new challenge — an amendment to the Prescription Drug Act could exempt its big three rivals from providing a so-called drug pedigree (an itinerary from factory to pharmacy) for each product that is shipped. The pedigree would be an onerous addition to Kinray's operations.

EXECUTIVES

President and CEO: Stewart Rahr
CFO: Howard B. Hirsch
EVP Sales: Michael Rothstein
EVP Sales: Tom Pelizza
EVP and Director Data Processing: Casey Bruno
EVP Operations: Lenny Romano
VP Generic Sales and Business Development: Jean Kappes
VP Information Technology: Mikhail (Mike) Rapoport
VP and General Manager: Bill Bodinger
Director Genetic TeleSales: Mark Lieberman

LOCATIONS

HQ: Kinray Inc.
152-35 10th Ave., Whitestone, NY 11357
Phone: 718-767-1234   **Fax:** 718-767-4388
Web: www.kinray.com

COMPETITORS

AmerisourceBergen
Amexdrug
Cardinal Supply Chain Pharmaceutical
H. D. Smith Wholesale Drug
McKesson
PSS World Medical
Quality King

HISTORICAL FINANCIALS

Company Type: Private

Income Statement

FYE: December 31

	REVENUE ($ mil.)	NET INCOME ($ mil.)	NET PROFIT MARGIN	EMPLOYEES
12/07	4,800	—	—	1,000
12/06	4,400	—	—	1,000
12/05	4,000	—	—	800
12/04	3,510	—	—	1,000
12/03	2,910	—	—	700
Annual Growth	13.3%	—	—	9.3%

Revenue History

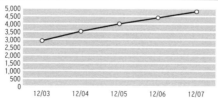

Kirkland & Ellis

Known for its work in cases that go to trial, law firm Kirkland & Ellis maintains a variety of practices aimed mainly at corporate clients. Besides litigation, the firm's core practice areas include corporate transactions, intellectual property, restructuring, and tax. Kirkland and Ellis represents public and private companies from a wide range of industries, as well as individuals and government agencies; over the years its clients have included companies such as Bank of America, General Motors, McDonald's, Motorola, and Siemens. Overall, Kirkland & Ellis has more than 1,400 lawyers in about 10 offices, mostly in the US but also in Europe and the Asia/Pacific region. The firm was founded in 1908.

EXECUTIVES

Chairman: Thomas D. Yannucci
Firm Administrator: Douglas (Doug) McLemore
CFO: Nicholas J. (Nick) Willmott, age 44
Chief Human Resources Officer: Gary Beu
CIO: Steve Novak
Chief Marketing Officer: Karen Braun
Manager Public Relations: Brian D. Pitts

LOCATIONS

HQ: Kirkland & Ellis LLP
Aon Center, 200 E. Randolph Dr., Chicago, IL 60601
Phone: 312-861-2000   **Fax:** 312-861-2200
Web: www.kirkland.com

Selected Office Locations

Chicago	New York
Hong Kong	Palo Alto, CA
London	San Francisco
Los Angeles	Washington, DC
Munich, Germany	

COMPETITORS

Baker & McKenzie	Latham & Watkins
Cravath, Swaine	Mayer Brown
DLA Piper	McDermott Will & Emery
Holland & Knight	Sidley Austin
Jenner & Block	Skadden, Arps
Jones Day	

HISTORICAL FINANCIALS

Company Type: Partnership

Income Statement

FYE: January 31

	REVENUE ($ mil.)	NET INCOME ($ mil.)	NET PROFIT MARGIN	EMPLOYEES
1/07	1,310	—	—	3,350
1/06	1,145	—	—	3,200
1/05	970	—	—	—
1/04	725	—	—	—
1/03	611	—	—	—
Annual Growth	21.0%	—	—	4.7%

Revenue History

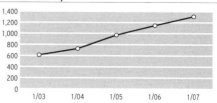

Knight inc

Knight (formerly Kinder Morgan) pipes in profits by operating 37,000 miles of natural gas pipelines in the US and Canada. The company also distributes natural gas to more than 1.1 million customers, primarily in the Midwest, and operates gas-fired power plants along its pipelines. Through Kinder Morgan Management, it controls Kinder Morgan Energy Partners, which transports refined products and operates 165 terminals that handle coal, petroleum coke, and other materials. In 2007 chairman and CEO Richard Kinder, who owns 31% of the company, led a group of investors in taking Kinder Morgan private and changed its name to Knight.

Kinder Morgan, formed in 1997 when Richard Kinder and William Morgan bought an Enron pipeline unit, expanded dramatically in 1999 through a reverse merger with troubled natural gas pipeline giant K N Energy.

In 2005 the company acquired Vancouver-based Terasen for a reported $3.1 billion in cash and stock and assumed $2.5 billion in debt. Kinder Morgan also purchased the Black Marlin Pipeline, a 38-mile long pipeline system that runs from southern Oklahoma to northern Texas. The company also plans to expand its storage capacity throughout the southern Rocky Mountain region of the US. Kinder Morgan has sold its TransColorado Gas Transmission subsidiary, which operates a 300-mile long interstate pipeline, to Kinder Morgan Energy Partners for $275 million.

In 2006 the company sold its US retail natural gas distribution and related operations for $710 million. In 2007 it sold Terasen Inc. to Fortis Inc. for approximately $3.2 billion.

In 2008 Knight sold 80% of its natural gas pipeline business segment to Myria Acquisition for $5.9 billion but remains the operator of these pipelines.

EXECUTIVES

Chairman and CEO: Richard D. (Rich) Kinder, age 63, $1 pay
President and Director: C. Park Shaper, age 39, $1,250,000 pay
President Gas and COO: Steven J. (Steve) Kean, age 46
VP Investor Relations and CFO: Kimberly A. (Kim) Dang, age 38
VP, General Counsel, and Secretary: Joseph Listengart, age 39, $1,175,000 pay
VP Corporate Development and Treasurer: David D. Kinder, age 33
VP Business Development, Natural Gas Pipelines: Scott E. Parker, age 47, $850,000 pay
VP; President, Retail: Daniel E. Watson, age 49
VP Human Resources and Administration: James E. Street, age 51
VP Corporate Communications: Larry S. Pierce
VP and CIO: Henry W. Neumann Jr.
President, Gas Pipelines, West Region: Mark Kissel
President, Power: Paul R. Steinway
President, Texas Intrastate Pipeline Group: Tom Martin
President, Kinder Morgan Canada: Ian D. Anderson, age 50
Investor Relations: Mindy Mills
Auditors: PricewaterhouseCoopers LLP

LOCATIONS

HQ: Knight Inc.
500 Dallas St., Ste. 1000, Houston, TX 77002
Phone: 713-369-9000 **Fax:** 713-369-9100
Web: www.kindermorgan.com

Knight operates pipelines and facilities throughout the continental US and Canada.

2007 Proforma Sales

	% of total
US	98
Canada	2
Total	**100**

PRODUCTS/OPERATIONS

2007 Proforma Sales

	% of total
Natural gas sales	57
Transportation & storage	32
Oil & product sales	9
Other	2
Total	**100**

Selected Operations and Subsidiaries

Kinder Morgan Canada
Kinder Morgan Energy Partners, L.P.
  CO2 Pipelines
  Bulk Terminals
  Natural Gas Pipelines
  Product Pipelines
Kinder Morgan Management, LLC
Kinder Morgan Retail Energy Services Company
Natural Gas Pipeline Company of America

COMPETITORS

Atmos Energy
Buckeye Partners
Canadian Utilities
CenterPoint Energy
Duke Energy
El Paso
Koch Industries, Inc.
Plains All American Pipeline
TEPPCO Partners
TransMontaigne
Williams Companies

HISTORICAL FINANCIALS
Company Type: Private

Income Statement

	REVENUE ($ mil.)	NET INCOME ($ mil.)	NET PROFIT MARGIN	EMPLOYEES
12/07	11,500	—	—	7,600
12/06	11,846	—	—	8,602
12/05	1,586	—	—	8,481
12/04	1,165	—	—	6,072
12/03	1,098	—	—	5,530
Annual Growth	**79.9%**	**—**	**—**	**8.3%**

FYE: December 31

Revenue History

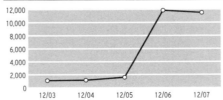

Knowledge Learning

Curious kids are welcome at Knowledge Learning Corporation. Its KinderCare Learning Centers provide day care and educational programs for more than 300,000 children throughout the US. The company provides care for children from their infancy to primary school years, including back-up child care, before- and after-school care, and summer camps. It operates about 2,000 community centers as 600 school-partnership sites, as well as 130 corporate child care centers for *FORTUNE* 500, mid-sized, and small companies; local and state governments; hospitals; and universities. The company made an unsolicited bid of some $186 million to buy for-profit school operator Nobel Learning Communities, which is mulling the offer.

In 2006 the company acquired Education Station, a provider of No Child Left Behind services to public schools, from Educate, Inc. The company also offers online high school courses for teenagers and young adults through Keystone National High School.

Knowledge Learning Corporation acquired KinderCare Learning Centers in 2005 and re-branded most of its early childhood and school-age centers in 2007. Previously operating under some 90 brand names (including Children's World Learning Centers, Magic Years Learning Centers, and Mulberry Child Care and Preschool), its centers now operate as KinderCare Learning Centers.

EXECUTIVES

President and COO: Elanna S. Yalow
EVP and CFO: Mark D. Moreland, age 43
EVP and CIO: John R. Hnanicek, age 36
EVP Human Resources: Donna J. Lesch
EVP and General Counsel: John Sims
SVP Marketing and Business Development: Dan Frechtling
SVP Education and Training: Sharon Bergen
SVP Real Estate Development: Bill Robards
VP Operations, CCLC: Sheila Niehaus
President, Knowledge Learning Corporation School Partnerships: Marcy Suntken

LOCATIONS

HQ: Knowledge Learning Corporation
650 NE Holladay St., Ste. 1400, Portland, OR 97232
Phone: 503-872-1300 **Fax:** 503-872-1349
Web: www.knowledgelearning.com

Knowledge Learning Corporation has operations in 32 US states.

PRODUCTS/OPERATIONS

Selected Services

Back-up child care
Child care consulting
Corporate discounts
Curriculum
  Creativity & imagination
  Mathematics
  Motor development
  Reading & language development
  Scientific discovery
  Social & emotional development
  Technology
Distance learning
Kindergarten
On-site care for children from infant through school age

COMPETITORS

A.B.C. Learning Centres
Bright Horizons Family Solutions
Child Development Schools
Edison Learning
Imagine Schools
Kaplan
Learning Care Group
New Horizon
Nobel Learning Communities

HISTORICAL FINANCIALS

Company Type: Private

Income Statement

	ESTIMATED REVENUE ($ mil.)	NET INCOME ($ mil.)	NET PROFIT MARGIN	EMPLOYEES
12/07	1,620	—	—	42,000
12/06	1,550	—	—	41,000
12/05	1,654	—	—	41,000
Annual Growth	(1.0%)	—	—	1.2%

FYE: December 31

Revenue History

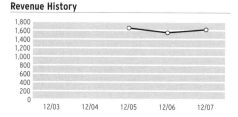

Koch Foods

Kids, always ready with a joke, ask why the chicken crossed the road. But it's you who should cross the road — to get to Koch Foods — because the company is ready with a whole henhouse full of chicken products. It is one of the top chicken producers in the US and its products include value-added fresh and frozen chicken products, including chicken tenderloins, tenders, strips, boneless breasts, and wings, along with diced and pulled white and dark meat, and whole and whole cut-up chickens. Its customers include companies in the retail food and food service sectors throughout the country and overseas.

Starting out as a one-room chicken deboner and cutter, Koch Foods has grown to a be a full-service chicken producer through acquisitions, including slaughtering plants and feed mills. The company's latest purchase was in 2006, when Koch closed on a $58 million deal for Alabama-based chicken processor Sylvest Farms.

EXECUTIVES

President and CEO: Joseph C. (Joe) Grendys
CFO: Mark Kaminsky
Director Sales and Marketing: Michael Lazarus

LOCATIONS

HQ: Koch Foods Incorporated
1300 W. Higgins Rd., Park Ridge, IL 60068
Phone: 847-384-5940 **Fax:** 847-384-5961
Web: www.kochfoods.com

COMPETITORS

Allen Family Foods
Barber Foods
Bell & Evans
Brakebush Brothers
Cagle's
Coleman Natural Foods
Cooper Farms
Empire Kosher Poultry
Fieldale Farms
Foster Farms
Hormel
Loggins Meat
Mountaire Farms

New Market Poultry
Northwestern Meat
O.K. Foods, Inc.
OSI Group
Perdue Incorporated
Petaluma Poultry
Pilgrim's Pride
Raeford Farms
Sanderson Farms
SYSCO
Townsends
Tyson Foods
Wayne Farms LLC

HISTORICAL FINANCIALS

Company Type: Private

Income Statement

	REVENUE ($ mil.)	NET INCOME ($ mil.)	NET PROFIT MARGIN	EMPLOYEES
12/07	1,800	—	—	14,000
12/06	1,800	—	—	8,000
12/05	1,400	—	—	7,500
Annual Growth	13.4%	—	—	36.6%

FYE: December 31

Revenue History

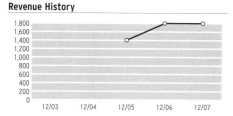

Koch Industries

Following the assimilation of forest products giant Georgia-Pacific (for a reported $21 billion), Koch Industries has become a real paper tiger. Koch (pronounced "coke") is one of the largest private companies in the US. Koch Industries' operations include refining and chemicals, process equipment, and technologies; fibers and polymers; commodity and financial trading; and forest and consumer products. Its Flint Hills Resources subsidiary owns three refineries that process 800,000 barrels of crude oil daily. Koch operates crude gathering systems and pipelines across North America as well as cattle ranches in Kansas, Montana, and Texas. Brothers Charles and David Koch control the company.

Koch's numerous subsidiary companies leverage capabilities such as its proprietary Market Based Management system; innovation; and a high level of operational, trading, transaction, and public sector skills to create long-term value for customers.

HISTORY

Fred Koch grew up poor in Texas and worked his way through MIT. In 1928 Koch developed a process to refine more gasoline from crude oil, but when he tried to market his invention, the major oil companies sued him for patent infringement. Koch eventually won the lawsuits (after 15 years in court), but the controversy

made it tough to attract many US customers. In 1929 Koch took his process to the Soviet Union, but he grew disenchanted with Stalinism and returned home to become a founding member of the anticommunist John Birch Society.

Koch launched Wood River Oil & Refining in Illinois (1940) and bought the Rock Island refinery in Oklahoma (1947). He folded the remaining purchasing and gathering network into Rock Island Oil & Refining (though he later sold the refineries).

After Koch's death in 1967, his 32-year-old son Charles took the helm and renamed the company Koch Industries. He began a series of acquisitions, adding petrochemical and oil trading service operations.

During the 1980s Koch was thrust into various arenas, legal and political. Charles' brother David, also a Koch Industries executive, ran for US vice president on the Libertarian ticket in 1980. That year the other two Koch brothers, Frederick and William (David's fraternal twin), launched a takeover attempt, but Charles retained control, and William was fired from his job as VP.

In a 1983 settlement Charles and David bought out the dissident family members for just over $1 billion. William and Frederick continued to challenge their brothers in court, claiming they had been shortchanged in the deal (the two estranged brothers eventually lost their case in 1998, and their appeals were rejected in 2000).

Despite this legal wrangling, Koch Industries continued to expand, purchasing a Corpus Christi, Texas, refinery in 1981. It expanded its pipeline system, buying Bigheart Pipe Line in Oklahoma (1986) and two systems from Santa Fe Southern Pacific (1988).

In 1991 Koch purchased the Corpus Christi marine terminal, pipelines, and gathering systems of Scurlock Permian (a unit of Ashland Oil). In 1992 the company bought United Gas Pipe Line (renamed Koch Gateway Pipeline) and its pipeline system extending from Texas to Florida.

To strengthen its engineering services presence worldwide, Koch acquired Glitsch International (a maker of separation equipment) from engineering giant Foster Wheeler in 1997. It also acquired USX-Delhi Group, a natural gas processor and transporter.

In 1998 Koch bought Purina Mills, the largest US producer of animal feed, and formed the KoSa joint venture with Mexico's Saba family to buy Hoechst's Trevira polyester unit. (Koch acquired the Saba family's stake in KoSa in 2001.) Lethargic energy and livestock prices in 1998 and 1999, however, led Koch to lay off several hundred employees, sell its feedlots, and divest portions of its natural gas gathering and pipeline systems. Purina Mills filed for bankruptcy protection in 1999 (later, it emerged from bankruptcy and held an IPO in 2000, and was acquired by #2 US dairy co-op Land O'Lakes in 2001).

William Koch sued Koch Industries in 1990, claiming the company had underreported the amount of oil purchased on US government and Native American lands. A jury found for William, but he, Charles, and David agreed to settle the case in 2001 — and sat down to dinner together for the first time in 20 years.

In other legal matters, in 2000 Koch agreed to pay a $30 million civil fine and contribute $5 million toward environmental projects to settle complaints over oil spills from its pipelines in the 1990s. The company agreed to pay $20 million in 2001 to settle a separate environmental case concerning a Texas refinery.

The company acquired INVISTA in 2004 for $4.2 billion and merged it with its KoSa unit. In 2005 SemGroup acquired all of Koch Materials Company's US and Mexico asphalt operations, and ONEOK, Inc. acquired the natural gas liquids businesses owned by several Koch companies.

In 2005 a Koch subsidiary completed the $21 billion acquisition of Georgia-Pacific.

EXECUTIVES

Chairman and CEO: Charles G. Koch, age 72
Vice-Chairman: Joseph W. (Joe) Moeller, age 65
President, COO, and Director:
  David L. (Dave) Robertson, age 46
CFO and Director: Steve Feilmeier
EVP and Director: David H. Koch, age 68
EVP and Director: Richard Fink
EVP Operations, and Director: James L. (Jim) Mahoney
SVP Corporate Strategy: John C. Pittenger
SVP and General Counsel: Mark Holden
VP Business Development: Ron Vaupel
Controller: Richard Dinkel
Treasurer: David May
Communication Coordinator and Public Affairs:
  Patti Parker
Communication Director: Melissa Cohlmia
CEO Koch Heat Transfer: John Rosso
President and COO Koch Chemical Technology Group:
  Robert (Bob) DiFulgentiz
President, Koch Financial Corporation:
  Randall A. (Randy) Bushman
President and COO, Flint Hills Resources: Brad Razook
President, Koch Carbon, LLC: Steve Tatum
President, Koch Nitrogen Company: Steve Packebush
President, Koch Supply & Trading: Steve Mawer
President, Koch Genesis Company, LLC:
  Timothy J. Cesarek, age 42
President, Koch Pipeline Company: Bob O'Hair

LOCATIONS

HQ: Koch Industries, Inc.
  4111 E. 37th St. North, Wichita, KS 67220
Phone: 316-828-5500   **Fax:** 316-828-5739
Web: www.kochind.com

Koch Industries has operations in Argentina, Australia, Belgium, Brazil, Canada, China, the Czech Republic, France, Germany, India, Italy, Japan, Luxembourg, the Netherlands, Poland, South Africa, Spain, Switzerland, the UK, the US, and Venezuela.

PRODUCTS/OPERATIONS

Selected Operations

Flint Hills Resources (formerly Koch Petroleum, crude oil, petrochemicals, and refined products)
Georgia-Pacific Corporation
Koch Chemical Technology Group (specialty equipment and services for refining and chemical industry)
  Iris Power Engineering, Inc.
  The John Zink Company
  Koch-Glitsch, Inc.
  Koch Heat Transfer Group (formerly Brown Fintube Company)
  Koch Membrane Systems Inc.
  Koch-Partners
  Koch Modular Process Systems, LLC
  Quest Tru-Tec Services (formerly Tru-Tec Services)
Koch Financial Corp.
Koch Genesis Company (investment in noncore businesses)
Koch Mineral Services (bulk ocean transportation and terminalling and trading)
  Koch Fertilizer Storage & Terminal Co.
  Koch Nitrogen Co.
Koch Pipeline Co. LP
Koch Specialty Chemicals (high-octane missile fuel)
Koch Supply & Trading, LLC
Matador Cattle Co.

COMPETITORS

AbitibiBowater
ADM
AEP
Ashland
Avista
BP
Cargill
CenterPoint Energy
Chevron
ConocoPhillips
ContiGroup
Duke Energy
Dynegy
Enron
Exxon
Gypsum Products
Hesperia Holding
Imperial Oil

International Paper
Kimberly-Clark
King Ranch
Marathon Oil
Motiva Enterprises
Occidental Petroleum
OfficeMax
Peabody Energy
PEMEX
PG&E
Royal Dutch Shell
Shell Oil Products
Smurfit-Stone Container
Southern Company
SUEZ-TRACTEBEL
Sunoco
Weyerhaeuser
Williams Companies

HISTORICAL FINANCIALS

Company Type: Private

Income Statement

FYE: December 31

	REVENUE ($ mil.)	NET INCOME ($ mil.)	NET PROFIT MARGIN	EMPLOYEES
12/07	98,000	—	—	80,000
12/06	90,000	—	—	80,000
12/05	80,000	—	—	80,000
12/04	40,000	—	—	30,000
12/03	40,000	—	—	30,000
Annual Growth	25.1%	—	—	27.8%

Revenue History

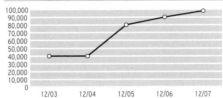

Kohler Co.

Kohler's profits are in the toilet, literally. The company makes bathroom and kitchen products — from toilets and baths to showers and sinks — under the names Kohler, Hytec, and Sterling. It also makes furniture under the names Baker and McGuire, as well as ceramic, stone, and mosaic tile under the brand Ann Sacks. Lesser-known operations include Kohler's manufacturing of small engines, generators, and power supplies for both consumer and industrial applications. Kohler's real estate operations include Destination Kohler, a resort in Wisconsin, and Old Course Hotel Golf Resort and Spa in Scotland. Chairman Herbert Kohler Jr. and his sister Ruth Kohler, grandchildren of the founder, control Kohler.

Long renowned as a leader in bath and kitchen design and technology, privately held Kohler is not content to sit on its, *ahem*, laurels. The company continues to innovate within the industry, designing a "bathroom of the future," which features a digitally controlled shower system that offers 22 different body spray options at the touch of a button. Its Hatbox toilet combines a minimalist "tankless" design with powerful

flushing capabilities. A handful of its toilet products also incorporate water-efficient design and use at least 20% less water than standard 1.6 gallon toilets.

Like any good three-headed giant, Kohler's other two business segments are also expanding. The company continues to seek and form joint ventures to market and sell its engine products overseas, especially in China where it has a strong foothold. Through acquisitions of such companies as Lombardini Srl, Kohler's Global Power Group subsidiary makes further headway into European and North African markets.

On the real estate front, Kohler is planning to expand its hospitality business by opening its first day spa in the suburbs of Chicago. It will pair the spa with a Kohler retail store, selling some of the same equipment and bath fixtures used in the spa. If successful, it plans to replicate the model in other markets. In 2008 the company acquired Mark David, a maker of upscale seating for the hospitality sector. Mark David was added to its Interiors Group.

HISTORY

In 1873, 29-year-old Austrian immigrant John Kohler and partner Charles Silberzahn founded Kohler & Silberzahn in Sheboygan, Wisconsin. That year they purchased a small iron foundry that made agricultural products with $5,000 from Kohler's father-in-law. In 1880, two years after Silberzahn left the firm, its machine shop was destroyed by fire.

The company introduced enameled plumbing fixtures in the rebuilt factory in 1883. The design caught on, and the business sold thousands of sinks, kettles, pans, and bathtubs. By 1887, when Kohler was incorporated, enameled items accounted for 70% of sales. By 1900 the 250-person company received 98% of its sales from enameled iron products. That year, shortly after John Kohler began building new facilities near Sheboygan (which later became the company village of Kohler), he died at age 56. More trouble followed: Kohler's new plant burned down in 1901, and two of the founder's sons died — Carl at age 24 in 1904 and Robert at age 35 in 1905.

Eldest surviving son Walter built a boarding hotel to house workers and introduced other employee-benefit programs. He also set up company-paid workmen's compensation before the state made it law in 1917.

By the mid-1920s, when Kohler premiered colors in porcelain fixtures and added brass fittings and vitreous china toilets and washbasins to its line, it was the #3 plumbing-product company in the US. As a testament to the design quality of its products, Kohler items were displayed at the New York Museum of Modern Art in 1929. The company also began developing products that would grow in importance in later decades: electric generators and small gasoline engines. During the 1950s Kohler's engines virtually conquered Southeast Asia, where they were used to power boats, drive air compressors, and pump water for rice paddies in Vietnam and Thailand. While strikes against Kohler in 1897 and 1934 had been resolved quickly, a 1954 strike against the firm lasted six years. The strike gave Kohler the dubious honor of enduring the longest strike in US history.

Small-engine use grew in the US in the 1960s, and Kohler's motors were used in lawn mowers, construction equipment, and garden tractors. Modern products include small 4-31 hp engines and generator sets up to 2,800 kW. Kohler also offers uninterruptible power systems through Kohler Rental Power.

The founder's last surviving son, Herbert (a child from John Kohler's second marriage), died in 1968. Under the leadership of Herbert's son Herbert Jr. (appointed chairman 1972), Kohler expanded its operations and began to develop its resort business in the US with the restoration of The American Club hotel (1981); it bought Sterling Faucet (1984), Baker Furniture (1986), Knapp & Tubbs (1986), and Jacob Delafon (1986). Subsequent acquisitions have included Sanijura (bathroom furniture, France) in 1993, Osio (enamel baths, Italy) in 1994, Robern (mirrored cabinets) in 1995, Holdiam (baths, whirlpools, and sinks, France) in 1995, and Canac (cabinets, Canada) in 1996.

The Interiors Group got its start with the 1986 acquisition of Baker Furniture. Today, the division includes Milling Road Furniture, Dapha, Ltd. (custom upholstery), McGuire Furniture (rattan, teak, bamboo, and Oriental hardwoods), and Ann Sacks (tile and stone).

The company entered a growing plumbing market in China through four joint ventures formed in that country in 1996 and 1997. In 1998 several family and non-family shareholders claimed a reorganization plan unfairly forced them out and undervalued their stock. Legal battles over the stock's fair price continued in 1999, and a settlement was reached in 2000 that granted shareholders a fair price and Herbert Jr. and his sister Ruth gained firm control of the company. Herbert reorganized the company and vowed it would never go public.

In 2001 the company sued Canada-based Kohler International Ltd. for trademark infringement. In the fall of 2002, Kohler and about 3,450 United Auto Workers (UAW) union members who worked at the company's Village of Kohler and Town of Mosel plants agreed on a five-year labor contract that called for increases in wages and benefits.

Kohler expanded its resort business internationally in 2004 by purchasing the world-renowned Old Course Hotel Golf Resort and Spa in St. Andrews, Scotland, along with Golf Resorts International (GRI), Limited.

EXECUTIVES

Chairman and President: Herbert V. Kohler Jr., age 65
SVP Finance and CFO: Jeffrey P. Cheney
SVP Human Resources: Laura Kohler
VP Hospitality and Real Estate: Alice Edland
VP Marketing, Fixtures: Mike Chandler
President, Engine Business: James Doyle, age 56
President, Global Power Group:
Richard J. (Dick) Fotsch, age 52
Director; President, Kitchen and Bath Group:
David Kohler, age 41

LOCATIONS

HQ: Kohler Co.
444 Highland Dr., Kohler, WI 53044
Phone: 920-457-4441   **Fax:** 920-457-1271
Web: kohlerco.com

Kohler Co. operates 44 manufacturing plants, 26 subsidiaries and affiliates, and sales offices worldwide.

PRODUCTS/OPERATIONS

Selected Operations

Engines
  Commercial turf equipment engines
  Consumer lawn and garden equipment engines
  Industrial, construction, and commercial equipment engines
  Recreational equipment engines
Furniture
  Baker Furniture
  McGuire Furniture Company
  Milling Road Furniture
Generators
  Kohler rental power
  Marine generators
  Mobile generators
  On-site power systems
    Automatic transfer switches
    Switchgear
  Residential generators
  Small business generators
Kitchen and bath products
  Cabinets and vanities
    Canac (bathroom cabinetry)
    Robern (lighting and mirrored bath cabinetry)
    Sanijura (vanities and other bath furniture)
  Plumbing products
    Jacob Delafon (bathtubs, faucets, lavatories, and toilets)
    Kohler (bath and shower faucets, baths, bidet faucets, bidets, body spa systems, glass showers and shower doors, kitchen and bathroom sinks and faucets, master baths, toilets, toilet seats, vanities, whirlpool baths)
    Kallista (bathroom and kitchen sinks and faucets)
    Sterling (bathing fixtures, faucets, sinks, tub/shower enclosures, vitreous china bath fixtures)
  Tile and stone products
    Ann Sacks (art tile, glazed tile, knobs and pulls, mosaics, terra cotta)
Real estate and hospitality (Destination Kohler)
  The American Club (resort hotel)
  Blackwolf Run golf course
  Golf Resorts International, Limited (Scotland)
  Inn on Woodlake
  Kohler Stables
  Kohler Waters Spa
  Old Course Hotel Golf Resort and Spa (Scotland)
  Riverbend (private club)
  River Wildlife
  The Shops at Woodlake Kohler
  Whistling Straits golf course

COMPETITORS

Armstrong World Industries
Bassett Furniture
Black & Decker
Briggs & Stratton
Carlson Companies
Chicago Faucet
Crane Co.
Crossville
Dal-Tile
Elkay Manufacturing
Geberit
Gerber Plumbing Fixtures
Grohe
Honda
Iberia Tiles
Jacuzzi Brands
Klaussner Furniture
Leggett & Platt
Masco
Moen
Mueller Industries
NIBCO
Price Pfister
Starwood Hotels & Resorts
Tecumseh Products
TOTO
Trane Inc.
Waxman
Yamaha

HISTORICAL FINANCIALS

Company Type: Private

Income Statement

FYE: December 31

	ESTIMATED REVENUE ($ mil.)	NET INCOME ($ mil.)	NET PROFIT MARGIN	EMPLOYEES
12/07	5,230	—	—	32,000
12/06	5,000	—	—	33,000
12/05	3,000	—	—	31,000
12/04	3,000	—	—	28,000
12/03	3,005	—	—	25,000
Annual Growth	14.9%	—	—	6.4%

Revenue History

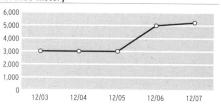

KPMG International

Businesses all over the world count on KPMG for accounting. KPMG is the smallest, yet one of the most geographically dispersed of accounting's Big Four, which also includes Deloitte Touche Tohmatsu, Ernst & Young, and PricewaterhouseCoopers. KPMG, a cooperative that operates as an umbrella organization for its member firms, has organized its structure into three operating regions: the Americas; Australia and Asia/Pacific; and Europe, Middle East, South Asia, and Africa. Member firms' offerings include audit, tax, and advisory services; KPMG focuses on clients in such industries as financial services, consumer products, and government.

KPMG, which operates worldwide, is focusing its growth on the BRIC countries (Brazil, Russia, India, and China), as are many of its member firms' clients.

HISTORY

Peat Marwick was founded in 1911, when William Peat, a London accountant, met James Marwick during an Atlantic crossing. University of Glasgow alumni Marwick and Roger Mitchell had formed Marwick, Mitchell & Company in New York in 1897. Peat and Marwick agreed to ally their firms temporarily, and in 1925 they merged as Peat, Marwick, Mitchell, & Copartners.

In 1947 William Black became senior partner, a position he held until 1965. He guided the firm's 1950 merger with Barrow, Wade, Guthrie, one of the US's oldest firms, and built its consulting practice. Peat Marwick restructured its international practice as PMM&Co. (International) in 1972 (renamed Peat Marwick International in 1978).

The next year several European accounting firms led by Klynveld Kraayenhoff (the Netherlands) and Deutsche Treuhand (Germany) began forming an international accounting federation. Needing an American member, the Europeans encouraged the merger of two American firms founded around the turn of the century, Main

Lafrentz and Hurdman Cranstoun. Main Hurdman & Cranstoun joined the Europeans to form Klynveld Main Goerdeler (KMG), named after two of the member firms and the chairman of Deutsche Treuhand, Reinhard Goerdeler. Other members were C. Jespersen (Denmark), Thorne Riddel (Canada), Thomson McLintok (UK), and Fides Revision (Switzerland).

Peat Marwick merged with KMG in 1987 to form Klynveld Peat Marwick Goerdeler (KPMG). KPMG lost 10% of its business as competing client companies departed. Professional staff departures followed in 1990 when, as part of a consolidation, the firm trimmed its partnership rolls.

In the 1990s the then-Big Six accounting firms all faced lawsuits arising from an evolving standard holding auditors responsible for the substance, rather than merely the form, of clients' accounts. KPMG was hit by suits stemming from its audits of defunct S&Ls and litigation relating to the bankruptcy of Orange County, California (settled for $75 million in 1998). Nevertheless KPMG kept growing; it expanded its consulting division with the acquisition of banking consultancy Barefoot, Marrinan & Associates in 1996.

In 1997, after Price Waterhouse and Coopers & Lybrand announced their merger, KPMG and Ernst & Young announced one of their own. But they called it quits the next year, fearing that regulatory approval of the deal would be too onerous.

The creation of PricewaterhouseCoopers (PwC) and increasing competition in the consulting sides of all of the Big Five brought a realignment of loyalties in their national practices. KPMG Consulting's Belgian group moved to PwC and its French group to Computer Sciences Corporation. Andersen nearly wooed away KPMG's Canadian consulting group, but the plan was foiled by the ever-sullen Andersen Consulting group (now Accenture) and by KPMG's promises of more money. Against this background, KPMG sold 20% of its consulting operations to Cisco Systems for $1 billion. In addition to the cash infusion, the deal allowed KPMG to provide installation and system management to Cisco's customers.

Even while KPMG worked on the IPO of its consulting group (which took place in 2001), it continued to rail against the SEC as it called for relationships between consulting and auditing organizations to be severed. In 2002 KPMG sold its British and Dutch consultancy units to France's Atos Origin.

In 2003 the SEC charged US member firm KPMG L.L.P. and four partners with fraud in relation to alleged profit inflation at former client Xerox in the late 1990s. (In 2005 the accounting firm paid almost $22.5 million, including a $10 million civil penalty, to settle the charges.)

KPMG exited various businesses around the globe during fiscal 2004, including full-scope legal services and certain advisory services, to focus on higher-demand services.

EXECUTIVES

Chairman; Chairman and CEO, KPMG L.L.P.:
Timothy P. (Tim) Flynn, age 48
Deputy Chairman; Chairman, Asia Pacific and Co-Chairman, China and Hong Kong: John B. Harrison, age 52
CEO: Michael P. (Mike) Wareing
Managing Partner, Global Markets: Alistair Johnston
Global Head of Citizenship and Diversity:
Lord Michael Hastings
Head, Global Indirect Tax: Neil D. Austin, age 56
Head, Leadership Development: Akber Pandor
Head, Transition Services: David Wilkinson
Head, Tax: Uday Ved

CIO; Global Managing Partner, Audit and Advisory Services Center: Stuart V.M. Campbell, age 55
Chairman, Americas Region: John B. Veihmeyer, age 49
COO Americas; Executive Vice Chairman, Operations, KPMG L.L.P.: Jack T. Taylor, age 55

LOCATIONS

HQ: KPMG International
Burgemeester Rijnderslaan 10-20,
1185 MC Amstelveen, The Netherlands
Phone: +31-20-656-7890 **Fax:** +31-20-656-7700
US HQ: 3 Chestnut Ridge Road, Montvale, NJ 07645
US Phone: 201-307-7000 **US Fax:** 201-830-8617
Web: www.kpmg.com

2007 Sales

	$ mil.	% of total
Europe, Middle East & Africa	10,670	54
Americas	6,590	33
Asia/Pacific	2,550	13
Total	**19,810**	**100**

PRODUCTS/OPERATIONS

2007 Sales by Function

	$ mil.	% of total
Audit	9,390	47
Advisory	6,430	33
Tax	3,990	20
Total	**19,810**	**100**

2007 Sales by Industry Group

	$ mil.	% of total
Financial Services	4,860	24
Industrial Markets	4,800	24
Information, Communication & Entertainment	3,960	20
Infrastructure, Government & Healthcare	3,900	20
Consumer Markets	2,290	12
Total	**19,810**	**100**

Selected Services

Audit services
  Financial statement audit
  Internal audit services
Tax services
  Corporate and business tax
  Global tax
  Indirect tax
  Personal tax
Advisory services
  Audit support services
  Financial risk management
  Information risk management
  Process improvement
  Regulatory and compliance

Selected Industry Specializations

Consumer and industrial markets
  Consumer markets
    Consumer products
    Food and beverage
    Retail
  Industrial markets
    Chemicals and pharmaceuticals
    Energy and natural resources
    Industrial and automotive products
Financial services
  Banking
  Insurance
Infrastructure, government, and health care
  Building, construction, and real estate
  Funding agencies
  Government
  Health care
  Transportation
Information, communications, and entertainment
  Business services
  Communications
  Electronics
  Media
  Software

COMPETITORS

Aon
Bain & Company
Baker Tilly International
BDO International
Booz Allen
Deloitte
Ernst & Young Global
Grant Thornton International
H&R Block
Hewitt Associates
Marsh & McLennan
McKinsey & Company
PricewaterhouseCoopers
Towers Perrin
Watson Wyatt

HISTORICAL FINANCIALS

Company Type: Partnership

Income Statement

FYE: September 30

	REVENUE ($ mil.)	NET INCOME ($ mil.)	NET PROFIT MARGIN	EMPLOYEES
9/07	19,810	—	—	123,322
9/06	16,880	—	—	112,795
9/05	15,690	—	—	103,621
9/04	13,440	—	—	93,983
9/03	12,160	—	—	93,470
Annual Growth	**13.0%**	—	—	**7.2%**

Revenue History

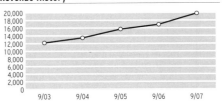

Kronos Incorporated

You won't ever catch Kronos taking a nap in the company supply closet. The company's Workforce Central systems collect attendance data and automatically post it to payroll. Kronos data collection systems keep track of factory production and labor hours. It also makes labor management analysis software and payroll processing applications. Kronos sells its products through its own sales force and through an alliance with payroll service company ADP. The company focuses on the health care, manufacturing, government, retail, and hospitality markets. Kronos was acquired by an investment group led by private equity firm Hellman & Friedman in 2007.

In addition to Hellman & Friedman, technology investment specialist JMI Equity funded the transaction, which was valued at approximately $1.8 billion.

Kronos customers include Banner Health, the city of Orlando, Georgia-Pacific, IKEA, and Quantas Airways. The company has broadened its service offerings and developed Web-based versions of its software. Kronos has also been using technology acquisitions to add payroll processing and human resources capabilities to its time and attendance systems.

In early 2005 Kronos spent about $17 million to acquire the assets of NexTime, a Kronos distributor in the southeastern US, strengthening its presence in the enterprise health care market. Later that year, the company acquired the assets of CTR, a Kronos reseller in Pennsylvania, for about $31 million.

The acquisitions kept on coming in 2006. Kronos acquired TimeWorks, a software developer specializing in the gambling industry. It also bought the assets of Compu-Cash Systems, a Las Vegas-based Kronos distributor, and Atlanta-based workforce analytics consulting firm ClarityMatters. In 2006 Kronos acquired Unicru, a provider of hiring management software, for approximately $150 million in cash. It also purchased the labor management business of SmartTime Software. Kronos acquired Deploy Solutions, a developer of recruiting and hiring software, in 2007.

Kronos generates most of its sales in the US, but the company markets its products worldwide. It expanded its operations into China with the opening of a Beijing-based office in 2006. The following year it launched an office in Bangalore, India.

EXECUTIVES

Chairman: Mark S. Ain, age 64, $576,000 pay
CEO and Director: Aron J. Ain, age 50
President: Paul A. Lacy, age 61, $528,000 pay
CFO: Mark V. Julien, $234,893 pay
Chief Administrative Officer:
  Charles T. (Charlie) Dickson, age 51
SVP Engineering and CTO: Peter C. George, age 46,
  $360,000 pay
SVP Corporate Strategy: James (Jim) Kizielewicz,
  age 46, $434,787 pay (prior to promotion)
VP International Operations: Mick Adamson
VP North American Sales: John O'Brien
VP Human Resources: Patrick J. (Pat) Moquin
VP and General Counsel: Alyce Moore
Senior Director, Corporate Communications:
  Michele Glorie
Auditors: Ernst & Young LLP

LOCATIONS

HQ: Kronos Incorporated
  297 Billerica Rd., Chelmsford, MA 01824
Phone: 978-250-9800   **Fax:** 978-367-5900
Web: www.kronos.com

PRODUCTS/OPERATIONS

Selected Products
Kronos iSeries Central (workforce management for IBM
  iSeries platform)
Workforce Central (process automation and workforce
  performance optimization suite)

COMPETITORS

Alphameric
Ceridian
JDA Software
Lawson Software
Navtech
NETtime Solutions
Northgate Information Solutions
Oracle
Replicon
Sage Group
Sandata Technologies
SAP
Technical Difference
Ultimate Software

The Krystal Company

The Krystal Company is a fast-food gem of the South. The company's chain of about 400 restaurants in almost a dozen southern states are known for their petite, square hamburgers (what Northerners might call a Slyder). In addition, Krystal's menu includes chicken sandwiches (Krystal Chik), chili, corn dogs, breakfast sandwiches, and dessert items. The company also sells its burgers through several grocery chains. More than 230 Krystal locations are company-owned, while the rest are franchised. The chain got its start in 1932 when R.B. Davenport, Jr. and J. Glenn Sherrill opened up shop in Chattanooga, Tennessee. It is owned by Port Royal Holdings, which is controlled by former CEO Philip Sanford.

Much like its Northern doppelgänger White Castle, Krystal has been more focused on maintaining customer loyalty and less on rapid expansion outside its core markets. It has been slowly expanding, mostly through a small number of new corporate-run locations.

EXECUTIVES

Chairman: Andrew G. Cope, age 66
President and CEO: James F. (Fred) Exum Jr., age 51
EVP and CFO: James W. (Jim) Bear, age 62
SVP Administration: Michael C. Bass, age 61
VP and CIO: David R. Reid
VP Franchise Division: Alan R. Wright
VP Purchasing and Quality Assurance: Gloria Daniels
VP Real Estate: Dennis B. Bookwalter
VP Marketing: Brad Wahl
VP Development: Bob Marshall
Director Marketing: John Wolf
Director Advertising: Howard Curtis
Director Research and Development: Becky Conner
Director Real Estate: David Snider
Controller: Scott Cochran
Auditors: Ernst & Young LLP

LOCATIONS

HQ: The Krystal Company
  1 Union Sq., Chattanooga, TN 37402
Phone: 423-757-1550   **Fax:** 423-757-5610
Web: www.krystal.com

COMPETITORS

American Dairy Queen
Arby's
Back Yard Burgers
Bojangles'
Burger King
Cajun Operating Company
Captain D's
Checkers Drive-In
Hardee's
Jack in the Box
Jack's Family Restaurants
McDonald's
Sonic Corp.
Wendy's
Whataburger
White Castle
YUM!

HISTORICAL FINANCIALS
Company Type: Private

Income Statement

	REVENUE ($ mil.)	NET INCOME ($ mil.)	NET PROFIT MARGIN	EMPLOYEES
			FYE: Sunday nearest December 31	
12/07	441	—	—	—
12/06	446	—	—	—
12/05	423	—	—	—
12/04	415	—	—	—
12/03	247	—	—	7,056
Annual Growth	15.6%	—	—	—

Revenue History

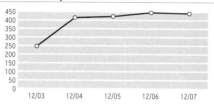

K-VA-T Food Stores

What do you call a chain of supermarkets in Kentucky, Virginia, and Tennessee? How about K-VA-T Food Stores? K-VA-T is one of the largest grocery chains in the region, with about 95 supermarkets primarily under the Food City banner (and a handful of Super Dollar Supermarkets). Originally a Piggly Wiggly franchise with three stores, K-VA-T was founded in 1955. It has expanded by acquiring stores from other regional food retailers, opening new stores, and adding services such as about 70 pharmacies, 50 Gas'N Go gasoline outlets, and banking. Its Food City Distribution Center provides warehousing and distribution services. The founding Smith family owns a majority of K-VA-T; employees own the rest of the company.

The company purchased eight BI-LO supermarkets in Tennessee in March 2006. The locations, acquired from C&S Wholesale, were quickly converted to the Food City label.

Food City is unique in its partnerships with local food product producers. In 2008 the company added products from regional Tennessee favorite Lay's Meats, following similar deals with a local bread company and ice cream company.

Jack C. Smith, founder and chairman, died in March 2007.

EXECUTIVES

President and CEO: Steven C. (Steve) Smith, age 50
SVP and COO: Jesse A. Lewis
**SVP Finance and Administration, CFO, Secretary, and
  Treasurer:** Robert L. Neeley
SVP Marketing: Tom Hembree
EVP Operations: Jody Helms
EVP Knoxville Division: John Jones
EVP Merchandising and Marketing: Richard Gunn
EVP Tri-Cities Division: Johnny Cecil
VP Human Resources: Donnie Meadows
VP Research and Real Estate: Lou Scudere
VP Store Planning and Development: Don Smith
VP Community and Government Relations:
  Bob Southerland
General Counsel and Risk Management: Charlie Fugate
Controller: Anne Overbay

LOCATIONS

HQ: K-VA-T Food Stores, Inc.
201 Trigg St., Abingdon, VA 24211
Phone: 276-628-5503 **Fax:** 276-623-5440
Web: www.foodcity.com

2007 Stores

	No.
Tennessee	60
Virginia	22
Kentucky	12
Total	**94**

PRODUCTS/OPERATIONS

Selected Departments

Bakery/Deli
Café
Dairy
Dry goods
Floral
Frozen foods
Gasoline
Meat
Pharmacy
Produce
Seafood
Video

Selected Services

Banking
Money orders
Party planning
Photo processing
Postage stamps

COMPETITORS

A&P
Alex Lee
Associated Wholesale Grocers
BI-LO
Costco Wholesale
Earth Fare
Food Lion
Houchens
Ingles Markets
Kroger
The Pantry
Ruddick
SUPERVALU
Target
Ukrop's Super Markets
Wal-Mart

HISTORICAL FINANCIALS

Company Type: Private

Income Statement

FYE: December 31

	REVENUE ($ mil.)	NET INCOME ($ mil.)	NET PROFIT MARGIN	EMPLOYEES
12/07	1,650	—	—	12,000
12/06	1,570	—	—	11,500
12/05	1,400	—	—	11,000
12/04	1,310	—	—	10,400
12/03	1,200	—	—	10,000
Annual Growth	**8.3%**	**—**	**—**	**4.7%**

Revenue History

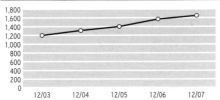

La Madeleine

This company hopes its crème brulee, croissants, and quiche prove as memorable as Proust's famous teacake. La Madeleine operates a chain of more than 60 la Madeleine Bakery, Café & Bistro casual dining locations in six states, offering French country cuisine for breakfast, lunch, and dinner. The restaurants, which welcome patrons with such interior appointments as a stone hearth and handcrafted wood tables, use a cafeteria-style serving line and limited table service. Each location also sells a variety of fresh baked goods. French native Patrick Leon Esquerré started the business in 1983. La Madeleine is owned by a group of investors including Paris-based restaurant operator Groupe Le Duff.

With food service veteran Greg Buchanan at the helm (formerly with Darden and Carlson Restaurants), the company has laid plans to expand to more than 100 restaurants during the next five years. It is also exploring the possibility of franchising new locations to accelerate the chain's growth.

In addition to physical expansion, the company has been focused on improvements to its menu, adding new crepe items for breakfast, lunch, and dinner in 2006. Looking to beef up its lunch offerings, La Madeleine rolled out more roast beef, chicken, and turkey sandwiches during 2007.

Groupe Le Duff, which operates and franchises La Brioche Dorée bistros and Pizza Del Arte quick service restaurants in France, acquired its stake in La Madeleine in 2001 for about $60 million.

EXECUTIVES

Chairman and CEO: Jean-Roch Vachon, age 63
COO: Philip (Phil) Costner
CFO: William (Bill) Schaffler
VP and General Counsel: Harry Martin
Senior Director Culinary: Susan Dederan
Senior Director Information Systems Support: George Popson
Senior Director Marketing: Hal Gronfein
Director Human Resources: Tina Hebert
Recruiting Manager: Jeff Erts

LOCATIONS

HQ: La Madeleine, Inc.
6688 North Central Expwy., Ste. 700,
Dallas, TX 75206
Phone: 214-696-6962 **Fax:** 214-692-8496
Web: www.lamadeleine.com

La Madeleine operates more than 60 restaurants in Georgia, Louisiana, Maryland, Texas, Virginia, and Washington, DC.

Selected Markets

Atlanta
Austin, TX
Baton Rouge, LA
Dallas
Fort Worth, TX
Houston
New Orleans
San Antonio, TX
Washington, DC

COMPETITORS

ABP Corporation
Applebee's
Atlanta Bread
Benihana
Brinker
BUCA
California Pizza Kitchen
Carlson Restaurants
CBC Restaurant
Cheesecake Factory
Consolidated Restaurant Operations
Darden
Einstein Noah Restaurant Group
Houlihan's
Landry's
Marie Callender
Mimi's Cafe
OSI Restaurant Partners
Panera Bread
P.F. Chang's
Ruby Tuesday

Lake Area Corn Processors

Lake Area Corn Processors produces ethanol and its byproduct, distillers grains, which are used in livestock feed. Through its Dakota Ethanol unit, the company produces about 50 million gallons of ethanol per year. Dakota Ethanol had worked in tandem with Broin Companies, a manufacturer of ethanol processing plants, until Lake Area Corn Processors bought out Broin's minority stake in Dakota Ethanol in 2006. The following year the company acquired a stake in its ethanol distributor, Renewable Products Marketing Group. Lake Area Corn Processors is owned by its 1,000 members.

EXECUTIVES

Chairman and CEO: Douglas L. (Doug) Van Duyn, age 54
Vice Chairman: Dale L. Thompson, age 59
CFO and Director: Brian D. Woldt, age 42
Treasurer and Director: Ronald C. Alverson, age 55
Secretary and Director: Randy Hansen, age 48
General Manager: Scott Mundt, age 45
Auditors: McGladrey & Pullen, LLP

LOCATIONS

HQ: Lake Area Corn Processors, LLC
46269 S. Dakota Hwy. 34, Wentworth, SD 57075
Phone: 605-483-2676 **Fax:** 605-483-2681
Web: www.dakotaethanol.com

PRODUCTS/OPERATIONS

2007 Sales

	$ mil.	% of total
Sales	102.9	99
Incentive income	0.8	1
Total	**103.7**	**100**

2007 Sales

	% of total
Ethanol	89
Distillers grains	11
Total	**100**

COMPETITORS

Abengoa Bioenergy
ADM
Badger State Ethanol
Cargill
Golden Grain
Little Sioux
Corn Processors
VeraSun
Williams Companies

HISTORICAL FINANCIALS
Company Type: Private

Income Statement				FYE: December 31
	REVENUE ($ mil.)	NET INCOME ($ mil.)	NET PROFIT MARGIN	EMPLOYEES
12/07	104	18	17.4%	39
12/06	104	46	44.3%	39
12/05	80	11	13.6%	38
12/04	84	8	8.9%	38
12/03	69	5	6.6%	38
Annual Growth	10.6%	40.6%	—	0.7%

2007 Year-End Financials

Debt ratio: —
Return on equity: 31.7%
Cash ($ mil.): —

Current ratio: —
Long-term debt ($ mil.): —

Net Income History

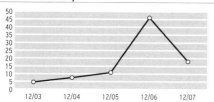

Land O'Lakes

Land O'Lakes butters up its customers, and shows you what life is like if everyone cooperates. Owned by and serving more than 7,000 dairy farmer members and 1,300 community cooperatives, Land O'Lakes is one of the largest dairy co-ops in the US (along with Dairy Farmers of America and California Dairies). It provides its members with wholesale fertilizer and crop protection products, seed, and animal feed. Its oldest and best known product, LAND O' LAKES butter, is the top butter brand in the US. Land O'Lakes also produces packaged milk, margarine, sour cream, and cheese. The co-op's animal-feed division, Land O'Lakes Purina Feed, is a leading animal and pet food maker.

Land O'Lakes also owns egg producer MoArk. (MoArk sold its liquid egg products operations to Golden Oval Eggs in 2006.) In addition, the company's subsidiary, Land O'Lakes Finance, provides financing services for beef, dairy, pork, and poultry producers.

In 2007 the company sold its international cheese and protein operations (known as CPI) to Saputo Cheese USA for about $216 million. The sale included the Golden Valley Dairy Products cheese manufacturing and cut-and-wrap operations. The deal also included a long-term milks agreement, making Land O'Lakes the sole milk supplier for CPI.

Also in 2007 Land O'Lakes and CHS realigned the businesses of their 50-50 joint venture Agriliance in 2007, with CHS acquiring its crop-nutrients wholesale products business and Land O'Lakes acquiring the crop-protection products business. The two companies are looking for a buyer for the one remaining Agriliance operation, retail agronomy.

Outside of the US, Land O'Lakes has taken aim at the largest emerging market: China, where the company is working to establish the Land O'Lakes brand of cheese and cultured dairy products in supermarkets.

HISTORY

In the old days, grocers sold butter from communal tubs and it often went bad. Widespread distribution of dairy products had to await the invention of fast, reliable transportation. By 1921 the necessary transportation was available. That year about 320 dairy farmers in Minnesota formed the Minnesota Cooperative Creameries Association and launched a membership drive with $1,375, mostly borrowed from the US Farm Bureau.

The co-op arranged joint shipments for members, imposed strict hygiene and quality standards, and aggressively marketed its sweet cream butter nationwide, packaged for the first time in the familiar box of four quarter-pound sticks. A month after the co-op's New York sales office opened, it was ordering 80 shipments a week.

Minnesota Cooperative Creameries, as part of its promotional campaigns, ran a contest in 1924 to name that butter. Two contestants offered the winning name — Land O'Lakes. The distinctive Indian Maiden logo first appeared about the same time, and in 1926 the co-op changed its name to Land O'Lakes Creameries. By 1929, when it began supplying feed, its market share approached 50%.

During WWII civilian consumption dropped, but the co-op increased production of dried milk to provide food for soldiers and newly liberated concentration camp victims.

In the 1950s and 1960s Land O'Lakes added ice cream and yogurt producers to its membership and fought margarine makers, yet butter's market share continued to melt. The co-op diversified in 1970 through acquisitions, adding feeds and agricultural chemicals. Two years later Land O'Lakes threw in the towel and came out with its own margarine. Despite the decreasing use of butter nationally, the co-op's market share grew.

Land O'Lakes formed a marketing joint venture, Cenex/Land O'Lakes Agronomy, with fellow co-op Cenex in 1987. As health consciousness bloomed in the 1980s, Land O'Lakes launched reduced-fat dairy products. It also purchased a California cheese plant, doubling its capacity. Land O'Lakes began ramping up its international projects at the same time: It built a feed mill in Taiwan, introduced feed products in Mexico, and established feed and cheese operations in Poland.

In 1997 the co-op bought low-fat cheese maker Alpine Lace Brands. Land O'Lakes took on the eastern US when it merged with the 3,600-member Atlantic Dairy Cooperative (1997), and it bulked up on the West Coast when California-based Dairyman's Cooperative Creamery Association joined its fold (1998).

During 2000 the co-op sold five plants to Dean Foods with an agreement to continue supplying the plants with raw milk. Also in 2000 Land

O'Lakes combined its feed business with those of Farmland Industries to create Land O'Lakes Farmland Feed, LLC, with a 69% ownership. That same year, Land O'Lakes and CHS joined their agronomy operations to create a 50-50 joint venture, Agriliance LLC.

In late 2001 the company spent $359 million to acquire Purina Mills (pet and livestock feeds). Purina Mills was folded into Land O'Lakes Farmland Feed and, as part of the purchase, Land O'Lakes increased its ownership of the feed business to 92%. In 2004 it purchased the remaining 8%.

To take advantage of its nationally recognized brand, Land O'Lakes formed an alliance with Dean Foods in 2002 to develop and market value-added dairy products.

Exiting the meat business, Land O'Lakes sold its swine operations in 2005 to private pork producer Maschhoff West LLC for an undisclosed sum. That same year it sold its interest in fertilizer manufacturer CF Industries. Long-time president and CEO Jack Gherty retired that year; he was replaced by Chris Policinski. In 2006 the company acquired 100% ownership of MoArk.

EXECUTIVES

Chairman: Peter (Pete) Kappelman, age 45
First Vice Chairman: Ronnie Mohr, age 59
President and CEO: Chris Policinski, age 49, $750,000 pay
EVP; COO, Dairy Foods Industrial: Alan Pierson, age 57
EVP; COO, Dairy Foods Value-Added: Steve Dunphy, age 50
EVP; COO, Feed: Fernando J. Palacios, age 48, $445,303 pay
EVP, Land O'Lakes Ag Business Development and Member Services: David L. (Dave) Seehusen, age 61, $265,700 pay
EVP; COO, Seed Division: Mike Vandelogt, age 53
EVP; COO, Crop Protection Products: Rodney (Rod) Schroeder, age 52
SVP and CFO: Daniel E. Knutson, age 51, $451,690 pay
SVP and General Counsel: Peter S. Janzen, age 48, $352,008 pay
SVP Corporate Strategy and Business Development: Jean-Paul (JP) Ruiz-Funes, age 50
SVP Corporate Marketing Strategy: Barry Wolfish, age 51
VP Human Resources: Karen Grabow, age 58
VP Public Affairs: James D. (Jim) Fife, age 58
Secretary and Director: Douglas (Doug) Reimer, age 57
Director, Corporate Communications: Lydia Botham
Auditors: KPMG LLP

LOCATIONS

HQ: Land O'Lakes, Inc.
4001 Lexington Ave. North, Arden Hills, MN 55112
Phone: 651-481-2222   **Fax:** 651-481-2000
Web: www.landolakesinc.com

PRODUCTS/OPERATIONS

2007 Sales

	% of total
Dairy foods	47
Feed	34
Seed	10
Layers	6
Agronomy	3
Total	**100**

Selected Brands

Alpine Lace (low-fat cheese)
CROPLAN GENETICS (crop seed)
LAND O' LAKES (consumer dairy products)
Land O'Lakes (animal feed)
New Yorker (cheese)

Dairy Products

Butter
Cheese
Flavored butter
Light butter
Margarine
Milk
Sour cream

Selected Joint Ventures

Advanced Food Products (35%, with Bongrain, S.A.)
Agriliance LLC (50%, with CHS, Inc.)

COMPETITORS

ADM	Kraft Foods
AMPI	Michael Foods Egg
Blue Seal Feeds	Products
Breeder's Choice	Michael Foods, Inc.
California Dairies Inc.	Monsanto Company
Cal-Maine Foods	MSC
Cargill	National Dairy Holdings
ConAgra	Nestlé
Dairy Farmers of America	Nestlé Purina PetCare
Darigold, Inc.	Nestlé USA
Dean Foods	Northwest Dairy
Doane Pet Care	Pioneer Hi-Bred
Fonterra	Prairie Farms Dairy
Foremost Farms	Rose Acre Farms
Frontier Agriculture	Royal Canin
Hartz Mountain	Saputo
Hill's Pet Nutrition	Sargento
HP Hood	Schreiber Foods
Iams	Syngenta Seeds
Keller's Creamery	Unilever
Kent Feeds	

HISTORICAL FINANCIALS

Company Type: Cooperative

Income Statement

FYE: December 31

	REVENUE ($ mil.)	NET INCOME ($ mil.)	NET PROFIT MARGIN	EMPLOYEES
12/07	8,925	164	1.8%	8,700
12/06	7,275	89	1.2%	8,500
12/05	7,557	129	1.7%	7,500
12/04	7,677	21	0.3%	8,000
12/03	6,321	84	1.3%	8,000
Annual Growth	9.0%	18.3%	—	2.1%

2007 Year-End Financials

Debt ratio: 59.3%
Return on equity: 16.6%
Cash ($ mil.): —
Current ratio: —
Long-term debt ($ mil.): 612

Net Income History

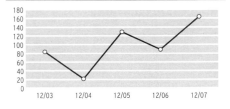

Landmark Communications

Once a leading diversified media conglomerate, Landmark Communications is in the process of selling its portfolio of newspapers and other regional publications. Its flagship subsidiary, The Weather Channel Companies, was sold in 2008 to NBC Universal and a group of private equity firms, while its remaining properties were transferred to affiliate Landmark Media Enterprises. Those remaining properties up for sale include three major daily newspapers (*The Virginian-Pilot*, *News & Record*, and *The Roanoke Times*) in North Carolina and Virginia, as well as more than 50 community papers in about 15 states. Landmark is owned by chairman Frank Batten Jr. and his family.

With the newspaper industry in wide decline due to waning advertising revenue and reader interest, Landmark announced a strategic review in early 2008 that led to a decision to break-up the company's holdings. The announcement came a little more than a year after Landmark split up its holdings in Trader Publishing with co-owner Cox Enterprises in 2006 as part of an effort to reduce its exposure to the volatile classified advertising business. Landmark kept Trader's real estate, apartment, employment, and recreational holdings and put them into a new company, Dominion Enterprises.

Landmark sold digital marketing unit Q Interactive to merchant banking firm Intrepid Investments. NBC Universal in partnership with private equity firms Bain Capital and The Blackstone Group acquired The Weather Channel for about $3.5 billion. Landmark had launched the 24-hour cable weather channel in 1982.

Batten family scion Frank Batten Sr. is known for his support of education, having donated more than $220 million to various schools, mostly in Virginia. In 2007 he gave $100 million to the University of Virginia to start the Frank Batten School of Leadership and Public Policy.

EXECUTIVES

Chairman and CEO: Frank Batten Jr.
Vice Chairman: Richard F. Barry III
President and COO: S. Decker Anstrom, age 57
EVP and CFO: Teresa F. Blevins
EVP, Landmark Publishing Group and Publisher, The Viginian-Pilot: R. Bruce Bradley
EVP, Corporate Secretary, and Corporate Counsel: Guy Friddell III
EVP, Human Resources: Charlie W. Hill
VP, Tax, Audit, and Analysis: Colleen R. Pittman
President, Landmark Interactive: Michael W. Alston
President and Publisher, Landmark Community Newspapers: Michael G. (Mike) Abernathy
President, Landmark Education Services: Dan Sykes
President and CEO, Trader Publishing Company: Conrad M. Hall
President, WSI: Mark Gildersleeve

LOCATIONS

HQ: Landmark Communications, Inc.
150 W. Brambleton Ave., Norfolk, VA 23510
Phone: 757-446-2010   **Fax:** 757-446-2489
Web: www.landmarkcom.com

PRODUCTS/OPERATIONS

Selected Operations

Daily newspapers
   News & Record (Greensboro, NC)
   The Roanoke Times (Virginia)
   The Virginian-Pilot (Norfolk)
Military publications
   The Bayonet (Columbus, GA)
   The Flagship (Hampton Roads, VA)
   Jet Observer (Virginia Beach, VA)
   RotoVue (Jacksonville, NC)
   Sentinel (Killeen, TX)
Other businesses
   Alliant Cooperative Data Solutions (database marketing)
   BusinessBroker.net (real estate)
   Capital-Gazette Communications (community newspapers)
   Continental Broadband (managed data network services)
   Franchise Solutions (business opportunity network)
   Landmark Community Newspapers

COMPETITORS

Cox Newspapers
Data Transmission Network
Gannett
Journal Broadcast Group
McClatchy Company
Media General
Meredith Corporation
New York Times
Sinclair Broadcast Group
Tribune Company
Washington Post

HISTORICAL FINANCIALS

Company Type: Private

Income Statement

FYE: December 31

	ESTIMATED REVENUE ($ mil.)	NET INCOME ($ mil.)	NET PROFIT MARGIN	EMPLOYEES
12/07	1,400	—	—	7,500
12/06	1,750	—	—	12,000
12/05	1,719	—	—	11,750
Annual Growth	(9.8%)	—	(20.1%)	

Revenue History

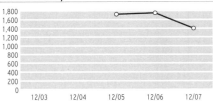

Latham & Watkins

Latham & Watkins' founders Dana Latham and Paul Watkins flipped a coin in 1934 to determine which of their names would go first on the law firm's shingle. From that coin toss, the firm has grown into one of the largest in the US and boasts more than 2,100 lawyers in some two dozen offices around the world, from Europe to Asia. Latham & Watkins organizes its practices into five main areas: corporate; environment, land, and resources; finance; litigation; and tax. The firm has counted companies such as Amgen, Time Warner Inc., and Morgan Stanley among its clients.

In an effort to expand globally in both leading and emerging financial, commercial, and regulatory capitals, Latham & Watkins is relocating some of its US and UK partners to the Middle East. The firm announced plans to open at least three offices in the Gulf region to support cross-border mergers and acquisitions and other corporate finance deals, particularly between London and the Middle East.

EXECUTIVES

Chairman and Managing Partner: Robert M. (Bob) Dell
Vice Chairman and Chief Operating Partner:
 Mark E. Newell
COO: LeeAnn Black
CFO: Grant Johnson
CIO: Kenneth L. Heaps
Chief Human Resources Officer: Mimi A. Krumholz
Chief Marketing Officer: Despina Kartson
Chief Real Estate and Facilities Officer: James E. Dow
Chief Administrative Officer: Wendy E. Ward
Chief Attorney Development Officer: Ann Huang Miller
Global Recruiting Manager: Skip Horne
Vice Chair, Global Tax Department: Daniel Friel
Global Chair, Finance Department: David Heller
Director Global Public Relations and Communications:
 Geoff Burt

LOCATIONS

HQ: Latham & Watkins LLP
 885 3rd Ave., New York, NY 10022
Phone: 212-906-1200   **Fax:** 212-751-4864
Web: www.lw.com

PRODUCTS/OPERATIONS

Selected Practice Areas
Antitrust and competition
Appellate
Banking
Benefits and compensation
Communications
Company representation
Corporate finance
Employment law
Energy and natural resources
Entertainment, sports, and media
Environmental litigation
Environmental regulatory
Environmental transactional support
French practice
Gaming, hotels, and hospitality
German practice

Government contracts
Government relations
Greater China practice
Health care and life sciences
Insolvency
Insurance coverage litigation
Intellectual property, media, and technology
International dispute resolution
International tax
Investment and strategic ventures
Israel practice
Italian practice
Land use
Latin American practice
Life sciences
Mergers and acquisitions
Outsourcing
Private equity
Private equity finance
Pro bono
Product liability and mass torts
Project finance
Public and tax-exempt finance
Public international law
Real estate
REITs
Scandinavian practice
Securities litigation and professional liability
Spanish practice
Stock options timing
Structured finance and securitization
Tax controversy
Tax-exempt organizations
Technology transactions
Transactional tax
Venture and technology
White collar and government investigations

COMPETITORS

Baker & McKenzie
Clifford Chance
Davis Polk
Gibson, Dunn & Crutcher
Holland & Knight
Kirkland & Ellis
O'Melveny & Myers
Paul, Hastings
Ropes & Gray
Simpson Thacher
Skadden, Arps
Sullivan & Cromwell
Weil, Gotshal

HISTORICAL FINANCIALS
Company Type: Partnership

Income Statement

	REVENUE ($ mil.)	NET INCOME ($ mil.)	NET PROFIT MARGIN	EMPLOYEES	FYE: December 31
12/07	2,005	—	—	—	
12/06	1,624	—	—	4,500	
12/05	1,413	—	—	4,234	
Annual Growth	19.1%	—	—	6.3%	

Revenue History

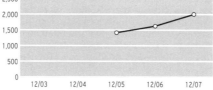

Laureate Education

If higher education is a matter of degrees, Laureate must be hot. Laureate Education, formerly Sylvan Learning Systems, provides full-time and working adult career education through online and campus-based programs in Asia, the Americas, and Europe. Laureate's educational institutions offer more than 100 bachelor's, master's, and doctoral degrees and specializations to a combined enrollment of more than 240,000. Students can earn degrees in areas such as business, education, hospitality management, law, and medicine. Laureate's Canter unit provides professional development and training programs for teachers. An investment group headed by chairman and CEO Douglas Becker owns the company.

Strong profits have allowed the company to aggressively expand its operations and build its collection of private universities around the world. In 2006 Laureate bought out Chilean partner Indeco (and its Ecuadorean subsidiary), and the following year it acquired Mexico's Universidad Valle del Bravo, adding five campuses and some 4,500 students. In early 2008 it took a 76%-stake in German college BiTS and it now plans to acquire a controlling stake in INTI College in Malaysia.

The company also has expanded in Mexico and Latin America with the acquisition of Costa Rica-based universities Universidad Latina de Costa Rica and Universidad Americana, and Mexican private university Universidad Tecnologica de Mexico (UNITEC). In 2008 the company expanded its stake in the Brazilian university Anhembi-Morumbi and plans to buy Faculdade Boa Viagem. The acquisitions are in line with Laureate's goal of having 100,000 college students in Brazil over the next few years.

Management took the company private in a leveraged buyout in 2007. According to its chairman, the move will allow it to expand in China, South Korea, and India.

EXECUTIVES

Chairman and CEO: Douglas L. (Doug) Becker, age 42, $1,450,000 pay
President and COO: Neal S. Cohen, age 48
EVP and CFO: Eilif Serck-Hanssen
EVP Corporate Operations: Daniel M. Nickel, $360,000 pay
SVP Education and Academic and Quality and University Network Programs and Partnerships:
 Joseph D. Duffey
SVP and Chief Accounting Officer: Amit Rai
SVP and General Counsel: Robert W. (Bob) Zentz
President, Latin America Operations:
 William C. (Bill) Dennis Jr., $1,216,000 pay
President, Laureate Online Education: Paula R. Singer, $660,750 pay
Director Investor Relations and Corporate Communications: Christopher (Chris) Symanoskie
Director Public Relations: Ana Sánchez
Auditors: Ernst & Young LLP

LOCATIONS

HQ: Laureate Education, Inc.
650 S. Exeter St., Baltimore, MD 21202
Phone: 410-843-6100
Web: www.laureate-inc.com

PRODUCTS/OPERATIONS

Selected Operations

Online
Canter & Associates
National Technological University (NTU)
Walden University
Campus-based
Asia
Les Roches Jin Jiang International Hotel
Management School
Central America
Universidad del Valle de México
Universidad Interamericana de Costa Rica
Universidad Interamericana de Panama
Universidad Latinoamericana de Ciencia y
Tecnología (ULACIT)
Europe
Cyprus College
Ècole Centrale D'Electonique
Ècole Supérieure du Commerce Extérieur
Glion Institute of Higher Education
Les Roches Hotel Management School
Les Roches Marbella
Universidad Europea de Madrid
South America
Universidade Anhembi Morumbi
Universidad Nacional Andrés Bello
Universidad Peruana de Ciencias Aplicadas
Universidad Privada del Norte (UPN)

COMPETITORS

Apollo Group
Berlitz
Corinthian Colleges
DeVry
ITT Educational
PLATO Learning
Strayer Education

HISTORICAL FINANCIALS

Company Type: Private

Income Statement

	REVENUE ($ mil.)	NET INCOME ($ mil.)	NET PROFIT MARGIN	EMPLOYEES
				FYE: December 31
12/07	1,420	—	—	28,500
12/06	1,146	—	—	23,000
12/05	875	—	—	22,800
12/04	648	—	—	17,534
12/03	473	—	—	13,374
Annual Growth	31.6%	—	—	20.8%

Revenue History

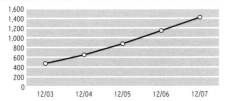

Leading Edge Brands

Leading Edge Brands is a soft drink marketer and manufacturer offering consumer products in the Caribbean, Mexico, the South Pacific, and the US. It owns the Frostie root beer brand, which dates back to 1936. The company also sells bottled water under the Heaven's Rain label. The company was founded in 1997 after acquiring the Kist and Flavette brand names from Monarch Beverage. That was followed by the purchase from Monarch of the Frostie label in 2000.

EXECUTIVES

CEO: Webb Stickney
President, Beverage Group: Tab Baxley
VP, Sales: Johnny Baird
Auditors: BDO Dunwoody LLP

LOCATIONS

HQ: Leading Edge Brands, LLC
4001 Central Pointe Pkwy., Temple, TX 76504
Phone: 254-770-6110   **Fax:** 254-770-6119
Web: www.leadingedgebrands.com

PRODUCTS/OPERATIONS

Selected Brands

Flavette
Frostie
Heaven's Rain
ignite
Kist
Tampico

COMPETITORS

Clearly Canadian	Hansen Natural
Coca-Cola	Jones Soda
Cott	Nestlé Waters
Danone Water	PepsiCo
Dr Pepper Snapple Group	Reed's

Lefrak Organization

Horace Greeley said, "Go west, young man!" and The Lefrak Organization listened — at least, if you take the famous *New Yorker* comic strip's view that you're in the Midwest once you cross the Hudson. The Lefrak Organization is a real estate development company and one of the US's largest private landlords, managing hundreds of apartment buildings (affordable and upscale) in New York, New Jersey, and more recently California, as well as millions of square feet of commercial space. Lefrak's office and retail holdings include its flagship office tower at 40 West 57th Street in midtown Manhattan, home to such tenants as Bank of America, Nautica, and Wells Fargo. Still family-owned and run, Lefrak was founded in 1901.

The Lefrak Organization has developed property in New Jersey since 1995, focusing solely on the $10 billion mixed-use Newport in Jersey City. The 600-acre community of apartments, shopping centers, hotels, and office buildings

sits on the Hudson River waterfront overlooking Lower Manhattan. The company has built office towers (occupied by CIGNA, U.S. Trust, and UBS Financial Services, among others) on the site, and plans for further developments are under way. When completed, the development will include 9,000 apartment units and 9 million sq. ft. of commercial space.

Although the company has sold some of its older working-class apartment buildings in Queens and Brooklyn, Lefrak reportedly has no plans to sell its flagship residential development, the 5,000-unit LeFrak City in Queens, which has been home to successive waves of ethnic groups and working- and middle-class tenants.

However, the organization is branching out beyond New York in an atttempt to diversify geographically, for the first time buying office buildings in Beverly Hills, California and a development site on Hollywood Boulevard, which it plans to turn into a luxury high-rise apartment complex. It is also actively looking for a big development site in London. Lefrak's commercial properties generate almost half its revenues.

In addition to real estate, The Lefrak Organization has holdings in oil and gas exploration and wind energy generation through its Lefrak Oil and Gas Organization Inc. (LOGO).

HISTORY

Harry LeFrak and his father Aaron came to the US from Palestine (or France — there are many conflicting versions of the LeFrak family history — Aaron's father Maurice is said to have been a developer there in the 1840s) around 1900. They began building tenements in Brooklyn's Williamsburg neighborhood to house the flood of immigrants then pouring into New York City.

In 1901, Harry and Aaron started what is now known as The Lefrak Organization. It diversified into glass and for some time provided raw material for the workshops of Louis Comfort Tiffany. After WWI the glass factory was sold, and the company expanded into Brooklyn, where it developed housing and commercial space in Bedford-Stuyvesant, among other areas.

Samuel, Harry's son, began working in the business early, assisting tradesmen at building sites. He then attended the University of Maryland, and shunning a future career in dentistry (family lore claims his left-handedness would have required special tools), returned to the business. Samuel's first project was a 120-unit apartment building in Brooklyn's Midwood — it was 1938, and he was 20 years old and still a university student.

During WWII, the firm built camps and housing for the Army. After the war, business took off, as the company began building low-cost housing. Samuel took over the company in 1948. To keep costs down, Samuel bought clay and gypsum quarries, forests, and lumber mills and cement plants, eventually achieving 70% vertical integration of his operations. This included the creation of in-house architectural, engineering, and construction departments that handled all aspects of building the Lefrak empire's properties — from initial designs to general contracting — from the ground up.

The 1950s building boom was in part spurred by new laws in New York authorizing the issue of state bonds for financing low-interest construction loans, which Lefrak used to build more than 2,000 apartments in previously undeveloped coastal sections of Brooklyn. At its peak,

Lefrak turned out an apartment every 16 minutes for rents as low as $21 per room.

In 1960 Lefrak broke ground for LeFrak City, a 5,000-apartment development built on 40 acres in Queens (after four years of negotiations with the trustees of the William Waldorf Astor estate over the sale price — $6 million), which featured air-conditioned units and rented for $40 per room.

The next decade brought a real estate slump that endangered the organization's next project, Battery Park. Lefrak issued public bonds to save it. Samuel also picked up a few more properties during this period, and he capitalized the "F" in his family name but not the company name. (He later said that he did this to distinguish himself from other Lefraks at his club who had been posted for nonpayment of dues, though a conflicting story states that his mother's French-born physician originally capitalized the "F" on Samuel's birth certificate.)

Samuel's son Richard became president of the company in 1975. Richard oversaw an even bigger project: the 600-acre Newport City development, begun in 1989 with plans for some 10,000 apartments and retail and commercial space.

Meanwhile, Lefrak City had "turned," as its original Jewish occupants sought greener fields. As occupancy dropped, the company relaxed its tenant screening, and the development deteriorated (it was subsequently tagged "Crack City"). In the 1990s, however, it began attracting a mix of African, Jewish, and Central Asian immigrants, whose tightly knit communities improved the development's safety and equilibrium.

Construction of the company's Newport project continued throughout the 1990s with construction of office buildings, apartments, and a hotel (completed in 2000) on the site. As a tight Manhattan office market drove up lease prices, Lefrak's new offices across the Hudson attracted companies in the finance and insurance sectors. Lefrak filled about 3 million sq. ft. in its Newport development during 1999 and 2000.

In 2001 the company's Gateway complex in Battery Park City was damaged in the World Trade Center terrorist attack. The tenants threatened a rent strike, prompting Lefrak to lower rents to compensate for the difficulties attributed to living near the site.

Samuel LeFrak died in April 2003 at the age of 85.

EXECUTIVES

Chairman, President, and CEO: Richard S. LeFrak, age 62
Managing Director: Harrison LeFrak
Managing Director: James (Jamie) LeFrak
EVP and Chief Investment and Financial Officer: Richard N. Papert
SVP Marketing and Public Relations: Edward Cortese
SVP Development: Marsilia (Marcy) Boyle
SVP and General Manager: Charles J. Mehlman
SVP, Finance and Accounting: Judy Wortsmann
SVP Construction and Engineering: Anthony Scavo
VP Commercial: Irwin Granville
VP Asset Management: Mitchell Ingerman
Assistant VP Human Resources and Administration: John Farrelly
CIO: Robert A. Brennan
General Counsel: Arnold S. Lehman
Director, Residential Leasing: Michael Bass
Auditors: Ernst & Young LLP

LOCATIONS

HQ: Lefrak Organization Inc.
 40 W. 57th St., New York, NY 10019
Phone: 212-708-6600   **Fax:** 212-708-6641
Web: www.lefrak.com

The Lefrak Organization operates primarily in New Jersey, New York, and California.

Selected Properties

Commercial space
 Jersey City, NJ
  Newport development
 New York City (Manhattan)
  40 W. 57th St.
  Gateway Plaza at Battery Park City
  James Tower
Residential apartments
 Jersey City, NJ
  Atlantic
  East Hampton
  James Monroe
  Presidential Plaza
  Riverside
  Southampton
  Towers of America
 New York City (Manhattan)
  Gateway Plaza at Battery Park City
 New York City (Queens)
  LeFrak City
Residential co-op properties
 New York City (Brooklyn)
  Bay Ridge
  Bensonhurst
  Flatbush
  Park Slope
  Sheepshead Bay
 New York City (Queens)
  Elmhurst
  Flushing
  Forest Hills
  Key Gardens
  Rego Park
  Woodside
Retail
 Jersey City, NJ
  Newport Centre Mall

PRODUCTS/OPERATIONS

Selected Operations

Energy
 Lefrak Oil & Gas Organization
Entertainment
 Lefrak Entertainment Company
Real estate
 Commercial properties
 Residential apartments
 Residential co-op properties
 Retail properties
Telecommunications
 Newport Telephone Company, Inc.

COMPETITORS

AIMCO	Grenadier
Alexander's	Helmsley Enterprises
Apollo Advisors	Mack-Cali
AvalonBay	Macklowe Properties
Boston Properties	Silverstein Properties
Centerline Capital Group	SL Green Realty
Durst Organization	Tishman
Equity Office Properties	The Trump Organization
Equity Residential	Vornado Realty
Forest City Ratner	Witkoff Group

Leprino Foods

Don't try to butter up Leprino Foods — it's into mozzarella with a capital "M." The company is a worldwide leader in mozzarella making. It sells its mozzarella to pizza purveyors large and small, including powerhouses like Domino's, Papa John's, and Pizza Hut, as well as to food manufacturers. Leprino's other products include whey protein concentrate and lactose for use in animal feeds, yogurt, baby formula, and baked goods. Supplied by the nation's large dairy co-ops, Leprino hitches its sales to the continuing rise in the global popularity of pizza. The company has a joint venture located in the UK called Glanbia Cheese with Glanbia. It is also a top maker of pizza cheese in Europe.

In addition to mozzarella, the company makes reduced-fat cheddar, reduced-fat Monterey Jack, and queso cheeses.

One of the company's top customers is the world's largest food company, Nestlé, which uses Leprino's products for manufacturing Hot Pockets and Stouffer's microwave pizzas.

Headquartered in Denver, Leprino has 10 cheesemaking sites in the US. Overseas, it has two plants in the UK. Italian immigrant Michael Leprino Sr. founded the company in 1950. It is still owned and managed by the Leprino family. Company chairman billionaire James Leprino is listed in the *Forbes* 400.

EXECUTIVES

Chairman: James Leprino, age 70
President: Larry Jensen
SVP, Administration: Ron Klump
SVP, Quality Assurance and Research and Development: Richard Barz
SVP, Sales and Marketing: Robert D. (Bob) Boynton
SVP, Production Operations: Bob DeLong
SVP, People Development: Bradley (Brad) Olsen
SVP, Procurement, Logistics, and Business Development: Mike Reidy
VP and Controller: Paul Adams

LOCATIONS

HQ: Leprino Foods Company
 1830 W. 38th Ave., Denver, CO 80211
Phone: 303-480-2600   **Fax:** 303-480-2605
Web: www.leprinofoods.com

COMPETITORS

Agri-Mark
AMPI
Bel Brands USA
Century Foods
Crystal Farms Refrigerated Distribution Company
Ellsworth Cooperative
F. Cappiello Dairy Products
Foremost Farms
Great Lakes Cheese
Kraft Foods
Main Street Ingredients
Saputo
Sargento
Schreiber Foods
Sorrento Lactalis
Tate & Lyle

Les Schwab Tire Centers

If you need new tires after heeding Greeley's advice, go to Les Schwab Tire Centers. And it doesn't hurt that the owner wrote the bible of tire retailing: *Pride in Performance — Keep It Going.* Les Schwab Tire Centers prides itself on continued customer service; it sells tires and batteries and does alignment, brake, and shock work at about 410 stores in California, Idaho, Montana, Nevada, Oregon, Utah, Alaska, and Washington. With a story that rivals Moses', late founder Les Schwab was reared in a logging camp and went to school in a converted boxcar. In 1952 he bought a tire shop that grew into Les Schwab Tire Centers. The firm, owned by Schwab's family, plans to open about 20 stores a year.

In December 2006 Dick Borgman, an attorney and 16-year veteran of the company, succeeded founder Les Schwab as CEO of the tire chain. Schwab died in May 2007 at age 89. Chairman Phil Wick plans to retire at the end of 2008 after a 40-year career with the firm. Borgman will add the chairman's title at that time.

The U.S. Equal Employment Opportunity Commission (EEOC) in mid-2006 sued Les Schwab Tire Centers charging that the company violated federal law by failing to hire, train, and promote women into management jobs.

The company trails rivals Discount Tire Co. and Tire Kingdom in sales.

EXECUTIVES

Chairman: Philip (Phil) Wick
CEO: Dick Borgman
CFO: Tom Freedman
VP Advertising and Marketing: Brian Capp
Director Development: Dave Husk
Director Human Resources: Jodie Hueske

LOCATIONS

HQ: Les Schwab Tire Centers
646 NW Madras Hwy., Prineville, OR 97754
Phone: 541-447-4136   **Fax:** 541-416-5488
Web: www.lesschwab.com

COMPETITORS

Advance Auto Parts
AutoZone
BFS Retail & Commercial
Bridgestone Americas
Commercial Tire
CSK Auto
Discount Tire
Goodyear
Pep Boys
Sears
TBC
TCI Tire Centers
Wal-Mart

HISTORICAL FINANCIALS

Company Type: Private

Income Statement

FYE: December 31

	REVENUE ($ mil.)	NET INCOME ($ mil.)	NET PROFIT MARGIN	EMPLOYEES
12/07	1,480	—	—	7,900
12/06	1,360	—	—	7,700
12/05	1,200	—	—	6,000
12/04	1,150	—	—	5,800
12/03	1,000	—	—	6,000
Annual Growth	10.3%	—	—	7.1%

Revenue History

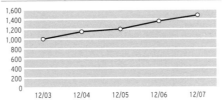

Leslie's Poolmart

Leslie's Poolmart is the big fish of pool product retailers. The company sells pool chemicals, cleaning and testing equipment, covers, and recreational items through about 575 stores in some 35 states, mostly in Arizona, California, Florida, and Texas. It also sells through catalogs and its Web site. Leslie's makes chlorine tablets and repackages other chemicals to be sold under the Leslie name. (Leslie's brand products account for nearly 40% of sales.) Pool chemicals, major equipment, and parts account for a majority of sales. Founded in 1963, Leslie's went private in a 1997 management LBO backed by Leonard Green & Partners, which owns more than 80% of the company.

The company locates its stores in an area with a high number of swimming pools. Its stores are found in strip malls or in freestanding sites near other retail traffic. It generally draws its customers from a five-mile trade area.

Leslie's Poolmart maintains a more-than-7-million-address mailing list, which includes some 90% of residential ground pools in the US.

EXECUTIVES

Chairman and CEO: Lawrence H. Hayward, age 53, $1,059,850 pay
President, COO, and Director: Michael L. Hatch, age 54, $356,282 pay
EVP, CFO, and Director: Steven L. Ortega, age 46, $620,641 pay
SVP Store Operations: Brian P. Agnew, age 42
SVP Commercial, Service, and Logistics: Rick D. Carlson, age 43, $238,688 pay
SVP and CIO: Janet I. McDonald, age 50, $263,728 pay
Auditors: Ernst & Young LLP

LOCATIONS

HQ: Leslie's Poolmart, Inc.
3925 E. Broadway Rd., Ste. 100, Phoenix, AZ 85040
Phone: 602-366-3999   **Fax:** 602-366-3934
Web: www.lesliespool.com

2007 Stores

	No.
California	128
Texas	105
Florida	66
Arizona	61
New York	22
Georgia	22
New Jersey	21
Pennsylvania	18
Nevada	17
Ohio	10
Connecticut	9
Missouri	8
Louisiana	8
Massachusetts	7
Michigan	7
Oklahoma	7
Virginia	7
Indiana	7
Maryland	6
Tennessee	6
Alabama	5
Illinois	5
Kentucky	4
North Carolina	4
South Carolina	3
Other states	14
Total	**577**

COMPETITORS

Home Depot
Keller Supply
Kmart
Pacific Sands
Paddock Pool
Pelican Sport Center
Pool Corp.
Target
Wal-Mart

HISTORICAL FINANCIALS

Company Type: Private

Income Statement

FYE: Saturday nearest September 30

	REVENUE ($ mil.)	NET INCOME ($ mil.)	NET PROFIT MARGIN	EMPLOYEES
9/07	469	32	6.9%	2,200
9/06	441	21	4.7%	2,201
9/05	389	(4)	—	2,026
9/04	356	16	4.6%	1,892
9/03	327	10	3.1%	2,006
Annual Growth	9.4%	33.0%	—	2.3%

Net Income History

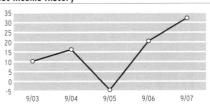

Levi Strauss

Levi Strauss & Co. (LS&CO.) strives to provide the world's casual workday wardrobe, inside and out. LS&CO., a top maker of brand-name clothing globally, sells jeans and sportswear under the Levi's, Dockers, and Levi Strauss Signature names in more than 110 countries. It also markets men's and women's underwear and loungewear. Levi's jeans — department store staples — were once the uniform of American youth, but LS&CO. has been working to reconnect with the niche and expand outside the US. It transformed its product offerings to include wrinkle-free and stain-resistant fabrics used in the making of some of its Levi's and Dockers slacks. The Haas family (relatives of founder Levi Strauss) owns LS&CO.

The Levi's brand accounted for 73% of the manufacturer's 2007 sales. That's up from 71% in 2005. Sales of products with the Dockers label, which represented 21% in 2007, have experienced similar increases, up from 19% in 2005. The company's Signature by Levi Strauss & Co. brand, however, has seen a dip in the past two years, accounting for 6% in 2007, down from 10% in 2005.

Levi Strauss overhauled its marketing strategy by expanding its products portfolio. Rather than relying on its basic one or two styles and brands, Levi's hoped to regain some of the market share lost to VF Corporation (maker of Lee and Wrangler) and others over the past decade. It's also finding sales gains in Asia/Pacific and European markets, as its sales in North America remain lackluster.

Specifically, Levi's Superlow jeans and Levi Strauss Signature jeans were created for the mass market, although their distribution in the US was short-lived. Dockers Flat Front Mobile pants (with secret pockets for cell phones, PDAs, and other gadgets) and Dockers Go Khaki pants (with Stain Defender, a Teflon treatment preventing stains) target the 25-to-39 age group. Undaunted by a slate of disappointing and stale brands, Levi Strauss revamped a number of its basic products, including Levi's 501, 550, and 515. In 2006 it debuted denim and other items made from organic materials. J.C. Penney Company represented 9% of 2007 sales; retailer Target carries Levi's Signature line.

Through licensing deals the company has extended its reach into other niche markets in recent years. Through a licensing agreement with Delhi, India-based M&B Footwear, LS&CO. launched men's and women's casual shoes and sneakers. LS&CO., under license by Signature Apparel Group, added Levi-brand underwear and loungewear to its portfolio.

Philip Marineau retired at the end of 2006. John Anderson, president of LS&CO.'s Asia Pacific Division and head of the firm's global supply chain unit, replaced Marineau as president and CEO.

In December 2007 Levi Strauss chairman Robert Haas announced plans to retire after 18 years in that role. His successor was Dryer's ice cream executive T. Gary Rogers.

HISTORY

Levi Strauss arrived in New York City from Bavaria in 1847. In 1853 he moved to San Francisco to sell dry goods to the gold rushers. Shortly after, a prospector told Strauss of miners' problems in finding sturdy pants. Strauss made a pair out of canvas for the prospector; word of the rugged pants spread quickly.

Strauss continued his dry-goods business in the 1860s. During this time he switched the pants' fabric to a durable French cloth called serge de Nimes, soon known as denim. He colored the fabric with indigo dye and adopted the idea from Nevada tailor Jacob Davis of reinforcing the pants with copper rivets. In 1873 Strauss and Davis produced their first pair of waist-high overalls (later known as jeans). The pants soon became *de rigueur* for lumberjacks, cowboys, railroad workers, oil drillers, and farmers.

Strauss continued to build his pants and wholesaling business until he died in 1902. Levi Strauss & Co. (LS&CO.) passed to four nephews who carried on their uncle's jeans business while maintaining the company's philanthropic reputation.

After WWII Walter Haas and Peter Haas (a fourth-generation Strauss family member) assumed leadership of LS&CO. In 1948 they ended the company's wholesaling business to concentrate on Levi's clothing. In the 1950s Levi's jeans ceased to be merely functional garments for workers: They became the uniform of American youth. In the 1960s LS&CO. added women's attire and expanded overseas.

The company went public in 1971. That year it added a women's career line and bought Koret sportswear (sold in 1984). By the mid-1980s profits declined. Peace Corps-veteran-turned-McKinsey-consultant Robert Haas (Walter's son) grabbed the reins of LS&CO. in 1984 and took the company private the next year. He also instilled a touchy-feely corporate culture often at odds with the bottom line.

In 1986 LS&CO. introduced Dockers casual pants. The company's sales began rising in 1991 as consumers forsook designer duds of the 1980s for more practical clothes. LS&CO. says seven out of every 10 American men own a pair of Dockers. However, LS&CO. missed out on the birth of another trend: the split between the fashion sense of US adolescents and their Levi's-loving, baby boomer parents.

In 1996 the company introduced Slates dress slacks. That year LS&CO. bought back nearly one-third of its stock from family and employees for $4.3 billion. Grappling with slipping sales and debt from the buyout, in 1997 LS&CO. closed 11 of its 37 North American plants, laying off 6,400 workers and 1,000 salaried employees; it granted generous severance packages even to those earning minimum wage.

In 1998, citing improved labor conditions in China, LS&CO. announced it would step up its use of Chinese subcontractors. Further restructuring added a third of its European plants to the closures list that year. LS&CO.'s sales fell 13% in fiscal 1998. The next year LS&CO. closed 11 of 22 remaining North American plants. It also unleashed several new jeans brands that eschewed the company's one-style-fits-all approach of old.

In 1999 Haas handed his CEO title to Pepsi executive Philip Marineau.

In April 2002 LS&CO. announced it would close six of its last eight US plants and cut 20% of its worldwide staff (3,300 workers). In September 2003 it cut another 5% of its global staff (650 workers). That month the company opened its first girls-only store, located in Paris. In December LS&CO. replaced CFO Bill Chiasson with an outside turnaround specialist.

EXECUTIVES

Chairman: T. Gary Rogers, age 65
President, CEO, and Director: R. John Anderson, age 56, $1,493,951 pay (prior to promotion)
SVP and CIO: David G. Bergen
SVP and General Counsel: Hilary K. Krane, age 44
SVP Strategy and Worldwide Marketing and Global Marketing Officer: Lawrence W. (Larry) Ruff, age 51
SVP; President, Asia/Pacific: Alan Hed, age 48
SVP and President, Levi Strauss North America: Robert L. Hanson, age 44, $1,285,569 pay
SVP Dockers Men's Merchandising, Design, and Licensing: Jim Tibbs
SVP; President, Levi Strauss Europe: Armin Broger, age 46
SVP Global Sourcing: David Love, age 45
SVP Worldwide Human Resources: Cathleen L. Unruh, age 59
SVP and General Manager, Signature by Levi Strauss & Co. Brand, US: Susan Brennan
VP Global Tax Department: Paul Smith
VP Global Corporate Communications: Dan Chew
VP Finance, Levi Strauss North America: Mary Boland, age 50
VP Marketing Dockers Brand: Sherri Phillips
VP, Controller, and Interim CFO: Heidi L. Manes, age 36
Director Worldwide and U.S. Communications: Jeff Beckman
President, Levi's Retail, US: Mark Breitbard
President, Levi's Wholesale, US: Loreen Zakern
Auditors: PricewaterhouseCoopers LLP

LOCATIONS

HQ: Levi Strauss & Co.
1155 Battery St., San Francisco, CA 94111
Phone: 415-501-6000 **Fax:** 415-501-7112
Web: www.levistrauss.com

2007 Sales

	% of total
North America	59
Europe	23
Asia/Pacific	19
Corporate	(1)
Total	**100**

PRODUCTS/OPERATIONS

2007 Sales

	% of total
Levi's brand	73
Dockers brand	21
Levi Strauss Signature brand	6
Total	**100**

Selected Brand Names

501
505
Dockers
Dockers K-1
Dockers Premium
Dockers Recode
Dress Mobile
Flat Front Mobile
Go Khaki
Levi's
Levi's Engineered
Levi's Red
Levi's Silvertab
Levi's Type 1
ProStyle
Pure Blue
Red Tab
Superlow

COMPETITORS

Abercrombie & Fitch	Limited Brands
adidas	Liz Claiborne
American Eagle Outfitters	Macy's
Benetton	Nautica Enterprises
Blue Holdings	NIKE
Calvin Klein	OshKosh B'Gosh
Diesel SpA	Oxford Industries
Eddie Bauer	Perry Ellis International
Fast Retailing	Phillips-Van Heusen
Fruit of the Loom	Playtex
FUBU	Polo Ralph Lauren
The Gap	Sean John
Guess?	Sears
Haggar	Target
Hugo Boss	Tommy Hilfiger
J. C. Penney	True Religion Apparel
J. Crew	Under Armour
Jockey International	VF
Joe's Jeans	Victoria's Secret Stores
Jones Apparel	Wacoal
Kmart	Wal-Mart
Kohl's	Warnaco Group
Lands' End	

HISTORICAL FINANCIALS

Company Type: Private

Income Statement

FYE: Last Sunday in November

	REVENUE ($ mil.)	NET INCOME ($ mil.)	NET PROFIT MARGIN	EMPLOYEES
11/07	4,266	460	10.8%	11,550
11/06	4,107	239	5.8%	10,680
11/05	4,125	156	3.8%	9,635
11/04	4,073	30	0.7%	8,850
11/03	4,091	(349)	—	12,300
Annual Growth	**1.1%**	**—**	**—**	**(1.6%)**

Net Income History

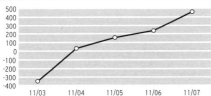

Liberty Media

Liberty Media takes the freedom to arrange its varied businesses as it pleases. The holding company comprises publicly traded Liberty Capital Group, Liberty Entertainment Group, and Liberty Interactive Group. The arrangement effectively splits the fast-growing video and online commerce operations and the company's less robust cable TV and entertainment businesses. (The company is spinning off its Liberty Entertainment unit.) Liberty Media's biggest holding, the QVChome shopping network, falls under the Liberty Interactive umbrella, as does e-tailer Provide Commerce. Movie channel Starz Media and the Atlanta Braves baseball team both belong to Liberty Capital, while Liberty Entertainment is the receptacle for a stake in DIRECTV. Liberty Media is chaired by John Malone.

Over the past few years, Liberty Media has made several attempts to simplify its structure through a variety d spinoffs, asset sales, acquisitions, and the formation of a third tracking stock. Whether it has succeeded is open to debate.

Liberty Media adopted its present three-part structure in early 2008 when Liberty Capital spawned Liberty Entertainment. Liberty Entertainment, which also houses subsidiaries Starz Entertainment and FUN Technologies, was formed following Liberty Media's exchange in February 2008 of a 41% stake in The DIRECTV Group for its 16% stake in News Corp. (valued at more than $10 billion). Liberty Media had agreed back in late 2006 to swap its stake in News Corp. for the now 48% stake (and controlling interest) in the satellite-TV company, as well as three regional sports networks and $465 million in cash.

Liberty Media announced in September 2008 that it would spin off its Liberty Entertainment unit, in order to give the parent company greater flexibility to focus on other objectives.

What remains of Liberty Capital includes Liberty Media's minority investments in Time Warner and Sprint Nextel.

Unaffected by the 2008 reorganization is Liberty Interactive, whose holdings include about 24% of online travel firm Expedia and Bodybuilding.com, which it bought in January 2008. Later in the year, Liberty bought online party and costume seller Celebrate Express to combine with Buyseasons (acquired in 2006). The deal furthers Liberty's strategy of acquiring niche e-commerce businesses. Liberty Interactive also owns a majority voting stake (62%) in Barry Diller's Internet conglomerate IAC/InterActiveCorp. (In August 2008, however, IAC spun off several of its companies, reducing Liberty's voting interest to 30% in the four separate companies.)

The company's TruePosition unit, which supplies mobile-phone location equipment, won a permanent injunction in August 2008 that prohibits rival Andrew Corp. from marketing products that infringe on a US patent. The US district court adjusted downward a more than $45 million jury award to give TruePosition slightly more than $23 million and denied Andrew's bid for a new trial.

Liberty Media has operations in Europe and Asia through its various subsidiaries.

EXECUTIVES

Chairman: John C. Malone, age 67, $627,600 pay
President, CEO, and Director: Gregory B. (Greg) Maffei, age 48, $1,625,000 pay
EVP, General Counsel, and Secretary: Charles Y. Tanabe, age 56
SVP: Mark D. Carleton, age 48
SVP: Michael P. Zeisser, age 43
SVP and Controller: Christopher W. (Chris) Shean, age 43, $700,000 pay
SVP Tax Strategy, Planning, and Compliance: Albert E. Rosenthaler, age 49, $681,000 pay
SVP and Treasurer: David J. A. Flowers, age 54, $668,000 pay
VP Business Development: John A. Orr
VP Investor and Media Relations: Michael Erickson
Auditors: KPMG LLP

LOCATIONS

HQ: Liberty Media Corporation
   12300 Liberty Blvd., Englewood, CO 80112
Phone: 720-875-5400   **Fax:** 720-875-5401
Web: www.libertymedia.com

PRODUCTS/OPERATIONS

2007 Sales

	$ mil.	% of total
Interactive Group		
QVC	7,397	79
Corporate & other	405	4
Capital Group		
Starz Entertainment	1,066	11
Starz Media	254	3
Corporate & other	301	3
Total	**9,423**	**100**

Selected Subsidiaries and Investments

Capital Group
   Atlanta National League Baseball Club, Inc.
   Leisure Arts, Inc.
   Starz Media, LLC
   TruePosition, Inc. (89%, wireless technology services)
   WFRV and WJMN Televisions Station, Inc.
Entertainment Group
   FUN Technologies, Inc. (53%, online and interactive casual games and sports content)
   GSN, LLC
   Starz Entertainment, LLC
   The DIRECTV Group, Inc. (48%, satellite-TV operator)
   WildBlue Communications, Inc.
Interactive Group
   Backcountry.com, Inc.
   Bodybuilding.com, LLC
   BuySeasons, Inc. (100%, online costume and party supply retail)
   Celebrate Express (100%, online costume and party supply retail)
   Provide Commerce, Inc. (100%, e-commerce)
   QVC (98%, home shopping network)

COMPETITORS

1-800-FLOWERS.COM	NBC
American Express	NDS Group
Blue Sky Studios	Orbitz Worldwide
Comcast	Oxygen Media
Cox Communications	Pixar
Disney	priceline.com
Disney Studios	Rainbow Media
DreamWorks	Teleflora
Fox Entertainment	Time Warner
FTD	Travelocity
Hallmark	Turner Broadcasting
Hearst Corporation	Twentieth Century Fox
HSN	ValueVision Media
KaBloom	Viacom

HISTORICAL FINANCIALS

Company Type: Holding company

Income Statement

FYE: December 31

	REVENUE ($ mil.)	NET INCOME ($ mil.)	NET PROFIT MARGIN	EMPLOYEES
12/07	9,423	2,114	22.4%	19,000
12/06	8,613	840	9.8%	14,765
12/05	7,960	—	—	13,660
12/04	7,051	—	—	—
12/03	3,230	—	—	—
Annual Growth	**30.7%**	**151.7%**	**—**	**17.9%**

2007 Year-End Financials

Debt ratio: 58.8%
Return on equity: 10.3%
Cash ($ mil.): 3,135
Current ratio: 1.82
Long-term debt ($ mil.): 11,524

Net Income History

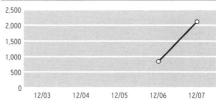

Liberty Mutual

Boston boasts of baked beans, the Red Sox, and the Liberty Mutual Group. Liberty Mutual Holding is the parent company for the Liberty Mutual Group and its three principal mutual insurance companies, Liberty Mutual Insurance, Liberty Mutual Fire Insurance, and Employers Insurance Company of Wausau. Liberty Mutual is one of the top property/casualty insurers in the US and among the top 10 providers of automobile insurance. The company also offers homeowners' insurance and commercial lines for small to large companies. Liberty Mutual Group is a diversified global insurer with operations throughout the world.

The company's Personal Market group offers property/casualty insurance, including private auto and homeowners' insurance. Much of its new business comes from its relationships with affinity groups such as credit unions, employers, and professional and alumni associations.

The Commercial Markets division provides commercial property/casualty products. The division includes the National Market unit, which serves large businesses, and the Business Market unit, serving midsized businesses. The Commercial Markets division also includes Liberty Mutual Property (commercial property coverage) and Group Market (group disability products and administration).

The Agency Markets division is focused on small and midsized employers and individuals. It operates through smaller regional businesses as well as Summit Holding Southeast and Liberty Mutual Surety. Commercial customers account for more than 80% of Agency Markets' business, with workers compensation premiums accounting for more than 40% of its total premiums.

The company's distribution strategy has shifted away from its direct sales force, and into a diversified blend of independent and exclusive agents, brokers, direct-response call centers, and the Internet.

Liberty's International unit has grown in importance as part of a planned long-term expansion outside of the US. The International division includes local companies that offer personal and commercial insurance to local markets in more than 20 countries and Liberty International Underwriters, which provides specialty commercial lines worldwide.

Back in the US, the company aims to bolster its Agency Markets division. It acquired property/casualty insurer Ohio Casualty for $2.6 billion in 2007. In 2008 Liberty Mutual spent $6.3 billion to acquire Safeco, then folded it into its Agency Markets division as well. That deal gave the company a greater share of the West Coast markets.

HISTORY

The need for financial aid to workers injured on the job was recognized in Europe in the late 19th century but did not make its way to the US until a workers' compensation law for federal employees was passed in 1908. Massachusetts was one of the first states to enact similar legislation. Liberty Mutual was founded in Boston in 1912 to fill this newly recognized niche.

Liberty Mutual followed the fire insurance practice of taking an active part in loss prevention. It evaluated clients' premises and procedures and recommended ways to prevent accidents. The company rejected the budding industry practice of limiting medical fees, instead studying the most effective ways to reduce the long-term cost of a claim by getting the injured party back to work.

In 1942 the company acquired the United Mutual Fire Insurance Company (founded 1908, renamed Liberty Mutual Fire Insurance Company in 1949). The next year it founded a rehabilitation center in Boston to treat injured workers and to test treatments.

In the 1960s and 1970s, Liberty Mutual expanded its line to include life insurance (1963), group pensions (1970), and IRAs (1975).

Seeking to increase its national presence, the company formed Liberty Northwest Insurance Corporation in 1983. It continued expanding its offerings, with new subsidiaries in commercial, personal, and excess lines and, in 1986, by moving into financial services by buying Stein Roe & Farnham (founded 1958).

The expansion/diversification strategy seemed to work. Earnings between 1984 and 1986 more than tripled. Then the downturn: Recession was followed by a string of natural disasters, and Liberty Mutual's income fell sharply between 1986 and 1988. In 1992 and 1993 the firm lost suits to Coors and Outboard Marine for failing to back those companies in environmental litigation cases.

Liberty Mutual gained a foothold in the UK in 1995 when it received permission to invest in a Lloyd's of London syndicate management company. In 1997 Liberty Mutual acquired bankrupt workers' comp provider Golden Eagle Insurance of California; the next year the firm bought Florida's Summit Holding Southeast. Mutual funds were also on the shopping list: Purchases included Société Générale's US mutual funds unit, led by international money dean Jean-Marie Eveillard.

In 1999 the company bought Guardian Royal Exchange's US operations. In a new international initiative that year, Liberty Mutual bought 70% of Singapore-based insurer Citystate Holdings (to be renamed Liberty Citystate) as its foothold in Asia.

The company's diversification efforts included Liberty International, which expanded operations in such countries as Canada, Japan, Mexico, Singapore, and the UK. The company also grew its international presence in areas such as China and southern Europe.

Slumping property/casualty lines and the events of September 11 hit Liberty Mutual in 2001 (the company paid out some $500 million in claims). In 2001 and 2002 the company reorganized into a mutual holding company structure with its three principal operating companies (Liberty Mutual Insurance, Liberty Mutual Fire Insurance, and Employers Insurance Company of Wausau) each becoming separate stock insurance companies and Liberty Mutual Holding Company as the parent.

Strengthening its personal lines business, Liberty Mutual in 2003 bought Prudential's domestic property/casualty operations. The deal included some 1,400 Prudential agents which were added to the company's distribution mix.

Hurricane-related losses totaled $1.5 billion in 2005, but were offset by nice returns from the company's investments that same year.

EXECUTIVES

Chairman, President, and CEO: Edmund F. (Ted) Kelly, age 61
EVP Personal Markets: J. Paul Condrin III
EVP Liberty International: Thomas C. Ramey
EVP and Chief Investment Officer: A. Alexander Fontanes
EVP Agency Markets: Gary R. Gregg
EVP Commercial Markets: David H. Long
SVP and CFO: Dennis J. Langwell
SVP and CIO: Stuart M. McGuigan, age 49
SVP and General Counsel: Christopher C. Mansfield
SVP and Corporate Actuary: Robert T. Muleski
SVP Human Resources and Administration: Helen E. R. Sayles
SVP Communications Services: Stephen G. Sullivan
VP and Comptroller: John D. Doyle
VP and Secretary: Dexter R. Legg
VP and Treasurer: Laurance H. S. Yahia
VP and Manager External Relations: John Cusolito
VP, Assistant Treasurer, and Director Investor Relations, Liberty Mutual Group: Matthew T. Coyle
Auditors: Ernst & Young LLP

LOCATIONS

HQ: Liberty Mutual Holding Company Inc.
175 Berkeley St., Boston, MA 02116
Phone: 617-357-9500   **Fax:** 617-350-7648
Web: www.libertymutual.com

PRODUCTS/OPERATIONS

2007 Sales

	$ mil.	% of total
Premiums earned	21,887	84
Net investment income	2,885	11
Net realized investment gains	436	2
Fees & other revenues	753	3
Total	**25,961**	**100**

2007 Sales

	$ mil.	% of total
Commercial markets	6,489	25
Liberty International	6,148	24
Personal markets	5,829	23
Agency markets	5,569	21
Other revenues	1,926	7
Total	**25,961**	**100**

Selected Subsidiaries and Affiliates

Liberty International
 Liberty ART SA (Argentina)
 Liberty Direct (Poland)
 Liberty Insurance Pte. Ltd. (Singapore)
 Liberty International Underwriters (LIU)
 Liberty Seguros (Brazil)
 Liberty Seguros SA (Colombia)
 Seguros Caracas de Liberty Mutual C.A. (Venezuela)
 Seker Sigorta A.S. (Turkey)
Liberty Mutual Group Inc.
 America First Insurance
 Colorado Casualty
 Employers Insurance Company of Wausau
 Golden Eagle Insurance Co.
 Hawkeye-Security Insurance
 Indiana Insurance Company
 Montgomery Mutual Insurance Company
 Peerless Insurance
 Summit Holding Southeast
 Wausau Insurance Companies

COMPETITORS

ACE Limited	MassMutual
AIG	MetLife
Allianz	Northwestern Mutual
Allstate	Progressive Corporation
Chubb Corp	State Farm
Citigroup	Travelers Companies
CNA Financial	Unum Group
The Hartford	W. R. Berkley
ING	Zurich Financial Services
Lincoln Financial Group	

HISTORICAL FINANCIALS

Company Type: Mutual company

Income Statement
FYE: December 31

	ASSETS ($ mil.)	NET INCOME ($ mil.)	INCOME AS % OF ASSETS	EMPLOYEES
12/07	94,679	1,518	1.6%	41,000
12/06	85,498	1,626	1.9%	39,000
12/05	78,824	1,027	1.3%	39,000
12/04	72,359	1,245	1.7%	38,000
12/03	64,422	851	1.3%	38,000
Annual Growth	10.1%	15.6%	—	1.9%

2007 Year-End Financials

Equity as % of assets: 13.1%
Return on assets: 1.7%
Return on equity: 13.1%
Long-term debt ($ mil.): —
Sales ($ mil.): 25,961

Net Income History

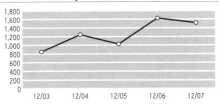

Life Care Centers

Life Care Centers of America is a privately owned operator of retirement and health care centers. The company manages more than 270 facilities throughout 28 states — including retirement communities, assisted-living facilities, and nursing homes — and provides specialized services such as home health care, as well as occupational, speech, and physical therapies. Additional services include adult day care, hospice, short-term care, and wound care. In addition, Life Care operates centers specifically for people with Alzheimer's disease or related dementia.

Founder Forrest Preston opened his first center in 1970. The company has expanded its network by leasing facilities from companies like Health Care REIT and through new facility construction. Some of Life Care's facilities are operated by affiliate Century Park Associates.

EXECUTIVES

Chairman: Forrest L. Preston
President: Beecher Hunter
COO: Cathy Murray
Controller: Steve Ziegler
SVP Information Systems and CIO: Terry Leonard
SVP Clinical Services: Dee McCarthy
SVP Life Care Home Health: Christopher Mitchell
VP Training and Professional Development: Michelle Talbert
VP and Integrity Services Officer: Gerald Webb
VP Training and Professional Development: Michelle Meadows
Director Public Relations and Editor: Cari Shanks
Treasurer: Lisa Lay

LOCATIONS

HQ: Life Care Centers of America
3570 Keith St. NW, Cleveland, TN 37312
Phone: 423-476-3254   **Fax:** 423-476-5974
Web: www.lcca.com

COMPETITORS

Advocat
Amedisys
Assisted Living Concepts
Capital Senior Living
Emeritus Corporation
Golden Horizons
Kindred Healthcare
Manor Care
Mariner Health Care
Merrill Gardens
National HealthCare
Regency Nursing and Rehabilitation
Res-Care
Sava
Skilled Healthcare Group
Sun Healthcare
Sunrise Senior Living

HISTORICAL FINANCIALS

Company Type: Private

Income Statement
FYE: December 31

	REVENUE ($ mil.)	NET INCOME ($ mil.)	NET PROFIT MARGIN	EMPLOYEES
12/07	2,120	—	—	31,153
12/06	2,050	—	—	30,000
12/05	1,957	—	—	30,000
12/04	1,800	—	—	40,000
12/03	1,600	—	—	30,000
Annual Growth	7.3%	—	—	0.9%

Revenue History

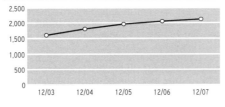

Lifetime Entertainment

Lifetime Entertainment Services hopes viewers make a long-term commitment to its television programs. The company operates three cable-TV networks (Lifetime, Lifetime Movie Network, Lifetime Real Women) focused on serving female viewers with original movies, talk shows, and syndicated shows. Its Lifetime channel reaches more than 95 million US households. Lifetime Entertainment also offers lifestyle and entertainment content online. The company was formed by the merger of channels Daytime and Cable Health Network in 1984. It's jointly owned by Walt Disney (through Disney ABC Cable) and publishing giant Hearst.

Lifetime scored a major coup in 2008 when it inked a deal with The Weinstein Company to air the show *Project Runway*, which had become a hit on Bravo. NBC Universal, the parent of Bravo, has filed a lawsuit to halt the deal, however.

With Lifetime's audience share continuing to slip, the network brought in Andrea Wong, previously head of alternative programming at ABC, to replace Betty Cohen as CEO in 2007. Cohen had been tapped to the top post in 2005 after a stint at Turner Broadcasting, replacing longtime chief Carole Black.

The company is still banking, though, on original programming. Lifetime has been steadily increasing its production budget for movies and primetime programming; however, its attempts at creating a hit series have been met with little success so far. Lifetime Entertainment is also making investments in digital media, acquiring ParentsClick Network in 2008.

EXECUTIVES

President and CEO: Andrea Wong, age 41
EVP and CFO: James Wesley
EVP Digital Media and Business Development: Dan Suratt
EVP Legal, Business Affairs, and Human Resources: Patricia (Pat) Langer
EVP Marketing and Enterprise Development: Martha Pease
EVP Public Affairs and Corporate Communications: Meredith Wagner
EVP Entertainment: JoAnn Alfano
EVP Research: Mike Greco
EVP Distribution: Lori Conkling
EVP Ad Sales: Debbie Richman
SVP Business Affairs and General Counsel: Linda Rein
SVP Marketing: Karen Cartales
SVP Public Affairs and Corporate Communications: Toby Graff
Co-Chief Marketing Officer: Bob Bibb
Co-Chief Marketing Officer: Lewis (Lew) Goldstein
President, Distribution and Business Development: Louise Henry Bryson

LOCATIONS

HQ: Lifetime Entertainment Services
309 W. 49th St., New York, NY 10019
Phone: 212-424-7000   **Fax:** 212-957-4449
Web: www.lifetimetv.com

PRODUCTS/OPERATIONS

Selected Operations

Lifetime Glam Network (Web sites)
Lifetime Movie Network
Lifetime On Demand
Lifetime Radio for Women (syndicated radio programming)
Lifetime Real Women (cable TV network)
Lifetime Television Network (cable TV network)

COMPETITORS

A&E Networks
Bravo Company
Crown Media
Discovery Communications
E! Entertainment Television
Harpo
iVillage
Martha Stewart Living
MTV Networks
Oxygen Media
Scripps Networks
Turner Broadcasting
USA Network
WE: Women's Entertainment

Lifetouch Inc.

When it's picture day at school and the kids are all lined up with new haircuts and scrubbed faces, odds are good that their toothy grins are directed at someone from Lifetouch. One of the largest US portrait photographers, employee-owned Lifetouch also runs about 600 photography studios inside J. C. Penney and Target stores across the nation. In addition, Lifetouch takes baby, family, business, and sports portraits; publishes church directories and yearbooks; and offers event digital imaging (which combines photography, graphics, and text), CD business imaging, and video production services. The firm operates in the US and Canada. Lifetouch was founded in 1936 as National School Studios.

Lifetouch also operates about 20 FLASH! Digital Portraits locations in malls in 10 states.

The company's SmileSafe Kids Program allows Lifetouch to send portraits and pictures of missing children to the authorities when needed (and when authorized by the children's parents), 24 hours a day, 7 days a week.

In mid-2006, Lifetouch bought the North American school photography operations of yearbook and class rings designer Jostens. The acquisition solidifies Lifetouch's leadership position in the North American school photography sector.

EXECUTIVES

Chairman Emeritus: Richard P. Erickson
Chairman and CEO: Paul Harmel
SEVP: Jake Barker
CFO: Randolph (Randy) Pladson
VP Administration: Ted Koenecke

LOCATIONS

HQ: Lifetouch Inc.
  11000 Viking Dr., Ste. 400, Eden Prairie, MN 55344
Phone: 952-826-4000   **Fax:** 952-826-4557
Web: www.lifetouch.com

PRODUCTS/OPERATIONS

Selected Products and Services
Business portraits
Church directories
Church family portraits
Family portraits
Infant portraits
Preschool portraits
School portraits
Senior/graduation portraits
Sports portraits
Yearbooks

Divisions
Lifetouch Canada Inc.
Lifetouch Church Directories and Portraits Inc.
Lifetouch Development Inc. (special event photography at malls, business portraits, and video production)
Lifetouch National School Studios Inc. (school pictures)
Lifetouch Portrait Studios Inc. (in J. C. Penney and Target stores)
Lifetouch Publishing Inc. (school yearbooks)
Media Productions (produces videos)

COMPETITORS

Cherry Hill Photo   Harris Connect
CPI Corp.   Olan Mills
H Tempest Limited   Walsworth

L.L. Bean

With L.L. Bean, you can tame the great outdoors — or just look as if you could. The outdoor apparel and gear maker mails more than 200 million catalogs per year. L.L. Bean's library includes about 10 specialty catalogs offering products in categories such as children's clothing, fly-fishing, outerwear, sportswear, housewares, footwear, camping and hiking gear, and the Maine hunting shoe upon which the company was built. L.L. Bean also operates about a dozen retail stores and some 15 factory outlets throughout the Northeast. In addition, it sells online through English- and Japanese-language Web sites. L.L. Bean was founded in 1912 by Leon Leonwood Bean and is controlled by his descendants.

From a pair of waterproof hunting boots L.L. Bean built a direct selling empire based on catalogs mailed out under some 60 different titles and advertising 16,000 products. Today, Web sales and a growing number of retail stores are contributing more to Bean's revenue. L.L. Bean's flagship store in Freeport, Maine (known by locals as "the Bean") attracts 3 million visitors annually and is open 24 hours a day, 365 days a year. Maine's most famous retailer has been increasing its presence outside its home state, with stores in Connecticut, Maryland, Massachusetts, New Hampshire, New Jersey, New York, Pennsylvania, and Virginia. Beyond the East Coast, Bean is mining the Midwest for sales with a pair of stores in the Chicago area slated to open in the fall of 2008. The company has set a target of 32 retail stores across the US by 2012.

Amid losses, the retailer has exited the Japanese market after opening several retail stores there. L.L. Bean also plans to scale back the number of catalog titles it offers.

L.L. Bean's famous customer service is exemplified by its liberal return policies and perpetual replacement of the rubber soles of its Maine Hunting Shoe. The company also offers seminars and events on such topics as fly fishing, sea kayaking, and outdoor photography.

HISTORY

Leon Leonwood Bean started out as a storekeeper in Freeport, Maine. Tired of wet, leaky boots, he experimented with various remedies and in 1911 came up with the Maine Hunting Shoe, a boot with rubber soles and feet and leather uppers. It became his most famous product.

From its outset in 1912, Bean's company was a mail-order house. The first batch of boots was a disaster: Almost all of them leaked. But Bean's willingness to correct his product's defects quickly, at his own expense, saved the company.

Maine's hunting licensing system, implemented in 1917, provided the company with a mailing list of affluent recreational hunters in the Northeast, and that year Bean opened a showroom to accommodate the customers stopping by his Freeport workshop.

Bean cultivated the image of the folksy Maine guide, offering durable, comfortable, weather-resistant clothes and reliable camping supplies. In 1920 Bean built a store on Main Street in Freeport. L.L. Bean continued to grow and add products, even during the Depression, and sales reached $1 million in 1937.

During WWII Bean helped design the boots used by the US military, and his company manufactured them, thus remaining afloat as the war years and rationing brought cutbacks in materials and outdoor activities. He began keeping the retail store open 24 hours a day in 1951, noting that he had "thrown away the keys." Bean added a women's department three years later.

Sales rose to $2 million in the early 1960s and were at $4.8 million when Bean died in 1967 at age 94. (He had resisted growing the business bigger, saying, "I'm eating three meals a day; I can't eat four.") The new president was Bean's grandson Leon Gorman, who had started with L.L. Bean in 1960. His early attempts at updating the mailing operations (mailing labels typed by hand and correspondence kept in cardboard boxes) had been vetoed by his grandfather. Gorman brought in new people and made improvements, including automating the mailing systems, improving the manufacturing systems, and targeting new, nonsporting markets (like women's casual clothes).

L.L. Bean continued its transition by targeting more of its classic customer profile — upper-middle-class college graduates — and sales grew about 20% annually for most of the 1980s. By 1989, however, sales had slowed and growth flattened as the national economy slumped and imitators carried away market share.

Unsolicited catalog orders had been coming in from Japan since the late 1980s, so in 1992 L.L. Bean began a joint venture with Seiyu and Matsushita Electric Industrial (now named Panasonic Corporation). Their first store opened that year (the company opened a catalog and service center in Japan in 1995). L.L. Kids began in 1993.

In 1996 the company began an online shopping service. Sparked by the success of its L.L. Kids division, which grew 300% in four years, the company opened a separate children's store in Freeport the next year. The company opened its second full-line store in 2000 near Washington, DC.

L.L. Bean veteran Chris McCormick was named president and CEO in May 2001; Gorman remained chairman. McCormick is the first person outside of the Bean family to head the company.

In January 2002 L.L. Bean laid off 175 employees (about 4% of its workforce); in early 2003 it cut about 500 more jobs and offered an early retirement program which was accepted by an additional 200 employees.

In July 2004 L.L. Bean settled lawsuits filed against Atkins Nutritionals Inc. and Gevalia Kaffe, accusing those companies of using pop-up ads on Bean's Web site without its permission. The amount of the settlement was not disclosed.

EXECUTIVES

Chairman: Leon A. Gorman
President and CEO: Christopher J. (Chris) McCormick
SVP and COO: Bob Peixotto
SVP and CFO: Mark Fasold
SVP Corporate Marketing: Steve Fuller
SVP Retail: Ken Kacere
VP Merchandising: George Kiesewetter
VP Card Services: Shawn Gorman
VP E-Commerce: Mary Lou Kelley
VP Human Resources: Martha Cyr
Chief Merchandising Officer: Fran Philip
Chief Retail Officer: Edward R. (Ed) Howell
PR Spokesman: Rich Donaldson
Senior Product Developer: Sandra Rossi
Director Design: Jim Hauptman

LOCATIONS

HQ: L.L. Bean, Inc.
3 Campus Dr., Freeport, ME 04033
Phone: 207-552-3028 **Fax:** 207-552-3080
Web: www.llbean.com

PRODUCTS/OPERATIONS

Selected Catalogs

Corporate Sales (custom embroidered clothing and
luggage)
Fly Fishing (equipment, outer wear, and accessories)
Home (linens, pillows, and decorating)
L.L. Bean
L.L. Bean Hunting
L.L. Bean: Everyday Adventures (women's yoga and
fitness products)
Outdoor Discovery Schools (classes and symposiums)
Outdoors (seasonal outdoor wear and accessories)
Traveler (clothing, luggage, and accessories)

Selected Products

Home and garden accessories
Men's, women's, and children's casual apparel
Outdoor classes
Outer wear
Shoes and boots
Sports gear and apparel
Travel apparel and luggage

COMPETITORS

Abercrombie & Fitch	Macy's
American Eagle Outfitters	Nautica Enterprises
Bass Pro Shops	Norm Thompson
Cabela's	North Face
Coldwater Creek	Orvis Company
Coleman	OshKosh B'Gosh
Columbia Sportswear	Patagonia, Inc.
Dillard's	Polo Ralph Lauren
Eddie Bauer Holdings	Redcats
Fast Retailing	REI
Foot Locker	Sara Lee
The Gap	Sears
J. C. Penney	Sports Authority
J. Crew	Sportsman's Guide
J. Jill Group	Talbots
Johnson Outdoors	Target
Lands' End	Timberland
Levi Strauss	Tommy Hilfiger

Lone Star Steakhouse

There are actually two stars in this steakhouse
constellation. Lone Star Steakhouse & Saloon
owns and operates more than 150 steakhouse
restaurants offering mesquite-grilled steaks,
ribs, chicken, and fish dishes. The casual dining
spots, found in 30 states, are punctuated by Texas
paraphernalia, neon beer signs, and country
music. The company also runs the Texas Land &
Cattle Steak House chain, which has more than
30 locations in Texas and six other states.
Founded by Jamie Coulter in 1992, Lone Star
Steakhouse is owned by Dallas-based private equity firm Lone Star Funds.

The company, which was taken private in 2006
through a $586 million buyout, has been strug-
gling against stiff competition in the steakhouse
segment. With new CEO Marc Buehler, previously with Tony Roma's operator Romacorp,
Lone Star is focused on driving additional traffic to its restaurants by updating its décor and

menu. It has also taken steps to return to profitability by closing several underperforming locations. More than 40 restaurants were closed in
2007 following the going-private transaction,
and an additional 20 units were shuttered the
next year.

Lone Star Steakhouse had operated two upscale dining chains, Del Frisco's Double Eagle
Steak Houses and Sullivan's Steakhouse, previous to the buyout. Lone Star Funds spun off the
high-end restaurants as Del Frisco's Restaurant
Group in 2007.

Lone Star Funds also owns supermarket
chains BI-LO and Bruno's.

EXECUTIVES

CEO: Marc A. Buehler, age 38
Interim CFO: Ed Barton
SVP Human Resources and Training: Pat Barth
SVP Operations: Ryan Franklin
SVP Operations, Texas Land & Cattle: Mario Cernadas
VP Purchasing: Ed Patton
VP Marketing: Tim Schroder
Auditors: Ernst & Young LLP

LOCATIONS

HQ: Lone Star Steakhouse & Saloon, Inc.
224 E. Douglas, Ste. 700, Wichita, KS 67202
Phone: 316-264-8899 **Fax:** 316-264-5988
Web: www.lonestarsteakhouse.com

COMPETITORS

Brinker	Logan's Roadhouse
Carino's Italian Grill	Metromedia Restaurant
Carlson Restaurants	Group
CBRL Group	OSI Restaurant Partners
Cheesecake Factory	Romacorp
Darden	Ruby Tuesday
Hooters	Texas Roadhouse
Houlihan's	

Long & Foster

Long & Foster wants to be your one-stop shopping center, at least when it comes to buying a
home. Flagship subsidiary Long & Foster Real
Estate is one of the largest residential real estate
brokerage firms in the mid-Atlantic. Some
16,000 agents represent Long & Foster Real Estate in nearly 240 sales offices, primarily in the
Washington, DC/Baltimore, Maryland metropolitan area. The company also operates in
Delaware, New Jersey, North Carolina, Pennsylvania, Virginia, and West Virginia. Other subsidiaries provide such products and services as
commercial brokerage, homeowners insurance,
title insurance, and mortgage financing. Long &
Foster Real Estate was founded in 1968.

Long & Foster has expanded and entered new
markets by opening new offices and by acquiring smaller brokerages. Among its latest strategic acquisitions are Fiola Blum in Maryland and
Realty Executives J&J Realty in New Jersey
(2007), Fonville Morisey Realty in North Carolina's Triangle area (2006), and Boone & Company in southwest Virginia (2004).

EXECUTIVES

Chairman and CEO: P. Wesley Foster Jr.
President and COO: Brenda Shipplett
EVP: Mary K. Weddle, age 58
SVP and CFO: Bruce Enger
**SVP and General Manager, Baltimore and Southern
Pennsylvania:** Alice Burch
**SVP and Regional Manager, Southern Maryland and
Prince George's County:** Hattie Scott
VP, Career Development: Jackie Thiel
VP Corporate Relocation: Pandra D. Richie
President, Affiliated Business: David H. Stevens
President, Long & Foster Financial Services:
George T. Eastment III
President, Long & Foster Settlement Services:
Michael (Mike) Maddiex
President, Mid-States Title Insurance Agency:
Susan Holler
President, Prosperity Mortgage: Herb Engler
President, Long & Foster Insurance Agency:
James Maiden

LOCATIONS

HQ: The Long & Foster Companies, Inc.
11351 Random Hills Rd., Fairfax, VA 22030
Phone: 703-359-1500 **Fax:** 703-591-6978
Web: www.longandfoster.com

PRODUCTS/OPERATIONS

Selected Subsidiaries

Long & Foster Institute of Real Estate, Inc.
Long & Foster Insurance Agency, Inc.
Long & Foster Real Estate, Inc.
Long & Foster Settlement Services
Prosperity Mortgage Company
Vision Relocation Group

COMPETITORS

Century 21
Coldwell Banker
Corus Home Realty
Donohoe Companies
NRT Inc.
Prudential Fox Roach
The Prudential Real Estate Affiliates
RE/MAX
Weichert Realtors
ZipRealty

Los Angeles Clippers

Forget about tall ships, this team is interested
in tall centers. The Los Angeles Clippers professional basketball team joined the National Basketball Association in 1970 as the Buffalo Braves
before moving west in 1978. Known as the San
Diego Clippers, the team relocated to Los Angeles in 1984 and now plays in the Staples Center
with its division rival Los Angeles Lakers. Attendance for Clippers games has generally been
eclipsed by the more popular team, due mostly
to a string of unsuccessful seasons. Real estate
magnate Donald Sterling has owned the franchise since 1981.

EXECUTIVES

Owner and Chairman: Donald T. Sterling
EVP: Andy Roeser
SVP Marketing and Sales: Carl Lahr
Head Coach and General Manager: Mike Dunleavy,
age 54

Assistant General Manager: Neil Olshey
VP Communications: Joe Safety
VP Finance: Donna Johnson
VP Marketing and Broadcasting: Christian Howard
General Counsel: Bob Platt
Director of Communications: Rob Raichlen
Director of Community Relations and Player Programs: Denise Booth
Director of Corporate Sales: Greg Flaherty
Director of Sponsorship Sales: Chris Beyer

LOCATIONS

HQ: Los Angeles Clippers
Staples Center, 1111 S. Figueroa St., Ste. 1100,
Los Angeles, CA 90015
Phone: 213-742-7500   **Fax:** 213-742-7570
Web: www.nba.com/clippers

The Los Angeles Clippers play at the 18,997-seat capacity Staples Center in Los Angeles.

COMPETITORS

Golden State Warriors
Los Angeles Lakers
Phoenix Suns
Sacramento Kings

Los Angeles Kings

These Kings have yet to be crowned Stanley Cup champions. The Los Angeles Kings Hockey Club entered the National Hockey League in 1967 and has made just one appearance in the Stanley Cup finals. Led by the great Wayne Gretzky, the team reached the championship in 1993 but lost to the Montreal Canadiens in seven games. Despite the lack of championships, the franchise has not been too overshadowed by its Staples Center brethren, the title-laden Los Angeles Lakers, and continues to draw decent crowds. The team is owned by Denver billionaire Philip Anschutz and Los Angeles developer Edward Roski, who bought the team in 1995. The partners also own the Staples Center and a minority stake in the Lakers.

The Los Angeles hockey franchise was first awarded to Jack Kent Cooke (one-time owner of both the Los Angeles Lakers and the Washington Redskins) and played in the LA Forum for most of its history. Anschutz, who also controls Regal Entertainment and holds stakes in a host of other businesses through his Anschutz Company, and Roski acquired the team from Jeffrey Sudikoff and Joseph Cohen for about $110 million. After buying the club, they built the $300 million Staples Center in 1999 with the help of media giant News Corp. (Anschutz and Roski bought the media titan's 40% stake in the arena in 2004.)

EXECUTIVES

Owner: Philip F. Anschutz, age 67
Owner: Edward P. (Ed) Roski Jr.
CEO/Governor: Timothy J. (Tim) Leiweke
President and General Manager: Dean Lombardi, age 45
President, Business Operations: Shawn Hunter, age 38
EVP and CFO: Dan Beckerman
EVP and Chief Administrative Officer: Kevin McDowell
EVP and General Counsel: Ted Fikre
VP Communications and Broadcasting: Michael Altieri, age 39
VP Sales and Marketing: Chris McGowan
Director of Amateur Scouting: Al Murray

Director of Communications: Jeff Moeller
Director of Pro Scouting and European Evaluation: Rob Laird
Manager of Communications: Mike Kalinowski

LOCATIONS

HQ: The Los Angeles Kings Hockey Club LP
1111 S. Figueroa St., Ste. 3100,
Los Angeles, CA 90015
Phone: 213-742-7100   **Fax:** 213-742-7296
Web: www.lakings.com

PRODUCTS/OPERATIONS

Championship Trophies
Clarence S. Campbell Bowl (1993)

COMPETITORS

Anaheim Ducks
Dallas Stars
Phoenix Coyotes
San Jose Sharks

HISTORICAL FINANCIALS
Company Type: Private

Income Statement

FYE: July 31

	REVENUE ($ mil.)	NET INCOME ($ mil.)	NET PROFIT MARGIN	EMPLOYEES
7/07	84	—	—	—
7/06	82	—	—	—
7/05	0	—	—	—
7/04	80	—	—	—
7/03	78	—	—	—
Annual Growth	1.9%			

Revenue History

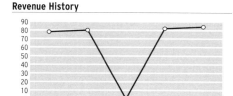

Los Angeles Lakers

These Lakers can be found navigating the choppy waters of the National Basketball Association. The Los Angeles Lakers professional basketball franchise is one of the most popular and successful teams in the NBA, earning 14 championship titles since joining the league in 1949. The team was founded in 1947 as the Minnesota Lakers of the National Basketball League and moved to California in 1960. Its roster has included such Hall of Fame players as Kareem Abdul-Jabbar, Wilt Chamberlain, Earvin "Magic" Johnson, and Jerry West. The franchise has been controlled by real estate mogul Jerry Buss since 1979; billionaire Philip Anschutz, developer Edward Roski, and Magic Johnson also own minority stakes in the team.

Lakers fans are once again rooting for a winner after the team hit a rough patch following its loss to the Detroit Pistons in the 2004 NBA

Finals. Head coach Phil Jackson is back at the helm after a brief retirement (he signed a three-year, $30 million contract to return in 2005 and inked a two-year, $24 million extension in 2007) and with the help of star player and MVP Kobe Bryant the team earned a Western Conference title in 2008. (The Lakers fell to the Boston Celtics in that year's NBA Finals, however.)

Despite the team's ups and downs, the Lakers continue to be a huge draw at Los Angeles' Staples Center, where the team boasts such celebrities as Denzel Washington and Jack Nicholson among its fan base.

Buss and his investors sold the Los Angeles Sparks of the WNBA to a local investment group led by Carla Christofferson and Katherine Goodman for $10 million in 2006.

HISTORY

The Los Angeles Lakers basketball team traces its roots to the Detroit Gems, a defunct franchise acquired for $15,000 by a group including Max Winter (later the first president of the Minnesota Vikings), Ben Berger, and Maurice Chalfen. Renamed the Minneapolis Lakers, the team joined the National Basketball League (NBL) in 1947 and with the help of center George Mikan won the league championship in its first year. The team switched leagues the following season to the Basketball Association of America (BAA) and won that championship as well. The BAA and NBL merged to form the National Basketball Association (NBA) after that season, and the Lakers won the NBA's first championship in 1949. The team went on to win three straight NBA titles from 1952-54.

Berger and Chalfen sold the team to businessman Bob Short in 1957 for $150,000. With the team struggling and attendance lagging, Short decided to move the Lakers to Los Angeles in 1960. Stars Elgin Baylor and Jerry West helped the team rebound and reach the NBA finals six times in the 1960s; however, they lost each time to their archrivals, the Boston Celtics. Jack Kent Cooke bought the team from Short for $5 million in 1965, and the Lakers moved to their new arena, the Forum, in 1967. Center Wilt Chamberlain joined the team in 1968, but the Lakers didn't win an NBA title as an LA team until 1972 (against the Knicks).

In 1979 real estate tycoon Jerry Buss bought the Lakers, the Forum, and the Los Angeles Kings from Cooke (who also owned the Washington Redskins) for $67.5 million. Led by Kareem Abdul-Jabbar, Magic Johnson, and slick-haired coach Pat Riley, the Lakers won two NBA titles in the early 1980s and persevered twice during a new series of title bouts with rival Boston. The team earned its fifth NBA title that decade in 1988, the same year Buss sold the Los Angeles Kings.

Riley stepped down after the 1990 season, and in late 1991 Magic Johnson announced he was HIV positive and retired. The loss was huge, and in 1994 the team missed the playoffs for the first time in almost 20 years. (Johnson also bought 5% of the team that year.) The Lakers signed center Shaquille O'Neal to a $120 million, seven-year contract and drafted 18-year-old guard Kobe Bryant in 1996. The next year saw the inaugural season of the NBA's sister league (literally), the Women's NBA (WNBA). Buss became owner of the Los Angeles Sparks. (He sold the women's basketball franchise to a local investment group in 2006.) Kings owners Philip Anschutz and Edward Roski bought 25% of the Lakers from Buss in 1998.

Buss sold the Forum in 1999, and the Lakers began the 1999-2000 season in the new $300 million Staples Center (built by Anschutz and Roski, which was what gave them their stake in the Lakers). After two consecutive sweeps out of the playoffs, the team in 1999 hired Phil Jackson, the cerebral head coach who led the Chicago Bulls to six NBA titles. The move immediately paid off as Jackson guided the Lakers, led by O'Neal and sharpshooter Bryant, to three straight championships between 2000 and 2002. In 2000 Jerry West retired from the franchise after 40 years as a player, coach, and front-office executive.

In 2003 the Lakers were booted from the playoffs in the second round. Future hall of famers Gary "The Glove" Payton and Karl "The Mailman" Malone signed with the team later that year in the hopes of winning a title. The move made the Lakers one of the most star-studded teams in NBA history, and though it gained a berth in the NBA Finals, the Lakers were thoroughly dominated in the championship series by the Detroit Pistons.

The team retooled in the off season and saw Jackson resign, O'Neal and Payton traded, and Malone opting out of his contract to become a free agent. The team hired former Houston Rockets head coach Rudy Tomjanovich to replace Jackson. Bryant re-signed with LA to the tune of $136 million over seven years.

Tomjanovich quit the coaching game in 2005 and the team lured Phil Jackson out of retirement with a three-year, $30 million coaching contract. After three years of either missing the playoffs or exiting in the first round, the Lakers returned to the NBA Finals in 2008; however, the team fell to the Eastern Conference champion Celtics in six games.

EXECUTIVES

Chairman, President, and Majority Owner; Chairman, Los Angeles Sparks: Jerry Buss
CEO: Frank Mariani
EVP Basketball Operations and General Manager: Mitch Kupchak
Assistant General Manager: Ronnie Lester
EVP Business Operations and Alternate Governor: Jeanie Buss
Head Coach: Phil Jackson, age 63
SVP Finance and CFO: Joe McCormack
VP Player Personnel: Jim Buss
VP Broadcasting and Marketing: Keith Harris
VP Public Relations: John Black
Executive Director of Corporate Sponsorships: Ron Rockoff
Director, Payroll and Personnel: Diane Rogers

LOCATIONS

HQ: The Los Angeles Lakers, Inc.
555 N. Nash St., El Segundo, CA 90245
Phone: 310-426-6000   **Fax:** 310-426-6115
Web: www.nba.com/lakers

The Los Angeles Lakers play at the 18,997-seat capacity Staples Center in Los Angeles.

PRODUCTS/OPERATIONS

Championship Titles

NBA Finals (1949-50, 1952-54, 1972, 1980, 1982, 1985, 1987-88, 2000-02)
NBA Western Conference (1972-73, 1980, 1982-85, 1987-89, 1991, 2000-02, 2004, 2008)
NBA Western Division (1951, 1953-54, 1962-63, 1965-66, 1969)
NBA Central Division (1950)
National Basketball League
NBL Finals (1947)

COMPETITORS

Golden State Warriors
Los Angeles Clippers
Phoenix Suns
Sacramento Kings

HISTORICAL FINANCIALS

Company Type: Private

Income Statement   FYE: July 31

	REVENUE ($ mil.)	NET INCOME ($ mil.)	NET PROFIT MARGIN	EMPLOYEES
7/07	170	—	—	—
7/06	167	—	—	—
7/05	156	—	—	—
7/04	170	—	—	—
7/03	149	—	—	—
Annual Growth	3.4%	—	—	—

Revenue History

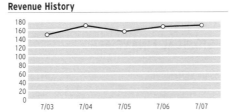

Love's Travel Stops

If you're a trucker or RVer on the road, all you need is Love's. Love's Travel Stops & Country Stores operates more than 200 travel stop locations throughout a swath of about 35 states from California to Virginia, including convenience stores in Colorado, Kansas, New Mexico, Oklahoma, and Texas. Each travel stop includes a convenience store, a fast-food restaurant, such as Taco Bell or Subway, and gas outlets for cars, trucks, and RVs. The travel stops also provide shower rooms, laundry facilities, game rooms, and mail drops. Love's Travel Stops & Country Stores is owned by the family of CEO Tom Love, who founded the company in 1964.

Love's has entered the Iowa market with a store in Newton. The company adds about 18 locations a year, on average.

EXECUTIVES

Chairman and CEO: Tom Love
President, Love's Development Companies: Greg Love
President, Love's Operating Companies: Frank Love
EVP and CFO: Doug Stussi
EVP Operations: Tom Edwards
VP Accounting: Shane Wharton
VP and CIO: Jim Xenos
VP Construction and Environmental Compliance: Terry Ross
VP Human Resources: Kevin Asbury
Director, Legal Services: Amy Guzzy
Director, Marketing: Mark Romig
Director, Public Relations: Jenny Love Meyer
Director, Sales: Don Van Curen

LOCATIONS

HQ: Love's Travel Stops & Country Stores, Inc.
10601 N. Pennsylvania Ave.,
Oklahoma City, OK 73120
Phone: 405-751-9000   **Fax:** 405-749-9110
Web: www.loves.com

COMPETITORS

7-Eleven	Pilot Corporation
Allsup's	Racetrac Petroleum
Chevron	Rip Griffin Truck Service
Exxon	Royal Dutch Shell
E-Z Mart Stores	Stuckey's
Flying J	TravelCenters of America
Marathon Oil	Valero Energy
Petro Stopping Centers	Walgreen

HISTORICAL FINANCIALS

Company Type: Private

Income Statement   FYE: December 31

	REVENUE ($ mil.)	NET INCOME ($ mil.)	NET PROFIT MARGIN	EMPLOYEES
12/07	7,000	—	—	6,000
12/06	6,330	—	—	5,600
12/05	3,807	—	—	4,400
12/04	2,210	—	—	3,800
12/03	1,900	—	—	3,500
Annual Growth	38.5%	—	—	14.4%

Revenue History

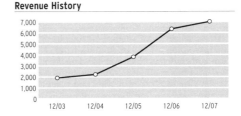

Lower Colorado River Authority

The stars at night may be big and bright, but more than one million people deep in the heart of Texas still need electricity from the Lower Colorado River Authority (LCRA). Serving more than 50 counties along the lower Colorado River from Central Texas' Hill Country to the Gulf of Mexico, the not-for-profit, state-run entity supplies wholesale electricity to more than 40 retail utilities (primarily municipalities and cooperatives). It operates three fossil-fuel powered plants and six hydroelectric dams that give it a capacity of about 2,300 MW; it also purchases electricity from Texas wind farms. The LCRA provides water and wastewater utility services to more than 30 communities as well.

Founded by the Texas Legislature in 1934, the LCRA has pursued two complementary goals — providing reliable, low-cost utility and public services, and ensuring the protection of the area's natural resources. In the latter role, the LCRA owns or operates more than 40 public recreation areas comprising more than 16,000 acres; it also monitors the water quality of the lakes formed by its dams.

EXECUTIVES

Chair: Rebecca A. Klein
Vice Chair: Clayborne Nettleship
CEO and General Manager: Thomas G. Mason
Assistant General Manager and COO:
  Marcus W. Pridgeon
Assistant General Manager and Chief Administrative Officer: Rick Bluntzer
Interim CFO and Treasurer: Brady Edwards
Director and Secretary: Linda C. Raun
Chief Risk Officer and Chief Engineer:
  Paul D. Thornhill
Executive Manager, LCRA Transmission Services:
  Ross Phillips
Executive Manager Corporate Services and CIO:
  Christopher Kennedy
Executive Manager Business Development:
  Frank C. McCamant
Executive Manager Corporate Communications:
  Robert Cullick
Executive Manager Federal Affairs:
  Michele (Missy) Mandell
Executive Manager Wholesale Power: Don Kuehn
Executive Manager Water Services: Suzanne Zarling
Manager Public Affairs: Bob Peck
Executive Director, Colorado River Foundation:
  Anita Mennucci
Auditors: Deloitte & Touche LLP

LOCATIONS

HQ: Lower Colorado River Authority
  3700 Lake Austin Blvd., Austin, TX 78703
Phone: 512-473-3200   **Fax:** 512-473-3298
Web: www.lcra.org

PRODUCTS/OPERATIONS

2007 Sales

	% of total
Electric	92
Water, wastewater & irrigation	5
Other	3
Total	**100**

Selected Subsidiaries and Affiliates

GenTex Power Corporation (power generation)
LCRA Transmission Services Corporation (power
  transmission services)

COMPETITORS

AEP
Brazos Electric
El Paso Electric
Energy Future
Entergy
ONEOK
Pedernales Electric
Southwest Water

HISTORICAL FINANCIALS

Company Type: Government-owned

Income Statement

FYE: June 30

	REVENUE ($ mil.)	NET INCOME ($ mil.)	NET PROFIT MARGIN	EMPLOYEES
6/07	1,079	44	4.0%	3,600
6/06	1,045	26	2.5%	2,200
6/05	803	41	5.2%	2,200
6/04	694	34	5.0%	2,224
6/03	643	23	3.5%	2,211
Annual Growth	**13.8%**	**17.7%**	**—**	**13.0%**

2007 Year-End Financials

Debt ratio: —   Current ratio: —
Return on equity: 5.8%   Long-term debt ($ mil.): —
Cash ($ mil.): —

Net Income History

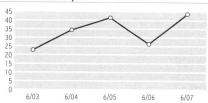

| | 6/03 | 6/04 | 6/05 | 6/06 | 6/07 |

Loyola University

Loyola University is a Jesuit, Catholic university with a reach that extends beyond the Windy City. In addition to its three Chicago-area campuses, the university also maintains an undergraduate campus in Italy and a study center in Beijing, China. Loyola University's more than 15,000 students can choose from about 70 undergraduate, 85 master's, 30 doctoral, and three professional degree programs. Notable alumni include actor Bob Newhart, writer Sandra Cisneros, and CNN-TV correspondent Susan Candiotti. Established in 1870 by a group of Jesuit priests, the university turned its medical center into a separate subsidiary in 1995.

EXECUTIVES

Chairman: Michael R. Quinlan, age 63
Vice Chair: William J. Hank
President and Trustee: Rev Michael J. Garanzini
Provost: Christine M. Wiseman
Associate Provost: John P. Pelissero
Associate Provost, International Initiatives and Academic Services: Patrick Boyle
Dean Of Students: Jane F. Neufeld
VP Finance, CFO, and Treasurer: William G. (Bill) Laird
VP Strategic Capital Planning and Chief of Staff:
  Wayne F. Magdziarz
VP and General Counsel: Ellen K. Munro
VP Public Affairs: Philip (Phil) Hale
VP Human Resources: Thomas M. (Tom) Kelly
VP Information Technology and Services and CIO:
  Susan M. Malisch
VP Marketing and Communication: Kelly Shannon

LOCATIONS

HQ: Loyola University Chicago
  6525 N. Sheridan Rd., Chicago, IL 60626
Phone: 773-274-3000   **Fax:** 312-915-6455
Web: www.luc.edu

PRODUCTS/OPERATIONS

Selected Schools and Colleges

College of Arts and Sciences
Graduate School of Business
Institute of Pastoral Studies
School of Business Administration
School of Communication
School of Continuing and Professional Studies
School of Education
School of Law
School of Nursing
School of Social Work
Stritch School of Medicine
The Graduate School

LPL Financial

LPL Financial (formerly Linsco/Private Ledger) is one of the largest independent brokerage firms in the US. The company's more than 10,000 advisors offer stocks and bonds, mutual funds, annuities, insurance, and other investments, as well as trust, research, and financial planning services. As an independent, LPL doesn't sell its own investment products, but provides access to those of other firms. It operates more than 6,500 offices in all 50 states and the District of Columbia. LPL expanded its client base with its 2006 purchase of UVEST Financial Services, which provides independent brokerage services to more than 300 regional and community banks and credit unions throughout the US.

In 2004 LPL acquired The Phoenix Companies' broker/dealer operations (WS Griffith Securities and Main Street Management), boosting its broker ranks and offering Phoenix the chance to sell its products through LPL's network.

The company acquired three broker-dealers from Pacific Life in 2007 — Mutual Service Corp., Associated Financial Group, and Waterstone Financial Group. The deal gave it another 2,200 brokers and around $350 million in sales.

EXECUTIVES

Chairman and CEO: Mark S. Casady
Vice Chairman: James S. (Jim) Putnam
President and COO: Esther Stearns
CFO: Robert J. Moore, age 46
Managing Director, Chief Investment Officer, and Chief Economist: Lincoln Anderson
Managing Director and Chief Risk Officer:
  Steven (Steve) Black
Managing Director and General Counsel:
  Stephanie L. Brown
Managing Director; President, Independent Advisor Services: Bill Dwyer
Managing Director, Strategic Planning: Mark G. Lopez
Managing Director and Chief Compliance Officer:
  Joseph Tuorto
Managing Director, Organizational Strategy:
  Gina Cannella
Managing Director; Chief of Staff, Independent Advisor Services: Rochelle Putnam
Managing Director, Broker/Dealer Support Services:
  Mark Helliker, age 45
Managing Director, Human Capital: Denise Abood
EVP and Head of National Sales: Jonathan Eaton
EVP, Operations: Amy Wong
EVP, Corporate Marketing: Kandis Bates
President, LPL Financial Institution Services:
  Dan Arnold

LOCATIONS

HQ: LPL Financial Corp.
  9785 Towne Centre Dr., San Diego, CA 92121
Phone: 858-450-9606   **Fax:** 858-546-8324
Web: www.lpl.com

COMPETITORS

Ameriprise
Charles Schwab
Edward Jones
Merrill Lynch
Morgan Keegan
Morgan Stanley
Raymond James Financial
UBS Financial Services
Wachovia Securities

HISTORICAL FINANCIALS

Company Type: Private

Income Statement

	REVENUE ($ mil.)	NET INCOME ($ mil.)	NET PROFIT MARGIN	EMPLOYEES
12/07	2,718	61	2.2%	2,621
12/06	1,740	34	1.9%	2,200
12/05	1,407	43	3.1%	1,200
12/04	1,157	35	3.1%	—
Annual Growth	32.9%	20.0%	—	47.8%

FYE: December 31

2007 Year-End Financials

Debt ratio: —
Return on equity: 8.9%
Cash ($ mil.): —

Current ratio: —
Long-term debt ($ mil.): —

Net Income History

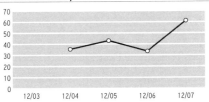

Lucasfilm Ltd.

The Force is definitely with Emperor George Lucas. With three of the 20 highest-grossing movies of all time, Lucasfilm is one of the most successful independent movie studios in the history of film. Owned by filmmaker George Lucas (the brains behind the *Star Wars* and *Indiana Jones* films), Lucasfilm's productions have won 19 Academy Awards. Its most recent movie is 2008's *Indiana Jones and the Kingdom of the Crystal Skull* (in partnership with Paramount); 1999's *Episode I — The Phantom Menace* is Lucasfilm's biggest money-maker, with a gross of more than $920 million worldwide. Other subsidiaries in the Lucas empire are responsible for licensing, special effects, and software. Lucasfilm was created in 1971.

Lucasfilm consists of LucasArts (video games), special effects house Industrial Light & Magic (ILM), Skywalker Sound, Lucas Licensing (consumer products), Lucas Online (e-commerce, news, and information), and Lucasfilm Animation (digitally animated feature films and television productions). The divisions are all housed under one roof at the Letterman Digital Arts Center at the Presidio, a former Army base in San Francisco.

The company has a presence in Asia with its Lucasfilm Animation Singapore. The unit, which produces digital animation for movies, television, and games, is 75% owned by Lucasfilm. The remainder is held by a Singapore state-led consortium.

The final sequel to the *Star Wars* series, *Episode III — Revenge of the Sith,* was a box office hit, earning a whopping $50 million in its first day of release. An all-new *Star Wars: The Clone Wars* animated adventure from Lucasfilm Animation premiered in summer 2008. And while audiences flocked to see *Indiana Jones*

and the Kingdom of the Crystal Skull in 2008, the movie only came in third place at the box office that summer (it was beat by the breakout hits *Dark Knight* and *Iron Man*).

HISTORY

After attending film school at the University of Southern California, George Lucas started his career as a documentary filmmaker, chronicling the production of Francis Ford Coppola's *Finian's Rainbow* in 1968. The two men became fast friends and founded American Zoetrope in 1969, which two years later released Lucas' feature film debut, the science-fiction film *THX 1138* (a full-length version of a student film he made at USC). The film flopped, and Coppola went into production on *The Godfather*. Lucas left American Zoetrope and created his own company, Lucasfilm, in 1971.

Two years later Lucas released *American Graffiti* through Universal Pictures (with some financial help from Coppola). The film was a smash hit; it raked in $115 million in the US and made him a millionaire before the age of 30. It also gave him the clout to try and get his most ambitious project off the ground, a space opera called *Star Wars*. Universal, frustrated with cost overruns on *Graffiti*, wanted no part of Lucas' seemingly ridiculous idea, so he went to 20th Century Fox, which agreed to finance the $10 million film. Lucas gave up his directing fee for a percentage of the box-office take and all merchandising rights. He created Industrial Light & Magic (ILM) and Sprocket Systems (later Skywalker Sound) in 1975 to produce the visual and sound effects needed for the film.

Star Wars cost about $12 million and almost everyone involved was sure it would bomb. Released in 1977, the movie shattered every box-office record, and the merchandising rights Lucas obtained made him a multimillionaire. With his take from *Star Wars,* Lucas was able to finance the film's sequel, *The Empire Strikes Back* (1980), out of his own pocket, meaning he would receive most of the profits (it grossed more than $220 million domestically). Lucasfilm's next production was *Raiders of the Lost Ark* (1981), directed by Lucas' friend Steven Spielberg. It went on to gross more than $380 million worldwide.

The next year Lucas began developing the THX sound system in preparation for the 1983 release of the third *Star Wars* film, *Return of the Jedi* (which hauled in more than $260 million domestically). He also founded LucasArts in 1982 to develop video games. Lucasfilm completed Skywalker Ranch (a facility housing many of its various companies in Marin County, California) in the mid-1980s and filled out the decade with two *Raiders* sequels — *Indiana Jones and the Temple of Doom* (1984, $333 million worldwide) and *Indiana Jones and the Last Crusade* (1989, $495 million worldwide).

Lucasfilm reorganized in 1993 by spinning off LucasArts into a separate subsidiary. Lucasfilm won local government approval to build an $87 million film studio near Skywalker Ranch in 1996, and the following year it re-released the *Star Wars Trilogy* to theaters with new special effects in celebration of the 20th anniversary, adding another $250 million to its take. Anticipating the release of the first of three prequels to the *Star Wars Trilogy*, Lucasfilm started signing marketing agreements in 1998 (including deals with Hasbro and Pepsi) that resulted in advance licensing of nearly $3 billion.

Star Wars: Episode I — The Phantom Menace opened in May 1999 and has grossed about $920 million worldwide (it finished its initial run second only to *Titanic*). Later in 1999 Lucas announced plans to develop a $250 million digital arts center at the old Presidio army base in San Francisco to house ILM, LucasArts, Lucas Online, Lucas Licensing, THX, and the George Lucas Educational Foundation (completed in 2005).

In 2002 Lucas spun off digital sound systems firm THX as an independent company. The next film in the *Star Wars* series, *Episode II — Attack of the Clones*, also opened that year. The following year the company formed its Lucasfilm Animation unit to create digitally animated feature films and television productions. The 2003 release of Lucasfilm's *The Adventures of Indiana Jones: The Complete DVD Movie Collection* made record-breaking sales.

The company hit gold again with the DVD release of the *Star Wars Trilogy* in 2004. In 2005 Lucasfilm released the third *Star Wars* movie, *Episode III — Revenge of the Sith*. Also that year the company opened its Letterman Digital Arts Center at the Presidio.

EXECUTIVES

Chairman: George W. Lucas Jr.
President and COO: Micheline (Mich) Chau
VP and General Manager, Lucasfilm Animation: Gail Currey
VP and General Manager, Skywalker Sound: Glenn Kiser
Director Communications: Lynne Hale
Director Content Management Marketing and Head of Fan Relations: Steve Sansweet
General Counsel: David J. Anderman
Chief Administrative Officer: Jan van der Voort
CTO: Richard Kerris
President, LucasArts: Darrell Rodriguez
President, Industrial Light and Magic: Chrissie England
President, Lucas Licensing: Howard Roffman

LOCATIONS

HQ: Lucasfilm Ltd.
1110 Gorgas Ave., San Francisco, CA 94129
Phone: 415-662-1800
Web: www.lucasfilm.com

PRODUCTS/OPERATIONS

Selected Productions

American Graffiti (1973)
Howard the Duck (1986)
Indiana Jones and the Kingdom of the Crystal Skull (2008)
Indiana Jones and the Last Crusade (1989)
Indiana Jones and the Temple of Doom (1984)
Labyrinth (1986)
More American Graffiti (1979)
Radioland Murders (1994)
Raiders of the Lost Ark (1981)
Star Wars: Episode I — The Phantom Menace (1999)
Star Wars: Episode II — Attack of the Clones (2002)
Star Wars: Episode III — Revenge of the Sith (2005)
Star Wars: Episode IV — A New Hope (1977)
Star Wars: Episode V — The Empire Strikes Back (1980)
Star Wars: Episode VI — Return of the Jedi (1983)
Star Wars: The Clone Wars (2008)
Tucker: The Man and His Dream (1988)
Willow (1988)
The Young Indiana Jones Chronicles (1992-96, TV movies)

COMPETITORS

Disney Studios	New Line Cinema
DreamWorks	Paramount Pictures
Fox Filmed Entertainment	Pixar
Lionsgate	Sony Pictures
MGM	Universal Studios

MA Laboratories

If you need a computer part, just ask your MA. Distributor MA Laboratories provides computer resellers and systems integrators with more than 3,000 computer-related products. MA Labs specializes in memory modules but sells just about everything commonly found in or near a computer, including hard drives, motherboards, CD-ROMs, and video cards. Other products include monitors, software, fax modems, network cards, digital cameras, notebook computers, and accessories. Among MA's suppliers are 3Com, Advanced Micro Devices, Hewlett-Packard, IBM, Intel, Microsoft, Sony, and Toshiba. MA Labs was founded in 1983 by owner and CEO Abraham Ma.

EXECUTIVES

President and CEO: Abraham Ma
MIS Manager: Michael Ma
Business Development: Patrick Lai
Marketing Manager: Zak Wood

LOCATIONS

HQ: MA Laboratories, Inc.
2075 N. Capitol Ave., San Jose, CA 95132
Phone: 408-941-0808   **Fax:** 408-941-0909
Web: www.malabs.com

PRODUCTS/OPERATIONS

Selected Products

CD and DVD drives
Computer components (keyboards, cooling fans, and other devices)
Data storage
Digital cameras
Hard drives
Input/output cards
Memory
Modems
Monitors
Motherboards
Multimedia (speakers, scanners, and other devices)
Networking
Notebook computers and accessories
Printers
Processors
Software
Video cards

Services

Technical support

COMPETITORS

Agilysys	Merisel
Arrow Electronics	N.F. Smith
Avnet	Super Micro Computer
Bell Microproducts	Tech Data
Ingram Micro	Viking InterWorks
Kingston Technology	Wintec

HISTORICAL FINANCIALS

Company Type: Private

Income Statement

FYE: December 31

	REVENUE ($ mil.)	NET INCOME ($ mil.)	NET PROFIT MARGIN	EMPLOYEES
12/07	2,000	—	—	1,200
12/06	1,500	—	—	1,000
12/05	1,200	—	—	600
Annual Growth	29.1%	—	—	41.4%

Revenue History

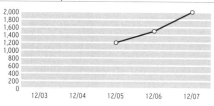

M. A. Mortenson

M. A. Mortenson Company is leaving its footprints all over the country. One of the largest builders in the US, with operations in 48 states, its design/build projects include the FedExForum, home of the NBA's Memphis Grizzlies, and the Walt Disney Concert Hall, home of the Los Angeles Philharmonic Orchestra. Besides its company projects group, Mortenson also has operations in biofuels and energy construction, targeting the growing renewable energy sector with projects including wind farms and biofuel facilities. Other construction ranges from real estate development and health care and government facilities. The family-owned company was founded in 1954 by M. A. Mortenson Sr., whose son now serves as chairman.

Its Mortenson China subsidiary, which was established in 2003, acts as a bridge between the West and East, facilitating the building process for western companies that are adding plants and operations in China. A recent project in the country includes building 150 learning centers for Disney as the iconic company strives to provide English education in China.

EXECUTIVES

Chairman: M. A. Mortenson Jr.
President and CEO: Thomas F. (Tom) Gunkel
SVP and CFO: Sandra Sponem
SVP: Paul I. Cossette
SVP Administration: Paul V. Campbell
SVP Energy Group: Thomas W. (Tom) Wacker
SVP Operations: Bradley C. (Brad) Funk
SVP: Daniel L. (Dan) Johnson
SVP: David C. Mortenson
SVP: John V. Wood
SVP Business Development: Robert J. Nartonis
VP Strategic Marketing: James P. Lesinski
VP Human Resources: Daniel R. (Dan) Haag
VP and Senior Counsel: Dwight Larson
VP Controller and Chief Accounting Officer: William Patt
Corporate Secretary and Director Financial Planning: Mark A. Mortenson
Senior Communications Specialist: Kim Kaisler
Auditors: Deloitte & Touche LLP

LOCATIONS

HQ: M. A. Mortenson Company
700 Meadow Ln. North, Minneapolis, MN 55422
Phone: 763-522-2100   **Fax:** 763-287-5430
Web: www.mortenson.com

PRODUCTS/OPERATIONS

Selected Services

Construction management
Design/build delivery
Engineering, procurement, and construction (EPC)
General contracting
Maintenance and operations
Planning
Preconstruction services
Program management
Project development
Turnkey construction

COMPETITORS

Barton Malow
Bechtel
Bovis Lend Lease
Brasfield & Gorrie
C. G. Schmidt
FaulknerUSA
Fluor
Gilbane
The Haskell Company
Hensel Phelps Construction
Hoffman Corporation
Hunt Construction
KBR
McCarthy Building
Miron Construction
Parsons Corporation
Pepper Construction
Perini
Skanska
Turner Corporation
Walbridge Aldinger
Walsh Group
Whiting-Turner
Zachry Group

HISTORICAL FINANCIALS

Company Type: Private

Income Statement

FYE: December 31

	REVENUE ($ mil.)	NET INCOME ($ mil.)	NET PROFIT MARGIN	EMPLOYEES
12/07	2,140	—	—	2,700
12/06	1,410	—	—	2,200
12/05	1,200	—	—	1,700
12/04	1,100	—	—	1,700
12/03	1,103	—	—	1,800
Annual Growth	18.0%	—	—	10.7%

Revenue History

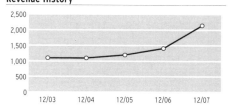

MacAndrews & Forbes

Through MacAndrews & Forbes Holdings, financier Ron Perelman is focused on cosmetics and cash. The holding company has investments in an array of public and private companies, most notably Revlon (one of the top cosmetics companies in the US) and M&F Worldwide (licorice flavors and financial products). Perelman is intent on reversing the fortunes of Revlon, which he has controlled since 1985. He made a hefty sum when Consolidated Cigar Holdings (the #1 US cigar maker) was sold to French tobacco maker Seita. Perelman acquired a majority stake in AM General, maker of Humvee and HUMMER vehicles through MacAndrews AMG Holdings. It bought The Rank Group's Deluxe Film operation for some $750 million.

With an 83% stake in Panavision (the top provider of cameras for shooting movies and TV shows) through its investment firm PX Holding, MacAndrews & Forbes' purchase of Deluxe Film (which has operations in Hollywood, Rome, and London) in 2006 pairs well in the company's portfolio alongside cosmetics. MacAndrews & Forbes' other holdings include the drug-development company TransTech Pharma (in which it is the largest shareholder) and privately held Allied Security, one of the biggest providers of security guards and systems. The company struck a deal in 2008 to sell Allied Security to the Blackstone Group for up to $750 million.

Perelman's holdings have dwindled in value since 1999. Most of the investor's business strategy involves improving his cash position and paying down debt — hence his IPO of Revlon (1996), the sale of The Coleman Company to American Household (formerly Sunbeam Corp., 1998), and the sale of two of Revlon's noncore units. Perelman has committed a $215 million debt-and-equity funding package to rescue Revlon, which is struggling with debt and dwindling market share.

Perelman's sale of The Coleman Company — in the late 1990s — is helping the investor improve his cash flow today. In his suit against Morgan Stanley, Perelman alleged that the investment bank withheld its knowledge of Sunbeam's accounting fraud when Perelman sold The Coleman Company to Sunbeam in 1998 for about $1.5 billion. Perelman's investment (he held 14.1 million shares of Sunbeam stock as part of the sale) later tanked as news broke of the accounting irregularities. Despite an attempt to settle the dispute with Morgan Stanley in 2003 for $20 million, Perelman took the bank to court and was awarded more than $1.5 billion in damages by a Florida jury in mid-2005.

Adding some more companies to the mix, MacAndrews & Forbes acquired the data management business of Pearson PLC for $225 million in 2008, which will be operated by its Scanton testing unit. In 2007 the company bought John H. Harland for $1.7 billion, which was paired with MacAndrews & Forbes' Clarke American unit.

HISTORY

Ron Perelman grew up working in his father's Philadelphia-based conglomerate, Belmont Industries, but he left at the age of 35 to seek his fortune in New York. In 1978 he bought 40% of jewelry store operator Cohen-Hatfield Industries. The next year Cohen-Hatfield bought a minority stake in MacAndrews & Forbes (licorice flavoring). Cohen-Hatfield acquired MacAndrews & Forbes in 1980.

In 1984 Perelman reshuffled his assets to create MacAndrews & Forbes Holdings, which acquired control of Pantry Pride, a Florida-based supermarket chain, in 1985. Pantry Pride then bought Revlon for $1.8 billion with the help of (convicted felon) Michael Milken. After Perelman acquired Revlon, he added several other cosmetics vendors, including Max Factor and Yves Saint Laurent's fragrance and cosmetic lines.

In 1988 MacAndrews & Forbes agreed to invest $315 million in five failing Texas savings and loans (S&Ls), which Perelman combined and named First Gibraltar (sold to BankAmerica, now Bank of America, in 1993). The next year MacAndrews & Forbes bought The Coleman Company, a maker of outdoor equipment.

With a growing reputation for buying struggling companies, revamping them, and then selling them at a higher price, Perelman bought Marvel Entertainment Group (Marvel Comics) in 1989 and took it public in 1991. That year he sold Revlon's Max Factor and Betrix units to Procter & Gamble for more than $1 billion.

MacAndrews & Forbes acquired 37.5% of TV infomercial producer Guthy-Renker and SCI Television's seven stations and merged them to create New World Television. That company was combined with TV syndicator Genesis Entertainment and TV production house New World Entertainment to create New World Communications Group, which Perelman took public in 1994.

Subsidiaries Mafco Worldwide and Consolidated Cigar Holdings merged with Abex (aircraft parts) to create Mafco Consolidated Group in 1995. Following diminishing comic sales, Perelman placed Marvel in bankruptcy in 1996 and subsequently lost control of the company.

In 1997 First Nationwide bought California thrift Cal Fed Bancorp for $1.2 billion. In addition, Perelman sold New World to Rupert Murdoch's News Corp.

In 1998 Perelman orchestrated a $1.8 billion deal in which First Nationwide merged with Golden State Bancorp to form the US's third-largest thrift. Sunbeam Corp. (now American Household) bought Perelman's stake in Coleman that year, making Perelman a major American Household shareholder. Also in 1998 MacAndrews & Forbes bought a 72% stake in Panavision (movie camera maker, later increased to 91%), invested in WeddingChannel.com (sold in 2006), and sold its 64% stake in Consolidated Cigar to French tobacco giant Seita.

Perelman's stock in American Household was rendered worthless when the company initiated bankruptcy proceedings in February 2001. (It would emerge from bankruptcy, however, in December 2002.) He also was sued by angry shareholders after the board of M&F Worldwide, the licorice company he controls, bought Perelman's stock in Panavision at more than five times its market value. In order to settle the litigation surrounding the purchase, in 2002 M&F agreed to return Perelman's 83% stake in Panavision to Mafco. Golden State Bancorp also left the MacAndrews fold in 2002 when it was acquired by Citigroup.

MacAndrews & Forbes Holdings acquired Allied Security, the largest independent provider of contract security services and products in the US, from Gryphon Investors in February 2003 for an undisclosed sum.

EXECUTIVES

Co-Chairman and CEO: Ronald O. (Ron) Perelman, age 65
Co-Chairman; President and CEO, Panavision: Robert L. (Bob) Beitcher
Vice Chairman and Chief Administrative Officer: Barry F. Schwartz, age 59
SVP Corporate Communications: Christine Taylor
VP: Matthew Adam Drapkin
VP and Controller: Norman J. Ginstling
President, MacAndrews & Forbes Acquisition Holdings: Samuel L. (Sam) Katz

LOCATIONS

HQ: MacAndrews & Forbes Holdings Inc.
35 E. 62nd St., New York, NY 10065
Phone: 212-572-8600 **Fax:** 212-572-8400
Web: www.macandrewsandforbes.com

PRODUCTS/OPERATIONS

Selected Holdings

AM General (majority stake, multipurpose and military vehicles)
American Household (minority stake, small appliances and Coleman camping gear)
Deluxe Film (film production)
M&F Worldwide Corp. (minority stake, licorice extract)
Revlon Inc. (majority stake, cosmetics and personal care products)
TransTech Pharma (drug development company)

COMPETITORS

Alberto-Culver	iRobot
Alticor	Johnson & Johnson
Avon	Kellwood
BAE Systems	Lockheed Martin
Body Shop	L'Oréal USA
Boeing	LVMH
Chattem	Mary Kay
Colgate-Palmolive	Procter & Gamble
The Dial Corporation	Ulta
Estée Lauder	Unilever
General Dynamics	

MacArthur Foundation

Granted, The John D. and Catherine T. MacArthur Foundation gives away a lot of money. With some $7 billion in assets, the private foundation issued some $267 million in grants in 2007 to groups and individuals working to improve the human condition. Its two primary programs are Human and Community Development (affordable housing, education reform, mental health) and Global Security and Sustainability (world peace, population reduction, conservation, human rights). The foundation also funds special initiatives and awards $500,000 MacArthur Fellowships to a variety of individuals.

Since making its first grant in 1978, The John D. and Catherine T. MacArthur Foundation has distributed about $3.7 billion.

The John D. and Catherine T. MacArthur Foundation was established in 1978 after the death of billionaire John D. MacArthur. The foundation supports projects worldwide. Along with such organizations as The Rockefeller Foundation and The Andrew W. Mellon Foundation, it is a member of The Partnership for Higher Education in Africa.

HISTORY

The John D. and Catherine T. MacArthur Foundation was established by an eccentric billionaire who enjoyed making money more than spending it. MacArthur, one of the three richest men in the US at the time of his death, made a fortune after he bought Bankers Life and Casualty Company of Chicago and sold mail-order insurance at the end of the Depression. He later became the largest landowner in Florida.

To avoid paying taxes, MacArthur used most of his $2.5 billion estate to establish a foundation named after himself and his second wife. After MacArthur's death in 1978, the foundation's board of trustees found no guidelines other than a brief statement: "I figured out how to make the money; you fellows will have to figure out how to spend it."

Soon after the foundation began making fellowship awards, it became known as one of the more eccentric of large US foundations. Its MacArthur Fellows program provides so-called "genius-grants" ($500,000 paid out over five years); recipients have included a cartoonist and a rare-books binder. Critics argue that such money might be better spent on other programs.

In 1997 the foundation reorganized under two integrated programs — Human and Community Development and Global Security and Sustainability — in an effort to unify its grant-making. It diversified its holdings in 1998 by selling nearly 15,000 acres of land in Florida. The following year Adele Simmons stepped down as president after a decade with the foundation; she was replaced by Jonathan Fanton, former president of the New York City-based New School for Social Research.

EXECUTIVES

Chairman and Director: Robert E. Denham, age 63
President and Director: Jonathan F. Fanton
VP and CFO: Marc P. Yanchura
VP and Chief Investment Officer: Susan E. Manske
VP, General Counsel, and Assistant Secretary:
  Joshua J. Mintz
VP: Arthur M. Sussman
VP Program on Global Security and Sustainability:
  Barry F. Lowenkron
VP General Program: Elspeth A. Revere
VP Public Affairs: Andrew Solomon
VP Program on Human and Community Development:
  Julia M. Stasch
**Associate VP Institutional Research and Grants
  Management:** Richard J. Kaplan
CIO: Sharon Burns
Director Finance and Tax: George B. Ptacin
Secretary: Elizabeth T. Kane
Senior Advisor to the President: William E. Lowry

LOCATIONS

HQ: The John D. and Catherine T. MacArthur
  Foundation
  140 S. Dearborn St., Ste. 1200, Chicago, IL 60603
Phone: 312-726-8000   **Fax:** 312-920-6258
Web: www.macfound.org

PRODUCTS/OPERATIONS

2006 Grants

	$ mil.	% of total
Global security & sustainability	85.4	36
Human & community development	78.6	34
General program	58.9	25
MacArthur Fellows program	12.0	5
Total	**234.9**	**100**

MacDermid, Incorporated

MacDermid's brood of specialty chemicals is too broad to pigeonhole. The company makes a range of chemicals used in electronics (for etching and to imprint electrical patterns on circuit boards), graphic arts (for image transfers), metal and plastics finishing, and oil and gas exploration. It markets and produces more than 5,000 proprietary chemical compounds used for cleaning, coating, electroplating, etching, mechanical galvanizing, and rust retarding applications. MacDermid also distributes chemical supplies of other companies and produces horizontal processing equipment used in circuit board production and chemical machining.

MacDermid has been run by the Leever family for nearly half a century. Daniel Leever, chairman and CEO like his father before him, has helped lift MacDermid's status to that of a global player in the specialty chemicals industry. In mid-2006 Leever, with the financial backing of Court Square Capital Partners, bid to buy MacDermid outright, planning to take the company private. The company's board agreed to the deal, and it closed in the spring of 2007.

For several years in the early part of the decade, the company was focused on growth through acquisitions and even hired a CFO, John Malfettone, who had experience in acquisitions through his past job at GE Capital. Although MacDermid largely accomplished its goal, many of the acquired businesses had difficulty in assimilating, and the company has decided to postpone further acquisitions (as a result, Malfettone left MacDermid in 2004).

The company reviewed several potential purchases during 2004, but was unable to find one that met its increased standards. Still interested in adding to its portfolio in 2005, the company found an acquisition candidate that it felt had excellent growth prospects, Autotype International, a maker of specialty coated film products for electronic and printing applications.

EXECUTIVES

Chairman and CEO: Daniel H. Leever, age 59,
  $761,824 pay
**EVP Advanced Surface Finishing and Printing
  Solutions Segments, Asia:** Peter Kukanskis,
  $332,750 pay
SVP Finance and Treasurer:
  Gregory M. (Greg) Bolingbroke, age 58, $278,937 pay
VP, Corporate Secretary, and General Counsel:
  John L. Cordani, age 44, $296,910 pay
Director Human Resources: Gary St. Pierre
Assistant Treasurer and Risk Manager:
  Frank J. Monteiro, age 37
President, Offshore Solutions: Mark R. Hollinger,
  age 50
VP Business Development, Offshore Solutions:
  Steve E. Racca Jr.
Auditors: Grant Thornton LLP

LOCATIONS

HQ: MacDermid, Incorporated
  1401 Blake St., Denver, CO 80202
Phone: 720-479-3060   **Fax:** 720-479-3087
Web: www.macdermid.com

MacDermid has manufacturing and sales operations in Asia, Australia, Europe, and North America.

COMPETITORS

BASF Catalysts
Cabot
Clariant
Croda
Day International
Elementis
Evonik Degussa
Infineum
Lubrizol
OM Group
Presstek
Rhodia
Rohm and Haas
W. R. Grace

HISTORICAL FINANCIALS

Company Type: Private

Income Statement

FYE: December 31

	REVENUE ($ mil.)	NET INCOME ($ mil.)	NET PROFIT MARGIN	EMPLOYEES
12/06	818	52	6.3%	2,900
12/05	738	47	6.4%	2,800
12/04	661	53	8.1%	2,362
12/03	620	56	9.1%	2,359
12/02	688	9	1.4%	3,166
Annual Growth	4.4%	53.2%	—	(2.2%)

2006 Year-End Financials

Debt ratio: 72.5%
Return on equity: 13.9%
Cash ($ mil.): 125
Current ratio: 3.13
Long-term debt ($ mil.): 301

Net Income History

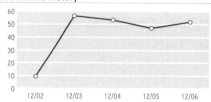

Main Street America

Who's your main insurance man? The Main Street America Group provides a range of personal and commercial property/casualty products including coverage for small and midsized businesses and individual auto and homeowners insurance plans. The company operates through its flagship subsidiary NGM Insurance, as well as its Old Dominion Insurance, MSA Insurance, and Main Street America Assurance businesses. Its Information Systems and Services Corporation offers third-party administration services such as broker management, policy processing, and underwriting services. Main Street America sells its products through more than 1,300 independent agents, primarily along the East Coast.

The company started out as National Grange Mutual Insurance in 1923 in New Hampshire. Since that time the company has expanded, and in 2005 it changed its corporate structure to that of a mutual insurance holding company.

Aiming to become a super-regional company, the company has expanded beyond its East Coast origins. In 2008 the firm entered the Michigan auto insurance market by acquiring Great Lakes Casualty Insurance.

Main Street America operates in about 20 states; primary markets include Connecticut, Florida, Massachusetts, New York, Pennsylvania, and Virginia.

The company also is expanding through new product offerings. Personal Auto MVP, a product offering multi-variable auto products, was launched in 2007. It also plans to expand its business owners' and commercial auto offerings.

EXECUTIVES

Chairman: Philip D. Koerner
President, CEO, and Director: Thomas M. Van Berkel
EVP Corporate Strategic Support: Jeanne H. Eddy
SVP and CFO: Edward J. Kuhl
SVP and General Counsel: Susan E. Mack
SVP Human Resources: Antonia (Toni) Porterfield
SVP Insurance Operations: Bill Anderson
SVP Field Operations: Doug Eden
VP Market Research: Stephen D. Canty
VP and CIO: Joel Gelb
VP and Corporate Actuary: Ed Lotkowski
VP Claims: Mike Lancashire
VP Commercial Lines: Henry Pippins
VP Internal Audit: Geof Molina
VP Legal and Secretary: William C. McKenna
Auditors: Ernst & Young LLP

LOCATIONS

HQ: The Main Street America Group
    4601 Touchton Rd., East, Ste. 3400,
    Jacksonville, FL 32246
Phone: 904-380-7281   **Fax:** 904-380-7244
Web: www.msagroup.com

PRODUCTS/OPERATIONS

2007 Written Premiums

	% of total
Commercial multiple peril	32
Private passenger auto	25
Commercial auto	14
Homeowners	13
Other lines	16
Total	**100**

Selected Subsidiaries

Great Lakes Casualty Insurance Company
Informations Systems and Services Corporation
Main Street America Assurance Company
MSA Information Systems and Services Corporation
MSA Insurance Company
NGM Insurance Company
Old Dominion Insurance Company

COMPETITORS

ACE Limited
AIG
Allstate
American Family Insurance
American Financial
Arrowpoint Capital Corp.
Cincinnati Financial
Farmers Group
Fireman's Fund Insurance
GEICO
The Hartford
Liberty Mutual
Progressive Corporation
Prudential
Safeco
State Farm
Travelers Companies

HISTORICAL FINANCIALS

Company Type: Mutual company

Income Statement

FYE: December 31

	ASSETS ($ mil.)	NET INCOME ($ mil.)	INCOME AS % OF ASSETS	EMPLOYEES
12/07	1,795	88	4.9%	—
12/06	1,641	74	4.5%	—
Annual Growth	**9.4%**	**19.7%**	**—**	**—**

2007 Year-End Financials

Equity as % of assets: 34.5%   Long-term debt ($ mil.): —
Return on assets: 5.1%   Sales ($ mil.): 839
Return on equity: 15.0%

Net Income History

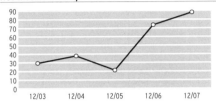

MAINES Paper & Food Service

A lot of restaurants look to this main middle man to get their supplies. MAINES Paper & Food Service is one of the leading foodservice distributors in the US, with about 10 distribution centers serving customers in more than 35 states. It provides fresh produce, beef, and seafood, as well as dry goods and a variety of non-food items to restaurants, convenience stores, health care and educational institutions. It also offers equipment and kitchen supplies, as well as logistics and quality assurance services. The family-owned company was founded in 1919 by Floyd Maines.

MAINES is a leading supplier for quick-service restaurants and chains; #2 hamburger outlet Burger King is one of its largest customers. In 2008 it added the Roy Rogers family dining chain to its customer roll.

EXECUTIVES

Co-Chairman: William R. (Bill) Maines
Co-Chairman: David J. Maines
President and CEO: Christopher (Chris) Mellon
COO: Terry Walsh
VP Decision Support: Bill Kimler
VP Information Technology: Joseph Oaks
Director Human Resources: Stephanie Wyatt
President, Corporate Park: Patrick (Pat) Lappin
Division President, New England Facility: Mike DiLarso
Division President, Farmingdale Facility:
  Mark Eisenberg
Division President, Oakwood Facility: Dennis Kee

LOCATIONS

HQ: MAINES Paper & Food Service Inc.
    101 Broome Corporate Pkwy., Conklin, NY 13748
Phone: 607-779-1200
Web: www.maines.net

COMPETITORS

Agar Supply
Ben E. Keith
Clark National
Gordon Food Service
McLane Foodservice
Meadowbrook Meat

Performance Food
Reinhart FoodService
Services Group of America
SYSCO
UniPro Foodservice
U.S. Foodservice

HISTORICAL FINANCIALS

Company Type: Private

Income Statement

FYE: December 31

	REVENUE ($ mil.)	NET INCOME ($ mil.)	NET PROFIT MARGIN	EMPLOYEES
12/07	2,400	—	—	2,000
12/06	2,020	—	—	1,950
12/05	1,950	—	—	1,950
Annual Growth	**10.9%**	**—**	**—**	**1.3%**

Revenue History

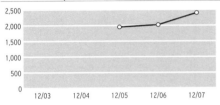

Major League Baseball

It may be the national pastime, but Major League Baseball (MLB) is also a big business. MLB runs the game of professional baseball and oversees 30 franchises in 28 cities. Each team operates as a separate business, but each is regulated and governed by MLB. The league sets official rules, regulates team ownership, and collects licensing fees for merchandise. It also sells national broadcasting rights and distributes fees to the teams. (Regional broadcast rights are held by each franchise.)

Professional baseball finds itself at its height of popularity and financial stability, with revenue growing at a faster pace than the National Football League, the most popular sports enterprise in the US. A big reason for MLB's growth has been the increasing parity between teams, a result of the collective bargaining agreement (CBA) between the league and the MLB Players Association that enforces a luxury tax on teams with higher payrolls. Shifting some money from large market teams such as the New York Yankees and Boston Red Sox to the smaller markets has helped such franchises as the Milwaukee Brewers and Colorado Rockies remain competitive, ensuring higher ticket sales all around.

MLB has also done a good job translating the nationwide popularity of baseball into revenue through broadcasting rights agreements. The league reached a new seven-year TV deal with FOX Broadcasting in 2006 worth $1.8 billion for a slate of regular-season games, one League Championship Series, and the World Series. Turner Broadcasting, a unit of Time Warner, also entered into separate seven-year deals worth a total of about $850 million to show baseball's other LCS and all the Division Series playoff games, along with more than 25 regular season contests. (Walt Disney's ESPN, meanwhile, kicked off an eight-year, $2.4 billion rights deal for regular season games in 2006.)

The league's interactive media arm, MLB Advanced Media, has borne fruit in the form of subscription-based Internet audio and video broadcasts of out-of-market games. MLB is also preparing to launch The Baseball Channel on cable and satellite for the 2009 season. The new broadcast offering, set to be carried by DIRECTV and iN DEMAND, will feature subscription access to out-of-market games.

MLB still faces the challenge posed by performance-enhancing drugs. Several high-profile players have been suspended in recent years after testing positive for steroids and rumors persist that many others continue to use banned substances. Prompted by the book *Game of Shadows*, an exposé on the alleged use of steroids and human growth hormones by former San Francisco Giants slugger Barry Bonds, MLB in 2006 established an independent commission led by former Senator George Mitchell to investigate the use of illegal performance-enhancing drugs in baseball.

Bud Selig, the former owner of the Brewers, was named interim commissioner in 1992 and took the job permanently six years later.

HISTORY

The first baseball team to field professional players was the Cincinnati Red Stockings (now the Cincinnati Reds) in 1869. Teams in Boston, New York City, and Philadelphia followed suit. In 1876 eight professional teams formed the National League. Competing leagues sprang up and folded, but Ban Johnson's Western League (formed in 1892) seized on territory abandoned by the National League in 1900 and began luring National League players with higher salaries. Renamed the American League, it also began drawing away fans. The two leagues agreed to join forces in 1903 by having their champions meet in the World Series.

The sport flourished until the "Black Sox" scandal of 1919, in which eight Chicago White Sox players were accused of taking bribes to throw the World Series. The owners hired Judge Kenesaw Mountain Landis as baseball's first commissioner in 1921 to clean up the game's image. He served until his death in 1944. A joint committee of owners and players introduced more reforms in 1947, including a player pension fund.

The players formed the Major League Baseball Players' Association (MLBPA) in 1954 and signed the first collective-bargaining agreement with the owners in 1968. The players called their first strike in 1972, a 13-day walkout that won an improved pension plan. They won the right to free agency in 1976; another seven-week strike interrupted the 1981 season.

Salary increases slowed, and the free agent market dried up in the mid-1980s, prompting the MLBPA to sue the owners for collusion. The owners agreed to a settlement of $280 million in 1990. Commissioner Fay Vincent resigned in 1992 after the owners effectively removed all power from the commissioner's office. An executive council of owners led by Milwaukee Brewers owner Bud Selig took control.

Prompted by the owners' decision to unilaterally restrict free agency and withdraw salary arbitration, the players started a 232-day strike in August 1994 that forced the cancellation of the World Series and stretched into the 1995 season. Revenue and income plummeted. Play resumed in 1995 when the owners and the MLBPA approved a new collective-bargaining agreement. Selig stepped down from the Brewers in 1998 to become the game's ninth commissioner.

Sweeping changes took place in 2000 when owners, who had voted the previous year to eliminate the American and National League offices, thus centralizing power with the commissioner's office, agreed to restore the "best interests of baseball" powers to the commissioner, giving Selig full authority to redistribute wealth, block trades, and fine teams and players.

In 2004 Bob DuPuy was named president and COO of the league replacing Paul Beeston, who resigned after talks over a new collective-bargaining agreement stalled. A new labor agreement was eventually reached in 2002, however, avoiding another players' strike. The new agreement pushed back the league's contraction plans until 2006 (those plans were eventually shelved altogether) and also enacted a luxury tax on teams with high payrolls, redistributing the money to small-market franchises.

Tokyo-based advertising giant Dentsu agreed to pay $275 million in 2003 for the right to broadcast MLB games in Japan. The following year MLB struck a $650 million broadcasting deal with XM Satellite Radio. Allegations about the use of performance enhancing drugs began to dominate the headlines in 2004 following a grand jury investigation of a California pharmaceuticals company. The flap over steroid use led to MLB implementing a tougher drug testing policy in 2005.

EXECUTIVES

Commissioner: Allan H. (Bud) Selig, age 74
President and COO: Robert A. (Bob) DuPuy, age 60
EVP Administration and CIO: John McHale Jr.
EVP Baseball Operations: Jimmie Lee Solomon
EVP Business: Timothy J. (Tim) Brosnan
EVP Finance and CFO: Jonathan D. Mariner, age 53
EVP Labor Relations and Human Resources: Robert D. (Rob) Manfred Jr.
Chief Legal Counsel: Thomas J. (Tom) Ostertag
SVP and General Counsel, Major League Baseball Properties: Ethan Orlinsky
SVP Advertising and Marketing: Jacqueline Parkes
SVP Baseball Operations: Joe Garagiola Jr.
SVP Corporate Sales and Marketing, Major League Baseball Properties: John S. Brody
SVP International Business Operations: Paul Archey
SVP Licensing: Howard Smith
SVP Media Relations: Richard (Rich) Levin
SVP Security and Facilities Management: Kevin M. Hallinan
SVP Club Relations: Phyllis Merhige
SVP Scheduling and Club Relations: Katy Feeney
VP Community Affairs: Thomas C. Brasuell
VP Public Relations: Patrick (Pat) Courtney
President and CEO, MLB Advanced Media: Robert A. (Bob) Bowman, age 53
Auditors: Deloitte & Touche LLP

LOCATIONS

HQ: Major League Baseball
245 Park Ave., 31st Fl., New York, NY 10167
Phone: 212-931-7800   **Fax:** 212-949-8636
Web: www.mlb.com

PRODUCTS/OPERATIONS

Major League Franchises

American League
  Baltimore Orioles (1954)
    St. Louis Browns (1902)
    Milwaukee Brewers (1901)
  Boston Red Sox (1901)
  Chicago White Sox (1901)
  Cleveland Indians (1915)
    Cleveland Spiders (1889)
  Detroit Tigers (1900)
  Kansas City Royals (1969, Missouri)
  Los Angeles Angels of Anaheim (2005)
    Anaheim Angels (1965, California)
    Los Angeles Angels (1961)
  Minnesota Twins (1961, Minneapolis)
    Washington Senators (1901; Washington, DC)
  New York Yankees (1913, New York City)
    New York Highlanders (1903, New York City)
    Baltimore Orioles (1901)
  Oakland Athletics (1968, California)
    Kansas City Athletics (1955, Missouri)
    Philadelphia Athletics (1901)
  Seattle Mariners (1977)
  Tampa Bay Rays (2007)
    Tampa Bay Devil Rays (1998)
  Texas Rangers (1972, Arlington)
    Washington Senators (1961; Washington, DC)
  Toronto Blue Jays (1977)

National League
  Arizona Diamondbacks (1998, Phoenix)
  Atlanta Braves (1966)
    Milwaukee Braves (1953)
    Boston Braves (1912)
    Boston Beaneaters (1883)
    Boston Red Stockings (1871)
  Chicago Cubs (1903)
    Chicago Orphans (1898)
    Chicago Colts (1894)
    Chicago White Stockings (1871)
  Cincinnati Reds (1866)
  Colorado Rockies (1993, Denver)
  Florida Marlins (1993, Miami)
  Houston Astros (1964)
    Houston Colt .45s (1962)
  Los Angeles Dodgers (1958)
    Brooklyn Dodgers (1890, New York)
  Milwaukee Brewers (1970; switched from American League, 1998)
    Seattle Pilots (1969)
  New York Mets (1962, New York City)
  Philadelphia Phillies (1883)
  Pittsburgh Pirates (1887)
  St. Louis Cardinals (1900)
    St. Louis Brown Stockings (1882)
  San Diego Padres (1969)
  San Francisco Giants (1958)
    New York Giants (1883, New York City)
  Washington Nationals (2004, Washington, DC)
    Montreal Expos (1969)

COMPETITORS

FIFA
Indy Racing League
Major League Soccer
NASCAR
NBA
NFL
NHL
PGA TOUR
World Wrestling Entertainment

HISTORICAL FINANCIALS

Company Type: Association

Income Statement

FYE: October 31

	REVENUE ($ mil.)	NET INCOME ($ mil.)	NET PROFIT MARGIN	EMPLOYEES
10/07	6,100	—	—	—
10/06	5,200	—	—	—
10/05	4,800	—	—	—
10/04	4,100	—	—	—
10/03	3,800	—	—	—
Annual Growth	12.6%	—	—	—

Revenue History

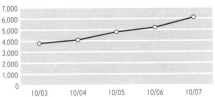

Manor Care

Manor Care is a lord of the manor in the nursing home kingdom. Operating as HCR Manor Care, the firm runs about 500 nursing homes, assisted living centers, and rehabilitation facilities in about 30 states. Its facilities, which operate under the names Heartland, ManorCare Health Services, and Arden Courts, provide not only long-term nursing care, but also rehabilitation services and short-term, post-acute care for patients recovering from serious illness or injury; many of them house special units for Alzheimer's patients. In addition to its nursing and assisted-living facilities, Manor Care offers hospice and home health care through offices across the US. It is owned by private equity firm The Carlyle Group.

Over the objections of the Service Employees International Union and some lawmakers, The Carlyle Group took Manor Care private in late 2007, in a deal worth about $6.3 billion.

In addition to its long-term care, hospice, and home health operations, Manor Care provides rehabilitation therapy at its own outpatient clinics, as well as third-party sites, such as schools, workplaces, and hospitals.

Manor Care gets most of its long-term care revenue from Medicare and Medicaid. In response to falling reimbursement rates, the company has shifted its focus to seeking out patients that require more complex care (over a shorter period of time) that is reimbursed at higher levels. This shift in patient mix has resulted in the growth of its post-acute business, which cares for patients recovering from chronic illness, serious injury, or surgery.

HISTORY

The new Manor Care has its roots in an Ohio lumber company bought by the Wolfe family in the mid-1940s. Over the next two decades the business diversified into mortgages and real estate development. By 1975 the company (renamed Wolfe Industries) had begun acquiring nursing homes. Wolfe spun off its non-nursing home interests in 1981 and created Health Care and Retirement Corporation of America (HCR) from what remained. HCR went public that year and continued making acquisitions.

Looking to diversify, glass and plastics maker Owens-Illinois bought HCR in 1984 and later added other health care operations, including long-term skilled nursing care, rehabilitation, and specialty care services. Owens-Illinois was taken private in a Kohlberg Kravis Roberts leveraged buyout in 1987; in 1991 HCR and related health care operations were sold to a group led by Paul Ormond, who had headed Owens-Illinois' health care business since 1986. Ormond took HCR public again that year.

HCR's acquisition strategy expanded to include partnerships and other ventures, as well as the opening of specialty units and the construction and development of new facilities. Under Ormond, HCR concentrated on attracting Medicare and private-pay patients, who were more profitable than Medicaid (i.e., public aid) patients.

As part of the effort to diversify beyond nursing homes, HCR in the 1990s added vision care (forming Vision Management Services to provide financing and management for eye-related medical practices, 1991), short-term rehabilitation, home health care (Heartland Home Health Services, 1991; enlarged through the acquisition of Allan Home Health Care and Hospice, 1995), and pharmacy services (through a joint venture to supply nursing homes, 1994).

In 1997 the company acquired MileStone Healthcare, a top provider of program management services for subacute care and acute rehabilitation programs. But it was still not enough. The company's 1998 purchase of larger rival Manor Care more than doubled its size, although related costs hammered earnings.

The next year the company took the more widely recognized Manor Care name. It partnered with Alterra Healthcare (formerly Alternative Living Services) to build and operate Alzheimer's and assisted-living residences and to provide management services for about 30 assisted-living and Alzheimer's care residences located outside Manor Care's core operating areas.

Also in 1999 Manor Care was hit with a suit by Genesis Health Ventures, claiming that it had bought Vitalink, a nursing home pharmacy services company, from Manor Care with the understanding that service contracts with Manor Care homes would remain in effect for several years (the new Manor Care terminated the contracts soon after the merger). The company also faced regulatory and legal actions in several states over infractions of patient care rules.

In 2000 Manor Care nixed separate buyout bids led by chairman Stewart Bainum and another management group. It also bought the percentage of In Home Health (a home health care provider) that it didn't already own and absorbed the firm into its own operations. That year the company opened 10 new Alzheimer's assisted living centers.

The Carlyle Group bought the company in 2007 with the understanding that its existing management team would stay on to continue operating the business.

EXECUTIVES

President and CEO: Paul A. Ormond, age 58, $2,761,531 pay
EVP and COO: Stephen L. Guillard, age 58
Group VP Hospice and Home Health Care: John K. Graham, age 47
VP and CFO: Steven M. (Steve) Cavanaugh, age 37
VP Procurement: R. Michael Ferguson
VP Information Services: Murry J. Mercier
VP Human Resources: Steven D. Spencer
VP and Controller: John I. Remenar
VP and General Manager, Assisted Living Division: Michael J. Reed, age 56
VP and General Counsel: Richard A. Parr II, age 49
Auditors: Ernst & Young LLP

LOCATIONS

HQ: Manor Care, Inc.
333 N. Summit St., Toledo, OH 43604
Phone: 419-252-5500   **Fax:** 419-252-5554
Web: www.hcr-manorcare.com

PRODUCTS/OPERATIONS

Selected Services

Assisted-living facilities
Dementia care
Home health care and hospice
Post-acute care
Outpatient rehabilitation centers
Skilled nursing care

COMPETITORS

Advocat
Amedisys
American HomePatient
Assisted Living Concepts
Emeritus Corporation
Extendicare
Five Star Quality Care
Genesis HealthCare
Gentiva
Golden Horizons
Kindred Healthcare
Life Care Centers
Mariner Health Care
National HealthCare
Regency Nursing and Rehabilitation
Skilled Healthcare Group
Sun Healthcare
Sunrise Senior Living
Ventas
VITAS Healthcare

HISTORICAL FINANCIALS

Company Type: Private

Income Statement

FYE: December 31

	REVENUE ($ mil.)	NET INCOME ($ mil.)	NET PROFIT MARGIN	EMPLOYEES
12/07	3,890	—	—	61,700
12/06	3,613	—	—	59,500
12/05	3,417	—	—	58,000
12/04	3,209	—	—	—
12/03	3,029	—	—	—
Annual Growth	6.5%	—	—	3.1%

Revenue History

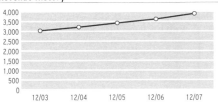

Maritz Inc.

Maritz may not *send* your employees on business trips, but it will still *motivate* them to go. The company designs employee incentive and reward programs (including incentive travel rewards) and customer loyalty programs, plans corporate trade shows and events, and also offers traditional market research services such as the creation of product launch campaigns. Its programs are designed to help its clients improve workforce quality and customer satisfaction. Subsidiaries and segments include Maritz Motivation, Maritz Research, Maritz Loyalty Marketing, and Maritz Travel. The company's Maritz Interactions segment designs special events and public relations programs for clients.

Maritz maintains a presence in more than 40 countries. Its customers include a majority of the *Forbes* 500 (automakers, financial corporations, pharmaceutical and technology companies).

Maritz expanded its product offerings and geographic reach in 2008 when it acquired Cascade Promotion Corporation, a marketing and fulfillment business operating out of Boston, Las Vegas, and St. Louis. With Cascade catering to the gaming and technology industries, the buyout also gave Maritz access to growing niche markets.

In 2006, chairman and CEO Steve Maritz controlled 60% of the company's shares while his brothers, Peter and Philip Maritz, held on to the remaining 40%. The brothers had repeatedly sued the company over the past few years in an effort to unload their shares at a price they deemed fair. The dispute stemmed partly from Maritz's 2002 purchase of incentive travel planner McGettigan (McGettigan worked primarily for the pharmaceutical industry), a transaction Peter and Philip called wasteful. The brothers claimed the acquisition's $48 million cost was $10 million higher than what was originally described to the company's board, and that the firm's shares declined in value as a result. After months of litigation, Steve Maritz finally bought out his brothers shares in September 2006, becoming the company's primary shareholder.

EXECUTIVES

Chairman and CEO: W. Stephen (Steve) Maritz, age 50
COO: Dennis Hummel
CFO: Rick Ramos
Chief Sales Officer: William P. (Scott) Bush
Chief Marketing Officer: Tim Rogers
Senior Executive and VP Development: John McArthur
Senior Executive, VP, and General Counsel:
John Risberg
VP People/Organization Development: Con McGrath
VP Public Relations and Corporate Communications:
Beth Rusert
VP and Group Executive, Maritz Travel and Maritz Interactions; President, Maritz Travel: Christine Duffy
VP and Group Executive, Maritz Learning and Maritz Research; President, Maritz Research:
Michael Brereton, age 48
VP and Group Executive, Maritz Motivation and Maritz Loyalty Marketing; CEO, Maritz Motivation:
Mike Donnelly
President, Maritz Learning: Brian Carlin
President, Maritz Interactions: Thom Casadonte

LOCATIONS

HQ: Maritz Inc.
1375 N. Highway Dr., Fenton, MO 63099
Phone: 636-827-4000   **Fax:** 636-827-3312
Web: www.maritz.com

PRODUCTS/OPERATIONS

Selected Services
Marketing Research
  Custom marketing research
  Customer satisfaction and customer value analysis
  Data collection (focus groups, telephone interviews)
  Maritz Polls and Maritz Research Reports
  Syndicated buyer research
  Telecommunications research
Performance Improvement
  Communications
  e-Learning
  Fulfillment
  Internet consulting
  Loyalty marketing
  Measurement and feedback
  Rewards and recognition
Travel
  Consulting services
  Corporate travel management
  Group travel services
  Travel award programs

COMPETITORS

ACNielsen	J.D. Power
Franklin Covey	JTB
Gallup	Landround
GiftCertificates.com	ORC
Harris Interactive	TNS North America
IMS Health	Custom
Information Resources	

Mark IV Industries

Mark IV Industries hits the mark with engineered components and systems for the automotive, industrial machinery, and transportation management markets. The company's Automotive OEM products include power transmission systems, air admission and cooling systems, and fluid handling systems. Mark IV's Industrial/Distribution unit makes small diesel and gasoline engines for industrial, agricultural, and marine uses; information display systems (for buses, aircraft, and railcars) and traffic management equipment, including electronic toll-collection systems; and belts and hoses for heavy-duty trucks as well as the automotive aftermarket. An affiliate of Sun Capital Partners controls Mark IV Industries.

Early in 2008 European private equity firm BC Partners sold its interest in Mark IV Industries to an affiliate of Sun Capital Partners. Details of the transaction were not released.

Mark IV's Automotive OEM and Industrial/Distribution divisions each account for about half of sales. Outside the US, Mark IV has a regional office in Turin, Italy. The company's automotive aftermarket products are marketed under the Dayco brand.

EXECUTIVES

CEO and Director: William P. Montague, age 61
VP, CFO, and Treasurer: Mark G. Barberio
VP and Chief Accounting Officer: Richard L. Grenolds
VP, Corporate Secretary, and Chief Tax Officer:
Edward R. Steele
General Manager, Power Transmission:
Maria Botto Micca
General Manager, Air Admission and Cooling:
Luc Schwab

CEO, Automotive OEM: Giuliano Zucco
President, Transportaion Technologies: Avi Zisman
President, Aftermarket: Dennis Welvaert

LOCATIONS

HQ: Mark IV Industries, Inc.
501 John James Audubon Pkwy.,
Amherst, NY 14226
Phone: 716-689-4972   **Fax:** 716-689-6098
Web: www.mark-iv.com

PRODUCTS/OPERATIONS

Selected Products
Automotive
  Power transmission
    Automatic tensioning devices
    Power transmission systems for accessory and camshaft drives
    Pulleys, idlers, brackets, and dampers
    Timing and poly-rib belts
  Platform
    Fuel filler systems and vapor recovery canisters
    Power steering, air conditioning, and oil cooling systems
  Air admission and cooling
    Air intake manifolds
    Brake fluid, surge, and power steering tanks and water pumps
    Engine cooling systems
Industrial and distribution
  Aftermarket
    Automotive belts and hoses
    Camshaft and accessory drive components
  Power Train
    Diesel and small gasoline engines
  Transportation technologies
    Bus, rail, aircraft, and stationary signs and lighting systems
    Intelligent Vehicle Highway Systems (IVHS)
    On-board vehicle location, monitoring, and information systems for railroads and mass transit
  Heavy duty
    Power transmission systems for accessory and camshaft drives

COMPETITORS

BorgWarner
Dana Corporation
Delphi Corp.
Eaton
Gates Corporation
Goodyear
Tomkins
Visteon

HISTORICAL FINANCIALS
Company Type: Private

Income Statement
FYE: Last day in February

	REVENUE ($ mil.)	NET INCOME ($ mil.)	NET PROFIT MARGIN	EMPLOYEES
2/08	1,394	—	—	4,632
2/07	1,200	—	—	4,600
Annual Growth	16.1%	—	—	0.7%

Revenue History

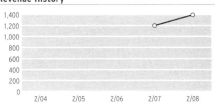

	2/04	2/05	2/06	2/07	2/08

Market Strategies International

Market Strategies International (MSI) offers full-service custom and syndicated research, as well as strategic consulting services to clients in such industries as energy, health care, financial services, information technology, and telecommunications. Its research specialties include customer satisfaction measurement, market segmentation, product and service evaluation, and e-commerce assessment. Founded in 1989, the firm has been steadily growing through acquisitions and operates out of several offices across the US and one in Canada.

In mid-2007, MSI expanded its geographic reach and broadened its customer base when it acquired Doxus, a research firm catering to the technology sector. After the acquisition, Doxus was reshuffled into MSI's Technology Industry Group division.

A few months after the buyout, MSI made another move to expand when it acquired Flake-Wilkerson Market Insights, a provider of customized market research targeting service industries such as travel, health care, and transportation. The buyout gives MSI access to Flake-Wilkerson's list of key telecommunications clients. Flake-Wilkerson was subsequently moved to MSI's Communications Industry Group division.

EXECUTIVES

Chairman and CEO: Andrew Morrison
Vice Chair: Karen E. Flake
President: Janice A. Brown
COO: Reginald (Reg) Baker
CFO: Philip (Phil) Giroux
SVP and Head, Global Life Sciences Division: Peter E. Carlin
SVP and Head, Energy and Usability Divisions: Christopher J. (Chris) Montaglione
SVP and Head, Financial Services Division: Mark Willard
SVP Communications Research Division: George Wilkerson
SVP Client Partnerships: Pamela S. (Pam) McGill
SVP Client Partnerships: Paul Donagher
VP, Human Resources: Margee Kaczmarek
Auditors: Plante & Moran, PLLC

LOCATIONS

HQ: Market Strategies International
20255 Victor Pkwy., Ste. 400, Livonia, MI 48152
Phone: 734-542-7600   **Fax:** 734-542-7620
Web: www.marketstrategies.com

COMPETITORS

Abt Associates	Maritz Research
Burke, Inc.	MORPACE
C&R Research	The Nielsen Company
Gallup	NPD
GfK AG	NRC
GfK NOP	ORC
Greenfield Consulting	Press Ganey
Harris Interactive	Synovate
IMS Health	Taylor Nelson
Ipsos	Walker Information
Kantar Group	

Marmon Group

With more monikers than most, The Marmon Group monitors a melange of more than 125 autonomous manufacturing and service companies. Marmon's manufacturing units make medical products, mining equipment, industrial materials and components, consumer products (including Wells Lamont gloves), transportation equipment, building products, and water-treatment products. Services include marketing and distribution. Overall, Marmon companies operate 250 facilities in more than 40 countries. Chicago's Pritzker family (owners of the Hyatt hotel chain) sold a 60% stake in The Marmon Group to Warren Buffett's Berkshire Hathaway for a reported $4.5 billion late in 2007.

For years the Pritzker family had been preparing a plan to break up The Marmon Group and divide it among heirs. An alternative to the breakup of the Marmon Group emerged when a buyer surfaced that had the experience — and the cash — to buy such an assemblage of diversified businesses all in one fell swoop. Of course that buyer was none other than Warren Buffett's Berkshire Hathaway. The Marmon Group initially sold a 60% stake to Berkshire Hathaway for about $4.5 billion. The remaining 40% will be acquired over the course of five to six years through staged acquisitions.

Each Marmon company works under its own management, and a small corporate office (fewer than 100 employees) oversees and pulls together the conglomerate, acting as combination CFO, tax lawyer, accountant, and broker to member companies.

HISTORY

Although the history of The Marmon Group officially begins in 1953, the company's roots are in the Chicago law firm Pritzker and Pritzker, started by Nicholas Pritzker in 1902. Through the firm the family made connections with First National Bank of Chicago, which A. N. Pritzker, Nicholas' son, used to get a line of credit to buy real estate. By 1940 the firm had stopped accepting outside clients to concentrate on the family's growing investment portfolio.

In 1953 A. N.'s son Jay used his father's connections to get a loan to buy Colson Company, a small, money-losing manufacturer of bicycles, hospital equipment, and other products. Jay's brother, Robert, a graduate of the Illinois Institute of Technology, took charge of Colson and turned it around. Soon Jay began acquiring more companies for his brother to manage.

In 1963 the brothers paid $2.7 million for about 45% of the Marmon-Herrington Company (whose predecessor, Marmon Motor Car, built the car that in 1911 won the first Indianapolis 500). The family now had a name for its industrial holdings — The Marmon Group.

It became a public company in 1966 when it merged with door- and spring-maker Fenestra. However, Jay began to take greater control of the group through a series of stock purchases, and by 1971 The Marmon Group was private once again.

A year earlier, in 1970, the group acquired a promising industrial pipe supplier, Keystone Tubular Service (which later became Marmon/Keystone). In 1973 Marmon began to acquire stock in Cerro Corp., which had operations in mining, manufacturing, trucking, and real estate; by 1976 the group had bought all of Cerro, thereby tripling its revenues. The brothers sold Cerro's trucking subsidiary, ICX, in 1977 and bought organ maker Hammond Corp., along with Wells Lamont, Hammond's glove-making subsidiary.

Marmon acquired conglomerate Trans Union in 1981. Trans Union brought many operations, including railcar and equipment leasing, credit information services, international trading, and water- and wastewater-treatment systems. In 1982 Jay acquired Ticketmaster (now a publically traded company).

The Pritzkers made a foray into the airline business in 1984 by buying Braniff Airlines. After unsuccessfully bidding for Pan Am in 1987, they sold Braniff in 1988. Disappointments in other Pritzker businesses didn't slow Marmon, which added to its transportation equipment business in 1984 with Altamil, a maker of products for the trucking and aerospace industries.

To mark its 40th anniversary, the company sponsored a car, the Marmon Wasp II, at the 1993 Indianapolis 500. That year the Pritzkers sold 80% of Ticketmaster to Microsoft co-founder Paul Allen but retained a minority interest. Marmon sold Arzco Medical Systems in 1995 and Marmon/Keystone acquired Anbuma Group, a Belgian steel tubing distributor.

The Anbuma purchase and Marmon/Keystone's 1997 acquisition of UK tube distributor Wheeler Group exemplified Marmon's practice of building strength through acquisitions in its established markets. In 1998 Marmon purchased more than 30 companies and opened a business development office in Beijing.

Marmon splashed out more than $500 million in 1999 to make 35 acquisitions, including Kerite (power cables), OsteoMed (specialty medical devices), and Bridport (medical and aviation products). Jay died that year, and the company announced that his title of chairman will not be filled.

In 2000 Marmon spent another $500 million on more than 20 acquisitions, buying operations engaged in the production of retail display equipment, tank containers, and metal products, among others.

Former Illinois Tool Works chief John Nichols took over the Marmon CEO responsibilities from Robert Pritzker in 2001. The company again went to ITW when Nichols retired at the end of 2005, hiring former vice chairman Frank Ptak.

Also in 2005, the company spun off Trans Union, the consumer credit information services provider. Penny Pritzker, the independent Trans Union's chairman, said that the separation would better allow the company to grow, as Trans Union is a technology and information company as opposed to Marmon's stable of manufacturing businesses. The Trans Union separation, however, served as a precursor to the decision to sell off the remainder of the Marmon Group companies in order to more easily divide the family holdings. Infighting among family members over the division of the family fortune began to intensify shortly after Jay's death in 1999.

EXECUTIVES

President and CEO: Frank S. Ptak, age 64
SVP and General Counsel: Robert W. (Bob) Webb, age 69
SVP and CFO: Robert K. Lorch, age 62
VP, Human Resources: Larry Rist
President, Marmon Retail Services LLC: Richard Winter
President, Marmon Distribution Services LLC: Norman E. Gottschalk Jr., age 63

President, Marmon Highway Technologies LLC:
  Kelly E. Dier
President, Marmon Wire and Cable LLC:
  Henry J. (Hank) West
President, Marmon Transportation Services LLC and
  Marmon Engineered Products: Kenneth Fischl, age 59
President, Marmon Water LLC: John Goody
President, Marmon Flow Products LLC: Gary Ewing
President, Marmon Industrial Companies LLC:
  Elwood (Woody) Petchel
Auditors: Ernst & Young LLP

LOCATIONS

HQ: The Marmon Group, LLC
  181 W. Madison St., 26th Fl., Chicago, IL 60602
Phone: 312-372-9500   Fax: 312-845-5305
Web: www.marmon.com

PRODUCTS/OPERATIONS

Selected Member Companies

Distribution Services
  Bushwick Metals
  Future Metals, Inc.
  Marmon/Keystone Corporation
Highway Technologies
  Fontaine Modification Co.
  Fontaine Trailer Co.
  Marmon-Herrington Co.
  Perfection Clutch
Industrial Products
  Amarillo Gear Co.
  Anderson Copper and Brass Co.
  Atlas Bolt & Screw Company
  MarCap Corp.
  Wells Lamont Corporation
Metal Products
  Cerro Fabricated Products
  Cerro Metal Products Co.
  Penn Aluminum International, Inc.
Retail Services
  Alexander-Otto Company
  L.A. Darling Co.
  Store Opening Solutions, Inc.
  Streater, Inc.
  Thorco Industries, Inc.
Transportation Services
  Exsif Worldwide, Inc.
  Penn Machine Company
  Railserve, Inc.
  Trackmobile, Inc.
  Union Tank Car Co.
Water Treatment Systems
  Ecodyne Limited
  EcoWater Systems LLC
  Graver Technologies LLC
Wire and Cable Products
  Cable USA, Inc.
  Comtran Corporation
  Hendrix Wire & Cable, Inc.
  The Kerite Co.
  Owl Wire and Cable, Inc.
  Rockbestos-Surprenant Cable Corp.

COMPETITORS

Alcatel-Lucent
Balfour Beatty
Eaton
Illinois Tool Works
ITT Corp.
LEONI
Masco
Nexans
Superior Essex
Terex
USG
Wolverine Tube

HISTORICAL FINANCIALS

Company Type: Private

Income Statement

FYE: December 31

	REVENUE ($ mil.)	NET INCOME ($ mil.)	NET PROFIT MARGIN	EMPLOYEES
12/06	6,990	—	—	21,500
12/05	5,900	—	—	21,500
12/04	6,400	—	—	22,000
12/03	5,560	—	—	28,000
12/02	5,756	—	—	30,000
Annual Growth	5.0%	—	—	(8.0%)

Revenue History

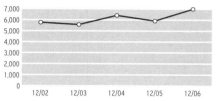

Mars, Incorporated

Mars knows chocolate sales are nothing to snicker at. The company makes such worldwide favorites as M&M's, Snickers, and the Mars bar. Its other confections include 3 Musketeers, Dove, Milky Way, Skittles, Twix, and Starburst sweets; Combos and Kudos snacks; Uncle Ben's rice; and pet food under the names Pedigree, Sheba, and Whiskas. Mars also provides office beverage services and makes drink vending equipment. The Mars family (including siblings and retired company CEO Forrest Mars Jr., chairman John Franklyn Mars, and VP Jacqueline Badger Mars) owns the highly secretive firm, making the family one of the richest in the US. In 2008 the company acquired the Wm. Wrigley Jr. Company.

Sweet deals are the name of the game in the confectionery sector and Mars' takeover of chewing gum giant, Wrigley (valued at some $23 billion) brought together two iconic US confectionery makers, both of which already have a substantial worldwide presence.

Mars acquired such well known brands as Altiods, Life Savers, and Creme Savers, along with the best-selling chewing gum brands Spearmint, Juicy Fruit, and Doublemint, plus a host of others. In addition both companies hope to realize cost savings in raw materials, especially at a time when commodity prices are rising. Together, the companies will also benefit from greater global marketing and distribution muscle.

The deal, which took Wrigley private and left it a stand-alone subsidiary of Mars, was partially financed by Warren Buffett's Berkshire Hathaway, which a owns stake in Wrigley as a result.

Two weeks after the aquisition was final, Mars yanked Wrigley CEO and president, William Perez, and replaced him with a Mars 19-year veteran, Dushan "Duke" Petrovich. Petrovich carries the title of president, Mars having eliminated the CEO position at Wrigley. Perez received a severance package of some $25 million (including $10.5 million in cash).

Mars makes non-chocolate confections including breath mints such as AquaDrops, and snack foods like Combos and Kudos. It also makes ice-cream versions of several of its candy bars. It swallows a large bite of the pet-food market with its Royal Canin, Pedigree, and Whiskas brands. In conjunction with Unilever, Mars' Pedigree dog food offers dairy-based Pedigree Ice Cream Sandwich Treats for Dogs. Mars' other brands include Uncle Ben's, Seeds of Change, and Flavia Beverage Systems.

HISTORY

Frank Mars invented the Milky Way candy bar in 1923 after his previous three efforts at the candy business left him bankrupt. After his estranged son, Forrest, graduated from Yale, Mars hired him to work at his candy operation. When Forrest demanded one-third control of the company and Frank refused, Forrest moved to England with the foreign rights to Milky Way and started his own company (Food Manufacturers) in the 1930s. He made a sweeter version of Milky Way for the UK, calling it a Mars bar. Forrest also ventured into pet food with the 1934 purchase of Chappel Brothers (renamed Pedigree). At one point he controlled 55% of the British pet food market.

During WWII Forrest returned to the US and introduced Uncle Ben's rice (the world's first brand-name raw commodity) and M&M's (a joint venture between Forrest and Bruce Murrie, son of Hershey's then-president). The idea for M&M's was borrowed from British Smarties, for which Forrest obtained rights (from Rowntree Mackintosh) by relinquishing similar rights to the Snickers bar in some foreign markets. The ad slogan "Melts in your mouth, not in your hand" (and the candy's success in non-air-conditioned stores and war zones) made the company an industry leader. Mars introduced M&M's Peanut in 1954. It was one of the first candy companies to sponsor a television show — Howdy Doody in the 1950s.

Forrest merged his firm with his deceased father's company in 1964, after buying his dying half-sister's controlling interest. (He renamed the business Mars at her request.) The merger was the end of an alliance with Hershey, who had supplied Frank with chocolate since his Milky Way inception.

In 1968 Mars bought Kal Kan. In 1973 Forrest, then 69 years old, delegated his company responsibilities to sons Forrest Jr. and John. Five years later the brothers, looking for snacks to offset dwindling candy resulting from a more diet-conscious America, bought the Twix chocolate-covered cookie brand. During the late 1980s they bought ice-cream bar maker Dove Bar International and Ethel-M Chocolates, producer of liqueur-flavored chocolates, a business their father had begun in his retirement.

Hershey in 1988 surpassed Mars as the largest candy maker in the US when it acquired Mounds, Almond Joy, and other US brands from Cadbury Schweppes (now Cadbury). In response to the success of Hershey's Symphony Bar, Mars introduced its dark-chocolate Dove bar in 1991.

The company entered the huge confectionery market of India in 1989 by building a $10 million factory there. In 1997 it launched new ad campaigns, including M&M's spots featuring a trio of animated M&M candies.

Forrest Sr. died in 1999, spurring rumors that Mars would go public or be sold. Instead, the company dismantled most of its sales force, opting to use less costly food brokers. Forrest Jr. retired the same year, leaving brother John Franklyn as president and CEO.

In 2000 the company established a subsidiary, Effem India, to market Mars' products in India. In 2003 Mars acquired French pet food producer Royal Canin. In 2004 the company appointed two co-presidents, Peter Cheney and Paul Michaels, leaving John Franklyn Mars as chairman. Cheney retired in 2005.

Responding to public concerns about healthy eating, Mars started phasing out its "king size" candy bars in 2005. Mars also jumped on the "chocolate as health food" bandwagon that year, introducing CocoaVia, a line of confections containing flavanols, which are said to have antioxidant qualities, and plant sterols, which the company claims is good for hearts and arteries.

Adding to its fast-growing pet-products sector, in 2006 Mars purchased dog-treat manufacturer S&M Nu Tec, maker of Greenies, a bone-shaped treat with a toothbrush on one end that is a hot item in the pet-product market.

Still barking up the pet-product tree, Mars acquired private-label dry pet food manufacturer Doane Pet Care Company that year as well. Doane's products are sold in the US and Europe.

EXECUTIVES

Chairman: John Franklyn Mars
President and CEO: Paul S. Michaels
EVP, Mars Nutrition for Health and Well-Being: Joseph (Joe) Perello
VP and General Manager, Mars Direct: Jim Cass
VP Small Outlet Sales, Masterfoods USA: Larry Lupo
VP Research and Development, U.S. Food: Mike Wilson
Chief Science Officer: Harold Schmitz
Global President, Mars Food: Brian Camastral
President, Mars Nutrition for Health and Well-Being: James (Jamie) Mattikow
President, Snackfoods, Masterfoods Europe: Andy Weston-Webb
President, Masterfoods Western Europe: Pierre Laubies
President, Mars North America: Bob Gamgort
President, Wm. Wrigley Jr. Company: Dushan (Duke) Petrovich, age 54
President Mars Drinks: Grant Reid
Controller, US Snackfoods: Brian Hart
Director Corporate and Regulatory Affairs, Asia/Pacific: Khaled Rabbani
Director Corporate Communications: Alison Clark

LOCATIONS

HQ: Mars, Incorporated
6885 Elm St., McLean, VA 22101
Phone: 703-821-4900   **Fax:** 703-448-9678
Web: www.mars.com

PRODUCTS/OPERATIONS

Selected Brands
Mars
  Beverages
    Flavia
  Ice cream bars
    3 Musketeers
    DoveBars
    Milky Way
    Snickers
  Main meals
    Dolmio
    Ebly
    Uncle Ben's
  Petcare
    Catscan
    Cesar
    Doane
    Frolic
    Pedigree
    Royal Canin
    Sheba
    Whiskas
  Snack foods
    3 Musketeers
    Altoids
    Bounty
    CocoaVia
    Combos
    Dove
    Kudo
    Life Savers
    M&M'S
    Marathon
    Milky Way
    Skittles
    Snickers
    Starburst
    Twix
Wrigley
  Domestic
    Big Red
    Doublemint
    Eclipse
    Everest
    Extra
    Freedent
    Hubba Bubba
    Juicy Fruit
    Orbit
    Squeeze Pop
    Winterfresh
    Wrigley's Spearmint
  International
    Airwaves
    Big Red
    Boomer
    Cool Air
    Doublemint
    Eclipse
    Excel
    Extra
    Hubba Bubba
    Juicy Fruit
    Orbit
    Pim Pom
    Solano
    Winterfresh
    Wrigley's Spearmint

COMPETITORS

Avani International Group
Barry Callebaut
Breeder's Choice
Butterfields Candy
Cadbury
Caribou Coffee
Chase General
Chupa Chups
Cloetta Fazer
Colgate-Palmolive
ConAgra
CSM
Endangered Species Chocolate
Ezaki Glico
Farley's & Sathers
Ferrara Pan Candy
Ferrero
Ford Gum & Machine Company
General Mills
Ghirardelli Chocolate
Gilster-Mary Lee
Godiva Chocolatier
Green Mountain Coffee
Grupo Corvi
Guittard
HARIBO
Harry London Candies
Heinz
Hershey
Hill's Pet Nutrition
Iams
International Flavors
Jelly Belly Candy
Just Born
Kent Gida
Kraft Foods
Laura Secord
Lindt & Sprüngli
McCormick & Company
Meiji Seika
Nestlé
Nestlé Purina PetCare
Perfetti Van Melle
PETCO (Holding)
PEZ Candy
Pfizer
Riviana Foods
Rocky Mountain Chocolate
Royal Cup Coffee
Russell Stover
S&D Coffee
See's Candies
Smucker
Spangler Candy
Starbucks
Strauss
SweetWorks
Tootsie Roll
Topps Company
Unilever
Upper Deck
World's Finest Chocolate

HISTORICAL FINANCIALS
Company Type: Private

Income Statement
FYE: December 31

	REVENUE ($ mil.)	NET INCOME ($ mil.)	NET PROFIT MARGIN	EMPLOYEES
12/07	25,000	—	—	48,000
12/06	21,000	—	—	40,000
12/05	18,000	—	—	40,500
12/04	18,000	—	—	39,000
12/03	17,000	—	—	31,000
Annual Growth	10.1%	—	—	11.6%

Revenue History

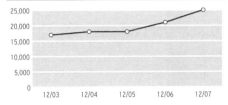

Mary Kay

Celebrating more than 40 years in business, Mary Kay is in the pink and in Avon's shadow as the US's #2 direct seller of beauty products. It offers more than 200 products in six categories: body care, color cosmetics, facial skin care, fragrance, nail care, and sun protection. More than 1.8 million independent sales consultants demonstrate Mary Kay products in the US and some 35 other countries. Consultants vie for awards each year, ranging from jewelry to the company's trademark pink Cadillac (first awarded in 1969). The company also founded the Mary Kay Ash Charitable Foundation in 1996 to fund cancer research and domestic violence programs. The family of founder Mary Kay Ash owns most of the company.

Founded by a woman for women, Mary Kay has an overwhelmingly female independent sales force. Although the company stands by Mary Kay's original goal of providing financial and career opportunities for women, much of the company's executive population is male. Ash's son Richard Rogers (executive chairman) runs the company alongside David Holl (president and CEO).

Mary Kay works hard to retain the feel of a small company, despite its more than 1.8-million-strong independent sales force and the firm's growing international reach. As part of this initiative, each beauty consultant receives the option to buy his or her own Web site to use for selling to clients. More than 90% of its revenue is generated through online orders by the company's independent sales force.

During her lifetime Mary Kay Ash was known for her religious nature as well as her generosity. She founded the Mary Kay Ash Charitable Foundation in 1996; by 2006 the foundation had awarded $8 million in grants to cancer researchers and US women's shelters. Mary Kay Ash suffered a debilitating stroke in 1996 and died on Thanksgiving Day 2001.

HISTORY

Before founding her own company in 1963, Mary Kay Ash worked as a Stanley Home Products sales representative. Impressed with the alligator handbag awarded to the top saleswoman at a Stanley convention, Ash was determined to win the next year's prize — and she did. Despite that accomplishment and having worked at Stanley for 11 years, a male assistant she had trained was made her boss after less than a year on the job. Tired of not receiving recognition, Ash and her second husband used their life savings ($5,000) to go into business for themselves. Although her husband died of a heart attack shortly before the business opened, Ash forged ahead with the help of her two grown sons.

She bought a cosmetics formula invented years earlier by a hide tanner. (The mixture was originally used to soften leather, but the tanner noticed how the formula made his hands look younger, and he began applying the mixture to his face, with great results.) Ash kept her first line simple — 10 products — and packaged her wares in pink to complement the typically white bathrooms of the day. Ash also enlisted consultants, who held "beauty shows" with five or six women in attendance. Mary Kay grossed $198,000 in its first year.

The company introduced men's skin care products in 1964. Ash bought a pink Cadillac the following year and began awarding the cars as prizes in 1969. (By 1981 orders were so large — almost 500 — that GM dubbed the color "Mary Kay Pink.")

Ash became a millionaire when her firm went public in 1968. Mary Kay grew steadily through the 1970s. Foreign operations began in 1971 in Australia, and over the next 25 years the company entered 24 more countries, including nations in Asia/Pacific, Europe, and Central and South America.

Sales plunged in the early 1980s, along with the company's stock prices (from $40 to $9 between 1983 and 1985). Ash and her family reacquired Mary Kay in 1985 through a $375 million LBO. Burdened with debt, the firm lost money in the late 1980s. Mary Kay took a number of steps to boost sales and income, doing a makeover on the cosmetics line and advertising in women's magazines again (after a five-year hiatus) to counter its old-fashioned image. The company also introduced recyclable packaging and lipstick in a tube (replacing brush-on palettes). In 1989 Avon rebuffed a buyout offer by Mary Kay, and both companies halted animal testing.

In 1993 Mary Kay opened a subsidiary in Russia, which later became the company's fourth-largest international market (behind Mexico, China, and Canada). Ash suffered a debilitating stroke in 1996.

In 1998 Mary Kay began selling through retail boutiques in China because of a government ban on direct selling. Changing with the times, Mary Kay added a white sport utility vehicle and new shades of pink to its fleet of 10,000 GM cars that year.

Chairman John Rochon was named CEO in 1999. Also in 1999 Mary Kay launched *Women & Success* (a magazine for consultants) and Atlas (its electronic ordering system).

In June 2001 Richard Rogers, now the company chairman and son of Ash, replaced Rochon as CEO. A month later Mary Kay introduced the Velocity Products line, targeting girls ages 14 to 24. Ash died on Thanksgiving Day 2001.

Mary Kay Poland, headquartered in Warsaw, became the company's 34th international market in mid-2003.

In 2006 Rogers became executive chairman and David Holl, previously president and COO, was named president and CEO.

EXECUTIVES

Executive Chairman: Richard R. Rogers
President and CEO: David B. Holl
EVP and CIO: Kregg Jodie
EVP, Global Manufacturing: Dennis Greaney
SVP, Finance: Terry Smith
SVP, General Counsel, and Secretary: Nathan P. Moore
SVP, Marketing: Rhonda Shasteen
SVP, Global Human Resources: Melinda Sellers
VP, Global Corporate Communications: Randall G. Oxford
VP, Government Relations: Anne Crews
VP, Information Technology: Karen Calvert
VP International Market Development and Sales Support: Murray Smith
VP Sales Development: Greg Franklin
President, US: Darrell Overcash
President, Mary Kay Europe: Tara Eustace
President, Mary Kay Greater China: Paul Mak

LOCATIONS

HQ: Mary Kay Inc.
   16251 Dallas Pkwy., Addison, TX 75001
Phone: 972-687-6300   **Fax:** 972-687-1611
Web: www.marykay.com

PRODUCTS/OPERATIONS

Selected Product Lines

Body care
Cosmetics
Facial skin care
Fragrances (men's and women's)
Men's skin care
Nail care
Nutritional supplements for men
Nutritional supplements for women
Sun protection

COMPETITORS

Alberto-Culver
Alticor
Avon
Bath & Body Works
BeautiControl
Body Shop
Clarins
Colgate-Palmolive
Coty Inc.
Dana Classic Fragrances
The Dial Corporation
DLI Holding
Estée Lauder
Helen of Troy
Intimate Brands
John Paul Mitchell
Johnson & Johnson
L'Oréal
Merle Norman
Murad, Inc.
Nu Skin
Perrigo
Procter & Gamble
Reliv'
Revlon
Schwarzkopf & Henkel
Scott's Liquid Gold
Shaklee
Shiseido
Sunrider
Unilever

HISTORICAL FINANCIALS

Company Type: Private

Income Statement				FYE: December 31
	REVENUE ($ mil.)	NET INCOME ($ mil.)	NET PROFIT MARGIN	EMPLOYEES
12/07	2,400	—	—	5,000
12/06	2,250	—	—	4,500
12/05	2,200	—	—	4,000
12/04	1,900	—	—	3,600
12/03	1,800	—	—	3,600
Annual Growth	7.5%	—	—	8.6%

Revenue History

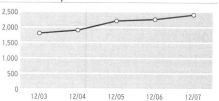

Maryland State Lottery

The Maryland State Lottery Agency offers players a variety of ways to amass a fortune. Among its games of chance are scratch-offs bearing titles such as Funky Monkey, Money Storm, 3 Bushels of Crabs, and Green Stuff. The agency's numbers games include Lotto, Pick 3, and Pick 4. Maryland State Lottery also participates in the multi-state Mega Millions lottery. The agency, which was created in 1973, distributes about 57% of its revenue as prizes; the rest goes to state-funded programs, retailers, and operational expenses. Proceeds from lottery sales helped build Camden Yards, home of Major League Baseball's Baltimore Orioles.

EXECUTIVES

Director: Buddy W. Roogow
Assistant Director and CFO: Gina M. Smith
Director Creative Services: Jill Q. Baer
Director Policy and Development: Paul Dorsey
Director Administration and Operations: Richard Chavis
Division Director, Product Development, Creative Services, and Research Division: Tracey Cohen
Director Communications: Carole Everett
Procurement Director: Robert Howells
Director Systems and Programming: Zechariah Way
Deputy Director and CIO: John Gallagher
Chief Security and Investigations: Nathaniel (Nate) Smoot
Principal Counsel: Robert T. Fontaine

LOCATIONS

HQ: Maryland State Lottery Agency
   1800 Washington Blvd., Ste. 330,
   Baltimore, MD 21230
Phone: 410-230-8800   **Fax:** 410-230-8728
Web: www.msla.state.md.us

PRODUCTS/OPERATIONS

Selected Games

Numbers games
  Keno
  Lotto
  Mega Millions
  Pick 3
  Pick 4
Scratch-off games
  3 Bushels of Crab
  Frozen Assets
  Funky Monkey
  Green Stuff
  Money Storm
  Poker Showdown
  Royal Riches
  Wild Cherries

COMPETITORS

Multi-State Lottery
New Jersey Lottery
Pennsylvania Lottery
Virginia Lottery

Mashantucket Pequot Tribal Nation

Mashantucket Pequot Tribal Nation (with roughly 700 members) has propelled itself from the depths of intense poverty to its lofty position as the wealthiest Native American tribe in the US. It owns and operates Foxwoods Resort Casino, one of the largest casinos in the world and, many believe, the most profitable. The complex offers more than 7,000 slot machines and some 400 gaming tables in six casinos, four hotels (Grand Pequot Tower, Great Cedar Hotel, Two Trees Inn, and MGM Grand), about 30 restaurants, live entertainment, and a string of retail shops. Foxwoods opened the MGM Grand at Foxwoods, a $700 million development project, in 2008.

In addition to its gaming operations, the Mashantucket Pequot Tribal Nation also owns Foxwoods Development Company, a developer and manager of hospitality related enterprises. Foxwoods Development Company holdings include Connecticut hotels and restaurants (Hilton Mystic, the Spa at Norwich Inn, and Randall's Ordinary), golf courses (Lake of Isles), and the five-story Mercantile building in Norwich, Connecticut.

The Mashantucket Pequot Tribal Nation has even established the Mashantucket Pequot Museum and Research Center dedicated to the tribe's life and history.

HISTORY

Once a powerful tribe, the Pequots were virtually wiped out in the 17th century by disease and attacks from colonists. More than 350 years later, Richard "Skip" Hayward, a pipefitter making $15,000 a year, led the fight for federal recognition of his nearly extinct Mashantucket Pequot tribe. He was elected tribal chairman in 1975, and the US government officially recognized the tribe in 1983.

The Indian Gaming Regulatory Act of 1988 opened the door for legal gambling on reservations, but tribes still had to negotiate with state governments for authorization. Hayward hired G. Michael "Mickey" Brown as a consultant and lawyer. Brown took the tribe's legal battle to the US Supreme Court, which eventually ruled that the Pequots could build a casino. When some 30 banks turned down the Pequots for a construction loan, Brown introduced Hayward and his tribe to Lim Goh Tong, billionaire developer of the successful Gentings Highlands Casino resort in Malaysia. Tong invested approximately $60 million, and the Foxwoods Casino opened in 1992.

Brown brought in Alfred J. Luciani to serve as president and CEO of Foxwoods. Luciani stayed less than a year, however, resigning because of what he called philosophical differences with tribe leadership. Brown took over as CEO in 1993. Although Foxwoods grew rapidly, Brown often wrestled with members of the tribal council over how the business should be run. The next year Brown rehired Luciani to oversee the development of the Grand Pequot Tower hotel.

Brown resigned and Luciani was fired in 1997 after it was revealed that Brown had not fully disclosed his ties with Lim Goh Tong and that, in 1992, Luciani had accepted a $377,000 loan from Gamma International, a vendor that provided keno services to Foxwoods. The Pequots considered these actions to be conflicts of interest. A new management team was brought in, and Floyd "Bud" Celey, a veteran of Hilton Hotels, was appointed CEO.

The Pequots opened the Mashantucket Pequot Museum and Research Center in 1998. When tribal elections were held later that year, Kenneth Reels was elected chairman of the Pequot's tribal governing body, ousting Hayward from the position he had held for more than 20 years. Hayward was elected vice chairman. Mashantucket Pequot Gaming Enterprise concentrated on improving financial accountability in 1999, and the tribe began cutting costs by shuttering unprofitable holdings, including Pequot River Shipworks, its shipbuilding business.

Former COO William Sherlock replaced Celey as CEO in 2000. That year the first of two books (the second was published in 2001), which questioned the tribe's legitimacy, created some controversy for the group. The books claimed that the government was duped into giving them more land for their reservation than they were entitled to, and sparked a series of lawsuits from neighboring communities.

A federal audit in 2000 revealed that the tribe's pharmaceutical firm was giving discount drugs intended for Native Americans to its non-Native American employees. In 2002 the tribe withdrew its application to annex 165 acres of land close to its Foxwoods Resort Casino, ending nearly 10 years of legal battles.

EXECUTIVES

Chairman: Michael J. Thomas, age 39
Vice Chairman: Kenneth M. (Ken) Reels
CEO: Patricia L. (Pat) Irvin, age 52
SVP Administration: Bruce Kirchner
SVP Property Marketing: Gary A. Borden
SVP Casino Marketing: Joseph C. Jimenez
SVP Human Resources: Joanne Franks
VP Finance: Mark Ford
VP Information Services: Brian Charette
VP Human Resources: Stephen E. (Steve) Heise
Interim President and Interim CEO, Foxwoods Resort Casino: Barry J. Cregan, age 54
President, Foxwoods Development: Gary D. Armentrout

VP Hotel Operations, Foxwoods Resort Casino: Edward Stanton
VP Entertainment and Sports, Foxwoods Resort Casino and MGM Grand at Foxwoods: Judy Alberti
VP Compliance, Foxwoods Resort Casino: John Perry
VP Development, Foxwoods Development: Nelson N. Parker II
VP Design and Construction, Foxwoods Development: Randee Bach
Secretary: Charlene Jones

LOCATIONS

HQ: Mashantucket Pequot Tribal Nation
  39 Norwich-Westerly Rd., Ledyard, CT 06339
Phone: 860-312-3000   **Fax:** 860-396-3599
Web: www.foxwoods.com

Mashantucket Pequot Tribal Nation has holdings in Connecticut and Rhode Island.

PRODUCTS/OPERATIONS

Selected Holdings

Foxwoods Resort Casino (Mashantucket, CT)
Hilton Mystic (Mystic, CT)
Lake of Isles (golf courses, Mashantucket, CT)
Mashantucket Pequot Museum and Research Center (Mashantucket, CT)
Mercantile Exchange Building (Norwich, CT)
Randall's Ordinary Inn (North Stonington, CT)
The Spa at Norwich Inn (Norwich, CT)

COMPETITORS

Connecticut Lottery
Harrah's Entertainment
Kerzner International
Mohegan Tribal Gaming Authority
New York State Lottery
Trump Resorts

Massachusetts Mutual Life Insurance

Massachusetts Mutual Life Insurance (MassMutual) is the flagship firm of the MassMutual Financial Group, a global organization of companies that provide financial services including life insurance, annuities, money management, and retirement planning. Founded in 1851, MassMutual's clients include individuals and businesses. The company also offers disability income insurance, long-term care insurance, structured settlement annuities, and trust services (through The MassMutual Trust Company). Other subsidiaries include OppenheimerFunds (mutual funds), Babson Capital Management (investor services), Baring Asset Management, and Cornerstone Real Estate Advisors (real estate investment management).

Like so many other insurance firms, MassMutual is eager to get on the financial services bandwagon. However, you won't catch the firm issuing stock to get the job done; its management and policyholders have reaffirmed their intention to keep MassMutual a mutual company despite the efforts of some policyholders. Also, the company doesn't seem too eager to throw out either the insurance baby or the bathwater — it has also reaffirmed its commitment to good old whole life insurance products and retirement income products

MassMutual International has established subsidiaries in Asia, Europe, and South America where it is focused on new product development (the majority of sales come from products or channels developed within the last couple of years) and broadened distribution.

HISTORY

Insurance agent George Rice formed Massachusetts Mutual in 1851 as a stock company based in Springfield. The firm converted to a mutual in 1867. For its first 50 years MassMutual sold only individual life insurance, but after 1900 it branched out, offering first annuities (1917) and then disability coverage (1918).

The early 20th century was rough on MassMutual, which was forced to raise premiums on new policies during WWI, then faced the high costs of the 1918 flu epidemic. The firm endured the Great Depression despite policy terminations, expanding its product line to include income insurance. In 1946 MassMutual wrote its first group policy, for Jack Daniel's maker Brown-Forman Distillers. By 1950 the company had diversified into medical insurance.

MassMutual began investing in stocks in the 1950s, switching from fixed-return bonds and mortgages for higher returns. It also decentralized and in 1961 began automating operations. By 1970 the firm had installed a computer network linking it to its independent agents. During this period, whole life insurance remained the core product.

With interest rates increasing during the late 1970s, many insurers diversified by offering high-yield products like guaranteed investment contracts funded by high-risk investments. MassMutual resisted as long as it could, but as interest rates soared to 20%, the company experienced a rash of policy loans, which led to a cash crunch. In 1981, with its policy growth rate trailing the industry norm, MassMutual developed new products, including some that offered higher dividends in return for adjustable interest on policy loans.

In the 1980s MassMutual reduced its stock investment (to about 5% of total investments by 1987), allowing it to emerge virtually unscathed from the 1987 stock market crash.

The firm changed course in 1990 and entered financial services. It bought a controlling interest in mutual fund manager Oppenheimer Management. MassMutual announced in 1993 that, with legislation limiting rates, it would stop writing new individual and small-group policies in New York.

The next year the company targeted the neglected family-owned business niche; in 1995 it sponsored the American Alliance of Family-Owned Businesses and rolled out new whole life products aimed at this segment. That year it bought David L. Babson & Company, a Massachusetts-based investment management firm, and opened life insurance companies in Chile and Argentina.

In 1996 MassMutual merged with Connecticut Mutual. It also acquired Antares Leveraged Capital Corp. (commercial finance) and Charter Oak Capital Management (investment advisory services). The next year MassMutual sold its Life & Health Benefits Management subsidiary.

Still in the mood to merge, the company entered discussions with Northwestern Mutual in 1998, but culture clashes terminated the talks. Also that year the company helped push through legislation that would allow insurers to issue stock through mutual holding companies, a move which MassMutual itself contemplated in 1999.

MassMutual expanded outside the US at the turn of the century. In 1999 it issued securities in Europe, opened offices in such locales as Bermuda and Luxembourg, and bought the Argentina operations of Jefferson-Pilot. A year later it expanded into Asia when it bought Hong Kong-based CRC Protective Life Insurance (now MassMutual Asia). In 2001 the company entered the Taiwanese market, buying a stake in Mercuries Life Insurance (now MassMutual Mercuries Life Insurance) and acquiring Japanese insurer Aetna Heiwa Life (a subsidiary of US health insurer Aetna).

Also in 2001 MassMutual policyholders defeated a proposal by some to convert the company to stockholder ownership.

The company's board of directors terminated former CEO Robert O'Connell in 2005, citing a laundry list of reasons that included using company assets improperly and the use of retaliatory behavior against employees. Stuart Reese was named his replacement.

MassMutual acquired the operations of Baring Asset Management from ING Groep in 2005 to boost its financial services portfolio.

EXECUTIVES

Chairman, President, and CEO: Stuart H. Reese
EVP and CFO: Michael T. Rollings, age 44
EVP Retirement Services; Chairman and CEO, MassMutual International LLC: Elaine A. Sarsynski, age 52
EVP, Chief Investment Officer, and Co-COO; Office of the CEO: Roger W. Crandall, age 43
EVP Retirement Services: Frederick C. Castellani
EVP, Chairman, President and CEO OppenheimerFunds, Inc: John V. Murphy
EVP and General Counsel: Mark D. Roellig, age 52
EVP U.S. Insurance Group and Co-COO: William Glavin, age 48
SVP and COO US Insurance Group: Michael R. Fanning, age 44
SVP and CFO, US Insurance Group: Gregory (Greg) Deavens
SVP Corporate Financial Operations: Richard D. Bourgeois
SVP; Managing Director and CEO, MassMutual Asia: Elroy Chan
SVP, Secretary, and Deputy General Counsel: Stephen L. Kuhn
SVP and General Auditor: Donald B. Robitaille
SVP, Corporate Human Resources: Debra A. Palermino
President and CEO, MassMutual Asset Finance: John Chipman
Public Relations Contact: Marty McDonough

LOCATIONS

HQ: Massachusetts Mutual Life Insurance Company
1295 State St., Springfield, MA 01111
Phone: 413-744-1000   **Fax:** 413-744-6005
Web: www.massmutual.com

PRODUCTS/OPERATIONS

2007 Sales

	$ mil.	% of total
Premium income	13,236	71
Net investment income	4,934	26
Fees & other income	574	3
Total	**18,744**	**100**

Selected Subsidiaries and Affiliates

Babson Capital Management LLC
Baring Asset Management Limited (UK)
C.M. Life Insurance Company
Cornerstone Real Estate Advisers LLC (real estate equities)
Fuh Hwa Securities Investment Trust Co., Ltd. (Taiwan)
MassMutual Asia Ltd. (Hong Kong)
MassMutual Europe S.A. (Luxembourg)
MassMutual International, Inc.
MassMutual Life Insurance Co. (Japan)
MassMutual Mercuries Life Insurance Co., Ltd. (Taiwan)
MML Bay State Life Insurance Company
MML Investors Services, Inc.
OppenheimerFunds, Inc. (mutual funds)
The MassMutual Trust Company, FSB

COMPETITORS

AIG
AIG American General
Allianz
Allstate
American Financial
AXA Financial
Charles Schwab
Citigroup
CNA Financial
Conseco
FMR
Genworth Financial
Guardian Life
The Hartford
John Hancock Financial Services
Liberty Mutual
Merrill Lynch
MetLife
Nationwide
New York Life
Northwestern Mutual
Principal Financial
Prudential
Savings Bank Life Insurance
TIAA-CREF
Torchmark
UBS Financial Services

HISTORICAL FINANCIALS

Company Type: Mutual company

Income Statement

FYE: December 31

	ASSETS ($ mil.)	NET INCOME ($ mil.)	INCOME AS % OF ASSETS	EMPLOYEES
12/07	131,491	201	0.2%	12,000
12/06	122,155	810	0.7%	12,000
12/05	113,552	753	0.7%	10,000
12/04	108,216	335	0.3%	10,000
12/03	96,779	461	0.5%	10,000
Annual Growth	8.0%	(18.7%)	—	4.7%

2007 Year-End Financials

Equity as % of assets: 6.1%   Long-term debt ($ mil.): —
Return on assets: 0.2%   Sales ($ mil.): 18,744
Return on equity: 2.7%

Net Income History

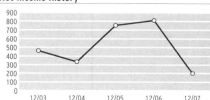

HOOVER'S HANDBOOK OF PRIVATE COMPANIES 2009

Massachusetts State Lottery

For a lucky few, the Commonwealth creates uncommon wealth. The Massachusetts State Lottery Commission operates several numbers games (Mass Cash, Cash Winfall, Megabucks), as well as a variety of scratch-off games. Massachusetts also participates in the 12-state Mega Millions lottery. State law requires that at least 45% of lottery proceeds must go to pay prizes, while a maximum of 15% can be used for operating expenses. The remainder of the commission's take is distributed throughout Massachusetts to fund such local services as fire and police protection, as well as for education. The Massachusetts State Lottery Commission was created in 1971.

EXECUTIVES

State Treasurer and Receiver General:
Timothy P. (Tim) Cahill, age 49
Executive Director: Mark J. Cavanagh, age 52
CFO: Edward Bartley
Chief of Staff: Al Grazioso
Assistant Executive Director MIS: Paul Mandeville
Assistant Executive Director Human Resources:
Michael T. Coughlin
Communications Director: Daniel L. (Dan) Rosenfeld

LOCATIONS

HQ: Massachusetts State Lottery Commission
60 Columbian St., Braintree, MA 02184
Phone: 781-849-5555   **Fax:** 781-849-5509
Web: www.masslottery.com

COMPETITORS

Connecticut Lottery
Maine State Lottery
Multi-State Lottery
New Hampshire Lottery
New York State Lottery
Vermont Lottery

Mayer Electric Supply

Mayer Electric Supply helps light up those southern nights. The company, founded in 1930, distributes electrical supplies from more than 50 locations in the southeastern US. Mayer Electric's line card includes some 22,000 products made by leading manufacturers such as 3M, GE, Littelfuse, and Schneider Electric. These products include factory automation systems, controls and switches, fire and safety products, lighting fixtures, motors, power tools, and wire and cable. The company supplies customers in such industries as construction, manufacturing, and utilities. Chairman Charles Collat and his family own Mayer Electric.

The company has widened its reach to Mississippi by acquiring Biloxi Electric Supply and opening a new branch in Gulfport.

In 2006 Mayer Electric acquired Jones & Lee Supply of Knoxville, Tennessee. Jones & Lee, a family business like Mayer, was founded in 1948

and employs 26 people. That year the company also bought the wholesale distribution operations of Higgins Electric in Dothan, Alabama.

In 2004 Mayer acquired Maddux Supply, an electrical products distribution company in North Carolina. The company has a Web portal at MyMayer.com.

EXECUTIVES

Chairman: Charles A. Collat Sr.
Vice Chairman: Nancy Collat Goedecke
President and CEO: Jim Summerlin
EVP and COO: Wes Smith
CFO: David L. Morgan
Director, Corporate Marketing:
W. Joseph (Joe) Llewellyn

LOCATIONS

HQ: Mayer Electric Supply Company Inc.
3405 4th Ave. South, Birmingham, AL 35222
Phone: 205-583-3500   **Fax:** 205-322-2625
Web: www.mayerelectric.com

Mayer Electric Supply has operations in Alabama, Florida, Georgia, Mississippi, North Carolina, South Carolina, Tennessee, and Virginia.

PRODUCTS/OPERATIONS

Selected Products

Ballasts	Fountains
Batteries	Lenses
Boxes	Lighting fixtures
Cable and wire	Locks
Conduit	Motors
Factory automation products	Plumbing products
	Terminal blocks
Fans	Tools
Fasteners	Transformers
Faucets	

COMPETITORS

Anixter International	Independent Electric
Consolidated Electrical	Rexel, Inc.
Crescent Electric Supply	WESCO International
Gexpro	Wholesale Supply Group
Graybar Electric	W.W. Grainger

HISTORICAL FINANCIALS
Company Type: Private

Income Statement
FYE: December 31

	REVENUE ($ mil.)	NET INCOME ($ mil.)	NET PROFIT MARGIN	EMPLOYEES
12/07	670	—	—	1,000
12/06	505	—	—	1,000
12/05	507	—	—	900
12/04	507	—	—	900
12/03	250	—	—	550
Annual Growth	27.9%	—	—	16.1%

Revenue History

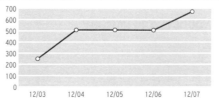

Mayo Foundation

Mayo can whip up a medical miracle. The not-for-profit Mayo Foundation for Medical Education and Research provides health care, most notably for complex medical conditions, through its renowned Mayo Clinic in Rochester, Minnesota. Other clinics are located in Arizona and Florida. The clinics' multidisciplinary approach to care attracts thousands of patients a year, including such notables as the late Ronald Reagan and the late King Hussein of Jordan. The Mayo Health System operates a network of affiliated community hospitals and clinics in Minnesota, Iowa, and Wisconsin. The Mayo Foundation also conducts research and trains physicians, nurses, and other health professionals.

In addition to the Mayo Clinics, the foundation operates other hospitals, including Saint Marys Hospital and Rochester Methodist Hospital in Rochester and Mayo Clinic Hospital in Phoenix. It sold St. Luke's Hospital in Jacksonville to the St. Vincent's Health System in 2005, but leased the facility until 2008 when the construction of its new 200-bed hospital on the Mayo Clinic Jacksonville campus was completed.

The Mayo Health System affiliated network includes about five clinics in Iowa, some 25 clinics and hospitals in Wisconsin, and about 35 facilities in Minnesota. At the University of Minnesota, the foundation's education programs include the Mayo School of Graduate Medical Education and the Mayo School of Health Sciences.

The company relies on private contributions, endowments, and grants to supplement funding for its operations and research programs. The foundation also commercializes medical technology, publishes medical literature, and invests in other medical startups to increase income. To manage its patient load, Mayo forms referral alliances with hospital groups, HMOs, and other organizations.

The Mayo Foundation dates back to a frontier practice launched by brothers William and Charles Mayo in 1863. The foundation bases its philosophy of putting the patient first and investing in education and research on the founding brothers' medical practices.

HISTORY

In 1845 William Mayo came to the US from England. He was a doctor, veterinarian, river boatman, surveyor, and newspaper editor before settling in Rochester, Minnesota, in 1863.

When a tornado struck Rochester in 1883, Mayo took charge of a makeshift hospital. The Sisters of St. Francis offered to replace the hospital that was lost in the disaster if Mayo would head the staff. He agreed reluctantly. Not only were hospitals then associated with the poor and insane, but his affiliation with the sisters raised eyebrows among Protestants and Catholics.

Saint Marys Hospital opened in 1889. Mayo's sons William and Charles, who were starting their medical careers, helped him. After the elder Mayo retired, the sons ran the hospital. Although the brothers accepted all medical cases, they made the hospital self-sufficient, attracting paying patients by pioneering in specialization at a time when physicians were jacks-of-all-medical-trades.

This specialization attracted other physicians, and by 1907 the practice was known as "the Mayo's clinic." The brothers, in association with the University of Minnesota, established the Mayo Foundation for Medical Research (now the Mayo Graduate School of Medicine), the world's first program to train medical specialists, in 1915.

In 1919 the brothers transferred the clinic properties and miscellaneous financial assets, primarily from patient care profits, into the Mayo Properties Association (renamed the Mayo Foundation in 1964). Under the terms of the endowment, all Mayo Clinic medical staff members became salaried employees. In 1933 the clinic established one of the first blood banks in the US. Both brothers died in 1939.

Part of the association's mission was to fund research. In 1950 two Mayo researchers won a Nobel Prize for developing cortisone to treat rheumatoid arthritis. The foundation opened its second medical school, the Mayo Medical School, in 1972.

As insurers in the 1980s pressured to cut hospital admissions and stays, the foundation diversified with for-profit ventures. In 1983 Mayo began publishing the *Mayo Clinic Health Letter,* its first subscription publication for a general audience, and the *Mayo Clinic Family Health Book.* It also began providing specialized lab services to other doctors and hospitals. The addition of Rochester Methodist Hospital (creating the largest not-for-profit medical group in the country) was also a response to financial pressures. Following the money south as affluent folks retired, the foundation opened clinics in Jacksonville (1986); Scottsdale, Arizona (1987); and in nearby Phoenix (1998).

Seeking to expand in its home market, Mayo in 1992 formed the Mayo Health System, a regional network of health care facilities and medical practices. In 1996 former patient Barbara Woodward Lips left $127.9 million to the foundation, the largest bequest in its history.

In the late 1990s the foundation increasingly looked to corporate partnerships to help defray costs and to expand research activities. In 1998 and 1999 Mayo boosted its presence overseas with nonmedical regional offices. Mayo scientists in 2000 announced they had regrown or repaired nerve coverings in mice; this type of damage in humans (caused by such conditions as multiple sclerosis) had been considered irreparable. The Mayo Foundation continues to push for breakthroughs in medical science.

EXECUTIVES

President and CEO, Mayo Clinic: Denis A. Cortese
CFO; Chair, Department of Finance, Mayo Clinic:
Jeffrey W. Bolton
VP and Chief Administrative Officer: Shirley A. Weis
Director Center for Individualized Medicine Research:
Franklyn G. Prendergast, age 62
Chairman, Department of Development: James P. Lyddy
Chairman, Human Resources: Marita Heller
**Secretary and Chairman, Legal Department, Mayo
Clinic:** Jonathan J. Oviatt
Medical Director for Development, Mayo Clinic:
John H. Noseworthy
Chairman Information Technology, Mayo Clinic:
Abdul Bengali
**Chairman, Department of Facilities and Systems
Support Services, Mayo Clinic Rochester:**
Craig A. Smoldt
Chief Administrative Officer, Mayo Clinic Rochester:
Jeffrey O. (Jeff) Korsmo
CEO, Mayo Clinic Jacksonville: George B. Bartley
CEO, Mayo Clinic Arizona: Victor F. Trastek
CEO, Mayo Clinic Rochester: Glenn S. Forbes
President and CEO, Franciscan Skemp Healthcare:
Robert E. Nesse
Auditors: Ernst & Young LLP

LOCATIONS

HQ: Mayo Foundation for Medical Education
and Research
200 1st St. SW, Rochester, MN 55905
Phone: 507-284-2511   **Fax:** 507-284-0161
Web: www.mayo.edu

Selected Locations and Affiliates
Arizona
   Mayo Clinic Hospital (Phoenix)
   Mayo Clinic Scottsdale
Florida
   Mayo Clinic Hospital (Jacksonville)
   Mayo Clinic Jacksonville
Iowa
   Amstrong Clinic (Armstrong)
   Decorah Clinic (Decorah)
   Lake Mills Clinic (Lake Mills)
   New Hampton Clinic (New Hampton)
   Franciscan Skemp Waukon Clinic (Waukon)
Minnesota
   Albert Lea Medical Center (Albert Lea)
   Austin Medical Center (Austin)
   Cannon Valley Clinic (Faribault)
   Fairmont Medical Center (Fairmont)
   Fountain Centers Rochester (Rochester)
   Franciscan Skemp La Crescent Clinic (La Crescent)
   Immanuel St. Joseph's (Mankato)
   Lake City Medical Center (Lake City)
   Mayo Clinic Rochester
   Rochester Methodist Hospital
   Saint Marys Hospital (Rochester)
   Springfield Medical Center (Springfield)
   Parkview Care Center (Wells)
   Wabasha Clinic (Wabasha)
Wisconsin
   Luther Midelfort (Eau Claire)
   Luther Midelfort Chippewa Valley (Bloomer)
   Luther Midelfort Northland (Barron)
   Red Cedar Medical Center (Menomonie)
   Franciscan Skemp Galesville Clinic (Galesville)
   Franciscan Skemp Holmen Clinic (Holmen)
   Franciscan Skemp Onalaska Clinic (Onalaska)

PRODUCTS/OPERATIONS

2007 Sales

	$ mil.	% of total
Medical services	5,730.2	83
Grants & contracts	310.1	5
Contributions	211.8	3
Return on investments	111.9	2
Premiums	87.3	1
Other	446.3	6
Total	**6,897.6**	**100**

COMPETITORS

Allina Hospitals
Ascension Health
Catholic Health Initiatives
Catholic Healthcare Partners
Detroit Medical Center
HCA
Health Management Associates
HealthSouth
Henry Ford Health System
Johns Hopkins Medicine
Memorial Sloan-Kettering
Methodist Hospital System
New York City Health and Hospitals
Rockefeller University
Rush System for Health
Scripps
SSM Health Care
Tenet Healthcare
Trinity Health (Novi)
Universal Health Services

HISTORICAL FINANCIALS
Company Type: Not-for-profit

Income Statement

	REVENUE ($ mil.)	NET INCOME ($ mil.)	NET PROFIT MARGIN	EMPLOYEES
12/07	6,898	—	—	54,914
12/06	6,289	—	—	52,194
12/05	5,802	—	—	45,000
12/04	5,354	—	—	—
12/03	4,822	—	—	42,620
Annual Growth	**9.4%**	**—**	**—**	**6.5%**

FYE: December 31

Revenue History

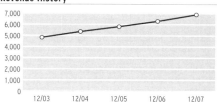

McCarthy Building Companies

A company that was in construction before Reconstruction, McCarthy Building Companies is one of the oldest privately held builders in the US. The general contractor and construction manager has projects worldwide and ranks among the top builders of health care and education facilities in the US. Contracts include heavy construction projects (bridges and water and waste-treatment plants), industrial projects (biopharmaceutical, food processing, and microelectronics facilities), commercial projects (retail and office buildings), and institutional projects (airports, schools, and prisons). Timothy McCarthy founded the firm in 1864. His great-grandson, Michael McCarthy, sold the firm to its employees in 2002.

McCarthy Building Companies' clients include Kaiser Permanente, California State University, and Bally's Casino Resort. Its projects include The Platinum condominium/hotel tower in Las Vegas and renovation and expansion of the National Baseball Hall of Fame and Museum in Cooperstown, New York.

Headquartered in Saint Louis, McCarthy Building Companies has offices in Newport Beach, San Francisco, Sacramento, and San Diego, California; Atlanta; Dallas; Las Vegas; and Phoenix.

EXECUTIVES

Chairman and CEO: Michael D. (Mike) Bolen
President and COO: Derek W. Glanvill
EVP, CFO, and Treasurer: George F. Scherer
SVP, General Counsel, and Secretary: James A. Staskiel
VP Information Technologies: Michael Oster
Director Corporate Communications:
Michael (Mike) Lenzen
Director Benefits and Compensation: Jan Schoemehl
**Director of Business Development, Research and
Laboratory Group:** Jim Contratto

Midwest Division President: Karl Kloster
Northern Pacific Division President: Richard A. Henry
California Region President: W. Carter Chappell, age 50
Nevada Division President: Randy Highland
Southwest Region President: Robert (Bo) Calbert
Texas Division President: Michael J. McWay
Auditors: Ernst & Young LLP

LOCATIONS

HQ: McCarthy Building Companies, Inc.
  1341 N. Rock Hill Rd., St. Louis, MO 63124
Phone: 314-968-3300   **Fax:** 314-968-4780
Web: www.mccarthy.com

Selected Services

Negotiated general contracting (preconstruction and
  construction phase services, self-performance of some
  work, in-house tradespeople conduct several tasks, and
  McCarthy controls cost, schedule, and quality)
Construction management (preconstruction and
  construction services; clients control cost, schedule,
  quality, constructability, startup, and warranties)
Hard bid (lump sum contract for services)
Design/build (single source contract for all services for
  planning, designing, constructing, and commission a
  project)
Construction management/general contracting
  (combining the two delivery methods as a result of
  contract negotiations)

COMPETITORS

Alberici	Hensel Phelps
Barton Malow	Korte
Bechtel	Perini
Bovis Lend Lease	Peter Kiewit Sons'
Centex	Primus Builders
Clayco	S. M. Wilson
DPR Construction	Skanska
Gilbane	Swinerton
HBE Corporation	Turner Corporation

McJunkin Red Man Holding Corporation

It's fitting that McJunkin Red Man is a pipeline
to parts and supplies for many oil and gas companies. The company is a distributor of steel pipe,
valves, and fittings, as well as drilling, electrical,
and mining supplies. It distributes gas and oil
products throughout the Appalachian basin and
across the US. Additional clients include power,
pulp and paper, mining, and automotive companies. McJunkin Red Man also supplies technical
support, storeroom management, and investment recovery services, as well as valve cleaning
and rebuilding services. In 2007 McJunkin Corporation merged with oilfield supplier Red Man
Pipe & Supply to form McJunkin Red Man.

McJunkin Red Man has expanded its product
portfolio to include 70,000 offerings and its distribution network to encompass more than 200
locations in about 30 states by entering new markets and through strategic acquisitions that
complemented its core activities. The company
is venturing into the international marketplace.
It has multiple branches in three western Canadian provinces, primarily in Alberta.

Founded in 1921, the firm is still partially
owned by descendants of the founding
McJunkin family — although Goldman Sachs
holds a substantial stake in the company. Following the investment by Goldman Sachs in
late 2006, CEO H. B. Wehrle III stated that
McJunkin would be a platform for further acquisitions, and that the stage was set for McJunkin
to become publicly traded.

In August 2007 McJunkin announced a
"merger-of-equals" agreement with Red Man Pipe
& Supply, which operated oilfield supply centers
in the US and Canada. The combined company
operates co-headquarters at the pre-merger
McJunkin and Red Man headquarters locations,
and Wehrle and Red Man CEO Craig Ketchum
served as co-CEOs following the merger.

In 2008, however, the company named former
Halliburton COO Andrew Lane as CEO. Ketchum
became chairman of McJunkin Red Man, while
Wehrle remained chairman of PVF Holdings LLC,
the majority shareholder of McJunkin Red Man
and an entity that is controlled by Goldman Sachs.

EXECUTIVES

Chairman: L. Craig Ketchum, age 51
CEO: Andrew R. (Andy) Lane, age 48
EVP and CFO: James F. (Jim) Underhill, age 53
EVP Branch Sales and Operations: Jeffrey Lang, age 52
EVP Canadian Operations and Business Development:
  J. M. (Dee) Paige, age 55
SVP, Midwestern Region: Scott Hutchinson
**SVP Sales and Marketing (Downstream and Gas
  Utilities):** Rory M. Isaac, age 58
SVP, Gulf Coast Region: Clyde Certain
SVP Sales and Marketing (Upstream): Randy K. Adams,
  age 51
SVP Integration: Matt Bailey
SVP Human Resources: David Lewis
**Senior Corporate VP, General Counsel, and Corporate
  Secretary:** Stephen W. Lake, age 44
Auditors: Ernst & Young LLP

LOCATIONS

HQ: McJunkin Red Man Holding Corporation
  835 Hillcrest Dr., Charleston, WV 25311
Phone: 304-348-5211   **Fax:** 304-348-4922
Web: www.mcjunkinredman.com

PRODUCTS/OPERATIONS

Selected Products

Carbon steel and corrosion-resistant fittings and flanges
  Buttweld
  Malleable iron fittings
  Pressure
Carbon steel pipe
  Grooved
  Beveled
  Threaded
  Coupled
  Plain end
  Seamless
Electrical products
  Conduit and channel
  Conveyor belt fasteners
  Insulating products
  Lighting, lamps, and ballasts
  Motors and motor controls
  Panelboards and switches
  Transformers
  Wire, cord, and cable
Engineered products
  Gaskets
  Pressure power pumps
  Steam traps
  Tylok tube fittings
  Victaulic tube fittings

Gas distribution and transmission products
  Gas fittings
  Meter parts
  Meter risers
  Meters and meter valves
  Polyethylene and steel pipe
  Protection products
  Regulators and parts
  Saddle tees and tapping tees
  Squeeze tools
  Transitions
  Valve and curb boxes
  Valves, clamps, and couplings
Stainless steel and corrosion-resistant tubular products
  Plastic-lined
  Seamless
  Welded
Valves
  Ball valves
  Bellows-sealed valves
  Butterfly valves
  Cast steel valves
  Check valves
  Gate valves
  Forged steel valves
  Globe valves
  Knife gate valves
  Plug valves
  Stainless steel valves
Other products
  Chains
  Compounds and paint
  Fasteners
  Hand tools
  Tape and Teflon

COMPETITORS

Applied Industrial Technologies
Blue Tee
Consolidated Electrical
Ferguson Enterprises
HD Supply
Piping & Equipment
Shaw Group
Würth
Wilson
WinWholesale
Wolseley
W.W. Grainger

HISTORICAL FINANCIALS

Company Type: Private

	REVENUE ($ mil.)	NET INCOME ($ mil.)	NET PROFIT MARGIN	EMPLOYEES
Income Statement				FYE: December 31
12/07	2,268	64	2.8%	3,484
12/06	1,714	70	4.1%	1,467
12/05	1,446	53	3.6%	1,436
Annual Growth	25.2%	10.0%	—	55.8%

2007 Year-End Financials

Debt ratio: 70.1%   Current ratio: 2.34
Return on equity: 8.7%   Long-term debt ($ mil.): 849
Cash ($ mil.): 10

Net Income History

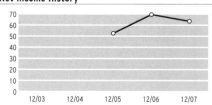

McKee Foods

When Little Debbie smiles up out of your lunch bag, you know you are loved. McKee Foods' Little Debbie is one of the US's best known brands of snack cakes, named for and featuring the smiling face of the company's founders' granddaughter. McKee also makes ready-to-eat cereals, granola, creme-filled cookies, crackers, and snack bars. Low prices and family packs of individually wrapped treats continue to drive sales. There are more than 160 varieties of Little Debbie snack packs. McKee's products are available in the US, Canada, and Mexico, as well as at US military commissaries around the world.

Product development is key in the highly competitive snack market, and McKee Foods steadily puts out offerings such as Fruit Jammers.

In addition to Little Debbie, the company's brand names include Sunbelt and Fieldstone Bakery (foodservice only). It also owns Blue Planet Foods, which makes toasted oats and other grain products under the Heartland brand name.

McKee has operations in Arkansas, Tennessee, and Virginia.

EXECUTIVES

Chairman: R. Ellsworth McKee
CEO: Jack C. McKee, age 70
President: Michael K. (Mike) McKee, age 46
CFO: Barry S. Patterson
EVP Sales and Marketing:
 Christopher T. (Chris) McKee, age 42
EVP Manufacturing; President, Blue Planet Foods:
 Russell E. (Rusty) McKee Jr.
VP Human Resources: Eva Lynne Disbro
VP Stuart Draft Operations: E. Ray Murphy
VP Transportation: Renee Tracy
Director Sales: Ed Hannah
Director Marketing: Barry Anthony
Corporate Communications and Public Relations Manager: Mike Gloekler

LOCATIONS

HQ: McKee Foods Corporation
 10260 McKee Rd., Collegedale, TN 37315
Phone: 423-238-7111 **Fax:** 423-238-7101
Web: www.mckeefoods.com

McKee Foods has baking facilities in Arkansas, Tennessee, and Virginia.

PRODUCTS/OPERATIONS

Selected Products

Fieldstone Bakery brand
 Cereals
 Cookies
 Granola
 Snack bars
Heartland brand
 Cereals
 Granola
 Granola bars
Little Debbie brand
 Brownies
 Coffeecake
 Cookies
 Crackers
 Seasonal snacks
 Snack cakes
Sunbelt brand
 Cereal bars
 Fruit snacks
 Granola bars

COMPETITORS

Chattanooga Bakery
Flowers Foods
General Mills
Interbake Foods
Interstate Bakeries
Kellogg
Kellogg U.S. Snacks
Lance Snacks
Otis Spunkmeyer
Pepperidge Farm
Sara Lee Food & Beverage
Tasty Baking
Voortman Cookies
Weston Foods

HISTORICAL FINANCIALS

Company Type: Private

Income Statement				FYE: Friday nearest June 30
	REVENUE ($ mil.)	NET INCOME ($ mil.)	NET PROFIT MARGIN	EMPLOYEES
6/08	1,100	—	—	6,000
6/07	1,000	—	—	6,000
6/06	1,000	—	—	6,000
6/05	1,000	—	—	6,000
6/04	1,000	—	—	6,000
Annual Growth	2.4%	—	—	0.0%

Revenue History

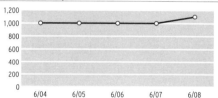

McKinsey & Company

One of the world's top management consulting firms, McKinsey & Company has about 90 offices in more than 50 countries around the globe. The company advises corporate enterprises, government agencies, and foundations on a variety of issues. It groups its practices into six main areas: business technology, corporate finance, marketing and sales, operations, organization, and strategy. McKinsey serves clients in numerous industry sectors, from automotive to high tech to telecommunications. Founded by James McKinsey in 1926, the company is owned by its partners.

McKinsey takes advantage of its global reach to gain business from multinational companies that want help in harmonizing their diverse operations. Toward that end, the firm aims to work collaboratively across its own organization, bringing together the work of multiple offices and practices on behalf of a single client.

In addition to being one of the oldest consulting firms, McKinsey is considered one of the most prestigious (along with Boston Consulting Group and Bain) as measured in surveys of aspiring consultants. Contributing to McKinsey's allure as an employer is the firm's network of 18,000-plus alumni, many of whom have been tapped for C-level jobs in the course of their careers. Alumni running companies, in turn, represent a potential source of business for the firm.

HISTORY

McKinsey & Company was founded in Chicago in 1926 by University of Chicago accounting professor James McKinsey. The company evolved from an auditing practice of McKinsey and his partners, Marvin Bower and A.T. Kearney, who began analyzing business and industry and offering advice. McKinsey died in 1937; two years later, Bower, who headed the New York office, and Kearney, in Chicago, split the firm. Kearney renamed the Chicago office A.T. Kearney & Co. (later acquired by Electronic Data Systems), and Bower kept the McKinsey name and built up a practice structured like a law firm.

Bower focused on the big picture instead of on specific operating problems, helping boost billings to $2 million by 1950. He hired staff straight out of prestigious business schools, reinforcing the firm's theoretical bent. Bower implemented a competitive up-or-out policy requiring employees who are not continually promoted to leave the firm.

The firm's prestige continued to grow during the booming 1950s along with demand for consulting services. Before becoming president in 1953, Dwight Eisenhower asked McKinsey to find out exactly what the government did. By 1959 Bower had opened an office in London, followed by others in Amsterdam; Dusseldorf, Germany; Melbourne; Paris; and Zurich.

In 1964 the company founded management journal *The McKinsey Quarterly*. When Bower retired in 1967, sales were $20 million, and McKinsey was the #1 management consulting firm. During the 1970s it faced competition from firms with newer approaches and lost market share. In response, then-managing director Ronald Daniel started specialty practices and expanded foreign operations.

The consulting boom of the 1980s was spurred by mergers and buyouts. By 1988 the firm had 1,800 consultants, sales were $620 million, and 50% of billings came from overseas.

The recession of the early 1990s hit white-collar workers, including consultants. McKinsey, scrambling to upgrade its technical side, bought Information Consulting Group (ICG), its first acquisition. But the corporate cultures did not meld, and most ICG people left by 1993.

In 1994 the company elected its first managing director of non-European descent, Indian-born Rajat Gupta. Two years later the traditionally hush-hush firm found itself at the center of that most public 1990s arena, the sexual discrimination lawsuit. A female ex-consultant in Texas sued, claiming McKinsey had sabotaged her career (the case was dismissed).

In 1998 McKinsey partnered with Northwestern University and the University of Pennsylvania to establish a business school in India. The following year graduating seniors surveyed in Europe, the UK, and the US named the company as their ideal employer.

Also in 1999 the company created @McKinsey to help "accelerate" Internet startups. The next year it increased salaries and offered incentives to better compete with Internet firms for employees. In 2001 the company expanded its branding business with the acquisition of Envision, a Chicago-based brand consultant.

Like its rivals in the consulting industry, McKinsey took a hit from the dot-com bust and the economic downturn of 2001 and 2002, as many companies were slower to sign up for costly long-term strategy consulting engagements and mergers and acquisitions work dried up.

In 2003 Ian Davis was elected as managing director of the firm, succeeding Gupta, who had served as McKinsey's top executive for nine years. (Managing directors serve for three years and are limited to three terms.) Davis had previously served as the head of the firm's UK office.

EXECUTIVES

Managing Director: Ian Davis, age 57
Chairman, Americas: Michael Patsalos-Fox
Chairman, Asia: Dominic Barton
Chairman, Europe, Middle East, and Africa:
  Robert Reibestein
Director, McKinsey Global Institute: Diana Farrell
Media Contact, Asia: Patricia Welch
Media Contact, McKinsey Global Institutue:
  Rebeca Robboy
Media Contact, UK: Andrea Minton Beddoes
Media Contact, North and South America:
  Simon London
Media Contact, Germany: Kai Peter Rath
Media Contact, Europe, Middle East, and Africa:
  Andrew Whitehouse
Manager Media Relations: Yolande Daeninck

LOCATIONS

HQ: McKinsey & Company
  55 E. 52nd St., 21st Fl., New York, NY 10022
Phone: 212-446-7000   **Fax:** 212-446-8575
Web: www.mckinsey.com

PRODUCTS/OPERATIONS

Selected Industry Practices

Automotive and assembly
Banking and securities
Business technology office
Chemicals
Consumer packaged goods
Electric power and natural gas
High tech
Insurance
Media and entertainment
Metals and mining
Payor/provider
Petroleum
Pharmaceuticals and medical products
Private equity
Pulp and paper
Retail
Social sector
Telecommunications
Travel infrastructure logistics

COMPETITORS

Accenture
A.T. Kearney
Bain & Company
BearingPoint
Booz Allen
Boston Consulting
Capgemini
Computer Sciences Corp.
Deloitte Consulting
EDS
ESource
IBM
PA Consulting
Perot Systems
PRTM Management
Roland Berger

HISTORICAL FINANCIALS
Company Type: Private

Income Statement
FYE: December 31

	ESTIMATED REVENUE ($ mil.)	NET INCOME ($ mil.)	NET PROFIT MARGIN	EMPLOYEES
12/07	5,330	—	—	15,600
12/06	4,370	—	—	14,190
12/05	3,800	—	—	12,900
12/04	3,150	—	—	12,100
12/03	3,000	—	—	11,500
Annual Growth	15.5%	—	—	7.9%

Revenue History

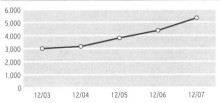

McWane, Inc.

As a leading manufacturer of fire hydrants, McWane is a good friend to both firefighters and dogs. Through its many divisions, McWane makes a variety of fluid control devices including fire hydrants, industrial valves, infrastructure pipes, and fittings. Its Amerex subsidiary is one of the world's leading makers of fire extinguishers and fire suppression systems. Through its Manchester Tank division, the company makes propane tanks used with gas grills and recreational vehicles. Its M&H Valve Company, which makes industrial valves used in waste-water equipment and fire hydrants, has been in operation since 1854. McWane was founded in 1921 and continues to be family-owned.

Over the years McWane has grown by acquiring troubled companies and turning them around with infusions of better equipment and streamlined management. It operates more than 25 manufacturing facilities in the US, Canada, and Australia. Recent growth into China includes the construction of a pipe manufacturing plant, as well as the forming of a joint venture with Xinxing Pipes.

Although the company touts its safety record and its commitment to environmental responsibility (it recycles the equivalent of 800,000 cars in scrap iron per year), McWane and several former employees have received various convictions and fines for violations of the Clean Air Act. In 2007 the company was fined $1.8 million for illegally dumping lead-contaminated waste between 2001 and 2004.

EXECUTIVES

Chairman: C. Phillip McWane, age 50
President: G. Ruffner Page Jr.
EVP Ductile Iron Pipe Group: Dennis R. Charko
SVP and CFO: Charles F. (Charley) Nowlin
SVP and General Counsel: James M. Proctor II
SVP, Compliance and Corporate Affairs: Michael C. Keel

VP and General Manager, Pacific States Cast Iron Pipe:
  John Balian
VP Sales, Tyler Pipe: Bob Sheehan
VP Human Resources and Community Affairs:
  Michelle Clemon
VP Environmental, Health, and Safety: Jitendra Radia

LOCATIONS

HQ: McWane, Inc.
  2900 Hwy. 280, Ste. 300, Birmingham, AL 35223
Phone: 205-414-3100   **Fax:** 205-414-3170
Web: www.mcwane.com

PRODUCTS/OPERATIONS

Selected Operations

Amerex Corporation (industrial and commercial fire
  extinguishers)
Anaco (couplings)
Atlantic States Cast Iron Pipe Company (ductile iron
  pipe)
Bibby-Ste-Croix (soil pipe, fittings, castings)
Canada Pipe Company Ltd. (cast iron pipe)
Clow Canada (valves and hydrants)
Clow Valve Company (fire hydrants and valves)
Clow Water Systems Company (ductile iron pipe and
  fittings)
Kennedy Valve Company (fire hydrants and valves)
Manchester Tank (pressure vessels, propane cylinders,
  tanks, torches)
M&H Valve Company (fire hydrants, gears and casings,
  stem guides, valves)
McWane International (international sales)
McWane Pipe Company (ductile iron pipe for municipal
  water infrastructure)
Pacific States Cast Iron Pipe Company (ductile iron pipe)
Tyler Pipe Company (soil pipe, cleanouts, drains, fittings,
  valves)
Union Foundry Company (ductile iron waterworks
  fittings)

COMPETITORS

Aluminum Precision	ITT Corp.
American Cast Iron Pipe	McJunkin Red Man
Ameron	Mueller Water Products
Citation Corporation	Northwest Pipe
Eaton	SPX
Evraz Steel Mills, Inc.	SSAB North America
Flowserve	Watts Water Technologies
Henry Technologies	

HISTORICAL FINANCIALS
Company Type: Private

Income Statement
FYE: December 31

	ESTIMATED REVENUE ($ mil.)	NET INCOME ($ mil.)	NET PROFIT MARGIN	EMPLOYEES
12/07	1,700	—	—	7,500
12/06	1,740	—	—	7,500
12/05	1,753	—	—	7,000
12/04	1,690	—	—	7,000
12/03	1,500	—	—	7,000
Annual Growth	3.2%	—	—	1.7%

Revenue History

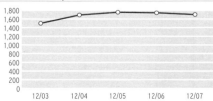

Meadowbrook Meat Company

What's on the menu at your favorite restaurant? Just ask Meadowbrook Meat Company, one of the largest privately owned foodservice distributors in the nation. The company specializes in providing food to national restaurant chains such as Arby's, Burger King, Captain D's, Chick-fil-A, and Darden Restaurants (Red Lobster, Olive Garden). Meadowbrook fills customer orders through a nationwide network of more than 30 distribution centers. J. R. Wordsworth founded the company about 50 years ago as a retail food distributor. It made the transition to its present role in restaurant food distribution after Wordsworth's children bought the business in the 1970s.

EXECUTIVES

Chairman, President, and CEO: Jerry L. Wordsworth
EVP and COO: Jim K. Sabiston
CFO: Jeffrey M. (Jeff) Kowalk
Executive Director Operations: Andy Blanton
Executive Director National Accounts: Mike Burk
Director Human Resources: Tim Ozment
Director Purchasing: Mitch Brantley
Director Quality Assurance: Samuel Richardson
Secretary and Treasurer:
  Debbie Wordsworth-Daughtridge
Controller: Ernest Avent
Executive Director National Accounts: Mike Burk

LOCATIONS

HQ: Meadowbrook Meat Company, Inc.
  2641 Meadowbrook Rd., Rocky Mount, NC 27801
Phone: 252-985-7200   **Fax:** 252-985-7247

COMPETITORS

Alex Lee	McLane Foodservice
Ben E. Keith	Nash-Finch
Clark National	Performance Food
Golden State Foods	Reyes Holdings
Gordon Food Service	SYSCO
MAINES	UniPro Foodservice
Martin-Brower	U.S. Foodservice

HISTORICAL FINANCIALS
Company Type: Private

Income Statement
FYE: December 31

	REVENUE ($ mil.)	NET INCOME ($ mil.)	NET PROFIT MARGIN	EMPLOYEES
12/07	5,500	—	—	3,400
12/06	5,200	—	—	3,400
12/05	4,964	—	—	3,000
12/04	4,800	—	—	3,500
12/03	4,744	—	—	3,500
Annual Growth	3.8%	—	—	(0.7%)

Revenue History

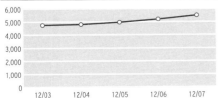

MediaNews Group

This company has part of the news media in its folds. MediaNews Group is one of the leading newspaper companies in the US with more than 60 daily papers serving markets in a dozen states. Its portfolio includes *The Denver Post, The Salt Lake Tribune*, and the *St. Paul Pioneer Press*, as well as Northern California newspapers the *Contra Costa Times* and the *San Jose Mercury News*. The papers boast a total circulation of about 2.5 million. In addition, MediaNews publishes about 100 non-daily newspapers and it operates a TV station in Anchorage, Alaska, along with four Texas radio stations. The company is owned by the families of vice chairman and CEO Dean Singleton and chairman Richard Scudder.

MediaNews has built its business through a series of acquisitions focused on creating newspaper clusters in specific markets, particularly in California, the Rocky Mountain region, and the Northeast. Several of its top papers are published through joint operating agency (JOA) agreements. *The Denver Post* is part of the Denver Newspaper Agency, a JOA with E. W. Scripps (owner of the *Rocky Mountain News*), while *The Salt Lake Tribune* is run under a JOA with The Deseret News Publishing Company (part of Deseret Management and owner of the *Deseret News*). In addition, the company has a 60% interest in a partnership with Gannett that operates newspapers in Texas, New Mexico, and Pennsylvania.

With the newspaper industry struggling, MediaNews sold a group of papers in Connecticut including the *Connecticut Post* to media giant Hearst. The disposal came a year after the company had acquired several newspapers including the *Monterey County Herald* and the *St. Paul Pioneer Press* from Hearst in exchange for a 30% stake in MediaNews' newspaper operations outside the San Francisco area. MediaNews and Hearst had joined together in 2006 to acquire those papers along with *San Jose Mercury News* and the *Contra Costa Times* from McClatchy.

The company has also been focused on expanding its digital media distribution operations to take advantage of increased ad spending online. It operates more than 70 Web sites in conjunction with its local papers. The company is also partnered with Yahoo's HotJobs to sell listings on the online classified company's site. The deal also allows the company to sell access to HotJobs' resume database.

EXECUTIVES

Chairman: Richard B. Scudder, age 95
Vice Chairman and CEO: William D. (Dean) Singleton, age 57, $1,260,625 pay
President: Joseph J. (Jody) Lodovic IV, age 47, $921,700 pay
EVP and Chief Marketing and Sales Officer: Mark J. Winkler, age 48
SVP New Business Development: Elizabeth A. (Liz) Gaier, age 43
SVP Operations: Anthony F. Tierno, age 63, $378,013 pay
SVP Circulation: Stephen M. (Steve) Hesse, age 60
VP and CFO: Ronald A. (Ron) Mayo, age 47
VP Human Resources: Charles M. Kamen, age 60
VP Sales: Michael R. (Mike) Petrak, age 50
Secretary: Patricia (Pat) Robinson, age 66
Treasurer: James L. McDougald, age 54
President and CEO, California Newspapers: Steven B. (Steve) Rossi, age 59

President and CEO, Los Angeles Newspaper Group: Edward R. (Ed) Moss, age 53
President, MediaNews Group Interactive: Oliver Knowlton, age 50
Auditors: Ernst & Young LLP

LOCATIONS

HQ: MediaNews Group, Inc.
  101 W. Colfax Ave., Ste. 1100, Denver, CO 80202
Phone: 303-954-6360   **Fax:** 303-954-6320
Web: www.medianewsgroup.com

PRODUCTS/OPERATIONS

Selected Operations

Newspapers
  Bennington Banner (Vermont)
  The Berkshire Eagle (Pittsfield, MA)
  Brattleboro Reformer (Vermont)
  Charleston Daily Mail (Charleston, WV)
  Daily Breeze (Torrance, CA)
  Daily News (Los Angeles)
  The Denver Post
  The Detroit News
  The Monterey County Herald (California)
  North Adams Transcript (Massachusetts)
  Press-Telegram (Long Beach, CA)
  St. Paul Pioneer Press
  The Salt Lake Tribune
  Sentinel & Enterprise (Fitchburg, MA)
  The Sun (Lowell, MA)
Other
  KLXK-FM (Breckenridge, TX)
  KROO-FM (Breckenridge, TX)
  KSWA-FM (Graham, TX)
  KTVA-TV (CBS; Anchorage, AK)
  KWKQ-FM (Graham, TX)

COMPETITORS

American City Business Journals
Freedom Communications
Gannett
Hearst Newspapers
McClatchy Company
New York Times
Philadelphia Media
Star Tribune
Tribune Company
Village Voice

HISTORICAL FINANCIALS
Company Type: Private

Income Statement
FYE: June 30

	REVENUE ($ mil.)	NET INCOME ($ mil.)	NET PROFIT MARGIN	EMPLOYEES
6/07	1,330	36	2.7%	12,700
6/06	836	1	0.1%	10,100
6/05	779	40	5.1%	10,000
6/04	754	28	3.7%	10,000
6/03	739	41	5.5%	10,700
Annual Growth	15.8%	(3.4%)	—	4.4%

2007 Year-End Financials

Debt ratio: —   Current ratio: —
Return on equity: 47.3%   Long-term debt ($ mil.): —
Cash ($ mil.): —

Net Income History

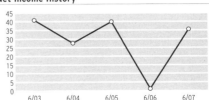

Medical Information Technology

Medical Information Technology (MEDITECH) prescribes a good dose of software to cure health care disorders. Founded in 1969, MEDITECH provides software and services for managing hospitals, ambulatory care centers, doctors' offices, long-term care facilities, nursing homes, and home health care agencies in North America and the UK. The company's software includes applications for patient identification and scheduling, patient care management, clinical information management, long-term and ambulatory care, behavioral health, and financial and reimbursement management. CEO Neil Pappalardo controls 37% of the company.

EXECUTIVES

Chairman and CEO: A. Neil Pappalardo, age 65, $1,060,921 pay
Vice Chairman: Lawrence A. (Larry) Polimeno, age 66, $680,921 pay
President and COO: Howard Messing, age 55, $814,921 pay
CFO, Treasurer, and Clerk: Barbara A. Manzolillo, age 55, $578,921 pay
SVP Product Development: Robert G. Gale, age 61
VP Client Service: Joanne Wood, age 54
VP Implementation: Steven B. (Steve) Koretz, age 55
VP Marketing: Hoda Sayed-Friel, age 49
VP Sales: Stuart N. (Stu) Lefthes, age 54, $592,921 pay
VP Technology: Christopher (Chris) Anschuetz, age 55
Marketing and Public Relations Contact: Paul Berthiaume
Auditors: Ernst & Young LLP

LOCATIONS

HQ: Medical Information Technology, Inc.
MEDITECH Circle, Westwood, MA 02090
Phone: 781-821-3000   **Fax:** 781-821-2199
Web: www.meditech.com

PRODUCTS/OPERATIONS

Selected Software Products

Ambulatory care applications
  Emergency department management
  Prescription management
Behavioral health applications
Clinical applications
  Anatomical pathology
  Blood bank
  Imaging and therapeutic services
  Laboratory
  Microbiology
  Pharmacy
Decision support applications
  Budgeting and forecasting
  Cost accounting
  Data archiving
  Data repository
  Executive support system
  Faxing
  Integrated communication system

Financial management applications
  Accounts payable
  Fixed assets
  General ledger
  Materials management
  Payroll/personnel
  Staffing and scheduling
Long-term care information system
Patient care management applications
  Patient care system
  Patient education suite
  Physician care manager
  Physician practice management
Patient identification and scheduling applications
  Case mix management
  Community-wide scheduling
  Enterprise patient index and medical records
  Operating room management
  Registration
Reimbursement applications
  Authorization and referral management
  Billing/accounts receivable

COMPETITORS

Alteer
AMICAS
CareCentric
Cerner
CPSI
Eclipsys
Health Management Systems
Healthvision
iSOFT Group
McKesson
Mediware
MedPlus
Misys Healthcare
NextGen
QuadraMed
Quality Systems
Siemens Healthcare
TriZetto

HISTORICAL FINANCIALS

Company Type: Private

Income Statement

FYE: December 31

	REVENUE ($ mil.)	NET INCOME ($ mil.)	NET PROFIT MARGIN	EMPLOYEES
12/07	376	89	23.5%	2,872
12/06	345	87	25.3%	2,566
12/05	305	78	25.5%	2,500
12/04	281	71	25.4%	2,100
12/03	271	67	24.9%	2,000
Annual Growth	8.6%	7.0%	—	9.5%

2007 Year-End Financials

Debt ratio: —
Return on equity: 21.4%
Cash ($ mil.): —
Current ratio: —
Long-term debt ($ mil.): —

Net Income History

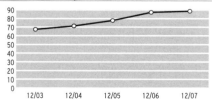

Medline Industries

When health care supplies are on the line, Medline Industries goes toe-to-toe with the bigger guns, selling more than 100,000 products. The family-owned company's catalog includes hospital furnishings, exam equipment, housekeeping supplies, and surgical gloves and garments. The firm manufactures and distributes health care products to customers including hospitals, extended care facilities, and home health providers. It also acts as a distributor for other manufacturers' products. In addition, Medline offers inventory and supply chain solutions for health care providers. Products are marketed by its more than 700 sales representatives through some 30 distribution centers in 20 countries.

The company manufactures a large number of the products it distributes; it also acts as a distributor for other products through partnerships with companies such as 3M. Medline also forms supply alliances with group hospital purchasing organizations such as Premier and Novation.

Medline continues to expand its product line through acquisitions, partnerships, and product innovations. In 2007 the company acquired the Curad first aid brand and related operations from Beiersdorf Inc.; it also launched a line of patient-lifting equipment. The following year Medline acquired Chester Packaging (formerly Chester Labs), a maker of liquid personal care, infection control, and diagnostic products.

In 2008 the company agreed to purchase the Carrington line of wound care products from DelSite, which is exiting the wound care market.

Owned by the Mills family, Medline traces its roots to Northwest Garment Factory, started by the current owners' great-grandfather in 1910.

EXECUTIVES

CEO: Charles N. (Charlie) Mills, age 46
COO: Jim Abrams
President: Andy Mills
SVP Corporate Sales: Tim Jacobson
VP Human Resources: Joseph Becker
VP National Accounts: Jack Hannemann
Group President, SPT, Anesthesia, OR: Tom Pistella
President, Dermal Management Systems: Jonathan Primer
President, Durable Medical Equipment Division: Dave Jacobs
President, Health Care National Accounts: Scott Sibigtroth
President, Medline Personal Care Division: Dan Love
President, General Line National Accounts: Kurt Krieghbaum
President, Operations: Bill Abington
President, Ready Care: Hunter Banks
President, Sales: Ray Swaback
Director Public Relations: Rebecca Hayne

LOCATIONS

HQ: Medline Industries, Inc.
1 Medline Place, Mundelein, IL 60060
Phone: 847-949-5500   **Fax:** 800-351-1512
Web: www.medline.com

PRODUCTS/OPERATIONS

Selected Products
Durable medical equipment (wheelchairs, beds, etc.)
Face masks
Gloves
Housekeeping
Incontinences
Isolation gowns
Prothrombin monitors
Surgery sterile (gloves, drapes, gowns)
Wound and skin care

Selected Corporate Programs
ACCESS
ACCESS O.R.
Medline Select
Patient-Home Direct
Physician-Office Direct
Prime Vendor
S.M.A.R.T.
Surgery Center Supply Management
Suture Control
TEXCAP
Truecost

COMPETITORS

3M Health Care
Bard
BD
Cardinal Health
Covidien
Hill-Rom
Hill-Rom Holdings
Invacare
Johnson & Johnson
Kimberly-Clark
Kinetic Concepts
McKesson
Owens & Minor
Patterson Companies
PSS World Medical
Sunrise Medical

HISTORICAL FINANCIALS

Company Type: Private

Income Statement

FYE: December 31

	REVENUE ($ mil.)	NET INCOME ($ mil.)	NET PROFIT MARGIN	EMPLOYEES
12/07	2,830	—	—	6,000
12/06	2,460	—	—	4,422
12/05	2,000	—	—	4,892
12/04	1,940	—	—	4,500
12/03	1,600	—	—	4,200
Annual Growth	15.3%	—	—	9.3%

Revenue History

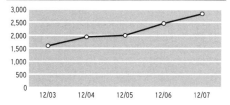

Meijer, Inc.

Meijer (pronounced "Meyer") is a giant of retailing in the Midwest. The company's huge grocery and general merchandise stores average 200,000 to 250,000 sq. ft. each (or about the size of four regular grocery stores) and stock about 120,000 items, including Meijer private-label products. Meijer operates about 180 locations; about half of its stores are in Michigan, while the rest are in Illinois, Indiana, Kentucky, and Ohio. Customers can choose from about 40 departments, including apparel, electronics, hardware, and toys. Most stores also sell gasoline, offer banking services, and have multiple in-store restaurants. Founder Hendrik Meijer opened his first store in 1934; the company is still family owned.

Although the discount superstore format is most often referred to in conjunction with its rival Wal-Mart, Meijer is its pioneer. But that hasn't stopped the world's #1 retailer from muscling in on Meijer's markets. Meijer is also facing increased pressure from warehouse club stores, drugstores, and supermarket chains, like Kroger, that are expanding in its markets.

The company's response has included cutting prices and renovating its stores. Indeed, to compete with the likes of Wal-Mart in the toy market, Meijer will cut prices on more than 300 toys for the 2008 holiday season. It also continues to grow. Meijer opened five stores in 2007 with seven more slated for the following year. Since 2000, Meijer has increased its presence in Illinois to about 15 stores, about a dozen of which are in Chicago's suburbs.

Late to the e-commerce party, Meijer in mid-2006 launched a specialty-foods shopping Web site offering some 40,000 hard-to-find items, including kosher, organic, and international foods. The following year it added general merchandise, including furniture, toys, and electronics to its Web offerings and now offers 100,000 products.

Meijer got into hot water in Michigan in 2008, when it was fined by the secretary of state for campaign law violations. The company was fined for various activities interfering with opposition to its planned big-box store in Acme Township.

HISTORY

Dutch immigrant and barber Hendrik Meijer owned a vacant space next to his barbershop in Greenville, Michigan. Because of the Depression, he couldn't rent it out. So in 1934 he bought $338.76 in merchandise on credit and started his own grocery store, Thrift Market, with the help of his wife, Gezina; son, Fred; and daughter, Johanna; he made $7 the first day. Meijer had 22 competitors in Greenville alone, but his dedication to low prices (he and Fred often traveled long distances to find bargains) attracted customers. In 1935, to encourage self-service, Meijer placed 12 wicker baskets at the front of the store and posted signs that read, "Take a basket. Help yourself."

A second store was opened in 1942. The company added four more in the 1950s. In 1962 Meijer — then with 14 stores — opened the first one-stop shopping Meijer Thrifty Acres store, similar to a hypermarket another operator had opened in Belgium a year earlier. By 1964, the year that Hendrik died and Fred took over, three of

these general merchandise stores were operating. The company entered Ohio in the late 1960s.

In the early 1980s Meijer bought 14 Twin Fair stores in Ohio and 10 in Cincinnati. But it sold the stores by 1987 after disappointing results. Meijer had greater success in Columbus, Ohio, where it opened one store that year and immediately captured 20% of the market. In 1988 the company began keeping most stores open 24 hours a day.

Meijer annihilated competitors in Dayton, Ohio, in 1991, when it opened four stores that year. The company entered the Toledo market in 1993 with four stores; after one year it had taken 11.5% of the market. A foray into the membership warehouse market was abandoned in 1993, just a few months after it began, when Meijer said it would close all seven SourceClubs in Michigan and Ohio.

The company entered Indiana in 1994, opening 16 stores in less than two years; it also reached an agreement with McDonald's to open restaurants in several stores. The first labor strike in Meijer's history hit four stores in Toledo that year, leading to pickets at 14 others. Union officials accused the company of using intimidation tactics by its hiring of large, uniformed men in flak jackets and combat boots as security guards. After nine weeks Meijer agreed to recognize the workers' newly attained union affiliation.

In 1995 the company opened 13 stores, including its first in Illinois. It reentered the Cincinnati market in 1996, announcing its opening of two new stores there by mailing 80,000 videos to residents. By the end of the year, Meijer had a total of five stores in Cincinnati and had entered Kentucky.

Meijer opened its first two stores in Louisville, Kentucky, in 1998. Meijer broke into the tough Chicago-area market with its first store in 1999.

The next year Meijer opened several "village-style" stores — scaled-down versions (about 155,000 sq. ft.) of its larger stores. Later in 2000 Meijer unveiled what it claimed was the largest superstore in North America. The 255,000-sq.-ft. behemoth (compared to a Wal-Mart Supercenter, which averages about 183,106 sq. ft.) features a gourmet coffee shop, a card shop, a bank open seven days a week, and restaurants serving pizza and sushi.

In February 2002 co-chairman Hank Meijer was named CEO, succeeding Jim McClean, who had run the company since 1999. The retailer launched a "reinvented superstore format" at six Dayton, Ohio-area stores in late 2002.

In 2003 Meijer eliminated about 350 jobs and opened two new stores. It also cut jobs — about 1,900 management positions — early the next year to become more efficient and competitive.

Larry Zigerelli was promoted from EVP of merchandising to president of the company in April 2005. He resigned in December citing personal reasons. Meijer opened about 10 stores in 2005. A year later, Meijer board member Mark Murray (formerly the president of Grand Valley State University) joined the company as president. (Co-CEOs Hank Meijer and Paul Boyer ran the grocery chain in the interim.) Boyer stepped down at the end of 2006, but remained on the executive board as vice chairman.

In 2007 the company launched a private-label organics brand in order to better compete with other supermarkets with similar offerings.

EXECUTIVES

Chairman Emeritus: Fred Meijer, age 84
Co-Chairman: Doug Meijer, age 50
Co-Chairman and CEO: Hendrik G. (Hank) Meijer,
  age 56
Vice Chairman: Paul Boyer, age 56
President and Director: Mark A. Murray, age 53
SVP, Finance and Administration, and CFO: Dan Webb
SVP, Human Resources and Government Relations:
  Brian Breslin
Group VP, Hardlines and Drug Store: Tim Lesneski
VP, Drug Store: Nat Love
VP, Human Resources: Karen Morris
VP, Merchandise Planning and Supply Chain:
  Tom Nakfoor
VP, Pharmacy Operations: Mike Major
VP, Real Estate: Mike Kinstle
Merchant Foods: Ralph Fischer
E-Commerce: Judith Clark
**Director, Marketing Strategy and Customer
  Relationship Management:** Michael Ross
Community Relations Manager: Steve VanWagoner
Senior Photo Buyer: Rob Shadowens

LOCATIONS

HQ: Meijer, Inc.
  2929 Walker Ave. NW, Grand Rapids, MI 49544
Phone: 616-453-6711   **Fax:** 616-791-2572
Web: www.meijer.com

2008 Stores

	No.
Michigan	93
Ohio	40
Indiana	27
Illinois	14
Kentucky	8
Total	**182**

PRODUCTS/OPERATIONS

Selected Meijer Store Departments

Apparel
Auto supplies
Bakery
Banking
Books
Bulk foods
Coffee shop
Computer software
Dairy
Delicatessen
Electronics
Floral
Food court
Gas station
Hardware
Health and beauty products
Home fashions
Jewelry
Lawn and garden
Music
Nutrition products
Paint
Pets and pet supplies
Pharmacy
Photo lab
Portrait studio
Produce
Service meat and seafood
Small appliances
Soup and salad bar
Sporting goods
Tobacco
Toys
Wall coverings
Wine

COMPETITORS

ALDI	Marsh Supermarkets
Busch's	Retail Ventures
Costco Wholesale	Roundy's Supermarkets
CVS Caremark	SAM'S CLUB
Dollar General	Schnuck Markets
Dominick's	Schottenstein Stores
Family Dollar Stores	Spartan Stores
Giant Eagle	SUPERVALU
Home Depot	Target
IGA	Walgreen
Kmart	Wal-Mart
Kohl's	Whole Foods
Kroger	

HISTORICAL FINANCIALS

Company Type: Private

Income Statement

FYE: January 31

	ESTIMATED REVENUE ($ mil.)	NET INCOME ($ mil.)	NET PROFIT MARGIN	EMPLOYEES
1/07	13,900	—	—	67,000
1/06	13,900	—	—	70,000
1/05	11,900	—	—	75,000
1/04	11,900	—	—	75,000
1/03	10,900	—	—	83,402
Annual Growth	**6.3%**	**—**	**—**	**(5.3%)**

Revenue History

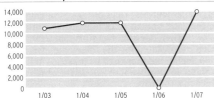

Melaleuca, Inc.

Idaho may be known for potatoes, but *Melaleuca alternifolia* — better known as the tea tree — is Melaleuca's preferred flora. Founded in 1985 to market a tea tree oil formulation called Melaleuca Oil, the Idaho Falls firm sells personal care products, cosmetics, household cleaning supplies, and vitamins directly to consumers through a network of sales representatives. Tea tree oil is a powerful antiseptic and antifungal agent used for skin care, as well as the treatment of a variety of ailments, insect bites, boils, and wounds. Melaleuca now sells more than 300 products, many of which are environmentally friendly and derived from natural ingredients, including tea tree oil.

The company, which operates two manufacturing centers in eastern Idaho, sells its products throughout Asia/Pacific, Europe, and North America. Melaleuca is rapidly expanding its international operations.

Charismatic CEO Frank VanderSloot, a devout Mormon with 14 children, encourages sales representatives to engage in a frugal lifestyle and supports causes that espouse traditional family values. The company offers Internet and phone service, health savings plans, discounted travel, mortgages, and other services to sales representatives.

EXECUTIVES

President and CEO: Frank L. VanderSloot, age 59
President, International and COO: McKay Christensen
CFO and Treasurer: Thomas K. (Tom) Knutson
SVP Sales: Jeff Hill
VP and General Counsel: Kenneth J. Sheppard
Secretary and Director: Allen Ball
Human Resources: Jann Nielson
Director Corporate Relations: Damond R. Watkins

LOCATIONS

HQ: Melaleuca, Inc.
  3910 S. Yellowstone Hwy., Idaho Falls, ID 83402
Phone: 208-522-0700   **Fax:** 208-535-2362
Web: www.melaleuca.com

PRODUCTS/OPERATIONS

Selected Products

Health
Daily Needs
Heart Health
Weight Management
Body
Bath and Shower
Hair Care
Lotions
Perfume
Shaving
Sun Care
Beauty
Accessories
Eyes
Lips
Nails
Home
Laundry
Cleansers
Pet Care
Dish Care
Kids
Accessories
Bath-Time Fun
Oral Hygiene
Children's Health
Medicine Cabinet
Acne Treatment System
Dry Skin Care
First Aid
Heartburn Relief
Sun Care
Business Tools
Brochures and flyers
Forms
Logo Merchandise
Product Training and Info
Publications
Tools for Rapid Growth

COMPETITORS

Amway
Avon
drugstore.com
Gaiam
Mary Kay
Pampered Chef
PartyLite Worldwide
Tupperware

HISTORICAL FINANCIALS
Company Type: Private

Income Statement
FYE: December 31

	REVENUE ($ mil.)	NET INCOME ($ mil.)	NET PROFIT MARGIN	EMPLOYEES
12/07	859	—	—	2,400
12/06	795	—	—	—
12/05	719	—	—	—
Annual Growth	9.3%	—	—	—

Revenue History

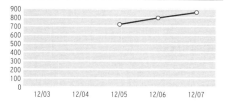

Memphis Grizzlies

The sweetest honey for these Grizzlies is an NBA championship. The Memphis Grizzlies professional basketball team joined the National Basketball Association as an expansion team in 1995. Originally located in Vancouver and controlled by Arthur Griffiths (who also owned the Vancouver Canucks hockey franchise), the team formed the new Canadian wing of the league along with the Toronto Raptors. The franchise was acquired by Chicago billionaire Michael Heisley in 2000 and relocated to Tennessee the following year. Fans have been filling more seats at home games due to the Grizzlies recent success in reaching the playoffs and the opening of the FedExForum in 2004.

Despite his relatively short tenure as a franchise owner, Heisley has been looking to sell his 70% stake in the franchise, though bidders have been few and far between. He had struck an agreement in 2006 with a group led by Brian Davis, a former Duke University basketball standout, that would have valued the Grizzlies at about $350 million, though that deal later fell through.

Heisley originally acquired control of the team for $160 million. (He has no ownership in the $300 million, publicly financed facility.)

EXECUTIVES

Majority Owner: Michael Heisley Sr.
President of Basketball Operations: Jerry West, age 70
Assistant General Manager: Tom Penn
Head Coach: Mike Fratello, age 57
SVP Business Operations: Mike Golub
SVP Broadcast: Randy Stephens
SVP Corporate Partnerships: Mike Redlick
SVP Ticket Sales and Services: Mike Levy
VP, Corporate Partnerships: Chad Bolen
VP Finance: Todd Kobus
Senior Director of Marketing Communications: Marla Taner
Director of Human Resources: Christy M. Haynes
Director of Player Personnel: Tony Barone, age 56
Director of Scouting: Tony Barone Jr., age 31

LOCATIONS

HQ: Memphis Grizzlies
191 Beale St., Memphis, TN 38103
Phone: 901-888-4667   **Fax:** 901-205-1235
Web: www.nba.com/grizzlies

The Memphis Grizzlies play at the 18,165-seat capacity FedExForum in Memphis.

COMPETITORS

Dallas Mavericks
Houston Rockets
New Orleans Hornets
San Antonio Spurs

HISTORICAL FINANCIALS
Company Type: Private

Income Statement
FYE: June 30

	REVENUE ($ mil.)	NET INCOME ($ mil.)	NET PROFIT MARGIN	EMPLOYEES
6/07	98	—	—	—
6/06	101	—	—	—
6/05	98	—	—	—
6/04	75	—	—	—
6/03	63	—	—	—
Annual Growth	11.7%	—	—	—

Revenue History

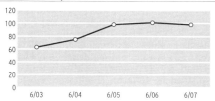

Menard, Inc.

If sticks and stones break bones, what can two-by-fours and two-inch nails do? That is what Menard is wondering now that its biggest rivals (#1 home improvement giant The Home Depot and #2 Lowe's) are hammering away at its home turf. The third-largest home improvement chain in the US, Menard has about 240 stores in Illinois, Indiana, Iowa, Michigan, Minnesota, Missouri, Nebraska, North and South Dakota, Ohio, and Wisconsin. The stores sell home improvement products, such as floor coverings, hardware, millwork, paint, and tools. Unlike competitors, all the company's stores have full-service lumberyards. Menard is owned by president and CEO John Menard, who founded the company in 1972.

Although Menard outlets are typically smaller than those of Home Depot, they offer a similar selection of products by building large warehouses adjacent to stores and then quickly restocking merchandise when it's sold. The company's products are laid out on easy-to-reach, supermarket-styled shelves. To help keep expenses low and prices cheap, Menard's Midwest Manufacturing (MM) division makes some of its merchandise, including doors and trusses. MM operates about a half a dozen plants in five Midwestern states that

make metal roofing and siding, doors, decking, trusses, and other building materials.

The company is increasing its average store size to more than 220,000 sq. ft. It has opened its largest store ever — 250,000 sq. ft. — in Minnesota and is expanding 30-40 stores. Most of the the company's new stores will be more than 200,000 sq. ft. Besides stocking hardware and building supplies these new megastores will include garden centers and sell a large range of home appliances.

In what may be a first for a home improvement chain, Menard has gotten into the business of residential real estate development with several large subdivisions either under construction or in the planning stages in Indiana and Illinois. The developments, situated on land near Menard stores, create a potential customer base among new homeowners and local builders.

In addition to billionaire founder John Menard, other family members are engaged in the chain's everyday operations. John Menard also owns Team Menard, an Indy car-racing team.

HISTORY

John Menard was the oldest of eight children on a Wisconsin dairy farm. To pay for attending the University of Wisconsin at Eau Claire, he and some fellow college students built pole barns in the late 1950s. Learning that other builders had trouble finding lumber outlets open on the weekends, Menard began buying wood in bulk and selling it to them. He added other supplies in 1960 and sold his construction business in 1970 as building supply revenues became his chief source of income.

He founded Menard in 1972 as the do-it-yourself craze was beginning, but he wanted an operation run more like mass merchandiser Target, with easy-to-reach shelves, wide aisles, and tile floors rather than the cold, cumbersome layout used by lumberyards. To realize that concept, Menard built warehouses and stockrooms behind the stores so he could restock merchandise quickly.

Menard's vision worked, and he began building his Midwestern empire, often acquiring abandoned retail sites that were inexpensive and in good locations. By 1986 Menard was in Iowa, Minnesota, North and South Dakota, and Wisconsin, and by 1990 it had 46 stores. In the early 1990s Menard began enlarging its operations to serve the ever-growing number of stores, opening a huge warehouse and distribution center and a manufacturing facility that made doors, Formica countertops, and other products. Menard entered Nebraska in 1990 and opened its first store in Chicago the next year. By 1992 there were more than 60 stores.

That year Menard made the National Enquirer with a story about the firing of a store manager who had built a wheelchair-accessible home for his 11-year-old daughter with spina bifida, violating a company theft-prevention policy forbidding store managers to build their own homes. The company insisted that the man was fired in part because of poor work performance.

Menard continued to expand to new areas, operating stores in Indiana and Michigan by 1992. As it continued expanding in the Chicago area, it offered varying store formats, ranging from a full line of building materials to smaller Menards Hardware Plus stores. By 1994 Menard had 85 stores, many bigger than 100,000 sq. ft.

In 1995 and 1996 the company was plagued with lawsuits filed by customers charging false arrest and imprisonment for shoplifting. An on-duty police officer apprehending a shoplifting suspect at a store was even stopped and searched.

Competition also heated up during that time. The Home Depot's push into the Midwest — including opening several stores directly across the street from Menard — spurred Menard to fight back by lowering prices and opening nearly 40 stores. The fight forced smaller chains like Handy Andy out of business.

In 1997 Menard and his company were fined $1.7 million after dumping bags of toxic ash from its manufacturing facility at residential trash pick-up sites rather than at properly regulated outlets (it had been fined for similar violations in 1989 and 1994). In response to a price war initiated by Home Depot, in 1998 Menard dropped sales prices by 10%.

In 1999 competitor Lowe's began moving into Menard's biggest market, Chicago. Menard began opening larger stores in 2000 (about 162,000 sq. ft., or some 74,000 sq. ft. bigger than the older stores). In 2001 it began beefing up its lines of home appliances, adding more washers, dryers, dishwashers, refrigerators, and ranges.

In January 2005 the Internal Revenue Service ruled the company owed $5.9 million in back taxes and fines because it paid John Menard too high a salary in 1998.

EXECUTIVES

President and CEO: John R. Menard Jr., age 68
COO: Scott Collette
VP Merchandise: Russ Raditke
CIO: Dave Wagner
Payroll Manager: Terri Jain
General Counsel: Rob Geske

LOCATIONS

HQ: Menard, Inc.
4777 Menard Dr., Eau Claire, WI 54703
Phone: 715-876-5911   **Fax:** 715-876-2868
Web: www.menards.com

PRODUCTS/OPERATIONS

Selected Operations
Menards (home improvement stores)
Midwest Manufacturing (product manufacturing)

Selected Departments
Appliances
Building materials
Electrical (wiring, lighting)
Floor coverings
Hardware
Lumberyard
Millwork (doors, cabinetry, molding)
Plumbing
Seasonal (Christmas, lawn, garden)
Tools
Wall coverings (wallpaper, paint)

COMPETITORS

84 Lumber	Seigle's
Ace Hardware	Sherwin-Williams
Carter Lumber	Stock Building Supply
Do it Best	Sutherland Lumber
Fastenal	True Value
Home Depot	Wal-Mart
Lowe's	WinWholesale
Sears	

Merisant Worldwide

With two major and some 18 regional brands and sales in some 90 countries, Merisant Worldwide has more than just an Equal share of the sweetener market. Fueled by the success of Canderel in Europe, Africa, and the Middle East, and Equal in NorthAmerica and the Asia/Pacific region, Merisant controls about one-fifth of the worldwide aspartame market. The Canderel and Equal brands of tabletop sweeteners account for 85% of the company's sales. Merisant's customers include retail grocery stores, pharmacies, food wholesalers, and food service distributors and operators.

In 2008 Merisant introduced PureVia brand tabletop sweetener. The product's active sweetening ingredient is Reb A (made by and supplied to Merisant by PureCircle), which is derived from the stevia plant. (Extracts of the stevia plant are said to be 200 times sweeter than sugar.) Concurrent with PureVia's introduction, Merisant partnered with PepsiCo, which will own the trademark for and use the sweetener in its beverages. Merisant's Whole Earth Sweetener subsidiary will distribute it for use as a table-top sweetener.

The company's largest challenge comes from Tate & Lyle's Splenda sweetener (made with sucralose), which received FDA approval in 1998 — nearly 20 years after Merisant's aspartame sweeteners. Merisant claims marketing of the rival Splenda product is misleading and in 2004 entered into a lawsuit to straighten the whole thing out. Tate & Lyle countered with a lawsuit of its own, filed by Johnson & Johnson subsidiary McNeil Nutritionals, which markets Splenda. The suits were confidentially settled in 2007.

However, Splenda remains Merisant's chief competition — during the years 2002 to 2007, Splenda's US retail grocery market share increased from some 15% to 61% and has surpassed that of Equal to become the #1 premium low-calorie sweetener in the US. Merisant has countered by promoting new uses for its products, increasing its pace of product innovation, and to begin offering private-label low-calorie sweeteners to its retail and foodservice customers.

The company did win a judicial victory of sorts, when, in 2007, a French court awarded Merisant France $54,000 in damages and ordered McNeil to amend its advertising claims in that country (*"Because it comes from sugar sucralose tastes like sugar"* and *"With sucralose: Comes from sugar and tastes like sugar"*) since they were found to violate French consumer-protection laws because they might lead consumers to believe that Splenda is a naturally occurring sugar, when, in fact, it is a synthetic compound.

A group of investors (including Pegasus Capital Advisors, MSD Capital, and Brener International) formed the company in 2000 when they bought the tabletop sweetener operations of biotech giant Monsanto. Monsanto's NutraSweet brand aspartame business — a supplier to Merisant — was later sold to J.W. Childs Associates. Pegasus Capital Advisors owns almost 89% of Merisant.

EXECUTIVES

Chairman, President, and CEO: Paul R. Block, age 51, $400,000 pay
EVP Global Commercial Director: Lee Van Syckle, $220,000
VP Business Development and General Counsel: Jonathan W. Cole, age 44, $275,000 pay pay
VP Marketing and Innovation: Sanjay Holay, age 51
VP Finance Planning and Analysis: Brian L. Alsvig, age 38
VP Finance Controller: Julie P. Wool
Global Director Human Resources: Carrie Murphy, age 49
Director Global IT: Keith Halvorsen
VP Global Operations: Angelo Di Benedetto, age 44
Auditors: BDO Seidman, LLP

LOCATIONS

HQ: Merisant Worldwide, Inc.
33 N. Dearborn St., Ste. 200, Chicago, IL 60602
Phone: 312-840-6000   **Fax:** 312-840-5541
Web: www.merisant.com

2007 Sales

	$ mil.	% of total
Europe, Africa & the Middle East	116.2	40
North America	115.5	40
Latin America	33.3	11
Asia/Pacific	25.2	9
Total	**290.2**	**100**

PRODUCTS/OPERATIONS

Selected Brands
Canderel (Belgium, France, Hungary, Mexico, the Netherlands, Portugal, South Africa, UK)
Chuker (Argentina)
Equal (Australia, Canada, Mexico, New Zealand, Puerto Rico, South Africa, US)
EqualSweet (Argentina, Mexico)
Misura (Italy)
Mivida (Italy)
PureVita (US)
Sucaryl (Argentina, Mexico)
Sweet Simplicity (US)
SweetMate (Mexico, US)

COMPETITORS

ADM
Ajinomoto
Alberto-Culver
Amalgamated Sugar
American Crystal Sugar
C&H Sugar
Cumberland Packing
Danisco A/S
Florida Crystals
Imperial Sugar
Johnson & Johnson
M A Patout
McNeil Ltd.
Michigan Sugar Company
Nippon Beet Sugar
NutraSweet
Südzucker
Sara Lee Food & Beverage
Sterling Sugars
Sugar Cane Growers Cooperative of Florida
Tate & Lyle
Tate & Lyle Ingredients
U.S. Sugar
Western Sugar Cooperative

HISTORICAL FINANCIALS

Company Type: Private

Income Statement

FYE: December 31

	REVENUE ($ mil.)	NET INCOME ($ mil.)	NET PROFIT MARGIN	EMPLOYEES
12/07	290	(13)	—	430
12/06	294	(52)	—	438
12/05	305	(17)	—	500
Annual Growth	(2.5%)	—	—	(7.3%)

2007 Year-End Financials

Debt ratio: —
Return on equity: —
Cash ($ mil.): —

Current ratio: —
Long-term debt ($ mil.): 540

Net Income History

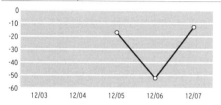

	12/03	12/04	12/05	12/06	12/07
0					
-10					
-20					
-30					
-40					
-50					
-60					

Merrill Corporation

Document services company Merrill is no relation to financial services giant Merrill Lynch, but the companies do share an interest in SEC paperwork. Through its transactional and compliance services segment, Merrill provides printing, distribution, and electronic processing of SEC filings and other documents related to corporate transactions. Merrill also handles documents used in litigation and in direct marketing. Customers come from the financial services, insurance, legal, and real estate industries. The company operates from more than 70 offices in the US and about 15 in other countries. Affiliates of DLJ Merchant Banking Partners, a unit of investment firm Credit Suisse, control a 58% stake in Merrill.

After acquiring litigation support provider WordWave in January 2006, Merrill reorganized its operations into four segments: legal solutions, marketing and communication solutions, transactional and compliance services, and other communications services.

The company has diversified beyond its traditional printing business and positioned itself as a business process outsourcing company. It sees growth opportunities in its legal solutions offerings, which include managing electronic data discovery, and in Merrill Datasite, which provides online hosting of documents related to mergers and acquisitions. In addition, Merrill is expanding geographically. In 2007 the company, through its WordWave subsidiary, acquired Sydney-based ComputerReporters, a provider of real-time and private reporting services to legal, corporate, and government clients. The acquisition followed WordWave's 2006 purchase of another Australian firm, Melbourne-based Court Recording Services, which does business in Australia and Hong Kong and offers similar services.

The company filed to go public in early 2006 but withdrew the offering in September 2007, citing adverse market conditions. Had the company completed the IPO it would have been Merrill's second go-round as a public company. The company's stock was publicly traded from 1986 to 1999, when Merrill went private in a recapitalization backed by DLJ, then known as Donaldson, Lufkin & Jenrette.

Chairman and CEO John Castro, who has served as CEO since 1984, owns 17% of Merrill.

EXECUTIVES

Chairman and CEO: John W. Castro
President and COO: Rick R. Atterbury
EVP and CFO: Robert H. (Bob) Nazarian, age 55
EVP and CTO: John R. Stolle, age 58
EVP General Counsel: Steven J. (Steve) Machov
EVP, Human Resources: Brenda J. Vale, age 43
EVP Global Marketing: Craig P. Levinsohn
Controller and Chief Accounting Officer: Kathy Miller
Treasurer: Dale S. Kopel, age 42
Auditors: PricewaterhouseCoopers LLP

LOCATIONS

HQ: Merrill Corporation
1 Merrill Cir., St. Paul, MN 55108
Phone: 651-646-4501 **Fax:** 651-646-5332
Web: www.merrillcorp.com

PRODUCTS/OPERATIONS

Selected Products and Services

Legal solutions
 Compliance and due diligence database
 Electronic discovery
 Litigation support
 Securities law database
Marketing and communications solutions
 Brand identity management
 Corporate identity materials
 Customer communications and packaged direct
  market programs
 Direct mail marketing collateral
Transaction and compliance services
 Document composition, filing, and printing
 Document hosting
 EDGAR filings
Other communications services
 Captioning
 Language translation
 Specialty printing

COMPETITORS

Applied Discovery
Bowne
Diebold
Harte-Hanks
IKON
IntraLinks
Kroll Ontrack
Lionbridge
Pitney Bowes
R.R. Donnelley
St Ives
Williams Lea
Workflow Management
Xerox

Metaldyne Corporation

You won't find much metal in a car's cockpit these days. To find Metaldyne's products, look under the hood or under the car. Metaldyne operates through three divisions: Chassis (ball joints, control arms, knuckles), Driveline (automatic transmission valve bodies, clutch modules, differential assemblies), and Engine (exhaust components and systems, powder metal parts, pulleys). Major customers include leading automakers such as Chrysler, Ford, GM, and Toyota, as well as suppliers like BorgWarner, Delphi, and Magna. Metaldyne is a subsidiary of Japan's Asahi Tec, a maker of aluminum and ductile automotive components, wheels, and electric power equipment.

Asahi Tec, which is controlled by New York investment concern Ripplewood Holdings LLC, acquired Metaldyne in 2007. The deal was valued at about $1.2 billion and the assumption of $824 million in debt. The joining of Metaldyne and Asahi Tec gives both companies better access to each other's home markets, and their combined efforts will provide for a more competitive footprint in Europe.

Since the acquisition, Asahi Tec has been working with Metaldyne to pay down debt and increase efficiency. Part of those efforts included the closure of facilities in Greenville, North Carolina, and Farmington Hills, Michigan, as well as the opening of a new facility in China. Asahi Tec has also worked to consolidate several corporate functions to eliminate redundancies.

Metaldyne continued to adjust its capacity in response to lower vehicle sales in North America, closing a third US-based manufacturing plant in 2008 and transferring the production lines to other facilities. It also plans to sell its Middleville, Michigan, and Niles, Illinois, facilities. Between 2005 and 2008, the company has reduced the number of its US manufacturing plants from 23 to 14. With 12 plants in Europe and 16 plants in Asia (including 13 that were owned by Asahi Tec already), Metaldyne has more equally divided its manufacturing operations geographically. Also in 2008 the company agreed to sell its GLO SrL operation in Italy to SKF.

Private equity firm Heartland Industrial Partners, which controlled Metaldyne before it was acquired by Asahi Tec, formed the company through the consolidation of MascoTech, Simpson Industries, and Global Metal Technologies.

EXECUTIVES

Chairman and CEO: Thomas A. (Tom) Amato
President and COO: Thomas V. (Tom) Chambers
CFO and Corporate Controller: Terry Iwasaki
EVP Human Resources and Metaldyne University:
 Kimberly A. (Kim) Kovac
VP Engineering, Chassis North America: Tom Worswick
VP Engineering and Sales, Powertrain Europe:
 Juergen C. Depp
VP Corporate Communications: Majorie (Marge) Sorge
VP Global Purchasing, Quality, and North American Sales: Linda Theisen
VP, Sales and Engineering, Asia: James (Jim) Hudak
VP Sales, Chassis North America:
 Christon (Chris) Franks
VP Sales and Engineering, Sintered Products:
 George Lanni
Auditors: KPMG LLP

LOCATIONS

HQ: Metaldyne Corporation
47603 Halyard Dr., Plymouth, MI 48170
Phone: 734-207-6200   **Fax:** 734-207-6500
Web: www.metaldyne.com

PRODUCTS/OPERATIONS

COMPETITORS

American Axle	Hayes Lemmerz
Delphi Corp.	Neapco LLC
EaglePicher Hillsdale	Visteon
GKN	ZF Friedrichshafen

HISTORICAL FINANCIALS

Company Type: Private

Income Statement

FYE: Sunday nearest March 31

	REVENUE ($ mil.)	NET INCOME ($ mil.)	NET PROFIT MARGIN	EMPLOYEES
3/08	1,842	(256)	—	6,300
3/07*	473	(92)	—	6,300
12/06	1,849	(181)	—	6,600
12/05	1,887	(262)	—	8,000
12/04	2,004	(28)	—	8,000
Annual Growth	(2.1%)	—	—	(5.8%)

*Fiscal year change

Net Income History

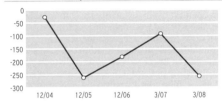

	12/04	12/05	12/06	3/07	3/08

Metro-Goldwyn-Mayer

The name is Mayer. Metro-Goldwyn-Mayer (MGM). The firm that runs MGM Studios and United Artists (UA) is the home of the valuable James Bond franchise. MGM makes and distributes movies (*The Nanny Diaries*) and TV shows (*Stargate Atlantis*) through MGM Studios, UA, and MGM Television; and DVDs through MGM Home Entertainment. Its MGM Networks' cable, satellite, and other channels distribute MGM titles. MGM houses one of the largest post-1948 film libraries in the world with some 4,000 titles — including the Bond and Pink Panther series as well as hits such as *Rain Man* and *Rocky*. It relies heavily on its library to generate revenue. MGM is owned by a consortium of investors led by Sony Corporation of America.

MGM has a distribution deal with Twentieth Century Fox Home Entertainment to distribute its movie library on video and DVD. In 2007 MGM adopted a strategy of focusing more on distributing films made by other studios.

In 2007 MGM had planned to emphasize its relationship with UA; the subsidiary had made a 2006 production partnership with Tom Cruise and Paula Wagner (Cruise's business partner at the time), in order to give MGM a boost with-some new star power. Cruise was no doubt happy to join UA after being booted from Paramount by Sumner Redstone in 2006. After the deal was sealed, in 2007 UA was enhanced with $500 million in financing from Merrill Lynch.

However, Wagner and Cruise failed to revitalize the studio; UA's sole release in 2007 — *Lions for Lambs* — flopped at the box office. Wagner subsequently left UA in 2008, while Cruise maintains his relationship with the company. The significantly slimmed down subsidiary is the subject of much speculation, as Cruise's role will not shift to that of a studio executive, and MGM seems unlikely to hire a successor for Wagner.

MGM has been expanding in other areas of the business. In 2008 the company announced plans to join Viacom and Lions Gate Entertainment in a joint venture to launch a premium pay TV channel that will directly compete with HBO, Showtime, and Starz. In addition, MGM has created a new-media division, MGM Worldwide Digital Media, to oversee the company's digital-distribution strategy.

Providence Equity Partners owns 29% of MGM; Texas Pacific Group owns 21%, Comcast Corporation and Sony each own 20%, and DLJ Merchant Banking Partners (part of CSFB Private Equity) owns 7%. Quadrangle Group is another shareholder (3%). Former owner billionaire Kirk Kerkorian had bought MGM three times since the late 1960s, most recently in 1996. Kerkorian had frequently tried to sell MGM to a variety of buyers including NBC, Pixar, and Time Warner. Eventually he sold it to the investment group made up of Sony and its equity partners, who bought the company for $4.8 billion (including $2 billion of MGM debt) in 2005.

HISTORY

Russian emigrant Louis B. Mayer started showing movies in a run-down theater outside Boston in 1907. After obtaining the New England distribution rights to D.W. Griffith's highly successful *Birth of a Nation* (1915), Mayer was flush with cash and left the theater business to start producing movies in Los Angeles. He founded Louis B. Mayer Pictures and began funding his own productions in 1918.

Theater chain owner Marcus Loew bought Metro Pictures in 1919. Frustrated with the lack of quality films coming from Metro, Loew proposed to buy Goldwyn Studios. Mayer wanted in on the deal and convinced Loew to make it a three-way merger. Metro-Goldwyn-Mayer was born in 1924, and Louis B. Mayer was head of the studio. Mayer ruled MGM with an iron fist and became the most powerful man in Hollywood during the 1930s and 1940s, guiding a firmament of stars including Clark Gable, Greta Garbo, and Judy Garland through a multitude of prestigious films such as *Ninotchka, The Wizard of Oz,* and *Gone With The Wind.*

After WWII, federal antitrust action forced movie companies to sell their theater chains. Despite successes such as *Singin' in the Rain,* MGM struggled. Mayer resigned under pressure in 1951 and died in 1957. By the end of the 1960s, MGM was faltering, while rival United

Artists (UA) found itself prospering with the emergence of its James Bond series (*Dr. No,* 1962) and five best picture winners in the 1960s.

Financier Kirk Kerkorian bought MGM in 1970, sold off many of its assets, and used the MGM name and lion logo for a new Las Vegas casino, the MGM Grand. Film production slowed to a crawl in the 1970s, and UA bought MGM's distribution rights in 1973. But UA's success collapsed after the box-office disaster *Heaven's Gate,* and MGM swooped in and purchased UA and its 900 titles, including the coveted James Bond franchise, in 1981 for $380 million.

The new MGM/UA was only five years old when Kerkorian sold it to Ted Turner, who promptly sold most of the studio assets and the MGM logo back to Kerkorian for $780 million that same year. Pathé (then led by Giancarlo Paretti) bought what was left of MGM in 1990, but by 1992 Crédit Lyonnais foreclosed and took control.

In 1996 the French bank put the studio on the block. That year Kerkorian (for a third time) and a group led by MGM chairman Frank Mancuso and Australian broadcaster Seven Network bought MGM with a winning $1.3 billion bid.

The company went public in 1997 and focused on bulking up its catalog of movies. It paid $573 million, including debt, for the 2,200-title Metromedia library.

The next year Kerkorian bought out Seven Network's 25% interest. Mancuso was replaced by president Alex Yemenidjian in 1999, and former Universal Pictures executive Chris McGurk became vice chairman and COO.

MGM also bought PolyGram's library of films from Seagram that year and won a crucial court battle with Sony Pictures Entertainment to maintain exclusive rights to James Bond. Continuing the shakeup, MGM restructured United Artists into a specialty film division.

In 2005 Kerkorian, yet again, sold MGM to a consortium of investors led by Sony Corporation of America (the other partners included Comcast, Texas Pacific Group, Providence Equity Partners, and DLJ Merchant Banking Partners). Yemenidjian and McGurk left the company following the deal. Former CFO Dan Taylor took over as president.

The company later that year named a new chairman and CEO, former Lionsgate and SBS Broadcasting executive Harry Sloan.

EXECUTIVES

Chairman and CEO: Harry E. Sloan
SEVP: Charles Cohen
EVP and CFO: Steve Hendry
EVP Corporate Communications: Jeff Pryor
EVP Consumer Products and Location Based Entertainment: Travis Rutherford
EVP Digital Distribution: Douglas A. (Doug) Lee
EVP, Secretary, and General Counsel: Scott Packman
EVP, General Manager, Home Entertainment: Blake Thomas
EVP MGM Networks: Bruce Tuchman
EVP Business and Legal Affairs: Ron Sufrin
EVP Worldwide Television Distribution: Joe Patrick
EVP Production: Cale Boyter
Chairperson, Worldwide Motion Picture Group: Mary Parent
President, Theatrical Marketing: Perry Stahman
President, MGM Entertainment Business Group and MGM On Stage: Darcie Denkert
President, Domestic Theatrical Distribution: Clark Woods
Co-President, Worldwide Television: Jim Packer
Co-President, Worldwide Television: Gary Marenzi
Manager Public Relations: Theo Dumont
Auditors: Ernst & Young LLP

HQ: Metro-Goldwyn-Mayer Inc.
    10250 Constellation Blvd., Los Angeles, CA 90067
Phone: 310-449-3000   **Fax:** 310-449-8857
Web: www.mgm.com

PRODUCTS/OPERATIONS

Selected Films

Annie Hall (1977)
The Apartment (1960)
Barbershop (2002)
Be Cool (2005)
Dances with Wolves (1990)
Gone With the Wind (1939)
In the Heat of the Night (1967)
James Bond (franchise)
Legally Blonde (2001)
Marty (1955)
Midnight Cowboy (1969)
Miss Potter (2006)
Mister Brooks (2007)
The Nanny Diaries (2007)
Pink Panther (franchise)
Platoon (1986)
Rain Man (1988)
Rebecca (1940)
Rocky (franchise)
The Silence of the Lambs (1991)
West Side Story (1961)
The Wizard of Oz (1939)

Selected Operations

MGM Consumer Products
MGM Distribution
MGM Home Entertainment
MGM Interactive (video games)
MGM Music (soundtracks)
MGM Networks
MGM Studios
MGM Television Entertainment
MGM Worldwide Television Distribution
United Artists

COMPETITORS

Disney Studios
Fox Filmed Entertainment
Lionsgate
Lucasfilm
Paramount Pictures
Universal Studios
Warner Bros.

HISTORICAL FINANCIALS

Company Type: Private

Income Statement

FYE: December 31

	ESTIMATED REVENUE ($ mil.)	NET INCOME ($ mil.)	NET PROFIT MARGIN	EMPLOYEES
12/06	1,460	—	—	400
12/05	1,430	—	—	445
Annual Growth	2.1%	—	—	(10.1%)

Revenue History

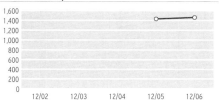

| | 12/02 | 12/03 | 12/04 | 12/05 | 12/06 |

Metromedia Company

Metromedia once had a lot of irons in a lot of fires but is juggling fewer and fewer. The holding company's units include Metromedia Restaurant Group, which owns or franchises Ponderosa and Bonanza steak restaurants; Metromedia Power, which offers electricity brokering service to businesses; and Metromedia Energy, an independent energy marketer. Metromedia Energy delivers more than 20 billion cu. ft. per year of commercial and industrial natural gas to customers in the Northeast, Midwest, and Mid-Atlantic. In recent years the company has divested many of its assets including telecommunications ventures in Europe and the former Soviet Union. Chairman John Kluge controls about 20% of Metromedia.

Metromedia sold its stake in Metromedia International Group, a holding company with interests in telecommunications ventures in Eastern Europe and the former Soviet Union, to Caucus-Com Ventures in 2007.

Two of the company's restaurant chains, Bennigan's Grill & Tavern and Steak & Ale, were forced to file for Chapter 7 bankruptcy in 2008 due to mounting losses. About 150 company-owned Bennigan's units and almost 60 Steak & Ale units (operated through S&A Restaurant Corp.) were closed; the Bennigan's brand and franchising rights were sold to Atlanta-based private equity firm Atalaya Capital Management. The chain had more than 150 franchised units still operating.

HISTORY

German immigrant John Kluge, born in 1914, came to Detroit at age eight with his mother and stepfather. He later worked at the Ford assembly line. At Columbia University he studied economics and (to the chagrin of college administrators) poker, building a tidy sum with his winnings by graduation. Kluge worked in Army intelligence during WWII. After the war he bought WGAY radio in Silver Spring, Maryland, and went on to buy and sell other small radio stations.

Kluge began to diversify, entering the wholesale food business in the mid-1950s. In 1959 he purchased control of Metropolitan Broadcasting, including TV stations in New York and Washington, DC, and took it public. He renamed the company Metromedia in 1960.

Metromedia added independent stations — to the then-legal limit of seven — in other major markets, paying relatively little compared to network affiliate prices. The stations struggled through years of infomercials but began to thrive in the late 1970s and early 1980s. Metromedia's stock price rose from $4.50 in 1974 to more than $500 in 1983. The company also acquired radio stations, the Harlem Globetrotters, and the Ice Capades.

In 1983 Kluge bought paging and cellular telephone licenses across the US. He later acquired long-distance carriers in Texas and Florida. In 1984 Metromedia went private in a $1.6 billion buyout and began to sell off its assets in 1985. It sold its Boston TV station to Hearst and its six other TV stations to Rupert Murdoch for a total of $2 billion. In 1986 it sold its outdoor advertising firm, nine of its 11 radio stations, and the

Globetrotters and Ice Capades. Kluge then sold most of the company's cellular properties to SBC Communications (now AT&T Inc.). In 1990 it sold its New York cellular operations to LIN Broadcasting and its Philadelphia cellular operations to Comcast.

Building what Kluge envisioned as his steak house empire, the firm bought the Ponderosa steak house chain (founded in the late 1960s) in 1988 from Asher Edelman and later added Dallas-based USA Cafes (Bonanza steak houses, founded 1964) and S&A Restaurant Corp. (Steak and Ale, founded 1966; Bennigan's, founded 1976). Also in 1988 Kluge rescued friend Arthur Krim, whose Orion Pictures was threatened by Viacom, by buying control of the filmmaker.

Kluge's grand steak house vision did not come to fruition. Increased competition squeezed profits at Ponderosa and Bonanza. The restaurant group also was plagued by management shakeups, aging facilities, food-quality issues, and even bad press. (Bennigan's was ranked the worst casual dining chain in the US in a 1992 Consumer Reports poll.)

In 1989 Kluge merged Metromedia Long Distance with the long-distance operations of ITT. Renamed Metromedia Communications in 1991, the company merged with other long-distance providers to become MCI WorldCom. (Kluge sold his 16% of MCI WorldCom to the public in 1995.)

Kluge created Metromedia International Group in 1995 by merging Orion Pictures, Metromedia International Telecommunications, MCEG Sterling (film and television production), and Actava Group (maker of Snapper lawn mowers and sporting goods — sold in 2002). Metromedia Restaurant Group announced a $190 million refinancing agreement for S&A Restaurant Corp. in 1998 to expand and refurbish its restaurants; it closed 28 unprofitable restaurants that year and launched a franchise program to grow its Bennigan's and Steak and Ale chains.

Metromedia expanded its Bennigan's units in South Korea in 1999 and the next year announced it would build 65 new restaurants in the US and expand to more than 200 units internationally. In 2001 Verizon Communications invested nearly $2 billion in Metromedia unit Metromedia Fiber Network (MFN), but MFN was forced into Chapter 11 bankruptcy the following year. It blamed lower than expected demand for its metropolitan Internet services due to stiff competition, which drove down prices.

MFN (now AboveNet) emerged from bankruptcy in 2002 with a new owner. Kluge resigned from the Metromedia Fiber Network board that year and also stepped down from the Metromedia International Group board.

In 2003 Metromedia sold a minority stake in its restaurant subsidiary to Irving, Texas-based Apex Restaurant Group, which assumed management of the chain operator.

Metromedia sold its stake in Metromedia International Group to CaucusCom Ventures in 2007.

EXECUTIVES

Chairman and President: John W. Kluge
EVP and General Partner: Stuart Subotnick, age 66
SVP Finance and Treasurer: Robert A. Maresca
SVP: Silvia Kessel
VP and Controller: David Gassler
Auditors: KPMG LLP

Metropolitan Transportation Authority

No Sigma Chi or Chi Omega chapter has anything on New York City's Metropolitan Transportation Authority (MTA) — it rushes millions of people every day. The largest public transportation system in the US, the government-owned MTA handles about 2.6 billion passenger journeys and carries more than 300 million vehicles a year. The MTA's New York City Transit Authority runs a fleet of buses in New York City's five boroughs, provides subway service to all but Staten Island, and operates the Staten Island Railway. Other MTA units offer bus and rail service to Connecticut and Long Island and maintain the Triborough system of toll bridges and tunnels.

The MTA, a public-benefit corporation chartered by the New York Legislature, is working to become more self-sufficient. It has attempted to cut expenses through more efficient administration and maintenance. But operating losses have persisted, and the MTA has increased fares and taken advantage of low interest rates to restructure its debt. The MTA also has considered bringing in cash by selling naming rights to subway stations, bus lines, bridges, and tunnels, as well as by expanding other corporate sponsorship and advertising opportunities. Leasing the right to build above railyards on Manhattan's West Side also is on the table.

At the same time, the agency has outlined a program of capital spending for several major enhancements to its system, including extending the Long Island Rail Road to Grand Central Station and creating a direct link between John F. Kennedy Airport and downtown Manhattan.

HISTORY

Mass transit began in New York City in the 1820s with the introduction of horse-drawn stagecoaches run by small private firms. By 1832 a horse-drawn railcar operating on Fourth Avenue offered a smoother and faster ride than its street-bound rivals.

By 1864 residents were complaining that horsecars and buses were overcrowded and that drivers were rude. (Horsecars were transporting 45 million passengers annually.) In 1870 a short subway under Broadway was opened, but it remained a mere amusement. Elevated steam railways were built, but people avoided them because of the smoke, noise, and danger from explosions. Cable cars arrived in the 1880s, and by the 1890s electric streetcars had emerged.

Construction of the first commercial subway line was completed in 1904. The line was operated by Interborough Rapid Transit (IRT), which leased the primary elevated rail line in 1903 and had effective control of rail transit in Manhattan and the Bronx. In 1905 IRT merged with the Metropolitan Street Railway, which ran most of the surface railways in Manhattan, giving the firm almost complete control of the city's rapid transit. Public protests led the city to grant licenses to Brooklyn Rapid Transit (later BMT), creating the Dual System. The two rail firms covered most of the city.

By the 1920s the transit system was again in crisis, largely because the two lines were not allowed to raise their five-cent fares. With the IRT and BMT in receivership in 1932, the city decided to own and operate part of the rail system and organized the Independent (IND) rail line. Pressure for public ownership and operation of the transit system resulted in the city's purchase of all of IRT's and BMT's assets in 1940 for $326 million.

In 1953 the legislature created the New York City Transit Authority, the first unified system. Then in 1968, two years after striking transit workers left the city in a virtual gridlock, the Metropolitan Transit Authority began to coordinate the city's transit activities with other commuter services.

The 1970s and 1980s saw the city's transit infrastructure and service deteriorate as crime, accidents, and fares rose. But by the early 1990s a modernization program had begun to make improvements: Subway stations were repaired, graffiti was removed from trains, and service was extended. By 1994 the agency said subway crime was down 50% from 1990, and ridership had increased.

The MTA set up a five-year plan in 1995 to cut expenses by $3 billion. Only 18 months later and already two-thirds of the way to reaching the goal, the authority said it would cut another $230 million and return the savings to customers as fare discounts. The agency agreed in 1996 to sell Long Island Rail Road's freight operations. The next year it began selling its one-fare/free-transfer MetroCard Gold.

In 1998 the MTA capital program completed the $200 million restoration of the Grand Central Terminal. The next year the MTA ordered 500 new clean-fuel buses. But the agency suffered a setback when New York State's $3.8 billion Transportation Infrastructure Bond Act, which included $1.6 billion for MTA improvements, was rejected by voters in 2000.

MTA subway lines in lower Manhattan suffered extensive damage from the September 11, 2001, terrorist attacks that destroyed the World Trade Center's twin towers. The attacks left the MTA, which was already seeking billions of dollars for improvements, faced with $530 million worth of damage.

Confronted with a budget gap for the 2003 fiscal year, the MTA authorized the sale of nearly $2.9 billion worth of bonds, the largest bond issue in the agency's history. The MTA had hoped the eventual proceeds from the bonds would help stave off a fare increase, but in 2003 the agency raised subway and bus fares from $1.50 to $2, among other fare and toll increases.

Angered by issues involving wage hikes, health care, retirement age, and pension costs, members of the Transportation Workers Union walked off the job mere days before Christmas in 2005. The strike stranded commuters and stymied New Yorkers eager to shop and celebrate during the holiday season. The strike was estimated to cause a loss of $300 million per day to the city. In the face of heavy fines, possible jail terms, and the growing ire of would-be commuters, the 33,000 striking union members agreed to go back to work without a contract after three days of picketing, and negotiations resumed.

EXECUTIVES

Chairman: Peter S. Kalikow
Vice Chairman: David S. Mack, age 66
Vice Chairman: Andrew M. Saul, age 61
Executive Director and CEO: Elliot G. (Lee) Sander
COO: Susan L. Kupferman
Director, Budgets and Financial Management:
  Gary M. Lanigan
Director, Special Project Development and Planning:
  William Wheeler
Deputy Executive Director, Administration:
  Linda Kleinbaum
Deputy Executive Director, Corporate and Community
  Affairs: Christopher P. Boylan
Deputy Executive Director and General Counsel:
  Catherine A. Rinaldi
Deputy Executive Director, Security:
  William A. Morange
President, MTA Bus Company: Thomas J. Savage
President, MTA Capital Construction:
  Mysore L. Nagaraja
President, MTA Long Island Bus: Neil S. Yellin
President, MTA Metro-North Railroad:
  Howard R. Permut
President, New York City Transit:
  Howard H. Roberts Jr., age 67
Auditors: Deloitte & Touche LLP

LOCATIONS

HQ: Metropolitan Transportation Authority
   347 Madison Ave., New York, NY 10017
Phone: 212-878-7000   **Fax:** 212-878-0186
Web: www.mta.info

PRODUCTS/OPERATIONS

Selected Operating Units

The Long Island Rail Road Company (MTA Long Island
  Rail Road)
Metro-North Commuter Railroad Company (MTA Metro-
  North Railroad)
Metropolitan Suburban Bus Authority (MTA Long Island
  Bus)
New York City Transit Authority (MTA New York City
  Transit)
Staten Island Rapid Transit Operating Authority (MTA
  Staten Island Railway)
Triborough Bridge and Tunnel Authority (MTA Bridges
  and Tunnels)

HISTORICAL FINANCIALS
Company Type: Government-owned

Income Statement				FYE: December 31
	REVENUE ($ mil.)	NET INCOME ($ mil.)	NET PROFIT MARGIN	EMPLOYEES
12/07	5,666	(66)	—	68,628
12/06	5,487	1,370	25.0%	67,457
12/05	5,198	397	7.6%	63,511
12/04	4,837	83	1.7%	63,604
12/03	4,523	651	14.4%	63,884
Annual Growth	5.8%	—	—	1.8%

Net Income History

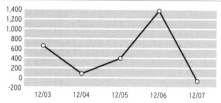

M-I L.L.C.

M-I, known as M-I Swaco, supplies drilling and completion fluids and additives to oil and gas companies in more than 70 countries worldwide. Its fluids cool and lubricate drill bits, remove rock cuttings, and maintain the stability of the wellbore. Through M-I's Swaco division, the company provides pressure control, rig instrumentation, and drilling waste management products and services. It is also a worldwide producer of barite and bentonite used by the oil and gas and industrial markets. M-I Swaco is a joint venture of Smith International (60%) and Schlumberger Limited (40%).

As a service provider to the global oil and gas industry, M-I Swaco does nearly two-thirds of its business outside the US. Specifically the company's African business is making great strides.

M-I Swaco ventured into the Scottish market in mid-2006 with the acquisition of Specialised Petroleum Services Group for about $165 million. That company provides wellbore clean-up products, primarily for the offshore drilling industry.

EXECUTIVES

President and CEO: Donald McKenzie
EVP, Product Segments: Chris Rivers
SVP, Production Technologies: John Kelly
SVP, North America Business Unit: Joe Bacho
SVP, South America Business Unit: Dave Chilton
SVP, Eastern Hemisphere North Business Unit: Curtis Bordelon
SVP, Eastern Hemisphere South Business Unit: Emad Kelada
VP, CFO and Treasurer: Frank Richter
VP, Research and Engineering: Jim Bruton
VP, Secretary and General Counsel: James Webster
VP, Human Resources: Brenda Beers-Reineke

LOCATIONS

HQ: M-I L.L.C.
  5950 N. Course Dr., Houston, TX 77072
Phone: 713-739-0222
Web: www.miswaco.com

COMPETITORS

Baker Petrolite
Champion Technologies
Nalco Energy Services

Miami Heat

Basketball is one hot property for this company. The Heat Group operates the Miami Heat professional basketball team, which joined the National Basketball Association as an expansion franchise in 1988. The team struggled to find success until 1995 when former Los Angeles Lakers coach Pat Riley came to Miami. However, it wasn't until 2006 that the Heat won its first NBA title with a roster that included another former Laker, Shaquille O'Neal, and such stars as Dwyane Wade. The family of Carnival CEO Micky Arison has controlled the basketball franchise since its founding.

After a disappointing 2007-08 season, Riley stepped down as head coach and appointed Erik Spoelstra as his replacement. Spoelstra previously served as head of scouting for the Heat. The coaching change was a repeat performance of 2003 when Riley resigned as head coach to become president (a title he still retains).

The former Lakers coach had returned to the bench in 2005 after Stan Van Gundy quit. Miami defeated the Dallas Mavericks in six games to win the championship that season. O'Neal was later traded to the Phoenix Suns during the 2007-08 season.

Family scion Ted Arison, who died in 1999, was the primary financial backer of the expansion franchise, along with Broadway producer Zev Buffman and Hall of Fame basketball player Billy Cunningham.

EXECUTIVES

Managing General Partner: Micky Arison, age 58
President: Pat Riley, age 63
President, Business Operations: Eric Woolworth
Head Coach: Erik Spoelstra
EVP and Chief Marketing Officer: Michael McCullough
EVP Heat Group Enterprises: Mike Walker
EVP and CFO: Sammy Schulman
EVP and General Counsel: Raquel Libman
EVP Sales: Stephen Weber
EVP; General Manager, AmericanAirlines Arena: Kim Stone
SVP and CIO: Tony Coba
SVP Basketball Operations: Andy Elisburg
VP Human Resources: Sonia Harty
VP Player Personnel: Chet Kammerer
Director, College and International Scouting: Adam Simon
Director, Pro and Minor League Scouting: Ed Maull
Manager Human Resources: Christine Machado Risso

LOCATIONS

HQ: The Heat Group
  AmericanAirlines Arena, 601 Biscayne Blvd.,
  Miami, FL 33132
Phone: 786-777-1000 **Fax:** 786-777-1615
Web: www.nba.com/heat

The Miami Heat play at 19,600-seat capacity AmericanAirlines Arena in Miami.

PRODUCTS/OPERATIONS

Championship Titles
NBA Champions (2006)
Eastern Conference Champions (2006)

COMPETITORS

Charlotte Bobcats
Hawks Basketball
Orlando Magic
Washington Wizards

HISTORICAL FINANCIALS
Company Type: Private

Income Statement				FYE: June 30
	REVENUE ($ mil.)	NET INCOME ($ mil.)	NET PROFIT MARGIN	EMPLOYEES
6/07	131	—	—	—
6/06	132	—	—	—
6/05	119	—	—	—
6/04	93	—	—	—
6/03	91	—	—	—
Annual Growth	9.5%	—	—	—

Revenue History

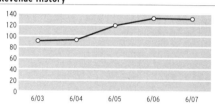

Michael Foods

It's not meat and potatoes but rather, poultry and potatoes at Michael Foods. The company is one of the leading US producers of shell eggs and value-added egg products (frozen, liquid, pre-cooked, dried). The food processor and distributor has other operations, but eggs account for almost 70% of its sales. The spuds come in with its Northern Star subsidiary, which pre-shreds and mashes potatoes. The company's Crystal Farms subsidiary packages and distributes cheese, butter, and other dairy products. Michael's customers include food processors, foodservice distributors, and retail grocery stores throughout North America, as well as internationally in the Far East, South America, and Europe.

Michael's other major subsidiaries include M.G. Waldbaum Company and Papetti's Hygrade Egg Products, Inc. (both make processed egg products).

The company's customers include foodservice companies SYSCO and U.S. Foodservice; national restaurant chains, such as Burger King, IHOP (owned by DineEquity), Sonic Corp., and Dunkin' Donuts; major retail grocery purveyors, such as SUPERVALU, Kroger, Publix, Albertsons, Costco, Wal-Mart, and Ahold; and major food-ingredient customers, including General Mills and Unilever Bestfoods North America.

About 30% of the company's egg needs are supplied by its own eggs, the remainder being purchased from third parties. Its laying barns, housing some 11.5 million producing hens, are located in Minnesota, Nebraska, and South Dakota. In addition the production of some 18 million hens is under long-term supply agreements and 14 million more are under shorter-term agreements.

Michael Foods ran "afowl" of the Humane Society in 2006, when the animal welfare organization charged the company with inhumane treatment of chickens, following the release of a secretly shot video, which showed dead and dying chickens stuck in cages at a Michael poultry production site. The surrounding brouhaha spurred Ben & Jerry's to drop Michael as its egg supplier. Whole Foods, Wild Oats, and Trader Joe's have also joined in the society's campaign to force Michael to change its chicken-raising practices.

The company sold its dairy products division (ice cream mixes, coffee creamers) to dairy giant Dean Foods in 2003 for $155 million.

Michael Foods is majority owned by private investment firm Vestar Capital Partners.

EXECUTIVES

Executive Chairman: Gregg A. Ostrander, age 55, $816,154 pay
Vice Chairman: John D. Reedy, $495,192 pay
President, CEO, and Director: David S. (Dave) Johnson, age 52
CFO: Mark Westphal, age 42
SVP Supply Chain and Logistics: James G. Mohr, age 56, $215,961 pay
SVP Operations and Supply Chain: Tom Jagiela
Treasurer and Secretary: Mark D. Witmer
VP Operations, Michael Foods Egg Products: Charles D. (Chuck) Bailey, $225,000 pay
President, Crystal Farms: Mark B. Anderson, age 47, $201,846 pay
Auditors: PricewaterhouseCoopers LLP

LOCATIONS

HQ: Michael Foods, Inc.
301 Carlson Pkwy., Ste. 400,
Minnetonka, MN 55305
Phone: 952-258-4000   **Fax:** 952-258-4911
Web: www.michaelfoods.com

PRODUCTS/OPERATIONS

2007 Sales

	$ mil.	% of total
Egg products	1,014.6	69
Crystal Farms	334.2	23
Potato products	119.0	8
Total	**1,467.8**	**100**

Selected Brands

Egg products
  All Whites
  Better n Eggs
  Broke N' Ready
  Canadian Inovatec
  Centromay
  Easy Eggs
  Emulsa
  Inovatec
  Michael Foods
  Papett's
  Quaker State Farms
Potato products
  Diner's Choice
  Farm Fresh
  Northern Star
  Simply Potatoes
Refrigerated distribution
  Crescent Valley
  Crystal Farms
  Farms Fresh
  Northern Star

Selected Products

Egg Products
  Dried eggs
  Egg substitutes
  Extended shelf-life liquid eggs
  Fresh eggs
  Frozen eggs
  Precooked eggs
Refrigerated distribution
  Bagels
  Butter
  Crystal Farms brand cheese
  Eggs
  Margarine
  Muffins
  Potato products
Refrigerated potato products
  Hash browns
  Mashed potatoes
  Specialty potato products

COMPETITORS

Bob Evans
Cal-Maine Foods
Cargill
ConAgra
Dairy Farmers of America
Golden Oval Eggs
Heinz
JR Simplot
Kraft Foods
Land O'Lakes
McCain Foods
Moark
Ore-Ida Foods, Inc.
Primera Foods
Reser's
Rose Acre Farms
Sargento
Sorrento Lactalis
Unilever

HISTORICAL FINANCIALS

Company Type: Private

Income Statement			FYE: Saturday nearest December 31	
	REVENUE ($ mil.)	NET INCOME ($ mil.)	NET PROFIT MARGIN	EMPLOYEES
12/07	1,468	28	1.9%	3,759
12/06	1,247	19	1.5%	3,875
12/05	1,243	39	3.1%	4,132
12/04	1,314	34	2.6%	3,897
12/03	1,325	(23)	—	3,806
Annual Growth	**2.6%**	**—**	**—**	**(0.3%)**

2007 Year-End Financials

Debt ratio: —   Current ratio: —
Return on equity: 8.1%   Long-term debt ($ mil.): —
Cash ($ mil.): —

Net Income History

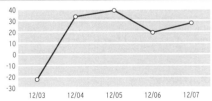

Michaels Stores

Michaels Stores is pretty crafty. The nation's #1 arts and crafts retailer owns and operates about 975 Michaels Stores canvassing the US and Canada. Michaels sells more than 40,000 products including art and hobby supplies, décor, frames, needlecraft kits, party supplies, seasonal products, and silk and dried flowers. Michaels also operates about 165 Aaron Brothers stores, mostly on the West Coast and Texas, which provide framing and art supplies. Artistree manufactures frames and molding for Michaels and Aaron Brothers stores. Michaels Stores was taken private in 2006 by the investment firms Bain Capital Partners, LLC, and The Blackstone Group.

The sale of the company, which closed in October 2006, valued the crafts retailer at $44 in cash per share, or more than $6 billion. Bain Capital and Blackstone acquired equal stakes in Michaels, while the company's senior management purchased a minority share.

A national chain in an industry where local shops and regional chains are typical, Michaels Stores is expanding. The company's management believes the North American market can support as many as 1,350 Michaels Stores, leaving plenty of room for future store growth. To that end, it plans to open between 45 and 50 Michaels Stores annually for the foreseeable future.

But not all of Michaels' businesses are growing. In late 2007 the company closed all 11 of its ReCollections stores, a scrapbooking retail concept launched by the company in 2003 to capitalize on the popularity of scrapbooking, and several Star Decorators Wholesale shops that offered wholesale merchandise to design professionals. The company said the move was made to focus on its core retail stores.

Michaels Stores' customers, who are predominantly married women, can order prints and posters, buy arts and crafts supplies, and find arts and crafts tips on the Michaels Web site. Employees teach in-store craft classes to generate interest and boost sales.

HISTORY

Michael Dupey founded Michaels arts and crafts store in 1973 by converting a Ben Franklin variety store in Dallas that was owned by his father. With dad footing the bill, Dupey opened several other stores in Texas, and by the early 1980s Michaels operated 11 stores.

Dupey wanted to buy the company from his father; the two could not agree on a price, however, so dad sold the chain in 1983 to Peoples Restaurants, which operated the Bonanza Steakhouse chain and was run by brothers Sam and Charles Wyly (later vice chairman and chairman, respectively). As part of the deal, Dupey was paid $1.2 million and was given ownership of two Dallas stores plus royalty-free licensing rights to Michaels stores in North Texas.

With 16 stores mostly in Texas, Peoples Restaurants spun off Michaels in 1984 to its shareholders. Michaels then acquired Montiel, a Colorado-based retailer with 13 stores. The next year the company acquired six retailers. In 1987 Michaels acquired Moskatel's, a 28-store chain based in California. By 1988 the company operated nearly 100 stores in 14 states.

Michaels had achieved the mass to attract the attention of big investors, and in 1989 it agreed to a $225 million LBO engineered in part by Acadia Partners, an investment group headed by Robert Bass. The group was unable to raise the junk-bond financing needed to acquire the company, and the deal fell apart in early 1990; Michaels took a $4 million charge for its effort.

That year the company hired Dupey, who had built his own Michaels-MJDesigns chain in the meantime, to assist it in selecting and marketing merchandise; it fired him in 1991, beginning a stormy relationship that played out in court. The company continued to open new stores and had 140 outlets by the end of 1991.

In 1992 Michaels began a drive to become the first national arts and crafts chain. It opened stores in new markets, including Iowa, Ohio, Oklahoma, Virginia, and Washington, and made its debut in Toronto.

Two years later Michaels acquired several chains in the West, including Oregon Craft & Supply, H&H Craft & Floral Company, and Treasure House. Its biggest acquisition that year, however, was its $92 million purchase of 101-store Leewards Creative Crafts, which gave it a total of 360 stores in 38 states. In 1995 Michaels acquired 71 Aaron Brothers specialty framing and art supply stores.

Ironically, the company's far-reaching expansion did not include its birthplace. After a three-year court battle proving even the crafts business has an ugly side, in 1996 Michaels was awarded the right to operate stores in its home market, the Dallas-Fort Worth area, and Dupey's Michaels-MJDesigns stores removed the Michaels name from its signs. (Dupey, in turn, was permitted to sell his assets without first getting right of approval from Michaels.)

Lowe's veteran Michael Rouleau became CEO of Michaels in 1996. Struggling to knit together its acquisitions, Michaels lost $31 million in fiscal 1997, its second straight loss. Rouleau refined the chain's merchandise (reducing noncore items like party supplies) and expanded its distribution system.

Michaels bought 16 stores (mainly in Maryland and Virginia) from bankrupt MJDesigns in 1999. To serve florists, interior decorators, and others, Michaels acquired a Dallas store in 2000, Star Wholesale Florist, and began operating it as Star Decorators' Wholesale Warehouse.

In June 2003 the company opened its first of two test stores in the Dallas-Fort Worth area. Called ReCollections, the stores are dedicated to helping "scrappers" make and compile scrapbooks. The second ReCollections opened in October 2003. Also in 2003 Michaels opened another Star Decorators' Wholesale Warehouse, in Atlanta.

In March 2006, Michaels Stores put itself up for sale. Concurrently, CEO Michael Rouleau retired after a decade with the company and was replaced by a pair of senior executives — Jeffrey N. Boyer and Gregory A. Sandfort — who were named co-presidents of Michaels Stores. In late October the company was taken private (and thus delisted from the New York Stock Exchange) by Bain Capital Partners, LLC, and The Blackstone Group in a deal that valued the firm at more than $6 billion.

In June 2007 Brian Cornell, a former Safeway and PepsiCo executive, joined Michaels as its new CEO. In late 2007 and early 2008 the company closed all of its ReCollections and Star Decorators Wholesale shops.

EXECUTIVES

CEO: Brian C. Cornell, age 48
President and COO: Shelley G. Broader, age 44
EVP and CFO: Elaine D. Crowley, age 49
EVP Supply Chain: Thomas C. DeCaro, age 53, $275,731 pay
SVP and CIO: Michael J. (Mike) Jones
SVP and Head of Strategic Planning and Initiatives: Jeffrey L. Wellen, age 43
SVP Marketing: David Abelman
SVP, General Counsel, Secretary: Mark V. Beasley, age 50
SVP Human Resources: Sue Elliott, age 53
SVP New Business Development: Duane E. Hiemenz, age 50
SVP New Ventures: J. Samuel Crowley, age 52
SVP Supply Chain Management: Stephen R. Gartner, age 53
SVP Finance and Treasurer: Lisa K. Klinger, age 48
VP Field Human Resources: Shawn Hearn
VP Finance, Principal Accounting Officer, and Controller: Richard Jablonski
President, Artistree: Mike Greenwood, age 56
Manager, Corporate Communications: Thomas J. (Tom) Clary
Auditors: Ernst & Young LLP

LOCATIONS

HQ: Michaels Stores, Inc.
  8000 Bent Branch Dr., Irving, TX 75063
Phone: 972-409-1300   **Fax:** 972-409-1556
Web: www.michaels.com

2008 Stores

	No.
US	
California	223
Texas	84
Florida	62
New York	45
Pennsylvania	39
Illinois	38
Michigan	37
Arizona	36
Georgia	33
Ohio	32
Virginia	32
Washington	32
North Carolina	29
Colorado	28
New Jersey	27
Maryland	23
Minnesota	23
Massachusetts	21
Missouri	18
Oregon	17
Nevada	17
Wisconsin	16
Indiana	14
Connecticut	12
Tennessee	12
Louisiana	11
Utah	11
Alabama	10
South Carolina	9
Kansas	8
Idaho	7
Iowa	7
Kentucky	7
Oklahoma	7
New Hampshire	6
Other states	39
Canada	67
Total	**1,139**

PRODUCTS/OPERATIONS

2008 Sales

	% of total
General & children's crafts	41
Home décor & seasonal	25
Picture framing	18
Scrapbooking	16
Total	**100**

Selected Merchandise

General crafts
  Apparel crafts
  Bakeware
  Beads
  Books and magazines
  Doll-making items
  Jewelry-making supplies
  Needlecraft items (knitting, needlepoint, embroidery, cross-stitch, crochet, rug-making, quilts, afghans)
  Paper crafting
  Plaster
  Rubber stamp supplies
  Scrapbooking supplies
  Wall décor (candles, containers, baskets, potpourri, other home decorating items)
  Wood and woodcraft items
Art supplies
  Acrylics
  Adhesives
  Brushes
  Canvases and other painting surfaces
  Easels
  Finishes
  Memory book materials
  Oil paints
  Pastels
  Sketch pads
  Stenciling materials
  Water colors
Picture framing
  Backing materials
  Custom framing
  Framed art
  Glass
  Mat boards
  Photo albums
  Ready-made frames
Silk and dried floral
  Artificial plants
  Dried flowers
  Floral arranging supplies
  Silk flowers and plants
Seasonal items
  Artificial trees
  Candles
  Christmas crafts
  Gift-making supplies
  Lights and ornaments
  Wreaths
Hobby, party, and candles
  Candle-making supplies
  Paint-by-number kits
  Party supplies (paper party goods, balloons, gift wrap, candy-making supplies, cake-decorating supplies)
  Plastic model kits
  Plush toys
  Soap-making supplies
  Wedding supplies (favors, flowers, headpieces, cake-decorating supplies)

COMPETITORS

A.C. Moore
Albecca
Cost Plus
Factory Card & Party Outlet
Garden Ridge
Hancock Fabrics
Hobby Lobby
HobbyTown USA
Home Interiors & Gifts
Jo-Ann Stores
Kirkland's
Kmart
Longaberger
Martha Stewart Living
Old Time Pottery
Party City
Pier 1 Imports
Pinnacle Frames
Target
Wal-Mart

HISTORICAL FINANCIALS

Company Type: Private

Income Statement
FYE: January 31

	REVENUE ($ mil.)	NET INCOME ($ mil.)	NET PROFIT MARGIN	EMPLOYEES
1/08	3,862	(32)	—	42,000
1/07	3,865	41	1.1%	43,100
1/06	3,676	131	3.6%	43,700
1/05	3,393	202	5.9%	41,100
1/04	3,091	178	5.8%	38,800
Annual Growth	5.7%	—	—	2.0%

2008 Year-End Financials

Debt ratio: —
Return on equity: —
Cash ($ mil.): —

Current ratio: —
Long-term debt ($ mil.): 3,741

Net Income History

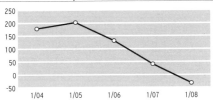

Michigan State University

The Spartan population is still growing today — in Michigan. With an enrollment of approximately 46,000 students, Michigan State University dominates the town of East Lansing. It offers more than 200 programs of study through 17 degree-granting colleges. Its research breakthroughs range from the cross-fertilization of corn in the 1870s to developing a top-selling anticancer drug in the 1960s. MSU was founded in 1855 as a land-grant college under the name Agricultural College of the State of Michigan. It became a full university a century later.

EXECUTIVES

Chairman: Joel I. Ferguson, age 69
Vice Chairperson: Melanie Foster
President: Lou Anna K. Simon
VP Academic Affairs and Provost: Kim Wilcox, age 51
Senior Associate Provost: June Youatt
Associate Provost and Dean, Graduate School: Karen L. Klomparens
Associate Provost and Dean, Undergraduate Studies: Douglas Estry
VP Finance and Operations and Treasurer: Fred L. Poston
VP Legal Affairs and General Counsel: Robert A. Noto
VP Research and Graduate Studies: J. Ian Gray
VP University Relations: Terry Denbow
Assistant VP, CFO, and Controller: David B. Brower
Assistant VP Human Resources: Brent Bowditch
Auditors: KPMG LLP

LOCATIONS

HQ: Michigan State University
438 Administration Bldg., East Lansing, MI 48824
Phone: 517-355-6550   **Fax:** 517-355-9601
Web: www.msu.edu

PRODUCTS/OPERATIONS

Selected Colleges

College of Agriculture and Natural Resources
College of Arts and Letters
College of Communication Arts and Sciences
College of Education
College of Engineering
College of Human Ecology
College of Human Medicine
College of Law (affiliated)
College of Music
College of Natural Science
College of Nursing
College of Osteopathic Medicine
College of Social Science
College of Veterinary Medicine
James Madison College
The Eli Broad College of Business
The Eli Broad Graduate School of Management

HISTORICAL FINANCIALS

Company Type: School

Income Statement
FYE: June 30

	REVENUE ($ mil.)	NET INCOME ($ mil.)	NET PROFIT MARGIN	EMPLOYEES
6/07	1,735	251	14.5%	10,900
6/06	1,601	197	12.3%	10,700
6/05	1,540	177	11.5%	10,500
6/04	1,448	—	—	
6/03	1,370	—	—	10,500
Annual Growth	6.1%	19.1%	—	0.9%

2007 Year-End Financials

Debt ratio: —
Return on equity: 10.5%
Cash ($ mil.): —

Current ratio: —
Long-term debt ($ mil.): —

Net Income History

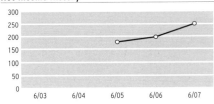

Micro Electronics

There's nothing small about the way Micro Electronics sets up shop. The company has more than 20 Micro Center computer retail stores, which operate in about 15 states. The stores range up to 62,000 sq. ft., contain nearly 36,000 products organized in about a dozen specialized departments (an approach it calls "dedicated departments"), and sell video game consoles, as well. Micro Electronics sells its own brands of notebook and desktop computers under the WinBook and PowerSpec names. Micro Center Online is the company's e-commerce operation and Redemtech recycles IT equipment. Micro Center was founded in 1979 by John Baker.

Micro Electronics maintains a loyal customer base, such as Apple's (which happens to do quite a bit of business with Micro Electronics), without spending money on expensive advertising.

Store departments include PCs (desktops, laptops), Macintosh computers, digital imaging (cameras, camcorders), hardware (monitors, printers, keyboards), accessories (memory, CD and DVD drives), The Game Room (game systems and games), and supplies (blank media, printer cartridges). It even has a BYOPC (Build Your Own PC) department where customers can build a computer from scratch.

In 2006 Micro Electronics launched a gaming department at its stores; a mail-in rebate promotion helped the firm get a foothold in the niche. The company opened its 21st location in Rockville, Maryland.

EXECUTIVES

Chairman, President, and CEO; President, Micro Center: Richard M. (Rick) Mershad
COO: Peggy Wolfe
CFO: James Koehler
VP Business Development: Kevin Hollingshead
VP Retail Marketing: Mike Papai
VP Merchandising: Kevin Jones
VP Retail Operations: Ralph Gilson
VP Retail Sales: Robert Demme
CIO: Misty Kuamoo
Director, Human Resources: Angie Miller
President, Redemtech: Robert Houghton

LOCATIONS

HQ: Micro Electronics, Inc.
4119 Leap Rd., Hilliard, OH 43026
Phone: 614-850-3000   **Fax:** 614-850-3001
Web: www.microelectronics.com

PRODUCTS/OPERATIONS

Selected Operations

Micro Center
Micro Center Online
PowerSpec PC
Redemtech
WinBook
WinBook Computer Corporation

Selected Products

Accessories
  Cables
  Furniture
Books
Communications
  Handhelds
  PDAs
  Phones
Computers
  Desktops
  Notebooks
Digital imaging
  Camcorders
  Cameras
  Printers
Macintosh products
  Computers
  Notebooks
Peripherals
  Keyboards
  Monitors
  Printers
Software
Supplies
  Blank media
  Media storage
  Paper
  Printer cartridges
Upgrades
  Drives (CD, DVD)
  Memory

MidAmerican Energy

There's a new kind of twister tearin' up Tornado Alley. MidAmerican Energy Holdings generates, transmits, and distributes electricity to 6.2 million customers, and distributes natural gas to some 700,000 customers in four Midwest states, primarily through subsidiary MidAmerican Energy Company. Its UK regional distribution subsidiaries, Northern Electric and Yorkshire Electricity, serve about 3.8 million electricity customers. MidAmerican Energy Holdings also has independent power production, real estate (HomeServices of America), and gas exploration, production, and pipeline operations. Warren Buffett's Berkshire Hathaway controls the company.

MidAmerican Energy Company distributes electricity in Iowa, South Dakota, and Illinois, and it distributes natural gas in those three states plus Nebraska. It also generates 4,500 MW of electricity (primarily from coal-fired plants) and sells wholesale energy to other utilities and marketers. MidAmerican Energy Holdings' residential real estate brokerage, HomeServices of America (formerly HomeServices.Com), operates in 19 states in the US. Subsidiary CalEnergy has more than 1,500 MW of gross capacity from independent power projects in the US and the Philippines.

MidAmerican Energy Holdings, which once focused on building and operating geothermal, hydroelectric, and natural gas power plants worldwide, now gets most of its revenues from its energy distribution operations. While deregulation led many regulated utilities into the independent power production business, MidAmerican Energy Holdings diversified by purchasing regulated utilities in the US and abroad. The company has also expanded its gas transportation operations through acquisitions; it operates nearly 18,000 miles of pipeline.

In 2006 the company acquired Oregon-based utility PacifiCorp for a reported $5.1 billion. MidAmerican Energy Holdings subsequently formed a holding company to serve approximately 3 million electric and natural gas customers.

In 2007 the company formed a joint venture company with American Electric Power to build and own new electric transmission assets within the Electric Reliability Council of Texas.

In 2008, in a move to expand its range of power holdings in the US, the company agreed to buy Constellation Energy.

HISTORY

Amid oil shortages, polluted air, and concerns about the safety of nuclear power plants, Charles Condy formed California Energy in 1971 to sell oil and gas partnerships and to consult on the development of geothermal power plants.

In 1978 Congress passed the Public Utility Regulatory Policies Act (PURPA) to wean the US from foreign oil by encouraging efficient use of fossil fuels and development of renewable and alternative energy sources. Grasping the potential of the changing energy environment, CalEnergy signed a 30-year deal with the US government in 1979 to develop the geothermal Coso Project, northeast of Los Angeles. In the 1980s CalEnergy focused entirely on geothermal development and started producing power at the Coso Project in 1987, the year the company went public.

Omaha, Nebraska-based construction firm Peter Kiewit Sons' injected some much-needed capital when it began buying a stake in the company in 1990. CalEnergy restructured in 1991, moving its headquarters from San Francisco to Omaha. It also acquired Desert Peak and Roosevelt Hot Springs geothermal areas in the US and made plans to enter markets in Asia. In 1993 the Philippine government contracted CalEnergy to develop geothermal projects. CalEnergy also obtained the rights to exploit geothermal fields in Indonesia. In 1994 the company opened a geothermal plant in Yuma, Arizona.

In 1996 CalEnergy doubled its size by acquiring rival Magma Power, and it began geothermal projects in the Salton Sea and the Imperial Valley in California. It also took advantage of the growing deregulation trend in the UK by acquiring a controlling stake in Northern Electric, a major British regional electricity company with about 1.5 million customers in northeast England and Wales.

Completing its transformation into a global power player, CalEnergy acquired gas plants in Poland and Australia in 1997. It also attracted 300,000 new gas customers in the UK. The company bought back Kiewit's stake that year. In 1998 CalEnergy subsidiary CalEnergy International Ltd. was part of a consortium (the PowerBridge Group) that won a contract to develop, synchronize, and transmit up to 1,000 MW of electricity from Lithuania to Poland, at an estimated cost of $400 million.

The next year CalEnergy bought MidAmerican Energy Holdings, an electric utility, for about $2.4 billion. CalEnergy then took the MidAmerican name and moved its headquarters to Des Moines, Iowa. Subsidiary MidAmerican Realty Services went public as HomeServices.Com; MidAmerican Energy Holdings retained a majority stake. In 2000 Warren Buffett's Berkshire Hathaway led an investor group, which included MidAmerican Energy Holdings CEO David Sokol, in purchasing MidAmerican Energy Holdings for about $2 billion and $7 billion in assumed debt.

In 2001 MidAmerican Energy Holdings bought out minority shareholders in HomeServices.Com, making it a wholly owned subsidiary. It also traded Northern Electric's electricity and gas retail supply operations for the distribution business of Yorkshire Electricity with Innogy (now RWE npower) in 2001.

The following year the company purchased The Williams Companies' Kern River Gas Transmission subsidiary, which operates a 926-mile interstate pipeline in the western US, in a $960 million deal. Also in 2002 MidAmerican Energy Holdings purchased the Northern Natural Gas pipeline from Dynegy for $928 million plus $950 million in assumed debt.

EXECUTIVES

Chairman: David L. Sokol, age 51, $14,600,000 pay
President, CEO, and Director; CEO, CE Electric UK; Chairman and CEO, PacifiCorp: Gregory E. (Greg) Abel, age 46, $14,190,000 pay
SVP and CFO: Patrick J. Goodman, age 41, $622,500 pay
SVP Communications, General Services, and Safety Audit and Compliance; SVP MidAmerican Energy Company: Keith D. Hartje, age 57
SVP and Chief Procurement Officer: P. Eric Connor, age 59
SVP, General Counsel, and Secretary: Douglas L. Anderson, age 49, $540,000 pay
SVP and Chief Administrative Officer: Maureen E. Sammon, age 43, $285,000 pay
SVP Environmental and Chief Environmental Counsel: Cathy Woollums
Chairman and CEO, HomeServices of America: Ronald J. (Ron) Peltier
President, MidAmerican Energy Company: William J. (Bill) Fehrman, age 46
President, MidAmerican Energy Pipeline Group; President, Northern Natural Gas: Mark A. Hewett
President, Rocky Mountain Power, PacifiCorp: A. Richard (Rich) Walje, age 56
President, Kern River Gas Transmission: Micheal G. Dunn
President, CalEnergy Generation U.S.: Stephen A. (Steve) Larsen
President, Pacific Power, PacifiCorp: Patrick (Pat) Reiten, age 46
Manager Communications: Mark Reinders
Auditors: Deloitte & Touche LLP

LOCATIONS

HQ: MidAmerican Energy Holdings Company
666 Grand Ave., Ste. 500, Des Moines, IA 50309
Phone: 515-242-4300 **Fax:** 515-281-2389
Web: www.midamerican.com

MidAmerican Energy Holdings has energy operations in the US (Alabama, Arizona, California, Florida, Georgia, Idaho, Illinois, Iowa, Kansas, Maryland, Minnesota, Missouri, Nebraska, North Carolina, Oregon, South Dakota, Texas, Utah, Washington, and Wyoming), as well as in the Philippines, Poland, and the UK.

PRODUCTS/OPERATIONS

2007 Sales

	$ mil.	% of total
MidAmerican Funding	4,267	35
PacifiCorp	4,258	34
HomeServices	1,500	12
CE Electric UK	1,079	9
Northern Natural Gas	664	5
Kern River	404	3
CalEnergy Generation		
Foreign	220	2
Domestic	32	—
Adjustments	(48)	—
Total	**12,376**	**100**

COMPETITORS

AES	International Power
Alliant Energy	Interstate Power and Light
Ameren	Lincoln Electric System
AmerenCILCO	Mirant
Basin Electric Power	National Power
Calpine	Nebraska Public Power
Dynegy	Nicor
Edison International	NRG Energy
El Paso	Scottish and Southern
Entergy	Energy

HISTORICAL FINANCIALS
Company Type: Subsidiary

Income Statement
FYE: December 31

	REVENUE ($ mil.)	NET INCOME ($ mil.)	NET PROFIT MARGIN	EMPLOYEES
12/07	12,376	1,189	9.6%	17,200
12/06	10,301	916	8.9%	17,800
12/05	7,116	563	7.9%	11,400
12/04	6,553	170	2.6%	11,540
12/03	6,145	416	6.8%	11,440
Annual Growth	19.1%	30.1%	—	10.7%

2007 Year-End Financials
Debt ratio: —
Return on equity: 13.7%
Cash ($ mil.): —
Current ratio: —
Long-term debt ($ mil.): —

Net Income History

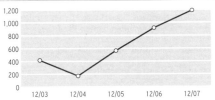

Midland Cogeneration Venture

Midland Cogeneration Venture has the power to go all the way (and the reputation to get away with it). The company, formerly Midland Nuclear Power Plant, operates one of the largest cogeneration power plants in the US (at one time the largest gas-fired steam recovery power plant in the world). Midland Cogeneration Venture, with a generating capacity of more than 1,560 MW, is responsible for about 10% of the electricity used in Michigan's lower peninsula. Midland Cogeneration Venture holds the distinction of being the first nuclear power plant that was converted to a conventional energy generating facility. It sells most of its capacity to Consumers Energy and Dow Chemical.

Midland Cogeneration Venture was jointly owned by CMS Energy (49%), El Paso Corporation (44%), and Dow Chemical (7%), but in 2006 CMS and El Paso sold their stakes to MCV Investors, Inc. which took the company private.

EXECUTIVES
President and CEO: Rodney E. Boulanger, age 60
VP and CFO: James M. Rajewski, age 50, $226,869 pay
VP and Treasurer: Laurie M. Valasek, age 40, $108,062 pay
VP, General Counsel, and Secretary: Gary Pasek, age 52, $279,692 pay
VP, Human Resources, Communications, and Public Affairs: Bruce C. Grant, age 59, $147,357 pay
VP Energy Supply and Marketing: Kevin R. Olling, age 43
Auditors: PricewaterhouseCoopers LLP

LOCATIONS
HQ: Midland Cogeneration Venture Limited Partnership
100 Progress Place, Midland, MI 48640
Phone: 989-839-6000   **Fax:** 989-633-7935

COMPETITORS
ITC Holdings Corp.
Lansing Board of Water and Light
Wolverine Power Supply

Midland Paper

Midland Paper Company (MPC) is a middleman for the paper industry. The firm distributes coated, uncoated, bond, specialty, and other types of paper produced by such manufacturers as Boise Cascade, Weyerhaeuser, and International Paper. It also sells packaging supplies and equipment and janitorial supplies. MPC distributes primarily to large companies that print trade books and catalogs. Founded in 1907 as a paper supplier to Chicago's graphic arts industry, the company now operates warehouses and sales offices in California, Connecticut, Illinois, Minnesota, New York, North Dakota, and Wisconsin.

EXECUTIVES
President and CEO: E. Stanton (Stan) Hooker III
VP and CFO: Ralph DeLetto
VP and COO: Michael Graves
Controller: Steven Pasek
President, Midland Paper National: Jim O'Toole
Corporate Credit Manager: Mari Fontana

LOCATIONS
HQ: Midland Paper Company Inc.
101 E. Palatine Rd., Wheeling, IL 60090
Phone: 847-777-2700   **Fax:** 847-777-2552
Web: www.midlandpaper.com

COMPETITORS
Bradner Central
Central National-Gottesman
Clifford Paper
Gould Paper
RIS the paper house
Unisource
West Coast Paper
xpedx

HISTORICAL FINANCIALS
Company Type: Private

Income Statement
FYE: December 31

	REVENUE ($ mil.)	NET INCOME ($ mil.)	NET PROFIT MARGIN	EMPLOYEES
12/07	700	—	—	—
12/06	700	—	—	—
12/05	629	—	—	375
12/04	560	—	—	—
12/03	500	—	—	300
Annual Growth	8.8%	—	—	11.8%

Revenue History

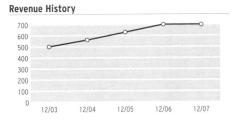

Midwest Research Institute

Midwest Research Institute (MRI) provides contract research services for government and private-sector clients in fields such as agricultural and food safety, analytical chemistry, biological sciences, energy, engineering, environment, health sciences, information technology, and national defense. The institute operates laboratories and agricultural research centers in Florida, Maryland, and Missouri. MRI also manages the US Department of Energy's National Renewable Energy Laboratory in Golden, Colorado. Work related to biological and chemical defense accounts for most of MRI's sales. The not-for-profit organization was founded in 1944.

EXECUTIVES
Chairman: Richard C. Green Jr.
Vice Chairman: William B. Neaves, age 65
President and CEO: James L. Spigarelli, age 65
SVP and Director Research Operations: Michael F. Helmstetter
SVP; Director, National Renewable Energy Lab: Dan E. Arvizu
VP and CFO: Fred Cornwell
General Counsel and Corporate Secretary: Jeanie Latz
Media Contact: Linda Cook

LOCATIONS
HQ: Midwest Research Institute
425 Volker Blvd., Kansas City, MO 64110
Phone: 816-753-7600   **Fax:** 816-753-8420
Web: www.mriresearch.org

PRODUCTS/OPERATIONS

2007 Sales

	% of total
Biological defense	40
Chemical defense	30
Food & agriculture	13
Life sciences	12
Infrastructure	4
Other	1
Total	**100**

HISTORICAL FINANCIALS
Company Type: Not-for-profit

Income Statement
FYE: June 30

	REVENUE ($ mil.)	NET INCOME ($ mil.)	NET PROFIT MARGIN	EMPLOYEES
6/07	272	6	2.2%	1,800
6/06	284	4	1.5%	1,800
6/05	292	4	1.5%	1,800
6/04	288	7	2.3%	1,500
6/03	270	(2)	—	1,200
Annual Growth	0.2%	—	—	10.7%

Net Income History

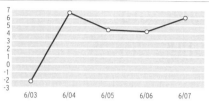

Milan Express Co.

This Milan Express is a trucking company from Tennessee, not a train from Rome. Milan Express provides less-than-truckload (LTL) and truckload freight transportation, along with logistics and warehousing and distribution services. (LTL carriers consolidate freight from multiple shippers into a single truckload.) Although its service territory ranges from Florida to Wisconsin, the company operates primarily in the southeastern and midwestern US. Tommy Ross, now the chairman of Milan Express, founded the company in 1969 to serve an 87-mile route between Memphis and Milan, Tennessee. The Ross family owns the company.

EXECUTIVES

Chairman: Tommy W. Ross
President: John W. Ross
VP and CFO: Bruce F. Kalem
VP Administration: Ed Wright
VP Corporate Services: Jim Szopinski
VP Distribution Services: Jeff Stinson
VP LTL Sales and Marketing: Mitch Anderson
VP Properties: Barry Jones
VP TLS Services: Mike Stone
VP Maintenance: Benny Page

LOCATIONS

HQ: Milan Express Co., Inc.
1091 Kefauver Dr., Milan, TN 38358
Phone: 731-686-7428   **Fax:** 731-686-8829
Web: www.milanexpress.com

COMPETITORS

AAA Cooper Transportation
Arkansas Best
Averitt Express
Celadon
C.H. Robinson Worldwide
Con-way Freight
Con-way Truckload
Covenant Transportation
Crete Carrier
Estes Express
FedEx Freight
GENCO Distribution System
J.B. Hunt
Landstar System
Old Dominion Freight
Saia, Inc.
Schneider National
Southeastern Freight Lines
Swift Transportation
UPS Freight
UPS Supply Chain Solutions
U.S. Xpress
USA Truck
Werner Enterprises
YRC Worldwide

HISTORICAL FINANCIALS
Company Type: Private

Income Statement
FYE: December 31

	REVENUE ($ mil.)	NET INCOME ($ mil.)	NET PROFIT MARGIN	EMPLOYEES
12/07	191	—	—	1,500
12/06	168	—	—	1,850
12/05	163	—	—	1,650
12/04	141	—	—	—
12/03	125	—	—	—
Annual Growth	11.3%	—	—	(4.7%)

Revenue History

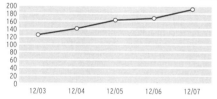

Milliken & Company

Making tennis balls feel soft and Jell-O puddings taste smooth and creamy are just two of the things that Milliken & Company does. One of the world's largest private textile companies, Milliken produces rugs and carpets, as well as synthetic fabrics used in such goods as apparel, automobiles, tennis balls, and specialty textiles. It also makes chemicals and petroleum products. Milliken's colorants infuse products such as Crayola markers, its clarifying agents make plastics clear, and its various other chemical products are used in the automotive, consumer products, and turf markets. Milliken operates more than 55 plants worldwide. The Milliken family controls the company.

Seth Milliken and William Deering founded the company in 1865. Seth's grandson, Chairman Roger Milliken, has led the company since 1947.

HISTORY

Seth Milliken and William Deering formed a company in 1865 to become selling agents for textile mills in New England and the southern US. Deering left the partnership, and in 1869 he founded Deering Harvester (now Navistar).

Milliken set up operations in New York before the turn of the century, began buying the accounts receivable of cash-short textile mill operators, and invested in some of the companies.

In his position as agent and financier, Milliken was able to spot failing mills. He bought out the distressed owners at a discount and soon became a major mill owner himself. In 1905 Milliken and his allies waged a bitter proxy fight and court case to win control of two mills, earning Milliken a fearsome reputation.

H. B. Claflin, a New York dry-goods wholesaler that also operated department stores, owed money to Milliken. When Claflin went bankrupt in 1914, Milliken got some of the stores, which became Mercantile Stores. The Milliken family retained about 40% of the chain (sold to Dillard's in 1998).

Roger Milliken, grandson of the founder, became the president of the company in 1947 and has ruled with a firm hand. He fired brother-in-law W. B. Dixon Stroud in 1955, and none of Roger's children, nephews, or nieces has ever been allowed to work for the company. The workers at Milliken's Darlington, South Carolina, mill voted to unionize in 1956. The next day Milliken closed the plant, beginning 24 years of litigation that ended at the US Supreme Court. Milliken settled with its workers for $5 million.

In the 1960s the company introduced Visa, a finish for easy-care fabrics. Milliken launched its Pursuit of Excellence program in 1981; the program stressed self-managed teams of employees and eliminated 700 management positions. Tom Peters dedicated his 1987 bestseller, *Thriving on Chaos,* to Roger.

Away from that limelight, Milliken is (and has always been) a secretive, closely held business. In 1989 that secrecy and family control were threatened when members of the Stroud branch of the family sued the company in the Delaware courts and then sold a small number of shares to Erwin Maddrey and Bettis Rainsford, executives of Milliken competitor Delta Woodside. The courts ruled in favor of Milliken in 1992; Maddrey and Rainsford were required to sign confidentiality agreements before receiving Milliken information. Roger financially backed opponents of NAFTA in 1993.

Milliken is known by competitors for its unofficial motto: "Steal ideas shamelessly." Woven-filament maker NRB sued Milliken in 1997 for corporate spying and the following year industrial textile maker Johnston Industries filed a similar lawsuit. Milliken settled both cases out of court.

In 1999 Milliken began using its Millitron dye technology to produce residential carpets and rugs. It also introduced new brands of patterned rugs (including Royal Dynasty, Prestige, American Heritage). In 2000 the company built a manufacturing facility in South Carolina to expand its production of Millard-brand clarifying agents. Milliken closed its Union and Saluda plants in 2004.

EXECUTIVES

Chairman: Roger Milliken, age 92
President and CEO: Ashley Allen, age 64
COO: Joe Salley, age 40
VP, Quality & Milliken University: Craig Long
VP Human Resources: Brad Kendall
Director Public Affairs: Richard Dillard
Director Safety and Health: Wayne Punch
President, Milliken Chemical: John Rekers

LOCATIONS

HQ: Milliken & Company
920 Milliken Rd., Spartanburg, SC 29303
Phone: 864-503-2020   **Fax:** 864-503-2100
Web: www.milliken.com

Milliken & Company has more than 60 manufacturing facilities worldwide, including operations in Belgium, Brazil, Denmark, France, Japan, Spain, the UK, and the US.

PRODUCTS/OPERATIONS

Selected Products
Chemicals
  Additives (antimicrobial agents, plastics additives)
  Carpet cleaner
  Coated products (extrusion coatings and composites, packaging systems)
  Colorants and tints (ClearTint, Liquitint, Palmer, Reactint)
  Elastomers
  Medical products
  Resin intermediates
  Specialty chemicals
  Textile chemicals (Lubestat, SynFac, SynStat, Versatint)
  Turf maintenance chemicals

Fabrics, carpet, and rugs
  Area rugs
  Automotive fabrics (upholstery and airbag fabrics)
  Carpet and carpet tiles
  Drapery fabrics
  Knit and woven apparel fabrics
  Table linen fabrics
  Upholstery fabric

COMPETITORS

Asahi Kasei
Beaulieu
Conso International
Dixie Group
Dow Chemical
DuPont
Guilford Mills
Interface, Inc.
International Textile Group
Johnston Textiles
Mohawk Industries
Mount Vernon Mills
Reliance Industries
Shaw Industries
Springs Global
SWIFT GALEY
W.L. Gore

Milwaukee Bucks

A herd of basketball fans gather around these Bucks. The Milwaukee Bucks professional basketball franchise joined the National Basketball Association in 1968 and earned a championship title just three years later with the help of Hall of Fame player Lew Alcindor (later Kareem Abdul-Jabbar). The team has made the NBA Finals only once since then (in 1974), but has generally been a contender for the postseason in recent years. Despite the Bucks' success on the court, the club has struggled with attendance at Milwaukee's aging Bradley Center. Wisconsin Senator Herb Kohl, whose family started the Kohl's department store chain, has owned the team since 1985.

Milwaukee enjoyed a string of playoff appearances under the direction of head coach George Karl, reaching the conference finals in 2001 (losing to the Philadelphia 76ers). Karl was fired in 2003, however, and the team has had up and down seasons since.

Terry Stotts became the Bucks ninth head coach in 2005 and the team again returned to the postseason, but it was promptly dumped from the tournament after a first round series loss to the Detroit Pistons. Stotts was fired midway through the 2006-07 season, with the team residing in last place in the Central Division.

In 2006 the Bucks announced a change to their uniforms, adopting a red-and-green color scheme to replace the purple-and-green uniforms they had used since 1993.

EXECUTIVES

President: Herb Kohl
General Manager: John Hammond
Head Coach: Scott Skiles, age 44
CFO: Mike Burr
VP Business Operations: John Steinmiller
Director Sales: Jim Grayson
Director Scouting: Billy McKinney
Director Basketball Operations: John Horst
Manager Equipment and Facilities: Dwayne Wilson
Manager Information Technology: Ron Kiepert
Head Athletic Trainer and Travel Coordinator: Marc Boff

LOCATIONS

HQ: Milwaukee Bucks, Inc.
Bradley Center, 1001 N. 4th St.,
Milwaukee, WI 53203
Phone: 414-227-0500   **Fax:** 414-227-0543
Web: www.nba.com/bucks

COMPETITORS

Cleveland Cavaliers
Chicago Bulls
Detroit Pistons
Indiana Pacers

HISTORICAL FINANCIALS

Company Type: Private

Income Statement

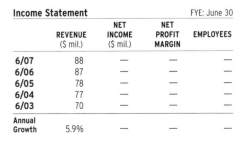

FYE: June 30

	REVENUE ($ mil.)	NET INCOME ($ mil.)	NET PROFIT MARGIN	EMPLOYEES
6/07	88	—	—	—
6/06	87	—	—	—
6/05	78	—	—	—
6/04	77	—	—	—
6/03	70	—	—	—
Annual Growth	5.9%	—	—	—

Revenue History

Minnesota Timberwolves

These wolves have basketball fans in the Twin Cities howling. The Minnesota Timberwolves franchise was awarded by the National Basketball Association to local businessmen Harvey Ratner and Marv Wolfenson in 1988, marking the return of NBA action to the Land of 10,000 Lakes for the first time since 1960 when the Minnesota Lakers moved to California to become the Los Angeles Lakers. The team has yet to win an NBA title but did advance to the Western Conference Finals in 2004. Glen Taylor, chairman of printing giant Taylor Corporation, led a group of 14 investors who bought the team in 1995.

EXECUTIVES

Owner: Glen A. Taylor
President: Rob Moor
General Manager: James (Jim) Stack
Head Coach: Randy Wittman, age 39
VP Basketball Operations: Kevin McHale, age 50
VP Communications: Ted Johnson
VP Fan Relations: Jeff Munneke
VP Marketing: Jason LaFrenz
Director of Finance: Peter Stene
Head Athletic Trainer: Gregg Farnam
Advance Scout: Brent Haskins
Scout: Zarko Durisic

LOCATIONS

HQ: Minnesota Timberwolves
600 1st Ave. North, Minneapolis, MN 55403
Phone: 612-673-1600   **Fax:** 612-673-1699
Web: www.nba.com/timberwolves

The Minnesota Timberwolves play at the 20,500-seat capacity Target Center in Minneapolis.

COMPETITORS

Denver Nuggets
Oklahoma City Thunder
Portland Trail Blazers
Utah Jazz

HISTORICAL FINANCIALS
Company Type: Private

Income Statement
FYE: June 30

	REVENUE ($ mil.)	NET INCOME ($ mil.)	NET PROFIT MARGIN	EMPLOYEES
6/07	103	—	—	—
6/06	103	—	—	—
6/05	101	—	—	—
6/04	97	—	—	—
6/03	85	—	—	—
Annual Growth	4.9%	—	—	—

Revenue History

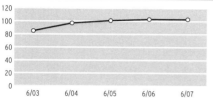

Minnesota Wild

Fans of this team are Wild about hockey, you might say. Minnesota Wild Hockey Club owns and operates the Minnesota Wild professional hockey franchise. The team joined the National Hockey League in the expansion of 2000 (along with the Columbus Blue Jackets), filling the void left after the Minnesota North Stars moved to Texas in 1993 to become the Dallas Stars. An investment group led by Robert Naegele Jr. helped bring hockey back to the Twin Cities. Former Nashville Predators owner Craig Leipold acquired control of the team from Naegele in 2008.

The Wild has been one of the most financially successful expansion franchises in NHL history, boasting a string of sellouts and a list of more than 7,500 people waiting for season tickets. The team has made three playoff appearances, never advancing past the first round.

Leipold, who sold the Preds to a group of Nashville businessmen for about $190 million in 2007, rejoined the ranks of NHL owners the following year when he purchased a 51% stake in the Minnesota team for $260 million. His Nashville franchise had struggled to build a fan base despite posting winning records and making the Stanley Cup playoffs three times since joining the league in 2001; Leipold claimed he lost about $70 million during the 2005-06 season.

Before starting the Nashville club in 1998, Leipold founded telemarketing firm Ameritel (later acquired by Convergys) and owned Rainfair Corporation, a maker of protective clothing that was sold to LaCrosse Footwear in 1996. His wife, Helen Johnson-Leipold, is CEO of outdoor equipment maker Johnson Outdoors and is part of the family that controls household products manufacturer S.C. Johnson & Son.

Former North Stars owner Norm Green — and NHL officials — drew the ire of Minnesota hockey fans when the Stars headed south for greener pastures in Dallas (where the franchise won its first Stanley Cup championship in 1999). Naegele and other investors, including Stanley Hubbard (CEO of Hubbard Broadcasting) and heirs of the Ordway family (early 3M investors), were awarded a new franchise for the Twin Cities market in 1997 as part of the league's expansion effort of the late 1990s.

EXECUTIVES

Owner: Craig L. Leipold
General Partner: Phil Falcone
President and General Manager: Doug Risebrough, age 54
Assistant General Manager, Hockey Operations: Tom Lynn, age 40
Assistant General Manager, Player Personnel: Tom Thompson, age 55
Head Coach: Jacques Lemaire, age 63
EVP and CFO: Pamela Wheelock
EVP: Matt Majka, age 48
VP Corporate Sales and Service: Tom Garrity, age 44
Amatuer Scouting Coordinator: Guy Lapointe, age 60
Player Development Coordinator: Barry MacKenzie, age 67
Director Professional Scouting: Blair Mackasey, age 52
Director Hockey Operations: Chris Snow, age 27

LOCATIONS

HQ: Minnesota Wild Hockey Club, LP
317 Washington St., St. Paul, MN 55102
Phone: 651-602-6000   **Fax:** 651-222-1055
Web: www.wild.com

The Minnesota Wild play at the 18,064-seat capacity Xcel Energy Center in St. Paul, Minnesota.

COMPETITORS

Calgary Flames
Colorado Avalanche
Edmonton Oilers
Vancouver Canucks

HISTORICAL FINANCIALS
Company Type: Private

Income Statement
FYE: June 30

	REVENUE ($ mil.)	NET INCOME ($ mil.)	NET PROFIT MARGIN	EMPLOYEES
6/07	78	—	—	—
6/06	71	—	—	—
6/05	0	—	—	—
6/04	71	—	—	—
6/03	79	—	—	—
Annual Growth	(0.3%)	—	—	—

Revenue History

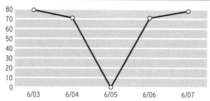

MITRE Corporation

The MITRE Corporation may not be able to cut perfect angles, but it can provide some fine systems engineering and information technology (IT) services. The not-for-profit organization develops, analyzes, and protects information systems for the US Department of Defense, the Internal Revenue Service, and the Federal Aviation Administration. MITRE's three Federally Funded Research and Development Centers (FFRDCs) provide such services as systems engineering, systems integration, and IT consulting. Founded in 1958 by a group of former MIT researchers, MITRE also designs surveillance and reconnaissance systems and provides air traffic management services.

EXECUTIVES

Chairman: James R. Schlesinger, age 79
Vice Chairman: Charles S. Robb
President, CEO, and Trustee; Director, DOD C3I Federally Funded Research and Development Center: Alfred Grasso
Director, SVP, and General Manager, Center for Advanced Aviation System Development: Agam N. Sinha
Director, SVP, and General Manager, Center for Enterprise Modernization and IRS Federally Funded Research and Development Center: Jason F. Providakes
SVP, CFO, and Treasurer: Mark W. Kontos
SVP and Corporate Chief Engineer: Louis S. Metzger
SVP and General Manager, Center for Integrated Intelligence Systems: Robert F. Nesbit
SVP and General Manager, Command and Control Center: David H. Lehman
VP and Chief Human Resources Officer: Lisa R. Bender
VP, General Counsel, and Corporate Secretary: Sol Glasner
VP and CIO: Robert A. Mikelskas
VP and CTO: Stephen D. Huffman
Director, Corporate Communications and Knowledge Services: Catherine L. Crawford
Auditors: PricewaterhouseCoopers LLP

LOCATIONS

HQ: The MITRE Corporation
202 Burlington Rd., Bedford, MA 01730
Phone: 781-271-2000   **Fax:** 781-271-2271
Web: www.mitre.org

PRODUCTS/OPERATIONS

Selected Practice Areas
Acquisition and systems analysis
Aviation systems, safety, and security
Command and control
Cybersecurity
Emerging technologies
Enterprise systems engineering
Global networking
Healthcare transformation
Homeland security
Intelligence, surveillance, and reconnaissance
Large-scale enterprise transformation

COMPETITORS

Battelle Memorial
QinetiQ
SAIC

HISTORICAL FINANCIALS
Company Type: Not-for-profit

Income Statement

				FYE: September 30
	REVENUE ($ mil.)	NET INCOME ($ mil.)	NET PROFIT MARGIN	EMPLOYEES
9/07	1,113	—	—	6,816
9/06	1,025	—	—	6,300
9/05	962	—	—	5,750
9/04	871	—	—	5,821
9/03	785	—	—	5,300
Annual Growth	9.1%	—	—	6.5%

Revenue History

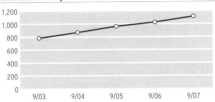

Modern Woodmen

No need to pitch a tent to have Modern Woodmen in your camp. One of the largest fraternal benefit societies in the US, Modern Woodmen of America provides annuities and life insurance to more than 750,000 members through some 1,500 agents. The group, founded in 1883, is organized into "camps" (or lodges) that provide social, recreational, and service — as well as financial — benefits to members. Founder Joseph Cullen Root chose the society's name to compare pioneering woodmen clearing forests to men using life insurance to remove financial burdens their families could face upon their deaths. Modern Woodmen offerings also include mutual funds, brokerage, and retirement and educational savings plans.

Modern Woodmen subsidiary MWA Financial Services, formed in 2001, is a securities broker/dealer. MWABank, inaugurated in 2003, offers retail banking services.

EXECUTIVES

President, CEO, and Director: W. Kenny Massey
National Secretary and Director: Gerald P. Odean
Investment Manager, Treasurer, and Director:
Nick S. Coin
Manager, Arkansas and Director: Albert T. Hurst Jr.
Public Relations Coordinator: Sharon K. Snawerdt
General Counsel and Director: Darcy G. Callas

LOCATIONS

HQ: Modern Woodmen of America
1701 1st Ave., Rock Island, IL 61201
Phone: 309-786-6481   **Fax:** 309-793-5547
Web: www.modern-woodmen.org

PRODUCTS/OPERATIONS

2007 Sales

	$ mil.	% of total
Premiums & other considerations		
Life & annuities	590.4	55
Other	6.1	1
Net investment income	435.0	41
Amortization of interest maintenance reserve	4.0	—
Other	30.1	3
Total	1,065.6	100

COMPETITORS

Allstate
Liberty Mutual
MassMutual
MetLife
Nationwide
New York Life
Northwestern Mutual
Prudential
Reliance Standard
State Farm
Thrivent Financial
Woodmen of the World

HISTORICAL FINANCIALS
Company Type: Not-for-profit

Income Statement

				FYE: December 31
	ASSETS ($ mil.)	NET INCOME ($ mil.)	INCOME AS % OF ASSETS	EMPLOYEES
12/07	8,318	97	1.2%	1,500
12/06	7,929	99	1.3%	1,500
Annual Growth	4.9%	(2.6%)	—	0.0%

2007 Year-End Financials

Equity as % of assets: 14.1%   Long-term debt ($ mil.): —
Return on assets: 1.2%   Sales ($ mil.): 1,066
Return on equity: 8.6%

Net Income History

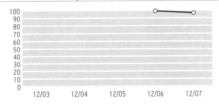

Mohegan Tribal Gaming Authority

The sun also rises at Mohegan Sun Casino, a complex run by the Mohegan Tribal Gaming Authority for the Mohegan Indian tribe of Connecticut. The Native American-themed Mohegan Sun Casino has more than 6,000 slot machines, some 300 tables, and simulcast horse race wagering. The facility also includes a 1,200-room luxury hotel, a 10,000-seat arena, a 350-seat cabaret, and dozens of stores and restaurants. The company also owns a horse racetrack, Mohegan Sun at Pocono Downs, in Pennsylvania. Gambling revenues go to the Mohegan Tribe and are used for cultural and educational programs. The tribe has lived as a community for hundreds of years in what is today southeastern Connecticut and has about 1,700 members.

In addition to operating casinos and hotels, the Mohegan Tribal Gaming Authority also owns the Connecticut Sun WNBA basketball team.

Other operations include subsidiaries that plan to assist the Cowlitz Indian Tribe of Washington and the Menominee Indian Tribe of Wisconsin to open casinos. The company has submitted proposals to co-develop gaming projects in New York and Kansas as well.

The company purchased Mohegan Sun at Pocono Downs (also known simply as Pocono Downs), from Penn National Gaming for $175 million in 2005. The following year the company announced plans for a $925 million expansion at Mohegan Sun Casino, including a new 1,000-room hotel and more gaming space.

In 2007 the Mohegan Tribal Gaming Authority expanded into golf with the acquisition of Pautipaug Country Club in Connecticut. It purchased the golf course for some $4.7 million and renamed it Mohegan Sun Country Club at Pautipaug.

EXECUTIVES

Chairman: Bruce S. (Two Dogs) Bozsum, age 47
Vice Chairwoman: Marilynn R. (Lynn) Malerba, age 55
CEO; President and CEO, Mohegan Sun:
Mitchell Grossinger Etess, age 46, $1,044,000 pay (prior to title change)
COO; EVP and COO, Mohegan Sun:
Jeffrey E. (Jeff) Hartmann, age 45, $967,000 pay (prior to title change)
CFO, MTGA and Mohegan Sun: Leo M. Chupaska, age 59, $741,000 pay (prior to title change)
SVP, Resort Operations: Gary S. Crowder, age 54
VP, Construction Management: Harry Coldreck
VP, Corporate Development: Paul Brody
VP, Corporate Finance: Peter J. Roberti
VP, Legal Administration: Michael J. Ciaccio
President and CEO, Pocono Downs: Robert J. Soper, age 35, $357,000 pay
Recording Secretary and Director: Allison D. Johnson, age 37
Treasurer and Director: William Quidgeon Jr., age 45
Public Relations Ambassador, Mohegan Tribe:
Jayne G. Fawcett, age 68
Auditors: PricewaterhouseCoopers LLP

LOCATIONS

HQ: Mohegan Tribal Gaming Authority
1 Mohegan Sun Blvd., Uncasville, CT 06382
Phone: 860-862-8000   **Fax:** 860-862-7824
Web: www.mtga.com

PRODUCTS/OPERATIONS

2007 Sales

	% of total
Gaming	83
Food & beverage	6
Hotel	3
Retail & other	8
Total	100

2007 Sales

	% of total
Mohegan Sun	88
Pocono Downs	12
Total	100

Table Games

Baccarat
Blackjack
Caribbean stud poker
Craps
Pai Gow poker
Roulette

COMPETITORS

Harrah's Entertainment
Mashantucket Pequot
Trump Resorts

HISTORICAL FINANCIALS
Company Type: Private

Income Statement
FYE: September 30

	REVENUE ($ mil.)	NET INCOME ($ mil.)	NET PROFIT MARGIN	EMPLOYEES
9/07	1,620	173	10.7%	10,400
9/06	1,426	155	10.9%	10,400
9/05	1,332	24	1.8%	10,600
9/04	1,257	103	8.2%	10,300
9/03	1,189	96	8.1%	11,100
Annual Growth	8.0%	15.9%	—	(1.6%)

2007 Year-End Financials
Debt ratio: —
Return on equity: 1,735.0%
Cash ($ mil.): —
Current ratio: —
Long-term debt ($ mil.): —

Net Income History

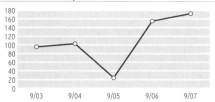

Momentive Performance Materials

Gathering momentum after its spin-off from General Electric, Momentive Performance Materials is ready to take on the world. The company manufactures silicones, quartz, and ceramic products for everything from adhesive labels to hair care products to pesticides. Silicone is prized for its ability to provide resistance (to heat, UV rays, and chemical reactions) and allow for different levels of lubricity and adhesion, therefore it is used by makers of a vast array of products. Its quartz and ceramic products go into semiconductors, cosmetics, and fiber optics. Created in 2006 after GE sold its former Advanced Materials unit to Apollo Management, the company operates globally through about 25 production plants.

When it was a part of GE the company had joint ventures with the likes of Bayer and Toshiba, but Momentive bought out its partners to prepare for its formation as a stand-alone company. It now serves companies as diverse as BASF, Lowe's, Motorola, and Unilever.

The silicones unit makes up the bulk of Momentive's business, accounting for just about 90% of sales. The company divides its global operations nearly equally among the Asia/Pacific region, Europe, and North America.

EXECUTIVES
Chairman: Joshua J. (Josh) Harris, age 43
President, CEO, and Director: Jonathan Rich, age 52
CFO: Steven Delarge, age 50
CTO: Eric Thaler, age 47
CIO: Jacky Wright, age 48
General Manager Global Operations: Joerg Krueger, age 44

General Counsel, Secretary, and Director: Douglas Johns, age 50
Manager Global Business Development: Mark Irwin, age 43
Manager Human Resources: Edward Stratton, age 49
President and CEO, Asia Pacific: Rachel Duan
President and CEO, Americas: Shawn Williams, age 44
President and CEO, Europe, Middle East, Africa and India: Ian Moore, age 48
President and CEO, Quartz: Raymond F. (Ray) Kolberg, age 46
Auditors: KPMG LLP

LOCATIONS
HQ: Momentive Performance Materials Inc.
22 Corporate Woods Blvd., Albany, NY 12211
Phone: 800-295-2392
Web: www.momentive.com

2007 Sales

	$ mil.	% of total
Europe	928.9	37
Asia/Pacific	758.9	30
US	688.6	27
Mexico & Brazil	83.1	3
Canada	78.3	3
Total	**2,537.8**	**100**

PRODUCTS/OPERATIONS

2007 Sales

	$ mil.	% of total
Silicones	2,264.3	89
Quartz	273.5	11
Total	**2,537.8**	**100**

COMPETITORS
3M
Dow Corning
Evonik Degussa
SABIC Innovative Plastics
Saint-Gobain Ceramics & Plastics
Shin-Etsu Chemical
Tosoh
Wacker Chemie

HISTORICAL FINANCIALS
Company Type: Private

Income Statement
FYE: December 31

	REVENUE ($ mil.)	NET INCOME ($ mil.)	NET PROFIT MARGIN	EMPLOYEES
12/07	2,538	(254)	—	5,117
12/06	2,414	(37)	—	4,982
12/05	2,342	74	3.2%	—
12/04	2,228	67	3.0%	—
Annual Growth	4.4%	—	—	2.7%

2007 Year-End Financials
Debt ratio: 959.8%
Return on equity: —
Cash ($ mil.): —
Current ratio: —
Long-term debt ($ mil.): 3,058

Net Income History

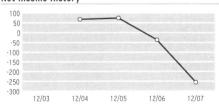

Monitronics International

Monitronics International keeps its employees on guard while its customers are away. The company provides alarm system monitoring services, which monitor signals arising from burglaries, fires, and other events, to nearly 500,000 customers throughout the US through its network of independent alarm dealers. The authorized dealers sell, install, and service security systems and related equipment to residential and commercial customers. Monitronics monitors its clients' accounts at the company's central monitoring station in Dallas. Investment firm ABRY Partners owns more than half of Monitronics, which was founded in 1994.

Monitronics offers its security service through subscriber accounts, which are purchased from dealers in the company's network. The company offers its dealers initial and ongoing training, marketing assistance, technical support, and discount pricing on equipment.

EXECUTIVES
Chairman: James R. (Jim) Hull, $733,427 pay
President, CEO, and Director: Michael R. Haislip, $350,057 pay
VP and CFO: Michael R. Meyers, $354,381 pay
VP and CIO: Charles Reilly
VP Customer Services: Rick L. Hudson, $155,143 pay
VP Finance and Treasurer: Stephen M. Hedrick
VP Operations and Secretary: Robert N. Sherman, $180,927 pay
VP Quality Assurance: Barry P. Johnson
Human Resources: T. Harmon
Auditors: Ernst & Young LLP

LOCATIONS
HQ: Monitronics International, Inc.
2350 Valley View Ln., Ste. 100, Dallas, TX 75234
Phone: 972-243-7443   **Fax:** 972-484-1393
Web: www.monitronics.com

PRODUCTS/OPERATIONS

Selected Products and Services
Access control
Burglar alarm systems
Latchkey services
Smoke/fire monitoring
Video monitoring

COMPETITORS
ADT Security
AlliedBarton Security
Brink's Home Security
C.O.P.S. Monitoring
Honeywell ACS
Protection One
Security Associates International

Motiva Enterprises

Making money is a major motive behind Motiva Enterprises, which operates the eastern and southeastern US refining and marketing businesses of Royal Dutch Shell's Shell Oil unit and Saudi Aramco. The company operates three refineries with a total capacity of 740,000 barrels a day, and it sells fuel at 7,900 Shell-branded gas stations. It also has stakes in 41 refined product storage terminals with an aggregate storage capacity of 19.8 million barrels. Motiva and sister company Shell Oil Products US (formerly Equilon), which operates in the West and Midwest, together make up the #1 US gasoline retailer. Motiva is a 50-50 joint venture of Shell and Saudi Aramco.

Motiva was formed in 1998 to combine the eastern and southeastern US refining and marketing businesses of Texaco, Shell Oil, and Saudi Aramco. Texaco and Saudi Aramco each owned 35% of Motiva, and Shell owned 30%. Texaco sold its stakes in Motiva (to Shell and Saudi Aramco) and Equilon (to Shell) to gain regulatory clearance to be acquired by Chevron. In 2002 Shell took full ownership of Equilon, which was renamed Shell Oil Products US.

In 2004 the company sold its Delaware refining complex to Premcor (now a part of Valero Energy) for $800 million.

In 2007 the company broke ground on a massive $7 billion refinery expansion in Port Arthur, Texas.

HISTORY

Although Motiva was not created until the late 1990s, two of its key players, Texaco and Saudi Aramco, had been doing business together in various ventures since 1936. But they had never tried anything on the scale of the Star Enterprise joint venture approved by Texaco CEO James Kinnear and Saudi Oil Minister Hisham Nazer in late 1988. The deal, valued at nearly $2 billion, was the largest joint venture of its kind in the US.

The agreement to create Star Enterprise sprang, in part, from Texaco's tumultuous ride following its purchase of Getty Oil in 1983. Texaco was sued by Pennzoil for pre-empting Pennzoil's bid for Getty, and Pennzoil won a $10.5 billion judgment in 1985. Texaco filed for bankruptcy in 1987 and eventually settled with Pennzoil for $3 billion.

In 1988 Texaco emerged from bankruptcy after announcing a deal with Saudi Aramco at a stockholder meeting. Texaco got a much-needed injection of cash, and Saudi Aramco gained a steady US outlet for its supply of crude. The Saudis had been at odds with their OPEC partners for several years, and in late 1985 then-Saudi Oil Minister Sheikh Yamani and Saudi Aramco began increasing production, leading to an oil price crash in 1986. Nazer replaced Yamani and changed Saudi Aramco's strategy. To secure market share, the Saudis started signing long-term supply contracts.

The deal with Texaco gave Saudi Aramco a 50% interest in Texaco's refining and marketing operations in the East and on the Gulf Coast — about two-thirds of Texaco's US downstream operations — including three refineries and its Texaco-brand stations. In return, the Saudis paid $812 million cash and provided three-fourths of Star's initial inventory, about 30 million barrels of oil. They also agreed to a 20-year, 600,000-barrel-a-day

commitment of crude. Each company named three representatives to Star's management.

The new company soon initiated a modernization and expansion program: It acquired 65 stations, built 30 new outlets, and remodeled another 172 during 1989. In 1994 the company began franchising its Texaco-brand Star Mart convenience stores. By mid-1995 it had sold 30 franchises.

Facing a more competitive oil marketing environment in the US, Shell Oil approached Texaco in 1996 with the possibility of merging some of their operations. In 1998 Shell and Texaco formed Equilon Enterprises, a joint venture that combined their western and midwestern refining and marketing activities.

Later that year Shell and Texaco/Saudi Aramco (Star Enterprises) formed Motiva to merge the companies' refining and marketing businesses on the East Coast and Gulf Coast. Shell and Texaco also formed two more Houston companies as satellite firms for Motiva and Equilon: Equiva Trading Company, a general partnership that provides supplies and trading services, and Equiva Services, which provides support services. Wilson Berry, the former president of Texaco Refining and Marketing, took over as CEO of Motiva.

In 1999 Motiva and Equilon together bought 15 product terminals from Premcor. To boost profits, the Motiva board appointed Texaco downstream veteran Roger Ebert as its new CEO in 2000, replacing Berry, who announced his resignation after a Motiva board meeting.

US government regulators in 2001 required that Texaco sell its Motiva and Equilon stakes in order to be acquired by Chevron. That year Texaco veteran John Boles replaced Ebert (who retired) as CEO. Shell and Saudi Aramco agreed to buy Texaco's stake in Motiva, and Shell agreed to buy Texaco's stake in Equilon. The deals were completed in 2002.

Boles retired in 2004.

EXECUTIVES

President and CEO: Bob Pease
CFO: Ronald Langan
VP Refining: Rudy Goetzee
VP Commercial Marketing and Distribution: Ralph Grimmer
VP Human Resources and Corporate Services: Elaine Guarrero
VP Services: John Kiappes
VP Supply: Brian Smith
VP Retail: Ian Sutcliffe
Chief Diversity Officer: John Jefferson
General Manager Wholesale: Hugh Cooley
Treasurer and Director of Finance: James B. Castles
General Counsel: Lynda Irvine
General Manager Business Development: Dan Grinstead
Regional Account Manager: Joe Ahern
Business Ventures and Ethanol Manager, North: John R. Gray
Business Development Manager, Northeast: Steve Johnson
Business Development Manager, South: Frank Rodriguez
Distribution Operations, Gulf Coast: Jon Seveney
Distribution Operations, Mid-Atlantic: Lynn Courvelle
Distribution Operations, Northeast: John Fuller
Media Relations Advisor: Karyn Leonardi-Cattolica

LOCATIONS

HQ: Motiva Enterprises LLC
700 Milam St., Houston, TX 77002
Phone: 713-277-8000
Web: www.motivaenterprises.com

Motiva operates gas stations in the northeastern and southeastern US. It has refineries in Convent and Norco, Louisiana; and Port Arthur, Texas.

Major Operations

Alabama
Arkansas
Connecticut
Delaware
Florida
Georgia
Louisiana
Maryland
Massachusetts
Mississippi
New Hampshire
New Jersey
New York
North Carolina
Pennsylvania
Rhode Island
Tennessee
Texas
Vermont
Virginia

COMPETITORS

7-Eleven
BP
CITGO
Cumberland Farms
Exxon
Gulf Oil
Marathon Petroleum
Racetrac Petroleum
Sunoco
Valero Energy
Wawa, Inc.

Mount Sinai Hospital

Mount Sinai Hospital opened its doors in 1919 with 60 beds to serve the burgeoning population of Eastern European immigrants in the Windy City. It is now a more than 430-bed teaching, research, and tertiary-care facility. Mount Sinai trains medical students from the Rosalind Franklin University of Medicine & Science. The hospital is a part of the Sinai Health System, which also includes the Schwab Rehabilitation Hospital, the Sinai Children's Hospital, the Sinai Medical Group's primary-care clinics, and the Sinai Community Institute's health, wellness, and educational programs.

EXECUTIVES

Chairman: Michael E. Traynor
President: Larry E. Volkmar
CFO: Charles (Chuck) Weis
VP, Corporate Services: David Hoekstra
VP, Medical Affairs: Maurice A. Scwartz
Auditors: Ernst & Young LLP

LOCATIONS

HQ: Mount Sinai Hospital
California Avenue at 15th Street, Chicago, IL 60608
Phone: 773-542-2000   **Fax:** 773-257-5145
Web: www.sinai.org

COMPETITORS

Northwestern Memorial HealthCare
Resurrection Health Care
University of Chicago Medical Center
Weiss Memorial Hospital

MTD Products

MTD Products wants to mow down its foes. The outdoor power equipment manufacturer makes walk-behind and tractor mowers, snow throwers, edgers, and tillers under the Cub Cadet, Bolens, McCulloch, White Outdoor, Yard-Man, and Yard Machines brands. Its Cub Cadet Commercial line is geared toward landscapers. In 2001 MTD bought the Troy-Bilt tiller and mower business from Garden Way, which filed for bankruptcy. MTD sells its products through home improvement and farm supply stores, big-box retailers, and hardware shops. MTD was formed in 1932 by German immigrants Theo Moll, Emil Jochum, and Erwin Gerhard as the Modern Tool and Die Company. The Moll family, including CEO Curtis Moll, owns MTD.

In November 2005 MTD Products formed a 50-50 joint venture with transmission manufacturer Torotrak. The entity, called Infinitrak LLC, combines Torotrak's technology and MTD's manufacturing and distribution expertise to reach the outdoor power equipment market. Manufacturing of IVT units, sold under the Infinitrak brand name, began in 2006. While MTD Products received the first Infinitrak units, it began selling to third parties in 2008. MTD Products has manufacturing facilities in Canada, Europe, and the US.

EXECUTIVES

Chairman and CEO: Curtis E. Moll, age 68
CFO: Jeff Deuch
EVP Marketing and Sales: Jean Hlay
EVP Operations and Global Supply: Theodore S. Moll, age 65
EVP Product Development: Hartmut Kaesgen
Director Health and Welfare: Fran Walsh

LOCATIONS

HQ: MTD Products Inc.
  5965 Grafton Rd., Valley City, OH 44280
Phone: 330-225-2600   **Fax:** 330-273-4617
Web: www.mtdproducts.com

COMPETITORS

Alamo Group	Emak Group
Black & Decker	Exmark Manufacturing
Blount International	Honda
Deere	Toro

Mutual of America Life Insurance

Mutual of America Life Insurance may be the saving grace for a lot of folks in the not-for-profit sector. The company provides retirement savings to employees of not-for-profit organizations who are excluded from Social Security and other retirement programs. Mutual of America still serves that market, but also offers its employee-sponsored retirement plans, savings plans, and insurance products to private-sector organizations (typically small to midsized businesses), and

direct to individual investors. The company has about $12 billion in assets under management.

Founded in 1945, Mutual of America and subsidiary Mutual of America Capital Management Corp. today provide products and services throughout the US via a network of more than 35 regional field offices.

EXECUTIVES

Chairman, President, and CEO: Thomas J. Moran, age 55
COO; Chairman, President, and CEO, Mutual of America Investment; Chairman and CEO, Mutual of America Capital Management: Manfred Altstadt
SEVP and General Counsel: Patrick A. Burns
SEVP and Chief Marketing Officer: William S. Conway
SEVP and CFO; Chairman, President, and CEO, Mutual of America Institutional Funds: John R. Greed
EVP, Corporate Secretary, and Assistant to the Chairman: Diane M. Aramony
EVP and Chief Actuary: Jeremy J. Brown
EVP Administrative Technical Services: Jared Gutman
EVP Human Resources and Corporate Services: Daniel J. LeSaffre
EVP and Treasurer: George L. Medlin
EVP and CIO: Joan M. Squires
EVP MIS Operations: Robert Giaquinto
EVP Sales Operations: William Rose
SVP Public Relations: James E. Flynn
Auditors: KPMG LLP

LOCATIONS

HQ: Mutual of America Life Insurance Company
  320 Park Ave., New York, NY 10022
Phone: 212-224-1600   **Fax:** 212-224-2539
Web: www.mutualofamerica.com

PRODUCTS/OPERATIONS

2007 Sales

	$ mil.	% of total
Premium & annuity considerations	1,388.4	77
Investment income	350.3	19
Separate account investment & administrative fees	50.5	3
Life & disability insurance premiums	16.9	1
Other	4.1	—
Total	**1,810.2**	**100**

COMPETITORS

AIG Retirement Services
American United Mutual
Ameriprise
Catholic Order of Foresters
Charles Schwab
FMR
MFS
National Life Insurance
Principal Financial
TIAA-CREF

HISTORICAL FINANCIALS

Company Type: Mutual company

Income Statement

FYE: December 31

	ASSETS ($ mil.)	NET INCOME ($ mil.)	INCOME AS % OF ASSETS	EMPLOYEES
12/07	13,021	8	0.1%	—
12/06	12,442	17	0.1%	—
Annual Growth	4.7%	(56.4%)	—	—

2007 Year-End Financials

Equity as % of assets: 6.4%	Long-term debt ($ mil.): —
Return on assets: 0.1%	Sales ($ mil.): 1,810
Return on equity: 0.9%	

Net Income History

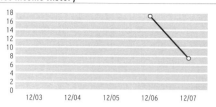

Mutual of Omaha

In the wild kingdom that is today's insurance industry, The Mutual of Omaha Companies wants to distinguish itself from the pack. The company provides individual, group, and employee benefits products through a range of affiliated companies. It offers health and accident coverage via subsidiary Mutual of Omaha Insurance; its United of Omaha Life Insurance unit offers life insurance and annuities. The firm also offers brokerage services, pension plans, and mutual funds through its Mutual of Omaha Investor Services business. Mutual of Omaha, which is owned by its policyholders, offers its products mainly through networks of independent agents.

Mutual of Omaha is exiting the health business in some areas and has sold off its employer-based group health coverage. It kept its employer-based life, disability, dental, and supplemental health coverage, but sold off the major medical coverage to Coventry Health Care in 2007. At the same time, the company launched its Medicare Supplement insurance products

Taking advantage of changes in regulatory restrictions, Mutual of Omaha is expanding into banking through acquisitions. Its key markets are rapidly growing cities where it already has high numbers of insurance customers. Operating as Mutual of Omaha Bank, it provides commercial and personal banking through more than a dozen locations in Nebraska and Colorado. The company intends to eventually offer Internet banking nationwide.

The company's sponsorship of the long-running television series *Mutual of Omaha's Wild Kingdom* introduced it to a generation of Americans. Recognizing that the connection remained strong, the company has revived the television series, which now runs on Discovery Communications' Animal Planet cable channel.

HISTORY

Charter Mutual Benefit Health & Accident Association got its start in Omaha, Nebraska, in 1909. A year later half of its founders quit, leaving a group headed by pharmaceuticals businessman H. S. Weller in charge. He tapped C. C. Criss as principal operating officer, general manager, and treasurer. Criss brought in his wife Mabel and brother Neil to help run the business.

Formed to offer accident and disability protection at a time when there were many fraudulent benefit societies, Charter Mutual Benefit Health faced consumer resistance that slowed growth in its first 10 years. By 1920 it was licensed in only nine states. Experience helped it refine its products and improve its policies' comprehensibility.

By 1924 the firm had more than doubled its penetration, gaining licensing in 24 states.

The US was nearing the depths of the Depression when Weller died in 1932. Criss succeeded him as president. The stock crash had brought a steep decline in the value of the firm's asset base, and premium income dropped (accompanied by an increase in claims). Even so, Mutual Benefit Health expanded its agency force, the scope of its benefits, and its operations. It went into Canada in 1935 and began a campaign to obtain licensing throughout the US.

By 1939 the company was licensed in all 48 states. During WWII it wrote coverage for civilians killed or injured in acts of war in the US (including Hawaii) and Canada. With paranoia running high and consumer goods in short supply, the insurance industry boomed during the war (and payouts on stateside act-of-war claims were low to nonexistent). Criss retired in 1949.

Gearing up its postwar sales efforts, in 1950 the company changed its name to Mutual of Omaha and adopted its distinctive chieftain logo. During the 1950s it added specialty accident and group medical coverage. In 1963 it made an advertising coup when it launched *Mutual of Omaha's Wild Kingdom*. Hosted by zoo director Marlin Perkins and, later, naturalist sidekick Jim Fowler, the show was one of the most popular nature programs of all time. Later that decade the company added investment management to its services.

Changes in the health care industry during the 1990s led Mutual of Omaha to de-emphasize its traditional indemnity products in favor of building managed care alternatives. In 1993 it joined with Alegent Health System to form managed care company Preferred HealthAlliance. Mutual of Omaha also stopped writing new major medical coverage in such states as California, Florida, New Jersey, and New York, where state laws made providing health care onerous. This led the company to cut its workforce by about 10% in 1996.

In 1999 it bought out Alegent's interest in their joint venture and entered the credit card business (offering First USA Visa cards). The firm also lifted its $25,000 limit for coverage of AIDS-related illnesses (its standard limit is $1 million); the company had been sued over the policy.

In the new millennium, the company enhanced its products targeted towards seniors, as well as introducing more flexible personal health care plans.

Focusing on its core individual and employer-based lines, in 2003 the company sold the renewal rights to all of its Omaha Property and Casualty Co. (OPAC) policies to Fidelity National Financial. After all the actual operations had been transferred, in 2005 the UK's Beazley Group bought up the OPAC operating license.

In 2006 the firm sold its innowave water purification subsidiary to Waterlogic International.

EXECUTIVES

EVP, CFO and Treasurer: David A. Diamond, age 52
Chairman and CEO; Chairman and CEO, United of Omaha Life Insurance Co.: Daniel P. (Dan) Neary, age 56
EVP Group Benefit Services: Daniel P. Martin
EVP and General Counsel: Thomas J. McCusker
EVP Customer Service: Madeline R. Rucker
EVP and Treasurer: Tommie D. Thompson
EVP Individual Financial Services; President, United World Life Insurance Co.: Michael C. (Mike) Weekly
EVP and Chief Investment Officer; President, Mutual of Omaha Investor Services: Richard A. (Rick) Witt
EVP Information Services: James Hanson

EVP Corporate Services and Human Resources: Stacy A. Scholtz
SVP, Group Health Plans: Joe Connolly
First VP and Regional Sales Officer: Mike Matlock
First VP, Health Networks: Kurt Irlbeck
First VP, Voluntary Benefits: Joan Malouf
President and CEO, Omaha Financial Holdings: Jeffrey R. (Jeff) Schmid
Market President, Mutual of Omaha Bank: Robert F. Strong
Auditors: Deloitte & Touche LLP

LOCATIONS

HQ: The Mutual of Omaha Companies
Mutual of Omaha Plaza, Omaha, NE 68175
Phone: 402-342-7600   **Fax:** 402-351-2775
Web: www.mutualofomaha.com

PRODUCTS/OPERATIONS

2007 Revenues

	$ mil.	% of total
Health & accident	2,023.7	48
Life & annuity	1,171.2	28
Net investment income	867.1	20
Net realized investment gains	17.1	—
Other	162.5	4
Total	**4,241.6**	**100**

Selected Subsidiaries and Affiliates

Companion Life Insurance Company (insurance in New York)
Mutual of Omaha Investor Services, Inc. (mutual funds)
Omaha Financial Holdings (banking)
United of Omaha Life Insurance Company
United World Life Insurance Company

COMPETITORS

Aetna
Allstate
Assurant
CIGNA
CNA Financial
Guardian Life
John Hancock Financial
Liberty Mutual
MassMutual
MetLife
New York Life
Northwestern Mutual
Prudential
State Farm
USAA

HISTORICAL FINANCIALS

Company Type: Mutual company

Income Statement

	ASSETS ($ mil.)	NET INCOME ($ mil.)	INCOME AS % OF ASSETS	FYE: December 31 EMPLOYEES
12/07	19,447	217	1.1%	—
12/06	19,008	166	0.9%	4,619
12/05	18,374	121	0.7%	5,053
12/04	18,540	125	0.7%	—
12/03	18,444	170	0.9%	5,847
Annual Growth	**1.3%**	**6.4%**	**—**	**(7.6%)**

2007 Year-End Financials

Equity as % of assets: 18.3%   Long-term debt ($ mil.): —
Return on assets: 1.1%   Sales ($ mil.): 4,242
Return on equity: 6.2%

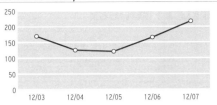

Net Income History

NAACP

The NAACP (National Association for the Advancement of Colored People) strives to ensure that all people are represented and have equal rights in American society and culture, regardless of race. The nation's oldest and largest civil rights organization, the group works via advocacy, education, and research, and it publishes the magazine *Crisis*. It registers African Americans to vote, encourages academic achievement among high school students, and works with inmates to promote education and reduce recidivism. Sources of support include contributions and membership dues. The NAACP was founded in 1909 by a group that included W.E.B. Du Bois and Ida B. Wells-Barnett.

Benjamin Jealous became president and CEO of the association in September 2008. Previously president of San Francisco-based Rosenberg Foundation, Jealous has logged several years of experience at Amnesty International (directing its US Domestic Human Rights program) and the National Newspaper Publishers Association (as well as the *Jackson Advocate*).

EXECUTIVES

Chairman: Julian Bond
Vice Chairwoman: Roslyn M. Brock
President and CEO: Benjamin T. (Ben) Jealous, age 35
COO: Rev Nelson B. Rivers III
CFO: J. Linloy Cox
Treasurer and Director: Francisco L. Borges, age 53
General Counsel and Director: Dennis C. Hayes
Chief Policy Officer: John H. Jackson
Chief Administrative Officer: Georgia A. Noone
Executive Director, Hollywood Bureau: Vicangelo (Vic) Bulluck
Director, Washington Bureau: Hilary O. Shelton

LOCATIONS

HQ: NAACP
4805 Mount Hope Dr., Baltimore, MD 21215
Phone: 410-580-5777   **Fax:** 410-585-1310
Web: www.naacp.org

PRODUCTS/OPERATIONS

Selected Programs

Civic engagement
Criminal justice
Economic empowerment
Education
Health
Research

NASCAR

In the race for riches in the sports world, NASCAR is on the right track. The National Association for Stock Car Auto Racing oversees one of the most popular and fastest-growing spectator sports in the US. NASCAR runs more than 100 races each year in three racing circuits: the Nationwide, Craftsman Truck, and its signature Sprint Cup Series. Featuring popular drivers such as Jeff Gordon and Dale Jarrett, the Sprint Cup draws millions of fans to the tracks each year. In addition to organizing and promoting the races, the association negotiates broadcast rights and licenses the NASCAR brand for merchandise. NASCAR was founded in 1948 by Bill France Sr. and is still owned by the France family.

Through various efforts, NASCAR has been expanding its fan base beyond its core audience of Southern white males to include more urban and female fans. The growing popularity of the sport has resulted in TV ratings that are second only to the National Football League, spurring a new $4.4 billion TV contract with Disney's ABC and ESPN, Time Warner's TNT, and News Corp's FOX and the SPEED channel that began in 2007 and runs through 2014. The increased coverage should help continue to propel stock car racing into new markets.

NASCAR's premier racing circuit was renamed the Sprint Cup Series in 2008 as part of a sponsorship deal with telecommunications giant Sprint Nextel. The series had previously been called the NEXTEL Cup before the 2005 merger between Sprint and Nextel Communications, which had inked a 10-year, $750 million marketing partnership with NASCAR in 2003.

Also helping expand the popularity of the sport has been the construction of new race courses away from the South. Coincidentally (or perhaps not), the France family also controls publicly traded International Speedway Corporation (ISC), the largest racetrack operator in the US, which now has facilities in Chicago and New York. The family's control of ISC has also created conflict, though, namely with rival Speedway Motorsports. The two sides butted heads most recently in 2004 when NASCAR pulled out of some smaller markets and scheduled more at ISC tracks, causing Speedway Motorsports to file a lawsuit charging NASCAR with antitrust violations. The two sides settled their dispute in 2005 when ISC agreed to sell its North Carolina Speedway to Speedway Motorsports.

For the 2008 racing season, NASCAR started using a new type of race car (dubbed "the car of tomorrow" while in development) that offers improved safety and performance, as well as lower costs.

HISTORY

Bill France Sr. founded the National Championship Stock Car Circuit (NCSCC) in 1947 as a place for ex-Prohibition-era moonshine runners to show off their driving skills. France, the son of a Washington, DC, banker, was a skilled mechanic and racecar builder. In 1934 he moved his family to Daytona Beach, Florida, which was nirvana for racecar drivers who used the hard beach as a speedway.

The City of Daytona Beach in 1938 approached France, who by then owned a successful gas station and mechanic shop frequented by racers, and asked him to organize a race. France

rounded up drivers and solicited local businesses to donate prizes such as beer and cigars. The event drew 4,500 fans. He organized another race the following year and turned a profit of a few thousand dollars.

WWII interfered with France's racing career when he was drafted and sent to work in a shipyard. Upon his return, lacking the money to put another race together in Florida, he sponsored a national championship race for stock cars (cars with standard auto bodies not specially designed for racing) in North Carolina. Since there was no national body governing the races and setting rules, France's championship idea drew little enthusiasm. So in 1947 he formed the NCSCC and set up a point system for drivers and a fund for prize money. Seeking to expand NCSCC's powers, France in 1948 gathered 35 prominent racing figures from all over the US, and they organized to form the National Association for Stock Car Auto Racing (NASCAR), of which France was elected president.

France tirelessly promoted the sport with the help of racetrack owners wanting NASCAR to make their races official, and as a result the sport grew rapidly in the 1950s and 1960s. Racetrack owners began upgrading their facilities or building new ones with paved tracks to replace the older dirt tracks. France in 1957 convinced Daytona Beach to allow him to replace the city's original beach track with a 2.5-mile paved raceway. It opened two years later to a crowd of 42,000.

In 1972, as France got more involved in operating specific tracks and having less time to focus on NASCAR, he passed the business on to his son, Bill France Jr., who signed R.J. Reynolds as a major sponsor in 1971. NASCAR held the Winston 500 (the first incarnation of the Winston Cup series) in Talladega, Alabama.

The company's first televised race, the Daytona 500, aired on the CBS Television Network in 1979 and drew about 16 million viewers. Cable sports network ESPN also began airing races in 1981. NASCAR came into its own as a major sports player in 2000 when NBC, FOX, and Turner Broadcasting agreed to pay the company $2.4 billion for the circuit's broadcasting rights until 2006. (FOX later extended its agreement until 2008.) And the inherent danger of stock car racing began to hit home with the racing-related deaths of popular drivers such as Adam Petty in 2000 and Dale Earnhardt in 2001.

In 2003 Bill France Jr. handed reins of the company to son Brian France by promoting him to chairman and CEO. (Bill Jr. remained as vice chairman.) Also that year R.J. Reynolds dropped out as the sponsor for the Winston Cup series after more than 30 years with the race. Cell phone company Nextel (now Sprint Nextel) took over as the new sponsor with the signing of a 10-year, $750 million deal. (The race series was renamed the Sprint Cup in 2008.)

The following year NASCAR announced that its Busch racing series would hold a race in Mexico City during the 2005 season, marking the first points-paying international event in about 50 years. Later that same year NASCAR signed a new $4.4 billion broadcasting contract with Disney's ABC and ESPN, Time Warner's TNT, and News Corp's FOX and SPEED Channel. Bill France Jr. died in 2007.

EXECUTIVES

Chairman and CEO: Brian Z. France, age 45
Vice Chairman, EVP, and Secretary:
  James C. (Jim) France
President and Director: Mike Helton

CFO: R. Todd Wilson, age 41
SVP; President, NASCAR Broadcasting and NASCAR Digital Entertainment: Paul Brooks, age 43
Chief Marketing Officer: Steve Phelps
General Counsel, Secretary, and Director:
  W. Garrett (Gary) Crotty, age 44
Treasurer: Tom Bledsoe
VP and Director: Lesa D. France Kennedy, age 46
VP Competition: Robin Pemberton, age 48
VP Corporate Administration: Ed Bennett
VP Corporate Communications: Jim Hunter
VP Corporate Marketing: Jim O'Connell
VP Finance: Doris Rumery
VP Broadcasting and New Media: Richard (Dick) Glover
VP Licensing and Consumer Products: Mark Dyer, age 48
VP Research and Development: Gary Nelson
VP Racing Operations: Steve O'Donnell
Director, Nextel Cup Series: John Darby
Director, Human Resources: Starr George
Director, Public Relations: Kerry Tharp
President and CEO, NASCAR Images: Jay Abraham

LOCATIONS

HQ: National Association for Stock Car
  Auto Racing, Inc.
  1801 W. International Speedway Blvd.,
  Daytona Beach, FL 32114
Phone: 386-253-0611   **Fax:** 386-681-4041
Web: www.nascar.com

PRODUCTS/OPERATIONS

NASCAR Championships

Driver
  Bobby Allison (1983)
  Buck Baker (1956-57)
  Kurt Busch (2004)
  Red Byron (1949)
  Dale Earnhardt (1980, 1986-87, 1990-91, 1993-94)
  Bill Elliott (1988)
  Tim Flock (1952, 1955)
  Jeff Gordon (1995, 1997-98, 2001)
  Bobby Isaac (1970)
  Dale Jarrett (1999)
  Ned Jarrett (1961, 1965)
  Jimmie Johnson (2006-07)
  Matt Kenseth (2003)
  Alan Kulwicki (1992)
  Bobby Labonte (2000)
  Terry Labonte (1984, 1996)
  Benny Parsons (1973)
  David Pearson (1966, 1968-69)
  Lee Petty (1954, 1958-59)
  Richard Petty (1964, 1967, 1971-72, 1974-75, 1979)
  Bill Rexford (1950)
  Tony Stewart (2002, 2005)
  Herb Thomas (1951, 1953)
  Rusty Wallace (1989)
  Darrell Waltrip (1981-82, 1985)
  Joe Weatherly (1962-63)
  Rex White (1960)
  Cale Yarborough (1976-78)
Automobile
  Buick (1981-83)
  Chevrolet (1957, 1960-61, 1973, 1976-77, 1979-80,
    1984-87, 1990-91, 1993-98, 2001, 2005-07)
  Chrysler (1954-56)
  Dodge (1966, 1970, 1974-75)
  Ford (1965, 1968-69, 1988, 1992, 1999, 2003-04)
  Hudson (1951-53)
  Oldsmobile (1949-50, 1958, 1978)
  Plymouth (1959, 1964, 1967, 1971-72)
  Pontiac (1962-63, 1989, 2000, 2002)

COMPETITORS

AFL
Indy Racing League
Major League Baseball
NBA
NFL
NHL
World Wrestling Entertainment

National Basketball Association

This league has the inside moves to score big with hoops fans. The National Basketball Association is one of the four major professional sports leagues in the US, with 30 teams representing 28 US markets and one in Canada. The NBA oversees the rules of the game and officiating, markets its teams and players, and regulates franchise ownership. It also licenses broadcasting rights and collects revenue from corporate sponsorships. In addition, the NBA operates the WNBA, a 14-team women's league; the NBA Development League for up-and-coming players; and NBA TV, a cable TV channel offering news, original programming, and live game broadcasts. The NBA was founded as the Basketball Association of America in 1946.

Professional basketball continues to be very popular and boasts a loyal fan base in many of its markets. Regular season attendance during the 2007-08 season dipped slightly from the record mark of more than 21.8 million set the previous year, but the league still managed to sell more than 90% of its seats for the fourth straight season. TV ratings also managed to tick upwards during 2008 after several seasons of stagnant viewership; a championship series between the Los Angeles Lakers and the Boston Celtics that season brought in the biggest television audience for the NBA Finals since 2004.

League officials have regularly downplayed sagging TV numbers, citing similar declines across the television spectrum due to the ever expanding universe of cable channels, but national fan interest in basketball has waned since the retirement of Michael Jordan in 2003. The association has been seeking a new star to replace His Airness as the face of the NBA.

Despite the lack of big audiences, longtime broadcast partners ABC and ESPN (both owned by Walt Disney) and Time Warner's TNT signed on to a new eight-year, $7.4 billion TV deal that runs through 2016.

The NBA is also looking outside the US for fans and possibly for expansion. In 2008 the league created NBA China to help spread professional basketball fever into the world's most populous country. ESPN, along with Bank of China and government-controlled Legend Holdings, acquired a 10% stake in the new business entity. Later that year, NBA China and Anschutz Entertainment Group (AEG; part of the Anschutz Company) inked a partnership to develop sports arenas throughout that country in an effort to spread the popularity of basketball.

Meanwhile, the league is making a concerted effort to expand its popularity in Europe through exhibition games against Euroleague teams and pre-season exhibition matches. The NBA has announced its intention to play regular-season games in London by 2012. It is also considering the possibility of creating an all-European division to compete in the NBA regular season.

HISTORY

Dr. James Naismith, a physical education teacher at the International YMCA Training School in Springfield, Massachusetts, invented basketball in 1891. Naismith nailed peach baskets at both ends of the school's gym, gave his students a soccer ball, and one of the world's most popular sports was born.

In the beginning many YMCAs deemed the game too rough and banned it, so basketball was limited to armories, gymnasiums, barns, and dance halls. To pay the rent for the use of the hall, teams began charging spectators fees for admission, and leftover cash was divided among the players. The first pro basketball game was played in 1896 in Trenton, New Jersey.

A group of arena owners looking to fill their halls when their hockey teams were on the road formed the Basketball Association of America in 1946. It merged with the National Basketball League in 1949 to form the 17-team National Basketball Association (NBA).

Six teams dropped out in 1950. The league got an unexpected boost the next year when a point-shaving scandal rocked college basketball. The bad publicity for the college game made the pros look relatively clean, and it helped attract more fans. Another boost came through innovation when the league introduced the 24-second shot clock in 1954, which sped up the game and increased scoring.

Basketball came into its own in the late 1950s and 1960s, thanks to the popularity of such stars as Wilt Chamberlain, Bill Russell, and Bob Cousy. A rival league, the American Basketball Association (ABA), appeared on the scene in 1967 with its red, white, and blue basketball. Salaries escalated as the two leagues competed for players. The NBA and ABA merged in 1976.

By the early 1980s the NBA was suffering major image problems (drugs, fighting, racial issues) and began to wane in popularity. The league was resuscitated by exciting new players such as Magic Johnson, Larry Bird, and Michael Jordan, and in 1984, a new commissioner, David Stern. Although increased commercialism drove some purists crazy, big-name players and big-time rivalries helped sell the NBA's most important commodity — sport as entertainment.

Stern went to work cleaning up the league's image and financial problems, pushing through a strict anti-drug policy and a salary cap (the first such cap in major US sports). The NBA added its first two non-US teams in 1995, the Toronto Raptors and the Vancouver Grizzlies. (The Grizzlies moved to Memphis in 2001.)

On July 1, 1998, the NBA owners voted to lock out players, leading to the first work stoppage in the NBA's 52-year history. The dispute lasted six months, and the NBA's 1998-99 season was pared down to 50 games from the standard 82.

Concerned with the rash of players either leaving college early or skipping it entirely for the NBA, the league announced the formation of a developmental league (akin to baseball's minor leagues) in 2000, which started play in 2001.

The following year the league signed a new TV contract, a six-year, $4.6 billion deal with Walt Disney's ABC and ESPN, and Time Warner's Turner Sports. Also in 2002, the Charlotte Hornets relocated to New Orleans after the franchise failed to attract a loyal following in North Carolina. The vacancy allowed the league to grant its 30th franchise, the Charlotte Bobcats, to Robert Johnson, making the founder of BET the first African-American owner of a major sports team.

The year 2008 saw the suspension of basketball in Seattle when SuperSonics owner Clay Bennett relocated his franchise to Oklahoma City to become the Oklahoma City Thunder. Under a settlement between the team and the city, Seattle was allowed to keep the Sonics name, colors, and history.

EXECUTIVES

Commissioner: David J. Stern, age 66
Deputy Commissioner and COO: Adam Silver
EVP Events and Attractions: Ski Austin
EVP Basketball Operations: Stu Jackson
EVP Business Affairs and General Counsel:
  William S. (Bill) Koenig
EVP Finance: Robert Criqui
**President Global Marketing Partnerships and
  International Business Operations:** Heidi J. Ueberroth,
  age 42
SVP Marketing: Carol Albert
SVP Marketing Communications: Michael Bass
SVP and Chief Intellectual Property Counsel:
  Ayala Deutsch
SVP Basketball Communications: Brian P. McIntyre
SVP and CIO: Michael S. Gliedman
SVP Facilities & Administration:
  Christopher J. (Chris) Russo
SVP Global Merchandising: Salvatore (Sal) LaRocca,
  age 40
SVP Referee Operations: Ronald L. Johnson
Chief Basketball Operations and Player Relations:
  Reneé Brown
Executive Counsel Business and Finance:
  Harvey E. Benjamin
President League and Basketball Operations:
  Joel M. Litvin
President Women's National Basketball Association:
  Donna G. Orender, age 49
President NBA Development League: Dan Reed
CEO NBA China: Timothy Y. (Tim) Chen, age 51

LOCATIONS

HQ: National Basketball Association, Inc.
  Olympic Tower, 645 5th Ave., New York, NY 10022
Phone: 212-407-8000   **Fax:** 212-754-6414
Web: www.nba.com

PRODUCTS/OPERATIONS

Teams
Atlanta Hawks (1968)
  St. Louis Hawks (1955)
  Milwaukee Hawks (1951)
  Tri-Cities Blackhawks (Moline, Illinois; 1946; joined
    the NBA from the National Basketball League in
    1949)
Boston Celtics (1946)
Charlotte Bobcats (North Carolina, 2004)
Chicago Bulls (1966)
Cleveland Cavaliers (1970)
Dallas Mavericks (1980)
Denver Nuggets (1974, joined the NBA from the
  American Basketball Association in 1976)
  Denver Rockets (1967)
Detroit Pistons (1957)
  Fort Wayne Pistons (1948, joined the NBA from the
    National Basketball League)
  Fort Wayne Zollner Pistons (Indiana, 1941)
Golden State Warriors (Oakland, 1971)
  San Francisco Warriors (1962)
  Philadelphia Warriors (1946)
Houston Rockets (1971)
  San Diego Rockets (1967)
Indiana Pacers (1967, joined the NBA from the American
  Basketball Association in 1976)
Los Angeles Clippers (1984)
  San Diego Clippers (1978)
  Buffalo Braves (New York, 1970)
Los Angeles Lakers (1960)
  Minneapolis Lakers (1947, joined the NBA from the
    National Basketball League in 1948)
Memphis Grizzlies (2001)
  Vancouver Grizzlies (1995)
Miami Heat (1988)
Milwaukee Bucks (1968)
Minnesota Timberwolves (1989)
New Jersey Nets (1977)
  New York Nets (1968, joined the NBA from the
    American Basketball Association in 1976)
  New Jersey Americans (1967)
New Orleans Hornets (2002)
  Charlotte Hornets (1988)

New York Knicks (1946)
Oklahoma City Thunder (2008)
Orlando Magic (1989)
Philadelphia 76ers (1963)
  Syracuse Nationals (1937, joined the NBA from the
    National Basketball League in 1949)
Phoenix Suns (1968)
Portland Trail Blazers (1970)
Sacramento Kings (1985)
  Kansas City Kings (1975)
  Kansas City-Omaha Kings (1972)
  Cincinnati Royals (1957)
  Rochester Royals (1945, joined the NBA from the
    National Basketball League in 1948)
San Antonio Spurs (1973, joined the NBA from the
  American Basketball Association in 1976)
  Dallas Chaparrals (1967)
Seattle SuperSonics (1967; suspended after 2007
  following relocation to Oklahoma City)
Toronto Raptors (1995)
Utah Jazz (1979)
  New Orleans Jazz (1974)
Washington Wizards (1997)
  Washington Bullets (1974)
  Baltimore Bullets (1963)
  Chicago Zephyrs (1962)
  Chicago Packers (1961)

COMPETITORS

AFL
FIFA
Major League Baseball
Major League Soccer
NASCAR
NFL
NHL
PGA
PGA TOUR
World Wrestling Entertainment

National Cancer Institute

Established in 1937, the National Cancer Institute (NCI) supports and conducts research, training, information dissemination about what causes cancer, ways to prevent the disease, and how it can be treated. As a component of the National Institutes of Health (itself one of eight agencies comprising the Public Health Service), the National Cancer Institute falls under the purview of the Department of Health and Human Services. The organization operates a variety of its own programs and supports the research and medical centers of others; about half of its budget is allotted for funding research project grants. The NCI is pursuing an ambitious goal of eliminating cancer-related death and suffering by 2015.

Pointing to recent reports, the NCI announced that the US in 2007 recorded the steepest decline in cancer deaths since the nation began to invest in cancer research and care in 1971.

One primary goal of the NCI is to educate Americans about cancer risks, including those that can be prevented through changes in lifestyle. The institute publishes pamphlets and brochures, such as its *American Journal of Public Health: Young Adult Tobacco Cessation* and *Pap Tests: Things to Know*, and fact sheets the likes of *Access to Investigational Drugs: Questions and Answers*.

EXECUTIVES

CEO: John R. Seffrin
Chief Medical Officer: Otis Webb Brawley
Director, Center for Cancer Research, Office of the Director and Chief, Laboratory of Biosystems and Cancer: J. Carl Barrett
Director, Division of Cancer Biology: Dinah S. Singer
Director, Division of Cancer Control and Population Sciences: Robert Croyle
Director, Division of Cancer Epidemiology and Genetics: Joseph F. Fraumeni Jr.
Director, Division of Cancer Prevention: Peter Greenwald
Director, Office of Cancer Survivorship: Julia H. Rowland
Director, Office of Centers, Training, and Resources: Ernest T. Hawk
Director, Office of Science Planning and Assessment: Cherie Nichols
Director, Office of Technology and Industrial Relations: Greg Downing
Director, Operations Research Office: Holly Massett
Executive Secretary: Sandy Koeneman

LOCATIONS

HQ: National Cancer Institute
  9000 Rockville Pike, Bethesda, MD 20892
Phone: 301-496-4000   **Fax:** 301-402-0601
Web: www.cancer.gov

National Distributing

National Distributing Company provides the liquid bottoms-up stuff for those suffering from parched throats in Georgia and New Mexico. National offers libations from companies such as distiller Brown-Forman and winemaker E & J Gallo, along with most other major alcoholic beverage makers. Following the combination of most of National's operations with those of distributor, Republic Beverage, to form RNDC Texas, LLC (also known as the Republic National Distributing Company) in 2007, National Distributing Company remained in business, but with operations in Georgia and New Mexico only.

In 1942 Chris Carlos and Al Davis joined forces to begin a distribution business that today is known as National Distributing Company. The Carlos and Davis families still operate the company.

EXECUTIVES

Chairman and CEO: Jay M. Davis
Vice Chairman and Secretary: Jerry Rosenberg
President and COO: John A. Carlos
EVP: Chris Carlos
President, Georgia: Fred Bleiberg
VP Sales, Atlanta Wholesale Wine: David Forman
District Manager: Kevin England
Division Manager: Carter Perks
Division Manager: Tom Copeland
Division Manager: A. J. Governale

LOCATIONS

HQ: National Distributing Company, Inc.
  1 National Dr. SW, Atlanta, GA 30336
Phone: 404-696-9440   **Fax:** 404-505-1013
Web: www.ndcweb.com

COMPETITORS

Bacardi USA
Constellation Brands
Gambrinus
Geerlings & Wade
Georgia Crown
Glazer's Wholesale Drug
Johnson Brothers
National Wine & Spirits
Premier Beverage
Southern Wine & Spirits
Sunbelt Beverage
Tarrant Distributors
W. J. Deutsch
Wirtz Corporation
Young's Market

National Football League

In the world of professional sports, the National Football League (NFL) blitzes the competition. The organization oversees America's most popular spectator sport, acting as a trade association for 32 franchise owners. The NFL governs and promotes the game, sets and enforces rules, and regulates team ownership. It generates revenue mostly through sponsorships, licensing of merchandise, and selling national broadcasting rights. The teams operate as separate businesses but share a percentage of their revenue. The NFL was founded as the American Professional Football Association in 1920, changing its name two years later.

The growing popularity of football has allowed the NFL to demand ever increasing rights fees from television and radio networks. Most fans get their games from CBS and FOX (owned by News Corp.), which show Sunday afternoon games under a combined $8 billion broadcasting deal that runs through 2011. NBC started showing a Sunday night game each week in 2006 through a six-year, $600 million broadcasting package. Meanwhile, Walt Disney's ABC transferred its venerable *Monday Night Football* broadcast to sister cable network ESPN that same year. (ABC had broadcast *MNF* since 1970.)

The NFL also has a relationship with direct satellite service provider DIRECTV, which offers games through its NFL Sunday Ticket package; the $3.5 billion broadcasting deal runs through 2010. In addition, games are distributed over terrestrial radio by Westwood One and through satellite radio broadcaster SIRIUS XM Radio.

While its relationship with broadcasters is very important to the continued well-being of the league, the NFL is also expanding its own NFL Network, a cable channel launched in 2003. The 24-hour football network began broadcasting a package of regular season contests on Thursday and Saturday nights in 2006.

The strength of football fandom has also translated into huge sales of licensed merchandise, from jerseys and caps to video games to every manner of trinket bearing the NFL emblem. The league gets more than $3 billion a year from licensed consumer products sales.

Making sure the league remains prosperous falls on the shoulders of commissioner Roger Goodell, who replaced the retiring Paul Tagliabue in 2006. Goodell must negotiate a settlement to the looming labor dispute between the team owners and the NFL Players Association. Owners in 2008 opted out of the final two years of a collective bargaining agreement struck in 2006, and now a new CBA must be enacted before the 2010 season in order to ensure labor peace. The last NFL players strike was in 1987.

Goodell is also guiding the league through an international expansion effort that has resulted in regular season games being played at London's Wembley Stadium. The NFL is also planning exhibition matches in China and other locations.

HISTORY

Descended from the English game of rugby, American football was developed in the late 1800s by Walter Camp, a player from Yale University who is generally credited with introducing new rules for downs and scoring. Professional teams sprang up in the 1890s, but football remained relatively unorganized until 1920, when George Halas and college star Jim Thorpe helped organize the American Professional Football Association. The new league featured 14 teams from the Midwest and East, including Halas' Staleys (now the Chicago Bears) and the Racine Cardinals (now the Arizona Cardinals). In 1922 the association changed its name to the National Football League.

The new league suffered many growing pains over the next decade, but by the 1930s the NFL had settled on 10 teams, including the Green Bay Packers (joined in 1921), the New York Giants (1925), and the Philadelphia Eagles (1933). Interest in the game remained somewhat regional, however, until the late 1940s and 1950s. In 1946 the Cleveland Rams moved to Los Angeles, and in 1950 the NFL expanded with three teams joining from the defunct All-American Football Conference. Television showed its potential in 1958 when that year's championship game, the first to be televised nationally, kept audiences riveted with an overtime victory by the Baltimore Colts (now the Indianapolis Colts) over the Giants. In 1962 the NFL signed its first league-wide television contract with CBS for $4.65 million.

The 1960s brought a new challenge in the form of the upstart American Football League (AFL). Concerned that the AFL would steal players with higher salaries and draw away fans, NFL commissioner Pete Rozelle negotiated a deal in 1966 to combine the leagues. That season concluded with the first AFL-NFL World Championship Game, which was renamed the Super Bowl in 1969. When the merger was completed in 1970, the new NFL sported 26 teams.

Football's popularity exploded during the 1970s, helped by the rise of franchise dynasties such as the Pittsburgh Steelers (four Super Bowl

wins that decade) and the Dallas Cowboys (five NFC titles). In 1982 the Oakland Raiders moved to Los Angeles after a jury ruled against the NFL's attempts to keep the team in Oakland. The decision prompted other teams to relocate in search of better facilities and more revenue. (The Raiders returned to Oakland in 1995.) Rozelle stepped down in 1989 and was replaced by Paul Tagliabue.

During the 1990s the league expanded to 30 teams, adding the Carolina Panthers and Jacksonville Jaguars in 1995. That same year the Rams abandoned Los Angeles to begin life as the St. Louis Rams. The next year Art Modell moved his Cleveland Browns franchise to Baltimore to become the Ravens. (The city of Cleveland held onto the rights to the Browns name and history and the franchise was revived in 1999.) The Houston Oilers defected to Tennessee in 1997 and were later renamed the Titans. The next year brought new television deals worth $17.6 billion over eight years.

The NFL made plans for new expansion in 1999, awarding a franchise to Robert McNair of Houston. Named the Houston Texans, the team began play in 2002. In 2003 the league launched its own television channel, the NFL Network.

The NFL and the NFL Players Association reached an accord on a new six-year collective bargaining agreement in 2006. The league shut down its NFL Europa development league the following year as international expansion began to focus on scheduling selected regular season NFL games outside of the US.

EXECUTIVES

Commissioner: Roger Goodell
CFO: Anthony Noto, age 39
EVP, Chief Administrative Officer, and General Counsel: Jeff Pash
EVP Communications and Public Affairs: Joe Browne
EVP Finance; President, Business Ventures: Eric P. Grubman
EVP Football Operations: Ray Anderson
EVP Player Programs: Harold R. Henderson
EVP Media: Steve Bornstein
SVP Business Affairs: Frank Hawkins
SVP Marketing and Consumer Products: Lisa Baird
SVP Corporate Development: Neil Glat, age 41
SVP Human Resources: Nancy Gill
SVP Marketing and Sales: Phil Guarascio
SVP Media and Operations; COO, NFL Films: Howard Katz
SVP Public Relations: Greg Aiello
VP Corporate Communications: Brian McCarthy
Senior Director New Media and Publishing: Evan Kamer
Senior Director Publishing and Direct Marketing: Bob O'Keefe
Director Marketing: Peter O'Reilly
Director Football Operations: Gene A. Washington, age 62
Director Strategic Insight and Marketing Information Management: Cary Meyers
President, NFL Films: Steve Sabol
Auditors: Deloitte & Touche LLP

LOCATIONS

HQ: National Football League
280 Park Ave., 15th Fl., New York, NY 10017
Phone: 212-450-2000   **Fax:** 212-681-7599
Web: www.nfl.com

PRODUCTS/OPERATIONS

Teams

Arizona Cardinals (1994, Phoenix)
    Phoenix Cardinals (1988)
    St. Louis Cardinals (1960)
    Chicago Cardinals (1922)
    Racine Cardinals (1901, Chicago)
    Morgan Athletic Club (1898, Chicago)
Atlanta Falcons (1966)
Baltimore Ravens (1996)
Buffalo Bills (1959, joined the NFL from the AFL in 1970, New York)
Carolina Panthers (1995; Charlotte, NC)
Chicago Bears (1922)
    Chicago Staleys (1921)
    Decatur Staleys (1920, Illinois)
Cincinnati Bengals (1968, joined the NFL from the AFL in 1970)
Cleveland Browns (1944, joined the NFL from the AAFC in 1950)
Dallas Cowboys (1960)
Denver Broncos (1959, joined the NFL from the AFL in 1970)
Detroit Lions (1934)
    Portsmouth Spartans (1930, Ohio)
Green Bay Packers (1919, Wisconsin)
Houston Texans (2002)
Indianapolis Colts (1984)
    Baltimore Colts (1953)
Jacksonville Jaguars (1995, Florida)
Kansas City Chiefs (1963, joined the NFL from the AFL in 1970)
    Dallas Texans (1959)
Miami Dolphins (1966, joined the NFL from the AFL in 1970)
Minnesota Vikings (1961, Minneapolis)
New England Patriots (1971; Foxboro, MA)
    Boston Patriots (1959, joined the NFL from the AFL in 1970)
New Orleans Saints (1967)
New York Giants (1925)
New York Jets (1959, joined the NFL from the AFL in 1970)
Oakland Raiders (1995, California)
    Los Angeles Raiders (1982)
    Oakland Raiders (1959, joined the NFL from the AFL in 1970)
Philadelphia Eagles (1933)
Pittsburgh Steelers (1940)
    Pittsburgh Pirates (1933)
St. Louis Rams (1995)
    Los Angeles Rams (1946)
    Cleveland Rams (1937)
San Diego Chargers (1961, joined the NFL from the AFL in 1970)
    Los Angeles Chargers (1959)
San Francisco 49ers (1946, joined the NFL from the AAFC in 1950)
Seattle Seahawks (1976)
Tampa Bay Buccaneers (1976)
Tennessee Titans (1998, Nashville)
    Tennessee Oilers (1997, Memphis)
    Houston Oilers (1959, joined the NFL from the AFL in 1970)
Washington Redskins (1937; Washington, DC)
    Boston Redskins (1933)
    Boston Braves (1932)

Selected Business Units

NFL Charities
NFL Enterprises (media development)
NFL Films (highlight packages)
NFL Network (24-hour cable network)
NFL Properties (licensing, marketing, promotions, and publishing)

COMPETITORS

AFL	NBA
FIFA	NHL
Major League Baseball	PGA
Major League Soccer	World Wrestling
NASCAR	Entertainment

HISTORICAL FINANCIALS
Company Type: Association

Income Statement

FYE: March 31

	REVENUE ($ mil.)	NET INCOME ($ mil.)	NET PROFIT MARGIN	EMPLOYEES
3/08	6,900	—	—	—
3/07	6,200	—	—	—
3/06	5,800	—	—	—
3/05	5,700	—	—	—
3/04	5,500	—	—	450
Annual Growth	**5.8%**	**—**	**—**	**—**

Revenue History

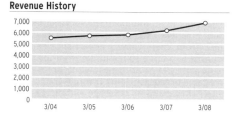

National Geographic Society

Still publishing its flagship *National Geographic* magazine, the not-for-profit National Geographic Society (NGS) has expanded into an array of venues to enhance our knowledge of the big blue marble. The NGS has staked claims in the worlds of television and the Web, as well as in book publishing and map-making. With News Corp., it operates the National Geographic Channel US, a cable channel that reaches about 64 million households. The NGS also supports geographic expeditions (it has funded more than 8,000 scientific research projects) and sponsors exhibits, lectures, and education programs. The NGS was founded in 1888, the year the first issue of *National Geographic* magazine was published.

Besides the award-winning *National Geographic* magazine, which has a circulation of some 8.5 million, the organization publishes several other magazines, including *National Geographic Adventure* and *National Geographic Kids*. As might be expected, the NGS's publishing operations are geographically diverse. *National Geographic* magazine is published in more than 25 local-language editions and has subscribers worldwide.

Also outside the US, the organization owns 25% of National Geographic Channels International (NGCI). (News Corp. owns the rest.) NGCI, one of the fastest-growing cable networks around the globe, reaches more than 250 million households in some 165 countries. The UK affiliate of National Geographic Channels is owned jointly by National Geographic (25%), News Corp. (25%) and satellite broadcaster BskyB (50%).

As competition from relative newcomers, such as Discovery Communications, intensifies, the diversification of the NGS has been accelerating. The organization bought educational and

English as a second language (ESL) publisher Hampton-Brown in February 2006. The next year it bought The Green Guide, publisher of an environment-oriented Web site and newsletter.

HISTORY

In 1888 a group of scientists and explorers gathered in Washington, DC, to form the National Geographic Society. Gardiner Greene Hubbard was its first president. The organization mailed the first edition of its magazine, dated October 1888, to 165 members. The magazine was clothed in a brown cover and contained a few esoteric articles, such as "The Classification of Geographic Forms by Genesis." The organization's tradition of funding expeditions began in 1890 when it sent geologist Israel Russell to explore Alaska. It began issuing regular monthly editions of *National Geographic* in 1896.

Following Hubbard's death in 1897, his son-in-law, inventor Alexander Graham Bell, became president. Aiming to boost the magazine's popularity, he hired Gilbert Grosvenor (who later married Bell's daughter) as editor. Grosvenor turned the magazine from a dry, technical publication to one of more general interest.

Under Grosvenor the magazine pioneered the use of photography, including rare photographs of remote Tibet (1904), the first hand-tinted colored photos (1910), the first underwater color photos (1920s), and the first color aerial photographs (1930).

The organization sponsored Robert Peary's trek to the North Pole in 1909 and Hiram Bingham's 1912 exploration of Machu Picchu in Peru. National Geographic expanded into cartography with the creation of a maps division in 1915. Grosvenor became president in 1920.

By 1930 circulation was 1.2 million (up from 2,200 in 1900). Grosvenor's policy of printing only "what is of a kindly nature . . . about any country or people" resulted in two articles that were criticized for their kindly portrayal of pre-war Nazi Germany (however, National Geographic maps and photographs were used by the US government for WWII intelligence). That policy eased over the years, and in 1961 a *National Geographic* article described the growing US involvement in Vietnam.

Grosvenor retired in 1954. His son Melville Bell Grosvenor, who became president and editor in 1957, accelerated book publishing with the first edition of *National Geographic Atlas of the World*. In addition, he created a film unit that aired its first TV documentary in 1965. Melville retired in 1967.

Melville's son Gilbert Melville Grosvenor took over as president in 1970. The organization debuted its *National Geographic Explorer* television series in 1985. National Geographic branched into commercial ventures in 1995 when it created subsidiary National Geographic Ventures to expand its presence on television, the Internet, maps, and retail. That same year the *National Geographic* magazine began international circulation.

Grosvenor became chairman in 1996, and Reg Murphy took over as president. Murphy shook up the organization by laying off nearly a quarter of its staff and stepping up its profit-making activities. In 1997 National Geographic branched into cable television when it partnered with Fox, NBC, and BskyB to launch outside the US the National Geographic Channels International (NGCI).

John Fahey replaced Murphy as president in 1998. That same year National Geographic released *Mysteries of Egypt*, its first IMAX-style film. The following year National Geographic unveiled its *Adventure* magazine. The organization began offering *National Geographic* on newsstands for the first time in 1999. In 2000 National Geographic Ventures acquired recreational topographic map company Wildflower Productions. As part of an agreement to buy 30% of travel portal iExplore, National Geographic also agreed to license the use of its name. In 2001 National Geographic Channel US, a cable channel, was launched as a joint venture with Fox parent News Corp.

In 2002 National Geographic began using IBM software and hardware to digitize thousands of its culture and nature images to sell online. That same year *National Geographic World,* a magazine for young people, became *National Geographic Kids*. The organization also began a literacy campaign that included *National Geographic Explorer* magazine and curriculum materials for classrooms. In 2003 it launched Hungarian-, Romanian-, Czech-, Croatian-, and Russian-language editions of *National Geographic* magazine.

EXECUTIVES

Chairman, National Geographic Society and Education Foundation: Gilbert M. Grosvenor, age 76
Vice Chairman: John R. (Reg) Murphy, age 76
President and CEO: John M. Fahey Jr.
EVP and CFO: Christopher A. Liedel
EVP and Secretary: Terrence B. (Terry) Adamson
EVP Mission Programs: Terry D. Garcia
EVP; President, Books and School Publishing: Nina A. Hoffman
EVP; President, Magazine Group: John Q. Griffin
EVP; President, National Geographic Enterprises: Linda Berkeley
SVP and Treasurer: H. Gregory Platts
SVP Communications: Betty Hudson
SVP Human Resources: Thomas A. (Tony) Sabló
SVP International Publishing: Robert W. (Rob) Hernandez
SVP Licensing: John Dumbacher
VP and Group Publisher, National Geographic Magazine: Stephen P. (Steve) Giannetti
Chairman, Committee for Research and Exploration: Peter Raven
Chairman, National Geographic Ventures: Dennis Patrick
President, National Geographic Television: Michael Rosenfeld
President, National Geographic Entertainment: David Beal
Executive Editor, National Geographic Magazine: Carolyn White
Publisher, National Geographic Adventure: Francis X. Farrell

LOCATIONS

HQ: National Geographic Society
1145 17th St. NW, Washington, DC 20036
Phone: 202-857-7000   **Fax:** 202-775-6141
Web: www.nationalgeographic.com

National Grape Cooperative

Well, of course grape growers want to hang out in a bunch! The more than 1,400 grower/owners who belong to the National Grape Cooperative Association harvest purple, red, and white grapes from almost 50,000 acres of vineyards in order to supply its wholly owned subsidiary Welch Foods. Welch's makes and sells juices, jams, and jellies under the Welch's and Bama brands. Other co-op products include fresh eating grapes, which are distributed by C.H. Robinson Worldwide, as well as dried fruit and frozen juice bars. National Grape Cooperative growers maintain vineyards in Pennsylvania, Michigan, New York, Ohio, Washington, and in Ontario, Canada.

Though jelly is a slowing market, new juice innovations, new packaging, and shelf-stable and single-serving products help drive sales at Welch's. Following the trend toward branded fresh produce, the Welch's logo appears on fresh grapes sold in grocery stores nationwide.

Top Welch's customers include US grocery giants Kroger, Publix, and Wal-Mart.

EXECUTIVES

President and Director: Randolph H. Graham
General Manager, COO, and Treasurer: Brent J. Roggie
First VP and Director: Joseph C. Falcone
Second VP and Director: James A. Schafer
Third VP and Director: Timothy E. Grow
Financial and Accounting Officer: Albert B. Wright III
Chief Legal Officer and Assistant Secretary:
  Vivian S. Y. Tseng
Secretary and Assistant Treasurer: Timothy A. Buss
Assistant Secretary: Richard H. Alpert
Assistant Secretary: Thomas A. Bockhorst
Assistant Secretary: Mathew A. Aufman
President and CEO, Welch Foods: David J. Lukiewski, age 53
Auditors: KPMG LLP

LOCATIONS

HQ: National Grape Cooperative Association, Inc.
  2 S. Portage St., Westfield, NY 14787
Phone: 716-326-5200   **Fax:** 716-326-5494
Web: www.nationalgrape.com

PRODUCTS/OPERATIONS

Selected Products
Bottled juices
Canned juices
Dried fruit
Fresh grapes
Frozen juices
Fruit juice bars
Fruit snacks
Jams
Jellies
Juice cocktails
Pourable concentrates
Preserves
Refrigerated juices
Single-serve juices
Sparkling juices

COMPETITORS

B&G Foods	Hansen Natural
Chiquita Brands	IZZE
Coca-Cola	Kraft Foods
Constellation Brands	Nestlé USA
Cranberries Limited	Ocean Spray
Del Monte Foods	PepsiCo
Dole Food	Procter & Gamble
Dr Pepper Snapple Group	Ralcorp
Ferolito, Vultaggio	Smucker
Fresh Del Monte Produce	Snapple
Goya	Tropicana

HISTORICAL FINANCIALS
Company Type: Cooperative

Income Statement   FYE: August 31

	REVENUE ($ mil.)	NET INCOME ($ mil.)	NET PROFIT MARGIN	EMPLOYEES
8/07	654	60	9.1%	1,200
8/06	600	31	5.2%	1,223
8/05	578	59	10.1%	1,382
8/04	583	75	12.9%	1,390
8/03	579	76	13.1%	1,350
Annual Growth	3.1%	(5.9%)	—	(2.9%)

2007 Year-End Financials

Debt ratio: 92.5%
Return on equity: 84.9%
Cash ($ mil.): —

Current ratio: —
Long-term debt ($ mil.): 53

Net Income History

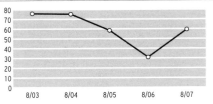

National Hockey League

Hockey is more than a cool sport for serious fans. The National Hockey League is one of the four major professional sports associations in North America, boasting 30 professional ice hockey franchises in the US and Canada organized into two conferences with three divisions each. The NHL governs the game, sets and enforces rules, regulates team ownership, and collects licensing fees for merchandise. It also negotiates fees for national broadcasting rights. (Each team controls the rights to regional broadcasts.) In addition, five minor and semi-pro hockey leagues also fly under the NHL banner. The league was organized in Canada in 1917.

Hockey continues to boast legions of fans dedicated to their local team; the league has set attendance records the past two seasons with more than 21 million fans going through arena turnstiles during the 2007-08 season. That, along with rising ticket prices, has led to consecutive seasons of revenue growth for the NHL, an impressive stat for a league that was closed for business the entire 2004-05 season due to a labor dispute between players and team owners.

The 2007-08 season also saw a turnaround on television, where hockey has traditionally struggled to find an audience. Ratings for games on NBC and cable sports channel VERSUS (owned by Comcast) ticked upwards for the first time, thanks in part to special events such as an outdoor game held on New Year's Day between the Buffalo Sabres and the Pittsburgh Penguins.

The uptick in ratings led NBC to renew its broadcasting deal with the league in 2008, retaining rights to a package of weekend regular season games and the playoffs through 2009. (The agreement, unique in the sports entertainment business, offers the league a share of revenue from each game's advertising sales as opposed to a large sum paid up front for rights to the games.) VERSUS, meanwhile, holds exclusive cable broadcast rights through 2011.

To help expand its coverage and increase the fan base, in 2007 it inked a deal with Web services startup NeuLion to broadcast live games to subscribers via the Internet.

With broadcasting and sponsorships on the rise, the league is hopeful that its teams will continue to thrive thanks to a new labor agreement reached in 2005. Many owners credit the leadership of commissioner Gary Bettman for holding the league together during the labor dispute and negotiating the new CBA.

The NHL commissioner still has his critics, though. Some continue to blame his expansion of the league into non-traditional markets far from its northern stronghold during the 1990s for the lack of US audience interest in the sport.

HISTORY

National Hockey League traces its heritage to 1893, when the Stanley Cup (donated by Lord Stanley, Governor General of Canada) was first awarded to the Montreal Amateur Athletic Association hockey club of the Amateur Hockey Association of Canada. The National Hockey Association (NHA) became the first professional league to award the Cup in 1910. Five years later the NHA agreed to send its champion to play against the top team of the Pacific Coast Hockey Association (founded in 1911) for bragging rights to the Cup.

The onset of WWI siphoned away players, and with infighting intensifying among the NHA's owners, the association decided to disband in 1917. Later that year Frank Calder, a British scholar and former sports journalist who came to Canada to be a soccer player, helped form the National Hockey League (NHL) and appointed himself president. The league originally consisted of five teams from the NHA that played a 22-game schedule.

The league's first dynasty emerged in the form of the original Ottawa Senators (the team went under in 1934; the expansion Senators joined the league in 1992), which won four Cups from 1920 to 1927. The 1920s saw continued expansion — the Boston Bruins became the first US team in the league in 1925 — but the NHL remained amorphous as many teams joined up and dropped out during the decade.

The sport lost most of its talent to the military during WWII, forcing teams to field players who were often too young, too old, or who were barely able to skate. The league almost shut down, but the Canadian government encouraged play to continue, claiming it boosted national morale.

In the post-war years, the NHL consisted of just six teams: the Boston Bruins, the Chicago Blackhawks, the Detroit Red Wings, the Montreal Canadiens, the New York Rangers, and the Toronto Maple Leafs, known as the Original Six. The Canadiens began their three-decade domination of the NHL during this time, winning 17 championships from 1946 to 1979.

The league began expanding in 1967 when six US-based franchises were added to form the West Division, while the Original Six were placed in the East Division. More teams were added through the 1970s, and in 1979 the league absorbed four franchises from its rival professional league, the World Hockey Association (founded in 1972).

At the beginning of the 1980s the NHL consisted of 21 teams, including 15 franchises in the US. The NHL's shift towards the US market became more concrete when the league's headquarters moved from Montreal to New York City later in the decade. But Canadian fans still had reason to cheer as Wayne Gretzky (The Great One) and the Edmonton Oilers won five Stanley Cup titles from 1984 to 1990.

Late that year, Gary Bettman, formerly assistant commissioner of the National Basketball Association, was hired as the NHL's first real commissioner. Under his leadership, the NHL began expanding to more southern locations in the US. The league's growth was temporarily slowed in 1994, however, by the first major labor dispute in NHL history. Team owners began a player lockout that delayed the start of the season until early 1995, but they ultimately failed in their goal of implementing a salary cap.

In 1998 NHL team owners agreed to a $600 million, five-year television contract with Walt Disney's ABC and ESPN starting with the 2000-01 season. That season also marked further expansion as the Minnesota Wild and the Columbus Blue Jackets took to the ice.

In 2003 hockey returned to its roots with the outdoor Heritage Classic between the Edmonton Oilers and the Montreal Canadiens in minus-1 degree weather that drew record crowds. The following year the NHL agreed to a two-year revenue-sharing deal to broadcast games on NBC.

EXECUTIVES

Commissioner: Gary B. Bettman, age 56
Deputy Commissioner: William L. (Bill) Daly
COO: John Collins, age 42
SEVP and CFO: Craig Harnett
SEVP and Director of Hockey Operations:
 Colin Campbell
SEVP Communications, Branding, Club Consulting, and Services: Ed Home
EVP Finance: Joseph DeSousa
EVP and General Counsel: David Zimmerman
EVP and General Counsel, NHLE: Richard Zahnd
EVP Marketing: Brian Jennings
EVP and CTO: Peter DelGiacco
SVP and Director Officiating, Toronto:
 Stephen Walkom
SVP Hockey Operations, Toronto: James (Jim) Gregory
SVP New Business Development and President, NHL Interactive CyberEnterprises: Keith Ritter
SVP Security: Dennis Cunningham
SVP Events and Entertainment and NHL International and Business Affairs: Kenneth (Ken) Yaffe

SVP Club Consulting and Services: Susan Cohig
SVP Communications: Bernadette Mansur
SVP Hockey Operations, Toronto: Mike Murphy
SVP Broadcasting: John Shannon
VP Administration and Human Resources:
 Debbie Jordan
Executive Director, NHL Players' Association:
 Paul Kelly, age 52
Auditors: Ernst & Young LLP

LOCATIONS

HQ: National Hockey League
 1185 Avenue of the Americas, 12th Fl.,
 New York, NY 10020
Phone: 212-789-2000   **Fax:** 212-789-2020
Web: www.nhl.com

PRODUCTS/OPERATIONS

Teams
Anaheim Ducks (2006)
 Mighty Ducks of Anaheim (1993, California)
Atlanta Thrashers (1999)
Boston Bruins (1924)
Buffalo Sabres (1970, New York)
Calgary Flames (1980, Alberta, Canada)
Atlanta Flames (1972)
Carolina Hurricanes (1997, Raleigh)
 Hartford Whalers (1975, Connecticut, joined the NHL from the World Hockey League in 1979)
 New England Whalers (1971, Boston)
Chicago Blackhawks (1926)
Colorado Avalanche (1995, Denver)
 Quebec Nordiques (1972; Quebec City, Quebec, Canada; joined the NHL from the World Hockey League in 1979)
Columbus Blue Jackets (2000, Ohio)
Dallas Stars (1993)
 Minnesota North Stars (1967, Minneapolis)
Detroit Red Wings (1926)
Edmonton Oilers (1973; Alberta, Canada; joined the NHL from the World Hockey League in 1979)
 Alberta Oilers (1972; Edmonton, Alberta, Canada)
Florida Panthers (1993, Miami)
Los Angeles Kings (1967)
Minnesota Wild (2000, St. Paul)
Montreal Canadiens (1909)
Nashville Predators (1998)
New Jersey Devils (1982, East Rutherford)
 Colorado Rockies (1976, Denver)
 Kansas City Scouts (1974)
New York Islanders (1972, Unionville)
New York Rangers (1926, New York City)
Ottawa Senators (1992; Ontario, Canada)
Philadelphia Flyers (1967)
Phoenix Coyotes (1996)
 Winnipeg Jets (1972; Manitoba, Canada; joined the NHL from the World Hockey League in 1979)
Pittsburgh Penguins (1967)
St. Louis Blues (1967)
San Jose Sharks (1991, California)
Tampa Bay Lightning (1992)
Toronto Maple Leafs (1927)
 Toronto St. Patricks (1919)
 Toronto Arenas (1917)
Vancouver Canucks (1947, joined the NHL from the Western Hockey League in 1970)
Washington Capitals (1974; Washington, DC)

COMPETITORS

AFL
CFL
FIFA
Indy Racing League
Major League Baseball
Major League Soccer
NASCAR
NBA
NFL
PGA
PGA TOUR

National Institutes of Health

The National Institutes of Health (NIH), through its own research and the distribution of grants, seeks to understand disease inside and out. Part of the US Department of Health and Human Services, the NIH is the government's main medical research entity. It comprises 27 institutes and centers covering every medical discipline, from general medical sciences to alternative therapies. The organization has nearly 6,000 scientists of its own and gives out some 50,000 grants to researchers at more than 3,000 universities, hospitals, and research labs in all 50 states. Among its vast array of projects, NIH has supported efforts to develop an AIDS vaccine, map human genetic variation, and study avian flu.

The history of the NIH began in an agency created by the federal government to check ship passengers coming into the country for signs of cholera and yellow fever. The NIH's predecessor, known as the Laboratory of Hygiene, used newfangled bacteriological methods to study infectious diseases in service of the public health. Today the NIH invests some $28 billion each year in medical research.

EXECUTIVES

Director: Elias A. Zerhouni
Principal Deputy Director, NIH: Raynard S. Kington
Director National Institute of General Medical Sciences: Jeremy M. Berg
Director NIH Clinical Center: John I. Gallin
Director National Institute of Nursing Research:
 Patricia A. Grady
Director National Library of Medicine:
 Donald A. B. Lindberg

LOCATIONS

HQ: National Institutes of Health
 9000 Rockville Pike, Bethesda, MD 20892
Phone: 301-496-4000   **Fax:** 301-496-7422
Web: www.nih.gov

PRODUCTS/OPERATIONS

Selected Institutes and Centers
Center for Information Technology (CIT)
Center for Scientific Review (CSR)
John E. Fogarty International Center (FIC)
National Cancer Institute (NCI)
National Center for Complementary and Alternative Medicine (NCCAM)
National Center for Research Resources (NCRR)
National Center on Minority Health and Health Disparities (NCMHD)
National Eye Institute (NEI)
National Heart, Lung and Blood Institute (NHLBI)
National Human Genome Research Institute (NHGRI)
National Institute of Allergy and Infectious Diseases (NIAID)
National Institute of Arthritis and Musculoskeletal and Skin Diseases (NIAMS)
National Institute of Biomedical Imaging and Bioengineering (NIBIB)
National Institute of Child Health and Human Development (NICHD)
National Institute of Deafness and Other Communication Disorders (NIDCD)
National Institute of Dental and Craniofacial Research (NIDCR)
National Institute of Diabetes and Digestive and Kidney Diseases (NIDDK)

National Institute of Environmental Health Sciences
  (NIEHS)
National Institute of General Medical Sciences (NIGMS)
National Institute of Mental Health (NIMH)
National Institute of Neurological Disorders and Stroke
  (NINDS)
National Institute of Nursing Research (NINR)
National Institute on Aging (NIA)
National Institute on Alcohol Abuse and Alcoholism
  (NIAAA)
National Institute on Drug Abuse (NIDA)
National Library of Medicine (NLM)
NIH Clinical Center (CC)

National Life Insurance

One nation, under insurance, with financial
security for all. National Life Group, the marketing name for National Life Insurance Company
and its affiliated companies, is a mutually-owned
insurer dating back to 1848. Today, National Life
Group offers a range of insurance and investment products throughout the US through its
namesake National Life Insurance Company and
other subsidiaries, including Equity Services (insurance broker/dealer), Life Insurance Company
of the Southwest (insurance and annuities), National Retirement Plan Advisors, Sentinel Asset
Management, and The Sentinel Companies (mutual funds).

National Life distributes its products through
a mix of both an internal career sales force and a
network of independent agents. The company
uses its NL Financial Alliance distribution arm to
target wealthy customers, while its Sentinel
brand of funds are distributed by its Sentinel Financial Services company.

National Life's Private Client Group was spun
off to management in 2004 and renamed Maple
Capital Management. In 2006 the company sold
off its American Guaranty & Trust subsidiary to
Royal Bank of Canada.

EXECUTIVES

Chairman, President, and CEO: Thomas H. MacLeay,
  age 58
EVP and CFO: Edward J. (Ed) Parry III
EVP; President and CEO, Sentinel Asset Management:
  Christian W. Thwaites
EVP Corporate Services and General Counsel:
  Michele S. Gatto
SVP and CIO: Joel Conrad
SVP and Chief Investment Officer:
  Thomas H. (Tom) Brownell
VP Human Resources: Bill Decker
President, Life & Annuity: Mehran Assadi
Auditors: PricewaterhouseCoopers LLP

LOCATIONS

HQ: National Life Insurance Company
  1 National Life Dr., Montpelier, VT 05604
Phone: 802-229-3333   **Fax:** 802-229-9281
Web: www.natlifeinsco.com

PRODUCTS/OPERATIONS

2007 Sales

	$ mil.	% of total
Investment income	758.1	55
Insurance premiums	322.3	23
Policy & contract charges	178.8	13
Mutual fund commissions & fee income	104.0	8
Change in value of trading equity securities	0.8	—
Net realized investment losses	(4.9)	—
Other	21.8	1
Total	**1,380.8**	**100**

Selected Subsidiaries

Equity Services, Inc.
Life Insurance Company of the Southwest
National Life Insurance Company
National Retirement Plan Advisors Inc.
The Sentinel Companies

COMPETITORS

AIG American General
AXA Financial
CIGNA
Citigroup
CNA Financial
FMR
John Hancock Financial Services
MassMutual
MetLife
Mutual of Omaha
New York Life
Ohio National
Pacific Mutual
Principal Financial
Prudential
Securian Financial
Sentry Insurance
Utica Mutual Insurance

HISTORICAL FINANCIALS

Company Type: Mutual company

Income Statement   FYE: December 31

	ASSETS ($ mil.)	NET INCOME ($ mil.)	INCOME AS % OF ASSETS	EMPLOYEES
12/07	15,511	109	0.7%	900
12/06	15,009	111	0.7%	900
12/05	14,035	98	0.7%	—
12/04	12,796	86	0.7%	—
12/03	12,034	77	0.6%	1,000
Annual Growth	6.6%	8.9%	—	(2.6%)

2007 Year-End Financials

Equity as % of assets: 9.4%   Long-term debt ($ mil.): —
Return on assets: 0.7%   Sales ($ mil.): 1,381
Return on equity: 7.7%

Net Income History

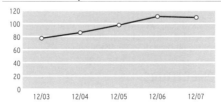

National Rural Utilities Cooperative

Cooperation may work wonders on *Sesame
Street*, but in the real world it takes money to pay
the power bill. The National Rural Utilities Cooperative Finance Corporation, or NRUCFC, provides financing for electrical and telephone
projects throughout the US. Owned by its more
than 1,500 members, most of which are electric
utility and telecommunications systems, the
NRUCFC supplements the government loans
that traditionally have fueled rural electric utilities by selling commercial paper, medium-term
notes, and collateral trust bonds for its loans.
The NRUCFC was formed in 1969 by the National Rural Electric Cooperative Association, a
lobby representing the nation's electric co-ops.

EXECUTIVES

Governor and CEO: Sheldon C. Petersen, age 55
President and Director: Roger Arthur, age 61
Secretary, Treasurer, and Director: Reuben McBride,
  age 61
SVP and CFO: Steven L. Lilly, age 58
SVP Corporate Relations: Richard E. Larochelle, age 55
SVP Credit Risk Management: John M. Borak, age 63
SVP Member Services and General Counsel:
  John J. List, age 61
SVP Operations: John T. Evans, age 58
SVP Rural Telephone Finance Cooperative:
  Lawrence Zawalick, age 50
VP and Director: Darryl Schriver, age 43
Acting Controller and Chief Accounting Officer:
  Robert Geier
Auditors: Deloitte & Touche LLP

LOCATIONS

HQ: National Rural Utilities Cooperative Finance
  Corporation
  2201 Cooperative Way, Herndon, VA 20171
Phone: 703-709-6700   **Fax:** 703-709-6780
Web: www.nrucfc.org

National Rural Utilities Cooperative Finance Corporation
provides financing throughout the US.

PRODUCTS/OPERATIONS

Selected Subsidiaries and Affiliates

National Cooperative Services Corporation (debt
  refinancing and lending to electric co-ops)

Rural Telephone Finance Cooperative (rural
  telecommunications lending)

COMPETITORS

AgFirst
AgriBank
GE

HISTORICAL FINANCIALS

Company Type: Cooperative

Income Statement   FYE: May 31

	ASSETS ($ mil.)	NET INCOME ($ mil.)	INCOME AS % OF ASSETS	EMPLOYEES
5/08	19,379	46	0.2%	231
5/07	18,575	12	0.1%	218
5/06	19,180	96	0.5%	210
5/05	20,046	123	0.6%	219
5/04	21,350	(178)	—	—
Annual Growth	(2.4%)	—	—	1.8%

Equity as % of assets: 3.4% Long-term debt ($ mil.): 12,063
Return on assets: 0.2% Sales ($ mil.): 1,106
Return on equity: 6.6%

Net Income History

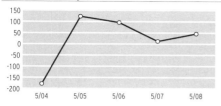

National Wine & Spirits

Bartender to the nation's breadbasket, National Wine & Spirits is one of the Midwest's largest wine and liquor distributors. Serving 36,000 locations with its fleet of 350 delivery vehicles, the company distributes to restaurants, liquor stores, and beverage retailers in Indiana and Michigan. The distributor carries more than 120,000 products and its suppliers include Fortune Brands (Jim Beam), Diageo (Bailey's), and Beringer Blass Wine Estates. CEO James LaCrosse and director Norma Johnston own National Wine & Spirits, which was founded in 1934.

Major changes among suppliers of distilled spirits have National Wine & Spirits and other alcohol distributors across the country re-evaluating how they do business.

For example, Diageo conducted a state-by-state review to determine the companies that have exclusive rights to distribute its products. In Illinois it had not granted such rights to National Wine & Spirits; in addition, two other suppliers (Future Brands and Canandaigua Wine Company) ended the company's Illinois distribution rights. As a result, National Wine & Spirits scaled back operations and about 300 jobs in that state, and formed a strategic alliance with Glazer's Wholesale Drug Company.

National sold its Illinois operations to Glazer's Wholesale Drug Company in 2006, effectively ending operations in that state. In 2007 the company acquired Michigan-based A.H.D. Vintners Ltd. and L&L Wine & Liquor Corp.

EXECUTIVES

Chairman, President, CEO, and CFO:
James E. LaCrosse, age 75, $450,000 pay
EVP, COO, and Director: John J. Baker, age 38, $520,000 pay
EVP Sales and Marketing: Gregory J. (Greg) Mauloff, age 56, $520,000 pay
Director; SVP Corporate Development and Fine Wine: Catherine M. LaCrosse, age 41
VP Human Resources and Development: Karin Lijana Matura
VP Information Systems: Dwight P. Deming
VP Corporate Operations: Steven A. Null
Corporate Controller, Treasurer, and Assistant Secretary: Patrick A. Trefun, age 48

LOCATIONS

HQ: National Wine & Spirits, Inc.
700 W. Morris St., Indianapolis, IN 46206
Phone: 317-636-6092 **Fax:** 317-685-8810
Web: www.nwscorp.com

PRODUCTS/OPERATIONS

Selected Spirits
Absolut Vodka
Bailey's
Beefeater
Belvedere Vodka
Bols
Bushmills
Captain Morgan Rum
Chivas Regal
Courvoisier Cognac
Cragganmore Single Malt
Glenfiddich Single Malt
Glenlivet Scotch
Glenmorangie
Grand Marnier
Hennessy Cognac
J & B
Jagermeister
Jameson Irish Whiskey
Jim Beam
Johnnie Walker
Kahlua
Knob Creek Bourbon
Macallan Single Malt
Maker's Mark
Malibu Rum
Patron
Sauza Tequila
Seagram's Gin

Selected Wines
Almaden
Arbor Mist
Beaulieu Vineyard
Beringer
Bolla
Buena Vista
Chateau St. Jean
Clos du Bois
Columbia
Dom Perignon
Falling Star
Fetzer
Inglenook
Jacob's Creek
Manischewitz
Moet & Chandon
Monkey Bay
Paul Masson
Penfolds
Real Sangria
Riunite
Rosemount Estate
Ruffino
Simi
Sonoma-Cutrer
Stag's Leap
Sterling
Stonehaven
Taylor
Vendange
Veuve Clicquot
Wild Horse

COMPETITORS

Constellation Brands
Georgia Crown
Glazer's Wholesale Drug
Johnson Brothers
National Distributing
Southern Wine & Spirits
Sunbelt Beverage

Nationwide Mutual Insurance

Call it truth in advertising — Nationwide Mutual Insurance Company has offices throughout the US. The company is a leading US property/casualty insurer that, though still a mutual firm, operates in part through its publicly held life insurance subsidiary Nationwide Financial Services. In addition to personal and commercial property/casualty coverage, life insurance, and financial services, Nationwide also offers such specialty lines as professional liability, workers' compensation, agricultural insurance and loss-control, pet insurance, and other coverage. The company sells its products through such subsidiaries as ALLIED Group, Nationwide Agribusiness Insurance, GatesMcDonald, and Scottsdale Insurance.

To enhance its focus on personal and small-business lines in the US, Nationwide bought specialty auto insurer THI from Prudential. Nationwide Financial also bought Provident Mutual Life Insurance (now Nationwide Financial Network); the acquisition made the company the fourth-largest US provider of variable life insurance. However, the insurance market in general is fairly mature, and the company sees more opportunities for growth from its financial services offerings — especially as Baby Boomers start looking at retirement.

In 2006 Nationwide Financial Services received approval to expand its services to include full-service online and telephone banking. Operating as Nationwide Bank, the business has added deposit products and ATM access for its insurance, mortgage, and financial services customers. The company also established its Nationwide Advantage Mortgage business, which provides both mortgages and home equity loans. Consumers can access its services online and through Nationwide agents.

Nationwide Mutual sold off the London-based arm of its Gartmore Investment Management subsidiary to Gartmore management and Hellman & Friedman LLC in 2006. Nationwide retained the US-based retail mutual-fund part of the business, changed its name to Nationwide Funds Group (NFG), and moved it under Nationwide Financial. However, in 2008 the company transferred NFG's active asset management business (with some 26 mutual funds) over to Aberdeen Asset Management.

In 2008 the company announced plans to take its majority owned subsidiary, Nationwide Financial Services, private in a $2.4 billion transaction to simplify the Nationwide group's ownership structure.

HISTORY

In 1919 members of the Ohio Farm Bureau Federation, a farmers' consumer group, established their own automobile insurance company. (As rural drivers, they didn't want to pay city rates.) To get a license from the state, the company, called Farm Bureau Mutual, needed 100 policyholders. It gathered more than 1,000. Founder Murray Lincoln headed the company until 1964.

The insurer expanded into Delaware, Maryland, North Carolina, and Vermont in 1928 and began selling auto insurance in 1931 to city folks. It expanded into fire insurance in 1934 and life insurance the next year.

During WWII growth slowed, although the company had operations in 12 states and Washington, DC, by 1943. It diversified in 1946 when it bought a Columbus, Ohio, radio station. By 1952 the firm had resumed expansion and changed its name to Nationwide.

The company was one of the first auto insurance companies to use its agents to sell other financial products, adding life insurance and mutual funds in the mid-1950s. Nationwide General, the country's first merit-rated auto insurance firm, was formed in 1956.

Nationwide established Neckura in Germany in 1965 to sell auto and fire insurance. Four years later the company bought GatesMcDonald, a provider of risk, tax, benefit, and health care management services. It organized its property/casualty operations into Nationwide Property & Casualty in 1979.

The company experienced solid growth throughout the 1980s by establishing or purchasing insurance firms, among them Colonial Insurance of California (1980), Financial Horizons Life (1981), Scottsdale (1982), and, the largest, Employers Insurance of Wausau (1985). Wausau wrote the country's first workers' compensation policy in 1911.

Earnings were up and down in the 1990s as the company invested in Wausau and in consolidating office operations. Nationwide set up an ethics office in 1995, a time of increased scrutiny of insurance industry sales practices, and made an effort to hire more women as agents. In 1996 the Florida Insurance Commission claimed the company discriminated against customers on the basis of age, gender, health, income, marital status, and location. Nationwide countered that the allegations originated from disgruntled agents.

In 1997 the company settled a lawsuit by agreeing to stop its redlining practices (it avoided selling homeowners' insurance to urban customers with homes valued at less than $50,000 or more than 30 years old, which allegedly discriminated against minorities). It also dropped a year-old sales quota system that was under investigation.

As the century came to a close, Nationwide began to narrow its focus on its core businesses. It spun off Nationwide Financial Services so the unit could have better access to capital, and it expanded both at home and abroad through such purchases as ALLIED Group (multiline insurance), CalFarm (agricultural insurance in California), and AXA subsidiary PanEuroLife (asset management in Europe). The company's discrimination woes came back to haunt it in 1999, and it created a $750,000 fund to help residents of poor Cincinnati neighborhoods buy homes.

Although Nationwide Financial and its Strategic Investments segment underperformed in 2002, the company swung to a net profit, helped in part by improved underwriting results by its insurance subsidiaries.

Nationwide and several other insurance companies were named in a series of lawsuits stemming from the aftermath of 2005's Hurricane Katrina. One suit alleged that prior to the natural disaster, insurance agents dissuaded their clients from purchasing flood insurance, and that the companies did not offer the full settlement amount to clients whose homes had been damaged by the storm surge of water. In one of the first lawsuits to be decided, the judge ruled in favor of Nationwide.

EXECUTIVES

CEO and Director: William G. (Jerry) Jurgensen, age 56
EVP and CFO: Lawrence A. (Larry) Hilsheimer, age 50
EVP, Chief Legal and Governance Officer: Patricia R. (Pat) Hatler, age 53
EVP and Chief Administrative Officer: Terri L. Hill, age 48
EVP and CIO: Michael C. Keller, age 48
EVP and Chief Marketing Officer: James R. (Jim) Lyski, age 45
SVP and Chief Investment Officer: Gail G. Snyder, age 53
VP Investor Relations: J. Mark Barnett
Assistant VP Corporate Communications: Joe Case
Chief Diversity Officer: Candice R. Barnhardt
Treasurer: Harry H. Hallowell, age 47
President and COO, Nationwide Financial Services, Inc.: Mark R. Thresher, age 51
President and COO, Property and Casualty Insurance Operations: Stephen S. (Steve) Rasmussen, age 55
President and COO, Scottsdale Insurance: Michael D. (Mike) Miller
Interim CEO, NWD Investment Group: John Grady
President, Nationwide Better Health: Holly Snyder
Auditors: KPMG LLP

LOCATIONS

HQ: Nationwide Mutual Insurance Company
1 Nationwide Plaza, Columbus, OH 43215
Phone: 614-249-7111 **Fax:** 614-854-3676
Web: www.nationwide.com

PRODUCTS/OPERATIONS

2007 Sales

	$ mil.	% of total
Premium & policy charges	17,688	78
Net investment income	3,579	16
Net realized gains on investments, hedging instruments & hedged items	337	1
Other income	1,193	5
Total	**22,797**	**100**

Selected Subsidiaries and Affiliates

Property and casualty
  Allied Property and Casualty Insurance Company
  Colonial County Mutual Insurance Company
  Depositors Insurance Company
  Farmland Mutual Insurance Company
  Nationwide Agribusiness Insurance Company
  Scottsdale Insurance Company
Life insurance and financial services
  Nationwide Financial Services, Inc.
  TBG Insurance Services Corp.
  Nationwide Life Insurance Company
  Nationwide Bank
  Nationwide Retirement Solutions, Inc.
  Pension Associates, Inc.
Asset management
  Nationwide Asset Management Holdings, LTD.
    Audenstar Limited
    NWD Investment Management, Inc.
Strategic investments
  GatesMcDonald & Company
  Nationwide Advantage Mortgage Company

COMPETITORS

ACE Limited	John Hancock Financial
AIG	Liberty Mutual
Allstate	MassMutual
American Financial	MetLife
AXA	New York Life
AXA Financial	Northwestern Mutual
Blue Cross	Pacific Mutual
CIGNA	Principal Financial
Citigroup	Prudential
CNA Financial	State Farm
GEICO	Travelers Companies
Guardian Life	UnitedHealth Group
The Hartford	USAA

HISTORICAL FINANCIALS

Company Type: Mutual company

Income Statement

FYE: December 31

	ASSETS ($ mil.)	NET INCOME ($ mil.)	INCOME AS % OF ASSETS	EMPLOYEES
12/07	161,090	1,994	1.2%	36,000
12/06	160,009	2,113	1.3%	36,000
12/05	158,258	1,149	0.7%	35,000
12/04	157,371	1,010	0.6%	32,933
12/03	147,934	653	0.4%	33,249
Annual Growth	**2.2%**	**32.2%**	**—**	**2.0%**

2007 Year-End Financials

Equity as % of assets: 9.9%
Return on assets: 1.2%
Return on equity: 12.2%
Long-term debt ($ mil.): —
Sales ($ mil.): 22,797

Net Income History

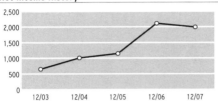

Navy Federal Credit Union

"Once a member, always a member," promises Navy Federal Credit Union (NFCU). This policy undoubtedly helped NFCU become one of the nation's largest credit unions, claiming more than 3 million members who can retain their credit union privileges even after discharge from the armed services. Formed in 1933, NFCU provides a variety of banking services to all Department of Defense uniformed personnel, reservists, national guard personnel, civilian employees, and contractors, as well as their families. NFCU offers checking, savings, and other deposit accounts; credit cards; insurance; investments; brokerage, trust services, and a variety of loans. It has about 150 branch locations in the US and overseas.

In 2008 the previously Navy and Marine Corps-only credit union extended its membership offering to all armed forces branches, including Army, Air Force, guard personnel, and all Department of Defense civilian workers and contractors on military installations.

In anticipation of an influx of members, NFCU announced plans to double its number of full-services branches by 2012. It added more than 30 in 2007 alone.

EXECUTIVES

Chairman: John A. Lockard
First Vice Chairman: Mary Jane Miller
Second Vice Chairman: Bruce B. Engelhardt
President, CEO, Treasurer, and Director: Cutler Dawson
COO: John R. Peden
CFO: Lauren D. Lloyd
EVP Lending: Mary McDuffie
SVP Marketing and Development: Patricia Schneck

VP Regulatory Compliance and Public Policy:
Bill Briscoe
VP Loan Servicing: Tisa Head
Secretary and Director: Kenneth R. Burns
Public Relations Manager: Jennifer Sadler
President and COO, Navy Federal Financial Group:
Thomas Lee
Auditors: PricewaterhouseCoopers LLP

LOCATIONS

HQ: Navy Federal Credit Union
820 Follin Ln., Vienna, VA 22180
Phone: 703-255-8000   **Fax:** 703-255-8741
Web: www.navyfcu.org

PRODUCTS/OPERATIONS

2007 Sales

	$ mil.	% of total
Interest		
Loans to members	1,661.5	70
Securities	220.8	9
Noninterest		
Check card interchange	109.9	5
Credit card interchange	98.2	4
Overdrawn check fees	95.4	4
Mortgage servicing	51.3	2
Mortgage origination	25.9	1
Other	110.3	5
Total	**2,373.3**	**100**

COMPETITORS

Bank of America
Citibank
JPMorgan Chase
USAA
Wachovia Corp

HISTORICAL FINANCIALS

Company Type: Not-for-profit

Income Statement				FYE: December 31
	ASSETS ($ mil.)	NET INCOME ($ mil.)	INCOME AS % OF ASSETS	EMPLOYEES
12/07	33,012	236	0.7%	7,000
12/06	27,122	402	1.5%	7,000
12/05	24,644	266	1.1%	—
Annual Growth	15.7%	(5.8%)	—	0.0%

2007 Year-End Financials

Equity as % of assets: 9.9%   Long-term debt ($ mil.): —
Return on assets: 0.8%   Sales ($ mil.): 2,373
Return on equity: 7.4%

Net Income History

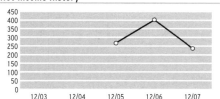

NBC Universal

This company's plumage spreads across TV, film, and the Internet. NBC Universal is a leading media conglomerate anchored by its flagship broadcast network NBC, with 230 affiliate stations and more than 25 owned and operated television stations. It also operates such cable channels as Bravo, USA Network, Oxygen, and 24-hour news channel MSNBC, as well as Spanish-language network Telemundo. In Hollywood, NBC Universal owns film studio Universal Studios, including its Universal Parks & Resorts theme park unit. The company's online operations include iVillage and a 50% stake in video site Hulu. Industrial giant General Electric owns 80% of NBC Universal; French utility operator Vivendi owns the rest.

The formation of NBC Universal in 2004 through the merger of NBC (previously wholly owned by GE) and Vivendi Universal Entertainment (VUE) was intended to create a multimedia titan with the means to produce and distribute content through a variety of channels. While that strategy remains in force, NBCU has trailed its media conglomerate rivals due mostly to poor ratings on television and uneven results at the box office.

Once the highest-rated network on TV, NBC has slipped to fourth-place among the national broadcasters. Trouble began at the Peacock network after such hit shows as *Friends* and *Frasier* ended their long runs in 2004, and new shows such as *Heroes, The Office,* and *My Name is Earl* have done little but stabilize the loss of audience share. NBC is looking to new programming chief Ben Silverman (founder of Reveille Productions) to revive the network's fortunes with a 52-week programming strategy that includes more replacement programs to cut down on the number of repeats.

Helping boost the company's broadcasting operation has been its portfolio of cable channels operated through NBC Universal Cable. USA has become one of the more popular general entertainment outlets on cable with popular reruns (*Law & Order: Special Victims Unit, House*) and successful original programming (*Burn Notice, Monk*), while Bravo has anchored its place in the reality-based TV niche with such hits as *Project Runway* and *Top Chef*. NBCU has also shepherded its SCI FI Channel to cult popularity status with such original programming as *Battlestar Galactica* and *Stargate Atlantis*.

NBCU in 2007 acquired the Oxygen network, a cable channel targeted towards women. The $875 million deal not only expanded its stable of non-broadcast networks, but also provides an opportunity for the company to cross-promote its women-oriented Web site iVillage, acquired the previous year for $600 million. Following the acquisitions, NBCU formed WomenNBCU to oversee its lifestyle and women entertainment outlets, and to consolidate advertising sales for those units; former Bravo head Lauren Zalaznick was tapped to lead the new division.

Adding to its already formidable news and information operations, NBCU in 2008 joined with private equity firms Bain Capital and The Blackstone Group to acquire The Weather Channel from Landmark Communications for

$3.5 billion. The deal added a popular cable property that reaches more than 95 million US homes, as well as the company's weather.com Web site and its audience of 40 million users. The Weather Channel operates as a separate entity managed by NBCU.

The company's Telemundo network continues to hold its place as the #2 Spanish-language broadcaster in the US, but it has struggled to compete against its chief rival Univision. The Latino network has been forced to cut jobs in a cost-saving effort and new shows, such as morning program *Cada Dia*, have been cancelled due to poor ratings. To expand its international operations, NBCU acquired Sparrowhawk Media, which operates the Hallmark Channel in 152 territories, for $350 million in 2007. The following year it purchased UK-based Carnival Film & Television.

At the box office, meanwhile, Universal Studios has turned in mostly lukewarm results the past few years, boasting only a handful of hit films such as *The Bourne Ultimatum, Knocked Up,* and *Mamma Mia!* to offset such recent flops as *Evan Almighty* and *Miami Vice*. The studio is hoping a distribution deal with Steven Spielberg's DreamWorks, inked in 2008, will help boost results in the future. Marc Shmuger and David Linde, who were installed as chairman and vice chairman, respectively, in 2006 after Stacey Snider left to head up DreamWorks, have been tasked with righting the ship at Universal.

NBCU has turned significant focus towards digital entertainment and online media distribution to capitalize on new technologies. In 2008 the company joined forces with News Corporation to launch the joint venture Hulu with some 250 TV programs and 100 full-length films. The move came after NBCU broke ties with Apple's iTunes store, through which it had been selling shows. (The two sides patched up their differences in 2008.) The company has also been investing in original video programming for the Web, as well as blog content and podcasts centered around its shows to further engage audiences.

Lightening the load at NBCU, the company in 2007 shed its investment in ION Media Networks, transferring its rights to a 35% stake in the network of UHF stations to hedge fund manager Citadel Investment Group. NBC had acquired its stake in ION (previously known as Paxson Communications) in 1999.

Also in 2007 Jeff Zucker was promoted to CEO of NBCU, replacing Robert Wright. Zucker previously served as head of NBC Universal Television; Wright had led the NBC network and later NBC Universal for more than 20 years.

EXECUTIVES

President and CEO: Jeffrey A. (Jeff) Zucker, age 42
EVP and CFO: Lynn Calpeter
EVP and CTO: Darren Feher
EVP and General Counsel: Richard (Rick) Cotton, age 60
EVP Administration: Jerry Petry
EVP Affiliate Relations: John Damiano
EVP Business Development: Bruce Campbell
EVP Communications: Cormac (Cory) Shields
EVP Entertainment Strategy and Programs: Ted Frank
EVP Sales and Marketing: Marianne Gambelli
EVP Strategic Partnership Group: Jay Linden
EVP Human Resources: Marc A. Chini
EVP Cable Ad Sales: Steven Mandala
EVP Television Networks Distribution: Henry Ahn

Chairman and CEO, Universal Parks & Resorts:
Thomas L. (Tom) Williams, age 60
Chairman, NBC Universal Sports and Olympics:
Dick Ebersol
Co-Chairman, Universal Pictures: David Linde
Co-Chairman, Universal Pictures: Marc Shmuger
President and COO, Universal Studios: Ron Meyer
President and COO, Universal Studios Hollywood:
Larry Kurzweil
President and General Manager, Universal Operations Group: Jim Watters
President, NBC TV Network and Media Works:
John W. Eck
Auditors: KPMG LLP

LOCATIONS

HQ: NBC Universal, Inc.
30 Rockefeller Plaza, New York, NY 10112
Phone: 212-664-4444   **Fax:** 212-664-4085
Web: www.nbcuni.com

PRODUCTS/OPERATIONS

Selected Operations

Digital media
  Hulu (50%)
  iVillage
  nbc.com
Feature films
  Focus Features
  Rogue Pictures
  Universal Pictures
  Universal Studios Home Entertainment
Television networks and production
  Cable channels
    Bravo
    Chiller
    CNBC
    MSNBC
    mun2
    Oxygen
    SCI FI Channel
    Sleuth
    Universal HD
    USA Network
    The Weather Channel
  NBC Television Network
  NBC Universal Television Distribution
  Telemundo
  Universal Media Studios
Television stations
  NBC
    KNBC (Los Angeles)
    KNSD (San Diego)
    KNTV (San Francisco)
    KXAS (Dallas)
    WCAU (Philadelphia)
    WMAQ (Chicago)
    WNBC (New York City)
    WRC (Washington, DC)
    WTVJ (Miami)
    WVIT (Hartford, CT)
  Telemundo
    KBLR (Las Vegas)
    KDEN (Denver)
    KHRR (Tucson, AZ)
    KMAS (Denver)
    KNSO (Fresno, CA)
    KSTS (San Francisco)
    KTAZ (Phoenix)
    KTMD (Houston)
    KVDA (San Antonio)
    KVEA (Los Angeles)
    KXTX (Dallas)
    WKAQ (Puerto Rico)
    WNEU (Boston)
    WNJU (New York)
    WSCV (Miami)
    WSNS (Chicago)
Universal Parks & Resorts (theme parks)

COMPETITORS

A&E Networks
CBS Corp
Discovery Communications
Disney
Lionsgate
MGM
News Corp.
Sony Pictures Entertainment
Time Warner
Univision
Viacom
Yahoo!

HISTORICAL FINANCIALS

Company Type: Subsidiary

Income Statement

	REVENUE ($ mil.)	NET INCOME ($ mil.)	NET PROFIT MARGIN	EMPLOYEES
12/07	15,416	—	—	—
12/06	16,188	—	—	—
12/05	14,689	—	—	—
12/04	12,886	—	—	—
12/03	14,433	—	—	—
Annual Growth	1.7%	—	—	—

FYE: December 31

Revenue History

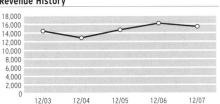

Nebraska Book

Nebraska Book Company (NBC) can help college students in the US and Canada with book learnin'. One of the largest textbook distributors in the US, NBC sells more than 6.8 million books annually and offers 108,000-plus titles. Its bookstores division operates about 260 bookstores on or adjacent to college campuses that sell new and used textbooks and other merchandise. NBC's Complementary Services unit provides education materials to students in private high schools, non-traditional colleges, and corporate and correspondence classes. Founded in 1915 as a single bookstore near The University of Nebraska, NBC also offers software for store management and WebPrism and CampusHub software for e-commerce.

The textbook company has grown its bookstores division through acquisitions and the opening of new stores. In late 2007 it acquired nine new bookstores. In 2006 NBC bought College Book Stores of America in a deal that practically doubled NBC's store count. College Book Stores of America kept its name and operates as a stand-alone business of NBC. Overall, the company has more than doubled the number of bookstore it operates since 2004.

Mark Oppegard, CEO of the company, promoted COO Barry Major to president and COO in September 2008. Investment firm Weston Presidio owns a controlling interest in the company.

EXECUTIVES

CEO and Director: Mark W. Oppegard, age 58, $295,007 pay
President, COO, and Director: Barry S. Major, age 51, $267,775 pay
SVP Finance and Administration, CFO, Treasurer and, Assistant Secretary: Alan G. Siemek, age 48, $197,773 pay
SVP College Bookstore Division: Robert A. (Rob) Rupe, age 60, $204,445 pay
SVP Complementary Services: Larry R. Rempe, age 60
SVP Textbook Division: Michael J. Kelly, age 50, $190,784 pay (prior to title change)
VP Corporate Communications: Sue Riedman
Corporate Administration: Mary Lockard
Human Resources: Melissa Kletchka
Marketing: Shane Jochum
General Merchandise College Bookstore Division: Jay Trent
CampusHub Textbook Division: Wendy Hicks
General Information Textbook Division: Frank Condello
Auditors: Deloitte & Touche LLP

LOCATIONS

HQ: Nebraska Book Company, Inc.
4700 S. 19th St., Lincoln, NE 68501
Phone: 402-421-7300   **Fax:** 800-869-0399
Web: www.nebook.com

PRODUCTS/OPERATIONS

2008 Sales

	$ mil.	% of total
Bookstore division	454.4	78
Textbook division	139.7	24
Complementary services	34.4	6
Adjustments	(47.1)	(8)
Total	**581.2**	**100**

COMPETITORS

Amazon.com
Barnes & Noble College Bookstores
Borders
Ecampus.com
Follett
MBS Textbook Exchange
Wal-Mart

HISTORICAL FINANCIALS

Company Type: Private

Income Statement

	REVENUE ($ mil.)	NET INCOME ($ mil.)	NET PROFIT MARGIN	EMPLOYEES
3/08	581	13	2.2%	3,400
3/07	544	13	2.3%	3,100
3/06	420	12	2.9%	2,900
3/05	402	14	3.4%	2,300
3/04	399	14	3.4%	2,500
Annual Growth	9.9%	(1.9%)	—	8.0%

FYE: March 31

2008 Year-End Financials

Debt ratio: —
Return on equity: 6.6%
Cash ($ mil.): —
Current ratio: —
Long-term debt ($ mil.): —

Net Income History

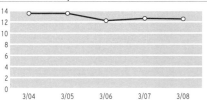

Neiman Marcus

Not for the faint of finances, Neiman Marcus department stores offer high-fashion, high-quality women's and men's apparel (from such labels as Chanel and Prada), accessories, fine jewelry, china, crystal, and silver. The Neiman Marcus Group operates some 40 Neiman Marcus stores in some 20 states and the District of Columbia, as well as two Bergdorf Goodman stores in New York City and two dozen Last-Call clearance centers that sell marked-down goods. Its mail-order business, Neiman Marcus Direct, distributes catalogs (which offer apparel, home furnishings, and gourmet foods) under the Neiman Marcus By Mail and Horchow names. The upscale retail chain was acquired by two private equity firms in 2005.

Texas Pacific Group (now TPG Capital) and Warburg Pincus LLC together paid about $5.1 billion ($100 per share in cash) for the company, beating out other joint bids by Kohlberg Kravis Roberts & Co. and Bain Capital Partners, and Thomas H. Lee Partners and The Blackstone Group.

Though fondly known as "Needless Markup," Neiman Marcus' success can be attributed in part to the lavish customer service upscale shoppers have come to expect. The company offers extravagant special events, one-of-a-kind items, and especially attentive salespeople. Customers (who tend to be older, affluent women prepared to purchase the best at any price) are often known by name and their needs are fastidiously met.

The luxury retailer is looking for growth outside its traditional markets, focusing on smaller enclaves of wealth scattered throughout the US. In 2008 Neiman's opened a store in Natick, Massachusetts. Future stores are slated to open in Seattle in 2009 and in Sarasota, Florida and Walnut Creek, California in 2010.

In a bid to appeal to the younger set, in 2006 Neiman's launched a retail concept called CUSP, a loft-like format (averaging 6,000 to 11,000 square feet) targeting fashion savvy 25- to 45-year-old women. There are currently five CUSP stores in operation. The stores' main brands are Diane von Furstenberg, Seven For All Mankind, and BCBG Max Azria. The company hopes to open as many as six new locations by 2010.

HISTORY

When Herbert Marcus, his sister Carrie Marcus Neiman, and her husband, A. L. Neiman, sold their sales promotion business in Atlanta, they chose to take $25,000 in cash instead of the Missouri or Kansas franchise rights for a new drink called Coca-Cola (which later prompted family members to joke that their company was founded on poor business judgment since no one recognized the drink's potential). The three moved to Dallas, and in 1907 they used their cash and the contributions of other relatives to open Neiman Marcus, a store for "fashionable women."

The three owners were determined to have a specialty store unlike any in the entire South — one that sold ladies' millinery and outergarments that were stylish, high quality, and ready-to-wear (a new concept). Neiman Marcus was an immediate success that showed a profit its very first year.

In 1928 Herbert bought out the Neimans. Also that year the store added men's fashions. Herbert's son Stanley, who started the extravagant Neiman Marcus Christmas catalog and oversaw the company's expansion into new markets, ran the stores from 1952 to 1979.

Retailer Carter Hawley Hale bought the chain in 1969 but did not keep up the stores in the customary manner. As a result, sales and the chain's reputation as upscale and unique suffered throughout the 1970s and into the 1980s. In 1979 Stanley's son Richard continued the family's reign, becoming the company's chairman and CEO.

As part of its 1987 restructuring, Carter Hawley Hale spun off the Neiman Marcus stores. At that time General Cinema traded its interest in Carter Hawley Hale for a controlling 44% of The Neiman Marcus Group. In addition to the Neiman Marcus stores, The Neiman Marcus Group included New York City's exclusive Bergdorf Goodman and the mainstream chain Contempo Casuals. Tailor Herman Bergdorf and his partner, Edwin Goodman, founded Bergdorf Goodman in New York in 1901. Carter Hawley Hale bought the high-end retailer in 1972.

The Neiman Marcus Group bought Horchow Mail Order of Dallas, a retailer of personal and home upscale decorative items, in 1988. That year Richard resigned as CEO and ended 81 years of family management of the 22-store chain.

An offer in 1990 by General Cinema (later renamed Harcourt Education in 2003 and Houghton Mifflin Harcourt in 2008) to buy the rest of The Neiman Marcus Group was rejected.

It bought Chef's Catalog, which sells high-dollar cookware, in 1998. That year the company also began testing The Galleries of Neiman Marcus, a new, smaller store format selling fine jewelry and gifts. In November the company acquired 51% of Gurwitch Products (formerly Gurwitch Bristow Products), makers of Laura Mercier cosmetics. Also in 1998 Robert Smith was promoted to CEO of The Neiman Marcus Group; his father, Richard, remained chairman. (The two also head up Harcourt.)

In February 1999 Neiman Marcus bought 56% of luxury handbag and accessories maker and retailer kate spade. In May Richard's son-in-law, Brian Knez, was named co-CEO. Later that year Harcourt spun off most of its Neiman Marcus stake to its own shareholders, who are led by the Smith family.

The company named co-CEOs Robert and Knez co-vice chairmen in February 2001 and appointed president and COO Burton Tansky CEO. Stanley Marcus, chairman emeritus of the company since 1975, died in early 2002 at the age of 96.

In 2004 the remainder of the company's The Galleries of Neiman Marcus stores shut down. In July 2005 the luxury retailer completed the sale of its private-label credit card business, which has about $525 million in accounts receivable, to HSBC Holdings for about $653 million. Under the terms of the deal, HSBC, one of the world's largest banks, will not sell the names of Neiman's 3 million credit card customers and Neiman's will continue to handle all dealings with cardholders. The purchase included the private-label credit card accounts of Neiman's Bergdorf Goodman subsidiary.

In 2006 the company sold kate spade to apparel giant Liz Claiborne for about $124 million.

EXECUTIVES

Chairman, President, and CEO:
Burton M. (Burt) Tansky, age 70, $2,990,000 pay
EVP; President and CEO, Neiman Marcus Stores:
Karen W. Katz, age 51, $1,409,086 pay
EVP, Women's Apparel, Neiman Marcus Stores:
Ann Stordahl
EVP and CFO: James E. Skinner, age 54, $918,000 pay
SVP and CIO: Phillip L. Maxwell
SVP and Director, Fashion Neiman Marcus Stores:
Ken Downing
SVP, Properties and Store Development: Wayne Hussey
SVP and General Merchandise Manager, Neiman Marcus Direct: Gerald Barnes
SVP and General Merchandise Manager, Neiman Marcus Stores: Jonathan Joselove
SVP, Human Resources: Marita O'Dea, age 57
SVP and General Counsel: Nelson A. (Tony) Bangs, age 55
SVP, Strategy, Business Development, and Multi-Channel Marketing: Steven P. Dennis, age 46
VP and General Merchandise Manager, Neiman Marcus Stores: Russ Patrick
VP and Controller: T. Dale Stapleton
VP, Public Relations and Fashion Presentation:
Gabrielle De Papp
VP Corporate Communications, The Neiman Marcus Group: Ginger Reeder
President and CEO, Bergdorf Goodman:
James J. (Jim) Gold, $720,000 pay
Auditors: Deloitte & Touche LLP

LOCATIONS

HQ: The Neiman Marcus Group, Inc.
1618 Main St., Dallas, TX 75201
Phone: 214-743-7600 **Fax:** 214-573-5320
Web: www.neimanmarcus.com

2008 Neiman Marcus Stores

	No.
Florida	7
Texas	7
California	5
Illinois	3
New Jersey	2
Arizona	1
Colorado	1
District of Columbia	1
Georgia	1
Hawaii	1
Massachusetts	2
Michigan	1
Minnesota	1
Missouri	1
Nevada	1
New York	1
North Carolina	1
Pennsylvania	1
Virginia	1
Total	**39**

PRODUCTS/OPERATIONS

2008 Stores

	No.
Neiman Marcus	39
Clearance Centers	24
Bergdorf Goodman	2
Total	**65**

2008 Sales

	$ mil.	% of total
Department stores	3,853.0	84
Direct marketing	747.5	16
Total	**4,600.5**	**100**

2008 Sales

	% of total
Women's apparel	36
Women's shoes, handbags & accessories	20
Men's apparel & shoes	12
Designer & precious jewelry	12
Cosmetics & fragrance	11
Home furnishings & decor	8
Other	1
Total	**100**

Selected Operations

Catalogs (Horchow, Neiman Marcus By Mail)
Retail stores (Bergdorf Goodman, Last Call Clearance
Centers, Neiman Marcus)

Selected Merchandise

Accessories
Children's apparel
China
Cosmetics
Crystal and silver
Decorative home items
Fine jewelry
Furs
Gift items
Gourmet foods
High-fashion women's and men's clothing
Shoes

COMPETITORS

AnnTaylor	Estée Lauder
Astor & Black	J. Crew
Barneys	Lands' End
Bloomingdale's	Macy's
Brooks Brothers	Nordstrom
Caché	Saks Inc.
DFS Group	Tiffany & Co.
Dillard's	Von Maur
Eddie Bauer Holdings	Williams-Sonoma

New Balance

New Balance Athletic Shoe runs on its every-man (and everywoman) appeal. Unlike its rivals, the firm shuns celebrity endorsers. Its lesser-known athletes show its emphasis on substance versus style. The approach attracts a clientele of Boomer jocks who are less fickle than the teens chased by other shoe firms. Founded in 1906 to make arch supports, New Balance is known for its wide selection of shoe widths. Besides men's and women's shoes for running, cross-training, basketball, tennis, hiking, and golf, the company offers fitness apparel and kids' shoes and owns leather boot maker Dunham. Chairman Jim Davis bought New Balance on the day of the 1972 Boston Marathon. The company appointed a new CEO in early 2007.

A former executive of brand behemoth Procter & Gamble, blades and battery leader Gillette, and poultry provider Tyson Foods, Robert DeMartini joined New Balance in April 2007 to breath new life and bring new blood into the company. (Davis had been at the helm for some 35 years.) DeMartini has logged more than 20 years of experience in sales, marketing, operations, and other areas at these consumer products companies. His hiring is the company's effort to step up its expansion pace and bring in younger and progressive management.

New Balance's products portfolio includes several brands, such as New Balance, Dunham, PF Flyers, Aravon, Warrior, and Brine. As companies such as Fila USA and Fila Retail are being bought out by investors and management, New Balance and its rivals are jockeying for second-tier positions, under goliaths Nike and adidas (which now owns Reebok).

The company's plans for the future include a push into new markets with the opening of some 20 new retail locations. It will also begin updating the brand by retrofitting about 50 stores a year.

New Balance also sees growth potential in its three apparel lines: fitness, running, and team apparel. It wants apparel to account for some 10% to 12% of its sales. The shoe company in mid-2006 acquired Massachusetts-based Brine Inc., a maker of soccer, lacrosse, field hockey, and volleyball apparel and equipment.

EXECUTIVES

Chairman: James S. (Jim) Davis, age 64
CEO: Robert T. DeMartini, age 47
President Emeritus: John E. Larsen
President and COO: Jim Tompkins
Vice Chairman and EVP Administration: Anne Davis
EVP and CFO: John Withee
VP Consumer Experiences: Paul Heffernan
EVP Global Quality Assurance and Product Integrity: Herb Spivak
EVP Global Footwear Product and Marketing: Joseph (Joe) Preston
EVP Manufacturing: John Wilson
VP and Treasurer: Alan Rosen
VP Corporate Human Resources: Carol O'Donnell
Marketing Manager: John Morgan
Corporate Communications: Amy Vreeland

LOCATIONS

HQ: New Balance Athletic Shoe, Inc.
Brighton Landing, 20 Guest St., Boston, MA 02135
Phone: 617-783-4000 **Fax:** 617-787-9355
Web: www.newbalance.com

PRODUCTS/OPERATIONS

Selected Brands

New Balance
Dunham
PF Flyers
Aravon
Warrior
Brine

COMPETITORS

adidas	Mizuno
ASICS	NIKE
Brooks Sports	PUMA
Converse	Roots Canada
Fila USA	Saucony
K-Swiss	Shoe Show

HISTORICAL FINANCIALS

Company Type: Private

Income Statement

FYE: December 31

	REVENUE ($ mil.)	NET INCOME ($ mil.)	NET PROFIT MARGIN	EMPLOYEES
12/07	1,630	—	—	2,800
12/06	1,550	—	—	2,800
12/05	1,540	—	—	2,800
12/04	1,400	—	—	2,600
12/03	1,200	—	—	2,600
Annual Growth	**8.0%**	**—**	**—**	**1.9%**

Revenue History

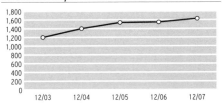

New Jersey Devils

These Devils make trouble for their opponents on the ice. The New Jersey Devils professional hockey team entered the National Hockey League in 1974 as the Kansas City Scouts and relocated to Colorado until it settled in the Garden State in 1982. A regular contender for the playoffs, it boasts three Stanley Cup championships, its last in 2003. The team was owned by uber-sports group YankeeNets (which also owned the New York Yankees and the New Jersey Nets), but former minority owner Jeffrey Vanderbeek and an investment group took it over in 2005.

Looking to boost home attendance and gate receipts, the team relocated from its former home at the Meadowlands in 2007 to take up residence at the Prudential Center in Newark, New Jersey. The Devils helped finance part of the $380 million arena, with the rest of the project being funded through public money.

New Jersey also hired Brent Sutter as head coach for the 2007-08 season, who brought a more open and offensive style to the normally defensive Devils squad. A veteran player with the Chicago Blackhawks and New York Islanders, Sutter is the third person to work behind the New Jersey bench in as many years.

EXECUTIVES

Chairman and Managing Partner: Jeffrey (Jeff) Vanderbeek, age 50
President, CEO, and General Manager: Louis A. (Lou) Lamoriello, age 65
SEVP and COO: Chris Modrzynski
Head Coach: Brent Sutter
EVP and CFO: Scott Struble
EVP: Peter S. McMullen
EVP Administration: Gordon Lavalette, age 45
EVP Hockey Operations and Director Scouting: David Conte, age 58
SVP Hockey Operations; General Manager, Lowell & Scout: Chris Lamoriello, age 33
SVP and General Counsel: Joseph C. Benedetti
SVP Facilities: Mark A. Gheduzzi
VP Ticket Sales and Customer Service: David Beck
VP Hockey Operations: Steve Pellegrini
VP Marketing and Community Development: Jeff Longo
Director Communications: Jeff Altstadter

LOCATIONS

HQ: New Jersey Devils
50 Rte. 120 North, East Rutherford, NJ 07073
Phone: 201-935-6050 **Fax:** 201-935-2127
Web: www.newjerseydevils.com

The New Jersey Devils play at the 17,625-seat capacity Prudential Center in Newark, New Jersey.

PRODUCTS/OPERATIONS

Championship Trophies
Stanley Cup (1995, 2000, 2003)
Prince of Wales Trophy (1995, 2000-01, 2003)

COMPETITORS

New York Islanders
New York Rangers
Philadelphia Flyers
Pittsburgh Penguins

HISTORICAL FINANCIALS
Company Type: Private

Income Statement   FYE: June 30

	REVENUE ($ mil.)	NET INCOME ($ mil.)	NET PROFIT MARGIN	EMPLOYEES
6/07	65	—	—	—
6/06	62	—	—	—
6/05	0	—	—	0
6/04	61	—	—	—
6/03	73	—	—	—
Annual Growth	(2.9%)	—	—	—

Revenue History

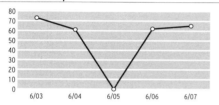

New Jersey Nets

This might be the most appropriately named team in professional sports. Nets Sports & Entertainment owns and operates the New Jersey Nets basketball team, a storied franchise of the National Basketball Association. That story has not always been so good, however; the team has yet to claim an NBA title and struggles with attendance at The IZOD Center (formerly Continental Airlines Arena). Organized by Arthur Brown in 1967 as the New Jersey Americans of the American Basketball Association, the team won two ABA titles as the New York Nets with the help of Julius "Dr. J" Erving. It returned to the Garden State and joined the NBA in 1976. New York real estate developer Bruce Ratner has owned the team since 2004.

Ratner paid about $300 million to purchase the team from Lewis Katz and Ray Chambers and plans to move the Nets to Brooklyn, New York. While construction of a proposed $550 million arena in the Atlantic Yards district has yet to be approved, the team agreed to a 20-year, $400 million naming rights with London-based

financial services giant Barclays in 2007. With construction delays mounting, however, the Nets renewed its lease at The IZOD Center in the Meadowlands through 2010.

The Atlantic Yards project is being developed by Forest City Enterprises, a real estate development company controlled by Ratner's family. The firm owns a 21% stake in the team.

EXECUTIVES

Principal Owner: Bruce C. Ratner, age 63
President and CEO: Brett Yormark
President, New Jersey Nets: Rod Thorn
General Manager: Ernest M. (Kiki) Vandeweghe III, age 50
Head Coach: Lawrence Frank
SVP and Chief Relationship Officer: Leo Ehrline
SVP; General Manager, Arena Operations: Alex Diaz
SVP and General Counsel: Jeff Gewirtz
SVP and CFO: Charlie Mierswa
VP Business and Entertainment Public Relations: Barry Baum
VP Basketball Operations: Bobby Marks
VP Public Relations: Gary Sussman
Director Scouting: Gregg Polinsky
Director Human Resources: Kimberly Blanco
Director Community Relations: Michele Alongi

LOCATIONS

HQ: Nets Sports & Entertainment, LLC
390 Murray Hill Pkwy., East Rutherford, NJ 07073
Phone: 201-935-8888   **Fax:** 201-935-1088
Web: www.nba.com/nets

The New Jersey Nets play at 20,049-seat capacity IZOD Center in East Rutherford, New Jersey.

PRODUCTS/OPERATIONS

Championship Titles
Eastern Conference Champions (2002-03)

COMPETITORS

Boston Celtics
New York Knicks
Philadelphia 76ers
Toronto Raptors

HISTORICAL FINANCIALS
Company Type: Private

Income Statement   FYE: June 30

	REVENUE ($ mil.)	NET INCOME ($ mil.)	NET PROFIT MARGIN	EMPLOYEES
6/07	102	—	—	—
6/06	93	—	—	—
6/05	87	—	—	—
6/04	93	—	—	—
6/03	94	—	—	—
Annual Growth	2.1%	—	—	—

Revenue History

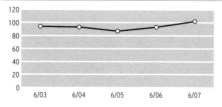

New NGC

When it comes to work, New NGC is always *board*. The company, the second-largest gypsum wallboard manufacturer in the US (behind USG Corporation), does business as National Gypsum Company. It sells wallboard under the Gold Bond, Durabase, and SoundBreak brand names. The company also produces other building products such as joint treatment compounds (ProForm), cement board (PermaBase), plaster, and framing systems. Its testing services division tests acoustical, fire, and structural properties of building materials. National Gypsum, which has more than 20 plants in the US and Mexico, sells its products worldwide to the construction industry. Delcor Inc., a subsidiary of Golden Eagle Industries, owns the company.

Growing sales in Latin America prompted National Gypsum to open its first cement board pant in Mexico in 2008. The joint venture with Panel Rey is called PermaBase de Américas. The new plant allows the company to streamline distribution in Mexico and reduce shipping and customs fees.

The company also is targeting its marketing toward Latinos around the world as well as in the US, where about half of drywall installers are Hispanic.

The housing slump in 2008 forced National Gypsum to close plants and cut jobs in the US.

EXECUTIVES

Chairman, President, and CEO:
Thomas C. (Tom) Nelson, age 45
SVP Manufacturing Operations and Engineering:
Gerard (Jerry) Carroll
SVP Sales and Marketing: Craig Weisbruch
VP and CFO: William D. (Bill) Parmelee
VP and General Counsel: Sam Schiffman
VP Human Resources: Nick Rodono
Director of Communications: Nancy H. Spurlock
Director of Marketing: David Drummond
Director of Purchasing: Raymond Syracuse
Auditors: PricewaterhouseCoopers LLP

LOCATIONS

HQ: New NGC, Inc.
2001 Rexford Rd., Charlotte, NC 28211
Phone: 704-365-7300   **Fax:** 800-329-6421
Web: www.nationalgypsum.com

New NGC operates plants, mines and quarries, paper mills, and research facilities in Canada and the US.

PRODUCTS/OPERATIONS

Selected Products and Brands
Ceiling systems (Gridstone, Seaspray, and Hi-Strength)
Cement board (PermaBase)
Gypsum wallboard (Gold Bond, Durabase, Hi-Impact, and SoundBreak)
Joint compounds, spray textures, and tape (ProForm and Easy Finish)
Manufactured housing products (wallboard, ceiling board, spray texture, and construction guides)
Plaster, plaster base, and finishes
Prefinished gypsum wallboard and panels (Durasan, Kal-Kote, and Uni-Kal)
Shaftwall and area separation wall (H-Stud systems)
Wallboard and plaster base (Hi-Abuse and Hi-Impact)

COMPETITORS

American Gypsum	Johns Manville
Eagle Materials	Lafarge North America
Gypsum Products	Temple-Inland
James Hardie Industries	USG

New Orleans Hornets

These Hornets are looking to sting their opponents on the basketball court. The New Orleans Hornets professional basketball team joined the National Basketball Association as the Charlotte Hornets in 1988 before moving from North Carolina to the Big Easy in 2002. During the 1990s the franchise was a perennial contender for the playoffs, but the team has yet to make an appearance in the NBA finals. Devastation from Hurricane Katrina in 2005 forced the Hornets to relocate its home games to Oklahoma City. (It plans on returning to the Crescent City for the 2007-2008 season.) George Shinn, who made his fortune building a network of for-profit schools, has controlled the franchise since its beginning.

Despite its losing record during the troubled 2005-06 season, the Hornets managed to draw sellout crowds at the Ford Center in its adopted home of Oklahoma City, prompting some to wonder if Shinn might relocate the team permanently. The NBA, however, had made a firm commitment to remain in New Orleans and held its 2008 All-Star game there.

Team president Paul Mott left the Hornets in 2006 after a year on the job.

EXECUTIVES

Owner: George Shinn
Minority Owner: Gary Chouest
President and COO: Hugh Weber
General Manager: Jeff Bower
Head Coach: Byron Scott, age 47
Executive Officer of the Board: Chad Shinn, age 28
EVP Business: Sam Russo
SVP Community Investment and External Affairs:
 Steve Martin
VP Marketing: Matt Biggers
VP Finance: Dan Crumb
VP and General Counsel: Richard House
Director Basketball Administration and Player
 Development: Andrew Loomis
Director Corporate Communications:
 Michael Thompson
Director Basketball Communications: Scott Hall
Director Human Resources: Donna Rochon

LOCATIONS

HQ: New Orleans Hornets
 1250 Poydras St., Fl. 19, New Orleans, LA 70113
Phone: 504-593-4700
Web: www.nba.com/hornets

COMPETITORS

Dallas Mavericks
Houston Rockets
Memphis Grizzlies
San Antonio Spurs

HISTORICAL FINANCIALS

Company Type: Private

Income Statement

FYE: June 30

	REVENUE ($ mil.)	NET INCOME ($ mil.)	NET PROFIT MARGIN	EMPLOYEES
6/07	91	—	—	—
6/06	83	—	—	—
6/05	78	—	—	—
6/04	80	—	—	—
6/03	80	—	—	—
Annual Growth	3.3%	—	—	—

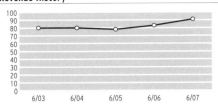

Revenue History

| 6/03 | 6/04 | 6/05 | 6/06 | 6/07 |

New York City Health and Hospitals

New York City Health and Hospitals Corporation (HHC) takes care of the Big Apple. HHC has facilities in all five boroughs of New York City. As one of the largest municipal health service systems in the US, HHC operates a health care network consisting of 11 acute care hospitals (including Bellevue, the nation's oldest public hospital), community clinics, diagnostic and treatment centers, long-term care facilities, and a home health care agency. HHC also provides medical services to New York City's correctional facilities and operates MetroPlus, a managed health care plan.

HHC is investing $1.2 billion to improve its facilities over a five-year period. The health care system has worked on expansion projects for the Lincoln Medical & Mental Health Center, Harlem Hospital Center, and the Kings County Hospital Center.

HISTORY

The City of New York in 1929 created a department to manage its hospitals for the poor. During the Depression, more than half of the city's residents were eligible for subsidized care, and its public hospitals operated at full capacity.

Four new hospitals opened in the 1950s, but the city was already having trouble maintaining existing facilities and attracting staff (young doctors preferred private, insurance-supported hospitals catering to the middle class). Meanwhile, technological advances and increased demand for skilled nurses made hospitals more expensive to operate. The advent of Medicaid in 1965 was a boon for the system because it brought in federal money.

In 1969 the city created the New York City Health and Hospitals Corporation (HHC) to manage its public health care system — and, it was hoped, to distance it from the political arena. But HHC was still dependent on the city for funds, arousing criticism from those who had hoped for more autonomy. A 1973 state report claimed "the people of New York City are not materially better served by the Health and Hospitals Corporation than by its predecessor agencies."

City budget shortfalls in the mid-1970s led to cutbacks at HHC, including nearly 20% of staff. Later in the decade several hospitals closed and some services were discontinued. Ed Koch became mayor in 1978 and gained more control over HHC's operations. Struggles between his administration and the system led three HHC presidents to resign by 1981. That year Koch crony Stanley Brezenoff assumed the post and helped transform HHC into a city pseudo-department.

The early 1980s brought greater prosperity to the system. Reimbursement rates and collections procedures improved, allowing HHC to upgrade its record-keeping and its ambulatory and psychiatric care programs. In the late 1980s sharp increases in AIDS and crack addiction cases strained the system and a sluggish economy decreased city funding. Criticism mounted in the early 1990s, with allegations of wrongful deaths, dangerous facilities, and lack of Medicaid payment controls. HHC lost patients to managed care providers, and revenues plummeted. In 1995 a city panel recommended radically revamping the system.

Faced with declining revenues and criticism from Mayor Rudolph Giuliani that HHC was "a jobs program," the company began cutting jobs and consolidating facilities in 1996. Under Giuliani's direction, HHC made plans to sell its Coney Island, Elmhurst, and Queens hospital centers. In 1997 the New York State Supreme Court struck down Giuliani's privatization efforts, saying the city council had a right to review and approve each sale. In 1998 Giuliani continued to seek to restructure HHC, and the agency itself contended it was making progress toward its restructuring goals, which were aimed at giving HHC more autonomy as well as more fiscal responsibility. In anticipation of a budget shortfall that year, the system laid off some 900 support staff employees. In 1999 the state court of appeals ruled HHC could not legally lease or sell its hospitals.

In 2000 HHC launched an effort to improve its physical infrastructure by beginning the rebuilding and renovation of facilities in Brooklyn, Manhattan, and Queens. The organization also began converting to an electronic (and thus more efficient) clinical information system. In 2001 HHC forged ahead with further restructuring initiatives. It introduced the Open Access plan, a cost-cutting measure designed to expedite the processes involved in outpatient visits.

In 2006 Mayor Michael Bloomberg committed $16 million in funds toward the treatment of those affected by exposure to toxic fumes and dust from the 2001 attacks on the World Trade Center. Together with the city, HHC established the WTC Environmental Health Center at Bellevue Hospital; treatment was made available at little or no charge to the patient.

EXECUTIVES

President and CEO: Alan D. Aviles
EVP, Medical and Professional Affairs:
 Ramanathan Raju
SVP Finance: Marlene Zurack
SVP, Central Brooklyn Family Health Network;
 Executive Director, Kings County Hospital Center:
 Jean G. Leon
SVP, Corporate Planning, Community Health, and
 Intergovernmental Relations: LaRay Brown
SVP, Facilities Development: Phillip W. Robinson
SVP, Generations Plus Northern Manhattan Health
 Network; Executive Director, Lincoln Medical and
 Mental Health Center and Metropolitan Hospital
 Center: Jose R. Sanchez
SVP, Medical and Professional Affairs: Van Dunn

SVP, North Bronx Healthcare Network; Executive
  Director, Jacobi Medical Center: William P. Walsh
SVP Operations: Frank J. Cirillo
SVP, Southern Brooklyn and Staten Island Health
  Network; Executive Director, Coney Island Hospital:
  Peter N. Wolf
SVP, South Manhattan Health Network; Executive
  Director, Bellevue Hospital Center: Lynda D. Curtis
SVP and General Counsel: Richard A. Levy
SVP, Central Brooklyn Family Health Network;
  Executive Director, Kings County Hospital Center:
  Iris Jimenez-Hernandez
CIO: Frances Pandolfi
Senior Assistant VP, Corporate Communications and
  Marketing: Ana Marengo
Auditors: KPMG LLP

LOCATIONS

HQ: New York City Health and Hospitals Corporation
    125 Worth St., Ste. 514, New York, NY 10013
Phone: 212-788-3321   Fax: 212-788-0040
Web: www.nyc.gov/html/hhc/html/home/home.shtml

HHC Networks

Central Brooklyn Family Health Network
  Dr. Susan Smith McKinney Nursing and
    Rehabilitation Center
  East New York Diagnostic & Treatment Center
  Kings County Hospital Center
Generations Plus Northern Manhattan Health Network
  Harlem Hospital Center
  Lincoln Medical and Mental Health Center
  Metropolitan Hospital Center
  Morrisania Diagnostic & Treatment Center
  Renaissance Health Care Network Diagnostic &
    Treatment Center
  Segundo Ruiz Belvis Diagnostic & Treatment Center
North Bronx Healthcare Network
  Jacobi Medical Center
  North Central Bronx Hospital
North Brooklyn Health Network
  Cumberland Diagnostic & Treatment Center
  Woodhull Medical and Mental Health Center
Queens Health Network
  Elmhurst Hospital Center
  Queens Hospital Center
South Brooklyn and Staten Island Health Network
  Coney Island Hospital
  Sea View Hospital Rehabilitation Center and Home
South Manhattan Healthcare Network
  Bellevue Hospital Center
  Coler-Goldwater Specialty Care and Nursing Facility
  Gouverneur Healthcare Services

COMPETITORS

Catholic Healthcare System
Columbia University
Cornell University
Lenox Hill Hospital
Memorial Sloan-Kettering
Montefiore Medical
Mount Sinai NYU Health
North Shore-Long Island Jewish Health System
NYU
Saint Vincent Catholic Medical Centers

New York Giants

It only seems natural that the Big Apple would
have a big football team. New York Football Giants owns and operates the New York Giants professional football team, one of the oldest and
most storied franchises in the National Football
League. Started in 1925, the team has played for
the league championship a record 18 times, winning seven titles, including three Super Bowl
championships. The Giants roster has included
such Hall of Fame players as Frank Gifford, Sam
Huff, Lawrence Taylor, and Y.A. Tittle. Tim Mara
paid $500 to found the franchise; the Mara and
Tisch families continue to control the team.

After an extended drought of playoff success,
Giants fans celebrated the team's third Super
Bowl title at the end of the 2007 season. New
York's previous championships had come under
head coach Bill Parcells in the late 1980s and
early 1990s.

The franchise reached an agreement in 2005
with the New Jersey Sports and Exposition Authority and real estate development firms The
Mills Corporation and Mack-Cali Realty to build
a new stadium at the Meadowlands. The $1.3 bil-
lion privately financed facility, planned for opening in 2010, is envisioned to have seating for
more than 82,500 spectators and will be part of
a larger development project to create a sports,
retail, and entertainment complex called Meadowlands Xanadu. The Giants also agreed to share
the new stadium with the New York Jets; the two
teams have called the Meadowlands home field
since 1984.

Team patriarch Wellington Mara (founder
Tim's son) died of cancer in late 2005. Robert
Tisch became sole CEO of the organization but
he also died of cancer three weeks later.

EXECUTIVES

Chairman and EVP: Steven (Steve) Tisch
President and CEO: John K. Mara, age 53
SVP and General Manager: Jerry Reese
SVP and Chief Marketing Officer: Mike Stevens
Assistant General Manager: Kevin Abrams
Head Coach: Thomas R. (Tom) Coughlin, age 62
VP and CFO: Christine Procops
VP Communications: Pat Hanlon
VP Marketing: Rusty Hawley
VP Player Evaluation: Chris Mara
Controller: Steve Hamrahi
Treasurer: Jonathan M. Tisch
Director of Administration: Jim Phelan
Director of Community Relations: Allison Stangeby
Director Pro Personnel: David Gettleman
Director of Public Relations: E. Peter John-Baptiste
CEO, The New Meadowlands Stadium: Mark Lamping

LOCATIONS

HQ: New York Football Giants, Inc.
    Giants Stadium, East Rutherford, NJ 07073
Phone: 201-935-8111   Fax: 201-935-8493
Web: www.giants.com

The New York Giants play at 80,242-seat capacity Giants
Stadium (The Meadowlands) in East Rutherford, New
Jersey.

PRODUCTS/OPERATIONS

Championship Titles

Super Bowl Championships
  Super Bowl XLII (2008)
  Super Bowl XXV (1991)
  Super Bowl XXI (1987)
NFC Championships (1986, 1990, 2000, 2007)
NFC Eastern Division Champions (1986, 1989, 1990,
  1997, 2000, 2005)
NFL Championships (1927, 1934, 1938, 1956)
NFL Eastern Conference Champions (1956, 1958-59,
  1961-63)
NFL East Division Champions (1933-35, 1938-39, 1941,
  1944, 1946)

COMPETITORS

Dallas Cowboys
Philadelphia Eagles
Washington Redskins

HISTORICAL FINANCIALS

Company Type: Private

Income Statement

	REVENUE ($ mil.)	NET INCOME ($ mil.)	NET PROFIT MARGIN	EMPLOYEES
2/08	214	—	—	—
2/07	195	—	—	—
2/06	182	—	—	—
2/05	175	—	—	—
2/04	154	—	—	—
Annual Growth	8.6%	—	—	—

FYE: February 28

Revenue History

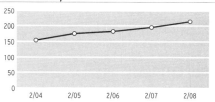

New York Islanders

These Islanders need to be surrounded by
frozen water to be successful. Gotham's other
hockey team, the New York Islanders entered
the National Hockey League in 1972 and dominated the league in the early 1980s: The franchise won four consecutive Stanley Cup titles
until its streak was ended in 1984 by the Wayne
Gretzky-led Edmonton Oilers. More recently, the
team has struggled on the ice, leading to a decline in ticket sales at Nassau Veterans Memorial Coliseum. Former CA executive Charles Wang
has owned the Islanders franchise and its home
arena since 2000.

The team's fortunes have been up and down
the past few years under the leadership of general manager Garth Snow. A disappointing 2007-
08 campaign led to the dismissal of head coach
Ted Nolan after two seasons behind the bench;
he had led the Isles to a post-season berth in his
inaugural year.

Snow, a former goalie for the Islanders, joined
the front office in 2006 replacing Mike Milbury

after more than a decade. He had hired Nolan to replace Steve Stirling.

Wang, who founded CA as Computer Associates before leaving in 2002, and partner Sanjay Kumar, who served as CEO until 2004, bought the Islanders from Steven Glückstern and Howard Milstein for about $190 million. Their relationship soured, however, and later unwound the partnership, leaving Wang in control of the franchise.

EXECUTIVES

Co-Owner: Charles B. Wang, age 61
Co-Owner: Sanjay Kumar, age 44
SVP and CFO: Arthur McCarthy
SVP Operations: Michael Picker
SVP Sales and Marketing: Paul Lancey
SVP Sports Properties: Mike Milbury, age 56
VP Corporate and Community Relations: Bill Kain
VP Marketing and Game Operations: Tim Beach
General Manager: Garth Snow
Director of Pro Scouting: Ken Morrow, age 41
Head Amateur Scout: Tony Feltrin, age 39
Media Relations Coordinator: Jim Morlock

LOCATIONS

HQ: New York Islanders Hockey Club, L.P.
1535 Old Country Rd., Plainview, NY 11803
Phone: 516-501-6700   **Fax:** 516-501-6762
Web: www.newyorkislanders.com

The New York Islanders play at the 16,234-seat capacity Nassau Veterans Memorial Coliseum in Uniondale, New York.

PRODUCTS/OPERATIONS

Championship Trophies
Stanley Cup (1980-83)
Prince of Wales Trophy (1982-84)
Clarence S. Campbell Bowl (1978-79, 1981)

COMPETITORS

New Jersey Devils
New York Rangers
Philadelphia Flyers
Pittsburgh Penguins

HISTORICAL FINANCIALS

Company Type: Private

Income Statement

	REVENUE ($ mil.)	NET INCOME ($ mil.)	NET PROFIT MARGIN	EMPLOYEES
8/07	60	—	—	—
8/06	56	—	—	—
8/05	0	—	—	—
8/04	64	—	—	—
8/03	56	—	—	—
Annual Growth	1.7%	—	—	—

FYE: August 31

Revenue History

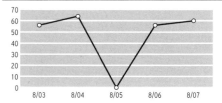

New York Life Insurance

New York Life Insurance has been in the Big Apple since it was just a tiny seed. The company (the top mutual life insurer in the US) is adding products but retaining its core business: life insurance and annuities. New York Life has added such products and services as mutual funds for individuals. It also offers its investment management services to institutional investors. Other lines of business include long-term care insurance and special group policies sold through AARP and other affinity groups or professional associations. The company, through New York Life International, is also reaching out geographically, targeting areas such as Mexico and India where the life insurance markets are not yet mature.

After state legislators failed to approve its proposed company restructuring, New York Life announced it would not follow its rivals in demutualizing for fear of being gobbled up in a merger. The insurer instead uses its considerable war chest to further expand its international operations — Asia and Latin America are major expansion targets, and sales growth in both regions has been rapid. It is also expanding its investment management operations through its New York Life Investment Management (mutual funds, group and individual retirement plans, college savings products). While other big-name insurers in the mature US market are only aiming for high net-worth individual customers, New York Life is also casting its nets a bit lower to catch middle-income consumers and creating products to lure younger families.

HISTORY

In 1841 actuary Pliny Freeman and 56 New York businessmen founded Nautilus Insurance Co., the third US policyholder-owned company. It began operating in 1845 and became New York Life in 1849.

By 1846 the company had the first life insurance agent west of the Mississippi River. Although the Civil War disrupted southern business, New York Life honored all its obligations and renewed lapsed policies when the war ended. By 1887 the company had developed its branch office system.

By the turn of the century, the company had established an agent compensation plan that featured a lifetime income after 20 years of service (discontinued 1991). New York Life moved into Europe in the late 1800s but withdrew after WWI.

In the early 1950s the company simplified insurance forms, slashed premiums, and updated mortality tables from the 1860s. In 1956 it became the first life insurer to use data-processing equipment on a large scale.

New York Life helped develop variable life insurance, which featured variable benefits and level premiums in the 1960s; it added variable annuities in 1968. Steady growth continued into the late 1970s, when high interest rates led to heavy policyholder borrowing. The outflow of money convinced New York Life to make its products more competitive as investments.

The company formed New York Life and Health Insurance Co. in 1982. It acquired MacKay-Shields Financial, which oversees its MainStay mutual funds, in 1984. The company's first pure investment product, a real estate limited partnership, debuted that year. (When limited partnerships proved riskier than most insurance customers bargained for, investors sued New York Life; in 1996 the company negotiated a plan to liquidate the partnerships and reimburse investors.)

Expansion continued in 1987 when New York Life bought a controlling interest in a third-party insurance plan administrator and group insurance programs. The company also acquired Sanus Corp. Health Systems.

New York Life formed an insurance joint venture in Indonesia in 1992; it also entered South Korea and Taiwan. The next year it bought Aetna UK's life insurance operations.

In 1994 New York Life grew its health care holdings, adding utilization review and physician practice management units. Allegations of churning (agents inducing customers to buy more expensive policies) led New York Life to overhaul its sales practices in 1994; it settled the resulting lawsuit for $300 million in 1995. Soon came claims that agents hadn't properly informed customers that some policies were vulnerable to interest-rate changes and that customers might be entitled to share in the settlement. Some agents lashed out, saying New York Life fired them so it wouldn't have to pay them retirement benefits.

As health care margins decreased and the insurance industry consolidated, New York Life in 1998 sold its health insurance operations and said it would demutualize — a plan ultimately foiled by the state legislature.

In 2000 the company bought two Mexican insurance firms, including Seguros Monterrey, the nation's #2 life insurer. It received Office of Thrift Supervision permission to open a bank, New York Life Trust Company. Also that year the company created a subsidiary to house its asset management businesses and entered the Indian market through its joint venture with Max India. In 2002 New York Life entered into a joint life insurance venture with China's Haier Group.

EXECUTIVES

Chairman: Seymour (Sy) Sternberg, age 65
Vice Chairman and Chief Investment Officer; Chairman, New York Life Investment Management: Gary E. Wendlandt, age 57
President and CEO: Theodore A. (Ted) Mathas, age 41
EVP and CFO: Michael E. Sproule
EVP, Chief Legal Officer, and General Counsel: Sheila K. Davidson
EVP; Chairman and CEO, New York Life International: Richard L. (Dick) Mucci, age 57
EVP; President and CEO, New York Life Investment Management: John Y. Kim, age 43
EVP and Chief Administrative Officer: Frank M. Boccio
SVP, Controller, and Chief Accounting Officer: John A. Cullen
SVP and Senior Advisor to the President: Solomon Goldfinger
SVP, Agency Department: Mark W. Pfaff
SVP, Deputy General Counsel, and Secretary: Susan A. Thrope
SVP, General Auditor, and Chief Privacy Officer: Thomas J. Warga
SVP and CIO: Eileen T. Slevin
SVP and COO, Life and Annuity: Christopher O. Blunt
SVP Individual Life: Jon Stenberg
Auditors: PricewaterhouseCoopers LLP

HQ: New York Life Insurance Company
    51 Madison Ave., Ste. 3200, New York, NY 10010
Phone: 212-576-7000   **Fax:** 212-576-8145
Web: www.newyorklife.com

New York Life Insurance Company operates in Argentina, China, Hong Kong, India, Mexico, the Philippines, South Korea, Taiwan, Thailand, the US, and Vietnam.

PRODUCTS/OPERATIONS

2007 Sales

	$ mil.	% of total
Premiums	9,879	47
Fees	956	4
Investment income	8,916	42
Investment gains	627	3
Other	745	4
Total	**21,123**	**100**

COMPETITORS

AIG American General
Allstate
American National Insurance
CIGNA
CNA Financial
Guardian Life
The Hartford
John Hancock Financial Services
MassMutual
MetLife
Mutual of Omaha
Northwestern Mutual
Principal Financial
Prudential
T. Rowe Price
TIAA-CREF
UBS Financial Services

HISTORICAL FINANCIALS

Company Type: Mutual company

Income Statement

FYE: December 31

	ASSETS ($ mil.)	NET INCOME ($ mil.)	INCOME AS % OF ASSETS	EMPLOYEES
12/07	198,383	1,497	0.8%	14,847
12/06	182,343	2,298	1.3%	13,580
12/05	168,865	855	0.5%	13,180
12/04	159,888	1,294	0.8%	12,650
12/03	144,699	1,120	0.8%	12,100
Annual Growth	8.2%	7.5%	—	5.2%

2007 Year-End Financials

Equity as % of assets: 10.2%   Long-term debt ($ mil.): —
Return on assets: 0.8%   Sales ($ mil.): 21,123
Return on equity: 7.7%

Net Income History

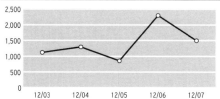

New York Power Authority

Question authority? Well, without question, authority for power lies in the Power Authority of the State of New York (commonly referred to as the New York Power Authority, or NYPA). The company generates and transmits more than 20% of New York's electricity, making it the largest state-owned public power provider in the US. It is also New York's only statewide electricity supplier. NYPA owns hydroelectric and fossil-fueled generating facilities (18 in total) that produce about 5,700 MW of electricity, and it operates more than 1,400 circuit-miles of transmission lines.

The authority sells power to government agencies, municipal systems, rural cooperatives, private companies, private utilities (for resale), and neighboring states. Its clients include some of the largest electricity users in the US, including the New York City government and the Metropolitan Transportation Authority. NYPA receives no state funds or tax credits. Instead, it finances new projects through bond sales.

Following its shift from a regulated monopoly to a competitor in an open power market, NYPA is aiming to grow by reducing the cost of the energy it provides and by developing electric transportation (such as electric cars) and other energy-efficiency projects, such as installing emergency power generators in metropolitan buildings. It is also working to improve the state's transmission grid and increase its generating capacity.

In 2008 the company began public hearings on renewing a long-term power contract with Alcoa involving supplying energy to the manufacturer's two facilities in Massena.

HISTORY

The Power Authority of the State of New York (aka New York Power Authority, or NYPA) was established in 1931 by Gov. Franklin Roosevelt to gain public control of New York's hydropower resources. The utility's major power plants came on line with the opening of the St. Lawrence-Franklin D. Roosevelt Power Project (1958) and the Niagara Power Project (1961). The Blenheim-Gilboa Pumped Storage Power Project opened in 1973.

In the mid-1970s NYPA shifted to nuclear power when it opened the James A. FitzPatrick Nuclear Power Plant (1975) and the Indian Point 3 Nuclear Power Plant (1976). The company then opened gas- and oil-powered plants: the Charles Poletti Power Project (1977) and the Richard M. Flynn Power Plant (1994).

In 1998 the authority allocated low-cost electricity to five companies that planned to invest $104 million in business expansions in western New York. The company suffered a loss in 1999 in part from reduced hydro generation and a drop in investment earnings. In 2000 NYPA sold its two nuclear plants (1,800 MW of capacity) to utility holding company Entergy for $967 million.

The company completed the installation of 11 gas-powered turbines at various locations in New York City and on Long Island in 2001; the program was initiated to prevent expected energy shortages that summer, but it also helped maintain power in areas of the city during the September 11 terrorist attacks.

EXECUTIVES

Acting Chairman: Michael J. Towsend
President and CEO: Richard M. Kessel
EVP and CFO: Joseph M. Del Sindaco
EVP, General Counsel, and Chief of Staff:
  Thomas J. Kelly
EVP Corporate Services and Administration:
  Vincent C. Vesce
EVP Energy Marketing and Corporate Affairs:
  Gil C. Quiniones
SVP, Energy Resource Management and Strategic Planning: William J. Nadeau
SVP, Energy Services and Technology:
  Angelo S. Esposito
SVP Public and Governmental Affairs: Brian Vattimo
SVP Marketing and Economic Development:
  James H. (Jim) Yates
SVP and Chief Engineer, Power Generation:
  Edward A. Welz
SVP, Transmission: Steven J. DeCarlo
VP and Controller: Arnold M. Bellis
VP and Chief Risk Officer, Energy Risk Assessment and Control: Thomas H. Warmath
VP Finance: Donald A. Russak
CIO: Dennis T. Eccleston
Corporate Secretary: Anne B. Cahill
Treasurer, Corporate Finance: Brian McElroy
Auditors: Ernst & Young LLP

LOCATIONS

HQ: Power Authority of the State of New York
    123 Main St., Ste. 10-B, White Plains, NY 10601
Phone: 914-681-6200   **Fax:** 914-681-6949
Web: www.nypa.gov

PRODUCTS/OPERATIONS

2007 Sales

	$ mil.	% of total
Power sales	2,430	84
Wheeling charges	327	11
Transmission charges	149	5
Total	**2,906**	**100**

Selected Operations

Transmission Control Facility
  Frederick R. Clark Energy Center (Oneida County)
Fossil-Fueled Plants
  Charles Poletti Power Project (New York City)
  Richard M. Flynn Power Plant (Suffolk County)
  PowerNow! Turbines (11 units in New York City and Long Island)
Hydropower Plants
  Blenheim-Gilboa Pumped Storage Power Project (Schoharie County)
  Niagara Power Project (Niagara County)
  St. Lawrence-Franklin D. Roosevelt Power Project (St. Lawrence County)
Small Hydropower Plants
  Ashokan Project (Ulster County)
  Crescent Plant (Albany and Saratoga Counties)
  Gregory B. Jarvis Plant (Oneida County)
  Kensico Project (Westchester County)
  Vischer Ferry Plant (Saratoga and Schenectady counties)

COMPETITORS

CH Energy
Con Edison
Dynegy
Enbridge
Energy East
Entergy
National Grid USA
Rochester Gas and Electric
TransCanada

HISTORICAL FINANCIALS

Company Type: Government-owned

Income Statement				FYE: December 31
	REVENUE ($ mil.)	NET INCOME ($ mil.)	NET PROFIT MARGIN	EMPLOYEES
12/07	2,906	235	8.1%	1,600
12/06	2,666	137	5.1%	1,600
12/05	2,506	—	—	1,600
12/04	2,215	—	—	1,600
12/03	2,215	—	—	1,600
Annual Growth	7.0%	71.5%	—	0.0%

2007 Year-End Financials

Debt ratio: —   Current ratio: —
Return on equity: 10.9%   Long-term debt ($ mil.): —
Cash ($ mil.): —

Net Income History

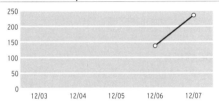

New York State Lottery

Winning the New York State Lottery could make you king of the hill, top of the heap. The New York State Lottery is one of the largest and oldest state lotteries in the US (only New Hampshire's lottery is older). It runs three jackpot, five daily, and about a dozen scratch-off games through retailers and online outlets. About a third of the lottery's revenue, or some $2 billion a year, goes to support New York State education. It also awards Leaders of Tomorrow scholarships to one eligible graduating senior from every public and private school in the state (provided they attend New York universities). The New York Lottery was established by the new state constitution passed in 1966.

The New York State Lottery has raised more than $30 billion for state educational programs since its inception. In addition to education, proceeds from the lottery have helped pay for the construction of New York City Hall, as well as bridges and roads for the state. It also sponsors the Empire State Games, an amateur athletic competition. The lottery returns more than half the money it takes in as prizes; 33% of sales go to aid education.

HISTORY

In the mid-1960s the New York state legislature succeeded in sending a lottery amendment to voters, and 60% of New Yorkers voted in favor of the amendment in 1966. Lottery sales began in 1967 with a raffle-style drawing game. In its first year of operation, the lottery contributed more than $26 million to the state's education fund.

New York introduced its first instant game in 1976, with sales topping $18 million the first week. The state debuted its six-of-six lotto game two years later. Sales were slow until 1981, when Louie "the Light Bulb" Eisenberg — the state's first lottery celebrity — won $5 million, the largest single-winner prize at that time.

GTECH Holdings won the contract to operate New York's lottery terminal sales in 1987. The Quick Pick option — through which a terminal chooses a player's numbers — was introduced in 1989, as was a new lotto game and the state's first online computer terminal game. Autoworker Antonio Bueti set a record for the largest individual prize, winning $35 million in 1990. A jackpot of $90 million was split among nine players in 1991.

Through the mid-1990s, however, lackluster lottery sales were blamed on the Persian Gulf War, the recession, and poor publicity. During 1993 and 1994 lottery management revamped the state's lottery infrastructure and redesigned some games. The investment paid off in October 1994 when lotto fever pushed a jackpot to $72.5 million. During the height of the frenzy, sales reached $46,000 a minute.

Quick Draw, which lets players choose numbers every five minutes, was added in 1995. Sales of the game topped $1 million on the second day, and soon it was grossing nearly $12 million a week. Real estate mogul Donald Trump unsuccessfully sued to stop Quick Draw, claiming that it was more addictive than (his) casinos and would encourage organized crime. That year the New York State Lottery became the first to reach $3 billion in sales in a single year.

In 1996 the state pulled its Quick Draw advertising after critics complained it encouraged compulsive gambling. Lottery officials replaced enticing ads with advertising stressing the lottery's benefits to state education. The lottery was the subject of a sting operation that year led by Governor George Pataki to crack down on lottery vendors selling tickets to minors. In 1997 the lottery spawned its own game show with the debut of *NY Wired*, a half-hour weekly program pitting vendor representatives against each other for cash prizes given to audience members and schools.

With sales slipping, the state left longtime ad partner DDB Needham Worldwide (now DDB Worldwide) in 1998 and signed a $28 million contract with Grey Advertising. Lottery director Jeff Perlee resigned the next year. He was replaced by Margaret DeFrancisco, who helped drum up sales with Millennium Millions, which paid out a record $100 million prize to Johnnie Ely, a cook from the South Bronx, on the eve of 2000. Two players shared a record $130 million jackpot later in the year.

After holding out for years, the New York legislature in late 2001 authorized a bill that would allow state residents to participate in the multistate Powerball lottery. In 2002 the New York Lottery joined with the nine-state Big Game Group to launch the Mega Millions game, which replaced the Big Game established in 1996. By 2005, Mega Millions had 12 participating states and New York had nine winners in the game.

EXECUTIVES

Executive Director: Gordon Medenica
Executive Deputy Director and Problem Gambling Awareness Coordinator: Susan E. Miller
Deputy Director and Director of Operations and Administration: Gardner S. Gurney
Director Drawings: Brad Smi
Director Human Resource Management: Lisa A. Fitzmaurice
Director Internal Audit: John R. McNulty
Director Marketing: Randall Lex
Director Communications: John E. Charlson
CIO: Ray Sestak
Acting General Counsel: Julie Barker
Auditors: KPMG LLP

LOCATIONS

HQ: New York State Lottery
   1 Broadway Center, Schenectady, NY 12301
Phone: 518-388-3300   **Fax:** 518-388-3403
Web: www.nylottery.org

PRODUCTS/OPERATIONS

2007 Revenue Allocation

	% of total
Prizes	55
Aid to Education	33
Commissions for Traditional Lottery Facilities	6
Commissions for Video Gaming Facilities	3
Other	3
Total	**100**

COMPETITORS

Connecticut Lottery
Massachusetts State Lottery
Multi-State Lottery
New Hampshire Lottery
New Jersey Lottery
Pennsylvania Lottery
Vermont Lottery

HISTORICAL FINANCIALS

Company Type: Government-owned

Income Statement				FYE: March 31
	REVENUE ($ mil.)	NET INCOME ($ mil.)	NET PROFIT MARGIN	EMPLOYEES
3/07	7,175	(27)	—	—
3/06	6,803	(73)	—	—
3/05	6,271	—	—	—
3/04	5,848	—	—	—
3/03	5,396	—	—	—
Annual Growth	7.4%	—	—	—

Net Income History

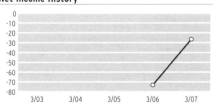

New York University

Higher education is at the core of this Big Apple institution. The setting and heritage of New York University (NYU) make it one of the nation's most popular educational institutions. With more than 50,000 students attending its 14 schools and colleges, NYU is among the largest private schools in the US. Its Tisch School of the Arts is well regarded, and its law school and Leonard N. Stern School of Business are among the foremost in the country. NYU occupies five major centers in Manhattan; its Washington Square campus is in the heart of Greenwich Village. The school was founded in 1831. Notable alumni include former Federal Reserve Chairman Alan Greenspan and film producer Oliver Stone.

NYU is one of the largest employers in New York City, with more than 16,000 employees. International students make up over 10% of the school's student body. Undergraduate tuition for the university runs more than $37,000 per year.

HISTORY

New York University was founded by several prominent New Yorkers in 1831. The school held its first classes the following year in rented rooms on the corner of Beekman and Nassau streets, then moved to a building in Washington Square in 1835. It established its law school that year. NYU started its school of medicine in 1841, followed by the school of engineering and science (1854). Postgraduate studies in arts and science (its first coeducational program) began in 1886.

NYU's enrollment jumped from fewer than 2,000 in 1900 to 28,000 in 1930. After a lull during the Depression and WWII, the campus boomed again in the postwar years. During the 1950s the university began focusing on improving academics rather than on increasing enrollment. It created a school of the arts in 1965, and in the early 1970s it completed the Elmer Holmes Bobst Library. However, a cash crunch during that decade almost forced the school into bankruptcy.

President Jay Oliva took the reins in 1981 and focused on transforming NYU from a largely commuter college into a global university. The school began a campaign to raise $1 billion in 1984, but earmarked the funds for campus improvements rather than swelling its endowment. During the late 1980s NYU opened several new dormitories and conference spaces. In 1994 British historian and collector Sir Harold Acton bequeathed to the school his Tuscany estate — five art-filled villas overlooking Florence, Italy.

In 1996 NYU's Medical Center began talks with Mount Sinai Medical Center aimed at merging their hospitals and medical schools. The talks fell apart in early 1997, but the following year the two sides agreed to merge hospitals and keep their medical schools distinct. Also in 1998 NYU formed NYU On-Line, Inc., a for-profit subsidiary to develop and sell specialized Internet courses to other schools, training centers, and students; the venture was subsequently folded in late 2001. During 1999 contributions to the school approached $250 million. That year, however, two upper-level school officials were fired following allegations of improper use of university money.

Oliva retired as president in 2002 and was replaced by John Sexton, former School of Law

dean. In 2004 Sexton announced that NYU would give $1 million to New York City toward renovation of Washington Square Park (the school annually gives some $200,000 for the park's ongoing maintenance).

EXECUTIVES

Chairman: Martin Lipton
Vice Chair: William R. Berkley, age 62
Vice Chair: Laurence D. Fink, age 53
Vice Chair: Kenneth G. Langone, age 72
Vice Chair: Larry A. Silverstein, age 71
Vice Chair: Anthony Welters, age 53
Vice Chair: Leonard A. Wilf
President: John E. Sexton, age 58
Provost: David W. McLaughlin
EVP: Michael C. Alfano, age 60
SVP Development and Alumni Relations:
  Debra A. LaMorte
SVP, Finance and Budget: Martin Dorph
SVP Health: Robert Berne
SVP, General Counsel, and Secretary of the University:
  Cheryl Mills
SVP University Relations and Public Affairs:
  Lynne P. Brown
VP Public Affairs: John Beckman
VP Student Affairs: Marc Wais
Chief of Staff and Deputy to the President: Diane C. Yu
Senior Director Human Resources: Kathleen Murray
Counselor to the President: Norman Dorsen
Auditors: KPMG LLP

LOCATIONS

HQ: New York University
  70 Washington Sq. South, New York, NY 10012
Phone: 212-998-1212   **Fax:** 212-995-4040
Web: www.nyu.edu

PRODUCTS/OPERATIONS

Selected Schools and Colleges
College of Arts and Science (founded 1832)
College of Dentistry (1865)
Courant Institute of Mathematical Sciences (1934)
Gallatin School of Individualized Study (1972)
Graduate School of Arts and Science (1886)
Leonard N. Stern School of Business (1900)
Robert F. Wagner Graduate School of Public Service
  (1938)
School of Continuing and Professional Studies (1934)
School of Law (1835)
School of Medicine (1841)
School of Social Work (1960)
Steinhardt School of Culture, Education, and Human
  Development (1890)
Tisch School of the Arts (1965)

New York Yankees

These Yanks are a big hit with New York baseball fans. The New York Yankees have won a record 26 World Series titles and 39 American League pennants, making the team the most successful professional sports franchise in history. That success and the team's association with sports icons including Babe Ruth, Lou Gehrig, Joe DiMaggio, and Mickey Mantle help make the Yankees one of the most popular teams in the world as well. At home in the Bronx, the club draws some of the largest crowds in Major League Baseball, while off the field the franchise generates huge sums from regional media deals. George Steinbrenner, who bought the team in

1973, also owns 60% of sports cable channel Yankee Entertainment & Sports.

Much to the dismay (or envy) of the rest of the league, the team is stocked full with such talented players as Derek Jeter, Hideki Matsui, and Alex Rodriguez, and (not surprisingly) has perennially had the highest payroll in baseball. For all that talent and money, however, the Yankees have not won a championship title since 2000, a fact that led to the ousting of longtime skipper Joe Torre after yet another early post-season exit in 2007. Former Florida Marlins manager Joe Girardi was hired as his replacement.

The change in the dugout coincided with a change in front office leadership as the aging Steinbrenner handed the reigns of daily responsibility to his sons Hank and Hal. The brothers drew some criticism from fans and the media for their handling of Torre's dismissal, but early indications are that they will continue to run the team much as their father had: During the off-season in 2007 they signed Rodriguez to a 10-year, $275 million contract extension.

Keeping the roster stocked with all-stars will be a high priority as the Yankees prepare to move into their new digs. Ground breaking on a new 51,000-seat, $1.3 billion stadium took place in 2006 across the street from The House that Ruth Built; the new facility is planned to be ready for the 2009 season.

One downside to all this free spending on talent is that under MLB's collective bargaining agreement, the franchise has to give a percentage of its excess payroll back to the league to be distributed to smaller-market teams. The Yankees are the only team to be hit with the luxury tax each year since the agreement was struck in 2002; its 2007 payment was more than $23 million.

HISTORY

Frank Farrell and Bill Devery purchased the Baltimore Orioles franchise (formed in 1901) in 1903 for $18,000 and brought the team to New York. Known as the Highlanders, the team played at Hilltop Park. In 1913 the team changed its name to the Yankees, and two years later it was bought by Jacob Ruppert and Tillinghast L'Hommedieu Huston. (Ruppert bought out Huston in 1922.)

The Yankees started down the path to greatness when they bought George Herman (Babe) Ruth from the Boston Red Sox for $125,000 in 1920. Three years later the team moved into Yankee Stadium. With icons such as Lou Gehrig (1923) and Joe DiMaggio (1936) joining the team, the Yankees won 14 American League pennants and 10 World Series titles by 1943.

The club changed hands again in 1945 when Dan Topping, Del Webb, and Larry MacPhail bought the team for almost $3 million. The Yankees continued to collect championship titles throughout the 1950s and into the next decade. CBS bought 80% of the team in 1964 for more than $11 million. Coincidentally, the Yankees didn't win another pennant for 12 years. However, a partnership led by Cleveland shipbuilder George Steinbrenner bought the team from CBS in 1973. With slugger Reggie Jackson, the Yankees won three consecutive pennants and back-to-back World Series over the Los Angeles Dodgers (1977, 1978). But trouble between the meddling Steinbrenner and his managers (notably Billy Martin) helped quiet things during the 1980s.

The Yankees returned to championship form in 1996 under manager Joe Torre. The team set an AL record for most wins in the regular season (114) in 1998 and swept the San Diego Padres to win the World Series. The following year the Yankees repeated as champions, sweeping Atlanta in the 1999 World Series. The team increased its financial clout later that year by merging with pro basketball's New Jersey Nets. The resulting holding company, YankeeNets, tried to form a cable network with IMG the following year, but MSG Network, which owned the rights to televise Yankee games, balked at the plan and won a ruling from the New York Supreme Court that ended the proposed partnership. Later in 2000 the Yankees won their third straight World Series title, defeating their crosstown rivals the New York Mets in the city's first Subway Series since 1956.

Putting its formidable wealth to good use, the Yankees signed star shortstop Derek Jeter to a 10-year, $189 million contract in early 2001. It also struck marketing and promotional relationships with local football franchise the New York Giants and Manchester United, the most successful soccer team in the UK.

The team finally lost a World Series, to the Arizona Diamondbacks, in 2001. The next year it launched the 60%-owned Yankees Entertainment & Sports cable channel. Reaching the World Series in 2003, the Yanks once again came up short, losing to the Florida Marlins. Later that year the Nets and Yankees dissolved their YankeeNets partnership. The following year, in an historic meltdown, the team won the AL East division title for the seventh year in a row but lost to the Boston Red Sox in the AL Championship Series. Boston went on to win the World Series for the first time in 86 years.

New York's postseason struggles continued in 2005 and 2006; despite a payroll hovering near $200 million, the Yankees were ejected from the postseason after divisional series losses each year. The team lost again in the playoffs in 2007, leading to the ouster of manager Torre. Former Marlins skipper Joe Girardi was hired as the new Yankees manager.

EXECUTIVES

Chairperson: George M. Steinbrenner III, age 78
Co-Chairperson: Henry G. (Hank) Steinbrenner
Co-Chairperson: Harold Z. (Hal) Steinbrenner
Vice Chairperson: Jessica Steinbrenner
Vice Chairperson: Joan Steinbrenner
Vice Chairperson: Jennifer Steinbrenner Swindal
President: Randy Levine
COO: Lonn A. Trost
SVP and General Manager: Brian Cashman
SVP Strategic Ventures: Martin (Marty) Greenspun
SVP Baseball Operations: Mark Newman
SVP Marketing: Deborah A. (Debbie) Tymon
SVP Corporate and Community Relations: Brian Smith
SVP Corporate Sales and Sponsorships: Michael Tusiani
SVP Business Development: Jim Ross
Manager: Joe Girardi
VP and Assistant General Manager: Jean Afterman
VP and CFO, Accounting: Robert Brown
VP and CFO, Financial Operations: Scott Krug
Senior Director Scoreboard and Broadcasting: Michael Bonner
Controller: Derrick Baio
Director Human Resources: Lea del Rosario

LOCATIONS

HQ: New York Yankees Partnership
Yankee Stadium, E. 161st St. and River Ave.,
Bronx, NY 10451
Phone: 718-293-4300   **Fax:** 718-293-8431
Web: newyork.yankees.mlb.com

The New York Yankees play at 57,545-seat capacity Yankee Stadium in Bronx, New York.

PRODUCTS/OPERATIONS

Championship Titles

World Series (1923, 1927-28, 1932, 1936-39, 1941, 1943, 1947, 1949-53, 1956, 1958, 1961-62, 1977-78, 1996, 1998-2000)
American League Pennant (1921-23, 1926-28, 1932, 1936-39, 1941-43, 1947, 1949-53, 1955-58, 1960-64, 1976-78, 1981, 1996, 1998-2001, 2003)
American League East Division (1976-78, 1980-81, 1994, 1996, 1998-2006)

COMPETITORS

Baltimore Orioles
Boston Red Sox
Tampa Bay Rays
Toronto Blue Jays

HISTORICAL FINANCIALS

Company Type: Private

Income Statement

FYE: December 31

	REVENUE ($ mil.)	NET INCOME ($ mil.)	NET PROFIT MARGIN	EMPLOYEES
12/07	327	—	—	—
12/06	302	—	—	—
12/05	277	—	—	—
12/04	264	—	—	—
12/03	238	—	—	—
Annual Growth	8.3%	—	—	—

Revenue History

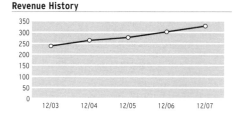

The Newark Group

The Newark Group is proof that one man's trash is another man's treasure. Founded in 1912, the company is a major producer of paper products from recycled materials. Its paperboard division recovers some 2.5 million tons of paper (corrugated containers, newspaper, and mixed paper) annually.

The Newark Group's converted products group operates in three segments: laminated products and graphicboard, tube and core manufacturing, and solidboard packaging. Brands include Fiberwrap (paperboard), NewEx (graphicboard), NewForm and Poli-NewForm (concrete forming tubes), and Fortex (coverboard).

The company operates more than 50 facilities in North America and Europe. Its operations are broken into three segments that include paperboard, converted products, and international.

With some 20 facilities devoted to it, the paperboard division is the largest of the three and accounts for more than half of the company's total sales. The paperboard segment essentially involves the collection of recovered paper from various sources. Discarded packaging from large retailers is the biggest contributor to the recovered paper operations, accounting for more than 40%. Industrial and other commercial customers account for about a third of the material while 12% and 9% come from small recycling companies and municipalities, respectively.

The converted paper operation supplies about 30% of the material used in the Newark Group's paperboard manufacturing, which is processed into various grades. Much of that paperboard ends up at one of the company's plants devoted to its next largest segment, converted products.

Accounting for nearly 30% of the company's sales, the converted products segment is responsible for making laminated and graphicboard products used for game boards and book covers. It also makes tubes and cores, around which paper, tape, and textiles can be wrapped, and solidboard, which is used to make packaging for produce and other food items.

The Newark Group's international segment oversees the paperboard and converted products operations at the company's seven European plants.

EXECUTIVES

Chairman, President, and CEO: Robert H. Mullen, age 55
Vice Chairman: Edward K. Mullen, age 85
SVP European Operations: William D. (Bill) Harper, age 65
SVP Paperboard Mills: Richard M. Poppe, age 53
SVP Converted Products: Philip B. Jones, age 59
VP and CFO: Joseph E. (Joe) Byrne, age 48
VP and Controller: Lynn M. Herro
VP, General Counsel, and Secretary: David Ascher, age 55
VP Human Resources: Carl R. Crook
Auditors: Deloitte & Touche LLP

LOCATIONS

HQ: The Newark Group, Inc.
20 Jackson Dr., Cranford, NJ 07016
Phone: 908-276-4000   **Fax:** 908-276-2888
Web: www.newarkgroup.com

2008 Sales

	$ mil.	% of total
North America		
US	800.3	78
Canada	12.9	1
Europe	215.7	21
Total	**1,028.9**	**100**

PRODUCTS/OPERATIONS

2008 Sales

	$ mil.	% of total
Paperboard	523.5	51
Converted Products	289.7	28
International	215.7	21
Total	**1,028.9**	**100**

Selected Products

Recycled Fibers
   Corrugated products
   Envelopes
   Newspapers
   Printing grades
   Roll stock

Recycled Paperboard
  Boxboard
  Clay-coated folding board
  Separator stock
  Tube and core grades

COMPETITORS

Caraustar
Carter Holt Harvey
Eagle Materials
Georgia-Pacific
Graphic Packaging Holding
Green Bay Packaging
International Paper
Oji Paper
Parsons & Whittemore
Rock-Tenn
Smurfit Kappa
Smurfit-Stone Container
Sonoco Products
Southern Container
Unipapel
Weyerhaeuser

HISTORICAL FINANCIALS
Company Type: Private

Income Statement

	REVENUE ($ mil.)	NET INCOME ($ mil.)	NET PROFIT MARGIN	EMPLOYEES
4/08	1,029	—	—	3,166
4/07	923	—	—	3,169
4/06	852	—	—	3,222
4/05	882	—	—	3,328
4/04	788	—	—	3,358
Annual Growth	6.9%	—	—	(1.5%)

FYE: April 30

Revenue History

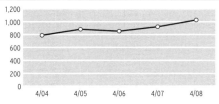

Newegg Inc.

Newegg caters to egghead types who build their own computers. The company, which prides itself on "fresh" offerings, is an online distributor of consumer electronics and computing products. It sells desktop and laptop computers along with all the related components to build or repair one yourself. Newegg also stocks digital cameras, networking devices, peripherals, DVDs, accessories, and software. The company's Web site carries products made by vendors including ATi, Canon, Sony, Toshiba, and Viewsonic. Newegg, founded in 2001, serves consumers, students, and corporate buyers among others.

The company claims more than 9 million registered users and is among the 400 most visited Web sites in the US. Newegg keeps customers happy by providing nearly 100% same day shipping from warehouses in California, Tennessee, and New Jersey.

Newegg also runs a Web site for its Chinese customers and nearly half of its employees are based in China. In 2007 the company launched a community site called Eggxpert.com, where amateur tech experts can share information and answer questions.

Company president Tally Liu was promoted to chairman and CEO of the Newegg in August 2008. Liu succeeded Fred Chang, a founder of the firm.

EXECUTIVES

Chairman and CEO: Tally C. Liu, age 55
Vice Chairman: Ken Lam
COO: George Jiao
EVP: S.C. Lee
VP Product Management, Home Entertainment, and Displays: Michael Amkreutz
VP Finance: Richard A. (Rick) Quiroga
VP Merchandising: Bernard Luthi
VP Consumer Electronics and Purchasing: Ron L. Bester
VP Marketing: Chad Chen
VP Business Development and Emerging Technologies: Anthony Chow
General Counsel: Lee Cheng
Marketing Manager: Bienca Yang
Public Relations Manager: Lora Ivanova

LOCATIONS

HQ: Newegg Inc.
  9997 E. Rose Hills Rd., Whittier, CA 90601
Phone: 909-395-9046   **Fax:** 909-395-8907
Web: www.newegg.com

COMPETITORS

Best Buy
CDW
Dell
Hewlett-Packard
Office Depot
PC Connection
PC Mall
Staples
Systemax
Wayside Technology Group

HISTORICAL FINANCIALS
Company Type: Private

Income Statement

	REVENUE ($ mil.)	NET INCOME ($ mil.)	NET PROFIT MARGIN	EMPLOYEES
12/07	1,900	—	—	1,500
12/06	1,500	—	—	1,500
12/05	1,300	—	—	1,200
12/04	1,000	—	—	—
Annual Growth	23.9%	—	—	11.8%

FYE: December 31

Revenue History

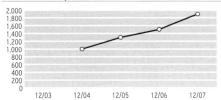

The Newton Group

The Newton Group, which operates as Strategic Products and Services (SPS), provides voice, data, and video networking services, including network design and installation, training, and technical support. It uses Avaya and Cisco equipment and serves enterprise customers from small businesses to multinational corporations. In addition to design and installation, SPS provides phone, Internet, and other data services through partnerships with such carriers as AT&T, Verizon, and XO Communications. Established in 1988, the company has offices throughout New England and the Midwest, as well as the Mid-Atlantic and South Atlantic states.

EXECUTIVES

Chairman, President, and CEO: John N. Poole
COO: James R. (Jim) Felicetti
VP Services and Operations: Nevelle R. (Vel) Johnson
CTO and VP Emerging Technologies: Michael W. (Mike) Taylor
VP Implementation Services: Ronald J. (Ron) Scavuzzo
VP Finance: Brian Crowe
VP Sales: James P. Maynard
Director Marketing: Theresa Goodreau
Human Resources and Administration: Sue Mullen

LOCATIONS

HQ: The Newton Group, Inc.
  3 Wing Dr., Ste. 100, Cedar Knolls, NJ 07927
Phone: 973-540-0600   **Fax:** 973-540-1221
Web: www.spscom.com

PRODUCTS/OPERATIONS

Selected Products and Services
Application integration
Cabling
Customer training
Data networking infrastructure
Disaster recovery support
Traditional PBX systems
Voice over Internet Protocol (VoIP)
Video and audio-conferencing

COMPETITORS

Altura Communication Solutions
Black Box
BT Global Services
Carousel Industries
CDW
CompuCom
Computer Design and Integration
EDS
MTM Technologies
Pomeroy IT
Software House
Unisys

HISTORICAL FINANCIALS

Company Type: Private

Income Statement

FYE: December 31

	REVENUE ($ mil.)	NET INCOME ($ mil.)	NET PROFIT MARGIN	EMPLOYEES
12/07	97	—	—	300
12/06	97	—	—	296
12/05	80	—	—	270
12/04	60	—	—	200
Annual Growth	17.4%	—	—	14.5%

Revenue History

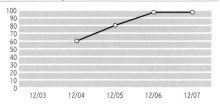

NewYork-Presbyterian Healthcare System

NewYork-Presbyterian Healthcare System serves New York City, as well as several counties in New York, Connecticut, and New Jersey. In fact, it serves nearly 25% of the patients located in the New York metropolitan area. The system, which maintains some 14,200 licensed beds, includes more than 30 hospitals. New York-Presbyterian Hospital is the system's flagship facility. All of its hospitals are affiliated with either Columbia University's College of Physicians and Surgeons or Cornell University's Weill Medical College. NewYork-Presbyterian Healthcare System also operates about 100 ambulatory sites, more than 15 nursing homes, and a few rehabilitation centers.

The NewYork-Presbyterian system has expanded its cardiac services by establishing cardiac-surgery programs at New York Methodist Hospital (Brooklyn), New York Hospital (Queens), St. Vincent's Hospital (Bridgeport, Connecticut), and The Valley Hospital (New Jersey).

EXECUTIVES

Chairman: John J. Mack, age 63
President and CEO: Herbert Pardes, age 74
EVP and COO: Steven J. (Steve) Corwin
EVP and CFO: Phyllis R. F. Lantos
SVP Strategy: Emme Deland
SVP and CIO: Aurelia G. Boyer
VP, System Development, and Director: Wayne Osten
VP Administration: Laurence J. Berger
VP and Chief Quality Officer: Eliot J. Lazar
Auditors: Ernst & Young LLP

LOCATIONS

HQ: NewYork-Presbyterian Healthcare System
525 E. 68th St., New York, NY 10065
Phone: 212-305-2500   **Fax:** 212-746-8235
Web: www.nypsystem.org

PRODUCTS/OPERATIONS

Facilities

Hospitals
 NewYork-Presbyterian Hospital
  The Allen Pavilion
  Children's Hospital of NewYork-Presbyterian
  NewYork-Presbyterian/Columbia
  NewYork-Presbyterian/Weill Cornell
  Westchester Division
 Bassett Healthcare
 The Brooklyn Hospital Center
 Holy Name Hospital
 Hospital for Special Surgery
 Lawrence Hospital Center
 New Milford Hospital
 New York Community Hospital
 New York Hospital Queens
 New York Methodist Hospital
 New York United Hospital Medical Center
 New York Westchester Square Medical Center
 Northern Westchester Hospital
 Nyack Hospital
 Orange Regional Medical Center
  Arden Hill Campus
  Horton Campus
 Palisades Medical Center
 The Rogosin Institute
 St. Barnabas Hospital--The Bronx
 St. Luke's Cornwall Hospital
 St. Vincent's Medical Center--Bridgeport
 South Nassau Communities Hospital
 Stamford Health System
 The Valley Hospital
 White Plains Hospital Center
 Winthrop-University Hospital
 Wyckoff Heights Medical Center
Long-Term Care Facilities
 Amsterdam Nursing Home
 Fort Tryon Center for Rehabilitation and Nursing
 Frankin Center for Rehabilitation and Nursing
 Friedwald Center for Rehabilitation and Nursing
 The Harborage at Palisades Medical Center
 Manhattanville Health Care Center
 Menorah Home and Hospital
 New York United Hospital Medical Center Skilled Nursing Pavilion
 St. Barnabas Nursing Home
 St. Mary's Hospital for Children--Queens
 Sea Crest Health Care Center
 Shore View Nursing Home
 The Silvercrest Center for Nursing and Rehabilitation
 Tandet Center for Continuing Care
Other Facilities
 The Burke Rehabilitation Hospital
 Community Healthcare Network
 Gracie Square Hospital
 Helen Hayes Hospital
 New York College of Podiatric Medicine & Foot Clinics of New York
 The Rogosin Institute

COMPETITORS

Beth Abraham Health Services
Bronx-Lebanon Hospital
Carilion Clinic
Continuum Health Partners
HCA
Jamaica Hospital Medical Center
Johns Hopkins Medicine
Mather Memorial Hospital
Mayo Foundation
Memorial Sloan-Kettering
Montefiore Medical
Mount Sinai NYU Health
New York City Health and Hospitals
North Shore-Long Island Jewish Health System
Partners HealthCare
Saint Barnabas
Saint Vincent Catholic Medical Centers
St. Luke's-Roosevelt Hospital

Noble Investment Group

Noble Investment Group holds its head high when walking through a hotel lobby. The company owns or manages more than 30 upscale hotels under the Starwood, Intercontinental Hotels Group, Hilton, Hyatt, and Marriott brands. Another sector of the Noble operation is its development arm, Noble Development Group, which develops hotels, convention centers, conference centers, and resorts; it also acquires existing hotel properties. In addition, the firm manages several golf courses and restaurants. Noble Investment Group was founded in 1979 by former chairman Dr. Bharat Shah. (Shah retired in 2005.)

EXECUTIVES

Senior Managing Principal and CEO:
 Mitesh B. (Mit) Shah
Managing Principle and COO: Robert J. (Bob) Morse
Managing Principal and CFO: James E. (Jim) Conley Jr.
Managing Principal and Chief Investment Officer:
 Rodney S. Williams
Managing Principal and Chief Development Officer:
 Mark Rafuse
Managing Principal Capital Markets, General Counsel, and Asset Management: Dave Weymer
Principal and EVP Strategic Investments:
 Benjamin Brunt
Principal and EVP Strategic Investments:
 Aditya (Adi) Bhoopathy
Principal and EVP Development: John I. Cooper
Principal and EVP Operations: Paul Burke
Principal and EVP Asset Management: Steven Nicholas
Principal and EVP Development: Kevin Grass
SVP Organizational Excellence and Human Resources:
 Robert J. (Bob) Mruz
VP Human Resources: David Kemp

LOCATIONS

HQ: Noble Investment Group, LLC
 1100 Monarch Tower, 3424 Peachtree Rd.,
 Atlanta, GA 30326
Phone: 404-262-9660   **Fax:** 404-262-9244
Web: www.nobleinvestment.com

COMPETITORS

APMC
Benchmark Hospitality
Ocean Properties

Noodles & Company

Forty lashes with a wet you-know-what if you don't like what this restaurant company offers. Noodles & Company operates and franchises more than 170 quick-casual restaurants in more than 15 states that feature noodle entrees in a variety of American, Asian, and Mediterranean flavors, from penne pasta to chicken noodle soup. The chain's menu includes noodle and vegetable bowls, soups, and green salads with pasta. It also offers "noodle-less" dishes, such as mixed grill and shrimp sauté. Most of the firm's outlets are company-owned. Chairman Aaron Kennedy, a former brand manager at PepsiCo who opened the first Noodles & Company location in 1995, owns the company with a group of private investors.

Having expanded primarily through opening corporate-owned locations, Noodles & Company has been ramping up its franchising operation to accelerate its growth. Kennedy stepped down as CEO in 2006 and turned the reigns over to company president Kevin Reddy, who previously worked for quick-casual restaurant operator Chipotle Mexican Grill.

EXECUTIVES

Chairman: Aaron Kennedy, age 44
President and CEO: Kevin Reddy
CFO and COO: Keith Kinsey
VP Franchise Initiatives: Wayne Humphrey
VP Human Resources: John R. Puterbaugh
VP Information Technology: John Lauderbach
VP Marketing: G. Dwayne Chambers
VP Development and Restaurant Support: Dawn Voss
VP Real Estate: Tim Mosbacher
VP Restaurant Development: Steve Cable
Director Marketing and Communications:
 Chad Gretzema
General Counsel: Vikki Wulf
Executive Chef: Ross Kamens
Corporate Communications Manager: Krista Koranda
Auditors: Deloitte & Touche

LOCATIONS

HQ: Noodles & Company
 520 Zang St., Broomfield, CO 80021
Phone: 720-214-1900　　**Fax:** 720-214-1934
Web: www.noodles.com

COMPETITORS

Café de Coral
California Pizza Kitchen
Camille's Sidewalk Cafe
Carlson Restaurants
CBC Restaurant
Chipotle
Einstein Noah Restaurant Group
Fresh Enterprises
Garden Fresh Restaurants
Panda Restaurant Group
Panera Bread
P.F. Chang's
Qdoba Restaurants

HISTORICAL FINANCIALS

Company Type: Private

Income Statement

FYE: December 31

	REVENUE ($ mil.)	NET INCOME ($ mil.)	NET PROFIT MARGIN	EMPLOYEES
12/07	130	—	—	4,500
12/06	115	—	—	3,900
12/05	106	—	—	3,000
12/04	90	—	—	3,000
12/03	70	—	—	2,100
Annual Growth	16.7%	—	—	21.0%

Revenue History

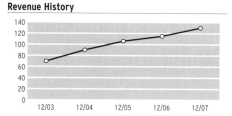

North Atlantic Trading Company

North Atlantic Trading Company might go up in smoke if not for some of its customers', er, joint ventures. Its North Atlantic Operating Company (NAOC), best known for its Zig-Zag brand of rolling papers, is a top importer and distributor of cigarette rolling papers in the US. NAOC also sells tobaccos, rolling machines, and similar accessories. North Atlantic Trading's National Tobacco subsidiary is a leading maker of chewing tobacco in the US on the strength of its top-selling Beech-Nut chaw, as well as Havana Blossom, Trophy, Stoker, and others. Chairman Thomas F. Helms Jr. owns about 49% of North Atlantic Trading.

The company's National Tobacco Company plans to shutter its tobacco manufacturing and distribution facility in Louisville, Kentucky, by the end of 2009. Production at the facility, which makes loose leaf tobacco, will be transferred to the company's Owensboro, Kentucky, plant under an agreement with Swedish Match North America.

EXECUTIVES

Chairman: Thomas F. Helms Jr., age 66, $482,000 pay
Vice Chairman: Jack Africk, age 79
President and CEO: Lawrence S. Wexler, age 54, $561,604 pay
SVP and CFO: Brian C. Harriss, age 58, $441,000 pay
SVP, General Counsel, and Secretary:
 James W. Dobbins, age 47, $300,423 pay
SVP, Market Planning and Strategy: James M. Murray, age 46
VP, Finance: Camilla Fentress
Auditors: McGladrey & Pullen, LLP

LOCATIONS

HQ: North Atlantic Trading Company, Inc.
 777 Post Rd., Ste. 304, Darien, CT 06820
Phone: 203-202-9547　　**Fax:** 230-656-3731
Web: www.zigzag.com

PRODUCTS/OPERATIONS

Selected Brands

Beech-Nut
Beech-Nut Wintergreen
Classic American Blend
Durango
Havana Blossom
Trophy
Zig-Zag

COMPETITORS

Altria	Reynolds S.A.
British American Tobacco	Swedish Match
Conwood	Swisher International
Imperial Tobacco	UST Inc.
Philip Morris USA	Vector Group
Reynolds American	

HISTORICAL FINANCIALS

Company Type: Private

Income Statement

FYE: December 31

	REVENUE ($ mil.)	NET INCOME ($ mil.)	NET PROFIT MARGIN	EMPLOYEES
12/07	123	—	—	299
12/06	118	—	—	299
12/05	117	—	—	289
12/04	115	—	—	296
12/03	102	—	—	292
Annual Growth	4.9%	—	—	0.6%

Revenue History

North Pacific Group

Paneling, poles, planks, pilings, and all, North Pacific Group (NOR PAC) is building on the construction industry. The firm is one of North America's largest wholesale distributors of building materials. Employee-owned since the 1986 retirement of its founder, Doug David, NOR PAC distributes wood, steel, agricultural, and food products from 30-plus locations. Wood products, which make up the majority of its business, include lumber, millwork, poles, and logs. NOR PAC sells its products to furniture makers, retailers, and metal fabricators. Though the company is part of an industry often at odds with environmentalists, it has made commitments to sustainable forestry practices. David founded NOR PAC in 1948.

In late 2006 North Pacific acquired Ohio-based North Santiam Lumber, a supplier of building materials to customers in Kentucky, Ohio, Pennsylvania, and West Virginia.

EXECUTIVES

President and CEO: Jay A. Ross
CFO and Treasurer: Christopher D. Cassard
SVP, Building Products Distribution: Tom Le Vere
SVP, Specialty Products: Kyle Burdick
SVP, Industrial Wood Products: Jack Clark
SVP, Building Materials East: Pat Heffernan
SVP, Commodity Products Distribution:
  Gregg Wilkinson
SVP HR: Tacy Lind
VP Marketing: Monique Bauer
Auditors: KPMG LLP

LOCATIONS

HQ: North Pacific Group, Inc.
  10200 SW Greenburg Rd., Portland, OR 97223
Phone: 503-231-1166   **Fax:** 503-238-2641
Web: www.north-pacific.com

PRODUCTS/OPERATIONS

Selected Products

Birdseed and grain seeds
Conventional and organic oils and vinegars
Decking, siding, and flooring
Domestic and imported hardwoods
Engineered wood products
Ingredients and processed foods
Laminate panels
Manufactured housings, fencing, siding, and shingles
Moulding, timbers, blanks, and cut stock
Plywood
Soil amendments: fertilizer, gypsum, and limestone
Steel, aluminum, and concrete poles
Wood poles and piling

COMPETITORS

ABC Supply
Arthur Lumber
Bradco Supply
Building Materials Holding
Georgia-Pacific
Guardian Building Products Distribution
Huttig Building Products
Louisiana-Pacific
MAXXAM
McFarland Cascade
PrimeSource Building
Sierra Pacific Industries
Simpson Investment
Temple-Inland
Weyerhaeuser

HISTORICAL FINANCIALS

Company Type: Private

Income Statement

	REVENUE ($ mil.)	NET INCOME ($ mil.)	NET PROFIT MARGIN	EMPLOYEES
12/07	1,200	—	—	780
12/06	1,200	—	—	769
12/05	1,232	—	—	813
12/04	1,450	—	—	862
12/03	1,200	—	—	800
Annual Growth	0.0%	—	—	(0.6%)

FYE: December 31

Revenue History

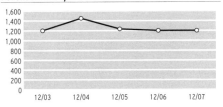

1,600	
1,400	
1,200	
1,000	
800	
600	
400	
200	
0	
	12/03 12/04 12/05 12/06 12/07

Northwest Community Healthcare

Northwest Community Healthcare has captured the hearts of northern Illinois. Located in Chicago's northwest suburbs, the health system includes the not-for-profit Northwest Community Hospital, a regional leader in providing all kinds of cardiac care, including open heart surgery, cardiac catheterization, and rehabilitation services. In fact, the nearly 500-bed hospital offers a comprehensive range of acute medical and surgical care. Through its ancillary facilities, Northwest Community Healthcare also operates primary and specialty physicians offices, an ambulatory surgery center, a home health agency, and diagnostic imaging services.

Founded in 1959, the hospital system began a $250 million expansion project in 2007 that will add some 200 rooms for critical care patients, new mothers, and people recovering from surgery. The project, expected to be completed in 2010, also includes an expansion of the hospital's emergency department.

EXECUTIVES

Chairman: Louis A. Gatta
Vice Chairman: Max Brittain Jr.
President, CEO, and Secretary: Bruce K. Crowther
EVP and COO: Michael B. Zenn
VP Human Resources: Mark Lusson
VP Information Technology and CIO: George Morris
VP Patient Services and Chief Nursing Officer:
  Dale E. Beatty
Media Relations Specialist: Blaine Krage
President, Medical Staff: Arnold P. Robin

LOCATIONS

HQ: Northwest Community Healthcare
  800 W. Central Rd., Arlington Heights, IL 60005
Phone: 847-618-1000   **Fax:** 847-577-4049
Web: www.nch.org

PRODUCTS/OPERATIONS

Selected Facilities

Adult Day Care Center (Arlington Heights)
Arlington Medical Offices (Arlington Heights)
Buffalo Grove Medical Offices (Buffalo Grove)
Buffalo Grove Treatment Center (Buffalo Grove)
Busse Center for Specialty Medicine (Arlington Heights)
Day Surgery Center (Arlington Heights)
Lake Zurich Treatment Center (Lake Zurich)
Northwest Community Hospital (Arlington Heights)
Palatine Medical Offices (Palatine)
Shaumburg Treatment Center (Schaumburg)
Shaumburg Imaging Center (Schaumburg)

COMPETITORS

Advocate Health Care
Advocate Lutheran General Hospital
Central DuPage Hospital
Evanston Northwestern Healthcare
Lake Forest Hospital Foundation
McDonough District Hospital
Provena Health
Resurrection Health Care
Rush System for Health
University of Chicago Medical Center

Northwestern Mutual Life Insurance

Even The Quiet Company has to toot its own horn. As one of the largest US life insurers, Northwestern Mutual Life holds more than $1 trillion in individual policies in force. Northwestern Mutual's 7,000 agents and financial professionals sell a lineup of life, disability, long-term care, and health insurance. It also offers retirement products, including fixed and variable annuities and mutual funds to a clientele of small businesses and prosperous individuals. Other lines of business include institutional asset manager Frank Russell Company, known for the Russell 2000 stock index, and brokerage and trust services through its investment services and wealth management subsidiaries.

Northwestern Mutual would "enter the 21st century as we left the 19th," according to former chairman and CEO John Ericson (who retired in mid-2001).

Well, not exactly. Although the company has resisted the industry trend of demutualizing and remains committed to ownership by its more than 3 million policyholders, Northwestern Mutual has reorganized to highlight its wealth management products. Life insurance still accounts for the majority of the company's revenue, though. The company targets wealthy individuals over 55.

HISTORY

In 1854, at age 72, John Johnston, a successful New York insurance agent, moved to Wisconsin to become a farmer. Three years later Johnston returned to the insurance business when he and 36 others formed Mutual Life Insurance (changed to Northwestern Mutual Life Insurance in 1865). From the beginning, the company's goal was to become better, not just bigger.

The company continued to offer level-premium life insurance in the 1920s, while competitors offered new types of products. This failure to rise to new demands brought a decline in market share that lasted into the 1940s.

Northwestern Mutual automated in the late 1950s. In 1962 it introduced the Insurance Service Account, whereby all policies owned by a family or business could be consolidated into one monthly premium and paid with preauthorized checks. In 1968 Northwestern Mutual inaugurated Extra Ordinary Life (EOL), which combined whole and term life insurance, using dividends to convert term to paid-up whole life each year. EOL soon became the company's most popular product.

Suffering from a low profile, in 1972 the insurer kicked off its "The Quiet Company" ad campaign during the summer Olympics. Public awareness of Northwestern Mutual jumped. But even in advertising, the company was staid; a revamped Quiet Company campaign made a return Olympic appearance 24 years later in another effort to raise the public's consciousness.

In the 1980s Northwestern Mutual began financing leveraged buyouts, gaining direct ownership of companies. Investments included two-thirds of flooring maker Congoleum (with other investors); it also bought majority interests in Milwaukee securities firm Robert W. Baird (1982) and mortgage guarantee insurer MGIC Investment (1985; later divested).

The firm stayed out of the 1980s mania for fast money and high-risk diversification. Instead, it devoted itself almost religiously to its core business, despite indications that it was a shrinking market.

In the early 1990s new life policy purchases slowed and the agency force declined — ominous signs, since insurers make their premium income on retained policies, and continued sales are crucial to growth. Northwestern Mutual reversed the trend, adding administrative support for its agents, using database marketing to target new customers, and increasing the cross-selling of products among existing customers. The result was a record-setting 1996.

With the financial services industry consolidating, Northwestern Mutual in 1997 moved into the mutual fund business by setting up its Mason Street Funds.

In the 1990s many large mutuals sought to demutualize, and in 1998 Northwestern Mutual, politically influential in Wisconsin, successfully lobbied for legislation to permit demutualization, citing the need to be able to move quickly in shifting markets.

The next year the company acquired Frank Russell Company, a pension management firm. The acquisition gave Northwestern Mutual a foothold in global investment management and analytical services (the Russell 2000 index).

In 2001 the firm opened Northwestern Mutual Trust, a wholly owned personal trust services subsidiary. In 2004 the employees of Robert W. Baird completed a buyback of Northwestern Mutual's stake in the firm.

EXECUTIVES

President, CEO, and Trustee: Edward J. Zore, age 63
EVP Investment Products and Services:
Gary A. Poliner, age 54
EVP and Chief Administrative Officer: Marcia Rimai, age 52
EVP Affiliate Investment: John E. Schlifske, age 48
SVP Insurance and Technology: Gregory C. Oberland, age 50
SVP Agencies: Todd M. Schoon
SVP and Chief Actuary: William C. Koenig, age 60
SVP Agency Services: Christina H. Fiasca, age 53
SVP Enterprise Operations and Chief Compliance Officer: Jean M. Maier, age 53
SVP and Chief Investment Officer: Mark G. Doll, age 58
SVP Life Product: Meridee J. Maynard, age 52
SVP Real Estate: David D. Clark, age 56
SVP Securities: Jeffrey J. Lueken, age 47
VP and CFO: Michael G. Carter, age 46
VP Corporate Affairs, and President's Assistant:
Gloster B. Current Jr., age 62

VP and Controller: John C. (Chris) Kelly, age 48
VP Human Resources: Susan A. Lueger, age 54
VP Communications: Kimberley Goode
VP Marketing: Conrad C. York
CIO: Timothy G. Schaefer
Auditors: PricewaterhouseCoopers LLP

LOCATIONS

HQ: The Northwestern Mutual Life Insurance Company
720 E. Wisconsin Ave., Milwaukee, WI 53202
Phone: 414-271-1444
Web: www.nmfn.com

PRODUCTS/OPERATIONS

2007 Sales

	$ mil.	% of total
Premiums	13,242	62
Investment income	7,568	35
Other income	545	3
Total	**21,355**	**100**

Selected Subsidiaries

Frank Russell Company
Northwestern Long Term Care Insurance Company
Northwestern Mutual Investment Services, LLC
Northwestern Mutual Wealth Management Company

COMPETITORS

AEGON USA
AIG
AIG American General
AllianceBernstein Holding
Allianz
AXA Financial
CIGNA
Citigroup
CNA Financial
Conseco
FMR
Genworth Financial
Guardian Life
The Hartford
ING
John Hancock Financial Services
Liberty Mutual
MassMutual
Merrill Lynch
MetLife
Morgan Stanley
MSCI
Mutual of Omaha
Nationwide
New York Life
Pacific Life
Principal Financial
Prudential
Sun Life
T. Rowe Price
TIAA-CREF

HISTORICAL FINANCIALS

Company Type: Mutual company

Income Statement

FYE: December 31

	ASSETS ($ mil.)	NET INCOME ($ mil.)	INCOME AS % OF ASSETS	EMPLOYEES
12/07	156,547	1,000	0.6%	4,983
12/06	145,102	829	0.6%	4,800
12/05	133,057	924	0.7%	4,800
12/04	123,957	817	0.7%	4,700
12/03	113,822	692	0.6%	4,500
Annual Growth	**8.3%**	**9.6%**	**—**	**2.6%**

2007 Year-End Financials

Equity as % of assets: 7.7% Long-term debt ($ mil.): —
Return on assets: 0.7% Sales ($ mil.): 21,355
Return on equity: 7.4%

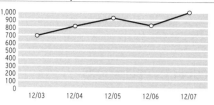

Net Income History

Northwestern University

What's NU? With its main campus in the Chicago suburb of Evanston, Northwestern University serves its 15,000 students through around a dozen schools and colleges such as the McCormick School of Engineering and Applied Sciences and the Medill School of Journalism. Its Chicago campus houses the schools of law and medicine, as well as several hospitals of the McGaw Medical Center. Faculty numbers around 2,500. Northwestern is home to several research centers, continuing education services, and community outreach programs; it has a branch in Qatar. It is the only private member of the Big 10 conference; varsity sports include baseball, football, basketball, and fencing.

Among Northwestern's top-ranked programs are its law school, medical school, and its engineering program. Its J. L. Kellogg Graduate School of Management consistently ranks among the nation's top five business schools by *Business Week* and *U.S. News & World Report*. Its prestigious journalism and drama programs produced such alumni as Charlton Heston, Gary Marshall, and Julia Louis-Dreyfus. Current US Supreme Court Justice John Paul Stevens is also a former Wildcat.

The school's endowment and other trust funds have swelled to around $6 billion, and it has exceeded its original Campaign Northwestern fundraising goal of $1 billion. The money is being used to increase endowment for student scholarships and fellowships, to help repair and build facilities, and to fund more faculty positions.

EXECUTIVES

President: Henry S. Bienen, age 68
Provost: Daniel H. Linzer, age 55
Associate Provost Faculty Affairs: John D. Margolis
Associate Provost University Enrollment:
Michael E. Mills
SVP Business and Finance: Eugene S. Sunshine
VP and CTO: Morteza A. Rahimi
VP and Chief Investment Officer: Will McLean
VP and General Counsel: Thomas G. Cline
VP Administration and Planning: Marilyn McCoy
VP Student Affairs: William J. Banis
VP University Relations: Alan K. Cubbage
Associate VP Finance and Controller: Ingrid S. Stafford, age 54
Director Media Relations: Charles R. Loebbaka
University Registrar: Patrick Martin
Auditors: Deloitte & Touche LLP

LOCATIONS

HQ: Northwestern University
633 Clark St., Evanston, IL 60208
Phone: 847-491-3741 **Fax:** 847-491-8406
Web: www.northwestern.edu

PRODUCTS/OPERATIONS

Selected Undergraduate Colleges and Schools

Medill School of Journalism
Robert McCormick School of Engineering and Applied
  Sciences
School of Communication
School of Education and Social Policy
School of Music
Weinberg College of Arts and Sciences

Graduate and Professional Schools

Feinberg School of Medicine
Interdisciplinary Biological and Life Sciences
J.L. Kellogg School of Management
McCormick School of Engineering and Applied Science
Medill School of Journalism
School of Communication (Speech)
School of Education and Social Policy
School of Law
School of Music

NTK Holdings

Chill, bro. NTK Holdings is a breath of fresh air in the home HVAC market. Through subsidiary Nortek, the company makes air conditioning, heating, ventilation, and home technology products for the residential and commercial construction, do-it-yourself, remodeling, and renovation markets. In addition to heating and air conditioning systems), NTK's wares include range hoods and other ventilation products, indoor air quality systems, lighting controls, and home entertainment system equipment. Products bear NTK's own brands (including Broan-NuTone), as well as such licensed names as Frigidaire, Maytag, and Westinghouse.

NTK has bought up several smaller companies since 2003 to build its home technology and other divisions. In 2007 alone it acquired the assets of residential gate and garage door maker Allstar Corporation, bought security systems designer International Electronics, purchased the assets of security products maker Aigis Mechtronics, and bought home subsystems (entertainment, security, climate control) firm HomeLogic. It plans to slow down the spending and focus on reducing costs by moving some production operations to China, Poland, and elsewhere. Sales outside of the US (primarily to Canada and European countries) account for some 20% of revenues.

NTK Holdings prepared itself for an IPO in 2006, but it withdrew its registration statement the following year amidst the troubled financial markets. NTK is controlled by Thomas H. Lee Partners and company management.

EXECUTIVES

Chairman, President, and CEO: Richard L. Bready, age 63
VP and Treasurer: Edward J. Cooney, age 60
VP, General Counsel, and Secretary: Kevin W. Donnelly, age 53
VP and CFO: Almon C. Hall III, age 61
Director, Human Resources: Jane White
Auditors: Ernst & Young LLP

LOCATIONS

HQ: NTK Holdings, Inc.
50 Kennedy Plaza, Providence, RI 02903
Phone: 401-751-1600 **Fax:** 401-751-4610
Web: www.nortek-inc.com

2007 Sales

	% of total
US	80
Other countries	20
Total	**100**

PRODUCTS/OPERATIONS

2007 Sales

	% of total
HVAC	41
Residential ventilation products	35
Home technology products	24
Total	**100**

Selected Products

Air Conditioning and Heating Products
  Commercial HVAC products
  Residential HVAC products
Residential Ventilation Products
  Exhaust fans
  Indoor air quality products
  Kitchen range hoods
Home Technology Products
  Audio/video distribution and control equipment
  Audio/video wall mounts and fixtures
  Lighting controls
  Power conditioners and surge protectors
  Security and access-control products
  Speakers and subwoofers
  Structured wiring

COMPETITORS

Carrier
Duchossois Industries
GE Security
Goodman Manufacturing
Johnson Controls
Lennox
Paloma
Trane Inc.

HISTORICAL FINANCIALS

Company Type: Private

Income Statement			FYE: December 31	
	REVENUE ($ mil.)	NET INCOME ($ mil.)	NET PROFIT MARGIN	EMPLOYEES
12/07	2,368	(7)	—	9,800
12/06	2,218	58	2.6%	9,800
12/05	1,959	57	2.9%	8,600
12/04	1,679	(47)	—	7,700
12/03	1,515	12	0.8%	7,450
Annual Growth	**11.8%**	**—**	**—**	**7.1%**

2007 Year-End Financials

Debt ratio: 2,159.0%
Return on equity: —
Cash ($ mil.): —
Current ratio: —
Long-term debt ($ mil.): 1,922

Net Income History

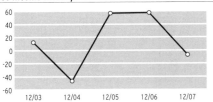

NUMMI

What do you get when a Japanese production process meets a California lifestyle? The answer is New United Motor Manufacturing, Inc. (NUMMI). The company, a 50-50 joint venture between General Motors (GM) and Toyota, makes Tacoma (formerly banded Hilux) pickup trucks and Corolla sedans for Toyota and the Vibe sport wagon for GM's Pontiac division. NUMMI can produce 250,000 cars and 170,000 pickups a year. Together GM and Toyota are researching alternative-fuel vehicles. Since its formation in 1984, NUMMI has produced more than 6.2 million vehicles.

NUMMI began as an experiment to see if Japanese management techniques emphasizing team decision-making would work in the US. The experiment has been a success story. Toyota's strategy to build more vehicles in the markets it serves (rather than transport them) helps the company reduce costs. NUMMI's production methods are considered to be among the world's most efficient.

EXECUTIVES

President and CEO: Kunihiko Ogura
VP, Human Resources: Robert McCullough
VP, Manufacturing Operations:
  Ernesto Gonzalez-Beltran
General Manager, CTO, Purchasing, and Corporate Planning: Linda McColgan
General Manager, Truck Organization: Walt Odisho
General Manager, Quality Control and Quality Assurance: Gary Workman

LOCATIONS

HQ: New United Motor Manufacturing, Inc.
45500 Fremont Blvd., Fremont, CA 94538
Phone: 510-498-5500 **Fax:** 510-770-4116
Web: www.nummi.com

PRODUCTS/OPERATIONS

Selected Models

Pontiac Vibe (sport wagon)
Toyota Corolla (sedan)
Toyota Tacoma (pickup)

COMPETITORS

AutoAlliance	Isuzu
Daimler	Kia Motors
Fiat	Mazda
Ford Motor	Nissan
Fuji Heavy Industries	Saab Automobile
Hindustan Motors	Suzuki Motor
Honda	Volkswagen
Hyundai Motor	

Nypro Inc.

Nypro is a real pro when it comes to injection molding. The company makes plastic parts used in devices that range from cell phones, electric razors, and seat belts to inkjet printer cartridges and personal computers. Customers in the electronics and telecommunications industries account for the largest part of Nypro's sales; the company serves clients in the industrial, consumer goods, automotive, packaging, and health care markets as well. Although custom-precision plastic-injection molding is Nypro's core business, the company also offers assembly services to other manufacturers. Major customers include Dell, Nokia, and Procter & Gamble. The company is owned by its employees.

Nypro's operations encompass more than 50 businesses that span nearly 20 countries. One of the challenges the company has faced is getting those operations to work together smoothly, so since 2004 it has focused on integrating its various businesses' communications, technologies, and supply chains.

The company has made significant strides; it surpassed an internal goal of reaching $1 billion in annual revenue in 2006. These increases in efficiencies have now become an integral part of the company's internal leadership development as well as the keystone of the products and services solutions it offers customers.

Chairman Gordon Lankton joined Nypro (then known as Nylon Products, Inc.) in 1962 as general manager and co-owner. He acquired the rest of the company in 1969. In 1998 Lankton sold the firm to Nypro's Employee Stock Ownership Plan (ESOP).

EXECUTIVES

Chairman: Gordon B. Lankton
President, CEO, and Director:
  Theodore E. (Ted) Lapres III
CFO and Chief Strategy Officer:
  James R. (Jim) Buonomo
Corporate VP, General Counsel, and Secretary:
  James W. (Jim) Peck
Corporate VP Consumer and Electronics:
  Louis (Lou) Gaviglia
Corporate VP, Global Engineering and Technology:
  Greg G. Adams
**Corporate VP, Human Resources and Organizational
  Development:** Ann S. Liotta
Corporate VP Healthcare: Stephen J. (Steve) Glorioso
President, Americas: Raymond S. (Ray) Grupinski
President, Nypro Medical Products Group:
  Thomas F. Taylor
Director Corporate Communications: Al Cotton
Auditors: PricewaterhouseCoopers LLP

LOCATIONS

HQ: Nypro Inc.
  101 Union St., Clinton, MA 01510
Phone: 978-365-9721   **Fax:** 978-368-0236
Web: www.nypro.com

COMPETITORS

Atlantis Plastics
Berry Plastics Corporation
Deswell
Formosa Plastics
Hoffer Plastics
Nagase
Sumitomo Heavy Industries
Toledo Molding and Die
Tuthill

HISTORICAL FINANCIALS
Company Type: Private

Income Statement
FYE: June 30

	REVENUE ($ mil.)	NET INCOME ($ mil.)	NET PROFIT MARGIN	EMPLOYEES
6/08	1,164	4	0.3%	18,000
6/07	1,106	18	1.7%	18,000
6/06	1,066	5	0.5%	17,000
6/05	729	17	2.4%	15,000
6/04	627	16	2.5%	—
Annual Growth	16.7%	(30.5%)	—	6.3%

2008 Year-End Financials

Debt ratio: —   Current ratio: —
Return on equity: 2.5%   Long-term debt ($ mil.): —
Cash ($ mil.): —

Net Income History

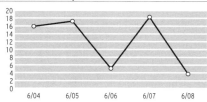

Oakland Raiders

Fighting under the silver and black Jolly Rodger, these Raiders are looking to plunder some treasure on the gridiron. The Oakland Raiders professional football team is one of the more storied franchises in the National Football League. Founded in 1960 as a charter member of the American Football League, the team played in the second Super Bowl between the rival leagues (losing to the Green Bay Packers) before joining the NFL in 1970. The franchise has since won three championship titles (its last in 1984). Over the years, Oakland has been home to such Hall of Fame players as Marcus Allen, Howie Long, and Jim Otto, as well as legendary head coach John Madden. Al Davis has run the team since 1972.

In 2007 Davis raised some additional capital for his football franchise by selling a 20% stake to outside investors, including David Abrams, Dan Goldberg, and Paul Leff. Through a settlement the previous year, Davis had gained a 30% stake owned by the family of E.J. McGah, one of the team's founders.

The Raiders have been on a downward trajectory since reaching the Super Bowl in 2003, where the team lost to the Tampa Bay Buccaneers. In 2008 head coach Lane Kiffin was fired shortly after the season began. The former University of Southern California assistant replaced Art Shell the previous season and had been the team's fourth head coach in five years.

In 2008 software company McAfee declined to renew its naming rights sponsorship with the Raiders home stadium, which reverted back to its original name of Oakland-Alameda County Coliseum. The company had originally entered into the naming rights deal in 1998 when it was known as Network Associates.

Davis, who served as Raiders head coach in the early 1960s and later helped negotiate the merger of the two rival football leagues as commissioner of the AFL, has been something of a thorn in the side of the NFL and a lightning rod for critics for many years. Unable to get concessions from Oakland for a new stadium, he proposed moving the Raiders to Los Angeles in 1980 but was blocked by the league. He later sued the NFL and won the right to relocate, but then returned the team to the Bay Area in 1995 when the City of Angels backed out of a new stadium deal. In recent years he has also filed unsuccessful lawsuits against the Carolina Panthers and the Buccaneers for trademark infringement.

EXECUTIVES

Owner: Al Davis
CEO: Amy Trask
CFO: Marc Badain
Interim Head Coach: Tom Cable
Technology: Tom Blanda
General Counsel: Jeff Birren
Director Public Relations: Mike Taylor
Director Football Development: Mark Jackson
College Scouting: Angelo Coia

LOCATIONS

HQ: The Oakland Raiders
  1220 Harbor Bay Pkwy., Alameda, CA 94502
Phone: 510-864-5000   **Fax:** 510-864-5160
Web: www.raiders.com

The Oakland Raiders play at 63,026-seat capacity Oakland-Alameda County Coliseum in Oakland, California.

PRODUCTS/OPERATIONS

Championship Titles
Super Bowl Championship
  Super Bowl XVIII (1984)
  Super Bowl XV (1981)
  Super Bowl XI (1977)
AFC Championship (1976, 1980, 1983, 2002)
AFC Western Division Champions (1970, 1972-76, 1983, 1985, 1990, 2000-02)
AFL Championship (1967)
AFL Western Division Champions (1967-69)

COMPETITORS

Denver Broncos
Kansas City Chiefs
San Diego Chargers

HISTORICAL FINANCIALS
Company Type: Private

Income Statement
FYE: June 30

	REVENUE ($ mil.)	NET INCOME ($ mil.)	NET PROFIT MARGIN	EMPLOYEES
6/08	205	—	—	—
6/07	189	—	—	—
6/06	171	—	—	—
6/05	169	—	—	—
6/04	149	—	—	—
Annual Growth	8.3%	—	—	—

Revenue History

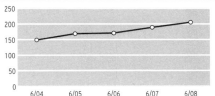

Obsidian Enterprises

The rubber meets the road at Obsidian Enterprises. The holding company's United Trailers and Classic Trailers subsidiaries make steel-framed trailers for hauling everything from race cars to ATVs. Obsidian's U.S. Rubber Reclaiming subsidiary reprocesses scrap tires and inner tubes to make reclaimed butyl rubber sheets that are used to make inner tubes and linings for tubeless tires. Obsidian also owns Pyramid Coach, which leases luxury buses to corporations and entertainers. Chairman and CEO Timothy Durham and other top executives own the company, which was taken private in 2006.

EXECUTIVES

Chairman and CEO: Timothy S. Durham, age 45, $185,000 pay
President and COO: Terry G. Whitesell, $185,000 pay
SEVP: Jeffrey W. Osler, $125,000 pay
EVP and CFO: Rick D. Snow
EVP Corporate Finance: Anthony P. Schlichte
VP Technology: Jonathan B. Swain
Corporate Administrative Services Manager: Elizabeth L. McClure
Corporate Accounting Manager: Erin Beesley
Marketing Communications Manager: Thetchen N. Price
Manager Corporate Manufacturing Services: Marc Kennedy
Executive Assistant: Shannon Frantz
Auditors: Somerset CPAs

LOCATIONS

HQ: Obsidian Enterprises, Inc.
111 Monument Cir., Ste. 4800,
Indianapolis, IN 46204
Phone: 317-237-4122   **Fax:** 317-237-0137
Web: obsidianenterprises.com

PRODUCTS/OPERATIONS

Selected Operations

Trailer and Related Transportation Equipment Manufacturing
  Classic Manufacturing, Inc. (steel-framed cargo and specialty trailers)
  United Trailers (steel-framed cargo, racing, and specialty trailers)
Butyl Rubber Reclaiming
  U.S. Rubber Reclaiming, Inc.
Coach Leasing
  Pyramid Coach, Inc.

COMPETITORS

Bayer AG
Exxon
Utilimaster
Wabash National
Wells Cargo

Ocean Spray Cranberries

Ocean Spray Cranberries transformed cranberries from turkey sidekick to the stuff of everyday beverages, cereal, and mixed drinks. Known for its blue-and-white wave logo, the company controls more than half of the US cranberry drink market. A cooperative owned by more than 700 cranberry and citrus growers in the US and Canada, it produces its line of juices by blending the cranberry with fruits ranging from apples to tangerines. It also makes other cranberry products (fresh berries, sauces, and snacks), grapefruit juice, and Ocean Spray Premium 100% juice drinks for both retailers and foodservice providers worldwide.

To expand beyond the berry's traditional role, Ocean Spray has turned the fruit into a chewy snack (Craisins), and cranberries now show up in co-branded cookies and cereal. It has also introduced a "white juice" made from pre-ripened cranberries that have a less tart taste. Promotional efforts have been aided by research showing that cranberry juice can reduce urinary tract infections and fight stomach ulcers.

The cooperative distributes internationally through partnerships with companies like Nestlé, Gerber, and even Sapporo in Japan. Closer ties to the alcoholic beverage industry came as the company expanded it reach with Absolut cranberry-flavored vodka. Ocean Spray also has a product deal with PepsiCo.

Ocean Spray's Ingredient Technology Group processes fruit into juice ingredients for food and beverage manufacturers.

HISTORY

Ocean Spray Cranberries traces its roots to Marcus Urann, president of the Cape Cod Cranberry Company. In 1912 Urann, who became known as the "Cranberry King," began marketing a cranberry sauce that was packaged in tins and could be served year-round. Inspired by the sea spray that drifted off the Atlantic and over his cranberry bogs, Urann dubbed his concoction Ocean Spray Cape Cod Cranberry Sauce.

It didn't take long for other cranberry growers to make their own sauces, and rather than compete, the Cranberry King consolidated. In 1930 Urann merged his company with A.D. Makepeace Company and with Cranberry Products, forming a national cooperative called Cranberry Canners. During the 1940s it added growers in Wisconsin, Oregon, and Washington and, to reflect its new scope, changed its name to National Cranberry Association.

Canadian growers were added to the fold in 1950. Urann retired in 1955, and two years later the co-op introduced its first frozen products. To take advantage of the popular Ocean Spray brand name, in 1959 the company changed its name to Ocean Spray Cranberries.

Two weeks before Thanksgiving that year, the US Department of Health mistakenly announced that aminotriazole, a herbicide used by some cranberry growers, was linked to cancer in laboratory rats. Sales of what consumers called "cancer berries" plummeted, and Ocean Spray nearly folded. However, the US government came to the rescue with subsidies in 1960, and the company stayed afloat.

The scare convinced Ocean Spray it needed to cut its dependence on seasonal demand, and it began to diversify more aggressively into the juice business, introducing a heavily promoted new line of juices blending cranberries with apples, grapes, and other fruits.

Ocean Spray allowed Florida's Indian River Ruby Red grapefruit growers to join the co-op in 1976. The company acquired Milne Food Products, a manufacturer of fruit concentrates and purees, in 1985, and three years later it signed a Japanese distribution deal.

To maintain its edge in a growing but increasingly competitive market, Ocean Spray automated plants and allied with food giants to create cranberry-flavored treats such as cookies (Nabisco, 1993) and cereal (Kraft Foods, 1996). In 1998 it unsuccessfully sued to block PepsiCo's purchase of juice maker Tropicana on grounds that it would interfere with PepsiCo's distribution of Ocean Spray's drinks. Ocean Spray also introduced a line of 100% juice blends to compete with rivals such as former co-op member Northland Cranberries (now Cranberries Limited).

Bumper harvests from 1997 through 1999 led to lower cranberry prices. As a result, in 1999 the company announced its third round of layoffs since 1997 (bringing the total to 500, or nearly one-fifth of its workforce). It also suspended its practice of buying back the stock of its growers, who must buy shares to join the co-op.

Amid criticism that it has been unable to compete effectively with for-profit rivals, Ocean Spray hired former Pillsbury executive Robert Hawthorne as CEO in 2000. Grower-owners voted not to explore a sale of the company at its 2001 annual meeting, a vote of confidence for the new management. The company supported a 32% crop reduction to help eliminate the crop surpluses that cause depressed prices.

In 2002 Hawthorne resigned. Barbara Thomas, a board member and former president of Warner Lambert's consumer health care division, was named interim CEO. She left the position in 2003 and was replaced by company president and COO Randy Papadellis.

In 2003 rival Northland made a cash and stock bid to take over the juice business of Ocean Spray. The company rejected the offer the same month. Upset by their lack of input in the decision, cranberry growers voted to revamp the Ocean Spray board, reducing its size from 15 to 12 members and keeping just three of the board's previous members. Soon after, Ocean Spray laid off about 60 people, including several executives.

In 2004 the cooperative nearly revamped its board a second time in one year to again increase input from membership. As a compromise, the cooperative returned the size of its board to 15 members. Seven of the members were considered "compromise" candidates that would bring "additional viewpoints" to the Board. In June cooperative members rejected a proposed joint venture with PepsiCo.

Rounding out a busy year, in September 2004 Ocean Spray settled an antitrust lawsuit filed by Northland Cranberries and Clermont, Inc. As part of the settlement, Ocean Spray agreed to purchase Northland's production plant and pay more than $5 million to buy eight of Northland's cranberry marshes in Wisconsin. The agreement also stipulated that Ocean Spray would make cranberry concentrate for Northland.

In 2005 it sold a fruit-processing facility in Vero Beach, Florida.

EXECUTIVES

President and CEO: Randy C. Papadellis, age 50
SVP, CFO, and Treasurer: Timothy C. (Tim) Chan, age 56
SVP and COO, Domestic: Kenneth G. (Ken) Romanzi, age 48
VP Operations: Michael (Mike) Stamatakos
VP, Human Resources and Organization Development: Katie Morey
Senior Corporate Communications Specialist: Denise Perry
Senior Manager, Corporate Communications: Chris Phillips
Public Relations Manager: Cindy Taccini
PR Specialist: Sharon Newcomb
Managing Director, Europe, Middle East, and Africa: Peter Patkowski, age 54
Auditors: Deloitte & Touche

LOCATIONS

HQ: Ocean Spray Cranberries, Inc.
1 Ocean Spray Dr., Lakeville-Middleboro, MA 02349
Phone: 508-946-1000   **Fax:** 508-946-7704
Web: www.oceanspray.com

PRODUCTS/OPERATIONS

Selected Products and Brands

Canned sauces
  Cran-Fruit Crushed Fruit
  Jellied Cranberry Sauce
  Whole Berry Cranberry Sauce

Craisins
  Cherry Flavor Sweetened Dried Cranberries
  Orange Flavor Sweetened Dried Cranberries
  Original Sweetened Dried Cranberries
  Trail Mix — Cranberry and Chocolate
  Trail Mix — Cranberry, Fruit and Nuts

Juice
  100% juice
  Cranberry blends
  Cranberry juice cocktails
  Diet juice drinks
  Grapefruit juice and juice drinks
  Light juice drinks
  Organics and naturals
  White cranberry juice drinks

Produce
  Fresh citrus
  Fresh cranberries
  Fresh grapefruit
  Refrigerated juices

COMPETITORS

Altria	Johnson Concentrates
Campbell Soup	Jugos del Valle
Chiquita Brands	Naked Juice
Clement Pappas & Co.	National Grape Cooperative
Cliffstar	Nestlé USA
Coca-Cola	Odwalla
Coloma Frozen Foods	Old Orchard
Cranberries Limited	PepsiCo Beverages North
Dole Food	America
Dr Pepper Snapple Group	Smucker
Florida's Natural	Sunkist
Fresh Del Monte Produce	Tampico Beverages
Hansen Natural	Tropicana
IZZE	Welch's
Jamba	Wells' Dairy

Oglethorpe Power

Much ogled, not-for-profit Oglethorpe Power Corporation is one of the largest electricity cooperatives in the US, with contracts to supply wholesale power to 38 member/owners (making up most of Georgia's electric distribution cooperatives) until 2025. Oglethorpe Power's member/owners, which also operate as not-for-profits, serve about 1.7 million residential, commercial, and industrial customers. The company has a generating capacity of more than 4,744 MW from fossil-fueled, nuclear, and hydroelectric power plants. In addition, Oglethorpe purchases power from other suppliers, and it markets power on the wholesale market.

Oglethorpe has stakes in 24 generating units. In 2007 Oglethorpe members Cobb EMC, Jackson EMC, and Sawnee EMC accounted for 13.3%, 12.3%, and 10.0% of Oglethorpe's total revenues, respectively.

EXECUTIVES

Chairman and At-Large Director: Benny W. Denham, age 77
Vice Chairman; Member Director (Group 4): J. Sam L. Rabun, age 76
President and CEO: Thomas A. (Tom) Smith, age 53, $526,693 pay
COO: Michael W. (Mike) Price, age 47, $291,332 pay
CFO: Elizabeth Bush (Betsy) Higgins, age 39, $281,949 pay
SVP Government Relations and Chief Administrative Officer: W. Clayton (Clay) Robbins, age 61
SVP Contracts, Operations, and Environmental: Clarence D. Mitchell
SVP External Relations and Member: William F. (Billy) Ussery, age 43
SVP Strategic Initiatives: George B. Taylor Jr.
SVP Plant Operations: James A. (Jim) Messersmith
VP Human Resources: Jami G. Reusch, age 45, $163,209 pay
VP and Controller: Brian Prevost, age 52
Director Public Relations: Greg Jones
Auditors: PricewaterhouseCoopers LLP

LOCATIONS

HQ: Oglethorpe Power Corporation
2100 E. Exchange Place, Tucker, GA 30084
Phone: 770-270-7600   **Fax:** 770-270-7872
Web: www.opc.com

PRODUCTS/OPERATIONS

2007 Sales

	$ mil.	% of total
Members	1,149.6	100
Non-members	1.6	—
Total	**1,151.2**	**100**

Member/Owners

Altamaha Electric Membership Corporation
Amicalola Electric Membership Corporation
Canoochee Electric Membership Corporation
Carroll Electric Membership Corporation
Central Georgia Electric Membership Corporation
Coastal Electric Membership Corporation (d/b/a Coastal Electric Cooperative)
Cobb Electric Membership Corporation
Colquitt Electric Membership Corporation
Coweta-Fayette Electric Membership Corporation

Diverse Power Incorporated, an Electric Membership Corporation (formerly Troup Electric Membership Corporation)
Excelsior Electric Membership Corporation
Grady Electric Membership Corporation
GreyStone Power Corporation, an Electric Membership Corporation
Habersham Electric Membership Corporation
Hart Electric Membership Corporation
Irwin Electric Membership Corporation
Jackson Electric Membership Corporation
Jefferson Energy Cooperative, an Electric Membership Corporation
Lamar Electric Membership Corporation
Little Ocmulgee Electric Membership Corporation
Middle Georgia Electric Membership Corporation
Mitchell Electric Membership Corporation
Ocmulgee Electric Membership Corporation
Oconee Electric Membership Corporation
Okefenoke Rural Electric Membership Corporation
Pataula Electric Membership Corporation
Planters Electric Membership Corporation
Rayle Electric Membership Corporation
Satilla Rural Electric Membership Corporation
Sawnee Electric Membership Corporation
Slash Pine Electric Membership Corporation
Snapping Shoals Electric Membership Corporation
Sumter Electric Membership Corporation
Three Notch Electric Membership Corporation
Tri-County Electric Membership Corporation
Upson Electric Membership Corporation
Walton Electric Membership Corporation
Washington Electric Membership Corporation

COMPETITORS

AGL Resources
FPL Group
MEAG Power
Progress Energy
PS Energy
Southern Company
TVA

HISTORICAL FINANCIALS

Company Type: Cooperative

Income Statement

FYE: December 31

	REVENUE ($ mil.)	NET INCOME ($ mil.)	NET PROFIT MARGIN	EMPLOYEES
12/07	1,151	19	1.7%	160
12/06	1,129	18	1.6%	161
12/05	1,170	18	1.5%	160
12/04	1,313	17	1.3%	168
12/03	1,204	17	1.4%	179
Annual Growth	(1.1%)	3.3%	—	(2.8%)

2007 Year-End Financials

Debt ratio: —   Current ratio: —
Return on equity: 0.5%   Long-term debt ($ mil.): —
Cash ($ mil.): —

Net Income History

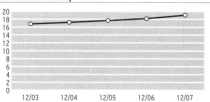

Ohio State University

The first student body of The Ohio State University (OSU) had 24 students. Today the school has around 60,000 at its flagship Columbus campus, consistently vying with Arizona State and U of Minnesota (Twin Cities) for the nation's largest campus in terms of enrollment. OSU also has four regional campuses and two agricultural institutes. Its approximately 3,500 regular and research faculty members offer instruction in around 160 undergraduate and 200 graduate programs. The colleges and schools range from the Austin E. Knowlton School of Architecture to the College of Medicine and Public Health to the Fisher College of Business. OSU was established in 1870 as Ohio Agricultural and Mechanical College.

Noteworthy university alumni include astronaut Nancy Sherlock Currie, golfer Jack Nicklaus, author John Jakes, and Olympian Jesse Owens.

The Ohio State University has campuses in Columbus, Lima, Mansfield, Marion, and Newark. It has two agricultural centers in Wooster and a freshwater biological field station (the Franz Theodore Stone Laboratory) on Gibraltar Island in Put-in-Bay harbor.

The school has an endowment of around $1.6 billion.

HISTORY

In 1870 the Ohio legislature, prompted by Governor Rutherford B. Hayes, agreed to establish the Ohio Agricultural and Mechanical College in Columbus on property provided by the Morrill Act of 1862 (the land-grant institution act, which gave land to states and territories for the establishment of colleges).

After a heated battle over whether the college should teach only agricultural and mechanical arts or foster a broad-based liberal arts curriculum, the college opened in 1873 offering agriculture, ancient languages, chemistry, geology, mathematics, modern languages, and physics courses. Two years later the school appointed its first female faculty member. The Ohio State University became the school's name in 1878; that year it graduated its first class. The next year OSU graduated its first female student.

OSU grew dramatically, adding schools of veterinary medicine (1885), pharmacy (1885), law (1891), and dairy sciences (1895). It awarded its first Masters of Arts degree in 1886.

The university continued to expand in the early 20th century, with enrollment surpassing 3,000 in 1908; by 1923 it had reached 10,000. New schools were added in education (1907), medicine and dentistry (1913), and commerce and journalism (1923). During WWI Ohio State designated part of its campus as training grounds and established the only college schools in the nation for airplane and balloon squadrons. Ohio Stadium was dedicated in 1922.

During the Great Depression, Ohio State cut back salaries and course offerings. In the 1940s the school geared for war once again by establishing radiation and war research labs, as well as programs and services for students who were drafted. OSU captured its first national football championship in 1942.

The 1950s ushered in the era of legendary OSU football coach Woody Hayes. Hayes led his beloved Buckeyes to three national championships and nine Rose Bowl appearances before he was discharged for striking a Clemson player in 1978. The 1950s also saw the addition of four regional campuses at Lima, Mansfield, Marion, and Newark.

In the early 1960s the university was engaged in internal free-speech battles. By the end of that decade, enrollment had surpassed 50,000. OSU opened its School of Social Work in 1976.

In 1986 OSU and rival Michigan shared the Big 10 football conference title. Enrollment at OSU topped 54,000 in 1990 but then began declining. In response, the university tried to cut costs and beef up revenues. One way was through alliances: In 1992 it teamed with research group Battelle to develop a testing system for new drugs for the Food and Drug Administration. But when more savings were needed in 1995-96, the university began streamlining operations, merging journalism and communications, and consolidating several veterinary departments. However, it also approved the creation of a new school of public health to provide education in environmental health, epidemiology, and health care management and financing.

But sports were not forgotten, and in 1996 OSU broke ground on the $84 million Schottenstein Center, a multipurpose facility for the university's basketball and ice hockey teams. In 1997 president Gordon Gee announced that he was leaving OSU for Brown University. The next year William Kirwan from the University of Maryland came on board as president.

In 2000 the university's "Affirm Thy Friendship" campaign came to a close. It increased OSU's endowment from $493 million in 1993 to $1.3 billion in 2000. In 2002 Kirwan stepped down and Karen Holbrook took over as president.

Ohio State won the national football championship in early 2003. The Buckeyes made it to the BCS championship game following the 2006 football season, only to be defeated by the #2-ranked Florida Gators. In 2007 Gordon Gee returned as president.

EXECUTIVES

Chairman: G. Gilbert Cloyd
Vice Chairman: Karen L. Hendricks, age 59
President: E. Gordon Gee, age 64
EVP and Provost: Joseph A. Alutto, age 66
SVP Business and Finance: William J. (Bill) Shkurti
SVP Government Affairs: Curt Steiner
SVP Research: Robert T. McGrath
SVP Health Sciences: Fred Sanfilippo
SVP University Development: Peter Weiler
SVP University Communications:
  Thomas (Tom) Katzenmeyer
VP and Chief Investment Officer: Jonathan D. Hook
VP and Executive Dean: Bobby D. Moser
VP and General Counsel: Christopher M. Culley
VP Student Affairs: Richard A. Hollingsworth
Associate VP Human Resources: Larry M. Lewellen
Secretary: David O. Frantz
Assistant to the President and Operations Director:
  Kate Wolford
Auditors: Deloitte & Touche LLP

LOCATIONS

HQ: The Ohio State University
  Enarson Hall, 154 W. 12th Ave.,
  Columbus, OH 43210
Phone: 614-292-3980   **Fax:** 614-292-0154
Web: www.osu.edu

PRODUCTS/OPERATIONS

Selected Colleges and Schools
Austin E. Knowlton School of Architecture
College of Biological Sciences
College of Dentistry
College of Education
College of Education and Human Ecology
College of Engineering
College of Food, Agricultural, and Environmental
  Sciences
College of Human Ecology
College of Humanities
College of Law
College of Mathematical and Physical Sciences
College of Medicine and Public Health
College of Nursing
College of Optometry
College of Pharmacy
College of Social and Behavioral Sciences
College of Social Work
College of the Arts
College of Veterinary Medicine
Graduate School
John Glenn School of Public Affairs
Max M. Fisher College of Business
Michael E. Moritz College of Law
School of Allied Medical Professions
School of Biomedical Science
School of Communication
School of Environment and Natural Resources
School of Music
School of Natural Resources
School of Public Health
University College

Oklahoma City Thunder

This team is causing a big noise in Oklahoma. Professional Basketball Club owns and operates the Oklahoma City Thunder, which relocated from Seattle for the 2008 season. The relocation deal struck between team owner Clay Bennett and the city gave Seattle rights to the old SuperSonics name, history, and colors. The Seattle team had originally been started by Sam Schulman and joined the National Basketball Association in 1967. It earned one NBA title in 1979. Bennett acquired the franchise in 2006 from a group led by Starbucks founder Howard Schultz.

The relocation settlement between the team and the city put an end to a long-running dispute over building a new sports facility to replace Seattle's KeyArena. Bennett, with the backing of the NBA, had insisted the aging arena was unfit for a professional basketball franchise to survive. (Schultz, in fact, claimed losses of about $60 million over five years when he sold the team.) The two parties could not come to an agreement, however, on public funding for a new building.

With its new name in place, the franchise will take up residence at Oklahoma City's Ford Center. An Oklahoma businessman, Bennett had helped negotiate a deal to temporarily relocate the New Orleans Hornets to the Ford Center in 2005 after Hurricane Katrina. He later led the $350 million acquisition of the SuperSonics.

Early in 2008 Professional Basketball Club sold its WNBA franchise, the Seattle Storm, for about $10 million to a local group of investors led by Anne Levinson, who previously served as Deputy Mayor of Seattle. The new ownership group, calling itself Force 10 Hoops, includes Microsoft executives Lisa Brummel and Dawn Trudeau.

EXECUTIVES

Chairman: Clayton I. (Clay) Bennett
EVP, Chief Administrative Officer, and CFO:
Danny Barth
VP Business Development: John Croley
VP Guest Relations: Pete Winemiller
SVP Ticket Sales and Services: Brian Byrnes
General Manager: Sam Presti
Assistant General Manager: Rich Cho
Head Coach: P.J. Carlesimo
Director Human Resources: Katy Semtner
Director Marketing: Ben Wilson
Director Corporate Communications: Tom Savage
Director Team Operations: Marc St. Yves

LOCATIONS

HQ: Professional Basketball Club, LLC
2 Leadership Square, 211 N. Robinson Ave., Ste. 300, Oklahoma City, OK 73102
Phone: 405-208-4800   **Fax:** 405-429-7900
Web: www.nba.com/thunder

The Oklahoma City Thunder play at the 19,599-seat capacity Ford Center in Oklahoma City.

COMPETITORS

Denver Nuggets
Minnesota Timberwolves
Portland Trail Blazers
Utah Jazz

HISTORICAL FINANCIALS

Company Type: Private

Income Statement

	REVENUE ($ mil.)	NET INCOME ($ mil.)	NET PROFIT MARGIN	EMPLOYEES
6/07	81	—	—	—
6/06	81	—	—	—
6/05	81	—	—	—
6/04	73	—	—	—
6/03	70	—	—	—
Annual Growth	3.7%	—	—	—

FYE: June 30

Revenue History

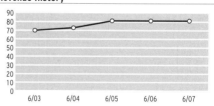

Old Dominion Electric

Ol' Virginny and neighboring states get power from Old Dominion Electric Cooperative, which generates and purchases electricity for its 12 member distribution cooperatives. These in turn serve nearly 550,000 customers in four northeastern states. The member-owned power utility has more than 2,000 MW of generating capacity from nuclear and fossil-fueled power plants and diesel generators; it purchases the remainder of its power from neighboring utilities and power marketers. Old Dominion transmits power to its members through the systems of utilities and transmission operators in the re-

gion. It also provides power to TEC Trading, a wholesale company also owned by the distribution cooperatives.

Old Dominion was organized in 1948 to identify new electric power sources for its growing member systems. It initially planned to build a power plant in 1949 but this plan fell through and the utility remained inactive until energy costs surged during the 1970s. From 1976 on Old Dominion has been serving its members' power supply needs by purchasing wholesale power and selling it to them at cost.

In 2008 the company's largest revenue contributor — Northern Virginia Electric Cooperative — renegotiated its wholesale supply agreement with Old Dominion, allowing it to seek supply from other sources.

As part of an energy diversification strategy, in 2008 the company signed a long-term contract with AES to purchase up to 70 MW of wind power.

EXECUTIVES

President and CEO: Jackson E. (Jack) Reasor, age 55
SVP and CFO: Robert L. (Bob) Kees, age 55
SVP, Accounting and Finance and Secretary:
Terri Young
SVP, Engineering and Operations:
Gregory W. (Greg) White
SVP Power Supply: Lisa D. Johnson, age 42
VP and Controller: Tom Smiley
VP, Engineering and Operations: Ken Alexander
VP, Finance: Lynn Maloney
VP Human Resources: Elissa Ecker, age 48
VP, Member and External Relations: John C. Lee Jr., age 47
VP, Power Supply Planning: Rick Beam
Human Resources Coordinator: Tammy Coburn
Auditors: Ernst & Young LLP

LOCATIONS

HQ: Old Dominion Electric Cooperative
4201 Dominion Blvd., Glen Allen, VA 23060
Phone: 804-747-0592   **Fax:** 804-747-3742
Web: www.odec.com

Old Dominion Electric Cooperative operates in Delaware, Maryland, Virginia, and West Virginia.

PRODUCTS/OPERATIONS

2007 Sales

	$ mil.	% of total
Northern Virginia Electric Cooperative	248.1	26
Rappahannock Electric Cooperative	184.4	19
Delaware Electric Cooperative	93.7	10
Other	436.9	45
Total	**963.1**	**100**

HISTORICAL FINANCIALS

Company Type: Cooperative

Income Statement

	REVENUE ($ mil.)	NET INCOME ($ mil.)	NET PROFIT MARGIN	EMPLOYEES
12/07	963	16	1.7%	101
12/06	818	21	2.6%	103
12/05	738	12	1.6%	83
12/04	589	12	2.1%	84
12/03	536	12	2.3%	82
Annual Growth	15.8%	7.2%	—	5.3%

FYE: December 31

2007 Year-End Financials

Debt ratio: —
Return on equity: 1.4%
Cash ($ mil.): —
Current ratio: —
Long-term debt ($ mil.): —

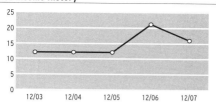

Old World Industries

Old World Industries is taking a progressive lead in the production of chemicals. The company is the #2 US antifreeze maker (after Honeywell, maker of Prestone) and the only vertically integrated antifreeze producer. Old World's antifreezes include Peak and Sierra (the latter is marketed to parents and pet owners as a safer alternative to other antifreezes), as well as private labels. Old World also makes deicers, pickup bed liners (Herculiner), windshield wiper blades, and spark plugs (SplitFire).

The company's chemicals unit is a leading maker of ethylene glycol (used in — no surprise — antifreeze), ethylene oxide, and liquid caustic soda.

Old World operates an online automotive parts store, 24-7Autoparts.com, where it sells its products as well as auto parts from other manufacturers. Chairman and CEO Tom Hurvis and Riaz Waraich own Old World.

EXECUTIVES

Chairman and CEO: J. Thomas (Tom) Hurvis
CFO: Tony Clesceri
Managing Director: Riaz Waraich
SVP Automotive Sales: Jerry Riccioni
SVP EO and Derivatives Division: Bruce Pullen
VP Marketing: Mark Kraus
Director, Human Resources: Vince Piat
CEO, Cachet Solutions: Mark S. Rangell, age 44
President, Industrial Chemicals Division:
James (Jim) Bryan
President, Consumer Products Division:
Richard (Rick) Jago
President, Ventum Energy: Bill Bippus

LOCATIONS

HQ: Old World Industries, Inc.
4065 Commercial Ave., Northbrook, IL 60062
Phone: 847-559-2000   **Fax:** 847-559-2266
Web: www.oldworldind.com

Old World Industries has a manufacturing plant in Pasadena, Texas, and offices in Northbrook, Illinois.

PRODUCTS/OPERATIONS

Selected Products

Antifreeze (Peak, Fleet, Sierra, private-label)
Chemicals (diethylene glycol, ethylene glycol, ethylene oxide, methanol, polyethylene glycol, triethylene glycol, and liquid caustic soda)
Deicer and ice remover (for windshields, streets, sidewalks, and runways)
Pickup bed liner (Herculiner)
Spark plugs and wire sets (SplitFire)
Windshield wiper blades (All Season, Max-Vision, Mr. Clean)

COMPETITORS

Arch Chemicals
Ashland
BASF SE
Dow Chemical
Durakon
Equistar Chemicals
Honeywell International
Lancaster Colony
Robert Bosch
Shell Chemicals

O'Melveny & Myers

O'Melveny & Myers has gotten used to playing the role of legal guardian angel. The firm is one of the oldest in Los Angeles, and over the years it has developed strong ties to the media and entertainment industries. Among its clients have been such leading players as Walt Disney, Sony Pictures Entertainment, and Time Warner. Besides entertainment and media law, O'Melveny & Myers' practice areas include labor and employment, intellectual property and technology, and venture capital litigation. The firm has more than 1,000 lawyers located in about a dozen offices worldwide. O'Melveny & Myers was founded in 1885.

EXECUTIVES

Chair: Arthur B. Culvahouse Jr.
Vice Chair: Robert E. (Bob) Willett
COO: Bruce A. Boulware
Chair, Strategic Counseling Practice:
   Thomas E. (Tom) Donilon
Chair, Partner Admissions Committee, Laterals:
   David A. Krinsky, age 59
Managing Director, Adversarial: Paul R. Covey
Managing Director, Finance: Peter J. Cyffka
Managing Director, Talent Development: Michelle Egan
Director Attorney Services: Teresa A. Doremus
Director Global Communications: John Buchanan
Director Marketing: Suzanne Donnels
Global Communications Administrator: Erika Tucker
Secretary, Office of the Chair: Maritza U. B. Okata

LOCATIONS

HQ: O'Melveny & Myers LLP
   400 S. Hope St., Los Angeles, CA 90071
Phone: 213-430-6000   **Fax:** 213-430-6407
Web: www.omm.com

PRODUCTS/OPERATIONS

Selected Practice Areas

Adversarial Practice
Antitrust/Competition
Appellate
Asia
Aviation
Business Restructuring and Reorganization
Capital Markets
Class Action Defense
China
Corporate Practice
Electronic Discovery and Document Retention
Employee Benefits/Executive Compensation
Entertainment and Media

Environmental Law and Natural Resources
Fund and Investment Management
Global Enforcement and Criminal Defense
Global Practice
Global Trade
Government Relations and Regulatory Practices
Health Care and Life Sciences
Insurance and Mass Torts
Intellectual Property and Technology
Japan
International Dispute Resolution and Arbitration
Labor and Employment Law
Legal Service Centers
Mergers and Acquisitions
Outsourcing
Private Equity
Project Development
Pro Bono
Real Estate
Securities Enforcement and Regulatory Counseling
Securities Litigation
Strategic Counseling
Tax
Telecommunications
Transactional Intellectual Property
Venture Capital and Emerging Technology
Venture Capital Litigation
White Collar Criminal Defense

COMPETITORS

Akin Gump
Baker & McKenzie
Bingham McCutchen
Davis Polk
Gibson, Dunn & Crutcher
Greenberg Glusker
Latham & Watkins
Morrison & Foerster
Munger, Tolles & Olson
Paul, Hastings
Pillsbury Winthrop Shaw Pittman
Skadden, Arps
Sullivan & Cromwell

HISTORICAL FINANCIALS
Company Type: Partnership

Income Statement

	REVENUE ($ mil.)	NET INCOME ($ mil.)	NET PROFIT MARGIN	EMPLOYEES
1/07	934	—	—	—
1/06	869	—	—	—
1/05	808	—	—	—
1/04	658	—	—	—
1/03	563	—	—	2,200
Annual Growth	13.5%	—	—	—

FYE: January 31

Revenue History

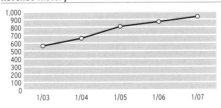

O'Neal Steel

O'Neal Steel has an angle on the steel industry. One of the US's leading metals service companies, O'Neal sells a full range of metal products — including angles, bars, beams, coil, pipe, plate, and sheet — made from steel, aluminum, brass, and bronze. The company operates throughout the US and in Europe and the Asia/Pacific region from about 70 facilities, offering such metal-processing services as forming, laser cutting, machining, plasma cutting, tube bending, and sawing. Founded by Kirkman O'Neal in 1921 in Alabama, the company has expanded largely through acquisitions. It is still owned and run by the O'Neal family.

O'Neal expanded in 2005 by acquiring Pennsylvania-based metals service center TW Metals and again in 2006 with the acquisition of metal services center Timberline Steel. In 2004, O'Neal bought Aerodyne Alloys, a supplier of cobalt, nickel-based alloys, stainless steel, and titanium to companies in the aerospace and energy industries.

EXECUTIVES

Chairman: Craft O'Neal
President and CEO: Bill Jones
EVP and COO: Holman Head
EVP and CFO: Mary Valenta
VP Human Resources: Shawn Smith
CIO: Michael (Mike) Gooldrup
Director Marketing: Henley Smith
President, Metal West: Terry Taft
President and CEO, TW Metal: Jack Elrod

LOCATIONS

HQ: O'Neal Steel, Inc.
   744 41st St. North, Birmingham, AL 35222
Phone: 205-599-8000   **Fax:** 205-599-8037
Web: www.onealsteel.com

PRODUCTS/OPERATIONS

Selected Products

Alloy bars
Coil
Cold finished bars
Grating
Hot rolled bars
Pipe
Structural shapes
Tubing

Selected Processing Services

Coil processing
Cutting
Forming
Machining
Notching
Punching and drilling
Rolling
Sawing
Shearing
Tube bending
Welding

COMPETITORS

A. M. Castle
Metals USA
Quanex Building Products
Reliance Steel
Russel Metals
Ryerson
SSAB North America
Worthington Industries

HISTORICAL FINANCIALS

Company Type: Private

Income Statement

FYE: December 31

	REVENUE ($ mil.)	NET INCOME ($ mil.)	NET PROFIT MARGIN	EMPLOYEES
12/07	2,440	—	—	4,400
12/06	2,300	—	—	4,300
12/05	1,600	—	—	3,700
Annual Growth	23.5%	—	—	9.0%

Revenue History

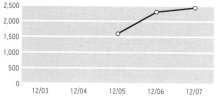

	12/03	12/04	12/05	12/06	12/07
2,500					
2,000					
1,500					
1,000					
500					
0					

Oneida

Oneida knows where the fish fork goes. Once one of the world's largest manufacturers of stainless steel and silver-plated flatware, Oneida now imports flatware, dinnerware, and glassware for both consumers and the food service and institutional markets. Metal products account for more than half of sales. Other tabletop products include cookware, china, and linens, as well as picture frames and accessories. Subsidiary Kenwood Silver operates about 15 Oneida outlet stores. Operating under the burden of substantial debt, Oneida filed for Chapter 11 bankruptcy protection in March 2006 and emerged six months later as a private company with new ownership.

The company's new shareholders are led by Quadrangle Group LLC and also include JPMorgan, Litespeed Partners LLC, and D. E. Shaw Laminar Portfolios, L.L.C.

Oneida serves both of its markets by selling its wares to department and discount store chains, mass merchandisers, specialty stores, catalog showrooms, restaurants, hotels, convention centers, airlines, hospitals, and others, as well as online. Oneida's products are sold in more than 75 countries.

James Joseph, an EVP since April 2005, succeeded Terry Westbrook as president in mid-2006. Joseph, nearly a 20-year veteran of the company, added the title of CEO in August 2007.

EXECUTIVES

President and CEO: James E. Joseph, $345,000 pay
COO and CFO: Andrew G. Church
EVP and Chief Global Supply Chain Officer:
W.Tim Runyan
Corporate SVP, Manufacturing and Engineering:
Harold J. DeBarr, age 59
SVP, Secretary, and General Counsel:
Catherine H. Suttmeier, age 48, $158,006 pay
SVP Supply Chain: Dominick J. Trapasso, age 51,
$176,922 pay
SVP Strategic Planning and Chief Marketing Officer:
David Sank
SVP Global Procurement: Bill Grannis
SVP Information Technology and CIO: Rob Hack

President, Foodservice Division: Foster Sullivan
President, Encore Promotions: Thomas E. Lowe, age 53
President, International Foodservice Division:
Gregory L. (Greg) Woodhall
President, Consumer: Timothy Shine
Corporate Public Relations: David Gymburch
Auditors: BDO Seidman, LLP

LOCATIONS

HQ: Oneida Ltd.
163-181 Kenwood Ave., Oneida, NY 13421
Phone: 315-361-3000   **Fax:** 315-361-3700
Web: www.oneida.com

PRODUCTS/OPERATIONS

2006 Sales

	% of total
Metalware	60
Dinnerware	33
Glassware	5
Other tabletop accessories	2
Total	**100**

Selected Brand Names

Buffalo China
Community
Delco
Heirloom
Oneida
Rego
Rogers
Sakura
Viners of Sheffield

Selected Products

Metalware
  Cookware
  Cutlery
  Stainless steel and silver-plated hollowware (bowls, trays, and tea and coffee sets)
  Stainless steel, silver-plated, and sterling silver flatware (forks, knives, spoons, serving pieces)
Dinnerware
  Bowls, cups, and mugs
  Domestic and imported china
  Ceramic, porcelain, and stoneware plates
  Serving pieces
Glassware (glass and crystal)
  Barware
  Decorative pieces
  Giftware
  Serveware
  Stemware
Other
  Bath, kitchen, and table linens
  Ceramic and plastic serveware
  Picture frames and decorative pieces

COMPETITORS

Anchor Hocking
ARC International
Brown-Forman
Carlsberg
Libbey
Lifetime Brands
Mikasa
Noritake
Pagnossin
Reed & Barton
Richard-Ginori 1735
Royal Doulton
Syratech
Vitro
Waterford Wedgwood
WKI Holding

Orlando Magic

This organization hopes to work a little voodoo on the basketball court. The Orlando Magic is a professional basketball franchise that joined the National Basketball Association in 1989. A surprising upstart, Orlando made its first playoff appearance in 1994 with the help of star center Shaquille O'Neal and reached the NBA Finals the following season, losing to the Houston Rockets in four games. (O'Neal left the following year to join the Los Angeles Lakers.) Founded by local businessman Jim Hewitt, the team holds court at Orlando's Amway Arena; the family of Amway co-founder Rich DeVos has owned the Magic through RDV Sports since 1991.

The team brought in Steve Van Gundy to be head coach in 2007 (following an aborted attempt to hire University of Florida basketball coach Billy Donovan). Van Gundy's inaugural season proved successful as Orlando made it to the second round of the 2008 NBA playoffs, its deepest penetration in post-season play in more than a decade.

Orlando began construction of a new events facility in 2008 that will serve as the future home of the Magic. The team plans to move into the $480 million arena for the 2010 season. Michigan-based direct-sales company Amway took over naming rights at Orlando's current arena in 2006 with a four-year deal that pays the city about $1.5 million each year. Previous named sponsor TD Waterhouse had let its naming deal run out after it was acquired by Ameritrade to become TD AMERITRADE.

Through RDV Sports, the DeVos family owns the RDV Sportsplex entertainment and fitness center. They previously owned the WNBA Orlando Miracle. (Sold in 2002, the team now competes as the Connecticut Sun.)

EXECUTIVES

Owner and Chairman: Richard (Rich) DeVos, age 82
President and CEO: Bob Vander Weide
COO: Alex Martins
CFO: Jim Fritz
SVP: Pat Williams, age 68
SVP Corporate Relationships: Jack Swope
SVP Business Development: Charles Freeman
General Manager: Otis Smith
Assistant General Manager: Dave Twardzik
Head Coach: Stan Van Gundy, age 49
VP Communications: Joel Glass
VP Corporate Partnerships: Cameron Scholvin
VP Human Resources and Administrative Services:
Audra Hollifield
Controller: Jeff Bissey

LOCATIONS

HQ: Orlando Magic, Ltd.
8701 Maitland Summit Blvd., Orlando, FL 32810
Phone: 407-916-2400   **Fax:** 407-916-2830
Web: www.nba.com/magic

The Orlando Magic play at the 17,519-seat capacity Amway Arena in Orlando, Florida.

PRODUCTS/OPERATIONS

Championship Titles

Eastern Conference Champions (1995)

COMPETITORS

Charlotte Bobcats
Hawks Basketball
Miami Heat
Washington Wizards

HISTORICAL FINANCIALS

Company Type: Private

Income Statement

	REVENUE ($ mil.)	NET INCOME ($ mil.)	NET PROFIT MARGIN	EMPLOYEES
6/07	92	—	—	—
6/06	89	—	—	—
6/05	82	—	—	—
6/04	78	—	—	—
6/03	80	—	—	—
Annual Growth	3.6%	—	—	—

FYE: June 30

Revenue History

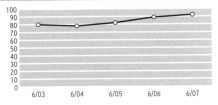

OSI Group

You might say a steady diet of red meat has made this company big and strong. OSI Industries (doing business as OSI Group) is one of the largest suppliers of meat products to foodservice operators. Through its operating companies, OSI provides a variety of beef, pork, and poultry products, including beef patties, hot dogs, sausages, bacon, and chicken nuggets. It has long been a supplier of beef to fast-food chain McDonald's. In addition, OSI offers contract manufacturing and packaging services for other food processors; it has more than 70 manufacturing facilities around the world. The company traces its roots to a family meat market started by Otto Kolschowsky.

OSI sold its Brazilian and European operations to Marfrig for almost $700 million in cash and stock in 2008; the deal included Northern Ireland-based poultry producer Moy Park.

EXECUTIVES

Chairman, President, and CEO: Sheldon (Shelly) Lavin
EVP and CFO: William J. (Bill) Weimer Jr.
SVP Americas and Asian Pacific Zones:
 David G. (Dave) McDonald
SVP European Zone: Douglas M. Gullang
SVP Business Development and Commercialization:
 Lynn Mulherin
VP, Treasurer, and Assistant Secretary:
 George Krzesinski
VP Information Technology: Stephen P. Burch
Director Human Resources: Mike Diaz

LOCATIONS

HQ: OSI Industries, LLC
 1225 Corporate Blvd., Aurora, IL 60504
Phone: 630-851-6600   **Fax:** 630-692-2340
Web: www.osigroup.com

COMPETITORS

Cargill Meat Solutions
Golden State Foods
Hormel
JBS
Keystone Foods
Lopez Foods
Perdue Incorporated
Pilgrim's Pride
Sanderson Farms
Sara Lee Food & Beverage
Smithfield Foods
Tyson Foods

HISTORICAL FINANCIALS

Company Type: Private

Income Statement

	ESTIMATED REVENUE ($ mil.)	NET INCOME ($ mil.)	NET PROFIT MARGIN	EMPLOYEES
12/07	4,620	—	—	22,000
12/06	4,200	—	—	20,500
12/05	4,000	—	—	19,738
12/04	3,400	—	—	—
12/03	3,200	—	—	12,000
Annual Growth	9.6%	—	—	16.4%

FYE: December 31

Revenue History

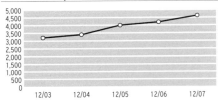

OSI Restaurant Partners

Peel back the layers of this bloomin' restaurateur, and you'll find more than a steakhouse. OSI Restaurant Partners is the #3 operator of casual-dining spots (behind Darden Restaurants and Brinker International), with more than 1,400 locations in the US and 20 other countries. Its flagship Outback Steakhouse chain boasts more than 950 locations that serve steak, chicken, and seafood in Australian-themed surroundings. OSI also operates the Carrabba's Italian Grill chain, with about 240 locations. Other concepts include Bonefish Grill, Fleming's Prime Steakhouse, and Cheeseburger In Paradise. Most of the restaurants are company owned. A group led by chairman Chris Sullivan took the company private in 2007.

Leading up to the management-led buyout, OSI's restaurants had been struggling with stagnant sales in part because of lower consumer spending on dining out. The company agreed to the $3.2 billion privatization deal to restructure its business away from the glare of Wall Street and securities regulators. Sullivan, along with co-founders Robert Basham and Tim Gannon, led the buyout backed by private equity firms Bain Capital and Catterton Partners.

The company sold 80% of its Lee Roy Selmon's business to a group led by the chain's namesake founder following the going-private transaction. The deal returned cash to OSI that it planned to use to pay down debt. The Southern-style comfort food chain had grown to a half-dozen units. OSI has indicated it might sell some of its other chains, including its interest in more than 20 Roy's restaurants serving Hawaiian-inspired dishes created by chef Roy Yamaguchi, that do not show potential for large-scale growth.

OSI had already been undergoing significant changes in the years before returning to private control. Formerly known as Outback Steakhouse, the company changed its name in 2006 in an effort to differentiate its corporate operations from that of its flagship chain and to signify its emergence as a leading multi-concept restaurant operator.

EXECUTIVES

Chairman: Chris T. Sullivan, age 60
Vice Chairman: Robert D. (Bob) Basham, age 59
CEO: A. William (Bill) Allen III, age 48
COO: Paul E. Avery, age 48
EVP and Chief Officer Legal and Corporate Affairs:
 Joseph J. Kadow, age 51
EVP and Chief Development Officer:
 Richard L. Renninger
EVP and Chief Brand Officer: Jody L. Bilney, age 46
SVP and CFO: Dirk A. Montgomery, age 44
SVP and Director: J. Timothy (Tim) Gannon, age 59
VP Public Relations: Stephanie L. Amberg
Manager Investor Relations: Lisa Hathcoat
President, Blue Coral Seafood & Spirits:
 Edna K. Morris, age 56
President, Bonefish Grill: John W. Cooper
President, Carrabba's Italian Grill:
 Steven T. (Steve) Shlemon, age 46
**President, Fleming's Prime Steakhouse and Wine Bar;
 President, Blue Coral Seafood & Spirits:**
 C.H. (Skip) Fox
President, Lee Roy Selmon's: Peter R. Barli
President, Outback International: Michael W. Coble,
 age 59
President, Roy's: Mark D. Running
Chef and Founder, Roy's: Roy Yamaguchi
President, Outback Steakhouse: Jeff Smith
Auditors: PricewaterhouseCoopers LLP

LOCATIONS

HQ: OSI Restaurant Partners, LLC
 2202 N. West Shore Blvd., Ste. 500,
 Tampa, FL 33607
Phone: 813-282-1225
Web: www.osirestaurantpartners.com

COMPETITORS

Applebee's
Brinker
Carlson Restaurants
Cheesecake Factory
Darden
Del Frisco's Restaurant
Hooters
McCormick & Schmick's
Ruby Tuesday
Ruth's Hospitality
Texas Roadhouse

HISTORICAL FINANCIALS

Company Type: Private

Income Statement

FYE: December 31

	REVENUE ($ mil.)	NET INCOME ($ mil.)	NET PROFIT MARGIN	EMPLOYEES
12/08	4,150	—	—	10,900

Oxbow Corporation

Oxbow is bullish on energy. The diversified firm's Oxbow Carbon unit markets and distributes coke, coal, petroleum, and carbon products and other commodities to power producers, refineries, and industrial manufacturers. Other company operations include Oxbow Mining, which operates a coal mine in Colorado, and Oxbow Realty Services, which develops and manages commercial and residential real estate projects. Oxbow also has stakes in independent geothermal and hydropower projects in Costa Rica. Oxbow is controlled by William Koch, an America's Cup winner who founded Oxbow in 1983 after being ousted from the family business (Koch Industries) by brothers Charles and David.

In 2007 Oxbow completed the acquisition of all of the assets of Great Lakes Carbon Income Fund (which indirectly holds the securities of GLC Carbon USA Inc).

EXECUTIVES

President and CEO: William I. (Bill) Koch
CFO and Director: Zachary K. Shipley
EVP, General Counsel, and Director:
 Richard P. Callahan
VP Human Resources: Kathy Flaherty
Director Corporate Communications: Brad Goldstein
President and COO, Oxbow Carbon and Minerals:
 Brian Acton
President, Gunnison Energy: Brad Robinson
President, Oxbow Mining: Jim Cooper
President, Oxbow Steel International: Ron Saca
Auditors: PricewaterhouseCoopers LLP

LOCATIONS

HQ: Oxbow Corporation
 1601 Forum Place, Ste. 1400,
 West Palm Beach, FL 33401
Phone: 561-697-4300   **Fax:** 561-697-1876
Web: www.oxbow.com

COMPETITORS

Alliance Resource
Arch Coal
Black Hills
CONSOL Energy
Drummond Company
Koch Industries, Inc.
Massey Energy
Peabody Energy
Westmoreland Coal

HISTORICAL FINANCIALS

Company Type: Private

Income Statement

FYE: December 31

	REVENUE ($ mil.)	NET INCOME ($ mil.)	NET PROFIT MARGIN	EMPLOYEES
12/07	3,400	—	—	1,200
12/06	1,600	—	—	800
12/05	1,300	—	—	800
Annual Growth	61.7%	—	—	22.5%

Revenue History

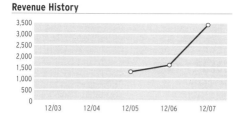

Pabst Brewing

The Pabst Brewing Company is a 19th-century brewer retooled for the 21st century. Pabst, founded in Milwaukee in 1844, today is a "virtual" brewer. It owns no brewery; instead, Pabst pays other brewers, such as MillerCoors and Lion Brewery, to brew the beers, while it retains the ownership and marketing of its some 85 brands (including Pabst Blue Ribbon, Blatz, Pearl, Lone Star, Old Milwaukee, Old Style, Schlitz, and Colt 45). With Woodridge, Illinois-based corporate headquarters Pabst Brewing is owned by the private group Kalmanovitz Charitable Trust.

Pabst's market share can't compare with those of the nation's top brewing giants, but its Pabst Blue Ribbon is enjoyed by rebel beer drinkers who resist the mass marketing of Pabst's rivals. The company ceased its brewing operations in 1996.

In 2006 the company moved its corporate headquarters from San Antonio to the Chicago suburb, Woodridge. Illinois is one of Pabst's largest markets.

EXECUTIVES

Chairman: Bernard Orsi
President and CEO: Kevin T. Kotecki, age 44
COO: James P. (Jim) Walter
CFO: William (Bill) Wolz
Chief Sales Officer: Abbott Wolfe
Chief Marketing Officer: Brad Hittle
CTO: Dave Meinz
VP and General Counsel: Yeoryios Apallas
VP Network Development: Richard Bartlett
VP Human Resources: Susan Lundquist

LOCATIONS

HQ: Pabst Brewing Company
 9014 Heritage Rd., Ste. 308, Woodridge, IL 60517
Phone: 630-972-3830
Web: www.pabst.com

PRODUCTS/OPERATIONS

Selected Brands

Ballentine
Black Label
Blatz
Champale
Colt 45
Country Club
Haffenreffer's Private Sock
Lone Star
McSorley's
National Bohemian Beer
Old Milwaukee
Old Style
Olympia
Pabst Blue Ribbon
Pearl
Piels
Rainier
Schaefer
Schlitz
Schmidt
Special Export
St. Ides
Stag
Stroh's

COMPETITORS

Anchor Brewing
Anheuser-Busch
Big Rock Brewery
Boston Beer
Breckenridge Brewery
Carlsberg
City Brewing Company
Constellation Brands
Craft Brewers Alliance
Flying Dog Brewery
Frederick Brewing
Gambrinus
Grupo Modelo
Heineken
Labatt
Lancaster Brewing Co.
Leinenkugel's
Lion Brewery
Massachusetts Bay Brewing
Molson Coors
New Belgium Brewing
Pyramid Breweries
Rheingold
Rogue Ales
SABMiller
Shipyard Brewing Company
Sierra Nevada
Stone Brewing
Stoudt's Brewing
Victory Brewing
Weyerbacher Brewing

Pacific Coast Building Products

Protecting Ronald Reagan's papers and propping up the San Francisco art world seems like a tall order, but Pacific Coast Building Products does both. The building materials manufacturer and distributor made roof tiles for Reagan's presidential library and concrete blocks for the San Francisco Museum of Modern Art. It sells building products for residential, commercial, and industrial construction to builders and contractors through about 10 subsidiaries in 10 Western states. Pacific Coast Building Products also provides services, such as roofing and insulation. The late Fred Anderson (father-in-law of president and CEO David Lucchetti) founded the company as Anderson Lumber in 1953; his family owns the firm.

EXECUTIVES

Chairman: James B. Thompson
President and CEO: David J. Lucchetti
CFO: Darren Morris
EVP: Dave Pringle
VP Marketing: George A. Foster
Managing Director Operational Services: Mark Ingram
Director Community Relations: Megan Vincent
Manager Marketing: Brian Opsal
Human Resources: Kimberly Bright

LOCATIONS

HQ: Pacific Coast Building Products, Inc.
 10600 White Rock Rd., Bldg. B, Ste. 100,
 Rancho Cordova, CA 95670
Phone: 916-631-6500   **Fax:** 916-631-6690
Web: www.paccoast.com

Pacific Coast Building Products has locations in Arizona, California, Colorado, Hawaii, Idaho, Montana, Nevada, Oregon, Utah, and Washington.

PRODUCTS/OPERATIONS

Selected Subsidiaries, Divisions, and Activities

Contracting
 Alcal Roofing, Waterproofing, and Insulation
  (installation and service of commercial and
  residential insulation, roofing, waterproofing)
 Arcade Insulation (installation and service of
  commercial and residential insulation)
Distribution
 Anderson Lumber (framing packages, including decks,
  doors, millwork, joists, paneling, plywood, particle
  board, lumber)
 Anderson Truss (roof and floor trusses, I-joists)
 Diamond Pacific (building products from lumber to
  paint, plus Keystone Retaining Wall Systems)
 Pacific Supply (brick, roofing materials, masonry,
  drywall, stucco products, acoustical ceiling products,
  insulation, pipes, waterproofing and coatings, tools
  and equipment)
 P.C. Wholesale (mill-direct shipments of lumber, sheet
  goods, i-joists, siding, and other wood products for
  large, high-volume projects)

Manufacturing
 Basalite Concrete Products (dry mixes, fences and wall
  systems, paving stones, retaining walls, structural
  block, garden products, stucco)
 Basalite Interlocking Paving Stones
 Gladding, McBean (clay, terra cotta, architectural
  pottery, roof tile)
 H.C. Muddox (brick, clay, stone products; flue liners;
  pool coping; glass block)
 Interstate Brick (brick, stone veneer, flue liners, glass
  brick)
 PABCO Gypsum (drywall)
 PABCO Roofing Products (asphalt roofing shingles)
Transportation
 Material Transport (fleet for transporting product and
  raw materials between various divisions)
 Pacific Coast Jet Charter, Inc. (charter jet and
  turboprop service throughout Western Hemisphere)

COMPETITORS

84 Lumber
ABC Supply
Building Materials Holding
Dixieline ProBuild
Georgia-Pacific
Guardian Building
 Products
HD Supply
Huttig Building Products
Lowe's
Pavestone
USG

Pacific Mutual

Life insurance is "alive and whale" at Pacific Mutual Holding. The mutual holding company's primary operating subsidiary, Pacific Life Insurance (whose logo is a breaching whale), is a top California-based life insurer. Lines of business include a variety of life insurance products for individuals and businesses; annuities and mutual funds geared to individuals and small businesses; management of stable value funds, annuity products, fixed income investments, and other investments for institutional clients and pension plans; and real estate investing (commercial mortgage loans). Additionally, its Aviation Capital Group subsidiary provides commercial jet aircraft leasing.

Major operating subsidiaries of Pacific Mutual Holding include mutual fund and annuities distribution network Pacific Select Distributors; Pacific Asset Funding, which provides trade financing and related services; and College Savings Bank, which offers a variety of college savings vehicles. In 2007 the company formed Pacific Asset Management to act as a third-party manager for structured credit transactions.

Pacific Mutual in 2008 sold its minority stake in Pacific Investment Management Company (PIMCO), a major investment management firm, for $288 million to PIMCO's majority-owner, insurance giant Allianz. It had already sold smaller chunks of its PIMCO stake to Allianz in 2005 and 2006.

The company has also been selling off some of its broker/dealer operations, excluding its Pacific Select operations.

Pacific Life policyholders own Pacific Mutual Holding Company, which was created in 1997 following a conversion to a mutual holding company structure. Pacific LifeCorp is the intermediate stock holding company, which owns 100% of Pacific Life and can take on outside capital funding (though it has not done so).

HISTORY

The Pacific Mutual Life Insurance began business in 1868 in Sacramento, California, as a stock company. Its board was dominated by California business and political leaders, including three of the "Big Four" who created the Central Pacific Railroad (Charles Crocker, Mark Hopkins, and Leland Stanford) and three former governors (Stanford, Newton Booth, and Henry Huntley Haight). Stanford (founder of Stanford University) was the company's first president and policyholder.

By 1870 Pacific Mutual Life was selling life insurance throughout most of the western US. Expansion continued in the early 1870s into Colorado, Kentucky, Nebraska, New York, Ohio, and Texas. The company ventured into Mexico in 1873 but sold few policies. It had more luck with China, accepting its first risk there in 1875, and in Hawaii, where it started business two years later. In 1881 Pacific Mutual Life moved to San Francisco.

Leland Stanford died in 1893. The eponymous university and Stanford's widow, though rich in assets, found themselves struggling through a US economic depression. The benefit from Stanford's policy kept the university open until the estate was settled.

In 1905 Conservative Life bought the firm. The Pacific Mutual Life name survived the acquisition just as its records survived the fire that ravaged San Francisco after the 1906 earthquake. Pacific Mutual Life then relocated to Los Angeles.

The company squeaked through the Depression after a flood of claims on its noncancellable disability income policies forced Pacific Mutual Life into a reorganization plan initiated by the California insurance commissioner (1936). After WWII, Pacific Mutual Life entered the group insurance and pension markets.

After 83 years as a stock company and an eight-year stock purchasing program, Pacific Mutual Life became a true mutual in 1959.

Pacific Mutual Life relocated to Newport Beach in 1972. During the 1980s it built up its financial services operations, including its Pacific Investment Management Co. (PIMCO, founded 1971). The company was in trouble even before the stock crash of 1987 because of health care costs and over-investment in real estate. That year it brought in CEO Thomas Sutton, who sold off real estate and emphasized HMOs and fee-based financial services.

In the 1990s the firm cut costs and increased its fee income. PIMCO Advisors, L.P. was formed in 1994 when PIMCO merged with Thomson Advisory Group. The merger gave Pacific Mutual Life a retail market for its fixed-income products, a stake in the resulting public company, and sales that offset interest-rate variations and changes in the health care system.

In 1997 the company assumed the corporate-owned life insurance business of failed Confederation Life Insurance; it also merged insolvent First Capital Life into Pacific Life as Pacific Corinthian Life. That year Pacific Mutual Life, which became Pacific Mutual Holding, became the first top-10 US mutual to convert to a mutual holding company, thus allowing it the option of issuing stock to fund acquisitions. Because the firm remained partially mutual, however, policyholders retained ownership but got no shares of Pacific LifeCorp, its new intermediate stock holding company.

To compete with such one-stop financial service behemoths as Citigroup, Pacific Mutual began selling annuities through a Compass Bank subsidiary in 1998. The next year it bought controlling interests in broker-dealer M.L. Stern and investment adviser Tower Asset Management. In 2000 the world's #2 insurer, Allianz, bought all of PIMCO Advisors (now Allianz Global Investors of America) other than the interest retained by Pacific Mutual when it spun off the investment manager. (Pacific Mutual gradually sold its holdings in the firm, and thus its stake in Pacific Investment Management Company, through sales to Allianz.)

Pacific Mutual Holding sharpened its focus on individuals and small businesses in 2001 with the sale of its reinsurance unit to what is now Scottish Re.

With its focus so firmly on life insurance, Pacific Life sold its group health insurance business (which included medical, dental, and life policies) to PacifiCare in 2005.

EXECUTIVES

Chairman, President, and CEO; President and CEO, Pacific Life Insurance Company: James T. (Jim) Morris, age 48
EVP and CFO: Khanh Tran, age 51
SVP Human Resources: Anthony J. Bonno
President and CEO, M.L. Stern & Co.: Milford L. (Mickey) Stern
Chairman and CEO, Pacific Select Group: Gerald W. (Bill) Robinson
Managing Director, Pacific Asset Funding: Robert G. Denhert
Group Managing Director and CEO, Aviation Capital Group: R. Stephen Hannahs
CEO, College Savings Bank: Gilbert S. Johnson
Auditors: Deloitte & Touche LLP

LOCATIONS

HQ: Pacific Mutual Holding Company
700 Newport Center Dr., Newport Beach, CA 92660
Phone: 949-219-3011
Web: www.pacificlife.com

PRODUCTS/OPERATIONS

2007 Revenues

	$ mil.	% of total
Net investment income	2,157	43
Policy fees & insurance premiums	1,792	35
Aircraft leasing	535	11
Investment advisory fees	327	6
Net realized investment gain (loss)	(28)	—
Other	266	5
Total	**5,049**	**100**

2007 Sales

	$ mil.	% of total
Life insurance	1,631	32
Annuities & mutual funds	1,248	25
Investment management	1,149	23
Aircraft leasing	611	12
Corporate & other	410	8
Total	**5,049**	**100**

Selected Products and Services

Life Insurance Division
Indexed universal life
Interest-sensitive whole life
Joint and last-survivor life
Term life
Universal life insurance
Variable universal life
Annuities and Mutual Fund Division
529 College savings plans
Individual(k) programs
Mutual funds
Small business 401(k) plans
Variable annuities

Investment Management Division
Fixed income investments
Funding agreements
High-yield and money market advisory
Private equity investments
Single premium group annuity contracts
Stable value products
Structured settlement annuities
Aircraft Leasing Division
Aircraft asset management for third-party financial institutions
Aircraft and aviation-related joint venture investments
Commercial jet aircraft for lease to airlines
Other products and services
Asset funding
Invoice discounting
Refinancing and re-factoring of accounts receivable
Revolving credit facilities
Structured trade finance facilities
Real estate services
Commercial mortgage-backed securities
Equity real estate properties and funds
Fixed-rate and floating-rate mortgage loans
REIT debt

COMPETITORS

AXA Financial
Boeing Capital
CIT Transportation Finance
Great-West Life Assurance
Guardian Life
Hartford Life
John Hancock Financial Services
Liberty Mutual
Life Investors Insurance
Lincoln Financial Group
MassMutual
MetLife
Mutual of Omaha
Nationwide
New York Life
Northwestern Mutual
Penn Mutual
Principal Financial
Prudential
StanCorp Financial Group
Travelers Companies
USAA

HISTORICAL FINANCIALS

Company Type: Mutual company

Income Statement

FYE: December 31

	ASSETS ($ mil.)	NET INCOME ($ mil.)	INCOME AS % OF ASSETS	EMPLOYEES
12/07	111,024	647	0.6%	2,800
12/06	99,346	614	0.6%	2,900
12/05	86,977	542	0.6%	3,100
12/04	77,137	540	0.7%	—
12/03	67,422	418	0.6%	—
Annual Growth	13.3%	11.5%	—	(5.0%)

2007 Year-End Financials

Equity as % of assets: 5.8%   Long-term debt ($ mil.): —
Return on assets: 0.6%   Sales ($ mil.): 5,049
Return on equity: 10.4%

Net Income History

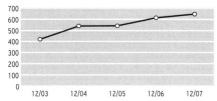

Palmetto Bancshares

If the palmetto is the official state tree of South Carolina, does that mean Palmetto Bancshares is the state's official bank? Palmetto Bancshares is the holding company for The Palmetto Bank, which operates about 40 full- and limited-service branches mostly in upstate South Carolina. Its offerings include checking, savings, and money market accounts; IRAs; and CDs. Loans secured by commercial real estate account for the largest portion of its loan portfolio, with single-family residential mortgages at a distant second. The Palmetto Bank also provides financial planning, trust, and brokerage services, plus bond, mutual fund, and annuity sales. It's been serving South Carolinians since 1906.

A group of about 17 officers and directors controls approximately 15% of Palmetto Bancshares, led by chairman and CEO Leon Patterson who owns about 9%.

EXECUTIVES

Chairman and CEO: L. Leon Patterson, age 66, $376,194 pay
President, COO, and Director; Chairman and CEO, The Palmetto Bank: Paul W. (Bill) Stringer, age 64, $351,930 pay
President and Chief Retail Officer, The Palmetto Bank: George A. (Andy) Douglas Jr., age 56, $150,000 pay
Treasurer; EVP, The Palmetto Bank: Ralph M. Burns III, age 57, $150,000 pay
EVP and Chief Credit Officer, The Palmetto Bank: W. Michael Ellison, age 55, $150,000 pay
EVP, The Palmetto Bank: Earle T. Harding, age 48
EVP, The Palmetto Bank: Hubert E. Tuttle III, age 39
EVP, The Palmetto Bank: Teresa W. Knight, age 52, $150,000 pay
EVP, The Palmetto Bank: Matthew I. Walter, age 42
SVP and CFO, Palmetto Bank: Lauren S. Greer
Auditors: Elliott Davis LLC

LOCATIONS

HQ: Palmetto Bancshares, Inc.
301 Hillcrest Dr., Laurens, SC 29360
Phone: 864-984-4551   **Fax:** 864-984-8415
Web: www.palmettobank.com

PRODUCTS/OPERATIONS

2007 Sales

	$ mil.	% of total
Interest		
Loans	78.4	78
Securities	4.4	4
Other	0.8	1
Noninterest		
Deposit account service charges	8.1	8
Trust, investment & brokerage services fees	3.1	3
Other	5.7	6
Total	**100.5**	**100**

COMPETITORS

Bank of America
BB&T
Community Capital
Community First Bancorp
First Citizens Bancorporation
First National Bancshares
First South Bancorp (NC)
First South Bancorp (SC)
GrandSouth Bancorporation
Peoples Bancorporation
Provident Community Bancshares
South Financial
Southern First Bancshares
Wachovia Corp

HISTORICAL FINANCIALS

Company Type: Private

Income Statement
FYE: December 31

	ASSETS ($ mil.)	NET INCOME ($ mil.)	INCOME AS % OF ASSETS	EMPLOYEES
12/07	1,248	16	1.3%	409
12/06	1,153	15	1.3%	400
12/05	1,075	14	1.3%	387
12/04	996	12	1.2%	374
12/03	898	11	1.2%	370
Annual Growth	8.6%	10.1%	—	2.5%

2007 Year-End Financials

Equity as % of assets: 8.8% Long-term debt ($ mil.): —
Return on assets: 1.3% Sales ($ mil.): 101
Return on equity: 15.2%

Net Income History

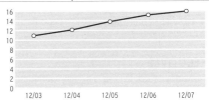

Pamida Stores

Pamida Stores Operating Co. offers more small-town values than a bandwagon of Republicans on the campaign trail. The rural retailer runs 200-plus Pamida general merchandise discount stores in about 15 states, mostly in the Midwest. The stores are located in small towns (5,500 people, on average), most of which are not served by mass merchandisers, such as Wal-Mart. Pamida's stores sell brand-name and private-label apparel, jewelry, health and beauty aids, housewares, electronics, and lawn and garden supplies. Most of its stores also sell groceries and two-thirds have in-store pharmacies. Formerly a division of ShopKo Stores, which bought Pamida in 1999, Pamida and ShopKo are now owned by Sun Capital Partners.

Sun Capital took ShopKo private in late 2005 and spun off Pamida in March 2007. (Pamida's first store opened in 1963 in Knoxville, Iowa, under the Quality Discount Center banner.)

Pamida hopes to add more than a dozen stores in 2008, including about 10 free-standing pharmacies. The retailer acquired five Medicine Chest Pharmacies in Iowa and Nebraska, which began operating under the Pamida banner in March 2005. The acquisition of local pharmacy chains (adding drugstores in states such as Michigan, South Dakota, and Missouri) is part of Pamida's ongoing effort in recent years to grow its stand-alone pharmacy business.

Michael J. Hopkins resigned as CEO of Pamida in January 2006 and was succeeded as president and CEO by Larry S. Johnson, a former executive of SAM'S CLUB. Johnson was succeeded in 2007 by Paul Rothamel, formerly of ShopKo.

EXECUTIVES

President and CEO: Paul Rothamel
VP Instore Operations: William (Bill) Young
VP Pharmacy Business Development:
James (Jim) Donatelle
Auditors: Deloitte & Touche LLP

LOCATIONS

HQ: Pamida Stores Operating Company, LLC
8800 F St., Omaha, NE 68127
Phone: 402-339-2400 **Fax:** 402-596-7330
Web: www.pamida.com

PRODUCTS/OPERATIONS

Selected Hardlines

Automotive accessories
Consumables
Electronics
Groceries
Hardware
Health and beauty aids
Housewares
Lawn and garden supplies
Linens
Paint
Seasonal merchandise
Toys

Selected Softlines

Clothing
Footwear
Jewelry and accessories

COMPETITORS

Big Lots	J. C. Penney
CVS Caremark	Kmart
Dollar General	Rite Aid
Dollar Tree	Sears
Duckwall-ALCO	Target
Family Dollar Stores	Tractor Supply
Fareway Stores	Walgreen
Farm King	Wal-Mart
Hy-Vee	

Panda Restaurant Group

This Panda certainly has food on its mind. Panda Restaurant Group is a leading quick-service restaurant operator with more than 1,100 Panda Express locations in about 35 states and Puerto Rico. The chain offers Asian-themed food primarily in high-traffic locations, including malls, airports, and sporting arenas. The company also runs almost 30 mall-based Hibachi-San outlets that offer a quick-service Japanese grill menu. For patrons looking for full-service dining, Panda Restaurants has a handful of Panda Inn branded units in California. The company is owned by the family of co-chairman Andrew Cherng, who opened the first Panda Inn location in 1973.

Where other restaurant operators have mostly failed, Panda Restaurant Group has succeeded in creating a nationwide chain of Chinese eateries, a feat made more impressive by the fact that the company does not have a full-scale franchising effort. (A small number of locations

are licensed to such food service operators as SSP America.) However, by owning and operating the vast majority of its restaurants, Panda has been able to maintain strict training and food quality standards.

The company similarly has no plans to tap into the public markets for investment capital. Still, Panda continues to expand at a rapid pace, adding more than 150 new locations each year, mostly in established markets.

In 2007 Panda sold its 40% stake in FoodBrand to food service operator HMSHost. A subsidiary of mall developer Mills Corporation, FoodBrand managed food court operations in several of Mills' malls in a half-dozen states.

EXECUTIVES

Co-Chairman: Andrew Cherng
Co-Chairman: Peggy T. Cherng, age 60
CEO: Thomas E. (Tom) Davin, age 50
CFO: John F. Theuer
Chief Marketing Officer: Glenn Lunde
EVP Restaurant Development: Kim Ellis
SVP Operations Support and Innovation: Larry Behm
SVP Information Systems: William Yu
VP Real Estate: David Landsberg
VP Operations: Stanley Liu
Chief People Officer: Linda Brandt
Executive Chef, Panda Inn: Sun-Fu Huang
Executive Chef, Panda Express: Andy Kao
General Counsel: Mike Wilkinson

LOCATIONS

HQ: Panda Restaurant Group, Inc.
1683 Walnut Grove Ave., Rosemead, CA 91770
Phone: 626-799-9898 **Fax:** 626-372-8288
Web: www.pandarg.com

COMPETITORS

AFC Enterprises	Jack in the Box
Arby's	Kahala
Burger King	L&L Hawaiian Barbecue
Café de Coral	McDonald's
Chick-fil-A	Quiznos
Chipotle	Sbarro
CKE Restaurants	Subway
Einstein Noah Restaurant Group	Wendy's
Fazoli's	YUM!

Parsons Brinckerhoff

After converting the US, Parsons Brinckerhoff is spreading its gospel around the globe. A leading transportation engineering firm, the company provides planning, design, construction management, and consulting services for infrastructure projects in about 80 countries worldwide. Organized into three divisions (the Americas, International, and Facilities), it specializes in transportation projects but also works in the environmental, energy, and telecommunications sectors. Founded in 1885 by William Barclay Parsons, the firm designed New York City's first subway. Employee-owned Parsons Brinckerhoff operates from about 150 offices globally.

Parsons Brinckerhoff has contributed to such landmark projects as the Cape Cod Canal, the Detroit-Windsor Tunnel, and the North American Air Defense Command (NORAD). In the 1890s it helped build the first railroad across

China, where the company still works on large infrastructure projects. It also has participated in the design of several of the world's leading public transit systems, including those in Atlanta, San Francisco, Singapore, and Taipei.

Other notable projects in which the globetrotter has been involved are Kuwait's Sabiya Power Station, Egypt's Greater Cairo Metro, Spain's Madrid-Barajas International Airport, and the controversial Central Artery/Tunnel in Boston.

In November 2005 Parsons Brinckerhoff and URS Corporation began joint construction of Santiago Calatrava's PATH terminal and a transportation hub at New York's World Trade Center Ground Zero. The project is expected to cost $2.2 billion and be completed around 2009.

The company is also partnering with Taylor Woodrow and others on bids for construction contracts for the 2012 Olympic Games in London.

EXECUTIVES

Chairman: Thomas J. (Tom) O'Neill
CEO: Keith J. Hawksworth
EVP, CFO, and Director: Richard A. (Rich) Schrader
EVP and Director Human Resources: John J. Ryan
SVP; President, Parsons Brinckerhoff Quade & Douglas: William D. (Bill) Smith
SVP; Chairman, PB Transit & Rail Systems; Northwest District Manager, Parsons Brinckerhoff Quade & Douglas: Anthony Daniels
SVP and National Strategic Sales Manager: Rick Cunningham
SVP and Controller: Andreas K. Rothe
Director Public Relations: Thomas W. (Tom) Malcolm
Human Resources Manager: Deborah Jasper
Auditors: Ernst & Young LLP

LOCATIONS

HQ: Parsons Brinckerhoff Inc.
1 Penn Plaza, New York, NY 10119
Phone: 212-465-5000   **Fax:** 212-465-5096
Web: www.pbworld.com

Parsons Brinckerhoff operates in three divisions: the Americas (North and South America); International (Europe, Africa, Middle East, Asia, Australia); and Facilities (facility operations and US federal government contracting).

PRODUCTS/OPERATIONS

Major Operations

Construction management
Design and engineering
E-Business and E-Media
Environmental
Management consulting
Operations and maintenance
Planning
Program management

Selected Subsidiaries

Parsons Brinckerhoff Limited (engineering services for infrastructure projects)
PB Asia
PB Australia
PBConsult Inc. (management consulting services)
PB Energy Storage Services (underground storage facilities construction)
PB PlaceMaking (transit development)
PB Power (energy consultancy services)
PB Telecommunications (engineering services for telecommunications networks)

COMPETITORS

AECOM
BE&K
Black & Veatch
CH2M HILL
Granite Construction
HNTB Companies
Jacobs Engineering
Louis Berger
Parsons Corporation
Skidmore Owings
Smith Management Construction
STS Consultants
STV
Tutor-Saliba
URS
Washington Division

Parsons Corporation

Almost evangelically, Parsons carries its message — and its engineering, procurement, and construction management services — worldwide. The company provides design, planning, and construction management through five main operating groups: water and infrastructure, construction, commercial technology, infrastructure and technology, and transportation. Parsons has designed power plants; built dams, resorts, and shopping centers; and provided environmental services such as the cleanup of hazardous nuclear wastes. Parsons has also added improvements to airports and rail systems, bridges, and highways. Government agencies and private industries are among the top customers of the employee-owned company.

Parsons has diversified in order to compete in every major region — and many major industries — of the world. Parsons Commercial Technology provides services to communications, industrial, and technology customers, including telecom carriers, equipment manufacturers, state and federal government agencies, pharmaceutical firms, defense contractors, and transportation agencies. Parsons Infrastructure & Technology provides construction-related services for environmental and chemical cleanup projects. Parsons Transportation builds, engineers, and manages the construction of projects for government and private clients.

Parsons is a participant in the US Army's program to develop alternative technologies for the destruction of chemical weapons. It also provides engineering management support for the construction of Russia's Chemical Weapons Destruction program. The group has had decades of experience internationally in infrastructure restoration, including work in Bosnia-Herzegovina and Kosovo.

But in war-torn Iraq, Parsons is running into trouble. The army has cancelled the remainder of a $70 million contract to build 20 hospitals in Iraq, due to performance problems with the construction. The company maintains, and an investigation supports, that the construction problems stemmed from mismanagement by the Army Corps of Engineers. Parsons was to design and build military, police, and security sites in Iraq as well as more than 1,000 education

and health facilities throughout the country. However, the US cancelled a $99 million prison contract as well, boding ill for the company's operations in Iraq.

HISTORY

Ralph Parsons, the son of a Long Island fisherman, was born in 1896. At age 13 he started his first business venture, a garage and machine shop, which he operated with his brother. After a stint in the US Navy, Parsons joined Bechtel as an aeronautical engineer. The company changed its name to Bechtel-McCone-Parsons Corporation in 1938. However, Parsons later sold his shares in that company and left in 1944 to start his own design and engineering firm, the Ralph M. Parsons Co., after splitting with partner John McCone (who later headed the CIA).

Parsons Co. expanded into the chemical and petroleum industries in the early 1950s. During that decade it oversaw the building of several natural gas and petroleum refineries overseas, including the world's largest, in Lacq, France.

In the early 1960s the company began working in Kuwait, which later proved to be one of its biggest markets. By 1969 Parsons had built oil refineries for all of the major oil companies, designed launch sites for US missiles, and constructed some of the largest mines in the world. In 1969 the company went public. With annual sales of about $300 million, it ranked second only to Bechtel in the design and engineering field. Ralph Parsons died in 1974.

The company built oil and gas treatment and production plants in Alaska in the 1970s and reorganized itself into The Parsons Corporation and RMP International in 1978. It went private in 1984 as The Parsons Corporation, taking advantage of a new tax law that favored corporations with employee stock ownership plans (ESOPs). Not all employees were happy, though. Several groups sued, maintaining that the plan disproportionately benefited executives, and that the buyout left the ESOP with all of the debt but no decision-making power. A Labor Department investigation later exonerated Parsons executives.

Parsons had just finished work on a power plant in Kuwait when Iraq invaded in 1990. Several employees were detained by the Iraqis but were released shortly before the Persian Gulf War. Two years later the company returned to Kuwait to rebuild some of the country's demolished infrastructure.

James McNulty, who had led the company's infrastructure and technology group, replaced Leonard Pieroni as CEO in 1996 after Pieroni died in a plane crash in Bosnia.

Parsons restructured in 1997 to focus on energy, transportation, and infrastructure projects. In 1999 Parsons was chosen to manage construction of a $5 billion refinery in Bahrain, a $1.4 billion gas plant in Saudi Arabia, and a $1 billion polyethylene project in Abu Dhabi.

Parsons partnered with TRW in 2000 to create TRW Parsons Management & Operations to bid on the DOE's Yucca Mountain site in Nevada, a potential repository for the US's high-level radioactive waste and spent nuclear fuel. It also was awarded a three-year contract to help rebuild the war-torn Serbian province of Kosovo and the next year was awarded a similar contract for Bosnia-Herzegovina.

In 2001 the company won a US Federal Aviation Agency contract to upgrade air traffic control towers and other equipment and systems, a contract that had been held by rival Raytheon since 1988. That year the company's joint venture with construction giant Fluor was awarded a contract to design and do engineering work for the first offshore oil field in Kazakhstan.

In 2002, Parsons completed construction of the Parsons Fabrication Facility as a part for the US Army's push for alternative methods of chemical weapons disposal.

Also that year, Parsons won a contract from Dallas Area Rapid Transit (DART) to provide systems engineering and construction management services for the second phase of the buildout for the light-rail system, the largest expansion of its kind in North America. In 2004 the Parsons' joint venture with Kellogg Brown & Root won a controversial defense contract for oil field and refinery engineering, construction, and maintenance in Iraq.

Another project for Parsons was the design and engineering support for construction of Carquinez Bridge near San Francisco, the first major suspension bridge to be built in the US in more than 35 years.

EXECUTIVES

Chairman: James F. (Jim) McNulty, age 66
Vice Chairman, EVP, Chief Risk Officer, and Special Assistant to the CEO: Curtis A. (Curt) Bower
CEO and Director: Charles L. (Chuck) Harrington
President and COO: John A. (Jack) Scott
EVP and CFO: George L. Ball
EVP, Parsons Water & Infrastructure:
  Martin N. (Marty) Fabrick
EVP, Parsons Construction Group:
  Stephen M. (Steve) Shive
SVP Government Relations: James E. Thrash
SVP, Secretary, and General Counsel:
  Clyde E. (Sonny) Ellis Jr.
SVP Government Relations: Andrew Bonds
SVP and Manager, International Division, Parsons Infrastructure and Technology Group:
  Earnest O. Robbins II
SVP, Rail and Transit: P. Takis Salpeas
VP Corporate Relations: Erin M. Kuhlman
VP Human Resources: David R. Goodrich
VP Safety: Andrew D. Peters
President, Transportation: James R. (Jim) Shappell
President, Construction: Andrew C. Albrecht
President, Infrastructure and Technology:
  Thomas L. (Tom) Roell
President, Water and Infrastructure:
  Richard N. (Rich) Wankmuller
President, Parsons Commercial Technology Group:
  Michael M. (Mike) Walsh

LOCATIONS

HQ: Parsons Corporation
  100 W. Walnut St., Pasadena, CA 91124
Phone: 626-440-2000   **Fax:** 626-440-2630
Web: www.parsons.com

PRODUCTS/OPERATIONS

Selected Markets and Services

Parsons Commercial Technology
  Advanced manufacturing
  Commercial facilities
  Data management services
  Educational facilities
  Entertainment
  Healthcare
  Industrial environmental remediation
  Life sciences
  Mission critical facilities
  Telecommunications
  Vehicle inspection and compliance
  Wireless telecommunications systems

Parsons Infrastructure and Technology
  Community relations
  Construction
  Construction management
  Design
  Engineering
  Estimating
  Operations
  Operator training
  Procurement
  Program management
  Start-up and operations
Parsons Transportation
  Aviation
  Bridges
  Highways
  Railroads
  Revenue collection & management systems
  Systems engineering
  Transportation consumer services
  Transportation planning
  Tunneling
  Urban Transit
Parsons Water and Infrastructure
  Biosolids management
  Combined sewer overflows
  Construction/Construction management
  Desalination and membrane technology
  Design-build
  Emergency response support
  Environmental planning and restoration
  Master planning
  Ocean outfalls
  Operations and maintenance
  Storm water management
  Utility tunneling
  Wastewater collection systems
  Wastewater treatment
  Water resources
  Water supply and pipelines

COMPETITORS

ABB
AECOM
ARCADIS
BE&K
Bechtel
Black & Veatch
Bouygues
Day & Zimmermann
Dick Corporation
Fluor
Foster Wheeler
Gilbane
Granite Construction
Halliburton
Hill International
HOCHTIEF
Hyundai Engineering
Jacobs Engineering
Kaiser Group
KBR
Layne Christensen
Lend Lease
Louis Berger
M. A. Mortenson
Michael Baker
Mott MacDonald
Paragon Project Resources
Peter Kiewit Sons'
RailWorks
RBF Consulting
Shaw Group
Technip
Telesource International
TIC Holdings
Turner Corporation
Tutor-Saliba
URS
Vecellio & Grogan
Washington Division

HISTORICAL FINANCIALS
Company Type: Private

Income Statement

	REVENUE ($ mil.)	NET INCOME ($ mil.)	NET PROFIT MARGIN	EMPLOYEES
12/07	3,600	—	—	11,500
12/06	2,710	—	—	11,500
12/05	3,000	—	—	11,600
12/04	1,990	—	—	10,000
12/03	1,651	—	—	9,000
Annual Growth	21.5%	—	—	6.3%

FYE: December 31

Revenue History

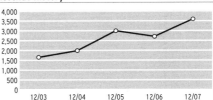

Paul, Hastings, Janofsky & Walker

Paul, Hastings, Janofsky & Walker has built a solid reputation in employment law, and over the years companies such as United Parcel Service and Hughes Aircraft have turned to the firm for its expertise in the field. With about 1,300 attorneys, Paul Hastings also practices in such areas as intellectual property, litigation, mergers and acquisitions, and real estate. Paul Hastings operates from about 20 offices, not only in the US but also in Europe and the Asia/Pacific region. The firm was founded in 1951; it adopted its current name in 1962.

EXECUTIVES

Chairman: Seth M. Zachary
Managing Partner: Greg M. Nitzkowski
Global Chairman, Litigation Department and Partner, Washington, DC: James D. (Jamie) Wareham
Chair, Corporate Department and Partner, Los Angeles: Robert A. Miller Jr.
Chair, Employment Law Department and Partner, Los Angeles: Nancy L. Abell
Chair, Real Estate Department and Partner, Los Angeles: Philip N. Feder
Chair, Tax Department: Douglas A. Schaaf
Chief Administrative Officer: Adam Norris
Chief Business Development and Marketing Officer: Meg Sullivan
Managing Director Diversity and Global Talent: Anton Mack
Director Public Relations: Eileen King

LOCATIONS

HQ: Paul, Hastings, Janofsky & Walker LLP
  515 S. Flower St., 25th Fl., Los Angeles, CA 90071
Phone: 213-683-6000   **Fax:** 213-627-0705
Web: www.paulhastings.com

PRODUCTS/OPERATIONS

Selected Practice Areas

Affordable housing and tax credits
Antitrust and competition
Appellate litigation
Asset securitization and structured finance
Banking and financial institutions
Bankruptcy litigation
Base realignment and closures
Class actions
Commercial leasing and sales leaseback
Copyright
Corporate
Counseling and preventive advice
Disaster mitigation
E-discovery
Employment class actions
Employment law
Employment litigation
Environmental law
ERISA, employee benefits, and executive compensation
Estate planning and probate
Finance and restructuring
Financial litigation
Financial services
Foreign corrupt practices act
Government affairs
Government contracts litigation
Immigration
Intellectual property
Intellectual property transactions and licensing
International arbitration
International employment law
International trade and export controls
Investment management
Labor/management relations
Land use
Leveraged finance
Litigation
Mergers and acquisitions
Patent litigation
Patent preparation and prosecution
Payment systems
Political risk and international trade credit insurance
Private equity
Private investment funds
Product liability and toxic tort
Project development and finance
Purchase and sale of non-performing loans
Real estate
Real estate acquisitions and dispositions
Real estate equity investments and joint ventures
Real estate finance
Real estate capital markets
Real estate litigation
Real estate restructuring and reorganization
Regulatory compliance
Restructuring
Securities finance and capital markets
Securities litigation and enforcement
Sustainability and global climate change
Tax advisory
Trade secrets
Trademark
White collar, internal investigations, and corporate governance

COMPETITORS

Baker & McKenzie
DLA Piper
Gibson, Dunn & Crutcher
Jones Day
Latham & Watkins
Littler Mendelson
Morrison & Foerster
O'Melveny & Myers
Orrick
Perkins Coie
Pillsbury Winthrop Shaw Pittman
Seyfarth Shaw
Skadden, Arps
Wilson Sonsini

HISTORICAL FINANCIALS

Company Type: Partnership

Income Statement

FYE: January 31

	REVENUE ($ mil.)	NET INCOME ($ mil.)	NET PROFIT MARGIN	EMPLOYEES
1/08	976	—	—	2,500
1/07	814	—	—	2,500
1/06	667	—	—	2,650
1/05	609	—	—	—
1/04	537	—	—	—
Annual Growth	16.1%	—	—	(2.9%)

Revenue History

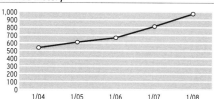

PBS

You might say these shows get a lot of public support. Public Broadcasting Service (PBS) is a non-profit organization that provides educational and public interest programming to more than 350 public TV stations in the US. In addition to such programs as *NOVA*, *This Old House*, and *Masterpiece Theatre*, it provides related services such as distribution, fundraising support, and technology development. PBS gets its revenue from underwriting, membership dues, federal funding (including grants from the not-for-profit Corporation for Public Broadcasting), royalties, license fees, and product sales. The organization was founded in 1969 to provide cultural and educational programming.

While PBS — and its federal funding — regularly finds itself caught in the crossfire between liberal and conservative political groups, supporters of the non-profit trumpet the benefits of publicly funded television programming created to serve groups often overlooked by commercial broadcasters. Children's programming and serious news shows such as *Frontline* and *The NewsHour with Jim Lehrer* are often touted as examples of how public broadcasting can fill voids left by the major networks.

Being supported by public stations and federal grants hasn't prevented PBS from pursuing additional support from corporate America, however. To augment federal funding, the organization courts underwriting dollars from corporations willing to foot the bill for such productions as Ken Burns' epic WWII documentary *The War*.

Meanwhile, PBS has been focused on new ways to distribute its programming. Adding to DVD sales, the organization has partnered with Apple to make certain programming available for purchase through its iTunes store.

EXECUTIVES

Chair: John E. Porter
General Vice Chair: Robert J. Flowers
Professional Vice Chair: Peter Frid
President, CEO, and Director: Paula A. Kerger
COO: W. Wayne Godwin
CFO and Treasurer; SVP, Corporate Services: Barbara L. Landes
SVP and Chief TV Programming Executive: John F. Wilson
SVP, General Counsel, and Corporate Secretary: Katherine Lauderdale
SVP PBS KIDS Next Generation Media: Lesli Rotenberg
SVP PBS Ventures: Andrew L. Russell
SVP Interactive: Jason Seiken
SVP Programming Services: Pat Hunter
SVP Education: Robert M. Lippincott
Chief Content Officer: John L. Boland
CTO: John McCoskey
Director Public Relations: Jenni Glenn
Auditors: BDO Seidman, LLP

LOCATIONS

HQ: Public Broadcasting Service
2100 Crystal Dr., Arlington, VA 22202
Phone: 703-739-5000　　**Fax:** 703-739-8495
Web: www.pbs.org

PRODUCTS/OPERATIONS

2007 Sales

	$ mil.	% of total
Underwriting	219.7	35
Member fees	165.6	27
Grants	115.9	18
Products	35.2	6
Royalties, license fees & other	87.7	14
Total	**624.1**	**100**

Selected Programming

Antiques Roadshow
Austin City Limits
Barney
Evening at Pops
Frontier House
Frontline
Great Performances
In The Mix
Juila Child: Lessons with Master Chefs
Live from Lincoln Center
Masterpiece Theatre
Mister Rogers' Neighborhood
MotorWeek
Mystery!
Nature
The NewsHour with Jim Lehrer
NOVA
NOW
P.O.V.
Reading Rainbow
Sesame Street
Teletubbies
This Old House
Victory Garden
Washington Week
ZOOM

COMPETITORS

A&E Networks
ABC
BBC Worldwide
CBS
Discovery Communications
FOX Broadcasting
HBO
NBC
Scripps Networks

HISTORICAL FINANCIALS

Company Type: Not-for-profit

Income Statement

FYE: June 30

	REVENUE ($ mil.)	NET INCOME ($ mil.)	NET PROFIT MARGIN	EMPLOYEES
6/07	624	102	16.3%	—
6/06	573	82	14.3%	—
6/05	532	—	—	—
6/04	517	—	—	507
6/03	498	—	—	—
Annual Growth	5.8%	24.1%	—	—

2007 Year-End Financials

Debt ratio: —   Current ratio: —
Return on equity: 32.4%   Long-term debt ($ mil.): —
Cash ($ mil.): —

Net Income History

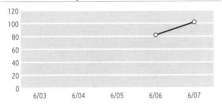

P.C. Richard & Son

P.C. Richard & Son aims to short out Circuit City. The family-owned company has about 50 electronics stores in the New York City area. P.C. Richard sells home electronics (DVD players, TVs), computers and appliances (microwaves, vacuum cleaners), and entertainment systems (portable electronics, video games, satellites). P.C. Richard also sells its wares online. In 2003 the company acquired the name, trademark, and customer lists of bankrupt electronics chain Nobody Beats The Wiz. Founded in 1909 by Dutch immigrant milkman and jack-of-all-trades Peter Christiään Richard as a hardware store, the firm is operated by fourth-generation Richard family members.

EXECUTIVES

CEO: Gary Richard
President: Gregg Richard
EVP: Peter Richard II
VP and CFO: Tom Pohmer
CTO: Chuck Fichtner
Director Human Resources: Bonni Rondinello
Manager Operations: Peter Richard III

LOCATIONS

HQ: P.C. Richard & Son
    150 Price Pkwy., Farmingdale, NY 11735
Phone: 631-843-4300   **Fax:** 631-843-4309
Web: www.pcrichard.com

PRODUCTS/OPERATIONS

Selected Products

Appliances
Camcorders
Cameras
Home office
Mobile
Portable electronics
Televisions
Vacuums
Video games

COMPETITORS

Best Buy
Circuit City
Harvey Electronics
J & R Electronics
Lowe's
REX Stores
Sears
Sixth Avenue Electronics
Wal-Mart

Pediatric Services of America

Pediatric Services of America (doing business as PSA HealthCare) knows there's no place like home, especially when you're a sick kid. The pediatric home health care company provides in-home nursing and related services for infants and children through offices in 18 states. The company also offers rehabilitation and nursing through day treatment centers in Florida and Georgia. Additionally, PSA HealthCare offers case management programs that coordinate services among insurers, doctors, and other health care providers. In 2007 private investment firm Portfolio Logic, which previously owned about 15% of PSA, took the firm private.

In 2006 PSA HealthCare sold its respiratory therapy and equipment business — which provided ventilators, oxygen systems, and other breathing equipment to children and adults — to Lincare. The company had previously sold its pharmacy business to Accredo Health for about $70 million.

The two divestitures allow PSA to focus exclusively on its core pediatric nursing business. It has been using the proceeds to acquire or establish in-home nursing branches in existing and new markets. In 2007, for example, it bought several private nursing businesses in Texas, as well as operations in Pennsylvania and Illinois.

EXECUTIVES

President, CEO, and Director: Daniel J. (Dan) Kohl, age 51, $582,400 pay
VP Human Resources: Wesley E. Debnam
VP Information Systems: Thomas D. (Tom) Zeimet
VP Business Development: Mark A. Kulick
VP, CFO, Secretary, and Treasurer: Lori J. Reel
VP Compliance: Dale Valentine
VP Operations, Private Duty Nursing, and Pediatric Day Treatment Centers for Medically Fragile Children: Elizabeth A. (Beth) Rubio
VP Reimbursement: Jeffrey K. (Jeff) Nickell
General Counsel and Chief Risk Officer: John R. Hamilton III
Auditors: Ernst & Young LLP

LOCATIONS

HQ: Pediatric Services of America, Inc.
    310 Technology Pkwy., Norcross, GA 30092
Phone: 770-441-1580   **Fax:** 770-263-9340
Web: www.psahealthcare.com

PSA HealthCare has branch offices in California, Colorado, Connecticut, Florida, Georgia, Illinois, Indiana, Louisiana, Massachusetts, New Jersey, New York, North Carolina, Oregon, Pennsylvania, South Carolina, Texas, Virginia, and Washington.

PRODUCTS/OPERATIONS

Selected Services

Pediatric private-duty nursing
    24/7 hourly private-duty care
    Care management
    Home health aids
    Medical social workers
    Speech, occupational, and physical therapy
Pediatric day treatment centers
    Care management
    Extended weekday day care
    Progress assessments
    Transportation services

COMPETITORS

Amedisys
American HomePatient
Gentiva
Home Health Corporation of America
National HealthCare
National Home Health
New York Health Care
Personal-Touch Home Care

Pella Corporation

Call Pella more practical than romantic; it can't make a window to your soul, but it can make windows for your house. Since the mid-1920s, Pella has designed, manufactured, and installed window and door products made from wood, vinyl, and fiberglass for construction and remodeling in the residential and commercial sectors. Many of its windows are energy efficient. Pella operates a nationwide network of stores and also sells its products through retailers in the US and Canada, as well as distributors in Asia, Mexico, Russia, the Middle East, and the UK. Do-it-yourselfers can find its windows and patio doors at such stores as Lowe's. Descendants of founder Pete Kuyper own Pella.

Pella was founded in 1925 as the Rolscreen Company. The company was named after its first product, a roll-up window screen. Updated in design, the patented Rolscreen insect screen still remains a popular product.

These days, the company is capitalizing on the "green craze" by continuing to develop window and door products that save energy and cut heating and cooling costs. That commitment has been recognized with an ENERGY STAR award by the US Department of Energy.

EXECUTIVES

Chairman: Charles (Charlie) Farver
President and CEO: Melvin R. (Mel) Haught
SVP, CFO, and Secretary: A. Jacqueline (Jackie) Dout, age 53
VP Human Resources: Karin Peterson
Corporate Public Relations: Kathy Krafka Harkema
Pella Corporation Sponsorships: Leanna Hafften
IT Supply Chain Manager: Peter Genheimer

LOCATIONS

HQ: Pella Corporation
102 Main St., Pella, IA 50219
Phone: 641-628-1000   **Fax:** 641-628-6070
Web: www.pella.com

Pella has manufacturing plants in Macomb, Illinois; Carroll, Pella, Shenandoah, and Sioux Center, Iowa; Columbia, South Carolina; Fairfield, Ohio; Gettysburg, Pennsylvania; Murray, Kentucky; Portland, Oregon; Tucson, Arizona; and Wylie, Texas. EFCO, a Pella company, makes commercial products in Monett, Missouri.

PRODUCTS/OPERATIONS

Selected Products

Doors
  Fiberglass
  Hinged patio
  Sliding patio
  Steel entry
  Storm door
Windows
  Angled
  Awning
  Bay/bow
  Casement
  Curved
  Double-hung
  Fixed
  Garden
  Single-hung
  Sliding
  Special (skylight)

Selected Brands

Architect
Designer Series
Pella Impervia
Proline
Vinyl by Pella
Pella Entry Door Systems

Selected Materials

Fiberglass
Steel
Vinyl
Wood

COMPETITORS

Andersen Corporation
Atrium Companies
Designer Doors
GBO
International Aluminum
JELD-WEN
Marshfield DoorSystems
NTK Holdings
Ply Gem
Sierra Pacific Industries
Silver Line Building Products
Simonton Windows, Inc.
Thermal Industries
Therma-Tru
Tomkins

Penn Mutual Life Insurance

Founded in 1847, Penn Mutual Life Insurance offers life insurance, annuities, and investment products and services. Its core product line includes life insurance every which way, disability income insurance policies, and a full range of deferred and immediate annuity products. It sells its policies through a national network of career and independent agents. Penn Mutual also distributes its own and third-party products through nationwide brokerage subsidiary Hornor, Townsend & Kent. Another broker/dealer subsidiary, Janney Montgomery Scott, operates in the Eastern US. In addition, the company provides trust services to individuals and institutions through The Pennsylvania Trust Company.

EXECUTIVES

Chairman, President, and CEO: Robert E. Chappell, age 63
EVP and CFO: Peter J. Vogt
EVP and Chief Investment Officer: Peter M. Sherman
EVP and Chief Marketing Officer: Eileen C. McDonnell
EVP Technology and Service Operations: Terry Ramey
SVP Market Conduct and General Auditor:
  Nina M. Mulrooney
SVP Human Resources: Edward F. Clemons
SVP and Treasurer: Barbara S. Wood
Managing Corporate Counsel and Secretary: Frank Best
President and CEO, Hornor, Townsend & Kent:
  Michelle Barry
President and CEO, Janney Montgomery Scott:
  Timothy C. (Tim) Scheve, age 50

LOCATIONS

HQ: The Penn Mutual Life Insurance Company
600 Dresher Rd., Horsham, PA 19044
Phone: 215-956-8000   **Fax:** 215-956-7699
Web: www.pennmutual.com

Penn Mutual Life Insurance operates throughout the US.

PRODUCTS/OPERATIONS

2007 Sales

	$ mil.	% of total
Premiums	444.8	31
Investment income	425.3	29
Other	577.5	40
Total	**1,447.6**	**100**

Selected Subsidiaries and Affiliates

Hornor, Townsend & Kent, Inc. (securities broker/dealer)
Independence Capital Management, Inc. (in-house asset management)
Janney Montgomery Scott LLC (securities brokerage)
The Pennsylvania Trust Company (investment advisory & trust services)

COMPETITORS

AEGON USA	Midland National Life
Aetna	Nationwide Financial
AIG	New York Life
American National	OM Financial
Insurance	Pacific Mutual
AXA Financial	Primerica
Erie Family Life Insurance	Protective Life
The Hartford	Prudential
ING Americas	Securian Financial
John Hancock Financial	Security Benefit Group
Manulife Financial	Sentry Insurance
MassMutual	TIAA-CREF
MetLife	Union Central

HISTORICAL FINANCIALS

Company Type: Mutual company

Income Statement

FYE: December 31

	ASSETS ($ mil.)	NET INCOME ($ mil.)	INCOME AS % OF ASSETS	EMPLOYEES
12/07	14,480	137	0.9%	3,000
12/06	14,082	145	1.0%	3,000
12/05	13,092	112	0.9%	—
12/04	14,251	137	1.0%	550
12/03	13,065	108	0.8%	1,100
Annual Growth	**2.6%**	**6.2%**	**—**	**28.5%**

2007 Year-End Financials

Equity as % of assets: 14.1%   Long-term debt ($ mil.): —
Return on assets: 1.0%   Sales ($ mil.): 1,448
Return on equity: 7.0%

Net Income History

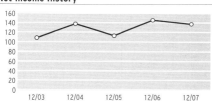

Pennsylvania Lottery

Even if they don't become millionaires, senior citizens in Pennsylvania can still benefit from the state lottery. Established in 1971, Pennsylvania Lottery proceeds (more than $16.5 billion raised since inception) are dedicated to programs geared toward seniors (property-tax relief, rent rebates, reduced-cost transportation, co-pay prescriptions). Proceeds also fund more than 50 Area Agencies on Aging across Pennsylvania. State law mandates that at least 40% of lottery proceeds must be awarded in prizes, and at least 30% must be used for benefit programs. Games range from the traditional Powerball to daily-wagering game Big 4. IGT Online Entertainment Systems operates the lottery's computer systems.

EXECUTIVES

Executive Director: Ed Mahlman
Executive Director, Administration and Finance:
  Tom Shaub
Executive Director, Marketing: Ed Trees

Director, Field Operations: Bob Siodlowski
Director, Product Delivery: Bill Powell
Director, Public Relations: Cris Stambaugh
Director, Research and Development: Drew Svitko
Director, Security: Jim Morgan
Deputy Director, Marketing: Connie Bloss
Division Chief, Computer Services: Byron Olenski
Press Secretary, Pennsylvania Lottery and Pennsylvania Department of Revenue: Steven L Kniley

LOCATIONS

HQ: The Pennsylvania Lottery
1200 Fulling Mill Rd., Ste. 1, Middletown, PA 17057
Phone: 717-702-8000   **Fax:** 717-702-8024
Web: www.palottery.state.pa.us

The Pennsylvania Lottery has offices throughout Pennsylvania in Clearfield, Erie, Harrisburg, Lehigh, Middletown, Philadelphia, Pittsburgh, and Wilkes-Barre.

PRODUCTS/OPERATIONS

2007 Game Sales

	$ mil.	% of total
Instant	1,706.8	55
Daily Number	416.1	13
Powerball	302.6	10
Big 4	270.3	9
Cash Five	186.1	6
Match 6	77.7	2
Powerplay	54.3	2
Mix & Match	26.7	1
Raffle	25.2	1
Treasure hunt	23.4	1
Total	**3,089.2**	**100**

Selected Games

Instant games (scratch-off tickets)
  Doughman Dollars
  Lifetime Riches
  Lucky Day
  Money Farm
  Santa's List
  Sleigh Ride Riches
  Triple 777
Numbers games
  Big 4 (daily)
  Cash 5 (daily)
  Daily Number (daily)
  Match 6
  Powerball
  Powerplay

COMPETITORS

Connecticut Lottery
Maryland State Lottery
Multi-State Lottery
New Jersey Lottery
New York State Lottery
Ohio Lottery
Virginia Lottery

HISTORICAL FINANCIALS

Company Type: Government-owned

Income Statement

FYE: June 30

	REVENUE ($ mil.)	NET INCOME ($ mil.)	NET PROFIT MARGIN	EMPLOYEES
6/08	3,089	928	30.0%	—
6/07	3,076	949	30.9%	—
6/06	3,070	965	31.4%	—
6/05	2,645	852	32.2%	—
6/04	2,352	817	34.7%	—
Annual Growth	7.1%	3.2%	—	—

Net Income History

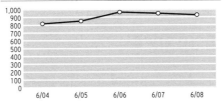

Pension Benefit Guaranty Corporation

Underfunded pension plans give PBGC the heebie-jeebies. The Pension Benefit Guaranty Corporation, or PBGC, itself operating at a multi-billion-dollar deficit, was set up to promote the growth of defined-benefit pension plans, provide payment of retirement benefits, and keep pension premiums as low as possible. The government agency protects the pensions of more than 34 million workers and monitors employers to ensure that plans are adequately funded. The agency receives no tax funds; its income is generated by insurance premiums paid by employers, investments, and assets recovered from terminated plans. The corporation was created by the Employee Retirement Income Security Act of 1974.

Insurance premiums paid by employers go into two programs: single-employer (about 28,800 pension plans) and multi-employer (some 1,540 pension plans under collective bargaining agreements that involve several unrelated employers). Employers pay about $8 per employee in the multi-employer plans and about $31 per employee for single-employer programs (plus a flat fee per $1,000 of unfunded vested benefits in underfunded plans).

PBGC terminates pension plans when it determines that a company can no longer pay benefits; it can take a portion of a company's assets to ensure that pension obligations are met. When PBGC takes over a failed plan, it pays each individual pensioner covered by the plan up to $50,000 annually.

Many companies are moving from traditional defined benefit pension plans to so-called defined contribution plans, usually reducing the benefits of long-time workers in the process. Workers and their advocates criticize the switched plans, but they don't come under PBGC's jurisdiction unless they fail.

HISTORY

The Employment Retirement Income Security Act (ERISA) of 1974 established the Pension Benefit Guaranty Corporation (PBGC) to protect workers' pension benefits. The poor economy of the day guaranteed PBGC plenty of business. By 1975 more than 1,000 companies were unable to meet pension obligations. Other companies tried to avoid entering the system by terminating their plans before a 1996 deadline; the Supreme Court in 1980 upheld PBGC's contention that these companies were obligated to pay benefits to vested workers.

ERISA's provisions initially let companies voluntarily terminate their plans by paying PBGC a portion of their assets; many companies took this route until Congress limited the provision. Pensions faced a new threat in the late 1980s, as many buyout deals were structured to use company pension plans as part of their funding; Congress put a stop to that practice in 1990.

Companies found themselves caught between conflicting requirements of the PBGC (ever watchful for underfunded pension plans) and the IRS (which penalized overfunded plans). PBGC's deficit grew as it took on more and more pension payment liabilities; companies continued to jeopardize plans by using funds for other purposes. On behalf of 40,000 workers, PBGC in 1988 sued companies that allegedly terminated their plans illegally between 1976 and 1981 (the suit was settled in 1995 for $100 million).

In 1989 new director James Lockhart began airing PBGC's plight, claiming that the pension system would follow the savings and loan industry into collapse. In the early 1990s his predictions seemed reasonable; PBGC's deficit was driven sky-high by such bankruptcies as Pan Am (1991), TWA, and Munsingwear (1992). Under Lockhart's guidance, the PBGC began publishing the "iffy fifty" — the 50 most underfunded pensions in the country.

Martin Slate succeeded Lockhart in 1993 and toned down the Chicken Little rhetoric, although that year PBGC announced that underfunding had nearly doubled between 1987 and 1992. Help arrived in the form of 1994's Retirement Protection Act, which put some teeth into pension laws. Under the reforms, PBGC required some employers to notify workers and retirees about the funding of their plans; it also changed the rules for annual reporting to the PBGC. The next year President Clinton vetoed the budget bill, which would have allowed companies to take money from their pension plans.

Slate died in 1997 and David Strauss took over. After two decades in the red, PBGC in 1998 marked its third consecutive year in the black. The organization was sued by several former Pan Am workers who claimed PBGC had shorted their benefits. That year PBGC announced that LTV, the giant steel company that went bankrupt in 1993, could resume monthly pension payments to retired workers.

In 1999 PBGC defended itself against critics who claimed it took too long to determine benefits from bankrupt companies and often required pensioners to repay thousands of dollars that had been paid in estimated benefits. A year later, with a $10 billion surplus under PBGC's belt, Strauss said that Congress should permit well-funded pensions a holiday from paying premiums.

PBGC experienced a string of losses in 2002, the largest in the single-employer programs; the agency recorded an $11 billion deficit the next year, primarily due to terminated pension plans. Posting a $23.5 billion deficit in 2004 prompted the government to create a plan to protect the agency from going bankrupt. Losses decreased slightly over the years, but by 2007, PBGC was still more than $13 billion in the red.

EXECUTIVES

Acting Inspector General: Deborah Stover-Springer
Chief of Staff: George Koklanaris
COO: Richard H. Macy
CFO: Patricia Kelly
Chief Management Officer: Stephen E. Barber
Chief Insurance Program Officer: Terrence M. Deneen
General Counsel: Judith R. Starr

Director, Budget Department: Henry R. Thompson
Director Contracts and Controls Review Department: Martin O. Boehm
Director, Benefits Administration and Payment Department (BAPD): Bennie Hagans
Director Facilities and Services Department (FASD): Patricia Davis
Director Strategic Planning and Evaluation Department (SPED): Wilmer Graham
Director, Legislative and Regulatory Department: John R. Hanley
Acting Director, Policy, Research, and Analysis Department (PRAD): David Gustafson
Director, Pension Benefit Guaranty Corporation: Charles E. F. Millard
Acting Director Department of Insurance Supervision and Compliance (DISC): Robert D. Bacon
Acting Director, Financial Operations Department (FOD): Walter A. Luiza
Acting Director Communications and Public Affairs Department (CPAD): Jeffrey Speicher
Director Procurement Department: Susan Taylor
Director Human Relations Department: Arrie Etheridge
CIO: Patsy A. Garnett

LOCATIONS

HQ: Pension Benefit Guaranty Corporation
1200 K St. NW, Washington, DC 20005
Phone: 202-326-4000   **Fax:** 202-326-4042
Web: www.pbgc.gov

PRODUCTS/OPERATIONS

2007 Sales

	% of total
Single-employer program	
Premium income	74
Investment income	23
Other income	1
Multi-employer program	
Premium income	1
Investment income	1
Total	**100**

HISTORICAL FINANCIALS

Company Type: Government agency

Income Statement

FYE: September 30

	REVENUE ($ mil.)	NET INCOME ($ mil.)	NET PROFIT MARGIN	EMPLOYEES
9/07	5,325	4,815	90.4%	—
9/06	9,526	4,230	44.4%	—
9/05	5,497	—	—	—
9/04	4,760	—	—	—
9/03	4,387	—	—	—
Annual Growth	**5.0%**	**13.8%**	**—**	**—**

Net Income History

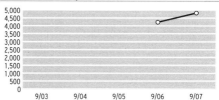

Penske Corporation

Penske, headed by race-car legend Roger Penske, appears to be on the right track as a diversified transportation firm. Penske is a partner with GE Equipment Management in Penske Truck Leasing, a commercial truck rental operation with about 200,000 vehicles at some 1,000 locations. Penske owns about 40% of publicly traded auto dealer Penske Automotive Group (formerly United Auto Group), which runs 300-plus franchised dealerships in some 20 states, Germany, Puerto Rico, and the UK. Through Penske Motor the company sells cars in California. Truck-Lite makes safety lights for boats, buses, cars, commercial trucks, construction equipment, and recreational vehicles. Roger Penske is the majority owner of the company.

Other Penske interests include Michigan-based DAVCO, a leader in Class 8 heavy duty diesel powered truck fuel-heater/water separators and filter systems; QEK Global Solutions, a provider of vehicle management services such as fleet planning and management; and logistics service provider Penske Logistics.

The company sold its 50% stake in Italy's VM Motori, which specializes in the design and production of diesel engines, to Russian auto maker GAZ Group in 2008.

Penske just can't seem to resist that new car smell. The company has sold its racetrack interests and upped its stake in Penske Automotive Group (PAG). Roger Penske personally visited most of PAG's dealerships to help return the chain to profitability. He now heads PAG.

Penske souped up its Penske Truck Leasing unit with the purchase of Rollins Truck Leasing, which was the US's third-largest truck rental and leasing player.

Penske is also a lead investment partner in Transportation Resource Partners, which is part of a group that acquired automotive component maker Autocam in 2004.

HISTORY

As a teen Roger Penske earned money by repairing and reselling cars. At 21 he entered his first auto race; he was running second when his car overheated. His winning ways, however, were soon apparent, and in 1961 *Sports Illustrated* named him race-car driver of the year.

Nonetheless, in 1965 Penske went looking for a day job. With a $150,000 loan from his father, he bought a Chevrolet dealership in Philadelphia and retired from racing to avoid loading his balance sheet with steep life-insurance premiums for the CEO. Penske teamed with driver Mark Donohue in 1966 to form the Penske Racing Team. Donohue died in a crash in 1975, but team Penske continued.

In 1969 Penske started a regional truck-leasing business, incorporated under the name Penske. The company established auto dealerships in Pennsylvania and Ohio in the early 1970s. In 1975 the company bought the Michigan International Speedway. Penske and fellow racing team owner Pat Patrick started the race-sponsoring organization Championship Auto Racing Teams (CART) in 1978.

In 1982 Penske's truck-leasing business formed a joint venture with rental company Hertz to form Hertz Penske Truck Leasing. Penske expanded its auto dealerships in the

1980s by acquiring dealerships in California, including Longo Toyota in 1985.

Racing legend Al Unser Sr. surprised Indy 500 watchers in 1987 by driving a car borrowed from an exhibition in a hotel lobby to a first-place finish for the Penske Racing Team.

In 1988 Penske bought 80% of GM's Detroit Diesel engine-making unit, which had a market share of only 3% and had lost some $600 million over the previous five years. Penske trimmed $70 million from the unit's budget by firing 440 salaried employees, streamlining manufacturing processes, and cutting administration expenses. Detroit Diesel's market share doubled in its first two years as a Penske unit. Also in 1988 Penske purchased Hertz's stake in Hertz Penske Truck Leasing, which it later combined with the truck-rental division of appliance maker General Electric to create Penske Truck Leasing.

By 1993 Detroit Diesel's market share had grown to more than 25%. That year the engine maker went public. Penske bought 860 Kmart auto centers for $112 million in 1995. The company's racing business, Penske Motorsports, went public in 1996, but Penske retained a 55% stake in the company. Also that year Penske bought Truck-Lite, Quaker State's automotive lighting unit.

Penske Truck Leasing formed Penske Logistics Europe in 1997 to offer information systems and other integrated logistics services on that continent. The next year it formed a logistics joint venture with Brazil-based Cotia Trading to serve US-based clients in the South American market, and Penske Logistics Europe opened a pan-European transport routing center in the Netherlands.

Penske sold its Penske Motorsports operations, which included racetracks in California, Michigan, North Carolina, and Pennsylvania, to International Speedway in 1999. The same year Penske invested about $83 million for a 38% stake in car retailer United Auto Group and Roger Penske became CEO of Penske. In 2000 the company sold its 48.6% stake in Detroit Diesel to Daimler AG.

The following year Penske Corp. added three additional dealerships. Later in 2001 Penske Truck Leasing acquired Rollins Truck Leasing (then the US's third-largest player behind Ryder and Penske) for $754 million.

After Kmart filed Chapter 11 early in 2002, Penske expressed a "wait and see" strategy about the fate of its Penske Auto Centers business. Later that year Penske's Truck-Lite Industries bought Federal-Mogul's lighting business for $23 million.

Early in April 2002 Penske had waited long enough, and didn't like what it saw. It closed its 560-plus Penske Auto Centers at Kmart locations nationwide.

In July 2007 Penske Corporation renamed two of its companies: United Auto Group changed its name to Penske Automotive Group, taking the name of the company's California auto dealership, which changed its name to Penske Motor Group.

EXECUTIVES

Chairman and CEO: Roger S. Penske, age 71
President and Director; Vice Chairman and President, Penske Automotive Group: Robert H. Kurnick Jr., age 47
EVP and CFO: J. Patrick Conroy
EVP: Walt Czarnecki
EVP, Administration: Paul F. Walters, age 63
VP: Tim Cindric

VP, Human Resources: Randall W. Johnson
Chairman, Truck-Lite, Inc.; Managing Partner, Transportation Resource Partners: Richard J. Peters, age 60
Managing Director, South America, Penske Logistics: Bill Scroggie
EVP, Penske Automotive Group, Eastern Region: Bernie Wolfe, age 53
VP Operations, Americas, Penske Logistics: Terry Miller
VP Sales, Strategic Accounts, Penske Logistics: Gary Franz
Director Communications: Randy Ryerson

LOCATIONS

HQ: Penske Corporation
2555 Telegraph Rd., Bloomfield Hills, MI 48302
Phone: 248-648-2000   **Fax:** 248-648-2525
Web: www.penske.com

PRODUCTS/OPERATIONS

Selected Subsidiaries and Affiliates

Davco Technologies, LLC (fuel filters and engine accessories)
Penske Automotive Group, Inc. (about 40%, retail auto sales)
Penske Motor (retail auto sales, California)
Penske Truck Leasing Co. LP (joint venture with GE Equipment Management, truck rental and leasing)
QEK Global Solutions (fleet and vehicle management services)
Truck-Lite Co., Inc. (automotive lighting)

COMPETITORS

AMERCO	Mack Trucks
Asbury Automotive	Navistar
AutoNation	PACCAR
Daimler	Prospect Motors
Fiat	Ryder System
General Motors	Sonic Automotive
Group 1 Automotive	Trailer Fleet Services
Isuzu	Volvo

Pepper Construction

Pepper Construction Group spices up the construction business with a little of this and a pinch of that. The construction operations of The Pepper Companies provide general contractor and construction management services for sectors including health care, retail, commercial, hotels, malls, and schools. Projects include the ape habitat at the Lincoln Park Zoo, with 29,000 sq. ft. of space complete with climbing vines and termite mounds. Pepper Environmental Technologies provides hazardous waste services. Stanley F. Pepper founded the company in Chicago in 1927; the group is owned and run by his family and employees of the firm.

The Pepper Companies formed Pepper Construction Group in 2000 to combine its construction assets. It has divisions in Illinois, Indiana, Ohio, and Texas.

The company's extensive list of clients includes UBS, Indiana University, and Galyan's.

EXECUTIVES

Chairman Emeritus: Richard S. Pepper
Chairman and CEO: J. David (Dave) Pepper II, age 46
CFO: Joel D. Thomason

SVP; President, Pepper Environmental Technologies: Richard H. (Rich) Tilghman
SVP Human Resources: John Beasley
VP IT: Howie Piersma
VP and Treasurer: Linda Nila
President and COO, Pepper Construction Company: Kenneth A. (Ken) Egidi
President, Pepper Construction Company of Indiana: William J. (Bill) McCarthy
President, Pepper-Lawson Construction: Paul E. Lawson
President, Pepper Construction Company of Ohio: Paul Francois
Project Executive: Dan Boland
Director Communications: Shannon Ghera

LOCATIONS

HQ: Pepper Construction Group, LLC
643 N. Orleans St., Chicago, IL 60610
Phone: 312-266-4700   **Fax:** 312-266-2792
Web: www.pepperconstruction.com

COMPETITORS

Barton Malow	Graycor
Bovis Lend Lease	M. A. Mortenson
C. G. Schmidt	Power Construction
Centex	Turner Corporation
Charles Pankow Builders	Walbridge Aldinger
Clark Enterprises	Walsh Group
Gilbane	

Perceptive Software

Perceptive hopes your company is receptive to its document management tools. The company provides software and services that companies use to manage documents, workflows, and other enterprise content. Its ImageNow software suite includes tools for document and content capture, integration, imaging, Web publishing, and workflow management. The company's customers have included Asante Health System, Georgia Tech, Novant Health, and Vassar College. Perceptive has technology alliances with such companies as Canon, Hewlett-Packard, IBM, Microsoft, Oracle, SAP, and Sun Microsystems.

Perceptive markets its ImageNow suite and other imaging and document management applications directly and through resellers and system integrators worldwide.

EXECUTIVES

President and CEO: Scott Coons
EVP Marketing and Communications: Cary DeCamp
EVP Sales and Alliances: Tim Helton
CFO: Eric J. Bur
VP Technical Services: Brent Flanders
VP Corporate Finance: Marjorie Adair
VP Professional Services: Patrick Kearney
Director, Human Resources: Susie Coultis
Director, Sales: David Lintz
Media Contact: Sherlyn Manson
Account Executive, Public Sector: Danny Schreiner

LOCATIONS

HQ: Perceptive Software, Inc.
22701 W. 68th Terrace, Shawnee, KS 66226
Phone: 913-422-7525   **Fax:** 913-422-3820
Web: www.imagenow.com

COMPETITORS

EMC	
Hyland Software	
Omtool	
Open Text	
Standard Register	
Streamline	

HISTORICAL FINANCIALS

Company Type: Private

Income Statement

FYE: June 30

	REVENUE ($ mil.)	NET INCOME ($ mil.)	NET PROFIT MARGIN	EMPLOYEES
6/07	48	—	—	500
6/06	35	—	—	400
6/05	26	—	—	—
Annual Growth	37.5%	—	—	25.0%

Revenue History

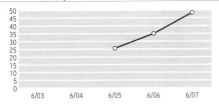

Perdue Incorporated

Chickens are always on the menu for this company. Perdue Incorporated is one of the largest poultry producers in the US with live production and processing facilities in about a dozen states. Its Perdue Farms division produces and packs more than 3 billion pounds of chicken and some 250 million pounds of turkey. Perdue sells poultry through retail outlets and to foodservice customers mostly in the eastern half of the country. It also exports products to about 50 countries. Through Perdue Agribusiness, the company processes grain for animal feed and pet food ingredients, and processes vegetable oils. Arthur Perdue started the family-owned business in 1920.

Perdue continues to strengthen its position in the consumer poultry market with new product innovations such as frozen and full-cooked poultry products designed for busy families. It has also responded to consumer concerns about food quality, trumpeting its "Farm-to-Fork" production and processing capabilities, as well as its antibiotic-free products.

James Perdue — like his father, Frank, before him — appears in the company's advertisements. Perdue produces its own breed of chicken, the skin of which is a distinct yellow color, resulting from a diet that includes marigold petals.

HISTORY

If asked which came first, the chickens or the eggs, the Perdue family will tell you the eggs did. Arthur Perdue, a railroad express worker, bought 23 layer hens in 1920 and started supplying the New York City market with eggs from a henhouse in his family's backyard in Salisbury, Maryland. His son Frank joined the business in 1939.

The Perdues sold broiling chickens to major processors, such as Swift and Armour, in the 1940s and pioneered chicken crossbreeding to develop new breeds. The family started contracting with farmers in the Salisbury area in 1950 to grow broilers for them. Frank became president of the company in 1952. The next year it began mixing its own feed.

Frank persuaded his father to borrow money to build a soybean mill in 1961. (Arthur had not willingly gone into debt in his previous 40-plus years in the poultry industry.) The soybean mill was part of Frank's plan to vertically integrate the company — with grain storage facilities, feed milling operations, soybean processing plants, mulch plants, hatcheries, and 600 contract chicken farmers — to counter the threat of processors buying chickens directly from farmers rather than through middlemen like the Perdues. To differentiate their products, the Perdue name was applied to packages on retail meat counters in 1968.

Two years later the company began a breeding and genetic research program. During the following years Frank transformed himself from country chicken salesman to media poultry pitchman when the company decided to use him as spokesperson in its print, radio, and TV ads. Catchy slogans ("It takes a tough man to make a tender chicken") combined with Frank's whiny voice and sincere face helped sales. As Perdue Farms expanded geographically into new eastern markets such as Philadelphia, Boston, and Baltimore, it acquired the broiler facilities of other processors.

In 1983 James Perdue, Frank's only son, joined the company as a management trainee. In 1984 Perdue added processors in Virginia and Indiana and introduced turkey products. Two years later it acquired Intertrade, a feed broker, and FoodCraft, a food equipment maker. However, after enjoying a rising demand for poultry by a health-conscious society in the 1970s and early 1980s, the company found its sales leveling off in the late 1980s. When North Carolina fined Perdue for unsafe working conditions in 1989, the company increased its emphasis on safety.

James, who had become chairman of the board in 1991, replaced his folksy father in 1994 as the company's spokesman in TV ads. In the early 1990s Perdue's management determined future sales growth lay in food service and international sales; therefore, the poultry company quietly began laying the groundwork to support these new markets.

Perdue launched its Cafe Perdue entree meal kits in 1997. The following year it purchased foodservice poultry processor Gol-Pak and, through a joint venture, opened a poultry processing plant in Shanghai, China.

Settlements to chicken catchers and line workers in 2001 and 2002 cost the company over $12 million in back wages. Also in 2002 Perdue announced it would be shuttering a deboning plant purchased only three years earlier. During 2003 the company started work on a new research and development facility in Salisbury, Maryland. In January 2004 Perdue purchased a poultry processing facility from competitor Cagle's, Inc.

Frank Perdue died in 2005. He was 84.

EXECUTIVES

Chairman and CEO: James A. (Jim) Perdue
SVP and CFO: Eileen F. Burza
SVP Retail Sales and Marketing: Steve Evans
VP Business Development: Steven M. (Steve) Schwalb
VP Deli Sales: Andrew (Andy) Seymour
VP Corporate Communications: Julie DeYoung
VP Corporate Research and Development: Dave Owens
VP Foodservice Sales and Marketing: Bernie McGorry
VP Supply Chain Management: Lester Gray
VP International: Carlos Ayala
VP Retail Marketing: John Bartelme
VP Human Resources: Robert H. (Rob) Heflin
CIO: Don Taylor
President and General Manager, AgriBusiness: Richard L. (Dick) Willey
President and General Manager, Food Products: J. Michael (Mike) Roberts
President Foodservice: Randall M. (Randy) Day
Chairman, Perdue Campaign: Gus Lebois

LOCATIONS

HQ: Perdue Incorporated
31149 Old Ocean City Rd., Salisbury, MD 21804
Phone: 410-543-3000   **Fax:** 410-543-3532
Web: www.perdue.com

PRODUCTS/OPERATIONS

Selected Poultry Products

Fresh Poultry
  Chicken parts
  Cornish hens
  Ground chicken
  Roasters and turkeys
  Seasoned chicken
  Skinless, boneless poultry cuts
  Turkey burgers
  Turkey sausage
Fully Cooked Poultry
  Cutlets
  Nuggets
  Rotisserie-style chicken
  Tenders
Other Products
  Pet food ingredients
  Vegetable oils

COMPETITORS

Butterball	Peco
Cagle's	Pilgrim's Pride
Hormel	Tyson Foods
Jennie-O	Wayne Farms LLC
OSI Group	West Liberty Foods

Performance Food

When it's time to eat out, Performance Food Group (PFG) delivers. The #3 broadline food service distributor in the US (behind SYSCO and U.S. Foodservice), PFG through 30 distribution centers supplies more than 68,000 national and private-label products to more than 41,000 restaurants, educational and health care facilities, and fast-food chain customers mostly in the eastern half of the country. Its subsidiary Vistar is a leading supplier of specialty foods for both food service and vending operators. The company was taken private in 2008 by The Blackstone Group and Wellspring Capital Management.

With the $1.3 billion buyout, PFG was merged with Colorado-based Vistar (which was already controlled by Blackstone) to create a giant in the food service distribution industry with tentacles reaching into several markets. While the combined business continues to operate under the PFG name, each unit maintains its own headquarters. George Holm, who headed Vistar, was named CEO for PFG following the going-private deal.

For PFG's broadline foodservice supply division, the focus has been on expanding the range of products it distributes to existing customers while improving margins. The division's customers include franchisees of such chains as Burger King, Popeyes Chicken & Biscuits, and Subway. It also serves contract foodservice operators, such as Compass Group USA.

The company's custom distribution segment, meanwhile, has been looking primarily to add new customers. In 2007 the company struck a deal to supply the O'Charley's casual dining chain. PFG's supplies more than a dozen chain restaurant operators, including Cracker Barrel, Outback Steakhouse, and T.G.I. Friday's.

HISTORY

Robert Sledd began working for his family's Taylor & Sledd food distribution business in 1974 and became president a decade later. In 1987, fearing that his family's business would be swallowed up in the ongoing consolidation of the food service industry, Sledd convinced his father, Hunter, to spin off their Richmond, Virginia-based Pocahontas Foods business and put him in charge, along with Robert's University of Tennessee fraternity brother and longtime friend, Michael Gray.

As part of the spinoff, Pocahontas merged with Caro Produce & Institutional Foods, which distributed produce in Texas and Louisiana. The company acquired Tennessee-based distributors Kenneth O. Lester Company and Hale Brothers in 1988 and 1989, respectively.

In 1991 the company changed its name from Pocahontas Foods to Performance Food Group (PFG). Although the company's name was different, its policy of growth by acquisition remained the same and PFG continued gobbling up distributors. That year PFG acquired B&R Foods, based in Tampa. The company continued to make acquisitions that expanded its market share in the South, including New Orleans distributor Loubat-L. Frank in 1992 and another Tennessee distributor, Hale of Summit Distributors, in 1993. That year the company offered its stock to the public for the first time.

Along with its aggressive consumption, PFG felt a burp in 1994 in the form of stunted profits and disappointing earnings. In what should have been the newly public company's salad days, PFG's performance was stifled by difficulties at its pre-cut salad plant and by rising labor and warehousing costs. As a result, the company's stock price plunged 66% at the end of 1994.

Undaunted, the company brought in new salad-making equipment and continued on its industry-consolidating course the next year. PFG acquired Atlanta's Milton's Food and North Carolina-based Cannon Food in 1995.

In 1996 PFG expanded its service in the Southwest with the acquisition of Texas distributor McLane Foodservice-Temple (now operating as Performance Food Group of Texas). Buoyed by solid growth in sales, the company made additional acquisitions in 1997, including Georgia's W.J. Powell, and its first foray into the Northeast, AFI Food Service.

The company grew internally in 1998 with the construction of distribution centers in Tennessee and Texas as well as its acquisition of Affiliated Paper Companies of Alabama and regional food distributor Virginia Food Service Group. In 1999 the company moved into the New England market when it bought NorthCenter Foodservice (Maine), and it expanded into custom-cut steaks when it bought State Hotel Supply Company and Nesson Meat Sales.

PFG continued to bulk up its broadline service when it acquired Carroll County Foods in 2000. Seeing the future in pre-cut salads and vegetables, the company purchased Dixon Tom-A-Toe (1999) and Redi-Cut Foods (2000). It also bought Empire Seafood Holding in 2001, doubling its seafood sales. That year Gray was promoted to CEO and PFG also bought Springfield Foodservice, a leading foodservice distributor in New England. The company then bought the largest independent fresh-cut produce processor in the US, Fresh Express.

In 2002 the acquisitions continued when in May PFG acquired Arkansas-based Quality Foods, which serves customers in Arkansas, Louisiana, Mississippi, Missouri, Oklahoma, Tennessee, and Texas. In July PFG acquired two foodservice distribution companies: Middendorf Meat, which specializes in custom-cut steaks, and Illinois-based Thoms-Proestler Co., which serves customers in Illinois, Indiana, Iowa, and Wisconsin. In October its Pocahontas Foods USA subsidiary acquired All Kitchens, a privately owned Idaho company, for $15.6 million.

In 2004 Gray left PFG and Sledd took over as chairman and CEO. The company sold its Fresh Express produce division the following year to Chiquita Brands International for $855 million. Steven Spinner was promoted from president and COO to succeed Sledd as CEO in 2006; Sledd remained as chairman.

PFG was taken private in 2008 by The Blackstone Group and Wellspring Capital Management for $1.3 billion. The deal also involved merging PFG's existing foodservice supply business with Vistar, a Colorado-based distributor of specialty foods for foodservice and vending operators. That same year George Holm became president and CEO.

EXECUTIVES

Chairman: Robert C. Sledd, age 55
President and CEO: George L. Holm
SVP and General Counsel: Joseph J. (Joe) Traficanti, age 56
SVP and CFO: John D. Austin, age 46, $567,760 pay
SVP and Controller: J. Keith Middleton, age 41, $341,664 pay
SVP and President and CEO, Customized Division: Thomas (Tom) Hoffman, age 68, $633,910 pay
SVP and Chief Human Resources Officer: Charlotte L. Perkins, age 49
SVP Broadline Operations: Joseph J. (Joe) Paterak Jr., age 56
VP and Treasurer: Jeffery W. (Jeff) Fender
CIO: Peter Giuffrida
Director, Corporate Communications: Cheryl R. Moore
Director, Investor Relations: Kevin P. Collier
Director, Risk Management: Sandy Black
Auditors: KPMG LLP

LOCATIONS

HQ: Performance Food Group Company
    12500 W. Creek Pkwy., Richmond, VA 23238
Phone: 804-484-7700   **Fax:** 804-484-7701
Web: www.pfgc.com

PRODUCTS/OPERATIONS

2007 Sales

	% of total
Center-of-the-plate	41
Frozen foods	19
Canned & dry groceries	16
Refrigerated & dairy products	11
Paper products & cleaning supplies	7
Produce	4
Equipment & supplies	1
Procurement, merchandising & other services	1
Total	**100**

Selected Private Labels

AFFLAB
Bay Winds
Brilliance
Empire's Treasure
First Mark
Guest House
Heritage Ovens
PFG Custom Meats
Raffinato
Village Garden

COMPETITORS

Alex Lee
Ben E. Keith
Gordon Food Service
Keystone Foods
MAINES
McLane Foodservice
Meadowbrook Meat Company
Services Group of America
SYSCO
UniPro Foodservice
U.S. Foodservice

HISTORICAL FINANCIALS
Company Type: Private

Income Statement			FYE: Saturday nearest December 31	
	REVENUE ($ mil.)	NET INCOME ($ mil.)	NET PROFIT MARGIN	EMPLOYEES
12/07	6,305	51	0.8%	7,200
12/06	5,827	43	0.7%	7,000
12/05	5,721	247	4.3%	7,000
12/04	6,149	53	0.9%	—
12/03	5,520	74	1.3%	—
Annual Growth	3.4%	(9.0%)	—	1.4%

2007 Year-End Financials

Debt ratio: 1.1%
Return on equity: 6.1%
Cash ($ mil.): 88
Current ratio: 1.36
Long-term debt ($ mil.): 10

Net Income History

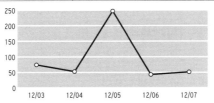

Peter Kiewit Sons'

Peter Kiewit Sons' has become a heavyweight in the heavy construction industry. The employee-owned general contractor has a breadth of expertise, building everything from roads and dams to high-rise office towers and power plants throughout the US and Canada. Its transportation projects, which include bridges, rail lines, airport runways, and mass transit systems, account for about 45% of sales. It also serves the oil and gas, electrical, power, and waterworks industries. Public contracts, most of which are awarded by government agencies, account for more than 60% of revenues. The company, also an owner of coal mines, is owned by current and former employees and Kiewit family members.

As a leader in construction in the transportation sector, Kiewit is responsible for several notable highway and bridge projects, from replacing a segment of the San Francisco-Oakland Bay Bridge Skyway to upgrading the Sea-to-Sky Highway between Vancouver and Whistler, British Columbia. Water supply and dam projects include the Olivenhain and East dams in California, underground storage tanks for the Hollywood Hills Quality Improvement Project, and an intake valve at Lake Mead in Nevada.

Peter Kiewit Sons' has also steadily built its expertise working on environmentally sensitive projects in the power sector. It has been contracted by Plutonic Energy Corporation and GE Energy Financial Services to work on one of British Columbia's largest renewable energy projects, building two hydroelectric powerhouses with intakes, penstocks, and a transmission line that will reduce dependence on non-renewable imported energy. The firm is working with the local Native American community, First Nations, creating jobs to help complete the project.

Like most in its industry, Kiewit frequently undertakes projects through joint ventures to spread risk and share resources; joint ventures account for more than one-quarter of its sales.

The company's mining operations include ownership of coal mines in Texas and Wyoming and management of two additional mines, all of which are surface mines.

HISTORY

Born to Dutch immigrants, Peter Kiewit and brother Andrew founded Kiewit Brothers, a brickyard, in 1884 in Omaha, Nebraska. By 1912 two of Peter's sons worked at the yard, which was named Peter Kiewit & Sons. When Peter Kiewit died in 1914, his son Ralph took over, and the firm took the name Peter Kiewit Sons'. Another son, Peter, joined Ralph at the helm in 1924 after dropping out of Dartmouth, and later took over.

During the Depression, Kiewit managed huge federal public works projects, and in the 1940s it focused on war-related emergency construction projects.

One of the firm's most difficult projects was top-secret Thule Air Force Base in Greenland, above the Arctic Circle. For more than two years 5,000 men worked around the clock, beginning in 1951; the site was in development for 15 years. In 1952 the company won a contract to build a $1.2 billion gas diffusion plant in Portsmouth, Ohio. It also became a contractor for the US interstate highway system (begun in 1956).

Peter Kiewit died in 1979, after stipulating that the largely employee-owned company should remain under employee control and that no one employee could own more than 10%. His 40% stake, when returned to the company, transformed many employees into millionaires. Walter Scott Jr., whose father had been the first graduate engineer to work for Kiewit, took charge. Scott made his mark by parlaying money from construction into successful investments.

When the construction industry slumped, Kiewit began looking for other investment opportunities, and in 1984 it acquired packaging company Continental Can Co. (selling off noncore insurance, energy, and timber assets). Continental was saddled with a 1983 class action lawsuit alleging that it had plotted to close plants and lay off workers before they were qualified for pensions. In 1991 Kiewit agreed to pay $415 million to settle the lawsuit. In the face of a consolidating packaging industry, the company sold Continental in the early 1990s.

In 1986 Kiewit loaned money to a business group to build a fiber-optic loop in Chicago; by 1987 it had launched MFS Communications to build local fiber loops in downtown districts. In 1992 Kiewit split its business into two pieces: the construction group, which was strictly employee-owned; and a diversified group, to which it added a controlling stake in phone and cable TV company C-TEC in 1993. That year Kiewit took MFS public; by 1995 it had sold all its shares, and the next year MFS was bought by telecom giant WorldCom.

In 1996 Kiewit assisted CalEnergy (now MidAmerican Energy) in a hostile $1.3 billion takeover of the UK's Northern Electric. Kiewit got stock in CalEnergy and a 30% stake in the UK electric company, all of which it sold to CalEnergy in 1998.

That year Kiewit spun off its telecom and computer services holdings into Level 3 Communications. Scott, who had been hospitalized the year before for a blood clot in his lung, stepped down as CEO, and Ken Stinson, CEO of Kiewit Construction Group, took over Peter Kiewit Sons'.

In 1999 Kiewit acquired a majority interest in Pacific Rock Products, a construction materials firm in Canada. Kiewit spun off its asphalt, concrete, and aggregates operations in 2000 as Kiewit Materials. Also that year the company created Kiewit Offshore Services to focus on construction for the offshore drilling industry. In 2001 the company acquired marine construction firm General Construction Company (GCC). The next year it expanded its offshore business further by buying a Canadian subsidiary from oil and gas equipment services company Friede Goldman Halter, which was trying to emerge from bankruptcy.

Kiewit made history in 2002 for the fastest completion of a project of its type when it completed the rebuilding of Webbers Falls I-40 Bridge in Oklahoma at the end of July. (The bridge had collapsed in May after being hit by a pair of barges, resulting in 14 fatalities.)

In 2004 Kiewit greatly increased its coal sales and reserves with the acquisition of the Buckskin Mine in Wyoming from Arch Coal.

Kiewit underwent a changing of the guard at the end of 2004, when 22-year veteran Bruce Grewcock took the reins as the company's fourth CEO since its founding. Stinson stayed on as the company's chairman.

EXECUTIVES

Chairman Emeritus: J. Walter (Walter) Scott Jr., age 76
Chairman: Kenneth E. (Ken) Stinson, age 65
President and CEO: Bruce E. Grewcock, age 53, $750,000 pay
EVP and Division Manager; EVP, Kiewit Corporation and Kiewit Construction; President, Gilbert Industrial Corp.: Scott L. Cassels, age 48
EVP and Division Manager and Director; EVP, Kiewit Corporation, Kiewit Construction, Kiewit Pacific Co., and Kiewit Western Co.: R. Michael Phelps, age 53, $322,700 pay
EVP; EVP, Kiewit Corporation and Kiewit Pacific Co.: Richard W. Colf, age 63, $416,000 pay
EVP: Douglas E. Patterson, age 55, $403,000 pay
SVP and CFO: Michael J. Piechoski, age 52, $236,600 pay
SVP, General Counsel, and Secretary: Tobin A. Schropp, age 44
Division Manager and Director; SVP, Kiewit Corporation, Kiewit Construction, and Kiewit Pacific Co.: Steven Hansen, age 60, $842,400 pay
Division Manager, VP, and Director; SVP, Kiewit Corporation; President, Kiewit Mining Group: Christopher J. Murphy, age 52
Division Manager and Director; SVP, Kiewit Corporation and Kiewit Construction; President, Kiewit Energy Group: Thomas S. Shelby, age 48
VP, Human Resources and Administration: John B. Chapman, age 61
VP and Treasurer: Ben E. Muraskin, age 42
Controller and Assistant Secretary; VP and Controller, Kiewit Corporation: Michael J. Whetstine, age 40
CEO, Kiewet Federal Group: Kirk R. Samuelson, age 49
President, Kiewit Engineering Co. (KECo): Gary Pietrok
Auditors: KPMG LLP

LOCATIONS

HQ: Peter Kiewit Sons', Inc.
3555 Farnam St., Omaha, NE 68131
Phone: 402-342-2052 **Fax:** 402-271-2939
Web: www.kiewit.com

Peter Kiewit Sons' US district and construction offices are located in Alaska, Arizona, Arkansas, California, Colorado, Florida, Georgia, Hawaii, Illinois, Kansas, Massachusetts, Nebraska, New Jersey, New Mexico, New York, Texas, and Washington. In Canada, the company has offices in Alberta, British Columbia, Ontario, and Quebec. The company's mining operations are in Texas and Wyoming.

PRODUCTS/OPERATIONS

Selected Subsidiaries and Affiliates

Ben Holt Company
Bighorn Walnut, LLC
Buckskin Mining Company
CMF Leasing Co.
Continental Alarm & Detection Company
Continental Fire Sprinkler Company
General Construction Company
Gilbert Central Corp.
Gilbert Industrial Corporation
Gilbert Network Services, L.P.
Gilbert/Healy, L.P.
Global Surety & Insurance Co.
GSC Atlanta, Inc.
GSC Contracting, Inc.
Guernsey Construction Company
KES Inc.
KiEnergy, Inc.

Kiewit Power Engineers (formerly Bibb and Associates)
KT Developers, LLC
KT Mining Inc.
Lac De Gras Excavation Inc.
Mass. Electric Construction Canada Co.
Mass. Electric Construction Co.
Mass. Electric Construction Venezuela, S.A.
Mass. Electric International, Inc.
MECC Rail Mexicana, S.A. de C.V.
Midwest Agencies, Inc.
Mission Materials Company
Seaworks, Inc.
Servitec de Sonora, S.A. de C.V.
Twin Mountain Construction II Company
V. K. Mason Construction Co.
Walnut Creek Mining Company

COMPETITORS

ABB
Ames Construction
Balfour Beatty Infrastructure
Bechtel
Black & Veatch
Bovis Lend Lease
CH2M HILL
Fluor
Foster Wheeler
Granite Construction
Halliburton
Hubbard Group
Jacobs Engineering
KBR
Lane Construction
Parsons Corporation
Perini
Raytheon
Skanska USA Civil
Turner Corporation
Tutor-Saliba
Walsh Group
Washington Division
Whiting-Turner
Williams Companies

HISTORICAL FINANCIALS

Company Type: Private

Income Statement				FYE: Last Saturday in December
	REVENUE ($ mil.)	NET INCOME ($ mil.)	NET PROFIT MARGIN	EMPLOYEES
12/07	6,200	—	—	15,000
12/06	5,049	—	—	14,700
12/05	4,145	—	—	14,500
12/04	3,352	—	—	14,000
12/03	3,375	—	—	15,000
Annual Growth	16.4%	—	—	0.0%

Revenue History

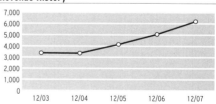

Petters Group Worldwide

Petters Group Worldwide is named for founder and chairman Tom Petters — not for what it does. It's a collection of some 20 companies, most of which make and market consumer products. Holdings include SoniqCast (maker of portable, WiFi MP3 devices), leading instant film and camera firm Polaroid (purchased for $426 million in 2005), Sun Country Airlines (acquired in 2006), and Enable Holdings (online marketplace and auction for consumers and manufacturers' overstock). It has a minority interest in Fingerhut (consumer products via its catalog and Web site). Tom Petters founded the company in 1988. In October 2008 Petters Group Worldwide filed for Chapter 11 bankruptcy protection.

The bankruptcy filing, which included the company's venture capital subsidiary Petters Co., came shortly after Petters Co. became the focus of a federal investigation. (Affidavits filed in support of federal search warrants outlined a case of allegedly massive fraud.) Tom Petters resigned as chairman and CEO of Petters Group Worldwide shortly before his arrest in early October.

Diversifying in late 2006 when it acquired the small Minnesota-based airline, Sun Country, Petters Group has added new local flights and aircraft. In late 2007 Petters Group bought out its joint venture partner in the airline, White Box Advisors, giving Petters Aviation more than 80% ownership of the carrier. (Sun Country filed for Chapter 11 bankruptcy protection about a week before its parent company.)

The company's SpringWorks division works as a technology incubator, bringing new technologies to the manufacturing process for Petters Consumer Brands products. Consumer Brands companies include Polaroid and Sunbeam.

Petters Group has manufacturing facilities in China, Japan, and Mexico as well as offices in Brazil, Hong Kong, Korea, and the US.

EXECUTIVES

President and COO: Mary L. Jeffries, age 50
EVP Finance, Tax and Treasury: James C. Wehmhoff
EVP Human Resources and Learning Center:
  Patricia Ann Hamm
Chief Customer Officer and EVP Sales and Marketing:
  Mike O'Shaughnessy
Chief Legal Officer: David Baer, age 34
Director, Corporate Communications: Andrea Miller
President and CEO, Sun Country Airlines:
  Stanley J. (Stan) Gadek, age 55
President, Petters Aviation; Vice Chairman, Sun Country Airlines: T. Jay Salmen

LOCATIONS

HQ: Petters Group Worldwide, LLC
  4400 Baker Rd., Minnetonka, MN 55343
Phone: 952-936-5000   **Fax:** 952-936-5048
Web: www.pettersgroup.com

PRODUCTS/OPERATIONS

Selected Brands
Consumer Brands
  2J Group
  Broadsign
  Celine Countryman
  John Porter
  Polaroid
  Sunbeam
  YFly
Retail Services and Distribution
  Campus Housing
  Fingerhut Direct Marketing
  Innovative Housing
  uBid.com
Other
  Sun Country Airlines

COMPETITORS

AMR Corp.	FUJIFILM
ARAMARK	Northwest Airlines
CBS Corp	Olympus
Daiko Advertising	Sony
Eastman Kodak	UAL
eBay	

HISTORICAL FINANCIALS
Company Type: Private

Income Statement
FYE: December 31

	ESTIMATED REVENUE ($ mil.)	NET INCOME ($ mil.)	NET PROFIT MARGIN	EMPLOYEES
12/06	2,300	—	—	3,200
12/05	2,200	—	—	3,200
Annual Growth	4.5%	—	—	0.0%

Revenue History

EXECUTIVES

Chairman and President: Jack C. Bendheim, age 61, $1,950,000 pay
CEO: Gerald K. Carlson, $1,044,000 pay
CFO: Richard G. Johnson, $411,917 pay
SVP, Human Resources: Daniel A. (Dan) Welch, age 55
SVP, General Counsel, and Corporate Secretary:
  Thomas G. Dagger
President, Specialty Chemicals Group:
  Daniel M. Bendheim
President, PhibroChem: Mike Giambalvo
President, Phibro Tech; President PhibroWood:
  W. Dwight Glover
President Animal Health Division: Larry Miller
President Prince Agri Products: Dean Warras
Auditors: PricewaterhouseCoopers LLP

LOCATIONS

HQ: Phibro Animal Health Corporation
  65 Challenger Rd., 3rd Fl.,
  RidgeField Park, NJ 07660
Phone: 201-329-7300   **Fax:** 201-329-7399
Web: www.pahc.com

Phibro Animal Health has operations in Asia, Europe, North America, and South America.

PRODUCTS/OPERATIONS

Principal Units and Products
Animal Health and Nutrition
  Agri-Tin
  Amprolium
  Animal feed ingredients
  Copper sulphate F.G.
  Nicarbazin
  Trace mineral premixes
  Trace minerals
  Ultra-flourish
Industrial Chemicals
  Alkaline etchant
  Calcium carbide
  Copper oxide
  Dicyandiamide
  Ferric chloride
  Fly ash
  Iron oxide
  Manganese dioxide
  Metal treatment
  Selenium disulfide
  Sodium flouride

Selected Subsidiaries
Ferro Metal and Chemical Corporation Limited (UK)
Koffolk, Ltd. (Israel)
PhibroChem, Inc.
Prince Mfg., LLC

COMPETITORS

Aceto
Akzo Nobel
Bayer Corp.
CFPI
Cognis
DuPont
MacDermid
Mitsui Chemicals
Sumitomo Chemical
Trans-Resources

Phibro Animal Health

Phibro Animal Health manufactures specialty chemicals for agricultural and industrial uses. Its largest segment by far, Animal Health and Nutrition, produces feed additives, including trace minerals, vitamins, and antibiotics. Its antibacterials protect against salmonellosis and fowl cholera. Phibro's Industrial Chemicals unit produces pigments, as well as minerals such as iron and manganese, which are used as colorants and in brick, masonry, and glass. Other subsidiaries include distributor PhibroChem and European specialty chemicals maker Ferro Metal & Chemical. The company operates worldwide. Chairman Jack Bendheim owns Phibro Animal Health.

Phoenix Coyotes

The desert heat hasn't stopped Arizona fans from howling for more. Coyotes Hockey owns and operates the Phoenix Coyotes professional hockey franchise, which draws respectable crowds at home despite a downward trend in wins over the past few seasons. The team began playing in 1972 as the Winnipeg Jets in the fledgling World Hockey League. Since joining the National Hockey League in 1979, it has made 14 playoff appearances but has yet to capture the Stanley Cup. A group led by trucking magnate Jerry Moyes and hockey great Wayne Gretzky owns the club.

The 2006-07 season marked a low point in the Coyotes short history as the team finished with its worst record since moving to Phoenix. Following the season, the franchise fired general manager Mike Barnett, along with several other front office executives. However, the team did announce that Gretzky would remain head coach for a third season. Don Maloney, formerly assistant general manager for the New York Rangers, was tapped as the team's new GM.

Glendale Arena, the team's home ice since 2003, was renamed Jobing.com Arena in 2006 after local online recruiting company Jobing.com agreed to a 10-year naming rights deal worth about $30 million.

Richard Burke and Steven Gluckstern bought the Jets in 1996 and moved the failing franchise to Phoenix. Gluckstern later sold his share to Burke in 1998 and bought the New York Islanders (now owned by Cablevision through subsidiary Madison Square Garden). Moyes and Gretzky (the Great One), along with real estate developer Steve Ellman, bought the franchise for $125 million in 2001. Ellman's involvement coincided with a larger deal that included not only the building of an arena for the Coyotes but also the surrounding Westgate City Center, a 223-acre mixed use real estate development.

In 2006 Ellman and Moyes agreed to split their holdings, with Ellman taking control of Westgate City Center and Moyes retaining control over the Coyotes. Gretzky remained a minority partner in both ventures.

EXECUTIVES

Chairman and Governor: Jeff A. Shumway, age 48
President, COO, and Alternate Governor: Douglas (Doug) Moss
Managing Partner, Alternate Governor, and Head Coach: Wayne Gretzky, age 43
EVP and CFO: Mike Nealy, age 44
EVP and Chief Marketing Officer: Michael (Mike) Bucek
EVP and Chief Communications Officer: Jeff Holbrook
SVP and General Manager, Arena Management Group: Jim Foss
VP and Controller: Joe Leibfried
VP and General Counsel: Steve Weinreich
General Manager and Head Coach, Arizona Sting: Bob Hamley
Executive Director Human Resources: Julie Atherton

LOCATIONS

HQ: Coyotes Hockey, LLC
6751 N. Sunset Blvd., Ste. 200, Glendale, AZ 85305
Phone: 623-772-3200   **Fax:** 623-872-2000
Web: www.phoenixcoyotes.com

The Phoenix Coyotes play at the 17,653-seat capacity Jobing.com Arena in Glendale, Arizona.

COMPETITORS

Anaheim Ducks
Dallas Stars
Los Angeles Kings
San Jose Sharks

HISTORICAL FINANCIALS
Company Type: Private

Income Statement

	REVENUE ($ mil.)	NET INCOME ($ mil.)	NET PROFIT MARGIN	EMPLOYEES
6/07	67	—	—	—
6/06	63	—	—	—
6/05	0	—	—	—
6/04	57	—	—	—
6/03	43	—	—	—
Annual Growth	11.7%	—	—	—

FYE: June 30

Revenue History

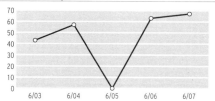

Phoenix Suns

These Suns give life to desert basketball fans. Suns Legacy Partners owns and operates the Phoenix Suns professional basketball team, which plays host at US Airways Center. The National Basketball Association franchise was awarded to businessman Richard Bloch in 1968 and fronted by investors such as Tony Curtis and Henry Mancini. Phoenix has reached the NBA Finals twice (the last time in 1993) but has yet to win a championship title. An investment group led by real estate executive Robert Sarver owns the team; former owner Jerry Colangelo remains as the team's chairman and CEO.

After leading the Suns to four straight playoff appearances without a trip to the NBA Finals, head coach Mike D'Antoni resigned at the end of the 2007-08 season to take the top coaching job with the New York Knicks.

Sarver, chairman of Western Alliance Bancorporation, ponied up a record $400 million for the team in 2004. Colangelo, who had owned the Suns since 1987, agreed to stay on as chairman and CEO through the 2007 season. He also lost control of the Arizona Diamondbacks baseball team in 2004.

EXECUTIVES

Chairman and CEO: Jerry J. Colangelo, age 68
Vice Chairman: Samuel S. (Sam) Garvin
President and COO: Rick Welts
Managing Partner: Robert Sarver
President, Basketball Operations and General Manager: Steve Kerr, age 43
Head Coach: Terry Porter
SEVP: Dick Van Arsdale, age 65
SEVP: Harvey Shank, age 62
EVP Finance and Administration: Jim Pitman, age 43

SVP and General Counsel: Jason Rowley
SVP; Executive Director, Phoenix Suns Charities: Thomas (Tom) Ambrose, age 60
VP Basketball Operations: David Griffin
VP Human Resources: Peter Wong
VP Player Programs: Mark West, age 47
Senior Director Marketing: Niki Adams
Director Sales and Development: Jeff Ianello
Director of Human Resources: Karen Rausch
Director Public Relations: Jamie Morris

LOCATIONS

HQ: Suns Legacy Partners, L.L.C.
201 E. Jefferson St., Phoenix, AZ 85004
Phone: 602-379-7900   **Fax:** 602-379-7990
Web: www.nba.com/suns

The Phoenix Suns play at 18,422-seat capacity US Airways Center in Phoenix.

PRODUCTS/OPERATIONS

Championship Titles
Western Conference Champions (1976, 1993)

COMPETITORS

Golden State Warriors
Los Angeles Clippers
Los Angeles Lakers
Sacramento Kings

Pinnacle Foods

Pinnacle Foods has a mouthful of big-name brands. The company produces grocery store staples such as Mrs. Butterworth's, Log Cabin, and Country Kitchen (syrup, pancake mixes); Duncan Hines (baking mixes); Lender's (bagels); Van de Kamp's and Mrs. Paul's (frozen seafood); Vlasic and Milwaukee's (pickles); Chef's Choice (frozen skillet meals); and Celeste (frozen pizza). Pinnacle has grown by buying well-known brands and then expanding those brand lines by adding new products. In 2007 Pinnacle was acquired by the Blackstone Group for some $2 billion in cash and assumed debt.

As a result of the merger, the company changed its name to Pinnacle Foods Finance. Former Kraft Foods CEO Roger Deromedi became Pinnacle's chairman. Jeffrey Ansell, a 25-year veteran of Procter & Gamble, was appointed as new CEO.

Now answerable to Blackstone, any acquisition plans are now subject to Blackstone's approval. In addition, as an investment company, Blackstone may buy businesses that are in competition with Pinnacle. The company incurred some $49 million in merger-related costs in 2007. That, along with increased slotting fees and a significant dip in the sales of its Open Pit brand barbecue sauce as well as a drop in its overall sales but particularly in its frozen foods segment, contributed to a sluggish year for Pinnacle.

The company distributes its products in Canada and the US to supermarket and other retail food outlets. It also sells through club stores, as well as the private-label, military, and food service channels; it has a product-development center in St. Louis.

Wal-Mart is the company's largest customer and accounted for 24% of its 2007 sales.

EXECUTIVES

Chairman: Roger K. Deromedi, age 54
CEO and Director: Jeffrey P. (Jeff) Ansell, age 48, $367,846 pay
President and Director: William (Bill) Toler, age 47, $405,394 pay
EVP and Chief Administrative Officer: Michael J. Cramer, age 55, $415,541 pay
EVP and CFO: Craig D. Steeneck, age 50, $367,404 pay
EVP Supply Chain and Operations: William Darkoch, age 57
SVP, Secretary, and General Counsel: M. Kelley Maggs, age 56
SVP, Frozen Dinners: Patrick (Pat) McAndrew
SVP, Treasurer, and Assistant Secretary: Lynne M. Misericordia, age 44
Auditors: PricewaterhouseCoopers LLP

LOCATIONS

HQ: Pinnacle Foods Finance LLC
1 Old Bloomfield Ave., Mt. Lakes, NJ 07046
Phone: 973-541-6620
Web: www.pinnaclefoodscorp.com

2007 Sales

	% of total
US	94
Canada	6
Total	**100**

PRODUCTS/OPERATIONS

2007 Sales

	$ mil.	% of total
Dry foods	863.9	59
Frozen foods	650.6	41
Total	**1,514.5**	**100**

Selected Brands

Appian Way
Armour
Aunt Jemima (frozen breakfasts only, licensed from The Quaker Oats Company)
Celeste
Duncan Hines
Grabwich
Hawaiian Bowls
Hearty Hero
Hungry-Man
Lenders
Log Cabin
Lunch Bucket
Milwaukee's
Mrs. Butterworth's
Mrs. Paul's
Open Pit
Snack'mms
Swanson (licensed from Campbell Soup Company)
Van de Kamp's
Vlasic

COMPETITORS

American Seafoods	Mt. Olive Pickle
B&G Foods	Nestlé
Campbell Soup	Nestlé USA
Chelsea Milling	Nippon Suisan Kaisha
ConAgra	Pacific Seafood
General Mills	PepsiCo
Gilster-Mary Lee	Red Chamber Co.
Gorton's	Rich Products
Goya	Sara Lee Food & Beverage
Heinz	Schwan's
High Liner Foods	Smucker
Hormel	StarKist
Icelandic USA	Thai Union
Interstate Bakeries	Trident Seafoods
Kellogg	Unilever
Kraft Foods	Weston Foods

HISTORICAL FINANCIALS

Company Type: Subsidiary

Income Statement

FYE: Last Sunday in December

	REVENUE ($ mil.)	NET INCOME ($ mil.)	NET PROFIT MARGIN	EMPLOYEES
12/07	1,515	(115)	—	3,100
12/06	1,442	34	2.4%	3,100
12/05	1,256	(43)	—	2,700
12/04*	511	(25)	—	2,600
7/04	756	(87)	—	—
Annual Growth	**19.0%**	**—**		**6.0%**

*Fiscal year change

Net Income History

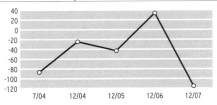

These Penguins do their thing on the ice in downtown Pittsburgh, not the Antarctic. The Pittsburgh Penguins hockey franchise represents the Steel City in the National Hockey League. The team, formed in 1967, brought home two Stanley Cup championships in 1991 and 1992 but has endured a long championship drought since. Despite its struggles on the ice, the Pens have remained popular among loyal fans, and the debut of rookie Sidney Crosby in 2006 has helped boost wins as well as ticket sales at Mellon Arena (better known as "The Igloo"). Legendary forward Mario Lemieux controls the team through the Lemieux Group.

In 2008 the team began construction on a new facility to replace Mellon Arena, the oldest rink in the NHL. The new $290 million arena is being funded partly through proceeds the state gets from slot machine casinos, with the team also contributing to the construction. The Pens hope to have the facility completed for the 2010 season.

While they await the new arena, fans are enjoying a resurgence of their Pens on the ice. Young stars such as Crosby, Evgeni Malkin, and Jordan Staal have re-energized the stands and helped make Pittsburgh a championship contender once again. In 2008 the team advanced to the Stanley Cup finals for the first time since 1992. The Pens' bid fell short, however, as they lost to the Detroit Red Wings in six games.

The current state of affairs is in stark contrast to the instability and uncertainty that has visited Pittsburgh hockey in the past. The Penguins were forced to declare bankruptcy in 1998 under previous owner Howard Baldwin. Lemieux, who had retired in 1997 after leading the team to its two championship titles, saved the club by rolling over nearly $30 million owed to him into an ownership bid. The Hall of Fame player resigned his position as governor of the club in 2000 to rejoin the team on the ice, scoring 35 goals in 43 games to take the Pens into the playoffs the following year. (Pittsburgh was eliminated by the New Jersey Devils in the Eastern Conference finals.)

Baldwin had helped form the New England Whalers of the World Hockey League (which joined the NHL in 1979 and became the Carolina Hurricanes) and later owned a stake in the Minnesota North Stars (now the Dallas Stars) before buying control of the Penguins in 1991 from Edward DeBartolo, Sr.

EXECUTIVES

Chairman: Mario Lemieux, age 43
CEO: Ken Sawyer
President: David Morehouse, age 46
EVP and General Manager: Ray Shero, age 45
Assistant General Manager: Chuck Fletcher, age 40
Head Coach: Michel Therrien, age 44
VP Communications and Marketing: Tom McMillan
VP Sales and Marketing: David Soltesz
VP and Controller: Kevin Hart
Senior Advisor of Hockey Operations: Ed (E.J.) Johnston
Director of Community Relations: Renee Petrichevich
Director of Entertainment: Paul Barto
Director of Marketing: Brian Magness

LOCATIONS

HQ: Pittsburgh Penguins
1 Chatham Center, Ste. 400, Pittsburgh, PA 15219
Phone: 412-642-1300   **Fax:** 412-642-1859
Web: www.pittsburghpenguins.com

The Pittsburgh Penguins play in 17,132-seat capacity Mellon Arena in Pittsburgh.

PRODUCTS/OPERATIONS

Championship Trophies

Stanley Cup (1991-92)
Prince of Wales Trophy (1991-92, 2008)
Presidents' Trophy (1993)

COMPETITORS

New Jersey Devils
New York Islanders
New York Rangers
Philadelphia Flyers

HISTORICAL FINANCIALS

Company Type: Private

Income Statement

FYE: June 30

	REVENUE ($ mil.)	NET INCOME ($ mil.)	NET PROFIT MARGIN	EMPLOYEES
6/07	67	—	—	—
6/06	63	—	—	—
6/05	0	—	—	—
6/04	52	—	—	—
6/03	57	—	—	—
Annual Growth	**4.1%**	**—**	**—**	**—**

Revenue History

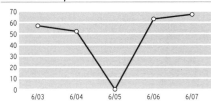

Pittsburgh Penguins

Pittsburgh Steelers

Pittsburgh Steelers Sports has forged a championship tradition in Steel Town. The company owns the Pittsburgh Steelers football franchise, which has won a record five Super Bowl titles (a mark it shares with the Dallas Cowboys and San Francisco 49ers). During the 1970s under head coach Chuck Noll, the team captured four titles with the help of such stars as Terry Bradshaw and Lynn Swann. The Steelers won its fifth title in 2006 under the direction of Noll's successor, Bill Cowher. Founded in 1933 as the Pirates, the football team (renamed in 1940) claimed winning seasons only eight times during its first 40 years. The family of chairman Dan Rooney (son of late team founder Art Rooney) owns the team.

The Rooney family is noted for its steady and stable management of the football franchise, illustrated in part by the fact that the team has had just three head coaches since the mid-1960s. Before he resigned following the 2006 season, Cowher boasted the longest tenure of any active head coach in the National Football League. He was replaced by Mike Tomlin, formerly an assistant with the Minnesota Vikings and Tampa Bay Buccaneers.

Steelers Sports has greatly improved its financial position since moving out of aging Three Rivers Stadium and into Heinz Field, a $244 million stadium opened in 2001. (Local condiment maker H. J. Heinz poured out $57 million for the naming rights.)

EXECUTIVES

Chairman: Daniel M. (Dan) Rooney
President: Arthur J. (Art) Rooney II, age 55
VP: John R. McGinley
VP: Arthur J. Rooney Jr.
Head Coach: Mike Tomlin
Director Business: Mark Hart
Director Football Operations: Kevin Colbert
Director Marketing: Tony Quatrini
Manager Public Relations and Media: Burt Lauten
Human Relations and Office Coordinator:
 Geraldine Glenn
Pro Personnel Coordinator: Doug Whaley
College Scouting Coordinator: Ron Hughes
Controller: Bob Tyler
Executive Director Stadium Management: Jim Sacco

LOCATIONS

HQ: Pittsburgh Steelers Sports, Inc.
 3400 S. Water St., Pittsburgh, PA 15203
Phone: 412-432-7800   **Fax:** 412-432-7878
Web: www.pittsburghsteelers.com

The Pittsburgh Steelers play at the 65,050-seat capacity Heinz Field in Pittsburgh.

PRODUCTS/OPERATIONS

Championship Titles
Super Bowl Championships
 Super Bowl XL (2006)
 Super Bowl XIV (1980)
 Super Bowl XIII (1979)
 Super Bowl X (1976)
 Super Bowl IX (1975)
AFC Championship (1974-75, 1978-79, 1995, 2005)
AFC North Division Champions (2002, 2004, 2007)
AFC Central Division Champions (1972, 1974-79, 1983-84, 1992, 1994-97, 2001)

COMPETITORS

Baltimore Ravens
Cincinnati Bengals
Cleveland Browns

HISTORICAL FINANCIALS
Company Type: Private

Income Statement
FYE: March 31

	REVENUE ($ mil.)	NET INCOME ($ mil.)	NET PROFIT MARGIN	EMPLOYEES
3/08	216	—	—	—
3/07	198	—	—	—
3/06	187	—	—	—
3/05	182	—	—	—
3/04	159	—	—	—
Annual Growth	8.0%	—	—	—

Revenue History

Plastipak Holdings

Plastipak likes to keep things bottled up. Doing business as Plastipak Packaging, the company manufactures plastic containers for four distinct industries: carbonated and noncarbonated beverages (soft drinks, bottled water, juice drinks, and beer); consumer cleaning (laundry detergent); food and processed juices (coffee creamers, relishes, and vegetable oils); and industrial, automotive, and agricultural (motor oil, antifreeze, windshield washer fluid). Plastipak Packaging makes high-density polyethylene (HDPE) resins and polyethylene terephthalate (PET) at its plants in the US, Europe, and South America. The Young family owns and runs Plastipak.

Plastipak has long enjoyed a close relationship with Procter & Gamble; Plastipak is the exclusive supplier of plastic containers for Procter & Gamble's liquid laundry detergents (Tide, Cheer, Era, and Gain) and other products like Bounce and Febreze; it has also been the largest supplier of plastic containers for Kraft Foods salad dressing, barbecue sauces, and grated cheeses.

The company's Whiteline subsidiary serves much of Plastipak's own transportation needs with a fleet of 300 tractors and 1,000 trailers. Its Clean Tech subsidiary, a plastics recycling firm, provides much of the company's raw material needs.

EXECUTIVES

Chairman, President, and CEO: William C. Young,
 $1,183,093 pay
VP, Finance; CFO, Treasurer, and Assistant Secretary:
 Michael J. Plotzke, age 48, $392,125 pay
VP, Controller and Strategic Operation Planning:
 Pradeep Modi, age 50
VP, International Sales and Marketing: Frank Pollock,
 age 50

VP, Operations and Manufacturing: William A. Slat,
 age 58, $390,475 pay
VP, Packaging Development: Richard Darr, age 56
VP, Product Supply: J. Ronald Overbeck, age 57
VP, Sales and Marketing: Gene W. Mueller, age 48,
 $364,835 pay
VP Human Resources: Renee Naud
CIO: David Daugherty, age 50
Corporate Legal Counsel and Secretary:
 Leann M. Underhill, age 60
President, Clean Tech: Thomas Busard, age 54,
 $355,647 pay
Auditors: Grant Thornton LLP

LOCATIONS

HQ: Plastipak Holdings, Inc.
 41605 Ann Arbor Rd., Plymouth, MI 48170
Phone: 734-455-3600   **Fax:** 734-354-7391
Web: www.plastipak.com

Plastipak has manufacturing facilities in Argentina, Brazil, the Czech Republic, Slovakia, and the US.

PRODUCTS/OPERATIONS

Selected Operations
Package development services
Plastic container manufacturing
 High-density polyethylene (HDPE) resins
 Polyethylene terephthalate (PET)
Technology licensing and equipment
 EXI-PAK preform over-molding process technology
  (employs multi-layer, barrier, and post-consumer
  plastic technologies in PET bottles)
 G.E.M. PAK container molding system

Selected Subsidiaries
Clean Tech, Inc.
LuxPet A.G./S.A.
Plastipak Packaging do Brasil, Ltda.
Plastipak Packaging, Inc.
Whiteline Express, Ltd.

COMPETITORS

Amcor
Ball Corporation
Consolidated Container
Constar International
Crown Holdings
DuPont Liquid Packaging Systems
Graham Packaging
Husky Injection Molding Systems
NOVAPAK
Owens-Illinois
Silgan

Plateau Systems

Plateau Systems wants to get your employees to peak performance. The company provides talent management systems designed to maximize workforce productivity. Its Plateau Talent Management suite includes performance management, compensation, succession planning, training, and compliance tools. Plateau targets corporations, not-for-profit organizations, and government agencies, particularly in regulated and training-intensive industries that require high levels of reliability from their employees. Its customers have included General Electric, the American Red Cross, and the US Air Force.

In 2007 the company purchased Nuvosoft, a provider of Web-based compensation management software. Plateau Systems has received investments from American International Group's AIG Horizon Partners, Euclid SR Partners, and Morgan Stanley.

EXECUTIVES

Chairman and CEO: Paul Sparta
President and COO: Brian F.X. Murphy
CFO: Stephen Blodgett
CTO: Edward (Ed) Cohen
EVP Global Operations: Shelly Heiden
SVP, Product Management and Alliances: Joe Herman
SVP Technical Integration and Quality Control: Hung Vu
SVP, Product Strategy: Bradley (Brad) Cooper
SVP Product Engineering: Sunil Chandran
SVP Marketing: Jeff Kristick
VP Quality Assurance and Corporate Security: Larry Thomas
Auditors: Ernst & Young

LOCATIONS

HQ: Plateau Systems Ltd.
4401 Wilson Blvd., Ste. 400, Arlington, VA 22203
Phone: 703-678-0000   **Fax:** 703-678-0001
Web: www.plateau.com

COMPETITORS

Futuremedia	OutStart
IBM	Saba Software
Mzinga	SAP
Oracle	SumTotal

Platinum Equity

Platinum Equity thinks the companies it buys are just precious. The firm invests in information technology and other firms, often buying units of large corporations. These companies usually offer legacy products and services and have well-established customer bases and distribution operations. It focuses on firms in such sectors as manufacturing, call center and help desk operations, data communications and networking, and software. Platinum Equity also looks for acquisitions as strategic add-ons to its portfolio companies, which have operations worldwide. Founder and CEO Tom Gores, who started Platinum in 1995, is the brother of Alec Gores, who founded another investment firm, Gores Technology Group.

In 2008, as part of its focus on the metals and manufacturing industries, Platinum Equity bought SCM Metal Products from Gibraltar Industries. SCM makes copper-based powder and pastes and copper oxide powders.

Later in 2008 the company bid to acquire a 40% stake in the Arena Football League for $100 million. The purchase would give Platinum Equity management control over the league.

Platinum Equity acquired WFI Government Services' wireless deployment business in 2007 for a reported $24 million. (The deal includes the rights to the Wireless Facilities name.) It also bought Ryerson Inc., a steel and metal processor, for $2 billion, taking it private.

Other recent acquisitions include Maxim Crane Works, Strategic Distribution, and the fastening systems business of Textron.

In 2006 Platinum Equity bought steel processor and distributor PNA Group from TUI; some two years later, it sold the firm to Reliance Steel & Aluminum for around $1.1 billion.

EXECUTIVES

Chairman and CEO: Tom T. Gores, age 43
CFO: Mary Ann Sigler
Partner, General Counsel, and Secretary: Eva M. Kalawski, age 53
EVP: Gary Newton, age 51
SVP Technology: Jim Hoffer
SVP Mergers and Acquisitions: E. James (Jim) Levitas
SVP Portfolio Sales and Marketing; CEO PEAK Technologies: Ross Young
VP Marketing Communications: Alanna Chaffin

LOCATIONS

HQ: Platinum Equity, LLC
360 N. Crescent Dr., South Bldg., Beverly Hills, CA 90210
Phone: 310-712-1850   **Fax:** 310-712-1848
Web: www.platinumequity.com

PRODUCTS/OPERATIONS

Selected Portfolio Companies

Acument Global Technologies
Advogent
Altura Communication Solutions
American Racing Equipment
Americatel Corporation
Broadleaf Logistics Company
Data2Logistics
DCA Services
DyStar
GeoLogic Solutions, Inc.
iET Solutions
Matrix Business Technologies
OVISO Manufacturing
PEAK Technologies
Ryerson, Inc
Strategic Distribution, Inc.
Turf Care Supply Corp.
USRobotics
WFI's Deployment Business

COMPETITORS

Apollo Advisors
Behrman Capital
CD&R
The Gores Group
HM Capital Partners
Hummer Winblad
KKR
Madison Dearborn
Thomas H. Lee Partners
TPG
Welsh Carson

HISTORICAL FINANCIALS

Company Type: Private

Income Statement				FYE: December 31
	REVENUE ($ mil.)	NET INCOME ($ mil.)	NET PROFIT MARGIN	EMPLOYEES
12/07	13,500	—	—	50,000
12/06	8,000	—	—	45,000
12/05	8,000	—	—	45,000
12/04	8,000	—	—	45,000
12/03	4,500	—	—	32,000
Annual Growth	31.6%	—	—	11.8%

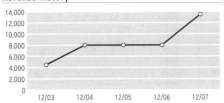

Revenue History

Pliant Corporation

Pliant is flexible when it comes to packaging. The company makes flexible packaging products and value-added films for the personal care, medical, agricultural, industrial, and food industries. Its specialty products include films used to make diapers, sterile films, and mulch films used for weed control. The company also produces industrial films such as stretch films (used to bundle palletized loads during shipping) and PVC films (used to wrap food products), along with engineered films, which are integrated into paper and foil packaging. Its printed products include bags and sheets for the packaging of consumer items. The company operates under the Stratum, Blockade, and Fresh View brands, among others.

The company filed for Chapter 11 bankruptcy protection early in 2006; it emerged later that year, after receiving new financing. Now JPMorgan Partners controls about 51% of the company.

Pliant, which has about 1 billion pounds of annual production capacity, operates more than 20 manufacturing and research and development facilities around the globe.

Established in 1992, the company has invested more than $158 million over the past several years to expand and upgrade its product offerings and information systems.

EXECUTIVES

Non-Executive Chairman: John D. Bowlin, age 57
President, CEO, and Director: Harold C. Bevis, age 48, $1,100,001 pay
EVP and COO: R. David Corey, age 59, $505,885 pay
SVP and CFO: Thomas C. Spielberger, age 46
SVP Technology and Innovation: Greg E. Gard, age 47
SVP Finance and Accounting: Joseph J. (Joe) Kwederis, age 61, $250,276 pay
SVP; President Engineered Film Groups: Kenneth J. (Ken) Swanson, age 41, $275,763 pay
SVP Business Development: Jim Kingsley, age 45
VP and General Manager, PVC Products: Robert J. (Bob) Maltarich, age 56, $263,210 pay
VP and General Manager, Printed Products: James L. (Jim) Kaboski, age 39, $295,102 pay
VP Operations: Marty DiPietro
VP and General Counsel: Stephen T. (Steve) Auburn, age 53
Auditors: Ernst & Young LLP

LOCATIONS

HQ: Pliant Corporation
1475 Woodfield Rd., Ste. 700, Schaumburg, IL 60173
Phone: 847-969-3300   **Fax:** 847-969-3338
Web: www.pliantcorp.com

Pliant Corporation has manufacturing facilities in Australia, Canada, Germany, Mexico, and the US.

PRODUCTS/OPERATIONS

2007 Sales

	$ mil.	% of total
Engineered films	347.2	32
Industrial films	317.2	29
Printed products	211.2	19
Specialty films	205.7	19
Corporate & other	15.7	1
Total	**1,097.0**	**100**

COMPETITORS

AEP Industries	Printpack
Atlantis Plastics	Reynolds Food Packaging
Bemis	Sealed Air Corporation
Griffon	Sigma Plastics
Pactiv	Spartech
Polymer Group	

HISTORICAL FINANCIALS

Company Type: Private

Income Statement

FYE: December 31

	REVENUE ($ mil.)	NET INCOME ($ mil.)	NET PROFIT MARGIN	EMPLOYEES
12/07	1,097	(12)	—	2,875
12/06	1,159	185	16.0%	3,073
12/05	1,073	(113)	—	2,940
12/04	969	(114)	—	3,025
12/03	929	(114)	—	3,250
Annual Growth	**4.2%**	**—**	**—**	**(3.0%)**

2007 Year-End Financials

Debt ratio: —
Return on equity: —
Cash ($ mil.): 7

Current ratio: 1.72
Long-term debt ($ mil.): 751

Net Income History

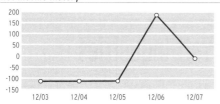

Port Authority of NY & NJ

The Port Authority of New York and New Jersey bridges the sometimes-troubled waters between the two states — and helps with many of the region's other transportation needs. The bistate agency operates and maintains airports, tunnels, bridges, a commuter rail system, shipping terminals, and other facilities within the Port District, an area surrounding the Statue of Liberty. A self-supporting public agency, the Port Authority receives no state or local tax money but relies on tolls, fees, and rents. Airport operations account for the majority of the agency's revenue. The governors of the two states each appoint six of the 12 members of the agency's board and review the board's decisions.

The Port Authority's facilities include such international symbols of transportation and commerce as the George Washington Bridge, the Holland and Lincoln tunnels, and LaGuardia and John F. Kennedy airports. The Port Authority Trans-Hudson (PATH) rapid-transit system provides commuter rail service between New York and New Jersey.

The World Trade Center was among the agency's most visible assets before its twin towers and much of the rest of the complex were destroyed in the terrorist attacks of September 11, 2001. The Port Authority is working with other agencies, government officials, and real estate interests on the rebuilding of the 16-acre site in Lower Manhattan.

Other key projects include a new commuter terminal under the Hudson River, improvements to the PATH rail system, and efforts to reduce flight delays at New York-area airports. At the same time, the agency is working to control costs.

To oversee its diverse operations, the Port Authority has a new executive director — its fourth since the September 11 attacks. Christopher Ward, who took over in May 2008, served as a port authority executive from 1997 to 2002 and is a veteran of several other public- and private-sector posts, mainly related to infrastructure management.

HISTORY

New York and New Jersey spent much of their early history fighting over their common waterways. In 1921 a treaty creating a single, bistate agency, the Port of New York Authority, was ratified by the New York and New Jersey state legislatures. The agency struggled at first, although its early projects, such as the Goethals Bridge (1928, linking Staten Island to New Jersey), were far from timid.

The agency merged with the Holland Tunnel Commission in 1930, which brought a steady source of revenue. In 1931 the George Washington Bridge (spanning the Hudson River from Manhattan to New Jersey) was completed. The Lincoln Tunnel (also linking Manhattan to New Jersey) opened in 1937.

After WWII the Port Authority broadened its focus to include commercial aviation. In 1947 the agency took over LaGuardia Airport, and the next year it dedicated the New York International Airport (renamed John F. Kennedy International Airport in 1963).

As trucking supplanted railroads in the late 1950s, The Port Authority experimented with more-efficient ways of transferring cargo. In 1962 it built the first containerport in the world. That year the agency acquired a commuter rail line connecting Newark to Manhattan, which became the Port Authority Trans-Hudson (PATH).

In the early 1970s the Port Authority completed the World Trade Center. The agency changed its name to The Port Authority of New York and New Jersey in 1972 to reflect its role in mass transit between the two states. Critics, however, frequently assailed the agency for inefficiency and pork-barrel politics. In 1993 terrorists detonated a truck bomb in one of the World Trade Center towers, but within a year the building had largely recovered.

George Marlin became executive director in 1995. He cut operating expenses for the first time since 1943 and through budget cuts and layoffs, saved $100 million in 1996 and avoided hikes in tolls and fares. A privatization proponent, Marlin sold the World Trade Center's Vista Hotel to Host Marriott and arranged for the sale of other non-transportation businesses. He stepped down in 1997, and Robert Boyle took the post. That year the agency broke ground on the $1.2 billion Terminal 4 at JFK International Airport.

In 1998 the Port Authority authorized a $930 million design and construction contract for a light-rail line to JFK International Airport. New York City mayor Rudolph Giuliani proposed legislation in 1999 to place the Port Authority's LaGuardia and JFK airports under City Hall jurisdiction.

An 18-month standoff between the governors of New York and New Jersey regarding disputes over leases and agency spending was settled in 2000, which allowed the Port Authority to move forward with projects that had been blocked. Also in 2000 Boyle announced plans to resign. Neil Levin, New York's state insurance superintendent and a former Goldman Sachs vice president, replaced him the next year.

After the Port Authority and Vornado Realty Trust in 2001 failed to finalize an agreement for Vornado to lease the World Trade Center, the Port Authority that year signed a 99-year, $3.2 billion deal to lease portions of the World Trade Center's office space to a group led by Silverstein Properties while leasing the retail space to Westfield America.

Less than two months later, on September 11, 2001, the World Trade Center's twin towers were destroyed when terrorists hijacked passenger jets and flew them into the buildings. Levin was killed, and 83 other Port Authority employees were listed as dead or missing.

The cleanup of the World Trade Center site, known as "Ground Zero," was completed in 2002, eight months after the attacks. In 2003 the Port Authority reopened the PATH rail station at the World Trade Center site. Construction of the World Trade Center Transportation Hub, intended to serve PATH, subway, and ferry passengers and aid in the economic development of Lower Manhattan, began in 2005.

To keep up with anticipated increases in air traffic, the Port Authority in 2007 took over the operating lease for Stewart International Airport in Newburgh, New York, about 70 miles north of Manhattan.

EXECUTIVES

Chairman: Anthony R. Coscia
Executive Director: Christopher O. (Chris) Ward
Deputy Executive Director: James P. (Jamie) Fox
Deputy Executive Director Operations:
 Ernesto L. Butcher
Deputy Executive Director, Capital Programs:
 William Goldstein
CFO: A. Paul Blanco
Inspector General: Robert E. Van Etten
Chief Administrative Officer: Louis J. LaCapra
Chief Engineer: Francis J. Lombardi
Chief of Staff: Edmond F. Schorno
Chief of Strategic Planning: Robert F. Lurie
Chief of Public and Government Affairs:
 Stephen Sigmund
Comptroller: Michael G. Fabiano
General Counsel: Darrell Buchbinder
Secretary: Karen E. Eastman
Director Development: Michael B. Francois
Director Government and Community Affairs:
 Shawn K. Laurenti
Director Public Affairs: John J. McCarthy
Director Engineering: Peter Zipf
Director, Office of Business and Job Opportunity:
 Lash Green
Acting Director Human Resources: Rosetta Jannotto
Auditors: Deloitte & Touche LLP

LOCATIONS

HQ: The Port Authority of New York and New Jersey
225 Park Ave. South, New York, NY 10003
Phone: 212-435-7000   **Fax:** 212-435-6670
Web: www.panynj.gov

PRODUCTS/OPERATIONS

2007 Sales

	$ mil.	% of total
Air terminals	1,918.0	60
Interstate transportation	850.2	27
Port commerce	236.0	7
Economic & waterfront development	103.6	3
World Trade Center	83.7	3
Total	**3,191.5**	**100**

Selected Operations

Air terminals
  Downtown Manhattan Heliport (New York)
  John F. Kennedy International Airport (New York)
  LaGuardia Airport (New York)
  Newark Liberty International Airport (New Jersey)
  Stewart International Airport (New York)
  Teterboro Airport (New Jersey)

Interstate transportation
  Bayonne Bridge (Staten Island to Bayonne, NJ)
  George Washington Bridge (Manhattan to Ft. Lee, NJ)
  George Washington Bridge Bus Terminal
  Goethals Bridge (Staten Island to Elizabeth, NJ)
  Holland Tunnel (Manhattan to Jersey City, NJ)
  Lincoln Tunnel (Manhattan to Union City, NJ)
  Outerbridge Crossing (Staten Island to Perth Amboy, NJ)
  Port Authority Bus Terminal (Manhattan)
  The Port Authority Trans-Hudson System (PATH, rail transportation between New York and New Jersey)

Port commerce
  Auto Marine Terminal (Bayonne, NJ)
  Brooklyn-Port Authority Marine Terminal (New York)
  Elizabeth Marine Terminal (New Jersey)
  Howland Hook Marine Terminal (New York)
  Port Newark (New Jersey)
  Red Hook Container Terminal (New York)

Economic and waterfront development
  Bathgate Industrial Park (Bronx, NY)
  Essex County Resource Recovery Center (municipal waste-to-energy electric generation plant; Newark, NJ)
  Hoboken South (mixed-use waterfront development, New Jersey)
  Industrial Park at Elizabeth (New Jersey)
  Newark Legal & Communications Center (office development, New Jersey)
  Queens West (mixed-use waterfront development, New York)
  The Teleport (communications center; Staten Island, NY)

HISTORICAL FINANCIALS

Company Type: Government agency

Income Statement   FYE: December 31

	REVENUE ($ mil.)	NET INCOME ($ mil.)	NET PROFIT MARGIN	EMPLOYEES
12/07	3,192	248	7.8%	7,128
12/06	3,039	200	6.6%	7,181
12/05	3,001	223	7.4%	7,194
12/04	2,865	264	9.2%	7,267
12/03	2,764	883	31.9%	7,000
Annual Growth	**3.7%**	**(27.2%)**	**—**	**0.5%**

2007 Year-End Financials

Debt ratio: —
Return on equity: 3.0%
Cash ($ mil.): —
Current ratio: —
Long-term debt ($ mil.): —

Net Income History

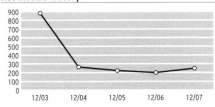

Portland Trail Blazers

This enterprise has opened a path for basketball fans in the Beaver State. Trail Blazers, Inc., owns and operates the Portland Trail Blazers professional basketball franchise, which claims just one championship title (in 1977) since joining the National Basketball Association in 1970. The team was started by Harry Glickman and has made two other NBA Finals appearances (its last in 1992). Trouble on and off the court in recent seasons has led to one of the lower attendance rates in the league. The team plays host at Portland's Rose Garden Arena. Microsoft co-founder Paul Allen, who owns the Seattle Seahawks, has controlled the team since 1988.

Allen has said he expects the Trail Blazers to lose about $100 million by 2009, in part because of the terms of the team's lease at the Rose Garden. After eyeing a sale of the team and its arena, Allen pulled out of negotiations in 2006.

With the team struggling near last place, president and general manager Steve Patterson unexpectedly quit the Trail Blazers halfway through the 2006-07 season. The team brought in former NIKE executive Larry Miller to help rebuild the franchise.

In addition to the Seahawks and Trail Blazers, Allen controls a portfolio of technology investments through Vulcan Inc.

EXECUTIVES

Chairman and Owner: Paul G. Allen, age 55
President: Larry G. Miller, age 59
COO: Mike Golub
General Manager: Kevin Pritchard
Head Coach, Portland Trail Blazers: Nate McMillan, age 44
SVP and CFO: Gregg M. Olson
SVP Business Affairs: J. E. Isaac
SVP and General Counsel: Michael (Mike) Fennell
SVP Marketing and Sales: Sarah Mensah
VP Community Relations: Traci Rose
VP Human Resources: Traci Reandeau
VP Marketing: Michele Daterman
VP Corporate Sales and Service: Jack Bradley
VP Communications: Cheri Hanson
Director Player Programs: Chris Bowles

LOCATIONS

HQ: Trail Blazers, Inc.
1 Center Ct., Ste. 200, Portland, OR 97227
Phone: 503-234-9291   **Fax:** 503-736-2194
Web: www.nba.com/blazers

The Portland Trail Blazers play at the 19,980-seat capacity Rose Garden Arena in Portland, Oregon.

PRODUCTS/OPERATIONS

Championship Titles

NBA Championship (1977)
Western Conference Champions (1977, 1990, 1992)

COMPETITORS

Denver Nuggets
Minnesota Timberwolves
Oklahoma City Thunder
Utah Jazz

HISTORICAL FINANCIALS

Company Type: Private

Income Statement   FYE: June 30

	REVENUE ($ mil.)	NET INCOME ($ mil.)	NET PROFIT MARGIN	EMPLOYEES
6/07	82	—	—	—
6/06	77	—	—	—
6/05	78	—	—	—
6/04	88	—	—	—
6/03	97	—	—	—
Annual Growth	**(4.1%)**	**—**	**—**	**—**

Revenue History

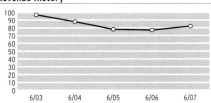

Pratt Industries

What do Burt Bacharach, Jay Leno, Muhammad Ali, and Ray Charles have in common? They have all headlined Pratt Industries (USA)'s customer appreciation parties. Pratt Industries (USA) lays claim to being the world's largest privately owned manufacturer of paper and packaging materials. Its products include container board and corrugated sheets. The company, which has plants in Australia, Mexico, and the US (in about 20 states in the South, East, and Midwest), was founded in 1948 by Leon Pratt, the grandfather of current chairman Anthony Pratt. Pratt Industries (USA) is controlled by Australian-based Pratt family vehicle, Visy Industries.

Between 2005 and 2006 the company has been growing primarily through acquisitions. It acquired corrugated paper product maker Love Box. Soon after, Pratt Industries (USA) purchased box plant General Corrugated and two additional corrugated mills through the acquisition of Merit Container.

While the company actively searches for possible acquisitions to grow its box and paper-making capacity, it has also developed several new production facilities, including a corrugating plant in Tennessee and a display facility in New York. Pratt is also focused on using 100% recycled materials in its products; it recycles about 1.5 million tons of waste paper per year. In 2008 the company broke ground on what will be Pratt Industries (USA)'s third 100% recycled containerboard mill. The new mill is located in Shreveport, Louisiana, and will produce 360,000 tons of recycled paper annually to supply the company's other operations. Its other two recycling mills are located in Georgia and New York.

EXECUTIVES

Chairman and CEO: Anthony Pratt
COO: Brian McPheely
EVP Commercial: Luis Henao
VP Sales: Haydn McLachlan
Manager Customer Tech Center: Glenn Rogers
Director, Human Resources: Jim Ross

LOCATIONS

HQ: Pratt Industries (USA)
  1800 C Sarasota Business Pkwy., Conyers, GA 30013
Phone: 770-918-5678   **Fax:** 770-918-5679
Web: www.prattindustries.com

COMPETITORS

Georgia-Pacific
Green Bay Packaging
International Paper
Interstate Resources, Inc.
Louisiana-Pacific
MeadWestvaco

Packaging Corp.
Smurfit Kappa
Smurfit-Stone Container
Southern Container
Temple-Inland
Weyerhaeuser

Pricewaterhouse-Coopers International

Not merely the firm with the longest one-word name, PricewaterhouseCoopers (PwC) is also one of the world's largest accounting firms, formed when Price Waterhouse merged with Coopers & Lybrand in 1998, passing then-leader Andersen. The accountancy has some 770 offices in 150 countries around the world, providing clients with services in three lines of business: Assurance (including financial and regulatory reporting), Tax, and Advisory. The umbrella entity for the PwC worldwide organization (officially PricewaterhouseCoopers International) is one of accounting's Big Four, along with Deloitte Touche Tohmatsu, Ernst & Young, and KPMG. PwC serves some of the world's largest businesses, as well as smaller firms.

PwC puts its heft to good use: Non-North American clients make up nearly two-thirds of the firm's sales. The company has expanded in developing economies, including Brazil, China, India, and Russia; business also got a temporary boost from the implementation of such new regulatory and financial reporting rules as the International Financial Reporting Standards and the Sarbanes-Oxley Act.

The company endured a two-month suspension in Japan in 2006 after three partners of its firm there were implicated in a fraud investigation involving a PwC client, Kanebo. To distance itself from the scandal, PwC's existing Japanese firm was renamed and a second firm was launched.

The next year US arm PricewaterhouseCoopers agreed to pay a whopping $225 million to settle a class-action lawsuit related to the Tyco International financial scandal.

The firm's bottom line changed significantly in 2002, when PwC sold its consulting arm to IBM. A separation had been under consideration for years in light of SEC concerns about conflicts of interest when firms perform auditing and consulting for the same clients. The collapse of Enron and concomitant downfall of Enron's auditor and PwC's erstwhile peer Andersen undoubtedly hastened plans to spin off PwC's consultancy via an IPO, which was scrapped in favor of the IBM deal.

Like the other members of the Big Four, PwC picked up business and talent as scandal-felled Andersen was winding down its operations in 2002. The former Andersen organization in China and Hong Kong joined PwC, accounting for about 70% of the approximately 3,500 Andersen alumni that came aboard.

HISTORY

In 1850 Samuel Price founded an accounting firm in London and in 1865 took on partner Edwin Waterhouse. The firm and the industry grew rapidly, thanks to the growth of stock exchanges that required uniform financial statements from listees. By the late 1800s Price Waterhouse (PW) had become the world's best-known accounting firm.

US offices were opened in the 1890s, and in 1902 United States Steel chose the firm as its auditor. PW benefited from tough audit requirements instituted after the 1929 stock market crash. In 1935 the firm was given the prestigious job of handling Academy Awards balloting. It started a management consulting service in 1946. But PW's dominance slipped in the 1960s, as it gained a reputation as the most traditional and formal of the major firms.

Coopers & Lybrand, the product of a 1957 transatlantic merger, wrote the book on auditing. Lybrand, Ross Bros. & Montgomery was formed in 1898 by William Lybrand, Edward Ross, Adam Ross, and Robert Montgomery. In 1912 Montgomery wrote *Montgomery's Auditing*, which became the bible of accounting.

Cooper Brothers was founded in 1854 in London by William Cooper, eldest son of a Quaker banker. In 1957 Lybrand joined up to form Coopers & Lybrand. During the 1960s the firm expanded into employee benefits and internal control consulting, building its technology capabilities in the 1970s as it studied ways to automate the audit process.

Coopers & Lybrand lost market share as mergers reduced the Big Eight accounting firms to the Big Six. After the savings and loan debacle of the 1980s, investors and the government wanted accounting firms held liable not only for the form of audited financial statements but for their veracity. In 1992 the firm paid $95 million to settle claims of defrauded investors in MiniScribe, a failed disk-drive maker. Other hefty payments followed, including a $108 million settlement relating to the late Robert Maxwell's defunct media empire.

In 1998 Price Waterhouse and Coopers & Lybrand combined PW's strength in the media, entertainment, and utility industries, and Coopers & Lybrand's focus on telecommunications and mining. But the merger brought some expensive legal baggage involving Coopers & Lybrand's performance of audits related to a bid-rigging scheme involving former Arizona governor Fife Symington.

Further growth plans fell through in 1999 when merger talks between PwC and Grant

Thornton International failed. The year 2000 began on a sour note: An SEC conflict-of-interest probe turned up more than 8,000 alleged violations, most involving PwC partners owning stock in their firm's audit clients.

As the SEC grew ever more shrill in its denunciation of the potential conflicts of interest arising from auditing companies that the firm hoped to recruit or retain as consulting clients, PwC saw the writing on the wall and in 2000 began making plans to split the two operations. As part of this move, the company downsized and reorganized many of its operations.

The following year PwC paid $55 million to shareholders of MicroStrategy Inc., who charged that the audit firm defrauded them by approving the client firm's inflated earnings and revenues figures.

The separation of PwC's auditing and consulting functions finally became a reality in 2002, when IBM bought the consulting business. (The acquisition took the place of a planned spinoff.)

In 2003 former client AMERCO (parent of U-Haul) sued PwC for $2.5 billion, claiming negligence and fraud in relation to a series of events that led to AMERCO restating its results. The suit was settled for more than $50 million the following year.

In 2005 PwC was ranked among the Top 10 companies in the US for working mothers by *Working Mother* magazine; it was given that honor again two years later.

EXECUTIVES

CEO and Global Board Member:
  Samuel A. (Sam) DiPiazza Jr.
Global Managing Partner, Advisory and Tax:
  Eugene (Gene) Donnelly
Global Managing Partner, Assurance:
  Robert (Rob) Ward
Global Managing Partner, Markets and Operations:
  Paul Boorman
Global Managing Partner, Human Capital:
  Richard L. (Rich) Baird
Global Managing Partner, Risk and Quality:
  Michael O. (Mike) Gagnon
Global Managing Partner Industries: Alec N. Jones
Global Managing Partner Public Policy and Regulatory Affairs: Richard R. Kilgust
Global Partner, Global Retail and Consumer and Global Board Member, China: Carrie Yu
Global Strategy Leader: Edgardo Pappacena
Global General Counsel: Javier H. Rubinstein
Director Global Public Relations: Mike Davies
Regional Marketing Director: Cynara Tan
Chairman and Senior Partner, UK: Kieran C. Poynter
Chairman and Senior Partner, US: Dennis M. Nally

LOCATIONS

HQ: PricewaterhouseCoopers International Limited
  300 Madison Ave., New York, NY 10017
Phone: 646-471-4000   **Fax:** 813-286-6000
Web: www.pwcglobal.com

PricewaterhouseCoopers has more than 770 offices in 150 countries.

2007 Sales

	% of total
Europe	
Western Europe	43
Central & Eastern Europe	3
North America & Caribbean	36
Asia	10
Australasia & Pacific Islands	4
Middle East & Africa	2
South & Central America	2
Total	**100**

PRODUCTS/OPERATIONS

2007 Sales by Industry

	% of total
Industrial products	22
Banking & capital markets	11
Investment management	11
Retail & consumer	11
Energy, utilities & mining	8
Technology	8
Insurance	5
Entertainment & media	5
Pharmaceuticals	4
Professional services	4
Government	3
Automotive	3
InfoComm	3
Health care	2
Total	**100**

2007 Sales

	% of total
Assurance	52
Advisory	25
Tax	23
Total	**100**

Selected Products and Services

Audit and assurance
  Actuarial services
  Assistance on capital market transactions
  Corporate reporting improvement
  Financial accounting
  Financial statement audit
  IFRS reporting
  Independent controls and systems process assurance
  Internal audit
  Regulatory compliance and reporting
  Sarbanes-Oxley compliance
  Sustainability reporting
Crisis management
  Business recovery services
  Dispute analysis and investigations
Human resources
  Change and program effectiveness
  HR management
  International assignments
  Reward
Performance improvement
  Financial effectiveness
  Governance, risk, and compliance
  IT effectiveness
Tax
  Compliance
  EU direct tax
  International assignments
  International tax structuring
  Mergers and acquisitions
  Transfer pricing
Transactions
  Accounting valuations
  Advice on fundraising
  Bid support and bid defense services
  Commercial and market due diligence
  Economics
  Financial due diligence
  Independent expert opinions
  Mergers and acquisitions advisory
  Modeling and business planning
  Post deal services
  Private equity advisory
  Privatization advice
  Project finance
  Public company advisory
  Structuring services
  Tax valuations
  Valuation consulting

COMPETITORS

Bain & Company
Baker Tilly International
BDO International
Booz Allen
Boston Consulting
Deloitte
Ernst & Young Global
Grant Thornton International
H&R Block
Hewitt Associates
KPMG
Marsh & McLennan
McKinsey & Company
Towers Perrin
Watson Wyatt

HISTORICAL FINANCIALS

Company Type: Partnership

Income Statement

FYE: June 30

	REVENUE ($ mil.)	NET INCOME ($ mil.)	NET PROFIT MARGIN	EMPLOYEES
6/07	25,150	—	—	146,767
6/06	21,986	—	—	142,162
6/05	18,998	—	—	130,203
6/04	16,283	—	—	122,471
6/03	14,683	—	—	122,820
Annual Growth	**14.4%**	—	—	**4.6%**

Revenue History

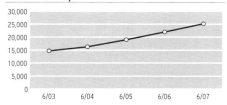

Princeton University

This prince's kingdom is covered with ivy. As a member of the Ivy League, Princeton University is one of an elite group of top-ranked schools in the northeast US. The research university offers degrees in 35 departments and has more than 7,000 students (4,900 undergraduates and 2,300 graduate students). More than half of its students receive financial aid. One of the US's richest universities (behind Harvard, Yale, and Texas), Princeton has an endowment of more than $10 billion.

The highly selective school admits about 10% of its total applicants. Nobel prize winners associated with Princeton include Woodrow Wilson (Princeton's president before becoming US president), writer Toni Morrison, and physicist Richard Feynman.

Princeton is loosely affiliated with the Institute for Advanced Study where Albert Einstein once taught.

Founded in 1746, Princeton is the fourth-oldest college in the nation. It was housed in Nassau Hall, which contained the entire college for nearly half a century. Nassau Hall served as the temporary capitol of the US in 1783.

EXECUTIVES

Chairman, Executive Committee: Stephen A. Oxman
Vice Chairman, Executive Committee: Dennis J. Keller, age 66
President and Trustee: Shirley M. Tilghman, age 60
Provost: Christopher L. Eisgruber
EVP: Mark Burstein
VP Development: Brian J. McDonald
VP Finance and Treasurer: Christopher McCrudden
VP Human Resources: Lianne Sullivan-Crowley
VP Information Technology and CIO: Betty Leydon
VP, Secretary, and Trustee: Robert K. Durkee
Dean of Admissions: Janet Lavin Rapelye
Dean of the College: Nancy Weiss Malkiel
Dean, Faculty: David P. Dobkin
Dean, Graduate School: William B. Russel
General Counsel: Peter G. McDonough
President, Princeton University Investment Co.: Andrew K. Golden
Auditors: Deloitte & Touche LLP

LOCATIONS

HQ: Princeton University
  1 Nassau Hall, Princeton, NJ 08544
Phone: 609-258-3000   **Fax:** 609-258-1301
Web: www.princeton.edu

PRODUCTS/OPERATIONS

Select Councils, Institutes, and Centers

Bendheim Center for Finance
Center for Migration and Development
Center for the Study of Religion
Council of the Humanities
Council on Science and Technology
Davis Center for Historical Studies
James Madison Program in American Ideals and Institutions
Lewis-Sigler Institute for Integrative Genomics
Liechtenstein Institute on Self-Determination
Princeton Environmental Institute (PEI)
Princeton Institute for International and Regional Studies (PIIRS)
Princeton Institute for the Science and Technology of Materials (PRISM)
Princeton Writing Program
Program of Freshman Seminars in the Residential Colleges
Program in Law and Public Affairs
Program in Neuroscience
University Center for Human Values

Printpack, Inc.

And that's a wrap! Printpack wraps its many types of flexible packaging around salty snacks, confections, baked goods, cookies, crackers, and cereal, as well as tissues and paper towels. The company's packaging includes plastic film, aluminum foil, metallized films, and paper with specialized coatings, as well as cast and blown monolayer and co-extruded films. Customers include Frito-Lay, Georgia-Pacific, General Mills, and Quaker Oats. Printpack manufactures packaging materials at about 25 plants in the US, Mexico, and the UK. The Love family owns and manages the company; Dennis Love, whose father founded the company, serves as Printpack's president.

The company has been experiencing some growth through acquisitions during its recent history. In 2006 it expanded its product portfolio when it snatched up the operations of Seal-it, which makes sleeved and flat heatshrink films used for labels on bottled beverages. Geographically, the company made significant steps towards increasing its presence in Latin America the following year when it acquired Mexican flexible package maker Grupo Industrial Plastico (GIPSA).

Printpack was founded by Erskine Love Jr. in 1956. By the early 1960s the company had established 50 to 60 accounts, including Frito-Lay and The Arkansas Rice Growers Co-op.

EXECUTIVES

Chairman: Gay M. Love, age 79
President, CEO, and Director: Dennis M. Love, age 52
VP, Finance and CFO: R. Michael Hembree, age 59
VP and General Counsel: Gray McCalley Jr.
VP, General Manager, and Director: James E. Love III, age 52
VP and General Manager: Michael A. Fisher, age 62
VP and General Manager: James J. Greco, age 66
VP and General Manager: John N. Stigler, age 61
VP, Technology and Support: Terrence P. Harper, age 50
VP Human Resources: Rick Williams
Treasurer and Assistant Secretary: Dave Kenny
Auditors: PricewaterhouseCoopers LLP

LOCATIONS

HQ: Printpack, Inc.
2800 Overlook Pkwy., NE, Atlanta, GA 30339
Phone: 404-691-5830   **Fax:** 404-699-7122
Web: www.printpack.com

Printpack operates 20 manufacturing plants in the US, Mexico, and the UK.

PRODUCTS/OPERATIONS

Selected Customers

ConAgra	Kellogg
Frito-Lay	Kodak
General Mills	Mars
Georgia-Pacific	Nabisco
Hershey	Nestlé
Hormel	Quaker Oats
Keebler	

COMPETITORS

AEP Industries	Pliant
Alcoa	PMC Global
Bemis	Reynolds Food Packaging
Exopack	Sealed Air Corporation
FlexSol Packaging	Tetra Pak
Madeco	

Pro-Build Holdings

Pro-Build Holdings is big and lumbering but it isn't unwieldy. Pro-Build is the nation's largest supplier of building materials to professional builders, contractors, and project-oriented consumers, serving customers through 10 regional brands. The company boasts more than 500 locations in 40 states, consisting of more than 450 lumber yards and dozens of truss plants, millwork shops, and wall panel plants. Services include installation, delivery, and manufacturing. The company's regional brands include The Contractor Yard, Dixieline Lumber, F.E. Wheaton, Strober Building Supplies, and U.S. Components.

Pro-Build got its start in 1997 when Fidelity Capital acquired The Strober Organization, then continued buying up professional building materials suppliers. Pro-Build then acquired Redmond, Washington-based Lanoga Corporation in February 2006 and merged it with Strober to form the nationwide professional building materials dealer chain.

Subsequent acquisitions included: drywall specialist Building Materials Wholesale/Retail of Charlotte, North Carolina; Rowley Building Products and its sister company, construction financing business Builder's Capital LLC; and Tulsa-based Hope Lumber and Supply Company.

It hasn't stopped growing. In 2008 Pro-Build acquired Wisconsin building supply business Big Buck Builders Supply, Ohio-based Khempco Building Supply, and others. It also bought the lumber business of Home Depot's supply operations that year, after Home Depot Supply was sold.

EXECUTIVES

Chairman: Paul L. Mucci
Vice Chairman: Frederick M. (Fred) Marino
CEO: Paul W. Hylbert Jr.
EVP Corporate Relations and COO: Ben Phillips
CFO: Thomas W. Ryan
SVP Market Development: Joseph (Joe) Todd
SVP Human Resources: John O'Loughlin
SVP Strategic Initiatives: William J. Myrick
SVP Corporate Development: George C. Finkenstaedt
VP Corporate Development: Michael Cassidy
VP and General Counsel: Mark B. Butterman
Director Marketing and Communications:
Carolyn Atkinson

LOCATIONS

HQ: Pro-Build Holdings Inc.
7595 Technology Way, 5th Fl., Denver, CO 80237
Phone: 303-262-8500
Web: www.pro-build.com

COMPETITORS

84 Lumber
ABC Supply
Building Materials Holding
HD Supply
Lowe's
PrimeSource Building

HISTORICAL FINANCIALS

Company Type: Private

Income Statement				FYE: December 31
	REVENUE ($ mil.)	NET INCOME ($ mil.)	NET PROFIT MARGIN	EMPLOYEES
12/07	5,000	—	—	17,000
12/06	5,960	—	—	16,640
12/05	5,700	—	—	12,790
Annual Growth	(6.3%)	—	—	15.3%

Revenue History

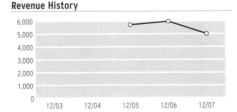

Professional Veterinary Products

Professional Veterinary Products, Ltd. (PVPL) wholesales and distributes pharmaceuticals and supplies to licensed veterinarians. The company carries more than 20,000 products from about 350 manufacturers, ranging from diagnostic equipment to animal identification tags. PVPL has two subsidiaries: Exact Logistics (distributes to other animal health companies) and ProConn (supplies products directly to the consumer). The company was founded by a group of veterinarians in 1982. PVPL says that even its telesales staff has experience in the field, with vet techs or others who have animal science degrees on the phones.

In 2007 the company launched a new online store and home delivery service called Vets First Choice. The service helps veterinarians by allowing their customers to order products online and improve compliance with doctor's orders.

PVPL distributes its products to its shareholders, as well as non-shareholder customers. Non-shareholders make up some 70% of sales.

PVPL has distribution centers in Kentucky, Nebraska, Pennsylvania, and Texas.

EXECUTIVES

Chairman: Amy L. Hinton, age 43
Vice Chairman: G.W. Buckaloo Jr., age 61
President and CEO: Lionel L. Reilly, age 65, $434,128 pay
EVP and COO: Stephen J. Price, age 49, $236,983 pay
VP and CFO: Neal B. Soderquist, age 53, $203,371 pay
VP Sales and Marketing: Daryl E. Schraad
VP Supply Chain: Jaime Meadows
VP People: Chris McGonigle
Auditors: Quick & McFarlin, P.C.

LOCATIONS

HQ: Professional Veterinary Products, Ltd.
10077 S. 134th St., Omaha, NE 68138
Phone: 402-331-4440   **Fax:** 402-331-8655
Web: www.pvpl.com

PRODUCTS/OPERATIONS

2007 Sales

	$ mil.	% of total
Wholesale distribution	338.5	98
Direct customer services	57.0	2
Logistics	0.3	—
Adjustments	(53.2)	—
Total	**342.6**	**100**

COMPETITORS

Animal Health International
Drs. Foster & Smith
FarmVet
IVESCO
Lambriar Animal Health
MWI Veterinary Supply
Patterson Companies
PETCO
PetMed
PetSmart
TW Medical
United Pharmacal

HISTORICAL FINANCIALS
Company Type: Private

Income Statement
FYE: July 31

	REVENUE ($ mil.)	NET INCOME ($ mil.)	NET PROFIT MARGIN	EMPLOYEES
7/07	343	2	0.7%	341
7/06	369	2	0.7%	350
7/05	387	3	0.6%	327
7/04	335	3	0.9%	307
7/03	299	3	1.1%	276
Annual Growth	3.5%	(6.9%)	—	5.4%

2007 Year-End Financials
Debt ratio: —
Return on equity: 11.3%
Cash ($ mil.): —
Current ratio: —
Long-term debt ($ mil.): —

Net Income History

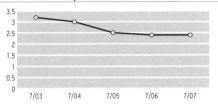

Promega Corporation

Promega helps researchers plumb the depths of the life sciences. The company sells more than 1,450 products that allow scientists to conduct various experiments in gene, protein, and cellular research. Its reagents and other goods fall into more than two dozen categories, including DNA and RNA purification, genotype analysis, protein expression and analysis, and DNA sequencing. Promega has branches in about a dozen countries around the world. The firm sells its products directly and through more than 50 distributors. Customers include academic, pharmaceutical, and clinical labs, as well as government agencies and energy and chemical companies.

Subsidiary Terso Solutions provides inventory management services, primarily through the PromegaExpress product management system, which directly ties stored products to automatic inventory controls.

EXECUTIVES
Chairman, President, and CEO:
  William A. (Bill) Linton, age 60
VP and CTO: Randall (Randy) Dimond
VP Finance and CFO: Laura Francis
VP Sales: Lisa Witte
Director Information Systems: Jeff Christopher
Director Marketing Communications: Roger Larrick
Manager Corporate Communications: Penny Patterson
Auditors: Ernst & Young LLP

LOCATIONS
HQ: Promega Corporation
  2800 Woods Hollow Rd., Madison, WI 53711
Phone: 608-274-4330   **Fax:** 608-277-2516
Web: www.promega.com

PRODUCTS/OPERATIONS

Selected Product Categories
Cellular Analysis
  Apoptosis
  Automation-robotics
  Cell viability
  Drug discovery
  Gene expression and reporter assays
  Immunological detection
  In-vitro toxicology
  Signal transduction
  Transfection
Genetic Identity
Genomics
  Automation-robotics
  Cloning
  DNA and RNA purification
  Electrophoresis
  Food and GMO testing
  Genotype analysis
  In-vitro transcription
  Microarrays
  Plant biotechnology
  Reverse transcription & cDNA synthesis
  RNA interference
  Sequencing
Proteomics
  Electrophoresis
  Gene expression and reporter assays
  Mutagenesis
  Protein interactions
  Protein expression and analysis
  RNA interference
  Transfection

COMPETITORS
Applied Biosystems
BD
Beckman Coulter
Invitrogen
QIAGEN
Roche Diagnostics
Siemens Healthcare
Sigma-Aldrich
Stratagene
Transgenomic

HISTORICAL FINANCIALS
Company Type: Private

Income Statement
FYE: December 31

	REVENUE ($ mil.)	NET INCOME ($ mil.)	NET PROFIT MARGIN	EMPLOYEES
12/07	220	—	—	920
12/06	200	—	—	911
12/05	175	—	—	850
12/04	170	—	—	755
12/03	156	—	—	758
Annual Growth	9.0%	—	—	5.0%

Revenue History

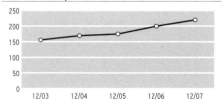

Providence Health & Services

Sisterhood is powerful in health care. Sponsored by two congregations of nuns — the Sisters of Providence and the Sisters of the Little Company of Mary — Providence Health & Services (through its Providence Health System division) operates more than 25 hospitals and dozens of other health facilities in five states in the western US. Its hospitals, nursing homes, and clinics are located in Alaska, California, Montana, Oregon, and Washington. All together, the system has more than 5,000 acute care beds and some 2,000 long-term care beds. The organization also provides health insurance for some 250,000 people through Providence Health Plans and offers subsidized housing for the low-income elderly and disabled.

In addition to its health care and housing operations, Providence Health & Services operates a small Catholic university in Great Falls, Montana, and a private high school in Burbank, California. In 2008 Providence Health bought the Tarzana campus of Encino-Tarzana Regional Medical Center from Tenet Healthcare.

The Sisters of Providence were founded in 1843 in Montreal. Their work in the US began in 1856, when five members of the order established a mission in what was then Washington Territory.

EXECUTIVES
Chairman: Kay Stepp
President and CEO: John F. Koster, age 57
EVP: Greg Van Pelt
SVP and CFO: Michael (Mike) Butler
SVP and Chief Medical Quality Officer: Keith I. Marton
SVP Mission Leadership: John O. (Jack) Mudd
SVP and Chief Administrative Officer: Jan Jones
VP Public Affairs: Chuck Hawley
VP Governance and Strategic Planning:
  Claudia Haglund
VP and CEO, Washington/Montana Region:
  John Fletcher
VP and Chief Executive, Alaska Region: Al Parrish
VP and Chief Executive, Oregon Region:
  Russ Danielson
VP and General Counsel, Legal Affairs:
  Jeffrey W. (Jeff) Rogers
VP and CIO: John Kenagy
Auditors: KPMG LLP

LOCATIONS
HQ: Providence Health & Services
  506 2nd Ave., Ste. 1200, Seattle, WA 98104
Phone: 206-464-3355   **Fax:** 206-464-3038
Web: www.providence.org

Selected Hospital Facilities
Alaska
  Providence Alaska Medical Center (Anchorage)
  Providence Kodiak Island Medical Center (Kodiak)
  Providence Seward Medical Center (Seward)
California
  Providence Saint Joseph Medical Center (Burbank)
  Providence Holy Cross Medical Center (Mission Hills)
  Little Company of Mary Hospital (Torrance)
  San Pedro Peninsula Hospital (San Pedro)

Montana
St. Joseph Medical Center (Polson)
St. Patrick Hospital (Missoula)
Oregon
Providence Hood River Memorial Hospital (Hood River)
Providence Medford Medical Center (Medford)
Providence Milwaukie Hospital (Milwaukie)
Providence Newberg Hospital (Newberg)
Providence Portland Medical Center (Portland)
Providence St. Vincent Medical Center (Porland)
Providence Seaside Hospital (Seaside)
Washington
Deer Park Hospital (Deer Park)
Holy Family Hospital (Spokane)
Mount Carmel Hospital (Colville)
Providence Centralia Hospital (Centralia)
Providence Everett Medical Center (Everett)
Providence St. Peter Hospital (Olympia)
Sacred Heart Medical Center (Spokane)
St. Joseph's Hospital (Chewelah)
St. Mary Medical Center (Walla Walla)

COMPETITORS

Adventist Health
Banner Health
Catholic Healthcare West
HCA
Legacy Health System
Los Angeles County Health Department
Memorial Health Services
PeaceHealth
Sutter Health
Tenet Healthcare

HISTORICAL FINANCIALS

Company Type: Not-for-profit

Income Statement				FYE: December 31
	REVENUE ($ mil.)	NET INCOME ($ mil.)	NET PROFIT MARGIN	EMPLOYEES
12/07	6,348	434	6.8%	45,000
12/06	5,821	348	6.0%	45,220
12/05	4,365	249	5.7%	47,572
12/04	4,021	382	9.5%	33,940
12/03	3,780	177	4.7%	32,526
Annual Growth	13.8%	25.2%	—	8.5%

2007 Year-End Financials

Debt ratio: —
Return on equity: 9.8%
Cash ($ mil.): —
Current ratio: —
Long-term debt ($ mil.): —

Net Income History

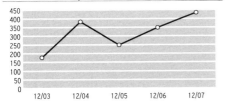

Publishers Clearing House

If your doorbell rings unexpectedly, it's probably just your mother-in-law stopping by for a chat. But it *could be* Publishers Clearing House (PCH) dropping by to let you know that you've won $10 million. PCH is one of the world's largest direct marketing organizations. Once known primarily for its magazines (and PCH giveaways), the company now makes most of its money from direct mail offerings for household items, personal care products, entertainment, collectibles, and food items in the US, the UK, and Canada. About half of the company's profits goes to charities. PCH was founded in 1953 by Harold and LuEster Mertz and is still owned largely by the charitable foundations established by the Mertz family.

In a bid to extend its reach into the virtual world in recent years, PCH acquired Mill Valley, California-based Blingo, an Internet search engine that tempts users with the chance to win instant prizes with each search they perform. With PCH's backing, Blingo offers prizes ranging from movie tickets, gift cards, new cars, big screen plasma TVs, $5,000 in cash, and more to fortunate Web surfers.

EXECUTIVES

Chairman: Robin B. Smith, age 66
President and CEO: Andy Goldberg
EVP: Deborah Holland
CFO: Rick Busch
SVP: Todd Sloane
Senior Director Consumer and Privacy Affairs:
Christopher L. Irving

LOCATIONS

HQ: Publishers Clearing House
382 Channel Dr., Port Washington, NY 11050
Phone: 516-883-5432   **Fax:** 516-767-4567
Web: www.pch.com

PRODUCTS/OPERATIONS

Selected Sources of Revenue

Magazines
Merchandise
pch.com
International

COMPETITORS

Amazon.com
Amazon.co.uk
Avon
EBSCO
Google
Home Interiors & Gifts
Lillian Vernon
Reader's Digest
Synapse Group
Time Inc.
Yahoo!

Publix Super Markets

Publix Super Markets tops the list of privately owned supermarket operators in the US. By emphasizing service and a family-friendly image over price, Publix has grown faster and been more profitable than Winn-Dixie Stores and other rivals. More than two-thirds of its 950 stores are in Florida, but it also operates in Alabama, Georgia, South Carolina, and Tennessee. Publix makes some of its own bakery, deli, and dairy goods, and many stores house pharmacies, and banks. The company also operates about a half dozen "Pix" convenience stores in the Sunshine State. Founder George Jenkins began offering stock to Publix employees in 1930. Employees own about 30% of Publix, which is still run by the Jenkins family.

The fast-growing grocer has opened about 125 supermarkets since 2003 and plans to open approximately 45 more stores in 2008. Also, Publix is converting the 49 Florida supermarkets it acquired from Albertsons to its own banner.

In 2007 the company launched a new store format called GreenWise Market (the name Publix has already given to its store-within-a-store natural/organic sections and private-label line of specialty foods) to court more health-conscious consumers and compete with national organic chains, such as Whole Foods. Three additional GreenWise stores are slated to open in 2008.

In addition to grocery stores, Publix also operates liquor stores next to about 35 of its supermarkets in Florida. Other ventures include its majority-owned restaurant chain Crispers in Florida. Currently, the soup-salad-and-sandwich chain operates about 40 locations.

To stay on top of the competitive Florida grocery market, Publix keeps up with national trends in grocery retailing. In 2007 it began offering free antibiotics at its 680-plus in-store pharmacies. The grocery chain also fills other generic prescriptions for $4 (upon customer request), thereby matching rival Wal-Mart's low-cost generic drug program. To better serve its Latino customers, Publix has launched its own line of pre-packaged Hispanic foods, including frozen plantains and ready-to-eat black beans. It also launched a Hispanic-themed format called Publix Sabor in 2005, which operates two stores in Miami.

HISTORY

George Jenkins, age 22, resigned as manager of the Piggly Wiggly grocery in Winter Haven, Florida, in 1930. With money he had saved to buy a car, he opened his own grocery store, Publix, next door to his old employer. The small store (named after a chain of movie theaters) prospered despite the Depression, and in 1935 Jenkins opened another Publix in the same town.

Five years later, after the supermarket format had become popular, Jenkins closed his two smaller locations and opened a new, more modern Publix Market. With pastel colors and electric-eye doors, it was also the first US store to feature air conditioning.

Publix Super Markets bought the All-American chain of Lakeland, Florida (19 stores), in 1944 and moved its corporate headquarters to that city. The company began offering S&H Green Stamps in 1953, and in 1956 it replaced its original supermarket with a mall featuring an enlarged Publix and a Green Stamp redemption center. Publix expanded into South Florida in the late 1950s.

As Florida's population grew, Publix continued to expand, opening its 100th store in 1964. Publix was the first grocery chain in the state to use bar-code scanners — all its stores had the technology by 1981. The company beat Florida banks in providing ATMs, and during the 1980s opened debit card stations.

Publix continued to grow in the 1980s, safe from takeover attempts because of its employee ownership. In 1988 it installed the first automated checkout systems in South Florida, giving patrons an always-open checkout lane.

Publix stopped offering Green Stamps in 1989, and most of the $19 million decrease in the chain's advertising expenditures was attributed to the end of the 36-year promotion. That year, after almost six decades, "Mr. George" — as founder Jenkins was known — stepped down as chairman in favor of his son Howard. (George died in 1996.)

In 1991 Publix opened its first store outside Florida, in Georgia, as part of its plan to become a major player in the Southeast. Publix entered South Carolina in 1993 with one supermarket; it also tripled its presence in Georgia to 15 stores.

The United Food and Commercial Workers Union began a campaign in 1994 against alleged gender and racial discrimination in Publix's hiring, promotion, and compensation policies.

Publix opened its first store in Alabama in 1996. That year a federal judge allowed about 150,000 women to join a class-action suit filed in 1995 by 12 women who had sued Publix, charging that the company consistently channeled female employees into low-paying jobs with little chance for good promotions. The case, which at the time was said to be the biggest sex discrimination lawsuit ever, was set to go to trial, but in 1997 the company paid $82.5 million to settle and another $3.5 million to settle a complaint of discrimination against black applicants and employees.

Publix promised to change its promotion policies, but two more lawsuits alleging discrimination against women and blacks were filed in 1997 and 1998. The suit filed on behalf of the women was denied class-action status in 2000. Later that year the company settled the racial discrimination lawsuit for $10.5 million. Howard Jenkins stepped down as CEO in mid-2001; his cousin Charlie Jenkins took the helm.

In 2002 Publix entered the Nashville, Tennessee, market with the purchase of seven Albertsons supermarkets, a convenience store, and a fuel center.

In February 2004 Publix acquired three Florida stores from Kash n' Karry, a subsidiary of Belgium's Delhaize Group. Also that year Publix became the majority owner of Crispers.

In April 2005 Publix introduced the Hispanic-themed Sabor format in Kissimmee, Florida.

In August 2007 the chain began offering seven popular antibiotics free at some 685 Publix Pharmacies. The drugs account for almost 50% of the generic, pediatric prescriptions filled at Publix. In 2007 Publix opened its first GreenWise Market in Palm Beach Gardens, Florida.

CEO Charlie Jenkins Jr. retired at the end of March 2008. Jenkins was succeeded by his cousin and Publix president Ed Crenshaw. In September Publix completed the roughly $500-million acquisition of 49 Albertsons stores in Florida.

EXECUTIVES

Chairman: Charles H. (Charlie) Jenkins Jr., age 64, $792,896 pay
Vice Chairman: Hoyt R. (Barney) Barnett, age 64, $401,694 pay
CEO and Director: William E. (Ed) Crenshaw, age 57, $663,152 pay
President: Randall T. (Todd) Jones Sr., age 46
CFO and Treasurer: David P. Phillips, age 48, $530,522 pay
SVP, General Counsel, and Secretary: John A. Attaway Jr., age 49
SVP and CIO: Laurie Z. Douglas, age 44
SVP: R. Scott Charlton, age 48
SVP: John T. Hrabusa, age 52
VP Manufacturing: Michael R. (Mike) Smith, age 48
VP Real Estate, Crispers: Cliff Wiley
VP Risk Management: Marc Salm
Assistant Secretary and Executive Director Publix Super Markets Charities: Sharon A. Miller, age 64
Director Marketing and Research: Mark Lang
Director Media and Community Relations: Maria Brous
Director Marketing and Advertising: Kevin Lang
Chairman and CEO, Crispers Restaurants: Ron Fuller
Auditors: KPMG LLP

LOCATIONS

HQ: Publix Super Markets, Inc.
3300 Publix Corporate Pkwy., Lakeland, FL 33811
Phone: 863-688-1188   **Fax:** 863-284-5532
Web: www.publix.com

2007 Supermarkets

	No.
Florida	665
Georgia	171
South Carolina	41
Alabama	29
Tennessee	20
Total	**926**

PRODUCTS/OPERATIONS

2007 Stores

	No.
Supermarkets	926
Crispers restaurants	41
Liquor stores	34
Pix convenience stores	5
Total	**1,006**

Selected Supermarket Departments

Bakery
Banking
Dairy
Deli
Ethnic foods
Floral
Groceries
Health and beauty care
Housewares
Meat
Pharmacy
Photo processing
Produce
Seafood

Foods Processed

Baked goods
Dairy products
Deli items

COMPETITORS

ALDI	Nash-Finch
BI-LO	The Pantry
Bruno's Supermarkets	Rite Aid
Costco Wholesale	Ruddick
CVS Caremark	Sedano's
IGA	Sweetbay
Ingles Markets	Walgreen
Kerr Drug	Wal-Mart
Kmart	Whole Foods
Kroger	Winn-Dixie

HISTORICAL FINANCIALS

Company Type: Private

Income Statement

FYE: Last Saturday in December

	REVENUE ($ mil.)	NET INCOME ($ mil.)	NET PROFIT MARGIN	EMPLOYEES
12/07	23,194	1,184	5.1%	144,000
12/06	21,820	1,097	5.0%	140,000
12/05	20,745	989	4.8%	135,000
12/04	18,686	819	4.4%	—
12/03	16,946	661	3.9%	—
Annual Growth	8.2%	15.7%	—	3.3%

2007 Year-End Financials

Debt ratio: —
Return on equity: 22.3%
Cash ($ mil.): 420
Current ratio: 1.18
Long-term debt ($ mil.): —

Net Income History

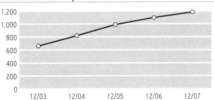

Purdue Pharma

Purdue Pharma has a prescription for what pains you. The company specializes in developing, manufacturing, and marketing sustained-release and long-acting treatments for chronic and severe pain. Its opioid drugs for pain relief include the controversial analgesic OxyContin (a controlled-release version of oxycodone) and slow-release morphine drug MS Contin. It is developing additional pain products through alliances with Labopharm and Shionogi. Purdue also sells a number of over-the-counter products, including hospital antiseptic Betadine and the Senokot line of laxatives. Purdue Pharma operates exclusively in the US market.

The company's OxyContin, hailed as a breakthrough pain therapy in the 1990s when it was approved, has since generated much controversy. While OxyContin pills are meant to be swallowed whole, with a time-release mechanism slowly delivering a potent opiate over twelve hours, illegal users of the drug found ways of crushing and then ingesting the powder to get a heroin-like high. As a result of its popularity as a street drug, the addictive OxyContin became known as "hillbilly heroin."

Purdue has taken steps to curb abuse of the painkiller, implementing a risk management program that included greater education efforts and collaboration with pharmacists and law enforcement agencies.

After prevailing in more than 400 civil cases regarding OxyContin, the company settled most of the remaining outstanding suits in early 2007. However, the company and several of its executives (some of them no longer with the company) pled guilty to federal charges that they misled the public and regulators about the drug's addictive qualities. As part of the settlement, Purdue agreed to pay about $600 million in fines.

In addition to settling its legal issues with OxyContin, Purdue is developing a second-generation version of the drug that it says is more resistant to abuse. The newer version includes a polymer that makes it harder to crush into powder or mix with water.

EXECUTIVES

Acting President; President, Purdue Pharma, Canada: John H. Stewart
EVP and CFO: Edward B. (Ed) Mahony
EVP and Chief Legal Officer: Howard R. Udell
EVP and Counsel to the Board of Directors: Stuart D. Baker
SVP Licensing and Business Development: James (Jim) Dolan
SVP Human Resources: David Long
SVP Technical Operations: Frederick (Fred) Sexton
VP IT Administration and CIO: Larry Pickett
VP Sales and Marketing: Russ Gasdia
VP, Chief Medical Officer, and Head of Clinical Research: Craig Landau
VP Project Management and Research Administration: William J. (Bill) Mallin
Group Executive Director Marketing: Michael Innaurato
Senior Director Public Affairs: James W. (Jim) Heins

LOCATIONS

HQ: Purdue Pharma L.P.
1 Stamford Forum, 201 Tresser Blvd.,
Stamford, CT 06901
Phone: 203-588-8000   **Fax:** 203-588-8850
Web: www.purduepharma.com

Purdue Pharma has facilities in Connecticut, New Jersey, North Carolina, and Rhode Island.

PRODUCTS/OPERATIONS

Selected Products

Over-The-Counter
  Betadine (antibiotic)
  Colace (laxative)
  Peri-Colace (stool softener)
  Senokot (laxative)
  Senokot-S (laxative)
  Slow-Mag (mineral supplement)
Prescription
  MS Contin (pain management)
  OxyContin (pain management)
  OxyFast (pain management)
  OxyIR (pain management)
  Uniphyl (asthma and other respiratory ailments)

COMPETITORS

Adolor
Alpharma
Cephalon
Elan
Endo Pharmaceuticals
GlaxoSmithKline
Johnson & Johnson
King Pharmaceuticals
Novartis
Pain Therapeutics
Schering-Plough
Watson Pharmaceuticals
Xanodyne Pharmaceuticals

Purity Wholesale Grocers

This company gets the goods to grocers at a discount. Purity Wholesale Grocers (PWG) is a leading secondary wholesaling company that distributes broadline grocery products, health and beauty care items, pharmaceutical products, dairy foods, and dry goods to small retailers across the country. It takes advantage of discounts granted to large wholesalers and retailers (and of the promotional pricing offered in certain regions) and passes those cost savings on to its customers. PWG supplies grocery chains, drugstores, and convenience stores. In addition, PWG offers online sourcing services that also help retailers find bargains. The company is owned by Jeff Levitetz, who founded PWG in 1982.

EXECUTIVES

Chairman: Jeffrey A. (Jeff) Levitetz, age 51
President: David Groomes
VP Accounting and Controller: Tom Jankus
VP Human Resources: Karen L. McGrath
President, Pinnacle Trading: Samuel T. (Sam) Reeves, age 73

LOCATIONS

HQ: Purity Wholesale Grocers, Inc.
5400 Broken Sound Blvd. NW, Ste. 100,
Boca Raton, FL 33487
Phone: 561-994-9360   **Fax:** 561-241-4628
Web: www.pwg-inc.com

PRODUCTS/OPERATIONS

Selected Operating Companies

American Wholesale Grocers
Pinnacle Trading
Purity Wholesale Grocers
Super Marketing
Supreme Distributors

COMPETITORS

Associated Wholesale Grocers
C&S Wholesale
Dot Foods
Eby-Brown
H.T. Hackney
McLane
Nash-Finch
SUPERVALU

Quad/Graphics, Inc.

Your mailbox may be filled with Quad/Graphics' handiwork. A leading US printing company, Quad/Graphics produces catalogs, magazines, books, direct mail, and other commercial material. The company offers a full range of services, including design, photography, desktop production, printing, binding, wrapping, distribution, and related software. At its 10 primary printing facilities, about half of which are in Wisconsin, the company has produced catalogs for the likes of Bloomingdale's and Victoria's Secret, books for National Geographic, and magazines such as *People*, *Newsweek*, and *Sports Illustrated*. Company employees and members of the founding Quadracci family own and run Quad/Graphics.

To grow, the company has been working to diversify beyond its core catalog and magazine printing business. To that end, Quad/Graphics combined its publishing-related software offerings to form a new business unit, QuadSystems, in 2006. Also that year Quad/Graphics bought Milwaukee-based direct mail business Openfirst in a deal that was projected to double the printing firm's direct mail division QuadDirect.

Following its December 2007 acquisition of Warsaw, Poland-based Winkowski, in August 2008 Quad/Graphics renamed the company QuadWinkowski and appointed as president Tom Frankowski, a 29-year veteran of Quad/Graphics US.

Quad/Graphics has been recognized as a good place to work. The company has provided on-site day care centers, health clubs, and medical clinics. In addition, it has sponsored sports leagues (softball, bowling), awarded college scholarships to employees' children, and offered interest-free auto loans. Quad/Graphics' Windhover Foundation supports social, cultural, and educational projects.

In addition to Wisconsin, the firm has printing plants in Georgia, Nevada, New York, Oklahoma, and West Virginia.

EXECUTIVES

President, CEO, and Director: J. Joel Quadracci
SVP Manufacturing; President, QuadWinkowski: Thomas J. (Tom) Frankowski
SVP Sales and Administration: David A. Blais
VP Customer Service: Ron Nash
VP Distribution: David (Dave) Riebe
VP Employee Services: Emmy M. LaBode
VP and General Counsel: Andy Schiesl
VP Information Systems and Infrastructure; President, QuadDirect: Steve Jaeger
Marketing Manager: Claire Ho
President, QuadCreative Group and Publisher, Milwaukee Magazine: Betty Ewens Quadracci
Chairman, QuadWinkowski: Tadeusz Winkowski

LOCATIONS

HQ: Quad/Graphics, Inc.
N63 W23075 State Hwy. 74, Sussex, WI 53089
Phone: 414-566-6000   **Fax:** 414-566-4650
Web: www.qg.com

PRODUCTS/OPERATIONS

Selected Services

Binding and finishing
Color correction
Design
Desktop production
Direct mailing
Imaging and photography
Ink jetting
Integrated circulation
Mailing and distribution
Mailing list management
Printing
Scanning

COMPETITORS

Arandell	Merrill
Brown Printing	Quebecor World
Cenveo	R.R. Donnelley
Consolidated Graphics	St Ives US Division
Dai Nippon Printing	Toppan Printing

HISTORICAL FINANCIALS

Company Type: Private

Income Statement

FYE: December 31

	REVENUE ($ mil.)	NET INCOME ($ mil.)	NET PROFIT MARGIN	EMPLOYEES
12/07	2,050	—	—	12,000
12/06	2,030	—	—	12,000
12/05	1,950	—	—	12,000
Annual Growth	2.5%	—	—	0.0%

Revenue History

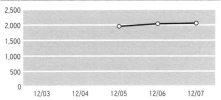

2,500				
2,000				
1,500				
1,000				
500				
0				
12/03	12/04	12/05	12/06	12/07

Quality King Distributors

Quality King Distributors rules a gargantuan gray market empire. It buys US name-brand OTC pharmaceutical and branded personal care products that have been exported to overseas markets, re-imports them, then sells them below suggested retail prices. The practice, deeply disliked by US manufacturers, has been ruled legal by the Supreme Court. Quality King distributes its products to pharmacy and grocery chains, grocery distributors, and wholesale clubs throughout the US. Subsidiary QK Healthcare distributes branded and generic prescription pharmaceuticals. Bernard Nussdorf and his wife Ruth founded Quality King in 1961 in Long Island, New York. The Nussdorf family still owns the company.

EXECUTIVES

Chairman and CEO: Glenn H. Nussdorf
COO: Marc Garrett
EVP: Michael W. Katz, age 60
VP Human Resources: Olga Lancaster
General Counsel: Alfred Paliani
Director Sales: Michael Ross

LOCATIONS

HQ: Quality King Distributors Inc.
2060 9th Ave., Ronkonkoma, NY 11779
Phone: 631-737-5555   **Fax:** 631-439-2388
Web: www.qkd.com

COMPETITORS

AmerisourceBergen
Apothecary Products
Cardinal Health
Imperial Distributors
Kinray
McKesson

QuikTrip Corporation

QuikTrip provides a quick fix for those on the go. QuikTrip (QT) owns and operates about 500 gasoline and convenience stores in nine states. QT stores, which average 4,200 to 5,000 sq. ft., feature the company's own QT brand of gas and diesel fuel, as well as brand-name beverages, candy, and tobacco, and QT's own Quik 'n Tasty and HOTZI lines of sandwiches. QT's 15-plus travel centers offer CAT scales, food, fuel, showers, and other services for truckers. The company's FleetMaster program offers commercial trucking companies detailed reports showing drivers' product purchases, amounts spent, and odometer readings. QT was co-founded in 1958 by chairman Chester Cadieux. His son Chet runs the company.

QuikTrip is remodeling stores and expanding its hot and cold beverage selection. The icy "Koolee," introduced in 1963, has been phased out and replaced by a frozen carbonated beverage called a Freezoni, available in seven flavors. More than 70% of the food products sold at QT stores are manufactured and distributed by its Quik 'n Tasty subsidiary.

The company recently opened several upscale, high-volume (capable of handling 120 cars per hour) car washes in Tulsa and Wichita, Kansas.

EXECUTIVES

Chairman, President, and CEO:
Chester (Chet) Cadieux III, age 41
SVP Store Operations: Mike Stanford
VP and CFO: Sandra J. (Sandi) Westbrook
VP Marketing: James (Jim) Denny
VP Finance and Treasurer: Paula Cotten
VP Operations Systems: Ron Jeffers
VP Human Resources: Kimberly (Kim) Owen
Director Real Estate: Rodney Loyd
Manager Public and Government Affairs:
Mike Thornbrugh

LOCATIONS

HQ: QuikTrip Corporation
4777 S. 129th East Ave., Tulsa, OK 74134
Phone: 918-615-7900   **Fax:** 918-615-7377
Web: www.quiktrip.com

PRODUCTS/OPERATIONS

2008 Stores

	No.
Convenience stores	483
Travel centers	17
Total	**500**

COMPETITORS

7-Eleven
Casey's General Stores
Chevron
CITGO
Couche-Tard
Exxon
E-Z Mart Stores
Krause Gentle
Motiva Enterprises
Racetrac Petroleum
Valero Energy

Quintiles Transnational

Quintiles Transnational has plenty to CRO about. One of the world's top contract research organizations (CROs), with offices in about 50 countries, it helps drug and medical device companies develop and sell their products. The firm provides a comprehensive range of clinical trials management services, including patient recruitment, data analysis, laboratory testing, and regulatory filing. Its consulting unit offers strategic advice at every stage of drug discovery and development, and its Innovex subsidiary is a contract sales organization providing sales personnel to promote approved products. An investment group led by founder and CEO Dennis Gillings took the firm private in 2003.

Additionally, the company provides financing and partnering support through its NovaQuest unit, which invests in client companies (either through cash or services) in return for royalties on sales of approved products. Quintiles launched the NovaQuest division in 2006. In 2007 it announced a major collaboration with ProStrakan, under which it is providing a US sales force to promote ProStrakan's Sancuso (a treatment for chemotherapy-induced nausea) in exchange for royalties.

Quintiles Transnational has been taking advantage of the growing demand for outsourced clinical development services, as belt-tightening pharma and biotech companies look to trim costs even as they are desperate to find and develop new products. The company has focused efforts on developing services that help its clients reduce risk and time-to-market. It established a joint venture with Thermo Fisher Scientific called Cenduit, for example, which helps control clinical trials costs by automating delivery of supplies, among other things. And in 2007 it acquired Eidetics, a company that helps drug companies collect and analyze data that is used at various decision-making junctures in the drug development process.

The company sold much of its preclinical services business, which provided services like toxicology testing and chemistry services, to Aptuit, in order to focus on its core clinical (i.e. human testing) services. It offers early-stage testing services to its clients through a continuing partnership with Aptuit.

In late 2007 Quintiles announced changes in its ownership structure: CEO Gillings, TPG Capital, and Temasek Holdings remain as investors, and Bain Capital and 3i join the investment group. JPMorgan Chase's One Equity Partners sold its stake in Quintiles. The new investment partnership is led by Gillings, Bain Capital, and TPG.

HISTORY

Quintiles was founded by Dennis Gillings, a British biostatistician who had worked with Hoechst (now part of Sanofi-Aventis) on data analysis in the 1970s. Gillings set up Quintiles (Quantitative Information Technology In The Life and Economic Sciences) in 1982 at the University of North Carolina, where he was then teaching. The company grew as drug companies began outsourcing some of the more irksome tasks of drug development. Quintiles went public in 1994.

Quintiles used the proceeds of the IPO to expand its health economics segment with the purchases of Benefit International (1995) and Lewin Group (1996). These purchases introduced the company to such new clients as governments and HMOs. Quintiles' 1996 purchase of Innovex (unrelated to the computer hardware maker of the same name) made it the world's largest CRO. The buying spree continued in 1997 and 1998. Among the purchases were some intended to strengthen Quintiles' marketing services (Data Analysis Systems Inc., Q.E.D. International, and France-based Serval). The firm also formed new collaborations with such academic research organizations as Johns Hopkins Medicine.

In 1999 Quintiles expanded its marketing arm with the purchase of Pharmaceutical Marketing Services (parent of the leading pharmaceuticals industry research company, Scott-Levin) and jumped headlong into data mining with its purchase of ENVOY — which processed insurance claims. Quintiles found the core business uninspiring and sold it to Healtheon (now Emdeon, formerly WebMD) the next year. But it kept rights to ENVOY's stream of treatment, outcome, and insurance data, gleaned from health care providers, hospitals, payers, and pharmacies — a treasure house of information useful to salespeople and health providers.

The company continued in 2000 to add offices in Europe, Asia, and Latin America. The company also opened additional offices in the US and Europe to help Japanese pharmaceutical companies market their products in those regions. Late in the year, Quintiles bought the clinical development unit of Pharmacia.

In 2001 Quintiles became embroiled in a legal dispute with WebMD involving the availability of data associated with ENVOY; the company challenged WebMD's efforts to withhold such data. The two companies settled the squabble later that year and agreed to sever all ties. Also in 2001 Quintiles streamlined operations and cut about 5% of its workforce.

The future of the CRO came into question at the end of 2002. Gillings presented the company with a buyout offer; he planned to take the company private so he could pursue a new growth strategy Wall Street would surely find risky. The board rejected that offer in October 2002, but it opened up an auction. Some leading equity firms reportedly made offers, but Gillings — with

backing from Blackstone Group and BANK ONE's One Equity Partners (now part of JPMorgan Chase) — placed another offer for Quintiles and won the prize in April 2003. Some five months later, Quintiles went private.

In 2005 Quintiles sold three business units — preclinical services, pharmaceutical sciences, and clinical trial supplies — to privately held Aptuit for $125 million. It made the sale in order to focus efforts on its core clinical-stage services.

EXECUTIVES

Chairman and CEO: Dennis B. Gillings, age 63
Vice Chairman Operations: Oppel Greeff
EVP Corporate Development: Ronald J. (Ron) Wooten
EVP and CIO: William R. Deam
EVP Strategic Business Partnerships and Customer Relationship: Derek M. Winstanly
SVP and Acting CFO: Mike Troullis
SVP Clinical Research Strategies; Managing Director, Quintiles Public Health and Government Services: Oren Cohen
SVP Communications and Patient Recruitment: David (Dave) Coman
SVP Global Marketing and Chief Marketing Officer: Millie Tan
Chief Administrative Officer: Mike Mortimer, age 44
Chief Medical and Scientific Officer: Christopher H. Cabell
VP Business Development: Matt Eberhart
VP Corporate Communications: Pat Grebe
President, Quintiles Global Commercialization: Hywel Evans
President, iGuard: Hugo Stephenson
Practice Leader, Market Access, US: John Doyle
Practice Leader, Product Development and Commercialization, US: Adrian McKerney
Practice Leader, Regulatory and Quality and Product Development and Commercialization, Europe: Jim Featherstone
Auditors: PricewaterhouseCoopers LLP

LOCATIONS

HQ: Quintiles Transnational Corp.
4709 Creekstone Dr., Ste. 200, Durham, NC 27703
Phone: 919-998-2000   **Fax:** 919-998-2094
Web: www.quintiles.com

PRODUCTS/OPERATIONS

Selected Products and Services
Continuing Medical Education (CME) program design
Contract sales services (Innovex)
Financing and partnering solutions (NovaQuest)
Product development services
  Biostatistics
  Central laboratory services
  Clinical pharmacology
  Data management
  Patient and investigator recruitment
  Phase I-III clinical trial design
  Regulatory services
Strategic consulting services

COMPETITORS

Covance
ICON
IMS Health
Kendle
MDS
PAREXEL
Pharmaceutical Product Development
PharmaNet Development Group
PRA International
Quest Diagnostics

HISTORICAL FINANCIALS
Company Type: Private

Income Statement
FYE: December 31

	REVENUE ($ mil.)	NET INCOME ($ mil.)	NET PROFIT MARGIN	EMPLOYEES
12/07	2,700	—	—	21,000
12/06	2,530	—	—	18,000
12/05	2,399	—	—	16,000
12/04	2,146	—	—	16,986
12/03	2,046	—	—	15,991
Annual Growth	7.2%	—	—	7.0%

Revenue History

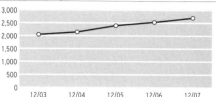

Racetrac Petroleum

RaceTrac Petroleum hopes it's a popular pit stop for gasoline and snacks in the Southeast. The company owns about 525 gas stations and convenience stores in about a dozen states under the RaceTrac and RaceWay names. (RaceWay stores are operated by independent contractors.) The chain plans to grow by adding between 35 and 45 new locations annually. Carl Bolch founded RaceTrac in Missouri in 1934. His son, chairman and CEO Carl Bolch Jr., moved the company into high-volume gas stations with long, self-service islands that can serve as many as two dozen vehicles at one time. RaceTrac's convenience stores sell fresh deli food and offer some fast-food fare. The Bolch family owns the company.

EXECUTIVES

Chairman and CEO: Carl E. Bolch Jr.
President: Max Lenker
CFO: Robert J. Dumbacher
SVP, Operations: Ben Tison
VP, Human Resources: Allison Moran

LOCATIONS

HQ: RaceTrac Petroleum, Inc.
3225 Cumberland Blvd., Ste. 100, Atlanta, GA 30339
Phone: 770-431-7600
Web: www.racetrac.com

COMPETITORS

7-Eleven
Chevron
Couche-Tard
Cumberland Farms
Exxon
E-Z Mart Stores
Gate Petroleum
Motiva Enterprises
The Pantry
Pilot Corporation
QuikTrip

HISTORICAL FINANCIALS

Company Type: Private

Income Statement

	REVENUE ($ mil.)	NET INCOME ($ mil.)	NET PROFIT MARGIN	EMPLOYEES
12/07	5,520	—	—	3,812
12/06	4,900	—	—	4,039
12/05	4,969	—	—	3,962
Annual Growth	5.4%	—	—	(1.9%)

FYE: December 31

Revenue History

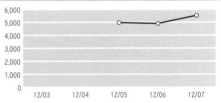

Radio Flyer

Radio Flyer makes those wittle wed wagons adults adore and kids covet. An icon of childhood play and imagination, the #18 Classic Red Wagon has rolled out of the plant for more than 70 years — an American toy industry record and the reason Radio Flyer owns a majority of the US market. The company also makes plastic wagons and models with oversized, terrain-friendly tires and wooden rails. Radio Flyer makes bikes and trikes for little tykes, in addition to scooters and pedal-powered cars. Italian immigrant Antonio Pasin made his first Liberty Coaster in 1917. He chose the name "Radio Flyer" in 1933 because it sounded futuristic. His grandchildren own and operate the company.

While many have an emotional attachment to the company's classic toys, Radio Flyer has continued to create new products designed for additional comfort and convenience. For example, its new "Ultimate Family Wagon" has a canopy, safety belts, removable storage areas, a tray table, and four cup holders. Its new award-winning Fold 2 Go Trike folds up for easy storage.

EXECUTIVES

Chairman: Mario Pasin
President and CEO: Robert Pasin
EVP and CFO: Paul Pasin
Human Resources Manager: Carol LaRocco

LOCATIONS

HQ: Radio Flyer Inc.
6515 W. Grand Ave., Chicago, IL 60707
Phone: 773-637-7100   **Fax:** 773-637-8874
Web: www.radioflyer.com

Radio Flyer sells its products in retail outlets throughout the US and Canada. It also has distributors in Asia, Australia, Europe, and South America.

PRODUCTS/OPERATIONS

Selected Products

Accessories
  Cooler pack
  Pads for wagon bed and sides
  Umbrella
  Wagon seat
  Wagon trailer
Kid's Wheelbarrow
Little Line (doll-sized)
  Little Red Wheelbarrow
  Little Red Scooter
  Little Red Tricycle
  Little Red Wagon
  Little Wood Sled
  Little Wood Wagon
Miniatures (Christmas ornaments, desk accessories)
Retro Red Line
  Classic Red Bicycle (training wheels)
  Classic Red Scooter
  Classic Red Tricycle
  Classic Red Tricycle with push handles
  My First Bicycle (training wheels)
Ride Ons
  Fold 2 Go Trike
  Little Red Fire Engine
  Little Red Roadster
  Little Red Scooter
  Radio Flyer Racer
  Speedy Pedal Car
Specialty Line
  Classic Rocking Horse
  Rolling Pony
  Tiny Trike (push-along wooden tricycle)
  Walker Wagon
Wagons
  All-Terrain Cargo Wagon (removable wooden sides)
  All-Terrain Discovery Wagon
  All-Terrain Steel and Wood Wagon
  All-Terrain Wood Wagon
  Big Red Classic ATW (all-terrain)
  Classic Red Wagon
  Discovery Wagon (plastic, includes storage compartment)
  My First Wagon
  Navigator Wagon (plastic, two-seater)
  Pathfinder Wagon (plastic, fold-up seats)
  Promotional Wagon
  Quad Shock Wagon (plastic, with Monroe shock absorbers)
  Sport Utility Wagon (wooden, all-terrain)
  Town and Country Wagon (removable wooden sides)
  Traditional Red Wagon
  Trailblazer Wagon (plastic)
  Trav-ler Wagon (wooden sides)
  Ultimate Family Wagon (plastic)
  Wagon-Barrow Utility Wagon (adult-oriented)

COMPETITORS

Deere
Hasbro
Little Tikes
Mattel
Pacific Cycle
Step 2

Raley's

Raley's has to stock plenty of fresh fruit and great wines — it sells to the people that produce them. The company operates about 130 supermarkets and larger-sized superstores, mostly in Northern California, but also in northern Nevada. In addition to its flagship Raley's Superstores, the company operates Bel Air Markets, Nob Hill Foods (an upscale Bay Area chain with about 25 locations), and about a half dozen discount warehouse stores under the Food Source banner in Northern California. Raley's stores typically offer groceries, natural foods, liquor, and pharmacies. Founded during the Depression by Thomas Porter Raley, the company is owned by Tom's daughter Joyce Raley Teel.

In August 2007 the company sold its 10 stores in New Mexico to Albertsons, thereby exiting the New Mexico market. Raley's said the sale will allow it to better focus on its core markets in Northern California, the Bay Area, and northern Nevada.

In mid-2006 the company launched an online shopping service in Sacramento. The service — called ecart — lets shoppers order and pay for groceries online, but pick up the orders at a pre-arranged time at the store. Rival Safeway's Internet grocery service offers home delivery.

EXECUTIVES

Co-Chairman and Owner: Joyce Raley Teel, age 73
Co-Chairman: James E. (Jim) Teel
President and CEO: William J. (Bill) Coyne
EVP and CFO: William Anderson
SVP, Store Operations: Rick Kaiser
SVP and CIO: Eric F. G. Wilson
SVP, Human Resources: Jeffrey D. Szczesny
SVP, Sales and Merchandising: Joel Barton
VP, Pharmacy and General Merchandise: Flint Pendergraft
VP, Real Estate: Kent Haggerty
General Counsel: Jennifer Crabb
Communications Specialist: Jennifer Ortega

LOCATIONS

HQ: Raley's
500 W. Capitol Ave., West Sacramento, CA 95605
Phone: 916-373-3333   **Fax:** 916-371-1323
Web: www.raleys.com

2007 Stores

	No.
California	116
Northern Nevada	13
Total	**129**

COMPETITORS

Andronico's Market
Costco Wholesale
Food 4 Less
Grocery Outlet
Kroger
Longs Drug
Lunardi's Super Market
Ralphs
Safeway
Save Mart
Trader Joe's
Wal-Mart
Whole Foods
WinCo Foods

Rand McNally

Rand McNally lets you know where you stand. The largest commercial mapmaker in the world, the company is famous for its top-selling flagship product, the *Rand McNally Road Atlas*. In addition, the company publishes *The Thomas Guide* map books and produces travel-related software (StreetFinder Wireless) and educational products for classrooms (*Goode's World Atlas*). It also makes commercial mileage and routing software for the transportation industry (IntelliRoute trucking software). Its Rand McNally Canada unit makes maps for the Canadian market. The company sells its products online and through some 60,000 retail outlets in the US. Rand McNally is majority-owned by private equity firm Leonard Green & Partners.

Although it created a Web site in 1996, the company didn't really begin focusing on the Internet until 1999, years later than online rivals such as MapQuest. Rand McNally relaunched its Web site and increased its Web and software product offerings in hopes of catching up with its online competitors.

Rand McNally also has started widening its map offerings to include more detailed tourist stops such as recommended lodging and restaurants. It also produces customized maps for customers.

HISTORY

Rand McNally was founded by William Rand and Andrew McNally in 1856. In 1864 the pair bought the job-printing department of the *Chicago Tribune* and expanded into the printing of railroad tickets and schedules. They published their first book, a Chicago business directory, in 1870. In 1872 the company printed its first map for the *Railway Guide*. Rand McNally later expanded into publishing paperback novels (popular among train travelers), and by 1891 annual sales topped $1 million.

During the 1890s McNally bought Rand's share of the business, and the company branched into printing school textbooks. Rand McNally's first photo auto guide was issued in 1907, and the company introduced its first complete US road atlas in 1924.

When Hitler invaded Poland in 1939, Rand McNally's New York stock of European maps sold out in one day. WWII necessitated the revision of a number of maps — a challenge that the company continued to face throughout the 20th century.

Although the company had abandoned adult fiction and nonfiction in 1914, it reentered the field in 1948 when a company official persuaded explorer Thor Heyerdahl to write a book for the company about his adventures. First published in 1950, Heyerdahl's *Kon-Tiki* sold more than a million copies in its first six years.

Rand McNally produced its first four-color road atlas in 1960, and during the 1970s it began publishing travel guides for Mobil Oil. The next decade the company published several new road atlases to fill the void created when gas stations discontinued their practice of giving away free road maps. Rand McNally sold its textbook publishing business to Houghton Mifflin in 1980, and five years later it began computerizing its cartography operation.

In 1993 the company acquired Allmaps Canada Limited (now Rand McNally Canada). It introduced *TripMaker,* a CD-ROM vacation-planning program, the next year. Also in 1994 Rand McNally won a contract to create maps for a *Reader's Digest* atlas. The company debuted its StreetFinder street-level software in 1995 and created its Cartographic and Information Services division in 1996. It also established a Web site that year.

The next year, as part of a plan to focus on mapmaking and providing geographic information, Rand McNally sold a number of its subsidiaries (Book Services Group, DocuSystems Group). AEA Investors bought a controlling interest in the company later in 1997, bringing an end to more than 140 years of McNally family control (though it did retain a minority stake). While Rand McNally was still profitable, the sale to AEA underscored the challenges facing the company: Growth in earnings had slowed, and technological changes (Internet maps and software) had altered the mapmaking industry.

Rand McNally expanded in 1999 with acquisitions of mapmakers Thomas Bros. Maps and King of the Road Map Service. Later that year Henry Feinberg resigned as chairman and CEO. Richard Davis was appointed CEO, and John Macomber became chairman.

In 2000 the company relaunched its Web site with additional trip planning capabilities. Also that year it became the primary North American distributor of *National Geographic* maps and COO Norman Wells replaced Davis as CEO.

In 2001 Michael Hehir was named CEO, Wells replaced Macomber as chairman, and Macomber remained as a director on the board. In 2003 Rand McNally filed for Chapter 11 bankruptcy protection. The company exited bankruptcy within two months, with buyout firm Leonard Green & Partners as its new majority owner. Also that year Hehir left the company and Allstate executive Robert Apatoff was named CEO. Wells was replaced by Peter Nolan, a managing partner at Leonard Green & Partners.

EXECUTIVES

Chairman: Peter J. Nolan, age 50
CEO: Robert Apatoff
COO: Mark Ogan
SVP and CFO: Norman Smagley, age 42
SVP and CTO: Ken Levin
SVP and Chief Marketing Officer: Betsy Owens
SVP Geographic Information Services: Joel Minster
SVP Supply Chain Management: Tom Anderson
VP Business and Specialty Sales: Donna Koppensteiner
VP Consumer Sales and Distribution:
  Dennis FitzPatrick
VP Consumer Sales: Jeff Ventura
VP Local Travel Marketing: Gary Lancina
VP National Travel Marketing: Kendra Ensor
VP New Products and Strategy: Alan Yefsky
Director Educational Publishing: Pat Riley
Director Internet: David Rickabaugh
Editorial Director: Laurie Borman
Director Sales, Transportation Division:
  Bernie Hockswender

LOCATIONS

HQ: Rand McNally & Company
  8255 N. Central Park Ave., Skokie, IL 60076
Phone: 847-329-8100   **Fax:** 800-934-3479
Web: www.randmcnally.com

PRODUCTS/OPERATIONS

Selected Products

Commercial Trucking Products
  IntelliRoute
  MileMaker
  Motor Carriers' Road Atlas
Consumer Products
  Children's Products
  Reference Maps and Books
  Road Atlases
    Motor Carriers' Road Atlases
    The Rand McNally Road Atlas Line
  Road and Street Maps
  Software
    StreetFinder
  Street Guides (street-level detail)
  Thomas Guides (spiral-bound format)
Educational Products
Online Business Locator
Wireless Products
  Mobile Travel Tools
  Rand McNally Traffic

COMPETITORS

AAA	Lonely Planet
Analytical Surveys	MapQuest
Avalon Travel Publishing	Michelin
DeLorme	National Geographic
ESRI	Pitney Bowes Software
Expedia	R. L. Polk
Globe Pequot	Vindigo
Google	Yahoo!

Randolph-Brooks Federal Credit Union

Randolph-Brooks Federal Credit Union brooks no interference with anyone who would come between it and its 260,000 members. Randolph-Brooks Federal Credit Union (RBFCU) provides deposit and lending services, making loans for homes, cars, education, and consumer goods. Other products offered by the credit union include credit cards, ATM cards, and foreign travel services. RBFCU has about 30 Texas locations in San Antonio, Austin, and nearby communities.

Through its subsidiary, Randolph Brooks Services Group, the credit union offers insurance, investment products, dental benefits, auto and home warranties, roadside assistance programs, and financial planning services.

Subsidiary Randolph Brooks Insurance Agency offers auto, home, and personal property insurance to members, while Randolph Brooks Title Company provides title settlement and insurance services.

The credit union opened in 1952 with a plan to serve military personnel stationed at Randolph Air Force Base.

EXECUTIVES

Chairman: Fred Walters
President: Randy Smith
SVP Finance: Jimmy O. Junkin
SVP Information Systems: Ron Freerking
SVP Planning and Marketing: John Kelly
VP Consumer Lending: Mark Sekula

LOCATIONS

HQ: Randolph-Brooks Federal Credit Union
Creswell Center, 1 Randolph Brooks Pkwy.,
Live Oak, TX 78233
Phone: 210-945-3333   **Fax:** 210-945-3764
Web: www.rbfcu.org

PRODUCTS/OPERATIONS

2007 Sales

	$ mil.	% of total
Interest		
Loans	95.1	49
Investments	48.3	25
Noninterest		
Fees	31.2	16
Other	20.6	10
Total	**195.2**	**100**

COMPETITORS

Bank of America
Compass Bancshares
Cullen/Frost Bankers
JPMorgan Chase
Regions Financial
SACU
SSFCU
Temple-Inland
Washington Mutual

HISTORICAL FINANCIALS

Company Type: Not-for-profit

Income Statement				FYE: December 31
	ASSETS ($ mil.)	NET INCOME ($ mil.)	INCOME AS % OF ASSETS	EMPLOYEES
12/07	2,952	36	1.2%	810
12/06	2,542	33	1.3%	736
12/05	2,380	35	1.5%	—
12/04	2,234	26	1.2%	—
12/03	2,088	22	1.1%	—
Annual Growth	9.1%	12.9%	—	10.1%

2007 Year-End Financials

Equity as % of assets: 12.1%   Long-term debt ($ mil.): —
Return on assets: 1.3%   Sales ($ mil.): 195
Return on equity: 10.8%

Net Income History

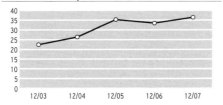

RBS Global

RBS Global manufactures power transmission components, drives, and conveying equipment, including bearings, chains, couplings, and other related products under the Rexnord name. Prominent brand names include TableTop and MatTop (flattop chains), Shafer and PSI (bearings), and Cartriseal (aerospace seals). The company also makes special components such as electric motor brakes, small mechanical power transmission components, and security systems for utility companies. In 2006 The Carlyle Group sold RBS Global to Apollo Management for about $1.8 billion. The US accounts for three-quarters of the company's sales.

In 2007 RBS Global/Rexnord acquired the Zurn Industries plumbing products business of Jacuzzi Brands for about $942 million in cash. The purchase price was financed through an equity investment by Apollo and its affiliates of approximately $290 million and debt financing of approximately $660 million.

In 2005 Rexnord acquired the Falk Corporation (gears and couplings) from Hamilton Sundstrand, a United Technologies Corporation subsidiary, for approximately $295 million.

An explosion at Falk's Milwaukee foundry killed three employees and injured dozens of people in late 2006. The building destroyed in the blast, believed to be caused by a propane leak, was a warehouse. The catastrophe temporarily suspended manufacturing operations at the Falk complex, raising industry concerns about how long Falk would be unable to produce and deliver its large industrial gears, castings, and couplings, which are widely used in construction and mining machinery. All employees were back to work about a month after the explosion.

Disasters have played a crucial role in the history of Falk, which was founded in 1856 as the Bavaria Brewery, on the site of the company's main plant in Milwaukee. Fires destroyed the brewery in 1889 and again in 1892, forcing the Falk family to sell the business to Frederick Pabst (of Pabst Brewing fame). Herman Falk, a son of the founder, eventually found his way into the cast-welding business, shaping and joining rails for railroad lines. The Falk company got into the foundry business in 1899 and went on to become a leading manufacturer of gears for steam turbines and other machinery. Sundstrand Corporation (now Hamilton Sundstrand) acquired Falk in 1968.

RBS Global, operating under the Rexnord, RBS Global, and Falk names, sells its products globally through more than 2,000 OEMs and more than 400 industrial distributors that operate through more than 2,200 branches. The company owns and operates about 50 manufacturing facilities and four repair facilities worldwide.

RBS Global derives more than half of its gear sales from replacement, or aftermarket, parts.

EXECUTIVES

Chairman: George M. Sherman, age 66
President, CEO, and Director: Robert A. Hitt, age 51, $739,316 pay
EVP: George C. Moore, age 53
SVP and CFO: Todd A. Adams, age 37
VP and General Counsel: Patricia (Patty) Whaley
President, Water Management Group: Alex P. Marini, age 61
Auditors: Ernst & Young LLP

LOCATIONS

HQ: RBS Global, Inc.
4701 W. Greenfield Ave., Milwaukee, WI 53214
Phone: 414-643-3000   **Fax:** 414-643-3078
Web: www.rexnord.com

RBS Global/Rexnord has manufacturing facilities in Australia, Brazil, Canada, China, France, Germany, Italy, the Netherlands, and the US.

2008 Sales

	$ mil.	% of total
US	1,392.1	75
Europe	285.2	15
Other regions	176.2	10
Total	**1,853.5**	**100**

PRODUCTS/OPERATIONS

2008 Sales

	$ mil.	% of total
Power transmission	1,342.3	72
Water management	511.2	28
Total	**1,853.5**	**100**

Selected Products

Aerospace bearings and seals
Couplings
Flattop chains
Gears
Industrial bearings
  Ball bearings
  Cylindrical bearings
  Filament and sleeves
  Roller bearings
Industrial chain products
  Engineered chain
  Roller chain
Special components
  Electric motor brakes
  Miniature mechanical power transmission components
  Security devices for utility companies
Water management (Zurn)
  Backflow preventers
  Chemical drainage systems
  Commercial brass faucets and valves
  Fire system valves
  Hydrants
  Interceptors
  Linear drainage systems
  Plumbing systems (PEX)
  Point drains
  Radiant heating systems (PEX)
  Relief valves
  Thermostatic mixing valves (Aqua-Guard)

COMPETITORS

A. O. Smith
Baldor Electric
Crane Co.
Emerson Electric
Habasit America
JTEKT
Kaydon
Kohler
MINEBEA
Moen
NSK
NTN
RBC Bearings
Regal Beloit
Reliance Electric
Renold
Rockwell Automation
Schaeffler
SKF
Sloan Valve
Solus Industrial Innovations
TB Wood's
Timken
Trane Inc.

HISTORICAL FINANCIALS
Company Type: Private

Income Statement
FYE: March 31

	REVENUE ($ mil.)	NET INCOME ($ mil.)	NET PROFIT MARGIN	EMPLOYEES
3/08	1,854	41	2.2%	7,400
3/07	1,256	3	0.2%	7,100
3/06	1,416	(17)	—	5,800
3/05	811	22	2.7%	5,680
3/04	713	14	2.0%	4,890
Annual Growth	27.0%	30.3%	—	10.9%

2008 Year-End Financials
Debt ratio: —
Return on equity: 5.7%
Cash ($ mil.): —
Current ratio: —
Long-term debt ($ mil.): —

Net Income History

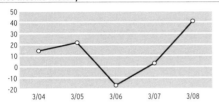

Reader's Digest

Eighty-million readers. Fifty editions. One undersized magazine. The Reader's Digest Association (RDA) is publisher of the world's #1 general-interest magazine, *Reader's Digest*, which is translated into some 20 languages. The company also uses its extensive consumer database of more than 130 million names (considered one of the best in the world) to market books (Reader's Digest Select Editions, how-to guides, cookbooks), special-interest magazines, music, videos, and financial and health products to customers in some 80 countries. Its Books Are Fun unit is a direct marketer of books and gifts. An investor group led by Ripplewood Holdings completed its $1.6 billion acquisition of the firm in 2007.

RDA has struggled to meet the challenges of a slowdown in advertising, a core publication that is not attracting young people (thus creating a stodgy image for the company), and regulatory changes in sweepstakes solicitations (on which the company relied for decades). To address these concerns, RDA eliminated its sweepstakes programs and is using alternate forms of marketing sources, including the Internet, direct mailings, and other methods. It restructured its books and entertainment division and ceased publication of *Walking* magazine. Reorganization at the company resulted in the loss of hundreds of jobs.

RDA is bulking up its online operations (including e-commerce) and has revamped *Reader's Digest* with a new cover and new features. In 2007 RDA added Weekly Reader Corporation's *Weekly Reader* to its portfolio through the acquisition of WRC Media, which it renamed RD School & Educational Services. The following year the company expanded its offerings with the launch of *Best Health* (a healthy lifestyle

magazine for Canadian women) and *Discovery Channel Magazine* in Asia (a collaboration with Discovery Communications).

Trying to reach a younger audience, the company has tapped popular Food Network star Rachael Ray for a new lifestyle magazine called *Every Day with Rachael Ray*. RDA boosted its food component further in 2006 with the purchase of Allrecipes.com, a food and cooking site. The acquisition makes RDA the world's #1 aggregator of food content in print and online. Further beefing up its food focused content, in 2008 the company launched *Healthy Cooking*, an offshoot of its *Taste of Home* title, that is focused on lighter food and nutrition-related topics.

The DeWitt Wallace-Reader's Digest Fund and the Lila Wallace-Reader's Digest Fund, named for the founders, once owned 50% of the company's voting shares. Responding to pressure from investors about the company's convoluted ownership structure, the DeWitt Wallace and Lila Wallace funds instituted a stock recapitalization plan and sold off their ownership stake in the company.

In a deal that then-CEO Eric Schrier called "a great opportunity," RDA agreed in late 2006 to a $1.6 billion takeover bid by an investor group led by Ripplewood Holdings. Subsequently Mary Berner succeeded Schrier as CEO of Reader's Digest, with Schrier becoming an industrial partner with Ripplewood and a consultant to Reader's Digest.

EXECUTIVES
Chairman: Harvey Golub, age 69
President, CEO, and Director: Mary G. Berner, age 49
Acting CFO and Director: Harris Williams, age 39
SVP Global Operations and Business Redesign and IT: Albert L. Perruzza, age 61, $509,015 pay
SVP Human Resources: Todd C. McCarty, age 42
VP and Editor-in-Chief, International Editions and Magazine Development: Frank Lalli, age 66
VP Global Communications and Chief Communications Officer: William K. (Bill) Adler, age 55
VP and Editor-in-Chief, International Editions and Magazine Development: Frank Lalli, age 66
VP Global Communications and Chief Communications Officer: William K. (Bill) Adler, age 55
Director Public Relations: Ellen Morgenstern
President, RD Europe; CEO, Direct Holdings US Corp: Michael A. Brennan, age 61, $579,794 pay
President and Publisher, Trade Publishing and Special Markets: Harold Clarke
President, Books are Fun: David A. Krishock, age 53
President, Global RDA Interactive: Jodi Kahn, age 44
President, Global Consumer Marketing: Dawn M. Zier, age 42
President, RD Canada and Latin America: Andrea C. Martin, age 48
President, RD Community; President and Group Publisher, Reader's Digest, Selecciones, and RD Large Print: Eva Dillon, age 51
President, RD Asia-Pacific: Paul Heath, age 48
President, Home & Garden and Health & Wellness: Alyce Alston, age 43
President, Food and Entertaining: Suzanne Grimes, age 49
Auditors: Ernst & Young LLP

LOCATIONS
HQ: The Reader's Digest Association, Inc.
Reader's Digest Rd., Pleasantville, NY 10570
Phone: 914-238-1000
Web: www.rd.com

PRODUCTS/OPERATIONS
2008 Sales

	$ mil.	% of total
Reader's Digest International	1,632.7	55
Reader's Digest US	836.0	29
School & Educational Services	458.1	16
Adjustments	(140.4)	—
Total	**2,786.4**	**100**

Selected Books and Home Entertainment Products
General-interest books (how-to and reference books, cookbooks, and children's books)
Reader's Digest Select Editions (popular fiction)
Recorded music (original and licensed recordings)
Series books (multiple volumes; seven languages)
TV movies and mini-series (developed with partner CBS)
Videocassettes and original video productions

Selected Magazines and Web Content
allrecipes.com
Backyard Living
Every Day With Rachael Ray
The Family Handyman
Light & Tasty
Reader's Digest
Reader's Digest Canada
Taste of Home
Weekly Reader

Other Businesses
Books are Fun, Ltd. (display marketer of books and gifts)
Fund-raising products and services

COMPETITORS
AARP
Advance Publications
Bauer Consumer Media
Deseret Management
F+W Publications
Hearst Magazines
K-tel
Lagardère Active
Martha Stewart Living
Meredith Corporation
Pearson
Rodale
Thomas Nelson
Time Inc.

Realogy Corporation

Realogy Corporation is all about keeping it real. The company is one of the biggest names in the real estate business you've never heard of. Instead, it operates through the names you *have* heard of: Century 21, Coldwell Banker, Sotheby's International Realty, and ERA. The company also licenses the Better Homes and Gardens brand from Meredith Corporation. Realogy has nearly 16,000 offices (more than 900 are company-owned) in nearly 90 countries. Besides its bread and butter of residential real estate and corporate relocation, it also offers title settlement and research through Title Resource Group. Domus Holding (an affiliate of Apollo Advisors) acquired Realogy for a reported $9 billion.

As with the rest of the real estate industry, Realogy was affected by the downturn in the housing market in 2007, with revenues sliding for the second straight year. However, the company feels that its size will help it weather the continuing downturn until the market improves.

Because Internet searches for homes has dramatically increased over the years, the company has made the decision to move away from traditional print marketing and put a greater emphasis on the Web. Its Openhouse.com site lists open houses around the country; in 2008 Prudential Realty signed a deal to provide a feed of its open house events to the site.

That year the company also took a stake in Century 21 China Real Estate, an independently owned firm that franchises the Century 21 name. China's growing middle class is spurring the growth of homeownership in the country.

Realogy was spun off from Avis Budget Group (formerly Cendant) in 2006.

EXECUTIVES

Chairman: Henry R. Silverman, age 67
President and CEO: Richard A. Smith, age 54
EVP, CFO, and Treasurer: Anthony E. Hull, age 49
EVP and Chief Administrative Officer:
David J. Weaving, age 41
EVP, General Counsel, and Secretary: Marilyn J. Wasser, age 52
SVP, Chief Accounting Officer, and Controller:
Dea Benson, age 53
SVP Corporate Communications: Mark Panus
SVP Human Resources: Marie R. Armenio
Investor Relations: Alicia Swift
Auditors: Deloitte & Touche LLP

LOCATIONS

HQ: Realogy Corporation
1 Campus Dr., Parsippany, NJ 07054
Phone: 973-407-2000 **Fax:** 973-407-7004
Web: www.realogy.com

PRODUCTS/OPERATIONS

2007 Sales

	$ mil.	% of total
Gross commission income	4,513	76
Service revenue	838	14
Franchise fees	424	7
Other	192	3
Total	**5,967**	**100**

Selected Subsidiaries

Century 21
Coldwell Banker
Coldwell Banker Commercial
ERA
Sotheby's International Realty

COMPETITORS

Advantis	Jones Lang LaSalle
CB Richard Ellis	LandAmerica Financial
Cushman & Wakefield	Group
Draper and Kramer	Prudential Connecticut
First American	RE/MAX
Grubb & Ellis	SIRVA
HomeServices	Weichert Realtors
Investors Title	ZipRealty
John L. Scott Real Estate	

HISTORICAL FINANCIALS

Company Type: Private

Income Statement

FYE: December 31

	REVENUE ($ mil.)	NET INCOME ($ mil.)	NET PROFIT MARGIN	EMPLOYEES
12/06	6,492	365	5.6%	8,500

Red Apple Group

Red Apple Group sells more than just apples in the Big Apple. Subsidiary United Refining, which processes 70,000 barrels of oil a day, distributes fuel to its 370 Country Fair, Red Apple Food Marts, and/or Kwik Fill branded gas stations/convenience stores in New York, Pennsylvania, and Ohio. Red Apple controls Gristede's Foods, a leading New York City supermarket chain. It also has real estate, aircraft leasing, and newspaper operations. CEO John Catsimatidis owns the Red Apple Group, which lost out to Russian oil giant LUKOIL in a bid to acquire East Coast gasoline retailer Getty Petroleum Marketing.

EXECUTIVES

Chairman, President, and CEO, Red Apple Group and Gristede's Foods; Chairman and CEO, United Refining Company: John A. Catsimatidis, age 59
President and COO, United Refining: Myron L. Turfitt, age 56

LOCATIONS

HQ: Red Apple Group, Inc.
823 11th Ave., New York, NY 10019
Phone: 212-956-5803 **Fax:** 212-247-4509
Web: www.jacny.com

The Red Apple Group operates gasoline stations in New York, Ohio, and Pennsylvania. It owns commercial property in Florida, New Jersey, New York, and the US Virgin Islands. The company also operates supermarkets in the New York City area.

COMPETITORS

7-Eleven	Man-dell
A&P	Motiva Enterprises
Ahold USA	Pathmark
D'Agostino Supermarkets	Sunoco
Getty Petroleum Marketing	TOTAL
Hess Corporation	Wakefern Food
King Kullen Grocery	

Red Chamber Co.

Ahoy, there, matey! The Red Chamber Group doesn't actually *catch* fish and other seafood, but it does almost everything else. A major North American seafood supplier, Red Chamber imports, exports, and processes various fish (catfish, cod, haddock, tuna, tilapia, swordfish, halibut, mahi-mahi, orange roughy, perch, pollock, and salmon), as well as oysters, octopus, lobster, shrimp, scallops, mussels, crab, surimi, and squid. Brands include such names as Captain Neptune, Mermaid Princess, and Fisherman's Choice. Red Chamber, which started as a small family-owned restaurant in Los Angeles, has grown to include companies such as Tampa Bay Fisheries, OFI Markesa International, Mid-Pacific Seafoods, and Neptune Foods.

In addition, the company's portfolio includes specialty operations such as the Ice Creamery and California Specialty Cheese.

Red Chamber operates processing facilities on the East and West coasts, and in other countries, and it can store more than 60 million pounds of seafood at its cold-storage facilities located throughout the US.

EXECUTIVES

Co-Chairman: Shan Chun Kou
Co-Chairman: Shu Chin Kou
President: Ming Bin Kou
EVP and CFO: Ming Shin Kou
SVP: Tony Neves
President, OFI Markesa International: Brent Church
President, Neptune Foods: Howard Choi

LOCATIONS

HQ: Red Chamber Co.
1912 E. Vernon Ave., Vernon, CA 90058
Phone: 323-234-9000 **Fax:** 323-231-8888
Web: www.redchamber.com

PRODUCTS/OPERATIONS

Selected Brands

Captain Neptune	Ocean Cafe
Cienna	Ocean Superior
Farmex	Pacific Gourmet
Fisherman's Choice	Pacific Harvest
Fresh From the Seas	Seaquel
Markesa	Sierra
Neptune	Sonoma
Ocean Bistro	

COMPETITORS

Alaska Seafood	Morey's Seafood
Alaskan Leader Fisheries	Nippon Suisan Kaisha
American Seafoods	North Coast Fisheries
Bumble Bee	North Pacific Seafoods
Chicken of the Sea	Ocean Beauty Seafoods
Fishhawk Fisheries	Orca Bay Seafoods
Gorton's	Pacific Seafood
Icelandic Group	Peter Pan Seafoods
Icelandic USA	StarKist
Kyokuyo	Trident Seafoods
Maruha Nichiro	

Red Cross

A specialist in dealing with events beyond its control, The American Red Cross offers disaster relief and other humanitarian services through more than 700 chapters nationwide. Although it was chartered by Congress in 1905, the American Red Cross isn't a government agency. The not-for-profit organization relies on the efforts of about 1 million volunteers. Aside from helping victims of about 70,000 disasters large and small each year, the American Red Cross teaches CPR and first aid courses, provides counseling for US military personnel, and maintains some of the largest blood and plasma banks nationwide. The group is a member of the International Red Cross and Red Crescent Movement.

Gulf Coast hurricanes Katrina, Rita, and Wilma in 2005 required major mobilizations for the American Red Cross and its volunteers. More than 4 million people received emergency assistance, and more than $2.1 billion was donated for hurricane victims.

Criticism of the group's handling of hurricane relief efforts, however, led to the resignation in December 2005 of CEO Marsha Evans. Biomedical services EVP John McGuire served as interim CEO for more than a year before Mark Everson, head of the Internal Revenue Service, was chosen to lead the group. Everson left the organization in 2007, however, after it was discovered by company officials that he had had an inappropriate relationship with a female subordinate. The organization named general counsel Mary Elcano as interim CEO and president.

In 2008 the organization announced that Gail McGovern would take over as president and CEO. McGovern, who'd been a Harvard business professor and has experience as a business executive, is expected to bring stronger finance and management skills to the job.

To fund its activities, the American Red Cross relies largely on its biomedical operation, which supplies blood and tissue to some 3,000 hospitals. Corporate, foundation, and individual donations, along with grants from organizations such as the United Way, account for most of the rest of its revenue.

In the years since the September 11, 2001, terrorist attacks, the organization has been engaged in a campaign to raise the nation's emergency preparedness, both for government agencies and for individuals.

HISTORY

The Red Cross traces its start to a trip made in 1859 by Jean-Henri Dunant, a Swiss businessman. Dunant was traveling in northern Italy when he saw the aftermath of the Battle of Solferino — 40,000 dead or wounded troops, left without help. He published a pamphlet three years later calling for the formation of international volunteer societies to aid wounded soldiers.

In 1863 a five-member committee (including Dunant) formed the International Committee of the Red Cross in Geneva. Delegates of 16 countries attended the first conference, which resulted in the formation of national Red Cross societies across Europe. A red cross on a white background (the reverse of the Swiss flag) was chosen as the organization's symbol; the Red Crescent symbol was added in 1876 by Muslim relief workers during the Russo-Turkish War. In 1864 the group's principles were codified into international law — initially signed by 12 nations — through the first Geneva Convention.

Clara Barton, famous for her aid to soldiers during the US Civil War, learned about the Red Cross when she assisted with relief efforts during the Franco-Prussian War (1870-71). After the war, Barton returned home and persuaded Congress to support the Geneva Convention. In 1881 she and some friends founded the American Association of the Red Cross, with the first chapter in Dansville, New York. The US signed the Geneva Convention in 1882.

Barton soon expanded the Red Cross' mission to include aiding victims of natural disasters. The group received a congressional charter in 1905, making it responsible for providing assistance to the US military and disaster relief in the US and overseas. Membership soared during WWI as the number of chapters jumped from 107 to 3,864, and volunteers from the US and other nations served with the armed forces in Europe. After the war, the American Red Cross

helped refugees in Europe, recruited thousands of nurses to improve the health and hygiene of rural Americans, and provided food and shelter to millions during the Depression.

The Red Cross established its first blood center, in New York's Presbyterian Hospital, in 1941. During WWII the American Red Cross again mobilized massive relief efforts. At home, volunteers taught nutrition courses, served in hospitals, and collected blood.

In 1956 the Red Cross began research to increase the safety of its blood supply. It also continued to provide assistance during natural disasters, as well as during the Korean and Vietnam Wars and other US military conflicts.

During the 1980s the Red Cross was criticized for moving too slowly to improve testing of its blood supply for the HIV virus. Elizabeth Dole, named the organization's president in 1991, reorganized the blood collection program.

In 1997 HemaCare settled a blood-product-pricing lawsuit against the Red Cross without disclosing terms. In 1999 Dole resigned to make a bid for the US presidency in 2000 (she later dropped out of the race). Dole was succeeded by Dr. Bernadine Healy, a former dean of the Ohio State University College of Medicine and the first physician to head the association.

The mission of the American Red Cross was highlighted after the 2001 terrorist attacks on New York City and Washington, DC, gaining praise for its quick response immediately afterwards. Donations made to the Red Cross specifically for the September 11 victims and their families amounted to about $1 billion. The group drew criticism, however, over a proposal to use some donations for a blood bank reserve instead of it all going to families of those killed and injured in the attacks. Amid the controversy, Healy was given her walking papers.

General Counsel Harold Decker was tapped to replace Healy at the end of 2001. That year the FDA announced that the Red Cross had failed to be in compliance with safety laws in its blood collection program, despite being under a consent decree since 1993. The American Red Cross appointed Marsha Johnson Evans as president and CEO in 2002.

In 2005 the organization announced a termination of its tissue programs to concentrate on disaster relief. The same year the FDA slapped the Red Cross with a $3.4 million fine for mishandling blood products after the government agency picked up 135 unsafe blood distributions.

EXECUTIVES

Chairman: Bonnie McElveen-Hunter, age 58
President and CEO: Gail J. McGovern, age 56
COO: Kevin M. Brown
Chief of Staff and Chief Strategist: James E. Starr
CFO: Robert P. (Bob) McDonald
EVP Chapter and International Operations:
R. Alan McCurry
EVP Biomedical Services: John F. McGuire
General Counsel and Corporate Secretary:
Mary S. Elcano
Acting SVP Communications and Marketing:
Patrick (Pat) McCrummen
SVP Enterprise Risk: Leigh A. Bradley
SVP Human Resources and Chief Diversity Officer:
D. Eric (Rick) Pogue
SVP Operations Biomedical Services: William F. Moore
SVP Information Technology and CIO: Steven I. Cooper
SVP Quality and Regulatory Affairs:
C. William (Bill) Cherry
SVP: Kathleen E. Loehr

VP Communication and Marketing: Brian McArthur
Chief Development Officer: Jeffrey T. (Jeff) Towers
Chief Public Affairs Officer: Suzanne (Suzy) DeFrancis
Chief Audit Executive: Dale P. Bateman
Chief Operations Support: Sean P. McLaughlin
National Chair Volunteers: Kathryn A. Forbes
Auditors: KPMG LLP

LOCATIONS

HQ: The American National Red Cross
2025 E St. NW, Washington, DC 20006
Phone: 202-303-4498
Web: www.redcross.org

PRODUCTS/OPERATIONS

Selected Programs and Services

Biomedical services
  Blood
  Clinical services
  Plasma
  Testing
Disaster relief
Health and safety services
  Care giving and babysitting
  CPR training
  First aid
  Lifeguard training
  Swimming lessons
  Youth programs
Community services
  Food and nutrition
  Homeless shelters
  Hospitals and nursing homes
  Senior services
  Transportation services
Military services
  Counseling
  Emergency communications
  Financial assistance
  Veterans services

HISTORICAL FINANCIALS

Company Type: Not-for-profit

Income Statement

FYE: June 30

	REVENUE ($ mil.)	NET INCOME ($ mil.)	NET PROFIT MARGIN	EMPLOYEES
6/07	3,175	39	1.2%	35,000
6/06	6,009	539	9.0%	35,000
6/05	3,919	445	11.4%	35,000
6/04	3,092	34	1.1%	—
6/03	3,034	—	—	40,000
Annual Growth	1.1%	4.2%	—	(3.3%)

2007 Year-End Financials

Debt ratio: —
Return on equity: 1.2%
Cash ($ mil.): —

Current ratio: —
Long-term debt ($ mil.): —

Net Income History

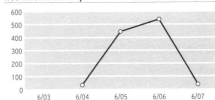

The Regence Group

The Regence Group is the health care king of the Northwest, operating the largest group of Blue Cross Blue Shield companies in the northwestern US. Through its subsidiary companies, Regence BlueCross BlueShield of Oregon, Regence BlueShield (select areas of Washington), Regence BlueCross BlueShield of Utah, and Regence BlueShield of Idaho, the company provides health insurance products to some 3 million members through a network composed of about 40,000 providers.

Subsidiary offerings include individual and group medical, vision, and dental plans and pharmacy benefits management services. Subsidiary Regence Life & Health Insurance provides life, disability, and short-term medical insurance. Another subsidiary, Asuris Northwest Health, serves 40,000 members in eastern Washington. Asuris is not affiliated with Blue Cross Blue Shield.

Although it faces stiff competition, The Regence Group has decided to remain not-for-profit. The company's strategy for remaining competitive consists of consolidating operations, upgrading the company's information technology infrastructure, and deploying new health insurance products. It also promotes wellness programs for its members.

The company enhanced its technology platform in 2008 by participating as a minority investor in Apax Partners' $1.2 billion acquisition of billing systems and process management services firm TriZetto Group.

EXECUTIVES

President and CEO: Mark B. Ganz, age 47
EVP and Chief Marketing Executive: Mohan Nair
EVP Health Care Operations: Bill Barr
EVP Corporate Services and Chief Legal Officer:
 Kerry E. Barnett
SVP, CFO, and Treasurer: Steven L. (Steve) Hooker
SVP and CIO: Cheron Vail
SVP Health Care Services: David Clark
SVP Enterprise Program Management: Jo Anne Long
Chief Medical Officer: Dennis Chong
President, Regence BlueShield of Idaho: John Stellmon
President, Regence BlueCross BlueShield of Oregon:
 J. Bart McMullan Jr.
President, Regence BlueCross BlueShield of Utah:
 D. Scott Ideson
President and CEO, Regence Life & Health Insurance:
 John C. Fick
Auditors: Deloitte & Touche LLP

LOCATIONS

HQ: The Regence Group
 200 SW Market St., Portland, OR 97201
Phone: 503-225-5221   **Fax:** 503-225-5274
Web: www.regence.com

PRODUCTS/OPERATIONS

Selected Subsidiaries

Asuris Northwest Health
Regence BlueCross BlueShield of Oregon
Regence BlueCross BlueShield of Utah
Regence BlueShield of Idaho
Regence BlueShield (Washington)
Regence Life and Health

COMPETITORS

BEST Life
CIGNA
First Choice Health
Group Health Cooperative (Puget Sound)
Kaiser Foundation Health Plan
Molina Healthcare
Premera Blue Cross
UnitedHealth Group

HISTORICAL FINANCIALS

Company Type: Not-for-profit

Income Statement				FYE: December 31
	REVENUE ($ mil.)	NET INCOME ($ mil.)	NET PROFIT MARGIN	EMPLOYEES
12/07	8,372	155	1.9%	7,500
12/06	7,551	241	3.2%	6,000
Annual Growth	10.9%	(35.6%)	—	25.0%

2007 Year-End Financials

Debt ratio: —   Current ratio: —
Return on equity: 7.7%   Long-term debt ($ mil.): —
Cash ($ mil.): —

Net Income History

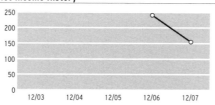

REI

Outdoor gear and clothing from Recreational Equipment, Inc. (REI) outfits everyone from mountain climbers to mall walkers. The company is the nation's largest consumer cooperative with more than 3 million members. Through some 100 outlets in more than 25 states, REI sells high-end gear, clothing, and footwear (including private-label goods) for outdoor activities such as climbing, kayaking, and skiing, as well as for hiking, bicycling, and camping. The company also repairs gear, and it sells merchandise online and through occasional catalogs. Its travel service, REI Adventures, offers trips such as cycling the Alps, sea kayaking Costa Rica, and hiking New Zealand. Climbers Lloyd and Mary Anderson formed REI in 1938.

REI's community and environmental involvement includes youth program support, community service, and designating a portion of its operating budget to environmental restoration projects. Through its partnership with US Bank (a subsidiary of U.S. Bancorp) the company offers members the REI Visa card.

REI stores feature product demonstrations, educational seminars, and gift registries. The company's MSR (Mountain Safety Research) subsidiary makes mountaineering equipment, outdoor clothing, and camping products. Customers can become co-op members by paying a one-time fee; its privileges include getting about 10% of their annual purchases refunded in the form of patronage dividends.

In 2005 former president and CEO Dennis Madsen retired. He had joined the company as a stockroom clerk when he was 17 years old. Sally Jewell, REI's COO, was named as new CEO and president.

HISTORY

Lloyd Anderson founded REI in his Seattle garage in 1938 along with his wife, Mary, and 23 other mountain climbers looking for high-quality mountaineering equipment at low prices. Uncomfortable about making money off of his friends, Anderson formed a co-op, returning a portion of the profits to its members. REI's first retail location (opened in 1944 in the back of a Seattle gas station) consisted of three shelves of Army surplus items. The company did not hire its first full-time employee until 1953.

Growth was slow yet steady. In 1971 the company operated one store; by 1983 REI had grown to seven stores with several additional product lines and a catalog business. That year Wally Smith became the company's CEO.

REI benefited from the growing interest in outdoor activities, expanding to 17 stores in 13 states in 1987. By 1991, when it built its first distribution center, REI had 27 stores in 16 states. The co-op reached for a new frontier in 1996 when it began selling on the Internet. It launched its REI-Outlet.com Web site in 1998 to sell discounted merchandise, and began a Japanese retail Web site in 1999. Also in 1999 REI decided to scale back its catalog mailings and focus instead on e-commerce. Smith, who grew the company from 9 to 54 stores during his 17-year reign, retired in early 2000 and was replaced by COO Dennis Madsen, a 34-year company veteran.

In 2000 the co-op rankled its rank and file when it moved its manufacturing operations to Mexico and closed its fleece-manufacturing subsidiary, Thaw. Also that year the company opened its first international location in Tokyo, but ended up closing the store and shutting down the Japanese Web site in 2001.

The company was named to *FORTUNE*'s "100 Best Companies" list for the sixth year in a row in 2003. It made the list again the next year, ranking 24th. In 2005 REI broke into the top 10 with a #9 ranking. Madsen retired in 2005 and was replaced by Sally Jewell.

In late 2007 REI opened a second distribution center. The first outside its home state, the new 520,000-square-foot facility in rural Bedford, Pennsylvania, will supply about a third of the company's stores and help it grow in the East, South, and Midwest.

EXECUTIVES

Chairman: Douglas W. (Doug) Walker
Vice Chairman: Anne V. Farrell
President, CEO, and Director: Sally Jewell
SVP, CFO, and Chief Administrative Officer:
 Brad Johnson
SVP Merchandising and Marketing: Matt Hyde
SVP Sales, Distribution, and Store Development:
 Brian Unmacht
VP Distribution: Clark Koch
VP Human Resources: Michelle Clements
VP E-Commerce and Web Strategy: Brad Brown
VP Logistics and Distribution: David Presley
VP Merchandising: Angela Owen
VP Public Affairs: Michael Collins
VP Real Estate: Jerry Chevassus
VP Marketing: Tom Vogl
VP General Counsel, and Corporate Secretary:
 Catherine Walker
VP REI Gear and Apparel: Lee Fromson

Regional VP Retail Stores — Midwest/East Region:
Janet Hopkins
Regional VP Retail Stores — Western Region:
Tim Spangler
Manager Public Relations: Randy Hurlow
CIO: Jeff Zon
Director Research and Development: Kevin Myette
Director Store Development: Dean Iwata
Auditors: Grant Thornton LLP

LOCATIONS

HQ: Recreational Equipment, Inc.
6750 S. 228th St., Kent, WA 98032
Phone: 253-395-3780   Fax: 253-891-2523
Web: www.rei.com

2007 Stores

	No.
California	25
Washington	9
Colorado	7
Texas	6
North Carolina	5
Oregon	6
Massachusetts	4
Washington, DC	4
Georgia	4
Maryland	3
Minnesota	3
Arizona	2
Illinois	3
Michigan	3
Nevada	2
Pennsylvania	2
Utah	2
Virginia	2
Wisconsin	2
Alaska	1
Connecticut	1
Idaho	1
Missouri	1
Montana	1
New Jersey	1
New Mexico	1
Tennessee	1
Rhode Island	1
Total	**103**

PRODUCTS/OPERATIONS

Selected Products and Services

Bicycles and accessories
Books and maps
Camping gear
Canoes, kayaks, and related gear
Climbing gear
Clothing (children's, men's, and women's)
Fitness gear
Footwear
Gift registry
Racks (bike, boat, and ski mounts)
REI repair service
Sleeping bags
Snow sports gear
Tents
Travel accessories

COMPETITORS

Academy Sports &	Joe's Sports
Outdoors	Johnson Outdoors
Bass Pro Shops	Lands' End
Big 5	L.L. Bean
Cabela's	Olympia Sports
Campmor	Orvis Company
Dick's Sporting Goods	Patagonia, Inc.
Eastern Mountain Sports	Sport Chalet
Eddie Bauer	Sports Authority
Eddie Bauer Holdings	Sportsman's Guide
Hibbett Sports	Sportsman's Warehouse

HISTORICAL FINANCIALS

Company Type: Cooperative

Income Statement

FYE: December 31

	REVENUE ($ mil.)	NET INCOME ($ mil.)	NET PROFIT MARGIN	EMPLOYEES
12/07	1,342	41	3.1%	10,000
12/06	1,182	40	3.4%	8,000
12/05	1,022	33	3.2%	8,000
12/04	888	25	2.8%	6,500
12/03	805	19	2.4%	—
Annual Growth	**13.6%**	**21.3%**	**—**	**15.4%**

2007 Year-End Financials

Debt ratio: —   Current ratio: —
Return on equity: 10.5%   Long-term debt ($ mil.): —
Cash ($ mil.): —

Net Income History

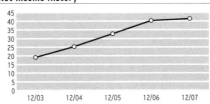

Reichhold, Inc.

Founded in 1927 by namesake Henry Reichhold to make auto paints, Reichhold has expanded its product line and geographic scope. The company makes resins used in coatings (powder coating, epoxy, and radiation-cured resins), synthetic latex (used in textiles, carpets, and paper products), and gel coats and bonding agents for the composites industry (to make tubs and showers, in marine applications, and to provide corrosion-resistance). The specialty-latex is made by a joint venture with Dow Chemical called Dow Reichhold Specialty Latex. Reichhold had been a subsidiary of Dainippon Ink and Chemicals (DIC) until 2005 when executives and DIC reached an agreement to take Reichhold private through a management buyout.

Reichhold reached back in time a little bit in early 2004 when it named two company veterans, John Gaither and Doug Frey, to its executive management. A year later Gaither and the management team he assembled negotiated a deal with DIC to buy Reichhold and take it private. Gaither had approached DIC with an offer to buy the company in 2004, when Dainippon countered with its own offer for Gaither to come on as chief executive. Given a year, DIC had evidently changed its mind and agreed to Gaither's proposal.

Reichhold has subsidiaries and investments in China, Europe, Latin America, the United Arab Emirates, and the US.

EXECUTIVES

Chairman, President, and CEO: John S. Gaither
CFO and Treasurer: Roger Willis
EVP Global Composites: Douglas E. (Doug) Frey
SVP Corporate Services: Mitzi A. Van Leeuwen
SVP Global Coatings: Rodney Biddle
SVP Operations and Supply Chain: Bill Branson
General Counsel: Edward R. (Ed) Leydon

Director, North American Coatings Sales:
Randy Vasseur
Director, Business Management: Bill Schramm
Director, North America Coatings Business:
Tony Rende
Corporate and Marketing Communications Manager:
H. Phil Bridges
President, Dow Reichhold Specialty Latex:
Jeffrey (Jeff) Welker

LOCATIONS

HQ: Reichhold, Inc.
2400 Ellis Rd., Durham, NC 27703
Phone: 919-990-7500   Fax: 919-990-7749
Web: www.reichhold.com

COMPETITORS

BASF SE
Dow Chemical
DuPont
LANXESS Corp.
PPG

The Related Group

Florida's skyline is only getting higher thanks to The Related Group. The real estate company develops and builds luxury condominiums, with 55,000 residential units under its belt throughout the state. Its portfolio includes $10 billion worth of developments, including Miami residential projects such as the Trump Towers and Icon Brickell, as well as the St. Regis Bal Harbour hotel, which it is co-developing with Starwood Hotels & Resorts. The Related Group operates several divisions covering construction, property management, and mortgage services. The company was founded in 1979 by chairman and CEO Jorge M. Pérez, whom *TIME* Magazine once named one of the 25 most influential Hispanics in the US.

The Related Group's Miami office is complemented by another in New York, which is responsible for high-end residential developments such as The Park Imperial and Astor Place. It is also developing and financing affordable housing units in New York City, Boston, Chicago, and Los Angeles.

The Related Group also made a move on Las Vegas, saying it would construct the 11-tower Las Ramblas condo resort (to be backed by actor George Clooney and nightclub owner Rande Gerber). However, it ultimately sold the property on which Las Ramblas was to be built because of rising construction costs. The company attributed the project's demise to taking on a market — casino resort versus residential — that was less familiar territory.

But Related bounced back with development plans that are taking it beyond the Silver State. The company announced it would invest $1 billion in Mexico real estate projects through 2009, specifically developments in tourist locales such as Acapulco, Cabo San Lucas, and Playa del Carmen. It is also eyeing locations in Costa Rica, Panama, Colombia, Argentina, and Uruguay for possible projects.

EXECUTIVES

Chairman and CEO: Jorge M. Perez, age 58
EVP and COO: Matthew J. (Matt) Allen
EVP: Roberto S. Rocha
EVP: Joyce Bronson
EVP: Bill Thompson
SVP: Oscar A. Rodríguez
SVP: Barbara Salk
VP: Carlos Rosso
VP: R. Lee Hodges
VP Construction: Jim M. Werbelow
Manager Communications: Leah Weatherspoon

LOCATIONS

HQ: The Related Group
   315 S. Biscayne Blvd., Miami, FL 33131
Phone: 305-460-9900   **Fax:** 305-460-9911
Web: www.relatedgroup.com

COMPETITORS

American Invsco
Colonial Development
Goldfield
Opus South
Stiles
Turnberry Associates

HISTORICAL FINANCIALS

Company Type: Private

Income Statement				FYE: December 31
	REVENUE ($ mil.)	NET INCOME ($ mil.)	NET PROFIT MARGIN	EMPLOYEES
12/07	1,250	—	—	450
12/06	1,400	—	—	—
12/05	3,200	—	—	—
Annual Growth	(37.5%)	—	—	—

Revenue History

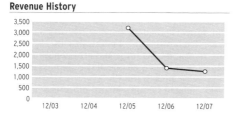

Remington Arms

They aim to arm at Remington Arms. The company makes shotguns and rifles, ammunition, and gear under the Remington brand. As the only US company to produce both guns and ammo, Remington is a top US seller of rifles and ammo and a top seller of shotguns. Wal-Mart accounts for some 17% of the company's revenue. Other mass merchandisers, as well as sporting goods shops, sell Remington. The firm was founded in 1816 by Eliphalet Remington II, who took his first orders upon winning second place in a shooting contest with a gun he built. Remington was acquired by private investment firm Cerebus Capital Management in 2007.

Remington has been expanding its product offerings. The company has increased its imported product offerings to include centerfire rifles, muzzleloaders, and rimfire rifles. It also began offering surveillance technology products through a distribution agreement.

Saying it was seeking capital to grow its business internationally, Remington agreed to the 2007 acquisition by Cerebus, which paid some $370 million for it, including the assumption of $252 million in debt.

That same year, in a joining of two venerable companies founded in the 19th century, Remington announced the acquisition of Marlin Firearms. The deal added Marlin's shoulder-arm long gun and lever-action rifle products to Remington's offerings. (The deal closed in 2008.)

About half of Remington's revenue is generated from firearm sales; the rest comes from ammunition. And most (88%) of the company's sales are logged within the US.

EXECUTIVES

President, CEO, and Director:
   Thomas L. (Tommy) Millner, age 54, $528,000 pay
COO: Theodore H. (Ted) Torbeck, age 51
CFO, Secretary, and Treasurer: Stephen P. Jackson Jr., age 38, $233,333 pay (prior to promotion)
CTO: John M. Dwyer Jr., age 49, $181,500 pay
CIO: Jeff Costantin, age 47
VP, Sales and Marketing, Firearms: Don H. Campbell, age 62, $165,000 pay
VP, Sales and Marketing, Law Enforcement, Federal and Military: Robert M. Pantle, age 50
President, Global Sales and Marketing:
   E. Scott Blackwell, age 46
Auditors: Grant Thornton LLP

LOCATIONS

HQ: Remington Arms Company, Inc.
   870 Remington Dr., Madison, NC 27025
Phone: 336-548-8700   **Fax:** 336-548-7801
Web: www.remington.com

2007 Sales

	$ mil.	% of total
Domestic	406.6	88
Foreign	57.4	12
Total	**489.0**	**100**

PRODUCTS/OPERATIONS

2007 Sales

	$ mil.	% of total
Firearms	219.2	45
Ammunition	248.2	50
Other	21.6	5
Total	**489.0**	**100**

COMPETITORS

Alliant Techsystems
American Ammunition
Browning Arms
Colt Defense
Colt's
Fabbrica D'Armi Pietro Beretta
Mossberg
Olin
Ruger
Savage Arms
Winchester Ammunition

HISTORICAL FINANCIALS

Company Type: Subsidiary

Income Statement				FYE: December 31
	REVENUE ($ mil.)	NET INCOME ($ mil.)	NET PROFIT MARGIN	EMPLOYEES
12/07	489	(2)	—	2,550
12/06	446	0	0.1%	2,150
12/05	410	(17)	—	2,200
12/04	393	(4)	—	2,400
12/03	361	(3)	—	2,184
Annual Growth	7.9%	—	—	3.9%

Net Income History

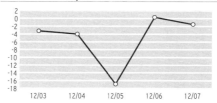

The Renco Group

Renco Group is a holding company for a diverse bunch of businesses. Its AM General subsidiary (a joint venture with Ronald Perelman's MacAndrews & Forbes Holding) makes the HUMVEE, an extra-wide, all-terrain vehicle used by the military, and the HUMMER, the HUMVEE's civilian counterpart. Renco Steel and Baron Drawn Steel manufacture, fabricate, and distribute steel. Other Renco Group companies include Doe Run, the world's #2 lead smelter; Unarco Material Handling, which makes racks and systems for warehouses; and US Magnesium. It lost control of WCI Steel (now called Severstal Warren) when that company emerged from Chapter 11 bankruptcy protection in 2006. The company is owned by industrialist Ira Rennert.

In 2008 Renco set up a new subsidiary, called Inteva Products, to acquire Delphi's interiors and closures business for just more than $100 million. Those operations serve the automotive industry (making instrument panels, cockpits, and door modules and latches) and give Inteva a global manufacturing presence, which includes more than 15 facilities worldwide.

EXECUTIVES

Chairman and CEO: Ira L. Rennert, age 73
VP Finance; VP Finance and CFO, Renco Steel:
   Roger L. Fay
VP: Ari Rennert
President and CEO, AM General:
   James A. (Jim) Armour, age 64
President, Baron Drawn Steel: Timothy J. (Tim) Dillon
President and CEO, Doe Run: A. Bruce Neil
President, Unarco Material Handling: Gary Slater
President and CEO, US Magnesium: Michael H. Legge
President, Doe Run Peru: Juan Carlos Huyhua

LOCATIONS

HQ: The Renco Group Inc.
   30 Rockefeller Plaza, New York, NY 10112
Phone: 212-541-6000   **Fax:** 212-541-6197
Web: www.rencogroup.net

PRODUCTS/OPERATIONS

Selected Subsidiaries
AM General (manufactures the High Mobility
 Multipurpose Wheeled Vehicle known as the HUMVEE
 and the HUMMER, and diesel engines)
Baron Drawn Steel (cold-drawn steel bar producer)
Doe Run Company (lead smelter)
Inteva Products (automotive interior and closure
 products)

COMPETITORS

AK Steel Holding Corporation
Ford Motor
Robert Bosch
RSR
United States Steel

Research Triangle Institute

Pythagoras would find a happy home among the scientists at Research Triangle Institute. Operating mainly under its trade name, RTI International, the not-for-profit enterprise conducts research in such areas as advanced technologies, environmental resources, and medicine. It provides such services as certification, and materials testing, as well as software used in laboratories and research projects. Primarily serving the federal government, RTI International offers analytical perspectives on public policy and has more than 2,600 researchers working in offices around the world. Duke University, North Carolina State University, and the University of North Carolina at Chapel Hill established RTI in 1958.

RTI International's main clients are the Department of Health and Human Services and the US Agency for International Development; both agencies collectively accounted for more than 60% of the institute's revenue in 2006.

EXECUTIVES

Chairman: Earl Johnson Jr.
President, CEO, and Governor: Victoria F. Haynes,
 age 60
EVP and CFO: James J. (Jim) Gibson
EVP International Development Group:
 Ronald W. (Ron) Johnson
EVP Science and Engineering Group: Satinder K. Sethi
EVP Social and Statistical Sciences: E. Wayne Holden
EVP Strategic Planning: Adam Saffer
SVP Operations: Lon E. (Bert) Maggart
SVP, Secretary, and Chief Legal Officer: J. Scott Merrell
SVP Human Resources and Corporate Affairs:
 Lorena K. Clark
SVP RTI Health Solutions: Allen W. Mangel
VP and COO, International Development Group:
 Lisa J. Gilliland
VP, Treasurer, and Chief Risk Officer: E. Ward Sax
VP and Corporate Controller: Stephen P. Snyder
VP and CIO: David Roseberry
Director Communications: Patrick Gibbons

LOCATIONS
HQ: Research Triangle Institute
 3040 Cornwallis Rd.,
 Research Triangle Park, NC 27709
Phone: 919-541-6000   **Fax:** 919-541-5985
Web: www.rti.org

PRODUCTS/OPERATIONS

Selected Research Areas
Advanced technology
 Aerospace and defense
 Auditory prosthesis research
 Contamination control
 Energy technology
 Information technology
 Nanotechnology
 Semiconductors
 Technology assisted learning
 Technology commercialization and policy
 Thermoelectrics
Drug discovery and development
 Bioassays
 Chemical synthesis and characterization
 Chemoinformatics
 Clinical trials
 Drug design and synthesis
 Drug metabolism and pharmacokinetics
 General chemistry support
 Natural products chemistry
 Proteomics
 Therapeutic outcomes and safety
 Toxicology services
Economic and social development
 Crime and justice
 Economic development and technology
 Environment and natural resource management
 Public utilities and infrastructure
Education and training
 Adult education
 Disability policy and programs
 Elementary and secondary education
 Family and early childhood
 International education policy and systems
 Postsecondary education
 Technology assisted learning
Environment and natural resources
 Air, water, and land resources
 Energy and the environment
 Environmental and natural resource economics
 Environmental chemistry and toxicology
 Environmental information systems
 Management and engineering
 Measurement and monitoring
 Policies and regulations
 Risk management
Health
 Communication and education
 Health and the environment
 Health behaviors and interventions
 Health care access
 Health economics
 Genetics, proteomics, and bioinformatics
 Special populations
 Therapeutic outcomes and safety
International development
 Democratic governance
 Education
 Environmental management
 Financial systems
 Health
 Information and communication technology

HISTORICAL FINANCIALS
Company Type: Not-for-profit

Income Statement
FYE: September 30

	REVENUE ($ mil.)	NET INCOME ($ mil.)	NET PROFIT MARGIN	EMPLOYEES
9/07	613	24	3.8%	2,678
9/06	546	20	3.6%	2,641
9/05	468	15	3.3%	2,500
9/04	510	17	3.4%	2,500
9/03	333	10	3.1%	2,301
Annual Growth	16.4%	22.9%	—	3.9%

2007 Year-End Financials
Debt ratio: —   Current ratio: —
Return on equity: 14.1%   Long-term debt ($ mil.): —
Cash ($ mil.): —

Net Income History

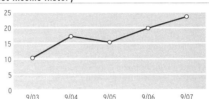

Reyes Holdings

Reyes Holdings has a grip on two things that are complementary — food and beer. The company is a leading food and beverage wholesale distributor serving customers throughout the US, Canada, and Latin America. Its Martin-Brower Company is a leading supplier of both food and non-food products for the McDonald's restaurant chain. Its Reinhart FoodService is also a leading foodservice supplier with about 20 distribution centers. The top beer distributor in the US, Reyes Holdings operates about a dozen distribution facilities through subsidiaries Premium Distributors of Virginia, Chicago Beverage System, and California's Harbor Distributing. Co-chairmen Chris Reyes and Jude Reyes founded the company in 1976.

Reyes Holdings grew to be a leader in the distribution business largely through acquisitions, a strategy it continues to follow today. During 2007 it acquired Dearing Beverage Company, a Virginia-based beer wholesaler, while Reinhart FoodService purchased the distribution operations of Iowa-based meat processor Harker's Distribution. The following year Reinhart acquired Missouri-based Banta Foods, and it has agreed to purchase The IJ Company.

The Reyes family started the business when it bought a Schlitz distributorship in Chicago. The company expanded into food distribution with the 1998 acquisition of Martin-Brower.

EXECUTIVES

Co-Chairman: J. Christopher (Chris) Reyes, age 54
Co-Chairman: M. Jude Reyes, age 53
EVP, Business Development: Dean H. Janke
EVP: James Reyes, age 45

SVP: Richard F. (Dick) Strup
SVP and CFO: Daniel P. (Dan) Doheny
SVP and CIO: Joe Crenshaw
SVP Operations; COO, Reyes Beer Division:
  Raymond M. (Ray) Guerin
VP, Human Resources: Jeff Carlsen
VP; CEO, Reyes Beer Division: David K. (Duke) Reyes,
  age 41
CEO, Reinhart FoodService Inc.: Mark Drazkowski

LOCATIONS

HQ: Reyes Holdings LLC
  9500 W. Bryn Mawr Ave., Ste. 700,
  Rosemont, IL 60018
Phone: 847-227-6500   **Fax:** 847-227-6550
Web: www.reyesholdings.com

PRODUCTS/OPERATIONS

Selected Operations

Beverage distribution
  Chicago Beverage System
  Gate City Beverage Distributors (Indio, CA)
  Harbor Distributing (Anaheim, California)
  Lee Distributors (Charleston, SC)
  Premium Distributors of Maryland (Frederick)
  Premium Distributors of Virginia (Chantilly)
  Premium Distributors of Washington, DC

Food distribution
  Martin-Brower
  Reinhart FoodService (LaCrosse, Wisconsin)

COMPETITORS

Alex Lee
Anderson-DuBose
Atlantic Dominion
Barton Inc.
Clark National
Glazer's Wholesale Drug
Golden State Foods
Gordon Food Service
Jordano's
Keystone Foods
Liquid Investments
McLane Foodservice
Meadowbrook Meat Company
Performance Food
Republic National Distributing Company
Sunbelt Beverage
SYSCO
U.S. Foodservice

HISTORICAL FINANCIALS

Company Type: Private

Income Statement

	REVENUE ($ mil.)	NET INCOME ($ mil.)	NET PROFIT MARGIN	EMPLOYEES
12/07	10,100	—	—	8,700
12/06	8,400	—	—	8,000
12/05	7,266	—	—	7,200
12/04	5,076	—	—	—
12/03	4,630	—	—	4,100
Annual Growth	21.5%	—	—	20.7%

FYE: December 31

Revenue History

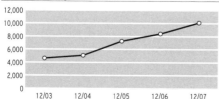

Riceland Foods

Riceland Foods is ingrained in the marketing and milling business. The agricultural cooperative markets rice, soybeans, and wheat grown by its 9,000 member-owners who farm in Arkansas, Louisiana, Mississippi, Missouri, and Texas. One of the world's leading rice millers, Riceland sells long-grain, brown, and wild rice; flavored rices; and rice-based meal kits (under the Riceland name, as well as private labels). Its customers include grocery retailers and foodservice, and food manufacturing companies. The co-op also makes edible oil and processes soybeans, bran, and lecithin, and it supplies rice bran and hulls to pet-food makers and to livestock farmers as feed and bedding products.

In addition to being a leader in rice milling, it is a major soybean processor. Riceland's milled soybean customers include poultry, catfish, and livestock producers in the southern and southwestern US.

Established in 1921, the co-op produces more than 125 million bushels of grain a year. Riceland markets its products throughout the US and overseas.

EXECUTIVES

Chairman: Thomas C. (Tommy) Hoskyn
President and CEO: K. Daniel (Danny) Kennedy, age 49
VP and CFO: Harry E. Loftis
VP International Rice Marketing: Terry Harris
VP Research: Don McCaskill
VP Corporate Communications and Public Affairs:
  Bill J. Reed
VP Soybean and Grain Procurement and Marketing:
  John B. Ruff
VP Commodity Operations: Scott Gower
Manager Sales, Private Label: Randy Johnson

LOCATIONS

HQ: Riceland Foods, Inc.
  2120 S. Park Ave., Stuttgart, AR 72160
Phone: 870-673-5500   **Fax:** 870-673-3366
Web: www.riceland.com

PRODUCTS/OPERATIONS

Selected Riceland Consumer Brands and Products

Broccoli & Cheese Rice N Easy Mix
Chicken Rice Mix Rice N Easy Mix
Extra Long Grain Rice
Jasmine Rice
Long Grain & Wild Mix Rice N Easy Mix
Long Grain Rice
Natural Brown Rice
Plump & Tender Medium Grain Rice
Rice Bran Oil
Riceland GOLD
Riceland GOLD Perfected
Saffron Yellow Rice N Easy Mix
Spanish Rice Mix Rice N Easy Mix

COMPETITORS

AarhusKarlshamn	Goya
American Rice	JFC International
Cereal Byproducts	Lotus Foods
CHS	Mars, Incorporated
Connell Company	Producers Rice Mill
Ebro Puleva	Riviana Foods
Farmers' Rice Cooperative	Specialty Rice
Farmers Rice Milling	

Rich Products

Starting in 1945 with "the miracle cream from the soya bean," Rich Products has grown from a niche maker of soy-based whipped toppings and frozen desserts to a major US frozen foods manufacturer. Since the 1960s the company has developed other products, such as Coffee Rich (non-dairy coffee creamer). It has expanded its product line to include frozen bakery and pizza doughs and ingredients for the foodservice and in-store bakery markets, plus seafood and barbecue. Rich Products markets more than 2,000 products in about 70 countries and has manufacturing facilities across the US and around the world.

In a move to expand its health and wellness offerings, Rich Products acquired GLP Free Manufacturing, a maker of gluten-free baked goods, in 2007.

The Rich family, through its Rich's Entertainment Group, owns the Buffalo Bisons, the Jamestown Jammers, and the Wichita Wranglers minor-league baseball teams. It also owns and operates a number of catering operations and restaurants in New York and Florida through its Be Our Guest group.

In addition, the family owns a corporate and leisure travel management and event-planning business called The Travel Team; Roar Logistics, which offers truck and rail shipping solutions; and the Palm Beach National Gold & Country Club.

EXECUTIVES

Chairman; Co-Chairman, Rich Products of Canada:
  Robert E. (Bob) Rich Jr., age 67
Vice Chairman; President, Rich's Entertainment Group:
  Melinda R. (Mindy) Rich, age 50
President, CEO, and Director:
  William G. (Bill) Gisel Jr., age 55
EVP and CFO: James (Jim) Deuschle
EVP and Chief Administrative Officer:
  Maureen O. Hurley
SVP and CIO: Paul Klein
SVP and General Counsel: Jill Bond
SVP Procurement: William V. Gillmore
VP Communications: Dwight Gram
VP International Human Resources: Judy Campbell
Senior Marketing Manager: Jennifer Meetz
Public Relations: Lisa Texido
President, Foodservice Division: Dennis Janesz
President, Consumer Brands Division: Jack C. Kilgore
President, Foodservice Division, North American Business Group: Ted Rich
Group President, North America Business Group:
  Richard M. Ferranti
Group President, International Business Group:
  Kevin R. Malchoff

LOCATIONS

HQ: Rich Products Corporation
  1 Robert Rich Way, Buffalo, NY 14213
Phone: 716-878-8000   **Fax:** 716-878-8765
Web: www.richs.com

PRODUCTS/OPERATIONS

Selected Products

Appetizers
Bagels
Barbecue
Brownies
Cakes
Cheesecakes
Donuts
Dough
  Bread
  Cookie
Dry Mixes
Eclairs and puffs
Fillings
Frozen seafood
Icings
Italian specialties
Mini desserts
Muffins
Pies
Pizza dough
Pretzels
Pudding
Sweet rolls
Topping
  On-top topping
  Prewhipped topping
  Ready-to-whip topping

COMPETITORS

Campbell Soup
ConAgra
Dawn Food Products
Dean Foods
Gorton's
Heinz
Hormel
Kraft Foods
Michael Foods, Inc.
Nestlé
Pinnacle Foods
Ralcorp
Sara Lee Food & Beverage
Schwan's

HISTORICAL FINANCIALS

Company Type: Private

Income Statement				FYE: December 31
	REVENUE ($ mil.)	NET INCOME ($ mil.)	NET PROFIT MARGIN	EMPLOYEES
12/07	2,650	—	—	7,200
12/06	2,400	—	—	6,500
12/05	2,500	—	—	7,000
12/04	2,100	—	—	6,500
12/03	1,910	—	—	6,500
Annual Growth	8.5%	—	—	2.6%

Revenue History

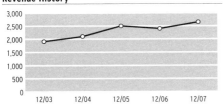

Richards Group

For The Richards Group every day is brand new. The independent advertising agency specializes in creating loyalty for its customers' brands through marketing, public relations, and sales promotions. Services include creating company or product names and inventing corporate identities, as well as graphic design, packaging, and interactive marketing services. Founded by Stan Richards in 1965, The Richards Group builds brand awareness using a variety of methods, ranging from print ads to employee uniform design. It has molded the public's perception of brands such as Amstel Light, Motel 6 (with spots featuring Tom Bodett), Chick-fil-A, and Red Lobster.

EXECUTIVES

Principal: Stan Richards, age 69
CFO: Stephen W. Kay
Creative Group Head and Creative Director: Terence Reynolds
Director of Print Services: Michael Hatley
Public Relations: Katie Myers

LOCATIONS

HQ: The Richards Group, Inc.
  8750 N. Central Expwy., Ste. 100, Dallas, TX 75231
Phone: 214-891-5700   **Fax:** 214-891-5230
Web: www.richards.com

COMPETITORS

Burrell Communications	Martin
Corporate Branding	MQ&C
Doner	Ogilvy & Mather
Fallon Worldwide	Publicis & Hal Riney
Goodby, Silverstein	SicolaMartin
GSD&M Idea City	TBWA Worldwide
Landor	TM Advertising
Lee Tilford Agency	TracyLocke
Leo Burnett	Williams

HISTORICAL FINANCIALS

Company Type: Private

Income Statement				FYE: December 31
	REVENUE ($ mil.)	NET INCOME ($ mil.)	NET PROFIT MARGIN	EMPLOYEES
12/07	166	—	—	700
12/06	160	—	—	684
12/05	148	—	—	657
12/04	100	—	—	—
12/03	114	—	—	—
Annual Growth	9.9%	—	—	3.2%

Revenue History

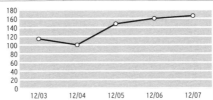

Ritz Camera Centers

Ritz Camera Centers, begun as a one-man portrait studio in 1918, has become the largest photographic chain in the US. Its nearly 1,200 stores nationwide offer one-hour photofinishing, cameras, film, and photographic and optical products and services. Stores operate under names such as Ritz Camera, Wolf Camera, Kits Camera, Inkley's, and The Camera Shop; the company also sells online. Subsidiary Boater's World Marine Centers has about 250 stores across the US that offer gear and clothing for fishing and boating. Chairman and CEO David Ritz owns Ritz Camera; he is also chairman of affiliate Ritz Interactive. His cousin, Chuck Wolf, owned Wolf Camera (#2 photo chain in the US), which Ritz Camera bought in 2001.

EXECUTIVES

Chairman and CEO; Chairman, Ritz Interactive: David M. Ritz
CFO: Curtis J. (Curt) Scheel, age 48
EVP: Richard Tranchida
Director of Human Resources: Alan MacDonald
Manager, Public Relations and Communications, Ritz Interactive: Mark Malkin

LOCATIONS

HQ: Ritz Camera Centers, Inc.
  6711 Ritz Way, Beltsville, MD 20705
Phone: 301-419-0000   **Fax:** 301-419-2995
Web: www.ritzcamera.com

PRODUCTS/OPERATIONS

Selected Merchandise and Services

Boater's World Marine Centers
  Apparel
  Electronics
  Fishing gear
    Bait tanks
    Bait well pumps
    Downriggers
    Nets and traps
    Outriggers
    Preserved bait and chum
    Rods, reels, and combos
    Tackle
  Watersports gear
    Kneeboards
    Life jackets
    Pool floats
    Snorkeling and dive gear
    Tubes
    Wakeboards
    Water skis
Ritz Camera Centers
  Albums and frames
  Batteries
  Binoculars
  Camera accessories
  Camera attachments
  Cameras
  Cellular phones
  Darkroom equipment and supplies
  Digital imaging accessories
  Digital imaging services
  Film and processing
  Lenses
  Memory
  One-hour photofinishing
  Personalized photo products
  Printers and scanners
  Projectors and accessories
  Studio lighting and accessories
  Telescopes

COMPETITORS

Best Buy
Circuit City
Costco Wholesale
CVS Caremark
MarineMax
MOTO Franchise
PhotoWorks
Target
Walgreen
Wal-Mart
West Marine

HISTORICAL FINANCIALS

Company Type: Private

Income Statement

FYE: December 31

	REVENUE ($ mil.)	NET INCOME ($ mil.)	NET PROFIT MARGIN	EMPLOYEES
12/07	1,180	—	—	10,150
12/06	1,150	—	—	10,150
12/05	1,185	—	—	10,700
12/04	1,190	—	—	10,700
12/03	1,100	—	—	10,700
Annual Growth	1.8%	—	—	(1.3%)

Revenue History

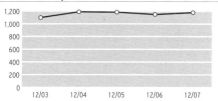

RNDC Texas

RNDC Texas, LLC (also known as Republic National Distributing Company) is one of the largest distributors of wine and spirits in the US (right up there with big-boys like Charmer Sunbelt), serving 18 US states and Washington, DC. It operated as the Republic Beverage Company until 2007, when it combined its operations with most of those of National Distributing (National retained the Georgia and New Mexico territories). Prior to this most recent expansion, RNDC was already growing; it formed partnerships with the operations of the Naifeh family (Oklahoma), Hertz (the southeast), and United Distillers (Nebraska), as well as acquiring a 50% stake in Alliance Wine and Spirits (Alabama).

The company began life with the combination of the Goldring and Block families' beverage distributorships. The families agreed in 2005 to merge their wine and spirits wholesaling companies and to use the Republic Beverage name at all of their locations, which included Arizona, Alabama, Louisiana, Mississippi, and Texas.

In 2006, just prior to joining forces with National Distributing, the company acquired SODAK Distributing Company of South Dakota, Congress Distribution of North Dakota, and Kentucky's Horizon Wine and Spirits.

EXECUTIVES

Partner: Edward L. (Eddie) Block
Partner: Alan W. Dreeben
Partner: Jeffrey (Jeff) Goldring
President: Thomas (Tom) Cole
CFO: Paul Fine
Corporate VP Finance and Accounting: Bill Blackwell
Corporate VP: Josh Zeller
Corporate VP National Accounts, Off-Premise: Greg Bowdish
Corporate VP Operations: Steve Feldman
Corporate VP Human Resources: James (Jim) Soggs
Corporate VP Wine: Peter Madden
Chief Administrative Officer: Greg Johnson
Corporate Director Employee Communications and Public Relations: Candice Gulden

LOCATIONS

HQ: RNDC Texas, LLC
   8045 Northcourt Rd., Houston, TX 77040
Phone: 832-782-1000   **Fax:** 832-782-1010
Web: www.rndc-usa.com

Republic Beverage Company has operations in Alabama, Arizona, Kentucky, Louisiana, Mississippi, Nebraska, North Carolina, North Dakota, South Dakota, Oklahoma, Texas, Virginia, and West Virginia.

COMPETITORS

Ben E. Keith
Constellation Brands
Gambrinus
Glazer's Wholesale Drug
National Wine & Spirits
Southern Wine & Spirits
Sunbelt Beverage

Robert W. Baird & Co.

Employee-owned Robert W. Baird & Co. brings midwestern sensibility to the high-flying world of investment banking. A subsidiary of Baird Holding Company (along with London-based sibling Robert W. Baird Ltd.), the company offers wealth management, asset management, and middle-market investment banking services to corporate, institutional, and wealthy individual clients in the US, Europe, and Asia. Robert W. Baird operates in five business segments: private wealth management (about 45% of sales), equity capital markets, private equity, fixed income capital markets, and asset management. It has some $73 billion in assets under management.

In 2008 Baird turned to the East for its fortunes. The company's private equity group opened an office in China, hoping to capitalize (pun intended) on China's expanding business-friendly environment. Baird's China outpost will focus on small, high-growth businesses that have been overlooked by other venture capitalists. It also expanded its investment banking operations in Shanghai and Hong Kong.

The company in 2007 launched a corporate restructuring business as part of its investment services division; it provides financing and advisory services to distressed companies.

Baird, founded in 1919, had been majority-owned by Northwestern Mutual since 1982. However, employees bought back the company's stock in a series of purchases that culminated in 2004.

EXECUTIVES

Chairman, President, and CEO: Paul E. Purcell, age 62
Vice Chairman: C. H. Randolph (Randy) Lyon
Vice Chairman and Managing Director: Richard F. (Dick) Waid
Managing Director and Chief Operations and Information Officer: Russell P. (Russ) Schwei
Managing Director and CFO: Leonard M. (Len) Rush
Managing Director and Chief Human Resources Officer: Leslie H. Dixon
Managing Director, General Counsel, and Secretary: Glen F. Hackmann
Managing Director, Private Wealth Management: Michael J. (Mike) Schroeder
Managing Director and Director of Research: Robert J. (Bob) Venable
Director Marketing: Brenda F. Skelton, age 52
Managing Director and Director of Investment Banking: Steven G. Booth
Auditors: PricewaterhouseCoopers

LOCATIONS

HQ: Robert W. Baird & Co. Incorporated
   777 E. Wisconsin Ave., Milwaukee, WI 53201
Phone: 414-765-3500
Web: www.rwbaird.com

Robert W. Baird & Co. has offices in the US (Atlanta; Chicago; Boston; Madison and Milwaukee, WI; Nashville, TN; New York; Philadelphia; and Washington, DC); Europe (Frankfurt, Hamburg, and London); and Asia (Beijing, Hong Kong, and Shanghai).

PRODUCTS/OPERATIONS

2007 Sales

	$ mil.	% of total
Private wealth management	339.0	47
Equity capital markets	224.0	31
Fixed-income capital markets	57.0	8
Private equity	47.0	6
Asset management	14.5	2
Other	47.5	6
Total	**729.0**	**100**

COMPETITORS

Broadpoint Securities	Oppenheimer Holdings
Cowen Group	Piper Jaffray
FAF Advisors	Raymond James Financial
Friedman, Billings,	Ryan Beck
Ramsey Group	Stifel Financial
Greenhill	SWS Group
Jefferies Group	Thomas Weisel Partners
Mesirow Financial	

HISTORICAL FINANCIALS

Company Type: Private

Income Statement

FYE: December 31

	ASSETS ($ mil.)	NET INCOME ($ mil.)	INCOME AS % OF ASSETS	EMPLOYEES
12/07	1,752	—	—	2,161
12/06	1,681	—	—	2,061
12/05	1,312	—	—	2,094
12/04	1,332	—	—	2,177
12/03	1,130	—	—	2,168
Annual Growth	11.6%	—	—	(0.1%)

Asset History

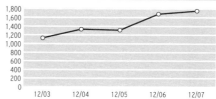

Robert Wood Johnson Foundation

The Robert Wood Johnson Foundation uses its wealth to improve your health. The foundation is the nation's largest charitable organization devoted exclusively to health care issues. It awards grants for programs that address such problems as health care quality and coverage, childhood obesity, and addiction prevention and treatment. In addition, the Robert Wood Johnson Foundation supports efforts to improve health care for vulnerable populations and to help recruit, develop, and retain health care workers. Established in 1972, the foundation has an endowment of more than $9 billion.

The Robert Wood Johnson Foundation awarded nearly 930 grants and contracts in 2006, extending some $403 million in funding for projects that improve health and health care in the US.

Investments in the infrastructure of the public health care system and in disease prevention have gained importance for the foundation, particularly in light of a shift in government priorities toward issues such as the threat of bioterrorism.

The foundation's founder and namesake, Robert Wood Johnson, endowed the organization with stock in his family's business, health care products conglomerate Johnson & Johnson.

HISTORY

Robert Wood Johnson took control of his family's health care products company, Johnson & Johnson, in 1932. Deeply concerned about corporate responsibility, he urged other corporate leaders to embrace philanthropy and set out his principles in a pamphlet called *Try Reality* (1935). He launched the Johnson Foundation in 1936, putting his words into action. The organization went nationwide in 1972 and was renamed The Robert Wood Johnson Foundation in honor of its founder, who had died in 1968 and bequeathed $1.2 billion in stock as an endowment.

The foundation began tackling the issue of terminal care in the late 1980s, seeking ways to improve the quality of care for dying patients. In 1987 it released its first forecast regarding the future of health care, which warned that the US government should adopt a national health care policy. Dr. Steven Schroeder was tapped to lead the Johnson Foundation in 1990. One year later, the foundation adopted a health reform initiative designed to help states analyze ways to increase health coverage.

In 1994 the Johnson Foundation bought airtime on NBC for a debate on national health care; despite the fact that NBC News crafted the program's content, some Republican officials questioned the foundation's impartiality because it had participated in First Lady Hillary Clinton's task force on health care. As managed-care practices increased in 1998, the foundation doubled the amount it would give for proposals to enhance the patient-provider relationship.

In 1999 the foundation embarked on a plan to address the issue of uninsured individuals in the US. The same year chairman Sidney Wentz stepped down and was replaced by former Johnson & Johnson vice chairman Robert Campbell. In 2000 the Johnson Foundation began a three-year drive to inform parents of ways they can obtain health insurance for their children. At the beginning of 2001, Johnson family member Robert Wood Johnson IV was named to the foundation's board. Later that year the Johnson Foundation committed $100 million to Faith in Action, a faith-based volunteer effort that addresses the needs of the chronically ill. In late 2002 Risa Lavizzo-Mourey became president and CEO when Steven Schroeder retired after leading the foundation for 12 years.

Chairman Robert Campbell retired in 2005; Thomas Kean, a former New Jersey governor and president of Drew University, was selected as his replacement.

EXECUTIVES

Chairman: Thomas H. (Tom) Kean, age 72
President, CEO, and Trustee: Risa J. Lavizzo-Mourey, age 53
SVP and Director, Health Care Group: John R. Lumpkin
CFO and Treasurer: Margaret H. (Peggi) Einhorn
Chief Investment Officer: Brian S. O'Neil
Chief Learning Officer: Robert G. Hughes
VP Communications: David J. Morse
VP, General Counsel, and Secretary: Katherine Hatton
VP Human Resources and Administration:
  David L. Waldman
VP Information Technology: Albert O. Shar
VP National Program Affairs: Peter Goodwin
**Chief of Staff and Special Advisor to the
  President/CEO:** Calvin Bland
Controller: Mary E. Castria
Director Information Center: Hinda F. Greenberg
Director Public Affairs: Adam M. Coyne
Director National Program Affairs: Rona Smyth Henry
Director IT Infrastructure and Operations:
  David Binder
Director Facilities Management: John M. D'Allessio
**Communications Officer and Director Policy
  Connections:** Maureen M. Cozine
Human Resources Officer: Pat A. McFadzean
Auditors: PricewaterhouseCoopers LLP

LOCATIONS

HQ: Robert Wood Johnson Foundation
  Route 1 and College Road East,
  Princeton, NJ 08543
Phone: 609-452-8701   **Fax:** 609-627-6422
Web: www.rwjf.org

PRODUCTS/OPERATIONS

Selected Programs

Human capital (recruitment, development, and
  retention of health care workers)
New Jersey
Pioneer (research and development)
Targeted
  Addiction prevention and treatment
  Childhood obesity
  Coverage
  Disparities (access to health care)
  Nursing
  Public health
  Quality health care
  Tobacco use and exposure
Vulnerable populations

HISTORICAL FINANCIALS

Company Type: Foundation

Income Statement

	REVENUE ($ mil.)	NET INCOME ($ mil.)	NET PROFIT MARGIN	EMPLOYEES
12/07	1,259	—	—	—

FYE: December 31

Rock Bottom Restaurants

When you reach this Rock Bottom, you'll find a warm meal and craft-brewed beers waiting. Rock Bottom Restaurants operates and franchises about 130 eateries and brew pubs across the US, including its flagship Rock Bottom Restaurant & Brewery and Old Chicago pizzerias. The company's brew pub locations, which also operate under such names as ChopHouse & Brewery and Walnut Brewery, offer fish, pasta, and meat, plus a variety of microbrews produced on the premises. Its pizzerias feature deep-dish, Chicago-style pizza and more than 110 different brands of beer. About 100 restaurants are company-owned, while the rest are franchised. Chairman Frank Day opened the first Old Chicago restaurant in 1976.

A slowing economy has put the brakes on expansion plans, which had called for new corporate units, as well as additional franchising agreements. Trying to boost the bottom line by cutting costs, Rock Bottom Restaurants trimmed about a third of its headquarters staff in late 2007. Day was tapped to serve as CEO the following year after Ned Lidvall and two other top executives resigned. Lidvall had been promoted to the top post in 2001.

Day had taken the company private in 1999.

EXECUTIVES

Chairman and CEO: Frank B. Day, age 73
SVP Brewery Division: Ted E. Williams
SVP Old Chicago Division: Gary B. Foreman
SVP Development and Old Chicago Franchising:
  Buck Warfield
VP Franchise Operations: Tom Lund
VP Information Technology: Jeff Gengler
VP Legal: Doug Christman
VP Operations, Brewery Division: Eliot J. Hermanson
VP Purchasing and Supply Chain Management:
  Maryanne Rose
Marketing and Public Relations Director:
  Marilyn Davenport
Brewery Operations Director: Kevin Reed

LOCATIONS

HQ: Rock Bottom Restaurants, Inc.
  248 Centennial Pkwy., Ste. 100,
  Louisville, CO 80027
Phone: 303-664-4000   **Fax:** 303-664-4197
Web: www.rockbottomrestaurantsinc.com

PRODUCTS/OPERATIONS

Selected Operations

ChopHouse & Brewery
Old Chicago (pizzeria and grill)
Rock Bottom Restaurant & Brewery
Sing Sing (dueling piano bars)
Walnut Brewery

COMPETITORS

Applebee's
BJ's Restaurants
Brinker
Carlson Restaurants
Cheesecake Factory
Damon's
Darden
Fox & Hound Restaurant
Gordon Biersch
Hillstone Restaurant
  Group
Hooters
OSI Restaurant Partners
P.F. Chang's
Romacorp
Ruby Tuesday
Uno Restaurants

HISTORICAL FINANCIALS
Company Type: Private

Income Statement
FYE: December 31

	REVENUE ($ mil.)	NET INCOME ($ mil.)	NET PROFIT MARGIN	EMPLOYEES
12/07	306	—	—	7,500
12/06	283	—	—	7,000
12/05	275	—	—	7,200
12/04	266	—	—	7,000
12/03	250	—	—	6,800
Annual Growth	5.2%	—	—	2.5%

Revenue History

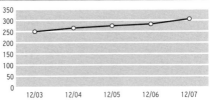

Rockefeller Foundation

The Rockefeller Foundation (established in 1913) is one of the oldest private charitable organizations in the US. It supports grants, fellowships, and conferences for programs that try to identify and alleviate need and suffering worldwide. These programs (or themes) include initiatives to foster fair implementation of health care, job opportunities for America's urban poor, creative expression through the humanities and arts, and agricultural policies that ensure food distribution to people in developing countries. An additional theme, global inclusion, serves a connection between the foundation's other programs and as an effort to make sure that poor people benefit from increases in global trade.

Outside North America, the Rockefeller Foundation concentrates its efforts in eastern and southern Africa and in Southeast Asia.

The foundation maintains no ties to the Rockefeller family or its other philanthropies. An independent board of trustees sets program guidelines and approves all expenditures.

HISTORY

Oil baron John D. Rockefeller, one of America's most criticized capitalists, was also one of its pioneer philanthropists. Before founding The Rockefeller Foundation in 1913, he funded the creation of The University of Chicago (with $36 million over a 25-year period) and formed organizations for medical research (1901), the education of southern African-Americans (1903), and hookworm eradication in the southern US.

Rockefeller turned the control of the foundation over to his son John D. Rockefeller Jr. in 1916. The younger Rockefeller separated the foundation from the family's interests and established an independent board. (The board later rejected a proposal from John Sr. to replace school textbooks that he claimed promoted Bolshevism.)

In the mid-1920s the foundation started conducting basic medical research. In 1928 it absorbed several other Rockefeller philanthropies,

adding programs in the natural and social sciences and the arts and humanities. During the 1930s the foundation developed the first effective yellow fever vaccine (1935), continued its worldwide battles against disease, and supported pioneering research in the field of biology. Other grants supported the performing arts in the US and social science research. During WWII it supplied major funding for nuclear science research tools (spectroscopy, X-ray diffraction).

After the war, with an increasing number of large public ventures modeled after the foundation (e.g., the UN's World Health Organization) taking over its traditional physical and natural sciences territory, the organization dissolved its famed biology division in 1951. The following year emphasis swung to agricultural studies under chairman John D. Rockefeller III. The organization took wheat seeds developed at its Mexican food project to Colombia (1950), Chile (1955), and India (1956); a rice institute in the Philippines followed (1960). The Green Revolution sprouted 12 more developing-world institutes.

In the 1960s the foundation began dispatching experts to African and Latin American universities in an effort to raise the level of training at those institutions. The long bear market of the 1970s caused the foundation's assets to drop to a low of $732 million (1977).

In 1990 the organization set up the Energy Foundation, a joint effort with the the Pew Charitable Trusts and the MacArthur Foundation, to explore alternate energy sources.

In the mid-1990s the Republican-led Congress launched three probes into the foundation and several other not-for-profits over allegations of political activities that could jeopardize their tax status.

In 1998 Gordon Conway, a British agricultural ecologist, became the foundation's 12th (and first non-US) president. He implemented a retooling of the organization's programs in 1999. He also led an effective campaign against bioengineering giant Monsanto's (now part of Pfizer) plan to market "sterile seeds" that do not regenerate. In 2000 James Orr, one of the foundation's board members and CEO of Boston's United Asset Management Corporation, succeeded Alice Ilchman as the organization's chairman.

The foundation pledged $5 million for disaster relief efforts in New York City following the September 11 terrorist attacks in 2001. The Rockefeller Foundation launched a multi-year initiative to promote fair intellectual-property policies to the poor the following year.

Conway retired from the foundation at the end of 2004; former University of Pennsylvania president Judith Rodin was named as his successor.

EXECUTIVES

Chairman: James F. (Jim) Orr III, age 64
COO: Peter Madonia
President: Judith (Judy) Rodin, age 63
CFO: Ellen Taus, age 49
Treasurer and Chief Investment Officer: Donna J. Dean
CTO: Fernando Mola-Davis
Director Communications: Peter Costiglio
VP Research and Evaluation: David J. Jhirad, age 59
VP Foundation Initiatives: Darren Walker
General Counsel and Corporate Secretary: Shari L. Patrick
Chief Media Strategist: Teresa Wells
Director Human Resources: Samantha H. Gilbert, age 45
Associate VP and Managing Director: Janice M. Nittoli
Associate VP and Managing Director: Maria Blair
Managing Director Grants Management and Assistant General Counsel: Pamela Foster

Managing Director: Gary H. Toenniessen
Managing Director: Robert M. (Bob) Buckley, age 60
Managing Director: Antony Bugg-Levine
Managing Director: Claudia Juech
Managing Director: Nick Turner
Managing Director: Ariel Pablos-Mendez
Managing Director: Ruben Puentes
Auditors: Deloitte & Touche LLP

LOCATIONS

HQ: The Rockefeller Foundation
420 5th Ave., New York, NY 10018
Phone: 212-869-8500   **Fax:** 212-764-3468
Web: www.rockfound.org

PRODUCTS/OPERATIONS

Selected Initiatives
American workers
Climate change resilience
Green revolution
Global health
Rebuilding New Orleans

HISTORICAL FINANCIALS
Company Type: Foundation

Income Statement
FYE: December 31

	REVENUE ($ mil.)	NET INCOME ($ mil.)	NET PROFIT MARGIN	EMPLOYEES
12/07	478	—	—	158
12/06	474	—	—	158
12/05	344	—	—	174
12/04	368	—	—	—
12/03	586	—	—	212
Annual Growth	(5.0%)	—	—	(7.1%)

Revenue History

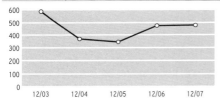

Roll International

Wonderful is the state of Stewart and Lynda Resnick's eclectic empire, Roll International. The company's holdings include POM Wonderful, marketer of the hip and trendy pomegranate juice with its distinctive, bulbous bottle. The company also owns the hip and trendy water bottler FIJI Water Company. More mundane, but no less important on its balance sheet is Teleflora, the largest flower-delivery service in the US. Roll also owns Paramount Farms, the world's largest grower, processor, and supplier of almonds and pistachios, and Paramount Citrus, a leading producer of fresh citrus fruits.

In 2008 Mr. Resnick, along with Los Angeles businessman and entrepreneur Selim K. Zilkha, formed a 50-50 joint venture (Jatropha Farm) with Global Clean Energy Holdings in order to commercialize a renewable, alternate energy source. The venture will acquire and develop raw land in the State of Yucatan in Mexico in order to grow japropha (*Jatropha curcas*) trees. The fruit and seeds of the trees, which are not edible and are not grown as a food crop, are to be made into oil for use as biomass, biodiesel, or feedstock.

Things get a little nuts at Roll. The company's Paramount Farms unit harvests more than 30,000 acres of pistachios and 40,000 acres of almonds every year. After processing, they're sold under the Sunkist and Everybody's Nuts brand names. Paramount also offers private-label products.

Out on the rest of the back forty is the Resnicks' other farming operation — Paramount Citrus. Its fruit is the bounty of 30,000 acres of navel and Valencia oranges, lemons, and Clementine mandarins. Paramount's Delano, California, processing plant is one of North America's largest orange and lemon packing operations.

The couple began planting 6,000 acres of pomegranate trees in 1996, and as the trees begin to bear fruit, so the Resnicks began promoting them to consumers. Pomegranate juice is advertised as a source of antioxidants, and Paramount Farms' ad campaigns play upon the fruit's supposed age-defying attributes with slogans like, "The pomegranate is 5,000 years old. Drink it and you will be, too."

Aside from fruit sales to grocery stores, the pomegranate juice, marketed through Roll's POM Wonderful unit, has become quite the rage. It made its debut at a 2003 Victoria's Secret lingerie show where "Sexy Flirts" (sugar-rimmed glasses of POM and vodka) were served. It was also the official cocktail (aka, Pomtinis) of the 2005 Oscars awards ceremony in Hollywood.

Last but not least on Roll's roster is FIJI Water, which the company acquired in 2004. Founded in 1998, FIJI's premium (and premium-priced) water is sourced from an artesian aquifer in Balsalt, Colorado. It is distributed throughout the world.

EXECUTIVES

Co-Chairman, President, and CEO; Co-Chairman and CEO, Teleflora; President, Paramount Farms: Stewart A. Resnick
Co-Chairman: Lynda R. Resnick
SVP and Chief Tax Officer: Jordan P. Weiss

LOCATIONS

HQ: Roll International Corporation
11444 W. Olympic Blvd., 10th Fl.,
Los Angeles, CA 90064
Phone: 310-966-5700   **Fax:** 310-914-4747

COMPETITORS

1-800-FLOWERS.COM	Martha Stewart Living
Agriflora	Naked Juice
Blue Diamond Growers	National Grape Cooperative
Calcot	Nestlé Waters
Clearly Canadian	Nestlé Waters North
Coca-Cola	America
Danone Water	Odwalla
Diamond Foods	Organic Bouquet
Dole Food	PepsiCo
Dr Pepper Snapple Group	Polar Beverages
Ferolito, Vultaggio	Primex International
Florida's Natural	Red Bull
Fresh Bouquets	South Beach Beverage
Frito-Lay	Stewart & Jasper Orchards
FTD Group	Sugar Foods
Fuze Beverage	Sun Growers
Golden West Nuts	Sunny Delight
Great Western Juice	Sun-Rype
Hansen Natural	SunWest Foods
Impulse Energy USA	Sweet Leaf Tea
Inventure	Tejon Ranch
IZZE	Tree Top
J & J Snack Foods	Tropicana
KaBloom	Veryfine
King Ranch	Warrell Corporation
Kraft Foods	Welch's
Lance Snacks	

HISTORICAL FINANCIALS

Company Type: Private

Income Statement				FYE: December 31
	ESTIMATED REVENUE ($ mil.)	NET INCOME ($ mil.)	NET PROFIT MARGIN	EMPLOYEES
12/07	1,980	—	—	3,714
12/06	1,430	—	—	2,596
12/05	1,479	—	—	2,685
Annual Growth	15.7%	—	—	17.6%

Revenue History

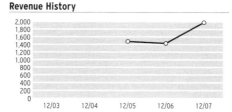

Rooms To Go

Need that sofa, recliner, table, and lamp in a hurry? Rooms To Go — with about 150 stores in nine Southern states — has transformed itself into the top-selling furniture retailer in the US. The company markets its limited selection of furniture to brand-conscious, time-pressed customers. It packages low- to moderately priced furniture and accessories and offers discounts for those willing to buy a roomful. Rooms To Go also operates a Rooms to Go Kids chain with more than 20 stores. CEO and owner Jeffrey Seaman and his father, Morty, founded the firm in 1991 after selling Seaman Furniture Company.

RTG expanded its operations in Louisiana in mid-2006 by purchasing five stores from Kirschman's, which had been in business for 92 years before Hurricane Katrina hit in 2005. As with other acquisitions, the company plans to remodel the stores and reopen them as its own format. The company enlisted the help of Great American Group soon thereafter to liquidate Kirschman's inventory.

In late 2007 RTG announced it would build a distribution center near Houston and will open seven to eight stores in the region by 2010. Its first Houston-area store, a 35,000-sq.-ft. showroom, opened in March 2008.

Rooms To Go (RTG) won the bidding war for bankrupt Atlanta-based Rhodes Furniture in 2005, which helped the company expand into northern Florida. RTG converted Rhodes' 50 stores in Florida, Alabama, and Georgia to the RTG format and sold the remaining stores to other furniture retailers.

In 2005 Rooms To Go teamed up with supermodel Cindy Crawford to launch the Cindy Crawford Home furniture line, which did about $50 million in sales in its first year. Her success led to an expansion of the line into kids' furniture. By 2008 her furniture lines were expected to reach $250 million in sales.

EXECUTIVES

CEO: Jeffrey (Jeff) Seaman
President and COO: Stephen (Steve) Buckley
CFO: Lewis Stein
CIO: Russ Rosen
SVP: Gary Cacioppo
VP Direct Marketing: Janis Altshuler
VP International: Jeff Knott
VP Human Resources: Linda Garcia

LOCATIONS

HQ: Rooms To Go, Inc.
11540 Hwy. 92 East, Seffner, FL 33584
Phone: 813-623-5400   **Fax:** 813-620-1717
Web: www.roomstogo.com

COMPETITORS

Bassett Furniture
Bombay Brands
Ethan Allen
Eurway
Furniture.com
Gabberts Furniture & Design Studio
Havertys
IKEA
J. C. Penney
Lack's Stores
La-Z-Boy
Pier 1 Imports
Rowe Fine Furniture
Sears

HISTORICAL FINANCIALS
Company Type: Private

Income Statement
FYE: December 31

	REVENUE ($ mil.)	NET INCOME ($ mil.)	NET PROFIT MARGIN	EMPLOYEES
12/07	1,750	—	—	7,000
12/06	1,760	—	—	7,500
12/05	1,600	—	—	6,500
12/04	1,400	—	—	6,000
12/03	1,400	—	—	5,700
Annual Growth	5.7%	—	—	5.3%

Revenue History
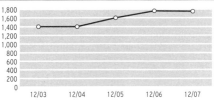

PRODUCTS/OPERATIONS

Subsidiaries
Manhattan Construction Company
  Cantera Concrete Company
  M. J. Lee Construction Company
  Manhattan Environmental
OAI Electronics, Inc.
Rooney Insurance Agency, Inc.

COMPETITORS

Austin Industries
Barton Malow
Bechtel
Beck Group
Fluor
Foster Wheeler
Hensel Phelps Construction
Jacobs Engineering
Kraft Construction
M. A. Mortenson
Siemens Corp
Skanska USA Building
Turner Corporation
Washington Division

Rooney Holdings

Film star Mickey isn't the only Rooney to get his act together. Rooney Holdings (formerly Rooney Brothers), through Manhattan Construction and other subsidiaries, builds hospitals, government buildings (George Bush Presidential Library in Texas), bridges (through M.J. Lee Construction), and sports arenas (Reliant Stadium in Houston). It offers construction management, general contracting, and design/build services in the US, Mexico, Central America, and the Caribbean. It also operates an insurance agency and manufactures electronics.

The family-owned group was formed in 1984 to acquire Manhattan Construction Company, which was founded by patriarch L. H. Rooney in 1896. Former CEO L. Francis Rooney III was named US ambassador to the Vatican in 2005.

Rooney Holdings' Manhattan Construction subsidiary is building the new stadium for the Dallas Cowboys, which is expected to be complete in 2009.

EXECUTIVES

Chairman and CEO: L. Francis Rooney III
CEO Hope Lumber: James (Jim) Cavanaugh
CFO and Chief Administrative Officer: Kevin P. Moore
VP Information Technology: Duwayn Anderson
VP Administration: Jackie Proffitt
Manager, Human Resources, Hope Lumber: Bill Vogt
Auditors: Hogan & Slovacek

LOCATIONS

HQ: Rooney Holdings, Inc.
1400 Gulf Shore Blvd. North, Ste. 184,
Naples, FL 34102
Phone: 239-403-0375 **Fax:** 239-403-0316
Web: www.rooneybrothers.com

Rooney Holdings has offices in Naples, Florida, and Tulsa, Oklahoma, as well as Santa Fe, Mexico.

Roseburg Forest Products

With roots in a Depression-era sawmill, Roseburg Forest Products has branched out with a comprehensive line of wood products. Formed in 1936, the company produces specialty panels (melamine, particleboard, and vinyl laminates), engineered wood products (joists, beams, and rimboards), and plywood products such as siding and concrete-forming panels. Its standard lumber offerings include pine, Douglas fir, and hemlock products. Roseburg manages some 750,000 acres in northern California and southern Oregon.

Heirs of philanthropist Kenneth Ford, who established the Ford Family Foundation, own Roseburg Forest Products. Allyn Ford, Kenneth's son, is chairman, president, and CEO of the company.

In 2006 the company bought half a dozen particleboard plants in the southeastern US from Georgia-Pacific, raising its profile nationally. Roseburg was hurt in 2008 when a local short-line railroad in Oregon shut down, raising the company's shipping costs by as much as $2 million annually.

EXECUTIVES

Chairman, President, and CEO: Allyn Ford
CFO: Bob Desrochers
VP: Lindsay Crawford
VP Engineering: Bill Randles
VP Sales and Marketing: J. Ray Barbee
VP Human Resources: Hank Snow
Logistics/Transportation Manager: Josh Renshaw
Controller: Jeff Groom
CIO: Dan Coyle

LOCATIONS

HQ: Roseburg Forest Products Co.
10599 Old Hwy. 99 South, Dillard, OR 97432
Phone: 541-679-3311 **Fax:** 541-679-9543
Web: www.rfpco.com

PRODUCTS/OPERATIONS

Selected Products
Engineered Wood
  Beams
  Columns
  Headers
  Joists
  Rimboard
  Underlayment
Lumber
  Douglas fir
  Hemlock/white fir
  Pine
  Premier stud
Plywood and Particleboard Products
  Concrete forming
  Industrial grades
  Medium-density overlay
  Sanded fir plywood
  Sheathing
  Siding
  Superply
  Underlayment
Specialty Panels
  Melamine
  Shelving
  Vinyl laminates

COMPETITORS

Boise Cascade
Columbia Forest Products
Georgia-Pacific
Hampton Affiliates
Louisiana-Pacific
MAXXAM
Potlatch
Sierra Pacific Industries
Simpson Investment
Weyerhaeuser

HISTORICAL FINANCIALS
Company Type: Private

Income Statement
FYE: December 31

	REVENUE ($ mil.)	NET INCOME ($ mil.)	NET PROFIT MARGIN	EMPLOYEES
12/07	1,300	—	—	3,800
12/06	1,100	—	—	3,900
12/05	1,162	—	—	3,650
Annual Growth	5.8%	—	—	2.0%

Revenue History
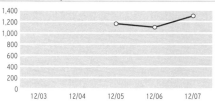

Rotary International

The rotary phone may be a thing of the past, but Rotary International and its more than 1.2 million members are still going strong. The service organization is made up of more than 32,000 clubs in some 200 countries and territories worldwide. Rotary service projects are intended to alleviate problems such as disease, hunger, illiteracy, poverty, and violence. Grants from the Rotary Foundation support the group's efforts. Along with its service projects, Rotary aims to promote high ethical standards in the workplace. Membership in Rotary clubs is by invitation; each club strives to include representatives from major businesses, professions, and institutions in its community. Rotary was founded in 1905.

As it enters its second century, Rotary has chosen the eradication of polio as its top priority. Other goals include expanding internationally and increasing the diversity of the organization's membership. Rotary International began admitting women to its clubs in 1989. It now counts more than 145,000 female members.

The Rotary name arose from the early practice of rotating meetings among members' offices.

HISTORY

On February 23, 1905, lawyer Paul Harris met with three friends in an office in Chicago's Unity Building. Inspired by the fellowship and tolerance of his boyhood home in Wallingford, Vermont, Harris proposed organizing a men's club to meet periodically for the purpose of camaraderie and making business contacts. The new endeavor was organized as the Rotary Club of Chicago and had 30 members by the end of the year.

As additional clubs followed, the organization assumed its role as a civic and service organization (the installation of public comfort stations in Chicago's City Hall was one of its first projects). At the first convention of the National Association of Rotary Clubs in 1910, Harris was elected president. International clubs soon followed, and by 1921 there were Rotary clubs on six continents.

In 1932, while struggling to revive a company with financial difficulties, Rotarian Herbert Taylor devised a statement of business ethics that later became the Rotarian mantra. Taylor's "4-Way Test" consisted of the following questions: "Is it the truth? Is it fair to all concerned? Will it build goodwill and better friendships? Will it be beneficial to all concerned?"

During WWII Rotary clubs promoted war relief and peace fund efforts. Following WWII the clubs assisted in efforts to aid refugees and prisoners of war. The extent of Rotarian involvement in international issues became clear when 49 members assisted in drafting the United Nations Charter in 1945.

The first significant contributions to The Rotary Foundation followed Harris' death in 1947. These funds formed the bedrock for the foundation's programs, and in 1965 the foundation created its Matching Grants and Group Study Exchange programs. Rotary International also welcomed younger members in the 1960s by creating its Interact and Rotaract clubs in 1962 and 1968, respectively.

The largest meeting of Rotarians occurred in 1978 when almost 40,000 members attended the organization's Tokyo convention. But controversy was fast approaching the male-only organization. In 1978 a California Rotary club defied the male-only requirement and admitted two women. Claiming that the club had violated the organization's constitution, Rotary International revoked the club's charter. A lengthy court battle ensued, and a series of appeals landed the issue on the docket of the US Supreme Court. In 1987 the court ruled that the all-male requirement was discriminatory. Two years later Rotary International officially did away with its all-male status.

In the 1990s membership in Rotary clubs grew, but at a slower pace than in the organization's past. Mary Wolfenberger was appointed the organization's first female CFO in 1993 (she resigned in 1997). In 1998 Rotary International joined with the United Nations to launch a series of humanitarian service projects in developing areas. In 1999 the organization spearheaded events to help flood victims in North Carolina and refugees in the Balkans. In 2000 the group created a program specializing in peace and conflict resolution. Rotary International established its first Internet-based Rotary club in early 2002. Also that year the group founded the Rotary Centers for International Studies, which selects 70 scholars a year to participate in a master's-level peace studies program.

In addition to celebrating its 100th anniversary in 2005, the organization awarded grants in Sudan and Indonesia to stop polio, and assisted victims of the tsunami that struck Southeast Asia at the end of that year.

EXECUTIVES

President: Wilfrid J. (Wilf) Wilkinson
General Secretary: Edwin H. (Ed) Futa
Treasurer: Ian Riseley
President Elect: Dong Kurn Lee
Auditors: Deloitte & Touche LLP

LOCATIONS

HQ: Rotary International
1 Rotary Center, 1560 Sherman Ave.,
Evanston, IL 60201
Phone: 847-866-3000   **Fax:** 847-328-8281
Web: www.rotary.org

PRODUCTS/OPERATIONS

Selected Programs
Educational programs
  Ambassadorial Scholarships
  Grants for University Teachers
  Group Study Exchange (GSE)
  Rotary World Peace Scholarships
Humanitarian grants
  Discovery Grants
  Grants for Rotary Volunteers
  Matching Grants
  New Opportunities Grants
  Peace Program Grants
PolioPlus Program
  Polio Eradication Advocacy
  Polio Eradication Private Sector Campaign
  PolioPlus Partners

HISTORICAL FINANCIALS
Company Type: Not-for-profit

Income Statement

	REVENUE ($ mil.)	NET INCOME ($ mil.)	NET PROFIT MARGIN	EMPLOYEES
6/07	92	—	—	—
6/06	79	—	—	—
6/05	79	—	—	—
6/04	80	—	—	—
6/03	61	—	—	600
Annual Growth	11.2%	—	—	—

FYE: June 30

Revenue History

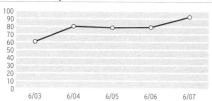

Roundy's Supermarkets

If you live in Wisconsin, you can probably find one of these grocery stores right round the corner. Roundy's Supermarkets owns and operates more than 150 grocery stores in Wisconsin and Minnesota under the names Pick 'n Save, Copps Food Center, and Rainbow Foods. The company also operates Metro Market, a smaller-format store concept in Milwaukee that specializes in gourmet foods and features an in-store cafe. In addition to its retail operations, Roundy's has three distribution centers that serve a small number of independent grocers, as well as its own stores. Founded in 1872 by a partnership that included Judson Roundy, the company is owned by private equity firm Willis Stein & Partners.

Once a major food distributor in the Midwest, Roundy's has been shedding its wholesale operations to concentrate on its retail businesses. To that end, the regional grocery chain acquired five Jewel-Osco stores in the Milwaukee market from its rival SUPERVALU in early 2007 and reopened them as Pick 'n Save stores in February. Roundy's is entering the Chicago market in 2008 with plans to open 15 to 25 stores in the Windy City by 2013.

In 2006 Roundy's CEO Robert Mariano said he expected the company's capital structure to change in the near future. Chicago-based Willis Stein, which bought Roundy's for $750 million in 2002, has a track record of holding its acquisitions for five years. The regional supermarket chain has been reported to be on or off the block since mid-2007. Among the rumored potential buyers is Safeway, the owner of Chicago's Dominick's chain.

HISTORY

Migration from the eastern US and overseas was boosting Milwaukee's ranks when William Smith, Judson Roundy, and Sidney Hauxhurst formed grocery wholesaler Smith, Roundy & Co. in 1872. Smith left the firm in 1878 for his first of two terms as Wisconsin's governor, and

William Peckham joined the enterprise, which was then renamed Roundy, Peckham & Co. Two years later Charles Dexter joined the company, by then operating in five Midwestern states and running a manufacturing business.

The wholesaler became Roundy, Peckham & Dexter Co. in 1902, following the death of Hauxhurst (Roundy died in 1907). The company introduced its first private-label product — salt — in 1922. In 1929 Dexter (then 84) came up with a plan to publicize the Roundy's name by handing out cookbooks that called for the company's goods.

Roy Johnson, who joined the company in 1912, was named president near the end of the Depression. In the 1940s the wholesaler acquired smaller companies in the region. The company became Roundy's in 1952 when Roundy, Peckham & Dexter was bought by a group comprising hundreds of Wisconsin grocery retailers. Johnson remained head of the new company until his death in 1962. James Aldrich led the company for the next 11 years.

In 1970 Roundy's started Insurance Planners, which offered insurance to retailers. Vincent Little became president of the company in 1973. Two years later Roundy's began a real estate subsidiary (Ronco Realty) and opened its first Pick 'n Save Warehouse Food store.

The company expanded in the mid-1980s through the purchase of distributors. But expansion hurt profits, and dividends were suspended in 1984 and 1985. In the late 1980s several Pick 'n Save stores opened throughout Wisconsin and other Midwestern states. Owners grew suspicious of Little's accounting practices and the special treatment given a Roundy's-owned store run by his son, and in 1986 they forced him out of his president and CEO positions. John Dickson replaced him.

By 1994 Pick 'n Save had vastly upgraded its image — one store sold $1,000 cognac and featured an $18,000 cappuccino machine. However, sales dropped off for the third straight year. COO Gerald Lestina was named CEO in 1995, replacing Dickson, who continued as chairman. Dickson died later that year.

Roundy's did not pay its members a dividend in 1995 as it made an effort to offset losses in Michigan and Ohio. To ease those losses, in 1997 the company closed 12 poorly performing stores in those states. A year later a fire destroyed its Evansville, Indiana, warehouse; the company rebuilt the facility in 1999. Also in 1999 Roundy's purchased three supermarkets in Indiana from Kroger and The John C. Groub Company.

The Mega Marts and Ultra Mart chains, which together operate 24 Pick 'n Save stores, primarily in Wisconsin, were acquired by Roundy's in 2000. In 2001 Roundy's launched an online shopping service, called Pick 'n Save Online Shopping, in two test stores in Wisconsin (the plan was eventually scuttled). Also in 2001 the company purchased its competitor, The Copps Corporation, acquiring 21 stores in north and central Wisconsin and a wholesale business that distributes to retailers in Wisconsin and northern Michigan. Chicago-based Willis Stein & Partners bought Roundy's in 2002 for $750 million.

In 2003 Roundy's purchased the Hopkins, Minnesota-based Rainbow Foods supermarket chain for $121.5 million from Fleming Companies Inc., a Texas-based wholesaler and retailer. Dale Riley, who had been hired to revitalize Roundy's flagging Minnesota Rainbow Food chain, resigned in 2004 after a year on the job.

That year the company closed its distribution operations in Illinois.

Nash Finch bought Roundy's wholesale food distribution operations in Westville, Indiana, and Lima, Ohio, as well as two Ohio retail stores for about $225 million in 2005.

EXECUTIVES

Chairman and CEO: Robert A. (Bob) Mariano, age 58
EVP and CFO: Darren W. Karst
EVP Operations: Donald S. (Don) Rosanova
Group VP Human Resources: Colleen J. Stenholt
Group VP IT and Business Process Excellence: John W. Boyle
Group VP Legal, Risk, and Treasury: Edward G. (Ed) Kitz
Group VP Retail Operations and Customer Satisfaction: Gary L. Fryda
Group VP Sales and Marketing: Ronald (Ron) Cooper
Group VP Real Estate: Michael J. (Mike) Schmitt
Group VP Merchandising and Procurement: Donald G. (Don) Fitzgerald
VP, General Merchandising: David Acchione
VP and General Manager, Rainbow Foods: Mark Beaty
Director, Communications: Lynn Guyer
Director, Floral: Kathy Hession
Director, Public Affairs: Vivian King

LOCATIONS

HQ: Roundy's Supermarkets, Inc.
875 E. Wisconsin Ave., Milwaukee, WI 53202
Phone: 414-231-5000 **Fax:** 414-231-7939
Web: www.roundys.com

PRODUCTS/OPERATIONS

Selected Operations

Retail grocery stores
  Copps Food Center
  Pick 'n Save
  Rainbow Foods
Wholesale food distribution

COMPETITORS

ALDI
Costco Wholesale
Cub Foods
Fresh Brands
Hy-Vee
IGA
Kroger
Wal-Mart

HISTORICAL FINANCIALS

Company Type: Private

Income Statement			FYE: Saturday nearest December 31	
	REVENUE ($ mil.)	NET INCOME ($ mil.)	NET PROFIT MARGIN	EMPLOYEES
12/07	4,000	—	—	21,000
12/06	3,620	—	—	21,000
12/05	3,700	—	—	21,000
12/04	4,777	—	—	21,855
12/03	4,383	—	—	19,999
Annual Growth	(2.3%)	—	—	1.2%

Revenue History

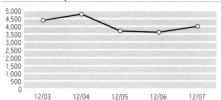

Russell Stover

For Russell Stover Candies, life really *is* a box of chocolates. The largest US maker of boxed chocolates is protecting its sweet position. And while boxed chocolates, such as the Whitman Sampler, are its, well, bread and butter, the company also sells bagged and individually wrapped candies. It offers sugar-free candy, including a sugarless version of Millionaires. Russell Stover's candies are sold by more than 70,000 supermarkets, card and gift shops, drugstores, department stores, and mass merchandisers in all 50 US states and Puerto Rico, and more than 50 other countries, including Canada and the UK. The company also operates some 50 Russell Stover Candies retail stores in the US.

Faced with growing competition as the big boys like The Hershey Company and Mars invaded the boxed-chocolate arena, the company countered with new products, including candy bars, bagged candy, and low-carb items. It manufactures almost 100 million pound of chocolate every year.

It markets to younger customers through the use of licensed characters in conjunction with its chocolate products, and has introduced a Private Reserve line of upscale chocolates. Its Whitman's division is selling candy in conjunction with Weight Watchers. In addition to being one of the top chocolate makers in the US, the company is the country's largest producer of hand-dipped chocolates.

Russell Stover has also joined foreign chocolatiers who sell their candy in the US, as well as other US confections in the production of premium chocolate, with a line of goodies with names such as German Black Forest Truffle, Vanilla Bean Brulee Chocolate, and Private Reserve Mocha Ganache.

The Ward family purchased Russell Stover Candies in 1960. Co-presidents and brothers Tom and Scott Ward lead the company today.

EXECUTIVES

Co-President and COO: Thomas S. (Tom) Ward, age 49
Co-President: Scott H. Ward, age 50
COO: Dan Trott
CFO and Chief Administrative Officer: Richard S. (Dick) Masinton
SVP Administration: Paul R. Billington
SVP Finance: Curtis Scholz
SVP and Chief Marketing Officer: Mark Sesler
SVP Human Resources: Robinn S. Weber
SVP Logistical Operations: Garry Willenbrink
SVP Manufacturing: Harold Wattjes
SVP Operations: Mark Frame
VP Advertising and Public Relations: John O'Hara

LOCATIONS

HQ: Russell Stover Candies Inc.
4900 Oak St., Kansas City, MO 64112
Phone: 816-842-9240 **Fax:** 816-561-4350
Web: www.russellstover.com

PRODUCTS/OPERATIONS

Selected Products

Almond Delights
Assorted Chocolates
Butterscotch Buttons
Caramels
Cherry Cordials
Chocolate Covered Nuts
Cinnamon Buttons

French Chocolate Mints
Fruit Flavored Jellies
German Black Forest Truffle Bar
Lemon Sour Wedges
Millionaires
Miniature Chocolates
Mint Patties
Orange Patties
PB & Grape Jelly Cup
PB & Red Raspberry Cup
Pecan Delights
Root Beer Barrels
Sugar Free Milk Chocolate
Toasted South Seas Coconut
Toffee
Traditional S'mores Candy Bar
Triple Chocolate Mousse Candy Bar
Truffles
Urban Assorted Chocolates
Vanilla Bean Brulee Chocolate Candy Bar

COMPETITORS

Anthony-Thomas Candy	Jelly Belly Candy
Asher's Chocolates	Just Born
Barry Callebaut	Laura Secord
Betsy Ann Candies	Lindt & Sprüngli
Cadbury	Mars, Incorporated
Chase General	Nestlé
Dynamic Chocolates	Perfetti Van Melle
Endangered Species	Purdy's Chocolates
Chocolate	Rocky Mountain Chocolate
Ferrero	See's Candies
Ghirardelli Chocolate	Sherwood Brands
Godiva Chocolatier	The Sweet Shop USA
Guittard	Tootsie Roll
Harry London Candies	World's Finest Chocolate
Hershey	Zachary Confections

Rutgers University

Rutgers University offers undergraduate and graduate degrees from more than two dozen schools and colleges on three campuses (Camden, Newark, and New Brunswick/Piscataway). Notable alumni include actors James Gandolfini and Calista Flockhart. Rutgers has more than 50,000 students and some 2,500 faculty members. Founded in 1766 as Queen's College, the university was the colonies' eighth institution of higher education. The name was changed in 1825 to honor Revolutionary War hero and alumnus Colonel Henry Rutgers.

EXECUTIVES

President: Richard L. McCormick, age 59
Provost, Camden Campus: Roger J. Dennis
Provost, Newark Campus: Steven J. Diner
EVP Academic Affairs: Philip Furmanski
SVP Administration and CFO: Jeffrey C. Apfel
VP and University Counsel: Jonathan R. Alger
VP Student Affairs: Gregory S. Blimling
Auditors: KPMG LLP

LOCATIONS

HQ: Rutgers, The State University of New Jersey
    83 Somerset St., New Brunswick, NJ 08901
Phone: 732-932-4636   **Fax:** 732-932-8060
Web: www.rutgers.edu

PRODUCTS/OPERATIONS

Selected Colleges and Schools

Camden College of Arts & Sciences
College of Nursing, Newark Campus
Cook College, New Brunswick/Piscataway Campus
Ernest Mario School of Pharmacy, New
    Brunswick/Piscataway Campus
Graduate School, Camden
Rutgers Business School, Newark and New
    Brunswick/Piscataway Campuses
School of Criminal Justice, Newark Campus
School of Management and Labor Relations, New
    Brunswick/Piscataway Campus

Ryerson Inc.

Ryerson has a heart of steel. A distributor and processor of metals, the company offers its customers steel products (carbon, stainless, and alloy), aluminum, copper, and industrial plastics. It buys bulk metal products (in sheets, bars, and other forms) from metal producers and processes them into smaller lots to meet the specifications of its customers — machine shops, fabricators, metal producers, and machinery makers. Ryerson has facilities in the US and Canada and joint ventures in China, India, and Mexico. In 2005 Ryerson purchased Integris Metals for $640 million. Two years later Platinum Equity bought Ryerson for $2 billion, taking it private.

Ryerson bought Integris from joint venture partners Alcoa and BHP Billiton. Following full integration of the acquired company, Ryerson changed its name from Ryerson Tull.

In 2006 Ryerson acquired Lancaster Steel Service Company, which operates in Upstate New York. The acquired company, which was renamed Ryerson Lancaster, distributes all manner of steel product and also provides processing services.

Early the next year, amid shareholder unrest, the company postponed its annual meeting. The move was designed, in part, to ward off a proxy fight for control of the Board. Ryerson's Board of Directors announced that it would review its strategic alternatives, which meant it would look for someone to buy the company. Cue private equity groups.

Platinum Equity moved in on Ryerson in the middle of 2007 with its offer to take the publicly traded company private. The $2 billion offer included assumed debt.

HISTORY

In 1893 eight partners purchased used steelmaking machinery from bankrupt Chicago Steel and established Inland Steel in the Chicago Heights, Illinois, area. Eight years later the Lake Michigan Land Company offered 50 acres to any company that would spend $1 million to develop it by building an open-hearth steel mill. Inland raised the money and built Indiana Harbor Works.

Inland grew and in 1916 expanded to meet the steel demands of WWI. After the war Inland began producing rails (1922). During the Depression years, Inland turned out tinplate and steel sheet used in consumer goods. In 1931 the company, under chairman L. E. Block, built plants to make strip, sheet, and plate steel. It moved into steel warehousing in 1935, buying

Joseph T. Ryerson & Son, a Chicago-based metal processor. Inland also bought Wilson & Bennett Manufacturing (later renamed Inland Steel Containers) in 1939. Inland manufactured armor during WWII, and after the war it expanded its rolling mills.

Inland became a billion-dollar company in 1966. The 1970s brought a steel boom, but when the party ended in the 1980s, the firm suffered large losses. Inland reorganized in 1986 as a holding company to separate its steel-manufacturing operations from its more profitable distribution division. The company also acquired J.M. Tull Metals from Bethlehem Steel.

Inland entered into joint ventures with Nippon Steel in 1987 and 1989 to build and operate a cold-rolling mill (I/N Tek, 60%-owned) and a coating facility (I/N Kote, 50%). Inland ceased making structural steel that year.

In 1994 the company formed Inland International and created a service center joint venture (Ryerson de Mexico) with Mexico's #1 steelmaker, Altos Hornos de Mexico. The following year quality problems and a derailed cost-reduction program forced Maurice Nelson to retire after three-and-a-half years as president and CEO of subsidiary Inland Steel Company; Dale Wiersbe, a 26-year company veteran, took over. The company combined its Ryerson and Tull operations and sold the public a 13% stake in Ryerson Tull.

In 1997 Inland Steel inked a deal with Tata Steel, the flagship of India's Tata conglomerate, to process steel in that country. That year Ryerson Tull (87% owned by Inland) acquired Thypin Steel, a US distributor of carbon and stainless-steel products. Inland sold its Inland Steel Company to Ispat International for $1.4 billion in 1998.

Inland Steel Industries acquired the rest of its Ryerson Tull subsidiary in 1999 and adopted the name Ryerson Tull for the company. Also in 1999 Ryerson Tull bought Washington Specialty Metals, which operates metal service centers that specialize in stainless steel, to boost its market share over 10%. The purchase added to Ryerson Tull's expansion of the specialty metals group, the company's single-largest product area. Despite the growth, slumping steel prices industrywide and weakness in the US manufacturing sector caused Ryerson Tull's profits to plunge by 90% in 1999 compared to its previous year.

In 2000 Ryerson Tull sold its 50% interest in Ryerson de México to its partner in the Altos Hornos de México joint venture. That year Ryerson Tull closed its coil processing facility in Minnesota and a metal service center in Texas. In December 2001 the company sold its subsidiary, Ryerson Industries de Mexico, S.A. de C.V., to Grupo Collado. It also stopped operations of its Internet steel marketplace, MetalSite.

As part of the company's continuing restructuring plan, Ryerson Tull sold off its Emeryville, California, service center for about $12 million in 2002. In 2003 Ryerson Tull formed a joint venture with G. Collado S.A. de C.V. to expand its services in Mexico. The following year, Ryerson Tull acquired J&F Steel, a carbon flat-rolled processor and subsidiary of Arcelor, for approximately $55 million. In early 2005 Ryerson Tull bought out Integris Metals, which was a joint venture of Alcoa and BHP Billiton, for around $410 million.

The following year the company dropped the latter half of its name and became simply Ryerson, Inc.

EXECUTIVES

CEO: Stephen E. Makarewicz, age 60, $562,433 pay
EVP and CFO: Terence R. (Terry) Rogers, age 47
President, Global Accounts: James M. Delaney, age 49
President, Ryerson Canada: Michael L. Whelan
VP International; President and CEO VSC, Ryerson China Limited: Frank Muñoz
VP Marketing: Patti Buckland
Sales Manager: Timothy Farrell
Auditors: Ernst & Young LLP

LOCATIONS

HQ: Ryerson Inc.
  2621 W. 15th Place, Chicago, IL 60608
Phone: 773-762-2121   **Fax:** 773-762-0437
Web: www.ryerson.com

Ryerson Tull maintains facilities throughout the US and in Canada. The company has stakes in joint ventures in China, India, and Mexico.

PRODUCTS/OPERATIONS

Selected Products

Alloy steel
Aluminum
Brass & copper
Carbon steel
Industrial plastics
Nickel alloys
Stainless steel

COMPETITORS

A. M. Castle
AK Steel Holding Corporation
Allegheny Technologies
Blue Tee
Commercial Metals
Empire Resources
Kreher Steel
Metals USA
Olympic Steel
O'Neal Steel
Reliance Steel
Rio Tinto Alcan
Steel Technologies
Sumitomo Metal Industries
Worthington Industries

HISTORICAL FINANCIALS

Company Type: Private

Income Statement				FYE: December 31
	REVENUE ($ mil.)	NET INCOME ($ mil.)	NET PROFIT MARGIN	EMPLOYEES
12/06	5,909	72	1.2%	5,700
12/05	5,781	98	1.7%	5,800
12/04	3,302	55	1.7%	—
12/03	2,189	(14)	—	—
12/02	2,097	(96)	—	3,600
Annual Growth	29.6%	—	—	12.2%

2006 Year-End Financials

Debt ratio: 173.4%   Current ratio: 4.13
Return on equity: 12.0%   Long-term debt ($ mil.): 1,125
Cash ($ mil.): 55

Net Income History

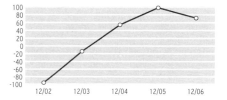

Sabre Holdings

Sabre Holdings has cut itself a huge slice of the travel reservations industry pie. Used by travel agencies worldwide to book airline tickets, rental cars, hotel reservations, and cruise/tour packages, the Sabre system is the world's #1 computerized travel reservation system. Individual consumers make travel plans using the company's Travelocity Web site (among the leaders of online travel services). The company also owns lastminute.com, which gives it a significant travel presence in Europe. In 2007 Sabre was acquired by private equity groups Silver Lake Partners and Texas Pacific Group for $4.5 billion.

Other key brands within the Sabre network include GetThere (offers business travel reservation technology), SynXis (provider of reservation management services to thousands of hotels), and TRAMS Marketing Alliance (promotional services provider targeting the leisure travel industry). Through Sabre Airline Solutions, the company offers software and services used by airlines and airports to help manage their operations.

Sabre, an acronym for Semi-Automated Business Research Environment, was established in 1996. AMR, American Airlines' parent company, developed Sabre and spun off its 83% stake to AMR shareholders in 2000.

EXECUTIVES

Chairman, President, and CEO:
  Michael S. (Sam) Gilliland, $794,231 pay
EVP and CFO: Jeffery M. Jackson, $469,115 pay
EVP and General Counsel: David A. Schwarte, $361,423 pay
EVP; President and CEO, Travelocity:
  Michelle A. Peluso, $441,346 pay
EVP and Group President, Sabre Travel Network and Sabre Airline Solutions: Thomas (Tom) Klein, $441,346 pay
EVP Human Resources: Paul G. Rostron
SVP; President, Airline Products and Services, Sabre Airline Solutions: Stephen M. (Steve) Clampett
SVP Government Affairs: Bruce J. Charendoff
SVP Product and Solutions Development:
  Sara Garrison
SVP Corporate Communications: Al Comeaux
CIO: Barry Vandevier
CTO: Robert Wiseman
President and General Manager, SynXis: Scott Alvis
Manager Investor Relations: Margaret Kim
Auditors: Ernst & Young LLP

LOCATIONS

HQ: Sabre Holdings Corporation
  3150 Sabre Dr., Southlake, TX 76092
Phone: 682-605-1000
Web: www.sabre-holdings.com

PRODUCTS/OPERATIONS

Selected Products and Services

IgoUgo.com (online travel community)
Jurni Network (offline travel agency consortium)
Sabre Airline Solutions (technology development and consulting services)
Sabre Travel Network (sales of travel-related products and services)
SynXis (reservation management system for hotels)
Travelocity.com (online travel reservation service for individual consumers)
  lastminute.com (European online travel services)
  Travelocity Business (travel service available for corporations and business travelers)
  Zuji (online travel company for Asia/Pacific)

COMPETITORS

Amadeus
American Express
Carlson Companies
Expedia
Lufthansa
Pegasus Solutions
priceline.com
Travelport

HISTORICAL FINANCIALS

Company Type: Private

Income Statement				FYE: December 31
	REVENUE ($ mil.)	NET INCOME ($ mil.)	NET PROFIT MARGIN	EMPLOYEES
12/07	3,000	—	—	9,000
12/06	2,824	—	—	9,000
12/05	2,521	—	—	8,800
12/04	2,131	—	—	6,700
12/03	2,045	—	—	6,200
Annual Growth	10.1%	—	—	9.8%

Revenue History

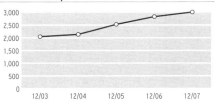

Sacramento Kings

These Kings hold court on the hardwood. The Sacramento Kings professional basketball team is one of the oldest franchises in the National Basketball Association, taking the court for the first time in New York as the Rochester Royals in 1945. Les Harrison started the team and coached the Royals to an NBA title in 1951, the only championship in the franchise's history. Afterward, the club turned vagabond and was known variously as the Cincinnati Royals, the Kansas City-Omaha Kings, and the Kansas City Kings until Gregg Lukenbill bought the team and moved it to Sacramento, California, in 1985. Brothers Joe and Gavin Maloof bought the team in 1998 through their Maloof Sports and Entertainment.

In 2006 the City of Sacramento agreed to foot part of the bill to construct a new arena for the Kings to replace the aging ARCO Arena. The Maloof family plans to contribute money as well, but negotiations continue about where to build such an arena. Some had feared the Maloofs would move their team to Las Vegas if a new arena deal couldn't be hammered out.

In 2006 the team struggled through its first losing season since 1998, leading to the ouster of head coach Eric Musselman in 2007. Reggie Theus, formerly head coach at New Mexico State, was tabbed to be the new head coach. A former NBA player, Theus was part of the Kings squad the team's first year in Sacramento.

In addition to the Kings, the Maloof brothers own the Sacramento Monarchs of the WNBA as well as the ARCO Arena both teams share. The Maloofs, whose family fortune was built through the Joe G. Maloof & Co. liquor distributorship, also own the Palms Casino Hotel in Las Vegas.

EXECUTIVES

Co-Owner: Gavin Maloof
Co-Owner: Joe G. Maloof
President: John Thomas
President, Basketball Operations: Geoff Petrie
Head Coach: Reggie Theus
SVP Business Operations: John Rienhart
SVP Arena Services: Mark Stone
SVP Strategic Alliances: Tom Hunt
VP Basketball Operations: Wayne Cooper
VP Human Resources: Donna Ruiz
VP Marketing, Brand Development, and Monarchs Business Operations: Danette Leighton
VP Media Relations and Basketball Operations: Troy Hanson
Director Player Personnel and TV Color Analyst: Jerry Reynolds
Director Scouting: Scotty Stirling

LOCATIONS

HQ: Sacramento Kings
ARCO Arena, 1 Sports Pkwy.,
Sacramento, CA 95834
Phone: 916-928-0000 **Fax:** 916-928-8109
Web: www.nba.com/kings

The Sacramento Kings play at the 17,317-seat capacity ARCO Arena in Sacramento, California.

PRODUCTS/OPERATIONS

Championship Titles
NBA Championship (1951)
Western Division Champions (1951)

COMPETITORS

Golden State Warriors
Los Angeles Clippers
Los Angeles Lakers
Phoenix Suns

HISTORICAL FINANCIALS

Company Type: Private

Income Statement FYE: June 30

	REVENUE ($ mil.)	NET INCOME ($ mil.)	NET PROFIT MARGIN	EMPLOYEES
6/07	128	—	—	—
6/06	126	—	—	—
6/05	119	—	—	—
6/04	118	—	—	—
6/03	102	—	—	—
Annual Growth	**5.8%**	—	—	—

Revenue History

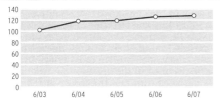

Saint Barnabas Health Care System

No one cares for New Jersey's health the way Saint Barnabas Health Care System does. Saint Barnabas Health Care System (SBHCS) is the state's largest private hospital network. The system includes seven hospitals, four outpatient centers, nine nursing and rehabilitation centers, two assisted living facilities, ambulatory care facilities, geriatric centers, a state-wide behavioral health network, and home care and hospice programs. To top it off, SBHCS has an alliance with The Mount Sinai Health System in New York, including the Mount Sinai Medical Center. SBHCS is the state's second-largest employer.

SBHCS hospitals include the 465-bed Clara Maass Medical Center, the 585-bed Community Medical Center in Toms River, the 350-bed Kimball Medical Center in Lakewood, the 530-bed Monmouth Medical Center in Long Branch, the 670-bed Newark Beth Israel Medical Center, the 645-bed Saint Barnabas Medical Center in Livingston, and the 200-bed Union Hospital.

In 2006 several whistleblowers accused SBHCS of fraudulently overbilling the federal Medicare program by $500 million over the course of eight years. Because of a loophole in the Medicare system that allows for extra reimbursement where medical charges are particularly high, SBHCS was able to draw from a pool of Federal funds that Congress set aside for such cases (called "outliers"). The move shortchanged other hospitals nationwide; it also affected tens of thousands of Medicare patients, many of them already uninsured and less able to pay artificially inflated bills. The "outliers" pool was created as an incentive for hospitals to ensure the continued treatment of patients with particularly costly illnesses.

Some of SBHCS' hospitals are the largest Medicare providers in the country.

SBHCS was able to settle the allegations out of court. Included in the settlement is the requirement that SBHCS' Medicare billing be monitored by an outside third party for six years. It must also pay back $265 million. The hospital did not admit any wrongdoing.

Later two New England-based small hospitals filed a class action lawsuit against SBHCS, claiming that SBCHS' abuse of the Medicare system forced them to pay more into the program. The two hospitals named plaintiffs in the lawsuit represented 4,000 hospitals across the country. The courts dismissed the suit, saying that the plaintive hospitals were not in competition with SBHCS for federal Medicare funds.

EXECUTIVES

President and CEO: Ronald J. Del Mauro
EVP; Executive Director and CFO, Community Medical Center: Mark Pilla
EVP; Director, Quality Institute: Fred M. Jacobs
VP Corporate Finance: Thomas G. Scott
VP Public Relations and Marketing: Ellen Greene
Corporate VP: Robert Carretta
Executive Director, Newark Beth Israel Medical Center: John A. Brennan
Executive Director, Clara Maass Medical Center: Thomas A. Biga
Executive Director, Kimball Medical Center: Joseph (Joe) Hicks
Executive Director, Monmouth Medical Center: Frank J. Vozos

LOCATIONS

HQ: Saint Barnabas Health Care System
368 Lakehurst Rd., Ste. 203, Toms River, NJ 08755
Phone: 732-557-3900
Web: www.sbhcs.com

COMPETITORS

Atlantic Health
Englewood Hospital and Medical Center
Hackensack University Medical Center
Robert Wood Johnson University Hospital
Solaris Health System
St. Joseph's Healthcare System
Trinitas Hospital
University of Medicine and Dentistry of New Jersey
The Valley Hospital

St. Louis Blues

With no championship title to call their own, St. Louis hockey fans have been singing the blues for a long time. The St. Louis Blues entered the National Hockey League in 1967 but has yet to capture a Stanley Cup championship despite perennial playoff appearances. (The Blues made its last finals appearance in 1970, losing to the Boston Bruins.) Still, the team has typically enjoyed one of the highest attendance levels in the league at St. Louis' Scottrade Center. An investment group led by former New York Knicks president Dave Checketts acquired the team and the arena from Bill Laurie and his wife Nancy (daughter of Wal-Mart founder James "Bud" Walton) in 2006.

Checketts, who was also formerly the CEO of Madison Square Garden (which oversees both the Knicks and the New York Rangers, in addition to their historic home venue), bought the team through Sports Capital Partners along with Dean Howes, Mike McCarthy, and Ken Munoz. The group, which owns Real Salt Lake of Major League Soccer, paid about $150 million for the hockey franchise.

With the team struggling at the start of the 2006-07 season, the Blues replaced head coach Mike Kitchen with former Los Angeles Kings coach Andy Murray. Kitchen had spent two seasons behind the bench for St. Louis.

The Lauries, who acquired the team in 1999, put the Blues up for sale in 2005 during the labor lockout that forced cancellation of the 2004-05 season. When hockey resumed in 2005, the Blues struggled early in the season, leading the Lauries to sell off much of the team's talent to reduce expenses while awaiting an offer on the franchise. As a result, St. Louis' string of playoff appearances came to an end in 2006.

EXECUTIVES

Chairman: David W. (Dave) Checketts, age 53
Vice Chairman: Michael McCarthy
President, Hockey Operations: John Davidson
Head Coach: Andy Murray, age 57
SVP and General Manager: Larry Pleau, age 61
SVP Finance and Hockey Administration: Jerry Jasiek
SVP Sales and Marketing: Eric Stisser
VP Player Personnel: Doug Armstrong, age 43
Director Amateur Scouting: Jarmo Kekalainen
Director Professional Scouting: Kevin McDonald

LOCATIONS

HQ: St. Louis Blues Hockey Club L.L.C.
Scottrade Center, 1401 Clark Ave.,
St. Louis, MO 63103
Phone: 314-622-2500   **Fax:** 314-622-2582
Web: www.stlouisblues.com

COMPETITORS

Chicago Blackhawks
Columbus Blue Jackets
Detroit Red Wings
Nashville Predators

HISTORICAL FINANCIALS

Company Type: Private

Income Statement   FYE: June 30

	REVENUE ($ mil.)	NET INCOME ($ mil.)	NET PROFIT MARGIN	EMPLOYEES
6/07	66	—	—	—
6/06	66	—	—	—
6/05	0	—	—	—
6/04	66	—	—	—
6/03	67	—	—	—
Annual Growth	(0.4%)	—	—	—

Revenue History

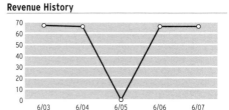

Salt River Project

One of the US's largest government-owned utilities, Salt River Project (SRP) provides Phoenix with two types of currents: electric and water. Electricity comes from the Salt River Project Agricultural Improvement and Power District, a political subdivision of the State of Arizona that has a generating capacity of 7,500 MW and distributes power to more than 900,000 homes and businesses. The district also sells excess power to wholesale customers. Water comes from the Salt River Valley Water Users' Association, a private firm that delivers about 1 million ac.-ft. of water to residents and agricultural irrigators per year; the association also operates dams, canals, reservoirs, and wells in its service area.

SRP was established in 1903 as the first multipurpose reclamation project authorized under the National Reclamation Act.

EXECUTIVES

Chairman and President: John M. Williams Jr.
VP: David Rousseau
General Manager: Richard H. Silverman
Associate General Manager, Commercial and Customer Services and CFO: Mark B. Bonsall
Associate General Manager, Power, Construction, and Engineering Services: David G. Areghini
Associate General Manager, Public and Communications Services: D. Michael Rappoport

Associate General Manager, Water Group: John F. Sullivan
Associate General Manager, Environmental, Human Resources, Land, Risk Management, and Telecom Services: Richard M. Hayslip
Corporate Counsel: Jane D. Alfano
Corporate Secretary: Terrill A. Lonon
Corporate Treasurer: Steven J. Hulet
Auditors: PricewaterhouseCoopers LLP

LOCATIONS

HQ: Salt River Project
1521 N. Project Dr., Tempe, AZ 85281
Phone: 602-236-5900   **Fax:** 602-236-4423
Web: www.srpnet.com

SRP provides electricity and water to Avondale, Chandler, Gilbert, Glendale, Mesa, Peoria, Phoenix, Scottsdale, Tempe, and Tolleson, and only electricity to Apache Junction, Fountain Hills, Guadalupe, Paradise Valley, and Queen Creek in Arizona.

PRODUCTS/OPERATIONS

2008 Sales

	$ mil.	% of total
Electric		
Retail	2,212.8	81
Wholesale & other electric	512.0	18
Water	14.3	1
Total	**2,739.1**	**100**

Selected Subsidiaries

Salt River Project Agricultural Improvement and Power District (electric utility)
New West Energy Corporation (energy support services)
Papago Park Center, Inc. (real estate facility management)
SRP Captive Risk Solutions, Ltd. (domestic captive property, boiler, and machinery insurer)
Salt River Valley Water Users' Association

COMPETITORS

American States Water
American Water
Calpine
PacifiCorp
PG&E
Pinnacle West
PNM Resources
Sempra Energy
Sierra Pacific Resources
Southwest Gas
UniSource Energy
Xcel Energy

HISTORICAL FINANCIALS

Company Type: Government-owned

Income Statement   FYE: April 30

	REVENUE ($ mil.)	NET INCOME ($ mil.)	NET PROFIT MARGIN	EMPLOYEES
4/08	2,739	232	8.5%	4,431
4/07	2,631	466	17.7%	4,388
4/06	2,522	426	16.9%	4,328
4/05	2,252	363	16.1%	4,336
4/04	2,077	112	5.4%	4,300
Annual Growth	7.2%	19.9%	—	0.8%

2008 Year-End Financials

Debt ratio: —   Current ratio: —
Return on equity: 6.2%   Long-term debt ($ mil.): —
Cash ($ mil.): —

Net Income History

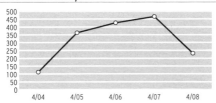

Salvation Army

Battling to provide social services, The Salvation Army is more than 4 million strong — including some 3.5 million registered volunteers. Its Christian faith-based programs assist alcoholics, drug addicts, the homeless, the elderly, prison inmates, people in crisis, and the unemployed through offerings such as community centers, housing facilities, and rehabilitation centers. The organization also provides disaster relief services. Overall, it serves more than 35 million people a year, including more than 63 million meals. The US organization is a unit of the London-based Salvation Army, which oversees activities in more than 100 countries. US operations began in 1880.

The organization's structure incorporates both church and military themes. In the US, it is organized into four regional commands. Its 3,600-plus US officers, who are also ordained ministers, are expected to wear their uniforms at all times and to work full-time for The Salvation Army. They receive no salary; instead, they are provided with room and board and given a limited stipend. Reporting to the officers of the US organization are more than 110,000 soldiers, or lay members. Before joining the organization as a soldier, one must agree to avoid gambling, debt, and profanity, as well as alcohol, tobacco, and recreational drugs.

In addition, The Salvation Army counts nearly 415,000 US members, or adherents — people who consider the organization to be their church.

Ringing bells at Christmas is just one of the ways The Salvation Army raises money. Besides cash dropped into red kettles, the group receives donations in response to direct mail campaigns; gifts from companies, foundations, and individuals; and fees from government agencies for providing social services under contract.

HISTORY

William Booth (1829-1912) started preaching the gospel as a Wesleyan Methodist in the UK, but the church expelled him because he insisted on preaching outside and to everyone, including the poor. In 1865 he moved to the slums of London's East End and attracted large crowds with his volatile sermons. Opposition to his message of universal salvation for drunks, thieves, prostitutes, and gamblers often caused riots. In fact, the first women in the organization wore bonnets designed with a dual purpose in mind — warmth and protection from flying objects.

At a meeting in 1878, a sign was used referring to the "Salvation Army." Booth adopted the reference as both the name and the style of his organization. Members became soldiers, evangelists were officers, and Booth was referred to as "General." Prayers became knee drills, and contributions were called cartridges.

The Salvation Army marched across the Atlantic to the US in 1880, led by seven women and one man. Women have always played an active role in the Salvation Army, both as officers and soldiers. Booth's wife, Catherine Mumford, was a leading suffragette, and Booth advocated equal rights for women.

In 1891 a crab pot was placed on a San Francisco street to collect donations, with a sign reading "Keep the Pot Boiling." The idea led to the Salvation Army's annual Christmas kettle program. During WWI the organization became famous for the doughnuts that it served the doughboys fighting on the front lines.

After some internal dissention, The Salvation Army took its only public political stance in 1928, with the endorsement of Herbert Hoover for his support of Prohibition during his presidential campaign. The charity opened its first home for alcoholics in 1939, in Detroit.

After WWII The Salvation Army began using such radio and TV programs as *Heartbeat Theater* and *Army of Stars* to spread its message.

Over the years The Salvation Army has provided assistance to victims of hurricanes, floods, and earthquakes. Volunteers rendered almost 70,000 service hours in the aftermath of the Oklahoma City bombing in 1995, counseling more than 1,600 victims and family members, helping with funeral arrangements, and providing food, clothing, and travel assistance. Indicative of the organization's readiness and extensive reach, its volunteers were helping victims in Guam within minutes of the 1997 Korean Air plane crash. The Salvation Army was quickly on the scene after a Jonesboro, Arkansas, shooting incident in 1998 when four students and one teacher were killed by fellow students. Late that year the organization received the largest donation in its history — $80 million from Joan Kroc, wife of McDonald's co-founder Ray Kroc.

In 2000 the organization initiated a major reform by allowing officers to marry outside the ranks. After the September 11 attacks in 2001, The Salvation Army provided assistance to rescue workers and families affected by the tragedy through its Disaster Relief Fund.

Joan Kroc left The Salvation Army $1.5 billion in 2003. The money was earmarked for construction of community centers modeled on one in San Diego named for her and her husband. By 2006, plans were under way to build community centers in Atlanta, Honolulu, Phoenix, and San Francisco.

EXECUTIVES

Chairman National Advisory Board: Robert J. (Rob) Pace
Commissioner (National Commander): Israel L. Gaither
Commissioner (National President of the Women's Ministries): Eva D. Gaither
Commissioner (Central Territory): Kenneth Baillie
Commissioner (Eastern Territory): Lawrence Moretz
Commissioner (Southern Territory): Maxwell Feener
Commissioner (Western Territory): Philip Swyers
General (International Director): Shaw Clifton
National Chief Secretary: David Jeffrey
Director Territorial Public Relations: Andrew Burditt

LOCATIONS

HQ: The Salvation Army
615 Slaters Ln., Alexandria, VA 22313
Phone: 703-684-5500 **Fax:** 703-684-3478
Web: www.salvationarmyusa.org

PRODUCTS/OPERATIONS

Selected Services
Alcohol and drug treatment centers
Clinics and hospitals
Convalescent homes
Counseling
Crisis counseling
Disaster services
Food distribution centers
Handicapped housing
Homeless shelters
Human trafficking awareness and eradication
Institutes for the blind
Leprosy clinics
Military canteens and hostels
Nurseries and day care centers
Occupational centers
Prison ministry
Probation housing
Refugee centers
Science and trade schools
Student housing
Welfare aid

Sammons Enterprises

Sammons Enterprises summons its revenues from several sources. The diversified holding company's interests include life insurance and financial services (Midland National Life Insurance, North American Company for Life and Health Insurance, and Sammons Annuity Group) and heavy equipment sales and rentals (Briggs Equipment). Sammons Enterprises also owns The Grove Park Inn Resort in Asheville, North Carolina. The late Charles Sammons, an orphan who became a self-made billionaire philanthropist (despite never attending college), founded the company in 1962 to consolidate his already varied holdings. His estate still owns the company, and his widow, Elaine Sammons, serves as chairman.

The company's list of partially owned holdings runs the range from real estate investments to oilfield suppliers. Sammons holds an interest in North American Technologies Group's Tie Tek unit, which supplies railroad ties. It prefers to invest in companies that have strong employee-ownership programs.

Sammons Enterprises continues to grow and is eyeing the life sciences and health care industry as possible expansion areas.

EXECUTIVES

Chairman: Elaine D. Sammons
CEO: Robert W. (Bob) Korba, age 63
President: Dave Sams
SVP and CFO: Darron Ash
SVP, Secretary, and General Counsel: Heather Kreager
VP: Bob Kendall
VP and Treasurer: Pamela (Pam) Doeppe
Chairman and CEO, Sammons Financial Group: Michael M. (Mike) Masterson
President and COO, Sammons Financial Group: John J. Craig
President and CEO, Grove Park Inn Resort & Spa: J. Craig Madison
President and CEO, Briggs International: David (Dave) Bratton
Auditors: PricewaterhouseCoopers LLP

LOCATIONS

HQ: Sammons Enterprises, Inc.
5949 Sherry Ln., Ste. 1900, Dallas, TX 75225
Phone: 214-210-5000 **Fax:** 214-210-5099
Web: www.sammonsenterprises.com

PRODUCTS/OPERATIONS

Selected Subsidiaries
Wholly Owned
Briggs Construction Equipment, Inc.
Midland National Life Insurance Company
North American Company for Life and Health Insurance
Sammons Annuity Group
Sammons Corporate Markets Group
SRI Ventures LLC
The Grove Park Inn Resort & Spa
Partially Owned
Eiger Venture, Inc.
iSECUREtrac
Ocular LCD, Inc.

COMPETITORS

CNH	New York Life
Deere	Principal Financial
MetLife	Prudential
NES Rentals	United Rentals

HISTORICAL FINANCIALS
Company Type: Private

Income Statement

	REVENUE ($ mil.)	NET INCOME ($ mil.)	NET PROFIT MARGIN	EMPLOYEES
				FYE: December 31
12/07	3,375	—	—	4,300
12/06	2,560	—	—	4,500
12/05	2,400	—	—	3,491
12/04	2,200	—	—	3,290
12/03	1,969	—	—	3,250
Annual Growth	14.4%	—	—	7.2%

Revenue History

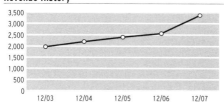

San Antonio Spurs

Basketball fans hardly need to be prodded to root for this team. The San Antonio Spurs professional basketball franchise was formed by Bob Folsom in 1967 as the Dallas Chaparrals of the American Basketball Association. The team moved to San Antonio in 1973 and joined the National Basketball Association when the leagues merged in 1976. The Spurs boast four NBA championship titles, its last in 2007. Peter Holt, whose family owns a statewide Caterpillar dealership (Holt CAT), has controlled the team since 1996. He also owns the San Antonio Silver Stars of the WNBA and the San Antonio Rampage of the Arena Football League.

In 2006 the name of the team's home arena was changed from SBC Center to AT&T Center after its corporate sponsor, SBC Communications, changed its name to AT&T. The company bought the naming rights under a 20-year, $40 million marketing deal. The publicly financed $180 million facility was built in 2002.

The Spurs franchise won its fourth NBA title in 2007, sweeping the Cleveland Cavaliers in four games. In 2008, however, the team's bid to reach the final round for a second consecutive year was thwarted by the Los Angeles Lakers.

EXECUTIVES

Chairman and CEO: Peter M. Holt
SVP and General Manager: R. C. Buford
Head Coach: Gregg Popovich, age 59
EVP Business Operations: Russ Bookbinder
EVP Finance and Corporate Development: Rick A. Pych
SVP Broadcasting: Lawrence Payne
VP Public Affairs and Corporate Administration: Leo Gomez
VP Community Relations: Alison Fox
VP Finance: Lori Warren
VP Human Resources: Paula Winslow
VP Marketing: Bruce Guthrie
VP Sales: Joe Clark
VP; General Manager, AT&T Center: John Sparks
Director of Pro Player Personnel: Dell Demps
Director Basketball Operations: Rob Hennigan
Auditors: Ernst & Young

LOCATIONS

HQ: San Antonio Spurs LLC
    1 AT&T Center Pkwy., San Antonio, TX 78219
Phone: 210-444-5000   **Fax:** 210-444-5100
Web: www.nba.com/spurs

The San Antonio Spurs play at the 18,797-seat capacity AT&T Center in San Antonio.

PRODUCTS/OPERATIONS

Championship Titles
NBA Champions (1999, 2003, 2005, 2007)
Western Conference Champions (1999, 2003, 2005, 2007)

COMPETITORS

Dallas Mavericks
Houston Rockets
Memphis Grizzlies
New Orleans Hornets

HISTORICAL FINANCIALS
Company Type: Private

Income Statement

FYE: June 30

	REVENUE ($ mil.)	NET INCOME ($ mil.)	NET PROFIT MARGIN	EMPLOYEES
6/07	131	—	—	—
6/06	122	—	—	—
6/05	121	—	—	—
6/04	108	—	—	—
6/03	105	—	—	—
Annual Growth	5.7%	—	—	—

Revenue History

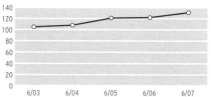

San Jose Sharks

Here's a team hockey fans can sink their teeth into. The San Jose Sharks professional hockey franchise represents the San Francisco Bay Area in the National Hockey League, having joined as an expansion team in 1991. Despite some success in reaching the playoffs the past several years, fans are still waiting for an appearance in the Stanley Cup finals. The team plays host at HP Pavilion, affectionately known as "The Shark Tank." George and Gordon Gund, former owners of the Cleveland Cavaliers, were originally awarded the NHL franchise; Silicon Valley Sports & Entertainment, an investment group led by veteran sports executive Greg Jamison, has owned the team since 2002.

Despite playing in California far from the more hockey-fertile regions in the North, the Sharks have built a strong following in the Bay Area thanks to the team's success in reaching the playoffs in recent years. During the 2007-08 season, San Jose earned its fourth consecutive postseason appearance, but was bounced from the tournament in the second round for the third year running. Head coach Ron Wilson was replaced by Todd McLellan, formerly an assistant with the Detroit Red Wings.

The team and its home arena are operated through Silicon Valley Sports & Entertainment (SVS&E), a marketing and facilities management business that also operates Sharks Ice (the team's practice rink), the Worcester Sharks of the American Hockey League, and the San Jose Stealth professional lacrosse team. SVS&E also handles marketing and merchandising for the Sharks.

Jamison previously worked for the Dallas Mavericks and Indiana Pacers before joining the Sharks organization in 1993. He eventually rose to become president of the team before leading the $80 million buyout. The Gund family, which also owned the Minnesota Stars (now the Dallas Stars) continues to own a small stake in the franchise.

EXECUTIVES

President and CEO: Greg Jamison, age 57
EVP and CFO: Charles (Charlie) Faas, age 48
EVP and General Counsel: Don Gralnek, age 62
EVP and General Manager: Doug Wilson
EVP and General Manager, HP Pavilion at San Jose: Jim Goddard, age 59
EVP Business Operations: Malcolm Bordelon, age 49
Head Coach: Todd McLellan
VP and Assistant General Manager: Wayne Thomas, age 60
VP Sales and Marketing: Kent Russell, age 50
Director Scouting: Tim Burke
Director of Hockey, Sharks Ice at San Jose and Fremont: Robert Savoie
Director of Communications and Internet Services: Roger Ross
Human Resources Manager: Cathy Chandler
Public Relations Manager: Jim Sparaco

LOCATIONS

HQ: San Jose Sharks, LLC
    525 W. Santa Clara St., San Jose, CA 95113
Phone: 408-287-7070   **Fax:** 408-999-5797
Web: www.sjsharks.com

The San Jose Sharks play at the 17,496-seat capacity HP Pavilion in San Jose, California.

COMPETITORS

Anaheim Ducks
Dallas Stars
Los Angeles Kings
Phoenix Coyotes

HISTORICAL FINANCIALS
Company Type: Private

Income Statement

FYE: July 31

	REVENUE ($ mil.)	NET INCOME ($ mil.)	NET PROFIT MARGIN	EMPLOYEES
7/07	72	—	—	—
7/06	69	—	—	—
7/05	0	—	—	—
7/04	74	—	—	—
7/03	65	—	—	—
Annual Growth	2.6%	—	—	—

Revenue History
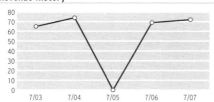

Sandia National Laboratories

Sandia stands for national security. Established in 1945 as part of the Manhattan Project, Sandia National Laboratories performs research and development primarily related to national security and defense. Its focus is nuclear weapons systems research, but Sandia also performs nonproliferation assessments, infrastructure assurance, and other research and development on such topics as energy and environmental technologies and economic competitiveness. Sandia's recent duties have expanded to combat terrorism, aid homeland security, and support US military in Afghanistan and Iraq. A part of the US Department of Energy, Sandia is operated by Lockheed Martin.

Sandia National Laboratories has facilities in Albuquerque, New Mexico, and Livermore, California; a rocket launch range in Kauai, Hawaii; and additional operations in New Mexico, Nevada, Texas, and Washington, DC.

EXECUTIVES

President and Laboratories Director: Thomas O. (Tom) Hunter
EVP and Deputy Laboratory Director: John H. Stichman
EVP and Deputy Director; Director, Nuclear Weapons Program: Joan B. Woodard, age 55
SVP and Deputy Laboratories Director for Integrated Technologies and Systems: Alton D. (Al) Romig Jr.

VP Business Management and CFO:
Francisco A. (Frank) Figueroa
VP, General Counsel, and Corporate Secretary:
Elizabeth D. (Becky) Krauss
VP and Principal Scientist: Gerold (Gerry) Yonas
VP Human Resources: Kimberly S. Adams
VP Science and Technology and Partnerships:
J. Pace VanDevender
Executive Staff Director: Carol A. Yarnall

LOCATIONS

HQ: Sandia National Laboratories
1515 Eubank Blvd. SE, Albuquerque, NM 87123
Phone: 505-845-0011   **Fax:** 505-844-1120
Web: www.sandia.gov

PRODUCTS/OPERATIONS

Selected Operations

Defense Systems and Assessments
  C3ISR (Command, Control, Communication,
    Intelligence, Surveillance & Reconnaissance)
  Integrated Military Systems for Missile Defense &
    Strike Systems
  Complex Adaptive Systems (e.g., Robotics)
  System-Level Modeling and Simulation
  Homeland Defense & Force Protection
  Science & Technology Products

Energy and Infrastructure Assurance
  Enhance the safety of energy and other critical
    infrastructures

Homeland Security

Nonproliferation
  Supporting treaty verification with other countries
  Creating new technologies for aircraft and satellites to
    detect proliferation activities
  Working with the former Soviet Union to safely
    manage nuclear materials from dismantled weapons
    systems
  Enhancing nuclear, chemical, and biological weapon
    proliferation detection capabilities
  Developing physical security technologies, including
    entry-control devices and electronic monitoring

Nuclear Weapons
  Enhance the capabilities of radiation-hardened
    microelectronics to address national security issues
  Develop advanced simulation and computing
    capabilities to model the entire nuclear weapon
    lifecycle
  Deliver advanced robotics systems to monitor
    proliferation activities, clean up hazardous sites, and
    disassemble old munitions
  Improve the methods and practices used to support
    product delivery
  Incorporate pulsed power technology into defense
    applications
  Develop distributed information systems for the
    nuclear weapons complex

Science, Technology & Engineering
  Aerospace Engineering
  BioScience & Technology
  Combustion, Chemical, & Plasma Sciences
  Data Instrumentation / Telemetry
  Directed Energy
  Electromechanical Components / Firing Sets
  Energy System & Environmental Characterization
  Environmental Remediation Systems
  Gas Transfer Systems
  GeoSciences
  Intelligence Technologies & Assessments
  Pulsed Power
  Radars
  Radiation Effects Science
  Remote Sensing & Satellite Systems
  Stockpile Surety & Analysis
  Stockpile Surveillance
  Systems Data Exploitation & Information
    Technologies
  System Performance Assessment
  Test Ranges / Facilities/Readiness
  Transportation Materials Management
  Weapon Engineering / Design

SAS Institute

Don't talk back to this company about business intelligence. SAS (pronounced "sass"), the world's largest privately held software company, is a leader in the market for business analytics, data warehousing, and data mining software used to gather, manage, and analyze enormous amounts of corporate information. Clients such as Air France and the US Department of Defense use its software to find patterns in customer data, manage resources, and target new business. Founded in 1976, SAS also offers industry-specific integrated software and support packages. CEO James Goodnight owns about two-thirds of the company; co-founder and EVP John Sall owns the remainder.

SAS has expanded its core business intelligence product line with such offerings as financial management software and marketing automation and analysis applications.The company has also worked closely with strategic partners such as Teradata and Accenture to integrate its software with their offerings.

The company serves more than 44,000 customers (including 96 of the top 100 *FORTUNE* Global 500 companies) from about 400 offices worldwide. In 2007 SAS's annual revenues topped the $2 billion mark for the first time in company history.

In 2008 the company acquired IDeaS Revenue Optimization, a provider of revenue management software for the hospitality industry. That year SAS also purchased Teragram, a text mining and natural language processing technology provider.

Known for its tight-knit community, SAS offers its employees perks including on-site childcare centers, cafeterias, exercise facilities, walking trails, and a health care center.

EXECUTIVES

CEO: James H. (Jim) Goodnight
EVP, EMEA and Asia/Pacific Operations:
 Mikael Hagström
EVP: John P. Sall
SVP and CTO: Keith V. Collins
SVP and Chief Marketing Officer: Jim Davis
SVP and CFO: Don Parker
SVP and SAS Fellow: Allan Russell
**SVP Americas; President, SAS Canada and SAS
 Americas Subsidiaries:** Carl Farrell
VP, General Counsel, and Secretary: John Boswell
VP and Chief Accounting Officer: David Davis
VP Information Technology and CIO: Suzanne Gordon
VP Human Resources: Jennifer Mann, age 37
Manager Corporate Public Relations: Beverly Brown

LOCATIONS

HQ: SAS Institute Inc.
 100 SAS Campus Dr., Cary, NC 27513
Phone: 919-677-8000   **Fax:** 919-677-4444
Web: www.sas.com

2007 Sales

	% of total
EMEA	45
Americas	44
Asia/Pacific	11
Total	**100**

PRODUCTS/OPERATIONS

2007 Sales by Industry

	% of total
Financial services	42
Government	14
Services	11
Communications	8
Health & life sciences	8
Other industries	17
Total	**100**

Selected Software

Customer relationship management
  Credit analysis
  Customer interaction management
  Customer retention
  Customer segmentation management
Data analysis
Data mining
Data warehousing
E-commerce
Enterprise performance management
  Balanced score card reporting
Experimental design
Financial management
  Activity-based management
  Forecasting
  Planning and budgeting
Human resources management
Information technology systems management
  Cost management
  Resource optimization
  Security management
Project planning and management
Quality improvement
  Warranty analysis
Risk management
Statistical analysis

COMPETITORS

Actuate	Lawson Software
AngossSoftware	Microsoft
Business Objects	MicroStrategy
CA, Inc.	Oracle
Cognos	SAP
Fair Isaac	SPSS
IBM	Sybase
Information Builders	Teradata
Insightful	

HISTORICAL FINANCIALS

Company Type: Private

Income Statement

FYE: December 31

	REVENUE ($ mil.)	NET INCOME ($ mil.)	NET PROFIT MARGIN	EMPLOYEES
12/07	2,150	—	—	10,737
12/06	1,900	—	—	10,027
12/05	1,680	—	—	10,000
12/04	1,530	—	—	9,528
12/03	1,340	—	—	9,306
Annual Growth	**12.5%**	—	—	**3.6%**

Revenue History

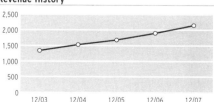

Sauder Woodworking

Sauder Woodworking takes the fear out of furniture and makes furniture for the God-fearing. The firm is the #1 US maker of ready-to-assemble (RTA) furniture (ahead of Bush Industries and O'Sullivan Industries) and, through Sauder Manufacturing, is also a top maker of church furniture and institutional seating. The company's RTA products include computer workstations, desks, entertainment centers, and wardrobes. Sauder's products are sold through retailers in more than 70 countries. Sauder acquired Progressive Furniture, which makes fully assembled furniture, in 2001. The company was founded in 1934 by Erie Sauder and is still family owned and operated.

From its struggling rival O'Sullivan, Sauder purchased the company's intellectual property, which included O'Sullivan's name, patents, and certain product drawings. As part of the deal, which was inked in early 2007, Sauder also inherited O'Sullivan's licensing agreement to make Coleman-branded garage storage products.

Soon after its O'Sullivan deal, Sauder announced in July 2007 plans to phase out domestic production of laminate and veneer bedroom pieces at its Progressive division. Due to stale sales, the company also exited its upscale Royal Patina line, which it bought in 2005.

In 2006 Sauder merged the sales and marketing operations for two of its business units — Studio RTA and Sauder RTA — to create operational efficiencies. Sauder sold its subsidiary Archbold Container, maker of corrugated packaging and displays, to Green Bay Packaging in mid-2005.

EXECUTIVES

Chairman: Maynard Sauder, age 75
President and CEO: Kevin J. Sauder, age 47
EVP Finance and CFO: Arnold Moshier
EVP Marketing and Sales: John D. Yoder
EVP Operations: Garrett Tinsman
SVP Sauder RTA Sales: Brent Gingerich
VP Human Resources: Steve Webster
VP Supply Chain Management: David K. Yoder
VP Engineering: Dan Sauder
Marketing Director: Michael (Mike) Lambright
Design Team Head: Doug Krieger
President, Studio RTA: Bob Hughes
President, Progressive Furniture: Dan Kendrick

LOCATIONS

HQ: Sauder Woodworking Co.
502 Middle St., Archbold, OH 43502
Phone: 419-446-2711   **Fax:** 419-446-3692
Web: www.sauder.com

PRODUCTS/OPERATIONS

Selected Furniture Products

Bedroom
Entertainment
Kitchen/Utility
Office/Computer
Shelving/Storage

Selected Subsidiaries

Archbold Container Corporation (manufacturer of corrugated packaging, packaging materials, and point-of-purchase displays)
Historic Sauder Village (history museum focused on the founding settlers of northwest Ohio)

Progressive Furniture (manufacturer and importer of solid wood, veneered, and laminate furniture)
Sauder Manufacturing Company (manufacturer of institutional seating)
Studio RTA (importer and distributor of RTA furniture)

COMPETITORS

Bassett Furniture
Bush Industries
Chromcraft Revington
DMI Furniture
Dorel Industries
Furniture Brands
Haworth, Inc.
Herman Miller
HNI
IKEA
Stanley Furniture
Steelcase

HISTORICAL FINANCIALS

Company Type: Private

Income Statement				FYE: December 31
	REVENUE ($ mil.)	NET INCOME ($ mil.)	NET PROFIT MARGIN	EMPLOYEES
12/07	700	—	—	2,700
12/06	700	—	—	3,400
12/05	730	—	—	3,400
12/04	750	—	—	4,000
12/03	700	—	—	3,500
Annual Growth	0.0%	—	—	(6.3%)

Revenue History

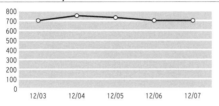

SavaSeniorCare

SavaSeniorCare operates about 190 skilled nursing and assisted living facilities in some two dozen states. The company provides health care, rehabilitation, physical therapy, and daily living assistance, as well as help with dementia and respiratory and intravenous therapy. SavaSeniorCare either owns, leases, or subleases the facilities through third parties (including Mariner Health Care). The company's SavaSeniorCare Administrative Services unit provides its properties with support services, including human resources, financial services, IT, compliance, legal, and risk management.

EXECUTIVES

Chairman: Leonard Grunstein, age 56
President: Tony Ogolsby
EVP Audit and Compliance: Brent A. Snelgrove
EVP Human Resources and Risk Management:
L. Scott Bardowell
EVP and General Counsel: Stefano M. Miele
SVP and CIO: Julie D. Purcell
VP and Controller: Robert M. Lyle
VP Real Estate and Associate General Counsel:
Annaliese (Nan) Impink

LOCATIONS

HQ: SavaSeniorCare, LLC
1 Ravinia Dr., Ste. 1400, Atlanta, GA 30346
Phone: 770-829-5100   **Fax:** 770-393-8054
Web: www.savaseniorcare.com

COMPETITORS

Advocat
Brookdale Senior Living
Catholic Healthcare Partners
Extendicare
Golden Horizons
HCA
Kindred Healthcare
Life Care Centers
Manor Care
National HealthCare
Omnicare
RehabCare
Signature HealthCARE
Skilled Healthcare Group
Sun Healthcare
Sunrise Senior Living
Tenet Healthcare

HISTORICAL FINANCIALS

Company Type: Private

Income Statement				FYE: December 31
	ESTIMATED REVENUE ($ mil.)	NET INCOME ($ mil.)	NET PROFIT MARGIN	EMPLOYEES
12/07	1,270	—	—	22,000
12/06	1,200	—	—	23,368
12/05	1,160	—	—	23,673
Annual Growth	4.6%	—	—	(3.6%)

Revenue History

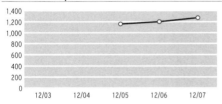

Save Mart Supermarkets

Save Mart Supermarkets is an even bigger wheel in the California grocery business now that it has doubled in size as a result of its recent acquisition of 132 Albertsons supermarkets in northern California and Nevada. A sponsor of the NASCAR Toyota/Save Mart 350, the company now operates about 250 grocery stores in northern and central California and Nevada. About half of the locations house in-store pharmacies. Its supermarkets and warehouse stores operate under the Save Mart Supermarkets, S-Mart, Lucky, and FoodMaxx names. Save Mart also owns distributor SMART Refrigerated Transport. CEO Robert Piccinini owns most of Save Mart, which was founded in 1952 by his father, Mike Piccinini, and uncle, Nick Tocco.

The grocery chain has converted most of the Albertsons stores it acquired in February 2007 to the Save Mart banner. (The remaining former Albertsons stores took on the resurrected Lucky Stores banner and FoodMaxx name.) Along with the supermarkets, Save Mart also purchased two distribution centers and division offices in California from Albertsons. The deal transformed Save Mart into the second largest California-based grocer, after Safeway. The Albertsons purchase also added more than 75 in-store pharmacies to Save Mart's operations.

After a big year in 2007, Save Mart announced plans to open only three new stores in 2008, all with pharmacies.

Save Mart also owns and operates Yosemite Wholesale Warehouse and Yosemite Advertising and is a partner in Super Store Industries.

The chain has been trying out different formats, including an upscale prototype with its own coffeehouse and expanded offerings of ethnic and organic foods, and its popular private-label salad mix line, Fresh Favorites.

Save Mart grew its sales and store count in 2003 with the acquisition of 25 Food 4 Less stores from bankrupt grocery distributor Fleming Companies, which were quickly converted to the FoodMaxx banner. The grocery chain has also been adding to its real estate holdings with the purchase of two shopping centers in Fresno and Visalia, California in mid-2004 and early 2005, and the purchase of four stores from rival Ralphs Grocery Co.

Save Mart president and COO Bob Spengler retired at the end of 2005, but came back in fall 2006 to help the company with the Albertsons deal. He retired again in early 2008.

EXECUTIVES

Chairman and CEO: Robert M. (Bob) Piccinini
COO: Steve Junqueiro
Acting CFO: Steve Ackerman
Chief Administrative Officer: Mike Silveira
VP Merchandising and Marketing: Cecil Russell
VP Fresh: Rick Smith
President, FoodMaxx: Art Patch

LOCATIONS

HQ: Save Mart Supermarkets
1800 Standiford Ave., Modesto, CA 95350
Phone: 209-577-1600   **Fax:** 209-577-3857
Web: www.savemart.com

PRODUCTS/OPERATIONS

2008 Stores

	No.
Save Mart	124
Lucky	72
FoodMaxx	44
S-Mart Foods	8
Total	**248**

COMPETITORS

Costco Wholesale
Longs Drug
Raley's
Ralphs
Rite Aid
Safeway
Target
Trader Joe's
Vons
Wal-Mart

Sbarro, Inc.

Sbarro lends an Italian flavor to that great American innovation, the shopping mall. The company operates and franchises more than 1,000 cafeteria-style Italian-food stands across the US and more than 40 other countries. Serving pizza, pasta entrees, and salads, Sbarro's units are typically found in high-traffic locations, such as malls, airports, and toll-road rest areas. The company owns and operates more than 500 locations, while the rest of the chain is operated by franchisees. Sbarro also sells its sauces through select locations. The late Gennaro Sbarro, with his wife Carmela, started the business in 1954; the Sbarro family sold the company to private equity firm MidOcean Partners in 2007.

Following the $450 million buyout, MidOcean has been funding further expansion of the chain, mostly through franchising. During 2007 the number of franchised locations grew by more than 45 (about 20 locations closed; another dozen were acquired by the company), while Sbarro opened 20 new corporate units. The chain's expansion efforts are being led by CEO Peter Beaudrault, who was brought in from Hard Rock Cafe by the Sbarro clan in 2004 to revitalize the sagging business.

In addition to its mall-based quick service restaurants, the company has more than 80 free-standing locations. It has also been branching out into the full-service dining sector through a small number of Carmela's of Brooklyn casual-dining units.

The Sbarro family originally took the company private for almost $390 million in 1999.

EXECUTIVES

Chairman, President, and CEO: Peter J. Beaudrault, age 53, $620,595 pay
SVP Operations: Jim Kelbaugh
SVP Operations: Randy Jones
VP and CFO: Anthony J. Puglisi, age 59
VP Franchise Development and Support Services: William J. Vetter
General Counsel and Secretary: Stuart M. Steinberg, age 51
CIO: Richard Guariglia
President, Business Development and Corporate VP: Anthony J. Missano, age 49
President, Franchise Development: John Brisco
Auditors: PricewaterhouseCoopers LLP

LOCATIONS

HQ: Sbarro, Inc.
401 Broadhollow Rd., Melville, NY 11747
Phone: 631-715-4100   **Fax:** 631-715-4197
Web: www.sbarro.com

2007 Locations

	No.
US	
New York	74
Florida	71
California	69
Ohio	40
Illinois	38
Pennsylvania	34
Virginia	28
Minnesota	25
Massachusetts	24
Michigan	24
New Jersey	24
Texas	24
North Carolina	21
Georgia	19
Maryland	19
Nevada	18
Missouri	15
Tennessee	14
Connecticut	13
Washington	13
Arizona	11
Kentucky	9
Mexico	9
Oklahoma	9
Wisconsin	9
South Carolina	8
Utah	8
Alabama	7
Colorado	7
Indiana	7
Iowa	7
Louisiana	7
Oregon	7
Other states	52
International	266
Total	**1,030**

PRODUCTS/OPERATIONS

2007 Sales

	$ mil.	% of total
Restaurants	342.9	96
Franchising	15.5	4
Other	0.3	—
Total	**358.7**	**100**

2007 Locations

	No.
Franchised	524
Company-owned	506
Total	**1,030**

COMPETITORS

AFC Enterprises
Arby's
Burger King
Cajun Operating Company
California Pizza Kitchen
Chick-fil-A
CiCi Enterprises
CKE Restaurants
Dairy Queen
Fazoli's
Galardi Group
Kahala
McDonald's
Nathan's Famous
Noble Roman's
Panda Restaurant Group
Pizza Hut
Pizza Inn
Quiznos
Subway
Wendy's
YUM!

HISTORICAL FINANCIALS

Company Type: Private

Income Statement

	REVENUE ($ mil.)	NET INCOME ($ mil.)	NET PROFIT MARGIN	EMPLOYEES
			FYE: Sunday nearest December 31	
12/07	359	(30)	—	5,400
12/06	350	10	2.8%	8,000
12/05	349	1	0.4%	5,500
12/04	349	(4)	—	6,500
12/03	332	(17)	—	5,600
Annual Growth	1.9%	—	—	(0.9%)

2007 Year-End Financials

Debt ratio: 243.5%
Return on equity: —
Cash ($ mil.): —
Current ratio: —
Long-term debt ($ mil.): 330

Net Income History

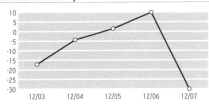

S.C. Johnson

S.C. Johnson & Son helped to replace the fly-swatter with the spray can. The firm is one of the world's largest makers of consumer chemical products, including Brise, Drano, Edge, Fantastik, Glade, Kabbikiller, Mr. Muscle, OFF!, Pledge, Raid, Scrubbing Bubbles, Saran, Shout, Vanish, Windex, and Ziploc. With operations on six continents, its international business generates some 60% of sales. The founder's great-grandson and once one of the richest men in the US, Samuel Johnson died in 2004. His immediate family owns about 60% of S.C. Johnson; descendants of the founder's daughter own about 40%. President, CEO, and director Bill Perez left for Nike in late 2004 and chairman Dr. Fisk Johnson replaced him as CEO.

Many of S.C. Johnson's products have been and remain top sellers in their market categories. The company has operations in more than 70 countries and its products are available in more than 110. In 2006 *Working Mother* magazine again recognized S.C. Johnson as one of the 100 best companies for working mothers.

The company's commercial products division (Johnson Wax Professional and Johnson Polymer) was spun off as a private company owned by the Johnson family. The company also has sold most of its personal care line.

HISTORY

Samuel C. Johnson, a carpenter whose customers were as interested in his floor wax as in his parquet floors, founded S.C. Johnson in Racine, Wisconsin, in 1886. Forsaking carpentry, Johnson began to manufacture floor care products. The company, named S.C. Johnson & Son in 1906, began establishing subsidiaries worldwide in 1914. By the time Johnson's son and successor,

Herbert Johnson, died in 1928, annual sales were $5 million. Herbert Jr. and his sister, Henrietta Lewis, received 60% and 40% of the firm, respectively. The original section of S.C. Johnson's headquarters, designed by Frank Lloyd Wright and called "the greatest piece of 20th-century architecture" in the US, was finished in 1939.

In 1954, with $45 million in annual sales, Herbert Jr.'s son Samuel Curtis Johnson joined the company as new products director. Two years later it introduced Raid, the first water-based insecticide, and soon thereafter, OFF! insect repellent. Each became a market leader. The company unsuccessfully attempted to diversify into paint, chemicals, and lawn care during the 1950s and 1960s. The home care products segment prospered, however, with the introduction of Pledge aerosol furniture polish and Glade aerosol air freshener.

After Herbert Jr. suffered a stroke in 1965, Samuel became president. In 1975 the firm banned the use of the chlorofluorocarbons (CFCs) in its products, three years before the US government banned CFCs. Samuel started a recreational products division that was bought by the Johnson family in 1986. That company went public in 1987 as Johnson Worldwide Associates, with the family retaining control.

The company launched Edge shaving gel and Agree hair products in the 1970s but had few products as successful in the 1980s. It moved into real estate with Johnson Wax Development (JWD) in the 1970s, but sold JWD's assets in the late 1980s.

S. Curtis Johnson, Samuel's son, joined the company in 1983. In 1986 S.C. Johnson bought Bugs Burger Bug Killers, moving into commercial pest control; in 1990 it entered into an agreement with Mycogen to develop biological pesticides for household use.

In 1993 it bought Drackett, bringing Drano and Windex to its product roster along with increased competition from heavyweights such as Procter & Gamble and Clorox. That year S.C. Johnson sold the Agree and Halsa lines to DEP. In 1996 it launched a line of water-soluble pouches for cleaning products that allow work to be done without touching hazardous chemicals. President William Perez became CEO the next year (and left in late 2004 to become president, CEO, and director of Nike, Inc.).

S.C. Johnson bought Dow Chemical's DowBrands unit, maker of bathroom cleaner (Dow), plastic bags (Ziploc), and plastic wrap (Saran Wrap), for $1.2 billion in 1998. It then sold off other Dow brands (cleaners Spray 'N Wash, Glass Plus, Yes, and Vivid) to the UK's Reckitt & Colman to settle antitrust issues.

A year later S.C. Johnson sold its skin care line, including Aveeno, to health care products maker Johnson & Johnson, and spun off its commercial products unit as a private firm owned by the Johnson family. Boosting its home cleaning line, in 1999 it introduced two new products: AllerCare (for dust mite control) and Pledge Grab-It (electrostatically charged cleaning sheets).

In 2000 S.C. Johnson pulled its AllerCare carpet powder and allergen spray from store shelves after some consumers had negative reactions to the fragrance additive in the products. That year H. Fisk Johnson succeeded his father (who became chairman emeritus) as chairman.

In 2001 the company was fined $950,000 for selling banned Raid Max Roach Bait traps in New York after agreeing to pull them from store shelves. Also that year S.C. Johnson's Japanese

subsidiary agreed to buy that country's leading drain cleaner brand, Pipe Unish, from Unicharm.

In October 2002 the company acquired the household insecticides unit of German drug giant Bayer Group for $734 million. The following year S.C. Johnson invested in Karamchand Appliances Private Limited, which owns India's second-leading insect control brand *AllOut*.

Chairman emeritus Samuel C. Johnson died in May 2004 at the age of 76. Chairman Dr. Fisk Johnson became CEO of the company again in late 2004.

EXECUTIVES

Chairman and CEO: H. Fisk Johnson
President, Americas: Pedro Cieza
President, Asia: Steven P. Stanbrook, age 50
President, Europe, Africa, and Near East Region (EurAFNE): Patrick J. O'Brien
President, North America: David L. (Dave) May
EVP and CFO: W. Lee McCollum, age 58
EVP, Worldwide Corporate and Environmental Affairs: Jane M. Hutterly
EVP, Worldwide Human Resources: Gayle P. Kosterman
SVP, New Products: Gregory J. (Greg) Barron
SVP, General Counsel, and Secretary: David Hecker
SVP, Worldwide Manufacturing and Procurement: Darcy D. Massey
VP and Corporate Treasurer: William H. Van Lopik
VP and General Manager, Mexico and Central America: Eduardo Ortiz-Tirado
VP and Group Managing Director, Europe: Filippo Meroni
VP and CIO: Mark H. Eckhardt
VP, Global Environmental and Safety Actions: Scott Johnson
VP, North American Sales: Darwin Lewis
VP, Marketing Services: Patricia Penman
VP, Global Public Affairs and Communications: Kelly M. Semrau

LOCATIONS

HQ: S.C. Johnson & Son, Inc.
1525 Howe St., Racine, WI 53403
Phone: 262-260-2000   **Fax:** 262-260-6004
Web: www.scjohnson.com

PRODUCTS/OPERATIONS

Selected Products and Brands

Air Care
  Air freshener (Glade, Glade Duet)
  Pillow and mattress covers (AllerCare)
Home Cleaning
  Bathroom/drain (Drano, Scrubbing Bubbles, Vanish)
  Cleaners (Fantastik, Windex, Windex Multi-Surface Cleaner with Vinegar)
  Floor care (Pledge, Pledge Grab-It, Johnson)
  Furniture care (Pledge, Pledge Wipes, Pledge Grab-it Dry Dusting Mitts)
  Laundry/carpet care (Shout)
Home Storage
  Plastic bags (Ziploc)
  Plastic wrap (Handi-Wrap, Saran Wrap)
Insect Control
  Insecticides (Raid, Raid Max)
  Repellents (Deep Woods OFF!, OFF!, OFF! Mosquito Lamp, OFF! Skintastic)

COMPETITORS

3M	Henkel Corp.
Alticor	IWP International
Blyth	Procter & Gamble
Church & Dwight	Reckitt Benckiser
Clorox	Shaklee
Colgate-Palmolive	Unilever
Dow Chemical	Yankee Candle
DuPont	

Scarborough Research

Scarborough Research provides marketing research studies for 75 local markets that delve into more than 1,700 consumer research topics such as lifestyle, home improvement, demographics, and travel. The company's more than 3,500 clients include the media, ad agencies, and sports teams. Its specialized services include Hispanic market research and custom analytics (helping clients better read customer data and make decisions based on that data). The company is a joint venture of marketing research firms Arbitron and Nielsen (formerly VNU). Scarborough Research was founded in 1975 and was originally developed as a newspaper measurement tool.

EXECUTIVES

President and CEO: Robert L. (Bob) Cohen
EVP Research: Gregg Linder
EVP and Director Sales: Steve Seraita
SVP Sales, U.S. Media Services, Arbitron: Carol Hanley
SVP Print and Internet Sales: Gary A. Meo
SVP Radio, Sports Marketing, and Outdoor Media: Howard Goldberg
SVP Human Resources: Debbie Morisie
SVP Television: Cheryl Greenblatt
VP and CFO: David Reifer
VP Marketing and Communications: Deirdre McFarland

LOCATIONS

HQ: Scarborough Research
770 Broadway, New York, NY 10003
Phone: 646-654-8400 **Fax:** 646-654-8450
Web: www.scarborough.com

COMPETITORS

Edison Media Research
GfK NOP
International Demographics
Kantar Group
Mediamark
ORC
Taylor Nelson
Zogby

HISTORICAL FINANCIALS

Company Type: Joint venture

Income Statement

FYE: December 31

	REVENUE ($ mil.)	NET INCOME ($ mil.)	NET PROFIT MARGIN	EMPLOYEES
12/07	65	—	—	—
12/06	61	—	—	—
12/05	56	—	—	—
12/04	55	—	—	—
12/03	50	—	—	—
Annual Growth	6.7%	—	—	—

Revenue History

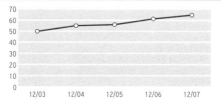

Schneider National

If you think that's the Great Pumpkin behind you on the highway, look again. With its signature bright-orange fleet of about 14,000 tractors and 40,000 trailers, Schneider National is one of the top truckload carriers in the US. The company's Schneider National Carriers unit provides truckload service throughout North America, including one-way van, dedicated, expedited, regional, and bulk freight transportation. The company also offers intermodal service, in which it arranges the transportation of freight by multiple methods, such as road and rail. It has a fleet of some 11,000 intermodal containers. Subsidiary Schneider Logistics offers supply chain management services.

Not content to rely on its signature nationwide truckload business, Schneider National in 2008 began offering regional freight hauling in the western US. The company hopes the new business will be able to take advantage of increased demand for short-haul transportation services. In addition, Schneider National has been working to strengthen its intermodal business, and it has entered China's domestic logistics services market.

At the same time, the company has been moving to divest noncore operations. In 2006 the company sold Schneider Payment Services, its freight bill payment business, to a unit of U.S. Bancorp, and sold glass transporter Schneider Specialized Carriers to flatbed carrier Maverick USA.

Schneider National is known for being an early adopter of new transportation technology — it was one of the first carriers to link all its trucks by two-way satellite. The company has been recognized for a pioneering trailer-tracking system that uses wireless networks, global positioning units, and sensors in order to keep closer track of shipments.

Chairman and former CEO Don Schneider, son of the company's founder, is among its shareholders, but he doesn't disclose how much of the company he owns.

HISTORY

A. J. "Al" Schneider bought a truck in 1935 with money earned from selling the family car. He drove the truck for three years, got another, and then leased them both to another firm. Becoming general manager of Bins Transfer & Storage in 1938, Schneider bought the company that year and changed the name to Schneider Transport & Storage. In 1944 Schneider stopped storing household goods and continued as an intrastate carrier in Wisconsin through the 1950s, transporting food and household goods. The Interstate Commerce Commission granted its first interstate license to Schneider in 1958.

Al's son Donald joined the company as general manager in 1961, and in 1962 the company dropped "Storage" from its name to become Schneider Transport. The 1960s also saw the first of many acquisitions. Donald became CEO in 1973, overseeing more acquisitions and the creation of Schneider National as a holding company for the organization. Donald also saw to the installation of computerized control systems, the first of many technical innovations Schneider would use in its trucks.

With the Motor Carrier Act's passage in 1980, restrictions eased and interstate shipping opened up. Schneider (and its competitors) saw the sky as the limit and founded Schneider Communications, a long-distance provider, in 1982. Eager to escape the Teamsters' thrall but choosing not to go head-to-head with the powerful union, Schneider formed Schneider National Carriers as a nonunion company out of three 1985 acquisitions, which signed on new recruits, while Schneider Transport remained unionized. Schneider focused on guaranteeing on-time delivery in the deregulated market: In 1988 Schneider became the first trucking company to install a satellite-tracking system in its trucks, setting the industry standard.

Schneider further expanded its services in the 1990s, starting with Schneider Specialized Services for carrying difficult items. It moved into Canada and Mexico in 1991. By 1993 some two-thirds of *FORTUNE* 500 companies used Schneider, and the company formed Schneider Logistics to help companies streamline their shipping operations. It sold Schneider Communications to Frontier Communications in 1995. The company moved into Europe in 1997.

It continued buying other US trucking firms, including Landstar Poole and Builder's Transport (both in 1998), mainly to acquire their drivers for its expanding fleet. In 1999 Schneider acquired the glass-transportation business of A. J. Metler & Rigging.

In 2000 Schneider acquired the freight payment services of Tranzact Systems and boosted its e-commerce offerings through alliances with ContractorHub.com and Paperloop.com. The company also made plans to spin off Schneider Logistics and sell part of it to the public, but unfavorable market conditions put the IPO on hold. Schneider added expedited services to its portfolio in 2001 to provide time-definite delivery in Canada, Mexico, and the US.

Christopher Lofgren's promotion to president and CEO in 2002 made him the first person outside the founding family to lead Schneider National.

The company enhanced its intermodal business in 2005 when Schneider Logistics acquired American Port Services, a provider of transloading services — moving freight from one mode of transportation to another — at several key US ports.

EXECUTIVES

Chairman: Donald J. (Don) Schneider, age 68
Vice Chairman and Secretary: Thomas A. (Tom) Gannon
President and CEO: Christopher B. (Chris) Lofgren, age 49
EVP and CIO: Judith A. (Judy) Lemke
EVP Sales, Marketing, and Customer Service: Steve Matheys
SVP Enterprise Sales: Dan Van Alstine
SVP Global Business Development: Brian Bowers
VP Commercial Operations, Intermodal: Jim Van Hefty
VP Enterprise Recruiting: Rob Reich
VP Human Resources: Tim Fliss
VP International, Schneider Logistics: John Ferguson
VP Litigation: Frank Stackhouse
VP Product Management: Bob Grawien
VP Safety and Driver Training: Don Osterberg
VP Sales, Mexico: Will Chang
VP Sales, Regional Client Group: Greg Sanders
VP Technology Services: Paul Mueller
President, Intermodal: Bill Matheson
President, Schneider Logistics: Thomas I. (Tom) Escott
President, Truckload: Mark Rourke
Manager, Public Relations: Janet Bonkowski

LOCATIONS

HQ: Schneider National, Inc.
3101 S. Packerland Dr., Green Bay, WI 54306
Phone: 920-592-2000 **Fax:** 920-592-3063
Web: www.schneider.com

COMPETITORS

Burlington Northern
 Santa Fe
C.H. Robinson Worldwide
Con-way Inc.
Crete Carrier
CSX
DHL
Expeditors
J.B. Hunt
Landstar System
Menlo Worldwide

Norfolk Southern
Pacer Global Logistics
Penske
Ryder System
Swift Transportation
Union Pacific
UPS Supply Chain
 Solutions
U.S. Xpress
Werner Enterprises

HISTORICAL FINANCIALS

Company Type: Private

Income Statement				FYE: December 31
	REVENUE ($ mil.)	NET INCOME ($ mil.)	NET PROFIT MARGIN	EMPLOYEES
12/07	3,400	—	—	22,216
12/06	3,700	—	—	21,600
12/05	3,500	—	—	20,000
12/04	3,200	—	—	20,000
12/03	2,900	—	—	20,733
Annual Growth	4.1%	—	—	1.7%

Revenue History

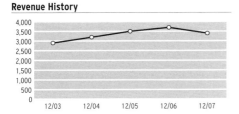

Schnuck Markets

If you'll meet me in St. Louis, then chances are there'll be a Schnucks in sight. The region's largest food chain, Schnuck Markets operates about 100 stores, mostly in the St. Louis area, but also in other parts of Missouri and in Illinois, Indiana, Iowa, Mississippi, Tennessee, and Wisconsin. All stores offer a full line of groceries, and most have pharmacies, video rental outlets, in-store banking, and florist shops. Although most stores operate under the Schnucks banner, the company also runs about a half dozen Logli supermarkets and a Sentry Drug in Illinois. The company acquired 12 Seessel's stores in Memphis from Albertsons in 2002. Founded in 1939, the company is owned by the Schnuck family.

Schnuck Markets expanded into Iowa with a 63,000-sq.-ft. store in Bettendorf in 2005.

In early 2007 Schnuck Markets lowered prices on some 10,000 items in 68 of its stores in the St. Louis and Springfield, Illinois markets, adopting an everyday-low-price strategy associated with, most notably, rival Wal-Mart Stores.

Schnuck pharmacies will begin offering free supplies of some antibiotics to customers.

Schnuck's announcement came about a year after Wal-Mart announced plans to offer about 150 generic medications for $4.

The regional grocery chain is expanding its Schnucks Express fuel centers, which sell convenience foods as well as gas. To that end, in May 2007 Schnuck acquired two Fill 'n Station convenience stores and converted them to the Schnuck Express banner.

EXECUTIVES

Chairman and CEO: Scott C. Schnuck, age 58
President: Todd R. Schnuck, age 48
SVP, Marketing and Merchandising: Randy Wedel
SVP, Store Operations: William (Bill) Bredenkoetter
SVP, Manufacturing and Logistics: Richard (Rick) Frede
VP, Finance: Gary Meyer
VP Center Store: Lori Caster
VP, Human Resources: Janice Rhodes
VP, Produce: Michael (Mike) O'Brien
VP, Shopping Center Development: Mark Schnuck
Secretary and General Counsel: Mary Moorkamp
Treasurer: David Bell
Controller: Stephen J. Hinderberger
Director, Communications: Lori Willis

LOCATIONS

HQ: Schnuck Markets, Inc.
11420 Lackland Rd., St. Louis, MO 63146
Phone: 314-994-9900 **Fax:** 314-994-4465
Web: www.schnucks.com

COMPETITORS

7-Eleven
Associated Wholesale Grocers
CVS Caremark
Dierbergs Markets
Dominick's
Hy-Vee
Kmart
Kroger
Meijer
SUPERVALU
Walgreen
Wal-Mart

Schreiber Foods

If you order cheese on your burger at the drive-thru, you might well get a taste of Schreiber Foods. The processor is a major supplier of the cheese used on hamburgers by US fast-food restaurants. Schreiber produces primarily private-label processed and natural cheese, and dairy ingredients for food retailers, food service distributors, and food manufacturers. It does offer a few of its brands for retail sale, including American Heritage and Cooper. The company has bought up smaller cheese operations to expand its geographic reach and is now a leading US private-label cream cheese maker.

In addition to cheese, the company offers its customers such services as category management, risk management, vendor managed inventory (VMI), and supply chain management.

Schreiber Foods has cheese production facilities in Arizona, Georgia, Missouri, Nebraska, Pennsylvania, Tennessee, Texas, Utah, and Wisconsin, as well as in Brazil, Germany, India, and Mexico. It counts among its customers Safeway, Weight Watchers, and Wal-Mart.

Schreiber owns and operates Capri Packaging, which offers flexible film structures and packaging solutions. It also owns Green Bay Machinery, a manufacturer of extruders and other equipment for processing cheese.

Founded in 1945, Schreiber opted in 1999 to transfer its ownership into an employee stock-ownership plan.

EXECUTIVES

Chairman: Larry P. Ferguson
President and CEO: David P. Pozniak
CFO: Brian Liddy
SVP Foodservice Sales: Mike Haddad
VP Industrial & Regulatory Affairs: Deborah A. Van Dyk
VP Information Services and CIO: Tom Andreoli
VP and General Counsel: Jerry Smyth
VP International Operations: Helmut Felder
VP Education and Community Relations: Nancy Armbrust
President, Yogurt Division: Dan LaValley

LOCATIONS

HQ: Schreiber Foods Inc.
425 Pine St., Green Bay, WI 54301
Phone: 920-437-7601 **Fax:** 920-437-1617
Web: www.schreiberfoods.com

PRODUCTS/OPERATIONS

Selected Cheese Brands

Food service brands
 Clearfield
 LaFeria
 Lov-It
 Menu
 Raskas
 Ready-Cut
 School Choice
 Schreiber

Retail brands
 American Heritage
 Cooper

Selected Subsidiaries

Capri Packaging (packaging films)
Green Bay Machinery (cheese slicing and wrapping
 equipment)

COMPETITORS

Ampac
AMPI
APW Wyott Foodservice Equipment
Barry-Wehmiller
Bel Brands USA
BelGioioso Cheese
Bongrain
Carlisle Companies
Carlisle FoodService
Dairy Farmers of America
Darigold, Inc.
Dover Corporation
Exopack
Foremost Farms
Fromageries Bel
Gencor Industries
Great Lakes Cheese
Hiland Dairy
Kraft Foods
Land O'Lakes
Leprino Foods
Letica
Marathon Cheese
PrimeSource FoodService
Rexam
Saputo
Sargento
Southern Film Extruders
Toyo Seikan Kaisha

Schwan Food

Frozen pizza is the flashy part of The Schwan Food Company. With well-known pizza brands such as Tony's, Red Baron, and Freschetta, the company is one of the top frozen pizza makers in the US, along with Kraft Foods. Schwan is also a top supplier to the institutional frozen-pizza market and has operations in more than 50 countries worldwide. But pizza isn't the only slice of the company's revenue — its core business is a fleet of more than 6,000 home-delivery trucks. Schwan delivers casseroles, ice cream, and frozen foods to homes in the continental US. The family of late founder Marvin Schwan owns the company.

President and CEO Lenny Pippin, who had been with the company since 1999, resigned unexpectedly in February 2008. Greg Flack, president of the company's global consumer brands division, was named interim leader. Schwan gave no reason for Pippin's departure.

With its unintentionally retro-hip bright yellow-gold freezer delivery trucks (the company calls the color Inca Gold), Schwan is definitely cool, both temperature-wise and customer-wise. The company maintains a home-delivery system that brings some 400 frozen food products directly to customers in all the US mainland states. Orders can include bagels or pancakes, and Schwan's ice cream has a devoted following.

The company's Salina, Kansas, facility is the world's largest frozen pizza manufacturing plant. If you laid all the pepperoni that Schwan uses in a year end to end, it would stretch from New York City to Los Angeles. In addition to its US pizza market, Schwan sells Chicago Town pizzas in Western Europe and supplies schools and other institutional cafeterias with frozen pizza and sandwiches. Its foodservice group serves health care facilities, public and private schools and universities, chain restaurants, and convenience stores.

In conjunction with its Red Baron pizza brand, Schwan owned and operated the #1 civilian airshow act in the world, featuring the Red Baron Stearman Squadron, a formation aerobatics team that performs using vintage Stearman biplanes. However, in 2007 the company refocused its Red Baron marketing program and retired the squadron, which had performed for 28 years.

The Schwan family is notoriously secretive (Marvin Schwan himself gave no interviews after 1982).

HISTORY

Paul Schwan bought out his partner in their dairy in 1948 and began manufacturing ice cream using his own recipes. His son, Marvin Schwan, made deliveries for the dairy for a few years. After attending a two-year college, Marvin came back in 1950 to work at the dairy full-time. Two years later he began using his delivery experience to take advantage of the increase in homes with freezers. He bought an old truck for $100 and began a rural route selling ice cream to farmers. He quickly developed a loyal customer base and expanded to two routes the following year.

In the 1960s the company diversified with two acquisitions: a prepared sandwich company and a condensed fruit juice company. A new holding company, Schwan's Sales Enterprises, was established in 1964. Schwan's began delivering pizza the next year. Paul died in 1969.

Deciding that frozen pizza was not a fad, Marvin bought Kansas-based Tony's Pizza in 1970 and quickly rose to the top of the new industry. In the late 1970s Schwan's entered the commercial leasing business, and it later added more leasing companies under the Lyon Financial Services umbrella (sold 2000).

The company entered the institutional-pizza market in the mid-1980s and bought out competitors Sabatasso Foods and Better Baked Pizza. Schools liked Schwan's use of their government surplus cheese to make pizzas, which the company then sold to the schools at a discount.

In 1992 the company bought two Minnesota-based food companies: Panzerotti, a stuffed pastry business, and Monthly Market, a specialty retailer that sells groceries to fund-raising groups. It also began selling its pizzas in the UK. The next year Schwan's bought Chicago Brothers Frozen Pizza, a San Diego-based company specializing in deep-dish pizza.

Marvin died of a heart attack in 1993 at age 64, with his worth estimated at more than $1 billion. The previous year he had willed two-thirds of the company's stock to a charitable Lutheran trust, which was to be bought out by Schwan's after his death. In 1994 his brother Alfred, and Marvin's friend Lawrence Burgdorf made arrangements to have the company repurchase the foundation's shares for a total of $1.8 billion. But Marvin's four children filed a lawsuit in 1995 against their uncle and Burgdorf over the action. They claimed the men did not have the financial health of the company at heart and were divided in their loyalty. The children, on the other hand, were called money-hungry and callous to their father's last wishes. (The case was settled in 1997, but no information was released.)

In 1994 more than 200,000 people in 28 states contracted salmonella food poisoning after eating *E. coli*-tainted Schwan's ice cream. The company's insurance company eventually paid out nearly $1 million to about 6,000 affected customers in exchange for their signing releases promising they would not sue Schwan's.

Lenny Pippin became the company's fourth CEO in 1999, replacing Alfred, who stayed on as chairman. Schwan's exited the Canadian market at the end of 1999 due to perennial losses. In 2000 Schwan's introduced irradiated frozen ground-beef patties, struck an agreement with another company to electronically pasteurize some of its products.

The company began a reorganization of its business units and changed its name from Schwan's Sales Enterprises to The Schwan Food Company in early 2003. Also in 2003 Schwan acquired the frozen-dessert business of Mrs. Smith's Bakeries from Flowers Foods for $240 million in cash. Flowers retained the frozen bread and roll dough segment of Mrs. Smith.

The company was forced to recall more than 350,000 pounds of products in 2005 because they might have contained glass fragments. The recalled products, which were manufactured at Schwan's Minh plant in Pasadena, Texas, and were distributed to food stores nationwide and purchased by the federal school lunch program, included eggrolls, pizza twists, and tacos.

Later in 2005, Schwan acquired Canadian company T&N Foods (frozen pizza, bread products). In 2006, it acquired Hollywood, Florida-based wholesale appetizer company, Holiday Foods.

EXECUTIVES

Chairman: Alfred Schwan
CEO, President, and COO: Gregory D. (Greg) Flack
SEVP Finance and CFO: Bernadette M. Kruk
SEVP; President, Schwan's Venture Group:
 David A. (Dave) Bunnell
EVP Administration; President, Schwan's Development Corporation: William O. McCormack
EVP Administration and General Counsel:
 Brian R. Sattler
SVP Product and Market Strategy: Kristy Griffin
SVP and Chief Human Resources Officer: Arnie Strebe
SVP and COO, Schwan's Global Home Service:
 Bruce Saugstad
SVP Marketing and Supply Chain: Brian Nau
SVP, Chief Strategy and Marketing Officer:
 Yvonne La Penotiere
SVP Information Services and CIO:
 Kathleen (Kate) McNulty
President, Schwan's Consumer Brands Europe:
 John M. Beadle
President, Schwan's Global Home Service:
 Lawrence A. (Larry) Oberkfell
President, Schwan's Global Supply Chain:
 Douglas J. (Doug) Olsem
President, Holiday Foods: Emily Zecchino
President, Schwan's Food Service: Mark Jansen
President, Schwan's Home Service: Scott McNair
President, Schwan's Consumer Brands North America:
 Mark Dalrymple

LOCATIONS

HQ: The Schwan Food Company
 115 W. College Dr., Marshall, MN 56258
Phone: 507-532-3274   **Fax:** 507-537-8226
Web: www.theschwanfoodcompany.com

PRODUCTS/OPERATIONS

Selected Consumer Brands

Asian Sensations (frozen Asian foods)
Chicago Town (frozen pizza and ready meals)
Edward's Fine Foods (desserts)
Freschetta (frozen pizza)
Larry's (frozen potato side dishes)
Mrs. Smith's (bakery)
Red Baron (frozen pizza)
Tony's (frozen pizza)
Wolfgang Puck (frozen pizza)

COMPETITORS

Ben & Jerry's
Blue Bell
ConAgra
Cuisine Solutions
DineWise
Domino's
Dreyer's
FreshDirect
Heinz
Kraft Foods
Kraft North America
Little Caesar's
McLane Foodservice
Michelina's
MyWebGrocer
Nash-Finch
Nation Pizza Products
Nestlé
Nestlé USA
Omaha Steaks
On-Cor Frozen Foods
Overhill Farms
Papa John's
Peapod
Performance Food
Pinnacle Foods
Southern Foods
Stefano Foods
SYSCO
U.S. Foodservice
YUM!

HISTORICAL FINANCIALS
Company Type: Private

Income Statement				FYE: December 31
	REVENUE ($ mil.)	NET INCOME ($ mil.)	NET PROFIT MARGIN	EMPLOYEES
12/07	3,300	—	—	22,000
12/06	3,500	—	—	22,000
12/05	3,375	—	—	22,000
Annual Growth	(1.1%)	—	—	0.0%

Revenue History

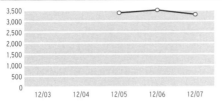

Schwarz Paper

Schwarz Paper Company is not just about paper: the diversified printing, packaging, paper, and distribution company sells a wide array of products, including bags, boxes, tissue paper, gift wrap, and other packaging materials used by retailers (such as The Gap and McDonald's) for promotional purposes. The company's commercial packaging unit provides inventory management and distribution of corrugated packaging, tapes, strapping, tubes, cushioning, and cleaning supplies. Its printing division prints tray liners, placemats, store fixtures, and point-of-purchase displays for customers including restaurants and airlines. Chairman Andrew McKenna Sr. (also chairman of McDonald's) owns the company.

Andrew McKenna Sr. has been with the national distributor of paper packaging and allied products since 1955. He became the president of Schwarz Paper in 1964.

The company was founded in 1907 as small store in Chicago providing paper and packaging supplies to other local businesses. The 100 year-old company has since expanded its operations across North American and into Europe and the Pacific Rim, and it has embraced 21st Century technologies to better manage its customers' supply, logistics, and inventory management needs.

EXECUTIVES
Chairman: Andrew J. (Andy) McKenna Sr., age 78
CEO: Christopher J. Donnelly
President: Andrew J. (Andy) McKenna Jr., age 50
EVP and CFO: Warren J. Kelleher
EVP and Chief Administration Officer: Louis M. DeRose
SVP Human Resources: Susan H. Bondy
VP Distribution: Kevin T. Hourican
VP Inventory Management: Bruce B. Barton
VP and CIO: Jean A. Luber
VP Sales and Marketing: Paul Frantz
Treasurer: Susan L. Donatello
Auditors: Deloitte & Touche

LOCATIONS
HQ: Schwarz Paper Company
8338 Austin Ave., Morton Grove, IL 60053
Phone: 847-966-2550   **Fax:** 847-966-1271
Web: www.schwarz.com

PRODUCTS/OPERATIONS

Selected Products
Appliances
Furniture
Grocery packaging
Health and beauty products
HR forms, business forms, and ID
Janitorial equipment
Leather and shoe care
Lighting and electrical fixtures
Maintenance equipment
Marking systems
Material handling equipment
Office supplies
Protective packaging
Retail display equipment
Retail packaging
Safety and security wear
Tape
Tools

COMPETITORS

3M
Bunzl Distribution USA
Graphic Packaging Holding
Hood Packaging
International Paper
Menasha Packaging
Packaging Dynamics
Unisource
xpedx

HISTORICAL FINANCIALS
Company Type: Private

Income Statement				FYE: September 30
	ESTIMATED REVENUE ($ mil.)	NET INCOME ($ mil.)	NET PROFIT MARGIN	EMPLOYEES
9/07	450	—	—	—
9/06	440	—	—	—
9/05	416	—	—	350
9/04	400	—	—	350
Annual Growth	4.0%	—	—	0.0%

Revenue History

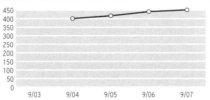

Scottrade, Inc.

Scottrade offers low-cost trading in stock, bonds, options, mutual funds, and exchange-traded funds (ETFs) to consumers, with transactions handled in real time. Customers can trade online via the company's Scottrade, Scottrader, and ScottradeELITE Web-based platforms, as well as by phone, wireless device, or through a broker at one of the firm's more than 350 branch offices in nearly all 50 states. The company also offers certificates of deposit, individual retirement accounts, and Coverdell education savings accounts. Scottrade is controlled by founder and CEO Rodger Riney.

Scottrade also offers a Chinese trading platform for customers in the US, China, Hong Kong, and Taiwan. Scottrade Chinese includes translated market news and research reports. The company is also eyeing potential expansion into Europe.

The company continues to expand its brick-and-mortar branch system as a means to attract and satisfy customers who prefer face-to-face interaction. Despite the expense of the branch network, the company maintains its discount pricing.

In 2006 the company put its name on the St. Louis Blues hockey arena (now known as Scottrade Center).

EXECUTIVES
Founder, President, and CEO: Rodger O. Riney, age 62
CFO and Treasurer: Ron Wiese
Chief Administrative Officer: Jane Wulf
Chief Marketing Officer: Chris X. Moloney
CTO: Joan Albeck
CIO: Ian Patterson
Executive Director Branch Administration: Kristie Mayer
Executive Director Legal and Compliance: Andy Small
Executive Director Operations: Catherine (Cathy) Maher
Executive Director Branch Administration and Corporate Communication: Mary Koomar
Director Business and Product Development: Steve Walkenbach
President, Scottrade Bank: Joe Pope

LOCATIONS
HQ: Scottrade, Inc.
12800 Corporate Hill Dr., St. Louis, MO 63131
Phone: 314-965-1555   **Fax:** 314-543-6222
Web: www.scottrade.com

COMPETITORS

Charles Schwab
E*TRADE Financial
FMR
Merrill Lynch
optionsXpress
ShareBuilder
Siebert Financial
Stifel Financial
T. Rowe Price
TD Ameritrade
The Vanguard Group

HISTORICAL FINANCIALS

Company Type: Private

Income Statement

FYE: September 30

	REVENUE ($ mil.)	NET INCOME ($ mil.)	NET PROFIT MARGIN	EMPLOYEES
9/07	1,030	—	—	2,000
9/06	796	—	—	1,640
9/05	464	—	—	1,383
9/04	348	—	—	1,000
9/03	223	—	—	1,000
Annual Growth	46.6%	—	—	18.9%

Revenue History

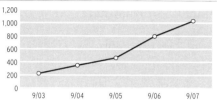

The Scoular Company

It's a grind and at the Scoular Company, that's a good thing. The company is best known for buying, selling, storing, handling, and transporting agricultural products (mainly grains) worldwide. It deals in the mainstays of farming: corn, hay, millet, rice, sorghum, soybeans, and wheat and gets them where they need to go. The company's other divisions offer fishmeal products for farm animal, pet, and aquaculture feeds, ingredients for food manufacturing, truck freight brokering, and livestock marketing. Scoular has operations in more than 50 countries throughout North and South America, Africa, Europe, and Asia.

Company services include bagging, blending, cleaning, containerizing, organic certification, packaging, sorting, sourcing, and storage. It also offers risk management and transportation and logistics. Container and vessel transportation, as well as rail, truck, and barge transportation are available.

Scoular serves customers in the aquaculture, flour milling, food processing and manufacturing, grain production, industrial ag processing, livestock feeding and manufacturing, pet food manufacturing, and renewable fuels sectors.

Founded in 1892 to run grain elevators, Scoular is employee owned.

EXECUTIVES

Chairman: Marshall E. Faith
President and CEO: Randal L. (Randy) Linville
COO: Robert (Bob) Ludington
SVP Asset, Resource, and Risk Management: John M. Heck
SVP Enterprise Systems and Technology: David M. Faith
SVP Flour Mill Markets: Charles (Chuck) Elsea
SVP Industrial Markets: Eric H. Jackson
SVP Producer Markets: George V. Schieber
SVP, Secretary, and General Counsel: Joan C. Maclin
VP and Chief Accounting and Control Officer: Randall Foster
Director Human Resources: Yvonne Lutz

LOCATIONS

HQ: The Scoular Company
2027 Dodge St., Omaha, NE 68102
Phone: 402-342-3500 **Fax:** 402-342-5568
Web: www.scoular.com

PRODUCTS/OPERATIONS

Selected Products and Services

Bakery meal
Barley
Beet pulp
Citrus
Corn gluten
Corn (yellow and white)
Cottonseed
Fats and oils
Freight (containers and rail)
Hay
Hominy
Hulls
Millet
Oats
Proteins (animal, dairy, marine, vegetable, and wet pet)
Rice hulls
Sorghum
Soybeans
Specialty food ingredients
Specialty pet-food ingredients
Wheat (durum, hard red winter, soft red winter, hard red spring, and white)

COMPETITORS

ADM
Ag Processing
AGRI Industries
Bartlett and Company
Bunge Limited
Cargill
CHS
DeBruce Grain
Excel Maritime Carriers
GROWMARK
Southern States
TBS International
TORM

Securian Financial

After 125 years of being in business, Minnesota Mutual felt secure enough to change its name to Securian Financial Group. The company still operates through its subsidiary Minnesota Life which offers individual and group life and disability insurance and annuities, as well as retirement services and mortgage life insurance. Other subsidiaries include Securian Financial Services which, along with Advantus Capital Management, offers mutual funds, institutional asset management, trust services, and annuity and retirement plans. The company was founded in 1880 and restructured as a mutual holding company in 2005.

Securian Financial has announced that it intends to acquire Maryland-based Capital Financial Group and its H. Beck securities broker-dealer business. While Capital Financial Group will operate as a independent business, it will serve to expand Securian's reach across the US.

EXECUTIVES

Chairman and CEO: Robert L. Senkler
President and Director: Randy F. Wallake
EVP, General Counsel, Secretary, and Director: Dennis E. Prohofsky
SVP and CFO: Gregory S. Strong
SVP, Financial Services: John F. Bruder
SVP, Human Resources and Corporate Services: Keith M. Campbell
SVP, Group Insurance: James E. Johnson
SVP, Retirement Services: Bruce P. Shay
SVP and General Counsel: Dwayne C. Radel
SVP and Chief Investment Officer: David Kuplic
Auditors: KPMG LLP

LOCATIONS

HQ: Securian Financial Group, Inc.
400 Robert St. North, St. Paul, MN 55101
Phone: 651-665-3500 **Fax:** 651-665-4488
Web: www.securian.com

PRODUCTS/OPERATIONS

2007 Revenues

	$ mil.	% of total
Premiums	1,505.6	53
Net investment income	546.2	19
Policy & contract fees	486.6	17
Commission income	89.7	3
Net realized investment gains	52.7	2
Finance charge income	49.8	2
Other	121.5	4
Total	**2,852.1**	**100**

COMPETITORS

AIG American General
American United Mutual
Conseco
COUNTRY Financial
Guardian Life
MetLife
National Western
Nationwide Life Insurance
New York Life
Northwestern Mutual
Pacific Mutual
Protective Life
Prudential
Torchmark

HISTORICAL FINANCIALS

Company Type: Private

Income Statement

FYE: December 31

	ASSETS ($ mil.)	NET INCOME ($ mil.)	INCOME AS % OF ASSETS	EMPLOYEES
12/07	26,644	207	0.8%	5,000
12/06	25,631	179	0.7%	5,000
12/05	23,435	186	0.8%	5,000
12/04	21,929	137	0.6%	5,000
12/03	20,799	44	0.2%	4,400
Annual Growth	6.4%	46.9%	—	3.2%

2007 Year-End Financials

Equity as % of assets: 10.5%
Return on assets: 0.8%
Return on equity: 7.6%
Long-term debt ($ mil.): —
Sales ($ mil.): 2,852

Net Income History

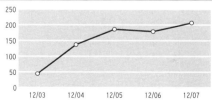

SemGroup, L.P.

SemGroup likes to stay in the middle of North America's stream of oil and gas. Through its SemCrude subsidiary, the company moves about 541,000 barrels of crude oil a day across the US, and operates more than 2,400 miles of pipeline in Oklahoma and Texas. Through its SemStream subsidiary, the company delivers natural gas liquids (NGLs), propane, and feedstock supplies to customers in 46 states. It also distributes refined petroleum products through its SemFuel unit. SemGas operates 800 miles of natural gas gathering pipeline. SemMaterials makes asphalt products. SemGroup Energy provides gathering, transporting, terminalling, and storage of crude oil in Oklahoma, Kansas, and Texas.

SemGroup serves customers in the US, Canada, Mexico, Wales, Switzerland and Vietnam.

The company is a major consolidator in the midstream industry. In 2005 its acquisitions included Central Alberta Midstream (Central), the fuel business of Halron Oil Company, and the asphalt operations of Koch Materials Company. In 2006 it acquired Petroplus International's Milford Haven storage terminal in the UK, and in 2007 it purchased the propane assets of Black Mountain Gas Co., a subsidiary of Southwest Gas Corp.

In 2008 SemGroup reported that it was experiencing liquidity issues.

EXECUTIVES

Acting President and CEO: Terry Ronan
EVP Strategic Development: W. James McCarthy
EVP and COO, SemGroup, SemCrude, and Seminole Canada Energy; President and CEO, SemGroup Energy Partners: Kevin L. Foxx, age 51
EVP Corporate Development, North America: Tim Purcell
SVP Eastern Canada: Darin Holst
VP Financial Services: Don Spaugy
VP Human Resources: Laura M. Lundquist
Corporate Controller and Chief Accounting Officer: Mark Lietzke
Treasurer: Alisa Perkins
Chief Restructuring Officer: Lisa J. Donahue, age 43

LOCATIONS

HQ: SemGroup, L.P.
2 Warren Place, 6120 S. Yale Ave., Ste. 700, Tulsa, OK 74136
Phone: 918-388-8100 **Fax:** 918-524-8290
Web: www.semgrouplp.com

SemGroup operates primarily in Kansas, Louisiana, Oklahoma, and Texas in the US, as well as in the Canadian provinces of Alberta, British Columbia, Manitoba, Ontario, Quebec, and Saskatchewan.

PRODUCTS/OPERATIONS

Selected Subsidiaries
SemCanada, L.P.
  SemCams
  Seminole Canada Energy Company
  Seminole Canada Gas Company
SemCrude, L.P.
SemFuel, L.P.
SemGas, L.P.
SemMaterials, L.P.
SemStream, L.P.

COMPETITORS

Duke Energy
Dynegy
Enbridge
Enterprise Products
TEPPCO Partners

HISTORICAL FINANCIALS

Company Type: Private

Income Statement				FYE: December 31
	REVENUE ($ mil.)	NET INCOME ($ mil.)	NET PROFIT MARGIN	EMPLOYEES
12/07	14,200	—	—	2,272
12/06	14,745	—	—	1,872
12/05	20,174	—	—	—
12/04	12,574	—	—	—
12/03	8,317	—	—	—
Annual Growth	14.3%	—	—	21.4%

Revenue History

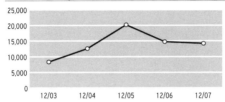

Seminole Electric Cooperative

This Seminole is not only a native Floridian, but it has also provided electricity in the state since 1948. Seminole Electric Cooperative generates and transmits electricity for 10 member distribution cooperatives that serve 1.7 million residential and business customers in 46 Florida counties. Seminole Electric has more than 2,100 MW of primarily coal-fired generating capacity (but with some natural gas and nuclear power generation, too). The cooperative also buys electricity from other utilities and independent power producers, and it owns about 350 miles of transmission lines.

Seminole Electric was formed to aggregate the power demands of its members and is governed by a board of trustees representing the 10 member utilities. The cooperative built its first power plant in the 1970s.

EXECUTIVES

President, Board of Trustees: Mal Green
EVP and General Manager: Timothy S. Woodbury
Assistant General Manager, CFO, and Assistant Secretary/Treasurer: John W. Geeraerts
SVP Operations and Assistant Secretary/Treasurer: Floyd J. Welborn
SVP Strategic Services: Michael P. Opalinski

VP, Administration: Savino (Al) Garcia
VP, Board of Trustees: Robert W. Strickland
Senior Director Corporate Compliance and Risk Management: Thomas H. Turke
Director Strategic Planning and Legislative Affairs: Lane T. Mahaffey
Director System Operations: Steven R. (Steve) Wallace
Secretary and Treasurer: Malcolm V. Page
Auditors: PricewaterhouseCoopers LLP

LOCATIONS

HQ: Seminole Electric Cooperative, Inc.
16313 N. Dale Mabry Hwy., Tampa, FL 33618
Phone: 813-963-0994 **Fax:** 813-264-7906
Web: www.seminole-electric.com

PRODUCTS/OPERATIONS

Members
Central Florida Electric Cooperative
Clay Electric Cooperative
Glades Electric Cooperative
Lee County Electric Cooperative
Peace River Electric Cooperative
Sumter Electric Cooperative
Suwannee Valley Electric Cooperative
Talquin Electric Cooperative
Tri-County Electric Cooperative
Withlacoochee River Electric Cooperative

COMPETITORS

Duke Energy
Florida Power & Light
Florida Public Utilities
FPL Group
JEA
Progress Energy
Southern Company
TECO Energy

HISTORICAL FINANCIALS

Company Type: Cooperative

Income Statement				FYE: December 31
	REVENUE ($ mil.)	NET INCOME ($ mil.)	NET PROFIT MARGIN	EMPLOYEES
12/07	1,210	11	0.9%	484
12/06	1,173	14	1.2%	482
12/05	1,080	6	0.6%	477
12/04	897	2	0.3%	468
12/03	799	2	0.3%	465
Annual Growth	11.0%	45.6%	—	1.0%

2007 Year-End Financials
Debt ratio: 1,120.3%   Current ratio: —
Return on equity: 10.5%   Long-term debt ($ mil.): 1,214
Cash ($ mil.): —

Net Income History

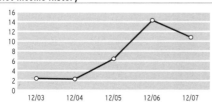

Sensata Technologies

Sensata Technologies has taken more than nine decades to become, it hopes, an overnight sensation. Founded in 1916 as General Plate Co., providing gold plate for jewelers, the company is a leading supplier of electrical and electronic sensors and controls. The business became part of Texas Instruments in 1959 and operated as TI's Sensors & Controls unit before going independent in a $3 billion buyout by Bain Capital in 2006. Sensata manufactures products used in aircraft, appliances, automotive engines, climate control systems, industrial equipment, and lighting to control and regulate their operation, based on changes in air flow, pressure, temperature, and other variable conditions.

The company gets more than half of its sales from international customers.

Sensata's products include the Klixon line of circuit breakers, motor protectors and controls, pressure and limit switches, printed circuit boards, and thermostats. The products help keep engines, motors, and other equipment from overheating and catching fire.

General Plate merged in 1931 with Spencer Thermostat Co., forming what was then called Metals & Controls Corp., which was absorbed by TI 28 years later.

TI divested the Sensors & Controls business because it said the products were not strategically related to its lines of analog semiconductors, digital signal processors, and radio-frequency identification (RFID) tags. The RFID products had been part of Sensors & Controls, but TI decided to hold on to that line, as RFID is becoming more widely used to track inventory and shipments by retailers, such as Wal-Mart Stores, and government entities, like the Department of Defense.

In late 2006 Sensata acquired the First Technology Automotive and Special Products (FTAS) business of Honeywell International for $90 million. FTAS manufactures automotive sensors, electromechanical control devices, and crash switch devices for automotive OEMs, Tier I automotive suppliers, large-vehicle and off-road OEMs, and industrial manufacturers.

In 2007 the company acquired the SMaL Camera Technologies subsidiary of Cypress Semiconductor for about $11 million in cash. SMaL Camera provides cameras and camera subsystems to automotive advanced driver assistance systems for such customers as Bosch and Delphi.

Also that year Sensata acquired Airpax for nearly $277 million, adding a complementary product line of magnetic circuit breakers and thermal sensors.

The company says its corporate moniker comes from the Latin word *sensata*, which means "those things gifted with sense."

EXECUTIVES

Chairman and CEO: Thomas (Tom) Wroe Jr.
EVP and COO: Martha Sullivan
EVP, CFO, and Director: Jeff Cote
SVP Corporate Services: Robert (Bob) Kearney
SVP and Human Resources: Donna Kimmel
SVP Global Operations: Dick Dane
SVP Sensors Business: Steve Major
SVP Controls Business: Jean-Pierre Vasdeboncoeur
VP and CIO: Aaron Weis
VP and General Counsel: Steve Reynolds
Investor Relations: Patty Campanile
Director Media Relations: Linda Megathlin

LOCATIONS

HQ: Sensata Technologies, Inc.
529 Pleasant St., Attleboro, MA 02703
Phone: 508-236-3800
Web: www.sensata.com

Sensata Technologies has manufacturing facilities in Brazil, China, the Dominican Republic, Japan, Malaysia, Mexico, the Netherlands, South Korea, and the US, with sales offices around the world.

2007 Sales

	$ mil.	% of total
Americas	685.4	49
Asia/Pacific	363.4	26
Europe	355.2	25
Total	**1,404.0**	**100**

PRODUCTS/OPERATIONS

2007 Sales

	$ mil.	% of total
Sensors	874.4	62
Controls	529.6	38
Total	**1,404.0**	**100**

COMPETITORS

ABB
Analogic
AREVA T&D
Atmel
Avago Technologies
Bourns
Cooper Industries
DENSO
Eaton
Fairchild Semiconductor
Freescale Semiconductor
Honeywell International
Infineon Technologies
Interconnect Devices
Legrand
Maxim Integrated Products
Motorola, Inc.
Murata Manufacturing
National Semiconductor
Navico
OmniVision Technologies
Pixelplus
Robert Bosch
Schneider Electric
Siemens Energy & Automation
Stoneridge
Technitrol
Tyco Electronics
Vishay Intertechnology

HISTORICAL FINANCIALS

Company Type: Private

Income Statement

FYE: December 31

	REVENUE ($ mil.)	NET INCOME ($ mil.)	NET PROFIT MARGIN	EMPLOYEES
12/07	1,404	(253)	—	14,246
12/06	1,174	(167)	—	10,100
12/05	1,061	143	13.5%	10,303
Annual Growth	15.1%	—	—	17.6%

Net Income History

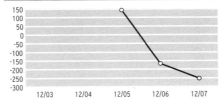

Sentara Healthcare

Health care's a beach for Sentara Healthcare. The not-for-profit organization operates a network of hospitals and other health facilities in the coastal Hampton Roads area of southeastern Virginia. The system includes seven acute care hospitals housing a total of more than 1,700 beds; one of the hospitals, Sentara Norfolk, includes a dedicated cardiac hospital with more than 100 beds. In addition to its acute care facilities, Sentara Healthcare operates several outpatient care facilities, as well as nursing homes, rehab centers, and medical practices. Its Optima Health unit provides HMO coverage and other health insurance products to about 350,000 Virginians.

EXECUTIVES

CEO: David L. Bernd
President and COO; Acting Administrator, Sentara Norfolk General Hospital: Howard P. Kern
SVP and CFO: Robert A. (Rob) Broerman
SVP Managed Care; President, Sentara Health Plans: Michael M. Dudley
SVP; President, Sentara Peninsula Region: Kenneth M. (Ken) Krakaur
VP; President, Sentara Life Care: Mary L. Blunt
VP and CIO: Bertram S. (Bert) Reese
VP Human Resources: Michael V. (Mike) Taylor
VP System Development: Vicky G. Gray
Chief Medical Officer: Gary R. Yates
Director Community Relations and Advocacy: Sandra Miller
Manager Public Relations: Emma Inman

LOCATIONS

HQ: Sentara Healthcare
6015 Poplar Hall Dr., Norfolk, VA 23502
Phone: 757-455-7540   **Fax:** 757-455-7964
Web: www.sentara.com

PRODUCTS/OPERATIONS

Selected Facilities

Sentara Bayside Hospital (Virginia Beach, VA)
Sentara CarePlex Hospital (Hampton, VA)
Sentara Leigh Hospital (Norfolk, VA)
Sentara Norfolk General Hospital (Norfolk, VA)
Sentara Obici Hospital (Suffolk, VA)
Sentara Virginia Beach General Hospital (Virginia Beach, VA)
Sentara Williamsburg Regional Medical Center (Williamsburg, VA)

COMPETITORS

Bon Secours Health
Carilion Clinic
Novant Health
Wake Forest University Baptist Medical Center

Sentry Insurance

Vigilant for its policyholders, Sentry Insurance (of the famous Minuteman statue logo) offers a variety of insurance products, including auto, homeowners, and other property/casualty lines, as well as life and annuities. The mutual company (owned by its policyholders) offers individual and family coverage through several subsidiaries. Sentry Insurance also provides specialized insurance to businesses of all sizes, including manufacturers and retailers. The company's Sentry Equity Services offers mutual fund services through its Sentry Fund. Formerly named Hardware Mutual, Sentry Insurance was founded in 1904 to provide insurance to members of the Wisconsin Retail Hardware Association.

Sentry Insurance has offices throughout the US. Subsidiaries include Parker Centennial Assurance, Dairyland Insurance, Middlesex Insurance, and Sentry Life Insurance.

In 2005 Sentry Insurance acquired ALF Insurance Agency, one of its brokerage partners. With about 15 Michigan locations, ALF continues to operate as an independent agency and sell other companies' products.

The Farm Equipment Manufacturers Association gives Sentry Insurance an exclusive endorsement as a recommended insurance provider. The company works with a number of other member groups to create insurance programs, including Business Technology Association, Industrial Supply Association, and Power Transmission Distributors Association.

EXECUTIVES

Chairman, President, and CEO: Dale R. Schuh
SVP Business Products: Jim Clawson
SVP and Treasurer: William J. Lohr
VP Human Resources: Joe Fritzsche
VP Investments: Jim Weishan
VP, Secretary, and General Counsel: William M. O'Reilly
VP Finance: Michael Zimmer
Auditors: PricewaterhouseCoopers

LOCATIONS

HQ: Sentry Insurance
1800 North Point Dr., Stevens Point, WI 54481
Phone: 715-346-6000   **Fax:** 715-346-7516
Web: www.sentry.com

PRODUCTS/OPERATIONS

Selected Subsidiaries

Dairyland Insurance Company
Middlesex Insurance Company
Parker Centennial Assurance Company
Patriot General Insurance Company
Sentry Aviation Services, Inc.
Sentry Casualty Company
Sentry Equity Services, Inc.
Sentry Life Insurance Company
Sentry Select Insurance Company

COMPETITORS

AIG	Nationwide
Allstate	New York Life
Badger Mutual	Penn Mutual
CIGNA	Progressive Corporation
CNA Financial	Prudential
GEICO	State Farm
MetLife	Travelers Companies

HISTORICAL FINANCIALS
Company Type: Mutual company

Income Statement
FYE: December 31

	REVENUE ($ mil.)	NET INCOME ($ mil.)	NET PROFIT MARGIN	EMPLOYEES
12/07	2,588	306	11.8%	—
12/06	2,626	262	10.0%	—
12/05	1,987	—	—	—
12/04	2,213	—	—	—
12/03	2,088	—	—	4,400
Annual Growth	5.5%	16.6%	—	—

Net Income History

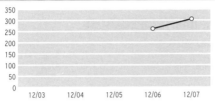

Sequa Corporation

Jet engine repair, airbag inflators, cigarette lighters, and tuxedos. Sounds like a shopping list for James Bond, but it's a partial list of Sequa's businesses. Its largest unit, aerospace, includes Chromalloy Gas Turbine, which makes and repairs jet engine parts for airlines and other customers. Other operations include an automotive unit, which makes airbag inflators and car cigarette lighters, and a metal-coatings unit, which makes coatings for building products. Other Sequa units make offset web printing equipment (MEGTEC Systems) and men's formalwear (After Six). In 2007 the company was bought out by The Carlyle Group in a deal valued at about $2.7 billion.

No one told Sequa that diversified collections of industrial operations went out of style about the time Sean Connery stopped playing James Bond. Of course, no one told General Electric, either.

Sequa tweaks its business mix from time to time, but the company continues to keep its fingers in multiple pies. Sequa is counting on its aerospace business to continue to drive revenue growth.

In 2008 Sequa sold its specialty chemicals unit, Warwick International (which makes bleach activators), for £129 million in an MBO backed by Close Brothers Private Equity.

HISTORY

Sequa Corporation began in 1929 from the merger of five firms: George H. Morrill Co. (1840), Sigmund Ullman Co. (1861), Fuchs & Lang Manufacturing (1871), Eagle Printing Ink (1893), and American Printing Ink (1897). Founded as General Printing Ink Corp., it specialized in making ink for news, letterpress, and lithographic printing. It also made lithographic machines and supplies.

Although the company's units competed against each other in the 1930s, they managed to stay profitable during the Depression. General Ink bought four firms in 1945 and, to reflect its expanding interests, changed its name to Sun Chemical Corp. More acquisitions followed over the next few years. By 1950 Sun had formed seven divisions.

The growth turned out to be too much, too soon, however. In 1954 Sun consolidated into three groups: chemicals; graphic arts; and waterproofing, paints, and product finishing. Norman Alexander became Sun's president in 1957. A research program began in 1960, and Sun spent much of the next decade expanding abroad and diversifying its product line.

In 1972 Sun entered the auto parts industry when it bought Standard Kollsman Industries. Sun's expansion in the late 1970s established subsidiaries in Bermuda, Chile, and Panama. The company initiated a takeover attempt in 1979 by buying 5% of diversified Chromalloy American. By 1980 Sun was the #1 world producer of printing inks, and by 1982 it had acquired 36% of Chromalloy. Also that year Alexander became Sun's CEO.

Sun itself became a takeover target in 1986, as Dainippon Ink and Chemicals tried to buy it. Alexander refused and upped his ownership in Sun to 47%. He sold the company's graphic arts unit to Dainippon later that year and used the proceeds to buy the rest of Chromalloy. Sun's 1987 purchase of Atlantic Research Corp. (ARC; rocket motors) was the impetus to rename itself Sequa Corporation, to reflect a shift in focus from chemical to military products.

Sales skyrocketed until 1990, but post-Cold War cutbacks dealt Sequa a financial blow. In the next several years it dumped about half a dozen divisions and cut its workforce in half. In 1996 ARC won a contract to make rocket motors for missiles used on Canadian, NATO, and US fighter planes.

Sequa bought TEC Systems (web press products) in 1997 and merged it with MEG, its French auxiliary press equipment division, to form MEGTEC Systems. Sequa sold its Northern Can Systems unit, a maker of easy-open can lids. It initiated major layoffs at MEGTEC in 1998 and sold its Sequa Chemicals unit to GenCorp for $108 million. That year ARC became the sole owner of its former joint venture, Bendix Atlantic Inflator Co.; it was renamed Atlantic Research Automotive Products Group.

In 1999 Sequa paid $13 million for Thermo Fibertek's Thermo Wisconsin unit, which supplies the US process and printing industries with continuous process dryers, air-pollution control equipment, and other specialty products. Sequa planned to combine the unit with its MEGTEC Systems. That year Sequa won a seven-year $10.1 billion contract to repair military aircraft for the US Air Force. The company acquired metal can machinery maker Formatec Tooling Systems in 2000.

In early 2002 Sequa reported a record fourth-quarter loss for 2001. The loss was largely related to cost-cutting measures and environmental remediation. Late in 2002, Sequa acquired Pacific Gas Turbine, an airplane engine overhaul business. The next year Sequa sold the propulsion business of its ARC unit for about $133 million. Sequa kept ARC's automotive business.

Late in 2004 Sequa sold its Sequa Can Machinery operations to Stolle Machinery Company.

EXECUTIVES

Chairman: Gail Binderman, age 67
Vice Chairman and CEO: Martin Weinstein, age 72, $845,252 pay
COO; CEO, Chromalloy Gas Turbine:
Armand F. Lauzon Jr., age 45
EVP and CFO: Kenneth J. Binder, age 55
SVP and Corporate Secretary: John J. Dowling III, age 57, $312,076 pay
SVP Metal Coating: Gerard M. Dombek, age 55, $334,083 pay
VP and Controller: Donna Costello, age 35
VP and Treasurer: James P. Langelotti, age 47
VP, Corporate Communications: Linda G. Kyriakou
VP, Corporate Development and Strategic:
Robert D. DeVito
VP, Environmental, Safety, and Health:
Robert L. Iuliucci
VP Taxes: Michael Blickensderfer, age 48
VP Human Resources: Leonard P. Pasculli, age 53
Corporate Communications: Mary Rotondi
Corporate Secretary: Diane C. Bunt
Managing Director and CEO, Warwick International:
Robert F. (Bob) Ellis, age 55, $374,189 pay
President and General Manager, After Six:
Kathleen Peskens, age 47
President and General Manager, Megtec: Mohit Uberoi
President and General Manager, ARC Automotive:
John Skaldan
Auditors: KPMG

LOCATIONS

HQ: Sequa Corporation
200 Park Ave., New York, NY 10166
Phone: 212-986-5500 **Fax:** 212-370-1969
Web: www.sequa.com

PRODUCTS/OPERATIONS

Selected Subsidiaries and Operations

Aerospace
Chromalloy Gas Turbine Corporation (jet aircraft engine repair and manufacture)
Automotive
ARC Automotive, Inc. (airbag inflators)
Casco Products (automotive cigarette lighters and power outlets)
Metal Coatings
Precoat Metals (protective and decorative coatings for steel and aluminum)
Industrial Machinery
MEGTEC Systems, Inc. (air flotation dryers, auxiliary equipment for web offset printing)
Other
After Six (men's apparel under the After Six, John Galenté, and Raffinati labels)

COMPETITORS

AAR Corp.
Autoliv
Ball Corporation
Barnes Group
Clinical Data
Dover Corporation
GE
GenCorp
General Magnaplate
Goss International
Honeywell International
Jason Incorporated
Nippon Kayaku
Pratt & Whitney
Raytheon
Rolls-Royce
Spar Aerospace
Valspar

HISTORICAL FINANCIALS

Company Type: Private

Income Statement

FYE: December 31

	REVENUE ($ mil.)	NET INCOME ($ mil.)	NET PROFIT MARGIN	EMPLOYEES
12/07	1,960	—	—	10,000
12/06	2,184	—	—	10,155
12/05	1,998	—	—	9,700
12/04	1,864	—	—	9,100
12/03	1,666	—	—	—
Annual Growth	**4.2%**	**—**	**—**	**3.2%**

Revenue History

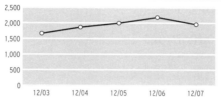

ServiceMaster

ServiceMaster merrily mows, scrubs, sprays, and trims. A giant in its industry, the company serves more than 10 million commercial and residential customers in the US and around the world with housecleaning, termite and pest control, landscape maintenance, and plumbing and drain services.

Its best-known consumer brands include Merry Maids, Terminix, TruGreen LawnCare, and Rescue Rooter. The TruGreen Companies and ServiceMaster Clean provide similar services to commercial clients. Its AmeriSpec division provides home inspections, while American Home Shield provides warranty contracts for home systems and appliances.

ServiceMaster was acquired by an investment firm for about $5.5 billion in July 2007. The price of the buyout by private equity firm Clayton, Dubilier & Rice included about $800 million in ServiceMaster debt.

Under its new owners, ServiceMaster has been working to improve the results of its business, in which the TruGreen and Terminix segments make up about 75% of sales. Most of the company's businesses, including TruGreen and Terminix, operate through company-owned branches. However, Merry Maids primarily franchises its units, and American Home Shield operates through a network of independent real estate brokers, who sell the service, and subcontractors, who perform the work.

ServiceMaster hopes to improve performance in its more than 5,500 service centers by centralizing some administrative functions (payroll and accounts receivable, for instance) and freeing the branch locations to focus on customer service and employee care. At the same time, in 2008 ServiceMaster will be focusing its efforts on restructuring, in order to cut down on costs and optimize its organizational structure. This process will involve reducing its work force, shutting down several centers or offices, and outsourcing certain business functions to third parties.

Servicemaster also has been moving to divest noncore operations, and in 2008 the company sold its InStar Services Group, a contractor that specializes in disaster recovery services, to private equity firm BlackEagle Partners. In 2006 ServiceMaster sold its American Mechanical Services and American Residential Services units, the latter to Caxton-Iseman Capital and Royal Palm Capital Partners for about $115 million.

Firmly rooted in religion, the company's name reflects both its business focus and its Christian credo of "Service to the Master."

EXECUTIVES

Chairman and CEO: J. Patrick (Pat) Spainhour, age 58
SVP and CFO: Steven J. (Steve) Martin, age 44
SVP and Corporate Controller: David Martin
SVP and General Counsel: Greer McMullen
SVP and Corporate Treasurer: Mark Peterson
SVP Corporate Strategy and Marketing: Jim Kunihiro
SVP Human Resources: Lisa V. Goettel, age 44
VP Corporate Communications: Pete Tosches
CIO: Dan Marks
President and COO, American Home Shield/AmeriSpec: David J. (Dave) Crawford
President and COO, ServiceMaster Clean and Furniture Medic: Michael M. (Mike) Isakson, age 54
President and COO, Terminix International:
Thomas G. (Tom) Brackett
President, TruGreen Landcare:
Richard A. (Rick) Ascolese, age 54
Auditors: Deloitte & Touche LLP

LOCATIONS

HQ: The ServiceMaster Company
860 Ridge Lake Blvd., Memphis, TN 38120
Phone: 901-597-1400 **Fax:** 630-663-2001
Web: www.servicemaster.com

PRODUCTS/OPERATIONS

2007 Sales

	$ mil.	% of total
TruGreen LawnCare	1,099.0	33
Terminix	1,091.5	33
American Home Shield	541.0	16
TruGreen LandCare	411.9	12
Other	213.4	6
Total	**3,356.8**	**100**

Selected Consumer Services

American Home Shield (warranty and service contracts)
AmeriSpec (home inspections)
Furniture Medic (on-site furniture repair, restoration)
Merry Maids (housecleaning)
ServiceMaster Clean (commercial and residential cleaning, disaster restoration, carpet cleaning)
Terminix (commercial and residential pest control)
TruGreen LandCare (landscape maintenance)
TruGreen LawnCare (commercial and residential lawn, tree, and shrub care)

COMPETITORS

ABM Industries	ISS A/S
Allstate	Liberty Mutual
American Family	Maid Brigade
Insurance	Maid to Perfection
ARAMARK	MaidPro
Arrowpoint Capital Corp.	Maids International, Inc.
Brickman	Molly Maid
Chemed	Mutual of Omaha
Cincinnati Financial	Orkin, Inc.
Comfort Systems USA	Rentokil Initial
Davey Tree	Scotts Miracle-Gro
Dwyer Group	Service Experts
Ecolab	Servpro Industries
FirstService	Sodexo USA
Hanover Insurance	Stanley Steemer
Hanover Insurance	State Farm
The Hartford	UGL Unicco
Infinity Property	ValleyCrest Companies
& Casualty	Vario Construction

HISTORICAL FINANCIALS
Company Type: Private

Income Statement				FYE: December 31
	REVENUE ($ mil.)	NET INCOME ($ mil.)	NET PROFIT MARGIN	EMPLOYEES
12/07	3,357	(42)	—	29,000
12/06	3,429	170	4.9%	32,000
12/05	3,240	199	6.1%	39,000
12/04	3,759	331	8.8%	38,000
12/03	3,569	(225)	—	40,000
Annual Growth	(1.5%)	—	—	(7.7%)

Net Income History

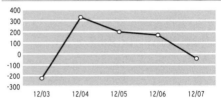

Services Group of America

Although its name is rather vague, Services Group of America specializes in food. Its subsidiary, Food Services of America, is a food service distributor that supplies hospitals, restaurants, and schools in 15 western states through nine distribution centers. It also serves customers nationally through its membership in Distribution Market Advantage, an alliance of 14 food service suppliers. The company's Systems Services of America subsidiary (formerly McCabe's Quality Meats) serves fast-food chains and casual-dining restaurants; other operations include Amerifresh (fresh produce) and S&P Meats (fresh and frozen boxed meat). Services Group of America was founded in 1985 by chairman Thomas Stewart.

EXECUTIVES

Chairman and CEO: Thomas J. (Tom) Stewart, age 64
President and COO: Peter Smith
CFO: Jim Keller
SVP and Chief Merchandising Officer, Food Services of America: Scott Bixby
VP, Corporate Communications: Gary L. Odegard
Director, Human Resources: Ira Duden
Director, Marketing: Donna Baraya
Treasurer: John Andersen
President, Food Services Of America: Tom Staley

LOCATIONS

HQ: Services Group of America, Inc.
16100 N. 71st St., Ste. 400, Scottsdale, AZ 85255
Phone: 480-927-4000   **Fax:** 480-927-4299
Web: www.fsafood.com

COMPETITORS

Gordon Food Service
McLane Foodservice
Meadowbrook Meat Company
Nash-Finch
Performance Food
Smart & Final
SYSCO
UniPro Foodservice
U.S. Foodservice

Shamrock Foods

You might say this company is milking the foodservice distribution business for all its worth. Shamrock Foods is a major foodservice supplier that also owns one of the largest dairy operations in the southwest. Its distribution business supplies food and related products to restaurants and institutional foodservice operators in intermountain states of the western US through three distribution centers. Sister company Shamrock Farms, with more than 10,000 cows, produces and distributes a full line of dairy products, including milk, ice cream, and cottage cheese.

In 2006 the company expanded its foodservice distribution operations with the acquisition of DPI Southwest, one of the regional operating units of wholesaler Distribution Plus. The deal added a new distribution facility in Albuquerque, New Mexico, to its Phoenix and Denver operations.

Founded in 1920 as a mom-and-pop dairy, Shamrock Foods is still owned and operated by the founding McClelland family.

EXECUTIVES

Chairman and CEO: Norman McClelland
President and COO: Kent McClelland
SVP and CFO: F. Phillips (Phil) Giltner III
SVP and General Manager, Dairy Division: Michael Krueger
SVP and General Manager, Colorado Foods Division: Kent Mullison
SVP and General Manager, Arizona Foods Division: Larry F. Yancy
VP Human Resources: Robert (Bob) Beake
CIO: Rob Baxter

LOCATIONS

HQ: Shamrock Foods Company
5080 N. 40th St,, Ste. 400, Phoenix, AZ 85009
Phone: 602-477-2500
Web: www.shamrockfoods.com

PRODUCTS/OPERATIONS

Selected Brands and Products

Aspen Gold butter alternative
Brickfire Bakery Cookies
Bountiful Harvest vegetables
Chef Mark
Cobblestone Market meats and cheeses
Culinary Secrets spices
Emerald Valley Ranch meats
Hidden Bay seafood
Markon First Crop fruits and vegetables
Ready-Set-Serve fruits and juices
Pierportsseafood
Ridgeline Coffee
San Pablo Mexican foods
Shamrock Farms dairy products
SilverBrook chicken fillets
Smart Source fruits and vegetables
Trescerro Coffee
Trifoglio Italian foods
Villa Frizzoni pastas and Italian specialties
Xtreme liquid shortening

COMPETITORS

C&S Wholesale
California Dairies Inc.
Dairy Farmers of America
Dean Foods
Land O'Lakes
McLane
Meadowbrook Meat Company
Nash-Finch
Performance Food
SYSCO
U.S. Foodservice

Sheetz, Inc.

You might say Sheetz is to the convenience store business what Wal-Mart is to discount shopping. Noted for being exceptionally large (stores average 4,200 sq. ft., nearly twice the size of the average 7-Eleven, but new stores are planned to be 4,700 sq. ft.), Sheetz stores sell groceries, fountain drinks, baked goods, made-to-order sandwiches and salads, and self-service car washes, as well as discount gas and cigarettes. The company operates about 350 combination convenience stores and gas stations, mostly in Pennsylvania, but also in five other states (Maryland, North Carolina, Ohio, Virginia, and West Virginia). Founded in 1952 by Bob Sheetz, the company is owned and run by the Sheetz family.

In July 2008 the chain launched its Sheetz Bros. Kitchen business. The 140,000-sq.-ft. commissary will supply Sheetz's 350 stores with baked goods and prepared foods.

Increasing convenience is a priority at Sheetz stores. The company has begun installing gas machines that accept paper money at the pump, eliminating the walk inside for drivers on the go.

To court the Starbucks crowd, Sheetz has added made-to-order espressos, cappuccinos, lattes, and mochas to its coffee menu. The company has installed Sheetz Bros. Coffeez counters with touch-screen ordering systems in all of its stores.

In 2006 the company began selling ethanol-based alternative fuel at select stores in the Pittsburgh area and is expanding the number of locations selling ethanol fuel.

Sheetz is also going beyond traditional convenience store fare at locations in Altoona, Pennsylvania, and Raleigh, North Carolina. The two new convenience restaurants are twice the size of a typical Sheetz store and have fried chicken, soups, salads, and pizza, in addition to sandwiches, on the menu. The stores seat about 50 people. In 2007 Sheetz began selling beer and malt-based coolers at the Altoona location. (Sheetz already has licenses to sell alcohol in about 100 of its stores in Maryland, Ohio, West Virginia, Virginia, and North Carolina.)

EXECUTIVES

Chairman: Stephen G. (Steve) Sheetz, age 60
President and CEO: Stanton R. (Stan) Sheetz, age 52
EVP Marketing: Louie Sheetz
EVP Finance and Store Development:
 Joseph S. (Joe) Sheetz
EVP Distribution and Sheetz Bros. Kitchen: Ray Ryan
EVP Petroleum Supply: Mike Lorenz
VP and General Counsel: R. Michael (Mike) Cortez
VP Operations: Travis Sheetz
VP Human Resources: Stephanie Hoover
Director, Brand Development: Colleen Devorris
Director, Corporate Information Technology:
 George Medairy

LOCATIONS

HQ: Sheetz, Inc.
 5700 6th Ave., Altoona, PA 16602
Phone: 814-946-3611   **Fax:** 814-946-4375
Web: www.sheetz.com

PRODUCTS/OPERATIONS

Selected Products

Burgerz
Coffeez
Cupo'ccino
Dot'z Bakery items
MTO (Made to Order) sandwiches
Nachos
Saladz
Schmuffin breakfast sandwiches

COMPETITORS

7-Eleven
BP
Cumberland Farms
Exxon
Giant Eagle
Kroger
Motiva Enterprises
Starbucks
Sunoco
Uni-Marts
Wawa, Inc.

ShopKo Stores

Rather than be a jack-of-all-retailing-trades across the country, ShopKo Stores is content to concentrate on a limited product range in a few regions of the US. The company operates about 135 ShopKo discount stores and several ShopKo Express Rx drugstore outlets in about a dozen states throughout the Midwest, Mountain, and Pacific Northwest regions. Instead of offering a watered-down selection of many retail categories, it focuses on popular, higher-margin categories such as casual apparel, health and beauty items, and housewares. Most ShopKo stores have optical centers and pharmacies. The company was taken private in 2005 by an affiliate of private investment firm Sun Capital Partners.

ShopKo's deal with Sun Capital, which valued the retailer at about $29 per share, closed in late December 2005. ShopKo terminated a previous agreement to be acquired by Minneapolis-based private equity firm Goldner Hawn Johnson & Morrison (GHJ&M) for about $1 billion. Investors were unhappy with the original GHJ&M offer, which was later raised twice to $25.50 per share. (Sun Capital purchased Mervyns from discount giant Target in 2004.)

Following the transaction, Sun Capital separated ShopKo from its rural cousin, Omaha-based Pamida, which operates more than 200 stores primarily in the Midwest. The firm also recruited Mike MacDonald from Carson Pirie Scott department store chain as its new CEO.

ShopKo sold most of its real estate assets to Spirit Finance in a deal that valued the land under the 112 ShopKo and 66 Pamida locations at about $815 million in mid-2006. The retailer is leasing the stores back from the real estate investment trust.

Sales at ShopKo's optical centers and pharmacies are growing. Its optometrists perform in-store eye exams and prescribe correctional lenses, most of which are made in the company's optical laboratory and in some 83 in-store finishing labs. Pharmacy and eye care centers represent about 30% of ShopKo sales. The company is rolling out health clinics in select locations in a partnership with Medical Marts Group.

Payless ShoeSource operates shoe departments (through a licensing agreement) in every ShopKo store.

HISTORY

Chicagoan James Ruben moved to Green Bay, Wisconsin, and opened the first ShopKo there in 1962. While other discounters crowded around major metro areas, Ruben saw the value potential in smaller markets and set up his stores in such locations. ShopKo focused on male consumers, with most of its goods in the hardlines segment, which includes sporting goods and automotive parts. Ruben soon expanded into Michigan and had annual sales of $41 million by the end of the decade.

ShopKo Stores was acquired by SUPERVALU, one of the US's biggest food wholesalers, in 1971. That year ShopKo became one of the first discounters to offer pharmacies at its stores; it also opened its tenth store. SUPERVALU was a hands-off parent and allowed store managers to select their own merchandise lines, which led to a merchandise shift toward housewares and clothing

during the 1970s. By 1977, with 21 stores, ShopKo surpassed $100 million in sales.

The company began offering in-store eye exams (in addition to selling eyeglasses) in 1978. ShopKo's strong growth continued, and by 1984 it ran 39 stores, mostly in Minnesota, Nebraska, and Wisconsin, but also in three other Upper Midwest states. Bitten by Horace Greeley's "Go West" spirit, ShopKo entered Montana and Idaho in 1986 and Utah in 1988. That year, with 87 stores, sales hit the billion-dollar mark.

Wal-Mart had become the proverbial 800-lb. gorilla by the middle of the 1980s, though, and ShopKo set up a special task force in 1986 to figure out how not to get squashed. Executives realized that ShopKo couldn't compete on price and decided instead to become strong where Wal-Mart was weak and to stay out of the ring when outmatched.

The ribbon on ShopKo's 100th store was cut in 1990, and the company's 1991 figures attest to its health at the time: It was eighth among the US's discount chains in sales but second in profits. In 1991 SUPERVALU made Dale Kramer ShopKo's president and CEO; it then spun the company off to the public, retaining a 46% stake. ShopKo also began remodeling its stores, giving the chain a more upscale image.

In 1993 ShopKo created ProVantage Health Services to offer prescription benefit management and mail-order pharmacy services. It soon added vision benefit management through a network of 4,500 eye care practitioners. ShopKo supplemented its retail health offerings by acquiring Bravell (1995, claims management) and a division of United Wisconsin Insurance Company (1996, vision benefit management).

 In 1997 SUPERVALU sold its 46% stake in ShopKo, and the company purchased 19 Penn-Daniels stores (two were closed, and 17 Jacks stores, mostly in Iowa and Illinois, were converted to the ShopKo banner in 1998).

In 1999 the firm spun off ProVantage to the public, retaining a 70% stake. ShopKo then acquired Pamida Holdings (about 160 small-town discount stores) for $375 million including debt.

In 2000 ShopKo sold its ProVantage stake to drugmaker Merck for $222 million and bought the 49-store P.M. Place Stores discount chain for $22 million. Later that year the company opened 56 additional Pamida stores. In 2001 ShopKo closed more than 20 low-performing stores in seven states and cut about 2,500 jobs.

In April 2002 president and CEO William Podany resigned and was replaced by vice chairman Jeffrey Girard as interim CEO. In September ShopKo launched in-store Urbanology shops offering home furnishings (including neon wall clocks, candles, and furry pillows) and fashion accessories targeted to the Generation Y market. Sam Duncan (formerly president of Fred Meyer Stores) joined the company as its new chief executive the following month.

In 2004 Girard resigned as the vice chairman, finance and administration. Duncan resigned in 2005 following the announcement of the pending acquisition by GHJ&M. That December ShopKo stock was delisted from the NYSE following the completion of the acquisition of the company by an affiliate of investment firm Sun Capital Partners. Following the transaction, Sun Capital separated ShopKo Stores from its Pamida division, which now operates independently. Michael MacDonald, from a Saks division, was appointed chairman and CEO in May 2006.

In March 2008 the company opened its first new store to be built in six years.

EXECUTIVES

Chairman and CEO: Michael R. (Mike) MacDonald
SVP Store Operations: Douglas McHose
SVP Retail Health: Michael J. Bettiga
SVP Property Development: Rodney D. Lawrence, age 47
SVP Merchandise Support: Jack Ingersoll
SVP Marketing: Jack Mullen
SVP and General Merchandise Manager, Hardlines and Home: Rod Ghormley
SVP and CIO: Tammy Hermann, age 39
SVP and General Merchandise Manager, Apparel and Accessories: Jill Soltau
VP Advertising: Kathy Friedland-Howard, age 43
VP Merchandise Planning and Support: Randy Roiko
VP Real Estate: Steve Cogan, age 47
VP and General Counsel: Peter G. Vandenhouten
VP HR: Sara Stensrud
VP Store Planning and Design: Jane VanAuken
VP and Controller: Mary Meixelsperger
CTO and VP Ecommerce: Ray Petersen
Director of Corporate Communications: John Vigeland
Auditors: Deloitte & Touche LLP

LOCATIONS

HQ: ShopKo Stores, Inc.
700 Pilgrim Way, Green Bay, WI 54304
Phone: 920-429-2211   **Fax:** 920-429-4799
Web: www.shopko.com

PRODUCTS/OPERATIONS

Selected Retail Merchandise

Hardlines
Automotive
Candy
Electronics
Furniture
Greeting cards and gift wrap
Health and beauty aids
Home entertainment products
Home textiles
Household supplies
Housewares
Lawn and garden products
Music/videos
Seasonal goods
Small appliances
Snack foods
Sporting goods
Toys

Softlines

Accessories
Apparel
Cosmetics
Jewelry
Shoes

COMPETITORS

Best Buy
Big Lots
Blue Cross (MI)
Costco Wholesale
CVS Caremark
Dollar Tree
Duckwall-ALCO
Family Dollar Stores
Gottschalks
J. C. Penney
Kmart
Kohl's
LensCrafters
Sears
Target
TJX Companies
Walgreen
Wal-Mart

HISTORICAL FINANCIALS

Company Type: Private

Income Statement

	REVENUE ($ mil.)	NET INCOME ($ mil.)	NET PROFIT MARGIN	EMPLOYEES
1/07	2,200	—	—	16,000

FYE: Last Saturday in January

Sidley Austin

Sidley Austin aims to be a one-stop shop for large and small businesses, government agencies, and individuals needing legal help. The firm's 1,600-plus lawyers practice in a wide range of areas from some 15 offices in the US, Europe, and the Asia/Pacific region. Sidley focuses on business transactions and litigation, and the firm's geographic diversity enables it to handle multinational matters. Sidley traces its roots to a firm founded in 1866.

Sidley took its modern form in 2001 when Chicago-based Sidley & Austin (founded by Norman Williams and John Thompson in 1866) merged with New York-based Brown & Wood (established in 1914). The combined firm was known as Sidley Austin Brown & Wood until 2006, when it changed its name to Sidley Austin.

EXECUTIVES

Chairman, Executive Committee: Thomas A. Cole
Chairman, Management Committee: Charles W. Douglas
Vice Chairman, Management Committee:
Theodore N. Miller
Executive Director: Timothy Bergen
CIO: Nancy Karen
Director Marketing: Janet Zagorin
Director Human Resources: Michael Prapuolenis
Controller: Christian Cooley
Partner: Peter D. Keisler

LOCATIONS

HQ: Sidley Austin LLP
1 S. Dearborn St., Chicago, IL 60603
Phone: 312-853-7000   **Fax:** 312-853-7036
Web: www.sidley.com

Sidley Austin has offices in Chicago, Dallas, Los Angeles, New York, San Francisco, and Washington, DC. Outside the US, the firm has offices in Beijing, Brussels, Frankfurt, Geneva, Hong Kong, London, Shanghai, Singapore, and Tokyo.

PRODUCTS/OPERATIONS

Selected Practice Areas

Alternative dispute resolution
Antitrust
Automotive safety litigation and regulation
Banking and financial transactions
Canada
China
College and university law
Communications
Corporate
Corporate reorganization and bankruptcy

Corporate/securities
Employee benefits
Employment and labor
Energy
Environmental
European Union law
Financial institutions
Food and drug
General appellate
Government contracts
Government relations
Health care
Hong Kong corporate finance
Immigration
Information law and privacy
Insurance
Insurance corporate practice
Intellectual property
International investment funds
International trade and dispute resolution
Investment company and investment adviser
Investment products and derivatives
Latin America
Litigation
London transactional practice
Postal services practice
Privacy, data protection, and information security
Private clients, trusts, and estates
Pro bono
Project finance
Public finance
Real estate
Religious institutions
Securities enforcement
Securitization and structured finance
Tax

COMPETITORS

Baker & McKenzie
Clifford Chance
Jones Day
Kirkland & Ellis
Latham & Watkins
Mayer Brown
McDermott Will & Emery
Morgan, Lewis
Shearman & Sterling
Skadden, Arps
Sullivan & Cromwell
Weil, Gotshal
White & Case

HISTORICAL FINANCIALS

Company Type: Partnership

Income Statement

	REVENUE ($ mil.)	NET INCOME ($ mil.)	NET PROFIT MARGIN	EMPLOYEES
12/07	1,386	—	—	—
12/06	1,247	—	—	3,806
12/05	1,124	—	—	3,585
Annual Growth	11.0%	—	—	6.2%

FYE: December 31

Revenue History

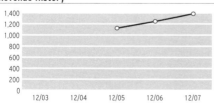

Sierra Club

Take a hike with the Sierra Club. The Sierra Club promotes outdoor activities and environmental activism on both the local and national level through political lobbies, education, outings, and publications. The club's more than 1.3 million members are organized into state and regional chapters throughout the US and Canada. Sierra Club publishes books, calendars, *SIERRA* magazine, and *The Planet,* an activist newsletter. Its current issues are smart energy solutions, clean water, stopping commercial logging in national forests, ending sprawl, and protecting wetlands. The group was founded in 1892 by naturalist John Muir.

The organization's youth program, "Building Bridges to the Outdoors," focuses on giving inner-city children access to nature experiences. The program's motto is "No child will be left inside."

EXECUTIVES

Executive Director: Carl Pope
Director: Larry Fahn
National Press Secretary: David Willett
President: Robbie Cox
VP: Robin Mann
Secretary: Sanjay Ranchod
Treasurer: Joni Bosh
Auditors: KPMG

LOCATIONS

HQ: Sierra Club
   85 Second St., 2nd Fl., San Francisco, CA 94105
Phone: 415-977-5500   **Fax:** 415-977-5799
Web: www.sierraclub.org

HISTORICAL FINANCIALS

Company Type: Not-for-profit

Income Statement

	REVENUE ($ mil.)	NET INCOME ($ mil.)	NET PROFIT MARGIN	EMPLOYEES
12/06	92	—	—	400
12/05	82	—	—	330
Annual Growth	11.6%	—	—	21.2%

FYE: December 31

Revenue History

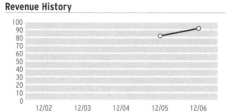

Sierra Pacific Industries

Sierra Pacific Industries (SPI) isn't your run-of-the-mill company. SPI owns and manages about 2 million acres of timberland in California and harvests about 1% of that each year. The company produces millwork, lumber and wood fiber products, fencing, aluminum-clad and wood patio doors, and windows. SPI operates cogeneration plants that recycle wood waste into electricity for its plants; excess electricity is sold to local energy service providers. It also develops residential and commercial real estate. SPI traces its roots to the late 1920s when it was founded by R. H. "Curly" Emmerson, father of CEO "Red" Emmerson. The third generation of the Emmerson family owns and operates SPI.

Protests in the 1980s against logging on public land prompted the company to begin buying its own forested areas, a practice the company continues. In 2001 Sierra Pacific sold 30,000 acres of timberland (on the North Fork of the American River) in the Sierra Nevada mountain range to the Trust for Public Land for preservation.

The Sierra Pacific Foundation is a company enterprise that was established and funded in 1979 by "Curly" Emmerson. The foundation annually provides, among other things, more than $367,000 in scholarships to dependent children of SPI employees.

SPI also operates the Eureka Dock facility on Humboldt Bay in Eureka, California, to serve its own shipping needs, as well as those of other California sawmills.

Recognizing that some of its acquired land tracts are better suited for residential or commercial development than for growing trees, SPI has moved into property development. The company develops both residential and commercial properties.

In 2007 the company paid $13 million in fines to settle air quality violations in California.

EXECUTIVES

President: A. A. (Red) Emmerson
VP Financial: Mark Emmerson
VP Sales and Marketing: George Emmerson
CTO: Steve Gaston
Director, Human Resources: Ed Bond
Manager, Equipment Sales: Gary Morgan
Manager, Lumber Sales: Terry Kuehl
President, Sierra Pacific Foundation:
   Carolyn Emmerson Dietz

LOCATIONS

HQ: Sierra Pacific Industries
   19794 Riverside Ave., Anderson, CA 96007
Phone: 530-378-8000   **Fax:** 530-378-8109
Web: www.spi-ind.com

Sierra Pacific Industries has operations in Northern and Central California.

PRODUCTS/OPERATIONS

Selected Products

Aluminum-clad windows and doors
Cedar fencing
Chips for pulp mills
Decorative bark
Dimension lumber
Douglas Fir timbers
Millwork
Poles
Shavings for particleboard
Wood windows and doors

COMPETITORS

Andersen Corporation
Atrium Companies
CraftMaster
EFCO
GBO
Georgia-Pacific
Hampton Affiliates
Harvey Industries
International Paper
Kolbe & Kolbe
Liaison Technologies
Louisiana-Pacific
Marshfield DoorSystems
MAXXAM
MI Windows and Doors
North Pacific Group
Pella
Plum Creek Timber
Pope & Talbot
Potlatch
Roseburg Forest Products
Silver Line Building Products
Simonton Windows, Inc.
Simpson Investment
Storey Sawmill
Therma-Tru
TRACO
Tumac Lumber
VELUX
W. L. Butler
Western Forest Products
Weyerhaeuser

HISTORICAL FINANCIALS

Company Type: Private

Income Statement

	ESTIMATED REVENUE ($ mil.)	NET INCOME ($ mil.)	NET PROFIT MARGIN	EMPLOYEES
12/07	1,010	—	—	4,400
12/06	1,350	—	—	3,900
12/05	1,570	—	—	4,000
12/04	1,500	—	—	3,600
12/03	1,400	—	—	3,600
Annual Growth	(7.8%)	—	—	5.1%

FYE: December 31

Revenue History

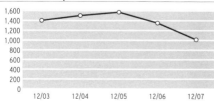

Sigma Plastics

The plastic sheeting and film business is not Greek to Sigma Plastics. Having grown through acquisitions, the company (one of the largest of its kind in North America) produces plastic film and sheet for industrial, institutional, and government markets. Subsidiary Alpha Industries and its associated companies, including Beta, Epsilon, and Omega, make plastic film and bags for dry cleaners, grocers, and retailers, as well as for the food service, health care, janitorial, industrial packaging, lodging, and safety industries. Sigma Plastics manufactures its diverse range of plastic products on 700 extrusion lines at its North American plants. Chairman and CEO Alfred Teo owns the company.

Singapore-born and China-raised Alfred Teo founded Sigma Plastics (as Sigma Extruding) in 1979. He came to the US in 1968, and after graduating from college (with a degree in business and accounting) was assigned by his accounting firm to monitor the books of Blue Star Packaging, a plastics manufacturing company.

In mid-2006 Teo pleaded guilty in a US federal court to five counts of securities fraud connected with insider trading violations at two companies unrelated to Sigma Plastics. Teo was sentenced early in 2007 to serve 30 months in prison. Alfred's son, Mark Teo, has replaced his father to lead the company.

There has been speculation about the future of the company with its acquisitive leader behind bars, but the company has maintained its practice of buying struggling competitors. In mid-2007 it acquired Allied Extruders Long Island City, giving Sigma an additional 80,000-sq.-ft. facility that makes specialty films for the food packaging industry.

EXECUTIVES

Chairman and CEO: Alfred S. Teo, age 62

LOCATIONS

HQ: Sigma Plastics Group
Page & Schuyler Ave., Bldg. #8,
Lyndhurst, NJ 07071
Phone: 201-933-6000 **Fax:** 201-933-6429
Web: www.sigmaplastics.com

COMPETITORS

AEP Industries
Atlantis Plastics
Bemis
Berry Plastics Corporation
DuPont
Huntsman International
Inteplast
Pactiv
Pliant
Raven Industries
Sealed Air Corporation
Sonoco Products
Spartech
Tyco

Simmons Bedding

Simmons Bedding sleeps tight as one of the top US mattress makers, along with Sealy and Serta. The firm, founded by Zalmon Simmons in 1870 and formerly known as THL Bedding Holding Company, makes mattresses and accessories under the BackCare, Beautyrest, Deep Sleep, Natural Care, HealthSmart, and Simmons labels, among others. It licenses its names for retail stores, beds, and sleeping aids makers, and sells its products through more than 12,200 furniture outlets, department stores, and specialty shops. Simmons operates 12 World of Sleep shops. It sold its 55 Sleep Country USA stores and bought Simmons Canada in 2006, as well as memory foam manufacturer Comfor Products in 2007.

Simmons also distributes mattresses and other bedding to the hospitality industry (Starwood Hotels, La Quinta, Best Western) and to government agencies. Starwood's Westin properties promotes its Heavenly Bed, which is the Simmons Beautyrest.

Simmons makes most of its revenue through wholesale sales of its innerspring mattresses. To secure a foothold in the North American bedding market, Simmons in late 2006 completed a buy-out of its former subsidiary, Simmons Canada, in a deal valued at about $120 million. (In 1990 Simmons had sold its Canadian rights to make and sell products to a group led by Simmons Canada executives.)

Looking to extend its reach into memory foam products and chase after rival Tempur-Pedic's share of that niche of the market, Simmons bought Comfor Products, which makes and markets the Comfor-Pedic line of mattresses. The company was founded as Industrial Rubber & Supply and has been manufacturing foam products for more than 60 years. As part of the agreement, Simmons plans to retain Comfor Product's headquarters near Seattle. The deal allows Simmons to leverage Comfor Products' foam mattress capabilities and expand its specialty sleep unit, which is anchored by the Simmons Natural Care line of latex mattresses.

Simmons, wanting to streamline its operations and benefit from a good customer relationship, sold off one of its holdings in mid-2006. Simmons generated some $55 million by selling its Sleep Country USA unit to California's Sleep Train, one of its top customers. As part of a related deal, Simmons stands to pocket up to $300 million through a multi-year supply partnership with Sleep Train/Sleep Country USA.

The executive suite at Simmons is showing some worn carpet. In 2006 Simmons hired Gary Matthews, who had logged experience at Sleep Innovations, Bristol-Myers Squibb, Derby Cycle, and Guinness, to work alongside chairman and CEO Charlie Eitel as Simmons' president. Matthews' tenure at the top was short-lived, however. He resigned in May 2007 and Eitel took over operations and announced that the company would not replace Matthews. Steve Fendrich, who joined the company in January 2008 as its president and COO reporting to Eitel, was promoted in October 2008 to run the company. Eitel, in turn, was named vice chairman.

THL Bedding (a holding of Thomas H. Lee Partners) bought Simmons in 2003 for about $1.1 billion. THL owns 71% of Simmons, while Fenway Partners Capital Fund holds a stake of about 9%.

EXECUTIVES

Chairman and CEO: Stephen G. (Steve) Fendrich, age 47
Vice Chairman: Charles R. (Charlie) Eitel, age 58
EVP, CFO, Assistant Treasurer, Assistant Secretary, and Director: William S. Creekmuir, age 53
EVP Operations: Robert (Rob) Burch, age 52
EVP, General Counsel, and Secretary: Kristen K. McGuffey, age 43
EVP Human Resources and Assistant Secretary: Kimberly A. Samon, age 41
EVP Marketing and International Licensing: Timothy F. (Tim) Oakhill, age 46
SVP and CIO: W. Wade Vann, age 51
SVP Technical Services: Robert M. Carstens, age 41
SVP Western Manufacturing: Tom Burns
SVP Eastern Manufacturing: Robert Ballard
SVP Sales Operations: Brad Hill
VP Credit Services: Tom Brkanovic
VP Corporate Controller and Assistant Secretary: Mark F. Chambless, age 51
General Manager Simmons Kids: George Bureau
President, Specialty Products: Scott Smalling
Auditors: PricewaterhouseCoopers LLP

LOCATIONS

HQ: Simmons Company
1 Concourse Pkwy., Ste. 800, Atlanta, GA 30328
Phone: 770-512-7700 **Fax:** 770-392-2560
Web: www.simmons.com

2007 Sales

	% of total
Domestic, including Puerto Rico	89
Canada	11
Total	**100**

PRODUCTS/OPERATIONS

Selected Brands

Advanced Pocketed Coil
BackCare
BackCare Kids
Beautyrest
Beautyrest Black
Comfor-Pedic
Deep Sleep
Pocketed Coil
Simmons

COMPETITORS

1800mattress.com
Aero Products International
Comfortaire
J. C. Penney
King Koil
Mattress Giant
Premier Bedding Group
Restonic Mattress
Sealy
Sears
Select Comfort
Serta
Spring Air
Tempur-Pedic

HISTORICAL FINANCIALS

Company Type: Private

Income Statement			FYE: Last Saturday in December	
	REVENUE ($ mil.)	NET INCOME ($ mil.)	NET PROFIT MARGIN	EMPLOYEES
12/07	1,127	24	2.1%	3,800
12/06	962	48	5.0%	3,300
12/05	855	3	0.4%	3,000
12/04	870	25	2.8%	3,300
12/03	806	(41)	—	3,200
Annual Growth	8.7%	—	—	4.4%

Debt ratio: —
Return on equity: 14.1%
Cash ($ mil.): —

Current ratio: —
Long-term debt ($ mil.): —

Net Income History

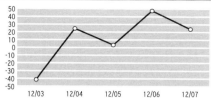

Simpson Investment

Holding company Simpson Investment Company is one of the oldest privately owned forest products companies in the northwestern US. It owns Simpson Timber Company, which makes Douglas fir and hemlock lumber used in home construction. Its Simpson Paper Company subsidiary, through Simpson Tacoma Kraft, produces unbleached kraft pulp and linerboard used in packaging such as boxes and grocery bags, and recycles more than 500 tons of waste paper daily. Simpson Door Company makes interior and exterior wood doors. Simpson Investment has been in business since 1890.

EXECUTIVES

President: Ray Tennison
CFO: Allan F. Trinkwald
Director, Human Resources: Clifford (Cliff) Slade
Environmental Manager, Simpson Tacoma Kraft Company, LLC: Greg Narum

LOCATIONS

HQ: Simpson Investment Company
917 E. 11th St., Tacoma, WA 98421
Phone: 253-779-6400   **Fax:** 253-280-9000
Web: www.simpson.com

PRODUCTS/OPERATIONS

Selected Subsidiaries

Simpson Door Company (interior and exterior wood doors)
Simpson Paper Company
    Simpson Tacoma Kraft Company, LLC (bleached and unbleached kraft pulp and linerboard)
Simpson Timber Company (dimension lumber)

COMPETITORS

Georgia-Pacific
International Paper
Louisiana-Pacific
North Pacific Group
OfficeMax
Rayonier
Roseburg Forest Products
West Fraser Timber
Weyerhaeuser

Sinclair Oil

Way out west, where fossils are found, brontosaur signs appear all 'round. They belong to Sinclair Oil's more than 2,600 service stations and convenience stores in 21 western and midwestern US states. The company also operates three oil refineries, pipelines, exploration operations, and a trucking fleet, all in the western US. It owns the Grand America Hotel, the Little America hotel chain, and two ski resorts (Sun Valley in Idaho and Snowbasin in Utah). Snowbasin was a venue of the 2002 Winter Olympics. The man behind all of this is Earl Holding, whose storied company, founded by Harry Sinclair, was a central figure in the infamous Teapot Dome scandal.

When Harry Sinclair set up his namesake exploration and production company in 1916, it was the largest oil independent in the US mid-continent, and sold some 33,000 barrels a day. Imprisoned for seven months in 1929 for refusing to answer questions from senators regarding his lucrative oil contracts with the government-owned Teapot Dome properties, Sinclair subsequently built Sinclair Oil into an industry giant. Earl Holding acquired the major surviving refining and marketing assets of the company in 1976.

EXECUTIVES

Chairman: R. Earl Holding
President and CEO: Peter M. Johnson
EVP Operations: Kevin Brown
SVP Marketing: Bud Blackmore
VP Finance and Treasurer: Charles Barlow
VP Government Relations: Clint Ensign
General Manager Retail: Larry Rogers
Regional Manager: Dalton Kehlbeck
Manager, Real Estate: Mark London
Auditors: PricewaterhouseCoopers LLP

LOCATIONS

HQ: Sinclair Oil Corporation
550 E. South Temple, Salt Lake City, UT 84102
Phone: 801-524-2700   **Fax:** 801-524-2880
Web: www.sinclairoil.com

Sinclair Oil's operations include marketing offices, refineries, trucking terminals, and Little America hotels and resorts throughout the western US.

PRODUCTS/OPERATIONS

Selected Operations

Oil and gas (exploration, marketing, pipelines, product terminals, refineries, service stations, trucking)
Little America Hotels & Resorts
    Grand America Hotel (Salt Lake City)
    Little America hotel chain (Arizona, Utah, Wyoming)
    Snowbasin (Utah) and Sun Valley (Idaho) ski resorts
    The Westgate Hotel (San Diego)

COMPETITORS

Avis Budget
BP
ConocoPhillips
Exxon
Hilton Hotels
Marriott
Royal Dutch Shell
Vail Resorts
Valero Energy
Winter Sports

HISTORICAL FINANCIALS

Company Type: Private

Income Statement

FYE: December 31

	ESTIMATED REVENUE ($ mil.)	NET INCOME ($ mil.)	NET PROFIT MARGIN	EMPLOYEES
12/07	7,000	—	—	7,000
12/06	6,800	—	—	7,000
12/05	5,600	—	—	7,000
12/04	3,950	—	—	7,000
12/03	2,900	—	—	7,000
Annual Growth	24.6%	—	—	0.0%

Revenue History

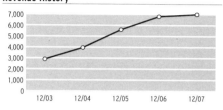

SIRVA, Inc.

Whether you're moving across the street, across town, or across the ocean, SIRVA will get your belongings where they need to be. One of the world's largest relocation and moving services companies, SIRVA operates in more than 40 countries. Its North American brands include Allied Van Lines, Global Van Lines, and North American Van Lines; it uses brands such as Allied Pickfords and Pickfords in other regions. Relocation services, delivered under contracts with employers to manage employee moves, account for more than half of SIRVA's sales. The company and its US subsidiaries emerged from Chapter 11 bankruptcy protection in May 2008.

SIRVA cited weakness in the US housing market, which has slowed demand for moving and relocation services, when it filed for Chapter 11 protection in February 2008. (Operations outside the US were not included in the filing.) In addition, delays in submitting financial reports between 2005 and 2007 as a result of an internal review of financial controls drove up SIRVA's borrowing costs. The voluntary bankruptcy filing came in conjunction with an agreement between the company and its lenders to restructure the company's debt; as a result of the company's financial restructuring, SIRVA's stock stopped trading publicly.

Before its Chapter 11 filing, SIRVA had been divesting noncore operations in order to focus on its relocation business. The company sold its moving services operations in several European countries to TEAM Group in separate deals in 2007 and 2008. The divested businesses still use SIRVA's Allied brand, as TEAM Allied, and participate in Allied's international network. SIRVA sold its business services division in the UK and Ireland to Crown Worldwide Holdings Ltd. for $87 million in March 2006, and the previous year the company sold its SIRVA Logistics unit.

SIRVA intends to maintain its broad geographic scope, however. The company hopes to grow by selling more packages of relocation and moving services to multinational companies.

Relocation services include help with home sales, purchases, and mortgages, in addition to arranging the transportation of employees' household goods.

SIRVA is operating under new leadership as it strives to move back toward profitability. After five years as the company's top executive, SIRVA president and CEO Brian Kelley resigned in 2007 to take a job at Coca-Cola North America. SIRVA board member Robert Tieken, a former CFO of Goodyear, was named interim CEO during the restructuring period. In mid-2008 Wes Lucas, a former head of Sun Chemical, came on board as the new CEO.

Two funds affiliated with investment firm Clayton, Dubilier & Rice together control a 33% stake in SIRVA. Another investment firm, ValueAct Capital, owns about 21%.

EXECUTIVES

Chairman: Kevin Dowd
CEO and Director: Wes W. Lucas
CFO: Nate Arnett
SVP, General Counsel, and Secretary: Eryk J. Spytek, age 40
SVP Global Sales: Timothy P. (Tim) Callahan, age 46, $431,848 pay
SVP, Treasurer, and Investor Relations:
 Douglas V. Gathany, age 52
SVP Human Resources: René C. Gibson, age 41
VP Client Technology: Brian Richards
VP and General Manager, International Moving Services: Andrew Coolidge
Chief Accounting Officer: Daniel P. Mullin, age 49
Manager Marketing Communication: Laura Trotter
President and Managing Director, Europe:
 Kevin D. Pickford, age 51
President, Global Relocation: Michael B. McMahon, age 44
President, Relocation Solutions, Asia/Pacific:
 K. Allen Chan, age 52
President, North American Moving Services:
 Michael T. Wolfe, age 37
President, Global Relocation Services: Deborah L. Balli
Auditors: PricewaterhouseCoopers LLP

LOCATIONS

HQ: SIRVA, Inc.
 700 Oakmont Ln., Westmont, IL 60559
Phone: 630-570-3000   **Fax:** 630-468-4761
Web: www.sirva.com

PRODUCTS/OPERATIONS

2007 Sales

	$ mil.	% of total
Global relocation services	2,395	60
Moving services		
North America	1,231	31
Europe & Asia/Pacific	344	9
Total	**3,970**	**100**

COMPETITORS

AMERCO
Atlas World Group
Bekins
GMAC Global Relocation
Graebel
Penske Truck Leasing
Prudential
Realogy
UniGroup
Weichert Relocation

HISTORICAL FINANCIALS
Company Type: Private

Income Statement   FYE: December 31

	REVENUE ($ mil.)	NET INCOME ($ mil.)	NET PROFIT MARGIN	EMPLOYEES
12/07	3,970	(413)	—	3,800
12/06	3,865	(55)	—	4,630
12/05	3,681	(265)	—	5,930
12/04	3,476	(69)	—	7,580
12/03	2,350	19	0.8%	—
Annual Growth	**14.0%**	**—**	**—**	**(20.6%)**

2007 Year-End Financials

Debt ratio: —   Current ratio: 0.63
Return on equity: —   Long-term debt ($ mil.): 2
Cash ($ mil.): 91

Net Income History

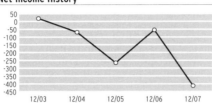

EXECUTIVES

Chairman: Ronald B. (Ron) Ashworth
President and CEO: John Sullivan
SVP and CFO: James R. Jaacks
SVP: Myra K. Aubuchon
SVP: Robert E. (Bob) Schimmel
SVP: Lynn Britton
VP and General Counsel: Philip Wheeler
VP Healthcare Solutions: Shannon Sock
VP Human Resources: Anthony D. (Tony) Kinslow
VP Medical Services: Jolene Goedken
VP and CIO: Michael (Mike) McCurry
VP, Mission and Ethics: Brian O'Toole
VP Managed Care: Robert R. (Bob) Vogel
VP Patient Financial Services: Sheri Beekman
Chief Development Officer: Bruce Bartoo
Chief Communications Officer:
 Barbara W. (Barb) Meyer

LOCATIONS

HQ: Sisters of Mercy Health System
 14528 S. Outer Forty Dr., Ste. 100,
 Chesterfield, MO 63017
Phone: 314-579-6100   **Fax:** 314-628-3723
Web: www.mercy.net

PRODUCTS/OPERATIONS

Selected Service Units and Subsidiaries

Mercy Health Plans

Mercy Health System of Kansas
 Mercy Health Center (Fort Scott)
 Mercy Hospital (Independence)
 Mercy Physician Group

Mercy Health System of Northwest Arkansas
 Mercy Health Center (Bentonville)
 Mercy Medical Clinics
 St. Mary's Hospital (Rogers)

Mercy Health System of Oklahoma
 Mercy Health Center (Oklahoma City)
 Mercy Health Network (clinics, Oklahoma City)
 Mercy Memorial Health Center (Ardmore)
 Oklahoma Heart Hospital (Oklahoma City)
 Southern Oklahoma Physician Hospital Organization (Ardmore)

Mercy Ministries of Laredo (Laredo, TX)

St. Edward Mercy Health Network (Arkansas)
 Health Point Physician Hospital Organization (Fort Smith)
 Mercy Hospital of Scott County (Waldron)
 Mercy Hospital/Turner Memorial (Ozark)
 Mercy Medical Group
 Mercy Northside Clinic (Fort Smith)
 North Logan Mercy Hospital (Paris)
 St. Edward Mercy Medical Center (Fort Smith)

St. John's Health System (Missouri)
 St. John's Clinic
 St. John's Home Care
 St. John's Hospital (Springfield)
 St. John's Hospital-Aurora (Aurora)
 St. John's Hospital-Berryville (Berryville)
 St. John's Hospital-Cassville (Cassville)
 St. John's Hospital-Lebanon (Lebanon)
 St. John's Mercy Villa
 St. John's St. Francis Hospital (Mountain View)

St. John's Mercy Health Care (Missouri)
 St. John's Mercy Medical Group (St. Louis)
 St. John's Mercy Hospital (Washington)
 St. John's Mercy Medical Center (Creve Coeur)

St. Joseph's Mercy Health Center (Arkansas)
 St. Joseph's Mercy Health Center (Hot Springs, AR)

Sisters of Mercy Health System

Not to be confused with the goth rock band of the same name, *this* Sisters of Mercy provides a range of health care and social services through its network of facilities and service organizations in seven states. The organization operates nearly 20 acute care hospitals (including one specialty heart hospital) with some 4,000 licensed beds in Arkansas, Missouri, Kansas, and Oklahoma. Its hospital groups include facilities such as nursing homes, medical practices, and outpatient centers. Additionally, Sisters of Mercy Health System runs health outreach organizations in Louisiana, Mississippi, and Texas; and its for-profit Mercy Health Plans offers managed health plans, primarily in Arkansas, Missouri, and Texas.

The organization's outreach efforts include Mercy Ministries of Laredo, a group providing primary health care and social services to residents of Laredo, Texas. It had previously owned a hospital system in Laredo (formerly known as Mercy Health Center), but sold the system to Community Health Systems.

In New Orleans, Sisters of Mercy sponsors Mercy Family Center, a mental health service provider, and in Mississippi, it funds a health care advocacy group.

The organization was founded by the Sisters of Mercy of the St. Louis Regional Community in 1986.

COMPETITORS

Baptist Health (Arkansas)
BJC HealthCare
CHRISTUS Health
Community Health Systems
HCA
INTEGRIS Health
Lester E. Cox Medical Centers
MedCath
Saint Luke's Health System
Shawnee Mission Medical Center
Sisters of Charity of Leavenworth
SSM Health Care
St. Anthony's Medical Center
St. Vincent Health System
Tenet Healthcare
Universal Health Services

HISTORICAL FINANCIALS
Company Type: Not-for-profit

Income Statement
FYE: June 30

	REVENUE ($ mil.)	NET INCOME ($ mil.)	NET PROFIT MARGIN	EMPLOYEES
6/07	3,654	68	1.9%	28,000
6/06	3,580	46	1.3%	29,500
6/05	3,247	56	1.7%	29,100
6/04	3,003	—	—	26,000
6/03	2,722	—	—	26,000
Annual Growth	7.6%	10.4%	—	1.9%

2007 Year-End Financials

Debt ratio: —
Return on equity: 2.8%
Cash ($ mil.): —
Current ratio: —
Long-term debt ($ mil.): —

Net Income History

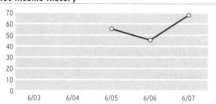

Sitel Corporation

When businesses need a little help in taking care of their customers, teleservices company Sitel (formerly ClientLogic) wants to be there. The company is a leading provider of business process outsourcing (BPO) services related to customer care. Its offerings include customer acquisition, back-office processing, collections, and technical support. It operates from more than 145 facilities in about 30 countries around the world. The former ClientLogic expanded significantly in 2007 when it acquired larger rival SITEL; the combined company then changed its name to Sitel. Canadian investment company Onex owns a controlling stake in Sitel.

The former ClientLogic paid about $472 million for SITEL, which before the deal ranked behind only Convergys and TeleTech Holdings among US teleservices providers. To focus on its teleservices operations, ClientLogic sold its Columbus, Ohio-based fulfillment business to distribution company Innotrac in October 2006.

The new Sitel traces its roots to Buffalo, New York-based Upgrade Corp. of America, which was founded by Ronald Schreiber and Jordan Levy. Upgrade (later known as SOFTBANK Services Group) marketed software upgrades for such clients as Microsoft. It was acquired in 1998 by Onex and merged with North Direct Response to create ClientLogic.

EXECUTIVES

Chairman: Harvey Golub, age 69
President and CEO: David E. Garner
Global CFO: Patrick Dupuis, age 45
EVP Global Sales and Marketing Officer: Julie M. Casteel
EVP Fulfillment: Thomas O. (Tom) Harbison
SVP Marketing and Public Relations: Amit Shankardass
VP Marketing: Andrew Kokes
Chief Global Information Officer: Eric A. Blassberg
Chief Human Resources Officer: Michael Wellman
Chief Legal Officer and Secretary: David Beckma
President, EMEA: Dale W. Saville, age 60
CEO, India: Neeraj Khanna
Auditors: PricewaterhouseCoopers LLP

LOCATIONS

HQ: Sitel Corporation
3102 West End Ave., Ste. 1000, Nashville, TN 37203
Phone: 615-301-7100   **Fax:** 615-301-7150
Web: www.sitel.com

PRODUCTS/OPERATIONS

Selected Products and Services

Back-office processing
 Catalog services
 eCommerce services
 Order and payment processing
 Rebate processing activities
Customer acquisition
 Database management
 Inbound sales
 Lead generation
 Order taking
 Outband sales
 Subscription renewals
Customer care
 Account change
 Billing information
 Investor inquiries
 Loyalty clubs
 Repeat purchases
 Up-selling/cross-selling
 Warranty calls
Risk management
 Credit activation
 Disaster prevention and recovery
 Property recovery
Technical support
 Corporate help desk
 Hardware and software support
 Internet support
 PC/server support
 Troubleshooting
 Warranty and post warranty

COMPETITORS

Accenture	ICT Group
Affiliated Computer Services	NCO
	StarTek
APAC Customer Services	Sykes Enterprises
Computer Sciences Corp.	Teleperformance
Convergys	TeleTech
EDS	West Corporation
IBM Global Services	Wipro Technologies

HISTORICAL FINANCIALS
Company Type: Private

Income Statement
FYE: December 31

	REVENUE ($ mil.)	NET INCOME ($ mil.)	NET PROFIT MARGIN	EMPLOYEES
12/07	1,700	—	—	66,000
12/06	749	—	—	67,000
12/05	715	—	—	22,000
12/04	562	—	—	20,300
12/03	433	—	—	14,400
Annual Growth	40.8%	—	—	46.3%

Revenue History

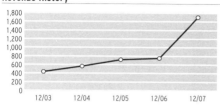

Skadden, Arps

Have you heard about the law firm that sued the business information publisher for a profile that opened with a wickedly clever lawyer joke? Neither have we, and we would like to keep it that way. Skadden, Arps, Slate, Meagher & Flom, a leading US law firm and one of the largest in the world, has some 2,000 attorneys in more than 20 offices around the globe, from Boston to Beijing and from London to Los Angeles. The firm is best known for its work in mergers and acquisitions, corporate restructuring, and corporate finance, but it represents businesses in a wide variety of practice areas, including intellectual property and litigation. Skadden was founded in 1948.

Skadden has worked for a number of FORTUNE 500 companies. High-profile clients have included JPMorgan Chase and State Farm, as well as Arcelor, Merrill Lynch, and Toshiba.

Over the years Skadden has grown organically rather than by merging with other firms. The New York office is the firm's largest, but offices outside the US have been growing faster.

EXECUTIVES

Managing Director: Earle Yaffa
Executive Partner: Robert C. Sheehan
Executive Partner: Eric J. Friedman, age 43
Corporate Partner: Joseph H. Flom
CFO: Noah J. Puntus
Senior Partner, Corporate Practice: Roger S. Aaron
Chief Administrative Officer: Laurel E. Henschel
Senior Director: Carol A. Sawdye
Director Professional Personnel and Associate Development: Jodie R. Garfinkel
Director Associate Relations, Alumni Relations, and Attorney Recruiting: Carol Lee H. Sprague
Director Marketing and Business Development: Sally J. Feldman
CTO: Harris Z. Tilevitz
Managing Attorney: Robert Abrams

LOCATIONS

HQ: Skadden, Arps, Slate, Meagher & Flom LLP
4 Times Sq., New York, NY 10036
Phone: 212-735-3000   **Fax:** 212-735-2000
Web: www.skadden.com

PRODUCTS/OPERATIONS

Selected Practice Areas

Alternative dispute resolution
Antitrust
Appellate litigation and legal issues
Asia
Australia and New Zealand
Banking and institutional investing
Brazil
Canada
CFIUS
China
Communications
Complex mass torts and insurance litigation
Consumer financial services enforcement and litigation
Corporate
Corporate compliance programs
Corporate finance
Corporate governance
Corporate restructuring
Crisis management
Derivative financial products, commodities, and futures
Employee benefits and executive compensation
Energy project finance and development
Energy regulatory
Environmental
Environmental litigation
Europe
European Union/international competition
Financial institutions
Financial services
Foreign corrupt practices act defense
Franchise law
Gaming
Government contract disputes
Government enforcement and white collar crime
Health care
Health care enforcement and litigation
Health care fraud and abuse
Hong Kong
India
Information technology and e-commerce
Insurance
Intellectual property and technology
International arbitration
International law and policy
International tax
International trade
Investment management
Israel
Italy
Japan
Labor and employment law
Latin America
Lease financing
Litigation
Mergers and acquisitions
Outsourcing
Patent and technology litigation and counseling
Pharmaceutical, biotechnology, and medical device licensing
Political law
Private equity
Private equity funds
Pro bono
Public policy
Real estate
Real estate investment trusts
Russia and CIS
Securities enforcement and compliance
Securities litigation
Sports
Structured finance
Tax
Tax controversy and litigation
Trademark, copyright, and advertising litigation and counseling
Trusts and estates
Utilities mergers and acquisitions

COMPETITORS

Baker & McKenzie
Clifford Chance
Davis Polk
Gibson, Dunn & Crutcher
Jones Day
Kirkland & Ellis
Latham & Watkins
Mayer Brown
McDermott Will & Emery
O'Melveny & Myers
Shearman & Sterling
Sidley Austin
Sullivan & Cromwell
Wachtell, Lipton
Weil, Gotshal
White & Case
WilmerHale

HISTORICAL FINANCIALS
Company Type: Partnership

Income Statement   FYE: December 31

	REVENUE ($ mil.)	NET INCOME ($ mil.)	NET PROFIT MARGIN	EMPLOYEES
12/07	2,170	—	—	4,721
12/06	1,850	—	—	4,520
12/05	1,610	—	—	4,400
Annual Growth	16.1%	—	—	3.6%

Revenue History

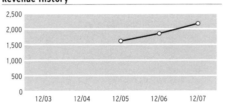

2,500				
2,000				
1,500				
1,000				
500				
0	12/03	12/04	12/05	12/06	12/07

Smart & Final

Smart & Final caters to caterers — as well as small businesses, restaurants, and even concession stands in the western US. Its 280-plus non-membership warehouse stores stock, on average, 8,000 items, including groceries, paper products, cleaning supplies, and restaurant equipment, in bulk sizes and quantities. The stores operate under the Smart & Final and Cash & Carry names in urban and suburban areas in Arizona, California, Idaho, Nevada, Oregon, and Washington, as well as northern Mexico. Once a foodservice operator, Smart & Final left that business to focus on its retail operations. Smart & Final is owned by an affiliate of the private equity firm Apollo Management.

France's Casino Guichard-Perrachon sold its majority stake in the retailer to Apollo Management for $813 million in May 2007. In October of the same year Apollo acquired 35 Henry's Farmers and Sun Harvest stores in California and Texas from Whole Foods Market for about $166 million. The stores, which Whole Foods acquired when it bought Wild Oats Markets, will join the Smart & Final chain.

Smart & Final also operates stores under the Smart Foodservice Cash & Carry name. The stores carry a broad range of restaurant-quality food, foodservice supplies, and culinary equipment.

Encouraged by strong sales since it jettisoned its foodservice operations, Smart & Final plans to dramatically increase the number of new stores it opens, possibly adding as many as 90 additional outlets by the end of the decade. The company plans to begin opening smaller stores (16,000 to 17,000 sq. ft., on average) in some noncore markets.

It operates its Mexico stores under a joint venture agreement with the operators of Calimax, a major grocery store chain in northwest Mexico.

The company was founded in 1871 in Los Angeles as the Hellman-Haas Grocery Company. It later took the names of subsequent owners J. S. Smart and H. D. Final.

EXECUTIVES

Chairman: Ross E. Roeder, age 70
President, CEO, and Director: Etienne Snollaerts, age 51, $1,027,888 pay
SVP and CFO: Richard N. Phegley, age 50, $368,047 pay
SVP, General Counsel, and Secretary: Donald G. Alvarado, age 52, $342,888 pay
SVP Store Operations: Timothy M. Snee, age 53
SVP Human Resources and Administration: Jeff D. Whynot, age 50
SVP Marketing and Buying: Norah Morley, age 54
SVP Supply Chain: C. Marie Robinson, age 39
VP Controller and Chief Accounting Officer: Richard A. Link, age 51
VP and Treasurer: Jan P. Berger
Auditors: Ernst & Young LLP

LOCATIONS

HQ: Smart & Final Inc.
600 Citadel Dr., Commerce, CA 90040
Phone: 323-869-7500   **Fax:** 323-869-7868
Web: www.smartandfinal.com

PRODUCTS/OPERATIONS

Private Labels

Chef's Review
First Street Deli
La Romanella (Italian food products)
Montecito (Hispanic food products)
ProPride
Rushing Springs (bottled water)
Snack'rs (snacks)

Selected Products

Beverages
Candy
Delicatessen products
Fresh meats
Fresh produce
Frozen and refrigerated foods
Janitorial supplies
Paper products
Party supplies
Restaurant equipment
Snacks
Tobacco

COMPETITORS

Costco Wholesale
Performance Food
Ralphs
Safeway
SAM'S CLUB
Save Mart
Stater Bros.
SYSCO
Trader Joe's
U.S. Foodservice
Wal-Mart

HISTORICAL FINANCIALS
Company Type: Private

Income Statement			FYE: Sunday nearest December 31	
	REVENUE ($ mil.)	NET INCOME ($ mil.)	NET PROFIT MARGIN	EMPLOYEES
12/07	2,300	—	—	6,200
12/06	2,105	—	—	5,910
12/05	2,003	—	—	5,870
12/04	1,956	—	—	5,370
12/03	1,730	—	—	5,060
Annual Growth	7.4%	—	—	5.2%

Revenue History

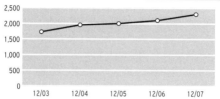

SMDK Corp.

SMDK (formerly SmartDisk) eliminates digital device divides. The company holds patents related to the portable data transfer and mass storage devices for removable memory modules. Once a maker of a wide range of data storage products, including USB- and FireWire-based personal storage drives, SMDK sold virtually all of its assets to Verbatim in 2007. Its business model now focuses on generating income from its patent portfolio. SMDK filed intellectual property lawsuits against eight companies — Audiovox, Coby Electronics, Creative Technology, Phison, Seiko Epson, THOMSON, TIC Computer, and Vosonic — in 2008.

After operating for a number of years as a public company, the company opted to go private in 2003.

In 2005 it acquired the business and certain assets of Zio, a supplier of digital media readers, mobile telephone accessories, and video editing products.

In 2007 the company changed its name to SMDK after selling its assets to Verbatim.

EXECUTIVES
Chairman: Addison M. Fischer
President and CEO: Michael S. Battaglia
CFO: Andrew Warner, age 39
VP Marketing and National Accounts: Charles Klinker
VP North American Sales: Stephen McLaughlin
VP Product Development: Steve Armfield
VP National Accounts: Brian Arensberg
Auditors: Ernst & Young LLP

LOCATIONS
HQ: SMDK Corp.
  27499 Riverview Center Blvd., Ste. 242,
  Bonita Springs, FL 34134
Phone: 239-425-4000   **Fax:** 239-425-4009
Web: www.smdkcorp.com

COMPETITORS
EZQuest	SCM Microsystems
Fujitsu Computer Products	Seagate Technology
Hewlett-Packard	Sony
Hitachi Global Storage	Soyo Group
Imation	STEC
I/OMagic	TEAC
Iomega	Toshiba
LaCie	Western Digital
Quantum Corporation	Yamaha
SanDisk	

HISTORICAL FINANCIALS
Company Type: Private

Income Statement			FYE: December 31	
	REVENUE ($ mil.)	NET INCOME ($ mil.)	NET PROFIT MARGIN	EMPLOYEES
12/06	44	(3)	—	—
12/05	46	(2)	—	—
12/04	39	(1)	—	—
12/03	29	(4)	—	—
12/02	41	(17)	—	45
Annual Growth	1.7%	—	—	—

Net Income History

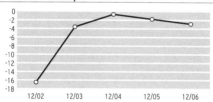

SmithGroup, Inc.

SmithGroup is the oldest continuously practicing architectural and engineering firm in the US. Founded in 1853 in Detroit by architect Sheldon Smith, the firm partnered with engineers in 1907 to become one of the first multidisciplinary firms in the country. Formerly known as Smith, Hinchman & Gryllis, it influenced the skyline of Detroit with structures like the Guardian, Penobscot, and Buhl buildings. The group also offers planning and consulting services and has 10 offices across the US. It targets the office, research, education, health care, technologies, and cities and communities markets.

SmithGroup's projects include the Providence Saint Joseph Medical Center in Burbank, California; the Smithsonian Institution's National Museum of the American Indian; and the US Arid-Land Agricultural Research Center in Maricopa, Arizona. The firm also was chosen to create a master plan for Indiana University.

Industry trends have led SmithGroup to build more and more environmentally friendly structures. The company is among other architects and engineers who are Leadership in Energy and Environmental Design certified.

In 2008 SmithGroup teamed with landscape architects JJR to create a joint studio dedicated to urban design, planning, and landscape architecture in Washington, DC.

EXECUTIVES
Chairman: David R. H. King
President and CEO: Carl Roehling
COO: Randal (Randy) Swiech
CFO: Russell (Russ) Sykes
VP and Director, Human Resources:
  Edward (Ed) Dodge
VP: Juhee Cho
VP: William Loftis
Corporate Marketing Director: Susan Arneson
Leader, Washington and Raleigh: Hal Davis
Leader, Los Angeles and San Francisco: Jim Hannon

LOCATIONS
HQ: SmithGroup, Inc.
  500 Griswold St., Ste. 1700, Detroit, MI 48226
Phone: 313-983-3600   **Fax:** 313-983-3636
Web: www.smithgroup.com

COMPETITORS
Carter & Burgess	RTKL Associates
Einhorn Yaffee	Skidmore Owings
Gensler	Syska Hennessy
Leo A Daly	URS

HISTORICAL FINANCIALS
Company Type: Private

Income Statement			FYE: December 31	
	REVENUE ($ mil.)	NET INCOME ($ mil.)	NET PROFIT MARGIN	EMPLOYEES
12/07	148	—	—	800
12/06	144	—	—	800
12/05	132	—	—	800
12/04	116	—	—	800
Annual Growth	8.6%	—	—	0.0%

Revenue History

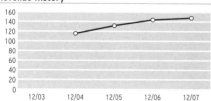

Smithsonian Institution

The Smithsonian Institution wears many hats, from the one worn by Harrison Ford in the Indiana Jones movies to the one worn by Abraham Lincoln the night he was assassinated. One of the world's leading cultural institutions, the Smithsonian houses more than 137 million pieces in 19 museums and galleries, most of which are on the National Mall in Washington, DC. Some 24 million people every year view the Smithsonian's exhibits on art, music, TV and film, science, history, and other subjects. Admission to all but one of the Smithsonian's facilities is free; only the Cooper-Hewitt, National Design Museum in New York charges admission. The Smithsonian receives about 80% of its funding from the federal government.

The Smithsonian's exhibits display items such as the Declaration of Independence, the ruby slippers worn by Judy Garland in *The Wizard of Oz*, and the Wright Brothers' first airplane. Along with its museums and galleries, the Smithsonian also operates the National Zoo and a handful of research facilities.

A board of regents that includes the vice president and the chief justice of the US, six members of Congress, and nine private citizens leads the institution. The board has named Patty Stonesifer, former CEO of the Bill & Melinda Gates Foundation, as its new leader effective January 2009. Stonesifer has been a member of the board since 2001.

Lawrence Small, the Smithsonian's secretary (or CEO), resigned under pressure in March 2007 amid criticism of his spending practices. Cristián Samper, director of the Smithsonian's National Museum of Natural History, was named acting secretary. A report on the matter issued by the Smithsonian in June said its Board of Regents failed to provide the oversight that might have prevented Small's extravagant spending.

After a 10-month delay, The Smithsonian Channel debuted in September 2007. The new television unit is a joint venture between the museum and Showtime Networks. The launch had been delayed in part because the unit, Smithsonian Networks LLC, changed its business plan to become a 24-hour, high-definition channel in response to changing industry demands, instead of starting with on-demand video, as originally planned. The new channel is operating solely as a high-definition channel on DirecTV.

An estimated $2.5 billion is needed to fund extensive maintenance and repair projects at the Smithsonian.

HISTORY

English chemist James Smithson wrote a proviso to his will in 1826 that would lead to the creation of the Smithsonian Institution. When he died in 1829, he left his estate to his nephew, Henry James Hungerford, with the stipulation that if Hungerford died without heirs, the estate would go to the US to create "an Establishment for the increase and diffusion of knowledge among men." Hungerford died in 1835 without any heirs, and the US government inherited more than $500,000 in gold.

Congress squandered the money after it was received in 1838, but perhaps feeling pangs of guilt, covered the loss. The Smithsonian was finally created in 1846, and Princeton physicist Joseph Henry was named as its first secretary. That year it established the Museum of Natural History, the Museum of History and Technology, and the National Gallery of Art. The Smithsonian's National Museum was developed around the collection of the US Patent Office in 1858. The Smithsonian continued to expand, adding the National Zoological Park in 1889 and the Smithsonian Astrophysical Observatory in 1890.

The Freer Gallery, a gift of industrialist Charles Freer, opened in 1923. The National Gallery was renamed the National Collection of Fine Arts in 1937, and a new National Gallery, created with Andrew Mellon's gift of his art collection and a building, opened in 1941. The Air and Space Museum was established in 1946.

More museums were added in the 1960s, including the National Portrait Gallery in 1962 and the Anacostia Museum (exhibits and materials on African-American history) in 1967. The Kennedy Center for the Performing Arts was opened in 1971. The Collection of Fine Arts was renamed the National Museum of American Art and the Mu-

seum of History and Technology was renamed the National Museum of American History in 1980.

The Smithsonian placed its first-ever contribution boxes in four of its museums in 1993.

A planned exhibit featuring the *Enola Gay* — the plane that dropped the atomic bomb on Hiroshima — created a firestorm in 1994 with critics charging that the exhibit downplayed Japanese aggression and US casualties in WWII. The original exhibit was canceled in 1995, the director of the Air and Space Museum resigned, and a scaled-down version of the exhibit premiered. In 2004 the exhibit attracted more protestors, prompting Smithsonian officials to evacuate and temporarily close the museum.

Large contributions from private donors continued in the 1990s; the Mashantucket Pequot tribe gave $10 million from its casino operations in 1994 for the Smithsonian's planned American Indian museum and prolific electronics inventor Jerome Lemelson donated $10.4 million in 1995. The museum celebrated its sesquicentennial in 1996 amid news that $500 million in repairs were needed over the next 10 years.

California real estate developer Kenneth Behring gave the largest cash donation ever to the museum in 1997 — $20 million for the National Museum of Natural History. Short of funds, the Smithsonian had to cut back on its 150th anniversary traveling exhibit that year. The Smithsonian announced a $26 million renovation for the National Museum of Natural History in 1998. Two years later Behring quadrupled his record-breaking 1997 donation of $20 million by giving $80 million to the National Museum of American History. Catherine Reynolds withdrew most of her $38 million gift in 2002 after the Smithsonian Institution refused to implement her ideas for an exhibit at the National Museum of American History.

The National Museum of the American Indian opened on the National Mall in 2004.

EXECUTIVES

Chairman: Roger W. Sant
CFO: Alice Collier Maroni
CIO: Ann Speyer
General Counsel: John E. Huerta
Secretary: G. Wayne Clough, age 66
Treasurer: Sudeep Anand
Comptroller: Andrew J. Zino
Director Communications and Public Affairs: Evelyn S. Lieberman
Director Human Resources: James Douglas
Director Investments: Amy Chen
Director National Collections: Bill Tompkins
Smithsonian Inspector General: Anne Sprightley Ryan
President, Smithsonian Enterprises and President and Publisher, Magazine Publishing: Tom Ott
Auditors: KPMG LLP

LOCATIONS

HQ: Smithsonian Institution
1000 Jefferson Dr. SW, Washington, DC 20560
Phone: 202-633-1000
Web: www.si.edu

PRODUCTS/OPERATIONS

Selected Museums and Research Centers

Anacostia Museum & Center for African American History and Culture
Archives of American Art
Arthur M. Sackler Gallery and Freer Gallery of Art
Arts and Industries Building
Center for Folklife and Cultural Heritage
Conservation and Research Center
Cooper-Hewitt, National Design Museum (New York)

Hirshhorn Museum and Sculpture Garden
National Air and Space Museum
National Museum of African Art
National Museum of American History
National Museum of Natural History
National Museum of the American Indian
National Museum of the American Indian George Gustav Heye Center (New York)
National Portrait Gallery
National Postal Museum
National Zoological Park
Smithsonian American Art Museum and Renwick Gallery
Smithsonian Astrophysical Observatory
Smithsonian Center for Latino Initiatives
Smithsonian Center for Materials Research and Education
Smithsonian Environmental Research Center (SERC)
Smithsonian Institution Building (The Castle)
Smithsonian Museum Conservation Institute
Smithsonian Tropical Research Institute

HISTORICAL FINANCIALS
Company Type: Not-for-profit

Income Statement				FYE: September 30
	REVENUE ($ mil.)	NET INCOME ($ mil.)	NET PROFIT MARGIN	EMPLOYEES
9/07	989	220	22.2%	6,300
9/06	979	146	14.9%	6,300
9/05	986	246	24.9%	6,300
9/04	904	147	16.3%	—
9/03	691	140	20.3%	—
Annual Growth	9.4%	12.0%	—	0.0%

2007 Year-End Financials

Debt ratio: —
Return on equity: 9.2%
Cash ($ mil.): —
Current ratio: —
Long-term debt ($ mil.): —

Net Income History

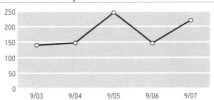

	9/03	9/04	9/05	9/06	9/07
250					
200					
150					
100					
50					
0					

Soave Enterprises

Soave Enterprises is suave enough to manage multiple lines of business. The company's wide-ranging interests are divided into four main industries: real estate (residential and industrial development); auto dealerships; beer distribution; plus a catch-all diversified holdings group that includes businesses ranging from waste collection and transportation to scrap metals processing, as well as units engaged in hydroponic tomato gardening and taxi services. The bulk of Soave's operations are in Michigan. President and CEO Anthony Soave, who founded the company in 1961, owns Soave Enterprises.

In 2005 Soave Enterprises teamed up with longtime auto parts professional Bill Wild to form Parts Galore, a Michigan-based self-service, used auto parts retail chain.

EXECUTIVES

Chairman, President, and CEO: Anthony L. Soave, age 69
EVP and Director: Yale Levin
SVP, CFO, and Director: Michael L. Piesko
SVP and Director: Michael D. Hollerbach
SVP and Director: Kathleen B. McCann
VP, Real Estate Group: Dan Roma
Treasurer: Richard T. Brockhaus
Corporate Controller: Bryan T. Susko
Secretary and Senior Counsel: Bryant M. Frank
Corporate Director Human Resources: Marcia K. Moss
President, Soave Automotive Group: Marion Battaglia

LOCATIONS

HQ: Soave Enterprises L.L.C.
   3400 E. Lafayette St., Detroit, MI 48207
Phone: 313-567-7000   **Fax:** 313-567-0966
Web: www.soaveenterprises.com

COMPETITORS

Continental Motors
David J. Joseph
KB Home
Lennar
OmniSource
Republic Services
Russ Darrow
The Ryland Group
Schnitzer Steel
Steel Technologies
Tang Industries
Waste Management

HISTORICAL FINANCIALS

Company Type: Private

Income Statement

	REVENUE ($ mil.)	NET INCOME ($ mil.)	NET PROFIT MARGIN	EMPLOYEES
12/07	1,770	—	—	2,200
12/06	1,630	—	—	2,450
12/05	1,500	—	—	2,601
12/04	1,610	—	—	2,556
12/03	1,100	—	—	2,400
Annual Growth	12.6%	—	—	(2.2%)

FYE: December 31

Revenue History

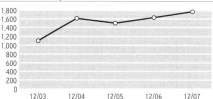

Software House

Software House International (SHI) wants to put computer products in houses across the globe. The company distributes more than 100,000 hardware and software products from suppliers such as Adobe, Hewlett-Packard, Lenovo, McAfee, and Microsoft. SHI also offers professional services such as application development, asset and lifecycle management, product procurement, systems integration, and training. The company serves enterprise, government, and education customers worldwide. Clients have included Bank of America, Boeing, and Merrill Lynch. SHI was founded in 1989.

EXECUTIVES

President and CEO: Thai Lee, age 50
CFO: Paul Ng
Enterprise Solutions Program Champion: Caroline Change
Human Resources: Michael Haluska

LOCATIONS

HQ: Software House International, Inc.
   2 Riverview Dr., Somerset, NJ 08873
Phone: 732-764-8888   **Fax:** 732-764-8889
Web: www.shi.com

PRODUCTS/OPERATIONS

Selected Services

Application development
Asset management
Contract staffing
Desktop installation
E-commerce
Network consulting
Security management
Systems integration
Technical support

COMPETITORS

Agilysys
Arrow Electronics
ASI Computer Technologies
Austin Ribbon & Computer
Avnet
Azlan Group
Bell Microproducts
CDW
CompuCom
Computacenter
Electrograph Systems
Ingram Micro
Insight Enterprises
Merisel
Morse
SARCOM, Inc.
Softmart
Supercom
Tech Data

HISTORICAL FINANCIALS

Company Type: Private

Income Statement

	REVENUE ($ mil.)	NET INCOME ($ mil.)	NET PROFIT MARGIN	EMPLOYEES
12/07	2,330	—	—	1,000
12/06	2,230	—	—	1,000
12/05	2,051	—	—	1,000
Annual Growth	6.6%	—	—	0.0%

FYE: December 31

Revenue History

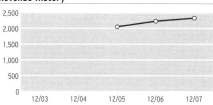

Solae, LLC

Solae mixes up its products and its ownership. Formed as a joint venture between DuPont and Bunge Limited in 2003, Solae develops, makes, and markets soy-based food ingredients. With more than 3,500 customers in 80 countries across the globe, the company manufactures soy protein that is used in a variety of beverages and meatless foods (V8 Splash smoothies, Gardenburgers, Mori-Nu non-dairy pie-fillings and pudding mixes, and Yves Veggie Cuisine deli slices and hot dogs). In addition to soy products for use in the food and beverage sectors, Solae makes soy-based polymers for use by makers of coated paper and paperboard.

Solae has a partnership with Chinese meat processor Henan Luohe Shineway Industry Group to expand its soy-processing production in that country. The company renamed all of its lecithin products to Solec Soy Lecithin in order to improve customer recognition.

Adding to its meat-replacement manufacturing capabilities and offerings, in 2007 the company purchased the soy protein product line (including the Prolisse brand) from Cargill. That same year Solae entered into a collaborative agreement with food-ingredient company Senomyx to develop flavor ingredients to enhance the taste of soy proteins.

The company has experienced rising costs for soy-protein manufacturing and materials, and in 2005 Solae exited the soy isoflavone business when it sold its global isoflavone business to Archer Daniels Midland.

Solae's products are used in four sectors of the food-manufacturing industry: by meat and poultry, consumer food, nutritional, and dairy-alternative companies.

DuPont owns 72% of Solae; Bunge owns the remaining 28%.

EXECUTIVES

Chairman: Craig F. Binetti, age 52
CEO: Torkel Rhenman
VP and CFO: Steven W. (Steve) Fray, age 41
VP, Global Marketing and Strategy: David A. Hollinrake
VP, Global Marketing and Business Development: Garnet Pigden
VP, Human Resources: Mark Nechita, age 43
VP, New Business Development: Paul Graham
VP, Research and Development: Jonathan (Jon) McIntyre
VP and CIO: George Tomko
VP, Operations and Commodity Business: Paul Bossert Jr.
Director, Corporate Communications: Geri Berdak

LOCATIONS

HQ: Solae, LLC
   4300 Duncan Ave., St. Louis, MO 63110
Phone: 314-659-3000   **Fax:** 314-659-5749
Web: www.solae.com

PRODUCTS/OPERATIONS

Selected Soy Products

Fibers
Industrial polymers
Lecithins
Protein concentrates
Protein isolates

COMPETITORS

ADM
Ag Processing
Cargill
Carolina Soy
Central Soya
CHS
US Soy

HISTORICAL FINANCIALS

Company Type: Joint venture

Income Statement

FYE: December 31

	REVENUE ($ mil.)	NET INCOME ($ mil.)	NET PROFIT MARGIN	EMPLOYEES
12/07	1,000	—	—	3,500
12/06	1,000	—	—	3,500
12/05	1,000	—	—	3,000
12/04	800	—	—	3,000
Annual Growth	7.7%	—	—	5.3%

Revenue History

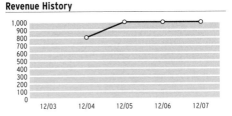

Solo Cup

Solo Cup married a Sweetheart, but kept its own name. Solo Cup — which makes disposable cups, plates, containers, cutlery, and the like — has bought and absorbed rival SF Holdings, parent company of disposable product maker Sweetheart Holdings (Sweetheart Cup). Solo Cup's plastic, paper, and foam items are sold through retailers and foodservice distributors around the world, then used and thrown away by consumers. In addition to typical disposables, Solo also makes specialty party supplies, upscale disposable products, and plastic and paper packaging for snack food and dairy product manufacturers.

The company's purchase of Sweetheart was completed in 2004; by the end of 2006, though, it had proven to be less than a sweetheart of a deal. While the marriage of Solo and Sweetheart created a company with more than 30 manufacturing facilities in North America (including more than 20 from the Sweetheart side) and combined sales of $2 billion, Solo was unable in the early years of the merger to realize the cost savings that it projected when it acquired Sweetheart.

The Sweetheart purchase was helped along by a $220 million investment in Solo from equity firm Vestar Capital Partners in exchange for a minority stake in the new company. Late in 2006, Vestar exercised its right — linked to the company's ongoing weak financial performance — to

take over the Solo board. Therefore, while the founding Hulseman family still holds a majority ownership stake in the firm, it no longer maintains majority operating control.

Early in 2007 the company sold six US factories for $130 million to reduce debt and subsequently leased back the plants for 20 years. As part of another cost-cutting effort, Solo sold Hoffmaster operations to private equity firm Kohlberg & Co., for about $170 million. Hoffmaster makes tableware such as place mats and napkins, primarily for hotels. Additional efforts to cut debt include the sale of its uncoated white paper plate operations to AJM Packaging and the planned closure of two plants, one in Massachusetts and one in Illinois.

Besides its North American facilities in the US, Canada, and Mexico, Solo also operates factories in the UK, Japan, and Panama. Sales to foodservice distributors such as Sysco and Bunzl and food chains such as Starbucks and McDonald's account for 80% of the company's sales. Solo Cup also serves consumer outlets such as supermarkets, dollar stores, and warehouse clubs.

Leo Hulseman founded the Paper Container Manufacturing Company in 1936; ten years later the company renamed itself Solo Cup, after the cone-shaped paper cup that made it famous.

EXECUTIVES

Chairman Emeritus: Robert L. Hulseman, age 75, $1,100,000 pay
Chairman: Kevin A. Mundt, age 54
President, CEO, and Director: Robert M. Korzenski, age 53, $611,250 pay
EVP Supply Chain: Thomas A. Pasqualini, age 50, $465,625 pay
EVP Human Resources, General Counsel, and Secretary: Jan Stern Reed, age 48, $542,062 pay
EVP and CFO: Robert D. Koney Jr., age 51
SVP Foodservice Sales and Marketing: Malcolm Simmonds, age 45
SVP Operations: Peter J. Mendola, age 51
SVP and CIO: Robert Fronberry, age 53
SVP Consumer Sales and Marketing: Steven J. Jungmann, age 44
Auditors: KPMG LLP

LOCATIONS

HQ: Solo Cup Company
1700 Old Deerfield Rd., Highland Park, IL 60035
Phone: 847-831-4800   **Fax:** 847-579-3245
Web: www.solocup.com

2007 Sales

	% of total
North America	95
Europe	4
Other regions	1
Total	**100**

PRODUCTS/OPERATIONS

2007 Sales

	$ mil.	% of total
Foodservice	1,728.8	80
Consumer	377.5	20
Total	**2,106.3**	**100**

Selected Products

Cold cups, lids, and straws
Cutlery
Dinnerware
Doilies
Fluted/Bakery products
Food containers
Hot cups and lids
Napkins
Paper plates, bowls, and cups
Placemats
Plastic plates, bowls, cups, lids, deli, and food containers
Portion cups
Specialty tabletop disposables
Tablecovers

Selected Brands

Creative Expressions (specialty tabletop products)
Flex-E-Form (paper packaging for frozen foods)
Flexstyle (paper packaging for frozen foods)
Mtrene (plastic packaging products for refrigerated foods)
Sensations (premium solid-color disposable tabletop products)
Sensations Café Collection (European-style paper napkins and dinner napkins)
Solo
Solo All Occasions (paper plates)
Solo Classic Colors (plastic plates, bowls, and cups)
SoloGrips (ergonomic plastic cups, plates, and tableware)
Solo Ultra Clear (clear cups)
Solo Ultra Colors (transparent colored cups and plates)
Ultra Sensations (Linen-Like table covers and dinner napkins; metallic silver cutlery)

COMPETITORS

American Greetings
Amscan
Berry Plastics
Dart Container
Dopaco
Dover Industries
Georgia-Pacific
Huhtamäki
International Paper
Pactiv
Rexam
Reynolds Food Packaging
WinCup

HISTORICAL FINANCIALS

Company Type: Private

Income Statement

FYE: December 31

	REVENUE ($ mil.)	NET INCOME ($ mil.)	NET PROFIT MARGIN	EMPLOYEES
12/07	2,106	68	3.2%	8,700
12/06	2,490	(373)	—	11,500
12/05	2,432	(19)	—	12,000
12/04	2,116	(50)	—	11,500
12/03	880	(3)	—	—
Annual Growth	24.4%	—	—	(8.9%)

2007 Year-End Financials

Debt ratio: 878.7%   Current ratio: —
Return on equity: 136.9%   Long-term debt ($ mil.): 756
Cash ($ mil.): —

Net Income History

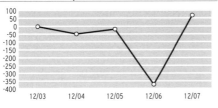

South Carolina Public Service Authority

Someone's got to turn on those bright lights in the big city — and in the small cities, too. South Carolina Public Service Authority, known as Santee Cooper (after two interconnected river systems), provides wholesale electricity to 20 cooperatives and two municipalities that serve more than 625,000 customers in South Carolina. It directly retails electricity to 155,000 customers. One of the largest US state-owned utilities, Santee Cooper operates in all 46 counties in South Carolina and has interests in power plants (fossil-fueled, nuclear, and hydroelectric) that give it 5,100 MW of generating capacity. The Santee Cooper Regional Water System distributes water to 125,000 consumers in the state.

The $48.2 million Santee Cooper project (55% federal loan and 45% federal grant), which connected the Santee and Cooper rivers and established hydroelectric dams and a transmission grid, began to generate electricity for the first time in 1942.

EXECUTIVES

Chairman: O. L. Thompson
First Vice Chairman: G. Dial Dubose
Second Vice Chairman: Clarence Davis
President and CEO: Lonnie N. Carter
EVP and COO: Bill McCall Jr.
EVP and CFO: Elaine G. Peterson
SVP and General Counsel: Jim Brogdon Jr.
SVP, Corporate Services:
 Rennie M. (R. M.) Singletary III
SVP, Generation: Maxie C. Chaplin
SVP, Power Delivery: Terry L. Blackwell
VP, Corporate Communications and Media Relations:
 Laura G. Varn
VP, Human Resource Management: W. Glen Brown Jr.
Treasurer: H. Roderick (Rod) Murchison
Corporate Secretary: Pamela J. Williams
Auditors: Deloitte & Touche LLP

LOCATIONS

HQ: South Carolina Public Service Authority
 1 Riverwood Dr., Moncks Corner, SC 29461
Phone: 843-761-8000   **Fax:** 843-761-7060
Web: www.santeecooper.com

COMPETITORS

Delmarva Power
Dominion Resources
Duke Energy
E.ON U.S.
Florida Public Utilities
Memphis Light
North Carolina Electric Membership
Progress Energy
PS Energy
SCANA
TVA
Utilities, Inc.

Southeastern Freight Lines

Less-than-truckload (LTL) carrier Southeastern Freight Lines hauls freight throughout the southern US with a fleet of about 2,700 tractors and 7,850 trailers. (LTL carriers consolidate freight from multiple shippers into a single truckload.) Southeastern Freight Lines operates from a network of about 75 terminals in about a dozen states, plus Puerto Rico and the US Virgin Islands. Through partnerships with other carriers, including A. Duie Pyle, Dayton Freight, and Oak Harbor Freight Lines, Southeastern Freight Lines provides service throughout the US and Canada. Southeastern Freight Lines is controlled by the Cassels family, which also owns truckload carrier G&P Trucking.

To attract additional business, Southeastern Freight Lines has been building out its network of service centers. Although the company continues to concentrate on its core territory, the new facilities allow Southeastern Freight Lines to offer next-day service to additional markets within its home region. The company opened terminals in Texas and Arkansas during 2007.

EXECUTIVES

Chairman: W. T. Cassels Jr.
President: W. T. (Tobin) Cassels III
SVP Corporate Planning and Development:
 Braxton Vick
SVP Finance: Russ Burleson
SVP Operations: Rick Toburen
SVP Sales and Marketing: Mike Heaton
VP Management Information Systems: Dave Robinson
VP Quality and Human Resources: David Scoggins

LOCATIONS

HQ: Southeastern Freight Lines, Inc.
 420 Davega Rd., Lexington, SC 29073
Phone: 803-794-7300   **Fax:** 803-794-8131
Web: www.sefl.com

COMPETITORS

AAA Cooper Transportation
Arkansas Best
Averitt Express
Con-way Freight
Estes Express
FedEx Freight
Old Dominion Freight
Saia, Inc.
UPS Freight
YRC Worldwide

HISTORICAL FINANCIALS
Company Type: Private

Income Statement
FYE: December 31

	REVENUE ($ mil.)	NET INCOME ($ mil.)	NET PROFIT MARGIN	EMPLOYEES
12/07	730	—	—	6,800
12/06	711	—	—	6,800
12/05	648	—	—	6,000
12/04	546	—	—	6,000
12/03	484	—	—	—
Annual Growth	10.8%	—	—	4.3%

Revenue History

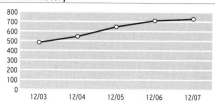

Southern Wine & Spirits

Fueled by alcohol and nicotine, Southern Wine & Spirits of America brews up market dominance. The firm is the #1 US distributor of wine and spirits. It represents more than 1,500 wine, beer, and spirits suppliers from around the world, offering some 5,000 different brands. The company ships more than 70 million cases a year and has operations in nearly 30 US states. Southern Wine & Spirits of America imported products include Grolsch and Steinlager beers; cigars, such as Don Diego and Montecristo; and nonalcoholic beverages, including Clamato and Rose's Lime Juice. Southern Wine & Spirits of America was founded in Florida in 1968.

The company does business in "control states" (those US states which control and regulate the sale of alcohol through a monopoly) through Southern Wine/Spirits West, a joint venture with Alaska Distributors Co. of Seattle, Washington. Southern Wine/Spirits West operates across the control states of Idaho, Montana, Oregon, Utah, Washington, and Wyoming.

Southern Wine & Spirits of America is also a licensed permittee in Nebraska and Texas.

EXECUTIVES

**Chairman and CEO; Chairman, Southern/Glazer's
 Distributors of America:** Harvey R. Chaplin, age 79
**President and COO; CEO, Southern/Glazer's
 Distributors of America:** Wayne E. Chaplin, age 52
EVP and General Manager: Brad Vassar, age 50
EVP Spirits: Rodolfo A. (Rudy) Ruiz, age 59
SVP Human Resources: W. Michael Head, age 58
First VP and Treasurer: Steven R. Becker
VP, Secretary, and Chief Administrative Officer:
 Lee F. Hager
VP Category Management and Business Intelligence:
 Thomas McDevitt
VP Finance and Administration: John R. Preston, age 61
Director Mixology: Francesco Lafranconi
Chairman and CEO, Lauber Imports: Ed Lauber

LOCATIONS

HQ: Southern Wine & Spirits of America, Inc.
 1600 NW 163rd St., Miami, FL 33169
Phone: 305-625-4171   **Fax:** 305-625-4720
Web: www.southernwine.com

PRODUCTS/OPERATIONS

Selected Products

Beer
Cigars
Nonalcoholic beverages and mixes
Spirits
Wines

COMPETITORS

Altadis	National Distributing
Bacardi	National Wine & Spirits
Banfi Vintners	Rémy Cointreau
Ben E. Keith	Sunbelt Beverage
Constellation Brands	Synergy Brands
Geerlings & Wade	Topa Equities
Georgia Crown	UST Inc.
Glazer's Wholesale Drug	Wirtz Corporation
Johnson Brothers	Young's Market

HISTORICAL FINANCIALS
Company Type: Private

Income Statement
FYE: December 31

	REVENUE ($ mil.)	NET INCOME ($ mil.)	NET PROFIT MARGIN	EMPLOYEES
12/07	8,300	—	—	10,300
12/06	6,980	—	—	10,300
12/05	6,500	—	—	10,300
12/04	5,500	—	—	—
12/03	5,400	—	—	8,000
Annual Growth	11.3%	—	—	6.5%

Revenue History

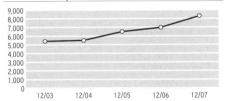

Southwire Company

Southwire hopes everyone's cable-ready. One of the world's largest cable and wire manufacturers, Southwire makes building wire and cable, utility cable products, industrial power cable, telecommunications cable, copper and aluminum rods, and cord products. The company also provides engineering and machining and fabrication services, as well as electronic inventory management. Southwire customers include building contractors, utility companies, and OEMs in the areas of automotive, electrical, appliances, and industrial equipment. Founded in 1950 by Roy Richards Sr. (the chairman's father), Southwire is owned by the Richards family.

Southwire will continue to build on its core operations, as evidenced by its purchase of General Cable Corporation's building wire assets, which made Southwire one of North America's largest producers of building wire. The company has also expanded its base of operations into Asia and Europe, but continues to focus on the North American market.

In 2006 Southwire acquired the wire and cable assets of Essex Electrical Products from Alpine Group for $27 million; it also purchased the CableTech cable and wire operation of GenTek. The previous year, Southwire acquired Decorp (later renamed FlatWire Technologies), a maker of surface-mounted wiring products, and Alflex, which manufactured metal-clad cable and flexible conduit products.

The company is working with American Superconductor, Consolidated Edison, and the Department of Homeland Security to develop surge-suppressing superconductor cable, which is being used to develop more secure power systems in areas such as New York City. Similarly, the company has teamed up with Entergy and NKT to begin a massive modernization of the electric grid across the US under a plan financed by the US Department of Energy.

EXECUTIVES

Chairman: Roy Richards Jr.
President and CEO: Stuart Thorn
EVP, Finance and CFO: J. Guyton Cochran Jr.
EVP, Human Resources: Michael R. (Mike) Wiggins
EVP, Operations: Jeff Herrin
EVP, Legal and Corporate Secretary: Floyd Smith
SVP and President, OEM Division: Norman Adkins
SVP, Research and Development: Vince Kruse
President, Energy: Charlie Murrah
President, Electrical: Jack Carlson
President, SCR: Will Berry
Manager, Communications: Gary Leftwich

LOCATIONS

HQ: Southwire Company
    1 Southwire Dr., Carrollton, GA 30117
Phone: 770-832-4242
Web: www.southwire.com

PRODUCTS/OPERATIONS

Selected Products
Aluminum rod
Building wire (copper, aluminum)
Communication cable
Copper rod
Electrical wire and cable
Flexible conduit section
Flexible cord
High voltage cable
Magnet wire
Specialty wire
Transit cable
Wire-making machinery

COMPETITORS

AFC Cable
Alcatel-Lucent
Alpine Group
Andrew Corporation
Anixter International
Balfour Beatty
Belden
Bridon
Capro
Carlisle Companies
Corning
Driver-Harris
Encore Wire
Freeport-McMoRan
General Cable
Hitachi Cable
Hubbell
International Wire
IRCE
Nexans
OFS BrightWave
Rio Tinto Alcan
Sumitomo Electric
Superior Essex
SWCC SHOWA
Volex

HISTORICAL FINANCIALS
Company Type: Private

Income Statement
FYE: December 31

	REVENUE ($ mil.)	NET INCOME ($ mil.)	NET PROFIT MARGIN	EMPLOYEES
12/07	4,980	—	—	4,200
12/06	4,900	—	—	4,108
12/05	3,200	—	—	4,180
12/04	2,200	—	—	3,600
12/03	1,500	—	—	3,100
Annual Growth	35.0%	—	—	7.9%

Revenue History

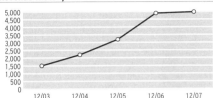

Spectrum Health System

Spectrum Health is a regional health system serving western Michigan. The not-for-profit health network features over half a dozen hospitals with some 2,000 beds; most of the hospitals operate under the Spectrum Health name. Residents and visitors to the area can also access Spectrum Health through its more than 140 service sites, which include urgent care centers, primary care physician offices, community clinics, rehabilitation and other outpatient facilities, and continuing care residences and services for the elderly. The health system also operates Priority Health, a health plan with about 560,000 members.

Spectrum Health was formed through the 1997 merger of Blodgett Hospital and Butterworth Hospital. Kent Community Hospital joined the organization in 1999, and the United Memorial Health System (Kelsey Hospital and United Hospital) became a member in 2003.

The company began construction on a new 14-story building for the Helen DeVos Children's Hospital in 2006; the facility is scheduled to open in 2010.

In 2007 Priority Health acquired Michigan insurance provider Care Choices, adding 120,000 members to its system.

EXECUTIVES

President and CEO: Richard C. (Rick) Breon
EVP and CFO: Michael P. (Mike) Freed
SVP: John Mosley
SVP and CIO: Patrick O'Hare
SVP, Human Resources: Daniel Oglesby
SVP, System Quality: John Byrnes
VP, Patient Care Services and Chief Nursing Officer:
    Shawn M. Ulreich
General Counsel: David Leonard
CEO, Spectrum Health — Reed City Campus:
    Tom Kaufman
President, Blodgett Hospital: Jim Wilson, age 52

President and CEO, Priority Health:
  Kimberly K. (Kim) Horn
President, Helen DeVos Children's Hospital:
  Robert Connors
President, Spectrum Health Hospitals:
  Matt Van Vranken
Auditors: Ernst & Young LLP

LOCATIONS

HQ: Spectrum Health System
    100 Michigan St. NE, Grand Rapids, MI 49503
Phone: 616-391-1774   **Fax:** 616-391-2780
Web: www.spectrum-health.org

PRODUCTS/OPERATIONS

2007 Sales

	$ mil.	% of total
Health plan	1,223.1	53
Hospital and physician services	960.8	41
Continuing care and home health	75.8	3
Investment income	17.2	1
Other	45.5	2
Total	**2,322.4**	**100**

Selected Operations

Helen DeVos Children's Hospital (Grand Rapids)
Priority Health (managed care plans)
Spectrum Health Blodgett Hospital (Grand Rapids)
Spectrum Health Butterworth Hospital (Grand Rapids)
Spectrum Health Continuing Care (long-term,
    rehabilitative, skilled nursing, and home health care)
Spectrum Health Kent Community Campus (Grand
    Rapids)
Spectrum Health Reed City Hospital (Reed City)
Spectrum Health Special Care Hospital (Grand Rapids)
Spectrum Health United Memorial
    Kelsey Hospital (Lakeview)
    United Hospital (Greenville)

COMPETITORS

Battle Creek Health System
Bay Regional Medical Center
Borgess Health
Bronson Healthcare
Covenant HealthCare
Munson Healthcare
Sheridan Community Hospital
Zeeland Community Hospital

HISTORICAL FINANCIALS

Company Type: Not-for-profit

Income Statement

	REVENUE ($ mil.)	NET INCOME ($ mil.)	NET PROFIT MARGIN	EMPLOYEES
6/07	2,322	185	8.0%	14,400
6/06	2,103	90	4.3%	14,400
6/05	1,932	65	3.4%	14,400
6/04	1,868	—	—	14,000
6/03	1,538	—	—	14,000
Annual Growth	10.9%	68.1%	—	0.7%

2007 Year-End Financials

Debt ratio: —   Current ratio: —
Return on equity: 15.9%   Long-term debt ($ mil.): —
Cash ($ mil.): —

Net Income History

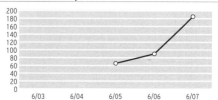

Sports Authority

Are you gonna argue with The Sports Authority? Now get in there and buy a StairMaster . . . or some cleats . . . or a basketball! The #1 US sporting goods chain (with more than 400 stores in 45 states), The Sports Authority sells sports equipment, general merchandise, shoes, and apparel, with a focus on premium brands. It also has an online store. The company's 2003 merger with Gart Sports (owner of the Sportmart and Oshman's chains) marked a major consolidation in the sporting goods retail industry, with the merged company coming out on top. Senior managers of The Sports Authority, together with an investor group led by Leonard Green & Partners, took the company private in 2006.

Following its merger with Gart Sports, the combined entity became known as The Sports Authority (TSA). As a result of a major rebranding effort, all the retailer's stores now operate under the Sports Authority nameplate. (Previously, TSA operated stores under the Sports Authority, Gart Sports, Oshman's, and Sportmart banners.) In the two years before it went private, the sporting goods chain invested heavily in closing and repositioning stores and remerchandising those that remained, to achieve a consistent look. It also adopted a new game plan: to court customers willing to pay full price. To that end, TSA adopted Gart Sports' emphasis on stocking premium brands in categories such as apparel, fitness, footwear, golf, and team sports.

With its rebranding, remerchandising, and remodeling efforts behind it, TSA has returned to opening new stores. In 2007 the company opened more than 25 new locations and has plans for about 40 new stores in 2008, including locations in Alaska, California, Florida, and Hawaii. The new stores range in size between 42,000 square feet and 50,000 square feet.

Many TSA stores also rent winter sports equipment, including skis and snowboards.

EXECUTIVES

Chairman and CEO: John D. (Doug) Morton, age 57
President: David J. (Dave) Campisi, age 52
**Vice Chairman, CFO, Chief Administrative Officer, and
  Treasurer:** Thomas T. Hendrickson, age 53
EVP and COO: Greg A. Waters, age 47
EVP Human Resources: Kerry M. Sims, age 50
EVP, General Counsel, and Secretary:
  Nesa E. Hassanein, age 55
Auditors: Deloitte & Touche LLP

LOCATIONS

HQ: The Sports Authority, Inc.
    1050 W. Hampden Ave., Englewood, CO 80110
Phone: 303-789-5266   **Fax:** 303-863-2240
Web: www.sportsauthority.com

PRODUCTS/OPERATIONS

Merchandise Categories

Athletic and active apparel
Athletic and active footwear
Fitness sports
Golf clubs and equipment
Outdoor sports
Recreational sports
Winter sports

COMPETITORS

Academy Sports & Outdoors	Golfsmith
Bass Pro Shops	Hibbett Sports
Big 5	J. C. Penney
Cabela's	Joe's Sports
Chick's	Kmart
Christy Sports	Lands' End
Costco Wholesale	L.L. Bean
Dick's Sporting Goods	Modell's
Dunham's	Nevada Bob's
Eastern Mountain Sports	Olympia Sports
Eddie Bauer	REI
Edwin Watts Golf	Scheels
Finish Line	Sears
Foot Locker	Sport Chalet
Gander Mountain	Target
Golf Galaxy	Wal-Mart
	West Marine

HISTORICAL FINANCIALS

Company Type: Private

Income Statement

FYE: Saturday nearest January 31

	REVENUE ($ mil.)	NET INCOME ($ mil.)	NET PROFIT MARGIN	EMPLOYEES
1/08	2,980	—	—	15,825
1/07	2,740	—	—	14,586
1/06	2,509	—	—	14,300
1/05	2,436	—	—	15,000
1/04	1,760	—	—	17,000
Annual Growth	14.1%	—	—	(1.8%)

Revenue History

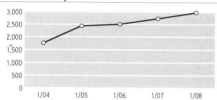

Spring Air

Spring Air is calling you to bed. The mattress company offers the Back Supporter, Four Seasons, Nature's Rest, and Chattan & Wells collections, featuring amenities such as asthma- and allergy-sensitive fabrics and silk and wool blend mattresses to control body temperature. Selling products worldwide through furniture retailers, department stores, and bedding stores, Spring Air is a leading mattress manufacturer (among Sealy, Serta, and Simmons Bedding). Spring Air was founded in 1926 by mattress innovator Francis Karr, who introduced an offset-coil that adjusts to a sleeper's weight. It merged with its largest licensee, Florida-based Consolidated Bedding, and folded in a half-dozen other licensees in mid-2007.

The resulting entity was headed by Robert Hellyer, a veteran of both Simmons Bedding and Sealy's Stearns & Foster division.

455

Spring Air and Consolidated Bedding consummated the deal to streamline their operations, as well as consolidate their research and development, sales, and marketing efforts. It also places the merged company in a position to maintain and build on its status as a leading mattress brand. As part of the deal, Spring Air gained manufacturing facilities in Alabama, Colorado, Georgia, Massachusetts, Utah, and Washington.

Blaming a challenging business climate, the company chose in 2008 to close two manufacturing plants (Phoenix, St. Louis) and move its headquarters from the Chicago area to Tampa, Florida. In September Hellyer resigned as CEO. Initially EVP Kevin Damewood and COO Steve Cumbow filled in for Hellyer as chief executive, but that didn't last long. By October 2008, Damewood had left and Cumbow was named interim CEO.

The company is also looking to India for future growth. Wanting to capture a piece of the Indian bedding market, which is valued at $400 million, Spring Air worked a deal with its Middle East licensee, W.J. Towell & Co. Through a joint venture called Spring Air India, the company hopes to produce 500 pieces daily from three manufacturing plants by 2010, as well as operate some 30 retail showrooms under the Spring Air brand name.

EXECUTIVES

Chairman: Michael Michienzi
Acting CEO: Steve Cumbow
SVP Manufacturing: Jan Wettergren
SVP Human Resources: Greg Moore
SVP Sales (Lacey, WA and Salt Lake City): Charles Dietiker
SVP Sales, (Columbus, OH and Dallas): Chad Megard
SVP Sales (Los Angeles): Howard Glant
SVP Sales (Chelsea, MA, New Brunswick, NJ, Atlanta, and Tampa): Robert Patten
VP Merchandising: Richard Fleck
VP Human Resources: Katie Sems

LOCATIONS

HQ: Spring Air Company
500 S. Falkenburg Rd., Tampa, FL 33619
Phone: 813-651-2233
Web: www.springair.com

PRODUCTS/OPERATIONS

Selected Collections

Back Supporter
ComfortFlex
Four Seasons
Posture Comfort

COMPETITORS

Sealy
Select Comfort
Serta
Simmons Bedding
Tempur-Pedic

HISTORICAL FINANCIALS
Company Type: Private

Income Statement

FYE: December 31

	REVENUE ($ mil.)	NET INCOME ($ mil.)	NET PROFIT MARGIN	EMPLOYEES
12/07	650	—	—	3,100
12/06	649	—	—	3,100
12/05	638	—	—	3,100
12/04	619	—	—	—
Annual Growth	1.6%	—	—	0.0%

Revenue History

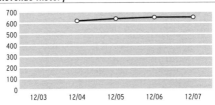

SRI International

With *BusinessWeek* magazine calling SRI International "Silicon Valley's soul," the not-for-profit think tank ponders advances in biotechnology, chemicals and energy, computer science, electronics, and public policy — and ways to commercialize those advances. SRI focuses on technology research and development, business strategies, and issues analysis. It has patents and patent applications in such areas as information sciences, software development, communications, robotics, and pharmaceuticals. SRI's clients have included Visa, Samsung, NASA, and the US Department of Defense. Originally founded in 1946 as Stanford Research Institute, SRI became fully independent of Stanford University in 1970.

The organization has conceived such innovations as the computer mouse, magnetic encoding for checks, and high-definition television, not to mention some of the foundations of personal computing, the Internet, and stealth technology. Its 1,400 employees (including about 600 scientists and researchers) work at research centers worldwide.

SRI's for-profit subsidiary the Sarnoff Corporation was formed in 1942 as RCA Laboratories. Formerly a unit of General Electric and gifted to SRI in 1987, Sarnoff specializes in creating and commercializing electronic, biomedical, and information technologies. SRI and Sarnoff together have spun off about two dozen companies.

In order to complement its biosciences division, SRI bought Quality Clinical Labs (QCL) in mid-2006. QCL is a California-based clinical pathology analysis center, specializing in clinical hematology and chemistry evaluations.

EXECUTIVES

Chairman: Samuel H. Armacost, age 68
President, CEO, and Director: Curtis R. Carlson, age 60
SVP and CFO: Thomas J. Furst
VP Biosciences Division: Walter H. Moos, age 53
VP Corporate and Marketing Communications: Alice R. Resnick
VP Engineering and Systems Division: John W. Prausa
VP Human Resources: Jean E. (Jeanie) Tooker
VP Information and Computing Sciences Division: William Mark
VP Legal and Business Affairs and General Counsel: Richard Abramson
VP Policy Division: Dennis Beatrice
VP Ventures and Strategic Programs: Norman D. Winarsky
Auditors: PricewaterhouseCoopers LLP

LOCATIONS

HQ: SRI International
333 Ravenswood Ave., Menlo Park, CA 94025
Phone: 650-859-2000   **Fax:** 650-326-5512
Web: www.sri.com

PRODUCTS/OPERATIONS

Selected Research Areas

Automation and robotics
Automotive and commercial equipment technologies
Chemistry, materials, and applied physics
Communications
Defense and intelligence
Homeland defense and national security
Information science and software development
Medical devices
Product engineering
Pharmaceutical services
Policy
Sensors and measurement systems

COMPETITORS

Aerospace Corporation
Battelle Memorial
Bayer Corp.
CACI International
Charles Stark Draper Laboratory
DaVinci Institute
DuPont
Kendle
LECG
MIT
MITRE
PAREXEL
Quintiles Transnational
RAND
Research Triangle Institute
Southwest Research Institute
Teknowledge
University of California
Wellcome Trust
Westat

HISTORICAL FINANCIALS
Company Type: Not-for-profit

Income Statement

FYE: December 31

	REVENUE ($ mil.)	NET INCOME ($ mil.)	NET PROFIT MARGIN	EMPLOYEES
12/07	450	—	—	1,600
12/06	411	—	—	1,400
12/05	286	—	—	1,400
Annual Growth	25.4%	—	—	6.9%

Revenue History

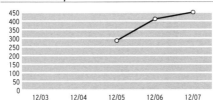

Stanford University

Prospectors panning for gold in higher education can strike it rich at Stanford University. The school is one of the premier educational institutions in the US, boasting respected programs in business, engineering, law, and medicine, among others. The school serves more than 19,700 students and has about 1,000 faculty members. A private institution, Stanford supports its activities through a $17 billion endowment, one of the largest in the US. The university was established in 1885 by Leland Stanford Sr., who made his fortune selling provisions to California gold miners. Leland Sr. and his wife, Jane, founded the school in memory of their son, Leland Jr., who died of typhoid at age 15.

Stanford is also widely recognized as one of the top US research universities and sports a host of laboratories and research centers, including the Stanford Institute for Economic Policy Research and the Stanford Linear Accelerator Center. Its faculty members include around 20 Nobel Prize winners, a handful of Pulitzer Prize winners, and around 20 National Medal of Science winners.

The university has received sizable donations from notable alumni such as Jerry Yang (co-founder of Yahoo!), Charles Schwab, Texas billionaire Robert Bass, and William Hewlett (of Hewlett-Packard, who has since died). The $400 million gift by the Hewlett Foundation is the largest in university history.

HISTORY

In 1885 Leland Stanford Sr. and his wife, Jane, established Leland Stanford Junior University in memory of their son Leland Jr., who had died of typhoid at age 15. Stanford made his fortune selling provisions to California gold miners and as a major investor in the Central Pacific Railroad, one of the two companies that built the first transcontinental railway. It was Stanford who connected the tracks laid eastward by Central Pacific and westward by Union Pacific with a gold railway spike in 1869. He also served as California's governor and as a US senator.

The Stanfords donated more than 8,000 acres of land from their own estate to establish an unconventional university, one that was coeducational and nondenominational with a focus on preparing students for a profession. Stanford opened its doors in 1891 to a freshman class of 559 students. It awarded its first degrees four years later, and among the graduates was future US president Herbert Hoover.

Leland Stanford Sr. died in 1893, and in 1903 Jane Stanford turned the university over to the board of trustees. After weathering significant damage in 1906 from the Great San Francisco Earthquake, the university established a law school in 1908 and its medical school five years later. During WWI the university mobilized half of its students into the Students' Army Training Corps. The School of Education was established in 1917, followed by the School of Engineering and Graduate School of Business eight years later. In 1933 a rule limiting the number of women admitted to Stanford was abolished.

Wallace Sterling, who became president of the university after WWII, initiated the transformation of Stanford into a world-class institution with a reputation for teaching and research. Under Sterling the university initiated development on the Stanford Research Park.

In 1958 Stanford opened its first overseas campus (near Stuttgart, Germany), and the Stanford Medical Center was completed the following year. The university created a computer science department in 1965 and two years later opened the Stanford Linear Accelerator Center dedicated to physics research.

Donald Kennedy became president in 1980. The next year students voted to abandon the university's official mascot, the "Indians," in response to concerns raised by Native American students. The nickname "Cardinal" was adopted in its place. The term refers to the school's color, cardinal red.

Also during Kennedy's tenure, it was revealed that Stanford had overcharged the Office of Naval Research for indirect costs associated with research. The scandal led to Kennedy's resignation in 1992, and in 1994 the Office of Naval Research and the university settled a related lawsuit for $1.2 million and a stipulation that Stanford had not committed any wrongdoing. Gerhard Casper succeeded Kennedy as president.

In 1997 Stanford and the University of California at San Francisco combined their teaching hospitals in a public/private merger. Two years later after the controversial experiment had harmed both hospitals' financial picture, the merger was terminated, and the two hospitals agreed to go their separate ways.

In 1999 Casper announced his intention to resign as president. The school tapped provost John Hennessy as his replacement. Soon after his appointment in 2000, Hennessey launched a campaign to raise $1 billion. Former Stanford professor and Netscape co-founder Jim Clark donated $150 million later that year to support Stanford's biomedical engineering and sciences program. The school also launched a new company, SKOLAR, which developed an online search engine for the medical industry.

EXECUTIVES

President: John L. Hennessy, age 55
Provost: John W. Etchemendy
Vice Provost Graduate Education: Patricia Gumport
Vice Provost and Dean Research: Ann M. Arvin
Vice Provost Undergraduate Education: John Bravman
VP Business Affairs and CFO:
  Randall S. (Randy) Livingston, age 54
VP and General Counsel: Debra Zumwalt
VP Public Affairs: David Demarest
VP Development: Martin Shell
Associate VP and Director University Communications:
  Alan Acosta
Dean Graduate School of Business:
  Robert L. (Bob) Joss, age 66
Executive Director Human Resources: Diane Peck
Executive Director Information Technology Services:
  Bill Clebsch
Student Affairs Officer Career Development Center:
  Beverley Principal
**University Librarian and Director Academic
  Information Resources, Library:** Micheal A. Keller
Auditors: PricewaterhouseCoopers LLP

LOCATIONS

HQ: Stanford University
  655 Serra St., Stanford, CA 94305
Phone: 650-723-2300   **Fax:** 650-725-0247
Web: www.stanford.edu

PRODUCTS/OPERATIONS

Selected Schools

Undergraduate
  School of Earth Sciences
  School of Engineering
  School of Humanities and Sciences
Graduate
  School of Business
  School of Earth Sciences
  School of Engineering
  School of Education
  School of Humanities and Sciences
  School of Law
  School of Medicine

Selected Interdisciplinary Research Centers

Alliance for Innovative Manufacturing at Stanford
Center for Computer Research in Music and Acoustics
Center for Integrated Facility Engineering
Center for Integrated Systems

Selected Laboratories, Centers, and Institutes

Center for Research on Information Storage Materials
Center for the Study of Language and Information
Edward L. Ginzton Laboratory
Institute for International Studies
Institute for Research on Women and Gender
John and Terry Levin Center for Public Service and
  Public Interest Law
Stanford Center for Buddhist Studies
Stanford Humanities Center
Stanford Institute for Economic Policy Research
W.W. Hansen Experimental Physics Laboratory

Selected Medical Research Facilities

Center for Biomedical Ethics
Center for Research in Disease Prevention
Human Genome Center
Richard M. Lucas Center for Magnetic Resonance
  Spectroscopy & Imaging
Sleep Disorders Center

Other Selected Research Facilities

Hoover Institution on War, Revolution and Peace
Hopkins Marine Station
Martin Luther King, Jr. Papers Project
Stanford Linear Accelerator Center

Staple Cotton Cooperative

Get some new cotton underwear for a gift? Chances are Staple Cotton Cooperative Association (Staplcotn) grew the cotton your new skivvies are made of. Most of the co-op's yield is sold to the US textile industry to make men's knit underwear, T-shirts, sheets, towels, and denim. Founded in 1921 by Mississippi cotton producer Oscar Bledsoe and 10 other Delta growers, Staplcotn sells almost 4 million bales of cotton annually, both domestically and overseas. It serves its approximately 4,600 member/owners in 10 southern states. The co-op's Stapldiscount unit offers members low-interest loans for equipment, buildings, and land. Staplcotn has 14 regional offices in six states and 16 warehouses in three states.

Staplcotn's customers include Fruit of the Loom, Levi Strauss, and Hanes.

EXECUTIVES

Chairman; Chairman, Stapldiscount: Ben Lamensdorf
President, CEO, and Director; President and CEO, Stapldiscount: Woods E. Eastland
VP and CFO: Charles Robertson
VP, Cotton Services: Sterling P. Jones
VP, Human Resources, and Secretary: Eugene A. (Gene) Stansel Jr.
VP, Marketing: Meredith B. Allen
VP, Sales Operations: David C. Camp
VP, Systems and Controls: L. A. (Larry) Gnemi
VP, Warehousing: Shane Stephens
VP and COO, Stapldiscount: J. D. Hoover
General Counsel: Kenneth E. Downs

LOCATIONS

HQ: Staple Cotton Cooperative Association
214 W. Market St., Greenwood, MS 38930
Phone: 662-453-6231   **Fax:** 662-453-4622
Web: www.staplcotn.com

COMPETITORS

Alabama Farmers Cooperative
Calcot
Cargill
Dunavant Enterprises
International Cotton Marketing
JB Cotton
J.G. Boswell Co.
King Ranch
Plains Cotton
Southern States
Tennessee Farmers Co-op
Weil Brothers Cotton

State Farm Mutual Automobile Insurance

Like an enormous corporation, State Farm is everywhere. The leading US personal lines property/casualty company (by premiums), State Farm Mutual Automobile Insurance Company is the #1 provider of auto insurance. It also is the leading home insurer and offers non-medical health and life insurance through its subsidiary companies. Its products are marketed via some 17,000 agents in the US and Canada. Competition has increased with the fall of barriers between the banking, securities, and insurance industries. State Farm's efforts to diversify include a federal savings bank charter (State Farm Bank) that offers consumer and business loans through its agents and by phone, mail, and the Internet.

The company also established itself as a financial services provider in 1999, and its mutual funds have since built up $3.9 billion in assets. However, insurance is still its main source of income. And, while State Farm already insures 15% of the automobiles on US roads, it is scrambling to hang on to that much while attempting to grab an even larger portion of the pie. Competition and market weakness has spurred the company to refocus its efforts on the segment.

Meanwhile, homeowners insurance has been a thornier issue. State Farm still insures more than 20% of the single-family homes in the US, but the insurer stopped writing new homeowners policies in some 15 states in an effort to improve profitability.

Hurricanes Katrina, Wilma, and Rita brought State Farm customer claims totaling $6.3 billion in property and casualty losses. For residents along the Gulf Coast, at first it seemed like State Farm would stay put. However, as the claims keep rolling in, the company has rewritten its underwriting guidelines to limit its risk. New homeowner policies in places such as New Orleans will have steeper deductibles and less coverage, and the company has completely stopped offering new homeowners and commercial property policies in the state of Mississippi.

A quieter problem looms ahead for the company's future: its aging agency force is readying for retirement, and fewer younger agents are signing up to sell insurance. It is an industry-wide trend that State Farm is addressing with more aggressive recruitment efforts.

Since its founding, the group's companies have been run by only two families: the Mecherles (1922-54) and the Rusts (1954-present).

HISTORY

Retired farmer George Mecherle formed State Farm Mutual Automobile Insurance in Bloomington, Illinois, in 1922. State Farm served only members of farm bureaus and farm mutual insurance companies, charging a one-time membership fee and a premium to protect an automobile against loss or damage.

Unlike most competitors, State Farm offered six-month premium payments. The insurer billed and collected renewal premiums from its home office, relieving the agent of the task. In addition, State Farm determined auto rates by a simple seven-class system, while competitors varied rates for each model.

State Farm in 1926 started City and Village Mutual Automobile Insurance to insure nonfarmers' autos; it became part of the company in 1927. Between 1927 and 1931 it introduced borrowed-car protection, wind coverage, and insurance for vehicles used to transport schoolchildren.

State Farm expanded to California in 1928 and formed State Farm Life Insurance the next year. In 1935 it established State Farm Fire Insurance. George Mecherle became chairman in 1937, and his son Ramond became president. In 1939 George challenged agents to write "A Million or More (auto policies) by '44." State Farm saw a 110% increase in policies.

During the 1940s State Farm focused on urban areas after most of the farm bureaus formed their own insurance companies. In the late 1940s and 1950s, it moved to a full-time agency force. Homeowners coverage was added to the insurer's offerings under the leadership of Adlai Rust, who led State Farm from 1954 until 1958, when Edward Rust took over. He died in 1985; his son Edward Jr. currently holds the top spot.

Between 1974 and 1987 the insurer was hit by several gender-discrimination suits (a 1992 settlement awarded $157 million to 814 women). State Farm has since tried to hire more women and minorities.

Serial disasters in the early 1990s, including Hurricane Andrew and the Los Angeles riots, proved costly. The 1994 Northridge earthquake alone generated more than $2.5 billion in claims and contributed to a 72% decline in earnings.

State Farm — the top US home insurer since the mid-1960s — canceled 62,500 residential policies in South Florida in 1996 to cut potential hurricane loss an estimated 11%. In response, Florida's insurance regulators rescinded a previously approved rate hike. That year the company agreed to open more urban neighborhood offices to settle a discrimination suit brought by the Department of Housing and Urban Development, which accused State Farm of discriminating against potential customers in minority-populated areas.

Legal trouble continued. In 1997 State Farm settled with a California couple who alleged the company forged policyholders' signatures on forms declining coverage and concealed evidence to avoid paying earthquake damage claims. That year a policyholder sued to keep State Farm from "wasting company assets" on President Clinton's legal defense against Paula Jones' sexual harassment charges (Clinton held a State Farm personal liability policy).

Relations with its sales force already rocky, State Farm in 1998 proposed to reduce up-front commissions and cut base pay in favor of incentives for customer retention and cross-selling. Reduced auto premiums and increased catastrophe claims from across the US eroded State Farm's bottom line that year. A federal thrift charter obtained in 1998 let the company launch banking operations the next year.

In 2000 the company was hit with a class-action lawsuit about its denial of personal-injury claims; previous suits had been individual cases. In 2002 State Farm Indemnity, the company's auto-only New Jersey subsidiary, withdrew from the Garden State's auto insurance market but began phasing back into the market in 2005.

Like all reinsurers, State Farm's reinsurance business was tested by the 2005 hurricane season. It underwrote losses of $2.8 billion.

EXECUTIVES

Chairman and CEO: Edward B. (Ed) Rust Jr., age 57
Vice Chairman, CFO, and Treasurer: Michael L. Tipsord
Vice Chairman and Chief Administrative Officer: James E. (Jim) Rutrough
Vice Chairman and Chief Agency and Marketing Officer: Michael C. Davidson
SEVP Financial Services: Jack W. North
EVP, General Counsel, and Secretary: Kim M. Brunner
EVP: Brian V. Boyden
EVP: Barbara Cowden
EVP: William K. (Bill) King
EVP: Willie G. Brown
EVP: Deborah Traskell
SVP Investments: Paul N. Eckley
VP Marketing: Pam El
VP Mortgages and Real Estate: David C. Graves
VP Fixed Income: Donald E. (Don) Heltner
VP Claims: Susan Hood
VP Agency: Craig Allen
VP Agency Recruiting: Carra Simmons
VP Human Resources: Mary Schmidt
VP Strategic Resources: Laurette Stiles
VP Securities Products: Philip Hawkins
President and CEO, State Farm Bank: Stanley R. (Stan) Ommen
Auditors: PricewaterhouseCoopers LLP

LOCATIONS

HQ: State Farm Mutual Automobile Insurance Company
1 State Farm Plaza, Bloomington, IL 61710
Phone: 309-766-2311 **Fax:** 309-766-3621
Web: www.statefarm.com

PRODUCTS/OPERATIONS

Selected Subsidiaries

State Farm Bank, FSB
State Farm County Mutual Insurance Company of Texas
(high-risk auto insurance)
State Farm Fire and Casualty Company (homeowners,
boat owners, and commercial insurance)
State Farm Florida Insurance Company (homeowners
and renters insurance)
State Farm General Insurance Company (property
insurance)
State Farm Indemnity Company (auto insurance in New
Jersey)
State Farm Investment Management Corp
State Farm Life and Accident Assurance Company
State Farm Life Insurance Company
State Farm Lloyds
State Farm VP Management Corp

COMPETITORS

AIG
Allstate
American Family Insurance
Berkshire Hathaway
CNA Financial
COUNTRY Financial
GEICO
GMAC Insurance
The Hartford
Liberty Mutual
MetLife
Nationwide
Philadelphia Consolidated
Progressive Corporation
Prudential
Safeco
Torchmark
USAA
W. R. Berkley

HISTORICAL FINANCIALS

Company Type: Mutual company

Income Statement				FYE: December 31
	REVENUE ($ mil.)	NET INCOME ($ mil.)	NET PROFIT MARGIN	EMPLOYEES
12/07	61,600	5,460	8.9%	68,000
12/06	60,500	5,320	8.8%	68,000
12/05	59,200	3,240	5.5%	79,200
12/04	58,800	5,300	9.0%	79,200
12/03	56,100	2,800	5.0%	79,000
Annual Growth	2.4%	18.2%	—	(3.7%)

Net Income History

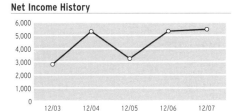

State University of New York

SUNY days are ahead for many New Yorkers seeking higher education. With an enrollment of more than 420,000 students, The State University of New York (SUNY) is vying with California State University System for the title of largest university system in the US. Most students are residents of New York State (about 40% of all New York State high school graduates enroll at SUNY institutions). SUNY maintains 64 campuses around the state, including four university centers, 13 university colleges, 30 community colleges, eight technical colleges, two medical centers, and colleges of ceramics and optometry.

Offering more than 7,600 degree and certificate programs, SUNY confers some 80,000 diplomas each year, including nearly 14,000 post-graduate degrees.

HISTORY

The State University of New York was organized in 1948, but it traces its roots back to several institutions founded in the 19th century. In 1844 the New York state legislature authorized the creation of the Albany Normal School, which was charged with educating the state's secondary school teachers. Two years later the University of Buffalo was chartered to provide academic, theological, legal, and medical studies. More normal schools later were founded between 1861 and 1889 in Brockport, Buffalo, Cortland, Fredonia, Geneseo, New Paltz, Oneonta, Oswego, Plattsburgh, and Potsdam.

In the early 1900s the state established several agricultural colleges, including schools in Canton (1907), Alfred (1908), Morrisville (1910), Farmingdale (1912), and Cobleskill (1916). New York also set up several schools as units of Cornell University, including colleges of veterinary medicine (1894), agriculture (1909), home economics (1925), and industrial and labor relations (1945).

After WWII, veterans began to fill US colleges and universities, taking advantage of the GI Bill to secure a college education. The legislature set up SUNY in 1948 to consolidate 29 institutions under a single board of trustees charged with meeting the growing demand. The board coordinated the state colleges into a single body and established four-year liberal arts colleges, professional and graduate schools, and research centers. During the 1950s and 1960s new campuses were created at Binghamton, Stony Brook, Old Westbury, Purchase, and Utica/Rome, and enrollment began to take off, jumping from 30,000 in 1955 to 63,000 in 1959.

By the early 1970s SUNY had more than 320,000 students at 72 institutions. But budget constraints later that decade led to higher tuition, reduced enrollment goals, and employment cutbacks. In 1975 eight New York City community colleges were transferred to City University. SUNY's enrollment began growing again during the 1980s, reaching more than 400,000 by 1990. Early in the decade, the institution began implementing SUNY 2000, a plan that called for increasing access to education and diversifying undergraduate studies. Following his election in 1994, Governor George Pataki proposed more than $550 million in cuts to the SUNY system.

In 1997 John Ryan replaced Thomas Bartlett as chancellor. The following year SUNY became the exclusive sponsor of The College Channel, a guide to colleges and college life aimed at high school juniors and seniors and broadcast by PRIMEDIA's Channel One. In 1999 the governor's budget director, Robert King, was named chancellor to replace the retiring Bartlett. King challenged SUNY administrators and the state to increase levels of funding to help keep the university competitive against other top-flight institutions. In 2000 SUNY faced rising budget shortfalls at its teaching hospitals, in part because money was being siphoned off to other areas. That year King announced a set of initiatives to raise an additional $1.5 billion in federal research grants and $1 billion in private donations over five years.

King retired as the university's chancellor in June 2005.

EXECUTIVES

Interim Chancellor: John B. Clark
Provost and Vice Chancellor for Academic Affairs: Risa I. Palm
Vice Chancellor for Community Colleges: Dennis Golladay
Vice Chancellor and Secretary; President, Research Foundation: John J. O'Connor
Senior Associate and Vice Chancellor for University Relations: Michael C. Trunzo
University Counsel and Vice Chancellor for Legal Affairs: Nicholas Rostow
Associate Vice Chancellor for Finance and Administration, Chief of Staff, and Chief of Human Resources: Curtis L. Lloyd
Assistant Vice Chancellor for Employee Relations: Raymond (Ray) Haines
University Controller: Patrick J. Wiater
University Auditor: Michael Abbott
Program Director, Office of Business and Industry Relations: Peter Thomas
Director of Employee Relations: Liesl K. Zwicklbauer
Director Legislative Relations: James J. Campbell
Director University Relations: Stacey Hengsterman
General Manager Construction Fund: Philip Wood
Auditors: KPMG LLP

LOCATIONS

HQ: The State University of New York
State University Plaza, 353 Broadway,
Albany, NY 12246
Phone: 518-443-5555 **Fax:** 518-443-5322
Web: www.suny.edu

PRODUCTS/OPERATIONS

Selected Institutions

Colleges of Technology
Alfred State
Canton
Cobleskill
Delhi
Farmingdale State
Maritime College
Morrisville State
SUNYIT
Doctoral Degree-Granting Institutions
College of Agriculture and Life Sciences at Cornell
University
College of Ceramics at Alfred University
College of Human Ecology at Cornell University
College of Industrial and Labor Relations at Cornell
University
College of Optometry
College of Veterinary Medicine at Cornell University
Downstate Medical Center (Brooklyn)
School of Industrial and Labor Relations at Cornell
University
Upstate Medical University (Syracuse)

Stater Bros.

Stater Bros. has no shortage of major league rivals, operating in the same Southern California markets as Kroger-owned Ralphs and Safeway-owned Vons. Stater Bros. Holdings operates about 165 full service Stater Bros. Markets in some six counties, primarily in the Riverside and San Bernardino areas. About 25 of the regional chain's grocery stores host Super Rx Pharmacies. The grocery chain also owns and operates Heartland Farms, provider of Knudsen Dairy products to Southern California and one of the state's largest milk processors. Founded in 1936 by twin brothers Leo and Cleo Stater, Stater Bros. is owned by chairman and CEO Jack Brown through La Cadena Investments.

Competition from the grocery giants, and the purchase of stores from Albertsons, have put a strain on the company's profits. To distinguish itself from rivals, the chain refuses to offer promotional games and frequent shopper cards, boasting everyday low prices and chainwide temporary price reductions (called Stater Savers) instead. Stater Bros. is bracing itself for intense competition from Wal-Mart and SAM'S CLUB stores, which are becoming more common in the area. To better compete with Wal-Mart, Stater Bros.'s Super RX Pharmacy locations began offering generic drugs for $4 per prescription in July 2008.

Stater Bros. Holdings is the largest privately held supermarket chain in Southern California. The company plans to open three to six new stores per year. The firm opened a new distribution center on the site of its new corporate headquarters in San Bernardino in September 2008.

HISTORY

In 1936, at age 23, Cleo Stater and his twin brother Leo mortgaged a Chevrolet to make a down payment on a modest grocery store where Cleo had been working for five years in their hometown of Yucaipa, California. Later that year the brothers bought their second grocery in the nearby community of Redlands. Their younger brother Lavoy soon joined them to help build the company. In 1938 the brothers opened the first Stater Bros. market in Colton; by 1939 they had a chain of four stores.

The small, family-owned grocery chain continued to grow. In 1948 Stater Bros. opened its first supermarket (which was several times larger than its other stores and had its own parking lot) in Riverside. By 1950 the company had 12 stores.

Stater Bros. consolidated its offices and warehouse in Colton in the early 1960s and continued its expansion into nearby communities. By 1964 it operated 27 supermarkets in 18 cities in Los Angeles, Orange, Riverside, and San Bernardino counties. In 1968 the brothers sold the company's 35 stores to Long Beach, California-based petroleum services provider Petrolane for $33 million. Lavoy succeeded Cleo as president.

As a division of Petrolane, Stater Bros. kept growing. In the 1970s the company introduced a new store design that expanded sales area but required less land and a smaller building. The number of stores more than doubled (to over 80) between 1968 and 1979, when Lavoy retired.

Ron Burkle, VP of Administration for Petrolane, and his father, Joe, president of Stater Bros., attempted to buy the chain for $100 million in 1981. Infuriated by the low bid, Petrolane fired Ron and demoted his father, who left that year. Jack Brown was named president in his place. Petrolane sold the chain in 1983 to La Cadena Investments, a private company that included Brown and other top Stater Bros. executives.

Leo died in 1985. That year the company went public to reduce debt from the 1983 LBO and to provide funds for an extensive expansion plan. It also incorporated as Stater Bros. Inc. In 1986 a proxy fight for control of the company erupted between Brown's La Cadena group and chairman Bernard Garrett, who owned about 41% of Stater Bros. Brown had been suspended as president and CEO (Joe Burkle returned in his place), but Los Angeles-based investment firm Craig Corp. bought Garrett's stake and Brown returned; he was later elected chairman. That year Stater Bros. also became a co-owner in Santee Dairies with Hughes Markets (now part of Kroger).

The next year Craig and Stater Bros. executives took the grocery chain private again. Burkle bought a 9% stake in Craig in 1989 through Yucaipa Capital Partners. Also in 1987 Craig reduced its stake in Stater Bros., transferring some stock to La Cadena. Stater Bros. Holdings was created as a parent company for the grocery chain.

Stater Bros. expressed an interest in buying rival Alpha Beta stores when they were put up for sale, but Yucaipa Companies bought them in 1991. Craig considered selling its stake in Stater Bros. in 1992; it finally sold its half of the company to La Cadena in 1996.

In 1999 Stater Bros. acquired 33 Albertsons and 10 Lucky stores, as well as one store site. (The FTC required Albertsons to sell the stores in order to acquire American Stores, Lucky's parent.) The acquisition and the early retirement of debt resulted in its 1999 losses. In September 2001 company co-founder Cleo Stater died.

In early 2002 the company announced a partnership with Krispy Kreme Doughnuts to offer the treats at selected Stater Bros. supermarkets. In 2003, Stater Bros. introduced Topco private-label brand merchandise in its stores.

In February 2004 Santee Dairies became a wholly owned subsidiary of Stater Bros. when the grocery chain acquired Kroger's 50% stake in the operation.

Stater Bros. sales rose by about 5% during a four-and-a-half month long strike by employees of rivals Albertsons, Kroger, and Vons. The dispute, which diverted shoppers from those stores to Stater Bros. markets, ended in March 2004. In October Don Baker was promoted to president and COO of Stater Bros. Previously, Baker was EVP and COO of the company.

In mid-2006 the company launched a new line of 100-plus natural and organic products called "Full Circle." In September Jim Lee replaced Baker as president and COO of the regional grocery chain.

In September 2007 the grocery chain moved its headquaters to the site of the former Norton Air Force Base in San Bernardino.

EXECUTIVES

Chairman and CEO: Jack H. Brown, age 68, $1,551,000 pay
Vice Chairman: Thomas W. Field Jr., age 74
President and COO: James W. (Jim) Lee, age 56, $314,000 pay (prior to promotion)
EVP and CFO: Phillip J. (Phil) Smith, age 60, $277,000 pay
EVP, Retail Operations and Administration: George Frahm, age 54
EVP, Marketing: Dennis L. McIntyre, age 47, $295,000 pay
VP, Corporate Affairs: Susan Atkinson
VP, Human Resources: Jerry Finazzo
VP, Produce: Roger Schroeder
Secretary and Director: Bruce D. Varner, age 71
Director, Grocery: Tom Finn
Director, Sales and Marketing: Cindy Schmitz
Auditors: Ernst & Young LLP

LOCATIONS

HQ: Stater Bros. Holdings Inc.
   301 S. Tippecanoe Ave., San Bernardino, CA 92408
Phone: 909-733-5000   **Fax:** 909-733-3930
Web: www.staterbros.com

2008 Stores

	No.
San Bernardino County	51
Riverside County	46
Orange County	30
Los Angeles County	26
San Diego County	10
Kern County	2
Total	**165**

PRODUCTS/OPERATIONS

Selected Departments and Products

Bakery
Dairy products
Delicatessen
Floral
Fresh produce
Frozen foods
General merchandise
Health & beauty aids
Liquor
Meats
Pharmacy
Seafood

COMPETITORS

Arden Group
Costco Wholesale
Longs Drug
Ralphs
SAM'S CLUB
Save Mart
Smart & Final
Tesco
Trader Joe's
Vons
Walgreen
Wal-Mart
Whole Foods

HISTORICAL FINANCIALS

Company Type: Private

Income Statement				FYE: Last Sunday in September
	REVENUE ($ mil.)	NET INCOME ($ mil.)	NET PROFIT MARGIN	EMPLOYEES
9/07	3,674	49	1.3%	18,000
9/06	3,508	26	0.7%	17,800
9/05	3,372	26	0.8%	16,300
9/04	3,705	72	1.9%	15,700
9/03	2,754	10	0.4%	13,500
Annual Growth	7.5%	48.7%	—	7.5%

Net Income History

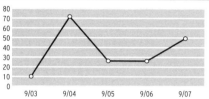

Station Casinos

When the train pulls out of this station, you might find you've left a little money behind. Station Casinos owns and operates nine hotel casinos in the Las Vegas area under the Station and Fiesta brand names, targeting mainly local gamblers. It also operates eight smaller casinos in the Vegas area. Properties include 50% interests in Green Valley Ranch Resort Spa Casino, Barley's Casino & Brewing Company, The Greens Gaming and Dining, and Renata's Casino. The company also manages the Thunder Valley Casino in Sacramento, California, for the United Auburn Indian Community. Investment firms Eurazeo and Colony Capital, along with Frank Fertitta III (CEO) and his brother Lorenzo (president), own the company.

Station's properties feature hotels, as well as slot machines, table games, and amenities such as restaurants and entertainment. While its Vegas properties are all much smaller than the glitzy operations on the Las Vegas Strip, Station dominates in the market for local gamblers, which the company feels is a more stable business than relying on the tourist trade.

The company in 2007 was acquired by a private equity investor group that includes members of the founding Fertitta family for about $5.4 billion. The Fertitta brothers are also majority owners of Ultimate Fighting Championship, which stages mixed martial arts fights in arenas across the country.

EXECUTIVES

Chairman, President, and CEO: Frank J. Fertitta III, age 46, $2,156,250 pay
Vice Chairman: Lorenzo J. Fertitta, age 39, $1,667,500 pay
EVP and Chief Development Officer: Scott M. Nielson, age 50, $920,000 pay
EVP, General Counsel, and Secretary: Richard J. Haskins, age 44
EVP, Chief Accounting Officer, and Treasurer: Thomas M. Friel, age 44

VP Human Resources: Valerie Murzl
Director Corporate Communications: Lori Nelson
Manager Public Relations: Morgan Gaspard
Auditors: Ernst & Young LLP

LOCATIONS

HQ: Station Casinos, Inc.
1505 S. Pavilion Center Dr., Las Vegas, NV 89102
Phone: 702-495-3000   **Fax:** 702-495-3530
Web: www.stationcasinos.com

PRODUCTS/OPERATIONS

2007 Sales

	$ mil.	% of total
Casino	1,031.0	66
Food and beverage	248.6	16
Room	112.4	7
Management fees	87.8	6
Other	77.3	5
Adjustments	(110.1)	—
Total	**1,447.0**	**100**

Selected Casino Operations

Barley's Casino & Brewing Company (50%; Henderson, NV)
Boulder Station (Las Vegas)
Fiesta Casino Hotel (Las Vegas)
Green Valley Ranch Station Casino (50%; Henderson, NV)
The Greens Gaming and Dining (50%; Henderson, NV)
Palace Station (Las Vegas)
Red Rock Casino, Resort and Spa (Las Vegas)
The Reserve Hotel and Casino (Henderson, NV)
Santa Fe Station (Las Vegas)
Sunset Station (Las Vegas)
Texas Station (Las Vegas)
Wild Wild West Gambling Hall & Hotel (Las Vegas)
Wildfire Casino (Las Vegas)

COMPETITORS

Ameristar Casinos
Boyd Gaming
Harrah's Entertainment
Las Vegas Sands
MGM MIRAGE
Pinnacle Entertainment

HISTORICAL FINANCIALS

Company Type: Private

Income Statement				FYE: December 31
	REVENUE ($ mil.)	NET INCOME ($ mil.)	NET PROFIT MARGIN	EMPLOYEES
12/07	1,447	(376)	—	14,500
12/06	1,339	110	8.2%	14,600
12/05	1,109	162	14.6%	11,500
12/04	987	66	6.7%	10,800
12/03	858	44	5.2%	10,300
Annual Growth	14.0%	—	—	8.9%

Net Income History

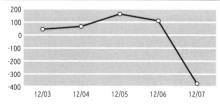

Stewart & Stevenson

Houstonian Stewart & Stevenson helps its customers quench their thirst for Texas Tea. The company is a leading supplier of equipment used in oilfield services. Stewart & Stevenson operates three divisions: Equipment (oil well stimulation, coil tubing, engines, and material-handling equipment), Aftermarket Parts and Service (parts and service for customers in oil and gas, marine, power generation, mining, and construction industries), and Rental (rental of generators, material-handling equipment, and air compressors). Customers in the oil and gas services industry include Schlumberger, Weatherford International, and BJ Services. Chairman Hushang Ansary controls the company.

In 2006 Stewart & Stevenson Services sold essentially all of its equipment, aftermarket parts and services, and rental operations to Houston businessman Hushang Ansary for about $277 million. Ansary then formed a new company, Stewart & Stevenson LLC.

In 2007 the company acquired Canada-based oil services equipment manufacturer Crown Energy Technologies for $70.5 million.

EXECUTIVES

Chairman: Hushang Ansary, age 80, $2,500,000 pay
Vice Chairman: Frank C. Carlucci, age 77
CEO and Director: Robert L. (Bob) Hargrave, age 66, $44,383 pay (partial-year salary)
President, COO, and Director: Gary W. Stratulate, age 51, $1,000,000 pay
VP Human Resources: Charles T. Hatcher
VP, CFO, and Secretary: Jeffery W. (Jeff) Merecka, age 41, $488,462 pay
VP Domestic Sales and Aftermarket: Kenneth W. Simmons, age 53
Auditors: Ernst & Young LLP

LOCATIONS

HQ: Stewart & Stevenson LLC
1000 Louisiana St., Ste. 5900, Houston, TX 77002
Phone: 713-751-2700   **Fax:** 713-751-2601
Web: www.stewartandstevenson.com

2008 Sales

	$ mil.	% of total
US	1,020.0	76
Other countries	315.4	24
Total	**1,335.4**	**100**

PRODUCTS/OPERATIONS

2008 Sales

	$ mil.	% of total
Equipment	930.4	70
Aftermarket parts & service	376.3	28
Rental	28.7	2
Total	**1,335.4**	**100**

COMPETITORS

Aggreko
Caterpillar
Cummins
Halliburton
Hertz
National Oilwell Varco
Twin Disc
United Rentals
ZF Friedrichshafen

HISTORICAL FINANCIALS
Company Type: Private

Income Statement
FYE: January 31

	REVENUE ($ mil.)	NET INCOME ($ mil.)	NET PROFIT MARGIN	EMPLOYEES
1/08	1,335	92	6.9%	3,374
1/07	942	42	4.4%	3,185
1/06	691	11	1.6%	2,230
1/05	549	6	1.1%	—
1/04	498	(34)	—	—
Annual Growth	28.0%	—	—	23.0%

2008 Year-End Financials
Debt ratio: 166.1%
Return on equity: 68.0%
Cash ($ mil.): 15
Current ratio: 2.53
Long-term debt ($ mil.): 291

Net Income History

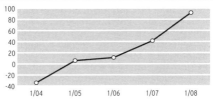

Stewart's Shops

I scream, you scream, we all scream for Stewart's ice cream — especially if we live in upstate New York or Vermont, home to nearly 320 Stewart's Shops. Formerly known as Stewart's Ice Cream Company, Stewart's Shops runs a chain of convenience stores selling more than 3,000 different products, including dairy items, groceries, food to go (soup, sandwiches, hot entrees), beer, gasoline, and, of course, ice cream. In addition the company has roughly 100 rental locations (including banks, hair salons, and apartments) adjacent to its shops. The founding Dake family owns about two-thirds of the company; employee compensation plans own the rest.

Stewart's makes its own ice cream — more than 50 flavors, both hand-dipped and packaged — and dairy products, and it has several private-label products. It also sells national brands.

EXECUTIVES
Chairman: William (Bill) Dake, age 69
President: Gary C. Dake, age 47
SVP: Nancy Trimbur
Treasurer: David A. Farr
Director, HR: Jim Botch
Director, Marketing and Public Relations: Susan Law Dake

LOCATIONS
HQ: Stewart's Shops Corp.
2907 Rte. 9, Ballston Spa, NY 12020
Phone: 518-581-1200 **Fax:** 518-581-1209
Web: www.stewartsicecream.com

PRODUCTS/OPERATIONS

Selected Products and Services
Automated Teller Machines (ATMs)
Beer
Dairy products
Food to go
Gasoline
Groceries
Hand-dipped ice cream
Lottery sales
Packaged ice cream
Rental properties
Soda

COMPETITORS
7-Eleven	Kroger
Ben & Jerry's	Pathmark
Cumberland Farms	Penn Traffic
Exxon	Royal Ahold
Golub	Sunoco
Hannaford Bros.	TravelCenters of America

HISTORICAL FINANCIALS
Company Type: Private

Income Statement
FYE: Last Sunday in December

	REVENUE ($ mil.)	NET INCOME ($ mil.)	NET PROFIT MARGIN	EMPLOYEES
12/07	1,000	—	—	3,800
12/06	1,000	—	—	3,800
12/05	1,023	—	—	4,000
Annual Growth	(1.1%)	—	—	(2.5%)

Revenue History

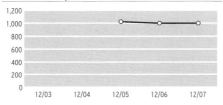

Structure Tone

Structured to set the right tone for its clients, The Structure Tone Organization develops commercial, industrial, and institutional properties for clients around the world. Active in the US, the UK, and Asia, the firm provides general contracting, construction management, and project management services for building construction, interior fit-outs and renovations, and infrastructure upgrades. Affiliates include construction management and construction services firms Constructors & Associates, Pavarini Construction, and Pavarini McGovern. Lewis Marino and Patrick Donaghy, whose families now own the company, founded Structure Tone in 1971 to focus on building interiors.

The Structure Tone Organization has completed a wide variety of projects, including academic facilities, broadcast studios, government facilities, museums, and research and development labs.

EXECUTIVES
Chairman: James K. Donaghy
Vice Chairman: Brian M. Donaghy
CEO: Robert W. Mullen
President: Anthony M. Carvette
CFO: Brett A. Phillips
EVP and Secretary: John T. White
EVP: Michael Neary
SVP Human Resources: Robert (Bob) Yardis
VP Marketing: Robin Malacrea
VP Information Technology: Terrence Robbins
CEO, Pavarini McGovern: Eric McGovern

LOCATIONS
HQ: The Structure Tone Organization
770 Broadway, New York, NY 10003
Phone: 212-481-6100 **Fax:** 212-685-9267
Web: www.structuretone.com

The Structure Tone Organization and its affiliates have US offices in Arlington, Virginia; Austin, Dallas, Houston, and San Antonio, Texas; Boston; Lyndhurst and Princeton, New Jersey; Miami Lakes, Florida; New York City (2); Philadelphia; and Stamford, Connecticut. It has international offices in Hong Kong and London.

PRODUCTS/OPERATIONS

Selected Sectors
Broadcast and media
Commercial
Educational
Entertainment
Financial
Government
Health care
Hospitality
Interiors
Law
Mission critical
Non-profit
Parking structures
Residential

COMPETITORS
Bovis Lend Lease	PCL
Clark Enterprises	Perini
Devcon Construction	Peter Kiewit Sons'
DPR Construction	Skanska USA Building
Foster Wheeler	Tishman
Gilbane	Turner Corporation
HRH Construction	Walsh Group
Hunt Construction	Washington Division
Opus Corp.	

Subway

You don't have to go underground to catch this Subway. Doctor's Associates operates the Subway chain of sandwich shops, the second-largest quick service chain behind McDonald's. It boasts more than 29,000 locations in 85 countries, with more US locations than the Golden Arches. Virtually all Subway restaurants are franchised and offer such fare as hot and cold sub sandwiches, turkey wraps, and salads. Subways are located in freestanding buildings, as well as in airports, convenience stores, sports facilities, and other locations. Doctor's Associates is owned by co-founders Fred DeLuca and Peter Buck, who opened the first Subway in 1965.

The national focus on healthy eating habits and the fast food industry has benefited the Subway chain greatly in recent years, and the company continues to tout the health benefits of its sandwiches over traditional burgers and fries. Its poster boy for weight loss, Jared Fogle, continues to be a focus for much of Subway's marketing campaign to get consumers to move away from fatty fast food.

The downside to this trend has been increasing competition in the healthy dining market. Quiznos, the company's main rival in the sub sandwich game, has been focused on expanding its own footprint of franchised outlets while mounting an aggressive advertising effort to steal away consumers. McDonald's and other fast food giants have also been adding healthier items to their menus over the years.

While keeping its competitors at bay, Subway has been focused on new menu items in an effort to increase business during the evening eating segment. During 2008 the company began promoting foot long subs to drive additional traffic to its restaurants, and Subway continues to market its toasted sandwiches as a dinner alternative.

The company's success also stems in part from its attractiveness to franchisees. With a low initial franchise cost and simple operations (minimum space requirements and little on-site cooking), the chain has been one of the fastest-growing franchises in the world. Subway surpassed 21,000 locations in the US in 2007.

EXECUTIVES

President: Frederick A. (Fred) DeLuca, age 60
VP Purchasing: Dennis Clabby
VP Operations: Millie Shinn
Chief Marketing Officer: Bill Schettini
CTO: Thys Van Hout
Director Brand Management: Michelle Cordial
Director Corporate Communications: Michele DiNello
Director Franchise Sales: Don Fertman
Director International: Patricia Demarais
President, Subway Development Corporation:
  Deep Dhindsa
President and CEO, Subway Independent Purchasing Cooperative: Jan Risi
SVP and Chief Administrative Officer, Subway Franchisee Advertising Fund Trust: Steven Safier

LOCATIONS

HQ: Doctor's Associates Inc.
  325 Bic Dr., Milford, CT 06461
Phone: 203-877-4281   **Fax:** 203-876-6674
Web: www.subway.com

COMPETITORS

AFC Enterprises
Arby's
Burger King
Cajun Operating Company
Chick-fil-A
CKE Restaurants
Dairy Queen
Jack in the Box
McDonald's
Quiznos
Wendy's
YUM!

Suffolk Construction

The bricks are being laid at Suffolk Construction. The company provides general contracting, construction management, preconstruction, and design/build services in the public and private sectors to automotive, education, health care, retail, and assisted living clients across the US. Commercial and residential projects include universities, senior housing facilities, hotels, corporate offices, and retail stores. Penske Automotive Group, Harvard University, and Boston Medical Center are among the firm's clients. Suffolk Construction is owned by president and CEO John Fish, whose family has been in the construction business for four generations. It was founded in 1982 and also operates in Florida and California.

A top Boston contractor, Suffolk Construction has annual sales of more than $1 billion.

In an effort to keep growing despite a downturn in the residential market, Suffolk restructured its Florida division in West Palm Beach into four business units. That division expects to reach $500 million in gross billings by 2012 by focusing on building more schools, biotechnology labs, and health care facilities, rather than residences. Particularly in Florida, with its large aging and senior populations, health care and assisted living are considered crucial growth sectors. Suffolk will compete in this market with such companies as Balfour Beatty Construction (ranked #1 in gross billings), Moss & Associates (#2), and Coastal Construction (#3).

EXECUTIVES

Chairman, President, and CEO: John F. Fish
EVP and CFO: Michael (Mike) Azarela
General Manager Florida: Rex B. Kirby
General Manager, California: David Cavecche
General Manager Group 1: Jeff Gouveia
General Manager Group 2: Joseph Murray
General Manager Group 3: Mark L. DiNapoli
General Counsel: Robert V. Lizza
VP, Human Resources: Susan O'Connor
Auditors: Ziner, Kennedy, & Lehan LLP

LOCATIONS

HQ: Suffolk Construction Company, Inc.
  65 Allerton St., Boston, MA 02119
Phone: 617-445-3500   **Fax:** 617-445-2343
Web: www.suffolkconstruction.com

Suffolk Construction has offices in Boston; Irvine and San Francisco, California; Falls Church, Virginia; and Miami, Naples, Sarasota, and West Palm Beach, Florida. It has projects throughout the US.

COMPETITORS

Balfour Construction
Bovis Lend Lease
Centex
Clark Enterprises
Coastal Construction
DooleyMack
Kraus-Anderson
McCarthy Building
Modern Continental Companies
Pepper Construction
Perini
Swinerton
Turner Corporation
Walsh Group
Whiting-Turner

SunGard Data Systems

Just about every financial services company under the sun relies on SunGard Data Systems. A majority of all Nasdaq trades pass through SunGard's investment support systems, which banks, stock exchanges, mutual funds, insurance companies, governments, and others use for transaction processing, asset management, securities and commodities trading, and investment accounting. SunGard provides business continuity, managed information technology, and professional services for businesses that rely on information resources. SunGard, which also offers higher education and public sector administrative systems, serves more than 25,000 customers in 50 countries

The company operates in four primary segments: Financial Systems, Higher Education, Public Sector, and Availability Services.

Its Financial Systems segment offers more than 50 software brands used by financial services firms, corporate and government treasury departments, and energy companies to automate the securities trading and portfolio and asset management processes. In 2007 SunGard acquired Aceva Technologies, a provider of credit and collections software.

SunGard's Higher Education and Public Sector Systems divisions serve higher education institutions, state and local governments, and not-for-profit organizations with over 30 products used for enterprise planning and administration functions.

Its Availability Services segment provides standby services for business continuity and disaster recovery functions, encompassing more than 4,000,000 sq. ft. of operational and computer hardware space and a 25,000 mile global network. In 2007 SunGard moved to boost this segment with the acquisition of managed hosting services provider VeriCenter.

The company has traditionally been very acquisitive: In 2006 and 2007 the company made more than 20 acquisitions throughout Europe, Asia, and North America.

HISTORY

When Philadelphia-based Sun Company in 1983 shifted focus from its computer disaster recovery services business in favor of its oil-related operations, the subsidiary's founder and president, John Ryan, led a group of New York investment bankers in a leveraged buyout for $19 million. They changed the name to SunGard Data Systems, providing IBM mainframe users with disaster recovery services through four operating subsidiaries in California, Illinois, North Carolina, and Pennsylvania.

By 1985 half of sales came from financial processing and software development services. In 1986 SunGard went public and reached profitability on revenues of $70 million. That year former US Air Force pilot and IBM salesman James Mann, who joined SunGard after the buyout in 1983, was named chairman and CEO.

SunGard acquired four more companies in 1987, including Devon International, whose CEO, Cristóbal Conde, went on to launch SunGard's trading systems division in 1990 and became the company's president in 2000. The acquisition also marked SunGard's first expansion overseas.

SunGard grew rapidly in the early 1990s through acquisitions, mostly in the area of data recovery. By 1993, sales had eclipsed $380 million. Two years later SunGard entered the health care information systems market with the acquisitions of Intelus Corporation and MACESS (later renamed SunGard Workflow Solutions).

Propelled by 12 more acquisitions in 1997, including risk management software maker Infinity Financial Technology, SunGard reached $1 billion in sales in 1998. By the following year its focus had shifted toward providing software for asset management and trade execution to financial services companies. The strategy paid off; nearly 70% of all 1999 trades on the Nasdaq exchange were supported by SunGard software. Among its acquisitions that year was life insurance and pension software specialist FDP.

In 2000 SunGard realigned operations as part of a companywide move to better integrate and brand its 50 subsidiaries. The next year the company acquired Bridge Information Systems' PowerPartner financial information management software for $165 million.

In 2001 SunGard entered into a bidding war with Hewlett-Packard for Comdisco's computer services operations, eventually purchasing the business for about $850 million.

In 2003 the company completed nine acquisitions. Most notably, it spent $159 million to acquire Caminus, a provider of commodity trading software for the global energy industry, in order to grow its SunGard Trading and Risk Systems unit; it bought UK-based insurance and government software maker Sherwood International in order to expand SunGard Insurance Systems; and it spent $121 million to buy public sector software maker H.T.E., which became part of the SunGard Higher Education and Public Sector Systems segment. SunGard's acquisition spree continued into 2004: the company further expanded its Higher Education and Public Sector segment with its $590 million purchase of Systems & Computer Technology (now SunGard SCT) and its purchase of Collegis, a provider of information technology services for higher education.

In 2004 SunGard sold its Brut subsidiary, which operates the Brut ECN alternative electronic trade-execution system, to Nasdaq for about $190 million in cash. Also that year, the company announced that it would spin off its Availability Services disaster recovery division as a separate, publicly traded company, but it canceled those plans after it agreed to be taken private.

In 2005 a group of seven private investment firms — Silver Lake Partners (lead investor), Bain Capital, The Blackstone Group, GS Capital Partners, Kohlberg Kravis Roberts & Co., Providence Equity Partners, and Texas Pacific Group — acquired SunGard Data Systems for about $11.3 billion.

EXECUTIVES

Chairman: Glenn H. Hutchins, age 52
Director: James L. (Jim) Mann, age 73
Vice Chairman: Till M. Guldimann, age 58
President, CEO, and Director: Cristóbal I. (Cris) Conde, age 47, $3,022,081 pay
EVP; Acting Group CEO, SunGard Higher Education: Michael K. Muratore, age 62, $1,933,786 pay

SVP Corporate Development: Richard C. Tarbox, age 55, $1,263,043 pay
SVP and Chief Marketing Officer: Brian Robins, age 49
SVP Finance and CFO: Michael J. Ruane, age 54
SVP Legal and General Counsel: Victoria E. Silbey, age 44
SVP Human Resources and Chief Human Resources Officer: Kathleen A. Weslock, age 52
VP and Controller: Karen M. Mullane, age 43
CEO, Delphi: Martin Walsh
Auditors: PricewaterhouseCoopers LLP

LOCATIONS

HQ: SunGard Data Systems Inc.
680 E. Swedesford Rd., Wayne, PA 19087
Phone: 484-582-2000   **Fax:** 610-225-1120
Web: www.sungard.com

PRODUCTS/OPERATIONS

2007 Sales

	$ mil.	% of total
Financial Systems	2,500	51
Availability Services	1,448	30
Higher Education	543	11
Public Sector Systems	410	8
Total	**4,901**	**100**

2007 Sales

	$ mil.	% of total
Services	4,363	89
License & resale fees	395	8
Reimbursed expenses	143	3
Total	**4,901**	**100**

Selected Products

BondMaster (interest and principal payments management systems)
BrokerWare (customer relationship management)
eTreasury (online cash management)
EXPEDITER (online mutual funds processing)
Investment support systems
    Asset management
    Banking and treasury
    Brokerage and execution
    Investor accounting
    Public sector
    Risk and derivatives
MINT (standardized messaging implementation)
Network Trade Model (XML-based data sharing between trading systems)
SunGard Transaction Network (financial services firm trade processing exchange)

Selected Services

Application service processing
Business continuity (on-site and remote disaster recovery)
Collocation application hosting
Consulting
Data center outsourcing
Private network access
Training
Web hosting

COMPETITORS

ADP
Advent Software
Bloomberg L.P.
DST
EDS
First Data
Fiserv
IBM
Jack Henry
Merrill Lynch
Misys
Morgan Stanley
Reuters

HISTORICAL FINANCIALS

Company Type: Private

Income Statement

FYE: December 31

	REVENUE ($ mil.)	NET INCOME ($ mil.)	NET PROFIT MARGIN	EMPLOYEES
12/07	4,901	(60)	—	17,900
12/06	4,323	(118)	—	16,600
12/05	4,002	117	2.9%	15,000
12/04	3,180	454	14.3%	13,000
12/03	2,955	370	12.5%	10,000
Annual Growth	**13.5%**	**—**	**—**	**15.7%**

Net Income History

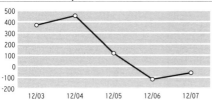

Sunkist Growers

Perhaps the US company least susceptible to an outbreak of scurvy among its employees, Sunkist Growers is an agricultural cooperative owned by some 6,000 California and Arizona citrus farmers. Sunkist markets fresh oranges, lemons, limes, grapefruit, and tangerines in the US and overseas. Fruit that doesn't meet fresh market standards is turned into juices, oils, and peels for use in food products. Sunkist is one of the most recognized brand names in the US and the world; through licensing agreements, the name appears worldwide on beverages and other products, from vitamins to candy, soda to pistachios.

The cooperative's seasonal citrus includes mandarin oranges, clementine oranges, and tangelos.

Sunkist is one of the 10 largest marketing cooperatives in the US, and it is the largest marketing cooperative in the worldwide fruit and vegetable industry.

It has licensing agreements with many food companies, including Dr Pepper/Snapple, Frasier & Neave, General Mills, Jelly Belly, and Morinaga Milk.

HISTORY

Sunkist Growers was founded in the early 1890s as the Pachappa Orange Growers, a group of California citrus farmers determined to control the sale of their fruit. Success attracted new members, and in 1893 the Southern California Fruit Exchange was born. The name "Sunkissed" was coined by an ad copywriter in 1908, and it was soon reworked into "Sunkist" and registered as a trademark, becoming the first brand name for a fresh produce item. Eventually the co-op renamed itself after its popular brand: It became Sunkist Growers in 1952. Sunkist began licensing its trademark to other companies in the early 1950s.

As early as 1916, efforts to increase citrus consumption included designing and marketing glass citrus juicers and encouraging homemakers to "Drink an Orange." The co-op also promoted the practice of putting lemon slices in tea or water and funded early research on the health benefits of vitamins (vitamin C in particular). In 1925 tissue wrappers gave way to stamping the Sunkist name directly on each piece of fruit.

Although Sunkist pioneered bottled orange juice in 1933, its juice marketing efforts were never as successful as those of its Florida competitors. Florida oranges are drippy and dowdy and thus better suited for juicing. Capitalizing on this aspect, Florida growers dominated the market for fresh and frozen juice.

In 1937 Congress created a system of citrus shipment quotas and limits (known as "marketing orders") that ultimately proved most beneficial to large citrus cooperatives. By the early 1990s the marketing order system was under political attack, and in 1992 the Justice Department filed civil prosecution against Sunkist, alleging that the co-op had reaped unfair extra profits by surpassing its lemon shipment limits. In 1994, after much legal wrangling, the quotas were abolished and the Justice Department dropped its case against Sunkist.

Inconveniently warm weather and increasing competition from imported citrus marked the harvests of 1996. That year the co-op had trouble maintaining discipline among its members; some undercut Sunkist price levels, while others flooded the market to sell their fruit at the higher early market prices, creating a supply surplus. Also that year the co-op relinquished the marketing of all Sunkist juices in North America to Florida-based Lykes Bros. in a licensing agreement.

The co-op agreed in 1998 to distribute grapefruit from Florida's Tuxedo Fruit, providing Sunkist with a winter grapefruit supply and increasing its year-round consumer a-peel. Also in 1998 Russell Hanlin, Sunkist president and CEO since 1978, was succeeded by Vince Lupinacci. Lupinacci, who had held positions with Pepsi and Six Flags, became the first person from outside the citrus business to hold Sunkist's top post.

In 1998 the company sold 90 million cartons of fresh citrus — the greatest volume in its history — despite increased competition from imported Latin American, South African, and Spanish crops, a damaging California freeze, and the ill effects of *El Niño*. The next year production was almost halved because of adverse weather.

Lupinacci resigned in 2000, citing personal and family reasons. Chairman emeritus James Mast then took the helm as acting president. Although the company grew its market through exports to China in 2000, its profits were squeezed that year by increasing foreign competition, a citrus glut, and lessened demand. In mid-2001 Jeff Gargiulo replaced Mast as Sunkist's president and CEO.

Sunkist formed a joint venture with strawberry shipper Coastal Berry Co. in 2003 to market strawberries under the Sunkist label year-round. (Coastal Berry's president and CEO John Gargiulo and Sunkist's former president and CEO Jeff Gargiulo are brothers.) Also that year Sunkist began offering pre-cut bagged fruit to retail customers and restaurants in order to keep up with a changing market and consumer demand.

In retrospect, 2006 was an eventful year for Sunkist. The co-op's largest producer and 16-year-member Paramount Citrus Association left the organization. In addition, chairman and CEO David Krause stepped down and president Jeff

Gargiulo left the company. Krause was replaced as chairman by Nicholas Boznick, president of produce grower/packer Richard Bagdasarian, Inc. Sunkist veteran and former president of Fruit Growers Supply Company, Timothy Lindgren was appointed president and CEO.

And, citing expense as the determining factor, the co-op discontinued marketing berries (strawberries, blueberries, and raspberries) in 2006.

EXECUTIVES

Chairman: Nicholas L Bozick
President and CEO: Timothy J. (Tim) Lindgren
Vice Chairman: Craig Armstrong
Vice Chairman: Mark D. Gillette
Vice Chairman: John M. Grether
EVP: Russell L. (Russ) Hanlin II
SVP Corporate Relations and Administration:
 Michael J. (Mike) Wootton
VP and CFO: Richard G. French
VP Law and General Counsel: Thomas M. (Tom) Moore
VP Human Resources: John R. McGovern
VP Citrus Juice and Oils Business: Ted R. Leaman III
VP Sales and Marketing: Kevin P. Fiori
Corporate Secretary: John Caragozian
Managing Director, Sunkist Global:
 Michael (Mike) Nomoto
Director Corporate Communications: Claire H. Smith
Director Domestic Sales: Mark Tompkins
Director Business Development: Brian Slagel
Director of Foodservice Sales: Bruce Simmons
Manager of National Sales Accounts: Lance McMillan
Auditors: Moss Adams, LLP

LOCATIONS

HQ: Sunkist Growers, Inc.
 14130 Riverside Dr., Sherman Oaks, CA 91423
Phone: 818-986-4800   **Fax:** 818-379-7405
Web: www.sunkist.com

PRODUCTS/OPERATIONS

2007 Sales

	$ mil.	% of total
Fresh fruit	805	81
Fruit products	72	7
Other	117	12
Total	**994**	**100**

Selected District Exchanges, Local Associations, and Licensed Packers

Allied Citrus Exchange, Inc.
 Marlin Packing Company
 Mesa Citrus Growers
Blue Banner Fruit Exchange
 Blue Banner Company, Inc.
 National Organic Packing Company
California Citrus Growers Exchange
 Golden Valley Citrus, Inc.
 Pfeiffer's Coalifornia Custom Packing, Inc.
 Porterville Citrus, Inc.
Central California Citrus Exchange
 Gillette Citrus, Inc.
 McKinney Packing, Inc.
 Sierra Citrus Association
Kaweah-Oxnard Fruit Exchange
 Oxnard Lemon Company
Klink Citrus Exchange
 Klink Citrus Association
Mid California Citrus Exchange
 Exeter-Ivanhoe Citrus Association
 Harding & Leggett, Inc.
 Orange Cove-Sanger Citrus Association
Mission Exchange, Inc.
 Mission Citrus
 Yuma Mesa Fruit Growers Association

Riverside Arlington Heights Fruit Exchange
 California Citrus Cooperative
 Euclid Packing Co-op, LP
 Redlands Foothill Groves
 Richard Bagdasarian, Inc.
Saticoy Fruit Exchange
 Saticoy Lemon Association
Southern California Citrus Exchange
 RBI Packing, LLC
Tulare County Fruit Exchange
 Kern Ridge Growers, LLC
 Magnolia Citrus Association
 San Antonio Orchard Company, LLC
Ventura County Citrus Exchange
 Baird-Neece Packing Corporation
 The Ventura Pacific Company, Inc.
Ventura County Fruit Exchange
 Limoneira Company
Villa Park Citrus Exchange
 The Villa Park Orchards Association, Inc.
Visalia Fruit Exchange
 Visalia Citrus Packing Group

COMPETITORS

Alico	Ocean Spray
Chiquita Brands	Odwalla
Coca-Cola	Old Orchard
Dole Food	PepsiCo
Dundee Citrus Growers	Silver Springs
Faygo	Snapple
Florida's Natural	South Beach Beverage
Fresh Del Monte Produce	Southern Gardens Citrus
Great Western Juice	Sunny Delight
Hansen Natural	Tree Top
IZZE	Tropicana
Lake Placid Groves	UniMark Group
Louis Dreyfus Citrus	Vitality Foodservice
Mott's	Welch's
Naked Juice	

HISTORICAL FINANCIALS

Company Type: Cooperative

Income Statement

FYE: October 31

	REVENUE ($ mil.)	NET INCOME ($ mil.)	NET PROFIT MARGIN	EMPLOYEES
10/07	994	5	0.5%	—
10/06	1,115	(7)	—	—
10/05	1,005	(1)	—	—
10/04	975	(9)	—	—
10/03	942	27	2.9%	—
Annual Growth	**1.3%**	**(35.5%)**	**—**	**—**

2007 Year-End Financials

Debt ratio: —   Current ratio: —
Return on equity: 7.6%   Long-term debt ($ mil.): —
Cash ($ mil.): —

Net Income History

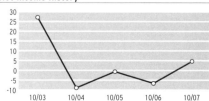

Super Center Concepts

Super Center Concepts is big on superlatives as well as groceries. One of the largest independently owned chain of grocery supercenters in Southern California, Super Center Concepts operates more than 30 outlets under the Superior Grocers banner. The grocery retailer has continued to expand, in spite of operating in the super competitive supercenter market where it competes with national chains including Wal-Mart and Costco Wholesale. The stores sell name brand and private label merchandise in the traditional grocery departments (produce, meat, bakery), as well as offering services such as check cashing and money orders. The first Superior Super Warehouse opened in Los Angeles in 1981.

EXECUTIVES

President: Mimi R. Song, age 47
CFO: Bill Cote
EVP: Marie Song
SVP, Operations: Phil Lawrence
Director, Risk Management: Cris Nunez

LOCATIONS

HQ: Super Center Concepts, Inc.
15510 Carmenita Rd., Santa Fe Springs, CA 90670
Phone: 562-345-9000   **Fax:** 562-345-9052
Web: superiorgrocers.com

COMPETITORS

Albertsons
Costco Wholesale
Food 4 Less
Gigante
Ralphs
Stater Bros.
Target
Vons
Wal-Mart
WinCo Foods

HISTORICAL FINANCIALS

Company Type: Private

Income Statement

FYE: December 31

	REVENUE ($ mil.)	NET INCOME ($ mil.)	NET PROFIT MARGIN	EMPLOYEES
12/07	969	—	—	4,700
12/06	916	—	—	4,000
12/05	789	—	—	3,900
Annual Growth	10.9%	—	—	9.8%

Revenue History

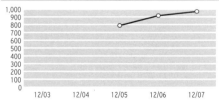

Sutherland Lumber

They are in a Southern state of mind at Sutherland Lumber. The company operates more than 65 lumber and home improvement stores in about 15 states, primarily in the southern and southwestern US. Sutherland's stores range in size from 50,000 to 190,000 sq. ft. They sell lumber, paints, tools, and building packages for houses, sheds, garages, and farm buildings. In addition, the stores sell lawn and garden equipment, plumbing supplies, and materials for hobbies and crafts. The company, which is owned and operated by the Sutherland family, was founded in 1917 to supply Oklahoma farmers with building materials. The Sutherland family is divided over how the company should be run and litigation has been filed.

EXECUTIVES

CEO and CFO: Steve Scott
President and CEO, Housemart.com:
Chris Sutherland Jr.

LOCATIONS

HQ: Sutherland Lumber Company, L.P.
400 Main St., Kansas City, MO 64111
Phone: 816-756-3000   **Fax:** 816-756-3594
Web: www.sutherlands.com

COMPETITORS

84 Lumber
Ace Hardware
Amazon.com
Do it Best
Foxworth-Galbraith Lumber
Handy Hardware Wholesale
Home Depot
Hope Lumber & Supply
Lowe's
McCoy Corp.
Menard
National Home Centers
True Value

HISTORICAL FINANCIALS

Company Type: Private

Income Statement

FYE: December 31

	ESTIMATED REVENUE ($ mil.)	NET INCOME ($ mil.)	NET PROFIT MARGIN	EMPLOYEES
12/07	1,070	—	—	2,140
12/06	1,180	—	—	2,300
12/05	1,100	—	—	2,400
Annual Growth	(1.4%)	—	—	(5.6%)

Revenue History

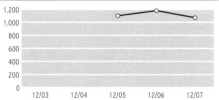

Sutter Health

Sutter Health is one of the nation's largest not-for-profit health care systems. It was organized in 1996 through the merger of Sutter Health and California Healthcare System. Today the company caters to residents of more than 100 Northern California communities. Its services are provided through the firm's approximately 3,500 affiliated doctors, from facilities of various types, including more than 25 acute care hospitals, home health/hospice networks, medical groups, occupational health services centers, and skilled nursing facilities. Sutter Health's network also boasts several research institutes.

To prevent its San Francisco-based St. Luke's Hospital from shuttering its doors, Sutter Health merged St. Luke's Hospital into its healthier California Pacific Medical Center in 2006. St. Luke's serves many of the city's uninsured and low-income population.

EXECUTIVES

Chairman: Jim Gray
President, CEO, and Director: Patrick E. (Pat) Fry
SVP and CFO: Robert D. (Bob) Reed, age 55
SVP and General Counsel: Gary F. Loveridge
SVP; President and CEO, Palo Alto Medical Foundation: David Druker
SVP and Chief Medical Officer: Gordon C. Hunt Jr.
SVP Strategy and Organization Development: Peter Anderson
SVP; Executive Officer, Sutter Medical Network: Jeffrey Burnich
VP Communications and Marketing: Bill Gleeson
Chief Medical Officer, Sutter North Medical Foundation, Brownsville: John Rose
Auditors: Ernst & Young LLP

LOCATIONS

HQ: Sutter Health
2200 River Plaza Dr., Sacramento, CA 95833
Phone: 916-733-8800   **Fax:** 916-286-6841
Web: www.sutterhealth.org

Hospitals

Alta Bates Summit Medical Center (Berkeley, Oakland)
California Pacific Medical Center (San Francisco)
Eden Medical Center (Castro Valley)
Kahi Mohala (Ewa, HI)
Marin General Hospital (Greenbrae)
Memorial Hospital Los Banos (Los Banos)
Memorial Medical Center (Modesto)
Menlo Park Surgical Hospital
Mills-Peninsula Health Services (Burlingame)
Novato Community Hospital (Novato)
Sutter Amador Hospital (Jackson)
Sutter Auburn Faith Hospital (Auburn)
Sutter Coast Hospital (Crescent City)
Sutter Davis Hospital (Davis)
Sutter Delta Medical Center (Antioch)
Sutter Lakeside Hospital (Lakeport)
Sutter Maternity & Surgery Center of Santa Cruz
Sutter Medical Center (Sacramento)
Sutter Medical Center of Santa Rosa
Sutter Roseville Medical Center
Sutter Solano Medical Center (Vallejo)
Sutter Tracy Community Hospital (Tracy)

COMPETITORS

Adventist Health
Catholic Healthcare West
HCA
Memorial Health Services
Providence Health & Services
Stanford University Medical
Tenet Healthcare

HISTORICAL FINANCIALS

Company Type: Not-for-profit

Income Statement

FYE: December 31

	REVENUE ($ mil.)	NET INCOME ($ mil.)	NET PROFIT MARGIN	EMPLOYEES
12/07	7,651	—	—	44,828
12/06	7,258	—	—	43,139
12/05	6,663	—	—	43,139
12/04	6,280	—	—	—
12/03	5,672	—	—	41,000
Annual Growth	7.8%	—	—	2.3%

Revenue History

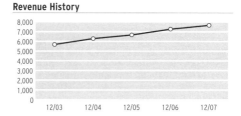

	12/03	12/04	12/05	12/06	12/07

Swagelok Company

With sales partners worldwide, Swagelok has to speak many languages, *fluidly*. The company makes fluid system components, which include plug, pinch, and radial diaphragm valves; sanitary fittings; and welding systems. Its products are used in the oil and gas, power, chemical, food and beverage, and semiconductor industries, as well as by bioprocess and pharmaceuticals research companies. Swagelok has more than 200 manufacturing, research, sales, and distribution facilities in nearly 60 countries. Founded in 1947 by Fred Lennon in his kitchen, the company is still controlled by the Lennon family.

Swagelok is expanding the product base in its biopharmaceutical line of valves and related supplies through the introduction of new equipment and acquisitions. The company has also expanded its line of pressure gauges.

Swagelok formed a new subsidiary, Swagelok Technology Services Company, in 2007 to market and commercialize the company's SAT12 metals surface enhancement heat-treatment process. Swagelok also acquired the assets of Hy-Level Industries (now Swagelok Hy-Level Company) to enhance its fluid systems offerings that year.

In 2008 the company bought the assets of Coreflex LLC, a manufacturer of hose products for biopharmaceutical and semiconductor applications. Also that year Swagelok acquired Plant Support and Evaluations Inc. (PSE), a provider of training services for evaluating compressed-air, condensate, and steam systems; PSE was renamed Swagelok Energy Advisors, Inc.

EXECUTIVES

President and CEO: Arthur F. (Art) Anton, age 50
CFO: Frank J. Roddy
VP Corporate Communications: Franziska H. Dacek
VP Distributor Support: Hans J. Goemans
VP Engineering: David H. Peace
VP Human Resources: James L. (Jim) Francis
VP Customer Service: David E. O'Connor
VP Marketing: Michael R. Butkovic
VP Operations: Michael F. Neff
VP Distributor Support: Sylvie A. Bon, age 48
President, Swagelok Capital Projects Company (SCPC): Reid Wayman
President, Swagelok Semiconductor Services Company: Philip I. Roberts

LOCATIONS

HQ: Swagelok Company
29500 Solon Rd., Solon, OH 44139
Phone: 440-248-4600   **Fax:** 440-349-5970
Web: www.swagelok.com

PRODUCTS/OPERATIONS

Selected Products

Filters
Fittings
Gauges
Hoses
Leak detectors
Lubricants and sealants
Manifolds
Quick connects
Regulators
Sample cylinders
Tube benders and cutters
Valves
Weld systems

COMPETITORS

CIRCOR International
Crane Co.
Dover Corporation
IMI
ITT Corp.
McJunkin Red Man
Precision Castparts
Shaw Group
SPX
T3 Energy Services
Tyco
Watts Water Technologies

HISTORICAL FINANCIALS

Company Type: Private

Income Statement

FYE: December 31

	ESTIMATED REVENUE ($ mil.)	NET INCOME ($ mil.)	NET PROFIT MARGIN	EMPLOYEES
12/07	1,300	—	—	4,000
12/06	1,100	—	—	3,300
12/05	1,000	—	—	3,000
Annual Growth	14.0%	—	—	15.5%

Revenue History

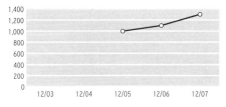

	12/03	12/04	12/05	12/06	12/07

Swift Transportation

Swift, but within the speed limit, truckload carrier Swift Transportation hauls freight such as building materials, paper products, and retail merchandise throughout the US and in Mexico. The company operates a fleet of about 18,000 tractors and 49,000 trailers from a network of about 30 terminals. Its services include dedicated contract carriage, in which drivers and equipment are assigned to a customer long-term. Besides standard dry vans, Swift's fleet includes refrigerated, flatbed, and other specialized trailers, as well as about 5,800 intermodal containers. CEO Jerry Moyes owns the company, which he founded in 1966, took public, and took private again in 2007.

Moyes took the company private by buying the 61% of Swift that he and his family didn't already own. His bid valued the carrier at about $2.7 billion, including some $330 million in assumed debt. Along with taking full ownership, Moyes took over as CEO, a position he had held for many years before stepping down in 2005 as part of an executive succession plan.

With Moyes in the driver's seat once again, Swift continues to concentrate on regional routes rather than long hauls. The company does offer transcontinental van service, but the shorter routes that are Swift's bread and butter help the company retain drivers and keep costs low.

Over the years Swift has worked to grow by selling more services to its large customers and by taking advantage of the trend among shippers toward outsourcing of transportation functions. Major customers have included Wal-Mart and Lowe's. Swift also has expanded its intermodal service, in which the company handles pickup and delivery of shipping containers transported by rail. Besides Swift, Moyes owns temperature-controlled carrier Central Refrigerated Service and less-than-truckload carrier Central Freight Lines.

EXECUTIVES

CEO: Jerry C. Moyes, age 62
EVP and CFO: Ginnie Henkels
EVP Business Transportation: Chad E. Killebrew
EVP Sales: Richard Stocking
EVP Western Region: Rodney K. Sartor
EVP, Swift Intermodal: Mark Young
EVP, Eastern Region: Kenneth C. (Ken) Runnels
VP and Corporate Controller: Bryan R. Schumaker
VP and General Counsel: Stephen J. Beaver
Director Financial Reporting and SEC Compliance: Cary Flanagan
Auditors: KPMG LLP

LOCATIONS

HQ: Swift Transportation Co., Inc.
2200 S. 75th Ave., Phoenix, AZ 85043
Phone: 602-269-9700   **Fax:** 623-907-7380
Web: www.swifttrans.com

COMPETITORS

Comcar
Covenant Transportation
Crete Carrier
CRST International
Heartland Express
J.B. Hunt
Knight Transportation
Landstar System
Schneider National
Universal Truckload Services
U.S. Xpress
Werner Enterprises

HISTORICAL FINANCIALS

Company Type: Private

Income Statement

FYE: December 31

	REVENUE ($ mil.)	NET INCOME ($ mil.)	NET PROFIT MARGIN	EMPLOYEES
12/07	3,270	—	—	21,900
12/06	3,173	—	—	21,900
12/05	3,198	—	—	21,900
12/04	2,826	—	—	23,000
12/03	2,398	—	—	21,000
Annual Growth	8.1%	—	—	1.1%

Revenue History

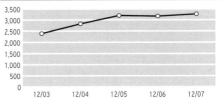

Swinerton Incorporated

Swinerton is building up the West just as it helped rebuild San Francisco after the 1906 earthquake. The construction group, formerly Swinerton & Walberg, builds commercial, industrial, and government facilities, including resorts, subsidized housing, public schools, Hollywood soundstages, hospitals, and airport terminals. Through its subsidiaries, Swinerton offers general contracting and design/build services, as well as construction and program management. It also provides property management for conventional, subsidized, and assisted living residences. The employee-owned company, which has expanded in the past decade in the Northwest and Southwest, traces its family tree to 1888.

Swinerton takes environmental stewardship to heart. As one of the top waste-reducing companies in California, Swinerton employs green building construction and design practices to conserve resources, reduce waste, and create healthier environments. The company's own headquarters building in San Francisco received Gold LEED-EB (Leadership in Energy & Environmental Design for Existing Buildings) certification from the U.S. Green Building Council.

EXECUTIVES

Chariman: Gordon W. Marks
CEO: Michael (Mike) Re
President: Jeffrey C. (Jeff) Hoopes
EVP and Co-COO: Charles P. (Charlie) Kuffner
EVP and COO: Gary J. Rafferty
EVP, Secretary, and General Counsel: Luke P. Argilla
SVP and CIO: Lucille (Luci) Morris-Tyndall
VP and CFO: Linda G. Showalter
VP Community Relations: Charles (Rick) Moore
VP and Director Human Resources: Brenda Reimche
National Marketing Director: Mark Gudenas
Auditors: PricewaterhouseCoopers

LOCATIONS

HQ: Swinerton Incorporated
260 Townsend St., San Francisco, CA 94107
Phone: 415-421-2980   **Fax:** 415-984-1204
Web: www.swinerton.com

Swinerton has offices in California, Colorado, Connecticut, Florida, Hawaii, New Mexico, Oregon, Texas, and Washington.

PRODUCTS/OPERATIONS

Selected Projects

Port of Oakland headquarters
deYoung Museum
Dreamworks Animation Campus

Selected Companies

Harbison-Mahony-Higgins Builders, Inc. (HMH, general contracting)
Lyda Swinerton Builders (general contracting)
Swinerton Builders (general contracting)
Swinerton Management & Consulting (property assessment)
Swinerton Property Services (property management)
William P. Young Construction (engineering and civil construction)

COMPETITORS

A.G. Spanos
Bechtel
Beck Group
Bovis Lend Lease
Charles Pankow Builders
Cordoba
Devcon Construction
DPR Construction
Gilbane
Hathaway Dinwiddie Construction
Hensel Phelps Construction
JCM Partners
J.F. Shea
Kitchell
Menas Realty
Rudolph & Sletten
S. J. Amoroso Construction
Skanska USA Building
Sundt
Turner Corporation
Tutor-Saliba
Webcor Builders
Western National Group
Whiting-Turner

HISTORICAL FINANCIALS

Company Type: Private

Income Statement

FYE: December 31

	REVENUE ($ mil.)	NET INCOME ($ mil.)	NET PROFIT MARGIN	EMPLOYEES
12/07	1,993	—	—	1,300
12/06	1,680	—	—	1,260
12/05	1,830	—	—	1,450
12/04	1,840	—	—	1,450
12/03	2,751	—	—	1,331
Annual Growth	(7.7%)	—	—	(0.6%)

Revenue History

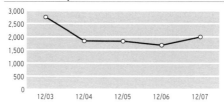

Symetra Financial

Symetra Financial provides a symmetrical offering of life insurance, annuities, retirement plans, financial advisory services, and employee benefits to some 3 million customers throughout the US. Affiliate Symetra Life Insurance Company offers insurance and retirement products to individuals and families, as well as to employers and benefit plan sponsors. Those products include life and health coverage, annuities, IRAs, retirement plans, mutual fund investments, group benefits plans, worksite life insurance, and stop loss products. Symetra was established in 1957.

In 2007 the company filed to go public, but later in the year, it announced plans to postpone its IPO because of unfavorable market conditions.

Symetra Financial was spun off from former parent Safeco in 2004, when the latter decided to focus on property/casualty insurance and let go of its life and investments operations. An investor group led by Berkshire Hathaway and White Mountains Insurance Group paid some $1.4 billion for the group; each company owns about 25% of the company.

EXECUTIVES

Chairman: David T. Foy, age 42
President, CEO, and Director:
Randall H. (Randy) Talbot, age 54
EVP and COO: Roger F. Harbin, age 58
EVP and CFO: Magaret A. Meister, age 43
EVP 403(b)/457: Scott L. Bartholomaus
SVP, General Counsel, and Secretary: George C. Pagos, age 58
SVP Group Division: Michael W. Fry
SVP Life and Annuities Division, Symetra Life Insurance: Richard J. Lindsay, age 50
SVP Enterprise Development: Jennifer V. Davies, age 50
SVP, Financial Institutions Distribution:
Roderick J. (Rod) Halvorson
VP and Chief Compliance Officer: Michele M. Kemper
VP Corporate Marketing and Investor Relations:
Jim Pirak
VP Human Resources: Christine A. (Chris) Katzmar, age 49
Auditors: Ernst & Young LLP

LOCATIONS

HQ: Symetra Financial Corporation
777 108th Ave., Ste. 1200, Bellevue, WA 98004
Phone: 425-256-8000   **Fax:** 425-256-5737
Web: www.symetra.com

PRODUCTS/OPERATIONS

2007 Sales

	$ mil.	% of total
Net investment income	973.6	61
Premiums	530.5	34
Other revenues	68.7	4
Net realized investment gains	16.8	1
Total	**1,589.6**	**100**

Selected Subsidiaries and Affiliates

Employee Benefit Consultants, Inc.
First Symetra National Life Insurance Company of New York
Medical Risk Managers
Symetra Investment Services Inc.
Symetra Life Insurance Company

COMPETITORS

AEGON USA	John Hancock Financial
Aetna	MassMutual
Aflac	MetLife
AIG	Mutual of Omaha
Allstate	Nationwide
Annuity and Life Re	New York Life
COUNTRY Financial	Northwestern Mutual
Guardian Life	Prudential
The Hartford	TIAA-CREF
HCC Insurance	Zurich Financial Services
ING Americas	

HISTORICAL FINANCIALS

Company Type: Private

Income Statement

FYE: December 31

	ASSETS ($ mil.)	NET INCOME ($ mil.)	INCOME AS % OF ASSETS	EMPLOYEES
12/07	19,560	167	0.9%	1,250
12/06	20,115	160	0.8%	1,200
12/05	20,980	146	0.7%	1,200
12/04	22,181	56	0.3%	1,500
Annual Growth	(4.1%)	43.8%	—	(5.9%)

2007 Year-End Financials

Equity as % of assets: 6.6%
Return on assets: 0.8%
Return on equity: 12.8%
Long-term debt ($ mil.): —
Sales ($ mil.): 1,590

Net Income History

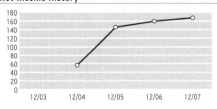

LOCATIONS

HQ: Synagro Technologies, Inc.
1800 Bering Dr., Ste. 1000, Houston, TX 77057
Phone: 713-369-1700 **Fax:** 713-369-1750
Web: www.synagro.com

COMPETITORS

American Water
BioMedical Technology Solutions
Ecology and Environment
N-Viro International
Siemens Water Technologies
TRC Companies
Wheelabrator

HISTORICAL FINANCIALS

Company Type: Private

Income Statement

FYE: December 31

	REVENUE ($ mil.)	NET INCOME ($ mil.)	NET PROFIT MARGIN	EMPLOYEES
12/06	346	8	2.3%	966
12/05	338	(10)	—	982
12/04	326	13	4.0%	964
12/03	299	7	2.4%	973
12/02	273	11	4.1%	960
Annual Growth	6.1%	(7.9%)	—	0.2%

2006 Year-End Financials

Debt ratio: 153.0%
Return on equity: 4.4%
Cash ($ mil.): 2
Current ratio: 1.46
Long-term debt ($ mil.): 279

Net Income History

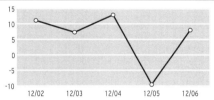

EXECUTIVES

Chairman: Claus Christiansen
CEO: Hervé Girsault
Chief Medical Officer: Charles G. Peterfy
VP and General Manager, Biochemical Markers:
Patrick Garnero
VP General Counsel and Secretary: Aaron C. Timm
Executive Director, Business Development: Steve Kahn
Senior Director, Project Management: Carmen Sosa
Scientific Director, Osteoporosis: Thomas (Tom) Fuerst
Director, Global Compliance and Quality Control:
Mikhail Mineyev
Director, Operational Support Planning: Nick Donovan
Corporate Marketing and Communications:
Natalie A. Cummins
CEO, Synarc Clinical Research Centers:
Jean-Claude Provost
Auditors: Deloitte & Touche

LOCATIONS

HQ: Synarc Inc.
575 Market St., 17th Fl., San Francisco, CA 94105
Phone: 415-817-8900 **Fax:** 415-817-8999
Web: www.synarc.com

COMPETITORS

Acurian	eResearchTechnology
Applied Biosystems Inc.	Pacific Biometrics
Bio-Imaging Technologies	Pharmaceutical Product
Covance	Development
DATATRAK International	Quintiles Transnational

Synagro Technologies

"Waste not" could be the motto of Synagro Technologies, which converts sewage sludge into marketable products. The company collects biosolids created by the treatment of wastewater at municipal and industrial plants throughout the US. Synagro makes money by drying, pelletizing, composting, and incinerating the biosolids and by transporting them for land application. The company also cleans out sewage lagoons and designs biosolids recycling systems. GTCR Golder Rauner owned 18.5% of Synagro before the 2007 acquisition of Synagro by The Carlyle Group for $462 million.

Synagro has grown through acquisitions. The company serves approximately 600 municipal and industrial water and wastewater treatment accounts and has operations in 33 US states and Washington, DC.

EXECUTIVES

CEO and President: Robert C. (Bob) Boucher Jr., $1,006,150 pay
SEVP and CFO: J. Paul Withrow, $818,846 pay
EVP and General Counsel: Alvin L. Thomas II, $212,491 pay
Sales and Marketing, Class A Processing:
Andrew Bosinger

Synarc Inc.

You put up the compounds, Synarc puts up the trials. The biomedical testing and contract research organization provides medical imaging, subject recruitment, and biomechanical marker services to drug development companies in around 200 trials around the world. A subsidiary of Center for Clinical and Basic Research (CCBR), the company operates clinical research centers in Brazil, China, and countries in Europe. Clinical areas include oncology, arthritis, cardiovascular disease, neurology, orthopedics, and osteoporosis. The company was formed in 1998 through a merger of three university research programs and three commercial operations.

In 2006 Synarc acquired Danish clinical trials specialist Center CCBR; in 2008 the Danish firm returned the favor, backed by Danish investors. Danish scientist and Synarc co-founder Claus Christiansen was named chairman.

TA Delaware

Automakers do a lot of leaning on TA Delaware (formerly Tower Automotive) for their metal stampings and engineered assemblies. TA's products include body structures and assemblies (body pillars, roof rails); lower vehicle frames and structures (pickup and SUV full frame assemblies); complex body-in-white assemblies (front and rear floor pan assemblies); chassis modules (axle assemblies); and suspension components (control arms, spring and shock towers). TA's largest customers include Ford Motor, General Motors, Honda, and Volkswagen. Struggling financially, TA filed for Chapter 11 bankruptcy protection in 2005; it emerged from Chapter 11 in 2007.

Between 2001 and 2005 TA was riding high with a big backlog of fresh business. During this time the company reorganized its North American operations to tighten capacity and reduce costs. But events conspired to undermine TA's efforts. Starting in 2004 rising steel prices, production cuts among key customers, and high costs associated with program launches created a liquidity crisis leading to the bankruptcy filing in 2005.

The company has gotten a tighter reign on costs and has its eye on incremental organic growth. TA is also capturing more business from outside Detroit, which takes advantage of the company's substantial global footprint.

In 2007 private equity group Cerberus Capital Management bought the company. Shortly after the transaction was completed, the company's name was changed from Tower Automotive to TA Delaware, Inc.

EXECUTIVES

Chairman: Daniel Ajamian
Vice Chairman: Rande Somma
President and CEO: Mark Malcolm
COO: Mike Rajkovic
EVP and CFO: Jim Gouin
SVP Global Human Resources: William R. (Bill) Cook
President, Americas: D. William (Bill) Pumphrey, age 48, $545,067 pay
President, International: Gyula Meleghy, age 52, $493,344 pay
Auditors: Deloitte & Touche LLP

LOCATIONS

HQ: TA Delaware, Inc.
  27175 Haggerty Rd., Novi, MI 48377
Phone: 248-675-6000   **Fax:** 248-675-6494
Web: www.towerautomotive.com

PRODUCTS/OPERATIONS

Selected Products

Body Structures and Assemblies
  Body pillars
  Heavy-truck frame rails
  Intrusion beams
  Light-truck frames
  Parcel shelves
  Roof rails
  Side sills
Lower Vehicle Frames and Structures
  Automotive engine cradles
  Cross members
  Floor pan components
  Pickup truck and SUV full frames
Chassis Modules and Systems
  Axle assemblies
  Front and rear structural suspension modules/systems
Complex Body-in-White Assemblies
  Door/pillar assemblies
  Front and rear floor pan assemblies
Suspension Components
  Control arms
  Spring/shock towers
  Suspension links
  Track bars
  Trailing axles
Other Products
  Heat shields
  Precision stampings

COMPETITORS

A.G. Simpson
American Axle & Manufacturing
ArvinMeritor
Benteler Automotive
Boler
cosma international
Dana Corporation
Kalamazoo Fabricating
KTH Parts
KUO
Lydall
Magna International
Midway Products Group
Midwest Stamping
Noble International
Noble Metal Processing
Norstar Founders
Ogihara America
Shiloh Industries
Sypris Solutions
Talon
T.J.T.
Visteon
Wagon plc
Winnebago

HISTORICAL FINANCIALS

Company Type: Private

Income Statement

	REVENUE ($ mil.)	NET INCOME ($ mil.)	NET PROFIT MARGIN	EMPLOYEES
12/07	2,500	—	—	11,000
12/06	2,539	—	—	10,477
12/05	3,284	—	—	—
12/04	3,179	—	—	—
12/03	2,816	—	—	—
Annual Growth	(2.9%)	—	—	5.0%

FYE: December 31

Revenue History

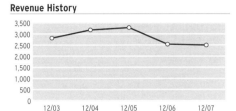

Tang Industries

Although it's probably not a good source of Vitamin C, Tang Industries *is* a diversified holding company. Its largest subsidiary, National Material, is a metal fabricating and distributing company that provides stamped steel products and recycles and trades aluminum and scrap metal. It operates throughout North America and in China. National Material subsidiary SKD Automotive Group makes stamped and welded vehicle components, including chassis, structural, and suspension components. Tang also has investments in pharmaceuticals and real estate. It was founded in 1960 by Cyrus Tang after he bought a small metal-stamping shop that has grown into National Material.

EXECUTIVES

Chairman, President, and CEO: Cyrus Tang
VP, Legal and Administration and General Counsel, National Material LP: Vytas P. Ambutas
CFO and Assistant Treasurer: Kurt R. Swanson

LOCATIONS

HQ: Tang Industries, Inc.
  8960 Spanish Ridge Ave., Las Vegas, NV 89148
Phone: 702-734-3700   **Fax:** 702-734-6766
Web: www.tangindustries.com

Tang Industries operates from facilities in Canada, China, Mexico, and the US.

PRODUCTS/OPERATIONS

Selected Operations

National Material, LP (industrial manufacturing)
  Maryland Pig Services (pig iron processing)
  Metal Resources International (importing, exporting, and trading steel, nonferrous metals, and advanced materials)
  SKD Automotive (stamped and welded automotive components)
  Taber Extrusions (extruded aluminum)

COMPETITORS

Alcoa
Commercial Metals
Metalcraft
OmniSource
Ryerson

HISTORICAL FINANCIALS

Company Type: Private

Income Statement

	REVENUE ($ mil.)	NET INCOME ($ mil.)	NET PROFIT MARGIN	EMPLOYEES
12/07	1,650	—	—	3,600
12/06	1,650	—	—	3,200
12/05	1,500	—	—	3,200
Annual Growth	4.9%	—	—	6.1%

FYE: December 31

Revenue History

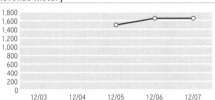

Tastefully Simple

Taste buds get the Tupperware treatment at Tastefully Simple. The company promotes its line of gourmet soups, dips, desserts, and convenience foods through in-home parties where attendees can taste prior to buying. Its standard food items range in price from $4.99 for beer bread mix to $41.99 for a large gift pack. Most items cost $7 to $8. Many are ready-to-eat, while others require only one or two additional ingredients to prepare. Tastefully Simple has about 25,000 sales representatives in all 50 US states, and it buys its products from specialty food vendors. Partners Jill Blashack Strahan and Joani Nielson founded the fast-growing company in 1995. CEO Blashack Strahan owns about 70% of Tastefully Simple.

EXECUTIVES

President and CEO: Jill Blashack Strahan, age 48
COO: Joani Nielson
CFO: Rick Miller
VP Information Systems: Peter Bellavance
VP Marketing: Jennifer Panchenko
VP Organizational Effectiveness: Theresa Moberg
VP Team Relations: Edgar F. Timberlake
Chief Legal Officer: Christy Caspers
Director, Business Development: John Richard Verhaeghe
Communication Senior Lead: Lynn Grueneich

LOCATIONS

HQ: Tastefully Simple, Inc.
  1920 Turning Leaf Ln., SW, Alexandria, MN 56308
Phone: 320-763-0695   **Fax:** 320-763-2458
Web: www.tastefullysimple.com

PRODUCTS/OPERATIONS

Selected Products

Beer bread
Cherry almond sauce
Chili mix
Corn and black bean salsa
Cranberry orange bread and muffin mix
Creamy wild rice soup
Dips
Dried tomato garlic pesto
Fudge brownies
Fudgy popcorn
Honey mustard
Marinara sauce
Party nut mixes
Potato cheddar soup
Pretzels
Raspberry salsa
Red pepper and onion preserves
Shortbread cookie mix
Spinach artichoke ball
Sweet pepper jalapeño jam

COMPETITORS

Fingerhut
Harry & David Holdings
Pampered Chef
Trader Joe's

HISTORICAL FINANCIALS

Company Type: Private

Income Statement

FYE: December 31

	REVENUE ($ mil.)	NET INCOME ($ mil.)	NET PROFIT MARGIN	EMPLOYEES
12/07	138	—	—	300
12/06	120	—	—	300
12/05	110	—	—	300
12/04	123	—	—	311
12/03	114	—	—	293
Annual Growth	5.0%	—	—	0.6%

Revenue History

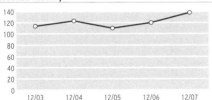

Taylor Corporation

The pleasure of your presence is big business to the Taylor Corporation. One of the holding company's largest businesses is Carlson Craft, a leading printer of invitations and related material for weddings and other special events. Other Taylor units provide business cards and stationery, greeting cards (Current USA), marketing communications products, and promotional items, along with other commercial printing services. Overall, Taylor's operations include more than 100 companies that do business throughout North America and in Europe. Chairman

Glen Taylor, majority owner of the NBA's Minnesota Timberwolves, has assembled the company from acquisitions, starting with Carlson Craft in 1975.

Recent acquisitions include the July 2008 purchase of Interprise Software Systems International, a developer of scalable software solutions for businesses, by Taylor's Services and Technology division. In June the firm's Print Craft unit bought the assets of Litho Express, which makes packaging for CDs, DVDs, and more. In April, Taylor's Current USA subsidiary acquired catalog and online gifts and home decor retailer Lillian Vernon out of bankruptcy.

The company merged three of its custom printing brands (Carlson Craft Business Solutions, Regency, Label Works) into one new unified brand called Navitor in fall 2007.

EXECUTIVES

Chairman: Glen A. Taylor
President and CEO: Jean M. Taylor, age 45
CFO: Tom Johnson
Chief Administrative Officer and General Counsel: Greg Jackson
EVP: Ron Hoffmeyer
EVP: Steven Singer
EVP: Colleen R. Willhite
VP: Todd Alexander
CIO: Jeff Eceles

LOCATIONS

HQ: Taylor Corporation
1725 Roe Crest Dr., North Mankato, MN 56003
Phone: 507-625-2828   **Fax:** 507-625-2988
Web: www.taylorcorp.com

COMPETITORS

American Achievement
American Greetings
BCT International
Champion Industries
CSS Industries
Hallmark
Quad/Graphics
Quebecor World
R.R. Donnelley

HISTORICAL FINANCIALS

Company Type: Private

Income Statement

FYE: December 31

	ESTIMATED REVENUE ($ mil.)	NET INCOME ($ mil.)	NET PROFIT MARGIN	EMPLOYEES
12/07	1,700	—	—	12,500
12/06	1,700	—	—	15,000
12/05	1,706	—	—	15,000
12/04	1,600	—	—	15,000
12/03	1,400	—	—	14,220
Annual Growth	5.0%	—	—	(3.2%)

Revenue History

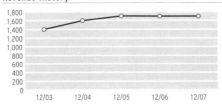

Teacher Retirement System of Texas

T is for Texas and teachers, too. The Teacher Retirement System (TRS) of Texas provides retirement, health care, and other benefits to educators and other employees of the Lone Star State's more than 1,000 independent public school districts, as well as universities, community colleges, junior colleges, and medical and dental schools. TRS serves more than 1.2 million active and retired members with more than $100 billion under management in its pension trust fund; almost two-thirds of that is invested in domestic and international equities. In 2007 the company added hedge funds to its investment mix despite the risk, and divested holdings in companies that do business in Iran at the behest of Texas lawmakers.

In 2007 TRS successfully sued Qwest Communications and received a $62 million settlement against the telecom for alleged securities fraud that dated back to 2005.

TRS was established in 1936 and had just 38,000 members its first year. In the beginning, the fund was limited to investing in government and municipal bonds.

EXECUTIVES

Chairman: Jarvis V. Hollingsworth
Vice Chairman: Linus D. Wright
Executive Director: Ronnie G. Jung
COO: Patricia O. (Pattie) Featherston
CFO: Tony C. Galaviz
Chief Benefit Officer: Marianne Woods Wiley
General Counsel: Conni H. Brennan
Chief Investment Officer: T. Britton (Britt) Harris IV
Director Human Resources: Annette Dominguez
Director Communications: Howard Goldman
Director ActiveCare: Bob Jordan
Director Information Technology: Amy L. Morgan
Director Governmental Relations: Ray Spivey
Director Special Projects: Betsey Jones
Auditors: Maxwell Locke & Ritter LLP

LOCATIONS

HQ: Teacher Retirement System of Texas
1000 Red River St., Austin, TX 78701
Phone: 512-542-6400   **Fax:** 512-542-6426
Web: www.trs.state.tx.us

COMPETITORS

FMR
TIAA-CREF
UTA

HISTORICAL FINANCIALS

Company Type: Government agency

Income Statement

FYE: August 31

	ASSETS ($ mil.)	NET INCOME ($ mil.)	INCOME AS % OF ASSETS	EMPLOYEES
8/07	135,813	11,890	8.8%	—
8/06	113,872	6,531	5.7%	—
8/05	106,825	9,505	8.9%	—
8/04	97,569	6,570	6.7%	—
8/03	87,930	5,937	6.8%	—
Annual Growth	11.5%	19.0%	—	—

2007 Year-End Financials

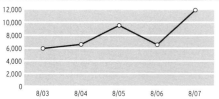

Equity as % of assets: 82.6%   Long-term debt ($ mil.): —
Return on assets: 9.5%   Sales ($ mil.): 18,002
Return on equity: 11.2%

Net Income History

Team Health

There's no "I" in Team Health, a leading provider of clinical outsourcing services to hospitals and physicians groups across the US. The company's main business is providing outsourced physician staffing and administrative services to hospital emergency rooms. It handles everything from doctor recruitment and medical training programs, to billing, payroll processing, and claims management. It provides similar program management services for hospital-affiliated radiology, anesthesiology, and pediatrics groups, as well as inpatient care (hospitalist) programs. Team Health contracts with some 600 hospitals and affiliated clinics in 45 states. It was acquired in 2005 by The Blackstone Group.

Previously, the company was owned by an investor group consisting of Madison Dearborn Partners, Cornerstone Equity Investors, Beecken Petty O'Keefe & Company, and members of the management team.

Team Health operates through a regionalized organizational structure, with management sites across the country that deliver services locally but which are supported by integrated information systems and procedures.

In addition to its program management services, the company has an array of other clinical outsourcing options, including medical call center services, locum tenens placement (through subsidiary Daniel & Yeager), teleradiology, and military medical facility staffing (through Spectrum Healthcare Resources).

The company sees opportunities for growth in the pressures hospitals face to control costs while maintaining high quality service. It intends to capitalize on those pressures with its outsourcing offerings and to use its established market position in emergency room program management to grow its business in other clinical areas, such as radiology, anesthesiology, and pediatrics. Additionally, the company looks to increase market share by acquiring complementary businesses in the fragmented clinical outsourcing industry. In 2006 it acquired Florida Acute Care Specialists, a hospitalist program management company operating primarily in Florida.

EXECUTIVES

Chairman and CEO: Lynn Massingale, age 55
President and COO: Greg Roth, age 51
CFO: David P. Jones, age 40
EVP and General Counsel: Robert C. (Bob) Joyner, age 60
EVP, Spectrum Healthcare Resources: George Tracy
SVP Business Development and Marketing: Michael J. (Mike) Shea
SVP HCFS: Ron Matthews
SVP Mergers and Acquisitions: Kit Crews
Corporate VP Human Resources: Lisa Courtney
Chief Compliance Officer: Stephen Sherlin, age 62
Chief Information Officer: Harry Herman
Chief Medical Officer: Gar LaSalle
Auditors: Ernst & Young LLP

LOCATIONS

HQ: Team Health, Inc.
  1900 Winston Rd., Ste. 300, Knoxville, TN 37919
Phone: 865-693-1000   **Fax:** 865-539-3073
Web: www.teamhealth.com

PRODUCTS/OPERATIONS

Selected Services

Coding and billing services
Locum tenens (temporary physician placement)
Medical call center services
Military treatment facilities management
Physician recruitment
Program management services
  Anesthesiology
  Emergency medicine
  Hospital medicine (coordination of care for
    hospitalized patients)
  Pediatrics
  Radiology
Teleradiology (electronic radiology image exchange and
  interpretation)

Selected Subsidiaries

After Hours Pediatrics, Inc.
Daniel & Yeager, Inc.
Medical Management Resources, Inc.
Spectrum Healthcare Resources, Inc.
TeamHealth Radiology, Inc.

COMPETITORS

CHG Healthcare
EmCare
Emergency Medical Services
IPC The Hospitalist Company
McKesson
Orion HealthCorp
Pediatrix Medical
RehabCare
Sheridan Healthcare
Sterling Healthcare
UCI

HISTORICAL FINANCIALS

Company Type: Private

Income Statement

FYE: December 31

	REVENUE ($ mil.)	NET INCOME ($ mil.)	NET PROFIT MARGIN	EMPLOYEES
12/07	1,232	—	—	5,900
12/06	1,570	—	—	5,600
12/05	1,613	—	—	5,600
12/04	1,572	—	—	5,800
12/03	1,479	—	—	6,700
Annual Growth	(4.5%)	—	—	(3.1%)

Revenue History

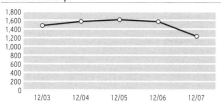

Teamsters

One of the largest and best-known labor unions in the US, the International Brotherhood of Teamsters has 1.4 million members. The Teamsters represents workers in some 20 industry sectors, including trucking, warehousing, parcel delivery, industrial trades, and government. More than 200,000 of the union's members are employees of package delivery giant United Parcel Service. Besides negotiating labor contracts with employers on behalf of its members, the union oversees pension funds and serves as an advocate in legislative and regulatory arenas. The union and its affiliates have about 1,900 local chapters in the US and Canada, including about 475 Teamsters locals. The Teamsters union was founded in 1903.

Teamsters chief James P. Hoffa (son of presumed-dead union leader Jimmy Hoffa) is working to improve the union's image after implementing ethics policies aimed at rooting out internal corruption and ties to organized crime. Hoffa, first elected in 1998, wants the Teamsters to police themselves and to put an end to the government supervision under which the union has operated since 1989.

The Teamsters have packed up and moved out from under the AFL-CIO umbrella and joined fellow unions Unite Here (textile, hotel, and restaurant workers), Service Employees International (SEIU), United Food and Commercial Workers, and others in the rival Change to Win Coalition. The group hopes to reverse the decline of labor jobs and union membership in the US by focusing its time and money on recruiting rather than on participating in political campaigns. Other key issues for Change to Win include health care, immigration, and retirement security.

HISTORY

Two rival team-driver unions, the Drivers International Union and the Teamsters National Union, merged to form the International Brotherhood of Teamsters in 1903. Led by Cornelius Shea, the Teamsters established headquarters in Indianapolis. Daniel Tobin (president for 45 years, starting in 1907) demanded that union locals obtain executive approval before striking. Membership expanded from the team-driver base, prompting the union to add Chauffeurs, Stablemen, and Helpers to its name (1909).

Following the first transcontinental delivery by motor truck (1912), the Teamster deliverymen traded their horses for trucks. The union then recruited food processing, brewery, and farm workers, among others, to augment Teamster effectiveness during strikes. It joined the American Federation of Labor in 1920.

Until the Depression the Teamsters was still a small union of predominantly urban deliverymen. Then Farrell Dobbs, a Trotskyite Teamster from Minneapolis, organized the famous Minneapolis strikes in 1934 to protest local management's refusal to allow the workers to unionize. Workers clashed with police and National Guard units for 11 days before management acceded to the workers' demands. The strikes demonstrated the potential strength of unions, and Teamsters membership swelled. Although union power ebbed during WWII, the union continued to grow. It moved its headquarters to Washington, DC, in 1953.

The AFL-CIO expelled the Teamsters in 1957 when Teamster ties to the mob became public during a US Senate investigation. New Teamsters boss Jimmy Hoffa eluded indictment and took advantage of America's growing dependence on trucking to negotiate the powerful National Master Freight Agreement (1964). Hoffa also organized industrial workers. He used a union pension fund to make mob-connected loans and was later convicted of jury tampering and sent to prison. In 1975, four years after his release, Hoffa vanished without a trace and is believed to have been the victim of a Mafia hit.

The Teamsters rejoined the AFL-CIO in 1987 and the following year settled a racketeering lawsuit filed by the US Justice Department by allowing government appointees to discipline corrupt union leaders, help run the union, and oversee its elections. The election of self-styled reformer Ronald Carey in 1991 (he received 49% of the vote) seemed to portend real changes for the union; each of his six predecessors had been accused of or imprisoned for criminal activities. However, membership dropped by 40,000 in both 1991 and 1992.

Carey won re-election as union president in 1996 over rival, and son of former boss Jimmy Hoffa, James P. Hoffa (whom Carey accused of having ties to organized crime). A 15-day strike by the Teamsters' UPS employees in 1997 led to the delivery company's agreement to combine part-time jobs into 10,000 new full-time positions. That year Carey's re-election was overturned amid a campaign finance investigation that netted guilty pleas from three Carey associates, and the Teamsters leader was disqualified from running for re-election in 1998. Carey was officially expelled from the Teamsters by the federal government, and Hoffa won the 1998 election over Tom Leedham (who was backed by the union's reform wing).

Promising to fight corruption, Hoffa hired former federal prosecutor Edwin Stier and several former FBI agents to help him operate Project RISE (respect, integrity, strength, and ethics), a new in-house anti-corruption program. In 2002 the union began lobbying against plans to allow Mexican trucking companies to transport goods across the US.

In 2005 the Teamsters joined four other unions representing more than 5 million workers to call for sweeping reform in the AFL-CIO. They released a proposal to revitalize the labor movement by focusing on growth and empowerment. When AFL-CIO president John Sweeney failed to heed their calls, the Teamsters joined the Service Employees International Union in boycotting the umbrella group's annual convention and joining the Change to Win Coalition.

EXECUTIVES

General President: James P. (Jim) Hoffa, age 67
General Secretary and Treasurer:
 C. Thomas (Tom) Keegel
General Counsel: Bradley T. Raymond
Director, Accounting and Budget Department:
 Mitzi Montemore
Director, Affiliates and Automated Records Department: Hollis Hypes
Director, Capital Strategies Department: Carin Zelenko
Director, Communications Department: Bret Caldwell
Director, Training and Development Department:
 Cynthia Impala
Director, Economics and Contracts Department:
 Jim Kimball
Director, Government Affairs Department: Mike Mathis
Director, Human Rights Commission:
 Cheryl L. Johnson
Director, Organizing Department: Jeff Farmer
Director, Safety and Health Department: LaMont Byrd
Director, Information Systems Department:
 David Gormley
Director, Express Division: Bill Hamilton
Strategic Organizing Coordinator: Iain Gold
Department for Retiree Affairs: Edgar A. Scribner

LOCATIONS

HQ: International Brotherhood of Teamsters
 25 Louisiana Ave. NW, Washington, DC 20001
Phone: 202-624-6800   **Fax:** 202-624-6918
Web: www.teamster.org

2007 Membership

	% of total
United States	
Central	32
East	28
West	26
South	7
Canada	7
Total	**100**

PRODUCTS/OPERATIONS

Trade Divisions

Airline
Bakery and Laundry
Brewery and Soft Drink
Building Material and Construction
Carhaul
Dairy
Food Processing
Freight
Graphic Communications
Industrial Trades
Motion Picture and Theatrical Trade
Newspaper, Magazine, and Electronic Media
Parcel and Small Package
Port
Public Services
Rail
Solid Waste
Tankhaul
Trade Show and Convention Centers
Warehouse

Tekni-Plex, Inc.

Combining packaging technology with a modicum of complexity, Tekni-Plex manufactures packaging, packaging products, and tubing products for the food, health care, and consumer industries. The company's packaging segment makes foam egg cartons, pharmaceutical blister films, poultry and meat processing trays, closure liners, foam plates, and aerosol and pump packaging components. Its tubing products division manufactures irrigation hoses, garden hoses, medical tubing, and pool and vacuum hoses. Tekni-Plex also makes vinyl resins and recycled PET used in a variety of industrial products.

Originally the General Felt Products division of Standard Packaging Corp., the company was spun off as Tekni-Plex in 1967. The company's current management took control of Tekni-Plex in 1994.

The company provides its services through nearly 20 operating companies in North America. It began expanding internationally in the late 1990s when it acquired PurePlast in Canada and Tri-Seal International and NATVAR in Singapore. Those operations were combined to form Tekni-Plex, Inc. (Singapore).

In 2000 it expanded into Latin America and Asia (through a partnership with Japan-based Sun A. Kaken). It strengthened its Asian foothold in 2006 when it formed Tekni-Plex Technologies (Suzhou) in China.

EXECUTIVES

CEO: Paul J. Young
CFO: Robert M. Larney, age 57
SVP International Sales: Michael Franklin
VP Human Resources: Joe Bruno
Chief Restructuring Officer: James (Jim) Mesterharm
Auditors: BDO Seidman, LLP

LOCATIONS

HQ: Tekni-Plex, Inc.
 260 N. Denton Tap Rd., Coppell, TX 75019
Phone: 972-304-5077
Web: www.tekni-plex.com

Tekni-Plex has manufacturing facilities in Argentina, Belgium, Canada, China, Italy, the UK, and the US.

2007 Sales

	$ mil.	% of total
US	642.0	83
Europe	105.4	14
Canada	17.3	2
China & Argentina	8.6	1
Total	**773.3**	**100**

PRODUCTS/OPERATIONS

2007 Sales

	$ mil.	% of total
Packaging	405.4	52
Tubing products	205.6	27
Other	162.3	21
Total	**773.3**	**100**

Selected Products

Consumer Packaging and Products
  Garden hose
  Irrigation hose
  Precision tubing and gaskets
Healthcare
  Blister packaging
  Cap liners and seals
  Coated film
  Co-extrusions
  Flexible film
  Laminations
  Medical tubing
  Rigid packaging film
  Semi-rigid film
  Vinyl compounds
Food Packaging
  Egg cartons
  Processor trays
Specialty Resins and Compounds
  Vinyl resins

COMPETITORS

Crown Holdings
Huntsman International
Pactiv
RPC Group
Sealed Air Corporation
Smurfit-Stone Container
Sonoco Products
Teknor Apex

HISTORICAL FINANCIALS

Company Type: Private

Income Statement				FYE: Friday nearest June 30
	REVENUE ($ mil.)	NET INCOME ($ mil.)	NET PROFIT MARGIN	EMPLOYEES
6/07	773	(61)	—	3,200
6/06	743	(84)	—	3,100
6/05	696	(82)	—	3,250
6/04	636	(55)	—	3,200
6/03	611	3	0.6%	3,300
Annual Growth	6.1%	—	—	(0.8%)

Net Income History

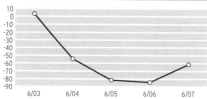

Teknor Apex

Teknor Apex is no retread. At least not any longer. Founded in 1924 as a tire distributor and retreader, Teknor Apex has sold off those assets to concentrate on chemicals, plastic, and rubber. The company has seven divisions that provide chemicals (plasticizers and toll compounding), garden hoses, rubber (custom mixing and molding of rubber compounds), specialty compounding (custom thermoplastic compound manufacturing and toll compounding of plastics), Teknor Color Company (color concentrates for plastics), thermoplastic elastomers, and vinyl (custom PVC compounds). The founding Fain family owns a controlling interest.

The company is broadening its technology base as well as its geographic reach. Chem Polymer, its wholly owned subsidiary in the UK, was purchased in 2004. It makes specialty compounds for glass fiber, flame retardants, and other items. Teknor Apex is also exploring the uses of flexible PVC and alternate extrusion methods.

EXECUTIVES

President and CEO: Jonathan D. Fain
CFO: James E. Morrison
Treasurer: Edward Massoud
EVP: Bertram M. Lederer
EVP and Secretary: Herbert Malin
SVP, Manufacturing: William (Bill) Murray
VP, Business Development: Robert S. Brookman
VP, Human Resources: Margaret North
President, Chem Polymer U.S.: Evan DeWulf
Manager, Corporate Marketing Communications: Sandra L. (Sandy) Hopkins

LOCATIONS

HQ: Teknor Apex Company
505 Central Ave., Pawtucket, RI 02861
Phone: 401-725-8000   **Fax:** 401-725-8095
Web: www.teknorapex.com

Teknor Apex has operations in Singapore, the UK, and the US.

PRODUCTS/OPERATIONS

Selected Products and Services

Chemicals and Colorants
  Color concentrates
  Custom compounds
  Dry colors
  High-performance colors
  Plasticizers (trimellitates, adipates, phthalates, sebacates, and azelates)
  Pulverized colors
  PVC compounds
  Thermoplastic elastomers
Garden Hose Products
  Cord, hose, and rope organizers
  Residential and commercial hoses
Rubber Products
  Custom rubber mixing
  Custom rubber molding

COMPETITORS

Atlantis Plastics
BASF SE
DuPont
GLS
PMC Global
PolyOne
RB Rubber
Spartech
Tekni-Plex
Vulcan International
Yule Catto

Temple University

Temple University, part of Pennsylvania's Commonwealth System of Higher Education, has four campuses in the Philadelphia area, as well as campuses in Tokyo and Rome and educational programs in China, Greece, France, Israel, and the UK. More than 34,000 students are enrolled in Temple's 17 schools and colleges. Temple's Health Sciences Center includes Temple University Hospital and schools that teach medicine and dentistry. Its Tyler School of Art will relocate from the Elkins Park campus to a modern facility on the main campus in 2009. After the move Temple plans to sell the 12-acre Elkins Park property. Dr. Russell Conwell founded the institution in 1884 and it was incorporated as Temple University in 1907.

EXECUTIVES

President: Ann Weaver Hart, age 59
Provost: Ira M. Schwartz
SVP Government, Community, and Public Affairs: Kenneth (Ken) Lawrence Jr.
VP, CFO, and Treasurer: Martin Dorph
VP Computer and Information Services: Timothy C. O'Rourke
VP Development and Alumni Affairs: Stuart P. Sullivan
Controller: Frank P. Annunziato
Chief Communications Officer: Mark Eyerly
Director Purchasing: Theresa (Terry) Burt
University Counsel: George E. Moore
Auditors: Deloitte & Touche LLP

LOCATIONS

HQ: Temple University
1801 N. Broad St., Philadelphia, PA 19122
Phone: 215-204-7000   **Fax:** 215-204-4403
Web: www.temple.edu

HISTORICAL FINANCIALS

Company Type: School

Income Statement				FYE: June 30
	REVENUE ($ mil.)	NET INCOME ($ mil.)	NET PROFIT MARGIN	EMPLOYEES
6/07	1,903	119	6.2%	7,996
6/06	1,789	(2)	—	—
6/05	1,821	113	6.2%	—
6/04	1,732	79	4.6%	—
6/03	1,668	162	9.7%	—
Annual Growth	3.3%	(7.5%)	—	—

2007 Year-End Financials

Debt ratio: —
Return on equity: 9.3%
Cash ($ mil.): —
Current ratio: —
Long-term debt ($ mil.): —

Net Income History

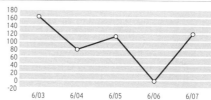

Tenaska, Inc.

Tenaska is tenacious when it comes to producing and selling energy. The employee-owned company is a top natural gas marketer in the US (selling or managing more than 1.8 trillion cu. ft. of natural gas a year); it also trades and markets electricity (including renewable energy) and develops, owns, or operates 23 generating plants in 11 US states and an investment in Bolivia, totaling approximately 35,000 MW of capacity. It directly owns some 6,800 MW of capacity in the US. Other operations include fuel supply, biofuels development, power transmission, and gas transportation contracting.

Tenaska was founded in 1987 by CEO Howard Hawks and EVP Thomas Hendricks. Its strategy is to build on core strengths while adapting to current market conditions.

In 2006 its Tenaska Power Fund unit acquired InfrastruX Group for $275 million and also acquired 3,145 MW of natural gas-fired generation assets from Constellation Energy for $1.6 billion.

In 2008 Tenaska's biofuels unit acquired Edible Oil Marketing, LLC, an Omaha-based biodiesel and vegetable oil marketing and trading company.

EXECUTIVES

Co-Founder, Chairman, and CEO; Chairman, Tenaska Capital Management: Howard L. Hawks
CFO: Jerry K. Crouse
Co-Founder and EVP; Vice Chairman, Tenaska Capital Management: Thomas E. (Tom) Hendricks
President and CEO, Operations Group: Michael C. (Mike) Lebens
President and CEO, Business Development: David G. Fiorelli
EVP: Ronald N. Quinn
EVP Corporate Investments: Michael F. (Mike) Lawler
EVP: Larry V. Pearson
SVP Power Marketing: Kevin R. Smith
VP Operations: Todd S. Jonas
VP Business Development: Ronald R. Tanner
VP Engineering and Construction: Nicholas N. Borman
VP and Controller: Timothy G. Kudron
VP Finance and Treasurer: Gregory A. Van Dyke
VP Strategy: David W. Kirkwood
Director, Government and Public Affairs: Jana M. Martin

LOCATIONS

HQ: Tenaska, Inc.
1044 N. 115th St., Ste. 400, Omaha, NE 68154
Phone: 402-691-9500 **Fax:** 402-691-9526
Web: www.tenaska.com

Tenaska owns operating power projects in Alabama, Georgia, Oklahoma, Texas, Virginia, and Washington in the US, as well as in Bolivia.

PRODUCTS/OPERATIONS

Selected Subsidiaries

Tenaska BioFuels, LLC (biofuels)
Tenaska Capital Managment. LLC (asset management)
Tenaska Marketing Canada (gas marketing)
Tenaska Marketing Ventures (gas marketing)
Tenaska Power Services Co. (power marketing)

COMPETITORS

AES	Exxon
BP	International Power
Calpine	Mirant
Chevron	NRG Energy
ConocoPhillips	Reliant Energy
Covanta	Sempra Energy
Edison Mission Energy	Shell Oil
El Paso	

HISTORICAL FINANCIALS

Company Type: Private

Income Statement

FYE: December 31

	REVENUE ($ mil.)	NET INCOME ($ mil.)	NET PROFIT MARGIN	EMPLOYEES
12/07	11,600	—	—	624
12/06	8,700	—	—	569
12/05	10,000	—	—	550
12/04	6,670	—	—	500
12/03	5,600	—	—	475
Annual Growth	20.0%	—	—	7.1%

Revenue History

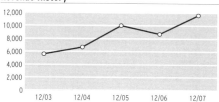

Texas A&M University System

Everything is bigger in Texas, even its universities. With over 100,000 students at nine institutions, The Texas A&M University System ranks among the largest in the US. Its flagship school at College Station is well known not only for its programs in engineering and agriculture, but also for its long-held traditions and school spirit. Other system institutions include Tarleton State University and Prairie View A&M. The system also runs seven state extension agencies and a health sciences center. Texas A&M was founded in 1876 as the Agricultural and Mechanical College of Texas. The A&M system was formed in 1948; it is funded in part by a state endowment (shared with the University of Texas).

Flagship Texas A&M in College Station is the largest campus in the university system, with an enrollment of about 46,500 students. Its campus is home to the George Bush Presidential Library Center, which opened in 1997.

At about 2,000 members, A&M's Corps of Cadets (commonly referred to as "the Corps") remains the largest uniformed body of students in the nation outside the US service academies.

In the wake of a bonfire collapse which took the lives of 12 students in 1999, Texas A&M has been charged by outsiders with trying to conceal its own involvement in the accident. Still others have called on Texas A&M to loosen some of its traditions. However, the school, students, and alumni have all stood fast against the tide of pressure. Texas A&M has embarked on a 20-year mission to renovate its facilities and secure status as a top public university.

EXECUTIVES

Chairman: Bill Jones
Vice Chairman: John D. White
Chancellor: Michael D. (Mike) McKinney, age 56
President: Elsa A. Murano, age 48
Interim EVP and Interim Provost: Jerry R. Strawser
EVP Operations: H. Russell Cross
Chief Marketing Officer: Steven B. Moore
VP Finance and CFO: Terry A. Pankratz
VP and Associate Provost Diversity: Tito Guerrero III
VP and Associate Provost for Information Technology: Pierce E. Cantrell Jr.
VP Institutional and Federal Affairs: Michael G. O'Quinn
VP Student Affairs: Dean L. Bresciani
VP Development and Strategic Outreach: Chad E. Wootton
VP Marketing and Communications: Jason D. Cook
Auditors: Texas State Auditor

LOCATIONS

HQ: The Texas A&M University System
A&M System Bldg., 200 Technology Way, Ste. 2043, College Station, TX 77845
Phone: 979-458-6000 **Fax:** 979-458-6044
Web: tamusystem.tamu.edu

PRODUCTS/OPERATIONS

Selected Texas A&M University System Components

Health Science Center
  Baylor College of Dentistry
  College of Medicine
  College of Nursing
  Graduate School of Biomedical Sciences
  Institute of Biosciences and Technology
  Irma Lerma Rangel College of Pharmacy
  School of Rural Public Health
State Agencies
  Texas Agricultural Experiment Station
  Texas Cooperative Extension
  Texas Engineering Experiment Station
  Texas Engineering Extension Service
  Texas Forest Service
  Texas Transportation Institute
  Texas Veterinary Medical Diagnostic Laboratory
Universities
  Prairie View A&M University
  Tarleton State University
  Texas A&M International University
  Texas A&M University
  Texas A&M University-Commerce
  Texas A&M University-Corpus Christi
  Texas A&M University-Kingsville
  Texas A&M University-Texarkana
  West Texas A&M University

HISTORICAL FINANCIALS
Company Type: School

Income Statement
FYE: August 31

	REVENUE ($ mil.)	NET INCOME ($ mil.)	NET PROFIT MARGIN	EMPLOYEES
8/07	1,605	(18)	—	26,876
8/06	1,485	136	9.1%	26,000
8/05	1,526	(909)	—	26,000
8/04	1,323	(882)	—	24,500
8/03	1,257	—	—	38,500
Annual Growth	6.3%	—	—	(8.6%)

Net Income History

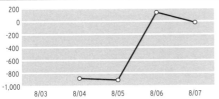

Texas Lottery

The Texas Lottery Commission hopes to have the eyes of Texans watching the lotto jackpot. The Texas Lottery Commission oversees one of the country's largest state lotteries, which has pumped more than $14 billion into state coffers since its inaugural in 1991. About 58% of lottery sales are paid out in prize money, while 30% goes to the state's Foundation School Fund; the remainder covers administration costs and commissions to retailers. The lottery offers numbers games and several instant-win games sold through grocery stores, gas stations, and liquor and convenience stores. Each store earns a small commission on tickets it sells.

A bit of luster has returned to the Lone Star State's lottery following slumping sales in 1998 and again in 2000. In 2005 and 2006 the lottery contributed more than $1 billion to the Foundation School Fund. However, lottery officials say certain lottery games will need continued tweaking to maintain consumer interest and that steady growth in sales cannot be guaranteed.

The Texas Lottery Commission offers numbers games (Lotto Texas, Pick 3, Cash 5, and Texas Two Step) in addition to Mega Millions, a multistate lottery game. Instant-win games are scratch-off cards sold under names like Super Lucky 7's, Blackjack Doubler, and Deuces Wild. The lottery commission also has a division that supervises charitable bingo games in the state of Texas.

HISTORY

A state lottery had been an issue in Texas for years before it was discussed in earnest in the mid-1980s. Falling oil and gas revenue had plunged the state into a recession, raising the specter of tax increases. In 1985 the state budget had a shortfall of $1 billion; that figure tripled by 1987. Adding fuel to the fire, the Texas Supreme Court ruled in 1989 that Texas had to change the way it funded public schools to avoid penalizing poor school districts. The ruling forced the state to seek new sources of revenue. In 1991 Gov. Ann Richards called a special session of the legislature to deal with the fiscal crisis, and House Bill 54 was passed, creating the state lottery. The measure was approved by 64% of voters.

In May 1992 Richards bought the symbolic first ticket at an Austin feed store (it was not a winner). Fourteen hours later Texans had spent nearly $23 million on tickets — breaking the California Lottery's first-day sales record — and had won $10 million in prizes. More than 102 million tickets were sold the first week. GTECH Holdings was awarded a five-year contract that year for lotto operations. Lotto Texas started in November with a winner taking nearly $22 million. By the end of the year, lotto sales in Texas had topped $1 billion. In its first 15 months, it contributed $812 million to the state's coffers.

In March 1994 five winners split a record $77 million jackpot. By that autumn sales from the lottery's beginning had surpassed $5 billion. In November a Mansfield, Texas, gas station owner picked up the largest single-winner jackpot, $54 million. By the end of 1994, Texas had the largest state lottery in the US. Cumulative sales topped $8 billion in mid-1995. In its first 37 months of operation, the Texas Lottery contributed $2.5 billion to the state's general fund. Cash 5 debuted that year, and instant ticket vending machines were installed at some sites.

In 1996 lottery director Nora Linares was dismissed following allegations that one of her friends received $30,000 from GTECH as a "hunting consultant." When a GTECH official was convicted in New Jersey of taking kickbacks from a lobbyist, questions were raised concerning payments to GTECH's Texas lobbyist, former Texas Lt. Gov. Ben Barnes. In 1997 Texas canceled its contract with GTECH to operate the lottery through 2002 and reopened bidding; GTECH filed suit to enforce the contract. Executive director Lawrence Littwin later was dismissed by the commission. Littwin sued GTECH, claiming the company had gotten him fired (the case was settled in 1999). Linda Cloud, his replacement, reinstated GTECH's contract. That year the Texas Legislature voted to increase the amount going to the state and to reduce prize payouts.

Lottery sales fell sharply in 1998, due in part to the reduced prize money. To combat suffering sales, the legislature reversed itself the next year and restored the level of prize payouts. The commission proposed lengthening the odds of winning to create larger jackpots, but public outcry scuttled the plan. In 2000 the commission agreed to change the wording on its scratch tickets after a San Antonio College professor and his students argued that breaking even is not winning.

The following year it introduced its first new lottery game in about three years, Texas Two Step, and discontinued Texas Million following slumping sales. It also changed its Lotto Texas game so that customers must match six numbers out of 54 numbers instead of 50. The extra four numbers changed the odds of winning from about one in 16 million to one in 26 million. The game was changed again in 2003 to a two-field game where players first select five numbers out of 44, and then select one number from a second field of 44. The new game has changed the odds of winning the jackpot to one in 48 million, while the odds of winning any prize have changed from one in 71 to one in 57.

EXECUTIVES

Executive Director: Anthony J. Sadberry
Deputy Executive Director: Gary Grief
Financial Accounting and Reporting Manager: Benito (Ben) Navarro
General Counsel: Kimberly (Kim) Kiplin
Director Lottery Operations: Michael Anger
Director Enforcement: James (Jim) Carney
Director Administration: Michael (Mike) Fernandez
Director Media Relations: Robert Heith
Director Internal Audit: Catherine Melvin
Director Charitable Bingo Operations: Phil Sanderson
Director Human Resources: Janine Mays
Director Governmental Affairs: Nelda Treviño
Manager Drawings and Validations, Lottery Operations: Robert Barnett
Manager Facilities: Vince Devine
Manager Support Services: Toni Erickson
Manager Information Resources: Joan Kotal
Manager Advertising and Promotions, Lottery Operations: Ray Page
Manager Retailer Services, Lottery Operations: Ed Rogers
Controller: Kathy Pyka
Auditors: Maxwell Locke & Ritter LLP

LOCATIONS

HQ: Texas Lottery Commission
611 E. Sixth St., Austin, TX 78701
Phone: 512-344-5000   **Fax:** 512-344-5080
Web: www.txlottery.org

COMPETITORS

Louisiana Lottery
Multi-State Lottery
New Mexico Lottery Authority

HISTORICAL FINANCIALS
Company Type: Government-owned

Income Statement
FYE: August 31

	REVENUE ($ mil.)	NET INCOME ($ mil.)	NET PROFIT MARGIN	EMPLOYEES
8/07	3,775	4	0.1%	—
8/06	3,776	(60)	—	—
8/05	3,663	(14)	—	—
8/04	3,489	20	0.6%	—
8/03	3,132	(11)	—	—
Annual Growth	4.8%	—	—	—

2007 Year-End Financials
Debt ratio: —
Return on equity: 12.8%
Cash ($ mil.): —
Current ratio: —
Long-term debt ($ mil.): —

Net Income History

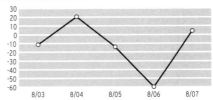

Thomas Nelson

Thomas Nelson's psalm of success comes straight from the Good Book. Considered the world's top commercial publisher of Christian-related materials, it produces about 10 major Bible translations in the English language, as well as biblical reference products, including commentaries, help texts, and study guides. In addition, Thomas Nelson publishes religious and inspirational titles by authors such as Max Lucado and John Eldredge. The company also hosts inspirational conferences (Women of Faith) and is a leading producer of Christian-oriented and family-focused products for adults and children, including books and games, and audio, video, and CD-ROM materials. Thomas Nelson became a private company in 2006.

The company's products are distributed through Christian and general bookstores, mass merchandisers, and by direct marketing to consumers via direct mail, telemarketing, conferences, and the Internet.

Cable veteran Leo Hindery and his private equity investment firm InterMedia Partners and its subsidiary Faith Media took Thomas Nelson private in a $473 million buyout deal in 2006.

Going against industry standards, the company eliminated its more than 20 imprints in early 2007 as part of its "One Company" initiative, instead putting all of its books under one brand and its publishing functions into consumer categories. As part of the initiative, Thomas Nelson began using a single strategy for all of its non-fiction books, combining two non-fiction units into one.

EXECUTIVES

Chairman: Sam Moore, age 77, $739,300 pay
(prior to title change)
President and CEO: Michael S. (Mike) Hyatt, age 52,
$549,565 pay
EVP and CFO: Joe L. Powers, age 62, $319,474 pay
EVP and Chief Live Events Officer: Mary Graham
EVP and Chief Publishing Officer:
Tamara L. (Tami) Heim
EVP and Chief Sales Officer: Mark Schoenwald,
$293,625 pay
EVP Ministry Sales and World Publishing: Ted Squires
EVP and Chief Service Officer: Vance Lawson, age 49,
$262,289 pay
**SVP Backlist Development and Strategic Publishing
Process:** Pete Nikolai
**SVP; Publisher, Reference, Electronic, and Nelson
Impact:** Wayne Kinde
SVP; Publisher, Thomas Nelson Family Entertainment:
Dan Lynch
SVP; Publisher, Nelson Books and Business:
Brian Hampton
SVP; Group Publisher, Non-Fiction Trade Book Group:
David Moberg
VP Human Resources: Jim Thomason
Auditors: KPMG LLP

LOCATIONS

HQ: Thomas Nelson, Inc.
501 Nelson Place, Nashville, TN 37214
Phone: 615-889-9000   **Fax:** 615-391-5225
Web: www.thomasnelson.com

PRODUCTS/OPERATIONS

Selected Books
Anchored in Love (John Carter Cash)
Every Day Deserves a Chance (Max Lucado)
Get Out of That Pit (Beth Moore)
Inside My Heart (Robin McGraw)
It's All About Him (Denise Jackson)
On the Move (Bono)
One Minute Wellness (Dr. Ben Lerner)
Talent Is Never Enough (John C. Maxwell)
Ten Tortured Words (Stephen Mansfield)
The Great Bird Flu Hoax (Dr. Joseph Mercola)
The Ransomed Heart (John Eldredge)
You Are Captivating (Stasi Eldredge)
Winning With People (John C. Maxwell)

Selected Bible Editions
International Children's Bible
King James Version
New American Bible
New American Standard Bible
New Century Version
New King James Version
New Living Translation
New Revised Standard Version
Revised Standard Version, Catholic Edition

Selected Children's Titles
Adventures in Odyssey
Bibleman
Buginnings
God's Kids Worship
Hermie and Friends
Jacob's Gift
Just in Case You Ever Wonder
Just Like Jesus for Tweens
Wally McDoogle series
Wemmicks

COMPETITORS

Baker Publishing
Beliefnet
Courier Corporation
Deseret Management
Guideposts
Integrity Media
R. B. Pamplin
Salem Communications
Standex
Tyndale House Publishers
Zondervan

Thorntons Inc.

Fill 'er (and you) up at Thorntons. Kentucky's largest privately owned corporation, Thorntons operates more than 150 QuickCafé & Market convenience stores and gas stations in Connecticut, Illinois, Indiana, Kentucky, and Ohio. Through wholly owned subsidiary Thornton Transportation, the company distributes its own fuel and operates a river bulk storage terminal. The chain is focusing on high-margin items such as sandwiches, doughnuts and gourmet coffee to boost sales. The family-owned and -operated company was co-founded in 1971 by namesake and chairman James H. Thornton and is run by his son CEO Matt Thornton.

Thorntons recently introduced CornerMarkets, convenience stores that offer shoppers a greater grocery selection, and Subworks, a proprietary food program that allows customers to order sandwiches and other fresh food via a touch-screen menu.

The company, which holds about a 20% market share in the Louisville, Kentucky, area, is growing at a pace of about a dozen stores per year.

EXECUTIVES

CEO: Matt Thornton
President and COO: William (Graham) Baughman
CFO: Christopher (Chris) Kamer
EVP: Brenda Stackhouse
SVP Retail Sales and Marketing: Tony Miller
VP Construction and Environmental Concerns:
Eric Zoph
VP and General Counsel: David Bridgers
VP Information Technology Services: Tony Harris
Associate General Counsel: Shelly Gibson

LOCATIONS

HQ: Thorntons Inc.
10101 Linn Station Rd., Ste. 200,
Louisville, KY 40223
Phone: 502-425-8022   **Fax:** 502-327-9026
Web: www.thorntonsinc.com

2008 Stores

	No.
Kentucky	54
Illinois	51
Indiana	30
Ohio	15
Connecticut	4
Total	**154**

COMPETITORS

7-Eleven
Chevron
Exxon
Kroger
Speedway SuperAmerica

Thrivent Financial

The Spirit moved Aid Association for Lutherans (AAL) to merge with Lutheran Brotherhood and form a new entity, christened Thrivent Financial for Lutherans. The fraternal benefit society now includes nearly 3 million members, and brings under one steepled roof more than $70 billion in assets under management. Individuals and congregations that become members can shop for life insurance, mutual funds, bank and trust services (through Thrivent Financial Bank), and other financial services. Thrivent Financial, which operates all over the US, has nearly $160 billion in life insurance in force. The company also supports three separate foundations, which contributed more than $27 million in 2006 to charitable causes.

EXECUTIVES

Chairman, President, and CEO: Bruce J. Nicholson,
age 62
EVP and Chief Administrative Officer:
Jon M. Stellmacher
**EVP Field Distribution; President, Thrivent Investment
Management:** James A. (Jim) Thomsen
EVP Marketing and Products: Pamela J. (Pam) Moret

SVP and CFO: Randall L. (Randy) Boushek
SVP and CIO: Holly J. Morris
SVP and Chief Investment Officer:
  Russell W. (Russ) Swansen
SVP, General Counsel, and Secretary:
  Teresa J. (Terry) Rasmussen
SVP Communications: Marie A. Uhrich
SVP Fraternal Operations: Bradford L. (Brad) Hewitt
SVP Human Resources: Prof Jennifer H. Martin, age 59
President and CEO, Thrivent Financial Bank:
  Todd H. Sipe
Auditors: Ernst & Young LLP

LOCATIONS

HQ: Thrivent Financial for Lutherans
    4321 N. Ballard Rd., Appleton, WI 54919
Phone: 612-340-7000   Fax: 800-205-8348
Web: www.thrivent.com

COMPETITORS

American Express
Citigroup
ELCA Board of Pensions
FMR
MetLife
Modern Woodmen
New York Life
Security Benefit Group
State Farm
TIAA-CREF

HISTORICAL FINANCIALS

Company Type: Not-for-profit

Income Statement

FYE: December 31

	ASSETS ($ mil.)	NET INCOME ($ mil.)	INCOME AS % OF ASSETS	EMPLOYEES
12/07	53,474	391	0.7%	—
12/06	52,539	524	1.0%	—
12/05	50,816	522	1.0%	—
12/04	56,750	488	0.9%	2,676
12/03	52,667	252	0.5%	2,979
Annual Growth	0.4%	11.6%	—	(10.2%)

2007 Year-End Financials

Equity as % of assets: 8.3%   Long-term debt ($ mil.): —
Return on assets: 0.7%   Sales ($ mil.): 6,081
Return on equity: 9.1%

Net Income History

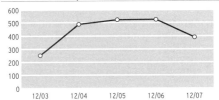

TIAA-CREF

It's punishment enough to write the name once on a blackboard. Teachers Insurance and Annuity Association — College Retirement Equities Fund (TIAA-CREF) is one of the largest, if not longest-named, private retirement systems in the US, providing for more than 3 million members of the academic community and for investors outside academia's ivied confines. It also serves institutional investors. TIAA-CREF's core offerings include financial advice, investment information, retirement accounts, pensions, annuities, individual life and disability insurance, tuition financing, and trust services (through TIAA-CREF Trust). The system, a not-for-profit organization, also manages a line of mutual funds.

TIAA-CREF is one of the nation's heftiest institutional investors, with more than $435 billion in assets under management, and it has not been afraid to throw its weight around corporate boardrooms. The organization is known for active and choosy investing and is a vocal critic of extravagant executive compensation packages.

In 2006 TIAA-CREF bought Kapsick & Company, which manages planned giving assets for colleges, universities, and other not-for-profits. The acquisition makes the system the largest provider of such services in the US. TIAA-CREF also owns one of the nation's largest portfolios of real estate investments.

HISTORY

With $15 million, the Carnegie Foundation for the Advancement of Teaching in 1905 founded the Teachers Insurance and Annuity Association (TIAA) in New York City to provide retirement benefits and other forms of financial security to educators. When Carnegie's original endowment was found to be insufficient, another $1 million reorganized the fund into a defined-contribution plan in 1918. TIAA was the first portable pension plan, letting participants change employers without losing benefits and offering a fixed annuity. The fund required infusions of Carnegie cash until 1947.

In 1952 TIAA CEO William Greenough pioneered the variable annuity, based on common stock investments, and created the College Retirement Equities Fund (CREF) to offer it. Designed to supplement TIAA's fixed annuity, CREF invested participants' premiums in stocks. CREF and TIAA were subject to New York insurance (but not SEC) regulation.

During the 1950s, TIAA led the fight for Social Security benefits for university employees and began offering group total disability coverage (1957) and group life insurance (1958).

In 1971 TIAA-CREF began helping colleges boost investment returns from endowments, then moved into endowment management. It helped found a research center to provide objective investment information in 1972.

For 70 years retirement was the only way members could exit TIAA-CREF. Their only investment choices were stocks through CREF or a one-way transfer into TIAA's annuity accounts based on long-term bond, real estate, and mortgage investments. In the 1980s CREF indexed its funds to the S&P average.

By 1987's stock crash, TIAA-CREF had a million members, many of whom wanted more protection from stock market fluctuations. After the crash, Clifton Wharton (the first African-American to head a major US financial organization) became CEO; the next year CREF added a money market fund, for which the SEC required complete transferability, even outside TIAA-CREF. Now open to competition, TIAA-CREF became more flexible, adding investment options and long-term-care plans.

John Biggs became CEO in 1993. After the 1994 bond crash, TIAA-CREF began educating members on the ABCs of retirement investing, hoping to persuade them not to switch to flashy short-term investments and not to panic during such cyclical events as the crash.

In 1996 it went international, buying interests in UK commercial and mixed-use property. TIAA-CREF filed for SEC approval of more mutual funds in 1997. Although federal tax legislation took away TIAA-CREF's tax-exempt status in 1997, the change was made without decreasing annuity incomes for the year.

The status change let TIAA-CREF offer no-load mutual funds to the public in 1998. A trust company and financial planning services were added; all new products were sold at cost, with TIAA-CREF waiving fees. TIAA-CREF in 1998 became the first pension fund to force out an entire board of directors (that of sputtering cafeteria firm Furr's/Bishop's). Also that year TIAA-CREF's crusade to curb "dead hand" poison pills (an antitakeover defense measure) found favor with the shareholders of Bergen Brunswig (now AmerisourceBergen), Lubrizol, and Mylan Laboratories.

Biggs retired in 2002 and was succeeded by Herbert Allison. In 2008 Roger Ferguson took over as CEO.

EXECUTIVES

Chairman: Ronald L. Thompson, age 57
Vice Chairman: Frances Nolan
President and CEO: Roger W. Ferguson Jr., age 57
EVP, Asset Management; CEO, Teachers Advisors and
  TIAA-CREF Investment Management: Scott C. Evans
EVP and CFO: Georganne C. Proctor, age 51
EVP and CTO: Susan S. Kozik
EVP and General Counsel: George W. Madison
EVP, Human Resources: Dermot J. O'Brien
EVP and Chief Institutional Development and Sales
  Officer: Bertram L. Scott, age 56
EVP Public Affairs and Marketing:
  I. Steven (Steve) Goldstein
EVP, Risk Management: Erwin W. Martens
EVP and Head of Fixed Income and Real Estate:
  John A. Somers
EVP Technology and Operations: Cara L. Schnaper
EVP Individual Client Services; President, TIAA-CREF
  Individual & Institutional Services: Maliz E. Beams,
  age 52
SVP Marketing and Advertising: Jamie DePeau
SVP and Head of Corporate Governance: John C. Wilcox
VP and Corporate Secretary: E. Laverne Jones
Chief Investment Officer: Edward J. Grzybowski
Chairman, President, and CEO, TIAA-CREF Life
  Insurance: Bret L. Benham
President, TIAA-CREF Trust Company: Dale Keyser

LOCATIONS

HQ: Teachers Insurance and Annuity Association —
    College Retirement Equities Fund
    730 3rd Ave., New York, NY 10017
Phone: 212-490-9000   Fax: 212-916-4840
Web: www.tiaa-cref.org

PRODUCTS/OPERATIONS

Selected Subsidiaries and Units

Kapsick & Company
Teachers Personal Investors Services, Inc. (mutual fund management)
TIAA-CREF Individual & Institutional Services, Inc. (broker-dealer)
TIAA-CREF Life Insurance Company (insurance and annuities)
TIAA-CREF Trust Company, FSB (trust services)
TIAA-CREF Tuition Financing, Inc. (state tuition savings program management)

Selected Mutual Funds

Bond
Bond Plus II
Equity Index
Growth & Income
High-Yield II
Inflation-Linked Bond
International Equity
Large-Cap Growth
Large-Cap Value
Managed Allocation II
Mid-Cap Growth
Mid-Cap Value
Money Market
Real Estate Securities
Short-Term Bond II
Small-Cap Equity
Social Choice Equity
Tax-Exempt Bond II

COMPETITORS

Aetna	JPMorgan Chase
AIG	MassMutual
AIG Retirement	Merrill Lynch
Ameriprise	MetLife
AXA Financial	New York Life
Bank of New York Mellon	Northwestern Mutual
Berkshire Hathaway	Principal Financial
CalPERS	Prudential
Charles Schwab	T. Rowe Price
CIGNA	US Global Investors
Citigroup	USAA
FMR	The Vanguard Group
John Hancock Financial	

HISTORICAL FINANCIALS

Company Type: Private

Income Statement

FYE: December 31

	REVENUE ($ mil.)	NET INCOME ($ mil.)	NET PROFIT MARGIN	EMPLOYEES
12/07	13,187	1,465	11.1%	7,500
12/06	12,378	3,453	27.9%	5,500
12/05	11,703	1,878	16.0%	5,500
12/04	10,864	540	5.0%	6,000
12/03	12,815	504	3.9%	6,000
Annual Growth	0.7%	30.6%	—	5.7%

Net Income History

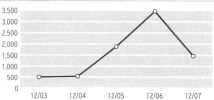

TIC Holdings

TIC Holdings doesn't flinch when it comes to heavy industrial construction projects. The holding company offers services including civil engineering, heavy equipment erection, pipeline construction, and electrical installation. Primary subsidiary TIC — The Industrial Company provides industrial services in the US through about a half dozen regional units; Western Summit Constructors focuses on water and wastewater projects. TIC International operates in North America, Asia, Africa, and Europe. The company is ranked among the leading industrial process and power contractors. TIC Holdings was founded in 1974 and is owned by management.

EXECUTIVES

Chairman: Ronald W. (Ron) McKenzie
President and CEO: Gary B. McKenzie
COO: John Paul
EVP Internal Controls and Risk Management: Ernie Wright
EVP Human Resources and Organizational Development: Victoria Humphrey
EVP Corporate Development: Brad Lawson
SVP TIC Global: John Roos
VP Strategic Growth: Mike Ross
VP Finance and CFO: James F. (Jim) Kissane
VP Corporate Business Development: David Scott
President, TIC Infrastructure and Western Summit Constructors: Terry J. Carlsgaard
President, TIC Diversified: Leroy Meador

LOCATIONS

HQ: TIC Holdings, Inc.
2211 Elk River Rd., Steamboat Springs, CO 80477
Phone: 970-871-7209   **Fax:** 970-879-5052
Web: www.tic-inc.com

TIC Holdings has offices in Arizona, California, Colorado, Georgia, Michigan, Nevada, New Mexico, Texas, and Wyoming. It has international offices in Mexico and Canada.

PRODUCTS/OPERATIONS

Selected Subsidiaries

TIC — The Industrial Company
  Canyon Valley Electric
  ERS Constructors
  TIC Marine and Heavy Civil Group/ Savannah Operations
  TIC International, Inc.
    MexTICa, S. de R.L. de C.V.
    TIC Canada
  TIC Maintenance
    Gulf States, Inc.
    Testronics, Inc.
  TIC The Industrial Company Wyoming, Inc.
Western Summit Constructors, Inc.

COMPETITORS

Aker Solutions	McDermott
Bechtel	Parsons Corporation
Black & Veatch	PCL Construction
Chicago Bridge & Iron	Enterprises
Day & Zimmermann	Peter Kiewit Sons'
Dick Corporation	Shaw Group
Earth Tech	Skanska
Fluor	Turner Corporation
Foster Wheeler	Washington Division
Gilbane	Whiting-Turner
Lummus Technology	Zachry Group
M. A. Mortenson	

HISTORICAL FINANCIALS

Company Type: Private

Income Statement

FYE: December 31

	REVENUE ($ mil.)	NET INCOME ($ mil.)	NET PROFIT MARGIN	EMPLOYEES
12/07	2,000	—	—	9,000
12/06	1,700	—	—	9,000
12/05	1,224	—	—	9,000
Annual Growth	27.8%	—	—	0.0%

Revenue History

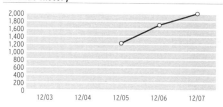

Tillamook County Creamery Association

Hoping to put its name on the map in more ways than one, Tillamook County Creamery Association (TCCA) has a reputation for making cheese. The cooperative, also known as Tillamook Cheese, manufactures dairy products including butter, ice cream, fluid milk, sour cream, yogurt, and yogurt smoothies, but most of its production is devoted to cheddar cheese. It does, however, make other cheeses, including colby, jack, and Swiss.

Tillamook products are available thoughout the US. The co-op is owned by some 130 dairy farmers in and around Tillamook County, Oregon. TCCA was founded in 1909 when 10 farmers consolidated their cheese manufacturing operations.

EXECUTIVES

Chairman and Secretary: Rick Godinho
President and CEO: Harold G. M. Strunk
VP Finance and CFO: Don Desjarlais, age 52
VP Sales and Marketing: Jay Allison
VP Member Relations and Public Affairs: Mark Wustenberg
Director Marketing: Kathy Holstad
Director Information Technology: Steve Burge

LOCATIONS

HQ: Tillamook County Creamery Association
4175 Hwy. 101 North, Tillamook, OR 97141
Phone: 503-815-1300   **Fax:** 503-842-6039
Web: www.tillamookcheese.com

PRODUCTS/OPERATIONS

Selected Products

Cheese
  Cheddar
  Kosher
  Medium
  Reduced fat
  Sharp
  Smoked
  Special Reserve Extra Sharp
  Vintage White Extra Sharp Vintage White Medium
Other cheeses
  Colby
  Colby Jack
  Monterey Jack
  Pepper Jack
  Mozzarella
Other products
  Butter
  Ice cream
  Sour cream
  Yogurt

COMPETITORS

Agri-Mark
American Milk Products
AMPI
Bel Brands USA
BelGioioso Cheese
Ben & Jerry's
Blue Bell
Brewster Dairy
California Dairies Inc.
Cheesemakers, Inc.
Crystal Farms Refrigerated Distribution Company
Dairy Farmers of America
Darigold, Inc.
Dean Foods
Dreyer's
Ellsworth Cooperative
Friendly Ice Cream
Great Lakes Cheese
Guida's
Hiland Dairy
HP Hood
Kraft Foods
Land O'Lakes
Leprino Foods
Marathon Cheese
Maryland & Virginia Milk Producers
Organic Valley
Prairie Farms Dairy
Saputo
Saputo Cheese USA Inc.
Sargento
Swiss Valley Farms
Swiss-American
United Dairy Farmers
Wells' Dairy

HISTORICAL FINANCIALS

Company Type: Cooperative

Income Statement				FYE: December 31
	REVENUE ($ mil.)	NET INCOME ($ mil.)	NET PROFIT MARGIN	EMPLOYEES
12/07	382	—	—	650
12/06	326	—	—	650
12/05	309	—	—	650
12/04	309	—	—	650
12/03	270	—	—	470
Annual Growth	9.1%	—	—	8.4%

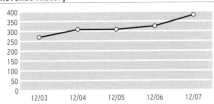

Revenue History

Tishman Realty & Construction

Tishman Realty & Construction is an immigrant success story writ large. The company builds and manages office, hospitality, recreational, industrial, and other property for itself and for others. It offers third-party developers a full menu of real estate design, construction, management, and other real estate and construction services. High-profile projects handled by the company include Disney World's EPCOT Center, Madison Square Garden, the ill-fated World Trade Center (as well as building the Freedom Tower on the same site), and Chicago's John Hancock Center. The Tishman family — scions of immigrant founder Julius Tishman, who began building tenements in 1898 — own Tishman Realty & Construction.

Affiliates of Tishman Realty & Construction include Tishman Construction, which provides development and construction services; Tishman Technologies, which equips buildings with data and communications infrastructure; and Tishman Hotel & Realty, which provides construction management and financial and property management services for hospitality and retail space. Tishman Realty & Construction typically handles all aspects of projects from feasibility, design, and financing to property and asset management.

Former CEO John Tishman expanded the company beyond its Big Apple origins, most notably through a partnership with the Walt Disney Company to build hotels and theme parks in Florida. Among the company's completed non-New York projects are the Dolphin and Swan hotels at Disney's EPCOT Center, the Sheraton Chicago Hotel & Towers, and the Westin Rio Mar Beach Resort & Casino in Puerto Rico.

HISTORY

Julius Tishman escaped the Russian pogroms of the late 19th century by emigrating to the US in 1885. Five years later he opened a store in Newburgh, New York. In 1898, as eastern European immigrants inundated New York City, Tishman began building tenements on the Lower East Side. He named his business Julius Tishman & Sons. By the 1920s, the firm had moved uptown and upscale, building luxury apartment buildings. The firm went public in 1928 as Tishman Realty & Construction, with the family retaining an ownership stake. Julius was chairman; son David was CEO.

The pitfalls of going public were soon obvious. The offering raised less than $2 million, not enough to finance projects, and because the stock market favored profit generation over asset appreciation, the company was undervalued. When the Depression hit, David's involvement as a director of the Bank of the United States and the family's participation in bad loans made by the bank forced the firm to sell assets. Tishman's lenders, including insurer Metropolitan Life, took over some of its buildings, leaving the firm to manage them. In the 1930s and 1940s, the company focused mainly on managing its properties. It continued its construction operations on a contract basis for the Federal Housing Authority.

After WWII, Tishman moved away from residential development and into office construction. Meanwhile, David's younger brothers Paul and Norman began jockeying for position to replace him as CEO; in 1948 David chose Norman to succeed him (Paul resigned to form his own construction company). A nephew, John, became head of the firm's construction arm.

By the early 1950s, Tishman had moved into management and leasing services and expanded nationally, opening offices in Chicago and Los Angeles. In 1962 David relinquished his chairmanship to Norman, who was in turn replaced as CEO by his brother Bob. Under Bob's leadership, Tishman divested residential properties to focus on office space, mostly company-owned.

In 1972 the company completed the World Trade Center complex, including twin 110-story towers, which were then the tallest buildings in the world. The iconic structures stood more than 1,300 feet above Manhattan until they collapsed as a result of the September 11 terrorist attacks in 2001.

Tishman was hit hard by recession in the 1970s. In 1976 Bob took the company private again, selling off the firm's New York assets, and split the company into Tishman Speyer Properties (headed by Bob and son-in-law Jerry Speyer); Tishman Management and Leasing (now part of Grubb & Ellis); and Tishman Realty & Construction (headed by John and promptly bought by the Rockefeller Center Corporation).

John Tishman bought back Tishman Realty & Construction in 1980 and steered it into high-profile partnerships with the likes of the Walt Disney Company. He also added project management and real estate financial services to his company's repertoire and continued to take part in highly visible construction projects.

Since the late 1990s, Tishman's major projects have centered around the revitalization efforts of Times Square and 42nd Street in New York City — including the construction of 4 Times Square (the Condé Nast building), 3 Times Square (Reuters America headquarters), and E Walk, a mixed-use entertainment and retail center.

EXECUTIVES

Chairman and CEO: Daniel R. Tishman
Vice Chairman; Chairman and CEO, Tishman Hotel & Realty LP: John A. Vickers
COO: Jay Badame
CFO: Frank Beck
EVP, Estimating: Bill Endres
EVP and Regional Manager, Tishman Construction Corporation of New Jersey and Tishman Construction Corporation of Pennsylvania: Edward J. (Ed) Cettina
EVP and Regional Manager, Tishman Construction Corporation of Washington, DC: Stephen H. Dalton
EVP and Regional Manager, Tishman Construction Corporation of Illinois: James E. McLean
EVP, Tishman Technologies Corporation: Ronald H. Bowman Jr.
EVP, Tishman Technologies: Richard O. Blackman
EVP, Tishman Technologies: Joseph B. Ryan Jr.

EVP, Tishman Interiors: Vincent Piscopo
EVP, Tishman Technologies and Tishman Construction: John Krush
SVP Corporate Relations: Richard M. Kielar
SVP and General Counsel: Linda Christensen Sjogren
President, Tishman Construction Corporation of Nevada and Tishman Construction Corporation of New England: Daniel P. McQuade
President and CEO, Tishman Real Estate Services: Joseph J. Simone
President, Tishman Construction Corporation of New York: John T. Livingston
President, Tishman Realty Corp.: William J. Sales

LOCATIONS

HQ: Tishman Realty & Construction Co., Inc.
666 5th Ave., 38th Fl., New York, NY 10103
Phone: 212-399-3600   **Fax:** 212-739-7065
Web: www.tishman.com

PRODUCTS/OPERATIONS

Selected Subsidiaries

Tishman Construction Corporation
Tishman Hotel & Realty LP
Tishman Interiors Corporation (interior build-out and renovation)
Tishman Technologies Corporation

COMPETITORS

Bovis Lend Lease	Jones Lang LaSalle
CB Richard Ellis	Lefrak Organization
Cushman & Wakefield	Lincoln Property
Forest City Ratner	Trammell Crow Company
Gilbane	The Trump Organization
Grubb & Ellis	Turner Construction
JMB Realty	Witkoff Group

Topa Equities

Holding company Topa Equities casts a wide net. Owned by John Anderson, Topa has about 40 businesses involved in auto dealerships, beer distribution, insurance, real estate, and more. Topa's beverage operations include Ace Beverage, Mission Beverages, and Paradise Beverages; the firm dominates the Hawaiian beer market. Brands sold include all major US brews and leading US imports, including Guinness, Heineken, and InBev products. Anderson started in 1956 as a distributor of Hamm's beer. UCLA's Anderson School of Business, to which Anderson donated $15 million, is named for him.

EXECUTIVES

Chairman, President, and CEO: John E. Anderson Sr., age 90
President and CEO, Topa Insurance: Noshirwan Marfatia
President, Topa Properties: Steven D. Morton
VP, CFO, and Treasurer, Topa Insurance: Daniel Sherrin
VP Commercial Lines, Topa Insurance: Larry Esposito
VP, Topa Properties: Elsbeth M. Rowaan
Director Human Resources, Topa Insurance: William Robinson
Underwriting Manager, Commercial Lines and Package and Property, Topa Insurance: Al Ridge
EVP, Ace Beverage: John Anderson Jr.

LOCATIONS

HQ: Topa Equities, Ltd.
1800 Avenue of the Stars, Ste. 1400,
Los Angeles, CA 90067
Phone: 310-203-9199   **Fax:** 310-557-1837
Web: www.topa.com

COMPETITORS

Beauchamp Distributing
Constellation Brands
Glazer's Wholesale Drug
Reyes Holdings
Southern Wine & Spirits
Western Beverage Company

HISTORICAL FINANCIALS

Company Type: Private

Income Statement

FYE: December 31

	REVENUE ($ mil.)	NET INCOME ($ mil.)	NET PROFIT MARGIN	EMPLOYEES
12/07	1,200	—	—	2,133
12/06	1,210	—	—	2,295
12/05	1,202	—	—	2,318
12/04	1,120	—	—	2,298
12/03	1,056	—	—	2,278
Annual Growth	3.2%	—	—	(1.6%)

Revenue History

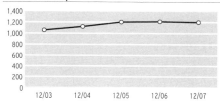

Topco Associates

Topco Associates is a top company in terms of private-label procurement. Topco uses the combined purchasing clout of more than 60 member companies (mostly supermarket operators and foodservice suppliers) to wring discounts from wholesalers and manufacturers. Topco distributes more than 5,000 private-label items, including fresh meat, dairy and bakery goods, and health and beauty aids, to some 10,000 retail locations. Its brands include Food Club, Shurfine, and a line of "Top" labels such as Top Crest. In 2001 Topco Associates, Inc., merged operations with Shurfine International to form Topco Associates LLC.

In addition to procurement services, Topco helps its members contain costs through financial services programs and other business services. It also helps members market their own store brands.

HISTORY

Food Cooperatives was founded in Wisconsin in 1944 to procure dairy bags and paper products during wartime shortages. A few years later it merged with Top Frost Foods, with which it had some common members. In 1948 the name

Topco Associates was adopted (created by combining the word "Top" from Top Frost with the "Co" in Cooperatives). The member companies involved in the merger included Alpha Beta, Big Bear Stores, Brockton Public Market, Fred Meyer, Furr's, Hinky Dinky, Penn Fruit Company, and Star Markets.

Topco initially sold basic commodities to private-label retailers. It added fresh produce in 1958 and expanded its product line further in 1960, moving into general merchandise, health and beauty care items, and store equipment. In 1961, when the company moved its headquarters to Skokie, Illinois, revenues topped the $100 million mark. In the 1960s other leading supermarkets, including Giant Eagle, King Soopers, McCarty-Holman, and Tom Thumb, joined Topco.

Also that decade it came under attack from the Justice Department when it was accused of antitrust activity in granting its members exclusive distribution rights for Topco-branded products. In 1972 the Supreme Court ruled against Topco. It then agreed to sell products under the private labels of its members.

In the late 1970s the company introduced Valu Time, the first nationally marketed line of branded generic products. This concept was then adopted by many US supermarkets. By 1979 Topco surpassed $1 billion in annual revenues.

By the end of the 1980s, Topco's membership had expanded to include Randall's, Riser Foods, Pueblo International, Schnuck Markets, and Smith's Food & Drug Centers. In 1988 it introduced World Classics, a premium line of high-volume, high-margin products promoted as national brands.

During the early 1990s Topco ran through a number of CEOs. In 1990 Robert Seelert replaced 10-year CEO Marcel Lussier. In 1992 John Beggs took over, and the next year Steven Rubow was handed the reins.

The early 1990s also saw rapid growth, with 20 new members bringing the company's total to 46 by 1995 (its membership later declined in number through acquisition and consolidation). Topco also expanded internationally, with the membership of Oshawa Group in Canada and the associate membership of SEIYU in Japan in 1995. Also that year the company lured upscale Kings Super Markets away from distributor White Rose.

Topco began offering members utility accounting and natural gas services through Illinova Energy Partners in 1998. The company expanded its Top Care line of personal care products in 1999, using a variety of packaging designed to resemble several name brands within a single category. Rubow retired late that year and was replaced by Steve Lauer. Topco took aim at consumers who prefer natural foods in 2000, launching the Full Circle line of organically grown items.

In November 2001 Topco combined operations with co-op operator Shurfine International and re-formed as a limited liability company. Topco Associates, Inc., and Shurfine International became holding companies with stakes in Topco Associates LLC. Lauer, the CEO of Topco Associates, Inc., was named president and CEO of the new company. In 2004 IGA became a member of Topco.

The company formed TopSource, a subsidiary to focus on not-for-resale goods and services, after acquiring BrainTree Sourcing from Ahold USA.

EXECUTIVES

Chairman: Steven C. (Steve) Smith, age 50
President and CEO: Steven K. (Steve) Lauer
EVP and Chief Procurement Officer: Frank Muschetto
SVP and CFO: Randall (Randy) Skoda
SVP Account Management: Ian Grossman
SVP Top Source Not-For-Resale: Nancy McDermott
SVP Account Management: Kenneth H. Guy
SVP Center Store Program Management:
  Daniel F. Mazur
SVP Account Management: John P. Stanhaus
SVP World Brands and Foodservice:
  Michael F. Ricciardi
Director Dry Grocery and Oils: Kathy Babiarz
Director Frozen Foods: Charlie Conrads
Director General Merchandise: Debbie Dietke
**Director Can Goods, Snack Foods, and Organic
  Grocery:** Chuck Harris
Director Media Relations: Annette McMillan
Director Non-Foods: Norm Spencer
Director Creative Services: Karen Vorwald
Director Corporate Communications: Virginia V. Mann
Manager Human Resources: Dennis Pieper
Auditors: KPMG LLP

LOCATIONS

HQ: Topco Associates LLC
  7711 Gross Point Rd., Skokie, IL 60077
Phone: 847-676-3030   **Fax:** 847-676-4949
Web: www.topco.com

PRODUCTS/OPERATIONS

Selected Private-Label Brands

Food Club
Full Circle
Paws Premium
Paws Professional
Top Care
Top Crest
Valu Time
World Classics Trading Company

COMPETITORS

Associated Wholesale Grocers	McLane
	Nash-Finch
C&S Wholesale	SUPERVALU
Central Grocers	Wakefern Food
Certified Grocers Midwest	Wal-Mart
Kroger	Western Family

HISTORICAL FINANCIALS
Company Type: Cooperative

Income Statement   FYE: December 31

	REVENUE ($ mil.)	NET INCOME ($ mil.)	NET PROFIT MARGIN	EMPLOYEES
12/07	8,800	—	—	400
12/06	7,348	—	—	360
12/05	5,600	—	—	310
12/04	5,000	—	—	—
12/03	4,600	—	—	400
Annual Growth	17.6%	—	—	0.0%

Revenue History

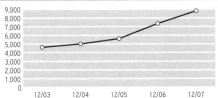

Towers Perrin

Refusing to live in an ivory tower, this company aims to offer practical advice. One of the leading management consulting firms in the world, Towers Perrin serves major enterprises — including most of the *FORTUNE* 1,000 — across a broad span of industries. The firm divides its service offerings into two main buckets: human capital, which includes human resources consulting practices related to issues such as benefits, compensation, and workforce effectiveness; and risk and financial services, which includes several practices related to insurance issues. Its Tillinghast unit provides consulting services for insurance companies. Towers Perrin, which is owned by its partners, was established in 1934.

The firm takes advantage of its global reach to pitch its services to multinational enterprises. It has offices and alliance partners throughout the Americas, the Asia/Pacific region, and Europe.

At the same time, Towers Perrin has been working to grow via tuck-in acquisitions. The company expanded its enterprise risk management practice in June 2006 by acquiring consulting firm Risk Capital Management Partners. It also boosted its financial services product portfolio in early 2007 when it acquired MGMC, Inc., a firm that provides market research and advisement services mostly to investment and commercial banks.

EXECUTIVES

Chairman and CEO: Mark Mactas
Global CEO and Managing Director, Reinsurance:
  William (Bill) Eyre Jr.
CFO: Robert G. (Bob) Hogan
Chief Administrative Officer and CIO: Tony Candito
General Counsel and Secretary: Kevin Young
Managing Director, Human Capital Group:
  Jim Foreman
**Managing Director, Tillinghast and Towers Perrin
  Reinsurance:** Patricia L. (Tricia) Guinn
Marketing Director, HR Services: Sharon Wunderlich
Executive Compensation and Rewards, HR Services:
  Gary Locke
Health and Welfare, HR Services: Dave Guilmette
Retirement, HR Services: Steve Kerstein

LOCATIONS

HQ: Towers Perrin
  1 Stamford Plaza, 263 Tresser Blvd.,
  Stamford, CT 06901
Phone: 203-326-5400   **Fax:** 203-326-5499
Web: www.towersperrin.com

PRODUCTS/OPERATIONS

Selected Services

Human Capital
  Actuarial consulting
  Executive compensations
  Health and welfare
  HR function effectiveness
  Mergers, acquisitions, and restructuring
  Research and surveys
  Retirement
  Total rewards effectiveness
  Workforce effectiveness
Risk and Financial
  Actuarial consulting
  Enterprise risk management
  Financial modeling
  Insurance consulting
  Mergers, acquisitions, and restructuring
  Reinsurance
  Retirement risk solutions

COMPETITORS

Accenture	Gallup
Aon	Hewitt Associates
A.T. Kearney	HR Solutions
Bain & Company	KPMG
Benecon Group	Marsh & McLennan
Booz Allen	McKinsey & Company
Boston Consulting	PricewaterhouseCoopers
Deloitte	Right Management
Drake Beam Morin	Watson Wyatt
Ernst & Young Global	

HISTORICAL FINANCIALS
Company Type: Private

Income Statement   FYE: December 31

	REVENUE ($ mil.)	NET INCOME ($ mil.)	NET PROFIT MARGIN	EMPLOYEES
12/07	1,570	—	—	6,232
12/06	1,420	—	—	5,484
12/05	1,410	—	—	5,171
12/04	1,620	—	—	7,827
12/03	1,500	—	—	8,384
Annual Growth	1.1%	—	—	(7.1%)

Revenue History

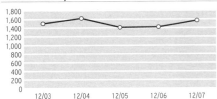

Toys "R" Us

Kids rule the aisles while parents tag along for the ride at Toys "R" Us. The company is one of the world's largest toy retailers, but it has lost its top position in the US to retailing behemoth Wal-Mart. Toys "R" Us sells its wares through 1,500-plus stores in the US and abroad, and Web sites. In addition to about 585 US namesake stores selling toys, games, and other items for kids, Toys "R" Us sells infant and toddler apparel, furniture, and feeding supplies at some 260 Babies "R" Us stores in more than 40 states. The company is owned by KKR, Bain Capital, and real estate firm Vornado Realty Trust, which together took the toy seller private in a $6.6 billion deal in 2005.

Store growth overseas is outpacing growth at home. In Canada and more than 30 other foreign countries, Toys "R" Us operates, licenses, and franchises more than 700 stores. Major markets include Japan, Canada, and the UK. The first Toys "R" Us store opened in Shanghai in late 2006, and the company now operates four stores in China.

The toy seller's CEO, former Target Vice Chairman Gerald L. Storch, succeeded John Eyler, who resigned when Toys "R" Us went private. He is charged with winning back market share from discounters, including his former employer Target. To that end, Storch has focused on making Toys "R" Us a leaner, more efficient retailer. The toy seller has also emphasized customer service and stocked up on top-selling and proprietary items (like special Barbie dolls available only at its stores) for its busy holiday season. It has also made a concerted effort to clean up its stores and reduce clutter to make shopping easier and more enjoyable.

Trying a new approach, Toys "R" Us has started converting some locations to combination Toys "R" Us and Babies "R" Us stores (placing the two formats side-by-side), hoping to give parents a one-stop shopping destination.

Along with the rest of the toy industry, Toys "R" Us had its hands full with recall concerns in 2007. The toy retailer took steps to help consumers find recall items by listing them on its Web site. It also plans to mandate that all toy vendors show proof that toys have been properly safety tested.

HISTORY

Charles Lazarus entered retailing in 1948, adding his $2,000 savings to a $2,000 bank loan to convert his father's Washington, DC, bicycle repair shop into a kids' furniture store. Customers persuaded him to add toys, and he renamed the store Children's Bargain Town. Lazarus later changed the format in 1957 and changed the company's name to Toys "R" Us.

By 1966 sales had reached $12 million. He sold his company to discounter Interstate Stores for $7.5 million, with the condition that he would retain control of the toy operation. By 1974 Lazarus' division had expanded to 47 stores and $130 million in annual sales, but the parent had filed for bankruptcy.

In 1978, Lazarus raised Interstate from the dead, or at least pulled them out of bankruptcy and into his control. With 72 toy stores (and 10 Interstate stores) and a 5% toy market share, it posted $349 million in sales that year. The company went public in 1978.

From 1978 to 1983 earnings grew 40% annually, market share climbed to 12.5%, and the number of toy stores reached 169. The company opened several Kids "R" Us clothing stores in 1983, copying the toy stores' discount formula. The following year the store expanded internationally, with locations in Canada and Singapore. Toys "R" Us entered the Japanese market in 1991.

Toys "R" Us pushed rivals Child World and Lionel into bankruptcy in 1992. In 1993 Toys "R" Us continued its international expansion before Lazarus stepped aside as CEO in 1994. The company opened its first franchise (in Dubai, United Arab Emirates) in 1995. The toy seller paid $376 million for Baby Superstore in 1997 to strengthen its fledgling Babies "R" Us (launched the previous year); by 1998 Babies "R" Us had become the largest US baby store chain.

Trouble came in 1997 when a federal judge decided Toys "R" Us violated trade laws by conspiring with manufacturers to keep toys priced artificially high and out of warehouse clubs like Costco. Toys "R" Us appealed, then settled with the FTC for $40.5 million, including $27 million in donated toys.

In 1998 president and COO Bob Nakasone became CEO, and the company began selling online and launched its first mail-order catalog. Toys "R" Us cut inventory by more than $560 million, closed almost 100 stores to consolidate some distribution and administration operations, and took a restructuring charge of almost $500 million.

Toys "R" Us was passed in US toy sales in 1999 by Wal-Mart. Later that year, as Toys "R" Us struggled to win back lost market share and after seven straight quarters of earnings decline, CEO Nakasone left the company.

In early 2000 the company hired John Eyler away from FAO Schwarz as president and CEO. That year Toys "R" Us sold 32% of its Japanese subsidiary, Toys – Japan, to the public, retaining a 48% stake. toysrus.com, haunted by its failure to deliver toys in time for Christmas 1999, launched a co-branded Internet store (toys, video games) with Amazon.com later in 2000. (The partnership came to a bitter end in 2006 after a lengthy court fight that stemmed from Amazon.com's decision to sell toys on its site from other distributors. Toys "R" Us now has full control over its Web operations.)

In 2002 the company said it would close 37 Kids "R" Us stores and 27 of the non-remodeled stores, in many cases converting nearby stores to the combo format; it also said it would cut 1,900 jobs. Weak holiday sales and continued competition from mass retailers prompted the company to lay off 700 of its management and supervisory employees in late January 2002.

Citing continued sales declines in some of its freestanding operations, the company closed the majority of its 146 Kids "R" Us clothing stores and all 36 Imaginarium stores in early 2004. The company sold 124 of the Kids "R" Us stores for $197 million to Office Depot.

In 2005 two private investment firms (KKR and Bain Capital) and a real estate company (Vornado Realty Trust) bought Toys "R" Us for $6.6 billion. At that time, CEO John Eyler and COO Christopher Kay both left the company.

In 2006 former Target Vice Chairman Gerald L. Storch joined Toys "R" Us as the company's new CEO. In its first store closings since going private, the company shuttered 75 of its toys stores in 2006, and converted a dozen others to its Babies "R" Us format. As a result of the closings some 3,000 employees lost their jobs.

EXECUTIVES

Chairman and CEO: Gerald L. (Jerry) Storch, age 51, $1,000,000 pay
EVP and COO: Claire H. Babrowski, age 51
EVP and CFO: F. Clay Creasey Jr., age 59, $346,154 pay
EVP; President, Toys "R" Us North America: Ronald D. (Ron) Boire, age 47, $1,168,269 pay
EVP Human Resources: Daniel Caspersen, age 55, $320,192 pay
SVP, General Counsel, and Corporate Secretary: David J. Schwartz
SVP Logistics: Michael C. Jacobs
SVP Marketing, Toys "R" Us, U.S.: Greg Ahearn
SVP Taxes: Peter W. Weiss
SVP Global Product Development and SVP, General Merchandise Manager, Toys "R" Us International: Joan W. Donovan
Manager Corporate Communications: Jennifer Albano
President, Babies "R" Us: Deborah M. (Deb) Derby, age 44, $547,115 pay
President, Toys "R" Us Japan: Monika Merz
President, Toys "R" Us Continental Europe: Antonio Urcelay, age 56
President, Toys "R" Us, Canada: Kevin Macnab
SVP and Chief Merchandising Officer, Toys "R" Us U.S.: Karen Dodge
Auditors: Deloitte & Touche LLP

LOCATIONS

HQ: Toys "R" Us, Inc.
1 Geoffrey Way, Wayne, NJ 07470
Phone: 973-617-3500   **Fax:** 973-617-4006
Web: www.toysrus.com

2008 Stores

	No.
Toys "R" Us (US)	585
Toys "R" Us (International)	715
Babies "R" Us	260
Total	**1,560**

2008 Toys "R" Us US Locations

	No.
California	71
Florida	41
Texas	41
New York	37
Pennsylvania	31
Illinois	27
Ohio	27
New Jersey	25
Michigan	21
Georgia	19
Virginia	19
Maryland	14
Massachusetts	14
North Carolina	13
Tennessee	12
Washington	12
Indiana	11
Missouri	11
Arizona	10
Connecticut	9
Wisconsin	9
Louisiana	8
Alabama	7
Kentucky	7
Minnesota	7
South Carolina	7
Iowa	6
Oregon	6
Colorado	5
New Hampshire	5
Oklahoma	5
Utah	5
Other states	43
Total	**585**

2008 Toys "R" US International Locations

	No.
Japan	168
United Kingdom	73
Canada	67
Germany	58
Spain	42
France	37
Turkey	35
Australia	32
Israel	24
South Africa	18
Netherlands	16
Taiwan	15
Austria	13
Denmark	13
Sweden	13
Malaysia	10
Hong Kong	9
Saudi Arabia	9
Norway	8
Portugal	8
Singapore	7
Switzerland	6
Thailand	6
Philippines	6
United Arab Emirates	5
China	4
Finland	4
Other countries	9
Total	**715**

PRODUCTS/OPERATIONS

2008 Sales

	$ mil.	% of total
Toys "R" Us (US)	5,955	43
Toys "R" Us (International)	5,344	39
Babies "R" Us	2,495	18
Total	**13,794**	**100**

2008 Sales

	% of total
Juvenile	32
Learning	20
Entertainment	17
Core toy	17
Seasonal	13
Other	1
Total	**100**

COMPETITORS

Best Buy	KB Toys
Build-A-Bear	Kids Stuff
The Children's Place	Kmart
Circuit City	Learning Express
Costco Wholesale	Macy's
Discovery Toys	Mothercare
Disney	OshKosh B'Gosh
Excelligence Learning	Parent Company
GameStop	Sears
The Gap	Target
Gymboree	Wal-Mart
Hamleys	

HISTORICAL FINANCIALS

Company Type: Private

Income Statement

FYE: Saturday nearest January 31

	REVENUE ($ mil.)	NET INCOME ($ mil.)	NET PROFIT MARGIN	EMPLOYEES
1/08	13,794	153	1.1%	72,000
1/07	13,050	109	0.8%	59,000
1/06	9,932	427	4.3%	63,000
1/05	11,100	252	2.3%	97,000
1/04	11,566	88	0.8%	113,000
Annual Growth	**4.5%**	**14.8%**	**—**	**(10.7%)**

2008 Year-End Financials

Debt ratio: —
Return on equity: —
Cash ($ mil.): —
Current ratio: —
Long-term debt ($ mil.): 5,824

Net Income History

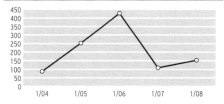

TPG Capital

Yee-haw! Let's round us up some LBOs! TPG Capital, also known as Texas Pacific Group, has staked its claim on the buyout frontier. The company, which does not get involved in the day-to-day operations of the companies in which it invests, usually holds onto an investment for at least five years, although consistent moneymakers may be kept indefinitely. Notable holdings include stakes in Neiman Marcus, Ducati, Lenovo, SunGard Data Systems, and Aleris International. With KKR, the company bought electric company TXU (now Energy Future Holdings) in 2007 for some $45 billion, including debt, in one of the largest buyouts in history. TPG amassed $15 billion for a Texas-sized buyout fund in 2006.

TPG is considering raising a relatively meager $1 billion for its latest fund, to the dismay of some investors. Co-founder and partner David "Bondo" Bonderman, known for turning around Continental Airlines, has traditionally adhered to the "bigger is better" model of investing, but TPG believes that the market for massive deals is becoming oversaturated and that midsized firms are ripe for the picking.

However, the company isn't exactly walking the talk yet. Working with Apollo Management and Northwest Airlines, respectively, TPG closed an approximately $28 billion purchase of Harrah's Entertainment and acquired Midwest Air Group for some $450 million in early 2008.

That year the company agreed to buy 25% of Israeli food and beverage company Strauss Group for $288 million. The deal gives it the option to buy another 10% at about its current valuation. It teamed up with Global Infrastructure Partners to place a hostile bid for Australia's Asciano Group, a year after the port and freight rail concern was spun off from Toll Holdings. It also agreed to buy a 23% stake in troubled British Bank Bradford & Bingley but withdrew its offer after the bank's credit rating dropped.

In addition to the massive TXU deal, TPG in 2007 joined with GS Capital Partners to buy telecommunications giant ALLTEL for nearly $25 billion. (The investment firms are seeing a rapid return on the investment: They are selling ALLTEL to Verizon Wireless for $28.1 billion.) Also, with Silver Lake Partners, TPG acquired telecom equipment maker Avaya for more than $8 billion.

TPG was in on several other gargantuan deals in 2006. It is part of a Blackstone Group-led consortium that acquired Freescale Semiconductor for $17.6 billion. TPG teamed with three other firms to buy Biomet for almost $11 billion. Also that year TPG bought the consumer packaging division of Smurfit-Stone (since renamed Altivity Packaging) and, along with Leonard Green & Partners, purchased the PETCO pet store chain. TPG also joined with Thomas H. Lee Partners and other investors to buy Spanish-language broadcaster Univision, and it allied with Silver Lake Partners in a buyout of travel-booking firm Sabre Holdings. It divested holdings in Burger King and J. Crew through IPOs that year.

TPG has invested extensively in Europe, where deals have included the turnaround of Punch Taverns. Other European investments include UK retailer Debenhams (with CVC Capital Partners); restaurant, pub, and hotel chain Scottish & Newcastle (with CVC and Blackstone Group); German bathroom fixtures manufacturer Grohe Water Technology; and luxury brand Bally Management.

Affiliated funds include the Newbridge partnerships (overseas investments) and TPG-Axon (hedge fund). Newbridge, which is also owned by Blum Capital Partners, has taken a share of China-based Shenzhen Development Bank in a landmark foreign investment in mainland China. TPG's venture capital affiliate, TPG Growth, specializes in telecommunications and technology companies.

Boasting more than $50 billion of capital under management, the company has about 15 offices worldwide.

EXECUTIVES

Managing Partner: David Bonderman, age 65
Managing Partner: James G. (Jim) Coulter, age 49
Managing Partner: William S. Price III, age 48
CFO: John E. Viola
COO: Thomas E. (Tom) Reinhart
Partner, Operations: Richard W. (Dick) Boyce, age 54
Partner, Investor Relations: Jamie Gates
VP and General Counsel: David A. Spuria

LOCATIONS

HQ: TPG Capital
301 Commerce St., Ste. 3300,
Fort Worth, TX 76102
Phone: 817-871-4000   **Fax:** 817-871-4001
Web: www.texaspacificgroup.com

TPG Capital has US offices in Fort Worth, Texas; Menlo Park, California; New York; San Francisco; and Washington, DC. It operates international offices in Hong Kong, London, Luxembourg, Melbourne, Moscow, Mumbai, Shanghai, Singapore, and Tokyo.

COMPETITORS

AEA Holdings	HM Capital Partners
Apollo Advisors	Jordan Company
Bain Capital	Kelso & Company
Berkshire Hathaway	Keystone Group
Blackstone Group	KKR
The Carlyle Group	Oaktree Capital
CD&R	Sevin Rosen
Goldman Sachs	Silver Lake Partners
Haas Wheat	Thomas H. Lee Partners
Heico Companies	Wingate Partners

Transammonia, Inc.

Fertilizers, liquefied petroleum gas (LPG), and petrochemicals form the lifeblood of international trader Transammonia. The company trades, distributes, and transports these commodities around the world. Transammonia's fertilizer business includes ammonia, phosphates, and urea. Its Sea-3 subsidiary imports and distributes propane to residential, commercial, and industrial customers in the northeastern US and Florida. The Trammochem unit trades in petrochemicals, specializing in aromatics, methanol, methyltertiary butyl ether (MTBE), and olefins. Trammo Petroleum trades oil products including gasoline, heating oil, jet fuel, and naphtha from its office in Houston.

Transammonia was founded in 1965 as an international ammonia trader. It branched into fertilizer merchandising and trading in 1967, LPG trading in 1978, and petrochemicals trading in 1987.

EXECUTIVES

Chairman and CEO: Ronald P. Stanton
SVP and CFO: Edward G. Weiner
CIO: Benjamin Tan
Director Human Resources: Marguerite Harrington

LOCATIONS

HQ: Transammonia, Inc.
   320 Park Ave., New York, NY 10022
Phone: 212-223-3200   **Fax:** 212-759-1410
Web: www.transammonia.com

Transammonia operates offices in Africa, Asia, Europe, North America, and South America.

PRODUCTS/OPERATIONS

Major Subsidiaries
Sea-3 (liquefied propane)
Trammo Gas (LPG)
Trammo Petroleum (crude oil and oil products)
Trammochem (petrochemicals)
Transammonia (fertilizers)

COMPETITORS

Cargill   HELM
CF Industries   Magellan Midstream
ConAgra   Norsk Hydro ASA
Dynegy   Terra Industries

HISTORICAL FINANCIALS

Company Type: Private

Income Statement   FYE: December 31

	REVENUE ($ mil.)	NET INCOME ($ mil.)	NET PROFIT MARGIN	EMPLOYEES
12/07	8,300	—	—	330
12/06	5,430	—	—	347
12/05	6,059	—	—	301
12/04	5,340	—	—	296
12/03	4,000	—	—	300
Annual Growth	20.0%	—	—	2.4%

Revenue History

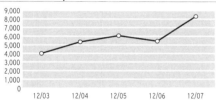

TransPerfect Translations

You pick the language, or languages, and TransPerfect Translations will aim to get your message through. In addition to translation and interpretation, the company offers services such as document management, multicultural marketing, and subtitling and voice-over work. Its network of translators can handle more than 100 languages. TransPerfect does much of its work for law firms and corporate legal departments; it also draws customers from industries such as advertising, financial services, information technology, and retail. Clients have included American Express, Exxon Mobil, and Jones Day. TransPerfect was founded in 1992.

EXECUTIVES

Co-CEO: Elizabeth (Liz) Elting, age 42
Co-CEO: Phil Shawe
COO: Roy B. Trujillo
CTO: Mark Hagerty
CIO: Yu Kai Ng
SVP Global Sales: Brooke Christian
VP Corporate Strategy: Michael Sank
VP European Operations: Angela O'Sullivan
VP Global Production: Mark Peeler
VP US Sales: Kevin Obarski
VP Quality Systems; President, Crimson Life Sciences Division: Marc H. Miller
President, TransPerfect Deposition Services: Stewart I. Edison
President, TransPerfect Diversity and Inclusion Consulting: Michael Davis
President, TransPerfect Document Management: Steven R. Kaplan

LOCATIONS

HQ: TransPerfect Translations, Inc.
   3 Park Ave., 39th Fl., New York, NY 10016
Phone: 212-689-5555   **Fax:** 212-689-1059
Web: www.transperfect.com

PRODUCTS/OPERATIONS

Selected Services
Translation
Interpretation
Transcription
Typesetting and graphics
Voice-overs and subtitling
Staffing solutions
Multicultural marketing
Document management
Diversity and inclusion consulting
Deposition services

COMPETITORS

Albors & Associates
ALT Services
Eclipse Translations
JLS Language Corporation
Linguistic Systems
Lionbridge

HISTORICAL FINANCIALS

Company Type: Private

Income Statement   FYE: December 31

	REVENUE ($ mil.)	NET INCOME ($ mil.)	NET PROFIT MARGIN	EMPLOYEES
12/07	156	—	—	800
12/06	113	—	—	600
12/05	100	—	—	500
12/04	50	—	—	250
Annual Growth	46.1%	—	—	47.4%

Revenue History

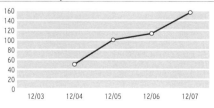

TransUnion LLC

TransUnion makes sure those past-due student loan bills follow you across the country. The firm is one of the three major consumer credit reporting agencies (the others are Experian and Equifax) that lenders use to help determine a borrower's creditworthiness. Combining technology with analysis, the company combats fraud and facilitates credit transactions between businesses and consumers by maintaining credit histories of more than 500 million people in around 35 countries. TransUnion also provides risk management services, insurance credit information, and real estate information services. The company's TrueCredit subsidiary helps consumers protect and improve their credit ratings via its Web site.

The company has services and solutions for industries including banking, real estate, health care, insurance, collections, communications, and tenant screening.

Along with rival Equifax, TransUnion was sued in 2007 for deliberately leaving discharged debt on some debtors' credit reports, in violation of state and federal laws.

Previously a member of the Pritzker family-owned Marmon Group since 1981, TransUnion was spun off in 2005. Its new parent company, TransUnion Corp., is also owned by the Pritzkers. The spinoff followed a series of squabbles over the Pritzker family fortune.

EXECUTIVES

President and CEO: Siddharth N. (Bobby) Mehta, age 48
COO: David Emery
CFO: S. Allen Hamood
Corporate General Counsel: John W. Blenke
EVP Consumer Solutions: Mark Marinko
EVP, Human Resources: Mary Krupka
EVP and CIO: Peter Hoversten
EVP Global Analytics and Decisioning: Wilbert P. Noronha
VP Corporate Affairs and Consumer Education: Colleen Ryan
Senior Director Global Public Relations: Clifton O'Neal
President, International: Andrew Knight
President, U.S. Information Services: Jeffrey (Jeff) Hellinga

LOCATIONS

HQ: TransUnion LLC
   555 W. Adams St., Chicago, IL 60661
Phone: 312-258-1717   **Fax:** 312-466-8385
Web: www.transunion.com

PRODUCTS/OPERATIONS

Selected Services
Business
   Collections
   Credit reporting
   Fraud and identity management
   Marketing
   Risk management
Consumer
   Credit dispute investigation
   Credit monitoring
   Credit reports
   Fraud victim assistance

COMPETITORS

ChoicePoint
Equifax
Experian Americas
Kroll Factual Data
Moody's

HISTORICAL FINANCIALS

Company Type: Private

Income Statement				FYE: December 31
	REVENUE ($ mil.)	NET INCOME ($ mil.)	NET PROFIT MARGIN	EMPLOYEES
12/07	1,200	—	—	4,000
12/06	1,200	—	—	4,100
12/05	1,140	—	—	4,100
12/04	1,000	—	—	4,000
Annual Growth	6.3%	—	—	0.0%

Revenue History

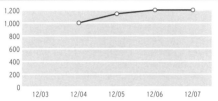

Tree Top

Tree Top stands tall in the nation's apple juice market. The cooperative's approximately 1,300 members grow and harvest about 450,000 tons of apples each year to make apple juice and cider. The co-op produces the Tree Top brand of apple juice, blended fruit juices, and applesauce (also under the Seneca brand). It also makes dried, frozen, and concentrated fruit products. Tree Top customers include retailers and distributors in 30 states. Tree Top also produces dehydrated and frozen fruit products for food manufacturers worldwide through its ingredient unit.

Tree Top's apple juice and cider account for the majority of its sales. The company has focused on growing markets by introducing new product lines including blended juices and flavored applesauce, and bagged fresh apple slices.

The company faces stiff competition from such beverage giants as Coca-Cola, PepsiCo, and Dr Pepper Snapple Group, which continually unveil new juices and other noncarbonated beverage products.

Tree Top also produces and sells a wide variety of bulk dried, chilled, and frozen apple and cherry products as ingredients, which are used by food manufacturers in such products as baked and frozen desserts, cold and hot cereals, yogurt, fruit fillings, and fruit smoothies.

The cooperative operates five production facilities (four in the state of Washington and one in southern California).

EXECUTIVES

Chairman: Fred Valentine
President and CEO: Tom Stokes, age 56
SVP Field Services: Lindsay Buckner, age 56

SVP Ingredient and Foodservice Sales: Tom Hurson, age 48
SVP Sales and Marketing: Dan Hagerty, age 46
VP Finance and CFO: John Wells, age 47
VP Engineering and Technical Support: Gerald (Jerry) Kobes, age 60
VP Human Resources: Nancy Buck, age 57
VP Operations: Berry Wright, age 59
Auditors: Moss Adams, LLP

LOCATIONS

HQ: Tree Top, Inc.
220 E. 2nd Ave., Selah, WA 98942
Phone: 509-697-7251　　**Fax:** 509-697-0421
Web: www.treetop.com

PRODUCTS/OPERATIONS

Selected Brands and Products

Consumer products
　Applesauce
　Apple slices
　Cider
　Flat fruit
　Juice
　　Orchard blends
　　Premium blends
　　Tree Top frozen juice concentrate
　　Three Apple Reserve
Ingredient Products
　Apple (dried, chilled, frozen, and concentrate)
　Cherry (dried, chilled, frozen, and concentrate)

COMPETITORS

Chiquita Brands	National Beverage
Coca-Cola	National Grape Cooperative
Coca-Cola North America	Ocean Spray
Cranberries Limited	Odwalla
Del Monte Foods	Old Orchard
Dole Food	PepsiCo
Dominion Citrus	Sun-Maid
Hansen Natural	Sun-Rype
Knouse Foods	Tropicana
Kraft Foods UK	Veryfine
Mott's	Welch's
Naked Juice	

HISTORICAL FINANCIALS

Company Type: Cooperative

Income Statement				FYE: July 31
	REVENUE ($ mil.)	NET INCOME ($ mil.)	NET PROFIT MARGIN	EMPLOYEES
7/07	284	—	—	836
7/06	290	—	—	1,000
7/05	258	—	—	—
7/04	266	—	—	—
Annual Growth	2.2%	—	—	(16.4%)

Revenue History

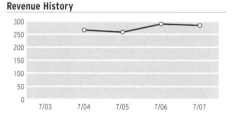

Tribune Company

Its roots are in print journalism, but the Tribune Company has branched beyond the written word to embrace virtually every aspect of modern media. One of the US's top newspaper publishers, it owns about 10 major daily newspapers, including the *Chicago Tribune*, the *Los Angeles Times,* and *Newsday* (Long Island). Tribune also owns 23 TV stations in about 20 markets, cable network Superstation WGN, and a stake in the Food Network (31%). The company's Tribune Media Services unit is a leading syndicator of news and other content. In addition, Tribune owns the Chicago Cubs baseball team, as well as a number of investments in online media. Real estate tycoon Sam Zell took the company private in 2007.

Tribune has been struggling against declining readership and advertising revenue for the past few years like many of its rivals in the newspaper business. Spurred by unhappy shareholders, the company undertook a lengthy review of its options before agreeing to the $8.2 billion going-private transaction. Zell, who controls Equity Group Investments, holds warrants entitling him to 40% of the business; an employee stock-ownership plan owns all the outstanding stock in Tribune.

Installing himself as chairman and CEO, Zell has announced several initiatives to help right the financial ship at the company, including staff cuts and redesigns of its newspapers to include fewer pages. It has also put up for sale some of its historic real estate holdings, including Times Mirror Square in Los Angeles (home of the *Times*) and Chicago's Tribune Tower, as well as the Cubs baseball team. In addition, Tribune has been looking at a spinoff of its TV stations.

In 2008 Tribune sold *Newsday* to cable system operator Cablevision for $650 million. In addition to the paper serving most of Long Island, the deal also included free weekly *amNewYork* and some community papers serving Staten Island. The company had already been paring down its operations in an effort to cut costs: It sold the New York City edition of its Spanish-language paper *Hoy* to ImpreMedia in 2006 and it sold two Connecticut papers to Hearst Newspapers.

The Robert R. McCormick Tribune Foundation, a charitable trust established in the name of the longtime Chicago Tribune publisher, had owned about 15% of the company. The Chandler family trust, which owned 20% of the company, had offered in 2006 to take Tribune private, but that bid was eventually rejected.

HISTORY

James Kelly, John Wheeler, and Joseph Forrest launched Tribune in 1847 when they created the *Chicago Daily Tribune*. Joseph Medill became part-owner and editor in 1855. The paper became the *Chicago Tribune* in 1860. Medill's grandsons, Robert McCormick and Joseph Patterson, took over in 1911.

McCormick built the *Tribune* into the self-proclaimed "World's Greatest Newspaper," whose acronym, WGN, became part of the company's subsequent radio-station call letters. Patterson went to New York in 1919 to found the *New York News* (later the *Daily News*).

In 1924 the company branched into broadcasting with radio station WGN. The station expanded into TV broadcasting in 1948, the same year the *Chicago Tribune* erroneously published its infamous "Dewey Defeats Truman" headline. McCormick died in 1955. The company continued adding to its stable of TV stations with purchases of several stations across the country.

Tribune added professional baseball to its portfolio when it bought the Chicago Cubs from William Wrigley (of chewing gum fame) in 1981. It branched into entertainment programming by launching Tribune Entertainment the following year. The company went public in 1983. A protracted strike at the *Daily News* prompted Tribune to sell the newspaper in 1991.

Tribune stepped up its diversification efforts during the 1990s, branching into educational publishing and building its Internet portfolio. In 1995 the company took a 13% interest in the fledgling WB Network (it raised its stake to 25% three years later) and a 33% share of TV-station operator Qwest Broadcasting. John Madigan was appointed CEO in 1995 and became chairman the following year.

Tribune's 1997 purchase of Renaissance Communications added six additional TV stations to the fold. The company sold its legal publishers to Reed Elsevier (now called Reed Elsevier Group) for $1.1 billion. (The IRS said in 2001 that it was investigating tax payments associated with the deal.)

In 2000 Tribune acquired the remaining two-thirds of Qwest Broadcasting that it didn't already own. Later that year the company made waves in the newspaper industry when it acquired Times Mirror, publisher of the *Los Angeles Times,* for about $8 billion. Sharpening its focus on media, Tribune sold Tribune Education to McGraw-Hill and flight information services provider Jeppesen Sanderson to Boeing. The company also sold Times Mirror Magazines (later called Time4 Media; *Field & Stream, Popular Science*) to Time Inc. for $475 million. Tribune later acquired and merged CareerBuilder and CareerPath.com with Knight Ridder to launch online recruitment venture CareerBuilder.

Citing the "worst advertising environment since the Depression," Madigan announced cost-cutting measures in late 2001, including wage cuts and freezes. Later that year the company sold its three Denver radio stations to Entercom Communications. In 2002 the company bought *Chicago* magazine for $35 million from PRIMEDIA and picked up Indiana TV stations WTTK and WTTV from Sinclair Broadcasting for $125 million. Madigan relinquished his title to company executive Dennis FitzSimons in 2003. That year Tribune continued its aggressive growth of its TV unit and purchased TV stations KPLR in St. Louis and KWBP in Portland, Oregon, from ACME Communications.

In 2004 the company partnered with Comcast and Chicago sports teams on a regional sports network called Comcast Sports Network that debuted the same year. Also in 2004 Tribune admitted that it had overstated circulations for its *Newsday* and *Hoy* New York properties. The Audit Bureau of Circulations sanctioned the publisher for the violations.

In 2006 the company switched about 15 of its stations to a new TV network called The CW, launched that year by CBS Corp. and Warner Bros. Entertainment. Real estate tycoon Sam Zell took Tribune private for $8.2 billion the following year, installing himself as chairman and taking over as CEO from FitzSimons.

Tribune sold its *Newsday* paper and some other titles serving the New York City area to Cablevision for $650 million in 2008.

EXECUTIVES

Chairman and CEO: Samuel (Sam) Zell, age 66
COO: Randy Michaels, age 56
CFO: Chandler Bigelow, age 39
EVP and Chief Administrative Officer:
  Gerald A. (Gerry) Spector, age 62
EVP Interactive and Broadcast Sales: John Hendricks
EVP and General Counsel: Donald J. (Don) Liebentritt, age 57
EVP, Multi-Media Sales Group (MSG): Carolyn Gilbert
EVP, Tribune Publishing: Robert (Bob) Gremillion, age 54
EVP, Tribune Broadcasting: Raymond J. Schonbak
SVP Corporate Relations: Ruthellyn Musil, age 56
SVP Development: Thomas D. (Tom) Leach, age 47
SVP Corporate Relations: Gary Weitman
SVP and Chief Innovation Officer: Lee Abrams, age 55
VP, Deputy General Counsel, and Corporate Secretary:
  David P. (Dave) Eldersveld
VP Human Resources Operations: Susan Mitchell, age 43
President, Tribune Broadcasting: Ed Wilson
Publisher and CEO, Baltimore Sun:
  Rondra J. (Ronnie) Matthews
President, CEO, and Publisher, Newsday:
  Timothy P. Knight, age 43
President and CEO, Tribune Media Services:
  David D. Williams, age 59
President, Tribune Publishing and Publisher, Chicago Tribune Company: Scott C. Smith, age 58
President, Tribune Interactive: Marc Chase
President and Publisher, Los Angeles Times:
  Eddy W. Hartenstein, age 57
Auditors: PricewaterhouseCoopers LLP

LOCATIONS

HQ: Tribune Company
  435 N. Michigan Ave., Chicago, IL 60611
Phone: 312-222-9100   **Fax:** 312-222-1573
Web: www.tribune.com

PRODUCTS/OPERATIONS

2007 Sales

	$ mil.	% of total
Publishing	3,664.6	72
Broadcasting & entertainment	1,398.4	28
Total	**5,063.0**	**100**

Selected Operations

Daily newspapers
  The Baltimore Sun
  Chicago Tribune
  Daily Press (Newport News, VA)
  The Hartford Courant (Hartford, CT)
  Los Angeles Times
  The Morning Call (Allentown, PA)
  Orlando Sentinel (Florida)
  South Florida Sun-Sentinel (Fort Lauderdale, FL)
Other publishing
  Chicago (magazine)
  El Sentinel (Spanish-language newspaper; Fort Lauderdale and Orlando, FL)
  Hoy (Spanish-language newspaper, Chicago and Los Angeles)
  Red Eye (free daily, Chicago)

TV stations
  KCPQ (FOX, Seattle)
  KDAF (CW, Dallas)
  KHCW (CW, Houston)
  KMYQ (MyNetworkTV, Seattle)
  KPLR (CW, St. Louis)
  KRCW (CW; Portland, OR)
  KSWB (CW, San Diego)
  KTLA (CW, Los Angeles)
  KTXL (FOX; Sacramento, CA)
  KWGN (CW, Denver)
  WDCW (CW; Washington, DC)
  WGN (CW, Chicago)
  WGNO (ABC, New Orleans)
  WNOL (CW, New Orleans)
  WPHL (MyNetworkTV, Philadelphia)
  WPIX (CW, New York)
  WPMT (FOX; Harrisburg, PA)
  WSLF (CW, Miami)
  WTIC (FOX; Hartford, CT)
  WTTV (CW, Indianapolis)
  WTXX (CW, Hartford, CT)
  WXIN (FOX, Indianapolis)
  WXMI (FOX; Grand Rapids, MI)
Other broadcasting
  CLTV News (cable news channel, Chicago)
  Superstation WGN (cable)
  Tribune Entertainment (syndicated TV programming)
  WGN-AM (radio station, Chicago)
Other operations and investments
  CareerBuilder (online recruitment, 31%)
  Chicago National League Ball Club (Chicago Cubs)
  Classified Ventures (online advertising and services, 28%)
  Comcast SportsNet Chicago (regional sports network, 25%)
  Metromix (online entertainment guides, 50%)
  Tribune Media Services (content syndication)
  Topix.net (online news aggregation, 34%)
  TV Food Network (cable channel, 31%)
  Zap2it.com (online entertainment news)

COMPETITORS

A. H. Belo
ABC
Belo Corp.
CBS
Chicago Reader
Daily News
Fox Entertainment
Freedom Communications
Gannett
Hearst Newspapers
LIN TV
McClatchy Company
MediaNews
NBC
New York Times
News Corp.
Sun-Times
Washington Post

HISTORICAL FINANCIALS

Company Type: Private

Income Statement				FYE: Last Sunday in December
	REVENUE ($ mil.)	NET INCOME ($ mil.)	NET PROFIT MARGIN	EMPLOYEES
12/07	5,063	87	1.7%	19,600
12/06	5,518	594	10.8%	21,000
12/05	5,596	535	9.6%	22,400
12/04	5,726	556	9.7%	23,200
12/03	5,595	891	15.9%	23,800
Annual Growth	(2.5%)	(44.1%)	—	(4.7%)

2007 Year-End Financials

Debt ratio: —
Return on equity: 21.6%
Cash ($ mil.): 233

Current ratio: 0.63
Long-term debt ($ mil.): 11,840

Net Income History

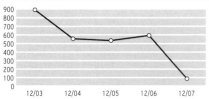

Trinity Capital

Trinity Capital is the holding company for Los Alamos National Bank, which operates four offices in Los Alamos, Santa Fe, and White Rock, New Mexico. A loan office is located in Albuquerque and the company plans to grow in that market. The bank was founded in 1963 to serve the scientific community that developed in the area as a result of the development of the atomic bomb. It offers a range of standard deposit and lending services. Real estate loans, including commercial mortgages, residential mortgages, and construction loans, make up more than 80% of the company's loan portfolio. Trinity Capital also has divisions that offer financial advice, mutual funds, title insurance, and real estate appraisal services.

EXECUTIVES

Chairman: Jeffrey F. Howell, age 55
Vice Chairman: Robert P. Worcester, age 61
President, CEO, and Director; Chairman and CEO, Los Alamos National Bank and Title Guaranty & Insurance: William C. Enloe, age 59, $364,839 pay
CFO; VP and CFO, Los Alamos National Bank: Daniel R. Bartholomew, age 42, $124,600 pay
Secretary and Director; President and Chief Administrative Officer, Los Alamos National Bank: Steve W. Wells, age 52, $242,438 pay
Auditors: Moss Adams, LLP

LOCATIONS

HQ: Trinity Capital Corporation
1200 Trinity Dr., Los Alamos, NM 87544
Phone: 505-662-5171   **Fax:** 505-662-0329
Web: www.lanb.com

PRODUCTS/OPERATIONS

2007 Sales

	% of total
Interest	
Loans, including fees	83
Investment securities	5
Other	2
Noninterest	
Mortgage servicing fees	2
Gain on sale of loans	2
Service charges on deposits	2
Loan & other fees	3
Other	1
Total	**100**

COMPETITORS

Bank of America
BOK Financial
First State Bancorporation

HISTORICAL FINANCIALS

Company Type: Private

Income Statement

FYE: December 31

	ASSETS ($ mil.)	NET INCOME ($ mil.)	INCOME AS % OF ASSETS	EMPLOYEES
12/07	1,380	13	1.0%	271
12/06	1,359	10	0.8%	269
12/05	1,244	12	1.0%	260
12/04	1,080	10	1.0%	271
12/03	1,007	13	1.3%	282
Annual Growth	**8.2%**	**0.8%**	**—**	**(1.0%)**

2007 Year-End Financials

Equity as % of assets: 5.2%
Return on assets: 1.0%
Return on equity: 19.8%

Long-term debt ($ mil.): —
Sales ($ mil.): 108

Net Income History

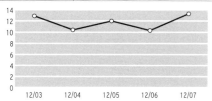

Trinity Health

One of the largest Catholic health care systems in the US, Trinity Health runs more than 40 hospitals and has nearly 400 outpatient facilities, as well as nursing homes, senior living facilities, home health agencies, and hospice programs. Its Trinity Continuing Care Services subsidiary operates nearly 20 long-term care facilities for seniors, and its Trinity Health International unit provides consulting, training, and other assistance to hospitals worldwide. Trinity Health has facilities in seven states with a combined 8,000 acute care and long-term care beds. Catholic Health Ministries sponsors the organization.

The organization's facilities in Iowa (Mercy Health Network) are a joint venture between Trinity Health and Catholic Health Initiatives.

In 2007 Trinity Health sold its stake in Michigan's St. Joseph's Healthcare (located in Clinton Township) to its joint-venture partner in the enterprise, Henry Ford Health System.

Trinity Health is really more of a duo than a trio: The not-for-profit company is the result of a coupling between Mercy Health Services and Holy Cross Health System.

EXECUTIVES

Chairman: Patrick G. Hays
Vice Chairman: Lawrence D. (Larry) Damron, age 61
President, CEO, and Director: Joseph R. Swedish
SVP and CFO: Edward Chadwick, age 47
SVP and General Counsel: Daniel G. (Dan) Hale
SVP, Mission Integration: Sister M. Gretchen Elliott
SVP, Diversity and Inclusion: VeLois Bowers

SVP and CIO: Paul Browne
SVP, Patient Care and CNO: Joy Gorzeman
Chief Development Officer: Mary D. Szymanski
SVP Strategic Planning and Marketing: Preston Gee
Auditors: Deloitte & Touche LLP

LOCATIONS

HQ: Trinity Health
27870 Cabot Dr., Novi, MI 48377
Phone: 248-489-5004   **Fax:** 248-489-6039
Web: www.trinity-health.org

Selected Operations

California
Saint Agnes Medical Center (Fresno)
Idaho
Saint Alphonsus Regional Medical Center (Boise)
Indiana
Saint Joseph Regional Medical Center (South Bend)
Iowa
Mercy Health Network (Des Moines)
Maryland
Holy Cross Hospital (Silver Spring)
Michigan
Battle Creek Health System
Mercy General Health Partners (Muskegon)
Mercy Hospital (Cadillac)
Mercy Hospital (Grayling)
Mercy Hospital (Port Huron)
Saint Mary's Health Care (Grand Rapids)
Saint Joseph Mercy Health System (Ann Arbor)
St. Joseph Mercy Oakland (Pontiac)
St. Mary Mercy Hospital (Livonia)
Trinity Health International (Farmington Hills)
Ohio
Mount Carmel Health System (Columbus)

COMPETITORS

Amedisys
Ascension Health
Detroit Medical Center
HCA
Henry Ford Health System
Hospice of Michigan
Johns Hopkins Medicine
Mayo Foundation
MedStar Health

Memorial Hospital & Health System
Odyssey HealthCare
OhioHealth
St. Luke's Health System
VITAS Healthcare
William Beaumont Hospital

True Temper Sports

True Temper's golf shafts have probably withstood many golf course temper tantrums. The firm primarily makes golf shafts and bicycle tubing, forks, and seat posts. Its steel manufacturing facility in Mississippi makes steel products for the bicycle, automobile, and golfing industries and its composite production facility in Guangzhou, China, make graphite golf shafts and hockey sticks. True Temper's golf shafts are used by club makers such as Callaway, Golfsmith, TaylorMade, and Mizuno. Members of management, along with Gilbert Global Equity Partners, bought the firm from Cornerstone Equity Investors in 2004. It bought CN Precision in 2007 to boost its manufacturing in China.

The company is spreading more of its manufacturing operations into China. In 2007 True Temper acquired a start-up steel golf shaft facility in Suzhou, China; operations began ramping up in 2008.

Strengthening its non-golf holdings, the company plans to further develop partnerships with firms in the hockey and cycling fields.

EXECUTIVES

Co-Chairman: Steven J. Gilbert, age 59
Co-Chairman: Steven Kotler, age 60
President, CEO, and Director: Scott C. Hennessy, age 48, $435,833 pay
SVP and COO: Fred H. Geyer, age 46, $225,833 pay
SVP, Global Distribution and Sales: Adrian H. McCall, age 49, $192,915 pay
VP, CFO, and Treasurer: Jason A. Jenne, age 37, $162,915 pay
VP, Engineering, Research, and Development: Graeme Horwood, age 62
VP, Human Resources: Stephen M. Brown, age 41
VP, Operations: L. Gene Pierce, $168,333 pay
VP, Sales: Raeford P. Lucas, age 41
Director, Marketing: Chad Hall, age 32
Auditors: KPMG LLP

LOCATIONS

HQ: True Temper Sports, Inc.
8275 Tournament Dr., Ste. 200, Memphis, TN 38125
Phone: 901-746-2000   **Fax:** 901-746-2160
Web: www.truetemper.com

2007 Sales

	$ mil.	% of total
US	75.0	65
International	41.2	35
Total	**116.2**	**100**

PRODUCTS/OPERATIONS

2007 Sales

	$ mil.	% of total
Golf shaft	102.8	88
Performance sports	13.4	12
Total	**116.2**	**100**

COMPETITORS

Aldila
Cannondale
Graphite Design

HISTORICAL FINANCIALS

Company Type: Private

Income Statement   FYE: December 31

	REVENUE ($ mil.)	NET INCOME ($ mil.)	NET PROFIT MARGIN	EMPLOYEES
12/07	116	(34)	—	807
12/06	108	(11)	—	821
12/05	118	(1)	—	734
12/04	98	(20)	—	649
12/03	116	11	9.4%	—
Annual Growth	**0.0%**	**—**	**—**	**7.5%**

2007 Year-End Financials

Debt ratio: 447.8%   Current ratio: —
Return on equity: —   Long-term debt ($ mil.): 260
Cash ($ mil.): —

Net Income History

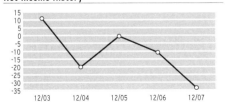

True Value

To survive against home improvement giants such as The Home Depot and Lowe's, True Value (formerly TruServ) is relying on the true value of service. Formed by the merger of Cotter & Company (which was the supplier to the True Value chain) and ServiStar Coast to Coast, the cooperative serves some 5,400 retail outlets (down from nearly 7,200 in 2001), including its flagship True Value hardware stores. The company sells home improvement and garden supplies, as well as appliances, housewares, sporting goods, and toys. Members use the Taylor Rental, Grand Rental Station, Home & Garden Showplace, Induserve Supply, and other banners. True Value also manufactures its own brand of paints and applicators.

The merger of Cotter & Company and ServiStar Coast to Coast (operator of Coast to Coast and ServiStar hardware stores, most of which converted to the True Value banner) gave members — many of them mom-and-pop outlets — more buying clout to compete against the do-it-yourself mega-retailers, plus retail advice and advertising support. True Value has been growing its business in the rental and maintenance, repair, and operation (MRO) arenas, and has resumed supplying lumber and building materials. (The company sold its lumber and building materials business in 2000.) At the store level, True Value has been developing "lite" or smaller versions of its signature programs, such as Platinum Paint Shop, for the co-op's stores (more than half) that are less than 6,000 sq. ft.

Outside the US the company serves about 700 stores in more than 50 countries.

HISTORY

Noting that hardware retailers had begun to form wholesale cooperatives to lower costs, John Cotter, a traveling hardware salesman, and associate Ed Lanctot started pitching the wholesale co-op idea in 1947 to small-town and suburban hardware retailers, and by early 1948 they had enrolled 25 merchants for $1,500 each. Cotter became chairman of the new firm, Cotter & Company.

The co-op created the Value & Service (V&S) store trademark in 1951 to emphasize the advantages of an independent hardware store. Acquisitions included the 1963 purchase of Chicago-based wholesaler Hibbard, Spencer, Bartlett, giving Cotter 400 new members and the well-known True Value trademark, which soon replaced V&S signs. Four years later Cotter broadened its focus by buying the General Paint & Chemical Company (Tru-Test paint). The V&S name was revived in 1972 for a five-and-dime store co-op, V&S Variety Stores.

In 1989 Cotter died and Lanctot retired. (Lanctot died in October 2003.) By 1989 there were almost 7,000 True Value Stores. Cotter moved into Canada in 1992 by acquiring hardware distributor and store operator Macleod-Stedman (275 outlets).

Juggling variety-store and hardware merchandise and delivering very small amounts of merchandise to a lukewarm co-op membership did not allow for economies of scale, so in 1995 the company quit its manufacturing operations and its US variety stores (though it still serves variety stores in Canada, operating as C&S Choices), tightened membership requirements, and introduced new services.

Two years later Cotter formed TruServ by merging with hardware wholesaler ServiStar Coast to Coast. ServiStar had its origins in the nation's first hardware co-op, American Hardware Supply, which was founded in Pittsburgh in 1910 by M. R. Porter, John Howe, and E. S. Corlett. By 1988, the year it changed its name to ServiStar, the co-op topped $1 billion in sales.

ServiStar expanded in the upper Midwest and on the West Coast in 1990 when it acquired the assets of the Coast to Coast chain (founded in 1928 as a franchise hardware store in Minneapolis); ServiStar brought Coast to Coast out of bankruptcy two years later, making it a co-op. Merging its 1992 acquisition of Taylor Rental Center with its Grand Rental Station stores in 1993 made ServiStar the #1 general rental chain. In 1996 it consolidated Coast to Coast's operations into its own and changed its name to ServiStar Coast to Coast.

President Don Hoye became CEO of the company in 1999. That year TruServ slashed 1,000 jobs and declared it would convert all its hardware store chains to the True Value banner. But TruServ lost $131 million in 1999 over bookkeeping gaffes, and co-op members received no dividends. Of 2,800 ServiStar dealers, only 1,900 raised the True Value flag. Others either declined to switch or were never offered the change because other True Value stores already shared their market area. In addition, stores began deserting the co-op because of inventory and other problems. In late 2000 the company sold its lumber and building materials business.

As competition continued to increase in 2001, the company was facing falling sales, lawsuits from shareholders, and accusations by retailers of unfair practices intended to pressure them into adopting the cooperative's flagship True Value banner. TruServ also had to confront a $200 million loan default. It made cuts in its corporate staff and divested its Canadian interests. In July 2001 Hoye resigned. The company's CFO and COO, Pamela Forbes Lieberman, was named the new CEO that November.

In April 2002 the company reported a net loss of $50.7 million during 2001, which it attributed to restructuring charges, inventory writedowns, and finance fees. TruServ, under SEC investigation for alleged inventory, accounting, and other internal-control problems, was one of several companies that failed in August 2002 to meet a government requirement to swear by their past financial results.

In January 2003 TruServ received about $125 million in financing from investment firm W. P. Carey & Co. in a sale-leaseback deal on seven of TruServ's distribution centers. In March 2003 TruServ settled the SEC's allegations, without admitting or denying them.

Lieberman resigned in November 2004. Director Thomas Hanemann was named interim CEO. TruServ changed its name to True Value in January 2005. In June 2005 Hanemann turned over the reins to Sears veteran Lyle G. Heidemann who joined True Value as its new president and CEO. In December 2005, the company sold its oil-based paint manufacturing operation in Chicago to Blackhawk/Halsted for about $10 million.

In 2007 True Value added more than 100 new stores in the US and experienced modest growth overseas. Also in 2007 the company launched its new store format, called Destination TrueValue.

EXECUTIVES

Chairman: Brian A. Webb
President, CEO, and Director: Lyle G. Heidemann,
 age 63, $955,527 pay (partial-year salary)
SVP and CFO: David A. (Dave) Shadduck, $469,191 pay
SVP and CIO: Leslie A. Weber
SVP and Chief Merchandising Officer: Michael Clark
SVP Logistics and Supply Chain Management:
 Stephen Poplawski
**SVP Human Resources, General Counsel, and
 Secretary:** Cathy C. Anderson, $445,457 pay
VP and Controller: Donald J. (Don) Deegan
VP and Corporate Treasurer: Barbara L. Wagner
VP Marketing: Carol Wentworth, age 48
VP Retail Finance: Jon Johnson
VP Retail and Specialty Businesses Development:
 Fred L. Kirst, age 54
VP Retail Growth: Mark Flowers
Director E-Business: Eric Lane
General Manager Rental: Tony Sabo
Auditors: PricewaterhouseCoopers LLP

LOCATIONS

HQ: True Value Company
 8600 W. Bryn Mawr Ave., Chicago, IL 60631
Phone: 773-695-5000   **Fax:** 773-695-6516
Web: www.truevaluecompany.com

PRODUCTS/OPERATIONS

2007 Sales

	$ mil.	% of total
Hardware	1,955.3	96
Paint manufacturing & distribution	85.3	4
Total	**2,040.6**	**100**

Selected Operations

Grand Rental Station (general rental)
Home & Garden Showplace (nursery and giftware)
Induserve Supply (commercial and industrial)
Party Central (parties and corporate events)
Taylor Rental (general rental)
True Value (hardware)

COMPETITORS

84 Lumber	Northern Tool
Ace Hardware	Orgill
Akzo Nobel	Reno-Depot
Benjamin Moore	Sears
Do it Best	Sherwin-Williams
Fastenal	Stock Building Supply
Home Depot	Sutherland Lumber
Kmart	United Rentals
Lowe's	Valspar
McCoy Corp.	Wal-Mart
Menard	

HISTORICAL FINANCIALS

Company Type: Cooperative

Income Statement

FYE: December 31

	REVENUE ($ mil.)	NET INCOME ($ mil.)	NET PROFIT MARGIN	EMPLOYEES
12/07	2,041	64	3.1%	3,000
12/06	2,050	73	3.6%	3,000
12/05	2,043	48	2.3%	2,800
12/04	2,024	43	2.1%	2,800
12/03	2,024	21	1.0%	3,000
Annual Growth	**0.2%**	**31.7%**	**—**	**0.0%**

2007 Year-End Financials

Debt ratio: 74.5%
Return on equity: 54.2%
Cash ($ mil.): 5
Current ratio: 1.37
Long-term debt ($ mil.): 99

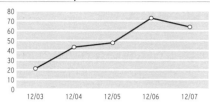

Net Income History

Truman Arnold

This jobber gets the job done by distributing wholesale petroleum across the US. Truman Arnold Companies (TAC) markets and distributes more than 100 million gallons of petroleum products a month to customers located in 48 states in the US through its TAC Energy subsidiary. Its TAC Terminals unit operates two major petroleum terminals in Arkansas. Through its TAC Air unit, the company offers fixed-based operations (FBO), including aircraft fueling, hanger, and ground transportation services, through 12 general aviation facilities in the US. The company also operates convenience stores and provides trucking, real estate, and construction services.

The family-owned and -operated company was founded in 1964 by Texarkana businessman Truman Arnold. The company expanded its FBO business through the acquisition of Cherokee Aviation in 2005. It opened its 12th FBO location in 2007, in Raleigh-Durham.

EXECUTIVES

Chairman: Truman Arnold
President and CEO: Gregory A. (Greg) Arnold
SVP and CFO: Steve McMillen
SVP and General Counsel: James (Jim) Day
VP, Aviation Division (TAC Air):
 Daniel A. (Danny) Walsh
VP and CIO: Michael Davis
VP, Trading and Supply: Tom Knight
VP, Terminal Services (TAC Energy): Benny Webb
Director Marketing: Jennifer Green
Director, Human Resources: Denny Peterson

LOCATIONS

HQ: Truman Arnold Companies, Inc.
 701 S. Robison Rd., Texarkana, TX 75501
Phone: 903-794-3835   **Fax:** 903-831-4056
Web: www.trumanarnoldcompanies.com

Truman Arnold Companies operates in 48 states in the US, as well as in five Canadian provinces.

COMPETITORS

Atlantic Aviation
Getty Petroleum Marketing
Gulf Oil
Million Air
SMF Energy
Sun Coast Resources
Warren Equities

The Trump Organization

The Trump Organization knows all about gilding the lily. Run by flamboyant, modern-day King Midas Donald Trump (and his hair), The Trump Organization owns several pieces of high-end real estate in the Big Apple. Properties include Trump International Hotel & Tower, Trump Tower, and 40 Wall Street. It also owns and operates hotels, resorts, residential towers, and golf courses in major US markets and abroad. Trump Organization owns 28% of Trump Entertainment Resorts, which owns and operates the Trump Taj Mahal, Trump Plaza, and Trump Marina casinos in Atlantic City, New Jersey. Together with NBC, Trump additionally owns the Miss USA, Miss Teen USA, and Miss Universe beauty pageants.

The Trump Organization depends heavily on (or succeeds in spite of, depending on your perspective) the fortunes of its founder, Donald Trump. The author of numerous books including *Think Like a Billionaire* and *The Art of the Deal* is renowned for setting up real estate partnerships in which other firms put up most of the cash while he retains most of the control.

He keeps himself in the public eye with the reality television show *The Apprentice*, in which aspiring moguls compete for a spot in his companies. The Donald even has a signature line: "You're fired!" and a signature move: the cobra — the hand motion he makes when axing a contestant. He has splashed his famous moniker — now trademarked — not just on buildings, but also water, vodka, restaurants, a university, a magazine, and more.

The firm plans to complete the Trump International Hotel & Tower Chicago at the site formerly leased by the *Chicago Sun-Times* in 2009. It has battled environmental groups opposing the planned development of a $2 billion champion-class golf course and resort in Scotland. The proposed project is located within a Site of Special Scientific Interest.

The Trump Organization has also teamed up with Irongate Capital Partners to build Trump International Hotel & Tower Waikiki in Hawaii. That deal is valued at an estimated $400 million.

The company is looking for a joint venture partner with which to enter an even more exotic market — India. The country has the world's second-fastest-growing economy, and Trump sees opportunity in the hotel market there.

Trump's foray into the mortgage market with Trump Mortgage hit a wall and it dissolved the unit. It reestablished its mortgage operations with an alliance with First Meridian Mortgage, creating a new entity called Trump Financial.

HISTORY

The third of four children, Donald Trump was the son of a successful builder in Queens and Brooklyn. After graduating from the Wharton School of Finance in 1968, his first job was to turn around a 1,200-unit foreclosed apartment complex in Cincinnati that his father had bought for $6 million with no money down. Managing the Cincinnati job gave Trump a distaste for the nonaffluent; he wanted to get to Manhattan to meet all the right people.

Operating as The Trump Organization, he took options on two Hudson River sites in 1975 for no money down and began lobbying the city to finance his construction of a convention center. The center was built, but not by Trump, who nevertheless got about $800,000 and priceless publicity. He and hotelier Jay Pritzker turned the Commodore Hotel near Grand Central Station into the Grand Hyatt Hotel in 1975.

In 1981 he built the posh Trump Tower on Fifth Avenue and proceeded to wheel and deal himself into 1980s folklore. In 1983 he joined with Holiday Inn to build the Trump Casino Hotel (now Trump Plaza) in Atlantic City using public-issue bonds (he bought out Holiday Inn's interest in 1986), and he bought the Trump Castle from Hilton in 1985. In 1987 he ended up with the unfinished Taj Mahal in Atlantic City, then the world's largest casino, after a battle with Merv Griffin for Resorts International (Griffin won). He bought the Plaza Hotel in Manhattan in 1988, and the Eastern air shuttle (renamed the Trump Shuttle) the next year.

As the 1990s dawned, though, Trump's balance sheet was loaded with about $3 billion in debt. Trump's 70 creditor banks consolidated and restructured his debt in 1990. In 1995 Trump formed Trump Hotels & Casino Resorts and took it public. He also paid a token $10 for 40 Wall St. The next year he sold his half-interest in the Grand Hyatt Hotel to the Pritzker family and unloaded more than $1.1 billion in debt by selling the Taj Mahal and Trump's Castle to Trump Hotels. That year Trump bought the Miss Universe, Miss USA, and Miss Teen USA beauty pageants.

In 1997 he published *The Art of the Comeback*, a follow-up to *The Art of the Deal* (1987), and started work on Trump Place, a residential development on New York's Upper West Side. He teamed with Conseco in 1998 to buy the famed General Motors Building for $800 million. In 1999 he began building the Trump World Tower — a 90-story residential building near the United Nations complex.

The following year Trump and publisher Hollinger International announced plans to transform the former riverfront headquarters of the Chicago Sun-Times into a residential and commercial development. Originally planned to be the world's tallest skyscraper, Trump decided to scale back the project in the wake of terrorist attacks on the World Trade Center; Hollinger sold its stake in the venture to Trump in 2004.

In 2002 Trump dumped his stake in the now-tallest building in New York City. His part of the Empire State Building leasehold brought in a paltry $2 million per year. He was also ordered by the courts to sell his 50% stake in the General Motors Building to co-owner Conseco; the two parties agreed to sell the building.

Trump ventured into reality television as the star and executive producer of *The Apprentice* in 2004. The show became a hit with viewers and critics (it garnered four Emmy Award nominations). Riding the wave of fascination with all things Donald, Trump published two more best-selling books (*How to Get Rich* and *Think Like a Billionaire*) that year.

In mid-2005 the Trump Organization and a group of investors sold a parcel of land and three buildings on the Manhattan waterfront to Extell Development Corp. and The Carlyle Group for about $1.8 billion. Later that year The Donald inked a deal with Nakheel, a developer in the United Arab Emirates, to develop resort destinations in the Middle East, including a $600 million high-rise in Dubai's ritzy Palm resort.

EXECUTIVES

Chairman and President: Donald J. Trump, age 61
EVP and COO: Matthew F. Calamari
EVP and CFO: Allen Weisselberg
EVP and General Counsel: Bernard Diamond
EVP and Assistant General Counsel: Jason Greenblatt
EVP Golf Course Development: Vincent Stellio
EVP Construction: Andrew Weiss
VP and Controller: Jeffrey McConney
EVP Development and Acquisitions:
 Donald J. Trump Jr.
VP Development: Jill Cremer
VP Media Relations and Human Resources:
 Norma Foerderer
VP Operations and Residential Buildings:
 Thomas Pienkos
VP Leasing and Insurance: Nathan Nelson, age 51
VP Real Estate Development and Acquisitions:
 Ivanka M. Trump, age 26
CEO, Trump Financial: David Brecher
President, Trump University: Michael W. Sexton

LOCATIONS

HQ: The Trump Organization
 725 5th Ave., New York, NY 10022
Phone: 212-832-2000   **Fax:** 212-935-0141
Web: www.trumponline.com

PRODUCTS/OPERATIONS

Selected Holdings
40 Wall Street (The Trump Building)
Mar-A-Lago (private club; Palm Beach, FL)
Miss Teen USA pageant
Miss Universe pageant
Miss USA pageant
Trump National Golf Club
Trump International Hotel and Tower
Trump Palace
Trump Park Avenue
Trump World (Seoul)
Trump World Tower

COMPETITORS

Boston Properties
Helmsley Enterprises
HKR International
Hyatt
Icahn Enterprises
Lefrak Organization
Marriott
Ritz-Carlton
Rockefeller Group International
Starwood Capital
Vornado Realty

HISTORICAL FINANCIALS

Company Type: Private

Income Statement

FYE: December 31

	REVENUE ($ mil.)	NET INCOME ($ mil.)	NET PROFIT MARGIN	EMPLOYEES
12/07	10,700	—	—	22,450
12/06	10,400	—	—	22,500
Annual Growth	2.9%	—	—	(0.2%)

Revenue History

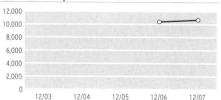

Trustmark Mutual Holding Company

Trustmark Mutual Holding, established in 1913 as the Brotherhood of All Railway Employees to provide disability coverage to railroad workers, is still administering benefits to workers across the US. Trustmark Mutual Holding operates through subsidiaries including Trustmark Group Insurance (group medical, dental, disability, and life insurance for larger employers), Starmark (employee benefits for smaller employers), and CoreSource (customized employee benefits for companies that self-fund). The company also offers voluntary insurance products (specialty products through voluntary payroll deductions), and health care plans created for affinity groups. Trustmark Mutual Holding is owned by its policyholders.

Trustmark's Disability Advisors offers employers disability claim management services.

The company is expanding its services through acquisitions. In 2008 Trustmark Mutual acquired Health Contact Partners, which operates a telephone call center for customers seeking health care information.

EXECUTIVES

Chairman: J. Grover Thomas Jr.
President and CEO: David M. McDonough
EVP CoreSource and Voluntary Benefit Solutions:
 Christopher J. (Chris) Martin
EVP and CFO: J. Brink Marcuccili
EVP, Affinity Markets, Trustmark Group Benefits and Starmark: Warren R. Schreier
SVP and General Counsel: Sara Lee Keller
SVP Human Resources and Corporate Communication:
 Kate Martiné, age 55
SVP Investments: Jerry Hitpas
SVP and COO, CoreSource: Paul Lotharius
SVP The Sentinel Group and Business Development:
 Julie M. Malida
VP Group Sales, Marketing, and Administration:
 David J. Meyer
VP and Medical Director: Deborah Y. Smart

LOCATIONS

HQ: Trustmark Mutual Holding Company
 400 Field Dr., Lake Forest, IL 60045
Phone: 847-615-1500   **Fax:** 847-615-3910
Web: www.trustmarkinsurance.com

COMPETITORS

Aetna
Aflac
Assurant Employee Benefits
Assurant Health
Blue Cross
CIGNA
Citigroup
Mutual of America
ULLICO

HISTORICAL FINANCIALS

Company Type: Mutual company

Income Statement

FYE: December 31

	REVENUE ($ mil.)	NET INCOME ($ mil.)	NET PROFIT MARGIN	EMPLOYEES
12/07	983	39	4.0%	2,400
12/06	1,101	111	10.1%	2,152
12/05	1,120	—	—	2,358
12/04	1,160	—	—	—
12/03	1,131	—	—	3,000
Annual Growth	(3.4%)	(64.8%)	—	(5.4%)

2007 Year-End Financials

Debt ratio: —
Return on equity: 8.7%
Cash ($ mil.): —
Current ratio: —
Long-term debt ($ mil.): —

Net Income History

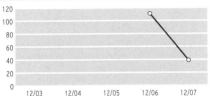

TTX Company

TTX keeps the railroad industry in the US and Canada chugging along by leasing railcars. Railroad operators often opt to lease railcars rather than buy them in order to be more nimble in adjusting to changes in demand. TTX's fleet of more than 210,000 railcars includes three types: intermodal, designed to carry shipping containers; autorack, for vehicles; and general use, for items such as lumber, steel, and farm and construction equipment. Its operations are supported by three maintenance divisions located in California, Florida, and South Carolina. TTX is owned by the largest US and Canadian railroads, which are also the company's main customers.

The company was originally formed in 1955 as Trailer Train by the Pennsylvania Railroad to supply affordable rail freight cars. Eventually, the Interstate Commerce Commission (now known as the Surface Transportation Board), the government regulatory agency responsible for rail transportation, sanctioned TTX's current operating structure. That structure allows major railroads to share the ownership and the use of equipment owned by TTX. Although ownership percentages have changed over the years, all owners share the same level of access to equipment and services that TTX offers. The fleet pool-like structure also gives TTX an edge over other rail equipment lessors because its customers are its shareholders. As such, increased profits are not the company's primary goal, and costs can be kept to a minimum.

EXECUTIVES

Chairman and CEO: Andrew F. Reardon, age 62
President and Director: Thomas F. Wells
SVP Law and Administration: Patrick B. Loftus
VP and CFO: Kathleen M. Savard
VP, Equipment: Robert J. Pokorski
VP, Fleet Management: Patrick J. Casey
VP Human Resources and Labor Relations:
Brian R. Powers
VP and Chief Information Officer: Bruce G. Schinelli
Controller: Margaret T. Kelleher
Corporate Secretary: Deborah S. Deppisch
Communications Director: Sara Lorenzo
Auditors: KPMG LLP

LOCATIONS

HQ: TTX Company
101 N. Wacker Dr., Chicago, IL 60606
Phone: 312-853-3223   **Fax:** 312-984-3790
Web: www.ttx.com

COMPETITORS

Andersons	Greenbrier
CIT Transportation Finance	Pioneer Railcorp
GATX	XTRA
Genesee & Wyoming	

HISTORICAL FINANCIALS

Company Type: Private

Income Statement

FYE: December 31

	REVENUE ($ mil.)	NET INCOME ($ mil.)	NET PROFIT MARGIN	EMPLOYEES
12/07	1,118	—	—	1,800
12/06	1,156	—	—	1,707
12/05	1,134	—	—	1,670
12/04	1,015	—	—	—
Annual Growth	3.3%	—	—	3.8%

Revenue History

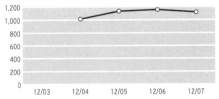

Tube City IMS

Tube City IMS can do just about anything with industrial leftovers. The company provides outsourced raw material procurement and post-production services that help steel mills profit from scrap. A major scrap metal broker, Tube City purchases more than 6 million tons of scrap annually from the likes of U.S. Steel and AK Steel. It also offers a host of pre-production material handling, scrap management, and scrap preparation services. Tube City's post-production services include material and product handling, co-product processing, and metal recovery. It also provides slag handling, metal recovery, and high-speed flame cutting to the steel industry. Canadian investment firm Onex owns Tube City IMS.

Wellspring Capital Management had acquired International Mill Service (IMS) and Tube City LLC in 2004; it then merged them to form Tube City IMS. It filed to take the company public in 2006. Before the public offering went through, however, Onex Corporation came in (allied with company management) to purchase Tube City.

The company operated both Tube City LLC and IMS as separate entities until the beginning of 2008, when the company merged the two units. The move consolidated operations into one unit called Tube City IMS, LLC. Later in 2008 the company acquired UK steel service center Hanson Resource Management. Tube City IMS wants Hanson to assist the company's other European operations.

Originally known as Tube City Iron & Metal, Tube City derives its name from the town of McKeesport, site of its original plant. McKeesport was nicknamed Tube City because it was home to a large steel tube mill run by U.S. Steel.

EXECUTIVES

Chairman and CEO: I. Michael Coslov, age 64, $1,678,462 pay
Vice Chairman and COO Tube City Division:
Joseph Curtin, age 60, $1,154,000 pay
EVP, General Counsel, and Secretary:
Thomas E. (Tom) Lippard, age 64, $797,693 pay
SVP, Optimization Group: Mike Mullen
SVP, CFO, and Treasurer: Daniel E. Rosati, age 44
Manager, Human Resources and Benefits Administrator: Jeannie DeCarlo
President and COO, IMS Division:
Raymond S. (Ray) Kalouche, age 44, $1,180,748 pay
President, Tube City Division: J. David Aronson, age 40, $1,097,693 pay
Auditors: Ernst & Young LLP

LOCATIONS

HQ: Tube City IMS Corporation
12 Monongahela Ave., Glassport, PA 15045
Phone: 412-678-6141   **Fax:** 412-678-2210
Web: www.tubecityims.com

Tube City IMS Corporation primarily operates in the US, though it also is active in Serbia and Slovakia.

PRODUCTS/OPERATIONS

Selected Services

Post-production
Co-product processing, metal recovery, and sales
Material handling and product handling
Pre-production
Material handling, scrap management, and scrap preparation
Raw materials optimization
Raw materials procurement

COMPETITORS

Aleris International
Commercial Metals
David J. Joseph
Edw. C. Levy
Harsco
Keywell
OmniSource
Sims Group

Tufts Associated Health Plans

One of Massachusetts leading health insurers, Tufts Associated Health Plans (which, with its subsidiaries, operates as Tufts Health Plan) provides medical coverage to about 700,000 members. The company offers HMO, PPO, and point-of-service plans to both employers and individuals, as well as Medicare Advantage plans for retirees. Several of its plans include consumer-directed products such as health savings accounts and health reimbursement accounts. The company's health care network includes some 85 hospitals and more than 20,000 doctors. With partner CIGNA, Tufts Health Plan also offers a nationwide health network called CareLink for multi-state employers.

In 2008 the company announced it would expand into the Rhode Island health care market, with plans to offer its PPO health plans beginning in 2009.

Like most managed health care companies, Tufts has worked to control medical costs while adding members and encouraging quality care. It has embraced the practice of "evidence-based medicine," encouraging standardized best practices among its providers, and it has implemented disease management programs for chronic illnesses like diabetes and chronic heart failure. It began expanding those disease management programs, which help members manage their illnesses in ways that hopefully prevent big and costly interventions, in 2005 through a partnership with Healthways.

Additionally, Tufts in 2007 introduced the My Wellness Plan, a set of online tools that, among other things, gives members access to health information, reminds them about prescription renewals, and helps them resolve claims.

EXECUTIVES

Chairman: Davey S. Scoon, age 61
Vice Chairman: David Green
President, CEO, and Director: James Roosevelt Jr.
COO: Thomas A. (Tom) Croswell
SVP and CFO: J. Andy Hilbert
SVP Operations and CIO: Tricia Trebino
SVP and Chief Medical Officer: Allen J. Hinkle, age 57
SVP Marketing, Product, and Strategy:
 Robert D. (Rob) Egan
SVP Sales and Client Services: Brian P. Pagliaro
SVP Human Resources, General Counsel, and Senior Compliance Officer: Lois Dehls Cornell
VP Communications: Patti Embry-Tautenhan

LOCATIONS

HQ: Tufts Associated Health Plans, Inc.
 705 Mt. Auburn St., Watertown, MA 02472
Phone: 617-972-9400
Web: www.tuftshealthplan.com

PRODUCTS/OPERATIONS

Selected Health Plans
Advantage HMO
Advantage PPO
Advantage Saver (high-deductible plan with health savings account)
CareLink (national network PPO, with CIGNA)
EPO Choice Copay (exclusive provider organization)

HMO Choice Copay (tiered provider network)
Navigator Choice (PPO)
Tufts Health Plan Medicare Preffered (HMO or private-fee-for-service Medicare plan)
Tufts Medicare Complement (supplemental Medicare coverage)

COMPETITORS

Aetna
Blue Cross (MA)
CIGNA
ConnectiCare
Fallon Community Health Plan
Harvard Pilgrim
Health New England
MVP Health Plan
Neighborhood Health Plan
Prudential
UnitedHealth Group

HISTORICAL FINANCIALS

Company Type: Not-for-profit

Income Statement

FYE: December 31

	REVENUE ($ mil.)	NET INCOME ($ mil.)	NET PROFIT MARGIN	EMPLOYEES
12/07	2,200	110	5.0%	—
12/06	1,900	78	4.1%	—
12/05	1,900	79	4.1%	—
12/04	2,100	28	1.3%	—
12/03	2,300	57	2.5%	2,500
Annual Growth	(1.1%)	17.9%	—	—

Net Income History

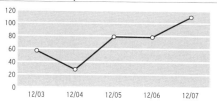

120				
100				
80				
60				
40				
20				
0	12/03	12/04	12/05	12/06	12/07

Turner Industries

Turner Industries does the heavy lifting for heavy industry. The company is a top US player in industrial construction, contract maintenance, and outsourcing. Its customers include oil refiners, petrochemical companies, power generators, and pulp and paper mills. Through its divisions, the group provides such services as scaffolding equipment rental, environmental remediation, heavy hauling and rigging, water treatment, pipe fabrication, and tank cleaning. Turner Industries also offers material management, training workshops, and staffing services. Bert Turner founded the company in Baton Rouge, Louisiana, in 1961. He died in 2008.

The company's bread and butter is the oil and gas industry, also Louisiana's economic mainstay. Turner Industries was hurt by Hurricane

Katrina in 2005, but added some 3,000 workers after the hurricane to cope with the cleanup and restoration.

Business continues to boom for Turner Industries, which has annual revenue at about $1.4 billion. Most of the industry's growth is fueled by manufacturers that upgrade plants and facilities.

In order to keep up with that growth and strengthen its work force, the company is building a new 20,000-sq. ft. training and recruiting facility near Baton Rouge.

EXECUTIVES

Chairman and CEO: Roland M. Toups
Vice Chairman and COO: Thomas H. Turner
VP Finance, CFO, Secretary, and Treasurer: Lester J. (Les) Griffon Jr.
VP Business Development and Marketing: Stephen M. Toups
General Counsel: John H. Fenner
Director Marketing: Tobie Craig
President, Construction Division: Donald L. (Don) McCollister
President, Equipment and Specialty Services Division: Davis J. Lauve
President, Maintenance and Turnarounds Division: Joseph W. (Billy) Guitreau
President, Pipe Fabrication Division: Robert L. (Bob) Pearson
Auditors: Postlethwaite & Netterville

LOCATIONS

HQ: Turner Industries Group, L.L.C.
 8687 United Plaza Blvd., 5th Fl.,
 Baton Rouge, LA 70809
Phone: 225-922-5050   **Fax:** 225-922-5055
Web: www.turner-industries.com

PRODUCTS/OPERATIONS

Selected Services
Construction
Contract maintenance
Environmental remediation
Equipment rental
Heat exchanger bundle extraction and cleaning
Heavy hauling
Hydroblasting and lancing
Painting and blasting
Petrochemical wastewater treatment construction and project management
Pipe fabrication and bending
Preventive maintenance
Project management
Procurement
Rigging
Scaffolding
Specialty welding
System integration
Tank cleaning
Turnarounds and shutdowns

COMPETITORS

ABB
Aker Solutions
APi Group
Austin Industries
BE&K
Bechtel
Black & Veatch
CH2M HILL
Chicago Bridge & Iron
Fluor
Foster Wheeler
Halliburton

HydroChem
Jacobs Engineering
McDermott
Parsons Corporation
Performance Contractors
Peter Kiewit Sons'
Philip Services
Shaw Group
TIC Holdings
Yates Companies
Zachry Group

HISTORICAL FINANCIALS

Company Type: Private

Income Statement

FYE: December 31

	REVENUE ($ mil.)	NET INCOME ($ mil.)	NET PROFIT MARGIN	EMPLOYEES
12/07	1,604	—	—	15,000
12/06	1,410	—	—	13,300
12/05	900	—	—	12,000
12/04	816	—	—	12,000
12/03	800	—	—	12,000
Annual Growth	19.0%	—	—	5.7%

Revenue History

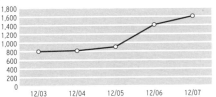

TVA

Although the Tennessee Valley Authority (TVA) may not be an expert on Tennessee attractions like Dollywood and the Grand Ole Opry, it is an authority on power generation. TVA is the largest government-owned power producer in the US, with 33,000 MW of generating capacity. Its power facilities include 11 fossil-powered plants, 29 hydroelectric dams, three nuclear plants, and six combustion turbine plants. The federal corporation transmits electricity to 158 local distribution utilities, which in turn serve 8.7 million consumers. It also provides power for industrial facilities and government agencies, and it manages the Tennessee River system for power production and flood control.

TVA is the sole power wholesaler, by law, in an 80,000-sq.-mi. territory that includes most of Tennessee and portions of six neighboring states (Alabama, Georgia, Kentucky, Mississippi, North Carolina, and Virginia). Generating and transmitting power to local distribution utilities accounts for 86% of TVA's sales.

Most of TVA's power comes from traditional generation sources, but the company is also exploring alternative energy technologies. It has developed solar, wind, and methane gas facilities, and it is offering green choice options through its distribution affiliates.

TVA has also agreed to produce tritium, a radioactive gas that boosts the power of nuclear weapons, for the US Department of Energy (a first for a civilian nuclear power generator). The company has made modifications at its Watts Bar and Sequoyah plants to produce and extract the gas; it provides the DOE with irradiation services through Watts Bar Unit 1. Sequoyah's services came online in 2007.

TVA's rates are among the nation's lowest, which would-be competitors attribute to its exemption from federal and state income and property taxes. To prepare for deregulation, the authority is trying to reduce its $25 billion debt.

HISTORY

In 1924 the Army Corps of Engineers finished building the Wilson Dam on the Tennessee River in Alabama to provide power for two WWI-era nitrate plants. With the war over, the question of what to do with the plants became a political football.

An act of Congress created the Tennessee Valley Authority (TVA) in 1933 to manage the plants and Tennessee Valley waterways. New Dealers saw TVA as a way to revitalize the local economy through improved navigation and power generation. Power companies claimed the agency was unconstitutional, but by 1939, when a federal court ruled against them, TVA had five operating hydroelectric plants and five under construction.

During the 1940s TVA supplied power for the war effort, including the Manhattan Project in Tennessee. During the postwar boom between 1945 and 1950, power usage in the Tennessee Valley nearly doubled. Despite adding dams, TVA couldn't keep up with demand, so in 1949 it began building a coal-fired unit. Because coal-fired plants weren't part of TVA's original mission, in 1955 a Congressional panel recommended the authority be dissolved.

Though TVA survived, its funding was cut. In 1959 it was allowed to sell bonds, but it no longer received direct government appropriations for power operations. In addition, it had to pay back the government for past appropriations.

TVA began to build the first unit of an ambitious 17-plant nuclear power program in Alabama in 1967. However, skyrocketing costs forced it to raise rates and cut maintenance on its coal-fired plants, which led to breakdowns. In 1985 five reactors had to be shut down because of safety concerns.

In 1988 former auto industry executive Marvin Runyon was appointed chairman of the agency. "Carvin' Marvin" cut management, sold three airplanes, and got rid of peripheral businesses, saving $400 million a year. In 1992 Runyon left to go to the postal service and was replaced by Craven Crowell, who began preparing TVA for competition in the retail power market.

TVA ended its nuclear construction program in 1996 after bringing two nuclear units on line within three months, a first for a US utility. The next year it raised rates for the first time in 10 years, planning to reduce its debt. In response to a lawsuit filed by neighboring utilities, it agreed to stop "laundering" power by using third parties to sell outside the agency's legally authorized area.

In 1999 the authority finished installing almost $2 billion in scrubbers and other equipment at its coal-fired plants so that it could buy Kentucky coal along with cleaner Wyoming coal. That year, however, the EPA charged TVA with violating the Clean Air Act by making major overhauls on some of its older coal-fired plants without getting permits or installing updated pollution-control equipment. It ordered TVA to bring most of its coal-fired plants into compliance with more current pollution standards. The next year TVA contested the order in court, stating compliance would jack up electricity rates.

TVA was fined by the US Nuclear Regulatory Commission in 2000 for laying off a nuclear plant whistleblower. Crowell resigned in 2001, and Glenn McCullough Jr. was named chairman; he served in that role until May 2005. He was replaced by Bill Baxter (who served until March 2006) and then by William Sansom.

EXECUTIVES

Chairman: William B. (Bill) Sansom, age 66
President and CEO: Tom D. Kilgore
COO: William R. (Bill) McCollum Jr.
EVP, TVA Nuclear and Chief Nuclear Officer: William R. (Bill) Campbell Jr.
EVP Fossil Power Group: Preston D. Swafford
EVP Financial Services, CFO, and Chief Risk Officer: Kimberly (Kim) Scheibe-Greene, age 37
EVP, General Counsel, and Secretary: Maureen H. Dunn
EVP Customer Resources: Kenneth R. Breeden
EVP Administrative Services and Chief Administrative Officer: John E. Long Jr.
EVP Power System Operations: Terry Boston
SVP Economic Development: John J. Bradley
SVP Pricing and Strategic Planning: Theresa A. Flaim
SVP Finance: John M. Hoskins
SVP Corporate Responsibility and Diversity, Chief Ethics and Compliance Officer, and External Ombudsman: Peyton T. Hairston Jr.
SVP, Office of Environment and Research: Bridgette K. Ellis
SVP Communications, Government, and Valley Relations: Emily J. Reynolds
SVP Fossil Engineering and Technical Services; Acting Manager, Resource Planning and System Forecasting: Marcia Cooper
VP, Controller, and Chief Accounting Officer: John M. Thomas III, age 45
Auditors: Ernst & Young LLP

LOCATIONS

HQ: Tennessee Valley Authority
400 W. Summit Hill Dr., Knoxville, TN 37902
Phone: 865-632-2101   **Fax:** 888-633-0372
Web: www.tva.gov

The Tennessee Valley Authority's service area covers most of Tennessee and parts of Alabama, Georgia, Kentucky, Mississippi, North Carolina, and Virginia.

PRODUCTS/OPERATIONS

2007 Sales

	$ mil.	% of total
Electricity sales		
Municipalities and cooperatives	7,774	84
Industries directly served	1,221	13
Federal agencies	112	1
Other revenue	137	2
Total	**9,244**	**100**

HISTORICAL FINANCIALS

Company Type: Government-owned

Income Statement

FYE: September 30

	REVENUE ($ mil.)	NET INCOME ($ mil.)	NET PROFIT MARGIN	EMPLOYEES
9/07	9,244	383	4.1%	12,013
9/06	9,175	329	3.6%	12,600
9/05	7,794	85	1.1%	12,703
9/04	7,533	386	5.1%	12,742
9/03	6,952	456	6.6%	13,000
Annual Growth	7.4%	(4.3%)	—	(2.0%)

2007 Year-End Financials

Debt ratio: —
Return on equity: 13.5%
Cash ($ mil.): —
Current ratio: —
Long-term debt ($ mil.): —

Net Income History

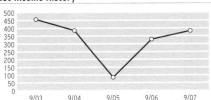

Ty Inc.

Take some fabric, shape it like an animal, fill it with plastic pellets, and you, too, could own luxury hotels. That's the lesson taught by Ty Warner, sole owner of Ty Inc., the firm behind Beanie Babies and their worldwide cult following — popular with kids and adults alike. Since 1993 Ty has produced more than 365 different Beanie Babies with colorful names such as McLucky the bear (current) and Cheeks the baboon (retired). Other products include Beanie Buddies (bigger versions of traditional Beanies), Ty Classics (stuffed animals), Ty Girlz (cloth dolls), and Bow Wow Beanies (pet toys). Beanie bucks enabled Warner to buy a half dozen luxury hotels (mostly in New York and California).

Ty's marketing smarts have kept Beanies popular for years rather than for a single holiday season, à la Furby or Tickle Me Elmo. The company limits production so that supply never outstrips demand, keeping only 40 or 50 Beanie Babies in circulation at any one time. Ty's "retirement" of a Beanie can cause its price among collectors to skyrocket from its $5-$7 retail debut to hundreds or even thousands of dollars.

Rather than flood the market with Beanies through the likes of Toys "R" Us and Wal-Mart, Ty sells them only through specialty toy and gift retailers.

In addition, the firm doesn't advertise, relying instead on the word of mouth that is rampant in Beanie culture. Books, magazines, newsletters, and Web sites stoke collectors' enthusiasm. This collectors' market — which Ty frowns upon (officially, anyway) — shows signs of fading, however.

Deciding to capitalize on a new market of young consumers who likely aren't familiar with its core product, the company launched Beanie Babies 2.0 in early 2008. The new Beanie Babies plushes come with a secret code that allows owners to access the online Beanie Baby world.

Knowing that online worlds for toys are becoming increasingly popular with today's youth, Ty also launched its line of cloth dolls Ty Girlz in 2007. The dolls come with passwords to an online world where users can interact with other Ty Girlz doll owners.

HISTORY

Ty Warner, the son of a plush-toy salesman, started his toy career selling stuffed animals to specialty shops for stuffed-bear manufacturer Dakin. Warner left Dakin in 1980, moved to Europe for a few years, and in the mid-1980s returned to the US and founded Ty Inc. The company first designed a line of understuffed Himalayan cats.

Beanie Babies first debuted at a 1993 trade show. In January 1994 the first nine Beanies went on sale — at prices low enough for kids to afford — in Chicago specialty stores. As Warner had learned at Dakin, selling stuffed animals through specialty retailers rather than through mass merchandisers meant bigger profits for suppliers and longer-term popularity. By 1995 there were about 30 different Beanies, and Ty's estimated sales were $25 million.

The popularity of Beanies exploded in 1996, first in the Midwest, then along the East Coast, and then across the US. By midyear, Beanies — plus the public's mania for getting them before they sold out — were receiving widespread media coverage. Ty heightened the frenzy among collectors when it started announcing Beanie retirements on its Web site in 1997.

That same year, McDonald's got on the bandwagon: The fast-food giant issued some 100 million "teenie" Beanie Babies in a Happy Meal promotion. McDonald's ran out of the toys and had to end the promotion early, causing a public relations mess. McDonald's doubled its toy order in 1998 and teamed up with Ty again in 1999 and 2000.

In 1998 Warner paid $10 million for a 7% stake in marketing company Cyrk. In return, Cyrk developed the Beanie Babies Official Club, which turned stores that sell Beanies into "official headquarters" offering club membership kits. Ty introduced its Attic Treasures and Beanie Buddies lines that year.

By spring 1998 Beanies had become a customs issue at the Canadian border, where Ty's limit of one imported Beanie per person into the US resulted in tears and fisticuffs. (The company later raised the personal limit to 30.) That summer the crowds at Major League Baseball games featuring Beanie giveaways were 26% bigger than average.

Warner bought the Four Seasons hotel in New York City in 1999. He also provided auditing documents and correspondence to *The New York Post* indicating that Ty had 1998 profits of more than $700 million — more than Hasbro and Mattel combined.

After an August 1999 announcement that it would retire the Beanies at the end of the year, the company held a New Year's vote to determine their fate. In the most shocking outcome since *Rocky IV*, the public voted overwhelmingly in favor of continuing the Beanies. Ty introduced its humanoid Beanie Kids line in early 2000. Later that year Warner bought the Four Seasons Biltmore Hotel and the San Ysidro Ranch — the hostelry where JFK and Jackie honeymooned; both are near Santa Barbara, California.

In 2001 Ty debuted its pre-teen Beanie Boppers (boy and girl dolls designed for kids from 8 to 12 years of age). To round out his Four Seasons Hotels and Coral Casino properties in California, in 2003 Warner purchased nearby Sandpiper Golf Course. Also that year, the Beanie Baby celebrated its 10th anniversary, and Ty marked the event with the introduction of the Decade Beanie Baby.

In 2008 the company introduced Beanie Babies 2.0, plush animals that come with codes to an online world where owners can interact with other Beanie owners.

EXECUTIVES

Chairman and CEO: H. Ty Warner
CFO: Richard Jeffrey
VP Sales: Johnathan Zaloum
Marketing Manager: Dana Scott-Turkovich

LOCATIONS

HQ: Ty Inc.
280 Chestnut Ave., Westmont, IL 60559
Phone: 630-920-1515   **Fax:** 630-920-1980
Web: www.ty.com

PRODUCTS/OPERATIONS

Selected Products

Baby Ty
Beanie Babies
Beanie Babies 2.0
Beanie Buddies
Bow Wow Beanies
Pinkies
Pluffies
Ty Classics
Ty Girlz

COMPETITORS

Aurora World	Nakajima USA
Build-A-Bear	North American Bear
Enesco	Russ Berrie
Gund	Sanrio
Hasbro	Simba Dickie Group
Manhattan Group	Vermont Teddy Bear
Mattel	

Unified Grocers

These grocers are unified in their purpose of stocking the shelves. Unified Grocers is a leading wholesale distributor that serves about 3,000 independent grocers, cash and carry outlets, and major grocery chains mostly in the western US through more than a dozen distribution centers. It offers more than 74,000 items to its members and non-member stores, including meat, dairy goods, fresh produce, general merchandise, and specialty items. The company sells goods under national brands, as well as such private labels as Cottage Hearth, Golden Creme, and Western Family. Unified Grocers boasts more than 500 member stores. The cooperative was formed in 1922 as Certified Grocers of California.

In addition to its core wholesale distribution business, Unified Grocers offers its customers such services as liability insurance, financing, and other support services. It also owns more than 15% of Western Family Foods, a distributor of private-label goods sold under the Western Family and Shurfine brands. The cooperative's largest customer, cash and carry warehouse operator Smart & Final, accounts for more than 10% of sales.

Expanding its number of store locations has helped drive wholesale volumes for Unified Grocers, and its perishable goods division has seen growth in the past few years. However, Unified Grocers is coming under increased pressure from the number of supercenters and discount grocers in its territory.

The company acquired Seattle-based Associated Grocers in 2007 for $40 million as part of an expansion effort.

HISTORY

Certified Grocers of California evolved from a group of 15 independent Southern California grocers that formed a purchasing cooperative in 1922 to compete against large grocery chains. Certified Grocers of California incorporated in 1925 and issued stock to 50 members.

The co-op merged with a small retailer-owned wholesale company called Co-operative Grocers in 1928. It acquired Walker Brothers Grocery in

1929 and nearly tripled the previous year's sales. By 1938 the co-op had grown to 310 members and 380 stores, and sales passed $10 million.

Certified launched a line of private-label products under the Springfield name in 1947. In the early 1950s it added nonfood items and began processing its own private-label coffee and bean products. The co-op added delicatessen items in 1956. During the 1960s and 1970s, Certified added a meat center, a frozen food and deli warehouse, a produce distribution center, a creamery, a central bakery, and a specialty foods warehouse.

In 1989 the co-op opened several membership warehouse stores called Convenience Clubs. The Save Mart and Boys Markets chains left the fold in 1991. The co-op lost about 30% of its business during the next two years, including the Bel Air and Williams Bros. chains. After disappointing returns, in 1992 Certified sold its warehouse stores, cut staff, and consolidated warehouses.

CFO (and former Atlantic Richfield executive) Al Plamann was appointed CEO in 1994, succeeding Everett Dingwell. In 1996 the co-op began to convert its customers' older retail stores to Apple Markets in Southern California. Revenues began to dip in 1997 as the result of reduced purchases from some supermarkets and the sale the previous year of one of its subsidiaries, Hawaiian Grocery Stores.

Member chain Stumps converted to the Apple Markets banner in 1998. Faced with a declining customer base, in 1999 Certified merged with United Grocers of Oregon to form Unified Western Grocers.

Dr. R. Norton, F. L. Freeburg, and A. C. Brinckerhoff founded United Grocers of Oregon in 1915 as a way for grocers in Portland to cooperate in purchasing merchandise. By the next year the co-op had 35 members. In the 1950s United formed a trucking department and established a general merchandise division. It also grew rapidly in the 1950s through acquisitions, buying Northwest Grocery Company and the Fridegar Grocery Company. In 1963 United formed its frozen food department when it purchased Raven Creamery.

By 1975 the company's Northwest Grocery Company subsidiary had 14 Cash and Carry warehouses that sold goods to small grocers and restaurants. In 1995 United bought California food distributor Market Wholesale. Three years later the company sold its Cash and Carry warehouse-style stores to Smart & Final.

Upon completion of the merger in 1999, Certified's president and CEO, Plamann, was named to head the new organization. Soon after, Unified consolidated warehouse operations, eliminated duplicate personnel, and combined its private labels. Also in 1999 the company acquired California-based Gourmet Specialties.

The next year it bought the specialty foods business of J. Sosnick and Son, another California company, and Central Sales of Washington State. The company attributed net losses during 2001 to delays in moving the source for northern California specialty merchandise from southern to northern California and to the costs of entering the Washington marketplace, among other factors.

In 2002 Unified closed seven retail stores in Northern California and Oregon (under the Apple Markets and SavMax Foods banners) that accounted for sales of about $140 million as part of its plan to reduce debt and focus on wholesaling. In 2003 the co-op sold or closed all 12 of its company-owned SavMax Foods stores as part of its plan to exit its unprofitable retail business and focus on its wholesale division (99% of total sales).

As part of an expansion effort, in 2007 Unified acquired Associated Grocers, a Seattle-based wholesale cooperative, for about $40 million. The following year the company changed its name to Unified Grocers as part of a corporate marketing campaign.

EXECUTIVES

Chairman: Louis A. (Lou) Amen, age 78
President and CEO: Alfred A. (Al) Plamann, age 65, $1,154,808 pay
EVP Finance and Administration and CFO: Richard J. Martin, age 62, $533,269 pay
EVP, General Counsel, and Secretary: Robert M. Ling Jr., age 50, $626,538 pay
EVP, Chief Marketing Officer, and Chief Procurement Officer: Philip S. Smith, age 57, $501,539 pay
SVP Distribution: Rodney L. Van Bebber, age 52
SVP Retail Support Services and Perishables; President, SavMax Foods: Daniel J. Murphy, age 61, $357,750 pay
SVP Sales: Joseph L. Falvey, age 47
VP Accounting and Chief Accounting Officer: Randall G. Scoville, age 47
VP; President, Pacific Northwest: Dirk T. Davis
VP, Human Resources: Donald E. (Don) Gilpin
VP and CIO: Gary S. Herman
VP and Treasurer: Christine Neal, age 54
VP, Manufacturing: John C. Bedrosian
VP, Real Estate: Gary C. Hammett
Auditors: Deloitte & Touche LLP

LOCATIONS

HQ: Unified Grocers, Inc.
5200 Sheila St., Commerce, CA 90040
Phone: 323-264-5200 **Fax:** 323-265-4006
Web: www.unifiedgrocers.com

PRODUCTS/OPERATIONS

2007 Sales

	$ mil.	% of total
Wholesale distribution	3,118.7	99
Insurance	26.6	1
Other	2.6	—
Adjustments	(14.5)	—
Total	**3,133.4**	**100**

COMPETITORS

Associated Food
Associated Wholesale Grocers
C&S Wholesale
Costco Wholesale
Eby-Brown
IGA
Kroger
McLane
Nash-Finch
Safeway
SUPERVALU
URM Stores
Wal-Mart

UniGroup, Inc.

Moving people's possessions has made many of UniGroup's companies household names. The company transports household goods and other items in more than 100 countries through subsidiaries United Van Lines and Mayflower Transit and a network of affiliates. The movers' operations are supported by UniGroup units such as Trans Advantage, which sells and leases trucks and trailers and provides moving supplies; UniGroup Worldwide UTS, which coordinates international moves; and Vanliner Group, which offers insurance to movers. Subsidiary Allegiant Move Management offers relocation management and assistance. UniGroup is owned by agents of United Van Lines and Mayflower Transit and by the company's senior executives.

In response to competition from companies such as PODS, which deliver storage containers to customers and then provide transportation and storage services, UniGroup has rolled out a similar offering, SAM (for Store and Move).

EXECUTIVES

Chairman and CEO: H. Daniel (Dan) McCollister
President and COO; CEO, United Van Lines: Richard H. (Rich) McClure
CFO: James G. (Jim) Powers
CIO: Randall C. (Randy) Poppell
SVP and Chief Marketing Officer: Stephan (Steve) Burkhardt
SVP Human Resources: Cathy Malear
VP Sales and Marketing: Casey P. Ellis
General Counsel: Jan R. Alonzo
Public Relations and Communications Manager: Jennifer Bonham
President and CEO, Transportation Services Group; President and COO, United Van Lines and Mayflower Transit: Patrick (Pat) Larch
President, Total Transportation Services: Patrick G. Baehler
President, UniGroup Worldwide: Michael Kranisky
President, Vanliner Group: Gale Preston
President, SAM Store and Move: Tom McCormick

LOCATIONS

HQ: UniGroup, Inc.
1 Premier Dr., Fenton, MO 63026
Phone: 636-305-5000 **Fax:** 636-326-1106
Web: www.unigroupinc.com

COMPETITORS

AMERCO
Atlas World Group
Bekins
Budget Rent A Car
Door To Door Storage, Inc.
Graebel
Penske Truck Leasing
PODS
Ryder System
SIRVA

HISTORICAL FINANCIALS

Company Type: Private

Income Statement

FYE: December 31

	REVENUE ($ mil.)	NET INCOME ($ mil.)	NET PROFIT MARGIN	EMPLOYEES
12/07	2,200	—	—	1,350
12/06	2,300	—	—	1,350
12/05	2,200	—	—	1,350
12/04	2,000	—	—	1,350
12/03	1,809	—	—	1,836
Annual Growth	**5.0%**	**—**	**—**	**(7.4%)**

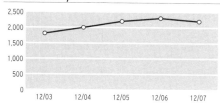

Unisource Worldwide

This company has a singular mission to distribute paper to North America. Unisource Worldwide is a leading distributor of paper products and other supplies, providing commercial printing and business imaging paper and specialty paper products though more than 100 distribution centers. Its offerings include ink jet and laser paper, Xerox paper, and toner cartridges, in addition to coated and uncoated commercial printing paper. Unisource also distributes packaging supplies (corrugated papers, foam and bubble sheeting), packaging systems (pallet systems, shrink packaging systems), and cleaning supplies and equipment. The company is 60%-owned by Bain Capital; paper manufacturer Georgia-Pacific owns about 40%.

In addition to its traditional distribution business, Unisource offers paper supply services to publishers and other commercial operators through its Websource paper brokerage. Its Rollsource unit specializes in business forms and products for customers in the direct mail industry. The company also sells retail paper products online and operates about 40 retail stores in nearly 20 states under the Paper Plus banner.

HISTORY

Tinkham Veale II, a mechanical engineer from Cleveland, got help from his father-in-law, A. C. Ernst of Ernst & Ernst accounting firm, to buy a stake in a prosperous engineered goods manufacturer in 1941. Veale retired at age 37 to breed and race horses. He invested his earnings, became a millionaire by 1951, and joined the board of Alco Oil and Chemical. In 1960 he and his associates formed a holding company, V & V Associates, and bought a large minority share in Alco.

Renamed Alco Chemical two years later, the company bought four fertilizer companies, and in 1965 (by then renamed Alco Standard) it merged with V & V Associates, which had stakes in machinery producers. At the helm, Veale implemented the partnership strategy that would serve Alco for 25 years: He bought small, privately owned companies, usually in exchange for cash and Alco stock, and let the owners continue to run them.

Alco took advantage of several Supreme Court antitrust decisions in the 1960s that forced papermakers to divest marketing companies acquired in the 1950s. Alco acquired Garrett-Buchanan of Philadelphia and Monarch Paper

in 1968 as the basis for its national paper distribution network. After acquiring other paper distributors, the company formed a distributor unit called Unisource. Veale brought in former Kimberly-Clark executive Ray Mundt in 1970 to guide the growing division. Unisource's profitability prompted Alco to enter other distribution businesses, including pharmaceuticals, hospital supplies, steel products, food service equipment, and liquor.

Alco also acquired several manufacturers (plastics, machinery, rubber, and chemicals), but they were not as prosperous. By 1981, with large warehouses and computerized ordering and delivery systems, Unisource was the most efficient, cost-effective distributor in the US. It continued to buy distributors, such as Saxon Industries (1984), an international paper seller valued at $378 million.

Mundt succeeded Veale as chairman two years later and switched Alco's focus to office products and paper distribution, eliminating seven divisions. In the 1990s Mundt oversaw a restructuring that included installing a state-of-the-art distribution software system across the network and consolidating the company's service center operations (Mundt cut Unisource's locations by half). He also expanded the supply products offered to include disposable paper and plastic supplies, packaging systems, and sanitary maintenance equipment in order to offset cyclical downturns in the paper market.

Unisource continued to grow, acquiring more than 40 companies (including 15 in Mexico) in fiscal 1996, and eventually accounting for 70% of Alco's revenues. In late 1996 Alco (which soon after became IKON Office Solutions) spun off Unisource Worldwide with Mundt as its chairman and CEO. The next year Unisource bought National Sanitary Supply (the #1 specialized distributor of sanitary maintenance supplies in the US) and 13 other companies (mostly supply systems). It also sold its $300 million grocery systems operation to Bunzl in 1997.

In 1998 the company announced a restructuring plan that included reducing its US workforce by 15% and cutting its number of distribution facilities almost in half (it took a $370 million charge for the year). Also that year Unisource divested its businesses in Mexico, where the economy was too uncertain.

In early 1999 Unisource agreed to be acquired by UGI Corporation, majority shareholder of AmeriGas Partners, the largest US propane distributor. However, UGI shares fell shortly after the offer, reducing the value of the deal. Georgia-Pacific made an unsolicited bid that Unisource couldn't refuse and the $1.2 billion deal was completed later that year. Unisource became the sole authorized distributor of Ecolab's Professional Products-branded janitorial supplies in 2001.

The next year Georgia-Pacific sold a 60% stake in the company to Bain Capital. It also sold 38 of Unisource's warehouses to Cardinal Capital Partners, which leased them back to the company. Unisource acquired paper broker Graphic Communications in 2003 and merged it with Websource, its existing paper brokerage division.

Al Dragone was named CEO in 2004.

The company sold its converting and manufacturing facility in Jacksonville, Florida, to Cardinal UniJax, LLC, in 2006.

EXECUTIVES

CEO: Allan (Al) Dragone, age 52
CFO: Gordon Glover
Chief Administrative Officer: John Sills
SVP and CIO: Tim Kutz
SVP Sales, Paper and Packaging: Glenn Barton
SVP Sales, Facility Supplies: Steve Topor
Corporate VP Sustainability: Nancy C. Geisler
VP, General Counsel, and Secretary: Zygmunt Jablonski
VP Marketing, Paper: Edward I. Farley
VP Marketing, Facility Supplies and Packaging: Timothy M. (Tim) O'Connor
VP Sourcing, Paper: Jeff Hederick
Director Corporate Communications: Kevin Feeney
President, Unisource Canada: Bruce Bond
President, Paper: Kenneth Winterhalter
Auditors: Ernst & Young LLP

LOCATIONS

HQ: Unisource Worldwide, Inc.
6600 Governors Lake Pkwy., Norcross, GA 30071
Phone: 770-447-9000   **Fax:** 770-734-2000
Web: www.unisourcelink.com

PRODUCTS/OPERATIONS

Selected Products

Envelopes, computer paper, and specialty paper
   Computer paper (blank and proprietary grades)
   Envelopes (mailing, shipping, commercial)
   Specialty products (engineering rolls, labels)
Facility supplies and equipment
   Production supplies (degreasers, work wear)
   Sanitary supplies and equipment (can liners, matting systems)
Packaging
   Case erecting, packaging, and sealing systems (case packers, gummed tapes)
   Case and pallet coding systems (ink jet printers, label materials)
   Packaging supplies (foam and bubble sheeting)
   Pallet unitization systems (conveyers, stretch films)
   Shrink packaging, bundling, bagging, and overwrapping systems
Printing papers
   Coated and uncoated sheet-fed papers
   Premium text, cover, and writing papers
   Uncoated and coated web papers
Specialty businesses
   Paper Plus (smaller orders of paper, packaging, and supplies)
   Rollsource (paper conversion to forms, direct mail)
   Websource (large web paper orders)

COMPETITORS

Bradner Central
Central National-Gottesman
Domtar
Ecolab
Gould Paper
International Paper
Katy Industries
Menasha
Midland Paper
Office Depot
OfficeMax
RIS the paper house
S.P. Richards
Staples
United Stationers
Weyerhaeuser

HISTORICAL FINANCIALS

Company Type: Private

Income Statement

FYE: Saturday nearest December 31

	REVENUE ($ mil.)	NET INCOME ($ mil.)	NET PROFIT MARGIN	EMPLOYEES
12/07	5,300	—	—	6,500
12/06	6,000	—	—	6,400
12/05	6,000	—	—	7,000
12/04	6,000	—	—	8,500
12/03	5,900	—	—	7,100
Annual Growth	(2.6%)	—	—	(2.2%)

Revenue History

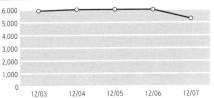

LOCATIONS

HQ: United Components, Inc.
14601 Hwy. 41 North, Evansville, IN 47725
Phone: 812-867-4156   **Fax:** 812-867-4157
Web: www.ucinc.com

2007 Sales

	$ mil.	% of total
US	822	85
Mexico	35	4
Canada	34	4
UK	14	1
France	9	1
Venezuela	6	1
Germany	4	—
Spain	4	—
Other countries	42	4
Total	**970**	**100**

PRODUCTS/OPERATIONS

2007 Sales

	% of total
Filtration products	40
Fuel products	24
Cooling products	21
Engine management products	15
Total	**100**

COMPETITORS

Affinia Group
BorgWarner
CLARCOR
Cummins
Dana Corporation
Delphi Corp.
DENSO
Magna International
Robert Bosch

HISTORICAL FINANCIALS

Company Type: Private

Income Statement

FYE: December 31

	REVENUE ($ mil.)	NET INCOME ($ mil.)	NET PROFIT MARGIN	EMPLOYEES
12/07	970	38	3.9%	5,200
12/06	906	(9)	—	5,200
12/05	1,009	(5)	—	6,200
12/04	1,027	31	3.0%	6,900
12/03	959	13	1.4%	6,500
Annual Growth	0.3%	30.8%	—	(5.4%)

2007 Year-End Financials

Debt ratio: —
Return on equity: 14.1%
Cash ($ mil.): —

Current ratio: —
Long-term debt ($ mil.): —

Net Income History

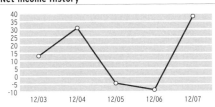

United Components

United Components, Inc. (UCI) might not bring together all the parts of an automobile, but the company has made a good start. UCI was formed by investment firm Carlyle Group in 2003 after it acquired the operations of several auto parts companies from UIS. UCI's component divisions include Airtex Products (fuel pumps and cooling systems), Champion Laboratories (oil, fuel, and air filters), Wells Manufacturing (engine management products), and ASC Industries (cooling systems, water pumps). UCI recently has been divesting non-core operations in the effort to achieve a more ideal product mix.

Building on current relationships, UCI has increased the number of products lines sold at AutoZone (already 28% of sales). Other customers include Advance Auto Parts, CARQUEST, and O'Reilly Automotive.

In 2006 UCI added to its water pump business with the acquisition of water pump manufacturer ASC Industries. Later that year the company sold its Pioneer and Neapco business units. Pioneer went to entrepreneur Doran Arad, and Neapco was sold to the division's senior management and a private investor group. The sales are part of UCI's efforts to focus on its core businesses.

To that same end, later in 2006 UCI sold its Flexible Lamps division (a maker of commercial vehicle lighting systems in the UK) for about $39 million to an affiliate of Truck-Lite Co.

EXECUTIVES

Chairman: David L. Squier, age 62
President, CEO and Director: Bruce M. Zorich, age 54, $560,833 pay
CFO and Director: Daniel J. (Dan) Johnston, age 50
VP and General Counsel: Keith A. Zar
VP Human Resources: Mike Malady
VP Sales and Marketing: Curtis Draper
VP, Traditional Markets: Bruce Tartaglione
VP Global Procurement: Tom Blackerby
Auditors: Grant Thornton LLP

United Supermarkets

From Muleshoe up to Dalhart and over to Pampa, United Supermarkets keeps the Texas Panhandle well fed. The grocer has more than 45 supermarkets, mostly in rural towns. Its stores feature deli, floral, and bakery shops, as well as groceries, pharmacies, and gas at some locales. Its larger Market Street format stocks more specialty foods. United Supermarkets runs its own distribution facility. H. D. Snell founded the firm in Sayre, Oklahoma, in 1916 as United Cash Store. He bucked the norms of the day by selling for cash — instead of on credit — at lower prices. United Supermarkets is owned and run by the Snell family. (Co-presidents Gantt and Matt Bumstead are the great-great-grandsons of the founder.)

The company is expanding its Market Street banner with two new locations slated to open in the Dallas-Fort Worth area in 2008, followed by three new stores in 2009. To promote its new small gourmet grocery format, called "A Taste of Market Street" — the company launched a "Free Fuel" promotion in September 2008 that credits customers with $0.10 off per gallon for every $25 spent in the store.

United Supermarkets has also broken ground on a 9,000-square-foot ice-making plant slated to open in Lubbock in the spring of 2009. The plant will be able to produce 5 million pounds of ice during peak selling periods (those hot, hot Texas summers).

In mid-2007 United Supermarkets acquired one of its major suppliers: Lubbock-based R.C. Taylor Distributing. The firm, which serves Texas and New Mexico, supplies convenience stores, grocery chains, independent grocers, and specialty stores.

In April 2007 the regional grocery chain became a member-owner of Topco Associates, which uses the combined purchasing clout of its 50-plus member companies (mostly supermarket operators and food service suppliers) to wring discounts from wholesalers and manufacturers.

The company, which opened its first Hispanic-themed Super Mercado store in 2001, shuttered two of the three stores in early 2007. The format was later renamed Amigos United.

EXECUTIVES

CEO: Dan Sanders
Co-President: R. Gantt Bumstead
Co-President and EVP, Customer and Community Service: Matt Bumstead
EVP and COO: Sidney Hopper
VP, Human Resources: Phil Pirkle
VP, Marketing: Renée Underwood
Chief Merchandising Officer: Wes Jackson
CIO: Peter Wellman
Director, Communications: Eddie Owens

LOCATIONS

HQ: United Supermarkets, Ltd.
7830 Orlando Ave., Lubbock, TX 79423
Phone: 806-791-7457   **Fax:** 806-791-7476
Web: www.unitedtexas.com

PRODUCTS/OPERATIONS

2008 Stores

	No.
United Supermarkets	40
Market Street	6
Amigos United	1
Total	**47**

COMPETITORS

Albertsons	IGA
Brookshire Grocery	Kroger
Dollar General	Minyard Group
Fiesta Mart	Randall's
H-E-B	Wal-Mart
Homeland Stores	

United Way

Where there's a will, there's a Way. United Way of America (UWA) unites about 1,300 local United Way organizations that work to raise money for charitable causes. Priorities are set by local organizations, but United Way groups tend to focus on helping children and families and on improving access to health care. Major recipients of United Way contributions have included American Cancer Society, Big Brothers/Big Sisters, Catholic Charities, Girl Scouts and Boy Scouts, and The Salvation Army, among others. United Way groups raise money primarily through an annual campaign conducted in workplaces. United Way organizations also receive government grants and corporate contributions.

Each of the UAW's local organizations is an independent entity governed by local volunteers. The UWA acts as a national services and training center that supports the local organizations with services, such as national advertising and research. Local organizations, in turn, support UWA with membership dues.

HISTORY

The first modern Community Chest was created in 1913, laying the foundation for the practice of allocating funds among multiple causes. Five years later, representatives from 12 fundraising organizations met in Chicago and established the American Association for Community Organizations, the predecessor of the present-day United Way. By 1929 more than 350 Community Chests had been established.

Payroll deductions for charitable contributions debuted in 1943. In 1946 the United Way's predecessor organization initiated a cooperative relationship with the American Federation of Labor and the Congress of Industrial Organizations (which merged to become the AFL-CIO in 1955); the two groups agreed to provide services to members of organized labor. (The relationship continues today, with the organizations collaborating on projects such as recruiting members of organized labor to lead health and human services organizations.)

The Uniform Federal Fund-Raising Program was created by order of President Dwight Eisenhower in 1957, enabling federal employees to contribute to charities of their choice. (The program later evolved into the Combined Federal Campaign.) Six years later Los Angeles became the first city to adopt the United Way name when more than 30 local Community Chests and United Fund organizations merged. The national organization, which had been operating under the United Community Funds and Councils (UCFCA) name, adopted the United Way of America (UWA) name in 1970. It established its headquarters in Alexandria, Virginia, the next year.

Congress made its first grant for emergency food and shelter to the private sector in 1983, and UWA was selected as its fiscal agent. UWA created its Emergency Food and Shelter National Board Program the same year. In 1984 UWA created the Alexis de Tocqueville Society to solicit larger donations from individuals (it attracted such members as Bill Gates and Walter Annenberg).

In 1992 William Aramony, UWA's president for more than two decades, resigned after coming under fire for his lavish expenditures. Former Peace Corps head Elaine Chao was tapped to replace him, and in 1995 Aramony was sentenced to seven years in prison for defrauding the organization of about $600,000. Former UWA CFO Thomas Merlo and Stephen Paulachak (former president of a UWA spinoff) were convicted on related charges. After four years spent burnishing UWA's tarnished image, Chao resigned in 1996 and was succeeded the next year by Betty Beene, who had served as CEO of the Tri-State United Way.

In an effort to stress the manner in which its local organizations benefit their communities, UWA launched a brand-initiative campaign in 1998. The following year UWA's local organization in Santa Clara, California, found itself in serious financial straits when donations began slipping despite its location in the wealthy Silicon Valley. Infoseek founder Steve Kirsch and Microsoft founder Bill Gates chipped in $1 million and $5 million, respectively, to help keep the organization afloat.

Beene, who drew the ire of some chapters for suggesting a national pledge-processing center and national standards, stepped down in January 2001. That same year UWA began funneling more funds into smaller community projects instead of national charities. In 2002 Brian Gallagher took over as president and CEO.

In the aftermath of Hurricane Katrina in 2005, UWA teamed up with the Red Cross and Salvation Army to form a Coordinated Assistance Network to address the needs of evacuees by providing emergency and recovery services.

EXECUTIVES

Chair: William G. (Bill) Parrett, age 63
President and CEO: Brian A. Gallagher, age 49
COO: Joseph V. Haggerty
Chief of Staff: Brian J. G. Lachance
EVP and CFO: Usha Chaudhary
EVP and Director, Center for Community Leadership: Brook Manville
EVP Brand Strategy and Marketing: Cynthia Round
EVP, Enterprise Services: Michael Schreiber
EVP Strategic Alliances and Inclusiveness: Deborah W. (Debbie) Foster
SVP, Community Impact: Alexander M. (Alex) Sanchez
Group VP, Investor Relations: Mary Kay Leonard
VP, Controller: Cynthia Smith
VP, Human Resources: Evelyn Amador
VP, Public Policy: Steve Taylor
VP Field and Media Communications: Del Galloway
General Counsel: Patti Turner
Secretary: Linda Chavez-Thompson, age 64
Director Media and Public Relations: Sally Fabens
Auditors: Ernst & Young LLP

LOCATIONS

HQ: United Way of America
701 N. Fairfax St., Alexandria, VA 22314
Phone: 703-836-7807   **Fax:** 703-683-7840
Web: www.liveunited.org

PRODUCTS/OPERATIONS

Selected Recipients

Big Brothers/Big Sisters
Catholic Charities
American Cancer Society
Girl Scouts
Boy Scouts

HISTORICAL FINANCIALS

Company Type: Not-for-profit

Income Statement

FYE: December 31

	REVENUE ($ mil.)	NET INCOME ($ mil.)	NET PROFIT MARGIN	EMPLOYEES
12/07	66	—	—	207
12/06	68	—	—	186
12/05	74	—	—	174
12/04	45	—	—	—
12/03	35	—	—	—
Annual Growth	17.2%	—	—	9.1%

Revenue History

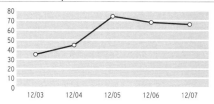

Universal Hospital Services

The yearning for medical equipment is universal, as Universal Hospital Services (UHS) well knows. Founded in 1939, the company leases movable medical equipment to hospitals and care providers from 80 sales and distribution offices across the US. It has a pool of more than 200,000 pieces of equipment in specialty areas such as critical care, monitoring, respiratory therapy, and newborn care. UHS's programs include the Asset Management Partnership, which supplies, maintains, manages, and tracks equipment for customers. The company also sells new and used equipment and disposable supplies, and it provides equipment maintenance services. In 2007 UHS was acquired by an affiliate of Bear Stearns for $712 million.

The company was previously controlled by leveraged buyout specialist J.W. Childs; other shareholders included equity firm The Halifax Group and members of UHS's management.

EXECUTIVES

Chairman Emeritus: David E. Dovenberg, age 63
Chairman and CEO: Gary D. Blackford, age 50,
$671,193 pay
EVP and COO: Timothy W. Kuck, age 50
EVP and CFO: Rex T. Clevenger, age 50, $465,361 pay
EVP Sales and Marketing: Jeffrey L. Singer, age 46,
$292,242 pay
SVP, Technology, Marketing, and Facilities:
David G. Lawson, age 51
SVP and General Counsel: Diana J. Vance-Bryan, age 52
SVP Human Resources and Development:
Walter T. Chesley, age 53
SVP, Medical Equipment Services: Timothy R. Travis
Auditors: PricewaterhouseCoopers LLP

LOCATIONS

HQ: Universal Hospital Services, Inc.
7700 France Ave., South, Ste. 275, Edina, MN 55435
Phone: 952-893-3200   **Fax:** 952-893-0704
Web: www.uhs.com

PRODUCTS/OPERATIONS

2007 Sales

	% of total
Medical equipment outsourcing	78
Technical & professional services	15
Medical equipment sales & remarketing	7
Total	**100**

COMPETITORS

Hill-Rom
Kinetic Concepts
Medline Industries
Owens & Minor
PSS World Medical

HISTORICAL FINANCIALS

Company Type: Private

Income Statement   FYE: December 31

	REVENUE ($ mil.)	NET INCOME ($ mil.)	NET PROFIT MARGIN	EMPLOYEES
12/07	264	(64)	—	1,318
12/06	225	0	0.0%	1,274
12/05	216	(2)	—	1,139
12/04	200	(4)	—	1,188
12/03	171	(20)	—	971
Annual Growth	**11.5%**	**—**	**—**	**7.9%**

Net Income History

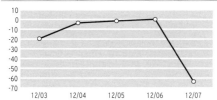

University of Alabama System

Students in the Heart of Dixie can choose from among three campuses overseen by The University of Alabama system. The flagship Tuscaloosa campus, created in 1936, offers more than 200 degree programs to more than 25,000 students. The University of Alabama at Birmingham offers nearly 140 degree programs and has an enrollment of more than 16,000 students; it is also home to the university's school of medicine and a 900-bed hospital. The system's Huntsville campus has about 7,000 students enrolled in its five colleges and graduate school. Each campus offers bachelor's, master's, and doctoral degree programs. The University of Alabama was founded in Tuscaloosa in 1831 as the state's first public university.

EXECUTIVES

Chancellor: Malcolm Portera, age 61
President, The University of Alabama: Robert E. Witt
Vice Chancellor Academic Affairs: Charles R. Nash
Vice Chancellor Financial Affairs: C. Ray Hayes
Vice Chancellor System Relations: Kellee Reinhart
Director Financial Operations: Stan Acker
Secretary and Executive Assistant to the Chancellor:
Michael A. Bownes
General Counsel: Ralph H. Smith II
General Auditor: Newt Hamner
Human Resources Generalist: Jon Garner
Coordinator Information Systems: Kim Thoma Bailey
President, The University of Alabama at Birmingham:
Carol Z. Garrison
President, The University of Alabama in Huntsville:
David B. (Dave) Williams
Auditors: KPMG LLP

LOCATIONS

HQ: The University of Alabama System
401 Queen City Ave., Tuscaloosa, AL 35401
Phone: 205-348-5861   **Fax:** 205-348-9788
Web: www.uasystem.ua.edu

PRODUCTS/OPERATIONS

Selected Colleges and Schools
The University of Alabama (Tuscaloosa)
Capstone College of Nursing
College of Arts and Sciences
College of Communication
College of Community Health Sciences
College of Continuing Studies
College of Education
College of Engineering
College of Human Environmental Sciences
Culverhouse College of Commerce and Business
Administration
Graduate School
School of Law
School of Social Work
The University of Alabama at Birmingham
School of Arts and Humanities
School of Business
School of Dentistry
School of Education
School of Engineering
School of Health Related Professions
School of Medicine
School of Natural Sciences and Mathematics
School of Nursing
School of Optometry
School of Public Health
School of Social and Behavioral Sciences

The University of Alabama in Huntsville
College of Administrative Science
College of Engineering
College of Liberal Arts
College of Nursing
College of Science
School of Graduate Studies

University of California

The University of California (UC) system has some 215,000 students at its 10 campuses (which include four law schools and five medical schools) located in Berkeley, Davis, Irvine, Los Angeles (UCLA), Merced (which opened in the fall of 2005 with an enrollment of 875 students), Riverside, San Diego, San Francisco, Santa Barbara, and Santa Cruz. The schools, with more than 120,000 faculty and staff, offer areas of study in more than 150 disciplines ranging from the arts to bioengineering. UC also operates three US Department of Energy research labs in California and New Mexico.

In the wake of the 1996 approval of California's Proposition 209, which eliminated state affirmative-action programs, enrollment of minorities and the hiring of female faculty both dropped in the UC system. To help restore minority admissions to pre-Prop 209 levels, UC guarantees admission to the top 4% of students at each California high school and operates outreach programs aimed at low-income students.

In 2004 the school agreed to raise the grade point level for students beginning in 2007 in order to shrink its pool of applicants to meet state guidelines. Opponents to the plan argued that the higher standards would unfairly reduce the enrollment of minority and disadvantaged students.

HISTORY

The founders of California's government provided for a state university via a clause in the state's constitution in 1849. The origins of the College of California, opened in Oakland in 1869, date back to the Contra Costa Academy, a small school established by Yale alumnus Henry Durant in 1853. Durant ran Contra Costa, and then the college, until 1872. Women were allowed to enter the school in 1870. The college moved to Berkeley and graduated its first class (12 men) in 1873.

As California's economy and population grew, so did its university system. Renamed University of California (UC) in 1879, it had 1,000 students by 1895. Agriculture, mining, geology, and engineering were among its first fields. A second campus was established at Davis in 1905, followed by campuses in San Diego (1912) and Los Angeles (1919).

The Depression brought cutbacks in funding for UC, but the system rebounded in the 1940s. It opened its fifth campus (Santa Barbara) in 1944, and during WWII it also began gaining recognition for research. Between 1945 and 1965 enrollment quadrupled, spurred by GI Bill-sponsored veterans and a population shift to the West. The state legislature formulated the Master Plan for Higher Education in 1960, which reorganized university administration and established admission requirements. Campuses were established at Irvine and Santa Cruz in 1965.

The first of several important demonstrations in the 1960s at UC Berkeley came in 1964 over the university's attempts to ban political activity on a strip of UC-owned land. The People's Park riot of 1969, touched off when UC tried to close a parcel of land in Berkeley that students had turned into a kind of playground for the counter-culture, left one dead and more than 50 wounded.

Aware of the changing demographics of its student body, especially its growing Asian enrollment (28% in 1990), UC Berkeley gave the chancellor's job to Chang-Lin Tien in 1990 — the first person of Asian descent to hold that position at a major US university (Tien served as chancellor until 1997). A California recession in the early 1990s resulted in budget cuts for UC. Strapped for cash, the university launched a for-profit entity in 1992 to tap its extensive library of patents.

UC San Diego chancellor Richard Atkinson succeeded Jack Peltason as UC president in 1995, the same year the UC Board of Regents approved a new campus — the university's 10th — in the San Joaquin Valley. That year it voted to phase out race- and sex-based affirmative action. The board, in an effort to be competitive with other top universities in recruiting faculty, voted to offer health benefits to the partners of gay employees in 1997. Also that year UC created the California Digital Library and began putting its library collection online.

Entrepreneur Alfred Mann donated $100 million to UCLA in 1998 for biomedical research. Also that year admissions of non-Asian-American minorities to the fall freshman classes of UCLA and UC Berkeley fell sharply. The following year the UC system began guaranteeing admission to the top 4% of students in each of the state's high schools. UC took some heat in 1999 and 2000 for two separate instances of security breaches at the Los Alamos National Laboratory.

Robert Dynes, previously chancellor of UC San Diego, became president of the UC system in October 2003. Mark Yudof became president in 2008.

EXECUTIVES

President: Mark G. Yudof, age 63
Executive Officer and Chief of Staff: Linda Fabbri
EVP Business Operations: Kathrine Lapp
SVP Chief Compliance and Audit Officer: Sheryl Vacca
Chief Investment Officer and Chief Investment Officer and Acting Treasurer of The Regents: Marie N. Berggren
General Counsel and Vice President Legal Affairs: Charles F. Robinson
Associate VP Human Resources and Benefits: Judith Boyette
Vice Provost Educational Relations: Joyce Justus
Vice Provost Academic Information and Strategic Services: Daniel Greenstein
Vice Provost for Research: Lawrence Coleman
Academic Senate Chair: Michael Brown
Chancellor University of California Davis: Larry N. Vanderhoef, age 66
Chancellor University of California San Francisco: J. Michael Bishop
Chancellor University of California Santa Cruz: George R. Blumenthal
Chancellor University of California San Diego: Marye Anne Fox
Chancellor University of California Berkeley: Robert J. Birgeneau, age 65

Chancellor University of California Irvine: Michael V. Drake
Chancellor University of California Santa Barbara: Henry T.Y. Yang
Acting Chancellor University of California Riverside: Robert D. Grey
Chancellor University of California Los Angeles: Gene D. Block
Chancellor University of California Merced: Sung-Mo (Steve) Kang, age 62
Auditors: PricewaterhouseCoopers LLP

LOCATIONS

HQ: University of California
 1111 Franklin St., Oakland, CA 94607
Phone: 510-987-0700   **Fax:** 510-987-0894
Web: www.universityofcalifornia.edu

Campuses

UC Berkeley
UC Davis
UC Irvine
UC Los Angeles (UCLA)
UC Merced
UC Riverside
UC San Diego
UC San Francisco
UC Santa Barbara
UC Santa Cruz

PRODUCTS/OPERATIONS

Department of Energy Laboratories

Ernest Orlando Lawrence Berkeley National Laboratory (Berkeley, CA)
Lawrence Livermore National Laboratory (Livermore, CA)
Los Alamos National Laboratory (New Mexico)

University of California, Davis

If you want to grow grapes and make wine in Napa Valley or Sonoma County, you might want to swing by the University of California, Davis (UC Davis) first. The school offers a wide variety of agricultural programs; its Viticulture and Enology department provides professional education for aspiring winemakers. Located between Sacramento and San Francisco, UC Davis has professional schools in education, law, business, medicine, and veterinary medicine. UC Davis enrolls more than 30,000, including about 4,100 graduate students. It was originally known as the University Farm School, and accepted its first students at its new campus in the town of Davisville (later changed to Davis) in 1909.

The California Legislature in 1905 authorized the establishment of a state agricultural college, and a 778-acre farm near the state capital was purchased the following year.

The first classes were held in 1908 for local farmers, and the first official class, which included students from the University of California at Berkeley, convened in January of 1909.

The school that became UC Davis was administratively tied to UC Berkeley for decades, before gaining its status as an independent university in 1959.

Davis had long been the largest campus in the UC system, at 5,300 acres, but the new University of California, Merced campus in the Central Valley has since surpassed it with more than 7,000 acres.

The university became part of US history and legal precedent in 1974, when Allan Bakke sued the UC regents to gain admission to UC Davis' School of Medicine, saying he was the victim of reverse racial discrimination. The US Supreme Court ruled in 1978 that race could be lawfully considered in college admissions.

EXECUTIVES

Chancellor: Larry N. Vanderhoef, age 66
Vice Chancellor Administration: Stan E. Nosek
Vice Chancellor Resource Management and Planning: John A. Meyer
Executive Vice Chancellor and Interim Provost: Barbara A. Horwitz
Vice Provost Undergraduate Studies: Patricia (Pat) Turner
Vice Chancellor University Relations: Beverly (Babs) Sandeen
Vice Chancellor Research: Barry M. Klein
Vice Chancellor Student Affairs: Fred Wood
Associate Vice Chancellor Finance and Controller: J. Michael Allred
Associate Vice Chancellor Human Resources: Karen Hull
Assistant Vice Chancellor University Communications: Lisa Lapin

LOCATIONS

HQ: University of California, Davis
 1 Shields Ave., Davis, CA 95616
Phone: 530-752-1011   **Fax:** 530-752-2400
Web: www.ucdavis.edu

HISTORICAL FINANCIALS

Company Type: School

Income Statement

	REVENUE ($ mil.)	NET INCOME ($ mil.)	NET PROFIT MARGIN	EMPLOYEES
6/07	2,571	—	—	30,086
6/06	2,380	—	—	30,000
Annual Growth	8.0%	—	—	0.3%

FYE: June 30

Revenue History

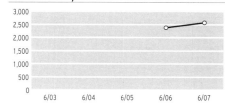

University of California, San Diego

Established in 1912 and a full university since 1961, the University of California at San Diego (UCSD) is a scientific powerhouse. Its faculty currently boasts five Nobel laureates, three National Medal of Science winners, and eight MacArthur Fellows (the "genius awards"). The university is home to the San Diego Supercomputer Center, the Scripps Institution of Oceanography, and the UCSD Medical Center, among other research organizations. With an enrollment of more than 20,000 students, UCSD has six undergraduate colleges as well as graduate and medical schools. The school is one of the ten campuses in the University of California System.

UCSD has one Pulitzer Prize and nine Nobel Prize winners, in addition to nine MacArthur "genius" awardees on its faculty. It is home to the Institute on Global Conflict and Cooperation and the California Institute for Information Technology and Telecommunications.

EXECUTIVES

Chancellor: Marye Anne Fox
Senior Vice Chancellor: Marsha A. Chandler, age 53
Acting Senior Vice Chancellor Academic Affairs: Marjorie C. Caserio
Vice Chancellor Business Affairs: Steven Relyea
Vice Chancellor Student Affairs: H. E. (Penny) Rue
Associate Vice Chancellor Academic Planning and Resources: David R. Miller
Associate Vice Chancellor University Communications: Stacie Spector
Assistant Vice Chancellor Program Planning and Undergraduate Education: Bonnie Horstmann
Assistant Vice Chancellor Administrative Computing and Telecommunications: Elazar C. Harel
Assistant Vice Chancellor Human Resources: Thomas R. Leet
Chief of Staff, Office of the SVCAA: Gillian Hemingway

LOCATIONS

HQ: University of California, San Diego
9500 Gilman Dr., La Jolla, CA 92093
Phone: 858-534-2230
Web: www.ucsd.edu

PRODUCTS/OPERATIONS

2005 Revenue

	$ mil.	% of total
Grants and contracts	660	33
Medical center	556	27
State educational appropriations	251	12
Student tuition and fees	176	9
Educational activities	163	8
Auxiliary enterprises	106	5
Private gifts	49	2
State financing appropriations	17	1
Investment income	15	1
Other	31	2
Total	**2,024**	**100**

Colleges

Earl Warren College
Eleanor Roosevelt College
John Muir College
Revelle College
Sixth College
Thurgood Marshall College

Schools and Divisions

Division of Arts and Humanities
Division of Biological Sciences
Division of Physical Sciences
Division of Social Sciences
Graduate School of International Relations and Pacific Studies
Graduate Studies and Research
Jacobs School of Engineering
Preuss School
School of Management
School of Medicine
School of Pharmacy and Pharmaceutical Sciences
Scripps Institution of Oceanography
UCSD Extension
UCSD Healthcare

University of Chicago

The University of Chicago ranks among the world's most esteemed major universities. It has an enrollment of nearly 14,000 students, some two-thirds of which are graduate students. The school's undergraduate branch offers a core curriculum based on the Great Books; students can choose from majors in about 50 areas. Among its graduate programs are the University of Chicago Law School and Graduate School of Business, both of which consistently rank in the top 10 by *U.S. News & World Report*. The U of C is associated with more than 80 Nobel Prize recipients including Enrico Fermi, Milton Friedman, and Saul Bellow. Founded in 1890 by John D. Rockefeller, the university has an endowment of about $4.8 billion.

The University of Chicago has steadfastly stood its ground against trendiness in education curricula. All students take courses that expose them to the social, biological, and physical sciences, as well as humanities, mathematics, and language. While the university's list of those who graduated is impressive, the list of those who did not is equally prominent, including Oracle's Larry Ellison and author Kurt Vonnegut.

Students attending the U of C study primarily at its 200-acre main campus on the South Side of Chicago, but the university's Graduate School of Business also maintains campuses in downtown Chicago, London, Paris, and Singapore. Among the many institutions affiliated with the U of C are the University of Chicago Hospitals and Health System, the Argonne National Laboratory, and the Yerkes Observatory. The University of Chicago Press, founded in 1892, is the largest university press in the US.

HISTORY

The University of Chicago took its name from the first U of C, a small Baptist school that operated from 1858-1886. The school, incorporated in 1890, was born when William Rainey Harper, the man who was to become the University's first president, convinced Standard Oil's John D. Rockefeller to provide a founding gift of $600,000. Members of the American Baptist Education Society chipped in another $400,000, and department store owner Marshall Field donated the land for the campus.

The university opened in 1892 with a faculty of 103 and 594 students. As it grew, the university took over property that had been used in the Columbian Exposition of 1892-93, eventually surrounding the fair's former midway. (The school's football team later earned the nickname "Monsters of the Midway" while being coached by the legendary Amos Alonzo Stagg; this was before withdrawing from intercollegiate play in 1939. Legend has it that the university retains the right to rejoin the Big Ten.)

Only four years after its founding, the university's enrollment of 1,815 exceeded Harvard's. By 1907, 43% of its 5,000 students were women. Robert Maynard Hutchins, president from 1929 to 1951, revolutionized the university and American higher education by insisting on the study of original sources (the Great Books) and competency testing through comprehensive exams. He organized the college and graduate divisions into their present structure, reaffirming the role of the university as a place for intellectual exploration rather than vocational training. In 1942 the U of C ushered in the nuclear age when Enrico Fermi created the first controlled nuclear chain reaction in the school's abandoned football stadium.

From the 1950s through the 1970s, the university purchased and restored Frank Lloyd Wright's famed Robie House and built the Joseph Regenstein Library (1970). In 1978 Hanna Holborn Gray became the first woman to be named president of a major university. Gray abolished the decade-old Lascivious Costume Ball, a major social event (some would say the only social event) at the university. Hugo Sonnenschein succeeded Gray in 1993. The beginning of his tenure coincided with a period of financial difficulty for the school as increases in costs outpaced revenue growth. In 1996 Sonnenschein announced plans to boost enrollment by as much as 30% in order to invigorate the school's finances.

U of C graduate and former professor Myron Scholes shared the Nobel Prize in economics in 1997. The next year the school announced plans for a $35 million athletics center to be named after Gerald Ratner, a former student who donated $15 million toward construction. The university later signed an agreement to supply content to Internet distance-learning startup UNext.com (now Cardean Learning Group), founded by trustee Andrew Rosenfield. (This agreement was controversial within the university community.) Cardean University, UNext.com's online university, began operating in 2000. Sonnenschein resigned in 2000 and was replaced by Don Randel, former provost of Cornell University. That year the University of Chicago Graduate School of Business opened a campus in Singapore, and U of C economist James Heckman was awarded the Nobel Prize for his work in microeconomics.

Don Randel stepped down as president in 2006 to become president of the Andrew W. Mellon Foundation. Robert Zimmer, previously provost at Brown University, was named his successor.

EXECUTIVES

Chairman: James S. Crown, age 54
President and Trustee: Robert J. (Bob) Zimmer
Provost: Thomas A. Rosenbaum
Dean, The College: John W. Boyer
University Secretary: David Fithian
SVP University Resources, Development, and Alumni Relations: Randy L. Holgate

VP Administration and CFO: Nim Chinniah
VP and CIO: Gregory A. (Greg) Jackson
VP and Chief Investment Officer: Peter D. A. Stein
VP and General Counsel: Beth A. Harris
VP University Relations and Dean, College Enrollment:
  Michael C. Behnke
VP Strategic Initiatives: David A. Greene
VP Research and National Laboratories: Donald H. Levy
VP Communications: Julie Peterson
VP Financial Strategy and Budget: Kermit Daniel
VP and Dean, Students at the University:
  Kimberly Goff-Crews
VP Development and Alumni Relations:
  Ronald J. Schiller
Auditors: KPMG LLP

LOCATIONS

HQ: The University of Chicago
    5801 S. Ellis Ave., Chicago, IL 60637
Phone: 773-702-1234   Fax: 773-702-4155
Web: www.uchicago.edu

The University of Chicago has campuses in the Hyde
Park area of Chicago and downtown Chicago, as well as
in London, Paris, and Singapore.

PRODUCTS/OPERATIONS

Selected Majors at The College (Undergraduate)

African and African American Studies
Ancient Studies
Art History
Biological Chemistry
Cinema and Media Studies
Classical Studies
Early Christian Literature
East Asian Languages and Civilization
English Language and Literature
Geographical Studies
Geophysical Sciences
Germanic Studies
History
History, Philosophy, and Social Studies of Science and
    Medicine
International Studies
Jewish Studies
Latin American Studies
Medieval Studies
Music
Near Eastern Languages and Civilizations
Physics
Political Science
Psychology
Public Policy Studies
Religion and the Humanities
Romance Languages and Literatures
Russian Civilization
Sociology
South Asian Languages and Civilizations
Visual Arts

Selected Affiliated Institutions

Argonne National Laboratory
Chapin Hall Center for Children
Consortium on Chicago School Research
Institute for Mind and Biology
University of Chicago Hospitals and Health System
Yerkes Observatory

Selected Graduate Schools and Programs

Divinity School
Graduate School of Business
Harris Graduate School of Public Policy Studies
Law School
Pritzker School of Medicine
School of Social Service Administration

University of Illinois

The log cabins that used to dot the landscape
in the Land of Lincoln have given way to the
three campuses of the University of Illinois. Established as a land grant institution in 1867, the
university has grown to include campuses in
Chicago, Springfield, and Urbana-Champaign.
Its roughly 70,000 students (a majority of whom
study at the main Urbana-Champaign campus)
can choose from more than 150 undergraduate
programs and more than 100 graduate and professional programs. The Urbana-Champaign
campus is the site of the National Center for Su-
percomputing Applications (which developed
Mosaic, the basis for popular Internet browsers
such as Netscape Navigator).

EXECUTIVES

President: B. Joseph White, age 60
Secretary: Michele M. Thompson
Executive Director Governmental Relations:
  Richard M. Schoell
Executive Director University Relations: Thomas Hardy
CFO and Comptroller: Walter Knorr
University Counsel: Thomas R. Bearrows
VP Academic Affairs: Mrinalini Chatta Rao
Interim Associate Vice President Human Resources:
  J. David Stewart
Chancellor, UI Chicago: Sylvia Manning
Interim Chancellor University of Illinois at Chicago:
  Eric A. Gislason
Chancellor, University of Illinois Springfield:
  Richard D. Ringeisen
Chancellor, UI Urbana-Champaign: Richard Herman
Chancellor, University of Illinois Chicago:
  Paula Allen-Meares
Auditors: BKD, LLP

LOCATIONS

HQ: University of Illinois
    108 Henry Administration Bldg., Urbana, IL 61801
Phone: 217-333-1000   Fax: 217-244-2282
Web: www.uillinois.edu

The University of Illinois has campuses in Chicago,
Springfield, and Urbana-Champaign, as well as health
professions sites and continuing education centers
throughout the state.

PRODUCTS/OPERATIONS

Selected Colleges and Instructional Units

College of Agricultural, Consumer and Environmental
    Sciences
College of Applied Life Studies
College of Business
College of Communications
College of Education
College of Engineering
College of Fine and Applied Arts
College of Law
College of Liberal Arts and Sciences
College of Medicine at Urbana-Champaign
College of Veterinary Medicine
Division of General Studies
Graduate School of Library and Information Science
Institute of Labor and Industrial Relations
School of Social Work

COMPETITORS

Bradley University	Northwestern University
City Colleges of Chicago	Southern Illinois
DePaul University	University
Indiana University	University of Chicago
Northern Illinois	
University	

University of Iowa Hospitals and Clinics

University of Iowa Hospitals and Clinics partners with the University of Iowa Roy J. and Lucille A. Carver College of Medicine and the
University of Iowa Physicians group practice organization to make up the University of Iowa
Health Care network. The organization provides
residents of the Hawkeye State with an acute
care hospital serving a variety of inpatient and
outpatient needs, including more than 200
health care specialties. The facility also houses
the Children's Hospital of Iowa and the Holden
Comprehensive Cancer Center. The health care
system, founded in 1898, has some 680 beds.

EXECUTIVES

CEO: Kenneth P. (Ken) Kates
Interim COO: Eric Dickson
CFO: Kenneth L. (Ken) Fisher
Chief of Staff: Eva Tsalikian
Senior Associate Director: John H. Staley
Associate Director and Legal Counsel:
  William W. Hesson
Associate Director, Children's Hospital of Iowa:
  John A. Brandecker
Associate Director and Chief Administrative Officer:
  Timothy M. Gaillard
CIO: L. Carmen
Joint Office for Marketing and Communications:
  D. Lundell
Joint Office for Marketing and Communications:
  S. McGauvran-Hruby
Associate VP Nursing and Chief Nursing Officer:
  Ann Williamson
Hospital Human Resources and Payroll: D. Leventry

LOCATIONS

HQ: University of Iowa Hospitals and Clinics
    200 Hawkins Dr., Iowa City, IA 52242
Phone: 319-356-1616   Fax: 319-384-7099
Web: www.uihealthcare.com/uihospitalsandclinics

PRODUCTS/OPERATIONS

Selected Centers

Holden Comprehensive Cancer Center
James A. Clifton Center for Digestive Diseases
University of Iowa Children's Hospital
University of Iowa Family Care
University of Iowa Heart and Vascular Center
University of Iowa Neurosciences
University of Iowa Sports Medicine
University of Iowa Weight Loss

COMPETITORS

Genesis Health System
Iowa Health System
Mercy Health Network
Regional Ventures

HISTORICAL FINANCIALS
Company Type: Not-for-profit

Income Statement
FYE: June 30

	REVENUE ($ mil.)	NET INCOME ($ mil.)	NET PROFIT MARGIN	EMPLOYEES
6/07	677	—	—	7,625
6/06	740	—	—	7,625
6/05	724	—	—	7,480
6/04	701	—	—	7,229
6/03	594	—	—	7,013
Annual Growth	3.3%	—	—	2.1%

Revenue History

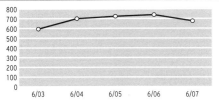

University of Kentucky

Kentucky knows bluegrass and basketball. Perennial basketball powerhouse The University of Kentucky (UK) has an enrollment of approximately 27,000 in about 20 colleges and schools. It offers more than 100 undergraduate majors and more than 100 graduate degree programs, including master's, doctoral, first professional, and post-doctoral programs. It confers some 5,500 degrees annually. UK also operates the The Albert B. Chandler Hospital. A public university and research institution, the school was founded in 1865 as the Agricultural and Mechanical College of the Kentucky University.

EXECUTIVES
Chairman: Mira S. Ball
Vice Chairman: Stephen P. Branscum
Trustee: James F. Hardymon, age 74
President: Lee T. Todd Jr., age 61
Provost: Kumble R. Subbaswamy
EVP Finance and Administration: Frank A. Butler
EVP Health Affairs: Michael Karpf
VP Student Affairs: Patricia S. Terrell
Treasurer: Marc A. Mathews
General Counsel: Barbara W. Jones
Secretary: Pamela Robinette May
Controller: Ronda S. Beck
Auditors: Deloitte & Touche LLP

LOCATIONS
HQ: The University of Kentucky
410 Administration Dr., Lexington, KY 40506
Phone: 859-257-9000   **Fax:** 859-257-1760
Web: www.uky.edu

PRODUCTS/OPERATIONS

Selected Colleges and Schools
College of Agriculture
College of Arts and Sciences
College of Communications and Information Studies
College of Dentistry
College of Design
College of Education
College of Engineering
College of Fine Arts
College of Health Sciences
College of Law
College of Medicine
College of Nursing
College of Pharmacy
College of Public Health
College of Social Work
Gatton College of Business and Economics
Graduate School
Martin School of Public Policy and Administration
Patterson School of Diplomacy and International Commerce

HISTORICAL FINANCIALS
Company Type: School

Income Statement
FYE: June 30

	REVENUE ($ mil.)	NET INCOME ($ mil.)	NET PROFIT MARGIN	EMPLOYEES
6/07	1,435	176	12.2%	13,500
6/06	1,333	239	17.9%	11,400
6/05	1,187	—	—	10,900
6/04	1,503	—	—	10,900
6/03	1,322	—	—	10,000
Annual Growth	2.1%	(26.5%)	—	7.8%

2007 Year-End Financials
Debt ratio: —   Current ratio: —
Return on equity: 8.0%   Long-term debt ($ mil.): —
Cash ($ mil.): —

Net Income History

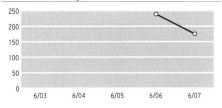

University of Louisville

This Louisville Slugger has hit a few out of the park, as well. Living up to its mandate by the Kentucky General Assembly to be a "preeminent metropolitan research university," the University of Louisville (U of L) is home to the first self-contained artificial heart implant and the first successful hand transplant. A major focus of the university is health care, and the University of Louisville Hospital is a part of the school's medical programs. U of L offers associate, baccalaureate, master's, professional, and doctorate degrees, as well as certificates in some 170 fields of study. It has more than 22,000 students enrolled in 12 colleges and schools on three campuses.

The origins of the University of Louisville date back to 1798 with a meeting to establish Jefferson Seminary, which didn't open its doors until 1813 and closed 16 years later. Subsequent incarnations eventually led to the creation of the University of Louisville in 1846.

EXECUTIVES
President: James R. Ramsey, age 59
EVP and Provost: Shirley C. Willihnganz
EVP Health Affairs: Larry N. Cook
VP Administration and Business Affairs: Larry L. Owsley
VP Finance: Michael J. Curtin
VP and Director Athletics: Tom Jurich
Associate VP Administration: Mitchell H. Payne
Associate VP Communications and Marketing: John Drees
Dean, University Libraries: Hannelore B. Rader
University Registrar and Director Enrollment Services: Kathleen Otto
Auditors: BKD, LLP

LOCATIONS
HQ: University of Louisville
2301 S. 3rd St., Grawemeyer Hall, Rm. 108, Louisville, KY 40292
Phone: 502-852-5555   **Fax:** 502-852-4337
Web: www.louisville.edu

HISTORICAL FINANCIALS
Company Type: School

Income Statement
FYE: June 30

	REVENUE ($ mil.)	NET INCOME ($ mil.)	NET PROFIT MARGIN	EMPLOYEES
6/07	868	—	—	6,138
6/06	769	—	—	5,949
6/05	430	—	—	5,764
6/04	384	—	—	5,521
6/03	328	—	—	5,100
Annual Growth	27.5%	—	—	4.7%

Revenue History

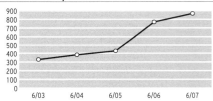

University of Michigan

Michigan — it's shaped like a mitten, and higher education fits the state like a glove. The University of Michigan has been a leader in that state's education effort since its founding in 1817. With more than 40,000 students and about 5,700 faculty members scattered across three campuses in Ann Arbor, Dearborn, and Flint, the university's diverse academic units span such areas of study as architecture, education, law, medicine, music, and social work. Notable alumni include the late President Gerald Ford (the university is home to the Gerald R. Ford Library and the Ford School of Public Policy) and playwright Arthur Miller. In addition to state funding, the university is supported by a $5.1 billion endowment.

The University of Michigan was founded in Detroit but moved to Ann Arbor in 1837. There are seven museums on campus — including the Museum of Art, the Exhibit Museum of Natural History (with a planetarium), and the Kelsey Museum of Archaeology — as well as the Nichols Arboretum and the Mattaei Botanical Gardens.

EXECUTIVES

President: Mary Sue Coleman, age 64
Provost and EVP Academic Affairs: Teresa A. Sullivan
EVP and CFO: Timothy P. (Tim) Slottow
EVP Medical Affairs; CEO, U-M Health System:
  Robert P. (Bob) Kelch
VP and Secretary: Sally J. Churchill
VP Government Relations: Cynthia H. Wilbanks
VP Student Affairs: E. Royster Harper
Interim VP and General Counsel: Gloria A. Hage
Associate VP and Chief Human Resource Officer:
  Laurita E. Thomas
Chief Investment Officer: L. Erik Lundberg
Treasurer: Gregory J. (Greg) Tewksbury
Director Public Affairs and Media Relations:
  Kelly Cunningham
Auditors: PricewaterhouseCoopers LLP

LOCATIONS

HQ: The University of Michigan
  3074 Fleming Administration Bldg.,
  Ann Arbor, MI 48109
Phone: 734-764-1817   **Fax:** 734-764-4546
Web: www.umich.edu

PRODUCTS/OPERATIONS

Selected Academic Units

Architecture and urban planning
Art and design
Business administration
Dentistry
Education
Engineering
Kinesiology
Law
Literature, science, and the arts
Medicine
Music
Natural resources and environment
Nursing
Pharmacy
Public health
Public policy
Social work

University of Minnesota

More than 65,000 students come seeking higher education in the Land of 10,000 Lakes. A major land grant university system, the University of Minnesota (U of M) offers undergraduate and graduate degrees in some 370 academic fields. It has some 4,000 faculty members. The university's Twin Cities campus, with about 50,000 students, ranks among the largest in the country in terms of enrollment. U of M serves additional students through campuses in Crookston, Duluth, Morris, and Rochester. The university was founded as a prep school in 1851 and became a land grant institution in 1867.

EXECUTIVES

Chairman: Patricia S. Simmons
President: Robert H. (Bob) Bruininks
SVP Academic Affairs and Provost:
  E. Thomas (Tom) Sullivan
SVP Health Sciences: Frank B. Cerra
SVP System Academic Administration: Robert J. Jones
VP, CFO, and Treasurer: Richard H. Pfutzenreuter
VP and Chief of Staff: Kathryn F. Brown
VP and Vice Provost Equity and Diversity:
  Nancy (Rusty) Barceló
VP Human Resources: Carol Carrier
Vice Provost; Dean, Graduate School: Gail Dubrow
Vice Provost Student Affairs: Gerald Rinehart
General Counsel: Mark B. Rotenberg
Director Communications: Lori Ann Vicich
Auditors: Deloitte & Touche LLP

LOCATIONS

HQ: University of Minnesota
  234 Morrill Hall, 100 Church St. SE,
  Minneapolis, MN 55455
Phone: 612-625-5000   **Fax:** 612-626-1693
Web: www.umn.edu

PRODUCTS/OPERATIONS

Selected Colleges and Schools

Carlson School of Management
Center for Allied Health Programs
College of Food, Agricultural, and Natural Resource
  Science
College of Biological Sciences
College of Continuing Education
College of Design
College of Education and Human Development
College of Liberal Arts
College of Pharmacy
College of Veterinary Medicine
Graduate School
Hubert H. Humphrey Institute of Public Affairs
Institute of Technology
Law School
Medical School
School of Dentistry
School of Nursing
School of Public Health

University of Missouri

Education isn't just for show in the Show Me State. The University of Missouri, founded in 1839, educates more than 60,000 students at four campuses and through a statewide extension program; about a quarter of the students are in graduate or professional programs. The university's campuses include flagship UM-Columbia (home to nearly 30,000 students, some 20 schools and colleges, and the University of Missouri Health Sciences Center), UM-Kansas City, UM-Rolla, and UM-St. Louis. Nicknamed "Mizzou," the University of Missouri has more than 7,400 faculty and members.

EXECUTIVES

Chairman and Director: Cheryl D. S. Walker
Vice Chairman and Director: Bo Fraser
President: Gary D. Forsee, age 58
EVP: Gordon H. Lamb
SVP Academic Affairs: Stephen W. Lehmkuhle
VP Finance and Administration:
  Natalie R. (Nikki) Krawitz
VP Government Relations: Stephen C. Knorr

VP Information Technology: Gary K Allen
VP Human Resources: Elizabeth Betsy Rodriguez
VP Research and Economic Development:
  Michael Nichols
General Counsel: Stephen J. Owens
Secretary: Kathleen M. Miller
Auditors: KPMG LLP

LOCATIONS

HQ: University of Missouri System
  1100 Carrie Francke Dr., Columbia, MO 65211
Phone: 573-882-2121   **Fax:** 573-882-2721
Web: www.umsystem.edu

PRODUCTS/OPERATIONS

Selected Colleges and Schools

Accountancy
Agriculture
Arts and Science
Business
Education
Engineering
Fine Arts
Food and Natural Resources
Health Professions
Honors College
Human Environmental Sciences
Information Science and Learning Technologies
Journalism
Law
Medicine
Music
Nursing
Public Affairs
Social Work
Veterinary Medicine

COMPETITORS

Missouri State University
Saint Louis University
Southeast Missouri State University
Washington University

University of Nebraska

The University of Nebraska has sprouted four campuses out in the fields of the Cornhusker State. Founded in 1869, the state university system offers bachelor's, master's, and doctoral degrees in such programs as agriculture, business, education, and engineering at its campuses in Kearney, Lincoln, and Omaha. The university's Medical Center in Omaha trains doctors, performs research, and is affiliated with a 700-bed teaching hospital. The University of Nebraska also operates research and extension services across the state. Nearly 47,000 students attend classes in the university system.

EXECUTIVES

President: James B. (J. B.) Milliken
EVP and Provost: Linda Pratt
VP Business and Finance: David E. Lechner
VP University Affairs: Peter G. (Pete) Kotsiopulos
VP and General Counsel: Joel D. Pedersen
Assistant Vice Chancellor: Deb Thomas
Assistant VP and Director Human Resources:
  Ed Wimes
Associate VP University Affairs and Director
  Governmental Relations: Ron Withem
Corporation Secretary: Donal Burns
CIO: Walter Weir
Director, University Communications: Meg Lauerman
Auditors: KPMG LLP

LOCATIONS

HQ: The University of Nebraska
3835 Holdrege St., Lincoln, NE 68583
Phone: 402-472-2111 **Fax:** 402-472-1237
Web: www.nebraska.edu

PRODUCTS/OPERATIONS

University Campuses

The University of Nebraska at Kearney
The University of Nebraska-Lincoln
The University of Nebraska Medical Center
The University of Nebraska at Omaha

Selected Colleges and Programs

Agricultural Science and Natural Resources
Architecture
Arts and Sciences
Business Administration
Dentistry (University of Nebraska Medical Center)
Engineering and Technology
Fine and Performing Arts
Graduate Studies
Human Resources and Family Science
Law
Medicine (University of Nebraska Medical Center)
Nursing (University of Nebraska Medical Center)
Pharmacy (University of Nebraska Medical Center)
Teachers College

COMPETITORS

Kansas State University
Oklahoma State
The University of Kansas
University of Missouri
University of Oklahoma
University of Wyoming

University of New Mexico

With around 26,000 students attending its main campus in Albuquerque, The University of New Mexico is most noted for its schools of medicine, law, and education. Nearly 7,000 additional students attend one of the school's four branches located around the northern part of the state at Taos, Los Alamos, Gallup, and Valencia. Through its eight schools and colleges, the university offers 145 bachelor's degrees, some 80 master's degrees, more than 40 doctorate degrees, and a variety of certificates and education specializations. UNM was founded in 1889.

In 2006 UNM agreed to purchase a new site for a campus in Rio Rancho. In addition to housing a new UNM campus, the university opened talks with rival New Mexico State University to include some of its specialized degree programs, including hotel and restaurant management, natural resource management, and agricultural programs.

EXECUTIVES

President: David J. Schmidly
President Staff Council: Loyola Chastain
University Secretary: Vivian Valencia
Financial Officer: Shelley Newman
EVP, Academic Affairs and Provost: Reed Dasenbrock
Deputy Provost: Richard Holder
Associate Provost Academic Affairs: Wynn Goering

Associate Provost Academic Affairs: Paul Nathanson
Vice Provost Extended University: Jeronimo Dominguez
Vice Provost Undergraduate Education: Peter White
Vice Provost Graduate Education and Dean Graduate Studies: Amy Wohlert
VP Student Affairs: Eliseo (Cheo) Torres
Associate VP and Director Human Resources: Susan A. Carkeek
Associate VP Development: Walt Miller

LOCATIONS

HQ: The University of New Mexico
1 University Hill NE, Albuquerque, NM 87131
Phone: 505-277-0111 **Fax:** 505-277-6686
Web: www.unm.edu

HISTORICAL FINANCIALS

Company Type: School

Income Statement

FYE: June 30

	REVENUE ($ mil.)	NET INCOME ($ mil.)	NET PROFIT MARGIN	EMPLOYEES
6/08	1,841	—	—	20,210
6/07	1,678	—	—	20,140
6/06	1,573	—	—	19,683
6/05	1,485	—	—	19,662
Annual Growth	7.4%	—	—	0.9%

Revenue History

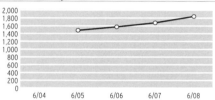

University of Pennsylvania

The University of Pennsylvania was founded by Benjamin Franklin when he had a little down time between establishing a country and experimenting with lightning. Since opening its doors to students in 1751, the Ivy League university has accumulated a notable list of accomplishments, including the creation of the first medical school in the US and the invention of the ENIAC computer. The university has about 24,000 students that pursue their studies in four undergraduate schools and a dozen graduate and professional schools, including the renowned Wharton School and the Annenberg School for Communications. Former president Judith Rodin was the first female to head an Ivy League university.

EXECUTIVES

President: Amy Gutmann
Provost: Ronald J. Daniels
EVP: Craig Carnaroli
EVP University of Pennsylvania Health System and Dean School of Medicine: Arthur H. Rubenstein, age 70
SVP and General Counsel: Wendy S. White

VP and Chief of Staff: Greg Rost
VP Development and Alumni Relations: John H. Zeller
VP Finance and Treasurer: Scott R. Douglass
VP Human Resources: John J. Heuer
VP University Communications: Lori Doyle
Secretary: Leslie Laird Kruhly
Auditors: PricewaterhouseCoopers LLP

LOCATIONS

HQ: The University of Pennsylvania
3451 Walnut St., Philadelphia, PA 19104
Phone: 215-898-5000 **Fax:** 215-898-9659
Web: www.upenn.edu

PRODUCTS/OPERATIONS

Selected Schools

Annenberg School for Communication
The College at Penn (School of Arts and Sciences)
Graduate School of Education
Graduate School of Fine Arts
Law School
School of Arts and Sciences
School of Dental Medicine
School of Engineering and Applied Science
School of Medicine
School of Nursing
School of Social Work
School of Veterinary Medicine
The Wharton School

University of Rochester

The buzz about the University of Rochester is music to some ears. The private, upstate New York institution is nationally recognized for its programs in medicine, engineering, and business, and its Eastman School of Music (founded by Eastman Kodak founder George Eastman) is one of the top music schools in the US. The university, which has an endowment of more than $1.5 billion, offers about 100 bachelor's, master's, and doctoral degrees to some 9,000 undergraduate and graduate students. Founded as a Baptist-sponsored institution in 1850, the university is nonsectarian today.

EXECUTIVES

President: Joel Seligman
Provost: Prof Charles E. Phelps, age 64
Vice Provost and Dean Administation, River Campus Libraries: Susan Gibbons
Vice Provost and CIO: David E. Lewis
Deputy President and Vice Provost, Faculty Development and Diversity: Lynne J. Davidson
Deputy President: Lamar R. Murphy
SVP Administration and Finance, CFO, and Treasurer: Ronald J. Paprocki
SVP Institutional Resources: Douglas W. Phillips
SVP and Chief Advancement Officer: James D. (Jim) Thompson
SVP Health Sciences; CEO, University of Rochester Medical Center: Bradford C. Berk
SVP and Dean, College Faculty: Peter Lennie
VP and General Secretary: Paul J. Burgett
VP and General Counsel: Sue S. Stewart, age 65
VP Communications: Bill Murphy
Auditors: PricewaterhouseCoopers LLP

LOCATIONS

HQ: University of Rochester
200 Administration Bldg., University of Rochester,
Rochester, NY 14627
Phone: 585-275-5931   **Fax:** 585-461-1046
Web: www.rochester.edu

PRODUCTS/OPERATIONS

Selected Facilities

Eastman School Campus
  Eastman School of Music
  Eastman Theater
  Memorial Art Gallery
Medical Center
  Eastman Dental Center
  School of Medicine and Dentistry
  School of Nursing
  Strong Memorial Hospital
Off Campus
  Cardiovascular Research Institute
  C.E.K. Mees Observatory (Bristol Hills, NY)
  Mt. Hope Campus
River Campus
  Margaret Warner Graduate School of Education and
    Human Development
  William E. Simon Graduate School of Business
    Administration
South Campus
  Center for Optoelectronics and Imaging
  Laboratory for Laser Energetics
  Nuclear Structure Research Laboratory

COMPETITORS

Albany College of Pharmacy
Colgate University
Cornell University
Medaille College
RIT
SUNY
SUNY Buffalo
UAlbany
Utica College

University of Southern California

This Trojan horse, filled with more than 33,000 students, is more than welcome at the University of Southern California (USC). Founded in 1880, the private university (whose mascot is a Trojan) grew up with the city of Los Angeles, and is one of the largest private employers in the city. Recognized for distinguished programs in fields such as business, engineering, film, law, medicine, public administration, and science, it offers approximately 150 undergraduate degree programs and more than 200 postgraduate degree programs. USC boasts 18 schools and a college of letters, arts, and sciences at two Los Angeles campuses.

The university's focus on fundraising under current president Steven Sample has quintupled USC's endowment since 1991.

Notable alumni include Marion Morrison (also known as John Wayne), who played tackle on the school's football team, and the first man on the moon, Neil Armstrong. Directors George Lucas and Robert Zemeckis are both USC film school graduates.

HISTORY

Los Angeles was still a frontier town when a diverse group of local citizens, led by Judge Robert Maclay Widney, established the University of Southern California in 1880 (early rules for students included a prohibition against carrying guns to class). But Los Angeles grew quickly, and USC grew with it. By 1910 the university had most of its major programs in place, including law and medical schools. During the 1920s USC established the nation's first school of international relations (1924) and offered the first degree in cinema (1929).

The end of WWII and the GI Bill brought a major increase in enrollment, forcing the university to expand. Some 50 new buildings were added in the 1950s and 1960s, and another 37 were begun or completed in the 1970s. The university started increasing its fund-raising efforts in the 1980s. Steven Sample became president in 1991 and secured hundreds of millions in donations over the course of the decade, including a $110 million grant in 1999 from the W.M. Keck Foundation for USC's School of Medicine.

USC was named 1999 college of the year by *Time* magazine and the *Princeton Review*.

EXECUTIVES

Chairman: Stanley P. Gold, age 65
Vice Chairman: Kathleen L. McCarthy
President and Trustee: Steven B. Sample, age 67
SVP Academic Affairs and Provost: C. L. Max Nikias
SVP University Relations: Martha Harris
SVP Administration: Todd R. Dickey
Associate SVP Alumni Relations: Scott Mory
Associate SVP Financial and Business Services:
  Robert V. Johnson
Associate SVP University Public Relations:
  Susan Heitman
VP Student Affairs: Michael L. Jackson
Interim VP Finance: Margo Steurbaut
Interim VP University Advancement: Courtney Surls
General Counsel and Secretary: Carol M. Amir
Treasurer: Ruth Wernig
University Controller: Erik Brink
Auditors: PricewaterhouseCoopers LLP

LOCATIONS

HQ: The University of Southern California
  University Park Campus, Los Angeles, CA 90089
Phone: 213-740-2311   **Fax:** 213-740-5229
Web: www.usc.edu

PRODUCTS/OPERATIONS

Selected Schools

Annenberg School for Communication
College of Letters, Arts and Sciences
Davis School of Gerontology
Gould School of Law
Graduate School
Keck School of Medicine
Leventhal School of Accounting
Marshall School of Business
Roski School of Fine Arts
Rossier School of Education
School of Architecture
School of Cinematic Arts
School of Dentistry
School of Pharmacy
School of Policy, Planning, and Development
School of Social Work
School of Theatre
Thornton School of Music
Viterbi School of Engineering

University of Texas System

These students are hooked on higher education. The University of Texas System runs nine universities throughout the Lone Star State with a total enrollment of more than 190,000 students, making it one of the largest university systems in the US. Its flagship Austin campus, with some 50,000 students, ranks as one of the nation's largest student populations (neck-and-neck with the main campuses at Ohio State and the University of Minnesota). UT also runs six health institutions, including four medical schools, and receives some $1.5 billion a year for research. Its $10 billion endowment fund (managed by the University of Texas Investment Management Co.) is the country's third largest (after Harvard and Yale).

Established in 1876, UT Austin opened in 1883. The UT System was formally organized in 1950.

The UT System launched a nearly $3 billion initiative to improve its science, engineering, health, and technology programs in 2006. The system received funding from government agencies, businesses, and individual donors for recruitment of faculty, equipment, renovation, and repair of facilities.

HISTORY

The Texas Declaration of Independence (1836) admonished Mexico for having failed to establish a public education system in the territory, but attempts to start a state-sponsored university were stymied until after Texas achieved US statehood and fought in the Civil War. A new constitution in 1876 provided for the establishment of "a university of the first class," and in 1883 The University of Texas (UT) opened in Austin. Eight professors taught 218 students in two curricula: academics and law.

The school's first building opened in 1884, and in 1891 the university's medical school opened in Galveston. By 1894 UT-Austin had 534 students and a football team. UT opened a Graduate School in 1910 and various other colleges over the years. The university added its first academic branch campus when the Texas State School of Mines and Metallurgy (opened in 1914 in El Paso) became part of the system in 1919.

UT's financial future was secured in 1923 when oil was found on West Texas land that had been set aside by the legislature as an education endowment. The income from oil production, as well as the proceeds of surface-use leases, became the Permanent University Fund (PUF), from which only interest and earnings on the revenues can be used: two-thirds by UT and one-third by Texas A&M University. UT continued to grow, thanks to the PUF, which topped $100 million by 1940.

UT sported the black eye of racial prejudice (as did many other institutions at the time) when it refused to admit Heman Sweatt, a black student, to its law school in 1946. The Supreme Court ordered UT to admit him in 1950, the same year the UT System was officially organized. Sixteen years later, in one of the nation's most highly publicized crimes, Charles Whitman killed 14 people and wounded 31 others with a high-powered rifle fired from atop the UT-Austin administration tower. The observation deck wasn't closed until

1975, however, after a series of suicides. (It was later reopened in 1999.)

In the meantime, UT added a medical center in Dallas and several graduate schools in Austin. The 1960s through the 1980s were a time of geographic expansion for the system as it absorbed other institutions, started several new campuses, and expanded its network of medical centers. In 1996 the UT System became the first public university to establish a private investment management company (University of Texas Investment Management Co.) to invest PUF money (by that time over $9 billion) and other funds.

The race issue reared its head again in 1996 when a Federal court ruled in the Hopwood decision (named for the plaintiff) that the UT System could no longer use race to determine scholarships and admissions. Minority enrollments declined the following year, prompting the Texas Legislature to enact a law granting admission to the top 10% of graduates from any Texas high school to the state university of their choice.

Chancellor William Cunningham announced plans in 2000 to expand the UT System by 100,000 students over the decade. After he resigned that year, R. D. Burck took over as his successor. In 2001 UT received a $50 million donation, the largest gift in its history, from Texas businessman and Minnesota Vikings owner Red McCombs. The following year Burck stepped down and was replaced by Mark Yudof, former president of the University of Minnesota.

Yudof stepped down as chancellor in the summer of 2008 and was succeeded by Kenneth Shine on an interim basis.

EXECUTIVES

Interim Chancellor: Kenneth I. Shine, age 73
Chairman: H. Scott Caven Jr.
Vice Chairman: Robert B. Rowling, age 54
Vice Chairman: James R. Huffines, age 57
Executive Vice Chancellor for Academic Affairs:
  David B. Prior
Executive Vice Chancellor Business Affairs:
  Scott C. Kelley
Vice Chancellor and General Counsel: Barry D. Burgdorf
Vice Chancellor Administration: Tonya M. Brown
Vice Chancellor External Relations: Randa S. Safady
Vice Chancellor for Governmental Relations:
  Barry McBee
Associate Vice Chancellor and CIO: Marg Knox
**Associate Vice Chancellor, Controller, and Chief Budget
  Officer:** Randy Wallace
Associate Vice Chancellor Finance: Philip R. Aldridge
General Counsel, Board of Regents:
  Francie A. Frederick
Director Public Affairs: Anthony P. de Bruyn
Auditors: Deloitte & Touche LLP

LOCATIONS

HQ: The University of Texas System
  601 Colorado St., Austin, TX 78701
Phone: 512-499-4200   **Fax:** 512-499-4215
Web: www.utsystem.edu

PRODUCTS/OPERATIONS

Selected Institutions
Academic Institutions
  The University of Texas at Arlington (established 1895;
    fall 2006 enrollment 24,825)
  The University of Texas at Austin (1883; fall 2006
    enrollment 49,697)
  The University of Texas at Brownsville (1991; fall 2006
    enrollment 15,677)
  The University of Texas at Dallas (1961; fall 2006
    enrollment 14,523)
  The University of Texas at El Paso (1914; fall 2006
    enrollment 19,842)
  The University of Texas-Pan American (Edinburg;
    1927; fall 2006 enrollment 17,337)
  The University of Texas of the Permian Basin (Odessa;
    1969; fall 2006 enrollment 3,462)
  The University of Texas at San Antonio (1969; fall 2006
    enrollment 28,379)
  The University of Texas at Tyler (1971; fall 2006
    enrollment 5,926)
Health Institutions
  The University of Texas Health Science Center at
    Houston (established 1972; fall 2006 enrollment
    3,651)
  The University of Texas Health Science Center at San
    Antonio (1959; fall 2006 enrollment 2,825)
  The University of Texas M.D. Anderson Cancer Center
    (Houston, 1941; fall 2006 enrollment 108)
  The University of Texas Medical Branch at Galveston
    (1891; fall 2006 enrollment 2,255)
  The University of Texas Southwestern Medical Center
    at Dallas (1943; fall 2006 enrollment 2,396)

University of Washington

The University of Washington (UW) is Husky indeed, with an enrollment of some 40,000 students. Founded in 1861 as the Territorial University of Washington, UW (pronounced "U-dub" by those on campus) has smaller branches in Tacoma and Bothell in addition to its main Seattle campus. The university, whose mascot is a Husky, offers undergraduate, graduate, and professional degree programs in some 150 fields of study at more than 15 schools and colleges. It also operates a health sciences center and an academic medical center, which includes the University of Washington Medical Center and Harborview Medical Center.

EXECUTIVES

President: Mark A. Emmert
EVP: Weldon E. Ihrig
Provost and EVP: Phyllis M. Wise, age 60
Interim Vice Provost: David Brown
Vice Provost Academic Personnel: Cheryl A. Cameron
Vice Provost Student Life: Eric Godfrey
SVP Financial and Facilities: V'Ella Warren
VP Human Resources: Mindy Kornberg
VP Minority Affairs and Vice Provost Diversity:
  Sheila Edwards Lange
Auditors: KPMG LLP

LOCATIONS

HQ: University of Washington
  Schmitz Hall, 1410 NE Campus Pkwy.,
  Seattle, WA 98195
Phone: 206-543-2100
Web: www.washington.edu

The University of Washington has campuses in Bothell, Seattle, and Tacoma, Washington.

PRODUCTS/OPERATIONS

Selected Schools and Colleges
College of Architecture and Urban Planning
College of Arts and Sciences
College of Education
College of Engineering
College of the Environment
College of Forest Resources
College of Ocean and Fishery Sciences
Daniel J. Evans School of Public Affairs
The Graduate School
Information School
Michael G. Foster School of Business
School of Dentistry
School of Law
School of Medicine
School of Nursing
School of Pharmacy
School of Public Health and Community Medicine
School of Social Work

University of Wisconsin

There is no School of Cheese in the University of Wisconsin System, but there are 13 four-year universities, 13 two-year campuses, and a statewide extension program. The University of Wisconsin System is one of the largest public university systems in the US, with more than 170,000 students. Its top school is the University of Wisconsin at Madison, which offers more than 400 undergraduate majors, master's degree programs, and doctoral programs to some 42,000 students. The system's other major campus is the University of Wisconsin at Milwaukee, with about 28,000 students.

Nearly one-quarter of the UW System's annual budget comes from state funds. Student fees, federal grants, fund raising, and other sources account for the remainder.

HISTORY

When Wisconsin became a state in 1848, its constitution called for the establishment of a state university. A board of regents was named, and it first established a preparatory school because regents felt Wisconsin's secondary schools were not advanced enough to prepare students for university studies. The school began classes in 1849 with 20 students in the Madison Female Academy Building. The University of Wisconsin's first official freshman class began studies in the fall of 1850. A campus was established a mile west of the state capitol in Madison. By 1854, when it held its first commencement (with two graduates), the school had 41 students.

Enrollment dipped during the Civil War (all but one of the school's senior class joined the army) but soon rebounded, and by 1870 the university had almost 500 students. Meanwhile, it established a school of agriculture (1866) and a school of law (1868). The state established normal schools (teachers colleges) in Platteville (1866), Whitewater (1868), Oshkosh (1871), and River Falls (1874).

There was also a teachers' course for women at the university in Madison. However, when John Bascom became president in 1874, he transformed the university into a truly coeducational institution, putting women "in all respects on precisely the same footing" with the men.

While the university at Madison remained Wisconsin's primary seat of learning, the state continued to establish normal schools. It opened institutions in Milwaukee (1885), Superior (1893), Stevens Point (1894), La Crosse (1909), and Eau Claire (1916). The nine normal schools eventually became a system of state colleges called Wisconsin State Universities.

The university at Madison also continued to grow, and by the late 1920s it had almost 9,000 students. WWII brought a drop in enrollment, but afterward it took off, jumping from about 7,000 in 1945 to over 22,000 by the late 1950s. The University of Wisconsin-Milwaukee branch was founded in 1956. Other branch campuses were established in Green Bay (1965) and Kenosha (1968).

The Madison campus became a focal point for student protests during the Vietnam War. Events came to a head in 1970 when President Fred Harrington resigned during a four-day standoff between students and the National Guard. War protesters also placed a bomb outside Sterling Hall, which housed the Army Math Research Center; the explosion killed one student and injured three others.

The state legislature merged the University of Wisconsin and the Wisconsin State Universities in 1971 to create The University of Wisconsin System.

EXECUTIVES

Chairman: David G. Walsh
Vice Chairman: Mark J. Bradley
President: Kevin P. Reilly
Executive SVP: Donald J. Mash
SVP Academic Affairs: Cora B. Marrett
VP Finance: Deborah A. Durcan
Associate VP University Relations: Margaret Lewis
Associate VP Human Resources: Alan Crist
Secretary: Judith A. Temby
Controller, Financial Services: D. Jeff Arnold
Controller, System Administration Accounting: Marc Messina
General Counsel: Patricia A. Brady
Executive Director of Communications and External Relations: David F. Giroux
Auditors: State of Wisconsin Legislative Audit Bureau

LOCATIONS

HQ: The University of Wisconsin System
Van Hise Hall, 1220 Linden Dr., Madison, WI 53706
Phone: 608-262-2321   **Fax:** 608-262-3985
Web: www.uwsa.edu

PRODUCTS/OPERATIONS

Four-Year Campuses

UW-Eau Claire	UW-Platteville
UW-Green Bay	UW-River Falls
UW-La Crosse	UW-Stevens Point
UW-Madison	UW-Stout
UW-Milwaukee	UW-Superior
UW-Oshkosh	UW-Whitewater
UW-Parkside	

Two-Year Colleges

UW-Baraboo/Sauk County
UW-Barron County
UW-Fond du Lac
UW-Fox Valley
UW-Manitowoc
UW-Marathon County
UW-Marinette
UW-Marshfield/Wood County
UW-Richland
UW-Rock County
UW-Sheboygan
UW-Washington County
UW-Waukesha

University of Wisconsin-Madison

The University of Wisconsin-Madison, the largest campus of the University of Wisconsin System, offers academic programs in more than 100 fields of study. UW-Madison offers about 8,000 courses in areas such as computer science, psychology, English, nursing, journalism, and art. The university, which offers bachelor's, master's, doctoral, and professional degrees, has an enrollment of more than 41,000 students and has about 2,000 faculty members. Its extracurricular activities include more than 600 clubs and student organizations. Resident undergraduate tuition and fees cost about $17,200. Wisconsin's first governor, Nelson Dewey, established the university in 1848.

Notable alumni include US Vice President Dick Cheney, novelist Joyce Carol Oates, and architect Frank Lloyd Wright. The university's students come from all the states in the US and abroad.

A decline in state funding, once its primary source of revenue, has led the university to rely more on tuition, federal and private grants, and auxiliary enterprises to fund its programs.

EXECUTIVES

Chancellor: Carolyn A. (Biddy) Martin
Vice Chancellor Administration: Darrell Bazzell
Vice Chancellor Research; Dean, Graduate School: Martin Cadwallader
Provost and Vice Chancellor for Academic Affairs: Patrick V. Farrell
Associate Vice President Academic and Student Services: Ronald M. Singer
Director Admissions: Robert A. Seltzer
Registrar: Joanne E. Berg
President and CEO, Wisconsin Alumni Association: Paula Bonner
Director Financial Aid: Susan E. Fischer

LOCATIONS

HQ: The University of Wisconsin-Madison
Van Hise Hall, 1220 Linden Dr., Madison, WI 53706
Phone: 608-263-2400   **Fax:** 608-262-3985
Web: www.wisc.edu

Univision Communications

Spanish-speaking Americans have a singular vision when it comes to watching TV — Univision Communications. The company is the leading Spanish-language broadcaster in the US with a portfolio of television and radio operations. Its runs the top-rated Univision network, carried by nearly 1,800 broadcast and cable affiliates, as well as sister networks TeleFutura and Galavisión. The company also owns and operates nearly 50 full-power TV stations and more than 20 low-power stations. Its Univision Radio division boasts about 70 stations. Univision was founded in 1961 as Spanish International Network. It is controlled by a group of private investment firms led by TPG Capital and Thomas H. Lee Partners.

In addition to being the #1 TV destination for Spanish-language speakers in the US, the company's Univision network ranks just behind the four main broadcast networks in the key 18-49 audience demographic. It has benefited from advertisers eager to reach the growing Hispanic population, a segment that has seen its buying power increase markedly over the past decade.

The company has been focused on improving efficiency within its advertising-driven broadcasting operations by reorganizing its sales force during 2007. As part of that effort, Univision in 2008 sold its music recording and publishing operation, Univision Music Group, to Universal Music Group for about $150 million.

The company was taken private in 2007 for about $12.3 billion (plus the assumption of some $1.4 billion in debt). The deal was a victory for CEO Jerrold Perenchio, who led the growth of the company and owned a 10% stake. The former talent agent and boxing promoter invested about $550 million into Univision in 1992. Rival broadcaster Grupo Televisa, which owned 10% of the company, also made a tidy profit from the deal, as did Cisneros Group, which had a small stake.

Following the going-private transaction Joe Uva was installed as Univision's new CEO. A veteran of the entertainment and media business, Uva formerly oversaw sales and marketing for several units at Time Warner's Turner Broadcasting subsidiary. He left his post as CEO at OMD Worldwide, one of the media buying agencies of advertising conglomerate Omnicom Group.

In addition, Univision owns 50% of TuTV, a joint venture with Grupo Televisa. TuTV distributes a handful of digital TV networks to the US market.

EXECUTIVES

CEO and Director: Joseph (Joe) Uva, age 52
President and COO: Ray Rodriguez, age 56
SEVP, CFO, and Chief Strategy Officer: Andrew W. (Andy) Hobson, age 46, $2,425,800 pay
EVP and General Counsel: C. Douglas Kranwinkle, age 67, $1,997,700 pay
EVP and Chief Strategy Officer: Cesar Conde
Chief Marketing Officer: Maryam Banikarim
SVP and Chief Accounting Officer: Peter H. Lori, age 42
SVP Business Affairs: Glenn A. Dryfoos
VP Integrated Sales and Marketing: Jeff Apodaca
VP Corporate Communications: Mónica Talán
VP Investor Relations: Diana M. Vesga

President and COO, Univision Radio: Gary B. Stone
President, Univision Television Station Group:
 Joanne Lynch
President, Television Station Group: Terry Mackin,
 age 50
President, Advertising Sales: David Lawenda, age 41
EVP Sales, Univision Network: Judy Kenny
SVP Programming and Promotions, Univision
 Network: Otto Padron
SVP and Operating Manager, Galavisión Network:
 Sebastian Trujillo
Auditors: Ernst & Young LLP

LOCATIONS

HQ: Univision Communications Inc.
 605 Third Ave., 12th Floor, New York, NY 10158
Phone: 212-455-5200   Fax: 212-867-6710
Web: www.univision.com

Selected Radio Markets

Albuquerque, NM
Austin, TX
Chicago
Dallas
El Paso, TX
Fresno, CA
Houston
Las Vegas
Los Angeles
McAllen, TX
Miami
New York City
Phoenix
San Antonio
San Diego
San Francisco

PRODUCTS/OPERATIONS

2007 Sales

	% of total
Television	77
Radio	21
Internet	2
Total	**100**

Selected Operations

Television networks
 Galavisión
 TeleFutura
 Univision
Univision Radio
Univision Online

COMPETITORS

ABC
CBS Corp
Cisneros Group
Clear Channel
Discovery Communications
Entravision
Fox Entertainment
Liberman Broadcasting
NBC
SIRIUS XM
Spanish Broadcasting
Telemundo Communications
Televisa
Turner Broadcasting
TV Azteca

HISTORICAL FINANCIALS

Company Type: Private

Income Statement

FYE: December 31

	REVENUE ($ mil.)	NET INCOME ($ mil.)	NET PROFIT MARGIN	EMPLOYEES
12/07	2,073	(248)	—	4,282
12/06	2,167	349	16.1%	4,233
12/05	1,953	187	9.6%	4,219
12/04	1,787	256	14.3%	4,400
12/03	1,311	155	11.9%	4,300
Annual Growth	**12.1%**	**—**	**—**	**(0.1%)**

Net Income History

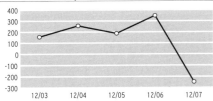

Uno Restaurants

It shouldn't be a surprise that Uno Restaurant Holdings thinks its pizza is numero uno. The company operates and franchises more than 200 Uno Chicago Grill restaurants in about 30 states and three other countries. Known for their deep-dish, Chicago-style pizza, the casual-dining spots also serve pasta, seafood, and sandwiches. About 120 locations are company-owned; the rest are franchised. Through subsidiary Uno Foods, the company also sells branded food products to airlines, hotels, supermarkets, and theaters. Ike Sewell opened the first Pizzeria Uno in Chicago in 1943. Uno Restaurants is owned by private equity firm Centre Partners Management; chairman emeritus Aaron Spencer also owns a significant stake.

The company is looking to expand both its company-owned operations and its franchising operations with plans to double the number of total locations by 2008. As part of that strategy, Uno Restaurants unveiled plans in 2007 to begin operating quick-service locations under the banner Uno Due Go. The new concept is designed for high-traffic locations such as airports and shopping malls.

The company's expansion plans are being bolstered by the investment of Centre Partners Management, which acquired its controlling stake in the company in 2005. Uno Restaurants is also working to increase its consumer products business. In addition to its flagship chain, the company owns one Mexican restaurant, Su Casa, in Chicago.

EXECUTIVES

Chairman Emeritus: Aaron D. Spencer, age 76
CEO: Frank W. Guidara, age 60
COO: Roger L. Zingle, age 54
EVP; President, Uno Foods: Alan M. Fox, age 60
SVP and CFO: Louie Psallidas
SVP Franchise Development: Jack G. Crawford
SVP Marketing: Richard K. Hendrie
SVP Purchasing, Design, and Construction:
 James T. (Jamie) Strobino
SVP and General Counsel: George W. Herz II, age 52
SVP Human Resources and Training: Roger C. Ahlfeld
SVP Operations: William J. (Bill) Golden
SVP Uno Foods: Charles J. Kozubal
Auditors: Ernst & Young LLP

LOCATIONS

HQ: Uno Restaurant Holdings Corp.
 100 Charles Park Rd., Boston, MA 02132
Phone: 617-323-9200   Fax: 617-218-5376
Web: www.unos.com

COMPETITORS

Applebee's
Back Bay Restaurant
Bertucci's Corp.
BJ's Restaurants
Brinker
BUCA
California Pizza Kitchen
Carino's Italian Grill
Carlson Restaurants
Cheesecake Factory
Darden
Famous Famiglia
OSI Restaurant Partners
Rock Bottom Restaurants
Ruby Tuesday
Sbarro

U.S. Central Federal Credit Union

U.S. Central Federal Credit Union is a cooperative "central bank" for a network of about 30 corporate credit unions. These, in turn, represent nearly 9,000 credit unions nationwide. U.S. Central performs a variety of liquidity and cash management functions, such as funds transfer, settlement services, risk management, and custody services. Subsidiary CU Investment Solutions provides investment advisory and brokerage services to the corporate credit unions, while its majority-owned Corporate Network eCom offers bill payment and technology services to the network and its members.

Another subsidiary, Charlie Mac (formerly Network Liquidity Acceptance Company), works as a liquidity facility by purchasing loans originated by credit unions.

U.S. Central's Network Financial Services provides electronic data transfer services and access to electronic forms, operational reports, and other information for credit unions.

EXECUTIVES

Chairman: Joseph P. Herbst
President and CEO: Francis Lee
EVP, Asset and Liability Management:
David (Dave) Dickens
EVP, Correspondent Services: Marcie Haitema
SVP and CFO: Kathryn (Kathy) Brick
SVP and General Counsel: François G. Henriquez II
SVP and CIO: Charles Troutman
SVP, Member Services and Communications:
Austin Braithwait
Chief Investment Officer: Connie Loveless
Treasurer: William A. Walby
Auditors: Ernst & Young LLP

LOCATIONS

HQ: U.S. Central Federal Credit Union
9701 Renner Blvd., Ste. 100, Lenexa, KS 66219
Phone: 913-227-6000 **Fax:** 913-227-6250
Web: www.uscentral.coop

PRODUCTS/OPERATIONS

Selected Subsidiaries and Affiliates

Charlie Mac LLC (formerly Network Liquidity
Acceptance Company, correspondent banking)
Corporate Network eCom LLC (87%; electronic billing
and technology services)
CU Investment Solutions, Inc. (formerly U.S. Central
Capital Markets, Inc.; brokerage and advising services
for member credit unions)
Network Financial Services, LLC (common trust fund,
file-switching service, and electronic information
exchange)

COMPETITORS

Elavon
First Data
Metavante

HISTORICAL FINANCIALS

Company Type: Cooperative

Income Statement

FYE: December 31

	REVENUE ($ mil.)	NET INCOME ($ mil.)	NET PROFIT MARGIN	EMPLOYEES
12/07	2,599	(51)	—	250
12/06	1,948	63	3.2%	250
12/05	1,224	59	4.8%	250
12/04	756	50	6.6%	250
12/03	710	69	9.7%	250
Annual Growth	38.3%	—	—	0.0%

Net Income History

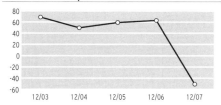

U.S. Foodservice

A lot of food services in the US would suffer without this company. U.S. Foodservice is the #2 food service supplier in the US (behind SYSCO), serving some 250,000 customers from its 70 distribution facilities. The company supplies restaurants, hotels, school, and other food service operators with a wide variety of food products, including canned and dry foods, meats, frozen foods, and seafood. It also distributes kitchen equipment and cleaning supplies among other non-food supplies. U.S. Foodservice distributes both national brand products and its own private labels. Private equity firms Kohlberg Kravis Roberts (KKR) and Clayton, Dubilier & Rice acquired the company in 2007.

U.S. Foodservice was purchased from Dutch food retail giant Royal Ahold for about $7.1 billion. The deal allowed the food distributor to expand its business with the help of new, deep pockets, while allowing Royal Ahold to focus on its core supermarket business.

By shedding U.S. Foodservice, the supermarket operator also hopes to recover from an accounting scandal that has embroiled the business since it acquired the US distributor in 2000. Following the $3.6 billion deal, federal investigators began reviewing accounting irregularities at the company and later brought charges against several former executives and suppliers, some of which are still pending.

US Foodservice, meanwhile, has announced an aggressive growth plan to open a new distribution center in Utah while expanding two existing facilities.

HISTORY

U.S. Foodservice has its origins in several different operations. The oldest part, Monarch Foods, dates back to 1853 and was an early food service distribution innovator. The Chicago-based company helped supply pioneers heading West and brought items to the Midwest, such as California oranges and imported teas.

Some 50 years later Scottish immigrant C. C. Pearce started Pearce-Young-Angel (PYA) with two mules, two wagons, and a 3,000-sq.-ft. warehouse in Columbia, South Carolina. The company became a produce supplier to independent grocers in the Carolinas and diversified into beer, becoming the exclusive distributor for Anheuser-Busch in the two states. PYA switched to wholesaling products to institutions, such as nursing homes, restaurants, and schools.

Consolidated Foods (now Sara Lee) acquired Monarch in 1946 and merged it with PYA in 1967, spinning off its Anheuser-Busch unit simultaneously. The Pearce family continued to manage both operations, and under their leadership PYA/Monarch grew from sales of about $100 million to about $3 billion. The southeastern division of the company (primarily the old PYA operations) maintained its lead as the #1 regional food distributor, but the northern division (primarily the old Monarch operations) was #3, behind SYSCO and Kraft. Sara Lee, which wanted all its business segments to be #1 or #2, decided it would keep the southeastern operations but dispose of the northern ones.

In 1989 James Miller (former CEO of U.S. Foodservice) led other managers in a $317 million LBO, acquiring 12 distribution centers in the Northeast and Midwest, then quickly selling

three of them. Miller and associates got 11% of the new company, JP Foodservice, while Sara Lee took 47% (sold 1996) and institutional investors got the rest. Heavily in debt, JP Foodservice (which took its name from the initials of the first names of two senior stockholders) lost $33 million over the next five years before becoming profitable in 1995.

JP Foodservice went public in 1994; its IPO raised $80 million to help with its expansion strategy of acquiring smaller distributors. After spending $350 million on several acquisitions in 1996, the company spent $1.4 billion the next year to buy Rykoff-Sexton. Saul E. Rykoff started that company in 1911 as S.E. Rykoff & Co. It went public in 1972 and acquired John Sexton & Co. from Beatrice Group in 1983. When purchased by JP Foodservice, Rykoff-Sexton had twice the sales of JP. Rykoff-Sexton moved the company into markets in the Southeast, as well as into Texas and California.

In early 1998 JP changed its name to U.S. Foodservice. Also that year the company acquired New York-based J.H. Haar & Sons and California-based Joseph Webb Foods. In 2000 U.S. Foodservice acquired Chicago-based meat cutter Stock Yards Packing. U.S. Foodservice was itself acquired for about $3.6 billion that year by Royal Ahold, becoming a subsidiary of its Ahold USA unit.

U.S. Foodservice purchased Parkway Food Service and Mutual Wholesale Co. (food distributors in Florida) in 2001, and later gained access to 21 new US markets by acquiring Alliant Exchange, the parent of Alliant Foodservice. The following year the company acquired Kansas City-based Lady Baltimore Foods, expanding its presence in Kansas and Missouri.

The discovery of massive accounting irregularities at the company led its Dutch parent in 2002 to report a $1.41 billion loss, which Royal Ahold attributed to special charges related to overstated profits at U.S. Foodservice. Royal Ahold attributed the scheme to inflate vendor rebates to two U.S. Foodservice managers who resigned. Founder and CEO of U.S. Foodservice James Miller also resigned and Robert Tobin, a member of Royal Ahold's supervisory board and former chairman and CEO of Stop & Shop, was named interim CEO. In all, the company's five most senior managers left U.S. Foodservice in the wake of the accounting scandal. Twenty more employees were suspended in 2003 as the investigation into the accounting scandal continued.

Talk that its Dutch parent would sell U.S. Foodservice was squelched that year when Royal Ahold announced the company would spend 18 to 24 months rebuilding its subsidiary before deciding its future. To that end, Lawrence S. Benjamin joined U.S. Foodservice as its new CEO. In 2004 the company hired two executives who specialize in corporate turnarounds to run its purchasing and marketing efforts.

That same year, Royal Ahold settled civil charges with the Securities and Exchange Commission and later paid $1.1 billion to settle a class-action lawsuit brought by shareholders. Federal prosecutors, however, brought charges against several former executives and suppliers, alleging that they played a role in the accounting fraud. Former CFO Michael Resnick pleaded guilty to charges of conspiracy in 2006.

Royal Ahold sold the company to private equity firms Kohlberg Kravis Roberts (KKR) and Clayton, Dubilier & Rice for about $7.1 billion in 2007.

EXECUTIVES

President and CEO: Robert (Bob) Aiken
CFO: Al Swanson
EVP Business Development: David Schreibman
SVP Information Systems: Rod Harris
SVP and Deputy General Counsel: Juliette Pryor
VP Corporate Communications: Kim Brown
General Counsel: David Eberhardt
Chief Human Resources Officer: Dave Esler
Chief Ethics, Diversity, and Accountability Officer:
  Cindy Hallberlin
President, Monarch Foods: Pat Mulhern
President, North Star Foodservice: Keith Campbell
President, Alliant Logistics: Mike Frank
President, North Region: Stuart Schuette
President, Southeast Region: Bob Stout
President, West Region: Gene Steffes
Auditors: Deloitte & Touche Accountants

LOCATIONS

HQ: U.S. Foodservice, Inc.
  9399 W. Higgins Rd., Rosemont, IL 60018
Phone: 847-720-8000   **Fax:** 847-720-8099
Web: www.usfoodservice.com

COMPETITORS

Ben E. Keith
Clark National
Edward Don
Foodbuy
Golden State Foods
Gordon Food Service
Keystone Foods
MAINES
Martin-Brower
McLane Foodservice
Meadowbrook Meat Company
Performance Food
Services Group of America
SYSCO
UniPro Foodservice

HISTORICAL FINANCIALS

Company Type: Private

Income Statement

FYE: Saturday nearest December 31

	REVENUE ($ mil.)	NET INCOME ($ mil.)	NET PROFIT MARGIN	EMPLOYEES
12/07	20,200	—	—	27,160
12/06	25,357	—	—	27,630
12/05	17,613	—	—	28,286
12/04	20,692	—	—	28,658
12/03	19,820	—	—	23,282
Annual Growth	0.5%	—	—	3.9%

Revenue History

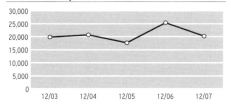

US Investigations Services

US Investigations Services (USIS) helps employers feel safe about their new hire decisions. One of the nation's largest investigations and support services firms, USIS completes security services for government agencies and private sector clients in human resources, insurance, and national security markets; it also provides background screening and risk management services for transportation, health care, financial, gaming, and retail industries. In addition to its investigative services, USIS provides staffing and training support for US government interests throughout the world. Formerly the Office of Federal Investigations (a US government agency), USIS was spun off as a private firm in 1996.

The company's operations center is located 200 feet underground in a mine that once held sensitive federal government records.

In 2008 USIS acquired HireRight, an employment background and drug screening services provider, for $249 million. The purchase expands the company's commercial services division.

Private equity firm Providence Equity Partners is a USIS investor.

EXECUTIVES

Chairman: Randy E. Dobbs
CEO: Michael G. Cherkasky, age 58
COO: William C. (Bill) Mixon
SVP and CFO: David A. Kaminsky
SVP Corporate Development: Philip T. Sweeney
SVP Human Resources: David Whitmore
Corporate VP Human Resources: Barbara M. Nieto,
  age 44
Corporate VP Financial Planning and Analysis:
  Bart Witteveen
VP and General Counsel: Keith R. Simmons
VP and Chief Technology and Information Officer:
  James J. Choi
President, National Security Division:
  Michael (Mike) Fraser
President, Commercial Services Division:
  Phillip C. McVey
President, Investigative Services Division:
  Christopher Tillery

LOCATIONS

HQ: US Investigations Services, LLC
  7799 Leesburg Pike, Ste. 1100 North,
  Falls Church, VA 22043
Phone: 703-448-0178   **Fax:** 703-448-1422
Web: www.usis.com

PRODUCTS/OPERATIONS

Selected Background Program Services

County court criminal record searches
Education history verification
Federal civil litigation record searches
In-person interviews
Military record verification
Motor vehicle record/driving history
Professional license/certification verification
Sexual offender records searches
Social security number trace and verification

Selected Clients

Government clients
  Department of Defense
  Department of Homeland Security
  Department of State
  Office of Personnel Management
Private-sector clients
  Briggs & Stratton
  Southwest Airlines
  U.S. Xpress

COMPETITORS

ADP Screening and Selection
ChoicePoint
Computer Sciences Corp.
Guardsmark
Kroll
TransNational Security

US Mint

The US Mint doesn't promote fresh breath, but it does make a pretty penny. Its primary mission is to produce an adequate volume of circulating coinage for the nation to conduct its trade and commerce. The Mint distributes coins and paper money to the Federal Reserve banks and branches, maintains custody of the Nation's gold and silver assets (worth more than $100 billion), and redeems and processes mutilated coins. It generates revenue by selling proof and uncirculated coins; commemorative medals; and platinum, gold, and silver bullion coins to the general public. Despite its standing as a government institution, the US Mint does turn a profit, which it transfers to the Treasury General Fund.

EXECUTIVES

Director: Edmund C. Moy
CFO: Patricia (Marty) Greiner
CIO: Jerry Horton
Associate Director Sales and Marketing: Gloria Eskridge
Field Chief Operations Fort Knox: Burt Barnes
Plant Manager Denver: David Croft
Plant Manager Philadelphia: Mark Landry
Plant Manager West Point: Ellen McCullom
Protection: Dan Shaver
Public Affairs: Michael White
Auditors: KPMG LLP

LOCATIONS

HQ: US Mint
  801 9th St., NW, Washington, DC 20220
Phone: 202-354-7222
Web: www.usmint.gov

The US Mint operates from facilities located across the US including its headquarters in Washington, DC; the US Bullion Depository in Fort Knox; and US Mints located in Denver; Philadelphia; San Francisco; and West Point, New York.

HISTORICAL FINANCIALS

Company Type: Government agency

Income Statement

FYE: September 30

	REVENUE ($ mil.)	NET INCOME ($ mil.)	NET PROFIT MARGIN	EMPLOYEES
9/07	2,635	—	—	—
9/06	2,324	—	—	—
9/05	1,771	—	—	—
9/04	1,650	—	—	—
Annual Growth	16.9%	—	—	—

Revenue History

U.S. Oil

Smitten with the oil distribution business, the founding Schmidt family own and operate U.S. Oil Co. The company supplies refined oil products to US residents in the Midwest, and does a lot more. In addition to the wholesale distribution of oil products (its largest revenue generator), the company operates gas stations, and installs gas pumps, tanks, and other petroleum-related equipment. It also provides plumbing, and HVAC services, operates a research laboratory for environmental analysis, collects used waste oil to be processed into burner fuel, and has a metal custom manufacturing unit.

U.S. Oil Co. was established in the 1950s as Schmidt Oil by the sons of local fuel distributor Albert Schmidt, who landed his first job in the oil business in 1923.

EXECUTIVES

Chairman: Thomas A. (Tom) Schmidt
President and CEO: John Schmidt
CFO, Secretary, and Treasurer: Paul Bachman
Director Information Systems: Fred Pennings
General Counsel: Marjorie Young
Director Safety and Risk Management: Tom Titzkowski
Director Human Resources: Lori Hoersch

LOCATIONS

HQ: U.S. Oil Co., Inc.
425 S. Washington St., Combined Locks, WI 54113
Phone: 920-739-6101 **Fax:** 920-788-0531
Web: www.usoil.com

U.S. Oil has operations in Illinois, Michigan, Minnesota, Missouri, and Wisconsin.

PRODUCTS/OPERATIONS

Major Operations

Design Air (heating and air conditioning equipment)
Express Convenience Centers (gas stations and car washes)
U.S. Custom Manufacturing (tube bending and fabrication)
U.S. Lubricants (motor oil and related products)
U.S. Petroleum Equipment — New (petroleum-related equipment installation)
U.S. Petroleum Equipment — Used (petroleum-related equipment installation)
U.S. Petroleum Laboratory (environmental and used oil testing and analysis)
U.S. Petroleum Operations (gasoline, fuel oil, and natural gas)
U.S. Tire & Exhaust (exhaust pipe manufacturing and auto parts distribution)

COMPETITORS

Apex Oil
Motiva Enterprises
Quality State Oil Company
Sunoco

US Oncology

US Oncology has got the backs (and the back offices) of medical oncologists across the US. The company provides management and support services to oncology practices and treatment centers throughout the US. It provides a comprehensive management offering, including billing, recruiting, data management, drug purchasing, and accounting. It also offers a separate drug purchasing service, negotiating prices with pharmaceutical and biotech companies for specialty cancer drugs and distributing them to client practices. Additionally, US Oncology helps its affiliate practices expand into full-fledged cancer treatment centers that offer diagnostic and therapeutic services, including radiation and chemotherapy.

US Oncology helped develop about 80 such cancer centers. The company provides development capital and shepherds its medical practices through the process of negotiating regulatory issues, building the facilities, and setting up operations.

Along with its services aimed at cancer doctors, the company serves pharmaceutical and biotechnology firms by designing and supervising cancer-related clinical trials. It enlists its affiliated physicians in the trials, thus giving them access to the latest available treatments.

US Oncology has several ongoing initiatives to enhance the quality and efficiency of the care it provides, including projects to offer new patient support services and to implement an oncology-specific electronic record-keeping system. The company wants to continue to expand its network of affiliated practices (which already includes some 1,200 doctors in more than 450 locations) and to grow its specialty pharmacy service. It began distributing oncology drugs

from its Fort Worth facility in 2005 and added a mail order service for orally administered cancer drugs in 2006.

In early 2008 long-time CEO Dale Ross resigned and was replaced by company president Bruce Broussard. Ross remained with US Oncology as executive chairman.

EXECUTIVES

Chairman: R. Dale Ross, age 61, $856,359 pay
Vice Chairman: Lloyd K. Everson, age 64, $363,125 pay
President, CEO, and Director: Bruce D. Broussard, age 45, $518,750 pay
EVP and COO: Glen C. Laschober, age 55
EVP and CFO: Michael A. (Mike) Sicuro, age 50
SVP Governmant Relations and Public Policy: Dan Cohen
SVP Human Resources: David Bronsweig
VP, Secretary, and General Counsel: Phillip H. Watts, age 42
Chief Accounting Officer: Vicki H. Hitzhusen, age 55
Marketing Communications Manager: Cara Heiman
Medical Director: Michael Kolodziej
Auditors: PricewaterhouseCoopers LLP

LOCATIONS

HQ: US Oncology, Inc.
16825 Northchase Dr., Ste. 1300, Houston, TX 77060
Phone: 832-601-8766
Web: www.usoncology.com

US Oncology operates in 37 states.

PRODUCTS/OPERATIONS

2007 Sales

	$ mil.	% of total
Pharmaceutical services	2,282.8	48
Medical oncology services	2,088.2	44
Cancer center services	349.9	7
Research & other services	51.2	1
Adjustments	(1,771.3)	—
Total	3,000.8	100

Selected Subsidiaries

AccessMed, LLC
Cancer Treatment Associates of Northeast Missouri, Ltd., LP
Colorado Cancer Centers, L.L.C.
Greenville Radiation Care, Inc.
Metropolitan Integrated Cancer Care, LCC
Oncology Rx Care Advantage, LP
Oregon Cancer Center, Ltd.
Physician Reliance Network, LLC
RMCC Cancer Center, LLC
SelectPlus Oncology, LLC
Southeast Texas Cancer Centers, LP
The Carroll County Cancer Center, LP
TOPS Pharmacy Services, Inc.
US Oncology Pharmaceutical Services, LLC
US Oncology Reimbursement Solutions, LLC
US Oncology Research, LLC
US Oncology Specialty, LP

COMPETITORS

Accredo Health	OnCure Medical
AmerisourceBergen	Orion HealthCorp
AmSurg	PAREXEL
Aptium Oncology	Pharmaceutical Product
BioScrip	Development
Cardinal Health	Quintiles Transnational
Caremark Pharmacy Services	Radiation Therapy Services
	RadNet
Covance	Sheridan Healthcare
Express Scripts	Sterling Healthcare
Gentiva	Symbion
InSight Health	United Surgical Partners
McKesson	Verispan
Medco Health	

HISTORICAL FINANCIALS

Company Type: Private

Income Statement

FYE: December 31

	REVENUE ($ mil.)	NET INCOME ($ mil.)	NET PROFIT MARGIN	EMPLOYEES
12/07	3,001	(35)	—	9,000
12/06	2,811	26	0.9%	8,600
12/05	2,519	31	1.2%	8,300
12/04	2,260	48	2.1%	—
12/03	1,966	71	3.6%	3,711
Annual Growth	11.2%	—	—	24.8%

Net Income History

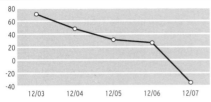

US Postal Service

The United States Postal Service (USPS) handles cards, letters, and packages sent from sea to shining sea. The USPS delivers more than 212 billion pieces of mail a year to some 148 million addresses in the US and its territories. The independent government agency relies on postage and fees to fund operations. Though it has a monopoly on delivering the mail, the USPS faces competition for services such as package delivery. The US president appoints nine of the 11 members of the board that oversee the USPS. The presidential appointees select the postmaster general and together they name the deputy postmaster general; the two also serve on the board.

A challenge for the agency is the growing use of the Internet, which has led to lower volume of some types of mail. To keep pace, the USPS has worked to gain delivery business generated by online shopping. The agency also is investing in the development of the Intelligent Mail Barcode, a mini-GPS system for tracking mail.

At the same time, the USPS is reducing its workforce through attrition and cutting hours of operation at some of its 36,000-plus post offices and other retail and delivery facilities. Transportation is a major expense for the agency, however, and high fuel prices have pumped up costs for operating the agency's 219,000 vehicles.

With an eye on its bottom line, the USPS has accelerated the pace of its rate increases. Between January 2006 and May 2008 the price of a first-class stamp went from 37 cents to 42 cents. However, USPS introduced a new concept in April 2007 — the Forever Stamp. The Liberty Bell-imaged stamp is sold at the same price as a first-class stamp but it can then be used, as the name says, forever, even as the price of first-class postage goes up.

The USPS was given some flexibility in setting rates, as well as some new restrictions, by the Postal Accountability and Enhancement Act of 2006, considered the farthest-reaching postal reform legislation since the agency became independent in 1970. The goal of the law was to enable the USPS adopt some private-sector management practices in order to ensure the agency's long-term financial health and to preserve universal mail service. Among the short-term effects of the legislation was a requirement that the agency pay into a new fund for retiree health benefits. The $5.4 billion payment caused the USPS to record a loss in 2007, the agency's first since 2002.

HISTORY

The second-oldest agency of the US government (after Indian Affairs), the Post Office was created by the Continental Congress in 1775 with Benjamin Franklin as postmaster general. The postal system came to play a vital role in the development of transportation in the US.

At that time, postal workers were riders on muddy paths delivering letters without stamps or envelopes. Letters were delivered only between post offices. Congress approved the first official postal policy in 1792: Rates ranged from six cents for less than 30 miles to 25 cents for more than 450. Letter carriers began delivering mail in cities in 1794.

First based in Philadelphia, in 1800 the Post Office moved to Washington, DC. In 1829 Andrew Jackson elevated the position of postmaster general to cabinet rank — it became a means of rewarding political cronies. Mail contracts subsidized the early development of US railroads. The first adhesive postage stamp appeared in the US in 1847.

Uniform postal rates (not varying with distance) were instituted in 1863, the year free city delivery began. The start of free rural delivery in 1896 spurred road construction in isolated US areas. Parcel post was launched in 1913, and new mail-order houses such as Montgomery Ward and Sears, Roebuck flourished.

The famous pledge beginning "Neither snow nor rain . . . " — not an official motto — was first inscribed at the main New York City post office in 1914. Scheduled airmail service between Washington, DC, and New York City began in 1918, stimulating the development of commercial air service. The ZIP code was introduced in 1963.

As mail volume grew, postal workers became increasingly militant under work stress. (Franklin's pigeonhole sorting method had barely changed.) A work stoppage in the New York City post office in 1970 spread within nine days to 670 post offices, and the US Army was deployed to handle the mail. Later that year the Postal Reorganization Act was passed. The new law established a board of governors to handle postal affairs and choose the postmaster general, who became CEO of an independent agency, the US Postal Service (USPS). The next year USPS negotiated the first US government collective-bargaining labor contract. Express mail service began in 1977, and USPS stepped up automation efforts.

In 1995 USPS launched Global Package Link, a program to expedite major customers' shipments to Canada, Japan, and the UK. The next year it overhauled rates, cutting prices for larger mailers who prepared their mail for automation and raising prices for small mailers who didn't.

Postmaster General Marvin Runyon — whose six-year tenure took the agency from the red into the black — retired in 1998 and was succeeded by USPS veteran William Henderson. The next year a one-cent hike in the price of first-class postage took effect. (Another one-cent increase took effect in 2001, and the rate rose once again the following year.) In a nod to the Internet, USPS in 1999 contracted with outside vendors to enable customers to buy and print stamps online.

In 2001 USPS formed a strategic alliance with rival FedEx through which FedEx agreed to provide air transportation for USPS mail, in return for the placement of FedEx drop boxes in post offices. Henderson stepped down at the end of May 2001, and EVP Jack Potter was named to replace him. That year several postal workers in a Washington, DC, branch office were exposed to anthrax-tainted letters.

Potter launched a series of cost-cutting programs, which together with rate increases enabled the USPS to post a profit in 2003 — the agency's first year in the black since 1999.

EXECUTIVES

Chairman: Alan C. Kessler
Vice Chairman: Carolyn Lewis Gallagher
Postmaster General, CEO, and Governor:
  John E. (Jack) Potter
Deputy Postmaster, COO, and Governor:
  Patrick R. Donahoe
EVP and CFO: Harold Glen Walker
EVP and Chief Human Resources Officer:
  Anthony J. (Tony) Vegliante
EVP and Chief Marketing Officer: Anita J. Bizzotto
SVP Intelligent Mail and Address Quality:
  Thomas G. (Tom) Day
SVP Operations: William P. (Bill) Galligan
SVP and General Counsel: Mary Anne Gibbons
SVP and Managing Director, Global Business:
  Paul Vogel
SVP Strategy and Transition: Linda A. Kingsley
SVP Customer Service: Stephen M. (Steve) Kearney
VP and Controller: Lynn Malcolm
VP Sales: Jerry W. Whalen
VP and Treasurer: Robert J. Pedersen
VP Public Affairs and Communications:
  Joanne Giordano
VP and CTO: George Wright
Chief Postal Inspector: Alexander Lazaroff
Judicial Officer: William Campbell
President, Shipping and Mailing Services Division:
  Robert F. Bernstock, age 57
Auditors: Ernst & Young LLP

LOCATIONS

HQ: United States Postal Service
  475 L'Enfant Plaza SW, Washington, DC 20260
Phone: 202-268-2500   **Fax:** 202-268-4860
Web: www.usps.com

PRODUCTS/OPERATIONS

2007 Sales

	$ mil.	% of total
First-class mail	37,564	50
Standard mail	20,779	28
Priority mail	5,233	7
Package services	2,306	3
Periodicals	2,188	3
International	2,036	3
Express mail	951	1
Other	3,916	5
Total	**74,973**	**100**

COMPETITORS

DHL
FedEx
UPS

HISTORICAL FINANCIALS

Company Type: Government agency

Income Statement

	REVENUE ($ mil.)	NET INCOME ($ mil.)	NET PROFIT MARGIN	EMPLOYEES
9/07	74,973	(5,142)	—	684,762
9/06	72,650	900	1.2%	696,138
9/05	69,907	1,445	2.1%	704,716
9/04	68,996	3,065	4.4%	707,485
9/03	68,529	3,868	5.6%	826,955
Annual Growth	2.3%	—	—	(4.6%)

FYE: September 30

2007 Year-End Financials

Debt ratio: —
Return on equity: —
Cash ($ mil.): —

Current ratio: —
Long-term debt ($ mil.): 618

Net Income History

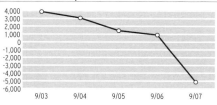

U.S. Xpress

U.S. Xpress Enterprises hopes customers find it x-ceptional. The company's truckload transportation units, led by flagship U.S. Xpress, provide medium- to long-haul service throughout North America, as well as regional service in the midwestern, southeastern, and western US. It also offers dedicated contract carriage, in which drivers and equipment are assigned to a customer long-term, and expedited freight hauling. Overall, the company's fleet includes about 7,500 tractors and 22,000 trailers. Customers include retailers, manufacturers, and other transportation companies. Co-chairmen and co-founders Patrick Quinn and Max Fuller own the company.

Quinn and Fuller took full ownership of U.S. Xpress Enterprises after their tender offer for shares they did not already own was completed in October 2007. When their takeover bid was announced in June 2007, Quinn and Fuller together controlled 42% of the company.

With Quinn and Fuller continuing at the wheel, U.S. Xpress Enterprises hopes to achieve profitable growth by allocating its assets efficiently among the different types of truckload transportation the company provides. It has seen strong growth in its dedicated services segment. Also, the company differentiates itself from competitors with a couple of expedited service offerings. Its "near airfreight" service uses teams of drivers on long-haul routes to compete with airfreight at lower costs, and its intermodal rail business involves contracting with railroads to move customers' freight on high-speed trains for less than the cost of over-the-road hauling.

The company has extended its reach by investing in regional truckload carriers. U.S. Xpress Enterprises owns controlling stakes in Arnold Transportation Services and Total Transportation of Mississippi, as well as minority interests

in Richmond, Virginia-based Abilene Motor Express and Duncan, South Carolina-based C&C Transportation. In late 2008, U.S. Xpress Enterprises also bought a 47% stake in Smith Transport, a truckload carrier owning 850 tractors and 3,000 trailers in the eastern US.

U.S. Xpress Enterprises' truckload transportation units account for the vast majority of the company's overall sales. Subsidiary Xpress Global Systems provides services such as less-than-truckload freight hauling, warehousing, and distribution to the floor-covering industry. In addition, U.S. Xpress Enterprises owns a minority stake in Transplace, a provider of transportation management and other logistics services.

EXECUTIVES

Co-Chairman, CEO, and Secretary: Max L. Fuller, age 55, $843,269 pay
Co-Chairman, President, and Treasurer: Patrick E. Quinn, age 61, $843,269 pay
EVP Operations and COO: Jeffrey S. (Jeff) Wardeberg, age 45, $417,500 pay
EVP Finance and CFO: Ray M. Harlin, age 58, $436,539 pay
EVP Operations: John White
SVP and General Manager, Dedicated Services Business Unit: William K. Farris, age 53, $214,200 pay
VP and General Counsel: Lisa M. Pate
VP and General Manager, Xpress Direct: William E. Fuller
VP Marketing Analysis and Sales Administration: Patrick Brian Quinn
Auditors: Ernst & Young LLP

LOCATIONS

HQ: U.S. Xpress Enterprises, Inc.
 4080 Jenkins Rd., Chattanooga, TN 37421
Phone: 423-510-3000   **Fax:** 423-510-3318
Web: www.usxpress.com

COMPETITORS

CEVA Logistics U.S.	Ryder System
Con-way Freight	Saia, Inc.
Covenant Transportation	Schneider National
Crete Carrier	Swift Transportation
Estes Express	Universal Truckload
Heartland Express	UPS Supply Chain
J.B. Hunt	Solutions
Knight Transportation	Werner Enterprises
Landstar System	

HISTORICAL FINANCIALS

Company Type: Private

Income Statement

	REVENUE ($ mil.)	NET INCOME ($ mil.)	NET PROFIT MARGIN	EMPLOYEES
12/07	1,510	—	—	10,885
12/06	1,472	—	—	10,885
12/05	1,164	—	—	8,269
12/04	1,106	—	—	—
12/03	931	—	—	—
Annual Growth	12.9%	—	—	14.7%

FYE: December 31

Revenue History

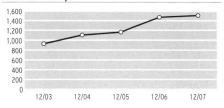

USAA

USAA has a decidedly military bearing. The mutual insurance company serves nearly 6 million member customers, primarily military personnel, military retirees, and their families. Its products and services include property/casualty (sold only to military personnel) and life insurance, banking, discount brokerage, and investment management. USAA relies largely on technology and direct marketing to sell its products, reaching clients via the telephone and Internet.

The company's USAA Alliance Services unit provides discount shopping (floral, jewelry, and home and auto safety items), and travel and delivery services to its members. Its USAA Real Estate division serves institutional and corporate customers with real estate development.

On average, members use five of the company's different products, and the company has begun tying its auto insurance rates to the number of products a member uses as well as how long they have held insurance with USAA.

The company is expecting its membership to continue growing, projecting it to nearly double by 2010. In an attempt to increase revenue, the company has entered new markets by making efforts to target people less affluent than military officers. At present, nearly 50% of its members are the grown children and grandchildren of people who have served in the military.

In recent years USAA has streamlined operations by reducing staff and closing down divisions (including mailing, printing, and information technology offices). Its efforts have rewarded members with lower prices.

HISTORY

In 1922 a group of 26 US Army officers gathered in a San Antonio hotel and formed their own automobile insurance association. The reason? As military officers who often moved, they had a hard time getting insurance because they were considered transient. So the officers decided to insure each other. Led by Major William Garrison, who became the company's first president, they formed the United States Army Automobile Insurance Association.

In 1924, when US Navy and Marine Corps officers were allowed to join, the company changed its name to United Services Automobile Association. By the mid-1950s the company had some 200,000 members. During the 1960s the company formed USAA Life Insurance Company (1963) and USAA Casualty Insurance Company (1968).

Robert McDermott, a retired US Air Force brigadier general, became president in 1969. He cut employment through attrition, established education and training seminars for employees, and invested in computers and telecommunications (drastically cutting claims-processing time). McDermott added new products and services, such as mutual funds, real estate investments, and banking. Under McDermott, USAA's membership grew from 653,000 in 1969 to more than 3 million in 1993.

During the 1970s, in an effort to go paperless, USAA became one of the insurance industry's first companies to switch from mail to toll-free (800) numbers. In the early 1980s the company introduced its discount purchasing program, USAA

Buying Services. In 1985 it opened the USAA Federal Savings Bank. USAA began installing an optical storage system in the late 1980s to automate some customer service operations.

McDermott retired in 1993 and was succeeded by Robert Herres. The following year USAA Federal Savings Bank began developing a home banking system, offering members information and services over advanced screen telephones provided by IBM.

In the early 1990s USAA's real estate activities increased dramatically. In 1995 USAA restructured its interest in the Fiesta Texas theme park in San Antonio in order to focus on previously developed properties in geographically diverse areas. That year Six Flags Theme Parks (now Six Flags, Inc.) assumed operation and management of Fiesta Texas (which purchased it from USAA in 1998).

In 1997 USAA began including enlisted military personnel as members. It also started to experiment with a "plain English" mutual fund prospectus. In 1998 USAA also began offering Choice Ride in Orlando, Florida. For about $1,100 per quarter and a promise not to drive except in emergencies, the pilot program provided 36 round trips and a 90% discount on car insurance, in hopes of keeping older drivers from unnecessarily getting behind the wheel.

Also in 1998, as part of its new Financial Planning Network, USAA began offering retirement and estate planning assistance aimed at 25- to 55-year-olds for a yearly $250 fee. In 1999 claims doubled largely due to the impact of Hurricane Floyd and spring hail storms hitting military communities in North Carolina and Virginia.

USAA also moved in 1999 to consolidate its customers' separate accounts (such as mutual fund holdings, stocks and bonds, and life insurance products) into one main account to strengthen customer relationships and reduce operational costs. The next year, after completing a number of technology projects, it laid off workers for the first time in its history.

In 2002, Robert Herres resigned as chairman and was succeeded by CEO Robert Davis. The next year the company saw increased sales and an improved net income thanks to a rebounding stock market and membership growth.

Robert Davis stepped down as chairman and CEO in 2007 and was replaced by John Moellering (chairman) and Joe Robles (CEO).

EXECUTIVES

Chairman: John H. Moellering
President and CEO: Josue (Joe) Robles Jr., age 62
CFO: Kristi A. Matus, age 39
EVP Enterprise Business Operations: S. Wayne Peacock
EVP, General Counsel, and Corporate Secretary: Steven A. Bennett
EVP People Services: Elizabeth D. (Liz) Conklyn
EVP Corporate Communications: Wendi E. Strong
SVP Information Technology and CIO: Greg Schwartz
SVP Claims Service: Ken Rosen
President, USAA Financial Services Group: Christopher W. Claus
President, USAA Property & Casualty Insurance Group: Stuart Parker
President, USAA Federal Savings Bank: F. David Bohne
Auditors: Ernst & Young LLP

LOCATIONS

HQ: USAA
   9800 Fredericksburg Rd., San Antonio, TX 78288
Phone: 210-498-2211
Web: www.usaa.com

USAA has major regional offices in Colorado Springs, Colorado; Las Vegas, Nevada; Norfolk, Virginia; Phoenix, Arizona; Sacramento, California; and Tampa, Florida. It operates international offices in London and Frankfurt, Germany.

PRODUCTS/OPERATIONS

2007 Revenues

	$ mil.	% of total
Insurance premiums	9,324	65
Fees, sales, & loan income	2,254	15
Investment income	1,825	13
Services & contractual income on securitizations	362	2
Real estate investment income	241	2
Other revenue	412	3
Total	**14,418**	**100**

COMPETITORS

AIG
AIG American General
Allstate
American Financial
AXA Financial
Berkshire Hathaway
Charles Schwab
Chubb Corp
CIGNA
Citigroup
GEICO
Guardian Life
The Hartford
John Hancock Financial Services
Liberty Mutual
MetLife
Mutual of Omaha
Nationwide
New York Life
Northwestern Mutual
Pacific Mutual
Prudential
State Farm
T. Rowe Price

HISTORICAL FINANCIALS

Company Type: Mutual company

Income Statement

FYE: December 31

	ASSETS ($ mil.)	NET INCOME ($ mil.)	INCOME AS % OF ASSETS	EMPLOYEES
12/07	67,177	1,855	2.8%	22,000
12/06	60,269	2,330	3.9%	22,000
12/05	51,038	1,388	2.7%	21,900
12/04	46,482	1,597	3.4%	21,000
12/03	41,044	1,501	3.7%	21,000
Annual Growth	**13.1%**	**5.4%**	**—**	**1.2%**

2007 Year-End Financials

Equity as % of assets: 21.4%   Long-term debt ($ mil.): —
Return on assets: 2.9%   Sales ($ mil.): 14,418
Return on equity: 13.5%

Net Income History

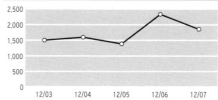

Valenti Management

Valenti Management owns and operates about 120 Wendy's fast food restaurants in Arkansas, Mississippi, Missouri, Pennsylvania, and Tennessee. The company's Valenti Southeast Management unit operates nine Chili's Grill & Bar casual-dining restaurants (franchised from Brinker International) in Alabama and Mississippi. In addition to its core restaurant operations, Valenti Management's Energy Master subsidiary manages several apartment buildings. The company was founded by CEO Darrell Valenti and his family in the 1970s.

The company has embarked on an aggressive expansion plan that calls for the opening of about 80 new locations in the next 10 years, making Valenti the largest Wendy's franchisee in the chain.

EXECUTIVES

President and CEO: Darrell J. Valenti
COO: Peter J. Grant
EVP and CFO: Steven (Steve) Nesbitt
SVP Real Estate and Development: Steven K. Underwood, age 46
Director IT: Pachy Torresola
Director Maintenance: Mike Smith
Director Marketing: Susie Temple
Director Operations, Region I: John Carlasare
Director Operations, Region II: Tim Driskill
Director Operations, Region III: Dan O'Donnell
Manager HR: Liz Butler

LOCATIONS

HQ: Valenti Management Inc.
   3450 Buschwood Park Dr., Ste. 195, Tampa, FL 33618
Phone: 813-935-8777   **Fax:** 901-684-1215
Web: www.valentifm.com

COMPETITORS

Back Yard Burgers	McDonald's
Burger King	Morgan's Foods
Cajun Operating Company	Paradise & Associates
Captain D's	Popeyes
Checkers Drive-In	Sonic Corp.
Chick-fil-A	Subway
Jack in the Box	West Quality Foods
K-MAC	YUM!
Krystal	

Vance Publishing

Does your pig need a new hairdo? Vance Publishing can help. The company publishes about 25 trade magazines serving a wide range of professionals, from beauticians (*Modern Salon*) to farmers (*Ag Professional*). It also publishes titles for woodworkers (*Wood & Wood Products*), farmers (*The Grower*), furniture retailers (*Residential Lighting*), and supermarket retailers (*Produce Merchandising*). With more than 117,000 subscribers, *Modern Salon* is Vance's highest circulation publication. The company — owned by the family of Herbert Vance, who founded it in

1937 — also provides custom publishing and research services, and invests in Internet ventures related to the industries it serves.

Vance's food and agriculture publications are organized under a unit called Food 360. The company's Interiors Media Group includes six trade titles: *Wood & Wood Products*, *Custom Woodworking Business*, *CLOSETS*, *Furniture Style*, *Residential Lighting*, and *Accessory Merchandising*. Its Salon group is devoted to titles such as *Modern Salon* and *Salon Today*.

Vance is focusing on product development in the digital media realm, as a way to quickly boost revenue growth. The company publishes Web versions of its print titles, including AgProfessional.com and ModernSalon.com.

EXECUTIVES

Chairman and CEO: William C. (Bill) Vance
President and COO: Peggy Walker
EVP: William P. (Bill) O'Neill
SVP, CFO, and Treasurer: Walter A. Kay
SVP Marketing: Steven U. (Steve) Lee
SVP Interiors and Events: Harry Urban
VP Publication Services: Mike Morgan
VP Business and Technology; VP and Group Publisher, Produce and Red Book: Leonard Timm
VP and Publishing Director, Protein: Cliff Becker Jr.
VP and Publishing Director, Salon Division: Robert (Bob) Bellew
VP and Publishing Director, Produce Division: Donald P. Ransdell
VP Human Resources and Facilities: Loreen Muzik
Director Research and Marketing: Judy Riggs

LOCATIONS

HQ: Vance Publishing Corporation
400 Knightsbridge Pkwy., Lincolnshire, IL 60069
Phone: 847-634-2600   **Fax:** 847-634-4379
Web: www.vancepublishing.com

PRODUCTS/OPERATIONS

Selected Publications

Ag Professional
Citrus & Vegetable Magazine
Custom Woodworking Business
Dairy Herd Management
Drovers (beef industry news)
Furniture Style
The Grower
Modern Salon
The Packer
Pork
Process (hair coloring magazine)
Produce Merchandising
Residential Lighting
Salon Today
Wood & Wood Products

COMPETITORS

Ascend Media
August Home Publishing
Fairchild Publications
Farm Journal
Hanley Wood
Lebhar-Friedman
Nielsen Business Media
Penton Media
Rodale
Watt Publishing

Vanderbilt University

The house that Cornelius built, Vanderbilt University was founded in 1873 with a $1 million grant from industrialist Cornelius Vanderbilt. The university's endowment has grown to close to $3 billion, and the school today is a haven for more than 11,500 students and some 2,600 full-time faculty. Vanderbilt offers undergraduate and graduate programs in areas such as education and human development, engineering, and the arts and sciences. The university has 10 schools and colleges; its Owen Graduate School of Management and its medical school rank near the top of national surveys. A major research university, Vanderbilt receives millions of dollars annually in sponsored awards to fund its facilities.

For its first 40 years of existence, Vanderbilt was under the auspices of the Methodist Episcopal Church, South. The Vanderbilt Board of Trust severed its ties with the church in 1914 after a dispute with the bishops over who would appoint University trustees.

EXECUTIVES

Chairman: Martha R. Ingram, age 72
Chancellor; Provost and Vice Chancellor for Academic Affairs: Nicholas S. Zeppos
Vice Chancellor Administration and CFO: Lauren J. Brisky, age 57
Vice Chancellor Health Affairs: Harry R. Jacobson, age 61
Vice Chancellor University Affairs, General Counsel, and Secretary: David Williams II
Vice Chancellor Investments: Mathew Wright
Interim Vice Chancellor Public Affairs: Beth Fortune
Executive Associate Vice Chancellor, Development and Alumni Relations: Robert L. Early
Associate Vice Chancellor Finance and Controller: Betty Price
Assistant Vice Chancellor Research Finance: Jerry Fife
Assistant Vice Chancellor Management Information Systems: Timothy R. (Tim) Getsay
Secretary of the Board: William W. Bain Jr.
Associate Provost; Dean, Students: Mark Bandas
Associate Provost, Faculty: Timothy P. McNamara
Interim Chief Human Resources Officer: Lenon Coleman
Auditors: KPMG LLP

LOCATIONS

HQ: Vanderbilt University
2201 West End Ave., Nashville, TN 37235
Phone: 615-322-7311
Web: www.vanderbilt.edu

PRODUCTS/OPERATIONS

Selected Schools and Colleges

Blair School of Music
College of Arts and Science
Divinity School
Graduate School
Law School
Owen Graduate School of Management
Peabody College of Education and Human Development
School of Engineering
School of Medicine
School of Nursing

HISTORICAL FINANCIALS

Company Type: School

Income Statement

FYE: June 30

	REVENUE ($ mil.)	NET INCOME ($ mil.)	NET PROFIT MARGIN	EMPLOYEES
6/07	2,733	692	25.3%	21,502
6/06	2,482	438	17.7%	20,571
6/05	2,230	—	—	19,703
6/04	1,971	—	—	18,551
6/03	1,799	—	—	17,700
Annual Growth	11.0%	57.9%	—	5.0%

2007 Year-End Financials

Debt ratio: —
Return on equity: 14.8%
Cash ($ mil.): —
Current ratio: —
Long-term debt ($ mil.): —

Net Income History

Vanderbilt University Medical Center

The Vanderbilt University Medical Center (VUMC) is one of the top health care organizations in the country, with its network of hospitals, outpatient centers, clinics, and specialty institutes. Its medical education programs train hundreds of doctors and nurses each year, and the center's Vanderbilt Clinic receives nearly 700,000 annual patient visits. Its Vanderbilt University Hospital, together with the clinic, has more than 800 beds. VUMC also boasts a children's hospital, a psychiatric hospital, a veterans' health facility, and a rehabilitation hospital, as well as a biomedical research center and the Vanderbilt-Ingram Cancer Center, a National Cancer Institute Comprehensive Cancer Center.

EXECUTIVES

Chairman: Edward G. Nelson, age 76
Executive Director and CEO, Vanderbilt University Hospital: Larry M. Goldberg
Vice Chancellor for Health Affairs and Director: Harry R. Jacobson, age 61
Associate Vice Chancellor for Research: Jeffrey R. Balser
Associate Vice Chancellor for Children's Services: Ian M. Burr
Associate Vice Chancellor for Medical Center Communications: Joel G. Lee
Associate Vice Chancellor for Clinical Affairs; Chief Medical Officer, Vanderbilt Medical Group: C. Wright Pinson
SVP and CFO: J. Richard Wagers
Chief Marketing Officer: Jill D. Austin
Dean, School of Medicine: Steven G. Gabbe
Dean, School of Nursing: Colleen Conway-Welch
Chief Nursing Officer and Director Patient Care Services, Vanderbilt University Hospital: Marilyn A. Dubree
Director News and Public Affairs: William N. Hance

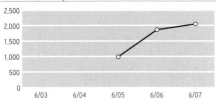
The Vanguard Group

If you buy low and sell high, invest for the long term, don't panic, and generally disapprove of those whippersnappers at Fidelity, then you may end up in the Vanguard of the financial market. The Vanguard Group offers individual and institutional investors a line of popular mutual funds and brokerage services. Claiming more than $1 trillion of assets under management, the firm is battling FMR (aka Fidelity) for the title of largest retail mutual fund manager on the planet. Vanguard's fund options include more than 180 stock, bond, mixed, and international offerings, as well as variable annuity portfolios; its Vanguard 500 Index Fund is one of the largest in the US.

In 2008 Vanguard joined the government's money-market insurance plan, designed to keep nervous investors from emptying their funds by safeguarding deposits.

The company is known as much for its puritanical thriftiness and conservative investing as for its line of index funds, which track the performance of such groups of stock as the S&P 500. Retired company founder John Bogle is sometimes derisively called "St. Jack" for his zealous criticism of industry practices, but the company's reputation for being squeaky clean

appears to have kept it unscathed by the mutual fund industry scandals of recent years.

Unlike other fund managers, Vanguard is set up like a mutual insurance company. The funds (and by extension, their more than 9 million investors) own the company, so fees are low to nonexistent; funds are operated on a tight budget so as not to eat into results. The company spends next to nothing on advertising, relying instead on strong returns and word-of-mouth.

And despite its no-broker, no-load background, Vanguard has developed cheap ways to dole out advice, especially through the use of toll-free numbers and the Internet and by quietly touting its online brokerage service.

HISTORY

A distant cousin of Daniel Boone, Walter Morgan knew a few things about pioneering. He was the first to offer a fund with a balance of stocks and bonds, serendipitously introduced early in 1929, months before the stock market collapsed. Morgan's balanced Wellington fund (named after Napoleon's vanquisher) emerged effectively unscathed.

John Bogle's senior thesis on mutual funds impressed fellow Princeton alum Morgan, who hired Bogle in 1951. Morgan retired in 1967 and picked Bogle to replace him. That year Bogle engineered a merger with old-school investment firm Thorndike, Doran, Paine and Lewis. After culture clashes and four years of shrinking assets, the Thorndike-dominated board fired Bogle, who appealed to the mutual funds and their separate board of directors. The fund directors decided to split up the funds and the advisory business.

Bogle named the fund company The Vanguard Group, after the flagship of Lord Nelson, another Napoleon foe. Vanguard worked like a cooperative; mutual fund shareholders owned the company, so all services were provided at cost. The Wellington Management Company remained Vanguard's distributor until 1977, when Bogle convinced Vanguard's board to drop the affiliation. Without Wellington as the intermediary, Vanguard sold its funds directly to consumers as no-load funds (without service charges). In 1976 the company launched the Vanguard Index 500, the first index fund. These measures attracted new investors in droves.

Vanguard rode the 1980s boom. Its Windsor fund grew so large the company closed it, launching Windsor II in 1985. Vanguard weathered the 1987 crash and began the 1990s as the US's #4 mutual fund company. The actively managed funds of FMR (better known as Fidelity), most notably its Magellan fund, led the market then. The retirement of legendary Magellan manager Peter Lynch and the fund's consequential underperformance spurred a rush to index funds. Vanguard moved up to #2.

Vanguard played against type in 1995 when it introduced the Vanguard Horizon Capital Growth stock fund, an aggressively managed fund designed to vie directly with Fidelity's funds. In 1997 Vanguard added brokerage services and began selling its own and other companies' funds on the Internet to allow clients to consolidate their financial activities. In 1998 Bogle passed the chairmanship to CEO John Brennan, a soft-spoken technology wonk. Morgan died that year at age 100.

Investors were ruffled when 70-year-old Bogle announced that corporate age limits would force him to leave the board of directors

at the end of 1999. (Bogle retains an office at Vanguard headquarters and remains popular on the speaker circuit.)

Despite Vanguard's stated commitment to the little guy, by late 2002 the company was forced to mitigate realities of the economy and started courting investors with bigger bankrolls; it also raised fees for some customers with smaller accounts.

EXECUTIVES

Chairman and CEO: John J. (Jack) Brennan, age 53
President and Director: F. William (Bill) McNabb III, age 50
Managing Director, Advice, Brokerage, and Retirement Services: R. Gregory Barton
Managing Director, Retail Investor Group: Mortimer J. (Tim) Buckley
Managing Director: James H. Gately
Managing Director, Human Resources: Kathleen C. Gubanich
Managing Director, Planning and Development Group: Michael S. Miller
Managing Director, Finance Group: Ralph K. Packard
General Counsel: Heidi Stam
Chief Investment Officer: George U. (Gus) Sauter
CIO: Paul Heller

LOCATIONS

HQ: The Vanguard Group, Inc.
100 Vanguard Blvd., Malvern, PA 19355
Phone: 610-648-6000   **Fax:** 610-669-6605
Web: www.vanguard.com

PRODUCTS/OPERATIONS

Selected Funds

500 Index Fund
Asset Allocation Fund
Balanced Index Fund
California Long-Term Tax-Exempt Fund
Capital Opportunity Fund
Capital Value Fund
Developed Markets Index Fund
Diversified Equity Fund
Emerging Markets Stock Index Fund
Energy Fund
European Stock Index Fund
Explorer Fund
Extended Market Index Fund
Federal Money Market Fund
Florida Long-Term Tax-Exempt Fund
FTSE Social Index Fund
Global Equity Fund
GNMA Fund
Growth and Income Fund
Growth Index Fund
Health Care Fund
High-Yield Corporate Fund
Inflation-Protected Securities Fund
Intermediate-Term Bond Index Fund
International Explorer Fund
International Growth Fund
International Value Fund
Large-Cap Index Fund
LifeStrategy Conservative Growth Fund
LifeStrategy Growth Fund
LifeStrategy Income Fund
Limited-Term Tax-Exempt Fund
Long-Term Bond Index Fund
Long-Term Treasury Fund
Massachusetts Tax-Exempt Fund
Mid-Cap Growth Fund
Morgan Growth Fund
New Jersey Long-Term Tax-Exempt Fund
New York Long-Term Tax-Exempt Fund
New York Tax-Exempt Money Market Fund
Ohio Long-Term Tax-Exempt Fund
Pacific Stock Index Fund
Pennsylvania Long-Term Tax-Exempt Fund
Precious Metals and Mining Fund
Prime Money Market Fund

PRIMECAP Fund
REIT Index Fund
Selected Value Fund
Short-Term Federal Fund
Short-Term Tax-Exempt Fund
Short-Term Treasury Fund
Small-Cap Growth Index Fund
STAR Fund
Strategic Equity Fund
Target Retirement 2010 Fund
Target Retirement 2015 Fund
Target Retirement 2020 Fund
Target Retirement 2025 Fund
Target Retirement 2030 Fund
Target Retirement 2035 Fund
Target Retirement 2040 Fund
Target Retirement 2045 Fund
Target Retirement 2050 Fund
Tax-Managed Capital Appreciation Fund
Tax-Managed Growth and Income Fund
Tax-Managed International Fund
Total Bond Market Index Fund
Total International Stock Index Fund
Total Stock Market Index Fund
U.S. Growth Fund
U.S. Value Fund
Value Index Fund
Wellesley Income Fund
Wellington Fund

COMPETITORS

AIG	Invesco Aim
AllianceBernstein	Janus Capital
American Century	Legg Mason
AXA Financial	MFS
BlackRock	Principal Financial
Charles Schwab	Putnam
FMR	T. Rowe Price
Franklin Resources	TIAA-CREF
Invesco	USAA

Vanguard Health Systems

Vanguard Health Systems hopes to lead the way to greater health care quality and profits. The company operates 15 for-profit acute care hospitals located in urban and suburban markets in Arizona, Illinois, Massachusetts, and Texas; all told, the hospitals have more than 4,000 licensed beds. The company's hospital systems generally include outpatient facilities and medical office buildings that form local health care networks providing a continuum of care. Vanguard also runs three managed health care plans that serve around 150,000 members in Arizona and Illinois. The Blackstone Group owns a majority stake in the company.

In order to focus on its four core markets, the company sold three Southern California hospitals to Prime Healthcare Services in 2006. It still owns two surgery centers in California, however.

The company's managed care operations include Phoenix Health Plan, a Medicaid managed care plan serving about 100,000 members in the Phoenix area, and MacNeal Health Providers, an organization affiliated with the company's Chicago-area facility MacNeal Hospital. Its third health plan, Abrazo Advantage, provides Medicare Advantage and prescription drug plans to Phoenix-area Medicare members who are also eligible for Medicaid.

Like most hospital operators, the company hopes to attract customers by providing high quality care, recruiting good doctors, and expanding its services. It particularly looks to add high-margin services in areas such as cardiology and orthopedics and to increase its hospitals' ability to offer private rooms.

The company completed a multi-million dollar expansion and renovation effort at six of its hospitals in the Phoenix and San Antonio markets during 2007. And it looks to selectively acquire additional facilities, both in its existing markets and in others that fit its preferred profile: struggling not-for-profits located in fast-growing and generally affluent urban and suburban areas.

Blackstone acquired its majority stake in the company from Morgan Stanley Capital Partners, which retains a minority interest. Chairman and CEO Charles Martin also holds about 7% of the company.

EXECUTIVES

Chairman and CEO: Charles N. (Charlie) Martin Jr., age 65, $1,562,088 pay
Vice Chairman: Keith B. Pitts, age 51, $921,328 pay
President and COO: Kent H. Wallace, age 53, $834,361 pay
EVP, CFO, and Treasurer: Phillip W. Roe, age 47
EVP: Joseph D. (Joe) Moore, age 61, $779,231 pay
EVP, Secretary, and General Counsel:
Ronald P. (Ron) Soltman, age 62, $688,170 pay
SVP and CIO: Alan N. Cranford
SVP and Chief Medical Officer: James Bonnette, age 55
SVP and Assistant General Counsel and Assistant Secretary: James H. (Jim) Spalding, age 49
SVP Human Resources: James Johnston, age 64
SVP Market Strategy and Government Affairs:
Reginald M. Ballantyne III, age 64
SVP, Controller, and Chief Accounting Officer:
Gary D. Willis, age 43
SVP, Controller, and Chief Accounting Officer:
Deanna L. Wise, age 39
Auditors: Ernst & Young LLP

LOCATIONS

HQ: Vanguard Health Systems, Inc.
20 Burton Hills Blvd., Ste. 100, Nashville, TN 37215
Phone: 615-665-6000   **Fax:** 615-665-6099
Web: www.vanguardhealth.com

Selected Facilities

Arrowhead Hospital (Phoenix)
Baptist Medical Center (San Antonio)
Louis A. Weiss Memorial Hospital (Chicago)
MacNeal Hospital (Chicago)
Maryvale Hospital (Phoenix)
MetroWest Medical Center-Framingham Union Hospital (Framingham, MA)
MetroWest Medical Center-Leonard Morse Hospital (Natick, MA)
North Central Baptist Hospital (San Antonio)
Northeast Baptist Hospital (San Antonio)
Paradise Valley Hospital (Phoenix)
Phoenix Baptist Hospital (Phoenix)
Southeast Baptist Hospital (San Antonio)
St. Luke's Baptist Hospital (San Antonio)
Saint Vincent Hospital at Worcester Medical Center (Worcester, MA)
West Valley Hospital (Phoenix)

PRODUCTS/OPERATIONS

2008 Sales

	$ mil.	% of total
Acute care services	2,340.5	84
Health plans	450.2	16
Total	**2,790.7**	**100**

COMPETITORS

Advocate Health Care
Banner Health
Blue Cross Blue Shield of Arizona
Catholic Healthcare West
CHRISTUS Health
Covenant Ministries
Essent Healthcare
John C. Lincoln Health Network
Massachusetts General Hospital
Methodist Healthcare System
Partners HealthCare
Rush System for Health
Universal Health Services
University Health System
WellGroup HealthPartners

HISTORICAL FINANCIALS

Company Type: Private

Income Statement

FYE: June 30

	REVENUE ($ mil.)	NET INCOME ($ mil.)	NET PROFIT MARGIN	EMPLOYEES
6/08	2,791	(1)	—	18,500
6/07	2,581	(133)	—	18,000
6/06	2,653	13	0.5%	19,500
6/05	2,269	(78)	—	19,000
6/04	1,783	40	2.2%	14,300
Annual Growth	**11.9%**	**—**	**—**	**6.6%**

Net Income History

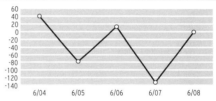

Varolii Corporation

Varolii makes sure customers and employees get the message. The company provides automated contact and notification software. Its products and services help client companies manage their interactions, contacting customers and employees via e-mail, fax, telephone, or instant messaging devices. Varolii provides applications designed to handle collections, customer service, customer retention, and business continuity. It targets customers in the communications, financial services, government, health care, insurance, transportation, and utilities sectors.

Formerly called PAR3 Communications, the firm acquired competitor EnvoyWorldWide, a provider of notification services for business continuity and emergency communications, in 2005.

The company changed its name to Varolii in 2007, the year it filed to go public. Citing unfavorable market conditions, Varolii withrew its IPO in 2008.

EXECUTIVES

President, CEO, and Director: Nicholas A. Tiliacos, age 53
CFO: John J. Flavio, age 60
EVP Sales, Marketing, and Business Development:
Jeffrey Read, age 38

EVP Professional Services, Technology, and Business Operations: Jean Francois Thions, age 69
SVP Marketing and Business Development: Pat Whelan
SVP Service Deployment: Michael Ho
VP Sales Eastern Region and General Manager: Steve H. Zirkel
VP and General Counsel: Jeff Shelby, age 42
CTO: Scott E. Sikora, age 39
Director, Corporate Communications: Robin Rees
Auditors: PricewaterhouseCoopers LLP

LOCATIONS

HQ: Varolii Corporation
821 2nd Ave., 10th Fl., Ste. 1000, Seattle, WA 98104
Phone: 206-902-3900   **Fax:** 206-902-3902
Web: www.varolii.com

COMPETITORS

724 Solutions
Adeptra
West Corporation

HISTORICAL FINANCIALS

Company Type: Private

Income Statement

FYE: December 31

	REVENUE ($ mil.)	NET INCOME ($ mil.)	NET PROFIT MARGIN	EMPLOYEES
12/07	68	(5)	—	287
12/06	51	(5)	—	251
12/05	30	(1)	—	144
12/04	16	(1)	—	81
Annual Growth	61.3%	—	—	52.5%

2007 Year-End Financials

Debt ratio: (10.3%)   Current ratio: —
Return on equity: —   Long-term debt ($ mil.): 3
Cash ($ mil.): —

Net Income History

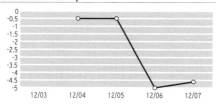

Vertrue Incorporated

Vertrue is all set to hook you up with the love of your life, or at least some discounts. The company markets membership programs offering discounts on financial services, health and dental care, travel, and other consumer products and services. Vertrue partners with companies such as credit card issuers, banks, direct-response TV advertisers, and retailers to market its membership programs. The company's personals business, Lavalife, provides Web and phone-based personals services to about 6 million members; it generates revenue by selling credits needed for romantics to interact with other lonely hearts. In August 2007, Vertrue was acquired by an investment group that included the company's management team.

With the assumption of debt, the buyers paid about $855 million for Vertrue. Besides com-

pany executives, the investor group included One Equity Partners and Rho Ventures.

The new owners took over a company that has been expanding via acquisitions. After buying Lavalife and Bargain Network in 2004, Vertrue purchased My Choice Medical Holdings in January 2005. The My Choice purchase allowed Vertrue to expand into direct and consumer services and it opens doors to the fast-growing cosmetic surgery market.

In addition to these operations, Vertrue's Coverdell subsidiary acts as a full-service marketing agency that markets insurance to banks. It has offices in Atlanta and Chicago.

Vertrue's largest single client, West Corporation, has sponsored a significant portion of the company's membership programs in the past.

EXECUTIVES

President, CEO, and Director: Gary A. Johnson, age 51, $1,372,160 pay
EVP Business Development: David Schachne, age 42
EVP Health and Insurance Services: Vincent DiBenedetto, age 49, $575,935 pay
SVP and Chief Marketing Officer: Jay Sung
SVP Human Resources: Monica Albano
General Counsel: George Thomas
President, Bargain Network: Thomas (Tom) Adams III
President, Neverblue Media: Todd Dunlop
President, Coverdell: Michael L. Owens
CEO, Lavalife: Marina Glogovac
Auditors: PricewaterhouseCoopers LLP

LOCATIONS

HQ: Vertrue Incorporated
20 Glover Ave., Norwalk, CT 06850
Phone: 203-324-7635   **Fax:** 203-674-7080
Web: www.vertrue.com

COMPETITORS

AARP
Access Plans
Affinion Group
American Automobile Association (AAA)
Costco Wholesale
eHarmony.com
FastCupid
Hospitality Marketing Concepts
Match.com
Passport Unlimited
Provell
Q Interactive
Rewards Network
SAM'S CLUB
Student Advantage
USAA

HISTORICAL FINANCIALS

Company Type: Private

Income Statement

FYE: June 30

	REVENUE ($ mil.)	NET INCOME ($ mil.)	NET PROFIT MARGIN	EMPLOYEES
6/07	800	—	—	2,500
6/06	659	—	—	2,371
6/05	580	—	—	2,281
6/04	489	—	—	1,616
6/03	457	—	—	1,410
Annual Growth	15.0%	—	—	15.4%

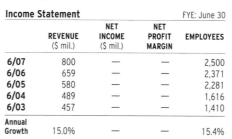

Revenue History

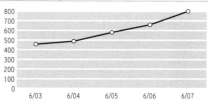

ViewSonic Corporation

ViewSonic has a display for every occasion. The company makes CRT and LCD computer displays, including the Pro Series for high-end computer-aided design, desktop publishing, and graphic design; the X and Graphics lines for consumers and businesses; and the E2, Optiquest, and Value Series for budget-minded buyers. ViewSonic also offers LCD TVs, LCD projectors, tablet PCs, and digital photo frames. ViewSonic sells directly and through resellers and distributors to consumer, corporate, government, and education customers. CEO James Chu, ViewSonic's majority owner, founded the company in 1987.

A leading provider of displays, ViewSonic has managed to hold its own in an industry where Asian giants such as NEC, Samsung, and Sony vie for market share.

ViewSonic filed to go public in 2007, but poor market conditions caused the company to withdraw its registration the following year.

EXECUTIVES

Chairman and CEO: James Chu, $347,442 pay
President, Global Products and Solutions: Heng-Chun Ho, age 54, $238,151 pay
CFO: Theodore R. (Ted) Sanders, age 53
VP, General Counsel, and Secretary: Robert J. Ranucci, age 42
VP Human Resources: Timothy Ashcroft
VP Sales, Americas: Brian Igoe
VP, Global Brand and Emerging Technologies: Jeff Volpe
VP Advanced Solutions and Emerging Technology: Michael Holstein, age 53
VP Sales, Consumer Electronics Products, ViewSonic Americas: Steve Woo
VP and Director, European Sales: Mel Taylor
Director, Public Relations: Duane Brozek
Auditors: Deloitte & Touche LLP

LOCATIONS

HQ: ViewSonic Corporation
381 Brea Canyon Rd., Walnut, CA 91789
Phone: 909-444-8888   **Fax:** 909-468-1240
Web: www.viewsonic.com

PRODUCTS/OPERATIONS

Selected Products

Digital photo frames
Digital signage
LCD projectors
LCD televisions
Monitors (CRT, LCD)
Tablet PCs

COMPETITORS

Acer	Panasonic corporation
Apple	Philips Electronics
BenQ	Planar Systems
Dell	Samsung Electronics
Fujitsu	Sharp Corp.
Gateway, Inc.	Sony
Hewlett-Packard	THOMSON
InFocus	Toshiba
LG Display	Victor Company of Japan
Mitsubishi Corp.	VIZIO
NEC	

HISTORICAL FINANCIALS

Company Type: Private

Income Statement

FYE: December 31

	REVENUE ($ mil.)	NET INCOME ($ mil.)	NET PROFIT MARGIN	EMPLOYEES
12/07	1,600	—	—	900
12/06	1,589	—	—	786
12/05	1,200	—	—	647
12/04	1,104	—	—	807
12/03	1,075	—	—	743
Annual Growth	10.5%	—	—	4.9%

Revenue History

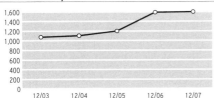

Visant Holding Corp.

Visant Holding is a real class act. Through its Jostens Scholastic, it provides school-related affinity products such as class rings and graduation items mostly to North American high schools and colleges. It also makes championship rings for professional sports and affinity rings for specialty markets. Its Jostens Yearbook segment makes and markets yearbooks to US middle and high schools and universities. Visant's Marketing and Publishing Services group produces advertising and direct marketing materials for the fragrance, cosmetics, and personal care markets, as well as the direct marketing sector. It also makes book covers for educational publishers. Visant is buying Phoenix Color Corp.

Once the deal, valued at $219 million, is final Visant plans to make Phoenix Color a wholly owned subsidiary. Visant stands to benefit from counting two Phoenix Color facilities — in Maryland and New Jersey — among its stable of book production plants.

Several acquisitions inked during the past couple years have helped Visant expand its products portfolio. Visant acquired the Dixon Web operation of Sleepeck Printing Company in 2006 and changed its name to Dixon Direct Corp. In a strategic move to expand its Marketing and Publishing Services segment, Visant in 2006 acquired Vertis, a fragrance sampling business, which operates as Arcade Marketing. In 2007

Visant bought Neff Holding and its subsidiary Neff Motivation, a provider of custom award programs and apparel, including chenille letters and letter jackets. The company operates as a direct subsidiary of Visant under the Neff brand name.

Visant was formed in 2004 through the consolidation of Jostens, Von Hoffmann, and Arcade. It has since sold off its Von Hoffmann business to R.R. Donnelley & Sons (in May 2007) for more than $412 million, as well as its Jostens Photography business.

Visant is controlled by Kohlberg Kravis Roberts & Co. and DLJ Merchant Banking Partners.

EXECUTIVES

Chairman, President, and CEO: Marc L. Reisch, age 52
VP Finance: Paul B. Carousso, age 38
VP, General Counsel, and Secretary: Marie D. Hlavaty, age 44
President and Chief Executive Officer, Jostens Group: Timothy M. Larson, age 34
Group President, Arcade and Lehigh Direct, and President, Chief Executive Officer, Arcade: John Van Horn, age 67
President, Arcade Marketing: Debra Leipman-Yale, age 50
Auditors: Ernst & Young LLP

LOCATIONS

HQ: Visant Holding Corp.
357 Main St., Armonk, NY 10504
Phone: 914-595-8200
Web: www.visant.net

PRODUCTS/OPERATIONS

2007 Sales

	$ mil.	% of total
Scholastic	465.4	37
Marketing & Publishing Services	434.1	34
Memory Book	372.1	29
Inter-segment eliminations	(0.1)	—
Total	**1,270.2**	**100**

COMPETITORS

American Achievement
Coral Graphic Services
Herff Jones
Walsworth

HISTORICAL FINANCIALS

Company Type: Holding company

Income Statement

FYE: December 31

	REVENUE ($ mil.)	NET INCOME ($ mil.)	NET PROFIT MARGIN	EMPLOYEES
12/07	1,270	155	12.2%	5,691
12/06	1,187	48	4.0%	5,096
Annual Growth	7.0%	221.9%	—	11.7%

2007 Year-End Financials

Debt ratio: —	Current ratio: —
Return on equity: 322.8%	Long-term debt ($ mil.): —
Cash ($ mil.): —	

Net Income History

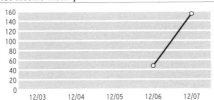

Vivid Entertainment

Vivid Entertainment Group, one of the world's top adult film producers, leaves little to the imagination. Fans of the form know the company best for its Vivid Girls, a gaggle of porn starlets such as Jenna Jameson, Briana Banks, and Lanny Barby, who are signed to exclusive contracts much like in the bygone days of the Hollywood studio system. Vivid sells its titles to the retail and rental markets and directly to consumers through its online mail-order site. Vivid also distributes the films to cable and satellite channels and offers its Internet subscribers pay-per-view access. Co-CEOs Steven Hirsch, David James, and Bill Asher own the company that Hirsch and James founded in 1984.

Leading the pack in the adult film industry, the company has been credited with bringing porn into the mainstream through its marketing efforts and by placing its actresses in mainstream films, television shows, and music videos. The company has also exposed itself to a more mainstream audience through licensing deals that stamp the Vivid brand on apparel, action figures, condoms, and an assortment of other products.

Licensing isn't the only area of expansion for Vivid. The company broadened its presence in a variety of additional media boudoirs. It has significantly boosted its Internet operations by making virtually all of its content available on its subscription-based Web site. Its book publishing achievements include *How to Have a XXX Sex Life: The Ultimate Vivid Guide* written by the Vivid Girls and produced by HarperCollins. Other publishing endeavors include a line of Vivid Girl comics from Avatar Press and a series of erotic novels from an imprint of Avalon Publishing.

Vivid received a bit of a shock in 2006 when rival Playboy acquired Club Jenna, the hardcore video production company founded and run by adult entertainment star Jenna Jameson. She had signed a long-term DVD distribution deal with Vivid and has been one of the company's more popular franchises. While the company will continue to distribute her videos under the deal that runs through 2014, Playboy now controls the Jenna Jameson brand as well as the several Web sites Club Jenna operates.

The company also made news in 2008 when it released a celebrity sex tape featuring what it claims is Jimi Hendrix in a tryst with two women. The release of the tape led the estate of Hendrix to challenge that the footage was actually of the guitar legend, but it could not prove its claim.

EXECUTIVES

Co-chairman and Co-CEO: William M. (Bill) Asher, age 45
Co-chairman, Co-CEO, and Custodian of Records: Steven Hirsch, age 47
Co-chairman, Co-CEO, and Custodian of Records: David James
VP Production and Licensing: Marci Hirsch
Press Office: Jackie Martin
National Sales Manager, Vivid Entertainment Group: David Peskin

LOCATIONS

HQ: Vivid Entertainment Group
3599 Cahuenga Blvd. W., Los Angeles, CA 90068
Phone: 323-845-4557   **Fax:** 323-436-2006
Web: www.vividentertainment.com

PRODUCTS/OPERATIONS

Selected Film Titles

Bad Girls
Bad Wives
Boiling Point
Briana Loves Jenna
Center Stage
Debbie Does Dallas . . . Again
Double Up
Fade To Black
Filthy Rich
Gettin' Lucky
The Good Time Girl
Hollywood Hostel
I Dream of Jenna
My Wife's Best Friend
Secrets and Lies
Sex at Six
Where the Boys Aren't

COMPETITORS

Beate Uhse
Digital Playground
LFP
New Frontier Media
Penthouse Media Group
Playboy
Private Media Group
Sin City
Wicked Pictures

Volunteers of America

There's a volunteer everywhere you look at Volunteers of America, a national faith-based organization that provides community-level human services to more than 2 million people a year. It works to help abused and neglected children, at-risk youth, disabled people, elderly people, the homeless, people with substance abuse problems, and prisoners and former prisoners. The group operates from more than 40 US offices; its offerings include a variety of residential facilities. It receives government grants as well as support from the public. Volunteers of America was organized in 1896 by Ballington and Maud Booth. Name sound familiar? Ballington Booth's father, William Booth, founded the Salvation Army.

EXECUTIVES

Chairman: Frances Hesselbein
Vice Chairman: Sandra Trice Gray
President and CEO: Charles W. Gould
EVP External Affairs: Jimmie Walton Paschall
EVP Operations and Strategic Development:
  Karen M. Dale
EVP Organizational Services and CFO:
  Rosemarie A. Rae
EVP and General Counsel: David T. Bowman
Treasurer: Robert E. Ransom
Secretary: Don Conley
Public Relations Manager: Julie Anderson

LOCATIONS

HQ: Volunteers of America
  1660 Duke St., Alexandria, VA 22314
Phone: 703-341-5000   **Fax:** 703-341-7000
Web: www.voa.org

HISTORICAL FINANCIALS

Company Type: Not-for-profit

Income Statement
FYE: June 30

	REVENUE ($ mil.)	NET INCOME ($ mil.)	NET PROFIT MARGIN	EMPLOYEES
6/07	851	30	3.5%	15,000
6/06	863	58	6.7%	15,000
6/05	842	—	—	15,000
Annual Growth	0.5%	(48.1%)	—	0.0%

2007 Year-End Financials

Debt ratio: 73.6%
Return on equity: 5.2%
Cash ($ mil.): —
Current ratio: —
Long-term debt ($ mil.): 436

Net Income History

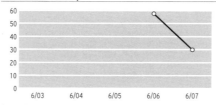

Vulcan Inc.

Even with all his Vulcan logic, could Spock invest like *this*? Brainy billionaire Paul Allen organizes his business and charitable ventures under Vulcan Inc. The firm includes Microsoft co-founder's remaining stake in the industry-defining juggernaut, as well as holdings in dozens of companies involved in technology, life sciences, multimedia, energy, and real estate. Portfolio holdings include stakes in DreamWorks SKG, Vulcan Energy, and Charter Communications. Vulcan Allen also owns two professional sports teams, the NBA's Portland Trail Blazers and the NFL's Seattle Seahawks, as well as interests in several charitable organizations.

Vulcan's charities support the arts, medical research, land conservation, and other causes. Allen, who co-founded Microsoft with Bill Gates, promotes a "wired world" vision, in which everyone is united through interconnecting communications, entertainment, and information systems. CEO Jody Patton, Allen's sister, oversees both his business and charitable ventures.

In 2007 the company joined a joint venture to acquire banks in the Southeast. Vulcan subsidiary Vulcan Sports Media in 2006 sold venerable sports publication *The Sporting News* to American City Business Journals.

HISTORY

Paul Allen and Bill Gates first worked together on computer projects as schoolmates in Seattle. They developed a program to determine traffic patterns and launched Traf-O-Data, an operation that failed because the state provided the information for free. When Allen saw an article on the MITS Altair 8800 minicomputer in 1975, the two realized it needed a simplified programming language to make it useful. They offered MITS a modified version of BASIC they had written for

---

Traf-O-Data. The company set them up in an office in Albuquerque, New Mexico. They then began their biggest collaboration of all: Microsoft. While Gates concentrated on business, Allen focused on technical issues.

They moved to Bellevue, a Seattle suburb, in 1979. The next year IBM asked them to create a programming language for a PC project. Allen bought Q-DOS (quick and dirty operating system) from Seattle Computer; the pair tweaked it and renamed it MS-DOS. Allen and Gates made a key decision to structure their contract with IBM to allow clones. They also helped design many aspects of the original IBM PC.

Allen developed Hodgkin's disease in 1982. Facing his own mortality, he ended his daily involvement in Microsoft (keeping a chunk of the company and a board seat) and began to play more (traveling and playing the electric guitar). With his cancer in remission in 1985, Allen founded multimedia software company Asymetrix. The next year he set up Vulcan to hold his diversified interests and Vulcan Ventures. He also began helping startups, indulging his interests (buying the NBA's Portland Trail Blazers in 1988 and donating some $60 million to build a museum honoring his musical idol, Jimi Hendrix, and other Pacific Northwest artists). He has also funded Seattle-area civic improvements.

In 1990 Allen hired William Savoy to help organize his finances; Savoy later became president of Vulcan Ventures. Seeing a need for more R&D in the US, Allen in 1992 started Interval Research. He also invested in America Online (sold 1994). In 1993 Allen bought 80% of Ticketmaster (sold 1997), and in 1995 he invested in DreamWorks SKG, the multimedia company of Steven Spielberg, Jeffrey Katzenberg, and David Geffen.

Allen made a rare buy outside the entertainment and high-tech worlds through a 1996 investment in power turbine maker Capstone Turbine. To prevent the Seattle Seahawks from moving to California, Allen bought the team in 1997 and made plans for a new stadium. He consolidated his management operations under Vulcan and dissolved Paul Allen Group (founded 1994), keeping Vulcan Ventures.

Allen moved into cable in 1998 and 1999; his Charter Communications eventually became the #4 US cable firm. In 1999 several Allen investments (Charter Communications, Vulcan Ventures, RCN, High Speed Access, and Go2Net) joined to form wired-world venture Broadband Partners.

In 2000 it was nearly impossible to ignore Allen's influence on Seattle as several major projects took shape or were completed, including the new Seahawks' arena, the Experience Music Project, and the renovation of a 90-year-old train station as part of a complex that includes Vulcan's new headquarters. That year he provided a $100 million infusion to struggling Oxygen Media. In 2001 Vulcan Ventures bought sports games Web site operator Small World Media to boost its sports holdings, which was later folded into the online fantasy sports operations of another Allen holding, *The Sporting News*, which was later sold.

Tech-boom losses accounted for only about 5% of Allen's portfolio, but things looked very bleak indeed in 2002 when the US attorney's office began investigating Charter Communications — for accounting irregularities. Four former executives were later indicted for fraud in 2003. Long-time right-hand man Bill Savoy left the firm that year; Savoy had overseen Vulcan's tech investments for more than a decade.

In late 2003, Allen began to restructure his holdings, dumping remaining unprofitable holdings (including RCN), and laying off many employees, including Savoy. TechTV was sold to Comcast in 2004; the network was merged in to Comcast's existing gaming and technology network, G4 TV. It is now called G4techTV.

Notable investments in 2004 include the acquisition of Plains Resources (now Vulcan Energy), which marked the company's first foray into the energy sector. Plains Resources owns 44% of Plains All American Pipeline, which provides oil and gas transportation services.

EXECUTIVES

Chairman: Paul G. Allen, age 55
President and CEO: Jo Allen (Jody) Patton, age 50
EVP, Investment Management: Lance Conn
EVP, Finance: Denise K. Fletcher, age 59
EVP, Legal and General Counsel: Bill McGrath
SVP, Business Operations, Major League Soccer Team: Gary Wright
VP, Corporate Communications: Steven C. Crosby
VP, Corporate Development and Operations: Denise Wolf
VP, Technology: Chris Purcell
VP, Media Development: Richard E. Hutton
VP, Real Estate Development: Ada M. Healey
VP, Paul G. Allen Family Foundation and Collections: Susan Coliton
VP, Design and Construction: Ray Colliver
VP, Tax: Bruce Lowry

LOCATIONS

HQ: Vulcan Inc.
505 5th Ave. South, Ste. 900, Seattle, WA 98104
Phone: 206-342-2000   **Fax:** 206-342-3000
Web: www.vulcan.com

PRODUCTS/OPERATIONS

Selected Holdings

Allen Institute for Brain Science
Audience (telecommunications audio)
Charter Communications (TV system)
Cinerama (movie theater, Seattle)
Digeo (interactive television)
DreamWorks SKG (entertainment company)
DrumCore (drum software and workstation)
Ember (wireless networking systems)
Experience Music Project (EMP, music museum, Seattle)
Flying Heritage Collection (WWII aircraft exhibit, Arlington, WA)
The Hospital (music, art, and film facility, London)
IntraPace (development of an endoscopically delivered pacemaker for treating obesity)
Laureate Education, Inc.
Makena Capital Management
Plains All American Pipeline
Portland Trail Blazers (professional basketball team)
PTC Theraputics (small molecule drugs)
Redfin (online real estate services)
Rose Garden (sports and entertainment arena)
Science Fiction Museum and Hall of Fame (Seattle)
Seattle Seahawks (professional football team)
Silvercrest Asset Management Group
SpaceShipOne (privately built spacecraft)
Vulcan Energy (formerly Plains Resources, oil and gas pipeline, transportation, and storage)
Vulcan Productions (independent film production company)
ZoomInfo (search engine focusing on people, companies, and relationships)

COMPETITORS

Accel Partners	KKR
Benchmark Capital	Kleiner Perkins
Blackstone Group	Matrix Partners
The Carlyle Group	MSD Capital
Draper Fisher Jurvetson	Platinum Equity
Equity Group Investments	SOFTBANK
Hummer Winblad	Thomas H. Lee Partners
IVP	The Trump Organization

VyStar Credit Union

The largest state-chartered financial institution in Florida, VyStar provides a galaxy of financial services from about two dozen locations in northeastern Florida. The credit union offers traditional banking services including deposit accounts, credit cards, and loans; its VyStar Financial Group subsidiary specializes in financial management and insurance services to members and nonmembers. Credit union membership is available to all who live or work in one of 15 area counties. Founded in 1952 (as Jax Navy Federal Credit Union) to serve those stationed at the Naval Air Station in Jacksonville, VyStar now boasts more than 350,000 members nationwide.

VyStar's loan portfolio consists largely of mortgages (48%) and automobile loans (28%); the credit union also services loans for others.

Residents and workers in Alachua, Baker, Bradford, Clay, Columbia, Duval, Flagler, Gilchrist, Levy, Marion, Nassau, Putnam, St. Johns, Union, and Volusia counties are eligible to join VyStar.

EXECUTIVES

Chairman: George R. Berry
Vice Chairman: Esther T. Schultz
President and CEO: Terry R. West
EVP and CFO: John H. Turpish
EVP and COO: Richard G. Alfirevic
SVP, Member Services: Randy Swift
SVP, Marketing and Planning: Judith T. Walz
SVP, Human Resources: Robert L. Davis
SVP Business Services: Joseph Nowland
SVP Risk Management: Raymond Ritoch
Chief Lending Officer: Kathryn Bonaventura
CIO: Terry L. Mayne
Secretary: P. Kem Siddons
Treasurer: Ralph R. Story
Auditors: Nearman, Maynard, Vallez, CPAs and Consultants, P.A.

LOCATIONS

HQ: VyStar Credit Union
4949 Blanding Blvd., Jacksonville, FL 32210
Phone: 904-777-6000   **Fax:** 904-908-2488
Web: www.vystarcu.org

COMPETITORS

Bank of America
BB&T
Compass Bancshares
SunTrust
Wachovia Corp

HISTORICAL FINANCIALS

Company Type: Not-for-profit

Income Statement

FYE: December 31

	ASSETS ($ mil.)	NET INCOME ($ mil.)	INCOME AS % OF ASSETS	EMPLOYEES
12/07	3,337	18	0.6%	1,100
12/06	3,169	22	0.7%	1,059
12/05	2,995	21	0.7%	1,000
12/04	2,852	17	0.6%	900
12/03	2,688	23	0.9%	—
Annual Growth	5.6%	(5.3%)	—	6.9%

2007 Year-End Financials

Equity as % of assets: 94.6%   Long-term debt ($ mil.): —
Return on assets: 0.6%   Sales ($ mil.): 238
Return on equity: 0.6%

Net Income History

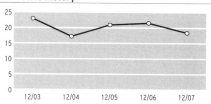

Waffle House

Don't look for pancakes at the Waffle House, because it doesn't serve 'em. The #2 family-style restaurant chain (behind Denny's) has more than 1,500 diners known for eggs, grits, waffles, and their famous "scattered, smothered, and covered" hash browns. In addition to day starters, the menu features T-bone steaks, cheeseburgers, and other sandwiches. Waffle House units are typically free standing, designed to resemble 1950s-style diners, and open 24 hours a day. They can be found in more than two dozen states, mostly in the South. The company operates more than 700 units and franchises the rest. Joe Rogers Sr., father of CEO Joe W. Rogers Jr., started the family-owned business with partner Tom Forkner in 1955.

An institution along southern highways, Waffle House has not been immune to the effects of rising food costs and a slowing economy. Two of the company's largest franchisees, Northlake Foods in Florida and Tennessee-based SouthEast Waffles, have been forced to file for bankruptcy during 2008. Together, the two businesses operated more than 250 stores.

The chain, which still only has a few locations outside its traditional Southern markets, has developed close relationships with food suppliers to serve exclusively Coca-Cola soft drinks, Minute Maid orange juice, and Heinz condiments. It also boasts several celebrities among its fans, including Britney Spears, running back Emmitt Smith, and actor Billy Bob Thornton.

HISTORY

Joe Rogers Sr. and Tom Forkner opened the first Waffle House restaurant on Labor Day, 1955, in Avondale Estates, Georgia. Rogers and Forkner based their restaurant's strategy on simple Southern cooking and low overhead. Little has changed at the Waffle House — the same black-on-yellow signs hang over each restaurant, and the menu could serve as a time capsule from 1955 (prices aside).

Joe Rogers Jr. became CEO in 1973. He built a reputation for management skills, establishing a rigorous training program for store managers and instituted incentive-based compensation in an effort to retain employees.

In 1981 the US Department of Labor took exception to the company's practice of paying inordinately low wages to restaurant managers who also served as cooks. The company won the case in 1983 and has since become tight-lipped about its operations.

In 1997 the Waffle House had another scrape with the law. A US district judge found the company guilty of sexual harassment and "egregious conduct" against a former human resources employee. The judge ordered the company to pay $8.1 million in damages. The following year Waffle House showed signs of rethinking its tight-lipped stance when it hired a public relations firm.

Waffle House's largest franchisee, Northlake Foods, was hit by a racial discrimination suit in 1999. Five African-American men alleged that they were denied service by a white cook at an Atlanta-area restaurant. Also that year a Waffle House waitress in Mobile, Alabama, won $10 million from a lottery ticket left by a customer as a tip. Four of her co-workers won a share in the winnings after demonstrating in court that the employees had a "share the wealth" agreement.

In 2000 the company found itself the subject of another race-related lawsuit when a manager said he was ordered to fire black employees in order to have the restaurant's staff reflect the racial makeup of its mostly white town. The following year a federal judge ordered Waffle House franchisee Treetop Enterprises to pay nearly $3 million to 125 employees who worked more than 80 hours a week despite allegedly being hired to work 53-hour weeks.

In 2003 and 2004 Waffle House faced more racial-discrimination lawsuits in five states, including Georgia. The company celebrated its 50th anniversary in 2005.

EXECUTIVES

Founder: Tom Forkner
Chairman and CEO: Joe W. Rogers Jr., age 61
President and COO: Bert Thornton
VP Advocacy: Don Balfour
VP Human Resources: Will Mizell
VP Public Relations and Marketing: Pat Warner
Media Contact: Kelly Thrasher

LOCATIONS

HQ: Waffle House, Inc.
5986 Financial Dr., Norcross, GA 30071
Phone: 770-729-5700   **Fax:** 770-729-5999
Web: www.wafflehouse.com

COMPETITORS

Bob Evans
Brinker
Buffets Holdings
Carlson Restaurants
CBRL Group
Darden
Denny's
DineEquity
Huddle House
OSI Restaurant Partners
Perkins & Marie Callender's
Ruby Tuesday
Shoney's
Steak n Shake

Wakefern Food

Some might say you aren't shopping right if you don't get your groceries from stores supplied by this company. Wakefern Food is one of the leading wholesale distribution cooperatives in the US, supplying groceries and other merchandise to a chain of nearly 200 ShopRite supermarkets in five eastern states. The company supplies both national brand and private-label products (ShopRite, Chef's Express, Readington Farms) to its member stores; Wakefern also offers advertising, merchandising, insurance, and other business support services. The co-op, which boasts more than 40 members, was founded by seven grocers in 1946.

While the ShopRite chain boasts a loyal following in its core markets, the supermarkets have been feeling the pinch from rivals in the price-competitive grocery business. The company is especially feeling pressure from non-supermarket chains such as Wal-Mart, CVS/Caremark, and Wawa.

The cooperative added to its footprint in 2007 when it acquired about 10 underperforming retail locations from Stop & Shop. The stores, located mostly in South Jersey, were rebranded under the ShopRite banner.

HISTORY

Wakefern Food was founded in 1946 by seven New York- and New Jersey-based grocers: Louis Weiss, Sam and Al Aidekman, Abe Kesselman, Dave Fern, Sam Garb, and Albert Goldberg (the company's name is made up of the first letters of the last names of first five of those founders). Like many cooperatives, the association sought to lower costs by increasing its buying power as a group.

They each put in $1,000 and began operating a 5,000-sq.-ft. warehouse, often putting in double time to keep both their stores and the warehouse running. The shopkeepers' collective buying power proved valuable, enabling the grocers to stock many items at the same prices as their larger competitors.

In 1951 Wakefern members began pooling their resources to buy advertising space. A common store name — ShopRite — was chosen, and each week co-op members met to decide which items would be sale priced. Within a year, membership had grown to over 50. Expansion became a priority, and in the mid-1950s co-op members united in small groups to take over failed supermarkets. One such group, called the

Supermarkets Operating Co. (SOC), was formed in 1956. Within 10 years it had acquired a number of failed stores, remodeled them, and given them the ShopRite name.

During the late 1950s sales at ShopRite stores slumped after Wakefern decided to buck the supermarket trend of offering trading stamps (which could then be exchanged for gifts), figuring that offering the stamps would ultimately lead to higher food prices. The move initially drove away customers, but Wakefern cut grocery prices across the board and sales returned. The company did embrace another supermarket trend: stocking stores with nonfood items.

The co-op was severely shaken in 1966 when SOC merged with General Supermarkets, a similar small group within Wakefern, becoming Supermarkets General Corp. (SGC). SGC was a powerful entity, with 71 supermarkets, 10 drugstores, six gas stations, a wholesale bakery, and a discount department store. Many Wakefern members opposed the merger and attempted to block the action with a court order. By 1968 SGC had beefed up its operations to include department store chains as well as its grocery stores. In a move that threatened to break Wakefern, SGC broke away from the co-op, and its stores were renamed Pathmark.

Wakefern not only weathered the storm, it grew under the direction of chairman and CEO Thomas Infusino, elected shortly after the split. The co-op focused on asserting its position as a seller of low-priced products. Wakefern developed private-label brands, including the ShopRite brand. In the 1980s members began operating larger stores and adding more nonfood items to the ShopRite product mix. With its number of superstores on the rise and facing increased competition from club stores in 1992, Wakefern opened a centralized, nonfood distribution center in New Jersey.

In 1995, 30-year Wakefern veteran Dean Janeway was elected president of the co-op. The company debuted its ShopRite MasterCard, co-branded with New Jersey's Valley National Bank, in 1996. The following year the co-op purchased two of its customers' stores in Pennsylvania, then threatened to close them when contract talks with the local union deteriorated. In 1998 Wakefern settled the dispute, then sold the stores.

The company partnered with Internet bidding site priceline.com in 1999, offering customers an opportunity to bid on groceries and then pick them up at ShopRite stores. Big V, Wakefern's biggest customer, filed for Chapter 11 bankruptcy protection in 2000 and said it was ending its distribution agreement with the co-op. In July 2002, however, Wakefern's ShopRite Supermarkets subsidiary acquired all of Big V's assets for approximately $185 million in cash and assumed liabilities.

Infusino retired in May 2005 after 35 years with Wakefern Food. He was succeeded by former vice chairman Joseph Colalillo.

EXECUTIVES

Chairman and CEO: Joseph S. (Joe) Colalillo, age 47
President and COO: Dean Janeway
CFO: Ken Jasinkiewicz
EVP, Marketing: Joseph Sheridan
SVP and CIO: Natan Tabak
VP, Corporate and Consumer Affairs: Mary Ellen Gowin
VP, Human Resources: Ernie Bell
VP, Corporate Merchandising and Advertising: Bill Crombie
VP, Information Services Division: Alan Aront
VP, Logistics: Pete Rolandelli

Director, Advertising: Karen McAuvic
Director, Marketing: Loren Weinstein
**Director Corporate Communications and Media
 Relations:** Karen Meleta
Director Wholesale Division: Dave Baer
Manager, Consumer Affairs: Cheryl Macik
President and COO, ShopRite Supermarkets:
 Kevin Mannix

LOCATIONS

HQ: Wakefern Food Corporation
 600 York St., Elizabeth, NJ 07207
Phone: 908-527-3300   **Fax:** 908-527-3397
Web: www.shoprite.com

COMPETITORS

A&P
Acme Markets
C&S Wholesale
CVS Caremark
IGA
Jetro Cash & Carry
Krasdale Foods
Stop & Shop
SUPERVALU
Wal-Mart
Wawa, Inc.

HISTORICAL FINANCIALS

Company Type: Cooperative

Income Statement				FYE: September 30
	REVENUE ($ mil.)	**NET INCOME** ($ mil.)	**NET PROFIT MARGIN**	**EMPLOYEES**
9/07	9,900	—	—	50,000
9/06	7,500	—	—	50,000
9/05	7,239	—	—	50,000
9/04	7,116	—	—	50,000
9/03	6,578	—	—	50,000
Annual Growth	10.8%	—	—	0.0%

Revenue History

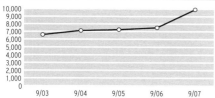

Walsh Group

The Walsh Group erects walls, halls, malls, and more. Operating through Walsh Construction and Archer Western Contractors, the group provides design/build, general contracting, and construction services for industrial, public, and commercial projects throughout the US. Walsh provides complete project management services, from demolition and planning to general contracting and finance. The company is a major player in bridge and highway construction, as well as in water treatment facilities; it also renovates and restores buildings. The Walsh family still owns the firm, founded in 1898.

EXECUTIVES

Chairman and CEO: Matthew M. Walsh
President; President, Walsh Construction:
 Daniel J. Walsh
CFO, Secretary, and Treasurer: Larry J. Kibbon
VP Business Development: Patrick M. Donley
Human Resources Manager: Rhonda Hardwick
Auditors: Wolf & Company, P.C.

LOCATIONS

HQ: The Walsh Group
 929 W. Adams St., Chicago, IL 60607
Phone: 312-563-5400   **Fax:** 312-563-5420
Web: www.walshgroup.com

The Walsh Group has regional offices in Arlington, Texas; Atlanta; Boston; Chicago; Detroit; Jacksonville, Florida; LaPorte, Indiana; Phoenix; Pittsburgh; Raleigh, North Carolina; Richmond, Virginia; and San Diego.

PRODUCTS/OPERATIONS

Projects

Airports
Athletic facilities
Bridges
Conference centers
Correctional facilities
Data centers
Educational facilities
Entertainment
Government
Health care
High rise residential
Highways and bridges
Hotels
Interiors
Laboratories
Parking garages
Renovations
Retail centers
Senior housing
Treatment plants
Warehouse and distribution

COMPETITORS

APAC
Bechtel
Black & Veatch
Bovis Lend Lease
Brasfield & Gorrie
C. G. Schmidt
CH2M HILL
Flatiron Construction
Fluor
Granite Construction
Hunt Companies
Hunt Construction
Jacobs Engineering
Lane Construction
McCarthy Building
Modern Continental Companies
MWH Global
Peter Kiewit Sons'
Skanska
TIC Holdings
Turner Corporation
Vecellio & Grogan

HISTORICAL FINANCIALS

Company Type: Private

Income Statement				FYE: December 31
	REVENUE ($ mil.)	**NET INCOME** ($ mil.)	**NET PROFIT MARGIN**	**EMPLOYEES**
12/07	3,600	—	—	10,500
12/06	2,900	—	—	6,000
12/05	2,335	—	—	5,000
12/04	1,955	—	—	4,200
12/03	1,725	—	—	3,750
Annual Growth	20.2%	—	—	29.4%

Revenue History

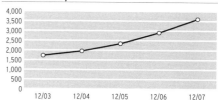

Warren Equities

Warren Equities fills car tanks and stomachs in the US Northeast. The holding company sells fuel and groceries from more than 300 Xtra Mart brand service stations and convenience stores from Maine to Virginia. Warren's distribution companies supply those stores, as well as independent outlets, with gasoline, grocery, and tobacco products. Other Warren companies trade and store petroleum, provide environmental testing services, and make promotional signs and clothing. Founder Warren Alpert's foundation gives annual grants to medical researchers. Alpert died in 2007. His last gift was a $100 million grant to the medical school at Brown Universtity.

Warren Alpert set up the company in 1950 after Standard Oil awarded him a distributorship. Over time, Alpert built Warren Equities into the holding company for wholesale and retail businesses.

EXECUTIVES

Chairman and CEO: Herbert (Herb) Kaplan
Vice Chairman: Edward M. Cosgrove
President and COO: August (Gus) Schiesser
EVP: Jeffery A. (Jeff) Walker
CFO and Treasurer: John T. Dziedzic
Controller and Assistant Treasurer: Richard J. Sawicki
Director Human Resources: Thomas (Tom) Palumbo

LOCATIONS

HQ: Warren Equities, Inc.
 27 Warren Way, Providence, RI 02905
Phone: 401-781-9900   **Fax:** 401-461-7160
Web: www.warreneq.com

Warren Equities operates in Connecticut, Maine, Maryland, Massachusetts, New Hampshire, New York, Pennsylvania, Rhode Island, and Virginia.

PRODUCTS/OPERATIONS

Major Subsidiaries

Drake Petroleum Company, Inc. (wholesale gasoline)
Warex Terminals Corporation (wholesale marketing)
Xtra Mart Convenience Stores (convenience stores)

COMPETITORS

7-Eleven
BP
Casey's General Stores
Crown Central
Cumberland Farms
Getty Petroleum Marketing
Global Partners
Motiva Enterprises
Sunoco
SUPERVALU
Wawa, Inc.

Washington Capitals

This company rules over hockey in the nation's capital. Lincoln Holdings owns and operates the Washington Capitals professional hockey franchise, which joined the National Hockey League in 1974. The team was founded by Washington Wizards owner Abe Pollin and has reached the Stanley Cup finals just once, losing to the Detroit Red Wings in 1998. Washington plays host at the Verizon Center, in which Lincoln Holdings owns a 45% stake. The group also owns the Washington Mystics WNBA and a 45% stake in the Wizards. Ted Leonsis, vice chairman of AOL, has controlled the hockey franchise since 1999.

The Caps made a return to the playoffs at the end of the 2007-08 season, ending a four-year drought that had drawn the ire of fans. The boost came thanks in part to Alexander Ovechkin, a top prospect from Russia who joined the team in 2005. The team had also hired Bruce Boudreau as head coach during that season, replacing longtime coach Glen Hanlon.

Lincoln Holdings got into the basketball business in 2005 when the group purchased the Mystics from Pollin's Washington Sports & Entertainment. Dr. Sheila Johnson, a co-founder of BET Holdings and a partner in Lincoln Holdings, was named president of the women's basketball team, becoming the first black woman to run a WNBA franchise.

Other investors in Lincoln Holdings include team president Dick Patrick and Capital One Financial chairman Richard Fairbank.

EXECUTIVES

Chairman: Ted Leonsis
President: Richard M. (Dick) Patrick
CFO: Ellen Folts
SVP and Chief Marketing Officer: Tim McDermott
VP and General Manager: George McPhee
Head Coach: Bruce Boudreau, age 53
VP Finance: Keith Burrows
VP Communications and Chief Communications Officer: Kurt Kehl
Senior Director of Operations: George Parr
Director of Player Personnel: Brian MacLellan
Director Scouting Operations: Kris Wagner
Director Media Relations: Nate Ewell

LOCATIONS

HQ: Lincoln Holdings LLC
627 N. Glebe Rd., Ste. 850, Arlington, VA 22203
Phone: 202-266-2200   **Fax:** 202-266-2360
Web: www.washingtoncaps.com

The Washington Capitals play in the 18,277-seat capacity Verizon Center in Washington, DC.

PRODUCTS/OPERATIONS

Championship Trophies

Prince of Wales Trophy (1998)

COMPETITORS

Atlanta Thrashers
Carolina Hurricanes
Florida Panthers
Tampa Bay Lightning

Washington Companies

Crossing the Delaware was the feat of one Washington, but traversing several industries is The Washington Companies' accomplishment. The group's activities include aviation technology, construction and mining, heavy equipment sales, marine transportation, and rail transportation. Seaspan International, one of the group's marine transportation units, is a leading Canadian tug and barge operator. (The group's containership operations have been spun off as Seaspan Corp.) Other affiliates include Montana Resources, which mines and mills copper and other minerals, and Montana Rail Link, which offers freight transportation. Billionaire Dennis Washington owns controlling stakes in all of the group's companies.

Although Dennis Washington's ownership stakes unite The Washington Companies, separate boards of directors and management teams oversee the individual companies under the group's umbrella. One of the companies, Washington Corporations, handles administrative functions for other companies in the group.

EXECUTIVES

Chairman: Dennis R. Washington, age 74
President; President, Washington Corporations: Lawrence R. (Larry) Simkins
CFO, Washington Marine Group: Nancy L. McKenzie
Director, Human Resources, Washington Corporations: Jon Barlow
Chairman and CEO, Aviation Partners; Chairman, Aviation Partners Boeing: Joseph (Joe) Clark
President, Modern Machinery: Brian Sheridan
President, Montana Resources: Rolin P. Erickson
President, Montana Rail Link: Thomas J. Walsh
President, Coast Engine and Equipment: David S. (Dave) Swanson
President and CEO, Aviation Partners Boeing: John R. Reimers
President, Envirocon: Jack Gilbraith
President, Seaspan International: Stephen A. (Steve) Frasher
President, Washington Development: Paul W. Keiper
President, Southern Railway of British Columbia: Frank J. Butzelaar

LOCATIONS

HQ: The Washington Companies
101 International Way, Missoula, MT 59808
Phone: 406-523-1300   **Fax:** 406-523-1399
Web: www.washcorp.com

PRODUCTS/OPERATIONS

Selected Operating Units

Aviation technology
   Aviation Partners, Inc. (develops and markets high-performance wingtips for jet industry)
Construction and mining
   Envirocon, Inc. (remediation, reclamation, and construction)
   Montana Resources, Inc. (mining and milling)
Heavy equipment sales
   Modern Machinery, Inc.
Marine transportation
   Norsk Pacific Steamship
   Seaspan Coastal Intermodal, Ltd.
   Seaspan International Ltd. (Canada)
   Washington Marine Group Shipyards
Rail transportation
   Montana Rail Link, Inc.
   Southern Railway of British Columbia Ltd. (SRY, Canada)
Real estate and professional services
   Washington Corporations (administrative services for group companies)
   Washington Development (oversees real estate transactions of group companies)

COMPETITORS

Alexander & Baldwin
APL
ASARCO
Canadian Pacific Railway
Crowley Maritime
Evergreen Marine
Freeport-McMoRan
Union Pacific

HISTORICAL FINANCIALS

Company Type: Group

Income Statement				FYE: December 31
	REVENUE ($ mil.)	NET INCOME ($ mil.)	NET PROFIT MARGIN	EMPLOYEES
12/07	4,300	—	—	1,900
12/06	1,700	—	—	4,300
12/05	1,300	—	—	4,100
Annual Growth	81.9%	—	—	(31.9%)

Revenue History

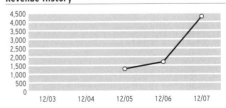

Wawa, Inc.

It's not baby talk — when folks say they need to go to the Wawa, they need groceries. Wawa runs 570-plus Wawa Food Markets in Delaware, Maryland, New Jersey, Pennsylvania, and Virginia. Wawa stores are noted for their coffee and their salad and deli offerings, including hoagie sandwiches; more than 200 stores sell gas. Unlike many convenience store chains, Wawa has its own dairy, supplying Wawa stores and about 1,000 hospitals, schools, and other institutions. The company opened its first store in 1964, but its roots go back to an iron foundry begun in 1803 by the Wood family; food operations began in 1902 when George Wood started a dairy in Wawa, Pennsylvania. The Wood family owns 52% of the company.

Howard Stoeckel succeeded Richard Wood as CEO of the company in January 2005 (Wood remained chairman). Stoeckel is the first non-family member to lead Wawa.

Wawa has been busy expanding its line of private-label foods and other merchandise in an effort to differentiate itself from its competition. Since the launch of its own brand of bottled water in 2004, the company has introduced about 300 packaged items, including candy, yogurt, and tea — under the Wawa label.

In mid-2006 the convenience store operator opened its first airport location at the Northeast Philadelphia Airport.

EXECUTIVES

Chairman: Richard D. (Dick) Wood Jr.
President and CEO: Howard B. Stoeckel
SVP Store Operations: David Johnston
VP, Procurement and Logistics: Jim Bluebello
Chief People Officer: Harry McHugh
Chief Marketing Officer: Carol Jensen
CIO: Neil McCarthy
Director, Food Service: Michael (Mike) Sherlock
Director, IT Architecture: Marty Maglio
Director, Store Operations Technology:
 John Cunningham
Manager, Public Relations: Lori Bruce

LOCATIONS

HQ: Wawa, Inc.
 260 W. Baltimore Pike, Red Roof, Wawa, PA 19063
Phone: 610-358-8000 **Fax:** 610-358-8878
Web: www.wawa.com

PRODUCTS/OPERATIONS

Selected Products and Private-Label Brands
Bakery (Wawa)
Cold beverages (Wawa)
Hoagies (Built-to-Order, Shorti)
Hot breakfast
 Coffee (Freshly Brewed Coffee)
 Hash browns
 Hot breakfast sandwiches (Sizzli)
Party platters
Ready-to-eat foods (Wawa Express)
Sides
Soups

Wawa Dairy Division
Products
 100% orange juice (All Florida)
 Butter
 Buttermilk
 Cappuccino
 Cottage cheese
 Cream cheese
 Eggs
 Fruit juices and drinks
 Half and half
 Ice cream mixes
 Margarine
 Milk (including lactose-free, chocolate, and
  strawberry)
 Non-dairy coffee blend
 Shakes
 Sour cream
 Spring water (Deer Park)
 Tea
 Whipping cream
 Yogurt (Dannon)
Customers
 Bakeries
 Colleges
 Hospitals
 Hotels
 Nursing homes
 Restaurants
 School districts
 Universities
 Wawa Food Markets

COMPETITORS

7-Eleven
A&P
Chevron
Cumberland Farms
Exxon
Foodarama Supermarkets
Genuardi's
Getty Realty
Hess Corporation
Kroger
Motiva Enterprises
Sheetz
Subway
Uni-Marts
Village Super Market
Warren Equities
Wegmans

HISTORICAL FINANCIALS
Company Type: Private

Income Statement
FYE: December 31

	REVENUE ($ mil.)	NET INCOME ($ mil.)	NET PROFIT MARGIN	EMPLOYEES
12/07	5,050	—	—	16,426
12/06	4,670	—	—	16,866
12/05	3,905	—	—	15,999
Annual Growth	13.7%	—	—	1.3%

Revenue History

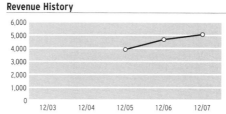

W. B. Doner & Company

This company brings marketing skills to the party. W. B. Doner & Company, which does business as Doner, is the largest independent advertising agency in the US, boasting a client roster that includes SIRIUS XM Radio and Mazda. It provides creative ad development and campaign management services, along with media planning and buying. Founded by Wilfred Broderick Doner in 1937, the firm has created classic campaigns for such customers as Timex ("Takes a licking and keeps on ticking") and Klondike Bar ("What would you do for a Klondike Bar?"). It is controlled by a management group that includes chairman and CEO Alan Kalter and vice chairmen John DeCerchio and Barry Levine.

Doner has picked up several top brands as clients, including Hotels.com (under Expedia) and Lexmark. It also struck a chord with its Mr. Six campaign for theme park operator Six Flags. In 2006, though, it lost a major account (valued at $135 million) for consumer electronics retailer Circuit City. Going forward, Doner plans to grow by expanding its interactive marketing and online advertising services and catering to new and emerging media channels.

In the US, Doner has offices in Cleveland, Detroit, Los Angeles, and Tampa. Internationally, the firm has facilities in Canada and in the UK, where it operates under the banner Doner Cardwell Hawkins.

EXECUTIVES

Chairman and CEO: Alan Kalter
Vice Chairman and CFO: H. Barry Levine
EVP and Chief Marketing Officer: James Ward
EVP and Chief Strategy Officer: David DeMuth
EVP and Director Operations: Sue Guise
EVP and General Manager, Direct: Ted Thompson
EVP and Chief Creative Officer: Rob Strasberg
EVP and Chief Media Officer: Greg Clausen
SVP and Chief Digital Officer: Brett Groom
Director Human Resources: Carol Cothern
President, Newport Beach: Tim Blett

LOCATIONS

HQ: W. B. Doner & Company
 25900 Northwestern Hwy., Southfield, MI 48075
Phone: 248-354-9700 **Fax:** 248-827-0880
Web: www.wbdoner.com

COMPETITORS

Arnold Worldwide
BBDO Detroit
Campbell Mithun
Campbell-Ewald
C-K
Deutsch, Inc.
Euro RSCG
Fallon Worldwide
GSD&M Idea City
Hill, Holliday
JWT
Leo Burnett
Martin Agency
Publicis USA
Saatchi & Saatchi
TBWA Worldwide
Team One
Wieden and Kennedy
Young & Rubicam

Webloyalty.com

Webloyalty.com offers services such as consumer membership programs for companies that are looking to garner better relationships with its customers. The company serves e-commerce, travel, and other fee-based Web sites by providing travel discounts and promotional offers on entertainment, retail merchandise, and home computer protection software seamlessly (Webloyalty sends the offers out but they are branded with the clients' Web site), building customer loyalty. Established in 1999, Webloyalty is owned by private equity firm General Atlantic LLC.

The company's business strategy involves expanding internationally into key markets involving savvy online communities. In mid-2007, Webloyalty opened its first office overseas, in London. The following year, it opened a new office in Paris (consumers shopping online in France now have the option to join its "Remises & Réductions" promotional program). The company plans to open an additional office in Germany in the future.

EXECUTIVES

CEO: Richard J. (Rick) Fernandes, age 49
President: Vincent R. D'Agostino
SVP Information Technology and Operations: Jeffrey Kendall
SVP Account Management: Eli Chalfin
SVP Business Development: Matt Gilbert
SVP Marketing: Martin Isaac
SVP Corporate Development and Corporate Marketing: David Lynch
SVP Finance: Gina Carey
SVP and General Counsel: Sloane Levy
CTO: Gary Cacace

LOCATIONS

HQ: Webloyalty.com, Inc.
   101 Merritt 7, 4th Fl., Norwalk, CT 06851
Phone: 203-846-3300   **Fax:** 203-846-4100
Web: webloyalty.com

COMPETITORS

Advantex Marketing International
Affinion Group
Loyaltyworks
Maritz Loyalty Marketing
Schoolpop
Synapse Group

HISTORICAL FINANCIALS

Company Type: Private

Income Statement

FYE: December 31

	REVENUE ($ mil.)	NET INCOME ($ mil.)	NET PROFIT MARGIN	EMPLOYEES
12/07	193	—	—	330
12/06	144	—	—	300
12/05	109	—	—	220
12/04	86	—	—	175
12/03	55	—	—	—
Annual Growth	36.6%	—	—	23.5%

Revenue History

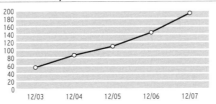

Wegmans Food Markets

One name strikes fear in the hearts of supermarket owners in New York, New Jersey, Pennsylvania, and now, Maryland and Virginia: Wegmans Food Markets. The grocery chain owns about 70 stores, but they are hardly typical. Much larger than most supermarkets (up to 160,000 sq. ft.), they offer specialty shops such as huge in-store cafes, cheese shops with some 400 different varieties, and French-style pastry shops. The company is known for its gourmet cooking classes and an extensive employee-training program. Wegmans closed its chain of Chase-Pitkin Home and Garden home-improvement stores in 2005. Founded in 1916, the company is owned and run by the family of founder John Wegman.

Former chairman Robert B. Wegman (who died in April 2006) stepped down as CEO of the company in January 2005 and was succeeded by his son Danny Wegman. Concurrently, Colleen Wegman, Danny Wegman's daughter, was named president of the grocery chain.

The company plans to open a second store in Maryland in 2009. (Its first supermarket in that state opened in 2005.) The chain debuted in Virginia in 2004, followed by a second store opening there in early 2005.

Wegmans has landed on *FORTUNE* magazine's list of the "100 Best Companies to Work For," in each of the past 10 years and captured the #1 spot in 2005.

To emphasize its commitment to health, Wegmans in early 2008 stopped selling cigarettes and other tobacco products.

Citing competition from national home improvement chains Home Depot and Lowe's, Wegmans has closed all 14 of its Chase-Pitkin Home and Garden Centers. (Chase-Pitkin employed 507 full-time and 1,660 part-time workers.)

EXECUTIVES

Chairman and CEO: Daniel R. (Danny) Wegman
President: Colleen Wegman, age 33
EVP Operations: Jack DePeters
SVP and CFO: James (Jim) Leo
SVP Consumer Affairs: Mary Ellen Burris
SVP Real Estate Development: Ralph Uttaro
SVP Syracuse Division: Shari Constantine
SVP Human Resources: Gerald Pierce
VP People: Karen Shadders
VP: Nicole Wegman
CIO: Donald (Don) Reeve

LOCATIONS

HQ: Wegmans Food Markets, Inc.
   1500 Brooks Ave., Rochester, NY 14603
Phone: 585-328-2550   **Fax:** 585-429-3285
Web: www.wegmans.com

2007 Stores

	No.
New York	48
Pennsylvania	12
New Jersey	7
Virginia	3
Maryland	1
Total	**71**

PRODUCTS/OPERATIONS

Selected Products and Operations

Asian foods
Bath and body
Bulk foods
Cheeses
Coffee/cappuccino Bar
Cooking classes
Deli
Dry cleaning
European bread bakery
Floral department
Food from around the world
Gift and fruit baskets
Kosher deli
Market café
Meat service
Nature's Marketplace (organic health and food items)
Organic produce
Pasta Station
Pharmacy
Photo processing and photo enlarging
Photocopies
Pizza Primo
Ready-to-cook meat and seafood
Rotisserie
Rug Doctor carpet cleaner rental
Seafood
Sub sandwiches
Sushi bar
UPS parcel service
Video player and game system rentals
Videos and DVDs
WKids Fun Center
Wokery

COMPETITORS

A&P	Penn Traffic
Foodarama Supermarkets	Safeway
Genuardi's	SUPERVALU
Giant Eagle	TOPS Markets
Giant Food Stores	Wal-Mart
Golub	Wawa, Inc.
IGA	Weis Markets

HISTORICAL FINANCIALS

Company Type: Private

Income Statement

FYE: December 31

	REVENUE ($ mil.)	NET INCOME ($ mil.)	NET PROFIT MARGIN	EMPLOYEES
12/07	4,500	—	—	37,602
12/06	4,100	—	—	35,798
12/05	3,800	—	—	35,000
12/04	3,600	—	—	32,000
12/03	3,300	—	—	32,000
Annual Growth	8.1%	—	—	4.1%

Revenue History

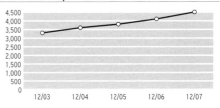

Weil, Gotshal & Manges

The seeds of today's Weil, Gotshal & Manges may have been planted in New York, but over the years the law firm's branches have spread far and wide. Founded in 1931, Weil Gotshal has more than 15 offices, not only in the US but also in Europe and the Asia/Pacific region. It has more than 1,200 lawyers overall. The firm maintains a full range of business-oriented practices, which it organizes into five main areas: business finance and restructuring; corporate; litigation and regulatory; tax; and trusts and estates. Clients have included CBS Broadcasting, General Electric, and HM Capital Partners.

EXECUTIVES

Chairman and CEO: Stephen J. Dannhauser
CFO: Norman W. LaCroix
Executive Director: David Strumeyer
Director Attorney Programs and Resources:
 Lisa I. Cuevas
Director Human Resources: Michael R. (Mike) Lewis
Director Marketing and Business Development:
 Mark P. Messing
Director Attorney Development: Sara B. Littauer
Director Global Diversity: Meredith Moore
Managing Partner Washington, DC; Co-Head, Products Liability and Mass Torts Practice Group:
 Michael J. (Mike) Lyle, age 44
Co-Head, Products Liability and Mass Torts Practice Group: Arvin Maskin
Manager Media Relations: Michael A. Ford
Corporate Department Business Manager: Kathie J. Lee
CIO: Ian M. Miller

LOCATIONS

HQ: Weil, Gotshal & Manges LLP
 767 5th Ave., New York, NY 10153
Phone: 212-310-8000   **Fax:** 212-310-8007
Web: www.weil.com

PRODUCTS/OPERATIONS

Selected Practice Areas

Business finance and restructuring

Corporate
 Banking and finance
 Capital markets
 Corporate governance
 Mergers and acquisitions
 Private equity
 Real estate transactions and finance
 Structured finance/derivatives

Litigation and regulatory
 Antitrust/competition
 Appellate
 Bankruptcy litigation
 Complex commercial litigation
 Employment
 Financial services
 Global dispute resolution
 Intellectual property and media
 International trade
 Patent appellate
 Patent litigation
 Product liability/mass tort/environmental
 Securities/corporate governance

Tax

Trusts and estates

COMPETITORS

Cleary Gottlieb	Sidley Austin
Clifford Chance	Simpson Thacher
Cravath, Swaine	Skadden, Arps
Paul, Weiss, Rifkind	Sullivan & Cromwell
Proskauer Rose	Wachtell, Lipton
Shearman & Sterling	White & Case

HISTORICAL FINANCIALS
Company Type: Partnership

Income Statement
FYE: December 31

	REVENUE ($ mil.)	NET INCOME ($ mil.)	NET PROFIT MARGIN	EMPLOYEES
12/07	1,175	—	—	—
12/06	1,050	—	—	2,800
12/05	1,017	—	—	3,000
Annual Growth	7.5%	—	—	(6.7%)

Revenue History

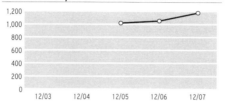

The Weitz Company

It took wits for The Weitz Company to become a top US general building contractor. Founded in 1855 by carpenter Charles H. Weitz, the company was run by the Weitz family for four generations before becoming employee-owned. It provides general contracting, construction management, and design/build services, constructing everything from office buildings, industrial plants, senior communities, and schools to hotels, golf courses, supermarkets, and malls. Weitz builds supermarkets and warehouse/distribution centers through its Hy-Vee Weitz unit.

Weitz affiliate companies go beyond the construction industry. Through subsidiaries the company offers construction products distribution, insurance, home security solutions, and document management services. Its capital resources group provides funding to developers and owners for various building projects.

Its 2006 acquisition of Miller/Watts Constructors increased Weitz's presence in the heavy engineering and military design/build fields.

EXECUTIVES

Chairman: Glenn H. De Stigter
President and CEO: Craig Damos
COO: Len Martling
CFO and Treasurer: Don Blum
SVP Human Resources: Kris Jensen
SVP: Larry Mohr
SVP, General Counsel, and Secretary: David Strutt
SVP, Weitz Senior Living: Fran Snook
VP Business Development: Clay Wells
CIO: Mark Federle

President, Rocky Mountain Division: Bill Hornaday
President, Iowa Division: Mike Tousley
President, Weitz Golf International: Greg Carlson
President, Kansas City Division: Radd Way
President, Southwest Division: Mike Bontrager
Auditors: KPMG Peat Marwick

LOCATIONS

HQ: The Weitz Company, LLC
 400 Locust St., Ste. 300, Des Moines, IA 50309
Phone: 515-698-4260   **Fax:** 515-697-5968
Web: www.weitz.com

PRODUCTS/OPERATIONS

Selected Subsidiaries

A+ Communications & Security/A+ Home Solutions
Capital Resources Group
Construction Products Distributors
Data Builder, Inc.
Hy-Vee Weitz Construction
Weitz Agricultural Services
Watts Constructors
Weitz Florida
Weitz Golf International
Weitz Industrial Services Group
Weitz Iowa
Weitz Rocky Mountain
Weitz Senior Living
Weitz Southwest

COMPETITORS

Barton Malow
Bovis Lend Lease
Brasfield & Gorrie
Centex
Charles Pankow Builders
Choate Construction
Clark Enterprises
Gilbane
Graycor
Hunt Construction
J. E. Dunn Construction
Miron Construction
Peter Kiewit Sons'
Skanska
Structure Tone
Sundt
Turner Corporation
Walsh Group
Whiting-Turner

HISTORICAL FINANCIALS
Company Type: Private

Income Statement
FYE: December 31

	REVENUE ($ mil.)	NET INCOME ($ mil.)	NET PROFIT MARGIN	EMPLOYEES
12/07	1,614	—	—	—
12/06	1,450	—	—	2,313
12/05	1,111	—	—	2,024
12/04	1,006	—	—	—
12/03	830	—	—	—
Annual Growth	18.1%	—	—	14.3%

Revenue History

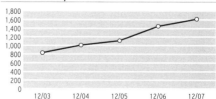

West Corporation

West Corporation keeps those phone lines buzzing. The company is one of the leading tele-services providers in the US with more than 30 call centers and seven automated voice and data centers around the country and abroad. It offers both inbound and outbound call handling for such things as customer support and technical assistance, as well as sales and marketing and order processing. It also offers automated and Web-based customer care programs for its customers. West additionally provides conference call services and it is one of the leading debt collections agencies in the country. In late 2006, an investment group led by Thomas H. Lee Partners and Quadrangle Group LLC acquired the company for $4.1 billion.

West Corp. has been diversifying its business through a series of acquisitions in recent years. Specifically, the company has been beefing up its conferencing segment, which includes an acquired business, Intercall, that accounts for more than 30% of West Corp.'s annual sales. In 2008 the company bolstered its conferencing operations even further when it bought France-based Genesys, a provider of Web-based conferencing services serving some 25 countries worldwide. Genesys will be integrated into Intercall's operations.

In 2006 West Corp. bought another prominent Web-conferencing services provider, Raindance Communications, for about $110 million. Further efforts by West Corp. to diversify its operations and revenue streams came later that year when it acquired 911 operations support business Intrado for about $465 million. It also snatched up InPulse Response Group, a sales outsourcer geared towards direct response marketers.

In 2007, AT&T accounted for about 15% of the company's total revenue.

HISTORY

After founding one of the first telemarketing firms in the nation in 1973 (called Mardex), and another one in 1978 (called WATS Marketing of America), Mary West founded her third company, West Telemarketing, in 1986 with Troy Eaden and other former WATS managers. Her husband, Gary, who had been chairman and CEO of WATS, joined the company in 1987. The company started its Omaha-based interactive services unit in 1989, and the following year it added an outbound call operation in San Antonio.

West Telemarketing and AT&T formed an alliance in 1990 to develop services based on interactive voice technology. The next year the company opened a second facility in San Antonio to process calls in Spanish. By 1994 West Telemarketing was processing more than 55 million calls a year.

The company went public as West TeleServices in 1996. It expanded by opening call centers in Arkansas, Illinois, Louisiana, and Nevada in 1998. The company's revenue stream took a blow in 1999 when AT&T, one of its largest clients, announced it would cut back its spending on telemarketing services. In 2000 West TeleServices unveiled its icare Web services program and the next year changed its name to West Corporation.

In response to changes in the telemarketing landscape, the company began diversifying its business through a series of acquisitions. It bought debt collection agency Attention in 2002

and the following year acquired teleconferencing firm Intercall for $340 million. West Corp. paid about $180 million for Worldwide Asset Management, beefing up its debt collection segment.

In 2006 West Corp. went private — it was acquired by an investment group featuring Thomas H. Lee Partners and Quadrangle Group LLC.

EXECUTIVES

Chairman and CEO: Thomas B. (Tom) Barker, age 53, $846,154 pay
President and COO: Nancee Shannon R. Berger, age 47, $548,077 pay
EVP Finance, CFO, and Treasurer: Paul M. Mendlik, age 53, $385,000 pay
EVP Administrative Services and Chief Administrative Officer; President, West Telemarketing: Jon R. (Skip) Hanson, age 41
EVP, General Counsel, and Secretary: David C. (Dave) Mussman, age 47
EVP Sales and Marketing: Michael M. (Mike) Sturgeon, age 46
EVP Corporate Development and Planning: David J. (Dave) Treinen, age 51
EVP, West Interactive: Pam Mortenson
President, InterCall: J. Scott Etzler, age 55, $425,000 pay
President, Intrado: George K. Heinrichs, age 49
President, West Asset Management: Michael E. (Mick) Mazour, age 48
President, West Communication Services: Steven M. Stangl, age 48, $397,116 pay
President, West Telemarketing: Mark V. Lavin, age 48
President, West Business Services: John Sanley
Director, Affirmative Action: Connie Hildabrand
Auditors: Deloitte & Touche LLP

LOCATIONS

HQ: West Corporation
11808 Miracle Hills Dr., Omaha, NE 68154
Phone: 402-963-1200 **Fax:** 402-963-1602
Web: www.west.com

PRODUCTS/OPERATIONS

2007 Sales

	$ mil.	% of total
Communications services	1,094.3	52
Conferencing services	727.8	35
Receivables services	283.5	13
Adjustments	(6.1)	—
Total	**2,099.5**	**100**

Selected Operations and Services

Communications
  Call center operations
  Customer relationship management
  Direct marketing
  Technical support
Conferencing
  Online training
  Teleconferencing
  Video conferencing
  Web conferencing
Receivables management
  Debt collection
  Debt purchasing
  Student loan collection

COMPETITORS

Accenture	Portfolio Recovery
ACT Teleconferencing	Premiere Global Services
APAC Customer Services	Rainmaker Systems
Asset Acceptance Capital	Sitel
Convergys	Sykes Enterprises
GC Services	Teleperformance USA
ICT Group	TeleTech
Infosys	TRG Customer Solutions
Medialink	Verizon Business
NCO	WebEx

HISTORICAL FINANCIALS

Company Type: Private

Income Statement

FYE: December 31

	REVENUE ($ mil.)	NET INCOME ($ mil.)	NET PROFIT MARGIN	EMPLOYEES
12/07	2,100	5	0.3%	42,000
12/06	1,856	69	3.7%	29,200
12/05	1,524	150	9.9%	28,100
12/04	1,217	113	9.3%	28,000
12/03	988	88	8.9%	24,000
Annual Growth	20.7%	(50.2%)	—	15.0%

Net Income History

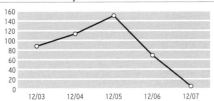

West Suburban Bancorp

As its name would indicate, West Suburban Bancorp provides banking services out in the *burbs*. West Suburban Bancorp is the holding company for West Suburban Bank, a community-oriented institution with about 40 branches serving Chicago's western suburbs. It offers personal and business deposit products such as checking, savings, and money market accounts, and certificates of deposit, as well as loan products including commercial, consumer, and home mortgage loans. Rounding out its offerings are Visa debit, credit, and gift cards, electronic banking, and investment and trust services offered through West Suburban Financial Services.

West Suburban Bancorp also runs an insurance agency, West Suburban Insurance Services, which offers auto, home, life, and major medical insurance, and a travel agency, Travel With West Suburban.

EXECUTIVES

Chairman, CEO, and VP; SVP Marketing, West Suburban Bank: Kevin J. Acker, age 58, $307,550 pay
President, CFO, and Director; SVP, Trust Officer, and Comptroller, West Suburban Bank: Duane G. Debs, age 51, $238,050 pay
COO; President, Trust Officer, and Director, West Suburban Bank: Keith W. Acker, age 58, $329,294 pay
VP; SVP Commercial Lending and Community Reinvestment Act Officer, West Suburban Bank: Michael P. Brosnahan, age 58, $253,728 pay
Chief Compliance Officer, West Suburban Bancorp and West Suburban Bank: David J. Mulkerin
Director Internal Audit; VP and Director Internal Audit, West Suburban Bank: Michael J. Lynch
Secretary and Treasurer; VP, Assistant Comptroller, and Investment Officer, West Suburban Bank: George E. Ranstead

SVP Business Development and Prepaid Solutions,
  West Suburban Bank: Daniel P. Grotto, $246,387 pay
SVP Consumer Lending, West Suburban Bank:
  James T. Chippas
VP Financial Analyst, Investment Officer, and
  Secretary, West Suburban Bank: Jay J. P. Greifenkamp
VP Human Resources, West Suburban Bank:
  Mary Ellen Condon

LOCATIONS

HQ: West Suburban Bancorp, Inc.
  711 S. Meyers Rd., Lombard, IL 60148
Phone: 630-629-4200   **Fax:** 630-629-0278
Web: www.westsuburbanbank.com

PRODUCTS/OPERATIONS

2007 Sales

	% of total
Interest	
Loans	63
Securities	15
Federal funds sold	2
Noninterest	
Prepaid solutions cards	10
Service fees on deposit accounts	5
Debit card fees	1
Bank-owned life insurance	1
Other	3
Total	**100**

COMPETITORS

AJS Bancorp	First Midwest Bancorp
American Chartered	Fort Dearborn Life
Bank of America	Harris Bankcorp
Bannockburn Travel	Marquette National
Management	MB Financial
Best Travel and Tours	Northern Trust
Citibank	Old Second Bancorp
Corporate Travel	Sammons Financial
Management	Taylor Capital
Fifth Third	U.S. Bancorp

HISTORICAL FINANCIALS

Company Type: Private

Income Statement   FYE: December 31

	ASSETS ($ mil.)	NET INCOME ($ mil.)	INCOME AS % OF ASSETS	EMPLOYEES
12/07	1,851	23	1.3%	616
12/06	1,877	25	1.4%	610
12/05	1,827	26	1.4%	616
12/04	1,748	24	1.4%	613
12/03	1,711	26	1.5%	629
Annual Growth	2.0%	(2.5%)	—	(0.5%)

2007 Year-End Financials

Equity as % of assets: 5.6%   Long-term debt ($ mil.): —
Return on assets: 1.3%   Sales ($ mil.): 136
Return on equity: 23.4%

Net Income History

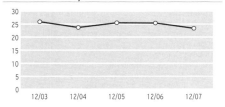

Western & Southern Financial

There's no need to stop and ask for directions if you're looking for a company that makes insurance and investments its cardinal concerns. Western & Southern, through its subsidiaries, offers a variety of life insurance products and annuities; accident and supplemental health coverage; mutual funds (Constellation family of funds) and other investment management products and services; and such financial services as mutual fund administration, trust services, financial advisory, and real estate development. The mutually owned company is licensed in most states and the District of Columbia. Western & Southern was founded in 1888.

Western & Southern Life Insurance provides whole life and cancer insurance products. Its Western-Southern Life Assurance subsidiary sells universal life and term insurance and annuities.

IFS Financial Services provides investment advisory, securities brokerage, and annuity products. Its Touchstone Advisors subsidiary offers a series of funds and annuities. Integrated Fund Services provides third-party administration for independent mutual funds.

Fort Washington Investment Advisors — which includes Todd Investment Advisors — manages private equity assets for corporate and government institutions and wealthy individuals; it has more than $29 billion under management.

Other divisions include Columbus Life Insurance, Integrity Life Insurance, Lafayette Life Insurance, and Eagle Realty Group (commercial real estate investment and management).

EXECUTIVES

Chairman, President, and CEO: John F. Barrett, age 58
SVP and CFO: Robert L. Walker
SVP and CIO: Clint D. Gibler
SVP and Chief Actuary: Nora E. Moushey
SVP and General Counsel: Donald J. Wuebbling
SVP, Corporate Financial Planning: Edward S. Heenan
SVP, Human Resources: Noreen Hayes
SVP, Insurance Operations: Constance M. Maccarone
SVP Special Projects: Carroll R. Hutchinson
VP and Treasurer: James J. (Jim) Vance
VP and CTO: Douglas Ross
VP and Medical Director: Keith T. Clark
VP Public Relations and Corporate Communications:
  Michael J. Laatsch
VP and Chief Underwriter: Keith W. Brown
Chairman Emeritus, Todd Investment Advisors:
  Bosworth M. Todd
Chairman, Todd Investment Advisors:
  Robert P. Bordogna
Auditors: Ernst & Young

LOCATIONS

HQ: Western & Southern Financial Group
  400 E. 4th St., Cincinnati, OH 45202
Phone: 513-629-1800   **Fax:** 513-629-1220
Web: www.westernsouthern.com

PRODUCTS/OPERATIONS

2007 Assets

	$ mil.	% of total
Investments		
Debt securities	20,758.9	63
Equity securities	2,795.8	8
Other invested assets	4,492.2	14
Other general account assets	2,296.4	7
Assets held in separate accounts	2,408.6	7
Total	**32,752.0**	**100**

2007 Sales

	$ mil.	% of total
Insurance premiums, product charges & other	928.2	33
Net investment income	1,449.2	52
Net realized investment gains	101.9	4
Other income	299.9	11
Total	**2,779.2**	**100**

Selected Subsidiaries and Affiliates

Columbus Life Insurance Company
  Capital Analysts Incorporated
Eagle Realty Group, LLC
Fort Washington Investment Advisors, Inc.
  Todd Investment Advisors, Inc.
IFS Financial Services, Inc.
  Touchstone Advisors, Inc.
  Touchstone Securities, Inc.
  W&S Financial Group Distributors, Inc.
Integrity Life Insurance Company
  National Integrity Life Insurance Company
The Lafayette Life Insurance Company
The Western and Southern Life Insurance Company
  Western-Southern Life Assurance Company

COMPETITORS

AEGON USA
Guardian Insurance and Annuity
Jackson National Life
Lincoln Financial Group
Nationwide Life Insurance
Phoenix Companies
Protective Life
Securian Financial
Security Benefit Group
Sentry Insurance

HISTORICAL FINANCIALS

Company Type: Private

Income Statement   FYE: December 31

	ASSETS ($ mil.)	NET INCOME ($ mil.)	INCOME AS % OF ASSETS	EMPLOYEES
12/07	32,752	365	1.1%	4,000
12/06	32,158	306	1.0%	4,000
12/05	30,764	268	0.9%	—
12/04	27,466	210	0.8%	—
12/03	26,306	190	0.7%	—
Annual Growth	5.6%	17.8%	—	0.0%

2007 Year-End Financials

Equity as % of assets: 15.1%   Long-term debt ($ mil.): —
Return on assets: 1.1%   Sales ($ mil.): 2,779
Return on equity: 7.2%

Net Income History

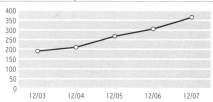

Whataburger

Fans of this chain know they can get quite a burger at the place with the orange and white roof. Whataburger Restaurants is a leading regional hamburger chain with more than 700 outlets in Texas and about 10 other states. The restaurants are typically open 24 hours a day and serve burgers and fries along with breakfast items (taquitos, pancakes), fajitas, chicken, and salads. Less than half of the company's restaurants are franchised. Loyal Whataburger fans can don the company's line of apparel sporting the chain's logo. The late Harmon Dobson founded the chain in Corpus Christi, Texas, in 1950. His family (including his son, chairman and CEO Thomas Dobson) continues to own the company.

Despite the fact that Whataburger has a much smaller presence than its national competitors, the chain continues to be a powerful player in its native Texas because of the intense loyalty of its customers. It continues to expand mostly through new franchising agreements.

In 2008 the company acquired its largest franchisee, Barrand, a Texas-based company with 47 Whataburger restaurants located in northeast Texas and the Florida Panhandle.

In 2007 Whataburger promoted company veteran Preston Atkinson to serve as president.

EXECUTIVES

Chairman and CEO: Thomas E. (Tom) Dobson, age 58
President and COO: Preston L. Atkinson
EVP: John M. (Mike) McLellan
VP Brand Management: Todd A. Coerver
VP Business Risks and Reporting: Jim Langenkamp
VP Property and Facilities: James G. Turcotte
VP Supply and Services: Dino Del Nano
VP Operations: Byron E. (Buddy) Reno
VP Human Resources: Marianne Dowdy
VP Stategic Planning: Rodney J. (Rod) Martin
Group Director Finance and Accounting: Ed Nelson
Director Communications: Pam Cox
Director Training and Development: Bill Adams
Director Marketing: Rich Scheffler
CIO: Karen H. Bird
Auditors: KPMG LLP

LOCATIONS

HQ: Whataburger Restaurants LP
1 Whataburger Way, Corpus Christi, TX 78411
Phone: 361-878-0650   **Fax:** 361-878-0473
Web: www.whataburger.com

COMPETITORS

AFC Enterprises
American Dairy Queen
Arby's
Burger King
Cajun Operating Company
Chick-fil-A
Jack in the Box
Krystal
McDonald's
Quiznos
Schlotzsky's
Sonic Corp.
Steak n Shake
Subway
Taco Bueno
Taco Cabana
Wendy's
YUM!

Wheaton Franciscan Services

Wheaton Franciscan Services (WFSI) is the parent company for more than 100 health care, housing, and social service organizations in Colorado, Illinois, Iowa, and Wisconsin. Through its Wheaton Franciscan Healthcare division, WFSI operates 15 hospitals including Affinity Health System, Marianjoy, Rush Oak Park Hospital, and United Hospital System. Its Franciscan Ministries division provides affordable housing units including assisted living facilities and housing for people living with HIV/AIDS. WFSI also includes home health agencies and physician offices. The health system was founded in 1983 and is sponsored by The Franciscan Sisters, Daughters of the Sacred Hearts of Jesus and Mary.

In 2008 the company completed construction on a new $90 million hospital facility in Franklin, Wisconsin. The Franklin Hospital provides emergency, surgery, imaging, and primary and specialty care.

EXECUTIVES

Chair: Joseph W. Lewis, age 72
President, CEO, and Director; President and CEO, Wheaton Franciscan Healthcare: John D. Oliverio
SVP and CFO: William H. Blum
SVP Mission Services: Terrance P. McGuire
SVP and CIO: Gregory A. Smith
SVP and Chief Administrative Officer: Jon L. Wachs
SVP, Human Resources: David A. Smith
SVP and General Counsel: Richard J. Canter
VP, Communications and Public Relations:
  Anne Ballentine
VP Strategic Planning: Abigail L. Navti
VP Organization and Leadership Development:
  Brenda Bowers

LOCATIONS

HQ: Wheaton Franciscan Services, Inc.
26 W. 171 Roosevelt Rd., Wheaton, IL 60189
Phone: 630-462-9271   **Fax:** 630-462-4977
Web: www.wfhealthcare.org/Wheaton

PRODUCTS/OPERATIONS

Selected Operations

Franciscan Ministries, Inc. (housing in Colorado,
  Illinois, Iowa, and Wisconsin)
Illinois
  Marianjoy Rehabilitation Hospital (Wheaton)
  Rush Oak Park Hospital (Oak Park)
Iowa
  Covenant Medical Center (Waterloo)
  Mercy Hospital (Oelwein)
  Sartori Memorial Hospital (Cedar Falls)
Wisconsin
  Affinity Health System (affiliated system)
    Calumet Medical Center (Chilton)
    Mercy Medical Center (Oshkosh)
    St. Elizabeth Hospital (Appleton)
  All Saints Hospital (Racine)
  Elmbrook Memorial Hospital (Brookfield)
  Franklin Hospital (Franklin)
  St. Francis Hospital (Milwaukee)
  St. Joseph Hospital (Milwaukee)
  United Hospital System, Inc. (affiliated system)
    Kenosha Medical Center (Kenosha)
    St. Catherine's Medical Center (Pleasant Prairie)
  Wisconsin Heart Hospital (Wauwatosa)

COMPETITORS

Alden Management Services
Elmhurst Memorial Healthcare
FHN
Froedtert Hospital
Hospital Sisters Health System
Kishwaukee Health System
Loyola University Health System
Rockford Health System
SwedishAmerican Health System

White & Case

One of the world's largest law firms, White & Case has buoyed its global reputation by establishing some 35 offices in locations spanning the US, Latin America, Europe, the Middle East, Africa, and Asia. It has some 2,300 lawyers overall. With the firm's global reach as its cornerstone, White & Case offers expertise in such areas as bankruptcy, corporate, intellectual property, litigation, project finance, and tax. The firm's client list has included major multinational companies such as Deutsche Bank, Royal Ahold, and Wal-Mart. White & Case was founded in 1901.

EXECUTIVES

Chairman: Hugh Verrier
COO: Gregory J. Dolan
CFO: Steve Wrede
Chief Administrative Officer: Richard M. McKenna
Chief Marketing Officer: Isabelle Young
Director Attorney Recruiting and Professional Development: Timm Whitney
Manager Legal Recruiting and Professional Development: Susanne L. Chapman
Manager Americas Media Relations:
  Nicholas (Nick) Clarke
Assistant Director Attorney Recruiting and Employment: Jane P. Stein

LOCATIONS

HQ: White & Case LLP
1155 Avenue of the Americas, New York, NY 10036
Phone: 212-819-8200   **Fax:** 212-354-8113
Web: www.whitecase.com

PRODUCTS/OPERATIONS

Selected Practice Areas

Antitrust
Asset Finance
Bank Advisory
Bank Finance
Banking
Capital Markets/Securities
Construction and Engineering
Corporate
Corporate Defense and Special Litigation
Energy, Infrastructure, and Project Finance
Environmental
European Union
Executive Compensation and Employee Benefits
Financial Restructuring and Insolvency
Global Equity Based Compensation
India
Insurance
Intellectual Property
International Arbitration
International Trade
Investment Funds
Labor, Employment, and Immigration Law
Latin America

Legislative/Law Reform
Litigation
Mergers and Acquisitions
Privacy
Private Clients
Private Equity
Privatization
Public Finance
Public International Law
Real Estate
Securitization
Sovereign
Tax
Technology
Telecommunications, Media, and Technology
Trade and Commodity Finance

COMPETITORS

Akin Gump	Latham & Watkins
Baker & McKenzie	Mayer Brown
Bryan Cave	Milbank, Tweed
Clifford Chance	Morgan, Lewis
Cravath, Swaine	Pillsbury Winthrop
Debevoise & Plimpton	Shaw Pittman
Dewey & LeBoeuf	Proskauer Rose
Freshfields	Sidley Austin
Holland & Knight	Skadden, Arps
Jones Day	Weil, Gotshal

HISTORICAL FINANCIALS
Company Type: Partnership

Income Statement				FYE: December 31
	REVENUE ($ mil.)	NET INCOME ($ mil.)	NET PROFIT MARGIN	EMPLOYEES
12/07	1,373	—	—	—
12/06	1,185	—	—	4,372
12/05	1,046	—	—	4,541
Annual Growth	14.6%	—	—	(3.7%)

Revenue History

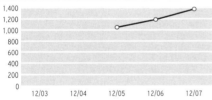

White Castle

The treasure room of this fast food fortress contains Slyders. White Castle System owns and operates more than 400 hamburger joints known for their little square burgers called Slyders. The meat patty is steamed over a bed of onions rather than grilled, and served on a steamed bun with a single slice of pickle. Patrons typically consume a sack of Slyders at a time. White Castle restaurants can be found in about a dozen states, primarily in the Midwest. The company also sells frozen Slyders through supermarket chains. The first fast food chain in

the US, White Castle was founded by Walter Anderson and real estate broker E. W. "Billy" Ingram in 1921. The Ingram family continues to control the company.

Little has changed at White Castle over the years, from its Slyders to its castle-shaped buildings, which has helped the chain establish strong loyalty among both customers and employees. Growth for the chain has been slow, however, due to the fact that the company does not franchise its restaurants. Yet change is slowly creeping into the mix at White Castle: The handful of new units it builds each year are now incorporating a slightly updated interior design. White Castle also sells branded items (caps, mugs, and shirts) to keep its loyal fans happy and engaged.

In addition to its hamburger business, White Castle System owns PSB Company, a subsidiary that makes metal products and equipment, including fixtures and cooking tools used at the company's restaurants. PSB also makes lawn spreaders under the PrizeLAWN brand.

EXECUTIVES

Chairman, President, and CEO:
Edgar Waldo (Bill) Ingram III, age 57
VP, CFO, and Treasurer: Russell (Russ) Meyer
VP, General Counsel, and Secretary: G. Roger Post
VP, Marketing and Site Development: Kim Kelly-Bartley
VP and General Manager, White Castle Distributing:
Rob Camp
VP, Assistant Secretary, and Corporate Counsel:
Nicholas W. Zuk
VP: Mike Smith
Assistant VP, Training and Human Resources:
John Kelley
Director, Human Resources: Heather Ward
Director, Marketing: Jamie Richardson
Director, Real Estate: Rob Albert
Director, Restaurant Operations: Lisa Ingram
Supervisor, Communications: Deborah P. Cline

LOCATIONS

HQ: White Castle System, Inc.
555 W. Goodale St., Columbus, OH 43215
Phone: 614-228-5781   **Fax:** 614-464-0596
Web: www.whitecastle.com

COMPETITORS

AFC Enterprises
American Dairy Queen
Arby's
Back Yard Burgers
Burger King
Cajun Operating Company
Checkers Drive-In
Chick-fil-A
Culver's
Hardee's
Jack in the Box
Krystal
McDonald's
Quiznos
Sonic Corp.
Subway
Wendy's
YUM!

Whiting-Turner Contracting

Whiting-Turner Contracting knows that in the construction industry you have to fish or cut bait. The employee-owned firm provides construction management, general contracting, and design/build services, primarily for large commercial, institutional, and infrastructure projects in the US. A key player in retail construction, the company also undertakes such projects as biotech cleanrooms, theme parks, educational facilities, stadiums, and corporate headquarters for such clients as AT&T and General Motors. Whiting-Turner Contracting has some 30 locations throughout the US. G. W. C. Whiting and LeBaron Turner founded the company in 1909 to build sewer lines.

Whiting-Turner Contracting's project portfolio includes the Joseph B. Whitehead Building at Emory University, Vanderbilt Hall at Yale University, and a vaccine facility at Chesapeake Biological Laboratories, Inc. Projects for the firm's hometown of Baltimore have included the city's convention center and Harborplace.

EXECUTIVES

President: Willard Hackerman
SEVP Finance and CFO: Charles A. (Chuck) Irish
SVP (Baltimore): Gino J. Gemignani
SVP (Irvine, California): Len Cannatelli Jr.
SVP (New Haven, Connecticut): Daniel (Dan) Bauer
SVP (Washington, DC/Bethesda, Maryland):
Richard L. Vogel Jr.
VP Marketing: David Boucher
Director Human Resources: Edward Spaulding
Auditors: PricewaterhouseCoopers LLP

LOCATIONS

HQ: The Whiting-Turner Contracting Company
300 E. Joppa Rd., Baltimore, MD 21286
Phone: 410-821-1100   **Fax:** 410-337-5770
Web: www.whiting-turner.com

The Whiting-Turner Contracting Company has offices in California, Colorado, Connecticut, Delaware, Florida, Georgia, Maryland, Massachusetts, Nevada, North Carolina, New Jersey, New York, Ohio, Pennsylvania, Texas, Virginia, and Washington, DC.

PRODUCTS/OPERATIONS

Selected Services
Construction management (at-risk or agency)
Design/build
General contracting
Preconstruction

Selected Markets
Biotechnology and pharmaceutical
Cleanroom and high-technology
Education
Entertainment
Health care
Industrial and manufacturing
Lodging and hospitality
Mission critical facilities
Offices and headquarters
Retail
Senior living
Sports
Warehouse and distribution

COMPETITORS

Barton Malow
Bechtel
Bovis Lend Lease
Choate Construction
Clark Enterprises
DPR Construction
Fisher Development
Fluor
Gilbane
Hensel Phelps Construction
Hoffman Corporation
Jacobs Engineering
JE Dunn Construction Group
Kitchell
McCarthy Building
Perini
Peter Kiewit Sons'
Simon Property Group
Skanska
Suffolk Construction
Swinerton
Turner Corporation
The Weitz Company, LLC

HISTORICAL FINANCIALS
Company Type: Private

Income Statement   FYE: December 31

	REVENUE ($ mil.)	NET INCOME ($ mil.)	NET PROFIT MARGIN	EMPLOYEES
12/07	3,970	—	—	2,200
12/06	3,340	—	—	1,900
12/05	3,066	—	—	1,700
12/04	2,620	—	—	1,600
12/03	1,876	—	—	1,352
Annual Growth	20.6%	—	—	12.9%

Revenue History

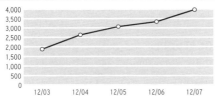

Wilbur-Ellis Company

Weed 'em and feed 'em could be the motto of Wilbur-Ellis Company. A distributor for major chemical companies, Wilbur-Ellis sells animal feed, fertilizer, insecticides, seed, and machinery through outlets in North America. Subsidiary Connell Brothers exports and distributes industrial chemicals throughout the Pacific Rim. Additionally, Wilbur-Ellis provides consulting, pesticide spraying, and other agriculture-related services. It also owns Knox McDaniel, a supplier of vitamin and mineral premix products in the western US. In addition to distribution in the US, Wilbur-Ellis exports its products to Canada and Pacific Rim countries.

The company also owns Brayton Chemicals, Harricros Chemicals, Tide Products, Tex-Ag Company, John Taylor Fertilizers, Soilserve, Willamette Seed Company, John Pryor Fertilizers, and the Olson Seed Company.

Continuing to grow, its recent acquisitions include Olson Seed and Knox McDaniel (2001), Hughtson Chemical (2004), and Ag Supply (2007). In 2007 the company's sales exceeded $2 billion.

Brayton Wilbur Sr. and Floyd Ellis founded the company in 1921 as a fish-oil supplier; it is still owned by the Wilbur family.

EXECUTIVES

Chairman: Herbert B. Tully
Vice Chairman: Carter P. Thacher, age 81
President and CEO: John P. Thacher
EVP Agribusiness Division: Daniel R. (Dan) Vradenburg
VP, Treasurer, and CFO: James D. Crawford
VP and General Counsel: William R. Sawyers, age 38
VP National Marketing and Supplier Relations: James M. (Jim) Loar
Controller: Charles Crume
Director Information Systems: Jerry Coupe
Director Human Resources: Tim McMullen
Director Credit: Robert Syron
President, Connell Bros.: Theodore L. (Ted) Eliot III
Auditors: Hood & Strong

LOCATIONS

HQ: Wilbur-Ellis Company
345 California St., 27th Fl.,
San Francisco, CA 94104
Phone: 415-772-4000   **Fax:** 415-772-4011
Web: www.wilbur-ellis.com

PRODUCTS/OPERATIONS

Selected Products and Services

Agribusiness Division
  Agricultural chemicals
  Fertilizers
  Fungicides
  Herbicides
  Insecticides
  Machinery
  Seed protectants
  Seed treatments
  Sprayers
Cascade & Great Lakes Packing Group
  Fruit anaysis
  Packaging products
  Post-harvest chemicals
Connell Bros. Division
  Industrial chemicals
Feed Division
  Aquaculture products
  Feed ingredients
  Food oils
  Forage products
  Pet food
Professional Products
  Forestry
    Fungicides
    Herbicides
  Golf
    Fungicides
  Landscape
    Fungicides
  Nursery/Greenhouse
    Fungicides
  Vegetation Management
    Selective and nonselective growth regulators

COMPETITORS

ADM	Crop Production Services
Ag Processing	Frontier Agriculture
AGRI Industries	Goulding Chemicals
Agrium	GROWMARK
Andersons	JR Simplot
Cargill	Land O'Lakes Purina Feed
CF Industries	Terra Industries
CHS	Western Farm Service
Corn Products	

HISTORICAL FINANCIALS
Company Type: Private

Income Statement   FYE: December 31

	REVENUE ($ mil.)	NET INCOME ($ mil.)	NET PROFIT MARGIN	EMPLOYEES
12/07	2,012	—	—	2,500
12/06	1,710	—	—	2,500
12/05	1,632	—	—	2,500
Annual Growth	11.0%	—	—	0.0%

Revenue History

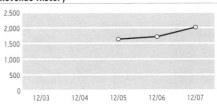

William Lyon Homes

William Lyon's compass is pointed due west. That's where the homebuilder and its joint venture partners construct single-family detached and attached homes. California accounts for nearly 70% of its closings, ahead of both Arizona and Nevada. The builder operates more than 60 sales locations and targets entry-level and move-up buyers. Homes range in price from about $75,000 to more than $1.7 million, and average $460,000. The company and its partners also control about 13,000 lots for development. Subsidiary William Lyon Financial Services (formerly known as Duxford Financial) offers loan and home financing services. Chairman William Lyon and family own the company.

Like other big domestic homebuilders, William Lyon Homes has been no stranger to the slow housing market. Its backlog consists of about 300 homes sold under sales contracts that have not yet closed. Because of decreased home orders and high cancellation rates in all but its California market, the company slashed its workforce by about 25% and sold properties in 10 communities for about $90 million in order to increase its cash.

EXECUTIVES

Chairman and CEO: William Lyon Sr., age 84
President, COO, and Director: Douglas F. Bauer, age 46
EVP, Chief Administrative Officer, and Director: William H. (Bill) Lyon Jr., age 34
EVP Business Development and Operations: Thomas J. (Tom) Mitchell, age 47
SVP and CFO: Michael D. Grubbs, age 49
SVP; President, Arizona Division: W. Thomas Hickcox, age 55
SVP; President, Nevada Division: Mary J. Connelly, age 56
SVP; President, San Diego Division: Larry I. Smith, age 53
SVP Finance: Richard S. Robinson, age 61
SVP, Corporate Controller, and Corporate Secretary: W. Douglass Harris, age 64
VP Operations: C. Dean Stewart
Human Resources Manager: Maureen Singer
President, William Lyon Financial Services: Mark A. Carver
Auditors: Ernst & Young LLP

LOCATIONS

HQ: William Lyon Homes
  4490 Von Karman Ave., Newport Beach, CA 92660
Phone: 949-833-3600   **Fax:** 949-476-2178
Web: www.lyonhomes.com

William Lyon Homes operates more than 60 sales locations in Arizona, California, and Nevada.

2007 Homes Sales by Region

	$ mil.	% of total
Southern California	780.2	71
Northern California	102.4	9
Arizona	134.1	12
Nevada	88.6	8
Total	**1,105.3**	**100**

PRODUCTS/OPERATIONS

2007 Sales

	$ mil.	% of total
Homes	1,002.5	91
Lots, land & other	102.8	9
Total	**1,105.3**	**100**

COMPETITORS

Barratt American
Beazer Homes
Capital Pacific
Centex
Corky McMillin
D.R. Horton
KB Home
Lennar
M.D.C.
Meritage Homes
The Ryland Group
Shapell Industries
Standard Pacific
Toll Brothers

HISTORICAL FINANCIALS

Company Type: Private

Income Statement   FYE: December 31

	REVENUE ($ mil.)	NET INCOME ($ mil.)	NET PROFIT MARGIN	EMPLOYEES
12/07	1,105	(349)	—	632
12/06	1,492	75	5.0%	730
12/05	1,856	191	10.3%	977
Annual Growth	**(22.8%)**	**—**	**—**	**(19.6%)**

Net Income History

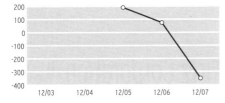

Williamson-Dickie Manufacturing

Appreciated by both the working class and the sophomore class, Williamson-Dickie Manufacturing makes Dickies-brand khaki pants, bib overalls, jeans, women's and children's apparel, and Workrite safety uniforms. It also makes apparel and footwear for work and outdoor use under the Kodiak and Terra names. Its work clothes, originally tailored for the blue-collar set, have come back into fashion with teens, which now account for a large portion of sales. Dickies products are sold worldwide through retailers, directly to businesses, and through its Work Authority stores. It was founded in 1922 by the Williamson family, which still owns the company. Dickies acquired Kodiak Group Holdings in April 2008.

Based in Canada, Kodiak Group Holdings makes and distributes work and outdoor footwear under the Kodiak and Terra brand names. The purchase allows Dickies to extend its reach into Canada and gives the company another brand that's just as rich in history as its own. As part of the agreement, Kodiak became a unit of Dickies, which will retain the Kodiak name, licensing program, and Work Authority stores in Canada.

EXECUTIVES

Chairman, President, and CEO: Philip C. Williamson
Vice Chairman: Gail Williamson-Rawl
CFO: Randy Teuber
EVP Human Resources: Marett Cobb
SVP Marketing and Merchandising: Tad Uchteman
Director Marketing: Jason Prior

LOCATIONS

HQ: Williamson-Dickie Manufacturing Company
  509 W. Vickery Blvd., Fort Worth, TX 76104
Phone: 866-411-1501   **Fax:** 817-877-5027
Web: www.dickies.com

PRODUCTS/OPERATIONS

Selected Brand Names

Dickies
Workrite
Kodiak
Terra

COMPETITORS

Carhartt	OshKosh B'Gosh
Fruit of the Loom	Phat
FUBU	Tommy Hilfiger
Levi Strauss	VF

HISTORICAL FINANCIALS

Company Type: Private

Income Statement   FYE: December 31

	ESTIMATED REVENUE ($ mil.)	NET INCOME ($ mil.)	NET PROFIT MARGIN	EMPLOYEES
12/07	1,100	—	—	4,160
12/06	1,100	—	—	4,160
12/05	1,102	—	—	4,160
Annual Growth	**(0.1%)**	**—**	**—**	**0.0%**

Revenue History

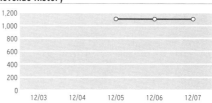

Wilson Sonsini

You might say these lawyers can get downright technical. Wilson Sonsini Goodrich & Rosati (WSGR) is one of the largest law firms in the US specializing in representing high-tech corporations. Its client roster includes several big Silicon Valley names, such as Apple Computer, Hewlett-Packard, and Sun Microsystems. WSGR has advised more than 350 clients on their IPOs in the last five years. It has also been involved in more than 1,000 M&A transactions in the last five years, including representing Avanex in the company's $200 million cross-border acquisition of the optical components division of Alcatel. The firm has about 650 lawyers at seven offices in the US and one in Shanghai. It was founded in 1961.

Other practice areas include antitrust and trade regulation, intellectual property, corporate finance, fund services, and wealth management.

WSGR rode high during the high-tech boom, collecting large fees and paying out large bonuses. The cooling of the sector has meant making some cutbacks, but the firm continues to grow and has an eye out for business in Europe and Asia (the company opened its Shanghai office in 2005).

It has also capitalized on industry consolidation by doing more merger and acquisition work and is garnering more non-tech clients such as Hasbro and Monaco Coach.

EXECUTIVES

Chairman: Larry W. Sonsini, age 67
Vice Chairman: Jeffrey D. (Jeff) Saper
CEO: John V. Roos
VP, Finance: Sunil Bhardwaj
VP, Information Services: Phillip Hoare
VP, Marketing: Courtney Chiang Dorman
General Counsel: Donald E. (Don) Bradley
Director, Attorney Recruiting and Retention:
  Carol A. Timm
Senior Director, Human Resources and Office Administration: Stacey Layzell
Senior Director, Professional Services: Chris Boyd

LOCATIONS

HQ: Wilson Sonsini Goodrich & Rosati
  650 Page Mill Rd., Palo Alto, CA 94304
Phone: 650-493-9300   **Fax:** 650-493-6811
Web: www.wsgr.com

Wilson Sonsini Goodrich & Rosati has offices in Austin, Texas; New York; Palo Alto, San Diego, and San Francisco, California; Reston, Virginia; Salt Lake City; and Seattle.

PRODUCTS/OPERATIONS

Selected Practice Areas

Antitrust law
Corporate and securities
Employment and employee benefits
Environmental law
Intellectual property
Litigation
Real estate
Tax law

COMPETITORS

Cooley Godward Kronish
DLA Piper
Fenwick & West
Heller Ehrman

Morrison & Foerster
Orrick
Perkins Coie

HISTORICAL FINANCIALS

Company Type: Partnership

Income Statement

FYE: January 31

	REVENUE ($ mil.)	NET INCOME ($ mil.)	NET PROFIT MARGIN	EMPLOYEES
1/08	531	—	—	—
1/07	460	—	—	—
1/06	412	—	—	—
1/05	382	—	—	—
1/04	387	—	—	—
Annual Growth	8.2%	—	—	—

Revenue History

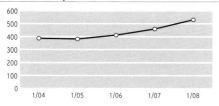

WinCo Foods

WinCo Foods isn't just big on self-service — it's giant. Inside the immense stores (average size is 90,000 sq. ft.) of this mostly employee-owned supermarket chain, customers shop for food in bulk and bag their own groceries. The company's 60-plus stores also feature pizza shops, bakeries, health and beauty products, and organic foods. WinCo Foods, formerly known as Waremart Foods, was renamed as a shortened version of "winning company." The name is also an acronym for its states of operation, which include Washington, Idaho, Nevada, California, and Oregon. Founded in 1968, WinCo Foods formerly operated stores under the Cub Foods and Waremart names. Employees, past and present, own nearly 90% of the company.

WinCo's long-held low-price, no-frills strategy has paid off despite the rise of Wal-Mart supercenters in its markets. The company is one of the few grocery chains known to match or beat Wal-Mart on price.

SUPERVALU, the nation's leading grocery wholesaler, sold its 25% stake in WinCo back to the company in April 2004.

EXECUTIVES

President, CEO, and Director: Steven Goddard
EVP and COO: Rich Charrier
EVP Finance and Director: Gary R. Piva
SVP Procurement: Dave Strausborger
VP Bulk Foods Operations: Dick Bryant
VP Information Technology: Glen Reynolds
VP Merchandising and Retail Pricing: Gary Kintz
VP Food Safety and Compliance: Alan Malone
VP Public and Legal Affairs: Michael (Mike) Read
VP Warehousing: Jim Parker
VP and Controller: Del Ririe
VP Labor and Human Resources: Valerie Davis

LOCATIONS

HQ: WinCo Foods, Inc.
650 N. Armstrong Place, Boise, ID 83704
Phone: 208-377-0110　　**Fax:** 208-377-0474
Web: www.wincofoods.com

2007 Stores

	No.
California	22
Oregon	16
Washington	10
Idaho	8
Nevada	2
Total	**58**

PRODUCTS/OPERATIONS

Selected Store Departments

Bakery
Bulk foods (more than 500 items)
Delicatessen
Fresh meat
Health and beauty aids
Organic products
Pizza shop
Produce
Seafood

COMPETITORS

Albertsons
ALDI
Associated Food
Associated Wholesale
Grocers
Costco Wholesale
Fred Meyer Stores

Haggen
Raley's
Safeway
Stater Bros.
Unified Grocers
Wal-Mart

WinWholesale

You Win some, you Win some more. So it goes for WinWholesale (formerly Primus). The company is invested in more than 470 small to medium-sized wholesale distributors in 40-plus states that sell plumbing, heating, air-conditioning, electrical, and other supplies to contractors and other professional customers. The companies are easily recognizable by their Win-prefixed names, such as Columbia Winnelson, Salt Lake Windustrial, and Dayton Winfastener. WinWholesale supports these companies with bulk purchasing, warehousing, accounting, and data processing. After operating as Primus for more than 40 years, the company (owned by heirs of the investors who founded it in 1956) changed its name to WinWholesale in 2004.

In 2005 WinWholesale acquired Virginia-based Noland Co., a wholesale distributor of plumbing, electrical, HVAC, mechanical equipment and supplies. Noland, which became a wholly owned subsidiary of WinWholesale, operates more than 100 distribution branches in about a dozen states, primarily in the South.

WinWholesale has been growing via acquisitions and by opening new locations, about a dozen new locations in 2008 alone.

EXECUTIVES

President and CEO: Richard W. (Rick) Schwartz
COO: Monte Salsman
CFO: Jack W. Johnston
EVP: Jack Osenbaugh
Regional VP, Central: Stan Reznicek
Regional VP, East: Calvin Grout
Regional VP, West: Steve Ford
VP Human Resources: Rhonda Binger
VP National Sales: Gary Benaszeski
VP Vendor Relations: Eddie Gibbs
VP Finance: Ward Allen
CTO: Jeffrey (Jeff) Dana
CIO: Steven L. Hangen
Secretary: Bruce Anderson
Director, Corporate Communications:
Steven B. (Steve) Edwards

LOCATIONS

HQ: WinWholesale Inc.
3110 Kettering Blvd., Dayton, OH 45439
Phone: 937-294-6878　　**Fax:** 937-293-9591
Web: www.winwholesale.com

PRODUCTS/OPERATIONS

Selected Businesses

Noland Company (wholesale distributor of plumbing, electrical, HVAC, and mechanical equipment and supplies)
Winair (heating, ventilation, air conditioning, and refrigeration)
Windustrial (industrial pipes and valves)
Winfastener (specialty fasteners)
Winlectric (electrical supplies and products)
Winnelson (plumbing)
Winpump (pumps and accessories)
Wintronic (electronic parts and equipment)
Winwaterworks (waterworks and utility supplies)

COMPETITORS

Fastenal
Ferguson Enterprises
Gensco
Groeniger & Company
Hajoca Corporation
HD Supply

Johnstone Supply
Lowe's
MSC Industrial Direct
Watsco
W.W. Grainger

Wirtz Corporation

Wirtz does it best on ice. The company owns the Chicago Blackhawks hockey team and is partnered with Jerry Reinsdorf, of the Chicago Bulls basketball team, in ownership of the United Center, where both sports teams play. Wirtz also owns and operates liquor distributorships, including Judge & Dolph, the largest distributor in Illinois and Wisconsin-based Edison, among others. Judge & Dolph owns the rights to distribute some key Diageo brands such as Crown Royal, Johnny Walker, J&B, and Tanqueray. President and CEO William Wirtz died in 2007; his eldest son, Rocky, took over management of the company.

The firm owns beverage interests in Wisconsin, Mississippi, Texas, Nevada, and Florida.

The Wirtz family gave thousands of dollars to Illinois state lawmakers in 1999 to pass legislation protecting liquor distributors by making it difficult for liquor producers to switch distributors. (The law later was declared unconstitutional.)

Arthur Wirtz (father of the late William Wirtz) founded the family-controlled empire in 1922.

EXECUTIVES

President and CEO: William Rockwell (Rocky) Wirtz, age 56
CFO: Max Mohler
VP; President, DeLuca Liquor and Wine: Ray Novell
VP Human Resources: Cindy Krch
Controller: Linda Bescalli

LOCATIONS

HQ: Wirtz Corporation
    680 N. Lakeshore Dr., 19th Fl., Chicago, IL 60611
Phone: 312-943-7000   **Fax:** 312-943-9017
Web: www.judgedolph.com

Wirtz operates liquor distributorships in Illinois, Iowa, Minnesota, Nevada, Texas, and Wisconsin.

PRODUCTS/OPERATIONS

Selected Operating Companies

Callison Distributing
Coors of Las Vegas
DeLuca Liquor & Wine, Ltd.
Edison
Griggs, Cooper & Company
Hawkeye Wine & Spirits Inc.
Judge & Dolph, Ltd.
Mark VII Distributors
Nevada Wine Agents
Silver State Liquor and Wine

COMPETITORS

Columbus Blue Jackets
Detroit Red Wings
Gambrinus
Georgia Crown
Glazer's Wholesale Drug
Johnson Brothers
Nashville Predators
National Distributing

National Wine & Spirits
Reyes Holdings
Southern Wine & Spirits
St. Louis Blues
Sunbelt Beverage
Tarrant Distributors
Young's Market

W. L. Gore & Associates

W. L. Gore & Associates would like your clothing to take a deep breath. The company makes a variety of fluoropolymer products; best known is its breathable, waterproof, and windproof GORE-TEX fabric. Product uses range from clothing and shoes to guitar strings, dental floss, space suits, and sutures. In addition to its apparel (popular among hikers and hunters), W. L. Gore makes insulated wire and cables, filtration products, and sealants. Fabrics are offered under such brands as GORE-TEX and WINDSTOPPER. The Gore family owns about 75% of the company; Gore associates own the rest.

Some of Gore's lesser known products include pipe bags (for making bagpipes), vacuum cleaner filters, and waterproof cast liners for broken limbs. Its GORE BIO-A helps regenerate and reinforce soft tissue in such medical procedures as hiatal hernia repair.

W. L. Gore is known for its unusual style of management — the lattice system. There is no fixed authority, as the company has "sponsors," not bosses, and all employees are considered associates. Company goals and tasks are determined by consensus.

The company launched a new branding campaign in 2008 for its GORE-TEX products. The campaign, which was launched a couple months before Gore celebrated its 50th anniversary, involves demonstrating how the various protective qualities of GORE-TEX emulate similar natural qualities found in wild animals like otters, wolves, butterflies, and fruit bats.

HISTORY

In 1941 Bill Gore, a DuPont scientist, started researching and developing plastics, polymers, and resins. One project at DuPont that Gore worked on was the development of a synthetic substance commonly known as teflon.

Seeing an untapped market for teflon-type products, Gore quit DuPont and in 1958 started his own business. He worked with his wife and his son Bob, a chemical engineering student. Bob helped him develop the company's first major product line — teflon-insulated electronic wires and cables.

With the success of its cables, the company was able to move out of the family basement and into a facility in Newark, Delaware. By 1965 Gore employed 200 people and soon implemented the lattice structure of management, eschewing demands for personal commitments and emphasizing cooperation and teamwork as paramount tenets of the business. A second plant was opened in Flagstaff, Arizona, in 1967.

Bob Gore, who had earned a doctorate in chemistry, hit the synthetic plastic motherlode in 1969. While experimenting with teflon, he discovered a way to stretch the material at microscopic levels, creating a fabric with holes large enough for body heat and moisture to escape, but small enough to deflect raindrops. Gore applied for a patent on its GORE-TEX fabric in 1970 and received it six years later. The company experienced an explosive period of growth as GORE-TEX found its way into space suits, sporting apparel, filters, and artificial arteries. Bob Gore became the company's president during this time.

By the 1980s GORE-TEX-related products generated the majority of sales. Globally, Gore operated about 30 plants, locating most in smaller cities since the Gores believed that small towns offered a better quality of life. Bill Gore died in 1986. The business continued and developed new uses for GORE-TEX. Various patent lawsuits emerged at the time, and when the company lost a case in 1990, Gore's exclusive patent on GORE-TEX ended, although it retained patents on certain products and processes.

The door was open for competition by 1993, but Gore still had the advantages of experience and a perception of higher quality and durability. It continued to introduce new uses for GORE-TEX, spooling out dental floss in 1993. The company also moved into the computer market that year by acquiring Supercomputer Systems.

Gore expanded its US medical product line in 1996 by marketing a membrane made from GORE-TEX-related material for use as a replacement for dura mater (the membrane that protects the brain and spinal cord) and in 1997 with the purchase of Prograft Medical.

In 1999 Gore introduced its REMEDIA catalytic filter system, which destroys carcinogenic dioxins and furans produced during industrial combustion by converting them into water and harmless chemicals.

The company exited the circuit packaging business in 2000 when it sold its Eau Claire, Wisconsin, plants to 3M. The following year Gore entered into a strategic agreement with Singapore-based photonic component manufacturer Flextronics Photonics to manufacture optical transmitter and receiver modules. In 2002 Gore sold its fiber optic operations to focus on electrical interconnects and materials. The next year Pall Corporation and Gore entered into a business alliance that allowed Pall rights to the GORE-TEX filter technology.

In 2005 Gore acquired Carmen AB, a Swedish manufacturer of hemocompatible surface coating for medical devices. In 2006 the company acquired Neural Intervention Technologies, a developer of medical devices that repair defective blood vessels. The following year the company acquired Amesil, a provider of reactive fluid transport, containment, and sampling services and products for the pharmaceutical industry.

EXECUTIVES

CEO: Terri Kelly, age 42
Medical Marketing Director: Thom O'Hara
Human Relations Chief: Donna Frey
Operations Leader, Shenzhen: Tom Zeng

LOCATIONS

HQ: W. L. Gore & Associates, Inc.
    555 Papermill Rd., Newark, DE 19711
Phone: 410-506-7787   **Fax:** 410-996-8585
Web: www.gore.com

PRODUCTS/OPERATIONS

Selected Divisions, Products, and Brands

Cables and cable assemblies
    Coaxial cable
    Fiber-optic cable
    Flat cable
    High data rate copper
    Hook-up wire
    Microwave/RF cable assemblies
    Round cable
Consumer products
    Canmore pipe pags
    CleanStream vacuum cleaner filters
    ELIXER guitar strings
    GLIDE dental floss
    GORE WINDSTOPPER fabrics
    GORE-TEX outerwear
    Procell cast liners
    ReviveX water and stain repellent
Electronics and electrochemical materials
    Acoustic protective covers
    Electronic packaging and materials
    Electronic security enclosures
    EMI/RFI shielding — GORE-SHIELD
    Fuel cell components
    Prepreg circuitboard substrates
    Thermal interface materials
Fabrics and fibers
    CROSSTECH fabrics
    Fire services and public safety fabrics
    GORE transparent screen fabric
    GORE-TEX BEST DEFENSE outerwear
    GORE-TEX fabrics
    Microwave fabrics
    Military fabrics
    Organic waste treatment fabrics
    Rope fiber
    Sewing thread and weaving fiber
    Tenara architectural fabric

Filtration
- CleanStream vacuum cleaner filters
- Disk drive filtration
- Industrial baghouse filters
- Industrial liquid filtration
- Microfiltration media

Medical and health care
- GLIDE floss
- GORE cast liner
- Implantable medical devices
    - GORE RESOLUT XT regenerative material
    - GORE subcutaneous augmentation material
    - GORE-TEX DualMesh biomaterial
    - GORE-TEX DualMesh PLUS biomaterial
    - GORE-TEX MycroMesh biomaterial
    - GORE-TEX MycroMesh PLUS biomaterial
    - GORE-TEX regenerative material
    - GORE-TEX stretch vascular graft
    - GORE-TEX suture
    - GORE-TEX vascular grafts
    - PRECLUDE dura substitute
    - PRECLUDE peritoneal membrane
    - SEAMGUARD staple line-reinforcement material

Sealants
- GFO fiber packing
- GFO marine service packing
- GORE gasket tape
- GORE GR sheet gasketing
- GORE joint sealant
- GORE valve stem packing
- ONE-UP pump diaphragms
- SEQUEL fiber packing

COMPETITORS

Belden	Milliken
Burlington WorldWide	Polartec, LLC
CardioTech	Superior Essex
Donaldson Company	Thoratec Corp
Kellwood	Timberland

World Wide Technology

World Wide Technology (WWT) has a broad view of its business. The company primarily provides such IT services as network design and installation, systems and application integration, and procurement. It also offers a range of Web-based products and services, including e-commerce systems development, order tracking, and catalog management. WWT serves businesses in the automotive, retail, and telecommunications industries, as well as government agencies. Top clients include Dell, the State of Missouri, and the State of Alaska. WWT was co-founded in 1990 by chairman David Steward and CEO Jim Kavanaugh.

Successful strategic partnerships with technology leaders including Cisco Systems and Hewlett-Packard and important contract wins, such as a seven year deal with NASA signed in 2007, have contributed to WWT's steady growth over the past several years. The company's sales more than tripled between 2002 and 2007.

EXECUTIVES

Chairman: David L. Steward, age 56
CEO: James P. (Jim) Kavanaugh
CFO: Thomas W. (Tom) Strunk
VP Business Strategy: Robert M. (Bob) Olwig
VP Professional Services: Matt Horner
VP Human Resources: Ann W. Marr
President, World Wide Technology:
 Joseph G. (Joe) Koenig
President and COO, Telcobuy.com: Mark J. Catalano

LOCATIONS

HQ: World Wide Technology, Inc.
 60 Weldon Pkwy., St. Louis, MO 63043
Phone: 314-569-7000   **Fax:** 314-569-8300
Web: www.wwt.com

PRODUCTS/OPERATIONS

Selected Services

Consulting
E-commerce management
Network design
Online procurement
Supply chain management
Systems integration

COMPETITORS

Accenture	HP Technology Solutions
Computer Sciences Corp.	Group
Dell	IBM Global Services
EDS	Perot Systems
Hewlett-Packard	Unisys

HISTORICAL FINANCIALS

Company Type: Private

Income Statement

FYE: December 31

	REVENUE ($ mil.)	NET INCOME ($ mil.)	NET PROFIT MARGIN	EMPLOYEES
12/07	2,500	—	—	1,100
12/06	2,100	—	—	1,050
12/05	1,800	—	—	1,030
12/04	1,400	—	—	—
12/03	1,100	—	—	650
Annual Growth	22.8%	—	—	14.1%

Revenue History

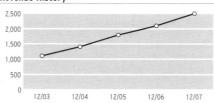

EXECUTIVES

CEO: George R. Melton
EVP and General Manager, Aerospace Group:
 Brent M. Bennitt
SVP and CFO: Dana P. Dorsey
SVP and General Manager, Life Sciences Group:
 Bob Ellis
SVP and General Manager, Test, Engineering and Research Group: Jim Neu
SVP Business Development: Drexel Smith
VP and CIO: Greg Burner
VP and Controller: Doug Van Kirk
VP Corporate Development: Roger Wiederkehr
VP Human Resources: Patti Robinson
Manager Corporate Communications: Dan Reeder

LOCATIONS

HQ: Wyle Laboratories, Inc.
 1960 E. Grand Ave., Ste. 900, El Segundo, CA 90245
Phone: 310-563-6800   **Fax:** 310-563-6850
Web: www.wylelabs.com

PRODUCTS/OPERATIONS

Selected Products and Operations

Life Sciences Systems and Services
- Aircrew performance
- Biotechnology
- Environmental research
- Medical operations and research
- Space flight hardware

Special test systems
- Acoustic test facilities
- Aero medical training
- Centrifuge test systems
- Space flight systems

Technical Support Services
- Calibration and repair services
- Computer system support
- Engineering services
- Laboratory services
- Logistics management
- Metrology management
- Weapons systems engineering

COMPETITORS

Bureau Veritas	Orbital Research
Exponent	SGS
Intertek	SRI International
National Technical Systems	

HISTORICAL FINANCIALS

Company Type: Private

Income Statement

FYE: December 31

	REVENUE ($ mil.)	NET INCOME ($ mil.)	NET PROFIT MARGIN	EMPLOYEES
12/07	800	—	—	4,200
12/06	500	—	—	3,000
12/05	500	—	—	3,000
12/04	450	—	—	3,000
12/03	200	—	—	1,500
Annual Growth	41.4%	—	—	29.4%

Revenue History

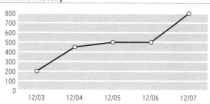

Wyle Laboratories

Wyle Laboratories provides engineering, testing, life cycle management, clinical health services, operations support, and other technical support services to clients in such industries as aerospace, life sciences, telecommunications, and transportation. In addition to serving commercial and industrial customers, the company is also a large government contractor, providing services to the various branches of the Department of Defense, as well as NASA. Founded in 1949 as a testing laboratory in California, Wyle Laboratories operates more than 40 facilities around the country through about 4,200 employees. It owns fellow government contractor Wyle Information Systems Group (formerly RS Information Systems).

In 2005 Wyle Laboratories expanded its research and testing capabilities when it acquired the aeronautics services business of General Dynamics. It completed the acquisition of RS Information systems in early 2008.

Yale University

What do President George W. Bush and actress Meryl Streep have in common? They are Yalies. Yale University is one of the nation's most prestigious private liberal arts institutions, as well as one of its oldest (founded in 1701). Its more than $22 billion endowment ranks second only to Harvard's in the US. Yale comprises an undergraduate college, a graduate school, and more than a dozen professional schools. Programs of study include architecture, law, medicine, and drama. Its 12 residential colleges (a system borrowed from Oxford) serve as dormitory, dining hall, and social center. The school has around 11,300 students and some 3,300 faculty members.

EXECUTIVES

President: Richard C. Levin, age 60
Provost: Andrew D. Hamilton
VP and Secretary: Linda Koch Lorimer, age 56
VP and General Counsel: Dorothy K. Robinson
VP, Finance and Administration: Shauna R. King, age 51
VP, Development: Ingeborg T. (Inge) Reichenbach
Associate Vice President and Chief Financial Officer: Gwendolyn Sykes
Associate VP and Chief Human Resources Officer: Robert Schwartz
Associate VP Administration: Janet E. Lindner
Dean, Undergraduate Admissions: Jeffrey Brenzel
Director Information Services and University CIO: Philip Long
Deputy Director Office of Public Affairs: Tom Conroy
Executive Director Yale Alumni Association: Mark Dollhopf
Auditors: PricewaterhouseCoopers LLP

LOCATIONS

HQ: Yale University
    246 Church St., New Haven, CT 06520
Phone: 203-432-2331   **Fax:** 203-432-2334
Web: www.yale.edu

PRODUCTS/OPERATIONS

Colleges and Schools

Graduate School of Arts and Sciences
Professional schools
    School of Architecture
School of Art
Divinity School
School of Drama
School of Engineering & Applied Science
School of Forestry & Environmental Studies
Law School
School of Management
School of Medicine
School of Music
School of Nursing
School of Public Health
Institute of Sacred Music
Yale College (undergraduate studies)

Residential Colleges

Berkeley College
Branford College
Calhoun College
Davenport College
Ezra Stiles College
Jonathan Edwards College
Morse College
Pierson College
Saybrook College
Silliman College
Timothy Dwight College
Trumbull College

Yankee Candle

While most Yankees are good at warming their homes, the ones at The Yankee Candle Company are also good at making their homes smell like Clean Cotton, Splash of Rain, or Home Sweet Home. The firm makes and sells candles, known for their burning longevity and strong smells — in scores of scents. It also sells candleholders, accessories, and dinnerware. Yankee Candle's products are sold by about 17,500 gift shops nationwide, as well as internationally through distributors. The company operates more than 450 namesake and Illuminations stores in 43 states, mostly in malls, and sells online and through catalogs. Private equity firm Madison Dearborn Partners acquired Yankee Candle in 2007 for $1.6 billion.

The company — founded in 1969 by Michael Kittredge, who made his first candle for his mother's Christmas gift — had hired Lehman Brothers that July to advise it on a possible sale of the company.

Yankee Candle is banking on future growth as part of Madison Dearborn. In recent years, the company has been adding to its brand portfolio and expanding its retail presence in the western US. Prior to being acquired, Yankee Candle in mid-2006 bought Candle Acquisition Co.'s Illuminations brand for about $22 million and folded it into its operations. As part of the deal, Yankee Candle picked up 15 Illuminations retail shops (located in California, Arizona, and Washington), as well as its consumer direct business.

Yankee Candle's target audience is women ranging in age from their early 20s into their 60s. Attempting to lure individuals outside of its core customer base, the company has introduced new products, such as electric devices that can be plugged into the wall and continuously dispense fragrance and "Car Jars" hanging tags (to scent the car).

Yankee Candle's Housewarmer and Country Kitchen candles, its core product, come in many different fragrances and a variety of sizes and shapes. Its signature style is a lidded jar. The company's 90,000-sq.-ft. flagship store in South Deerfield, Massachusetts, attracts more than 2.5 million tourists a year.

EXECUTIVES

Chairman, CEO, and Director: Craig W. Rydin, age 56, $1,201,243 pay
President, COO, and Director: Harlan M. Kent, age 45, $608,197 pay (prior to title change)
SVP Finance and CFO: Bruce L. Hartman, age 54
SVP Brand Marketing and Innovation: Richard R. (Rick) Ruffolo, age 40
SVP and General Counsel: James A. Perley, age 45
SVP Human Resources: Martha S. LaCroix, age 42
SVP Retail: Stephen (Steve) Farley, age 53, $401,724 pay (partial-year salary)
SVP Supply Chain: Paul J. Hill, age 53, $329,420 pay
SVP Wholesale Division: Mike Thorne, age 43
VP and General Merchandise Manager: Hope Margala Klein
CIO: Dennis Shockro
Head, Fragrance Committee: Bob Nelson
Director, Public Relations: Susan Stockman
Auditors: Deloitte & Touche LLP

LOCATIONS

HQ: The Yankee Candle Company, Inc.
    16 Yankee Candle Way, South Deerfield, MA 01373
Phone: 413-665-8306   **Fax:** 413-665-4815
Web: www.yankeecandle.com

PRODUCTS/OPERATIONS

Selected Products

Jar candles (3.7 oz., 14.5 oz., 22 oz.)
Kindle Candles (unscented wax for fire starters)
Samplers (votive candles for sampling fragrances)
Scented Ionic pillars (grooved candles)
Scented tea lights (small, scented candles in clear cups)
Standard pillars (scented and unscented)
Tapers (scented and unscented, the oldest style of candles)
Tart Warmers (white, unscented candles for potpourri pots)
Textured pillars (scented and unscented)
Wax Potpourri Tarts (scented wax without wicks used in potpourri pots)

COMPETITORS

American Greetings
Avon
Bath & Body Works
Blyth
The Dial Corporation
Faultless Starch
Human Pheromone Sciences
Lancaster Colony
Procter & Gamble
Reckitt Benckiser
S.C. Johnson
Target
Unilever
Wal-Mart

HISTORICAL FINANCIALS

Company Type: Subsidiary

Income Statement

	REVENUE ($ mil.)	NET INCOME ($ mil.)	NET PROFIT MARGIN	EMPLOYEES
				FYE: December 31
12/06	688	—	—	5,500
12/05	601	—	—	3,100
12/04	554	—	—	4,200
12/03	509	—	—	3,800
12/02	445	—	—	3,500
Annual Growth	11.5%	—	—	12.0%

Revenue History

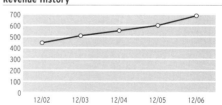

Yates Companies

The Yates Companies operates an extended family of construction companies, comprising W.G. Yates & Sons Construction (the largest of the group), Yates Electrical Division, Mississippi-based JESCO, and Tennessee-based Blaine Construction. The group provides a broad range of construction-related services, including engineering, electrical and mechanical construction, millwrighting, and steel fabrication. The Yates Companies operates mostly in the Southeast and along the East Coast. It has completed casino projects as well as federal contracts for military facilities. CEO William Yates Jr. co-founded the family-owned company in 1964 with his father, the late William Gully Yates.

EXECUTIVES

Chairman, President, and CEO:
William G. (Bill) Yates Jr., age 66
CFO and Treasurer: Marvin Blanks III
EVP and President, W.G. Yates & Sons:
William G. Yates III
VP, Business Development: Jody Tidwell
VP and General Counsel: Kenny Bush
Controller: Brandon Dunn
President, JESCO: Jerry Stubblefield
President, Blaine Construction: Dorman Blaine

LOCATIONS

HQ: The Yates Companies, Inc.
1 Gully Ave., Philadelphia, MS 39350
Phone: 601-656-5411   **Fax:** 601-656-8958
Web: yatescompanies.com

PRODUCTS/OPERATIONS

Selected Construction Categories and Services
Casino
Construction Management
Corporate
Design / Build
Electrical
Engineering
Environmental
Forest Products
General Construction
Heavy Commercial
Hospitality
Industrial
Institutional
Marine
Medical
Processing
Renovation
Resort
Retail
Utility

COMPETITORS

Brasfield & Gorrie
Choate Construction
Clark Enterprises
Fluor
Hunt Construction
Jacobs Engineering
JE Dunn Construction Group
Perini
Turner Corporation
Whiting-Turner

HISTORICAL FINANCIALS
Company Type: Private

Income Statement
FYE: December 31

	REVENUE ($ mil.)	NET INCOME ($ mil.)	NET PROFIT MARGIN	EMPLOYEES
12/07	1,980	—	—	8,000
12/06	2,240	—	—	8,000
12/05	1,761	—	—	8,000
12/04	1,440	—	—	6,000
12/03	1,100	—	—	4,500
Annual Growth	15.8%	—	—	15.5%

Revenue History

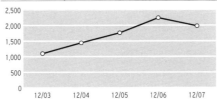

YMCA

A not-for-profit community service organization, YMCA of the USA assists the more than 2,600 individual YMCAs across the country and represents them on both national and international levels. Local YMCAs are leading providers of child care in the US; the facilities also offer programs in areas such as aquatics, arts and humanities, education of new immigrants, health and fitness, and teen leadership. Overall, YMCAs serve about 20 million people across the US. The first YMCA in the US was established in 1851 as an outgrowth of the YMCA movement launched by George Williams in the UK in 1844. Although YMCA stands for Young Men's Christian Organization, the organization's programs are open to all.

EXECUTIVES

Chairman: Ken Colloton
President and CEO: Neil Nicoll
SVP and Advisor CEO: Tom Craine
SVP and COO: Kent Johnson
SVP and CFO: Jim Mellor
SVP and Chief Innovation Officer: Lynne Vaughan
SVP and Chief Government Affairs Officer:
Audrey Tayse Haynes
SVP and Strategic Director Human Resources and Organizational Development: Elinor Hite
SVP and Chief Counsel: Angela Williams
SVP Advancement: Monica Elenbaas
VP and Chief Development Officer: Monique Hanson
National Director Staff Development: Terri Radcliff

LOCATIONS

HQ: YMCA of the USA
101 N. Wacker Dr., Chicago, IL 60606
Phone: 312-977-0031   **Fax:** 312-977-9063
Web: www.ymca.net

PRODUCTS/OPERATIONS

Selected YMCA Programs
Aquatics
Arts and humanities
Camping
Child-care
Community development
Family
Health and fitness
International
Older adults
SCUBA
Sports
Teen leadership

Young's Market

Although no longer young, Young's Market Company, founded in 1888, is in high spirits. The company is a major US supplier of alcoholic beverages; its customers are located in California, Arizona, and Hawaii. Young's Market distributes wine and liquors for Bacardi, Brown-Forman, and Rémy Contreau, among other domestic and foreign distillers and winemakers. In California it distributes wines of Brown-Forman's Sonoma-Cutter Vineyards. The Underwood family, relatives of the founding Young family, bought the company in 1990. The third generation of the family currently operates the company, with Jeff and Chris Underwood serving as co-presidents.

The company's domestic wines also include those of Sonoma Coast Vineyards and Silverado Vineyards. Its imports include Grant Burge Wines, Morey-Blanc, and House of Delamotte.

EXECUTIVES

Chairman and CEO: Vernon O. (Vern) Underwood, age 68
Co-President and COO: Jeffrey V. (Jeff) Underwood
Co-President and COO: Christopher (Chris) Underwood
EVP: Paul A. Vert
EVP and CFO: Dennis J. Hamann
EVP Operations: John Klein
VP Human Resources: Craig Matsuda
General Counsel: Donald (Don) Robbins
President, California Division: Dennis Barnett
Media Contact: Bob Paterson

LOCATIONS

HQ: Young's Market Company, LLC
2164 N. Batavia St., Orange, CA 92865
Phone: 714-283-4933   **Fax:** 714-283-6175
Web: www.youngsmarket.com

COMPETITORS

Beauchamp Distributing
Glazer's Wholesale Drug
Harbor Distributing
Johnson Brothers
Republic National Distributing Company
Southern Wine & Spirits
Sunbelt Beverage

Yucaipa Companies

Yucaipa has a hungry eye for picking out ripe bargains in different industries, but made its name with grocery stores. The investment company forged its reputation as the ultimate grocery shopper, executing a series of grocery chain mergers and acquisitions involving such companies as Fred Meyer, Ralphs, and Jurgensen's that put the company on the supermarket map. The Yucaipa Companies currently owns a stake in SUPERVALU, but sold its interest in Pathmark to A&P in 2007. The company's chairman, billionaire and former grocery store bag boy Ron Burkle, is a prominent Democratic activist and fundraiser.

Former president Bill Clinton has served as an advisor to — and was a high-profile investor in — Yucaipa, but cashed out his interest in order to avoid any conflicts with the presidential bid of wife Hillary.

Burkle, who also owns a significant stake in the NHL's Pittsburgh Penguins, made headlines in 2006 when he set up a sting to catch New York *Post* columnist Jared Paul Stern allegedly trying to extort some $200,000 from Burkle to keep him off the gossip page.

Yucaipa's portfolio also includes Piccadilly Restaurants, about a 20% stake in Simon Worldwide, and half of Alliance Entertainment (a distributor of music, videos, and games).

HISTORY

Ronald Burkle launched his career in the grocery industry as a bag boy at his dad's Stater Bros. grocery store. By age 28 Burkle had moved up to SVP of administration, but he was fired after botching a buyout of the company in 1981.

Burkle and former Stater Bros. colleagues Mark Resnik and Douglas McKenzie founded Yucaipa (named after Burkle's hometown of Yucaipa, California) in 1986 when they bought Los Angeles gourmet-grocery chain Jurgensen's. The next year Yucaipa bought Kansas-based Falley's, which had 20 Food 4 Less stores in California.

In 1989 Yucaipa merged with Breco Holding, operator of 70 grocery stores, and bought Northern California's Bell Markets. It acquired ABC Markets in Southern California in 1990. The next year the company bought the 142-store chain Alpha Beta. Thirty-six Yucaipa stores were damaged in the 1992 Los Angeles riots, but Yucaipa rebuilt, working with unions to keep workers employed until the stores were operational.

The company acquired the 28-store Smitty's Super Valu chain (now Fred Meyer Marketplace) in 1994. The following year Yucaipa bought the 70-year-old family-owned chain Dominick's Finer Foods. Later in 1995 Yucaipa's Food 4 Less chain merged with Los Angeles competitor Ralphs Grocery (founded in 1873 by George Ralphs), making Yucaipa #1 in Southern California.

Yucaipa sold Smitty's to Utah-based Smith's in 1996, acquiring a minority stake in Smith's (Burkle became Smith's CEO). Dominick's went public in 1996, and Yucaipa retained a minority stake. The next year Fred Meyer bought Smith's for $1.9 billion. Burkle became the acquired company's chairman, and Yucaipa gained a 9% interest in Fred Meyer.

In 1998 Fred Meyer bought Ralphs and 155-store Quality Food Centers (QFC). Yucaipa and Wetterau Associates, a management firm, bought Golden State Foods, giving Yucaipa a 70% stake in the McDonald's food supplier. Yucaipa sold Dominick's to Safeway.

After Kroger bought Fred Meyer in 1999, Yucaipa turned away from the consolidating grocery industry and moved into cyberspace. That year Burkle and former Walt Disney president Michael Ovitz launched CheckOut Entertainment Network, which operated CheckOut.com, an entertainment Web site at which Web surfers could buy books, music, and video games. Yucaipa hired Richard Wolpert, former president of Disney Online, to oversee its Internet and technology activities.

Yucaipa added to its portfolio in 1999 by taking stakes in GameSpy (online games), Talk City (later LiveWorld, online chat service), OneNetNow (online communities), ClubMom (Web site for mothers), and Cyrk (now Simon Worldwide, promotional marketing). Yucaipa also bought music, video, and games distributor Alliance Entertainment. The company also holds a minority stake in Simon Worldwide.

Music and video retailer Wherehouse Entertainment became a 50%-owner of CheckOut.com after it merged its online retailing operations with CheckOut.com in 1999. (As the Internet economy faltered, Yucaipa sold CheckOut.com in 2001.)

In 2000 the company digressed from its focus on the Web to invest in Kole Imports, an importer of merchandise sold in discount stores. Yucaipa sold its stakes in grocery distributor Fleming and discount retailer Kmart in 2001 before both companies crashed and burned into bankruptcy.

EXECUTIVES

Managing Partner: Ronald W. (Ron) Burkle, age 55
Partner: Steve Mortensen
Partner: Carlton J. Jenkins, age 52
Partner: Erika Paulson, age 34
Partner: Edward (Ed) Renwick, age 41
Partner: Scott Stedman
Partner: Nick Tasooji
Partner: Ira Tochner, age 46
Legal: Robert P. Bermingham
CFO: Lori Crawford
Public Relations and Corporate Communications:
 Frank Quintero

LOCATIONS

HQ: The Yucaipa Companies LLC
 9130 W. Sunset Blvd., Los Angeles, CA 90069
Phone: 310-789-7200   **Fax:** 310-228-2873

COMPETITORS

Bain Capital
Berkshire Hathaway
Blackstone Group
The Carlyle Group
HM Capital Partners
KKR
Leonard Green
Thomas H. Lee Partners
TPG

HISTORICAL FINANCIALS
Company Type: Private

Income Statement   FYE: December 31

	ESTIMATED REVENUE ($ mil.)	NET INCOME ($ mil.)	NET PROFIT MARGIN	EMPLOYEES
12/06	617	—	—	11,000

Zachry Group

All roads lead to — and from — Zachry. The holding company for Zachry Engineering and Capital Aggregates, Zachry constructs major highways in its native Texas, including portions of the Trans-Texas Corridor and other toll and non-toll transportation corridors. The company also builds and maintains power and chemical plants, cement and paper mills, refineries, roadways, dams, airfields, and pipelines, primarily in the Lone Star State. Zachry Engineering comprises the group's industrial, power plant, and refinery construction and maintenance. Capital Aggregates runs the company's highway construction operations. The Zachry family owns the firm, which was founded by H.B. Zachry in 1924.

In 2008 Zachry reorganized, eliminating its Zachry Construction subsidiary by folding its operations into Zachry Engineering. Company executives said that streamlining its structure would enable it to pursue contracts in the growing ethanol and nuclear markets, among others.

That year subsidiary Zachry American Infrastructure and its partner, Spanish construction firm ACS Infrastructure (a part of ACS) won the contract for building the I-69 portion of the Trans-Texas Corridor, which is being designed to move trucks to and from Mexico. The corridor is envisioned as around 4,000 miles of road that parallels existing highways and would have separate highways for trucks, cars, and rail as well as utility and other pipelines.

EXECUTIVES

Chairman: H. Bartell Zachry Jr.
CEO and Director: John B. Zachry, age 46
President, COO, and Director: David S. Zachry
SVP: Edward R. (Ed) Bardgett, age 65
SVP, Controller, and Director: Joe J. Lozano
SVP Corporate Business Development:
 Keith D. Manning
SVP and Manager, Power: Robert J. (Bob) Kalt
SVP Corporate Development: Kenneth A. (Ken) Oleson
SVP Finance and Director: D. Kirk McDonald
VP Administration, Accounting, and Director:
 Charles Ebrom
VP, General Counsel, Secretary and Director:
 Murray L. Johnston Jr.
VP Employee Relations: Stephen L. (Steve) Hoech
VP Community Relations: Cathy Obriotti Green
Treasurer: Gonzalo O. Ornelas
Director Public Affairs: Victoria Waddy
Auditors: Ernst & Young

LOCATIONS

HQ: Zachry Group
 527 Logwood Ave., San Antonio, TX 78221
Phone: 210-475-8000   **Fax:** 210-475-8060
Web: www.zachry.com

COMPETITORS

Aker Solutions	Jacobs Engineering
Alberici	KBR
APAC	M. A. Mortenson
Austin Industries	McCarthy Building
Barton Malow	MWH Global
Bechtel	Parsons Corporation
Black & Veatch	Peter Kiewit Sons'
Dick Corporation	Polysius
Fluor	Shaw Group
Foster Wheeler	Sumitomo Mitsui
Gilbane	TIC Holdings
Granite Construction	Turner Industries
Hensel Phelps	Washington Division
Hoffman Corporation	Williams Brothers
Holloman	

HISTORICAL FINANCIALS

Company Type: Private

Income Statement

FYE: December 31

	REVENUE ($ mil.)	NET INCOME ($ mil.)	NET PROFIT MARGIN	EMPLOYEES
12/07	2,188	—	—	11,500
12/06	1,660	—	—	14,000
12/05	1,175	—	—	12,000
12/04	966	—	—	9,096
12/03	1,007	—	—	12,000
Annual Growth	21.4%	—	—	(1.1%)

Revenue History

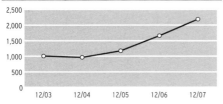

Zappos.com

If the shoe fits, wear it. If not, Zappos.com will gladly take it back at no cost to you. Zappos.com has become the #1 seller of shoes on the Internet (ahead of J.C. Penney) by stressing customer service. The e-tailer stocks 3 million pairs of shoes, handbags, and apparel and accessories, specializing in some 1,000 brands that are difficult to find in mainstream shopping malls. With only one Web site (and 7,000 affiliate partners), Zappos.com distributes stylish and moderately priced footwear, and more, to frustrated and shop-worn customers nationwide. The company was founded by Chairman Nick Swinmurn in 1999 following a mall-based shoe quest gone wrong.

Swinmurn's venture has paid off. Zappos.com has increased its sales from about $1.6 million in 2000 to more than $800 million in 2007. The firm, which has moved beyond shoes to boost sales, has set a goal of selling more than $1 billion in merchandise in 2008. To that end, Zappos.com is becoming an e-tailer that sells "anything and everything," adding apparel, bags, jewelry, watches, ties, eyewear and even electronics to its online store.

To ensure its share of the footwear and accessories market is in the bag and to reach a broader audience, Zappos.com acquired the assets of 6pm.com (formerly Shoedini.com), which specializes in peddling footwear and accessories online, from Denver-based eBags, Inc. in 2007. As part of the agreement, Zappos.com operates 6pm.com separately. Zappos.com was attracted to 6pm.com for its explosive growth; it quadrupled in size in three years.

The online shoe seller's success has attracted competition including IAC/InterActiveCorp's Shoebuy.com and Gap's Piperlime online shoe store, among others. Traditional shoe stores have also moved into the online space.

After decrying the shortcomings of bricks-and-mortar shoe stores, Zappos plans to open a pair of locations in Kentucky. Zappos currently operates an outlet store near its Bullitt County distribution center in Shepherdsville, Kentucky.

EXECUTIVES

CEO: Tony Hsieh
CFO and Director: Alfred Lin
SVP, Merchandising: Fred Mossler
VP, Marketing: Lisa Vagge

LOCATIONS

HQ: Zappos.com, Inc.
2280 Corporate Cir., Ste. 100, Henderson, NV 89074
Phone: 702-943-7777 **Fax:** 702-943-7778
Web: www.zappos.com

PRODUCTS/OPERATIONS

Selected Products

Apparel and accessories
Electronics
Eyewear
Handbags
Jewelry and watches
Shoes

COMPETITORS

Amazon.com	Macy's
Collective Brands	Nine West
DSW	Rack Room Shoes
Finish Line	Shoe Carnival
Foot Locker	shoebuy.com
The Gap	Target
IAC	TJX Companies
J. C. Penney	Wal-Mart

HISTORICAL FINANCIALS

Company Type: Private

Income Statement

FYE: December 31

	REVENUE ($ mil.)	NET INCOME ($ mil.)	NET PROFIT MARGIN	EMPLOYEES
12/07	840	—	—	1,300
12/06	597	—	—	1,000
12/05	370	—	—	800
12/04	135	—	—	243
12/03	72	—	—	134
Annual Growth	84.8%	—	—	76.5%

Revenue History

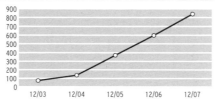

ZelnickMedia Corporation

Entertainment is big business for ZelnickMedia Corporation. Created by former BMG Entertainment (now Sony Music Entertainment) CEO Strauss Zelnick and with operations in the US, Europe, and Asia, ZelnickMedia owns completely, or has stakes in, a variety of media businesses. Holdings include in-flight catalogue publisher and marketer SkyMall, online gaming developer Arkadium, and market research firm OTX. ZelnickMedia serves its portfolio companies in either an advisory or management capacity. ZelnickMedia sold catalog retailer Lillian Vernon to Sun Capital Partners in 2006.

EXECUTIVES

CEO: Strauss Zelnick, age 50
Partner: Benjamin (Ben) Feder, age 44
Partner: Jim Friedlich
Partner: Seymour Sammell
Partner: Scott Siegler
Partner: Karl Slatoff, age 37
Partner: Jordan Turkewitz
Partner: Andrew Vogel, age 35

LOCATIONS

HQ: ZelnickMedia Corporation
19 W. 44th St., 18th Fl., New York, NY 10036
Phone: 212-223-1383 **Fax:** 212-223-1384
Web: www.zelnickmedia.com

PRODUCTS/OPERATIONS

Portfolio Companies

Advisory
  Arkadium (online gaming developer)
  Rights Group (wireless entertainment)
  Skymall, Inc. (catalog sales)
Managed
  Columbia Music Entertainment (Japan, music direct retailer)
  ITN Networks (national media sales)
  Naylor, Inc. (B2B media services for advertising, printing, and publishing industries)
  OTX (aka Online Testing Exchange, consumer market research)
  Take-Two Interactive Software, Inc. (entertainment hardware, software, and accessories)

COMPETITORS

ABRY Partners
Allen & Company
Audiolux
Benchmark Capital
Bertelsmann
CCMP Capital
Demand Media
Fox Interactive
WPP Group

Hoover's Handbook of

Private Companies

The Indexes

Index by Industry

ELECTRONICS

ENERGY & UTILITIES

ENVIRONMENTAL SERVICES
& EQUIPMENT

FINANCIAL SERVICES

FOOD

FOUNDATIONS

GOVERNMENT

HEALTH CARE

Index by Headquarters

Index of Executives

A

Aamodt, Patsy 52
Aaron, Roger S. 447
Abate, Peter 169
Abbot, John 249
Abbott, Henry J. 121
Abbott, Katherine L. 69
Abbott, Michael 459
Abbott, Todd A. 65
Abel, Gregory E. 325
Abeles, Jon C. 115
Abell, Nancy L. 376
Abelman, David 323
Abernathy, Michael G. 278
Abinder, Susan 243
Abington, Bill 312
Able, Brett W. 163
Abood, Denise 291
Abraham, Jay 335
Abrahamson, James R. 203
Abrams, Jim 312
Abrams, Kevin 351
Abrams, Lee 487
Abrams, Robert 447
Abrams, Sarah K. 187
Abramson, Richard (SRI
  International) 456
Abramson, Rick (Delaware North) 155
Accavitti, Michael J. 127
Acchione, David 420
Acheson, Eleanor D. 46
Achtenberg, Roberta 103
Acker, Keith W. 530
Acker, Kevin J. 530
Acker, Stan 500
Ackerman, Steve 429
Ackermann, Josef 136
Acosta, Alan 457
Acquaye, Robert S. 259
Acton, Brian 371
Adair, Ben 125
Adair, Marjorie 382
Adair, Tedd 243
Adams, Baine 91
Adams, Ben C. 68
Adams, Bill 532
Adams, Brady 210
Adams, Cathy C. 180
Adams, Clint B. 53
Adams, Edward 175
Adams, Greg G. 363
Adams, J. Phillip 186
Adams, Julie 69
Adams, Kimberly S. 427
Adams, Niki 387
Adams, Paul 281
Adams, Randy K. 308
Adams, Richard C. 72
Adams, Robert C. 145
Adams, Stephen 27
Adams, Thomas III 520
Adams, Todd A. 404
Adamski, Dave 227

Adamson, Geoff 208
Adamson, Mick 275
Adamson, Terrence B. 339
Adante, David E. 152
Adelman, Rick 240
Adelman, Warren J. 204
Adkins, Norman 454
Adler, William K. 405
Adusumilli, Sat 245
Aertker, Gayle 161
Afable, Mark V. 40
Affeldt, Eric L. 131
Africk, Jack 359
Afterman, Jean 356
Agarwal, Amit 141
Agnew, Brian P. 282
Agnew, Joe 189
Agostinelli, D. D. 62
Agre, Peter C. 167
Ahearn, Greg 483
Ahern, Joe 332
Ahlfeld, Roger C. 510
Ahmad, Asif 167
Ahmed, Mumtaz 156
Ahn, Henry 345
Ahrold, Robbin 98
Aibe, Sono 152
Aiello, Greg 338
Aijala, Ainar D. Jr. 156
Aiken, Robert 512
Ain, Aron J. 275
Ain, Mark S. 275
Ainley, Christopher J. 258
Ajamian, Daniel 470
Akers, Jeff 122
Akin, Steven P. 187
Akin, T.W. Hudson 126
Albano, Jennifer 483
Albano, Monica 520
Albeck, Joan 434
Alber, Michael J. 33
Alberici, John S. 30
Albert, Carol 336
Albert, Rob 533
Albert, Tom 184
Alberti, Judy 304
Albertson, Marty P. 218
Albrecht, Andrew C. 376
Album, Jeff 157
Aldred, Sophie 159
Aldridge, Philip R. 508
Alexander, Ashok 80
Alexander, Jean 18
Alexander, Jimmy 21
Alexander, Ken 367
Alexander, Leslie L. 240
Alexander, Lori 203
Alexander, Peter H. 207
Alexander, Todd 471
Alfano, Jane D. 424
Alfano, JoAnn 286
Alfano, Michael C. 355
Alfano, Michele D. 185
Alfirevic, Richard G. 523

Alger, Jonathan R. 421
Alic, James M. 25
Allbritton, Barbara B. 34
Allbritton, Robert L. 34
Alldian, David P. 90
Allen, A. William III 370
Allen, Andrew W. 55
Allen, Ashley 328
Allen, Barry 142
Allen, Craig 458
Allen, David W. 217
Allen, Gary K 505
Allen, Jane 156
Allen, Jim 30
Allen, Katherine 181
Allen, Kenneth 232
Allen, Matthew J. (Related Group) 410
Allen, Matthew N. (ICON Health) 244
Allen, Meredith B. 458
Allen, Paul G. 392, 523
Allen, Robert C. 122
Allen, Ward 536
Allen-Meares, Paula 503
Allison, Jay 479
Allred, J. Michael 501
Almeida, Butch 132
Almond, Stephen 156
Almquist, David C. 197
Alongi, Michele 349
Alonso, Gerardo L. 180
Alonzo, Jan R. 496
Alpert, Richard H. 340
Alpert, Theodore S. 25
Alston, Alyce 405
Alston, Michael W. 278
Alsvig, Brian L. 316
Altieri, Michael 289
Altman, Lawrence B. 238
Altman, Steven J. 143
Altman, Vicki S. 121
Altshuler, Janis 417
Altstadt, Manfred 333
Altstadter, Jeff 348
Alutto, Joseph A. 366
Alvarado, Donald G. 448
Alvarez, Michelle 18
Alvarez, Scott G. 182
Alverson, Ronald C. 276
Alvis, Scott 422
Amador, Evelyn 499
Amato, Thomas A. 317
Amberg, Stephanie L. 370
Ambrose, Thomas 387
Ambrosini, Robert P. 100
Ambutas, Vytas P. 470
Amen, Louis A. 496
Amendola, Michael 111
Ames, Larry 154
Amir, Carol M. 507
Amkreutz, Michael 357
Anand, Sudeep 450
Andereck, Mike 167
Anderman, David J. 292
Andersen, John 440

Anderson, Ann S. 87
Anderson, Bill (Main Street
  America) 296
Anderson, Brian 140
Anderson, Bruce 536
Anderson, Cathy C. 490
Anderson, Charles 48
Anderson, Charlotte Jones 149
Anderson, David R. 40
Anderson, Douglas (Carlson
  Companies) 109
Anderson, Douglas L. (MidAmerican
  Energy) 325
Anderson, Duwayn 418
Anderson, Gregory W. 88
Anderson, Ian D. 270
Anderson, Jarrett 116
Anderson, Joel R. 48
Anderson, John Jr. (Topa Equities) 481
Anderson, John E. Sr. (Topa
  Equities) 481
Anderson, John F. (Catholic Health
  Initiatives) 114
Anderson, John R. (Concentra) 136
Anderson, Julie 522
Anderson, Lee R. Sr. 50
Anderson, Lincoln 291
Anderson, Mark B. 322
Anderson, Mitch 327
Anderson, Peter 466
Anderson, R. John 283
Anderson, Ray 338
Anderson, Richard 173
Anderson, Scott R. 178
Anderson, Steve 177
Anderson, Tom 403
Anderson, Walter 23
Anderson, William (Raley's) 402
Andoga, James R. 63
Andoscia, Caroline 199
Andreassen, Inge 42
Andreoli, Tom 432
Andretta, Jay 123
Andrews, Bill 213
Andrews, Gloria Moore 105
Andrews, Paul 211
Andy, John 137
Anger, Laura 145
Anger, Michael 476
Angress, David 218
Angulo, Carlos 20
Annunziato, Frank P. 474
Ansary, Hushang 461
Anschuetz, Christopher 312
Anschutz, Philip F. 289
Ansell, Jeffrey P. 388
Anstrom, S. Decker 278
Antes, John D. 83
Anthony, Barry 309
Anthony, Tye 81
Antman, Karen H. 95
Anton, Arthur F. 467
Antoniou, Chris 251
Apallas, Yeoryios 371

Beasley, John 382
Beasley, Mark V. 323
Beatrice, Dennis 456
Beatty, Dale E. 360
Beaty, Mark 420
Beauchine, Fay 109
Beaudrault, Peter J. 429
Beaver, Stephen J. 467
Bechtel, Riley P. 75
Bechtel, Stephen D. Jr. 75
Beck, David (Golden Horizons) 205
Beck, David (New Jersey Devils) 348
Beck, Frank 480
Beck, Jim 196
Beck, Joseph 120
Beck, Ronda S. 504
Beck, S. Fred 244
Becker, Cliff Jr. 517
Becker, Dan 206
Becker, Douglas L. 279
Becker, Joseph 312
Becker, Robert G. 157
Becker, Russell 50
Becker, Steve (Golden State Foods) 206
Becker, Steven R. (Southern Wine & Spirits) 453
Becker, Tom 215
Becker, William L. 223
Beckerman, Dan 289
Beckert, Ellen 193
Beckett, Godfrey 92
Beckman, David 447
Beckman, Jeff 283
Beckman, Jerry 186
Beckman, John 355
Beckmann, James K. Jr. 55
Beddow, David L. 146
Bedrosian, John C. 496
Beekman, Sheri 446
Beeler, Ralph Brent 77
Beers-Reineke, Brenda 321
Beesley, Erin 364
Beglin, James 222
Beha, Ralph 109
Behm, Larry 374
Behnke, Michael C. 503
Behr, Joan 190
Beissner, Sheree 146
Beitcher, Robert L. 294
Belani, Rahul 138
Belechak, Joseph G. 168
Belek, Marilynn 157
Belfer, Barry 217
Belk, H. W. McKay 76
Belk, John R. 76
Belk, Thomas M. Jr. 76
Bell, Christy W. 238
Bell, David 432
Bell, Ernie 524
Bell, Stanley R. 91
Bell, Stephen M. 187
Bell, Thomas R. Jr. 185
Bellavance, Peter 470
Bellew, Robert 517
Bellini, Karen 222
Bellis, Arnold M. 353
Bena, John 153
Benaszeski, Gary 536
Bender, Lisa R. 329
Bendheim, Daniel M. 386
Bendheim, Jack C. 386
Bendler, Alison 71
Benedetti, Joseph C. 348
Bengali, Abdul 307
Benham, Bret L. 478
Benjamin, Harvey E. 336
Bennack, Frank A. Jr. 230
Bennet, Richard W. III 118
Bennett, Clayton I. 367
Bennett, David S. 244
Bennett, Dennis J. 185
Bennett, Ed 335
Bennett, Lerone Jr. 259

Bennett, Steven A. 516
Bennett, Tim 223
Bennich, Larry 30
Bennitt, Brent M. 538
Benson, Dea 406
Benson, Jared P. 210
Bentas, Lily Haseotes 146
Benusa, Gerry W. 40
Benzel, Craig 214
Benzon, Jessica 67
Berdak, Geri 451
Beré, David L. 161
Berens, Gregg 267
Berenson, Marvin 98
Berg, David A. 39
Berg, Jeremy M. 341
Berg, Joanne E. 509
Bergen, David G. 283
Bergen, Sharon 270
Bergen, Timothy 442
Berger, Dennis G. 118
Berger, Gary 41
Berger, Jan P. 448
Berger, Laurence J. 358
Berger, Nancee Shannon R. 530
Berggren, Marie N. 501
Bergland, Bruce W. 246
Bergman, Howard 158
Bergman, Michelle D. 166
Bergquist, Betty A. 40
Berk, Bradford C. 506
Berkeley, Linda 339
Berkery, Michael J. 42
Berkley, William R. 355
Berlind, Mark 61
Bermingham, Robert P. 541
Bernandes, Ricardo 103
Bernanke, Ben S. 182
Bernard, Dane 267
Bernard, Melissa 215
Bernd, David L. 437
Berne, Robert 355
Berner, Mary G. 405
Bernick, Alan 48
Berning, Melvin 17
Bernstein, Alison R. 190
Bernstock, Robert F. 514
Berry, G. Dennis 144
Berry, George R. 523
Berry, Philip A. 130
Berry, Will (Southwire) 454
Berry, William E. (American Tire) 43
Berryman, David H. 201
Berson, David 177
Berthiaume, Joanne 93
Berthiaume, Paul 312
Bertsch, Jan A. 127
Bescalli, Linda 537
Bescher, Jeff 22
Besser, David J. 145
Best, Frank 379
Best, J. Kirby 248
Bester, Ron L. 357
Bettiga, Michael J. 442
Bettman, Gary B. 341
Betts, Douglas G. 127
Beu, Gary 269
Bevilaqua, Joseph P. 235
Bevis, Harold C. 390
Beyer, Alana 253
Beyer, Chris 289
Beyer, Richard E. (JE Dunn Construction Group) 255
Beyer, Richard M. (Freescale Semiconductor) 194
Beyer, Tom 201
Beyle, Jeffrey L. 199
Bezney, Michael A. 115
Bhardwaj, Sunil 535
Bhoopathy, Aditya 358
Bhoumik, Sam 44
Bianchi, Franco 227
Bibb, Bob 286

Biddle, Rodney 409
Biehn, Doug 89
Bienen, Henry S. 361
Bierly, John 104
Bieszczat, Stephen L. 22
Biga, Thomas A. 423
Bigelow, Chandler 487
Biggers, Matt 350
Bikman, Samuel G. 207
Bilek, Glenn 152
Bilik, Jerry 184
Biljanic, Mary 124
Billet, Van 79
Billiel, Jack 241
Billington, Craig 132
Billington, Paul R. 420
Bilney, Jody L. 370
Binder, David 415
Binder, Jeffrey R. 82
Binder, Kenneth J. 439
Binderman, Gail 439
Bindon, James G. 192
Binetti, Craig F. 451
Binger, Rhonda 536
Binnicker, Chris 49
Bippus, Bill 367
Bird, Karen H. 532
Bird, Larry 246
Birden, Ray 196
Birgeneau, Robert J. 501
Birkins, Rod 161
Birmingham, Thomas 139
Birren, Jeff 363
Bishop, J. Michael 501
Bishop, Kay 63
Bishop, Stephen P. 213
Bishop, Warren 250
Bissett, William J. 155
Bissey, Jeff 369
Bitsoff, Jason 184
Bittenbender, Tom 219
Bitterle, Jim 201
Bitting, Stuart 153
Biunno, Susan 96
Bixby, Scott 440
Bizzotto, Anita J. 514
Black, Cathleen P. 230
Black, John 290
Black, Sandy 384
Black, Steven 291
Blackburn, B. 165
Blackburn, Lawrence M. 207
Blackerby, Tom 498
Blacketer, Rachel 126
Blackey, Brent G. 238
Blackford, Gary D. 500
Blackman, Richard O. 480
Blackman, Rolando 149
Blackmore, Bud 445
Blackwell, Bill 414
Blackwell, E. Scott 410
Blackwell, Terry L. 453
Blaine, Dorman 540
Blair, Maria 416
Blair, Robert 196
Blair, Sam 68
Blais, David A. 399
Blake, H. Scott 241
Blake, John C. 95
Blakely, Paul A. 100
Blakey, Jay B. 136
Blanchard, Dan 179
Blanco, A. Paul 391
Blanco, Kimberly 349
Bland, Calvin 415
Blanda, Tom 363
Blank, Joel 240
Blankley, Anthony 171
Blanks, Lance 117
Blanks, Marvin III 540
Blanton, Andy 311
Blashack Strahan, Jill 470
Blassberg, Eric A. 447

Blaszyk, Michael D. 116
Bledsoe, Tom 335
Bleiberg, Fred 337
Bleich, Jeffrey L. 103
Blenke, John W. 485
Blett, Tim 527
Blevins, Teresa F. 278
Blickensderfer, Michael 439
Blimling, Gregory S. 421
Blinn, Richard P. 197
Bliwise, Cherie 268
Block, Edward L. 414
Block, Gene D. 501
Block, Paul R. 316
Blodgett, Stephen 390
Blois, Tim 211
Bloom, Steven E. 175
Bloom, Ted 250
Bloomberg, Michael R. 85
Bloss, Connie 380
Blue, Greg 208
Bluebello, Jim 527
Bluhm, Robert 222
Blum, Don 529
Blum, William H. 532
Blumb, Jeff 214
Blumenthal, George R. 501
Blunt, Christopher O. 352
Blunt, Mary L. 437
Bluntzer, Rick 291
Blye, Colleen M. 114
Blythe, Roger E. Jr. 126
Boag, Simon 127
Boccio, Frank M. 352
Bockhorst, Thomas A. 340
Bodaken, Bruce G. 89
Bodal, Bernt O. 42
Bode, Ken A. 143
Bodenhamer, William H. Jr. 121
Bodenheimer, George W. 177
Bodenman, Brad D. 42
Bodie, Becky 205
Bodinger, Bill 269
Boe, Ralph 74
Boedeker, Bob 121
Boehm, Martin O. 381
Böer, Ralf-Reinhard 188
Boff, Marc 328
Bogan, Patti 128
Boggess, Mark J. 27, 193
Bohac, Don E. 220
Bohan, Lynne M. 241
Bohman, Daniel 186
Bohne, F. David 516
Boike, James E. 222
Boire, Ronald D. 483
Boisture, William W. Jr. 110
Boland, Dan 382
Boland, John L. 377
Boland, Mary 283
Bolbach, Cynthia J. 100
Bolch, Carl E. Jr. 401
Bolen, Chad 315
Bolen, Michael D. 307
Boler, John M. 91
Boler, Matthew J. 91
Boley, Carl 48
Bolhous, M. Kathleen 50
Bolingbroke, Gregory M. 295
Boller, Steve 151
Bollinger, Lee C. 134
Bolton, Jeffrey W. 307
Bon, Sylvie A. 467
Bonaventura, Kathryn 523
Bond, Bruce 497
Bond, Ed 443
Bond, James H. 121
Bond, Jill 412
Bond, Julian 334
Bonderman, David 484
Bonds, Andrew 376
Bondy, Susan H. 434
Bondy, Timothy J. 172

Buckingham, Lorie 65
Buckland, Patti 422
Buckley, Jean 162
Buckley, Michael A. 162
Buckley, Mortimer J. 518
Buckley, Robert M. 416
Buckley, Stephen 417
Buckman, Kurt 82
Buckman, Michael A. 74
Buckner, Lindsay 486
Buckner, William A. 108
Budde, Tom L. 188
Buehler, Marc A. 288
Buenrostro, Fred R. Jr. 105
Bufano, Kathryn 76
Buford, R. C. 426
Bugg-Levine, Antony 416
Buhr, James 71
Bujack, Denise A. 229
Bukowski, Gerard T. 102
Bullard, James B. 182
Bullen, Bruce M. 225
Bullock, Robert 122
Bulluck, Vicangelo 334
Bulman, Lyn 184
Bumgardner, Eunice L. 100
Bumgarner, Ron 95
Bumstead, Matt 498
Bumstead, R. Gantt 498
Bunce, Jode 170
Bundy, Steve 170
Bunnell, David A. 433
Bunsick, Robert 209
Bunt, Diane C. 439
Buonomo, James R. 363
Bur, Eric J. 382
Burch, Alice 288
Burch, Robert 444
Burch, Stephen P. 370
Burchard, Jacquie 153
Burchill, Jeffrey A. 180
Burd, Loretta M. 146
Burdick, Kyle 360
Burdick, Richard L. 95
Burdiss, James E. 27
Burditt, Andrew 425
Bureau, George 444
Burgay, Stephen P. 95
Burgdorf, Barry D. 508
Burge, Steve 479
Burgess, Maggie 54
Burgess, Matt 142
Burgett, Paul J. 506
Burgo, Raymond 200
Burk, Mike 311
Burke, Adam 236
Burke, Brian P. 47
Burke, James A. 174
Burke, Michael W. 30
Burke, Paul 358
Burke, Tim 426
Burke, Vince G. 222
Burkett, Johanna 68
Burkett, Kathleen 20
Burkhardt, Stephan 496
Burkhead, Jeffrey 106
Burkle, Ronald W. 541
Bürkner, Hans-Paul 94
Burleson, Russ 453
Burlingame, Keith 245
Burner, Greg 538
Burnett, Mark 131
Burnett, Nancy Packard 152
Burnich, Jeffrey 466
Burns, Baxter 175
Burns, Brent 257
Burns, Deborah 195
Burns, Donal 505
Burns, Jeff Jr. 259
Burns, Jim 121
Burns, Kenneth R. 345
Burns, Patrick A. 333
Burns, Ralph M. III 373

Burns, Robert E. 62
Burns, Sharon 295
Burns, Stephanie A. 163
Burns, Tom 444
Burr, Ian M. 517
Burr, Mike 328
Burrell, James 175
Burris, Mary Ellen 528
Burrows, Keith 526
Bursch, H. Dean 138
Burstein, Mark 394
Burt, Geoff 279
Burt, Theresa 474
Burtch, Douglas R. 97
Burwell, Sylvia Matthews 80
Burza, Eileen F. 383
Busard, Thomas 389
Busby, A. Patrick 175
Busch, Rick 397
Buser, Curt 110
Bush, Kenny 540
Bush, William P. 299
Bushman, Randall A. 272
Buss, Jeanie 290
Buss, Jerry 290
Buss, Jim 290
Buss, Timothy A. 340
Butcher, Ernesto L. 391
Butkovic, Michael R. 467
Butler, Adrian 120
Butler, Frank A. 504
Butler, Gary 99
Butler, Lisa M. 259
Butler, Liz 516
Butler, Mark 31
Butler, Michael 396
Butt, Charles C. 232
Butt, Stephen 232
Butterman, Mark B. 395
Buttress, Larry D. 92
Butts, Mike 165
Butzelaar, Frank J. 526
Byman, Nelson 254
Byrd, Warren 22
Byrne, Brian A. 19
Byrne, Joseph E. 356
Byrnes, Brian 367
Byrnes, John 454

C

Cabaniss, Wyman 33
Cabell, Christopher H. 401
Cable, Steve 359
Cabrera, Jose 151
Cabrera, Noel 62
Cacace, Gary 528
Cacioppo, Gary 417
Caddell, Douglas D. 188
Cadieux, Chester III 400
Cadwallader, Martin 509
Cahill, Anne B. 353
Cahill, Timothy P. 306
Cain, Brian 123
Calabrese, Jeannie L. 63
Calamari, Matthew F. 491
Calanca, Anthony 25
Calandro, Michele 86
Calbert, Michael M. 161
Calbert, Robert 308
Caldarello, Becky 170
Caldeira, Stephen J. 167
Caldwell, Bret 473
Califf, Robert 167
Calkins, Dan 150
Callahan, John W. 187
Callahan, Richard P. 371
Callahan, Timothy M. (Berwind) 79
Callahan, Timothy P. (SIRVA) 446
Callas, Darcy G. 330
Callison, Jack R. 52
Calloway, Gregory 41

Calo, Amber 142
Calpeter, Lynn 345
Calvert, Karen 303
Camastral, Brian 302
Camden, Hugh 178
Camerlo, James P. 148
Cameron, Cheryl A. 508
Cameron, Ian 59
Camp, David C. 458
Camp, Rob 533
Campanile, Patty 437
Campbell, Alan (Freescale Semiconductor) 194
Campbell, Allen J. (Cooper-Standard Automotive) 141
Campbell, Ben D. 207
Campbell, Brett 261
Campbell, Bruce 345
Campbell, Colin 341
Campbell, David A. (Energy Future) 174
Campbell, David K. (Boston University) 95
Campbell, Don H. 410
Campbell, Gary S. 114
Campbell, George Anthony 198
Campbell, James J. 459
Campbell, John (Anderson News) 48
Campbell, John B. (Ag Processing) 29
Campbell, John W. (Horizon Healthcare) 238
Campbell, Judy 150
Campbell, Keith (U.S. Foodservice) 512
Campbell, Keith M. (Securian Financial) 435
Campbell, Kevin P. 242
Campbell, Kirk 250
Campbell, Mary 150
Campbell, Paul V. 293
Campbell, Stuart V.M. 274
Campbell, Victor L. 227
Campbell, William (US Postal Service) 514
Campbell, William H. (Amtrak) 46
Campbell, William R. Jr. (TVA) 494
Campbell, William V. (Columbia University) 134
Campi, John P. 127
Campisi, David J. 455
Campos, Denise 258
Cancro, Lawrence C. 95
Candito, Tony 482
Cannatelli, Len Jr. 533
Cannella, Gina 291
Cannizzo, Gary 98
Cannon, Robert W. 83
Cannova, Laurie 66
Cansler, Vicki 229
Canter, Richard J. 532
Cantrell, Dawn 86
Cantrell, Pierce E. Jr. 475
Canty, Stephen D. 296
Capasso, John 113
Capellas, Michael D. 185
Capozzi, Vincent 225
Capp, Brian 282
Capps, W. Lee III 266
Caputo, Louise 120
Caracappa, Joe 106
Caragozian, John 465
Carano, Gary L. 128
Carano, Glenn T. 128
Carcone, John D. 192
Card, Robert G. 122
Carette, Yves 44
Carey, Gina 528
Carey, William C. 187
Cargill, Jerry 202
Cargill, John 237
Carkeek, Susan A. 506
Carlasare, John 516
Carlesimo, P.J. 367
Carleton, Mark D. 284

Carlile, Thomas E. 91
Carlin, Brian 299
Carlin, Peter E. 300
Carlisle, Rick 149
Carlos, Chris 337
Carlos, John A. 337
Carlsen, Jeff 412
Carlsgaard, Terry J. 479
Carlson, Brian 258
Carlson, Bruce W. 155
Carlson, Curtis R. 456
Carlson, Gerald K. 386
Carlson, Greg 529
Carlson, Jack 454
Carlson, Jeanne H. 88
Carlson, Mark 68
Carlson, Rick D. 282
Carlson, Robert F. 105
Carlson Gage, Barbara 109
Carlsson, Sören 211
Carlucci, Frank C. 461
Carlyle, Randy 47
Carmen, L. 503
Carmen, Robert G. 25
Carmignani, Jeff 244
Carnaroli, Craig 506
Carney, Brian P. 81
Carney, James 476
Carousso, Paul B. 521
Carper, Tad 117
Carr, Curtis 178
Carr, Lisa 154
Carretta, Robert 423
Carrico, Stephen J. 234
Carrier, Carol 505
Carrigan, Bob 250
Carroll, Charles A. 207
Carroll, Gerard 344
Carroll, James F. 148
Carroll, John 146
Carroll, Kathleen 59
Carroll, Matt 67
Carroll, Milton 229
Carson, Amanda 254
Carson, Ken 120
Carstens, Robert M. 444
Cartales, Karen 286
Carter, Bobbie 129
Carter, C. Michael 161
Carter, Ian R. 236
Carter, Lonnie N. 453
Carter, Mary D. 48
Carter, Michael G. 361
Carter, Rosalind Clay 17
Carter, William H. 235
Caruana, Maureen 264
Caruso, Joseph A. 217
Caruso, Thomas (Blue Tee) 90
Caruso, Tom (ADESA) 22
Carver, Mark A. 534
Carvette, Anthony M. 462
Casaccio, Anthony A. 249
Casadonte, Thom 299
Casady, Mark S. 291
Case, C. Wayne 220
Case, Joe 344
Casebeer, Steve 266
Caserio, Marjorie C. 502
Casey, Larry 267
Casey, Mabel 227
Casey, Patrick J. 492
Casey, Sister Juliana M. 113
Casey, T. Michael 257
Casey, Thomas J. 49
Cash, Carol Dalton 185
Cashion, Robert 226
Cashman, Brian 356
Caso, Laura 111
Caspers, Christy 470
Caspersen, Daniel 483
Cass, Jim 302
Cassard, Christopher D. 360

Collins, John (NHL) 341
Collins, Keith V. 427
Collins, Michael 408
Collins, Paul 209
Collins, Timothy R. 170
Colliver, Ray 523
Colloton, Ken 540
Colon, Conrad O. 210
Colony, Sandra D. 249
Colson, Rick 254
Colvin, Dwain S. 243
Coman, David 401
Combs, Sean 65
Comeaux, Al 422
Comer, Ruth 242
Compagno, Robert 184
Companion, Lydia 68
Conant, Douglas R. 136
Conatser, Lark 181
Conde, Cesar 509
Conde, Cristóbal I. 464
Condello, Frank 346
Condon, Kenneth G. 95
Condon, Mary Ellen 531
Condos, George M. 195
Condrin, J. Paul III 285
Conklin, Richard L. 83
Conkling, Lori 286
Conklyn, Elizabeth D. 516
Conley, Don 522
Conley, James E. Jr. 358
Conley, Michael P. 192
Conlon, John 44
Conlon, Richard 98
Conn, Lance 523
Connell, Margot 137
Connell, Sharon 39
Connelly, James M. 234
Connelly, Kevin 78
Connelly, Mary J. 534
Connelly, Michael D. 115
Conner, Becky 275
Conner, W. Theodore 63
Conner, Wayne J. 172
Connolly, Christine 161
Connolly, Joe 334
Connolly, John P. 156
Connor, P. Eric 325
Connors, Robert 455
Conrad, Christy 175
Conrad, Joel 342
Conrads, Charlie 482
Conroy, J. Patrick 381
Conroy, James 130
Conroy, John J. Jr. 67
Conroy, Mark S. 109
Conroy, Tom 539
Constantine, Shari 528
Conte, David 348
Conti, Caterina 49
Contratto, Jim 307
Conway, Paul D. 108
Conway, William A. (Henry Ford Health System) 234
Conway, William E. Jr. (The Carlyle Group) 110
Conway, William S. (Mutual of America) 333
Conway-Welch, Colleen 517
Cook, Cheryl 171
Cook, Jason D. 475
Cook, Julie 49
Cook, Larry N. 504
Cook, Linda 326
Cook, Marvin F. 95
Cook, Ralph K. 186
Cook, Thomas H. (Dow Corning) 163
Cook, Tom (Elkay Manufacturing) 172
Cook, William R. 470
Cooley, Christian 442
Cooley, Hugh 332
Coolidge, Andrew 446
Cooney, Edward J. 362

Coons, Margaret 238
Coons, Scott 382
Cooper, Bradley 390
Cooper, Dean 240
Cooper, Jim 371
Cooper, John I. (Noble Investment) 358
Cooper, John W. (OSI Restaurant Partners) 370
Cooper, Marcia 494
Cooper, Ronald 420
Cooper, Steven I. 407
Cooper, Wayne 423
Cooper, W.H. 46
Cope, Andrew G. 275
Cope, Roger J. 250
Copeland, David 219
Copeland, R. Jeffrey 115
Copeland, Richard P. 29
Copeland, Tom 337
Copp, Duke 214
Coppel, Ron 170
Copses, Peter P. 130
Corbin, Chuck 69
Corcoran, Elizabeth 66
Corcoran, Thomas A. 110
Cordani, John L. 295
Cordial, Michelle 463
Cordova, Stefano 78
Cords, Brian 190
Corey, R. David 390
Cormier, Ken 113
Cornell, Brian C. 323
Cornell, Terry 239
Cornwell, Fred 326
Corr, Thomas L. 198
Correa, Eduardo 107
Correa, Larry 183
Correale, Michael A. 44
Correy, Paula 242
Corrick, Tom 91
Corsano, Anthony 49
Corsi, John 122
Cortese, Denis A. 307
Cortese, Edward 281
Cortez, R. Michael 441
Corwin, Steven J. 358
Cosbey, John R. 152
Coscia, Anthony R. 391
Cosenza, G. Joseph 248
Cosgrove, Edward M. 525
Coslov, I. Michael 492
Cosmos, Bill 123
Cossette, Paul I. 293
Cost, Michael 97
Costantin, Jeff 410
Costello, Donna 439
Costiglio, Peter 416
Costner, Kathy M. 69
Costner, Philip 276
Cote, Bill 466
Cote, Jeff 437
Cothern, Carol 527
Cotta, Richard 102
Cotten, Paula 400
Cotter, Mary Carole 265
Cotterell, Samuel K. 91
Cotton, Al 363
Cotton, Richard 345
Coughlin, Michael T. 306
Coughlin, Thomas R. 351
Coulter, James G. 484
Coultis, Susie 382
Counce, J. Daniel 180
Countryman, Tom 152
Coupe, Jerry 534
Coursen, Sam 194
Courtney, Lisa 472
Courtney, Patrick 297
Courvelle, Lynn 332
Cova, Charles 116
Coventry, Bruce D. 127
Covert, Derek F. 116
Covey, Patrick M. 152

Covey, Paul R. 368
Covington, Monty 215
Cowan, R. Douglas 152
Coward, Michael 141
Cowden, Barbara 458
Cowfer, David 53
Cox, Gregg 54
Cox, J. Linloy 334
Cox, Pam 532
Cox, Robbie 443
Coy, Jerry 264
Coyle, Dan 418
Coyle, Frank A. 243
Coyle, Matthew T. 285
Coyne, Adam M. 415
Coyne, Frank 86
Coyne, William J. 402
Cozine, Maureen M. 415
Crabb, Jennifer 402
Craig, John J. 425
Craig, Tobie 493
Crain, Keith E. 145
Crain, Mary Kay 145
Crain, Merrilee P. 145
Crain, Rance E. 145
Craine, Tom 540
Cramer, Bonnie M. 18
Cramer, Michael J. (Pinnacle Foods) 388
Cramer, Mike (ICC Industries) 243
Cranch, Laurence E. 35
Crandall, Roger W. 305
Crandus, Shlomo Y. 192
Crane, Phillip 206
Crane, Robert M. 263, 264
Cranford, Alan N. 519
Craven, Pamela F. 65
Crawford, Catherine L. 329
Crawford, Colin 250
Crawford, David J. 439
Crawford, Jack G. 510
Crawford, James D. 534
Crawford, Jeffrey W. 21
Crawford, Lindsay 418
Crawford, Lori 541
Crayton, Raquel Graham 259
Creasey, F. Clay Jr. 483
Crecca, Paul J. 221
Creekmuir, William S. 444
Cregan, Barry J. 304
Cremer, Jill 491
Crenshaw, Joe 412
Crenshaw, William E. 398
Crews, Anne 303
Crews, Kit 472
Criqui, Robert 336
Crist, Alan 509
Croft, David 512
Croft, John 81
Croley, John 367
Crombie, Bill 524
Cromer, Donald L. 27
Cromwell, Ted 74
Cronin, Constance J. 234
Cronin, Tim 147
Crook, Carl R. 356
Crook, David 130
Cropper, Jon 65
Crosbie, William L. 46
Crosby, Steven C. 523
Croskey, Chuck 216
Cross, H. Russell 475
Cross, Marvin 117
Cross, Sue 59
Cross, Thomas 86
Crosson, Francis J. 263
Croswell, Thomas A. 493
Crotty, W. Garrett 335
Crouse, Jerry K. 475
Crowder, Gary S. 330
Crowe, Brian 357
Crowley, Elaine D. 323
Crowley, J. Samuel 323

Crowley, Jane Durney 115
Crown, James S. 502
Crowther, Bruce K. 360
Croyle, Robert 337
Crumb, Dan 350
Crume, Charles 534
Crusco, Kathleen M. 22
Cuban, Mark 149
Cubbage, Alan K. 361
Cuccorelli, Albert 101
Cuevas, Lisa I. 529
Cuffe, Michael 167
Cullen, John A. 352
Cullen, Karen 245
Culley, Christopher M. 366
Cullick, Robert 291
Cully, David K. 67
Culvahouse, Arthur B. Jr. 368
Cumbow, Steve 456
Cummings, Bruce 216
Cummings, John 42
Cummins, Natalie A. 469
Cundy, Deborah 109
Cunningham, Dennis 341
Cunningham, John 527
Cunningham, Kelly 505
Cunningham, Michael R. 128
Cunningham, Rick 375
Cunningham, Steve 86
Curley, Jay 87
Curley, Thomas 59
Curran, Chris 177
Curran, Terri 93
Curren, Vincent 143
Current, Gloster B. Jr. 361
Currey, Gail 292
Currie, Robert 258
Curtin, Brian 175
Curtin, John 137
Curtin, Joseph 492
Curtin, Michael J. 504
Curtin, Thomas A. Jr. 264
Curtis, Arnold 133
Curtis, Howard 275
Curtis, Lynda D. 351
Curtis-McIntyre, Amy 203
Cushman, Jeffrey D. 69
Cusolito, John 285
Cyffka, Peter J. 368
Cymerys, Edward C. 89
Cyr, Martha 287
Czarnecki, Walt 381
Czelusniak, Judith A. 85

D

D. S. Walker, Cheryl 505
Dacek, Franziska H. 467
Daeninck, Yolande 310
Dagenais, Mike 141
Dagger, Thomas G. 386
D'Agostino, Vincent R. 528
Dagot, Antoine 236
Dahlin, Richard L. 154
Dailey, Sean 124
Dake, Gary C. 462
Dake, William 462
Dale, Karen M. 522
Dale, Kenneth J. 59
Dalebout, William T. 244
D'Alessandro, D. Beatty 212
D'Alessandro, Dennis 159
Dallafior, Kenneth R. 88
D'Allessio, John M. 415
Dalpiaz, Paul 145
Dalrymple, John S. III 148
Dalrymple, Mark 433
Dalrymple, Rich 149
Dalton, Stephen H. 480
Daly, Ann 164
Daly, William L. 341
Damiano, John 345

Follett, Chuck 189
Follis, Russ 243
Folts, Ellen 526
Fong Goh, Mui 61
Fontaine, Bryan 93
Fontaine, Robert T. 303
Fontan, Julio Perez 126
Fontana, James C. 33
Fontana, Mari 326
Fontanes, A. Alexander 285
Fontham, Elizabeth T. H. 39
Foote, Jeff 186
Forbes, Glenn S. 307
Forbes, Kathryn A. 407
Ford, Allyn 418
Ford, Ian 107
Ford, Judith V. 29
Ford, Mark 304
Ford, Michael A. 529
Ford, Sabrina 179
Ford, Steve 536
Fordyce, Michael L. 114
Foreman, Gary B. 415
Foreman, Jim 482
Forkner, Tom 524
Forman, David 337
Forman, Gar 125
Formella, Nancy 151
Forquignon, Dirck 61
Forsee, Gary D. 505
Forst, Edward C. 226
Forster, Peter C. 131
Forsythe, Richard A. 192
Forte, Kate 223
Fortunato, Joseph 203
Fortune, Beth 517
Foskey, Andrew 254
Fosler, Gail D. 136
Foss, Jim 387
Foster, Deborah W. 499
Foster, George A. 372
Foster, Martin G. 229
Foster, Melanie 324
Foster, P. Wesley Jr. 288
Foster, Pamela 416
Foster, Randall 435
Foster, Richard M. 265
Foster, Ron 192
Fotiades, George L. 112
Fotsch, Richard J. 273
Fouad, Sam 176
Foulon, Koenraad C. 106
Fountain, W. Frank Jr. 127
Fournier, Steve 160
Fowler, June McAllister 83
Fox, Alan M. 510
Fox, Alison 426
Fox, Alissa 86
Fox, Brent 19
Fox, C.H. 370
Fox, Claudia K. 111
Fox, James P. 391
Fox, Kevin 150
Fox, Mary Anne (University of California) 501
Fox, Marye Anne (UC-San Diego) 502
Foxx, Kevin L. 436
Foy, David T. 468
Frahm, George 460
Frame, Mark 420
Frampton, Judith H. 225
Francavilla, Ben 46
France, Brian Z. 335
France, James C. 335
France Kennedy, Lesa D. 335
Francis, Charles P. 116
Francis, Dave 79
Francis, Gerard 85
Francis, James L. 467
Francis, Laura 396
Francis, Peter T. 258
Franck, John M. II 227
Franco, Robert M. 58

Francois, Michael B. 391
Francois, Paul 382
Francona, Terry John 95
Frank, Bryant M. 451
Frank, Craig T. 268
Frank, Darryl 164
Frank, Elaine S. 192
Frank, James S. 192
Frank, Lawrence 349
Frank, Mike 512
Frank, Peter 62
Frank, Susan C. 158
Frank, Ted 345
Frankenthaler, Stan 167
Franklin, Greg 303
Franklin, Michael 473
Franklin, Ryan 288
Frankowski, Thomas J. 399
Franks, Christon 317
Franks, Joanne 304
Franks, Mark 150
Frantz, David O. 366
Frantz, Paul 434
Frantz, Shannon 364
Franz, Gary 382
Frapwell, Dorothy J. 246
Frasch, Richard D. 108
Fraser, Bo 505
Fraser, Michael 512
Frasher, Stephen A. 526
Fratello, Mike 315
Fraumeni, Joseph F. Jr. 337
Fray, Steven W. 451
Frazier, Larry R. 123
Frazier-Coleman, Christie 71
Freadhoff, Chuck 106
Freake, Baxter 112
Frechtling, Dan 270
Frede, Richard 432
Fredeau, Michel 94
Frederick, Francie A. 508
Freed, Michael P. 454
Freedlund, Kurt 198
Freedman, Tom 282
Freeman, Bruce 254
Freeman, Charles 369
Freeman, Donald S. Jr. 193
Freeman, Randall J. 97
Freerking, Ron 404
Fremaux, Emmett H. 46
French, Richard G. 465
French, Tammy 42
Frennea, Robert 19
Frey, David 149
Frey, Donna 537
Frey, Douglas E. 409
Frey, James E. 30
Frey, Shellie 206
Fribourg, Paul J. 140
Frick, Jeffrey E. 135
Frid, Peter 377
Friddell, Guy III 278
Frieden, Sue 176
Friedenberg, Michael 250
Friedland-Howard, Kathy 442
Friedlich, Jim 542
Friedman, Alexander S. 80
Friedman, Brad H. 101
Friedman, Eric J. 447
Friedman, Joel 69
Friel, Daniel 279
Friel, Thomas M. 461
Fritsch, Doug 244
Fritz, Jerald N. 34
Fritz, Jim 369
Fritzsche, Joe 438
Frobes, Patricia 252
Froeschle, Thomas A. 93
Frommer, Andrew J. 66
Fromson, Lee 408
Fronberry, Robert 452
Frush, Karen 167
Fry, David 196

Fry, John 196
Fry, Michael W. 468
Fry, Patrick E. 466
Fry, Scott 33
Fry, William (H-E-B) 232
Fry, William R. (Fry's Electronics) 196
Fryda, Gary L. 420
Fudge, James 30
Fuerst, Thomas 469
Fugate, Charlie 275
Fuhrman, Susan H. 134
Fuhrmann, David E. 190
Fulkerson, William J. Jr. 167
Fuller, Bonnie 41
Fuller, John (Johnny Rockets) 258
Fuller, John (Motiva Enterprises) 332
Fuller, Kathryn S. 190
Fuller, Max L. 515
Fuller, Nick 204
Fuller, Ron 398
Fuller, Steve 287
Fuller, William E. 515
Fullerton, Andrew 96
Fulton, John 122
Fumagali, Oscar J. 97
Funk, Bradley C. 293
Funk, Robert A. 179
Funk, Roger C. 152
Furbush, Robert C. 95
Furmanski, Philip 421
Furst, Jack 95
Furst, Thomas J. 456
Furth, Mark 59
Furumasu, Brian 92
Fusco Nagle, Julie A. 192
Fuson, Rick 246
Fussner, Tom 24
Futa, Edwin H. 419

G

Gabbe, Steven G. 517
Gabriel, Nicholas M. 190
Gadek, Stanley J. 386
Gadiesh, Orit 66
Gafford, Ronald J. 63
Gage Lofgren, Diane 263
Gagnon, Michael O. 393
Gaier, Elizabeth A. 311
Gaillard, Timothy M. 503
Gaines, Gay Hart 143
Gaitanzis, Denise 196
Gaither, Eva D. 425
Gaither, Israel L. 425
Gaither, J. Michael 43
Gaither, John S. 409
Galaviz, Tony C. 471
Gale, Robert G. 312
Galin, Tomi 243
Gallagher, Brian A. 499
Gallagher, Carolyn Lewis 514
Gallagher, Catherine R. 137
Gallagher, Gavin L. 232
Gallagher, John 303
Gallant, Mark 62
Gallardo, Luis 156
Galligan, William P. 514
Gallin, John I. 341
Gallo, Dominic 219
Gallo, Joseph E. 169
Gallo, Robert J. 169
Gallo, Stephanie 169
Galloway, Caroline 201
Galloway, Del 499
Gallup, Derek 16
Galster, Mark 218
Gambelli, Marianne 345
Gambill, Mark J. 119
Gamble, John 30
Gamgort, Bob 302
Gammarino, Steve W. 86
Gamson, Peter 211

Gannon, J. Timothy 370
Gannon, Richard B. 138
Gannon, Thomas A. 431
Gantt, Michael 71
Ganz, Mark B. 408
Garagiola, Joe Jr. 297
Garanzini, Michael J. 291
Garboski, Mark 17
Garcia, Angel L. 21
Garcia, Daniel P. 263
Garcia, Linda 417
Garcia, Ray 20
Garcia, Savino 436
Garcia, Terry D. 339
Gard, Greg E. 390
Garding, Edward 186
Gardner, Brian E. 222
Gardner, John 196
Gardner, Max L. 252
Garfinkel, Jodie R. 447
Garland, Greg C. 123
Garland, Jerry 60
Garland, Todd 120
Garland, Trish 178
Garman, M. Lawrence 152
Garman, Scott 171
Garner, David E. 447
Garner, Jon 500
Garnero, Patrick 469
Garnett, Patsy A. 381
Garofalo, Donald L. 48
Garrett, Marc 400
Garrett, Melanie 74
Garrett, Tom 97
Garrison, Carol Z. 500
Garrison, Lynne 88
Garrison, Sara 422
Garrity, Tom 329
Garry, Mary Pat 158
Garthwaite, Thomas L. 113
Gartner, Stephen R. 323
Garvin, Samuel S. 387
Gary, Marc 187
Gasdia, Russ 399
Gaspard, Morgan 461
Gassler, David 319
Gaster, R. Scott 35
Gaston, Roger C. 65
Gaston, Steve 443
Gately, James H. 518
Gates, Jamie 484
Gates, Melinda F. 80
Gates, William H. III (Bill & Melinda Gates Foundation, Corbis) 80, 142
Gates, William H. Sr. (Bill & Melinda Gates Foundation) 80
Gathany, Douglas V. 446
Gats, Michael 147
Gatta, Louis A. 360
Gatto, Domenic 62
Gatto, Michele S. 342
Gaudio, Michael M. 44
Gaufin, Shirley 83
Gaumer, George M. 152
Gavales, Lisa A. 179
Gaviglia, Louis 363
Gay, R. Norwood III 63
Gayle, Jacob A. 190
Gaynor, Joseph P. III 208
Gearhart, Bruce 123
Gearhart, Michael 122
Gearon, Michael Jr. 61
Gedwed, William J. 229
Gee, E. Gordon 366
Gee, Preston 488
Geekie, Matthew W. 212
Geeraerts, John W. 436
Geffen, David 164
Gehron, John R. 223
Geier, B. Gwen 63
Geier, Frank 208
Geier, Robert 342
Geiger, Steve 109

Hoffman, Nina A. 339
Hoffman, Paul 242
Hoffman, R. Thomas 192
Hoffman, Rob 56
Hoffman, Telisha 68
Hoffman, Thomas 384
Hoffmeyer, Ron 471
Hogan, Robert G. 482
Hogan, Tim 174
Hogan, William P. 79
Hogel, Maureen L. 168
Hoggarth, Karen 256
Hohner, Joseph H. 88
Hoiberg, Dale 173
Holay, Sanjay 316
Holbrook, Jeff 387
Holden, E. Wayne 411
Holden, Mark 272
Holder, George 118
Holder, Richard 506
Holding, R. Earl 445
Holewinski, Paul P. 159
Holgate, Randy L. 502
Holl, David B. 303
Holland, Christopher S. 51
Holland, Deborah 397
Holland, John 268
Holland, Ken 245
Hollander, Ellie 18
Hollenhorst, Kathy 109
Holler, Susan 288
Hollerbach, Michael D. 451
Hollern, Michael P. 222
Holley, Jeffrey D. 146
Hollifield, Audra 369
Hollinger, Mark R. 295
Hollingshead, Kevin 324
Hollingsworth, Jarvis V. 471
Hollingsworth, Richard A. 366
Hollinrake, David A. 451
Hollocher, Richard 120
Holm, George L. 384
Holman, Bob 160
Holmberg, Gail J. 69
Holmes, Donald N. 121
Holmes, Walter 251
Holst, Darin 436
Holstad, Kathy 479
Holstein, Michael 520
Holt, Lewis P. 78
Holt, Peter M. 426
Holt, Wayne 30
Holwill, Richard 37
Home, Ed 341
Hommert, Douglas D. 49
Honce, Tom 59
Honeycutt, Gene 165
Honickman, Harold A. 238
Honickman, Jeffrey A. 238
Hood, Danny 74
Hood, Susan 458
Hook, Jonathan D. 366
Hooker, E. Stanton III 326
Hooker, Steven L. 408
Hooks, Brian 238
Hoopes, Jeffrey C. 468
Hoover, J. D. 458
Hoover, Stephanie 441
Hopkins, Janet 409
Hopkins, Sandra L. 474
Hoplamazian, Mark S. 203
Hopper, Sidney 498
Horn, Kimberly K. 455
Horn, Stephen 167
Hornaday, Bill 529
Horne, Skip 279
Horner, Jody 108
Horner, Matt 538
Horst, John 328
Horstmann, Bonnie 502
Horton, Chandler 267
Horton, Eustace M. 137
Horton, Jerry 512

Horwitz, Barbara A. 501
Horwood, Graeme 489
Hoskins, Jim 224
Hoskins, John M. 494
Hoskyn, Thomas C. 412
Hosokawa, Koichi 268
Hotarek, Brian W. 81
Hotze, Jim 109
Houghton, Robert 324
Houle, Patricia S. 96
Houmann, Lars D. 25
Houpt, Jeffrey L. 88
Hourican, Kevin T. 434
House, Richard 350
Houser, Mark A. 75
Hove, John N. 213
Hoversten, Peter 485
Howard, Christian 289
Howard, Deborah 215
Howard, Mark G. (Cumberland Farms) 146
Howard, Martin J. (Boston University) 95
Howard, Michael P. 54
Howard, Norman 265
Howe, Douglas T. 131
Howe, Richard W. 20
Howell, Edward R. 287
Howell, Jeffrey F. 488
Howell, Lloyd W. Jr. 93
Howells, Robert 303
Hower, Matthew J. 45
Howlett, Lori R. 70
Hoyt, Mark S. 107
Hrabusa, John T. 398
Hradil, Joe 96
Hsieh, Tony 542
Hsu, Daniel 268
Huang, Sun-Fu 374
Hubbard, R. Glenn 134
Hubbard, William 38
Hubbell, Kent L. 142
Hubel, William F. Jr. 129
Huber, Dan 192
Hudak, James 317
Hudak-Roos, Marty 206
Hudson, Betty 339
Hudson, Rick L. 331
Huerta, Elmer E. 39
Huerta, John E. 450
Hueske, Jodie 282
Huffines, James R. 508
Huffman, Stephen D. 329
Hufford, Bob 60
Hugh, Yoon J. 161
Hughes, Bob (Sauder Woodworking) 428
Hughes, Dale 144
Hughes, F. H. 212
Hughes, Gerald T. 240
Hughes, James M. 68
Hughes, John M. 41
Hughes, Michael P. 264
Hughes, Robert G. (Robert Wood Johnson Foundation) 415
Hughes, Ron 389
Hughes, Timothy W. 144
Hulet, Steven J. 424
Hull, Anthony E. 406
Hull, James R. 331
Hull, Karen 501
Hullinger, Norman 98
Hulseman, Robert L. 452
Hulsen, Mike 162
Hulst, Herman 176
Hummel, Dennis 299
Humphrey, Heather 153
Humphrey, James E. 48
Humphrey, Mike 153
Humphrey, Victoria 479
Humphrey, Wayne 359
Humphreys, William V. Sr. 129
Hunt, Gordon C. Jr. 466

Hunt, Hunter 242
Hunt, Kurt 193
Hunt, Martin 262
Hunt, Ray L. 242
Hunt, Robert 215
Hunt, Tom 423
Hunt, William J. 116
Hunter, Beecher 286
Hunter, Jim 335
Hunter, John E. 229
Hunter, Michael J. 137
Hunter, Pat 377
Hunter, Shawn 289
Hunter, Thomas O. 426
Huntsberry, Lisa 251
Huntsman, Peter R. 235
Hupp, Stephen E. 178
Hupp, William T. 178
Hurley, Brian J. 180
Hurley, Maureen O. 412
Hurlow, Randy 409
Hurson, Tom 486
Hurst, Albert T. Jr. 330
Hurstel, Pierre 176
Hurvis, J. Thomas 367
Huschitt, Erik 66
Husk, Dave 282
Hussey, Wayne 347
Hutchins, Glenn H. 464
Hutchinson, Carroll R. 531
Hutchinson, James 198
Hutchinson, Scott 308
Hutterly, Jane M. 430
Hutton, John W. 249
Hutton, Richard E. 523
Huyhua, Juan Carlos 410
Hyatt, Michael S. 477
Hyde, Matt 408
Hylbert, Paul W. Jr. 395
Hyman, Steven E. 226
Hynes, Toby 219
Hypes, Hollis 473
Hyson, Kevin 41

I

Iacobelli, Al 127
Ianello, Jeff 387
Iannini, Joe 96
Iannotti, Frank 44
Ibbotson, John 133
Ideson, D. Scott 408
Ienuso, Joseph A. 134
Igoe, Brian 520
Ihrig, Weldon E. 508
Iles, Martin 49
Iles, T. Randall 48
Ilitch, Atanis 245
Ilitch, Christopher 245
Ilitch, Marian 245
Ilitch, Matthew 245
Ilitch, Michael 245
Ill, Charles 65
Illich, Jim 75
Impala, Cynthia 473
Impicciche, Joseph R. 55
Impink, Annaliese 428
Incollingo, Gerry 101
Ing, Gayle M. 255
Ingerman, Mitchell 281
Ingersoll, Jack 442
Inglis, I. Martin 72
Ingram, David B. 247
Ingram, Edgar Waldo III 533
Ingram, John R. 248
Ingram, Lisa 533
Ingram, Mark 372
Ingram, Martha R. 248, 517
Ingram, Orrin H. II 248
Ingulsrud, Brian F. 39
Inkley, Robert L. 186
Inman, Emma 437

Innaurato, Michael 399
Inserra, Lawrence R. Jr. 249
Inserra, Theresa 249
Intrator, Tom 108
Iori, Ronald 51
Iotti, Robert 122
Irby, Edward C. Jr. 185
Irick, Shelton 54
Irion, Edward O. 148
Irish, Charles A. 533
Irish, George B. 230
Irlbeck, Kurt 334
Irvin, Patricia L. 304
Irvine, Lynda 332
Irving, Christopher L. 397
Irwin, Mark 331
Isaac, Carly 151
Isaac, J. E. 392
Isaac, Martin 528
Isaac, Rory M. 308
Isaacson, Dean B. 29
Isakson, Michael M. 439
Isgitt, Tim 143
Iske, Chad 158
Isler, Charles S. III 63
Itami, Steve 191
Iuliano, Robert I. 226
Iuliucci, Robert L. 439
Ivanikiw, Aleksei 70
Ivanova, Lora 357
Ivy, Christopher 203
Iwasaki, Terry 317
Iwata, Dean 409

J

Jaacks, James R. 446
Jablonowski, Bill 21
Jablonski, Richard 323
Jablonski, Zygmunt 497
Jackson, Darryl R. 127
Jackson, David 41
Jackson, Don 192
Jackson, Eric H. 435
Jackson, Greg (Taylor Corporation) 471
Jackson, Gregory A. (University of Chicago) 503
Jackson, James S. (Harman Management) 222
Jackson, Jeffery M. 422
Jackson, Jim (Bechtel) 75
Jackson, John H. 334
Jackson, Marc F. (HealthMarkets) 229
Jackson, Marianne 89
Jackson, Mark (Oakland Raiders) 363
Jackson, Michael L. (USC) 507
Jackson, Mike (ASI Computer Technologies) 57
Jackson, Phil 290
Jackson, Stephen P. Jr. 410
Jackson, Stu 336
Jackson, Wes 498
Jacob, Ken 93
Jacobs, Charles M. 155
Jacobs, Dave (Medline Industries) 312
Jacobs, David (Baker & McKenzie) 67
Jacobs, Fred M. 423
Jacobs, Howard 123
Jacobs, Irwin L. 197
Jacobs, Jeffrey P. 253
Jacobs, Jeremy M. Jr. (Delaware North) 155
Jacobs, Jeremy M. Sr. (Delaware North) 155
Jacobs, Louis M. 155
Jacobs, Marisa F. 130
Jacobs, Michael C. 483
Jacobs, Peter J. 33
Jacobs, Seth A. 89
Jacobson, Benjamin R. 78
Jacobson, Bill 66
Jacobson, Harry R. 517

Jacobson, Richard J. 144
Jacobson, Tim 312
Jaeger, Steve 399
Jagiela, Tom 322
Jago, Richard 367
Jahner, Floyd 149
Jain, Dinesh C. 249
Jain, Terri 316
James, David 521
James, Laura A. 27
Jamison, Greg 426
Jan Vandenakker, Gert 108
Janesz, Dennis 412
Janeway, Dean 524
Janiszewski, Charles A. 29
Janke, Dean H. 411
Jankus, Tom 399
Jannotto, Rosetta 391
Jansanti, Kristen 17
Jansen, Mark 433
Jansson, Dwain 56
Janz, Greta 192
Janzen, Peter S. 277
Jared, Donna 232
Jarrett, Madonna 156
Jasiek, Jerry 423
Jasinkiewicz, Ken 524
Jaspan, Stanley S. 188
Jasper, Deborah 375
Jaworowicz, Roman J. 79
Jealous, Benjamin T. 334
Jeffers, Ron 400
Jefferson, John 332
Jeffrey, David 425
Jeffrey, Richard 495
Jeffries, Mary L. 386
Jendrzejewski, George 91
Jenkin, Edward 128
Jenkins, Carlton J. 541
Jenkins, Charles H. Jr. 398
Jenkins, Sheila 259
Jenne, Jason A. 489
Jennifer, Jackie R. 238
Jennings, Brian 341
Jennings, Gary 60
Jensen, Carol 527
Jensen, Craig 193
Jensen, Kris 529
Jensen, Larry 281
Jent, Chris 117
Jergensen, Jace 244
Jernigan, Donald L. 25
Jerosko, Mark 81
Jesse, Sandra L. 87
Jewell, Sally 408
Jezerinac, Daniel E. 165
Jha, Praveen 180
Jhirad, David J. 416
Jiao, George 357
Jimenez, A. David 115
Jimenez, Augusto 165
Jimenez, Joseph C. 304
Jimenez, Roberto I. 144
Jimenez-Hernandez, Iris 351
Jochum, Shane 346
Jodie, Kregg 303
Johanson, Roy 46
John-Baptiste, E. Peter 351
Johns, Douglas 331
Johnson, Abigail P. 187
Johnson, Allison D. 330
Johnson, Barry P. 331
Johnson, Brad 408
Johnson, Bruce 106
Johnson, Carol (Chugach Electric) 128
Johnson, Carol M. (EBSCO) 170
Johnson, Cheryl L. 473
Johnson, Christopher 180
Johnson, Craig 219
Johnson, Dan (Baker & Taylor) 67
Johnson, Daniel (Georgia Lottery) 198
Johnson, Daniel L. (M. A. Mortenson) 293

Johnson, David S. 322
Johnson, Donna 289
Johnson, Earl Jr. 411
Johnson, Edward C. III 187
Johnson, Ernest R. 147
Johnson, Eunice W. 259
Johnson, Frederick M. 92
Johnson, Galen G. 108
Johnson, Gary A. 520
Johnson, Gilbert S. 373
Johnson, Glenn 111
Johnson, Gloria 101
Johnson, Grant 279
Johnson, Greg 414
Johnson, H. Fisk 430
Johnson, James E. (Securian Financial) 435
Johnson, James Thomas (FHLB Atlanta) 180
Johnson, Jennifer J. 182
Johnson, John (David Weekley Homes) 153
Johnson, John C. (Catholic Health East) 113
Johnson, John T. (Estes Express) 178
Johnson, Jon (True Value) 490
Johnson, Kathy Sellers 86
Johnson, Keith 106
Johnson, Kent 540
Johnson, Lisa (Denver Nuggets) 158
Johnson, Lisa D. (Old Dominion Electric) 367
Johnson, Michael 201
Johnson, Miriam 207
Johnson, Nevelle R. 357
Johnson, Peter M. 445
Johnson, Phil 59
Johnson, R. Milton 227
Johnson, Randall W. (Penske) 382
Johnson, Randy (Riceland Foods) 412
Johnson, Ray F. 27
Johnson, Richard G. (Phibro Animal Health) 386
Johnson, Richard P. (American Tire) 43
Johnson, Rick (Holiday Companies) 238
Johnson, Robert V. 507
Johnson, Ronald L. (NBA) 336
Johnson, Ronald W. (Research Triangle Institute) 411
Johnson, Samuel Curtis III 260
Johnson, Sandra K. 26
Johnson, Scott 430
Johnson, Spencer C. 88
Johnson, Stephen P. (Cornell University) 142
Johnson, Steve (Motiva Enterprises) 332
Johnson, Ted 328
Johnson, Tina 30
Johnson, Tom 471
Johnson, W. Jerry 33
Johnson Rice, Linda 259
Johnston, Alistair 274
Johnston, Daniel J. 498
Johnston, David 527
Johnston, Ed 388
Johnston, Jack W. 536
Johnston, James 519
Johnston, Murray L. Jr. 541
Johnstone, Sherry 105
Johnstone, William A. 153
Jolibois, Marcus 240
Joliet, Mariel A. 236
Joly, Gene 219
Joly, Hubert 109
Jonas, Todd S. 475
Jones, Aaron 154
Jones, Alec N. 393
Jones, Barbara W. 504
Jones, Barry 327
Jones, Betsey 471
Jones, Bill (O'Neal Steel) 368

Jones, Bill (Texas A&M) 475
Jones, Brad 254
Jones, Charlene 304
Jones, Christine N. 204
Jones, Dan 164
Jones, David C. (Dairy Farmers of America) 148
Jones, David P. (Team Health) 472
Jones, Donald G. 26
Jones, E. Laverne 478
Jones, Frances 183
Jones, Greg 365
Jones, Jan (Providence Health & Services) 396
Jones, Janis L. (Harrah's Entertainment) 224
Jones, Jerral W. (Dallas Cowboys) 149
Jones, Jerry Jr. (Dallas Cowboys) 149
Jones, Jill 120
Jones, Jimmy R. 63
Jones, John 275
Jones, Joy 59
Jones, Keith 240
Jones, Ken 81
Jones, Kevin 324
Jones, Larri Sue (Feed The Children) 183
Jones, Larry (Feed The Children) 183
Jones, Michael J. 323
Jones, Miles E. 154
Jones, Patricia P. 63
Jones, Philip B. 356
Jones, Randall T. Sr. (Publix) 398
Jones, Randy (Sbarro) 429
Jones, Richard 217
Jones, Robert A. (First Interstate) 186
Jones, Robert J. (University of Minnesota) 505
Jones, Ronald L. 154
Jones, Roy 117
Jones, Sandra 86
Jones, Sarah 154
Jones, Stephen 149
Jones, Sterling P. 458
Jones, Tracie 47
Jones-Barber, Carrie L. 154
Jordan, Bob 471
Jordan, Debbie 341
Jorge, Robert 206
Jorgenson, Mary Ann 235
Jorgenson, Richard T. 135
Joselove, Jonathan 347
Joseph, James E. 369
Joseph, Robert H. Jr. 36
Joseph, Sarah 240
Joss, Robert L. 457
Jost, Jerry 120
Josza, David 82
Joyner, David S. 89
Joyner, Robert C. 472
Juech, Claudia 416
Julien, Craig 121
Julien, Mark V. 275
Jung, John T. 33
Jung, Ronnie G. 471
Jungmann, Steven J. 452
Junkin, Jimmy O. 404
Junqueiro, Steve 429
Jura, James J. 58
Jurgens, Richard N. 242
Jurgensen, William G. 344
Jurich, Tom 504
Justus, Bill 153
Justus, Joyce 501
Juszkiewicz, Henry E. 201

K

Kabeche, Elias J. 97
Kaboski, James L. 390
Kacere, Ken 287
Kaczmarek, Margee 300

Kadow, Joseph J. 370
Kaesgen, Hartmut 333
Kahle, Rita D. 21
Kahn, Alan (JR Simplot) 262
Kahn, Alan J. (Central Parking) 121
Kahn, Eugene S. 130
Kahn, Jodi 405
Kahn, Steve 469
Kain, Bill 352
Kaiser, Laura S. 55
Kaiser, Rick 402
Kaisler, Kim 293
Kalawski, Eva M. 390
Kaleak, George T. 52
Kalem, Bruce F. 327
Kalikow, Peter S. 320
Kalinowski, Mike 289
Kalouche, Raymond S. 492
Kalt, Robert J. 541
Kalter, Alan 527
Kamen, Charles M. 311
Kamens, Ross 359
Kamer, Christopher 477
Kamer, Evan 338
Kaminsky, David A. 512
Kaminsky, Mark 271
Kamis, Dave 145
Kammerer, Chet 321
Kane, Elizabeth T. 295
Kaneb, Gary R. 241
Kaneb, John A. 241
Kang, Sung-Mo 501
Kao, Andy 374
Kaplan, Beth J. 203
Kaplan, Herbert 525
Kaplan, Lee R. 175
Kaplan, Richard J. 295
Kaplan, Steven R. 485
Kappelman, Peter 277
Kappes, Jean 269
Karcher, Kevin 123
Karen, Nancy 442
Karet, Laura 200
Karicher, Michael 205
Karl, George 158
Karmanos, Peter Jr. 111
Karpf, Michael 504
Karst, Darren W. 420
Karst, William B. 104
Kartson, Despina 279
Kasdin, Robert A. 134
Kashuba, Glen A. 82
Kasi, Srinandan 59
Kaskie, James R. 264
Kassing, Suzanne 162
Kates, Kenneth P. 503
Katz, Howard 338
Katz, Karen W. 347
Katz, Mark 177
Katz, Michael W. 400
Katz, Ronald C. 172
Katz, Samuel L. 294
Katz Armoza, Marcela 130
Katzenmeyer, Thomas 366
Katzman, David B. 117
Katzmar, Christine A. 468
Kauffman, Emma Jo 161
Kaufman, David S. 51
Kaufman, Tom 454
Kaufmann, Michael 157
Kautz, Karen 249
Kavanaugh, James P. 538
Kay, Stephen W. 413
Kay, Walter A. 517
Keady, Kurt J. 137
Kean, Steven J. 270
Kean, Thomas H. 415
Kearney, Patrick 382
Kearney, Robert 437
Kearney, Stephen M. 514
Kearns, Jim 37
Keating, John 108
Keating, Ronald C. 139

Kee, Dennis 296
Keefer, Elizabeth J. 134
Keegan, Brendan P. 69
Keegel, C. Thomas 473
Keel, Michael C. 310
Keeler, Mike 91
Keeler, Rick 102
Keeley, John 96
Keeney, Frank D. 49
Keeney, Thomas 252
Kees, Robert L. 367
Keglevic, Paul M. 174
Kehl, Kurt 526
Kehlbeck, Dalton 445
Keiper, Paul W. 526
Keiser, Ingrid 131
Keisler, Peter D. 442
Keith, Claudia 103
Keith, Tricia 88
Kekalainen, Jarmo 423
Kelada, Emad 321
Kelbaugh, Jim 429
Kelch, Robert P. 505
Kelleher, Margaret T. 492
Kelleher, Warren J. 434
Keller, Brian (Blue Cross and Blue
  Shield of Louisiana) 86
Keller, Bryan J. (Delaware North) 155
Keller, Dennis J. 394
Keller, Jim 440
Keller, Michael C. (Nationwide) 344
Keller, Micheal A. (Stanford
  University) 457
Keller, Sara Lee 491
Keller, Steven E. 27
Kellert, Bob 192
Kelley, Barbara M. 73
Kelley, James P. 137
Kelley, Joe 207
Kelley, John 533
Kelley, Mark A. (Henry Ford Health
  System) 234
Kelley, Mary Lou (L.L. Bean) 287
Kelley, Sadie 48
Kelley, Scott C. 508
Kelly, Christopher M. 93
Kelly, Daniel J. 40
Kelly, David 72
Kelly, Edmund F. 285
Kelly, John (M-I Swaco) 321
Kelly, John (Randolph-Brooks Federal
  Credit Union) 404
Kelly, John C. (Northwestern
  Mutual) 361
Kelly, Kevin T. 155
Kelly, Michael J. 346
Kelly, Patricia 380
Kelly, Paul 341
Kelly, Sally 112
Kelly, Stephen E. 72
Kelly, Terri 537
Kelly, Thomas J. (New York Power
  Authority) 353
Kelly, Thomas M. (Loyola
  University) 291
Kelly, William M. 90
Kelly-Bartley, Kim 533
Keltner, Thomas L. 236
Kemp, David 358
Kemp, Karen L. 155
Kemper, Michele M. 468
Kenagy, John 396
Kendall, Bob 425
Kendall, Brad 328
Kendall, Jeffrey 528
Kendrick, Dan 428
Kendrick, Katherine 164
Kennealy, William J. 207
Kennedy, Aaron 359
Kennedy, Brian A. 229
Kennedy, Christopher 291
Kennedy, Craig 175

Kennedy, James C. (Cox
  Enterprises) 144
Kennedy, James M. (Associated
  Press) 59
Kennedy, John C. 64
Kennedy, K. Daniel 412
Kennedy, Kim 89
Kennedy, Marc 364
Kennedy, Michael D. 122
Kennedy, Samuel 95
Kennedy, Thomas C. 236
Kenney, Anne R. 142
Kenny, Dave 395
Kenny, Judy 510
Kent, Harlan M. 539
Kerger, Paula A. 377
Kerin, Andrew C. 51
Kerle, Phillip 258
Kern, Howard P. 437
Kernan, Richard T. 165
Kerr, David J. 146
Kerr, Jim 153
Kerr, Robert K. Jr. 76
Kerr, Steve 387
Kerris, Richard 292
Kerstein, Steve 482
Kessel, Richard M. 353
Kessel, Silvia 319
Kessler, Alan C. 514
Kessler, Joseph 264
Kesteloot, Hendrick 112
Ketchum, L. Craig 308
Ketola, Todd 70
Kettenbach, Michael 157
Key, Billy 215
Keyes, Joseph 177
Keys, William M. 133
Keyser, Dale 478
Khalighi, Dar 42
Khanna, Neeraj 447
Khichi, Samrat 112
Kiappes, John 332
Kibbon, Larry J. 525
Kidd, Wyndham Jr. 229
Kieckhefer, Robert 229
Kielar, Richard M. 481
Kiepert, Ron 328
Kiesewetter, George 287
Kilgore, Jack C. 412
Kilgore, Tom D. 494
Kilgust, Richard R. 393
Killebrew, Chad E. 467
Killebrew, George 149
Killeen, Paul 205
Killen, James C. Jr. 34
Killian, Rex P. 55
Killingsworth, Cleve L. Jr. 87
Killingsworth, Kyle 213
Kim, Hyung Tai 55
Kim, John Y. 352
Kim, Margaret 422
Kimball, Bob 227
Kimball, Jim 473
Kimbrough, Mark 227
Kimler, Bill 296
Kimmel, Donna 437
Kimmel, Steve 33
Kinde, Wayne 477
Kinder, David D. 270
Kinder, Jacquelyn 113
Kinder, Richard D. 270
King, David L. (Associated
  Materials) 58
King, David R. H. (SmithGroup) 449
King, Donald R. 207
King, Edward M. 95
King, Eileen 376
King, Regina 192
King, Richie 192
King, Shauna R. 539
King, Thomas H. 36
King, Tim 99
King, Vivian 420

King, William K. 458
Kingsley, Jim 390
Kingsley, Linda A. 514
Kington, Raynard S. 341
Kinkela, David 210
Kinser, Dennis 60
Kinsey, Keith 359
Kinslow, Anthony D. 446
Kinstle, Mike 314
Kintz, Gary 536
Kintzinger, Douglas P. 256
Kiplin, Kimberly 476
Kiplinger, Austin H. 142
Kiraly, Thomas H. 136
Kirby, Phil 70
Kirby, Rex B. 463
Kirchner, Bruce 304
Kirkland, Moira 151
Kirkpatrick, Scott 240
Kirksey, Hugh 99
Kirkwood, David W. 475
Kirley, Tim 261
Kirsch, Nancy 253
Kirst, Fred L. 490
Kirwin, Paul S. 109
Kiser, Glenn 292
Kissane, James F. 479
Kissel, Mark 270
Kittoe, Larry 155
Kitz, Edward G. 420
Kitz, Jim 213
Kizielewicz, James 275
Klassy, Nathan 66
Kleffner, Gregory W. 266
Klegon, Frank O. 127
Klein, Barry M. 501
Klein, Bob 24
Klein, Hope Margala 539
Klein, John (Young's Market) 540
Klein, Jonathan D. (Getty Images) 199
Klein, Koos 237
Klein, Paul 412
Klein, Rebecca A. 291
Klein, Thomas 422
Kleinbaum, Linda 320
Kleiner, Madeleine A. 236
Kleinert, Chris 242
Kleinman, Ira D. 58
Kleinschmidt, Robert 109
Kleopfer, Stuart G. 82
Kletchka, Melissa 346
Klimstra, Cindy T. 119
Kline, Howard 266
Kline, Ronald L. 245
Klinger, Lisa K. 323
Klinker, Charles 446
Klipp, Todd L. C. 95
Klomparens, Karen L. 324
Kloster, Karl 308
Kluge, John W. 319
Klump, Ron 281
Klusmann, Neil W. 186
Kluts, Kevin 79
Knaack-Esbeck, Jane 242
Knafel, Sidney R. 249
Knapp, Ann H. 86
Knapp, Kevin 107
Knapstein, Annette S. 40
Knedlik, Ronald W. 32
Knee, Kevin 220
Kneeland, Paul 268
Knight, Andrew 485
Knight, Greg 158
Knight, Jeffrey A. 216
Knight, Lyle R. 186
Knight, Teresa W. 373
Knight, Timothy P. 487
Knight, Tom 490
Kniley, Steven L 380
Knorr, Stephen C. 505
Knorr, Walter 503
Knott, Jeff 417
Knowlton, Oliver 311

Knox, Marg 508
Knox, Robert A. 95
Knutson, Daniel E. 277
Knutson, Thomas K. 314
Kobes, Gerald 486
Kobus, Todd 315
Koch, Charles G. 272
Koch, Clark 408
Koch, Dan 162
Koch, David H. 272
Koch, Gary 60
Koch, Joseph T. 184
Koch, William I. 371
Koehler, James 324
Koenecke, Jane 251
Koenecke, Ted 287
Koeneman, Sandy 337
Koenig, Joseph G. 538
Koenig, Rachel 68
Koenig, William C. (Northwestern
  Mutual) 361
Koenig, William S. (NBA) 336
Koenig-Browne, Julie 20
Koerner, Philip D. 296
Koffinke, Doug 201
Kohl, Daniel J. 378
Kohl, Herb 328
Kohler, David 273
Kohler, Herbert V. Jr. 273
Kohler, Laura 273
Kohn, Donald L. 182
Kohrt, Carl F. 72
Kokes, Andrew 447
Kokinakis, George 257
Koklanaris, George 380
Kolberg, Raymond F. 331
Kolder, Kathryn 196
Kolka, Ronald E. 127
Koller, Kurt 66
Kolodziej, Michael 513
Kolsrud, David 66
Kolter, William C. 82
Komoroski, Len 117
Kompa, John 235
Koney, Robert D. Jr. 452
Kong, David T. 79
Konowitch, Paul A. 221
Kontos, Mark W. 329
Kontos, Tom 22
Koomar, Mary 434
Koontz, John 20
Koos, Thomas D. 253
Kopel, Dale S. 317
Kopfensteiner, Thomas R. 114
Koppensteiner, Donna 403
Koranda, Krista 359
Korba, Robert W. 425
Koretz, Steven B. 312
Korn, Allan M. 86
Kornberg, Mindy 508
Kornstein, Don R. 69
Korsmeyer, Mark 148
Korsmo, Jeffrey O. 307
Korzenski, Robert M. 452
Koslow, Steve 146
Koster, John F. 396
Koster, Steven 101
Kosterman, Gayle P. 430
Kostrinsky, Michael 224
Kosub, Suzanne C. 136
Kotal, Joan 476
Kotecki, Kevin T. 371
Kotlar, John M. 245
Kotler, Steven 489
Kotsiopulos, Peter G. 505
Kou, Ming Bin (Red Chamber Co.) 406
Kou, Ming Shin (Red Chamber
  Co.) 406
Kou, Shan Chun 406
Kovac, Kimberly A. 317
Kovaleski, Charles J. 63
Kowal, David 154
Kowalik, Ray 102

LeFrak, James 281
LeFrak, Richard S. 281
Lefthes, Stuart N. 312
Leftwich, Gary 454
Leftwich, Norma 240
Leftwich, Robin 252
Legg, Dexter R. 285
Legge, Michael H. 410
Lehman, Arnold S. 281
Lehman, David H. 329
Lehmkuhle, Stephen W. 505
Lehnhard, Mary Nell 86
Leibfried, Joe 387
Leighton, Danette 423
Leipman-Yale, Debra 521
Leipold, Craig L. 329
Leipzig, Frank 133
Leitzinger, James 66
Leiweke, Timothy J. 289
Lemaire, Andy 17
Lemaire, Jacques 329
Lemieux, Mario 388
Lemire, Catherine 66
Lemke, Judith A. 431
Lemonis, Marcus A. 27, 193
Lenderink, Gary B. 217
Lenker, Max 401
Lennie, Peter 506
Lenzen, Michael 307
Leo, James 528
Leon, Jean G. 350
Leonard, David 454
Leonard, Jeff 67
Leonard, Mary Kay 499
Leonard, Stephanie 135
Leonard, Terry 286
Leonardi-Cattolica, Karyn 332
Leonsis, Ted 526
Lepori, Stephanie D. 128
Lepre, Christopher M. 238
Leprino, James 281
LeResche, Steve 55
LeSaffre, Daniel J. 333
Lesch, Donna J. 270
Lescoe, Daniel 79
Lesesne, Joab M. III 144
Lesinski, James P. 293
Lesneski, Tim 314
L'Esperance, Thomas F. 35
Lesser, Rich 94
Lester, Jeffery H. 213
Lester, Ronnie 290
Letson, Steve 149
Lettes, Louis 137
Leung, Pete 99
Leutwyler, Ric 79
Leventry, D. 503
Levin, Ken 403
Levin, Richard (Major League
    Baseball) 297
Levin, Richard C. (Yale University) 539
Levin, Yale 451
Levine, H. Barry 527
Levine, Randy 356
Levinsohn, Craig P. 317
Levit, Max S. 215
Levitas, E. James 390
Levitetz, Jeffrey A. 399
Leviton, Gareth C. 218
Levitt, Arthur Jr. 110
Levitt, Wayne 196
Levy, Brian 73
Levy, Donald H. 503
Levy, Fiona Howard 126
Levy, Michael (CPB) 143
Levy, Mike (Memphis Grizzlies) 315
Levy, Richard A. 351
Levy, Sloane 528
Lewellen, Larry M. 366
Lewis, Angela 208
Lewis, Darwin 430
Lewis, David (McJunkin Red Man) 308

Lewis, David E. (University of
    Rochester) 506
Lewis, J. Lacey 144
Lewis, James 184
Lewis, Jesse A. 275
Lewis, Joseph W. 532
Lewis, Keith 267
Lewis, Margaret 509
Lewis, Michael R. 529
Lewis, Mitchell B. 178
Lewis, Renée Cogdell 259
Lewis, William R. 136
Lewison, Linda 109
Lex, Randall 354
Ley, Marc 252
Leydon, Betty 394
Leydon, Edward R. 409
Leyendekker, Gerben 102
Li, Ted 86
Liakopulos, Nick 244
Liang, Christine 57
Liang, Louise L. 263, 264
Liang, Marcel 57
Liberatore, Robert G. 127
Libman, Raquel 321
Liddy, Brian 432
Lieb, Jeanne R. 180
Liebentritt, Donald J. 487
Lieberman, Evelyn S. 450
Lieberman, Gerald M. 35
Lieberman, Mark 269
Liebert, Carl C. III 16
Liedel, Christopher A. 339
Lietzke, Mark 436
Ligmanowski, John 125
Lijana Matura, Karin 343
Liles, Bob 193
Lilly, Steven L. 342
Liming, Dave 45
Lin, Alfred 542
Lin, Gary H. 225
Lind, Tacy 360
Linda, Linda 501
Lindberg, Donald A. B. 341
Linde, David 346
Linden, Jay 345
Linder, Gregg 431
Lindner, Janet E. 539
Lindsay, Richard J. 468
Linebarger, Dale 54
Ling, Dennis 135
Ling, Robert M. Jr. 496
Link, Richard A. 448
Linneman, Stephen 102
Linnington, Max 85
Linsky, Melissa (Atlanta Spirit) 61
Linsky, Melissa L. (Haights Cross
    Communications) 221
Linton, William A. 396
Lintz, David 382
Linville, Randal L. 435
Linzer, Daniel H. 361
Liotta, Ann S. 363
Liotta, Charles 198
Lipman, Gustave K. 218
Lipman, Ira A. 218
Lipman, Joshua S. 218
Lipman, M. Benjamin 218
Lippard, Thomas E. 492
Lippincott, Robert M. 377
Lippleman, Stan 71
Lips, Paul 22
Lipstein, Steven H. 83
Lipton, Martin 355
Liroff, David B. 143
Lis, Frank 112
Lisman, Eric I. 25
List, John J. 342
Listengart, Joseph 270
Listi, Frank 206
Littauer, Sara B. 529
Little, Michael (Feld
    Entertainment) 184

Little, Mike (J.F. Shea) 256
Little, Robert R. 158
Litvin, Joel M. 336
Litzsinger, R. Mark 189
Litzsinger, Todd 189
Liu, Stanley 374
Liu, Tally C. 357
Lively, Dorvin D. 21
Livingston, John T. 481
Livingston, Randall S. 457
Livingstone, Bruce T. 199
Livingstone, Michelle 106
Lizza, Robert V. 463
Llewellyn, W. Joseph 306
Lloyd, Curtis L. 459
Lloyd, David G. 78
Lloyd, Lauren D. 344
Lloyd, Rjay 191
Loar, James M. 534
Lob, Dianne F. 36
Locilento, Arthur T. Jr. 197
Lock, Chris 161
Lockard, John A. 344
Lockard, Mary 346
Locke, Gary 482
Locke, Michael 203
Lockhart, Dennis P. 182
Lodovic, Joseph J. IV 311
Loebbaka, Charles R. 361
Loeffler, Robert D. 232
Loehr, Kathleen E. 407
Loepp, Daniel J. 88
Loesch, Mary Beth 22
Lofgren, Christopher B. 431
Loflin, Brian 243
Loftis, Harry E. 412
Loftis, William 449
Lofton, Kevin E. 114
Loftus, Patrick B. 492
Logan, Eric 223
Loggia, Joseph 25
Lohmann, Jack R. 198
Lohr, William J. 438
Lombardi, Dean 289
Lombardi, Francis J. 391
London, Debra K. 115
London, Mark 445
London, Simon 310
Lonergan, Edward F. 260
Long, Anne E. 126
Long, Bruce (UNICOR) 181
Long, Bruce C. (Guardian Life) 217
Long, Craig 328
Long, David (Purdue Pharma) 399
Long, David H. (Liberty Mutual) 285
Long, Jo Anne 408
Long, John (Dot Foods) 162
Long, John E. Jr. (TVA) 494
Long, Philip 539
Long, Randall 196
Long, Robert A. 255
Long, Ron 106
Long, Tim 262
Longo, Jeff 348
Longstreet, John H. 131
Lonon, Terrill A. 424
Loomis, Andrew 350
Loos, Steve 192
Looyenga, Roger L. 64
Lopez, Lucille 157
Lopez, Mark G. 291
Lopez, Roberto 20
Lorch, Robert K. 300
Lorenz, Mike 441
Lorenzo, Sara 492
Lori, Peter H. 509
Lorimer, Linda Koch 539
Loscocco, Peter F. 235
Lotharius, Paul 491
Lotkowski, Ed 296
Lotman, Herbert 267
Louis, Alex 251
Louttit, Gordon J. 27

Love, Bob 125
Love, Dan 312
Love, David 283
Love, Dennis M. 395
Love, Frank 290
Love, Gay M. 395
Love, Greg 290
Love, James E. III 395
Love, Nat 314
Love, Tom 290
Love Meyer, Jenny 290
Lovelace, Jason 107
Loveless, Connie 511
Loveman, Gary W. 224
Loveridge, Gary F. 466
Lovett, Michael F. 248
Lovlien, Thomas A. 91
Lowe, Thomas E. 369
Lowenkron, Barry F. 295
Lowery, Michael 112
Lowrey, Ray F. 120
Lowry, Bruce 523
Lowry, William E. 295
Loyd, Rodney 400
Lozano, Joe J. 541
Lozier, Bob 193
Luber, Jean A. 434
Lucas, George W. Jr. 292
Lucas, Raeford P. 489
Lucas, Richard M. 236
Lucas, Wes W. 446
Lucchetti, David J. 372
Lucchino, Larry 95
Luceri, Richard 257
Lucia, Marian M. 180
Luciano, Gene 123
Luck, David A. 19
Luck, Jo 232
Lucke, Kathi 89
Lucki, Anthony 240
Lucki, Donna 240
Ludgate, Allan C. 163
Ludington, Andrea J. 205
Ludington, Robert 435
Luebrecht, Donald E. 145
Lueger, Susan A. 361
Lueken, Jeffrey J. 361
Lugo, Miguel 210
Luis, Nelson 240
Luiza, Walter A. 381
Lukiewski, David J. 340
Lum, Donna 105
Lumpkin, John O. (Associated
    Press) 59
Lumpkin, John R. (Robert Wood
    Johnson Foundation) 415
Lund, Constance E. 43
Lund, Jay 48
Lund, Tom 415
Lundberg, L. Erik 505
Lunde, Glenn 374
Lundell, D. 503
Lundgren, David 146
Lundin, Leslie 249
Lundquist, Laura M. 436
Lundquist, Susan 371
Lunn, Randall R. 141
Luo, Jason 267
Lupia, Gene 122
Lupia, Jerry 101
Lupo, Larry 302
Lurie, Robert F. 391
Lusson, Mark 360
Lustig, Richard 138
Luther, Jon L. 167
Luther, Karen 139
Luthi, Bernard 357
Luthringer, Paul 230
Lutz, Yvonne 435
Lux, James D. 78
Lyddy, James P. 307
Lydon, Joseph J. 20
Lyle, Michael J. 529

May, Pamela Robinette 504
Mayer, John D. 93
Mayer, Kristie 434
Mayer, Lori 197
Mayer, Marc O. 36
Mayer, Nick 20
Maynard, James P. 357
Maynard, Meridee J. 361
Mayne, Terry L. 523
Mayo, Ronald A. 311
Mayorek, John 135
Mays, Bruce 149
Mays, Janine 476
Mazour, Michael E. 530
Mazur, Daniel F. 482
Mazzarella, Kathleen M. 212
Mazzuca, Robert J. 95
McAdam, Lowell C. 119
McAliley, Kevin M. 221
McAlister, G. Wayne 111
McAllister, Mike 74
McAndrew, Patrick 388
McAreavy, Michael J. 154
McArthur, Brian 407
McArthur, John 299
McAuvic, Karen 525
McBee, Barry 508
McBride, Reuben 342
McCabe, James B. 126
McCabe, Jerry A. 27
McCaffery, Gregory C. 100
McCaffery, Tom 89
McCall, Adrian H. 489
McCall, Bill Jr. 453
McCall, Bron 186
McCall, Jeff 248
McCall, Michael T. 174
McCalley, Gray Jr. 395
McCamant, Frank C. 291
McCann, Andy 242
McCann, Kathleen B. 451
McCarter, Kenneth J. 127
McCarthy, Arthur 352
McCarthy, Brian 338
McCarthy, Daniel W. 83
McCarthy, Dee 286
McCarthy, John J. 391
McCarthy, Kathleen L. 507
McCarthy, Michael (Albertsons) 31
McCarthy, Michael (Green Bay Packers) 214
McCarthy, Michael (St. Louis Blues) 423
McCarthy, Neil 527
McCarthy, W. James 436
McCarthy, William J. 382
McCarty, Todd C. 405
McCaskey, Raymond F. 229
McCaskill, Don 412
McCaslin, Teresa E. 140
McClain, Jackie 103
McClellan Upicksoun, Alma 52
McClelland, Kent 440
McClelland, Michael 79
McClelland, Norman 440
McClelland, Scott 232
McClure, Elizabeth L. 364
McClure, Gail D. 265
McClure, Polley Ann 142
McClure, Richard H. 496
McColgan, Linda 362
McCollister, Donald L. 493
McCollister, H. Daniel 496
McCollum, A. Michael 136
McCollum, W. Lee 430
McCollum, William R. Jr. 494
McConnell, Bill 123
McConnell, Donald P. 72
McConney, Jeffrey 491
McCormack, James F. 137
McCormack, Joe 290
McCormack, Terry R. 27
McCormack, William O. 433

McCormick, Christopher J. 287
McCormick, Richard L. 421
McCormick, Thomas H. (Chevy Chase Bank) 124
McCormick, Tom (UniGroup) 496
McCoskey, John 377
McCoy, Harvey 232
McCoy, John B. Jr. 72
McCoy, Kirk 184
McCoy, Marilyn 361
McCrobie, Mike 17
McCrudden, Christopher 394
McCrummen, Patrick 407
McCrystal, Carol A. 159
McCullom, Ellen 512
McCullough, Bob (H-E-B) 232
McCullough, Michael 321
McCullough, Robert (NUMMI) 362
McCurdy, Larry W. 27
McCurry, Michael 446
McCurry, R. Alan 407
McCusker, Thomas J. 334
McDermott, Nancy 482
McDermott, Tim 526
McDevitt, Thomas 453
McDonald, Brian J. 394
McDonald, D. Kirk 541
McDonald, David G. 370
McDonald, Janet (Ingram Industries) 248
McDonald, Janet I. (Leslie's Poolmart) 282
McDonald, Kevin 423
McDonald, Robert P. 407
McDonald, Scott 102
McDonnell, David C. 211
McDonnell, Eileen C. 379
McDonnell, Marge 219
McDonnell, Sue K. 163
McDonough, David M. 491
McDonough, Marty 305
McDonough, Maureen 48
McDonough, Peter G. 394
McDougal, Ranee 129
McDougald, James L. 311
McDowell, Kevin 289
McDuffie, Anthony D. 224
McDuffie, Mary 344
McElroy, Brian 353
McElroy, Greg 149
McElveen-Hunter, Bonnie 407
McElya, James S. 141
McFadzean, Pat A. 415
McFarland, Deirdre 431
McGarvie, Paul 267
McGarvy, Joyce 145
McGauvran-Hruby, S. 503
McGean, Jim 119
McGee, Mike 47
McGhee, John 92
McGill, Larry 206
McGill, Pamela S. 300
McGinley, John R. 389
McGinley, Mary Jo 113
McGinnis, Randall S. 148
McGivern, Arthur J. 21
McGonigle, Chris 395
McGorry, Bernie 383
McGovern, Eric 462
McGovern, Gail J. 407
McGovern, John R. 465
McGovern, Patrick J. 250
McGowan, Amy 181
McGowan, Chris 289
McGrath, Bill 523
McGrath, Con 299
McGrath, Karen L. 399
McGrath, Robert T. 366
McGrath, Thomas P. 176
McGuffey, Kristen K. 444
McGuigan, Stuart M. 285
McGuire, John F. 407
McGuire, Maureen 55

McGuire, Terrance P. 532
McHale, James E. 265
McHale, John Jr. 297
McHale, Kevin 328
McHose, Douglas 442
McHugh, Harry 527
McHugh, Joseph H. 46
McHugh, Robert 184
McIntire, Lee A. 122
McIntire, Lisa 196
McIntyre, Brian P. 336
McIntyre, Dennis L. 460
McIntyre, Jonathan 451
McKean, Kevin 138
McKee, Christopher T. 309
McKee, Jack C. 309
McKee, Joseph M. 123
McKee, Lynn B. 51
McKee, Michael D. (Irvine Company) 252
McKee, Michael K. (McKee Foods) 309
McKee, Paul Jr. 83
McKee, R. Ellsworth 309
McKee, Russell E. Jr. 309
McKeehan, Effie 164
McKelvy, Michael 122
McKenna, Andrew J. Jr. (Schwarz) 434
McKenna, Andrew J. Sr. (Schwarz) 434
McKenna, John F. 135
McKenna, Richard M. 532
McKenna, William C. 296
McKenzie, Donald 321
McKenzie, Ed 17
McKenzie, Gary B. 479
McKenzie, Michael K. 215
McKenzie, Nancy L. 526
McKenzie, Reggie 214
McKenzie, Ronald W. 479
McKenzie, Ryan 215
McKenzie-Swarts, Molly 236
McKeon, James V. III 197
McKerney, Adrian 401
McKewen, Darren P. 100
McKinley, Scott A. 32
McKinney, Billy 328
McKinney, Gary 154
McKinney, Jim 243
McKinney, Michael D. 475
McKinney, Michelle 19
McLachlan, Haydn 393
McLane, Drayton Jr. 95
McLarty, Thomas F. III 110
McLaughlin, Dan 153
McLaughlin, David W. 355
McLaughlin, Sean P. 407
McLaughlin, Stephen (SMDK) 449
McLaughlin, Stephen A. (Activant Solutions) 22
McLean, James E. 480
McLean, Margaret B. 122
McLean, Will 361
McLellan, John M. 532
McLellan, Todd 426
McLemore, Douglas 269
McLeod, Ian 208
McMahon, Michael B. (SIRVA) 446
McMahon, Michael P. (Day & Zimmermann) 154
McMeekin, Nancy 221
McMillan, Annette 482
McMillan, Lance 465
McMillan, Nate 392
McMillan, Tom 388
McMillen, Steve 490
McMullan, J. Bart Jr. 408
McMullan, W. Wesley 180
McMullen, Greer 439
McMullen, Peter S. 348
McMullen, Ronald B. 83
McMullen, Tim 534
McNabb, David W. 58
McNabb, F. William III 518
McNair, Scott 433

McNamara, Timothy P. 517
McNeive, Mike 61
McNiece, Andy 222
McNish, Russ 124
McNulty, James F. 376
McNulty, John R. 354
McNulty, Kathleen 433
McNutt, Robert 91
McParlan, Mike 50
McPhee, George 526
McPheely, Brian 393
McQuade, Daniel P. 481
McRee, Sandra K. 243
McRobbie, Michael A. 246
McSween, W. Scott 124
McTavish, Lori 127
McTernan, Bernita 116
McVey, Keshmira 92
McVey, Phillip C. 512
McWane, C. Phillip 310
McWay, Michael J. 308
Meacham, Phil 202
Mead, Dennis 106
Meador, Leroy 479
Meadows, Donnie 275
Meadows, Jaime 395
Meadows, Michelle 286
Mears, Phillip W. 114
Mecca, Gerald 198
Medairy, George 441
Medenica, Gordon 354
Medlin, George L. 333
Meetz, Jennifer 412
Megard, Chad 456
Megathlin, Linda 437
Mehigen, Karen M. 137
Mehlman, Charles J. 281
Mehta, Siddharth N. 485
Meidenbauer, Richard 33
Meier, Tom 263
Meijer, Doug 314
Meijer, Fred 314
Meijer, Hendrik G. 314
Meinig, Peter C. 142
Meinz, Dave 371
Mei-Pochtler, Antonella 94
Meissner, Jochen 208
Meister, Magaret A. 468
Meixelsperger, Mary 442
Meleghy, Gyula 470
Meleta, Karen 525
Melfi, Mitch H. 114
Mellinger, Kristin 52
Mellon, Christopher 296
Mellor, Jim 540
Melone, Anthony J. Sr. 119
Melton, George R. 538
Meltzer, Paul 249
Melvin, Catherine 476
Menard, Denice 254
Menard, John R. Jr. 316
Mendes, Tony 102
Mendillo, Jane 226
Mendler, Stacy 33
Mendlik, Paul M. 530
Mendola, Peter J. 452
Mennucci, Anita 291
Mensah, Sarah 392
Menuet, Beth 19
Menzies, Pamela Cash 259
Meo, Gary A. 431
Mercier, Murry J. 298
Mercurio, Joseph P. 95
Merdek, Andrew A. 144
Merecka, Jeffery W. 461
Meredith, Russ 37
Merhige, Phyllis 297
Meriam, Harold A. 233
Merinoff, Charles 123
Merks, Nic A. 93
Meroni, Filippo 430
Merrell, Brett L. 200
Merrell, J. Scott 411

Moss, Edward R. 311
Moss, Marcia K. 451
Mossler, Fred 542
Mosticchio, Dennis P. 217
Mostrom, Michael 44
Motel, George 96
Mott, Daniel C. 39
Mottola, Vincent 121
Moushey, Nora E. 531
Moy, Edmund C. 512
Moyes, Jerry C. 467
Mruz, Robert J. 358
Mucci, Paul L. 395
Mucci, Richard L. 352
Muchnick, Ed 118
Mudd, John O. 55, 396
Mueller, Charles E. Jr. 52
Mueller, Gene W. 389
Mueller, Paul 431
Muirhead, Sophia A. 136
Mulders, Abbe M. 163
Muldowney, Michael 240
Muleski, Robert T. 285
Mulherin, Lynn 370
Mulhern, Pat 512
Mulkeen, Niall 258
Mulkerin, David J. 530
Mullane, Karen M. 464
Mullen, Edward K. 356
Mullen, Jack 442
Mullen, Mike 492
Mullen, Patrick 209
Mullen, Richard 165
Mullen, Robert H. (The Newark
    Group) 356
Mullen, Robert W. (Structure
    Tone) 462
Mullen, Sue 357
Mulligan, Deanna M. 217
Mulligan, Donald 157
Mullin, Chris 206
Mullin, Daniel P. 446
Mullin, John 198
Mullins, Russell 213
Mullison, Kent 440
Mulrooney, Nina M. 379
Mulvey, Daniel B. 124
Mundt, Kevin A. 452
Mundt, Scott 276
Muniz, Priscilla 89
Munneke, Jeff 328
Munnelly, Joan E. 130
Muñoz, Frank 422
Munro, Ellen K. 291
Muraskin, Ben E. 385
Muratore, Michael K. 464
Murchison, H. Roderick 453
Murdoch, Cynthia M. 121
Murdock, David H. 161
Murphy, Bill 506
Murphy, Brian F.X. 390
Murphy, Carrie 316
Murphy, Christopher J. 385
Murphy, Daniel J. 496
Murphy, E. Ray 309
Murphy, Elizabeth A. 151
Murphy, Jeremiah T. 30
Murphy, John (Ernst & Young
    Global) 176
Murphy, John R. (National
    Geographic) 339
Murphy, John V. (MassMutual) 305
Murphy, Lamar R. 506
Murphy, Larry 20
Murphy, Mark (ClubCorp) 131
Murphy, Mark H. (Green Bay
    Packers) 214
Murphy, Mike 341
Murphy, Ronald H. 58
Murphy, Susan H. 142
Murrah, Charlie 454
Murray, Al 289

Murray, Andy 423
Murray, Cathy (Life Care Centers) 286
Murray, James M. 359
Murray, John M. 150
Murray, Joseph 463
Murray, Kathleen (NYU) 355
Murray, Kathy (ABC Supply) 19
Murray, Mark A. 314
Murray, William 474
Murtaugh, Philip F. 127
Murzl, Valerie 461
Musacchio, Robert A. 42
Muschetto, Frank 482
Musil, Ruthellyn 487
Mussman, David C. 530
Mustian, Lewis 178
Musumeche, Rocco 135
Muzik, Loreen 517
Myer, David F. 21
Myers, Katie 413
Myers, Margery B. 167
Myers, Thomas 98
Myette, Kevin 409
Myrick, William J. 395

N

Nachtigal, Jules 135
Nachtwey, Peter H. 110
Nadeau, William J. 353
Naegle, Debby 89
Nagaraja, Mysore L. 320
Naidoo, Vassi 156
Nail, George 196
Nair, Mohan 408
Nakfoor, Tom 314
Nakis, Dominic J. 26
Nally, Dennis M. 393
Napoli, Andy 146
Nardelli, Robert L. 127
Narea, Jaime 97
Nartonis, Robert J. 293
Narum, Greg 445
Nash, Charles R. 500
Nash, Ron 399
Nassetta, Christopher J. 237
Nathanson, Paul 506
Nau, Brian 433
Naud, Renee 389
Navarro, Benito 476
Navarro, Javier 61
Navarro, Richard J. 31
Navti, Abigail L. 532
Nay, Randall M. 159
Nazarian, Robert H. 317
Neal, Christine 496
Neal, Elise 19
Neal, James 232
Nealy, Mike 387
Neary, Daniel P. 334
Neary, Michael 462
Neaves, William B. 326
Nechita, Mark 451
Neeley, Robert L. 275
Neely, Alfred G. 52
Neff, Michael F. 467
Negri, Michael 209
Neidus, Stuart D. 49
Neil, A. Bruce 410
Neil, Robert F. 144
Nelms, Charlie 246
Nelson, Bob (Yankee Candle) 539
Nelson, Don (Golden State
    Warriors) 206
Nelson, Donnie (Dallas Mavericks) 149
Nelson, Ed (Whataburger) 532
Nelson, Edward G. (Vanderbilt
    University Medical Center) 517
Nelson, Elaine E. 63
Nelson, Gary 335
Nelson, Jim 215
Nelson, John (Follett) 189

Nelson, Joni C. (Ilitch Holdings) 245
Nelson, Linda 82
Nelson, Lori 461
Nelson, Marilyn Carlson 109
Nelson, Nathan 491
Nelson, Robert C. (Baker & Taylor) 67
Nelson, Shanna Missett 254
Nelson, Su Zan 136
Nelson, Thomas C. (AARP) 18
Nelson, Thomas C. (New NGC) 349
Nelson, Tom (Davidson
    Companies) 153
Neri, David 76
Nerland, Nairn 142
Nesbit, Robert F. 329
Nesbitt, Steven 516
Nesci, Mark A. 101
Nesse, Robert E. 307
Nettleship, Clayborne 291
Neu, Jim 538
Neubauer, Joseph 51
Neufeld, Jane F. 291
Neukom, William H. 38
Neumann, Henry W. Jr. 270
Neumann, Paul G. 114
Neves, Tony 406
Newbold, Michael 106
Newby, Jerry A. 33
Newcomb, Sharon 365
Newell, Mark E. 279
Newhouse, Donald E. 23
Newhouse, Samuel I. Jr. 23
Newhouse, Steven 23
Newman, Diane 41
Newman, Mark 356
Newman, Paul R. 167
Newman, Shelley 506
Newmier, Diana M. 154
Newsom, Charles R. 166
Newton, Anne 262
Newton, Gary 390
Newton, Richard Y. III 54
Newton, W. Keith 136
Newton, Younger D. II 126
Ng, Paul 451
Ng, Yu Kai 485
Nguyen-Phuong, Lam 106
Nicholas, Steven 358
Nicholls, Katherine 123
Nichols, Cherie 337
Nichols, Kenneth L. 21
Nichols, Michael 505
Nichols, Scott G. 95
Nicholson, Bruce J. 477
Nicholson, Pamela M. 175
Nick, Jerry 99
Nickel, Daniel M. 279
Nickell, Jeffrey K. 378
Nicksa, Gary W. 95
Nicol, Ron 94
Nicoll, Neil 540
Niehaus, Sheila 270
Niekamp, Randall W. 146
Nielsen, Nancy H. 42
Nielson, Jann 314
Nielson, Jeff 184
Nielson, Joani 470
Nielson, Scott M. 461
Nieto, Barbara M. 512
Nightingale, Paul C. 241
Nikias, C. L. Max 507
Nikolai, Pete 477
Nila, Linda 382
Nilekani, Nandan M. 136
Nishnick, Larry 141
Nitschke, Ken 105
Nittoli, Janice M. 416
Nitzkowski, Greg M. 376
Nix, Jack P. Jr. 255
Nobers, Jeff 17
Nobles, John E. 102
Noblitt, Niles L. 82
Nolan, David A. Jr. 82

Nolan, Frances 478
Nolan, Peter J. 403
Nolan, Robert 264
Noll, Jessica 139
Nollman, Mitch 93
Nomoto, Michael 465
Nook, Gregory E. 255
Noonan, Simon J. 97
Noone, Georgia A. 334
Nordyke, Greg 99
Norman, Andrew 165
Norman, Paul E. 92
Noronha, Wilbert P. 485
Norris, Adam 376
Norris, William 251
North, Jack W. 458
North, Margaret 474
Norton, David W. 224
Norton, Deborah A. 225
Nosek, Stan E. 501
Noseworthy, John H. 307
Notkin, Shelby 106
Noto, Anthony 338
Noto, Robert A. 324
Novak, Steve 269
Novell, Ray 537
Novelli, Bob 89
Novelli, William D. 18
Novelly, P. Anthony 49
Nowland, Joseph 523
Nowlin, Charles F. 310
Nugent, Nancy 25
Null, Steven A. 343
Nunez, Cris 466
Nusbaum, John 55
Nussdorf, Glenn H. 400
Nussdorf, Lawrence C. 131
Nuttall, Roger 193
Nuxoll, Erin 262
Nuzzo, Michael 203
Nye, Robert S. 238
Nyirjesy-Bragale, Christine 207

O

Oakes, Robert K. 44
Oakhill, Timothy F. 444
Oaks, Joseph 296
Obarski, Kevin 485
Obendorf, Steven E. 45
Oberdorf, Thomas 199
Oberkfell, Lawrence A. 433
Oberland, Gregory C. 361
Obert, Steve 47
O'Brien, Dermot J. 478
O'Brien, George G. 97
O'Brien, Jim 246
O'Brien, John 275
O'Brien, Kenneth 219
O'Brien, Michael 432
O'Brien, Morgan K. 168
O'Brien, Patrick J. 430
O'Brien, Peggy 143
O'Brien, Shelbie 25
O'Carroll, John 108
O'Connell, Barbara 201
O'Connell, Jim 335
O'Connell, John F. (Freeman
    Decorating Services) 193
O'Connell, John T. (Centric Group) 121
O'Conner, Nora 248
O'Conner, Patrick F. 229
O'Connor, David E. 467
O'Connor, John J. 459
O'Connor, Maureen K. 88
O'Connor, Stephen J. 201
O'Connor, Susan 463
O'Connor, Timothy M. 497
O'Dea, Marita 347
Odean, Gerald P. 330
Odegard, Gary L. 440
O'Dell, Julie 222

Stubblefield, Greg R. 175
Stubblefield, Jerry 540
Stubblefield, William 167
Stubbs, Timothy R.J. 245
Stubenhofer, Gerald J. Jr. 203
Stuckey, Bruce D. 190
Stump, David P. 58
Sturdevandt, Don 262
Sturgeon, Mark B. 24
Sturgeon, Michael M. 530
Stussi, Doug 290
Styrlund, Kenneth A. 255
Subbaswamy, Kumble R. 504
Subotnick, Stuart 319
Subramaniam, Shivan S. 180
Sucic, Nicholas R. 152
Sudderth, Gregory A. 88
Suever, Mike J. 241
Sufrin, Ron 318
Sullivan, Anne R. 134
Sullivan, Chris T. 370
Sullivan, E. Thomas 505
Sullivan, Foster 369
Sullivan, Jennifer 107
Sullivan, John (Sisters of Mercy Health
   System) 446
Sullivan, John F. (SRP) 424
Sullivan, Mark E. 93
Sullivan, Martha 437
Sullivan, Maureen 86
Sullivan, Meg 376
Sullivan, Michael B. 207
Sullivan, Stephen G. 285
Sullivan, Stuart P. 474
Sullivan, Teresa A. 505
Sullivan, Thomas 252
Sullivan-Crowley, Lianne 394
Sulmon, Bruno J. 163
Sumida, Glenn 42
Summer, Thomas S. 23
Summerfield, Judith 130
Summerlin, Jim 306
Sun, David 268
Sung, Jay 520
Sunshine, Eugene S. 361
Suntken, Marcy 270
Suratt, Dan 286
Surls, Courtney 507
Suscavage, Charles 251
Susienka, Cindy H. 205
Susko, Bryan T. 451
Sussman, Arthur M. 295
Sussman, Gary 349
Sutcliffe, Ian 332
Sutherland, Chris Jr. 466
Sutherland, George H. 99
Sutherland, L. Frederick 51
Sutter, Brent 348
Suttmeier, Catherine H. 369
Svitko, Drew 380
Swaback, Ray 312
Swafford, Preston D. 494
Swain, Jonathan B. 364
Swansen, Russell W. 477
Swanson, Al 512
Swanson, David S. 526
Swanson, Kenneth J. 390
Swanson, Kurt R. 470
Swartz, Richard 240
Swedish, Joseph R. 488
Sweeney, Gregory B. 99
Sweeney, John J. 28
Sweeney, Kelly 254
Sweeney, Matthew 250
Sweeney, Philip T. 512
Sweeris, Charles 89
Swider, John 41
Swiech, Randal 449
Swier, Ryan 57
Swift, Alicia 406
Swift, David L. 207
Swift, Randy 523
Swindal, Jennifer Steinbrenner 356

Swist, Bob 103
Swope, Jack 369
Swyers, Philip 425
Sykes, Dan 278
Sykes, Gwendolyn 539
Sykes, Rebecca 115
Sykes, Russell 449
Sylvan, Audrey E. 97
Symanoskie, Christopher 279
Symons, John 81
Syracuse, Raymond 349
Syron, Robert 534
Szczesny, Jeffrey D. 402
Szefel, Dennis J. 155
Szomjassy, Michael A. 122
Szopinski, Jim 327
Szymanski, Mary D. 488

T

Tabak, Natan 524
Tabinowski, Dale 245
Tabolt, David 67
Taccini, Cindy 365
Taft, Terry 368
Taich, Timothy F. 22
Takach, Tom 256
Takahashi, Tsuneo 194
Talán, Mónica 509
Talbert, Michelle 286
Talbert, Robin 18
Talbot, Randall H. 468
Talley, Joseph J. 39
Tamai, Tashiyuki 103
Tan, Benjamin 484
Tan, Cynara 393
Tan, Millie 401
Tanabe, Charles Y. 284
Tandy, Bradley J. 82
Taner, Marla 315
Tang, Cyrus 470
Tang, Paul C. 101
Tannenbaum, Richard 106
Tanner, David A. 140
Tanner, Harold 142
Tanner, Ronald R. 475
Tanner, Steven 20
Tansky, Burton M. 347
Tapp, Stephen 240
Tarapore, Kairus K. 121
Tarbox, Richard C. 464
Tarde, Merv 251
Tarr, David 203
Tartaglione, Bruce 498
Tartalia, Vince 57
Tasooji, Nick 541
Tassinari, Florence 195
Tassopoulos, Timothy P. 126
Tatlock, Anne M. 136
Tattrie, Amy 88
Tatum, Steve 272
Taus, Ellen 416
Tavares, Silvio 185
Taylor, Andrew C. 121, 175
Taylor, Beth A. 22
Taylor, Christine 294
Taylor, David 248
Taylor, Don 383
Taylor, George B. Jr. 365
Taylor, Glen A. 328, 471
Taylor, Gregory B. 265
Taylor, Jack T. 274
Taylor, Jean M. 471
Taylor, Jodi L. 139
Taylor, L. Edward 179
Taylor, Mark 102
Taylor, Mel 520
Taylor, Michael A. (FHC Health
   Systems) 185
Taylor, Michael V. (Sentara
   Healthcare) 437

Taylor, Michael W. (Strategic Products
   and Services) 357
Taylor, Mike (Oakland Raiders) 363
Taylor, Orlando L. 240
Taylor, Rob 97
Taylor, Ron 242
Taylor, Steve 499
Taylor, Susan 381
Taylor, Thomas F. 363
Taylor, Timothy G. 123
Taylor Kindle, Jo Ann 175
Tayman, William P. Jr. 143
Teaster, Michael D. 199
Teats, Aaron 47
Teel, James E. 402
Tegeder, David E. 29
Tehle, David M. 161
Tekunoff, Mark 268
Telfer, Martin 67
Tellado, Marta L. 190
Telles, Robert 141
Telliano, Steven 171
Temby, Judith A. 509
Temple, Jim 175
Temple, Susie 516
Templeton, Dave 91
Teneza, Gregory J. 36
Tennison, Ray 445
Tenny, Barron M. 190
Teo, Alfred S. 444
Terjeson, Steven R. 129
Terol, Alberto E. 156
Terrell, Patricia S. 504
Terry, Jim 95
Tersigni, Anthony R. 55
Tesch, Mary 128
Tesoriero, Joseph S. 161
Tessier, Zena 106
Tetnowski, Sonya 92
Teuber, Randy 535
Tewksbury, Gregory J. 505
Texido, Lisa 412
Thacher, Carter P. 534
Thacher, John P. 534
Thaler, Eric 331
Tharp, Christy 183
Tharp, Kerry 335
Theile, Barton C. 37
Theisen, Linda 317
Theiss, Jim 121
Theobald, Neil D. 246
Theriault, Bruce 143
Therrien, Michel 388
Theuer, John F. 374
Theus, Reggie 423
Thiel, Jackie 288
Thions, Jean Francois 520
Thomas, Alvin L. II 469
Thomas, Blake 318
Thomas, Daniel J. 136
Thomas, Deb 505
Thomas, Dennis 30
Thomas, George 520
Thomas, Herb 159
Thomas, J. Grover Jr. 491
Thomas, Jeff 232
Thomas, John (Sacramento Kings) 423
Thomas, John M. III (TVA) 494
Thomas, Kyle 185
Thomas, Larry 390
Thomas, Laurita E. 505
Thomas, Mary H. 224
Thomas, Michael J. 304
Thomas, Neil H. 165
Thomas, Peter 459
Thomas, Tommy 241
Thomas, Wayne 426
Thomason, Jim 477
Thomason, Joel D. 382
Thomasset, Paul 266
Thompson, Bill 410
Thompson, Brad 133
Thompson, Brian C. 147

Thompson, Chuck 50
Thompson, Dale L. 276
Thompson, Henry R. 381
Thompson, James B. (Pacific Coast
   Building Products) 372
Thompson, James D. (University of
   Rochester) 506
Thompson, Jeffrey 166
Thompson, John 170
Thompson, Michael 350
Thompson, Michele M. 503
Thompson, O. L. 453
Thompson, Robert K. 198
Thompson, Ronald L. 478
Thompson, Ted (Doner) 527
Thompson, Ted (Green Bay
   Packers) 214
Thompson, Tom (Minnesota Wild) 329
Thompson, Tommie D. (Mutual of
   Omaha) 334
Thoms, Jeffrey 35
Thomsen, James A. 477
Thomson, Glen 124
Thomson, Vincent 149
Thorn, Rod 349
Thorn, Stuart 454
Thornbrugh, Mike 400
Thorne, Mike 539
Thornhill, Paul D. 291
Thornton, Bert 524
Thornton, Matt 477
Thornton, Tom 34
Thorpe, James W. 161
Thorson, Alan G. 39
Thrailkill, John 139
Thrash, James E. 376
Thrasher, Kelly 524
Thresher, Mark R. 344
Thrope, Susan A. 352
Thum Suden, Paul 76
Thurgood, Keith L. 54
Thurk, Michael C. 65
Thurmond, William D. 54
Thwaites, Christian W. 342
Tibbils, Kent 57
Tibbs, Jim 283
Tidwell, Jody 540
Tierno, Anthony F. 311
Tietz, Jeff 184
Tigani, J. Paul 123
Tilearcio, Peter 209
Tilevitz, Harris Z. 447
Tilghman, Richard H. 382
Tilghman, Shirley M. 394
Tiliacos, Nicholas A. 519
Tillerson, Rex W. 95
Tillery, Christopher 512
Tilley, Daniel T. 131
Tillinghast, Marilyn 106
Tillman-Taylor, Susan 113
Timberlake, Edgar F. 470
Timm, Aaron C. 469
Timm, Carol A. 535
Timm, Dann 261
Timm, Leonard 517
Tindall, Robert J. 104
Tindell, Kip 139
Tindell, Sharon 139
Tinney, Joseph J. Jr. 51
Tinsman, Garrett 428
Tipsord, Michael L. 458
Tisch, Jonathan M. 351
Tisch, Steven 351
Tishman, Daniel R. 480
Tison, Ben 401
Titzkowski, Tom 513
Tobias, Maura C. 195
Toburen, Rick 453
Tochner, Ira 541
Todd, Bosworth M. 531
Todd, Joseph 395
Todd, Lee T. Jr. 504
Todorov, Kostadin 120

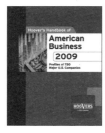

MAY 1 5 2009